THE LAW OF CONTRACT

AUSTRALIA
Law Book Co.
Sydney

CANADA and USA
Carswell
Toronto

HONG KONG
Sweet & Maxwell Asia

NEW ZEALAND
Brookers
Wellington

SINGAPORE AND MALAYSIA
Sweet & Maxwell Asia
Singapore and Kuala Lumpur

THE LAW
OF CONTRACT

by

SIR GUENTER TREITEL,
Q.C., D.C.L., F.B.A.

Honorary Bencher of Gray's Inn
Formerly Vinerian Professor of English Law

ELEVENTH EDITION

THOMSON

™

SWEET & MAXWELL

First edition 1962
Second edition 1966
Third edition 1970
Fourth edition 1975
Fifth edition 1979
Sixth edition 1983
Seventh edition 1987
Eighth edition 1991
Ninth edition 1995
Tenth edition 1999
Eleventh edition 2003

Published in 2003 by
Sweet & Maxwell Limited of
100 Avenue Road, London NW3 3PF
Computerset by Interactive Sciences,
Gloucester
Printed in England by MPG, Bodmin

A CIP catalogue record
for this book is available
from the British Library

ISBN 0 421 788402 (h/b)
ISBN 0 421 88 50X (p/b)
ISBN 0 421 788305 (ISE)

PREFACE

In the four years since the last edition of this book, many important changes in the law of contract have been made, both by legislation and by judicial decision. These changes have continued the trend of qualifying, or of engrafting exceptions on, previously existing rules. The result has been a further increase in the complexity of the subject and hence, unavoidably, in the length of the text.

The most important statutory change has been the enactment of the Contracts (Rights of Third Parties) Act 1999, though as this Act largely follows the structure of the 1998 Bill on the topic, discussed in the last edition of this book, only relatively minor changes in that discussion have been made. Other statutory changes with significant impact on contract law are the Limited Liability Partnerships Act 2000 (discussed particularly in the chapters on Capacity and Agency), the Financial Services and Markets Act 2000 and the Enterprise Act 2002. The effects of the last two Acts extend far beyond our topic: their main impact on it is that they have repealed (or led to the repeal of) much legislation affecting contract law that was formerly contained in the Financial Services Act 1986 and the Fair Trading Act 1973. Many further legislative changes are contained in secondary legislation. This edition takes account, in particular, of the many important changes made by the Unfair Terms in Consumer Contracts Regulations 1999 to the previous (1994) version of these Regulations, and of the entirely new body of rules introduced by the Sale and Supply of Goods to Consumers Regulations 2002. A glance at the table of Statutory Instruments will show how widespread the impact of the latter Regulations has been (even in a book that does not purport to be about sale of goods as a special contract) in introducing new concepts into English contract law. The same is true, if to a less significant extent, of the Consumer Protection (Distance Selling) Regulations 2000. This edition also attempts (with considerable trepidation on my part) to deal with the impact on the law of contract of electronic means of communication; it does so particularly, though not exclusively, in the light of relevant provisions of the Electronic Communications Act 2000 and of the Electronic Commerce (EC Directive) Regulations 2002.

Developments in the courts have continued at an accelerated pace: this edition takes account of more than 350 new cases. Among many decisions of the House of Lords which have called for substantial changes in the text, reference may here be made to *Johnson v Gore Wood* (on estoppels), *Director General of Fair Trading v First National Bank* (on unfair terms in consumer contracts), *Royal Bank of Scotland v Etridge* (on undue influence), *Alfred McAlpine Construction v Panatown* (on damages in respect of a third party's loss), *The Starsin* (on Himalaya Clauses), *Att-Gen v Blake* (on discretionary account of profits as a remedy for breach of contract) and *Farley v Skinner* (one of a group of cases on damages for non-pecuniary loss). A number of decisions of the lower courts also deserve special mention here: for example, *Baird Textile Holdings v Marks and Spencer* (raising many issues of contractual intention, consideration and estoppel), *Jennings v Rice (on proprietary estoppel)* and *The Great Peace* (on equitable relief for mistake).

Significant changes in the text have also been made where they were prompted by new reflections on points not directly affected by changes in the primary sources: this is, for example, true of the accounts of the various kinds of estoppel discussed in Chapter 3 and of the relationship between them. As a result of these and many other minor changes, about a quarter of the text is new.

My warm thanks are due to the staff of the Codrington Library of All Souls College for continuing to provide their usual excellent service in times of extreme difficulty (caused by building works there); and to the staff of the Underwood Law Library of Southern Methodist University for helping, during my visit at the proof correcting stage to the Law School there, to keep me in touch with current English materials. It is a pleasure also to thank Professor Colin Tapper and Dr Katharine Grevling, both of Magdalen College, for their continuing help with the retrieval of electronically stored information. I am grateful, too, to Andrew Turner for compiling the Index, Angela Foskett and Linda Gibbs for compiling the Tables of References and to Riaz Darr, Dan Leissner, Louise Etherington and Mark Ralph for help with cross-referencing.

The main work on this edition was completed in the first week of December 2002; later developments to March 2003 were (more briefly) incorporated at the proof stage. I am grateful to the publishers for making this possible and for their help in many other ways.

The first edition of this book was published over 40 years ago, and work on that edition had begun many years before then. For the whole of that time, I have found my work on the subject immensely enjoyable, largely because of the stimulus provided in this branch of the law by the subtlety and inventiveness of the courts, helped, no doubt, by the Bar. Nevertheless, and particularly while that enjoyment and my fascination with contract law have by no means diminished, I think that the time has come to pass the task to other hands. I am confident that it will be performed with distinction by Mr Edwin Peel, Fellow of Keble College, who has agreed to edit future editions; and I hope that he will find it as satisfying and enjoyable as I have done in writing this and the earlier editions.

GHT

April 28, 2003

CONTENTS

TABLE OF CASES

TABLE OF STATUTES

TABLE OF STATUTORY INSTRUMENTS

MISCELLANEOUS

CHAPTER ONE

INTRODUCTION[1]

A CONTRACT is an agreement giving rise to obligations which are enforced or recognised by law. The factor which distinguishes contractual from other legal obligations is that they are based on the agreement of the contracting parties. This proposition remains generally true, even though it is subject to a number of important qualifications.

The first such qualification is that the law is often concerned with the objective appearance, rather than with the actual fact, of agreement: a person is bound "whatever [his] real intention may be", if "a reasonable man would believe that he was assenting to the terms proposed by the other party and that other party upon that belief enters into a contract with him".[2] This objective principle is based on the needs of commercial convenience. Considerable uncertainty would result if A, after inducing B reasonably to believe that he (A) had agreed to certain terms, could then escape liability merely by showing that he had no "real intention" to enter into that agreement. The principle is an important one; but it would be wrong to say that the law of contract has no concern at all with actual agreement. This would put too much emphasis on the exceptional situation; for in most cases, the appearance corresponds with the fact of agreement. And the principle is not purely objective: A is not bound merely because "a reasonable man would believe that he was assenting to the terms proposed by the other party". In particular, there will be no contract if (in spite of the objective appearance of agreement) B *actually knows* that A in fact has *no* intention to contract with him, or to contract on the terms alleged.[3] A subjective element thus qualifies the objective principle; and this follows from the purpose of that principle, which is to protect B from the prejudice which he might suffer as a result of relying on a false appearance of agreement. There is clearly no need in this way to protect a party who knows that the objective appearance does not correspond with reality.[4] It also follows from the purpose of the objective principle that it will not apply where A's apparent assent is based on a mistake induced by B's negligence.[5] More generally, it may be said that the objective principle applies only where serious inconvenience would be caused by allowing a party to rely on his "real intention". In the interests of convenience the law may sometimes hold that there is a contract although there was not even the objective appearance of an agreement.[6] It does not follow that the law is not concerned with any sort of agreement at all: to allege that this was the position "would introduce into the law of contract a novel heresy".[7]

---

[1] See Hughes Parry, *The Sanctity of Contracts in English Law*.
[2] *Smith v Hughes* (1871) L.R. 6 Q.B. 597 at 607; see below, p.303 *Cambridge Nutrition Ltd v BBC* [1990] 3 All E.R. 523 at 542. Howarth, 100 L.Q.R. 265; Vorster, 103 L.Q.R. 274; Howarth, 103 L.Q.R. 527; Goddard, 7 *Legal Studies* 263; de Moor, 106 L.Q.R. 632.
[3] *e.g.* below, pp.8–9, 198, 307.
[4] For the further question whether the objective principle protects the "other party" where he has *no view* on the question whether the objective appearance corresponded with reality, see below, p.9.
[5] *e.g.*, below pp.309, 322; *cf. Norwich Union Fire Insurance Society Ltd v Price* [1934] A.C. 455 at 463.
[6] See below, p.41.
[7] *The Hannah Blumenthal* [1983] 1 A.C. 854 at 916–917.

The idea that contractual obligations are based on agreement must, secondly, be qualified because contracting parties are normally expected to observe certain standards of behaviour. These are the result of terms implied by law[8] into certain types of contract, for example, into contracts for the sale of goods or of employment. The parties may be able to vary or exclude some such terms by contrary agreement; but unless they do so they are bound by many duties to which they have not expressly agreed and of which they may have never thought. Agreement is not the *sole* factor which determines the legal effects of a contract once it is shown to exist. But it remains an important factor. For example, the intention of the parties determines whether a statement made at the time of contracting has contractual force or is a mere representation[9]; and it determines whether a term which is not expressly stated in the contract should be implied in fact, *i.e.* because the parties must have intended to incorporate it.[10] It has been suggested that in such cases the courts only *say* that the intention of the parties is the determining factor, but really apply rules based on various considerations of policy unconnected with that intention.[11] But a bare assertion that the relevant judgments do not mean what they say should not be accepted unless it is supported by argument. Such an argument can, perhaps, be based on the history of the doctrine of frustration, under which contracting parties may be discharged from liability by supervening events[12]: *e.g.* where such events make performance impossible. The doctrine was at one time justified by saying that the parties had impliedly agreed to be discharged in such circumstances; but many lawyers now prefer to say that the parties are discharged by operation of law, whether they would have agreed to discharge or not. This may be true; but the intention of the parties cannot for that reason be wholly disregarded. Before holding that parties are discharged, the court must find out what they contracted about: they may have deliberately taken the risk of supervening impossibility. The court must decide whether the parties contracted about a certainty or about a possibility; and it does so by ascertaining, as best it can, their intentions in the matter.

The idea that contractual obligations are based on agreement must, thirdly, be qualified in relation to the scope of the principle of freedom of contract.[13] In the nineteenth century, judges took the view that persons of full capacity should in general be allowed to make what contracts they liked: the law only interfered on fairly specific grounds such as misrepresentation, undue influence or illegality.[14] It did not interfere merely because one party was economically more powerful than the other and so able to drive a hard bargain. This attitude became particularly important when the courts recognised the validity of standard form contracts[15] drawn up by one party on terms designed to protect its interests at the expense of those of the other. This practice of contracting on standard terms is now very common; and it is arguable that a customer who contracts on such standard terms has them imposed on him, and does not really "agree" to them at all. This argument is particularly strong where standard terms are used by a monopoly supplier, or where all suppliers in a particular field use the same

---

[8] See below, pp.206 *et seq.*
[9] See below, p.353.
[10] See below, p.201.
[11] Atiyah, *An Introduction to the Law of Contract* (5th ed.), pp.20–21. (The point was more emphatically put in the 1st ed. at pp.13, 103).
[12] See below, Chap.20.
[13] For an historical account, see Atiyah, *The Rise and Fall of Freedom of Contract.*
[14] See below, Chaps 9, 10, 11.
[15] See below, Chap.7.

standard terms. The customer's only choice may then be between accepting those terms or doing without the goods or services in question; and often he cannot in practice do without. On the other hand, exact equality of bargaining power is probably rare; and there can be much dispute as to the precise degree of pressure which makes the difference between consent reluctantly given and a state of mind which cannot properly be described as consent at all. The amount of pressure which can be brought to bear on the customer does not depend solely on the respective wealth and power of the parties, but also on market conditions. In a buyer's market, an insistent private customer may be able to induce a normally powerful supplier to modify his standard terms, rather than lose a sale; while in a seller's market a customer may be ready to agree to any terms which the seller puts forward, or be willing to take his chance of the contents of any document put forward by the seller. A person may also agree to contract on a set of terms although he does not know in detail what they provide, *e.g.* where parties contract on terms settled by a trade association, or where a person takes employment on terms negotiated between employers and a trade union.[16] In such cases the parties would not deny that they *had* agreed to the terms whatever they might be.

Important inroads on the principle of freedom of contract have been made by legislation passed to redress some real or supposed imbalance of bargaining power. The contents of many contracts of employment are now regulated in some detail by legislation[17]; and many important aspects of the relationship of landlord and tenant are in the case of some tenancies controlled by legislation.[18] Under other statutes, terms are compulsorily implied into contracts and cannot be excluded by contrary agreement[19]; while the validity of standard form contracts is subject to severe legislative restrictions, especially in contracts between a commercial supplier of goods or services and a consumer.[20] In all these cases the main relationship between the parties is still based on agreement, but many of the obligations arising out of it are imposed or regulated by law.

But there are other cases in which the law plays so large, and the agreement of parties so small, a part that it becomes doubtful whether the relationship can still be called contractual. The agreement of the parties may create a status, such as marriage, the main legal incidents of which are fixed by law and cannot be varied by the parties at all.[21] Sometimes, the terms on which a person is employed (especially in the public service) are governed in part by legislation; and in one such case it was said that a claim under the "statutory scheme of employment"[22] could not "be dealt with as though it were an ordinary master and servant claim in which the rights of the parties were regulated solely by contract".[23] Similarly, a member of the armed forces is not in any contractual

---

[16] See below, p.213.

[17] See, *e.g.* Employment Rights Act 1996, s.86; National Minimum Wage Act 1998; Employment Relations Act 1999; Employment Act 2002.

[18] Rent Act 1977. It is, in general, impossible to "contract out" of the provisions of the Act: see, *e.g.* s.44(2). *cf.* Leasehold Reform Act 1967, s.23; *Johnson v Moreton* [1980] A.C. 37. Housing Act 1988, Pt I indicates some return to freedom of contract, but contrast Leasehold Reform, Housing and Urban Development Act 1993, s.93.

[19] *e.g.* Sex Discrimination Act 1975, s.8, amending Equal Pay Act 1970, s.1; *cf.* National Minimum Wage Act 1998, s.49.

[20] See below, pp.246 *et seq.*

[21] *Bellinger v Bellinger* [2001] EWCA Civ 1140; [2002] Fam. 150 at [99] ("marriage . . . is a matter of status and not for the parties alone to decide").

[22] *Barber v Manchester Regional Hospital Board* [1958] 1 W.L.R. 181 at 196.

[23] *Barber's Case*, above; for the effect of this distinction on remedies, see below, p.1030.

relationship with the Crown, even if he enlists voluntarily.[24] In a number of further borderline cases, the fact that many of the terms of the relationship are settled by law has not of itself been regarded as decisive. Thus on the one hand the relationship between a general medical practitioner and the health authority in whose area he worked under the National Health Service is not a contractual one.[25] On the other hand, it has been said that a consultant appointed to a post at a hospital under the National Health Service, works under "an ordinary contract between master and servant," although it is one with a "strong statutory flavour",[26] as it is governed by regulations made under statutory powers and having the force of law. Similarly, the relationship between the Crown and a lawyer employed in the Crown Prosecution Service is governed by contract in spite of the fact that such a lawyer has considerable independence (which the law would protect) in the exercise of his functions as a member of the Service.[27]

In the cases so far considered the parties are free to decide whether or not to enter into the relationship (though the law may fix some or all of its incidents); but there are other cases in which the law to some extent restricts even this freedom. For example, at common law a common innkeeper may be liable criminally[28] or in tort[29] for refusing, without sufficient excuse, to accommodate a guest. Injunctions may be granted and damages awarded against persons whose withholding of supplies from, for example, distributors amounts to an abuse of dominant position, contrary to European Community or United Kingdom competition law[30]; such remedies are also available against persons whose refusal to make certain contracts amounts to unlawful discrimination on grounds of race, sex or disability[31]; it is unlawful to refuse a person employment "because he is, or is not, a member of a trade union"[32]; and compensation is payable to a person who is excluded from a trade union (except on one of a number of specified

[24] See *Grant v S of S for India* (1877) 2 C.P.D. 445; *Mitchell v R* [1896] 1 Q.B. 121n.; *Leaman v R* [1920] 3 K.B. 663; *Kynaston v Attorney-General* (1933) 49 T.L.R. 300; dicta in *Owners of SS Raphael v Brandy* [1911] A.C. 413 at 415 perhaps suggest the contrary: *cf.* Mitchell, *Contracts of Public Authorities*, p.41. And see below, p.170.

[25] *Roy v Kensington and Chelsea and Westminster Family Practice Committee* [1992] 1 A.C. 624; *Wadi v Cornwall, etc. Family Practice Committee* [1985] I.C.R. 492 at 498; *Ealing, Hammersmith and Hounslow Family Health Services Authority v Shukla* [1993] I.C.R. 710.

[26] *Barber's Case*, above; *cf. R. v E Berkshire Health Authority, Ex p. Walsh* [1985] Q.B. 152; *R. v Derbyshire CC, Ex p. Noble* [1990] I.C.R. 808; *Associated British Ports v T & GWU* [1989] 1 W.L.R. 939; *cf.* the position of school teachers under Education Act 2002, s.122.

[27] *R. v Crown Prosecution Service, Ex p. Hogg, The Times,* April 14, 1994.

[28] See *R. v Ivens* (1835) 7 C. & P. 213.

[29] *Constantine v Imperial Hotels Ltd* [1944] K.B. 693.

[30] *Garden Cottage Foods Ltd v Milk Marketing Board* [1984] A.C. 130, where the prohibition in question was that contained in Art.86 of the European Community Treaty (now renumbered Art.82 in pursuance of European Communities (Amendment) Act 1998); for a similar prohibition in UK law, see Competition Act 1998, s.18, below, p.477.

[31] See Sex Discrimination Act 1975, Pts II and III and ss.65, 66 and 71 (as amended by Employment Act 1989, ss.1–9); Race Relations Act 1976, Pts II and III and ss.56, 57 and 62. Disability Discrimination Act 1995, ss.4, 5, 12 and 19; Sex Discrimination and Equal Pay (Miscellaneous Amendments) Regulations 1996 (SI 1996/438). Injunctions are not available under these Acts in the employment field: below, p.997. See also Courts and Legal Services Act 1990, s.64; Human Rights Act 1998, s.1 and Sch.1, Pt I, Art.14. By virtue of s.6, this prohibition makes unlawful only the activities of a "public authority" (including a court: s.6(3)(a)) and the question to what extent the Act gives rise to rights between private persons (the question of so-called "horizontal effect") remains as yet unresolved: see, *e.g.* Buxton, 116 L.Q.R. 48; Wade, *ibid.* 217; Hunt, *ibid.* 423; Bamforth, 117 L.Q.R. 34; [1999] C.L.J. 159; *RSPCA v Attorney-General* [2002] 1 W.L.R. 448. Such rights could also be affected in consequence of judicial declarations of incompatibility of other legislation with the Convention (to which the Act gives the force of law) under s.4 of the Act. For another suggestion as to possible effects of the Act on private contracts, see below, p.441.

[32] Trade Union and Labour Relations (Consolidation) Act 1992, s.137(1)(a); *cf. ibid.* s.138(1)(a); under s.140 the remedy (in the last resort) is by way of compensation. *cf.* Human Rights Act 1998, s.1 and Sch.1, Pt I, Art.11; but see above, n.31.

grounds).[33] Even at common law, a withholding of supplies may, in exceptional circumstances, be restrained by injunction[34]; and it is possible that a refusal to enter into a contract might similarly be restrained where it gave effect to a policy of discrimination even though it was not unlawful by statute; *e.g.* where a person was excluded from an association (and so deprived of the opportunity to do work available only to its members) on religious or political grounds that had no bearing on his competence to do the type of work in question.[35] In all these cases a relationship which results from some degree of legal compulsion is nevertheless regarded as contractual, because the parties still have considerable freedom to regulate its incidents. But there are other cases in which a relationship created by legal compulsion is clearly not contractual. A person whose property is compulsorily acquired against his will does not make a contract with the acquiring authority even though he receives compensation[36]; a patient who is treated in a hospital under the National Health Service is not considered to make a contract with the hospital authority[37]; nor does one to whom medicines are supplied under the Service make a contract to buy them, even if he pays a prescription charge[38]; and at common law, a person who posted a letter or parcel did not make a contract with the Post Office[39]; and the relations that now arise between such a person and a "universal [postal] service provider" appears similarly to be governed, not by contract, but by a scheme made under statute.[40] The borderline between the two classes of cases is by no means clearly defined: it is, for example, doubtful whether there is a contract between a patient and his doctor or dentist under the National Health Service, or between a client and his lawyer under the Legal Aid Scheme.[41] In the case of arrangements for the supply of gas, electricity or water, there may be a contract even though the supplier is bound by statute to make the supply, so long as the terms on which the supply is made are not also determined by

---

[33] Trade Union and Labour Relations (Consolidation) Act 1992, ss.174–177, as inserted by Trade Union and Employment Rights Act 1993, s.14; *cf.* Disability Discrimination Act 1995, s.13.

[34] *Acrow (Automation) Ltd v Rex Chainbelt Inc* [1971] 1 W.L.R. 1676.

[35] A suggestion based on *Nagle v Feilden* [1966] 2 Q.B. 633 (where the refusal was based on sex discrimination before that was made unlawful by statute); see below, p.474. Some support for this view may be given by Human Rights Act 1998, s.1 and Sch.1, Pt I, Arts 9 and 14; but see above, n.31. The availability of injunctive relief (apart from statute) against such refusal has been doubted: *R. v Disciplinary Committee of the Jockey Club, Ex p. Aga Khan* [1993] 1 W.L.R. 909 at 933.

[36] See *Sovmots Investments Ltd v S of S for the Environment* [1977] Q.B. 411 at 443, affirmed but without reference to this point [1979] A.C. 144. If a price is agreed after notice to treat, there is said to be a "statutory contract": *Munton v GLC* [1976] 1 W.L.R. 649; *cf. Harding v Metropolitan Ry* (1872) L.R. 7 Ch.App. 154 at 158. Even where this is not the case, the transaction may be regarded as a contract for the purpose of a particular statute: *Ridge Nominees v IRC* [1962] Ch. 376. A variety of techniques is used by legislation which entitles tenants to acquire the premises: contractual concepts are used by Landlord and Tenant Act 1987, Pt I and Leasehold Reform and Urban Development Act 1993, Pt I (see especially s.24(3)), while Pt III of the 1987 Act (above) (as amended by Leasehold Reform, Housing and Urban Development Act 1993, s.85) (above) and Housing Act 1985, Pt V use the concepts of compulsory purchase. Other statutes using non-contractual techniques are Access to Neighbouring Land Act 1992, s.3(2) (compensation for grant of access to land "without the consent" of the owner); New Roads and Street Works Act 1991, s.15 (liability for tolls).

[37] *Allen v Bloomsbury Health Authority* [1993] 1 All E.R. 651; see below, p.814; *cf.* also National Health Service and Community Care Act 1990, s.4(3), denying contractual status to arrangements for the provision of goods or services by one "health service body" to another under an "NHS contract".

[38] See *Pfizer Corp v Ministry of Health* [1965] A.C. 512; *Appleby v Sleep* [1968] 1 W.L.R. 948; *Re Medicaments Reference* [1970] 1 W.L.R. 1339.

[39] *Whitfield v Lord Le Despencer* (1778) Cowp. 754 at 764.

[40] Postal Services Act 2000, s.89; for exclusion and limitation of liability, see *ibid.* ss.90, 91.

[41] *cf.* Legal Aid Act 1988, ss.9(7), 24 and Sch.3, Pt 1, para.2(1); s.16(10) refers to a contract between the legally assisted person and *the Board* (not to one between that person and the legal adviser). For the power of barristers to make contracts for the provision of services as such, and for the power of the General Council of the Bar to prohibit or restrict such contracts, see Courts and Legal Services Act 1990, s.61.

legislation so as to leave no scope for bargaining between the supplier and the cus-tomer.[42]

In spite of the above qualifications, it remains broadly true that the law of contract is concerned with the circumstances in which agreements are legally binding. Thus it deals mainly with the two questions of agreement and legal effects or enforceability. The rules relating to offer and acceptance,[43] for instance, deal with the process of reaching agreement. Those relating to consideration and contractual intention[44] concern the requirements which must normally be satisfied before an agreement will be legally enforced; while the rules relating to misrepresentation and illegality[45] deal with the effect of special factors on account of which the law may refuse to enforce agreements which would, apart from such factors, be binding. The rules which limit the contractual capacity of certain individuals[46] are based partly on the view that certain classes of persons cannot form the requisite contractual intention, and partly on the view that it is undesirable to enforce agreements against them. The rules relating to mistake are based partly on the view that there is no agreement when the parties are at cross-purposes on a fundamental point,[47] and partly on the view that an agreement has no legal effect if both parties were under a fundamental mistake as to the subject-matter.[48] The rules relating to the contents of a contract, performance, breach and frustration[49] are again partly based on the agreement between the parties, and partly on rules of law which determine the precise legal effect of that agreement.

The bulk of the law of contract is concerned with the questions of agreement and legal enforceability; but a number of other topics also call for discussion. Thus the rules relating to plurality, third parties, assignment and agency[50] determine who is bound by, and entitled to the benefit of, a contract. The rules relating to remedies[51] assume the existence of an enforceable agreement, and deal with the methods of, and limits on, enforcement. These are in principle determined by law. Thus the agreement of the parties does not determine whether a contract is to be enforced specifically, or only by an award of damages; though that agreement may be relevant in determining the precise amount of damages which will be awarded for a breach of contract.

---

[42] See, for example, Electricity Act 1989, ss.16 and 17 (as substituted by Utilities Act 2000, s.44) and *ibid.* Sch.6 (as substituted by Utilities Act 2000, s.51 and Sch.4). The repeal of s.18 of the 1989 Act by s.45 of the 2000 Act, abolishing charges by reference to tariffs, appears to undermine the reasoning of *Norweb plc v Dixon* [1995] 1 W.L.R. 635, that there was no contract between the supplier and a "tariff" customer; see also the 2000 Act, s.108 and Sch.7, para.23(2): supplier deemed to have contracted with former tariff customers. The position appears to be the same with regard to the supply of gas: see the repeal by s.89 of the 2000 Act of Gas Act 1986, s.10(2), which appears to have assumed that there was no contract between the supplier and a domestic customer. In the case of water supplies, the relations between suppliers and domestic consumers appear to remain non-contractual as even the terms of such supply are regulated by legislation: see Water Industry Act 1991, ss.53, 54; contrast *ibid.* ss.55, 56 (terms of *bulk* supply to be determined by agreement or by the Director); see also Water Industry Act 1999; and *cf.* Competition and Services (Utilities) Act, ss.1, 44, also using non-contractual language in relation to the supply of water, gas and telephone services. In *Hamilton v Papkura DC* [2002] UKPC 9; *The Times*, March 5, 2002 the Privy Council regarded the relationship between a New Zealand local authority (which was under a statutory duty to supply water) and a person to whom the supply was made as contractual, but held there was no breach.
[43] See below, Chap.2.
[44] See below, Chaps 3, 4.
[45] See below, Chaps 9, 11; see also Chaps 10, 12.
[46] See below, Chap.13.
[47] See below, Chap.8, s.2.
[48] See below, Chap.8, s.1.
[49] See below, Chaps 6, 18, 19, 20.
[50] See below, Chaps 14 to 17.
[51] See below, Chap.21.

Remedies for breach of contract are discussed in Chapter 21; but one fundamental point relating to them must be made at this stage. Such remedies might attempt to do one of two things. First, they might attempt to put the injured party into the position in which he would have been if the contract *had never been made*. This would require the party in breach to restore anything that he had received under the contract, and also to compensate the injured party for any loss that he had suffered by acting in reliance on the contract. Such remedies are said to protect the injured party's *restitution* and *reliance* interests.[52] But remedies for breach of contract go beyond the pursuit of these objectives. Their distinguishing feature is that they seek to put the injured party into the position in which he would have been if the contract *had been performed*.[53] If, for example a seller agrees to sell goods for less than they are worth, and then fails to deliver them, he must compensate the buyer for not having received goods which are worth more than he had agreed to pay for them. Conversely, if a buyer contracts to buy goods for more than they are worth, and then fails to pay for them, he is liable for the agreed price[54]: it is quite immaterial that the value of the goods with which the seller has parted was lower than that price. What the law does in these cases is to protect the injured party's *expectation* interest.[55] Sometimes it does so directly, by actually ordering the party in breach to perform his part of the contract.[56] Sometimes it does so indirectly by ordering him to pay the injured party damages for *loss of his bargain*.

The result of awarding damages on this basis is to compensate the injured party, not because he is worse off than he was before the contract was made, but because the other party has failed to make him better off.[57] The law of contract takes this position in response to the needs of commercial certainty. It is probably going too far to say that business could not be carried on at all if the law did not protect the injured party's expectation interest. Some industries (such as the credit betting industry) are carried on without this, or indeed any other legally recognised, sanction.[58] But in relation to other spheres of commercial activity, such as share and commodity markets and the insurance industry (to take a few random examples)[59] the protection of expectations is of crucial importance. In these cases, that protection promotes stability and furthers one of the central purposes of the law of contract in providing the legal framework required for commercial relations.

---

[52] See below, pp.940–942.

[53] See below, pp.936–940.

[54] Assuming that the conditions stated on pp.1013–1019, below are satisfied.

[55] See below, pp.936–940.

[56] See below, pp.1019–1046.

[57] *South Australian Asset Management Corp v York Montague Ltd* [1997] A.C. 191 at 216.

[58] See below, pp.520–521.

[59] Another may be the sale of houses, where the fact that agreements "subject to contract" have no binding force has been strongly criticised: see below, p.52.

Chapter Two

AGREEMENT[1]

THE first requisite of a contract is that the parties should have reached agreement. Generally speaking, an agreement is made when one party accepts an offer made by the other. Further requirements are that the agreement must be certain and final; and special problems arise from conditional agreements.

SECTION 1. OFFER

1. Offer Defined

(1) The objective test

An offer is an expression of willingness to contract on specified terms, made with the intention that it is to become binding as soon as it is accepted by the person to whom it is addressed.[2] Under the objective test of agreement,[3] an apparent intention to be bound may suffice, *i.e.* the alleged offeror (A) may be bound if his words or conduct[4] are such as to induce a reasonable person to believe that he intends to be bound, even though in fact he has no such intention. This was, for example, held to be the case where a university offered a place to an intending student as a result of a clerical error[5]; and where a solicitor who had been instructed by his client to settle a claim for $155,000 by mistake offered to settle it for the higher sum of £150,000.[6] Similarly, if A offers to sell a book to B for £10 and B accepts the offer, A cannot escape liability merely by showing that his actual intention was to offer the book to B for £20, or that he intended the offer to relate to a book different from that specified in the offer.[7]

Whether A is actually bound by an acceptance of his apparent offer depends on the state of mind of the alleged offeree (B); to this extent, the test is not purely objective.[8] With regard to B's state of mind, there are three possibilities. First, B actually believes that A intends to be bound: here the objective test is satisfied so that B can hold A to his apparent offer even though A did not, subjectively, have the requisite intention.[9] The general view is that there is no further requirement that A must also be aware of B's state

---

[1] Winfield, 55 L.Q.R. 499; Kahn, 72 S.A.L.J. 246; Nussbaum, 36 Col.L.Rev. 920.

[2] *e.g. Storer v Manchester CC* [1974] 1 W.L.R. 1403; contrast *André & Cie v Cook Industries Inc* [1987] 2 Lloyd's Rep. 463; *Schuldenfrei v Hilton (Inspector of Taxes)* [1998] S.T.C. 404.

[3] See above, p.1; *First Energy (UK) Ltd v Hungarian International Bank Ltd* [1993] 2 Lloyd's Rep. 195 at 201; *Ignazio Messina & Co v Polskie Linie Oceaniczne* [1995] 2 Lloyd's Rep. 566 at 571; *Bowerman v Association of British Travel Agents Ltd* [1995] N.L.J. 1815.

[4] For offers made by conduct, see below, at nn.15 to 25; *The Aramis* [1989] 1 Lloyd's Rep. 213 (where the objective test was not satisfied) *G Percy Trentham Ltd v Archital Luxfer Ltd* [1993] 1 Lloyd's Rep. 25 at 27.

[5] *Moran v University College Salford (No.2), The Times*, November 23, 1993.

[6] *OT Africa Line Ltd v Vickers plc* [1996] 1 Lloyd's Rep. 700.

[7] *cf. Centrovincial Estates plc v Merchant Investors Assurance Co Ltd* [1983] Com.L.R. 158; cited with approval in *Whittaker v Campbell* [1984] Q.B. 318 at 327, in *The Antclizo* [1987] 2 Lloyd's Rep. 130 at 146, affirmed [1988] 1 W.L.R. 603, and in *OT Africa Line Ltd v Vickers plc* [1996] 1 Lloyd's Rep. 700 at 702.

[8] *The Hannah Blumenthal* [1983] 1 A.C. 854 at 924.

[9] *The Splendid Sun* [1981] 1 Q.B. 694, as explained in *The Hannah Blumenthal*, above; *Challoner v Bower* (1984) 269 E.G. 725; *The Multibank Holsatia* [1988] 2 Lloyd's Rep. 486 at 493.

of mind.[10] Secondly, B knows that, in spite of the objective appearance, A does not have the requisite intention: here A is not bound; the objective test does not apply in favour of B as he knows the truth about A's actual intention.[11] Thirdly, B has simply not formed any view about A's intention, so that B neither believes that A has the requisite intention nor knows that A does not have this intention: this situation has given rise to a conflict of judicial opinion. One view is that A is not bound: in other words, the objective test is satisfied only if A's conduct is such as to induce a reasonable person to believe that A had the requisite intention *and* if B actually held that belief.[12] The opposing view is that (in our third situation) A is bound: in other words, the objective test is satisfied if A's words or conduct would induce a reasonable person to believe that A had the requisite intention, so long as B does not actually know that A does *not* have any such intention.[13] This latter view no doubt facilitates proof of agreement, but it is hard to see why B should be protected in the situation to which it refers. Where B has no positive belief in A's (apparent) intention to be bound, he cannot be prejudiced by acting in reliance on it; and the purpose of the objective test is simply to protect B from the risk of suffering such prejudice.[14] The test embodies a principle of convenience; it is not based on any inherent superiority of objective over subjective criteria. It is therefore submitted that the objective test should not apply to our third situation since in it B's state of mind is such that there is no risk of his suffering any prejudice as a result of the objective appearance of A's intention.

(2) Conduct as an offer

An offer may be addressed either to an individual, or to a group of persons, or to the world at large; and it may be made expressly or by conduct. At common law, a person who had contracted to sell goods and tendered different goods (or a different quantity) might be considered to make an offer by conduct to sell the goods which he had tendered.[15] It seems that an offer to sell can still be made in this way, though by legislation against "inertia selling" the dispatch of goods without any prior request from the recipient may amount to a gift to him, rather than to an offer to sell.[16]

---

[10] The suggestion that A must be aware of B's state of mind was made by Lord Diplock in *The Hannah Blumenthal* [1983] 1 A.C. 854 at 916 but Lord Brightman's contrary view, expressed *ibid.* at 924 has been generally preferred: see *The Multibank Holsatia*, above, at 492.

[11] See above, p.1, *Ignazio Messina & Co v Polskie Linie Oceaniczne* [1995] 2 Lloyd's Rep. 566 at 571 ("not communicated to or otherwise apparent to the other party [B]"); *OT Africa Line Ltd v Vickers plc* [1996] 1 Lloyd's Rep. 700 at 703; and see the authorities cited in n.13, below.

[12] *The Hannah Blumenthal*, above, as interpreted in *The Leonidas D* [1985] 1 W.L.R. 925; Beatson, 102 L.Q.R. 19; Atiyah, *ibid.* p.392; *The Agrabele* [1987] 2 Lloyd's Rep. 223, esp. at 235; *cf. Cie. Française d'Importation, etc. SA v Deutsche Continental Handelsgesellschaft* [1985] 2 Lloyd's Rep. 592 at 597; *Amherst v James Walker Goldsmith and Silversmith Ltd* [1983] Ch.305.

[13] *The Golden Bear* [1987] 1 Lloyd's Rep. 330 at 341 (doubted on another point at p.32, below); this view was approved in *The Antclizo* [1987] 2 Lloyd's Rep. 130 at 143 but doubted *ibid.* at 147 (affirmed [1988] 1 W.L.R. 603 without reference to the point); and *semble* in *Floating Dock Ltd v Hong Kong and Shanghai Bank Ltd* [1986] 1 Lloyd's Rep. 65 at 77; *The Multibank Holsatia* [1988] 2 Lloyd's Rep. 486 at 492 ("at least did not conflict with [B's] subjective understanding"); *The Maritime Winner* [1989] 2 Lloyd's Rep. 506 at 515 (using similar language). A dictum in *The Amazonia* [1990] 1 Lloyd's Rep. 238 at 242 goes even further in suggesting that there may be a contract even though "*neither* [party] intended to make a contract".

[14] See above, p.1.

[15] *Hart v Mills* (1846) 15 L.J.Ex. 200; below, p.17; *cf. Steven v Bromley & Son* [1919] 2 K.B. 722; *The Saronikos* [1986] 2 Lloyd's Rep. 277.

[16] Consumer Protection (Distance Selling) Regulations 2000, SI 2000/2334 (implementing Dir.97/7 ([1997] O.J. L144/19)), regs 22 (amending Unsolicited Goods and Services Act 1971) and 24; *quaere* whether these provisions would apply where an order had been placed but the quantity sent grossly exceeded that ordered.

A number of cases raise the further question whether the "conduct" from which an offer may be inferred can take the form of inactivity. The issue in these cases was whether an agreement to submit a dispute to arbitration could be said to have been "abandoned" where, over a long period of time, neither party had taken any steps in the arbitration proceedings. In cases of "inordinate and inexcusable delay" of this kind, arbitrators now have a statutory power to dismiss the claim for want of prosecution[17]; and it is also open to the parties expressly to provide for "lapse" of the claim if steps in the proceedings are not taken within a specified period.[18] But, conversely, the statutory power to dismiss the claim for want of prosecution may be excluded by agreement,[19] and where it is so excluded the question of abandonment can still arise in the present context. Such a question could also arise in the context of the alleged abandonment of some other type of right or remedy,[20] to which no similar legislative provision extends. The arbitration cases indicate that, when inactivity is combined with other circumstances (such as destruction of relevant files),[21] it may, on the objective test, amount to an offer of abandonment, even though those other circumstances would not, of themselves, constitute evidence from which an offer could be inferred. But when inactivity stands alone, it is unlikely[22] to have this effect, for it is equivocal and explicable on other grounds, such as inertia or forgetfulness, or the simple tactical consideration that the party alleged to have made the offer does not wish to re-activate his opponent's counterclaims.[23] Consequently, it will not normally suffice to induce a reasonable person in the position of the other party to believe that an offer is being made[24]; and the mere fact that the other party nevertheless had this belief cannot suffice to turn the former party's inactivity into such an offer.[25]

2. Offer Distinguished from Invitation to Treat

When parties negotiate with a view to making a contract, many preliminary communications may pass between them before a definite offer is made. One party may simply respond to a request for information (*e.g.* by stating the price at which he might be

---

[17] Arbitration Act 1996, s.41(3), replacing Arbitration Act 1950, s.13A. Under s.13A it had been held that the court could take into account delay occurring before the section came into force: *The Boucraa* [1994] 1 A.C. 486; and that the court would (*mutatis mutandis*) apply the same principles to the power to dismiss arbitration proceedings as those which govern the dismissal of an action for want of prosecution: *James Lazenby & Co v McNicholas Construction Co Ltd* [1995] 1 W.L.R. 615.

[18] See the GAFTA arbitration rules referred to in *Cargill SpA v Kadinopoulos* [1992] 1 Lloyd's Rep. 1.

[19] Arbitration Act 1996, s.41(2) so provides.

[20] *cf. Amherst Ltd v James Walker Goldsmith & Silversmith Ltd* [1983] Ch.305; *Collin v Duke of Westminster* [1985] Q.B. 581; *MSC Mediterranean Shipping Co SA v BRE Metro Ltd* [1985] 2 Lloyd's Rep. 239; *Fenton Ins Ltd v Gothaer Versicherungsbank VVaG* [1991] 1 Lloyd's Rep. 172 at 180.

[21] *The Splendid Sun* [1981] Q.B. 694, as explained in *The Hannah Blumenthal* [1983] 1 A.C. 854 (though this explanation was doubted in *Cie. Française d'Importation, etc. SA v Deutsche Conti Handelsgesellschaft* [1985] 2 Lloyd's Rep. 592 at 599); *Tracomin SA v Anton C Nielsen* [1984] 2 Lloyd's Rep. 195 (as to which see below, p.33 n.64); *The Multibamk Holsatia* [1988] 2 Lloyd's Rep. 486; for the question whether such an offer can be *accepted* by inactivity, see below, p.31.

[22] *Unisys International Services Ltd v Eastern Counties Newspapers Group Ltd* [1991] 1 Lloyd's Rep. 538 at 553 suggests (with some scepticism) that the possibility cannot be wholly ruled out; *cf. The Boucraa* [1994] 1 A.C. 486 at 521, describing the "abandonment" approach as "largely useless in practice".

[23] *Unysis* case, above, at 553.

[24] *The Leonidas D* [1985] 1 W.L.R. 925; *Cie. Française d'Importation, etc. SA v Deutsche Conti Handelsgesellschaft* [1985] 2 Lloyd's Rep. 592; *The Antclizo* [1988] 1 W.L.R. 603; *The Agrabele* [1987] 2 Lloyd's Rep. 223; *The Maritime Winner* [1989] 2 Lloyd's Rep. 506; *contra, The Golden Bear* [1987] 1 Lloyd's Rep. 330 (*sed quaere*: the decision was in part based on the decision at first instance in *The Agrabele* [1985] 2 Lloyd's Rep. 496, but this was reversed on appeal: [1987] 2 Lloyd's Rep. 223); *The Ermoupolis* [1990] 1 Lloyd's Rep. 161 at 166; see also below, p.35.

[25] *The Antclizo* [1988] 1 W.L.R. 603; Davenport, 104 L.Q.R. 493.

prepared to sell a house[26]), or he may make such a request (*e.g.* where he asks a prospective supplier whether he can supply goods suitable for his purpose).[27] That party is then said to make an "invitation to treat": he does not make an offer but, invites the other party to do so. The question whether a statement is an offer or an invitation to treat depends primarily on the intention with which it was made. It follows from the nature of an offer as described above[28] that a statement is not an offer if it in terms negatives the maker's intention to be bound on acceptance: for example, if it expressly provides that he is *not* to be bound merely by the other party's notification of assent, but only when he himself has signed the document in which the statement is contained.[29] Apart from this type of case, the wording is not conclusive: a statement may be an invitation to treat, although it contains the word "offer".[30] Conversely, a statement may *be* an offer although it is expressed to be an "acceptance,"[31] or although it requests the person to whom it is addressed to *make* an "offer".[32]

The distinction between an offer and an invitation to treat is often hard to draw as it depends on the elusive criterion of intention. But there are certain stereotyped situations in which the distinction is determined, at least *prima facie*, by rules of law. It may be possible to displace these rules by evidence of contrary intention, but in the absence of such evidence they will determine the distinction between offer and invitation to treat, and they will do so without reference to the intention (actual or even objectively ascertained) of the maker of the statement. This is true, for example, in cases of auction sales and shop displays. These and other illustrations of the distinction will be discussed in the following paragraphs.

(1) Auction sales

At an auction sale, the general rule is that the offer is made by the bidder and accepted by the auctioneer when he signifies his acceptance in the customary manner, *e.g.* by fall of the hammer.[33] Before acceptance the bidder may withdraw his bid and the auctioneer may withdraw the goods. It seems, moreover, that the offer made by each bidder lapses[34] as soon as a higher bid is made. Thus if a higher bid is made and withdrawn the auctioneer can no longer accept the next highest.

When property is put up for auction subject to a reserve price, there is no contract if the auctioneer by mistake purports to accept a bid lower than the reserve price.[35] Where the auction is without reserve, there is no contract *of sale* between the highest bidder and the *owner* of the property if the auctioneer refuses to accept the highest bid.

---

[26] *Harvey v Facey* [1893] A.C. 552; *Gibson v Manchester CC* [1979] 1 W.L.R. 294; *cf. The Barranduna* [1985] 2 Lloyd's Rep. 419 (quotation of freight rates by carrier not an offer); *Michael Gerson (Leasing) Ltd v Wilkinson* [2000] Q.B. 514 at 530 ("I am willing to make an outright sale" for a specified price not an offer and, even if it was, it had not been accepted: see below, p.17).

[27] *Interfoto Picture Library Ltd v Stiletto Visual Programmes Ltd* [1989] Q.B. 433 at 436; *cf.* Electronic Commerce (EC Directive) Regulations 2002 (SI 2002/2013), reg.12: in electronic trading (*e.g.* on a website) an "'order' may be, but need not be, the contractual offer . . . " for certain purposes specified in those Regulations.

[28] See above, p.8 at n.2.

[29] *Financings Ltd v Stimson* [1962] 1 W.L.R. 1184.

[30] *Spencer v Harding* (1870) L.R. 5 C.P. 561; *Clifton v Palumbo* [1944] 2 All E.R. 497.

[31] *Bigg v Boyd Gibbins Ltd* [1971] 1 W.L.R. 913.

[32] *Harvela Investments Ltd v Royal Trust Co of Canada (CI) Ltd* [1986] A.C. 207.

[33] Sale of Goods Act 1979, s.57(2); *Payne v Cave* (1789) 3 T.R. 148; *British Car Auctions Ltd v Wright* [1972] 1 W.L.R. 1519.

[34] See below, p.43.

[35] *McManus v Fortescue* [1907] 2 K.B. 1; on a sale of land, it must be expressly stated whether the sale is with reserve or not: Sale of Land by Auction Act 1867, s.5.

But it has been held that the *auctioneer* is in such a case liable on a separate, or collateral, contract between him and the highest bidder that the sale will be without reserve.[36] Although a mere advertisement of an auction is not an offer to hold it,[37] the actual request for bids seems to be an offer by the auctioneer that he will on the owner's behalf accept the highest bid; and this offer is accepted by the bidding.[38]

(2) Display of goods for sale

The general rule is that a display of price-marked goods in a shop window is not an offer to sell goods but is an invitation to a customer to make an offer to buy.[39] Similarly, the display of goods on the shelves of a self-service shop is merely an invitation to treat; the customer makes an offer to buy when he presents the goods for payment; at this stage, the retailer may accept or reject it.[40] Similar principles would seem to apply where a supplier of goods or services indicates their availability on a website: that is, the offer would seem to come from the customer (*e.g.* when he clicks the appropriate "button") and it is then open to the supplier to accept or reject that offer.[41] There is judicial support for the view that an indication of the price at which petrol is to be sold at a filling station is likewise an invitation to treat,[42] the offer to buy being made by the customer and accepted by the seller's conduct in putting the petrol into the tank.[43] But this analysis hardly fits the now more common situation in which the station operates a self-service system[44]; for once the customer has put petrol into his tank, the seller has no effective choice of refusing to deal with him.

The general rule relating to shop and similar displays is well established, but the reasons given for it are not entirely convincing. One reason is that "a shop is a place for bargaining, not for compulsory sales".[45] But the modern English shop, in which goods are generally bought on the retailer's terms, is scarcely a place for bargaining; and even if the display of goods were an offer, any resulting sale would not be compulsory: the shopkeeper need not display goods which he does not want to sell. Another argument is that if the display were regarded as an offer, the retailer might be exposed to many actions for damages if more customers purported to accept than his stock could satisfy.[46] But such an offer could be construed as one which automatically expired when the retailer's stock was exhausted: this would probably be in keeping with the common

---

[36] *Warlow v Harrison* (1859) 1 E. & E. 309; *cf. Johnston v Boyes* [1899] 2 Ch.73 at 77; *Barry v Davies* [2001] 1 W.L.R. 1962. *Contra, Fenwick v Macdonald, Fraser & Co Ltd* (1904) 6 F. (Ct. of Sess.) 850; Slade, 68 L.Q.R. 238; Gower, 68 L.Q.R. 457; Slade, 69 L.Q.R. 21. Under the American Uniform Commercial Code (hereinafter referred to as U.C.C.) the goods may not be withdrawn once they have been put up, if the auction is without reserve: s.2–328(3).

[37] *Harris v Nickerson* (1873) L.R. 8 Q.B. 286.

[38] The question whether there is any consideration for the auctioneer's undertaking is discussed below, p.155.

[39] *Timothy v Simpson* (1834) 6 C.&P. 499; *Fisher v Bell* [1961] 1 Q.B. 394; (the actual decision has been reversed: Restriction of Offensive Weapons Act 1961, s.1; contrast Criminal Justice Act 1988, s.14A(1), as inserted by Offensive Weapons Act 1996, s.6, which refers only to selling); dicta in *Wiles v Maddison* [1943] 1 All E.R. 315 at 317, may perhaps suggest the contrary.

[40] *Pharmaceutical Society of Great Britain v Boots Cash Chemists Ltd* [1952] 2 Q.B. 795; [1953] 1 Q.B. 401; Unger, 16 M.L.R. 369; D.C.W., 10 N.I.L.Q. 117; Montrose, 10 N.I.L.Q. 178; and *cf. Lacis v Cashmarts Ltd* [1969] 2 Q.B. 400; *Davies v Leighton* [1978] Crim.L.R. 575.

[41] See below, p.17 for what *constitutes* an acceptance, and p.26, n.93 for the *time* of acceptance, in such cases.

[42] *Esso Petroleum v Commissioners of Customs & Excise* [1976] 1 W.L.R. 1 at 5, 6, 11; *Richardson v Worrall* [1985] S.T.C. 693 at 717.

[43] *Re Charge Card Services* [1989] Ch.497 at 512; for acceptance by conduct, see below, p.18.

[44] *cf.* below, p.14 at n.63.

[45] Winfield, 55 L.Q.R. 518.

[46] *Esso Petroleum* case above, n.42, at 11.

expectation of both retailer and customer. It has also been said that, if a display in a self-service shop were an offer, the undesirable result would follow that the customer would be bound to buy as soon as he picked up the goods to examine them.[47] But if the display were an offer, it could be argued that there was no acceptance until the customer did some less equivocal act, such as presenting the goods for payment.[48] Finally, it may be asked whether the general rule does not sometimes cause injustice. Customers may be induced by a window display to believe that they will be able to buy goods at exceptionally low prices and to wait outside the shop for many hours in reliance on that belief. Is it right to allow the retailer to go back on such a statement at the very moment when the customer demands the goods? It seems that the special terms of a display, or the circumstances in which it is made, may be evidence of intention to be bound and so displace the *prima facie* rule that the display is not an offer: thus in one case a notice in a shop window stating that "We will beat any TV . . . price by £20 on the spot" was described as "a continuing offer".[49] The customer might, indeed, still lose his bargain since the offer could be withdrawn at any time before it was accepted[50]; but if it is so withdrawn the person displaying the notice may incur criminal liability under legislation passed for the protection of consumers.[51]

(3) Advertisements and other displays

Advertisements of rewards for the return of lost or stolen property, or for information leading to the arrest or conviction of the perpetrator of a crime,[52] are invariably treated as offers: the intention to be bound is inferred from the fact that no further bargaining is expected to result from them. The same is true of other advertisements of unilateral contracts.[53] Thus in *Carlill v Carbolic Smoke Ball Co*,[54] an advertisement promising to pay £100 to any user of a carbolic smoke ball who caught influenza was held to be an offer. The intention to be bound[55] was made particularly clear by the statement that the advertisers had deposited £1,000 in their bank "shewing our sincerity". A case nearer the borderline was *Bowerman v Association of British Travel Agents Ltd*[56] where a package holiday had been booked with a tour operator who was a member of the defendant association (ABTA). A notice displayed on the tour operator's premises stated, *inter alia*, that in the event of the financial failure of an ABTA member before commencement of the holiday, "ABTA arranges for you to be reimbursed the money you have paid for your

---

[47] *Boots Case* [1952] 2 Q.B. 795 at 802.

[48] See *Lasky v Economic Grocery Stores*, 65 N.E. 2d 305 (1946). In *Gillespie v Great Atlantic & Pacific Stores*, 187 S.E. 2d. 441 (1972) and *Sheeskin v Giant Food Inc*, 318 A 2d. 874 (1974) acceptance was said to take place before the customer presented the goods for payment, but subject to his power to cancel before that point. In *R. v Morris* [1984] A.C. 320 taking goods off the shelf of a self-service store *and changing the price-labels* was held to be an "appropriation" within Theft Act 1968, s.3(1); but it does not follow that at this stage there would for the purpose of the law of contract be an acceptance even if the shelf-display amounted to an offer: see, *ibid.* at 334.

[49] *R. v Warwickshire CC, ex p. Johnson* [1993] A.C. 583 at 588.

[50] See below, p.41.

[51] Consumer Protection Act 1987, s.20(1): see *R. v Warwickshire CC, ex p. Johnson*, above; contrast *Link Stores Ltd v Harrow BC* [2001] 1 W.L.R. 1479. The section applies also to misleading price indications relating to the supply of services, accommodation and other facilities. Such misleading indications could conceivably amount to deceit.

[52] *e.g. Gibbons v Proctor* (1891) 64 L.T. 594; *Williams v Carwardine* (1833) 5 C. & P. 566; 4 B. & Ad. 621, below, p.35.

[53] See below, p.37, for the meaning of "unilateral contracts".

[54] [1893] 1 Q.B. 256.

[55] Contrast *Lambert v Lewis* [1982] A.C. 225 at 262, *per* Stephenson L.J. (affirmed without reference to this point [1982] A.C. 271).

[56] [1995] N.L.J. 1815.

holiday". A majority of the Court of Appeal held that these words constituted an offer from ABTA since, on the objective test,[57] they would reasonably be regarded as such by a member of the public booking a holiday with an ABTA member.

Advertisements of bilateral contracts are not often held to be offers since such advertisements do often lead to further bargaining, and since the advertiser may legitimately wish, before becoming bound, to assure himself that the other party is able to perform his part of any contract which may result. Thus a newspaper advertisement that goods are for sale is not an offer,[58] an advertisement that an auction sale will be held is not an offer to a person who comes to bid[59]; an advertisement that a scholarship examination will be held is not an offer to a candidate[60]; and the circulation of a price-list by a wine merchant is only an invitation to treat.[61] The same is probably true of a menu displayed, or handed to a customer, in a restaurant.[62] On the other hand, a notice at the entrance to an automatic car park may be an offer which can be accepted by driving in[63] and a display of deck chairs for *hire* has been held to be an offer.[64] No useful purpose is served by attempting to reconcile all the cases on this subject, since the question is one of intention in each case.[65]

(4) Timetables and passenger tickets

There is a remarkable diversity of views on the question just when a contract is made between a carrier and an intending passenger. It has been said that rail carriers made offers by issuing advertisements stating the times at and conditions under which trains would run[66]; and that a road carrier made offers to intending passengers by the act of running buses.[67] Such offers could be accepted by an indication on the part of the passenger that he wished to travel, *e.g.* by applying for a ticket or getting on the bus. Another view is that the carrier makes the offer at a later stage, by issuing the ticket; and that this offer is accepted by the passenger's retention of the ticket without objection,[68] or (even later) by claiming the accommodation offered in the ticket.[69] On this view the passenger makes no more than an invitation to treat when he asks for the ticket to be issued to him; and the offer contained in the ticket may be made to, and accepted by, the passenger even though the fare is paid by a third party (*e.g.* the passenger's employer[70]). Where the booking is made in advance, through a travel agent, yet a third view has been

---

[57] See above, p.8.

[58] *Partridge v Crittenden* [1968] 1 W.L.R. 1204; contrast *Lefkowitz v Great Minneapolis Surplus Stores* 86 N.W. 2d 689 (1957).

[59] *Harris v Nickerson* (1873) L.R. 8 Q.B. 286.

[60] *Rooke v Dawson* [1895] 1 Ch.480.

[61] *Grainger & Sons v Gough* [1896] A.C. 325; *quaere* whether a price-list sent on request to a single customer could be an offer.

[62] cf. *Guildford v Lockyer* [1975] Crim.L.R. 236.

[63] *Thornton v Shoe Lane Parking Ltd* [1971] 2 Q.B. 163 at 169.

[64] *Chapelton v Barry Urban DC* [1940] 1 K.B. 532.

[65] Contrast *Harvey v Facey* [1893] A.C. 552 with *Philp & Co v Knoblauch*, 1907 S.C. 994.

[66] *Denton v GN Ry* (1856) 5 E. & B. 860; *Thompson v LM&S Ry* [1930] 1 K.B. 41 at 47; perhaps because such carriers could not refuse to carry? See now Railways Act 1993, s.123.

[67] *Wilkie v LPTB* [1947] 1 All E.R. 258 at 259.

[68] *Thornton v Shoe Lane Parking Ltd* [1971] 2 Q.B. 163 at 169; *Cockerton v Naviera Aznar SA* [1960] 2 Lloyd's Rep. 450. Such acceptance would be by conduct rather than by silence: cf. below, p.35.

[69] *MacRobertson–Miller Airline Service v Commissioner of State Taxation* (1975) 8 A.L.R. 131; the principle resembles that stated in *Heskell v Continental Express Ltd* [1950] 1 All E.R. 1033 at 1037 in relation to carriage of goods by sea.

[70] *Hobbs v L&SW Ry* (1875) L.R. 10 Q.B. 111 at 119, as explained in the *MacRobertson–Miller* case above at 147; consideration for the promises of both parties would be provided on the principle of *Gore v Van der Lann* [1967] 2 Q.B. 31, below, p.157.

expressed: that the contract is concluded when the carrier indicates, even before issuing the ticket, that he "accepts" the booking[71] or when he issues the ticket.[72] On this view, it is the passenger who makes the offer. The authorities yield no single rule: one can only say that the exact time of contracting depends in each case on the wording of the relevant document and on the circumstances in which it was issued.

(5) Tenders

At common law, a statement that goods are to be sold by tender is not normally an offer, so that the person making the statement is not bound to sell to the person making the highest tender.[73] Similarly a statement inviting tenders for the supply of goods or for the execution of works is not normally an offer.[74] The offer comes from the person who submits the tender and there is no contract until the person asking for the tenders accepts[75] one of them. The preparation of a tender may involve considerable expense; but the tenderer normally incurs this at his own risk. The position is different where the person who invites the tenders states in the invitation that he binds himself to accept the highest offer to buy[76] (or, as the case may be, the lowest offer to sell or to provide the specified services).[77] In such cases, the invitation may be regarded *either* as itself an offer *or* as an invitation to submit offers coupled with an undertaking to accept the highest (or, as the case may be, the lowest) offer; and the contract is concluded as soon as the highest offer to buy (or lowest offer to sell, etc.) is communicated.[78] There is also an intermediate possibility. This is illustrated by a case[79] in which an invitation to submit tenders was sent by a local authority to seven selected parties; the invitation stated that tenders submitted after a specified deadline would not be considered. It was held that the authority was contractually bound to consider (though not to accept[80]) a tender submitted before the deadline.

The common law position stated above is in some situations modified by legislation, for example by regulations[81] which give effect to EC Council directives, the object of which is to prevent discrimination in the award of major contracts for public works, supplies and services in one Member State against nationals of another Member State. These regulations restrict the freedom of the body seeking tenders to decide which tender it will accept and provide a remedy in damages for a person who has made a tender and is prejudiced by breach of the rules.

---

[71] *The Eagle* [1977] 2 Lloyd's Rep. 70; *The Dragon* [1979] 1 Lloyd's Rep. 257 (affirmed [1980] 2 Lloyd's Rep. 415) *Oceanic Sun Line Special Shipping Co v Fay* (1988) 165 C.L.R. 97; *cf. The Anwar al Sabar* [1980] 2 Lloyd's Rep. 261 at 263 (carriage of goods by sea).

[72] *The Mikhail Lermontov* [1991] 2 Lloyd's Rep. 155 at 159, reversed on other grounds: *Baltic Shipping Co v Dillon* (1993) 176 C.L.R. 344.

[73] *Spencer v Harding* (1870) L.R. 5 C.P. 561.

[74] *ibid.* at 564.

[75] See below, p.21.

[76] *Spencer v Harding*, above, at 563.

[77] See *William Lacey (Hounslow) Ltd v Davis* [1957] 1 W.L.R. 932 at 939; *cf. MJB Enterprises Ltd v Defence Construction Ltd* (1999) 15 Const.L.J. 455: promise to accept lowest *compliant* tender broken by accepting lowest non-compliant one (Supreme Court of Canada).

[78] *Harvela Investments Ltd v Royal Trust of Canada (CI) Ltd* [1986] A.C. 207 at 224–225.

[79] *Blackpool and Fylde Aero Club Ltd v Blackpool BC* [1990] 1 W.L.R. 1195. No decision was reached on the quantum of damages: as to this, see below, p.955.

[80] *cf. Fairclough Building v Port Talbot BC* (1992) 62 B.L.R. 82.

[81] SI 1991/2679; SI 1991/2680, applied in *R. v Portsmouth CC, Ex p. Coles, The Times,* November 13, 1996; SI 1992/3279; SI 1993/3228 (as amended by SI 2000/2009), applied in *R. v S of S for the Environment, Ex p. Harrow LBC* [1996] E.G.C.S. 2; Craig in *Consensus ad Idem, Essays in the Law of Contract in Honour of Guenter Treitel* (Rose ed.), pp.148–151. See also Environmental Protection Act 1990, Sch.2, Pt II, applied in *R. v Avon CC, Ex p. Terry Adams Ltd, The Times,* January 20, 1994.

(6) Sales of shares

A company which, in commercial language,[82] makes an "offer to the public", asking them to subscribe for shares in it, does not in law offer to sell the shares. It invites members of the public to apply for them, reserving the right to decide how many (if any) to allot to each applicant.[83] But where a company makes a "rights" issue of shares to its existing shareholders, entitling each shareholder to buy a number of new shares in proportion to the shares he already holds, the letter informing the shareholder of his rights is regarded as an offer.[84] This letter will set out the precise rights of each shareholder, thus showing an intention on the part of the company to be bound, if the shareholder takes up his rights.

3. Where and When an Offer Takes Effect

In one sense an offer cannot take effect until it is received, for until the offeree knows about it he can take no action in reliance on it. But for the purpose of determining whether a contract can be sued on in a particular court it has been held that an offer sent through the post was made *where* it was posted.[85] The question *when* such an offer was made may also arise for the purpose of determining whether the offer has expired by lapse of time[86] before it was accepted. In *Adams v Lindsell*[87] an offer to sell wool was made by a letter which was misdirected. The letter reached the offerees two days late; and they immediately posted an acceptance which was held binding because the delay arose "entirely from the mistake of the [offerors]".[88] From this emphasis on the offerors' fault, it seems that the decision might have gone the other way if the delay had been due to some other factor, *e.g.* to an accident in the post. In such a case the time for acceptance probably runs from the moment at which the letter would, but for such accident, have reached the offeree's address. Even where the delay is due to the offeror's fault, the offer may have lapsed before its receipt by the offeree. Obviously, the offer could not be accepted if it reached the offeree only after the date expressly specified in it as the last date for acceptance. The position is probably the same where it is clear to the offeree that there has been such a long delay in the transmission of the offer as to make it obvious to the offeree that the offer was "stale" when it reached him.

SECTION 2. ACCEPTANCE

1. Acceptance Defined

An acceptance is a final and unqualified expression of assent to the terms of an offer. The objective test of agreement applies to an acceptance no less than to an offer.[89] On this test, a mere acknowledgment of an offer would not be an acceptance; nor would a person to whom an offer to sell goods had been made accept it merely by replying that it was

---

[82] And in the terminology of Companies Act 1985, ss.80(1), 742A (as inserted by Financial Services and Markets Act 2000 (Consequential Amendments and Repeals) Order 2001 (SI 2001/3649), para.29) and 744 and of Financial Services and Markets Act 2000, s.103(4).

[83] *e.g. Hebb's Case* (1867) L.R. 4 Eq. 9; *Harris' Case* (1872) L.R. 7 Ch.App. 587; *Wall's Case* (1872) 42 L.J.Ch. 372; *Nicol's Case* (1883) 29 Ch.D. 421 at 426; *National Westminster Bank plc v IRC* [1995] 1 A.C. 119 at 126; *cf. Wallace's Case* [1900] 2 Ch.671; *Rust v Abbey Life Ins Co* [1979] 2 Lloyd's Rep. 335.

[84] *Jackson v Turquand* (1869) L.R. 4 H.L. 305.

[85] *Taylor v Jones* (1871) 1 C.P.D. 87.

[86] See below, p.43.

[87] (1818) 1 B. & Ald. 681.

[88] *ibid.* at 683.

[89] See above, p.8; *Inland Revenue Commissioners v Fry* [2001] S.T.C. 1715 at [6, 7]; *cf.* in criminal law, *DPP v Holmes*, 152 J.P.N. 738.

his "intention to place an order"[90] or by asking for an invoice.[91] The mere acknowl-edgment of an offer, in the sense of a communication stating simply that the offer had been received, would likewise not be an acceptance. But an "acknowledgment" may by its express terms or, in a particular context by implication, contain a statement that the sender agreed to the terms of the offer and that he was therefore accepting it: this might, for example, be the effect of an "acknowledgment" of a customer's order in website trading.[92] Where the offer makes alternative proposals, the reply must make it clear to which of them the assent is directed. In one case an offer to build a freight terminal was made by a tender quoting in the alternative a fixed price and a price varying with the cost of labour and materials. The offeree purported to accept "your tender" and it was held that there was no contract as there was no way of telling which price term had been accepted.[93]

(1) Continuing negotiations

When parties carry on lengthy negotiations, it may be hard to say exactly when an offer has been made and accepted. As negotiations progress, each party may make concessions or new demands and the parties may in the end disagree as to whether they had ever agreed at all. The court must then look at the whole correspondence and decide whether, on its true construction, the parties had agreed to the same terms. If so, there is a contract even though both parties, or one of them, had reservations not expressed in the correspondence.[94] The court will be particularly anxious to reach such a conclusion where the performance which was the subject-matter of the negotiations has actually been rendered. In one such case, a building sub-contract was held to have come into existence (even though the parties had not yet reached agreement when the contractor began the work) as during its progress outstanding matters were resolved by further negotiations.[95] The contract may then be given retrospective effect so as to cover acts done before the final agreement was reached.[96]

Businessmen do not, any more than the courts, find it easy to say precisely when they have reached agreement, and may continue to negotiate after they appear to have agreed to the same terms. The court will then look at the entire course of the negotiations to decide whether an apparently unqualified acceptance did in fact conclude the agree-ment.[97] If it did, the fact that the parties continued negotiations after this point will not

---

[90] *OTM Ltd v Hydranautics* [1981] 2 Lloyd's Rep. 211 at 214.

[91] *Michael Gerson (Leasing) Ltd v Wilkinson* [2000] Q.B. 514 at 530 (where there was probably no offer: see above, p.11).

[92] In the Electronic Commerce (EC Directive) Regulations 2002, SI 2002/2013 (implementing most of the EC Directive 2000/31 on Electronic Commerce ([2000] O.J. L178/1)), reg.11, the words "acknowledge" and "acknowledgement" seem to be used in this sense.

[93] *Peter Lind & Co Ltd v Mersey Docks & Harbour Board* [1972] 2 Lloyd's Rep. 234.

[94] *Kennedy v Lee* (1817) 3 Mer. 441; *cf. Cie de Commerce, etc., v Parkinson Stove Co* [1953] 2 Lloyd's Rep. 487; B.S.E., 17 M.L.R. 476; *Port Sudan Cotton Co v Govindaswamy Chettiar & Sons* [1977] 2 Lloyd's Rep. 5; *Thoresen Car Ferries Ltd v Weymouth Portland BC* [1977] 2 Lloyd's Rep. 614; *OTM Ltd v Hydranautics* [1981] 2 Lloyd's Rep. 211 at 215; *The Bay Ridge* [1999] 2 All E.R. (Comm) 306.

[95] *G Percy Trentham Ltd v Archital Luxfer Ltd* [1993] 1 Lloyd's Rep. 25. The *Peter Lind* case, above, n.93, shows that the factor of performance of the work is not decisive, though it may (as in that case) give rise to a restitutionary claim: see below, p.1062.

[96] *G Percy Trentham* case, above at 27.

[97] *Hussey v Horne-Payne* (1878) 4 App.Cas. 311; *Bristol, Cardiff & Swansea Aerated Bread Co v Maggs* (1890) 44 Ch.D. 616; *British Guiana Credit Corporation v Da Silva* [1965] 1 W.L.R. 248; *Container Transport International Inc v Oceanus Mutual, etc. Association* [1984] 1 Lloyd's Rep. 476; *The Astyanax* [1985] 2 Lloyd's Rep. 109 at 112; *The Intra Transporter* [1986] 2 Lloyd's Rep. 132; *Pagnan SpA v Granaria BV* [1986] 1 Lloyd's Rep. 547; *Pagnan SpA v Feed Products Ltd* [1987] 2 Lloyd's Rep. 601 at 619; *Ignazio Messina & Co v Polskie Linie Oceaniczne* [1995] 2 Lloyd's Rep. 566; *The Frotanorte* [1996] 2 Lloyd's Rep. 461.

normally affect the existence of the contract[98]; it will do so only if the continuation of the negotiations can be construed as an agreement to rescind the contract. *A fortiori*, the binding force of an oral contract is not affected or altered merely by the fact that, after its conclusion, one party sends to the other a document containing terms significantly different from those which had been orally agreed.[99]

(2) Acceptance by conduct

An offer may be accepted by conduct, *e.g.* by supplying or despatching goods in response to an offer to buy them,[1] or by beginning to render services in response to an offer in the form of a request for them.[2] Similarly, an offer to supply goods (made by sending them to the offeree) can be accepted by using them.[3] Conduct will, however, only have this effect if the offeree did the act with the intention (ascertained in accordance with the objective principle[4]) of accepting the offer. Thus a buyer's taking delivery of goods after the conclusion of an oral contract of sale will not amount to his acceptance of written terms which differ significantly from those orally agreed and which are sent to him by the seller after the making of that contract but before taking delivery.[5] That conduct is then referable to the oral contract rather than to the attempted later variation. Nor is a company's offer to insure a car accepted by taking the car out on the road, if there is evidence that the driver intended to insure with another company.[6] *A fortiori*, there is no acceptance where the offeree's conduct clearly indicates an intention to reject the offer. This was the position in a Scottish case where a notice on a package containing computer software stated that opening the package would indicate acceptance of the terms on which the supply was made, and the customer returned the package unopened.[7]

Where it is alleged that an offer has been made, or accepted, by conduct it is often hard to say exactly what terms have been agreed. The difficulty may be so great as to lead to the conclusion that no agreement was reached at all.[8] But the court has considerable power to resolve uncertainties. If the offer is silent as to the rate of payment the court may imply a term that a reasonable amount should be paid.[9] Or the court may import into the contract the terms of another contract between the parties, or of a draft

---

[98] *Perry v Suffields Ltd* [1916] 2 Ch.187; *Davies v Sweet* [1962] 2 Q.B. 300; *Cranleigh Precision Engineering Ltd v Bryant* [1965] 1 W.L.R. 1293 *The Good Helmsman* [1981] 1 Lloyd's Rep. 377 at 409, 416.

[99] *Jayaar Impex Ltd v Toaken Group Ltd* [1996] 2 Lloyd's Rep. 437.

[1] *Harvey v Johnston* (1848) 6 C.B. 295 at 305; *cf. Steven v Bromley & Son* [1919] 2 K.B. 722 at 728; *The Saronikos* [1986] 2 Lloyd's Rep. 277; *Interfoto Picture Library Ltd v Stiletto Visual Programmes Ltd* [1989] Q.B. 433 at 436; *Re Charge Card Services* [1989] Ch.497 at 512; *Carlyle Finance Ltd v Pallas Industrial Finance Ltd* [1999] 1 All E.R. (Comm) 659 at 670; and see below, p.23.

[2] *The Kurnia Dewi* [1997] 1 Lloyd's Rep. 533.

[3] *Weatherby v Banham* (1832) 5 C. & P. 228; or even by using part of the goods: *cf. Hart v Mills* (1846) 15 L.J.Ex. 200. It is assumed that the goods are not "unsolicited" within legislation against "inertia selling".

[4] See above, p.8.

[5] *Jayaar Impex Ltd v Toaken Group Ltd* [1992] 2 Lloyd's Rep. 437.

[6] *Taylor v Allon* [1966] 1 Q.B. 304. The objective principle could not apply as the conduct alleged to constitute the acceptance had not come to the notice of the offeror; *cf.*, in another context, *Re Leyland Daf Ltd* [1994] 4 All E.R. 300, affirmed sub nom. *Powdrill v Watson* [1995] 2 A.C. 394.

[7] *Beta Computers (Europe) v Adobe Systems (Europe)* 1996 S.L.T. 604; even opening the package would not necessarily be an acceptance so as to incorporate the printed terms: see Tapper in *Consensus ad Idem, Essays in the Law of Contract in Honour of Guenter Treitel* (Rose ed.), pp.287–288.

[8] *Capital Finance Co Ltd v Bray* [1964] 1 W.L.R. 323.

[9] Sale of Goods Act 1979, s.8(2); Supply of Goods and Services Act 1982, s.15(1); *cf. Steven v Bromley & Son*, above; see below, p.52.

agreement between them,[10] or even of a contract between one of them and a third party.[11]

(3) Acceptance must be unqualified

A communication may fail to take effect as an acceptance because it attempts to vary the terms of the offer. Thus an offer to sell 1,200 tons of iron is not accepted by a reply asking for 800 tons[12]; an offer to pay a *fixed* price for building work is not accepted by a promise to do the work for a *variable* price[13]; an offer to *supply* goods is not accepted by an "order" for their "supply and installation".[14] Nor, generally, is an offer accepted by a reply which varies one of its other terms (*e.g.* that specifying the time of perform-ance)[15] or by a reply which is intended to introduce an entirely new term.[16] Such replies are not acceptances but counter-offers[17] which the original offeror can accept or reject.

The requirement that the acceptance must be unqualified does not, however, mean that there must be precise *verbal* correspondence between offer and acceptance. An acceptance could be effective even though it departed from the wording of the offer by making express some term which the law would in any case imply.[18] And a reply which adds some new provision by way of indulgence to the offeror (*e.g.* one allowing him to postpone payment) may be an acceptance. Conversely, an acceptance in which the acceptor asks for extra time to pay may be effective, so long as he makes it clear that he is prepared to perform in accordance with the terms of the offer even if his request is refused.[19] It is also possible for a communication which introduces a new term to amount at the same time to a firm acceptance and also to a further offer relating to the same subject-matter but emanating from the original offeree. In such a case, there will be a contract on the terms of the original offer, but none on the terms of the new offer unless that is, in turn, accepted.[20]

After parties have reached agreement, the offer and acceptance may be set out in formal documents. The purpose of such documents may be merely to record the agreed terms[21]; and where one of the documents performs this function accurately while the other fails to do so, the discrepancy between them will not prevent the formation of a

---

[10] *e.g. Brogden v Metropolitan Ry* (1877) 2 App.Cas. 666; contrast *D&M Trailers (Halifax) Ltd v Stirling* [1978] R.T.R. 468, *Jayaar Impex Ltd v Toaken Ltd* [1996] 2 Lloyd's Rep. 437, where the conduct of the buyer was referable to the earlier oral contract (above, n.5) rather than to the document sent by the seller, and *UK Safety Group Ltd v Heane* [1998] 2 B.C.L.C. 208.

[11] *e.g. Pyrene Co Ltd v Scindia Navigation Co Ltd* [1954] 2 Q.B. 402, see below, p.638.

[12] *Tinn v Hoffmann & Co* (1873) 29 L.T. 271; *cf. Holland v Eyre* (1825) 2 Sim. & St. 194; *Jordan v Norton* (1838) 4 M. & W. 155; *Harrison v Battye* [1975] 1 W.L.R. 58.

[13] *North West Leicestershire DC v East Midlands Housing Association* [1981] 1 W.L.R. 1396.

[14] *Butler Machine Tool Co Ltd v Ex-Cell-O Corp (England) Ltd* [1979] 1 W.L.R. 401.

[15] *ibid.*; *North West Leicestershire DC v East Midlands Housing Association* [1981] 1 W.L.R. 1396; *cf. Brinkibon Ltd v Stahag Stahl und Stahlwarenhandelsgesellschaft mbH* [1983] 2 A.C. 34.

[16] *Jackson v Turquand* (1869) L.R. 4 H.L. 305; *Northland Aircraft Ltd v Dennis Ferranti Meters Ltd* (1970) 114 S.J. 845; *Bircham & Co Nominees (No.2) Ltd v Worrell Holdings Ltd* [2001] EWCA Civ 725; (2001) 82 P. & C.R. 427 at [11]. Statements which are *not* intended to add new terms do not vitiate the acceptance: *Clive v Beaumont* (1847) 1 De G. & Sm. 397; *Simpson v Hughes* (1897) 66 L.J.Ch. 334; *Butler Machine Tool Co Ltd v Ex-Cell-O Corp (England) Ltd* [1979] 1 W.L.R. 401.

[17] *Jones v Daniel* [1894] 2 Ch.332; *Von Hartzfeld-Wildenburg v Alexander* [1912] 1 Ch.284; *Love & Stewart Ltd v S Instone & Co Ltd* (1917) 33 T.L.R. 457; *Lark v Outhwaite* [1991] 2 Lloyd's Rep. 132 at 139. For an exception, see Vienna Convention (below, p.29), Art.19(2).

[18] *Lark v Outhwaite*, above at 139.

[19] *cf. Global Tankers Inc v Amercoat Europa NV* [1975] 1 Lloyd's Rep. 666 at 671; *G Percy Trentham Ltd v Archital Luxfer Ltd* [1993] 1 Lloyd's Rep. 25 at 28.

[20] *The Master Stelios* [1983] 1 Lloyd's Rep. 356; *Society of Lloyd's v Twinn, The Times*, April 4, 2000.

[21] *e.g. OTM Ltd v Hydranautics* [1981] 2 Lloyd's Rep. 211 at 215; *cf.* below, p.54.

contract. In such a case, the court can rectify[22] the document which fails to record the agreed terms, and a contract will be on those terms.[23]

(4) The battle of forms

The growing use of printed contract forms by one or both parties has given rise to problems with regard to the rule that the acceptance must correspond to the offer. Two situations call for discussion.

First, A may make an offer to B by asking for a supply of goods or services. B may reply that he is willing to supply the goods or services on his "usual conditions". *Prima facie*, B's statement is a counter-offer which A is free to accept or reject, and he may accept it by accepting the goods or services. If he does so, there is a contract between A and B, though the question whether B's "usual conditions" form part of it may depend on a number of further factors which will be discussed in Chapter 7.[24]

Secondly, *each* party may purport to contract with reference to his own set of standard terms and these terms may conflict. In *BRS v Arthur V Crutchley Ltd*[25] the claimants delivered a consignment of whisky to the defendants for storage. Their driver handed the defendants a delivery note purporting to incorporate the claimants' "conditions of carriage". The note was stamped by the defendants: "Received under [the defendants'] conditions". It was held that this amounted to a counter-offer which the claimants had accepted by handing over the goods, and the contract therefore incorporated the defendants' and not the claimants' conditions.

This case gave some support to the so-called "last shot" doctrine: *i.e.* to the view that, where conflicting communications are exchanged, each is a counter-offer so that if a contract results at all (*e.g.* from an acceptance by conduct) it must be on the terms of the final document in the series leading to the conclusion of the contract.[26] But this view requires some modification in the light of *Butler Machine Tool Co Ltd v Ex-Cell-O Corporation (England) Ltd.*[27] In that case sellers offered to supply a machine for a specified sum. The offer was expressed to be subject to certain terms and conditions, including a "price escalation clause", by which the amount payable by the buyers was to depend on "prices ruling upon date of delivery". In reply, the buyers placed an order for the machine on a form setting out their own terms and conditions, which differed from those of the sellers in containing no price-escalation clause and in various other respects.[28] It also contained a tear-off slip to be signed by the sellers and returned to the buyers, stating that the sellers accepted the order "on the terms and conditions stated therein". The sellers did so sign the slip and returned it with a letter saying that they were "entering" the order "in accordance with" their offer. This communication from the sellers was held to be an acceptance of the buyers' counter-offer[29] so that the resulting contract was on the buyers' terms, and the sellers were not entitled to the benefit of the price escalation clause. The sellers' reply to the buyers' order did not prevail (though it was the "last shot" in the series) because the reference in it to the

---

[22] See below, p.321.

[23] *Domb v Isoz* [1980] Ch.548.

[24] See below, pp.216–221.

[25] [1967] 2 All E.R. 285 at 287; [1968] 1 W.L.R. 811 at 817; *cf. OTM Ltd v Hydranautics* [1981] 2 Lloyd's Rep. 211; *Muirhead v Industrial Tank Specialities Ltd* [1986] Q.B. 507 at 530; *Sauter Automation v Goodman (Mechanical Services)* (1984) 34 Build.L.R. 81.

[26] As in *Zambia Steel & Building Supplies Ltd v James Clark & Eaton Ltd* [1986] 2 Lloyd's Rep. 225.

[27] [1979] 1 W.L.R. 401, esp. at 405; Adams, 95 L.Q.R. 481; Rawlings, 42 M.L.R. 715.

[28] See above, p.19 at n.14 and 15.

[29] *per* Lawton and Buckley L.JJ.; Lord Denning M.R. also uses this analysis, but prefers the alternative approach of considering "the documents . . . as a whole": see at 405 and *cf.* below, p.47.

original offer was not made for the purpose of reiterating all the terms of that offer, but only for the purpose of identifying the subject-matter. It would, however, have been possible for the sellers to have turned their final communication into a counter-offer by explicitly referring in it, not only to the subject-matter of the original offer, but also to all its other terms. In that case no contract would have been concluded, since the buyers had made it clear before the machine was delivered that they did not agree to the "price escalation" clause.[30]

Thus it is possible by careful draftsmanship to avoid losing the battle of forms, but not (if the other party is equally careful) to win it. In the *Butler Machine Tool* case, for example, sellers' conditions included one by which their terms were to "prevail over any terms and conditions in Buyer's order"; but this failed (in consequence of the terms of the buyers' counter-offer) to produce the effect desired by the sellers.[31] The most that the draftsman can be certain of achieving is the stalemate situation in which there is no contract at all. Such a conclusion will often be inconvenient,[32] though where the goods are nevertheless delivered it may lead to a liability on the part of the buyers to pay a reasonable price.[33]

The above discussion is concerned with the effect of the submission of a document or documents containing terms *before* the alleged contract is made. The submission of such a document by one party *after* the making of the contract will not affect the existence of the contract,[34] nor will the terms of the document form part of the contract unless they are in turn accepted as variations of the contract, either expressly or by conduct.

(5) Acceptance of tenders

The submission of a tender normally amounts to an offer,[35] and the effect of an "acceptance" of the tender depends on the interpretation of the documents. Where, for example, a tender is submitted for the construction of a building, acceptance will normally create a binding contract unless it is expressly stipulated that there is to be no contract until certain formal documents have been executed.[36] But where a tender is made for an indefinite amount, *e.g.* for the supply of "such quantities (not exceeding 1,000 tons) as you may order" the person to whom the tender is submitted does not incur any liability merely by "accepting" it. He becomes liable only when he places an order for the goods[37]; and he is not bound to place any order at all (unless he has expressly or by necessary implication[38] indicated in his invitation for tenders that he would do so).[39] Once an order has been placed, the party who has submitted the tender is bound to fulfil it.[40] Whether he can withdraw before an order has been placed, or avoid liability with regard to future orders, depends on the interpretation of the tender. If it

---

[30] At 406, *per* Lawton L.J.

[31] *cf. Matter of Doughboy Industries Inc* 233 N.Y.S. 2d. 488 at 490 (1962): "The buyer and seller accomplished a legal equivalent to the irresistible force colliding with the immoveable object".

[32] It seems to have been rejected for this reason in *Johnson Matthey Bankers Ltd v State Trading Corp of India* [1984] 1 Lloyd's Rep. 427.

[33] *cf. Peter Lind & Co Ltd v Mersey Docks & Harbour Board* [1972] 2 Lloyd's Rep. 234, above, p.17; McKendrick, 8 O.J.L.S. 197.

[34] *Jayaar Impex Ltd v Toaken Group Ltd* [1996] 2 Lloyd's Rep. 437; *cf.* below, pp.52, 200.

[35] See above, p.15.

[36] See below, p.54.

[37] *Percival v London County Council Asylum, etc. Committee* (1918) 87 L.J.K.B. 677.

[38] *e.g. Sylvan Crest Sand & Gravel Co v US*, 150 F. 2d. 642 (1945).

[39] *cf. Harvela Investments Ltd v Royal Trust Co of Canada (CI) Ltd* [1986] A.C. 207.

[40] *Great Northern Ry v Witham* (1873) L.R. 9 C.P. 16; *cf.* a similar rule applied to "declarations" under an "open cover" insurance in *Citadel Insurance Co v Atlantic Union Insurance Co* [1982] 2 Lloyd's Rep. 543.

merely means "I will supply such quantities as you may order" he can withdraw before a definite order is placed.[41] But he will not be entitled to withdraw if the tender means "I hereby bind myself to execute any orders which you may place", and if there is some consideration for this undertaking.[42]

(6) Acceptance by tender

An invitation for tenders may, exceptionally, amount to an offer, *e.g.* where the person issuing the invitation binds himself to accept the highest tender to buy (or the lowest tender to sell).[43] The acceptance then takes the form of the submission of a tender; but difficulties can arise where several tenders are made and one (or more) of them takes the form of a so-called "referential bid". In *Harvela Investments Ltd v Royal Trust Co of Canada (CI) Ltd*[44] an invitation for the submission of "offers" to buy shares was addressed to two persons; it stated that the prospective sellers bound themselves to accept the "highest offer". One of the persons to whom the invitation was addressed made a bid of a fixed sum while the other submitted a "referential bid" undertaking to pay either a fixed sum or a specified amount in excess of the bid made by the other, whichever was the higher amount. It was held that this "referential bid" was ineffective and that the submission of the other bid had concluded the contract. The House of Lords stressed that the bids were, by the terms of the invitation, to be confidential, so that neither bidder would know the amount bid by the other. In these circumstances the object of the invitation, which was to ascertain the highest amount which each of the persons to whom it was addressed was willing to pay, would have been defeated by allowing it to be accepted by a "referential bid".

2. Communication of Acceptance

(1) General rule

The general rule is that an acceptance has no effect until it is communicated to the offeror.[45] One reason for this rule is the difficulty of proving an uncommunicated decision to accept "for the Devil himself knows not the intent of a man".[46] But this is not the sole reason for the rule, which applies even where the fact of acceptance could be proved with perfect certainty, *e.g.* where a person writes his acceptance on a piece of paper which he simply keeps[47]; where a company resolves to accept an application for shares, records the resolution, but does not communicate it to the applicant[48]; where a person decides to accept an offer to sell goods to him and instructs his bank to pay the seller, but neither he nor the bank gives notice of this fact to the seller[49]; or where a

---

[41] *Great Northern Ry v Witham*, above, at 19.

[42] *Percival v London County Council Asylum etc. Committee* (1918) 87 L.J.K.B. 677; *cf. Miller v F A Sadd & Son Ltd* [1981] 3 All E.R. 265. For an exception to the requirement of consideration in the law of insurance, see the *Citadel* case (above n.40) 546; see below, p.154.

[43] See above, p.15.

[44] [1986] A.C. 207.

[45] *M'Iver v Richardson* (1813) 1 M. & S. 557; *Mozley v Tinkler* (1835) C.M. & R. 692; *Ex p. Stark* [1897] 1 Ch.575; *Holwell Securities Ltd v Hughes* [1974] 1 W.L.R. 155 at 157; *The Leonidas D* [1985] 1 W.L.R. 925 at 937.

[46] *Anon.* (1478) Y.B. 17 Edw. IV Pasch, f.1–pl.2, cited in Fifoot, *History & Sources of the Common Law*, p.253.

[47] *Kennedy v Thomassen* [1929] 1 Ch.426; *Brogden v Metropolitan Ry* (1877) 2 App.Cas. 666 at 692.

[48] *Best's Case* (1865) 2 D.J. & S. 650; *cf. Gunn's Case* (1867) L.R. 3 Ch.App. 40.

[49] *Brinkibon v Stahag Stahl und Stahlwarenhandelsgesellschaft mbH* [1983] 2 A.C. 34.

person communicates the acceptance only to his own agent.[50] The main reason for the rule is that it could cause hardship to an offeror if he were bound without knowing that his offer had been accepted. It follows that there can be a contract if the offeror knows of the acceptance although it was not brought to his notice *by the offeree*.[51] However, there will be no contract if the communication is made by a third party without the authority of the offeree in circumstances indicating that the offeree's decision to accept was not yet regarded by him as irrevocable.[52]

For an acceptance to be "communicated" it must normally be brought to the notice of the offeror. Thus if an oral acceptance is "drowned by an aircraft flying overhead" or is spoken into a telephone after the line has gone dead, or is so indistinct that the offeror does not hear it, there is no contract.[53] The requirement of "communication" may, however, sometimes be satisfied even though the acceptance has not actually come to the notice of the offeror: *e.g.* where a written notice of acceptance is left at his address.[54]

(2) Exceptional cases

In a number of cases, an acceptance is, or may be, effective although it is not communicated to the offeror.

(a) COMMUNICATION TO OFFEROR'S AGENT. The effect of giving an acceptance to the agent of the offeror depends on the nature of the agent's authority.[55] If the agent has authority to *receive* the acceptance, it takes effect as soon as it is communicated to him, *e.g.* if acceptance of an offer made by a company is communicated to its managing director. But if the agent is only authorised to *transmit* the acceptance to the offeror, it may not take effect until the offeror receives it, *e.g.* if a written acceptance is given to a messenger.

(b) CONDUCT OF OFFEROR. An offeror may be precluded from denying that he received the acceptance if "it is his own fault that he did not get it", *e.g.* "if the listener on the telephone does not catch the words of acceptance, but nevertheless does not . . . ask for them to be repeated"[56]; or if the acceptance is sent during business hours by telex but is simply not read by anyone in the offeror's office when it is there transcribed on his machine.[57] If such a message is received out of business hours, it probably takes effect at the beginning of the next business day.[58]

(c) TERMS OF OFFER. An offer may expressly or impliedly waive the requirement that acceptance must be communicated. This is often the case where an offer invites acceptance by conduct. Thus where an offer to sell goods is made by sending them to the offeree, it may be accepted by simply using them without communicating this fact to the offeror.[59] Similarly, it seems that, where an offer to buy goods is made by asking the seller to supply them, it may be accepted by simply despatching the goods to the

---

[50] *Hebb's Case* (1867) L.R. 4 Eq. 9; *Kennedy v Thomassen* [1929] 1 Ch.426.

[51] *Bloxham's Case* (1864) 33 Beav. 529; (1864) 4 D.J. & S. 447; *Levita's Case* (1867) L.R. 3 Ch.App. 36.

[52] This seems to be the best explanation of *Powell v Lee* (1908) 99 L.T. 284.

[53] *Entores Ltd v Miles Far East Corp* [1955] 2 Q.B. 327 at 332.

[54] *cf.* below, p.41.

[55] *Henthorn v Fraser* [1892] 2 Ch.27 at 33.

[56] *Entores* case [1955] 2 Q.B. 327 at 333.

[57] *cf. The Brimnes* [1975] Q.B. 929.

[58] *The Pamela* [1995] 2 Lloyd's Rep. 249 at 252; *The Peter Schmidt* [1998] 2 Lloyd's Rep. 1.

[59] *Weatherby v Banham* (1832) 5 C. & P. 228; *cf. Minories Finance Ltd v Afribank Nigeria Ltd* [1995] 1 Lloyd's Rep. 134 at 140; and see above, p.9, n.15.

buyer.[60] And a tenant can accept an offer of a new tenancy by simply staying on the premises.[61]

Communication of acceptance is scarcely ever required in the case of an offer of a unilateral contract.[62] Thus in *Carlill v Carbolic Smoke Ball Co*,[63] the court rejected the argument that the claimant should have notified the defendants of her acceptance of their offer before starting to use the smoke ball. Similarly, where a reward is offered for the return of lost property the finder need not notify the owner in advance of his acceptance: he can accept by finding and returning the thing; and once he has found it the owner probably cannot withdraw.[64] Again, the contract which arises[65] between a bank which has issued a credit card to one of its customers and the retailer to whom the customer presents the card has been described as unilateral,[66] so that the bank's offer can be accepted by the retailer's dealing with the customer even before that acceptance is communicated to the bank.[67]

(d) ACCEPTANCE BY POST.[68] There are many possible solutions to the problem: when does a posted acceptance take effect? Such an acceptance could take effect when it is actually communicated to the offeror, when it arrives at his address, when it should, in the ordinary course of post, have reached him, or when it is posted. As the following discussion will show, each of these solutions is open to objections on the grounds of convenience or justice. This is particularly true where the acceptance is lost or delayed in the post.[69]

(i) *The posting rule.* What is usually[70] called the general rule is that a postal acceptance takes effect when the letter of acceptance is posted.[71] For this purpose a letter is posted when it is in the control of the Post Office,[72] or of one of its employees authorised to receive letters: handing a letter to a postman authorised to *deliver* letters is not posting.[73]

(ii) *Reasons for the rule.* Various reasons for the rule have been suggested. One is that the offeror must be considered as making the offer all the time that his offer is in the post, and that therefore the agreement between the parties is complete as soon as the acceptance is posted.[74] But this does not explain why posting has any significance at all:

---

[60] *cf.* UCC, s.2–206(1)(b); *Port Huron Machinery Co v Wohlers*, 221 N.W. 843 (1928); *The Kurnia Dewi* [1997] 1 Lloyd's Rep. 553 at 559.

[61] *Roberts v Hayward* (1828) 3 C. & P. 432; but not if the tenant disclaims the intention to accept: *Glossop v Ashley* [1921] 2 K.B. 451.

[62] For the meaning of "unilateral contract," see below, p.37.

[63] [1893] 1 Q.B. 256; see above, p.13.

[64] See below, pp.38–41.

[65] See below, p.81.

[66] *First Sport Ltd v Barclays Bank plc* [1993] 1 W.L.R. 1229 at 1234 (where the card had been stolen and been presented to the retailer by the thief).

[67] *ibid.* at 1234–1235.

[68] Gardner, 12 O.J.L.S. 170.

[69] See, for example below, after n.79.

[70] But see below, p.26.

[71] *Henthorn v Fraser* [1892] 2 Ch.27 33; *Adams v Lindsell* (1818) 1 B. & Ald. 681; *Potter & Sanders* (1846) 6 Hare 1; *Harris' Case* (1872) L.R. 7 Ch.App. 587; *cf.* in criminal law, *Treacy v DPP* [1971] A.C. 537 (blackmail); contrast *R. v Baxter* [1972] 1 Q.B. 1 (attempt to obtain by deception). For an application of the same principle to the now uncommon situation where the acceptance is contained in a telegram, see *Bruner v Moore* [1904] 1 Ch.305; *cf. Stevenson, Jacques & Co v McLean* (1880) 5 Q.B.D. 346; *Cowan v O'Connor* (1888) 20 Q.B.D. 640 (place of acceptance).

[72] *Brinkibon Ltd v Stahag Stahl und Stahlwarenhandelsgesellschaft mbH* [1983] 2 A.C. 34 at 41; the "Post Office" here refers to the provider of the universal postal service under the Postal Services Act 2000, by whatever name that provider may from time to time be known.

[73] *Re London & Northern Bank* [1900] 1 Ch.220.

[74] *Henthorn v Fraser* [1892] 2 Ch.27 at 31.

any other proof of intention to accept would equally well show that the parties were in agreement. Another suggested reason for the rule is that, if it did not exist "no contract could ever be completed by the post. For if the [offerors] were not bound by their offer when accepted by the [offerees] till the answer was received, then the [offerees] ought not to be bound till after they had received the notification that the [offerors] had received their answer and assented to it. And so it might go on *ad infinitum*".[75] But it would be perfectly possible to hold that the acceptance took effect when it came to the notice of the offeror, whether the offeree knew of this or not. Such a rule would not result in an infinity of letters. Yet another suggested reason for the rule is that the Post Office is the common agent of both parties, and that communication to this agent immediately completes the contract.[76] But the contents of a sealed letter cannot realistically be said to have been communicated to the Post Office, which in any case is at most an agent to *transmit* the acceptance, and not to *receive* it.[77] A mere delivery of the acceptance to such an agent does not of itself complete a contract.[78] Finally, it has been suggested that the rule minimises difficulties of proof: it is said to be easier to prove that a letter has been posted than that it has been received. But this depends in each case on the efficiency with which the parties keep records of incoming and outgoing letters.[79]

The rule is in truth an arbitrary one, little better or worse than its competitors. When negotiations are conducted by post, one of the parties may be prejudiced if a posted acceptance is lost or delayed; for the offeree may believe that there is a contract and the offeror that there is none, and each may act in reliance on his belief. The posting rule favours the offeree, and is sometimes justified on the ground that an offeror who chooses to start negotiations by post takes the risk of delay and accidents in the post; or on the ground that the offeror can protect himself by expressly stipulating that he is not to be bound until actual receipt of the acceptance.[80] Neither justification is wholly satisfactory, for the negotiations may have been started by the offeree[81]; and the offer may be made on a form provided by the offeree,[82] in which case he, and not the offeror, will for practical purposes be in control of its terms. The rule does, however, serve a possibly useful function in limiting the offeror's power to withdraw his offer at will[83]: it makes a posted acceptance binding although that acceptance only reaches the offeror after a previously posted withdrawal reaches the offeree.[84]

(iii) *Must be reasonable to use post*. The posting rule only applies when it is reasonable to use the post as a means of communicating acceptance. Generally an offer made in a letter sent by post may be so accepted; but it may be reasonable to accept by post even though the offer was not sent in this way. In *Henthorn v Fraser*[85] the mere fact that the parties lived at a distance justified acceptance by post of an oral offer. It would not

---

[75] *Adams v Lindsell* (1818) 1 B. & Ald. 681 at 683. This case is usually considered to be one of the early leading authorities in support of the "general rule"; but in fact the court does not mention the *posting* of the *acceptance* at all.

[76] *Household, etc. Insurance Co Ltd v Grant* (1879) 4 Ex.D. 216 at 220.

[77] *Henthorn v Fraser* [1892] 2 Ch.27 at 33.

[78] See above, p.23.

[79] See Winfield, 55 L.Q.R. 509.

[80] *Household, etc. Insurance Co Ltd v Grant* (1879) 4 Ex.D. 216 at 223.

[81] It is often hard to tell which party is offeror and which is offeree, especially if the final offer was a counter-offer (see above, p.19).

[82] See below, p.30.

[83] See below, p.41. In countries in which the acceptance is only effective when communicated a similar result is often reached by legally limiting the offeror's power to withdraw his offer.

[84] See below, p.41.

[85] [1892] 2 Ch.27.

normally be reasonable to reply by a posted letter to an offer made by telex[86] email or telephone. Nor would it be reasonable to accept by post if the acceptor knew that the postal service was disrupted.[87]

(iv) *Terms of the offer.* The posting rule can be excluded by the terms of the offer. This may be so even though the offer does not expressly provide when the acceptance is to take effect. In *Holwell Securities Ltd v Hughes*[88] an offer to sell a house was made in the form of an option expressed "to be exercisable by notice in writing to the Intending Vendor . . . " Such a notice was posted but did not arrive. It was held that there was no contract of sale as the terms of the offer, on their true construction, required the acceptance to be actually communicated.

(v) *Instantaneous and electronic communications.* The posting rule does not apply to acceptances made by some instantaneous mode of communication, *e.g.* by telephone or by telex.[89] The reason why the rule does not apply in such cases is that the acceptor will often know at once that his attempt to communicate was unsuccessful,[90] so that it is up to him to make a proper communication. But a person who accepts by letter which goes astray may not know of the loss or delay until it is too late to make another communication.[91] Fax messages seem to occupy an intermediate position. The sender will know at once if his message has not been received at all, and where this is the position the message should not amount to an effective acceptance. But if the message is received in such a form that it is wholly or partly illegible, the sender is unlikely to know this at once, and it is suggested an acceptance sent by fax might well be effective in such circumstances. The same principles should apply to other forms of electronic communication such as e-mail[92] or web-site trading[93]: here again the effects of unsuccessful attempts to communicate should depend on whether the sender of the message knows (or has the means of knowing) at once of any failure in communication.

(vi) *Applications of the posting rule.* Discussions of this subject sometimes start by stating the "general rule" that an acceptance takes effect when posted, and then proceed

---

[86] *cf. Quenerduaine v Cole* (1883) 32 W.R. 185 (telegram).

[87] *Bal v Van Staden* [1902] T.S. 128.

[88] [1974] 1 W.L.R. 155; *cf. New Hart Builders Ltd v Brindley* [1975] Ch.342.

[89] *Entores Ltd v Miles Far East Corp* [1955] 2 Q.B. 327; *Brinkibon Ltd v Stahag Stahl und Stahlwarenhandelsgesellschaft mbH* [1983] 2 A.C. 34; *cf. The Pendrecht* [1980] 2 Lloyd's Rep. 55 at 66; *Gill & Duffus Landauer Ltd v London Export Corp GmbH* [1982] 2 Lloyd's Rep. 627; *cf. The Pamela* [1995] 2 Lloyd's Rep. 249 at 252 (telexed notice withdrawing ship from charterparty). Such acceptances are therefore governed by the general rule stated at p.22, above, subject to exceptions (a) to (c) stated at pp.22–23, above. *cf.* (in tort) *Diamond v Bank of London and Montreal* [1979] Q.B. 333.

[90] See the *Entores* case, above, at 333 and the *Brinkibon* case, above, at 43.

[91] This would also be the position in the now uncommon case in which an acceptance by telegram or telemessage was dictated over the telephone and then went astray. It is submitted that the acceptance should therefore take effect when so dictated; for the contrary view, see Winfield, 55 L.Q.R. 449 at 455.

[92] For various possible times at which an email can be said to have been *received*, see Law Commission, *Electronic Commerce: Formal Requirements in Electronic Communications* (December 2001) §3.56; the present question is whether such a message may be effective *before* it is received. The Electronic Commerce (EC Directive) Regulations 2002 (SI 2002/2013), which implement most of EC Directive 2000/31 on Electronic Commerce [2000] O.J. L178/1, provide that the formal requirements contained in regs.9 and 11 do not apply to "contracts concluded exclusively by electronic mail or by equivalent individual communications": regs.9(4) and 11(3).

[93] The Law Commission paper (above, n.92) §3.37 regards "clicking on a website button" as satisfying the requirement of *signature* but does not state whether it is an offer or an acceptance, or specify *when* it takes effect. Art.11.1 of the Directive on Electronic Commerce (above) states that "the order and acknowledgement are deemed to be received when the parties to whom they are addressed are able to access them"; and almost identical language is used in reg.11(2)(a) of the Regulations cited in n.92, above. But this form of words does not of itself answer the question whether the contract may not be concluded even before that time.

to deduce various "consequences" from this rule. In fact few, if any, judges or writers have been prepared to follow all these deductions to their logical conclusions; and it would be more accurate to admit that there is no single or universal rule which determines the effect of a posted acceptance.[94] The effect of such an acceptance has to be considered *as against* various competing factors, such as withdrawal of the offer, loss or delay of the acceptance, subsequent revocation of the acceptance, previous rejection of the offer and so forth. Obviously, a rule laid down in a case concerning the effect of a posted acceptance as against a withdrawal of the offer is no real guide to the solution of the problem whether such an acceptance is effective as against a subsequent revocation of the acceptance. The English cases in fact only support three "consequences" of the posting rule. The first (and probably the most important[95]) is that a posted acceptance prevails over a previously posted withdrawal of the offer which had not yet reached the offeree when the acceptance was posted.[96] A second, and more controversial,[97] application of the rule is that an acceptance takes effect on posting even though it never reaches the offeror because it is lost through an accident in the post,[98] and the same rule probably applies where the acceptance is merely delayed through such an accident.[99] Thirdly, the contract is taken to have been made at the *time* of posting so as to take priority over another contract affecting the subject-matter made after the original acceptance had been posted but before it had reached the offeror.[1] Whether a posted acceptance should take effect against *other* competing factors is a question of policy and convenience.[2] The posting rule will not apply where it would lead to "manifest inconvenience and absurdity".[3] Its scope is determined by practical considerations rather than by "deductions" from a "general" rule.

(vii) *Misdirected acceptance.* A letter of acceptance may be lost or delayed because it bears a wrong, or an incomplete, address. Normally, such misdirection will be due to the carelessness of the offeree. Although there is no authority precisely in point,[4] it is submitted that the posting rule should not apply to such cases. Even if an offeror can be said to take the risk of accidents in the post, it would be unreasonable to impose on him the further risk of the offeree's carelessness.

It does not follow that a misdirected acceptance should necessarily take effect when received. For such a rule may actually favour the careless acceptor, *e.g.* when an offer is made to sell "at the market price prevailing when this offer is accepted," and the market falls after the misdirected acceptance has been posted. Moreover, the misdirection may be due to the fault of the offeror himself, *e.g.* if he makes the offer in a letter on which his own address is incompletely or illegibly written, or if he uses an out-of-date letter-

---

[94] See Evans, 15 I.C.L.Q. 553.

[95] See above, p.25 at n.83.

[96] *Harris' Case* (1872) L.R. 7 Ch.App. 587; *Byrne & Co v Leon van Tienhoven* (1880) 5 C.P.D. 344; *Henthorn v Fraser* [1892] 2 Ch.27; *Re London & Northern Bank* [1990] 1 Ch.200; for the contrary view, see *Rhode Island Tool Co v US*, 130 Ct.Cl. 698, 128 F.Supp. 417 (1955).

[97] See above, p.24.

[98] *Household, etc. Insurance v Grant* (1879) 4 Ex.D. 216, overruling *British and American Telegraph Co v Colson* (1871) L.R. 6 Ex. 108.

[99] See *Dunlop v Higgins* (1848) 1 H.L.C. 381, which would probably be followed in England though it is expressly restricted (at 402) to Scots law.

[1] *Potter v Sanders* (1846) 6 Hare 1. This application of the rule can perhaps be explained as a reward for the superior diligence of the first acceptor.

[2] *Brinkibon Ltd v Stahag Stahl und Stahlwarenhandelsgesellschaft mbH* [1983] 2 A.C. 34 at 41; *Gill & Duffus Landauer Ltd v London Export Corp GmbH* [1982] 2 Lloyd's Rep. 627 at 631.

[3] *Holwell Securities Ltd v Hughes* [1974] 1 W.L.R. 157 at 161.

[4] See, by way of analogy, *Getreide-Import Gesellschaft v Contimar, etc.* [1953] 1 W.L.R. 207 and 793.

head.[5] The better rule, therefore, seems to be that a misdirected acceptance takes effect (if at all) at the time which is least favourable to the party responsible for the misdirection.

(viii) *Garbled messages*. A message may be garbled as a result of some inaccuracy in transmission for which the sender is not responsible. This problem used to arise in the case of telegraphed messages and could still arise from the use of now more common modes of communication: *e.g.* where a telex or electronic message was corrupted in transmission without any fault on the part of the sender; and the discussion of garbled telegraphic messages in (and arising from) the older authorities may provide some guidance to the solution of such problems. In one such case, it was held that an offeror was not bound by a telegraphed offer which was garbled so as to indicate that he was placing an order for a different quantity of goods from that which he wished to buy.[6] But there is no English authority on the question whether an offeror would be bound where it was the acceptance rather than the offer which was garbled in this way. It is submitted that if the offeree sends a telegraphed message of acceptance in words corresponding to the offer, then (so long as it was reasonable for the offeree to accept in this way), the offeror would be bound by the acceptance and would not be entitled to treat it as a counter-offer. If an offeror takes the risk of such accidents in the post as loss or delay, he should similarly take the risk of errors in the transmission of a telegraphed message; for in each case the offeree will have no means of knowing that something has gone wrong until it is too late to make another, proper, communication.[7]

(ix) *Revocation of posted acceptance.* An offeree may, after posting an acceptance, attempt to revoke it by a later communication which reaches the offeror before, or at the same time as, the acceptance. There is no English authority on the effectiveness of such a revocation. One view is that the revocation has no effect, since, once a contract has been concluded by posting of the acceptance, it cannot be dissolved by the unilateral act of one party.[8] But this argument has little to commend it if (as has been suggested above) it is undesirable to resolve what are really issues of policy by making "logical" deductions from some "general" rule as to the effect of posted acceptances. As a matter of policy, the issue is whether the offeror would be unjustly prejudiced by allowing the offeree to rely on the subsequent revocation. On the one hand, it can be argued that the offeror cannot be prejudiced by such revocation as he had no right to have his offer accepted and as he cannot have relied on its having been accepted before he knew of the acceptance. Against this, it can be argued that, once the acceptance has been posted, the offeror can no longer withdraw his offer,[9] and that reciprocity demands that the offeree should likewise be held to his acceptance. For if the offeree could revoke the acceptance

---

[5] *cf. Townsend's Case* (1871) L.R. 13 Eq. 148, where the offeror gave his address as "36 Westland Row," omitting "Dublin." The actual reasoning of the case is obsolete since *Household, etc. Insurance v Grant* (1879) 4 Ex.D. 216. Fault of one party may not be the effective cause of the misdirection if the resulting error is obvious to the other party.

[6] *Henkel v Pape* (1870) L.R. 6 Ex. 7.

[7] *cf.* above, p.26.

[8] This view is sometimes said to be supported by *Wenckheim v Arndt* (N.Z.) 1 J.R. 73 (1873), where the defendant by letter accepted an offer of marriage; *her mother* sent a telegram purporting to cancel it. The actual decision was that the mother had no authority to act on behalf of her daughter in this way. The view stated in the text is supported by *Morrison v Thoelke*, 155 So. 2d 889 (1963) and by *A to Z Bazaars (Pty) Ltd v Minister of Agriculture* 1974 (4) S.A. 392(C) (discussed by Turpin, [1975] C.L.J. 25) but contradicted by *Dick v US*, 82 F.Supp. 326 (1949). It is also sometimes said to be contradicted by *Dunmore v Alexander* (1830) 9 Shaw 190, but the first letter was probably an offer; only the dissenting judge regarded it as an acceptance. See generally Hudson, 82. L.Q.R. 169. *cf. Kinch v Bullard* [1999] 1 W.L.R. 423 (notice which, by virtue of Law of Property Act 1925, s.196(3), had taken effect on being left at a person's place of abode, but without having been actually communicated to him, could not thereafter be withdrawn by sender).

[9] See above, p.26.

he would be able, without risk to himself, to speculate at the expense of the offeror. He could post his acceptance early in the morning of a working day and could, if the market moved against him, revoke his acceptance the same afternoon, while the offeror had no similar freedom of action. It has been suggested[10] that the offeror should take this risk just as much as he takes the risk of loss or delay; but here again it is submitted that while the offeror may take the risk of accidents in the post, he should not have to take risks due entirely to the conduct of the offeree.

So far, it has been assumed that it is in the offeror's interest to uphold the contract. But to hold the acceptance binding as soon as it was posted, in spite of an overtaking communication purporting to revoke it, might cause hardship to the *offeror*. This is particularly true where he had acted in reliance on the revocation. Suppose that A offers to sell B a car. After posting a letter of acceptance, B sends an overtaking telex, telling A to ignore that letter. On receipt of the telex, A sells the car to C. Could B change his mind yet again, and claim damages from A? There are several ways of avoiding such an unjust result. The first is to say that there had once been a contract but that it was later rescinded by mutual consent: B's telex was an offer to release A, which A accepted by conduct; communication of such acceptance could be deemed to have been waived. The second is to regard B's telex as a repudiation amounting to a breach of contract; and to say that, by "accepting" the breach, A has put an end to his obligations under the contract.[11] This analysis is preferable from A's point of view if the sale to C is for a lower price than that to B, for it would enable A to claim the difference from B as damages.[12]

An offeree who is bound by a contract made by an exchange of letters under the common law rules stated above may nevertheless have the "right to cancel" the contract under the Consumer Protection (Distance Selling) Regulations 2000 in circumstances to be more fully described below.[13] The legal consequences of the exercise of this right to cancel are, however, not entirely the same as those that would follow at common law if legal effect were given to the revocation of a posted acceptance.[14] For the purpose of the argument put forward above (that, if the revocation were effective, the offeree could speculate without risk to himself at the offeror's expense), it is also significant that the "right to cancel" under the Regulations does not (unless otherwise agreed) extend to contracts "for the supply of goods or services the price of which is dependent on fluctuations in the financial market which cannot be controlled by the supplier."[15]

(x) *International sales.* The Vienna Convention on Contracts for the International Sale of Goods, (which has not yet been ratified by the United Kingdom) governs not only the rights and duties of the parties to, but also the formation of, such contracts. Under the Convention, an offer takes effect when it "reaches" the offeree[16] and an acceptance when it "reaches" the offeror,[17] *i.e.* (in both cases) when it is communicated

---

[10] Hudson, 82 L.Q.R. 169, who also argues that the offeror can protect himself by stipulating that he is not to be bound till the acceptance reaches him, or that the offeree is to be bound as soon as he posts the acceptance.

[11] See below, p.849.

[12] See below, pp.859 *et seq. cf. Kinch v Bullard* [1999] 1 W.L.R. 423 at 430: purported withdrawal by sender of a notice after it had taken effect held ineffective against addressee (above, n.8) but said (at 430–431) to be effective against sender.

[13] See below, p.30.

[14] See below, p.30, n.21.

[15] Consumer Protection (Distance Selling) Regulations 2000 (SI 2000/2334 implementing Dir.97/7 ([1997] O.J. L144/19)), reg.13(1)(b).

[16] Art.15(1).

[17] Art.18(2).

to the addressee or delivered to his address.[18] Thus there is no contract if the acceptance is lost in the post; but if the acceptance is delayed in transmission, it is effective, unless the offeror informs the offeree promptly on its receipt that he regards the offer as having lapsed.[19] Once an offer has become effective, it cannot be revoked after the offeree has dispatched his acceptance[20]: this preserves the English position that a posted acceptance prevails over a previously posted withdrawal (referred to in the Convention as a revocation). An acceptance may be withdrawn by a communication which reaches the offeror before (or at the same time as) the acceptance would have become effective[21] if there had been no such withdrawal.

(xi) *Consumer's right to cancel distance contracts.* A contract made by (for example) exchange of letters, faxes or emails or by website trading falls within the definition of a "distance contract" within the Consumer Protection (Distance Selling) Regulations 2000 if it is one for the supply of goods or services by a commercial supplier to a consumer.[22] The Regulations do not specify when such a contract is made[23]; but if it has been made, they give the consumer the right to cancel it[24] by notice within a cancellation period specified in the Regulations (*e.g.* of seven working days from the consumer's receipt of the goods which have been supplied under it).[25] The contract, if so cancelled, is as a general rule "treated as if it had not been made"[26] but this general rule is qualified in various ways.[27] The effect of the exercise of the right to cancel is therefore not the same as the effect of saying that no contract has been concluded by (*e.g.*) exchange of letters under the common law rules of offer and acceptance discussed in above; on the contrary, the very concept of the consumer's "right to cancel" is based on the assumption that, as a matter of common law, a contract has come into the existence. Moreover, the *supplier* has no right to cancel under the Regulations, so that the question whether he has entered into the contract continues to be governed by the common law rules.

3. Prescribed Method of Acceptance

(1) Compulsory method

Where an offer states that it can only be accepted in a specified way, the offeror is not, in general, bound unless acceptance is made in that way. Thus if the offeror asks for the acceptance to be sent to a particular place an acceptance sent elsewhere will not bind

---

[18] Art.24.

[19] Art.21(2).

[20] Art.16(1); "dispatch" is not defined.

[21] Art.22.

[22] SI 2000/2334 (implementing Dir.97/7 ([1997] O.J. L144/19)); for definitions of "distance contract", "consumer" and "supplier", see reg.3; for a list of methods of communication by which such a contract may be made, see *ibid.* Sch.1. For contracts to which only part of the Regulations apply, see reg.6.

[23] This is also true of the Electronic Commerce (EC Directive) Regulations 2002 (implementing Dir.2000/31 ([2000] O.J. L178/1), below, p.187) which merely provide that in the case of, for example, a contract made on a web-site, "the order and the acknowledgement of receipt [of the order] will be deemed to be received when the parties to whom the are addressed are able to access them" (reg.11(2)(a)). The effect of acknowledgement of receipt of an order falls to be determined as a matter of common law: see the definition of acceptance at p.17, above. The provision of reg.11(2)(a) quoted in this note does *not*, in any event apply to "contracts concluded exclusively by exchange of electronic mail or by equivalent individual communications": reg.11(3).

[24] reg.10.

[25] reg.11(2).

[26] reg.10(2).

[27] See, *e.g.* reg.13 (exceptions to right to cancel); reg.17 (dealing with restoration of goods to the supplier after cancellation).

him[28]; nor, if he asks for an acceptance in writing, will he be bound by one that is oral.[29] The rule is particularly strict where the offer is contained in an option.[30] The offeror will, however, be bound if he acquiesces in the different mode of acceptance and so waives the stipulated mode. Alternatively, a contract may be concluded if the purported acceptance (which is ineffective as such for failure to comply with the stipulated method) can be regarded as a counter-offer and if that counter-offer is then accepted by the counter-offeree.[31] Since such acceptance may be effected by conduct,[32] the contract may be concluded without any further communication between the parties after the original, ineffective, acceptance.

Where the offeror prescribes a method of acceptance, he usually does so with some particular object in view, *e.g.* to secure a speedy acceptance, or one which will prevent disputes from arising as to the terms of the agreement. An acceptance which accomplishes that object just as well as, or better than, the stipulated method may, by way of exception to the general rule, bind the offeror.[33] For the purpose of this exception, it must first be determined what object the offeror had in view. If he says "reply by letter sent by return of post" this may simply mean "reply quickly": the words may "fix the time for acceptance and not the manner of accepting."[34] If so, a reply by telex would suffice. But such a reply would not suffice if the offer meant "reply quickly and by letter, I do not like telexes as they are often obscure".

The rules on this subject are based on two assumptions: that the offer is drawn up by the offeror and that stipulations as to the mode of acceptance are put into it for his benefit. In modern conditions, these assumptions are often untrue, for it is increasingly common for an offer to be made on a form provided or drafted by the offeree: *e.g.* where a customer submits a proposal to enter into a hire-purchase agreement; or where an offer is made on a form of tender provided by the offeree. Stipulations as to the mode of acceptance in such documents are usually intended for the protection and benefit of the *offeree*. If the offeree accepts in some other way, this will often be evidence that he has waived the stipulation; and it is submitted that the acceptance ought to be treated as effective unless it can be shown that failure to use the stipulated mode has prejudiced the offeror.[35]

(2) Alternative method: silence

An offer may specify, not that it *must*, but that it *may*, be accepted in a particular way. In cases of this kind, particular difficulty arises from provisions to the effect that the offeree may accept by silence.

---

[28] *Frank v Knight* (1937) O.Q.P.D. 113; *cf. Eliason v Henshaw* (1819) 4 Wheat. 225.

[29] *Financings Ltd v Stimson* [1962] 1 W.L.R. 1184 at 1186. Contrast *Hitchens v General Guarantee Corp* [2001] EWCA Civ 359, *The Times*, March 13, 2001 (where there was *no* requirement that the acceptance must be in writing).

[30] *Holwell Securities Ltd v Hughes* [1974] 1 W.L.R. 157.

[31] *Wettern Electric Ltd v Welsh Development Agency* [1983] Q.B. 796.

[32] As in the *Wettern Electricity* case, above; provided, however, that such conduct is accompanied by the requisite contractual intention: see *Harvela Investments Ltd v Royal Trust Co of Canada (CI) Ltd* [1986] A.C. 207; and below, p.171.

[33] *Manchester Diocesan Council for Education v Commercial and General Investments Ltd* [1970] 1 W.L.R. 242.

[34] *Tinn v Hoffmann & Co* (1873) 29 L.T. 271 at 278; *Manchester Diocesan Council for Education v Commercial & General Investments Ltd*, above; *cf. Edmund Murray v PSB Foundations* (1992) 33 Con.L.R. 1.

[35] See *Robophone Facilities v Blank* [1966] 1 W.L.R. 1423; *Carlyle Finance Ltd v Pallas Industrial Finance Ltd* [1999] 1 All E.R. (Comm) 659 at 670 (approving reasoning identical with that in the text above); *cf.* the *Manchester Diocesan* case, above, n.33. From this point of view, these cases are, it is submitted, to be preferred to *Financings Ltd v Stimson* [1962] 1 W.L.R. 1184.

(a) OFFEREE GENERALLY NOT BOUND. As a general rule, an offeree who simply does nothing on receipt of an offer which states that it may be accepted by silence is not bound. In *Felthouse v Bindley*[36] an uncle offered to buy his nephew's horse by a letter in which he said: "If I hear no more about him, I shall consider the horse mine." Later, the horse was, by mistake, included in an auction sale of the nephew's property. The uncle sued the auctioneer for damages for the conversion of the horse. It was held that, at the time of the auction, there was no contract for the sale of the horse to the uncle because "The uncle had no right to impose upon the nephew the sale of his horse . . . unless he chose to comply with the condition of writing to repudiate the offer . . . "[37] The reason for the rule is that it is, in general, undesirable to impose the trouble and expense of rejecting an offer on an offeree who does not wish to accept it. But in *Felthouse v Bindley* this was not the position. Before the auction, the nephew had told the auctioneer that he "intended to reserve" the horse for his uncle; and later correspondence showed that, at the time of the auction, the nephew did in fact wish to sell the horse to the uncle. In spite of this it was held that there was no contract because the nephew "had not communicated his intention to the uncle".[38] But the need to communicate an acceptance can be waived[39]; and it seems clear that the uncle's letter did waive it. In view of these facts, the actual decision is hard to support, but this is no criticism of the general rule laid down in the case.

The question whether silence can amount to an acceptance binding the offeree has also arisen in the cases, already discussed, in which the issue was whether an agreement to abandon an earlier agreement to submit a claim to arbitration could be inferred from inactivity, in the form of long delay in prosecuting the claim. Such a delay is now in certain circumstances a statutory ground for dismissing the claim for want of prosecution[40] but the statutory power to dismiss a claim on this ground can be excluded by agreement,[41] and similar questions of agreement to abandon *other* types of claim or remedy could still be governed by the common law principles developed in the arbitration cases. In these cases, it had been held that, even if one party's inactivity could be regarded as an offer to abandon the arbitration,[42] the mere silence or inactivity[43] of the other did not normally amount to an acceptance. For one thing, such inactivity was often[44] equivocal,[45] being explicable on other grounds (such as forgetfulness). For another, acceptance could not, as a matter of law, be inferred from silence alone[46] "save in the most exceptional circumstances".[47]

---

[36] (1862) 11 C.B.(N.S.) 869; affirmed (1863) New Rep. 401; Miller, 35 M.L.R. 489. *cf. Financial Techniques (Planning Services) v Hughes* [1981] I.R.L.R. 32 at 35.

[37] At 875.

[38] At 876.

[39] See above, p.24.

[40] Arbitration Act 1996, s.41(3).

[41] *ibid.* s.41(2).

[42] See above, p.10.

[43] For acceptance by silence *and conduct*, see below, p.33.

[44] But not always: see below, p.33 at n.52.

[45] e.g. *Jayaar Impex Ltd v Toaken Group Ltd* [1996] 2 Lloyd's Rep. 437 at 445.

[46] *The Leonidas D* [1985] 1 W.L.R. 925 at 927; *Rafsanjan Pistachio Producers Co-operative v Bank Leumi (UK) plc* [1992] 1 Lloyd's Rep. 513 at 542; *The Gas Enterprise* [1993] 2 Lloyd's Rep. 352 at 357 (affirmed without reference to this point *ibid.* at 364).

[47] *The Leonidas D*, above at 927; *Vitol SA v Norelf Ltd* [1996] A.C. 800 at 812. Such "exceptional circumstances" may be illustrated by *The Splendid Sun* [1981] Q.B. 694 (where acceptance may have been by conduct: below, p.35) though this case is hard to reconcile with *The Leonidas D*, above: see *The Antclizo* [1987] 2 Lloyd's Rep. 130 at 149 (affirmed [1988] 1 W.L.R. 603). *cf. Cie. Française d'Importation etc. v Deutsche Continental Handelsgesellschaft* [1985] 2 Lloyd's Rep. 592 at 598; *The Agrabele* [1987] 2 Lloyd's Rep. 223 at 224, 235. *The Golden Bear* [1987] 1 Lloyd's Rep. 330 is hard to reconcile with these cases and was apparently doubted in *The Antclizo*, above: see [1987] 2 Lloyd's Rep. 130 at 147.

(b) OFFEREE EXCEPTIONALLY BOUND? As the above reference to "exceptional circumstances" suggests, there may be exceptions to the general rule that an offeree is not bound by silence. If the offer has been solicited by the offeree, the argument that he should not be put to the trouble of rejecting it loses much of its force,[48] especially if the offer is made on a form provided by the offeree[49] and that form stipulates that silence may amount to acceptance.[50] Again, if there is a course of dealing between the parties, the offeror may be led to suppose that silence amounts to acceptance: *e.g.* where a retailer's offers to buy goods from a wholesaler have in the past been accepted as a matter of course by the despatch of the goods in question.[51] In such a case it may not be unreasonable to require the offeree to give notice of his rejection of the offer, especially if the offeror, in reliance on his belief that the goods would be delivered in the usual way, had forborne from seeking an alternative supply. On a somewhat similar principle, one party's wrongful repudiation of a contract may be accepted by the other party's failure to take such further steps in the performance of that contract as he would have been expected to take, if he were treating the contract as still in force.[52] There may also be "an express undertaking or implied obligation to speak"[53] arising out of the course of negotiations between the parties, *e.g.* "where the offeree himself indicates that an offer is to be taken as accepted if he does not indicate the contrary by an ascertainable time."[54] Failure to perform such an "obligation to speak" could be held to amount to an acceptance by silence. There is also the possibility that silence may constitute an acceptance by virtue of the custom of the trade or business in question.[55]

Where the offeree is under a "duty to speak", his failure to perform that duty may thus enable the *offeror* to treat that failure as an acceptance by silence. But it is not normally open to the *offeree* in such cases to treat his own silence (in breach of his duty to speak) as an acceptance.[56] This course would be open to him only in situations such as that in *Felthouse v Bindley*,[57] in which the offeror had indicated (usually in the terms of the offer) that he would treat silence as an acceptance.

Even where silence of the offeree does not amount to an acceptance, it is arguable that he might be liable on a different basis. In *Spiro v Lintern* it was said that "If A sees B acting in the mistaken belief that A is under some binding obligation to him and in a manner consistent only with such an obligation, which would be to B's disadvantage if A were thereafter to deny the obligation, A is under a duty to B to disclose the non-existence of the supposed obligation."[58] Although this statement was made with reference to wholly different circumstances,[59] it could also be applied to certain cases in which an offeror had, to the offeree's knowledge,[60] acted in reliance on the belief that his

---

[48] *cf. Rust v Abbey Life Ins Co* [1979] 2 Lloyd's Rep. 335.

[49] *cf.* above, p.30.

[50] As in *Alexander Hamilton Institute v Jones*, 234 Ill. App. (1924).

[51] As in *Cole-McIntyre-Norfleet Co v Holloway*, 141 Tenn. 679; 214 S.W. 87 (1919).

[52] *Vitol SA v Norelf Ltd* [1996] A.C. 800; see below, p.849.

[53] *The Agrabele* [1985] 2 Lloyd's Rep. 496, 509, *per* Evans J., whose statement of the relevant legal principles was approved on appeal, though the actual decision was reversed on the facts: [1987] 2 Lloyd's Rep. 223 at 225. The case concerned an alleged "abandonment" by delay of an agreement to submit a claim to arbitration; this situation would now be governed by Arbitration Act 1996, s.41(3).

[54] *Re Selectmove* [1995] 1 W.L.R. 474 at 478 (where the point was left open).

[55] *Minories Finance Ltd v Afribank Nigeria Ltd* [1995] 1 Lloyd's Rep. 134.

[56] *Yona International Ltd v La Réunion Française, etc.* [1996] 2 Lloyd's Rep. 84 at 110.

[57] See above, p.32, further discussed below.

[58] [1973] 1 W.L.R. 1002 at 1011.

[59] See below, p.716.

[60] See *Yona International Ltd v La Réunion Française, etc.* [1996] 2 Lloyd's Rep. 84 at 107 (where this requirement was not satisfied).

offer had been accepted by silence. The liability of the offeree would then be based on a kind of estoppel.[61] The application of this doctrine to cases of alleged acceptance by silence indeed gives rise to the difficulty that an estoppel can only arise out of a "clear and unequivocal"[62] representation, and that such a representation cannot generally be inferred from mere inactivity.[63] But this general rule does not preclude the application of the doctrine of estoppel to exceptional cases of the kind here under discussion, in which there are special circumstances which give rise to a "duty to speak", and in which it would be unconscionable for the party under that duty to deny that a contract had come into existence.

It is finally possible for the offeree to be bound by silence if the offeror, to the offeree's knowledge, actually performs in accordance with his offer and so confers a benefit on the offeree; though the better solution in this type of case would be to make the offeree restore the benefit rather than to hold him to an obligation to perform his part of a contract to which he had never agreed.

(c) OFFEROR BOUND? There is some authority for saying that the offeror cannot, any more than the offeree, be bound where the offeree simply remains silent in response to the offer,[64] and the case is not one of the exceptional ones discussed above[65] in which an offer can be accepted by silence. But it is submitted that the general rule laid down in *Felthouse v Bindley*[66] does not invariably lead to such a conclusion. For the object of this rule is to protect *the offeree* from having to incur the trouble and expense of rejecting the offer so as to avoid being bound. No such argument can normally be advanced for protecting the offeror. He may indeed be left in doubt on the question whether his offer has been accepted; but this is not a matter about which he can legitimately complain where he has drawn up his offer in terms which permit (and even encourage) acceptance by silence.[67] Thus it is submitted that the uncle in *Felthouse v Bindley* might have been bound if the nephew had resolved to accept the offer and had, in reliance on its terms, forborne from attempting to dispose of the horse elsewhere. This possibility has, indeed, been judicially doubted,[68] but in the case in which the doubt was raised it was not an express term of the offer that silence would be regarded as acceptance. Where the offeror has expressly formulated his offer in such terms, it is submitted that the offeree's silence in response to the offer should be capable of binding the offeror.

It is settled that a creditor can accept his debtor's offer to give additional security for a debt by simply forbearing to sue for the debt.[69] If such forbearance can be regarded as silence, this rule supports the view that acceptance by silence can bind the offeror. Another possible explanation of the rule is that a creditor who forbears accepts by conduct[70] rather than by silence.

---

[61] See below, pp.115, 403; *cf.* (in another context) *The Stolt Loyalty* [1993] 2 Lloyd's Rep. 281 at 289–291, affirmed without reference to this point, [1995] 1 Lloyd's Rep. 598. The case would not be one of estoppel by convention (below, p.119); for such estoppel is based on an *agreed* assumption of fact, while in cases of the present kind the question is whether there was any agreement.

[62] See below, pp.107, 403.

[63] See below, p.133.

[64] *Fairline Shipping Corp v Adamson* [1975] Q.B. 180 at 189.

[65] At nn.49–55.

[66] See above, p.31.

[67] This reasoning would, however, not apply where the terms of the offer had been drawn up by the *offeree*: *cf.* above, p.30.

[68] *Fairline Shipping Corp v Adamson* [1975] Q.B. 180 at 189.

[69] See below, p.90.

[70] See above, p.18.

(d) SILENCE AND CONDUCT. In *Roberts v Hayward*[71] a tenant accepted his landlord's offer of a new tenancy at an increased rent by simply staying on the premises. It was held that he had accepted the landlord's offer by silence; but it seems better to say that he accepted by conduct and that the landlord waived notice of acceptance.[72] Similarly an offer made *to* a landowner to occupy land under a licence containing specified terms may be accepted by the landowner's permitting the offeror to occupy the land.[73] An offeree is not, for the present purpose, "silent" merely because his acceptance is not expressed in words. The possibility of acceptance by conduct is, yet again, illustrated by the arbitration cases already mentioned, in which an agreement to abandon the proceedings was alleged to have arisen from delay in prosecuting them. As already noted, legislation has now dealt with the practical problems which used to arise from delay in the pursuit of arbitration claims,[74] but the reasoning of the arbitration cases could still apply where the legislative provisions have been excluded by agreement,[75] or where it was alleged that some other type of claim or remedy had been abandoned by tacit agreement. According to those cases, an offer of abandonment can be accepted by reacting to it, not merely by inactivity,[76] but also by some further conduct: *e.g.* by closing or disposing of relevant files.[77]

In *Rust v Abbey Life Ins Co*[78] the plaintiff applied and paid for a "property bond" which was allocated to her on the terms of the defendants' usual policy of insurance. After having retained this document for some seven months, she claimed the return of her payment, alleging that no contract had been concluded. The claim was rejected on the ground that her application was an offer which had been accepted by issue of the policy. But it was further held that, even if the policy constituted a counter-offer, this counter-offer had been accepted by "the conduct of the plaintiff in doing and saying nothing for seven months. . . . "[79] Thus mere inaction was said to be sufficient to constitute acceptance; and it seems to have amounted to no more than silence in spite of having been described as "conduct". The conclusion that it amounted to acceptance can, however, be justified in the circumstances. The negotiations had been started by the plaintiff[80] (the counter-offeree), and in view of this fact it was reasonable for the defendants to infer from her long silence that she had accepted the terms of the policy which had been sent to her and which she must be "taken to have examined".[81] The case thus falls within one of the suggested exceptions[82] to the general rule that an offeree is not bound by silence.

---

[71] (1828) 3 C. & P. 432.

[72] *cf.* above, p.23.

[73] *Wettern Electric Ltd v Welsh Development Agency* [1983] Q.B. 796.

[74] Arbitration Act 1996, s.41(3); above, p.31.

[75] *ibid.* s.41(2).

[76] See above, p.31; *cf. Collin v Duke of Westminster* [1985] Q.B. 581.

[77] See *The Splendid Sun* [1981] Q.B. 694 at 712, 713 ("closed their files"); *cf. ibid.* 706 ("did so act"); *The Multibank Holsatia* [1988] 2 Lloyd's Rep. 486 at 493 (where the offeree had destroyed relevant files, so that the case was not one of mere inaction). *Tracomin SA v Anton C Nielsen A/S* [1984] 2 Lloyd's Rep. 195 can be supported on the same ground even though it was based on the decision at first instance in *The Leonidas D* which was reversed on appeal: [1985] 1 W.L.R. 925, above, p.10. There seems to have been no "conduct" amounting to acceptance in *The Golden Bear* [1987] 1 Lloyd's Rep. 300.

[78] [1979] 2 Lloyd's Rep. 355.

[79] [1979] 2 Lloyd's Rep. 335 at 340, affirming [1978] 2 Lloyd's Rep. 386 at 393.

[80] *cf.* above, p.29 and *Vitol SA v Norelf Ltd* [1996] A.C. 800, above, p.33.

[81] *Yona International Ltd v La Réunion Française* [1996] 2 Lloyd's Rep. 84 at 110 (where no inference of assent could be drawn from silence).

[82] See above, pp.33–34.

4. Acceptance in Ignorance of Offer

(1) Generally ineffective

The general view is that acceptance in ignorance of an offer cannot create a contract since the parties must *reach* agreement: it is not enough that their wishes happen to coincide: the act or promise constituting the acceptance must be "given in exchange for the offer".[83] The same reasoning applies where a person once knew of the offer but had at the time of the alleged acceptance forgotten it.[84] Thus it has been held in other jurisdictions that a person who gives information for which a reward has been offered cannot claim the reward unless at the time of giving it he knew of the offer of reward.[85] The English case of *Gibbons v Proctor*[86] is sometimes thought to support the contrary view, but can be explained on the ground that the plaintiff did know of the offer of reward by the time the information was given on his behalf to the person named in the advertisement.[87]

In the reward cases just considered, it is hard to see what prejudice the offeror would suffer if he had to pay the reward to someone who had complied with the terms of the offer without being aware of it. The reasons for holding that there is no contract in such a case seem to be largely doctrinal; but more practical difficulties can arise where the acts alleged to amount to an acceptance can not only confer rights on the actor, but also deprive him of rights[88] or impose duties on him. This last possibility may be illustrated by reference to *Upton Rural DC v Powell*[89] where the defendant, whose house was on fire, telephoned the Upton police and asked for "the fire brigade". He was entitled to the service of the Pershore fire brigade free of charge as he lived in its district; but the police called the Upton fire brigade, in the belief that the defendant lived in that district. The latter fire brigade for a time shared this belief and thought "that they were rendering gratuitous services in their own area". It was held that the defendant was contractually bound to pay for these services. But even if the defendant's telephone call was an offer, it is hard to see how the Upton brigade's services, given with no thought of reward, could be an acceptance. It would have been better to give the claimants a restitutionary remedy than to hold that there was a contract. The case was concerned only with the rights of the fire brigade, but the fire brigade could also have owed more extensive duties as contractors than as volunteers. It may well be hard to subject a person who reasonably thinks that he is a volunteer to the more stringent duties of a contractor.[90]

(2) Cross-offers

The requirement that the offeree must know of the offer at the time of the alleged acceptance also accounts for the rule that there is no contract if two persons make identical cross-offers, neither party knowing of the other's offer when he makes his own,

---

[83] *R. v Clarke* (1927) 40 C.L.R. 227 at 233; *Tracomin SA v Anton C Nielsen* [1984] 2 Lloyd's Rep. 195 at 203; *Lark v Outhwaite* [1991] 2 Lloyd's Rep. 132 at 140.

[84] *R. v Clarke*, above, at 241.

[85] *Bloom v American Swiss Watch Co* (1915) A.D. 100; the American authorities are divided: see Corbin, *Contracts*, s.59.

[86] (1891) 64 L.T. 594, sub nom. *Gibson v Proctor*, 55 J.P. 616. See Hudson, 84 L.Q.R. 513.

[87] "The information ultimately reached Penn at a time when the plaintiff knew that the reward had been offered": 55 J.P. 616.

[88] *e.g. Tracomin SA v Anton C Nielsen* [1984] 2 Lloyd's Rep. 195 at 203.

[89] [1942] 1 All E.R. 220; Mitchell, 12 J.C.L. 78. For the fire brigade's duty apart from contract, see *John Munroe (Acrylics) Ltd v London Fire & Civil Defence Authority* [1997] 2 Lloyd's Rep. 161.

[90] *cf. BSC v Cleveland Bridge & Engineering Co Ltd* [1984] 1 All E.R. 504 at 510. *Quaere* what the position should be where one party thinks that he is giving or getting a gratuitous service while the other thinks that he is contracting.

e.g. if A writes to B offering to sell B his car for £5,000 and B simultaneously writes to A offering to buy the car for £5,000. If no further communication took place in such a case, the parties might well be in doubt as to whether there was indeed a contract between them; and the view that "cross offers are not an acceptance of each other"[91] can be supported on the ground that it tends to promote certainty.

(3) Motive for acceptance

A person who knows of the offer may do the act required for acceptance with some motive other than that of accepting the offer. In *Williams v Carwardine*[92] the defendant offered a reward of £20 to anyone who gave information leading to the conviction of the murderers of Walter Carwardine. The plaintiff knew of the offer, and, thinking that she had not long to live, signed a "voluntary statement to ease my conscience, and in hopes of forgiveness hereafter". This statement resulted in the conviction of the murderers. It was held that the plaintiff had brought herself within the terms of the offer and was entitled to the reward. Patteson J. said: "We cannot go into the plaintiff's motives".[93] Similarly, in *Carlill v Carbolic Smoke Ball Co*[94] the plaintiff recovered the £100, although her predominant motive in using the smoke ball was (presumably) to avoid catching influenza. But in the Australian case of *R. v Clarke*[95] a reward had been offered for information leading to the arrest and conviction of the murderers of two police officers. Clarke, who knew of the offer and was himself suspected of the crime, gave such information. He admitted that he had done so to clear himself of the charge, and with no thought of claiming the reward. His claim for the reward failed as he had not given the information "in exchange for the offer".[96] It seems that an act which is *wholly* motivated by factors other than the existence of the offer cannot amount to an acceptance,[97] but if the existence of the offer plays some part, however small, in inducing a person to do the required act, there is a valid acceptance of the offer.

5. Acceptance in Unilateral Contracts

(1) Classification

An offer of a unilateral contract is made when one party promises to pay the other a sum of money[98] if the other will do (or forbear from doing) something without making any promise to that effect: for example, when one person promises to pay another £100 if he will walk from London to York,[99] or find and return the promisor's lost dog, or give up smoking for a year.[1] The contract which arises in these cases is called "unilateral" because it arises without the offeree's having made any counter-promise to perform the required act or forbearance; it is contrasted with a bilateral contract, in which each party undertakes an obligation and in which acceptance, as a general rule, takes the form of a communication by the offeree of his counter-promise. The distinction between the two

---

[91] *Tinn v Hoffmann & Co* (1873) 29 L.T. 271 at 278.

[92] (1833) 5 C. & P. 566; 4 B. & Ad. 621; it must be assumed that the plaintiff knew of the offer: *Carlill v Carbolic Smoke Ball Co Ltd* [1892] 2 Q.B. at 489, n.2.

[93] 4 B. & Ad. at 623.

[94] [1893] 1 Q.B. 256.

[95] (1927) 40 C.L.R. 227; contrast *Simonds v US*, 308 F. 2d 160 (1962).

[96] At 233.

[97] *Lark v Outhwaite* [1991] 2 Lloyd's Rep. 132 at 140.

[98] Or to do some other act, or to forbear from doing something. In the text we shall deal only with the most common case of a promise to pay money.

[99] An old example: *Rogers v Snow* (1573) Dalison 94; *cf. Great Northern Ry v Witham* (1873) L.R. 9 C.P. 16 at 19. Its modern version is the "sponsored walk".

[1] *cf. Hamer v Sidway*, 124 N.Y. 538 (1881).

types of contract sometimes gives rise to difficulty,[2] because a contract may be in its inception unilateral, but become bilateral in the course of its performance.[3] For example, A may promise to pay B £1000 for some service (such as repainting A's house) which B does not promise to render. Here B would not be liable if he did nothing; but once he began the work (*e.g.* by stripping off the old paint) he might be held to have impliedly promised[4] to complete it, so that at this stage the contract would become bilateral[5] and both parties would be bound by it.

(2) General rules as to acceptance

Once a promise is classified as an offer of a unilateral contract, a number of rules apply to the acceptance of such an offer. First, the offer can be accepted by fully performing the required act or forbearance.[6] Secondly, there is no need to give advance notice of acceptance to the offeror.[7] And thirdly, the offer can, like all other offers, be withdrawn before it has been accepted. But there is much dispute as to the exact stage at which the offer is "accepted" so as to deprive the offeror of the power of withdrawal. It is probable that the offer can be accepted *only* by some performance and not by a counter-promise to walk to York, or to look for the lost dog, or to give up smoking; for such a counter-promise would not be what the offeror had bargained for. Thus the offeror could still withdraw after such a counter-promise had been made.

(3) Acceptance by part performance

It is less clear whether the offeror can still withdraw after the offeree has *partly* performed the required act or forbearance, *e.g.* if he has walked half-way to York or refrained from smoking for six months. The first problem (which will be discussed here) is whether the offeree has at this stage accepted the offer; the second (to be discussed in Chapter 3[8]) is whether he has provided consideration for the offeror's promise.

(a) IN GENERAL. According to one view, there is no contract until the required act or forbearance has been completed, and this is said to give effect to the intention of the parties, each of whom intends, until then, to reserve a *locus poenitentiae*.[9] But in most cases[10] it is unlikely that the offeree intends to expose himself to the risk of withdrawal

---

[2] See generally Llewellyn, 48 Yale L.J. 1, 799. *cf.* the American Law Institute's Restatement of the Law of Contracts (hereinafter called Restatement, *Contracts*) §12; the Restatement of the Law Second, Contracts (hereinafter called Restatement 2d., *Contracts*), §45 substitutes the term "option contract", without any very obvious increase in clarity.

[3] *cf. The Eurymedon* [1975] A.C. 154, 167–8 ("a bargain initially unilateral but capable of becoming mutual"). For this classification of the contract in that case, see further p.631, below.

[4] According to a dictum in *Little v Courage Ltd* (1995) 70 P. & C.R. 469 at 475, terms which impose legal obligations cannot be implied into a unilateral contract; but this view would not preclude such a contract from becoming bilateral after it had originally come into existence. See further p.205, below.

[5] See *The Unique Mariner* [1979] 2 Lloyd's Rep. 37 at 51–52; *The Kurnia Dewi* [1997] 1 Lloyd's Rep. 553 at 559; contrast *BSC v Cleveland Bridge & Engineering Co Ltd* [1984] 1 All E.R. 504 at 510–511 where such an implied promise was negatived by the fact that the terms of a bilateral contract were still under negotiation and were never agreed. It is not clear whether the situation discussed in *Offord v Davies* (1862) 12 C.B.N.S. 748 at 753 falls into the category of a unilateral or into that of a bilateral contract.

[6] See *Daulia Ltd v Four Millbank Nominees Ltd* [1978] Ch.231 at 238; *cf. Harvela Investments Ltd v Royal Trust of Canada (CI) Ltd* [1986] A.C. 207 at 224.

[7] *Carlill v Carbolic Smoke Ball Co* [1893] 1 Q.B. 256; *Bowerman v Association of British Travel Agents* [1995] N.L.J. 1815.

[8] See below, p.151.

[9] Wormser in *Selected Readings on the Law of Contracts*, p.307; but for the same writer's later views see 3 Jl.Leg.Educ. 146.

[10] For a possible exception, see below, p.39.

when he has partly performed and is willing and able[11] to complete performance for the sake of securing the promised benefit.[12] The general view is that it would cause hardship to the offeree to allow the offeror to withdraw in such a case; and most writers try to find some reason for saying that part performance prevents the offeror from withdrawing the offer. One possibility is to say that the offeror makes two offers: (1) the principal offer and (2) a collateral one to keep the principal offer open once performance has begun; this latter offer is accepted by beginning to perform.[13] But this analysis is artificial: it is more realistic to say that the principal offer itself is accepted by beginning to perform.[14] It has been objected that this cannot simply be asserted but must be explained.[15] The explanation appears to be that acceptance is no more (or less) than an unqualified expression of assent to the terms of the offer by words or conduct; and that the question whether an inference of such assent can be drawn from part performance is simply one of fact. The sight of a man walking northwards from London may or may not suggest that he does so in response to an offer to pay him £100 if he reaches York, but, if his conduct does clearly suggest this, there is no theoretical difficulty in saying that he has accepted the offer. Factual difficulties might, of course, arise in distinguishing between commencement of performance and mere preparation to perform. Thus it is probable that an offer of a reward for the return of lost property could still be withdrawn after someone had spent time looking for the property without success, but not after he had actually found it and was in the process of returning it to the owner.

Support for the above view is provided by *Errington v Errington*[16] where a father bought a house subject to a mortgage, allowed his son and daughter-in-law to live in it, and told them that, if they paid the mortgage instalments, the house would be theirs when the mortgage was paid off. The couple started to live in the house and paid some of the mortgage instalments; but they did not bind themselves to go on making the payments. It was held that this arrangement amounted to a contract which could not, after the father's death, be revoked by his personal representatives. Denning L.J. said:

"The father's promise was a unilateral contract—a promise of the house in return for their act of paying the instalments. It could not be revoked by him once the couple entered on performance of the act, but it would cease to bind him if they left it incomplete and unperformed, which they have not done."[17]

(b) CONTINUING GUARANTEES. The view that part performance of a unilateral contract can amount to an acceptance is further supported by the law relating to continuing guarantees. These may be divisible, where each advance constitutes a separate transaction; or indivisible *e.g.* where, on A's admission to an association, B guarantees all liabilities that A may incur as a member of the association.[18] If the guarantee is divisible,

---

[11] It is assumed that performance remains within the offeree's power. If not, the offeror can withdraw: see *Morrison SS Co v The Crown* (1924) 20 Ll.L.R. 283.

[12] Lord Diplock in the *Harvela* case [1986] A.C. 207 at 224 can be read as depriving the offeror of the power to withdraw as soon as his offer is *communicated* (*i.e.* before any performance); but in that case the offeree had completely performed the required act by making the requested bid.

[13] McGoveney, *Selected Readings*, p.300.

[14] Pollock, *Principles of Contract* (13th ed.), p.19; Ballantine, *Selected Readings*, p.312.

[15] McGoveney, above.

[16] [1952] 1 K.B. 290. The reasoning of this case was doubted, but not on this point, in *National Provincial Bank Ltd v Ainsworth* [1965] A.C. 1175 at 1239–1240, 1251–1252 and in *Ashburn Anstalt v Arnold* [1989] Ch.1, 17 (overruled on another point in *Prudential Assurance Co Ltd v London Residuary Body* [1992] A.C. 386): see below, p.559, n.7. See also *Beaton v McDivitt* (1988) 13 N.S.W.L.R. 162 at 175.

[17] [1952] 1 K.B. 290 at 295.

[18] As in *Lloyd's v Harper* (1880) 16 Ch.D. 290.

it can be revoked at any time with regard to future advances[19]; but an indivisible guarantee cannot be revoked after the creditor has begun to act on it by giving credit to the principal debtor.[20] This rule applies even though the contract of guarantee is unilateral in the sense that the creditor has not made any promise to the guarantor (in return for the guarantee) to give credit to the debtor.

(c) BANKERS' IRREVOCABLE CREDITS. This subject is more fully explained in Chapter 3.[21] Here it need only be said that the essence of the system is that a bank, on the instruction of its customer (usually a buyer of goods) notifies a third person (usually the seller) that it has opened an irrevocable credit in his favour, promising to pay him a stipulated sum if he will present certain specified documents to the bank. The general view is that the bank cannot revoke the promise once it has been notified to the seller; and, as the seller makes no promise *to the bank*, this result is sometimes explained in terms of a unilateral contract between these parties. In most cases there will be some act of part performance by the seller, *e.g.* in shipping the goods so as to procure the required documents. But the bank's promise is regarded as binding as soon as it is notified to the seller, *i.e.* before he has done any act in response to it. The binding force of such irrevocable credits is not, therefore, easily explicable in terms of acceptance of an offer.

(d) ESTATE AGENTS' CONTRACTS. Where an estate agent is engaged to negotiate the sale of a house, it is arguable that his client's promise to pay a commission on sale gives rise to a unilateral contract, for in one case of this kind it was said that "No obligation is imposed on the agent to do anything."[22] It is settled that the client (the offeror) can, without liability, revoke his instructions before a claim to commission has accrued, in spite of the fact that the agent (the offeree) has made considerable efforts to find a purchaser.[23] Hence these cases could be said to support the view that an offer of a unilateral contract can be withdrawn after part performance by the offeree. But the better explanation is that this is one of the exceptional cases in which, on the true construction of the offer, a *locus poenitentiae* is reserved to the client even after part performance by the agent. This view is supported by the fact that the right to revoke instructions exists even where the contract is bilateral because the agent has, expressly or by implication, made some promise, *e.g.* one to use his best endeavours to effect a sale[24] or one to bear advertising expenses.[25] Such promises have been found to exist where the agent has been appointed "sole agent", but in practice they are commonly made by other agents as well. A "sole agent" is entitled to damages if the client sells through another agent,[26] but not if he simply revokes his instructions or sells "privately", without the help of any agent at all.[27] These rules apply irrespective of the unilateral or bilateral nature of the contract; so that the estate agency cases shed little,

---

[19] As in *Offord v Davies* (1862) 12 C.B.N.S. 748.

[20] *Lloyd's v Harper*, above.

[21] See below, p.152.

[22] *Luxor (Eastbourne) Ltd v Cooper* [1941] A.C. 108 at 124. In fact the agent often does undertake to do something; see below, nn.24, 25. See generally Murdoch, (1975) 91 L.Q.R. 357.

[23] See below, p.742.

[24] *Christopher v Essig* [1958] W.N. 461; *John McCann & Co v Pow* [1974] 1 W.L.R. 1643 at 1647; *Wood v Lucy (Lady Duff-Gordon)*, 118 N.E. 214 (1917) (where such a promise was implied). On the question whether such a promise is sufficiently certain to have legal effect, see below, pp.48, 167.

[25] *cf. Bentall, Horsley & Baldry v Vicary* [1931] 1 K.B. 253.

[26] *Hampton & Sons Ltd v George* [1939] 3 All E.R. 627; *Christopher v Essig* [1958] W.N. 461, below, p.714.

[27] See below, p.744.

if any, light on the question of acceptance by part performance of unilateral contracts.

(e) EXTENT OF RECOVERY. Where a unilateral contract takes the shape of a promise to pay a sum of money, it is generally assumed that the promisee must either get nothing or the full sum. Perhaps some compromise is possible. Suppose the promisee has walked half-way to York before the offer is withdrawn. It is arguable that he should desist and recover his expenses, or a reasonable sum.[28] This might be fairer to both parties than the "all or nothing" solutions which are usually canvassed.[29]

SECTION 3. TERMINATION OF OFFER

1. Withdrawal

(1) Communication to offeree generally required

As a general rule, an offer can be withdrawn at any time before it is accepted.[30] It is not withdrawn merely by acting inconsistently with it, *e.g.* by disposing of the subject-matter.[31] Notice of the withdrawal must be given and must actually reach the offeree: mere posting will not suffice. In *Byrne & Co v Leon van Tienhoven*[32] an offer to sell tinplates was posted in Cardiff on October 1 and reached the offerees in New York on October 11, and they immediately accepted it by a telegram which they confirmed by a letter of October 15. Meanwhile, the offerors had on October 8 posted a letter withdrawing their offer, but that letter of withdrawal did not reach the offerees until October 20. It was held that there was a contract since the withdrawal had not been communicated when the offer was accepted.[33] Thus there was a contract in spite of the fact that the parties were demonstrably not in agreement, for when the offerees first knew of the offer, the offerors had already ceased to intend to deal with the offerees. The rule is based on convenience; for no one could rely on a postal offer if it could be withdrawn by a letter already posted but not yet received.

(2) Communication need not come from offeror

Although withdrawal must be communicated to the offeree, it need not be communicated by the offeror. It is sufficient if the offeree knows from any reliable source that the offeror no longer intends to contract with him. Thus in *Dickinson v Dodds*[34] it was held that an offer to sell land could not be accepted after the offeror had, to the offeree's knowledge, decided to sell the land to a third party. The decision is based on the fact that

---

[28] Unless the promisee has a "substantial or legitimate interest" in going on, this may be the law under the principles laid down in *White & Carter (Councils) Ltd v McGregor* [1962] A.C. 413, below, pp.1016–1019.

[29] Fuller & Perdue, 46 Yale L.J. at p.411.

[30] *Routledge v Grant* (1828) 4 Bing 653; *Offord v Davies* (1862) 12 C.B.N.S. 748; *Tuck v Baker* [1990] 2 E.G.L.R. 195; *Scammell v Dicker* [2001] 1 W.L.R. 631; *Bircham & Co Nominees (No.2) v Worrell Holdings* [2001] EWCA Civ 775; (2001) 82 P. & C.R. 472 at [24], [35]; *Dunmore v Alexander* (1830) 8 Shaw 190; *cf.* Defamation Act 1996, s.2(6). For a statutory exception, see Companies Act 1985, s.82(7); and see Vienna Convention (above, p.28) Art.16(2).

[31] *Adams v Lindsell* (1818) 1 B. & Ald. 681; *Stevenson, Jacques & Co v McLean* (1880) 5 Q.B.D. 346; contrary dicta in *Dickinson v Dodds* (1876) 2 Ch.D. 463 at 472 would no longer be followed.

[32] (1880) 5 C.P.D. 344. Under Consumer Credit Act 1974, s.69(1)(ii) and (7) posting is, exceptionally, sufficient.

[33] The same result would follow under Vienna Convention (above, p.28) Art.16(1), though under Arts 18(2) and 24 the contract would not be made until the acceptance was communicated to the offeror or delivered to his address.

[34] (1876) 2 Ch.D. 463; *cf. Cartwright v Hoogstoel* (1911) 105 L.T. 628.

there is in such a case no agreement between the parties. But this would be equally true if the offeree did not know of the withdrawal at all when he accepted the offer: yet in that case there is normally[35] a contract.[36] The rule that communication of withdrawal need not come from the offeror can be a regrettable source of uncertainty. It puts on the offeree the possibly difficult task of deciding whether his source of information is reliable, and it may also make it hard for him to tell exactly when the offer was withdrawn. In *Dickinson v Dodds*, for example, it is not clear whether this occurred when the offeree realised that the defendant had (a) sold the land to the third party, or (b) begun to negotiate with the third party, or (c) simply decided not to sell to the plaintiff. Certainty would be promoted if the rule were that the withdrawal must be communicated by the offeror, as well as to the offeree.

(3) Exceptions

The general rule that the withdrawal must be "brought to the mind of"[37] the offeree is subject to a number of exceptions. First, the requirement cannot be taken quite literally where an offer is made to a company whose mail is received, opened and sorted in different offices and then distributed to be dealt with in various departments. Is a letter withdrawing such an offer communicated when it is received, or when it is opened, or when it is actually read by the responsible officer?[38] In the interests of certainty it would probably be held that communication took place when the letter was "opened in the ordinary course of business or would have been so opened if the ordinary course was followed."[39] Secondly (as the concluding words of the passage just quoted suggest) the general rule may be displaced by the conduct of the offeree. A withdrawal which was delivered to the offeree's last known address would be effective if he had moved without notifying the offeror. Similarly, a withdrawal which had reached the offeree would be effective even though he had simply failed to read it after it had reached him: this would be the position where a withdrawal by telex or fax reached the offeree's office during business hours[40] even though it was not actually read by the offeree or by any of his staff till the next day.[41] Of course the withdrawal would not be effective in such a case, if it had been sent to the offeree at a time when he and all responsible members of his staff were, to the offeror's knowledge, away on holiday or on other business.[42] A third exception to the requirement that a withdrawal must be actually communicated relates to offers made to the public, *e.g.* of rewards for information leading to the arrest of the perpetrator of a crime. As it is impossible for the offeror to ensure that the notice of withdrawal comes to the attention of everyone who knew of the offer, it seems to be enough for him to take reasonable steps to bring the withdrawal to the attention of such persons, even though it does not in fact come to the attention of them all.[43]

---

[35] *i.e.* subject to the exceptions stated in the following paragraph.

[36] *Byrne & Co v Leon van Tienhoven* (1880) 5 C.P.D. 344, above, n.32.

[37] *Henthorn v Fraser* [1892] 2 Ch.27 at 32.

[38] *cf. Curtice v London, etc. Bank* [1908] 1 K.B. 291 at 300–301 (notice to countermand a cheque).

[39] *Eaglehill Ltd v J Needham (Builders) Ltd* [1973] A.C. 992 at 1011, discussing notice of dishonour of a cheque; *The Pamela* [1995] 2 Lloyd's Rep. 249 at 252; contrast *The Pendrecht* [1980] 2 Lloyd's Rep. 56 at 66 (telex notice of arbitration).

[40] For the effect of such messages when sent *out* of business hours, see above, p.22.

[41] *cf. The Brimnes* [1975] Q.B. 929 (notice withdrawing ship from charterparty).

[42] *cf. Brinkibon Ltd v Stahag Stahl und Stahlwarenhandelsgesellschaft mbH* [1983] 2 A.C. 34 at 42 (communication of acceptance).

[43] *Shuey v US*, 92 U.S. 73 (1875).

2. Rejection

An offer is terminated by rejection.[44] An attempt to accept an offer on new terms, not contained in the offer, may be a rejection of the offer accompanied by a counter-offer.[45] An offeree who makes such an attempt cannot later accept the original offer.[46] A communication from the offeree *may* be construed as a counter-offer (and hence as a rejection) even though it takes the form of a question as to the offeror's willingness to vary the terms of the offer.[47] But such a communication is not *necessarily* a counter-offer: it may be a mere inquiry[48] or request for information made without any intention of rejecting the terms of the offer. Whether the communication is a counter-offer or a request for information depends on the intention, objectively ascertained,[49] with which it was made. If, for example, an offer is made to sell a house at a specified price, an inquiry whether the intending vendor is prepared to reduce the price will not amount to a rejection if the inquiry is "merely exploratory."[50]

It seems that a rejection has no effect unless it is actually communicated to the offeror. There is no ground of convenience for holding that it should take effect when posted. The offeree will not act in reliance on it as he derives no rights or liabilities from it; and the offeror will not know that he is free from the offer until the rejection is actually communicated to him. Hence if a letter of rejection is overtaken by an acceptance sent by telex there should be a contract, provided that the offeree has made his final intention clear to the offeror. But once the rejection had reached the offeror he should not be bound by an acceptance posted after the rejection and also reaching the offeror after the rejection. To hold the offeror bound,[51] merely because the acceptance was *posted* before the rejection had reached him, could expose him to hardship, particularly when he had acted on the rejection, *e.g.* by disposing elsewhere of the subject-matter. If the offeree has posted a rejection and then wishes, after all, to accept the offer, he should ensure that his subsequently posted acceptance actually comes to the notice of the offeror before the latter receives the rejection.

3. Lapse of Time

An offer which is expressly stated to last for a fixed time cannot be accepted after that time; and an offer which stipulates for acceptance "by return" (of post) must normally[52] be accepted either by a return postal communication or by some other no less expeditious method. An offer which contains no express provision limiting its duration terminates after lapse of a reasonable time.[53] What is a reasonable time depends on such circumstances as the nature of the subject-matter and the means used to communicate the offer. Thus an offer to sell a perishable thing, or one whose price is liable to sudden fluctuations, would determine after a short time. The same is true of an offer made by telegram[54] or by some other at least equally speedy means of communication such as telex or fax.

---

[44] *Tinn v Hoffmann & Co* (1873) 29 L.T. 271 at 278.
[45] See above, p.20.
[46] *Hyde v Wrench* (1840) 3 Beav. 334.
[47] See the treatment in *Tinn v Hoffman* (1873) 29 L.T. 271 at 278 of the claimant's letter of November 27.
[48] *Stevenson Jacques & Co v Maclean* (1880) 5 Q.B.D. 346 at 349.
[49] See above, p.8.
[50] *Gibson v Manchester CC* [1979] 1 W.L.R. 294 at 302.
[51] Under the "posting rule", above, p.24.
[52] See above, p.30.
[53] *Ramsgate Victoria Hotel Co Ltd v Montefiore* (1866) L.R. 1 Ex. 109; *Cemco Leasing SpA v Rediffusion Ltd* [1987] F.T.L.R. 201.
[54] *Quenerduaine v Cole* (1883) 32 W.R. 185.

The period that would normally constitute a reasonable time for acceptance may be extended if the conduct of the offeree within that period indicates an intention to accept and this is known to the offeror. Such conduct would often of itself amount to acceptance, but this possibility may be ruled out by the terms of the offer, which may require the acceptance to be by written notice sent to a specified address.[55] In such a case the offeree's conduct, though it could not *amount* to an acceptance, could nevertheless prolong the time for giving a proper notice of acceptance. For the offeree's conduct to have this effect, it must be known to the offeror; for if this were not the case the offeror might reasonably suppose that the offer had not been accepted within the normal period of lapse, and act in reliance on that belief: *e.g.* by disposing elsewhere of the subject-matter.

4. Occurrence of Condition

An offer which expressly provides that it is to terminate on the occurrence of some condition cannot be accepted after that condition has occurred; and such a provision may also be implied. If an offer to buy or hire-purchase goods is made after the offeror has examined them, it may be an implied term of the offer that they should at the time of acceptance still be in substantially the same state as that in which they were when the offer was made. Such an offer cannot be accepted after the goods have been seriously damaged.[56] Similarly, an offer to insure the life of a person cannot be accepted after he has suffered serious injuries by falling over a cliff.[57] On the same principle, it is submitted that the offer which is made by bidding at an auction by implication provides that it is to lapse as soon as a higher bid is made.[58]

5. Death

One possible view is that the death of either party terminates the offer, as the parties can no longer reach agreement.[59] But there may be a contract in spite of a demonstrable lack of agreement if to hold the contrary would cause serious inconvenience.[60] In accordance with this principle, it is submitted that the death of either party should not of itself terminate the offer except in the case of such "personal" contracts as are discharged by the death of either party.[61]

(1) Death of an offeror

The effect of the death of the offeror has been considered in a number of cases concerning continuing guarantees. In general, a continuing guarantee, *e.g.* of a bank overdraft, is divisible[62]: it is a continuing offer by the guarantor, accepted from time to time as the banker makes loans to his customer. Each loan is a separate acceptance,

---

[55] As in *Manchester Diocesan Council for Education v Commercial and General Investments Ltd* [1970] 1 W.L.R. 241.

[56] *Financings Ltd v Stimson* [1962] 1 W.L.R. 1184.

[57] *Canning v Farquhar* (1885) 16 Q.B.D. 722 (the offer here came in the form of a counter-offer from the insurance company: see at 733); *Looker v Law Union & Rock Ins Co Ltd* [1928] 1 K.B. 554. Contrast p.292, n.63, below.

[58] See above, p.11.

[59] *Dickinson v Dodds* (1876) 2 Ch.D. 463 at 475.

[60] See above, p.41.

[61] *e.g.* contracts of employment or agency: below, p.750. Even in such cases the legal effects of saying that the offer was terminated, so that there was never any contract, would be likely to differ from those of saying that there had been a contract which had been discharged: *e.g.* the Law Reform (Frustrated Contracts) Act 1943 could apply to the latter, but not to the former, situation.

[62] See above, p.39.

turning the offer *pro tanto* into a binding contract. It seems that such a guarantee is not terminated merely by the death of the guarantor.[63] But it is terminated if the bank knows that the guarantor has died and that his personal representatives have no power under his will to continue the guarantee[64]; or if for some other reason it is inequitable for the bank to charge the guarantor's estate.[65] If the guarantee expressly provides that it can be terminated only by notice given by the guarantor *or his personal representatives*, the death of the guarantor, even if known to the bank, will not terminate the guarantee: express notice must be given.[66]

(2) Death of offeree

Two cases have some bearing on the effect of the death of the offeree. In *Reynolds v Atherton*[67] an offer to sell shares was made in 1911 "to the directors of" a company. An attempt to accept the offer was made in 1919 by the survivors of the persons who were directors in 1911 and by the personal representatives of those who had since died. The purported acceptance was held to be ineffective; and Warrington L.J. said obiter that an offer "made to a living person who ceases to be a living person before the offer is accepted . . . is no longer an offer at all". The actual ground for the decision, however, was that the offer had, on its true construction, been made to the directors of the company for the time being, and not to those who happened to hold office in 1911. In *Kennedy v Thomassen*[68] an offer to buy annuities was accepted by the solicitors of the annuitant after she had, without the solicitors' knowledge, died. This acceptance was held to be ineffective on the grounds that the solicitors' authority was terminated by their client's death and that the acceptance was made under a mistake.[69] Neither case supports the view that an offer can never be accepted after the offeree's death. It is submitted that, where an offer related to a contract which was not "personal",[70] it might, on its true construction, be held to have been made to the offeree or to his executors, and that such an offer could be accepted after the death of the original offeree.

6. Supervening Incapacity

(1) Mental patients

If an offeror became a mental patient he would not be bound by an acceptance made after this fact had become known to the offeree, or after the patient's property had been made subject to the control of the court. But the other party would be bound; and an offer made to a person who later became a mental patient could be accepted so as to bind the other party. These rules can readily be deduced from the law as to contracts with mental patients.[71]

---

[63] *Bradbury v Morgan* (1862) 1 H. & C. 249; *Harris v Fawcett* (1873) L.R. 8 Ch.App. 866 at 869; *Coulthart v Clementson* (1879) 5 Q.B.D. 42, at 46.
[64] *Coulthart v Clementson* (1879) 5 Q.B.D. 42.
[65] *Harris v Fawcett* (1873) L.R. 8 Ch.App. 866.
[66] *Re Silvester* [1895] 1 Ch.573.
[67] (1921) 125 L.T. 690; affirmed, (1922) 127 L.T. 189.
[68] [1929] 1 Ch.426.
[69] *cf.* below, p.286.
[70] See above, at n.61.
[71] See below, pp.557 *et seq.*

(2) Corporations

(a) COMPANIES GOVERNED BY THE COMPANIES ACT 1985. Such a company may lose its capacity to do an act by altering its memorandum of association.[72] If the company nevertheless entered into transactions after so losing its capacity to do so, those transactions were formerly *ultra vires* and void.[73] Now the general rule[74] is that acts done by the company can no longer be called into question on the ground that the company lacked capacity to do them by reason of anything in its memorandum[75]; and that, in favour of a person dealing with the company in good faith, the power of the board of directors to bind the company, or to authorise others to do so, is deemed to be free of any limitation under the company's constitution.[76] But a member of the company may bring proceedings to restrain the doing of acts beyond the company's capacity, or beyond the powers of the directors, except where such acts are done in fulfilment of legal obligations arising from previous acts of the company.[77] The effect of these provisions must be considered on offers made *to* and *by* the company.

(i) *Company as offeree.* A company may receive an offer to enter into a contract and then alter its memorandum so as to deprive itself of the capacity to enter into that contract. If it nevertheless accepts the offer, the acceptance is effective in favour of a person who deals with the company in good faith; but before the company has accepted the offer, it can be restrained from doing so in proceedings brought by one of its members.

(ii) *Company as offeror.* A company may make an offer to enter into a contract and then alter its memorandum and so deprive itself of the capacity to enter into that contract. An acceptance of that offer is nevertheless effective in favour of a person dealing with the company in good faith; but it is not entirely clear whether in this situation a member of the company could take proceedings to prevent the conclusion of the contract. Such proceedings lie only to restrain "the doing of an act"[78] by the company and since the relevant act on the company's part (*i.e.* the making of the offer) would already have been done when the company still had capacity to do it, there seems to be nothing for the member to restrain, unless holding the offer open could be described as a continuing act.

Of course, the company itself could normally withdraw the offer and would be likely to do so in pursuance of the policy which had led it to change its memorandum. But this possibility would not be open to the company where it had bound itself not to withdraw the offer, *i.e.* where it had granted a legally enforceable option[79]; and in such a case a member could not take proceedings to prevent the conclusion of the contract since such proceedings cannot be taken "in respect of an act to be done in fulfilment of a legal obligation arising from a previous act of the company"[80]: *i.e.* from the grant of the option.

(b) OTHER CORPORATIONS. Companies may also be incorporated by Royal Charter or by special legislation. Charter corporations have the legal capacity of a natural person so that an alteration of the charter would not affect the validity of an offer or acceptance

[72] See below, p.560.
[73] See below, p.560.
[74] See generally below, pp.561–563. For an exception, see Charities Act 1993, s.65.
[75] Companies Act 1985, s.35(1) (as substituted by Companies Act 1989, s.108).
[76] *ibid.* s.35A(1).
[77] *ibid.* ss.35(2), 35A(4).
[78] *ibid.*
[79] For legally enforceable options, see below, p.153, n.80.
[80] Companies Act 1985, ss.35(2), 35A(3) (as substituted by Companies Act 1989, s.108).

made by the corporation.[81] The legal capacity of corporations incorporated by special statute is governed by the statute, and acts not within that capacity are *ultra vires*[82] and void. An alteration of the statute could therefore prevent the company from accepting an offer made to it, and from being bound by the acceptance of an offer made by it, where the offer was made before the alteration came into effect. In practice, the problem is likely to be dealt with in the statute which changes the capacity of the corporation.

Limited liability partnerships incorporated under the Limited Liability Partnerships Act 2000[83] are bodies corporate[84]; but problems of the kind here under discussion cannot arise with regard to them as they have "unlimited capacity".[85]

SECTION 4. SPECIAL CASES

In some situations already discussed, the analysis of agreement into offer and acceptance gives rise to considerable difficulty,[86] and in others, to be discussed in this section, such analysis is impossible or highly artificial.[87] For this reason, it has been suggested that the analysis is "out of date"[88] and that "you should look at the correspondence as a whole and at the conduct of the parties and see therefrom whether the parties have come to an agreement".[89] The objection to this view, however, is that it provides too little guidance for the courts (or for the legal advisers of the parties) in determining whether agreement has been reached. For this reason, the situations to be discussed below are best regarded as exceptions[90] to a general requirement of offer and acceptance. This approach is supported by cases in which it has been held that there was no contract precisely because there was no offer and acceptance[91]; and by those in which the terms of a contract have been held to depend on the analysis of the negotiation into offer, counter-offer and acceptance.[92]

1. Multipartite Agreements

In *The Satanita*[93] the claimant and the defendant entered their yachts for a regatta. Each signed a letter, addressed to the secretary of the club which organised the regatta, undertaking to obey certain rules during the race. It was held that there was a contract

---

[81] See below, p.560; but members of a corporation could bring proceedings to restrain the conclusion of the contract: *ibid.*

[82] See below, p.563.

[83] See ss.2 and 3 of the Act.

[84] *ibid.* s.1(2).

[85] *ibid.* s.1(3).

[86] See above, pp.10, 16–17, 20–21.

[87] *Gibson v Manchester CC* [1978] 1 W.L.R. 520 at 523, reversed [1979] 1 W.L.R. 294; *cf. The Eurymedon* [1975] A.C. 154 at 167; Pollock, *Principles of Contract* (13th ed.), p.5.

[88] *Butler Machine Tool Co Ltd v Ex-Cell-O Corp (England) Ltd* [1979] 1 W.L.R. 401 at 404; *cf. Port Sudan Cotton Co v Govindaswamy Chettiar & Sons* [1977] 2 Lloyd's Rep. 5 at 10; *Interfoto Picture Library Ltd v Stiletto Visual Programmes Ltd* [1989] Ch.433 at 443.

[89] *Gibson v Manchester CC* [1978] 1 W.L.R. 520 at 523, reversed [1979] 1 W.L.R. 294.

[90] *Gibson v Manchester CC* [1979] 1 W.L.R. 294 at 297; *The Good Helmsman* [1981] 1 Lloyd's Rep. 377 at 409; *G Percy Trentham v Archital Luxfer Ltd* [1993] 1 Lloyd's Rep. 25 at 27, 29–30.

[91] *The Kapetan Markos NL (No.2)* [1987] 2 Lloyd's Rep. 323 at 331 ("What was the mechanism for offer and acceptance?"); *cf. The Good Helmsman* [1981] 1 Lloyd's Rep. 377 at 409; *The Aramis* [1989] 1 Lloyd's Rep. 213, Treitel [1989] L.M.C.L.Q. 162; *Taylor v Dickens* [1998] 1 FLR 806 at 818 (doubted on another point in *Gillett v Holt* [2001] Ch.210); *Schuldenfrei v Hilton* [1999] S.T.C. 821. The "offer and acceptance" analysis was also regarded as decisive in many of the arbitration cases discussed at pp.10, 30, above, though it was viewed with scepticism in *The Multibank Holsatia* [1988] 2 Lloyd's Rep. 486 at 491 and in *The Maritime Winner* [1989] 2 Lloyd's Rep. 506 at 515.

[92] *e.g.* The "battle of forms" cases discussed at pp.20–21, above.

[93] [1895] p.248; affirmed sub nom. *Clarke v Dunraven* [1897] A.C. 59; Phillips, 92 L.Q.R. 499.

between all the competitors on the terms of the undertaking, though it is not clear whether the contract was made when the competitors entered their yachts or when they actually began to race. In either event, it is difficult to analyse the transaction into offer and acceptance.[94] If the contract was made when the yachts were entered, one would have to say that the entry of the first competitor was an offer and that the entry of the next was an acceptance of that offer and (simultaneously) an offer to yet later competitors; but this view is artificial and unworkable even in theory unless each competitor knew of the existence of previous ones. It would also lead to the conclusion that entries which were put in the post together were cross-offers and thus not binding on each other.[95] If the contract was made when the race began, then it seems that each competitor simultaneously agreed to terms proposed by the officers of the club, and not that each proposed an identical set of terms amounting at the same time to an offer to the others and to an acceptance of the offers at that instant made by them. Even if the second view of the facts could be taken, the "offers" and "acceptances" would all occur at the same moment. Thus they would be cross-offers and would not create a contract. The competitors, no doubt, reached agreement, but they did not do so by a process which can be analysed into offer and acceptance. Similar reasoning would seem to apply to the contract which governs the legal relations between members of an unincorporated association.[96]

The above discussion is based on the assumption that all the parties to the alleged multilateral contract were willing to agree to the same terms. Where one of the negotiating parties had refused to accept one of the terms of the proposed contract, no multilateral contract would arise between that party and any of the others, unless the others agreed to be bound to that party on terms excluding the one rejected by him.[97]

2. Reference to Third Party

Where two negotiating parties reach deadlock, they may ask a third party to break it. If both simultaneously assent to a solution proposed by him, there is a contract, but it is again impossible to say which party has made the offer and which the acceptance.[98] The same is true where the parties negotiate through a single broker who eventually obtains their consent to the same terms.[99]

3. Sale of Land

There is some difficulty in analysing into offer and acceptance a transaction such as the sale of land where parties agree "subject to contract" so that they are not bound until formal contracts are exchanged.[1] Strictly an "offer" subject to contract does not satisfy the definition of offer[2] since the person making it has no intention to be bound immediately on acceptance. However, the *agreement* is made by the usual process: the

---

[94] cf. *Kingscroft Insurance Co Ltd v Nissan Fire and Marine Insurance Co Ltd* [2000] 1 All E.R. (Comm) 272 at 291 (admission of new members to an existing insurance pool analysed in terms of offer and acceptance).

[95] See above, p.37.

[96] See *Artistic Upholstery Ltd v Art Forma (Furniture) Ltd* [1999] 4 All E.R. 277, 285; below, p.543; though breach of the rules by one member may not, on their true construction, be actionable in damages at the suit of another: *Anderton v Rowland, The Times*, November 5, 1999.

[97] *Azov Shipping Co v Baltic Shipping Co* [1999] 2 Lloyd's Rep. 159 at 165.

[98] Pollock, *Principles of Contract* (13th ed.), p.5.

[99] *Pagnan SpA v Feed Products Ltd* [1987] 2 Lloyds's Rep. 601 at 616.

[1] See below, p.52.

[2] See above, p.8.

reason why parties are not bound until they exchange formal contracts is that the terms of their agreement expressly negative for the time being the intention to enter into legal relations.[3] Alternatively, a party can be regarded as making the offer when he submits a signed contract for exchange[4]; and this would be accepted when the exchange took place.

SECTION 5. CERTAINTY

An agreement is not a binding contract if it lacks certainty, either because it is too vague or because it is obviously incomplete.[5]

1. Vagueness

An agreement may be so vague that no definite meaning can be given to it without adding new terms. Thus in *G Scammell & Nephew Ltd v Ouston*[6] the House of Lords held that an agreement to buy goods "on hire-purchase" was too vague to be enforced, since there were many kinds of hire-purchase agreements in widely different terms, so that it was impossible to say on which terms the parties intended to contract. Similarly, agreements "subject to war clause",[7] "subject to strike and lockout clause",[8] and "subject to *force majeure* conditions"[9] have been held too vague, there being no evidence in any of the cases of a customary or usual form of such clauses or conditions.[10] Similar reasoning has sometimes been applied where agreements were made subject to the "satisfaction" of one party.[11] The problems arising from such provisions are discussed later in this Chapter.[12]

But the courts do not expect commercial documents to be drafted with strict precision, and will, particularly if the parties have acted on an agreement,[13] do their best to avoid striking it down on the ground that it is too vague.[14]

(1) Custom and trade usage

Apparent vagueness can be resolved by custom. Thus a contract to load coal at Grimsby "on the terms of the usual colliery guarantee" was upheld on proof of the terms usually contained in such guarantees at Grimsby.[15] It has similarly been held that an undertaking

---

[3] See below, p.150.

[4] See *Christie Owen & Davies v Rapacioli* [1974] Q.B. 781; *cf. Commission for the New Towns v Cooper (Great Britain) Ltd* [1995] Ch.259 at 285.

[5] Fridman, 76 L.Q.R. 521; Lücke, 6 Adelaide L.Rev. 1.

[6] [1941] A.C. 251.

[7] *Bishop & Baxter Ltd v Anglo-Eastern Trading Co* [1944] K.B. 12.

[8] *Love & Stewart Ltd v S Instone & Co* (1917) 33 T.L.R. 475.

[9] *British Electrical, etc. Industries Ltd v Patley Pressings Ltd* [1953] 1 W.L.R. 280.

[10] For further illustrations, see below, p.423.

[11] *Stabilad Ltd v Stephens & Carter Ltd (No.2)* [1999] 2 All E.R. (Comm) 651 at 659.

[12] See below, p.63.

[13] *Brown v Gould* [1972] Ch.53 at 57–58; *Tito v Waddell (No.2)* [1977] Ch.106 at 314; *The Tropwind* [1982] 1 Lloyd's Rep. 232; *Sudbrook Trading Estate Ltd v Eggleton* [1983] 1 A.C. 444; *The Mercedes Envoy* [1995] 2 Lloyd's Rep. 559 at 564.

[14] See *Rahcassi Shipping Co v Blue Star Line* [1969] 1 Q.B. 173; *Nea Agrex SA v Baltic Shipping Co Ltd* [1976] Q.B. 933; *Grace Shipping Inc v CF Sharpe & Co (Malaysia) Pte* [1987] 1 Lloyd's Rep. 207; *Deutsche Schachtbau-und-Tiefbohrgesellschaft mbH v Ras Al Khairah National Oil Co* [1990] 1 A.C. 295 at 306, reversed on other grounds *ibid.* at 329 *et seq.*; *Anangel Atlas Compania Naviera SA v Ishikawajima Harima Heavy Industries Co Ltd (No.2)* [1990] 2 Lloyd's Rep. 526 at 546; *The Star Texas* [1993] 2 Lloyd's Rep. 445 at 455.

[15] *Shamrock SS Co v Storey & Co* (1899) 81 L.T. 413; *cf. Hart v Hart* (1881) 18 Ch.D. 670; *Baynham v Philips Electronics (UK) Ltd*, The Times, July 19, 1995.

to grant a lease of a shop "in prime position" was not too uncertain to be enforced since the phrase was commonly used by persons dealing with shop property, so that its meaning could be determined by expert evidence.[16] And courts often enforce commercial contracts expressed in abbreviations whose meaning is certain and notorious.

(2) Reasonableness

In *Hillas & Co Ltd v Arcos Ltd*,[17] an agreement for the sale of timber "of fair specification", was made between persons well acquainted with the timber trade. The agreement was upheld as the standard of reasonableness could be applied to make the otherwise vague phrase certain since the words of the contract imported some objective standard for assessing the quality of the goods to be supplied. The case should be contrasted with one in which a supplier of clothing to a retail chain alleged that there was an implied contract between them not to terminate their long-standing relationship except on reasonable notice. One ground for rejecting the claim was that there were "no objective criteria by which the court could assess what would be reasonable either as to quantity or price."[18]

(3) Duty to resolve uncertainty

An agreement containing a vague phrase may be binding because one party is under a duty to resolve the uncertainty. In one case an agreement to sell goods provided for delivery "free on board . . . good Danish port". It was held that the agreement was not too vague: it amounted to a good contract under which the buyer was bound to select the port of shipment.[19]

(4) Meaningless and self-contradictory phrases

The court will make considerable efforts to give meaning to an apparently meaningless phrase[20]; but, even where these efforts fail, the presence of such phrases does not necessarily vitiate the agreement. In *Nicolene Ltd v Simmonds*[21] steel bars were bought on terms which were certain except for a clause that the sale was subject to "the usual conditions of acceptance". There being no such usual conditions, it was held that the phrase was meaningless, but that this did not vitiate the whole contract: the words were severable and could be ignored. A self-contradictory clause can be treated in the same way. Thus where an arbitration clause provided for arbitration of "any dispute" in London and of "any other dispute" in Moscow the court disregarded the clause and

---

[16] *Ashburn Anstalt v Arnold* [1989] Ch.1 at 27, overruled on another ground in *Prudential Assurance Co Ltd v London Residuary Body* [1992] A.C. 386.

[17] (1932) 147 L.T. 503 (and see below, p.55); *Sweet & Maxwell Ltd v Universal News Services Ltd* [1964] 2 Q.B. 699; cf. *Greater London Council v Connolly* [1970] 2 Q.B. 100; *Finchbourne Ltd v Rodrigues* [1976] 3 All E.R. 581; *Malcolm v Chancellor, Masters and Scholars of the University of Oxford, The Times*, December 19, 1990; *Hackney LBC v Jackson* [2001] L.&T. Rep. 7.

[18] *Baird Textile Holdings Ltd v Marks & Spencer plc* [2001] EWCA Civ 274; [2002] 1 All E.R. (Comm) 737, at [30].

[19] *David T Boyd & Co v Louis Louca* [1973] 1 Lloyd's Rep. 209; cf. *Siew Soon Wah v Yong Tong Hong* [1973] A.C. 831; *Pagnan SpA v Feed Products Ltd* [1987] 2 Lloyd's Rep. 601; cf. *Bulk Trading Co Ltd v Zenziper Grains and Feedstuffs* [2001] 1 Lloyd's Rep. 357 (seller's duty to specify place of delivery under f.o.t. contract).

[20] *The Tropwind* [1982] 1 Lloyd's Rep. 232.

[21] [1953] 1 Q.B. 543; discussed in *Heisler v Anglo-Dal Ltd* [1954] 1 W.L.R. 1273; cf. *Slater v Raw, The Times*, October 15, 1977; *The Scaptrade* [1981] 2 Lloyd's Rep. 425 at 432 (affirmed without reference to this point [1983] 2 A.C. 694), and see below, p.54.

determined the dispute itself.[22] Such cases show that the question whether a meaningless phrase vitiates the contract, or can be ignored, depends on the importance which the parties may be considered to have attached to it. If it is simply verbiage, not intended to add anything to an otherwise complete agreement, or if it relates to a matter of relatively minor importance, it can be ignored. But if the parties intend it to govern some vital aspect of their relationship, its vagueness will vitiate the entire agreement.

2. Incompleteness

(1) Agreement in principle only[23]

Parties may reach agreement on essential matters of principle, but leave important points unsettled, so that their agreement is incomplete. There is, for example, no contract if an agreement for a lease fails to specify the date on which the term is to commence.[24] Similarly, an agreement for the sale of land by instalments is not a binding contract if it provides for conveyance of "a proportionate part" as each instalment of the price is paid but fails to specify which part was to be conveyed on each payment.[25]

On the other hand, the agreement does not have to be worked out in meticulous detail.[26] Under the Sale of Goods Act 1979, an agreement for the sale of goods may be binding as soon as the parties have agreed to buy and sell, where the remaining details can be determined by the standard of reasonableness or by law. Even failure to fix the price is not necessarily fatal in such a case. S.8(2) of the Act provides that, if no price is determined by the contract, a reasonable price must be paid. Under s.15(1) of the Supply of Goods and Services Act 1982, a reasonable sum must similarly be paid where a contract for the supply of services fails to fix the remuneration to be paid for them.[27] These statutory provisions assume that the agreement amounts to a contract in spite of its failure to fix the price or remuneration. The very fact that the parties have not reached agreement on this vital point may indicate that there is *no* contract, *e.g.* because the price or remuneration is to be fixed by further agreement.[28] In such a case, the statutory provisions for payment of a reasonable sum do not apply. There may, however, be a claim for payment of such a sum at common law: for example, where work is done in the belief that there was a contract or in the expectation that the negotiations between the parties would result in the conclusion of a contract.[29] Such liability arises in restitution, in spite of the fact that there was *no* contract. It follows that the party doing the work, though he is entitled to a reasonable sum, is not liable in damages, *e.g.* for failing to do the work within a reasonable time.[30] If the claim arose under a contract by virtue of s.15(1) of the 1982 Act, the party doing the work would be both entitled and liable.

---

[22] *E R J Lovelock v Exportles* [1968] 1 Lloyd's Rep. 163; *cf. The Star Texas* [1993] 2 Lloyd's Rep. 445.

[23] Lücke, 3 Adelaide L.Rev. 46.

[24] *Harvey v Pratt* [1965] 1 W.L.R. 1025; and see *Re Day's Will Trusts* [1962] 1 W.L.R. 1419.

[25] *Bushwall Properties Ltd v Vortex Properties Ltd* [1976] 1 W.L.R. 591; Emery, [1976] C.L.J. 215; *cf. Hillreed Land v Beautridge* [1994] E.G.C.S. 55; *Avintar v Avill* 1995 S.C.L.R. 1012; *Hadley v Kemp* [1999] E.M.L.R. 589 at 628; *London & Regional Development Ltd v TBI plc Belfast International Airport Ltd* [2002] EWCA Civ 355.

[26] *First Energy (UK) Ltd v Hungarian International Bank Ltd* [1993] 2 Lloyd's Rep. 195 at 205.

[27] *cf.* at common law, *Way v Latilla* [1937] 3 All E.R. 759; *The Tropwind* [1982] 1 Lloyd's Rep. 232; *Michael Elliott & Partners v UK Land* [1991] 1 E.G.L.R. 39; and see, as to agents' commissions, below, p.740.

[28] *e.g. May & Butcher v R.* [1934] 2 K.B. 17n; *Courtney & Fairbairn Ltd v Tolaini Bros (Hotels) Ltd* [1975] 1 W.L.R. 297; Dugdale and Lowe [1976] J.B.L. 312; *Chamberlain v Boodle & King* [1982] 1 W.L.R. 1443 n.; *Russell Bros (Paddington) Ltd v John Elliott Management Ltd* (1995) 11 Const. L.J. 337; *Southwark LBC v Logan* (1996) 8 Admin.L.R. 315.

[29] See below, pp.988–989.

[30] *BSC v Cleveland Bridge & Engineering Co Ltd* [1984] 1 All E.R. 504.

Even an agreement for the sale of land dealing only with the barest essentials may be regarded as complete if that was the clear intention of the parties. Thus in *Perry v Suffields Ltd*[31] an offer to sell a public-house with vacant possession for £7,000 was accepted without qualification. It was held that there was a binding contract, in spite of the fact that many important points such as the date of completion[32] and the question of paying a deposit, were left open.[33] In another case[34] a buyer and seller of corn feed pellets had reached agreement on the "cardinal terms of the deal: product, price, quantity, period of shipment, range of loading ports and governing contract terms".[35] The agreement was held to have contractual force even though the parties had not yet reached agreement on a number of other important points, such as the loading port,[36] the rate of loading and certain payments (other than the price) which might in certain events become due under the contract. In all these cases, the courts took the view that the parties intended to be bound at once in spite of the fact that further significant terms were to be agreed later; and that even their failure to reach such agreement would not invalidate the contract unless without such agreement the contract was unworkable or too uncertain[37] to be enforced.

A distinction must finally be drawn between cases in which agreement on such matters as the price is required for the making, and those in which it is required for the *continued operation*, of a contract. The latter possibility is illustrated by a case[38] in which an agreement for the supply of services for 10 years fixed the fee to be paid only for the first of those two years. On the parties' failure to fix the fee in later years, it was held that they had intended to enter into a 10-year contract and that a term was to be implied into that contract for payment of a reasonable fee in those later years.

(2) Further agreement expressly required

An agreement may be incomplete because it expressly requires further agreement to be reached on points as yet left open.

(a) AGREEMENTS "SUBJECT TO CONTRACT". Agreements for the sale of land by private treaty are usually[39] made "subject to contract". Such an agreement is incomplete until the details of a formal contract have been settled and approved by the parties.[40]

---

[31] [1916] 2 Ch.187; *Elias v George Sahely & Co (Barbados) Ltd* [1982] 3 All E.R. 801.

[32] *cf. Storer v Manchester CC* [1974] 1 W.L.R. 1403.

[33] For the resolution of such points, see below, p.55.

[34] *Pagnan SpA v Feed Products Ltd* [1987] 2 Lloyd's Rep. 601.

[35] *ibid.* at 611.

[36] *cf.* above, p.50 at n.19.

[37] See above, p.48.

[38] *Mamidoil-Jetoil Arab Petroleum Co SA v Okta Crude Oil Refinery AD* [2001] EWCA Civ 406; [2001] 2 Lloyd's Rep. 76. For further proceedings arising out of the same contract, see [2003] 1 Lloyd's Rep. 1, below, p.58.

[39] Not always: *Storer v Manchester CC* [1974] 1 W.L.R. 1403; *Tweddell v Henderson* [1975] 1 W.L.R. 1496 at 1501–1502; *Elias v George Sahely & Co (Barbados) Ltd*, above.

[40] *Winn v Bull* (1877) 7 Ch.D. 29. *cf. The Nissos Samos* [1985] 1 Lloyd's Rep. 378 at 385; *The Intra Transporter* [1985] 2 Lloyd's Rep. 159 at 163, affirmed [1986] 2 Lloyd's Rep. 132; *The Junior K* [1988] 2 Lloyd's Rep. 583; (sale of ship and charterparty intended to be "subject to details" not binding before details settled); *cf. The CPC Gallia* [1994] 1 Lloyd's Rep. 68; Debattista, [1985] L.M.C.L.Q. 241; *Ronald Preston & Partners v Markheath Securities* [1988] 2 E.G.L.R. 23 (agreement to pay fee to estate agent "subject to contract" not legally binding); *Ignazio Messina & Co v Polskie Linie Oceaniczne* [1995] 2 Lloyd's Rep. 566; *Drake Scull Engineering Ltd v Higgs & Hill (Northern) Ltd* (1995) 11 Const.L.J. 214; *Regalian Properties plc v London Dockland Development Corp* [1995] 1 W.L.R. 212; *Enfield LBC v Arajah* [1995] E.G.C.S. 164; contrast *Prudential Assurance Co Ltd v Mount Eden Land Co Ltd* [1997] 1 E.G.L.R. 37 (consent to alterations given by landlord "subject to licence" held effective as the consent was a unilateral act, so that no question of agreement arose).

(i) *Requirement of exchange of contracts.* Even when the terms of the formal contract have been agreed, there is, where the agreement is subject to contract, no binding contract until there has been an "exchange of contracts".[41] It is also necessary (though not sufficient) for the formal requirements for contracts for the sale of land (which are described in Chapter 5) to be satisfied.[42] The formal requirement in cases of the present kind is that each party must sign a document containing all the terms which have been expressly agreed[43]; and the requirement of exchange traditionally refers to the handing over by each party to the other of one of these documents, or to their despatch by post; if the later method is adopted, the process is completed on the receipt of the second of the posted documents.[44] No doubt the mechanics of "exchange" will be suitably modified when the proposed system of electronic conveyancing is brought in to operation.[45] Before the "exchange," there is no uncertainty as to the terms of the agreement, but there is no contract because neither party intends to be legally bound until the "exchange of contracts" takes place.[46]

(ii) *Mitigations of the requirement.* The above state of the law, which enables either party with impunity to go back on a concluded agreement, has been described as "a social and moral blot on the law"[47]; and there are indications that the courts are prepared to mitigate the former strictness of the requirement of "exchange of contracts". Thus it has been held that the exchange may be effected by telephone or telex[48]; that certain technical slips in the process may be disregarded[49]; that exchange is not necessary where the parties use the same solicitor[50]; and (in Australia) that where the two parts do not match precisely there may nevertheless be a contract, the discrepancy being remedied by rectification.[51] The parties may also create a binding contract by a subsequent agreement to remove the effect of the words "subject to contract," thus indicating their intention henceforth to be legally bound.[52] Subsequent conduct may also give rise to liability on other grounds: where one party to the agreement encourages the other to believe that he will not withdraw, and the other acts to his detriment in reliance on that belief, the former may be liable on the basis of "proprietary estoppel".[53] In "a very strong and

---

[41] *Eccles v Bryant & Pollock* [1948] Ch.93; *Santa Fé Land Co Ltd v Forestal Land Co Ltd* (1910) 26 T.L.R. 534; *cf. Coope v Ridout* [1921] 1 Ch.291; *Chillingworth v Esche* [1924] 1 Ch.97; *Raingold v Bromley* [1931] 2 Ch.307; *D'Silva v Lister House Development Ltd* [1971] Ch.17.

[42] See below, p.163. A document setting out all the terms expressly agreed and signed by both parties would satisfy the *formal* requirements; but if it were expressed to be "subject to contract" it would not give rise to a contract till "exchange" had taken place.

[43] Law of Property (Miscellaneous Provisions) Act 1989, ss.2(1), (3).

[44] See *Commission for the New Towns v Cooper (Great Britain) Ltd* [1995] Ch.259 at 285, 289; *cf. ibid.* 293, 295.

[45] On the making of Orders under Land Registration Act 2002.

[46] See below, p.163.

[47] *Cohen v Nessdale* [1981] 3 All E.R. 118 at 128 (affirmed [1982] 2 All E.R. 97); *cf.* Law Commission Paper No.65.

[48] *Domb v Isoz* [1980] Ch.548. This relaxation refers only to the process of exchange. The formal requirements referred to at n.43 must also be satisfied.

[49] *Harrison v Battye* [1975] 1 W.L.R. 58.

[50] *Smith v Mansi* [1963] 1 W.L.R. 26; exchange is also unnecessary in the case of a deed, which takes effect as soon as it has been duly executed (below pp.158–159): *Vincent v Premo Enterprises Ltd* [1969] 2 Q.B. 609; *D'Silva v Lister House Development Ltd* [1971] Ch.17.

[51] *Sindel v Georgiou* (1984) 1454 C.L.R. 661; for rectification see below, p.321.

[52] *Law v Jones* [1974] Ch.112, as explained in *Daulia v Four Millbank Nominees* [1978] Ch.231 at 250; *Cohen v Nessdale* [1981] 3 All E.R. 118 at 127; [1982] 2 All E.R. 97 at 104; see also *Tiverton Estates Ltd v Wearwell* [1975] Ch.146; the subsequent agreement would now have to satisfy formal requirements more stringent than those in force at the time of the decisions cited in this note: see below, p.179.

[53] See the discussion at p.138, below of *Attorney-General of Hong Kong v Humphreys Estate (Queen's Gardens)* [1987] A.C. 114.

exceptional context"[54] the court may even infer that the parties intended to be legally bound when executing the original document, even though it is expressed to be "subject to contract". This was held to be the position where a document containing these words laid down an elaborate time-table, imposed a duty on the purchaser to approve the draft contract (subject only to reasonable amendments) and required him then to exchange contracts.[55] In these exceptional circumstances, the words "subject to contract" were taken merely to mean that the parties had not yet settled all the details of the transaction and therefore not to negative the intention to be bound.

(iii) *Exceptions to the requirement.* Agreements for the sale of land by auction or by tender are not normally made "subject to contract". The intention of the parties in such cases is to enter into a binding contract as soon as an offer to buy has been accepted. In one case[56] of a sale by tender, the words "subject to contract" were, by a clerical error, typed on one of the contractual documents. In these highly exceptional circumstances,[57] the words were held to be meaningless, so that there was a binding contract. This was also held to be the case where a notice exercising an option to purchase land was expressed to be "subject to contract", as the notice was clearly intended to give rise to a binding contract.[58]

(iv) *Collateral contract.* A party's freedom to withdraw from an agreement "subject to contract" may also be restricted by a collateral contract. For example a vendor who has agreed to sell land "subject to contract" may, either at the same time or subsequently, undertake not to negotiate for the sale of the land with a third party. Such a collateral agreement (sometimes called a "lock-out" agreement) must itself satisfy the requirement of certainty[59] and in *Walford v Miles*[60] it was held that this requirement had not been satisfied where the agreement failed to specify the time for which the vendor's freedom to negotiate with third parties was to be restricted. But in a later case[61] it was held that a vendor's promise not to negotiate with third parties *for two weeks* was sufficient to satisfy the requirement of certainty and so to give rise to a collateral contract.[62]

(b) EXECUTION OF FORMAL DOCUMENT REQUIRED. One possible effect of a stipulation that an agreement is to be embodied in a formal written document is that the agreement is regarded by the parties as incomplete, or as not intended to be legally binding,[63] until the terms of the formal document are agreed and the document is duly executed in accordance with the terms of the preliminary agreement (*e.g.* by signature).[64] A second possibility is that such a document is intended only as a solemn record of an

---

[54] *Alpenstow Ltd v Regalian Properties Ltd* [1985] 1 W.L.R. 721 at 730; Harpum, [1986] C.L.J. 356.
[55] *Alpenstow Ltd v Regalian Properties Ltd*, above.
[56] *Michael Richard Properties Ltd v St Saviour's Parish* [1975] 3 All E.R. 416; Emery, [1976] C.L.J. 28.
[57] See *Munton v GLC* [1976] 1 W.L.R. 649.
[58] *Westway Homes v Moore* (1991) 63 P. & C.R. 480.
[59] See above, p.48.
[60] [1992] 2 A.C. 128. See further p.59, below.
[61] *Pitt v PHH Asset Management Ltd* [1993] 1 W.L.R. 327; *cf. Tye v House* [1997] 2 E.G.L.R. 171.
[62] For the consideration for this promise, see below, p.154.
[63] *BSC v Cleveland Bridge & Engineering Co Ltd* [1984] 1 All E.R. 504; *Ignazio Messina Co v Polskie Linie Oceaniczne* [1995] 2 Lloyd's Rep. 566; *The Bay Ridge* [1999] 2 All E.R. (Comm) 306 at 323; *Galliard Homes Ltd v Jarvis Interiors Ltd* [2000] C.L.C. 411.
[64] *Okura & Co Ltd v Navara Shipping Corp SA* [1982] 2 Lloyd's Rep. 537; *cf. R. v Sevenoaks DC, Ex p. Terry* [1985] 3 All E.R. 226; *The Nissos Samos* [1985] 1 Lloyd's Rep. 378 at 385; *The Intra Transporter* [1985] 2 Lloyd's Rep. 159 at 163; affirmed [1986] 2 Lloyd's Rep. 132; *The Pina* [1992] 2 Lloyd's Rep. 103 at 107; *New England Reinsurance Corp v Messaghios Insurance Co SA* [1992] 2 Lloyd's Rep. 251; *Britvic Soft Drinks Ltd v Messer UK Ltd* [2001] 1 Lloyd's Rep. 20 at [64], affirmed on other grounds [2002] EWCA Civ 548; [2002] 2 All E.R. (Comm) 321.

already complete and binding agreement[65]: for example, a contract of insurance is generally regarded as complete as soon as the insurer initials a slip setting out the main terms of the contract, even though the execution of a formal policy is contemplated.[66] The question whether an agreement which expressly requires the execution of a formal document is incomplete depends on the purpose of the requirement in each case[67]; and there is no point multiplying examples.

Even where, under the principles here stated, the agreement has no contractual force, a party to it may be liable on other grounds: *e.g.* under a separate preliminary contract coming into existence when one party begins to render services requested by the other and entitling the former to a reasonable remuneration for those services[68]; or under a constructive trust.[69]

(c) TERMS LEFT OPEN. Parties may be reluctant to commit themselves to a rigid long-term contract, particularly when prices and other factors affecting performance are likely to fluctuate. They therefore attempt sometimes to introduce an element of flexibility into the agreement; a number of devices which have been used for this purpose call for discussion.

(i) *Terms "to be agreed"*. One possibility is to provide that certain matters (such as prices, quantities or delivery dates) are to be agreed later, or from time to time. The question whether the resulting agreement is a binding contract then depends primarily on the intention of the parties; and inferences as to this intention may be drawn both from the importance of the matter left over for further agreement, and from the extent to which the parties have acted on the agreement.

Sometimes such agreements have no contractual force. In *May & Butcher v R.*[70] an agreement for the sale of tentage provided that the price, dates of payment and manner of delivery should be agreed from time to time. The House of Lords held that the

---

[65] *Rossiter v Miller* (1878) 3 App.Cas. 1124; *cf. Fowle v Freeman* (1804) 9 Ves. 351; *Filby v Hounsell* [1896] 2 Ch.737; *Branca v Cobarro* [1947] K.B. 854; *E R Ives Investments Ltd v High* [1967] 2 Q.B. 379; *Elias v George Sahely & Co (Barbados) Ltd* [1982] 3 All E.R. 801; *The Blankenstein* [1985] 1 W.L.R. 435; *The Anemone* [1987] 1 Lloyd's Rep. 547; *Malcolm v Chancellor, Masters and Scholars of the University of Oxford, The Times,* December 19, 1990; *The Great Marine (No.2)* [1990] 2 Lloyd's Rep. 250, affirmed without reference to this point, [1991] 1 Lloyd's Rep. 421; *Jayaar Impex Ltd v Toaken Group Ltd* [1996] 2 Lloyd's Rep. 437; *The Kurnia Dewi* [1997] 1 Lloyd's Rep. 553 at 559. *cf. Crowden v Aldridge* [1993] 1 W.L.R. 433, applying the same principle to a document which was not a contract but a direction to trustees.

[66] *Ionides v Pacific Insurance Co* (1871) L.R. 6 Q.B. 674 at 684; *Cory v Patton* (1872) L.R. 7 Q.B. 304; *General Reinsurance Corp v Forsakringsaktiebolaget Fennia Patria* [1983] Q.B. 856; *Hadenfayre Ltd v British National Insurance Soc. Ltd* [1984] 2 Lloyd's Rep. 393; *The Zephyr* [1984] 1 Lloyd's Rep. 56 at 69–70 (reversed in part on other grounds [1985] 2 Lloyd's Rep. 529); *Youell v Bland Welch & Co Ltd* [1992] 2 Lloyd's Rep. 127 at 140–141; *HIH Casualty & General Insurance Ltd v New Hampshire Insurance* [2001] EWCA Civ 735; [2001] 2 All E.R. (Comm) at [86–87]; under Marine Insurance Act 1906, s.22, the contract is complete, though evidence of it may not be admissible: below, p.165. Under an "open cover" arrangement, it is not the initialling of the slip but the declaration of the insured that creates the obligation of the insurer: *Citadel Insurance Co v Atlantic Union Insurance Co* [1985] 2 Lloyd's Rep. 543.

[67] *Von Hatzfeldt-Wildenburg v Alexander* [1912] 1 Ch.284 at 288–289.

[68] *The Kurnia* [1997] 1 Lloyd's Rep. 553; *cf. Galliard Homes Ltd v Jarvis Interiors* [2000] C.L.C. 411, where the incomplete agreement expressly provided for such a remuneration in the events which happened.

[69] *Banner Homes Ltd v Luff Development Ltd* [2000] Ch.372 (party to joint venture agreement, which lacked contractual force, acquiring proposed subject-matter for himself); contrast *London & Regional Investments Ltd v TBI plc Belfast International Airport Ltd* [2002] EWCA Civ 355 (where such an agreement was expressly "subject to contract").

[70] [1934] 2 K.B. 17n.; *cf. British Homophone Ltd v Kunz* (1935) 152 L.T. 589; *The Shamah* [1981] 1 Lloyd's Rep. 40 at 83; *The Good Helmsman* [1981] Lloyd's Rep. 377 at 409. *Pancommerce SA v Veecheema BV* [1983] 2 Lloyd's Rep. 304 at 307; *The Gudermes* [1985] 2 Lloyd's Rep. 623.

agreement was incomplete as it left vital matters still to be settled. Had the agreement simply been silent on these points, they could perhaps have been settled in accordance with the provisions of the Sale of Goods Act 1979[71]; or by the standard of reasonableness[72]; but the parties showed that this was not their intention by providing that such points were to be settled by further agreement between them. It has similarly been held that a lease at "a rent to be agreed" was not a binding contract.[73] In these cases, the most natural inference to be drawn from the fact that the parties left such an important matter as the price to be settled by further agreement was that they did not intend to be bound until they had agreed on the price. Even where the points left outstanding are of relatively minor importance, there will be no contract if it appears from the words used or other circumstances that the parties did not intend to be bound until agreement on these points had been reached.[74] *A fortiori* they are not bound by a term requiring outstanding points to be agreed if that term forms part of an agreement which is itself not binding because it was made without any intention of entering into contractual relations.[75]

Where, on the other hand, it can be inferred that the parties intended to be bound immediately, in spite of the provision requiring further agreement, a binding contract can be created at once[76]; for the courts are "reluctant to hold void for uncertainty any provision that was intended to have legal effect".[77] This judicial attitude is illustrated by *Foley v Classique Coaches Ltd.*[78] The claimant owned a petrol-filling station and adjoining land. He sold the land to the defendants on condition that they should enter into an agreement to buy petrol for the purpose of their motor-coach business exclusively from him. This agreement was duly executed, but the defendants broke it, and argued that it was incomplete because it provided that the petrol should be bought "at a price agreed by the parties from time to time". The Court of Appeal rejected this argument and held that, in default of agreement, a reasonable price must be paid.[79] *May & Butcher v R.*[80] was distinguished on a number of grounds: the agreement in *Foley's* case was contained in a stamped document; it was believed by both parties to be binding and had been acted upon for a number of years; it contained an arbitration clause in a somewhat unusual

---

[71] See above, p.51.

[72] cf. *Mamidoil-Jetoil Greek Petroleum SA v Okta Crude Oil Refinery AD* [2001] EWCA Civ 406; [2001] 2 Lloyd's Rep. 76, esp. at [73]; *Malcolm v Chancellor, Masters & Scholars of the University of Oxford, The Times*, December 19, 1990.

[73] *King's Motors (Oxford) Ltd v Lax* [1970] 1 W.L.R. 426; cf. *King v King* (1981) 41 P. & C.R. 311 (rent review clause).

[74] *The Gladys* [1994] 2 Lloyd's Rep. 402; *Ignazio Messina & Co v Polskie Linie Oceaniczne* [1995] 2 Lloyd's Rep. 566.

[75] *Orion Insurance plc v Sphere Drake Insurance plc* [1992] 1 Lloyd's Rep. 239.

[76] *Pagnan SpA v Freed Products Ltd* [1987] 2 Lloyds's Rep. 601.

[77] *Brown v Gould* [1972] Ch.53 at 57–58; cf. *Smith v Morgan* [1971] 1 W.L.R. 803 at 807; *Snelling v John G Snelling Ltd* [1973] 1 Q.B. 87 at 93; *Queensland Electricity Generating Board v New Hope Colliery Pty Ltd* [1989] 1 Lloyd's Rep. 205 at 210.

[78] [1934] 2 K.B. 1.

[79] cf. *British Bank for Foreign Trade v Novinex* [1949] 1 K.B. 623; *Sykes (Wessex) Ltd v Fine Fare Ltd* [1967] 1 Lloyds's Rep. 53; *Beer v Bowden* [1981] 1 W.L.R. 522; *Thomas Bates & Sons Ltd v Wyndham's (Lingerie) Ltd* [1981] 1 W.L.R. 505 at 518–519; *The Tropwind* [1982] 1 Lloyd's Rep. 232 at 236; *Voest Alpine Intertrading GmbH v Chevron International Oil Co Ltd* [1987] 2 Lloyd's Rep. 547; *Granit SA v Benship International Inc* [1994] 1 Lloyd's Rep. 526; *Mitsui Babcock Energy Ltd v John Brown Engineering Ltd* (1996) 51 Const.L.R. 129; *Global Container Lines Ltd v State Black Sea Shipping Co* [1999] 1 Lloyd's Rep. 127 at 155; *Mamidoil-Jetoil* case above, n.72.

[80] See above, at n.70.

form which was construed to apply "to any failure to agree as to the price"[81]; and it formed part of a larger bargain under which the defendants had acquired the land at a price which was no doubt fixed on the assumption that they would be bound to buy all their petrol from the claimant.[82] While none of these factors in itself is conclusive,[83] their cumulative effect seems to be sufficient to distinguish the two cases.[84]

Thus an agreement is not incomplete *merely* because it calls for some further agreement between the parties.[85] Even the parties' later failure to agree on the matters left outstanding will vitiate the contract only if it makes the agreement "unworkable or void for uncertainty."[86] Often, the failure will not have this effect, for it may be possible to resolve the uncertainty in one of the ways already discussed, *e.g.* by applying the standard of reasonableness[87]; or by regarding the matter to be negotiated as of such subsidiary importance[88] as not to negative the intention of the parties to be bound by the more significant terms to which they have agreed.[89] There can be no doubt as to the commercial convenience of this approach. Commercial agreements are often intended to be binding in principle even though the parties are not at the time able or willing to settle all the details. For example, contracts of insurance may be made "at a premium to be arranged" when immediate cover is required but there is no time to go into all the details at once: such agreements are perfectly valid and a reasonable premium must be paid.[90] All this is not to say that the courts will hold parties bound when they have not yet reached substantial agreement[91]; but once they have reached such agreement it is not necessarily fatal that some points (even important ones) remain to be settled by further negotiation.

(ii) *Options and rights of pre-emption.* An option to purchase land "at a price to be agreed" is not a binding contract[92]; but such an option must be distinguished from a "right of pre-emption" by which a landowner agrees to give the purchaser the right to buy "at a figure to be agreed" should the landowner wish to sell.[93] An *option* has at least

[81] [1934] 2 K.B. 1 at 10; the clause covered disputes as to "the *subject matter or* construction of this agreement," while the arbitration clause in *May & Butcher v R.* covered "disputes with reference to or arising out of this agreement." For the distinction between the two forms of clause, see *Heyman v Darwins* [1942] A.C. 356 at 382, 392; *cf.* also *Vosper Thorneycroft Ltd v Ministry of Defence* [1976] 1 Lloyd's Rep. 58; *Queensland Electricity Generating Board v New Hope Collieries Pty Ltd* [1989] 1 Lloyd's Rep. 205.

[82] Scrutton L.J. said at 7 that he was glad to decide in favour of the plaintiff "because I do not regard the appellants' [defendants'] contention as an honest one".

[83] R.S.T.C., 49 L.Q.R. 316.

[84] *Foley's* case was approved by the House of Lords in *G Scammell & Nephew Ltd v Ouston* [1941] A.C. 251.

[85] *cf. Wilson Smithett & Cape (Sugar) Ltd v Bangladesh Sugar & Food Industries Ltd* [1986] 1 Lloyd's Rep. 378 at 386.

[86] *Pagnan SpA v Feed Products Ltd* [1987] 2 Lloyd's Rep. 601 at 619.

[87] See above, p.50; or by imposing on one party the duty to resolve the uncertainty: p.51 at n.19; *Pagnan SpA v Feed Products Ltd,* above.

[88] Though this point is not decisive: see above p.56, n.74.

[89] *Nelson v Stewart* (1991) S.L.R. 523.

[90] *Glicksten & Son Ltd v State Assurance Co* (1922) 10 Ll.L.R. 604; *cf.* Marine Insurance Act 1906, s.31(2); contrast *American Airline Inc v Hope* [1973] 1 Lloyd's Rep. 233, affirmed [1974] 2 Lloyd's Rep. 301 ("at an additional premium *and geographical area* to be agreed").

[91] See *Shakleford's Case* (1866) L.R. 1 Ch.App. 567; *Bertel v Neveux* (1878) 39 L.T. 257; *Loftus v Roberts* (1902) 18 T.L.R. 532; *The Intra Transporter* [1986] 2 Lloyd's Rep. 132; *Pagnan SpA v Granaria BV* [1986] 2 Lloyd's Rep. 547; *Alfred McAlpine Construction Ltd v Panatown Ltd* [2001] EWCA Civ 485; (2001) 67 Con.L.R. 224 at [35].

[92] See *Brown v Gould* [1972] Ch.52 (where, however, the option was binding as it specified *criteria* for determining the price: see below, p.58).

[93] *Pritchard v Briggs* [1980] Ch.339. For the purposes of the Landlord and Tenants (Covenants) Act 1995, " 'option' includes a right of first refusal:" s.1(6).

some of the characteristics of an offer[94] in that it can become a contract of sale when the purchaser accepts it by exercising the option; and it cannot have this effect where it fails to specify the price. A *right of pre-emption* is not itself an offer[95] but an undertaking to make an offer in certain specified future circumstances.[96] An agreement conferring such a right is therefore not void for uncertainty merely because it fails to specify the price. It obliges the land-owner to offer the land to the purchaser at the price at which he is prepared to sell; and if the purchaser accepts that offer there is no uncertainty as to price.[97] This is so even though the parties have described the right as an "option" when its true legal nature is that of a right of preemption.[98]

(iii) *Criteria or machinery specified in the agreement.* An agreement may fail to specify matters such as price or quality but lay down *criteria* for determining those matters. For example, in *Hillas & Co Ltd v Arcos Ltd*[99] an option to buy timber was held binding even though it did not specify the price, since it provided for the price to be calculated by reference to an official price list. Similarly, an option to renew a lease "at a rent to be fixed having regard to the market value of the premises" has been held binding as it provided a criterion (though not a very precise one) for resolving the uncertainty.[1] Even a provision that hire under a charterparty was in specified events to be "equitably decreased by an amount to be mutually agreed" has been held sufficiently certain to be enforced: it was said that "equitably" meant "fairly and reasonably"[2] and that a "purely objective standard has been prescribed."[3] Where, on the other hand, an agreement provided for payment of a fixed percentage of the "open market value" of shares in a *private* company, it was held that these words did not provide a sufficiently precise criterion since there was more than one formula for calculating the market value of shares in such a company.[4]

Alternatively, the agreement may provide *machinery* for resolving matters originally left open. Perhaps the most striking illustration of this possibility is provided by cases in which such matters are to be resolved by the decision of one party: for example a term, by which interest rates are expressed to be variable on notification by the creditor, is perfectly valid,[5] though the creditor's power to set interest rates under such a contract is limited by an implied term that he must not exercise it "dishonestly, for an improper purpose, capriciously or arbitrarily".[6] Similarly, an arbitration clause can validly provide for the arbitration to take place at one of two or more places to be selected by one of the parties.[7] Agreements are *a fortiori* not incomplete merely because they provide that

---

[94] See below, p.153 n.74; *Bircham & Co Nominees (No.2) Ltd v Worrell Holdings Ltd* [2001] EWCA Civ 775; (2001) P. & C.R. 427 at [41].

[95] *ibid.* at [16], [23].

[96] Similarly, a "lock-out agreement" (above, p.54) does not bind the promisor to sell to the promisee: it merely restricts his freedom to sell to someone else: see *Tye v House* [1997] 2 E.G.L.R. 171.

[97] *Smith v Morgan* [1971] 1 W.L.R. 803; *cf. Snelling v John G Snelling* [1973] 1 Q.B. 87 at 93; *Miller v Lakefield Estates Ltd* [1988] 1 E.G.L.R. 212 (where some doubts were expressed about *Smith v Morgan*).

[98] See *Fraser v Thames Television Ltd* [1984] Q.B. 44.

[99] (1932) 147 L.T. 503; *cf. Miller v F A Sadd & Son Ltd* [1981] 3 All E.R. 265; *Mamidoil-Jetoil Greek Petroleum Company S.A. v Okta Crude Oil Refinery AD* [2003] 1 Lloyd's Rep. 1, at [161–165].

[1] *Brown v Gould* [1972] Ch.53.

[2] *Didymi Corp v Atlantic Lines & Navigation Co Inc* [1988] 2 Lloyd's Rep. 108 at 116, 118.

[3] *ibid.* at 117.

[4] *Gilliatt v Sky Television Ltd* [2000] 1 All E.R. (Comm) 461.

[5] *Lombard Tricity Finance Ltd v Paton* [1989] 1 All E.R. 918. This position is preserved by Unfair Terms in Consumer Contracts Regulations 1999 (SI 1999/2083), reg.5(5) and Sch.2, para.2(b).

[6] *Paragon Finance Ltd v Staunton* [2001] EWCA Civ 1466 at [36]; [2001] 2 All E.R. (Comm) 1025; the power (to maintain interest rates at a level above that charged by other lenders) had in that case been validly exercised.

[7] *The Star Texas* [1993] 2 Lloyd's Rep. 445.

outstanding points shall be determined by arbitration[8] or by the valuation of a third party. The Sale of Goods Act 1979 provides that if the third party "cannot or does not make the valuation, the agreement is avoided"[9]; but an agreement is not necessarily ineffective merely because the agreed machinery fails to work. In *Sudbrook Trading Estate Ltd v Eggleton*[10] a lease gave the tenant the option to purchase the premises "at such price as may be agreed upon by two Valuers, one to be nominated by" each party. The landlord having refused to appoint a valuer, the House of Lords held that the option did not fail for uncertainty. It amounted, on its true construction, to an agreement to sell at a reasonable price to be determined by the valuers; and the stipulation that each party should nominate one of the valuers was merely "subsidiary and inessential".[11] So long as the agreed machinery (which fails to operate) is of this character,[12] the court can substitute other machinery: for example, it can itself fix the price with the aid of expert evidence. This is so not only where the agreed machinery fails because of one party's refusal to operate it,[13] but also where it fails for some other reason, such as the refusal of a designated valuer to make the valuation.[14]

(d) FACTS TO BE ASCERTAINED. An agreement is not ineffective on the ground of uncertainty merely because the facts on which its operation depend are not known when it is made: the requirement of certainty is satisfied if those facts become ascertainable and are ascertained (without the need for further negotiation) after the making of the agreement.[15]

(e) CONTRACT TO MAKE A CONTRACT In some cases of incomplete agreements it is said that there is a "contract to make a contract". This expression may refer to a number of different situations.

(i) *Agreement to execute formal document.* One possibility is that the parties may agree to execute a formal document incorporating terms on which they have previously agreed. Such a provision does not deprive the agreement of contractual force.[16] For example, in *Morton v Morton*[17] an agreement "to enter into a separation deed containing the following clauses" (of which a summary was then given) was held to be a binding contract. The grant of an option to purchase can similarly be described as a contract by which one party binds himself to enter into a further contract if the other so elects; and neither of these contracts is void for uncertainty.[18]

(ii) *Express agreement to negotiate.* A further possibility is that the parties have simply agreed to negotiate. In spite of dicta to the contrary,[19] it has been held that a mere agreement to negotiate is not a contract "because it is too uncertain to have any binding

---

[8] *Arcos Ltd v Aronson* (1930) 36 Ll.L.R. 108; *cf. Thomas Bates & Son Ltd v Wyndham's (Lingerie) Ltd* [1981] 1 W.L.R. 505, where a lease was rectified (below, p.321) to include such a clause; *Queensland Electricity Generating Board v New Hope Collieries Pty Ltd* [1989] 1 Lloyd's Rep. 205.

[9] Sale of Goods Act 1979, s.9(1); *cf. Pym v Campbell* (1856) 6 E. & B. 370.

[10] [1983] 1 A.C. 444; Robertshaw, 46 M.L.R. 493.

[11] *Re Malpas* [1985] Ch.42 at 50; *Tito v Waddell (No.2)* [1977] Ch.106 at 314; *Didymi Corp v Atlantic Lines & Navigation Co Inc* [1988] 2 Lloyd's Rep. 108 at 115.

[12] *i.e.* not if it is "an integral and essential part of the definition of the payments to be made": *Gilliatt v Sky Television Ltd* [2000] 1 All E.R. (Comm) 461 at 479.

[13] As in the *Sudbrook* case, above.

[14] As in *Re Malpas*, above.

[15] *Welsh Development Agency v Export Finance Ltd* [1992] B.C.L.C. 148.

[16] Subject to statutory exceptions: see Consumer Credit Act 1974, s.59.

[17] [1942] 1 All E.R. 273.

[18] See *The Messiniaki Bergen* [1983] 1 Lloyd's Rep. 424 at 426; and below p.153 n.74 for various views as to the nature of an option.

[19] *Chillingworth v Esche* [1924] 1 Ch.97 at 113; *Hillas & Co Ltd v Arcos Ltd* (1932) 147 L.T. 503 at 515. See F.P., 48 L.Q.R. 141; F.W. McC., *ibid.* 310; Williams, 6 M.L.R. 81.

force."[20] It therefore does not impose any obligation to negotiate, or to use best endeavours to reach agreement,[21] or to accept proposals that "with hindsight appear to be reasonable".[22]

(iii) *Implied agreement to negotiate.* Where an agreement is too uncertain to be enforced, this defect cannot be cured by implying into it a term to the effect that the parties must continue to negotiate in good faith. In *Walford v Miles*,[23] a "lock-out" agreement collateral to negotiations for the sale of a business lacked sufficient certainty because it failed to specify the time during which the vendors were not to negotiate with third parties[24]; and the House of Lords unanimously rejected the argument that a term should be implied requiring the vendors to continue to negotiate in good faith with the purchasers for so long as the vendors continued to desire to sell, since such a term was itself too uncertain to be enforced. The uncertainty lay in the fact that the alleged duty was "inherently inconsistent with the position of a negotiating party"[25] who must normally[26] be free to advance his own interests during the negotiations. The point is well illustrated by the facts of *Walford v Miles* itself, where the defendants had agreed subject to contract to sell a property to the purchasers for £2 million and had (in breach of the ineffective "lock-out" agreement) sold it to a third party for exactly that sum, and the purchasers then claimed damages of £1 million on the basis that the property was (by reason of facts known to them but not the defendants) worth £3 million. If a duty to negotiate in good faith exists, it must be equally incumbent on both parties, so that it can hardly require a vendor to agree to sell a valuable property for only two-thirds of its true value when the facts affecting that value are known to the purchaser and not disclosed (as good faith would seem to require) to the vendor. The actual result in *Walford v Miles* (in which the purchasers recovered the sum of £700 in respect of their wasted expenses as damages for misrepresentation,[27] but not the £1 million which they claimed as damages for breach of contract[28]) seems with respect, to be entirely appropriate on the facts, especially because the vendors reasonably believed themselves to be protected from liability in the principal negotiation by the phrase "subject to contract".

In *Walford v Miles* Lord Ackner, with whom all the other members of the House agreed, described as "unsustainable" the view expressed in an American case[29] "that an agreement to negotiate in good faith is synonymous with an agreement to use best

---

[20] *Courtney & Fairbairn Ltd v Tolaini Bros (Hotels) Ltd* [1975] 1 W.L.R. 297 at 301; *cf. Von Hatzfeldt-Wildenburg v Alexander* [1912] 1 Ch.284 at 249; *Malozzi v Carapelli SpA* [1976] 1 Lloyd's Rep. 407; *The Scaptrade* [1981] 2 Lloyd's Rep. 425 at 432 (affirmed without reference to this point [1983] 2 A.C. 694); *Nile Co for the Export of Agricultural Crops v H & J M Bennett (Commodities) Ltd* [1986] 1 Lloyd's Rep. 555 at 587; *The Jing Hong Hai* [1989] 2 Lloyd's Rep. 523 at 526; *Paul Smith Ltd v H & S International Holdings Inc* [1991] 2 Lloyd's Rep. 127 at 131; *Mamidoil-Jetoil Greek Petroleum SA v Okta Crude Oil Refining AD* [2001] EWCA Civ 406; [2001] Lloyd's Rep. 76, at [53], [59].

[21] *The Scaptrade*, (above, n.20) [1981] 2 Lloyd's Rep. at 432; *The Junior K* [1988] 2 Lloyd's Rep. 583. Contrast, in the United States, *Hoffman v Red Owl Stores Inc*, 133 N.W. 2d. 267 (1965).

[22] *Pagnan SpA v Granaria BV* [1985] 1 Lloyd's Rep. 256 at 270; affirmed [1986] 2 Lloyd's Rep. 547.

[23] [1992] 2 A.C. 128; Neill, 108 L.Q.R. 405.

[24] See above, p.54.

[25] [1992] 2 A.C. 128 at 138; *cf. Surrey C.C. v Bredero Homes Ltd* [1993] 1 W.L.R. 1361 at 1368 (doubted on other grounds in *Attorney-General v Blake* [2001] 1 A.C. 268 at 283, below, p.868); *Halifax Financial Services Ltd v Intuitive Systems Ltd* [1999] All E.R. (Comm) 303 at 311; *Baird Textile Holdings Ltd v Marks and Spencer plc* [2001] EWCA Civ 274; [2002] 1 All E.R. (Comm) 737 at [68].

[26] For an exception, see *Re Debtors (Nos.4449 and 4450 of 1998)* [1999] 1 All E.R. (Comm) 149 at 158 (Lloyds bound to negotiate in good faith with its names as it was "performing functions in the public interest within a statutory framework".

[27] See [1992] 2 A.C. 128 at 136.

[28] *ibid.* at 135.

[29] *Channel Home Centers Division of Grace Retail Corp v Grossman* 795 F.2d 291 (1986).

endeavours and, as the latter is enforceable so is the former".[30] He went on to say that "the reason why an agreement to negotiate, like an agreement to agree, is unenforceable is simply because it lacks the necessary certainty. The same does not apply to an agreement to use best endeavours".[31] This passage gives rise to a number of difficulties. The first arises from dictum in an English case[32] (which is cited with approval in *Walford v Miles*[33]) to the effect that an agreement to negotiate does not impose any obligation to use best endeavours to reach agreement; and this dictum certainly supports the view that an agreement to negotiate contains no *implied* term to use best endeavours. It may be that Lord Ackner's reference was to an *express* term to use best endeavours, or that he was simply prepared to assume (without deciding) that an agreement (express or implied) to use best endeavours might be legally enforceable and that he was concerned only to make the point that, even on that assumption, the same was not true of an agreement to negotiate in good faith. That explanation of Lord Ackner's statement in turn gives rise to the difficulty of distinguishing between the two types of agreement. One possibility is that an "agreement to negotiate" refers to the *formation* and one "to use best endeavours" to the *performance* of a contract, *e.g.* where an admitted contract between A and B requires A to use his best endeavours to make a computer software system supplied by A work, or procure C to enter into a contract with B. There is no doubt that such terms can impose a legal obligation on A.[34] But where the question is whether any contract has come into existence, later decisions support the view that an express agreement to use best or reasonable endeavours to agree on the terms of a contract is no more than an agreement to negotiate, lacking contractual force.[35] It may be that, while an agreement to use best endeavours could be interpreted as referring to the *machinery* of negotiation, one to negotiate in good faith is more plausibly interpreted as referring to its *substance*. A promise to use best endeavours might, for example, oblige a party to make himself available for negotiations, or at least not (*e.g.* by deliberately failing to pick up his telephone) to prevent the other from communicating with him.[35a] A promise to negotiate in good faith, on the other hand, would oblige a party not to take unreasonable or exorbitant positions during the negotiations; and it is the difficulty of giving precise content to this obligation, while maintaining each party's freedom to pursue his own interests, that makes such a promise too uncertain to be enforced.

In *Walford v Miles* the principal agreement was not legally binding because it was subject to contract, and the lock-out agreement was not legally binding because it specified no dates.[36] The case does not exclude the possibility that a different conclusion may be reached where the parties have reached agreement on all essential points so as to show that they do intend to be legally bound by the agreement, but have left other points open. The court may then imply a term that they are to negotiate in good faith

---

[30] [1992] 2 A.C. 128 at 138.

[31] *ibid.*

[32] *The Scaptrade* [1981] 2 Lloyd's Rep. 425 at 432 (and see above n.20); *cf. Little v Courage Ltd* (1995) 70 P. & C.R. 469 at 475.

[33] [1992] 2 A.C. 128 at 137.

[34] See *Watford Electronics Ltd v Sanderson Ltd* [2001] EWCA Civ 317; [2001] 1 All E.R. (Comm) 696 at [45]; and the estate agency cases discussed at p.38 above; *cf. Lambert v HTV Cymru (Wales) Ltd, The Times,* March 17, 1998.

[35] See *Little v Courage* (1995) 70 P. & C.R. 469 at 475; *London & Regional Investments Ltd v TBI plc Belfast International Airport Ltd* [2002] EWCA Civ 355 at [39].

[35a] Example based on *Nissho Iwai Petroleum Co Inc v Cargill International SA* [1993] 1 Lloyd's Rep. 80, where such conduct was held to amount to a breach of a party's duty to co-operate in the *performance* (not in the *formation*) of a contract. *cf. Re Debtors (Nos.4449 and 4450 of 1998)* [1999] 1 All E.R. (Comm) 149 at 158 (implied obligation to use "best endeavours" to conclude an agreement required the party "not unreasonably to frustrate" its conclusion).

[36] See above, p.54 at n.60.

so as to settle outstanding details which are to be incorporated in the formal document setting out the full terms of the contract between them.[37]

SECTION 6. CONDITIONAL AGREEMENTS

1. Classification

An agreement is conditional if its operation depends on an event which is not certain to occur. Discussions of this topic are made difficult by the fact that in the law of contract the word "condition" bears many senses: it is "a chameleon-like word which takes on its meaning from its surroundings."[38] At this stage, we are concerned with only one of these meanings; but to clear the ground it is necessary to draw a number of preliminary distinctions.

The word "condition" may refer either to an *event*, or to a *term* of a contract (as in the phrase "conditions of sale"[39]). Where "condition" refers to an event, that event may be either an occurrence which neither party undertakes to bring about, or the performance by one party of his undertaking. The first possibility is illustrated by a contract by which A is to work for B, and B is to pay A £50, "if it rains tomorrow". Here the obligations of both parties are contingent on the happening of the specified event which may therefore be described as a *contingent* condition. The second possibility is illustrated by the ordinary case in which A agrees to work for B at a weekly wage payable at the end of the week. Here the contract is immediately binding on both parties, but B is not liable to pay until A has performed his promise to work. Such performance is a condition of B's liability, and, as A has promised to render it, the condition may be described as *promissory*.[40] In this Chapter our concern is with contingent conditions; promissory conditions will be discussed in Chapter 18.[41]

Contingent conditions may be precedent or subsequent.[42] A condition is precedent if it provides that the contract is not to be binding until the specified event occurs. It is subsequent if it provides that a previously binding contract is to determine on the occurrence of the event: *e.g.* where A contracts to pay an allowance to B until B marries.[43]

2. Degrees of Obligation

Where an agreement is subject to a contingent condition precedent, there is, before the occurrence of the condition, no duty on either party to render the principal performance

---

[37] *Donwin Productions Ltd v EMI Films Ltd, The Times*, March 9, 1984 (not cited in *Walford v Miles* [1992] 2 A.C. 128).

[38] *The Varenna* [1984] Q.B. 599 at 618.

[39] *Property and Bloodstock Ltd v Emerton* [1968] Ch.94 at 118; *cf.* also below, pp.705, 731.

[40] For the distinction between *promissory* and *contingent* condition see Chalmers, *Sale of Goods* (18th ed.) Appendix 2, Note A; *Roadworks (1952) Ltd v Charman* [1994] 2 Lloyd's Rep. 99 at 103; *Total Gas Marketing Ltd v Arco British Ltd* [1998] 2 Lloyd's Rep. 209 at 215, 218.

[41] See below, pp.761–766; 788–805.

[42] Conditions precedent are also sometimes called "suspensive", and conditions subsequent "resolutive", conditions: see Treitel, *Remedies for Breach of Contract*, pp.262–263. In *Ignazio Messina & Co v Polskie Linie Oceaniczne* [1995] 2 Lloyd's Rep. 566 at 580 a condition there under discussion was said to be "a true condition subsequent or suspensive condition". "Subsequent" here seems to be a misprint for "precedent." The distinction between the two types of condition is not always clear-cut: see below at n.52.

[43] *cf. Brown v Knowsley BC* [1986] I.R.L.R. 102 (appointment to "last only as long as sufficient funds were provided" from specified sources), and (*semble*) *Gyllenhammar & Partners International v Sour Brodogra-devna Industria* [1989] 2 Lloyd's Rep. 403 (contract to "become null and void" if certain consents were not obtained) and *Jameson v CEGB* [2000] 1 A.C. 455 at 477 (settlement of a tort claim immediately binding but subject to an implied resolutive condition that it was to become void if the agreed amount was not paid).

promised by him: for example, a seller is not bound to deliver and a buyer is not bound to pay. Nor, in such a case, does either party undertake that the condition will occur. But an agreement subject to such a condition may impose some degree of obligation on the parties or on one of them. Whether it has this effect, and if so what degree of obligation is imposed, depends on the true construction of the term specifying condition.[44]

One possibility is that, before the event occurs, each party is free to withdraw from the agreement. In *Pym v Campbell*[45] an agreement for the sale of a patent was executed, but the parties at the same time agreed that it should not "be the agreement" unless a third party approved of the invention. He did not approve, and it was held that the buyer was not liable for refusing to perform. The written agreement was "not an agreement at all".[46] If this is taken literally, either party could have withdrawn even before the third party had given his opinion.

A second possibility is that, before the event occurs, the main obligations have not accrued; but that, so long as the event can still occur, one (or both) of the parties cannot withdraw. Thus in *Smith v Butler*[47] A bought land from B on condition that a loan to B (secured by a mortgage on the premises) would be transferred to A.[48] It was held that A could not withdraw before the time fixed for completion: he was bound to wait until then to see whether B could arrange the transfer. However, if it becomes clear that the condition has not occurred, or that it can no longer occur, within the time specified in the contract, the parties will be under no further obligations under the contract.[49] In such a case, the effect of the non-occurrence of the condition is that the parties are "no longer bound"[50] by the contract, or that the contract is "discharged."[51] What the parties have called a "condition precedent" can thus operate as, or have the effect of, a condition subsequent.[52]

A third possibility is that, before the event occurs, the main obligations have not accrued; but that in the meantime neither party must do anything to prevent the occurrence of the event. Thus in *Mackay v Dick*[53] an excavating machine was sold on condition that it could excavate at a specified rate on the buyer's property. The buyer's refusal to provide facilities for a proper trial was held to be a breach. Similarly, the seller would have been in breach, had he refused to subject the machine to a proper test. The same principle is illustrated by a case[54] in which a professional footballer was transferred for a fee, part of which was to be paid only after he had scored 20 goals. Before he had done so, the new club dropped him from their first team, and they were held to be in

---

[44] For special difficulties where the condition precedent is implied, see *Bentworth Finance Ltd v Lubert* [1968] 1 Q.B. 680; Carnegie, 31 M.L.R. 78.

[45] (1856) 6 E. & B. 370.

[46] *ibid.* at 374.

[47] [1900] 1 Q.B. 694, *cf. Felixstowe Dock & Ry Co v British Transport Docks Bd* [1976] 2 Lloyd's Rep. 656; *Alan Estates Ltd v W. G. Stores Ltd* [1982] Ch.511 at 520.

[48] On agreements "subject to finance", see Coote, 40 Conv. (N.S.) 37; Furmston, 3 O.J.L.S. 438, discussing *Meehan v Jones* (1982) 149 C.L.R. 571.

[49] *North Sea Energy Holdings NV v Petroleum Authority of Thailand* [1997] 2 Lloyd's Rep. 418 at 428–429 (affirmed on other grounds [1999] 1 Lloyd's Rep. 483).

[50] *Total Gas Marketing Ltd v Arco British Ltd* [1998] 2 Lloyd's Rep. 209 at 215.

[51] *ibid.* at 218.

[52] *ibid.* at 221, 224.

[53] (1881) 6 App.Cas. 251. The condition is described as subsequent in *Colley v Overseas Exporters* [1921] 3 K.B. 302 at 308. *cf.* also *Shipping Corp of India v Naviera Letasa* [1976] 1 Lloyd's Rep. 132; *CIA Barca de Panama SA v George Wimpey & Co Ltd* [1980] 1 Lloyd's Rep. 598 and *South West Trains Ltd v Wightman, The Times*, January 14, 1998; contrast *North Sea Energy Holdings NV v Petroleum Authority of Thailand* [1999] 1 Lloyd's Rep. 483 (duty to co-operate in bringing about the event negatived by terms of the contract).

[54] *Bournemouth & Boscombe Athletic FC v Manchester United FC, The Times*, May 22, 1980. *cf.* also below, p.744.

breach as they had not given the player a reasonable opportunity to score the 20 goals.

The duty not to prevent the occurrence of the condition has been explained as resting on an implied term and this explanation limits the scope of the duty in a number of ways. For example, the implied term may be only to the effect that a party will not *deliberately* prevent the occurrence of the condition[55]; or (even more narrowly) that he will not *wrongfully* do so.[56] The latter type of implication may allow a party to engage in certain kinds of deliberate prevention but not in others: for example, it may allow a company which has promised an employee the opportunity of earning a bonus to deprive him of that opportunity by going out of business, but not by simply dismissing him, before the bonus has become due.[57] The implied term can also be excluded by an express contrary provision,[58] in particular, by a provision making the operation of a contract depend on the "satisfaction" of one party with the subject-matter or other aspects relating to the other's performance. Thus it has been held that there was no contract where a house was bought "subject to satisfactory mortgage"[59]; and where a boat was bought "subject to satisfactory survey"[60] it was held that the buyer was not bound if he expressed his dissatisfaction,[61] in spite of the fact that such expression was a deliberate act on his part which prevented the occurrence of the condition. The same is true where goods are bought on approval and the buyer does not approve them,[62] and where an offer of employment is made "subject to satisfactory references," and the prospective employer does not regard the references as satisfactory.[63] There is some apparent conflict in the authorities on the question whether the law imposes any restriction on the freedom of action of the party on whose satisfaction the operation of the contract depends. In one case[64] a proposed royalty agreement relating to the use by a manufacturer of an invention was "subject to detailed evaluation of production and marketing feasibility" by the manufacturer. It was held that his discretion whether to enter into the contract was "unfettered by any obligation to act reasonably or in good faith"[65] and that, as his satisfaction had not been communicated[66] to the other party, the agreement had not acquired contractual force. On the other hand, where a ship was sold "subject to satisfactory completion of two trial voyages" it was said that such a stipulation was to be construed as "subject to bona fides".[67] The distinction between the two lines of cases turns, ultimately, on the construction of the agreement. Even if this requires the

---

[55] See *Blake & Co v Sohn* [1969] 1 W.L.R. 1412.

[56] See *Thompson v ASDA-MFI Group plc* [1988] Ch.241.

[57] Example based on *Thompson v ASDA-MFI Group plc*, above and below, p.744.

[58] See *Micklefield v SAC Technology Ltd* [1990] 1 W.L.R. 1002.

[59] *Lee-Parker v Izett (No.2)* [1975] 1 W.L.R. 775; distinguished in *Janmohammed v Hassam, The Times*, June 10, 1976.

[60] *Astra Trust Ltd v Adams & Williams* [1969] 1 Lloyd's Rep. 81 doubted in *The Merak* [1976] 2 Lloyd's Rep. 250 at 254 and in *Ee v Kahar* (1979) 40 P. & C.R. 223 (as to which see below, n.34).

[61] But if the buyer declared his satisfaction the seller would be bound even though the survey was not objectively satisfactory: *Graham v Pitkin* [1992] 1 W.L.R. 403 at 405.

[62] *cf.* Sale of Goods Act 1979, s.18, r.4.

[63] *Wishart v National Association of Citizens' Advice Bureaux* [1990] I.C.R. 794.

[64] *Stabilad Ltd v Stephens & Carter (No.2)* [1999] 2 All E.R. (Comm) 651.

[65] *ibid.* at 662.

[66] For the requirement of communication see *ibid.* at 660; the requirement may be satisfied by conduct from which satisfaction can be inferred, *e.g.* where a buyer of goods on approval retains them without notifying rejection for more than the stipulated or a reasonable time: Sale of Goods Act 1999, s.18, r.4(b).

[67] *The John S Darbyshire* [1977] 2 Lloyd's Rep. 457 at 464; *cf. BV Oliehandel Jongkind v Coastal International Ltd* [1983] 2 Lloyd's Rep. 463; *The Nissos Samos* [1985] 1 Lloyd's Rep. 378 at 385; contrast *The Junior K* [1988] 2 Lloyd's Rep. 583 at 589 (where the words were held to negative contractual intention). See also *El Awadi v Bank of Credit & Commerce International SA* [1990] 1 Q.B. 606 at 619; and in an analogous context, *The Product Star (No.2)* [1993] 1 Lloyd's Rep. 397 at 404.

discretion to be exercised in good faith, it does not follow that it must be exercised reasonably: the matter may be left to the relevant party's "subjective decision".[68] It has also been held that the party on whose satisfaction the operation of the contract depends must at least provide facilities for, or not impede, the inspection referred to in the agreement.[69] Of course if the result of the inspection is unsatisfactory, the principal obligation of the contract will not take effect.[70]

A fourth possibility is that, before the event occurs, the main obligations have not accrued but that one of the parties undertakes to use reasonable efforts to bring the event about (without absolutely undertaking that his efforts will succeed). This construction was applied, for instance, where land was sold subject to the condition that the purchaser should obtain planning permission to use the land as a transport depot: he was bound to make reasonable efforts to obtain the permission, but he was free from liability when those efforts failed.[71] Similarly, where goods are sold "subject to export (or import) licence", the party whose duty it is to obtain the licence[72] does not *prima facie* promise absolutely that a licence will be obtained,[73] but only undertakes to make reasonable efforts to that end.[74] The principal obligations to buy and sell will not take effect if no licence is obtained[75]; but if the party who should have made reasonable efforts has failed to do so he will be liable in damages,[76] unless he can show that any such efforts, which he should have made would (if made) have necessarily been unsuccessful.[77] The same principles have been applied where an agreement was made "subject to the approval of the court"; and where an agreement was made to assign a lease which could only be assigned with the consent of the landlord. In such cases the requisite approval or consent must be sought; but the main obligations do not accrue until the approval or consent is given,[78] and if it is refused the principal obligation will not take effect.[79]

---

[68] *Stabilad Ltd v Stephens & Carter Ltd (No.2)* [1999] 2 All E.R. (Comm) 651 at 659.

[69] *The Merak* [1976] 2 Lloyd's Rep. 250; *cf. Ee v Kahar* (1979) 40 P. & C.R. 223 (where the sale was simply "subject to survey"—omitting the word "satisfactory"—thus falling, it is submitted, within the principle of *Mackay v Dick*, above n.53).

[70] As in *The John S. Darbyshire* [1977] 2 Lloyd's Rep. 457.

[71] *Hargreaves Transport Ltd v Lynch* [1969] 1 W.L.R. 215 (condition not satisfied); *Richard West & Partners (Inverness) Ltd v Dick* [1969] 2 Ch.424 (similar condition satisfied); *cf. Fisher v Tomatousos* [1991] 2 E.G.L.R. 204; *Jolley v Carmel Ltd* [2000] 2 E.G.L.R. 153 (buyer who was required by the contract to make reasonable efforts to get planning permission under no duty to get it within a reasonable time); contrast *Tesco Stores Ltd v Gibson* (1970) 214 E.G. 835 (no obligation on purchaser to apply for planning permission).

[72] As to which party has this duty, see *H O Brandt & Co v H N Morris & Co* [1917] 2 K.B. 784; *A V Pound & Co v M W Hardy & Co* [1956] A.C. 588.

[73] The *prima facie* rule may be excluded by express words which do, on their true construction, impose an absolute duty; *e.g. Peter Cassidy Seed Co Ltd v Osuustukkukauppa* [1957] 1 W.L.R. 273; *C Czarnikow Ltd v Centrala Handlu Zagranicznego "Rolimpex"* [1979] A.C. 351 at 371; *Congimex Companhia Geral, etc. SARL v Tradax Export SA* [1983] 1 Lloyd's Rep. 250; *Pagnan SpA v Tradax Ocean Transport SA* [1987] 3 All E.R. 565; and, semble, *The Seaflower* [2001] 1 Lloyd's Rep. 341 (where the standard of duty imposed by a "guarantee" to get specified approvals was not discussed); Yates and Carter, 1 J.C.L. 57.

[74] *Re Anglo-Russian Merchant Traders and John Batt & Co (London) Ltd* [1917] 2 K.B. 679; *Coloniale Import-Export v Loumidis & Sons* [1978] 2 Lloyd's Rep. 560; *Overseas Buyers Ltd v Granadex SA* [1980] 2 Lloyd's Rep. 608; *Gamerco SA v ICM Fair Warning (Agency) Ltd* [1995] 1 W.L.R. 1226 at 1231. Where the contract is expressly subject to the approval of a public authority, there may not even be a duty to make reasonable efforts to secure that approval: see *Gyllenhammar Partners International v Sour Brodegradevna Industria* [1989] 2 Lloyd's Rep. 403.

[75] *Charles H Windschuegl Ltd v Alexander Pickering & Co Ltd* (1950) 84 Ll.L. Rep 89 at 92–93; *Brauer & Co (Great Britain) Ltd v James Clark (Brush Materials) Ltd* [1952] 2 All E.R. 497 at 501; *cf.* the cases on sales of goods "to arrive" discussed in Benjamin's *Sale of Goods* (5th ed.), §§ 21–022 to 21–027.

[76] *e.g. Malik v C.E.T.A.* [1974] 1 Lloyd's Rep. 279; *Agroexport v Cie. Européenne de Céréales* [1974] 1 Lloyd's Rep. 499.

[77] See Benjamin's *Sale of Goods* (6th ed.), § 18–293; *Overseas Buyers Ltd v Granadex SA*, above, at 612.

[78] *Smallman v Smallman* [1972] Fam. 25.

[79] *Shires v Brock* (1977) 247 E.G. 127.

It will be seen that in cases falling within the second, third and fourth categories discussed above, a distinction must be drawn between two types of obligation: the principal obligation of each party (*e.g.* to buy and sell) and a subsidiary obligation, *i.e.* one not to withdraw, not to prevent occurrence of the condition, or to make reasonable efforts to bring it about. One view is that the party who fails to perform the subsidiary obligation is to be treated as if the condition had occurred; and that he is then liable on the principal obligation. Thus in *Mackay v Dick*[80] the buyer was held liable *for the price*; but there was no discussion as to the remedy. In principle it seems wrong to hold him so liable, for such a result ignores the possibility that the machine might have failed to come up to the standard required by the contract, even if proper facilities for trial had been provided. It is submitted that the correct result in cases of this kind is to award *damages* for breach of the subsidiary obligation: in assessing such damages, the court can take into account the possibility that the condition might not have occurred, even if there had been no such breach.[81] To hold the party in breach liable for the full performance promised by him, on the fiction that the condition had occurred, seems to introduce into this branch of the law a punitive element that is inappropriate to a contractual action.[82] The most recent authorities rightly hold that such a doctrine of "fictional fulfilment" of a condition does not form part of English law.[83]

Where a condition is inserted entirely for the benefit of one party, that party may waive the condition. He can then sue[84] and be sued[85] on the contract as if the condition had occurred. Obviously this rule does not apply to cases falling within the first of the categories discussed above, in which there is no contract at all before the condition occurs.

---

[80] (1881) 6 App.Cas. 251, above, p.63.

[81] *Bournemouth & Boscombe Athletic FC v Manchester United FC*, *The Times*, May 22, 1980; *cf. The Blankenstein* [1985] 1 W.L.R. 435 (below, p.764); *Alpha Trading Ltd v Dunshaw-Patten Ltd* [1981] Q.B. 290 (below p.688); *George Moundreas & Co SA v Navimpex Centrala Navala* [1985] 2 Lloyd's Rep. 515; *The Energy Progress* [1993] 1 Lloyd's Rep. 355 at 358.

[82] *cf.* below, p.935.

[83] *Thompson v ASDA-MFI Group plc* [1988] Ch.241 at 266 (where the condition was said at 251 to be subsequent); *Little v Courage Ltd* (1995) 70 P. & C.R. 469 at 474.

[84] *Wood Preservation Ltd v Prior* [1969] 1 W.L.R. 1077; contrast *Heron Garages Properties Ltd v Moss* [1974] 1 W.L.R. 148.

[85] *McKillop v McMullan* [1979] N.I. 85.

CHAPTER THREE

CONSIDERATION[1]

SECTION 1. INTRODUCTION

1. General

IN English law, a promise is not, as a general rule, binding as a contract unless it is either made in a deed[2] or supported by some "consideration". The purpose of the requirement of consideration is to put some legal limits on the enforceability of agreements even where they are intended to be legally binding[3] and are not vitiated by some factor such as mistake, misrepresentation, duress or illegality.[4] The existence of such limits is not a peculiarity of English law: for example, in some civil law countries certain promises which in England are not binding for "want of consideration" cannot be enforced unless they are made in some special form, *e.g.* by a notarised writing.[5] The view was, indeed, at one time put forward that consideration was only evidence of the intention of the parties to be bound, and that (at any rate in the case of certain commercial contracts), such evidence could equally well be furnished by writing.[6] But the view that agreements (other than those contained in deeds), were binding without consideration merely because they were in writing was rejected in England over 200 years ago,[7] though it has been revived as a proposal for law reform.[8] The present position therefore is that English law limits the enforceability of agreements (not in deeds) by reference to a complex and multifarious body of rules known as "the doctrine of consideration".

This doctrine is based on the idea of reciprocity: "something of value in the eye of the law"[9] must be given for a promise in order to make it enforceable as a contract. An informal gratuitous promise therefore does not amount to a contract.[10] A person or body to whom a promise of a gift is made from purely sentimental or charitable motives gives nothing for the promise; and the claims of such a promisee are less compelling than those of a person who has given (or promised) some return for the promise.[11] The invalidity of informal gratuitous promises of this kind can also be supported on the ground that their enforcement could prejudice third parties such as creditors of the promisor.[12]

---

[1] Shatwell, 1 Sydney L.R. 289; Sutton, *Consideration Reconsidered*.

[2] See below, p.158.

[3] See below, Chap.4.

[4] See below, Chaps 8–11.

[5] See generally von Mehren, 72 Harv.L.Rev. 1009.

[6] *Pillans v Van Mierop* (1765) 3 Burr. 1663.

[7] *Rann v Hughes* (1778) 7 T.R. 350 n.; 4 Bro. P.C. 27. In the United States, writing is in a number of jurisdictions, at least for some purposes, regarded as a substitute for consideration: see *Farnsworth on Contracts* §2.18.

[8] See below p.160.

[9] *Thomas v Thomas* (1842) 2 Q.B. 851 at 859.

[10] *Re Hudson* (1885) 54 L.J. Ch. 811; *Re Cory* (1912) 29 T.L.R. 18; *Williams v Roffey Bros & Nicholls (Contractors) Ltd* [1991] 1 Q.B. 1 at 19.

[11] *cf.* Eisenberg, 47 U. of Chi.L.Rev. 1; 85 Cal.L.Rev. 821.

[12] *Eastwood v Kenyon* (1840) 11 A. & E. 438 at 451.

Such promises, too, may be rashly made[13]; and the requirements of executing a deed or giving value provide at least some protection against this danger.

The doctrine of consideration has, however, also struck at many promises which were not "gratuitous" in any ordinary or commercial sense. These applications of the doctrine were brought within its scope by stressing that consideration had to be not merely "something of value", but "something of value *in the eye of the law*".[14] The law in certain cases refused to recognise the "value" of acts or promises which might well be regarded as valuable by a layman. This refusal was based on many disparate policies; so that "promises without consideration" included many different kinds of transactions which, at first sight, had little in common.[15] It is this fact which is the cause of the very great complexity of the doctrine; and which has also led to its occasional unwarranted extensions and hence to demands for reform of the law.[16]

2. Definitions

(1) Benefit and detriment

The traditional definition of consideration concentrates on the requirement that "something of value" must be given and accordingly states that consideration is either some detriment to the promisee (in that he may give value) or some benefit to the promisor (in that he may receive value).[17] Usually, this detriment and benefit are merely the same thing looked at from different points of view. Thus payment by a buyer is consideration for the seller's promise to deliver and can be described as a detriment to the buyer or as a benefit to the seller; and conversely delivery by a seller is consideration for the buyer's promise to pay and can be described either as a detriment to the seller or as a benefit to the buyer. These statements relate to the consideration *for the promise of each party* looked at separately. For example, the seller suffers a "detriment" when he delivers the goods and this enables him to enforce the buyer's promise to pay the price. It is quite irrelevant that the seller has made a good bargain and so gets a benefit from the performance of the contract. What the law is concerned with is the consideration *for a promise*—not the consideration *for a contract*.

(a) EITHER SUFFICIENT. Under the traditional definition it is sufficient if there is either a detriment to the promisee or a benefit to the promisor. Thus detriment to the promisee suffices even though the promisor does not benefit[18]: for example, where A guarantees B's bank overdraft and the promisee bank suffers detriment by advancing money to B, then A is bound by his promise, even though he gets no benefit from the advance to B. One view indeed, was that "Detriment to the promisee is of the essence

---

[13] *Beaton v McDivitt* (1988) 13 N.S.W.L.R. 162 at 170. It is often easier to promise to make a gift than actually to make one.

[14] See above, at n.9; below, p.69.

[15] *cf.* Corbin, *Contracts*, Vol.I, p.489: "The doctrine of consideration is many doctrines."

[16] See below p.146.

[17] *Currie v Misa* (1875) L.R. 10 Ex. 153 at 162. See also *Barber v Fox* (1682) 2 Wms. Saund. 134, n.(e); *Cooke v Oxley* (1790) 3 T.R. 653 at 654; *Jones v Ashburnham* (1804) 4 East 455; *Bainbridge v Firmstone* (1838) 8 A. & E. 743 at 744; *Thomas v Thomas* (1842) 2 Q.B. 851 at 859; *Bolton v Madden* (1873) L.R. 9 Q.B. 55 at 56; *Gore v Van der Lann* [1967] 2 Q.B. 31 at 42; *Argy Trading Development Co Ltd v Lapid Developments Ltd* [1977] 1 W.L.R. 444 at 455; *Midland Bank & Trust Co Ltd v Green* [1981] A.C. 513 at 531; *R. v Braithwaite* [1983] 1 W.L.R. 385 at 391; *Johnsey Estates Ltd v Lewis Manley (Engineering) Ltd* [1987] 2 E.G.L.R. 69 at 70; *Guiness Mahon & Co Ltd v Kensington & Chelsea Royal BC* [1999] Q.B. 215 at 236; *Modahl v British Athletics Federation Ltd* [2001] EWCA Civ 1447; [2002] 1 W.L.R. 1192 at [50]; *cf. ibid.* at [103].

[18] *O'Sullivan v Management Agency & Music Ltd* [1985] Q.B. 428 at 459; *Re Dale* [1994] Ch. 31 at 38; *cf. Gill & Duffus SA v Rionda Futures Ltd* [1994] 2 Lloyd's Rep. 67 at 82.

of the doctrine, and benefit to the promisor is, when it exists, merely an accident".[19] But the view that benefit to the promisor is, on its own, sufficient to satisfy the requirement of consideration is supported by a number of cases[20] in which promises were enforced on the ground that such a benefit had been conferred, even though there was no apparent detriment to the promisee.

(b) BENEFIT AND DETRIMENT MAY BE FACTUAL OR LEGAL. The traditional definition of consideration lacks precision because the key notions of "benefit" and "detriment" are used in at least two senses. They may refer, first, to any act[21] which is of some value, or, secondly, only to acts, the performance of which is not already legally due from the promisee. In the first sense, there is consideration if a benefit or detriment is *in fact* obtained or suffered. When the words are used in the second sense this factual benefit or detriment is disregarded, and a notion of what may be called legal benefit or detriment is substituted.[22] Under this notion, the promisee may provide consideration by doing anything that he was not legally bound to do, whether or not it actually occasions a detriment to him or confers a benefit on the promisor; while conversely he may provide no consideration by doing only what he was legally bound to do, however much this may in fact occasion a detriment to him or confer a benefit on the promisor. The English courts have not consistently adopted either of these senses of the words "benefit" and "detriment." In some of the situations to be discussed in this Chapter, factual benefit is stressed[23] even though legal detriment may also have been present; while in others the absence of a legal detriment or benefit has in the past been regarded as decisive.[24] One modern authority[25] regards factual benefit to the promisor as sufficient in one such situation, even in the absence of a legal benefit to him or of a legal detriment to the promisee and it is possible (though far from certain) that this approach may spread to at least some[26] of the situations in which the courts have in the past insisted on legal benefit or detriment.

(2) Other definitions

The traditional definition of consideration in terms of benefit and detriment is sometimes regarded as unsatisfactory. One cause of dissatisfaction is that it is thought to be wrong to talk of benefit and detriment when both parties expect to, and actually may, benefit from the contract. But this reasoning falls, with respect, into the error of treating the subject-matter of the definition as the consideration *for a contract*,[27] when the definition is actually concerned with the consideration *for a promise*.[28] Another cause of dissatisfaction is the artificial reasoning that is sometimes necessary to accommodate decided cases within the traditional definition. Sir Frederick Pollock has, accordingly, described consideration as simply "the price for which the promise is bought".[29] This

---

[19] Holdsworth, *History of English Law*, Vol.8, p.11.

[20] *e.g.* below, pp.81, 92, 127, 129.

[21] Or forbearance, or promise to do or to forbear. For the sake of simplicity references in the text are confined to the doing of an act.

[22] Corbin, §172 rightly points out that use of this terminology does not explain *why* legal benefit or detriment is necessary; but the present point is simply that the terms are sometimes used in this sense.

[23] *e.g.* in *Bolton v Madden* (1873) L.R. 9 Q.B. 55, below, p.81.

[24] *e.g.* in some of the existing duty cases discussed on pp.92–95, below.

[25] *Williams v Roffey Bros & Nicholls (Contractors) Ltd* [1991] 1 Q.B. 1, below, p.95.

[26] *e.g.* to the variation cases discussed below, pp.101–102; but probably not to the forbearance to sue cases discussed below, pp.88–90.

[27] There are traces of this approach in *Williams v Roffey Bros & Nicholls (Contractors) Ltd* [1991] 1 Q.B. 1 at 23: "If both parties benefit from an agreement it is not necessary that each also suffered a detriment."

[28] See above, p.68.

[29] *Principles of Contract*, (13th ed.), p.133.

statement has been approved in the House of Lords[30]; but if it is to be regarded as a definition of consideration it is defective in being so vague as to give no help in determining whether consideration exists on a given set of facts. A view which leads to even more uncertainty is that consideration *"means* a reason for the enforcement of promises"[31]—that reason being simply "the justice of the case".[32] But "the justice of the case" is in almost all the decided cases highly debatable, so that the suggested definition provides no basis for formulating a coherent legal doctrine.[33] A modification of the suggested definition, describing consideration as "a reason for the recognition of an obligation"[34] is open to the same objection. Of course the traditional definition does not provide complete (or even a very high degree of) certainty. But it does state the doctrine in a way which gives some basis for predicting the course of future decisions; and it has more support in the authorities than any other definition. For these reasons it will be used in this Chapter.

(3) Mutual promises

So far we have discussed performance by one party as consideration for the promise of the other: for example, payment by a buyer as the consideration for the seller's promise to deliver, or delivery by a seller as consideration for the buyer's promise to pay. It is, however, also well settled that mutual promises can be consideration for each other. Hence if a seller promises to deliver goods in six months' time and the buyer to pay for them on delivery, there is an immediately binding contract from which neither party can withdraw, though, of course, performance cannot be claimed till the appointed time. Implied, no less than express, promises can constitute consideration for each other.[35]

Some difficulty has been felt in explaining the rule that mutual promises can be consideration for each other. At first sight, it might seem that the mere giving of a promise was not a detriment, nor its receipt a benefit, so as to make the counter-promise binding. It will not do to say that the person making the promise suffers a detriment because he is legally bound to perform it; for if this assumption is made about one of the promises, it must also be made of the other, so that the "explanation" assumes the very point in issue. Probably the reason for the rule is simpler. A person who makes a commercial promise expects to have to perform it (and is in fact under considerable pressure to do so). Correspondingly, one who receives such a promise expects it to be kept. These expectations, which can exist even where the promise is not legally enforceable,[36] are based on commercial morality, and can properly be called a detriment and a benefit; hence they satisfy the requirement of consideration in the case of mutual promises.

---

[30] *Dunlop Pneumatic Tyre Co Ltd v Selfridge Ltd* [1915] A.C. 847 at 855.

[31] Atiyah, *Consideration in Contracts: A Fundamental Restatement* (Canberra, 1971) p.60. For an earlier, similar statement, see Llewellyn, 40 Yale L.J. at 741 (1931)—"any sufficient justification for court enforcement"; but he makes no attempt to suggest that this actually is the law. For criticism of Atiyah's views, see Treitel, 50 A.L.J. 439. *cf. Colonia Versicherung AG v Amoco Oil Co* [1995] 1 Lloyd's Rep. 570 at 577 (affirmed without reference to this point [1997] 1 Lloyd's Rep. 261) where the words "(a) the reason for and (b) ample consideration for" a payment clearly treat these concepts as distinct.

[32] Atiyah (above, n.31), pp.52, 58.

[33] *cf.* the description of a similar concept as "potentially very confusing" in *Guiness Mahon & Co Ltd v Kensington & Chelsea Royal BC* [1999] Q.B. 215 at 236.

[34] Atiyah, *Essays in Contract*, pp.179, 183.

[35] *Thoresen Car Ferries Ltd v Weymouth Portland BC* [1977] 2 Lloyd's Rep. 614 at 619; *The Aramis* [1989] 1 Lloyd's Rep. 213 at 225 (where the claim failed for want of contractual intention). But a mere proposal falling short of a promise does not suffice: *The Kaliningrad and Nadezhda Krupskaya* [1995] 2 Lloyd's Rep. 35 at 39.

[36] *cf. Lipkin Gorman v Karpnale Ltd* [1991] 2 A.C. 548 at 581.

As a general rule a promise is regarded as consideration for a counter-promise only if its performance would also have been so regarded.[37] It follows that a mere promise to accept a gift cannot be consideration for the promise to make it. Similarly, we shall see that a debtor who actually pays part of a debt does not thereby provide consideration for the creditor's promise to release the balance[38] and the position is exactly the same if the debtor *promises* part payment in return for the creditor's counter-promise to accept the part payment in full settlement.

(4) Invented consideration

Normally, a party enters into a contract with a view to obtaining the consideration provided by the other: for example, the buyer wants the goods and the seller the price. In the United States it has been said that this is essential, and that "Nothing is consideration that is not regarded as such by both parties."[39] But English courts do not insist on this requirement and often regard an act or forbearance as the consideration for a promise even though it may not have been the object of the promisor to secure it.[40] They may also regard the possibility of some prejudice to the promisee as a detriment without regard to the question whether it has in fact been suffered.[41] These practices may be called "inventing consideration",[42] and the temptation to adopt one or the other of them is particularly strong when the act or forbearance which was actually bargained for cannot be regarded as consideration for some reason which is thought to be technical and without merit. In such cases the practice of inventing consideration may help to make the operation of the doctrine of consideration more acceptable; but the practice may also be criticised[43] on the ground that it gives the courts a wide discretion to hold promises binding (or not) as they please. Thus the argument that the promisee *might* have suffered prejudice by acting in reliance on a promise is in some cases made a basis of decision,[44] while in others precisely the same argument is rejected.[45] The courts have not been very consistent in the exercise of this discretion and its existence is a source of considerable uncertainty in this branch of the law.

---

[37] *Thorp v Thorp* (1702) 12 Mod. 445 at 449; *Re Dale* [1994] Ch. 31 at 38.

[38] See below, p.125.

[39] *Philpot v Gruninger* (1872) 14 Wall, 570 at 577; Restatement, *Contracts* §75(1); Restatement 2d, *Contracts* §71(1) and (2); Williston, *Contracts* (rev. ed.), Vol.1, at p.320; Corbin, *Contracts*, §172, is more sceptical. Restatement 2d, *Contracts* §72 also supports the converse proposition, namely that anything is consideration if it is bargained for, even if there is no element of benefit or detriment; but this is subject to important exceptions, especially where what is bargained for is the performance of an existing duty or the settlement of an invalid claim: §§73, 74: as to these topics, see below, pp.88–90, 92–98.

[40] See for example, below, pp.85–86, 155, 298; *cf. Pollway Ltd v Abdullah* [1974] 1 W.L.R. 493, discussed by Zuckerman, 38 M.L.R. 384; Thornely [1975] C.L.J. 26; *The Alev* [1989] 2 Lloyd's Rep. 138 at 147; *Moran v University College Salford (No.2)*, *The Times*, November 23, 1993.

[41] *e.g.* below, n.44.

[42] Atiyah, *Essays in Contract*, p.183 accuses me of having "invented the concept of invented consideration"; but all that I can claim to have invented is a phrase for describing what the courts sometimes actually do. The phrase does not imply approval of the practice: see below after n.43. Nor does the phrase necessarily imply inconsistency between decisions, as Atiyah suggests *ibid.*: courts could *consistently* hold that an act or forbearance was consideration although it was not the promisor's object to secure it. In fact, the decisions on the point are not perfectly consistent with each other: see below at nn.44 and 45; but that is hardly unusual in a common law system.

[43] Holmes, *The Common Law*, p.292. In the United States there is less need to invent consideration because of the existence of a broad doctrine of promissory estoppel: see below, p.118.

[44] *Shadwell v Shadwell* (1860) 9 C.B.(N.S.) 159 at 174: the consideration was said by Erle C.J. to consist of the possibility that the promisor "*may* have made a most material change in his position . . . ".

[45] In *Offord v Davies* (1862) 12 C.B.(N.S.) 748: the argument of counsel (at 750) that "the plaintiff *might* have altered his position in consequence of the guarantee" was rejected, Erle C.J. being again a member of the court. *cf.* also below p.84, n.67 and p.85, n.74, for refusal to "invent" consideration.

(5) Motive and consideration

In *Thomas v Thomas*[46] a testator shortly before his death expressed a desire that his widow should during her life have the house in which he lived, or £100. After his death, his executors "in consideration of such desire" promised to convey the house to the widow during her life or for so long as she should continue a widow, "provided nevertheless and it is hereby further agreed" that she should pay £1 per annum towards the ground rent, and keep the house in repair. In an action by the widow for breach of this promise, the consideration for it was stated to be the widow's promise to pay and repair. An objection that the declaration omitted to state part of the consideration, namely the testator's desire, was rejected. Patteson J. said: "Motive is not the same thing with consideration. Consideration means something which is of value in the eye of the law, moving from the plaintiff."[47] This remark should not be misunderstood: a common motive for making a promise is the desire to obtain the consideration; and an act or forbearance on the part of the promisee may fail to constitute consideration precisely because it was not the promisor's motive to secure it: for example, where A promises to give B £1,000 and B thereupon buys a diamond ring. What Patteson J. meant was that a motive for promising does not amount to consideration unless two further conditions are satisfied, *viz.*: (i) that the thing secured in exchange for the promise is "of some value in the eye of the law"[48]; and (ii) that it moves from the plaintiff.[49] Consideration and motive are not opposites; the former concept is a subdivision of the latter. The consideration for a promise is (unless it is nominal or invented)[50] always a motive for promising; but a motive for making a promise is not necessarily consideration for it in law. Thus the testator's desire in *Thomas v Thomas* was a motive for the executors' promise, but not part of the consideration for it. The widow's promise to pay and repair was another motive for the executors' promise and did constitute the consideration.

(6) Consideration and condition

Thomas v Thomas also illustrates the difference between consideration and condition[51]: the plaintiff's remaining a widow was not part of the consideration but a condition of her entitlement to enforce the executors' promise. Similarly, in *Carlill v Carbolic Smoke Ball Co*[52] the plaintiff provided consideration for the defendants' promise by using the smoke-ball; but her catching influenza was only a condition of her entitlement to enforce that promise. In these cases, the promisee can be said to have performed the condition, but such performance was not requested by the promisor.[53] Where the promisee's performance of the condition is (or can reasonably be regarded as having been) so requested, it can constitute consideration[54]: for example, where A promised B to convey

---

[46] (1842) 2 Q.B. 851.

[47] *ibid.* at 859. *cf. Hadley v Kemp* [1999] E.M.L.R. 589 at 625.

[48] See below, pp.83–98.

[49] See below, pp.80–83.

[50] See above, p.71, below, p.73. In *Thomas v Thomas* the consideration may not have been adequate, but it was not nominal: *cf.* below, p.74, and *Westminster City Council v Duke of Westminster* [1991] 4 All E.R. 136 at 146 (reversed in part on other grounds (1992) 24 H.L.R. 572).

[51] *i.e.* a *contingent* condition: see above, p.62.

[52] [1893] 1 Q.B. 256; above, p.13.

[53] For similar reasoning, see *Dickinson v Abel* [1969] 1 W.L.R. 295 where A promised to pay £10,000 to B if A succeeded (as he did) in buying Blackacre from X. This was said to be "nothing but a conditional promise without consideration" because B had not been requested to do anything to promote the sale by X to A.

[54] Williston, *Contracts*, rev. ed. §112; *cf. Ellis v Chief Adjudication Officer* [1998] 1 F.L.R. 184 where performance of the condition was no doubt requested but the actual decision was that an executed gift of a flat failed because the condition (that the donee should look after her mother there) had not been performed. The agreement in that case lacked contractual force for want of contractual intention: below, p.167.

a plot of land to B if B built a house on it, B could enforce the promise after he had built the house.[55] Similarly, where A promised to pay £3,000 to B if B established a school, in the running of which A was to take an active part, it was held that B had provided consideration by setting up the school[56]: a request that he should do so could be inferred from the fact that A had expressed his intention to take part in its management.

(7) Limited effects of promises without consideration

A promise that is not supported by consideration may nevertheless give rise to certain legal effects. In particular, English law places certain restrictions on the revocability of a promise where the promisee has acted on it in a way that the promisor could have anticipated but had not requested; and it may give a remedy against a promisor who would be unjustly enriched if he were allowed freely to revoke his promise after such action in reliance on it by the promisee. These limited legal effects of promises without consideration will be discussed later in this Chapter[57]: here it is only necessary to emphasise that they do not give such promises the full consequences of binding contracts. Thus the restrictions on their revocability may be only temporary[58] and breach of the promise may not entitle the injured party to the full loss of bargain damages normally awarded for breach of contract,[59] or may not entitle him to them as of right.[60] Only a promise supported by consideration (or one made in a deed) has these full contractual effects. "Contract" does not exhaust the category of promises or agreements having *some* legal effects[61]; it refers, more narrowly, to those promises or agreements leading to the full measure of enforceability to be discussed later in this book.[62] Moreover, while promises without consideration may have some legal effects, the promisee can still gain a number of important practical advantages by showing that he provided consideration. If the promise was supported by consideration, the promisee will not need to show action in reliance on the promise, or unjust enrichment of the promisor; the promise will not be revocable but enforceable according to its terms; and the promisee will be entitled to full loss of bargain damages as of right. The limited effects of promises without consideration may have mitigated some of the rigours of the strict doctrine; but they have not eliminated consideration as an essential requirement of a binding contract.[63]

SECTION 2. ADEQUACY

1. Consideration need not be Adequate

Under the doctrine of consideration, a promise has no contractual force unless *some* value has been given for it. But the courts do not, in general, ask whether adequate value

---

[55] See *Raffaele v Raffaele* [1962] W.A.R. 29; Allan, 79 L.Q.R. 239; *cf. Errington v Errington* [1952] 1 K.B. 290 (above, p.38); *The Castle Alpha* [1989] 2 Lloyd's Rep. 383 at 387. For the purpose of assessing VAT, a wider test (laid down by European Community Law), requiring only a "direct link" between performance and counter-performance, suffices: see *Rosgill Group Ltd v Customs & Excise Commissioners* [1997] 3 All E.R. 1012, though in that case the English test for what constitutes consideration was said at 1020 also to have been satisfied.

[56] *Re Soames* (1897) 13 T.L.R. 439.

[57] See below, pp.105–119, 130–149.

[58] See below, pp.111, 131–133, 142.

[59] See above, pp.6–7, below, Chap.21; *cf.* Restatement 2d, *Contracts* §90 ("the remedy . . . may be limited as justice requires").

[60] See below, p.144.

[61] *cf.* Duncanson, 39 M.L.R. 268.

[62] See below, Chap.21.

[63] See below, p.112.

has been given,[64] or whether the agreement is harsh or one-sided.[65] The reason for this is not that the courts *cannot* value the promise of each party: they have to do just this when assessing damages.[66] It is rather that they *should* not interfere with the bargain actually made by the parties. The fact that a person pays "too much" or "too little" for a thing may be evidence of fraud or mistake, or induce the court to imply a term as to the quality of the subject-matter or be relevant to the question whether a contract has been frustrated.[67] But it does not of itself affect the validity of the contract. This state of the law sometimes causes dissatisfaction, for example, when it is alleged that "excessive" profits have been made out of government contracts[68] or that "irrationally generous" payments had been made out of public funds[69] or when, in times of scarcity, it is said that "excessive" prices are charged for goods or services or accommodation. Such problems are, however, more appropriately dealt with by special legislation or by administrative measures than by the ordinary process of civil litigation. The courts are not well equipped to develop a system of price-control, and their refusal, as a general rule, to concern themselves with the adequacy of consideration is a reflection of this fact. At the same time, the general rule is subject to a number of exceptions, to be discussed later in this book.[70] These indicate that the courts are (even where the legislature has not intervened) by no means insensitive to the problem of unequal bargains; but in none of them is a promise held invalid *merely* because adequate value for it has not been given. Some additional factor is required to bring a case within one of the exceptions: for example, the existence of a relationship in which one party is able to take an unfair advantage of the other. The general rule remains that "no bargain will be upset which is the result of the ordinary interplay of forces".[71]

2. Nominal Consideration

(1) Sufficiency of nominal consideration

The rule that consideration need not be adequate makes it possible to evade the doctrine of consideration, in the sense that a gratuitous promise can be made binding by means of a nominal consideration, *e.g.* £1 for the promise of valuable property, or a peppercorn for a substantial sum of money. Such cases are merely extreme applications of the rule

---

[64] *Haigh v Brooks* (1840) 10 A. & E. 309 at 320; *Westlake v Adams* (1858) 5 C.B.(N.S.) 248 at 265; *Wild v Tucker* [1914] 3 K.B. 36 at 39; *cf. Langdale v Danby* [1982] 1 W.L.R. 1123; *CCC Films (London) Ltd v Impact Quadrant Films Ltd* [1985] Q.B. 16 at 27; *Brady v Brady* [1989] A.C. 755 at 775; *Normid Housing Association Ltd v R. John Ralphs* [1989] 1 Lloyd's Rep. 265 at 272; Barton, 103 L.Q.R. 118. The principle is recognised and, in general, preserved by Unfair Terms in Consumer Contracts Regulations 1999 (SI 1999/2083), reg.6(2)(b), below, p.271, n.77.

[65] *Gaumont-British Pictures Corp v Alexander* [1936] 2 All E.R. 1686 (where the 1999 Regulations, above, would not apply: Dir. 93/13, Recital 10 and below, p.278); *Midland Bank & Trust Co Ltd v Green* [1981] A.C. 513 at 532. *cf.* below, p.421 at n.99.

[66] See below, p.936.

[67] *e.g.* in the coronation cases, below pp.885–887.

[68] See [1964] Public Law 391; *cf.* the report into allegations of overcharging by Bristol Siddeley Engines Ltd (H.C. Paper 129, Session 1967–1968); see Turpin, 31 M.L.R. 241; Turpin, *Government Contracts*, pp.196 *et seq.*

[69] *Newbold v Leicester CC* [1999] I.C.R. 1182 at 1185 (upholding such a promise).

[70] See below, pp.75 at n.74, 419–421, 461, 1027–1029; Waddams, 39 M.L.R. 393; Tiplady, 46 M.L.R. 601. See also *Bankway Properties Ltd v Penfold Dunsford* [2001] EWCA Civ 538; [2001] 1 W.L.R. 1369 where a provision for rent increase in a shorthold tenancy far beyond the amount which (as the landlord knew) the tenant could possibly pay was held to be unenforceable as being inconsistent with the intention of the parties to create an assured tenancy.

[71] *Lloyds Bank Ltd v Bundy* [1975] Q.B. 326 at 336, *per* Lord Denning M.R.

that the courts will not judge the adequacy of consideration.[72] If, however, it appears on the face of the agreement that the consideration must as a matter of arithmetic be worth less than the performance of the counter-promise, there would seem to be no contract: for example, if A promised to pay B £100 in return for £1 to be simultaneously paid by B. It is assumed in the example that both sums are simply to be paid in legal tender. An agreement to exchange a specific coin or coins of a particular description for a sum of money greater than their face value (*e.g.* 20 shilling pieces bearing the date 1900 for £100) would be a good contract. The same would be true of an agreement to pay a sum in one currency in exchange for one payable in another, and of an agreement to pay a larger sum tomorrow in exchange for a smaller sum paid today.

Where an agreement is legally binding on the ground that it is supported by nominal consideration, the doctrine of consideration does not serve its main purpose, of distinguishing between gratuitous and onerous promises. But the law has no settled policy against enforcing all gratuitous promises. It refuses to enforce only *informal* gratuitous promises; and the deliberate use of a nominal consideration can be regarded as a form to make a gratuitous promise binding. In some cases it may, indeed, be undesirable to give nominal consideration the same legal effect as substantial consideration; but these cases are best dealt with by special rules.[73] Such rules are particularly necessary where the promise can cause prejudice to third parties. For example, the danger that company promoters might use the device of nominal consideration to the prejudice of shareholders is avoided by imposing fiduciary duties on the promoters.[74]

(2) Nominal distinguished from inadequate consideration

It is not normally necessary to distinguish between "nominal" and "inadequate" consideration, since both equally suffice to make a promise binding. The need to draw the distinction may, however, arise in some of the exceptional cases[75] in which the law treats promises or transfers supported only by nominal consideration differently from those supported by consideration which is substantial or "valuable" (even though it may be inadequate).

One view is that a nominal consideration is one which is of only token value,[76] while an inadequate consideration is one which has substantial value even though it is manifestly less than that of the performance promised or rendered in return. A second view is that "'Nominal consideration' and a 'nominal sum' appear . . . , as terms of art, to refer to a sum or consideration which can be mentioned as consideration but is not necessarily paid."[77] This was the view of Lord Wilberforce in *Midland Bank & Trust Co*

---

[72] Atiyah, *Essays in Contract*, p.194 argues that there is no logical connection between the two rules, relying on the fact that in many of the United States the courts recognise the principle that consideration need not be adequate, while rejecting the device of nominal consideration. The answer to this argument lies in Holmes' aphorism (The *Common Law*, p.1) that "the life of the law has not been logic: it has been experience": American courts which reject the device of nominal consideration do so on policy grounds which have nothing to do with logic.

[73] Thus a nominal consideration was disregarded in *Milroy v Lord* (1862) 4 D.F. & J. 264, discussed below, p.685 and for the purposes of the Law of Property Act 1925, "'valuable consideration' . . . does not include a nominal consideration in money"; s.205(1)(xxi).

[74] See below, p.399. For other ways of protecting third parties from being prejudiced by contracts made for inadequate consideration see Insolvency Act 1986, ss.238, 339, 423; Trustee Act 1925, s.13; Law of Property Act 1925, s.172; Local Government Act 1972, s.123(2); Inheritance (Provisions for Family and Dependants) Act 1975, ss.10(2)(b), 10(5)(b), 11(2)(c); *cf.* Companies Act 1985, ss.103, 320.

[75] See above at nn.73 and 74.

[76] This seems to be the sense in which 10s. was described as "nominal" consideration (for the assignment of a debt) in *Turner v Forwood* [1951] 1 All E.R. 746.

[77] *Midland Bank & Trust Co Ltd v Green* [1981] A.C. 513 at 532.

Ltd v Green,[78] where a husband sold a farm, said to be worth £40,000, to his wife for £500. It was held that the wife was, for the purposes of the Land Charges Act 1925, s.13(2), a "purchaser for money or money's worth" so that the sale to her prevailed over an unregistered option to purchase the land, which had been granted to one of the couple's sons.[79] It was not necessary to decide whether the consideration for the sale was nominal but Lord Wilberforce said that he would have had "great difficulty" in so holding; and that "To equate 'nominal' with 'inadequate' or even 'grossly inadequate' consideration would embark the law on inquiries which I cannot think were ever intended by Parliament"[80]: *i.e.* inquiries into the adequacy of the price. On the facts of the case the £500 was in fact paid and was more than a mere token, so that the consideration was not nominal on either of the two views stated above. But if the stated consideration had been only £1, or a peppercorn, it is submitted that it would have been nominal even if it had been paid, or delivered, in accordance with the intention of the parties. So to hold would not lead to enquiries as to the adequacy of consideration; for the distinction between a consideration that is a mere token and one that is inadequate (or even grossly inadequate) is, it is submitted, clear as a matter of common sense. Thus where the question was whether a lease amounted to a "disposition . . . for a nominal consideration"[81] it was said that "Any substantial value—that is, a value of more than, say, £5 . . . will prevent [the] disposition from being for a nominal consideration".[82] Such an approach gives rise to no more difficulty than the concept of a consideration which is "mentioned as a consideration but . . . not necessarily paid". That test would presumably make the question whether consideration was nominal turn on the intention of the parties; and, in the present context, this would be an even more than usually elusive criterion, since no guidance could be obtained from the terms of the contract, those terms being, in cases of this kind, often deliberately drafted so as to conceal the true nature of the transaction.

3. Attitude of Equity

Equity recognised the general rule that the validity of a contract could not be challenged merely on the ground of inadequacy of consideration.[83] But it sometimes refused specific performance, or set a contract aside, or even reopened it (*i.e.* varied its terms) on the ground that adequate value had not been given to a party who was thought to need special protection.[84]

Equity also refuses to aid a "volunteer"—*i.e.* a person who has given no substantial consideration but can nonetheless enforce a promise at law because it was made in a deed or supported by nominal consideration.[85] It was evidently thought that even such formal gratuitous promises did not deserve the same degree of enforcement as those for which substantial value had been given, and so the equitable remedy of specific performance is not available in respect of such a promise.[86] But while the equitable principle restricts the

---

[78] See above.

[79] For later successful proceedings by the son against his parents in conspiracy see [1982] Ch. 529.

[80] [1981] A.C. 513 at 532. In other legislative contexts such an inquiry may be intended: *e.g.* by use of the phrase "full and valuable consideration" in Inheritance (Provision for Family and Dependants) Act 1975, s.1(3).

[81] Within Law of Property Act 1925, s.84(7).

[82] *Westminster City Council v Duke of Westminster* [1991] 4 All E.R. 136 at 146, reversed in part on another ground (1992) 24 H.L.R. 572.

[83] See, *e.g. Cheale v Kenward* (1858) 3 D. & J. 27; *Townend v Toker* (1866) L.R. 1 Ch.App. 446.

[84] *Tennent v Tennents* (1870) L.R. 2 Sc. & Div. 6 at 9, below pp.419–421, 1027–1029.

[85] *Jefferys v Jefferys* (1841) Cr. & Ph. 138.

[86] See below, pp.1035–1037.

enforceability of gratuitous *promises*, it does not affect the validity of a *completed gift*.[87]

SECTION 3. PAST CONSIDERATION

1. General Rule

The consideration for a promise must be given in return for the promise. If A makes a present of a car to B and a year later B promises to pay A £500 there is no consideration for B's promise as A did not give B the car in return for it. This reasoning often applies where there is an interval of time between an act and the promise said to have been given in return for it. The alleged consideration is then said to be "past consideration" and therefore bad.[88] Thus if a thing is guaranteed *after* it has been sold there is no consideration for the guarantee.[89] Similarly, a promise to pay a sum of money may be made to an employee after his retirement or to an agent after the termination of the agency. If the sole consideration for the promise is the service previously rendered by the employee or agent under the terminated contract, it will be a past consideration so that the promise will not be contractually binding.[90] It will be so binding only if some consideration, other than the past service, has been provided by the promisee. Such other consideration may consist in his giving up rights which are outstanding (or are in good faith believed to be outstanding) under the original contract,[91] or in his promising or accomplishing some other act or forbearance not due from him under the original contract: for example, in his validly promising not to compete with the promisor.[92]

In determining whether consideration is past, the court is not, it is submitted, bound to apply a strictly chronological test. If the consideration and the promise are substantially one transaction, the exact order in which these events occur is not decisive.[93] A manufacturer's "guarantee" may be given to a customer after he has bought the goods. But the consideration for the guarantee would not be past if the sale and the giving of the "guarantee" were in substance a single transaction, as they would be if the customer at the time of the sale thought that he was buying a guaranteed product. Where the guarantee is a "consumer guarantee" within the Sale and Supply of Goods to Consumers Regulations 2002[94] it binds the guarantor by force of this legislation. For this purpose, the consumer need not show that he has provided consideration for the

---

[87] *T Choithram International SA v Pagarani* [2001] 1 W.L.R. 1; *Pennington v Waine* [2002] EWCA Civ 227; [2002] 1 W.L.R. 2075.

[88] *Dent v Bennett* (1839) 4 My. & Cr. 269; *Eastwood v Kenyon* (1840) 11 A. & E. 438.

[89] *Thorner v Field* (1612) 1 Bulst. 120; *Roscorla v Thomas* (1842) 3 Q.B. 234. In the latter case, an oral warranty had been given at the time of sale (see 11 L.J.Q.B. 214 and 6 Jur. 929) but was presumably regarded as "void" for want of written evidence: see below, p.176.

[90] *cf. Simpson v John Reynolds* [1975] 1 W.L.R. 617; *Murray v Goodhews* [1978] 1 W.L.R. 489, where payments made in such circumstances were for tax purposes held to be voluntary.

[91] *e.g. Bell v Lever Bros Ltd* [1932] A.C. 161 (where the value of the rights given up in return for the payment was uncertain in amount since it included not only future salary but also possible future commission).

[92] *cf. Wyatt v Kreglinger and Fernau* [1933] 1 K.B. 793, where the ex-employee's claim would have succeeded if the restraint undertaken by him had not been invalid (below, p.461).

[93] *Thornton v Jenkyns* (1840) 1 Man. & G. 166; *Tanner v Moore* (1846) 9 Q.B. 1; *National Westminster Bank v Cullinane, The Times*, October 27, 1982; *Westminster City Council v Duke of Westminster* [1991] 4 All E.R. 136 at 145, reversed in part on another ground (1992) 24 H.L.R. 572; and *cf.* the discussion of *Halifax BS v Edell* [1992] Ch. 436, below, p.587.

[94] SI 2002/3045, reg.15, implementing Dir. 1999/44, Art.7. For definitions of "consumer", "consumer guarantee" and "guarantor", see reg.2.

guarantor's promise; but the requirement of consideration continues to apply to guarantees which are *not* "consumer guarantees" within the Regulations.[95]

The question whether consideration is past is one of fact: the wording of the agreement is not decisive. Thus in *Re McArdle*[96] a promise made "in consideration of your carrying out" certain work was held to be gratuitous as the work had already been done. Conversely, a promise made "in consideration of your having today advanced . . . £750" has been held binding on proof that the advance was made at the same time as the promise.[97]

2. Past Acts or Promises requested by Promisor

A past act can be consideration for a promise if three conditions are satisfied: the act must have been done at the request of the promisor[98]; it must have been understood that payment would be made; and the payment, if it had been promised in advance, must have been legally recoverable.[99] In such a case the promisee is, quite apart from the subsequent promise, entitled to a reasonable sum for his services. The promise can be regarded either as fixing the amount of that sum[1] or as being given in consideration of the promisee's releasing his claim for such a payment.

On the other hand, a past service which was not done at the request of the promisor, or one for which payment was not expected, or one for which payment, though expected, is not legally recoverable, is no consideration for a subsequent promise to pay for it.[2]

The consideration for a promise by A can consist not only of a past *act* done by B at A's request, but also of an earlier *promise* made by B at A's request. Thus in *Pao On v Lau Yiu Long*[3] the claimants had promised the defendants that for one year they would not sell certain shares in a company of which the defendants were the principal shareholders. This promise had been made at the request of the defendants, who were anxious to prevent the value of their own holding from being depressed by a sudden sale of the claimants' shares. Later, the defendants gave the claimants a guarantee in which they promised to indemnify the claimants against any loss which they might suffer if, during the year, the shares fell in value.[4] The Privy Council rejected the argument that the consideration for the guarantee was past.[5] The claimants' promise not to sell the shares was good consideration for the guarantee; for although that promise had been made before the guarantee was given, it had been made at the defendants' request and on the understanding that the claimants were, in return for making it, to receive some

---

[95] *e.g.* where the buyer is not a "natural person" and so does not fall within the definition of "consumer" in reg.2.

[96] [1951] Ch. 669.

[97] *Goldshede v Swan* (1847) 1 Ex. 154. The burden of proving that the consideration was not past is on the person seeking to enforce the promise: *Savage v Uwechia* [1961] 1 W.L.R. 455.

[98] *Southwark LBC v Logan* (1996) 8 Admin.L.R. 315, where this requirement was not satisfied.

[99] *Re Casey's Patents* [1892] 1 Ch. 104 at 115–116; *cf. Lampleigh v Brathwait* (1615) Hob. 105.

[1] *Kennedy v Broun* (1863) 13 C.B.(N.S.) 677 at 740; *Rondel v Worsley* [1969] 1 A.C. 191 at 236, 278, 287.

[2] *Kennedy v Broun*, above; *Rondel v Worsley*, above: promise to pay barrister for past professional services not binding since he could not sue for his fees; see now Courts and Legal Services Act 1990, s.61. In *Arthur JS Hall Ltd v Simons* [2002] 1 A.C. 615 the House of Lords disapproved the reasoning of *Rondel v Worsley* so far as it relates to an advocate's immunity from liability for negligence in the conduct of civil or (by a majority) criminal proceedings. This disapproval therefore does not affect the point for which *Rondel v Worsley* is here cited, *i.e.* the common law rule that a barrister cannot sue for his fees. Reference to this point is made, perhaps with some scepticism, in the *Arthur JS Hall* case at 677 and 685.

[3] [1980] A.C. 614.

[4] This guarantee replaced an earlier agreement which was less favourable to the claimants.

[5] For the further argument that the consideration was no more than the promise to perform an existing contractual duty, see below, p.98.

form of protection against the risk (to which the promise exposed them) of a fall in the value of those shares.

3. Antecedent Debt

In a number of cases it has been held that the mere existence of an antecedent debt does not constitute "value" for a *transfer* by the debtor as it amounts only to past consideration.[6] These cases are not directly concerned with the question whether such an antecedent debt can constitute consideration for a later *promise* by the debtor: *e.g.* for one to pay higher interest or to pay early. But they may, by analogy, support the view that, where the only possible consideration for such a promise is an antecedent debt owed by the promisor to the promisee, then such consideration is past, so that the promise is not contractually binding.[7] In practice, however, the creditor (*i.e.* the promisee) will often provide consideration for such a promise by forbearing, on the strength of it, to sue for the debt.[8]

4. Moral Obligation

In the eighteenth and early nineteenth centuries, an attempt was made (originally by Lord Mansfield) to define consideration so as to include certain pre-existing "moral" obligations. In accordance with this theory it was held that an executor was personally liable on a promise to pay a legacy if he had sufficient assets of the deceased in his hands to pay his debts and legacies[9]; that a promise by a discharged bankrupt to pay a debt contracted before the discharge was binding[10]; and that a promise to pay a statute-barred debt[11] or one contracted during minority[12] was binding. In some of these cases, the consideration for the promise was said to be the "moral" obligation of the promisor to pay the debt.

In this context, the term "moral obligation" was used in a narrow sense. It was restricted to cases in which the promisor's previous obligation was not legally enforceable (or not enforceable in the particular court in which the action on the promise was brought[13]) because it suffered from some specific legal defect. It did not follow that any "moral" obligation was consideration. Thus in *Eastwood v Kenyon*[14] the guardian of a young girl had raised a loan to pay for her maintenance and education, and to improve her estate. After she had come of age and married; and her husband promised the guardian to pay the amount of the loan. In dismissing the guardian's action on this promise, the court rejected the argument that the husband's promise was binding merely because he was under a moral obligation to perform it. Lord Denman C.J. said that this argument would "annihilate the necessity for any consideration at all, inasmuch as the

---

[6] *Roger v Comptoir d'Escompte de Paris* (1869) L.R. 2 C.P. 393; *Re Barker's Estate* (1875) 44 L.J. Ch. 487; *Wigan v English & Scottish Law Life Assurance Society* [1909] 1 Ch. 291.

[7] *e.g. Hopkinson v Logan* (1839) 5 M. & W. 241 (promise fixing date of payment).

[8] See below, p.92.

[9] *Atkins v Hill* (1775) 1 Cowp. 284; *Hawkes v Saunders* (1782) 1 Cowp. 289, an alternative ground for the decision given by Buller J. was that the defendant's equitable (as opposed to "moral") obligation to pay the legacy was consideration for the promise.

[10] *Trueman v Fenton* (1772) 2 Cowp. 544.

[11] *Hyeling v Hastings* (1699) 1 Ld. Raym. 389.

[12] See below, p.508; *cf. Lee v Muggeridge* (1813) 5 Taunt. 36 (promise by a woman after her husband's death to pay debt incurred during marriage); for attempts to restrict or define the doctrine, see *Littlefield v Shee* (1831) 2 B. & Ad. 811; *Meyer v Haworth* (1838) 8 A. & E. 467.

[13] As in *Hawkes v Saunders*, above, n.9.

[14] (1840) 11 A. & E. 438.

mere fact of giving a promise creates a moral obligation to perform it".[15] The moral obligation to *perform* a promise cannot be the consideration for it even in the most general sense: it cannot be the reason for *making* the promise. The case also shows that the mere existence of an antecedent moral obligation (in the ordinary sense of the phrase) to reimburse the guardian did not amount to consideration for the husband's promise. From this point of view, the case provides the classic illustration of the requirement that the consideration for a promise must not be past.

Many of the cases in which promises were held binding under the old "moral obligation" theory would now go the other way. For example, an executor who has assets of the deceased in his hands is no longer personally liable on a promise to pay legacies[16]; a promise by a discharged bankrupt to pay in full debts incurred before his discharge is binding only if supported by fresh consideration[17]; and the same is true of a promise to pay a debt after it has become statute-barred.[18]

On the other hand, a promise by an adult to pay a debt (or to perform some other obligation) contracted during minority is enforceable[19]; and *Eastwood v Kenyon*[20] did not purport to overrule the "moral obligation" theory in its original narrow sense, that a promise to perform an earlier obligation which suffered from some specific legal defect might be binding. In this sense the theory was restated by Lord Denman himself only two years after his decision in *Eastwood v Kenyon*[21] and applied 23 years later in a case[22] that was mentioned with approval by Scrutton L.J. in 1918.[23] In this narrow sense, the "moral obligation" theory may still survive, though its scope has been restricted and the label has become unfashionable.

5. Statutory Exceptions

There are two exceptions to the rule that past consideration is no consideration.

First, an "antecedent debt or liability," though normally a past consideration,[24] is good consideration for a bill of exchange.[25]

Secondly, the Limitation Act 1980[26] provides that, where a debtor in a writing signed by him[27] "acknowledges" a debt, it shall be deemed to have accrued on and not before the date of the acknowledgment. An "acknowledgment" need not take the form of a promise[28]; but if it does take this form the promise can extend the period of limitation even though the only consideration for it was the antecedent debt, and thus past. Further acknowledgments made within such an extended period or periods have the same effect.[29] But once the debt has become statute-barred the right to sue for it cannot

---

[15] *ibid.* at 450; *cf. Monkman v Stephenson* (1840) 11 A. & E. 411 at 416.
[16] Williams, Mortimer and Sunnucks, *Executors and Administrators and Probate* (17th ed.), p.714.
[17] *Jakeman v Cook* (1878) 4 Ex.D. 26; *Re Bonacina* [1912] 2 Ch. 394; *Wild v Tucker* [1914] 3 K.B. 36.
[18] Limitation Act 1980, s.29(7); *cf.* as to time bars imposed by contract, *The Ion* [1980] 2 Lloyd's Rep. 245 at 249.
[19] See below, p.549.
[20] (1840) 11 A. & E. 438.
[21] *Roscorla v Thomas* (1842) 3 Q.B. 234 at 237.
[22] *Flight v Reed* (1863) 1 H. & C. 703.
[23] *J Evans & Co v Heathcote* [1918] 1 K.B. 418 at 437.
[24] See above, p.78.
[25] Bills of Exchange Act 1882, s.27(1)(b). Such consideration is not *necessarily* past: it might consist of forbearance of the creditor to sue for the debt or in his treating the bill as conditional payment: see *Currie v Misa* (1875) L.R. 10 Ex. 153 and *cf.* below, pp.86, 698.
[26] s.27(5).
[27] *ibid.* s.30(1).
[28] An admission of liability suffices: *Surrendra Overseas Ltd v Government of Sri Lanka* [1977] 1 W.L.R. 481; *cf. Re Overmark Smith Warden Ltd* [1982] 1 W.L.R. 1195.
[29] Limitation Act 1980, s.29(7).

be revived by any subsequent acknowledgment[30]: to this extent, the old "moral obligation" theory as applied to statute-barred debts[31] has been reversed.

SECTION 4. CONSIDERATION MUST MOVE FROM THE PROMISEE

1. Promisee must provide Consideration

The rule that consideration must "move from the promisee"[32] means that a person to whom a promise was made can enforce it only if he himself provided the consideration for it. He has no such right if the consideration moved from a third party. Thus if A promises B to pay £10,000 to B if C will paint A's house, and C does so, B cannot enforce A's promise (unless, of course, B had procured, or undertaken to procure, C to do the work). The promisee need not, however, provide the whole consideration for the promise: thus he can enforce a promise, the consideration for which was provided partly by himself and partly by his agent or partner or by some other co-promisee.[33]

2. Consideration need not move to Promisor

While consideration must move from the promisee, it need not move to the promisor.[34] It follows that the requirement of consideration may be satisfied where the promisee suffers some detriment at the promisor's request, but confers no corresponding benefit on the promisor. Thus the promisee may provide consideration by giving up a job[35] or the tenancy of a flat,[36] even though no direct benefit results to the promisor from these acts. Consideration may also move from the promisee without moving to the promisor where the promisee at the promisor's request confers a benefit on a third party, *e.g.* by entering into a contract with the third party.[37] This possibility is illustrated by the case in which goods are bought and paid for by the use of a cheque card or credit card. The issuer of the card makes a promise to the supplier of the goods that the cheque will be honoured or that the supplier will be paid; and the supplier provides consideration for this promise by supplying the goods to the customer.[38] In the case of the credit card transaction, there is also consideration in the shape of the discount allowed by the supplier of the goods to the issuer of the card: this is both a detriment to the supplier and a benefit to the issuer.[39]

---

[30] *ibid.*
[31] See above, p.79.
[32] *Barber v Fox* (1682) 2 Wms.Saund. 134, n.(e); *Thomas v Thomas* (1842) 2 Q.B. 851 at 859; *Tweddle v Atkinson* (1861) 1 B. & S. 393 at 398, 399; *Pollway Ltd v Abdullah* [1974] 1 W.L.R. 493 at 497; *cf. Dickinson v Abel* [1969] 1 W.L.R. 295; *Customs & Excise Commissioners v Telemed* [1992] S.T.C. 89; for criticism of a contrary dictum, see below, p.578.
[33] *Jones v Robinson* (1847) 1 Ex. 454; *Fleming v Bank of New Zealand* [1900] A.C. 577. For the position where the *whole* consideration is provided by a co-promisee, see below, p.577.
[34] *Re Wyvern Developments Ltd* [1974] 1 W.L.R. 1097; *cf. Barclays Bank plc v Weeks, Legg & Dean* [1998] 3 All E.R. 213 at 220–221.
[35] *Jones v Padavatton* [1969] 1 W.L.R. 628.
[36] *Tanner v Tanner* [1975] 1 W.L.R. 1346; contrast *Horrocks v Forray* [1976] 1 W.L.R. 230; *Coombes v Smith* [1986] 1 W.L.R. 808.
[37] See *International Petroleum Refining Supply Ltd v Caleb Brett & Son Ltd* [1980] 1 Lloyd's Rep. 569 at 594 (where the promisor benefited indirectly since promisor and third party were associated companies); *cf.* also *The Chemical Venture* [1993] 1 Lloyd's Rep. 509 at 522 (payments made by charterer to crew regarded as consideration for promise by shipowner to charterer).
[38] See *R. v Lambie* [1982] A.C. 449; *Re Charge Card Services Ltd* [1987] Ch. 150, affirmed [1989] Ch. 497.
[39] *Customs & Excise Commissioners v Diner's Club Ltd* [1989] 1 W.L.R. 1196 at 1207.

3. Benefit to Promisor sufficient

The requirement that consideration must move from the promisee at first sight supports the view that the essence of consideration is detriment to the promisee. But the requirement may be satisfied, even though the promisee in fact suffers no detriment, if he confers a benefit on the promisor, or on a third party at the promisor's request. This was the position in *Bolton v Madden*,[40] where the claimant and defendant were entitled, as subscribers to a charity, to vote on the disposition of its funds. The claimant promised to vote at one meeting for a person whom the defendant wished to benefit, and the defendant promised in return to vote at the next meeting for a person whom the claimant wished to benefit. In an action on the defendant's promise, it was argued that there was no consideration for it as the claimant "incurred neither trouble nor prejudice".[41] But it was held the that consideration had moved from the claimant when he had at the defendant's request conferred a benefit on a third party. It could be argued that the claimant had suffered a legal detriment[42] by voting in accordance with his promise as he was not previously bound to do so. But this was not the basis of the decision. The possibility that consideration may consist in benefit to the promisor is further illustrated by *Edmonds v Lawson*,[43] where the relationship between a pupil barrister and the members of the chambers at which she had accepted an offer of pupillage was held to be contractual even though she paid no pupillage fee. The requirement of consideration was satisfied in that her (and other pupils') agreement to accept pupillage "provide[d] a pool of selected candidates who can be expected to compete with each other for recruitment as tenants",[44] and in that "chambers may see an advantage in developing close relationships with pupils who plan to practise as employed barristers or over-seas".[45] Both these factors stress the benefit to the promisors (the members of the chambers), moving from the promisee (the pupil barrister) even though no detriment was suffered by her.

The view that consideration can move from the promisee though he in fact suffers no detriment is, supported by two further rules to be discussed later in this Chapter. The first is that performance of an existing contractual duty (or a promise to perform such a duty) can constitute consideration if it benefits the promisor[46]: this benefit "moves" from the promisee in that it is conferred by him, even though it may cause him no detriment[47] in the sense that he was already bound to do the acts in question. The second is that a composition agreement between a debtor and his creditors is binding[48] because it benefits the creditors; and this benefit can be said to "move" from the debtor in that his co-operation is essential to the making and performance of the composition agreement. It could be said that the debtor suffers a legal detriment by signing the

---

[40] (1873) L.R. 9 Q.B. 55.
[41] *ibid*. at 57.
[42] See above, p.69.
[43] [2000] Q.B. 501.
[44] *ibid*. at 515.
[45] *ibid*.
[46] See below, pp.95, 98.
[47] *Williams v Roffey Bros & Nicholls (Contractors) Ltd* [1991] 1 Q.B. 1 at 16.
[48] See below, p.129, the application of this rule in *West Yorks Darracq Agency Ltd v Coleridge* [1911] 2 K.B. 326 is hard to support, since there the creditors got nothing and so received no benefit. The consideration was said at 329 to be benefit to the debtor, but he was the person *to* whom the promise was made, and benefit to the promisee is obviously no consideration. If it were, there would be consideration for every gratuitous promise.

agreement when he is not bound to do so. But the rule is not based on this invented consideration.[49] It is based on benefit to the promisors.[50]

4. Contracts (Rights of Third Parties) Act 1999

Under this Act, a term in a contract between A (the promisor) and B (the promisee) is, in specified conditions, enforceable by a third party, C, against A. The Act is more fully discussed in Chapter 15[51]; the only points to be made here are that C is not prevented from enforcing the term by the fact that no consideration for A's promise moved from him,[52] and that C's right to enforce that promise can be described as a quasi-exception to the rule that consideration must move from the promisee.[53] It is not a true exception to the rule since in the case put the promisee is B, who must provide consideration for A's promise.

SECTION 5. CONSIDERATION MUST BE OF SOME VALUE

1. Must be of Economic Value

An act, forbearance or promise will amount to consideration only if the law recognises that it has some economic value. It may have such value even though the value cannot be precisely quantified. But "natural affection of itself is not a sufficient consideration",[54] and the same is true of other merely sentimental motives for promising. This is the reason why in *Thomas v Thomas*[55] the desire of the testator that his widow should live in his house was not part of the consideration for the executors' promise that she might do so. Similar reasoning may also explain the decision in *White v Bluett*[56] that a son had not provided consideration (for his father's promise not to sue him on a promissory note) by promising not to bore his father with complaints.

2. Illusory Consideration

A promise may appear to be made for some consideration which is illusory and which must therefore be disregarded.

One such situation can arise when the alleged consideration consists of a promise, the performance of which is, to the knowledge of both parties, impossible. For example, a promise by A to pay B £100 in return for B's promise to let A have all the wine in B's cellar would probably be regarded as a gratuitous promise if, when the promise was made, both A and B knew[57] that there was no wine in the cellar. The position would be different if B's promise were to deliver the *future* contents of the cellar. In that case, A

---

[49] See above, p.71. The creditors do not bargain for the debtor's signature but for a dividened. If the debtor's signature were the consideration it could equally well be so regarded in a composition with a single creditor, but this would be contrary to *Foakes v Beer* (1884) 9 App.Cas. 605, below, p.125.

[50] See below, p.129.

[51] See below, pp.651 *et seq.*

[52] Law Com. No. 242 (on which the Act is based) §6.8.

[53] See below, pp.656–657.

[54] *Bret v JS* (1600) Cro.Eliz. 756; *Mansukhani v Sharkey* [1992] 2 E.G.L.R. 105.

[55] (1842) 2 Q.B. 851; above, p.72.

[56] (1853) 23 L.J.Ex. 36. Pollock C.B. said at 37 that the son had "no right" to bore his father with complaints; but the son certainly had no legal duty not to do this and it is arguable that his forbearance did amount to consideration. Perhaps the decision can be explained on the ground that the father, in spite of his promise, retained the note.

[57] There could be a good contract if the parties were in doubt on this point: see *Smith v Harrison* (1857) 26 L.J. Ch. 412, below, p.294.

would be buying the chance of the cellar's containing wine[58]; and the value of that chance would be illusory only if the question whether any wine was to be put into the cellar had been left entirely to B's discretion.[59]

A second situation in which consideration would be illusory is where the promisee would have accomplished the act or forbearance anyway, even if the promise had not been made. This will be the position if A promises to pay B, who happens to be fond of port, £5 if B will drink the glass of port that he has just poured for himself; or if C promises D, who has religious objections to smoking, £5 if he will not smoke for a week. Since "it is no consideration to refrain from a course of conduct which it was never intended to pursue",[60] such promises would not be legally binding. But where the promise provided *an* inducement for the act or forbearance, the requirement of consideration would be satisfied even though there were also other inducements operating on the mind of the promisee.[61] It seems that the burden of proving that the requested act or forbearance would have been accomplished, even if the promise had not been made, is on the promisor.[62]

Consideration would again be illusory where it was alleged to consist of a promise the terms of which left performance entirely to the discretion of the promisor.[63] A person does not provide consideration by promising to do something "if I feel like it", or "unless I change my mind"; and the same principle may apply in analogous cases. Thus a promise may be illusory if it is accompanied by a clause effectively[64] excluding all liability of the promisor for breach.[65] And a promise to buy "so much coal as I may decide to order" would be an illusory consideration for the seller's counter-promise to deliver, which could therefore not be enforced.[66] On the other hand, if the promise were to buy "so much of the coal *that I require* as I may order from you", the court could give reality to the promise by implying a term into it to the effect that at least a reasonable part of any requirements which the promisor actually turned out to have must be ordered from the promisee. Equally a buyer would provide consideration by promising to buy from the seller "*all* the coal I require"; for in such a case, even if the buyer does not promise to have any requirements, he does at least give a definite undertaking not to deal with anybody else.[67] Similarly, a promise which is subject to cancellation by A may nevertheless constitute consideration for a counter-promise from B where A's power to

---

[58] *cf. Brady v Brady* [1989] A.C. 755 at 774 ("at the date of the promise").

[59] See below at n.63.

[60] *Arrale v Costain Civil Engineering Ltd* [1976] 1 Lloyd's Rep. 98 at 106; *cf. Colchester BC v Smith* [1991] Ch. 448 at 489, affirmed on other grounds [1992] Ch. 421; *Beaton v McDivitt* (1988) 13 N.S.W.L.R. 162.

[61] *Brikom Investments Ltd v Carr* [1979] Q.B. 467 at 490.

[62] *cf.* the analogous rule in cases of "proprietary estoppel" (below, p.141): *Greasley v Cook* [1980] 1 W.L.R. 1306; and misrepresentation (below, p.342): *Smith v Chadwick* (1884) 9 App.Cas. 187 at 196.

[63] *Stabilad Ltd v Stephens & Carter Ltd (No.2)* [1999] 2 All E.R. (Comm) 651 at 659. Such promises may also give rise to problems of contractual intention: see below, p.167.

[64] See below, Chap.7. If the clause were ineffective (*e.g.*, under Unfair Terms in Consumer Contracts Regulations 1999 (SI 1999/2083), Sch.2, para.1(c) or (f)), this fact would give reality to an otherwise illusory promise.

[65] *Firestone Tyre & Rubber Co Ltd v Vokins* [1951] 1 Lloyd's Rep. 32; *cf.* the discussion of *The Cap Palos* [1921] p.458, in the *Suisse Atlantique Case* [1967] 1 A.C. 361 at 432.

[66] See *Wickham & Burton Coal Co v Farmer's Lumber Co* 189, 179 N.W. 417 (1923); for an exception, see *Citadel Insurance Co v Atlantic Union Insurance Co* [1982] 2 Lloyd's Rep. 543; below, p.154.

[67] The validity of "requirement" contracts is assumed in such cases as *Metropolitan Electric Supply Co v Ginder* [1901] 2 Ch. 799 and *Dominion Coal Co Ltd v Dominion Steel & Iron Co Ltd* [1909] A.C. 293. Similarly, a contract by a manufacturer to sell his entire output to a particular buyer is binding even though he does not bind himself to have any output: see, for example, *Donnell v Bennett* (1883) 22 Ch.D. 835 and *cf. Thames Tideway Properties Ltd v Serfaty* [1999] 2 Lloyd's Rep. 110 at 127; Howard, 2 U. of Tas.L.R. 446; Adams, 94 L.Q.R. 73. For the possible illegality of such promises, see below, pp.468–472.

cancel is limited by the express terms of the promise, *e.g.*, where it can be exercised only within a specified time. Such a limitation on the power to cancel may also be implied, so that (for example) A could not cancel after B had begun to perform his counter-promise. A's promise would then constitute consideration, so that B would be liable if he failed to complete the performance. Finally, the objection that a promise amounts only to illusory consideration on the grounds here discussed can be removed if the promise is performed: such actual performance can constitute consideration even though the person who has rendered it was not legally obliged to render it.[68]

3. Trivial Acts or Objects

Since consideration need not be adequate, acts or omissions of very small value can be consideration. Thus it has been said that there was consideration for a promise to give a man £50 "if you will come to my house"[69]; that the act of executing a deed could be consideration for a promise to pay money although the deed was void[70]; that the execution of a will by A could be consideration for B's promise to make (and not to revoke) a similar will, even though the will made by A is revocable[71]; that to give up a piece of paper without reference to its contents was consideration[72]; that even to show a person a document was consideration[73]; and that the mere act of conducting negotiations can satisfy the requirement of consideration, even though that act does not commit the promisee to bringing the negotiations to a successful conclusion.[74]

On the same principle, objects of trifling value can constitute consideration. In *Chappell & Co Ltd v Nestlé Co Ltd*,[75] chocolate manufacturers sold gramophone records for 1s. 6d. plus three wrappers of their 6d. bars of chocolate. It was held that the delivery of the wrappers formed part of the consideration, though the wrappers were of little value and were in fact thrown away. If the delivery of the wrappers formed part of the consideration it could, presumably, have formed the whole of the consideration, so that a promise to deliver records for wrappers alone would have been binding. This case should be contrasted with *Lipkin Gorman v Karpnale Ltd*,[76] where gaming chips supplied by a gaming club to one of its members (and then lost by the member in the course of the gaming) were held not to constitute consideration for the money which the member had paid for them. One reason for this view appears to have been that

---

[68] *Cambridge Nutrition Ltd v BBC* [1990] 3 All E.R. 523 at 538; *Stabilad Ltd v Stephens & Carter Ltd (No.2)* [1999] 2 All E.R. (Comm) 651 at 660.

[69] *Gilbert v Ruddeard* (1608) 3 Dy. 272b (n); *cf. Denton v GN Ry* (1856) 5 E. & B. 860.

[70] *Westlake v Adams* (1858) 5 C.B.(N.S.) 248; perhaps there was also an element of compromise in this case: *cf.* below, p.88.

[71] *Re Dale* [1994] Ch. 31 at 38. Contrast *Re Goodchild* [1997] 1 W.L.R. 1216 where a mere "common understanding" (as opposed to definite mutual promises) did not suffice to make B's promise irrevocable, but some effect was given to it by an order in favour of the intended beneficiary under the Inheritance (Provision for Dependants) Act 1975; *cf. Taylor v Dickens* [1998] 1 F.L.R. 806, the reasoning of which was doubted on other grounds in *Gillett v Holt* [2001] Ch. 210.

[72] *Haigh v Brooks* (1839) 10 A. & E. 309 at 334; contrast *Foster v Dawber* (1861) 6 Ex. 839.

[73] *Sturlyn v Albany* (1587) Cro.Eliz. 67; *March v Culpepper* (1628) Cro.Car. 70. Contrast *Re Charge Card Services Ltd* [1987] Ch. 150 at 164, affirmed [1989] Ch. 497 (production of charge card and signature of voucher not the consideration for a supply of goods, evidently because such "consideration" would be blatantly "invented": above, p.71).

[74] *Sepong Engineering Construction Co v Formula One Management Ltd* [2000] 1 Lloyd's Rep. 602 at 611; but damages for breach of the resulting contract would be no more than nominal: *cf.* below, p.955.

[75] [1960] A.C. 87.

[76] [1991] 2 A.C. 548.

"the chips themselves were worthless"[77]; but this is equally true of the wrappers in the *Chappell* case. Another seems to have been that the chips "remained the property of the club"[78]; but this again would not of itself be decisive, for the transfer of possession (no less than that of ownership) can constitute consideration.[79] A third reason for the view that the chips were not consideration for the money may be that the parties did not so regard the transaction: they regarded the chips as merely "a convenient mechanism for facilitating gambling",[80] and the case may be one in which the court refused to "invent" consideration[81] (by regarding something as consideration which was not so regarded by the parties) even though this course was technically open to it. This refusal appears to have been based on the context in which the question arose. The issue was not whether the club could sue the member on any promise made by him: it arose because the money paid by the member to the club had been stolen; and the club, which had received the money in good faith, argued that it had given valuable consideration for it, so as to defeat the true owner's claim for the return of the money. This explanation of the case derives some support from Lord Goff's discussion of a hypothetical case of tokens supplied by a department store in exchange for cash. He said that "by receiving the money in these circumstances the store does not *for present purposes* give valuable consideration for it"[82]; yet he also accepted that (in the store example) "an independent contract is made for the chips when the customer originally obtains them at the cash desk".[83] The question whether a party has provided consideration may thus receive one answer when it arises for the purpose of determining the enforceability of a promise, and a different and narrower one when it arises for the purpose of determining whether a transaction has adversely affected the rights of an innocent third party.[84] It was the desire to protect the victim of the theft which led the House of Lords in the *Lipkin Gorman* case to reject the, no doubt somewhat technical, argument that the chips constituted consideration for the money.

The *Lipkin Gorman* case gives rise to further difficulty because the chips were supplied on the terms that they could be used, not only for gaming, but also to purchase refreshments at the club. There was no evidence of their having been used for this purpose,[85] but Lord Templeman said that "neither the power to buy refreshments nor the exercise of that power could constitute consideration for the receipt [by the club] of £154,693", (the sum lost by the member of the club).[86] One possible interpretation of this passage is that the supply of refreshments could not constitute consideration for £154,693 since the disparity in value was too great; but this would be inconsistent with the principle that consideration need not be adequate. It is submitted that the preferable explanation of Lord Templeman's statement is that the chips were simply "treated as currency"[87] in the club and could be used for a variety of transactions. The reason why the supply of refreshments was not consideration for the face value of the chips lost at play was simply that these transactions were entirely separate ones.

---

[77] *ibid.* at 561.
[78] *ibid*; and see 575.
[79] *Bainbridge v Firmstone* (1838) 8 A. & E. 743.
[80] *Lipkin Gorman's* case at 575.
[81] See above, p.71.
[82] *Lipkin Gorman's* case, at 577; italics supplied; *cf.* above, p.70.
[83] *Lipkin Gorman's* case at 576.
[84] See above, p.67.
[85] *Lipkin Gorman's* case at 569.
[86] *Lipkin Gorman* case at 567.
[87] *ibid.*, at 561.

4. Gift of Onerous Property

A promise to give away onerous property is binding if the donee promises in return to discharge obligations attached to it. Thus a promise to give away a leasehold house is binding if the donee promises to perform the donor's covenants under the lease, *e.g.* to repair, to insure and to pay rent[88]; a promise to give away a freehold house is binding if the donee promises to pay outstanding mortgage instalments or other charges[89]; and a promise to give away partly paid-up shares in a company is binding if the donee promises to pay further calls which may be made on the shares.[90] If the property is worth more than the obligations attached to it, there will be an element of gift in such transactions; and safeguards are provided by law to ensure that this aspect of it does not prejudice certain categories of third parties, such as creditors of the promisor.[91]

5. Compromise and Forbearance to Sue

Three situations call for discussion. In the first, a person promises not to enforce a *valid* claim; in the second the claim that he promises not to enforce is *invalid or doubtful*; and in the third he simply *forbears in fact* from enforcing a claim, without making any *promise* to forbear.

(1) Valid claims

A promise not to enforce a valid claim[92] is clearly good consideration for a promise given in return.[93] If, for example, A is injured by the admitted negligence of B, they can validly compromise the claim, A's promise not to sue B constituting the consideration for B's promise to pay the agreed compensation. Similarly, a creditor to whom a sum of money has become due may promise to give the debtor extra time to pay in return for the debtor's promise to pay higher interest or to give additional security. In such a case there is good consideration for the debtor's promise: he benefits by getting extra time to pay, while the creditor suffers a detriment in that he is, for a time, kept out of his money.[94] There is such benefit to the debtor and detriment to the creditor even if the creditor promises to forbear for only a limited time; and if no time is specified, the court will infer that he undertook to forbear for a reasonable time.[95] The principles just stated apply, not only to a promise not to enforce a claim, but also to a promise to abandon a good defence[96]; and to a promise to abandon a particular remedy, *e.g.* to one to abandon arbitration proceedings.[97]

Although a promise to release a valid claim is thus supported by consideration, the court may protect the party granting the release on other grounds. This possibility is

---

[88] *Price v Jenkins* (1877) 5 Ch.D. 619; *Johnsey Estates Ltd v Lewis Manley (Engineering) Ltd* [1987] 2 E.G.L.R. 69; *Westminster City Council v Duke of Westminster* [1991] 4 All E.R. 136, reversed in part on other grounds (1992) 24 H.L.R. 572. In so far as *Thomas v Thomas* (1842) 2 Q.B. 851, above, p.68, takes a contrary view, it seems to be inconsistent with *Price v Jenkins* (where the "case which is not reported" mentioned at 620 closely resembles *Thomas v Thomas*).

[89] *Merritt v Merritt* [1970] 1 W.L.R. 1121.

[90] *Cheale v Kenward* (1858) 3 D. & J. 27.

[91] Insolvency Act 1986, ss.238, 339; above, p.75, n.74; *Re Kumar* [1993] 1 W.L.R. 224.

[92] For promises to abandon defences and remedies, see below at nn.96 and 97.

[93] *e.g. Greene v Church Commissioners for England* [1974] Ch. 467; *cf. Centrovincial Estates plc v Merchant Investors Assurance Co Ltd, The Times*, March 8, 1983 (as to which see above, p.8, n.7); *The Attika Hope* [1988] 1 Lloyd's Rep. 439 at 442 (forbearance to sue third party).

[94] *Crowther v Farrer* (1850) 15 Q.B. 677.

[95] *Payne v Wilson* (1827) 7 B. & C. 423; *Oldershaw v King* (1857) 2 H. & n.517.

[96] See *Banque de l'Indochine v J H Rayner (Mincing Lane) Ltd* [1983] Q.B. 711.

[97] *The Leonidas D* [1985] 1 W.L.R. 925 at 933, where there was no such abandonment: see above p.10.

illustrated by *Bank of Credit and Commerce International SA v Ali*[98] where an employee, on being dismissed for redundancy, promised in return for certain payments to release all claims against the employers "of whatever nature that exist or may exist". At the time of the release, claims for "stigma damages" were believed not to be available to employees for breach of their employment contracts, but the availability of such claims was established by a later decision of the House of Lords.[99] It was held by the House of Lords in the present case that the general words of the release (quoted above) were not sufficiently clear to show "that the parties intended to provide for the release of rights and surrender of claims which they could never have had in contemplation at all".[1] It is implicit in this reasoning that the possibility of releasing such a claim is not ruled out as a matter of law: the court is simply "slow to infer that a party intended to surrender rights and claims of which he was unaware and could not have been aware".[2] The crucial points in *Ali's* case seems to have been that *neither* party could have been aware of the possibility that the employee might, in law, have had a claim for stigma damages. If the *employer* had been aware of this possibility, it is far from clear that the employee would have succeeded on the issue of *construction*. There is, however, the further possibility that the amount of a settlement may be affected by the fact that "the party to whom the release was given [B] knew that the other party [A] had or might have a claim [beyond the one he thought he was releasing] *and knew also* that the other party was ignorant of this".[3] B's taking the release "without disclosing the existence of the claim or possible claim" would then be "unacceptable sharp practice"[4] and there is judicial support for the view that the law should on this ground grant relief to A,[5] *i.e.* allow him to pursue the claim which he had unwittingly abandoned.

(2) Invalid and doubtful claims

(a) CLAIMS KNOWN TO BE INVALID. It used to be thought that a promise by A not to enforce a claim which was invalid was no consideration for a promise given by B in return, since B, if he was not liable, did not benefit from A's promise not to sue him, while A lost nothing by giving up a worthless right.[6] This reasoning still applies where the sole[7] consideration provided by A is his forbearance to enforce a claim which is clearly invalid and which he either knows to be invalid or does not believe to be valid. Thus a promise by a bookmaker not to sue his client for the amount of lost bets[8] is no consideration for a promise made in return by the client.[9]

---

[98] [2001] UKHL 8; [2001] I.C.R. 337.

[99] *Malik v Bank of Credit and Commerce International* [1998] A.C. 20, below, p.991.

[1] [2001] I.C.R. 337 at [19]. This reasoning does not apply to an arbitration clause in a contract since the very purpose of such a clause is "to provide machinery for the resolution of disputes which may arise in the future": *Capital Trust Investment Ltd v Radio Design TJAB* [2002] EWCA Civ 135; [2002] 2 All E.R. 159 at [50]. Contrast also, on the issue of construction, *Mostcash plc v Fluor Ltd* [2002] EWCA Civ 975, [2002] B.L.R. 411.

[2] [2001] I.C.R. 377 at [10]. Lord Hoffmann dissented.

[3] *ibid.* at [32], italics supplied.

[4] *ibid.* at [32]. in *Ali's* case there was no such knowledge on B's part.

[5] *ibid. per* Lord Nicholls. Lord Bingham left the point open: *ibid.* at [20].

[6] *Jones v Ashburnham* (1804) 4 East 455.

[7] The position is different where there is also other consideration: *The Siboen and the Sibotre* [1976] 1 Lloyd's Rep. 293 at 334.

[8] For the invalidity of the bookmaker's claim, see below, p.520.

[9] *Hyams v Coombes* (1912) 28 T.L.R. 413; *Burrell & Sons v Leven* (1926) 42 T.L.R. 407; *Poteliakhoff v Teakle* [1938] 2 K.B. 816; *cf. Edwards v Baugh* (1843) 11 M. & W. 641; *Goodson v Baker* (1908) 98 L.T. 415, *contra,* seems wrong.

(b) DOUBTFUL CLAIMS. Where the claim is doubtful in law, a promise to abandon it involves the possibility of detriment to the potential claimant and of benefit to the other party. Such a promise is therefore good consideration for a counter-promise given by the latter party: *e.g.* for one to pay a sum of money to the party promising to abandon the claim.[10]

(c) CLAIMS WRONGLY BELIEVED TO BE VALID. A promise by A to abandon a claim is also good consideration for a counter-promise made by B, even though A's claim is *clearly* bad in law, if it is believed by A to be a valid one.[11] One reason which has been given for this rule is that otherwise "in no case of a doubtful claim could a compromise be enforced"[12]; but this does not explain why the rule applies where A's claim is not merely "doubtful" but *clearly* bad. Another suggested reason for the rule is that A suffers detriment because "he gives up what he believes to be a right of action"[13]; but, in general, consideration must be something of value, not something believed to be of value. In fact A would be worse off, if he did not forbear, for he would lose his action and the costs. A further suggestion is that A suffers detriment in that it becomes more difficult to get up his case, the longer he waits[14]; this is a possible detriment (even though his action is bound to fail) as the failure may be more expensive than it would have been, had he sued promptly. A may also suffer detriment if as a result of the agreement he loses the right to sue a third party who is liable on the original cause of action.[15] A's forbearance can also be said to confer a benefit on B since "instead of being annoyed with an action, he [B] escapes from the vexations incident to it".[16] There is some difficulty in relying on this benefit as the consideration for B's counter-promise, since it may also exist where A's claim is *known* to be bad, in which case the compromise is not binding.[17] Perhaps this last rule is based on public policy rather than on want of consideration. As Tindal C.J. said in *Wade v Simeon*[18]: "It is almost *contra bonos mores* and certainly contrary to the principles of natural justice that a man should institute proceedings against another when he is conscious that he has no good cause of action". If compromises of such claims were upheld, improper pressure might be brought to bear on persons who "owed" void debts.

The rule that a promise by A to abandon a claim which is clearly bad, but believed to be valid, is good consideration for a counter-promise from B is subject to a number of safeguards. There must be a "reasonable claim",[19] (*i.e.* one made on reasonable grounds) and A must honestly believe that his claim had at any rate a fair chance of success.[20] He must not conceal from B any facts which, if known to the latter, would

---

[10] *Haigh v Brooks* (1839) 10 A. & E. 309; *cf. Colchester BC v Smith* [1992] Ch. 421; *Colonia Versicherung AG v Amoco Oil Co* [1995] 1 Lloyd's Rep. 570 at 577 (affirmed without reference to this point [1997] 1 Lloyd's Rep. 261).

[11] *Cook v Wright* (1861) 1 B. & S. 559; *Callisher v Bischoffsheim* (1870) L.R. 5 Q.B. 449; *Holsworthy Urban DC v Holsworthy Rural DC* [1907] 2 Ch. 62; *cf. Horton v Horton* [1961] 1 Q.B. 215; *Freedman v Union Group plc* [1997] E.G.C.S. 28.

[12] *Callisher v Bischoffsheim*, above, at 451.

[13] *ibid.* at 452.

[14] *Cook v Wright*, above, at 569.

[15] *ibid.* at 569–570.

[16] *Callisher v Bischoffsheim*, above, at 452; *cf. Pitt v P.H.H. Asset Management Ltd* [1994] 1 W.L.R. 327 at 332, but in this case it is not clear that the party forbearing in fact believed in the validity of his claim. See also *Mousaka Inc v Goldon Seagull Maritime Inc* [2002] 1 Lloyd's Rep. 797 at [14] ("commercial benefit").

[17] See above, n.9.

[18] (1846) 2 C.B. 548, 564; *cf. Edwards v Baugh* (1843) 11 M. & W. 641, 646.

[19] *Cook v Wright*, above, at 569.

[20] *Callisher v Bischchoffsheim*, above, at 452.

enable him to resist the claim.[21] And he must show that he seriously intended to enforce the claim.[22]

The cases in the present group all concern claims the validity of which was doubtful in law. It seems that the same rules apply where the claim was doubtful because of a dispute about the facts. A settlement based on a simple *mistake* of fact made by both parties might be void for mistake.[23] But it will not be void on this ground where both parties knowingly take the risk that the actual facts may turn out to be different from the facts as they were supposed to be. This element of risk is always present when parties negotiate a settlement on disputed facts.

(d) EXECUTED COMPROMISES. The preceding discussion is concerned with the enforceability of an agreement to compromise a claim. Different problems can arise after such an agreement has been *performed*, generally by payment of the amount which one party has agreed to pay under the compromise. Even if there was, under the rules discussed above, no consideration for that party's promise, he will not be entitled to the return of the payment if it was made "to close the transaction"[24]: in such a case the payment is treated as if it were an executed gift.[25] To give rise to a claim for repayment, it will be necessary to establish other circumstances than lack of consideration: *e.g.* that the payment was made under duress.[26]

(3) Actual forbearance

A person may forbear from enforcing a claim without expressly promising to do so. The question then arises whether this actual forbearance is consideration for some promise or act of the other party, for example for a promise by him to give security, or for giving the security. Sometimes actual forbearance may be evidence of an implied promise to forbear.[26a] Thus the acceptance of a cheque in payment of a debt may be evidence of a promise not to sue the debtor so long as the cheque is not dishonoured, or at least for a reasonable time.[27]

But even where no promise to forbear (express or implied) has been made, an actual forbearance may constitute consideration. In *Alliance Bank v Broom*[28] the defendant owed £22,000 to his bank, which pressed him to give some security. He promised to do so, but the bank made no counter-promise not to sue him. It was held that there was consideration for the defendant's promise as the bank had given, and the defendant received, "some degree of forbearance".[29] On the other hand, in *Miles v New Zealand*

---

[21] *Miles v New Zealand Alford Estate Co* (1886) 32 Ch.D. 267 at 284; *Colchester BC v Smith* [1992] Ch. 421 at 435. The discussion at nn.3 to 5, above is concerned with the different problem of non-disclosure *by B* of the existence of a *valid* claim against himself.

[22] *Cook v Wright*, above, at 569; *The Proodos C* [1980] 2 Lloyd's Rep. 390 at 392.

[23] *e.g. Gloyne v Richardson* [2001] EWCA Civ 716; [2001] 2 B.C.L.C. 669 at [39]; below, Chap.8; Andrews [1989] L.M.C.L.Q. 431; *Grains & Fourrages SA v Huyton* [1997] 1 Lloyd's Rep. 628, where there was no compromise since both parties wished from the start to achieve the same result but were mistaken only as to the effect of the steps they had taken to achieve it.

[24] *Woolwich Equitable BS v IRC (No.2)* [1993] A.C. 70 at 165.

[25] *ibid.*, citing *Maskell v Horner* [1915] 3 K.B. 106 at 120.

[26] See below, p.405.

[26a] *Re Wyvern Developments Ltd* [1974] 1 W.L.R. 1097; *Thornton Springer v NEM Insurance Co Ltd* [2000] 2 All E.R. 489 at 516.

[27] *Baker v Walker* (1845) 14 M. & W. 465; *Elkington v Cooke-Hill* (1914) 30 T.L.R. 670.

[28] (1864) 2 Dr. & Sm. 289; *cf.* also *Brikom Investments Ltd v Carr* [1979] Q.B. 467 at 490.

[29] At 292.

Alford Estate Co[30] a company had bought land and then became dissatisfied with the purchase. The vendor later promised to make certain payments to the company, and it was alleged that the consideration for this promise was the company's forbearance to take proceedings to rescind the contract. A majority of the Court of Appeal held that there was no consideration for the vendor's promise as no proceedings to rescind were ever intended; and Cotton L.J. added that "it must be shown that there was something which would bind the company not to institute proceedings".[31] Bowen L.J. dissented from this proposition,[32] relying on *Alliance Bank v Broom*; but it may be possible to reconcile the cases by reference to the types of claim forborne. A bank to which £22,000 is owed is virtually certain to take steps to enforce its claim, but a dissatisfied purchaser of land is much less certain to take proceedings for rescission. It may, therefore, be reasonable to say that an actual forbearance can amount to consideration in relation to the former type of claim, but that a promise to forbear is necessary where it is problematical whether the claim will ever be enforced at all. A promise to forbear is also, of course, necessary where that is what the debtor bargains for.

Where the consideration consists of a *promise* to forbear which specifies no time the creditor must forbear for a reasonable time.[33] There is no such requirement where the consideration consists of *actual forbearance*: here it is enough that the debtor had "a certain amount of forbearance".[34]

A forbearance amounts to consideration only for a promise or performance that is induced by it. In *Wigan v English & Scottish Law Life Assurance Society*[35] a debtor executed a mortgage of an insurance policy in favour of his creditor. It was held that the creditor, who knew nothing of the mortgage, had not provided consideration for it merely by having forborne to sue for his antecedent debt. But Parker J. added[36] that the creditor would have provided consideration if he had been told of the mortgage and if, "on the strength of" it, he had actually forborne to sue for the debt. The crucial question, therefore, is whether the creditor has forborne "on the strength of" the debtor's act or promise. He will clearly have done so where the debtor has *expressly* requested the forbearance[37] but in *Alliance Bank v Broom*[38] the bank's forbearance was held to constitute consideration even though the defendant had not expressly requested it. The case has been explained on the ground that the debtor had impliedly requested forbearance.[39] But where the forbearance is not requested either expressly or by implication, it is no consideration. In *Combe v Combe*[40] a husband during divorce proceedings promised to pay his wife an annual allowance. In an action to enforce this promise, the wife argued, *inter alia*, that she had given consideration for it by forbearing to apply to the court for a maintenance order. But her argument was rejected as she had not forborne at the husband's request.[41]

---

[30] (1886) 32 Ch.D. 267; *cf. Hunter v Bradford Property Trust Ltd*, 1970 S.L.T. 173.

[31] (1886) 32 Ch.D. 267 at 285.

[32] *ibid.* at 291; his view was approved by Lord Macnaghten in *Fullerton v Provincial Bank of Ireland* [1903] A.C. 309 at 314.

[33] See above, p.87.

[34] *Alliance Bank v Broom* (1864) 2 Dr. & Sm. 289 at 292.

[35] [1909] 1 Ch. 291: *cf.* above, p.78.

[36] At 298.

[37] *Crears v Hunter* (1887) 19 Q.B.D. 341 at 344.

[38] (1864) 2 Dr. & Sm. 289.

[39] *Fullerton v Provincial Bank of Ireland* [1903] A.C. 309 at 313.

[40] [1951] 2 K.B. 215.

[41] *Quaere* whether such a request should not have been implied.

6. Performance of Existing Duty[42]

Much difficulty arises in determining whether a person who does, or promises to do, what he was already under a legal duty to do thereby provides consideration for a promise made to him. As he was already legally bound to do the act, he suffers no legal detriment.[43] But he may suffer a factual detriment if he actually does the act: this may be more troublesome to him than to pay damages. The promisor may also get a factual benefit, as damages might not fully compensate him for the loss which he would suffer if the duty were broken. Denning L.J. has therefore said that the performance of an existing duty, or the promise to perform it, was of itself good consideration.[44] This radical view has not been accepted; but the requirement of consideration in this group of cases has been mitigated by recognising that it can be satisfied where the promisee has conferred a factual (as opposed to a legal) benefit on the promisor.[45]

(1) Duty imposed by law

The question whether a person can enforce a promise made to him in return for performing, or promising to perform, a duty imposed by law (as opposed to one imposed by contract) has received a variety of answers.

(a) PUBLIC POLICY. One group of cases denies the enforceability of such promises. Thus a public officer cannot enforce a promise to pay him money for doing his duty as such,[46] and generally a person does not provide consideration by forbearing to engage in a course of conduct that is criminal.[47] Enforcement of such promises would tend to encourage an undesirable form of extortion; and it is this ground of public policy, rather than want of consideration, that accounts for most of the authorities in this group.

(b) PERFORMANCE OF THE DUTY AS CONSIDERATION. Promises to pay rewards for information that might lead to the arrest of a felon were often enforced[48] though, till 1968, a person who had such information was bound to communicate it to the police, and indeed committed an offence[49] if he failed to do so. Public policy was not offended by the enforcement of such promises, as they might induce people to look for the information and so promote the interests of justice. These cases show that an act may constitute consideration even though there is a public duty to do it. The contrary view

---

[42] Davis, 6 C.L.J. 202; Reynolds and Treitel, 7 Malaya Law Rev. 1; Aivazian, Trebilcock & Penny, 22 Osgoode Hall L.J. 173; Hooley, [1991] J.B.L. 195; Halston, 107 L.Q.R. 649.

[43] See above, p.69.

[44] *Ward v Byham* [1956] 1 W.L.R. 496 at 498; *Williams v Williams* [1957] 1 W.L.R. 148 at 151.

[45] See below, pp.95, 98.

[46] *Wathen v Sandys* (1811) 2 Camp. 640; *Morris v Burdett* (1808) 1 Camp. 218; *Bilke v Havelock* (1813) 3 Camp. 374; *Morgan v Palmer* (1825) 2 B. & C. 729 at 736 (where the actual decision was that money paid to the official was recoverable by the payee as having been extorted from him *colore officii*: see *Woolwich Equitable BS v IRC (No.2)* [1993] A.C. 70 at 155 at 165, 181, 198).

[47] *Brown v Brine* (1875) L.R. 1 Ex.D. 5 (forbearance to commit criminal libel).

[48] *England v Davidson* (1840) 11 A. & E. 856; *Neville v Kelly* (1862) 12 C.B.(N.S) 740; *Bent v Wakefield and Barnsley Union Bank* (1878) 4 C.P.D. 1. Contrast *Maryland Casualty Co v Matthews*, 209 F.Supp. 822 (1962) where a similar claim *by a detective* failed on grounds of public policy.

[49] *i.e.* misprision of felony: *Sykes v DPP* [1962] A.C. 528. This offence was abolished by Criminal Law Act 1967, s.1. The offence of concealing an arrestable offence created by s.5(1) of that Act is narrower in scope than the former offence of misprision of felony; it is committed only if the person withholding the information accepts or agrees to accept some consideration (other than making good the loss) for not disclosing it. *cf.* below, p.445. For the definition of "arrestable offence," see now Police & Criminal Evidence Act 1984, s.24, as amended by Police Act 2002, s.48.

is, indeed, supported by *Collins v Godefroy*[50] where an attorney who had been sub-poenaed to give evidence was promised a guinea a day for attendance. This was held to be "a promise without consideration" as he was already bound to attend. But the reasoning is hard to reconcile with the reward cases just mentioned; and the actual decision has long ceased to represent the practice in such cases.[51] A subpoena must be accompanied by a tender of "conduct money"[52]; this includes the reasonable expenses of attending the trial, and, in certain cases, compensation for loss of time. Expert witnesses can validly contract for payment[53]; and it seems that all witnesses who attend in a professional capacity, whether they are strictly expert witnesses or not, are entitled to compensation for loss of time.

(c) OTHER CONSIDERATION. A person can provide consideration by doing, or promis-ing, *more* than he is by law obliged to do. Thus in *Glasbrook Bros Ltd v Glamorgan CC*[54] mine-owners who feared violence from strikers asked, and promised to pay, for a greater degree of police protection than the police reasonably thought necessary. It was held that the police authority had provided consideration for this promise by giving the extra protection, and that accordingly the promise was enforceable. The position in cases of this kind is now regulated by statute. S.25(1) of the Police Act 1996 provides that payment can be claimed for "special police services" rendered at the "request" of the person requiring them. Such a request can be implied from conduct, *e.g.* where a person organises an event which cannot safely take place without such special services. On this reasoning, a football club has been held liable to a police authority for the cost of policing matches played on its ground.[55] Such liability arises irrespective of contract.

In *Ward v Byham*[56] the father of an illegitimate child promised to pay its mother £1 per week "providing you can prove that [the child] is well looked after and happy, and also that she is allowed to decide for herself whether or not she wishes to come and live with you". The mother began to look after the child, and it was held that she could enforce the father's promise although she was under a statutory duty to maintain the child. One basis of the decision is that the mother had provided consideration by showing that she had made the child happy, etc.: in this way she can be said to have done more than she was required by law to do, and to have conferred a factual benefit on the father or on the child,[57] even though she may not have suffered any detriment.[58] But if a son's promise not to bore his father is not good consideration,[59] it is hard to see why a mother's promise to make her child happy should stand on a different footing. There is, with respect, force in Denning L.J.'s view, that the mother provided consideration by merely performing her legal duty to support the child. There was certainly no ground of public policy for refusing to enforce the promise.

---

[50] (1831) 1 B. & Ad. 950; *cf. Willis v Peckham* (1820) 1 Br. & B. 515; *Thoresen Car Ferries Ltd v Weymouth Portland BC* [1977] 2 Lloyd's Rep. 614 at 619.

[51] *Re Working Men's Mutual Society* (1882) 21 Ch.D. 831; *Chamberlain v Stoneham* (1889) 24 Q.B.D. 113.

[52] Supreme Court Act 1981, s.36(4). A subpoenaed witness (other than an expert witness) is not entitled to more than this and if he threatens to withhold or alter his evidence unless he is paid more he may be guilty of blackmail: *R. v Clear* [1968] 1 Q.B. 670; *semble* the same result could be reached under Theft Act 1968, s.21.

[53] *Goulden v White Barca* [2000] 1 W.L.R. 167.

[54] [1925] A.C. 270; *cf. Thoresen Car Ferries v Weymouth Portland BC* [1977] 2 Lloyd's Rep. 614 at 619 (A's promise to *make use* of B's services for which he was under a legal duty to *pay* held to constitute consideration for B's counter-promise).

[55] *Harris v Sheffield United FC Ltd* [1988] Q.B. 77.

[56] [1956] 1 W.L.R. 496.

[57] Consideration need not move to the promisor (the father); above, p.81.

[58] *Williams v Roffey Bros & Nicholls (Contractors) Ltd* [1991] 1 Q.B. 1 at 13.

[59] *White v Bluett* (1853) 23 L.J. Ex. 36; above, p.83.

(2) Duty imposed by contract with promisor

When A was bound by contract with B to do, or to forbear from doing, something, the law at one time took the view that A's performance of that duty (or his promise to perform it) was no consideration for a new promise by B. Later authority has qualified that view but the extent of the qualification is uncertain. The cases fall into three groups.

(a) CASES IN WHICH THERE WAS NO CONSIDERATION. The view that there was no consideration for B's new promise was first established in cases in which seamen who had bound themselves to serve for a voyage were promised higher wages by the masters of their ships if they performed their duty by working the ships home. It was held that these promises were not binding. Originally this conclusion was based on the ground of public policy that the enforcement of such promises might lead the men to refuse to perform their original contracts unless they were promised extra pay.[60] But according to one of the reports of *Stilk v Myrick*[61] such reasoning was doubted in that case, where the claim for extra pay was instead rejected on the ground that the men had provided no consideration by doing only what they were already bound to do; and this is the explanation of such cases which is now commonly accepted.[62] On the same principle, a promise to pay an extra charge for the carriage of goods to the agreed destination cannot be enforced by the carrier[63]; and a debtor's promise to pay in stated instalments a debt that is already due is no consideration for the creditor's promise not to take bankruptcy proceedings in respect of the debt.[64]

The public policy explanation of the rule, stated above,[65] was always open to the objection that it was based on a danger that was not more than hypothetical: in the cases on seamen's wages,[66] for example, there was no evidence of any refusal on the men's part to perform their original contracts. Even where there is such evidence, the argument is much reduced in importance now that the law has come to recognise that such a refusal may amount to economic duress.[67] Where the refusal *does* amount to duress, a promise induced by it can be avoided (and money paid in pursuance of it be recovered back) on that ground.[68] This is true even where the promise *is* supported by consideration: for example, because the promisee has undertaken, not merely to perform his duties under the original contract, but also to render some additional performance.[69] If, on the other hand, the promisee's refusal to perform the original contract does *not* amount to duress, it has been held that the promise cannot be impugned merely on the ground that the

---

[60] *Harris v Watson* (1791) Peake 102; *cf. Scotson v Pegg* (1861) 6 H. & n.295 at 299.

[61] That in (1809) 2 Camp. 317; the other report, in 6 Esp. 129, does not mention consideration and makes the decision turn on public policy. Both grounds are stated in *Harris v Carter* (1854) 3 E. & B. 559.

[62] *Harrison v Dodd* (1914) 111 L.T. 47; *Swain v West (Butchers) Ltd* [1936] 3 All E.R. 261; *The Atlantic Baron* [1979] Q.B. 705 at 712; *Pao On v Lau Yiu Long* [1980] A.C. 614 at 633; *Sybron Corp v Rochem Ltd* [1984] Ch. 112 at 129; *The Alev* [1989] 1 Lloyd's Rep. 138 at 147; *Hadley v Kemp* [1999] E.M.L.R. 586 at 626.

[63] *The Proodos C* [1980] 2 Lloyd's Rep. 390; *cf. Atlas Express Ltd v Kafco (Importers and Distributors) Ltd* [1989] Q.B. 833.

[64] *Vanbergen v St. Edmund's Properties Ltd* [1933] 2 K.B. 223.

[65] See above, at n.60.

[66] See above, at nn.60 and 61.

[67] See below, pp.405–407.

[68] As in *The Universe Sentinel* [1983] 1 A.C. 366; *B & S Contracts & Designs v Victor Green Publications* [1984] I.C.R. 419, below, p.405; *Atlas Express Ltd v Kafco (Importers and Distributors) Ltd* [1989] Q.B. 833; and in *T A Sundell & Sons Pty Ltd v Emm Yannoulatos (Overseas) Pty Ltd* [1956] 56 S.R. (N.S.W.) 323. The position would have been the same in *The Atlantic Baron* [1975] Q.B. 705 if the victim of the duress had not affirmed the contract.

[69] *e.g. The Atlantic Baron* [1979] Q.B. 705; below, p.96 at n.85; *The Alev* [1989] 1 Lloyd's Rep. 138.

refusal amounted to an abuse by the promisee of a dominant bargaining position.[70] To allow a promise to be invalidated on this ground alone would introduce an intermediate category of promises unfairly obtained; and this would (in the words of Lord Scarman) "be unhelpful because it would render the law uncertain".[71]

The now more generally held view is that the new promises in the present group of cases are unenforceable for want of consideration; and the reason for this view seems to have been that the promisee suffered no legal detriment[72] in performing what was already due from him, nor did the promisor receive any legal benefit in receiving what was already due to him. But this reasoning takes no account of the fact that the promisee may in fact suffer a detriment: for example, the wages that a seaman could earn elsewhere may exceed those that he would earn under the original contract together with the damages that he would have to pay for breaking it. Conversely, the promisor may in fact benefit from the actual performance of what was legally due to him: in *Stilk v Myrick* the master got his ship home and this may well have been worth more to him than any damages that he could have recovered from the crew.

(b) FACTUAL BENEFIT TO PROMISOR. The foregoing discussion shows that a new promise by B in consideration of A's performing his duty to B under an earlier contract between them is not necessarily obtained by duress; and that A's performance of the duty may in fact benefit B. Where both these conditions are satisfied, it has been held that A can enforce B's new promise.

In *Williams v Roffey Bros & Nicholls (Contractors) Ltd*[73] B had engaged A as carpentry sub-contractor, for the purpose of performing a contract between B and X to refurbish a number of flats. The amount payable by B to A under the subcontract was £20,000 but B later promised to make extra payments to A, who undertook no additional obligation in return.[74] B made this new promise because B's own surveyor recognised that the originally agreed sum of £20,000 was too low, and because B feared that A (who was in financial difficulties) would not be able to complete his work on time, and so expose B to penalties for delay under his contract with X. It was held that B's promise to make the extra payments to A was supported by consideration in the shape of the "practical benefits"[75] obtained by B from A's performance of his duties under the original contract between them.[76] Since no allegation of duress on A's part had been made by B, the new promise by B to pay extra could not be avoided on this ground. There had been no threat by A to break his original contract; indeed, the initiative for the agreement containing the promise of extra pay seems to have come from B.

---

[70] *Pao On v Lau Yiu Long* [1980] A.C. 614 at 632.

[71] *ibid.* at 634. This statement was made in a case involving three parties, but it is of general application: *Williams v Roffey Bros & Nicholls (Contractors) Ltd* [1991] 1 Q.B. 1 at 15.

[72] See above, p.69.

[73] [1991] 1 Q.B. 1; Adams and Brownsword, 53 M.L.R. 536; Chen-Wishart, 14 N.Z.U.L.R. 270; Hird and Blair [1996] J.B.L. 254.

[74] The payments under the original contract were found to be due in unspecified instalments while those under the new promise were due as each flat was completed, but no attempt was made to argue that this change in the times when payment was due *might* have been to A's disadvantage and therefore provided consideration. There is perhaps a hint to this effect in Russell L.J.'s judgment at 19. Similar reasoning is one basis of *Anangel Atlas Compania Naviera SA v Ishikawajima-Harima Heavy Industries Co Ltd (No.2)* [1990] 2 Lloyd's Rep. 526, where "promisor" and "promisee" appear to have been transposed in a passage at p.588.

[75] [1991] 1 Q.B. 1 at 11; *cf. ibid.* at 19, 23. See also *Simon Container Machinery Ltd v Emba Machinery A.B.* [1998] 2 Lloyd's Rep. 428 at 435.

[76] In fact, B did not secure the whole of this benefit, but this was because B's wrongful failure to make the extra payments justified A's refusal to continue with the work: see below, p.787.

The element of factual benefit which was stressed in the *Williams* case has also been regarded as consideration where a person performs (or promises to perform) a contractual duty owed to a third party[77]; and the *Williams* case is to be welcomed in bringing the two-party cases in line with those involving three parties.[78] But it is by no means clear how the case is, from this point of view, to be reconciled with *Stilk v Myrick* and with the line of more recent decisions which have followed that case.[79] As has been suggested above, the master in *Stilk v Myrick* also obtained a factual benefit (in getting his ship home); and such a factual benefit will very often be obtained by B where he secures actual performance from A (as opposed to having to sue him for non-performance of the original contract).

In the *Williams* case, *Stilk v Myrick* was not overruled; indeed Purchas L.J. described it as a "pillar stone of the law of contract".[80] But he added that the case might be differently decided today[81]; while Glidewell L.J. said that the present decision did not "contravene" but did "refine and limit"[82] the principle of the earlier case; and Russell L.J. said that the "rigid approach" to consideration in *Stilk v Myrick* was "no longer necessary or desirable."[83] The conclusion which may tentatively be drawn from these statements is that the factual benefit to B in securing A's performance of the earlier contract will normally suffice to constitute consideration. The insistence in the earlier cases on the stricter requirement of legal benefit or detriment is no longer justified (if it ever was) by the need to protect B from the undue pressure that A might exert by refusing to perform his original contract; for this need can now be met by the expanding concept of duress. This provides a more satisfactory solution of the present problem since it invalidates promises only where actual duress is established. Where this is not the case, and the promisee has in fact conferred a benefit on the promisor by performing the original contract, then the requirement of consideration is satisfied and there seems to be no good reason for refusing to enforce the new promise.

(c) OTHER CONSIDERATION. The promisee may provide other consideration for the new promise by doing, or promising to do, more than he was bound by the original contract to do. Thus a seaman is entitled to extra wages if, during the voyage, he is promoted and so undertakes additional duties.[84] The same principle was applied where shipbuilders claimed an increase in the agreed price for a supertanker on the ground that the currency in which that price was to be paid had been devalued. The contract required the builders to give a performance guarantee, and it was held that they had provided consideration for the prospective owners' promise to pay the price increase by making a corresponding increase in their performance guarantee.[85]

---

[77] See below, p.98.

[78] In *Stilk v Myrick* above, p.94 the distinction was ignored: no one even asked whether the original contract was with the promisor (the master) or with a third party (the shipowner). It is clear from the report in Espinasse that the action was brought against the master. *cf.* also *Turner v Owen* (1862) 3 F. & F. 176; *B & S Contracts & Designs v Victor Green Publications Ltd* [1984] I.C.R. 419.

[79] See above, p.94.

[80] [1991] 1 Q.B. 1 at 20.

[81] *ibid.* at 21. But he was not prepared to accept *Watkins v Carrig* 21 A 2d. 591 (1941), where a contractor who had agreed to do excavating work unexpectedly struck hard rock and was held entitled to enforce a promise to pay nine times the originally agreed sum. That case was said not to represent English law in *The Atlantic Baron* [1979] Q.B. 705 at 714, *cf.* also *Finland SS Co Ltd v Felixstowe Dock Ry Co* [1980] 2 Lloyd's Rep. 390.

[82] [1991] 1 Q.B. 1 at 16.

[83] *ibid.* at 18.

[84] *Hanson v Royden* (1867) L.R. 3 C.P. 47; *semble*, such extra pay is recoverable notwithstanding failure to comply with the formal requirements now contained in Merchant Shipping Act 1995, s.25; *cf.* below, p.176, n.5.

[85] *The Atlantic Baron* [1979] Q.B. 705; Coote [1980] C.L.J. 40; Adams, 42 M.L.R. 557.

The promisee similarly provides other consideration where, before the new promise is made, circumstances arise which justify his refusal to perform the original contract. Thus the crew of a ship may be justified in refusing to complete a voyage because so many of their fellows have deserted that completion will involve hazards of a kind not originally contemplated. If they are induced to go on by a promise of extra pay, they do something which they were not bound to do, and can recover the extra pay.[86] The same principle applies where the contract is determined by notice or by mutual consent. Thus a promise to pay an employee higher wages after he has lawfully determined his contract by notice is binding. Or the parties might agree to rescind the contract and substitute a new one, at a higher rate of pay[87]; though such a transaction might be hard to distinguish from a simple promise to pay higher wages for continuing to work under the original contract.[88] If the original contract is void, voidable or unenforceable, performance of the work specified would, it seems, be consideration for a promise of extra pay; and if the original contract was in fact good but was believed to be defective, then the new promise might be binding on the analogy of the rule that forbearance to litigate an invalid claim may amount to consideration.[89] A final possibility is that the contract may provide, expressly or by implication, for revision of pay scales from time to time; and in such a case an agreement to pay higher (or to accept lower) wages would clearly be binding.[90]

(3) Duty imposed by contract with a third party

Two problems arise under this heading. The first is whether, if A is under a contractual duty to B, the *performance* of this duty can constitute consideration for a promise made to A by C. The second is whether A's *promise* to perform his contractual duty to B can constitute consideration for a counter-promise made to A by C.

(a) PERFORMANCE OF THE DUTY. Three mid-nineteenth century cases give some support to the view that A's actual performance of a contractual duty owed by him to B can constitute consideration for a promise later made by C to A.[91] These cases are, however, less than wholly conclusive, since in two of them[92] A did or may have done *more* than he was bound by the original contract with B to do (and so have provided additional consideration for C's promise); while in the third[93] the decision was reached only by a majority who make no reference to the fact that A was already under a contractual duty

---

[86] *Hartley v Ponsonby* (1857) 7 E. & B. 872; *O'Neil v Armstrong, Mitchell & Co* [1895] 2 Q.B. 418; *Palace Shipping Co v Caine* [1907] A.C. 386; *Liston v SS Carpathian (Owners)* [1915] 2 K.B. 42.

[87] See *Schwartzreich v Bauman-Basch Inc* 131 N.E. 887 (1921); Dekoven, 35 U. of Chi.L. Rev. 173.

[88] *cf.* below, pp.101, 189.

[89] See above, pp.88–89; *E. Hulton & Co v Chadwick Taylor Ltd* (1918) 34 T.L.R. 230 at 231.

[90] e.g. *Pepper & Hope v Daish* [1980] I.R.L.R. 13; *cf. Lombard Tricity Finance Ltd v Paton* [1989] 1 All E.R. 98 (credit agreement providing for increases in interest rates to be made by lender).

[91] For the contrary view, see *McDevitt v Stokes* 192 S.W. (1917). In *Pfizer Corp v Ministry of Health* [1965] A.C. 512, Lord Reid said that there was no contract where a chemist supplied drugs to a patient under the National Health Service in return for a prescription charge, because the chemist is "bound by his contract with the appropriate authority to supply the drug . . . " (at 536). But it seems from the context that Lord Reid was considering whether the relationship was consensual (above, p.5) and was not thinking of the problem of consideration.

[92] *Scotson v Pegg* (1861) 6 H. & n.295; *Chichester v Cobb* (1866) 14 L.T. 433. The question in these cases was whether A provided consideration for C's promise by performing a contractual duty owed by A to B. There is no doubt that C's promise to perform a duty owed by B to A (or the performance of such a promise) can constitute consideration for a promise (express or implied) by A to C: see, *e.g. Brandt v Liverpool, etc. SN Co* [1924] 1 K.B. 575; *The Aramis* [1989] 1 Lloyd's Rep. 213 at 225 (where C's claim failed for want of contractual intention: below, p.169).

[93] *Shadwell v Shadwell* (1860) 9 C.B.(N.S.) 159. *cf. De Cicco v Schweitzer* 117 N.E. 807 (1917).

to B to render the performance in question,[94] and the view of the dissentient, that C's later promise to A was not binding for want of contractual intention, has been approved in a twentieth-century case.[95] The view that performance of a contractual duty owed to a third party can constitute consideration for a promise is, however, supported by *The Eurymedon*.[96] A (a firm of stevedores) had unloaded goods from B's ship. Some of these belonged to C who, for present purposes,[97] may be taken to have promised A not to sue him for damaging the goods. It was held that A had provided consideration for this promise by unloading the goods even if he was already bound[98] by a contract with B to unload them.

(b) PROMISE TO PERFORM THE DUTY. It was at one time thought that a mere promise to perform a contractual duty owed to a third party could not constitute consideration. Thus in *Jones v Waite*[99] it was said that a promise by A to C that A will pay a debt owed by A to B is no consideration for a promise made by C to A. This view seems to be based on the idea that A suffers no (legal) detriment by promising to pay a debt that he was already bound to pay; nor did it appear that C gained any benefit as a result of the promise. It is, however, possible for C to gain such a benefit: for example, where C promises A some benefit in return for A's promise not to carry out his intention of breaking a contract with B, a company in which C has an interest. This was the position in *Pao On v Lau Yiu Long*[1] where A, having entered into a contract with a company (B), refused to perform it unless C, who were shareholders in the company, guaranteed A against loss which might be incurred as a result of the performance of one of the terms of that contract. The guarantee was given in consideration of A's promise to perform their contractual obligations to the company; and was held binding[2] on the ground that "A promise to perform, or the performance of, a pre-existing contractual obligation to a third party can be valid consideration".[3] This view seems, with respect, to be preferable to that expressed in *Jones v Waite*; for the guarantee was certainly not gratuitous in a commercial sense.

It will, of course, be open to the promisor to avoid liability if he can show that the promisee's refusal to perform the contract with the third party amounted to duress[4] not merely with regard to the third party, but also with regard to the promisor himself.

---

[94] *i.e.* to marry B. Such a promise would no longer have contractual force: see Law Reform (Miscellaneous Provisions) Act 1970, s.1.

[95] *Jones v Padavatton* [1969] 1 W.L.R. 328 at 333.

[96] [1975] A.C. 154; followed in *The New York Star* [1981] 1 W.L.R. 138 and *The Antwerpen* [1994] 1 Lloyd's Rep. 213; *cf. The Mahkutai* [1996] A.C. 650 at 664.

[97] For a discussion of this point, see below, pp.631–634.

[98] A question may arise as to whether A has indeed performed or begun to perform his contract with B: *The Rigoletto* [2000] 2 Lloyd's Rep. 532 at 542–545.

[99] (1839) 5 Bing. N.C. 341, 351, affirmed on another ground (1842) 9 Cl. & F. 107; contrast *Morton v Burn* (1837) 7 A. & E. 19 (promise to pay assignee).

[1] [1980] A.C. 614.

[2] For rejection of the argument that the consideration was past, see above, p.78.

[3] [1980] A.C. 614 at 632. *cf. Scotson v Pegg* (1861) 6 H. & N. 295 at 301. In *The Eurymedon*, above, at 183, a promise to perform a contractual duty owed to a third party is said to be consideration because it is a *benefit* to the promisee. This is puzzling at first sight, since consideration must be a detriment to the promisee or a benefit to the promisor. The reference, however, is to a case in which A's promise to C is said to be the consideration for C's counter-promise to A, and it is the consideration for C's counter-promise which is in issue. In relation to the counter-promise, C is the promisor, and the benefit that he gets from A's promise satisfies the orthodox test of consideration for C's counter-promise. *cf.* the words "for the benefit of the shipper" (*i.e.* the promisor) at p.182; and above, p.68.

[4] See above, pp.94–95.

SECTION 6. RESCISSION AND VARIATION

A contract may be rescinded or varied by subsequent agreement. The object of rescission is to release the parties from the contract, while that of variation is to alter some term of the contract. Such subsequent agreements give rise to problems of consideration, which will be discussed here, and to problems of form, to be discussed in Chapter 5. One aspect of the consideration problem has already been dealt with in our discussion of the question whether the performance by A of his obligations under the old contract could be consideration for a new promise from B.[5] Our present problem is whether there is consideration for a promise by B to accept in discharge of A's obligations some performance *other* than that originally undertaken by A, or to grant A a total release from the contract. Even if there is no such consideration B's subsequent promise may, nevertheless, have some limited legal effect either as a waiver or in equity.[6]

1. Rescission

An agreement to rescind a contract will generate its own consideration whenever each party has outstanding rights under the contract against the other. This is most obviously true where the contract is wholly executory and neither party is in breach.[7] Thus a contract for the sale of goods to be delivered and paid for on a future day can be rescinded by mutual consent at any time before the day fixed for performance. A contract can similarly be rescinded by agreement after both parties have broken it.[8] And a partly executed contract can be rescinded by agreement so long as there are outstanding obligations on both sides: thus a lease for seven years can be rescinded by mutual consent after it has run for three years. In all these cases there is consideration for the rescission in that each party promises to give up his rights against the other under the original contract. It is, of course, essential, that *each* party should make such a promise. If only one party does so, the other making no counter-promise, the former party's promise will be "entirely unilateral and unsupported by any consideration".[9]

An agreement to rescind a contract may also fail to generate its own consideration (and so lack contractual force) where only one party has outstanding rights under the contract. This will often be the position where the contract has been wholly executed by that party. Suppose that goods are sold and delivered but not paid for, and the parties then agree to "rescind" the contract. If the agreement means that the buyer is to return the goods and to be released from his liability to pay the price, there is good consideration for the promise of each party. But if it simply means that the buyer is not to pay the price, it is a gratuitous promise by the seller.[10] Conversely, goods may be sold, delivered and paid for, but turn out to be defective. Here an agreement to "rescind" would be a gratuitous promise if it simply released the seller from his liability under the original contract for the defects. Similarly, A may agree to sell goods to B for cash on delivery on a future day. If, when that day came, B tendered the price but A failed to deliver the

---

[5] See above, pp.94–98.
[6] See below, pp.102–119; 130–134.
[7] *Foster v Dawber* (1851) Ex. 839 at 850; *cf. The Trado* [1982] 1 Lloyd's Rep. 157.
[8] *e.g. Morris v Baron & Co* [1918] A.C. 1.
[9] *Collin v Duke of Westminster* [1985] Q.B. 581 at 598.
[10] *Commissioner of Stamp Duties v Bone* [1977] A.C. 511 at 519. ("A debt can only be truly released and extinguished by agreement for valuable consideration or under seal.") This rule seems with respect, to have been overlooked in a dictum in *Brikom Investments Ltd v Carr* [1979] Q.B. 467 at 488 according to which "waiver" of instalments of rent could extinguish the tenant's liability to pay. The landlord's actual promise in that case was supported by consideration: above, p.90; below, p.102.

goods, A would be liable in damages; and a rescission of the contract at this stage would be gratuitous if it merely released A from that liability. This is what is meant by the statement that rescission after breach requires separate consideration.[11]

That statement must, however, be qualified where the contract is a continuing one, such as one to deliver goods by instalments. An agreement to "rescind" such a contract after one defective instalment had been delivered and paid for would not be a gratuitous release of the seller from his liability for the defects, for he would be giving up his rights to have future instalments accepted and paid for. It is only where the defect is of such a kind as to give the buyer the right as a matter of law to treat the contract as repudiated[12] that the seller may be said to give up nothing in return for the buyer's promise not to sue for the defect. Even in such a case, however, this result would not necessarily follow; for so long as the seller in good faith believed that the contract remained binding he would provide consideration by forbearing to enforce it.[13]

Where the rescinding agreement does not generate its own consideration, it must be supported by separate consideration: there must, in technical language, be not only accord but also satisfaction. Thus a buyer of goods may agree to release a seller who has become liable in damages for non-delivery, if the seller will pay him £50. The agreement to release the seller is the accord; payment of the £50 is the satisfaction.[14] On payment of the £50, the seller is released from his liability in damages.

It was formerly said that an executory accord, i.e. one which had not yet been followed by satisfaction, had no effect: that it neither released the party in breach nor gave the other party any new right of action.[15] But it is settled that an executory accord can be enforced by the party to whom the satisfaction was offered,[16] and it may release the party by whom it was offered if that party's *promise* to perform his part of the accord has, on the true construction of the accord, been accepted by the injured party in discharge of his original cause of action.[17] Even where the injured party has not accepted the wrongdoer's promise in settlement of the cause of action, a question can arise as to the time at which the accord takes effect. In the absence of an express provision in it on the point, the accord releases the original cause of action at the time of the accord,[18] subject only to the implied condition subsequent[19] that it will be retrospectively avoided on the wrongdoer's failure to perform it in accordance with its terms. On such failure, the original liability will therefore revive. The parties may, of course, also agree to make performance of the accord a condition precedent to discharge. If they do so, the party originally in breach will not be discharged by the accord so long as it remains executory; he will be discharged only on giving the agreed satisfaction.[20]

---

[11] *Atlantic Shipping & Trading Ltd v Louis Dreyfus & Co* [1922] 2 A.C. 250 at 262.

[12] See below, pp.759 *et seq.*

[13] See above, pp.88–89.

[14] *British-Russian Gazette Ltd v Associated Newspapers Ltd* [1933] 2 K.B. 616 at 643. Mere acceptance of a cheque sent in full settlement is not conclusive evidence of such an agreement: *Stour Valley Builders v Stuart, The Times*, February 23, 1993, following *Day v McLea* [1889] 2 Q.B. 610; *Inland Revenue Commissioners v Fry* [2001] S.T.C. 1715 at [12]. See also *Clarke v Nationwide BS* (1998) 76 P. & C.R. D5 (acceptance of cheque sent "as a gesture of goodwill" not an accord).

[15] *Bayley v Homan* (1837) 3 Bing.N.C. 915; *cf. Morris v Baron & Co* [1918] A.C. 1 at 36.

[16] *Henderson v Stobart* (1850) 5 Ex. 99.

[17] *Elton Cop Dyeing Co v Broadbent & Son Ltd* (1919) 89 L.J.K.B. 186; *cf. Cartwright v Cooke* (1832) 3 B. & Ad. 701; *Crowther v Farrer* (1850) 15 Q.B. 677.

[18] *Jameson v CEGB* [2000] 1 A.C. 455 at 477, where the original liability arose in tort; and see p.572, below.

[19] *ibid.*; for the distinction between conditions precedent and subsequent, see above, p.63.

[20] *cf. Johnson v Davies* [1999] Ch. 117 at 128 (a case, not of accord and satisfaction at common law, but of a "voluntary arrangement" under the Insolvency Act 1986, Pt VIII).

There is one long-established exception to the rule that accord without satisfaction does not discharge a contract after breach. If the holder of a bill of exchange or promissory note at or after its maturity absolutely, unconditionally and in writing renounces his rights against any person liable on the bill or note, the latter is discharged.[21] The exception provides a comparatively simple way of evading the general rule: the creditor can take a bill or note in satisfaction of the debt and then renounce it.

2. Variation

Four situations call for discussion.

First, a variation of a contract may amount to a rescission of the old contract followed by the making of a new one relating to the same subject-matter. The question whether there is consideration for the rescission then depends on the principles just discussed.[22] If there is consideration for the rescission there is also consideration for the new promises. "The same consideration which existed for the old agreement is imported into the new agreement, which is substituted for it."[23]

Secondly, the parties may agree to vary their contract in a way that can benefit either party. Such a variation again normally generates its own consideration. This is the position if a lease is varied by altering the date on which notice of termination can be given[24]; or if a contract of sale is varied by altering the currency in which payment is to be made.[25] In the latter case, it would make no difference that the new currency was later devalued in relation to the old, for at the time of the variation it could not be certain how the two currencies would move in relation to each other: hence either party *might* benefit from the variation. If a variation is, taken as a whole, capable of benefiting either party, the requirement of consideration will be satisfied even though a particular term of the variation is for the sole benefit of one.[26] A variation does not, however, generate its own consideration if, though capable of benefiting either party, it is in fact made wholly for the benefit of one. For example, a variation as to the place at which a debt is to be paid may benefit either party and thus provide consideration for a promise by the creditor to accept part payment in full settlement. But it will not have this effect if it is introduced solely for the benefit of the debtor.[27] Similarly, an agreement to reduce the quantity of goods to be delivered and paid for under a contract for the sale of goods may benefit either party; but if it is made purely for the seller's convenience it will not be consideration for the buyer's promise to accept the smaller quantity; nor conversely.[28]

Thirdly, the parties may agree to vary the contract in a way that can confer a legal benefit[29] on only one party. In some situations, it is settled that such a variation does not generate its own consideration: thus a promise by a creditor to accept part payment of a debt in full settlement is not binding unless it is supported by some separate consideration.[30] Such separate consideration could be provided by some further variation which may benefit the creditor: for example, by a debtor's promise to make the part

---

[21] Bills of Exchange Act 1882, s.62.

[22] See above, pp.99–102.

[23] *Stead v Dawber* (1839) 10 A. & E. 57 at 66.

[24] *Fenner v Blake* [1900] 1 Q.B. 427.

[25] *W J Alan & Co Ltd v El Nasr Export & Import Co* [1972] 2 Q.B. 189; *Woodhouse AC Israel Cocoa Ltd SA v Nigerian Produce Marketing Co* [1972] A.C. 741 at 757.

[26] *Ficom SA v Sociedad Cadex Ltda* [1980] 2 Lloyd's Rep. 118 at 132.

[27] *Vanbergen v St. Edmund's Properties Ltd* [1933] 2 K.B. 233; *cf. Continental Grain Export Corp v STM Grain Ltd* [1979] 2 Lloyd's Rep. 460 at 476.

[28] *ibid.*

[29] See above, p.69.

[30] See below, p.125.

payment *before* the day when the debt becomes due.[31] In other situations, it is arguable[32] that the variation may be supported by consideration if, though capable of conferring a legal benefit on only one party, it can also confer a factual benefit[33] on the other, *e.g.* where a buyer's promise to pay more than the originally agreed price secures eventual delivery when strict insistence on the original contract would have led to nothing but litigation.

Fourthly, there is the apparently paradoxical possibility that the parties may agree to vary a contract even before that contract has been concluded. This may be the position where A and B negotiate on the basis of formal documents and A represents that the proposed contract will be on terms less favourable to himself than those set out in the documents. If the documents are nevertheless executed without alteration, the representation may then be enforceable as a collateral contract. The consideration for the promise contained in A's representation is provided by B when he executes the documents (and so enters into the principal contract) at the request of A and in reliance on the representation. In *Brikom Investments Ltd v Carr*[34] landlords of blocks of flats, negotiated with their tenants for the sale of long leases of the flats on terms requiring the tenants to contribute to the cost of (*inter alia*) roof maintenance. At the time of the negotiations, the roof was in need of repairs, and the landlords promised to execute these "at our own cost". It was held that one of the tenants had provided consideration for this promise by executing the agreement for the lease, and the lease itself; and that the promise was accordingly binding as a collateral contract. It followed that the landlords could not enforce the term in the lease under which the tenant would (but for the collateral contract) have been liable to contribute to the cost of the roof repairs.[35] Greater difficulty would have arisen if the tenant had already executed the documents *before* the landlord's promise had been made,[36] for in that case the execution of the documents would have been past consideration.[37] The tenants could, however, have succeeded, even in such a case, on an alternative ground. The landlords had been guilty of unreasonable delay in executing the repairs, and the tenants would, by forbearing to take proceedings in respect of that breach,[38] have provided consideration for the landlords' promise to bear the cost of the repairs.

3. Waiver[39]

(1) At common law

Where a party promises to relinquish some or all of his rights under a contract, he is sometimes said to have "waived" those rights. Unfortunately, however, "the word

---

[31] See below, p.127.

[32] On the analogy of the reasoning of *Williams v Roffey Bros & Nicholls (Contractors) Ltd* [1991] 1 Q.B. 1, above, p.95.

[33] See above, p.69.

[34] [1979] Q.B. 467.

[35] This was agreed by all members of the Court of Appeal. For other grounds for the decision, see below, pp.130, 133.

[36] From the grounds of appeal as stated at 472–473 of the report, it seems that the tenants relied on representations made *before* the main contracts were concluded; *cf.* the statement at 490 that the landlords' promise was made "at the time when the leases were granted." According to Lord Denning M.R. at 480 "some of the tenants" had *already* signed agreements for leases when the representations were made; but that does not seem to have been the position with regard to any of the cases before the court.

[37] See above, p.77.

[38] See [1979] Q.B. 467 at 490; *cf.* above, p.90. Delay in *executing* the repairs was a breach irrespective of the question of who was to *pay* for them.

[39] Ewart, *Waiver Distributed*; Wilben and Villiers, *Waiver Variation and Estoppel*; Cheshire and Fifoot, 63 L.Q.R. 283; Stoljar, 35 Can.Bar.Rev. 485; Dugdale and Yates, 39 M.L.R. 681.

'waiver' . . . covers a variety of situations different in their legal nature. . . . "[40] Of the many senses in which it is used, three are relevant to the present discussion.[41]

(a) TO MEAN RESCISSION. Sometimes "waiver" means total rescission of the contract: "The waiver spoken of in the case is an entire abandonment and dissolution of the contract."[42] This usage assumes that the rescission is supported by consideration.[43] It has been judicially criticised so far as it refers to a purported release without consideration. "To say that a claim is to be waived is incorrect. If a right has accrued, it must be released or discharged by deed or upon consideration."[44]

(b) TO MEAN VARIATION. Sometimes, "waiver" refers to a variation which is supported by consideration and is therefore binding as a contract.[45] It is also used to refer to a variation which, though supported by consideration, is for some other reason *not* contractually binding. This usage occurs in the context of the rule that a contract which is required to be in, or evidenced in, writing can be rescinded but not varied orally.[46] In such cases, the ineffective oral variation is sometimes referred to as a "waiver". so as to contrast it with an effective rescission followed by the making of a substituted contract on new terms: "There was no fresh agreement . . . which can be regarded as having been substituted for the original written contract. There was nothing more than a waiver by the defendants of a delivery by the plaintiff in [the originally stipulated month]".[47]

(c) TO MEAN FORBEARANCE. A variation may not be contractually binding for want of consideration or of contractual intention, or because it fails to comply with a legal requirement that it must be in, or evidenced in, writing.[48] It may nevertheless have certain limited legal effects, which are sometimes said to arise because one party has "waived" his rights. To distinguish such arrangements from contractually binding variations, they will here be referred to as "forbearances".[49] Their effects are as follows:

(i) The party requesting the forbearance cannot refuse to accept the varied performance. Thus, if a seller at the request of the buyer delivers late, the buyer cannot refuse to accept on the ground that delivery was made after the time specified in the original contract.[50]

---

[40] *The Laconia* [1977] A.C. 850 at 871; *cf. Kammins Ballrooms Co Ltd v Zenith Investments (Torquay) Ltd* [1971] A.C. 850 at 882–883; *The Athos* [1983] 1 Lloyd's Rep. 127 at 134; *The Kanchenjunga* [1990] 1 Lloyd's Rep. 391 at 397; *Oliver Ashworth (Holdings) Ltd v Ballard (Kent) Ltd* [2000] Ch. 12 at 28; *The Happy Day* [2002] EWCA Civ 1068, [2002] 2 Lloyd's Rep. 487, at [64].
[41] For further senses, see below pp.752–753.
[42] *Price v Dyer* (1810) 17 Ves. 356 at 364.
[43] See above, p.99.
[44] *Atlantic Shipping & Trading Co Ltd v Louis Dreyfus & Co* [1922] 2 A.C. 250 at 262; *cf. The Ion* [1980] 2 Lloyd's Rep. 245 at 249.
[45] *Semble*, this is the sense in which the word is used by Roskill and Cumming-Bruce L.JJ. in *Brikom Investments Ltd v Carr* [1979] Q.B. 467 at 488, 491; for the consideration for the "waiver", see above p.102; *cf. Shamsher Jute Mills Ltd v Sethia (London) Ltd* [1987] 2 Lloyd's Rep. 388 at 392. In *Royal Boskalis Westminster NV v Mountain* [1997] 2 All E.R. 929, "waiver" is similarly used to refer to a variation which would have been contractually binding if it had not been vitiated by duress and illegality. Only Phillips L.J. took the view that there was no "meaningful" consideration. "Meaningful" here seems to mean no more than "adequate"; for it appears from the facts stated at 934 and 958–959 that in the subsequent agreement each party gave up rights existing under the original contract.
[46] See below, p.190.
[47] *Hickman v Haynes* (1875) L.R. 10 C.P. 598 at 604.
[48] See below, pp.189–190.
[49] *cf. The Kanchenjunga* [1990] 1 Lloyd's Rep. 391 at 397.
[50] *Hickman v Haynes*, above; *Levey & Co v Goldberg* [1922] 1 K.B. 688; *cf. British and Beningtons Ltd v NW Cachar Tea Co* [1923] A.C. 48.

(ii) If the varied performance is actually made and accepted, neither party can claim damages on the ground that performance was not in accordance with the original contract. Thus, in the above example the seller who delivers late, or the buyer who takes delivery late, is not liable in damages. But if the contract is not performed at all, the damages are assessed on the footing that the breach took place at the end of the extended period.[51]

(iii) The cases that give rise to the greatest difficulty are those in which the party *granting* the forbearance refuses to perform, or to accept performance, in accordance with it.

Suppose, for example, that a buyer agrees, at the seller's request, to accept late delivery. The buyer cannot then claim damages for the seller's failure to deliver within the contract period[52]; but a further set of problems can arise if, after expiry of that period but within the extended period, the seller tenders delivery, and the buyer refuses to accept it. One possible view is that the seller cannot derive rights from a forbearance which is not binding as a contract, and that therefore he is not entitled to damages for the buyer's refusal to take delivery within the extended, but outside the original, contract period. A claim for such damages was accordingly rejected in *Plevins v Downing*,[53] where the agreement to extend the delivery dates had no contractual force since it was oral when it should, as the law then stood, have been evidenced in writing[54] and since it was probably unsupported by consideration, having been made at the request, and for the sole benefit, of the seller.[55]

But in many cases the party for whose benefit the forbearance was granted was allowed to enforce the contract in accordance with the new terms. In *Hartley v Hymans*[56] a buyer of cotton agreed to allow the seller to make late delivery. It was held that he was liable in damages for peremptorily refusing to take delivery after the period originally specified in the contract had expired. Similarly, a party may acquiesce in a method of payment other than that specified in the contract so as to indicate that the new method is to become the "accepted method."[57] He cannot then refuse to perform his part simply because the other party has not performed his obligation to pay strictly in accordance with the terms originally agreed[58]; nor can he peremptorily require performance strictly in accordance with those terms.[59] In these cases it is sometimes said that there is no variation of the contract, but only a variation of the mode of performance; or that there is no variation, but only a waiver[60] in the sense of forbearance.

Such a forbearance differs from a variation which is supported by consideration in that it does not *irrevocably* alter the rights of the parties under the original contract. The party granting the forbearance *can generally retract it*, provided that he gives reasonable

---

[51] *Ogle v Vane* (1868) L.R. 3 Q.B. 272.

[52] *cf. The Kanchenjunga* [1989] 1 Lloyd's Rep. 354 at 358, affirmed [1990] 1 Lloyd's Rep. 391.

[53] (1876) 1 C.P.D. 220.

[54] For this reason alone, the variation could not then have been enforced as a contract: below, p.190.

[55] See above, p.101.

[56] [1920] 3 K.B. 475; *cf. Tyers v Rosedale & Ferryhill Iron Co* (1875) L.R. 10 Ex. 195; *Besseller Waechter Glover & Co v South Derwent Coal Ltd* [1938] 1 K.B. 408; and see *Leather Cloth Co v Hieronimus* (1875) L.R. 10 Q.B. 104 (variation of route of shipment).

[57] *The Scaptrade* [1981] 2 Lloyd's Rep. 425 at 431 (where this requirement was not satisfied), affirmed without reference to this point [1983] 2 A.C. 694; *Hazel v Akhtar* [2001] EWCA Civ 1883, *The Times*, January 7, 2002 (landlord tolerating habitually late payment of rent).

[58] *Panoutsos v Raymond Hadley Corp of NY* [1917] 2 K.B. 473; *Tankexpress A/S v Cie Financière Belge des Petroles, SA* [1949] A.C. 76; *Plasticmoda Soc v Davidsons (Manchester) Ltd* [1952] 1 Lloyd's Rep. 527.

[59] *Mitas v Hymans* [1951] 2 T.L.R. 1215.

[60] *e.g.* in *Plevins v Downing* (1876) 1 C.P.D. 220 at 225; *Besseller Waechter Glover & Co v South Derwent Coal Co Ltd* [1938] 1 K.B. 408 at 416; *The Kanchenjunga*; [1990] 1 Lloyd's Rep. 391 at 397–398.

notice of his intention to do so to the party for whose benefit it was granted.[61] Thus, in *Charles Rickards Ltd v Oppenhaim*[62] a contract for the sale of a car provided for delivery on March 20. The car was not delivered on that day but the buyer continued to press for delivery and finally told the seller on June 29 that he must have the car by July 25 at the latest. It was held that the buyer could not have refused peremptorily to accept the car merely because the original delivery date had gone by, as he had continued to press for delivery; but that he could refuse on the seller's failure to comply with a notice to deliver within a reasonable time. Here the notice did give the seller a reasonable time to deliver, so that the buyer was justified in refusing to take the car after July 25. *A fortiori*, the buyer could have refused to take delivery if the original delivery date had been extended only for a fixed time and if delivery had not been made by the end of that time.[63]

A forbearance may, however, become irrevocable as a result of subsequent events: for example if a buyer indicates that he is willing to accept goods of a different quality from those contracted for, and the seller, in reliance on that assurance, so conducts himself as to put it out of his power to supply goods of the contract quality within the contract period.[64]

The distinction between a forbearance and a variation is sometimes said to depend on the intention of the parties[65]: a statement is a forbearance if the party making it intends to reserve a power to retract; but a variation if he intends permanently to abandon his rights under the contract. The courts were, however, anxious to avoid the unjust effects of the rules as to variations that were not contractually binding for lack of consideration or failure to comply with formal requirements. Hence they often interpreted a subsequent agreement as a forbearance, so as to give it at least some legal effects.

(2) In equity[66]

The common law rules as to waiver in the sense of forbearance are defective in two ways. First, they rest on the tenuous distinction between forbearance and variation, which can be deduced from the judgments, but does not provide any very solid basis for distinguishing between the actual decisions. It is hard to see, for instance, why the buyer in *Plevins v Downing*[67] was allowed to reject late delivery, while the buyer in *Hartley v Hymans*[68] was not allowed to do so. Secondly, the common law rules produced the paradoxical result that, the more a party purported to bind himself by a subsequent agreement, the less he was likely to be bound. An attempt permanently to renounce a right would be a variation, and ineffective for want of writing or consideration. But an attempt to suspend a right would be effective, to a limited extent, as a forbearance.

(a) HUGHES V METROPOLITAN RY. Equity devised a more satisfactory approach to the problem by concentrating, not on the intention of the party granting the forbearance,

---

[61] *Banning v Wright* [1972] 1 W.L.R. 972, 981. *Ficom SA v Sociedad Cadex Ltda.* [1980] 2 Lloyd's Rep. 118 at 131; *Bremer Handelsgesellschaft mbH v Raiffeisen Hauptgenossenschaft EG* [1982] 1 Lloyd's Rep. 599.

[62] [1950] 1 K.B. 616; *cf. Cape Asbestos Co Ltd v Lloyds Bank Ltd* [1921] W.N. 274 at 276; *Bird v Hildage* [1948] 1 K.B. 91; *State Trading Corp of India v Cie Française d'Importation et de Distribution* [1983] 2 Lloyd's Rep. 679 at 681.

[63] *cf. Nichimen Corp v Gatoil Overseas Inc* [1987] 2 Lloyd's Rep. 46, where similar fixed term extensions were granted by a seller.

[64] *Toepfer v Warinco AG* [1978] 2 Lloyd's Rep. 569 at 576.

[65] *Stead v Dawber* (1839) 10 A. & E. 57 at 64.

[66] Denning, 15 M.L.R. 1; Wilson, 67 L.Q.R. 330; Sheridan, 15 M.L.R. 325; Gordon [1963] C.L.J. 222; Wilson [1965] C.L.J. 93; Thompson [1983] C.L.J. 257; Spence, *Protecting Reliance*.

[67] (1876) 1 C.P.D. 220; above, p.104.

[68] [1920] 3 K.B. 475; above, p.104.

but on the conduct of that party and on its effect on the position of the other party. The leading case is *Hughes v Metropolitan Ry*,[69] where a landlord had given his tenant notice requiring him to do repairs within six months. During the six months he began to negotiate with the tenant for the purchase of his lease. When the negotiations broke down, he immediately claimed to forfeit the lease on the ground that the tenant had not done the repairs. The claim was rejected, Lord Cairns saying that if one party leads the other "to suppose that the strict rights arising under the contract will not be enforced, or will be kept in suspense or held in abeyance, the person who otherwise might have enforced those rights will not be allowed to enforce them where it would be inequitable having regard to the dealings which have thus taken place between the parties".[70] The landlord had by his conduct led the tenant to suppose that during the negotiations he would not enforce his right to forfeit. Hence he could not forfeit immediately the negotiations broke down: he had to give the tenant a reasonable time from that date to do the repairs. This equitable doctrine can now be applied to arrangements which might formerly have been regarded as variations ineffective at common law for want of consideration.[71] For reasons to be discussed later in this Chapter[72] the doctrine is often (if somewhat misleadingly) referred to as "equitable" or "promissory" estoppel.

(b) RELATIONSHIPS WITHIN THE DOCTRINE. The rights which the equitable doctrine prevents a promisor or representor from enforcing normally arise out of a contract between him and the other party. But the doctrine can also apply where the relationship giving rise to rights and duties is non-contractual: *e.g.* to prevent the enforcement of a liability imposed by statute[73]; or to prevent a man from ejecting a woman, with whom he had been cohabiting, from the family home.[74] On the other hand, it has been said that the doctrine "has no application as between a landowner and a trespasser".[75] Hence the mere fact that a landowner has for some time failed or neglected to enforce his rights against a trespasser does not prevent him from later doing so without notice.

It has been suggested that the doctrine can apply even where, before the making of the promise or representation, there is no legal relationship of any kind between the parties[76]; or where there is only a putative contract between them: *e.g.* where the promisee is induced to believe that a contract into which he had undoubtedly entered was between him and the promisor, when in fact it was between the promisee and another person.[77] But it is submitted that these suggestions mistake the nature of the doctrine, which is to restrict the enforcement by the promisor of previously existing rights against the promisee. Such rights can arise only out of a legal relationship existing between these parties before the making of the promise or representation. To apply the

---

[69] (1877) 2 App.Cas. 439.

[70] *ibid.* at 448. *cf. Smith v Lawson* (1998) 75 P. & C.R. 466, below p.115.

[71] *e.g. Charles Rickards Ltd v Oppenhaim* [1950] K.B. 616 (where both common law and equitable principles were applied). The principle in *Hughes v Metropolitan Ry* was said in *Brikom Investments Ltd v Carr* [1979] Q.B. 467 at 489 to be "an illustration of *contractual* variation of strict contractual rights." This description was apt on the facts of that case, where the promise not to enforce such rights was supported by consideration: above, p.102. But the principle stated in *Hughes v Metropolitan Ry* applies even in the absence of such consideration: *cf.* below, p.133.

[72] See below, p.114.

[73] *Durham Fancy Goods Ltd v Michael Jackson (Fancy Goods) Ltd* [1968] 2 Q.B. 839.

[74] *Maharaj v Chand* [1986] A.C. 898.

[75] *Morris v Tarrant* [1971] 2 Q.B. 143 at 160; *cf. Burrows v Brent LBC* [1996] 1 W.L.R. 1448 at 1458, where no attempt was made to invoke the doctrine in favour of a "tolerated trespasser".

[76] See *Evenden v Guildford City FC* [1975] Q.B. 917 at 924, 926 (actual decision overruled in *Secretary of State for Employment v Globe Elastic Thread Co Ltd* [1980] A.C. 506); *cf.* in Australia, *Waltons Stones (Interstate) Ltd v Maher* (1988) 164 C.L.R. 387; below, p.118.

[77] *The Henrik Sif* [1982] 1 Lloyd's Rep. 456 at 466; the actual decision can perhaps be explained as one of liability for actionable non-disclosure: below, p.400.

doctrine where there was no such relationship would contravene the rule (to be discussed below) that the doctrine creates no new rights.[78]

(c) WHEN APPLICABLE. The operation of the doctrine is subject to the following requirements:

(i) *A "clear" or "unequivocal" promise or representation.* There must be a promise (or an assurance or representation in the nature of a promise)[79] which is intended to affect the legal relationship between the parties[80] and which indicates that the promisor will not insist on his strict legal rights,[81] arising out of that relationship, against the promisee. Here, as elsewhere,[82] the law applies an objective test. It is enough if the promise induces the promisee reasonably to believe that the other party will not insist on his strict legal rights.[83] A mere threat to do something is not sufficient, nor, probably, is a representation or promise by a person that he *will* enforce a legal right: thus the doctrine does not apply where A tells B that he will exercise his right to cancel a contract between them unless by a specified date B has paid sums due under the contract to A.[84]

The promise or representation must be "clear" or "unequivocal," or "precise and unambiguous." This requirement seems to have originated in the law relating to estoppel by representation[85] and it is now frequently stated in relation to "waiver"[86] and "promissory estoppel."[87] It does not mean that the promise or representation must be

---

[78] See below, p.111. Some doubt as to the correctness of *The Henrik Sif*, above, is expressed by Webster J. (who decided the case) in *Shearson Lehman Hutton Inc v MacLaine Watson & Co Ltd* [1989] 2 Lloyd's Rep. 570 at 596, 604, though the decision was approved on another point in *The Stolt Loyalty* [1993] 2 Lloyd's Rep. 281 at 289–291, affirmed without reference to this point [1995] 1 Lloyd's Rep. 599; see also *Orion Finance Ltd v J D Williams & Co Ltd* [1997] C.L.Y. 986, where no estoppel arose in the absence of a previous legal relationship; *Baird Textile Holdings Ltd v Marks & Spencer plc* [2001] EWCA Civ 274; [2002] 1 All E.R. (Comm) 737, at [89] apparently doubting some of the reasoning in *The Henrik Sif*, but not the outcome since there was undoubtedly "a legal relationship . . . whoever were the parties thereto" (though the difficulty remains that the first defendants, against whom the doctrine was said to operate, were not parties to that relationship).

[79] *James v Heim Galleries* (1980) 256 E.G. 819 at 821; *Collin v Duke of Westminster* [1985] Q.B. 581 at 595.

[80] *Spence v Shell* (1980) 256 E.G. 55 at 63; *Central London Property Trust Ltd v High Trees House Ltd* [1947] K.B. 130 at 134; *Baird Textile Holdings Ltd v Marks & Spencer plc*, above, n.78, at [94].

[81] Or that he will not rely on an available defence: *cf.* below, pp.115, 403.

[82] See above, pp.1, 8.

[83] *Bremer Handelsgesellschaft mbH v Vanden Avenne-Izegem P.V.B.A.* [1978] 2 Lloyd's Rep. 109 at 126; *Bremer Handelsgesellschaft mbH v Mackprang Jr* [1979] 1 Lloyd's Rep. 221 (both these cases concerned "waiver"; *cf.* below, n.86).

[84] *Drexel Burnham Lambert International NV v El Nasr* [1986] 1 Lloyd's Rep. 356.

[85] *Low v Bouverie* [1891] 3 Ch. 82 at 106; *Woodhouse AC Israel Cocoa Ltd SA v Nigerian Produce Marketing Co Ltd* [1972] A.C. 741; *The Shakleford* [1978] 2 Lloyd's Rep. 155 at 159; below, p.402.

[86] *Finagrain SA Geneva v p.Kruse Hamburg* [1976] 2 Lloyd's Rep. 508 at 534; *The Laconia* [1977] A.C. 850 at 871; *Bremer Handelsgesellschaft mbH v Vanden Avenne-Izegem PVBA* [1978] 2 Lloyd's Rep. 109 at 126; *The Mihalios Xilas* [1979] 1 W.L.R. 1018 at 1024; *Avimex SA v Dewulf & Cie.* [1979] 2 Lloyd's Rep. 57 at 67; *Bremer Handelsgesellschaft GmbH v Westzucker GmbH* [1981] 1 Lloyd's Rep. 207 at 212; *Prosper Homes v Hambro's Bank Executor & Trustee Co* (1979) 39 P. & C.R. 395; *Bremer Handelsgesellschaft mbH v Finagrain Cie. Commerciale Agricole & Financière SA* [1981] 2 Lloyd's Rep. 259 at 266; *The Rio Sun* [1981] 2 Lloyd's Rep. 489 and [1982] 1 Lloyd's Rep. 404; *The Athos* [1983] 1 Lloyd's Rep. 127 at 134–135; *Bremer Handelsgesellschaft mbH v Deutsche Conti-Handelsgesellschaft mbH* [1983] 1 Lloyd's Rep. 689; for the analogy between waiver and the equitable doctrine here under discussion, see above, p.106; below, p.117.

[87] *BP Exploration Co (Libya) Ltd v Hunt (No.2)* [1979] 1 W.L.R. 783 at 812 (affirmed without reference to this point [1983] 2 A.C. 352); *Spence v Shell* (1980) 256 E.G. 55 at 63; *James v Heim Galleries* (1980) 256 E.G. 819 at 821; *The Post Chaser* [1981] 2 Lloyd's Rep. 695 at 700; *The Scaptrade* [1983] Q.B. 529 at 534–535 ("equitable estoppel") (affirmed without reference to this point [1983] A.C. 694); *Goldsworthy v Brickell* [1987] Ch. 378 at 410; *Hiscox v Outhwaite (No.3)* [1991] 2 Lloyd's Rep. 524 at 535; *Rowan Companies Inc v Lambert Eggink Offshore Transport Consultants* [1999] 2 Lloyd's Rep. 443 at 448 and *Thameside MBC v Barlow Securities Group Services Ltd* [2001] EWCA Civ 1; [2001] B.L.R. 113 (where this requirement was not satisfied).

express[88]: in *Hughes v Metropolitan Ry*[89] itself the landlord made no express promise that he would not enforce his right to forfeit the lease; but an implication of such a promise fairly arose from the course of the negotiations between the parties. There is some support for the view that the promise must have the same degree of certainty as would be needed to give it contractual effect if it were supported by consideration.[90] Thus if the statement could not have contractual effect because it was too vague,[91] or if it was insufficiently precise to amount to an offer,[92] or if it does not amount to an unqualified acceptance,[93] it will not bring the equitable doctrine into operation.[94]

The purpose of the requirement that the promise or representation must be "clear" or "unequivocal" is to prevent a party from losing his legal rights merely because he has granted some indulgence by failing throughout to insist on strict performance of a contract[95]; or because he has offered some concession in the course of negotiations for the settlement of a dispute arising out of the contract[96] or merely because he has declared his willingness to continue such negotiations.[97] Thus the requirement was not satisfied where one of the parties to such negotiations throughout insisted on strict compliance with the terms of the contract.[98] Nor was it satisfied where he accepted less than that to which he was entitled but did so subject to an express reservation of his rights.[99] Failure, in the course of negotiations of this kind, to object to a defect or deficiency in performance is likewise insufficient if the injured party did not know and could not reasonably have known of it[1] or if full performance remained possible and continued to be demanded by that party.[2] On the other hand, failure to object to a known defect or deficiency within a reasonable time of its discovery[3] may be regarded as an unequivocal indication of the injured party's intention not to insist on his strict legal

---

[88] *Spence v Shell* (1980) 256 E.G. 55 at 63.

[89] (1877) 2 App.Cas. 439; *cf. The Post Chaser* [1981] 2 Lloyd's Rep. 695 at 700.

[90] *The Winson* [1980] 2 Lloyd's Rep. 213 at 222; reversed on other grounds [1982] A.C. 939; *Drexel Burnham Lambert International NV v El Nasr* [1986] 1 Lloyd's Rep. 357; *The Antclizo* [1987] 2 Lloyd's Rep. 130 at 142 (affirmed [1988] 1 W.L.R. 603); *Baird Textile Holdings Ltd v Marks & Spencer* [2001] EWCA Civ 274; [2002] 1 All E.R. (Comm) 737, at [38], [54]; *cf.* above, p.48 for the requirement of certainty.

[91] See above, p.48.

[92] See above, p.8.

[93] *Azov Shipping Co v Baltic Shipping Co* [1999] 2 Lloyd's Rep. 159 at 173, a case of estoppel by representation, to which the requirement of a clear and unequivocal representation also applies: see below, p.403. For the requirement of an "unqualified" acceptance, see above, p.18.

[94] *The Winson* [1980] 2 Lloyd's Rep. 213 at 223; reversed on other grounds [1982] A.C. 939.

[95] *The Scaptrade* [1981] 2 Lloyd's Rep. 425 at 431, [1983] Q.B. 529 at 535 affirmed [1983] 2 A.C. 694; *cf. Cape Asbestos Co Ltd v Lloyds Bank Ltd* [1921] W.N. 274 at 276; *Bunge SA v Compagnie Européenne des Céréales* [1982] Lloyd's Rep. 306; *Bremer Handelsgesellschaft mbH v Raiffeisen Hauptgenossenschaft E.G.* [1982] 1 Lloyd's Rep. 599; *Bremer Handelsgesellschaft mbH v Bunge Corp* [1983] 1 Lloyd's Rep. 476.

[96] *cf. London & Clydebank Properties v HM Investment Co* [1993] E.G.C.S. 63.

[97] *Seechurn v Ace Insurance SA* [2002] EWCA Civ 67; [2002] 2 Lloyd's Rep. 390, esp. at [55].

[98] *V Berg & Son Ltd v Vanden Avenne-Izegem PVBA* [1977] 1 Lloyd's Rep. 500; *cf. Edm J M Mertens & Co PVBA v Veevoeder Import Export Vimex BV* [1979] 2 Lloyd's Rep. 372.

[99] *Finagrain S.A. Geneva v p.Kruse Hamburg* [1976] 2 Lloyd's Rep. 508; *cf. Cook Industries Inc v Meunerie Liègeois SA* [1981] 1 Lloyd's Rep. 359 at 368; *Bremer Handelsgesellschaft mbH v Deutsche Conti Handelsgesellschaft mbH* [1983] 2 Lloyd's Rep. 45; *Peter Cremer v Granaria BV* [1981] 2 Lloyd's Rep. 583; *cf. The Winson* [1980] 2 Lloyd's Rep. 213 (as to which see n.90, above).

[1] *Avimex SA v Dewulf & Cie.* [1979] 2 Lloyd's Rep. 57.

[2] *The Mihalios Xilas* [1979] W.L.R. 1018; *Bremer Handelsgesellschaft mbH v C Mackprang Jr* [1981] 1 Lloyd's Rep. 292 at 299; *Bremer Handelsgesellschaft mbH v Westzucker GmbH* [1981] 1 Lloyd's Rep. 207 at 212–213; *Peter Cremer v Granaria BV* [1981] 2 Lloyd's Rep. 583; *The Post Chaser* [1981] 2 Lloyd's Rep. 695 at 700.

[3] See *The Laconia* [1977] A.C. 850 (where retention of an under-payment accepted without authority by the payee's bank was held not to amount to a waiver); *The Superhulls Cover Case (No.2)* [1990] 2 Lloyd's Rep. 431 (where the deficiency was not known).

rights.[3a] The position seems to be the same where the defect or deficiency, though not actually known to the injured party, was obvious or could have been discovered by him, if he had taken reasonable steps.[4] But where more than one matter is in dispute between the parties, "emphatic reliance upon some important disputed point does not by itself . . . imply any unequivocal representation that compliance with other parts of the bargain is thereby waived".[5]

Although a promise or representation may be made by conduct, mere inactivity will not normally suffice for the present purpose since "it is difficult to imagine how silence and inaction can be anything but equivocal".[6] Unless the law took this view, mere failure to assert a contractual right could lead to its loss; and the courts have on a number of occasions rejected this clearly undesirable conclusion. Thus it has been held that there is "no ground for saying that mere delay, however lengthy, destroys the contractual right"[7]; and that the mere failure to prosecute a claim regarded by both parties as hopeless did not amount to a promise to abandon it.[8] The only circumstances in which "silence and inaction" can have this effect are the exceptional ones (discussed elsewhere in this book[9]) in which the law imposes a duty to disclose facts or to clarify a legal relationship and the party under the duty fails to perform it.

(ii) *Reliance.* The requirement of reliance means that the promise or representation must in some way have influenced the conduct of the party to whom it was made. Although the promise need not form the sole inducement,[10] it must (it is submitted) be *some* inducement. Hence the requirement would not be satisfied if it could be shown that the other party's conduct was not influenced by the promise at all,[11] so that he was not in any way prejudiced by it.[12] But if this is a matter of "mere speculation",[13] or if the

---

[3a] *e.g. Bremer Handelsgesellschaft mbH v Vanden Avenne-Izegem PVBA* [1978] 2 Lloyd's Rep. 109; *Hazel v Akhtar* [2001] EWCA Civ 1883; *The Times*, January 7, 2002.

[4] See *Bremer Handelsgesellschaft mbH v C. Mackprang Jr.* [1979] 1 Lloyd's Rep. 221, where there was a division of opinion on the point in the Court of Appeal. Contrast, for a different type of waiver, pp.815–816, below.

[5] *The Athos* [1983] 1 Lloyd's Rep. 127 at 135; *Rafsanjan Pistachio Producers Co-operative v Bank Leumi (UK) plc.* [1992] 1 Lloyd's Rep. 513 at 542.

[6] *The Leonidas D* [1985] 1 W.L.R. 925 at 937; *cf. Cook Industries v Tradax Export SA* [1983] 1 Lloyd's Rep. 327 at 332 (affirmed [1985] 2 Lloyd's Rep. 454); *The August P Leonhardt* [1985] 2 Lloyd's Rep. 28 at 33; *MSC Mediterranean Shipping Co SA v BRE Metro Ltd* [1985] 2 Lloyd's Rep. 239; *Cie. Française d'Importation, etc., v Deutsche Continental Handelsgesellschaft* [1985] 2 Lloyd's Rep. 592 at 598; *The Antclizo* [1986] 1 Lloyd's Rep. 181 at 187 (affirmed [1988] 1 W.L.R. 603); *The Superhulls Cover Case (No.2)* [1990] 2 Lloyd's Rep. 431 at 452; and see above, p.10.

[7] *Amherst v James Walker Goldsmith & Silversmith Ltd* [1983] Ch. 305 at 315; *cf.*, in another context, *The Nai Genova* [1984] 1 Lloyd's Rep. 353 at 365.

[8] *Collin v Duke of Westminster* [1985] Q.B. 581.

[9] See below, pp.392–400, above, p.33; see, for example, *The Lutetian* [1982] 2 Lloyd's Rep. 140 at 158; *The Stolt Loyalty* [1993] 2 Lloyd's Rep. 281 at 289, 291, affirmed (without reference to the point here under discussion) [1995] 1 Lloyd's Rep. 559; and see *Petrotrade Inc v Stinnes Handel GmbH* [1995] 1 Lloyd's Rep. 142 at 151, where the statement that there may be a representation by "conduct (including silence)" evidently refers to the exceptional situations described in the text above.

[10] *cf.* below, p.340.

[11] See *Fontana NV v Mautner* (1979) 254 E.G. 199; *Raiffeisen Hauptgenossenschaft v Louis Dreyfus & Co* [1981] 1 Lloyd's Rep. 345 at 352; *Cook Industries Ltd v Meunerie Liègeois SA* [1981] 1 Lloyd's Rep. 359 at 368; *The Scaptrade* [1983] Q.B. 529 at 536, affirmed without reference to this point [1983] 2 A.C. 694; *Bremer Handelsgesellschaft mbH v Bunge Corp* [1983] 1 Lloyd's Rep. 476; *Bremer Handelsgesellschaft mbH v Deutsche-Conti Handelsgesellschaft mbH* [1983] 1 Lloyd's Rep. 689; *Lark v Outhwaite* [1991] 2 Lloyd's Rep. 132 at 142; *The Nerano* [1996] 1 Lloyd's Rep. 1; *Rowan Companies Inc v Lambert Eggink Offshore Transport Consultants* [1999] 2 Lloyd's Rep. 443 at 449.

[12] *Ets Soules & Cie. v International Trade Development Co Ltd* [1980] 1 Lloyd's Rep. 129; *The Multibank Holsatia* [1988] 2 Lloyd's Rep. 486 at 493.

[13] *Brikom Investments Ltd v Carr* [1979] Q.B. 467 at 482.

promise or representation "was one of the factors . . . relied upon",[14] it would form a sufficient inducement. In other words, where the promisee has, after the promise, conducted himself in the way intended by the promisor, it will be up to the promisor to establish that the conduct was not induced by the promise.[15]

There is sometimes said to be a further requirement, namely that the promisee must have suffered some "detriment" in reliance on the promise.[16] This may mean that the promisee must have done something which he was not previously bound to do and as a result have suffered loss, *e.g.* by incurring expenditure in reliance on the promise. The alleged requirement of "detriment" in this sense is based on the analogy of estoppel by representation.[17] But that analogy is (as we shall see)[18] inexact; and the equitable doctrine can clearly operate even though there is no "detriment" in this sense.[19] It is enough if the promisee has altered his position in reliance on the promise so that it would be inequitable to allow the promisor to act inconsistently with it.[20] Thus the requirement can be satisfied if the promisee has forborne from taking steps to safeguard his legal position (as in *Hughes v Metropolitan Ry*[21] itself); or if he has performed or made efforts to perform the original obligation as altered by the promise (for example, where a seller who has been promised extra time for delivery continues to make efforts to perform after the originally agreed delivery date has gone by).

(iii) *Inequitable.* It must be "inequitable" for the promisor to go back on the promise. This requirement cannot be defined with anything approaching precision, but the underlying idea is that the promisee must have acted in reliance on the promise in one of the ways just described, so that he can no longer be restored to the position in which he was before he took such action.[22] If the promisee can be restored to that position, it will not be inequitable for the promisor to go back on the promise. In one case[23] the promisor re-asserted his strict legal rights only two days after the promise had been made. It was held that this was not "inequitable", since the promisee had not, in this short period, suffered any prejudice: he could be, and was, restored to exactly the position in which he had been before the promise was made. Sometimes, moreover, extraneous circumstances will justify the promisor in going back on the promise without notice. In *Williams v Stern*[24] the plaintiff gave the defendant a bill of sale of furniture as security for a loan; the bill entitled the defendant to seize the furniture if the plaintiff defaulted in paying instalments due under it. When the fourteenth instalment became due, the plaintiff asked for extra time, and the defendant said that he "would not look

---

[14] *ibid.* at 490 (*per* Cumming-Bruce L.J., whose decision was based on the different ground discussed above, p.101).

[15] *cf.* the similar rule in cases of "proprietary estoppel" stated below, p.141.

[16] *e.g. Fontana NV v Mautner* (1979) 254 E.G. 199; *Meng Long Development Pte Ltd v Jip Hong Trading Co Pte Ltd* [1985] A.C. 511 at 524. *cf.* Wilson, 67 L.Q.R. 344.

[17] See below, p.403; *Carr v L & NW Ry* (1875) L.R. 10 C.P. 310 at 317.

[18] See below, pp.114–115.

[19] *W J Alan & Co Ltd v El Nasr Export & Import Co* [1972] 2 Q.B. 189 at 213.

[20] *James v Heim Galleries* (1980) 256 E.G. 819 at 825; *The Post Chaser* [1981] 2 Lloyd's Rep. 695 at 701; *The Superhulls Cover Case (No.2)* [1990] 2 Lloyd's Rep. 431 at 454; *cf. Seechurn v Ace Insurance SA* [2002] EWCA Civ 67, [2002] 2 Lloyd's Rep. 390, at [25], leaving open the question whether further "detriment" is required.

[21] (1877) 2 App.Cas. 439; above p.105.

[22] *Maharaj v Chand* [1986] A.C. 898.

[23] *The Post Chaser* [1981] 2 Lloyd's Rep. 693; *cf. Bremer Handelsgesellschaft mbH v Bunge Corp* [1983] 1 Lloyd's Rep. 476 at 484; *Bremer Handelsgesellschaft mbH v Deutsche-Conti Handelsgesellschaft mbH* [1983] 1 Lloyd's Rep. 689; *The Trado* [1982] 1 Lloyd's Rep. 157 at 160; *Banner Industrial & Commercial Properties Ltd v Clark Patterson* [1990] 2 E.G.L.R. 139; *Transatlantico de Commercio SA v Incrobasa Industrial e Commercio Brazileira SA* [1995] 1 Lloyd's Rep. 215 at 219.

[24] (1879) 5 Q.B.D. 409.

to a week". Three days later he seized the furniture because he had heard that the plaintiff's landlord intended to distrain it for arrears of rent. It was held that the defendant's seizure was justified. There was no consideration for his promise to give time, nor did *Hughes v Metropolitan Ry*[25] apply. Brett L.J. said: "Has there been any misconduct on the part of the defendant? I think not: it appears that a distress by the plaintiff's landlord was threatened; and under those circumstances I do not blame the defendant for changing his mind."[26] His conduct was not "inequitable".

(d) EFFECT GENERALLY SUSPENSORY. The equitable doctrine, like the common law doctrine of waiver,[27] does not extinguish, but only suspends, rights. In *Hughes v Metropolitan Ry* the landlord was not forever prevented from enforcing the covenant: he could have enforced it on giving reasonable notice requiring the tenant to do the repairs.[28] This aspect of the doctrine was stressed in *Tool Metal Manufacturing Co Ltd v Tungsten Electric Co Ltd*,[29] where a licence for the use of a patent provided that the licensees should pay "compensation" if they manufactured more than a stated number of articles incorporating the patent. In 1942 the owners of the patent agreed to suspend the obligation to pay "compensation" until a new agreement was made. They later gave notice to end the suspension. It was held that they were once again entitled to the payments after the expiry of a reasonable time from the giving of notice. The reason for this rule is that, in equity, the effect of the representation is to give the court a discretion to do what is equitable in all the circumstances[30]; and in the cases just discussed it would not be equitable (or in accordance with the intention of the parties) wholly to extinguish the representor's (or promisor's) rights.

Subsequent events may, however, in exceptional circumstances, give the doctrine an extinctive effect. They can, most obviously, lead to this result where they make it impossible for the promisee to perform his original obligation. In *Birmingham & District Land Co v L & NW Ry*[31] a building lease bound the tenant to build by 1885. The lessor agreed to suspend this obligation; but in 1886, while the suspension was still in force, the land was compulsorily acquired by a railway company, so that performance of the tenant's obligation became impossible. The tenant recovered statutory compensation from the railway company on the footing that the building lease was still binding; but clearly his obligation to build was wholly extinguished. Even where performance of the original obligation has not become literally impossible, the doctrine may sometimes have an extinctive effect. For example, in *Ogilvy v Hope-Davies*[32] a vendor of land indicated on August 15 that he would not insist on the contractual completion date of August 30. It was held that no question of reinstating the contractual completion date could arise "because the time was far too short".[33] The doctrine has an extinctive effect in such cases because subsequent events, or the passage of time, though not making performance

---

[25] (1877) 2 App.Cas. 439; above, p.105.

[26] At 413; *cf.* also *Southwark LBC v Logan* (1996) 8 Admin.L.R. 315.

[27] *i.e.* in the sense of forbearance, above, p.102.

[28] No reference to this point was made in *Smith v Lawson* (1998) 75 P. & C.R. 446 (below, p.115), probably because no attempt was made by the promisor to give notice of any intention to resume his strict legal rights.

[29] [1955] 1 W.L.R. 761; *cf. Banning v Wright* [1972] 1 W.L.R. 972 at 981, *The Post Chaser* [1981] 2 Lloyd's Rep. 695 at 701; *The Kanchenjunga* [1990] 1 Lloyd's Rep 391 at 399; *Hazel v Akhtar* [2001] EWCA Civ 1883, *The Times*, January 7, 2002, at [43].

[30] *Roebuck v Mungovin* [1994] 2 A.C. 224 at 235.

[31] (1888) 40 Ch.D. 268. *cf. Durham Fancy Goods Ltd v Michael Jackson (Fancy Goods) Ltd* [1968] 2 Q.B. 839.

[32] [1976] 1 All E.R. 683; *The Ion* [1980] 2 Lloyd's Rep. 245; *Voest Alpine Intertrading GmbH v Chevron International Oil Co* [1987] 2 Lloyd's Rep. 547 at 560.

[33] *Ogilvy v Hope-Davies* [1976] 1 All E.R. 683 at 696.

of the original obligation impossible, have made it highly inequitable to require such performance even after reasonable notice.[34]

(e) CREATES NO NEW RIGHTS. The equitable doctrine prevents the enforcement of existing rights, but it does not create entirely new rights or extend the scope of existing ones. This was decided in *Combe v Combe*,[35] where a husband during divorce proceedings promised to pay £100 per annum to his wife who, in reliance on this promise, forbore from applying to the court for maintenance. This forbearance did not constitute consideration for the husband's promise.[36] It was held that the equitable doctrine did not entitle the wife to recover the promised payments; nor is there any support in English cases for the view that it could create a cause of action in the narrower sense of "limiting recovery to reliance loss".[37] The view that the doctrine gave rise to no new rights came to be associated with its description as a kind of estoppel (known as "promissory estoppel"[38]) and hence with the rule, established in relation to another kind of estoppel (known as "estoppel by representation"[39]), that "you cannot found a cause of action on an estoppel".[40] It will be submitted below[41] that the analogy between the two kinds of estoppel is (to say the least) imperfect and that it does not satisfactorily account for the rule that "promissory estoppel" gives rise to no new rights. The more plausible explanation for this restriction on the scope of the equitable doctrine is that the restriction is needed to prevent that doctrine from coming into head–on collision with the rules which lay down the requirements for the creation of a binding contract. The significant point in the present context is that the restriction preserves consistency between the equitable doctrine and the rule that a promise is not binding as a contract unless it is supported by consideration or made in a deed.[42] *Combe v Combe* has likewise been relied on in support of the view that the equitable doctrine could not give rise to a cause of action on a promise which lacked contractual force for want, not of consideration, but of certainty and contractual intention.[43] There seems, with respect, to be no reason in principle for distinguishing for the present purpose between promises which lack contractual effect for want of consideration and those which lack such effect for some other reason: the danger of collision between the equitable principle and the requirements for the creation of a contract exists, whatever the reason may be why a

---

[34] See *Maharaj v Chand* [1986] A.C. 898; *cf. W J Alan & Co Ltd v El Nasr Export & Import Co* [1972] Q.B. 189 (where the actual decision was that there was a variation supported by consideration: above, p.101).

[35] [1951] 2 K.B. 215. The point had been foreshadowed in *Central London Property Trust Ltd v High Trees House Ltd* [1947] K.B. 130 at 134.

[36] See above, p.91.

[37] *Baird Textile Holdings Ltd v Marks & Spencer plc* [2001] EWCA Civ 274; [2002] 1 All E.R. (Comm) 737, at [99]; for the difficulty of distinguishing in that case between reliance and expectation loss, see *ibid.* at [81], [82]; for the distinction in general, see below, pp.937 to 941.

[38] See above, p.106.

[39] See below, p.403.

[40] *Low v Bouverie* [1891] 3 Ch. 82 at 101; *cf. ibid.* at 105; below, p.403.

[41] See below, p.108, esp. n.47a.

[42] This appears to be the point that Denning L.J. had in mind in *Combe v Combe* [1951] 2 K.B. 215 at 219 when he said that he did not want the equitable principle to be "stretched too far lest it be endangered". *cf. Brikom Investments Ltd v Carr* [1979] Q.B. 467 at 486; *Tool Metal Manufacturing Co Ltd v Tungsten Electric Co Ltd* [1955] 1 W.L.R. 761 at 764; *Beesly v Hallwood Estates Ltd* [1960] 1 W.L.R. 549 at 561; *Drexel Burnham Lambert International NV v El Nasr* [1986] 1 Lloyd's Rep. 357 at 365 contrast *Vaughan v Vaughan* [1953] Q.B. 762 at 768; Denning, 15 M.L.R. 1.

[43] *Baird Textile Holdings Ltd v Marks & Spencer plc*, above, n.37, where *Combe v Combe* is cited at [34], and [87] in support of the view stated in the text above; though an alternative explanation for the result in the *Baird* case may be that, in the absence of certainty or contractual intention, the requirements for the operation of the equitable doctrine are simply not satisfied (above, pp.107–109), so that no question can arise as to its effects.

particular promise lacks contractual force.[44] The view that the equitable doctrine does not create new causes of action seems, indeed, to have been doubted[45] or ignored[46] by dicta in later cases; but the promises in these cases created new rights on the orthodox ground that they were supported by consideration.[47] *Combe v Combe* therefore still stands as the leading English[48] authority for the proposition that the doctrine creates no new rights and this proposition has been reaffirmed in a number of later cases.[49]

It appears to follow from this proposition that the equitable doctrine would not enable employees in a case like *Stilk v Myrick*[50] to recover the extra pay which they had been promised. It could, indeed, be argued[51] that in such a case the cause of action was the original contract of employment and that the subsequent agreement fell within the principle stated by Denning L.J. in *Combe v Combe* that consideration was not necessary for the "modification or discharge"[52] of a contract where the conditions required for the operation of the equitable doctrine were otherwise satisfied. This argument may derive some judicial support from a dictum that promissory estoppel "may enlarge the effect of an agreement"[53]; for this could mean that a promise of extra pay on facts such as those of *Stilk v Myrick* could create a cause of action even though it was not supported by consideration. This view is, however, hard to reconcile with the treatment of *Stilk v Myrick* in *Williams v Roffey Bros*[54] and with the fact that the decision in the latter case was based, not on estoppel,[55] but on the ground that the promise of extra pay there was supported by consideration. It is submitted that, when in *Combe v Combe* Denning L.J.

---

[44] In *Azov Shipping Co v Baltic Shipping Co* [1999] 2 Lloyd's Rep. 159 at 175 it is suggested that the rule that promissory estoppel gives rise to no cause of action "is limited to the protection of consideration" and has "no general application in the field of estoppel". The estoppel there under discussion was estoppel by representation, and the suggestion is, with respect, hard to reconcile with the statements in *Low v Bouverie* [1891] 3 Ch. 82 at 101, 105 referred to in n.40 above. Similar difficulty arises from the more tentative suggestion in *Thornton Springer v NEM Insurance Ltd* [2000] 2 All E.R. 489 at 519 that estoppel could lead to the "enforcement of the promise" where no contract was concluded for want of acceptance of an offer, though not where there was no contract for want of consideration. The former situation is one of estoppel by convention (as to which see below, p.119); and it is also, with respect hard to see why one answer should be given to the question whether the rule in *Combe v Combe* applies where the promise lacks contractual force for want of consideration and a different one where it lacks such force for want of an effective acceptance. Such a distinction seems also to be inconsistent with the readiness of the Court of Appeal in the *Baird* case (above at n.43) to apply the rule in *Combe v Combe* to an alleged promise which lacked contractual force for some reason other than want of consideration.

[45] *Re Wyvern Developments Ltd* [1974] 1 W.L.R. 1097 at 1104–1105; Atiyah, 38 M.L.R. 65 and see Allan, 79 L.Q.R. 238. The point was left open in *The Henrik Sif* [1982] 1 Lloyd's Rep. 456 at 466–468 (as to which see above, p.107 n.78).

[46] *Evenden v Guildford City FC* [1975] Q.B. 917 at 924, 926; Napier, [1976] C.L.J. 38; and see next note.

[47] e.g. *Secretary of State for Employment v Globe Elastic Thread Co Ltd* [1980] A.C. 506, overruling *Evenden's* case, above. Lord Wilberforce remarked at 518 that "To convert this [contract] into an estoppel is to turn the doctrine of promissory estoppel . . . upside down."

[48] For other jurisdictions, see below, p.118.

[49] *Argy Trading Development Co Ltd v Lapid Developments Ltd* [1977] 1 W.L.R. 444 at 457; *Aquaflite Ltd v Jaymar International Freight Consultants Ltd* [1980] 1 Lloyd's Rep. 36; *The Proodos C* [1980] 2 Lloyd's Rep. 390 at 394; *James v Heim Galleries* (1980) 256 E.G. 819 at 821; *Brikom Investments Ltd v Seaford* [1981] 1 W.L.R. 863; *cf. Taylors Fashions Ltd v Liverpool Victoria Trustees Co Ltd* [1982] Q.B. 133 n. at 152; *Baird Textile Holdings Ltd v Marks & Spencer plc*, above, n.43.

[50] (1809) 2 Camp. 317; 6 Esp. 129; above, p.94.

[51] See *Hiscox v Outhwaite (No.3)* [1991] 2 Lloyd's Rep. 524 at 535.

[52] [1951] 2 K.B. 215 at 219.

[53] *Baird Textile Holdings Ltd v Marks & Spencer plc* [2001] EWCA Civ 274, [2002] 1 All E.R. (Comm) 737, at [88].

[54] *Williams v Roffey Bros & Nicholls (Contractors) Ltd* [1991] 1 Q.B. 1, above, p.95.

[55] Though there are references to estoppel in that case at 13 ("not yet fully developed") and 17–18 (this reference seems to be to estoppel by convention, the relevance of which to the case is doubted at p.123, n.43, below).

used the phrase "modification or discharge" he had in mind a modification which *reduced* a party's obligations.[56] To apply it to a case in which it had the effect of *increasing* them necessarily amounts to giving the other party a new cause of action on a promise for which he has not provided any consideration; and *Combe v Combe* decides that this is not the effect of the equitable doctrine here under discussion.[57] A cause of action on a promise unsupported by consideration could, however, arise under other equitable doctrines: *e.g.* under the doctrine of "proprietary estoppel" to be discussed later in this Chapter.[58]

The essentially defensive nature of the equitable doctrine here under discussion is sometimes expressed by saying that it operates as a shield and not as a sword.[59] In other words, its normal effect is merely to protect the promisee against enforcement of the original obligation. But the metaphor is apt to mislead,[60] for the equitable doctrine can assist a claimant no less than a defendant. For example, a creditor may threaten to seize property on which a debt is secured, after having indicated that he would not insist on punctual payment. In such a case the debtor will, if the requirements of the equitable doctrine[61] are satisfied, be able to restrain the creditor's threatened seizure by injunction.[62] Similarly, a seller may tender goods after the originally agreed delivery date, in reliance on the buyer's promise to accept late delivery. If the buyer without justification refuses to accept the delivery, the seller will be entitled to damages.[63]

The equitable doctrine can also assist the promisee as claimant in that it may prevent the promisor from relying on a defence which would, but for the promise, have been available to him: *e.g.* the defence that a claim which the promisee has made against him is time-barred,[64] or that the claim has been satisfied,[65] or that the contractual document suffers from some minor formal defect, the effect of which is not specified by the statute imposing the formal requirement.[66] In such cases, the doctrine will, once again, enable the promisee to win an action which, but for the doctrine, he would have lost. But the promisee's cause of action will have arisen independently of the promise which brought the equitable doctrine into operation: the effect of the doctrine is merely to prevent the promisor from relying on some circumstance which would, if the promise had not been made, *have destroyed the promisee's original cause of action*. This situation must be distinguished from that in which the promisor's "defence" is that (apart from the promise) the promisee's alleged *cause of action never existed at all*. It is submitted that the equitable doctrine should not prevent the promisor from relying on a "defence" of this

---

[56] As in *Central London Property Trust Ltd v High Trees House Ltd* [1947] K.B. 130, below p.130, this being the case under discussion in *Combe v Combe*, above, at 219.

[57] *The Proodos C* [1980] 2 Lloyd's Rep. 390.

[58] See below, pp.134–149, especially at p.147.

[59] *Combe v Combe* [1951] 2 K.B. 215 at 224; *The Proodos C* [1980] 2 Lloyd's Rep. 390 at 391 ("time-honoured phrase"); *Lark v Outhwaite* [1991] 2 Lloyd's Rep. 132 at 142; *Hiscox v Outhwaite (No.3)* [1991] 2 Lloyd's Rep. 524 at 535.

[60] *Azov Shipping Co v Baltic Shipping Co* [1999] 2 Lloyd's Rep. 159 at 175 ("largely inaccurate"); *Baird Textile Holdings Ltd v Marks & Spencer plc* [2001] EWCA Civ 274; [2001] 1 All E.R. (Comm) 737 at [52] ("misleading aphorism").

[61] *i.e.* those discussed at pp.107–111, above.

[62] Such a claim would have succeeded in *Williams v Stern* (1879) 5 Q.B.D. 409 (above, p.104), if the creditor's conduct had been "inequitable."

[63] *cf. Hartley v Hymans* [1920] 3 K.B. 475, applying the corresponding doctrine of common law forbearance (above, p.104); *Johnson v Gore-Wood* [2001] 1 All E.R. 481 at 508. And see Jackson, 81 L.Q.R. 223.

[64] See *The Ion* [1980] 2 Lloyd's Rep. 245; *Hazel v Akhtar* [2002] EWCA Civ 1883; *The Times*, January 7, 2002 at [25]. *Commonwealth of Australia v Verwayen* (1990) 170 C.L.R. 394 (discussed by Spence, 107 L.Q.R. 221) can be explained on this ground: see *Baird Textile Holdings Ltd v Marks & Spencer plc*, above, n.60 at [98].

[65] *cf.* below, p.403.

[66] *Shah v Shah* [2001] EWCA Civ 527; [2001] 4 All E.R. 138 at [31] (a case of estoppel by representation).

kind. If the doctrine were allowed to operate in this way, it would give the promisee a new cause of action based on the promise, even though the promise was not supported by consideration; and such a result would be inconsistent with the essentially defensive nature of the doctrine.[67]

This doctrine may also, somewhat paradoxically, deprive a promisee of a defence. This was the position in *Smith v Lawson*[68] where a lessor told the lessee that he would not trouble to collect the small rent which the lessee had previously paid. It was held that the lessee's rent-free occupation did not amount to adverse possession since the lessor was precluded by the doctrine of promissory estoppel from obtaining possession on the ground of non-payment of rent and that therefore the lessee could not rely on her occupation to defeat the lessor's claim for a declaration that he remained freehold owner of the land.

(f) ANALOGY WITH ESTOPPEL. The equitable doctrine has certain features in common with the doctrine of estoppel by representation.[69] Each is based on a representation followed by reliance on the part of the representee, and each is defensive in nature in that neither is capable in itself of giving rise to new rights. But there are also many differences between estoppel by representation and the equitable doctrine, even though the latter is now often referred to as a kind of estoppel.[70] These differences are reflected in the statement of Millett L.J. that "the attempt . . . to demonstrate that all estoppels . . . are now subsumed in the single and all-embracing estoppel by representation and that they are all governed by the same principle[71]" has "never won general acceptance".[72] The various kinds of estoppel discussed in this book[73] are linked only by the broadest of general principles, that a person's taking of inconsistent positions is in some situations to be discouraged by law; in this sense it can be said that "unconscionability . . . provides the link between them".[74] But they nevertheless have "separate requirements and different terrains of application"[75] and therefore "cannot be accommodated within a single principle".[76] An important difference between the two types of estoppel at this stage under discussion[77] relates to the nature of the representations required to bring them into operation. A representation of *intention* or a *promise* suffices for the purpose of the equitable doctrine; for this reason, and because the doctrine was developed in

---

[67] *cf.* the criticism (above, p.107) of *The Henrik Sif* [1982] 1 Lloyd's Rep. 456.

[68] (1998) 75 P. & C.R. 466.

[69] See below, p.403.

[70] Below, n.78.

[71] The reference seems to be to Lord Denning M.R.'s statement in *Amalgamated Investment & Property Co Ltd v Texas Commerce International Bank Ltd* [1982] 2 Q.B. 73 at 122 ("one general principle shorn of limitations"). The passage containing these words is cited with apparent approval by Lord Bingham in *Johnson v Gore Wood & Co* [2001] 1 All E.R. 481 at 501 but it is not clear whether this citation (a) is part of Lord Bingham's *ratio* in that case or (b) the apparent approval is shared by Lords Hutton and Cooke who agree generally with the part of Lord Bingham's speech in which it occurs; *cf.* also the reference, in another context, to a possible "move to a more uniform doctrine of estoppel" in *Scottish Equitable plc v Derby* [2001] EWCA Civ 369 at [48]; [2001] 3 All E.R. 818.

[72] *First National Bank plc v Thomson* [1996] Ch. 231 at 236; *cf. The Indian Endurance (No.2)* [1998] A.C. 878 at 913; *National Westminster Bank plc v Somer* [2001] 1 All E.R. 198 at [38], [39] dicta in *Baird Textile Holdings Ltd v Marks & Spencer plc* [2001] EWCA Civ 274; [2002] 1 All E.R. (Comm) 737 at [38, 50, 83, 84] perhaps incline in the other direction but cannot be regarded as conclusive.

[73] *i.e.*, estoppel by representation (below, p.403) promissory estoppel (discussed here), estoppel by convention (below, pp.119 *et seq.*) and proprietary estoppel (below, pp.134 *et seq.*).

[74] *Johnson v Gore Wood & Co* [2001] 1 All E.R. 481 at 508.

[75] *The Indian Endurance (No.2)* [1998] A.C. 878 at 914, distinguishing between estoppels by convention and by acquiescence.

[76] *Johnson v Gore Wood & Co* [2001] 1 All E.R. 481 at 508.

[77] *i.e.*, estoppel by representation and promissory estoppel.

equity, it is often referred to as "promissory" or "equitable" estoppel.[78] True estoppel by representation, on the other hand, cannot be based on a representation of intention, but only on one of *existing fact*. This rule was laid down in *Jorden v Money*,[79] where it was held that a representation by a creditor that he *would not* enforce a bond did not give rise to such an estoppel. This difference between estoppel by representation and the equitable doctrine cannot be explained by saying that the requirement of a representation of existing fact did not exist in equity but only at common law.[80] *Jorden v Money* was an appeal from the Court of Appeal in Chancery and was, no less than *Hughes v Metropolitan Ry*,[81] decided on equitable principles; and the requirement of a representation of existing fact is stated in many equity cases.[82] There are, moreover, other significant differences between the two doctrines. The equitable doctrine may operate even though there is no such "detriment" as is required to bring the doctrine of estoppel by representation into play.[83] And the effect of the equitable doctrine is only to suspend rights,[84] while estoppel by representation, where it operates, has a permanent effect. There is, finally, a difference in the legal nature of the two doctrines. Estoppel by representation prevents a party from establishing *facts*: *i.e.* from alleging that the facts represented by him are untrue, even where that is actually the case.[85] The equitable

---

[78] *e.g. Woodhouse AC Israel Cocoa Ltd v Nigerian Produce Marketing Co Ltd* [1972] A.C. 741 at 758; *Ogilvy v Hope-Davies* [1976] 1 All E.R. 683 at 689; *Ets. Soules & Cie v International Trade Development Co Ltd* [1980] 1 Lloyd's Rep. 129 at 133; *The Ion* [1980] 2 Lloyd's Rep. 245 at 250; *Peter Cremer v Granaria BV* [1981] 2 Lloyd's Rep. 583 at 587; *The Post Chaser* [1981] 2 Lloyd's Rep. 695 at 700; *The Kanchenjunga* [1990] 1 Lloyd's Rep. 391 at 398; *Roebuck v Mungovin* [1994] 2 A.C. 224 at 235. Contrast *Brikom Investments Ltd v Carr* [1979] Q.B. 467 at 485, 489, where Roskill L.J. prefers to refer simply to the principle of *Hughes v Metropolitan Ry* (1877) 2 App.Cas. 439. *Amherst v James Walker Goldsmiths & Silversmiths Ltd* [1983] Ch. 305 at 316 somewhat puzzlingly seems to distinguish between "promissory" and "equitable" estoppel. Terminological difficulty is compounded by the occasional use of the phrase "equitable estoppel" to refer to true estoppel by representation: see below, n.80.

[79] (1854) 5 H.L.C. 185; criticised by Jackson, 81 L.Q.R. 84; *cf.* Halliwell, 5 L.S. 15. Atiyah (above, p.70, n.31, pp.56–61), argues that *Jorden v Money* does not support the proposition for which it is usually cited, but that there was a contract in the case, which was unenforceable for want of written evidence. But no such contract was alleged by the claimant: as Lord Cranworth said at 215, "it is put entirely on the ground of misrepresentation." The orthodox view is also unequivocally supported by Lord Selborne (who was counsel in *Jorden v Money*) in his speech in *Maddison v Alderson* (1883) 8 App.Cas. 467, 473. For more recent statements of the rule that there must be a representation of fact see *Argy Trading Development Co Ltd v Lapid Development Ltd* [1977] 1 W.L.R. 444 at 450; *Spence v Shell* (1980) 256 E.G. 55 at 63; *TCB Ltd v Gray* [1986] Ch. 621 at 634, affirmed [1987] Ch. 458; *Roebuck v Mungovin* [1994] 2 A.C. 224 at 235; so-called "estoppel by convention" (below, p.119) is similarly based on an assumption as to an *existing* state of fact or (at least to some extent) of "law" see below, p.119 at n.56 and p.111 at n.69a.

[80] Estoppel by representation of fact (below, p.403) was recognised at common law at least as long ago as *Freeman v Cooke* (1848) 2 Ex. 654; but sometimes this form of estoppel is confusingly referred to as "equitable estoppel": *e.g.* in *Lombard North Central plc v Stobart* [1990] Tr.L.R. 105 at 107. In that case, an estoppel arose from a finance company's statement that no more than £1,003 was due under a conditional sale, when the actual sum due was nearly five times as much. This statement was clearly a representation of *fact* rather than a *promise*.

[81] (1877) 2 App.Cas. 439; above, p.105.

[82] *Pigott v Stratton* (1859) 1 D.F. & J. 33 at 51; *Citizens' Bank of Louisiana v First National Bank of New Orleans* (1873) L.R. 6 H.L. 352 at 360; *Maddison v Alderson* (1883) 8 App.Cas. 467 at 473; *Chadwick v Manning* [1896] A.C. 231 at 238.

[83] See above, p.110.

[84] See above, p.111.

[85] This point accounts for the rule that estoppel *by representation* does not give rise to a cause of action: below p.403. If, for example, A represents to B that B's goods are in C's possession, the fact that A is estopped from denying the truth of that representation does not turn A into a bailee of those goods. The rule that *promissory* estoppel does not give rise to a cause of action is based on different grounds explained at p.112, above.

doctrine, by contrast, has nothing to do with proof of facts; it is concerned with the *legal effects* of a promise. There was, for example, no dispute about facts, in *Hughes v Metropolitan Ry*[86]: the issue was not whether the repairs had been done or whether the landlord had promised or represented that he would not forfeit the lease; it was simply whether he was (to some extent, at least) bound by that promise.

(g) ANALOGY WITH WAIVER. It is submitted that the characteristics just described indicate that the equitable doctrine is not truly analogous with estoppel by representation. As Denning J. (a leading proponent of the modern equitable doctrine) has pointed out, the authorities which support it "although they are said to be cases of estoppel, are not really such".[87] The doctrine has closer affinities with the common law rules of waiver in the sense of forbearance: both are based on promises, or representations of intention; both are suspensive (rather than extinctive) in effect and both are concerned with the legal effects of promises rather than with proof of disputed facts. The main difference between them is that the equitable doctrine avoids the difficulties encountered at common law in distinguishing between a variation and a forbearance.[88]

There is now much judicial support for these submissions. Lord Pearson has said that "promissory estoppel" was "far removed from the familiar estoppel by representation of fact and seems . . . to be more like waiver of contractual rights".[89] In many later cases "waiver" and "promissory estoppel" (or the rule in *Hughes v Metropolitan Ry*)[90] are treated as substantially similar doctrines.[91] The two expressions have been judicially described as "two ways of saying exactly the same thing"[92]; and, although the use of terminology has not been wholly consistent,[93] the courts often use the two expressions interchangeably when discussing situations in which it is alleged that one party has indicated that he will not enforce his strict legal rights against the other. This usage

---

[86] (1877) 2 App. Cas. 439, above, p.105. The application of the principle of this case in *Central London Property Trust Ltd v High Trees House Ltd* [1947] K.B. 130 (below p.131) likewise did not give rise to any dispute about facts.

[87] *Central London Property Trust Ltd v High Trees House Ltd* [1947] K.B. 130 at 134; below, p.121.

[88] See above, pp.103–105.

[89] *Woodhouse AC Israel Cocoa Ltd v Nigerian Produce Marketing Co Ltd* [1972] A.C. 741 at 762.

[90] (1877) 2 App.Cas. 439; above, p.105.

[91] *Ogilvy v Hope-Davies* [1976] 1 All E.R. 683 at 688–689; *Finagrain SA Geneva v p.Kruse Hamburg* [1976] 2 Lloyd's Rep. 508 at 534; *Bremer Handelsgesellschaft mbH v C. Mackprang Jr* [1979] 1 Lloyd's Rep. 221 at 226; *Brikom Investments Ltd v Carr* [1979] Q.B. 467 at 488, 489, 490; *Bremer Handelsgesellschaft mbH v Westzucker GmbH* [1981] 1 Lloyd's Rep. 207 at 212–213; *Bremer Handelsgesellschaft mbH v Mackprang Jr* [1981] 1 Lloyd's Rep. 292 at 298; *Bremer Handelsgesellschaft mbH v Bunge Corp.* [1983] 1 Lloyd's Rep. 476 at 484; *BICC Ltd v Burndy Corp.* [1985] Ch. 232 at 253; *The Chemical Venture* [1993] 1 Lloyd's Rep. 509 at 521.

[92] *Prosper Homes v Hambro's Bank Executor & Trustee Co* (1979) 39 P. & C.R. 395 at 401; *The Nerano* [1996] 1 Lloyd's Rep. 1 at 6.

[93] For suggestions that "waiver" may be distinguishable from the equitable doctrine, see *W J Alan & Co Ltd v El Nasr Export Co* [1972] 2 Q.B. 189 at 212; *The Ion* [1980] 2 Lloyd's Rep. 245 at 249–250; *Brikom Investments Ltd v Carr* [1979] Q.B. 467 at 485, 489 (perhaps because there the "waiver" amounted to a variation supported by consideration). In *The Superhulls Cover Case (No.2)* [1990] 2 Lloyd's Rep. 431 at 449 "waiver" is distinguished from "equitable estoppel" on the ground that the former doctrine requires the party who is alleged to have lost his rights to know the material facts, while the latter is not subject to any such requirements. But when "waiver" is said to be subject to this requirement, the reference is to "waiver" in the sense of election between remedies (below, p.811) and not to "waiver" in the sense of relinquishing rights; and it is this latter type of waiver which is here under discussion. The reference in *Union Eagle Ltd v Golden Achievements Ltd* [1997] A.C. 514 at 518 to "waiver or estoppel" is likewise to election between remedies. This was also the type of "waiver" under consideration in *Oliver Ashworth (Holdings) Ltd v Ballard (Kent) Ltd* [2000] Ch. 12 at 27, 28 and in *The Happy Day* [2002] EWCA Civ 1068, [2002] 2 Lloyd's Rep. 487 at [67].

indicates that the equitable doctrine is more closely akin to waiver (in the sense of forbearance) than to true estoppel by representation of fact.

(h) DISTINGUISHED FROM PROMISES SUPPORTED BY CONSIDERATION. Under the equitable doctrine, certain limited effects are given to a promise without consideration. But it is nevertheless in the interests of the promisee to show, if he can, that he did provide consideration so that the promise amounted to a contractually binding variation. Such proof will free him from the many rules that restrict the scope of the equitable doctrine: he need not then show that he has "relied" on the promise, or that it would be "inequitable" for the other party to go back on it; the variation will permanently affect the rights of the promisor and not merely suspend them (unless it is expressed so as to have only a temporary effect); and a contractual variation can not only reduce or extinguish existing rights but also create new ones. Where parties agree to modify an existing contract, the equitable doctrine (and its common law counterpart of waiver) may have reduced, but they have by no means eliminated, the practical importance of the doctrine of consideration.

(i) OTHER JURISDICTIONS. The English view that the doctrine of promissory estoppel gives rise to no cause of action has not been followed in other common law jurisdictions. In the United States, a similar doctrine has long been regarded as being capable of creating new rights, though both the existence and the content of the resulting rights are matters for the discretion of the courts.[94] A line of Australian cases likewise supports the view that promises or representations which, for want of consideration or of contractual intention, lack contractual force may nevertheless be enforceable as if they were binding contracts. The leading Australian case is *Waltons Stores (Interstate) Ltd v Maher*,[95] where A, a prospective lessor of business premises, did demolition and building work on the premises while the agreement for the lease lacked contractual force because it was still subject to contract[96]; he had done so to meet the prospective lessee's (B's) requirements and on the assumption, of which B must have known, that a binding contract would come into existence. B withdrew from the agreement (relying on his solicitor's advice that he was not bound by it); and it was held that he was estopped from denying that a contract had come into existence and that the agreement for the lease was therefore specifically enforceable against him. The reasoning of the High Court is complex, but the basis of the decision appears to be that B had knowingly induced A to believe that a binding contract would come into existence by exchange of contracts[97] and to act in reasonable reliance on that belief. In English law, such reliance is, in appropriate circumstances, capable of giving rise to a variety of remedies, even where the promise or representation which induces it lacks contractual force. Sometimes the remedy may be the enforcement of the promise according to its terms, as in cases of proprietary estoppel (to be discussed later in this Chapter)[98]; sometimes it may be an award of the reasonable value of work done in the belief that a contract had, or would, come into existence.[99] Neither of these remedies would have been available in the *Waltons Stores* case since

---

[94] *Restatement*, Contracts §90 and *Restatement 2d*, Contracts §90. In English law, the need to use the doctrine to give rise to a cause of action is less acute than in the US, where the courts are less ready than the English courts to "invent" consideration (above, p.71).

[95] (1988) 164 C.L.R. 387; Duthie, 104 L.Q.R. 362; Sutton, 1 J.C.L. 205.

[96] See above, p.52.

[97] For this requirement, see above, p.53.

[98] *e.g.*, in *Dillwyn v Llewelyn* (1862) 4 D.F. & G. 517, below, p.135.

[99] *e.g.*, in *William Lacey (Hounslow) Ltd v Davis* [1954] 1 Q.B. 428; *Countrywide Communications Ltd v ICL Pathways Ltd* [2000] C.L.C. 325; *cf.* below, p.989.

proprietary estoppel does not arise where work is done on the promisee's (rather than on the promisor's) land[1] and a claim for the reasonable value of the claimant's work is not available where he is aware of the fact that no binding agreement has come into existence and so takes the risk that the negotiations may fail.[2] Even where the second of these objections can be overcome (*e.g.* on the ground that the work was done at the request of the promisor or as a result of his assurance that an exchange of contracts would take place) it does not follow that the appropriate remedy is enforcement of the contract in its terms: if the basis of the Australian doctrine is reliance induced by the promisor, compensation for reliance loss would appear to be the more appropriate remedy. The Australian doctrine also gives rise to the difficulties that there appear to be no clear limits to its scope, and that this lack of clarity is a regrettable source of uncertainty. The doctrine is, moreover, hard to reconcile with a number of fundamental principles of English law, such as the non-enforceability of informal gratuitous promises (even if relied on)[3] and the rule that there is no right to damages for a wholly innocent non-contractual misrepresentation.[4] While on the facts of some of the cases in which the Australian doctrine has been applied the same conclusions would probably be reached in English law on other grounds,[5] the broad doctrine remains, in the present context, inconsistent with the view that the English doctrine of promissory estoppel (like that of estoppel by representation)[6] does not give rise to a cause of action in the sense of entitling the promisee to enforce a promise in its terms, even though it was unsupported by consideration. It is true that other forms of estoppel, such as proprietary estoppel, may produce this result; but the scope of that doctrine is limited in many important ways[7] and the law would present an incongruous appearance if those limits could be outflanked simply by invoking the broader Australian doctrine.

(j) DISTINGUISHED FROM ESTOPPEL BY CONVENTION. Estoppel by convention may arise where both[8] parties to a transaction "act on an assumed state of facts or law,[9] the assumption being either shared by both or made by one and acquiesced in by the other".[10] The parties are then precluded from denying the truth of that assumption, if

---

[1] See below, p.139; proprietary estoppel would also probably have been excluded on the ground that the prospective lessor had no belief that a right had been or would be created in his favour while the agreement remained "subject to contract": see *Attorney-General of Hong Kong v Humphreys Estates (Queens Gardens)* [1987] 1 A.C. 114; this obstacle can be overcome if one party induces the other to believe that he will not withdraw: see *ibid.* at 124; but this qualification can scarcely enable the party *by* whom the interest in property is to be created to rely on proprietary estoppel.

[2] *Regalian Properties plc v London Dockland Development Corp* [1995] 1 W.L.R. 212.

[3] See above, p.67.

[4] *e.g.*, *Oscar Chess Ltd v Williams* [1957] 1 W.L.R. 370, below, p.354.

[5] See, for example, *Commonwealth of Australia v Verwayen* (1990) 179 C.L.R. 394, which could be explained in English law on the ground stated in n.64 on p.114, above.

[6] *Low v Bouverie* [1891] 3 Ch. 82; *Clipper Maritime Ltd v Shirlstar Container Transport Ltd (The Anemone)* [1987] 1 Lloyd's Rep. 547 at 557.

[7] *e.g.* by the requirements that the promisee must believe that legal rights have been, or will be, created in his favour, and that these are rights in or over the promisor's land: see below, pp.138–140.

[8] There can be no such estoppel where one party is not yet in existence: see *Rover International Ltd v Cannon Film Sales Ltd* [1987] B.C.L.C. 540, revsd. in part on other grounds [1989] 1 W.L.R. 912 (company not yet formed: see below, pp.734–736).

[9] See below, p.121.

[10] *The Indian Endurance (No.2)* [1998] A.C. 878 at 913; Spencer Bower and Turner, *Estoppel by Representation* (3rd ed. 1977), p.157; for qualification of this formulation, see *The Vistafjord* [1988] 2 Lloyd's Rep. 343 at 351; and see *Shearson Lehman Hutton Inc v Maclaine Watson & Co Ltd* [1989] 2 Lloyd's Rep. 570 at 596; *Phillip Collins Ltd v Davis* [2000] 3 All E.R. 808 at 823 (where there was no common assumption or acquiescence); Dawson, 9 *Legal Studies* 16.

it would be unjust or "unconscionable"[11] to allow them (or one of them) to go back on it.[12] Such an estoppel differs from estoppel by representation and from promissory estoppel[13] in that it does not depend on any "clear and unequivocal" representation or promise[14]: it can arise where the assumption was based on a mistake spontaneously made by the party relying on it, and acquiesced in by the other party. Estoppel by convention has also been said to arise out of an express agreement by which the parties had compromised a disputed claim[15]; but where such a compromise is supported by consideration in accordance with the principles discussed earlier in this Chapter[16] it is binding as a contract,[17] so that there is, it is submitted, no need to rely on estoppel by convention in order to establish the facts in dispute.

(i) *Requirements.* Estoppel by convention was discussed in *Amalgamated Investment & Property Co Ltd v Texas Commerce International Bank Ltd*,[18] where A had negotiated with the X Bank for a loan to B (one of A's subsidiaries) for the purpose of acquiring and developing a property in the Bahamas. It was agreed that the loan was to be secured by a mortgage on that property and also by a guarantee from A. In the guarantee, A promised the X Bank, in consideration of the Bank's giving credit to B, to "pay you . . . all moneys . . . due . . . *to you*" from B. This was an inappropriate form of words since the loan to B was made, not directly by the X Bank, but by one of its subsidiaries, the Y Bank, with money provided by the X Bank: hence, if the guarantee were read literally, it would not apply to the loan since no money was due from B to the X Bank. The Court of Appeal, however, took the view that this literal interpretation would defeat the intention of the parties, and held that, on its true construction, the guarantee applied to the loan made by the Y Bank.[19] But even if the guarantee did not, on its true construction, produce this result, A was estopped from denying that the guarantee covered the loan by the Y Bank, since, when negotiating the loan, A and the X Bank had assumed that the guarantee did cover it; and since the X Bank continued subsequently to act on that assumption[20] in granting various indulgences to A in respect of the loan to B and of another loan made directly by the X Bank to A. It made no difference that the assumption was not induced by any representation[21] made by A but originated in the

---

[11] *Crédit Suisse v Borough Council of Allerdale* [1995] 2 Lloyd's Rep. 315 at 367–370, affirmed on other grounds [1997] Q.B. 362.

[12] *The Vistafjord* [1988] 2 Lloyd's Rep. 343, 352; *Hiscox v Outhwaite* [1992] 1 A.C. 562, affirmed on other grounds *ibid.* 585; *Republic of India v India SS Co Ltd (No.2)* [1998] A.C. 878 at 913.

[13] *cf.* above p.115 at nn.71 and 73 for the distinction between various kinds of estoppel.

[14] *Troop v Gibson* (1986) 277 E.G. 1134; *Baird Textile Holdings Ltd v Marks & Spencer plc* [2001] EWCA Civ 274, [2002] 1 All E.R. (Comm) 737 at [84]; in *Commercial Union Assurance plc v Sun Alliance Assurance Group plc* [1992] 1 Lloyd's Rep. 475 at 481 estoppel by convention was rejected on the ground that the evidence did not "clearly and unequivocally establish the agreement of the parties on the relevant conventional interpretation"; but this statement seems to relate to quantum of proof rather than to the definition of the facts to be proved.

[15] *Colchester BC v Smith* [1992] Ch. 421 at 434.

[16] See above, p.87.

[17] *Colchester BC v Smith*, above, at 435.

[18] [1982] Q.B. 84.

[19] *cf.* on the issue of construction, *TCB Ltd v Gray* [1987] Ch. 458; *Bank of Scotland v Wright* [1990] B.C.C. 663.

[20] Contrast *Crédit Suisse v Borough Council of Allerdale* [1996] 2 Lloyd's Rep. 315 at 367, where this requirement was not satisfied as the conduct of the party alleged to be estopped had not "influenced the mind" of the other party; affirmed on other grounds [1997] Q.B. 362.

[21] A dictum in the *Crédit Suisse* case, above, at 367 which appears to treat representation as a requirement of estoppel by convention is, with respect, inconsistent with the treatment of that doctrine in the *Amalgamated Investment* case.

X Bank's own mistake: the estoppel was not one by representation but by convention.[22] The same principle was applied in *The Vistafjord*[23] where an agreement for the charter of a cruise ship had been negotiated by agents on behalf of the owners. Both the agents and the owners throughout believed that commission on this transaction would be payable under an earlier agreement but, on its true construction, this agreement gave no such rights to the agents. It was held that estoppel by convention precluded the owners from relying on the true construction of the earlier agreement, so that the agents were justified in retaining the amount of the commission out of sums received by them from the charterers.

To give rise to an estoppel by convention, the mistaken assumption of the party claiming the benefit of the estoppel must, however, have been shared or acquiesced in by the party alleged to be estopped; and both parties must have conducted themselves on the basis of such a shared assumption: the estoppel "requires communications to pass across the line between the parties. It is not enough that each of two parties acts on an assumption not communicated to the other".[24] Such communication may be effected by the conduct of one party, known to the other.[25] But no estoppel by convention arose where each party spontaneously made a different mistake and there was no subsequent conduct by the party alleged to be estopped from which any acquiescence in the other party's mistaken assumption could be inferred.[26] Nor can a party (A) invoke such an estoppel to prevent the other (B) from denying facts alleged to have been agreed between A and B if A has later withdrawn from that agreement; for in the light of A's withdrawal it is no longer unjust to allow B to rely on the true state of affairs.[27]

(ii) *Assumption of law*. It is often said that the assumption giving rise to an estoppel by convention can be one of "fact of law".[28] The point of reference to "law" in this formulation appears to be to include within the scope of the doctrine assumptions about the construction of a contract[29]; for, since the construction of a contract is often said to be a matter of "law",[30] all such assumptions would be excluded from the scope of the doctrine (and its scope be unduly narrowed) if it did not include at least assumption of this kind. The question whether estoppel by convention could be based on assumptions of "law" in a wider sense was the subject of conflicting views in *Johnson v Gore-Wood*

---

[22] *cf. The Leila* [1985] 2 Lloyd's Rep. 172; and see below, n.26.

[23] [1988] 2 Lloyd's Rep. 343; *Thornton Springer v NEM Insurance Co Ltd* [2000] 2 All E.R. 489 at 516–518; *cf.* also *Kenneth Allison Ltd v A.E. Limehouse & Co* [1992] 2 A.C. 105 at 127, *per* Lord Goff. The other members of the House of Lords took the view that there was an actual agreement (to accept service of a writ) which was legally effective even though the requirements of the Rules of the Supreme Court (with regard to personal service) had not been complied with.

[24] *The Captain Gregos (No.2)* [1990] 2 Lloyd's Rep. 395 at 405, following *The August P Leonhardt* [1985] 2 Lloyd's Rep. 28 at 35; *Hiscox v Outhwaite (No.3)* [1991] 2 Lloyd's Rep. 524 at 533; *The Indian Endurance (No.2)* [1998] A.C. 878 at 913.

[25] As in *The Vistafjord* [1988] 2 Lloyd's Rep. 343 at 351 ("very clear conduct crossing the line . . . of which the other party was fully cognisant").

[26] *The August P Leonhardt* [1985] 2 Lloyd's Rep. 28, reversing [1984] 1 Lloyd's Rep. 332, which had been followed in *The Leila*, above, n.22. The status of *The Leila* is therefore in doubt but the two cases can be reconciled on the ground that in *The Leila* there was, while in *The August P Leonhardt* there was not, conduct by the party alleged to be estopped from which acquiescence in the other party's mistaken belief could be inferred.

[27] *Gloyne v Richardson* [2001] EWCA Civ 716, [2001] 2 B.C.L.C. 669 at [41].

[28] *Amalgamated Investment* case [1982] 2 Q.B. 84 at 122, 126; *The Vistafjord* [1988] 2 Lloyd's Rep. 343 at 351; *Shearson Lehman Hutton Inc v Maclaine Watson & Co Ltd* [1989] 2 Lloyd's Rep. 570 at 596; *The Indian Endurance (No.2)* [1988] A.C. 878 at 913.

[29] Such an assumption could also be called one of "private right" and hence of fact: below, pp.314, 334.

[30] See below, pp.334, 923.

& Co.[31] In that case a company had brought a claim for professional negligence against a firm of solicitors who were told that a further claim based on the same negligence would be made against them by the company's managing director. The company's claim was settled on terms which limited some of the director's personal claims against the solicitor and when the director later brought other claims against the solicitors, it was held that this was not an abuse of process. Lord Bingham based this conclusion in part[32] on estoppel by convention: in his view, the terms of the settlement were based on the common assumption that it would not be an abuse of process for the director to pursue the claims which he had in fact brought; and it would be unfair to allow the solicitors to go back on this assumption. All the members of the House of Lords agreed with Lord Bingham's conclusion that there was no abuse of process; but Lord Goff was "reluctant to proceed on estoppel by convention"[33] as the common assumption was in his view one of law, a type of assumption which in his view did not give rise to this form of estoppel; while Lord Millett was equally reluctant to "put it on the ground of estoppel by convention" as he had "some difficulty in discerning a common assumption".[34] Lord Millett's difficulty is an entirely factual one but Lord Goff's raises a more difficult issue of principle. Support for the view that estoppel by convention can be based on a common assumption of law is admittedly based only on dicta[35]; but it is arguable that those dicta gain support from cases concerned with mistakes (and possibly misrepresentations) of law. In these fields, the distinction between matters of "law" and of "fact" has proved hard to draw and is now, at least in some context, discredited.[36] On the other hand, the extension of estoppel by convention to *all* common assumptions of "law" could undermine the security of commercial transactions by allowing a party to resist enforcement merely on account of an assumption as to the *legal effect* of a contract the terms or meaning of which were not in dispute; and this is a type of assumption which, on the authorities, does not give rise to such an estoppel.[37]

(iii) *Effect of estoppel by convention.* The effect of this form of estoppel is to preclude a party from denying the agreed or common assumption of fact or as to the meaning of a document[38] or (at least to the extent suggested above[39]) of law. One such assumption may be that a particular promise has been made[40]: thus it is possible to describe the result in the *Amalgamated Investment & Property* case by saying that A was estopped from denying that it had promised the X Bank to repay any sum left unpaid by B to the Y Bank. But, although estoppel by convention may thus take effect in relation to a promise, it is quite different in its legal nature[41] from promissory estoppel. In cases of promissory estoppel, the promisor or representor is not estopped from denying that the promise or representation *has been made*: on the contrary, this must be proved to establish that kind of estoppel, which is concerned with the *legal effects* of a promise that has been shown to exist. Where, on the other hand, the requirements of estoppel by convention are satisfied, then this type of estoppel operates to prevent a party from

---

[31] [2001] 1 All E.R. 481.

[32] See *ibid.* at 501–502 for an alternative ground for Lord Bingham's decision. Lords Cooke and Hutton agreed with Lord Bingham on the "abuse of process' point but without referring to estoppel by convention.

[33] *ibid.* at 508.

[34] *ibid.* at 527.

[35] See above, p.119 at n.9; above, n.28.

[36] See below, pp.313–314, 333.

[37] See below, p.124.

[38] *Amalgamated Investment & Property* case [1982] 2 Q.B. 84 at 126, 130.

[39] See above, pp.121–122.

[40] Such an assumption is one of fact (and not as to the future).

[41] See above, p.116.

denying a *fact*,[42] *i.e.* that the assumed promise *has been made*, or that a promise contains the assumed term: it does not specify the *legal effects* of the assumed promise or term.[43] In the *Amalgamated Investment & Property* case, once A was estopped from denying the *existence* of the promise described above, no question arose as to its legal *validity*. There could be no doubt that that promise was supported by consideration[44]: this was provided by the X Bank in making funds available to the Y Bank to enable it to make a loan to B, and in inducing the Y Bank to make that loan.[45] Where the assumed promise is one that would, if actually made, have been unsupported by consideration, both types of estoppel can, however, operate in the same case: estoppel by convention to establish the existence of the promise, and promissory estoppel to determine its legal effect.[46]

Estoppel by convention does not operate prospectively, so that "once the common assumption is revealed to be erroneous the estoppel will not apply to future dealings".[47]

(iv) *Whether estoppel by convention can create new rights.* We have seen that promissory estoppel does not "create new causes of action where none existed before"[48]; and the same principle applies to estoppel by representation.[49] Estoppel by convention resembles estoppel by representation in that it can prevent a party from denying existing *facts*, and one would therefore expect estoppel by convention to operate only where its effect was defensive in substance. The question whether estoppel by convention is so limited was discussed in the *Amalgamated Investment & Property* case where, however, it was not necessary to decide the point. The action was brought because the X Bank had sought to apply money due from it to A under another transaction in discharge of A's alleged liability under A's guarantee of B's debt. Hence the effect of the estoppel was to provide the X Bank with a defence to A's claim for a declaration that it was not entitled to apply the money in that way. Eveleigh L.J. said: "I do not think that the bank could have succeeded in a claim on the guarantee itself."[50] Brandon L.J. seems to have taken the view that the bank could have sued on the guarantee, but to have based that view on the ground that the loan agreement between A and the X Bank imposed an obligation on A to give the guarantee: hence it was that agreement, and not the estoppel, which would have given rise to the X Bank's cause of action, if it had sued on the guarantee.[51] Lord Denning M.R. expressed the principle of estoppel by convention in such a way as to enable it to give rise to a cause of action[52]; but he was alone in stating the principle so

---

[42] In this respect its legal nature resembles that of estoppel by representation: see above, p.116.

[43] *The Vistafjord* [1988] 2 Lloyd's Rep. 343 at 351 ("not dependent on contract but on common assumption"). For this reason the citation in *Williams v Roffey Bros & Nicholls (Contractors) Ltd* [1991] 1 Q.B. 1 at 17–18 of the *Amalgamated Investment & Property* case seems, with respect, to be of doubtful relevance. In the *Williams* case there was no doubt that the promise had been made; and the actual decision was that it was supported by consideration and thus binding contractually: above, p.95.

[44] This was also true in *The Vistafjord* [1988] 2 Lloyd's Rep. 343, above, p.121.

[45] It is enough that consideration moved from the promisee (the X Bank): above, p.81.

[46] *e.g.* (apparently) *Troop v Gibson* (1986) 277 E.G. 1134.

[47] *Hiscox v Outhwaite* [1992] A.C. 562 at 575, *per* Lord Donaldson M.R. (affirmed *ibid.* at 585 on other grounds); *Phillip Collins Ltd v Davis* [2000] 3 All E.R. 808 at 823.

[48] *Combe v Combe* [1951] 2 K.B. 215 at 219; above, p.112.

[49] See above, p.112; below, p.403.

[50] [1982] Q.B. 84 at 126.

[51] *ibid.* at 132. For a different interpretation of Brandon L.J.'s judgment, see *Baird Textile Holdings Ltd v Marks & Spencer plc* [2001] EWCA Civ 274; [2002] 1 All E.R. (Comm) 737, at [84]. The alleged estoppel in the *Baird* case was regarded at first instance as one "by convention" (at [20]) but it is far from clear whether the Court of Appeal so regarded it.

[52] [1982] Q.B. 84 at 122. A similar view may be hinted at in *Williams v Roffey Bros & Nicholls (Contractors) Ltd* [1991] 1 Q.B. 1 at 17–18; but see above, n.43.

broadly.[53] In *The Vistafjord*[54] the estoppel similarly operated defensively. This factor was not stressed in the judgments, but there is no suggestion in them that in this respect estoppel by convention differs from estoppel by representation, which does not, of itself, give rise to a cause of action.[55] It is indeed, possible for estoppel by convention (as it is for promissory estoppel[56] and estoppel by representation) to deprive the defendant of a *defence* and so to enable the claimant to win an action which otherwise he would have lost[57]; but even in such cases the estoppel does not create the cause of action, for the *facts giving rise to* the cause of action exist independently of the estoppel.[58] No other authority squarely supports the view that estoppel by convention can, of itself, create a new cause of action; and the present position seems to be that it cannot, any more than promissory estoppel or estoppel by representation, produce this effect.[59]

(v) *Invalidity of assumed term.* A party is not liable on the basis of estoppel by convention where the alleged agreement would, if concluded, have been ineffective for want of contractual intention,[60] or on account of a formal defect[61] (other than a minor one[62]) or where the term in respect of which such an estoppel is alleged to operate would, if actually incorporated in the contract, have been invalid[63]; nor does such an estoppel prevent a party from relying on the true legal effect (as opposed to the meaning[64]) of an admitted contract merely because the parties have entered into it under a mistaken view as to that effect.[65]

---

[53] *Keen v Holland* [1984] 1 W.L.R. 251 at 261–262. In *Wilson Bowden Properties Ltd v Milner & Bardon* [1996] C.L.Y. 1229 the cause of action arose out of the undisputed contract and not out of the estoppel.

[54] [1988] 2 Lloyd's Rep. 343; above, p.112. In *Shearson Lehman Hutton Inc v Maclaine Watson & Co Ltd* [1989] 2 Lloyd's Rep. 570 the estoppel would likewise (if supported on the facts) have operated defensively. *cf. Mitsui Babcock Energy Ltd v John Brown Energy Ltd* (1996) Const.L.R. 125 at 185–186 where the estoppel, if it had been necessary to invoke it, would have restricted the claimant's rights.

[55] See below, p.403.

[56] See above, pp.115.

[57] This was the effect of the estoppel in *The Amazonia* [1990] 1 Lloyd's Rep. 238, where it operated to prevent a party from relying on facts giving rise to a mistake nullifying consent (below, p.286) and where the effect of allowing him to rely on those facts would have been to bar the other party's claim by lapse of time. For the possibility that estoppel by convention may deprive a party of a defence, see also *Azov Shipping Co v Baltic Shipping Co* [1999] 1 Lloyd's Rep. 159 at 175–176; semble this is subject to the limitation discussed with regard to promissory estoppel at p.114, above.

[58] *cf. Johnson v Gore Wood & Co* [2001] 1 All E.R. 481 (above, pp.121–122) where the estoppel likewise did not create the cause of action, which was based on the alleged negligence of the defendant solicitors; it merely helped to dispose of the defendants' objection that the action to enforce that claim was an abuse of process.

[59] *Russell Bros (Paddington) Ltd v John Elliott Management Ltd* (1995) 11 Const.L.J. 377. Contrast dicta in *Thornton Springer v NEM Insurance Co Ltd* [2000] 2 All E.R. 489 at 516–518, which seem to assume that estoppel by convention can give rise to new rights. This aspect of the case gives rise to the same difficulty as that discussed in relation to promissory estoppel at p.113, above. The actual decision in the *Thornton Springer* case was that there was a contract supported by consideration in the form of "an implied promise not to take proceedings" (at 516): see above, p.90.

[60] *Orion Insurance plc v Sphere Drake Insurance* [1992] 1 Lloyd's Rep. 239.

[61] *Yaxley v Gotts* [2000] Ch. 162 at 182.

[62] *cf. Shah v Shah* [2001] EWCA Civ 527, [2001] 4 All E.R. 138, at [31] (deed signed but not in presence of attesting witness); contrast *ibid.* at [28] (deed not signed at all). The case was one of estoppel by representation.

[63] See *Keen v Holland* [1984] 1 W.L.R. 251; *Godden Merthyr Tydfil Housing Association* (1997) 74 P. & C.R. D1; contrast *The Amazonia* [1990] 1 Lloyd's Rep. 238 (illegality under foreign law).

[64] See above, p.121.

[65] *Keen v Holland*, above, n.63; *cf. The Nile Rhapsody* [1992] 2 Lloyd's Rep. 399 at 408, affirmed, on another ground [1994] 1 Lloyd's Rep. 382.

4. Part Payment of a Debt

(1) General rule

The general rule of common law is that a creditor is not bound by an undertaking to accept part payment in full settlement of a debt. An accrued debt can be discharged only by accord and satisfaction.[66] A promise by the debtor to pay part of the debt provides no consideration for the accord, as it is merely a promise to perform part of an existing duty owed to the creditor. And the actual part payment is no satisfaction under the rule in *Pinnel's* case that "Payment of a lesser sum on the day in satisfaction of a greater sum cannot be any satisfaction for the whole."[67] This rule was approved by the House of Lords in *Foakes v Beer*.[68] Mrs Beer had obtained a judgment against Dr Foakes for £2,090 19s. Sixteen months later Dr Foakes asked for time to pay. Thereupon the parties entered into a written agreement[69] under which Mrs Beer undertook not to take "any proceedings whatsoever" on the judgment, in consideration of an immediate payment by Dr Foakes of £500 and on condition[70] of his paying specified instalments "until the whole of the said sum of £2,090 19s. shall have been paid and satisfied". Some five years later, when Dr Foakes had paid £2,090 19s., Mrs Beer claimed £360[71] for interest on the judgment debt. The House of Lords upheld her claim, and the actual decision does not appear to be unjust; for it seems that Mrs Beer intended only to give Dr Foakes time to pay, and not to forgive interest.[72]

The rule in *Pinnel's* case may sometimes have served the useful purpose of protecting a creditor against a debtor who had too ruthlessly exploited the tactical advantage of being a potential defendant in litigation.[73] For example, in *D & C Builders Ltd v Rees*[74] the claimants had done building work for the defendant and had presented an account of which some £482 was outstanding. Six months after payment had first been demanded, the defendant's wife (acting on his behalf) offered the claimants £300 in full settlement. They accepted this offer as they were in desperate straits financially; and there was some evidence that the defendant's wife knew this.[75] It was held that the claimants were entitled to the balance; and a majority[76] of the Court of Appeal based their decision on the rule in *Pinnel's* case.

On the other hand, it is arguable that the function of protecting the creditor in such a situation is now satisfactorily performed by the expanding concept of economic duress,[77] while the rule in *Pinnel's* case is open to two main objections. First, it applies

---

[66] See above, p.100.

[67] (1602) 5 Co.Rep. 117a; *Cumber v Wane* (1721) 1 Stra. 426; *McManus v Bark* (1870) L.R. 5 Ex. 65; *Underwood v Underwood* [1894] p.204; *Tilney Engineering v Admos Knitting Machinery* [1987] 2 C.L. 21; *Re Broderick* (1986) 6 N.I.J.B. 36.

[68] (1884) 9 App.Cas. 605; Dixon, *Jesting Pilate*, 159–165.

[69] Drawn up by Dr Foakes' solicitor: (1884) 9 App.Cas. 625.

[70] Dr Foakes made no promise to pay the instalments.

[71] *Beer v Foakes* (1883) 11 Q.B.D. 221 at 222.

[72] Lords Fitzgerald and Watson thought that the agreement did not, on its true construction, cover interest. Lords Selborne and Blackburn sympathised with this view but felt unable to adopt it as the operative part of the document was too "clear" to be controlled by the recitals.

[73] As Dr Foakes appears to have done. Kelly, 27 M.L.R. 540, argues that there is consideration in giving up this advantage, as there is in the compromise of a disputed claim. This may be so, but a compromise is only binding if there is a *bona fide* dispute as to liability (above, p.90) and there was no such dispute in *Foakes v Beer*.

[74] [1966] 2 Q.B. 617; Chorley, 29 M.L.R. 165; Cornish, 29 M.L.R. 428.

[75] [1966] 2 Q.B. 617 at 622.

[76] Lord Denning M.R. based his decision on a different ground: see below, pp.134–135.

[77] *cf.* above, p.95 and below, pp.405–407. A debtor who by any deception dishonestly induces the creditor to accept part payment of a debt in full settlement may also be guilty of an offence under Theft Act 1978, s.2: see Treitel in *Essays in Memory of Sir Rupert Cross*, pp.90–92.

to all agreements to accept part payment of debts in full settlement, even though some such agreements are perfectly fair and reasonable transactions.[78] Secondly, as Lord Blackburn said in *Foakes v Beer*, part payment is often in fact more beneficial to the creditor than strict insistence on his full legal rights.[79] A factual benefit[80] of a similar kind has been accepted as sufficient consideration for a promise to make an extra payment for the performance of an existing contractual duty owed by the promisee to the promisor[81]; and the law would be more consistent, as well as more satisfactory in its practical operation, if it adopted the same approach to cases of part payment of a debt. Agreements of the kind here under discussion would then be binding unless they had been made under duress. But the rule in *Foakes v Beer* is open to challenge only in the House of Lords.[82] In the meantime, its operation is mitigated by limitations on its scope at common law and by evasions of it in equity.

(2) Common law limitations

(a) DISPUTED CLAIMS. The general rule does not apply where the creditor's claim (or its amount) is disputed in good faith.[83] In such cases, the value of the claim is doubtful and the debtor accordingly provides consideration by paying something, even though it is less than the amount claimed. It makes no difference that the amount paid is small in relation to the amount claimed, or that the creditor has a good chance of succeeding on the claim; for the law will not generally investigate the adequacy of consideration.[84]

Where the defendant admits liability for less than the amount claimed, payment of the smaller sum is no consideration for the claimant's promise to accept that payment in full settlement of the larger claim. The rule in *Foakes v Beer* applies since, once a binding admission has been made to pay the smaller sum, the payment of it amounts to no more than the performance of what, at that stage, is legally due from the defendant.[85]

(b) UNLIQUIDATED CLAIMS. The general rule applies only if the original claim is also a "liquidated" one, *i.e.* a claim for a fixed sum of money, such as one for money lent or for the agreed price of goods[86] or services. It does not apply to "unliquidated" claims[87] such as claims for damages or for a reasonable remuneration (where none is fixed by the contract). In such cases, the claim is of uncertain value; and even if the overwhelming

---

[78] *e.g.* on the facts of *Central London Property Trust Ltd v High Trees House Ltd* [1947] K.B. 130; below, pp.130–131.

[79] (1884) 9 App.Cas. 605 at 617–620.

[80] See above, p.69.

[81] *Williams v Roffey Bros & Nicholls (Contractors) Ltd* [1991] 1 Q.B. 1, above, p.95.

[82] See *Re Selectmove Ltd* [1995] 1 W.L.R. 474 where the Court of Appeal refused to apply the principle of the *Williams* case; above in the present context; Peel, 110 L.Q.R. 353.

[83] *Cooper v Parker* (1885) 15 C.B. 822; *Re Warren* (1884) 53 L.J. Ch. 1016; *Anangel Atlas Compania Naviera SA v Ishikawajima Harima Heavy Industries Co Ltd (No.2)* [1990] 2 Lloyd's Rep. 526 at 544; for other consideration in this case, see *ibid.* at 545 and below, p.117; *Huyton SA v Peter Cremer GmbH* [1999] 1 Lloyd's Rep. 620 at 629.

[84] See above, p.73. But the fact that the sum received is much smaller than that claimed may be evidence that the recipient has not accepted it in full settlement: *Rustenburg Platinum Mines Ltd v Pan Am* [1979] 1 Lloyd's Rep. 19.

[85] *Ferguson v Davies* [1997] 1 All E.R. 315, *per* Henry L.J.; Evans L.J.'s judgment is based on the ground that, as a matter of construction, the claimant had not accepted the smaller sum in full settlement. Aldous L.J. agreed with both the other judgments.

[86] A claim may be "liquidated" even though it is disputed and even though the dispute relates to its amount: *e.g.* where it is for the price of goods and the buyer alleges short delivery: *The New Vanguard* [1994] 1 W.L.R. 1634.

[87] *Wilkinson v Byers* (1834) 1 A. & E. 106; *Ibberson v Neck* (1886) 2 T.L.R. 427.

probability is that it is worth more than the sum paid, the possibility that it may be worth less suffices to satisfy the requirement of consideration.

An originally unliquidated claim may later become liquidated by act of the parties. For example, in *D & C Builders v Rees*[88] it does not seem that the contract fixed the price of the work to be done by the claimants. When they presented their account they had only an unliquidated claim (for a reasonable remuneration); and if at this stage they had accepted £300 in full settlement they would not have been protected by the rule in *Foakes v Beer*. That rule only became applicable because the defendant had, by retaining the account without protest, impliedly agreed that it correctly stated the sum due, and so turned the claim into a liquidated one.[89]

A creditor may have two claims against the same debtor, one of them liquidated and the other unliquidated; or a single claim which is partly liquidated and partly unliquidated. A promise by the creditor to release the *whole* claim will not be binding if the debtor pays no more than the liquidated amount and if his liability to pay this amount is undisputed. For example, in *Arrale v Costain Civil Engineering Ltd*[90] an employee was injured at work. Legislation in force at the place of work gave him an undisputed right against the employers to a fixed lump sum of £490 and it was assumed that he also had a common law right to sue the employers in tort for unliquidated damages.[91] It was held that any promise[92] which he might have made not to pursue the common law claim was not made binding by the employers' payment of the £490. They had not provided any consideration for such a promise since, in making that payment, they merely did what they were already bound to do.[93]

(c) VARIATIONS IN DEBTOR'S PERFORMANCE. Consideration for a creditor's promise to accept part payment in full settlement can be provided by the debtor's doing an act that he was not previously bound by the contract to do.[94] For example, payment of a smaller sum at the creditor's request before the due day is good consideration for a promise to forego the balance, since it is a benefit to the creditor to receive (and a corresponding detriment to the debtor to make) such early payment.[95] The same applies, *mutatis mutandis*, where payment of a smaller sum is made at the creditor's request at a place different from that originally fixed for payment,[96] or in a different currency.[97] Again, payment of a smaller sum accompanied at the creditor's request by the delivery of a chattel is good consideration for a promise to forego the balance: "The gift of a horse, hawk or robe, etc., in satisfaction is good. For it shall be intended that a horse, hawk or robe, etc., might be more beneficial than the money. . . . ".[98]

---

[88] [1966] 2 Q.B. 617; above, p.125.

[89] *cf. Amantilla v Telefusion* (1987) 9 Con. L.R. 139, where a builder's *quantum meruit* claim which had not been disputed was treated as "liquidated claim" for the purpose of Limitation Act 1980, s.29(5)(a).

[90] [1976] 1 Lloyd's Rep. 98; *cf. Rustenburg Platinum Mines Ltd v Pan Am* [1979] 1 Lloyd's Rep 19 at 24.

[91] *cf.* below, p.206.

[92] Lord Denning M.R. and Stephenson L.J. took the view that no such promise had been made.

[93] *Per* Stephenson and Geoffrey Lane L.JJ. Lord Denning M.R. based his decision on a different ground: below, p.134.

[94] *e.g. Re William Porter & Co* [1937] 2 All E.R. 261: *Ledingham v Bermejo Estancia Co Ltd* [1947] 2 All E.R. 748.

[95] *Pinnel's* case, above, p.125.

[96] *ibid.*

[97] *cf.* above, p.101.

[98] *Pinnel's* case, above. Many cases formerly supported the view that part payment by a negotiable instrument, made at the request of the creditor and accepted by him in full settlement, discharged the debt. But these cases were overruled in *D & C Builders Ltd v Rees* [1966] 2 Q.B. 617.

(d) OTHER BENEFIT TO CREDITOR. We have seen that a promise to pay a supplier of services more than the agreed sum for performing his part of the contract can be supported by consideration in the form of a benefit in fact obtained by the other party as a result of his obtaining the promised performance.[99] Conversely, a promise by the supplier to accept less than the agreed sum may be supported by a similar consideration. The mere receipt of the smaller sum cannot, indeed, constitute the consideration: that possibility is precluded by *Foakes v Beer*.[1] But the performance by the debtor of *other* obligations under the contract may confer such a benefit on the creditor and so satisfy the requirement of consideration. This possibility is illustrated by the *Anangel Atlas*[2] case, where a shipbuilder's promise to reduce the price which the buyers had agreed to pay was held to have been supported by consideration, and one way in which the buyers had provided consideration was by accepting delivery on the day fixed for such acceptance. Even if the buyers were already bound to take delivery on that day, they had conferred a benefit on the shipbuilder by so doing since they were "core customers"[3] and their refusal to take delivery might have led other actual or potential customers to cancel (or not to place) orders.

(e) FORBEARANCE TO ENFORCE CROSS-CLAIM. The debtor may have a cross-claim against the creditor; and forbearance to enforce such a claim can constitute consideration for the creditor's promise to accept part payment in full settlement. For example, where a landlord promises to accept part payment of rent in full settlement, the tenant may provide consideration for this promise by forbearing to sue the landlord for breach of the latter's obligation to keep the premises in repair.[4]

(f) PART PAYMENT BY THIRD PARTY. Part payment by a third party, if accepted by the creditor in full settlement of the debtor's liability,[5] is a good defence to a later action by the creditor against the debtor for the balance.[6]

It is generally agreed that this rule does not depend on any contract between debtor and creditor, so that it can apply even though no promise was made to the debtor and no consideration moved from him. The rule has therefore been explained on other grounds. One such ground is that it would be a fraud on the third party to allow the creditor to sue the debtor for the balance of the debt.[7] The difficulty with this reasoning is that the mere breach of a promise does not usually amount to fraud at common law; it only has this effect if the promisor had no intention of performing the promise when he made it.[8] A second reason for the rule is that the court will not help the creditor to break his contract with the third party by allowing him to recover the balance of the debt from the debtor. On the contrary, it has been held that where A (the creditor) contracts with B (the third party) not to sue C (the debtor), and A nevertheless does sue C, B can

---

[99] *Williams v Roffey Bros & Nicholls (Contractors) Ltd* [1991] 1 Q.B. 1, above, p.95.
[1] (1884) 9 App.Cas. 605, above, p.125.
[2] *Anangel Atlas Compania Naviera SA v Ishikawajima-Harima Heavy Industries Co Ltd (No.2)* [1990] 2 Lloyd's Rep. 526. For other consideration in that case, in the form of reducing "a previously ill-defined understanding" to "precise terms," and so setting a potential dispute, see *ibid.* at 544.
[3] *ibid.* at 544.
[4] *Brikom Investments Ltd v Carr* [1979] Q.B. 467; as explained above, p.102.
[5] See below, pp.699–700 for this requirement.
[6] *Welby v Drake* (1825) 1 C. & p.557; *Cook v Lister* (1863) 13 C.B.(N.S.) 543 at 595.
[7] See the authorities cited in n.6, above.
[8] See below, pp.331–332.

intervene so as to obtain a stay of the action.[9] A third explanation is suggested by *Hirachand Punamchand v Temple*,[10] where the defendant was indebted to the claimant on a promissory note. The claimant accepted a smaller sum from the defendant's father in full settlement. It was held that he could not later sue the defendant for the balance of the debt, because the promissory note was extinct: the position was the same as if the note had been cancelled.[11] This reasoning again does not depend on any contract between the claimant and the defendant, for the cancellation of a promissory note can release a person liable on it irrespective of contract and without consideration.[12] Under the Contracts (Rights of Third Parties) Act 1999, the debtor may also, if the requirements of the Act are satisfied,[13] be able to take the benefit of any term in the contract between the creditor and the person making the payment which may exclude the debtor's liability for the balance; and he will be able to do so without having to show that he provided any consideration for the creditor's promise to accept the part payment in full settlement.[14]

(g) COMPOSITION AGREEMENTS. A debtor who cannot pay all his creditors in full may be able to induce them to agree with himself and each other to accept a dividend in full settlement of their claims.[15] A creditor who has accepted a dividend under such an agreement cannot sue the debtor for the balance of his original demand.[16] If the debtor fails to pay the agreed dividend, the original debt revives.[17]

One reason why such composition agreements are binding is again said to be that a creditor who sued for the balance of his debt would commit a fraud on the others.[18] On this view it is unnecessary to look for any consideration moving from the debtor. Another possible reason for the rule is that the debtor may be prejudiced by forbearing to have himself adjudicated bankrupt. But it is hard to see how this can be consideration if the debtor's whole object in agreeing to the composition was to avoid bankruptcy.[19] And if such a forbearance were consideration for a composition with several creditors, why is it not consideration for a composition with one? The same objection applies to the theory that the debtor can provide consideration by the act of executing the composition agreement. The debtor may, however, provide consideration by procuring a third party to act as surety for his promise to pay the dividend.[20] A final justification for the rule, stated in some of the relevant judgments, is that there is consideration for the creditors' promise to forgo the balance since each creditor benefits from the arrangement: he is

---

[9] *Snelling v John G Snelling Ltd* [1973] 1 Q.B. 87, distinguishing *Gore v Van der Lann* [1967] 2 Q.B. 31, where no promise was made not to sue C; *cf. South West Trains Ltd v Wightman*, *The Times*, January 14, 1998.

[10] [1911] 2 K.B. 330.

[11] At 336. *cf.* in the case of joint debts, the reasoning of *Johnson v Davies* [1999] Ch. 117 at 130.

[12] See above, p.101.

[13] See below, pp.651 *et seq.*

[14] See above, p.83, below, p.656. For the purposes of the Act, it is the debtor who is the "third party".

[15] Provision for publicity and substantial agreement among creditors is made by the Deeds of Arrangement Act 1914 (repealed in part by Insolvency Act 1985, s.235 and Sch.10, Pt III and amended by Insolvency Act 1986, s.439(2)). *Oral* agreements are not caught by the 1914 Act; *Hughes & Falconer v Newton* [1939] 2 All E.R. 869. "Voluntary arrangements" under Insolvency Act 1986, Pts I and VIII can, by virtue of ss.5(2) and 260(2), bind even a creditor who did not attend the meeting or dissented from the proposal "as if he were a party to the arrangement:" see *Johnson v Davies* [1999] Ch. 117 at 138; *cf. Re Cancol Ltd* [1996] 1 All E.R. 37. And see *Re a Debtor (No.259 of 1990)* [1990] 1 W.L.R. 226.

[16] *Good v Cheesman* (1831) 2 B. & Ad. 328; *Boyd v Hind* (1857) 1 H. & n.938; the bare *agreement* to pay a dividend may operate as satisfaction, if the parties so intend: *Bradley v Gregory* (1810) 2 Camp. 383.

[17] *Evans v Powis* (1847) 1 Ex. 601.

[18] *Wood v Roberts* (1818) 2 Stark. 417; *Cook v Lister* (1863) 13 C.B.(N.S.) 543 at 595.

[19] *cf.* above, p.83. The position might be different if the debtor really did intend to go into bankruptcy and the creditors dissuaded him by promising to accept part payment in full settlement.

[20] As in *Bradley v Gregory* (1810) 2 Camp. 383.

certain to get some payment, while in the scramble for priority which would take place if there were no composition agreement he might get nothing at all.[21]

(h) COLLATERAL CONTRACT. An agreement to accept part payment of a debt in full settlement may take effect as a collateral contract if the requirements of contractual intention and consideration are satisfied. This was the position in *Brikom Investments Ltd v Carr*[22] where a tenant's liability to contribute to the maintenance costs of a block of flats was held to have been reduced by a collateral contract under which the landlord undertook to execute certain roof repairs at his own expense.[23] The landlord's claim for contribution in this case was probably unliquidated; but the principle seems to be equally applicable where a creditor enters into a collateral contract to accept part payment in full settlement of a liquidated claim.

(3) Equitable evasion

The common law limitations can (with one exception[24]) be explained on the ground that there was, in the situations covered by them, some consideration for the creditor's promise to accept the part payment in full settlement. They assume the continued existence of the general, if often inconvenient, rule that, in the absence of such consideration, the creditor's promise was not binding. Equity went further: it made two attempts to evade that rule even where there was no consideration for the creditor's promise.

(a) EQUITABLE RELEASE. A number of early cases may support the view that in equity a creditor could release a debt by simply saying that he had done so, or was doing so.[25] Other cases, on the contrary, hold that a release was not good in equity unless it was also good at law.[26] A possible distinction between the two lines of cases is that in the first the creditor says "I hereby release the debt", while in the second he says "I promise not to sue the debtor".[27] The former statement could be regarded as a completed gift of the debt by the creditor to the debtor[28] and the latter as a mere promise not to sue (which would not be binding without consideration). But the distinction is tenuous, and it is doubtful whether the doctrine of equitable release, if it was ever established, has survived *Jorden v Money*.[29]

---

[21] *Good v Cheesman* (1831) 2 B. & Ad. 328 at 334; *Garrard v Woolner* (1832) 8 Bing. 258 at 265; *West Yorks Darracq Agency Ltd v Coleridge* [1911] 2 K.B. 326 is an unwarranted extension of the principle since the creditor got nothing: above, p.83, n.55. Even in such cases, the debtor may get the benefit of the agreement if, when he is sued by one creditor, another is entitled to, and does, intervene to stay the action under *Snelling v John G Snelling Ltd* [1973] 1 Q.B. 87, above, p.129, n.9. The debtor will not, however, be able to avoid the requirement of consideration by relying on the Contracts (Rights of Third Parties) Act 1999 (above, n.13) since this applies only in favour of "a person who is *not* a party" to the contract (s.1(1)); and in the case of a composition agreement the debtor typically *will* be a party.

[22] [1979] Q.B. 467.

[23] For the consideration supporting this promise, see above p.102, for other grounds for the decision, see below, p.133.

[24] *i.e.* cases of part payment by a third party: above, p.128. The debtor does also not need to provide consideration where he can rely on the Contracts (Rights of Third Parties) Act, 1999: above at n.14.

[25] *Wekett v Raby* (1724) 2 Bro.P.C. 386; *Richards v Syms* (1740) 2 Eq.Ca.Abr. 617; *Eden v Smyth* (1800) 5 Ves. 341; *Flower v Marten* (1837) 2 My. & Cr. 459.

[26] *Cross v Sprigg* (1849) 6 Hare 552 (reversed on other grounds: 2 Mac. & G. 113); *Major v Major* (1852) 1 Drew. 165; *Luxmore v Clifton* (1867) 17 L.T. 460.

[27] See *Reeves v Bryner* (1801) 6 Ves. 516, distinguishing *Eden v Smyth*, above.

[28] *cf. Gray v Barton*, N.Y. 68 (1873). If a creditor can make a gift of a debt to a third party by assignment (below, pp.631 *et seq.*) why should he not be able to make such a gift to the debtor?

[29] See above, p.116.

(b) EQUITABLE FORBEARANCE. Under the equitable doctrine of *Hughes v Metropolitan Ry*[30] a promise by a contracting party not to enforce his legal rights has (even where it is not supported by consideration) at least a limited effect in equity. Before 1946, this doctrine had not been applied where a creditor's promise to accept part payment of a debt in full settlement was not supported by any consideration moving from the debtor.[31] Such an extension of the rule seemed to be barred by *Foakes v Beer*.[32] The possibility of making the extension was, however, suggested in *Central London Property Trust Ltd v High Trees House Ltd*.[33] In 1937 block of flats had been let to the defendants for 99 years at a rent of £2,500 per annum. In 1940 the landlords agreed to reduce the annual rent to £1,250 as many of the flats were unlet because of war-time conditions. After the end of the war, the landlords demanded the full rent for the last two quarters of 1945 and Denning J. upheld their claim on the ground that, as a matter of construction, the 1940 agreement was intended to apply only while the war-time conditions lasted. But he also said that the landlords would have been precluded by the equitable doctrine of *Hughes v Metropolitan Ry*[34] from suing for the full rent for the period which *was* covered by the 1940 agreement. He added: "The logical consequence no doubt is that a promise to accept a smaller sum, if acted upon, is binding notwithstanding the absence of consideration."[35] The requirements and effects of the equitable doctrine have already been discussed.[36] Three points give rise to particular difficulty in its application to cases of part payment of a debt.

(i) *Effect generally suspensory.* The first difficulty is to reconcile the remarks of Denning J. in the *High Trees* case with *Foakes v Beer*.[37] If the claimant in *Foakes v Beer* could go back on her promise not to ask for interest, why could not the landlords in the *High Trees* case go back on their promise not to ask for the full rent in, say, 1941, when war-time difficulties of letting still prevailed? One possibility is to say that "that aspect was not considered in *Foakes v Beer*"[38] which was decided without reference to equity, and is therefore "no longer valid"[39]; but this is unsatisfactory, as the rule that part payment of a debt was no discharge was clearly recognised in equity.[40] Another possibility, and one which does less violence to the authorities, is to say that the creditor's right to the balance of his debt is not extinguished but only suspended.[41] This is generally the sole consequence of the principle in *Hughes v Metropolitan Ry*[42] and in

---

[30] (1877) 2 App.Cas. 439; above, p.105.

[31] The doctrine had been applied in *Buttery v Pickard* (1946) 62 T.L.R. 241 to a landlord's promise to accept payment of part of the rent in full settlement, but in that case consideration did move from the tenant in the shape of her forbearance to exercise her contractual right to terminate the lease (though this was not the *ratio decidendi* of the case).

[32] (1884) 9 App.Cas. 605; above, p.110.

[33] [1947] K.B. 130; Denning, 15 M.L.R. 1; Wilson, 67 L.Q.R. 330; Sheridan, 15 M.L.R. 325; Bennion, 16 M.L.R. 441; Guest, 30 A.L.J. 187; Turner, 1 N.Z.U.L.R. 185; Campbell, *ibid.* 232.

[34] See above, p.105.

[35] [1947] K.B. 130 at 134; *cf. Combe v Combe* [1951] 2 K.B. 215 at 220.

[36] See above, pp.105–119.

[37] (1884) 9 App.Cas. 605, above, p.125.

[38] *High Trees* case, above, at p.146; this sentence does not occur in any of the other reports of the case ([1947] L.J.R. 77; (1946) 175 L.T. 333; (1946) 62 T.L.R. 557; [1956] 1 All E.R. 256n.) The argument, with respect, lacks plausibility since *Hughes v Metropolitan Ry*, above n.34, had been decided only seven years before *Foakes v Beer* and Lords Selborne and Blackburn heard the appeals in both cases.

[39] *Arrale v Costain Civil Engineering Ltd* [1976] 1 Lloyd's Rep. 98 at 102.

[40] *Bidder v Bridges* (1887) 37 Ch.D. 406; *Re Warren* (1884) 53 L.J.Ch. 1016.

[41] *Ajayi v R T Briscoe (Nig) Ltd* [1964] 1 W.L.R. 1326, 1330; Unger, 28 M.L.R. 231; *cf. Re Venning* [1947] W.N. 196; Gordon [1963] C.L.J. 222, arguing that the equitable principle is limited to relief against forfeiture. But see Wilson [1965] C.L.J. 93.

[42] See above, p.111.

the present context it would give effect to the intention of the parties where the purpose of the arrangements was to give the debtor extra time to pay,[43] rather than to extinguish part of the debt. Of course, where the intention is to extinguish, and not merely to suspend, the creditor's right to the balance, the suggestion that the creditor is permanently bound by his promise not to sue for the balance[44] may seem to be an attractive one.[45] But such an extension of the principle of *Hughes v Metropolitan Ry* would require the overruling of *Foakes v Beer*. It is, no doubt, with such difficulties in mind that Lord Hailsham L.C. has said that the *High Trees* principle "may need to be reviewed and reduced to a coherent body of doctrine by the courts".[46]

For the present the better view is that the principle only suspends rights; but the meaning of this statement is not entirely clear where the debtor is under a continuing obligation to make a series of payments, *e.g.* of rent under a lease,[47] or of royalties under a licence to use a patent,[48] or of instalments under a hire-purchase agreement.[49] In such cases the statement may mean one of two things: first, that the creditor is entitled to payment in full only of amounts which fall due *after* the expiry of a reasonable notice of the retraction of his promise[50]; or, secondly, that he is then entitled, not only to future payments in full, but also to the unpaid balance of *past* ones. Of course the second of these views might sometimes be at variance with the intention of the parties at the time of the promise.[51] On the other hand it is hard to see why a debtor whose liability accrues from time to time should, for the present purpose, be in a more favourable position than one whose liability is to pay a single lump sum; nor is it clear which of the two views should apply where a debtor who owed a lump sum undertook to pay it off in instalments and the creditor first made, and then gave reasonable notice revoking, a promise to accept reduced instalments. In such a case, it is at least arguable that the intention of the creditor is only to give extra time for payment. Hence the total debt remains due, and the only effect of the promise is to extend the period over which it is to be repaid.[52]

There may, however, be exceptional cases where the creditor's right is wholly extinguished. We have seen that a forbearance cannot be retracted where subsequent events,

---

[43] *e.g.* in *Ajayi v R T Briscoe (Nig) Ltd*, above: see below, n.51. This seems also to have been the position in *Foakes v Beer*, above.

[44] Originally made by Lord Denning in the *High Trees* case at 134 and repeated by him in *D & C Builders Ltd v Rees* [1966] 2 Q.B. 617 at 624. *cf. W J Alan & Co Ltd v El Nasr Export & Import Co* [1972] 2 Q.B. 189, 213; and *ibid.* 218 at 220; but in that case there was consideration: above, p.101.

[45] Provided that there was no duress: *cf.* above, p.94; below, p.137.

[46] *Woodhouse AC Israel Cocoa Ltd v Nigerian Produce Marketing Co Ltd* [1972] A.C. 741 at 758; *cf. Baird Textile Holdings Ltd v Marks & Spencer plc* [2001] EWCA Civ 274; [2002] 1 All E.R. (Comm) 737, at [48] ("not yet fully developed").

[47] As in the *High Trees* case.

[48] As in the *Tool Metal* case [1955] 1 W.L.R. 761; above, p.111.

[49] As in *Ajayi v R T Briscoe (Nig) Ltd* [1964] 1 W.L.R. 1326.

[50] *Banning v Wright* [1972] 1 W.L.R. 972 at 981; *cf. W J Alan & Co Ltd v El Nasr Export & Import Co* [1972] 2 Q.B. 189 at 213. This view is apparently regarded as correct in the *Tool Metal* case, above; but the case is not conclusive as the liability of the licensee to make the payments *during* the suspension period was not directly considered by the House of Lords.

[51] This would be so in cases like the *High Trees* and *Tool Metal* cases—but not in a case like *Ajayi v R T Briscoe (Nig) Ltd*, above, n.49 as the promise there "was not intended to be irrevocable": *Meng Long Development Pte Ltd v Jip Hong Trading Pte Ltd* [1985] A.C. 511 at 524. *J T Sydenham & Co Ltd v Enichem Elastometers Ltd* [1989] 1 E.G.L.R. 257 at 260 (discussed by Cartwright, [1990] C.L.J. 13) purports to give the "estoppel" an extinctive effect; but the amount of rent due in that case was in dispute, so that the actual decision is explicable on the ground stated at p.126, above.

[52] *Hardwick v Johnson* [1978] 1 W.L.R. 683 (where the creditor was said at 699 to have agreed to "postpone" the debtor's obligation to pay instalments).

or the passage of time, make it highly inequitable[53] to require performance of the original obligation, even after reasonable notice. This principle could be applied to cases of the present kind, so that the creditor's right to the balance might be extinguished if, in reliance on that promise, the debtor had undertaken new commitments in relation to the subject-matter: *e.g.* if the tenant in the *High Trees* case had used the rebate to modernise the flats.[54]

The creditor's right was also held to have been wholly extinguished in *Brikom Investments Ltd v Carr*.[55] In that case, long leases of flats provided that the tenants should pay (*inter alia*) contributions in respect of certain expenses incurred by the landlords on repairs. During negotiations leading to the execution of the leases, the landlords had promised to put the roof into repair "at our own cost". This was held to amount to a collateral contract[56] with one of the original tenants, precluding the landlords from enforcing against her the provision in the lease requiring her to contribute to the cost of the roof repairs. It was further held that claims for contributions to the cost of those repairs could not be made against assignees and sub-assignees of original tenants, even though there were no collateral contracts with these persons. Lord Denning M.R. based this conclusion on the *High Trees* principle which, in his view, was available not only between the original parties, but also in favour of, and against, their assigns.[57] The extinctive effect of the principle in these circumstances can perhaps be supported on the ground that the original tenants, the assignees and the sub-assignees had all, in reliance on the landlord's promise, undertaken fresh commitments by entering into long leases of the flats. Alternatively, the case can be treated, not as one of "promissory estoppel",[58] but as one of "waiver".[59] The latter expression here seems to refer to a variation supported by consideration[60]; for the consideration provided by the tenants[61] could equally support the landlords' promise whether that promise was regarded as a collateral contract[62] or as a variation of the principal contract itself. On this interpretation of the case, it is possible to account for the extinctive effect of the landlord's promise even on the liability of the assignees and sub-assignees. The variation was supported by consideration and so extinguished the liability of the original tenants to contribute to the cost of the repairs in question; and once it had been so extinguished it was not revived on assignment of the leases.

(ii) *Reliance.* One difficulty which has been felt about the *High Trees* case is that a tenant who is bound to pay £2,500 per annum for 99 years suffers no "detriment", in the sense in which that word is used in the law of estoppel,[63] by paying half that rent for part of the period. Ingenious attempts have been made to find some "detriment" in the

---

[53] See above, p.111 at n.34.

[54] *cf.* Mitchell, 2 Univ. of Western Australia Annual Law Review 245 at 251. The principle is somewhat similar to that which underlies the defence of "change of position" in an action for the recovery of money paid; for recognition of this defence, see *Lipkin Gorman v Karpnale Ltd* [1991] 2 A.C. 548; below, p.537.

[55] [1979] Q.B. 467.

[56] See above, p.102.

[57] [1979] Q.B. 467 at 484–485.

[58] *ibid.* at 485, 491.

[59] *ibid.* at 488, 490.

[60] *cf.* above, p.102.

[61] See above, p.102. Roskill L.J. at 489 refers to *Hughes v Metropolitan Ry* (1877) 2 App.Cas. 439 (above p.100) as stating a principle of "contractual variation of strict contractual rights." It is respectfully submitted that this phrase should be interpreted to refer to *variations of contracts*, rather than to *contractually binding variations*; for the *Hughes* principle clearly applies to variations which are not contractually binding (but revocable on reasonable notice) because they are not supported by consideration.

[62] See above, p.102.

[63] *cf.* above, p.111.

case[64]; but Lord Denning himself has said extra-judicially that there was none.[65] Nor is the requirement mentioned in the *High Trees* case itself, or in later statements of the principle.[66] And if such "detriment" is not necessary for the purpose of the rule in *Hughes v Metropolitan Ry*[67] it is hard to see why it should be necessary for the purpose of its offshoot, the *High Trees* rule. All that is necessary is that the tenant should have acted in reliance on the promise in such a way as to make it inequitable for the landlord to act inconsistently with it. This requirement was satisfied on the facts of the *High Trees* case, no less than on those of *Hughes v Metropolitan Ry*.

(iii) *Inequitable.* When the debtor makes the part payment in reliance on the creditor's promise, it becomes *prima facie* "inequitable" for the creditor peremptorily to go back on his promise. But other circumstances may indicate that it would not be "inequitable" for the creditor to reassert his claim for the full amount[68]: this would, for example, be the position where the debtor had failed to perform his promise to pay the smaller amount.[69] It has been suggested that another such circumstance may be the conduct of the debtor in obtaining the promise. Thus in *D & C Builders Ltd v Rees*[70] Lord Denning M.R. held that the *High Trees* principle did not apply because the builders' promise to accept £300 in full settlement of their claim for £482 had been obtained by taking undue advantage of their desperate financial position. The difficulty with this reasoning is that most debtors who offer part payment in full settlement try to exert some form of "pressure" against their creditors. The law now recognises that it is possible for such pressure to amount to duress[71]; and where it has this effect the promise should clearly not bring the *High Trees* principle into operation. Where, on the other hand, there is no duress, the operation of the *High Trees* principle should not be excluded merely because it could be said that the creditor's promise had, in some sense, been "improperly obtained." Such an intermediate category between promises obtained by duress and those not so obtained should, here as elsewhere,[72] be rejected as "unhelpful because it would make the law uncertain".[73]

SECTION 7. PROPRIETARY ESTOPPEL

Proprietary estoppel is said to arise in certain situations in which a person has done acts in reliance on the belief that he has, or that he will acquire, rights in or over another's land. Usually, but not invariably, these acts consist of erecting buildings on, or making other improvements to, the land in question. Where the requirements of proprietary estoppel are satisfied, the landowner is precluded from denying the existence of the rights in question, and may indeed be compelled to grant them. Because the estoppel precludes him from denying the existence of rights in property, it has come to be known

---

[64] *e.g.* Wilson, 67 L.Q.R. 330 at 344.

[65] 15 M.L.R. 1, 6–8.

[66] *e.g.* in *Combe v Combe* [1951] 2 K.B. 215 at 220. See also p.110, *et seq.*, above.

[67] See above, p.111.

[68] *cf.* above, pp.111–112.

[69] *cf. Re Selectmove* [1995] 1 W.L.R. 474 at 481, where the debtor's promise was not to pay *less* but to pay *late*; and see *Burrows v Brent LBC* [1996] 1 W.L.R. 1448, where decision was based on lack of contractual intention so that neither consideration nor the equitable doctrine was discussed.

[70] [1966] 2 Q.B. 617. Winder, 82 L.Q.R. 165; above, p.114. *cf. Arrale v Costain Civil Engineering Ltd* [1976] 1 Lloyd's Rep. 98 at 102.

[71] See above, pp.94–95; below, pp.405–407.

[72] See above, p.98.

[73] *Pao On v Lau Yiu Long* [1980] A.C. 614 at 634; *cf. Huyton SA v Peter Cremer GmbH* [1999] 1 Lloyd's Rep 620, where the requirement of consideration was satisfied (above, p.115) but there was no duress (below, p.405). It was said at 629 that "the submissions relating to consideration and duress inter-relate".

as "proprietary estoppel".[74] It is distinct[75] from promissory estoppel, both in the conditions which must be satisfied before it comes into operation and in its effects. But under both doctrines some legal effects are given to promises which are not contractually binding for want of consideration; and it is this aspect[76] of proprietary estoppel which calls for discussion in the present Chapter.

1. Nature and Scope of the Doctrine

Proprietary estoppel operates in a variety of cases so disparate that it has been described as "an amalgam of doubtful utility."[77] The cases can be divided broadly into two categories.

In the first, one person acts under a mistake as to the existence or as to the extent of his rights in or over another's land. Even though the landowner did not induce mistake, he might be prevented from taking advantage of it, particularly if he "stood by" knowing of the mistake, or actively encouraged the mistaken party to act in reliance on his mistaken belief.[78] These cases of so-called "acquiescence"[79] do not raise any questions as to the enforceability of promises and therefore do not call for further discussion in this Chapter.[80]

In the second group of cases, there is not merely "acquiescence" by the landowner, but "encouragement"[81]: that is, conduct by the landowner, or a representation by him, from which a promise to the other party (the promisee) can be inferred[82] to the effect that the promisee has a legally enforceable[83] interest in the land or that one will be created in his favour. If the other party acts in reliance on such a promise, the question will arise to what extent the promise can be enforced, even though it may not be supported by consideration, or fail to satisfy the other requirements (such as those of certainty or form[84]) of a binding contract.

(1) Bases of liability

(a) EXPENDITURE ON ANOTHER'S LAND IN RELIANCE ON A PROMISE. In *Dillwyn v Llewelyn*[85] a father executed a memorandum "presenting" a named estate to his son "for

---

[74] *Jones v Jones* [1977] 1 W.L.R. 438 at 442; *Pascoe v Turner* [1979] 1 W.L.R. 431 at 436; *Re Sharpe* [1980] 1 W.L.R. 219 at 233; *Greasley v Cooke* [1980] 1 W.L.R. 1306 at 1311; *cf. Midland Bank plc v Cooke* [1995] 4All E.R. 564 at 573 ("equities in the nature of an estoppel").

[75] *Fontana NV v Mautner* (1980) 254 E.G. 199 at 207; and see below, p.146.

[76] For wider discussions, see Davies, 8 Sydney L.Rev. 200 and 7 Adelaide L.Rev. 200; Moriarty, 100 L.Q.R. 376; Smith in *Consensus ad Idem: Essays in the Law of Contract in Honour of Guenter Treitel* (ed. Rose), p.235.

[77] *Amalgamated Investment & Property Co Ltd v Texas Commerce International Bank Ltd* [1982] Q.B. 84 at 103.

[78] *Wilmott v Barber* (1880) 15 Ch.D. 96; *cf. Taylors Fashions Ltd v Liverpool Victoria Trustee Co Ltd* [1982] Q.B. 133n.

[79] *Wilmott v Barber* (1880) 15 Ch.D. 96 at 105.

[80] Nor do they call for discussion in Chap.8, since the mistake is not one that prevents the formation of a contract, or is alleged to do so.

[81] *Ramsden v Dyson* (1866) L.R. 1 H.L. 129 at 170. Contrast *Attorney-General of Hong Kong v Humphreys Estate (Queen's Gardens)* [1987] A.C. 114, where there was no encouragement.

[82] See *Lloyd's Bank plc v Rosset* [1991] 1 A.C. 107 and *Keelwalk Properties Ltd v Waller* [2002] EWCA Civ 1076 at [63] (where this requirement was not satisfied).

[83] See *Coombes v Smith* [1986] 1 W.L.R. 808 (where there was no belief in the existence of a *legally enforceable* right; *cf. Brinnand v Ewens* (1987) 19 H.L.R. 415.

[84] See, for example, below, p.136, n.91.

[85] (1862) 4 D.F. & G. 517; Allan, 79 L.Q.R. 238.

the purpose of furnishing himself with a dwelling house". The son spent £14,000 in building a house on the land; and it was held (after the father's death) that he was entitled to have the fee simple of the estate conveyed to him. Many latter cases similarly give some degree of legal enforceability to a promise by a landowner in reliance on which the promisee has spent money on making improvements to the promisor's land: for example, where a mother purported to make a gift of a cottage to her son "provided he did it up" and the son incurred considerable expense in doing so[86]; where A built a bungalow on B's land in reliance on B's promise that A could stay there for the rest of his life[87]; where A spent money on extending or improving B's house in reliance on a similar promise by B[88]; where, in reliance on such a promise, A actually did the work of improvement him- or herself[89]; and where a tenant, whose lease had been terminated, spent money on improving the premises in reliance on the landlord's promise to grant him a new lease.[90] The most obvious explanation of such cases is that in them the landowner would be unjustly enriched if he were allowed to disregard his promise and to take back the land after he had induced the promisee to make improvements to it. This explanation is, perhaps, reflected in statements found in some modern cases that the liability is based on "an implied or constructive trust."[91] But the discussion which follows will show that the doctrine can apply even where there is no enrichment of the kind just described, or indeed of any kind at all.[92] Unjust enrichment therefore cannot provide complete explanation of the doctrine.

(b) OTHER ACTS DONE IN RELIANCE ON THE PROMISE. Improvement to the promisor's land is not a necessary condition for the operation of proprietary estoppel. The doctrine can apply also where the promisee has conferred some other benefit on the promisor[93] and even where no benefit at all is received by the promisor. This appears from one of the illustrations given by Lord Westbury in *Dillwyn v Llewelyn*: if "A gives a house to B, but makes no formal conveyance, and the house is afterwards included, with the knowledge of A, in the marriage settlement of B, A would be bound to complete the title

---

[86] *Voyce v Voyce* (1991) 62 P. & C.R. 290.

[87] *Inwards v Baker* [1965] 2 Q.B. 507.

[88] *Hussey v Palmer* [1972] 1 W.L.R. 1286; *Pascoe v Turner* [1979] 1 W.L.R. 431; *Durant v Heritage* [1994] E.G.C.S. 134; *semble* spending money on mere maintenance would not suffice: *Griffiths v Williams* [1978] E.G. Digest of Cases 919.

[89] *Eves v Eves* [1975] 1 W.L.R. 1338; *Jones v Jones* [1977] 1 W.L.R. 438; *Ungurian v Lesnoff* [1990] Ch. 206; *Clough v Kelly* (1996) 72 P. & C.R. D22 (where the claimant had also spent money on the premises).

[90] *J T Developments v Quinn* (1991) 62 P. & C.R. 33.

[91] *Sen v Headley* [1991] Ch. 425 at 440; *Re Dale* [1994] Ch. 31, 47; *Lloyd's Bank plc v Carrick* [1996] 4 All E.R. 632 at 640 cf. *Drake v Whipp* (1996) 28 H.L.R. 531; *Yaxley v Gotts* [2000] Ch. 162 at 176, 193; *Banner Homes Group plc v Luff Developments Ltd* [2000] Ch. 372 at 382. The agreements (if any) in these last two cases lacked contractual force, not for want of consideration, but in *Yaxley v Gotts* on account of failure to comply with the formal requirements imposed by Law of Property (Miscellaneous Provisions) Act 1989, s.2 (below, pp.178, 179) and in the *Banner Homes* case for incompleteness (above, p.55).

[92] *Canadian Pacific Railway v The King* [1931] A.C. 414; *Armstrong v Sheppard & Short* [1959] 2 Q.B. 384.

[93] e.g. *Tanner v Tanner* [1975] 1 W.L.R. 1346 (services rendered to promisor in managing his property); *Greasley v Cooke* [1980] 1 W.L.R. 1306 (personal and nursing services); *Wayling v Jones* (1993) 69 P. & C.R. 170 (services rendered for virtually no pay); *Campbell v Griffin* [2001] EWCA Civ 999; [2001] W.T.L.R. 981 (lodger caring for elderly couple); *Jennings v Rice* [2002] EWCA Civ 159; [2002] W.T.L.R. 367 (below, p.144); cf. *Plimmer v Mayor of Wellington* (1884) 9 App.Cas. 699 and *E. R. Ives Investments Ltd v High* [1967] 2 Q.B. 379 (where the landowner benefited from improvements to his land but also—and more significantly—in other ways); *Grant v Edwards* [1986] Ch. 638 at 657; *Maharaj v Chand* [1986] A.C. 898 (where, because of local legislation, proprietary estoppel was not argued); *Re Basham* [1986] 1 W.L.R. 1498; contrast *Howard v Jones* (1988) 19 Fam. L. 231 (contribution to running cost of *another* property insufficient).

of the parties claiming under the settlement."[94] Similarly, the doctrine operated in the absence of any expenditure on the promisor's land in *Crabb v Arun DC*.[95] In that case A (a local authority) by its conduct represented to B that B had a right of way from his land over adjoining land owned by A. In reliance on that representation, B sold part of his own land, so that the only access from the remainder to the nearest public highway was by means of the right of way across A's land. It was held that B had a right to cross A's land for the purpose of access to his retained land. Detrimental reliance by the promisee here gave rise to a proprietary estoppel even though no benefit was conferred on the promisor.[96]

(c) ALTERNATIVE EXPLANATION: CONTRACT. In *Dillwyn v Llewelyn* Lord Westbury, while referring to the parties to the transaction as "donor" and "donee" also said that the son's expenditure "supplied a valuable consideration originally wanting"[97] and, in discussing a hypothetical example similar to the facts of the case before him, he concluded "that the donee acquires a right from the subsequent transaction to call upon the donor to perform that contract and to complete the imperfect donation".[98] These passages may suggest that he regarded the memorandum as a kind of unilateral contract[99] by which the father promised to convey the land if the son built a house on it. The terms of the memorandum make it improbable that a modern court would so regard it; it is more likely that these terms would now be regarded as negativing contractual intention.[1] However, in a number of later cases the rights of a person who had expended money on the property of another have been explained as being based on contract[2]; and often such an explanation was sufficiently plausible to make reliance on a doctrine of proprietary estoppel unnecessary.[3] A unilateral contract to transfer an interest in land has been held to arise out of a promise to make the transfer if the promisee would pay instalments due under a mortgage on the house[4]; it can equally arise out of a promise to make the transfer if the promisee will make improvements to the land, or indeed do any other act.[5]

---

[94] (1862) 4 D.F. & G. 517 at 521.

[95] [1976] Ch. 179. The case was described in *Amalgamated Investment & Property Co Ltd v Texas Commerce International Bank Ltd* [1982] Q.B. 84 at 121 as one of "estoppel by convention"; but this would require a dealing between A and B on the basis of common assumption (above, p.120), while in *Crabb's* case the dealing was between B and a purchaser from him. In *Waltons Stores (Interstate) Ltd v Maher* (1988) 64 C.L.R. 387, 403 *Crabb's* case was described as one of "promissory estoppel" (see above, p.116); but the requirements of that doctrine (in particular, the requirement of a pre-existing legal relationship: above, p.105) were not satisfied in *Crabb's* case, and the effect of the estoppel differed from promissory estoppel in giving rise to a new right: *cf.* above, pp.105–106.

[96] *cf. Hammersmith & Fulham BC v Top Shop Centres Ltd* [1990] Ch. 237.

[97] (1862) 4 D.F. & G. 517 at 521.

[98] *ibid.* at 521.

[99] See above, p.37.

[1] *cf.* below, p.164.

[2] *e.g. Plimmer v Mayor of Wellington* (1884) 9 App.Cas. 699 as explained in *Canadian Pacific Railway v The King* [1931] A.C. 414 at 428; *Eves v Eves* [1975] 1 W.L.R. 1338; *Tanner v Tanner* [1975] 1 W.L.R. 1346; *cf. Re Sharpe* [1980] 1 W.L.R. 219 at 224; and see *E R Ives Investments Ltd v High* [1967] 2 Q.B. 379 (where there was a contract between the defendant and the claimant's predecessor in title).

[3] See *Lloyd's Bank plc v Carrick* [1996] 4 All E.R. 632, where the existence of a contract of sale precluded reliance by the purchaser on proprietary estoppel, even though that contract was, as against a bank to which the property had been charged as security, void for non-registration. Contrast *Yaxley v Gotts* [2000] Ch. 162 at 179, where there was *no* such contract but, at most, an agreement lacking contractual force.

[4] *Errington v Errington* [1952] 1 Q.B. 290; see above, p.39, n.16, for authorities doubting this case on other points.

[5] *e.g. Tanner v Tanner* [1975] 1 W.L.R. 1346; merely to maintain the house in repair could be sufficient for the present purpose, even if it did not suffice to raise a proprietary estoppel: above p.136, n.88.

But there are, it is submitted, obstacles to treating all cases of proprietary estoppel as depending on contract.[6] One is that the promises in cases of this kind are often made in a family context, without contractual intention. Another is that the promise may lack consideration because the party relying on the estoppel made no counter-promise and so incurred no obligation, and that the arrangement was one in which it would not be in accordance with the intention of the parties to treat it as a unilateral contract.[7] A third is that the terms of the alleged contract are often too vague to satisfy the requirement of certainty.[8] This point accounts for the view of the Court of Appeal that there was no contract in *Crabb v Arun DC*[9]: there may have been an implied promise to grant the claimant some right of way across the defendants' land, but no financial or other terms were specified in that promise, so that it would not (even if supported by consideration) have been sufficiently certain to give rise to a contract. Moreover, many arrangements which can give rise to proprietary estoppel are made without any attempt to comply with the stringent formal requirements for the making of contracts for the disposition of interests in land.[10] Failure to comply with these requirements does not prevent such arrangements from giving rise to a proprietary estoppel,[11] but it does prevent them from taking effect as contracts. The possibility of explaining proprietary estoppel on the basis of contract is therefore in practice likely to be restricted to cases where the arrangement does *not* purport to dispose of an interest in land, *e.g.* where it amounts to no more than a promise to grant a licence to occupy the land.[12]

(2) Conditions of liability

(a) KINDS OF PROMISES CAPABLE OF GIVING RISE TO A PROPRIETARY ESTOPPEL. A promise may give rise to a proprietary estoppel even though it is not express but is implied: for example, from the fact that the parties acted on the common assumption that one of them was to have the right to reside on the other's property.[13] The promise must be of such a kind that it is reasonable for the promisee to rely on it; the promisor must have intended the promisee would so to rely on it[14]; and it must induce the promisee to believe that a legal right has been, or will be, created in his favour; though there is no further requirement that this belief must be legally well founded.[15] There can

---

[6] *cf. Beaton v McDivitt* (1988) 13 N.S.W. L.R. 162 at 170–171.

[7] *J T Developments v Quinn* (1991) 62 P. & C.R. 33.

[8] See above, p.49. See *Gillett v Holt*, above, at 230; *Banner Homes Group plc v Luff Developments Ltd* [2000] Ch. 372; *Jennings v Rice* [2002] EWCA Civ 159; [2002] W.T.L.R. 367, at [10], [49, 50].

[9] [1976] Ch. 179; Atiyah, 92 L.Q.R. 174, criticises the view that there was no contract but the argument is based on the fallacy that, merely because a promise has *some* legal effects, it must necessarily have *all* the effects of a contract: *cf.* above, p.73, and below, p.148; Millett, 92 L.Q.R. 342; Duncanson, 39 M.L.R. 268.

[10] Law of Property (Miscellaneous Provisions) Act 1989, s.2(1)–(3). Previously the contract could be *made* informally, but Law of Property Act 1925, s.40 (replacing part of Statute of Frauds 1677, s.4 and now repealed) had required either a note or memorandum in writing as evidence of the contract, or "part performance" of the contract: The latter requirement could be satisfied by the conduct of the promisee giving rise to proprietary estoppel. *cf.* the reference to "part performance" in *Dillwyn v Llewelyn* (1862) 4 D.F. & G. 517 at 521.

[11] See below, p.180.

[12] The earlier legislation referred to in n.10, above, did not apply to a licence to occupy land: *Wright v Stavert* (1860) 2 E. & E. 721; *cf. Taylor v Waters* (1816) 7 Taunt. 374 (licence to use opera box). The position seems to be the same under Law of Property (Miscellaneous Provisions) Act 1989, s.2(6).

[13] *e.g. Re Sharpe* [1980] 1 W.L.R. 219.

[14] *Gillett v Holt* [2001] Ch. 210 at 228.

[15] *ibid.* at 229.

normally be no such belief, and hence no proprietary estoppel, if the promise expressly disclaims legal effect: for example, in one case[16] it was held that no proprietary estoppel arose out of an agreement for the transfer of a number of flats "subject to contract", it being well known that the effect of these words was to negative the intention to be legally bound.[17] The promisee may have formed "the confident and not unreasonable hope"[18] that the promise would not be withdrawn; but no *belief* to this effect had been encouraged[19] by the promisor or relied on by the promisee. It seems that a proprietary estoppel could arise out of such an agreement if one of the parties *did* encourage such a belief in the other and the other acted to his detriment in reliance on that belief.[20] Similar reasoning applies where the promise in terms reserves a right to the promisor wholly to revoke the promise. Thus where a landowner promised her part-time gardener to leave him her house in her will but told him "not to count his chickens before they were hatched," it was held that no proprietary estoppel arose when, after having made a will in his favour, she then revoked it and made another leaving the property to someone else: in these circumstances it was not unconscionable for the landowner to revoke the promise.[21] The position is the same where the promise, even though it does not in terms reserve a power of revocation, is in its nature revocable and this is a matter of common knowledge so that the promisee must be taken to have been aware of the risk of its being revoked. This will often be the position where the promise is one to make a will in favour of the promisee; but it does not follow as a matter of law that such a promise cannot give rise to proprietary estoppel. In *Gillett v Holt*[22] the claimant had worked for nearly 40 years in the defendant's farming business in reliance on the defendant's frequently repeated promises to leave him the bulk of his estate, and had in various other ways relied on those promises. It was held that the promises were "more than a statement of revocable intention",[23] and that they were capable of giving rise, and did give rise, to a proprietary estoppel.

The rights which the promisee believes to have been created must, as a general rule, be rights in or over the property of the promisor. Thus a representation by a planning authority to the effect that a landowner does not need permission to carry

---

[16] *Attorney-General of Hong Kong v Humphreys Estates (Queen's Gardens)* [1987] 1 A.C. 114; the case was said in *Waltons Stores (Interstate) Ltd v Maher* (1988) 164 C.L.R. 387 at 404 to be "not a case of proprietary estoppel" but (apparently) one of *promissory* estoppel. But most of the authorities relied on in the *Humphreys Estates* case were cases of proprietary estoppel; the leading cases on promissory estoppel were not cited; and if the requirements of encouragement and reliance had been satisfied the estoppel would have created a new right, which in English law is not the effect of promissory estoppel: above, p.111. *cf. Salomon v Akiens* [1993] 1 E.G.L.R. 10 (no proprietary estoppel arising from agreement "subject to lease"); *Pridean Ltd v Forest Taverns* (1998) P. & C.R. 477 (no proprietary estoppel arising from work done during negotiations which failed to lead to a contract); *Edwin Shirley Productions v Workspace Management Ltd* [2001] 23 E.G. 158 (negotiations "subject to contract" and "without prejudice" held not to give rise to proprietary estoppel); *London & Regional Investments Ltd v TBI plc Belfast International Airport Ltd* [2002] EWCA Civ 355 (no estoppel or constructive trust where agreement was "subject to contract").

[17] See above, p.52; below, p.163.

[18] [1987] 1 A.C. 114 at 124.

[19] *cf.* above, p.136; *Brinnand v Ewens* (1987) 19 H.L.R. 415; and (in a different context) *Kelly v Liverpool Maritime Terminals* [1988] I.R.L.R. 310, where authorities on proprietary estoppel are cited in a case unconnected with property.

[20] This is assumed in *Attorney-General of Hong Kong v Humphreys Estate (Queen's Gardens)* above n.16, where the Privy Council at 124 stress that there had been *no* such encouragement.

[21] *Taylor v Dickens* [1998] F.L.R. 806, as explained in *Gillett v Holt* [2001] Ch. 210 at 227.

[22] [2001] Ch. 210.

[23] *ibid.* at 228.

out development on his *own* land is not capable of giving rise to a proprietary estoppel.[24] The promisor may, however, make two promises, of which the first relates to the promisor's land while the second relates to that of the promisee; and the two promises may be so closely linked as to form in substance a single transaction. If the doctrine of proprietary estoppel applies to that transaction as a whole, then it can provide the promisee with a remedy in respect of the second promise even though that promise, standing alone, could not have given rise to proprietary estoppel because it related only to the promisee's land. In one case,[25] for example, A promised B (1) to sell blackacre to B to enable B to build on it, and (2) to buy whiteacre from B so that B could pay for the building operations on blackacre. B carried out the building work envisaged in the first of A's promises and it was held that the doctrine of proprietary estoppel provided B with a remedy in respect of the second promise (which had no contractual force), even though that promise related only to B's land. But it was recognised that the doctrine could not have applied to the second promise if it had stood alone and not formed part of a transaction also relating to A's land.[26] It could not, for example, have applied if A had simply made a non-contractual promise to B to buy whiteacre from B, knowing that B intended to use the proceeds of the sale to buy shares from C, and if B had then entered into a contract to that effect with C. Normally, the doctrine applies to promises to *grant* rights in land *to* the promisee;[27] it only applies to promises to *acquire* such rights *from* him where they are inextricably linked with promises of the former kind.

(b) SUBJECT MATTER OF THE PROMISE. In the cases to which the doctrine has so far been applied, the subject-matter of the promise has always been (or at least included[28]) land. The question whether a promise can give rise to a proprietary estoppel where its subject-matter is property of some other kind remains an open one.[29] Even if the doctrine is extended to such promises, its scope will in one respect remain narrower than that of so-called promissory estoppel[30]: the promise must relate to the acquisition of an interest in the property which is the subject-matter of the promise. It is not enough that the promise should in some other way relate to property: for example, the doctrine of proprietary estoppel would not apply on the facts of *Central London Property Trust v High Trees House Ltd.*[31]

(c) DETRIMENTAL RELIANCE. The promisee must have relied on the promise or

---

[24] *Western Fish Products Ltd v Penwith DC* [1981] 2 All E.R. 204 (decided in 1978); *cf. Lloyd's Bank plc v Carrick* [1996] 4 All E.R. 632 (above, p.137 n.3).

[25] *Salvation Army Trustee Co v West Yorks Metropolitan CC* (1981) 41 P. & C.R. 179.

[26] *ibid.* at 191. The case was approved but distinguished in *Attorney-General of Hong Kong v Humphreys Estate (Queen's Gardens)* [1987] A.C. 114 at 126–127.

[27] For the possibility that the doctrine may *prevent* A from asserting rights in B's property against C, a purchaser of that property: see *J S Bloor (Measham) Ltd v Calcott (No.2)*, *The Times*, December 12, 2001.

[28] See *Re Basham* [1986] 1 W.L.R. 1498.

[29] *Western Fish Products Ltd v Penwith DC* [1981] 2 All E.R. 204 at 217; *cf.* the reference *ibid.* at 218, and in *Crabb v Arun DC* [1976] Ch. 179 at 187, to the decision of the Court of Appeal in *Moorgate Mercantile Co v Twitchings* [1976] Q.B. 225; that decision was reversed by the House of Lords: [1977] A.C. 890. For the view that proprietary estoppel is limited to cases where the subject-matter of the promise is land, see *Baird Textile Holdings Ltd v Marks & Spencer plc* [2001] EWCA Civ 274; [2001] 1 All E.R. (Comm) 737, at [97].

[30] See above, pp.105–118, 130–134.

[31] [1947] K.B. 130; above, pp.130–131.

representation to his detriment.[32] The requirement has been doubted[33] but in the absence of any such reliance it is hard to see why failure to perform a merely gratuitous promise should be regarded as giving rise to any legal liability. The element of detrimental reliance is necessary to satisfy "the essential test of unconscionability"[34] on which the operation of proprietary estoppel depends; and the existence of the requirement is further supported by the rules (to be discussed below) as to the revocability of the promise.[35] The detriment must be "substantial", *i.e.* such as to make it "unjust or inequitable to allow the assurance to be disregarded"[36]; and the question whether it has this character is to be judged "as at the moment when the person who has given the assurance seeks to go back on it".[37]

Where a promise has been made which is capable of inducing detrimental reliance, and which is in fact followed by such reliance, the question may arise whether the promise actually did induce the reliance. The burden on this issue is on the promisor: that is, it is up to the promisor, in order to escape liability, to show that the promisee would have done the acts in question anyway, even if the promise had not been made.[38] The position appears to be different where a proprietary estoppel arises because both parties have acted under a mistake as to their rights in the land.[39] Here it seems to be up to the party relying on the proprietary estoppel to show that his conduct in relation to the property was in fact induced by his belief that he had an interest in it.[40]

(d) WHETHER RELIANCE MUST RELATE TO SPECIFIC PROPERTY. The authorities are divided on the question whether, to give rise to a proprietary estoppel, the reliance must relate to identifiable property. According to one case, the promisee's conduct must relate to "some specific asset" in which an interest is claimed; so that proprietary estoppel did not arise merely because B rendered services to A in the expectation of receiving some indeterminate benefit under A's will.[41] But in another case reliance on a similar expectation (induced by A's promise) was held sufficient even though it did not relate to any "particular property".[42] The latter case can perhaps be explained on the ground that the promise did to some extent identify the property.[43] It is submitted that the view

---

[32] This was the view of the majority of the Court of Appeal in *Greasley v Cooke* [1980] 1 W.L.R. 1306; the requirement is assumed to exist in *Taylors Fashions Ltd v Liverpool Victoria Trustees Co Ltd* [1982] Q.B. 133 n and stated in *Grant v Edwards* [1986] Ch. 638 at 657; *cf. Lloyds Bank Plc v Rosset* [1991] 1 A.C. 107 at 132; *Hammond v Mitchell* [1991] 1 W.L.R 1127. The fact that there was no such reliance was one reason why the claim based on proprietary estoppel failed in *Western Fish Products Ltd v Penwith DC*, above: see [1981] 2 All E.R. 204 at 217, in *Coombes v Smith* [1986] 1 W.L.R. 808, in *Attorney-General of Hong Kong v Humphreys Estate (Queen's Gardens)* [1987] A.C. 114, in *Mecca Leisure v The London Residuary Body* [1988] C.L.Y. 1375, in *Jones v Stones* [1999] 1 W.L.R. 1739 and in *Jennings v Rice* [2002] EWCA Civ 159; [2002] W.T.L.R. 367 at [21], [49].

[33] By Lord Denning M.R. in *Greasley v Cooke*, above at p.1311. The argument may be influenced by the analogy of promissory estoppel (see above, p.110); but the two doctrines are distinct: below, p.146.

[34] *Gillett v Holt* [2001] Ch 210 at 232; *Jennings v Rice* [2002] EWCA Civ 159; [2002] W.T.L.R. 367 at [21], [49].

[35] See below, p.142.

[36] *Gillett v Holt*, above, n.34, at 232.

[37] *ibid.*

[38] *Greasley v Cooke*, above; *cf. Grant v Edwards* [1986] Ch. 638; *Re Basham* [1986] 1 W.L.R. 1498; *Hammersmith & Fulham BC v Top Shop Centres Ltd* [1990] Ch. 237; *Wayling v Jones* (1993) 69 P. & C.R. 170 at 172.

[39] See above, pp.134–136.

[40] *Taylors Fashions Ltd v Liverpool Victoria Trustees Co Ltd* [1982] Q.B. 133 note; *cf. Coombes v Smith* [1986] 1 W.L.R. 808.

[41] *Layton v Martin* [1986] 2 F.L.R. 277.

[42] *Re Basham* [1986] 1 W.L.R. 1498 at 1508.

[43] By referring to the promisor's cottage. In *Gillett v Holt* [2001] Ch. 210 the property was likewise identified, if not very precisely; *cf. Jennings v Rice*, above, n.32 at [50], where the promise again related in part to the promisor's house.

that the promise must relate to identified or identifiable property is to be preferred; for, without some such limitation on its scope the doctrine of proprietary estoppel could extend to any gift promise on which the promisee had relied to his detriment. Such a very broad doctrine would be fundamentally inconsistent with the doctrine of consideration[44] and, indeed, with the rule that the doctrine of *promissory* estoppel gives rise to no new rights.[45]

2. Effects of the Doctrine

(1) Revocability

Proprietary estoppel will not arise at all where the promise to confer a benefit on the promisee is revocable in the sense that it reserves a power to the promisor wholly to deprive the promisee of that benefit.[46] But even where the promise does not allow the promisor to do this, and so is capable of giving rise to a proprietary estoppel, the extent of the promisee's rights under the estoppel may be limited by terms of the promise giving the promisor a power of putting an end to those rights. Thus if the landowner promises to allow the promisee to stay on the land "until I decide to sell", then the promisee cannot, merely by spending money on improvements to the land, acquire any right to stay there for a longer period.[47] Even where the promise is not expressed to be revocable, it can be revoked before the promisee has acted on it. Thus in *Dillwyn v Llewelyn*[48] the father could have revoked his promise before the son had started to build on the land[49] and in *Crabb v Arun DC*[50] the promise to grant a right of way could have been revoked before the promisee had, by selling off part of his land, made it impossible for himself to obtain access to the retained land except by means of the promised right of way. In this respect proprietary estoppel resembles so-called promissory estoppel (under which promises are similarly revocable[51]) and differs from contractually binding promises which are not revocable unless they expressly or impliedly so provide. The cases of proprietary estoppel assume that once the promisee has acted on the representation, he cannot be restored to his original position. Where he has made improvements to land, this will generally be the case. Where a restoration of the status quo is physically possible, it seems that a promise giving rise to a proprietary estoppel could be revoked even after the promisee had acted on it, provided that the promisor in fact restored the promisee to the position in which he was before he had acted in reliance on the promise.

A promise which has given rise to proprietary estoppel may also be none the less revocable, because the court considers it appropriate in this way to limit the effects to be given to the promise.[52]

(2) Operation of proprietary estoppel

Where the conditions required to give rise to a proprietary estoppel have been satisfied, the effect of the doctrine is said to be to confer an "equity" on the promisee. Two further

---

[44] See, *e.g.* above, p.67.
[45] See above, p.111.
[46] See above, pp.138–140.
[47] *E & L Berg Homes v Gray* (1979) 253 E.G. 473.
[48] (1862) D.F. & G. 517; above, p.136.
[49] *cf. Pascoe v Turner* [1979] 1 W.L.R. 431 at 435 (where before the promisee's action in reliance on the promise she was said to be only a licensee at will).
[50] [1976] Ch. 179; above, pp.136–137.
[51] See above, p.111.
[52] See below, p.143, at n.60.

questions then arise: namely, what is the extent of that "equity", and what are the remedies for its enforcement.[53] In practice these questions tend to merge into each other; but an attempt to deal with them in turn will be made in the following discussion.

(a) EXTENT OF THE EQUITY. At one extreme, the promisee may be entitled to conveyance of the fee simple in the property which is the subject-matter of the promise, as in *Dillwyn v Llewelyn*.[54] On the other hand, in *Inwards v Baker*,[55] where a son had also built a house for himself at his father's suggestion on the latter's land, the result of the estoppel was only to entitle the son to occupy the house for life. Similar results were reached in a number of later cases in which the promisee made improvements to the promisor's property (or otherwise acted to his detriment) in reliance on a promise, or common understanding, that the promisee would be entitled to reside there for as long as he or she wished to do so[56]; or for some shorter period: *e.g.* until her children had left school[57]; or that a lease of the premises, to which the promise related, would be granted to him.[58] *Dillwyn v Llewelyn* can be reconciled with these cases by reference to the terms of the respective promises, which may be expressed either as an outright gift of the property or merely as an assurance that the promisee would be entitled to reside in the property for the specified period. Another way of giving effect to a promise of the latter kind is by the grant of a long, non-assignable lease at a nominal rent, on terms that ensured that the right of occupation was personal to the promisee.[59] In other cases, not concerned with rights of personal occupation but with the right to keep and use structures on promisor's land, the promisee has been held entitled only to a revocable licence.[60]

Where the circumstances are such as to give rise to an estoppel against the landowner, the estoppel is equally available against a third party who claims later to have obtained title to the land by way of gift from the landowner.[61]

The estoppel may operate conditionally where the promisee has acted in reliance on the promise but the terms of the promise show that the promisor did not intend to give up his title gratuitously. This was the position in *Lim Teng Huan v Ang Swee Chuan*[62] where A built a house on land jointly owned by him and L, who had agreed that he was to have no title to the house and would exchange his share in the land for other land. The arrangement had no contractual force as the other land was not identified with sufficient certainty; and it was held that L was estopped from asserting title to the house but that he was entitled to be compensated for the loss of his share in the land.

Similarly, where the promise is one to allow the promisee access to his own land over that of the promisor, the effect of the proprietary estoppel will be to entitle the promisee to an easement or licence on terms.[63] Such terms, if not agreed between the parties, may be imposed by the court: they can specify the extent of the permitted user as well as any

---

[53] *Crabb v Arun DC* [1976] Ch. 179 at 193, *per* Scarman L.J.

[54] (1862) D.F. & G. 517; *Durant v Heritage* [1994] E.G.C.S. 134; or, in the exceptional cases discussed on p.140 above, at n.25 and n.27, to orders enforcing the promises made in those cases.

[55] [1965] 2 Q.B. 507; Maudsley, 81 L.Q.R. 183.

[56] *Jones v Jones* [1977] 1 W.L.R. 438; *Re Sharpe* [1980] 1 W.L.R. 219; *Greasley v Cooke* [1980] 1 W.L.R. 1306.

[57] *Tanner v Tanner* [1975] 1 W.L.R. 1346 (where there was a contract: *cf.* above, p.137); *Yaxley v Gotts* [2000] Ch. 162 (where the remedy was based on constructive trust).

[58] *J T Developments v Quinn* (1991) 62 P. & C.R. 33.

[59] *Griffiths v Williams* [1978] E.G. Digest of Cases 919; *cf. Jones v Jones* [1977] 1 W.L.R. 438.

[60] *Canadian Pacific Railway v The King* [1931] A.C. 414; *Armstrong v Sheppard & Short* [1959] Q.B. 384.

[61] *Voyce v Voyce* (1991) 62 P. & C.R. 290.

[62] [1991] 1 W.L.R. 113.

[63] *E R Ives Investments Ltd v High* [1967] 2 Q.B. 379; *Crabb v Arun DC* [1976] Ch. 179.

payment that the promisee may be required to make for the exercise of the right.[64] However, an order for such payment was held not to be appropriate in one case, because the promisor had already obtained other benefits under the agreement.[65] It may also be inappropriate for other reasons, as the following discussion of the promisee's remedy will show.

(b) REMEDY. The remedy in cases of proprietary estoppel is "extremely flexible", its object being "to do what is equitable in all the circumstances".[66] Although the court thus has a considerable discretion with regard to the remedy in cases of proprietary estoppel, that discretion is not a "completely unfettered"[67] one and a "principled approach"[68] must be taken to its exercise. In giving effect to the "equity"[69] account must be taken, not only of the claimant's expectations "but also of the extent of his detrimental reliance"[70]; and "there must be proportionality between the expectation and the detriment".[71] For the purpose of achieving such "proportionality" regard must be had to the degree of precision of the promise giving rise to the expectation. Where this amounts to an assurance that an interest in specific property will be transferred in return for specified acts, then an order for the specific enforcement of that promise (once the acts have been done) may be the appropriate remedy.[72] Where, on the other hand, the terms of the promise are less precise, amounting only to an assurance that some indeterminate benefit will be conferred on the promisee, so that the expectations reasonably arising from it are, at least objectively, uncertain, then the court will not give effect in full to expectations which the promisee may in fact have formed if they are "uncertain or extravagant or out of all proportion to the detriment which the claimant has suffered".[73] In such cases, compensation in money is likely to be the more appropriate remedy. That compensation must be proportionate to the detriment, but need not be its precise equivalent[74]: the fact that the detriment was incurred in response to a promise indicating (though in vague terms) some higher level of recompense is also to be taken into account. The balancing of such factors is illustrated by *Jennings v Rice*[75] where the claimant had worked as gardener-handyman for an elderly widow for some 17 years without pay and had also provided personal care for her in the years of increasing frailty towards the end of her life. He had done so in response to her statements that "he would be alright" and that "all this will be yours one day".[76] The latter statement referred to her house and its contents, valued on her death at £435,000 out of a total estate of £1.285 million. The Court of Appeal upheld an award of £200,000 as being properly proportionate to the detriment suffered by the claimant in reliance on the assurances given to him.

Apart from the terms of the promise and the extent of the promisee's reliance on them, the court may also take into account the conduct of the promisor after the facts giving rise to the estoppel. Thus in *Crabb v Arun DC*[77] the defendants acted without

---

[64] *Crabb v Arun DC*, [1976] Ch. 179 at 199.
[65] *E R Ives Investments Ltd v High* [1967] 2 Q.B. 379.
[66] *Roebuck v Mungovin* [1994] 2 A.C. 224 at 235; cf. the remedy granted in *Gillett v Holt* [2001] Ch. 210.
[67] *Jennings v Rice* [2002] EWCA Civ 159; [2002] W.T.L.R. 367 at [43].
[68] *ibid.*
[69] See above, p.143.
[70] *Jennings v Rice*, above, at [49].
[71] *ibid.* at [36]; cf. *ibid.* at [56] ("proportionality (between remedy and detriment)").
[72] *ibid.* at [45].
[73] *ibid.* at [50].
[74] *ibid.* at [51].
[75] See above, at n.67.
[76] At [9].
[77] [1976] Ch. 179.

warning in blocking the claimants' access to his land. In view of this "high-handed-ness"[78] and the resulting loss to the claimant, he was not required to make the payment that would otherwise have been a condition of the exercise of the right of way. Similarly, in *Pascoe v Turner*[79] a proprietary estoppel arose when a man told a woman with whom he had formerly cohabited that the house in which they had lived was hers, and she later spent some £230 of her limited resources on repairs and improvements to it. The Court of Appeal relied on the man's "ruthlessness"[80] in seeking to evict the promisee as a ground for ordering him to convey the fee simple to her. The submission that she should have no more than an irrevocable licence to occupy the house was rejected since this would not protect her against a bona fide purchaser from the promisor. The result seems, with respect, unduly punitive; and intermediate possibilities (such as granting the promisee a long lease[81]) were not put before the court.

Pascoe v Turner illustrates the possibility that the grant of an irrevocable licence to remain on the property may constitute an unsatisfactory remedy because it will not adequately secure the promisee's possession. It may also be unsatisfactory on account of its inflexibility: thus in *Inwards v Baker*[82] the remedy would have been of no use to the promisee, had he wanted to move elsewhere; nor would his dependants have had any remedy had he died shortly after completing the house. In such cases a remedy by way of compensation in money would be more satisfactory for the promisee; and it would also have the advantage for the promisor that dealing with the property would not be impeded for an indefinite time.[83] Such a remedy was granted in *Dodsworth v Dodsworth*[84] where the promisees spent £700 on improvements to the promisor's bungalow in reliance on an implied promise (not intended to have contractual force) that they could live there as if it were their home. The Court of Appeal held that to give the promisees a right of occupation for an indefinite time would confer on them a greater interest than had been contemplated by the parties; and that the most appropriate remedy was to repay them their outlay on improvements. Compensation in money will also be the more appropriate remedy where, as a practical matter, the promise which gives rise to the estoppel cannot be specifically enforced; for example, where its performance would involve occupation of premises by, and co-operation between, members of a family who later quarrel,[85] or between a couple whose relationship has broken down.[86] Where there is evidence that the improved property has increased in value by reason of market fluctuations, it is submitted that the amount recoverable by the promisee should be increased correspondingly; conversely it should be reduced where the market value of the property has declined.[87]

---

[78] *ibid.* at 199; *cf. ibid.* at 189.

[79] [1979] 1 W.L.R. 431; Sufrin, 42 M.L.R. 574.

[80] At 439; *cf.* the reference in *Gillett v Holt* [2001] Ch 210 at 235 to the promisee's "bitter humiliation" on being summarily dismissed and made the subject of a police investigation for allegations of dishonesty which the promisor made no attempt to justify at the trial of the civil action.

[81] As in *Griffiths v Williams* [1978] E.G. Digest of Cases 919.

[82] [1965] 2 Q.B. 507.

[83] *cf.* criticisms of the law by Browne-Wilkinson J. in *Re Sharpe* [1980] 1 W.L.R. 219 at 226.

[84] [1973] E.G. Digest of Cases 233; to the extent that the reasoning is based on the provisions of Settled Land Act 1925, s.1, it is criticised in *Griffiths v Williams* [1978] E.G. Digest of Cases 919; *cf. Campbell v Griffin* [2001] EWCA Civ 990; [2001] W.T.L.R. 981; *Jennings v Rice* [2002] EWCA Civ 159; [2002] W.T.L.R. 367.

[85] *Burrows and Burrows v Sharp* (1991) 23 H.L.R. 82; *cf. Baker v Baker* (1993) 25 H.L.R. 408. (where the action was for damages).

[86] *Clough v Kelly* (1996) 72 P. & C.R. D22.

[87] *cf. Cheese v Thomas* [1994] 1 W.L.R. 129, a case of undue influence.

In *Dodsworth v Dodsworth*[88] the court awarded compensation even though, when the action was brought, the promisee was still in possession of the improved property. More commonly this form of remedy is granted where the promisee is no longer in possession, having either left voluntarily[89] or been lawfully ejected as a result of legal proceedings.[90] Where the promisee has been wrongly ordered to give up possession, compensation in money is similarly available,[91] though in such a case the court may alternatively order the promisee to be put back into possession of the premises.[92] The compensation has been assessed in a variety of ways: at the cost of improvements made with the promisee's money[93]; at a proportionate interest in the property[94]; or at the reasonable value of the right of occupation, based (presumably) on the cost to the promisee of equivalent alternative accommodation.[95] The flexibility of the remedy also enables the court to combine monetary compensation with specific relief: for example, in *Gillett v Holt*[96] the promisee was awarded part of the property to which the promise referred, together with a cash payment to compensate him for his exclusion from the farming business on that property.

The court may, finally, deny the promisee a remedy where, on balance, greater hardship would be produced by giving effect to the promise than by allowing the promisor to go back on it. This was the position in *Sledmore v Dalby*,[97] where the promisee had contributed to major improvements to the property but at the time of the proceedings had already enjoyed 20 years' rent-free occupation and was gainfully employed, while the promisor was a widow living on social security benefits. The promisee's claim to be entitled to a licence for life to stay in the house was in these circumstances rejected and the promisor was held entitled to possession.

(3) Proprietary and promissory estoppels contrasted[98]

Proprietary and promissory estoppels have a number of points in common. Both can arise from promises[99]; consideration is not, while action in reliance is, a necessary condition for their operation[1]; and both are, within limits, revocable.[2] But there are also important differences between the two doctrines.

The scope of proprietary is in two respects narrower than that of promissory estoppel. First, proprietary estoppel is restricted promises relating to property (generally the land) of another. Promissory estoppel may, on the other hand, arise (if other necessary conditions are satisfied[3]) out of *any* promise that strict legal rights will not be enforced: there is no need for those rights to relate to land or other property. Secondly proprietary estoppel requires the promisee to have acted to his detriment,[4] while promissory estoppel may operate even though the promisee merely performs a pre-existing duty and

---

[88] [1973] E.G. Digest of Cases 233.
[89] As in *Hussey v Palmer* [1972] 1 W.L.R. 1286 and *Eves v Eves* [1975] 1 W.L.R. 1338.
[90] As in *Plimmer v Mayor of Wellington* (1884) 9 App.Cas. 699.
[91] *Tanner v Tanner* [1975] 1 W.L.R. 1346 (where there was a contract).
[92] *ibid.*
[93] *Hussey v Palmer* [1972] 1 W.L.R. 1286; *Burrows and Burrows v Sharp* (1991) 23 H.L.R. 82.
[94] *Eves v Eves* [1975] 1 W.L.R. 1338.
[95] *Tanner v Tanner* [1975] 1 W.L.R. 1346; *Baker v Baker* (1993) 25 H.L.R. 408.
[96] [2001] Ch. 210.
[97] (1996) 72 P. & C.R. 196.
[98] Evans [1988] Conv. 346.
[99] See above, **pp.**107, 116, 131, 136. For use of the expressions "promissory estoppel" see above, p.116.
[1] See above, pp.109, 131, 141.
[2] See above, pp.111, 131, 142.
[3] See above, pp.107–111, 130–134.
[4] See above, p.141.

so suffers no detriment in the sense of doing something that he was not previously bound to do.[5] This difference between the two doctrines follows from the fact that promissory estoppel is (unlike proprietary estoppel) concerned only with the variation or abandonment of rights arising out of a pre-existing legal relationship between promisor and promisee.

On the other hand, the scope of proprietary is in two respects wider than that of promissory estoppel. First, promissory estoppel arises only out of a representation or promise that is "clear" or "precise and unambiguous".[6] Proprietary estoppel, on the other hand, can arise where there is no actual promise: for example, where one party makes improvements to another's land under a mistake[7] and the other either knows of the mistake[8] or seeks to take unconscionable advantage of it.[9] Secondly (and more significantly), while promissory estoppel is essentially defensive in nature,[10] proprietary estoppel can give rise to a cause of action.[11] The promisee is not merely entitled to raise the estoppel as a defence to an action of trespass or to a claim for possession: the court can make an order for the land to be conveyed to him,[12] or for compensation[13] or for such other remedy as appropriate.[14] Although the authorities support this second distinction between the two kinds of estoppel, they do not make any attempt to explain or justify it. It is submitted that the explanation is in part historical and terminological. Proprietary estoppel was originally explained in terms of *acquiescence*[15] or *encouragement*.[16] Hence no conflict with the requirement that *promises* must be supported by consideration was perceived; or where it was perceived the facts were said to give rise to a contract.[17] Promissory estoppel, on the other hand, dealt principally with the renegotiation of contracts; it obviously depended on giving binding effect to promises, and it did so in the context of releases and variations, in which the common law requirement of consideration had long been established.[18] The rule that promissory estoppel gives rise to no cause of action was evolved to prevent what would otherwise be an obvious conflict between the doctrines of promissory estoppel and consideration. In cases of proprietary estoppel there was no such conflict where liability was based on "acquiescence"; and where it was based on "encouragement" the conflict, though sometimes real enough, was at least less obvious. There are, moreover, two aspects of proprietary estoppel which help to justify the distinction. These are that the acts done by the promisee are not ones which he was under any previous legal obligation to perform; and that generally their effect would be unjustly to enrich the promisor if he were allowed to go back on his promise.[19] In these respects, the facts on which proprietary estoppel is based provide

---

[5] See above, p.110.

[6] See above, p.107.

[7] See above, pp.134–136.

[8] *Wilmott v Barber* (1880) 15 Ch.D. 96 at 105 (the claim in that case failed as the party against whom it was made did not know of the extent of his own rights or of the other party's mistake).

[9] *Taylors Fashions Ltd v Liverpool Victoria Trustees Co Ltd* [1982] Q.B. 133 n.

[10] See above, pp.111–114.

[11] *Crabb v Arun DC* [1976] Ch. 179 at 187; *Taylors Fashions Ltd v Liverpool Victoria Trustees Co Ltd* [1982] Q.B. 133n. at 148; *Durant v Heritage* [1994] E.G.C.S. 134, where the words "promissory estoppel" appear to be a misprint for "proprietary estoppel."

[12] *e.g. Dillwyn v Llewelyn* (1862) 4 D.F. & G. 517.

[13] *e.g. Eves v Eves* [1975] 1 W.L.R. 1338.

[14] See above, pp.144–146.

[15] *Wilmott v Barber* (1880) 15 Ch.D. 96 at 105.

[16] *Ramsden v Dyson* (1866) L.R. 1 H.L. 129 at 170.

[17] *Dillwyn v Llewelyn* (1862) 4 D.F. & G. 517 at 522; above, pp.136–138.

[18] See above, pp.99–102.

[19] See the reference to the landowner's "profit" in *Ramsden v Dyson* (1866) L.R. 1 H.L. 129 at 141 and *cf.* above, pp.136–137.

more compelling grounds for relief[20] than those commonly found in cases of promissory estoppel.

While the two doctrines are in these respects distinct it can also be argued that they have a common basis, namely that it would be unconscionable for the promisor to go back on his promise after the promisee has acted on it; and that the precise labels to be attached to them are "immaterial".[21] It is perhaps for these reasons that the distinction between the two kinds of estoppel was described as "not . . . helpful" by Scarman L.J. in *Crabb v Arun DC*.[22] That decision was, in a later case, said to illustrate "the virtual equation of promissory estoppel and proprietary estoppel",[23] perhaps because it extended the operation of proprietary estoppel beyond the situations originally within its scope, namely those in which the promisor would be unjustly enriched by the work done by the promisee on the land unless some legal effect were given to the promise. Nevertheless it is submitted that the doctrines are distinct in the respects stated above.[24] Attempts to unite them by posing "simply" the question whether it would be "unconscionable",[25] for the promisor to go back on his promise are, for reasons given earlier in this Chapter,[26] unhelpful[27]; and they are also open to the objection that they provide no basis on which a legal doctrine capable of yielding predictable results can be developed.

(4) Proprietary estoppel and contract contrasted

We have seen that some cases which have been said to support the doctrine of proprietary estoppel can be explained on the alternative basis that there was a contract between the parties.[28] But this explanation will not cover all the cases; for proprietary estoppel can operate even though the conditions required for the creation of a contract are not satisfied. The need to discuss the doctrine in this Chapter arises precisely because a promise can give rise to a proprietary estoppel even though it is not supported by consideration; and a promise can also give rise to such an estoppel even though it cannot take effect as a contract because it is not sufficiently certain or because it fails to comply with formal requirements. Moreover, the effect of a proprietary estoppel differs from that of a contract. Sometimes, indeed, the result of a proprietary estoppel is to give effect to the promise in the terms in which it was made[29]; but such a result does not

---

[20] See Fuller and Eisenberg, *Basic Contract Law* (3rd ed.), p.70: "Unjust enrichment presents a more urgent case for judicial intervention than losses through reliance which do not benefit the defendant." *cf.* Fuller and Perdue, 46 Yale L.J. 52, 56 (1936).

[21] *Taylors Fashions Ltd v Liverpool Victoria Trustee Co Ltd* [1982] Q.B. 133 n.at 153, where, however, a distinction is also drawn between "promissory estoppel" and the principle in *Ramsden v Dyson* (1866) L.R. 1 H.L. 129 (*i.e.* proprietary estoppel).

[22] [1976] Ch. 179 at 193.

[23] *Taylors Fashions Ltd v Liverpool Victoria Trustees Co Ltd* [1982] Q.B. 133 n.at 153. The use of "promissory estoppel" to describe a typical *proprietary* estoppel situation in *Griffiths v Williams* [1978] E.G. Digest of Cases 919 at 921 may be a misprint.; *cf.* also above, p.137, n.95.

[24] At nn.11 to 22.

[25] *Taylors Fashions Ltd v Liverpool Victoria Trustees Co Ltd* [1982] Q.B. 133 n. at 155; *cf. Habib Bank Ltd v Habib Bank AG Zürich* [1981] 1 W.L.R. 1265 at 1285; *Amalgamated Investment & Property Co Ltd v Texas Commerce International Bank Ltd* [1982] Q.B. 84 at 104, 122.

[26] See above, p.115.

[27] *cf. Haslemere Estates Ltd v Baker* [1982] 1 W.L.R. 1009 at 1119 where Megarry V.-C., rejecting the argument that proprietary estoppel arises "whenever justice and good conscience requires it," said "I do not think that the subject is as wide and indefinite as that". Dicta emphasising the flexibility of the *remedy* (above, p.144) must be read subject to the requirement to adopted a "principle approach" (*ibid.*) to this aspect of the doctrine; and they should, in any event, not be taken to refer also to *conditions of liability*.

[28] See above, p.137.

[29] *e.g. Dillwyn v Llewelyn* (1862) 4 D.F. & G. 517.

follow as of right. We have seen that the promisee's rights may depend, not only on the terms of the promise and on the extent to which he has acted on it, but also on the subsequent conduct of the promisor. Thus in *Crabb v Arun DC* the promisee would have had to make some payment for the right of way but for the "high-handedness"[30] of the promisor; and in *Pascoe v Turner* the promisee would not have been entitled to the fee simple of the house (but only to an irrevocable licence for life) if the promisor had not shown a "ruthless"[31] determination to evict her. The rights arising under a binding contract are fixed at its formation and not subject to such variation in the light of the court's approval or disapproval of the subsequent conduct of one of the parties. For this reason, and because proprietary estoppel may be revocable,[32] it will generally be more advantageous to a party to show the existence of a binding contract (if he can) than to rely on a proprietary estoppel.

SECTION 8. SPECIAL CASES

1. Defective Promises[33]

Mutual promises are generally consideration for each other,[34] but difficulty is sometimes felt in treating a promise as consideration for another if the first promise suffered from some defect by reason of which it was not legally binding. The law on this topic is based rather on expediency than on any supposedly logical deductions which might be drawn from the doctrine of consideration. The question whether a defective promise can constitute consideration for a counter-promise depends on the policy of the rule of law making the former promise defective.

(a) POLICY CONSIDERATIONS. One group of cases concerns contracts made between persons, one of whom lacks contractual capacity.[35] A minor can enforce a promise made to him under such a contract, even though the only consideration for that promise is his own promise, which does not bind him by reason of his minority.[36] The same rule applies to contracts with mental patients.[37] The reason for these rules is that it is the policy of the law to protect the person under the incapacity, and not the other party, who is therefore not allowed to rely on that incapacity. A contrasting group of cases concerns promises which are illegal. Obviously the illegal promise cannot be enforced; and if both promises are illegal the consequence that neither can be enforced follows from the policy of the invalidating rule rather than from the fact that an illegal promise cannot constitute consideration.[38] But in some cases of illegal contracts the illegality affects the promise or promises of only one party: this is, for example, often the position where the contract is in restraint of trade. In such a case, the party who makes the illegal promise cannot enforce the counter-promise (*e.g.* to pay a sum of money) if the illegal promise constitutes the sole consideration for the counter-promise.[39] Indeed, the position is the same if the illegal promise is the *main* consideration for the counter-promise, even though

---

[30] [1976] Ch. 179 at 199.
[31] [1979] 1 W.L.R. 431 at 438.
[32] See above, p.142.
[33] Treitel, 77 L.Q.R. 83.
[34] See above, pp.70.
[35] See Chap.13 below.
[36] *Holt v Ward Clarencieux* (1732) 2 Stra. 937; below, p.549.
[37] See below, p.557.
[38] As suggested in *Nerot v Wallace* (1789) 3 T.R. 17 at 23.
[39] *e.g. Wyatt v Kreglinger & Fernau* [1933] 1 K.B. 793.

there was also some other consideration for it.[40] The reason for this rule lies in the policy of the law to discourage illegal bargains.

(b) PERFORMANCE OF DEFECTIVE PROMISE. Where a defective *promise* does not amount to consideration its *performance* can nevertheless sometimes provide consideration for the counter-promise. For example, a mere promise to negotiate has no contractual force[41] and so cannot constitute consideration for a counter-promise; but actually carrying on the negotiations can satisfy the requirement of consideration.[42] A similar principle accounts for the rule that a victim of misrepresentation, duress or undue influence can sue but not be sued: by suing, he affirms the contract, makes his own promise binding on himself, and so supplies consideration for the other party's promise. But where the promise of one party is illegal, even its performance does not entitle that party to enforce the counter-promise,[43] for the law must not give him any incentive to perform the illegal promise.

(c) PROMISE DEFECTIVE BY STATUTE. Where one of the promises is defective by statute, the terms of the statute may solve the problem whether the person giving the defective promise can sue on the counter-promise.[44] Thus a party who gives a promise which is defective under s.4 of the Statute of Frauds 1677, or under s.34 of the Matrimonial Causes Act 1973, may, in spite of not being bound by that promise, be entitled to enforce the counter-promise[45]; and this may be so even though for other purposes (such as the validity of a disposition) a promise, precisely because it is defective by statute, does amount to consideration.[46] Where a statute invalidates a promise but does not provide for the effect of its invalidity on the other party's promise, it seems that the invalid promise is not good consideration[47]; but, unless the promise is illegal, the party giving it can sue on the counter-promise if he actually performs his own promise.[48]

(d) BOTH PROMISES DEFECTIVE BY STATUTE. A statute may also invalidate *both* promises: this is the position with regard to wagering contracts which are "null and void" under s.18 of the Gaming Act 1845.[49] Performance of one such promise clearly would not make the other enforceable[50]; but the question whether performance of the void promise could constitute consideration might also arise in another context, for example in the context of the question whether the performance amounted to consideration for the purpose of a rule of law by which a transfer or disposition of property was effective only if made for valuable consideration. This was the question which arose in

---

[40] See *Goodinson v Goodinson* [1954] 2 Q.B. 118; the actual decision is obsolete in view of Matrimonial Causes Act 1973, s.34, below, p.118.

[41] See above, pp.59–62.

[42] *Sepong Engineering Construction Co Ltd v Formula One Management Ltd* [2000] 1 Lloyd's Rep. 602 at 611, where it was also said that damages for breach of the resulting contract would be no more than nominal: below, p.890. The same reasoning applied when, before the Corporate Bodies Contracts Act 1960, unsealed promises made by a corporation did not bind it: see *Fishmongers' Co v Robertson* (1843) 5 Man. & G. 131; *Kidderminster Corp v Hardwick* (1873) L.R. 9 Ex. 13.; *cf. Re Dale* [1994] Ch. 31 at 38.

[43] *e.g. Wyatt v Kreglinger & Fernall* [1933] 1 K.B. 793.

[44] See *Laythoarp v Bryant* (1836) 2 Bing.N.C. 735.

[45] See below, pp.183, 447. For more elaborate provisions of this kind, see Financial Services and Markets Act 2000, ss.20, 26–30.

[46] *Re Kumar* [1993] 1 W.L.R. 224, where a void promise was held not to constitute consideration for the purpose of protecting third parties under Insolvency Act 1986, s.339 (above, p.75).

[47] *Clayton v Jennings* (1760) 2 W.Bl. 706.

[48] This, it is submitted, is the best justification for *Rajbenback v Mamon* [1955] 1 Q.B. 283; see 77 L.Q.R. 95. For another view, see Unger 19 M.L.R. 99.

[49] See below, p.520.

[50] *cf.* above at n.43.

Lipkin Gorman v Karpnale Ltd,[51] where stolen money was used by the thief for gambling at a club of which he was a member, and it was held that the club had not received the money for valuable consideration so as to be entitled, as against the owner of the money, to retain it. We have already noted that the club did not provide consideration for the payment by exchanging the money for gaming chips.[52] The present point is that the club did not provide consideration for the payments made to it by the member by allowing him to gamble and promising to pay, or actually paying him, the amount of any bets which he had won. The club's *promise* to pay did not amount to consideration since it was void under s.18 of the 1845 Act. Nor did *performance* of that promise constitute consideration; for such a payment was said by Lords Templeman and Goff to be treated in law as a completed voluntary gift to the winner.[53] To treat the payment of losses as gifts may not be easy to reconcile with the "common sense approach"[54] used in the same case to rebut the argument that the club had provided consideration for the payments by supplying the member with gaming chips. In another part of his speech Lord Goff said that "the practical business position is that if the casino does not pay winnings when they are due it will simply go out of business. So the obligation in honour to pay winnings is an obligation which, in business terms, the casino has to comply with".[55] Conversely, a member who did not pay losses when due would no doubt be excluded from the club. It is scarcely realistic to describe payments made under such pressures as voluntary gifts. But the view that the club did not provide consideration by paying bets which it had lost can be explained by reference to the context in which it arose: it helped to protect the victim of the theft,[56] or at least formed the first step in a line of reasoning which enabled the House of Lords to split the loss between the victim of the theft and the equally innocent recipient of the money.[57]

2. Unilateral Contracts[58]

In the case of a unilateral contract the promisee clearly provides consideration if he completes the required act or forbearance (such as walking to York or not smoking for a year).[59] This amounts in law to a detriment to the promisee; and the promisor may also obtain a benefit: *e.g.* where he promises a reward for the return of lost property and it is actually returned to him. But it has been suggested that if the promisee has begun, but not yet completed, the required act or forbearance the promisor can still withdraw. At this stage, there is said to be no consideration for the promise, since the promisee is not bound to complete performance.[60] But it may in law be detriment to walk part of the way to York, or to forbear from smoking for part of the year. Questions of fact may, indeed, arise in determining whether performance has actually begun, particularly where the stipulated performance was a forbearance; but if an actual forbearance *to sue* can

---

[51] [1991] 2 A.C. 548; below, p.535.
[52] See above, p.86.
[53] [1991] 2 A.C. 548 at 562, 565, 577.
[54] [1991] 2 A.C. 548 at 576.
[55] *ibid.* at 581.
[56] See above, p.86.
[57] See below, p.537.
[58] See above, pp.37 *et seq.*
[59] See above, p.38; *Marshall v N M Financial Management Ltd* [1997] 1 W.L.R. 1527 at 1533. For controversy whether the act must be "requested" by the promisor in cases of unilateral contracts, see A.L.G., 67 L.Q.R. 456; Smith, 69 L.Q.R. 99; A.L.G., 69 L.Q.R. 106.
[60] Wormser, in *Selected Readings on the Law of Contracts*, at p.307; but for the same writer's later views, see 3 Jl.Leg.Educ. 146.

constitute good consideration,[61] it must in principle be possible to tell when a forbearance has begun. Thus commencement of performance (whether of an act or of a forbearance) may provide consideration for the promise and so deprive the promisor of the power to withdraw it. Of course, the promisor's liability to pay the amount promised (*e.g.* the £100 for walking to York) does not accrue before the promisee has fully performed the required act or forbearance. The present point is merely that, after part performance by the promisee, the promisor cannot withdraw his promise with impunity.

It has been suggested that a unilateral contract may be made as soon as the offer is received by the offeree[62]; and this could be interpreted to mean that the contract was binding even before the offeree had acted on the offer in any way. But at this stage the offeree has clearly not provided any consideration, and in the case in which the suggestion was made no problem of consideration arose as the offeree had completed the required act[63] before any attempt to withdraw the offer was made. Except in the case of bankers' irrevocable credits (to be discussed below), the better view is that an offer of a unilateral contract is not binding on receipt, but only when the offeree has begun to render the required performance.

3. Bankers' Irrevocable Credits

Contracts for the international sale of goods often provide for payment by irrevocable credit.[64] The buyer instructs his bank to open an irrevocable credit in favour of the seller; and the bank then notifies the seller that such a credit has been opened in his favour, and that he will be paid, usually when he tenders specified shipping documents to the bank. The general view is that the bank is bound by this arrangement and is not entitled to withdraw simply because the shipping documents have not yet been tendered.[65] But it is very doubtful whether at this stage there is any consideration, moving from the seller, for the bank's promise to him.[66]

One view is that the bank makes an offer of a unilateral contract, for which the seller provides consideration by performing his contract with the buyer.[67] As in the case of other unilateral contracts, steps taken in the performance would be enough, *e.g.* beginning to manufacture the goods. If the seller already had the goods when he received notification of the credit one could find consideration in his forbearing to make other attempts to dispose of them. Another view is that, because the seller is not bound to deliver the goods to the buyer until he receives notification of the credit, his becoming

---

[61] See above, p.90.

[62] *Harvela Investments Ltd v Royal Trust Co of Canada (CI) Ltd* [1986] 1 A.C. 207 at 224 ("when the invitation was received").

[63] By submitting the requested bid: *cf.* above, p.21.

[64] See generally *Guaranty Trust Co of NY v Hannay* [1918] 2 K.B. 623 at 659.

[65] See *Hamzeh Malas & Sons v British Imex Industries Ltd* [1958] 2 Q.B. 127 at 129 (where there was consideration of the most orthodox kind, the seller having paid the bank a confirmation commission: see *British Imex Industries Ltd v Midland Bank Ltd* [1958] 1 Q.B. 542 at 544); *W J Alan & Co Ltd v El Nasr Export & Import Co* [1972] 2 Q.B. 189 at 208; *cf. ibid.* at 218; *Offshore International SA v Banco Central SA* [1977] 1 W.L.R. 399 at 401; *Trendtex Trading Corp v Central Bank of Nigeria* [1977] Q.B. 529 at 551; *The American Accord* [1983] 1 A.C. 168 at 183; *Jaks (UK) Ltd v Cera Investment Bank SA* [1998] 2 Lloyd's Rep. 89 at 94.

[66] Davis, *The Law Relating to Commercial Credits* (3rd ed.), Chap.7; Gutteridge & Megrah, *The Law of Bankers' Commercial Credits* (7th ed.), pp.26 *et seq.*; Ellinger, *Documentary Letters of Credit*, pp.39 *et seq*; *Benjamin's Sale of Goods* (6th ed.), §§23–131 to 23–135.

[67] *cf. Guaranty Trust Co of NY v Hannay* [1918] 2 K.B. 623 at 659; *Urquhart Lindsay & Co v Eastern Bank* [1922] 1 K.B. 318 at 321; above, p.40.

so bound on such notification is the consideration for the bank's promise.[68] But as the seller's becoming bound in this way does not result from any act (or even forbearance) by him at this stage, it is hard to see how it can amount to consideration for the promise by the bank. Yet another suggestion is that the seller might provide consideration by forbearing to sue the buyer for the price. But the bank would not, on this view, be bound before the seller had acted, or forborne, in some such way. The widely held commercial view is that the bank is bound as soon as the seller is notified of the credit. If (as seems probable) this view also represents the law, it is best regarded as exception to the doctrine of consideration.[69] A final possibility is that the seller might be able to make a claim, as a third party, to enforce a term of the contract between the buyer and the bank, under the Contracts (Rights of Third Parties) Act 1999. Such a claim could succeed even though no consideration for the bank's promise had moved from the seller[70]; but it would in a number of ways[71] be less secure than one available at common law.

4. Firm Offers

A "firm" offer is one containing a promise not to revoke it for a specified time. Such a promise is not binding unless the offeree has provided some consideration for it. Thus in *Dickinson v Dodds*[72] it was held that an offer to sell land "to be left over until Friday"[73] could be withdrawn on Thursday. Consideration for such a promise is most obviously provided if the offeree pays (or promises to pay) a sum of money for it and so buys an option.[74] It may also be provided by some other promise: for example, in the case of an offer to sell a house, the offeree may provide consideration for the offeror's promise to hold the offer open, by promising to apply for a mortgage on the house; and, in the case of an offer to buy shares, the offeree may provide consideration for the offeror's promise not to revoke the offer for a specified time, by promising not to dispose of those shares elsewhere during that time. The performance of the offeree's promises in such cases could likewise provide consideration for the offeror's promise to keep the offer open. In one case a vendor of land entered into a so-called "lock-out" agreement[75] by which he

---

[68] The suggestion is sometimes said to be supported by dictum in *Dexters Ltd v Schenker & Co* (1923) 14 Ll.L. Rep. 586 at 588; but the judgment does not purport to go beyond *Urquhart Lindsay & Co v Eastern Bank*, above, n.67. The seller does not *promise* the bank to perform his contract with the buyer, so that cases such as *Pao On v Lau Yiu Long* [1980] A.C. 614 (above, p.98) do not help with the problem of consideration for the bank's promise to him.

[69] *cf.* in the United States, U.C.C. ss.5–105.

[70] See above, p.83.

[71] It would be subject to any defences which the bank might have against the buyer: see s.3(2) of the 1999 Act, below, p.660 and to rescission or variation by agreement between the buyer and the bank of the contract between them, to the extent permitted by s.2(1), below, p.657.

[72] (1876) 2 Ch.D. 463; *cf. Cooke v Oxley* (1790) 3 T.R. 653; *Routledge v Grant* (1828) 4 Bing. 653; *Head v Diggon* (1828) 3 M. & Ry. 97.

[73] *Quaere* whether this meant that the offer would not be withdrawn before Friday, or only that it should lapse on Friday and not before. The latter interpretation was given to a stipulation that an offer should be "open all Monday" in *Stevenson, Jacques & Co v McLean* (1880) 6 Q.B.D. 346.

[74] The legal characteristics of such an option have been variously described: (1) as a contract: *Greene v Church Commissioners for England* [1974] Ch. 467 at 476, 478 (disapproving a dictum in *Beesly v Hallwood Estates Ltd* [1960] 1 W.L.R. 549 at 555, actual decision affirmed [1961] Ch. 549); though not one of sale: *Chippenham Golf Club v North Wilts Rural DC* (1992) 64 P. & C.R. 527; (2) as a transaction which, even though it is not a contract, gives rise to an interest in property: *Re Button's Lease* [1964] Ch. 263 at 270–271; *Armstrong & Holmes Ltd v Holmes* [1994] 1 All E.R. 826; (3) as a unilateral contract: *United Scientific Holdings Ltd v Burnley B.C.* [1978] A.C. 904 at 945; *Little v Courage Ltd*, (1995) 70 P. & C.R. 469 at 474; (4) as a conditional contract: *Bircham & Co Nominees (No.2) Ltd v Worrell Holdings Ltd* [2001] EWCA Civ 773; (2001) 82 P. & C.R. 427 at [45]; and (5) as being *sui generis*: *Spiro v Glencrown Properties* [1991] Ch. 537 at 544. And see Mowbray, 74 L.Q.R. 242; Lücke, 3 Adelaide L.Rev. 200.

[75] See above, p.53.

promised a prospective purchaser not to consider other offers if that purchaser would exchange contracts within two weeks; and it was said that "the promise by the [purchaser] to get on by limiting himself to just two weeks"[76] constituted consideration for the vendor's promise not to consider other offers. Such a "lock out" promise is not strictly a firm offer since it does not prevent the vendor from deciding not to sell at all; but the reasoning quoted above could apply to the case of a firm offer. On the facts of the case from which it is taken, the reasoning gives rise to some difficulty since it does not appear that the purchaser there made any *promise* to exchange contracts within two weeks. It seems more plausible to say that the vendor's promise had become binding as a unilateral contract under which the purchaser had provided consideration by actually making efforts to meet the deadline, even though he had not promised to do so. Similar reasoning can apply if a seller of land promises to keep an offer open for a month, asking the buyer during that period to raise the necessary money. If the buyer makes efforts to that end (without actually promising to do so) it is arguable that he has by part performance accepted the seller's offer of a unilateral contract to keep the principal offer open. On the other hand the equitable doctrine of *Hughes v Metropolitan Ry*[77] will not avail the offeree since it does not create new causes of action where none existed before.[78] Nor does it seem likely that an offeree who suffers loss as a result of the withdrawal of the offer will be able to claim damages in tort[79] for misrepresentation.[80]

The rule in *Dickinson v Dodds* can lead to inconvenience, so much so that there are some situations in which it has been said that "the market would disdain"[81] to take the point that there was no consideration for a promise to keep an offer open. In the case of certain international sales, the rule is rejected by the Vienna Convention on Contracts for the International Sale of Goods.[82] It is also subject to a common law exception in the law of insurance where an underwriter who initials a slip under an "open cover" arrangement is regarded as making a "standing offer" which the insured can accept from time to time by making "declarations" under it. The underwriter's commitment is regarded as binding even though there is no consideration for his implied promise not to revoke the "standing offer".[83] But even with these mitigations, the rule can still cause hardship to an offeree who has acted in reliance on the assurance that the offer will be kept open for a stated time. Such hardship can, for example, arise where a builder submits a tender in reliance on offers from sub-contractors, expressed to remain "firm" for a fixed period,[84] and those offers are withdrawn within that period but after his

---

[76] *Pitt v PHH Asset Management Ltd* [1994] 1 W.L.R. 327 at 332; MacMillan, [1993] C.L.J. 392; for other consideration in this case, see above, p.90; *Tye v House* [1997] 2 E.G.L.R. 171.

[77] (1877) 2 App.Cas. 439; above, p.105.

[78] See above, p.111.

[79] *cf. Holman Construction Ltd v Delta Timber Co Ltd* [1972] N.Z.L.R. 1081; and see *Blackpool and Fylde Aero Club Ltd v Blackpool BC* [1990] 1 W.L.R. 1195 at 1202.

[80] *i.e.* under *Hedley Byrne & Co Ltd v Heller & Partners Ltd* [1964] A.C. 465; below, p.344.

[81] *Jaglom v Excess Insurance Co Ltd* [1972] 2 Q.B. 250 at 258; *cf. County Ltd v Girozentrale Securities* [1996] 3 All E.R. 834 where an "offer to subscribe" for shares was described at 837 as "not legally binding but regarded by City convention as binding in honour unless some unforeseen exceptional circumstances supervened." It seems that the "commitment" (*ibid.*) was given, not to the company, but to the underwriter, or by prospective investors to each other, so that the principles discussed at pp.15–16 above did not apply. For the view that the statement in *Jaglom's* case was not an offer, but an acceptance (and binding as such) see *General Reinsurance Corp v Forsakringsaktiebolaget Fennia Patria* [1983] Q.B. 856 at 863–864.

[82] See above, p.29, Art. 16(2); *cf.* U.C.C. s.2–205, limiting the period of irrevocability to three months on the theory that unlimited irrevocability could unreasonably prejudice the offeror.

[83] *Citadel Insurance Co v Atlantic Union Insurance Co* [1982] 2 Lloyd's Rep. 543 at 546.

[84] For conflicting American authorities, see *James Baird Co v Gimbel Bros* 64 F. 2d. 344 (1933); *Drennan v Star Paving Co* 51 Cal. 2d. 409, 333 p.2d. 757 (1958). For a review of Canadian authorities, see *Northern Construction Co v Gloge Heating & Plumbing* [1986] 2 W.W.R. 649, holding a sub-contractor bound by his offer.

tender has been accepted. On the other hand, the rule does sometimes provide necessary protection for the offeror: *e.g.* when an offer is made by a customer on a form provided by a supplier and expressed to be irrevocable; or when the period of irrevocability is not specified so that the offeror is left subject to an indefinite obligation without acquiring any corresponding right. Any further development of the law on the point will require a balancing of these conflicting factors.[85]

5. Auction Sales Without Reserve[86]

Where goods are put up for auction without reserve, there is no contract *of sale* if the auctioneer refuses to knock the goods down to the highest bidder; but the auctioneer is liable to the highest bidder on a separate promise that the sale will be without reserve.[87] It is arguable that there is no consideration for this promise as the highest bidder is not bound by his unaccepted bid.[88] But it has been held that the bidder suffers a detriment by bidding on the strength of the promise, for he runs the risk of being bound by a contract of sale[89]; and the auctioneer benefits as the bidding is driven up.[90] Hence there is consideration for the separate promise, and it makes no difference to the auctioneer's liability *on this promise* that he would not be liable if he did not put the goods up for sale at all (since an advertisement of an auction is not an offer to hold it)[91] or that there was no contract *of sale* because of his refusal to accept the highest bid.[92]

6. Novation of Partnership Debts

When the composition of a partnership changes, it is usual to arrange that liability for the debts owed by the existing partners should be transferred by novation[93] to the new partners. Two situations may be considered.

(1) A and B are in partnership; A retires and C is admitted as a new partner; it is agreed between A, B and C, and the creditors of the old firm of A and B, that A shall cease to be liable for the firm's debts, and that C shall undertake such liability. The result is that the creditors can sue C and can no longer sue A. They provide consideration for C's promise to pay by abandoning their claim against A; and A provides consideration for their promise to release him by procuring a substitute debtor, C.

(2) A and B are in partnership; A retires; it is agreed between A, B and the creditors of the firm that A shall cease to be liable and that B shall be solely liable. It seems that the creditors cannot sue A, but it is hard to see what consideration moves from him. In one case it was said that there was consideration in that a remedy against a single debtor

---

[85] See Law Commission Working Paper 60 (1975).

[86] See also above, p.11.

[87] *Warlow v Harrison* (1859) 1 E. & E. 309; approved in *Harris v Nickerson* (1873) L.R. 8 Q.B. 286 at 288; *Johnston v Boyes* [1899] 2 Ch. 73 at 77.

[88] For discussion of this point, see Slade, 68 L.Q.R. 238; Gower, *ibid.* 457; Slade, 69 L.Q.R. 21.

[89] An "invented" consideration: see above, p.71.

[90] *Barry v Davies* [2000] 1 W.L.R. 1962 at 1967.

[91] *Harris v Nickerson* (1873) L.R. 8 Q.B. 286; above, p.12.

[92] See above, p.11.

[93] See below, p.673; *cf.* Partnership Act 1890, s.17(3). Problems of the kind here discussed do not arise in the same form in the case of a limited liability partnership incorporated under the Limited Liability Partnership Act 2000 since the liabilities of the partnership are those of the body corporate incorporated under ss.1–3 of that Act; these are not affected by a change in the membership of that body. S.6(3) of the Act deals with the different question of the extent to which acts of a person who has ceased to be a member can still impose liability on the partnership.

might be easier to enforce than one against several, all of whom are solvent[94]; thus the creditors benefit by the release of A. This is a possible, if invented[95] consideration.

7. Gratuitous Bailments

A gratuitous bailment may be for the benefit of either the bailee or the bailor.

The first possibility is illustrated by *Bainbridge v Firmstone*[96] where the defendant asked for, and received, permission from the plaintiff to weigh two boilers belonging to the plaintiff. In performing this operation, the defendant damaged the boilers; and he was held liable for breach of his promise to return them in good condition. The court rejected the argument that, as the defendant was not paid to weigh, or look after, the boilers, there was no consideration for his promise. Patteson J. said: "I suppose the defendant thought he had some benefit; at any rate there is a detriment to the plaintiff from his parting with the possession for even so short a time."[97] It is more doubtful whether there would be any consideration moving from the defendant for any promise by the plaintiff to allow the defendant to have possession of the boilers. A mere promise by the defendant to return the boilers might not suffice as it would only be a promise to perform a duty imposed by law on all bailees; but a promise to repair the boilers or to improve them in some way would probably be regarded as consideration moving from the defendant.[98]

The second possibility, *i.e.* that of a bailment for the benefit of the bailor, arises where A undertakes the safekeeping of B's chattel without reward. Here B's parting with the possession is hardly a detriment to him; and A's duty to look after the thing[99] does not arise out of a contractual promise made by him but is imposed by the general law. It follows that A's *only* duty is that imposed by the law.[1] Thus A is under no obligation before he actually receives the thing; and if he promised to do anything which went beyond the duty imposed by law (for example, to keep the thing in repair) he would be bound by this promise only if B had provided some consideration for it apart from the delivery of the chattel.[2] To constitute such consideration, it is not necessary to show that A profited from the transaction; thus it is enough if B reimburses (or promises to reimburse) any expenses that A has incurred for the purpose of performing his promise.[3]

8. Gratuitous Services

Normally, a promise to render services without reward is not binding contractually as no consideration for it is provided by the promisee. For example, where A gratuitously promises B to insure B's property but fails to do so, A is not liable to B for breach of contract if the property is lost or damaged.[4] It may sometimes be possible to find

---

[94] *Lyth v Ault* (1852) 7 Ex. 669; *Thompson v Percival* (1834) 5 B. & Ad. 925 is based on reasoning which is obsolete after *D & C Builders Ltd v Rees* [1967] 2 Q.B. 617.

[95] See above, p.71.

[96] (1838) 8 A. & E. 743.

[97] *ibid.* at 744.

[98] *cf. Verrall v Farnes* [1966] 1 W.L.R. 1254, a case relating to land; followed in *Mitton v Farrow* (1980) 255 E.G. 449.

[99] For this duty see *Coggs v Bernard* (1703) 2 Ld.Raym. 909; *Mitchell v London Borough of Ealing* [1979] Q.B. 1; *Port Swettenham Authority v T W Wu & Co* [1979] A.C. 580 at 590.

[1] *Morris v C W Martin Ltd* [1966] 1 Q.B. 716 at 731; *The Agia Skepi* [1992] 2 Lloyd's Rep. 467 at 472.

[2] *cf. Charnock v Liverpool Corporation* [1968] 1 W.L.R. 1498; below, p.584.

[3] *CCC Films (London) Ltd v Impact Quadrant Films Ltd* [1985] Q.B. 16 at 27.

[4] *Argy Trading & Development Co Ltd v Lapid Developments Ltd* [1977] 1 W.L.R. 444; *cf.* the New York case of *Thorn v Deas* 4 Johns. 84 (1809); more recent American authorities are divided: Corbin, *Contracts*, s.205, n.54.

consideration in an indirect benefit which the promisor obtains from the arrangement: *e.g.* in the form of favourable publicity.[5]

Even where the promise is not supported by consideration, the promisor may be liable in tort for negligence if he actually renders the gratuitous services but does so without due care and so causes loss. A banker who gives a negligent credit reference may be liable on this ground even though he makes no charge to the person to whom the information is given.[6] Similarly, where A gratuitously promised B to insure B's property and did so negligently, so that the policy did not cover the loss which occurred, A was held liable to B in tort.[7] In one case, a person was even held liable in tort for negligently giving free advice to a friend in connection with the purchase of a second-hand car which turned out to be seriously defective.[8]

The most important distinction between the two groups of cases discussed above is that between non-feasance and misfeasance in the performance of a promise to render gratuitous services. For this purpose, non-feasance means complete failure to pursue a *promised course of action*, while misfeasance means carelessness in the pursuit of that course of action, leading to failure to achieve a *promised result*. The first group of cases shows that non-feasance does not (in the absence of consideration[9]) make the promisor liable in contract, while the second shows that misfeasance can make the promisor liable in tort. There is no liability in tort for simply doing nothing after having promised to render services gratuitously; for to impose such liability would amount to holding "that the law of England recognises the enforceability of a gratuitous promise. On the face of it, this would be inconsistent with fundamental principle."[10] In cases of such pure non-feasance, the promisee will therefore have a remedy only if he can show that he provided consideration for the promise. Even in the case of misfeasance he may be in a better position with regard to damages if he can show that the promise had contractual force.[11]

In *Gore v Van der Lann*[12] a corporation issued a free travel pass to the claimant who "in consideration of my being granted a free pass" undertook that the use of the pass

---

[5] *cf. De la Bere v Pearson* [1908] 1 K.B. 280 at 287.

[6] See *Hedley Byrne & Co Ltd v Heller & Partners Ltd* [1964] A.C. 465; *cf.* below, p.344.

[7] *Wilkinson v Coverdale* (1793) 1 Esp. 75.

[8] *Chaudhry v Prabhakar* [1989] 1 W.L.R. 29 where the defendant conceded that he owed a duty of care to the claimant and two members of the Court of Appeal seem to have regarded this concession as correct; Brown [1989] L.M.C.L.Q. 148. Contrast *Henderson v Merrett Syndicates Ltd* [1995] 2 A.C. 145 at 181, suggesting that there may be no liability in respect of services rendered on "an informal occasion."

[9] Or of privity of contract: see *The Rebecca Elaine* [1999] 2 Lloyd's Rep. 1 at 5.

[10] *The Zephyr* [1985] 2 Lloyd's Rep. 529 at 538, disapproving the contrary view expressed at first instance [1984] 1 Lloyd's Rep. 58 at 85 and there based on authorities which were all cases of misfeasance. *The Zephyr* itself was also such a case: [1984] 1 Lloyd's Rep. at 79, 86 ("he was making the position steadily worse"). *A fortiori*, there is no liability in tort for pure omission where *no* promise has been made: see *Reid v Rush & Tompkins Group plc* [1990] 1 W.L.R. 212 and *Van Oppen v Clerk to the Bedford Charity Trustees* [1990] 1 W.L.R. 235, though in the latter case it was said at 260 that a voluntary assumption of responsibility by one party followed by reliance on it by the other might in exceptional cases give rise to such liability. The scope of this exception is not clear; in the last two cases it was held that there was *no* duty on respectively an employer and a school to advise an employee or the parents of a pupil to insure against forseeable risks of injury; *cf. Outram v Academy Plastics Ltd* [2001] I.C.R. 367 at 372: generally no liability in tort "for pure omission", the omission taking the form of an employer's failure, without breach of contract, to advise an employee as to his membership of the employer's pension scheme. Liability in tort for pure omission may exceptionally arise where there is a "duty to act": see *White v Jones* [1995] 2 A.C. 207 at 261, 268, 295 (below, p.616); but it is submitted that no such duty would be imposed by merely making gratuitous promise.

[11] *cf.* below, pp.359–362.

[12] [1967] 2 Q.B. 31; Harris, 30 M.L.R. 584; Odgers, 86 L.Q.R. 69; and see below, p.171, on the issue of contractual intention.

by her should be subject to certain conditions. One of these was that neither the corporation nor its servants were to be liable to her for loss or injury suffered while she was boarding, alighting from, or being carried in, the corporation's vehicles. The claimant was injured while boarding a corporation bus; and it was held that the issue and acceptance of the free pass amounted to a contract.[13] Willmer L.J. said that "Each party gave good consideration by accepting a detriment in return for the advantages gained."[14] The parties were, as a result of the issue of the pass, brought into a relationship of passenger and carrier which gave rise to duties independently of contract; and it was the promise not to enforce these obligations which constituted the consideration moving from the claimant. In the absence of such a relationship, a promise not to sue for defective performance would not amount to consideration for a promise to render a gratuitous service. Thus if A promised to carry B's goods to London free of charge and B promised not to sue A for negligently damaging them on the way, A would not be under any contractual liability for failing to pick up the goods. But he might be liable if he did pick them up and then unloaded them short of the agreed destination.

SECTION 9. PROMISES IN DEEDS

Consideration is not necessary for the validity of a promise in a deed. The binding force of such a promise does not depend on contract at all. Thus it can take effect although the person in whose favour it was made did not know of it.[15] To take effect as a deed, an instrument must make it clear on its face that it is intended to be a deed and must be validly executed as such.[16] At common law, execution of an instrument as a deed had to be under seal, but in many cases the requirement of sealing has been abolished by legislation. Sealing is no longer necessary in the case of an instrument executed as a deed by an individual.[17] To be validly executed as a deed, such an instrument must be signed[18] by or at the direction of the person making it in the presence of one attesting witness if it is signed by that person or of two such witnesses if it is signed as his direction[19]; it must also be delivered.[20] Sealing is also no longer necessary for the execution of a deed by a company incorporated under the Companies Acts: a document signed by a director and secretary, or by two directors, of such a company and expressed to be executed by the company has the same effect as if executed under the common seal of the company[21]; and (even if the company has no common seal[22]) a document executed by the company which makes it clear on its face that it is intended to be a deed has effect upon delivery

---

[13] This contract was void, so far as it purported to exclude liability for personal injury, by virtue of s.151 of the Road Traffic Act 1960, now Public Passenger Vehicles Act 1981, s.29; below, p.249.

[14] [1967] 2 Q.B. 31 at 42.

[15] *Hall v Palmer* (1844) 3 Hare 532; *Macedo v Stroud* [1922] 2 A.C. 330.

[16] Law of Property (Miscellaneous Provisions) Act 1989, s.1(2); Virgo and Harpum, [1991] L.M.C.L.Q. 209.

[17] 1989 Act, above, s.1(1)(b).

[18] Making one's mark suffices: *ibid.*, s.1(4).

[19] *ibid.*, s.1(3)(a). In *Shah v Shah* [2001] EWCA Civ. 527; [2001] 4 All E.R. 138 it was held that, though the requirement of signing was "fundamental" (at [28]), the requirement of the attesting witness' presence at the time of the signature was not; and that the maker of the instrument could be estopped from denying that the latter requirement was satisfied where, by delivering the Instrument, he had unambiguously represented that the instrument had been validly executed.

[20] Law of Property (Miscellaneous Provisions) Act 1989, s.1(3)(b).

[21] Companies Act 1985, s.36A(4) (as inserted by Companies Act 1989, s.130(1)). The subsection can apply where a document purporting to be sealed is not properly sealed: *OTV Birwelco Ltd v Technical & General Guarantee Co* [2002] EWHC 2240 (TCC); [2002] 4 All E.R. 668 at [70].

[22] See *ibid.*, s.36A(3).

as a deed.[23] Similar rules apply to charities incorporated under the Charities Act 1993.[24] When the system of electronic conveyancing envisaged by the Land Registration Act 2002 is brought into operation, certain electronic documents relating to the transfer of interests in land[25] are also to be regarded as deeds "for the purposes of any enactment".[26] The common law requirements of sealing and delivery continue to apply to the execution of deeds by corporations where it has not been relaxed by statutory provisions of the kind here described.

The common law requirement of sealing has been laxly interpreted. There need be no actual seal: it is enough if the document indicates where the seal is meant to be, and is signed with the intention of executing it as a deed.[27]

Delivery does not mean transfer of possession, but conduct indicating that the person who has executed the deed intends to be bound by it.[28] Delivery can be effected by giving the deed to the beneficiary, or to a third person to hold for him, but it is perfectly possible for the grantor to "deliver" the deed and yet keep possession of it.[29] A deed sealed by a corporation is deemed, in favour of a purchaser, to have been duly executed if certain statutory requirements are satisfied.[30] In such a case there is no separate requirement of "delivery". In the case of a document executed by a company incorporated under the Companies Acts, the rules just stated apply even if the document is *not* sealed: in favour of a purchaser, a document is deemed to have been duly executed if it purports to be signed by a director and the secretary or by two directors; and where the document makes it clear on its face that it is intended to be a deed, it is deemed to have been delivered upon its being executed.[31] Similar rules apply to charities incorporated under the Charities Act 1993.[32]

A document may be executed as a deed and delivered with the intention that it is to take effect only on the occurrence of some condition. The document is then said to be delivered as an escrow.[33] It will become effective as a deed only if the condition occurs; though it may then relate back to the date of the original delivery. For example, if the document is a lease, rent under it is payable from that date, unless the document specifies some other date.[34] Even before the occurrence of the condition, the document has some legal effect; it cannot be revoked by the grantor so long as it remains possible for the condition to occur.[35] The document will, however, cease to have this effect if the condition fails to occur within the time specified for its occurrence by the document.[36]

---

[23] *ibid.*, s.36A(5).

[24] Charities Act 1993, ss.50, 60.

[25] See below, p.178.

[26] Land Registration Act 2002, s.91(5); Companies Act 1985, s.36A(4) (above n.21) is modified accordingly by Land Registration Act 2002, s.91(9).

[27] *First National Securities Ltd v Jones* [1978] Ch. 109; Hoath, 43 M.L.R. 415. Contrast *TCB Ltd v Gray* [1987] Ch. 48; *Rushingdale SA v Byblos Bank SAL* 1985 P.C.C. 342.

[28] *Xenos v Wickham* (1866) L.R. 2 H.L. 296; *cf. Beesly v Hallwood Estates Ltd* [1960] 1 W.L.R. 549 at 562; affirmed [1961] Ch. 105; *Vincent v Premo Enterprises (Voucher Sales) Ltd* [1969] 2 Q.B. 609; Yale [1970] C.L.J. 52.

[29] *Doe v Knight* (1826) 5 B. & C. 671.

[30] Law of Property Act 1925, s.74(1); *D'Silva v Lister House Developments Ltd* [1971] Ch. 17.

[31] Companies Act 1985, s.36A(5) and (6), as inserted by Companies Act 1989, s.130(1).

[32] Charities Act 1993, s.60(7) and (8).

[33] See, for example, *Davy Offshore Ltd v Emerald Field Contracting Ltd* [1992] 2 Lloyd's Rep. 142 at 155.

[34] *Alan Estates Ltd v W G Stores Ltd* [1982] Ch. 511.

[35] *ibid.* at 520–521 and 527 rejecting a dictum in *Terrapin International Investments v IRC* [1976] 1 W.L.R. 665 at 669 that before the condition is fulfilled the escrow has "no effect whatsoever"; *cf.* above, p.63.

[36] *Glessing v Green* [1975] 1 W.L.R. 863.

Where no such time is specified, a term is likely to be implied that the condition must be fulfilled within a reasonable time.[37]

It is sometimes difficult to distinguish between a deed which has not been delivered at all and one which has been delivered as an escrow.[38] The distinction depends on the intention of the grantor. If he reserves an overriding power to recall the deed at his discretion, it is not delivered as an escrow but is simply an undelivered deed.[39]

SECTION 10. PROPOSALS FOR REFORM

The doctrine of consideration has attracted much criticism on general and on particular grounds. It has been said that the doctrine is an historical accident; that foreign systems do without it; and that it can easily be evaded, *e.g.* by the device of nominal consideration.[40] But these criticisms fail to come to grips with the fundamental question: whether it is desirable to enforce informal gratuitous promises. So long as the rights and interests of third parties are adequately protected,[41] the enforcement of such promises may do no harm. On the other hand English law does recognise, in the deed, a perfectly safe and relatively simple means of making gratuitous promises binding. Many such promises are in fact made by deed for tax purposes; and for this reason the legal enforceability of promises to give money to charitable institutions presents no serious problem in England.[42] Moreover, the small amount of extra effort, which the execution of a deed requires the promisor to make, may be a useful safeguard against rash promises.[43] The availability of the deed does not solve the problem of action in reliance on an *informal* gratuitous promise; but where there is such action the court may be able to invent consideration, or to give at least some effect to the promise under the doctrine of waiver or in equity.[44]

The doctrine can also cause inconvenience where the law for some reason treats a promise as not being supported by consideration even though the parties reasonably regard it as having been made for value.[45] This is particularly true in the existing duty cases, and in the cases on part payment of a debt. In those cases the doctrine of consideration may indeed at one time have performed a useful function in protecting a promisor against undue pressure or other undesirable conduct on the part of the promisee.[46] But this function is now more satisfactorily provided by the expanding notion of duress,[47] and the authorities have recognised this point, by holding that the requirement of consideration can be satisfied by the performance of, or the promise to perform, an existing duty, even if it causes no legal detriment to the promisee, so long

---

[37] *Alan Estates Ltd v W G Stores Ltd* [1982] Ch. 511 at 520.

[38] See *Vincent v Premo Enterprises (Voucher Sales) Ltd* [1969] 2 Q.B. 609; *Kingston v Ambrian Investments Ltd* [1975] 1 W.L.R. 161.

[39] *Windsor Refrigerator Co Ltd v Branch Nominees Ltd* [1961] Ch. 88 at 102; actual decision reversed on other grounds [1961] Ch. 375.

[40] See above, p.74.

[41] *cf.* above, p.74; *Eastwood v Kenyon* (1840) 11 A. & E. 438 at 450 and *Horrocks v Forray* [1976] 1 W.L.R. 230 (where a finding that there was no consideration helped to protect the creditors of the alleged promisor).

[42] There appear to be only two reported cases in which such claims failed for want of consideration; *Re Hudson* (1885) 54 L.J.Ch. 811 and *Re Cory* (1912) 29 T.L.R. 18.

[43] *cf.* below, p.176.

[44] See above, pp.71, 105–118, 130–134.

[45] *e.g.* above, pp.91–96, 125–126.

[46] See above, pp.91–92, 94, 125–126.

[47] See above, pp.94–95; below, p.405.

as it results in a factual benefit to the promisor.[48] On the other hand, the function of the doctrine in providing protection against the different risk of being bound by rashly made gratuitous promises remains an important one and must be taken into account in formulating proposals for reform.

A number of such proposals were made in 1937 by the Law Revision Committee.[49] Detailed discussion of these proposals no longer seems to be appropriate since some of them have been overtaken by later developments in the law[50] and since proposals for reform, if now revived, would no doubt differ substantially[51] from those made in 1937. Two central questions remain: first, whether the law should protect the promisor and third parties by retaining restrictions on the enforceability of gratuitous promises; and secondly, to what extent the law should protect a promisee who has reasonably acted in reliance on a promise which is not supported by consideration. So far as the second question is concerned, the present law amounts to a compromise solution,[52] giving the promisee *some* remedy on the ground of such reliance. This compromise could be carried further[53] by providing that the promisee, while not necessarily entitled in full to the promised performance,[54] should at least be compensated to the extent to which he has been prejudiced as a result of his reliance on the promise.[55]

---

[48] *Pao On v Lau Yiu Long* [1980] A.C. 614, above, p.98; *Williams v Roffey Bros & Nicholls (Contractors) Ltd* [1991] 1 Q.B. 1, above, p.95.

[49] 6th Interim Report, Cmnd. 5449; Hamson, 54 L.Q.R. 233; Hays, 41 Col.L.Rev. 849; Chloros, 17 I.C.L.Q. 137; Beatson, [1992] C.L.P. 1.

[50] *e.g.* in the cases on existing duties as consideration, on promissory estoppel and on proprietary estoppel.

[51] Contrast the Committee's recommendations that "firm offers" should be binding with the more sophisticated proposals, on this subject in Law Commission, Working Paper 60 (1975), above, p.155.

[52] See above, pp.105–132, 130–149.

[53] *e.g.* by allowing "promissory estoppel" (above, p.116) to give rise to a cause of action or by extending the categories of cases covered by proprietary estoppel (above, p.134).

[54] The qualification would not preclude such enforcement at the discretion of the court, as at present in cases of proprietary estoppel: above, p.144.

[55] *cf.* p.41, above, and *Restatements, Contracts*, §90. Restatement 2d, *Contracts*, §90 imposes somewhat less stringent conditions and concludes: "The remedy . . . may be limited as justice requires."

CHAPTER FOUR

CONTRACTUAL INTENTION

AN agreement, though supported by consideration, is not binding as a contract[1] if it was made without any intention of creating legal relations.

SECTION 1. ILLUSTRATIONS

1. Mere Puffs

A statement inducing a contract may be so vague, or so clearly one of opinion, that the law refuses to give it any contractual effect.[2] Even a statement that is perfectly precise may nevertheless not be binding if the court considers that it was not seriously meant. Thus in *Weeks v Tybald*[3] the defendant "affirmed and published that he would give £100 to him that should marry his daughter with his consent". The court held that "It is not reasonable that the defendant should be bound by such general words spoken to excite suitors." Similarly, in *Lambert v Lewis*[4] a manufacturer stated in promotional literature that his product was "foolproof" and that it "required no maintenance". These statements did not give rise to a contract between the manufacturer and a dealer (who had bought the product from an intermediary) as they were "not intended to be, nor were they, acted on as being express warranties".[5]

2. Other Statements Inducing a Contract

A statement inducing a person to enter into a contract may be *either* "mere representation" *or* a term of the contract. The distinction between these categories turns on the intention with which the statement was made.[6] In most cases on this subject the question is merely as to the *contents* of a contract which is proved or admitted to exist. But sometimes the test of intention determines the very existence of the contract itself. This happens when a statement inducing a principal contract for some reason cannot take

---

[1] For enforcement on other grounds, see *John Fox v Bannister King & Rigbeys* [1988] Q.B. 925 at 928.
[2] See below, p.330.
[3] (1605) Noy 11; *cf Dalrymple v Dalrymple* (1811) 2 Hag.Con. 54 at 105.
[4] [1982] A.C. 225; affirmed, so far as the manufacturer's liability was concerned, but on other grounds, *ibid.* at 271.
[5] [1982] A.C. 225 at 262; contrast *Carlill v Carbolic Smoke Ball Co Ltd* [1893] 1 Q.B. 256 and *Bowerman v Association of British Travel Agents* [1995] N.L.J. 1815, above, p.13. Under s.14(2D) of the Sale of Goods Act 1979, as inserted by Sale and Supply of Goods to Consumers Regulations 2002, SI 2002/3045, reg.3, implementing Directive 1999/44, a commercial seller of goods to a buyer who deals as consumer may be liable if the goods lack a quality claimed for them in "public statements on the *specific* characteristics of the goods made about them by the seller, the producer or his representative in advertising or labelling". Statements such as those made in *Lambert v Lewis*, above, would probably not be sufficiently "specific" for this purpose. Similar provisions apply to contract for the supply of goods other than contracts of sale: see Supply of Goods and Services Act 1983, s.4(2B), as inserted by reg.7 of the Regulations cited above.
[6] See below, pp.352, *et seq.*

effect as one of its terms, but only as collateral contract.[7] In *Heilbut, Symons & Co v Buckleton*[8] the claimant said to the defendants' manager that he understood the defendants to be "bringing out a rubber company." The manager replied that they were, on the strength of which statement the claimant applied for, and was allotted, shares in the company. It turned out not to be a rubber company and the claimant alleged that the defendants had warranted that it was a rubber company. It was held that nothing said by the defendants' manager was intended to have contractual effect. "Not only the terms of such contracts, but the existence of an *animus contrahendi* on the part of all the parties to them must be clearly shewn".[9] It follows that an oral statement made in the course of negotiations will not take effect as a collateral contract where the terms of the main contract show that the parties did not intend the statement to have such effect. This was, for example, the position where the main contract contained an "entire agreement" clause: this showed that statements made in the course of negotiations were to "have no contractual force".[10]

3. Intention Expressly Negatived

An agreement has no contractual force if it expressly negatives the intention to be legally bound.[11] It is a question of construction whether a particular provision has this effect.[12]

(1) Honour clauses

In *Rose & Frank Co v J R Crompton & Bros Ltd*[13] an agency agreement provided: "This arrangement is not entered into, nor is this memorandum written, as a formal or legal agreement, and shall not be subject to legal jurisdiction in the Law Courts . . . but is only a definite expression and record of the purpose and intention of the . . . parties concerned, to which they each honourably pledge themselves. . . . " These words were held to negative contractual intention, so that the agreement did not amount to a legally binding contract. On the other hand, contractual intention was not negatived where an arbitration clause in a reinsurance contract provided that "this treaty shall be interpreted as an honourable engagement rather than as a legal obligation . . . " The contract as a whole was clearly intended to be legally binding and the purpose of the words quoted

---

[7] See below, pp.180, 199–200, 356–357, 582–584. Under reg.15(1) of the Regulations referred to in n.5, above, a "consumer guarantee" given on the sale or supply of goods to a consumer is "takes effect as a contractual obligation owed by the guarantor"; it seems so to take effect by force of the Regulations, without regard to the issue of contractual intention.

[8] [1913] A.C. 30. A decision described as "catastrophic" by Atiyah in *The Rise and Fall of Freedom of Contract* at p.772, but followed by the House of Lords in *IBA v EMI Electronics Ltd* (1980) 14 Build. L.R. 1 (below, p.578); *cf Strover v Harrington* [1988] Ch. 390 at 410; *Ignazio Messina & Co v Polskie Linie Oceaniczne* [1995] 2 Lloyd's Rep. 566 at 581. The Regulations referred to in nn.5 and 7, above would not now apply on facts such as those of any of the cases cited in this note.

[9] At 47; *Unit Construction Co Ltd v Liverpool Corp* (1972) 221 E.G. 459; *The Kapetan Markos NL (No.2)* [1987] 2 Lloyd's Rep. 323 at 332. For possible effects of the Misrepresentation Act 1967, s.2 on such statements, see below, p.356.

[10] *Inntrepeneur Pub Co (GL) v East Crown Ltd* [2000] 2 Lloyd's Rep. 611 at 614; *cf White v Bristol Rugby Club Ltd* [2002] I.R.L.R. 204.

[11] e.g. *Broadwick Financial Services Ltd v Spencer* [2002] EWCA Civ 35; [2002] 1 All E.R. (Comm) 446 at [27].

[12] *R. v Lord Chancellor's Departments, Ex p. Nangle* [1991] I.C.R. 743.

[13] [1925] A.C. 445; [1923] 2 K.B. 261; *County Ltd v Girozentrale Securities* [1996] 3 All E.R. 834; *cf.* similar provisions in football pool coupons: *Jones v Vernon's Pools* [1938] 2 All E.R. 464; *Appleson v Littlewoods* [1939] 1 All E.R. 464; *Guest v Empire Pools* (1964) 108 S.J. 98. In Scotland, it has been argued that such honour clauses in football coupons may be unreasonable and hence ineffective: *Ferguson v Littlewoods Pools* 1997 S.L.T. 309 at 314–315.

was merely to free the arbitrator "to some extent from strict legal rules"[14] in interpreting the agreement.

(2) Agreement subject to contract

Agreements for the sale of land by private treaty are commonly made "subject to contract". These words normally negative contractual intention, so that the parties are not bound until formal contracts are exchanged.[15] It is a crucial part of this process of "exchange" that the parties should intend by it to bring a legally binding contract into existence.[16]

(3) Other phrases

The words "ex gratia" in a promise to make a payment to a dismissed employee have been held not to negative contractual intention: they merely mean that the employers did not admit any pre-existing liability to make the payment.[17] Contractual intention was likewise not negatived where a shipowner, during negotiations for a charterparty said "we are fixed in good faith".[18] If these words had any effect, they amounted merely to a "collateral understanding"[19] that account should be taken of damage to the vessel, of which both shipowner and charterer were aware.

4. Social and Domestic Arrangements

Many social arrangements do not amount to contracts because they are not intended to be legally binding. "The ordinary example is where two parties agree to take a walk together, or where there is an offer and an acceptance of hospitality."[20] Similarly it has been held that the winner of a competition held by a golf club could not sue for his prize where "no one concerned with that competition ever intended that there should be any legal results flowing from the conditions posted and the acceptance by the competitor of those conditions"[21]; that the rules of a competition organised by a "jalopy club" for charitable purposes did not have contractual force[22]; that "car pool" and similar arrangements between friends or neighbours did not amount to contracts even though one party contributed to the running costs of the other's vehicle[23]; that an agreement between members of a group of friends relating to musical performances by the group

---

[14] *Home Insurance Co v Administratia Asigurarilor* [1983] 2 Lloyd's Rep. 674 at 677; *cf. Overseas Union Ins Ltd v International Ins Ltd* [1988] 2 Lloyd's Rep. 65; *Home & Overseas Ins Co Ltd v Mentor Ins (UK) Ltd* [1989] 1 Lloyd's Rep. 473.

[15] See above, p.52. *Rose & Frank Co v JR Crompton & Bros Ltd* [1923] 2 K.B. 261 at 294.

[16] *Commission for the New Towns v Cooper (GB) Ltd* [1995] Ch. 259 at 295.

[17] *Edwards v Skyways Ltd* [1964] 1 W.L.R. 349; it was admitted that there was consideration moving from the employee.

[18] *The Mercedes Envoy* [1995] 2 Lloyd's Rep. 559.

[19] *ibid.*, at 612.

[20] *Balfour v Balfour* [1919] 2 K.B. 571 at 578; *Rose & Frank Co v JR Crompton & Bros Ltd* [1923] 2 K.B. 261 at 293; *Wyatt v Kreglinger & Fernau* [1933] 1 K.B. 793 at 806.

[21] *Lens v Devonshire Club* (1914) *The Times*, December 4; referred to in *Wyatt's* case, above, from which the quotation in the text is taken.

[22] *White v Blackmore* [1972] 2 Q.B. 651.

[23] *Coward v MIB* [1963] 1 Q.B. 259; overruled, but not on the issue of contractual intention, in *Albert v MIB* [1972] A.C. 301; *Buckpitt v Oates* [1968] 1 All E.R. 1145, criticised on this point by Karsten, 32 M.L.R. 88. The actual decisions are obsolete by reason of Road Traffic Act 1988, ss.145 to 149; *cf.* also s.150. But an issue of contractual intention might still arise if one party to such an arrangement simply failed to turn up at the agreed time. For another context in which sharing of expenses did not give rise to an inference of contractual intention, see *Monmouth CC v Marlog, The Times*, May 4, 1994.

was not intended to have contractual effect[24]; and that the provision of free residential accommodation for close friends did not amount to a contract as it was an act of bounty, done without any intention to enter into legal relations.[25]

For the same reason, many domestic arrangements lack contractual force. In *Balfour v Balfour*[26] a husband who worked abroad promised to pay an allowance of £30 per month to his wife, who had to stay in England on medical grounds. The wife's attempt to enforce this promise by action failed for two reasons: she had not provided any consideration, and the parties did not intend the arrangement to be legally binding. On the second ground alone, most domestic arrangements between husband and wife are not contracts. Atkin L.J. said: "Those agreements, or many of them, do not result in contracts at all . . . even though there may be what as between other parties would constitute consideration for the agreement. . . . They are not contracts . . . because the parties did not intend that they should be attended by legal consequences. . . . "[27] It has been said that the facts of *Balfour v Balfour* "stretched that doctrine to its limits"[28]; but the doctrine itself has not been judicially questioned and the cases provide many other instances of its application.[29] It does not of course prevent a husband from making a binding contract with his wife: he can be her tenant[30]; and binding separation agreements are often made when husband and wife agree to live apart.[31] Similarly, where a man before marriage promised his future wife to leave her a house if she married him, she was able to enforce the promise although it was made informally and in affectionate terms.[32]

Such issues of contractual intention can also arise between parents and children. An informal promise by a parent to pay a child an allowance during study is not normally a contract, though it may become one, if, for example, it is part of a bargain made to induce the child to give up some occupation so as to enter on some particular course of study.[33] Similarly, where a mother bought a house as a residence for her son and daughter-in-law on the terms that they should pay her £7 per week to pay off the purchase price, this was held to amount to a contractual licence which the mother could not revoke so long as either of the young couple kept up the payments.[34] On the other hand, there is normally no contract where a mother agrees to nurse her child who has fallen ill or been injured, even though performance of the agreement makes it necessary

---

[24] *Hadley v Kemp* [1999] E.M.L.R. 589 at 623.

[25] *Heslop v Burns* [1974] 1 W.L.R. 1241.

[26] [1919] 2 K.B. 571; Hedley, 5 O.J.L.S. 391.

[27] At p.627: it would clearly be undesirable to enforce such agreements in accordance with their original terms, however much the position of the parties had changed; *cf. Gould v Gould* [1970] 1 Q.B. 275 where it was held by a majority that there was no contractual intention where a husband on leaving his wife promised to pay her £15 per week so long as he could manage it; Ingman [1970] J.B.L. 109.

[28] *Pettitt v Pettitt* [1970] A.C. 806 at 816.

[29] e.g. *Gage v King* [1961] 1 Q.B. 188; *Spellman v Spellman* [1961] 1 W.L.R. 921; *cf. Lloyds Bank plc v Rosset* [1991] 1 A.C. 107.

[30] *Pearce v Merriman* [1904] 1 K.B. 80; contrast *Morris v Tarrant* [1971] 2 Q.B. 143.

[31] e.g. *Merrit v Merrit* [1970] 1 W.L.R. 1121; *Re Windle* [1975] 1 W.L.R. 1628 (doubted in *Re Kumar* [1993] 1 W.L.R. 224); *Tanner v Tanner* [1975] 1 W.L.R. 1346 (where the parties were not married) as explained in *Horrocks v Forray* [1976] 1 W.L.R. 230; *cf.* below, p.440.

[32] *Synge v Synge* [1894] 1 Q.B. 466; *cf. Jennings v Brown* (1842) 9 M. & W. 496 (promise to discarded mistress).

[33] See *Jones v Padavatton* [1969] 1 W.L.R. 328 at 333; *cf. Shadwell v Shadwell* (1860) 9 C.B. N.S. 159.

[34] *Hardwick v Johnson* [1978] 1 W.L.R. 683 *per* Roskill and Browne L.JJ.; Lord Denning M.R. thought that there was no contract but reached the same conclusion on other grounds; *cf. Collier v Holinshead* (1984) 272 E.G. 941.

for her to give up her job.[35] Conversely, it has been held that the gift of a flat by a mother to her daughter on condition that the daughter should look after the mother there did not amount to a contract because it was not intended to have contractual force.[36]

The principle of *Balfour v Balfour* can also apply where persons other than husband and wife share a common household. While that household is a going concern, many arrangements will be made about running it from day to day, and it is unlikely that these will be intended to be legally binding. But this may not be true of the financial terms which form the basis on which the household was established. In one case a young couple were induced to sell their house, and move in with their elderly relations, by the latters' promise to leave them a share of the proposed joint home. The argument that this promise was not intended to be legally binding was rejected as the young couple would not have taken the important step of selling their own house on the faith of a merely social arrangement.[37] Similar reasoning was used in a later case[38] in which a man promised a woman that the house in which they had lived together (without being married) should be available for her and the couple's children. It was held that the promise had contractual force because, in reliance[39] on it, the woman had moved out of her rent-controlled flat. In another case of this kind,[40] the fact that the promisee had helped to improve the property was relied on to support the conclusion that an express or implied promise, giving her an interest in the property, had contractual force. Formal requirements for contracts for the disposition of interests in land (imposed in 1989)[41] make it unlikely[42] that such an arrangement could now take effect as such a contract, but legal effect could be given to it by holding that it had taken effect by way of constructive trust.[43]

In view of the informality of many house-sharing arrangements, it may be hard in a particular case to say just what obligation is created. In *Hussey v Palmer*[44] a lady spent £600 on having a room added to her son-in-law's house, on the understanding that she could live there for the rest of her life. When she left voluntarily, about a year later, it was held that there was no contract *of loan* in respect of the £600[45] but there probably was a contract to allow her to live in the room for the rest of her life.

---

[35] If there is very clear evidence of contractual intention there may be a binding contract, as in *Haggar v de Placido* [1972] 1 W.L.R. 716. But in practice such "contracts" were made only as devices to enable the value of the mother's services to be recovered from a tortfeasor who had injured the child, and for this purpose they are now unnecessary: *Donnelly v Joyce* [1974] Q.B. 454.

[36] *Ellis v Chief Adjudication Officer* [1998] 1 F.L.R. 184 at 188.

[37] *Parker v Clark* [1960] 1 W.L.R. 286; *cf. Schaefer v Schuhman* [1972] 1 W.L.R. 1286; *Lee*, 88 L.Q.R. 320; *Tanner v Tanner* [1975] 1 W.L.R. 1346; *Nunn v Dalrymple*, *The Times*, August 3, 1989.

[38] *Tanner v Tanner* [1975] 1 W.L.R. 1346.

[39] Contrast *Horrocks v Forray* [1976] 1 W.L.R. 320 and *Coombes v Smith* [1986] 1 W.L.R. 808, where there was no such reliance and hence no contract.

[40] *Eves v Eves* [1975] 1 W.L.R. 1338 at 1345, *per* Browne L.J. and Brightman J.

[41] Law of Property (Miscellaneous Provisions) Act 1989, s.2, below, p.179.

[42] *e.g. Taylor v Dickens* [1998] 1 FLR 806 at 809; the reasoning of this case was doubted, but not on this point, in *Gillett v Holt* [2001] Ch. 210 at 227. S.2(1) of the 1989 Act (above) requires the contract to be made in writing by incorporating all its "expressly agreed" terms in a document; and if the promise in *Eves v Eves*, *supra*, n.40, was indeed implied it could be argued that there were no "expressly agreed" terms.

[43] *Eves v Eves* [1975] 1 W.L.R. 1338 at 1342, *per* Lord Denning M.R.: *cf. Grant v Edwards* [1986] Ch. 638; *Lloyds Bank plc v Rosset* [1991] 1 A.C. 107 at 127 contrast *Burns v Burns* [1984] Ch. 317; Lowe and Smith, 47 M.L.R. 341; Dewar, *ibid.* p.735. The formal requirements imposed by the 1989 Act (above, n.41) do not apply to "the creation or operation of . . . constructive trusts": s.2(5).

[44] [1972] 1 W.L.R. 1286.

[45] But she recovered the £600 on equitable grounds; *cf. Re Sharpe* [1980] 1 W.L.R. 219, where there was both a loan and an equitable right in the lender, and *Briggs v Rowan* [1991] E.G.C.S. 6.

An agreement between persons who share a common household may have nothing to do with the management of the household. In *Simpkins v Pays*[46] three ladies who lived in the same house took part in a fashion competition run by a newspaper, agreeing to pool their entries and to share the prize which any entry might win; and the agreement to share was held to be legally binding.

5. Agreements Giving Wide Discretion to One Party

Contractual intention may be negatived where the terms of a promise leave its performance entirely to the discretion of the promisor.[47] In *Taylor v Brewer*[48] the claimant agreed to do work for a committee who resolved that he should receive "such remuneration . . . as should be deemed right." His claim for a reasonable remuneration for work done failed: the promise to pay was "merely an engagement of honour".[49] This case is now more often distinguished than followed,[50] but its reasoning would still be followed if the wording made it clear that the promise was not intended to be legally binding.[51] *A fortiori*, there is no contract where performance by *each* party was left to that party's discretion.[52] Where, however, an agreement is clearly intended to have contractual effect, there is judicial support for the view that a discretion conferred by it on one party cannot "however widely worded . . . be exercised for purposes contrary to those of the instrument by which it is conferred".[53]

An agreement may give one party a discretion to rescind. That party will not be bound if his promise means "I will only perform if I do not change my mind." But the power to rescind may be inserted only as a safeguard in certain eventualities which are not exhaustively stated: for example, a contract for the sale of land may entitle the vendor to rescind if the purchaser persists in some requisition or objection which the vendor is "unable *or unwilling* to satisfy." In such a case there is a contract and the court will control the exercise of the power to rescind by insisting that the vendor must not rescind "arbitrarily, or capriciously, or unreasonably. Much less can he act in bad faith."[54]

6. Letters of Intent or of Comfort[55]

An issue of contractual intention may arise where parties in the course of negotiations exchange "letters of intent" or where one party gives to the other a "letter of comfort".

---

[46] [1955] 1 W.L.R. 975.

[47] *cf.* above, p.83 for the question whether such a promise can constitute consideration for a counter-promise.

[48] (1813) 1 M. & S. 290; *cf. Shallcross v Wright* (1850) 12 Beav. 558; *Roberts v Smith* (1859) 28 L.J.Ex. 164; *Robinson v Commissioners of Customs & Excise*, *The Times*, April 28, 2000.

[49] 1 M. & S. at p.291.

[50] See below, p.740; *cf. Re Brand Estates* [1936] 3 All E.R. 374.

[51] *cf. Re Richmond Gate Property Co Ltd* [1965] 1 W.L.R. 335; below, p.741.

[52] *Carmichael v National Power plc* [1999] 1 W.L.R. 2042.

[53] *Equitable Life Assurance Society v Hyman* [2002] 1 A.C. 408 at 460 *per* Lord Cooke, giving this as an alternative ground for the decision while also accepting the "implied term" reasoning on which the other members of the House based their decision: below, p.212.

[54] *Selkirk v Romar Investments Ltd* [1963] 1 W.L.R. 1415 at 1422. For the possible effects of Unfair Contract Terms Act 1977, s.3(2)(b)(ii) and of Unfair Terms in Consumer Contracts Regulations 1999 (esp. Sch.2, para.1(c)), see below, pp.252, 275. In the cases of agreements subject to the "satisfaction" of one party, there is no general rule requiring that party to act in good faith or reasonably: see *Stabilad Ltd v Stephens & Carter Ltd* [1999] 2 All E.R. (Comm) 651 at 622, above, p.64; such agreements can be distinguished from contracts which give one party a discretion to rescind since the exercise of such a discretion deprives the other party of rights under an existing contract, while in the "satisfaction" cases there is no such contract unless the party's satisfaction is communicated to the other.

[55] Lake & Draetta, *Letters of Intent* (2nd ed.); Furmston, Poole & Norisada, *Contract Formation and Letters of Intent*.

The terms of such documents may negative contractual intention.[56] This was, for example, held to be the case where a company had issued a "letter of comfort" to a lender in respect of a loan to one of its subsidiaries.[57] The letter stated that "it is our policy that [the subsidiary] is at all times in a position to meet its liabilities in respect of the loan." This was interpreted to be no more than a statement of the company's present policy: it was not an undertaking that the policy would not be changed, since neither party had intended the statement to take effect as a contractual promise. On the other hand, where the language of such a document does not in terms negative contractual intention, it is open to the courts to hold the parties bound by the document; and they will, in particular, be inclined to do so where the parties have acted on the document for a long period of time or have expended considerable sums of money in reliance on it.[58] The fact that the parties envisage that the letter is to be superseded by a later, more formal, contractual document does not, of itself, prevent it from taking effect as a contract.[59]

7. Collective Agreements

Agreements as to rates of wages and conditions of work are commonly reached after collective bargaining between trade unions and employers or associations of employers. The general common law view was that such collective agreements were *prima facie* not intended to be legally binding[60] as between the trade unions and the employers.[61] The Trade Union and Labour Relations (Consolidation) Act 1992 goes further in providing that a collective agreement[62] is *"conclusively* presumed not to have been intended by the parties to be a legally enforceable contract" unless it is in writing and expressly provides the contrary (in which case the agreement is conclusively presumed to have been intended by the parties to be a legally enforceable contract).[63] To displace the presumption that a collective agreement is not intended to be a legally binding contract, the agreement must provide that it was intended to be *legally* binding. The presumption is

---

[56] *Snelling v John G Snelling Ltd* [1973] Q.B. 87; *cf. Montreal Gas Co v Vesey* [1900] A.C. 595; *BSC v Cleveland Bridge & Engineering Ltd* [1984] 1 All E.R. 504; *Monk Construction v Norwich Union Life Assurance Society* (1992) 62 B.L.R. 107.

[57] *Kleinwort Benson Ltd v Malaysian Mining Corp* [1989] 1 W.L.R. 379; Reynolds, 104 L.Q.R. 353; Davenport [1988] L.M.C.L.Q. 290; Prentice, 105 L.Q.R. 346; Ayres and Moore, [1989] L.M.C.L.Q. 281; Tyree, 2 J.C.L. 279.

[58] *cf. Turriff Construction Ltd v Regalia Knitting Mills* (1971) 22 E.G. 169 (letter of intent held to be a collateral contract for preliminary work); *Wilson Smithett & Cape (Sugar) Ltd v Bangladesh Sugar and Food Industries Ltd* [1986] 1 Lloyd's Rep. 378 (letter of intent held to be an acceptance); *Chemco Leasing SpA v Rediffusion* [1987] 1 F.T.L.R. 201 (letter of intent held to be an offer but to have lapsed before acceptance).

[59] See above, p.55.

[60] Kahn-Freund in (ed.) Flanders and Clegg, *The System of Industrial Relations in Great Britain*, Chap.2; and in (ed.) Ginsberg, *Law and Opinion in England in the 20th Century*, p.215; Grunfeld, *Modern Trade Union Law*, pp.219–220; Wedderburn, *The Worker and the Law* (3rd ed.), pp.318–322; Report of the Royal Commission on the Trade Unions and Employers' Associations (Cmnd. 3623, 1968) §§470–471 *Ford Motor Co Ltd v AEF* [1969] 1 W.L.R. 339; Selwyn, 32 M.L.R. 377; Hepple [1970] C.L.J. 122; Lewis, 42 M.L.R. 613.

[61] For the position between employer and employee where the terms of a collective agreement are incorporated in individual contracts of employment, see below, pp.213–214.

[62] As defined by s.178(1) and (2) of the 1992 Act.

[63] s.179(1) and (2); *The Universe Sentinel* [1983] A.C. 366 at 380. *The Rosso* [1982] 2 Lloyd's Rep. 120; *cf. Cheall v APEX* [1983] 1 A.C. 180 at 189 (inter-union agreement); provisions making collective agreements legally binding are said to be rare: see *Commission of the European Communities v United Kingdom* [1984] I.C.R. 192, 195.

not displaced by a statement that the parties shall be "bound" by the agreement, for this may mean that they are to be bound in honour only.[64]

8. Other Cases

The cases in which there is no intention to create legal relations cannot be exhaustively classified. Contractual intention may be negatived by many factors other than those listed above: for example, by evidence that "the agreement was a goodwill agreement . . . made without any intention of creating legal relations"[65]; that it was a sham, made with "no intention . . . to create legal relations"[66]; that the parties had not yet completed the contractual negotiations[67]; and, where a landlord had agreed not to enforce an order for possession against a tenant who had fallen into arrears with her rent, it was held that as the parties "plainly did not intend"[68] the agreement to have contractual force, but intended it merely to turn the tenant into a "tolerated trespasser".[69]

A number of cases support the view that an arrangement which was believed simply to give effect to pre-existing rights was not a contract because the parties had no intention to enter into a *new* contract[70]; this may be true even where the contract giving rise to those rights had been discharged, so long as the parties believed that it was still in existence.[71] But contractual intention is not negatived where the conduct of the parties to an earlier contract makes it clear that they intended not merely to give effect to that contract but also to enter into a new contract containing additional terms[72]; nor is contractual intention necessarily negatived where the conduct of only *one* party to the alleged new contract consisted of his performance of an earlier contract between him and a third party.[73]

The context in which an agreement is made may negative contractual intention. For example, in one case a statement was made on behalf of the Government in time of war that a certain neutral ship would be allowed to leave a British port if specified conditions were met. It was held that the statement did not have contractual force as it was "merely an expression of intention to act in a particular way in a certain event".[74] And in *President of the Methodist Conference v Parfitt*[75] it was held that the appointment of a person as a Minister of the Methodist Church did not give rise to a contract as the relationship was not one "in which the parties intended to create legal relations between

---

[64] *NCB v NUM* [1986] I.C.R. 736.

[65] *Orion Ins Co plc v Sphere Drake Ins plc* [1990] 1 Lloyd's Rep. 465 at 505, affirmed [1992] 1 Lloyd's Rep. 239; *cf. County Ltd v Girozentrale Securities* [1996] 3 All E.R. 834 at 837; *Clarke v Nationwide Building Society* (1998) 76 P. & C.R. D5.

[66] *The Ocean Enterprise* [1997] 1 Lloyd's Rep. 449 at 484; *Hitch v Stokes* [2001] EWCA Civ 63; [2001] S.T.C. 214.

[67] *The Bay Ridge* [1999] 2 All E.R. (Comm) 306 at 329.

[68] *Burrows v Brent LBC* [1996] 1 W.L.R. 1448 at 1454. *cf. Stirling v Leadenhall Residential 2 Ltd* [2001] EWCA Civ 1011; [2001] 3 All E.R. 645: agreement as to *rate* at which payments under a court order for rent arrears were to be made held not to give rise to a new tenancy.

[69] [1996] 1 W.L.R. at 1455.

[70] *Beesly v Hallwood Estates Ltd* [1960] 1 W.L.R. 549 at 558, affirmed on other grounds [1961] Ch. 105; *cf., Harvela Investments Ltd v Royal Trust Co of Canada (CI) Ltd* [1986] A.C. 207. See also *The Aramis* [1989] 1 Lloyd's Rep. 213, Treitel, [1989] L.M.C.L.Q. 162; *The Gudermes* [1993] 1 Lloyd's Rep. 311; *The Happy Day* [2002] EWCA Civ 1068; [2002] 2 Lloyd's Rep. 487 at [63].

[71] *GF Sharp & Co v McMillan* [1998] I.R.L.R. 632.

[72] *The Amazonia* [1990] 1 Lloyd's Rep. 238 at 241–242; *cf.* the *Stirling* case, above, n.68, where a new tenancy was held to arise on the parties' subsequent agreement to *increase* the rent.

[73] *Pyrene v Scindia Navigation Co Ltd* [1954] 2 Q.B. 402; *The Eurymedon* [1975] A.C. 514; *The Captain Gregos (No 2)* [1990] 2 Lloyd's Rep. 395 (so far as it relates to B.P.'s claim). *cf. Halifax Building Society v Edell* [1992] Ch. 436, discussed below. p.587.

[74] *Rederiaktiebolaget Amphitrite v R.* [1921] 2 K.B. 500 at 503.

[75] [1984] Q.B. 368.

themselves so as to make the agreement . . . enforceable in the courts".[76] At one time, it was thought that the relationship between the Crown and one of its civil servants was not contractual because the Crown did not, when the relationship was entered into, have the necessary contractual intention.[77] But in one of the cases which supported that view it was said that there was evidence that the Crown was reconsidering its position on the point[78]; and more recently it has been held[79] that the requirement of contractual intention was satisfied in spite of the fact that the terms of appointment stated that "a civil servant does not have a contract of employment" but rather "a letter of appointment". These words were not sufficient to turn a relationship which, apart from them, had all the characteristics of a contract into one which was binding in honour only. It has been said that a police constable was a person who "holds an office and is not therefore strictly an employee"[80]; and that there is "no contract between a police officer and a chief constable".[81] But it does not follow that the relationship is binding in honour only: the resulting relationship is "closely analogous to a contract of employment"[82] so that duties analogous to those arising out of such a contract may be owed to the constable.

Contractual intention may be negatived by the vagueness of a statement or promise. Thus, in one case a promise by a husband to allow his deserted wife to stay in the matrimonial home was held to have no contractual force because it did not state for how long or on what terms she could stay there: this showed that it was "not intended by him, or understood by her, to have any contractual basis or effect".[83] So, too, the use of deliberately vague language was held to negative contractual intention where a property developer reached an "understanding" with a firm of solicitors to employ them in connection with a proposed development, but neither side entered into a definite commitment.[84] The assumption in all these cases was that the parties had reached agreement, and in them lack of contractual intention prevented that agreement from having legal effect. Vagueness may also be a ground for concluding that the parties had never reached agreement at all.[85] This issue is separate from that of contractual intention, which strictly speaking concerns only the *effect* of an agreement which is first shown to exist.[86] But the two issues are related in borderline cases in which the question whether an agreement exists depends on the degree of vagueness or on whether the vagueness can be resolved, *e.g.* by applying the standard of reasonableness; for in such

---

[76] *ibid.* at 378; approved in *Davies v Presbyterian Church of Wales* [1986] 1 W.L.R. 323 (no contract of employment between pastor and Presbyterian Church); Woolman, 102 L.Q.R. 356; *cf. Santokh Singh v Guru Nanak Gurdwara* [1990] I.C.R. 309; *Diocese of Southwark v Coker* [1998] I.C.R. 140; and see *Birmingham Mosque Trust v Alavi* [1992] I.C.R. 435.

[77] See *R. v Civil Service Appeal Board, ex p. Bruce* [1988] I.C.R. 649, affirmed on other grounds [1989] I.C.R. 171; *McLaren v Home Office* [1990] I.C.R. 824.

[78] *R. v Civil Service Appeal Board, ex p. Bruce*, above, at 659.

[79] *R. v Lord Chancellor's Department, ex p. Nangle* [1991] I.C.R. 743; *cf.* Trade Unions and Labour Relations (Consolidation) Act 1992 ss.62(7), 245: "deemed [for certain purposes] to constitute a contract".

[80] *White v Chief Constable of the South Yorkshire Police* [1999] A.C. 455 at 481.

[81] *ibid.* at 497.

[82] *ibid.*; see also *Waters v Commissioner of Police to the Metropolis* [2000] 1 W.L.R. 1607 at 1616.

[83] *Vaughan v Vaughan* [1953] 1 Q.B. 762 at 765; *cf. Booker v Palmer* [1942] 2 All E.R. 674; *Horrocks v Forray* [1976] 1 W.L.R. 230; *Jones v Padavatton* [1969] 1 W.L.R. 328; *Windeler v Whitehall* [1990] 2 FLR 505; and see *Gould v Gould* [1970] 1 Q.B. 275; *Layton v Morris, The Times,* December 11, 1985.

[84] *J H Milner & Son v Percy Bilton Ltd* [1966] 1 W.L.R. 1582; *cf. Baird Textile Holdings Ltd v Marks & Spencer plc* [2001] EWCA Civ 274; [2002] 1 All E.R. (Comm) 737, at [10, 46, 47, 73, 76].

[85] See above, pp.46–47.

[86] See *Re Goodchild* [1997] 1 W.L.R. 1216, where it is said at 1226 that one of the parties to alleged mutual wills "regarded the arrangement as irrevocable, but . . . [the other] did not"; *cf. Taylor v Dickens* [1998] 1 FLR 806, criticised, but not on the issue of contractual intention, in *Gillett v Holt* [2000] Ch. 210 at 227.

cases "the absence of any intention to create legal relations"[87] may be a ground for holding that no agreement ever came into existence.

The fact that a statement was made in jest or anger may also negative contractual intention. Thus in *Licenses Insurance Corporation v Lawson*[87a] the defendant was a director of two companies, A and B. The former company held shares in the latter and resolved, in the defendant's absence, to sell them. At a later meeting this resolution was rescinded after a heated discussion during which the defendant said that he would make good any loss which A might suffer if it kept the shares in B. It was held that the defendant was not liable on this undertaking. Nobody at the meeting regarded it as a contract; it was not recorded as such in the minute book; and the defendant's fellow-directors at most thought that he was bound in honour.

There are conflicting decisions on the question whether the issue and acceptance of a free travel pass amounts to a contract. In *Wilkie v LPTB*[88] it was held that such a pass issued by a transport undertaking to one of its own employees did not amount to a contract. But the contrary conclusion was reached in *Gore v Van der Lann*[89] where the pass was issued to an old age pensioner. This conclusion was based on the ground that an application for the pass had been made on a form couched in contractual language; and *Wilkie's* case was distinguished on the ground that the pass there was issued to the employee "as a matter of course . . . as one of the privileges attaching to his employment".[90] But as the pass in *Gore's* case was issued expressly on the "understanding" that it constituted only a licence subject to conditions the distinction seems, with respect, to be a tenuous one.

9. Proof of Contractual Intention

The question of contractual intention is, in the last resort, one of fact.[91] In deciding it, a distinction must be drawn between implied and express agreements.[92] Claims based on *implied* agreements are approached on the basis that "contracts are not lightly to be implied" and that the court must therefore be able "to conclude with confidence that . . . the parties intended to create contractual relations".[93] The burden of proof on this issue is on the proponent of the implied contract, and in a number of cases claims or defences based on implied contracts have been rejected precisely on the ground that contractual intention had not been shown by that party to exist.[94] But where a claim is based on a proved or admitted *express* agreement the courts do not require, in addition, proof that parties to an ordinary commercial relationship actually intended to be bound.[95] On the

---

[87] *Baird Textile Holdings Ltd v Marks & Spencer plc*, above, n.84 at [30]; and see above, p.50.

[87a] (1896) 12 T.L.R. 501.

[88] [1947] 1 All E.R. 258.

[89] [1967] 2 Q.B. 31; above, p.157.

[90] [1967] 2 Q.B. 31 at 41.

[91] See *Zakhem International Construction Ltd v Nippon Kohan KK* [1987] 2 Lloyd's Rep. 596.

[92] For judicial recognition of the distinction, see *Baird Textile Holdings Ltd v Marks & Spencer plc* [2001] EWCA Civ 274; [2002] 1 All E.R. (Comm) 737, at [61]; *Modahl v British Athletics Federation Ltd* [2001] EWCA Civ 1447; [2002] 1 W.L.R. 1477 at [102] (where the burden of proof referred to at n.94 below, was held to have been discharged).

[93] *Blackpool and Fylde Aero Club v Blackpool BC* [1990] 1 W.L.R. 1195 at 1202; *cf.* the *Baird Textile* case, above, n.92, at [20, 21, 30, 62] (where the burden of proof was not discharged).

[94] *The Kapetan Markos NL (No.2)* [1987] 2 Lloyd's Rep. 323; *The Aramis* [1989] 1 Lloyds Rep. 213; *The Gudermes* [1993] 1 Lloyd's Rep. 311; in some of these cases rights and liabilities under shipping documents would now arise by virtue of Carriage of Goods by Sea Act 1992, ss.2, 3.

[95] Certain regulated agreements under the Consumer Credit Act 1974 must contain the following notice: "This is a Hire-Purchase Agreement regulated by the Consumer Credit Act 1974. Sign it only if you want to be legally bound by its terms." (Consumer Credit (Agreements) Regulations 1983 (SI 1983/1553)).

contrary, the onus of proving that there was no such intention "is on the party who asserts that no legal effect was intended, and the onus is a heavy one".[96] In deciding whether the onus has been discharged, the courts will be influenced by the importance of the agreement to the parties, and by the fact that one of them has acted in reliance on it.[97] Contractual intention is not negatived merely by the fact that the parties were companies in the same group and that the terms of their agreement "might not in practice be strictly enforced between them".[98]

The test of contractual intention is normally an objective one,[99] so that where, for example, an agreement for the sale of a house is *not* "subject to contract",[1] both parties are likely to be bound even though one of them subjectively believed that he would not be bound till the usual exchange of contracts had taken place.[2] But the objective test is here (as elsewhere)[3] subject to the limitation that it does not apply in favour of a party who knows the truth. Thus in the example just given the party who did not intend to be bound would not be bound if his state of mind was actually known to the other party.[4] Nor could a party who did not in fact intend to be bound invoke the objective test so as to hold the other party to the contract[5]: to apply that test in such a case would pervert its purpose, which is to protect a party who has relied on the objective appearance of consent from the prejudice which he would suffer if the *other* party could escape liability on the ground that he had no real intention to be bound. Nor does the objective test apply where the parties have expressed their actual intention in the document alleged to constitute the contract: the question whether they intended the document to have contractual effect then becomes one "of construction of the documents as a whole what effect is to be given to such a statement".[6] The objective test, in other words, merely prevents a party from relying on his *uncommunicated* belief as to the binding force of the agreement. The incidence of the burden of proof and the objective test may explain two

---

[96] *Edwards v Skyways Ltd* [1964] 1 W.L.R. 349 at 355; *cf. The Polyduke* [1978] 1 Lloyd's Rep. 211; *Financial Techniques (Planning Services) Ltd v Hughes* [1981] I.R.L.R. 32. *The Zephyr* [1985] 2 Lloyd's Rep. 529, 537 (disapproving [1984] 1 Lloyd's Rep. 58 at 63–64); *Yani Haryanto v ED & F Man (Sugar) Ltd* [1986] 2 Lloyd's Rep. 44; *Orion Ins Co plc v Sphere Drake Ins plc* [1992] 1 Lloyd's Rep. 239 at 263 (where the burden was discharged); *Mamidoil-Jetoil Greek Petroleum Company S.A. v Okta Oil Refinery AD* [2003] 1 Lloyd's Rep. 1, at [159].

[97] See above, p.166; *Kingswood Estate Co Ltd v Anderson* [1963] 2 Q.B. 169; *cf. South West Water Authority v Palmer* (1982) 263 E.G. 438.

[98] *The Marine Star (No.2)* [1994] 2 Lloyd's Rep. 629 at 632, reversed on other grounds [1996] 2 Lloyd's Rep. 383.

[99] See above, pp.1, 8; *Ignazio Messina & Co v Polskie Linie Oceaniczne* [1995] 2 Lloyd's Rep. 566 at 579 (where, on the objective test there was no contractual intention); *Bowerman v Association of British Travel Agents* [1995] N.L.J. 1815; *The Bay Ridge* [1999] 2 All E.R. (Comm) 306 at 327; *London Baggage (Charing Cross) v Railtrack plc* [2000] EGCS 57; *Edmonds v Lawson* [2000] Q.B. 501; *Baird Textile Holdings Ltd v Marks & Spencer plc* [2001] EWCA Civ 274; [2002] 1 All E.R. (Comm) 737. If the agreement is intended to give rise to legal relations, its precise legal *effects* are similarly not determined by the subjective intentions of the parties or one of them: see *Street v Mountfort* [1985] A.C. 809 where an agreement was held as a matter of law to take effect as a lease even though the lessor clearly intended it to take effect only as a licence. *cf. AG Securities v Vaughan* [1990] 1 A.C. 417; contrast *Ogwr BC v Dykes* [1989] 1 W.L.R. 295; *Monmouth BC v Marlog, The Times*, May 4, 1994; *Bruton v Quadrant Housing Trust* [1997] N.L.J. 1385. See also *Crowden v Aldridge* [1993] 1 W.L.R. 433, applying the objective test of intention to produce legal consequences to a non-contractual direction to executors in favour of a third party. *Quaere* whether, in the absence of reliance on the direction, the policy which justifies the objective test in a contractual context extends to the situation which arose in this case.

[1] See above, p.52.

[2] *Tweddell v Henderson* [1975] 1 W.L.R. 1496; *Storer v Manchester CC* [1974] 1 W.L.R. 1403 at 1408.

[3] See above, p.9.

[4] *Pateman v Pay* (1974) 263 E.G. 467.

[5] *Lark v Outhwaite* [1991] 2 Lloyd's Rep. 132 at 141.

[6] *R. v Lord Chancellor's Department, Ex p. Nangle* [1991] I.C.R. 743 at 751.

controversial decisions, in each of which there was a difference of opinion on the issue of contractual intention.

The first is *Esso Petroleum Ltd v Commissioners of Customs and Excise*.[7] Esso supplied garages with tokens called "World Cup coins", instructing them to give away one coin with every four gallons of petrol sold. The scheme was advertised by Esso and also on posters displayed by the garages. By a majority of four to one, the House of Lords held that there was no "sale" of the coins; but the majority was equally divided on the question whether there was any contract at all with regard to the coins. Those who thought that there was a contract[8] relied on the incidence of the burden of proof, and on the point that "Esso envisaged a bargain of some sort between the garage proprietor and the motorist".[9] But this point relates rather to the intention of Esso than to that of the alleged contracting parties. With regard to *their* intention, it is submitted that the more realistic view is that contractual intention was negatived by the language of the advertisements (in which the coins were said to be "going free"), and by the minimal value of the coins.

The second case is *J Evans & Son (Portsmouth) Ltd v Andrea Merzario Ltd*.[10] The representative of a firm of forwarding agents told a customer, with whom the firm had long dealt, that henceforth his goods would be packed in containers and assured him that these would be carried *under* deck. About a year later, such a container was carried *on* deck and lost. At first instance,[11] Kerr J. held that the promise was not intended to be legally binding since it was made in the course of a courtesy call, not related to any particular transaction, and indefinite with regard to its future duration. The Court of Appeal, however, held[12] that the promise did have contractual force, relying principally on the importance attached by the customer to the carriage of his goods under deck, and on the fact that he would not have agreed to the new mode of carriage but for the promise. The case is no doubt a borderline one, but it is submitted that Kerr J.'s view accords more closely with the objective test of contractual intention. In most cases, that test prevents the *promisor* from relying on his subjective intention not to enter into a contractual undertaking. But it should equally prevent the *promisee's* subjective intention (if not known to the promisor) from being decisive. The Court of Appeal appears with respect to have attached too much weight to the customer's subjective state of mind, and too little weight to the circumstances in which the promise was made.

SECTION 2. INTENTION AND CONSIDERATION

In the United States, the view has been put forward by Williston[13] that "the common law does not require any positive intention to create a legal obligation as an element of contract". No one disputes that an agreement is not a contract if the parties expressly provide that it is not to be legally binding. But it is said that an agreement containing no such provision will generally be a contract although no positive intention to create a legal obligation existed in the minds of the parties. This theory can be interpreted in two ways.

---

[7] [1976] 1 W.L.R. 1; Atiyah, 39 M.L.R. 335.

[8] Lords Simon and Wilberforce. Lord Fraser, who dissented on the main issue, took the same view.

[9] [1976] 1 W.L.R. 1 at 6.

[10] [1976] 1 W.L.R. 1078; Adams, 40 M.L.R. 227; *cf. El Awadi v Bank of Credit and Commerce International* [1990] 1 Q.B. 606 at 617.

[11] [1975] 1 Lloyd's Rep. 162.

[12] [1976] 1 W.L.R. 1078.

[13] Williston, *Contracts*, Section 21; Tuck, 21 Can.B.Rev. 123; Shatwell, 1 Sydney L.R. at p.293; Unger, 19 M.L.R. 96. Hedley, 5 O.J.L.S. 391.

The first interpretation simply emphasises the rule as to burden of proof (as applied to express promises) and the objective test, stated above.[14] Thus Williston says: "If, under the circumstances, a reasonable person would understand[15] the words used as importing that the speaker promised to do something if given a requested exchange therefor, it is immaterial what intention the offeror may have had." This statement is no doubt true in the case of an ordinary commercial contract; but it is harder to apply where words are spoken in jest or in anger.[16] Williston admits that there is no contract in such cases; and this admission can perhaps be explained on the ground that a person to whom a promise is made in *obvious* jest or anger would know that it was not intended to be binding, so that the objective test would not be satisfied. Another difficulty is that Williston's test is, if taken quite literally, wide enough to cover ordinary social and domestic arrangements. Williston sees no reason why these "should not create a contract, if the requisites for the formation of a contract exist". No doubt it is possible that in exceptional circumstances and by use of clear words acceptance of an invitation to a party could create a contract. But would it do so *merely* because "the speaker promised to do something if given a requested exchange therefor?" Would acceptance of an invitation to a bottle-party normally create a contract? And can Williston's view be reconciled with the "car pool" cases[17] mentioned above?

The second, and more extreme, version of the theory is that there is no requirement of contractual intention at all. A promise is binding if it is supported by consideration; nothing else is necessary. Social and domestic arrangements are not contracts, even if they involve reciprocal promises or performances, because the promise of one party is not given as the price for the other's: there is no bargain. "The family circle differs from the market place in that it is not the setting for bargaining but for an exchange of gifts or gratuitous services".[18] This is said to be the true basis of *Balfour v Balfour.*[19] But this view merely makes the requirement of intention part of the definition of consideration: one cannot tell whether mutual promises constitute a bargain or an "exchange of gifts" without regard to the intention of the parties. Nor can one on this view explain why mere puffs or statements made in jest or anger do not give rise to contractual obligations; why a defendant who concedes that there was consideration has any case left to argue on the issue of intention[20] or why there was no contract in *Heilbut, Symons & Co v Buckleton*[21]; and why claims or defences based on implied contracts have been rejected precisely because contractual intention had not been established.[22] It is finally inconsistent with a number of cases in which there was agreement and consideration,[23] and the conclusion that the agreement did not amount to a contract was based solely on the ground that the parties did not intend that it should give rise to legal relations between them.

---

[14] See above, pp.171–172.

[15] See *Edwards v Skyways Ltd* [1964] 1 W.L.R. 349 at 356 for the difficulties which may arise in determining this question, especially where one of the parties is a corporation.

[16] See above, p.171.

[17] See above, p.164.

[18] Unger, *loc. cit.*; *cf.* Hepple [1970] C.L.J. 122.

[19] [1919] 2 K.B. 571.

[20] As in *Edwards v Skyways Ltd* [1964] 1 W.L.R. 349; *cf. Re Beaumont* [1980] Ch. 444 at 453, recognising that consideration may be provided "under a contract *or otherwise*".

[21] [1913] A.C. 30; above, p.149.

[22] See above, p.171.

[23] *e.g. President of the Methodist Conference v Parfitt* [1984] Q.B. 368 at 378; *R. v Civil Service Appeal Board Ex p. Bruce* [1988] I.C.R. 649 at 659, 665 (affirmed on other grounds [1989] I.C.R. 171); *The Aramis* [1989] 1 Lloyd's Rep. 213.

It is submitted that neither version of the theory is satisfactory. Many of the decisions discussed in this Chapter are expressly based on the absence of an intention to create legal relations, and cannot be satisfactorily explained in any other way. They show that such intention is recognised by English law as a separate requirement for the formation of contracts.[24]

---

[24] For recent judicial support for this view, see *Baird Textile Holdings Ltd v Marks & Spencer plc* [2001] EWCA Civ 274; [2002] 1 All E.R. (Comm) 737 at [30], [59].

CHAPTER FIVE

FORM

SECTION 1. GENERAL RULE

A LEGAL system is said to require that a contract shall be made in a certain form if it lays down the manner in which the conclusion of the contract must be marked or recorded. In modern legal systems, such formal requirements generally consist of writing, sometimes with additional requirements, *e.g.* those of a deed or (in some countries) of authentication by a notary. It has even been said that consideration is a form,[1] but more usually "form" refers to requirements which have nothing to do with the contents of an agreement. In this sense consideration is not generally a form, though the giving of peppercorn to make a gratuitous promise binding might be so regarded.[2]

Form may be *sufficient* to make a promise binding, as we have seen in discussing the effect of a gratuitous promise made in a deed.[3] But in this Chapter we shall discuss cases in which form is a *necessary* requirement which must be satisfied (granted that there is agreement, consideration and contractual intention) before the contract is fully effective. Such a requirement may serve one or more of several purposes. First, it promotes certainty, as it is usually relatively easy to tell whether the required form has been used. A requirement of writing also simplifies the problem of ascertaining the contents of the agreement. Secondly, form has a cautionary effect: a person may hesitate longer before executing a deed than he would before making an oral promise. Thirdly, form has a protective function: it is used to protect the weaker party to a contractual relationship by ensuring that he is provided with a written record of the terms of the contract. For example, an employee must be informed in writing of the particulars of his employment,[4] and a tenant must (in certain cases) be given a rent-book containing certain particulars of his tenancy.[5] Both the second and the third purposes of form are illustrated by the elaborate formal requirements that protect a debtor under certain consumer credit agreements. He must be given a document to be signed by him inside a "signature box"; this must contain a notice warning him that he is signing a consumer credit agreement. A similar box must contain a notice telling him of his statutory right

---

[1] Holmes, *The Common Law*, p.273: "Consideration is a form as much as a seal." See also Fuller, 41 Col.L.Rev. 799.

[2] See *The Alev* [1989] 1 Lloyd's Rep. 138 at 147.

[3] See above, p.158.

[4] Employment Rights Act 1996, s.1; see also ss.2–4; these provisions give effect to EC Council Directive 91/533; the actual contract need not be in writing. Machinery for securing compliance with these sections is provided by s.11.

[5] Landlord and Tenant Act 1985, s.4; the actual lease is not required by this Act to be in writing. Failure to comply with s.4 is an offence under s.7 of the Act; but does not make the contract invalid: *Shaw v Groom* [1970] 2 Q.B. 504; *cf.* Estate Agents Act 1979, s.18 below, p.743, for information which estate agents must give to their clients; Consumer Protection (Distance Selling) Regulations 2000, SI 2000/2334, regs 7 and 8; these Regulations implement Dir.97/7/EC. See also Electronic Commerce (EC Directive) Regulations 2002, SI 2002/2013, reg.9 implementing Dir.2000/31/EC (below, p.170), requiring specified information to be given *before* the conclusion of a contract to which the Regulations apply; this requirement does not apply to contracts made exclusively by email: reg.9(4).

of cancellation.[6] It is scarcely fanciful to suggest that these boxes fulfil in a modern context some of the functions formerly performed by use of the seal. Form may finally serve what has been called a "channelling" purpose[7]: that is, the use of a certain form may help to distinguish one type of transaction from another.

Form has, on the other hand, the disadvantage that it is time-consuming and clumsy and that it is a source of technical pitfalls. Even the relatively simple requirement of writing is open to these objections and has therefore been regarded as inconvenient from a commercial point of view. Thus the general rule is that contracts can be made quite informally.[8]

SECTION 2. STATUTORY EXCEPTIONS

The general rule is subject to many exceptions. These now all depend on legislation dealing with specific types of contracts. Some such contracts must be made by deed, some must be in writing, and others must be evidenced by a note or memorandum in writing. No attempt can be made in this book to give a complete list of these exceptions. A few illustrations must suffice; after these have been discussed, an attempt will be made to consider the impact on this subject of contracting by electronic means.

1. Contracts which must be made by Deed

A lease for more than three years must be made by deed.[9] If it is not so made, it is "void for the purpose of creating a legal estate".[10] But it operates in equity as an agreement for a lease,[11] which can be specifically enforced if it complies with the formal requirements (to be discussed below)[12] for contracts for the disposition of interests in land. Thus between the parties to the lease lack of a deed is not fatal. But, unless the tenant has registered the lease as a land-charge or, in the case of registered land, is in actual occupation, he can be turned out by a third party to whom the landlord has sold the land.[13]

2. Contracts which must be in Writing

(1) Illustrations of such contracts

Under nineteenth century legislation, contracts which must be in writing include bills of exchange, promissory notes[14] and bills of sale.[15] More recent statutes impose the requirement of writing on regulated consumer credit agreements and on most contracts for the sale or other disposition of interests in land.

---

[6] Consumer Credit (Agreements) Regulations (1983 SI No. 1553), Sch.5, made under Consumer Credit Act 1974, s.60. They apply where the price is under £25,000: below, pp.178–179.

[7] Von Mehren, 72 H.L.R. 1009 at 1017.

[8] *Beckham v Drake* (1841) 9 M.& W. 79 at 92.

[9] Law of Property Act 1925, ss.52, 54(2); and see above, p.159 at n.25.

[10] *ibid.*, s.52.

[11] *Walsh v Lonsdale* (1882) 21 Ch.D. 9.

[12] Below, pp.179–181.

[13] At present under Law of Property Act 1925, s.199(1)(i); Land Charges Act 1925, ss.10(1) Class (iv); 13(2); Land Registration Act 1925, s.70(1)(g), to be superseded by Land Registration Act 2002, Sch.3, para.2.

[14] Bills of Exchange Act 1882, ss.3(1), 17(2).

[15] Bills of Sale Act 1878 (Amendment) Act 1882.

Under the Consumer Credit Act 1974, regulated consumer credit agreements, and certain other agreements[16] are "not properly executed"[17] unless certain formalities are complied with. A regulated consumer credit agreement is one by which a creditor provides an individual debtor with credit[18] not exceeding £25,000.[19] Both parties must sign a document in the form prescribed by government regulations.[20] This must legibly set out all the express terms of the contract[21] and contain a notice of the debtor's statutory right to cancel during the "cooling off" period (where this applies),[22] as well as certain other information.[23] A copy must also be given to the debtor.[24]

Under s.2 of the Law of Property (Miscellaneous Provisions) Act 1989, most contracts for the sale or disposition of an interest in land[25] must be "made in writing".[26] All the terms[27] expressly[28] agreed by the parties must be incorporated in the document (or in each document, where contracts are exchanged).[29] The terms may be incorporated either by being set out in the document, or by reference.[30] The document (or documents) must also be signed "by or on behalf of"[31] each party[32]; this requirement of signature is no longer satisfied (as it was earlier under legislation superseded by s.2 of the 1989 Act[33]) by merely typing a party's name and address on the document.[34] The requirement of writing does not apply to short leases for less than three years, to sales at public auctions or to transactions in certain forms of investment securities (*e.g.* unit trust investing in land).[35]

---

[16] Such as consumer hire agreements (s.15) and security instruments (s.105).

[17] s.61(1).

[18] As defined by s.9.

[19] s.8; Consumer Credit (Further increase of Monetary Amounts) Order 1998 (SI 1998/996); certain agreements are exempt under s.16 of the 1974 Act.

[20] s.61(1)(a); for exceptions, see **s.74**; *cf.* above, p.176.

[21] s.61(1)(b) and (c).

[22] s.64(5); for "cooling off" periods, see below, p.428.

[23] Consumer Credit Act 1974, s.55(1).

[24] ss.62, 63.

[25] As defined in Law of Property (Miscellaneous Provisions) Act 1989, s.2(6); for application to mortgages, see *United Bank of Kuwait v Sahib* [1997] Ch. 107, not cited in *Target Holdings Ltd v Priestley* (2000) 79 P. & C.R. 305, where s.2 was held not to apply to the disposition itself, as opposed to the contract for the disposition. A "lock-out" agreement is not within the section: *Pitt v PHH Asset Management Ltd* [1993] 1 W.L.R. 327.

[26] s.2(1). When the system of electronic conveyancing envisaged by Pt 8 of the Land Registration Act 2002 is introduced, s.2 of the 1989 Act will be superseded by Rules to be made under that Part.

[27] See *Enfield LBC v Arajah* [1995] E.G.C.S. 164 (where only the *main* terms were set out in the document).

[28] This word makes it unnecessary to set out *implied* terms in the document.

[29] Law of Property (Miscellaneous Provisions) Act 1989, s.2(1). An agreement reached in pre-exchange correspondence between the parties will not satisfy s.2(1) where no single document contains all the terms expressly agreed or is signed by both parties; nor will such correspondence amount to an "exchange" since this process refers to exchange of the formal documents described at p.52 above: see *Commission for the New Towns v Cooper (Great Britain) Ltd* [1995] Ch. 259 at 285, 293 disapproving the concession to the contrary which had apparently been accepted in *Hooper v Sherman* [1995] C.L.Y. 840.

[30] s.2(2). *cf. Record v Bell* [1991] 1 W.L.R. 853, where this requirement was not satisfied, but there was a collateral contract (below, p.179).

[31] Signature by an agent who is liable and entitled under the contract suffices: *Braymist v Wise Finance Co Ltd* [2002] EWCA Civ 127; [2002] 2 All E.R. 333; below, p.680.

[32] s.2(3). In the case of an option to purchase, the agreement granting the option is within the section, but the notice exercising it is not, and so does not have to be signed by the vendor: *Spiro v Glencrown Properties Ltd* [1991] Ch. 537.

[33] *i.e.* Law of Property Act 1925, s.40, in turn superseding the relevant part of Statute of Frauds 1677, s.4; for the authorities on what amounts to "signature" under this legislation, see below, p.183.

[34] *Firstpost Homes Ltd v Johnson* [1995] 1 W.L.R. 1567, where it is said at 1576 that "signed" in s.2 of the 1989 Act should be given the meaning which "the ordinary man would understand it to have."

[35] s.2(5).

(2) Effect of non-compliance

Failure to comply with the statutory requirements just described can produce a variety of legal consequences.

A bill of sale is void unless it is in writing in the statutory form.[36] But if the sort of promise which is normally contained in a bill of exchange or promissory note is made orally, it can result in a perfectly valid contract. The contract is not invalid[37] but will not have the legal and commercial characteristics[38] of a bill or note.

In the case of regulated consumer credit agreements, the 1974 Act provides an intermediate solution. An agreement which is not properly executed can be enforced *against the debtor* "on an order of the court only".[39] In the absence of such an order, no restitutionary remedy is available against the borrower at common law since the award of such a remedy to the lender would be inconsistent with the legislative scheme that, in the case of an improperly executed document, "subject to the enforcement powers of the court, the debtor should not have to pay".[40] No enforcement order can be made against the debtor if the agreement has not been signed by him,[41] or (in the case of a cancellable agreement) if the debtor has not been given a copy or notice of his right to cancel.[42] In the case of other formal defects, the court has a wide discretion. It can take into account the prejudice caused to the debtor and the degree of culpability of the creditor[43]; order enforcement conditionally or subject to variations[44]; reduce the amount payable by the debtor[45]; or enforce the agreement as if it did not include a term omitted from the document signed by the debtor.[46] This flexible approach goes far to meet the objection that formal requirements can give rise to unmeritorious defences based on technical slips.[47]

S.2 of the Law of Property (Miscellaneous Provisions) Act 1989 requires a contract for the sale or other disposition of an interest in land to be "made in writing". The effect of these words is that the contract does not come into existence if the parties fail to comply with the statutory formal requirements.[48] This could cause hardship where one party has partly performed[49] such a contract, or otherwise acted in reliance on it, *e.g.* by

---

[36] See above, at n.15.

[37] *Hitchens v General Guarantee Corp* [2001] EWCA Civ 359, *The Times*, March 13, 2001.

[38] See below, pp.691–693.

[39] s.65(1). The defective agreement is thus unenforceable only and not void: *Reg. v Modupe* [1991] C.C.L.R. 29.

[40] *Dimond v Lovell* [2002] 1 A.C. 384 at 398.

[41] s.127(3). In *Wilson v First County Trust* [2001] EWCA Civ 633; [2001] Q.B. 407 the court made a declaration under s.4 of the Human Rights Act 1998 that s.127(3) of the Consumer Credit Act 1974 was incompatible with provisions of the European Convention on Human Rights, which have the force of law by virtue of s.1(1) of the 1998 Act. It is part of the reasoning of this case that s.127(3) does not invalidate, but merely makes unenforceable (without scope for judicial discretion) a contract which fails to comply with the requirements of the subsection and may do so even though the failure, *e.g.* to include one of the "prescribed terms" in a document signed by the debtor, causes him little or no prejudice. See further n.48, below.

[42] s.127(4).

[43] s.127(1)(i).

[44] s.127(1)(ii).

[45] s.127(2); *National Guardian Mortgage Corp v Wilks* [1993] CCLR 1.

[46] s.127(5).

[47] *cf.* Mobile Homes Act 1983, s.1, under which the court can order the site-owner to comply with the formal requirements imposed by the Act.

[48] Since no contract comes into existence where s.2 of the 1989 Act is not complied with, the reasoning of *Wilson v First County Trust*, above n.41, does not apply to failure to comply with s.2 of the 1989 Act: it is an essential part of the reasoning of *Wilson's* case that s.127(3) of the Consumer Credit Act did *not* make the contract void (but made it only unenforceable).

[49] s.2 has been held not to apply where the contract was fully performed: *Tootal Clothing v Guinea Properties Management* (1992) 64 P. & C.R. 452.

making improvements to the land in question. But such hardship can be avoided by other judicially developed doctrines, such as proprietary estoppel or constructive trust.[50] Under these doctrines, the court can make an order for the transfer of the land to the party who has acted in reliance on the contract.[51] But the remedy is limited in various ways[52] and does not necessarily lead to enforcement of the contract as such.[53] In this respect the position of the party who has acted in reliance on the defective contract is now less favourable than it was before the 1989 Act.[54] Where the document fails to include *all* the terms on which the parties are alleged to have orally agreed, a number of possibilities call for discussion. If the failure was due to parties' having *deliberately* omitted the term from the written document, then it will not be a term expressly agreed so as to form part of the contract, so that its omission will not affect the validity of the contract as set out in the document.[55] If the failure was due to a mistake in recording those terms, it may be possible to rectify the document, *i.e.* to bring it into line with what was actually agreed.[56] If the failure is due to some other cause, it is sometimes possible to treat the omitted term as a separate or "collateral" contract, independent of the (main) contract set out in the document,[57] which will then satisfy the requirements of s.2. The omitted term cannot, however, be so treated if it is intended to form part of the main contract[58]: *e.g.* if it is so "interwoven with the substance of the transaction"[59] as to form an essential part of it; for to treat a document as sufficient even though it omitted such a term would be inconsistent with the statutory requirement that the document must incorporate all the expressly agreed term. It seems that a term can for the present purpose be treated as a collateral contract only if it was intended to take effect as an independent contract, separate from that set out in the document. If it can be so treated, two consequences follow. First, a document which omits the term can nevertheless satisfy the statutory requirement of incorporating *all* the express terms of the main contract. Secondly, the collateral contract is binding, even if oral, so long as it is not itself one which is required to be in writing,[60] and so long as evidence of it is admissible under the parol evidence rule.[61]

---

[50] See above, pp.134–149, 166 n.43. The concluding words of s.2(5) of Law of Property (Miscellaneous Provisions) Act 1989 are intended to preserve these rules: see Law Com. No. 164 paras 4.3, 5.4 and 5.5; *Yaxley v Gotts* [2000] Ch.162 at 193, referring with apparent approval to the view stated in the text above.

[51] See above, pp.142–143.

[52] *ibid.*; *cf.* also above, p.145.

[53] See above, p.149.

[54] Under Law of Property Act 1925, s.40 (re-enacting part of s.4 of the Statute of Frauds 1677 and now repealed) failure to comply with the statutory requirement of written evidence only made the contract unenforceable; and "part performance" (below, p.184) enabled the party so performing to enforce the contract.

[55] *Grossman v Hooper* [2001] EWCA Civ 615, [2001] 2 E.G.L.R. 82.

[56] See *Commission for the New Towns v Cooper (GB) Ltd* [1995] Ch.259. For the conditions in which rectification is available, see below, pp.321–326; the possibility of rectification is recognised by Law of Property (Miscellaneous Provisions) Act 1989, s.2(4), which provides that the contract is deemed to come into being at such time as may be specified in the court order rectifying the document. See also Law Com. No.164, para.5.6.

[57] *e.g. Record v Bell* [1991] 1 W.L.R. 853.

[58] *Grossman v Hooper*, above, n.55, at [21].

[59] *Preece v Lewis* (1963) 186 E.G. 113, decided under Law of Property Act 1925, s.40 (above, n.54) but, *semble*, equally applicable under Law of Property (Miscellaneous Provisions) Act 1989, s.2(1); *Godden v Merthyr Tydfil Housing Association* (1997) 74 P. & C.R. D1; see also Law Com. No. 164, paras 5.7, 5.8.

[60] *Angell v Duke* (1875) L.R. 10 Q.B. 174 (and see next note); *Record v Bell* [1991] 1 W.L.R. 853.

[61] See below, pp.199–200; in *Angell v Duke*, above, the evidence of the collateral contract was later rejected under the parol evidence rule: (1875) 32 L.T. 320.

3. Contracts which must be Evidenced in Writing

(1) In general

Some statutes do not require contracts to be made in writing, but only to be evidenced by a written document. A contract of marine insurance, for example, is "inadmissible in evidence" unless it is embodied in a marine policy signed by the insurer.[62] This is not a requirement of the making or validity of such a contract: it is enough if the policy is executed *after* the making of the contract. Other statutory provisions are less exacting; they are satisfied if there is merely a "note or memorandum" in writing. The Statute of Frauds 1677 applied this requirement to six classes of contracts. Its object was to prevent fraudulent claims based on perjured evidence; but it sometimes gave rise to technical defences which had little merit, so that it was restrictively interpreted by the courts. This process can be illustrated by reference to contracts of guarantee, the only type of contract to which the formal requirements imposed by the Statute still apply.[63]

(2) Contracts of guarantee

(a) DEFINITION. S.4 of the Statute of Frauds provides: "No action shall be brought . . . whereby to charge the defendant upon any special promise to answer for the debt, default or miscarriage of another person" unless there is written evidence of the promise. This provision applies whether the liability guaranteed is contractual or tortious.[64] But it does not apply in the following cases.

(i) *Promise to debtor.* The Statute applies only where the defendant's promise to pay the debt is made to the creditor. It does not apply where that promise is made to the debtor.[65]

(ii) *Indemnity.* The Statute applies to a guarantee, but not to an indemnity. A guarantee is a promise to pay another's debt if he fails to pay. An indemnity is a promise to indemnify the creditor against loss arising out of the principal contract.[66] In the case of a guarantee the liability of the principal debtor is primary and that of the guarantor only secondary; thus if for some reason the principal debtor is not liable, the guarantor is not liable either. A promise to indemnify creates primary liability which arises even though the promisee has no enforceable rights under the principal contract.[67]

It follows from the nature of a guarantee that there can be no guarantee if there never was a principal debtor: *e.g.* if A promises to pay B for doing work for C, which C has not ordered so that C is not liable to pay B for it.[68] Nor is a contract a guarantee if there once was a principal debtor, but if the whole object of the new contract is that his liability should cease and the liability of the new promisor be substituted for it. Thus a promise by a father to pay his son's creditor, if the creditor will release the son, is an indemnity.[69] But a promise may be an indemnity in spite of the fact that there is a principal debtor whose liability continues. This is the position if the person making the promise

---

[62] Marine Insurance Act 1906, ss.22 and 24.

[63] For the repeal of other relevant provisions contained (or formerly contained) in the Statute, see Law Reform (Enforcement of Contracts) Act 1954; Law of Property (Miscellaneous Provisions) Act 1989, ss.2(8) and 4, Sch.2.

[64] *Kirkham v Marter* (1819) 2 B. & Ald. 613.

[65] *Eastwood v Kenyon* (1840) 11 A. & E. 438.

[66] *Birkmyr v Darnell* (1704) 1 Salk. 27; *Argo Caribbean Group v Lewis* [1976] 2 Lloyd's Rep. 289; *cf.* below, p.396.

[67] *Yeoman Credit Ltd v Latter* [1961] 1 W.L.R. 828; in Consumer Credit Act 1974, s.189(1), "security" includes both guarantee and indemnity.

[68] *Lakeman v Mountstephen* (1874) L.R. 7 H.L. 17.

[69] *Goodman v Chase* (1818) 1 B. & Ald. 297.

undertakes not merely to pay if the principal debtor fails to do so, but "to put the [creditor] in funds in any event".[70]

It can hardly be said that there is less danger of perjury in the case of an indemnity than in the case of a guarantee. The distinction between them has accordingly been criticised for having "raised many hair-splitting distinctions of exactly that kind which bring the law into hatred, ridicule and contempt by the public".[71] It can only be explained historically as a device for restricting the scope of the Statute of Frauds.

(iii) *Part of larger transaction.* The Statute applies to a guarantee which stands alone but not to one which is part of a larger transaction. It did not, for example, apply where the defendant introduced clients to a firm of stockbrokers on the terms that he was to receive half the commissions earned, and to pay half the losses incurred, by the stockbrokers on transactions with such clients.[72] The promise to pay losses was enforceable, though oral, as it formed part of a larger transaction in which the defendant was interested otherwise than as guarantor. Similarly the guarantee given by a *del credere* agent is not within the Statute. Such an agent guarantees the solvency of the third party between whom and his principal he makes a contract: that is, he promises the principal to pay if the third party does not. The main object of a *del credere* agency is to enable the principal to sell and the agent to earn his commission. "Though it may terminate in a liability to pay the debt of another, that is not the immediate object for which the consideration is given."[73] On the wording of the Statute, it is hard to justify the special treatment of these cases. Perhaps it could be said that such promises are more likely to be made than purely disinterested guarantees: hence there is less danger of perjury.

(iv) *Protection of property.* A guarantee is not within the Statute if it is given to protect some proprietary interest of the guarantor. Thus A may buy goods from B which are held by C as security for a debt owed by B to C. If A induces C to deliver the goods to him by promising to pay B's debt in case B does not pay it, A's promise is not within the Statute.[74] The main object of A's promise is said to be to protect his own property and not to guarantee B's debt. This rule may again be justified on the ground that such promises are more likely to be made than purely disinterested guarantees. But if this is so, it is hard to see why the rule is restricted to cases in which the interest is strictly proprietary. The rule has, for example, been held not to apply where the guarantee was given to protect the assets of a company in which the guarantor was a substantial shareholder or debenture holder.[75] It was said that to enforce an oral guarantee in such a case would amount to repealing the Statute.[76] But this is also true where the interest protected is a strictly proprietary one.

So many subtle distinctions have been drawn to whittle away the application of the Statute to contracts of guarantee that it seems a pity that this part of the Statute has not been replaced by legislation which more effectively furthers its purpose of protecting guarantors. The requirement of written evidence is scarcely an effective means of

---

[70] *Guild & Co v Conrad* [1894] 2 Q.B. 885 at 892; *cf. Thomas v Cook* (1828) 8 B. & C. 728; *Wildes v Dudlow* (1874) L.R. 19 Eq. 198; *Re Hoyle* [1893] 1 Ch. 84.

[71] *Yeoman Credit Ltd v Latter* [1961] 1 W.L.R. 828 at 835; *cf. Actionstrength Ltd v International Glass Engineering Co* [2001] EWCA Civ 1477; [2002] 4 All E.R. 468, at [52] ("overburdened with fine distinctions").

[72] *Sutton & Co v Grey* [1894] 1 Q.B. 285.

[73] *Couturier v Hastie* (1852) 8 Ex. 40 at 56, reversed on another point: (1856) 5 H.L.C. 673, below, p.295.

[74] *Fitzgerald v Dressler* (1859) 7 C.B.(N.S.) 374.

[75] *Harburg India Rubber Comb Co v Martin* [1902] 1 K.B. 778; *Davys v Buswell* [1913] 2 K.B. 47; *The Anemone* [1987] 1 Lloyd's Rep. 547.

[76] *Harburg* case, above, at 787.

providing such protection, since it can be satisfied by a standard form of guarantee drafted by a bank to protect its own interests rather than those of the guarantor.[77] Even if the requirement of written evidence did protect the guarantor, it would not do so very effectively, for it can fairly easily be evaded by drawing up the contract as one of indemnity.

(b) TYPE OF EVIDENCE REQUIRED. Contracts within the Statute of Frauds must be evidenced by a signed note or memorandum in writing. The exact nature of the evidence required was not specified by the Statute, but the following rules were later laid down by Parliament and by the courts. Many of the relevant cases concern contracts to which the Statute no longer applies; but the principles to be derived from them still apply, where appropriate, to contracts of guarantee.

(i) *Parties.* The memorandum must identify the parties by naming or describing them,[78] and state the capacity in which they contract.[79] It may sufficiently describe the parties without actually naming them. For example, a party can even be sufficiently described by a pronoun.[80]

(ii) *Consideration.* The memorandum of guarantee need not state the consideration for the guarantee.[81]

(iii) *Terms.* The memorandum must contain all the material terms of the contract.[82] There is some authority for the view that if a term has been omitted from the memorandum the claimant may waive the term if it is solely for his benefit and not of major importance, and enforce the contract without the term.[83] Conversely, if the omitted term is for the benefit of the defendant, the claimant may be able to enforce the contract on agreeing to perform it.[84]

(iv) *Signature.* The memorandum must be signed by the party to be charged or by his agent lawfully authorised[85] to sign for him.

The requirement that the memorandum must be "signed" is liberally interpreted. A party need not sign his full name: initials will do.[86] The signature may be printed,[87] and may be in any part of the document, not necessarily at the bottom.[88] It may be put on the document before the contract was made so long as it is "recognised" at the time of

---

[77] See below, p.244. In relation to regulated agreements, statutory protection is provided by Consumer Credit Act 1974, Pt VIII and s.127.

[78] *Williams v Jordan* (1877) 6 Ch.D. 517 ("Sir" not sufficient); *Re Lindrea* (1913) 109 L.T. 623 (first name sufficient); *cf. UCB Corporate Services Ltd v Clyde & Co* [2000] 2 All E.R. (Comm) 257 where the guarantor was not named or otherwise identified.

[79] *Vandenbergh v Spooner* (1866) L.R. 1 Ex. 316; *Newell v Radford* (1867) L.R. 3 C.P. 52; *Dewar v Mintofi* [1912] 2 K.B. 373.

[80] *Carr v Lynch* [1900] 1 Ch.613.

[81] Mercantile Law Amendment Act 1856, s.3.

[82] *Hawkins v Price* [1947] Ch. 645; *cf. Beckett v Nurse* [1948] 1 K.B. 535; *Tweddell v Henderson* [1975] 1 W.L.R. 1496; *Marshall v Berridge* (1881) 19 Ch.D. 233; *Edwards v Jones* (1921) 124 L.T. 740; *State Bank of India v Kaur, The Times,* April 24, 1995; *MP Services v Lawyer* (1996) P. & C.R. D49.

[83] *North v Loomes* [1919] 1 Ch. 378; *Beckett v Nurse* [1948] 1 K.B. 535; *Turner v Hatton* [1952] 1 T.L.R. 1148. The point was not argued in *Tweddell v Henderson* [1975] 1 W.L.R. 1496.

[84] *Martin v Pycrofi* (1852) 2 D.M. & G. 785; *Scott v Bradley* [1971] Ch.850 (refusing to follow *Burgess v Cox* [1951] Ch. 383 on this point).

[85] Many cases on this point concern the authority of auctioneers and are obsolete now that no formal requirements apply either to sales of goods (Law Reform (Enforcement of Contracts) Act 1954) or to sales of land by public auction (Law of Property (Miscellaneous Provisions) Act 1989, s.2(5)(b)).

[86] *Chichester v Cobb* (1866) 14 L.T. 433; *Hill v Hill* [1947] Ch. 231 at 240.

[87] *Schneider v Norris* (1814) 2 M. & S. 286; *cf. Godwin v Francis* (1870) L.R. 5 C.P. 295 (telegram).

[88] *Ogilvie v Foljambe* (1817) 3 Mer. 53; *Durrell v Evans* (1862) 1 H. & C. 174; *Evans v Hoare* [1892] 1 Q.B. 593.

contracting. Thus a form printed before the contract is made and bearing one party's name is "signed" by that party if he at the time of contracting submits it to the other party for signature: he thereby "recognises" his own "signature".[89] These rules are lax, but a document is not signed by a party merely because his name occurs somewhere within it: the signature must authenticate the whole document. Thus if a memorandum is headed "Articles of Agreement between A & B" and concludes "As witness our hands . . . " the parties must actually subscribe: the mention of their names at the beginning is clearly not intended as a signature.[90] A party is not considered to have signed a document merely because he adds his signature to it as witness to the signature of the other party.[91]

The writing need be signed only by "the party to be charged". Thus the contract can be enforced against a party who has signed by one who has not.[92]

(v) *Memorandum need not be prepared as such.* The memorandum need not be prepared for the purpose of satisfying the statutory requirements of written evidence. A writing which comes into existence before an action is brought[93] on the contract will suffice so long as it acknowledges or recognises the existence of the contract.[94] Thus an offer signed by one party and orally accepted by the other,[95] a recital or disposition in a will,[96] a letter written by one of the parties to his own agent[97] and pleadings in a previous action between different parties[98] have been held sufficient. A letter repudiating liability is a sufficient memorandum if it admits the terms of the contract but denies the construction put upon them by the other party; but not if it denies that a contract was ever made on the terms alleged.[99]

(vi) *Joinder of documents.* Where no single document fully records the transaction it may be possible to produce a sufficient memorandum by joining together two or more documents.

Joinder is, in the first place, possible where one document expressly or impliedly *refers* to another transaction. If that transaction is also recorded in a document, and that document was in existence when the first was signed[1] the two documents can be joined.[2] Joinder may be effected via an intermediate document: *e.g.* where the first sets out the terms of the guarantee, the second referred to those terms and the third (which is signed

---

[89] *Schneider v Norris,* above; *Evans v Hoare,* above; *Cohen v Roche* [1927] 1 K.B. 169; *Leeman v Stocks* [1951] Ch. 941.

[90] *Hubert v Treherne* (1842) 3 Man. & G. 743.

[91] *Gosbell v Archer* (1835) 1 A. & E. 500.

[92] *Laythoarp v Bryant* (1836) 2 Bing.N.C. 735; *cf. The Maria D* [1992] 1 A.C. 21 (signature by agent sufficient although he was not liable on the main contract); as to specific performance, see below, p.1028.

[93] See *Lucas v Dixon* (1889) 22 Q.B.D. 357; *Farr, Smith & Co v Messers* [1928] 1 K.B. 397.

[94] *Tweddell v Henderson* [1975] 1 W.L.R. 1496.

[95] *Reuss v Picksley* (1866) L.R. 1 Ex. 342; *Lever v Koffler* [1901] 1 Ch. 543; *Parker v Clark* [1960] 1 W.L.R. 286.

[96] *Re Hoyle* [1893] 1 Ch. 84; *Schaefer v Schuhmann* [1972] A.C. 572; contrast *Maddison v Alderson* (1883) 8 App.Cas. 467, where there was probably no contract at all.

[97] *Gibson v Holland* (1865) L.R. 1 C.P. 1.

[98] *Grindell v Bass* [1920] 2 Ch. 487. The position is probably different where reliance is placed on pleadings in an earlier action between the *same* parties; *Hardy v Elphick* [1974] Ch. 65.

[99] See *Buxton v Rust* (1872) L.R. 7 Ex. 279; *Thirkell v Cambi* [1919] 2 K.B. 591; *cf. Dobell v Hutchison* (1835) 3 A. & E. 355.

[1] For recognition of, and an exception to, this requirement, see *Re Danish Bacon Co Ltd v Staff Pension Fund* [1971] 1 W.L.R. 248, a case arising under Law of Property Act 1925, s.53(1)(c).

[2] *Long v Millar* (1879) 4 C.P.D. 450; *cf. Reading Trust Ltd v Spero* [1930] 1 K.B. 492; *Holiday Credit Ltd v Erol* [1977] 1 W.L.R. 704; *Elias v George Sahely & Co (Barbados) Ltd* [1983] 1 A.C. 646, where joinder is said at 655 to be possible even though the second document has no contractual force.

by the guarantor) refers to the second.[3] Even where there is no express reference in one document to the other, they can be joined if, on placing them side by side, it becomes obvious without the aid of oral evidence that they are connected.[4] It seems that the original and the photocopy of a document (one signed by one party and the other by the other) could be joined on this ground.[5] But if the document signed by the defendant contains no reference to another document or transaction, and if the connection between the two documents can be established only by oral evidence, joinder is not permitted.[6]

(c) EFFECT OF NON-COMPLIANCE. Failure to comply with the requirements just described does not make the contract void[7] but only unenforceable.[8] The contract can be *made* orally, but it can be enforced by action only if a note or memorandum of it exists, signed by the party against whom enforcement is sought. As the contract is not void, money paid or property transferred under it cannot be recovered back merely because the contract is not evidenced in writing.[9] For example, a guarantor could not recover back from the creditor money which he had paid or property which he had deposited under a guarantee of which there was no sufficient note or memorandum. Similarly, a security given for the guarantor's performance would not be void merely because the guarantee was unenforceable: thus an action could be brought on a cheque given to the creditor in payment of sums due from the debtor.[10]

The Statute of Frauds could cause hardship to a party who had wholly or partly performed a contract which was unenforceable for want of written evidence. To meet this hardship, Equity developed the doctrine of part performance, under which the party who had rendered such performance could enforce the contract in spite of the lack of a proper note or memorandum.[11] This doctrine was applied almost exclusively to contracts for the sale or other disposition of interests in land. S.2(1) of the Law of Property (Miscellaneous Provisions) 1989 Act now requires such contracts to be *made* (and not merely to be *evidenced*) in writing.[12] The result of failure to comply with the subsection is that no contract comes into existence, and since there can be no part performance of a non–existent contract, it is submitted[13] that the doctrine can no longer apply in cases of such failure. The doctrine of part performance was in the past restricted to contracts which were specifically enforceable in Equity, or, perhaps more narrowly, to contracts for the disposition of interests in land.[14] Contracts of guarantee would hardly ever (if at all) fall within even the broader of these two formulations. The normal remedy against a

---

[3] *The Anemone* [1987] 1 Lloyd's Rep. 547.

[4] *Sheers v Thimbleby* (1879) 13 T.L.R. 451; *cf. Burgess v Cox* [1951] Ch. 383 (disapproved on another point in *Scott v Bradley* [1971] Ch. 850).

[5] *Stokes v Whicher* [1920] 1 Ch. 411, 419 (top and carbon copies).

[6] *Timmins v Moreland Street Property Co* [1958] Ch. 110; *cf. Boydell v Drummond* (1809) 11 East 192; contrast *Stokes v Whicher* [1920] 1 Ch. 411; *Pearce v Gardner* [1899] 1 Q.B. 688.

[7] For the now rejected view that the contract was void, see dicta in *Carrington v Roots* (1837) 2 M. & W. 248 at 255, 257.

[8] *Leroux v Brown* (1852) 12 C.B. 801; *Elias v George Sahely & Co (Barbados) Ltd* [1983] 1 A.C. 646 at 650.

[9] *Thomas v Brown* (1876) 1 Q.B.D. 714.

[10] *Low v Fry* (1935) 152 L.T. 585.

[11] See the discussion on pp.144–146 of the 7th edition of this book.

[12] See above, p.179.

[13] Notwithstanding a dictum to the contrary in *Sing v Beggs* (1996) 71 P. & C.R. 120 at 122. For other devices by which hardship to a party who has acted in reliance on the supposed contract can be avoided, see above, p.179.

[14] See *Britain v Rossiter* (1879) 11 Q.B.D. 123; *McManus v Cooke* (1887) 35 Ch.D. 681.

guarantor would be a common law action for the amount which he had promised to pay, and not a claim for specific performance.[15] Accordingly, the doctrine of part performance has not in the past been applied to contracts of guarantee.[16] The possibility of its being so applied in the future cannot be categorically ruled out,[17] since it is conceivable that a contract of guarantee might, in exceptional circumstances, be specifically enforceable[18]; if so, acts done by the creditor in reliance on the guarantee might be regarded as sufficient part performance. But the possibility seems to be a remote one, and the safest conclusion is that it is highly unlikely that the doctrine will be applied to contracts of guarantee.

4. Formal Requirements and Electronic Documents

Many problems arise in determining whether the formal requirement of "writing", or of a "document", or of a "signature" are satisfied in the case of contracts made electronically. The Law Commission has advised[19] that where commercial contracts[20] are made by email or by trading on a website, the requirement of writing[21] will normally be satisfied, though this will not be true of electronic data interchange[22]: the distinction is based on the point that in the first two of these situations, but not in the third, the terms of the transaction will be produced (on screen or in printed out copies) in visible form.[23] It has also been held that electronically stored information can, in law, constitute a "document".[24] The requirement of "signature" *can* likewise be satisfied in the case of electronic documents: *e.g.* by a digital signature, by typing a name into an electronic document or even by clicking on a website button.[25] Whether the requirement is *actually* so satisfied depends in these cases on the common law test of what constitutes a signature: *i.e.* on whether the act in question was done with the intention of authenticating the electronic document.[26] Under s.7 of the Electronic Communications Act 2000, "electronic signatures" are admissible in evidence; but this provision does not specify the *effect* of such signatures, which continues to depend on the common law "authentication" test stated above. S.8 of the Act also empowers the appropriate Minister by order to modify existing legislation (such as the legislation discussed in this Chapter) so as to authorise the use of electronic communications for the purpose of (*inter alia*) "the doing of anything which under . . . such [legislation] is required to be or may be authorised by

---

[15] The common law remedy would normally be "adequate" and so exclude specific performance: below, p.1026. A debtor's promise to give security may be specifically enforceable because damages for breach of it may be hard to quantify (below, p.1021); but no such difficulty arises in quantifying the liability of the guarantor.

[16] *cf. Maddison v Alderson* (1883) 8 App.Cas. 467 at 490.

[17] The point was left open in *The Anemone* [1987] 1 Lloyd's Rep. 546 at 557.

[18] *e.g.* if the principal debt were one to pay an annuity to a person other than the promisee, as in *Beswick v Beswick* [1968] A.C. 58; *cf.* below, pp.1021, 1026, 1038. The Contracts (Rights of Third Parties) Act 1999 will not, in a case of this kind, deprive the promisee of his remedy of specific performance: see s.4 of that Act below, p.665.

[19] In its paper on *Electronic Commerce: Formal Requirements in Commercial Contracts* (December 2001).

[20] The paper (above) does not deal with transactions relating to land; as to the use of electronic documents in this context, see above, p.178.

[21] Within Interpretation Act 1978, Sch.1.

[22] Law Commission, above, n.1, §§3.9, 3.23.

[23] *ibid.* §§3.14, 3.20.

[24] *Victor Chandler International v Customs & Excise Commissioners* [2000] 1 W.L.R. 1296.

[25] Law Commission, above, n.1, §§3.31–3.34, 3.36, 3.39.

[26] *cf.* above, p.184.

a person's signature or seal, or is required to be delivered as a deed or witnessed."[27] The Law Commission has (with respect) rightly advised that, since electronic communications will in most cases be capable of satisfying the requirements of writing and signature, legislation of the kind envisaged by s.8 "is not only unnecessary but risky,"[28] legislation should be attempted only where it was "context specific"[29] *i.e.* where it was needed to create "absolute certainty"[30] in some particular context.[31] Art.9 of the Directive of the European Parliament and Council on Electronic Commerce[32] (the Electronic Commerce Directive, 2000) obliges Member States to "ensure that their legal system allows contracts to be concluded by electronic means" and that "the legal requirements applicable to the contractual process neither create obstacles for the use of electronic contracts nor result in such contracts being deprived of their legal effectiveness on account of their having been made by electronic means".[33] Legislation to implement Art.9 will not be necessary[34] where present formal requirements of writing and signature can (as will commonly be the case) be satisfied by electronic means; the need for it is likely to arise where statutory requirements can be satisfied only by the use of paper documents: *e.g.* where legislation requires one party to send specified contractual particulars to the other by post.[35] The obligations imposed by Art.9 are, moreover, subject to a number of exceptions, the most important of which, in the present context, relate to (1) "contracts that create or transfer rights in real estate, except for rental rights;"[36] and (2) "contracts of suretyship granted on collateral securities furnished by persons acting outside their trade, business or profession".[37] If, and so far as, the United Kingdom chooses to rely on these exceptions, it will not (so far as they permit) be required to modify existing legislation imposing formal requirements on contracts for the sale of interests in land and on contracts of guarantee and will, moreover, be free to impose further formal requirements on such contracts where they are made electronically. It follows that, to this extent, the provisions for the use of electronic documents to be made under the Land Registration Act 2002 and in delegated legislation to be made under it[38] will not need to comply Art.9; and that nothing in that Article prevents the United Kingdom from imposing legislative restrictions on the efficacy of electronic contracts of guarantee of the kind there specified. The latter point is of some general interest in relation to what we have called the cautionary and protective functions of form[39]: if a guarantor could incur liability by simply clicking on the appropriate part of a website, then these functions would lose much of their efficacy,[40] at least if the guarantor were a person skilled in the use of this technology.

---

[27] s.8(2)(c).

[28] Law Commission, above n.1, §3.43: general provisions might be inappropriate for specific legislative requirements of form.

[29] Law Commission, above n.1, §3.43.

[30] *ibid.*

[31] *e.g.*, that of electronic conveyancing: above, p.178; and see above n.20.

[32] Dir.2000/31.

[33] Art.9.1.

[34] Parts of Dir.2000/13 (but not Art.9) are implemented by the Electronic Commerce (EC Directive) Regulations 2002 (SI 2002/2013).

[35] *e.g.*, Consumer Credit Act 1974, ss.63(3), 64(2).

[36] Art.9.2(a).

[37] Art.9.2(c). Art.9.2(b) also allows Member States to retain requirements of notarial attestation for contracts within the Directive: *cf.* Recital 36 and Art.6.5(d).

[38] See above, p.178.

[39] See above, p.176.

[40] Law Commission, above, n.1, §3.46.

SECTION 3. FORMAL REQUIREMENTS FOR RESCISSION AND VARIATION

So far this Chapter has dealt with formal requirements for the making, proof or enforceability of a contract. It is finally necessary to consider the impact of form where a contract which complies with such a requirement, or which is (though it is not required to be) made by deed or in writing, is rescinded or varied by subsequent agreement of the parties.[41] Our present concern is with formal requirements for such agreements. They also give rise to problems of consideration, which have been discussed in Chapter 3.[42]

1. Rescission

The general principle is that formal requirements which apply to the making of a contract do not apply to its rescission by mutual consent. For example, a contract of guarantee can be rescinded orally[43]; and the same appears to be true of a contract for the disposition of an interest in land.[44] Somewhat greater difficulty arises where the rescinding agreement is itself a contract which is subject to formal requirements. Suppose, for example, that A in writing guarantees X's debt to B and that the guarantee is later rescinded by an oral agreement by which A guarantees Y's debt to B. The oral agreement is a valid contract[45] so that the guarantee of X's debt is rescinded, but B cannot enforce[46] the guarantee of Y's debt since that guarantee is not evidenced in writing. The position is less certain where the original contract is one which must be *made* (and not merely evidenced) in writing and where the rescinding agreement is also such a contract: for example, where both agreements are contracts for the disposition of an interest in land and the first does, but the second does not, comply with the formalities required for the making of such contracts.[47] The second agreement is not itself a valid contract to make the new disposition; and one possible view is that that agreement, not having been properly "made",[48] is totally ineffective and so cannot operate even to rescind the first. An alternative (and, it is submitted, a preferable) view is that the second agreement is merely ineffective as a contract for the disposition of an interest in land. On this view, it can nevertheless amount to an agreement, supported by good consideration,[49] to rescind the first contract.[50] Hence the first contract is rescinded but the second is not binding.

---

[41] Our concern here is with this type of rescission. Formal requirements are sometimes imposed where a contract is "rescinded" *without* the consent of a party because of his failure in performance: below, p.723 n.34.

[42] See above, pp.99–102.

[43] *cf. Morris v Baron & Co* [1918] A.C. 1.

[44] Law of Property (Miscellaneous Provisions) Act 1989, s.2(1) (above, p.178) provides that such a contract shall be "*made* in writing" and says nothing about how it can be *unmade*. *cf. McCausland v Duncan Lawrie Ltd* [1997] 1 W.L.R. 38 at 48 ("rescission . . . may well be capable of being done otherwise than in writing").

[45] See above, p.185.

[46] See *Morris v Baron & Co*, above; *Goman v Salisbury* (1648) 1 Vern. 240.

[47] See above, n.44.

[48] Law of Property (Miscellaneous Provisions) Act 1989, s.2(1).

[49] See above, p.101.

[50] The mere rescission of a contract for the disposition of an interest in land does not itself appear to amount to a "disposition": see the definition of "disposition" in the Law of Property Act 1925, s.205(1)(ii), incorporated into the Law of Property (Miscellaneous Provisions) Act 1989 by s.2(6) of the latter Act.

At common law, a deed could only be rescinded by deed,[51] but this rule did not apply in equity, which now prevails.[52]

2. Variation

Difficult problems used frequently to arise out of oral variations of contracts which had to be evidenced in writing. Many of the cases concerned contracts which no longer need to be so evidenced,[53] or which must now be made in writing[54]; but the rules laid down in them continue to apply to contracts which still have to be in, or evidenced in, writing.[55]

An oral variation of a contract which had to be evidenced in writing could be regarded as a rescission of the old contract, followed by the making of a new one affecting the same subject-matter. If so, the old contract was effectively rescinded, but the new one could not be enforced for want of writing.[56] Alternatively, it could be said that the parties had simply tried to vary a term of, or to add one to, the original contract. If so, the original contract remained in force, but the variation, being oral, could not be enforced by action.[57] In this sense, a contract which had to be *evidenced in writing* could not be varied orally. For example, a written guarantee may provide that the guarantor is to be liable only if the creditor gives him notice of the debtor's default within one week of its occurrence. If the guarantor then says orally that he will not insist on this requirement, that oral variation does not have contractual force.[58] The position is the same where a contract which must be *made* in writing is varied in a way that does not satisfy the statutory formal requirements, for example, where a contract for the sale of land[59] which was made in a document signed by both parties is varied in a material respect by an exchange of letters each of which is signed by only one party. In one case[60] such a variation substituted an earlier completion date for that specified in the original contract; and it was held that the vendor could not insist on the earlier date.

In the above examples, the result would have been the same if the subsequent oral agreement had been regarded as a rescission: the guarantor or purchaser would not have been *liable* on the original contract because it was rescinded, nor under the new agreement because it was oral. But the distinction between (on the one hand) a rescission followed by a new agreement and (on the other) a variation would have been crucial if an attempt had been made, not to enforce the subsequent agreement, but to assert rights under the original one.[61] Had the subsequent agreement been a rescission, such an attempt would have failed. Had it been a variation, the attempt would *prima facie* have succeeded since the original agreement would have remained in force,[62] and the subsequent oral agreement would not have been effective to vary it, though it might have

---

[51] *West v Blakeway* (1841) 2 Man. & G. 729; *Spence v Healey* (1853) 8 Ex. 668. The rule applied whether or not the contract was by law required to be made by deed.

[52] *Berry v Berry* [1929] 2 K.B. 316 at 319.

[53] *i.e.* since the Law Reform (Enforcement of Contracts) Act 1954: above, p.181.

[54] Law of Property (Miscellaneous Provisions) Act 1989, s.2(1).

[55] See above, pp.177–186.

[56] *Morris v Baron & Co* [1918] A.C. 1. *Robinson v Page* (1826) 3 Russ. 114; *Tyers v Rosedale & Ferryhill Iron Co Ltd* (1875) L.R. 10 Ex. 195.

[57] But it may provide a defence: *Re a Debtor (No.517 of 1991)*, *The Times*, November 25, 1991.

[58] Example based on *Goss v Nugent* (1835) 5 B. & Ad. 58, where the contract was one for the disposition of an interest in land which then required only to be evidenced (not made) in writing.

[59] Law of Property (Miscellaneous Provisions) Act 1989, s.2, above, p.178.

[60] *McCausland v Duncan Lawrie Ltd* [1997] 1 W.L.R. 38.

[61] *e.g.* if in *Goss v Nugent*, above, n.30, the *purchaser* had been suing to enforce the original contract.

[62] *Robinson v Page* (1826) 3 Russ. 114; *Tyers v Rosedale & Ferryhill Iron Co Ltd* (1875) L.R. 10 Ex. 195.

had some effect as a waiver (in the sense of forbearance), or in equity,[63] if the necessary requirements[64] for invoking these doctrines were satisfied.[65]

Whether a subsequent agreement is a rescission or a variation depends on the extent to which it departs from the original contract. It is a rescission if it alters the original contract in some essential way; but if it does not go "to the very root of the original contract"[66] it is only a variation. The distinction is one of degree. In *Morris v Baron & Co*[67] a dispute arising out of a contract for the sale of goods (which then had to be evidenced in writing) was orally compromised: it was agreed that the buyer should have extra time to pay and that he should have an option whether he would take the goods not yet delivered. This compromise was held to be a rescission as it dealt with an essential matter, the quantity of goods to be delivered. On the other hand, alterations in the place and time of delivery have been held to be variations only, so that the original contracts could still be enforced.[68]

The foregoing discussion concerns contracts which are subject to some formal requirement imposed by law. If, however, a contract which is not subject to any such legal requirement merely happens to have been executed in writing or by deed, it can be varied informally. At common law, indeed, a deed could not be varied except by another deed; but this rule did not apply in equity which now prevails. Accordingly it was held in *Berry v Berry*[69] that a separation agreement which had been made by deed (though there was no legal requirement for it to be so made) could be varied by a subsequent agreement that was not made by deed. Later cases apply this rule where the original contract *was* by law required to be made by deed.[70] These decisions are hard to reconcile with the reasoning of cases which hold that a contract required to be evidenced or made in writing cannot be varied orally.[71] They are best explained on the ground that, though the variations were not contractually binding, they nevertheless had a limited effect under the rules of waiver in the sense of forbearance,[72] or in equity.[73]

---

[63] See above, pp.103 *et seq.*

[64] See above, pp.106–111.

[65] *McCausland v Duncan Lawrie Ltd* [1997] 1 W.L.R. 38 at 49–50.

[66] *British and Beningtons Ltd v NW Cachar Tea Co* [1923] A.C. 48 at 68.

[67] [1918] A.C. 1.

[68] *e.g.* the *British and Beningtons* case, above; *Hickman v Haynes* (1875) L.R. 10 C.P. 598; *The Arawa* [1980] 2 Lloyd's Rep. 135; *cf. United Dominions Corp (Jamaica) Ltd v Shoucair* [1969] 1 A.C. 340 (temporary variation in rate of interest held not to amount to rescission of a mortgage).

[69] [1929] 2 K.B. 316.

[70] *Plymouth Corporation v Harvey* [1971] 1 W.L.R. 549 (lease for seven years), and possibly *Mitas v Hyams* [1951] 2 T.L.R. 1215 (where the length of the lease is not stated).

[71] *e.g. Morris v Baron & Co* [1918] A.C. 1; *McCausland v Duncan Lawrie Ltd* [1997] 1 W.L.R. 38.

[72] See above, p.103.

[73] See above, pp.105 *et seq.*

CHAPTER SIX

THE CONTENTS OF A CONTRACT

THE contents of a contract depend primarily on the words used by the parties in entering into the contract: these make up its express terms. A contract may, in addition, contain terms which are not expressly stated, but which are implied, either because the parties so intended, or by operation of law, or by custom or usage.

SECTION 1. EXPRESS TERMS

Where a contract is made orally, the ascertainment of its terms raises in the first place the pure question of fact: what did the parties say? Once this has been determined, a further question can arise as to the meaning of the words used. In answering this question, the court applies the objective test of agreement.[1] Under that test, a party cannot enforce the contract in the sense which he gave to the words, if that sense differs from the one which the other party reasonably gave to them.[2]

Further problems of ascertaining or proving express terms can arise where the contract is, or appears to have been, reduced to writing.

1. Joinder of Documents

(1) Incorporation by express reference

The terms of a contract may be contained in more than one document. One of these may expressly refer to another, *e.g.* where a contract is made subject to standard terms settled by a trade association. Those terms are then incorporated by reference into the contract; if there are several editions of the standard terms, the contract is *prima facie* taken to refer to the most recent edition.[3] It may also incorporate amendments validly made by the association.[4]

The parties may purport to incorporate one document in another by express reference, not realising that the terms of the two documents conflict. In *Adamastos Shipping Co v Anglo-Saxon Petroleum Co*[5] clause 1 of a charterparty provided: "This bill of lading shall have effect subject to the Carriage of Goods by Sea Act of the United States 1936, which shall be deemed to be incorporated herein. . . . " The object of this clause was to reduce the shipowner's duty to provide a seaworthy ship from the absolute duty existing at common law to that of due diligence imposed by the Act.[6] But s.5 of the Act stated that its provisions "shall not be applicable to charterparties. . . . " Two difficulties arose out of this contract. First, the parties had described their contract as "this bill of lading" when it was a charterparty; but, as this was a simple mistake, it was held that the phrase

---

[1] See above, pp.1, 8.
[2] *Eyre v Measday* [1986] 1 All E.R. 488; *Thake v Maurice* [1986] Q.B. 644; *Grubb* [1986] C.L.J. 197; below, p.841.
[3] *Smith v South Wales Switchgear Ltd* [1978] 1 W.L.R. 165.
[4] *Shearson Lehman Hutton Inc v Maclaine Watson & Co* [1989] 2 Lloyd's Rep. 570 at 589; *cf. The Marinor* [1996] 1 Lloyd's Rep. 301.
[5] [1959] A.C. 133; applied in *The Oceanic Amity* [1984] 2 All E.R. 140.
[6] *cf.* Carriage of Goods by Sea Act 1971, s.3 and Sch., Art.III.(1)(a).

could be taken to mean "this charterparty." Secondly, the parties had apparently provided that the charterparty was to take effect subject to an Act which expressly provided that it did *not* apply to charterparties. The House of Lords could have held the whole contract meaningless, or rejected clause 1 of the charterparty, or rejected s.5 of the United States Act. The House chose the last course, and so gave effect to the intention of the parties that there should be a contract under which the shipowner was only bound to use due diligence to provide a seaworthy ship. The case is a good illustration of the anxiety of the courts to make sense, if possible, of loosely and sometimes carelessly drafted commercial documents.

(2) No express reference

A contract may be contained in several documents even though one does not expressly refer to the other. Suppose, for example, that a series of dealings takes place under a "master contract", a separate document being executed each time an individual contract is made. All these contracts may be subject to the master contract, even though they do not refer to it.[7] Similarly, a policy of insurance can be read together with the rules of the mutual insurance society which had issued it,[8] although the policy does not expressly refer to the rules[9]; and a contract to purchase securities may be held to incorporate the terms of a prospectus on the faith of which they were bought.[10] Such incorporation without express reference appears to depend on the intention of the parties, determined in accordance with the objective test of agreement.

2. The Parol Evidence Rule

(1) Statement of the rule

The parol evidence rule states that evidence cannot be admitted (or, even if admitted, cannot be used) to add to, vary or contradict a written instrument.[11] In relation to contracts, the rule means that, where a contract has been reduced to writing, neither party can rely on extrinsic evidence of terms alleged to have been agreed, *i.e.* on evidence not contained in the document. Although the rule is generally stated as applying to *parol* evidence, it applies just as much to other forms of extrinsic evidence. Of course, if a contractual document incorporates another document by reference, evidence of the second document is admissible, but the rule prevents a party from relying on evidence that is extrinsic to both documents.[12]

There are obvious grounds of convenience for the application of the parol evidence rule to contracts: certainty is promoted by holding that parties who have reduced a contract to writing should be bound by the writing and by the writing alone.[13] On the other hand, the parol evidence rule will commonly be invoked where a dispute arises after the time of contracting as to what was actually said at that time; and in such cases

---

[7] *Panorama Developments (Guildford) Ltd v Fidelis Furnishing Fabrics Ltd* [1971] 2 Q.B. 711.

[8] *Edwards v Aberayron Insurance Society Ltd* (1876) 1 Q.B.D. 563.

[9] For difficulties relating to joinder where contracts have to be evidenced in writing, see above, p.185.

[10] *Jacobs v Batavia & General Plantations Trust Ltd* [1924] 1 Ch. 287; affirmed [1924] 2 Ch. 329; another possible explanation of the case is that there was a collateral contract: below, p.199.

[11] *Jacobs v Batavia & General Plantations Trust Ltd* [1924] 1 Ch. 287 at 295; *Rabin v Gerson Berger Association Ltd* [1986] 1 W.L.R. 526 at 531, 537; *The Nile Rhapsody* [1992] 2 Lloyd's Rep. 349 at 407, affirmed [1994] 1 Lloyd's Rep. 382; *Orion Ins Co v Sphere Drake Ins plc* [1992] 1 Lloyd's Rep. 239 at 273; *W F Trustees Ltd v Expo Safety Systems Ltd, The Times,* May 24, 1993.

[12] *Jacobs v Batavia & General Plantations Trust Ltd,* above.

[13] *Rabin v Gerson Berger Association Ltd* [1986] 1 W.L.R. 526 at 534, 537 *AIB Group plc v Martin* [2001] UKHL 63; [2002] 1 W.L.R. 94 at [4].

one of the parties could feel aggrieved if evidence on the point were excluded merely because the disputed term was not set out in the contractual document.[14] Evidence extrinsic to the document is therefore admitted in a number of situations (to be discussed below) which fall outside the scope of the rule.

(2) Cases in which extrinsic evidence is admissible

(a) WRITTEN AGREEMENT NOT THE WHOLE AGREEMENT. When a contract is reduced to writing, there is a presumption that the writing was intended to include all the terms of the contract; but this presumption is rebuttable.[15] If the written document was not intended to set out all the terms on which the parties had actually agreed, extrinsic evidence is admissible. In *Allen v Pink*[16] the buyer of a horse received a note as follows: "Bought of G. Pink, a horse for the sum of £7 2s. 6d. G. Pink." Evidence of an oral warranty that the horse would go quietly in harness was admitted as the note was "meant merely as a memorandum of the transaction, or as an informal receipt for the money, not as containing the terms of the contract itself". This case should be contrasted with *Hutton v Watling*[17] where a document was headed "To sale of a business," set out a number of terms, contained a receipt for the price of the goodwill, and was signed over a 6d. stamp. In an action by the purchaser to enforce one of the clauses of the written document, the vendor argued that the document was only a memorandum of a provisional agreement for the sale of goodwill, which had already been fully performed. Evidence to this effect was held inadmissible as the document was not intended to be a mere memorandum but a "true record of the contract".[18] It seems that a document which is intended simply to form a record of a previously concluded contract will *prima facie* be a mere memorandum[19]; while a document the execution of which marks the actual conclusion of a contract is more likely to be taken to contain all the terms of the contract.

It has been argued that the right of a party to rely on extrinsic evidence in the present group of cases turns the parol evidence rule (as applied to contracts) into "no more than a circular statement".[20] For if the rule applies only where the written document is intended to contain *all* the terms of the contract, evidence of other terms would be useless even if admitted (since they would not form part of the contract); while the rule never prevents a party from relying on evidence of terms which *were* intended to be part of the contract. Accordingly, on this view, no injustice is caused by the operation of the

---

[14] Contrast *AIB Group plc v Martin*, above at [4] with *ibid.* at [44] on the question whether this was the position in that case.

[15] *Gillespie Bros & Co v Cheney, Eggar & Co* [1896] 2 Q.B. 59 at 62.

[16] (1838) 4 M. & W. 140; *cf. Harris v Rickett* (1859) 4 H. & N. 1; *Malpas v L & S W Ry Co* (1866) L.R. 1 C.P. 336; *Roe v R A Naylor Ltd* (1918) 87 L.J.K.B. 958; *J Evans & Son (Portsmouth) Ltd v Andrea Merzario* [1976] 1 W.L.R. 1078 at 1083; *Yani Haryanto v E D & F Man (Sugar) Ltd* [1986] 2 Lloyd's Rep. 44 at 46–47; *Anangel Atlas Compania Naviera SA v Ishikawajima-Harima Heavy Industries Co Ltd (No.2)* [1990] 2 Lloyd's Rep. 526 at 545; *Guardian Ocean Cargoes Ltd v Banco do Brasil* [1991] 2 Lloyd's Rep. 68 at 80, affirmed [1994] 2 Lloyd's Rep. 152; *The Riza and Sun* [1997] 2 Lloyd's Rep. 314 at 319–320.

[17] [1948] Ch. 398.

[18] [1948] Ch. 398 at 404.

[19] This view would account for the special position of bills of lading: as to this see *The Ardennes* [1951] 1 K.B. 55; but for the need to protect third parties to whom such documents are transferred, see *Leduc v Ward* (1888) 20 Q.B.D. 475; *Carver on Bills of Lading*, (1st ed., 2001), §3–004 to 3–009.

[20] Law Commission Report on *The Parol Evidence Rule* (Law Com. No.154), para.2.7; Marston [1986] C.L.J. 192; *Wild v Civil Aviation Authority* (unrep.) (1987) C.A.T. No.85/N3/4250, *per* Ralph Gibson L.J.; *cf.* the reference to the Law Commission's analysis of "the rule, if rule it be" by Beldam L.J. in *Youell v Bland Welch & Co Ltd* [1992] 2 Lloyd's Rep. 127 at 140.

rule.[21] There is much force in this view in cases in which, at the time of contracting, both parties actually shared a common intention with regard to the term in question. But in most cases in which the rule is invoked this is not the position: the dispute arises precisely because the parties had different intentions, and one alleges, while the other denies, that terms not set out in the document were intended to form part of the contract. In such cases, the court will attach importance to the appearance of the document: if it *looks* like a complete contract to one of the parties taking a reasonable view of it, then the rule will prevent the other party from relying on extrinsic evidence to show that the contract also contained other terms.[22] This result has been described as being simply an application of the objective test of agreement[23]; but, even if it can be so regarded, it is such a common and frequently recurring application of this test as to amount to an independent rule. In cases of the present kind, moreover, the law goes beyond the normal objective test. That test normally requires the party relying on it to prove that he reasonably believed that the other party was contracting on the terms alleged.[24] Where a document *looks* like a complete contract, the party relying on it does not have to prove that he had such a belief: he can rely on a presumption to that effect which it is up to the other party to rebut.[25] As laymen are known to attach greater importance than the law does to writing in a contractual context, it will be hard for the party relying on extrinsic evidence to rebut the presumption that the written document was an exclusive record of the terms agreed. Moreover, the objective test normally prevents a party from relying on his "private but uncommunicated intention as to what was to be agreed".[26] The presumption which applies in the case of an apparently complete contractual document goes beyond this: it prevents a party from relying on evidence of intention that was not "private and uncommunicated" at all, but simply not recorded in the document. For these reasons, it is submitted that the admissibility of extrinsic evidence, where it is proved that the document was not in fact intended to contain all the terms of the contract, does not turn the rule into a merely "circular statement".[27] Whether it also supports the conclusion that the rule is not one that "could lead to evidence being unjustly excluded"[28] is perhaps more doubtful. The primary purpose of the rule, like that of the objective test of agreement, is to promote certainty, sometimes even at the expense of justice.[29] Where the parties have brought into being an apparently complete contractual document, the rejection of evidence of extrinsic terms that were actually agreed may cause injustice to the party relying on those terms, while the reception of such evidence may cause injustice to the other party, if he reasonably believed that the document formed an exclusive record of the contract.[30] The question is which, on balance, is the greater injustice. Where the evidence is rejected because the party relying on it cannot overcome the presumption arising from the fact that the document *looks* like a complete contract, the greater injustice would appear to lie in the exclusion of the evidence; for the presumption seems to be based on

---

[21] Law Com. No.154, above; and see also para.1.7.

[22] Wedderburn [1959] C.L.J. 58, 62.

[23] Law Com. No.154, above, para.2.14, 2.17.

[24] See above, pp.1, 8.

[25] See above, p.193 at n.15.

[26] Law Com. No.154, above, para.2.14; *cf.* above, p.172.

[27] *cf.* the authorities cited in n.11 on p.192 above.

[28] Law Com. No.154, para.2.7.

[29] *AIB Group plc v Martin* [2001] UKHL 63; [2002] 1 W.L.R. 94 at [4].

[30] For the rejection of evidence in such circumstances, see *Hutton v Watling* [1948] Ch. 398 at 404; and *cf. Rabin v Gerson Berger Association Ltd* [1986] 1 W.L.R. 526 where the rule was applied to a declaration of trust but said at 536 to apply to contracts.

the nature and form of the document, rather than on any actual belief of the party relying on it, that it formed an exclusive record of the contract.[31]

(b) VALIDITY. The rule prevents a party from relying on extrinsic evidence only as to the *contents* of the contract, and not as to its *validity*. Such evidence can therefore be used to establish the presence or absence of consideration or of contractual intention,[32] or some invalidating cause such as incapacity, misrepresentation, mistake[33] or *non est factum*.[34] Evidence has similarly been held admissible to show that provisions in an agreement purporting to be a licence to occupy a room (as opposed to a lease of it) were a "mere sham"[35] in that they had failed to state the parties' true intention and had been inserted simply in an attempt to evade the Rent Act.

(c) IMPLIED TERMS. The rule prevents a party from relying on extrinsic evidence only as to the express terms of the contract. Where the contract is silent on a matter on which a term is normally implied by law, parol evidence may be given to support, or to rebut, the usual implication. Thus a buyer of coal can show that he made known to the seller the particular purpose for which he required the coal, so as to raise the implication that he relied on the seller's skill and judgment.[36] Conversely, a person who takes out a policy of marine insurance can show that the insurer knew the ship to be unseaworthy, and so negative the usual implied warranty of seaworthiness.[37]

(d) ORAL WARRANTIES. Where parties enter into a written contract of sale, the rule would *prima facie* prevent the buyer from relying on evidence of oral undertakings as to the quality of the subject-matter; but this application of the rule is subject to two qualifications. First, an exclusion clause contained in a written contract can be over-ridden by an express oral warranty given at the time of sale.[38] Secondly, an oral statement of fact may operate as a misrepresentation in spite of its purported incorporation into the contract as a warranty[39]; and where this is the case, the oral statement can be used as evidence, not of the contents of the contract, but of an invalidating cause.

(e) OPERATION OF THE CONTRACT. Extrinsic evidence can be used to show that the contract does not yet operate, or that it has ceased to operate. Thus in *Pym v Campbell*[40] a written agreement for the sale of a patent was drawn up, and evidence was admitted of an oral stipulation that the agreement should not *become operative* until a third party had approved of the invention. It seems from the reasoning of the court that evidence

---

[31] The Law Commission had, before publishing the Report referred to in n.20, above, provisionally recommended the abolition of the rule: Law Commission Working Paper No.76 (1976); *cf.* Administration of Justice Act 1982, s.21 (making extrinsic evidence admissible in certain cases for interpretation of wills).

[32] *Clever v Kirkman* (1876) 33 L.T. 672; *Zahem International Construction Ltd v Nippon Kohan K.K.* [1987] 2 Lloyd's Rep. 596; *Kleinwort Benson Ltd v Malaysian Mining Corp* [1989] 1 W.L.R. 379 at 392; *Orion Ins Co plc v Sphere Drake Ins plc* [1992] 1 Lloyd's Rep. 239; *Carmichael v National Power plc* [1999] 1 W.L.R. 2042.

[33] *Campbell Discount Co v Gall* [1961] 1 Q.B. 431 reversed on other points, by Consumer Credit Act 1974, s.56 and by *Branwhite v Worcester Works Finance Ltd* [1969] 1 A.C. 552; below, pp.707, 1058.

[34] *Roe v R A Naylor Ltd* (1918) 87 L.J.K.B. 958 at 964; below, p.326.

[35] *AG Securities v Vaughan* [1990] 1 A.C. 417 at 469, 475; *Mikeover v Brady* [1989] 3 All E.R. 618 at 625; *cf. Chase Manhattan Equities Ltd v Goodman* [1991] BCLC 897.

[36] *Gillespie Bros. & Co v Cheney, Eggar & Co* [1896] 2 Q.B. 59.

[37] *Burges v Wickham* (1863) 3 B. & S. 669; Blackburn J. dissented on this point.

[38] See below, p.241.

[39] Misrepresentation Act 1967, s.1(a); below, p.375.

[40] (1856) 6 E. & B. 370. According to this report a new trial was sought on the ground of misdirection; but the other reports (25 L.J.Q.B. 277; 2 Jur.(N.S.) 641 and 4 W.R. 528) are probably more accurate in stating that it was sought on the ground of improper reception of evidence.

of an oral stipulation that the agreement should *cease to bind* if the third party disapproved of the invention would not have been admissible. On the other hand, evidence is admissible to show that a written contract has been varied or rescinded.[41] It is not easy to deduce from the purpose of the parol evidence rule why evidence should be admissible in the first and third, but not in the second of these cases.

(f) EVIDENCE AS TO PARTIES. Extrinsic evidence can be used to identify the parties[42] and to show in what capacities the parties contracted. Thus in *Newell v Radford*[43] the written record of a contract read "Mr. Newell, 32 sacks of culasses at 39s. 280lbs., to await orders. John Williams." Evidence was admitted that Newell was a baker and Williams' principal a flour dealer, so as to show which party was buyer and which seller.

Where a person contracts ostensibly as principal evidence is admissible to prove that he really acted as another's agent so as to entitle the latter to sue[44] unless such evidence contradicts the express description of the agent in the contract.[45] As the ostensible contracting party is in such cases personally liable even if he acted as agent, the evidence would not normally relieve him from liability. But in *Wake v Harrop*[46] an agent signed a charterparty on behalf of the charterer, but so as to make himself personally liable. He did so after an oral agreement with the shipowner that he should not be personally liable. It was held that the agent could rely on the oral agreement, if not at law, at any rate by way of equitable defence. Conversely, where a person contracted on the face of the document as agent evidence was held to be admissible of his contemporaneous statements that he intended to undertake personal liability.[47]

(g) DEFENCE TO SPECIFIC PERFORMANCE. Failure to perform an oral promise may be available as a defence when the party who made it claims specific performance of the written agreement.[48] Alternatively, in such a case, the court may have a discretion to order specific performance on the terms that the claimant performs the oral undertaking.[49] Where, as in the authorities which support these propositions, the contract was one for the disposition of an interest in land, it now generally has to be made in writing by incorporating *all* its express terms in a contractual document.[50] Failure to incorporate the oral promise would therefore prevent the contract from coming into existence,[51] and would lead to the dismissal of a claim (whether for specific performance or for damages) on that ground, unless the promise could be said to take effect only as a collateral contract.[52] But the reasoning of the older authorities would still apply where specific

---

[41] *Morris v Baron & Co* [1918] A.C. 1; *Goss v Nugent* (1833) 5 B. & Ad. 58 at 65. It does not, of course, follow from the admissibility of evidence of a variation that the variation can be enforced: as to this, see above, pp.188, 190.

[42] *OTV Birwelco Ltd v Technical & General Guarantee Co Ltd* [2002] EWHC 2240 (TCC); [2002] 4 All E.R. 668, at [22].

[43] (1867) L.R. 3 C.P. 52; *cf. The Riza and Sun* [1997] 2 Lloyd's Rep. 314 at 320.

[44] *Humfrey v Dale* (1857) 7 E. & B. 266; affirmed (1858) E.B. & E. 1004.

[45] See, p.727.

[46] (1861) 6 H. & N. 768; affirmed 1 H. & C. 202.

[47] *Sun Alliance Pensions Life & Investment Services Ltd v RJL* [1991] 2 Lloyd's Rep. 410.

[48] *Martin v Pycroft* (1852) 2 D.M. & G. 785, 795; *cf. Scott v Bradley* [1971] Ch. 850.

[49] See *London & Birmingham Ry v Winter* (1840) Cr. & Ph. 57.

[50] Law of Property (Miscellaneous Provisions) Act 1989, s.2(1), above, p.178. Before this section came into force, the contract only had to be evidenced in writing, and failure to comply with this requirement did not prevent enforcement if there had been "part performance" by the claimant: above, p.185.

[51] See above, p.179.

[52] *ibid.*; below, p.199.

performance was sought of a contract which was in fact in writing, even though there was no legal requirement to this effect.[53]

(h) AID TO CONSTRUCTION. Where the words of the contract are "clear", extrinsic evidence cannot be used to explain their meaning,[54] unless they have a special meaning by custom.[55] Extrinsic evidence can, on the other hand, be used to explain words or phrases which are ambiguous,[56] or which, if taken literally, make no sense,[57] or conflict with others in the same document,[58] as well as technical terms. Evidence is likewise admissible of the factual background (or "matrix"[59]) to the negotiations insofar as this sheds light on the meaning of the words used.[60]

Even where extrinsic evidence is normally admissible as an aid to construction, its use for this purpose is subject to a number of restrictions. First, evidence of *prior negotiations* is generally inadmissible, being unhelpful since "It is only the final document which records a consensus".[61] Evidence of a prior *contract* between the parties may be admissible as part of the "factual matrix"[62] surrounding the contract in issue, though if that contract was intended to supersede the prior one, then evidence of the prior contract is either inadmissible[63] or, even if admissible, "of little relevance".[64] If the final document contains ambiguous expressions, evidence of precontract communications is however admissible to show that the parties had attached an agreed meaning to these expressions.[65] Secondly, evidence of the *conduct* of the parties *after* the making of the contract will not be admitted on the issue of construction. For if such evidence were admitted the undesirable result might follow "that a contract meant one thing the day it was signed but, by reason of subsequent events, meant something different a month

---

[53] *e.g.* if it was a lease for less than three years (above, p.178) or a contract for the sale of "unique" goods (below, pp.1022, 1023).

[54] *Bank of New Zealand v Simpson*, [1900] A.C. at 189; *Edward Lloyd Ltd v Sturgeon Falls Pulp Co* (1901) 85 L.T. 162; *Lovell & Christmas Ltd v Wall* (1911) 104 L.T. 85.

[55] See below, p.198.

[56] *Robertson v Jackson* (1845) 2 C.B. 412; *Bank of New Zealand v Simpson* [1900] A.C. 182; *cf. Scarfe v Adams* [1981] 1 All E.R. 843; *Pao On v Lau Yiu Long* [1980] A.C. 614 at 631; *Forsikringsaktieselskapet Vesta v Butcher* [1989] A.C. 582 at 909–910; *Shearson Lehman Hutton Inc v Maclaine Watson & Co Ltd* [1989] 2 Lloyd's Rep. 570 at 591; *Anangel Atlas Compania Naviera SA v Ishikawajima-Harima Heavy Industries (No.2)* [1990] 2 Lloyd's Rep. 526 at 554.

[57] *The Sounion* [1987] 1 Lloyd's Rep. 230 ("grates and stoves" on ships which no longer carried such implements).

[58] *e.g. Mannai Investment Co Ltd v Eagle Star Life Assurance Co* [1997] A.C. 749; *BOC Group plc v Centeon LLC* [1999] 1 All E.R. (Comm) 970 at 979.

[59] *Prenn v Simmonds* [1971] 1 W.L.R. 1381 at 1384.

[60] *Prenn v Simmonds* [1971] 1 W.L.R. 1381 at 1385; *Reardon Smith Line Ltd v Hansen Tangen* [1976] 1 W.L.R. 989 at 996; *Youell v Bland Welch & Co Ltd* [1992] 2 Lloyd's Rep. 127 at 133; *Scottish Power plc v Britoil (Exploration) Ltd, The Times*, December 2, 1997 (urging a restrictive use of evidence for this purpose); *Simon Container Machinery Ltd v Emba Machinery A.B.* [1998] 2 Lloyd's Rep. 428 at 435.

[61] *Prenn v Simmonds* [1971] 1 W.L.R. 1381 at 1384; *Arrale v Costain Civil Engineering Ltd* [1976] 1 Lloyd's Rep. 49; *The Ionio* [1985] 2 Lloyd's Rep. 271 at 274; *Youell v Bland Welch & Co Ltd* [1992] 2 Lloyd's Rep. 127 at 133; *cf. Rabin v Gerson Berger Association Ltd* [1986] 1 W.L.R. 526; *Mannai Investment Co Ltd v Eagle Star Life Assurance Co Ltd* [1997] A.C. 749 at 779; *Investors Compensation Scheme Ltd v West Bromwich B.S.* [1998] 1 W.L.R. 896 at 913.

[62] *HIH Casualty & General Insurance Ltd v New Hampshire Insurance Co* [2001] 2 All E.R. (Comm) 39, [2001] EWCA Civ 735 at [83].

[63] *Youell v Bland Welch & Co Ltd* [1992] 2 Lloyd's Rep. 127 at 141 (insurance slip inadmissible on construction of later policy; for the binding force of the slip, see above, p.54).

[64] *HIH Casualty Case*, above, n.62 at [83] (where the prior contract was not intended to be superseded by the later one).

[65] *The Karen Oltman* [1976] 2 Lloyd's Rep. 708; *cf. The Pacific Colocotronis* [1981] 2 Lloyd's Rep. 40.

or a year later".[66] Such evidence may be admissible to show what the terms of the original contract were,[67] or that the written terms were a "mere sham",[68] or that the contract had been varied by subsequent agreement,[69] or to raise an estoppel[70]; but it cannot be used to elucidate the original meaning of the contract. Thirdly, it has been said that evidence of the "parties' intentions"[71] will not be admitted on the issue of construction. What seems to be meant is that the purposes of the parties,[72] or the subjective intention of one of them[73] (not known to the other[74]) will not be considered. So far as their intentions relate (for example) to the identity of the subject-matter, evidence of them is no doubt admissible.[75]

(i) TO PROVE CUSTOM. Evidence of custom is admissible "to annex incidents to written contracts[76] in matters with respect to which they are silent".[77] It is generally said that the evidence can be used to add to, but not to contradict, the written contract. Thus the evidence cannot be used where the custom, if actually written into the contract, would make it "insensible or inconsistent".[78] For example, where a charterparty provided that expenses of discharging should be borne by the *charterer* "as customary", a custom that they were to be borne by the *shipowner* was held to be inconsistent with the charterparty[79]; and where a bill of lading provided for "freight payable in London" this was held to be inconsistent with a custom that it was payable *in advance* in London.[80] But where a bill of lading provided for freight at a specified rate, evidence of a customary

---

[66] *James Miller & Partners v Whitworth Street Estates (Manchester) Ltd* [1970] A.C. 583 at 603, 606; *Wickman Ltd v Schuler AG* [1974] A.C. 325; *cf. Houlder Bros & Co Ltd v Commissioners of Public Works* [1908] A.C. 276 at 285; *The Good Helmsman* [1981] 1 Lloyd's Rep. 377 at 416; *Macedonia Maritime Co v Austin Pickersgill Ltd, The Times*, January 26, 1989; *Porteus v Element Books Ltd* [1996] C.L.Y. 1029. For an exception, see *Wilson v Maynard Shipbuilding Consultants A.B.* [1978] Q.B. 665 at 675–676.

[67] *Ferguson v Dawson & Partners (Contractors) Ltd* [1976] 1 W.L.R. 1213; *Mears v Safecar Securities Ltd* [1983] Q.B. 54 at 77; *Carmichael v National Power plc* [1999] 1 W.L.R. 2042 at 2050–2051; *cf.* above, p.193.

[68] See above, p.195 at n.35.

[69] *McCausland v Duncan Lawrie Ltd* [1997] 1 W.L.R. 38 at 49.

[70] *James Miller & Partners Ltd v Whitworth Street Estates (Manchester) Ltd* [1970] A.C. 583 at 611, 615; *cf. Amalgamated Investment & Property Co Ltd v Texas Commerce International Bank Ltd* [1982] Q.B. 84 at 119.

[71] *Prenn v Simmonds*, above, n.59 at 1385; *Pritchard v Briggs* [1980] Ch. 338; *The Good Helmsman* [1981] 1 Lloyd's Rep. 377 at 416; *The Scaptrade* [1981] 2 Lloyd's Rep. 425 at 432, affirmed without reference to this point [1983] 2 A.C. 694; *Rabin v Gerson Berger Association Ltd* [1986] 1 W.L.R. 526 at 533; *Transpetrol Ltd v Transol Olieprodukten Nederland BV* [1989] 1 Lloyd's Rep. 309 at 310; *New Hampshire Insurance Co Ltd v MGN, The Times*, July 25, 1995; *Investors Compensation Scheme Ltd v West Bromwich BS* [1998] 1 W.L.R. 896 at 913 ("subjective intent"); *The Red Sea* [1999] 1 Lloyd's Rep. 28 at 30 ("subjective intention" as opposed to "objective meaning"); *AIB Group plc v Martin* [2001] UKHL 63; [2001] 1 W.L.R. 99, at [4]. This restriction on the admissibility of such evidence cannot be avoided "as it were by the backdoor" by invoking the doctrine of estoppel by convention (above, p.119): *Phillip Collins Ltd v Davis* [2000] 3 All E.R. 808 at 824.

[72] *Prenn v Simmonds*, above, n.59 at 1385.

[73] *Scottish Power plc v Britoil (Exploration) Ltd, The Times*, December 2, 1997; *Zoan v Rouamba* [2000] 1 W.L.R. 1509 at [43].

[74] *ibid.*, at [42], distinguishing the *Mannai* case (above, p.197, n.58) where the mistake in the tenant's notice was obvious to the landlord.

[75] See below at n.84.

[76] Including those made by deed: *Wigglesworth v Dallison* (1779) 1 Doug. 201.

[77] *Hutton v Warren* (1836) 1 M. & W. 466 at 475.

[78] *Humfrey v Dale* 7 E. & B. 266, 275; affirmed (1858) E.B. & E. 1004.

[79] *Palgrave Brown & Son Ltd v SS Turid (Owners)* [1922] 1 A.C. 397; *cf. Mowbray Robinson & Co v Rosser* (1922) 91 L.J.K.B. 524.

[80] *Krall v Burnett* (1877) 25 W.R. 305; advance freight would be payable even though the ship failed to reach the contractual destination: below, p.917.

deduction of interest was held merely to add to the contract since the discount was calculated on the contract rate of freight.[81] In such borderline cases, the distinction between customs which add to and those which contradict the written contract is largely one of emphasis.

Custom can also be used as an aid to construction.[82] For this purpose, evidence of custom is admissible even though it contradicts the ordinary meaning of the words used in the contract *e.g.*, to show that "1,000 rabbits" meant "1,200 rabbits."[83]

(j) To IDENTIFY THE SUBJECT-MATTER. Extrinsic evidence is admissible to identify the subject-matter of a contract: for example, to show that "your wool" meant not only wool produced by the claimant but also wool produced on a neighbouring farm[84]; and to define the exact area of land conveyed where the conveyance fails to make this clear.[85] Similarly, such evidence is admissible to define the extent of a party's obligations under a contract: *e.g.* to show that a contract to pump oil out of a stranded tanker obliged the party rendering the service to take away only so much oil as was necessary to avert the risk of pollution[86]; or to show whether a guarantee related to one debt only or was a continuing one,[87] or to which of a number of transactions a guarantee related.[88] Where a lease contains a covenant to repair, evidence can similarly be given as to the character of the premises in order to determine the extent of the obligation imposed by the covenant.[89]

(k) RECTIFICATION A document may be meant to record a previous oral agreement, but fail accurately to do so. Such a document can sometimes be rectified, *i.e.* brought into line with the previous oral agreement.[90] When this is done evidence of the previous oral agreement must inevitably be admitted. This does not mean that a party can claim rectification merely by alleging that terms which were in fact agreed were not incorporated in the document. The remedy of rectification is based on a *mistake* in the recording of a previous oral agreement.[91] In most of the cases in which the parol evidence rule is invoked the parties make no such mistake: they know perfectly well that the extrinsic term is not incorporated in the document, so that rectification is not available.

(l) COLLATERAL AGREEMENTS. Even where extrinsic evidence cannot be used to vary, add to or contradict the terms of a written agreement, it may be possible to show that the parties made two related contracts, one written and the other oral. In *Mann v Nunn*[92] the claimant orally agreed to take a lease of the defendant's premises if the defendant would first do certain repairs. A written agreement was later executed, but did not refer to the defendant's promise to do the repairs. The claimant was nonetheless able to

---

[81] *Brown v Byrne* (1854) 3 E. & B. 703.

[82] *e.g. Norden Steam Co v Dempsey* (1876) 1 C.P.D. 654; *cf. Robertson v Jackson* (1845) 2 C.B. 412.

[83] *Smith v Wilson* (1832) 3 B. & Ad. 728.

[84] *Macdonald v Longbottom* (1859) 1 E. & E. 977.

[85] *Scarfe v Adams* [1981] 1 All E.R. 843; *cf. Freeguard v Rogers, The Times,* October 27, 1998.

[86] *The Pacific Colocotronis* [1981] 2 Lloyd's Rep. 40; *cf. Essex CC v Ellam* [1989] 2 All E.R. 494 (evidence admissible as to legal nature of payments made under covenant).

[87] *Heffield v Meadows* (1869) L.R. 4 C.P. 595.

[88] *Perrylease Ltd v Imecar Ltd* [1988] 1 W.L.R. 463.

[89] *Burges v Wickham* (1863) 3 B. & S. 669 at 698.

[90] See below, p.321 *et seq.*

[91] See below, p.321; *cf. Rabin v Gerson Berger Association Ltd* [1986] 1 W.L.R. 526, 534; *The Riza and Sun* [1997] 2 Lloyd's Rep. 314 at 320.

[92] (1874) 30 L.T. 526; *cf. Walker Property Investments (Brighton) Ltd v Walker* (1947) 177 L.T. 204.

enforce this promise. "The parol agreement neither alters nor adds to the written one, but is an independent agreement."[93]

Thus evidence is admissible if it proves an "independent agreement"; but it is often hard to say whether the evidence has this effect or whether it varies, or adds to, the terms of the main contract. The test seems to be whether the evidence relates to a term which would go to the essence of the whole transaction: if so, it cannot be regarded as evidence of a collateral contract and will be inadmissible.[94]

In *Mann v Nunn* the lease contained no provisions as to putting the premises in repair, so that the landlord's promise merely *added* to it. According to two later cases, evidence of a collateral contract is inadmissible if it *varies* or *contradicts* a term actually set out in the main written contract. In the first,[95] a lease of a furnished house specified the furniture to be included. Evidence of a collateral agreement, made before the lease, to put in more furniture, was held inadmissible. In the second,[96] rent under a lease was payable quarterly in advance. Evidence of a collateral agreement allowing the tenant (in effect) to pay the rent in arrear was similarly held inadmissible.

On the other hand, in *City & Westminster Properties* (1934) *Ltd v Mudd*[97] a lease contained a covenant to use the premises for business purposes only. The tenant had been induced to sign it by an oral assurance that the lessors would not object to his continuing to reside on the premises (as he had done in the past). In spite of the fact that this assurance contradicted the lease, evidence of it was held admissible to prove a collateral contract. The case is hard to distinguish from the cases discussed above[98]; and it is arguable that evidence of a collateral contract should not, any more than evidence of custom,[99] be allowed to contradict the main written contract. But evidence of custom is meant to elucidate the meaning of the written document itself, and it could hardly do this by introducing contradictory terms. Evidence of a collateral agreement is not meant to determine the content or meaning of a written document, but to give effect to an independent agreement. There is no compelling reason why this agreement should not contradict the written document.

It can be argued that the collateral contract device largely destroys the parol evidence rule, especially if *Mudd*'s case is right. But some limitations on this device are imposed by the requirements that a statement operates as a collateral contract only if intended to be legally binding and supported by separate consideration.[1] Such consideration will often be provided by the promisee's act of entering into the main contract.[2] But this act could not be consideration for the collateral promise if that promise was made *after* the conclusion of the main contract; for in that case the consideration would be past and hence of no effect in law.[3]

---

[93] *Mann v Nunn*, above, at 527. For other requirements of collateral contracts, see above, pp.162, 180–181, below, pp.356–357.

[94] *e.g. The Nile Rhapsody* [1992] 2 Lloyd's Rep. 399 at 407, affirmed [1994] 1 Lloyd's Rep. 382; *Mitchill v Lath* 160 N.E. 646 (1928) *cf.* in the context of formal requirements *ante*, pp.180–181.

[95] *Angell v Duke* (1875) 32 L.T. 320; for previous proceedings in this case, see (1875) L.R. 10 Q.B. 174; above, p.181.

[96] *Henderson v Arthur* [1907] 1 K.B. 10.

[97] [1959] Ch. 129; *cf. Couchman v Hill* [1947] K.B. 554, where one reason for the decision was that the oral warranty was a collateral contract; and *Brikom Investments Ltd v Carr* [1979] Q.B. 467 (above, p.102), where no point as to admissibility of evidence seems to have been taken.

[98] The fact that the tenant actually *refused* to sign the lease until he was given the oral assurance may distinguish *Mudd*'s case from *Angell v Duke* and *Henderson v Arthur* above, at nn.95, 96.

[99] See above, p.198.

[1] See above, p.102; *post*, p.356.

[2] *e.g.* in *City of Westminster Properties (1934) Ltd v Mudd* [1959] Ch. 129.

[3] See above, p.77.

(m) CONSIDERATION. In *Turner v Forwood*[4] a person assigned a debt due to him from a company to one of its directors by a deed stated to have been made for a nominal consideration. It was held that evidence was admissible to show that there was a substantial consideration for the assignment.[5] This evidence did not really contradict the deed as the nominal consideration was mentioned only as a matter of form.[6] Where an agreement states a substantial consideration, evidence of *additional* consideration is also admissible, so long as it does not contradict that stated in the written agreement.[7]

SECTION 2. IMPLIED TERMS[8]

Implied terms may be divided into three main[9] groups. The first consists of terms implied in fact, that is, terms which were not expressly set out in the contract, but which the parties must have intended to include. The second consists of terms implied in law, that is, terms imported by operation of law, although the parties may not have intended to include them. The third consists of terms implied by custom.

1. Terms Implied in Fact

(1) Officious bystander test

One test for the implication of a term in fact is the "officious bystander" test. This has been stated by MacKinnon L.J. as follows: "*Prima facie* that which in any contract is left to be implied and need not be expressed is something so obvious that it goes without saying; so that, if while the parties were making their bargain, an officious bystander were to suggest some express provision for it in the agreement, they would testily suppress him with a common 'Oh, of course!' "[10] For example, in one case[11] a vendor of land undertook that, if he later *sold* certain adjoining land, he would give the purchaser the "first refusal" of it. A term was implied to prevent the vendor from defeating the purchaser's expectation by disposing of the land to a third party by way of *gift*.

(2) Business efficacy test

A second test for the implication of a term in fact is that of "business efficacy." Lord Wright has described such a term as one "of which it can be predicated that 'it goes

---

[4] [1951] 1 All E.R. 746.

[5] *cf.* above, p.75.

[6] *i.e.* to avoid the implication of a use: *Cross and Tapper on Evidence* (9th ed.), p.656.

[7] *Pao On v Lau Yiu Long* [1980] A.C. 614 at 631.

[8] Lücke, 5 Adelaide L.Rev. 31.

[9] See below, p.211 for cases not falling readily into anyone of these groups.

[10] *Shirlaw v Southern Foundries (1926) Ltd* [1939] 2 K.B. 206 at 227 (affirmed [1940] A.C. 701); *cf. Comptoir Commercial Anversois v Power, Son & Co* [1920] 1 K.B. 868 at 899–900; MacKinnon L.J.'s test is viewed with some scepticism in *The Manifest Lipkowy* [1989] 2 Lloyd's Rep. 138 at 142, but (*semble*) approved *ibid.* at 143. In *The Bonde* [1991] 1 Lloyd's Rep. 136 at 145 and in *North Sea Energy Holdings NV v Petroleum Authority of Thailand* [1997] 2 Lloyd's Rep. 418 at 431 (affirmed [1999] 1 Lloyd's Rep. 483) the officious bystander is, unusually, regarded as answering, rather than as posing, the question assumed to have been put; *cf. The Rio Assusu* [1999] 1 Lloyd's Rep. 115 at 126.

[11] *Gardner v Coutts & Co* [1968] 1 W.L.R. 173, distinguished in *Nicholson v Markham* [1997] C.L.Y. 4255 on the ground stated below, p.204 at n.33; *cf. Vosper Thorneycroft v Minister of Defence* [1976] 1 Lloyd's Rep. 58; *Essoldo v Ladbroke Group, The Times*, December 26, 1976; *Bournemouth & Boscombe Athletic FC v Manchester United FC, The Times*, May 22, 1980; *Fraser v Thames Television Ltd* [1984] Q.B. 44 at 57; *The Dadomar General T.J. Park* [1986] 2 Lloyd's Rep. 68.

without saying,' some term not expressed but necessary to give the transaction such business efficacy as the parties must have intended".[12] It is sometimes also said that all implied terms are subject to a requirement of "necessity",[13] as if that were an additional requirement, but in the present context "necessity" seems to be no more than a part of (or perhaps an alternative to[14]) the "business efficacy"[15] test as stated by Lord Wright.

The relationship between the "officious bystander" and "business efficacy" tests is, however, not entirely clear.[16] One view is that *both* tests must be satisfied: in other words, that the party seeking to establish the term must show "that the implication was necessary, that the contract would have made no sense without it, *and* that the term was omitted . . . because it was so obvious that there was no need to make it explicit".[17] But if it can be established, as a matter of fact, that both parties regarded the term as obvious and would have accepted it, had it been put to them at the time of contracting, that should suffice to support the implication of the term in fact[18]; for the purpose of such an implication is simply "to give effect to the intention of the parties."[19] A second view is that it is sufficient to satisfy *either* test, so that "a term will be implied only where it is necessary in a business sense to give efficacy to a contract *or* where the term is one which the parties must obviously have intended."[20] This view in turn gives rise to difficulty where it is clear that one party (at least) would *not* have agreed to the term, even though the other (or the court) would have regarded it as necessary to give business efficacy to the contract. In such a case, the implication would clearly not "give effect to the intention of the parties",[21] so that there would to be no room for an implication in fact. It is submitted that, in the present context, "business efficacy" (or "necessity"[22])

---

[12] *Luxor (Eastbourne) Ltd v Cooper* [1941] A.C. 108 at 137; *cf. Comptoir Commercial Anversois v Power, Son & Co* [1920] 1 K.B. 868 at 899–900; *Barclays Bank plc v Taylor* [1989] 1 W.L.R. 1066 at 1074; *The Star Texas* [1993] 2 Lloyd's Rep. 444 at 451; Burrows, 3 N.Z.U.L.R. 121.

[13] *Luxor* case, above, at 125; *Anderson v Corporation of Lloyd's (No.2)* [1992] 1 Lloyd's Rep. 620 at 627; *Hughes v Greenwich LBC* [1994] A.C. 170 at 179; *Baker v Black Sea & Baltic Insurance Co Ltd* [1998] 1 W.L.R. 974 at 980 (but see *ibid.* at 978).

[14] See *Cox v Bankside* [1995] 2 Lloyd's Rep. 436 at 466.

[15] See above at n.12: "*necessary* to give . . . business efficacy"; *cf. Friend's Provident Life Office v Hillier Parker May & Rowden* [1995] 4 All E.R. 260 at 279 ("business necessity"); *Insurance Co v Lloyd's Syndicate* [1995] 1 Lloyd's Rep. 273 at 275; *Flementatos Maritimos SA v Effjohn International BV* [1995] 1 Lloyd's Rep. 311 at 314–315; *The Aegean Sea* [1998] 2 Lloyd's Rep. 39 at 65.

[16] See *Suriya & Douglas v Midland Bank plc* [1999] 1 All E.R. (Comm) 612 at 615.

[17] *Stubbs v Trower Still and King* [1987] I.R.L.R. 321 at 324 (emphasis added); *McAuley v Bristol CC* [1992] Q.B. 134 at 147; *Association of British Travel Agents v British Airways plc* [2000] 1 Lloyd's Rep. 169 at 175, affirmed [2000] 2 Lloyd's Rep. 209; *BP v Hastings* (1978) 52 A.L.J.R. 20 at 26.

[18] *Aspden v Webbs Poultry & Meat Group (Holdings) Ltd* [1996] I.R.L.R. 521.

[19] *Luxor (Eastbourne) Ltd v Cooper* [1941] A.C. 108 at 137.

[20] *The Manifest Lipkowy* [1989] 2 Lloyd's Rep. 138 at 143 (emphasis added) and 144; *cf. The C Joyce* [1986] 2 All E.R. 177 at 182; *Barrett v Lounava (1982) Ltd* [1990] 1 Q.B. 348 at 355: *The Choko Star* [1990] 1 Lloyd's Rep. 516 at 524, 526; *The Wardens, etc. of Mercers v New Hampshire Insurance Co* [1992] 2 Lloyd's Rep. 365 at 370; *Cox v Bankside* [1995] 2 Lloyd's Rep. 437 at 457, 466; *Coca Cola Financial Corp v First International Ltd* [1996] 2 Lloyd's Rep. 274 at 277; *The Kurnia Dewi* [1997] 1 Lloyd's Rep. 553 at 559 ("and/or"); *Clarion Ltd v National Provident Association* [2000] 1 W.L.R. 1888 at 1896; *Weldon v GRE Linked Life Assurance Ltd* [2000] 2 All E.R. (Comm) 914 at 919; *Ministry of Defence v County and Metropolitan Homes (Rissington) Ltd*, *The Times*, November 9, 2002. In *Ashmore v Corporations of Lloyd's (No.2)* [1992] 2 Lloyd's Rep. 620 at 626 the "business efficacy" and "officious bystander" tests are described as two tests of "implications in fact" and it is said that "both depend upon the presumed joint intention of the parties."

[21] *Luxor (Eastbourne) Ltd v Cooper*, above at n.11; *cf. The Gudermes* [1993] 1 Lloyd's Rep. 311 at 323.

[22] See *Kumar v AGF Insurance Ltd* [1998] 4 All E.R. 788 at 793–794; [1999] 1 W.L.R. 1747 at 1752.

is merely a practical test for determining the intention of the parties: in most cases, it can be assumed that they would have agreed to a term which is necessary to make their agreement work. This seems to be the meaning of Lord Wright's statement (quoted above) in which the two tests are stated in apposition and evidently regarded as meaning much the same thing[23]; and most of the authorities with which the following discussion is concerned are based on the assumption that a term cannot be implied in fact where the evidence actually negatives the "officious bystander" test.[24] In the absence of such evidence, it seems that satisfaction of either the "officious bystander" or the "business efficacy" test will suffice for the implication of a term in fact.

(3) Reasonableness

The fact that a particular implication is reasonable may be evidence that the parties would have agreed to it; if so, the "officious bystander test" is satisfied,[25] and the same fact may help to satisfy the "business efficacy" test.[26] But the courts will not imply a term in fact merely because it would be reasonable to do so[27]; "they will not . . . improve the contract which the parties have made for themselves, however desirable the improvement might be".[28] At most, the fact that the alleged term was *unreasonable* may lead to a refusal to imply a term on the ground that the party objecting to the implication would not have agreed to it.[29] The standard of reasonableness may also be used in interpreting *express* terms that are imprecise or ambiguous[30]; but the test for implying a new term in fact is to ask whether the parties would have agreed to it—not whether it would have been reasonable for them to have done so.

---

[23] *cf. K C Sethia (1944) Ltd v Partabmull Rameshwar* [1950] 1 All E.R. 51 at 59 (affirmed [1951] 2 Lloyd's Rep. 89): "unless, considering the matter from the point of view of business efficacy, it is clear that both parties intended a given term to operate"; *The Good Luck* [1989] 2 Lloyd's Rep. 238 at 268 (reversed on other grounds [1992] 1 A.C. 233): "what would the parties, if asked, have said, *also known* as the business efficacy test" (emphasis added); *The Bonde* [1991] 1 Lloyd's Rep. 136 at 145. *McClory v Post Office* [1992] I.C.R. 758 at 764 ("often a different way of saying the some thing"); *Flementatos Maritimos SA v Effjohn International BV* [1995] 1 Lloyd's Rep. 311 at 315 (regarding the "officious bystander" test as an application of the "business efficacy" test); *Ali Shipping Corp v Shipyard Trogir* [1998] 2 All E.R. 136 at 147. See also *The Island Archon* [1994] 2 Lloyd's Rep. 227 where Evans L.J. at 237 based the implication in part on "business efficiency" while Nicholls V.-C. at 237 based it on the ground they "the contracting parties must have so intended."

[24] *Clarion Ltd v National Provident Association* [2000] 1 W.L.R. 1888 at 1897; see also *Ali v Christian Salveson Food Services Ltd* [1997] 1 All E.R. 721 at 725, where "no reliance was placed on "the business efficacy test; *Kumar v AGF Insurance Ltd* [1998] 4 All E.R. 788 at 793–794, where the test of "necessity" is evidently regarded as the equivalent of the "officious bystander" test.

[25] *Paragon Finance Ltd v Staunton* [2001] EWCA Civ 1466 at [36]; [2001] 2 All E.R. (Comm) 1025.

[26] *Weldon's* case, above, n.20 at 919.

[27] *Reigate v Union Manufacturing Co (Ramsbottom) Ltd* [1918] 1 K.B. 592 at 605; *Bandar Property Holdings Ltd v J S Darwen (Successors) Ltd* [1968] 2 All E.R. 305; *Lupton v Potts* [1969] 1 W.L.R. 1749; *Liverpool City Council v Irwin* [1977] A.C. 239; *Duke of Westminster v Guild* [1985] Q.B. 688 at 698; *The Mammoth Pine* [1986] 3 All E.R. 767 at 770. *McAuley v Bristol CC* [1992] Q.B. 134 at 146; *The Island Archon* [1994] 2 Lloyd's Rep. 227 at 237; *Friends' Provident Life Office v Hillier Parker May & Rowden* [1995] 4 All E.R. 260 at 279; *Insurance Co v Lloyd's Syndicate* [1995] 1 Lloyd's Rep. 273 at 275; *cf.* Lord Simonds' warning in *Scruttons Ltd v Midland Silicones Ltd* [1962] A.C. 446 at 467 that the process of implication is one "against the abuse of which the courts must keep constant guard;" and see *White v Reflecting Roadstuds Ltd* [1991] I.C.R. 733.

[28] *Trollope & Colls Ltd v NW Metropolitan Hospital Board* [1973] 1 W.L.R. 601 at 609; *cf. Johnson v Davies* [1999] Ch.117 at 128.

[29] *Suriya & Douglas v Midland Bank plc* [1999] 1 All E.R. (Comm) 615 (see especially at 615); *cf. Times Newspapers Ltd v George Weidenfeld & Nicholson Ltd* [2002] F.S.R. 29.

[30] *Paula Lee Ltd v Robert Zehil & Co Ltd* [1983] 2 All E.R. 390; *cf.* above, p.50.

(4) Factors negativing implication in fact

It follows from the nature of the process of implication in fact that a term cannot be implied in fact if it actually conflicts with the express terms of the contract.[31] The courts are also reluctant to imply such a term "where the parties have entered into a carefully drafted written contract containing detailed terms agreed between them;"[32] or where the express terms of the agreement embody the outcome of negotiations to settle a "bitter and contentious" dispute between them.[33] Although the contrary is sometimes suggested,[34] the test of implication under the officious bystander test is subjective: what would the parties have agreed?—not what would reasonable persons in their position have agreed? This view is supported by the fact that attempts to imply terms in fact may fail for one of two further reasons.

(a) IGNORANCE OF ONE. First, one of the parties may simply not know of the matter to be implied or of the facts on which the implication is to be based.[35] For example, the terms of an agreement between one of the contracting parties and a third party cannot be implied in fact[36] into the contract in question if the other party to that contract was unaware of the existence or terms of the agreement; for if that party were asked whether he had agreed to the incorporation of the agreement, his reply would more probably be a puzzled "what's that?" than a testy "oh, of course".[37] Again, in *K C Sethia (1944) Ltd v Partabmull Rameshwar*[38] sellers of Indian jute to Italian buyers could not perform their contract because they failed to obtain a quota for shipment to Italy. They argued that the contract was impliedly "subject to quota," and one reason why the argument was rejected was that the buyers did not know that the sellers had no quota for Italy.

(b) DIVERGENT VIEWS. Secondly, the parties may have different views with regard to the alleged term.[39] Where their interests are opposed, an implication that may be

---

[31] *Duke of Westminster v Guild* [1985] Q.B. 688 at 700. *cf. Johnstone v Bloomsbury Health Authority* [1992] Q.B. 333, *per* Legatt L.J. and Browne-Wilkinson V.-C.; *McClory v Post Office* [1992] I.C.R. 758; *Yorkshire Water Services Ltd v Sun Alliance & London Insurance plc* [1997] 2 Lloyd's Rep. 21 at 33; *Courage Ltd v Crehan* [1999] U.K.C.L.R. 110; [1999] 2 E.G.L.R. 145; *Times Newspaper Ltd v George Weidenfeld & Nicholson Ltd* [2002] F.S.R. 463 at 473.

[32] *Shell UK Ltd v Lostock Garages Ltd* [1976] 1 W.L.R. 1187, 1200; *Duke of Westminster v Guild* [1985] Q.B. 688; *Ali v Christian Salveson Food Services Ltd* [1997] 1 All E.R. 721 at 726; contrast *Associated Japanese Bank (International) v Crédit du Nord SA* [1989] 1 W.L.R. 255; *The Maira (No.3)* [1988] 2 Lloyd's Rep. 126, reversed on other grounds [1990] 1 A.C. 637; for some difference of judicial opinion on the point, see *Turner v Stevenage BC* [1997] 2 Lloyd's Rep. 129 at 133, 134–135.

[33] *Nicholson v Markham* [1997] C.L.Y. 4255.

[34] *e.g. The Dadomar General T.J. Park* [1986] 2 Lloyd's Rep. 68 at 70 ("reasonable men faced with the suggested term . . . "); *McAuley v Bristol CC* [1992] Q.B. 134 at 147; *BP v Hastings* (1978) 52 A.L.J.R. 20 at 26, PC; the phrase "presumed intention" in *Hughes v Greenwich LBC* [1994] 1 A.C. 170 at 179 is more equivocal. *cf. Fal Bunkering of Sharjah v Grecale Inc of Panama* [1990] 1 Lloyd's Rep. 369 at 372–373 (where both tests would have led to the same result).

[35] *McCutcheon v David MacBrayne Ltd* [1964] 1 W.L.R. 125 at 128, 134.

[36] For implication of such terms by custom, see below, pp.213–214.

[37] *Spring v NASDS* [1956] 1 W.L.R. 585 at 599 (inter-union agreement on transfer of members not incorporated in membership contract; see now Trade Union and Labour Relations (Consolidation) Act 1992 s.174 as substituted by Trade Union and Employment Rights Act 1993, s.14); *cf. Spence v Cosmos Air Holidays Ltd, The Times,* December 6, 1989; *Wilson v Best Travel* [1993] 3 All E.R. 353.

[38] [1950] 1 All E.R. 51 (affirmed [1951] 2 Lloyd's Rep. 89).

[39] *Attica Sea Carriers Corp v Ferrostaal Poseidon Bulk Reederei GmbH* [1976] 1 Lloyd's Rep. 250; *Frobisher (Second Investments) Ltd v Kiloran Trust Co Ltd* [1980] 1 W.L.R. 425; *Tadd v Eastwood* [1985] I.C.R. 132; *Nutting v Baldwin* [1995] 1 W.L.R. 201 at 211 (no implied term that financial hardship should excuse members of an association from paying subscriptions); *Quinn v Calder Industrial Materials Ltd* [1996] I.R.L.R. 126 (no term to be implied from practice of employer to make enhanced redundancy payments).

regarded as obvious by one party may well be unacceptable to the other. For example, in *Luxor (Eastbourne) Ltd v Cooper*[40] the defendant had employed an estate agent to sell two cinemas and promised to pay him a commission "on completion of sale". Before the agent had effected a sale, the defendant sold the cinemas himself. It was held that no term could be implied to the effect that the defendant should not (except for good cause) refuse to sell to a person introduced by the agent, since it was not clear that both parties would have agreed to such a term. Similarly, in *Shell UK Ltd v Lostock Garages Ltd*[41] a written contract provided that Shell should supply petrol and oil to the defendant garage, which undertook, *(inter alia)* to buy such goods solely from Shell.[42] During a price war, Shell reduced the price of petrol to neighbouring garages, so that the defendant could trade only at a loss. A majority of the Court of Appeal refused to imply a term that Shell should not "abnormally discriminate" against the defendant. One ground for rejecting the implication was that Shell would not have agreed to it[43]; another was that the alleged implication was too vague.[44] The complexity of the alleged term may be yet a further ground for saying that the "officious bystander" test is not satisfied.[45] Even where both parties accept that *some* term should be implied, an implication in fact may still fail because they disagree as to the exact formulation of that term.[46]

The view that both parties must have intended to agree to the implication also explains cases in which the courts have refused to imply a term in agency agreements that the principal would not, by going out of business, deprive the agent of a chance of earning his commission.[47] On the other hand, where a seller's agent had negotiated a sale of particular goods, a term was implied that the seller would not, by breaking that contract of sale, deprive the agent of his right to commission.[48] This implied term made the seller liable to the agent only if he broke one particular contract of sale, without otherwise restricting his freedom to go out of business. This made it less likely that he would have refused to agree to the term if it had been put to him at the time when the agency agreement was made.

(c) UNILATERAL CONTRACTS. The need for the agreement of both parties to the implication also seems to be the basis for the view that it is "impossible to imply terms (. . . which impose legal obligations) . . . into a unilateral contract"[49]; for, where such an

---

[40] [1941] A.C. 108; *cf. Lonrho v Shell Petroleum Co* [1981] Com.L.R. 74 (affirmed without reference to the point [1981] 2 All E.R. 456); *Chorley BC v Ribble Motor Services* (1997) 74 P. & C.R. 182; *Kumar v AGF Insurance Ltd* [1998] 4 All E.R. 788 at 793; *Suriya & Douglas v Midland Bank plc* [1999] 1 All E.R. (Comm) 612 at 617.

[41] [1976] 1 W.L.R. 1187; Russell, 40 M.L.R. 582; *cf. Courage Ltd v Crehan*, above, n.31.

[42] See below, p.469 as to such agreements.

[43] *cf. The Good Luck* [1989] 2 Lloyd's Rep. 238 at 273 (reversed on other grounds [1992] 1 A.C. 233); *The Gudermes* [1993] 1 Lloyd's Rep. 311 at 323.

[44] *cf. Watford BC v Watford Rural DC* (1986) 86 L.G.R. 524 at 529; *Paul Smith Ltd v H & S International Holdings Inc* [1991] 2 Lloyd's Rep. 127 at 131; *Walford v Miles* [1992] 2 A.C. 128 (above, p.56); *Coca Cola Financial Corp v Finsat International Ltd* [1996] 2 Lloyd's Rep. 274 at 277; *Yorkshire Water Services Ltd v Sun Alliance & London Insurance plc* [1997] 2 Lloyd's Rep. 21 at 31–32.

[45] *Ashmore v Corporation of Lloyd's (No.2)* [1992] 2 Lloyd's Rep. 620 at 628.

[46] *Abbott v Sullivan* [1952] 1 K.B. 189; *Trollope & Colls Ltd v NW Metropolitan Hospital Bd* [1973] 1 W.L.R. 601 at 609, 610.

[47] *Rhodes v Forwood* (1876) 1 App.Cas. 256; *cf. Hamlyn & Co v Wood* [1891] 2 Q.B. 488; *Lazarus v Cairn Line Ltd* (1912) 106 L.T. 378; *cf. Sun Alliance Pensions Life & Investment Services Ltd v RJL* [1991] 2 Lloyd's Rep. 40. Contrast cases in which the principal has *expressly* promised to stay in business: *Reigate's Case* [1918] 1 K.B. 592; *cf. Ogdens Ltd v Nelson* [1905] A.C. 109.

[48] *Alpha Trading Ltd v Dunshaw-Patten* [1981] Q.B. 290; *post*, p.744. Contrast *The Manifest Lipkowy* [1989] 2 Lloyd's Rep. 138 where it was held that no such term could be implied in an arrangement between a seller and the *buyer's* agent that the commission was to be deducted from the proceeds of sale.

[49] *Little v Courage Ltd* (1995) 70 P. & C.R. 469 at 474.

implied term would impose obligations on both parties,[50] it would destroy the unilateral nature of the contract and therefore it would not be accepted by the promisee. But it is not obvious why such reasoning should preclude the implication of a term which imposed an obligation only on the *promisor*. Nor does the reasoning exclude the possibility of implying a term which imposed an obligation on the *promisee* in cases (of the kind discussed in Chapter 2[51]) in which an originally unilateral contract becomes bilateral in the course of its performance.

2. Terms Implied in Law[52]

Many of the obligations arising out of particular types[53] of contracts are, at any rate presumptively, determined by rules of law; and some such obligations are said to be the result of implied terms. For example, in a contract of employment the employee impliedly undertakes that he is reasonably skilled,[54] that he will faithfully serve his employer[55] and not act against the employer's interests,[56] and that he will indemnify his employer against liabilities incurred by the employer as a result of his wrongful acts.[57] The employer, for his part, impliedly undertakes that he will not require the employee to do any unlawful act,[58] that he will provide safe premises,[59] that he will take reasonable care not to endanger the employee's health[60]; and that he will not without reasonable cause conduct himself so as to destroy or seriously damage the relationship of trust and confidence between himself and the employee.[61] Similarly, a surgeon carrying out an operation impliedly undertakes to exercise due care and skill, but he does not impliedly guarantee that the operation will achieve the desired result.[62]

Many terms which are implied in law have been put into statutory form. For example, a number of important terms implied into contracts for the sale of goods are stated in ss.12 to 15 of the Sale of Goods Act 1979,[63] and similar terms are implied by statute into hire-purchase agreements,[64] other contracts for the supply of goods[65] and contracts for

---

[50] The only term which, in *Little v Courage Ltd*, the court was prepared to imply (or to read into the contract as a matter of construction) did not impose any obligation on either party: see below, p.811.

[51] See above, p.38.

[52] There is no scope for an implication of this kind where the contract does not fall within any "particular generic type": *Clarion Ltd v National Provident Association* [2000] 2 All E.R. 265 at 273; [2000] 1 W.L.R. 1888 at 1897.

[53] Peden, 117 L.Q.R. 190.

[54] *Harmer v Cornelius* (1858) 5 C.B.(N.S.) 236.

[55] *Hivac Ltd v Park Royal Scientific Instruments Ltd* [1946] Ch. 169; *cf. Secretary of State v ASLEF (No.2)* [1972] 2 Q.B. 455; *Faccenda Chicken Ltd v Fowler* [1987] Ch. 117.

[56] *Wessex Dairies Ltd v Smith* [1935] 2 K.B. 80; *Sanders v Parry* [1967] 1 W.L.R. 753.

[57] *Lister v Romford Ice & Cold Storage Co Ltd* [1957] A.C. 555; below, p.209.

[58] *Gregory v Ford* [1951] 1 All E.R. 121.

[59] *Matthews v Kuwait Bechtel Corp* [1959] 2 Q.B. 57; Webber, (1959) 22 M.L.R. 521; Jolowicz [1959] C.L.J. 163. See also Employers' Liability (Defective Equipment) Act 1969.

[60] *Johnstone v Bloomsbury Area Health Authority* [1992] 2 Q.B. 333.

[61] *Malik v BCCI* [1998] A.C. 20; for restrictions on the scope of this term, see *University of Nottingham v Eyett* [1999] I.C.R. 721.

[62] *Eyre v Measday* [1986] 1 All E.R. 488; *Thake v Maurice* [1986] Q.B. 644; below, p.781. In determining whether he has *expressly* given such a guarantee, the court will apply the objective test: above, p.191.

[63] As amended by Sale and Supply of Goods Act 1994, ss.1, 7 and Sch.2. For further amendments of some of the implied terms as to quality in the Sale of Goods Act 1979 and the Acts of 1973 and 1982 referred to in nn.64 and 65 below, see Sale and Supply of Goods to Consumer Regulations 2002, SI 2002/3045, regs. 3, 8 and 14.

[64] Supply of Goods (Implied Terms) Act 1973, ss.8–11, as substituted by Consumer Credit Act 1974, s.112 and Sch.4, para.35 and amended by Sale and Supply of Goods Act 1994, s.7 and Sch.2 and see above, n.63.

[65] Supply of Goods and Services Act 1982, ss.2–5, 7–10, as amended by Sale and Supply of Goods Act 1994, s.7 and Sch.2 and see above, n.63.

the supply of services.[66] The power to exclude these terms is now severely restricted by legislation.[67]

Detailed discussion of the terms implied by law into particular types of contracts will be found in specialist works on such contracts. But points of general interest arise out of the distinction between terms implied in fact and terms implied in law, and out of the legal nature of terms of the latter kind.

(1) Terms implied in law distinguished from terms implied in fact

The implication of a term in fact is usually based on the inference that the parties intended to incorporate the term into their contract[68]; but no such inference is necessary for the implication of a term in law.[69] This point can be illustrated in a number of ways.

(a) COMPLEXITY. Some statutory implied terms, such as the implied term as to fitness for a particular purpose set out in s.14(3) of the Sale of Goods Act 1979,[70] are extremely complex. If an officious bystander tried to read, and explain, this subsection to a chemist and an intending buyer of a hot-water bottle, he might be testily suppressed, but scarcely with a common "of course". And the question whether any, and if so what, term is to be implied at common law often turns on distinctions which are so subtle that they can scarcely be based on the intention of the parties.[71]

(b) CITATION OF AUTHORITIES. The question whether any, and if so what, term should be implied in law is often decided exclusively by the citation of earlier cases.[72] This is done to determine an issue of "pure law"[73] and not to ascertain the intention of the parties.

(c) NEGATIVING THE IMPLICATION. A term implied in law can generally[74] be excluded by a definite contrary agreement,[75] but it is not necessarily excluded by circumstances which would prevent the implication of a term in fact. In *Sterling Engineering Co Ltd v Patchett*[76] it was held to be an implied term in a contract of service between an inventor and his employers that the inventor was trustee of his inventions and of the resulting patents for the employers. It was further held that this implied term could not be excluded by a mere "understanding" to the contrary, though obviously the term could not have been *implied in fact* if such an "understanding" had been proved. *A fortiori*, an

---

[66] Supply of Goods and Services Act 1982, ss.13–14.

[67] See below, p.251 *et seq.*

[68] This is true though the implication of even such terms may be a question of "law" in the sense of an *inference* based on primary facts: see *O'Brien v Associated Fire Alarms* [1968] 1 W.L.R. 1916; *cf.* below, p.836.

[69] For the distinction between the two processes, see *The Dadomar General TJ Park* [1986] 2 Lloyd's Rep. 68 at 70; *The Choko Star* [1990] 1 Lloyd's Rep. 516 at 526; *McAuley v Bristol CC* [1992] Q.B. 134 at 147; *Ashmore v Corp of Lloyd's (No.2)* [1992] 2 Lloyd's Rep. 620 at 626; *McClory v Post Office* [1992] I.C.R. 758 at 764; *Scally v Southern Health & Social Services Board* [1992] 1 A.C. 294 at 307; *The Star Texas* [1993] 2 Lloyd's Rep. 445 at 451; *Timeload Ltd v British Telecommunications plc* [1995] E.M.L.R. 459 at 467; *Ali Shipping Corp v Shipyard Trogir* [1998] 2 All E.R. 136 at 146–147; *Equitable Life Assuance Society v Hyman* [2002] 1 A.C. 408 at 459.

[70] As amended: see above, p.206, n.63.

[71] See, *e.g.* the contrast between *Young & Marten Ltd v McManus Childs Ltd* [1969] 1 A.C. 454 and *Gloucestershire CC v Richardson* [1969] 1 A.C. 480.

[72] *e.g. Yeoman Credit Ltd v Apps* [1962] 2 Q.B. 508.

[73] *Malik v BCCI* [1998] A.C. 20 at 46.

[74] *i.e.* subject to exceptions such as those discussed at pp.251–252, 254–255 and 270–271, below.

[75] *e.g. The Berge Sund* [1993] 2 Lloyd's Rep. 453; *The Spiros C* [2000] 2 Lloyd's Rep. 319 at 335.

[76] [1955] A.C. 534.

express term will exclude a term implied in law (just as it will exclude one implied in fact[77]) if the two terms are in conflict with each other.[78] Whether there is such a conflict will depend on the construction of the express term.[79]

(2) Implied terms as legal duties

The implication of a term implied in law is simply a way of specifying some of the duties which *prima facie* arise out of certain types of contracts, or, as it has been put, "legal incidents of those . . . kinds of contractual relationship".[80] It has indeed been said of such terms that "the test of implication is necessity" rather than "the imposition of a term".[81] One possible view is that "necessity" here means the same thing as it does in relation to terms implied in fact: in other words, that it refers to the requirement that the implication must be necessary to give business efficacy to the contract.[82] But in the context of terms implied in fact the reason for this requirement is that it provides evidence of common intention: the parties are assumed to have agreed to a term, without which their contract would not work. In the context of terms implied in law the courts do not look for any such evidence of common intention; and it is submitted that, in such a context, the test of "necessity" (if appropriate at all[83]) has a different shade of meaning from that which it has in formulations of the business efficacy test.[84] The House of Lords has distinguished "between the search for an implied term necessary to give business efficacy to a particular contract and the search, based on wider considerations, for a term which the law will imply as a necessary incident of a definable category of contractual relationship".[85] In accordance with this test, it has for example been held that it was an implied term in a contract of employment that the employer should inform the employees of steps which they were entitled to take to enhance their pension rights.[86] Such an implication was not necessary to give business efficacy to any individual employment contract, but it was a necessary aspect of employment relationships generally. "Necessity" in the sense in which the requirement is used in applying the "business efficacy" test similarly cannot justify the complex implied term of fitness of goods for a particular purpose, set out in s.14(3) of the Sale of Goods Act 1979: it is perfectly possible to imagine a workable contract of sale which did not contain such a term. In other contracts, moreover, terms have been implied in law in spite of the fact that the implication was *not* necessary to give business efficacy to the contract.[87] In many cases of this kind, the same process can with equal plausibility be described either as the

---

[77] See above, p.186, n.31.

[78] *e.g. Eagle Star Life Assurance Co Ltd v Griggs and Miles* [1998] 1 Lloyd's Rep. 256.

[79] *Johnstone v Bloomsbury Health Authority* [1992] 1 Q.B. 333.

[80] *Mears v Safecar Securities Ltd* [1983] Q.B. 54 at 78; *Johnstone v Bloomsbury Health Authority* [1992] Q.B. 333 at 343; *The Kriti Rex* [1996] 2 Lloyd's Rep. 171 at 191; *Ali Shipping Corp v Shipyard Trogir* [1998] 2 All E.R. 136 at 146 ("attaching as a matter of law"); *Johnson v C.E.G.B.* [2000] 1 A.C. 455 at 477–478.

[81] *Tai Hing Cotton Mill Ltd v Liu Chong Hing Bank Ltd* [1986] A.C. 80 at 104–105; *Reid v Rush & Tompkins Group plc* [1990] 1 W.L.R. 212 at 220; *Barrett v Lounava (1982) Ltd* [1990] 1 Q.B. 348 at 358–359; *Ashmore v Corp of Lloyd's (No.2)*, above, n.69. *cf.* Landlord and Tenant (Covenants) Act 1995, s.2(1)(b), distinguishing covenants which are "implied" from those which are "imposed by law."

[82] See above, p.201; *Clarion Ltd v National Provident Association* [2000] 1 W.L.R. 1888 at 1897.

[83] *Timeload Ltd v British Telecommunications Ltd* [1995] E.M.L.R. 459 at 467; *cf.* below, p.210 at n.6.

[84] *cf.* the reference to the two types of implication depending "*in one form or another* on a test of necessity" in *Baker v Black Sea & Baltic General Insurance Co* [1998] 1 W.L.R. 974 at 980 (italics supplied), where the alleged term was one "implied by law" (*ibid.* at 983).

[85] *Scally v Southern Health & Social Services Board* [1992] 1 A.C. 294 at 307; *Malik v BCCI* [1998] A.C. 20 at 45; *cf. The Foresight Driller II* [1995] 1 Lloyd's Rep. 251 at 266, treating "general principle" and "business efficacy" as *separate* grounds for implying a term.

[86] *Scally's* case, above.

[87] See *Liverpool City Council v Irwin* [1977] A.C. 239 at 255, below p.210.

implication of a term in law or as the imposition of a legal duty. In one case concerning a landlord's duty to repair the outside of the premises the court indiscriminately refers to an "implied term" and to an "implied obligation"[88] which must be "imposed on"[89] the landlord. Where a term is imposed in law, the two processes are, as a practical matter, indistinguishable. It is, for example, commonly said that a landlord *impliedly covenants* that his tenant shall have quiet possession, and that the tenant is under an *obligation* not to commit waste.[90] One could just as well say that the landlord was under an obligation to let the tenant have quiet possession, and that the tenant impliedly covenanted not to commit waste. Again, it is said that if a party enters into an arrangement which can take effect only if a given state of circumstances continues, he impliedly promises not to put an end to it.[91] But in a case in which this rule was applied, Lord Atkin said: "Personally I should not so much base the law on an implied term, as on a positive rule of the law of contract that conduct of either promisor or promisee which can be said to amount to himself 'of his motion' bringing about the impossibility of performance is in itself a breach."[92]

This point would not be worth stressing if the true nature of the inquiry before the court were not sometimes obscured by the use of the expression "implied term" to refer to the imposition of a legal duty, and by the failure to distinguish between terms implied in fact and terms implied in law. In *Lister v Romford Ice and Cold Storage Co Ltd*[93] a lorry driver injured a third party by negligent driving in the course of his employment. The third party recovered damages from the employers, who obtained judgment for an indemnity from the driver on the ground that he had broken the implied term in the contract of employment to drive with proper care.[94] The driver in turn argued that the contract also contained an implied promise by the employers. This was formulated in various ways: as a promise to indemnify the driver against liability to third parties if the employers were insured, or if they were required by law to be insured, or if they ought as reasonable and prudent persons to have been insured. The House of Lords, by a majority, held that no such term could be implied. Some of the reasons given by the majority are reasons against the implication of a term *in fact*. The implication was not "precise and obvious"[95]; it was not necessary to give business efficacy to the contract[96];

---

[88] *Barrett v Lounava (1982) Ltd* [1990] 1 Q.B. 348 at 359; *cf. Imperial Group Pension Trust Ltd v Imperial Tobacco Ltd* [1991] 1 W.L.R. 589, 597 ("I will call this implied term 'the implied obligation of good faith'"); *Scally v Southern Health & Social Services Board* [1992] 1 A.C. 294 at 307B ("terms which the law will imply"), 307D ("necessary . . . to imply an obligation").

[89] *Barrett v Lounava (1982) Ltd* [1990] 1 Q.B. 348 at 358; *cf. Spring v Guardian Insurance plc* [1995] 2 A.C. 296 at 353 ("imposing a duty").

[90] See Megarry and Wade, *Law of Real Property* (6th ed.), pp.702, 860, 881.

[91] *Stirling v Maitland* (1864) 5 B. & S. 840.

[92] *Southern Foundries (1926) Ltd v Shirlaw* [1940] A.C. 701 at 717; *cf. The Dadomar General TJ Park* [1986] 2 Lloyd's Rep. 68 at 70; *Nisho Iwai Petroleum Co Inc v Cargill International SA* [1993] 1 Lloyd's Rep. 80; *The Energy Progress* [1993] 1 Lloyd's Rep. 355; *Spring v Guardian Insurance* [1995] 2 A.C. 296 at 320; *Grant v Cigman* [1996] B.C.L.C. 24.

[93] [1957] A.C. 555.

[94] Employers' insurers have agreed not to make such claims against employees, so that the decision has little practical effect. See 272 L.T. 67 for a summary of the report of an Interdepartmental Committee set up in 1957. *Semble*, the validity of the alleged term would not be affected by Unfair Contract Terms Act 1977, s.4 (below, p.255) since that section does not seem to apply to *implied* promises to indemnify or to cases where the liability to indemnify arises from the negligence of the promisor himself. Nor would the term be affected by the Unfair Terms in Consumer Contracts Regulations 1999, since these do not apply to contracts of employment: see below, p.278; nor does it seem that they apply to *implied* terms. For an unsuccessful attempt by a third party to claim the indemnity, see *Morris v Ford Motor Co Ltd* [1973] Q.B. 792.

[95] [1957] A.C. 555 at 574.

[96] *ibid.* at 583.

and it was not clear that both parties would have agreed to it.[97] But many terms implied *in law* would fail to pass these tests. Whether such terms should be implied is not a question of intention, but one of policy: "*Should* one imply [the alleged] term . . . ?"[98] In fact the House of Lords in *Lister's* case was to a large extent concerned with considerations of policy. The argument that seems to have weighed most heavily with the majority was that it would be undesirable to allow a driver to recover an indemnity from his employer as he might then drive less carefully. Considerations of this kind always influence the implication of terms in law; but they have nothing to do with the intention of the parties, and hence with the implication of terms in fact.

The distinction between the two types of implication is clearly drawn in the later case of *Reid v Rush & Tompkins Group plc*,[99] where an employee was injured, while working abroad, as a result of the fault of a third party who could not be traced. He argued that his contract of employment contained an implied term obliging his employers to warn him to insure against such risks; but the argument was rejected on two separate grounds. First, no such term *could* be implied in fact since it would not have been agreed by the parties. And secondly, no such term *should* be implied in law by the court as the exact scope of such an implication raised issues of policy which could be resolved only by the legislature. It is, conversely, possible for both tests to support the conclusion that a term should be implied,[1] in which case the implication can be said to arise both in fact and in law.

There are, however, also cases in which, though no term can be implied in fact, it may be desirable to attach certain "legal incidents"[2] to a contract, or, in other words, to impose a legal duty. This point has sometimes been overlooked,[3] so that it was occasionally held that no terms *should* be implied in law merely because none *could* be implied in fact. But such reasoning would now be inconsistent with *Liverpool City Council v Irwin*.[4] The House of Lords there held that it was an implied term of a lease of a maisonette in a Council block that the landlord should take reasonable care to keep the common parts of the block in a reasonable state of repair. The term was clearly not implied in fact: the "officious bystander" test was not satisfied[5]; nor was the implication necessary to give business efficacy to the contract.[6] The implication arose because the nature of the relationship made it desirable to place some obligation on the landlord as to the maintenance of the common parts of the premises. It amounted to the imposition of a legal duty, in spite of the fact that no term could be implied in fact.[7]

---

[97] *ibid.* at 578.

[98] *Rockeagle Ltd v Alsop Wilkinson* [1992] Ch. 47 at 51. Where this test as well as that for the implication of a term in fact is satisfied (as in *St Albans City and District Council v International Computers Ltd* [1996] 4 All E.R. 481) failure to distinguish between them causes no harm in the result.

[99] [1990] 1 W.L.R. 212; *cf. Galaxy Energy International Ltd v Bayoil SA* [2001] 1 All E.R. (Comm) 289 at 295, where an "implication of law" is supported by reference to the "officious bystander" test, which is, strictly speaking, apposite only to the implication of a term in fact: above pp.201–202 and also at n.97 above.

[1] See *The Island Archon* [1994] 2 Lloyd's Rep. 227 at 237, where Evans L.J. regards the implication as justified "first by business efficacy" (*i.e.* in fact: above, p.201) and "secondly . . . [as] an implication of law."

[2] Above, at p.208 at n.80.

[3] *e.g.* in *Abbott v Sullivan* [1952] 1 K.B. 189 where, it is submitted, a term might well have been implied in law (though on the principle stated at pp.204–205 above, none could be implied in fact). *The Aramis* [1989] 1 Lloyd's Rep. 213 is open to criticism on similar grounds: see Treitel, [1989] L.M.C.L.Q. 162. *cf. John v Rees* [1970] Ch. 345 where a term was implied in law.

[4] [1977] A.C. 239; MacIntyre [1977] C.L.J. 15; *Duke of Westminster v Guild* [1985] Q.B. 688 at 697–698; *Sim v Rotherham MBC* [1987] Ch. 216 at 245; *cf. King v Northamptonshire DC, The Times*, December 3, 1991 ("implied obligation").

[5] At pp.283–290. This was also the position in *Barrett v Lounava (1982) Ltd* [1990] 1 Q.B. 348 (where a term was nevertheless implied in law).

[6] [1977] A.C. 239 at 255.

[7] *cf. McAuley v Bristol CC* [1992] Q.B. 134.

In deciding whether to imply a term in law, the courts are guided by general policy considerations affecting the type of contract in question[8]; and to this extent considerations of reasonableness and fairness may enter into the implication of such terms.[9] It has, indeed, been suggested that, even in this type of case, the test of implication is "necessity, not reasonableness".[10] But it has been submitted above that terms are sometimes implied in law even though the test of "necessity" is not satisfied[11]; they are implied because the court considers that specified duties ought to be attached to the type of contractual relationship in question. Such decisions are based on considerations of "justice and policy"[12]; and the distinction between such considerations and "reasonableness" is at best an elusive one.[13] Nor, it is submitted, are decisions of such policy issues helped by distinguishing between what is reasonable and what is necessary; in the context of terms implied in law, that distinction appears to be no more than one of degree.[14] The principle that reasonableness is not of itself a ground for implying a term is entirely appropriate when the court is being asked to imply a term *in fact* into an individual contract,[15] but is, it is submitted, not one which should preclude the implication of terms *in law* into contracts of a particular type.

(3) Doubtful cases

(a) CLASSIFICATION PROBLEMS Sometimes it is not clear whether a particular term is implied in fact or in law. In *The Moorcock*[16] the defendants owned a wharf and made a contract to allow the claimants to unload their ship at the wharf. The ship was damaged by settling at low water on a ridge of hard ground. It was held that the defendants were liable for this damage as they were in breach of an implied term that they would take reasonable care to see that the berth was safe. The case is generally regarded as the leading authority on terms implied in fact, but some passages in the judgment also refer to terms implied in law. Lord Esher M.R. said that it must be implied that the defendants had "undertaken to see that the bottom of the river is reasonably fit, or at all events that they have taken reasonable care to find out that the bottom of the river is reasonably fit for the purpose. . . . "[17] Had these alternatives been put to the parties, they might well have disagreed. This suggests that the term was implied, not in fact, but in law. Again, in a famous passage, Bowen L.J. said: "An implied warranty, or, as it is called,

---

[8] *The Star Texas* [1993] 2 Lloyd's Rep. 445.

[9] *cf. Re Charge Card Services Ltd* [1989] Ch. 497 at 513 ("What is the fair term to imply"); *Motis Exports Ltd v Dampskibsselskapet AF 1912* [1999] 1 Lloyd's Rep. 837 at 842, ("both reasonable and necessary"), affirmed without reference to this point: [2000] 1 Lloyd's Rep. 211; *The Spiros C* [2000] 2 Lloyd's Rep. 319 at 333 (using the same words); *Galaxy Energy International Ltd v Bayoil SA* [2001] 1 All E.R. (Comm) 289 at [27] ("necessary and reasonable"). The reference in these dicta seems to be to terms implied *in law* since reasonableness is neither a necessary or a sufficient condition for the implication of a term *in fact*: see above, p.203. The use in them of the word "necessary" gives rise, in the context of terms implied in law, to difficulties already mentioned: see p.208; see also text at n.6 above.

[10] *Scally v Southern Health and Social Services Board* [1992] 1 A.C. 294 at 307; *cf. The Choko Star* [1990] 1 Lloyd's Rep. 516 at 526; *Ashmore v Corporation of Lloyd's* [1992] 2 Lloyd's Rep. 620 at 630; *The Star Texas* [1993] 2 Lloyd Rep. 445 at 451; *Spring v Guardian Insurance plc.* [1995] 2 A.C. 296 at 339, 354; *The Island Archon* [1994] 2 Lloyd's Rep. 227 at 237, above, p.208 at nn.81–82.

[11] See above, p.208.

[12] *The Star Texas*, see above, n.8 at 491.

[13] *cf.* Lord Radcliffe's observation in *Davis Construction Ltd v Fareham Urban DC* [1956] A.C. 696 at 728 (more fully quoted at p.921 *post*) that "the fair and reasonable man . . . represents no more than an anthropomorphic conception of justice").

[14] *cf.* above, p.208, n.85.

[15] See above, pp.203–204.

[16] (1889) 14 P.D. 64.

[17] *ibid.* at 67.

a covenant in law . . . is in all cases founded on the presumed intention of the parties *and upon reason. . . .* In business transactions such as this, what the law desires to effect by the implication is to give such business efficacy to the transaction as must have been intended at all events by both parties who are businessmen."[18] The two italicised phrases show that Bowen L.J. was not exclusively concerned with the actual intention of the parties, on which terms implied in fact are based; and it does not seem that the "officious bystander" test[19] was satisfied. The most that could have been implied in fact was that the wharf-owner was to be under *some* obligation in relation to the safety of the berth; but the intention of the parties was not decisive in defining the precise extent of that obligation. To the extent that the implication was based on objective criteria of reasonableness, *The Moorcock* therefore resembles terms implied in law; but it differs from the category of terms implied in law discussed above, in that the implication related to a particular transaction rather than to a type of contract.

(b) IMPUTED INTENTION It has been submitted above that a term cannot be implied in fact where it is shown that one party would *not* have agreed to it[20]; and this submission appears to be supported by many cases in which the courts have indeed refused to imply terms on the ground that the officious bystander test had not been satisfied.[21] There is, however, also House of Lords authority that a term can be implied on the basis of an intention *imputed* to the parties.[22] Such an implication differs from an implication in fact as it "is not critically dependent on proof of an actual intention of the parties",[23] while on the other hand the term is not one "implied by law in the sense of incidents impliedly annexed to particular forms of contract".[24] A term of this kind was implied in *Equitable Life Assurance Society v Hyman*[25] where a provision incorporated in a life assurance policy gave the insurer a discretion, with regard to bonus declarations. This discretion was not fettered by the express term of the contract, but its exercise was nevertheless held to be restricted, so that it could not be so exercised as to conflict with the contractual rights of a group of policy holders. It is not entirely clear whether this conclusion is based on the process of implication or on that of construction or interpretation[26]; but the former seems to be the more probable view.[27] If so, the case appears to illustrate a type of implied term which does not fall precisely within the categories of terms implied in fact or in law; for this type of implication does not either give effect to the actual intention of the parties[28] or attach legal incidents to a particular type of contract.[29] The implication in the *Equitable Life* case was made as a matter of law but into an individual contract (it being irrelevant for the purposes of the reasoning in the

---

[18] (1889) 14 P.D. 64 at 68 (italics supplied).

[19] See above, p.202.

[20] See above, pp.204–205 at nn.39–43.

[21] See above, p.204 at nn.35–38.

[22] *Equitable Life Assurance Society v Hyman* [2002] 1 A.C. 408; *cf.* the reference to what parties "must have" intended and to their "presumed" intention: pp.202–203 at nn.20 and 23, p.204, n.34.

[23] *ibid.*, at 459.

[24] *ibid.*, at 458.

[25] See above, n.22.

[26] Lord Steyn, with whose speech all the other members of the House of Lords agreed, distinguished at 458 "between the processes of interpretation and implication"; at 459 he says that "the enquiry is entirely constructional in nature".

[27] In the rest of the paragraph in which the words quoted at the end of n.26 occur, Lord Steyn he reverts to the language of implication. The exact difference between "interpretation" and a "constructional" inquiry is not made clear. For the distinction between "implication" and "interpretation", see also *Mousaka Inc v Golden Seagull Maritime Inc* [2002] 1 Lloyd's Rep. 797 at [7].

[28] See above, p.202, n.21.

[29] See p.208, n.80 and n.24, above.

case that many policy holders were affected by the outcome). A term will be implied on the basis only if the implication is "strictly necessary"[30] or "essential to give effect to the *reasonable* expectations of the parties"[31]; and the "strict" necessity seems to override the fact that the implication corresponded with the *actual* expectations of only *one* of the parties. In this respect, the requirements of the present hybrid type of implied term are more stringent than those of the categories, discussed earlier in this Chapter,[32] of terms implied in fact and terms implied in law. The process of implication on the basis of imputed intention is to be "sparingly and cautiously used"[33] and the special circumstance calling for its use in the *Equitable Life* case seems to be that, without the implication, the insurers would have been able to exercise their discretion in conflict with the policyholder's contractual rights against the Society. The decision gives no further guidance as to other circumstances in which terms will be implied on the basis of a merely imputed intention.[34]

3. Custom or Usage

We have seen that evidence of custom is admissible to add to, but not to contradict, a *written* contract.[35] Further, *any* contract (whether written or not) may be deemed to incorporate any relevant and notorious[36] custom of the market, trade or locality in which it is made, unless the custom is inconsistent with the express (or necessarily implied) terms, or with the nature, of the contract.[37] In cases of such inconsistency the custom is said to be "unreasonable", and binds a party only if he knew of it. A custom which is "reasonable" binds both parties, whether they knew of it or not.[38] It is sometimes said that the incorporation of custom into a contract is based on the presumed intention of the parties,[39] but this is a somewhat unrealistic view. For the question whether a custom binds depends on whether it is "reasonable", and this question can give rise to complex issues of law and fact on which the parties are unlikely to have a common (or any) view.[40]

The terms of collective agreements between trade unions and employers may be incorporated in the employment contracts of individual employees by express reference,[41] or by being acted on over a period of time.[42] Between employer and union, such agreements normally have no contractual force because they are not intended to be legally binding.[43] But when their terms are incorporated in individual contracts of

---

[30] [2002] 1 A.C. 408 at 459.

[31] *ibid.*

[32] See above, pp.202–203, 208.

[33] [2002] 1 A.C. 408 at 459.

[34] It is one of the paradoxes of the decision that its reasoning relied on the phrase "intention imputed" in *Luxor (Eastbourne) Ltd v Cooper* [1941] A.C. 108 at 137, where the result was to *reject* the implication precisely because it was not clear that both parties would have agreed to it: see above, p.204–205.

[35] See above, p.198.

[36] See *Turner v Royal Bank of Scotland* [1999] 2 All E.R. (Comm) 664, where this requirement was not satisfied.

[37] Such inconsistency was one ground why the alleged custom was not incorporated in the contract in *Danowski v Henry Moore Foundation* [1996] E.M.L.R. 364.

[38] *Reynolds v Smith* (1893) 9 T.L.R. 494 for other illustrations, see below, pp.711–712.

[39] *e.g.* in *Produce Brokers Co Ltd v Olympia Oil & Cake Co Ltd* [1916] 1 A.C. 314 at 324.

[40] *cf. The Maira (No.3)* [1990] 1 A.C. 637 at 681.

[41] *Hooker v Lange, Bell & Co* [1937] 4 L.J.N.C.C.R. 199; *Camden Exhibition & Display Ltd v Lynott* [1966] 1 Q.B. 555. Special requirements exist for the incorporation of "no strikes" clauses in collective agreements into employment contracts: Trade Union and Labour Relations (Consolidation) Act 1992, s.180(1) and (2).

[42] *NCB v Galley* [1958] 1 W.L.R. 16.

[43] See above, p.168.

employment, those terms can, if so intended,[44] become legally binding between employer and employee.[45] It has, moreover, been suggested that the terms of collective agreements may be incorporated in contracts of employment as "crystallised custom".[46] The "custom" may be incorporated even in contracts with employees who are not members of the union which has negotiated the agreement,[47] so long as there is some evidence of intention to incorporate it.[48] Once the terms of the collective agreement have been incorporated in the contract of employment, the employee can enforce rights under that contract, even after the collective agreement itself has, as between the union and the employer, been brought to an end.[49]

Terms may also be implied by trade usage.[50] For example, where the owner of a crane hired it out to a contractor who was also engaged in the same business, it was held that the hirer was bound by the owner's usual terms though these were not actually communicated at the time of contracting.[51] They were, however, based on a model supplied by a trade association; and references in the judgment to the fact that they were reasonable and prevalent in the trade[52] suggest that they were incorporated on a principle similar to that which applies to customary terms.

---

[44] See *NCB v NUM* [1986] I.C.R. 736 where this intention was said to have been negatived. *cf. Hulland v Saunders* [1945] K.B. 78 (parties contracting out of collective agreement).

[45] *Robertson v British Gas Corp* [1983] I.C.R. 351; *Marley v Forward Trust Group* [1986] I.C.R. 891; *Alexander v Standard Telephone and Cables Ltd* [1990] I.C.R. 291 at 303 (where the intention was later found to have been negatived: see [1991] I.R.L.R. 286).

[46] Kahn-Freund in Flanders & Clegg (ed.), *The System of Industrial Relations in Great Britain*, Chap.2, p.58, and in Kahn-Freund (ed.), *Labour Relations and the Law*, pp.26–27; Wedderburn, *The Worker and the Law* (2nd ed.), pp.188–197.

[47] Gayler & Purvis, *Industrial Law* (2nd ed.), p.353.

[48] *Young v Canadian Northern Ry* [1931] A.C. 83.

[49] *Gibbons v Associated British Ports Authority* [1985] I.R.L.R. 376.

[50] See *Baker v Black Sea & Baltic General Insurance Co Ltd* [1998] 2 All E.R. 833 for proof of such usage.

[51] *British Crane Hire Corp Ltd v Ipswich Plant Hire Ltd* [1975] Q.B. 303; *The Ulyanovsk* [1990] 1 Lloyd's Rep. 425 at 431; *Harlow & Jones Ltd v American Express Bank Ltd* [1990] 2 Lloyd's Rep. 343. And see generally Hoggett, (1970) 33 M.L.R. 518.

[52] [1975] Q.B. 303 at 311, 313; contrast *Salsi v Jetspeed* [1977] 2 Lloyd's Rep. 57 (where there was no evidence of usage).

CHAPTER SEVEN

STANDARD FORM CONTRACTS[1]

CONTRACTUAL terms are often set out in standard forms which are used for all contracts of the same kind, and are only varied so far as the circumstances of each contract require. Such terms may be settled by a trade association for use by its members for contracting with each other or with members of the outside public. Standard contract forms are even provided by legislation[2] or under statutory authority.[3]

One object of these standard forms is to save time. The work of insurers, carriers and bankers, for example, would become impossibly complicated if all the terms of every contract they made had to be newly settled for each transaction.[4] Standard form contracts are also a device for allocating contractual risks: they can be used to determine in advance who is to bear the expense of insuring against those risks[5]; and they also facilitate the quotation of differential rates: *e.g.* where a carrier's form provides for goods to be carried either at his or at the customer's risk, and the charge is adjusted accordingly. Between businessmen bargaining at arm's length such uses of standard forms can be perfectly legitimate[6]; and this may be true even where the party to whom the standard terms are presented is a private consumer who has or is likely to have insured against the loss which has occurred.[7] But a less defensible object of the use of standard terms has been the exploitation or abuse of the superior bargaining power of commercial suppliers when contracting with such consumers. The supplier could draft the standard terms in ways highly favourable to himself, both by means of clauses which *excluded or limited his liability* for failure to perform or for defective performance, and by provisions which *conferred rights* on him under the contract. In cases concerning exemption clauses, the courts were to a considerable extent able to redress the balance in favour of the parties prejudicially affected by standard form contracts; but they were less inclined to do so where standard terms conferred rights on the supplier. In both fields, legislative intervention has become increasingly important. The most important legislative provisions are contained in the Unfair Contract Terms Act 1977,[8] and in the

---

[1] Prausnitz, *The Standardisation of Commercial Contracts*; Coote, *Exception Clauses;* Yates and Hawkins, *Standard Business Contracts*; Lawson, *Exclusion Clauses and Unfair Contract Terms* (3rd ed.).

[2] *e.g.* Companies' Articles of Association: see Companies Table A–F Regulations (SI 1985/805) as amended by Companies Table A–F (Amendment) Regulations (SI 1985/1052) and by Companies Act (Electronic Communications) Order 2000 (SI 2000/3373).

[3] *e.g.* the Statutory Form of Conditions of Sale made by the Lord Chancellor under s.46 of the Law of Property Act 1925.

[4] *cf.* also Schmitthoff, 17 I.C.L.Q. 551.

[5] See *The Maratha Envoy* [1978] A.C. 1 at 8; *Photo Production Ltd v Securicor Transport Ltd* [1980] A.C. 827 at 843, 851; *cf. A Schroeder Music Publishing Co Ltd v Macaulay* [1974] 1 W.L.R. 308 at 316.

[6] See *Marston Excelsior Ltd v Arbuckle Smith & Co Ltd* [1971] 1 Lloyd's Rep. 70 at 95; *Photo Production* case above, at 851; *Ailsa Craig Fishing Co Ltd v Malvern Fishing Co Ltd* [1983] 1 W.L.R. 964 at 966. In some cases liability is even limited by statute: *e.g.* Carriage of Goods by Sea Act 1971, Sch. Art.IV. 5; Merchant Shipping Act 1995, ss.185, 186 and Sch.7.

[7] *e.g.* in the car-park cases, such as *Hollins v J Davy Ltd* [1963] 1 Q.B. 844. Contrast *Mendelssohn v Normand Ltd* [1970] 1 Q.B. 177 (where luggage stolen from a parked car did not belong to the owner of the car).

[8] See below, pp.246–266.

Unfair Terms in Consumer Contracts Regulations 1994.[9] The 1977 Act deals almost[10] exclusively with exemption clauses; it makes some such clauses ineffective and subjects others to a requirement of reasonableness. The 1999 Regulations deal with standard terms in contracts between commercial sellers and suppliers on the one hand and consumers on the other, and provide that such terms do not bind the consumer if they are "unfair." In a significant number of cases, however, standard form contracts are not affected by these legislative provisions[11] and continue to be governed by rules of common law. These rules therefore still call for discussion, even though many of the cases from which they are derived would now be differently decided under those legislative provisions,[12] or under other legislation to be described later in this Chapter.[13] For the most part, the common law rules are concerned with the efficacy of exemption clauses; but it will be necessary also to consider the common law approach to other types of standard terms.

SECTION 1. EXEMPTION CLAUSES AT COMMON LAW

A party who wishes to rely on a clause excluding or limiting liability[14] must show that the clause has been incorporated in the contract, and also that, on its true construction, it covers both the breach which has occurred and the resulting loss or damage. Even if he can show these things, he may still find that the clause is invalid or inoperative.

1. Incorporation in the Contract

An exemption clause can be incorporated in the contract by signature, by notice,[15] or by course of dealing.

(1) Signature

A person who signs a contractual document is bound by its terms even though he has not read them. In *L'Estrange v F Graucob Ltd*[16] the proprietress of a café bought an automatic cigarette vending machine. She signed, but did not read, a sales agreement which contained an exemption clause "in regrettably small print".[17] It was held that she was bound by the clause, so that she could not rely on defects in the machine, either as a defence to a claim for part of the price, or as entitling her to damages. It would have

---

[9] See below, pp.266–283.

[10] The exception is s.4, which deals with indemnity clauses; for the close relationship of some such clauses with exemption clauses, see below, p.255.

[11] See below, pp.264–266, 277–280.

[12] See above at nn.8 and 9.

[13] See below, pp.283–285.

[14] For the distinction between these and certain other kinds of clauses, see below, pp.237–238.

[15] These are alternative ways of incorporating the clause so that the rules as to incorporation by notice do not apply to terms set out in signed contracts: *HIH Casualty & General Insurance Ltd v New Hampshire Insurance Co* [2001] 2 All E.R. (Comm) 39; [2001] EWCA Civ 735 at [209].

[16] [1934] 2 K.B. 394; *Levison v Patent Steam Cleaning Co Ltd* [1978] Q.B. 69; *The Polyduke* [1978] 1 Lloyd's Rep. 211; *Singer (UK) Ltd v Tees & Hartlepool Port Authority* [1988] 2 Lloyd's Rep. 164 at 166; for criticism, see *McCutcheon v David MacBrayne Ltd* [1964] 1 W.L.R. 125 at 133; *cf.* Spencer [1973] C.L.J. 104; Samek, 52 Can.Bar Rev. 351.

[17] [1934] 2 K.B. 394 at 405. For the relationship between the rule in this case and Unfair Terms in Consumer Contracts Regulations 1999, Sch.2, para.1(i), see below pp.276–277; on the facts of *L'Estrange v F Graucob Ltd*, the Regulations would not apply as the buyer was not a "consumer:" see below, p.269.

made no difference had she been a foreigner who could not read English.[18] A party is, however, bound by terms of which he was unaware only if the document which he has signed was one which could reasonably have been expected to contain contractual terms. Where, for example, a hirer of machinery together with a driver had signed weekly time-sheets, it was held that he was not bound by terms printed on these sheets since their purpose was merely to record the hours worked and not to vary the terms of the earlier oral contract of hire.[19] It has been further suggested that "in some extreme circumstances even signature might not be enough", so that a term which was "particularly onerous or unusual"[20] would not be incorporated unless, in addition to the signature, steps were taken to draw the attention of the signer[21] to such a term.

(2) Notice[22]

If the exemption clause is set out, or referred to,[23] in a document which is simply handed by one party to the other, or displayed where the contract is made, it will be incorporated in the contract only if the latter party either knew that the document contained (or was likely to contain) such a clause,[24] or if reasonable notice of its existence is given to that party. Whether such notice has been given depends on the following factors.

(a) NATURE OF THE DOCUMENT. An exemption clause is not incorporated in the contract if the document in which it is set out (or referred to) is not intended to have contractual force: for example, if the document is a mere receipt for payment.[25] On the other hand, the mere fact that a document is called a "receipt" will not prevent it from having contracted effect.[26] A document will have such effect if the party to whom it was handed knew that it was intended to be a contractual document or if it was handed to him in such circumstances as to give him reasonable notice of the fact that it contained conditions.[27] It will also be contractual if it is obvious to a reasonable person that it must have been intended to have this effect. This will be the case if the document is of a kind that generally contains contractual terms.[28] Whether a document falls into this class depends on current commercial practice, which may vary from time to time.[29]

(b) DEGREE OF NOTICE. The party relying on the exemption clause need not show that he actually brought it to the notice of the other party, but only that he took reasonable steps to do so. The test is whether the former party took such steps[30]—not whether the latter should, in the exercise of reasonable caution, have discovered or read

---

[18] *The Luna* [1920] p. 22; *cf. Barclays Bank plc v Schwartz*, *The Times*, August 2, 1995. The signer might be able to rely on the doctrine of *non est factum* (below, p.326), but if this applied there would be no contract at all.

[19] *Grogan v Robin Meredith Plant Hire*, *The Times*, February 20, 1996; *cf.* below, at n.25.

[20] *Ocean Chemical Transport Inc v Exnor Craggs Ltd* [2000] 1 Lloyd's Rep. 446 at 454.

[21] *i.e.*, in accordance with the requirements stated under heading (ii) on p.219, below.

[22] Clarke [1976] C.L.J. 451.

[23] For the sufficiency of incorporation by reference, see *Circle Freight International Ltd v Mideast Gulf Exports* [1988] 2 Lloyd's Rep. 427; *cf.* above, p.191.

[24] *Lacey's Footwear (Wholesale) Ltd v Bowler Insurance Ltd* [1997] 2 Lloyd's Rep. 369 at 378.

[25] *Chapelton v Barry Urban D.C.* [1940] 1 K.B. 532; *cf. Henson v London & North Eastern Ry* [1946] 1 All E.R. 653; *The Eagle* [1977] 2 Lloyd's Rep. 70; Clarke [1978] C.L.J. 22.

[26] *Harling v Eddy* [1951] 2 K.B. 739 at 746; *Parker v South Eastern Ry* (1877) 2 C.P.D. 416; *The Polyduke* [1978] 1 Lloyd's Rep. 211.

[27] *Watkins v Rymill* (1883) 10 Q.B.D. 178.

[28] *Nunan v Southern Ry* [1923] 2 K.B. 703 at 707; *Thompson v London, Midland & Scottish Ry* [1930] 1 K.B. 41 at 46.

[29] For changing views on the status of railway cloakroom tickets, contrast *Parker v South Eastern Ry*, above, n.26, at 424 with *Alexander v Railway Executive* [1951] 2 K.B. 882 at 886.

[30] *Parker v SE Ry* (1877) 2 C.P.D. 416 at 424; *cf. Burnett v Westminster Bank Ltd* [1966] 1 Q.B. 742.

the clause.[31] Where the clause is printed on a ticket, it is not enough to show that the party to whom it was handed knew that there was writing on the ticket,[32] for the writing might not have been intended to have contractual effect. Nor is one party's reference in a telephone conversation to his own standard terms sufficient notice of those terms if the other party has no knowledge or means of knowledge of them.[33] The question whether adequate notice has been given turns principally on two factors: the steps taken to give notice and the nature of the exempting conditions.

(i) *Steps taken to give notice.* Where the notice is contained in a contractual document it is normally sufficient for the exempting condition to be prominently set out or referred to on the face of the document. In *Thompson v LM & S Ry*[34] the claimant asked her niece to buy a railway excursion ticket for her. The ticket (which cost 2s. 7d.) had on its face the words "see back" and on the back a statement that it was issued subject to the conditions set out in the company's time-tables,[35] which could be bought for 6d. These conditions included an exemption clause. The claimant could not read the words on the ticket as she was illiterate; and the jury found that the defendants had not taken reasonable steps to bring the conditions to the claimant's notice. But the Court of Appeal held that there was no evidence to support this finding as the notice was clear and as the ticket was a common form contractual document. Hence the exemption clause was held to be incorporated in the contract. The case is an extreme one since the time-table cost nearly a fifth of the fare paid by the claimant and was evidently a volume of some size, the exemption clause being set out on its 552nd page.[36] The likelihood of its being bought (let alone read) by an excursion passenger was, to say the least, remote; and it seems probable that the steps taken to incorporate the clause would not now be regarded as sufficient.[37] The principle that such a clause can be incorporated by reference[38] nevertheless seems to be a sound one. Many common contractual documents would become impossibly bulky if that principle were to be rejected. In a more recent case,[39] the rules of a newspaper "scratch card" competition were referred to on the card and had been set out in copies of the paper. It was held that they were incorporated in the contract between the owners of the paper and a competitor, even though they had not been read by the competitor.

On the other hand, the clause is unlikely to be incorporated if there are no words on the face of the document drawing attention to it,[40] or if words on the front of the document refer to terms on the back but the back is blank (only the front having been transmitted by fax),[41] or if the words are made illegible by a date stamp,[42] or if the exemption clause is buried in a mass of advertisements.[43] It is not necessary, *as a matter*

---

[31] *Parker v SE Ry* (1877) 2 C.P.D. 416; *cf. Birch v Thomas* [1972] 1 W.L.R. 294, a case that would now fall within Road Traffic Act 1988, s.149; *cf.* also *ibid.* s.150.

[32] This was the majority view in *Parker v SE Ry*, above. Bramwell L.J. dissented on this point.

[33] *Jayaar Impex Ltd v Toaken Group Ltd* [1996] 2 Lloyd's Rep. 437.

[34] [1930] 1 K.B. 41; *cf. Hood v Anchor Line* [1918] A.C. 837.

[35] For the effect on such a term of Unfair Terms in Consumer Contracts Regulations 1999, Sch.2, para.1(i), see below, pp.276–277.

[36] [1930] 1 K.B. 41 at 46.

[37] *cf. The Mikhail Lermontov* [1990] 1 Lloyd's Rep. 579 at 594, affirmed [1991] 2 Lloyd's Rep. 155 though reversed on other grounds sub nom *Baltic Shipping Co v Dillon* (1993) 176 C.L.R. 344.

[38] *cf. Smith v South Wales Switchgear Ltd* [1978] 1 W.L.R. 165 (indemnity clause).

[39] *O'Brien v MGN Ltd, The Times,* August 8, 2001, [2001] EWCA Civ 1279; [2002] C.L.C. 33.

[40] *Henderson v Stevenson* (1875) L.R. 2 Sc. & Div. 470 (where dicta that the ticket was not a contractual document are not *ratio: Harris v GW Ry* (1876) 1 Q.B.D. 515 at 532); *Richardson, Spence & Co v Rowntree* [1894] A.C. 217.

[41] *Poseidon Freight Forwarding Co Ltd v Davies Turner Southern Ltd* [1996] 2 Lloyd's Rep. 388.

[42] *Sugar v London, Midland & Scottish Ry* [1941] 1 All E.R. 172.

[43] *Stephen v International Sleeping Car Co Ltd* (1903) 19 T.L.R. 620.

of law, to print words such as "see back" or "see inside" on the face of the document.[44]

In *Thompson's* case, the illiteracy of the claimant was treated as immaterial; but the position would probably be different where the party relying on the clause knew or should have known of the other party's disability. In an earlier case[45] some reliance was placed on the fact that the other party was a steerage passenger and so could not have been expected to read clauses in small print. Extra steps may have to be taken to bring the notice home to a person suffering from a *known* disability: for example translating it to a party who is known not to understand the language in which it is expressed, if such a step is reasonably practicable.[46] A person trying to incorporate the terms of a document should, however, beware of translating only part of it; for by doing this he may suggest that the rest is of no importance and so be unable to rely on it.[47]

(ii) *Nature of the clause.* The more unusual or unexpected a particular term is, the higher will be the degree of notice required to incorporate it. If the clause is of such a nature that the party adversely affected would not normally expect it, then the other party will not be able to incorporate it by simply handing over or displaying a document containing the clause. He must go further and "make it conspicuous"[48] or take other special steps to draw attention to it. For example, a person who drives his car into a car-park might expect to find in his contract a clause excluding the proprietor's liability for loss of or damage to the car. But in *Thornton v Shoe Lane Parking Ltd*[49] the car-park ticket referred to a condition purporting to exclude liability for *personal injury*.[50] It was held that adequate notice of this condition had not been given, even though the steps taken by the proprietor might have been sufficient to incorporate the more usual clauses excluding or limiting liability for property damage. As Denning L.J. had said in an earlier case: "Some clauses I have seen would need to be printed in red ink on the face of the document with a red hand pointing to it before the notice could be held to be sufficient."[51]

(c) TIME OF NOTICE. The steps required to give notice of an exemption clause must be taken before or at the time of contracting. In *Olley v Marlborough Court*[52] the claimant booked a room in the defendants' hotel. She later saw a notice in her bedroom exempting the defendants from liability for articles lost or stolen unless handed to the management for safe custody. It was held that, as the contract had been made at the reception desk when the defendants agreed to accept the claimant as a guest and as the notice in the

---

[44] *Burke v South Eastern Ry* (1879) 5 C.P.D. 1.

[45] *Richardson, Spence & Co v Rowntree* [1894] A.C. 217.

[46] *Geier v Kujawa, Weston & Warne Bros Transport* [1970] 1 Lloyd's Rep. 364; the notice in that case would now be invalid under Road Traffic Act 1988, s.149.

[47] *H Glynn (Covent Garden) Ltd v Wittleder* [1959] 2 Lloyd's Rep. 409.

[48] *Crooks v Allen* (1870) 5 Q.B.D. 38 at 40.

[49] [1971] 2 Q.B. 163; *cf. The Eagle* [1977] 2 Lloyd's Rep. 70; *Interfoto Picture Library Ltd v Stiletto Visual Programmes Ltd* [1989] Q.B. 433, discussed at p.245, below; *Shearson Lehman Hutton Inc v Maclain Watson & Co Ltd* [1989] 2 Lloyd's Rep. 570 at 612; *Villela v MFI Furniture Centres Ltd* [1999] I.R.L.R. 468 at 473; Chandler and Holland, 104 L.Q.R. 359; McLean, [1988] C.L.J. 172; Macdonald [1988] J.B.L. 375 and 8 *Legal Studies* 48; Swanton, 1 J.C.L. 223.

[50] Where the injury is caused *by negligence* such a provision is now ineffective: below, pp.249, 274.

[51] *J Spurling Ltd v Bradshaw* [1956] 1 W.L.R. 461 at 466. Contrast *Ocean Chemical Transport Inc v Exnor Cragg Ltd* [2000] 1 Lloyd's Rep. 446 at 454 ("neither onerous nor unusual"); *O'Brien v MGN Ltd* [2001] EWCA Civ 1279; [2002] C.L.C. 33 at [21] (term not "onerous or outlandish").

[52] [1949] 1 K.B. 532; *cf. The Eagle* [1977] 2 Lloyd's Rep. 70; *The Dragon* [1979] 1 Lloyd's Rep. 257, affirmed without reference to this point [1981] 1 W.L.R. 120; *Jayaar Impex Ltd v Toaken Group Ltd* [1996] 2 Lloyd's Rep. 437; *Oceanic Sun Line Special Shipping Co v Fay* (1988) 165 C.L.R. 197. And *cf.*, in the context of a hospital "refusal" form, *Re T* [1993] Fam. 95.

bedroom could not have been seen by the claimant until later, its terms were not incorporated in the contract.

(3) Course of dealing

Parties may for some time have dealt with each other on terms that exempted one of them from liability and that were usually incorporated by signature or notice. On the occasion in question, however, the usual document may by some oversight not have been handed over or signed at the time of contracting; and the question then arises whether the usual exemption clause is nevertheless incorporated in that particular transaction. A negative answer to this question was suggested by Lord Devlin in *McCutcheon v David MacBrayne Ltd* where he said: "Previous dealings are relevant only if they prove knowledge of the terms, *actual and not constructive, and consent to them.*"[53] But this view is inconsistent with at least one earlier case[54]; and the House of Lords has held that if there has been a long consistent course of dealing on terms incorporating an exemption clause, then those terms may apply to a particular transaction even though in relation to it the usual steps to incorporate the clause have not been taken.[55] Of course the terms will not apply if the transaction in question was not part of a *consistent* course of dealings[56]; if the transactions were spread over a long period of time and their number was so small that they could not be said to give rise to a course of dealing[57]; if the steps necessary to incorporate the clause had never been taken at any stage of the dealings between the parties[58]; or if the terms of each transaction in the series had been separately negotiated and expressly agreed between the parties.[59]

The fact that there has been a long course of dealing may also be relevant to the degree of notice required when the party claiming the benefit of a clause seeks to alter it to his own advantage. As the other party is reasonably entitled to assume that the course of dealing is continuing on the accustomed terms, it seems that special steps would have to be taken to draw his attention to any such alteration.[60]

The course of dealing referred to in the present discussion is one between the parties to the contract.[61] A term may also be implied into a contract because of a general course

---

[53] [1964] 1 W.L.R. 125 at 134 (italics supplied).

[54] *J Spurling Ltd v Bradshaw* [1956] 1 W.L.R. 461.

[55] *Hardwick Game Farm v Suffolk Agricultural, etc. Association* [1969] 2 A.C. 31 at 90, 104, 105, 113, 130; and see *Britain & Overseas Trading (Bristles) v Brookes Wharf and Bull Wharf* [1967] 2 Lloyd's Rep. 51; *SIAT di dal Ferro v Tradax Overseas SA* [1978] 2 Lloyd's Rep. 470, affirmed [1980] 1 Lloyd's Rep. 53; *George Mitchell (Chesterhall) Ltd v Finney Lock Seeds Ltd* [1983] Q.B. 284 at 295, affirmed without reference to this point [1983] 2 A.C. 803; *Circle Freight International Ltd v Mideast & Gulf Exports Ltd* [1988] 2 Lloyd's Rep. 427.

[56] *McCutcheon v David MacBrayne Ltd*, above, n.53, can be explained on the ground that the parties contracted sometimes on one set of terms and sometimes on another. *cf.* also *Burnett v Westminster Bank Ltd* [1966] 1 Q.B. 742, and *Mendelssohn v Normand Ltd* [1970] 1 Q.B. 177.

[57] On this question, contrast *Hollier v Rambler Motors (A.M.C.) Ltd* [1972] 2 Q.B. 71 (three or four transactions in five years not sufficient) and *Metaalhandel JA Magnum BV v Ardfields Transport Ltd* [1988] 1 Lloyd's Rep. 197 at 203 ("isolated affairs") with *The Havprins* [1983] 2 Lloyd's Rep. 356 at 362 (three transactions in five years sufficient, though incorporation was "not by course of dealing alone") and with the *Hardwick Game Farm* case, above, n.55, (three or four contracts a month for three years held to be sufficient).

[58] *Smith v Taylor* [1966] 2 Lloyd's Rep. 231.

[59] *Johnson Matthey Bankers Ltd v State Trading Corp of India* [1984] 1 Lloyd's Rep. 427 at 433.

[60] See *Pancommerce Co SA v Veecheema BV* [1983] 2 Lloyd's Rep. 304 at 305 ("in bold type"); and contrast *Burnett v Westminster Bank Ltd* [1966] 1 Q.B. 742 with *Re Bond Worth Ltd* [1980] Ch. 228. In the last two cases the actual issue was as to the variation of a continuing contract: sufficient notice had been given in the first, but not in the second case.

[61] Or between one of them and a group of companies to which the other belongs, as in the *SIAT* case, above, n.55, and in *The Raphael* [1982] 2 Lloyd's Rep. 42.

of dealing amounting to a trade custom or usage.[62] Such an implication can arise even though the parties to the particular contract in question have not previously dealt with each other. It seems that exemption clauses, no less than other types of terms, can be incorporated in this way.

2. Construction

Under this heading we shall first discuss the general principle that contract terms are construed *contra proferentem*; we shall then consider two special applications of that principle to cases in which a party relies on an exemption clause to protect him from liability for negligence or for certain particularly serious breaches.

(1) Contra proferentem rule

In relation to exemption clauses, the principle of construction *contra proferentem* means that such a clause is construed strictly against the party at whose instigation it was included in the contract and who now seeks to rely on it.[63] Thus a provision that a seller gives "no *warranty*, express or implied" does not protect him from liability for breach of *condition*[64]; a clause protecting him from liability for breach of *implied* conditions and warranties does not cover breach of an *express* term of the contract[65]; a provision in a hire-purchase agreement that "no warranty, condition or description or representation *is* given" does not exclude liability for breach of a collateral undertaking *previously* given,[66] and a clause excluding the right to *rescind* a contract does not affect the right to *damages*[67] (nor conversely).[68]

Ambiguous words in exemption clauses are construed in the way least favourable to the party relying on them.[69] In *Houghton v Trafalgar Insurance*[70] a five-seater car was involved in an accident while carrying six people. The driver's insurance policy exempted the insurers from liability for damage caused "whilst the car is carrying any *load* in excess of that for which it was constructed". The insurers were held liable as the clause did not extend to cases where the car was carrying too many *passengers*. Similarly, in *Beck & Co v Szymanowski*[71] a contract for the sale of cotton provided that "The *goods delivered* shall be deemed to be in all respects in accordance with the contract", unless

---

[62] *British Crane Hire Corp Ltd v Ipswich Plant Hire Ltd* [1975] Q.B. 303; above, p.214. The dispute concerned an indemnity clause, but the principle seems equally applicable to exemption clauses: *cf. Smith v South Wales Switchgear Ltd* [1978] 1 W.L.R. 165; *Victoria Fur Traders v Roadline UK Ltd* [1981] 1 Lloyd's Rep. 571.

[63] In the present context, this formulation necessarily refers to the same party, even though in other contexts this may not be the case: see *Youell v Bland Welch & Co Ltd* [1992] 2 Lloyd's Rep. 127 at 134.

[64] *Wallis, Son & Wells v Pratt & Haynes* [1911] A.C. 394; *Harling v Eddy* [1951] 2 K.B. 739; for the distinction between conditions and warranties, see below, pp.788 *et seq.*; for statutory restrictions on exemption clauses in contracts for the sale of goods, see below, pp.250–251; 254–255.

[65] *Andrews Bros (Bournemouth) Ltd v Singer & Co Ltd* [1934] 1 K.B. 17; *cf. Laceys Footwear (Wholesale) Ltd v Bowler International* [1997] 2 Lloyd's Rep. 369 at 379; contrast *British Fermentation Products Ltd v Compair Reavell Ltd* [1999] 2 All E.R. (Comm) 389, where *other* words in a clause referring to implied terms extended its scope to express terms.

[66] *Webster v Higgins* [1948] 2 All E.R. 127; *cf. J Evans & Son (Portsmouth) Ltd v Andrea Merzario Ltd* [1976] 1 W.L.R. 1078, 1084; *Thomas Witter Ltd v BTP Industries Ltd* [1996] 2 All E.R. 573 at 595–597.

[67] *Toomey v Eagle Star Insurance Co* [1995] 2 Lloyd's Rep. 89.

[68] See below, p.238.

[69] *cf. Morris v C W Martin & Sons Ltd* [1966] 1 Q.B. 716; below, p.641, *Ackerman v Protius Services* [1988] 2 EGLR 259. Where an exemption clause is subject to the statutory reasonableness test, it may fail to satisfy that test on account of its obscurity and be ineffective on that ground: see below, p.259.

[70] [1954] 1 Q.B. 247.

[71] [1924] A.C. 43.

the buyer gave notice of a complaint within 14 days of the arrival of the goods. This clause did not prevent the buyers from claiming damages for *short delivery*: "The damages are claimed not in respect of goods delivered but in respect of goods which were not delivered."[72]

Although the *contra proferentem* rule applies to all exemption clauses, the courts do not apply it with the same rigour to clauses which merely limit liability as they do to those which purport totally to exclude it[73]; for while it is thought to be "inherently improbable" that the injured party will agree to a total exclusion of the other party's liability "there is no such high degree of improbability that he would agree to a limitation of . . . liability."[74]

The *contra proferentem* rule is intended to protect the injured party but it may sometimes paradoxically have the opposite effect. For example, where an exemption clause is subject to a legislative requirement of reasonableness, it may, on a narrow construction of its words, satisfy that requirement while, on a wider construction, it would not have done so. If the narrow construction suffices to protect the alleged wrongdoer, it will be in his interest to rely on that construction to prevent the clause from being struck down for unreasonableness.[75]

(2) Negligence

Legislation has severely restricted the effectiveness of clauses purporting to exempt a party from liability for negligence[76]; and the negligence of the party in breach may also support the conclusion that the statutory requirement of reasonableness has not been satisfied.[77] But even where it remains possible to exclude liability for negligence,[78] "clear words" must be used for this purpose, since the courts regard it as "inherently improbable that one party to a contract should intend to absolve the other party from the consequence of his own negligence".[79] The requirement is most obviously satisfied where the exemption clause expressly refers to negligence: *i.e.* uses the word "negligence"[80] or some synonym for it.[81] It *may* be satisfied, even though there is no such

---

[72] *ibid.* at 50, *cf. Connaught Restaurants Ltd v Indoor Leisure Ltd* [1994] 1 W.L.R. 501.

[73] *Ailsa Craig Fishing Co Ltd v Malvern Fishing Co* [1983] W.L.R. 964; Palmer, 45 M.L.R. 327; *George Mitchell (Chesterhall) Ltd v Finney Lock Seeds Ltd* [1983] 2 A.C. 803 at 814; *Ocean Chemical Transport Inc v Exnor Cragg Ltd* [2000] 1 Lloyd's Rep. 446 at 452; *BHP Petroleum Ltd v British Steel plc* [2000] 2 All E.R. (Comm) 133 at 149; *ibid.* at 143 is more sceptical.

[74] *Ailsa Craig* case, above, at 970.

[75] As in *Watford Electronics Ltd v Sanderson Ltd* [2001] 1 All E.R. (Comm) 696, [2001] EWCA Civ 317, below. See also below p.284, n.22 for another illustration of the same paradox; for a legislative provision which is designed to prevent it from arising, see Unfair Terms in Consumer Contracts Regulations 1999 (SI 1999/2083), reg.7(2), below, p.280, n.86.

[76] Unfair Contract Terms Act 1977, s.2; below, pp.250, 252; *cf.* Unfair Terms in Consumer Contracts Regulations 1999, Sch.2, para.1(a) and (b).

[77] *George Mitchell (Chesterhall) Ltd v Finney Lock Seeds Ltd* [1983] 2 A.C. 803; below, p.228.

[78] As it is at common law: *cf. Armitage v Nurse* [1997] 2 All E.R. 705 at 712.

[79] *Gillespie Bros Ltd v Roy Bowles Transport Ltd* [1973] Q.B. 400 at 419; *cf. Sonat Offshore SA v Amerada Hess Development Ltd* [1988] 1 Lloyd's Rep. 145 at 157. This rule of construction has been said not to apply to a clause excluding the right to avoid (*i.e.* to rescind) a contract for misrepresentation, as opposed to one excluding the right to damages: *HIH Casualty & General Insurance v Chase Manhattan Bank* [2001] EWCA Civ 125; [2001] 1 Lloyd's Rep. 483 at [114]; such a right to rescind is equally available for innocent and for negligent misrepresentation.

[80] *e.g. Spriggs v Sotheby Parke Bernet & Co* [1986] 1 Lloyd's Rep. 487; *Henderson v Merrett Syndicates Ltd* [1995] 2 A.C. 145 at 183; *Monarch Airlines Ltd v Luton Airport* [1998] 1 Lloyd's Rep. 403.

[81] *Canada SS Lines Ltd v The King* [1952] A.C. 192 at 208.

express reference to negligence, if the words are nevertheless wide enough to cover negligence: *e.g.* if the clause exempts a party from "all liability whatsoever".[82] But whether such general words *actually are* effective to exclude liability for negligence depends on a further distinction: namely that between cases in which, but for the clause, the party relying on it may be liable irrespective of negligence, and those in which his only possible liability is for negligence.[83]

(a) PARTY LIABLE IRRESPECTIVE OF NEGLIGENCE. If there is a realistic possibility (as opposed to a merely fanciful one[84]) that a party can be made liable irrespective of negligence, an exemption clause in general terms will not normally be construed so as to cover liability for negligence.[85] For example, a common carrier of goods is strictly liable if they are lost or damaged. A clause exempting him from liability "for loss or damage"[86] would be construed to refer to his strict liability only. The position is the same where it is doubtful in law whether the party relying on the clause is liable irrespective of negligence: here again a clause which does not refer to negligence will not *prima facie* be construed to exempt him from liability for negligence.[87] But in all the situations just described it is not absolutely necessary to refer expressly to negligence; for the rule is one of construction only and "should not be applied rigidly or mechanically so as to defeat [the] intentions [of the parties]".[88] Thus in one case[89] a charterparty provided that the shipowners were to be liable *only* for negligent stowage, want of personal diligence in making the ship seaworthy, and personal default. It was held that by accepting liability *only* for these three causes the shipowners had excluded liability for negligence of the crew resulting in the stranding of the ship. In another case[90] a clause excluded liability for loss or damage "however caused which can be covered by insurance". This was similarly held to cover negligence even though the party relying on the clause could have been liable (as a common carrier) irrespective of negligence.

The fact that the clause only *limits* (and does not wholly *exclude*) liability is also relevant to the issue of construction. Thus a seller is strictly liable for defects in goods; so that *prima facie* general words would not exclude liability for defects due to his negligence. But where a seller of seeds undertook to replace defective seeds or to refund the price paid for them, it was held that a clause excluding "all [further] liability" did, as a matter of construction, apply where the seller was negligent in supplying seeds

---

[82] *Canada SS Lines Ltd v The King*, above, at 208; such general words do not amount to an *express* reference to negligence: see *Smith v South Wales Switchgear Ltd* [1978] W.L.R. 165 at 173 and *Smith v UMB Chrysler (Scotland)* 1978 S.C.(H.L.) 1 at 12, disapproving dicta in *Gillespie v Roy Bowles Transport Ltd* [1973] Q.B. 400 at 420, 421; *The Raphael* [1982] 2 Lloyd's Rep. 42.

[83] *Canada SS Lines Ltd v The King* [1952] A.C. 192 at 208.

[84] See *Hair & Skin Trading Co Ltd v Norman Airfreight Carriers Ltd* [1974] 1 Lloyd's Rep. 442; *Gallagher v BRS* [1974] 2 Lloyd's Rep. 440 at 448; *Smith v South Wales Switchgear Ltd* [1978] 1 W.L.R. 165 at 178; *The Raphael*, above, n.82; *Cert plc v George Hammond plc* [1999] 2 All E.R. (Comm) 976 at 988.

[85] *Canada SS Lines Ltd v The King* [1952] A.C. 192, esp. at 208; *White v J Warwick & Co Ltd* [1953] 1 W.L.R. 1285; Gower, 17 M.L.R. 155; *Toomey v Eagle Star Insurance Co* [1995] 2 Lloyd's Rep. 89. *Cf. EE Caledonia Ltd v Orbit Valve Co Europe* [1994] 1 W.L.R. 221; *The Fiona* [1994] 2 Lloyd's Rep. 506; *Shell Chemical UK Ltd v P & O Tankers Ltd* [1995] 1 Lloyd's Rep. 297 (indemnity clause).

[86] *Rutter v Palmer* [1922] 2 K.B. 87; *cf. Dorset CC v Southern Felt Roofing Co* (1990) 9 Tr.L.R. 96; *The Fantasy* [1991] 2 Lloyd's Rep. 391, affirmed without reference to this point [1992] 1 Lloyd's Rep. 235.

[87] *The Emmanuel C* [1983] 1 Lloyd's Rep. 310; *The Oceanic Amity* [1984] 2 All E.R. 140 at 151.

[88] *The Golden Leader* [1980] 2 Lloyd's Rep. 573 at 574; *cf. HIH Casualty & General Insurance v Chase Manhattan Bank* [2001] EWCA Civ 735; [2001] 2 All E.R. (Comm) 39 at [137].

[89] *The Golden Leader*, above.

[90] *Joseph Travers & Sons Ltd v Cooper* [1915] K.B. 73; *cf. The Danah* [1993] 1 Lloyd's Rep. 351 at 354; and see *A E Farr Ltd v Admiralty* [1953] 1 W.L.R. 965.

which were defective; and one reason given for this conclusion was that the rules limiting the scope of exemption clauses in cases of negligent breach "cannot be applied in their full rigour to limitation clauses".[91] The question in all the above cases is whether the intention of one party to exclude liability for negligence has been made sufficiently clear to the other. An express reference to negligence is the safest, but not the only, way of achieving this result.

(b) PARTY LIABLE ONLY FOR NEGLIGENCE. Where a contracting party is liable only for negligence, the rule of construction discussed above obviously does not apply. It follows that in such cases an exemption clause in general terms (*i.e.* one not specifically referring to negligence) *can* cover negligence.[92] It used, moreover, to be thought that, in cases of this kind, a clause in general terms necessarily *did* cover negligence, since "it would otherwise lack subject-matter"[93]: it would have no effect if it did not exclude the only liability which the defendant could incur. But this reasoning no longer prevails. Even where the defendant's only liability is for negligence, the clause must make it clear that liability is to be excluded. It may do so by general words not containing any express reference to negligence.[94] But in *Hollier v Rambler Motors (AMC) Ltd*[95] a customer's car had been left with the defendants for repair and was damaged in a fire caused by their negligence. It was held that they could not rely on a provision[96] that they were "not responsible for damage caused by fire to customer's cars on the premises". This was so even though they were liable for such damage only if the fire was due to their negligence: the provision merely operated as a warning to the customer that the garage proprietors were not liable for loss caused by a fire which was *not* due to their negligence. Obviously, however, a clause cannot be construed merely as such a warning if it expressly exempts a party from liability for negligence.[97]

Even where a defendant is liable only for negligence and clearly intends to exclude that liability, general words may fail to protect him. In *Re Polemis*[98] a clause in a charterparty provided that liability for fire should be *mutually* excepted, *i.e.* that neither shipowner nor charterer should be liable for fire. The shipowner was a common carrier and therefore liable without negligence. Thus the clause would not exempt him from liability for negligence, but only from strict liability. In view of this, it was held that the

---

[91] *George Mitchell (Chesterhall) Ltd v Finney Lock Seeds Ltd* [1983] 2 A.C. 803 at 814; but the fact that the seller was negligent was relevant for the purpose of the statutory reasonableness test: below p.260.

[92] *e.g. J Archdale Ltd v Comservices Ltd* [1954] 1 W.L.R. 459; *White v Blackmore* [1972] 2 Q.B. 651; *Scottish Special Housing Association v Wimpey Construction UK Ltd* [1986] 1 W.L.R. 995; *Rutter v Palmer* [1922] 2 K.B. 87; *cf. Levison v Patent Steam Carpet Cleaning Co Ltd* [1978] Q.B. 69 at 83–84; *The Raphael* [1982] 2 Lloyd's Rep. 42; *BHP Petroleum Ltd v British Steel Ltd* [2000] 2 All E.R. (Comm) 133 (where the duties of the party in breach were partly strict and partly duties of diligence); *Co-operative Retail Services Ltd v Taylor Young Partnerships Ltd* [2002] UKHL 17; [2002] 1 W.L.R. 1419 at [42–44].

[93] *Alderslade v Hendon Laundry* [1945] K.B. 189 at 192; *cf. Gibaud v Great Eastern Ry* [1921] 2 K.B. 426; *The Ballyalton* [1961] 1 W.L.R. 929.

[94] *Alderslade v Hendon Laundry Ltd* [1945] K.B. 189, as explained in *Hollier v Rambler Motors (AMC) Ltd* [1972] 2 Q.B. 71; *Hair & Skin Trading Co Ltd v Norman Airfreight Carriers Ltd* [1974] 1 Lloyd's Rep. 442; *Cert plc v George Hammond plc* [1999] 2 All E.R. (Comm) 976. For similar construction of indemnity clauses, see *Gillespie Bros & Co Ltd v Roy Bowles Transport Ltd* [1973] Q.B. 400, *Arthur White (Contractors) Ltd v Tarmac Civil Engineering Ltd* [1967] 1 W.L.R. 1506 and *Thompson v T Lohan (Plant Hire) Ltd* [1987] 1 W.L.R. 649; *HIH Casualty* case, above, n.88, at [138] and *cf. The Super Servant Two* [1990] 1 Lloyd's Rep. 1 at 8 (similar construction of cancellation clause).

[95] [1972] 2 Q.B. 71; *cf. Olley v Marlborough Court* [1949] 1 K.B. 532.

[96] Which was actually not incorporated in the contract: above, p.220 at n.57.

[97] *Spriggs v Sotheby Parke Bernet & Co* [1986] 1 Lloyd's Rep. 487.

[98] [1921] 3 K.B. 560.

clause did not exempt the charterer from liability for negligence either, although he was liable only for negligence.

(3) Seriousness of breach

Before exemption clauses were subject to legislative control, the courts were reluctant to allow a party to rely on such a clause in respect of a breach that was particularly serious. Effect was given to this policy by two techniques. One was to construe the clause narrowly, so that it would not apply where such a serious breach had occurred, unless the intention that it should apply in spite of the gravity of the breach was made very clear. Another was to say that, as a matter of substantive law, it was impossible by any clause (however widely drafted) to exclude liability for certain breaches which were "fundamental".[99] This "substantive doctrine" of fundamental breach was developed by the courts mainly as a device for protecting consumers. But it was not restricted to consumer cases; and, when applied to commercial transactions negotiated at arm's length, it was liable to upset perfectly fair bargains for the reasonable allocation of contractual risks. When, in the *Suisse Atlantique* case[1] in 1966, an attempt was made to apply the doctrine in such a context, the House of Lords rejected the view that the doctrine was one of substantive law and held that it was one of construction only, so that liability for even a fundamental breach could be excluded so long as the words of the clause were sufficiently clear. In the following years the lower courts were reluctant to accept this position, no doubt because they feared that it would weaken the doctrine of fundamental breach as a consumer-protecting device. But the substantive doctrine was no longer needed for this purpose once the effectiveness of exemption clauses came to be restricted by legislation[2]; and, where these restrictions did not apply, it was desirable, in the interests of commercial certainty, to allow the parties to allocate risks between themselves by clearly drafted exemption clauses.[3] In the *Photo Production*[4] case in 1980 the House of Lords therefore reasserted the view that the doctrine of fundamental breach was a rule of construction only. That view was again affirmed by the House of Lords in the *George Mitchell* case in 1983, where Lord Bridge said that the *Photo Production* case had given "the final quietus to the doctrine that a 'fundamental breach' of contract deprived the party in breach of the benefit of clauses in the contract excluding or limiting his liability".[5]

In the course of the development just described, the House of Lords overruled a small number of cases that were consistent only with the substantive doctrine[6]; but it did not cast doubt on many other decisions in which the seriousness of the breach had been a ground for holding that an exemption clause afforded no protection. A difficult question is therefore left unresolved as to the status of these decisions. One view is that they are all obsolete, as the question whether a clause applies to a particular breach simply depends in each case on whether the words of the clause are sufficiently clear to cover that breach. On this view, nothing more need or can be said about "fundamental breach"

---

[99] *e.g. Karsales (Harrow) Ltd v Wallis* [1956] 1 W.L.R. 936; and see Grunfeld, 24 M.L.R. 62; Guest, 77 L.Q.R. 98; Montrose [1964] C.L.J. 60 at 254.

[1] [1967] 1 A.C. 361 discussed at p.234, below.

[2] *Photo Production Ltd v Securicor Transport Ltd* [1980] A.C. 827 at 843.

[3] *ibid.*

[4] See above; discussed below at p.234.

[5] *George Mitchell (Chesterhall) Ltd v Finney Lock Seeds* [1983] 2 A.C. 803 at 813; *cf. The Antares* [1987] 1 Lloyd's Rep. 424 at 428.

[6] *i.e. Charterhouse Credit Co Ltd v Tolly* [1963] 2 Q.B. 683 ("though the result might have been reached on construction of the contract": *Photo Production* case, above, at 845); *Harbutt's "Plasticine" Ltd v Wayne Tank Co Ltd* [1970] 1 Q.B. 477; *Wathes (Western) Ltd v Austins (Menswear) Ltd* [1976] 1 Lloyd's Rep. 14.

than that all exemption clauses are to be construed *contra proferentem*,[7] and that, the more serious the breach is, the less likely it is that the clause will apply. A second view is that the earlier cases are to be reinterpreted rather than rejected or ignored. In support of this view, it can be said that some of the earlier judgments explicitly proceeded on the basis that the rule was one of construction,[8] while others, though originally based on the substantive doctrine, were later explained as illustrations of the rule of construction,[9] or on other special grounds.[10] For these reasons, it is submitted that the second view is to be preferred. The cases concerning serious breaches resemble those (discussed above) concerning negligent breaches: they can be regarded as illustrations of the *contra proferentem* rule, but they amount to particular or special applications of that rule and therefore still provide guidance on the scope and effects of the rule of construction which applies where the breach is of a certain degree of seriousness. They can be said to give rise to a presumption or *prima facie* rule that general words will not exclude liability for certain very serious breaches; but they recognise that this presumption or rule can be displaced if the words of the clause are sufficiently clear. At the same time, the practical importance of the cases on this topic is likely to be confined to situations in which the validity of the exemption clause is not affected by the legislation to be considered later in this Chapter.[11] If under this legislation the clause is ineffective or not binding on the injured party, the outcome of the case will not depend on whether the clause covers the breach; and if the clause is subject to a statutory requirement of reasonableness, the outcome is more likely to depend on the question whether that requirement is satisfied than on the construction of the clause.[12]

In the following discussion, we shall first describe the breaches to which the rule of construction applies, bearing in mind that the occurrence of such a breach does not *necessarily* lead to the conclusion that the clause will not cover it: there is only a presumption that it will be construed so as not to have this effect, and this presumption can be overcome if the words of the clause are sufficiently clear. It will then be necessary to consider the exact effects (or present operation) of the rule of construction.

(a) SCOPE OF THE RULE. For the purpose of the rule of construction, a breach may be a serious one either because of the nature of the term broken, or because of the consequences of the breach, or because of the manner in which the breach was committed.

(i) *Nature of the term broken.* The legal consequences of a breach often depend on the nature of the term broken. The leading distinction is between three categories of terms known respectively as conditions, warranties and intermediate terms. This distinction is discussed in Chapter 18[13] here it need only be said that breach of condition of itself gives the injured party the right to rescind the contract while breach of warranty or of an intermediate term does not have this effect. But the law recognises yet a further category,

---

[7] See above, p.221.

[8] *Gibaud v GE Ry* [1921] 2 K.B. 426: see the *Suisse Atlantique* case [1967] 1 A.C. 361 at 412; and see the judgment of Pearson L.J. in *UGS Finance Ltd v National Mortgage Bank of Greece* [1964] 1 Lloyd's Rep. 446 at 453.

[9] *e.g. Levison v Patent Steam Cleaning Co* [1978] Q.B. 69: see the *Photo Production* case [1980] A.C. 827 at 845, 846; and *cf.* the *Charterhouse* case, above, n.6.

[10] *i.e.* the deviation cases: see below pp.228–231, 240.

[11] See below, pp.246, *et seq.*

[12] *e.g.* in *George Mitchell (Chesterhall) Ltd v Finney Lock Seeds Ltd* [1983] 2 A.C. 803, below, pp.227–228, 261.

[13] See below, pp.788–805.

the so-called "fundamental term," which is "narrower than a condition of the contract"[14] and it is this category of fundamental term that is significant for the present purpose. Such a term is one that specifies the essential purpose of the contract, so that breach of the term turns the performance rendered into one which is not merely defective, but essentially different from that promised: for example, where a person who had contracted to sell peas instead delivered beans[15]; or where a seller of mahogany logs instead delivered pine logs.[16] In a number of cases exemption clauses have been held not to cover breaches of this kind. It has, for example, been held that a seller of "foreign refined rape oil" could not rely on an exemption clause where what he delivered was not "foreign refined rape oil"[17]; that a seller of a new car would be in breach of a fundamental term if he delivered a second-hand car[18]; and that a shipowner who had contracted with a tour operator to provide cruise accommodation was not protected by an exemption clause when he substituted an inferior ship and a much less attractive itinerary.[19]

The same principle of construction can apply where what is supplied is not literally a different thing from what was bargained for, but is so seriously defective as to be different in substance.[20] In *Pinnock Bros v Lewis & Peat Ltd*[21] copra cake was sold "not warranted free from defect" but was so adulterated by castor beans as to poison the cattle to which it was fed. It was held that "where a substance quite different from that contracted for has been delivered, that clause has no application, as such a difference of substance cannot be said to constitute a 'defect'". On the other hand, a party does not lose the protection of an exemption clause merely because his performance suffers from a defect that entitles (or would, but for the clause, have entitled) the other party to reject the defective performance. Thus a seller of "mahogany logs equal to sample" would not be in breach of a fundamental term (but only in breach of condition[22]) if he delivered mahogany logs that were not equal to sample.[23] Similarly, the supplier of a motor vehicle which corresponds with the contractual description does not commit a breach of a fundamental term merely because he breaks some implied undertaking as to the fitness of the vehicle for the purpose for which it was supplied.[24]

In these cases of defective performance, it is often hard to tell whether the performance rendered is so essentially different from that promised as to amount to a breach of a fundamental term. This depends on the answer to a preliminary question of construction: what is the essence of the bargain that the parties have made?[25] The "peas and

---

[14] *Per* Devlin J. in *Smeaton Hanscomb & Co Ltd v Sassoon I Setty & Co (No.1)* [1953] 1 W.L.R. 1468 at 1470; *R W Green Ltd v Cade Bros Farms* [1978] 1 Lloyd's Rep. 602. A passage in *Photo Production Ltd v Securicor Transport Ltd* [1980] A.C. 827 at 849–850, can be interpreted as treating the two concepts as identical (*cf.* below, p.229, n.46) but only for the purpose of the rule that breaches of both give rise to a right to rescind: see below, p.806. It is respectfully submitted that Devlin J. was correct in treating them as distinct for the *present* purpose, *i.e.* the construction of an exemption clause.

[15] See *Chanter v Hopkins* (1838) 4 M. & W. 399 at 404; for a modern application, *cf. The Bow Cedar* [1980] 2 Lloyd's Rep. 601.

[16] *Smeaton Hanscomb & Co Ltd v Sassoon I Setty & Co (No.1)* [1953] 1 W.L.R. 1468 at 1470.

[17] *Nichol v Godts* (1854) 10 Ex. 191; *cf. Wieler v Schilizzi* (1856) 17 C.B. 619.

[18] *Andrews Bros (Bournemouth) Ltd v Singer & Co* [1934] 1 K.B. 17, as explained in *Karsales (Harrow) Ltd v Wallis* [1956] 1 W.L.R. 17.

[19] *Anglo-Continental Holidays Ltd v Typaldos Lines* [1967] 2 Lloyd's Rep. 61.

[20] *cf. Topfell Ltd v Galley Properties Ltd* [1979] 1 W.L.R. 446 at 450 (vendor of a house not protected where he failed to give vacant possession); and see below, pp.771–773.

[21] [1923] 1 K.B. 690.

[22] See above, p.226; below, p.792; Sale of Goods Act 1979, s.15(2) and (3), as amended by Sale and Supply of Goods Act 1994 s.7 and Sch.2.

[23] *Smeaton Hanscomb & Co Ltd v Sassoon I Setty & Co (No.1)* [1953] 1 W.L.R. 1468 at 1470.

[24] *Astley Industrial Trust Ltd v Grimley* [1963] 1 W.L.R. 584.

[25] See Melville, 19 M.L.R. 26; Unger [1957] J.B.L. 30.

beans" example may be contrasted with a case put by Lord Devlin: "If an anxious hostess is late in the preparation of a meal, she can perfectly well say: 'Send me peas or if you haven't got peas send beans, but for heaven's sake send something.' That would be a contract for peas, beans or anything else *ejusdem generis* and is a perfectly sensible contract to make."[26] In such a case, the supplier would not have been in breach at all if he had sent beans; but more difficulty arises where the supplier is undoubtedly in breach and the question is whether that breach makes the article supplied as different from that contracted for as peas are from beans. This question gave rise to much difference of judicial opinion in *George Mitchell (Chesterhall) Ltd v Finney Lock Seeds Ltd*[27] where the defendants agreed to sell to the plaintiffs 30 lbs of "a cabbage seed"[28] which was later invoiced to them as "Finney's Late Dutch Special," a variety of winter white cabbage. It was "common ground . . . that the seed agreed to be sold was seed for a winter white cabbage"[29] and "conceded that what was supplied was not the winter white cabbage which to everybody's knowledge was what the plaintiffs had ordered and the defendants had agreed to sell."[30] As a result of this breach, the plaintiffs' crop failed, being fit for neither human nor animal consumption, and the question was whether the performance rendered was essentially or fundamentally different from that promised. This depended on how the defendants' essential or fundamental obligation under the contract was to be described. Was it an obligation to deliver "cabbage seed" or one to deliver "vegetable seed" or simply one to deliver "seed"? Parker J.[31] and a majority of the Court of Appeal held that the essential obligation was one to deliver vegetable seed and that a clause limiting the sellers' liability did not cover their breach of that obligation. Oliver L.J. said: "what was delivered to the plaintiffs simply was not fulfilment of the contract, even a defective fulfilment, any more than delivery of a motor bicycle would be a fulfilment of a contract for the sale of a car".[32] But the House of Lords held that the clause did as a matter of construction cover the breach (though it did not in the end protect the defendants as it failed to satisfy the statutory requirement of reasonableness[33]). Lord Bridge said: "In my opinion this is not a 'peas and beans' case at all"[34]: in other words, he seems to have regarded the defendants' essential obligation as one simply to deliver "seed". Such a narrow view of a party's essential obligation obviously extends the scope of exemption clauses for it increases the range of cases in which a breach can be described as giving rise to defective performance, as opposed to a failure to perform an essential obligation.

(ii) *Deviation and analogous rules.* In a contract for the carriage of goods by sea, the term as to the route is regarded as fundamental, so that the benefit of an exemption clause is normally lost by a carrier who has without justification[35] deviated, *i.e.* departed

---

[26] [1966] C.L.J. at 212.

[27] [1981] 1 Lloyd's Rep. 476 (Parker J.); [1983] Q.B. 284, CA; [1983] 2 A.C. 803, HL.

[28] [1981] 1 Lloyd's Rep. 476 at 477.

[29] *ibid.*

[30] *ibid.* At first instance counsel for the defendant further conceded that he would not be able to rely on the clause limiting the defendant's liability "if what had been delivered had been beetroot seed or carrot seed" and "that to get within any distance of success he must establish that what was delivered was cabbage seed": [1981] 1 Lloyd's Rep. 476 at 479. This concession was withdrawn on appeal: [1983] Q.B. 284 at 303.

[31] [1981] 1 Lloyd's Rep. 476 at 480.

[32] [1983] Q.B. 284 at 305.

[33] See below, p.260.

[34] [1983] 2 A.C. 803 at 813.

[35] See *Kish v Taylor* [1912] A.C. 604 at 617; Carriage of Goods by Sea Act 1971, Sch., Art.IV 4: deviation may be justified for the purpose of saving life or property at sea, or if it is "reasonable".

from the agreed or usual route.[36] The same is true where a warehouseman has stored the goods in a place other than that agreed[37]; and where a bailee such as a cleaner or carrier has in the course of unauthorised subcontracting parted with the possession of goods entrusted to him.[38] On the other hand, such a person will not lose the protection of an exemption clause merely because he has broken some other term such as a carrier's undertaking to supply a seaworthy ship[39]; or a warehouseman's undertaking to exercise reasonable care in looking after the goods.[40] The reason for the distinction is sometimes said to be that the terms as to the route and as to the place where the goods are to be stored are fundamental,[41] while the other terms mentioned are not. The special importance of the term as to route has been explained on the ground that the owner of the goods may lose his insurance cover if the ship departs from the agreed route[42]: it is therefore thought necessary to give him a remedy against the carrier (in spite of the exemption clause) as if the latter were an insurer. In fact the goods-owner may not suffer the hardship on which the rule is based, since his insurance policy may provide that he is to be "held covered" in case of deviation at a premium to be arranged.[43] The special rule as to the effects of deviation has accordingly been criticised.[44] It can be explained either as an application of the rule of construction normally applied to breach of a fundamental term,[45] or as a rule which, on account of its historical and commercial background, must be treated as *sui generis*.[46]

Once a term has been identified as fundamental, the next question is whether that term has been broken. For this purpose it is first necessary to construe that term to see

---

[36] *Joseph Thorley Ltd v Orchis SS Co Ltd* [1907] 1 K.B. 660; *James Morrison & Co Ltd v Shaw Savill & Albion Co Ltd* [1916] 2 K.B. 783; *Stag Line Ltd v Foscolo, Mango & Co Ltd* [1932] A.C. 328. For the application of the same principle to unauthorised carriage on deck, see *J Evans & Sons (Portsmouth) Ltd v Andrea Merzario* [1976] 1 W.L.R. 1078, and *The Chanda* [1989] 2 Lloyd's Rep. 494; but contrast (in cases of a *statutory* limitation of liability), *The Antares (No.2)* [1987] 1 Lloyd's Rep. 424, where dicta at p.430 suggest that on deck carriage is no longer regarded as a special case. *cf. L & NW Ry v Neilson* [1922] 2 A.C. 263 (carriage by land).

[37] *Woolf v Collis Removal Services* [1948] 1 K.B. 11 at 15; *cf. United Fresh Meat Co Ltd v Charterhouse Cold Storage Ltd* [1974] 2 Lloyd's Rep. 286; *cf. The OOCL Bravery* [2000] 1 Lloyd's Rep. 394 at 401 (parking container lorry in street instead of in secured depot).

[38] *Davies v Collins* [1945] 1 All E.R. 247; *Garnham, Harris & Elton Ltd v Alfred W Ellis (Transport) Ltd* [1967] 1 W.L.R. 940.

[39] *The Europa* [1908] P. 84; *Kish v Taylor* [1912] A.C. 604. But if the unseaworthiness *causes* the loss, the carrier cannot rely on the exceptions provided under the Carriage of Goods by Sea Act 1971: see *Maxine Footwear Ltd v Canadian Government Merchant Marine Ltd* [1959] A.C. 589; but he can rely on the *limitation* so provided: *The Happy Ranger* [2002] EWCA Civ 694; [2002] 2 All E.R. (Comm) 694 at [38].

[40] *J Spurling Ltd v Bradshaw* [1956] 1 W.L.R. 461; *Kenyon Son & Craven Ltd v Baxter Hoare & Co Ltd* [1971] 1 W.L.R. 519; *cf. Mayfair Photographic Supplies Ltd v Baxter Hoare & Co Ltd* [1972] 1 Lloyd's Rep. 410.

[41] See *Smeaton Hanscomb & Co v Sassoon I Setty* [1953] 1 W.L.R. 1468 at 1470, describing deviation as a breach of a fundamental term.

[42] See *Hain SS Co v Tate & Lyle Ltd* (1936) 41 Com.Cas. 350 at 354. For the significance of this point, see further, p.240, below.

[43] See *State Trading Corp of India v S. M. Golodetz Ltd* [1989] 2 Lloyd's Rep. 277 at 289. But such clauses may fail to provide satisfactory protection: for example, in *Vincentelli v Rowlett* (1911) 16 Com.Cas. 310 the insurer "arranged" the premium at an amount equal to the loss. *Quaere*, whether such conduct is consistent with Marine Insurance Act 1906, s.31(2) under which such a premium must be reasonable.

[44] *Farr v Hain SS Co (The Tregenna)* 121 F 2d. 940 at 944 (1941). This case arose from the same facts as *Hain SS Co v Tate & Lyle Ltd*, above; *cf.* Livermore, 2 J.C.L. 241.

[45] *The Antares* [1987] 1 Lloyd's Rep. 424 at 430; *State Trading Corp of India v S M Golodetz Ltd* [1989] 2 Lloyd's Rep. 277 at 289.

[46] *Photo Production Ltd v Securicor Transport Ltd* [1980] A.C. 827 at 845 *per* Lord Wilberforce; *cf. ibid.* at 850, where Lord Diplock treats deviation as a breach of "condition": as to this see above, p.227, n.14. Contrast Devlin J.'s description of deviation (in the passage referred to in n.41, above) as a breach of a fundamental term.

what obligation it imposes. Thus a warehouseman commits a breach of a fundamental term if he stores the goods elsewhere than at the agreed place. But the court cannot apply the rule that, *prima facie*, exemption clauses are not to be construed so as to cover such a breach until it has first determined exactly where the goods were to be stored. In *Gibaud v GE Ry*[47] a contract to store a bicycle in a railway station cloakroom was interpreted as one to store in the cloakroom or in any convenient place nearby. Accordingly, an exemption clause was held to apply when the bicycle was stolen, even though it had been stored in the station hall and not in the cloakroom.

A similar principle applies in the deviation cases. In determining the content of the carrier's obligation as to route, the court will have regard not only to the agreed or usual route (if any)[48] but also to any liberty to deviate given by the contract of carriage. But because of the actual or assumed importance of the term specifying the route, such liberties are restrictively construed. In *Glyn v Margetson*[49] a contract for the carriage of oranges from Malaga to Liverpool gave the carrier a wide liberty to deviate. It was held that this provision did not apply where the ship first went east from Malaga, retraced her course, and then made for Liverpool. The general words of the clause were to be limited with reference to "the main object and intent"[50] of the contract—in this case a voyage from Malaga to Liverpool. The clause only justified the carrier in calling at ports *on the route* between those places. Such a restrictive interpretation can to some extent be overcome by permitting the carrier to call at any port "although in a contrary direction to or out of or beyond the route." In *Connolly Shaw Ltd v A/S Det Nordenfjeldske D/S*[51] a deviation clause containing these words was included in a contract for the carriage of lemons from Palermo to London. It was held that the clause justified deviation to Hull, involving a delay of three days on a voyage of 22 days. But it would not have justified a deviation to Vladivostock, though that was literally within its terms. It gave the carrier only such liberties as could be used "without frustrating the contract".[52]

Clauses permitting a change of route in circumstances beyond the control of the parties are more generously construed. In *G H Renton & Co v Palmyra Trading Corporation of Panama*[53] timber was shipped from Canada for carriage to London or Hull; if strikes prevented discharge at these ports, "the Master may discharge the cargo at . . . any other convenient port." Strikes at London and Hull made discharge at those ports impossible, and the master discharged the cargo at Hamburg. It was held that the carriers were entitled to rely on the clause; for it only applied in a specified emergency and did not enable them to alter the contractual destination at will.

Where the carrier departs from the agreed or usual route and cannot justify that departure by a deviation clause or otherwise,[54] he normally loses the protection of other exemption clauses in the contract. This rule is quite different in nature from that which applies in the supply of goods and similar cases discussed above.[55] In those cases, the term is regarded as fundamental because the effect of its breach is that the injured party receives a performance essentially different from that promised. In the deviation cases, by contrast, the courts are not concerned with the *effect* of the breach: *any* departure from the agreed route "however for practical purposes irrelevant"[56] normally deprives

---

[47] [1921] 2 K.B. 426; contrast *Davies v Collins* [1945] 1 All E.R. 247; below, p.757.
[48] See *Frenkel v MacAndrew & Co Ltd* [1929] A.C. 545.
[49] [1893] A.C. 351.
[50] *ibid.* at 355.
[51] (1934) 49 Ll.L.R. 183.
[52] *ibid.* at 190.
[53] [1957] A.C. 149; and see below, p.238.
[54] See above, p.228 n.35.
[55] See above, pp.226–228.
[56] *Suisse Atlantique* case [1967] 1 A.C. 361 at 423.

the shipowner of the benefit of the exemption clause. Yet it can hardly be said that a voyage actually accomplished after a minor deviation is essentially different from the voyage bargained for. According to *Joseph Thorley Ltd v Orchis SS Co Ltd*, it is, moreover, irrelevant that the deviation did not cause, or increase the risk of, loss. In that case,[57] a cargo of beans was damaged through being mixed with poisonous earth. The carrier lost the benefit of his exemption clause because he had deviated, though the deviation had not caused the loss.[58] And in *James Morrison & Co v Shaw, Savill & Albion Co Ltd*[59] a ship was sunk by enemy action while deviating. The shipowner lost the benefit of his exemption clause even though the ship *might* just as probably have been sunk on her proper route. He would only have been protected had he been able to show that the loss *must* have occurred anyway, *i.e.* even if the ship had not deviated.

The deviation cases do, however, have one thing in common with the supply of goods cases: the *manner* in which the breach is committed is irrelevant. In the supply of goods cases, this point is assumed without argument; and in the deviation cases, so long as the carrier's act is voluntary,[60] it makes no difference that the deviation was quite innocent. In *L & NW Ry v Neilson*[61] the label came off a vanload of theatrical properties and its contents were despatched to various wrong destinations by a stationmaster. In spite of the fact that he had acted under an honest mistake, the railway company lost the protection of its exemption clause. From this point of view, the supply of goods, deviation and analogous cases may be contrasted with the next group to be discussed.

(iii) *Manner of breach.* The courts are reluctant to construe exemption clauses so as to apply to acts amounting to a *deliberate* disregard of the main purpose of the contract. They assume that "the parties never contemplated that such a breach should be excused or limited."[62] In accordance with this assumption, it has been held that a tug-owner could not rely on a clause which protected him from liability for "omission" and "default," where he had deliberately abandoned the tow[63]; and that a carrier of goods by sea could not rely on a clause, which protected him from liability after the goods were "discharged," where he had delivered the goods to a person who, as the carrier knew, had no authority to receive them.[64]

The former substantive doctrine of fundamental breach was often invoked in cases in which a bailee of goods had delivered them to the wrong person. It was held that exemption clauses did not apply where the misdelivery was deliberate[65] or reckless,[66] but could apply where it was merely negligent.[67] Thus the manner of breach was the crucial

---

[57] [1907] 1 K.B. 660. For criticism, see *Carver on Bills of Lading* (1st ed., 2001), §§9–059, *et seq.*

[58] *Aliter* if loss is due to inherent vice or the nature of the goods themselves: *Internationale Guano etc v Robert MacAndrew & Co* [1909] 2 K.B. 360.

[59] [1916] 2 K.B. 783.

[60] See *Rio Tinto Co Ltd v Seed Shipping Co Ltd* (1926) 24 Ll.L.Rep. 321 at 326, where there was in fact no departure from the route.

[61] [1922] 2 A.C. 263. The deviation was no doubt "deliberate" (at 274) in the sense that the defendants' servant knew where he was sending the goods: but it was not "deliberate" in the sense that he knew he was sending them to a wrong destination. *cf.* below, p.232.

[62] *Suisse Atlantique* case [1967] 1 A.C. 361 at 435; *cf. ibid.* at 394, 397.

[63] *The Cap Palos* [1921] P. 458.

[64] *Sze Hai Tong Bank Ltd v Rambler Cycle Co Ltd* [1959] A.C. 576; so far as *contra, Chartered Bank of India v British India Steam Navigation Co Ltd* [1909] A.C. 369 would no longer be followed: see Guest, 77 L.Q.R. 98, 116–118; Wedderburn [1990] C.L.J. 11; *The Ines* [1995] 2 Lloyd's Rep. 144 at 152; *Motis Exports Ltd v Dampskibsselskapet AF 1912* [2000] 1 Lloyd's Rep. 211.

[65] *Alexander v Railway Executive* [1951] 2 K.B. 882.

[66] *J Spurling Ltd v Bradshaw* [1956] 1 W.L.R. 461 at 466; *cf. United Fresh Meat Co Ltd v Charterhouse Cold Storage Ltd* [1974] 2 Lloyd's Rep. 286 at 291.

[67] *Hollins v J Davy Ltd* [1963] 1 Q.B. 844; Guest, (1963) 26 M.L.R. 301; *cf. Gallagher v BRS* [1974] 2 Lloyd's Rep. 446; *The New York Star* [1981] 1 W.L.R. 138.

point, since the term broken and the consequences of the breach were (in these misdelivery cases) always the same: because of delivery to the wrong person, the goods were lost to the owner. The cases, in which the decisive factor was the manner of breach, gave rise to much difficulty. For one thing, a "deliberate" breach was hard to define[68]; for another it was puzzlingly held that a deliberate misdelivery by an employee did not deprive the employer of the protection of an exemption clause where the employee had acted with the intention of defrauding his employer.[69] The need for "reconciling" the cases has largely disappeared now that each must be explained as turning on the construction of the clause. The fact that the breach was deliberate would be a ground[70] for holding that the clause was not intended to cover the breach; but it would no longer be a decisive ground. Thus an exemption clause may apply to a breach in spite of the fact that it is deliberate if it is of only trivial importance: "for example, a deliberate delay of one day in unloading."[71] This may be so even where a deliberate but trivial breach gives rise to unexpectedly serious consequences.[72]

(iv) *Consequences of breach.* Even though a breach is not deliberate, or one of a fundamental term, it may still, by reason of its practical consequences be sufficiently serious to attract the operation of the rule of construction. Failure to perform at the agreed time is always a breach of the same term; but an exemption clause may be construed so as to cover only slight delays and not those that are so prolonged as to cause serious prejudice to the injured party.[73] Again, goods supplied under a contract of sale or hire-purchase may not be fit for the particular purpose for which the customer has acquired them. The supplier is not, merely because he has failed to perform the implied condition as to fitness,[74] in breach of a fundamental term[75] but in a number of cases it has been held that he was not protected by an exemption clause because the defect was so serious as to make the thing practically useless for the customer's purposes.[76] The same result was reached where the proprietor of a parking garage had undertaken to keep a car which had been parked there locked, but left it unlocked, so that the customer's luggage was stolen.[77] In all these cases, the crucial factor was not the nature of the term broken, but the consequence of the breach: for this reason, it was the *breach*, rather than the *term broken*, that was described as fundamental.[78]

The rule of construction most clearly applies where the breach is such that the defective performance becomes "totally different from what the contract contem-

---

[68] Probably it meant delivery "to someone known to have no right" to the goods: *Hollins v J Davy Ltd* (above) at 856.

[69] *John Carter (Fine Worsteds) Ltd v Hanson Haulage (Leeds) Ltd* [1965] 2 Q.B. 495—a case now to be "treated with caution": *W & J Lane v Spratt* [1970] 1 All E.R. 162 at 172. *cf.* also *Levison v Patent Steam Carpet Cleaning Co Ltd* [1978] Q.B. 82 (where, on such facts, there is said to be a fundamental breach).

[70] e.g. *The Cap Palos* [1921] P. 458; *Sze Hai Tong Bank Ltd v Rambler Cycle Co Ltd* [1959] A.C. 576; above at n.64.

[71] *Suisse Atlantique* case [1967] 1 A.C. 361 at 435.

[72] e.g. *Photo Production Ltd v Securicor Transport Ltd* [1980] A.C. 827 at 840 (fire started deliberately but without the intention of burning down the factory: see below, p.236, n.24).

[73] See, e.g. *Bontex Knitting Works Ltd v St John's Garage* [1943] 2 All E.R. 690; [1944] 1 All E.R. 381; *Suisse Atlantique* case [1967] 1 A.C. 361; *cf. Brandt v Liverpool, etc. SN Co Ltd* [1924] 1 K.B. 575 at 597, 601.

[74] See above, p.207, below, p.251.

[75] See above, p.228.

[76] *Yeoman Credit Ltd v Apps* [1962] 2 Q.B. 508; *Farnsworth Finance Facilities Ltd v Attryde* [1970] 1 W.L.R. 1053.

[77] *Mendelssohn v Normand Ltd* [1970] 1 Q.B. 177; Treitel, 32 M.L.R. 685.

[78] For the distinction between breach of a fundamental term and fundamental breach, see the *Suisse Atlantique* case [1967] 1 A.C. 361 at 393, 421; *United Fresh Meat Co Ltd v Charterhouse Cold Storage Ltd* [1947] 2 Lloyd's Rep. 286; *cf.* (in the context of stipulations as to time) *United Scientific Holdings Ltd v Burnley BC* [1978] A.C. 904 at 945.

plates".[79] But the examples given in the preceding paragraph show that the rule can apply even where the breach does not make the performance *totally* different from that promised: it is sometimes enough if the breach causes *serious* prejudice to the injured party. Thus the rule was applied against suppliers of motor vehicles that were seriously defective,[80] even though they could still be described as the motor vehicles that were, under the contracts, to be supplied.[81] It has further been suggested that the rule of construction applies whenever the breach "entitles the injured party to treat it as repudiatory and rescind a contract".[82] This may merely refer to the general principle that an injured party wishing to rescind a contract on account of the other party's breach must show that the breach was a "serious" one.[83] But there are many exceptions to this principle: for example, a party may be entitled to rescind for breach of condition even though the breach does not cause him serious prejudice, or indeed any prejudice at all[84]; and the rule of construction with which we are here concerned would not apply merely because there had been a breach of condition.

It is impossible to define with precision the degree of seriousness of the prejudice (resulting from the breach) that is required to bring the rule of construction into operation. One can only say that the court's reluctance to construe a clause so as to apply to a particular breach will, in general, be directly proportioned to the gravity of that breach. The point may be illustrated by reference to *Kenyon Son & Craven Ltd v Baxter Hoare & Co Ltd*[85] where nuts stored in a warehouse were seriously damaged by rats as a result of the warehouseman's "gross and culpable" failure to take care to prevent such damage. It was held that the warehouseman was protected by an exemption clause which, on its true construction, covered the events which had occurred; but Donaldson J. said that clause would not have protected the warehouseman if he had stored the nuts in the open or in an area which was prohibited by the contract.[86]

(b) NATURE OF THE RULE. At this stage, it is necessary to discuss general statements of the rule, to illustrate its operation, and to consider a possible limitation on its scope.

(i) *General statements.* Where a breach falls within the scope of the rule of construction, the effect of the rule is that an exemption clause will cover the breach only if it is "most clearly and unambiguously expressed",[87] so that general words which can fairly be said to apply only to less serious breaches will be construed so as not to cover the serious breach which has occurred.[88] It would, indeed, be wrong "to create ambiguities by strained construction".[89] But general words which at first sight appear to cover even the most serious breach may not be construed in this sense, if to give them this effect

---

[79] *Suisse Atlantique* case [1967] 1 A.C. at 393.

[80] *Yeoman Credit Ltd v Apps* [1962] 2 Q.B. 508; *Farnsworth Finance Facilities Ltd v Attryde* [1970] 1 W.L.R. 1053.

[81] Thus in *Yeoman Credit Ltd v Apps*, above, it was held that there was a fundamental breach but *no* "total failure of consideration": *cf.* below, p.1055.

[82] *Suisse Atlantique* case, [1967] 1 A.C. 361 at 397.

[83] See below, p.769. Lord Diplock in the *Photo Production* case [1980] A.C. 827 at 849 and in *The Afovos* [1983] 1 W.L.R. 12 at 195, 202 uses "fundamental breach" to refer to this type of breach.

[84] See below, pp.791, 793.

[85] [1971] 1 W.L.R. 519; Legh-Jones and Pickering, 86 L.Q.R. 513.

[86] [1971] 1 W.L.R. 519 at 532.

[87] *Ailsa Craig Fishing Co Ltd v Malvern Fishing Co Ltd* [1983] 1 W.L.R. 964 at 966.

[88] *e.g. Levison v Patent Steam Cleaning Co* [1978] Q.B. 69, now said to be explicable on construction in *Photo Production Ltd v Securicor Transport Ltd* [1980] A.C. 827 at 845–846.

[89] *Ailsa Craig* case, above, at 966; *Photo Production Ltd v Securicor Transport Ltd* [1980] A.C. 827 at 851; *George Mitchell (Chesterhall) Ltd v Finney Lock Seeds Ltd* [1983] 2 A.C. 803 at 814; *Singer (UK) Ltd v Tees & Hartlepool Port Authority* [1988] 2 Lloyd's Rep. 164 at 169; *The Ines* [1995] 2 Lloyd's Rep. 144 at 151.

"would lead to an absurdity, or because it would defeat the main object of the contract or perhaps for some other reason".[90] For example, a carrier who had undertaken to deliver goods to one person could not rely on such general words if he deliberately delivered the goods to another person, or threw them into the sea.[91] In such cases it is said that the exemption clause "cannot be taken to refer" to the "total breach"[92]; or that the courts "lean against"[93] such a construction, while not wholly ruling out the possibility of its being achieved by sufficiently clear words.[94] According to another formulation of the rule, there is a "strong, though rebuttable, presumption that in inserting a clause of exclusion or limitation . . . the parties are not contemplating breaches of fundamental terms".[95]

(ii) *Illustrations of breaches covered.* An important element in the formulation of the rule just quoted is that the presumption is rebuttable. One way of rebutting it is to provide expressly that the clause is to cover loss or damage caused by fundamental breach: such words can, for example, protect a bailee from liability even for deliberate misdelivery by his employees.[96] But such an express reference to fundamental breach is by no means the only way of rebutting the presumption. It can also be rebutted if the court is for some other reason satisfied that the clause was intended to cover the breach which has occurred. In a number of cases, the House of Lords has therefore given effect to clauses excluding or restricting liability in spite of the seriousness of the breach. In the *Suisse Atlantique*[97] case, the liability of charterers for delays was limited to $1000 per day by a demurrage clause even though it was accepted[98] that the delays which had taken place were so long as to amount to a "fundamental breach".[99] In the *Photo Production*[1] case a security firm which had been engaged to safeguard a factory was protected by an exemption clause which was "clearly and fairly susceptible of one meaning only",[2] even though the firm's breach resulted in the total destruction of the factory by fire. In the *Ailsa Craig*[3] case, a security firm was likewise protected by a clause limiting its liability to £1,000, even though the firm had committed a "total" breach of its undertaking to provide a continuous security service for fishing boats, leading to a loss valued at £55,000. As the potential loss which might be caused by the breach was very great in proportion to the sums that could be charged for the service, and as the loss suffered was likely to have been covered by insurance, it was not inherently improbable that the owners of the boats should have agreed to the limitation of liability.

The same approach to the construction of exemption clauses is yet again illustrated by *George Mitchell (Chesterhall) Ltd v Finney Lock Seeds Ltd*,[4] where a contract for the sale of winter white cabbage seed contained a clause limiting the sellers' liability for defects to the return of the price (some £200) or to replacing the defective seed. The clause expressly provided that, except to the extent just stated, the sellers excluded "all

---

[90] *Suisse Atlantique* case [1967] 1 A.C. 361 at 398.

[91] *Sze Hai Tong Bank Ltd v Rambler Cycle Co Ltd* [1959] A.C. 576 at 587.

[92] *Suisse Atlantique* case [1967] 1 A.C. 361 at 432.

[93] *Motis Exports Ltd v Dampskibsselskapet AF 1912* [2000] 1 Lloyd's Rep. 211 at 216.

[94] *ibid.* at 217.

[95] [1967] 1 A.C. 361 at 427.

[96] See *The Antwerpen* [1994] 1 Lloyd's Rep. 213, where the *general* words of clause 4 were said at 246 not to be sufficient to cover the breach but the *express* reference to fundamental breach in clause 8(3) did produce this effect.

[97] [1967] 1 A.C. 371; Drake, 30 M.L.R. 531; Fridman, 7 Alberta L.Rev. 281; Treitel, 29 M.L.R. 546.

[98] [1967] 1 A.C. 371 at 419, 430.

[99] *ibid.* p.433.

[1] [1980] A.C. 827; below, p.239.

[2] [1980] A.C. 827 at 851; *Swiss Bank Corp v Brink's-Mat Ltd* [1986] 2 Lloyd's Rep. 79 at 92.

[3] [1983] 1 W.L.R. 964; Palmer, 45 M.L.R. 322.

[4] [1983] 2 A.C. 803; Clarke [1983] C.L.J. 32; Adams, 46 M.L.R. 147.

liability for any loss or damage" and for consequential loss or damage "arising from the use of any seeds ... supplied by us ... or any failure in the performance of or any defect in any seed supplied by us". The actual decision was that this clause did not protect the sellers as it failed to comply with the statutory requirement of reasonableness.[5] But the House of Lords also held that the clause did, as a matter of construction, cover the breach which occurred even though the breach was of a most serious kind in that the seed supplied was "in no commercial sense vegetable seed at all"[6] so that the farmers who had bought it suffered total crop failure and a loss valued at over £60,000. Lord Bridge said that the clause, read as a whole, "unambiguously" limited the sellers' liability and that it was "only possible to read an ambiguity into it by the process of strained construction"[7] which had been deprecated in the *Ailsa Craig* and *Photo Production* cases.[8] The adoption of such a "strained construction" would come "dangerously near to reintroducing by the back door the doctrine of 'fundamental breach' which this House in the *Photo Production* case had so forcibly evicted from the front".[9]

(iii) *Illustrations of breaches not covered.* The four House of Lords cases just considered show that clear words in an exemption or limitation clause can cover even a very serious breach; but one feature of the *George Mitchell* case perhaps deserves some emphasis. It will be recalled that Lord Bridge described the case as "not a 'peas and beans' case at all. The relevant condition applies to 'seeds',"[10] and seeds had indeed been supplied. If the articles supplied had been plastic pellets designed for roof insulation but resembling seeds in appearance, no "strained construction" would have been necessary to hold that the clause did not apply: the things supplied would simply not have been "seeds". In theory the sellers could have drafted a clause to cover even such a breach but in practice they would find it difficult to persuade a court that a clause "unambiguously" had such a very wide ambit. This kind of difficulty may be illustrated by contrasting the *George Mitchell* case with the later decision of the House of Lords in *The TFL Prosperity.*[11] In that case, a clause in a charterparty exempting the shipowner from liability for "damage" was held not to cover the economic loss suffered by the charterer by reason of the fact that the ship was not of the dimensions specified in the contract. The effect of construing the clause so as to cover this kind of loss would, in the words of Lord Roskill, have been that "the charter virtually ceases to be a contract . . . and becomes no more than a statement of intent by the owners in return for which the charterers are obliged to pay large sums of hire, though if the owners fail to carry out their promises as to description or delivery, [the charterers] are entitled to nothing in lieu"[12]; and he rejected that construction on the ground that it did not accord with "the true common intention of the parties".[13] The same principle of construction has been held to deprive a carrier of goods by sea of the benefit of exemption clauses where he had undertaken to carry the goods *under* deck but had, by wrongfully carrying them *on* deck, exposed them to

---

[5] See below, p.260.
[6] [1981] 1 Lloyd's Rep. 476 at 478; *cf.* above, pp.227–228.
[7] [1983] 2 A.C. 803 at 814. All the other members of the House of Lords agreed with Lord Bridge's speech.
[8] See above, p.233 at n.89.
[9] [1983] 2 A.C. 803 at 813.
[10] *ibid.* and see above, p.228.
[11] [1984] 1 W.L.R. 48.
[12] *ibid.* at 58–59.
[13] *ibid.* at 59. *cf.* in different contexts, *cf. Bishop v Bonham* [1988] 1 W.L.R. 742; *Bovis Construction (Scotland) Ltd v Whatlings Construction Ltd* 1995 S.L.T. 1339, HL; contrast *Great North Eastern Ry Ltd v Avon Insurance plc* [2001] EWCA Civ 780; [2001] 2 All E.R. (Comm) 526, at [31].

significantly greater risks of loss or damage.[14] But cases of this kind also illustrate the possibility that the principle can be displaced by sufficiently clear language[15]; and there are conflicting decisions on the question whether it is displaced by the words "in any event" in a clause which merely limits, without wholly excluding, the carrier's liability for such a breach.[16]

(iv) *Total breach.* In discussing the scope of the rule of construction, we distinguished between breaches that caused *serious* prejudice and those that made performance *totally* different from that bargained for.[17] Clear words can, no doubt, exclude liability for serious breaches, but it is less certain whether the same is true where the words purport to cover breaches that are indeed total. Two suggestions in the *Suisse Atlantique* case bear on the point.

The first suggestion was made by Lord Wilberforce, when he said that the court could refuse to apply an exemption clause literally if to give effect to the clause would be to "deprive one party's stipulation of all contractual force".[18] The clause might then turn the party's promise into one to perform only if he felt like it; and a promise of this kind might not amount to a contract at all on the ground that it was illusory.[19] Such a situation should be contrasted with that in the *Ailsa Craig* case[20] where the clause was expressed to cover "failure in the provision of services." It was held to apply even on the assumption that the failure was "total"[21]; but the clause only *limited* the defendants' liability, and therefore did not make their promise illusory. If an exemption clause would, on its literal meaning, make a promise illusory, the court might reject that meaning; but such a decision could be explained on the ground that the court was rejecting the literal meaning of the clause so as to give effect to the construction of the contract as a whole.

The second suggestion is based on Lord Reid's statement in the *Suisse Atlantique* case, that an exemption clause might "apply to at least *some cases* of fundamental breach without being so widely drawn that it can be cut down by applying the ordinary principles of construction".[22] The words here italicised suggest that there might be *other* cases in which this would not be true: for example, if a shipowner to whom goods had been entrusted for carriage deliberately threw them into the sea,[23] if the defendants in the *Photo Production* case had deliberately burnt down the factory[24] or if the defendants in the *George Mitchell* case had supplied plastic pellets instead of seeds. In such cases the

---

[14] *The Kapitan Petko Voivoda* [2002] EWHC (Comm) 1306; [2002] 1 All E.R. (Comm) 560, at [27], so far as it relates to the carrier's *exemptions* from liability.

[15] *The Antares* [1987] 1 Lloyd's Rep. 424 (time bar discharging carrier "in any event . . . from all liability whatsoever").

[16] Contrast *J Evans & Son (Portsmouth) Ltd v Andrea Merzario Ltd* [1976] 1 W.L.R. 1078; *The Chanda* [1987] 2 Lloyd's Rep. 494 and *The Pembroke* [1995] 2 Lloyd's Rep. 290 (carrier's liability not limited) with *The Kapitan Petko Voivoda* [2002] EWHC (Comm) 1306; [2002] 1 All E.R. (Comm) 560, at [28] (carrier's liability limited).

[17] See above, p.233.

[18] *Suisse Atlantique* case [1967] 1 A.C. 361 at 432.

[19] See above, pp.83, 167, *cf. Firestone Tyre & Rubber Co Ltd v Vokins & Co Ltd* [1951] 1 Lloyd's Rep. 32 at 39: "It is illusory to say—'we promise to do a thing but we are not liable if we do not do it.'" The *TFL Prosperity*, above, p.235, n.11, goes further in that the owner was, even on his own argument, bound to supply *some* ship.

[20] [1983] 1 W.L.R. 964.

[21] *ibid.* at 971.

[22] [1967] A.C. 361 at 399.

[23] *cf.* above, p.232.

[24] This was not the position: see [1980] A.C. 827 at 840 where Lord Wilberforce says that, though the fire was started deliberately by one of the defendants' employees, "it was not established that he intended to burn down the factory."

court might refuse to give effect to the clause (even if it was literally wide enough to cover the breach) because to do so would "lead to an absurdity".[25]

(c) CLAUSES TO WHICH THE RULE APPLIES. The principles of strict construction which operate in cases of serious breach apply to clauses that limit,[26] as well as to those that wholly exclude, liability; but they do not apply to limitation clauses "in their full rigour".[27] Thus in the *Ailsa Craig*[28] case the House of Lords emphasised that the clause was not one of total exclusion; and this was also true of the clause in the *Suisse Atlantique*[29] case. To put the point in another way, the presumption that the clause is not intended to cover the breach is weaker in the case of a clause which merely limits than in the case of one which wholly excludes liability. Of course the presumption can be rebutted even in a case of the latter kind.[30]

Exclusion and limitation clauses must be distinguished from clauses that fix damages in advance.[31] The distinction can be illustrated by reference to the *Suisse Atlantique*[32] case where a further ground for the decision was that the purpose of the demurrage clause was not to limit damages but rather to fix in advance the damages payable in the event of certain breaches.[33] Under a limitation clause the owners would have recovered such loss as they could prove, with an upper limit of $1,000 per day. Under the demurrage clause they were entitled to $1,000 per day even if they could not prove any loss at all, or only a smaller loss. In the circumstances, the clause operated to limit the liability of the charterers; but it differed from a limitation clause in that it was capable of benefiting either party. Therefore there was less need to apply strict rules of construction to it.[34]

This is also true of arbitration clauses.[35] Although such clauses may be said to exclude a remedy (in restricting a party's right to sue on the contract in a court of law),[36] their main purpose is not to deprive a party of rights to compensation, but to set up machinery for determining these rights. The same is true of a clause which merely prevents a party from asserting his rights by some specified procedure: *e.g.* by way of set-off (as opposed to cross-action).[37]

---

[25] *Suisse Atlantique* case [1967] 1 A.C. 361 at 398. The substantive doctrine also finds a, perhaps unintended, echo in the passage from *Equitable Life Assurance Society v Hyman* [2000] All E.R. 961 at 971 quoted on p.167 above, at n.53.

[26] See *Bovis Construction (Scotland) Ltd v Whatlings Construction Ltd* 1995 S.L.T. 1339.

[27] *George Mitchell* case [1983] 2 A.C. 803 at 814; *cf.* above, p.202, 204; *The Happy Ranger* [2002] EWCA Civ 694; [2002] 2 All E.R. (Comm) 24 at [38].

[28] [1983] 1 W.L.R. 964.

[29] [1967] 1 A.C. 361.

[30] As, for example, in the *Photo Production* case [1980] A.C. 827.

[31] See below, pp.999 *et seq.* Such clauses in contracts with consumers can fall within the Unfair Terms in Consumer Contracts Regulations 1999 (see Sch.2, para.1(e)); but those Regulations are not restricted in their operation to exemption clauses: see below, p.268.

[32] [1967] 1 A.C. 361.

[33] [1967] 1 A.C. 361 at 395, 421, 435–436.

[34] *Semble* the rule does not apply to qualifications of provisions *increasing* a party's normal liability: *Adams v Richardson & Starling Ltd* [1969] 1 W.L.R. 1465.

[35] *Woolf v Collis Removal Service* [1948] 1 K.B. 11. *cf.* Unfair Contract Terms Act 1977, s.13(2). Contrast Unfair Terms in Consumer Contracts Regulations 1994, Sch.3, para.1(q), and see above n.31.

[36] See below, p.447.

[37] *The Fedora* [1986] 2 Lloyd's Rep. 441; but the *contra proferentem* rule (above, p.221) was applied to such a clause in *Connaught Restaurants Ltd v Indoor Leisure Ltd* [1994] 1 W.L.R. 501 and in *Esso Petroleum Ltd v Milton* [1997] 1 W.L.R. 938. *cf.* also Unfair Terms in Consumer Contracts Regulations 1999 Sch.2 para.1(b), (under which a clause "inappropriately excluding" a consumer's right of set-off is *prima facie* unfair); and see above n.31.

Clauses which assume that there has been a breach and exclude or limit liability must be distinguished from those which define a contracting party's duty.[38] For example, a building contract may provide for completion by a fixed date and contain an "exception" for delays caused by strikes. This may only be another way of saying that the builder will complete by the agreed date, if strikes do not prevent him from doing so: he is under no higher duty.[39] The clause in *G H Renton & Co v Palmyra Trading Corporation*[40] permitting discharge at ports other than London or Hull was of the same nature. In these cases, failure to complete on the day named, or to get to the specified ports, is *not a breach at all*.[41] On the other hand, a clause which provided that a builder was not to be liable for loss or damage due to his defective workmanship would be an exemption clause, for it would be absurd to suppose that a building contract should impose no duty at all with respect to the standard of workmanship.[42] This is all the more obvious where the clause only limits, and does not wholly exclude, liability. The rule of strict construction applies to exemption clauses, but it has been said that it does not apply to clauses which merely define the duties of a contracting party.[43] In borderline cases the distinction between the two types of clauses will not be easy to draw; but one important test is whether the events in which a clause is expressed to operate are beyond the control of the party relying on it. If they are, the clause is likely to be regarded as a provision defining the contractual duty rather than as an exemption clause.[44]

(d) EFFECTS OF AFFIRMATION OR RESCISSION. A serious breach of the kind here under discussion normally gives the injured party two remedies: he can claim damages, and he can rescind (or terminate) the contract.[45] An exemption clause may affect one or both of these remedies. If it is so worded as to exclude or restrict only the injured party's right to *damages*, it will not affect that party's remedy by way of *rescission* at all. This is true even though the clause is, as a matter of construction, held to apply to the serious breach that has occurred. Thus in the *Suisse Atlantique*[46] case the clause covered the serious breach which had occurred, and so limited the shipowners' damages; but it did not deprive them of their right to rescind the contract by sailing their ship away. Conversely, a contract may contain a non-rejection or non-cancellation clause which excludes the right to rescind but makes no reference to damages. Such a clause may take away the right to rescind even for a very serious breach, but it would not prevent the injured party from claiming damages.[47]

The right to rescind may be lost by affirmation; and it was held to have been so lost in the *Suisse Atlantique* case when the shipowners, with knowledge of the existence of that right, took no steps to rescind the charterparty.[48] The case therefore supports the

---

[38] See *The London Lion* [1980] 2 Lloyd's Rep. 456 at 468; *The Saudi Prince* [1988] 1 Lloyd's Rep. 1.

[39] *Semble*, the position is the same under Unfair Contract Terms Act 1977, s.3(2)(b)(i). See further, below, p.248.

[40] [1957] A.C. 149; above, p.229.

[41] *The Angelia*, [1973] 1 W.L.R. 210 at 230, disapproved, but on another point, in *The Nema* [1982] A.C. 724; below, p.898.

[42] *cf.*, in another context, *The Union Amsterdam* [1982] 2 Lloyd's Rep. 832 at 836.

[43] *The Angelia*, above, at 231; *Kenyon Son & Craven Ltd v Baxter Hoare & Co* [1971] 1 W.L.R. 519 at 522; *cf. The Gudermes* [1993] 1 Lloyd's Rep. 311 at 328 (oil to be carried on a ship known to have no means of heating it).

[44] *The Angelia*, above, at 231; contrast *Blackburn v Liverpool, etc. SN Co* [1902] 1 K.B. 290 ("exception" expressly including negligence).

[45] See below, pp.843 *et seq.*

[46] [1967] 1 A.C. 361; above, p.234.

[47] *cf. Toomey v Eagle Star Insurance Co* [1995] 2 Lloyd's Rep. 89.

[48] [1967] 1 A.C. 361 at 395, 398, 409, 410, 437.

view[49] that affirmation after a serious breach does not affect the operation of an exemption clause which is expressed so as to exclude or restrict only *the right to damages* for that breach[50]: that right continues, after affirmation, to depend on the construction of the clause.

The position was formerly thought to be different if the injured party did not affirm the contract but rescinded it on account of the serious breach. It was argued that, by rescinding, the injured party could bring the whole contract to an end; and that in this way he could get rid of an exemption clause even though the clause, on its true construction, excluded or restricted his right to damages for the breach.[51] But this view was rejected in *Photo Production Ltd v Securicor Transport Ltd*,[52] where defendants had agreed to provide a "night patrol service" for the claimants' factory for a weekly charge of £8 15s. One of their employees started a small fire which got out of control so that the factory, worth £650,000, was destroyed. The contract contained an exemption clause which, on its true construction, applied to this breach, in spite of the seriousness of its effects.[53] The House of Lords held that the claimants could not get rid of the clause by electing to rescind the contract; for to allow their claim on this ground would have amounted to a reintroduction of the "substantive doctrine" after its rejection in the *Suisse Atlantique* case. The effect of the claimants' election to rescind was to put an end to obligations of further performance *after* that election.[54] But it did not operate retrospectively so as to deprive the defendants of the protection of the clause with respect to loss suffered *before* that election had been made.

Where a party exercises his right to rescind for breach, he may, however, be *prima facie* entitled to damages not only in respect of past loss but also in respect of prospective loss, *i.e.* loss which he will suffer after rescission, as a result of the other party's wrongful repudiation.[55] Suppose, for example, that in the *Suisse Atlantique* case the shipowners had justifiably rescinded when only half the period of the charter had expired, and that they had found alternative employment for the ship for the rest of that period. They would then, but for any exemption clauses, have been entitled to damages in respect of (i) detention of the ship before rescission and (ii) loss suffered thereafter if the alternative employment of the ship was less profitable than that under the original contract. The demurrage clause limited the damages for the past loss recoverable under the first head, but it did not even purport to affect the damages for prospective loss recoverable by reason of wrongful repudiation under the second head. When Lord Reid said that the shipowners would have been entitled to damages over and above the agreed demurrage if, instead of affirming the charterparty, they had justifiably terminated it,[56] he was (it is submitted) referring to this prospective loss. It should be emphasised that the demurrage clause did not cover this type of loss but only damages for detention

---

[49] This view is also supported by *Chandris v Isbrandtsen-Moller Inc* [1951] 2 K.B. 240; reversed on another ground [1951] 1 K.B. at 256. For the apparently contrary decision in *Charterhouse Credit Ltd v Tolly* [1963] 2 Q.B. 683, see above, p.225, n.6.

[50] *cf.* Unfair Contract Terms Act 1977, s.9(2); below, p.261.

[51] *e.g. Harbutt's "Plasticine" Ltd v Wayne Tank Co Ltd* [1970] 1 Q.B. 447, overruled in *Photo Production Ltd v Securicor Transport Ltd* [1980] A.C. 827.

[52] [1980] A.C. 827. Guest, 96 L.Q.R. 324; Sealy [1980] C.L.J. 252; Palmer and Yates [1981] C.L.J. 108; Nicol and Rawlings, 43 M.L.R. 567.

[53] See above, p.234.

[54] [1980] A.C. 827 at 844–845, 849–850.

[55] See below, pp.850–852.

[56] [1967] 1 A.C. 361 at 398, *cf. ibid.* 419 and 437. It does not seem that Lord Wilberforce intended to cast doubt on this dictum when in the *Photo Production* case at 842 he criticised a different passage of Lord Reid's speech.

under the first head. If an exemption clause on its true construction did cover prospective loss under the second head, it is submitted that the injured party could not, by
simply rescinding the contract on account of the breach, get rid of the clause so as to
recover full damages in respect of loss of this kind. To allow him to do so would not,
indeed, infringe the general principle that rescission for breach has no retrospective
effect on the operation of exemption clauses; but it would be inconsistent with the
rejection of the substantive doctrine of fundamental breach. This submission is supported by a dictum of Lord Diplock in the *Photo Production* case that liability for such
loss can be "excluded or modified by express words".[57] Clauses which regulate "the
manner in which liability . . . is to be established",[58] *e.g.* by limiting the time within
which a claim must be made, similarly continue to govern the future relations of the
parties even after rescission for serious breach.[59] Arbitration clauses likewise survive
such rescission.[60]

To the general rule that termination does not retrospectively deprive a party of the
benefit of exemption clauses, there is or may be an exception. In the deviation cases, it
is commonly held that the carrier is deprived of the benefit of exemption clauses in
respect of loss which has occurred before the owner of the goods elected to terminate the
contract.[61] One possible explanation for this state of the law is that it follows from the
special considerations which affect deviation. We have seen that one reason for classifying deviation as a breach of a fundamental term is that it deprives the cargo-owner of his
insurance cover[62]; and since it so deprives him automatically and "as from the time of
the deviation,"[63] the same reasoning would seem to support the view that deviation
deprives the carrier of the benefit of exemption clauses in the contract of carriage
from the same time and with the same retrospective effect. Alternatively, it can be argued
that the cargo-owner may well intend the shipowner to be deprived of such protection
from the time at which the insurance cover is lost and not from some later time at which
he learns of the deviation and elects to terminate the contract of carriage. On this view,
the deviation cases could be "assimilated into the general law of contract[64]: that is, they
could be explained as turning on the construction of the contract. It would follow that
a shipowner would not be retrospectively deprived of the protection of an exemption
clause *merely* because the ship had deviated: he would be so deprived only where the
clause was, on its true construction, intended to have such retrospective effect. Yet
another possibility is to regard the deviation cases as exceptional or *sui generis*.[65]
Whichever may be the true explanation, the authority of the deviation cases was
expressly recognised in the *Photo Production* case.[66]

(e) BURDEN OF PROOF. An exemption clause may, as a matter of construction, be held
not to cover certain serious breaches, and it may be alleged that the loss which has been

[57] [1980] A.C. 827 at 849.
[58] *The New York Star* [1981] 1 W.L.R. 138 at 145.
[59] *ibid. cf.* the discussion of "ancillary" obligations at p.850, below.
[60] *Heyman v Darwins Ltd* [1942] A.C. 356.
[61] See the authorities cited at pp.228–229, above.
[62] See above, p.229.
[63] Marine Insurance Act 1906, s.46(1). For the principle that discharge is automatic (*i.e.* without any election
   on the part of the insurer), see *The Good Luck* [1992] A.C. 233, below, p.846. That case was concerned with
   the effect on the contract of insurance of breach of warranty under s.33(3) of the 1906 Act; but the crucial
   words of that subsection ("the insurer is discharged from liability as from the time of . . . ") are identical
   with the corresponding words of s.46(1), above, which deal with the effect on that contract of deviation.
[64] *The Antares (No.2)* [1987] 1 Lloyd's Rep. 424 at 430; *State Trading Corporation of India v S M Golodetz Ltd*
   [1989] 2 Lloyd's Rep. 277 at 289; *cf. ibid.* at 287.
[65] *Photo Production* case, [1980] A.C. 827 at 845; *cf. ibid.* at 850.
[66] *ibid.*; see n.65 above, p.229.

suffered is due to such a breach. The question then arises whether it is up to the claimant to show that the breach which has occurred was of this kind or whether it is up to the defendant to show that the loss was not due to a breach of this kind (but to one that is covered by the clause).

This question has arisen in a number of cases in which goods were lost by a bailee to whom they had been entrusted for storage, carriage or cleaning. On the one hand, it can be argued that the bailee should not have the burden of proving that the loss was not due to the serious breach alleged, as it is notoriously difficult to prove a negative. On the other hand there is the argument that the result in these cases generally depends on the *manner* of the breach[67]; that the bailee will generally be in a better position than the bailor to know how the goods were lost; and that the bailor should not have the burden of proving facts peculiarly accessible to the other party. After some conflict in the authorities, the latter argument has prevailed, so that the burden is on the bailee to show that the breach was not so serious as to fall outside the scope of the exemption clause.[68]

The above cases all concern breaches by bailees of their duty with regard to the safekeeping of the goods. They do not necessarily apply where the breach consists of delay in performance and is alleged to be serious because of its *consequences*.[69] In such cases it is probably the claimant who has the burden of proving that the delay is so serious as not to be covered by the clause. This is consistent with the principle of the bailment cases; for the consequences of the breach on the claimant's position would be a matter peculiarly within *his* (rather than the defendant's) knowledge.

3. Other Common Law Limitations

Even if an exemption clause on its true construction covers the breach that has occurred, its effectiveness is subject to a number of further common law limitations. These are much reduced in importance by the legislative limitations to be discussed later in this Chapter[70]; but they retain their practical importance in cases to which those limitations do not apply.[71]

(1) Misrepresentation as to contents

In *Curtis v Chemical Cleaning & Dyeing Co Ltd*,[72] the claimant took a dress to the defendants to be cleaned. She signed a receipt after being told that it exempted the defendants from liability for certain specified kinds of damage, when it actually exempted them for liability "for any damage, however arising". It was held that the defendants could not rely on the clause as they had induced the claimant to sign the

---

[67] See above, pp.231–232.

[68] *Levison v Patent Steam Cleaning Co Ltd* [1978] Q.B. 68, following *Woolmer v Delmer Price Ltd* [1955] 1 Q.B. 291, and distinguishing *Hunt & Winterbotham (West of England) Ltd v B.R.S. (Parcels) Ltd* [1962] 1 Q.B. 617. See also *J Spurling Ltd v Bradshaw* [1956] 1 W.L.R. 461 at 466, 470; and *cf. United Fresh Meat Co Ltd v Charterhouse Cold Storage Ltd* [1974] 2 Lloyd's Rep. 286 (deterioration of goods in a warehouse); Handford, 38 M.L.R. 577; Males [1978] C.L.J. 24. Contrast, in Australia, *The Antwerpen* [1994] 1 Lloyd's Rep. 213. The normal rule as to burden of proof in such cases may be reversed by the terms of the contract: see *Thames Tideway Properties Ltd v Serfaty* [1999] 2 Lloyd's Rep. 110.

[69] *e.g.* in cases like the *Suisse Atlantique* case, [1967] 1 A.C. 361; above, p.234.

[70] See below, pp.246–285.

[71] See below, pp.264–266, 277–280. Theoretically, the common law limitations could be used to impugn a clause which satisfied the legislative tests of reasonableness (below, pp.252–256) and fairness (below, pp.271–279); but in practice it is unlikely that these tests could be satisfied where one of the common law limitations applied.

[72] [1951] 1 K.B. 805; *cf. Horry v Tate & Lyle Refineries Ltd* [1982] 2 Lloyd's Rep. 416 at 422.

receipt by misrepresenting its contents. Denning L.J. said[73] that mere failure to draw attention to the existence or extent of the exemption clause might in some circumstances amount to misrepresentation.

(2) Overriding undertaking

An exemption clause in a document with reference to which the parties contract can be overridden by an express inconsistent undertaking given at or before the time of contracting. Thus a buyer of goods by auction can recover damages for breach of an oral undertaking given at the time of sale although the printed conditions of sale exempt the seller from all liability for defects.[74] To bring this rule into operation, there must be an "express specific oral promise"[75] which is inconsistent with the exemption clause: a party is not prevented from relying on a clause merely because no reference was made to it at the time of contracting, so that (in this sense) it can be said to be inconsistent with the terms expressly agreed. Where a series of contracts is made under a master agreement, an obligation imposed by that agreement may similarly override an exemption clause contained in a written document evidencing the terms of the particular contract in question.[76]

(3) Excluding liability for fraud

The common law power to exclude liability for misrepresentation *inducing* a contract[77] has been limited by s.3 of the Misrepresentation Act 1967[78]; but that section does not affect contractual provisions purporting to exclude liability for fraud in the *performance* of a contract. It seems unlikely that such a provision would now be regarded as effective. In *Tullis v Jacson*[79] the parties to a building contract agreed to submit disputes to the arbitration of an architect, whose award was to be final, and not to be set aside for "any pretence, suggestion, charge or insinuation of fraud". An attempt to challenge the award on the ground that it was not made in good faith failed because of this provision. But this decision has been judicially criticised[80] and is in any event limited in two ways. Such a clause would not protect a party from liability for his *own* fraud[81]; and although it is in principle possible to exclude liability for the fraud of an agent, even this cannot be done by general words.[82] Only "the clearest possible wording"[83] will exclude even such

---

[73] [1951] 1 K.B. 805 at 809.

[74] *Couchman v Hill* [1947] K.B. 554; *Harling v Eddy* [1951] 2 K.B 739; these cases can also be explained on another ground: above, p.183; *cf. Brikom Investments Ltd v Carr* [1979] Q.B. 467 at 480; *BCT Software Solutions Ltd v Arnold Laver & Co Ltd* [2002] EWHC 1298, Ch; [2002] 2 All E.R. (Comm) 85.

[75] *George Mitchell (Chesterhall) Ltd v Finney Lock Seeds Ltd* [1983] Q.B. 284 at 309, affirmed without reference to this point [1983] 2 A.C. 803.

[76] *Gallagher v BRS Ltd* [1974] 2 Lloyd's Rep. 440; *J Evans & Son (Portsmouth) Ltd v Andrea Merzario* [1976] 1 W.L.R. 1078; *cf. Mendelssohn v Normand Ltd* [1970] 1 Q.B. 177.

[77] See *Toomey v Eagle Star Insurance Co* [1995] 2 Lloyd's Rep. 89, where the clause on its true construction was held not to cover *negligent* misrepresentation.

[78] See below, p.385.

[79] [1892] 3 Ch. 441. In so far as this case decides that the architect's decision was final *on a point of law*, it will not be followed: *Re Davstone Estates Ltd's Leases* [1969] 2 Ch. 378.

[80] *Czarnikow v Roth, Schmidt & Co* [1922] 2 K.B. 478 at 488.

[81] *S Pearson & Son Ltd v Dublin Corporation* [1907] A.C. 351 at 353, 362; *Shipskreditforeningen v Emperor Navigation* [1998] 1 Lloyd's Rep. 67 at 76; *cf. Garden Neptune Shipping Ltd v Occidental Worldwide Investment Corp* [1990] 1 Lloyd's Rep. 330 at 335.

[82] *S Pearson & Son Ltd v Dublin Corporation*, above; *Walker v Boyle* [1982] 1 W.L.R. 495. *cf. Schneider v Heath* (1813) 3 Camp. 506 and *Re Englefield Holdings* [1962] 1 W.L.R. 1119; *Thomas Witter Ltd v TBP Industries Ltd* [1996] 2 All E.R. 573 at 598.

[83] *HIH Casualty & General Insurance v Chase Manhattan Bank* [2001] EWCA Civ 1250; [2001] 2 Lloyd's Rep 483, at [110].

liability: that is, there must be an "express reference to fraud" or "language which is in every way the equivalent of such express reference."[84]

(4) Excluding liability for breach of certain fiduciary duties

The promoter of a company is under a fiduciary duty to the company not to make a profit out of the promotion without disclosing it to the company.[85] He cannot contract out of this duty.[86] It is submitted that any contract term by which a person who was under a fiduciary duty attempted to exempt himself from liability for a deliberate breach of that duty would be similarly ineffective.[87]

(5) Excluding "natural justice"

Where members of an association agree to submit certain disputes to a domestic tribunal, that tribunal is *prima facie* bound by certain rules of "natural justice". It must give each party a fair hearing and a chance to rebut the case that is made against him; and its members must not have any pecuniary interest in the dispute or any other interest which is likely to bias them.[88] In a number of cases[89] Lord Denning M.R. has said that a provision in the rules of an association would be void if it purported to oust the rules of "natural justice."

(6) Unreasonableness

It is sometimes said that exemption clauses may be held invalid on the ground that they are "unreasonable in themselves or irrelevant to the main purpose of the contract"[90] or "so unreasonable that no-one could contemplate that they exist".[91] Unreasonableness of the latter kind can certainly be relevant to the process of incorporation of a clause in a contract, in the sense that the degree of notice required for this purpose increases in proportion to the unusualness of the clause.[92] Some dicta go further and suggest that even a properly incorporated clause can be invalid on the ground of unreasonableness[93]

---

[84] *ibid.* at [159].

[85] See Gower, *Modern Company Law* (6th ed.), pp.297, 133 *et seq.*

[86] *Gluckstein v Barnes* [1900] A.C. 240. This rule is quite independent of the statutory provisions referred to at p.399, below.

[87] Contrast *Bogg v Raper, The Times,* April 22, 1998 (liability for *negligence* of a solicitor as a trustee of a will drawn up by himself effectively excluded).

[88] See de Smith, Woolf and Jowell, *Judicial Review of Administrative Action* (5th ed.), Chaps 7 to 12, for a full account of these rules.

[89] *Lee v Showmen's Guild* [1952] 2 Q.B. 329; *Bonsor v Musicians' Union* [1954] Ch. 479 (dissenting): the majority decision was reversed by the House of Lords [1956] A.C. 104, without reference to this point. *cf. Edwards v SOGAT* [1971] Ch. 354 at 382; *Enderby Town FC Ltd v The FA Ltd* [1971] Ch. 591 at 606; *Breen v AEU* [1971] 2 Q.B. 175 at 190; and see *London Export Corp v Jubilee Coffee Roasting Co* [1958] 1 W.L.R. 661. For the contrary view, see *Maclean v The Workers' Union* [1929] Ch. 602 at 603; *cf. Russell v Duke of Norfolk* [1949] 1 All E.R. 109, where a majority of the Court of Appeal held that an undertaking to observe the rules of natural justice could not be implied into a contract the terms of which gave the domestic tribunal an absolute discretion. See also *Fontaine v Chesterton* (1968) S.J. 690, discussed in *John v Rees* [1970] Ch. 345 at 398–400.

[90] *Watkins v Rymill* (1883) 10 Q.B.D. 178 at 189.

[91] *Thompson v London, Midland & Scottish Ry* [1930] 1 K.B. 41 at 56.

[92] See above, p.219; *cf.* (in relation to terms *other* than exemption clauses) below, p.246.

[93] See Lord Denning M.R. in *Thornton v Shoe Lane Parking Ltd* [1971] 2 Q.B. 163 at 170; *Gillespie Bros & Co Ltd v Roy Bowles Transport Ltd* [1973] Q.B. 400 at 416; *Levison v Patent Steam Carpet Cleaning Co Ltd* [1978] Q.B. 68 at 69; *Re Brocklehurst (dec'd)* [1978] Ch. 14 at 31 (dissenting); *Standard Chartered Bank Ltd v Walker* [1982] 1 W.L.R. 1410 at 1416.

or unfairness.[94] But no decision squarely supports this view, which is also rejected in other dicta.[95]

Many exemption clauses are now subject to a requirement of reasonableness under the Unfair Contract Terms Act 1977 or to one of fairness under the Unfair Terms in Consumer Contracts Regulations 1999.[96] One possible view is that the courts might rely by way of analogy on these requirements so as to develop similar requirements at common law. But such a development would be open to the objection that it would extend the requirements precisely to cases from which the legislator had deliberately excluded them; and it is submitted that the better view is that the existence of the legislative requirements has reduced both the need for, and the likelihood of, the recognition of unreasonableness or unfairness as grounds for the invalidity of exemption clauses[97] at common law.[98]

(7) Third parties

The question whether exemption clauses can protect or prejudice third parties is discussed in Chapter 15.[99]

SECTION 2. OTHER STANDARD TERMS AT COMMON LAW

The problem raised by standard terms is by no means confined to exemption clauses. It can arise also where such terms confer rights on the party relying on them, or where they restrictively define the other party's rights under the contract (other than those based on the former party's breach).

The first of these possibilities is illustrated by cases which raise the question at what stage an estate agent is entitled to his commission. This question is more fully discussed in Chapter 17[1]; here it need only be noted that the courts have tried, by various more or less strained constructions, to uphold the principle that no commission is payable if no sale takes place (unless the sale falls through because of the client's default). But in the end the courts were unable to maintain this principle in the teeth of clearly worded contracts entitling the agent to his commission whether a sale resulted from his efforts or not.[2] The second possibility is illustrated by standard terms in contracts of insurance which may make statements by the assured the basis of the contract even though they are of little importance in relation to the risk. The effect of such clauses is that the insurer can repudiate liability for some quite trivial misstatement.[3]

---

[94] *Laceys Footwear (Wholesale) Ltd v Bowler International Ltd* [1997] 2 Lloyd's Rep. 369 at 384–385, *per* Brooke L.J.; the majority based their decision on the construction of the clause: see above, **p.221**.

[95] *Van Toll v South Eastern Ry* (1862) 12 C.B.N.S. 75 at 85; *Grand Trunk Ry of Canada v Robinson* [1915] A.C. 740 at 747; *Luddit v Ginger Coote Airways Ltd* [1947] A.C. 233 at 242.

[96] See below, pp.252–258, 271–279.

[97] For other standard terms, see below, p.246.

[98] *Clark v West Ham Corp* [1909] 2 K.B. 858 is best explained as turning on the construction of the relevant statute.

[99] See below, pp.626 *et seq.*

[1] See below, pp.742–744.

[2] Note, however, the view of Lord Denning M.R. in *Jaques v Lloyd D George & Partners Ltd* [1968] 1 W.L.R. 625, stated below, p.743, n.24. The Estate Agents Act 1979, s.18 has done nothing to resolve the problem; it merely requires the agent to inform the client of the circumstances in which commission will become due. If the agent complies with the requirements imposed by or under the Act, the Unfair Terms in Consumer Contracts Regulations 1999 seem to be excluded: see reg.4(2)(a).

[3] See below, p.396. The Unfair Contract Terms Act 1977 does not alter this position: below p.264; the Unfair Terms in Consumer Contracts Regulations 1999 might apply as contracts of insurance are not specifically excepted from their operation; see further below, p.272.

To a limited extent the courts have been able to protect the weaker contracting party in some such situations. They have, for example, held that the rules which govern the incorporation of exemption clauses[4] and some of the rules which govern their construction[5] also apply to certain standard terms[6] which purport to confer rights on the party relying on those terms. Such reasoning also forms one basis of *Interfoto Picture Library Ltd v Stiletto Visual Programmes Ltd*.[7] In that case, the defendants (an advertising agency) had hired photographic transparencies from the claimants under a contract allegedly incorporating the terms of the claimants' delivery note, which had been sent with the goods. One of these terms purported to make the defendants liable for a "holding charge" of £5 per day (an unusually high rate)[8] for each transparency retained for more than 14 days. In holding that the defendants were not liable to pay this charge, both members of the Court of Appeal regarded it as crucial that the claimants had failed to take reasonable steps to bring the term to the attention of the defendants. But while Dillon L.J. drew from this failure the orthodox conclusion that the term had not been incorporated in the contract,[9] it is less clear exactly why Bingham L.J. regarded the failure as vital. It seems that he so regarded it (even on the assumption, that the terms of the delivery note *had* been incorporated into the contract),[10] because, on account of the failure, it would not be "fair to hold [the defendants] bound by the condition in question".[11] He went on to suggest that "this may yield a result not very different from the civil law principle of good faith, at any rate so far as the formation of the contract is concerned".[12] The reference here to "formation" seems to indicate that Bingham L.J. was, after all, concerned with the incorporation of the clause and perhaps intended to make the point that "this unreasonable and extortionate clause"[13] was not incorporated *merely* because the formal requirements of offer and acceptance had been satisfied[14]: there must, in addition, be "fair" notice, and the degree of notice required increases with the unusualness or unreasonableness of the clause.[15] But once the requisite degree of notice has been given, the English common law does not, as a general rule, control the *substance* of the clause; it does not impose any further requirement that contracts must be reasonable or that contractual rights must be exercised reasonably.[16] The rejection by

---

[4] See above, pp.216–220.

[5] See above, pp.220 *et. seq.* Obviously, the rules governing cases of serious breach (above, pp.225–241) cannot apply where there is no breach.

[6] *e.g.* indemnity clauses: above, p.218, n.38 and some clauses conferring rights to be paid: *Sonat Offshore SA v Amerada Hess Development Ltd* [1988] 1 Lloyd's Rep. 191.

[7] [1989] Q.B. 433.

[8] *ibid.* at 436: a reasonable rate would have been £3.50 per transparency per week.

[9] See above, p.219.

[10] [1989] Q.B. at 445: "I do not think that the defendants could successfully contend that [the conditions] were not incorporated in the contract."

[11] *ibid.*; *cf. Timeload Ltd v British Telecommunications plc* [1995] E.M.L.R. 459 at 468; contrast *Nutting v Baldwin* [1995] 1 W.L.R. 201 at 211, where the term was "neither onerous nor unusual;" *cf.* above, p.219, n.51.

[12] [1989] Q.B. 433 at 445; this approach was favoured by Brooke L.J. in *Laceys Footwear (Wholesale) Ltd v Bowler International Ltd* [1997] 2 Lloyd's Rep. 369 at 384 (where the clause in question was a limitation clause).

[13] [1989] Q.B. 433 at 445. *Semble*, it does not for this purpose suffice merely that the clause was *unusual*: *HIH Casualty & General Insurance Ltd v New Hampshire Insurance Co* [2001] EWCA Civ 735; [2001] 2 All E.R. (Comm) 39, at [211].

[14] *cf.* above, p.47.

[15] See above, p.219.

[16] See, for example *Margaronis Navigation Agency Ltd v Henry W Peabody of London Ltd* [1965] 1 Q.B. 300; *Innisfail Laundry v Dawe* (1963) 107 S.J. 437; for exceptions, see above, pp.65, 168, and below, pp.1009–1010; and *cf. Paula Lee Ltd v Robert Zehil & Co Ltd* [1983] 2 All E.R. 390; *Walkinshaw v Dinitz* [2001] 1 Lloyd's Rep. 632 at 649, affirmed [2002] 2 Lloyd's Rep. 165.

the courts of the substantive doctrine of fundamental breach[17] can be said to support this general common law rule. In a number of situations to be discussed later in this Chapter, standard terms other than exemption clauses are now subject to legislative control; and the need for such legislation seems to be based on the assumption that, at common law, the principle of freedom of contract as a general rule applies[18] to cases of the kind discussed in this Section.

There may, however, be highly exceptional cases in which the common law is prepared to recognise exceptions to its general rule. It has, for example, been said that a term in a contract for the deposit of goods at a railway station would be void for unreasonableness if it provided that £1,000 was to be forfeited if the goods were not collected within 48 hours.[19] The far-fetched nature of the example suggests that this common law exception to the general rule is not likely to have much practical importance. The invalidity of penalty clauses[20] could be regarded as another common law exception to the general rule; but this exception is limited in scope, as a clause is penal only if it requires a payment[21] to be made *on breach*: not if it specifies some other event on which the payment is to be made.[22]

SECTION 3. LEGISLATIVE LIMITATIONS ON EFFECTIVENESS OF STANDARD TERMS

The most important legislative limitations on the effectiveness of standard terms are now contained in the Unfair Contract Terms Act 1977 and in the Unfair Terms in Consumer Contracts Regulations 1999. These two sets of provisions overlap, so that some types of terms are governed by both of them and others by one though not by the other.[23] The resulting structure is complex and proposals to simplify it by combining the two sets of rules into a single legislative scheme are under consideration by the Law Commissions.[24] In the present Section, we shall deal only with one technique of control (used by this and other legislation), which is to deprive certain exemption clauses and standard terms of their legal force. Other legislative techniques will be considered in the next Section of this Chapter.

1. The Unfair Contract Terms Act 1977[25]

The Act deals almost exclusively with exemption clauses in contracts[26]; it makes some such clauses ineffective in all circumstances and others ineffective unless they comply with a requirement of reasonableness.

---

[17] See above, pp.225–226.

[18] *cf.* below, pp.395–396, 422–423.

[19] *Parker v South Eastern Ry* (1876) 2 C.P.D. 416 at 428.

[20] See below, pp.999 *et seq.*

[21] Or some other performance: below, p.1003.

[22] See below, pp.1004–1006; in the example in *Parker's* case, above at n.19, it seems that failure to collect the goods is not a breach, so that the clause is not a penalty.

[23] See further p.267 below.

[24] Law Commission Consultation Paper No.166, Scottish Law Commission Discussion Paper No.119 (2002).

[25] Thompson, *Unfair Contract Terms Act 1977*; Coote, (1978) 41 M.L.R. 312; Sealy [1978] C.L.J. 15; Reynolds, [1978] 1 L.M.C.L.Q. 201; Adams and Brownsword, 104 L.Q.R. 94.

[26] See above, p.216 n.10. The Act also deals with certain notices not having contractual effect, *e.g.* in ss.2 and 11(3). Attempts by such notices to exclude or restrict tort liability are beyond the scope of this book.

(1) Preliminary definitions

The operation of the Act depends on a number of preliminary definitions.

(a) "BUSINESS LIABILITY" AND "DEALING AS CONSUMER". The Act defines "business liability" as "liability for breach of obligations or duties arising (a) from things done or to be done by a person in the course of a business (whether his own business or another's); or (b) from the occupation of premises used for business purposes of the occupier".[27] Such a person will in the following discussion be called B.

A person "deals as consumer" if he does not make (or hold himself out as making) the contract in the course of a business *and* the other party does make the contract in the course of a business.[28] For this purpose, a contract is made "in the course of" a business only if it forms part of the *regular* course of dealing of that business.[29] In the case of contracts for the supply of goods, it is also except where the goods are supplied to an individual,[29a] necessary for the goods to be of a type ordinarily supplied for private use or consumption.[30] A buyer of goods is not to be regarded as dealing as consumer, (a) if he is an individual and the goods are second hand goods sold at public auction which individuals have the opportunity of attending in person; or (b) if he is not an individual and the goods are sold by auction or competetive tender.[31] In the following discussion a person who deals as consumer will be called C.

Generally, contracts will be made between B and C, or between B1 and B2. It is, however, impossible to have a contract between two persons each of whom deals as consumer, since it is part of the definition of dealing as consumer that one party does, while the other does not, make the contract in the course of a business. If, for example, a

---

[27] s.1(3). "Business" includes a profession and activities of government departments or local or public authorities: s.14. Liability to persons gaining access to premises for recreational or educational purposes is excepted, in certain circumstances, by Occupiers' Liability Act 1984, s.2

[28] s.12(1)(a) and (b). The EC Directive on the Sale of Consumer Goods and Associated Guarantees (Dir. 1999/44) defines "consumer" more narrowly to mean "any natural person who, in the contracts covered by this Directive, is acting for purposes not related to his trade, business or profession". The Regulations which implement this Directive in the UK use similar language in defining "consumer" as "any natural person who, in contracts covered by these Regulations, is acting for purposes which are outside his trade, business or profession" (Sale and Supply of Goods to Consumers Regulations 2002, SI 2002/3045, reg.2). But the techniques adopted by these Regulations to give effect to the new rights specified in the Directive are (1) to widen the scope of one the statutorily implied terms as to quality, where the person to whom the goods are supplied "deals as consumer" (regs.3, 7, 9, 10 and 13) and (2) to give certain additional remedies or rights to such persons where the supplier is in breach of certain statutorily implied terms or of an express term (regs.5 and 9). The expression "dealing as consumer" is defined in the relevant statutes by cross-reference to the Unfair Contract Terms Act 1977: see Sale of Goods Act 1979, s.61(5A), Supply of Goods and Services Act 1982, s.18(4), Supply of Goods (Implied Terms) Act 1973, s.11A(4). The reference is to s.12 of the 1977 Act, which is amended by the 2002 Regulations but not so as to restrict the definition of consumer, even in contracts for the supply of goods, to natural persons: see text at nn.29a and 30, below. Hence "dealing as consumer" in the Acts above referred to seems to have a wider meaning than that of "consumer" in the Regulations.

[29] *R & B Customs Brokers Ltd v United Dominions Trust Ltd* [1988] 1 W.L.R. 321 (company held to have dealt as consumer in buying a car for use of one of its directors, having only made two or three such purchases in the past); Price, 52 M.L.R. 245; Jones and Harland, 2 J.C.L. 266. The amendment to s.12(1)(c) referred to in n.24 below does not affect this position: it merely removes the requirement that the goods must be of a type ordinarily supplied for private use or consumption from cases in which the buyer, etc. is a natural person. Contrast the interpretation in *Stevenson v Rogers* [1991] 1 All E.R. 613 of "course of business" in Sale of Goods Act 1979, s.14(2).

[29a] s.12(1A), as inserted by Sale and Supply of Goods to Consumers Regulations 2002 (SI 2002/3045), reg.14(2).

[30] s.12(1)(c) as amended by Sale and Supply of Goods to Consumers Regulations 2002 (SI 2002/3045), reg.14(2).

[31] s.12(2), as substituted by Sale and Supply of Goods to Consumer Regulations 2002 (SI 2002/3045), reg.14(3).

car were sold "privately" (neither buyer nor seller acting in the course of a business) there would be no dealing as consumer. However, a person can deal as consumer in disposing of goods, no less than in acquiring goods or services: for example, if the "private" (non-business) owner of a car transferred it to a car dealer in part-exchange for a new car, he would deal as consumer in relation to the first as well as to the second vehicle.

(b) EXCLUDING OR RESTRICTING LIABILITY. Many sections of the Act limit the effectiveness of clauses that "exclude or restrict" liability. To the same extent these sections also prevent a party from doing certain analogous things: for example, from imposing a short time limit within which claims must be brought, or from excluding a particular remedy (such as rejection or set-off)[32] without affecting another (such as damages).[33] Other clauses which do not in terms exclude or restrict liability may nevertheless have this effect in substance. For example, a provision in a contract between X and Y that Y will indemnify X for any liability which X may incur to Y is in substance a clause excluding X's liability to Y and will be treated as such for the purposes of the Act.[34] A clause requiring an employee to work such long hours as would lead to injury to his health could likewise be regarded as one which exempted the employer from liability which, but for the clause, he would incur in respect of the injury.[35] On the other hand, a valid agreed damages clause[36] is probably not subject to the Act, for such a clause may extend as well as restrict liability. An agreement in writing to submit present or future differences to arbitration is not to be treated as excluding or restricting liability.[37]

In two cases, the Act prevents a party from excluding or restricting *duties* (as opposed to *liabilities*): namely where a provision purports to exclude (i) the duty of care giving rise to liability in negligence[38] or (ii) the duties arising out of terms implied by statute in contracts for the supply of goods.[39] Apart from these cases, the Act does not strike at provisions which exclude or restrict duties. Thus a provision purporting to exclude or restrict a seller's duty as to the fitness of goods for a particular purpose would only be effective to the extent permitted by the Act[40]; but the effectiveness of a clause qualifying a provision as to the time of delivery (*e.g.* by making it "subject to strikes" or "subject to availability") would not be governed by the Act.[41]

At common law a distinction is sometimes drawn between clauses which exclude or restrict liability and those which prevent it from arising[42] and in some cases this distinction is no doubt relevant for the purposes of the Act. For example, if a seller of goods expressly warned the buyer *not* to use goods for a specified purpose, any implied term of fitness for that particular purpose would be negatived, and the warning would not be subject to the Act.[43] But to give such effect to all provisions which might at

---

[32] *Stewart Gill Ltd v Horatio Myer & Co Ltd* [1992] Q.B. 600; *Esso Petroleum Ltd v Milton* [1997] 1 W.L.R. 938; *Schenkers Ltd v Overland Shoes Ltd* [1998] 1 Lloyd's Rep. 499; *cf. BOC Group plc v Centeon plc* [1999] 1 All E.R. (Comm) 970.

[33] s.13(1).

[34] *Phillips Products Ltd v Hyland* [1987] 1 W.L.R. 659, below, p.256.

[35] *Johnstone v Bloomsbury Health Authority* [1992] Q.B. 333.

[36] See above, p.237; below, p.999. For the position under the Unfair Terms in Consumer Contracts Regulations 1999, see p.268 below.

[37] s.13(2). Contrast the position under the Unfair Terms in Consumer Contracts Regulations 1999, below, p.269.

[38] See the reference to ss.2 and 5 in s.13(1).

[39] See the reference to ss.6 and 7 in s.13(1).

[40] See s.6(1) and (2).

[41] s.3(2)(b)(ii) would not apply to such a clause: see below, p.253.

[42] *cf.* above, p.238.

[43] *Wormell v RHM Agriculture (East) Ltd* [1987] 1 W.L.R. 1091; *cf. Harlingdon & Leinster Enterprises Ltd v Christopher Hull Fine Art Ltd* [1990] 1 All E.R. 737 at 753, and the examples given at p.238, above.

common law prevent liability from arising would, it has been said, "emasculate"[44] the Act. In *Smith v Eric S Bush*[45] the House of Lords has therefore held that a clause purporting to exclude responsibility for negligence on the part of the valuer of a house was subject to the test of reasonableness under the Act. The decision was based on s.13(1) of the Act, by which a term purporting to exclude the duty of care giving rise to liability in negligence is to be treated as a term excluding or restricting liability. In order to determine whether such a duty existed, the court must disregard the term purporting to exclude it, and ask itself whether, but for the existence of the term, there would have been such a duty; if so, the effectiveness of term is then subject to the restrictions imposed by the Act. It seems likely that the courts will also "look behind" certain other clauses which are similarly being used in an obvious attempt to evade the Act.[46]

(2) Ineffective terms

In the following cases, attempts to exclude or restrict liability are wholly ineffective under the 1977 Act or under other legislation.

(a) NEGLIGENCE LIABILITY: DEATH OR PERSONAL INJURY. By s.2(1) of the 1977 Act, B[47] cannot by any contract term or notice exclude or restrict his[48] liability for death or personal injury[49] resulting from negligence[50] to any person (whether C or not). Provisions excluding *strict* liability for death or personal injury are not affected by s.2(1). Under other legislation, any provision in a contract for the carriage of passengers by rail[51] or by road in a public service vehicle[52] is void if it purports to negative or limit the liability of the carrier in respect of the death or personal injury of the passenger. These Acts do not expressly refer to negligence, but since the carrier is not liable in the absence of negligence[53] their scope is restricted to negligence liability.

S.2(1) does not apply where death or personal injury results from a breach of contract or duty which can be, and is, committed without negligence: for example, where a seller supplies defective goods to a buyer, where a producer incurs "product liability" in respect of defective products, or where a person who does work for the provision of a dwelling fits defective components.[54] Clauses purporting to exclude liability for such

---

[44] *Smith v Eric S Bush* [1990] 1 A.C. 831 at 848.
[45] See above, n.44; *cf. Davies v Parry* [1988] 1 E.G.L.R. 147.
[46] *cf.* below, p.386. *Smith v Eric S. Bush*, above, deals only with clauses purporting to exclude the duty of care giving rise to liability in negligence. It seems that the "but for" test there formulated would not apply to sale of goods cases such as *Wormell v RHM Agriculture (East) Ltd*, above, n.43: in order to determine for what "particular purpose" goods had been bought, a warning such as the one given in that case would, it is submitted, have to be taken into account. For possible application of the Unfair Terms in Consumer Contracts Regulations 1999, see below, pp.273–274.
[47] See s.1(3).
[48] s.2 does not prevent a contracting party from excluding or restricting the liability of a *third* party: *The Chevalier Roze* [1983] 2 Lloyd's Rep. 438 at 442. For the effect of the section on indemnity clauses, see below, p.256.
[49] As defined by s.14.
[50] As defined by s.1(1). "Negligence" is there stated to include "breach . . . of any obligation, arising from the . . . terms . . . of a contract, to take reasonable care . . . ;" for the purpose of this definition the court must apply the "but for" test (above, n.46), *i.e.* it must disregard a clause the effect of which is (or would be, if the clause were valid) to exclude liability for such a breach: *Phillips Products Ltd v Hyland* [1987] 1 W.L.R. 659.
[51] Transport Act 1962, s.43(7).
[52] Public Passenger Vehicles Act 1981, s.29. *cf.* also Financial Services and Markets Act 2000, s.253 (dealing with purely financial loss).
[53] *Readhead v Midland Ry* (1869) L.R. 4 Q.B. 376; *Barkway v S. Wales Transport Co Ltd* [1950] 1 All E.R. 392 at 403–404.
[54] For strict liability in such cases, see below, p.839.

breaches may, however, be ineffective under other provisions of the Act,[55] or under other Acts.[56]

(b) "GUARANTEES" OF CONSUMER GOODS. S.5 deals with provisions in "guarantees" of goods of a type ordinarily supplied for private use or consumption. It does not apply between the parties to the contract for the supply of the goods[57]: exemption clauses in such contracts are regulated by ss.6 and 7. It is aimed at the relations between manufacturer and customer under so-called manufacturers' guarantees.[58]

The section defines a "guarantee" as a written promise or assurance that defects will be made good.[59] It provides that B[60] cannot by means of such a guarantee exclude or restrict liability for loss or damage that arises from defects in the goods while in "consumer use" and results from the negligence of a person concerned in the manufacture or distribution of the goods.[61] Goods are in "consumer use" when a person is using them or has them in his possession otherwise than *exclusively* for the purpose of a business. Thus generally s.5 will apply only between B and C. But it may also apply in certain other circumstances: for example, where a car is bought in the course of a business (so that the buyer does not deal as consumer) and used partly for business and partly for private purposes.

Under the Sale and Supply of Goods to Consumers Regulations 2002, a "consumer guarantee" relating to goods supplied to a consumer "takes effect . . . as a contractual obligation owed by the guarantor."[62] The Regulations do not themselves[62a] prohibit exclusion or restriction of liability *under the guarantee*: *e.g.* by terms imposing a short time limit, or a low financial limit, on claims under the guarantee; but it seems that, if the "consumer guarantee" were also a "guarantee" within s.5 of the 1997 Act, then the validity of such terms would be open to attack under that section.[62b] Terms limiting the "duration" of the guarantee itself,[62c] or restricting the consumer's right under it to one to the return of the price,[62d] seem however, to be authorised under the Regulations, so that their validity is not open to attack under the Act.[62e] The definition of a "consumer guarantee" in the Regulations differs significantly from that of a "guarantee" in the Act: in particular, the "consumer" under the Regulations must be a "natural person"[62f]; the "guarantor" may be the other party to the contract for the supply of the goods to the consumer[62g]; and there is no requirement of "consumer use" in the Regulations.

---

[55] *e.g.* ss.6, 7.
[56] Defective Premises Act 1972, s.1(1) ("proper materials") and s.6(3). Consumer Protection Act, 1987, ss.5 and 7(1); below, p.252.
[57] s.5(3).
[58] See above, p.77 and below, p.582.
[59] s.5(2)(b); making good is defined so as to include payment of compensation.
[60] See s.1(3).
[61] s.5(1). Consumer Protection Act 1987, s.7 (below, p.252) could also apply to such a guarantee.
[62] SI 2002/3045 (implementing Directive 1999/44), reg.15(1).
[62a] For such a prohibition, see Directive 1999/44, Art.7.
[62b] Thus securing compliance with Art.7, above.
[62c] SI 2002/3045, reg.15(2) ("duration").
[62d] *ibid.* reg.2 (definition of "consumer guarantee").
[62e] Unfair Contract Terms Act 1977, s.29, below p.266.
[62f] Reg.2 (definition of "consumer").
[62g] Reg.2 (definition of "guarantor").

(c) SALE OF GOODS AND HIRE-PURCHASE. S.6(1) provides that liability for breach of the undertakings as to title implied by statute[63] into contracts for the sale or hire-purchase of goods cannot be excluded or restricted by reference to any contract term. S.6(2) lays down the same rule, but only "as against a person dealing as consumer", in relation to the statutorily implied terms as to correspondence of the goods with description or sample, and as to their quality or fitness for a particular purpose.[64]

As a general principle the only types of terms made completely ineffective by the Act are those purporting to exclude or restrict "business liability".[65] S.6(4), however, provides that the liabilities referred to "in this section" are not only "business liabilities . . . but include those arising under any contract of sale of goods or hire-purchase agreement". It follows that a private (non-business) seller cannot exclude or restrict liability for breach of the implied undertakings as to title. At first sight, s.6(4) suggests that an attempt by a private seller to exclude or restrict liability for breach of the implied undertakings as to correspondence with description, etc., (referred to in s.6(2)) is equally ineffective. But s.6(2) applies only "as against a person dealing as consumer", and a person can so deal only if "the other party does make the contract in the course of a business".[66] Since a private seller does not contract "in the course of a business", it seems that a person who buys from such a seller does not "deal as consumer" and is not protected by s.6(2); he is protected only by the requirement of reasonableness.[67] In some cases, indeed, the statutorily implied term only arises at all where the supplier acts in the course of a business. This is true of the implied terms as to satisfactory quality and fitness for a particular purpose.[68] Here the private supplier is never subject to the statutorily implied term at all, and so the issue of the validity of a clause excluding liability for breach of it cannot arise.[69]

(d) OTHER CONTRACTS FOR THE SUPPLY OF GOODS. S.7 deals with contracts for the supply of goods other than contracts of sale and hire purchase: for example, contracts of exchange, pledge or hire. By statute, such contracts contain implied terms as to title, correspondence with description or sample, quality and fitness for a particular purpose.[70] As against C, B[71] cannot, in such contracts, exclude or restrict liability in respect of the failure of the goods to correspond with their description or with a sample, or in

---

[63] By Sale of Goods Act 1979, s.12 and Supply of Goods (Implied Terms) Act 1973, s.8 as substituted by Consumer Credit Act 1974, s.192 and Sch.4, para.35. For amendments of the 1979 and 1973 Acts, see Sale and Supply of Goods Act 1994 s.7 and Sch.2.

[64] By Sale of Goods Act 1979, ss.13–15 and Supply of Goods (Implied Terms) Act 1973, ss.9–11 as substituted by Consumer Credit Act 1974, s.192 and Sch.4, para.35; for amendments see above n.63; *Hughes v Hall and Hall* [1981] R.T.R. 430. The Regulations referred to in n.62 above make further amendments to s.14 of the 1979 Act (reg.3) and confer additional rights or remedies on buyers who deal as consumers (Sale of Goods Act 1979 ss.48A–48D, as inserted by reg.5 of those Regulations). It seems that these new provisions are subject to s.6(2) of the Unfair Contract Terms Act 1977. For the meaning of the phrase "dealing as consumer" for this purpose see above, p.247, n.28. Similar amendments are made by the same Regulations to the Sale of Goods (Implied Terms) Act 1973 below, n.68) and to the Supply of Goods and Services Act 1982 (below n.70; see regs.7, 9, 10 and 13).

[65] See s.1(3) of the 1977 Act.

[66] s.12(1)(b).

[67] s.6(3), below, p.254.

[68] Sale of Goods Act 1979, s.14(2) (as substituted by Sale and Supply of Goods Act 1994, s.1) and (3); Supply of Goods (Implied Terms) Act 1973, s.10(2) and (3) as substituted by Consumer Credit Act 1974, s.192 and Sch.4, para.35. For further amendments of the 1979 and 1973 Acts, see above n.64.

[69] See further below, pp.254–255.

[70] Supply of Goods and Services Act 1982, ss.2–5, 7–10, as amended by Sale and Supply of Goods Act 1994 s.7 and Sch.2. For further amendments of the 1982 Act, see above n.64.

[71] Unfair Contract Terms Act 1977, s.1(3).

respect of their quality or fitness for a particular purpose.[72] So far as liability for breach of the implied terms as to title is concerned, a distinction must be drawn. Such liability cannot be excluded by B[73] where the contract is one by which he transfers or agrees to transfer the property in the goods to another (not necessarily C): this rule would, for example, apply to a contract of exchange. But where the contract is not one by which property is transferred or to be transferred (*e.g.* where it is one of pledge or hire) attempts by B[74] to exclude or restrict such liability are subject only to the test of reasonableness.[75]

(e) PRODUCT LIABILITY. Under Pt I of the Consumer Protection Act 1987, producers, and certain other persons engaged in the distribution, of products which are defective, in the sense of being unsafe, are liable if the defect causes death or personal injury or certain kinds of damage to property. S.7 of the 1987 Act provides that such "product liability" (which arises without proof of negligence and irrespective of contract) cannot be limited or excluded by any contract term, notice or other provision.

(f) DANGEROUS GOODS. Under Pt II of the Consumer Protection Act 1987, it is an offence to supply goods which do not comply with a general safety requirement laid down by the Act and in safety regulations made under the Act. Failure to perform an obligation imposed by such a regulation gives a civil remedy to any person who may be affected by a contravention of the obligation; and the resulting liability cannot be excluded by any contract term, notice or other provision.[76]

(g) DISTANCE SELLING. The Consumer Protection (Distance Selling) Regulations 2000 provide, that in "distance contracts" between a commercial supplier of goods or services and a consumer, the consumer must be given specified information and is to have a right to cancel within a specified period and with specified consequences.[77] The Regulations also specify the time within which such contracts must be performed by the supplier, as well as certain legal consequences of his failure to perform it.[78] A term in such a contract is void if and to the extent it is inconsistent with a provision for the protection of the consumer contained in the Regulations.[79]

(3) Terms subject to the requirement of reasonableness[80]

In the following cases, exemption clauses are, under the 1977 Act, subject to the requirement of reasonableness. Where the requirement applies, the burden of showing (and of pleading[81]) that it is satisfied lies on the party so claiming.[82]

(a) NEGLIGENCE LIABILITY: HARM OTHER THAN DEATH OR PERSONAL INJURY. By s.2(2) the requirement applies to a contract term or notice by which B[83] seeks to exclude or restrict his[84] liability for negligence[85] giving rise to loss or damage other than death

---

[72] *ibid.* s.7(2).
[73] ss.1(3) and 7(3A), as inserted by Supply of Goods and Services Act 1982, s.17(2).
[74] Unfair Contract Terms Act 1977, s.1(3).
[75] *ibid.* s.7(4), as amended by Supply of Goods and Services Act 1982, s.17(3).
[76] Consumer Protection Act 1987, ss.10, 41(1) and (4).
[77] SI 2000/2334 (implementing Dir.97/7), regs 7–18.
[78] *ibid.* regs 19, 20. "Consumer" is defined in reg.3(1).
[79] *ibid.* reg.25.
[80] Brown and Chandler, 109 L.Q.R. 41.
[81] *Sheffield v Pickfords Ltd* [1997] C.L.C. 648.
[82] Unfair Contract Terms Act 1977, s.11(5).
[83] s.1(3).
[84] See above, p.249, n.48. For the effect of the section on indemnity clauses, see below, p.256.
[85] As defined by s.1(1).

or personal injury. The subsection does not apply to provisions excluding or restricting *strict* liability[86]; on the other hand it is not confined to cases where the other party deals as consumer. In both these respects, it resembles s.2(1).

(b) CONSUMER CONTRACTS AND STANDARD FORM CONTRACTS. S.3 applies to two situations: to any contract between B and C[87]; and to a contract in which a party (not necessarily C) deals with B on the latter's "written standard terms of business".[88] In such cases B cannot "by reference to any contract term", except insofar as it satisfies the requirement of reasonableness, do any of the following three things:

(i) Under s.3(2)(a) B cannot exclude or restrict any liability in respect of his own breach. "Any liability" here includes strict liability[89] for breach of contract.

(ii) Under s.3(2)(b)(i) B cannot "claim to be entitled . . . to render a contractual performance substantially different[90] from that which was reasonably expected of him". It has been held that a clause giving a lender power to vary interest rates did not fall within s.3(2)(b)(i) since the exercise of that power was not a "contractual performance."[91] Where a term in a contract for services entitles the provider to change those services, the questions what the recipient reasonably expected and whether the change is substantial can obviously give rise to difficult questions of fact and degree.[92] It seems that s.3(2)(b)(i) could apply to provisions in a contract between a carrier and a tour operator purporting to entitle the carrier to change the advertised route, accommodations or means of transport.[93] B could not rely on the provision even though he was not actually obliged to render the performance expected: the criterion is the reasonable expectation of the other party, not the obligation of B under the contract. There would, however, be no such reasonable expectation where the contract made it clear that, while B would endeavour to provide a particular service, he also reserved the right to substitute a reasonable alternative.[94]

---

[86] See above, p.249. A contract term or notice purporting to exclude certain types of property damage is ineffective irrespective of reasonableness: Consumer Protection Act 1987, ss.5, 7(1), above.

[87] An employee was held to have dealt as consumer with his employer for the purpose of s.3 in *Brigden v American Express Bank Ltd* [2000] I.R.L.R 94.

[88] s.3(1). This part of the section does not generally apply to specially negotiated contracts: *The Flammar Pride* [1990] 1 Lloyd's Rep. 434 at 438; but it does apply even though "there has been negotiation over those terms" if the terms in question "remained effectively untouched by those negotiations:" *St Albans City & District Council v International Computers Ltd* [1996] 4 All E.R. 491. Where a party makes use of a standard form drafted by a trade association or similar body, the terms of that form are that party's "standard terms" only if he "invariably or at least usually" contracted on those terms: *British Fermentation Products Ltd v Compare Reavell Ltd* [1999] 2 All E.R. (Comm) 389 at 401. For an exception to the requirement that, between parties acting in the course of a business, the contract must be on written standard terms, see Late Payment of Commercial Debts (Interest) Act 1998, s.14(2), below, p.995.

[89] See below, p.838.

[90] In *Brigden v American Express Bank Ltd* [2000] I.R.L.R. 94 a clause in a contract of employment providing for dismissal by notice without going through the normal disciplinary procedures in the case of an employee of less than two years' standing was held not to fall within s.3(2); the reference seems to be to s.3(2)(b)(i).

[91] *Paragon Finance Ltd v Staunton* [2001] EWCA Civ 1466; [2001] 2 All E.R. (Comm) 102, at [75].

[92] Contrast *Timeload Ltd v British Telecommunications plc* [1995] E.M.L.R. 459 with *Zokoll Group Ltd v Mercury Communications Ltd* [1999] E.M.L.R. 385.

[93] e.g. it would apply to a situation such as that which arose in *Anglo-Continental Holidays Ltd v Typaldos Lines (London) Ltd* [1967] 2 Lloyd's Rep. 61. A contract of this kind between the tour operator and consumer would be governed by Package Travel, Package Holidays and Package Tours Regulations 1992 (SI 1992/3288) (below p.261); under reg.12; where the "organiser" is "constrained" to alter "an essential term" of the contract the consumer is entitled to cancel the contract. For the relationship between such legislation and the Unfair Terms in Consumer Contracts Regulations 1999, see below, p.277.

[94] *Duffy v Newcastle United Football Club Ltd, The Times*, July 7, 2000.

(iii) Under s.3(2)(b)(ii) B cannot "claim to be entitled . . . in respect of the whole or any part of his contractual obligation to render no performance at all". This would apply where an agreement is on its true construction held to impose a contractual obligation but gives or purports to give B a wide discretion whether to perform at all or to the full extent promised. The criterion is not (as it is under s.3(2)(b)(i)) what the other party reasonably expects: it is the obligation undertaken by B. If the "contract term" gave B a totally free discretion whether to perform or not, there might be no "contractual obligation" on B at all; and in such a case the requirement of reasonableness need not be satisfied.[95] S.3(2)(b)(ii) would also not apply to a clause defining B's duty[96] in such a way that in the circumstances which have occurred no duty arose; e.g. where B promised to perform "subject to strikes" and strikes have prevented performance.

In a number of other situations, the scope of s.3(2)(b)(ii) is harder to determine. A contract may provide that B is entitled to cancel it by giving notice, or on the occurrence of specified events: e.g. on the other party's failure to perform (whether or not it amounts to a breach) or on some other event, such as the other party's death.[97] Or it may require B to perform only when the other party's performance has been rendered in full, or when some prescribed part of the performance has been rendered.[98] For example, a building contract may provide that nothing is to be paid till the work is completed, or that instalments of the price are to be paid only when specific parts of the work had been done. Such provisions might at first sight appear to be literally within s.3(2)(b)(ii); but it does not seem to have been the purpose of that enactment to alter the law as to cancellation clauses of the kind mentioned above,[99] or as to the effect of the other party's breach on the obligations of B. It is submitted that the scope of the enactment must be narrowed by a restrictive interpretation of the opening words of s.3(2), according to which B cannot do the three things specified in the subsection "by reference to any contract term". These words should be taken to mean "by reference *only* to such a term"—not by reference to it combined with other circumstances justifying B's refusal, such as a failure by the other party to perform his part.[1]

(c) SUPPLY OF GOODS. By s.6(3), the requirement of reasonableness applies to a term in a contract for the sale or hire-purchase of goods purporting to exclude or restrict liability for breach of the statutorily implied terms[2] as to correspondence of the goods with description or sample, or as to their quality or fitness for a particular purpose, where the buyer or hire-purchaser deals otherwise than as consumer.[3] A similar rule is laid down by s.7(3) with regard to terms in other contracts for the supply of goods (such as contracts of hire or exchange) purporting to exclude liability for breach of similar terms implied by law in such contracts.[4] S.7 applies only to terms purporting to exclude or restrict "business liability"[5] so that s.7(3) is restricted to the case where the supplier

---

[95] For the position under Unfair Terms in Consumer Contracts Regulations 1994, Sch.3 para.1(c), see below, p.274.

[96] See above, p.248; s.3 is *not* referred to in s.13(1).

[97] See below, p.778.

[98] See below, **pp.**782–788.

[99] The view that s.3(2)(b)(ii) does not apply to such cancellation clauses is supported by the *Paragon Finance* case, above, n.91, at [76–77]; the question was left open in *Timeload Ltd v British Telecommunications plc* [1995] E.M.L.R. 459 at 468.

[1] For the position under Unfair Terms in Consumer Contracts Regulations 1999, Sch.2, para.1(o), see below, p.276.

[2] See above, p.250, n.56.

[3] See above, p.250 for the position where he deals as consumer.

[4] See above, p.251 at n.63.

[5] s.1(3).

acts in the course of a business and the acquirer does not deal as consumer.[6] S.6 is however not restricted to the case where the supplier acts in the course of a business.[7] A term by which a private seller seeks to exclude or restrict liability for breach of the statutorily implied terms (even against a buyer who acts in the course of a business) is therefore under s.6(3) subject to the requirement of reasonableness. However, the statutorily implied terms as to satisfactory quality or fitness for a particular purpose arise only where the supplier acts in the course of a business.[8] A private supplier is under no liability in respect of such matters unless he gives an express undertaking. There is nothing in the Act to prevent him from restricting his liability for breach of such an *express* undertaking, *e.g.* by limiting his liability to a specified sum. In this respect he is in a better position than a business supplier, whose right so to limit his liability for breach of an express term may be subject to the requirement of reasonableness under s.3, *e.g.* if he deals on his "written standard terms of business."

We have seen that B cannot exclude or restrict his liability for breach of the implied terms as to title in contracts of sale and hire purchase, and in certain other contracts under which he transfers or agrees to transfer the property in goods[9] (such as contracts of exchange). In contracts for the transfer or supply of goods which fall outside this group, s.7(4)[10] applies the requirement of reasonableness to terms by which B seeks to exclude or restrict such liability: this would, for example, be the position in contracts of pledge,[11] or hire. As s.7 applies only to "business liability",[12] a private supplier's right to exclude or restrict liability in respect of defects of title in contracts of this kind is in no way affected by the Act. This is also true where a private supplier enters into a contract (other than one of sale or hire-purchase) by which he transfers or agrees to transfer the property in goods: for example, where the contract is one of exchange.[13] Where, on the other hand, the contract is one of sale or hire-purchase, a term by which even a private supplier seeks to exclude or restrict liability for breach of the implied undertakings as to title is simply ineffective,[14] without regard to its reasonableness.

(d) INDEMNITY CLAUSES. A contract may provide that if one party incurs a liability under it, whether to the other party or to a third party, then the other party shall indemnify the first against such liability. For example, a contract for the hire of a vehicle with a driver may contain a clause by which the hirer promises to indemnify the owner for any injury, loss or damage caused by the negligence of the driver.

S.4 of the Act applies the requirement of reasonableness to a contract term by which C undertakes to indemnify another person in respect of a business liability[15] incurred by the other for negligence or breach of contract. The operation of the section, and its relationship to other provisions of the Act, can best be explained by distinguishing between two situations, based on the example just given.

---

[6] *e.g.*, *Stewart Gill Ltd v Horatio Myer & Co Ltd* [1992] Q.B. 600.

[7] s.6(4).

[8] Sale of Goods Act 1979 s.14(2) and (3); Supply of Goods (Implied Terms) Act 1973, s.10(2) and (3), as substituted by Consumer Credit Act 1974, s.192 and Sch.4, para.35. For amendments, see Sale and Supply of Goods Act 1994, s.7 and Sch.2 and Sale and Supply of Goods to Consumers Regulations 2002, (SI 2002/3045), above p.250, n.64.

[9] See above, pp.250, 251, 252.

[10] As amended by Supply of Goods and Services Act 1982, s.17(3).

[11] See Supply of Goods and Services Act 1982, s.1(2)(e).

[12] Unfair Contract Terms Act 1977, s.1(3).

[13] The restriction on the effectiveness of terms excluding liability for breach of the implied terms as to title in such contracts is imposed by Unfair Contract Terms Act 1977, s.7(3A) (above, p.231, n.66) which, like the rest of s.7 only applies to "business liability": s.1(3).

[14] s.6(1); above, pp.250, 251.

[15] s.1(3).

(i) *Injury, loss or damage caused to a third party.* Where the driver negligently injures, or causes loss or damage to, a third party, s.4 subjects the indemnity clause to the requirement of reasonableness, but only if the hirer dealt as consumer. The clause is therefore not subject to the requirement of reasonableness, under s.4, if the contract of hire was between B1 and B2. Nor is the clause treated as an exemption clause for the purposes of the Act, since it does not "exclude or restrict" the liability of the owner to the third party: it simply determines by whom (as between owner and hirer) that liability is to be borne.[16] It follows that s.2 does not apply and that the clause is neither ineffective (in case of personal injury)[17] nor subject to the requirement of reasonableness (in case of other loss or damage).[18] S.4 likewise does not apply to an indemnity clause in a contract between two parties neither of whom acts in the course of a business, since neither party to such a contract "deals as consumer".[19] Here again the clause is not subject to s.2, both because it is not an exemption clause and because s.2 is restricted to "business liability".[20] The clause is likewise not an exemption clause for the purpose of other restrictions (already discussed)[21] imposed by the Act on the operation of exemption clauses.

(ii) *Injury, loss or damage caused to indemnifier.* Where (in our example) the driver negligently injures, or causes loss or damage to, the hirer himself, s.4 again subjects the indemnity clause to the requirement of reasonableness if the hirer dealt as consumer. In addition, the clause is regarded as an exemption clause for the purposes of the Act since there is no difference of substance between the owner's saying to the hirer "I am not liable to you" and his saying "you must indemnify me against any damages which I may have to pay to you".[22] The clause is therefore subject not only to s.4 but also to other provisions of the Act, for example to s.2. This point is significant for two reasons. First, in cases of personal injury the clause is not merely subject to the requirement of reasonableness, as it would be if s.4 alone applied: the clause is simply ineffective under s.2(1). Secondly, in cases of other loss or damage the requirement of reasonableness must be satisfied, not only in contracts between B and C, as would be the case if s.4 alone applied: it must be satisfied also in contracts between B1 and B2, since s.2 applies even in favour of a person who does not deal as consumer. An indemnity clause in the present type of case will likewise be treated as an exemption clause for the purpose of other restrictions (already discussed)[23] imposed by the Act on the operation of exemption clauses.

(e) MISREPRESENTATION. The 1977 Act[24] amends s.3 of the Misrepresentation Act 1967, which had originally applied a requirement of reasonableness to terms excluding or restricting liability for misrepresentation. Such terms are now subject to the requirement of reasonableness as newly defined by the 1977 Act. The requirement applies to all contracts, and is not restricted to "business liabilities" or to contracts in which one party "deals as consumer." It is further discussed in Chapter 9.[25]

---

[16] *Thompson v T Lohan (Plant Hire) Ltd* [1987] 1 W.L.R. 649; Sealy [1988] C.L.J. 6; Adams and Brownsword [1988] J.B.L. 146; *cf. The Caspar Trader* [1991] 2 Lloyd's Rep. 550.
[17] Unfair Contract Terms Act 1977, s.2(1), above, p.250.
[18] *ibid.* s.2(2), above, p.252.
[19] See above, p.247.
[20] Unfair Contract Terms Act 1977, s.1(3).
[21] *e.g.* those imposed by ss.6 and 7, above, pp.251–252, 254–255.
[22] *Phillips Products Ltd v Hyland* [1987] 1 W.L.R. 659.
[23] See n.21, above.
[24] s.8.
[25] See below, p.385.

(4) Partly effective terms

Under the 1977 Act, a term may be partly effective and partly ineffective. There are two types of situations in which this may be the position.

First, a clause may be drafted so as to exclude or restrict both a liability which cannot be excluded or restricted at all, and one which can be excluded by a provision which satisfies the requirement of reasonableness or by one which is effective subject only to common law restrictions. A clause may, for example, purport to limit the liability of a seller of goods for *any* breach to the return of the contract price. Such a provision is wholly ineffective to protect him from liability for breach of the implied undertaking as to title.[26] But this does not make the clause entirely void.[27] Thus the seller could rely on it to limit his liability for some other breach: for example, for breach of the statutorily implied terms as to quality if the buyer was not dealing as consumer and the clause satisfied the requirement of reasonableness.[28] He could similarly rely on it to limit liability for late delivery (or simple non-delivery) subject only to common law restrictions.[29] These conclusions follow from the fact that the Act nowhere invalidates contractual provisions as such: it simply says that specified liabilities cannot be excluded or restricted "by reference" to them.

Secondly, the Act provides that terms subject to the requirement of reasonableness are ineffective "except in so far as",[30] or effective "only in so far as",[31] they satisfy the requirement of reasonableness. In most cases, the term will either satisfy the requirement (and so be effective) or fail to satisfy it (and so be ineffective). But the words "in so far as" make it possible for the court to hold one part of a term valid and another invalid. Thus where a clause in a contract for the sale of goods imposed a short time limit on all claims and also limited the seller's liability to the amount of the contract price, it was held that the first part of the clause was reasonable, and the second unreasonable.[32]

In the situation just described, what appears to be a single clause is treated as severable and the court, having severed the clause, then determines separately the reasonableness of each of its parts. Where a clause (or a severable part of one) is unreasonable, the court will not modify it so as to make it reasonable: *e.g.* by allowing a limitation of liability where the contract had provided for total exclusion,[33] or by striking out an unreasonably low limitation in the contract and substituting a higher one that the court regarded as reasonable. Similarly, where a clause excluded a customer's right to "any payment, credit, set-off [or] counterclaim" it was held that the clause was unreasonable as a whole, and that it could not be severed so as to exclude only the right of set-off.[34] To do any of these things would be inconsistent with the wording of s.11(1) of the 1977 Act, under

---

[26] s.6(1).

[27] *cf. George Mitchell (Chesterhall) Ltd v Finney Lock Seeds Ltd* [1983] Q.B. 284 at 303, 309 decided under an earlier and now superseded statutory requirement of reasonableness and affirmed without reference to this point in [1983] 2 A.C. 803.

[28] s.6(3).

[29] Such breaches are not covered by s.6. If the buyer was not dealing as consumer and the seller was not dealing on his written standard terms of business, the Act would not apply to such a case: see below, p.264.

[30] ss.2(2), 3(2), 4(1), and 7(4).

[31] ss.6(3) and 7(3).

[32] *R W Green Ltd v Cade Bros Farms* [1978] 1 Lloyd's Rep. 602, decided under an earlier and now superseded statutory requirement of reasonableness.

[33] *George Mitchell (Chesterhall) Ltd v Finney Lock Seeds Ltd* [1983] 2 A.C. 803 at 816; *cf. Esso Petroleum Ltd v Milton* [1997] 1 W.L.R. 938.

[34] *Stewart Gill Ltd v Horatio Myer & Co Ltd* [1992] Q.B. 600; Hedley, [1992] C.L.J. 418; *cf. Shipskreditforeningen v Emperor Navigation* [1998] 1 Lloyd's Rep. 67 at 75 (applying the same principle for the purpose of Misrepresentation Act 1967, s.3, below, p.387).

which the requirement of reasonableness "is that the term shall have been a fair and reasonable one to be included." This means that the reasonableness test has to be applied to the term actually in the contract (or to each such term, if the contract contains more than one) and not to some other term which in the court's view might reasonably have been included.

(5) Rules relating to reasonableness

A judicially administered requirement of reasonableness is open to the objection that it is a source of uncertainty.[35] To meet this objection, the Act lays down a rule as to the time for determining reasonableness and it also provides guidelines for this purpose. In addition, the Act lays down two rules as to the effects of breach on the requirement; their object is to prevent undue restrictions on its scope.

(a) TIME FOR DETERMINING REASONABLENESS. The question whether a contract term satisfies the requirement is determined by reference to the time at which the contract was made.[36] If the term was a fair and reasonable one to be included having regard to the circumstances which were or should reasonably have been known to or in the contemplation of the parties *at that time*, its effectiveness will not be impaired by subsequent events.

(b) GUIDELINES. S.11(4) of the Act lays down two guidelines for determining the reasonableness of provisions limiting a person's liability to a specific sum of money: regard is to be had to (a) the resources which that person could expect to be available to him for the purpose of meeting the liability, and (b) how far it was open to him to cover himself by insurance.[37] Under the second of these guidelines, a clause limiting the liability of a manufacturer for defects would not be reasonable if he could have insured against the liability without materially raising the price of his product (particularly if it would have been difficult or virtually impossible for the customer to have insured against the loss)[38] or if he actually had so insured.[39] On the other hand, a clause limiting the liability of a person engaged in the storage or carriage of goods would be reasonable if he had little knowledge of the nature or value the goods, and if the goods could be more cheaply insured by their owner than by the bailee.[40] In applying the second guideline, the court considers the *availability* of insurance to the defendant, rather than his *actual* insurance position.[41] The two guidelines stated in s.11(4) do not contain an exhaustive list of factors to be taken into account in deciding whether a limitation clause satisfies a

---

[35] Treitel, *Doctrine and Discretion in the Law of Contract*, pp.13–19. For the American experience under UCC ss.2–302, see Leff, 115 U. of Pa L.Rev. 485; Ellinghaus, 78 Y.L.J. 757. For a legislative attempt to square this circle, see Late Payments of Commercial Debts (Interest) Act 1998, s.9(1)(b) and 9(3)(a).

[36] 1977 Act, s.11(1). In the case of a non-contractual notice (above, pp.247, 249, 252) the relevant time is the time when the liability arose or but for the notice would have arisen: s.11(3): see *Monarch Airlines Ltd v London Luton Airport* [1998] 1 Lloyd's Rep. 403; *First National Commercial Bank v Loxleys, The Times*, November 14, 1996.

[37] s.11(4). The subsection is in terms applicable only to terms which *limit* (as opposed to those which wholly *exclude*) liability: *The Flammar Pride* [1990] 1 Lloyd's Rep. 434 at 438; but the guidelines in question can be applied by analogy to clauses of the latter kind: see below, p.260 at n.57.

[38] *Salvage Association v CAP Services* [1995] F.S.R. 654.

[39] *George Mitchell (Chesterhall) Ltd v Finney Lock Seeds Ltd* [1983] A.C. 803 at 817, decided under earlier and now superseded legislation not containing this guideline; *St Albans City and District Council v International Computers Ltd*, [1995] F.S.R. 686, reversed but not on the application of the reasonableness test [1996] 4 All E.R. 481.

[40] *Singer (UK) Ltd v Tees & Hartlepool Port Authority* [1988] 2 Lloyd's Rep. 164.

[41] *ibid.* at 169; *The Flammar Pride* [1990] 1 Lloyd's Rep. 434 at 439; *Monarch Airlines Ltd v London Luton Airport* [1998] 1 Lloyd's Rep. 403 at 413.

reasonableness test. A negative answer to this question may, for example be given because of the "insufficient clarity"[42] of the clause.

Where a term in a contract for the supply of goods is subject to the requirement of reasonableness under ss.6 or 7,[43] the Act provides five further guidelines.[44] These include the strength of the bargaining positions of the parties relative to each other,[45-47] whether the customer "received an inducement to agree to the term" (*e.g.* in the form of a lower price), whether he could have bought elsewhere without being subjected to a similar term, and the customer's knowledge or means of knowledge of the existence and extent of the terms.[48] Under these guidelines, the fact that the contract was in a standard form settled after negotiations between trade associations to which both parties belonged is relevant to the issue of reasonableness; for it helps to show that its terms were "not imposed by the strong upon the weak."[49] *A fortiori*, terms are unlikely to be struck down for unreasonableness under the Act where the contract in which they are contained was made between commercial companies "of equal bargaining power"[50] after negotiations in which each party had made concession to the other.[51] In the interests of certainty, an "entire agreement" clause in such a contract is also like to satisfy the test of reasonableness.[52] But where the term has *not* been the subject of negotiation it may be struck down, even in a contract between such parties, if its effect is to "contradict a fundamental assumption that all parties have made in this respect"[53]: *e.g.*, where a seller of ingredients to a manufacturer of beverages supplied a defective ingredient which made the resulting product unsaleable.

These statutory guidelines no doubt help to reduce the uncertainty to which the requirement of reasonableness gives rise; but the restrictions on their scope are hard to understand. Thus it is not easy to see why the strength of the bargaining positions of the parties is relevant only in contracts for the supply of goods; nor why the five guidelines[54] which can apply where a seller delivers goods of the wrong *quality*[55] do not also apply where he delivers goods of the wrong *quantity*.[56] The courts have remedied this defect in the wording of the Act by treating the guidelines as being of general application, so

---

[42] *Overseas Medical Supplier Ltd v Orient Transport Services Ltd* [1999] 2 Lloyd's Rep. 273 at 280. This lack of clarity may, alternatively, be a ground for holding that, as a matter of construction, the clause does not cover the breach: see above p.221.

[43] See above, pp.254–255.

[44] s.11(2) and Sch.2.

[45-47] *cf. Thames Tideway Properties Ltd v Serafty* [1999] 2 Lloyd's Rep. 110 at 110.

[48] The question whether a term has been incorporated in the contract is, however, a separate question, as is recognised by the concluding words of s.11(2).

[49] *R W Green Ltd v Cade Bros Farms Ltd* [1978] 1 Lloyd's Rep. 602 at 607; above, n.98; *The Zinnia* [1984] 2 Lloyd's Rep. 211; *Schenkers Ltd v Overland Shoes Ltd* [1998] 1 Lloyd's Rep. 499; *cf. British Fermentation Products Ltd v Compair Reavell Ltd* [1999] 2 All E.R. (Comm) 389; contrast *George Mitchell (Chesterhall) Ltd v Finney Lock Seeds Ltd* where the conditions were not negotiated by the National Farmers Union but simply introduced by seed merchants without objection from farmers: see [1983] 2 A.C. 803 at 817.

[50] *Watford Electronics Ltd v Sanderson Ltd* [2001] EWCA Civ 317 at [55]; [2001] 1 All E.R. (Comm) 696; *cf.* below, p.388 for the same approach to the test of reasonableness under Misrepresentation Act 1967, s.3.

[51] *Watford Electronics* case, above.

[52] *ibid.* at [39].

[53] *Britvic Soft Drinks Ltd v Messer UK Ltd* [2002] EWCA Civ 548; [2002] 2 All E.R. (Comm) 321 at [26]; *Bacardi Martini Beverages Ltd v Thomas Hardy Packaging Ltd* [2002] EWCA Civ 549 [2002] 2 Lloyd's Rep. 379 at [26].

[54] See above, n.44.

[55] The requirement of reasonableness applies to terms purporting to exclude or restrict B's liability in such cases if the buyer does not deal as consumer: s.6(3).

[56] The requirement of reasonableness applies to terms purporting to exclude or restrict B's liability in such cases if the contract is made on his "written standard terms of business": s.3.

that, for example, the guidelines stated in relation to contracts for the supply of goods can be applied by analogy to other types of contracts.[57]

Even in relation to the situations covered by them, the statutory guidelines are by no means exhaustive; indeed it has been said that it is "impossible to draw up an exhaustive list of factors to be taken into account when a judge is faced with this very difficult question".[58] In *Smith v Eric S Bush*[59] the House of Lords held that a term purporting to exclude the liability for negligence of surveyors (engaged by a building society) to buyers of dwelling houses did not satisfy the reasonableness test. The principal factors leading to this conclusion were that there was no equality of bargaining power, that the houses were of modest value so that it was not reasonable to expect the buyers to commission their own structural survey, and that the surveyors could easily have insured against the risk without unduly increasing their charges.[60] On the other hand, a disclaimer might be reasonable if the task undertaken had been one of great difficulty and complexity; if the value of the subject-matter had been very high, so that insurance against professional liability would have been very expensive or impossible to obtain[61]; or if it would have been reasonable for the injured party to have taken steps to discover the truth. Thus the requirement of reasonableness was held to have been satisfied where an estate agent disclaimed liability in respect of representations as to area made to the prospective purchaser who later contracted to buy the property in question for £875,000[62]: in such a transaction the purchaser could be expected to make his own investigations before exchanging contracts. The availability to the *other* party of an opportunity of discovering the defect in respect of which he is seeking to exclude liability can likewise be relevant to the issue of reasonableness. Thus where the seller of a car was a company which had been brought into the transaction purely to provide finance, it was said that the test of reasonableness would have been satisfied (if the buyer had not dealt as consumer)[63] because the company had never seen the car.[64] It has also been said that the courts should not be "too ready" to hold a term unreasonable by reference to "remote contingencies" to which the term, if taken literally, might apply but which the parties had not in fact intended to cover.[65]

(c) NATURE OF DECISION ON REASONABLENESS. A decision on the issue of reasonableness is not merely an exercise of judicial discretion[66]; for it involves the application of statutory and judge-made guidelines. Nevertheless in the *George Mitchell* case Lord Bridge described such a decision as one on which there "will sometimes be room for a legitimate difference of judicial opinion"; and as one with which an appellate court should not interfere "unless satisfied that it proceeded on some erroneous principle or

---

[57] *Singer (UK) Ltd v Tees & Hartlepool Port Authority* [1988] 2 Lloyd's Rep. 164 at 169; *The Flammar Pride* [1990] 1 Lloyd's Rep. 434 at 439; *Overseas Medical Supplies Ltd v Orient Transport Services Ltd* [1999] 2 Lloyd's Rep. 273 at 276–277; *cf. Monarch Airlines Ltd v London Luton Airport* [1998] 1 Lloyd's Rep. 403; *Schenkers Ltd v Overland Shoes Ltd* [1998] 1 Lloyd's Rep. 499 at 500.

[58] *Smith v Eric S Bush* [1990] 1 A.C. 831 at 858.

[59] [1990] 1 A.C. 831; Kaye, 52 M.L.R. 841; for other factors relevant to the issue of reasonableness, see *George Mitchell (Chesterhall) Ltd v Finney Lock Seeds Ltd* [1983] 2 A.C. 803, decided under an earlier (now superseded) statutory reasonableness test; *Overseas Medical* case, above n.57, at 280.

[60] *Smith v Eric S Bush* [1990] 1 A.C. 831 at 851–854, 858–859.

[61] *ibid.* at 859.

[62] *McCullagh v Lane Fox & Partners Ltd* [1996] 1 E.G.L.R. 35.

[63] See above, p.247.

[64] *R & B Customs Brokers Ltd v United Dominions Trust Ltd* [1988] 1 W.L.R. 321 at 332.

[65] *Shipkreditforeningen v Emperor Navigation* [1998] 1 Lloyd's Rep. 67 at 75–77 (where the question of reasonableness arose under Misrepresentation Act 1967 s.3, below, p.385).

[66] *George Mitchell (Chesterhall) Ltd v Finney Lock Seeds Ltd* [1983] 2 A.C. 803 at 816. *cf. Comemsco Ltd v Contrapol* (unrep.) referred to by Kerr L.J. in [1983] Q.B. 284 at 315.

was plainly and obviously wrong".[67] These remarks are intended to restrict, but not to rule out, the possibility of successful appeals on the issue of reasonableness. An appeal may, for example, succeed where the trial judge has held the clause to be unreasonable by attributing to it a wider meaning than that which, in the view of the appellate court, it could, on its true construction, bear.[68]

(d) EFFECTS OF RESCISSION OR AFFIRMATION. S.9(1) of the Act provides that effect may be given to a term which satisfies the requirement of reasonableness even though the contract has been terminated; while s.9(2) provides that the requirement of reasonableness is not excluded by affirmation of the contract.[69]

(e) EFFECT OF SERIOUSNESS OF BREACH. Earlier in this Chapter, we saw that the question whether exemption clauses covered certain particularly serious breaches was one of construction.[70] If the clause does not cover such a breach, no issue of reasonableness will arise; but even if the clause does cover the breach it may still fail to satisfy the requirement of reasonableness, as in the *George Mitchell* case.[71] Hence reasonableness under the Act and the rules of construction applicable at common law remain separate requirements of the effectiveness of exemption clauses.[72] Although the importance of the rule of construction will thus be reduced where the clause is subject to the statutory requirement of reasonableness, factors similar to those relevant for construction purposes have been taken into account in determining issues of reasonableness. Thus clauses have been held unreasonable on the ground that, if valid, they would operate "in respect of matters which the parties would have regarded as fundamental".[73] It is arguable that the concept of fundamental breach here makes its reappearance for a purpose that differs both from the former substantive doctrine[74] and from the rule of construction.[74a] That rule also differs from the statutory requirement of reasonableness in that reasonableness is determined by reference to the time of contracting,[75] while the question whether a clause covers a particular breach may depend on the manner in which the breach has been committed, or on its consequences,[76] and these circumstances can be known only at or after the time of breach.

(6) Restrictions on evasions

The Act invalidates two possible devices for evading its provisions.

(a) SECONDARY CONTRACT. The first such device is that the term restricting or excluding liability may be contained, not in the principal contract itself, but in another

---

[67] [1983] 2 A.C. 803, 810; *Phillips Products Ltd v Hyland* [1987] 1 W.L.R. 659 at 669; *St Albans City & District Council v International Computers Ltd* [1996] 4 All E.R. 481; *Schenkers Ltd v Overland Shoes Ltd* [1998] 1 Lloyd's Rep. 499; *Overseas Medical Supplies Ltd v Orient Transport Services Ltd* [1999] 2 Lloyd's Rep. 273 at 276.

[68] *Watford Electronics Ltd v Sanderson Ltd* [2001] EWCA Civ 317; [2001] 1 All E.R. (Comm) 696.

[69] *cf.* the common law position, above, pp.238–240.

[70] See above, **pp.225–241.**

[71] [1983] 2 A.C. 803: see above p.258 at n.39; *Lease Management Services v Purnell Secretarial Services* [1994] Tr. L.R. 337.

[72] See the *George Mitchell* case, above, and *R W Green Ltd v Cade Bros Farms Ltd* [1978] 1 Lloyd's Rep. 602. *Semble* the decision in the *Overseas Medical* case, above, could have been based on construction, though it was actually based on failure to satisfy the reasonableness test.

[73] *Bacardi-Martini Beverages Ltd v Thomas Hardy Packaging Ltd* [2002] EWCA Civ 549; [2002] 2 All E.R. (Comm) 335 at [26]; *cf.* above, p.259 at n.53.

[74] Above, p.225.

[74a] Above, pp.225, 233.

[75] See above, p.258.

[76] See above, pp.231–233.

(secondary) contract. To meet this possibility, s.10 provides that "A person is not bound by any contract term prejudicing or taking away rights of his which arise under, or in connection with the performance of, another contract,[77] so far as those rights extend to the enforcement of another's liability which this Part of this Act[78] prevents[79] that other from excluding or restricting." Unfortunately, the terminology of s.10 differs from that used elsewhere in the Act,[80] and this fact gives rise to a number of difficulties of interpretation.

S.10 refers to a contract term "prejudicing or taking away rights", not to one "excluding or restricting liability". The statutory explanation of the latter phrase[81] therefore does not apply to s.10. In particular, it is by no means clear whether the section would cover a secondary contract excluding a particular *remedy*, or one imposing onerous conditions (such as short time limits) on the enforcement of a liability; or whether it would apply to a subsequent agreement to submit disputes under the original contract to arbitration.[82]

The exact scope of s.10 is also in doubt in relation to consumer contracts and contracts on written standard terms. S.3(2) applies the requirement of reasonableness to terms in such contracts which (a) exclude or restrict liability for breach, or (b) purport to entitle a party to render a performance substantially different from that reasonably expected of him, or to render no performance at all. Clearly, a secondary contract seeking to achieve result (a) is within s.10 and thus ineffective. But is the same true of a secondary contract seeking to achieve result (b)? The concluding words of s.10 give rise to a difficulty because the rights affected by the secondary contract must "extend to the enforcement of another's *liability* which . . . this Act prevents the other from excluding or restricting". S.3(2) appears to contrast terms *excluding or restricting liability* with terms purporting to *entitle a party to render a performance substantially different*, etc. It is at least doubtful whether s.10 is apt to cover a secondary agreement having the latter effect.

S.10 does not apply to a contract by which the parties to an earlier contract, containing terms which would be subject to the Act, reach a settlement of disputes which have arisen between them under the original contract. The argument that such a settlement was a secondary contract within s.10 has been rejected on the ground that there was no hint in the legislative history that the section was intended to strike at such genuine out of court settlements.[83] On the contrary, the legislative history indicates that, in using the phrase "another's liability" s.10 refers to the liability of a third party,[84] so that the section "does not apply where the parties to both contracts are the same".[85] The point of the section is to deal with the case in which a contract between X and Y provides

---

[77] s.10 does not apply where a contract between A and B takes away A's right to sue a third party, C, *in tort*, since A's right against C does not arise "under . . . another contract:" *The Chevalier Roze* [1983] 2 Lloyd's Rep. 438 at 422.

[78] *i.e.* Pt I, which extends to England and Wales and to Northern Ireland.

[79] *i.e.* (*semble*) not only by making it totally ineffective but also by subjecting it to the requirement of reasonableness.

[80] Perhaps because s.10 was introduced at a late stage in the Parliamentary proceedings on the Act.

[81] s.13(1) above, pp.247–248.

[82] See s.13(2) which, unlike s.10, uses the standard terminology of the Act—"excluding or restricting liability."

[83] *Tudor Grange Holdings Ltd v Citibank NA* [1992] Ch. 53 at 65–67; Brown, 108 L.Q.R. 233; Cumberbatch, 55 M.L.R. 866.

[84] (1977) 385 H.L. Cols. 57–59, 511–514.

[85] *Tudor Grange* case, above, at 66.

that Y is not to exercise rights against Z under a separate contract between Y and Z.[86] The latter contract may not contain any exemption clause but be of such a kind that, if it did contain such a clause, that clause would be subject to the Act. At common law, Z could not as a general rule rely on the clause in the contract between X and Y as he was not a party to it[87]; and the statutory right to rely on it, which Z may have under the Contracts (Rights of Third Parties) Act 1999, will be of no avail to him where the clause is ineffective under the Unfair Contract Terms Act 1977.[88] The purpose of s.10 of the 1977 Act is to prevent X from enforcing against Y a clause in the contract between X and Y which provides that Y is not to sue Z under the contract between Y and Z and which would have been ineffective under that Act if it had been contained in the contract between Y and Z. Even apart from s.10 such a proceeding might not be open to X unless X could show that he had a sufficient interest[89] in Z's immunity from being sued by Y. The view that s.10 does not apply where the parties to both contracts are the same (even though it is acknowledged that the words of the section are capable of covering such a case[90]) has also been supported by the argument that, between the parties to the original contract, s.10 would be unnecessary since the secondary contract, no less than the original one, would be subject to the requirement of reasonableness under ss.2 and 3 of the Act.[91] But this reasoning seems to overlook the possibility that the secondary contract may be subject only to the requirement of reasonableness (*e.g.*, under s.3), while the original contract might be one in which the exemption clause was simply ineffective: *e.g.* under s.6(2) where it excluded or restricted liability for defects in goods sold to a consumer. In such a case to give effect to the secondary contract, even between the parties to the original contract, could significantly reduce the protection which the Act intends to give to the consumer under the original contract.

The view that s.10 does not apply where the parties to both contracts are the same would also help to solve the problem of the renegotiation of a contract before any dispute under it has arisen. A contract may, for example, contain a term limiting the liability of a party to it, and that term may be subject to, and satisfy, the requirement of reasonableness. The parties may later agree on a lower limit of liability which would also (had it been originally incorporated in the contract) have satisfied that requirement. If that later agreement were within s.10, it would be totally ineffective and incapable of being validated by being shown to be reasonable. This—surely undesirable—result can be avoided by arguing *either* that s.10 does not apply between the parties to the original contract *or* that the later agreement is a variation of the original contract, so that the terms of that later agreement do not prejudice rights which "arise under *another* contract." The new limit of the defaulting party's liability would thus be subject to the same requirement of reasonableness as the term which originally limited that liability.

(b) CHOICE OF LAW CLAUSES. A second possible way of evading the Act is to provide that a contract which would otherwise be subject to its provisions shall be governed by the law of a foreign country (which imposes no such restriction on the effectiveness of contract terms). By s.27(2), the Act applies, even though the contract contains such a clause, where the clause was "imposed" wholly or mainly to evade the Act; and also where one of the parties dealt as consumer, was habitually resident in the United

---

[86] See the example given in 385 H.L. Col. 57, on which the discussion in the *Tudor Grange* case above at 66 seems to have been based; reference to the Parliamentary report would now be authorised by *Pepper v Hart* [1993] A.C. 593.

[87] See below, p.626.

[88] See below, p.660.

[89] See below, p.603.

[90] *Tudor Grange* case, above, at 66.

[91] *ibid.*, at 67.

Kingdom, and the essential steps necessary for the making of the contract were taken there. Further restrictions on the efficacy of choice of law clauses are contained in the Unfair Terms in Consumer Contracts Regulations 1999, to be considered later in this Chapter,[92] and in the EC Convention on the Law Applicable to Contractual Obligations (also known as the Rome Convention), which has the force of law in the United Kingdom.[93] Art.5 of the Convention provides that, where specified conditions are satisfied,[94] such a clause in a contract for the supply of goods or services[95] to a consumer is not to have the effect of depriving the consumer of mandatory rules[96] of law of the country of his habitual residence.

(7) Situations not covered by the Act

These fall into two categories: those which are not within the scope of the provisions of the Act, and those which would be within the scope of its provisions if they were not specifically excepted.

(a) CASES NOT WITHIN THE SCOPE OF THE ACT. Contract terms excluding or restricting the liability of a person not acting in the course of a business are generally unaffected by the Act. The Act only limits such a person's right to exclude or restrict certain liabilities arising out of contracts for the sale and hire purchase of goods[97] and for misrepresentation.[98] Even terms excluding or restricting business liability may be outside the scope of the Act: this is the position where a contract between B1 and B2, not made on written standard terms of business,[99] excludes or restricts a liability other than one for breach of the implied terms in contracts for the supply of goods dealt with in ss.6 and 7 of the Act.[1] For example, a clause by which B1 excluded or limited liability to B2 for delay in delivering goods, or for short delivery or for an express undertaking as to quality going beyond those implied by law, would not be affected by the Act.

(b) CASES SPECIFICALLY EXCEPTED. Some or all of the provisions of the Act do not apply in the following cases.

(i) *The principal group* of contracts excepted[2] from some of the provisions of the Act is listed in Sch.1.

Para.1 of the Schedule lists a number of contracts to which ss.2, 3 and 4 do not apply. In the excepted cases, contract terms[3] excluding or restricting liability for negligence, terms in consumer contracts and provisions in written standard terms of business and indemnity clauses are not subject to the provisions of those sections. The contracts within para.1 of the Schedule are contracts of insurance and any contract "so far as it

---

[92] See below, p.283.

[93] Contracts (Applicable Law) Act 1990, s.2 and Sch.1, as amended by SI 1994/1900.

[94] See Art.5(2); these conditions relate mainly to the place where the steps leading to the conclusion of the contract are taken.

[95] With certain exceptions specified in Art.5(4) (contracts of carriage and contracts of service where the services are to be performed exclusively in a country other than that of the consumer's habitual residence).

[96] *i.e.* "rules of . . . law . . . which cannot be derogated from by contract:" Art.3(3).

[97] ss.6(1) and 6(4) above, pp.251, 254–255.

[98] s.8 below, pp.385–389.

[99] See s.3(1).

[1] See above, pp.251, 254–255; it is assumed that there is no "product liability" (above, p.252).

[2] By s.1(2).

[3] s.2 also deals with certain notices not having contractual effect, but the wording of s.1(2) ("in relation to contracts") indicates that the exclusions in Sch.1 only apply to contract terms.

relates to" the creation, transfer or termination of an interest in land[4] or in any patent, trade mark,[5] copyright or other intellectual property; the formation, dissolution or constitution of a company or the rights or obligations of its members; and the creation or transfer of securities or any right or interest in securities. Contracts of insurance are *wholly* excepted, but a contract falling within the other categories is only excepted "*so far as* it relates to" the matter specified.[6] Where a contract relates to such matters and also to others, the specified sections are excluded with regard to the former: *e.g.* they do not apply to a share option[7] contained in a contract of employment.[8] In the case of a contract for the transfer of an interest in land, it has been held that a clause in a lease by which rent was payable "without any deduction or set-off whatsoever" was excepted from ss.2, 3 and 4 since the tenant's covenant to pay rent was "an integral part of the creation of the interest in land".[9] This reasoning gives some support to the view that provisions in the lease which do not "relate to" the transfer would not be so excepted.

Para.2 of the Schedule lists three contracts: contracts of marine salvage or towage, charterparties of ships or hovercraft, and contracts for the carriage of goods by ship or hovercraft.[10] These contracts are subject to s.2(1), which provides that B[11] cannot by any contract term exclude or restrict his liability for death or personal injury resulting from negligence. But they are excepted from the remainder of s.2, as well as from ss.3 and 4, except in favour of C. Since some contracts within this group may involve the hire of a chattel[12] they are also excepted from s.7 which limits the extent to which liability for breach of certain implied terms in such contracts can be excluded or restricted.[13]

Para.3 of the Schedule deals with the case where goods are carried by ship or hovercraft under a contract which either specifies that means of carriage only for part of the journey[14] or makes no provision for the means of carriage. Such contracts may not be contracts *for* the carriage of goods by ship or hovercraft, but are nevertheless excepted from the operation of ss.2(2), 3 and 4 in the same way as such contracts.

By para.4 of the Schedule, ss.2(1) and (2) do not apply to contracts of employment "except in favour of the employee". The liability of the employee for negligence can therefore be restricted or excluded; but the employer cannot exclude or restrict such liability as against the employee. Since s.2 applies only to "business liability" the need for para.4 may not at first sight be apparent. But "business liability" includes liability for breach of a duty arising from things done in the course of *another* person's business[15] so

---

[4] A provision in a lease for the payment without set-off of a service charge to a management company has been held to fall within this exception and so not to be subject to the requirement of reasonableness under the 1977 Act: *Unchained Growth III plc v Granby Village (Manchester) Management Co* [2000] 1 W.L.R. 739.

[5] See Trade Marks Act 1994, s.106(1) and Sch.4, para.1.

[6] *Salvage Association v CAP Financial Services* [1995] F.S.R. 654.

[7] *Micklefield v SAC Technology* [1990] 1 W.L.R. 1002.

[8] As to which see Sch.1, para.4, below.

[9] *Electricity Supply Nominees Ltd v IAF Group Ltd* [1993] 1 W.L.R. 1059 at 1063; for the treatment of provisions excluding set-off as exemption clauses under the Act, see above, p.247. In *Connaught Restaurants Ltd v Indoors Leisure Ltd* [1994] 1 W.L.R. 501 no attempt was made to rely on the Act, perhaps because the conditions for the applicability of s.3 (above, p.252) were not satisfied; but the tenant succeeded on the construction of the lease: see above, p.221.

[10] See, for example *The European Enterprise* [1989] 2 Lloyd's Rep. 185. Certain contracts for the carriage of goods by sea also come within the excepting provisions of s.29, below, p.266.

[11] s.1(3).

[12] *e.g.* a demise charterparty.

[13] See above, pp.251–252, 254–255.

[14] This situation commonly arises where the goods are carried in a container from one inland destination to another in an overseas country.

[15] s.1(3).

that liability incurred by an employee (whether to his employer or to a third party) can be a "business liability." Moreover, "business" includes profession[16] so that an employee who in the course of his employment exercises a profession could incur a "business liability" which, but for para.4, would attract the operation of s.2(1) and (2).

Para.5 of the Schedule excepts from s.2(1) the validity of a discharge and indemnity given on or in connection with an award of compensation for pneumoconiosis.[17]

(ii) *Contracts for the international supply of goods.* In such contracts,[18] none of the limits "imposed by this Act" on contract terms which exclude or restrict liability apply.[19] However, it seems that the limits contained in s.3 of the Misrepresentation Act 1967 do apply: they were not "imposed by this [*i.e.* the 1977] Act" even though the 1977 Act amends s.3 of the Misrepresentation Act.[20]

Under the Unfair Contract Terms Act, the requirement of reasonableness sometimes applies to terms which do not "exclude or restrict" liability; for example, it applies to terms entitling a party to render a performance substantially different from that reasonably expected of him, or to render no performance at all,[21] and to indemnity clauses.[22] Where such terms or clauses are contained in a contract for the international supply of goods, the requirement of reasonableness does not apply.[23]

(iii) *Contractual provisions authorised or required under legislation or international agreements.* An increasingly common technique for controlling exemption clauses (and other contract terms) is found in international conventions, for example those regulating the international carriage of goods and passengers. Many such conventions have been given the force of law by statute.[24] These conventions often lay down a limitation of liability and then provide that any attempt at further reduction in the contract is void. This position is preserved by the 1977 Act.[25]

(iv) *Choice of law clauses.* The Act is intended to deal with contracts having some substantial connection with some part of the United Kingdom. A contract may be governed by English law though its connection with England is tenuous (or even non-existent); this can happen if it contains an express term that it is to be governed by English law. S.27(1)[26] accordingly provides that ss.2 to 7 do not apply where a contract is governed by the law of a part of the United Kingdom only by choice of the parties and would apart from that choice have been governed by the law of some country outside the United Kingdom. The point is of considerable commercial importance as contracts

---

[16] s.14.

[17] This matter is governed by an agreement originally made between the NCB and the NUM: HL, Deb., Vol.384, col.518.

[18] As defined by s.26(3) and (4); see *Ocean Chemical Transport Inc v Exnor Craggs* [2000] 1 Lloyd's Rep. 446 at 451. Generally such contracts will be between persons acting in the course of a business, but this is not an essential part of the definition. A contract for the sale of goods can fall within s.26 in respect of maintenance obligations imposed on the seller: *Amin Flight Authority v BAE Systems plc* [2002] EWCA 2481 (Comm), [2003] 1 Lloyd's Rep. 50 at [27].

[19] s.26(1).

[20] s.8, above, p.256.

[21] See s.3(2)(b), above, pp.252–254.

[22] See s.4, above, p.255.

[23] s.26(2).

[24] *e.g.* Carriage by Air Act 1961, Sch.1, Arts 22, 23(1) and 32; Carriage of Goods by Road Act 1965, Sch. Arts 23, 41; Carriage of Goods by Sea Act 1971, Sch. Arts III. 8 and IV. 5; Carriage by Railway Act 1972, Sch. Arts 6(2), 7 and 10; Carriage of Passengers by Road Act 1974, Sch., Arts 13, 16 and 23(1) (not yet fully in force); International Transport Conventions Act 1983, s.1; Merchant Shipping Act 1995, ss.183 and 184 and Sch.6, Pt I, Arts 7, 8, 18 and Pt III (not yet fully in force: for transitional provisions, see Unfair Contract Terms Act 1977, s.28).

[25] s.29. Certain contracts for the carriage of goods by sea are within both this exception and the somewhat more restricted exception of Sch.1, para.2(c), above, p.265.

[26] As amended by Contracts (Applicable Law) Act 1990, s.5 and Sch.4.

having no substantial connection with England are quite commonly made subject to English law by choice of the parties.[27]

2. The Unfair Terms in Consumer Contracts Regulations 1999

(1) General

These Regulations[28] give effect to an EC Council Directive[29] which is intended to promote the harmonisation of the laws of member states so as to ensure that contracts with consumers do not include terms which are unfair to the consumer.[30] They supersede earlier Regulations made in 1994[31] to give effect to the same Directive; and it will be necessary from time to time in the following discussion to refer to differences between them and the 1994 Regulations. The 1999 Regulations apply in relation to "unfair terms" which have not been "individually negotiated"[32] in contracts concluded between a seller or a supplier and a consumer. Their central provision is that if such terms are "unfair", then they shall not be binding on the consumer.[33]

(2) Relation with Unfair Contract Terms Act 1977

The Regulations operate side by side with the Unfair Contract Terms Act, so that it is possible for a term to be valid under the Regulations and not under the Act, and conversely. Or, to put the same point in another way, a party wishing to rely on a contract term will have to satisfy the requirements of both sets of rules. The scope of the Regulations, however, differs significantly from that of the Act, so that often only one set of rules will apply.

In some respects, the Regulations are or may be narrower in scope than the Act. First, the Regulations strike only at contract terms,[34] while some of the provisions of the Act apply also to notices (not forming part of any contract) purporting to exclude or restrict liability.[35] Secondly, the Regulations apply only to any terms which have "not been individually negotiated".[36] Only one provision of the Act is restricted to the situation in which a party deals on the other party's "written standard terms of business".[37] The other provisions of the Act can apply to individually negotiated contracts (or to notices given to individuals), though in practice they will no doubt most commonly apply to terms or notices in standard form. Thirdly, the Regulations apply only where one party

---

[27] See *Shipskreditforeningen v Emperor Navigation* [1998] 1 Lloyd's Rep. 67 at 78.

[28] SI 1999/2083, as amended by Unfair Terms in Consumer Contracts (Amendment) Regulations 2001 (SI 2001/1186).

[29] 93/13/EEC. For the construction of legislation based on such Directives, see *Litster v Forth Dry Dock & Engineering Co Ltd* [1990] 1 A.C. 546 at 559, adopting a "purposive" construction, "even though perhaps it may involve some departure from the strict and literal application of the words which the legislature has elected to use." *cf. Three Rivers DC v Bank of England (No.2)* [1996] 2 All E.R. 563.

[30] 93/13/EEC, Recital 4.

[31] SI 1994/3159.

[32] SI 1999/2083, regs 3(1) (definition of "unfair terms") and 5(1). The combined effect of these two provisions appears to be that the 1999 Regulations apply *only* to terms which have *not* been "individually negotiated". This point was more clearly expressed in reg.3(1) of the 1994 Regulations. The Directive (above n.29) on which the Regulations are based is stated in Recital 12 to cover "only contractual terms which have not been individually negotiated" but gives Member States the option of extending its protection beyond such terms. That option seems not to have been exercised by the United Kingdom in 1999 Regulations.

[33] SI 1999/3159, reg.8(1).

[34] *ibid.* regs 4(1) and 8(1).

[35] ss.2(1), 5(1), 11(3) and 11(4).

[36] Reg.5(1) and see n.32, above.

[37] s.3(1).

acts for purposes relating to his business and the other is a consumer[38] while some of the provisions of the Act apply where both parties act, or where neither party acts, in the course of a business. Fourthly, it is arguable that the Regulations apply only to a restricted range of contracts[39] while at least some of the provisions of the Act[40] apply to contracts generally. This difference between the two sets of rules (if it exists) is, however, much reduced by the list of contracts specifically excepted from the Act.[41] In respect of some of these exceptions,[42] indeed, the scope of the Act may actually be narrower than that of the Regulations.

In one significant respect, the scope of the Regulations is, on the other hand, clearly wider than that of the Act. With the exception of s.4, which deals with indemnity clauses, the Act is concerned only with exemption clauses, that is, with clauses which have the effect of excluding or restricting liability or of excluding or restricting an obligation or a duty. The scope of the Regulations includes such clauses but also extends beyond them to clauses which can confer rights on the party relying on them. This is clear not only from the operative parts of the Regulations, which refer generally to "an unfair term in a contract",[43] but also from the list of illustrations given in the Regulations of terms which may (though they will not necessarily) be regarded as unfair.[44] The list includes terms which allow the seller to retain sums paid by the consumer if the latter decides not to conclude or perform the contract, terms which require the consumer to pay a disproportionately high amount of compensation if he fails to perform his obligations, terms which automatically extend a fixed-term contract if the consumer does not give notice of termination, and terms which enable sellers or suppliers to increase their charges.[45] None of these provisions would fall within the 1977 Act since they are all terms which confer rights on the supplier and not terms which exclude or restrict his liability.

(3) Definitions

The Regulations contain a series of definitions comparable to those (already discussed)[46] in the 1977 Act.

(a) "SELLER" OR "SUPPLIER". The Regulations define this expression to mean "any natural or legal person who, in contracts covered by these Regulations, is acting for the purposes of his trade, business or profession . . . "[47] The words "contracts covered by these Regulations" here refer to contracts between such a seller or supplier and a consumer, containing terms which have not been "individually negotiated".[48] The definition however, perhaps deliberately, maintains an enigmatic silence as to the subject-matter of such contracts: in other words, it leaves open the question what it is that the seller must sell or the supplier supply. The 1994 Regulations answered these questions by defining seller as a person who sold "goods" and a supplier as one who supplied

---

[38] Regs 8(1), 3(1) (definition of "seller or supplier").

[39] See the discussion of the meaning of "seller" and "supplier" at p.268, below.

[40] *e.g.* ss.2 and 3.

[41] Above, pp.264–266.

[42] In particular, that relating to contracts for the transfer of interests in land: see above p.265, below, pp.278–279.

[43] reg.5(1); *cf.* reg.4(1).

[44] 1999 Regulations, Sch.2.

[45] *ibid.*, para.1(d), (e), (h), (l); below, p.275–276.

[46] See above, pp.246–248.

[47] reg.3(1).

[48] See regs 3(1) (definition of "unfair terms"), 4(1); for exceptions, see below, p.278.

"goods or services".[49] These words appear to have been intended to reflect the frequent use of the phrase "goods or services" in the Directive[50] on which the 1994 Regulations were, and the 1999 Regulations are, based and in the light of which the Regulations are to be interpreted[51]; and they have indeed survived in some of the provisions of the 1999 Regulations.[52] It seems that they were dropped from the definition of "seller or supplier" in the 1999 Regulations so as to leave open the question whether those Regulations could apply to contracts for the disposition of interests in land and similar problems could arise in relation to contracts for the transfer of interests in intellectual property or for the creation or issue of certain financial securities.[53] No doubt some aspects of such contracts would fall within the concept of "services" within the Directive and the Regulations (where they still use this term[54]); but this argument would not apply to a simple contract for the sale of land which did not oblige the vendor to do anything except to convey his interest to the purchaser. There is as yet no English authority on the point whether such a contract would fall within the Regulations.[55]

(b) "CONSUMER". This expression is defined[56] to mean "any natural person who, in making contracts covered by these Regulations,[57] is acting for purposes which are outside his trade, business or profession". The definition differs in various ways from the definition of "dealing as consumer" in the 1977 Act. First, it is not part of the definition under the Regulations (as it is under the Act) that the other party must make the contract in the course of a business; but this is a point of no significance as the Regulations have no effect on the contract unless the other party[58] acts for purposes relating to his trade, business or profession.[59] Secondly, the Regulations as a general rule[60] include only natural persons in the definition of consumer, while under the Act a corporation can deal as consumer in relation to a contract not made in the course of a business: *e.g.* if a company not engaged in the entertainment business hired musicians for social purposes of one of its staff.[61] Thirdly, a person is not to be regarded as dealing as a consumer for the purposes of the Act if he is an "individual"[62] and the goods are second hand goods sold at public auction which individuals have the opportunity of attending in person,[63] but a person who buys in this way may be a "consumer" within the Regulations. Finally, under the Act a person deals as consumer only if "he neither

---

[49] 1994 Regulations, reg.2(1).

[50] Dir 93/13 Recitals 2, 5, 6, 16, 18, 19 and Art.4(1); *cf.* Recitals 7 and 9 ("goods and services"), and see Recital 1, below, p.278, p.279.

[51] See below, p.278 n.65.

[52] reg.6(1), 6(2)(b). See also Sch.1, para.1(c), (f), (e), and (m); *cf. ibid.*, para.1(k) ("product or service").

[53] Such contracts are excepted from the scope of the Unfair Contract Terms Act 1977: above, pp.264 *et seq.*

[54] See above, n.50.

[55] See further pp.278–279, below.

[56] reg.3(1).

[57] *cf.* above at n.48.

[58] *i.e.*, the seller or supplier: see reg.4(1).

[59] See the definitions of "seller or supplier", above.

[60] Exceptionally, for the purposes of Arbitration Act 1996 the Regulations are extended by ss.89–91 to consumer arbitration agreements so that such an agreement is unfair even though the consumer is a legal (as opposed to a natural) person where the amount claimed is £5,000 or less: Arbitration Agreements (Specified Amounts) Order 1999 (SI 1999/2167).

[61] The amendment of s.12(1)(c) of the 1977 Act discussed at p.227, above relates only to contracts for the supply of *goods* and so would not affect the example given in the text.

[62] There seems to be no significant distinction between "an individual" and a "natural person" within the definition of "consumer" reg.3(1), above, after n.56.

[63] 1977 Act, s.12(2), as substituted by Sale and Supply of Goods to Consumers Regulations 2002 (SI 2002/3045), reg. 14(3).

makes the contract in the course of a business nor holds himself out as doing so",[64] while under the Regulations a person is a consumer if in making the contract he "is acting for purposes which are outside his trade, business or profession".[65] These differences between the definitions in the Regulations and the Act should, however, be considered against the background of the relative scope of the two legislative regimes. The Regulations have effect only on contracts with consumers while many of the Act's provisions apply even where both parties act in the course of a business. It is often only the *degree* of control which is affected under the Act by the distinction between such a transaction and one in which one party deals as consumer, so that, for example, an exemption clause in a consumer transaction will be simply ineffective, while one in a business transaction will be subject to the requirement of reasonableness.

A person may be a consumer for the purposes of the Regulations even in relation to a transaction of considerable value: *e.g.*, in one case, to a contract to acquire foreign currency worth $7million.[66] The value of the transaction appears likewise to be no bar to a person's dealing as consumer for the purposes of the 1977 Act.

(c) TERM NOT INDIVIDUALLY NEGOTIATED. The Regulations apply only[67] to terms which have not been individually negotiated; and they provide that a term "shall always be regarded as not having been individually negotiated where it has been drafted in advance *and* the consumer has therefore not been able to influence the substance of the term".[68] This definition does not require the term to have been drafted by the seller or supplier: it would cover a term drafted by a trade association for use by its members. The requirement that the term must have been drafted "in advance" prompts the question: in advance of what? The most obvious answer appears to be "in advance of the conclusion of the contract"; but this is unsatisfactory because all the terms of a contract will normally be drafted before the contract is made. "In advance" is therefore perhaps more appropriately taken to mean "in advance of the negotiations leading to the conclusion of the contract," so that it is *because* of the time at which the term was drafted that the consumer could not influence its substance.[69] Where a term has been negotiated between organisations representing on the one hand sellers or suppliers and on the other hand consumers, it would appear not to be "individually" negotiated but the fact that the term has been negotiated between such organisations will no doubt be relevant to the issue of its fairness.

Where one or more terms (or aspects of a particular term) have been individually negotiated, but the rest of the contract has not been so negotiated, the Regulations will apply to the rest of the contract if, viewed as a whole, it is a "pre-formulated standard contract".[70] The burden of proof on the issue whether a term was individually negotiated is on the seller or supplier who seeks to rely on the term.[71] A similar issue may arise under s.3 of the Unfair Contract Terms Act 1977 which applies where one party deals on the other's written standard terms. The section, however, lays down no rule as to the burden of proof on this issue; though other sections of the Act do require the party relying on an exemption clause to show (where these points are relevant) that the term was reasonable or that the other party was not dealing as consumer.[72]

---

[64] s.12(1)(a).
[65] reg.3(1).
[66] *Standard Bank of London Ltd v Abelowolakis* [2000] I.L.Pr. 766.
[67] See above, p.267, n.32.
[68] reg.5(2) (italics supplied).
[69] See the word "therefore" in the definition quoted at n.68, above.
[70] reg.5(3).
[71] reg.5(4).
[72] ss.11(5) and 12(3).

(d) UNFAIRNESS AND GOOD FAITH. The definition of an "unfair term"[73] is the aspect of the Regulations which is likely to give rise to the greatest difficulty in their practical operation. Two ideas are central to the definition: the term must be "contrary to the requirement of good faith" and it must be one which "causes a significant imbalance in the parties' rights and obligations arising under the contract to the detriment of the consumer." These requirements standing alone would clearly be a source of considerable uncertainty, and the courts and the Regulations have sought in a number of ways to reduce this uncertainty.

(i) *Factors relevant to "significant imbalance".* First, the Regulations direct the court, in deciding the issue of "significant imbalance", to take into account or to refer to a number of factors.[74] One such factor is "the nature of the goods or services for which the contract was concluded" so that, for example, a term which was not fair in a contract for the sale of new goods might be fair if the goods were sold as being second-hand. The court is also directed to refer "to all the circumstances attending the conclusion of the contract" as at the time of its conclusion: here the fact that the consumer had examined goods before deciding to buy them would be relevant; and in a contract for the supply of services it would be relevant that, when the contract was made, the consumer was in a position to appreciate the risk that the services might fail to achieve the desired purpose.[75] It is significant that the Regulations refer at this point to the time of the conclusion of the contract, thus supporting the view that the issue of fairness (like that of reasonableness under the 1977 Act[76]) is to be determined by reference to the time of contracting. Finally, the court is directed to take into account "all the other terms of the contract or of another contract on which it is dependent". The point here is that a term which might, standing alone, appear to be unfair could be fair having regard to the structure or system of rights and immunities created by the contract as a whole. It might, for example, be fair for a supplier who undertook liabilities beyond those imposed under a particular type of contract at common law to require notice of claims in respect of such liabilities to be given within a period shorter than the normal period of limitation for claims of the kind in question. The words "or of another contract on which it is dependent" would apply similar reasoning to the case in which the particular contract in question was made under a "master contract" governing a series of transactions between the parties.

(ii) *"Core provisions."* Secondly, the Regulations are not intended to operate as a mechanism of quality or price control.[77] Reg.6(2) accordingly provides that "In so far as it is in plain intelligible language, the assessment of fairness of a term shall not relate (a) to the definition of the main subject-matter of the contract, or (b) to the adequacy of the price or remuneration, as against the goods or services supplied in exchange." This

---

[73] In regs 5(1) and 6(1).

[74] *ibid.*

[75] *e.g.* where a ticket was bought to view an event, the parties knowing of a risk that it might be called off, as in the renegotiated term in *Clark v Lindsay* (1902) 88 L.T. 198 (below, p.288, n.17), where that term would now be regarded as having been "individually negotiated" within reg.5(2).

[76] s.11(1).

[77] This sentence is cited with apparent approval in *Director General of Fair Trading v First National Bank plc* [2001] UKHL 52; [2002] 1 A.C. 481, at [12] by Lord Bingham, with whose reasoning all the other members of the House of Lords agreed. Lord Roger, however, at [64] expresses "no concluded view" on the question whether, under the Regulations, it is open to the court to consider "whether there is an equivalence between the services or goods and the consideration for them". He suggests that to regard this point as relevant "would seem to be inconsistent with the reference to the price/quality ratio' in the nineteenth recital" of the Directive (above p.267, n.29) to which the Regulations give effect. This recital is not easy to interpret but it seems to mean that this ratio is not relevant to the fairness of the price term itself (first sentence) though it may be relevant to the fairness of *other* terms of the contract (second sentence).

provision may be compared with a number of common law principles discussed else-where in this book. The most important of these principles is that the court will not, as a general rule, investigate the adequacy of consideration.[78] A term is not unfair for the purposes of the Regulations merely because it fixes a price or remuneration which may be regarded as "excessive" by the application of some objective standard of valuation.[79] Conversely, the Regulations leave it open to the parties to define the subject-matter of the contract: in this respect, they resemble the common law rules discussed earlier in this Chapter,[80] under which there would be no breach at all, even though the subject-matter was in some objective sense defective, if what was supplied was what the parties had contracted about: *e.g.* where the contract was simply to supply "seed" rather than "cabbage seed" and the seed, when planted, disappointed the buyer's expectation of yielding a crop of cabbages.[81] Similarly, in the case of the hostess who asked a supplier to "send me peas or if you haven't got peas send me beans, but for heaven's sake send something",[82] the term allowing the supplier to make such a choice would not appear to fall within the Regulations. The term would not be even *prima facie* unfair (as one enabling the seller unilaterally to alter the characteristics of the product to be provided[83]) since this product was defined by the contract not as "peas" but as "peas or beans or something". A further group of terms excluded from control on the principle of reg.6(2) consists of terms in insurance contracts which "clearly define or circumscribe the insured risk and the insurer's liability".[84] This exclusion is, however, narrower in scope than the exclusion of "any contract of insurance" from the 1977 Act.[85] Terms in an insurance contract, other than those which define its subject-matter, would therefore be within the Regulations, though not within the Act. This would, for example, be true of a clause requiring the consumer to give notice of claims within an unreasonably short period: such a clause could be *prima facie* unfair on the ground that it "hindered" the consumer's right to take legal action.[86]

Reg.6(2) is of crucial importance in recognising the parties' freedom of contract with respect to the essential features of their bargain. It is limited by the words of the Regulation to cases in which the term in question is "expressed in plain, intelligible language." Hence an obscurely expressed price term which, on its true construction, but unexpectedly, entitled the supplier to make additions to a price prominently stated elsewhere in the contractual document could, by reason of its obscurity, be an "unfair" term. The courts are, moreover, reluctant to give too wide a scope to the concept of a "core provision" since the effect of doing this would be to except too great a range of contract terms from the scope of the Regulations so that their object would be "plainly frustrated".[87] A term which specifies payments to be made by the consumer is not necessarily one which relates to "the adequacy of the price or remuneration" within reg.6(2)(b).[88] The point may be illustrated by reference to a consumer credit agreement, in which a term specifying the rate of interest would no doubt fall within these words;

---

[78] See above, p.74.

[79] *cf.* below, p.422.

[80] See above, p.228.

[81] Example based on the *George Mitchell* case [1983] 2 A.C. 803, above, p.235.

[82] See above, p.228.

[83] Within reg.5(2) and Sch.2, para.1(k).

[84] See Dir.93/13, Recital 19.

[85] 1977 Act, Sch.1, para.1(a). This provision also excludes contracts "to pay an annuity on a human life;" the Regulations do not except such contracts.

[86] 1999 Regulations, Sch.2, para.1(q).

[87] *Director General of Fair Trading v First National Bank plc* [2001] UKHL 52; [2002] 1 A.C. 481, [12]; *cf. ibid.* at [34].

[88] Formerly reg.3(2)(b) of the 1994 Regulations considered in the case cited in n.87, above.

but the House of Lords has held[89] that they did not cover a term requiring the debtor to pay interest on outstanding amounts, even after judgment had been given against him for the principal sum, since this term was "ancillary"[90] to his principal obligation. The term was therefore subject to the Regulations, though it was upheld as being neither "unfair" nor "contrary to the requirement of good faith" since, when the contract was made,[91] neither party would have supposed that the lender "would willingly forgo any part of its principal or interest".[92]

The requirement of considering the adequacy of the price or remuneration "as against"[93] the subject-matter of the contract could similarly restrict the concept of a "core provision" and hence of reg.6(2). The point may be illustrated by reference to the case in which a contract for the hire of goods for a fixed period provides that the hirer is to pay a "holding charge" if he retains the goods after the end of the stipulated period.[94] Although such a provision could be described as the "price" of an option to extend the period of hire,[95] it could also be regarded as "ancillary"[96] to the main object of the contract; or as fixing the "price," not of what was to be supplied, but of the option described above. The provision would then be subject to the Regulations and, if the charge were unusually high, the term requiring it to be paid could be regarded as "unfair" within them. Indeed, the example comes very close to one of the illustrations given in Sch.2 of *prima facie* unfair terms.[97]

(iii) *Good faith.* Thirdly, the requirement of good faith has been described in the House of Lords as "one of fair and open dealing".[98] Openness here refers to the way in which terms are set out: they must be "expressed fully, clearly and legibly, containing no concealed pitfalls or traps" and giving due "prominence to terms which might operate disadvantageously to the customer".[99] Fairness refers to the substance of the contract and requires the supplier not "whether deliberately or unconsciously, [to] take advantage of the consumer's necessity, indigence, lack of experience, unfamiliarity with the subject-matter of the contract, [or] weak bargaining position".[1] The Directive on which the Regulations are based further lists, among factors relevant to good faith, "the strength of the bargaining positions of the parties, whether the consumer had an inducement to agree to the term and whether the goods or services were supplied to the special order of the consumer".[2] It is probably impossible to achieve greater precision in formulating such an essentially flexible requirement.

(iv) *Examples of unfair terms.* Finally, the Regulations contain (in Sch.2) a long and elaborate list of terms "which *may* be regarded as unfair",[3] this list in effect provides

---

[89] *Director General of Fair Trading v First National Bank plc*, above.

[90] *ibid.* at [12].

[91] See reg.6(1) (formerly reg.4(2) of the 1994 Regulations).

[92] *Director General of Fair Trading v First National Bank plc*, above, n.87 at [20].

[93] reg.6(2)(b).

[94] See *Interfoto Picture Library Ltd v Stiletto Visual Programmes Ltd* [1989] Q.B. 433, above, p.245.

[95] *cf.* below, p.1004.

[96] Above, at n.90.

[97] Sch.2, para.1(h), above, p.268 at n.45.

[98] *Director General of Fair Trading v First National Bank plc* [2001] UKHL 52; [2002] 1 A.C. 481 at [17].

[99] *ibid.*

[1] *ibid.*

[2] Dir.93/13, Recital 16. These guidelines were formerly contained in Sch.2 of the 1994 Regulations (above, p.267) but they are not reproduced in the 1999 Regulations. To some extent they form the basis of the judicial guidelines summarised in the text above. They also resemble the guidelines for applying the reasonableness test contained in Sch.2 of the Unfair Contract Terms Act 1977. The further statement in Recital 16, above, that the requirement of good faith may be satisfied by "dealing fairly and equitably with the consumer" seems to be more in the nature of a restatement that a guidelines for its operation.

[3] Reg.5(5), emphasis added.

further guidelines. It is "indicative and non-exhaustive",[4] so that, on the one hand, a term is not unfair merely because it is of a type included in the list; and, on the other hand, a term may be unfair even though it does not fall within, or closely resemble, any such type of term.

It will be convenient to refer to terms included in the list as "*prima facie* unfair terms". Some of the *prima facie* unfair terms listed in Sch.2 would also be classified as exemption clauses within the 1977 Act. Like the Act, Sch.2 distinguishes between clauses which exclude or limit liability for death or personal injury and other clauses excluding or limiting rights: any term of the former kind is *prima facie* unfair,[5] while in the case of a term of the latter kind there is the additional requirement that it must "inappropriately" exclude or limit the consumer's rights.[6] The list in Sch.2 also includes terms "limiting" the seller's or supplier's obligation to respect commitments undertaken by his agents[7]: such terms would clearly be regarded as an exemption clause under the Act. The fact that the Schedule at this point refers only to terms "limiting" the obligation would not preclude a clause which *excluded* it from being also regarded as *prima facie* unfair: this follows from the fact that the list is not exhaustive.

Terms "excluding or hindering"[8] the consumer's right to take legal action or exercise any other legal remedy are included in the list of *prima facie* unfair terms. In this context, the list refers, in particular, to terms "requiring the consumer to take disputes exclusively to arbitration not covered by legal provisions."[9] At first sight, this goes beyond the Act, which, while recognising that a term excluding or restricting a remedy may be an exemption clause,[10] expressly excepts arbitration agreements from this category.[11] The reference to arbitration clauses in Sch.2 is, however, restricted by the words "not covered by legal provisions" and the purpose of this restriction may be to narrow the category of *prima facie* unfair arbitration clauses to those in which the parties have agreed to exclude the powers of the courts to control the arbitrator's decision. In English law, the effectiveness of such a stipulation is subject to limitations which, in the case of a "domestic arbitration agreement", make the stipulation ineffective if it is contained in the original contract between the seller or supplier and the consumer.[12] Other types of terms listed in Sch.2, which would also be governed by the 1977 Act, are clauses entitling the seller or supplier to dissolve the contract at his discretion where the same facility is not granted to the consumer,[13] to terminate a contract of indeterminate duration without reasonable notice (except on serious grounds),[14] to alter the terms of the contract unilaterally without a valid reason which is specified in the contract[15] or to alter unilaterally without a valid reason any characteristic of the product or service to be provided[16]: all such terms could be subject to the requirement of reasonableness under s.3 of the 1977 Act.[17] Yet other terms listed in Sch.2 which would be classified as

---

[4] *ibid.*

[5] Sch.2, para.1(a).

[6] *ibid.* para.1(b). There is no reference to negligence in these illustrations.

[7] *ibid.* para.1(n).

[8] *ibid.* para.1(q).

[9] *ibid.*, para.1(q); the Arbitration Agreements (Specified Amounts) Order 1999 (SI 1999/2167), makes an arbitration agreement with a consumer unfair where less than £5,000 is claimed.

[10] 1977 Act s.13(1).

[11] *ibid.*, s.13(2).

[12] Arbitration Act 1996, s.87, below, p.447.

[13] Sch.2, para.1(f); *cf.* 1977 Act s.3(2)(b)(ii).

[14] Sch.2, para.1(g), subject to *ibid.* para.2(a) and (c); *cf.* 1977 Act s.3(2)(b)(i).

[15] Sch.2, para.1(k); *cf.* 1977 Act, s.3(2)(6)(ii).

[16] Sch.2, para.1(j), subject to *ibid.* para.2(b) and (c); *cf.* 1977 Act s.3(2)(b)(i).

[17] See above, pp.252–254. There is no reference in the last illustration to termination *for breach* by the consumer; as to this, see above, pp.253–256.

exemption clauses under the Act are terms which make the seller's or supplier's commitments subject to compliance with a particular formality,[18] and terms giving him the right to determine whether the goods or services supplied are in conformity with the contract, or giving him the exclusive right to interpret the contract[19]: all such terms could be treated, for the purpose of the 1977 Act, as exemption clauses on the ground that they made the enforcement of the seller's or supplier's liability "subject to restrictive or onerous conditions" within s.13 of that Act.

Sch.2 also refers to many varieties of terms which would not be regarded as exemption clauses under the Act or at common law,[20] and it is this aspect of the Schedule which is significant in indicating the potentially wide scope of the Regulations. The list in Sch.2 in particular includes many types of terms which confer rights (other than rights of cancellation) on the seller or supplier.

Some such clauses might, indeed, be ineffective at common law on grounds discussed elsewhere in this book. This might, for example, be true of a term making an agreement binding on the consumer while making performance by the seller or supplier subject to a condition depending on his own will alone[21]: at common law there might in such a case be no consideration for the consumer's promise so long as the seller's or supplier's promise remained executory.[22] Similarly, the list includes a term requiring the consumer, when in breach, to pay a disproportionately high sum in compensation[23]: at common law, such a term is likely to be invalid as a penalty.[24] The same might be true of terms entitling the seller to forfeit a deposit paid by the consumer[25]: these again might in certain circumstances be invalid as penalties at common law.[26]

A significant number of *prima facie* unfair terms listed in Sch.2 are, however, of a kind that has not, apart from the Regulations been subjected to legal control, at least as a matter of general principle, either at common law or by legislation (other than legislation applying to specific types of contract). One type of term within this group is that automatically extending a contract of fixed duration unless the consumer gives notice to terminate it, where the time for giving such notice is unreasonably early[27]: in contracts outside the scope of the Regulations, there appears to be no ground on which the validity of such a term could be called into question at common law or under the 1977 Act. The same is true of another type of *prima facie* invalid term listed in Sch.2, *i.e.* one "providing for the price of goods to be determined at the time of delivery"[28] or one providing for the price of goods or services to be increased without giving the consumer the right to cancel if the final price is too high in relation to the originally agreed price.[29] There is no reason to suppose that such a clause is open to attack at common law and even its *prima facie* invalidity under the Regulations is extensively qualified in relation to transactions in which the price is linked to stock exchange fluctuations or which contain

---

[18] Sch.2, para.1(n); it is not clear whether the concluding words of this illustration are limited to commitments undertaken by agents.

[19] Sch.2, para.1(*m*).

[20] This is also true of other legislation designed to prevent avoidance by contract of a legislative scheme: *e.g.*, Landlord and Tenant (Covenants) Act 1995. s.25(1)(a).

[21] Sch.2, para.1(c). Terms conferring such rights can be exemption clauses under s.3 the 1977 Act: see text at n.13 above.

[22] See above, p.83.

[23] Sch.2, para.1(e).

[24] See below, p.999.

[25] Sch.2, para.1(d).

[26] See below, p.1008.

[27] Sch.2, para.1(h).

[28] Sch.2, para.1(l).

[29] *ibid.*

other indexation clauses; and in relation to contracts for the purchase of foreign currency or instruments expressed in foreign currency.[30] Yet another type of *prima facie* unfair term is that obliging the consumer "to fulfil all his obligation where the seller or supplier does not perform his".[31] A clause excluding the consumer's right of set-off would no doubt be regarded as an exemption clause for the purposes of the 1977 Act[32]; but the same would not be true of a clause which so defined the consumer's obligation that he had *no* right of set-off but only a cross-claim for damages in respect of the other party's default.[33] Again, a term is *prima facie* invalid within Sch.2 if it gives the seller or supplier "the possibility of transferring his rights and obligations under the contract where this may serve to reduce the guarantees for the consumer without the latter's agreement".[34] At common law the seller or supplier could not strictly transfer his obligations, though he might arrange for them to be vicariously performed,[35] and he could certainly transfer his rights by assignment[36]; and these powers would not seem at common law to be limited by the possibility that this would impair the consumer's guarantees. A term expressly limiting the effectiveness of guarantees given by the seller or supplier would no doubt be subject to control as an exemption clause, but that is not the type of term here under consideration. Yet another *prima facie* invalid term is one which has the object or effect of "irrevocably binding the consumer to terms with which he had no real opportunity of becoming acquainted before the conclusion of the contract".[37] This may already represent the common law position with regard to the incorporation of standard terms by notice[38]; but at first sight, it differs strikingly from the common law rule governing the incorporation of such terms by signature. The latter common law rule is, however, concerned with the effect of signature,[39] rather than with terms specifying that effect. If a consumer signed a document containing a term incorporating by reference conditions set out in another document, then *that term* could be *prima facie* unfair under the Regulations if the other document was not readily accessible to the consumer.

(4) Excluded terms

(a) STATUTORY OR REGULATORY PROVISIONS. The Regulations do not apply to contractual terms which reflect "mandatory statutory or regulatory provisions".[40] The effect of these words is that the Regulations do not apply to terms which a contract is by other legislation required to contain.[41] The 1977 Act is subject to similar, but more broadly expressed, limitation: it does not apply to contractual provisions "*authorised or required*"[42] by legislation. The use of the word "mandatory"[43] in the Regulations seems to mean that the exception in them does not extend to provisions which are merely authorised but not required by other legislation; though the fact that they are so authorised would no doubt be taken into account in determining whether they were

---

[30] Sch.2, para.2(c) and (d).
[31] Sch.2, para.1(o).
[32] See above, pp.247–248.
[33] See below, p.763.
[34] Sch.2, para.1(p).
[35] See below, p.757.
[36] See below, Chap.16.
[37] Sch.3, para.1(i).
[38] See above, pp.217–219.
[39] See above, p.197.
[40] reg.4(2)(a).
[41] *e.g.*, below, p.285.
[42] s.29(1)(a).
[43] Above, at n.40.

"unfair". For example, the Consumer Credit Act 1974 at least by implication authorises a term in a regulated hire-purchase agreement requiring the hirer on exercising his right to cancel to make a minimum payment not exceeding on half of the hire-purchase price.[44] If that sum is excessive, the hirer can seek relief by way of reduction of the minimum payment under the 1974 Act[45]; and an undesirable conflict would be created between that Act and the Regulations if, under them, such a term were held to be "unfair" (and so not bringing at all on the hirer).

(b) INTERNATIONAL CONVENTIONS. The Regulations also do not apply to contractual terms which reflect "the provisions or principles of international conventions to which the Member States or the Community are party".[46] Again this exclusion resembles a similar limitation on the scope of the 1977 Act.[47] The exclusion is, however, wider than that contained in the Act in two respects. First, it refers to international conventions to which the Member States or the Community are party (while the Act refers only to international agreements to which the United Kingdom is a party). Secondly, the Regulations refer to "the provisions *or principles*" of such conventions, so that a term based on the principles of a relevant convention would not be governed by the Regulations even though the contract in which the term was contained was not governed by the convention: *e.g.* where a term in a contract for the domestic carriage of goods was based on the principles of a convention which in terms governed only international carriage.

Unlike the 1977 Act,[48] the Regulations contain no exception for international supply contracts; but it seems that contracts governed by the Vienna Convention on Contracts for the International Sale of Goods[49] would fall within the present exception. The point is not likely to be of major importance since the Regulations apply only to consumer contracts, and these will only rarely (if ever) be governed by the Convention.[50] But where the Convention does govern such contracts, the parties are allowed by it to "derogate" from or vary its provisions,[51] and thus a seller can exclude or restrict liability which, but for such derogation, would be imposed on him by the Convention. This appears to be one of the "principles" of the Convention, so that the Regulations would not apply to a term of this kind in such a contract.

(5) Excluded contracts

(a) CONTRACTS SPECIFICALLY EXCLUDED. The Directive on which the Regulations are based lists a number of contracts which "must be excluded from this Directive".[52] This list was reproduced in the 1994 Regulations[53] but is no longer contained in the 1999 Regulations. It is, nevertheless, arguable that contracts in this list remain outside the scope of the Regulations since, by force of the Directive, they are not contracts under which there is a sale or supply of the kind contemplated by it[54] to the consumer.[55] The

---

[44] s.100(1).

[45] s.100(3), below, p.1005.

[46] reg.4(2)(b); for definitions of "Member States" and "the Community," see reg.3(1).

[47] s.29(1)(b).

[48] 1977 Act s.26.

[49] See above, p.29.

[50] Art.2(a) of the Vienna Convention; Art.1, referring to "places of business," may suggest that the Convention does not apply to consumer contracts at all.

[51] Art.6 of the Vienna Convention.

[52] Dir.93/13, Recital 10.

[53] SI 1994/3159, reg.3(1) and Sch.1(a) to (e).

[54] *i.e.*, contracts for sale or supply of "goods" (or "products") and for the supply of services (*sc. to* the consumer): see above p.269 n.50.

[55] *cf. Chitty on Contracts* (28th ed.), §15–021.

most important of the contracts excluded by the Directive are contracts "relating to employment".[56] This exclusion differs from the corresponding provision of the 1977 Act, some of the provisions of which do not extend to contracts of employment "except in favour of the employee".[57] Under the Directive, even the employee cannot rely on the unfairness of a term against the employer: the problems arising from such terms are left to be dealt with by employment law or perhaps by collective bargaining. The Directive also excludes "contracts relating to succession rights" or to "any contract relating to rights under family law"[58]; but these exceptions are unlikely to be of great practical importance in English law, which seems to provide no examples of such contracts being made between a seller or supplier acting in the course of business and a consumer. The Directive finally excludes "contracts relating to the incorporation and organisation of companies or partnership agreements."[59] This resembles a similar exclusion from the operation of the 1977 Act.[60] The question whether the Regulations apply to dealings in company shares after their issue is part of the wider problem (to be discussed below) whether certain contracts, though not specifically excluded, are nevertheless unaffected by the Regulations because they fall outside their inclusive provisions.

(b) CONTRACTS NOT COVERED BY THE INCLUSIVE PROVISIONS. It will be recalled that the 1977 Act excludes certain types of contracts from its scope and, in particular, that it excludes any contract "so far as it relates to" the creation of an interest in land or in intellectual property.[61] The 1999 Regulations contain no such exclusions, though under the 1994 Regulations it was arguable that such contracts were impliedly excluded by the definitions of a "seller" as a person who sold "goods" and of a "supplier" as one who supplied "goods or services."[62] This argument is no longer available now that the definition of "seller or supplier" in the 1999 Regulations[63] has ceased to tell us what it is that must be sold or supplied. But, as we have noted in discussing that definition,[64] the Directive on which those Regulations are based, and which must be taken into account in interpreting them,[65] contain many references to "goods or services"[66]; and the Regulations themselves contain two such references.[67] These references do not, however, conclude the question whether contracts for the sale of interests in land are excluded by the use of the word "goods" since in EC Directives and in legislation based on them this word does not necessarily bear the same meaning as that normally given to it in English law[68]; indeed, the view that in the Directive it bears a wider meaning is supported by some of the items in the list of *prima facie* unfair terms annexed to the

---

[56] Dir.93/13, Recital 10.

[57] 1977 Act, Sch.1, para.4.

[58] Dir.93/13, Recital 10.

[59] *ibid.*

[60] 1977 Act, Sch.1, para.1(d).

[61] Unfair Contract Terms Act 1977, Sch.1, para.1(b) and (c).

[62] 1994 Regulations, reg.2(1).

[63] 1999 Regulations, reg.3(1).

[64] See above, p.269.

[65] Case C14/83 *Von Colson and Kamman v Land Nordrhein Westfalen* [1984] E.C.R. 1891; Craig and De Búrca, *E.U. Law* (2nd ed. 1998); *Chitty on Contracts* (28th ed.), §15–006.

[66] Dir.93/13, Recitals 2, 5, 6, 16, 18, 19 and Art.4(1); *cf.* Recitals 7 and 9 ("goods and services").

[67] reg.6(1) and 6(2)(b).

[68] Dir.97/7 on protection of consumers in respect of "distance contracts" applies to "contracts concerning goods and services" but finds it necessary specifically to *except* "contracts concluded for the construction and sale of immovable property . . . except for rental", This Directive has been implemented in the UK by the Consumer Protection (Distance Selling) Regulations 2000 (SI 2000/2334) under which a "distance contract" is likewise one "concerning goods or services" (reg.3(1)) and contracts "for the sale or disposition of an interest in land except for a rental agreement" are specifically excepted (reg.5(1)(a)). In Enterprise Act 2002, s.232(2)(a), "goods include buildings or other structures" but not, it seems, the land itself.

Directive and reproduced in the Regulations.[69] Some aspects of contracts for the sale of land could clearly come within the Directive (and hence of the Regulations) as contracts for the supply of "services": this would, for example be true of a covenant in such a contract to keep the subject-matter in repair or to render some other service in relation to it; but this reasoning would not apply to a simple contract for the conveyance of freehold land, containing no such additional undertakings.[70] Most contracts for the sale of private dwellings would not be covered by the Regulations because in them the seller, as well as the buyer, would act in a "private" capacity, *i.e.*, not "for the purposes relating to his trade, business or profession".[71] But the seller would be likely so to act where he was a developer selling to a "private" buyer (who would be likely to fall within the definition of "consumer"). The question whether in such circumstances a simple contract for the sale of the freehold to the buyer would fall within the Regulations is one that awaits judicial determination in England.[72] As a matter of policy it can be argued, on the one hand, that there is no good reason why such a seller should not be subject to the Regulations; and, on the other, that the buyer has less need than the normal consumer of their protection since in such a transaction he is likely to be represented by his own solicitor. The latter consideration would not apply to what is now probably the most common type of contract for the "sale" of intellectual property to a consumer *i.e.*, to one licensing him to use computer software; but as such contracts often also involve the transfer of a moveable physical object it seems that they would be contracts for the sale of supply of "goods or services" within the Directive and hence be covered by the Regulations.[73] Contracts of insurance are excluded from the scope of the 1927 Act[74]; but they are within the scope of the Directive[75] and hence (again) of the Regulations.

The failure of the 1999 Regulations to specify what it is that must be sold as supplied, coupled with the references noted above in the Directive and in the Regulations, to "goods" and "services"[76] gives rise to yet more difficulty in relation to certain other kinds of transactions which are not transactions in "goods" within other statutory definitions of that expression.[77] Of these, the best known is that in the Sale of Goods Act 1979, which provides that, in that Act, the word "goods" includes "all personal chattels *other than things in action or money*"[78]; and this definition is followed or adopted by many other statutes which have as at least one of their objects the protection of consumers.[79] The Vienna Convention on Contracts for the International Sale of Goods similarly does not apply to sales of "stocks, shares investment securities and money".[80] In the Regulations, however, some of the illustrations of *prima facie* unfair terms are evidently

---

[69] See the Annex to Dir.93/13 and Sch.2 of the 1999 Regulations. Some illustrations of contracts which are assumed in these lists to be within the Directive and the Regulations are discussed in the paragraph that follows in the text below.

[70] The reference in Recital 1 of Dir.93/13 to "goods" which "move freely" is scarcely appropriate to such contracts.

[71] 1999 Regulations, reg.3(1).

[72] For the view that such contracts should be covered by the 1994 Regulations, see Attew, 58 M.L.R. 696; *cf.* Bright and Bright, 111 L.Q.R. 655; *Chitty on Contracts* (28th ed.), §§15–012, 15–013.

[73] See *St Albans City & District Council v International Computers* [1996] 4 All E.R. 481 *per* Sir Iain Glidewell; the question in that case was discussed in relation to the Unfair Contract Terms Act 1977 and the buyer was not a "consumer".

[74] 1977 Act, Sch.1, para.1(a).

[75] See the reference to "insurance contracts" in Recital 19 of the Directive.

[76] See n.66, above.

[77] See *Benjamin's Sale of Goods* (6th ed.), §1–079.

[78] Sale of Goods Act 1979, s.62(1).

[79] *e.g.* Consumer Credit Act 1974, s.189(1); Unfair Contract Terms Act 1977, ss.14, 25; Supply of Goods and Services Act 1982, s.18.

[80] Art.2(d).

based on the assumption that certain transactions in securities could fall within the scope of the Regulations.[81] The assumption is not easy to reconcile with the references to "goods" and "services" in the Directive and in the Regulations[82] since the subject-matter of such a contract does not seem to be covered by either of these expressions. A similar difficulty arises from the assumption that contracts for the purchase or sale of foreign currency can fall within the Regulations.[83] It is not impossible for "goods" to be defined so as to include money[84]; but usually money, when used as a medium of exchange, is not regarded as falling within the definition of goods.[85] It seems highly unlikely that a person who in the course of business supplied English money in exchange for foreign currency would be regarded as a seller of goods; and it seems probable that the same is true of the converse situation, where the seller supplied foreign currency in exchange for English money. Such transactions can be brought within the scope of the Regulations only by arguing that the expression "goods" in them and in the Directive is used in an unusual and extended sense.

(6) Drafting and interpretation

Regulation 7 provides that "(1) A seller or supplier shall ensure that any written term of a contract is expressed in plain, intelligible language" and "(2) If there is doubt about the meaning of a written term, the interpretation most favourable to the consumer shall prevail . . . "[86] The restriction of these requirements to terms in writing indicates that oral contracts are covered by the Regulations[87] but (curiously) they are not required to be in plain or intelligible language. Failure to express a written term "in plain, intelligible language" does not of itself make the term even *prima facie* unfair. In this respect the present requirement is weaker than that already noted, by which a term defining the price or subject-matter of the contract must be in "plain intelligible language"[88]: here the sanction for failure to comply with the requirement is that the term may be considered unfair. The words of reg.7(2), quoted above appear to be no more than a legislative formulation of the *contra proferentem* principle.[89] No doubt this will most commonly apply to terms which are not drafted in plain, intelligible language; but it does not appear to be restricted to such terms. Language which is plain and intelligible may nevertheless be ambiguous; the fascination of oracular statements lies precisely in the fact that they combine these qualities.

(7) Effects of unfairness

(a) UNFAIR TERM NOT BINDING ON CONSUMER. Reg.8(1) provides that "an unfair term in a contract concluded with a consumer by a seller or supplier shall not be binding on the consumer". The exact legal consequence of this regulation will depend on the nature of the unfair term. If that term is one excluding or limiting the liability of the seller or supplier, or the rights of the consumer,[90] the latter will be able to enforce those rights as if the term had not been included in the contract. If the unfair term is one

---

[81] Sch.2, para.2(c).

[82] Above, nn.66 and 67.

[83] *ibid.*

[84] See Theft Act 1968, s.34(2)(b).

[85] Mann, *Legal Aspects of Money* (5th ed.), 24–26.

[86] The concluding words of reg.7(2) make this provision inapplicable to proceedings for injunctions under reg.12 to prevent the continued use of unfair terms.

[87] *cf.* Dir.93/13, Recital 11.

[88] reg.3(2), above, p.271.

[89] See above, p.221.

[90] Under Sch.2, para.1(a) and (b).

conferring rights on the seller or supplier (such as one extending a contract of fixed duration without giving the consumer a reasonable opportunity of cancelling it)[91] these rights will not arise. If effect has been given to such rights, reg.8(1) may require those effects to be undone: for example, where the term was unfair because it permitted the seller or supplier to retain sums paid by the consumer,[92] any such sums, if paid, would have to be restored. It is only the consumer who is not bound by the unfair term. The other party is so bound: for example, he may be bound by a term extending a contract of fixed duration[93] if the consumer should wish to enforce that term.

(b) REST OF CONTRACT GENERALLY UNAFFECTED. In general, the fact that the unfair term does not bind the consumer does not affect the binding force, even on the consumer, of the rest of the contract: for example, the fact that he is not bound by an exemption clause does not relieve him from liability for the price (though such liability may be reduced to the extent that a breach covered by the ineffective clause has caused him loss). The point is put beyond doubt by reg.8(2), which provides that "the contract shall continue to bind the parties if it is capable of continuing in existence without the unfair term." The reason for the concluding words of this provision is that sometimes an invalid term goes so much to the heart of the contract that the effect of its not being binding on the consumer is likely to be that the consumer is not bound by the contract at all. This would, for example, be the position where the term was unfair because it irrevocably bound the consumer "to terms with which he had no real opportunity of becoming acquainted before the conclusion of the contract".[94] If that term was not binding on the consumer, it would seem to follow that the terms to which it referred[95] were not binding on him either; and if those terms contained the whole or the essential part of the contract he would not be bound by any part of that contract. The other party would, however, be so bound if the consumer wished to enforce the contract: the argument that the consumer had provided no consideration because his own promises were not binding would probably be rejected on the ground that it was not the policy of the Regulations to protect the other party.[96] The question whether a term goes so much to the heart of the contract that the effect of its not being binding on the consumer is to relieve him of all obligations under the contract is obviously in borderline cases one of degree. The point may be illustrated by reference to a term which is *prima facie* unfair because it provides for the price of goods to be determined at the time of delivery without giving the consumer the right to cancel if that price is "too high in relation to the price agreed [if any?] when the contract was concluded".[97] One possible consequence of the consumer's taking the point that the term is not binding is that the contract contains no price term and is therefore not binding on him at all; another is that the contract contains no price term but remains in being as one under which a reasonable price must be paid; and a third is that the contract remains in being as one under which the originally agreed price (if any) must be paid. No doubt the result will depend on the exact wording of the price term; but, subject to this point, it is submitted that the "reasonable price" solution will normally achieve the most satisfactory balance between the interests of the parties. There is, of course, nothing to prevent the consumer from enforcing the contract according to its terms where it is in his interest to do so.

---

[91] Under Sch.2, para.1(h).
[92] Under Sch.2, para.1(d).
[93] See Sch.2, para.3(g).
[94] See Sch.2, para.1(i).
[95] See above, p.276.
[96] See above, p.149.
[97] See Sch.2, para.1(l), above, pp.275–276.

(c) COMPARISON OF EFFECTS OF UNFAIRNESS WITH 1977 ACT. The 1999 Regulations differ from the 1977 Act in that they lay down a single criterion (that of fairness[98]) on which the effectiveness of a term depends. Under that Act, by contrast, there are two possibilities: a term may be simply ineffective, or effective only insofar as it complies with the requirement of reasonableness. No difficulty arises from this difference in the situations (already discussed[99]) in which a term falls only within the scope of the Regulations or only within the scope of the Act. But where the same term falls within both legislative schemes there is the possibility that it may satisfy the requirements of the one but not those of the other. For example, a contract for the sale of goods to a consumer may contain a term limiting the seller's liability for breach of the terms implied by the Sale of Goods Act 1979 as to the quality of the goods. Such a term may be fair under the Regulations (which list among *prima facie* unfair terms those "*inappropriately* excluding or limiting"[1] the consumer's rights in respect of such terms) but it is simply ineffective under the Act.[2] Again, under the Regulations a term excluding or limiting liability for death or personal injury is only *prima facie* unfair,[3] while under the Act such a term is (if the defendant was negligent) simply ineffective.[4] The two schemes may also lead to different results where the same term is subject to a requirement of reasonableness under the Act and to one of fairness under the Regulations. No doubt in most cases a term which satisfied one of these requirements would also satisfy the other; but it is possible to imagine situations in which this might not be true, particularly where the guidelines for determining reasonableness under that Act differ from those for determining fairness under the Regulations.[5] A contract for the supply of services to a consumer might, for example, contain a term limiting the supplier's liability for breach to a specified sum of money, and this term might satisfy the requirement of reasonableness[6] under one of the guidelines applicable under the 1977 Act to such terms: *e.g.*, on the ground that the supplier could not have insured against the breach without materially raising his charges.[7] But this guideline has no counterpart in the Regulations so that under them the term in question could nevertheless be an unfair one. In all such cases, in which the term falls within both the Act and the Regulations, the party relying on the term will have to show that the term satisfies the requirements of both these legislative schemes.

(8) Restriction on evasion

Like the 1977 Act,[8] the Regulations protect the consumer against the risk of being deprived of his protection under them by means of a choice of law clause: they apply "notwithstanding any contract term which applies or purports to apply the law of a non-Member State, if the contract has a close connection with the territory of the Member States".[9] Thus the Regulations cannot be excluded by a term specifying a law applicable *only* by virtue of being so specified, but they can be excluded by a term specifying a law which would or might have applied even in absence of the term. Art.5 of the Rome

---

[98] reg.8.
[99] See above, pp.267 *et seq.*
[1] Sch.2, para.1(b).
[2] s.6(1).
[3] Sch.2, para.1(a).
[4] s.2(1).
[5] See above, p.273.
[6] Imposed by s.3 of the 1977 Act.
[7] *ibid.*, s.11(4), above, p.259.
[8] s.27(2), above, p.263.
[9] reg.7; for the definition of "Member State," see reg.3(1).

Convention (which has already been discussed[10]) gives similar protection to the consumer. The Regulations differ from the Act in that they do not except from their operation contracts governed by the law of a part of the United Kingdom only by virtue of the choice of the parties[11]; a consumer contract is perhaps thought unlikely to contain such a choice of law clause.

SECTION 4. OTHER LEGISLATIVE TECHNIQUES

Simply to deprive an exemption clause of legal validity might be a wholly ineffective means of control, particularly in cases between consumers on the one hand and commercial suppliers of goods and services on the other. If, for example, a contract contained an invalid exemption clause the consumer might believe that he was bound by it and so not pursue his claim. Even if he did make a claim, the supplier might settle it so as to avoid a judicial declaration of invalidity, and then continue to use the clause. To remedy this situation other legislative techniques have been devised.

1. Supervised Bargaining

This technique requires the bargain to be made under the supervision of the court or some administrative body. For example, the Landlord and Tenant Act 1985 provides that in certain leases covenants by the landlord to repair are implied.[12] These can be excluded but only by a court order made with the consent of both parties.[13] The court's supervision ensures that no unfair advantage is taken of the tenant.

2. Administrative Control

This technique involves the intervention of a public authority[14]; it was used by the Fair Trading Act 1973 in provisions to be replaced by the relevant sections of the Enterprise Act 2002[15] when those sections are brought into force. Under these sections, one of the functions of the Office of Fair Trading is to promote "good practice for the carrying out of activities"[16]: *e.g.* by making "arrangements for approving consumer codes".[17–21] Delegated legislation[22] made under the 1973 Act (and to be continued in force under the Act of 2002) also makes it an offence for a person who sells goods in the course of a business to a consumer to apply (or to purport to apply) to the transaction an exemption clause which would be void under the statutory provisions discussed earlier in this Chapter.[23] However, under s.26 of the 1973 Act the mere fact that such an offence has been committed does not make "a contract . . . void or unenforceable": the point of the section seems to be that the *whole contract* is not invalid, so that the supplier can enforce

---

[10] See above, p.263.

[11] 1977 Act, s.27(1), above, p.266.

[12] s.11; *cf.* Housing Act 1988, s.16.

[13] Landlord and Tenant Act 1985, s.12.

[14] *cf.* National Minimum Wage Act 1998, s.20.

[15] See especially ss.8 and 10.

[16] *ibid.*, s.8(1).

[17–21] *ibid.*, s.8(2).

[22] Consumer Transactions (Restrictions on Statements) Order 1976 (SI 1976/1813) as amended by Consumer Transactions (Restrictions on Statements) (Amendment) Order 1978 (SI 1978/127). For a successful prosecution, see *Hughes v Hall & Hall* [1981] R.T.R. 430. The *contra proferentem* rule (above, p.221) can here operate *in favour* of the proponent of the clause: see *Cavendish Woodhouse v Mancy* (1984) 82 L.G.R. 376 where no offence was committed by a seller of furniture "as seen," since these words did not exclude liability but only confirmed that the customer had seen the goods. *cf.* above, p.224.

[23] See above, pp.248–252. (completely ineffective terms).

other provisions in it. For example, if the goods were not seriously defective he could sue for the price in spite of the fact that the contract contained a punishable exemption clause.

The technique of administrative control is also used by the Unfair Terms in Consumer Contracts Regulation 1999, which impose on the Office of Fair Trading[24] ("OFT") a duty to consider any complaint made to it that any contract term drawn up for general use is unfair[25]; a similar duty is imposed on certain "qualifying bodies" (listed in the Regulations) which have agreed to consider such complaints.[26] If it appears to the OFT (or to the qualifying body) that the term is unfair, the OFT (or that body after due notice to it) may apply to the court for an injunction to restrain the use of the term, and the court may grant the injunction on such terms as it thinks fit.[27] The OFT and most of the qualifying bodies are also empowered to obtain information about the terms and use of any "pre-formulated contract in dealings with consumers",[28] and it is envisaged that the OFT and qualifying bodies may obtain undertakings from or on behalf of any person (such as a seller or supplier) as to the continued use of terms which it or the qualifying body considers to be unfair in contracts with consumers.[29] These provisions appear to be intended to promote negotiations between, on the one hand, the OFT and qualifying bodies, and, on the other, commercial sellers and suppliers or their trade associations. Such "pre-emptive challenges"[30] may well have greater practical effect than private litigation, initiated by consumers, in controlling unfair standard terms in consumer contracts.[31]

3. Prescribing the contents of a contract

This is another common method of controlling contracts of a particular type. It is well illustrated by the elaborate system of legislative control which exists in relation to regulated consumer credit agreements. To a considerable extent, the contents of such agreements are prescribed by the Consumer Credit Act 1974 and by delegated legislation[32]: the debtor is given a cooling-off period[33]; the creditor's power to terminate on the death of the debtor is restricted[34] and he can terminate for default only after giving a notice calling on the debtor to make good the default[35]; the debtor has the right to

---

[24] See Enterprise Act 2002, s.2(3), substituting the OFT for the reference in the regulations to the Director General of Fair Trading, an office which is abolished by s.2(2) of that Act.

[25] reg.10.

[26] reg.11; "qualifying bodies" include a number of public bodies whose functions include the protection of consumers (Sch.1, Pt 1) and the Consumers' Association (Sch.1, Pt 2).

[27] reg.12. cf. Consumer Protection (Distance Selling) Regulations 2000 (SI 2000/2334), reg.27 (enforcement by injunction may be sought by the Director General or other enforcement authority). These Regulations implement Dir.97/7; Late Payment of Commercial Debts Regulations 2002 (SI 2002/1674), reg.3, implementing Dir.2000/35.

[28] reg.13(3); the Consumers' Association is not given this power: see reg.13(2).

[29] regs 10(3) and 11(2). For further powers of the Director General, going beyond the control of exemption clauses, see the Stop Now Orders (EC Directive) Regulations 2001 (SI 2001/1422) implementing Dir.1998/27, as amended by the Electronic Commerce (EC Directive) Regulations 2002 (SI 2002/2013), reg.16.

[30] *Director General of Fair Trading v First National Bank plc* [2001] UKHL 52; [2002[1 A.C. 481, at [33].

[31] Under the 1999 Regulations, there are no criminal sanctions for the use of such terms: contrast the position under the 1977 Act, stated at n.22 above.

[32] See above, pp.177–178.

[33] s.67. cf. Consumer Protection (Cancellation of Contracts Concluded away from Business Premises) Regulations 1987, SI 1987/2117, implementing Council Dir.85/577; *Chiron Corp v Murex Diagnostics Ltd* [1995] All E.R. (EC) 88; Dir.97/7 of the European Parliament and of the Council on the Protection of Consumers in respect of Distance Contracts, Art.6.

[34] s.86.

[35] s.87.

make early payment and thereby to earn certain rebates[36]; and in the case of a regulated hire-purchase agreement he can terminate in certain circumstances on making prescribed payments.[37] Any term in such an agreement is void to the extent of its inconsistency with any such legislative provision for the protection of the debtor.[38] A number of other types of contracts are subject to similar detailed legislative control. These include contracts for the provision of package travel and similar facilities to consumers,[39] contracts with consumers concluded away from the trader's business premises,[40] and "distance contracts" with consumers.[41] A similar principle has been laid down by legislation regulating electronic commerce.[42] Where the customer places his order by "technological means"[43] (*e.g.* on a website) the service provider must make available to him "accessible"[44] means allowing the customer to identify and correct input errors before placing the order. Failure to comply with this requirement gives the customer the right to rescind the contract unless the court orders otherwise.[45]

---

[36] ss.94, 95.

[37] ss.99, 100.

[38] s.173.

[39] Package Travel, Package Holidays and Package Tours Regulations 1992 (SI 1992/3288) (which compulsorily imply terms into such contracts and restrict the other party's ability to exclude his liability to the consumer).

[40] Consumer Protection (Cancellation of Contracts Concluded away from Business Premises) Regulations 1987 (SI 1987/2117), implementing Dir.85/577.

[41] Consumer Protection (Distance Selling) Regulations 2000 (SI 2000/2334), reg.10, implementing Dir.97/7.

[42] Electronic Commerce (EC Directive) Regulations 2002 (SI 2002/2013) implementing most of Dir.2000/31.

[43] SI 2002/2013, reg.11(1); contrast use of the phrase "electronic means" in reg.9(1).

[44] *ibid.* reg.11(1)(b).

[45] *ibid.* reg.15.

CHAPTER EIGHT

MISTAKE[1]

IN *Bell v Lever Bros Ltd*,[2] Lord Atkin said: "If mistake operates at all, it operates so as to negative or in some cases to nullify consent." Mistake *negatives* consent where it puts the parties at cross-purposes so as to prevent them from reaching agreement, *e.g.* because they intend to contract about different things. It *nullifies* consent where the parties reach an agreement which is based on a fundamental mistaken assumption made by both of them, *e.g.* where a contract is made to paint a portrait of someone who, unknown to either party, has just died. At law, the effect of mistake is to make a contract void[3]; but this rule is confined within very narrow limits. It is thought to be in the interests of commercial convenience that, in general, apparent contracts should be enforced. Equity sometimes gives relief for mistakes which have no effect at common law; but recent authority[4] has considerably restricted the scope of such relief. Certain special rules apply to documents mistakenly signed.

SECTION 1. MISTAKE NULLIFYING CONSENT

1. Fundamental Mistake at Common Law

Consent may be nullified if both parties make a *fundamental* mistake of fact.[5] In such cases, the extreme injustice of holding one of the parties to the contract outweighs the general principle that apparent contracts should be enforced. The following types of mistake can be "fundamental" for this purpose.

(1) Mistake as to the existence of the subject-matter

Consent is nullified where both parties are mistaken as to the existence of the subject-matter. Thus it has been held that a separation deed between a man and a woman, who

---

[1] Champness, *Mistakes in the Law of Contract*; Palmer, *Mistake and Unjust Enrichment*; Stoljar, *Mistake and Misrepresentation*; Lawson, 52 L.Q.R. 79; Tylor, 11 M.L.R. 257; Wade, 7 C.L.J. 361; Grunfeld, 13 M.L.R. 50; 15 M.L.R. 297; Slade, 70 L.Q.R. 385; Atiyah, 73 L.Q.R. 340; Atiyah and Bennion, 24 M.L.R. 421; Shatwell, 33 Can. Bar Rev. 164; Bamford, 72 S.A.L.J. 166, 282; Stoljar, 28 M.L.R. 265; Sutton, 7 N.Z.U.L.R. 40 (discussing possible reforms); Cartwright, 103 L.Q.R. 594; Smith, 110 L.Q.R. 400; other articles dealing specifically with mistakes as to identity are cited below, p.300.
[2] [1932] A.C. 161 at 217.
[3] *Associated Japanese Bank* (*International*) *Ltd v Crédit du Nord SA* [1989] 1 W.L.R. 255 at 268. In *Re Goldcorp Exchange Ltd* [1995] 1 A.C. 74 at 103 it is tentatively suggested that a contract which is not void for mistake can "perhaps" be "set aside at common law or under statute." The reference to "statute" may be to the New Zealand Contractual Mistakes Act 1977 (the suggestion being made in a Privy Council appeal from that country); and "common law" may be used here simply by way of contrast to "statute" rather than to equity.
[4] *The Great Peace* [2002] EWCA Civ 1407; [2002] 4 All E.R. 689, below, p.319.
[5] Not of law: *British Homophone Ltd v Kunz* (1932) 152 L.T. 589 at 593; *cf. Gee v News Group Newspapers, The Times*, June 8, 1990. The rule does not apply where the mistake is one as to *foreign* law, which is treated as a matter of fact in English courts: *The Amazonia* [1990] 1 Lloyd's Rep. 236. Since relief for mistakes of law may be more widely available in equity than at common law, it is convenient to defer discussion of the nature and effects of the distinction (in the present context) between such mistakes and mistakes of fact to pp.313–316 below.

mistakenly thought that they were married to each other, was void, because it purported to deal with a marriage which did not exist[6]; and that a contract to buy an annuity was void where, at the time of the contract, the annuitant had died, so that the annuity no longer existed.[7] Contracts for the sale of non-existent goods illustrate the same point, but give rise to further difficulties, which are discussed below.[8]

(2) Mistake as to the identity of the subject-matter

Such a mistake usually arises where one party intends to deal with one thing and the other with a different thing. Here consent is negatived,[9] and not nullified. Consent could, however, be nullified if *both* parties thought that they were dealing with one thing when they were in fact dealing with another.[10]

Mistake as to a fundamental quality of the subject-matter may sometimes be regarded as affecting the identity of the subject-matter; this possibility is discussed below.[11]

(3) Mistake as to the possibility of performing the contract

Consent may be nullified if both parties believe that the contract is capable of being performed when this is not the case.

(a) PHYSICAL IMPOSSIBILITY. In *Sheikh Bros Ltd v Ochsner*[12] a contract was made for the exploitation of sisal, growing on land belonging to A. The contract provided that B was to cut and process the sisal and to deliver an average of 50 tons of sisal fibre per month to A. It was held that the contract was void because (contrary to the parties' belief) the land was not capable of producing 50 tons of fibre per month.

(b) LEGAL IMPOSSIBILITY. A contract may be void if it provides for something to be done which cannot, as a matter of law, be done. For example, a person cannot acquire property which he already owns, and Lords Atkin and Wright have said that, if he purports to do so in the mistaken belief that the property belongs to the other contracting party, the contract is void.[13] On the other hand, a contract is not void merely because it purports to dispose of property which belongs to a third party,[14] for in such a case the vendor might be able to acquire the property and then make a proper transfer.

One special case of legal impossibility is illegality. A contract involving the commission of a crime is often illegal.[15] The contract may be illegal even though both parties believe it to be lawful, so that in a sense they were under a mistake as to the legal possibility of performing it. Persons may, moreover, agree to do what is the *actus reus* of

---

[6] *Galloway v Galloway* (1914) 30 T.L.R. 531.

[7] *Strickland v Turner* (1852) 7 Ex. 208.

[8] See below, pp.295–298.

[9] See below, pp.303–304.

[10] cf. *Diamond v British Columbia Thoroughbred Breeders' Society* (1966) 52 D.L.R. (2d) 146, where two horses at an auction were confused by the auctioneer *and* by the bidders; but the court held that the difference was one of quality only: *sed quaere*. See also *Grains & Fourrages SA v Huyton* [1997] 1 Lloyd's Rep. 628.

[11] See below, pp.288 *et seq.*

[12] [1957] A.C. 136; applying the principles laid down in *Bell v Lever Bros Ltd* [1932] A.C. 161.

[13] *Bell v Lever Bros Ltd* [1932] A.C. 161 at 218; *Norwich Union Fire Insurance Society Ltd v Price* [1934] A.C. 455 at 463. The proposition supported by these dicta remains valid even though, to the extent that they are based on *Cooper v Phibbs* (1867) L.R. 2 H.L. 149, they may involve a misinterpretation of that case: see Matthews, 105 L.Q.R. 599. For the view that the contract in that case should now be regarded as void, see also *The Great Peace* [2002] EWCA Civ 1407; [2002] 4 All E.R. 689, at [126]–[128] (though it may not have been so regarded at the time: see *ibid.*, at [110]).

[14] *Bell v Lever Bros Ltd*, above; *Clare v Lamb* (1875) L.R. 10 C.P. 334.

[15] See below, pp.430 *et seq.*

crime, but may not commit a crime if they do the act because they lack *mens rea*. Such an agreement might not be illegal, but would probably be void for legal impossibility.

(c) COMMERCIAL IMPOSSIBILITY. In *Griffith v Brymer*[16] a contract was made for the hire of a room on June 26, 1902, the day fixed for the coronation of King Edward VII, for the purpose of viewing the coronation procession. The contract was held void[17] because, when it was made, the decision to postpone the coronation had (unknown to the parties) already been taken. Performance may have been physically and legally possible, but its commercial object was defeated. It could also be said that the parties had made a mistake about a quality of the subject-matter. On this view, the present status of the decision[18] depends on the discussion that follows.

(4) Mistake as to quality

Where the subject-matter of the contract lacks some quality which it is believed to have, the first question is whether the quality forms part of the contractual description of the thing. If it does and "the article does not answer the description of that which is sold",[19] the contract is valid and the party who gave the description is in breach.[20]

If there is no contractual misdescription, the general rule is that mistake as to quality does not nullify consent. This is so whether the mistake prejudices the buyer (so that he pays "too much") or the seller (so that he charges "too little"). In *Scott v Littledale*[21] a contract for the sale of tea was held valid in spite of a mistake as to its quality and hence as to its value. The same rule applies where the mistake affects, not the value of the subject-matter, but its utility to the buyer. In *Harrison & Jones v Bunten & Lancaster*[22] a contract was made for the sale of " 'Sree' brand Calcutta kapok." It was held that the contract was valid even though both parties believed such kapok to be pure, when in fact it was impure, and therefore of no use to the buyer.[23] The position is, *a fortiori*, the same where the mistake merely makes the subject-matter less useful to the acquirer than it was believed to be. In *The Great Peace*[24] a ship had been chartered for a minimum period of five days to provide escort services to another, which was in distress at sea, in the mistaken belief, apparently shared by charterer and shipowner,[25] that the chartered ship was "in close proximity" to the one in distress or that the former was "the closest

---

[16] (1903) 19 T.L.R. 434; *cf.* below, p.885.

[17] So that the hirer recovered back the money he had paid for the room. This appears to be the only reported "Coronation Case" in which the hirer of a room or seat was held entitled to recover back his money. Contrast *Clark v Lindsay* (1903) 88 L.T. 108, where a similar claim was rejected as the contract, though made in ignorance of the postponement, was later varied, after the parties had discovered the truth, so as to allow the hirer to use the room on the day of the postponed procession, which turned out to be a much less attractive event than that originally planned. *cf.* also below, p.910.

[18] The case is cited with apparent approval in *The Great Peace* [2002] EWCA Civ 1407; [2002] 4 All E.R. 689, at [67].

[19] *Gompertz v Bartlett* (1853) 2 E. & B. 849 at 853; *cf. Gurney v Womersley* (1854) 4 E. & B. 133. Contrast *Harlingdon and Leinster Enterprises Ltd v Christopher Hull Fine Art Ltd* [1991] 1 Q.B. 564, where a false attribution, made in good faith, was held not to form part of the contractual description on the sale of a painting by one art dealer to another.

[20] *Gompertz v Bartlett*, above.

[21] (1858) 8 E. & B. 815; *cf. Hall v Conder* (1857) 2 C.B.(N.S.) 22; *Pope & Pearson v Buenos Ayres New Gas Co* (1892) 8 T.L.R. 758; *cf. William Sindall plc v Cambridgeshire CC* [1994] 1 W.L.R. 1016.

[22] [1953] 1 Q.B. 646.

[23] It is not clear whether *both* parties thought that the kapok was pure, but this was assumed: see [1953] 1 Q.B. 646 at 657.

[24] *The Great Peace* [2002] E.W.C.A. Civ 1407; [2002] 4 All E.R. 689.

[25] See *ibid.*, at [162] ("common assumption of both parties"); from the statement of facts at [8], [9], the exact state of the shipowner's mind is less clear.

vessel" to the latter.[26] This mistake did not make the contract void since the chartered ship could, in spite of it, have reached the scene of the casualty to "provide several days of escort service".[27]

It does not follow from these illustrations of the general rule that a mistake as to quality can *never* make a contract void at law. In *Kennedy v Panama, etc. Royal Mail Co*,[28] the claimant applied for shares in a company on the faith of an untrue statement (made in good faith) that the company had secured a contract to carry mail for the New Zealand Government. The shares were allotted to him, and the actual decision was that the resulting contract between him and the company was valid.[29] But in reaching this conclusion Blackburn J. referred to the Roman doctrine of *error in substantia*, by which mistakes as to quality may make a contract void if they relate to the "substance" of the subject-matter, *e.g.* to the metal of which a thing is made.[30] He added that: "the principle of our law is the same as that of the civil law; and the difficulty in every case is to determine whether the mistake or misapprehension is as to the substance of the whole consideration, going, as it were, to the root of the matter, or only to some point, even though a material point, an error as to which does not affect the substance of the whole consideration".[31] This principle did not help the claimant as he got the very shares he bargained for and as his mistake did not affect the substance of the whole transaction. But it may be[32] possible to infer from Blackburn J.'s approval of the Roman texts that, in his view, mistake as to quality could in some cases make a contract void in English law.

Whether this view is correct depends on the decision of the House of Lords in *Bell v Lever Bros Ltd*[33] Bell and Snelling had agreed with Lever Bros to serve for five years as chairman and vice-chairman of a company controlled by Lever Bros. Before the end of this period Lever Bros wished to terminate these service contracts, and the parties entered into compensation agreements under which Bell and Snelling received between them £50,000 for loss of office. Lever Bros then discovered that Bell and Snelling had broken their service contracts in a way which would have justified their summary dismissal without compensation.[34] It was found that Bell and Snelling had forgotten about these breaches of the service contracts when the compensation agreements were made, so that they were not guilty of fraudulent concealment.[35] The remaining issue was whether the compensation agreements were void for mistake, so as to entitle Lever Bros to recover back the £50,000 which they had paid under those agreements.[36] They had made the compensation agreements in the belief that the service contracts still bound

---

[26] *ibid.*, at [8], [9]. The mistake arose from information supplied to the charterer by a third party. If this had been accurate, the two ships would have been only 35 miles apart (see the judgment of Toulson J. at first instance at [21]). In fact, the distance between them was 410 miles: Toulson J. at [20]; CA at [16].

[27] *ibid.*, at [165]. This conclusion was supported *ibid.* by the fact that the charterers themselves did not regard the contract as affected by the mistake immediately on discovery of the truth. They sought to cancel only when a third ship (which happened also to be under charter to the charterers) came on the scene and was able to provide the escort services.

[28] (1867) L.R. 2 Q.B. 580. Contrast *Emmerson's Case* (1866) L.R. 1 Ch. App. 433 (where special statutory provisions affected the result).

[29] There being then no remedy for innocent misrepresentation at common law: below, pp.366, 369.

[30] Lawson, 52 L.Q.R. 79; De Zulueta, *The Roman Law of Sale*, p.26. The Romans did not call such an error one of "quality" but an English lawyer could so describe it.

[31] *Kennedy v Panama, etc Royal Mail Co*, above at 588.

[32] The point is not clear: see *The Great Peace* [2002] EWCA Civ 1407; [2002] 4 All E.R. 689, at [59].

[33] [1932] A.C. 161.

[34] See below, p.745; the harshness of this rule may account for the eventual decision in the case. *cf.* below, p.320, n.22.

[35] Nor were they under any duty to disclose their breaches of duty: *cf.* below, p.400.

[36] See below, p.1058.

them when in fact they were terminable. They had paid £50,000 to get rid of Bell and Snelling, when they might have got rid of them for nothing. Wright J. and a unanimous Court of Appeal held that the compensation agreements were void as Lever Bros had made them under a fundamental mistake. But the House of Lords, by a narrow majority, reversed this decision. The mistake related only to a quality of the service contracts (which were the subject-matter of the compensation agreements), and was not fundamental. Lord Atkin said: "The contract released is the identical contract in both cases,[37] and the party paying for release gets exactly what he bargained for".[38] Lord Thankerton stressed that mistake even as to a fundamental quality was of no effect unless it related to some assumption which *both* parties regarded as essential. In his view there was nothing to show that Bell and Snelling regarded the binding force of the service contracts as vital: only Lever Bros did so.[39]

The mistake in this case gave rise to a belief that subject-matter which was actually worthless had a value of £50,000. It might be thought that if such a mistake is not fundamental, no mistake as to quality can ever have this effect; but once one accepts the principle that a mere mistake as to value is not fundamental, the size of that difference cannot be decisive. *Bell v Lever Bros Ltd* has indeed been described as "a quite exceptional case"[40]; and dicta in it do recognise that some mistakes as to quality may be fundamental. Lord Atkin said that mistake as to quality "will not affect assent unless it is the mistake of both parties, and is as to the existence of some quality which makes the thing without the quality essentially different from the thing as it was believed to be".[41] Lord Thankerton said that a mistake as to subject-matter must relate to "something which both must necessarily have accepted in their minds as an essential and integral element of the subject-matter".[42]

These are stringent requirements, which make the common law doctrine of mistake "markedly narrower in scope than the civilian doctrine"[43] referred to by Blackburn J. in the dictum cited above.[44] It follows that generally a mistake as to quality will not make a contract void. According to Lord Atkin, it would not have this effect if a man bought a horse mistakenly believed to be sound; if he bought a dwelling-house mistakenly believed to be inhabitable; if he bought a garage on a road which was about to be starved of all traffic by the construction of a by-pass; and (most difficult of all): "A buys a picture from B; both A and B believe it to be the work of an old master and a high price is paid. It turns out to be a modern copy. A has no remedy in the absence of representation or warranty"[45] *i.e.* the contract is valid. The same view was taken in *Leaf v International Galleries*,[46] where it was said[47] that a contract for the sale of a picture

---

[37] *i.e.* whether the service contracts were binding on Lever Bros or terminable by them. *cf. Robert A Munro & Co Ltd v Meyer* [1930] 2 K.B. 312.

[38] *Bell v Lever Bros Ltd*, above, at 223. It was particularly important for Lever Bros to get rid of Bell and Snelling by May 1, 1929, but this fact is not stressed in the speeches of Lords Atkin and Thankerton.

[39] At 235.

[40] *Associated Japanese Bank (International) Ltd v Crédit du Nord SA* [1989] 1 W.L.R. 255 at 267.

[41] [1932] A.C. 161 at 218.

[42] *ibid.* at 256.

[43] *Associated Japanese Bank* case, above n.40, at, 268, approved in *The Great Peace* [2002] EWCA Civ 1407, [2002] 4 All E.R. 689, at [90]–[91].

[44] See above, at n.31.

[45] [1932] A.C. 161 at 224. Contrast *Smith v Zimbalist*, 2 Cal.App. 2d 234; 38 P. 2d 170 (1934) (violins mistakenly believed to be by Stradivarius and Guarnerius: held buyer not liable for the price on grounds of mistake *and* breach of warranty).

[46] [1950] 2 K.B. 86.

[47] *ibid.* at 89; below, pp.292–294. *cf. Harlingdon and Leinster Enterprise Ltd v Christopher Hull Fine Art Ltd* [1991] 1 Q.B. 564, where the buyer's claim (which failed) was based solely on breach; no attempt was made to base it on mistake as to the authenticity of the picture; Lawrenson, 54 M.L.R. 122.

would not be void if the parties mistakenly believed that it was by Constable. Similarly it was held in *Solle v Butcher*[48] that a lease was not void because the parties mistakenly believed the premises to be free from rent control; in *Magee v Pennine Insurance Co Ltd*[49] it was said that a compromise of a claim under an insurance policy was not void because the parties mistakenly believed that the policy was valid when in fact it was voidable[50]; in *F E Rose (London) Ltd v W H Pim Jnr & Co Ltd*[51] it was said that a contract for the sale of horse-beans would not be void because the parties believed that they were dealing with a type of horse-beans more valuable than those with which they had actually dealt; in *Oscar Chess Ltd v Williams* it was said that a contract for the sale of a car would not be void because the parties made a mistake as to its age, so that the buyer paid more than he would have done, had he known the truth[52]; and in *Naughton v O'Callaghan* a horse sold by auction with a false pedigree was said to be "a different animal altogether",[53] but it was not suggested that the contract was void.

But according to other dicta and decisions a mistake as to quality can sometimes make a contract void. Thus it has been said that a contract for the sale of land believed to be freehold could be avoided if it turned out to be leasehold[54]; and where a chalet on a caravan site was sold in the mistaken belief that it was a chattel which could be sold separately from its pitch, it was said that the sale was void.[55] In *Bell v Lever Bros Ltd* Greer L.J. said in the Court of Appeal that a contract for the sale of a horse, believed to be a racehorse, would be void if it turned out to be a carthorse[56]: it may be significant that Lord Atkin, in his example of the *unsound* horse,[57] did not contradict this suggestion. Similarly, in *Scott v Coulson*[58] a policy on the life of one Death was sold for £460 on the assumption that Death was alive. The price paid was therefore fixed in relation to the surrender value of the policy. In fact Death was dead, so that the policy had matured and was worth £777. The vendor successfully claimed to have the contract set aside and Vaughan Williams L.J. said[59] that it was void at law. Again, in the *Associated Japanese Bank*[60] case payments to be made by the lessee under a purported sale and lease-back of machinery were guaranteed by the defendant. In fact no such machinery existed, so that the lease was voidable for fraud; and it was said that the guarantee was void for mistake. And in *Nicholson & Venn v Smith-Marriott*[61] the defendants put up for auction table napkins "with the crest of Charles I and the authentic property of that monarch". On the faith of this description the lot was bought for £787 10s., but the napkins were Georgian and worth £105 only. The buyer recovered damages for breach of contract but Hallett J. also said that the contract might have been treated by the

---

[48] [1950] 1 K.B. 671.

[49] [1969] 2 Q.B. 507; 85 L.Q.R. 454; Harris, 32 M.L.R. 688.

[50] For the relief given in the last two cases on equitable grounds see now below, pp.317–320.

[51] [1953] 2 Q.B. 450 at 459.

[52] [1957] 1 W.L.R. 370 at 373. *cf. Wood v Boynton*, 64 Wis. 265; 25 N.W. 42 (1885) (sale of uncut stone believed to be a topaz for $1: in fact it was a diamond worth $700: held, contract valid). Contrast Restatement, *Contracts*, §503, Ill. 3, but see Restatement 2d, *Contracts* §154 Ill. 3.

[53] [1990] 3 All E.R. 191 at 197.

[54] *Durham v Legard* (1835) 34 Beav. 611 at 613, possibly expressing a purely equitable view.

[55] *Nutt v Read* (2000) 32 H.L.R. 761.

[56] [1931] 1 K.B. 557, 597. *cf. Sherwood v Walker*, 66 Mich. 568; 33 N.W. 919 (1887) (sale of cow, believed to be barren, for no more than $80; in fact she was a breeder worth at least $750: held, contract invalid).

[57] [1932] A.C. 161 at 224; above, n.45.

[58] [1903] 2 Ch. 249.

[59] *ibid.* at 252. *Cf. Gloyne v Richardson* [2001] EWCA Civ 716; [2001] B.C.L.C. 669, at [41] (agreement made in mistaken belief that option had been exercised).

[60] *Associated Japanese Bank (International) Ltd v Crédit du Nord SA* [1989] 1 W.L.R. 255; Treitel 104 L.Q.R. 501; Cartwright [1988] L.M.C.L.Q. 300; Marston [1989] C.L.J. 173.

[61] (1947) 177 L.T. 189.

buyer[62] as void for mistake. The transaction could be regarded in two ways. The parties may have intended to buy and sell antique table linen: in this case a mistake as to its exact age, provenance or value would not be fundamental. Alternatively, the parties may have intended to buy and sell a Carolean relic; in this case their mistake would be fundamental and make the contract void.

The cases and examples concerning mistakes as to quality cannot be perfectly reconciled; but there is a principle which runs through them. A thing has many qualities. A car may be black, old, fast and so forth. For any particular purpose one or more of these qualities may be uppermost in the minds of the persons dealing with the thing. Some particular quality may be so important to them that they actually use it to *identify* the thing. If the thing lacks that quality, it is suggested that the parties have made a fundamental mistake, even though they have not mistaken one thing for another, or made a mistake as to the existence of the thing.[63] The matter may be tested by imagining that one can ask the parties, immediately after they made the contract, what its subject-matter was. If, in spite of the mistake, they would give the right answer the contract is valid at law. Thus in *Bell v Lever Bros Ltd*, the parties would have said, quite rightly: "We are contracting about a service agreement". In *Nicholson & Venn v Smith-Marriott* they might have said, rightly, "We are contracting about antique table linen," in which case the contract would be valid; or they might have said, wrongly, "We are contracting about a Carolean relic," in which case the contract would be void. Most of the cases and illustrations given above can be explained in this way; but three of them give rise to particular difficulty.

The first is *Scott v Coulson*, where the subject-matter of the contract would no doubt have been described as "an insurance policy" so that the contract ought to have been valid at law. The view that the contract was void is also very hard to reconcile[64] with *Bell v Lever Bros Ltd*. If the difference between a binding and a terminable contract is not fundamental, why is there a fundamental difference between a contingent and an accrued debt?[65]

A second source of difficulty is that the contract of guarantee in the *Associated Japanese Bank* case was held to be *void*. The subject-matter of that contract was not the machinery, but the lease, and this contract was not void but only voidable for fraud. Yet the compensation agreements in *Bell v Lever Bros Ltd* were held *valid* even though their subject-matter, too, consisted of the earlier service contracts which were also terminable but not void. One possible way of distinguishing the cases is to say that the lease in the *Associated Bank* case was voidable for fraud, so that it was liable to be rescinded *ab initio*,[66] while the factor vitiating the service agreements in *Bell v Lever Bros Ltd* was breach, which entitled the employers to rescind them by dismissing the employees, but

---

[62] It may be objected that Hallett J. held the contract *valid* by giving the buyer damages. But where one party negligently causes the other to make a mistake, the former cannot rely on the mistake to escape liability: *McRae v Commonwealth Disposals Commission* (1951) 84 C.L.R. 377 at 408; below, p.298.

[63] Contrast p.44, above. The rule that deterioration of the subject matter after offer may preclude acceptance is distinct from the principles discussed in this Chapter. It operates even though the parties at the time of the formation of the alleged contract were perfectly well aware of the true facts; and it may operate even though the change is not "fundamental" in our present sense: for example, the sale of a life-insurance policy would probably not be void for mistake merely because at the time of sale the person insured had (unknown to the parties to the sale) suffered serious injury. For another view, see Atiyah, 2 Ottawa L.Rev. 337 at 339.

[64] *The Great Peace* [2002] EWCA Civ 1407; [2002] 4 All E.r. 689, at [87].

[65] In *Bell v Lever Bros Ltd* [1932] A.C. 161 at 236 Lord Thankerton regards the contract in *Scott v Coulson* as one for the sale of a non-existent subject matter. But it is hard to see in what sense a policy of insurance ceases to exist when it matures.

[66] See below, pp.369–372.

not with retrospective effect[67]: hence the mistake in the former case could be said to be more serious than that in the latter case. Another is that in the *Associated Japanese Bank* case the guarantee was part of a composite transaction intended to raise money on the security of the alleged machinery, so that "the analogy of the classic *res extincta* cases . . . [was] fairly close".[68] Hence the crucial fact was that guarantor and lessor both mistakenly believed that *the machinery* existed: this was more important than their state of mind as to the legal effect of the fraud on *the lease*.

The third source of difficulty is Lord Atkin's example of a modern copy bought for a high price in the belief that it is an old master, supported by dicta in *Leaf v International Galleries*.[69] The assumption behind these statements seems to be that the parties would identify the subject-matter simply as "a picture"; but this seems to be a questionable assumption. Suppose that A has just paid B £10 million for what both believe to be a painting by Rembrandt. If A were asked "what have you just bought?" he would almost certainly reply "a Rembrandt"—not "a picture." With the greatest respect, this type of case stands on a different level from Lord Atkin's other examples.[70] Nor are the dicta in *Leaf v International Galleries* conclusive, for the buyer there sought only to rescind the contract for misrepresentation and did not claim that it was void for mistake.[71] It is submitted that, on the bare facts given by Lord Atkin, the contract should be held void. Of course in practice the facts of cases of this kind are likely to be more complex. On the one hand, it may be a term of the contract that the picture is authentic, in which case the seller is liable for breach of contract[72] so that no question of mistake will arise. On the other hand, a picture may be sold speculatively, in which case the contract will be valid and the seller will not be in breach, even though the buyer's belief in the authenticity of the picture turns out to be incorrect. Between these extremes lies the large group of cases in which both parties may believe the picture to be authentic but in which there can be no certainty on the point; scholarly or expert opinion as to the authenticity of a picture may vary from time to time.[73] In cases within this group, it has been held that the seller does not impliedly undertake that the picture is genuine (at least

---

[67] See below, pp.849–850; *cf.* above, pp.238–240.

[68] *Associated Japanese Bank (International) Ltd v Crédit du Nord SA* [1989] 1 W.L.R. 255 at 269.

[69] [1950] 2 K.B. 86. *cf.* also *Hindle v Brown* (1907) 98 L.T. 44, where only misrepresentation was discussed.

[70] See above, p.290. The answer to the question "what have you just bought?" would in those cases be: "a horse," "a house," and "a garage."

[71] Nor did he claim damages for breach of warranty, though Denning and Jenkins L.JJ. thought that this remedy was open to him. The receipt described the picture as "One original oil painting Salisbury Cathedral by J. Constable, £85": [1950] 1 All E.R. at 694. *cf.* also 66 T.L.R. (Pt.1) 1031 at 1032. The only report which says that there was a representation that the picture was by "*John* Constable" is that in the *Law Reports*, where the statement is that of the reporter and not of any member of the court. In the usage of art auctioneers "John Constable" would mean that the picture was considered to be the work of the famous painter, but "J. Constable" would not; and the seller may have been adopting this usage. The All E.R. and T.L.R. reports seem to be preferable, for it is hard to imagine that a dealer would have been prepared to give a contractual undertaking that the picture was "by John Constable" when the price was as low as £85. *cf. Harlingdon and Leinster Enterprises Ltd v Christopher Hull Fine Art Ltd* [1991] 1 Q.B. 564 at 578, stating that, at least between art dealers, the principle of *caveat emptor* applied. In *Peco Arts Inc v Hazlitt Gallery Ltd* [1983] 1 W.L.R. 1315 the buyer claimed no more than the return of the price plus interest; it seems that any claim for damages for breach of contract or for misrepresentation would have been statute-barred. *cf.* the newspaper report of *de Balkany v Christie's, The Times*, January 12, 1995.

[72] As in *Peco Arts Inc v Hazlitt Gallery Ltd* [1983] 1 W.L.R. 1315 (where it was a term of the contract that the subject matter of the sale was a drawing by J.A.D. Ingres, but it turned out to be a copy). The seller admitted liability to return the price as money paid under "a common mistake of fact"; the only issue was whether the claim was statute-barred. A seller who knows that his attribution is false may be guilty of an offence under the Trade Descriptions Act 1968: *May v Vincent* (1991) 10 Tr.L.R. 1.

[73] See *Firestone & Parson Inc v Union League of Philadelphia* 672 F. Supp. 819 (1987), affirmed 833 F. 2d. 304; *cf. Luxmoore-May v Messenger May Baverstock* [1990] 1 W.L.R. 1009 at 1028.

where the sale is by one dealer to another, and the seller indicates that he is not an expert on the work of the artist in question[74]; and it is submitted that the element of uncertainty would make it equally inappropriate to regard such a case as one in which the contract was void for mistake.

The suggested test for determining whether a mistake is fundamental, presupposes that both parties would give the same answer to the question "what are you contracting about?" If they would give different answers, the mistake, whatever else its effect may be, will not *nullify* consent. A seller may intend to sell antique table linen and the buyer to buy a Carolean relic. If the parties are thus at cross-purposes consent may be *negatived*. The question whether the buyer could rely on the mistake as making the contract void at law would then depend on factors discussed later in this Chapter.[75]

(5) Mistake as to quantity

Mistake as to quantity has generally been dealt with in equity; but it may also be capable of invalidating a contract at law. In *Cox v Prentice*[76] a silver bar was sold under a mistake as to its weight. The buyer (who was the party prejudiced by the mistake) obtained a verdict for damages for the difference in value between the weight of the bar as it was, and as it was believed to be. The court added that the buyer could have recovered back the price he paid for the bar, which may suggest that he had the option of treating the contract as void for mistake.[77] Similarly, Lord Atkin in *Bell v Lever Bros Ltd* said: "I agree that an agreement to take an assignment of a lease for five years is not the same thing as to take an assignment of a lease for three years, still less a term for a few months,"[78] though it is not clear from the context whether Lord Atkin thought that such a mistake could make a contract void. And in *Barrow, Lane & Ballard Ltd v Phillips & Co Ltd*[79] a contract for the sale of an "indivisible parcel" of 700 bags of nuts was held to be void because, unknown to the parties, only 591 bags were in existence.

2. Cases in which a Fundamental Mistake Does Not Nullify Consent

In two situations, a contract may not be void, even though the parties have made a fundamental mistake of fact.

(1) Construction of the contract

When a contract is made on the basis of a fundamental assumption which turns out to be false, there are in theory four possible solutions: that neither party shall be bound, or that one shall be bound, or that the other shall be bound, or that both shall be bound.

In the cases of fundamental mistake so far discussed, the first solution has been applied, so that neither party could enforce the contract, and money paid under it could be recovered back. In such cases the contract may properly be called void.[80] But where the parties intend to adopt one of the other solutions the contract is, generally speaking, perfectly valid. Thus, contracts of marine insurance may contain a "lost or not lost" clause: the effect of this is that both parties are bound although the thing insured had

---

[74] *Harlingdon and Leinster Enterprises Ltd v Christopher Hull Fine Art Ltd* [1991] 1 Q.B. 564.

[75] See below, pp.303–306 *et seq.*

[76] (1815) 3 M. & S. 344; *cf. Devaux v Connolly* (1849) 8 C.B. 640 at 659.

[77] As to this option, see below, p.298.

[78] [1932] A.C. 161 at 223.

[79] [1929] 1 K.B. 574.

[80] *Norwich Union Fire Insurance Society Ltd v Price* [1934] A.C. 455 at 463; *Barclays Bank Ltd v W J Sims & Cooke (Southern) Ltd* [1980] Q.B. 677, 695 ("void for mistake").

(unknown to them) perished at the time of the contract.[81] That is, the insurer has to pay on the policy if the loss is covered by it; and the person insured has to pay the premium even though the loss is caused by an excepted peril, *i.e.* by one not covered by the policy. Similarly, a sale of "my title, *if any*" to specified land could bind both parties even though the seller had no title (unless he knew this fact)[82]; and the same is true where a contract for the sale of land limits the vendor's liability for defects of title to incumbrances known to him, and it turns out that his title was subject to an easement of which he was unaware.[83]

In these cases the express terms of the contract dealt with the possibility that certain assumed facts might not exist; but in others more difficult questions of construction may arise. Two cases concerning mining leases illustrate the point. In one the tenant promised to dig at least 1,000 tons of clay and to pay a royalty of 2s. 6d. per ton, but there was not so much clay in the land. It was held that the tenant was not liable in respect of the deficiency: he had not warranted that enough clay could be extracted from the land.[84] In the other the tenant of a coal mine agreed to raise a minimum quantity of coal and to pay a minimum rent *in any event*. He was held liable to pay this rent, though there was not so much coal in the mine, because the parties had appreciated the risk and had thrown it on the tenant.[85]

A similar question of construction arose in *Couturier v Hastie*,[86] where a contract was made for the sale of "a cargo of about 1,180 quarters of Salonika Indian corn of fair average quality when shipped, per the '*Kezia Page*' . . . free on board, and including freight and insurance, to a safe port in the United Kingdom, payment at two months from this date upon handing over shipping documents." Before the contract was made, the cargo had, unknown to the parties, become overheated and been sold at Tunis to prevent further deterioration. The seller argued that the buyer was nevertheless liable for the price: what he had bought was an interest in a maritime adventure, or such rights as the seller had under the shipping documents, against which payment was to be made.[87] But the House of Lords rejected this argument and held that the buyer was not liable. Lord Cranworth L.C. said: "The whole question turns upon the construction of the contract . . . Looking to the contract . . . alone it appears to me clearly that what the parties contemplated . . . was that there was an existing something to be sold and bought."[88] The contract was for the sale of existing goods—not for the sale of the goods *or* the documents representing them. A similar issue may arise in relation to an accessory contract. The actual decision in the *Associated Japanese Bank* case[89] was accordingly based on the ground that the guarantee contained an express or implied undertaking in favour of the guarantor that the machinery was in existence; and as the machinery did not exist the guarantor was not liable.

In these cases the non-existence of the underlying subject-matter merely absolved the party prejudiced by that fact from liability, but it may as a matter of construction also impose a liability on the other party. This was the position in *McRae v Commonwealth*

---

[81] *cf.* Marine Insurance Act 1906, Sch.1, r.1.
[82] See *Smith v Harrison* (1857) 26 L.J.Ch. 412.
[83] *William Sindall plc v Cambridgeshire CC* [1994] 1 W.L.R. 1016 at 1035. Such a provision amounts to an allocation of risk of the defect.
[84] *Clifford v Watts* (1870) L.R. 5 C.P. 577.
[85] *Bute v Thompson* (1844) 13 M. & W. 487.
[86] (1856) 5 H.L.C. 673; Atiyah, 73 L.Q.R. 487.
[87] This would normally have satisfied the buyer, as he could have claimed the insurance money. But if the contract was indeed void (below at n.95) the buyer would not have acquired any rights by virtue of it under the "shipping documents," including the insurance policy.
[88] *Couturier v Hastie*, above, at 681.
[89] *Associated Japanese Bank (International) Ltd v Crédit du Nord SA* [1989] 1 W.L.R. 255, above, p.291.

Disposals Commission,[90] where the defendants purported to sell the wreck of an oil tanker, said to be lying on the Jourmand Reef, and to contain oil. The buyers sent out an expedition to salvage the tanker but found that there was not and never had been any such tanker. The High Court of Australia held that the defendants had impliedly undertaken that there was a tanker there[91]; and that, being in breach of this undertaking, they were liable in damages.

Thus there may be a good contract about a non-existent subject-matter if on the true construction of the contract the risk of non-existence is thrown on one party.[92] In *Couturier v Hastie* the risk was not thrown on the buyer: he was not liable for the price. It is more doubtful whether the risk was thrown on the seller, *i.e.* whether the buyer could have claimed damages for non-delivery. In *McRae's* case the court thought that *prima facie* the seller in *Couturier v Hastie*, had promised that the goods were in existence[93]: on this view, the contract in that case was not void and the seller could have been held liable on it. But in *Barrow, Lane & Ballard Ltd v Phillips & Co Ltd*,[94] Wright J. said "Where a contract relates to specific goods which do not exist, the case is not to be treated as one in which the seller warrants the existence of those specific goods, but as one in which there has been failure of consideration and mistake." The English courts would probably adopt this approach. *Prima facie* a seller would not be held to undertake that the goods existed, any more than the buyer would bind himself to pay for them in any event. Thus, neither party is bound and the contract can properly be called void. This explains why the contract in *Couturier v Hastie* has for long been regarded as void[95] for mistake, although the words "void" and "mistake" do not occur in any of the judgments. Similarly, in the *Associated Japanese Bank*[96] case Steyn J., having rejected the claim against the guarantor on the issue of construction, considered the alternative argument based on mistake and held that the claim also failed on this further and *separate* ground. Mistake and construction are thus not necessarily mutually exclusive concepts. Construction will displace mistake (as a ground of invalidity) only where it is clear from the words of the contract or from the surrounding circumstances that one party or the other promised to undertake responsibility in any event.

In *McRae's* case the tanker never existed; in *Couturier v Hastie* the goods originally existed but had, before the contract was made, "perished" as a commercial entity. This distinction, unimportant in principle, gives rise to difficulty because s.6 of the Sale of Goods Act 1979 provides that "Where there is a contract for the sale of specific goods, and the goods without the knowledge of the seller have perished at the time when the contract is made, the contract is void." At first sight this section prevents the buyer from recovering damages even though the seller has expressly guaranteed that the goods exist, and the seller from recovering the price or damages even though the buyer has expressly promised to pay whether or not the goods exist. The problem may be of more theoretical than practical interest, for it does not seem that contracts on such terms are at all common. In practice the more important question is whether s.6 would apply where the contract was *either* a sale of alternatives (*e.g.* of the goods *or* the shipping documents

---

[90] (1951) 84 C.L.R. 377 and see below, p.941.

[91] *cf.* the explanation of *McRae's* case in *The Great Peace* [2002] EWCA Civ 1407; [2002] 4 All E.R. 689, at [76]–[77].

[92] *cf. Kalsep Ltd v X-Flow BV, The Times*, May 3, 2001.

[93] *McRae's* case (1951) 84 C.L.R. 377 at 407.

[94] [1929] 1 K.B. 574 at 582; above, p.294. *Cf. Bell v Lever Bros* [1932] A.C. 161 at 217 *per* Lord Atkin: "void if in fact the article had perished before the date of the sale".

[95] See Sale of Goods Act 1979, s.6, originally enacted in 1893, and discussed below. *Cf. The Great Peace* [2002] EWCA Civ 1407, [2002] 4 All E.R. 1407, [2002] 4 All E.R. 689, at [51]–[53].

[96] [1989] 1 W.L.R. 255, above, p.292.

representing them[97]) *or* simply one of the documents. Probably s.6 would not apply as such transactions would, in the events which had happened, be sales of things in action and not of goods at all.[98]

If the parties are conscious of a doubt as to the existence of the goods, and one of them expressly undertakes to bear the risk that they may not exist, there seems to be no strong reason against upholding the contract. But in view of s.6 some ingenuity is required to reach this result. One possible argument is that s.6 is only a rule of construction which can be ousted by proof of contrary intention.[99] But many other sections of the Act expressly provide that they are subject to contrary agreement and there is no such provision in s.6.[1] Another possibility is to say that the main contract is void but that the seller can be held liable on a collateral contract that the goods do exist. But if nothing had been done under the main contract it would be hard to find any consideration for the seller's promise under the collateral contract. It is just possible that such consideration could be found in the buyer's act of purporting to enter into the main contract, especially if it involved the execution of a document.[2] There is even more difficulty in seeing how the buyer's promise to pay can be expressed as a collateral contract, for it seems to be merely a reiteration of his principal obligation under the main contract. It is finally possible that a seller who warrants that goods exist may be liable in damages for negligent misrepresentation[3]; but the damages on such a claim would be differently assessed from those for breach of contract,[4] and the claim would fail if the seller was wholly innocent.[5]

(2) Conduct of the parties

A party may be liable, even where he did not expressly or impliedly take the risk of the mistake, if he was at fault in inducing the mistake in the mind of the other party. This was a further ground for the decision in *McRae's* case,[6] where it was said that a party could not rely on a mistake consisting "of a belief which is . . . entertained without any

---

[97] But for this possibility, *Couturier v Hastie* would scarcely have reached the House of Lords. The writer is not aware of any English case in which the court was called upon to consider a simple *sale* of goods "lost or not lost" at the time of the contract unless the buyer was entitled under the contract to documents giving him rights against the carrier or insurer in respect of the loss of the goods in certain events.

[98] See the definition of "goods" given in s.61(1) of the Sale of Goods Act 1979. The normal contract for the sale of goods on c.i.f. terms is not regarded as a sale of documents but as a sale of goods to be performed by the delivery of documents: see *Arnhold Karberg & Co v Blythe, Green Jourdain & Co* [1916] 1 K.B. 495 at 510, 514; and other authorities cited in Benjamin's *Sale of Goods* (6th ed.), §19–008. *Couturier v Hastie* provides an early illustration of a c.i.f. contract.

[99] Atiyah, 73 L.Q.R. 340.

[1] s.55(1) provides that "Where any right, duty or liability would arise under a contract of sale of goods by implication of law, it may (subject to the Unfair Contract Terms Act 1977) be negatived or varied by express agreement . . . ." But this does not affect the present problem, since the effect of s.6 is that *no* "right, duty or liability would arise" and that there is *no* contract of sale. Atiyah (above) argues that under s.6 liability might arise to restore the price; but this would hardly be a liability which "would arise under a contract of sale."

[2] *cf.* above, p.84. Such a consideration would be blatantly invented (above, p.71).

[3] At common law, if there was a "special relationship" (below, p.345); and possibly under s.2(1) of the Misrepresentation Act 1967 (below, p.350). But that subsection only applies "Where a person has entered into a contract . . . " and it is not clear whether these words cover the case where the "contract" is wholly void.

[4] See below, p.359. *cf.* the damages recovered in *McRae's* case (below, p.941).

[5] See below, pp.366, 367–368.

[6] (1951) 84 C.L.R. 377.

reasonable ground, and . . . deliberately induced by him in the mind of the other party."[7]
In such a situation one party may be able to rely on the mistake while the other cannot.
Thus in *Nicholson & Venn v Smith-Marriott*[8] the buyer could have relied on mistake to
recover back his money while the defendant could not have relied on it to resist the
buyer's claim for damages.

SECTION 2. MISTAKE NEGATIVING CONSENT

Mistake negatives consent where the parties are so much at cross-purposes that they do
not reach agreement. This may happen where one party is mistaken about the identity
of the other, where one party intends to deal with one thing and the other with a
different one, or where one party intends to deal on one set of terms and the other on
a different set of terms. A mistake as to the other party or as to the subject-matter of the
contract has no effect unless it is fundamental, and it is this requirement which links the
present group of cases with those in which consent is nullified.

The mere existence of a mistake which negatives consent does not make a contract
void. The mistake must also induce the contract, and be operative. In many cases, the
last requirement will not be satisfied, so that there will often be a contract in spite of the
fact that consent was negatived.

1. Types of Mistake

(1) Mistake as to the person[9]

(a) REQUIREMENT OF FUNDAMENTAL MISTAKE. A mistake is fundamental, so that
consent is negatived, if one party is mistaken as to the *identity* of the other. In *Cundy v
Lindsay*[10] claimants received an order for handkerchiefs from a dishonest person called
Blenkarn, who gave his address as 37, Wood Street, Cheapside. He signed his name to
make it look like "Blenkiron & Co", a respectable firm known by reputation to the
claimants and carrying on business at 123, Wood Street. The claimants sent the goods
to "Blenkiron & Co, 37, Wood Street," where Blenkarn took possession of them. He did
not pay for the goods and he later sold them to the defendants. It was held that there was
no contract between the claimants and Blenkarn, as the claimants did not intend to deal
with him but with someone else. Thus no property in the handkerchiefs passed to
Blenkarn,[11] so that he could pass none to the defendants, who were accordingly liable for
conversion.

But a mistake by one party as to an *attribute* of the other will not as a general rule put
the parties so seriously at cross-purposes as to negative consent. In *King's Norton Metal*

---

[7] (1951) 84 C.L.R. 377 at 408; *cf. The Great Peace* [2002] EWCA Civ 1407, [2002] 4 All E.R. 689, at [76]–[77].
In *Associated Japanese Bank (International) Ltd v Crédit du Nord SA* [1989] 1 W.L.R. 255 at 268 Steyn J.
carries the principle further by omitting the second requirement (*i.e.* that of inducement) stated in the
passage quoted in the text above from *McRae's* case. That principle should be distinguished from "estoppel
by convention" as applied in cases such as *Amalgamated Investment & Property Co Ltd v Texas Commerce
International Bank Ltd* [1982] Q.B. 84; above, p.110. The mistake in that case related to the existence of a
promise which, if made, was undoubtedly a valid contract, and not to facts on which the validity of that
contract depended.

[8] (1947) 177 L.T. 189; above, p.291.

[9] Goodhart, 57 L.Q.R. 228; Williams, 23 Can.Bar Rev. 271 at 380; Wilson, 17 M.L.R. 515; Unger, 18 M.L.R.
259; Smith & Thomas, 20 M.L.R. 38.

[10] (1878) 3 App.Cas. 459; *cf. Baillie's Case* [1898] 1 Ch. 110; *Shogun Finance Ltd v Hudson* [2001] EWCA Civ
1001 [2002] Q.B. 834.

[11] *cf.* below, p.371.

Co Ltd v Edridge, Merrett & Co Ltd[12] the claimants received an order for wire from "Hallam & Co" which was made on the letter-head to appear as a substantial firm having a large factory in Sheffield and depôts in various other places. In fact "Hallam & Co" consisted solely of an impecunious rogue called Wallis. The claimants sent the goods to "Hallam & Co" on credit. Wallis took possession of them, failed to pay, and sold them to the defendants. It was held that the claimants had contracted with "the writer of the letters".[13] Thus property in the goods passed to Wallis, so that he could pass it to the defendants, who were accordingly not liable for conversion. As Wallis and "Hallam & Co" were one and the same person, the claimants had not made any mistake as to the identity, but only one as to the credit-worthiness, of the other contracting party, whom they identified as the writer of the letter. The essential point is that "Hallam & Co" *was* Wallis, just as much as "Currer Bell" *was* Charlotte Brontë.

In both the above cases, the dispute was between one of the contracting parties and a third party who later acquired the subject-matter. The effect of holding the contract void was to prejudice the third party even though he might have acted in the most perfect good faith. A recommendation by the Law Reform Committee to reverse this result so as to protect the third party[14] has not been implemented by legislation; but the courts have provided such protection by confining the category of mistakes as to identity within narrow limits. This in turn can cause hardship to the mistaken party who may (as in *Cundy v Lindsay*) be an equally innocent dupe of the other party to the alleged contract. The mistaken party is not likely to suffer such hardship where the dispute is between the contracting parties themselves; for if the mistake is induced by the other party's misrepresentation, the mistaken party will be entitled to rescind the contract for that misrepresentation.[15] He will need to rely on mistake as such only[16] where the mistake arises without any misrepresentation.[17]

Where a contract is in writing, the parties to that contract are *prima facie*[18] the persons described as such in the writing. In *Hector v Lyons*[19] a father conducted negotiations for the purchase of a house, and, when these were successfully concluded, instructed his solicitors to draw up the contract in the name of his son (who was a minor) as purchaser. Contracts were duly exchanged naming the son as purchaser and it was held that the father could not enforce the contract against the vendor, even though the vendor believed that she was dealing with the father. It was said that the identity of vendor and purchaser was established by the terms of the written contract. Similar reasoning was applied in *Shogun Finance Ltd v Hudson*[20] where a rogue (X) obtained possession of a car by pretending to be Y, producing a driving licence in Y's name and forging Y's signature to a hire-purchase agreement purporting to be between Y and Z. A majority of the Court of Appeal held that X was not a party to the agreement, so that a person who in good faith later bought the car from X acquired no title to it.[21] Equally, Y was not liable on the agreement as his signature to it was forged nor, as the contract was procured by

---

[12] (1897) 14 T.L.R. 98.

[13] *ibid*. at 99.

[14] 12th Report Cmnd.2958 (1966), para.15; for adverse comment on the failure to implement the recommendation, see *Shogun Finance Ltd v Hudson* [2001] EWCA Civ 1000; [2002] Q.B. 834 at [51].

[15] See below, pp.369 *et seq*.

[16] Contrary authorities such as dicta in *Gordon v Street* [1899] 2 Q.B. 641 and the decision in *Sowler v Potter* [1940] 1 K.B. 271 are no longer law: see *Gallie v Lee* [1969] 2 Ch. 17 at 33, 41, 45, affirmed without reference to this point [1971] A.C. 1004; *Lewis v Averay* [1972] 1 Q.B. 198 at 206.

[17] *e.g.* in *Craven-Ellis Ltd v Canons Ltd* [1936] 2 K.B. 403, below, p.302.

[18] Subject to the possible application of the principles of agency (below, pp.727–729).

[19] (1989) 58 P. & C.R. 156.

[20] [2001] EWCA Civ 1000; [2002] Q.B. 834.

[21] Under Hire-Purchase Act 1964, s.27.

fraud, could Y have acquired rights under the contract.[22] It is less clear whether, in *Hector v Lyons*, where there was no fraud, there was a contract between the vendor and the son. It is arguable that the vendor had made a mistake as to the identity of the other party: she believed that the other party was the father when actually it was the son. But it does not follow that there was no contract between the vendor and the son since that mistake, even if fundamental, would not have been operative (unless it was known[23] to the son). Hence it seems that the vendor could have been held liable in damages to the son.[24]

(b) MISTAKE INTER PRAESENTES. The difficulty of deciding whether the mistake is one of attribute or of identity is particularly acute where the parties who are alleged to have contracted have come physically face to face. In *Phillips v Brooks Ltd*,[25] a rogue called North entered a shop and asked to see pearls and rings. He selected (*inter alia*) a ring worth £450, produced a chequebook, claimed to be Sir George Bullough (a wealthy man known by name to the shopkeeper) and gave Sir George's address. The shopkeeper checked this address in a directory, and then allowed North to take away the ring in exchange for a cheque, which was dishonoured. North later pledged the ring with the defendant. The shopkeeper claimed that there was never any contract between him and North, so that the latter had no title to the ring which he could pass to the defendant. But Horridge J. held that the shopkeeper had "contracted to sell and deliver [the ring] to the person who came into his shop . . . who obtained the sale and delivery by means of the false pretence that he was Sir George Bullough".[26] The shopkeeper's mistake was not one of identity. "His intention was to sell to the person present and identified by sight and hearing."[27] Lord Haldane has explained the decision on the alternative ground that the sale was concluded before any mention was made of Sir George Bullough, and that the mistake only induced the shopkeeper to let North take the ring away on credit.[28] But this explanation was rejected in a later judicial discussion of the case[29]; and it is only doubtfully consistent with the reported facts. North made an offer to buy when he selected the ring[30]; and it is not clear whether he said that he was Sir George Bullough before or after the offer was accepted.[31]

The same result was reached in *Lewis v Averay*,[32] where a person had advertised his car for sale and was visited by a rogue who falsely claimed to be a well-known actor called Richard Greene. By this pretence the rogue induced the seller to sell the car to him on credit and to let him take it away in exchange for a cheque, which was dishonoured. The seller claimed the car from the defendant, who had bought it in good faith from the rogue; but the claim failed as the contract between the seller and the rogue was not void

---

[22] For the reasons given at p.723, below, Y could not have ratified X's act of forging his signature; nor does there seem to be any good reason why Y might want to do so.

[23] See below, pp.307–309; the other conditions there discussed, in which a mistake negativing consent may be operative, were plainly not satisifed.

[24] See below, p.545–546. As the son was a minor, the remedy of specific performance was not available to him, nor was he liable on the contract: *ibid.*

[25] [1919] 2 K.B. 243; *cf. Dennant v Skinner* [1948] 2 K.B. 164.

[26] [1919] 2 K.B. 243 at 246.

[27] *ibid.* at 247.

[28] *Lake v Simmons* [1927] A.C. 487 at 501.

[29] *Lewis v Averay* [1972] 1 Q.B. 198 at 206.

[30] See above, p.12.

[31] Three of the reports of the case (88 L.J.K.B. 952, 35 T.L.R. 470 and 24 Com.Cas. 263) suggest that North said he was Sir George Bullough as soon as he entered the shop; while two ([1919] 2 K.B. 243, 121 L.T. 249) suggest that he said this a little later.

[32] [1972] 1 Q.B. 198; A.L.G. 88 L.Q.R. 161; Turpin [1972] C.L.J. 19; *cf.* (in criminal law) *Whittaker v Campbell* [1984] Q.B. 319.

for mistake. The presumption that the seller intended to contract with the person physically before him had not been overcome[33]: his mistake was not one of identity[34] but as to the credit-worthiness of the other party.[35]

It does not follow from *Phillips v Brooks* or *Lewis v Averay* that there can be no fundamental mistake as to the person merely because the parties alleged to have contracted were in each other's presence. There may, in the first place, be such a mistake where A induces B to deal with him by pretending to act as agent for C, while in fact intending to contract on his own behalf.[36] In such a case it could be said that there was no mistake as to the identity of A, but rather one as to the capacity in which he purported to contract.[37] Secondly, a mistake about a person who was present could be one of identity where he had adopted a physical disguise: for example, where A induced B to deal with him by disguising himself as C, and C was personally known to B, so that B thought that A was C. And there are, thirdly, other exceptional circumstances in which a mistake about a person present at the time of the alleged contract can be one as to his identity. This possibility is illustrated by *Ingram v Little*,[38] where the owners of a car had, again, advertised it for sale and been visited by a rogue who falsely claimed to be "P. G. M. Hutchinson of Stanstead House, Stanstead Road, Caterham." They agreed to sell the car to him on credit, but only after one of them had checked in a telephone directory that there was a person of that name living at that address. The rogue later sold the car to the defendants from whom the owners claimed it when the rogue's cheque was dishonoured. A majority of the Court of Appeal upheld the claim on the ground that the owners had intended to deal with the Hutchinson of Stanstead House and not with the person before them *as such*. The case was doubted in *Lewis v Averay*,[39] though it can be supported on its special facts: *i.e.* on the ground that the owners had refused to clinch the deal until they had consulted the telephone directory.[40]

(c) DISTINCTION BETWEEN IDENTITY AND ATTRIBUTE. The above discussion shows that it may be difficult to say precisely what mistake has been made: *i.e.* whether B thought that A was C, as opposed to merely thinking that A was not A or making a mistake about A's credit-worthiness. In other cases, it may be clear what mistake has been made, but disputed whether it should be described as one of identity or attribute. This possibility is illustrated by *Lake v Simmons*.[41] A woman called Esmé Ellison told a jeweller that she was married to one Van der Borgh (with whom she was in fact living as his mistress); and that he wanted to give her a necklace which he wished to see on approval. The jeweller let her have possession of the necklace and entered it in his book as being out on approval to Van der Borgh. Esmé Ellison absconded with the necklace, and the actual decision was that the jeweller had not "entrusted" the necklace to her as

---

[33] [1972] 1 Q.B. 198 at 208, 209.

[34] Lord Denning M.R. said at 207 that there *was* a mistake of identity but that it did not make the contract void. With respect, this approach cannot be reconciled with *Cundy v Lindsay* (1878) 3 App.Cas. 459, above, p.298.

[35] [1972] 1 Q.B. at 209.

[36] *Hardman v Booth* (1863) 1 H. & C. 803; *cf. Higgons v Burton* (1857) 26 L.J.Ex. 342. Contrast *Citibank NA v Brown Shipley & Co Ltd* [1991] 2 All E.R. 690 (identity of person acting as mere messenger not fundamental).

[37] *cf. Ingram v Little* [1961] 1 Q.B. 31 at 50, 66.

[38] [1961] 1 Q.B. 31.

[39] [1972] 1 Q.B. 198 at 206, 208 (Megaw L.J.).

[40] *ibid.* at 208 (Phillimore L.J.); *cf. Shogun Finance Ltd v Hudson* [2001] EWCA Civ 1001, [2002] Q.B. 834 at [45] *per* Dyson L.J.; contrast *ibid.* at [18] *per* Sedley L.J. (dissenting), who would have brought the case within *Phillips v Brooks*, above, p.300; Brooke L.J. left the point open. The actual decision of the majority was based on the ground stated at p.299–300, above.

[41] [1927] A.C. 487.

a "customer" within the terms of an insurance policy.[42] Lord Haldane also said that there was no contract, since there was no *consensus*. The jeweller "thought that he was dealing with a different person, the wife of Van der Borgh. . . . He never intended to contract with the woman in question."[43] "Nothing short of a belief in her *identity as a wife* who was transacting for her husband as the real customer would have induced the [jeweller] to act as he did."[44] One possible interpretation of these remarks is that Esmé Ellison's "identity as a wife" was important in inducing a mistake as to the *capacity* in which she dealt: the jeweller intended to deal with her as agent for Van der Borgh, while she intended to contract (if at all) on her own behalf.[45] A second possibility is that the jeweller's mistake was one as to her *identity*[46]: he identified her as the wife of Van der Borgh and not by the more usual process of sight and hearing. This possibility raises the question how the distinction between identity and attributes should in this context be drawn.

It is submitted that the test formulated for the purpose of defining fundamental mistakes as to the subject-matter[47] should also (with appropriate modifications) be applied in the present context. A person may be identified by reference to any one of his attributes. If a mistake is made as to that attribute,[48] there can be said to be a mistake as to identity. This is the basis of the second possible explanation of Lord Haldane's remarks in *Lake v Simmons*. It is also supported by a dictum of Greene L.J. in *Craven-Ellis v Canons Ltd*,[49] where a director's service agreement was held "void *ab initio*" as neither he nor those who appointed him had the necessary qualification shares. One reason for this conclusion was that the agreement was made "under a mistake as to the present existence of an essential fact recognised by the law as the foundation of the contract".[50] Other hypothetical cases can be imagined which would come within the same principle. A college may hold a private dance and intend to sell tickets only to past or present members. In such a case the identifying attribute of an applicant for tickets might be his or her membership of the college.

The principle, then, is that a mistake as to *the* attribute by which a person is identified is in law regarded as a mistake of identity. In applying this principle, the law indeed makes certain *prima facie* assumptions about the way in which a person is identified: *e.g.* that a person physically present is identified by sight and hearing, and an unknown correspondent as "the writer of this letter". The situations discussed above show that these assumptions can be displaced by showing that the mistaken party identified the other party in some other, unusual way. But one attribute on which the mistaken party cannot in law rely for this purpose is that of the credit-worthiness of the other party, about whom no other mistake is made.[51] In deciding whether the other party is credit-worthy, the mistaken party takes a business risk. It would be undesirable to allow an error of judgment on such a point to negative consent.

---

[42] As to this point, contrast *John Rigby (Haulage) Ltd v Reliance Marine Insurance Co* [1956] 2 Q.B. 468.
[43] *Lake v Simmons* [1927] A.C. 487 at 500.
[44] *ibid.* at 502 (italics supplied).
[45] As in *Hardman v Booth* (1863) 1 H. & C. 803; above, p.301 at n.36.
[46] *Citibank N A v Brown Shipley & Co Ltd* [1991] 2 All E.R. 690 at 700.
[47] See above, pp.291–292.
[48] Contrast *Sunderland Association Football Club v Uruguay Montevideo Football Club* [2001] 2 All E.R. (Comm) 828 at 830 (mistake as to the division in which a football club competed not one of identity).
[49] [1936] 2 K.B. 403.
[50] *ibid.* at 413.
[51] *e.g.*, *King's Norton Metal Co Ltd v Edridge Merrett & Co* (1897) 14 T.L.R. 98, above, p.298–299; contrast *Shogun Finance Ltd v Hudson* [2001] EWCA Civ 1001 at [45]–[46], where a borrower by fraudulently impersonating another person procured a loan on the basis of a credit reference relating to that person.

(d) WHETHER ONE PERSON MUST BE MISTAKEN FOR ANOTHER. In most cases of mistaken identity, one person is mistaken for another *existing* person; but this does not seem to be a necessary requirement. If, in *Ingram v Little*,[52] it had been shown that Mr P G M Hutchinson had died six months before the transaction, this would have made no difference to the process by which the owners of the car identified the rogue; and it ought not to have affected the decision. If B thinks that A is C, there can be a mistake as to identity so long as C is or was a distinct entity from A (as opposed to a mere alias[53]) and is so regarded by B.

(e) UNDISCLOSED PRINCIPALS. A person who knows that another is unwilling to contract with him may employ an agent to make the contract without disclosing the existence of the principal. In some such cases the undisclosed principal is not allowed to intervene and take the benefit of the contract. But the contract is not void since the agent can (fraud apart) enforce it. These cases are discussed in Chapter 17.[54]

(2) Mistake as to the subject-matter

Consent is negatived if one party intends to deal with one thing, and the other with a different one. This principle may have been applied in *Raffles v Wichelhaus*,[55] where a seller of "125 bales of Surat cotton . . . to arrive *ex Peerless* from Bombay" tendered cotton from a ship called *Peerless* which had sailed from Bombay in December. The buyer refused to accept the goods, alleging that he had intended to buy the cotton shipped on another *Peerless* which had sailed from Bombay in October: thus it was argued that there was no agreement between the parties. On a claim by the seller, judgment was given for the buyer but, as no reasons were stated, it is hard to tell whether the ground of decision was that there was *no* contract,[56] or that there *was* a contract to deliver cotton from the October *Peerless* which could not be performed by delivering cotton from the December *Peerless*.[57]

Consent was clearly negatived in *Falck v Williams*.[58] A and B were negotiating about two charterparties: one to carry shale from Sydney to Barcelona, and one to carry copra from Fiji to Barcelona. B's agent sent a coded telegram intending to confirm the copra charter, but the telegram was ambiguous and was understood by A to refer to the shale charter. It was held that there was no contract. Similarly, consent is negatived if a buyer at an auction thinks that the lot for which he is bidding consists of hemp when it consists of hemp and tow.[59]

On the other hand, consent is not generally negatived by a mere mistake as to quality: thus it was held in *Smith v Hughes*[60] that if a person buys oats, thinking that they are old, from a seller who knows that they are new, there is a good contract. Similarly, a contract for the sale of goods is not void merely because the seller, under a mistake as to the quality of the goods, charges a lower price than he would have done, had he known the

---

[52] [1961] 1 Q.B. 31.

[53] As in *Collings v Lee* [2001] 2 All E.R. 332, where no attempt was made that the contract was void for mistake.

[54] See below, pp.727–730.

[55] (1864) 2 H. & C. 906.

[56] *Smith v Hughes* (1871) L.R. 6 Q.B. 597 at 609; *O T Africa Line Ltd v Vickers plc* [1996] 1 Lloyd's Rep. 700 at 703. There was no allegation that the seller intended to deal with the cargo of the December rather than the October *Peerless*. The case was decided on a demurrer so that the facts were never proved.

[57] *Van Praagh v Everidge* [1902] 2 Ch. 266 at 269. On this view the buyer could have got damages for the seller's failure to deliver cotton from the October *Peerless*.

[58] [1900] A.C. 176.

[59] *Scriven Bros & Co v Hindley & Co* [1913] 3 K.B. 564.

[60] (1871) L.R. 6 Q.B. 597.

truth.[61] In such cases, the parties are at cross-purposes, but not to such an extent that they are not in agreement at all. A mistake as to quality can negative consent only if it is a mistake as to a fundamental quality by which the thing is identified.[62]

(3) Mistake as to the terms of the contract

Consent is negatived if the parties intend to contract on different terms, *e.g.* if A sells goods to B for so many "pounds" intended by A to mean sterling and by B to mean a different currency[63]; or if A intends to sell rabbit skins at a fixed price per piece when B intends to buy at the same price per pound, there being about three pieces to the pound.[64]

Mistakes as to the person and mistakes as to the subject-matter negative consent only if they are fundamental. There seems to be no such requirement where the mistake is as to the terms of the contract. A sale of oats is not void merely because they are believed by one party to be old but known by the other to be new. The mistake is as to the subject-matter and is not fundamental.[65] But according to *Smith v Hughes*[66] a sale of oats believed by the buyer to be *warranted* to be old and not intended by the seller to be so warranted may be void for mistake. The mistake is as to a term of the contract and negatives consent although the term relates to a quality of the subject-matter which is not fundamental. This distinction seems to be generally accepted, but the reason for it is not easy to see. If a quality is not fundamental, a mistake as to its existence does not destroy consent. Why should consent be destroyed by mistake as to a warranty of that same quality? Is it really true, in the latter case, that the parties have not agreed at all? An alternative explanation for this aspect of *Smith v Hughes* will be put forward later in this Chapter.[67]

2. Mistake must Induce the Contract

A mistake negatives consent only if it induced the mistaken party to enter into the contract. If that party takes the risk that the facts are not as he supposed them to be,[68] or if he is simply indifferent as to the matter to which the mistake relates, the validity of the contract is not affected. For example, in *Mackie v European Assurance Soc*[69] the claimant took out an insurance policy through an agent, believing that the agent was acting for one company when in fact he was acting for another. It was held that the policy with the latter company was not void for mistake. The claimant's intention "was not to

---

[61] *Dip Kaur v Chief Constable of Hampshire* [1981] 1 W.L.R. 578; but the invalidity of the contract is not decisive for the purpose of criminal liability: *R. v Morris* [1984] A.C. 320; *Dobson v GAFLAC* [1990] Q.B. 274.

[62] As defined above, pp.291–292. *The Kaliningrad and Nadezhda Krupskaya* [1997] 2 Lloyd's Rep. 35 at 39 is, with respect, hard to reconcile with the usual interpretation of the requirement that the mistake must be "fundamental."

[63] See *Woodhouse A C Israel Cocoa Ltd v Nigerian Produce Marketing Co* [1972] A.C. 741 at 768; *cf. Felthouse v Bindley* (1862) 11 C.B.(N.S.) 869 ("30" intended to mean pounds by buyer but guineas by seller); *Smidt v Tiden* (1874) L.R. 9 Q.B. 446.

[64] *Hartog v Colin & Shields* [1939] 3 All E.R. 566.

[65] See above, after n.60.

[66] (1871) L.R. 6 Q.B. 597; *cf. London Holeproof Hosiery Co Ltd v Padmore* (1928) 44 T.L.R. 499; *Sullivan v Constable* (1932) 49 T.L.R. 369.

[67] See below, pp.308–309.

[68] *Wales v Wadham* [1977] 1 W.L.R. 199 at 220; (approved on the issue of mistake in *Jenkins v Livesey* [1985] A.C. 424); *cf.* above, pp.294–295, 296–297.

[69] (1869) 21 L.T. 102; *cf. Fellowes v Gwydyr* (1829) 1 Russ. & My. 83.

remain uninsured for one hour and in what office it was was a secondary consideration, provided it would meet its engagements and was able to do so".[70]

This case should be contrasted with *Boulton v Jones*.[71] Boulton had just bought a shop from one Brocklehurst when the defendant sent his servant to the shop with an order, addressed to Brocklehurst, for a quantity of pipe hose. Boulton supplied the goods, no doubt thinking that the defendant did not care from whom he obtained them. The defendant was apparently satisfied with the goods and used them. He had clearly made a fundamental mistake, in that he thought he was dealing with Brocklehurst when he dealt with Boulton. Ordinarily, that mistake would have had no effect, since it would not matter to the defendant whether the goods were supplied by Boulton or by Brocklehurst. But Brocklehurst owed money to the defendant, who had intended to set off this debt against the price of the goods. He could thus show that it was important for him to contract with Brocklehurst rather than with Boulton. It was therefore held that there was no contract so that the defendant was not liable for the price of the goods.[72] To have held him liable would have been unjust as it would have deprived him of the benefit of his set-off against Brocklehurst. But the result of holding him not liable was almost equally unjust. The defendant got the goods for nothing but retained his right to sue Brocklehurst for the amount which the latter owed him. It seems that on such facts the defendant should be under some quasi-contractual liability,[73] or that he should at least be bound to transfer his claim against Brocklehurst to the supplier.[74]

In a number of English cases, reference has been made to the following passage from the French writer Pothier: "Whenever the consideration of the person with whom I am willing to contract enters as an element into the contract which I am willing to make, error in regard to the person destroys my consent and consequently annuls the contract. . . . On the contrary, when the consideration of the person with whom I thought I was contracting does not enter at all into the contract, and I should have been equally willing to make the contract with any person whatever as with him with whom I thought I was contracting, the contract ought to stand." This passage has sometimes been interpreted to mean that mistake will make a contract void if it relates to a personal attribute of the other party, but for the existence of which the mistaken party would not have contracted.[75] If it means this, it does not represent English law,[76] for a mistake must be fundamental, and a mistake as to the person is fundamental only if one person is mistaken for another or if the mistake relates to *the* attribute by which a person is identified.[77] But it seems that the purpose of the passage is not to define when a mistake is fundamental but to distinguish between cases in which it does, and those in which it does not, induce the contract. This is made clear by the examples given by Pothier: a contract by which an artist is commissioned to paint a picture is void if mistakenly made with the wrong artist; but a contract to sell a book is not void simply because the bookseller thinks he is contracting with Peter when in fact he is contracting with Paul. In both cases the mistake is fundamental, one person being mistaken for another. The difference between them is that in the first case the mistake induces the contract, while in the second it does not. Nor would a mistake induce the contract where it related, not

---

[70] (1869) 21 L.T. at p.105.

[71] (1857) 2 H. & N. 564; L.J.Ex. 117; 6 W.R. 107.

[72] cf. *Westminster CC v Reema Construction (No.2)* (1992) 24 Con.L.R. 26 (no *liability* of successor in business under contract with predecessor).

[73] cf. below, p.1063.

[74] Goff and Jones, *The Law of Restitution* (6th ed.), pp.132, 591.

[75] e.g. in *Sowler v Potter* [1940] 1 K.B. 271 at 274; see above, p.300, n.16 as to this case.

[76] *Lewis v Averay* [1972] 1 Q.B. 198 at 206.

[77] See above, p.301.

to the person with whom the mistaken party believed that he was negotiating, but only to an intermediary through whom the contract was to be performed. Thus if A believes that he is contracting with B and has indeed entered into a contract with B, that contract is not void merely because A is induced to deliver its subject-matter to C by C's fraudulent pretence that he is a messenger authorised by B to receive it.[78] Such a case differs from *Lake v Simmons*[79] where the jeweller thought that he was dealing with the wife of Van der Borgh: Esmé Ellison in that case did not purport to act as a mere messenger for her alleged husband, but falsely claimed to be negotiating as his wife and on his behalf.

The requirement that the mistake must induce the contract applies not only to mistake as to the person but also to other types of mistake. If in *Raffles v Wichelhaus*[80] both ships *Peerless* had sailed from Bombay on the same day and had arrived at the same time, it might not have mattered to the buyer which cargo he got. In that case he could not have escaped liability by saying that he intended to buy the cargo in the one ship while the seller intended to sell the cargo in the other.

3. When Mistake is Operative

(1) Contract generally valid

A mistake which negatives consent does not necessarily make the contract void. On the contrary, the general rule is that a party is bound, in spite of his mistake: this follows from the objective principle,[81] under which one party (A) is often bound if his words or conduct are such as to induce the other party (B) reasonably to believe that A was assenting to the terms proposed by B.[82] This principle is sometimes regarded as a kind of estoppel by representation. But such estoppel operates only in favour of a person who acts on a representation to his detriment[83]; while a person who invokes the objective principle need only show that he has entered into the contract in reliance on the appearance of the agreement created by the other's conduct. He need not show that he has, as a result of entering into that contract, suffered any actual detriment.[84]

The operation of the objective principle is most easily illustrated by the case of a person who by mistake bids for the wrong lot at an auction. Although the parties may

---

[78] *Citibank NA v Brown Shipley & Co Ltd* [1991] 2 All E.R. 690.

[79] [1927] A.C. 487, above, p.301.

[80] (1864) 2 H. & C. 906; *cf. Ind's Case* (1872) L.R. 7 Ch.App. 485 (validity of share transfer not affected by which shares the transferee gets, so long as he gets the quantity contracted for).

[81] See above, pp.1, 8.

[82] *Smith v Hughes* (1871) L.R. 6 Q.B. 597, 607; *OT Africa Line Ltd v Vickers plc* [1996] 1 Lloyd's Rep. 700. This principle contains no requirement of negligence and is in this respect wider in scope than that which prevents a mistake which *nullifies* consent from being operative on account of the conduct of one of the parties: above, p.297.

[83] See below, p.403; such detrimental reliance is also necessary for "estoppel by convention," discussed above at p.110. Reliance, though not "detriment" is also necessary for "promissory" estoppel: above p.111.

[84] Williston, in *Selected Readings on the Law of Contracts*, p.119; Atiyah's contrary suggestion in 94 L.Q.R. 193 at 202 is inconsistent with the cases discussed in the following paragraph, and with *Centrovincial Estates plc v Merchant Investors Assurance Co Ltd*, [1983] Com.L.R. 158. That decision is described by Atiyah in his *Introduction to the Law of Contract* (5th ed.), p.462 as "absurd and unjustifiable"; but it has on a number of occasions been cited with approval: see *Whittaker v Campbell* [1984] Q.B. 318 at 327; *The Antclizo* [1987] 2 Lloyd's Rep. 130 at 146 (affirmed [1988] 1 W.L.R. 603); *OT Africa Line Ltd v Vickers plc* [1996] 1 Lloyd's Rep. 700 at 704. In further support of his view, Atiyah relies (102 L.Q.R. 363) on *The Hannah Blumenthal* [1983] 1 A.C. 854, above, p.11. But the principal question in that case was whether A's conduct had induced B reasonably to believe that A was making an offer to B. Conduct amounting to reliance (not necessarily detrimental) by B is *one* way in which such an offer can be accepted (above, pp.18, 35), but it is not the *only* way: an express acceptance in so many words would be equally effective.

not be *ad idem*,[85] (as they intended to deal with different things), the bidder is prevented by the objective principle from relying on the mistake and so from saying that the contract is void.[86] The same principle applies to mistakes as to the person[87] and as to the terms of the contract. Thus a seller who, as a result of some miscalculation, offers goods at a price lower than that which he would have asked but for the mistake cannot, after the offer has been accepted, generally rely on the mistake to make the contract void.[88] Similarly, where a landlord as a result of a clerical error offers to grant a tenancy at a rent of £1,000 per month, he cannot, after the offer has been accepted, escape from the transaction merely by showing that his real intention was to make the offer at a rent of £2,000 per month.[89] The position is the same where a person signs a document under some other mistake about its terms or legal effects: he cannot, in general, say that the contract is void because of his mistake.[90]

(2) Exceptional cases in which mistake is operative

Where the objective principle applies, the contract is valid in spite of the existence of a mistake, so that it is unnecessary to go into the difficult question whether the mistake is fundamental. That question need only be answered in the following three exceptional situations, in which the objective principle does not apply, so that the mistake is *operative*.

(a) AMBIGUITY. There may be such ambiguity in the circumstances that a reasonable person could not draw any relevant inference from them at all. In *Raffles v Wichelhaus*[91] a reasonable person could not have deduced with which cargo the parties intended to deal. Similarly, if parties stipulate for the payment of freight "per charterparty" but there are two charterparties in the case, providing for payment of different rates of freight, the reasonable person cannot put any definite interpretation on the promises.[92] In these cases, therefore, the mistake is operative and makes the contract void.

(b) MISTAKE KNOWN TO OTHER PARTY. The objective principle applies where A's words or conduct induce B reasonably to believe that A is contracting with him; but it does not apply where B actually knows that (in spite of the objective appearance) A has no such intention.[93] It follows that the objective principle will not apply, and that the mistake will be operative, if A's mistake is known to B. This is the reason why the contract in *Cundy v Lindsay*[94] was void. Lindsays may have behaved so as to induce a reasonable person to believe that they were dealing with Blenkarn, but the mistake was operative as Blenkarn knew that they had no such intention. The case would have been different if Blenkarn had written to Lindsays in good faith and they had misread his signature for "Blenkiron & Co." In such a case, Lindsays could not have relied on their mistake, had they simply sent the goods to Blenkarn's address, unless it had been clear

---

[85] *Van Praagh v Everidge* [1903] 1 Ch.434.

[86] *Robinson, Fisher & Harding v Behar* [1927] 1 K.B. 513.

[87] *Cornish v Abington* (1859) 4 H. & N. 549; *Re Reed* (1876) 3 Ch.D. 123, so far as *contra*, seems wrong.

[88] This would have been the position in *Hartog v Colin & Shields* [1939] 3 All E.R. 566 (below, p.309) if the court had not taken the view that the claimant must have known of the defendant's mistake.

[89] *Centrovincial Estates plc v Merchant Investors Assurance Co Ltd*, above n.84.

[90] *Blay v Pollard & Morris* [1930] 1 K.B. 628; cf. *L'Estrange v F Graucob Ltd* [1934] 2 K.B. 394, a case of ignorance rather than mistake.

[91] (1864) 2 H. & C. 906 ("a case of latent ambiguity": *The Great Peace* [2002] EWCA Civ 1407; [2002] 4 All E.R. 689, at [29]); cf. *Hickman v Berens* [1895] 2 Ch.638.

[92] *Smidt v Tiden* (1874) L.R. 9 Q.B. 446.

[93] See above, pp.11–12.

[94] (1878) 3 App.Cas. 459.

to Blenkarn from the contractual documents that they did not intend to deal with him but with Blenkiron & Co.[95]

In *Boulton v Jones* the defendant's order was addressed to Brocklehurst, so that Boulton knew it was not meant for him. It is not clear whether he also knew *why* the order was not meant for him, *i.e.* whether he knew that Brocklehurst owed money to Jones.[96] Probably such knowledge is not essential to make the contract void. A person who accepts an offer knowing that it is addressed to another must take the risk that the mistake may turn out to be material.

The rule that a mistake of one party is operative if known to the other is further illustrated by *Smith v Hughes*.[97] Oats were bought by sample, the buyer thinking that they were old when, in fact, they were new. He refused to accept them, as he had no use for new oats. In an action for the price, the trial judge told the jury to find for the buyer (1) if the word "old" had been used in the negotiations, *i.e.* if the oats had been *expressly described* as old; or (2) if "the [seller] believed the [buyer] to believe, or to be under the impression, that he was *contracting for the purchase of old oats*". The jury found for the buyer, but did not say which of these two questions they had answered in his favour. If they thought that the word "old" had been used, their verdict was clearly correct. But they might have based their verdict on their answer to the second question, so that the court had to decide whether this question was correctly formulated.

If the buyer's mistake had been *as to the subject-matter*, it could not in law negative consent at all because it was not fundamental.[98] The seller's knowledge of the buyer's mistake would not alter this. But if the mistake had been *as to the terms of the contract* it could negative consent although it was not fundamental.[99] There would have been such a mistake if the buyer believed that the seller had *warranted* the oats to be old, while the seller intended to sell without warranty. *Prima facie* this mistake would not be operative: the objective principle would apply, the buyer having behaved so as to induce the seller reasonably to believe that the buyer was buying oats of the same quality as those in the sample. The mistake would be operative only if the seller knew of the buyer's mistake—*i.e.* if he knew that the buyer believed he was buying the oats with a warranty that they were old.[1] Thus if the buyer thought the oats *were old* there was a good contract even if the seller knew of this mistake; but if the buyer thought the oats were *warranted to be old* and the seller knew of this, quite different, mistake the contract was void. The court ordered a new trial because the direction to the jury did not clearly distinguish between the two mistakes which the buyer might have made.

It has been suggested above[2] that it is hard to see why a mistake as to a warranty of quality should negative consent when a mistake as to the existence of the quality itself does not have this effect. The distinction is based on *Smith v Hughes*; and it is submitted that if the buyer did believe the oats to have been warranted old, and the seller knew this, the buyer could have been absolved from liability on an alternative ground. In such a case it could be said that there *was* a contract under which the seller was bound by the warranty that the oats were old, because he had behaved so as to induce the buyer

---

[95] *cf. The Unique Mariner* [1978] 1 Lloyd's Rep. 438 at 451–452.

[96] The only report of the case which suggests that Boulton did know this is in 6 W.R. 107, where counsel for the defendants says at 108: "The plaintiff knew that Brocklehurst was indebted to the defendants . . . ."

[97] (1871) L.R. 6 Q.B. 597.

[98] See above, p.304.

[99] See above, p.304.

[1] *cf. Hartog v Colin & Shields* [1939] 3 All E.R. 566 (below, p.309).

[2] See above, p.304.

reasonably to believe that he was contracting on those terms.[3] Breach of the warranty that the oats were old could have justified the buyer's refusal to accept new oats.[4]

(c) MISTAKE NEGLIGENTLY INDUCED. A mistake is operative where one party has negligently led the other to make it. In *Scriven Bros v Hindley & Co*[5] the defendant at an auction bid for two lots believing that both were lots of hemp, whereas one was a lot of hemp and tow. Normally, he could not have relied on this mistake,[6] but he was able to do so in this case because the mistake was caused by the misleading nature of the catalogue and by the conduct of one of the seller's servants. This principle is distinct from that which applies in cases of ambiguity.[7] Where a mistake is negligently induced, the circumstances need not be so perfectly ambiguous as to make each party's view of the contract equally tenable. If auction particulars are so obscure as to lead a purchaser to make a mistake, the mistake will be operative even though the particulars, properly interpreted, can only bear the meaning intended by the vendor.[8]

(3) Mistake may operate against one party only

If A's mistake is deliberately induced by B, then A can treat the contract as void, but it does not follow that B can do so. It seems probable that in *Cundy v Lindsay* Blenkarn could have been sued for the price of the handkerchiefs.[9] The same may be true even where B does not in any way bring about A's mistake. In *Hartog v Colin & Shields*[10] the defendants intended to offer hare skins for sale at a stated price "per piece", but inadvertently offered to sell at that price "per pound". A pound contained, on average, three pieces. The claimant purported to accept this offer. It was held that there was "no contract"[11] as the claimant must have known of the defendants' mistake in expressing their offer.[12] But it is possible that the defendants could have held the claimant liable on his acceptance if a fall in the market had made them wish to do so.

4. Theoretical Basis

It has been suggested[13] that the cases discussed in this Section do not depend on mistake at all, but on the rule that there is no contract if offer and acceptance do not correspond. If, for example, contract notes are exchanged by which A agrees to sell "St. Petersburgh clean hemp ex *Annetta*" but B agrees to buy "Riga Rhine hemp ex *Annetta*",[14] then it is as plausible to say that there is no contract because offer and acceptance do not

---

[3] This is the argument of counsel for the buyer as reported in 40 L.J.Q.B. at p.223. But in the *Law Reports*, counsel is reported as saying: "The parties were not *ad idem*" (p.600).

[4] It is true that under the Sale of Goods Act 1979, s.11 refusal to accept is (as a general rule) justified only by a breach of *condition* and not by one of *warranty* (below, p.788 *et seq.*). But in 1871 these words were probably not used in their present sense: see below, p.790; *cf. Hardwick Game Farm v Suffolk Agricultural, etc. Association* [1969] 2 A.C. 31 at 83.

[5] [1913] 3 K.B. 564.

[6] See above, p.307. *cf. Lloyd's Bank v Waterhouse* [1993] 2 FLR 97, 123.

[7] See above, p.307.

[8] *cf. Swaisland v Dearsley* (1861) Beav. 430, in equity, but *Scriven Bros & Co v Hindley & Co* [1913] 3 K.B. 564 shows that the common law is the same.

[9] So in the agency situation discussed at p.301, above, the agent might have been liable: *cf. Bell v Balls* [1897] 1 Ch. 663 at 669.

[10] [1939] 3 All E.R. 566.

[11] *ibid.* at 567.

[12] *cf. Watkin v Watson-Smith, The Times*, July 3, 1986.

[13] Slade, 70 L.Q.R. 385; Shatwell, 33 Can.Bar Rev. 164; Atiyah, 2 Ottawa L.Rev. 337, esp. at 344–350 and *Essays in Contract*, pp.253–260; *cf. Whittaker v Campbell* [1984] Q.B. 319 at 327—but in that case the mistake was as to attribute only, and so not fundamental: see *ibid.* at 329.

[14] As in *Thornton v Kempster* (1814) 5 Taunt. 786.

correspond as it is to say that there is no contract because the parties intended to deal with different things.

But there are also difficulties in the way of this "offer and acceptance" theory.[15] It clearly does not mean that there is a good contract merely because the express words of the offer correspond with those of the acceptance. In *Raffles v Wichelhaus*,[16] there was, so far as appears from the report, no lack of verbal correspondence between offer and acceptance, and yet (on one view of the case) there was no contract.

Another version of the same theory is that the full terms of the offer, as intended by the offeror, must correspond with the full terms of the acceptance, as intended by the offeree. But on this view it is hard to see why some discrepancies prevent the formation of a contract, while others do not. Two cases may be contrasted. In the first, A intends to sell oats which are new; B intends to buy oats which are old. In the second, A intends to sell cotton ex *Peerless* (December); B intends to buy cotton ex *Peerless* (October). The contract in the first case is expressed to be for "oats" and in the second for "cotton ex *Peerless*." In both cases offer and acceptance correspond verbally. In neither case would they correspond if each party expressed his full intention. Yet in the first case there is a good contract, while in the second there is none. This version of the "offer and acceptance" theory makes no allowance for the crucial distinction between mistakes which are fundamental and those which are not.

A third version of the theory is that the required correspondence is between offer and acceptance *as construed by the court*. On this view *Raffles v Wichelhaus* can be explained on the ground that offer and acceptance were so ambiguous that the court could not, in the context, determine their meaning at all. But this version of the theory makes it hard to explain the distinction drawn in *Smith v Hughes* between a mistake as to the age of the oats and a mistake as to a warranty as to their age; and, more generally, to say why offer and acceptance should have been held to correspond in some of the cases discussed in this Section, but not in others. It seems that this version of the "offer and acceptance" theory still raises the same difficulties as those which arise under the doctrine of mistake. If the offer and acceptance correspond verbally, the court is unlikely to hold that they do not correspond on their true construction unless the parties are very seriously at cross-purposes; and such a process of construction would not appear to differ substantially from the application of the principle of fundamental mistake.[17]

SECTION 3. MISTAKE IN EQUITY

The common law of mistake can be a source of hardship in a number of situations. First, a contract may be held valid because of the narrow common law definition of a "fundamental" mistake. The result is that a person may have to pay for something that he does not want[18] or for something that is nearly worthless.[19] Secondly, a contract may be valid at common law, in spite of the existence of a fundamental mistake, because of

---

[15] *cf.* Devlin L.J. (dissenting) in *Ingram v Little* [1961] 1 Q.B. 31.

[16] (1864) 2 H. & C. 906; above, pp.303, 307.

[17] Atiyah, above, n.13 at pp.350 and 260, suggests that the courts are "in fact using" the construction technique and not the mistake technique, citing *Sullivan v Constable* (1932) 48 T.L.R. 369. On the other hand, it seems that the mistake technique was used in *Dennant v Skinner* [1948] 2 K.B. 164 and in *Lewis v Averay* [1972] 1 Q.B. 198. It is also accepted in the Law Reform Committee's 12th Report Cmnd. 2958 (1966), para.15. The difficulty of determining which technique was used by the majority in *Ingram v Little* [1961] 1 Q.B. 31 may support the view expressed in the text that there is little (if any) practical difference between them.

[18] *e.g. Smith v Hughes* (1871) L.R. 6 Q.B. 597 (assuming that the only mistake was as to the age of the oats).

[19] *e.g. Bell v Lever Bros Ltd* [1932] A.C. 161.

the objective principle. Here again the mistaken party can suffer hardship through being held to a contract which he did not intend to make[20] though this hardship must be weighed against that which the other party might suffer if the contract were held invalid.[21] In both these situations, the common law emphasises the needs of commercial certainty, sometimes at the expense of the demands of justice in individual cases. Thirdly, an innocent third party may suffer hardship where the contract is *void* at common law, as in *Cundy v Lindsay*.[22]

Equity deals only to a very limited extent with the hardship which the mistaken party can suffer under the objective principle[23]; and it provides no relief against the hardship to third parties that can arise when the contract is void at law. It has been concerned mainly with the first of the above hardships: that is, it has given relief for certain kinds of mistake which do not make the contract void at law. Three kinds of relief were at one time available for this purpose. First, equity could refuse specific performance (or grant that remedy only on terms); secondly, it could rescind the contract, again on terms; and thirdly, it could rectify a contractual document where a mistake had been made, not in the formation, but in the recording, of a contract. Considerable powers of adjustment were available where relief could be given on terms; but this flexibility[24] has been much reduced now that the Court of Appeal[25] has rejected the former view[26] that rescission on terms could be ordered in equity where a contract was made under a mistake which was not "fundamental" in the narrow common law sense. The position that there is no such power to rescind must now be accepted, at least until the issue arises in the House of Lords. The reasons for this development are discussed later in this Chapter; here it must be stressed that it affects only *rescission* and has no effect on equitable relief for mistake by way of refusal of specific performance (or the granting of that remedy on terms) or of rectification. It also gives rise to a problem as to the status of the previous authorities concerning rescission on terms. One of these has been disapproved[27] but this disapproval does not expressly extend to later cases[28] exercising the power to rescind or to earlier cases[29] in which equitable relief was given by way of (or amounting to) rescission.[30] Such cases still serve to illustrate the *types* of mistake for which equity can give relief[31]; though they are no longer reliable as to the *form* of relief given in them, unless, where this amounted to rescission, it could be justified on grounds other than mistake.[32]

To the extent that equity has given, and still gives, relief for mistakes which do not make the contract void at law, it sacrifices the requirement of certainty which is emphasised by the common law. Here (as elsewhere in the law of contract[33]) rules which

---

[20] *cf.* below, p.317.

[21] The other party can, however, invoke the objective principle even though he has not suffered any detriment by relying on the appearance of agreement induced by the conduct of the mistaken party: above, p.306.

[22] (1878) 3 App.Cas. 459; for a proposal for reform, see above, p.298.

[23] Below, pp.318, 322; *cf.* above p.306.

[24] The statutory powers of adjustment available in cases of frustration (below, pp.911–917) do not apply to cases of mistake: *e.g.* the defendant in a case like *Griffith v Brymer* (1903) 19 T.L.R. 434 (above, p.288) would not, even now be able to invoke these powers in respect of his expenses.

[25] In *The Great Peace* [2002] E.W.C.A. Civ 1407, [2002] 4 All E.R. 689, below, p.319.

[26] Usually thought to have originated in *Solle v Butcher* [1950] 1 K.B. 671, below, p.318.

[27] *Solle v Butcher*, above: see *The Great Peace*, above, at [160].

[28] *i.e.*, cases after *Solle v Butcher*, above; for such cases see below, p.318, n.1.

[29] *i.e.*, cases before *Solle v Butcher*, above; some of these cases are discussed at pp.318–319, below.

[30] See, for example, *Re Garnett* (1885) 31 Ch.D. 1; *Allcard v Walker* [1896] 2 Ch. 369.

[31] Below, pp.316–317.

[32] *e.g. Torrance v Bolton* (1872) L.R. 8 Ch. App. 118 (perhaps explicable on the ground of misrepresentation); *Colyer v Clay* (1843) 7 Beav. 188 (where it was conceded that the contract could not stand); and see below, pp.312, 313, nn.42 and 43.

[33] *e.g.* below, p.778.

are intended to achieve certainty can lead to results, the justice of which is open to question; and English law presents, or has presented, an incongruous appearance, with the common law striving for certainty while equity tried to promote justice. It may be that the common law approach the mistake has over-stressed the need for certainty. This is suggested by the fact that the American rules on this subject are much closer to those of English equity than to those of the English common law,[34] and do not seem to have caused widespread inconvenience. Nor has such inconvenience resulted from the rule that a contract can be set aside for even a wholly innocent misrepresentation.[35] Yet from the representor's point of view this rule creates almost as much uncertainty as would a broad doctrine of mistake.

At first sight, it may seem odd still to provide a separate discussion of mistake in equity. A more satisfactory approach, it might be thought, would simply be to look at each mistake situation and to ask whether the law (including equity) provided any relief.[36] But this approach would not help towards an understanding of the present law, because equitable remedies for mistake differ from those available at common law in being not only more flexible but also discretionary. Even today it is therefore not enough to know that there is *some* remedy for mistake in a given case. It can still make a practical difference whether the remedy is available at common law (because the contract is void) or in equity (even though the contract is not void).

1. Types of Mistake Dealt With in Equity

(1) Mistake of fact

(a) MISTAKE NOT FUNDAMENTAL. Equity may give relief to a person who has made a mistake which is not fundamental in the narrow common law sense: for example to a purchaser who buys under a mistake as to the vendor's title,[37] though at law the contract would be valid unless the title happened to be in the purchaser himself.[38] Similarly, equity may give relief if a vendor intends to sell property subject to a right of way or a mortgage, but the purchaser believes he is buying without incumbrance.[39] Conversely, equitable relief can be given to a vendor who sells property to which he has a greater right than he thinks he has: *e.g.* if he thinks that he has only a half-share in property when he is in fact entitled to the whole.[40] Other cases in which equitable relief may be given for mistakes that are not fundamental in the common law sense are considered later in this Chapter in the discussion of the various forms which such relief can take.[41]

(b) MISTAKE AS TO VALUE. Occasionally, equity has intervened even where a mistake has been made by a vendor which merely affects the value of the thing sold.[42] Similarly,

---

[34] See Williston, *Contracts*, rev. ed., §1544; *cf.* his criticism in §1570, n.3 of *Bell v Lever Bros Ltd*; Restatement 2d, *Contracts*, §§152, 153.

[35] See below, Chap.9.

[36] Phang, 9 Legal Studies 291; Burrows, 2002 O.J.L.S. 1.

[37] *Hitchcock v Giddings* (1817) 4 Price 135 (Court of Exchequer, stating equitable principles).

[38] See above, p.287.

[39] *Manser v Back* (1848) 6 Hare 433; *Torrance v Bolton* (1872) L.R. 8 Ch.App. 118; but not if the mistake is trivial or the risk of it is allocated by the contract: *William Sindall plc v Cambridgeshire CC* [1994] 1 W.L.R. 1016.

[40] *Colyer v Clay* (1843) 7 Beav. 188.

[41] *e.g.* below, pp.316–317.

[42] *Cocking v Pratt* (1749) 1 Ves.Sen. 400; *cf.* cases of "surprise" (below, pp.420, 1027) such as *Evans v Llewellin* (1787) 1 Cox CC 333 and *Walters v Morgan* (1861) 3 D.F. & J. 718; *Bettyes v Maynard* (1882) 46 L.T. 766; *Scott v Coulson* [1903] 2 Ch. 249, above, p.267 may be explained as a case of relief for such a mistake as to value.

in *Re Garnett*[43] a testator left half his estate to his sister and the other half to be shared equally between his nieces, who lived with the sister. The nieces later released their shares to the sister in consideration of a payment of £10,500. The releases were set aside on the ground that the shares of the nieces were worth over £15,000. However, where a contract price is fixed by the valuation of a third party, equity will not intervene merely because that valuation is too high[44] or too low. The remedy (if any) of the party prejudiced by the mistake is against the valuer.[45]

(c) NO RELIEF FOR MISTAKE AS TO EXPECTATION. Equity can grant relief for a mistake as to facts existing at the date of the contract; but not for "one which related to the expectation of the parties".[46] The distinction is illustrated by *Amalgamated Investment & Property Co Ltd v John Walker & Sons Ltd*[47] where a contract was made for the sale of a London warehouse which the purchaser (to the vendor's knowledge) intended to redevelop. Before the contract was made, a government official had decided that the warehouse ought to be listed as a building of special architectural or historic interest. But the actual listing took place only after the conclusion of the contract; its effect was to make it harder to obtain permission to redevelop. If such permission were refused the value of the property would be reduced by some £1,500,000 below the contract price of £1,710,000. The Court of Appeal held that equity could not intervene[48] merely because the purchaser mistakenly believed that the property was "suitable for and capable of being developed".[49] No doubt the official's decision, if known, would have affected the negotiations; but that decision did not amount to a listing, and therefore did not affect the quality of the subject-matter at the time of contracting. It only affected the extent of the risk that permission to redevelop might be refused—a risk which would have existed, though to a lesser extent, quite apart from any question of listing. It follows, *a fortiori*, that relief will not be given for a mistake which relates neither to subject-matter nor to the terms of contract, but only to "the commercial advantage which the contract gave"[50] to the mistaken party.

(2) Mistake of law

At common law, the traditional view is that a mistake can affect the validity of a contract only if it is one of "fact" as opposed to one of "law",[51] and this view has been said also to apply in equity.[52] But the distinction between these two categories of mistake is not always easy to draw[53] or to justify[54]; and in *Kleinwort Benson Ltd v Lincoln C C*[55] the

---

[43] (1885) 31 Ch.D. 1; *cf. Jones v Rimmer* (1880) 14 Ch.D. 588 (where the mistake was induced by a misleading omission in auction particulars).

[44] *Campbell v Edwards* [1976] 1 W.L.R. 403; *cf. Jones v Sherwood Computer Services Ltd* [1992] 1 W.L.R. 277; contrast *Macro v Thompson* [1996] B.C.C. 707 (expert valuing assets of wrong company).

[45] If he is negligent: below, p.345.

[46] *Amalgamated Investment & Property Co Ltd v Walker & Sons Ltd* [1977] 1 W.L.R. 164 at 172. For a similar distinction in the law relating to restitution of money paid under a mistake, see *Dextra Bank & Trust Co Ltd v Bank of Jamaica* [2001] 1 All E.R. (Comm) 193 at 2002.

[47] See above; Brownsword, 40 M.L.R. 467.

[48] Whether by rescission or by refusal of specific performance; rescission is now ruled out by the development described at p.319, below.

[49] [1977] 1 W.L.R. at p.171.

[50] *Clarion Ltd v National Provident Association* [2000] 1 W.L.R. 1888 at 1905.

[51] See above, p.286, n.4.

[52] *Midland Great Western Ry of Ireland v Johnson* (1858) 6 H.L.C. 798 at 810–811.

[53] See *Friendly Provident Life Office v Hilliers Parker May & Rowden* [1997] Q.B. 85. *cf.* below, pp.333–335 for a similar distinction in the law of misrepresentation.

[54] *cf. Avon CC v Howlett* [1983] 1 W.L.R. 605 at 620; *Woolwich Equitable Building Society v IRC (No.2)* [1993] A.C. 70 at 154, 199.

[55] [1999] 2 A.C. 349; below, p.1059.

House of Lords held that the analogous right to recover back money paid under a mistake existed even where the mistake was one of law, the mistake there being that contracts under which moneys had been paid to local authorities were valid when actually they were beyond the powers of those authorities and therefore void. Neither this result nor the reasoning on which it was based directly settles the present question, whether a mistake can make a contract void at law or be a ground for relief in equity if it is one as to some point of law *other* than the validity of the contract itself.[56] But it does seem to be probable that the principle of the *Kleinwort Benson* case will be extended to cases of this kind, so that a mistake will not be precluded from affecting the validity of a contract (even at law) merely because it is one of law. Since, however, there can be no certainty that this further step will be taken,[57] an account must still be given of cases in which relief has been given in equity for certain types of mistakes which under the common law, as it now stands, would not affect the validity of a contract because they were mistakes of law.

(a) PRIVATE RIGHT. A mistake as to private right can make a contract void, even at law if it results in an attempt by a person to buy his own property.[58] Such a mistake may be based on a pure mistake of fact, *e.g.* where A is wrongly thought to be older than B. More usually, the mistake arises out of the misconstruction of a document, such as a will or settlement.[59] It may also result from a mistake about the law, *e.g.* as to the age at which a person can marry or make a will, or as to the contractual capacity of a person under a disability. In such cases the mistake seems to be a pure mistake of law, though, like many mistakes of law, it may affect private rights.

(b) PURE MISTAKE OF LAW. There is some support for the view that equity can relieve against a pure mistake of law of the kind last mentioned, even though it does not result in an attempt by a person to buy his own property. In *Allcard v Walker*[60] a married woman executed a settlement containing a covenant to settle after-acquired property. As the law then stood, a married woman could not bind herself by such a covenant. In later divorce proceedings she agreed to an order varying the settlement, mistakenly believing that the settlement and the covenant were valid. It was held that the order could be set aside on terms. Since orders made by consent may for this purpose have the effect of contracts,[61] the case supports the view that equity can give relief to a party who has entered into a contract under a pure mistake of law. Stirling J., apart from affirming this proposition, also said that the mistake was one as to private right: he relied on the analogy of *Cooper v Phibbs*,[62] where equitable relief was granted to a person who had taken a lease of land to which he was already entitled beneficially, though not at law, neither party being at the time of the transaction aware of the true state of the title. The

---

[56] As, for example, in *Solle v Butcher* [1950] 1 K.B. 671, below, pp.316, 334.

[57] According to a dictum in *S v S* [2002] N.L.J. 398, the *Kleinwort Benson* decision was "specific to the law of restitution and was not intended to apply across the board of every branch of law".

[58] *cf.* above, p.287.

[59] As in *Cooper v Phibbs* (1877) L.R. 2 H.L. 149; regarded in *Kleinwort Benson Ltd v Lincoln City Council* [1999] 2 A.C. 349 at 407 as an exception to the rule that relief was not available for mistake of law.

[60] [1896] 2 Ch.369; *cf. Stone v Godfrey* (1854) 5 D.M. & G. 76 at 90; *Re Saxon Life Assurance Soc* (1862) 2 J. & H. 408 at 412 (affirmed 1 D.J. & S. 29). In *Gibson v Mitchell* [1990] 1 W.L.R. 1304 the court puzzlingly distinguishes at 1309 between a mistake of law as to the "effect" and "consequences" of the transaction. The actual decision is based on the Variation of Trusts Act 1958.

[61] *Huddersfield Banking Co Ltd v Henry Lister & Son Ltd* [1895] 2 Ch.273; *cf. Sport International Bussum BV v Inter-Footwear Ltd* [1984] 1 W.L.R. 776. But a "consent" order may be merely one to which a party submits without objection in which case it does not have the effect of a contract: *Siebe Gorman & Co Ltd v Pneupac Ltd* [1982] 1 W.L.R. 185; and in matrimonial proceedings consent orders are not now regarded as contracts: *Thwaite v Thwaite* [1982] Fam. 1; *Jenkins v Livesey* [1985] A.C. 424.

[62] (1867) L.R. 2 H.L. 149; Matthews, 105 L.Q.R. 599.

mistake in that case, however, was one as to the construction of the documents on which the title to the land depended,[63] while that in *Allcard v Walker* was one as to the general law which then governed the contractual capacity of married women. In *Solle v Butcher*[64] it seems to have been assumed by all the members of the court that relief for a mistake of pure law was not available even in equity; the court was divided only on the question whether the mistake was one of law.

(c) MISTAKE AS TO CONSTRUCTION. Law and equity can give relief where a contract is made under a mistake as to private rights arising out of a misconstruction of earlier documents that specify those rights. Equity can also sometimes give relief where one of the parties has misinterpreted the contract itself. The mere fact that A has misinterpreted the contract does not entitle him to enforce it against B in the sense in which A understood it[65]; and, in general, the court will specifically enforce the contract, properly interpreted, at the suit of either A[66] or B.[67] But the court can, in its discretion, refuse B specific performance on the ground that A has misinterpreted the contract[68]; and if A's mistake is induced (even innocently) by B, A may be entitled to have the contract set aside.[69]

A mistake as to the *contents* of a contract is clearly one of fact.[70] Action in reliance on such a mistake may give rise to an estoppel by convention. The requirements and effects of such an estoppel are discussed in Chapter 3[71]; they differ from the kind of relief with which we are concerned in this Chapter. Such relief is sought by a party who wishes to claim relief *against* enforcement of the contract. Estoppel by convention is, on the other hand, invoked by a party who seeks to *rely*[72] on the contract, as understood by him. This accounts for the fact that the requirements of such an estoppel are more stringent than those of relief for mistake. Estoppel by convention requires action in reliance on an agreed but mistaken assumption; usually this takes the form of acts done in the performance of the contract. There is no such requirement where a party merely seeks to resist the enforcement of a contract on the ground of mistake: he need show no more than that he entered into the contract under the mistake, and that it falls into one of the categories (discussed above) for which equity gives relief.

(d) MISTAKEN INFERENCES. Many cases involve an inquiry into the physical circumstances from which some inference then has to be drawn. The physical circumstances are called the primary facts of the case and the inference is called a secondary fact. Questions of secondary fact are for some purposes treated as questions of law and for others as questions of fact.[73]

The cases of mistake dealt with at common law involve mistakes as to primary facts or as to private rights. But equity goes further and gives relief against mistakes of

---

[63] It made no difference that one of these was a private Act of Parliament: *cf.* below, p.334 n.37.

[64] [1950] 1 K.B. 671; below, p.317; disapproved in *The Great Peace* [2002] EWCA Civ 1407; [2002] 4 All E.R. 689, but not on this point.

[65] *Midland Great Western Ry of Ireland v Johnson* (1858) 6 H.L.C. 798.

[66] *Berners v Fleming* [1925] Ch.264.

[67] *Powell v Smith* (1872) L.R. 14 Eq. 85; *Hart v Hart* (1881) Ch.D. 670.

[68] *Watson v Marston* (1853) 4 D.M. & G. 230.

[69] *Wilding v Sanderson* [1897] 2 Ch.534; *Faraday v Tamworth Union* (1917) 86 L.J. Ch. 436. Rescission in these cases could now be explained on the ground of misrepresentation, as the reference in *Wilding v Sanderson* to *Stewart v Kennedy* (1890) 15 App.Cas. 108 suggests.

[70] See below, p.333.

[71] See above, p.119.

[72] Though probably only by way of defence: see above, pp.123–124.

[73] *cf.* below, p.836, *Benmax v Austin Motor Co Ltd* [1955] A.C. 370.

secondary fact, or mistaken inferences. In *Solle v Butcher*[74] a flat was extensively altered and then let. Both landlord and tenant mistakenly thought that, as a result of the alterations, the flat had changed its "identity", so that it was no longer subject to the Rent Acts. In the Court of Appeal, the mistake was variously described as one of fact, as to private rights, or of law.[75] It is submitted that it is best described as a mistake of secondary fact. The parties were under no mistake as to the primary facts: they knew what work had been done in the flat. Their mistake was as to the inference to be drawn from those facts and this mistake could be a ground for equitable relief. The actual form of relief granted was by way of rescission on terms in favour of the landlord, and this would no longer be available.[76] But it seems that if the tenant had claimed specific performance, then relief by way of refusal of this remedy (or by granting it only on terms) would still be available to the landlord.[77]

2. Forms of Equitable Relief

(1) Refusal of specific performance

Refusal of specific performance is the most freely available form of equitable relief for mistake. It leaves the contract enforceable at law, so that it does not seriously prejudice the interests of certainty.

(a) ABSOLUTE REFUSAL. Specific performance will clearly be refused where the contract is *void* at law, *e.g.* where a person contracts to buy his own property[78] or where one party, to the knowledge of the other, makes a mistake as to the terms of the contract[79]; or as to its binding force.[80]

Specific performance may also be refused where the contract is *valid* at law because the mistake is not one of fact, or not fundamental,[81] or not operative by reason of the objective principle.[82] Thus in *Day v Wells*[83] the defendant instructed an auctioneer to sell cottages thinking that he had told the auctioneer to put a reserve price on them. The auctioneer sold without reserve, at a lower price, and it was held that the defendant could not be compelled to perform specifically. Similarly, in *Wood v Scarth*[84] a landlord agreed to let a public house, intending to take a premium but failing to say so. He successfully resisted a claim for specific performance, though he was later held liable in damages at law.[85]

Where the contract is valid, refusal of specific performance is a matter for the discretion of the court. In exercising that discretion, the court must weigh the hardship of granting the remedy against the uncertainty caused by refusing it. Two cases may be contrasted. In *Malins v Freeman*[86] the defendant at an auction bid for one lot under the mistaken impression that he was bidding for another. Although he was clearly liable at

---

[74] [1950] 1 K.B. 671; disapproved, but not on this point, in *The Great Peace* [2002] EWCA Civ 1407; [2002] 4 All E.R. 689.
[75] *ibid.* at 685, 693, 705 (Jenkins L.J. dissenting).
[76] *The Great Peace* [2002] EWCA Civ 1407; [2002] 4 All E.R. 689, below, p.319.
[77] Below, under next heading.
[78] *Jones v Clifford* (1876) 3 Ch.D. 779.
[79] *Webster v Cecil* (1861) 30 Beav. 62. It seems reasonable to deduce from the report that the claimant knew of the defendant's mistake; but this fact is not actually stated.
[80] *Pateman v Pay* (1974) 232 E.G. 457.
[81] *e.g. Jones v Rimmer* (1880) 14 Ch.D. 588.
[82] See above, pp.306–307.
[83] (1861) 30 Beav. 220.
[84] (1855) 2 K. & J. 33.
[85] (1858) 1 F. & F. 293.
[86] (1837) 2 Keen 25.

law,[87] it was held that specific performance should not be ordered against him. But in *Tamplin v James*[88] the defendant at an auction bid for an inn and a shop mistakenly believing that the lot included a certain garden. The Court of Appeal ordered specific performance, stressing the uncertainty which would result from allowing the defendant to rely on his own mistake. James L.J. said that a defendant could rely on a mistake to which the claimant had not contributed only "where a hardship amounting to injustice would have been inflicted upon him by holding him to his bargain, and it was unreasonable to hold him to it".[89] The two cases may be reconciled by saying that it is a "hardship amounting to injustice" to force a person to take one property when he thinks he has bought another, but not to force a person to take a property which is less extensive than he thought.

Since the object of refusing specific performance is to avoid hardship to the party prejudiced by the mistake, it follows that, where the contract is valid at law, only that party can rely on the mistake. Thus if A thinks that he is buying more than B intends to sell, A can specifically enforce the contract for the smaller quantity intended by B.[90] But where the contract is void at law, neither party can specifically enforce it[91] unless the circumstances are such that, even at law, one party, but not the other, can rely on the mistake.[92]

(b) SPECIFIC PERFORMANCE ON TERMS. Equity can take a middle course between refusing specific performance and granting it in spite of the mistake: it can, where the contract is valid at law, grant specific performance on terms. Thus in *Baskcomb v Beckwith*[93] an estate was sold in lots, on the terms that the purchaser of each lot should covenant not to build a public house on it. The vendor kept one of the lots himself, and proposed to build a public house there, but the plan of the lots did not make this clear. It was held that the vendor could specifically enforce the contract but only if he covenanted not to build a public house on the land retained by him. Similarly, equity can order specific performance with compensation, *i.e.* abatement or increase of the purchase price, where the value of the property sold is less or greater than supposed because of some misdescription of the property.[94]

(2) No rescission in equity for mistake

Two questions call for discussion. The first is whether a contract which is *valid* at law can be rescinded in equity for mistake; the second is whether this remedy is available where the mistake makes the contract *void* at law. Both questions must (though for different reasons) be answered in the negative.

(a) CONTRACT VALID AT LAW. A contract may, in spite of the mistake, be valid at law either because the mistake is not *fundamental* or because the mistake is, under the objective principle, not *operative*.[95] It will be convenient to begin by discussing the second (relatively uncontroversial) situation.

---

[87] See above, p.307.
[88] (1880) 15 Ch.D. 215; *cf. Calverley v Williams* (1790) 1 Ves.Jun. 209.
[89] *Tamplin v James*, above, at 221; *cf. Stewart v Kennedy* (1890) 15 App.Cas. 75 at 105.
[90] *Preston v Luck* (1884) 27 Ch.D. 497.
[91] *Higginson v Clowes* (1808) 15 Ves. 516 (vendor's claim); *Clowes v Higginson* (1813) 1 v & B. 524 (purchaser's claim).
[92] See above, p.309.
[93] (1869) L.R. 8 Eq. 100.
[94] See below, p.771.
[95] Above, p.306.

(i) *Mistake not operative.* Here equity may refuse specific performance against the mistaken party,[96] leaving the other to his remedy at law. But it will not rescind[97] and so deprive the other party of his remedy at law on the contract; for to take this step would subvert the certainty which the objective principle is intended to promote.

Accordingly, equity will, in general, follow the common law rule that a mistake is not operative if the mistaken party, A, has so conducted himself as to induce the other party, B, reasonably to believe that A has agreed to the terms proposed by B. In particular, a person cannot have a contract set aside because of a mistake which he made because he failed to act with due diligence.[98]

(ii) *Mistake not fundamental: Solle v Butcher.* A line of twentieth century cases supported the view that a contract could be rescinded on terms on the ground that it was made under a mistake, even though the mistake was not fundamental in the narrow common law sense and so did not affect the validity of the contract at law. The leading case was *Solle v Butcher*[99] where a flat had been let for £250 per annum, both parties mistakenly believing that it was free from rent control, when in fact it was subject to the Rent Acts and to a standard rent of £140 per annum. Had the landlord realised this, he could, before granting the lease, have increased the rent to about £250 per annum, on account of the work done by him to the flat; but he had no right to make such an increase during the currency of a lease already granted. The tenant claimed a declaration that the standard rent was £140 per annum and repayment of the excess; the landlord claimed rescission of the lease. It was held that the lease could be rescinded, though it was valid at law. As it would have caused considerable hardship to the tenant to turn him out of the flat, the court gave him the option of staying on if he paid the standard rent plus the amount by which the landlord could have increased it, had he been aware of the true position when he granted the lease.

(iii) *Criticism.* In the 50 years after *Solle v Butcher*, the equitable power to rescind contracts for mistakes which did not invalidate them at law was exercised in a number of first instance and Court of Appeal decisions.[1] No doubt the reason why the courts continued to use this equitable power was that, in mitigating the narrow common law definition of mistake, rescission in equity could "on occasion be the passport to a just result".[2] But in one of these cases[3] Winn L.J. dissented on the ground that the majority view (that the contract should be rescinded) was inconsistent with the refusal of the

---

[96] Above, p.316.

[97] *Riverlate Properties Ltd v Paul* [1975] Ch. 133; below, p.298. In *OT Africa Line Ltd v Vickers Ltd* [1996] 1 Lloyd's Rep. 700, the court was prepared at 704 to assume that a contract could be rescinded for mistake "where it is simply inequitable for one party to hold the other to a bargain objectively made". But this assumption is, with respect, inconsistent with the *Riverlate Properties* case, which was not cited and it would seriously subvert the certainty which the objective principle is intended to promote. The actual decision in the *OT Africa Line* case was that there had been no "inequitable" conduct, so that the contract was upheld.

[98] *Attorney-General v Tomline* (1877) 7 Ch.D. 388; *Soper v Arnold* (1877) 37 Ch.D. 96; 14 App.Cas. 429. For the common law position, *cf.* above, pp.297–298.

[99] [1950] 1 K.B. 671, above, p.316.

[1] *Peters v Batchelor* (1950) 100 L.J. News 715; *Laurence v Lexcourt Holdings Ltd* [1978] 1 W.L.R. 1128; *Grist v Bailey* [1967] Ch. 532 (the last two cases were doubted in *William Sindall plc v Cambridgeshire CC* [1994] 1 W.L.R. 1016 at 1035 on the ground that the risk of mistake had been allocated by the contract); *Magee v Pennine Insurance Co Ltd* [1969] 2 Q.B. 507; *Nutt v Read* (2000) 32 H.L.R. 761; *The Times*, December 3, 1999; *West Sussex Properties Ltd v Chichester DC*, June 28, 2000, CA. These are described in *The Great Peace* [2002] E.W.C.A. Civ 1407; [2002] 4 All E.R. 689, at [153] and [157] as a "small number" and "a handful" of cases; and although these statements are true in absolute terms, the number of such cases in relation to those in which contracts were impugned on the ground of mistake in the same period is by no means insignificant.

[2] *West Sussex Properties* case, above, at [42].

[3] *Magee's* case, above.

House of Lords in *Bell v Lever Bros Ltd*[4] to grant relief for mistake; and no satisfactory way was ever found of explaining the relationship between that leading case and the equitable jurisdiction to rescind.[5] One view was that the equitable jurisdiction could have been exercised in Bell v Lever Bros Ltd if an attempt had been made to invoke it; but some of the relevant equity cases were cited to,[6] and equitable principles were discussed by, the House of Lords.[7] A second view was that the exercise of the equitable jurisdiction depended on relative degrees of "fault" so that rescission would not be ordered in favour of a party who was himself at fault,[8] while conversely it could be ordered against one who had acted improperly in inducing the mistake,[9] or whose insistence on his legal rights after becoming aware of the mistake was unconscientious.[10] The difficulty with this view was that, since there was no definition of "fault" for this purpose, it did little to clarify the scope of the jurisdiction. A third view was that the common law rules laid down in *Bell v Lever Bros Ltd* determined the rights of the parties, while the equitable jurisdiction entitled the court to vary these at its discretion, so that equity "supplemented"[11] the common law; but the difficulty with this view lay in the failure of the relevant cases to formulate any principles governing the equitable discretion.

(iv) *The Great Peace.* At one time it seemed that, in spite of the criticisms summarised in the preceding paragraph, the courts had accepted the existence of the equitable jurisdiction,[12] though without giving any clear answer to the question just when a contract which was valid at law could be rescinded in equity. The issue arose again in *The Great Peace*[13] where, as will be recalled, it was held that a charterparty was not void at law[14] by reason of a mistake as to the "proximity" of the chartered ship to the vessel to which she was to render escort services. The Court of Appeal further held that there was no power to rescind the charterparty in equity. It did so on the ground that *Solle v Butcher* was inconsistent with *Bell v Lever Bros Ltd*[15] and that there was, therefore, no equitable power to rescind a contract which, in spite of the mistake was "valid and enforceable on ordinary principles of contract law".[16] Only by taking this view could

---

[4] [1932] A.C. 161.

[5] A.L.G. 66 L.Q.R. 169; Atiyah & Bennion, 24 M.L.R. 421 at 439.

[6] *e.g. Harris v Pepperell* (1867) L.R. 5 Eq. 1; *Paget v Marshall* (1884) 28 Ch.D. 255. As to these cases, see below p.322; *cf. Associated Japanese Bank International Ltd v Crédit du Nord SA* [1989] 1 W.L.R. 255 at 256.

[7] See the discussion in *Bell v Lever Bros Ltd*, above of *Cooper v Phibbs* (1872) L.R. 2 H.L. 149 and the discussion of the latter case in *The Great Peace* [2002] E.W.C.A. Civ 1407; [2002] 4 All E.R. 689, at [100] *et seq.*

[8] [1950] 1 K.B. at 693; *cf. Harrison & Jones Ltd v Bunten & Lancaster Ltd* [1953] 1 Q.B. 646 at 654 (equitable relief refused as neither party at fault); *Laurence v Lexcourt Holdings Ltd* [1978] 1 W.L.R. 1128 (relief granted as party prejudiced by mistake was not, while the other party was, at fault); *The Lloydiana* [1983] 2 Lloyd's Rep. 313 at 318 (relief refused as mistake entirely due to fault of allegedly mistaken party); *Associated Japanese Bank International Ltd v Crédit du Nord SA* [1989] 1 W.L.R. 255 at 270 (equitable relief would have been available, had the contract not been void at law, as claimant was "not at fault in any way").

[9] *e.g. Cocking v Pratt* (1749) 1 VEs.Sen. 400; *Evans v Llewellin* (1787) 1 Cox C.C. 333; *Torrance v Bolton* (1872) L.R. 8 Ch. App. 118; *cf. Beauchamp v Winn* (1873) L.R. 6 H.L. 223 AT 233.

[10] *e.g. Hitchcock v Giddings* (1817) 4 Price 135; *Bettyes v Maynard* (1882) 46 L.T. 766, but see *Riverlate Properties Ltd v Paul* [1975] Ch.133 at 140–141.

[11] *Associated Japanese Bank (International) Ltd v Credit du Nord SA* [1989] 1 W.L.R. 255 at 267, describing this as "an entirely sensible and satisfactory state of the law."

[12] See the dictum quoted in n.11, above.

[13] [2002] E.W.C.A. Civ 1407, [2002] 4 All E.R. 689.

[14] Above, p.288.

[15] *The Great Peace*, above n.13, at [157], [160].

[16] *ibid.* at [161].

"coherence . . . be restored to this area of our law"[17] which had been thrown into "confusion"[18] by *Solle v Butcher* and later cases which had exercised the jurisdiction to rescind. What lies at the heart of this reasoning is the need for doctrinal consistency, rather than any attempt to evaluate past exercises of the equitable jurisdiction on their merits.[19] With regard to the latter point, the judgment merely hints that there is "scope for legislation to give greater flexibility to our law of mistake than the common law allows".[20] At this stage, two further possibilities cannot be ruled out. The first is that the House of Lords might yet disagree with the Court of Appeal on the issue of discretionary relief for mistake,[21] and the second (no doubt more remote) one is that the House might even review the narrowness of the scope of mistake at common law as laid down in *Bell v Lever Bros Ltd*.[22] With regard to *The Great Peace* itself, it may be relevant to note that the question of equitable relief arose in the context of a charterparty, that this is a type of contract in which certainty (which would be subverted by the exercise of a discretion to rescind) is of paramount importance,[23] and that on the facts there was said to be "no injustice in the result".[24]

(b) CONTRACT VOID AT LAW. The cases which formerly supported the existence of an equitable power to set contracts aside on terms must at first sight have been restricted to contracts which were valid at law.[25] Where the contract is void at law, it can simply be ignored; there is nothing to "set aside" and hence no power to impose terms: "It is axiomatic that there is no room for rescission of a contract which is void."[26] There are, however, two apparent difficulties in the way of this view.

The first arises from *Cooper v Phibbs*.[27] In that case A was the legal owner of land to which B was beneficially entitled in equity. A improved the land and later agreed to grant a lease of it to B, together with other land of which A was both legal and beneficial owner. It was held that the agreement must be set aside for mistake (neither party having been aware of B's entitlement to part of the land); and that B could get back rent which he had paid under the agreement. But B had to compensate A for the improvements, and to pay a reasonable rent for that part of the land in which he had no interest when the agreement was made. *Cooper v Phibbs* is now regarded as a case of a contract which was

---

[17] *ibid.* at [157].

[18] *ibid.*

[19] See the dictum referred to at n.11, above.

[20] *The Great Peace*, above at [161], referring to the analogy of the Law Reform (Frustrated Contracts) Act 1943. If such legislation following the principle of equitable intervention in mistake cases, it would differ in nature from the 1943 Act. This assumes that the contract *is* discharged by the supervening event; equitable intervention assumes that the contract is *not* made void by the mistake.

[21] In another branch of contract law, the House of Lords has been prepared to mitigate a common law rule by a discretion based on equitable analogies: see *Attorney-General v Blake* [2001] 1 A.C. 168, below, p.930.

[22] [1932] A.C. 161. The decision was reached by a majority of three to two, reversing the unanimous view of the judges in the courts below. Perhaps the majority in the House of Lords used the narrow definition of mistake to mitigate the severity of the rule that the breaches by the employees justified their summary dismissal without compensation (below, p.777), particularly at a time when a less serious view was taken of those breaches than might now be the case; *cf.* Treitel, 104 L.Q.R. 501 at 505. For doubts about the merits of the case, see also above, p.312 n.34 and (perhaps) p.290 at n.40.

[23] See the judgment of Toulson J. in *The Great Peace*, Transcript, November 9, 2001, at [126], affirmed on appeal; *cf.* below p.780.

[24] [2002] E.W.C.A. Civ 1407; [2002] 4 All E.R. 689, at [166]. *Cf.* above, p.289, n.27. The outcome was that the owners recovered five days' hire even though the charterers had cancelled only about two hours after the chartered ship had changed course towards the stricken vessel: see [15], [21]. There was no discussion as to the remedy and it is arguable that, on receipt of the charterer's cancellation, the owners should have mitigated by resuming their original course: see below, pp.1015–1019.

[25] *Ingram v Little* [1961] 1 Q.B. 31 at 62.

[26] *The Great Peace* [2002] E.W.C.A. Civ 1407; [2002] 4 All E.R. 689 at [96].

[27] (1867) L.R. 2 H.L. 149.

void at law[28]; and this view of the case may give rise to the impression that equity can impose terms even where the contract is void at law. But the actual decision in *Cooper v Phibbs* was that the agreement "ought to be set aside",[29] this form of relief begin then thought to be necessary because the legal title to the land was not vested in B.[30] It is, moreover, submitted that, in imposing terms on B (which in any event he did not contest)[31] the court gave effect to obligations that were based, not on any purported contract, but on general principles of equity or restitution. The crucial point was not that A and B had purported to enter into a contract under a mistake, but that A had conferred benefits on B, by the retention of which (without compensating A for them) B would be unjustly enriched.[32] *Cooper v Phibbs* does not support the view that equity can impose terms merely because parties have entered into a void contract.

The second difficulty arises from a number of statements by Lord Denning to the effect that the contract in cases such as *Cundy v Lindsay*[33] would now be voidable in equity.[34] The attraction of this view is that it would enable the court in such cases to protect innocent third parties. But he has also said that there was "no contract at all"[35] in *Cundy v Lindsay*; and this view is certainly the more consistent with the decision. Unless *Cundy v Lindsay* is reversed by legislation or by the House of Lords, there can be nothing to rescind in such a case.

(3) Rectification

Contracting parties may execute a document purporting to contain the terms previously agreed between them. If, as a result of a mistake, the document fails to contain all those terms, or contains different terms, the court may rectify it, that is, order its wording to be changed so as to bring it into line with the earlier agreement[36]; alternatively, the court may treat the document as having been so rectified without making a formal order for its rectification.[37] Having been developed in equity, rectification is a discretionary remedy.[38] It is available where there has been a mistake, not in the *making*, but in the *recording*, of a contract: "Courts of equity do not rectify contracts; they may and do rectify instruments."[39] Rectification can be ordered although the contract is one which

---

[28] See above, p.287.

[29] (1867) L.R. 2 H.L. at 167, 173.

[30] See Matthews, 105 L.Q.R. 599. *The Great Peace*, above, n.26 at [109] and [110].

[31] (1867) L.R. 7 H.L. 149 at 154.

[32] *cf.* below, p.382 in respect of the improvements and below, p.1063 in respect of the rent (showing that even where a contract is void there may be liability at law in respect of benefits obtained under it).

[33] (1878) 3 App.Cas. 459; above, p.298.

[34] *Solle v Butcher* [1950] 1 K.B. 671 at 692; *Lewis v Averay* [1972] 1 Q.B. 198 at 207; and see his statement in *Magee v Pennine Insurance Co Ltd* [1969] 2 Q.B. 507 at 514, that "a common mistake, even on a most fundamental matter, does not make a contract void at law: but makes it voidable in equity." This view would very much increase the scope of the equitable jurisdiction but it appears to be inconsistent with many of the cases discussed in Sections 1 and 2 of this Chapter. *cf. Associated Japanese Bank (International) Ltd v Crédit du Nord SA* [1989] 1 W.L.R. 255 at 266, describing Lord Denning's view as an "individual opinion."

[35] *Gallie v Lee* [1969] 2 Ch. 17 at 33 (affirmed [1971] A.C. 1004).

[36] *Murray v Parker* (1854) 19 Beav. 305; *Crane v Hegeman-Harris Co Inc* [1939] 1 All E.R. 662, affirmed [1939] 4 All E.R. 68; for a passage omitted from these reports, see [1971] 3 All E.R. 245; *The Rhodian River* [1984] 1 Lloyd's Rep. 373.

[37] *The Nile Rhapsody* [1994] 1 Lloyd's Rep. 382; *OTV Birwelco Ltd v Technical & General Guarantee Co Ltd* [2002] EWHC 2240 (TCC); [2002] 4 All E.R. 668, at [39].

[38] *Re Butlin's S.T.* [1976] Ch.251 at 263.

[39] *Mackenzie v Coulson* (1869) L.R. 8 Eq. 369, 375; *The Olympic Pride* [1980] 2 Lloyd's Rep. 67 at 72. The point seems to have been overlooked in *McAuley v Bristol CC* [1992] Q.B. 134, where the phrase "rectify a . . . contract" occurs at p.147.

must be in, or evidenced in, writing.[40] The availability of the remedy depends on the following rules.

(a) MISTAKE OF BOTH PARTIES OR KNOWN TO ONE.

(i) *Mistake of one party generally insufficient.* A contractual document[41] can, in general, be rectified only if it fails to record the intention of *both* parties. Thus if A lets a house to B and both agree that the rent is to be £200 per month, the lease can be rectified if by mistake it states the monthly rent to be only £100. But if all the time A intended to charge £200 while B intended to pay only £100 the lease could not be rectified to conform with A's intention,[42] for this would force on B a contract to which he had never agreed. Rectification could, however, be ordered if B, when he executed the lease, knew of, or wilfully shut his eyes to,[43] A's mistake,[44] or if B was guilty of fraud[45] or other unconscionable conduct: for example, if he intended A to be mistaken as to the construction of the document and prevented A from discovering the mistake by making "false and misleading statements" during the negotiations.[46] In such cases, the remedy would cause no injustice to B.

Some cases formerly supported the view that, where the intention of only one party (A) was inaccurately recorded, the court could force the other (B) to choose between having the contract rescinded or having it rectified.[47] These cases have, however, been overruled[48] since they conflicted with the objective principle[49] in that they deprived B of a bargain on terms which had every appearance of being offered to him. A is accordingly bound by the terms of the contract as recorded in the document.

(ii) *One party indifferent.* In *Van der Linde v. Van der Linde*[50] the court refused to rectify a covenant so as to achieve the tax advantage which the covenantor had intended (but failed) to secure. One reason for the refusal was that there was not sufficient evidence of mistake; another was that the covenantee had no view as to "the intention of the document".[51] In *Whiteside v Whiteside*[52] the court likewise refused to rectify a covenant made for (but failing to achieve) the same purpose, partly because there was no evidence of the *common* intention of the parties, and partly because there was no issue between them: the covenantor went on paying the covenantee (his wife) as if the

---

[40] *Olley v Fisher* (1886) 34 Ch.D. 367; *Johnson v Bragge* [1901] 1 Ch.28; *USA v Motor Trucks Ltd* [1924] A.C. 196; *May v Platt* [1900] 1 Ch. 616, if *contra*, is not law: *Craddock Bros v Hunt* [1923] 2 Ch. 136; Law Com.No.164, para.5, 6. The position was different before the Judicature Act 1873: *Woollam v Hearn* (1802) 7 Ves. 211; *Squire v Campbell* (1836) 1 My. & Cr. 459; but s.24(7) of that Act altered the law. See now s.49 of the Supreme Court Act 1981.

[41] A voluntary settlement can be rectified on account of a mistake of the settlor alone: *Re Butlin's S T* [1976] Ch.251.

[42] *Faraday v Tamworth Union* (1917) 86 L.J.Ch. 436; *W. Higgins Ltd v Northampton Corp.* [1927] 1 Ch.128; *cf. Lloyd v Stanbury* [1971] 1 W.L.R. 535; *The Nai Genova* [1984] 1 Lloyd's Rep. 353; *The Ypatia Halcoussi* [1985] 2 Lloyd's Rep. 364 at 370; *Thomas Witter Ltd v TBP Industries Ltd* [1996] 2 All E.R. 573 at 601.

[43] *Commission for the New Towns v Cooper (Great Britain) Ltd* [1995] Ch. 259 at 280.

[44] *Garrard v Frankel* (1862) 30 Beav. 445, 451; *A Roberts & Co Ltd v Leicestershire CC* [1961] Ch.555, discussed by R.E.M., 77 L.Q.R. 313; *The Olympic Pride*, above n.39 at 72; *Thomas Bates & Son Ltd v Wyndham's (Lingerie) Ltd* [1981] 1 W.L.R. 505.

[45] *Blay v Pollard & Morris* [1930] 1 K.B. 628 at 633.

[46] *Commission for the New Towns v Cooper (Great Britain) Ltd* [1995] Ch. 259 at 280.

[47] *Harris v Pepperell* (1867) L.R. 5 Eq. 1; *Paget v Marshall* (1884) 28 Ch.D. 255.

[48] *Riverlate Properties Ltd v Paul* [1975] Ch.133.

[49] See above, p.306; *Commission for the New Towns v Cooper (Great Britain) Ltd* [1995] Ch. 259 at 277.

[50] [1947] Ch. 306.

[51] *ibid.*, at 312.

[52] [1950] Ch. 65; *cf. Rabin v Gerson Berger Assocation Ltd* [1986] 1 W.L.R. 526 at 534 (where no claim for rectification was made); *Sherdley v Sherdley* [1986] 1 W.L.R. 732 at 744, reversed on other grounds [1988] A.C. 213; *Racal Group Services v Ashmore* [1995] S.T.C. 1151.

covenant had been rectified. But such an issue can be manufactured by simply refusing to make a single payment. If the document in fact fails to express the intention of the parties, rectification can be ordered even though there is no dispute between them *inter se*, but only one between them and the Revenue authorities.[53]

(iii) *Customary terms.* A document may be rectified if it fails to record terms implied by custom into an agreement even though there is no evidence that the parties actually intended such terms to be incorporated. Thus in *Caraman, Rowley & May v Aperghis*[54] sellers were prevented by war from performing a contract for the sale of sultanas. Similar contracts normally contained a *"force majeure"* clause which would have protected the sellers; but in this case the clause was inadvertently left out. It was held that the contractual document could be rectified by the inclusion of a *"force majeure"* clause, whether or not the buyer knew that such a clause was usual. In such a case the customary term is, by implication, part of the *contract*[55] even though the *document* is not rectified. But it may be convenient to have the document rectified, especially if the contract is a long-term one, or if it affects, or is likely to come into the hands of, a third party.

(b) TYPES OF MISTAKE. Rectification is most frequently ordered where the terms of a document do not correspond with those of the agreement between the parties, *e.g.* where the rent is misstated in a lease, or the area of land to be conveyed is misstated in a conveyance.[56] For this purpose, "the agreement" refers to the terms actually agreed between the parties. Thus where those terms were accurately recorded in a lease it was held that rectification was not available merely because they had not been correctly stated in the earlier written agreement for the lease.[57] The only "mistake" of the parties was as to the effect of that written agreement, and to rectify the lease would have defeated, rather than given effect to, the intention of the parties.

Rectification is also available where a person who intends to sign a document in one capacity does so in another, *e.g.* where the name of a person to whom a bill of exchange is meant to be payable is put in as drawer instead of as payee.[58] The court may also rectify a document executed under a mistake as to its meaning or legal effect[59]; but such a mistake will not be a ground for rectification if the true legal effect of the document was fully explained to the party claiming to have made the mistake.[60] A mere misnomer can sometimes be corrected as a matter of construction, in which case there may be no need to rectify the document.[61] The same is true of other mistakes as to the construction of the document: *e.g.* of mistakes as to the subject-matter covered by it. For example, A may believe that the document relates to X alone and B allege that it relates to X and Y. If A succeeds on the issue of construction, rectification is strictly unnecessary[62] (though it

---

[53] *Re Colebrook's Conveyances* [1973] 1 W.L.R. 1379; *cf. Re Slocock's Will Trust* [1979] 1 All E.R. 359; *Seymour v Seymour, The Times,* February 16, 1989; *Lake v Lake* [1989] S.T.C. 865.
[54] (1923) 40 T.L.R. 124.
[55] See above, p.213.
[56] *e.g. Murray v Parker* (1854) 19 Beav. 305; *Beale v Kyte* [1907] 1 Ch.564; *Blacklocks v J B Developments (Godalming) Ltd* [1982] Ch. 183.
[57] *London Regional Transport v Wimpey Group Services* (1987) 53 P. & C.R. 356.
[58] *Druiff v Parker* (1868) L.R. 5 Eq. 131 *cf. Co-operative Bank plc v Tipper* [1996] 4 All E.R. 366 (guarantor's name mistakenly inserted as borrower's).
[59] *Re Colebrook's Conveyances* [1973] 1 W.L.R. 1379; *cf. Jervis v Howle & Talke Colliery Ltd* [1937] Ch.67, following *Burroughes v Abbott* [1922] 1 Ch.86; *Tucker v Bennett* (1887) 38 Ch.D. 1; *Re Butlin's S T* [1976] Ch. 251. No claim for rectification was made in *Keen v Holland* [1984] 1 W.L.R. 251 (where a mistake as to legal effect was held not sufficient to give rise to an estoppel by convention: above, p.125).
[60] *Constantinidi v Ralli* [1953] Ch. 427.
[61] *Nittan UK Ltd v Solent Steel Fabrications Ltd* [1981] 1 All E.R. 633; *Porteus v Element Books Ltd* [1996] C.L.Y. 1029; or even to treat the document as rectified (above p.296).
[62] *cf. Mangistaumunaigaz Oil Production Association v United World Trade Inc* [1995] 1 Lloyd's Rep. 617.

may be convenient[63]); but even if B succeeds on the issue of construction, rectification will be available to A if the case was one of the exceptional ones (described above[64]) in which the remedy can be granted in spite of the fact that the mistake was that of one party only.[65]

(c) PRIOR CONTRACT NOT NECESSARY. The court can rectify a document which was preceded by a *concluded agreement* or (still less stringently) a "continuing common intention"[66] even though there was no prior *binding contract*,[67] for example, because the prior agreement was binding in honour only.[68] In *Joscelyne v Nissen*[69] an agreement for the transfer of a business and premises was negotiated between a father and daughter, it being understood that the father should continue to live in the premises and that the daughter should pay his gas and electricity bills. No provision for such payments was made in the formal contract finally executed. Rectification was ordered even though, before execution of the document, the agreement between the parties had no contractual force. It was enough that there was "some outward expression of accord" and that this was "adhered to in intention by the parties to the subsequent written contract".[70] On the other hand, a document cannot be rectified to bring it into line with mere steps in the antecedent negotiations,[71] for these may not have led to a concluded agreement on the particular point, or, if they did, that agreement may not have been maintained till the execution of the document.

(d) DOCUMENT ACCURATELY RECORDING PRIOR AGREEMENT. It follows from the principle that equity rectifies instruments and not contracts[72] that a document which accurately records a prior agreement cannot be rectified merely because that agreement was made under some mistake. In *F E Rose (London) Ltd v W H Pim, Jnr & Co Ltd*[73] the claimants had received an order from a customer for "Moroccan horsebeans described here as feveroles" and asked the defendants (their suppliers) what "feveroles" were. The defendants replied that feveroles were just horsebeans and orally agreed to sell "horsebeans" to the claimants. When this contract was reduced to writing, the goods were again described as "horsebeans." In fact there were three types of Moroccan horsebeans: feves, feveroles and fevettes. The defendants supplied feves, which were less valuable than feveroles. It was held that the written contract could not be rectified by inserting

---

[63] See above, after n.55.

[64] At nn.43–46.

[65] *Commission for the New Towns v Cooper (Great Britain) Ltd* [1995] Ch. 259.

[66] *The Olympic Pride* [1980] 2 Lloyd's Rep. 67 at 72; *The Pina* [1991] 1 Lloyd's Rep. 246 at 250, affirmed [1992] 2 Lloyd's Rep. 103 on the ground that there was no need to rectify the *prior* non-contractual document as it had no legal force; *Grand Metropolitan plc v William Hill Group plc* [1997] 1 B.C.L.C. 390.

[67] For the now rejected contrary view, see *Mackenzie v Coulson* (1869) L.R. 8 Eq. 369 at 375.

[68] *Eagle Star, etc., Insurance Co v Reiner* (1927) 43 T.L.R. 259; *cf. Symington & Co v Union Insurance Society of Canton* (1928) 34 Comm.Cas. 233.

[69] [1970] 2 Q.B. 86; Bromley, 87 L.Q.R. 532; Kavanagh, 34 M.L.R. 102; *cf. Wilson v Wilson* [1969] 1 W.L.R. 1470; *Michael Richards Properties v St Saviour's Parish* [1975] 3 All E.R. 416 at 423; *The Olympic Pride*, above n.66, at 72.

[70] [1970] 2 Q.B. 86 at 99; *Shipley Urban DC v Bradford Corp* [1936] Ch.375 at 396; *cf. Crane v Hegeman-Harris Co Inc* [1939] 1 All E.R. 662 at 664–665; criticised in *F E Rose (London) Ltd v W H Pim, Jnr., & Co Ltd* [1953] 2 Q.B. 450 at 461; distinguished in *Ashville Investments Ltd v Elmer Contractors Ltd* [1989] Q.B. 488 at 516, and in *Ethiopian Oilseeds & Pulses Corp v Rio del Mar Foods Inc* [1990] 1 Lloyd's Rep. 86; approved in *Joscelyne v Nissen* [1970] 2 Q.B. 86; *Earl v Hector Whaling* [1961] 1 Lloyd's Rep. 459 at 470. The requirement of "outward expression of accord" is inappropriate where the mistake is that of the common agent of the parties in drawing up the instrument in such a way as to fail to give effect to the common intention of the parties: *Mace v Rutland House Textiles Ltd*, *The Times* January 11, 2000.

[71] *Lovell & Christmas Ltd v Wall* (1911) 104 L.T. 85 at 88.

[72] See above, p.321.

[73] [1953] 2 Q.B. 450; *cf. The Ypatia Halcoussi* [1985] 2 Lloyd's Rep. 364 at 371.

"feveroles" after "horsebeans," as it accurately recorded the previous oral agreement.[74]

(e) CLEAR EVIDENCE. When rectification is claimed, the court has to guard against two dangers. The first is that the remedy may result in imposing on a party terms to which he might not in fact have agreed. The second is that the "certainty and ready enforceability [of written agreements] would be hindered by constant attempts to cloud the issue by reference to precontract negotiations".[75] For these reasons, rectification will be ordered only if there is strong and convincing evidence that the document failed accurately to record the intention of the parties.[76] The court is, in particular, reluctant to rectify a contract solely on the oral evidence of the party claiming rectification[77] but there is no absolute rule against rectification on such evidence.[78] The requirement of clear evidence seems to be less strict when rectification is sought of a voluntary deed, or of a voluntary provision in a deed.[79]

(f) EXECUTED CONTRACTS. Although the contrary has been suggested[80] execution (i.e., performance) of a contract is no bar to rectification. Thus leases and conveyances can be rectified on the ground that they are inconsistent with the contracts which preceded them.[81] Any other view would conflict with the whole concept of rectification, for the formal document which it is sought to rectify often *is* the execution of the prior contract.

(g) RESTITUTIO IN INTEGRUM IMPOSSIBLE. Impossibility of restoring the parties to the position in which they were before the contract is, in general, no bar to rectification. For example, a marriage settlement can be rectified after the marriage has taken place.[82]

(h) LIMITATIONS ON THE REMEDY.

(i) *Lapse of time.* A claim for rectification is barred by lapse of time. It is not clear whether time begins to run when the contract was made[83] or when the mistake is discovered[84] or when it should by the exercise of reasonable diligence have been

---

[74] The contract was not void for mistake: above, p.290. Nor could the claimants rescind for misrepresentation as they had resold the horsebeans: *cf.* below, p.378, but they might now be able to claim damages under Misrepresentation Act 1967, s.2(1) (below, p.350). They might also (as Denning L.J. suggested) be able to claim damages for breach of a collateral warranty, if the necessary *animus contrahendi* on the part of the seller could be shown (above, p.149, below, pp.356–357).

[75] *The Olympic Pride* [1980] 2 Lloyd's Rep. 67 at 73.

[76] *Fowler v Fowler* (1859) 4 D. & J. 250 at 265; *Fredensen v Rothschild* [1941] 1 All E.R. 430 at 436; *Joscelyne v Nissen* [1970] 2 Q.B. 86; *Ernest Scragg & Sons Ltd v Perseverence Banking & Trust Co* [1973] 2 Lloyd's Rep. 101; *The Olympic Pride*, above, n.75, at 73; *Blacklocks v J B Developments (Godalming) Ltd* [1982] Ch. 183 at 191; *Cambro Contractors Ltd v John Kennedy Sales Ltd, The Times*, April 14, 1994. On the question whether the evidence must come up to the standard required in criminal cases contrast *Earl v Hector Whaling* [1961] 1 Lloyd's Rep. 459 at 468, 470; and *Mangistaumunaigaz Oil Production Association v United Trade Inc* [1995] 1 Lloyd's Rep. 617 at 621 with *The Pina* [1991] 1 LLoyd's Rep. 246 at 250, affirmed on other grounds [1992] 2 Lloyd's Rep. 103; *Pappadakis v Pappadakis* [2000] W.T.L.R. 719; *Luk Leamington Ltd v Whitmarch plc* [2002] 1 Lloyd's Rep. 6 at 18–19.

[77] *Tucker v Bennett* (1887) 38 Ch.D. 1; *Fredensen v Rothschild*, above; *Thomas Bates & Son Ltd v Wyndham's (Lingerie) Ltd* [1981] 1 W.L.R. 505 at 514, 521.

[78] *Cook v Fearn* (1878) 48 L.J.Ch. 63.

[79] See *Hanley v Pearson* (1879) 13 Ch.D. 545.

[80] *e.g.* in *May v Platt* [1900] 1 Ch. 616, criticised in *Thompson v Hickman* [1907] 1 Ch.550.

[81] *e.g. Murray v Parker* (1854) 19 Beav. 305; *Cowen v Truefitt Ltd* [1899] 2 Ch.309; *Stait v Fenner* [1912] 2 Ch. 504.

[82] *Cook v Fearn* (1878) 48 L.J. Ch. 63; *Johnson v Bragge* [1901] 1 Ch.28.

[83] *Bloomer v Spittle* (1872) L.R. 13 Eq. 427.

[84] *Beale v Kyte* [1907] 1 Ch. 564.

discovered. The last view probably applies in cases of innocent misrepresentation[85]; and there seems to be no good reason for applying a different rule where rectification is claimed.

(ii) *Third party rights*. The right to claim rectification, like the other equitable rights, can be asserted against a purchaser with notice of the mistake,[86] but not against a bona fide purchaser for value without notice.[87]

(iii) *Judgment*. A claim for rectification is barred by a judgment in proceedings in which the issue of rectification could have been (though it was not) raised.[88] But judgment in proceedings in which the question of rectification could *not* have been raised is no bar to a later claim for rectification.[89]

(iv) *Assignment*. It has been suggested that, even where a contracting party can claim rectification, a person to whom he assigns his rights cannot do so.[90] The basis for this suggestion seems to be that in such circumstances rectification might produce an undeserved windfall for the assignee.

(v) *Instruments which cannot be rectified*. The articles of association of a company cannot be rectified once they have been registered, even if they contain a simple clerical error.[91] To allow rectification would cut across the scheme laid down by the Companies Acts for the registration and alteration of such documents.

In *Phillipson v Kerry*[92] it was held that a deed poll cannot be rectified, though, if executed under a mistake, it can be set aside. One possible reason for this rule, given in the judgment, is that a voluntary gift cannot be rectified. But as it is now clear that a voluntary deed *inter partes* can be rectified,[93] there does not seem to be any convincing reason for the rule.

The court cannot rectify a settlement which is binding, not as a contract, but by virtue of a court order.[94] If a mistake is made in drawing up such an order, it is more appropriate to ask the court which made the order to vary it than to ask another court to rectify it.

SECTION 4. DOCUMENTS MISTAKENLY SIGNED

1. Development

As a general rule, a person is bound by his signature to a document whether he reads it or understands it, or not. But at the end of the sixteenth century an exception to this rule was established. It was held in *Thoroughgood's* Case[95] that if a person who could not read executed a deed after it had been incorrectly read over to him, he was not bound by it. He could plead *non est factum*: it is not my deed.

---

[85] See below, p.385.
[86] *Craddock Bros. v Hunt* [1923] 2 Ch. 136; *Blacklocks v J B Developments (Godalming) Ltd* [1982] Ch. 183.
[87] *Smith v Jones* [1954] 1 W.L.R. 1089; *cf. Garrard. v Frankel* (1862) 30 Beav. 445.
[88] *Caird v Moss* (1886) 33 Ch.D. 22.
[89] *Crane v Hegeman-Harris Co Inc* [1939] 4 All E.R. 68 (above, p.321, n.36).
[90] *Napier v Williams* [1911] 1 Ch. 361; the actual decision would now be different because of Law of Property Act 1925, s.82. Where the assignment forms part of a conveyance, the assignee can claim rectification by virtue of Law of Property Act 1925, s.63(1): *Boots the Chemist v Street* (1983) 268 E.G. 817; *Berkley Leisure Group Ltd v Williamson* [1996] E.G.C.S. 18.
[91] *Scott v Frank F Scott (London) Ltd* [1904] Ch. 794.
[92] (1863) 32 Beav. 628.
[93] *Bonhote v Henderson* [1895] 1 Ch.742; *Re Butlin's S.T.* [1976] Ch.251; *Re Slocock's Will Trust* [1979] 1 All E.R. 359.
[94] *Mills v Fox* (1887) 37 Ch.D. 153.
[95] (1584) 2 Co.Rep. 9a; *cf. Hitchman v Avery* (1892) 8 T.L.R. 698; *Lloyds Bank plc v Waterhouse* [1993] 2 FLR 97 at 108.

In the nineteenth century, it was settled that this doctrine was no longer confined to persons who were unable to read. The reason for this extension of the doctrine was the insistence on the requirement of *consensus ad idem* in contract. A person who signed a document without being aware of its nature was not bound because "the mind of the signer did not accompany the signature".[96] But if too wide a scope were given to this reasoning, it could lead to results that were inconsistent with the objective principle[97] and with the general common law requirement that a mistake must be fundamental if it is to negative consent.[98]

The objective principle does not operate in favour of a person who *knows* of the mistake of the signer[99]; and if that person has induced the mistake by some mis-representation about the document which is alleged to contain the contract between him and the signer, then the signer will be entitled to avoid the contract on that ground.[1] Often, however, the document purports to be a contract between the signer and someone other than the fraudulent party. For example, A may induce B to sign a guarantee of A's bank overdraft by representing that it is an insurance proposal. Here the document is an apparent contract, not between A and B, but between B and *the bank*, which may reasonably believe that B has assented to the terms of the document. As the bank is not responsible for the fraud of A, B's only hope is to plead *non est factum*; but success of the plea would deprive the bank of the protection of the objective principle.

Even if the document is an apparent contract only between A and B, the latter may try to invoke the doctrine of *non est factum* because it may provide a better remedy for him than rescission on the ground of A's fraud. This will be the position where B has under the contract parted with property and an innocent third party has later acquired an interest in that property for value.[2] If the doctrine of *non est factum* applies, the contract will be void so that B will be entitled to the return of the property; while if the contract is only voidable for A's fraud the third party will be protected. In cases of mistaken identity, the courts have in many cases protected such innocent third parties by a strict insistence on the requirement that the mistake must be fundamental[3]; and a similar requirement has restricted the scope of the *non est factum* defence.[4]

2. Scope of the Doctrine

(1) Persons to whom the plea is available

The nineteenth century extension of the doctrine to persons who could read has been called "one of the less happy developments in our law"[5] and it has been suggested that the doctrine should not apply in favour of such persons if they were of full age and capacity.[6] But this very narrow view has not prevailed. In *Gallie v Lee* Lord Reid said that the doctrine may apply to "those who are permanently or temporarily unable through no fault of their own to have without explanation any real understanding of the purport of a particular document, whether that be from defective education, illness or

---

[96] *Foster v Mackinnon* (1869) L.R. 4 C.P. 704 at 711; *cf.* (in criminal law). *R. v Davies* [1982] 1 All. E.R. 513 at 516.

[97] See above, p.306.

[98] See above, p.299, but see p.304.

[99] See above, p.307.

[1] See below, p.369; *Lloyds Bank plc v Waterhouse* (above n.95) at 111.

[2] As in *Gallie v Lee* [1971] A.C. 1004, below, p.328.

[3] See above, pp.299 *et seq.*

[4] *Norwich and Peterborough BS v Steeds (No.2)* [1993] 1 All E.R. 330 at 337.

[5] *Gallie v Lee* [1969] 2 Ch.17 at 43 *per* Salmon L.J.

[6] *ibid.* at 36–37.

innate incapacity",[7] and to these must be added persons who have been tricked into signing the document.[8] The doctrine may thus apply not only to the blind or illiterate but also to persons who are senile, of very low intelligence or ignorant of the language in which the document is expressed. But it will not normally protect literate persons of full capacity.[9]

(2) Serious mistake required

In their desire to restrict the scope of the doctrine, the courts have insisted that the plea of *non est factum* is available only where the mistake of the signer was a serious one. Formerly, they gave effect to this policy by drawing a distinction between the "character"[10] of a document and its "contents".[11] But in *Gallie v Lee*[12] the House of Lords rejected this distinction as unworkable,[13] and put in its place the requirement that the difference between the document as it was and as it was believed to be must be radical or substantial or fundamental.[14] Under this test, the seriousness of the mistake is to be judged by "difference in practical result" rather than by "difference in legal character".[15] The facts of the case were that a widow of 78 wanted to help her nephew Parkin to raise money on the security of her leasehold house, provided that she could continue to live there rent free for the rest of her life. Parkin did not want the loan to be in his own name, or to become owner of the house as he feared that this would enable his wife (from whom he was separated) to enforce her claim for maintenance against him. He therefore arranged that the money should be raised through an intermediary called Lee on a mortgage of the house; and as a first step in this scheme a document was prepared which was in fact an assignment on sale of the lease to Lee for £3,000. The widow did not read this document as her glasses were broken, but she signed it after being told by Lee that it was a deed of gift to Parkin (who witnessed the document). Lee mortgaged the house to a building society, but did not pay over the money so raised either to Parkin or to the widow. It was held that the widow was not protected by the doctrine of *non est factum* as her mistake was not sufficiently serious. She believed that the document would enable her nephew to raise money on the security of the house, and the document was in fact designed to achieve this purpose, though by a different process from that contemplated by her.[16]

(3) Mistake as to identity

We have seen that consent may be negatived, so as to make a contract void, where A deals with B in the mistaken belief that B is C.[17] But if A signs a document expressed to be in favour of B, the defence of *non est factum* is not open to A merely because A thought that the party named in the document was C. Thus in *Gallie v Lee*[18] the defence failed

---

[7] [1971] A.C. 1004 at 1016.

[8] *ibid.* at 1025.

[9] [1971] A.C. 1004 at 1016, 1025.

[10] *e.g. Foster v Mackinnon* (1869) L.R. C.P. 704.

[11] *e.g. Howatson v Webb* [1907] 1 Ch. 537; affirmed [1908] 1 Ch. 1.

[12] [1971] A.C. 1004.

[13] *Muskham Finance Ltd v Howard* [1963] 1 Q.B. 904 is, for example, hard to reconcile with *Howatson v Webb*, above. See also *Gallie v Lee* [1969] 2 Ch. 17 at 31–32, *per* Lord Denning M.R.

[14] [1971] A.C. 1004 at 1017, 1019, 1021, 1026, 1034.

[15] *ibid.* at 1017.

[16] *cf. Mercantile Credit Ltd v Hamblin* [1965] 2 Q.B. 242; *Avon Finance Co v Bridger* [1985] 2 All E.R. 281. For a difference of judicial opinion on a similar point, see *Lloyds Bank plc v Waterhouse* [1993] 2 FLR 97.

[17] *e.g. Cundy v Lindsay* (1873) 3 App.Cas. 459; above, p.299.

[18] [1971] A.C. 1004; *cf. Howatson v Webb* [1907] 1 Ch. 535; affirmed [1908] 1 Ch. 1. For discussion of the mistaken identity point, see *Gallie v Lee* [1969] 2 Ch. 17 at 44.

even though the widow thought that she was making a gift to Parkin when in fact she was making a conveyance to Lee. The reason for this rule may be that the mistaken party can discover the mistake by reading the document.

(4) Ignorance

The plea of *non est factum* is not normally open to a person who is merely ignorant of (as opposed to mistaken about) what he is signing[19]: for example, to one who signs a document in the belief that it is "only a form" without having any precise idea as to its nature.[20] Similarly, in *Gillman v Gillman*[21] a wife, shortly before her husband left her, signed a document which was in fact a separation deed. She did not know this when she signed it, but neither had she any definite idea as to what it was that she was signing. It was held that she was bound by the deed.

(5) Mistake as to capacity

The rule just stated is subject to an exception where a person signs a document under a mistaken belief as to the capacity in which he signs. Thus in *Lewis v Clay*[22] the defendant was induced to sign two promissory notes by the fraudulent representation that his signature was required as a witness and that the documents were of a private nature. The plea of *non est factum* succeeded even though the defendant could not say precisely what type of document he thought he had signed.

(6) Carelessness

Carelessness of the signer excludes the doctrine of *non est factum*. This was a second ground for the decision in *Gallie v Lee*[23]: the widow could not rely on the doctrine as she had been careless in signing the document without reading it. For the same reason, a person cannot rely on the doctrine if he signs a document containing blanks which are later filled in otherwise than in accordance with his instructions.[24]

In this context, the standard of care cannot be that of the reasonable person, for such a person will not normally be able to rely on the doctrine of *non est factum* at all.[25] One has to assume that the person relying on the doctrine falls within the class of persons to whom it is available, and then to ask whether that person took such care as one so disadvantaged could have been expected to take. In *Gallie v Lee* itself, this test was not satisfied; for, although the widow could not be expected to follow the intricacies of conveyancing, she could at least be expected to make sure that the person named in the document as transferee was the person intended by her. It does not follow that failure to read the document will exclude the plea of *non est factum* in all cases: the plea might, for example, still be available if reading the document would not have revealed its true character to a person of the signer's limited capabilities.[26]

---

[19] *Norwich and Peterborough BS v Steeds (No.2)* [1993] 1 All E.R. 330 at 338–339.

[20] *Hunter v Walters* (1871) L.R. 7 Ch.App. 75; *cf. National Provincial Bank of England v Jackson* (1886) 33 Ch.D. 1.

[21] (1946) 174 L.T. 272; *cf. Mercantile Credit Co Ltd v Hamblin* [1965] 2 Q.B. 242 (but in that case the signer escaped liability on another ground).

[22] (1897) 67 L.J.Q.B. 224.

[23] [1971] A.C. 1004; overruling *Carlisle & Cumberland Banking Co v Bragg* [1911] 1 K.B. 489. See also *Vorley v Cooke* (1857) 1 Giff. 230 at 236, *Hunter v Walters* (1871) L.R. 7 Ch.App. 75 at 87; *Lewis v Clay* (1897) 67 L.J.Q.B. 224 at 226; *Howatson v Webb* [1908] 1 Ch. 1; *Crédit Lyonnais v F T Barnard & Associates* [1976] 1 Lloyd's Rep. 557. *Avon Finance Co v Bridger* [1985] 2 All E.R. 281; *PB Leasing Ltd v Patela Patel* [1995] C.C.L.R. 82.

[24] *United Dominion's Trust Ltd v Western* [1976] Q.B. 513; Marston, [1976] C.L.J. 218.

[25] See above, pp.327–328.

[26] [1971] A.C. 1004 at 1023; *cf. Lloyd's Bank plc v Waterhouse* [1993] 2 FLR 97.

CHAPTER NINE

MISREPRESENTATION[1]

OUR concern in this Chapter is with the remedies available to a person who has been induced to enter into a contract by a statement which is misleading. These remedies are available only if the statement is of a kind which the law recognises as giving rise to liability, and if certain general conditions of liability are satisfied. The representee may then be able to claim damages or to rescind the contract or to do both these things. Similar remedies may also in certain cases be available where there has been mere non-disclosure of material facts, as opposed to active misrepresentation.

SECTION 1. MEANING OF "REPRESENTATION"[2]

The general rule is that no relief will be given for a misrepresentation as such unless it is a statement of *existing fact*. There may, therefore, be no remedy if the statement falls into one of the following categories.

1. Mere Puffs

These are statements which are so vague that they have no effect at law or in equity. To describe land as "fertile and improvable" is mere sales talk which affords no ground for relief.[3] But there is a liability for more precise claims, *e.g.* that use of a carbolic smoke-ball will give immunity from influenza.[4] The distinction is between indiscriminate praise, and specific promises or assertions of verifiable facts.

2. Statements of Fact and of Opinion or Belief

Even where a statement is not so vague as to be a mere puff, it may nevertheless have no legal effect because it is not a positive assertion that the fact stated is true, but only a statement of the maker's opinion or belief. Assertions that an anchorage was safe and that a piece of land had the capacity to support 2,000 sheep have been held to be of this character[5]; for in each case, the party making the statement had (as the other party knew) no personal knowledge of the facts on which it was based: it was understood that he could only state his belief. If that party has or professes to have some special knowledge or skill as to the matter stated, the statement is likely to be treated as one of fact.[6] A statement that the representor had been informed of a particular fact has also been held

---

[1] Allen, *Misrepresentation*; Cartwright, *Misrepresentation*.
[2] Our concern is with the common law meaning of this expression. For the wider meaning of "representation" in Consumer Credit Act 1974, s.67, see *Moorgate Services Ltd v Kabir, The Times*, April 25, 1995.
[3] *Dimmock v Hallett* (1866) L.R. 2 Ch.App. 21; *cf.* above, p.162.
[4] *Carlill v Carbolic Smoke Ball Co* [1893] 1 Q.B. 256.
[5] *Anderson v Pacific Fire & Marine Insurance Co* (1872) L.R. 7 C.P. 65; *Bissett v Wilkinson* [1927] A.C. 177.
[6] *e.g. Esso Petroleum Co Ltd v Mardon* [1976] Q.B. 801, below, p.338; *Box v Midland Bank Ltd* [1979] 2 Lloyd's Rep. 391 (reversed as to costs only [1981] 1 Lloyd's Rep. 434); *Thomas Witter Ltd v TBP Industries Ltd* [1996] 2 All E.R. 573 at 594–595; *Parks v Esso Petroleum Co Ltd* [1999] C.M.L.R. 455, affirmed on other grounds [2000] Eu.L.R. 25.

to be a representation, not merely that the representator had been so informed, but that the fact existed.[7]

A statement may, in terms, be one of opinion or belief, but by implication involve a statement of fact. Thus it is a misrepresentation of fact for a person to say that he holds an opinion which he does not hold, *e.g.* to say that he thinks a picture is a Rembrandt when he thinks it is a copy.[8] And if the facts on which an opinion is based are particularly within the knowledge of the person stating the opinion, he may be taken to have represented that those facts exist. For example, where the vendor of a house describes it as "let to a most desirable tenant", when the tenant has for long been in arrears with his rent, he misrepresents a fact, "for he impliedly states that he knows facts which justify his opinion".[9] The same principle applies where a person honestly makes a statement of belief but fails to check the facts on which it appears to be based, when he could easily have done so.[10]

3. Representations as to the Future

A representation as to the future does not, of itself, give rise to any cause of action[11] unless it is binding as a contract. Thus if A induces B to lend him money by representing that he will not borrow from anybody else, and then does borrow elsewhere, he is not liable to B unless the representation is a term of the contract of loan or amounts to a collateral contract.[12]

A person who promises to do something may simply be making a statement as to his future conduct; if so, he does not misrepresent a fact merely because he fails to do what he said he would do.[13] But he may also be making a statement of his present intention; if so, he does misrepresent a fact if, when he made the statement, he had no such intention. The courts tend to construe statements as to the future in the second of these two ways in order to protect the interests of persons deceived by them.[14] In *Edgington v Fitzmaurice*[15] the directors of a company procured a loan of money to their company by representing that the money would be used to improve the company's buildings and to expand its business. In fact the directors intended to use the money to pay off the company's existing debts. They were held liable to the lender in deceit. Bowen L.J. said: "There must be a mis-statement of an existing fact; but the state of a man's mind is as

---

[7] *Sirius International Ins Corp v Oriental Assurance Corp* [1999] 1 All E.R. (Comm) 699; presumably the latter representation arose by implication from the former.

[8] *Jendwine v Slade* (1797) 2 Esp. 571 at 573; *Brown v Raphael* [1958] Ch. 636 at 641; contrast *Harlingdon and Leinster Enterprises Ltd v Christopher Hull Fine Art Ltd* [1991] 1 Q.B. 564.

[9] *Smith v Land & House Property Corp* (1884) 28 Ch.D. 7 at 15.

[10] *Brown v Raphael* [1958] Ch. 636; contrast *Humming Bird Motors v Hobbs* [1986] R.T.R. 276 and *William Sindall plc v Cambridgeshire CC* [1994] 1 W.L.R. 1016, where the sellers where not negligent in stating their (mistaken) beliefs.

[11] It may be a ground for refusing specific performance: below, p.957. It may also, in combination with other circumstances, give rise to a proprietary estoppel: see above, pp.134–149

[12] *cf. Ex p. Burrell* (1876) 1 Ch.D. 537 at 552; *Strachan & Henshaw Ltd v Stein Industrie (UK) Ltd (No.2)* (1998) 87 B.L.R. 52. Failure to perform a promise is, similarly, not a false "statement" for the purpose of the Trade Descriptions Act 1968: *Beckett v Cohen* [1972] 1 W.L.R. 1593; *R. v Sunair Holidays Ltd* [1973] 1 W.L.R. 1105; unless the promise also contains a statement of present intention: see n.16, below.

[13] *The Seaflower* [2002] 2 Lloyd's Rep. 37 at 42; but the eventual outcome was that the representee was entitled to rescind *for breach*: *The Seaflower* [2001] 1 Lloyd's Rep. 341, below, p.798.

[14] *cf.* Theft Act 1968, s.15(4); Theft Act 1978, s.5(1); *R. v Gilmartin* [1983] Q.B. 953; *R. v Grantham* [1984] Q.B. 675.

[15] (1885) 29 Ch.D. 459.

much a fact as the state of his digestion. . . . A misrepresentation as to the state of a man's mind is, therefore, a mis-statement of fact".[16]

This principle is not restricted to statements of intention. A person may misrepresent a fact if he states an *expectation* or a *belief* which he does not hold as to some future event. The Marine Insurance Act 1906 provides that a marine policy can be avoided for an untrue representation of expectation or belief[17]; but that such a representation "is true if it be made in good faith".[18] These rules apply also to other types of insurance and under them a person would be guilty of misrepresentation if he stated a belief which he did not in fact hold. But the standard imposed by them is no more than one of honesty, so that where a representor made an honest statement of his knowledge and belief (which turned out to be wrong) as to the value of the contents of a house it was held that he was not guilty of misrepresentation: he was not required to show that he had reasonable grounds for making the statement.[19] In contexts other than that of insurance, however, a statement of expectation or belief may be held to contain an implied assertion that the representor did have reasonable grounds for making it. For example, a shipowner who in a charterparty says that his ship is "expected ready to load" at a particular port on or about a specified date impliedly represents that he honestly holds that belief, and that he does so on reasonable grounds. If he has no reasonable grounds for holding the belief, he misrepresents a fact.[20]

A person may similarly state his intention of doing something and thereby impliedly assert that he has reasonable grounds for thinking that he has the capacity to do it. There is no logical reason why such an implied assertion should not also be regarded as one of fact. It could further be argued that a person who incurs a debt may impliedly represent that he has reasonable grounds for thinking that he will be able to pay it[21]; and that, if he had no such grounds, the creditor should be able to rescind the contract. But the common understanding is that the creditor's only remedy (in the absence of fraud, such as an express misrepresentation as to solvency) is an action to recover the debt; and the whole scheme set up by the law of bankruptcy for the distribution of an insolvent debtor's estate would be seriously disrupted if some creditors could rescind (and so regain title to goods with which they had parted) on the ground that the debtor had, by merely incurring the debt, impliedly asserted that he had reasonable grounds for thinking that he would be able to pay. An implied assertion of this kind will not be a sufficient ground for rescinding a contract.[22]

A statement of intention may also be coupled with an *express* statement of existing fact. Thus a statement by A that he *had* sold flour and *would* pay over the proceeds to B is a misrepresentation of fact if A had made no such sale.[23]

---

[16] *ibid.* at 482; *cf. British Airways Bd v Taylor* [1976] 1 W.L.R. 13; *Smith Kline & French Laboratories Ltd v Long* [1988] 1 W.L.R. 1; *Kleinwort Benson Ltd v Malaysian Mining Corp* [1989] 1 W.L.R. 379 at 396; *East v Maurer* [1991] 1 W.L.R. 461 at 463; *Tudor Grange Holdings Ltd v Citibank N.A.* [1992] Ch. 53 at 67–68; *Goff v Gauthier* (1991) 62 P. & C.R. 388; *St. Paul Fire & Marine Ins v McConnell Dowell Contractors Ltd* [1995] 2 Lloyd's Rep. 116 at 125.

[17] s.20(1) and (3).

[18] *ibid.* s.20(5); *The Zephyr* [1985] 2 Lloyd's Rep. 529 at 538.

[19] *Economides v Commercial Union Assurance plc* [1998] Q.B. 587 rejecting (at 599, 606) so far as *contra*, dicta in *Highlands Insurance Co v Continental Insurance Co* [1987] 1 Lloyd's Rep. 109.

[20] *The Mihalis Angelos* [1971] 1 Q.B. 164 at 194, 205.

[21] See the authorities cited in n.14, above.

[22] *Amalgamated Metal Trading Ltd v DTI, The Times*, March 21, 1989.

[23] *Babcock v Lawson* (1880) 5 Q.B.D. 284; *cf. Ismail v Polish Ocean Lines Ltd* [1976] Q.B. 893: statement that goods *were* so packed that they *would* withstand the voyage; *The Siben* [1996] 1 Lloyd's Rep. 35 (representation that property *was or would be* acquired without encumbrance).

4. Statements of Fact and Law[24]

(1) Effect of the distinction

The traditional view is that a misrepresentation of law gives rise at common law neither to a right to rescind nor to a right to damages.[25] In equity, too, a money claim cannot be based on a misrepresentation of law[26]; and the same is probably true of claims for damages under the Misrepresentation Act 1967.[27] It is sometimes assumed that a misrepresentation of law is not even a ground for rescission in equity.[28] But this is more doubtful. It has been said that *wilful* misrepresentation of law is ground for equitable relief.[29] And equity gives relief for misrepresentation as to private rights[30] whether or not these are rightly called misrepresentation of fact.

The distinction between representations of fact and representations of law is (as the following discussion will show) sometimes hard to draw and its effects are hard to justify.[31] The House of Lords has held that *mistakes* of law, no less than mistakes of fact, can give rise to a claim for the return of money paid under a mistake.[32] Such a claim is analogous to one for the return of payments made under a contract which has been rescinded for misrepresentation, so that there is now a strong case for reconsidering the effects of the distinction in the context of restitution claims based on misrepresentation. The relationship between such restitution claims and claims for *damages* for misrepresentation is, perhaps, more distant; but even in the context of such a claim it is arguable that a person who has acted to his prejudice in reliance on a misrepresentation of law has as strong a claim for relief as one who is entitled to restitution because he has spontaneously made a mistake of law. The rules on this topic therefore seem to be ripe for reconsideration; but until this takes place[33] an account must still be given of the cases which analyse the distinction on the assumption that the representee's remedies are (to say the least) more restricted where the representation is one of law than where it is one of fact.

(2) Illustrations of the distinction

(a) POWERS OF COMPANIES. A number of cases deal with the question whether a misrepresentation by a director of a company as to its powers is one of law or one of fact. In one case directors represented that they had power under the private Act incorporating the company to issue new preference shares ranking *pari passu* with an existing issue. This was held to be a representation of law.[34] But in another case directors who had

---

[24] Hudson, 1958 S.L.T. 16.

[25] This is implicit in the authorities discussed below which illustrate the distinction.

[26] See *Rashdall v Ford* (1866) L.R. 2 Eq. 750; *Beattie v Ebury* (1872) L.R. 7 Ch.App. 777; *Eaglesfield v Londonderry* (1876) 4 Ch.D. 693.

[27] *André & Cie SA v Ets Michel Blanc & Fils* [1979] 2 Lloyd's Rep. 427 at 432, 434–435.

[28] *e.g.* in *Wauton v Coppard* [1899] 1 Ch. 92 and *Mackenzie v Royal Bank of Canada* [1934] A.C. 468. But in each of these cases the representation was held to be one of fact.

[29] *West London Commercial Bank v Kitson* (1884) 13 Q.B.D. 360 at 362–363; this formulation appears to exclude the possibility of relief for *negligent* misrepresentation of law. For certain purposes in the law of theft, a deliberate or reckless deception as to fact *or law* is sufficient: Theft Act 1968, s.15(4); Theft Act 1978, s.5(1).

[30] See below, p.336. *André & Cie SA v Ets Michel Blanc & Fils*, above, n.27, at 431, 432.

[31] See *André & Cie. SA v Ets Michel Blanc* [1997] 2 Lloyd's Rep. 427 at 431.

[32] *Kleinwort Benson Ltd v Lincoln CC* [1999] 2 A.C. 349; below, p.1059; *cf.* above, p.313.

[33] *cf.* above, p.314, n.57.

[34] *Beattie v Ebury* (1872) L.R. 7 Ch.App. 777.

power to borrow with the consent of the shareholders borrowed without such consent. It was held that they had impliedly made a representation of fact, *viz.*, that they had obtained the shareholders' consent.[35]

(b) EFFECT OF A DOCUMENT. A representation as to the effect of a document may be one as to its contents or one as to its meaning. In the former case, the representation is clearly one of fact.[36] A representation as to the meaning of a document whose contents are known may be one of law since for many purposes the construction of a document is a question of law[37]; but for the present purpose it is more likely to be treated as a representation of private right, and hence as one of fact.[38]

(c) EFFECT OF A STATUTE. A representation as to the meaning of an Act of Parliament is clearly one of law.[39] The same, it is submitted, is generally true of a representation as to the contents. One nineteenth century case[40] gives some support to the view that a representation as to the contents of a private Act is one of fact. But it is submitted that there is no longer any ground for distinguishing between private and public Acts for this purpose[41]; and that a representation as to the contents of any Act of Parliament would, like a representation as to its effects, be one of law.

(d) APPLICABILITY OF A RULE OF LAW. A statement that a statute or rule of common law applies to a known state of facts may be one of fact or of law according to the circumstances. Thus a statement that the Rent Acts applied to a house which was known to be in the occupation of the Crown was a misrepresentation of law, for it involved the erroneous proposition of law that the Rent Acts bound the Crown.[42] But a statement that the Rent Acts did not apply to a flat because its identity was wrongly thought to have been changed by work done to it was a misrepresentation of fact.[43] The proposition of law involved in this statement—that the Rent Acts did not apply where the identity of the flat had changed—was accurate. The only misrepresentation was one of fact, *viz.*, as to the change of identity.

(e) PRIVATE RIGHT. A representation as to private right is for the present purpose treated as one of fact.[44] Thus representations that A's shares are pledged to B, that C has

---

[35] *Cherry v Colonial Bank of Australasia* (1869) L.R. 3 P.C. 24; *cf. Firbank's Executors v Humphreys* (1886) 18 Q.B.D. 54. Now that a company incorporated under the Companies Acts is liable, to a person dealing with it in good faith, on a contract even though it is *ultra vires* (below, pp.561–563), the need for a remedy for misrepresentation is less acute; but the representee may still prefer rescission to enforcement.

[36] *Wauton v Coppard* [1889] 1 Ch. 92; *cf. Carmichael v National Power plc* [1999] 1 W.L.R. 2042 at 2050 (ascertainment of terms a question of fact).

[37] *Carmichael v National Power plc*, above, at 2049.

[38] See above, p.313; below, at n.44; *Horry v Tate & Lyle Refineries Ltd* [1982] 2 Lloyd's Rep. 417; *Cornish v Midland Bank plc* [1985] 3 All E.R. 513; in *National Westminster Bank plc v Morgan* [1985] A.C. 686 no claim based on misrepresentation was made.

[39] *cf. National Pari-Mutuel Association v R* (1930) 47 T.L.R. 110 (*mistake* of law).

[40] *West London Commercial Bank v Kitson* (1884) 13 Q.B.D. 360.

[41] Such a distinction may formerly have been based on the lack of publicity for private Acts; but it cannot be maintained after Interpretation Act 1889, s.9 (now Interpretation Act 1978, s.3). The question whether a representation as to the contents of a subordinate law is one of "law" might similarly depend on the question whether the law has been published under the Statutory Instruments Act 1946; but there seems to be no authority on the point.

[42] *Territorial & Auxiliary Forces Association v Nichols* [1949] 1 K.B. 35; see now Rent Act 1977, s.154. *cf. Harse v Pearl Life Assurance Co* [1904] 1 K.B. 558, below, p.493.

[43] *Solle v Butcher* [1950] 1 K.B. 671; above, p.316.

[44] *cf.* above, p.313 *André & Cie SA v Ets Michel Blanc & Fils* [1979] 2 Lloyd's Rep. 427 at 431, 432.

a patent in a certain invention and that D's product embodies E's invention have all been treated as representations of fact.[45]

(f) STATEMENTS OF LAW AND FACT. A statement may contain a misrepresentation of law and one of fact. If so, the availability of relief seems to depend on which part of the statement provided the representee's major inducement to enter into the contract.[46]

Sometimes the same statement may be one of law or fact, according to the circumstances. Thus the statement that A is unmarried is one of fact if it amounts to an assertion that A had never gone through a ceremony of marriage. If it amounts to an assertion that a ceremony in which A is known to have taken part was invalid, the following distinction has been drawn by Jessel M.R.: if the person making the statement tells "the whole story and all the facts" and *concludes* that A is still unmarried, the statement is one of law but if he simply says that A is single, he states a fact.[47] But it is hard to see the force of this distinction,[48] unless statements of the latter kind are regarded as analogous to statements as to private rights. The fact that in such borderline cases "representations of fact shade into representations of law"[49] gives further support to the view that the distinction between them is hard to justify on grounds of policy.

(g) REPRESENTATION OF FOREIGN LAW. In an English court, foreign law is a matter of fact.[50] A representation of foreign law is therefore regarded as one of fact.[51]

SECTION 2. GENERAL CONDITIONS OF LIABILITY

Where a representation does not have contractual force, it will give rise to the remedies discussed in Sections 3 and 4 of this Chapter only if it is unambiguous and material and if the representee has relied on it.

1. Unambiguous

A statement may be intended by the representor to bear a meaning which is true, but be so obscure that the representee understands it in another sense, in which it is untrue. In such a case the representor is not liable if his interpretation is the correct one[52]; and even if the court holds that the representee's interpretation was the correct one, the representor is not guilty of fraud.[53] This is so in spite of the fact that the representor's interpretation was an unreasonable one, so long as he honestly believed in it.[54] *A fortiori* the representee has no remedy in deceit if the representation is ambiguous and he did not in fact understand it in a different sense from that intended by the representor.[55] But

---

[45] *Mackenzie v Royal Bank of Canada* [1934] A.C. 468; *Begbie v Phosphate Sewage Co Ltd* (1875) L.R. 10 Q.B. 491; *Lyle-Mellor v Lewis* [1956] 1 W.L.R. 29; *cf. Taylors Fashions Ltd v Liverpool Victoria Trustee Co Ltd* [1982] Q.B. 133 (note), 158.

[46] *cf. Holt v Markham* [1923] 1 K.B. 504.

[47] *Eaglesfield v Londonderry* (1876) 4 Ch.D. 693 at 702–703.

[48] The Court of Appeal disagreed with Jessel M.R.'s conclusion that the mistake in *Eaglesfield's* case was one of law; but how much of his reasoning was disapproved is not clear.

[49] *Brikom Investments Ltd v Seaford* [1981] 1 W.L.R. 863 at 869; *cf. Amalgamated Investment & Property Co Ltd v Texas Commerce International Bank Ltd* [1982] Q.B. 84 at 122.

[50] Dicey and Morris, *The Conflict of Laws*, (12th ed.) Rule 18.

[51] *André & Cie. S.A. v Ets. Michel Blanc & Fils* [1979] 2 Lloyd's Rep. 427 at 431, 432.

[52] *McInerny v Lloyds Bank Ltd* [1974] 1 Lloyd's Rep. 246 at 254; contrast *Spice Girls Ltd v Aprilia World Service BV* [2002] EWCA Civ 15 at [67], where there was held to be *no* ambiguity in the representation.

[53] *Akerhielm v De Mare* [1959] A.C. 789; *Gross v Lewis Hillman Ltd* [1970] Ch. 445; and *cf.* below, p.394.

[54] *Quaere* whether it could make him liable in negligence: do *Hedley Byrne & Co Ltd v Heller & Partners Ltd* [1964] A.C. 465 and s.2(1) of the Misrepresentation Act 1967 apply to bad drafting?

[55] *Smith v Chadwick* (1884) 9 App.Cas. 187.

it does not follow from the fact that the representor was not guilty of fraud that the representee has no remedy at all. If he reasonably understood the ambiguous statement in a sense in which the representor did not mean it, and which was untrue, he can rely on it as a defence to specific performance.[56]

A representor is guilty of fraud if he makes an ambiguous statement intending it to bear a meaning which is to his knowledge untrue,[57] and if the statement is reasonably understood in that sense by the representee. In such a case it is no defence for the representor to show that, on its true construction, the statement bore a meaning that was in fact true.[58]

2. Material

A misrepresentation generally has no legal effect unless it is material.[59] That is, it must be one which would affect the judgment of a reasonable person in deciding whether, or on what terms, to enter into the contract; or one that would induce him to enter into the contract without making such inquiries as he would otherwise make.[60] Thus in a contract of insurance it is material that the subject-matter has been grossly overvalued[61] or that a previous proposal for insuring it has been declined[62]; in a contract for a loan of money it is material that the lender is a notoriously ruthless money-lender[63]; and in an auction sale of a house it is material who owns the house "as it was, to a certain extent, a guarantee as to the character of the sale".[64] Conversely, a representation as to the identity of the purchaser may be material where the vendor is willing to sell to X but not to Y. In such a case the vendor can rescind if the purchaser knows that the representation is material, even though he does not know why it is so regarded by the vendor.[65] A misrepresentation may be material although the representor in good faith thinks that it is not material.[66]

There are two exceptions to the requirement of materiality. First, a person who has successfully perpetrated a fraud cannot be heard to say that the representation which he used to achieve this end was immaterial.[67] Secondly, every representation is material if

---

[56] *New Brunswick & Canada Ry v Muggeridge* (1860) 1 Dr. & Sm. 363, 382; and see below, p.394.

[57] *Henry Ansbacher & Co Ltd v Binks Stern, The Times*, June 26, 1997.

[58] *The Siboen and the Sibotre* [1976] 1 Lloyd's Rep. 293 at 318.

[59] *McDowell v Fraser* (1779) 1 Dougl. 247 at 248, *per* Lord Mansfield; *Lonrho plc v Fayed (No.2)* [1992] 1 W.L.R. 1, 6; *cf.* (in cases of non-disclosure) below, pp.394–395.

[60] *Traill v Baring* (1864) 4 D.J. & S. 318 at 326; *Dimmock v Hallett* (1866) L.R. 2 Ch.App. 21 at 29, 30; Marine Insurance Act 1906, s.20(2), expressing the general law: *Locker & Woolf Ltd v W. Australian Insurance Co Ltd* [1936] 1 K.B. 408 at 414; *Industrial Properties Ltd v A E I Ltd* [1977] Q.B. 580 at 597, 601; *Highland Ins Co v Continental Ins Co* [1987] 1 Lloyd's Rep. 109; *Pan Atlantic Ins Co Ltd v Pine Top Ins Co Ltd* [1995] 2 A.C. 501; *St Paul Fire & Marine Insurance Co (UK) Ltd v McConnell Dowell Contractors Ltd* [1995] 2 Lloyd's Rep. 116 at 121; *cf. Walker v Boyle* [1982] 1 W.L.R. 495 at 503; *Geest plc v Fyffes plc* [1999] 1 All E.R. (Comm) 672 at 686; *The Mercadian Continent* [2001] EWCA Civ 1275; [2001] 2 Lloyd's Rep. 563, at [26].

[61] *Ionides v Pender* (1874) L.R. 9 Q.B. 531.

[62] *Locker & Woolf Ltd v W Australian Insurance Co Ltd*, above, n.60.

[63] *Gordon v Street* [1899] 2 Q.B. 641.

[64] *Whurr v Devenish* (1904) 20 T.L.R. 385.

[65] *Lonrho plc v Fayed (No.2)* [1992] 1 W.L.R. 1 at 5–6.

[66] *Lindenau v Desborough* (1828) 8 B. & C. 586; *Joel v Law Union & Crown Insurance Co* [1908] 2 K.B. 863 at 883; *cf.* (in criminal law) *R. v Millward* [1985] Q.B. 519.

[67] *Smith v Kay* (1859) 7 H.L.C. 750; *cf. Gordon v Street*, above, n.63; *Rafsanjan Pistachio Producers Co-operative v Bank Leumi (UK) plc* [1992] 1 Lloyd's Rep. 514 at 542; *Agapitos v Agnew* [2002] EWCA Civ 247; [2002] 1 All E.R. (Comm) 714, at [32, 33]. *Quaere* whether this strict rule would be applied to a negligent misrepresentation. A dictum in *Downs v Chappell* [1997] 1 W.L.R. 345 at 351 applies the requirement of materiality even in a case of fraud, but is *obiter* since it was not there suggested that the representation was not material.

the contract so provides. Thus if a policy of insurance provides that statements by the assured in the proposal form shall be the basis of the contract, or are warranted to be true, such statements are material,[68] however unimportant they may be in themselves.

It has also been said that materiality was not relevant where the claim was "not for misrepresentation" but for "negligence only".[69] This distinction was drawn in a case in which solicitors were held liable for failure to provide accurate information to a client who, in consequence, made a mortgage loan on a security which turned out to be inadequate. What the distinction seems to mean is that the client's claim was for breach of a contractual duty of care[70] and not for inducing the claimant by misrepresentation to enter into a contract with the defendant; and that materiality is not relevant to a claim of the former kind. It should not be taken to mean that "misrepresentation" and "negligence" are mutually exclusive categories[71] or that materiality is irrelevant to claims for negligent misrepresentation inducing a contract, whether with the representor or with a third party.

The requirement of materiality has been doubted[72]; but in evaluating these doubts a distinction should, it is submitted, be drawn between two reasons why the misrepresentation would not affect the judgment of a reasonable person. This may be the position either because of the *circumstances in which the representation was made*, or because of its *contents*. The first possibility is illustrated by *Museprime Properties Ltd v Adhill Properties Ltd*,[73] where a purchaser by auction of commercial property was allowed to rescind for a representation by the auctioneer that higher rents could still be negotiated, when in fact the rents had been fixed for the next rent review period. The court held that it was sufficient for the purchaser to show that his bid had actually been affected by the representation: he did not have to show that a reasonable bidder would have allowed it to affect his bid. The representation could certainly have affected the value of the property and was in this sense material. The only sense in which it was not material was that the representee had (and did not take) the opportunity of discovering the truth; but even though a reasonable person might have made use of such an opportunity, it is settled that a representee's failure to do so is no bar to relief for misrepresentation.[74] The case is, in other words, concerned with the question whether the representee could be taken to have *relied* on the representation (or had been *induced* by it to enter it into the contract); and this is distinct from the question of materiality.[75] The second of the two possibilities mentioned above arises where the matter misrepresented is not "material" because it had little (or only a trivial) effect on the value of the subject-matter. What is an "immaterial" representation (in this sense) can be illustrated by supposing that the auctioneer in the *Museprime* case had represented the tenant to be 40 years old when actually he was 39 or 41, that this representation had (for some reason) been a factor inducing the representee's successful bid, and that its falsity had caused no, or no substantial, loss to the representee. If the representor has made such a representation in good faith it is hard to see why a representee should be entitled to any relief when,

---

[68] *Andersen v Fitzgerald* (1853) 4 H.L.C. 484; *London Assurance v Mansel* (1879) 11 Ch.D. 363 at 368; and see below, p.396. Such clauses are not affected by the Unfair Contract Terms Act 1977: above, p.264; nor (*semble*) by the Unfair Terms in Consumer Contracts Regulations 1999: above, p.271.

[69] *Bristol & West B S v Mothew* [1998] Ch. 1 at 10–11.

[70] See below, p.890.

[71] See *Hedley Byrne & Co Ltd v Heller & Partners Ltd* [1964] A.C. 465; below p.344.

[72] Goff and Jones, *The Law of Restitution* (5th ed.), pp.272–273; *Chitty on Contracts*, (27th ed.), Vol.I, §6–022.

[73] [1990] 2 E.G.L.R. 196.

[74] See below, p.340.

[75] *The Mercadian Continent* [2001] 2 Lloyd's Rep. 563, [2001] EWCA Civ 1275 at [26].

by definition, the representation would not have influenced a reasonable person. Damages would be no more than nominal, and a claim to rescind for such a misrepresentation has been rejected as totally unmeritorious.[76] This conclusion could also be justified on the analogous ground that, in the example given above, the representation was "substantially correct"; and in determining whether it has this quality, the law applies the same test as that which determines whether a representation is material.[77]

3. Reliance

The person to whom the misrepresentation was made must have relied on it[78] in the sense that it must have induced him to enter into the contract.[79] He therefore cannot rescind, or claim damages, for misrepresentation if the representation did not come to his notice,[80] if he knew the truth,[81] if he took a deliberate risk as to the truth of the matter stated, if he would have entered into the transaction even though he had known the truth,[82] or if he relied on his own information.[83] If, however, a fraudulent representation has induced the representee to enter into the transaction, then it is no bar to a claim for damages that he would have acted in the same way even if the representation had not been made.[84]

(1) Truth known to agent

A person cannot get relief for misrepresentation if the truth, though not known to him, was known to his agent while acting within the scope of his authority.[85] But the principal

---

[76] *Industrial Properties Ltd v A E I Ltd* [1977] Q.B. 580; *Re a Company (No.001946 of 1991) Ex p. Fin Soft Holdings SA* [1991] B.C.L.C. 737 at 748; *cf.* Restatement 2d. *Contracts* §162, Ill. 4.

[77] See Marine Insurance Act 1906, s.20(4); *Avon Insurance plc v Swire Fraser Ltd* [2000] 1 All E.R. (Comm) 573 at 579.

[78] *Pan Atlantic Insurance Co Ltd v Pine Top Insurance Co Ltd* [1995] 2 A.C. 501; *Skipskreditforeningen v Emperor Navigation* [1998] 1 Lloyd's Rep. 67 at 73; *J. Jarvis & Sons Ltd v Castle Wharf Developments Ltd* [2001] EWCA Civ 19; [2001] Lloyd's Rep. P.N., at [62, 68]. Our concern in this Chapter is with representations inducing contracts. There is no requirement of reliance by the injured party where the misrepresentation is made *about* that party, so that he suffers loss as a result of the act or omission of a third party, as in *Spring v Guardian Assurance plc* [1995] 2 A.C. 296.

[79] *Pan Atlantic Insurance Co Ltd v Pine Top Insurance Co Ltd* [1995] 2 A.C. 501; *Avon Insurance plc v Swire Fraser Ltd* [2000] 1 All E.R. (Comm) 573 at 633; *cf. Spice Girls Ltd v Aprilia World Service BV* [2002] EWCA Civ 15 at [68–72]. In *Downs v Chappell* [1997] 1 W.L.R. 426 at 433. Hobhouse L.J. puzzlingly says that "reliance is not the correct criterion" (apparently of inducement) in "the tort of deceit" but later on the same page when dealing with "the tort of negligence", he states the test as one of "reliance". This distinction is accepted in *Bristol and West BS v Mothew* [1996] 4 All E.R. 698 at 705, where the test in a negligence case is said to be "not inducement but reliance"; for the view that the claim in that case was "not for misrepresentation", see above, p.317 at n.69; *cf.* also *Swindle v Harrison* [1997] 4 All E.R. 705 at 727 (stating the test of "inducement" in deceit).

[80] *Ex p. Biggs* (1859) 28 L.J.Ch. 50.

[81] *Eurocopy v Teesdale* [1992] B.C.L.C. 1067.

[82] *J E B Fasteners Ltd v Marks Bloom & Co* [1983] 1 All E.R. 583 (as to which see below, p.343); *The Lucy* [1983] 1 Lloyd's Rep. 188; *cf. Beaumont v Humberts* [1988] 2 E.G.L.R. 171. *Chase Manhattan Equities Ltd v Goodman* [1991] B.C.L.C. 897 at 930 (as to which see also below, p.488).

[83] *Jennings v Broughton* (1854) 5 D.M. & G. 126; *cf. Cooper v Tamms* [1988] 1 E.G.L.R. 257; *The Morning Watch* [1990] 1 Lloyd's Rep. 547 at 556; *Goodwill v Pregnancy Advisory Service* [1996] 1 W.L.R. 1397, below, p.617 (claimant relying on own doctor's advice); *Spice Girls Ltd v Aprilia World Service BV* [2002] EWCA Civ 15 at [29].

[84] *UCB Corporate Services Ltd v Williams* [2002] EWCA Civ 555, *The Times*, May 5, 2002.

[85] *Bawden v London Assurance* [1892] 2 Q.B. 534; *Strover v Harrington* [1988] Ch. 390; contrast *El Ajou v Dollar Holdings plc* [1994] 2 All E.R. 685 at 689, 702–705.

may get such relief if the agent found out the truth while acting for the other party,[86] or in fraud of the principal,[87] or in any way outside the scope of his authority.

(2) Testing accuracy

A person who himself tests the accuracy of the representation can be said to rely on his own judgment, rather than on the representation. Accordingly, he cannot obtain relief for innocent[88] (or probably for negligent[89]) misrepresentation. But this rule does not apply in cases of fraud. In *S. Pearson & Son Ltd v Dublin Corporation*[90] the claimants undertook to execute works for the corporation on the faith of plans supplied by it. The contract provided that the claimants should satisfy themselves of the accuracy of the plans.[91] It was held that this provision would not protect the corporation if the plans were fraudulent. It is not clear what steps, if any, the claimants took to test the accuracy of the plans. But it is submitted that if, in spite of taking some such steps, they had failed to discover the truth, the corporation should still have been liable on proof of fraud.

(3) Opportunity to find out the truth

A person may be entitled to relief even though he had, but did not take, the opportunity to test the accuracy of the representation.[92] This rule is most frequently applied to cases of fraud,[93] but *Smith v Eric S Bush*[94] shows that it can also apply where the misrepresentation was negligent. The claimants in that case had bought a house with the aid of a mortgage, relying on a valuation which had been negligently conducted by a surveyor engaged by the lender. Their claim against the surveyor succeeded in spite of the fact that they might have discovered the truth if they had conducted their own independent survey; for it was neither reasonable to expect them to take this step, nor likely that they would do so, since the house in question was one of modest value. But the House of Lords indicated[95] that the position might be different on the purchase of commercial or industrial premises, or even of residential property of high value. The principle appears to be that failure to make use of an opportunity to discover the truth

---

[86] *Newsholme v Road Transport Insurance Co Ltd* [1929] 2 K.B. 356; *The Hellespont Ardent* [1997] 2 Lloyd's Rep. 547 at 596.

[87] *Wells v Smith* [1914] 3 K.B. 722; *Group Josi Re v Wallbrook Insurance Co Ltd* [1996] 1 W.L.R. 1152.

[88] *Clarke v Mackintosh* (1862) 4 Giff. 134; *Redgrave v Hurd* (1881) 20 Ch.D. 1, 14, discussing *Attwood v Small* (1838) 6 Cl. & F. 232.

[89] *McInerny v Lloyds Bank Ltd* [1974] 1 Lloyd's Rep. 246 at 254.

[90] [1907] A.C. 351.

[91] For such provisions, see below, p.385.

[92] *Dobell v Stevens* (1825) 3 B. & C. 623; *Reynell v Sprye* (1852) 1 D.M. & G. 660; *Central Ry of Venezuela v Kisch* (1867) L.R. 2 H.L. 99; *Redgrave v Hurd* (1881) 20 Ch.D. 1; *Smith v Land & House Property Corporation* (1884) 28 Ch.D. 7; *Aaron's Reefs Ltd v Twiss* [1896] A.C. 273; cf. *The Arta* [1985] 1 Lloyd's Rep. 534; *Rignal Developments Ltd v Halil* [1988] Ch. 190 at 199, *aliter*, if a person reads a document revealing the truth, but simply fails to understand it: *Ex p. Briggs* (1866) L.R. 1 Eq. 483.

[93] *e.g.* *Gordon v Selico Ltd* (1986) 278 E.G. 53 at 61; *Strover v Harrington* [1988] Ch. 390 at 410; cf. *Commission for the New Towns v Cooper (Great Britain) Ltd* [1995] Ch. 259 at 282. *Horsfall v Thomas* (1862) 1 H. & C. 90, so far as *contra*, was doubted in *Smith v Hughes* (1871) L.R. 6 Q.B. 597 at 605; *Standard Chartered Bank v Pakistan National Shipping Co (No.3)* [2001] EWCA Civ 55; [2001] 1 All E.R. (Comm) 55 at [52].

[94] [1990] 1 A.C. 831; Allen, 105 L.Q.R. 511; Horton Rogers [1989] C.L.J. 366; cf. *Halifax B S v Edell* [1992] Ch. 426 at 454.

[95] cf. pp.854, 872 (dealing with the issue of reasonableness under the Unfair Contract Terms Act 1977); *Kijowski v New Capital Properties* (1990) 15 Con.L.R. 1; *McCullagh v Lane Fox & Partners* [1996] E.G.L.R. 35.

may defeat a claim for negligent misrepresentation where, but only where, it is reasonable to expect the representee to make use of the opportunity. An express warning to the representee not to rely on the representation could also negative liability for negligent misrepresentation.[96]

In *Redgrave v Hurd*,[97] it was held that an opportunity to discover the truth was no bar to relief even where the misrepresentation was innocent. In that case, a person was induced to buy a solicitor's practice and house by an innocent misrepresentation as to the value of the practice. He was allowed to rescind even though he had the opportunity of examining the accounts of the practice and so discovering the truth. It should, however, be noted that, when *Redgrave v Hurd* was decided, all misrepresentations which were not fraudulent were described as "innocent".[98] Now, the law distinguishes between negligent and wholly innocent misrepresentations[99]; and it further distinguishes between cases in which it was, and those in which it was not, reasonable for the representee to make use of an opportunity to discover the truth.[1] Where it *is* reasonable to expect the representee to make use of such an opportunity, and he fails to do so, the reasoning of *Smith v Eric S Bush*[2] indicates that a claim based on negligent misrepresentation will fail; and the position should, *a fortiori*, be the same where the misrepresentation is wholly innocent.[3] To this extent, it is submitted that the rule in *Redgrave v Hurd* no longer applies.[4] Where it is *not* reasonable to expect the representee to make use of the opportunity to discover the truth, and he fails to do so, the actual decision in *Smith v Eric S Bush* shows that a claim based on negligent misrepresentation can nevertheless succeed; but it is less clear whether the same result should follow where the misrepresentation was wholly innocent, so that both parties were equally innocent. *Redgrave v Hurd* stands as an authority for the proposition that, in the case last put, failure to make use of the opportunity to discover the truth is no bar to relief. It can be supported on the ground that there is actual, and reasonable, reliance on the misrepresentation in such a case.

(4) Representation addressed to another

A person may rely on a representation even though it was not made directly to him: *e.g.* where A makes a misrepresentation to B which later comes to the notice of C and

---

[96] *Hemmens v Wilson Browne* [1993] 4 All E.R. 826 at 839; *McCullagh v Lane Fox & Partners*, above. Such reasoning can also prevent a representation from being included in the contract as one of its terms: below, pp.353–354.

[97] (1881) 20 Ch.D. 1; *Laurence v Lexcourt Holdings Ltd* [1978] 1 W.L.R. 1128.

[98] Now that damages can be recovered for negligent misrepresentation the carelessness of the representee may be a ground for reducing the damages under the Law Reform (Contributory Negligence) Act 1945 (below, p.668): this possibility was recognised in *Gran Gelato Ltd v Richcliff (Group) Ltd* [1992] Ch. 560 at 573–574, where, however, the court refused to exercise its discretion under the 1945 Act. This Act would not apply where the misrepresentation was fraudulent: *Alliance & Leicester BS v Edgestrop* [1993] 1 W.L.R. 1462; *KCB Bank v Industrial Steels (UK) Ltd* [2001] 1 Lloyd's Rep. 370 at 377; *Standard Chartered Bank v Pakistan National Shipping Co* [2002] UKHL 43, [2003] 1 All E.R. 173; *cf. Corporacion Nacional del Cobrre de Chile v Sojemin Metah Ltd* [1997] 1 W.L.R. 1369. Nor would the 1945 Act affect a right to *rescind* for misrepresentation.

[99] See below, pp.350–351, 357.

[1] See above at n.88.

[2] *ibid.*

[3] *cf. McInerny v Lloyds Bank Ltd* [1974] 1 Lloyd's Rep. 246 at 254 and *The Nai Genova* [1984] 1 Lloyd's Rep. 353 at 365 (where the claimant's carelessness prevented him from relying on an estoppel).

[4] *cf. Archer v Brown* [1985] Q.B. 401 at 416 (doubting *Redgrave v Hurd* on another point).

induces C to contract with A. If A intended to bring about this result he is liable to C.[5]

A representation made by A to B may also make A liable to C where it was reasonable for A to anticipate that the representation would be passed on to C and that C would act on it in some way other than by entering into a contract with A.[6] This possibility is illustrated by cases such as *Smith v Eric S Bush*,[7] where a representation in a report as to the value or condition of a house was made by A to B, was then passed on by B to C, and induced C to buy the house from X. Where the contract induced by the misrepresentation is not made between A and C, it may be difficult to determine whether A owed any duty of care to C. This question is discussed later in this Chapter[8]; the present point is simply that the requirement of reliance on the representation may be satisfied even though the representation is not made directly by the representor to the representee.

Where A by misrepresentation induces B to buy something from him, he will not be liable to C merely because B repeats the misrepresentation when later reselling the subject-matter to C. In one such case it was held that the misrepresentation was "spent"[9] when the contract was made between A and B, so that C could not rely on it against A. He might, however, be able to do so if he could show that A knew that B intended to resell and was likely to repeat the misrepresentation on the occasion of the sale to C.[10]

(5) Other inducements

A person who relies on a misrepresentation can get relief although he also relied on other inducements. Thus in *Edgington v Fitzmaurice*[11] a lender was induced to lend money to a company by (i) the misrepresentations which have already been discussed,[12] and (ii) his mistaken belief that he would have a charge on the assets of the company. He was entitled to damages for deceit[13] even though he admitted that he would not have lent the money,

---

[5] *Pilmore v Hood* (1838) 5 Bing.N.C. 97; *cf. Langridge v Levy* (1837) 2 M. & W. 519; *Brikom Investments Ltd v Carr* [1979] Q.B. 467 at 485; *Standard Chartered Bank v Pakistan National Shipping Corp* [1995] 2 Lloyd's Rep. 365 at 378 (as to which see above, n.98); *Possfund Custodian Trustees Ltd v Diamond* [1996] 1 W.L.R. 1351. Contrast *Peek v Gurney* (1873) L.R. 6. H.L. 377 (but see Financial Services and Markets Act 2000, ss.90 and 86); and, in another context, *R. v Jockey Club, Ex p. R A M Racecourses Ltd* [1993] 2 All E.R. 225 at 228–239.

[6] But not in the absence of such circumstances: *The Zephyr* [1985] 2 Lloyd's Rep. 529 at 539 (and see below, p.608); *Bank Leumi Le Israel B M v British National Insurance Co* [1988] 1 Lloyd's Rep. 71 at 77; *cf. Beaumont v Humberts* [1988] 2 E.G.L.R. 171; *Goodwill v National Pregnancy Advisory Service* [1996] 1 W.L.R. 1397.

[7] [1990] 1 A.C. 831; *Yianni v Edwin Evans & Sons* [1982] Q.B. 438.

[8] See above, pp.345 *et seq.*

[9] *Gross v Lewis Hillman Ltd* [1970] Ch. 445 at 461.

[10] *ibid. cf. The Sennar (No.2)* [1985] 1 W.L.R. 490. *cf. Clef Aquitaine SARL v Laporte Materials (Barrow) Ltd* [2001] Q.B. 485, where the subject-matter was transferred by B to C by novation. A was a necessary party to this transaction (below, p.673) and knew that his representation would be passed on by B to C, those entities being under the same control.

[11] (1885) 29 Ch.D. 459; *The Siboen and the Sibotre* [1976] 1 Lloyd's Rep. 293 at 324; *Horry v Tate & Lyle Refineries Ltd* [1982] 2 Lloyd's Rep. 417 at 422; *KCB Bank v Industrial Steels (UK) Ltd* [2001] 1 Lloyd's Rep. 370 at 377; *BP Operating Co Ltd v Chevron Transport (Scotland)* [2001] UKHL 50; [2002] 1 All E.R. (Comm) 1 at [105]; *Spice Girls Ltd v Aprilia World Service BV* [2002] EWCA Civ 15 at [70]; *UCB Corporate Services Ltd v Williams* [2002] EWCA Civ 555; *The Times*, May 27, 2002; *cf.* (in cases of duress) *Barton v Armstrong* [1976] A.C. 104; *St Paul Fire & Marine Insurance Co (UK) Ltd v McConnell Dowell Contractors Ltd* [1995] 2 Lloyd's Rep. 116 at 125; and above, p.109.

[12] See above, p.331.

[13] See *Standard Chartered Bank v Pakistan National Shipping Co* [2002] UKHL 43, [2003] 1 All E.R. 173 at [17] for the view that the rule is "probably restricted" to cases of fraud.

had he not held this mistaken belief. The victim of a fraud can likewise recover damages in respect of his full loss even though that loss was caused partly by the deceit and partly by his own decision (not based on any mistaken belief by him) to take the course of action which led to his suffering the loss.[14] This rule has been applied even where the victim's motive for taking this course of action was his wish to deceive a third party.[15] It is an open question whether, in such a case, the loss so suffered should be apportioned between the victim and the original perpetrator of the fraud.[16]

But if a person to whom two statements, one true and one untrue, are made relies exclusively on the true one, he has no right to relief. Thus in *Heilbut, Symons & Co v Buckleton*[17] a person bought shares in a company after being told (i) that it was a rubber company (which was untrue), and (ii) that the defendants were "bringing it out" (which was true). One reason given by Lord Atkinson for dismissing the buyer's claim for damages was that the he had relied on the second statement to the exclusion of the first.

(6) Distinguished from materiality

The rule that the representee must rely on the representation is distinct from the requirement of materiality. Whether a representation is material depends, in general,[18] on the significance which a reasonable person would have attached to it. Whether the representee has relied on the representation depends on his actual state of mind. The mere fact that a representation is material gives rise to no "inference of law" that the representation was relied on.[19] For example, in *JEB Fasteners Ltd v Marks Bloom & Co*[20] the plaintiffs took over a company after seeing its accounts, which were inaccurate, having been negligently prepared by the defendants (a firm of accountants). A duty of care seems to have arisen because the accounts had been "impliedly confirmed directly to the plaintiff... with a particular transaction in contemplation",[21] and the misrepresentation was clearly material; but the plaintiffs' claim for damages was dismissed as they had placed no reliance on the accounts. Their object in taking over the company was to secure the services of two of its directors and they would have proceeded with the transaction even if the accounts had shown the company's true financial state. The distinction between the two requirements of materiality and reliance is further supported by the rule that the representee must show, not only that the representation was material, but also that it induced him to enter into the contract.[22]

The distinction is sometimes obscured by the use of the word "material" to mean "material to the representee". Thus in *Smith v Chadwick*[23] the representee bought shares in a company on the faith of a prospectus which contained the untrue statement that one Grieve was a director of the company. The representee's claim for damages was dismissed: the statement was "immaterial" as the representee had never heard of Grieve. It is more accurate to say that for this reason the representee did not rely on the

---

[14] *Standard Chartered Bank v Pakistan National Shipping Co (No.2)* [2000] 1 Lloyd's Rep. 218, reversed on another point [2002] UKHL 43 [2003] 1 All E.R. 173.

[15] *ibid.*

[16] [2000] 1 Lloyd's Rep. 218 at 230, 236.

[17] [1913] A.C. 30; above, p.162.

[18] See above, p.337.

[19] *Smith v Land & House Property Corp* (1884) 28 Ch.D. 7 at 16.

[20] [1983] 1 All E.R. 583, affirming [1981] 3 All E.R. 289. The question whether the defendants owed any duty to the plaintiffs was only discussed at first instance; on this point see below, p.347.

[21] *Al Saudi Banque v Clark Pixley* [1990] Ch. 313 at 335.

[22] *Pan Atlantic Ins Co Ltd v Pine Top Ins Co Ltd* [1995] 2 A.C. 501, disapproving *Container Transport International v Oceanus Mutual, etc., Insurance* [1984] 1 Lloyd's Rep. 476 on this point.

[23] (1884) 9 App.Cas. 187.

statement, which was clearly material in the sense that it could influence a reasonable person.

(7) Burden of proof

For the purpose of the requirement of reliance, the representee need only show that the representation was made and that it was capable of inducing the contract. The burden then passes to the representor to show that the representee would have entered into the contract anyway, even if the misrepresentation had not been made.[24]

SECTION 3. DAMAGES FOR MISREPRESENTATION[25]

In this Section, we shall discuss the five grounds on which damages can be recovered for misrepresentation, consider the relationship between them; and refer, in the context of misrepresentation, to the power of criminal courts to make compensation orders in criminal cases.

1. Fraud

At common law a person who suffers loss as a result of acting in reliance on a fraudulent statement can recover damages in an action of deceit. He can generally do this whether he rescinds the contract or not[26] though he cannot pursue both remedies if this results in his recovering twice over for the same loss.[27]

In *Derry v Peek*[28] the House of Lords held that a statement is fraudulent only if made (i) with knowledge of its falsity, or (ii) without belief in its truth, or (iii) recklessly,[29] not caring whether it is true or false. Fraud is a serious charge which must be clearly and distinctly proved.[30] A person who negligently makes a false statement will now often be liable in damages, but it may still be important that he is not guilty of fraud at common law. One reason for this is that the damages for fraud may not be the same as damages for negligence.[31] Another is that certain special rules may apply to rescission for fraud.[32]

A statement may be fraudulent although it was made without bad motive and without intention to cause loss: an "intention to deceive" suffices even though there is no

---

[24] *Smith v Chadwick* (1884) 9 App.Cas. 187 at 196.

[25] Greig, 87 L.Q.R. 179.

[26] *Newbigging v Adam* (1886) 34 Ch.D. 582 at 592; *Archer v Brown* [1985] Q.B. 401 at 415; *Tang Man Sit v Capacious Investments Ltd* [1996] A.C. 514 at 521. *cf.* Companies Act 1985, s.111A (as substituted by Companies Act 1989, s.131) overriding the former rule in *Houldsworth v City of Glasgow Bank* (1880) 5 App.Cas. 317 "at least in part:" *Soden v British & Commonwealth Holdings plc* [1998] A.C. 298 at 327.

[27] *Archer v Brown*, above, at 415.

[28] (1889) 14 App.Cas. 337 (actual decision was reversed by the Directors Liability Act 1890; see now Financial Services and Markets Act 2000, ss.90, 86); *Standard Chartered Bank v Pakistan National Shipping Corp (No.2)* [2000] 1 Lloyd's Rep. 218; and see n.33, below.

[29] Recklessness goes beyond mere carelessness: see *Thomas Witter Ltd v TBP Industries Ltd* [1996] 2 All E.R. 573 at 587; the statement made *ibid.* that "dishonesty" is a requirement of fraud, must be read subject to the qualification discussed at nn.33 and 34, below.

[30] *Wallingford v Mutual Society* (1880) 5 App.Cas. 685; for the standard of proof of fraud in civil cases, see *Hornal v Neuburger Products* [1957] 1 Q.B. 267; *Rafsanjan Pistachio Producers Co-operative v Bank Leumi plc* [1992] 1 Lloyd's Rep. 513 at 525 ("very heavy burden"); *Nsbuga v Commercial Union Co plc* [1998] 2 Lloyd's Rep. 682 at 686, 690; *The Grecia Express* [2002] 2 Lloyd's Rep. 88 at 98.

[31] See below, p.362.

[32] See below, pp.372–373, 379, 384; *cf.* p.358.

"intention to defraud".[33] Thus in *Polhill v Walter*[34] an agent purported to accept a bill of exchange on behalf of his principal, knowing that he had no authority to do so but believing that his principal would ratify. He was held liable in deceit. This case should be contrasted with *Angus v Clifford*.[35] The directors of a company which had bought a gold mine issued a prospectus containing extracts from an engineer's report said to have been "prepared for the directors". It had in fact been prepared for the sellers of the mine. The directors knew this, but were held not liable for fraud as they did not at the time of issuing the prospectus appreciate the importance of the words "prepared for the directors". Thus it seems that a person is not guilty of fraud if he knows that his statement is false but does not appreciate its materiality.

Responsibility for a statement may be divided between principal and agent or between several agents of the same principal. If an agent within the scope of his authority makes a statement which he knows to be false, the principal is liable for the fraud of the agent[36]; the agent is also liable for his own fraud.[37] If the agent who made the statement did not know that it was false, but the principal, or another agent did know this, the principal is in general not liable for fraud.[38] The *mens rea* required for fraud cannot be established by adding together the states of mind of several persons, each of whom is innocent. But if the principal or the second agent stood by, knowing that the representation was being made and that it was false, the principal would be guilty of fraud or liable for the fraud of the second agent.[39] In such a case the principal or second agent has *mens rea*, though he made no representation. The same rule should apply where the representation is innocently made by the principal, and the agent, acting within his authority, stands by knowing that the representation is going to be made and that it is false.

2. Negligence at Common Law

(1) Duty of care

A misrepresentation is negligent if it is made carelessly and in breach of a duty owed by the representor to the representee to take reasonable care that the representation is accurate. It used to be thought that such a duty could arise only where the relationship between representor and representee arose out of a pre-existing contract between them, or where it was "fiduciary".[40] But this narrow view was rejected in *Hedley Byrne & Co*

---

[33] *Standard Chartered Bank v Pakistan National Shipping Corp* [1995] 2 Lloyd's Rep. 365 at 375; see further [1998] 1 Lloyd's Rep. 656; *Standard Chartered Bank v Pakistan National Shipping Co (No.2)* [2000] 1 Lloyd's Rep. 218 at 221, 224 (reversed on another point [2002] UKHL 43, [2003] 1 All E.R. 173); *KCB Bank v Industrial Steels (UK) Ltd* [2001] 1 Lloyd's Rep. 370 at 374. "Dishonesty" seems to be used to mean no more than "intention to deceive" in *Armitage v Nurse* [1998] Ch. 241 at 251.

[34] (1832) 3 B. & Ad. 114; *cf. Foster v Charles* (1830) 6 Bing. 396; *Edgington v Fitzmaurice* (1885) 29 Ch.D. 459 at 481; *Watts v Spence* [1976] Ch. 165 at 176 (where fraud was not alleged).

[35] [1891] 2 Ch. 449.

[36] *S. Pearson & Son Ltd v Dublin Corporation* [1907] A.C. 351; *Briess v Woolley* [1954] A.C. 333; *cf. Rignal Developments Ltd v Halil* [1988] Ch. 190 at 198.

[37] *Standard Chartered Bank v Pakistan National Shipping Co* [2002] UKHL 43, [2003] 1 All E.R. 173; *Niru Battery Manufacturing Co v Milestone Trading Ltd* [2002] EWHC 1425; [2002] 2 All E.R. (Comm) 701 at [53].

[38] *Cornfoot v Fowke* (1840) 6 M. & W. 358; *Gordon Hill Trust Ltd v Segall* [1941] 2 All E.R. 379; *Armstrong v Strain* [1952] 1 K.B. 232; Devlin, 53 L.Q.R. 344; Gower, 15 M.L.R. 232. For liability in negligence, see below.

[39] *London County Freehold v Berkeley Property Co Ltd* [1936] 2 All E.R. 1039; *The Siboen and the Sibotre* [1976] 1 Lloyd's Rep. 293 at 321.

[40] *Nocton v Ashburton* [1914] A.C. 932.

Ltd v Heller & Partners Ltd.[41] The claimants in that case suffered loss as a result of having given credit to a firm called Easipower Ltd, in reliance on a reference carelessly given by Easipower's bank, who knew of the purpose for which the reference was required. The actual decision was that the bank was not liable because the reference had been given "without responsibility".[42] But the House of Lords made it clear that, had there been no such disclaimer, the bank would have owed to the claimants a duty to take reasonable care in the making of the statements contained in the reference.

(2) Relationships giving rise to the duty

(a) SPECIAL RELATIONSHIPS. A duty of the kind just described can arise at common law if there is a "special relationship" between the parties. The crucial question, therefore, is when such a relationship will come into existence; and two at first sight divergent approaches to this question are taken by the authorities.

(i) *The "threefold test"*. Under this test, there is a "special relationship" when three conditions are satisfied: it must be reasonably foreseeable by the representor that the representee will rely on the statement; there must be sufficient "proximity" between the parties; and it must be just and reasonable for the law to impose the duty.[43] It is obvious that these requirements are closely related, so much so that it has been said that they are "at least in most cases, merely facets of the same thing".[44] In the context of mis-representation, foreseeable reliance by the representee on the representor's statement or advice is the single most important requirement of the special relationship.[45] But while it is a necessary condition of liability in tort for misrepresentation inducing a contract,[46] it is not a sufficient one. Thus a purely social relationship will not normally suffice to give rise to a duty, so that no action normally lies at common law where a person suffers loss as a result of acting on careless friendly advice,[47] even if it is given by a professional person.[48] In such a case, it would not normally be just and reasonable to impose a duty. This would also be true where the representor had expressly warned the representee not to rely on his representation but to seek independent advice.[49]

On the other hand, there was a "special relationship" between the claimants and the bank in *Hedley Byrne*'s case,[50] and it is clear from dicta in that case, from earlier

---

[41] [1964] A.C. 465; *cf. White v Jones* [1995] 2 A.C. 207 at 274; Stevens, 27 M.L.R. 121; Payne, 6 Univ. of W. Australia L. Rev. 467; Honoré, 8 J.S.P.T.L. 284; Craig, 92 L.Q.R. 213.

[42] Such a provision would now be subject to the requirement of reasonableness by virtue of Unfair Contract Terms Act 1977, ss.2(1) and 13(1): see *Smith v Eric S Bush* [1990] 1 A.C. 831 at 875–876; *cf. McCullagh v Lane Fox & Partners Ltd* [1996] 1 E.G.L.R. 35; above, p.248. The Unfair Terms in Consumer Contracts Regulations 1999 would not have applied to the disclaimer in the *Hedley Byrne* case as these Regulations apply only to *contract terms* in *consumer* cases (above, p.267).

[43] *Smith v Eric S Bush* [1990] 1 A.C. 831 at 865; *Al Saudi Banque v Clark Pixley* [1990] Ch. 313; *Caparo Industries plc v Dickman* [1990] 2 A.C. 605 at 617–618; *cf. Yuen Kun Yeu v Attorney-General of Hong Kong* [1988] A.C. 175; *Davies v Radcliffe* [1990] 1 W.L.R. 821; *T v Surrey CC* [1994] 4 All E.R. 577; *Law Society v KPMG Peat Marwick* [2000] 1 W.L.R. 1921.

[44] *Caparo Industries plc v Dickman* [1900] 2 A.C. 605 at 632.

[45] *Murphy v Brentwood D C* [1991] 1 A.C. 398 at 480, 486–487.

[46] Though not of liability for negligence arising in other ways: see *White v Jones* [1995] 2 A.C. 207 at 268, 275; *Spring v Guardian Royal Insurance plc* [1995] 2 A.C. 296 at 344.

[47] [1964] A.C. 465 at 482; see *ibid.* p.531 for possible exceptions. In *Chaudhry v Prabakhar* [1989] 1 W.L.R. 29 (above, p.144) the existence of a duty was conceded; this concession was approved by two members of the Court, who, however, also recognised (at 36 and 34) that advice given in "family, domestic or social relationships" would not normally be actionable.

[48] *Mutual Life and Citizens' Assurance Co Ltd v Evatt* [1971] A.C. 793 at 806.

[49] *Hemmens v Wilson Browne* [1993] 4 All E.R. 826 at 839. But such a warning would not exclude liability for fraud: see above, p.339.

[50] [1964] A.C. 465 at 494, 502, 538, 539.

decisions which were overruled[51] or rehabilitated[52] by it, and from later cases, that a duty of care will often arise where the representor makes the representation while acting in some professional capacity. If he makes the representation to his own client, his duty of care with respect to its accuracy will generally be imposed by his contract with that client,[53] though a duty of care imposed by the general law (and giving rise to liability in tort) may exist side by side with such a contractual duty.[54] The more important point to be made here is that such a duty of care may also arise under the law of tort even though there is *no* contract between representor and representee. Thus the duty may be owed by accountants,[55] surveyors and valuers[56] even to persons other than their immediate clients who rely on their statements, where the conditions (stated above) which give rise to a duty of care are satisfied. A duty is more likely to arise in cases of this kind where the statement was made for the purpose of the transaction which it induced than where it was not so made. There was accordingly sufficient proximity between a surveyor and the prospective purchaser of a house, where the surveyor had been commissioned by a building society to report on the value of that house, knowing that his report would be passed on to the purchaser, where it was so passed on, and the house was bought in reliance on it.[57] Similarly, an accountant's report on the financial state of a company can give rise to liability to an intending lender to, or investor in, the company if it was made for the purpose of providing such a person with the information on which his decision whether to make the loan or investment is likely to be, and is in fact, based.[58] But the position is different where auditors are appointed by a company to enable the company to perform its statutory obligation to produce audited annual accounts. In such a case there is no sufficient proximity between those auditors and prospective lenders to, or investors in, the company, or even between the auditors and shareholders in the company

---

[51] *Candler v Crane, Christmas & Co* [1951] 2 K.B. 164.

[52] *Cann v Willson* (1883) 39 Ch.D. 39.

[53] See below, p.840.

[54] *cf. Henderson v Merrett Syndicates Ltd* [1995] 2 A.C. 145; and see below, pp.608, 986. This case was one of liability, not for negligent *statements*, but for negligently rendered *services*: below, p.348.

[55] See the overruling in *Hedley Byrne*'s case, above, of *Candler v Crane, Christmas & Co*, above.

[56] *Yianni v Edwin Evans & Son* [1982] Q.B. 438; *Smith v Eric S Bush* [1990] 1 A.C. 831; above, pp.339–340. For the personal liability of an employee of a firm of surveyors, see *Merrett v Babb* [2001] EWCA Civ 214; [2001] Q.B. 1174. For the liability in negligence of architects and valuers issuing certificates on which their clients pay, see *Sutcliffe v Thackrah* [1974] A.C. 727; *Campbell v Edwards* [1976] 1 W.L.R. 403; *Arenson v Arenson* [1977] A.C. 405. For similar liability of auditors, *cf. Burgess v Purchase & Sons Ltd* [1983] Ch. 216.

[57] *e.g. Yianni v Edwin Evans and Sons* [1982] Q.B. 438; *Davies v Parry* (1988) 20 H.L.R. 452; *Roberts v J Hampson & Co* [1990] 1 W.L.R. 94; *Smith v Eric S Bush* [1990] 1 A.C. 831, (where *Yianni*'s case is cited with approval at 852–853, 864, 875); contrast *Beaumont v Humberts* [1990] 2 E.G.L.R. 166.

[58] See n.55, above, *J E B Fasterners Ltd v Marks Bloom & Co* [1981] 3 All E.R. 583 (affirmed [1983] 1 All E.R. 583 on other grounds) is now explicable (if at all) only on the ground stated at p.342, above; *cf. J Jarvis & Sons Ltd v Castle Wharf Developments Ltd* [2001] EWCA Civ 19, [2001] Lloyd's P.N. 308 at [53] (duty owed by member of property developer's professional team to building contractor, but claim failed for want of reliance); *Caparo Industries plc v Dickman* [1990] 2 A.C. 605, 625, 647–648; *Morgan Crucible Co plc v Hill Samuel Bank Ltd* [1991] 1 All E.R. 148; *Barings plc v Coopers & Lybrand* [1997] 1 B.C.L.C. 427; *Bank of Credit and Commerce International (Overseas) Ltd v Price Waterhouse, The Times*, March 4, 1998; *Law Society v KPMG Peat Marwick* [2000] 1 W.L.R. 1921: auditors engaged by a firm of solicitors held to owe a duty of care to the Law Society (as trustee of its compensation fund) in respect of reports by statute to be sent to the Society and to be in breach of that duty in consequence of their failure to draw attention to the solicitors' failure to comply with the Society's account rules. Contrast *James McNaughton Paper Group v Hicks Anderson & Co* [1991] 1 All E.R. 134, where the circumstances in which the report was prepared negatived the duty; *Anthony v Wright* [1996] 1 B.C.L.C. 238 (auditor owing no such duty to a person who *had* invested money in the company).

who, in reliance on the accounts, buy additional shares.[59] The reason why no duty is owed to these persons is that the audited accounts are produced simply for the purpose of satisfying the statutory obligation described above, and not to induce the transactions in question. The same principle may limit the scope of the duty to the particular transaction for the purpose of which the statement was made. Thus where auditors employed by a company produced accounts which, as they knew, were to determine the price at which the claimants were to acquire a substantial shareholding in the company, the auditors were held to owe a duty to the claimants in respect of that purchase but not in respect of loans of money made to the company nor in respect of a further purchase of shares in the company made by the claimants over three years after the original transaction.[60]

(ii) *"Assumption of responsibility"*. In many of the relationships described above, the representor can be said to have voluntarily assumed responsibility, in the sense of having undertaken (though not contracted) to exercise care with regard to the accuracy of the representation. This factor of assumption of responsibility was referred to in *Hedley Byrne's* case[61] and is mentioned in a number of later cases as an ingredient of liability for negligent misrepresentation at common law.[62] Such references to assumption of responsibility are found also in cases in which liability in tort for economic loss was alleged to have arisen, not from negligent misrepresentation inducing the representee to enter into a contract, but in some other way: *e.g.* from the negligent performance of services,[63] or from negligently making a false statement *about* (rather than *to*) the person who suffers loss in consequence of its falsity.[64] Cases of this kind have been said to fall "within the extended *Hedley Byrne* principle",[65] and in them "assumption of responsibility" is both a necessary,[66] and (it seems) normally[67] a sufficient, condition of liability, displacing the

---

[59] *e.g. Al Saudi Banque v Clark Pixley* [1990] Ch. 313; *Caparo Industries plc v Dickman* [1990] 2 A.C. 605; Flemming, 106 L.Q.R. 349; *Esanda Finance Corp Ltd v Peat Marwick Hungerford (Reg)* [2000] Lloyd's P.N. 684 (High Court of Australia); *cf. Huxford v Stoy Hayward & Co* (1989) 5 B.C.C. 421 (auditors called in by company's bank held to owe no duty to shareholders); *The Morning Watch* [1990] 1 Lloyd's Rep. 547 (no duty owed to buyer of a yacht in respect of certificate issued by Lloyd's); *Berg Sons & Co Ltd v Adams* [1993] B.C.L.C. 1045; *The Sundancer* [1994] 1 Lloyd's Rep. 183; *Peach Publishing Ltd v Slater & Co* [1997] C.L.Y. 3 (purchaser advised by own solicitors and accountants); *cf. Abbott v Strong, The Times*, July 9, 1998 (no duty owed in respect of statements not known by plaintiff to have been made by defendant). Contrast *Law Society v KPMG Peat Marwick*, above, n.58, where the duty was owed to, and the loss suffered by, the very body to which the defendants' report was, by the statute, required to be made.

[60] *Galoo Ltd v Bright Grahame Murray* [1994] 1 W.L.R. 1360. *cf.*, in relation to false statements in a company prospectus, *Al Nabib Investments (Jersey) Ltd v Longcroft* [1990] 1 W.L.R. 1390; contrast *Possfund Custodian Trustees Ltd v Diamond* [1996] 1 W.L.R. 1351, where it was arguable such statements were intended to induce "after-market" purchases. These cases concerned common law liability, as opposed to liability under the statutory provisions now contained in Financial Services and Markets Act 2000, ss.90 and 86.

[61] [1964] A.C. 494 at 529. The test of such assumption of responsibility is objective: *Electra Private Equity Partners v KPMG Peat Marwick* [1999] Lloyd's Rep. P.N. 670.

[62] *Yuen Kun-yeu v Attorney-General of Hong Kong* [1988] A.C. 175 at 196; *Simaan General Contracting Co v Pilkington Glass Ltd (No.2)* [1988] Q.B. 758 at 784; *Chaudhry v Prabakhar* [1989] 1 W.L.R. 29 at 34; *Shearson Lehman Hutton Inc v Maclaine Watson & Co Ltd* [1989] 2 Lloyd's Rep. 570, 636; *First National Commercial Bank v Loxleys, The Times*, November 14, 1996.

[63] *Henderson v Merrett Syndicates Ltd* [1995] 2 A.C. 145 at 180, 181, 205; *White v Jones* [1995] 2 A.C. 207 at 256, 268–269; *cf. ibid.* 273 ("assumption of responsibility *for the task*"). The former immunity of advocates from liability for negligence in the conduct of litigation no longer exists: see *Arthur J S Hall & Co v Simons* [2002] 1 A.C. 615.

[64] *Spring v Guardian Insurance plc* [1995] 2 A.C. 296 at 324.

[65] *Williams v Natural Life Health Foods Ltd* [1998] 1 W.L.R. 830 at 835.

[66] *Williams v Natural Life Health Foods Ltd*, above.

[67] *i.e.* unless displaced by contractual arrangements between the parties: below p.608. *cf. Sumitomo Bank Ltd v Banque Bruxelles Lambert SA* [1997] 1 Lloyd's Rep. 487, treating "assumption of responsibility" as *one* basis of liability.

"threefold" test, so that this test need not be satisfied where there is such an assumption.[68] But opinion is divided as to the significance of "assumption of responsibility" in cases of the kind with which we are here concerned, that is, in cases of liability for alleged negligent misrepresentation inducing contracts and so causing loss to the representee.

One view is that the reference to such an assumption in *Hedley Byrne's*[69] case and in later cases[70] makes it an essential ingredient of liability for negligent misrepresentation[71]; but this view makes it hard to explain the fact that the "threefold test" (which is said to be *displaced* where there is an assumption of responsibility)[72] has been applied and developed precisely in a number of such cases.[73] A second view is that references to assumption of responsibility in some of the misrepresentation cases are merely descriptive of the relationships which have been held to give rise to the duty of care in them. Some of the misrepresentation cases can be reconciled with the first of these views only by a process of *ex post facto* rationalisation[74]; and it is submitted that the weight of authority favours the second view.[75] It should be added that, in a significant number of cases, the two views would lead to the same result[76] and can be regarded as alternative ways of reaching it: for example, it would be hard to establish that the representor had assumed responsibility where it would not be just and reasonable (within the "threefold test") to impose liability on him.[77]

(b) PROFESSIONAL SKILL. One feature of the relationships discussed above, in which the representor was held to owe a duty of care, was that he made the statement in the exercise of some professional skill. The absence of this factor was held to negative liability in *Mutual Life and Citizen's Insurance Co Ltd v Evatt*,[78] where a company carelessly gave misleading information about an associated company to a prospective investor in the latter company. As a result the investor suffered loss, but the majority of the Privy Council held that the first company was not liable in negligence as it was not and did not purport to be engaged in the business of giving skilled advice on investments.[79] The majority regarded this as an essential ingredient of liability[80]; but the

---

[68] *Henderson v Merrett Syndicates Ltd* [1995] 2 A.C. 145 at 181; *Williams v Natural Life Health Foods* [1998] 2 All E.R. 577 at 581.

[69] See above, n.61.

[70] See above, n.62.

[71] *e.g. McCullagh v Lane Fox & Partners Ltd* [1996] 1 E.G.L.R. 35 at 41, *per* Hobhouse L.J. relying on *Henderson v Merrett Syndicates Ltd* [1995] 2 A.C. 145 (though that was not a case of negligent misrepresentation).

[72] See above, at n.68.

[73] See above, p.346 n.43.

[74] *e.g. Anderson & Son Ltd v Rhodes (Liverpool) Ltd* [1967] 2 All E.R. 850; *Esso Petroleum Co Ltd v Mardon* [1976] Q.B. 801.

[75] *Smith v Eric S Bush* [1990] 1 A.C. 831 at 862, 871 and (*semble*); *Caparo Industries plc v Dickman* [1990] 2 A.C. 605 at 623, 628, 637; *The Morning Watch* [1990] 1 Lloyd's Rep. 547; *John W Pryke v Gibbs Hartley Cooper Ltd* [1991] 1 Lloyd's Rep. 602 at 616; *Reid v Rush and Tompkins Group plc* [1990] 1 W.L.R. 212 leaves the point open.

[76] See *Bank of Credit and Commerce International Ltd v Price Waterhouse*, 1998 P.N.L.R. 564; *cf. Weldon v GRE Linked Life Assurance Ltd* [2000] 2 All E.R. (Comm) 914 at 917, stating both tests; and (in another context) *Parkinson v St James & Seacroft University Hospital NHS Trust* [2001] EWCA Civ 530; [2002] Q.B. 266 at [17].

[77] *cf. The Nicholas H* [1996] A.C. 211 at 241–242, where Lord Steyn, having held that it was not just and reasonable to impose a duty of care, went on to say that the facts could not be "forced into even the most expansive view of the doctrine of voluntary assumption of responsibility".

[78] [1971] A.C. 793; A.L.G., 87 L.Q.R. 147; Rickford, 34 M.L.R. 328. The case is viewed with some scepticism in *Spring v Guardian Insurance plc* [1995] 2 A.C. 296 at 320.

[79] [1971] A.C. 793 at 809.

[80] *ibid.* at 805, 809.

prevailing view is that, so long as other conditions of liability are satisfied, the representor may be liable even though he was not in the business of giving advice[81] and even though the representee did not seek his advice (but only asked for information).[82] Thus in *Anderson & Sons Ltd v Rhodes (Liverpool) Ltd*[83] a commission agent made a representation to a seller of potatoes about the solvency of his principal, the buyer. It was held that the agent owed a duty of care to the seller.

(c) COMMERCIAL RELATIONSHIPS. A duty of care may exist at common law even in a purely commercial relationship, such as that of buyer and seller or landlord and tenant. For example, in *Esso Petroleum Co Ltd v Mardon*[84] a tenant was induced to take a lease of a petrol station from an oil company by a statement made by an experienced salesman on the company's behalf, as to the potential future turnover of the premises. As the tenant had relied on the salesman's superior knowledge and experience, it was held that the company was under a duty of care at common law. On the other hand there are many commercial relationships in which each party consciously relies on his own skill or judgment[85] or where it is reasonable for the representor to assume that the representee will be advised by his own experts.[86] In such cases there would be no duty of care at common law; though, even in the absence of a "special relationship", there can be liability in damages under the Misrepresentation Act.[87]

(3) Effects of negligence on other rules

The main importance of *Hedley Byrne*'s case lies in its recognition of liability in damages in tort for negligent misrepresentation; but it may also have a further, less easily predictable, impact on the law of misrepresentation. Before the decision, there was, for most purposes, no separate legal category of negligent misrepresentation. This state of affairs had an important influence on the development of the law relating to the effect of misrepresentation on contract. Many of the rules on this topic provided that one result should follow if the representation was fraudulent, and another if it was innocent.[88] For these purposes, "innocent" simply meant "not fraudulent".[89] The development which began with the *Hedley Byrne* case makes it necessary to accommodate

---

[81] The views of the minority in *Evatt's* case were preferred to those of the majority by Ormrod L.J. in *Esso Petroleum Co Ltd v Mardon* [1976] Q.B. 801 at 827 and by Lord Denning M.R. (dissenting) and Shaw L.J. in *Howard Marine & Dredging Co Ltd v A. Ogden & Sons (Excavations) Ltd* [1978] Q.B. 574 at 591, 600. The point was left open in *Caparo Industries plc v Dickman* [1990] 2 A.C. 605 at 637. The need for a professional relationship was emphasised in *Nitrigin Eirann Teoranta v Inco Alloys Inc* [1992] 1 W.L.R. 498 at 503 (not a case of misrepresentation.)

[82] *Box v Midland Bank Ltd* [1979] 2 Lloyd's Rep. 391 (reversed as to costs only [1981] 1 Lloyd's Rep. 434). Contrast *Royal Bank Trust Co (Trinidad) v John Robert Pampellone* [1987] 1 Lloyd's Rep. 218; *Civic Structures v Clark Quinney & Co* [1991] 2 E.G.L.R. 165: no liability for merely *passing on* information.

[83] [1967] 2 All E.R. 850; Dias [1967] C.L.J. 155; Dean, 31 M.L.R. 322; contrast *Jones v Still* [1965] N.Z.L.R. 1071; McKenzie, 29 M.L.R. 337.

[84] [1976] Q.B. 801; Gravells, 39 M.L.R. 462; *cf.* dicta in *Hedley Byrne*'s case [1964] A.C. 465 at 486, 514, 528–529; *Gran Gelato Ltd v Richcliff (Group) Ltd* [1992] Ch. 560 (claim against first defendant); *McCullagh v Lane Fox & Partners* [1996] 1 E.G.L.R. 35 at 42.

[85] *Oleificio Zucchi SA v Northern Sales Ltd* [1965] 2 Lloyd's Rep. 496 at 519; *cf. Jones v Still* [1965] N.Z.L.R. 1071; *Amalgamated Metal Trading Ltd v DTI*, The Times, March 31, 1989.

[86] *McInerny v Lloyds Bank Ltd* [1974] 1 Lloyd's Rep. 246.

[87] S.2(1), below; on the facts of *Esso Petroleum Co Ltd v Mardon*, above, n.84, there would now be liability under this provision, as well as at common law.

[88] See above, pp.334, 337, 339, 340; below, pp.364, 372, 373, 378.

[89] *cf.* above, p.340; below, p.357.

negligent misrepresentation within this scheme, and to ask whether, for the purpose of any given rule, negligence is to be treated in the same way as fraud, or in the same way as innocence, or in some third way. There is as yet little guidance as to how questions of this kind are going to be answered. The only thing that is certain is that a negligent misrepresentation resembles a fraudulent one in giving rise to a claim for damages.

3. Misrepresentation Act 1967, s.2(1)

This subsection creates a statutory liability for misrepresentation. It provides: "Where a person has entered into a contract after a misrepresentation has been made to him by another party thereto and as a result thereof he has suffered loss, then, if the person making the misrepresentation would be liable to damages in respect thereof had the misrepresentation been made fraudulently, that person shall be so liable notwithstanding that the misrepresentation was not made fraudulently, unless he proves that he had reasonable ground to believe and did believe up to the time the contract was made that the facts represented were true".

(1) Scope of the subsection

The statutory liability differs from common law liability for negligent misrepresentation in two ways.

First, it is not necessary under the subsection to ask whether there was a "special relationship", giving rise to a duty of care, between the parties[90]: it is enough if the representation is made by one contracting party to the other. For this reason, it has been said that the subsection imposes an "absolute obligation"[91]; but these words cannot be taken to refer to the *standard* of liability. This is far from "absolute", for under the concluding words of s.2(1), the representor can escape liability by proving that his belief in the truth of the facts stated was not formed carelessly. Liability under the subsection is in this respect "essentially founded on negligence".[92]

Secondly, the subsection reverses the burden of proof. At common law, the representee must prove negligence, while under the subsection the representor is liable "unless he proves that he had reasonable ground to believe and did believe up to the time the contract was made that the facts represented were true". The difficulty of discharging this burden is illustrated by a case in which, during negotiations for the hire of barges, the owner's agent mis-stated their deadweight capacity, relying on an erroneous statement in Lloyd's Register. It was held that the burden had not been discharged since the owner could have discovered the true state of affairs by looking at documents in his possession.[93] But where the representator had no such means of discovering the truth, the burden would probably be discharged if he could show that he was himself the victim of an earlier fraud and that he had innocently repeated a representation previously made

---

[90] *Howard Marine & Dredging Co Ltd v A Ogden & Sons (Excavations) Ltd* [1978] Q.B. 574 at 596; Sills, 96 L.Q.R. 15; Sealy [1978] C.L.J. 229; *Cemp Properties (UK) v Dentsply Research & Developments Corp* [1991] 2 E.G.L.R. 197.

[91] *The Skopas* [1983] 1 W.L.R. 857 at 861; *cf.* the *Howard Marine* case, above, at p.647.

[92] *Gran Gelato Ltd v Richcliff Group Ltd* [1992] Ch. 560 at 573; *cf. South Australia Asset Management Corp v York Montague Ltd* [1997] A.C. 191 at 216; *HIH Casualty & General Insurance v Chase Manhattan Bank* [2001] EWCA Civ 1250; [2001] 2 Lloyd's Rep. 483, at [117]; but see *HIH Casualty & General Insurance v New Hampshire Insurance Corp* [2001] EWCA Civ 735; [2001] 2 All E.R. (Comm) 39 at [137] (negligence said not to be part of the cause of action, but lack of negligence a defence).

[93] *Howard Marine* case, above; *cf. Walker v Boyle* [1982] 1 W.L.R. 495 at 509.

to him,[94] or that he had reasonably relied on an expert's report on the point in question,[95] or that he had made due enquiries before making the statement.[96] The subsection requires him to prove only that he had reasonable ground for his belief, so that his actual means of knowledge are relevant: accordingly, a layman may succeed in discharging the burden where an expert would fail.

Under the subsection, a contracting party can be held liable for a representation made on his behalf by his agent.[97] But the agent himself is not liable under the subsection,[98] though he will be liable in negligence at common law if the representee can establish that there was a "special relationship" between himself and the agent, and that the agent was in breach of the resulting duty of care; but the agent would not be so liable where the only special relationship was between his *principal* and the representee.[99] There are two further situations in which the subsection does not apply, though there may be liability in negligence at common law: namely, where (as in *Hedley Byrne's*[1] case) the representation is made by a stranger to the contract; and where the negotiations between representor and representee do not reach the stage of a concluded contract.

(2) The fiction of fraud

S.2(1) has the effect of imposing liability in damages for careless misrepresentation; but instead of simply providing that the representor shall be liable in damages[2] it says that he shall be so liable if he "would be liable to damages . . . had the misrepresentation been made fraudulently". This fiction of fraud seems to be quite unnecessary; and it may lead the courts to extend to cases within s.2(1) rules which have been developed in the context of fraudulent misrepresentation and which are wholly inappropriate where there is no actual fraud.[3] In the Parliamentary debates on the Act, Lord Reid suggested that the effect of the fiction might be to apply to the new cause of action the extended period of limitation which applies where an action is "based upon"[4] fraud. But he added that this result would be "rather unreasonable"[5] and a more recent dictum indicates that the fiction of fraud would not be applied to this situation.[6] Further support for the view that the fiction is not to be literally applied is provided by a case in which the Court of Appeal has held[7] that a principal may be liable under the subsection for his agent's misrepresentation even though there is no such shared responsibility for the statement as is required to make the principal liable in cases of fraud.[8] It is to be hoped that the courts

---

[94] As in *Oscar Chess Ltd v Williams* [1957] 1 W.L.R. 370; below, p.354; *cf. Humming Bird Motors v Hobbs* [1986] R.T.R. 276 below, p.356.

[95] *Cooper v Tamms* [1988] 1 E.G.L.R. 257.

[96] *William Sindall plc v Cambridgeshire CC* [1994] 1 W.L.R. 1016.

[97] *Gosling v Anderson* (1972) 223 E.G. 1743; *Howard Marine* case, above.

[98] *The Skopas* [1983] 1 W.L.R. 857; Owen [1984] C.L.J. 27.

[99] *Williams v Natural Life Health Foods Ltd* [1998] 1 W.L.R. 835; *J Jarvis & Sons Ltd v Castle Wharf Development Ltd* [2001] EWCA Civ 19; [2001] Lloyd's Rep. P.N. 308 (where the claim failed for want of reliance by the representee).

[1] See above, p.345; *Kleinwort Benson Ltd v Malaysian Mining Corp* [1989] 1 W.L.R. 379 at 386.

[2] *cf.* Financial Services and Markets Act 2000, s.90 ("is liable to pay compensation").

[3] See *Royscot Trust Ltd v Rogerson* [1991] 2 Q.B. 297 (below, p.362), where the court seems to have viewed such a result with equanimity.

[4] See now Limitation Act 1980, s.32(1).

[5] 274 H.L. 936.

[6] *Garden Neptune Shipping Ltd v Occidental Worldwide Investment Corp* [1990] 1 Lloyd's Rep. 330 at 335; *cf.* (in another context) *Mander v Evans* [2001] 1 W.L.R. 2378.

[7] *Gosling v Anderson* (1972) 223 E.G. 1743.

[8] See above, p.345.

will similarly reject certain other consequences[9] which could be deduced from the fiction of fraud.

(3) Effect of affirmation

The right to *rescind* a contract for misrepresentation can be lost by affirmation[10]; but affirmation does not deprive the representee of his right to damages under s.2(1). Such damages can therefore in principle be recovered if, after having entered into the contract, the representee discovers the truth and nevertheless performs the contract.[11] Of course the right to damages may be limited in such cases: *e.g.* if the matter to which the misrepresentation relates was so serious that the representee's performance with knowledge of the truth amounts to failure by him to mitigate his loss.[12]

4. Contractual Statements

So far, in this Section, we have assumed that the misrepresentation induces the representee to enter into the contract, but that it has not become a term of the contract or otherwise acquired contractual force. If the misrepresentation does have contractual force, the representee is entitled to recover damages for breach of contract. He may also be entitled to rescind the contract for breach or for misrepresentation. The relation between these various rights will be considered below[13]; our only concern here is with the right to damages. This differs in two ways from the rights to damages previously considered in this Section: it can arise without fraud or negligence, and it is governed by different rules as to assessment of damages and remoteness.[14] It also differs in a number of ways from the power of the court to award damages in lieu of rescission, which will be considered below.[15] That power is discretionary, while damages for breach of contract can be recovered as of right; a representee cannot rescind for misrepresentation *and* claim damages in lieu of rescission, while (if the misrepresentation has become a term of the contract) he may be able to rescind and claim damages for breach of contract[16]; a party who once had the right to rescind, but has lost it, may not be able to recover damages in lieu of rescission,[17] though he can clearly recover damages for breach of contract; and the two causes of action are, once again, governed by different rules as to assessment of damages and remoteness.

---

[9] *e.g.* the rule that a fraudulent statement need not be material (above, p.311), the rule in *S Pearson Ltd v Dublin Corp* [1907] A.C. 351 (above, p.339), and the rule that a person cannot exclude liability for his own fraud (above, p.242): see the *Garden Neptune* case, above, n.96. On the other hand the rule that a representation as to a third person's credit must be in writing to give rise to liability under Statute of Frauds Amendment Act 1828, s.6 applies only to *fraudulent* misrepresentation: *Banbury v Bank of Montreal* [1918] A.C. 626; and in *The Pacific Colocotronis* [1984] Q.B. 713 at 718–719 it seems to have been thought that the fiction of fraud applied in this context, for it was "common ground" that the requirement of writing equally applied for the purpose of an action under Misrepresentation Act 1967, s.2(1). And see below, p.335 as to damages under s.2(1).

[10] See below, p.383.

[11] *Production Technology Consultants v Barlett* [1986] 1 E.G.L.R. 82: *cf.* at common law *Arnison v Smith* (1889) 41 Ch.D. 348 (where, however, the claimants did not have full knowledge of their right to rescind and so could not be said to have affirmed).

[12] See below, p.980.

[13] See below, pp.359–361, 375–376.

[14] See below, pp.359–363.

[15] See below, pp.357–359.

[16] See below, p.375.

[17] See below, p.359.

For all these reasons it is still necessary to distinguish between contractual statements and "mere" representations inducing a contract,[18] though the provisions of the Misrepresentation Act as to damages will probably reduce the practical importance of the distinction. A contractual statement may either be a term of the main contract or a collateral contract.

(1) Term of main contract

Where a contract is in writing, a descriptive statement may actually be made in the contractual document. Such a statement will clearly be a contractual term if it is said to be the basis of the contract.[19] Subject to such express provisions, the question whether the statement is a term or a mere representation is one of construction.[20] The same is true where the statement is contained in a written offer, the acceptance of which concludes the contract.[21] Where a descriptive statement is contained in a contractual document it may[22] be a term even though it did not induce the party complaining of its untruth to enter into the contract,[23] and, indeed, even though he was at the time of contracting unaware of its existence.[24]

Often a statement inducing a contract will not be set out in the contractual document, but will be made during the negotiations leading up to the contract. The question whether such a statement was a mere representation or a term of the contract used to be treated as one of fact and left to the jury.[25] Cases of this kind are no longer tried by jury, but the orthodox view is that the question remains one of fact: with what intention was the statement made?[26] This intention would, in general, be objectively ascertained.[27] It is impossible to lay down any strict rules for determining when such an intention can be said to exist. But a number of guiding principles can be deduced from the cases.

(a) VERIFICATION. A statement is unlikely to be a term of the contract if the person making it expressly asks the other party to verify its truth. In *Ecay v Godfrey*[28] the seller of a boat said that it was sound but advised the buyer to have it surveyed. This advice negatived any intention to warrant the soundness of the boat. The same principle applies where the circumstances are such that the person to whom the statement was made would normally be expected to verify it. This is the reason traditionally given for the view that statements made by sellers of houses in pre-contract negotiations do not normally have contractual force: the buyer is expected to rely on a survey, commissioned by himself or his building society, for information with regard to the state of the premises.[29] It has indeed been held that, if the buyer relies on a survey negligently conducted by a surveyor commissioned by the building society he may have a right of action in tort against that surveyor, in spite of the fact that he might have discovered the

---

[18] Atiyah, 1971 Alberta L.Rev. 347, and *Essays in Contract* 275.

[19] *e.g. London Assurance v Mansel* (1879) 11 Ch.D. 363.

[20] *Behn v Burness* (1863) 1 B. & S. 751 at 754 (statement in charterparty as to position of ship).

[21] *The Larissa* [1983] 2 Lloyd's Rep. 325 at 330.

[22] Though reliance may be relevant in determining whether the statement was intended as a term: see *Harlingdon & Leinster Enterprises Ltd v Christopher Hull Fine Art Ltd* [1991] 1 Q.B. 564.

[23] *ibid.* at 574, 579, 584.

[24] *cf.* above, p.216: the principle of incorporation by signature can here work *in favour* of the signer.

[25] *e.g. Power v Barham* (1836) 4 A. & E. 473; *Miller v Cannon Hill Estates Ltd* [1931] 2 K.B. 113.

[26] *Howard Marine & Dredging Co Ltd v A. Ogden & Son (Excavations) Ltd* [1978] Q.B. 574 at 595.

[27] See above, pp.1, 11.

[28] (1947) 80 Ll.L.R. 286; *cf. Mahon v Ainscough* [1952] 1 All E.R. 337; *Eustace v Kempe-Roberts* [1964] C.L.Y. 3280.

[29] See *Longman v Blount* (1896) 12 T.L.R. 520; *Green v Symons* (1897) 13 T.L.R. 301; *cf. Terence Ltd v Nelson* (1937) 157 L.T. 254. Proposals for modifying this practice are under discussion.

truth by commissioning his own survey.[30] But that does not affect the present point, which is that the buyer normally has no cause of action *in contract* against the seller in respect of statements made by the latter about the condition of the property.

On the other hand, a statement is likely to be a term of the contract if it is intended to prevent the other party from finding out the truth, has this effect, and induces him to contract in reliance on it. This was, for example, said to be the position[31] where a buyer of a horse was about to examine it but was induced to buy without examination by the seller's statement that "You need not look for anything; the horse is perfectly sound. If there was anything the matter with the horse I should tell you". An earlier case,[32] in which a similar statement by a seller was held not to have contractual force, turns on the special facts that the sale was at Tattersall's and that sales there were known by both parties to be without warranty unless the contrary was expressly stated in the catalogue.

(b) IMPORTANCE. A statement is likely to be a term of the contract where its importance is such that, if it had not been made, the representee would not have entered into the contract at all.[33] Such a statement can be a term of the contract even though it conflicts with a previous written statement. Thus in *Couchman v Hill*[34] a heifer was put up for auction under printed conditions of sale which provided that no warranty was given. A bidder asked whether the heifer was in calf, adding that, if she were, he would not bid. He bought the heifer after being assured that she was not in calf, and it was held that this assurance was a term of the contract. On the other hand, in *Oscar Chess Ltd v Williams*,[35] where the defendant sold a car for £280 honestly describing it as a 1948 Morris 10 when it was in fact a 1939 model worth £175. The statement that the car was a 1948 model was held not to be a term of the contract. If in this case, the buyers had known the truth, they might still have bought the car (though for less money)[36] but if the buyer in *Couchman v Hill* had known the truth, he would not have bought at all.

(c) SPECIAL KNOWLEDGE. The question whether a statement is a contractual term or a mere representation may turn on the relative abilities of the parties to ascertain the truth of what was stated.[37] In *Oscar Chess Ltd v Williams* the seller was a private person to whom the car had been previously sold as a 1948 model, with a forged logbook. The main reason why his statement as to the age of the car was not a term of the contract was that he had no special knowledge as to the age of the car, while the buyers were car dealers, and so in at least as good a position as the seller to know whether the statement was true.[38] The case may be contrasted with *Dick Bentley Productions Ltd v Harold Smith (Motors) Ltd*[39] where a dealer sold a Bentley car, representing that it had only done

---

[30] *Smith v Eric S Bush* [1990] 1 A.C. 831; above, p.340.

[31] *Schwawel v Reade* [1913] 2 I.R. 64, HL.

[32] *Hopkins v Tanqueray* (1854) 15 C.B. 130.

[33] *Bannerman v White* (1861) 10 C.B.(N.S.) 844.

[34] [1947] K.B. 554. Alternatively, the statement was said to be a collateral contract: below, p.329; see also *Otto v Bolton* [1936] 2 K.B. 46.

[35] [1957] 1 W.L.R. 370.

[36] cf. *Moore v Khan Ghauri* [1991] 2 E.G.L.R. 9.

[37] cf. *Esso Petroleum Co Ltd v Mardon* [1976] Q.B. 801, where this test was applied to determine the existence of a collateral contract (below, p.356).

[38] cf. *Routledge v McKay* [1954] 1 W.L.R. 615; *Hummingbird Motors v Hobbs* [1986] R.T.R. 276 (below, p.356), where the seller was not a dealer, though he occasionally sold cars; and see *Harrison v Knowles & Foster* [1918] 1 K.B. 608; *The Larissa* [1983] 2 Lloyd's Rep. 325 at 330. Contrast *Beale v Taylor* [1967] 1 W.L.R. 1193; Koh, [1968] C.L.J. 11; this case is hard to reconcile with the *Oscar Chess* case, which was not cited to the court (the seller conducted his own case).

[39] [1965] 1 W.L.R. 623.

20,000 miles since being fitted with a replacement engine, when in fact it had done nearly 100,000 miles since then. He was clearly in a better position than the buyer to know whether the representation was true, and it was held to be a warranty. Salmon L.J. based this conclusion on the orthodox test of contractual intention,[40] while Lord Denning M.R. took the different view, that any inducing representation was *prima facie* a warranty, though the representor could "rebut this inference if he can show that it really was an innocent misrepresentation, in that he was in fact innocent of fault in making it, and that it would not be reasonable for him in the circumstances to be bound by it".[41] But the view that an inducing misrepresentation has contractual force unless the misrepresenter can disprove "fault" is hard to reconcile with cases in which representors have escaped liability for breach of contract without having disproved "fault"; and in some of these the representors were clearly careless.[42] The representor will often be careless where he is in a better position than the representee to know the truth, but *Gilchester Properties Ltd v Gomm*[43] shows that this fact is not, for the present purpose, decisive.[44] In that case, a statement by the vendor of a block of flats as to the rent at which the flats were let was held to have no contractual force, though obviously the vendor was in a better position than the purchaser to know the truth. Of course a representor who is guilty of "fault" may be liable for damages in tort at common law or under the Misrepresentation Act[45]; but such liability may differ in extent from liability for breach of contract.[46]

(d) OPINION. Statements of opinion which are so vague that they cannot be verified are mere puffs and have no legal effect. But a statement which is one of opinion in the sense that it states a fact which is difficult, but not impossible, to verify may be a term of the contract. In *Jendwine v Slade*[47] Lord Kenyon held that statements that two pictures were respectively by Claude Lorrain and Teniers were not warranties: the authenticity of pictures painted "some centuries back" could only be a matter of opinion. But later cases show that this is not an inflexible rule. In *Power v Barham*[48] it was held that a statement that certain pictures were by Canaletto could be a warranty, *Jendwine v Slade* being distinguished on the ground that Canaletto was "not a very old painter".[49] Similarly, in *Leaf v International Galleries*[50] the Court of Appeal indicated that a representation made in 1945 that a picture was a Constable could be a warranty; though the position will be different where the seller of a picture makes an attribution but expressly disclaims expert knowledge.[51] Nor will a statement be a warranty as to a quality if the statement is *expressly* one of opinion or belief. Thus where the seller of a car said that, to the best of his knowledge and belief, the odometer reading was correct,

---

[40] *ibid.* at 629.
[41] *ibid.* at 627–628. Contrast his dissenting judgment in *Howard Marine & Dredging Co Ltd v A Ogden & Son (Excavations) Ltd* [1978] Q.B. 574 at 591, applying the test of whether the statement was "intended to be binding".
[42] *e.g. Redgrave v Hurd* (1881) 20 Ch.D. 1; above, p.340.
[43] [1948] 1 All E.R. 493.
[44] See criticisms in *Heilbut, Symons & Co v Buckleton* [1913] A.C. 30 at 50 of *De Lassalle v Guildford* [1901] 2 K.B. 215 on this point.
[45] See above, pp.343–352.
[46] See below, pp.359–363; the claim in the *Dick Bentley* case was limited to £400.
[47] (1797) 2 Esp. 571; *cf. Gee v Lucas* (1867) 16 L.T. 357.
[48] (1836) 4 A. & E. 473.
[49] *ibid.* at 476. He had died in 1768.
[50] [1950] 2 K.B. 86. *Quaere*, however, whether there was such a warranty; above, p.293, n.63.
[51] *Harlingdon and Leinster Enterprises Ltd v Christopher Hull Fine Art Ltd* [1991] 1 Q.B. 564.

it was held that he had not given a warranty of such correctness, and that he was not liable merely because, unknown to him, the odometer had been tampered with before he had acquired the car.[52]

(2) Collateral contract[53]

It may not be possible for a statement made during the negotiations leading up to the contract to take effect as one of its terms. The contract may be in writing, so that extrinsic evidence cannot be used to add to it, or to vary it[54]; or the statement may be oral and the contract one which the law requires to be in, or evidenced in, writing.[55] In such cases[56] the oral statement may nevertheless be enforceable as a "collateral contract". There are then two contracts between the parties: the main (written) contract and the collateral (oral) contract, both relating to the same subject-matter. Thus in *De Lassalle v Guildford*[57] the intending lessee of a house refused to execute the lease unless the landlord first assured him that the drains were in good order. The landlord gave this assurance, which was not incorporated in the lease. He was nonetheless held liable, when the drains were found to be defective, for breach of a collateral contract. The statement made on behalf of the landlord in *Esso Petroleum Co Ltd v Mardon*,[58] was similarly held to amount to a collateral contract.

A statement can, it seems, take effect as a collateral contract only if two conditions are satisfied. First, it must have been intended to have contractual effect; and secondly there must be some indication that the parties intended it to take effect as a collateral contract and not simply as a term in the main contract. These requirements have already been discussed[59] and it will suffice here to recall the statement of principle by Lord Moulton in *Heilbut, Symons & Co v Buckleton*[60]: "There may be a contract the consideration for which is the making of some other contract. . . . Such collateral contracts, the sole effect of which is to vary or add to the terms of the principal contract, are therefore viewed with suspicion by the law . . . Not only the terms of such contracts but the existence of an *animus contrahendi* on the part of all the parties to them must be clearly shown".[61] It follows that statements made during negotiations leading up to the contract will not amount to a collateral contract if the main contract provides that they are *not* to have this effect.[62] Contractual intention may also be negatived by the fact that there was a

---

[52] *Humming Bird Motors v Hobbs* [1986] R.T.R. 276. Liability in negligence was also excluded; and the seller had not misrepresented his knowledge or belief: *cf.* above, p.331.

[53] Wedderburn [1959] C.L.J. 58.

[54] See above, pp.192, *et seq.*, especially at pp.199–200.

[55] *Angell v Duke* (1875) L.R. 10 Q.B. 174; *Jameson v Kinmell Bay Land Co Ltd* (1931) 47 T.L.R. 593; *Hill v Harris* [1965] 2 Q.B. 601; Law Com. No.164, paras 5.7–5.8; above, pp.179–180.

[56] See *J Evans & Son (Portsmouth) Ltd v Andrew Merzario Ltd* [1976] 1 W.L.R. 1078 at 1083.

[57] [1901] 2 K.B. 215; *cf. Wake v Renault (UK) Ltd, The Times*, August 1, 1996.

[58] [1976] Q.B. 801; above, p.349.

[59] See above, pp.179–180, 199–200.

[60] [1913] A.C. 30 at 47; above, p.162. In *J. Evans & Son (Portsmouth) Ltd v Andrea Merzario Ltd* [1967] W.L.R. 1078 at 1081 Lord Denning M.R. described "much of what was said in that case as entirely out of date"; *cf.* his dissenting judgment in *Howard Marine & Dredging Co Ltd v A Ogden & Sons (Excavations) Ltd* [1978] Q.B. 574 at 590. But, though damages may be recoverable under Misrepresentation Act 1967, s.2 for statements which do not satisfy Lord Moulton's test, that test remains good law so far as *contractual* liability is concerned: *IBA v EMI (Electronics) Ltd* (1980) 14 Build.L.R. 1 (below, p.584).

[61] *cf. Hill v Harris* [1965] 2 Q.B. 601.

[62] *Inntrepeneur Pub Co (GL) v East Crown Ltd* [2000] 2 Lloyd's Rep. 611 at 614 ("entire agreement" clause).

considerable interval of time between the making of the statement alleged to constitute the collateral contract and the conclusion of the main contract.[63]

In one respect a person who relies on a statement as a collateral contract is at first sight in a worse position than one who relies on it as a term of the main contract: since a collateral contract exists apart from the main contract, it must be supported by *separate* consideration. But this requirement would usually be satisfied by entering into the main contract. The only cases in which this analysis could give rise to difficulty are those in which the party relying on the collateral contract was already bound to enter into the main contract; *e.g.* where a lease was executed in performance of an agreement to enter into it.[64] Even in such cases, however, the act of entering into the main contract (*i.e.* the execution of the lease) would constitute consideration for the collateral contract if that act in fact conferred a benefit on the other party.[65]

The question whether evidence of a collateral contract is admissible if it actually *contradicts* the main written contract has been discussed in Chapter 6.[66]

5. Damages in Lieu of Rescission

(1) Misrepresentation Act 1967, s.2(2)

Before the Misrepresentation Act, damages could not be awarded for a wholly innocent misrepresentation (*i.e.* for one that was neither fraudulent nor negligent[67]) if it did not have contractual force.[68] The principal remedy for innocent misrepresentation was rescission, though when a contract was rescinded, the court could make some form of monetary adjustment by granting an "indemnity".[69] This position was unsatisfactory since, in cases of wholly innocent misrepresentation, the entire transaction would have to be set aside (even though the misrepresentation related to a matter of relatively minor importance), if any remedy at all were to be given to the representee. S.2(2) of the Misrepresentation Act partly cures this defect[70] by giving the court a discretionary power to declare the contract subsisting and to award damages in lieu of rescission. It provides: "Where a person has entered into a contract after a misrepresentation has been made to him otherwise than fraudulently, and he would be entitled, by reason of the misrepresentation, to rescind the contract, then, if it is claimed, in any proceedings arising out of the contract, that the contract ought to be or has been rescinded, the court or arbitrator may declare the contract subsisting and award damages in lieu of rescission, if of opinion that it would be equitable to do so, having regard to the nature of the misrepresentation and the loss that would be caused by it if the contract were upheld, as well as to the loss that rescission would cause to the other party".

---

[63] *ibid.*, at 617 (five years).

[64] See the discussion of *Brikom Investments Ltd v Carr* [1979] Q.B. 467, above, p.102.

[65] *Williams v Roffey Bros & Nicholls (Contractors) Ltd* [1991] 1 Q.B. 1; above, p.95.

[66] See above, pp.199, 200.

[67] See above, pp.340, 350.

[68] *Redgrave v Hurd* (1881) 20 Ch.D. 1, where the representor would now almost certainly be liable in damages for negligence at common law, or under Misrepresentation Act 1967, s.2(1): see *Archer v Brown* [1985] Q.B. 401 at 416; *cf.* above, p.340.

[69] See below, pp.366–368.

[70] See *Thomas Witter Ltd v BTP Industries Ltd* [1996] 2 All E.R. 573 at 589: the subsection "comes into play" where there is no right to damages either at common law (because the misrepresentation is not negligent) or under Misrepresentation Act 1967 (because the representor has discharged the burden of proof under s.2(1): above, p.351).

(2) Scope of the subsection

(a) DISCRETIONARY. The power to uphold the contract and to award damages in lieu of rescission is discretionary: neither party has a right to require its exercise. The concluding words of the subsection specify the factors which the court is to consider in deciding whether to exercise the power. It seems that the court can take into account the contents of the representation, and balance the interests of the parties in on the one hand seeking and on the other resisting rescission. Usually the representor will want to resist rescission and a number of factors are likely to affect the exercise of the discretion. On the one hand, the court is likely to uphold the contract (and so leave the representee to his remedy in damages) if the representation related to a relatively minor[71] matter and if the representor was not guilty of fault.[72] On the other hand, the "policing function"[73] of the remedy of rescission may also be taken into account: this was the ground on which the court refused to uphold a contract of reinsurance which had been induced by a broker's material misrepresentation.[74]

(b) IN LIEU OF RESCISSION. Damages under the subsection can be awarded only "in lieu of rescission", so that the representee cannot rescind *and* claim such damages.[75] If he rescinds on account of a wholly innocent misrepresentation[76] which has no con-tractual force,[77] any claim for monetary compensation will continue to be governed by the principles which determine the extent of an indemnity.[78] The misrepresentee can, however, still rescind *and* claim damages for fraud, since fraudulent misrepresentation is expressly excepted from the subsection; and there is nothing in the subsection to prevent him from rescinding *and* claiming damages for negligence at common law or under s.2(1).[79] The suggestion that the victim of an "innocent" misrepresentation can now rescind and claim damages under "section 2"[80] cannot, it is submitted, be interpreted to mean that the representee can rescind *and* claim damages under s.2(2) in spite of the fact that the representor was not negligent and has succeeded in discharging the burden of proof under s.2(1). Such an interpretation would be plainly inconsistent with the words of s.2(2), that the damages which can be awarded under it are "in lieu of rescission".

A further consequence of the rule that damages under the subsection are "in lieu of rescission" is more controversial. Such damages are available where a person "would be entitled, by reason of the misrepresentation, to rescind the contract". It is not clear from these words whether the court can award damages if the representee once had the right to rescind but had lost it[81] before the claim under s.2(2) was made; and conflicting views on the point have been expressed in decisions at first instance. On the one hand, the fact that the court's power is to award damages "in lieu of rescission", and the description of the factors to which the court is to have regard in determining whether to exercise its discretion, suggest that the court must have some real choice in the matter and therefore

---

[71] *William Sindall plc v Cambridgeshire CC* [1994] 1 W.L.R. 1016 at 1036, 1043.

[72] See *The Lucy* [1983] 1 Lloyd's Rep. 188 at 202.

[73] *Highlands Ins Co v Continental Ins Co* [1987] 1 Lloyd's Rep. 109 at 118.

[74] *ibid. cf. TSB v Camfield* [1995] 1 W.L.R. 430 at 439.

[75] *ibid.*; *HIH Casualty & General Insurance v Chase Manhattan Bank* [2001] EWCA Civ 1250; [2001] 2 Lloyd's Rep. 483 at [51].

[76] See above, at n.67.

[77] For "incorporated misrepresentations" see below, pp.359, 375–376.

[78] See below, pp.366–368.

[79] As in *F & H Entertainments v Leisure Enterprises* (1976) 240 E.G. 445; *cf. Atlantic Estates v Ezekiel* [1991] 2 E.G.L.R. 202 at 204.

[80] *Archer v Brown* [1985] Q.B. 401 at 415; the suggestion is *obiter* as the case was one of fraud, and "innocent" may have been intended simply to mean "not fraudulent".

[81] See below, pp.377–378.

support the view that damages in lieu cannot be awarded where the right to rescind has been lost.[82] On the other hand it is hard, as a matter of policy, to see why the factors which bar the right to rescind should limit the discretion to award damages. The intervention of third party rights, for instance, may make it highly inappropriate to rescind the contract,[83] but it does not follow that it should prevent the court from awarding monetary compensation to the representee.[84]

(c) INCORPORATED MISREPRESENTATION. A representation originally made to induce a contract may become a term of the contract by being subsequently incorporated in it; and this does not affect the right to rescind for misrepresentation.[85] In such cases the representee is entitled as of right to *damages* for breach of contract; this right is not subject to the discretion of the court. The question whether his right to "*rescind*" for breach of contract is affected by s.2(2) will be discussed below.[86]

6. Basis of Assessment and Remoteness

Where a representee claims damages, questions may arise as to the basis of assessment and remoteness. These questions are discussed generally in Chapter 21,[87] but some special factors relating to misrepresentation must be considered here.

(1) Basis of assessment

Liability for misrepresentation may arise in tort (where the representation is made fraudulently or negligently) or in contract (where the representation has contractual force). This distinction affects the assessment of damages in the most common case of misrepresentation: namely, where a seller represents that the subject-matter of a contract has a quality which in fact it lacks. The general principle is that in tort the claimant is entitled to such damages as will put him into the position in which he would have been if the tort had not been committed; while in contract he is entitled to be put into the position in which he would have been if the contract had been performed.[88] It is thought to follow that in tort the claimant is entitled to be put into the position in which he would have been if the representation *had not been made*, while in contract he is entitled to be put into the position in which he would have been if the representation *had been true*.[89] If the representation induces the claimant to buy something which, but for the misrepresentation, he would not have bought at all, it follows that the damages in tort are *prima facie*[90] the amount by which the actual value of the thing bought is less than

---

[82] *Zanzibar v British Aerospace (Lancaster House) Ltd* [2001] 1 W.L.R. 2333; *Floods of Queensferry Ltd v Shand Construction Ltd (No.3)* [2000] B.L.R. 81 at 93; the same assumption seems to underlie *The Lucy* [1983] 1 Lloyd's Rep. 188 at 201–202. But the right to damages *under s.2(1)* survives loss of the right to rescind by affirmation: above, p.352.

[83] The *third party* cannot invoke s.2(2): see *TSB Bank plc v Camfield* [1995] 1 W.L.R. 430.

[84] See *Thomas Witter Ltd v TBP Industries Ltd* [1996] 2 All E.R. 573 at 589–590.

[85] See below, p.375.

[86] See below, p.376.

[87] See below, pp.944–974.

[88] *McGregor on Damages* (16th ed.), §11.

[89] *Smith Kline French Laboratories Ltd v Long* [1989] 1 W.L.R. 1 at 6; *East v Maurer* [1991] 1 W.L.R. 461 at 464, 467, 468 (below, p.937); *Gran Gelato Ltd v Richcliff (Group) Ltd* [1992] Ch. 570 at 575; *Thomas Witter Ltd v BTP Industries Ltd* [1996] 2 All E.R. 573 at 606; *South Australia Asset Management Corp v York Montague Ltd* [1997] A.C. 191 at 216; *Avon Insurance plc v Swire Fraser Ltd* [2000] 1 All E.R. (Comm) 573 at 577–578.

[90] The value of an illegal part of the thing bought is not taken into account: *The Siben* [1996] 1 Lloyd's Rep. 35 at 63–64.

the price paid for it.[91] In contract, on the other hand, the damages are *prima facie* the amount by which the actual value of the thing bought is less than *the value which it would have had if the representation had been true*[92]; and this value is not relevant to the assessment of damages in tort for deceit.[93]

There is some conflict in the authorities as to which of these bases of assessment is to be adopted for the purpose of s.2(1) of the Misrepresentation Act 1967. One view is that damages under the subsection are to be assessed on a contractual basis[94]; but the more generally held view is that such damages are "the same as in an action of deceit",[95] *i.e.* that they are to be assessed on a tortious basis. It is submitted that the latter is the correct view since the reference to fraud in s.2(1) indicates that the statutory cause of action is tortious in nature. Accordingly, the tortious basis of assessment applies where the representee has received something which lacked a quality that it was represented to have.

A representation may have contractual force, but the contract may be to the effect, not that the representation is true, but that the representor has taken due care in making it. This was the position in *Esso Petroleum Co Ltd v Mardon*[96] where a tenant was induced to take a lease of a petrol station by a statement made on behalf of the landlord that the future annual turnover could be estimated at 200,000 gallons. The estimate had been carelessly made and the actual turnover was much lower. The landlord was held liable both for negligence at common law and for breach of collateral warranty.[97] But even on the latter basis the tenant did not recover damages for loss of his bargain[98] (*i.e.* for loss of the profit that he would have made if the turnover had been 200,000 gallons); for the warranty was not that 200,000 gallons would be sold but only that the estimate had been

---

[91] This rule is stated in many cases: see, for example, *Davidson v Tulloch* (1860) 3 Macq. 783 at 790; *Peek v Derry* (1887) 37 Ch.D. 541 at 578 (reversed on liability 14 App.Cas. 337); *Twycross v Grant* (1877) 2 C.P.D. 496 at 504; *Cackett v Keswick* [1902] 2 Ch. 456 at 468; *McConnel v Wright* [1903] 1 Ch. 546 at 554; *Broome v Speake* [1903] 1 Ch. 586 at 605, 623 (affirmed [1904] A.C. 342); *Stevens v Hoare* (1904) 20 T.L.R. 407; *Heineman v Cooper* [1987] H.L.R. 262; *Saunders v Edwards* [1987] 1 W.L.R. 1116 at 1121; *Strover v Harrington* [1988] Ch. 390 at 411; *Westgate v Bracknell DC* (1987) 19 H.L.R. 735; *Smith v Eric S Bush* [1990] 1 A.C. 831 at 851; *Hussey v Eels* [1990] 2 Q.B. 227 at 241; the assessment in *Roberts v J Hampson & Co* [1990] 1 W.L.R. 94 is (if correctly reported) hard to reconcile with the normal basis of assessment. The damages awarded "for loss of an expectation" in *White v Jones* [1995] 2 A.C. 207 at 269 would not extend to expectations created only by a misrepresentation of the kind here under discussion: see below, p.616. See *McGregor on Damages* (16th ed.), §1970; *Spencer Bower and Turner on Actionable Misrepresentation* (3rd ed.), pp.237–258.

[92] See, for example, Sale of Goods Act 1979, s.53(3); an alternative measure is the cost of making the defect good (below, p.944). For the measure of a price reduction under s.48c of the Act, as inserted by Sale and Supply of Goods to Consumers Regulations 2002, SI 2002/3045, reg.5, see below, p.952.

[93] *Smith New Court Securities Ltd v Scrimgeour Vickers (Asset Management) Ltd* [1997] A.C. 254 at 267 (*per* Lord Browne-Wilkinson) and 283 (*per* Lord Steyn) disapproving *Downs v Chappell* [1997] 1 W.L.R. 426 at 444 on this point; see also *South Australia Asset Management Corp v York Montague Ltd* [1997] A.C. 191 at 215–216 (*per* Lord Hoffmann) expressing no concluded view on the point.

[94] *Davis & Co (Wines) Ltd v Afa Minerva (E M I) Ltd* [1974] 2 Lloyd's Rep. 27 at 32.

[95] *F & H Entertainments Ltd v Leisure Enterprises Ltd* 240 E.G. 455 (the reference is simply to s.2, but it is clear from the context that subs. (1) is meant); *André & Cie SA v Ets Michel Blanc & Fils* [1977] 2 Lloyd's Rep. 166 at 181 (affirmed, without reference to this point [1979] 2 Lloyd's Rep. 427); *Cemp Properties (UK) v Dentsply Research & Development Corp* [1991] 2 E.G.L.R. 197; *Naughton v O'Callaghan* [1990] 3 All E.R. 191 at 196; *The Siben* [1996] 1 Lloyd's Rep. 35 at 63. *cf. Box v Midland Bank Ltd* [1979] 2 Lloyd's Rep. 391 (reversed as to costs only [1981] 1 Lloyd's Rep. 434); *Archer v Brown* [1985] Q.B. 401 at 426–427 (denying an item of loss of bargain damages); *Sharneyford Supplies Ltd v Edge* [1987] Ch. 305 at 303, disapproving a contrary dictum in *Watts v Spence* [1975] Ch. 165, 175 (the actual reasoning of these last two cases has been made obsolete by Law of Property (Miscellaneous Provisions) Act 1989, s.3, below, p.999); Taylor, 45 M.L.R. 139; Cartwright [1987] Conv. 423; Wadsley, 54 M.L.R. 698.

[96] [1976] Q.B. 801.

[97] See above, pp.349, 356.

[98] [1976] Q.B. 801 at 820.

prepared with due care.[99] In tort, the claimant clearly cannot recover damages for loss of his bargain, though he may be entitled to damages for loss of the chance of making profits out of *another* business in which he would have invested his money, had he not been induced by the misrepresentation to enter into the contract with the defendant.[1]

The distinction between the two bases of assessment can be hard to draw: where a seller's misrepresentation relates, not to some quality of the goods, but to the terms on which he deals with other customers. In the *Clef Aquitaine* case[2] the fraudulent representation by which A was induced to enter into a long-term distributorship with B (a manufacturer of damp-proofing materials) was that B did not sell goods of the same kind to other customers for prices lower than those payable by A under the agreement. As the goods had no readily ascertainable "particular value",[3] the normal deceit measure of damages (price less value) could not be applied. But it was held that A could recover, as damages for deceit, the difference between the prices payable by A under the agreement and the prices that A would have been able to negotiate for the purposes of that agreement, if the misrepresentation had not been made. If the representation had had contractual force, A could in contract have recovered damages in respect of lost or reduced profit on resales; and to the extent that A's tort damages reflected the fact that his profit margins on sales actually achieved were reduced by the fact that he had paid higher prices to B by reason of the misrepresentation, the tort damages that A recovered can be said to resemble contract damages.[4] But the latter would have included damages in respect of a reduction in the volume of A's resales by reason of the falsity of B's statement (if it had had contractual force) and such damages would not be recoverable under the tort formula applied in the *Clef Aquitaine* case. Moreover, under that formula, A recovered damages even though the transaction induced by the fraud did not cause him any overall loss[5]: the transaction remained profitable to A but he suffered loss because it was *less* profitable than it would have been, but for the representation. The same can, in theory, be true where the normal deceit formula of the "price less value" *can* be applied to goods bought for resale,[6] though in practice the representee is in such a case unlikely to be able to resell the goods for more than the price paid by him without being himself guilty of a further misrepresentation.

In the cases so far discussed, the misrepresentations were made *by* the seller and affected the price paid by the buyer. They may also be made *to* the seller and affect his willingness to contract with a particular buyer.[7] In one case,[8] manufacturers of pharmaceuticals were induced to sell tablets to a company by the defendant's representation that the company intended to resell them in Central Africa; in fact they were resold in Holland. If the sellers had known the truth, they would not have sold to the company; but that sale did not affect their capacity to supply other customers. In these circumstances, the proper way of putting the sellers into the position in which they would have been, if the representation had not been made, was to ensure that they should receive the market value of the tablets. As this value was not shown to exceed the contract price, the

---

[99] Contrast *Lion Nathan v CC Bottlers Ltd* [1996] 1 W.L.R. 1438 where the price of a business was based on the vendor's warranty that its achievable *profits* had been "calculated in good faith and on a proper basis".

[1] *East v Maurer* [1991] 1 W.L.R. 461, below p.938.

[2] *Clef Aquitaine SARL v Laporte Materials (Barrow) Ltd* [2001] Q.B. 488.

[3] *ibid.*, at 500; the reference seems to be to *market* value: *cf. ibid.*, at 513 and below, p.953.

[4] *cf. ibid.*, p.513 ("mimic reasoning more familiar in contract").

[5] This was the position in the *Clef Aquitaine* case, above, n.2.

[6] In the *Clef Aquitaine* case, the normal tort measure could *not* be applied for the reason given at n.3, above.

[7] *cf.* above, pp.274–278.

[8] *Smith Kline & French Laboratories Ltd v Long* [1989] 1 W.L.R. 1.

defendant was liable for no more than the contract price, less that part of it which had already been paid by the company.

There is, finally, the possibility that a misrepresentation relating to the value of the subject-matter may be made by a third party. For example, A may lend money to B on the security of B's property in reliance on a valuation of that property negligently made by C. Here the damages for which C is liable to A are based, not on the interest which B should have paid on the loan, but on the position in which A would have been if C had made the valuation with due care.[9] If on that assumption A would not have made the loan to B, he can recover from C not only loss of principal but also damages for loss of use of the money: *i.e.* what he would have earned by putting the money on deposit elsewhere, or by using it to enter into other transactions.[10] But C is not liable for any interest above normal market rates which B may have undertaken to pay to A.[11] This is so whether A's claim is brought in contract[12] or in tort since C in such case undertakes only to make the valuation with due care: he makes no promise or representation that B will perform his contractual obligations to A.[13]

(2) Remoteness

The fact that the subject-matter lacks a quality which it was represented to have may, apart from affecting its value, also cause the representee to suffer consequential loss. For example, where diseased cows are sold under representations of soundness and infect the buyer's other animals, he may be able to recover for the loss of those animals[14]; and where a business is sold under misrepresentations as to its profitability the buyer may be able to recover damages for losses suffered in the course of running the business.[15] Consequential losses can, however, be recovered only if they are not too remote[16]; and the rules as to remoteness are more favourable to the claimant in actions of deceit than they are in actions for breach of contract.[17] Lord Denning M.R. has said that "In contract the damages are limited to what may reasonably be supposed to have been in the contemplation of the parties. In fraud they are not so limited. The defendant is bound to make reparation for all the actual damage directly flowing from the fraudulent inducement. . . . It does not lie in the mouth of the fraudulent person to say that they could not reasonably have been foreseen".[18] A number of later dicta in the House of Lords similarly regard foreseeability as irrelevant in actions for deceit[19]; though it may,

---

[9] Not on the position in which A would have been had C's valuation been correct: *cf.* above at n.99.

[10] *First National Commercial Bank plc v Humberts* [1995] 2 All E.R. 673 at 677.

[11] *Swingcastle Ltd v Gibson* [1991] 2 A.C. 223.

[12] See below, pp.938–939 for the scope of C's duty where this arises under a contract between A and C.

[13] *Swingcastle v Gibson*, above, at 238. For the time at which the loss is suffered, see *First National Commercial Bank plc v Humberts* [1995] 2 All E.R. 673.

[14] *Mullett v Mason* (1866) L.R. 1 C.P. 559 (fraud); *Smith v Green* (1875) 1 C.P.D. 92 (breach of contract).

[15] *Doyle v Olby (Ironmongers) Ltd* [1969] 2 Q.B. 158; Treitel, 32 M.L.R. 526; *Hornal v Neuburger Products* [1957] 1 Q.B. 247 at 259; *cf. Naughton v O'Callaghan* [1990] 3 All E.R. 191. As to punitive damages, see below, p.937.

[16] See below, pp.965–974.

[17] Especially after *The Heron II* [1969] 1 A.C. 350, below, p.966. In *Archer v Brown* [1985] Q.B. 401 at 417–418 both tests were satisfied.

[18] [1969] 2 Q.B. 158 at 167; *cf. Thomas Witter Ltd v TBP Industries Ltd* [1996] 2 All E.R. 573 at 606 (where no consequential loss was claimed); *KCB Bank v Industrial Steels (UK) Ltd* [2001] 1 Lloyd's Rep. 370 at 377.

[19] *Smith New Court Securities Ltd v Scrimgeour Vickers (Asset Management) Ltd* [1997] A.C. 254 at 265, 267, *per* Lord Browne-Wilkinson, 269 *per* Lord Mustill, accepting "the irrelevance of foreseeability" though not regarding Lord Denning's judgment (above, n.18) as "an invariable guide". *cf.* also *South Australia Asset Management Corp v York Montague Ltd* [1997] A.C. 191 at 215; *Kuwait Airways Corp v Iraqi Airways Corp* [2002] UKHL 19; [2002] 1 All E.R. (Comm) 843 at [100].

with respect, be doubted whether a defendant would be liable, even in such an action, for loss of a *kind* that was totally unforeseeable.[20] The statement that "a wider test [of remoteness] applies in an action for deceit"[21] (than in one for negligence) carries with it the implication that *some* test of remoteness applies even in deceit.

In an action based on negligent misrepresentation at common law, the loss must be reasonably foreseeable, that being the general rule applied in actions for negligence.[22] This rule may be less favourable to the claimant than the rule in deceit but it is probably more favourable than the rule in a contractual action.[23] Where the action is brought under s.2(1) of the Misrepresentation Act, one possible view is that the deceit rule applies by virtue of the fiction of fraud.[24] Support for this view is provided by *Royscot Trust Ltd v Rogerson*,[25] where a car-dealer induced a finance company to enter into a hire-purchase agreement by misrepresenting the amount of the deposit paid by the customer, who later defaulted and sold the car to a third party.[26] The dealer was held liable to the finance company under s.2(1) for the balance due under the agreement on the ground that "the plain words"[27] of the subsection required the court to apply the deceit rule, under which the dealer was liable for "all the losses" suffered by the finance company "even if those losses were unforeseeable, provided that they were not otherwise too remote".[28] Later discussions of the *Royscot* case in the House of Lords somewhat pointedly refrain from expressing any concluded view as to its correctness[29]; and in one of these discussions the question whether the fraud rule should to applied to cases of "innocent misrepresentation under the Misrepresentation Act 1967"[30] is expressly left open by Lord Browne-Wilkinson. It is submitted that the words of the subsection are not so "plain"[31] as to compel the court to apply the fraud rule in the present context. We have seen that there are other contexts[32] in which the courts have not given a similar literal effect to the fiction of fraud, which could be interpreted to refer to the *existence* of liability, rather than to its extent. This view derives some support from the legislative history of the subsection.[33] It can also be supported on the policy ground that the

---

[20] *cf. Mullen v Mason* (1866) L.R. 1 C.P. 559 at 564; *Doyle v Olby (Ironmongers) Ltd* [1969] 2 Q.B. 158 at 169.

[21] *Smith New Court* case, above, at 852.

[22] *The Wagon Mound* [1961] A.C. 388; *cf. Esso Petroleum Co Ltd v Mardon* [1976] Q.B. 801 at 822. For a possible alternative explanation of the rule, see below, p.939.

[23] See *The Heron II* [1969] 1 A.C. 350; below, pp.966–969.

[24] See above, p.351.

[25] [1991] 2 Q.B. 297; Hooley, 107 L.Q.R. 547; *cf. Cooper v Tamms* [1988] 1 E.G.L.R. 256, 263; *Cemp Properties (UK) v Dentsply Research and Development Corp* [1991] 2 E.G.L.R. 97; *William Sindall plc v Cambridgeshire CC* [1994] 1 W.L.R. 1016 at 1037, 1043.

[26] Who obtained good title to the car.

[27] [1991] 2 Q.B. 297 at 306; *cf.* p.309.

[28] *ibid.* at 307. The concluding words of the quotation may refer to cases in which the loss is wholly different *in kind* from that which could have been foreseen.

[29] *Smith New Court Securities Ltd v Scrimgeour Vickers (Asset Management) Ltd* [1997] A.C. 254 at 267, 283. A dictum in *South Australia Asset Management Corp v York Montague Ltd* [1997] A.C. 191 at 216 states the fraud rule as applicable to claims under Misrepresentation Act 1967, s.2(1) but expresses no concluded view on the relevance of foreseeability (of whatever degree) and makes no reference to the *Royscot* case; that case is also viewed with considerable scepticism in *Avon Insurance plc v Swire Fraser Ltd* [2000] 1 All E.R. (Comm) 573 at 576; *cf. ibid.* at 633.

[30] *Smith New Court* case, above, at 267; the reference seems from the context to be to s.2(1), which imposes a species of liability for negligence (above, p.351).

[31] [1997] A.C. 254 at 283, referring to "the rather loose wording" of the 1967 Act.

[32] See above, p.352.

[33] *ibid.*; the Court of Appeal in the *Royscot Trust* case was not at liberty to consider this piece of legislative history, and even now it would not seem to be admissable under the rules laid down in *Pepper v Hart* [1993] A.C. 593 since the statement in question was not that of the promoter of the legislation.

severity of a rule which is justified in cases of actual fraud will often be inappropriate where the defendant is merely negligent.[34]

(3) Fluctuations in value

Some of the nineteenth century cases which had established the principle that damages in tort for misrepresentation were based on the difference between the price paid by the injured party and the actual value of the subject-matter[35] also supported the so-called "date of transaction"[36] rule, by which for this purpose the relevant value of the subject-matter was its value at the time of its transaction.[37] Thus if the claimant had been induced by fraud to pay £15 each for shares which at that time were worth no more than £10, the defendant was liable for £5 per share, but not for further loss suffered by reason of any later fall in the market value of the shares. Such further loss was irrecoverable because it was assumed either that it had not been caused by the wrong, or that the claimant's retention of the shares on a falling market amounted to a failure on his part to take reasonable steps to mitigate his loss.[38] The "date of transaction" rule continues to be recognised as the general rule[39]; but its inflexible application could lead to injustice where the defrauded party had acted reasonably in retaining the subject-matter after that date. Recent cases have therefore created exceptions to the general rule where the assumptions on which it is based are not in fact true. This may be so for a variety of reasons: the subject-matter may suffer from some hidden flaw, not known to the market,[40] so that its market value at the time of the transaction does not reflect its true value; or the plaintiff may "by reason of the fraud, [be] locked into the property"[41]; or the decline in value may have taken place before the plaintiff discovered the truth, so that the misrepresentation "continued to operate . . . so as to induce the plaintiff to retain"[42] the subject-matter. In such cases, his damages for deceit will be based on the difference between the price which he paid for the subject-matter and *either* the proceeds of his actual disposal of it,[43] *or* the proceeds which would have been realised by an earlier disposal of it which he should, acting reasonably, have made.[44] In a case of the latter kind, he will be compensated for loss due to the fall in the value of the subject-matter up to the time when it was reasonable for such a disposal to have been made, but not for loss due to any further fall in its market value after that time.[45] These rules resemble those which govern the time for assessment of damages and mitigation in cases of breach of contract.[46]

When the general "date of transaction" rule was first developed, liability in damages for misrepresentation existed only in cases of fraud,[47] and that rule must therefore have

---

[34] *cf. Shepheard v Broome* [1904] A.C. 342 at 345, 346, where the House of Lords protested against being compelled by statute to treat a person who was morally innocent as if he were guilty of fraud.

[35] See above, p.360.

[36] *Smith New Court Securities Ltd v Scrimgeour Vickers (Asset Management) Ltd* [1997] A.C. 254 at 283.

[37] *e.g. Twycross v Grant* (1877) 2 C.P.D. 469; *Peek v Derry* (1887) 37 Ch.D. 541; and (in the 20th Century) *McConnell v Wright* [1903] 1 Ch. 546.

[38] *cf.* see below, p.977 (mitigation by means of a substitute transaction).

[39] *Smith New Court* case, above, n.36, at 267, 284.

[40] *ibid.* at 267 ("pregnant with disaster").

[41] *ibid. per* Lord Browne-Wilkinson; *Standard Chartered Bank v Pakistan National Shipping Co (No.3)* [2001] EWCA Civ 55; [2001] 1 All E.R. (Comm) 822, at [37].

[42] *Smith New Court* case, above, at 267.

[43] As in the *Smith New Court* case, above, n.36; *cf. Naughton v O'Callaghan* [1990] 3 All E.R. 191.

[44] *Downs v Chappell* [1997] 1 W.L.R. 426 (as to which see also above, p.360, n.84).

[45] *Downs v Chappel*, above.

[46] See below, pp.957–960; *cf.* Lord Browne-Wilkinson's reference in the *Smith New Court* case [1997] A.C. 254 at 266 to *Johnson v Agnew* [1980] A.C. 367 at 401, cited on p.958, below.

[47] See above, p.345.

been restricted to such cases. The recent cases which have established exceptions to the general rule have likewise been cases in which the purchase of assets was induced by fraud[48]; and they do not settle the question how damages are to be assessed where the inducing representation is merely negligent. There is no doubt that the general "date of transaction" rule applies to such cases; the more difficult question is whether this is also true of the recently established exceptions to it. The answer to this question depends in part on the legal nature of the exceptions and in part on wider policy considerations. So far as the legal nature of the exceptions is concerned, they can be regarded as dealing *either* (like the general principle) with the issue of quantification *or* with the issue of remoteness.[49] If they deal with quantification, they should logically apply in cases of negligent, no less than in cases of fraudulent, misrepresentation. Quantification is simply the process of putting a monetary value on a loss in respect of which the defendant is found or admitted to be liable and for this purpose it is irrelevant to ask whether that loss arose as a result of fraud or of negligence. If, on the other hand, the exceptions deal with the issue of remoteness, (or, in other words, with the question, what limits the law should impose on the items of loss in respect of which the wrongdoer is to be held responsible) then there is (as our foregoing discussion of remoteness shows[50]) certainly support for the view that a person guilty of fraudulent misrepresentation is liable for a wider range of consequences than one who is merely negligent; and some reliance is placed on this distinction in one of the recent cases[51] in which it was held that a fraudulent defendant was not entitled to limit his liability by reference to the "date of transaction" rule. But it scarcely follows from such reasoning that the liability of a misrepresentor will necessarily be limited by that rule merely because he is guilty only of negligence and not of fraud. Some support for the view that it is not so limited is provided by another of the recent cases which have established the exceptions to the rule. In that case,[52] the representee alleged fraud against the seller of a business but only negligence against his accountants, and *both* these defendants were held liable for an amount by which the value of the business had fallen by reason of a general market decline between the time of the sale induced by the misrepresentation and the time when the representee, acting reasonably, should have disposed of the business. The case does not, however, conclude the issue since the accountants were "recklessly negligent"[53]; and recklessness suffices to give rise to liability in deceit even though it does not amount to actual dishonesty.[54] It remains, therefore an open question whether a representor who was merely negligent, but not reckless, would be liable for a fall in the value of the subject-matter due to factors (such as market movements) other than those to which the misrepresentation related. It is submitted (with some hesitation) that, since such loss of value is a kind of consequential loss,[55] the question should be treated as one of remoteness[56] rather than as one of quantification; and that the answer to it should depend on whether representor could

---

[48] This was true in *Downs v Chappell* [1997] 1 W.L.R. 426 even though fraud was alleged against only one of the defendants: see below, at n.52.

[49] For the difference between these two issues, see below, pp.944, 964, 973–974.

[50] See above, p.362.

[51] *Smith New Court* case [1997] A.C. 254 at 279; *cf. South Australia Asset Management Corp v York Montague Ltd* [1997] A.C. 191 at 215.

[52] *Downs v Chappell* [1997] 1 W.L.R. 426.

[53] *ibid.* at 431, 445. In contribution proceedings between the seller and the accountants, the degree of responsibility of these parties was held at 445 to be equal since, though the fault of the accountants was "less serious" than that of the seller, their misrepresentation "had a greater causative impact".

[54] See above, p.317.

[55] *Downs v Chappell* [1997] 1 W.L.R. 426 at 438.

[56] In *Downs v Chappel*, above, at 434 it was said that "No question of remoteness arises". This seems to mean that the test of remoteness was *satisfied*.

reasonably have foreseen that the representee would suffer a loss of value of the kind which in fact occurred after the time of the transaction.

(4) Misrepresentation Act 1967, s.2(2)

Under this subsection "damages" may be awarded in lieu of rescission even though the misrepresentation is wholly innocent[57] and even though it has no contractual force. There is, therefore, no reason for regarding these damages as being either tortious or contractual. They are really *sui generis*, and the subsection gives no clue as to the basis of assessment or as to the rules as to remoteness that govern an award under it. The legislative history gives some slight support to the view that the contractual basis was not to be applied[58]; and indeed it seems unreasonable to make a person who has not guaranteed the truth of his representations liable as if he had. On the other hand, a person should not actually profit from even a wholly innocent non-contractual misrepresentation; and accordingly he should be liable for the amount by which the actual value of what he has transferred is less than the price received by him.

So far as remoteness is concerned, there is nothing in the wording of the subsection[59] to suggest that the strict deceit rule applies, nor (as a matter of policy) should it apply against a misrepresentor who is wholly innocent; and it may be doubted whether he should be liable for consequential loss at all. The view that he should not be so liable can perhaps be supported by reference to s.2(3) which provides that damages may be awarded under subs.(2) against a person who is also liable under subs.(1), "but where he is so liable any award under the said subsection (2) shall be taken into account in assessing his liability under the said subsection (1)". It can be inferred from these words that damages under subs.(2) are meant to be less than damages under subs.(1). One possible explanation for this may be that remoteness is governed by the deceit rule under subs.(1) while under subs.(2) damages are limited by the contract rule of remoteness, which is more restrictive even than that applicable in tort to cases of negligence.[60] Dicta which support this view of the damages recoverable under s.2(2)[61] do not, however, rule out the possibility that such damages may be *less* than those recoverable in contract,[62] and they could be less if, under the subsection, consequential loss were not recoverable at all. If this view were to be accepted, a wholly innocent misrepresentor would be liable *only* for the amount by which the actual value was less than the price; while a negligent misrepresentor could be made liable for this amount under subs.(1) or (2), and, in addition, for consequential loss under subs.(1).[63]

7. Limit of the Right to Damages

(1) Cases in which damages cannot be recovered

Although the availability of damages for misrepresentation has been greatly extended by *Hedley Byrne*'s case and the Misrepresentation Act, there is still no *right* to damages for

---

[57] *i.e.* even though it is neither fraudulent nor negligent and even though the representor has discharged the burden of proof under s.2(1).

[58] At one stage an amendment was introduced to apply the contractual basis to actions under s.2(2): Standing Committee G, February 23, 1966. But it was withdrawn without discussion. The point made in n.33 above on p.363 applies here.

[59] *i.e.* there is no fiction of fraud so that the reasoning of the *Royscot* case [1991] 2 Q.B. 297, above, pp.362–363, (even if sound) does not apply.

[60] See below, pp.965–968.

[61] *William Sindall v Cambridgeshire CC* [1994] 1 W.L.R. 1016 at 1038, 1044.

[62] *ibid.* p.1038 ("not necessary . . . to discuss the circumstances in which they may be less").

[63] See *Thomas Witter Ltd v TBP Industries Ltd* [1996] 2 All E.R. 573 at 591.

a wholly innocent misrepresentation which has no contractual force. In the case of such a misrepresentation, the court has a discretionary power to award damages in lieu of rescission; but it cannot rescind the contract, or regard it as rescinded *and* award damages. If the representee wishes to rescind for a wholly innocent non-contractual misrepresentation, and if the court does not think it equitable to declare the contract subsisting and award damages in lieu of rescission, the old rule that damages cannot be recovered for innocent misrepresentation[64] will continue to apply. In such a case the representee may, however, have a remedy by way of an indemnity.

(2) Indemnity

In rescinding a contract, equity will so far as possible order each party to restore benefits received under the contract from the other. In the simplest case, the seller will have to restore the price and the buyer the thing sold. It is sometimes necessary, as part of the process of rescission, to go further and to order one party to "restore" a benefit not received directly by him. Suppose, for example, that a buyer rescinds after having, under the terms of the contract, paid the price to a third party. There is little doubt that in such a case rescission would entitle the buyer to recover the money so paid from the seller.[65]

On the same principle, the buyer can sometimes recover an "indemnity" in respect of certain expenses; while other expenses are regarded as damages and may therefore be irrecoverable in cases of wholly innocent non-contractual misrepresentation. The distinction can be illustrated by reference to *Whittington v Seale-Hayne*.[66] A tenant had taken a lease of premises for the purpose of breeding poultry; he had done so in reliance on a representation that the premises were in good sanitary condition. In fact the water supply was poisoned so that the tenant's manager became ill and most of the birds died. The landlord submitted to rescission and agreed to repay £20 in respect of rent and rates paid, and repairs done, by the tenant under the lease. On the other hand, claims for loss of profits and loss of stock were disallowed as they were clearly claims for damages. Further claims for removal expenses[67] and medical expenses were rejected on the same ground: they were not claims for an indemnity, since such claims could be allowed only in respect of expenses incurred in discharging obligations *created* by the contract.[68] The important distinction is that between the money spent on rates and repairs on the one hand, and the removal and medical expenses on the other. It is that the lease obliged the tenant to pay rates and to do repairs, but not to move in and employ a manager. The tenant's undertaking to pay rates and to do repairs was really *part of the price* for the lease of the premises. If the lease had provided that the landlord should do these things, he would no doubt have charged a higher rent, which he would clearly have had to restore. He was under a similar liability in respect of part of the price not paid directly to him, or not paid in cash. The tenant's removal and medical expenses could not be regarded in this way. On the facts of the case a claim for damages under s.2(1) of the Misrepresentation Act would now almost certainly succeed[69]; but if the defendant could discharge the burden of proof under that subsection[70] the representee would still be

---

[64] See above, p.357.

[65] Any question between seller and third party would not be the concern of the buyer.

[66] (1900) 82 L.T. 49; 16 T.L.R. 181; 44 S.J. 229.

[67] On this point, *cf. Redgrave v Hurd* (1881) 20 Ch.D. 1.

[68] For a possible extension of the right to necessary maintenance costs, see *Lagunas Nitrate Co v Lagunas Syndicate* [1899] 2 Ch. 392.

[69] *cf.* above, p.357, n.60.

[70] See above, p.351.

restricted to a claim for an indemnity. He could not rescind *and* get damages under s.2(2) of the Act.

The distinction between indemnity and damages, it is submitted, is that stated in the preceding paragraph, but there is thought to be some conflict of opinion on the point in *Newbigging v Adam*.[71] The representee was induced by the defendants' fraud to enter into a partnership with them and another person. On rescinding the contract of partnership he was clearly entitled to get back the money which he had paid for his share. The Court of Appeal held that he was also entitled to be indemnified against his liability to pay debts incurred by the partnership.[72] The crucial point is that it is a term of a contract of partnership, or a legal incident of it,[73] that each partner is liable for the partnership debts. Hence any partner who pays such debts performs an obligation *under that contract*, though it is also true that the debts arise under another contract (*i.e.* that with the creditor of the partnership). Accordingly Cotton L.J. said that the representee was entitled to an indemnity "against the obligations which he has *contracted under the contract which is set aside*".[74] Bowen L.J. similarly said that he was entitled to be restored to his original position "so far as regards the rights and obligations *created by the contract into which he has been induced to enter*".[75] Only Fry L.J. appears to state a broader view when he says that the representee is entitled to an indemnity not only against obligations "created by" the contract but also against such "obligations *entered into under the contract* as are within the reasonable expectation of the parties to the contract".[76] What seems to have troubled Fry L.J. is that the *debts of the partnership* were not "created by" the contract of partnership. But the representee's *liability to contribute to the payment of those debts* clearly was "created by" or "contracted under" that contract. In the context of *Newbigging v Adam*, it is submitted that Fry L.J.'s statement does not conflict with the distinction drawn above between indemnity and damages. The point can be illustrated by supposing that the tenant in *Whittington v Seale-Hayne*[77] had employed a builder to do the repairs and a furniture remover to move in his furniture. The debt to the builder would not of course have been "created by" the lease, but the tenant's obligation to repair was so created, thus entitling him to an indemnity against the cost of its performance: this would amount, *prima facie*, to the sum due to the builder. The debt to the furniture remover would simply have been incurred *in reliance* on the lease: it would obviously not have been "created by" the lease; nor even would it have been "entered into under" the lease within Fry L.J.'s formulation.

The grant of an indemnity amounts only to "working out the proper result of setting aside a contract in consequence of misrepresentation".[78] It is ancillary to rescission. It follows that, if the right to rescind is barred, the court cannot grant an indemnity unless the misrepresentor consents to rescission.[79] Where the right to rescind is barred, the court may[80] have no power to award damages in lieu of rescission; and if this is the position the victim of a wholly innocent misrepresentation might still be left, in such a case, without any remedy.

---

[71] (1886) 34 Ch.D. 582.

[72] In the House of Lords it was held that the question of indemnity did not arise because the debt in question was not enforceable against the firm: *Adam v Newbigging* (1888) 13 App.Cas. 308.

[73] *cf.* Partnership Act 1890, s.41.

[74] (1886) 34 Ch. 582 at 589 (italics supplied).

[75] *ibid.* at 592–593 (italics supplied).

[76] *ibid.* at 596 (italics supplied).

[77] See above, p.367.

[78] *Newbigging v Adam*, above, at 589.

[79] As in *Whittington v Seale-Hayne* (1900) 16 T.L.R. 181, where the right to rescind was probably barred by the execution of the lease; see now below, pp.376–377.

[80] See above, p.359.

8. Compensation Orders in Criminal Cases

Misrepresentation may involve criminal liability, for example, where a person obtains property, services or a pecuniary advantage by deception,[81] or where, in the course of a trade or business, he applies a false trade description to goods or makes a false statement as to the provision of services or accommodation.[82] The court by or before which such a person is convicted may order the offender to pay compensation "for any . . . loss or damage resulting from that offence . . . ".[83] Such an order may be made even though the conduct constituting the offence does not give rise to any civil liability in damages[84]: for example where a person is convicted under the Theft Act 1968 or 1978 on account of a misrepresentation of law.[85] In the more common case where the criminal conduct also involves civil liability, the making of a compensation order is no bar to later civil proceedings. The damages in those proceedings will be *assessed* on normal principles, without reference to the order; but, to prevent double recovery, the sum so assessed will be reduced by the amount paid under the compensation order.[86]

SECTION 4. RESCISSION FOR MISREPRESENTATION

1. Introduction

It is impossible to understand the authorities on this subject without referring to the difference between the rules of common law and equity before the Judicature Acts 1873–1875.

At common law the general rule was that a contract could be rescinded *for misrepresentation* only on the ground of fraud; but this requirement of fraud was subject to several qualifications. If an innocent misrepresentation became a term of the contract, it might give rise to a right to rescind the contract *for breach*.[87] If it led to a fundamental *mistake* it might make the contract void so that each party could, on returning what he had got under the contract, recover back what he had given. This was sometimes called "rescinding" the contract, though strictly there was no need to rescind since the contract was void *ab initio*.[88] Rescission was also available at common law in certain cases of *non-disclosure*.[89]

In equity, on the other hand, there was a general rule that a contract could be rescinded for "innocent misrepresentation"[90]; this phrase covered every misrepresentation which was not fraudulent, and so included negligent misrepresentation.[91] Now that

---

[81] Theft Act 1968, ss.15, 16; Theft Act 1978, ss.1, 5.

[82] Trade Descriptions Act 1968, ss.1, 14.

[83] Powers of Criminal Courts (Sentencing) Act 2000, s.130(1)(a). The power to make "reparation orders" against young offenders under s.73 of the 2000 Act does not appear to envisage the making of orders for monetary compensation. See also Financial Services and Markets Act 2000, s.397.

[84] *R. v Chappell, The Times*, May 26, 1986.

[85] Theft Act 1968, s.15(4); Theft Act 1978, s.5(1). For possible civil liability for such misrepresentations, see above, pp.332–335. For the court's power to make restitution orders in respect of goods which have been stolen, see Powers of Criminal Courts (Sentencing) Act 2000, s.148.

[86] Powers of Criminal Courts (Sentencing) Act 2000, s.134.

[87] See below, pp.758 *et seq.*

[88] See *Kennedy v Panama, etc. Royal Mail Co Ltd* (1867) L.R. 2 Q.B. 580 at 587, stating the common law position before the Judicature Acts.

[89] See below, p.401; see, for example, *Ionides v Pender* (1874) L.R. 9 Q.B. 531; the distinctions formerly drawn between various kinds of insurance are no longer of importance now that all policies can be rescinded in equity for innocent misrepresentation and non-disclosure: see *London Assurance v Mansel* (1879) 11 Ch.D. 363 at 367.

[90] See *Redgrave v Hurd* (1881) 20 Ch.D. 1.

[91] See above, pp.340, 350.

the equitable rule prevails, the distinction between rescission at common law and in equity is of small (if any) importance; but the fact that the distinction once existed may account for some of the surviving differences between rescission for fraudulent and for innocent misrepresentation.

2. Various Meanings of "Rescission"

Bowen L.J. once said that "A fallacy may possibly lurk in the use of the word 'rescission'"[92]; and it is a great pity that subsequent lawmakers have not taken this observation to heart. The Misrepresentation Act, in particular, uses the expressions "rescind", "rescinded" and "rescission" without attempting to define them. They have in the past been used in a number of senses, and it is impossible to say that one of these rather than another is the "correct" one: "there is no primary meaning".[93] The following distinctions, in particular, are relevant in this Chapter.

(1) Rescission for misrepresentation and for breach

Where a misrepresentation is not a term of the contract, the process which may be referred to as "rescission for misrepresentation" amounts to setting the contract aside for all purposes,[94] so as to restore, as far as possible, the state of things which existed before the contract.[95] Where, on the other hand, a misrepresentation has become a term of the contract[96] the victim of the misrepresentation may seek "rescission for breach", and this may also result in a restoration of the state of things which existed before the contract.[97] But there is a crucial difference between the two processes.[98] Rescission for misrepresentation involves an allegation that there was a defect in the *formation* of the contract; and if this allegation is substantiated it follows that the contract is avoided *ab initio*. Rescission for breach, on the other hand, involves an allegation that there was a defect in the *performance* of the contract; and the existence of such a defect does not lead to the conclusion that the contract should be treated as if it had never existed. It follows that a party who rescinds for breach can also claim damages for breach of the contract[99]; while one who rescinds for misrepresentation has, by treating the contract as if it never existed, *prima facie* lost the right to claim damages for its breach.[1] If such a conclusion were to cause hardship to the representee the court could exercise its discretion under s.2(2) of the Misrepresentation Act to declare the contract subsisting.[2]

(2) Rescinding and pleading misrepresentation as a defence

A party who "rescinds" a contract (whether for misrepresentation or for breach) may take active steps to this end: *e.g.* by seeking the cancellation of the contract, or a

---

[92] *Mersey Steel and Iron Co v Naylor Benzon & Co* (1882) 9 Q.B.D. 648 at 671.

[93] *Buckland v Farmar & Moody* [1979] 1 W.L.R. 221 at 232.

[94] *The Kanchenjunga* [1990] 1 Lloyd's Rep. 391 at 398 ("wipe it out altogether"); *cf. TSB Bank plc v Camfield* [1995] 1 W.L.R. 430 (no partial rescission); contrast *Bank Melli Iran v Samadi-Rad* [1995] 1 F.C.R. 465.

[95] A duty to restore a loan of money obtained by fraud may arise even before rescission: *Stanlake Holdings Ltd v Tropical Capital Investments Ltd, Financial Times*, June 25, 1991.

[96] See below, p.375.

[97] See below, p.1052.

[98] *Johnson v Agnew* [1980] A.C. 367 at 392–393; *cf. Buckland v Farmar & Moody* [1979] 1 W.L.R. 221, 232; *Eagle Star Ins Co Ltd v Provincial Ins plc* [1994] 1 A.C. 130 at 140; and, in cases of non-disclsoure, *The Star Sea* [2001] UKHL 1; [2001] 1 All E.R. (Comm) 193 at [52].

[99] See below, p.851.

[1] *cf.* the rule that a party cannot rescind in part while affirming some particular term of the contract: below, p.384.

[2] See above, p.358. See further below, p.377.

declaration of its invalidity, or the return of money or property with which he has parted under the contract, on restoring what he obtained under it. Alternatively he may simply rely on the misrepresentation (or breach) as a defence to an action on the contract; and this process is not necessarily governed by the same rules as the active process of rescission.[3]

3. Rescission for Misrepresentation

(1) Contract voidable

The general rule is that misrepresentation makes the contract voidable at the option of the representee.[4] In *Redgrave v Hurd*,[5] for instance, the defendant was induced to buy a solicitor's house and practice by an innocent misrepresentation as to the value of the practice. It was held that he could rescind the contract and so get back the deposit he had paid.

Misrepresentation makes a contract voidable but not void[6]; and this has important effects on property rights in the subject-matter,[7] both as between the parties and between one of them and a third party. When the contract is one involving the transfer of property in its subject-matter, then between the parties such property is transferred to the representor to the extent that the representee intended it to be so transferred[8]; and if the entire property has been so transferred, then it remains in the representor until rescission.[9] So far as third parties are concerned, we have seen that if a person obtains goods under a contract which is void for mistake, property in the goods may not pass to him so that the goods can be recovered by the owner from a third person into whose hands they have come.[10] But if a person obtains goods under a contract which is only voidable for misrepresentation, a voidable title passes to him and the former owner's right to avoid it is lost when an innocent third party for value acquires an interest in the goods.[11]

The position of the third party in such cases should be contrasted with that of a third party to whom a chose in action[12] is assigned. The assignee takes "subject to equities"[13] and one such "equity" is the possibility of rescission for misrepresentation. Thus if A induces B to sell him a gold watch on credit by some fraud (not giving rise to a fundamental mistake) and pledges the watch to C, C's right to retain the watch is not affected by A's fraud. But if A by fraud induces B to buy a worthless watch, said to be of gold, and assigns the benefit of B's promise to pay for it to C as security for a loan,

---

[3] See below, pp.372–373.

[4] *Clough v L & NW Ry* (1871) L.R. 7 Ex. 26 at 34; *Urquhart v Macpherson* (1878) 3 App.Cas. 831 at 838; *cf. Whittaker v Campbell* [1984] Q.B. 319 (where, however, the distinctions drawn in the law of contract were said at 329 not to be decisive in criminal law); *Killick v Roberts* [1991] 1 W.L.R. 1146.

[5] (1881) 20 Ch.D. 1.

[6] See the authorities cited in n.11 below; for a contrary dictum, see *Pilgrim v Rice-Smith* [1977] 1 W.L.R. 671 at 675; Phillips, 93 L.Q.R. 497; *Lonrho plc v Fayed (No.2)* [1992] 1 W.L.R. 1 at 7.

[7] *Lonrho plc v Fayed (No.2)*, above.

[8] See *Collings v Lee* [2001] 2 All E.R. 332 (legal title, but not equitable interest, transferred by house-owners to their agent who had fraudulently claimed to have found a purchaser for the house).

[9] Before rescission, the representor therefore does not hold the property as trustee for the injured party: *Bristol & West BS v Mothew* [1998] Ch. 1 at 22–23.

[10] *e.g. Cundy v Lindsay* (1878) 3 App.Cas. 459; above, p.299.

[11] *White v Garden* (1851) 10 C.B. 919; *Stevenson v Newnham* (1853) 13 C.B. 285; the third party must give value: *Scholefield v Templer* (1859) 4 D. & J. 429; and see generally above, pp.299–304.

[12] For the meaning of "chose in action", see below, p.671.

[13] See below, p.689; *cf.* Marine Insurance Act 1906, s.50(2); *William Pickersgill & Sons Ltd v London & Provincial Marine, etc. Insurance Co Ltd* [1912] 3 K.B. 614 (non-disclosure).

C's right to sue B is affected by A's fraud.[14] It looks at first sight strange that the third party's position should depend on whether the fraudulent person was buyer or seller. One reason for treating the two cases differently may be that the law gives greater protection to proprietary than to contractual rights; and this distinction could be justified by saying that the assignee of a chose in action takes a greater business risk than the pledgee of a chattel. But some cases will still cause difficulty. For example, a person may fraudulently induce a company to allot shares to him and then sell them to an innocent third party. It is disputed whether shares are to be regarded as choses in action or as property in possession,[15] and it is therefore not clear whether the third party would take subject to the company's "equity" of rescission, or whether the company's right to rescind would be barred by the third party's acquisition of a proprietary interest.

(2) Mode of rescission

A contract may be rescinded by bringing legal proceedings, or simply by giving notice to the other party, though, even in the latter case, legal proceedings may be necessary to work out the consequences of rescission. This is most obviously true where, as a result of rescission, a sum of money becomes due to the representee and the representor refuses to pay it. It may also be desirable to have a court order stating that a formal transaction (such as a lease or a transfer of shares) has been or ought to be set aside. Even in such a case rescission is the act of the representee and not that of the court, so that the time at which it takes effect is when the representee gives the notice or commences legal proceedings—not the time of the court's order.[16] In other cases no legal proceedings are necessary to give effect to the consequences of rescission: thus where goods have been obtained by fraud rescission can be effected by simply taking them back.[17]

All these modes of rescission involve some degree of notice to the representor; but it has been held that this is not always necessary. In *Car & Universal Finance Co Ltd v Caldwell*[18] the owner of a car was induced by fraud to sell it to a rogue who absconded and could not be traced. On discovering the fraud, the owner notified the police and the Automobile Association and asked them for help in recovering the car. It was held that these acts were enough to rescind the contract, so that an innocent third party who later bought the car got no title to it. It would no doubt be hard on the owner to hold that he could only rescind by communicating with the rogue, for this would deprive him of the right to rescind whenever the rogue disappears. But the actual decision is equally hard on the third party[19]; and the Law Reform Committee has recommended that it

---

[14] Good faith on the part of C is assumed in both examples.

[15] See Gower, *Modern Company Law* (6th ed.), pp.357–361. In *MCC Proceeds Inc v Lehman Bros International Europe* [1998] 4 All E.R. 675 at 686 share *certificates* were treated as chattels for the purpose of a claim in conversion (which failed) but Hobhouse L.J. said at 699 that the shares themselves were, for that purpose, choses in action.

[16] *Reese Silver Mining Co v Smith* (1869) L.R. 4 H.L. 64.

[17] *Re Eastgate* [1905] 1 K.B. 465, doubted but *semble* not on this point in *Re Goldcorp Exchange Ltd* [1995] 1 A.C. 74 at 103.

[18] [1965] 1 Q.B. 525.

[19] Such a third party may, in appropriate circumstances, be protected by s.25 of the Sale of Goods Act 1979: *Newtons of Wembley Ltd v Williams* [1965] 1 Q.B. 560; but the scope of this protection is limited: see Thornley [1965] C.L.J. 24. The Law Reform Committee has recommended that the rule in *Caldwell's* case should be reversed: 12th Report (1966) Cmnd. 2958, para.16; this is already the position in Scots Law: see *Macleod v Ker*, 1965 S.C. 253, where (without mentioning *Caldwell's* case) the Court of Session decided a very similar case in favour of the third party, saying at 257: "By no stretch of imagination could we treat an intimation to the police as of any materiality to found a plea of rescission of contract". See also *Young v D S Dalgleish & Son (Hawick)* 1994 S.C.L.R. 696.

should be reversed. It applies only where the representor has disappeared or for some other reason cannot be reached.[20]

The general principles governing the mode of rescission apply whether the representation is fraudulent or negligent or innocent. But in *Caldwell*'s case the Court of Appeal left open the question whether the rule there laid down applies where the misrepresentation is negligent. The question is perhaps academic since negligent representors are not likely to go into hiding; but it is submitted that the rule can be justified, if at all, only by the strong need to protect victims of fraud and that it should not be applied in cases of negligent or wholly innocent misrepresentation. It is also questionable whether the rule that a contract can be rescinded by simply taking back goods delivered under it should be applied except in cases of fraud.

(3) Misrepresentation as a defence

The operation of misrepresentation as a defence to an action to enforce the contract is illustrated by further reference to *Redgrave v Hurd*.[21] The purchaser there successfully relied on the misrepresentations as to the value of the practice by way of defence to the vendor's claim for specific performance.

Since this process of pleading misrepresentation as a defence is a form of "rescission"[22] it is, in general, subject to the requirement that the representee must return what he got under the contract.[23] But this requirement does not always apply where the representor is guilty of actual fraud. For example where a ship was insured after she had, to the knowledge of the assured, been lost, it was held that the insurer could repudiate liability under the policy on the ground of fraud, and also keep the premiums.[24] The result is to leave the insurer with a windfall; but the rule may perhaps be justified by the strong need to discourage fraud.[25] Even this justification is, however, hard to square with the further rule that, if the insurer takes the initiative by suing for rescission, he does have to return the premiums.[26] This is also the position where he relies on a negligent or wholly innocent misrepresentation as a defence[27]; unless the policy provides for forfeiture of premiums if *any* false statement is made in the proposal form.[28]

---

[20] *Empresa Cubana de Fletes v Lagonisi Shipping Co Ltd* [1971] 1 Q.B. 488 at 505 (actual decision overruled in *The Laconia* [1977] A.C. 850).

[21] (1881) 20 Ch.D. 1.

[22] See above, p.370.

[23] See above, p.370; below, p.378.

[24] See *Tyler v Horne* (1785) and *Chapman v Fraser* (1795), related in *Park on Marine Insurance* (8th ed.), pp.455, 456; *Feise v Parkinson* (1812) 4 Taunt. 639 at 641; *Anderson v Thornton* (1853) 8 Exch. 425 at 428. *Contra*, *Fowkes v Manchester, etc. Assurance* (1863) 3 B. & S. 917, 929, where Blackburn J. is reported to have said that in cases of *fraudulent* misrepresentation the premiums could be recovered back. But the corresponding passages in 11 W.R. 622, 623 and 8 L.T. 309, 311 refer to *innocent* misrepresentation; and these reports are to be preferred as they make the statement consistent with the earlier authorities, from which Blackburn J. showed no intention of departing. See also Marine Insurance Act 1906, s.84(1) and (3), restating the common law rule.

[25] If the assured could recover back the premiums, the only risk to which he would be exposed under the civil law would be that of not being able to sue on the policy; and where he had already lost the property this would be no risk at all.

[26] *Barker v Walters* (1844) 8 Beav. 92 at 96; *London Assurance v Mansel* (1879) 11 Ch.D. 363; *cf. The Litsian Pride* [1985] 1 Lloyd's Rep. 437 at 515 (disapproved on another point in *The Star Sea* [2001] UKHL 1, [2001] 1 All E.R. (Comm) 193; at [71]). *Quaere* whether an insurer who only claims a *declaration* that he is entitled to avoid the policy on the ground of fraud (as in *Fire, etc., Insurance v Greene* [1964] 2 Q.B. 687) must return the premiums.

[27] *Feise v Parkinson* (1812) 4 Taunt. 639; *Anderson v Thornton* (1853) 8 Exch. 425.

[28] *Kumar v Life Insurance Corp of India* [1974] 1 Lloyd's Rep. 147; Hasson, 38 M.L.R. 93. If the insured was a consumer, such a term might not bind the consumer if it was "unfair" within Unfair Terms in Consumer Contracts Regulations 1999, above, pp.271, 274.

A further situation in which a person can plead fraud as a defence without restoring what he has obtained under the contract is illustrated by *Berg v Sadler & Moore*.[29] The claimant was a retail tobacconist, and knew that the defendants (who were wholesalers) would not supply him as he had been put on a stop-list[30] for price-cutting. He therefore sent one Reece to the defendants to buy cigarettes, ostensibly in his own name. Reece paid with money supplied by the claimant but when the defendants discovered the true facts they refused to deliver the cigarettes or to pay back the price. It was held that the claimant was not entitled to the return of the price, so that (as in the insurance cases discussed above) the defendants were left with a windfall. The court justified this result on the ground that the claimant had been engaged in an attempt to perpetrate a *criminal* fraud; and the rule seems to be based on the supposed need to deter such fraud,[31] though it is far from clear why adequate deterrence is not provided by the criminal law. The rule would probably not apply where the fraud was not criminal: *e.g.* where a statement was made with knowledge of its falsity but without dishonest intent.[31a] The rule should certainly not apply where the misrepresentation was only negligent or where it was innocent.

(4) Application to sale of goods

It has been doubted whether the equitable remedy of rescission for innocent misrepresentation applies at all to a contract for sale of goods.[32] The remedy is not mentioned in the Sale of Goods Act 1979, and in *Re Wait* Atkin L.J. said that "the total sum of legal relations (meaning by the word 'legal' existing in equity as well as in common law) arising out of the contract for the sale of goods may well be regarded as defined by the Code".[33] S.62(2) of the Act indeed saves the rules of "common law so far as they are not inconsistent with the Act, but it has been held in other jurisdictions that "common law" here does not include equity, and that the equitable right to rescind a contract for the sale of goods for innocent misrepresentation has not (if it ever existed) survived the Act.[34] But it is submitted that this view should be rejected for the following reasons.

First: the Act plainly does not deal with every aspect of a contract for the sale of goods. It does not, for example, deal with assignment but clearly the benefit of a contract for the sale of goods can be assigned.[35] The Act can only deal exhaustively with the topics to which its enacting sections refer. One of those topics, admittedly, is remedies and Atkin L.J. has said that the rules contained in the Act as to (*inter alia*) the "remedies" of the parties appear to be "complete and exclusive statements of the legal relations both at law and in equity".[36] Even this may, with respect, be doubted. Breach of a contract for the sale of goods may be restrained by injunction,[37] and such a contract

---

[29] [1937] 2 K.B. 158; Allen, 54 L.Q.R. 201; Goodhart, *ibid.* 216; Treitel in *Essays in Memory of Sir Rupert Cross*, pp.107–108.

[30] This practice was made unlawful by Resale Prices Act 1976, Pt I, but that Act has (subject to transitional provisions) been repealed by Competition Act 1998, s.1.

[31] *South Australia Asset Management Corp v York Montague Ltd* [1997] A.C. 191 at 215; *Smith New Court Securities Ltd v Scrimgeoour Vickers (Asset Management) Ltd* [1997] A.C. 254 at 279; *cf. Direct Line Insurance v Khan* [2001] N.L.J. 485 (fraud relating to *part* of an insurance claim held to make insured liable to return the *whole* of the sum paid by the insurers); and see below, pp.438–439.

[31a] See *Polhill v Walter* (1832) 3 B. & Ad. 114, above, p.343.

[32] Atiyah, 22 M.L.R. 76; but see his *Sale of Goods* (10th ed.), pp.529–530.

[33] [1927] 1 Ch. 606 at 635.

[34] *Riddiford v Warren* (1901) 20 N.Z.L.R. 572; followed in *Watt v Westhoven* [1933] V.L.R. 458.

[35] *Re Wait* [1927] 1 Ch. 606 at 636.

[36] *ibid.*

[37] See below, p.1046.

may be rectified,[38] although these remedies are not mentioned in the Act. In any event, it seems that Atkin L.J. used the word "remedies" in the sense in which it is used in Pt VI of the Act, *i.e.* to mean remedies *for breach* of contract[39]; and rescission for misrepresentation is not such a remedy.[40] In an earlier case, Atkin J. himself had said that, if the seller had made a misrepresentation, the buyer "would be entitled to rescind the contract".[41]

Secondly: it is submitted that in s.62(2) "common law" does include equity. The subsection saves the rules of "common law . . . relating to the law of principal and agent and the effect of fraud, *misrepresentation*, duress or coercion, mistake, *or other invalidating cause*". Misrepresentation is here regarded as an invalidating cause distinct from fraud and mistake. But at common law an innocent misrepresentation did not invalidate a contract for the sale of goods,[42] unless it induced a fundamental mistake. Hence the saving of the rules as to the effect of misrepresentation can refer only to the rules of equity. Moreover, it would be strange if the Act saved the rules of common law, but not those of equity, relating to mistake and agency.

Thirdly: the authorities support the view that a contract for the sale of goods can be rescinded for innocent misrepresentation. In *Leaf v International Galleries*[43] and *Long v Lloyd*[44] the right to rescind such contracts for innocent misrepresentation was held to be barred—in the first case by lapse of time and in the second by acceptance.[45] The decision in each case was that the right to rescind had been lost: not that it never existed. In *Goldsmith v Roger*[46] a contract for the sale of a boat was induced by an innocent[47] misrepresentation of the buyer; and it was held that the seller could "rescind" in the sense of being able to rely on the misrepresentation as a defence.

Fourthly: if a contract for the sale of goods could not be rescinded for innocent misrepresentation the injured party would have no remedy at all for an innocent misrepresentation not incorporated in the contract. Such an unjust result ought not to be reached in the absence of a clear statutory provision to that effect.

4. Incorporated Misrepresentation

(1) Misrepresentation Act 1967, s.1(a)

S.1(a) provides that a person who has entered into a contract after a misrepresentation has been made to him shall be entitled to rescind notwithstanding that "the misrepresentation has become a term of the contract" if he would otherwise be entitled to rescind without alleging fraud. This right to rescind therefore survives[48] when a statement of fact (as opposed to a promise[49]) is made to induce a contract and later

---

[38] *e.g. Caraman, Rowley & May v Aperghis* (1928) 40 T.L.R. 124; the same assumption was made (though the claim for rectification failed) in *F E Rose (London) Ltd v W H Pim Jr & Co Ltd* [1953] 2 Q.B. 450, above, p.324.

[39] See the title of Pt VI of the Act and the sub-headings before ss.49 and 51.

[40] Unless Atkin L.J.'s remarks are interpreted in this way the first three sections of the Misrepresentation Act would not apply to contracts for the sale of goods; but obviously no court would reach this conclusion.

[41] *Re Harrison & Micks, Lambert & Co* [1917] 1 K.B. 755 at 761.

[42] See above, p.369. Negligent misrepresentation was not recognised as a separate category in 1893, when the Sale of Goods Act was originally passed.

[43] [1950] 2 K.B. 86.

[44] [1958] 1 W.L.R. 753.

[45] *cf.* below, pp.383–384.

[46] [1962] 2 Lloyd's Rep. 249.

[47] *i.e.* not fraudulent: *cf.* above, pp.340, 350, 369.

[48] For doubts on this point before the Act, see *Cie Française de Chemin de Fer Paris-Orléans v Leeston Shipping Co* (1919) 1 Ll.L.R. 235; *Pennsylvania Shipping Co v Cie Nationale de Navigation* (1936) 155 L.T. 294.

[49] See above, p.331.

becomes one of its terms. But s.1(a) does not take away any remedies for breach of contract; and the relation between these remedies and the statutory right to rescind is obscure.

Apart from the Misrepresentation Act, breach of contract gives rise sometimes to a right to damages for breach only, and sometimes to a right to damages and also to a right to "rescind for breach".[50] Where an incorporated misrepresentation gives rise to both these rights, they can presumably still be exercised independently of s.1 (and the right to rescind for breach is probably unaffected by s.2(2)).[51] Where the incorporated misrepresentation gives rise (apart from the Act) to a right to damages for breach only, the representee can ignore his right to rescind under the Act and claim damages for breach of contract. But it is not clear whether he can still claim such damages if he does "rescind" under s.1(a). If "rescind" here refers to "rescission for misrepresentation" it is arguable that such rescission destroys all outstanding liabilities under the contract, including liability in damages for its breach. This view might cause hardship where a representee had rescinded out of court (*e.g.* by returning defective goods) but the court could probably come to his rescue by declaring the contract subsisting under s.2(2) of the Act. It is true that damages in lieu of rescission under that subsection may be less than damages for breach of contract[52]; but one effect of declaring the contract subsisting might be to revive the right to damages for breach of contract, *i.e.* for the untruth of the incorporated misrepresentation.[53]

(2) Misrepresentation Act 1967, s.2(2)

This subsection, which gives the court a discretion to declare the contract subsisting, and award damages in lieu of rescission,[54] may limit the right to rescind for an incorporated misrepresentation. Where the representee does not rescind but simply claims damages for breach of contract, the subsection clearly has no effect, for the court's discretion depends on a claim having been made "that the contract ought to be or has been rescinded". Where the representee does claim "rescission" it is first necessary to ask what would be the effect of the incorporated misrepresentation viewed purely as a breach of contract. If its only effect as a breach would be to give rise to a right to damages, any claim to "rescind" must be a claim to "rescind for misrepresentation" which is subject to the discretion of the court, so that the court could refuse to allow rescission and confine the claimant to a claim for damages. If on the other hand, the effect of the incorporated misrepresentation as a breach would be to give rise to a right to damages and also to a right to "rescind for breach", the position is less clear. One view is that a representee who treats the contract as repudiated thereby claims "that the contract ought to be or has been rescinded"; and this view has the attraction that it enables the court to restrict the right to "rescind for breach" which has sometimes been exercised by parties who have not suffered any appreciable loss as a result of the breach.[55] On the other hand there is no hint in the legislative history of the Act that any such reform was intended; and if such a change in the law has been made it would be an extraordinarily partial one, for it would apply only to breaches resulting from representations *of fact* made before the contract (and not to breaches of *promises*). The better view

---

[50] See above, p.370; below, pp.758 *et seq.* For further remedies in consumer sales, see Sale of Goods Act 1979, ss.48A to 48F, as inserted by Sale and Supply of Goods to Consumers Regulations 2002, SI 2002/3045, reg.5.

[51] See the discussion under heading (2), below.

[52] See above, pp.365–366.

[53] A possibility which was overlooked in 30 M.L.R. at 372.

[54] See above, p.357.

[55] See, for example, below, pp.779, 794–795.

seems to be that "rescinded" in s.2(2) refers only to "rescission for misrepresentation" as the subsection deals with the case of a person "who is entitled, *by reason of the misrepresentation* to rescind the contract"; and that, accordingly, the right to "rescind for breach" is not subject to the discretion of that court.

SECTION 5. LIMITS TO THE RIGHT TO RESCIND

The right to rescind a contract may be barred by a number of factors. Before these are considered, two points must be made with regard to the effects of the Misrepresentation Act 1967.

1. Effects of Misrepresentation Act 1967

First, the Act has abrogated one restriction on the right to rescind. Before the Act, it had been held that certain contracts could not be rescinded for innocent misrepresentation after they had been "executed" (*i.e.*, performed). This rule applied, in particular, where a contract for the disposition of an interest in land was performed by execution of the conveyance or lease[56]; and where a contract for the sale of shares was performed by transfer of the shares.[57] Many applications[58] of the rule were hard to justify, and its scope was uncertain. It was reversed by s.1(b) of the Act, which provides that a person who would otherwise be entitled to rescind a contract for misrepresentation without alleging fraud[59] shall be so entitled notwithstanding that "the contract has been performed". The buyer of a house can therefore rescind for misrepresentation even after conveyance and even though the misrepresentation was wholly innocent.

Secondly, the right to rescind a contract for misrepresentation is now subject to the discretion of the court under s.2(2) of the Act.[60] In the case just put, of a house-purchaser claiming rescission for wholly innocent misrepresentation, the court might prefer to declare the contract subsisting and to award damages in lieu of rescission. For if (as would often be the case) the vendor had used the purchase-money to buy another house, rescission might cause him severe hardship. This would be a factor which the court could take into account under s.2(2), so that rescission would probably be allowed only where the buyer had suffered serious prejudice as a result of the misrepresentation. S.2(2) may, similarly, operate in cases which are not precisely covered by the bars to rescission but in which the court nevertheless considers that damages would be a more appropriate remedy than rescission. It is, however, still necessary to define the bars to rescission because if one of them has arisen the court has *no* discretion to allow rescission and, on one possible interpretation of s.2(2),[61] cannot award damages either.

---

[56] *Angel v Jay* [1911] 1 K.B. 666 (lease).

[57] *Seddon v North Eastern Salt Co* [1905] 1 Ch. 326.

[58] *e.g.* in the cases cited in the last two notes. The rule may have served some useful purpose in relation to contracts for the sale of land and to long leases: *cf.* Law Reform Committee 10th Report Cmnd. 1782 (1962) paras 6 and 7.

[59] The rule that an executed contract could not be rescinded never applied to cases of fraudulent misrepresentation, so that it was not necessary to change the law in such cases.

[60] See above, p.358. Rescission was said to be a discretionary remedy even before the 1967 Act: see *Spence v Crawford* [1939] 3 All E.R. 271 at 288; but this principle would be hard to apply to rescission by some extra-judicial act of the representee (above, pp.371–372); *cf. TSB Bank plc v Camfield* [1995] 1 W.L.R. 430 at 438.

[61] See above, p.359.

2. Bars to Rescission

(1) Restitution impossible

Normally, a party who wishes to rescind a contract for misrepresentation is required to restore to the other any benefits which he has obtained under the contract: for example, a buyer who wants to rescind with a view to getting back the price must give back the goods. If the benefit obtained is a sum of money[62] there is never any difficulty in complying with this requirement: the representee restores an equivalent sum. But, where he has obtained a benefit other than money, he may for some reason be unable to restore it; and this inability will sometimes bar his right to rescind.

(a) CHANGES MADE BY MISREPRESENTEE. Where a contract of sale has been induced by a misrepresentation of the seller, the buyer may lose the right to rescind if he has so changed the subject-matter that he can no longer restore what he obtained under the contract: for example, the buyer of an animal who has slaughtered it cannot rescind on returning the corpse.[63] Similarly, the purchaser of a business cannot get back his purchase-money after carrying on the business for four months and disposing of some of its assets,[64] or after changing a partnership into a limited company[65]; nor can the purchaser of a mine rescind after he has worked it out.[66] On the same principle a person cannot rescind after he has disposed of the subject-matter of the contract unless, perhaps, he has been able to get back that subject-matter or its substantial equivalent.[67]

(b) DETERIORATION OR DECLINE IN VALUE. In the cases discussed above, deterioration or decline in value barred the right to rescind because it was due to the acts of the representee. Where it is due to other causes, different rules apply. The right to rescind is clearly not barred where the subject-matter deteriorates precisely because it lacks a quality that it was represented to possess. Thus a person who is induced to enter into a partnership by a misrepresentation as to its solvency can still rescind after the bankruptcy of the firm.[68] The position is the same where the deterioration or decline in value is not related to the misrepresentation but is due to some external cause. In *Armstrong v Jackson*[69] a broker purported to buy shares for a client, but in fact sold his own shares to the client. Five years later, when the shares had fallen in value from nearly £3 to 5s., it was held that the client could rescind on account of the broker's breach of duty.[70] He still had the identical shares and was able to return them, together with the

---

[62] Or the release of an obligation to pay money, as in *The Siboen and the Sibotre* [1976] 1 Lloyd's Rep. 293; see esp. p.337.

[63] *Clarke v Dickson* (1858) E.B. & E. 148 at 155.

[64] *Sheffield Nickel Co Ltd v Unwin* (1877) 2 Q.B.D. 215; cf. *Thomas Witter Ltd v BTP Industries Ltd* [1996] 2 All E.R. 573 at 588.

[65] *Clarke v Dickson* (1858) E.B. & E. 148; *quaere* whether this is *per se* decisive; *Western Bank of Scotland v Addie* (1867) L.R. 1 Sc. & Div. 145 at 159.

[66] *Clarke v Dickson*, above; *Lagunas Nitrate Co v Lagunas Syndicate* [1899] 2 Ch. 392.

[67] e.g. where a buyer of shares has sold them but can re-acquire an equivalent quantity in the market. In *Smith New Court Securities Ltd v Scrimgeour Vickers (Asset Management) Ltd* the Court of Appeal seems to have taken the view that the buyer could not rescind in such a case: [1994] 1 W.L.R. 1271 at 1280; but on appeal Lord Browne-Wilkinson said that the law on the point would have to be "closely looked at hereafter:" [1997] A.C. 254 at 264. Some difficulty might arise where the representee had bought the subject matter back for less than the amount for which he had previously sold it, so that he would make an actual profit out of recission: see *Marr v Tumulty* 175 N.E. 356 (1931). Perhaps he could be required to account for any such profit as part of the process of rescission.

[68] *Adam v Newbigging* (1886) 34 Ch.D. 582; (1888) 13 App.Cas. 308.

[69] [1917] 2 K.B. 822.

[70] See below, p.745.

dividends he had received. McCardie J. said: "It is only... where the plaintiff has sustained loss by the inferiority of the subject-matter or a substantial fall in its value that he will desire to exert his power of rescission. . . . If mere deterioration of the subject-matter negatived the right to rescind, the doctrine of rescission would become a vain thing".[71]

Similarly, a contractual right to reject is not lost simply because the subject-matter deteriorates without the fault of the party claiming to rescind. In *Head v Tattersall*[72] the buyer of a horse was allowed to return it for breach of "warranty"[73] although it had been seriously injured through no fault of his. Bramwell B. added that the right to reject would not be lost if "the injury were caused by reason of a trial necessary to test the warranty".[74] It is submitted that these rules also apply where the buyer is induced to buy by a misrepresentation which has been incorporated in the contract.[75]

(c) CHANGES MADE BY MISREPRESENTOR. Where the misrepresentation is that of the seller, the question is whether the buyer (*i.e.* misrepresent*ee*) can rescind even though he cannot restore the subject-matter in its original state. A sale may also be induced by a misrepresentation on the part of the buyer, *e.g.* as to his solvency or as to the value of the subject-matter. The question then arises whether the seller's right to rescind is affected by some dealing with the subject-matter by the buyer (who in such a case is the misrepresent*or*). Obviously, the right may be so affected in a practical sense where the buyer consumes the property or so alters it that the seller has no interest in getting it back. As a matter of law, however, a buyer who is guilty of fraud cannot rely on his own dealings[76] with the subject-matter as a bar to the seller's right to rescind. In *Spence v Crawford*[77] A was induced by the fraud of B to enter into a contract by which (i) A sold to B shares in a company, and (ii) B undertook to relieve A of his liability under a guarantee of the company's bank overdraft, and to procure the release of securities deposited by A with the bank. A duly transferred the shares, while B relieved A of his liability to the bank and freed the securities by giving his own personal guarantee to the bank. The constitution of the company was later altered and some of the shares in it were sold. It was held that this dealing with the shares did not bar A's right to rescind. The question whether it would have had this effect if B's misrepresentation had been innocent was left open.[78]

(d) BENEFIT TO MISREPRESENTEE. The mere fact that the misrepresentee has received a benefit under the contract does not bar his right to rescind, if the misrepresentor has not been put to any expense in conferring that benefit. Thus in *Spence v Crawford* the fact that B had relieved A of his liability to the bank and freed his securities did not bar A's right to rescind. B was not put to any expense *by merely giving* the guarantee to the bank, nor was he ever asked to pay anything under it, as the company prospered. We shall see that B did suffer some loss as a result of giving his guarantee, but this did not bar A's claim to rescind as he was able to make allowance for it.[79]

---

[71] [1917] 2 K.B. 822 at 829.
[72] (1871) L.R. 7 Ex. 7.
[73] *i.e.* a "condition" in the modern terminology used at below, p.788.
[74] (1871) L.R. Ex. 7 at 12.
[75] *cf. Long v Lloyd* [1958] 1 W.L.R. 753 at 760.
[76] Nor on the other party's dealings at his request: *cf. Hulton v Hulton* [1917] 1 K.B. 813 (destruction of letters).
[77] [1939] 3 All E.R. 271.
[78] *ibid.* at 281. The effect of negligence in such a situation is also unclear.
[79] See below, p.381.

Conversely, if no benefit has been received by the representee, the right to rescind is not lost *merely* because the representor has acted on the contract to his prejudice. In *Mackenzie v Royal Bank of Canada*[80] a wife was induced by misrepresentation to deposit share certificates with a bank as security for the overdraft of a company controlled by her husband. She was able to rescind although the bank had, after the deposit, advanced further money to the company, for she had received no benefit from this payment. It is sometimes said that the object of rescission is to restore the parties to the situation in which they would have been if the contract had never been made,[81] but in the light of *Mackenzie*'s case such statements are not quite accurate. The essential point is that the representee should not be unjustly enriched at the representor's expense[82]; that the representor should not be prejudiced is a secondary consideration.

(e) PRECISE RESTITUTION IMPOSSIBLE. The general rule that a representee had to restore what he had got under the contract was very strictly applied at common law where a person sought the return of his money on rescission *for breach*. The rule was so strict that a person who had agreed to buy an interest in land lost the right to get his money back merely by going into possession under the contract. The benefit of even such temporary possession was thought to make restitution impossible.[83] The authorities supporting this rule were sometimes cited in cases of rescission *for misrepresentation*[84]; though it is by no means clear whether the strict common law rule ever extended to such cases. The point is no longer of any importance, since a more flexible rule was developed by equity in cases of misrepresentation, and this rule now prevails.

In equity a representee who is able to make substantial, though not precise, restitution can rescind if he returns the subject-matter of the contract in its altered state, accounts for any profits derived from it and makes allowance for deterioration caused by his dealing with it. Thus a person who has gone into possession under a contract to buy, or take a lease of, land can rescind[85] on terms of paying rent for the period of his occupation.[86] The court can also set off benefits received by one party against those received by the other.[87] Similarly, in *Erlanger v New Sombrero Phosphate Co*[88] a company bought and worked a phosphate mine, but did not so work it out as to make restitution utterly impossible. It was held that the company could rescind the sale for breach of fiduciary duty by one of its promoters on terms of returning the mine and accounting for the profits of working it. Lord Blackburn said that equity could "take account of profits and make allowance for deterioration.[89] And I think the practice has always been for a court of equity to give this relief whenever, by the exercise of its powers, it can do

---

[80] [1934] A.C. 468; *cf. TSB Bank v Camfield* [1995] 1 W.L.R. 430.

[81] *e.g. Gillett v Peppercorne* (1840) 3 Beav. 78 at 81.

[82] *Bouygues Offshore v Ultisol Transport Contractors* [1996] 2 Lloyd's Rep. 153 at 159.

[83] *Hunt v Silk* (1804) 5 East 449; *Blackburn v Smith* (1848) 2 Ex. 783 (both cases of pure breach); below, p.1061.

[84] *e.g.* in *Clarke v Dickson* (1858) E.B. & E. 148.

[85] *Redgrave v Hurd* (1881) 20 Ch.D. 1.

[86] *Hulton v Hulton* [1917] 1 K.B. 813 at 826. It seems that no such terms were imposed in *Redgrave v Hurd*, above, where the buyer got back the whole of his deposit in spite of having been in possession for a short time.

[87] *Hulton v Hulton* [1917] 1 K.B. 813.

[88] (1878) 3 App.Cas. 1218; *cf. Gillett v Peppercorne* (1840) 3 Beav. 78; *The Lucy* [1983] 1 Lloyd's Rep. 188 at 202.

[89] *cf. Cheese v Thomas* [1994] 1 W.L.R. 129, where rescission of a joint house purchase was claimed, not against the vendor, but by one of the joint purchasers against the other. The case was one of presumed undue influence (below, p.419) but the court relied on misrepresentation cases, such as *Newbigging v Adam* (1886) 34 Ch.D. 582.

what is practically just, though it cannot restore the parties precisely to the state they were in before the contract".[90]

These powers of adjustment are normally exercised where the misrepresentee is a buyer who claims back his money. They may also be available in the converse case where the misrepresentee is a seller who claims back his property, as in *Spence v Crawford*.[91] The fraudulent buyer in that case had performed his contractual undertaking to relieve the seller of certain obligations to a bank. He was asked by the bank to sell some stock to maintain his liquidity, and the sale resulted in a loss to him of £1,000. The final order made in that case was that the seller should recover back his shares plus the dividends received by the buyer; but that he should repay the purchase price plus interest, and make allowance in respect of part[92] of the £1,000 lost by the buyer on the sale of his stock.

(f) NATURE OF SUBJECT-MATTER. Restitution by the representee may be possible but the court may be unwilling to order it on account of the nature of the property. This was the position in *The Siben*[93] where a contract for the sale of property included an escort agency, the employees of which provided "sexual favours" for its clients. The sale had been induced by the vendor's fraudulent misrepresentations unrelated to this point; and a claim to rescind the contract was rejected on the ground that the court should not "make an order which would in principle have the effect of transferring an illegal business from one party to another".[94] This reasoning is not easy to reconcile with the principle that rescission is the act of the representee, not that of the court[95]; and the return of the illegal business would, moreover be merely a condition of any judgment which might have been given for the return of the price, so that there would have been no need to make an actual order for the return of that business.

(g) IMPROVEMENTS IN THE SUBJECT-MATTER. Two problems arise where dealings with the subject-matter have not decreased its value, but have improved it. The first is whether such dealings bar the right to rescind; the second is what allowance (if any) is to be awarded in respect of the improvements. These may be made either by the misrepresentee or by the misrepresentor.

(i) *Made by the misrepresentee.* One illustration of this possibility is provided by *Boyd & Forrest v Glasgow & SW Ry.*[96] Contractors alleged that they had been induced to enter into a contract to build a railway by misrepresentations as to the strata. After the railway had been built, they claimed to rescind, with a view to recovering a *quantum meruit* (exceeding the contract price) for the cost of the work. The claim failed on a number of grounds, one of which was that the right to rescind was barred since it was no longer possible to restore the railway company to its original position. This is an unusual application of the requirement of restoration, which normally prevents the representee from rescinding unless he can *give back* benefits that he has *received*. In this case, the requirement prevented rescission because the representee could not *take back* benefits that he had *conferred*.[97] The decision can be explained on the ground that it was not practicable to restore the parties to their pre-contract position, so that "rescission"

---

[90] (1878) 3 App.Cas. 1218 at 1278–1279; approved in *Guiness plc v Saunders* [1990] 2 A.C. 663 at 698, but distinguished as the agreement in the latter case was not voidable but void.

[91] [1939] 3 All E.R. 271; above, p.380.

[92] This seems to have been a compromise, adopted to avoid the need to take complicated cross-accounts.

[93] [1996] 1 Lloyd's Rep. 35; for further proceedings see [1996] 2 Lloyd's Rep. 667.

[94] [1996] 1 Lloyd's Rep. 35 at 62.

[95] See above, p.372.

[96] 1915 S.C.(H.L.) 20.

[97] For the suggestion that, in such cases, the representee may be able to "waive restitution due to him", see *Bouygues Offshore v Ultisol Transport Contractors* [1996] 2 Lloyd's Rep. 153 at 159.

made no practical sense. The more convenient remedy is damages and on such facts this would now generally be available under s.2(1) of the Misrepresentation Act.[98]

A second, and perhaps more common, illustration of this situation is provided by the case of a person who is induced by misrepresentation to buy something which he improves before discovering the truth. In such a case, the improvements probably do not bar the right to rescind; and their cost can often be claimed as damages.[99] Where the representation is wholly innocent and the contract has been rescinded, there will be no such claim[1]; but the representee might be able to set off the cost of the improvements against his liability[2] to make allowance for benefits received by him under the contract.[3]

(ii) *Made by the misrepresentor.* In *Spence v Crawford*[4] the fraudulent buyer was granted an allowance in respect of his loss on sale of stock. This loss did not produce any directly corresponding increase in the value of what he had bought; and it was incurred in consequence of something that he was *obliged* under the contract to do. It does not follow from the decision that a buyer who obtains property by misrepresentation can, if the seller claims rescission, insist on an allowance for improvements which he has made *without* being contractually bound to do so. It can be argued on the one hand that the seller would get a windfall if he did not have to pay anything for the improvements[5]; and on the other that he should not be forced to pay for improvements (which he may not want or be able to afford) as a condition of getting back his property. The better view, probably, is that if the seller claims rescission, he should have to make some allowance (based on increase in value rather than the cost of work to the buyer).[6] If the seller is unwilling or unable to pay the allowance he can generally fall back on his alternative remedy of damages.[7]

(2) Third party rights

The right to rescind a contract may be barred by the intervention of third party rights. For example, a person who has been induced by fraud to sell goods cannot rescind after the goods have been bought by an innocent third party, that is, by one without notice of the fraud.[8] On the same principle, a person cannot rescind an allotment of shares in a company after the company has gone into liquidation. At that point the rights of third parties intervene in that the assets of the company have to be collected for distribution among the company's creditors.[9] This should be contrasted with the rule in the bankruptcy of an individual that the trustee in bankruptcy takes the property "subject to equities", including the right of rescission. Thus in *Load v Green*[10] a seller was by fraud induced to sell goods to one Bannister, who became bankrupt. It was held that the seller could disaffirm the contract and recover the value of his goods from Bannister's trustee in bankruptcy. It is difficult to find any convincing reason for this distinction between winding up of insolvent companies and individual bankruptcy. It seems to be

---

[98] See above, p.350.
[99] See above, pp.345 *et seq.*
[1] See above, pp.366 *et seq.*
[2] See above, p.378.
[3] *cf. Cooper v Phibbs* (1867) L.R. 2 H.L. 149, above, pp.320–321.
[4] [1939] 3 All E.R. 271; above, pp.380, 381.
[5] *e.g., Williams v Logue*, 122 So. 490 (1929).
[6] *cf. Walker v Galt*, 171 F. 2d 613 (1948); *Cheese v Thomas* [1994] 1 W.L.R. 129 at 137.
[7] See above, pp.344 *et seq.*
[8] See above, p.371; and see below, p.424. *cf. Society of Lloyd's v Lyon, The Times,* August 11, 1997.
[9] *Re Scottish Petroleum Co* (1883) 23 Ch.D. 413.
[10] (1846) 15 M. & W. 216.

based on the assumption that third parties place greater reliance on a company's nominal share capital (especially if the company is a new one, or has just raised new capital) than on an individual's appearance of wealth.

A similar principle to that here under consideration can apply where a misrepresentation induces the representee to enter into a contract with a third party; for example, where A, by a misrepresentation addressed to B, induces the B to guarantee A's overdraft with the C bank. The bank's ability to enforce such a transaction depends on whether it is "put on enquiry"[11] as to the circumstances in which it was concluded. As in most of the recent cases of this kind the alleged vitiating factor has been undue influence (sometimes together with misrepresentation), a full discussion of the effect of such factors on the rights of the third party will be found in Chapter 10.[12]

(3) Affirmation

A contract cannot be rescinded for misrepresentation if the representee expressly or by conduct affirms it after discovering the truth.[13] Thus a person who is induced by misrepresentation to buy goods cannot rescind if, after discovering the truth, he uses them[14]; a person who is induced by misrepresentation to subscribe for shares in a company cannot rescind if, after discovering the truth, he accepts dividends, votes at meetings or tries to sell the shares[15]; a person who is induced by misrepresentation to take a lease cannot rescind if, after discovering the truth, he stays on and pays rent[16]; *a fortiori* a mining lease cannot be rescinded if, after discovering the truth, the lessee continues to work the mine.[17] Use of the subject-matter for the sole purpose of testing the accuracy of the representation does not, however, amount to affirmation.[18]

Affirmation may be inferred even from failure to rescind: for example, where a person wishes to rescind an allotment of shares in a company on the ground of misrepresentation. Such a person is not allowed to wait and see whether the company will prosper: he must not only tell the company that he rescinds but must also take steps to remove his name from the register of shareholders.[19]

On a principle analogous to affirmation[20] a person cannot set aside one term of a contract on the ground of fraud while affirming the rest. For example, a person who has been induced to enter into an agreement to take a lease by a misrepresentation relating to one of its terms cannot repudiate that term while affirming the rest of the lease.[21] Similarly, an insurance company can rescind a policy for non-disclosure, but it cannot repudiate a particular claim while purporting to recognise that the policy is still in force.[22] Nor is it open to the court at the request of the representor to restrict rescission

---

[11] *Royal Bank of Scotland v Etridge (No.2)* [2001] UKHL 44; [2002] 2 A.C. 773, at [44].

[12] Below, pp.424–427..

[13] *cf.* the loss of the right to rescind *for breach* on similar grounds: below, p.811.

[14] *United Shoe Machinery Co of Canada v Brunet* [1909] A.C. 330; *cf. Long v Lloyd* [1958] 1 W.L.R. 753; *Skipskreditforeningen v Emperor Navigation* [1998] 1 Lloyd's Rep. 67 at 73–74.

[15] *Western Bank of Scotland v Addie* (1867) L.R. 1 Sc. & Div. 145; *Scholey v Central Ry of Venezuela* (1870) L.R. 9 Eq. 266n.; *Ex. p. Briggs* (1866) L.R. 1 Eq. 483.

[16] *Kennard v Ashman* (1894) 10 T.L.R. 213.

[17] *Vigers v Pike* (1842) 8 Cl. & F. 562.

[18] *Long v Lloyd* [1958] 1 W.L.R. 753 (first trip); *cf. Lindsay Petroleum Co v Hurd* (1874) L.R. 5 P.C. 221 (sinking exploratory well no bar to rescission).

[19] *First National Reinsurance Co Ltd v Greenfield* [1921] 2 K.B. 260; for a qualification of this principle, see *Pawle's Case* (1869) L.R. 4 Ch.App. 487.

[20] *Urquhart v Macpherson* (1878) 3 App.Cas. 831.

[21] *Inntrepreneur Pub Co v Sweeney* [2002] EWHC 1060; [2002] E.G.L.R. 132.

[22] *West v National Motors & Accident Insurance Union Ltd* [1955] 1 W.L.R. 343. It is not clear why the company adopted this ambivalent attitude: see p.347 of the report. The result might have been different had fraud been alleged; above, p.373.

to the part of the contract to which the representation relates. If, for example, a guarantee is procured by a representation that it relates only to future debts, when in fact it relates to past and future debts, then the guarantee cannot be rescinded with regard to the past, but upheld with regard to the future debts: such a course would amount to remaking, not to rescinding the contract.[23]

A person can affirm only after he has discovered the truth. To hear rumours that the representation may be untrue is not, for this purpose, discovery of the truth.[24] But if the representee knows all the facts from which a reasonable person would deduce the truth, he may be taken to know it.[25]

Affirmation as a bar to the right to rescind *for misrepresentation* must be compared with certain bars to a buyer's right to rescind *for breach of condition*.[26] In *Leaf v International Galleries*[27] Denning L.J. said: "An innocent misrepresentation is much less potent than a breach of condition; and a claim to rescission for innocent misrepresentation must at any rate be barred when the right to reject for breach of condition is barred". The latter is barred by (*inter alia*) "acceptance", and this takes place (a) when the buyer intimates that he accepts the goods; or (b) when the goods have been delivered to him and he does any act inconsistent with the ownership of the seller; or (c) when after lapse of a reasonable time he retains the goods without intimating that he has rejected them.[28] In the first two cases, the buyer is not deemed to have accepted the goods until he has had a reasonable opportunity of examining them, and in the third the question whether he has had such an opportunity is material in determining whether a reasonable time has elapsed.[29] But in all three cases it is the opportunity of discovering the defect, rather that its actual discovery, which is the crucial factor, so that a buyer may "accept" without discovering the truth,[30] and a literal reading of Denning L.J.'s dictum would suggest that acceptance will always deprive him of the right to rescind for innocent misrepresentation. But it is submitted that the dictum must be read, according to its context, to refer to cases in which a claim to rescission is resisted on the ground of lapse of time. In other words, it means only that, where lapse of time amounts to acceptance, then it will also bar the right to rescind for misrepresentation. If the buyer, in ignorance of the true facts, "accepts" in some other way he may nevertheless be able to rescind for misrepresentation; and he may, by virtue of s.1(a) of the Misrepresentation Act, be able to do this even where the misrepresentation had been incorporated in the contract.

(4) Lapse of time

In cases of fraud or breach of fiduciary duty, lapse of time does not itself bar rescission. It is simply evidence of affirmation.[31] This view is supported by the rule that time begins

---

[23] *TSB plc v Camfield* [1995] 1 W.L.R. 430, citing *Barclays Bank plc v O'Brien* [1994] 1 A.C. 180 at 199; *De Molestina v Ponton* [2002] 1 Lloyd's Rep. 271 at 286–288 rejecting (as inconsistent with the above authorities) the contrary view taken in the Australian case of *Vadasz v Pioneer Concrete (SA) Pty Ltd* (1995) 184 C.L.R. 182; the conflict was left unresolved in *Far Eastern Shipping Co Public Ltd v Scales Trading Ltd* [2001] 1 All E.R. (Comm) 315.

[24] *Central Ry of Venezuela v Kisch* (1867) L.R. 2 H.L. 99.

[25] *Scholey v Central Ry of Venezuela* (1870) L.R. 9 Eq. 266n.; *Long v Lloyd* [1958] 1 W.L.R. 753 at 760. Contrast, in cases of breach, below, pp.814 *et seq.*

[26] See below, p.816.

[27] [1950] 2 K.B. 86, 90.

[28] Sale of Goods Act 1979, s.35(1) and (2), as substituted by Sale and Supply of Goods Act 1994, s.2.

[29] Sale of Goods Act 1979, s.35(4) and (5), as substituted by Sale and Supply of Goods Act 1994, s.2.

[30] *e.g.* where he has a reasonable opportunity of examining the goods but does not discover the truth.

[31] *Clough v LNW Ry* (1871) L.R. 7 Ex. 26, 35; *cf.* (in cases of breach) below, pp.814–815.

to run only from the discovery of the truth[32]; and by the rule that time spent in negotiations to settle the dispute does not bar rescission.[33]

In *Leaf v International Galleries*[34] the claimant was induced to buy a picture by the innocent misrepresentation that it was "by J. Constable".[35] Five years later he sought to rescind but it was held that his right to do so was barred by lapse of time. As rescission was sought promptly on discovery of the truth, the lapse of time was not evidence of affirmation, so that, even in the absence of such evidence, lapse of time is a bar to the right to rescind for *innocent* misrepresentation. The length of time required for this purpose seems to be such as would enable a reasonably diligent inquirer to discover the truth. This rule probably applies to a negligent misrepresentation in the same way as to a wholly innocent one.

SECTION 6. EXCLUDING LIABILITY FOR MISREPRESENTATION

The common law starts with the principle that contract terms which exclude liability for misrepresentation (including those which exclude the right to rescind)[36] are valid. Their effectiveness may, indeed, be limited by the general rules relating to exemption clauses, discussed elsewhere in this book.[37] In addition, s.3 of the Misrepresentation Act 1967[38] provides: "If a contract contains a term which would exclude or restrict (*a*) any liability to which a party to a contract may be subject by reason of any misrepresentation made by him before the contract was made; or (*b*) any remedy available to another party to the contract by reason of such a misrepresentation, that term shall be of no effect except in so far as it satisfies the requirement of reasonableness as stated in section 11(1) of the Unfair Contract Terms Act 1977; and it is for those claiming that the term satisfies that requirement to show that it does".

1. Scope of the Misrepresentation Act 1967, s.3

(1) Excluding or restricting liabilities or remedies

The section covers not only clauses excluding or limiting a party's liability but also certain analogous terms: for example clauses which impose a short time limit within which claims must be brought, or which exclude a particular remedy (such as rescission or set-off[39]) without affecting another (such as damages).[40] On the other hand, it probably does not cover a valid agreed damages clause, since this might in some circumstances extend rather than restrict liability.[41] Some terms which purport to define a duty rather than to exclude or restrict a liability[42] are probably outside the scope of the section: *e.g.* a term which indicates that the representor is in good faith passing on

---

[32] *Gillett v Peppercorne* (1840) 3 Beav. 78; *Armstrong v Jackson* [1917] 2 K.B. 822; *Lindsay Petroleum Co v Hurd* (1874) L.R. 5 P.C. 221 at 241; *Aaron's Reefs Ltd v Twiss* [1896] A.C. 273 at 287.

[33] *Erlanger v New Sombrero Phosphate Co* (1878) 3 App.Cas. 1218 at 1252.

[34] [1950] 2 K.B. 86.

[35] See above, p.294.

[36] *Toomey v Eagle Star Insurance Co* [1995] 2 Lloyd's Rep. 89.

[37] See especially above, p.242.

[38] As substituted by Unfair Contract Terms Act 1977, s.8(1). No attempt to invoke this section was made in *Toomey*'s case, above, n.36.

[39] *Skipskreditforeningen v Emperor Navigation* [1998] 1 Lloyd's Rep. 67 at 74.

[40] *cf.* above, p.248 for a similar definition in s.13 of the Unfair Contract Terms Act 1977. That definition only applies in terms for the purposes of Pt I of 1977 Act, which is not considered to include (though it amends) s.3 of the Misrepresentation Act 1967: see s.11(1) of the 1977 Act. An arbitration clause is excluded from the definition in s.13 of the 1977 Act, but may be covered by s.3 of the Misrepresentation Act.

[41] *cf.* above, p.248; below, pp.999–1007.

[42] See above, p.249.

information supplied to him by a third party, or (probably) one which indicates that a written document formed an exclusive record of the terms of the contract.[43] The same may be true of certain other terms which do not exclude or restrict liability but prevent it from arising. It seems, for example, that the section would not apply to a term in a contract made through an agent negativing his ostensible authority to make representation as to the subject-matter.[44] But it would be comparatively easy to evade s.3 if the courts were not to some extent prepared to look behind clauses purporting to "prevent liability from arising". It has therefore been held that a statement can take effect as a misrepresentation in spite of the fact that it is made in a document expressly warning the representee to make his own enquiries into its accuracy.[45] Similarly, a clause in an auctioneer's catalogue might provide that all representations in it were statements of opinion only. If the court, on applying the tests stated earlier in this Chapter,[46] concluded that such a representation would, but for the clause, be one of fact, it might well hold that the clause was within s.3.

The section applies to terms excluding or restricting "*any* remedy". This phrase obviously covers the normal remedies of damages and rescission. It probably also covers terms restricting or excluding the right to plead misrepresentation as a defence,[47] for this could be described as a "remedy" in a broad sense. Similarly, a term excluding or restricting the right to retake goods obtained by fraud[48] would be within the section.

(2) "Party to a contract"

The section applies only to provisions excluding or restricting the liability of a "party to a contract", and the subsequent words of the section show that this means *the* contract induced by the misrepresentation. The section therefore would not apply to disclaimers of liability in cases such as *Hedley Byrne & Co Ltd v Heller & Partners Ltd*[49] and *Smith v Eric S Bush*[50] since the contracts induced by the misrepresentations in those cases were not made with the representor but with a third person. Such disclaimers of liability for negligence in giving advice in the course of a business would, however, be subject to the test of reasonableness under the Unfair Contract Terms Act 1977.[51] The scope of that test is, however, as will be seen below, in several ways significantly narrower than that of s.3 of the Misrepresentation Act 1967.

---

[43] *McGrath v Shaw* (1989) 57 P. & C.R. 452. For further discussion of the question whether s.3 applies to such "entire agreement" clauses, see *Government of Zanzibar v British Aerospace Ltd* [2000] 1 W.L.R. 2333 at 2344–2347; *White v Bristol Rugby Club Ltd* [2002] I.R.L.R. 204 at [34, 35].

[44] See *Overbrooke Estates Ltd v Glencombe Properties Ltd* [1974] 1 W.L.R. 1335; Coote, [1975] C.L.J. 17; the amendments to s.3 made by the Unfair Contract Terms Act 1977, s.8(1) appears not to affect the point. *cf. Museprime Properties Ltd v Adhill Properties Ltd* [1990] 2 E.G.L.R. 196 at 200.

[45] *Walker v Boyle* [1982] 1 W.L.R. 495; *cf. Cremdean Properties Ltd v Nash* (1977) 244 E.G. 547; *South Western General Property Co Ltd v Marton* (1982) 263 E.G. 1090. The reasoning of *Smith v Eric S Bush* [1990] 1 A.C. 831 (above, p.250) might also be applied by analogy, even though it is not directly applicable to cases falling within s.3 of the 1967 Act since (i) it is based on the definition exemption clauses in s.13(1) of the Unfair Contract Terms Act 1977, and this definition does not apply for the purpose of 1967 Act; and (ii) the misrepresentation in that case did not induce any contract between misrepresentor and misrepresentee: *cf.* below, after n.49.

[46] See above, pp.330–331.

[47] See above, p.372.

[48] See above, p.372.

[49] [1964] A.C. 465; above, p.345. Nor would non-contractual disclaimers, such as that in *Hedley Byrne*'s case, be affected by the Unfair Terms in Consumer Contracts Regulations 1999: see above, p.347.

[50] [1990] 1 A.C. 831; above, p.249.

[51] *i.e.* under s.2(2) (above, p.252) and possibly under s.3(2) (above, pp.252–253).

(3) "By reason of any misrepresentation made"

The first requirement under this heading is the obvious one that there must be a representation; and this requirement may not be satisfied where a contractual document contains (1) a statement that would, standing alone, amount to a representation but (2) words denying that the maker of the statement represents the fact so (apparently) stated. This was, for example, the position where in a bill of lading the carrier stated the weight of goods shipped to be "11,000 tons" but also qualified this statement with the words "weight unknown". It was held that the carrier had not represented 11,000 to have been shipped[52]; and it seems to follow that the "weight unknown" provision would not be subject to the reasonableness test under s.3 of the 1967 Act.[53]

Where a misrepresentation has been made, s.3 clearly applies to terms excluding or restricting liability for mere misrepresentations.[54] It equally clearly does not apply to terms which exclude or restrict liability only for breaches of pure promises (as opposed to statements of fact) or for breaches of implied terms not dependent on statements of fact. Terms which exclude or restrict liability only for such breaches may be subject to the test of reasonableness under the Unfair Contract Terms Act 1977. But the scope of the test under that Act is limited[55]: it does not, for example, generally apply where the party relying on the clause has made the contract otherwise than in the course of a business, nor does it apply to certain specified contracts, such as contracts for the sale of houses.[56] The scope of s.3 of the Misrepresentation Act is not so limited; and the difference in the scope of the two Acts gives rise to two problems. In discussing these, we shall assume that the case is one in which the reasonableness test under the 1977 Act does not apply.

(a) INCORPORATED MISREPRESENTATION. Where a misrepresentation is incorporated in the contract, the right to rescind for misrepresentation is preserved by s.1(a), and a term purporting to exclude or restrict that right would be within s.3. But a term may purport to exclude or restrict liabilities or remedies available only because the representation has been incorporated in the contract: for example, it may provide that the representee is to recover no more than out-of-pocket expenses and is not to have damages for loss of his bargain.[57] It seems that such a term would not be within s.3, for the liability which it purported to exclude would arise, not by reason of the *making* of the representation, but by reason of its *incorporation* into the contract. This conclusion is, however, subject to the point next to be discussed.

(b) PROVISION APPLICABLE TO MISREPRESENTATION AND BREACH. A single term may exclude liability for misrepresentation *and* for breach of contract. A clause excluding liability "for all defects" would have this effect where some defects were merely represented not to exist while others amounted to breaches of contract. S.3 provides that where a term would exclude or restrict any liability for misrepresentation "*that term* shall be of no effect except in so far as" the test of reasonableness is satisfied. It seems to follow that the *whole* term may be subject to the reasonableness test and not only the part of it which excludes liability for misrepresentation, unless that part is severable,[58] in

---

[52] *The Mata K* [1998] 2 Lloyd's Rep. 614 (discussing earlier authorities on such "unknown" provisions).

[53] *Carver on Bills of Lading* (1st ed., 2001) §2–004.

[54] For the possible application of the section to cases of non-disclosure, see below, p.373.

[55] See above, pp.264–267.

[56] If the sale were a private sale, it would be completely outside the scope of the 1977 Act: above, p.264. Even if the seller acted in the course of a business, and the buyer dealt as consumer, the reasonableness test would not apply to the contract "so far as it relates to" the transfer of an interest in land: above, p.264.

[57] *cf.* above, pp.359–361.

[58] *cf.* above, pp.255–256.

which case the reasonableness of the part relating to breach would, if it fell within relevant provisions of the Unfair Contract Terms Act 1977,[59] have to be determined under that Act.[60] An unseverable term excluding liability for "misrepresentation" generally could be ineffective (if unreasonable) to exclude contractual liability for an incorporated misrepresentation.

(4) "Before the contract was made"

S.3 applies to terms excluding or restricting liability for misrepresentations made before the conclusion of the contract. It does not apply to terms excluding or restricting liability for misrepresentations made in the course of *performing* a contract. However, in general[61] such liability is likely to be incurred only by a person who acts in the course of a business and is negligent: *e.g.* by a negligent surveyor or valuer. In such a case, a term excluding or restricting liability is subject to the test of reasonableness under the Unfair Contract Terms Act 1977.[62] If the representation was fraudulent, a clause excluding liability for it is probably void at common law.[63]

2. The Reasonableness Test

S.3 applies "the test of reasonableness *as stated in section 11(1)* of the Unfair Contract Terms Act 1977" to terms excluding or restricting liability for misrepresentation. S.11(1) provides that, in order to determine whether the test of reasonableness is satisfied, regard is to be had to the time of contracting; this rule is expressly stated in s.11(1) to apply for the purposes of s.3 of the Misrepresentation Act 1967. The 1977 Act also lays down guidelines for determining reasonableness; these take effect under s.11(2) and 11(4) of that Act.[64] At first sight, none of these guidelines apply for the purpose of s.3 of the Misrepresentation Act, since s.3 of that Act refers only to s.11(1) of the 1977 Act, while s.11(2) of that Act contains no words that could be taken to refer to s.3 of the 1967 Act. However, the guidelines contained in s.11(4) are there said to apply where "the question arises (under this *or any other* Act) whether the term . . . satisfies the test of reasonableness". In view of the italicised words, those guidelines[65] are, it is submitted, applicable for the purpose of s.3 of the Misrepresentation Act. Even the guidelines referred to in s.11(2) apply by analogy to contracts which are not literally within the wording of the subsection[66]; and they could by a process of further analogous extension be applied to cases in which the reasonableness test applies by virtue only of s.3 of the 1967 Act. The statutory guidelines are, moreover, not exhaustive for the purpose of s.3: in this respect their position under this section is indistinguishable from that under the 1977 Act.[67]

A clause which had been "freely negotiated . . . between banks", excluding liability for non-disclosure has been held to satisfy the reasonableness test under s.3.[68] On the

---

[59] See above, pp.251–255.

[60] *Skipskreditforeningen v Emperor Navigation* [1998] 1 Lloyd's Rep. 67 at 75.

[61] For an exception, see *Chaudhry v Prabhakar* [1989] 1 W.L.R. 29. *Semble,* a disclaimer of liability in such a situation would not be subject to the reasonableness test under either Act.

[62] *i.e.* s.2(2) (above, p.231) and possibly s.3(2) (above, pp.251–253).

[63] See above, p.242; the point might be of some importance if the liability were not a "business liability" within the Unfair Contract Terms Act 1977.

[64] See above, pp.258–259.

[65] See above, p.259.

[66] See above, pp.259–260.

[67] See above, p.260.

[68] *National Westminster Bank v Utrecht-American Finance Co* [2001] EWCA Civ 658; [2001] 2 All E.R. (Comm) 7, at [59].

other hand, that test was not satisfied by a clause which, on its true construction, excluded liability for fraudulent representations.[69]

Under s.3 (as under the Unfair Contract Terms Act 1977)[70] the court will generally hold the term to be either wholly ineffective[71] or fully valid; but it can also, if the clause is severable, uphold it in part, *i.e.* "in so far as" it satisfies the test of reasonableness.[72]

3. Unfair Terms in Consumer Contracts Regulations 1999[73]

These Regulations have in some respects a narrower scope than s.3 of the Misrepresentation Act, 1967. They apply only where the party relying on the term is a seller or supplier acting for purposes relating to his trade, business or profession, where the other party is a consumer, and where the term in question is not individually negotiated.[74] None of these limitations applies to s.3 of the 1967 Act. For example, an individually negotiated term by which a private seller of land to a property developer excluded liability for misrepresentation could fall within s.3; but it would not fall within the Regulations because, (i) the seller did not act for purposes relating to any trade, etc., (ii) the buyer did so act, (iii) the term was individually negotiated and (possibly) (iv) the contract was one for the sale of land. On the other hand, s.3 applies only to terms "which would exclude or restrict" liability for misrepresentation, *i.e.* to exemption clauses; while under the Regulations terms other than exemption clauses may be struck down as unfair. Terms which are outside the scope of s.3 because they purport to define a duty, rather than to exclude or restrict a liability,[75] can therefore fall within the Regulations. Whether the Regulations do indeed apply to such terms, the effect of which is to protect the seller or supplier from liability for misrepresentation, is an open question. Such terms are not included in the list of *prima facie* unfair terms given in the Regulations,[76] but this point is not decisive as that list is "indicative and non-exhaustive".[77] In principle there is, it is submitted, no reason why terms of the present kind should not be regarded as "unfair" and hence not binding on the consumer.[78] There is also the point that some of the guidelines for determining the issue of reasonableness under the Act have no counterpart in the Regulations: this is, for example, true of the guidelines which apply under the Act to terms limiting liability to a specified sum of money.[79] It is therefore possible (if unlikely) for a term to be reasonable under the Act but nevertheless unfair under the Regulations, or conversely. The clause will protect the party guilty of the misrepresentation only if both sets of requirements are satisfied.[80]

---

[69] *Thomas Witter Ltd v TBP Industries Ltd* [1996] 2 All E.R. 573 at 598; *South West Water Services Ltd v International Computers Ltd* [1999] B.L.R. 420; contrast *Zanzibar v British Aerospace (Lancaster House) Ltd* [2001] 1 W.L.R. 2333 (clause on its true construction *not* covering fraud held to satisfy reasonableness test).

[70] See above, pp.252–254.

[71] See *Walker v Boyle* [1982] 1 W.L.R. 495; *cf. Howard Marine & Dredging Co Ltd v A Ogden & Sons (Excavations) Ltd* [1978] Q.B. 574.

[72] See above, p.258.

[73] See above, pp.267–283.

[74] See above, p.267, n.2b.

[75] See above, p.386.

[76] Sch.2, above, pp.273–277.

[77] reg. 5(5), above, p.273.

[78] reg. 8(1), above, p.280.

[79] Unfair Contract Terms Act 1977, s.11(4), applicable for the purposes of Misrepresentation Act 1967, s.3: above, p.388.

[80] *cf.* above, p.282.

SECTION 7. NON-DISCLOSURE

1. General Rule

(1) No duty of disclosure

As a general rule, a person who is about to enter into a contract is under no duty to disclose material facts known to him but not to the other party.[81] Thus it has been held that a landlord is not liable in deceit if before letting his house he fails to tell the tenant that it is in a ruinous condition[82]; and that a person who applies for the post of governess is not bound to divulge the fact that she is a divorcee.[83] Sometimes the rule may appear to operate harshly; but if a general duty of disclosure did exist it would be very hard to say exactly what must be disclosed in any particular case.

(2) Representation by conduct

A person may make a representation by conduct[84] and, if he fails to correct the impression given by his conduct, he cannot rely on the general rule that there is no duty of disclosure.[85] Active concealment of a defect amounts to misrepresentation[86]; and even conduct falling short of this may suffice. In the words of Blackburn J.: "The defendant, by taking the cow to a public market to be sold ... thereby furnishes evidence of a representation that, so far as his knowledge goes, the animal is not suffering from any infectious disease. . . . The case might be different where the sale takes place privately".[87]

(3) Latent defects

It has been said that a person must disclose latent defects in the subject-matter of the contract which are known to him.[88] But cases which may appear to support this view are best explained on the ground of active misrepresentation[89] by words or by conduct and the preferable view is that English law does not recognise any general duty to disclose known latent defects. In the dictum quoted above,[90] Blackburn J. based liability, not on any general duty to disclose latent defects, but on the defendant's conduct in taking the cow to market. The dictum was cited without comment in *Ward v Hobbs*[91] where pigs were taken to Newbury market and sold there "with all faults". The seller knew that the pigs were diseased but he did not disclose this fact to the buyer. It was held that the buyer had no remedy as there was no general duty to disclose known latent defects and as any representation which might be inferred from the seller's conduct in taking the

---

[81] *Norwich Union Life Insurance Co Ltd v Qureshi* [1999] 2 All E.R. (Comm) 707 at 717.

[82] *Keates v Cadogan* (1851) 10 C.B. 591.

[83] *Fletcher v Krell* (1872) 42 L.J.Q.B. 55; cf. *The Unique Mariner* [1978] 1 Lloyd's Rep. 438 at 449; *Lloyds Bank v Egremont* [1990] 2 FLR 351; *Suriya & Douglas v Midland Bank plc, The Times*, March 29, 1999.

[84] *Curtis v Chemical Cleaning & Dyeing Co Ltd* [1951] 1 K.B. 805 at 808; contrast *Geest plc v Fyffes plc* [1999] 1 All E.R. (Comm) 672 at 686 (where the conduct gave rise to no such inference).

[85] *Walters v Morgan* (1861) 3 D.F. & J. 718 at 723; *Spice Girls Ltd v Aprilia World Service BV* [2002] EWCA Civ 15 at [61–63].

[86] *Schneider v Heath* (1813) 3 Camp. 506; *Sybron Corp v Rochem Ltd* [1984] Ch. 112 at 130 ("covering up and deliberately concealing"); *Gordon v Selico Ltd* (1986) 278 E.G. 53.

[87] *Bodger v Nicholls* (1873) 28 L.T. 441, 445.

[88] *Horsfall v Thomas* (1862) 1 H. & C. 90 at 100.

[89] e.g. *Hill v Gray* (1816) 1 Stark. 434, as explained in *Keates v Cadogan* (1851) 10 C.B. at 600.

[90] See above, at n.87.

[91] (1878) 4 App.Cas. 13.

pigs to market was negatived by the words "with all faults". These words might, on such facts, now protect the seller only if they satisfied the legislative requirements of reasonableness or fairness.[92] Moreover, if the thing sold suffers from a latent defect of which the seller knows, and if that defect causes injury to the buyer, or harm to other property belonging to him, then the seller's failure to warn the buyer of the defect may make him liable in negligence; and it has been suggested that *Ward v Hobbs* may require reconsideration in the light of this possibility.[93] But there is such liability where the defect caused no loss to the buyer except in making the thing sold less valuable than he had supposed it to be.[94] Cases of this kind continue to be governed by the general rule that there is no duty of disclosure.

That general rule has been applied where land sold was subject to a latent physical defect[95]; and it has similarly been held that a vendor of a leasehold interest was not bound to disclose the fact that the organisation to which the premises were let had only a limited "life".[96] There is some support for the view that on a sale of land latent defects of title must be disclosed[97] but even here it seems that there is no general duty of disclosure,[98] and that an undisclosed defect of this kind is a ground for relief only if it is unusual,[99] or if it leads to a breach of contract[1] or to an operative mistake.[2] It can also, if known to the vendor, prevent him from relying on a term of the contract under which the purchaser is deemed to have made enquiries relating to the matter in question and to have knowledge of it.[3]

The general rule that there is no duty of disclosure also applies where the buyer knows (but the seller does not) of some latent quality which makes the subject-matter of the contract *more* valuable. Thus a contract for the sale of land is binding even though the buyer, but not the seller, knew that it contained valuable minerals.[4]

---

[92] See above, pp.252–253, 244 *et seq.*

[93] *Hurley v Dyke* [1979] R.T.R. 265 at 303. For a similar duty to disclose one's own *breach* where it may lead to danger, see below, p.400.

[94] *cf.* below, p.612. There is no such liability in tort even where (exceptionally) there *is* a duty of disclosure because the contract is *uberrimae fidei* (below, p.366): *Banque Keyser Ullmann SA v Skandia (UK) Insurance Co Ltd* [1990] 1 Q.B. 665 at 798–800; [1991] 2 A.C. 249 at 282 (where the decision was affirmed on other grounds). *A fortiori* there should be no liability in tort for mere non-disclosure where there is *no* duty of disclosure; and this is the situation under discussion at this point.

[95] *Shepherd v Croft* [1911] 1 Ch. 521.

[96] *Safehaven Investments Ltd v Springbok Ltd* (1996) 71 p.& C.R. 59.

[97] *Selkirk v Romar Investments Ltd* [1963] 1 W.L.R. 1415 at 1423; *F & H Entertainments Ltd v Leisure Enterprises Ltd* (1976) 120 S.J. 331, 240 E.G. 455; *Faruqi v English Real Estates* [1979] 1 W.L.R. 963; *William Sindall plc v Cambridgeshire CC* [1994] 1 W.L.R. 1016 at 1023.

[98] Megarry and Wade, *The Law of Real Property* (5th ed.), p.622, n.75. For criticisms, see *Let the buyer be well informed*: recommendations of the Conveyancing Standing Committee of the Law Commission.

[99] *Molyneux v Hawtrey* [1903] 2 K.B. 487; *cf. Carlish v Salt* [1906] 1 Ch. 335; *Celsteel Ltd v Alton House Holdings Ltd (No.2)* [1986] 1 All E.R. 598 at 607 (not reported on this point in [1986] 1 W.L.R. 666).

[1] *e.g. Flight v Booth* (1834) 1 Bing. N.C. 370; *Peyman v Lanjani* [1985] Ch. 457 at 496. Certain covenants for title are implied under Law of Property (Miscellaneous Provisions) Act 1994, Pt I.

[2] See above, Chap.8.

[3] *Rignall Developments Ltd v Halil* [1988] Ch. 190.

[4] *Smith v Hughes* (1871) L.R. 6 Q.B. 587 at 604; *quaere* whether the contract would be specifically enforced: below, p.1028. *cf.* also *Phillips v Homfray* (1871) L.R. 7 Ch.App. 770. For a statutory exception, see Criminal Justice Act 1993, Pt V, giving effect to E.C. Council Directive 89/592 EEC, and imposing criminal penalties on "insider dealing"; and see Insider Dealing (Securities and Regulated Markets) Amendment Order 1996 (SI 1996/1561). But the validity or enforceability of the resulting transaction is not affected: 1993 Act, s.63(2), the wording of which appears to reverse this aspect of *Chase Manhattan Equities Ltd v Goodman* [1991] B.C.L.C. 897; for the effect of this provision see further p.488 n.27 below. See also the powers to impose penalties for "market abuse" under Financial Services and Markets Act 2000, ss.118 and 123.

2. Exceptions

There are many important exceptions to the rule that there is no liability for non-disclosure. In these exceptional cases, a person is, in general, bound to disclose only facts which he knew (or which he would have known if he had not "wilfully shut his eyes" to them).[5] A person may, however, be under a duty to disclose facts which, though not known to him, were known to his agent, if that knowledge had been acquired within the scope of the agent's authority and if it was the agent's duty to communicate it to the principal.[6] He may also be under a duty to disclose facts which he ought to have known, if there is a "special relationship" between the parties within *Hedley Byrne & Co Ltd v Heller & Partners Ltd*.[7]

Where a duty of disclosure exists, it generally continues until the contract becomes legally binding.[8] But where a contract is regarded as binding as a matter of business the duty to disclose may cease at that point even though the contract is not yet binding in law. Thus in contracts of insurance the duty ceases when the insurer initials a slip saying that he will accept the risk, even where there is no legally binding contract until a policy is executed.[9] Conversely the duty may in a sense continue even after the conclusion of the contract. For example, a person who takes a fidelity bond for the honesty of one of his servants is under a continuing duty to disclose to the surety any acts of dishonesty on the part of the servant[10]; and the express or implied terms of a contract may impose a contractual duty of disclosure to be further discussed below.[11] Once the parties become engaged in hostile litigation, however, any continuing duties of disclosure are superseded by the rules of procedure which govern such litigation.[12] Failure to perform a continuing (post-contractual) duty of disclosure does not, moreover, vitiate the *formation* of the contract but amounts to a *breach* of one of its express or implied terms[13]; and this distinction has significant effects, to be discussed below,[14] on the remedies for this type of non-disclosure. In insurance contracts, the duty of disclosure also continues after the making of the original contract in the sense that its performance is a prerequisite to any renewal of the insurance.

The duty of disclosure exists in the following cases.

---

[5] *Blackburn, Low & Co v Vigors* (1887) 12 App.Cas. 531; *Economides v Commercial Union Assurance Co plc* [1998] Q.B. 587 at 602; *cf. William Sindall plc v Cambridgeshire CC* [1994] 1 W.L.R. 1016, (where the contract expressly restricted the duty in this way); *Simner v New India Assurance Co Ltd, The Times,* July 21, 1994; Marine Insurance Act 1906, s.18(1).

[6] *Proudfoot v Montefiore* (1867) L.R. 2 Q.B. 511; *Joel v Law Union and Crown Insurance Co* [1908] 2 K.B. 863.

[7] [1964] A.C. 465; above, p.345.

[8] *Container Transport International Inc v Oceanus Mutual, etc., Association* [1984] 1 Lloyd's Rep. 476 at 486, disapproved on another point in *Pan Atlantic Ins Co v Pine Top Inc Co* [1995] 2 A.C. 501 (below, pp.394–395, above, p.343).

[9] *Cory v Patton* (1872) L.R. 7 Q.B. 304; *Citadel Insurance Co v Atlantic Union Insurance Co* [1982] 2 Lloyd's Rep. 543 at 548. S.2(1) of the Misrepresentation Act (requiring belief in the truth of the "facts represented" up to the time that the contract was made) would not apply to pure non-disclosure: *cf.* below, pp.372–373.

[10] *Phillips v Foxall* (1872) L.R. 7 Q.B. 666; *cf. Roadworks (1952) Ltd v Charman* [1994] 2 Lloyd's Rep. 99 at 107–108.

[11] Below, p.400.

[12] *The Star Sea* [2001] UKHL 1; [2001] 1 All E.R. (Comm) 193, at [73–78]; *The Mercadian Continent* [2001] EWCA Civ 1275; [2001] 2 Lloyd's Rep. 563 at [22]; *Agapitos v Agnew* [2002] EWCA Civ 247; [2002] 1 All E.R. (Comm) 714 at [52].

[13] *cf.* above, p.370.

[14] See below, pp.401–402.

(1) Representation falsified by later events

A person may have to disclose material facts which come to his notice[15] before the conclusion of a contract if they falsify a representation previously made[16] by him. In *With v O'Flanagan*[17] negotiations for the sale of a medical practice were begun in January, when the practice was said to be worth £2,000. A contract of sale was made on May 1, by which time the practice had become worthless because of the intervening illness of the vendor. The contract was set aside on the ground that the vendor ought to have communicated this change of circumstances to the purchasers. But there would probably be no need to disclose minor variations in the income of the practice.[18] And there are obvious limitations on the scope of any duty of disclosure which may arise from a statement such as one as to a person's financial position, which can influence a series of transactions extending, perhaps, over many years. A time must come when the representation loses its force and the representee begins to rely rather on his own judgment.[19]

There are conflicting decisions on the question whether a duty of disclosure arises where during negotiations a party makes a representation as to his present intention but changes his mind before the conclusion of the contract. In *Traill v Baring*[20] an insurance company made a proposal for reinsurance to a second company, stating that it would retain part of the risk. This was its intention when it made the representation but before the proposal was accepted it disposed of that part of the risk. It was held that the "change of intention"[21] of the first company should have been disclosed to the second company. On the other hand, in *Wales v Wadham*[22] a husband who had left his wife made her an offer of financial provision after she had declared her intention of not remarrying. She accepted the offer after having decided to marry again. If the husband had known this, he would have made a lower offer; but it was held that the wife was not bound to disclose her change of mind. The duty of disclosing changed circumstances was said only to apply where the original representation was one of *fact*: not where it was one of *intention*.[23] The view that the wife was not bound to disclose her decision to remarry was disapproved by the House of Lords in *Jenkins v Livesey*,[24] but only on the ground that the agreement for financial provision had been embodied in a consent order made in matrimonial proceedings; and that parties seeking such an order were, by statute,[25] under a duty to make full and frank disclosure to the court which made the order. So far as common law liability for fraud and non-disclosure was concerned, *Wales v Wadham* was approved, though without any reference to *Traill v Baring*. It may be

---

[15] Or, which, if there is a "special relationship", should have come to his notice, had he exercised reasonable care.

[16] For this requirement, see *English v Dedham Vale Properties Ltd* [1978] 1 W.L.R. 93 at 104.

[17] [1936] Ch. 575; *cf. Traill v Baring* (1864) 4 D.J. & S. 318; *British Equitable Insurance Co v Great Western Ry* (1869) 38 L.J.Ch. 132; *Davies v London & Provincial Marine Insurance Co* (1878) 8 Ch.D. 469; *Brownlie v Campbell* (1880) 5 App.Cas. 925 at 950; *Zamir v S of S for the Home Dept.* [1980] A.C. 730 at 750; *Spice Girls Ltd v Aprilia World Service BV* [2002] EWCA Civ 15 at [51, 58]. In view of these authorities, *Turner v Green* [1895] 2 Ch. 205, where this point was not argued, cannot be supported. Contrast also *Thomas Witter Ltd v TBP Industries* [1996] 2 All E.R. 573 at 587 where there appears to have been no change in the facts but only one in their evaluation by the allegedly fraudulent party. And see Financial Services and Markets Act 2000, ss.81, 86.

[18] For the possible application of the Misrepresentation Act 1967, see below, p.401.

[19] *cf. Argy Trading Development Co Ltd v Lapid Developments Ltd* [1977] 1 W.L.R. 444 at 461–462.

[20] (1864) 4 D.J. & S. 318.

[21] *ibid.* at 326, 330.

[22] [1977] 1 W.L.R. 199.

[23] *ibid.* at 211.

[24] [1985] A.C. 424.

[25] Matrimonial Causes Act 1973, ss.23–25 (as amended by Family Law Act 1996, s.15 and Sch.2).

possible to reconcile these two decisions by saying that in *Traill v Baring* the first company had, before acceptance of its offer, not merely changed its mind but acted accordingly, while the wife in *Wales v Wadham* had not actually remarried when she accepted the husband's offer; or by saying that the wife's statement in the latter case was as to an intention so intrinsically likely to be changed that the husband should not have relied on the statement. Subject to these possible distinctions, it is submitted that the principle in *Traill v Baring* is to be preferred; for, in cases of this kind, what was originally a misrepresentation of intention becomes by the time of contracting one of fact, *viz.* as to the representor's state of mind at that time.[26] And there is no difficulty in specifying exactly what should be disclosed, so that the reason for the general rule against imposing a duty of disclosure does not apply.

(2) Statement literally true, but misleading

A person is guilty of misrepresentation, though all the facts stated by him are true, if his statement is misleading as a whole because it does not refer to other facts affecting the weight of those stated. In *Notts Patent Brick and Tile Co v Butler*[27] a purchaser of land asked the vendor's solicitor whether the land was subject to restrictive covenants. The solicitor replied that he was not aware of any, but failed to add that this was because he had not troubled to read the relevant documents. The solicitor's reply, though literally true, amounted to a misrepresentation entitling the purchaser to rescind.

The duty of disclosure in cases of this kind is narrower than that which exists in contracts *uberrimae fidei*.[28] The maker of a statement which is literally true but on the whole misleading is required to disclose only such facts as affect the weight of those stated[29]; he need not disclose further facts merely because they might reasonably be regarded by the representee as material.[30]

(3) Custom

In *Jones v Bowden*[31] pimento was sold after having been damaged by sea water. It was usual in the trade, when pimento had been so damaged, to declare this, but the seller failed to make such a declaration. He was held liable in deceit as, in view of the custom, his silence amounted to misrepresentation.

(4) Contracts *uberrimae fidei*

There is a duty to disclose material facts in contracts *uberrimae fidei* (*i.e.*, of "utmost good faith"[32]), in which one party is in a particularly strong position, and the other in a particularly weak one, to know the material facts.

---

[26] See above, p.331.
[27] (1886) 16 Q.B.D. 778; *cf. Tapp v Lee* (1803) 3 B. & p.367; *R. v Kylsant* [1932] 1 K.B. 442; *Faruqi v English Real Estates* [1979] 1 W.L.R. 963; *The Lucy* [1983] 1 Lloyd's Rep. 188 (where relief was denied as the requirement of reliance was not satisfied: above, p.340); *Cemp Properties (UK) Ltd v Dentsply Research & Development Corp* [1991] 2 E.G.L.R. 197; *Henry Ansbacher & Co Ltd v Binks Stern, The Times*, June 26, 1997.
[28] See below, pp.394–397.
[29] See the common law position with regard to company prospectuses, as stated in *New Brunswick and Canada Ry v Muggeridge* (1860) 1 Dr. & Sm. 363 at 381; approved in *Central Ry of Venezuela v Kisch* (1867) L.R. 2. H.L. 99; *cf. Dimmock v Hallett* (1866) L.R. 2 Ch.App. 21 at 28; *Oakes v Turquand* (1867) L.R. 2 H.L. 325. For statutory duties of disclosure in such cases, see below, p.399.
[30] *Aaron's Reefs Ltd v Twiss* [1896] A.C. 273 at 287.
[31] (1813) 4 Taunt. 847.
[32] Marine Insurance Act 1906, s.17.

(a) INSURANCE. "It has been for centuries in England the law in connection with insurance of all sorts, marine, fire, life, guarantee and every kind of policy, that, as the underwriter knows nothing and the man who comes to him to ask him to insure knows everything, it is the duty of the assured . . . to make a full disclosure to the underwriters, without being asked, of all the material circumstances".[33]

(i) *Material facts to be disclosed.* The assured must disclose all such facts as a prudent insurer would take into account in deciding whether or at what premium or on what conditions he would take the risk.[34] It is not necessary to show that, if such facts had been disclosed, the insurer would have declined to take the risk, or that he would have increased his premium[35]; but the non-disclosure must have been one of the factors which induced him to enter into the contract.[36] A policy of marine insurance can therefore be avoided if the assured conceals the real value of the cargo[37]; or if he fails to declare that it may be carried on deck (thus increasing the risk),[38] that the ship carrying the cargo had already been stranded,[39] or that she had been engaged in smuggling, so that those operating her faced criminal charges.[40] Similarly a policy of life insurance can be avoided if the assured fails to disclose a medical condition material to the risk,[41] or the fact that a number of other insurance offices had declined proposals to insure his life,[42] or that there was a doubt as to his mental health[43]; a policy of insurance on jewellery can be avoided if the insurer is not told that jewellery had on several occasions been stolen from the assured[44]; and a home contents insurance policy can be avoided by reason of the insured's failure to disclose that he had been convicted of obtaining money by deception.[45] A policy can also be avoided on the ground of non-disclosure of facts material to

---

[33] *Rozanes v Bowen* (1928) 32 Ll.L.R. 98 at 102.

[34] *Lambert v Co-operative Insurance Society Ltd* [1975] 2 Lloyd's Rep. 485; Marine Insurance Act 1906, s.18(2); *Woolcott v Sun Alliance, etc. Insurance Ltd* [1978] 1 W.L.R. 493 at 498; *Woolcott v Excess Insurance Co Ltd* [1979] 1 Lloyd's Rep. 231, [1979] 2 Lloyd's Rep. 210; *Container Transport International v Oceanus Mutual, etc., Association* [1984] 1 Lloyd's Rep. 476, disapproved on the point stated at n.36 in *Pan Atlantic Insurance Co Ltd v Pine Top Insurance Co Ltd* [1995] 1 A.C. 501; *Fraser Shipping Ltd v Cotton* [1997] 1 Lloyd's Rep. 565 at 589; Road Traffic Act 1988, s.152, as amended by Road Traffic Act 1991, s.48 and Sch.4, para.66. For criticism and proposals for reform, see Law Com. 104 paras 3.17–3.19, 4.43–4.53; *Pan Atlantic* case, above, at 528.

[35] *Pan Atlantic Insurance Co Ltd v Pine Top Insurance Co* [1995] 1 A.C. 501; *Aneco Reinsurance Underwriting v Johnson & Higgins* [1998] 1 Lloyd's Rep. 565 at 589.

[36] [1995] 1 A.C. 501 at 517–518, 549, 570, 571; *St Paul Fire & Marine Insurance Co (UK) Ltd v McConnell Dowell Contractors Ltd* [1995] 2 Lloyd's Rep. 116.

[37] *Ionides v Pender* (1874) L.R. 9 Q.B. 531.

[38] *Hood v West End Motor Car Packing Co* [1917] 2 K.B. 38.

[39] *Proudfoot v Montefiore* (1867) L.R. 2 Q.B. 511.

[40] *Inversiones Mannia SA v Sphere Drake Ins Co plc* [1989] 1 Lloyd's Rep. 69; *cf. The Moonacre* [1992] 2 Lloyd's Rep. 501 (failure to disclose forgery of insured's signature by broker, though this was done simply to save time).

[41] *Winter v Irish Life Assurance plc* [1995] 2 Lloyd's Rep. 274.

[42] *London Assurance v Mansel* (1879) 11 Ch.D. 363.

[43] *Lindenau v Desborough* (1828) 8 B. & C. 586.

[44] *Rozanes v Bowen* (1928) 32 Ll.L.R. 98; *cf. Pan Atlantic* case, above, n.35 and *Marc Rich & Co AG v Portman* [1997] 1 Lloyd's Rep. 225.

[45] *Galloway v Guardian Royal Exchange (UK) Ltd* [1999] L.R.L.R. 209 (where an additional ground for the decision was that the insured had made a fraudulent claim).

the risk[46] by the insurer,[47] *e.g.* if he accepts a premium for insuring a voyage which he knows to have been safely accomplished.

(ii) *Facts which need not be disclosed.* The assured need not disclose facts which the insurer himself knows or ought to know,[48] facts which diminish the risk, facts which both parties have equal means of knowing, "general topics of speculation",[49] and facts the disclosure of which is waived by the insurer.[50]

(iii) *Basis of contract clauses.* The duty of disclosure gives a generous measure of protection to insurers, but they often add that the accuracy and completeness of the answers given by the assured to questions in the proposal form shall be the basis of the contract.[51] The result is that quite unimportant misstatements or failure to disclose some quite trivial matter can vitiate a policy[52]; and this position has drawn strong judicial criticism[53] and the Law Commission has recommended that basis of the contract clauses should cease to have this effect.[54] Meanwhile, the courts do their best to protect policyholders by construing the basis of the contract clauses strictly against insurers.[55]

(iv) *Insurance distinguished from suretyship or guarantee.* A contract of insurance must be distinguished from a contract of suretyship or guarantee, since it is disputed whether the latter type of contract is *uberrimae fidei.*[56]

A promise to pay another person's debt if he fails to pay it is normally a contract of guarantee, but it is possible to insure against non-payment of a debt, or against some other breach of contract. In *Seaton v Heath*[57] A guaranteed a loan of £15,000 made by B to X. B then obtained a promise from C "in consideration of a premium of 50s. per cent". to "guarantee" A's solvency. The contract between B and C was held to be one of insurance. But in *Trade Indemnity Co Ltd v Workington Harbour Board*[58] A agreed to

---

[46] See *Banque Keyser Ullmann SA v Skandia (UK) Insurance Co Ltd* [1991] 2 A.C. 249 and *Norwich Union Life Insurance Co v Qureshi* [1999] 2 All E.R. (Comm) 707 at 714, 716 (where the facts in question were not so material).

[47] *Carter v Boehm* (1766) 3 Burr. 1905, 1909 and Marine Insurance Act 1906, s.17 ("either party"). No such duty is owed to, or by, an assignee of the policy: *The Good Luck* [1989] 2 Lloyd's Rep. 238 (reversed on other grounds [1992] 1 A.C. 233) or by a third party entitled to the benefit of the policy under the principle stated at 615, below: *Sumitomo Bank Ltd v Banque Bruxelles Lambert SA* [1997] 1 Lloyd's Rep. 487.

[48] Not facts coming to the notice of his agent while acting in fraud of the principal: *PCW Syndicates v PCW Reinsurers* [1996] 1 W.L.R. 1136.

[49] *Carter v Boehm*, above, at 1910.

[50] *Roberts v Plaisted* [1989] 2 Lloyd's Rep. 341; "waiver" here refers to failure to enquire into circumstances material to the risk when a reasonable insurer would make such enquiries: see *Container Transport International v Oceanus Mutual, etc., Association* [1984] 1 Lloyd's Rep. 476; *Marc Rich & Co AG v Portman* [1996] 1 Lloyd's Rep. 430 at 442, affirmed [1997] 1 Lloyd's Rep. 225.

[51] Hasson, (1971) 34 M.L.R. 29.

[52] *Dawsons Ltd v Bonnin* [1922] 2 A.C. 413.

[53] *Joel v Law Union & Crown Insurance Co* [1908] 2 K.B. 863 at 885; *cf. West v National Motor & Accident Insurance Union Ltd* [1955] 1 W.L.R. 343, 348; *The Star Sea* [2001] UKHL 1; [2001] 1 All E.R. (Comm) 193 at [50], quoted below, p.401 at n.8.

[54] Law Com. 104, para.7.4; *cf.* Law Reform Committee Fifth Report, Cmnd. 63 (1957). Contracts of insurance are excepted from the relevant provisions of the Unfair Contract Terms Act 1977: above, p.242. For the question whether "basis of contract" clauses are open to challenge under the Unfair Terms in Consumer Contracts Regulations 1994. The possibility is, in any event, restricted to consumer contracts.

[55] *Joel's* case, above, n.53.

[56] See below, p.397.

[57] [1899] 1 Q.B. 782; reversed on another ground [1900] A.C. 135.

[58] [1937] A.C. 1; *Trafalgar House Construction (Regions) Ltd v General Surety & Guarantee Co Ltd* [1996] A.C. 199.

build a dock for B. C gave B a "guarantee" of £50,000 that A would complete the work, and it was held that this was not a contract of insurance.

The distinction between the two types of contract is that a guarantor is usually provided by the debtor,[59] while an insurer is usually sought out by the creditor. Thus the creditworthiness of the debtor is a matter about which a guarantor is likely to know at least as much as the creditor[60]; while an insurer is likely to know less about it than the creditor, having probably had no previous dealings with the debtor. Hence a higher duty of disclosure is owed to the insurer.[61]

(v) *Source of duty of disclosure in insurance contracts.* In *William Pickersgill & Sons Ltd v London, etc., Insurance Co*[62] Hamilton J. said: "The rule imposing an obligation to disclose upon the intending assured does not rest upon a general principle of common law, but arises out of an implied condition, contained in the contract itself, precedent to the liability of the underwriter to pay". One possible interpretation of this dictum is that, in contracts of insurance, there is a *contractual* duty of disclosure based on an implied term in the contract. This duty, being mutual,[63] would rest on the underwriter no less than on the insured; and failure to perform it would amount to a breach of contract, giving rise to a right, not only to rescind the contract, but also to recover damages for its breach. But the prevailing view is that the duty "derives from a rule of law, not from the parties' agreement",[64] and that the "condition precedent" to which it gives rise is contingent only and not promissory.[65] That is, the party who fails to make the disclosure required of him cannot enforce the contract, but is not, merely on account of the non-disclosure, liable in damages for breach of the contract.[66] Nor does the non-disclosure give the other party a right to claim damages in tort for negligence. It has been said that the effect of allowing such a claim would be to undermine the general common law principle that there is no duty of disclosure in the negotiations leading to the conclusion of a contract.[67] That general principle is attenuated in insurance contracts only to the extent that the law provides a remedy by way of rescission for non-disclosure of material facts.

(b) FAMILY ARRANGEMENTS. There is a duty to make full disclosure in certain family arrangements, *e.g.* in agreements between members of a family for settling disputes as to the family property. Thus parties to an agreement for the division of the property of a

---

[59] *The Zuhal K* [1987] 1 Lloyd's Rep. 151 at 155.

[60] *e.g.* where the debtor is a company and the guarantor is one of its directors.

[61] *cf. Re Denton's Estate* [1904] 2 Ch. 178 at 188.

[62] [1912] 3 K.B. 614 at 621.

[63] See above, p.395.

[64] *The Star Sea* [2001] UKHL 1; [2001] 1 All E.R. (Comm) 193, at [46]; *Banque Keyser Ullmann SA v Skandia (UK) Insurance Ltd* [1988] 2 Lloyd's Rep. 513 at 549, affirmed [1991] 2 A.C. 249; *John W Pryke v Gibbs Hartley Cooper Ltd* [1991] 1 Lloyd's Rep. 602 at 615; *The Grecia Express* [2002] 2 Lloyd's Rep. 88.

[65] See above, p.62 for the distinction between contingent and promissory conditions.

[66] *Banque Keyser Ullmann SA v Skandia (UK) Insurance Co Ltd* [1990] 1 Q.B. 665 at 779–781; approved on this point [1991] 2 A.C. 249 at 288, where the case was affirmed on other grounds. *cf. March Cabaret Club & Casino Ltd v London Assurance* [1975] 1 Lloyd's Rep. 169 at 175; *The Good Luck* [1990] 1 Q.B. 818 at 888 reversed, on other grounds [1992] 1 A.C. 233; Clarke [1989] C.L.J. 363; Davenport [1989] L.M.C.L.Q. 251; *John W Pryke v Gibbs Hartley Cooper Ltd* [1991] 1 Lloyd's Rep. 602, 615; *Agnew v Landsförsäkringsbolagens AB* [2001] A.C. 223 at 246; *Norwich Union Life Insurance Co Ltd v Qureshi* [1999] 2 All E.R. (Comm) 707 at 716; *quaere* whether there is such liability where the non-disclosure is fraudulent: see *HIH Casualty & General Insurance v Chase Manhattan Bank* [2001] EWCA Civ 1250; [2001] 2 Lloyd's Rep. 483 at [52], [74] and [164].

[67] *Banque Keyser Ullmann SA v Skandia (UK) Insurance Co Ltd* [1990] 1 Q.B. 665, 801–802, as to which see above, n.66.

deceased member of the family must disclose to each other all facts known to them which bear on their rights to the estate, or on its value.[68]

(5) Contracts in which there is a limited duty of disclosure

In some cases there is a duty to disclose certain specified facts, or to disclose unusual facts.

(a) SURETYSHIP OR GUARANTEE. Contracts of suretyship or guarantee are sometimes said to be *uberrimae fidei*[69]; but the better view is that they do not fall into this category.[70] The creditor is bound only to disclose unusual circumstances, which the surety would not commonly expect.[71] A somewhat higher duty rests on an employer who takes a fidelity bond, by which the honesty of one of his employees is guaranteed, is under a somewhat higher duty: he must disclose to the surety any acts of dishonesty by the employee of which he has notice[72]; even if such acts occur after the execution of the bond.

(b) SALE OF LAND. Contracts for the sale of land are not *uberrimae fidei*,[73] so that there is in general no duty on a seller of land to disclose latent physical defects, but there may be a duty to disclose *unusual* defects of title which a reasonably prudent purchaser could not be expected to discover.[74]

(c) COMPROMISES. There can be a valid compromise of a claim which is bad in law if it is believed to be valid and is made in good faith. But the compromise is valid only if the person making the claim discloses to the other party all facts known to him which affect the validity of the claim.[75] Conversely, the party released may know that there are circumstances making the claim more valuable than the party granting the release believed to it to be, and that the latter party was unaware of those circumstances. Failure by the former party to disclose those circumstances may then be a ground on which the latter party can set the release aside.[76]

(d) EXEMPTION CLAUSES. In some cases failure to disclose or draw attention to the terms of a contractual document may (without affecting the validity of the contract as a whole) deprive one party of the benefit of an exemption clause.[77]

---

[68] *Gordon v Gordon* (1817) 3 Swan. 400; *Greenwood v Greenwood* (1863) 1 D.J. & S. 28. *cf. Tennent v Tennents* (1870) L.R. 2 Sc. & Div. 6. Contrast *Wales v Wadham* [1977] 1 W.L.R. 199, 218, above, p.393, where the rule did not apply as the parties bargained at arm's length, and *Crowden v Aldridge* [1993] 1 W.L.R. 433 at 442–443, where no dispute between members of a family existed before execution of the document in question.

[69] *Railton v Matthews* (1844) 10 Cl. & F. 934, 943; *March Cabaret Club & Casino Ltd v London Assurance* [1975] 1 Lloyd's Rep. 169 at 175; *Wales v Wadham* [1977] 1 W.L.R. 199 at 214.

[70] *Davies v London & Provincial Marine Insurance Co* (1878) 8 Ch.D. 469 at 475; *LGOC Ltd v Holloway* [1912] 2 K.B. 72 at 81, 83; *John W Pryke* case, above, n.66; *Geest plc v Fyffes plc* [1999] 1 All E.R. (Comm) 672 at 683; *Royal Bank of Scotland v Edridge (No.2)* [2001] UKHL 44; [2002] 2 A.C. 773 at [114]. The point was left open in *Mackenzie v Royal Bank of Canada* [1934] A.C. 468 at 475 and in *Trade Indemnity Co Ltd v Workington Harbour & Dock Board* [1937] A.C. 1 at 18.

[71] *National Provincial Bank of England Ltd v Glanusk* [1913] 3 K.B. 335 at 338; *Cooper v National Provincial Bank* [1946] K.B. 1 at 7; *Levett v Barclays Bank plc* [1995] 1 W.L.R. 1260.

[72] *LGOC Ltd v Holloway*, above.

[73] *Safehaven Investments Ltd v Springbok Ltd* (1996) 71 P. & C.R. 59 at 66.

[74] See above, p.392.

[75] See above, p.90.

[76] *Bank of Credit and Commerce International SA v Ali* [2001] UKHL 8; [2001] I.C.R. 337, at [32]; above, p.88.

[77] See above, p.241.

(6) Fiduciary relationship

A duty of disclosure may arise from the relationship of the parties. There is clearly such a duty where the relationship is one to which the equitable doctrine of undue influence applies.[78] The duty in such cases is indeed not discharged by mere disclosure; more stringent conditions must be satisfied before a person who is under the duty can take the benefit of a transaction with the person to whom the duty is owed.[79] But there are other cases in which a person is under a fiduciary duty which he can discharge merely by making full disclosure. This is the position between principal and agent,[80] partners,[81] and between a company and its promoters.[82] A company promoter owes no such common law duty to persons who subscribe for shares in the company on the faith of a prospectus or listing particulars issued by him,[83] but he does owe them an extensive statutory duty of disclosure.[84]

(7) Legislation

Under the Financial Services and Markets Act 2000, extensive duties of disclosure are imposed on persons who apply for an official listing of securities on the Stock Exchange, and on those who issue a prospectus inviting subscriptions for unlisted securities.[85]

Parties to matrimonial proceedings who seek a consent order from the Family Division for the settlement of their financial and proprietary arrangements must make full and frank disclosure of relevant circumstances to the court that is asked to make the order.[86]

(8) Duty to clarify legal relationship

A duty of disclosure may arise where A sees B acting in reliance on a view of a legal relationship between them which is to A's knowledge false.[87] In the authorities which support the existence of such a duty, the effect of its breach has simply been to give rise to an estoppel[88]; but it is conceivable that such a breach might also invalidate a contract.

---

[78] See below, pp.408–420.

[79] See below, p.420.

[80] e.g. *Armstrong v Jackson* [1917] 2 K.B. 822.

[81] Pollock, *Law of Partnership* (15th ed.), p.8.

[82] Gower, *Modern Company Law* (6th ed.), pp.133 *et seq.*; *Erlanger v New Sombrero Phosphate Co* (1879) 3 App.Cas. 1218.

[83] *Heyman v European Central Ry* (1868) L.R. 7 Eq. 154.

[84] Below. Breach of this duty gives rise to a right to damages against those responsible for the prospectus, but not to a right to rescind an allotment of shares: *Re South of England Natural Gas Co* [1911] 1 Ch. 573. This position seems to be unaffected by the Financial Services and Markets Act 2000, ss.90, 86.

[85] ss.80, 86; and see *Chase Manhattan Equities Ltd v Goodman* [1991] B.C.L.C. 897 for a discussion of the question to whom such a duty is owed. And see Public Offers of Securities Regulations 1995 (SI 1995/1537); Financial Services and Markets Act 2000 (Offer of Securities) Order 2001 (SI 2001/2598); above p.392 n.4.

[86] *Jenkins v Livesey* [1985] A.C. 424.

[87] *Bell v Marsh* [1903] 1 Ch. 528 at 541; *Spiro v Lintern* [1973] 1 W.L.R. 1002 at 1010–1011, quoted above, p.34; *The Henrik Sif* [1982] 1 Lloyd's Rep. 456; *The Lutetian* [1982] 2 Lloyd's Rep. 140 at 158; *The Stolt Loyalty* [1993] 2 Lloyd's Rep. 281 at 289 (affirmed without reference to this point [1995] 1 Lloyd's Rep. 599). Contrast *The Tatra* [1990] 2 Lloyd's Rep. 51 (where A had no such knowledge); *Rafsanjan Pistachio Producers Co-operative v Bank Leumi (UK) plc* [1991] 1 Lloyd's Rep. 513 at 542.

[88] See below, p.402. *cf.* also the cases of "estoppel by convention" discussed at p.110, above. In those cases, the mistake is shared by both parties, so that it is inappropriate to talk of a duty of disclosure: *cf.* above, p.392 at n.5.

(9) Duty of disclosure in performance of contract

So far, our main concern[89] has been with the exceptional cases in which a duty of disclosure may exist in the negotiations leading to the conclusion of a contract. The further question is whether a duty of disclosure can arise in the *performance* of an already concluded contract. At common law, there is no general duty of disclosure in cases of this kind: for example, a bank which has entered into a contract to provide banking services is under no duty to disclose to its customer (A) that it has made later contracts with other customers for the provision of substantially similar services on terms more favourable to the customers than those of its contract with A.[90] But there are many situations (which may be regarded as exceptions to the general principle) in which a duty of disclosure does arise in the course of the *performance* of an already existing contract.[91] For example, an employee may be bound to disclose breaches of duty of fellow-employees who have defrauded the employer[92]; though he is not normally bound to disclose his own breaches of duty,[93] let alone his intention to commit breaches of duty in the future.[94] A contracting party may, however, be under a duty to disclose his own breaches of the contract on the ground that they may lead to danger of physical injury to persons or to property.[95] A professional person may be under certain duties of disclosure towards the person who has engaged his services; but again these duties arise out of the contract (or relationship giving rise to liability in tort)[96] between them: their performance is not a prerequisite for its creation. Sometimes, failure to perform a duty of disclosure imposed by one contract may vitiate a second contract between the same parties: thus in one case it was held that an employee's failure to perform his duty under his contract of employment to disclose frauds being perpetrated by his subordinates on his employers entitled the employers to rescind an arrangement with the employee under which he had obtained considerable benefits on "early retirement".[97] Similarly, it has been suggested that, where a bank lends money on a mortgage to one of its customers, it is under a duty "to proffer to her some adequate explanation of the nature and effect of the document which she had come to sign".[98]

---

[89] Except on p.393 above, at nn.10 to 13.

[90] *Suriya & Douglas v Midland Bank plc* [1999] 1 All E.R. (Comm) 612.

[91] *The Star Sea* [2001] UKHL 1; [2001] 1 All E.R. (Comm) 193, at [50].

[92] *Sybron Corp v Rochem Ltd* [1984] Ch. 112 at 126–127, 129; Kerr L.J. treated the case as one of "covering up and deliberately concealing": *ibid.* at 130.

[93] *Bell v Lever Bros* [1932] A.C. 161; *Nottingham University v Fischel* [2000] I.C.R. 1462 ("moonlighting" in breach of contract of employment).

[94] *Horcal v Gatland* [1984] I.R.L.R. 288; *cf. Balston v Headline Filters* [1990] F.S.R. 385.

[95] *The Zinnia* [1984] 2 Lloyd's Rep. 211 at 218.

[96] See the discussion of the extent of a surgeon's duty of disclosure before carrying out an operation: *Sidaway v Bethlehem Royal Hospital* [1985] A.C. 871; and the duty of a doctor carrying out a vasectomy to warn the patient that sterility might not be permanent: *Thake v Maurice* [1986] Q.B. 644. Cases in which solicitors acting both for mortgage lender and borrowers were held liable to the lender for failing to disclose facts coming to their notice in the course of the transaction fall into the present category: see, for example, *Bristol & West Building Society v May, May & Merrimans* [1996] 2 All E.R. 801; *Mortgage Express Ltd v Bowerman* [1996] 2 All E.R. 836; contrast *National Home Loans Corp v Giffen Couch & Archer* [1997] 3 All E.R. 808 (where no duty of disclosure arose).

[97] *Sybron Corp v Rochem Ltd* [1984] Ch. 112; Honeyball [1983] C.L.J. 218.

[98] *Cornish v Midland Bank plc* [1985] 3 All E.R. 513 at 523, where the bank was found to be guilty of active misrepresentation. Contrast *Barclays Bank plc v Khaira*, *The Times*, December 19, 1991 (no such duty owed to a person who was not a customer of the bank).

3. Effects of Non-disclosure

(1) In general

In discussing the effects of non-disclosure two preliminary distinctions must be drawn. The first relates to what may be called the nature of the non-disclosure; the second relates to the time when the facts which were not disclosed should have been disclosed.

(a) NATURE OF NON-DISCLOSURE. Cases of liability for non-disclosure can be divided into two kinds. First, there are cases in which no misrepresentation has been made in so many words, but one can be inferred from conduct or from the surrounding circumstances, *e.g.* where a representation is falsified by later events, or where a statement is literally true but misleading, or where disclosure is required by custom.[99] Secondly, there are cases of what may be called "pure" non-disclosure, in which no such inference can be drawn, but the law nevertheless gives a remedy for non-disclosure, *e.g.* in contracts of insurance, or by statute.[1]

In the first of the above groups of cases, non-disclosure can give rise to the same remedies as active misrepresentation, that is, to a right to rescind the contract (in the sense of setting it aside *ab initio* for all purposes[2]) and to a common law right to damages for deceit, or for negligence (but not for breach of the rescinded contract). The position is more complex in the second group of cases, *i.e.* in those of "pure" non-disclosure. We have seen that failure to perform the duty of disclosure in contracts *uberrimae fidei* gives rise to a right to rescind, but not to one to damages either for breach of contract or for negligence at common law.[3] Conversely, breach of the statutory duty of disclosure imposed on persons issuing a company prospectus has been held to give rise to a right to damages, but not to one to rescind.[4] General statements about the effects of "pure" non-disclosure are best avoided: the effects depend on the purpose of the rule of law by which the duty of disclosure is imposed.

(b) PRE- AND POST-CONTRACT NON-DISCLOSURE. The remedy of rescission for non-disclosure, in the sense of setting the contract aside *ab initio*,[5] sometimes operates harshly: for example where this remedy is available to an insurer in respect of non-disclosure by the insured, which may be quite innocent. The courts have therefore mitigated the severity of the remedy by distinguishing between cases in which the non-disclosure occurred before, and induced the formation of, the contract, and those in which it occurred after the contract had been made and amounted to a breach of one of its terms.[6] Rescission *ab initio* (as for misrepresentation) is available (if at all)[7] only in cases of the former kind. Where the non-disclosure is post-contractual and amounts to a breach of the contract, the drastic effects of rescission *ab initio* would be "disproportionate" and "penal"[8]; and the injured party's remedies in respect of it depend on the rules relating to the effects of breach,[9] to be discussed later in this book.[10] These

---

[99] See above, pp.393–394.

[1] See above, pp.394, 399.

[2] See above, p.343 at n.94; the contract is voidable, not void: Marine Insurance Act 1906, s.17 ("may be avoided"); *The Grecia Express* [2002] 2 Lloyd's Rep. 88 at 127–128.

[3] See above, p.398.

[4] See above, p.399, n.84.

[5] See above, at n.2.

[6] See above, p.400 under heading (9).

[7] It may not be available even in such cases: see above, at n.4.

[8] *The Star Sea* [2001] UKHL 1; [2001] 1 All E.R. (Comm) 193, at [51].

[9] *ibid.*, at [50], [52].

[10] See below, pp.759 *et seq*, 849 *et seq*.

remedies are in one respect more extensive than those for pre-contractual non-disclosure: rescission for breach does not deprive the injured party of the right to damages for breach of the contract.[11] On the other hand, while the effect of rescission for pre-contractual non-disclosure is to "wipe [the contract] out altogether,[12] with retrospective effect, rescission for breach operates only with *prospective* effect[13]; and the remedy is, as a general rule,[14] available only in respect of a breach which causes serious prejudice to the injured party.[15] The rule that post-contractual non-disclosure has no retrospective effect is, however, subject to an exception in cases of fraud: if an insured person makes a fraudulent claim,[16] the insurer is entitled to reject not only that claim but also any lesser claim which the insured might honestly have made.[17] The exception has been explained on the ground that, if it did not exist, the insured would have nothing to lose (though he would incur the risk of a criminal penalty)[18] by putting forward a fraudulent claim.[19]

(2) Effects of Misrepresentation Act 1967

The Misrepresentation Act repeatedly uses the expression "misrepresentation made". This refers primarily to active misrepresentation and not to "pure" non-disclosure,[20] as described above. The Act therefore does not impose liability for such non-disclosure where none existed before.[21] Nor does it affect any liability for, or defence based on, such non-disclosure which did exist before the Act. It follows that liability in damages for "pure" non-disclosure could not arise under s.2(1); that the court has no discretion in cases of such non-disclosure to award damages in lieu of rescission under s.2(2); and that a term whose sole effect was to exclude or restrict liability for such non-disclosure is not affected by s.3.

On the other hand, the distinction between cases of "pure" non-disclosure, and those in which a misrepresentation, though not made in so many words, can be inferred from conduct, probably applies for the purposes of the Act. It is submitted that the Act would apply to cases of the latter kind,[22] *e.g.* where a representation had been made by conduct,[23] and where a representation had been made which was literally true but misleading because it was obscure or only told part of the truth.[24] It seems probable that the Act would also apply where the representation was true when it was made but was falsified by later events.[25] S.2(1) in particular might be thought to apply to such a case

---

[11] See below, p.851.

[12] *The Kanchenjunga* [1990] 1 Lloyd's Rep. 391 at 398, above, p.370.

[13] See below, p.850; *The Star Sea*, above, n.8, at [50].

[14] See below, p.778 *et seq.* for exceptions.

[15] See below, p.748; *The Mercadian Continent* [2001] EWCA Civ 1275; [2001] 2 Lloyd's Rep. 563 at [14].

[16] *i.e.* one of the *validity* of which depends on the false statement. The exception does not apply to false statements relating to other, and relatively minor, matters; *e.g.* in *The Mercadian Continent*, above n.15 it did not apply to a false statement affecting only the jurisdiction of the court called on to determine the validity of the claim, rather than that validity itself.

[17] *The Star Sea*, above, n.8, at [62].

[18] *cf.* above, p.374.

[19] *The Star Sea*, above, n.8, at [62].

[20] *HIH Casualty & General Insurance v Chase Manhattan Bank* [2001] EWCA Civ 1250; [2001] 2 Lloyd's Rep. 483, at [51]. The 1967 Act has not altered the common law meaning of "misrepresentation": *André & Cie SA v Ets Michel Blanc & Fils* [1979] 2 Lloyd's Rep. 427 at 435.

[21] *Banque Keyser Ullmann SA v Skandia (UK) Ins Co Ltd* [1990] 1 Q.B. 665 at 789–790, affirmed [1991] 2 A.C. 249.

[22] See Hudson, 85 L.Q.R. 524.

[23] See above, p.390.

[24] See above, p.394.

[25] See above, p.393.

as it requires the representor to show that he believed "up to the time the contract was made that the facts represented were true". It could be said that there was no "misrepresentation made" if the facts originally stated were then true; but the answer to this point may be that the representation can be treated as a continuing one and that it would become a *mis*representation when the falsifying event occurred. S.3 could also apply to a term which by general words excluded liability for all non-disclosure, since such words could cover cases in which a representation was inferred from conduct or the surrounding circumstances. In one case[26] a term containing such general words was assumed to be covered by s.3 but was held to satisfy the requirement of reasonableness. The question whether the section would apply to a term excluding liability only for "pure" non-disclosure was not discussed.

SECTION 8. MISREPRESENTATION AND ESTOPPEL

Under the doctrine of estoppel by representation[27]; a person who makes precise and unambiguous[28] representation[29] of fact[30] may be prevented from denying the truth of the statement if the person to whom it was made was intended to act on it, and did act on it to his detriment.[31] It is generally said that the doctrine does not give rise to a cause of action[32] but only to a defence. Thus if A agrees to let a house to B, representing that the drains are sound when they are not, B cannot rely on the doctrine of estoppel to found a claim for damages against A.[33] But the doctrine could provide B with a defence: for example, if A, immediately after the execution of the lease, brought an action for breach of covenant to repair.[34] Such a defence would be available even though B had affirmed (and not rescinded) the lease.

In addition to providing a defence to the representee, estoppel may remove one that would otherwise be available to the representor. Thus it may help a claimant no less than a defendant.[35] In *Burrowes v Lock*[36] a beneficiary under a trust fund proposed to assign

---

[26] *National Westminster Bank v Utrecht-American Finance Co*, [2001] 2 All E.R. (Comm) 7; [2001] EWCA Civ 658 at [59].

[27] In this Chapter our only concern is with this kind of estoppel. Estoppel by negligence is beyond the scope of this book. For the distinction, see *Moorgate Mercantile Co v Twitchings* [1977] A.C. 890. For promissory estoppel, estoppel by convention and proprietary estoppel, see above, pp.105–125, 130–149.

[28] See *Low v Bouverie* [1891] 3 Ch. 82, *Woodhouse AC Israel Cocoa Ltd v Nigerian Produce Marketing Co* [1972] A.C. 741 and *Phillip Collins Ltd v Davis* [2000] 3 All E.R. 808 at 805, where this requirement was not satisfied; *cf.* *The Junior K* [1988] 2 Lloyd's Rep. 583 at 589; *The Zhi Jiang Kou* [1991] 1 Lloyd's Rep. 493. It has been said that "reasonable clarity is sufficient": *The Shakleford* [1978] 2 Lloyd's Rep. 155 at 159.

[29] Non-disclosure or inaction will not normally suffice: *Laurie & Morewood v Dudin & Sons* [1926] 1 K.B. 223; *Moorgate Mercantile Co v Twitchings*, above, n.27; *The Nai Genova* [1984] 1 Lloyd's Rep. 353 at 363; *Tai Hing Cotton Mill Ltd v Liu Chong Hing Bank* [1986] A.C. 80 at 110, 392; *The Leonidas D* [1985] 1 W.L.R. 925; *The Tatra* [1990] 2 Lloyd's Rep. 51; *The Zhi Jiang Kou* [1991] 1 Lloyd's Rep. 493; *Orion Finance Ltd v J D Williams & Co Ltd* [1997] C.L.Y. 983.

[30] As distinct from one of law: see *Territorial & Auxiliary Forces Association v Nichols* [1949] 1 K.B. 35; *The Argo Hellas* [1984] 1 Lloyd's Rep. 296 at 304; (for this distinction, see further pp.333–335 above); and from a representation as to the future (or a promise): see above, pp.118, 331–332.

[31] *e.g.* *Lombard North Central plc v Stobart* [1990] Tr.L.R. 105. There is no further requirement that the reliance must be reasonable: *Downderry Construction Ltd v S of S for Transport, etc.* [2002] N.L.J. 108.

[32] *Low v Bouverie*, above, n.28; *The Anemone* [1987] 1 Lloyd's Rep. 546 at 557.

[33] Of course, there might be a claim for damages under one of the five heads discussed at pp.343–359 above.

[34] *cf.* *Oades v Spafford* [1949] 1 K.B. 74.

[35] *e.g.* *Cotterell v Leeds Day* [2001] W.T.L.R. 435 (estoppel depriving defendant of defence that claim was timebarred); *Shah v Shah* [2001] EWCA Civ 537; [2002] Q.B. 35 at [31] (defendant estopped from relying on fact that witness to a deed had not signed in his presence); *Aker Oil & Gas Technology UK Plc v Sovereign Corporate Ltd* [2002] C.L.C. 557; Jackson, 81 L.Q.R. 223; *cf.* above, p.115.

[36] (1805) 10 Ves. 470, as explained in *Low v Bouverie*, above; see Sheridan, *Fraud in Equity*, pp.31–36.

his share for value to a prospective lender, who, before advancing any money, asked the trustee whether the beneficiary had previously encumbered his share. The trustee replied that there was no encumbrance, having forgotten that 10 years earlier the beneficiary had in fact encumbered his share. It was held that the trustee was estopped from denying the truth of his statement. Thus he was liable to pay the assigned share to the assignee, free from the earlier encumbrance. The assignee here had an independent cause of action against the trustee based on the assignment; and the trustee was, by his representation, deprived of the defence that he was already bound to pay part of the fund to the previous encumbrancer. Similarly, a warehouseman may make a contractual promise to deliver goods out of his warehouse; and if the promise is coupled with an untrue statement about the goods (*e.g.* that they are in good condition, or in the warehouse, when they are not), he may be estopped from denying the truth of the statement.[37] The cause of action is based on the contractual promise, and the effect of the estoppel is simply to remove a defence.[38] And a person who has entered into a voidable contract may indicate that he is not going to exercise his power to avoid it. The effect of such a representation will be that he is bound by the contract without any power of avoidance[39]; and this result may be explained on the ground of either affirmation or estoppel. If the second explanation is adopted, it is again not the estoppel, but the contract, which constitutes the cause of action: the effect of the estoppel is simply to remove the power of avoidance.

---

[37] See *Coventry Shepherd & Co v GE Ry* (1883) 11 Q.B.D. 76; *cf. Alicia Hosiery Ltd v Brown Shipley & Co Ltd* [1970] 1 Q.B. 195, 206; *Griswold v Haven*, 25 N.Y. 595 (1862).

[38] *e.g. European Asian Bank v Punjab & Sind Bank* [1983] 2 All E.R. 508; *The Uhenbels* [1986] 2 Lloyd's Rep. 294 at 300.

[39] *Janred Properties Ltd v Ente Nazionale Italiano per il Turismo* [1989] 2 All E.R. 444.

CHAPTER TEN

DURESS AND UNDUE INFLUENCE[1]

THE consent of a contracting party may have been obtained by some form of pressure which the law regards as improper. The victim of such pressure may be entitled to relief under the common law of duress, and under the equitable rules of undue influence. He is also protected by certain special statutory provisions.

SECTION 1. DURESS AT COMMON LAW

A contract is voidable[2] at common law if it was made under duress. At one time the common law concept of duress was a very narrow one. It was restricted to actual or threatened physical violence to, or unlawful constraint of, the person of the contracting party[3] or of his employees for whom he is responsible.[4] This view was open to the objection that it failed to give due weight to the coercive effect of other illegitimate conduct or threats.[5] It was therefore rejected in *The Siboen and the Sibotre*,[6] where Kerr J. said that a plea of "compulsion or coercion" would also be available in other circumstances: *e.g.* where a person had been forced to enter into a contract under an imminent threat of having his house burnt down, or a valuable picture slashed.[7] His views have been accepted in later cases, so that the question is no longer what was threatened, but whether the effect of the threat was to bring about a "coercion of the will, which vitiates consent".[8] The view that consent is "vitiated" has been criticised[8a] but the criticism appears to be based on a misinterpretation of it: what it seems to mean is, not that consent is negatived, but that it has been improperly obtained.[9] In *The*

---

[1] Winder, 3 M.L.R. 97; 4 Conv. (N.S.) 274; Capper, 114 L.Q.R. 479.

[2] In *Barton v Armstrong* [1976] A.C. 104 certain deeds were declared "void" for duress; *cf.* Lanham, 29 M.L.R. 615. But the general view is that a contract procured by duress is only voidable: *Pao On v Lau Yiu Long* [1980] A.C. 614 at 634; *The Universe Sentinel* [1983] 1 A.C. 366 at 383, 400; *The Evia Luck (No.2)* [1992] 2 A.C. 152 at 168; *Deputy v Stapleford* 19 Cal. 302 (1861) (contract procured by flogging, etc., held "voidable"). A marriage is voidable for duress: Matrimonial Causes Act 1973, s.12(c).

[3] *Cumming v Ince* (1847) 11 Q.B. 112 at 120; the violence threatened had to be unlawful: *Biffin v Bignell* (1862) 7 H. & N. 877; *Smith v Monteith* (1844) 13 M. & W. 427. *cf. Latter v Bradell* (1880) 50 L.J.C.P. 166; (1881) 50 L.J.Q.B. 448.

[4] *cf. Gulf Azov Shipping Co Ltd v Idisi* [2001] 1 Lloyd's Rep. 727.

[5] Admiralty took a broader view in cases concerning salvage agreements: see *The Port Caledonia* [1903] p. 184.

[6] [1976] 1 Lloyd's Rep. 293. Beatson, 92 L.Q.R. 496; Beatson, *The Use and Abuse of Unjust Enrichment*, Chap.5.

[7] At p.335.

[8] *Pao On v Lau Yiu Long* [1980] A.C. 614 at 636; *cf. The Atlantic Baron* [1979] Q.B. 705; *The Proodos C* [1980] 2 Lloyd's Rep. 390 at 393; Coote [1980] C.L.J. 40; *Re T* [1993] Fam. 95 at 115–116.

[8a] Atiyah, 98 L.Q.R. 197; Beatson, *The Use and Abuse of Restitution*, pp.113 *et seq.*; *Crescendo Management Pty Ltd v Westpac Banking Corp* (1989–1990) 19 N.S.W.L.R. 40. The point is left open in *The Evia Luck (No.2)* [1992] 2 A.C. 152, 166.

[9] *cf. Huyton SA v Peter Cremer GmbH* [1999] 1 Lloyd's Rep. 620, at 638 (will said to be "deflected"; and *ibid.* at 642: same factors said to be relevant to "deflection" as to "coercion"). See also the reference, in the analogous case of undue influence, to an "overbearing" of the injured party's will: *Royal Bank of Scotland v Etridge (No.2)* [2001] UKHL 44; [2001] 4 All E.R. 449 at [103] and [162].

Universe Sentinel,[10] for example, trade union officials threatened to induce the crew of a ship to break their contracts of employment and so to prevent the ship from leaving port. In view of the "catastrophic"[11] financial consequences which the shipowners would suffer if these threats were carried out, it was conceded that they constituted "economic duress",[12] vitiating the shipowners' consent to an agreement to make certain payments to the union. To be capable of giving rise to such duress, the threat must be illegitimate[13] either because what is threatened is a legal wrong[14] (as in the examples so far given) or because the threat itself is wrongful (as in the case of the blackmailer's threat to disclose his victim's conduct to third parties[15]) or because it is contrary to public policy.[16] Whether the threat actually gives rise to duress must then be considered by reference to its coercive effect in each case: no particular type of threat is regarded either as *ipso facto* having such an effect, or as being incapable, as a matter of law, of producing it.

Even under this more flexible test, mere "commercial pressure"[17] will not suffice: it is, for example, not duress for a supplier of goods to refuse to continue to give credit to his customer unless the latter complies with a demand for payment made in good faith, even though the demand turns out to be unjustified.[18] Nor is a contract voidable for duress merely because a party is induced to enter into it by a threat to break an earlier contract.[19] The question whether a threat amounts to duress depends on its coercive effect in each case. Thus cases such as *D & C Builders v Rees*[20] have been explained[21] on the ground that the creditor's promise to accept part payment in full settlement had been obtained by duress. Similarly, in *B & S Contracts and Designs Ltd v Victor Green Publications Ltd*[22] a contractor who had undertaken to erect stands for an exhibition told his client, less than a week before the exhibition was due to open, that the contract would be cancelled unless the client paid an additional sum to meet claims which were being made against the contractor by his workforce. The consequence of not having the stands available in time would have been disastrous for the client in that it would have gravely damaged his reputation and might have exposed him to heavy claims for damages from exhibitors to whom space on the stands had been let. In these circumstances it was held

---

[10] [1983] 1 A.C. 366; Napier, [1983] C.L.J. 43; Jones, *ibid.* 47.

[11] [1983] 1 A.C. 366 at 383.

[12] *ibid. cf. The Evia Luck* [1992] 2 A.C. 152; *Woolwich Equitable BS v IRC (No.2)* [1993] A.C. 70 at 164; *Huyton SA v Peter Cremer GmbH* [1998] 1 Lloyd's Rep. 620 at 635.

[13] *ibid.*, at 636–638, 642.

[14] Hence a threat merely to exercise one's rights under a contract is not illegitimate: *The Olib*, [1991] 2 Lloyd's Rep. 108. *cf. Alf Vaughan & Co Ltd v Royscot Trust Ltd* [1999] 1 All E.R. (Comm) 856 (threat to recover goods from hirer not "illegitimate").

[15] [1983] 1 A.C. 366 at 401.

[16] *The Evia Luck (No.2)* [1990] 1 Lloyd's Rep. 319 at 329, affirmed [1992] 2 A.C. 152 (where the illegitimacy of the threat was no longer in dispute); *cf. The Evia Luck* [1986] 2 Lloyd's Rep. 165 at 178.

[17] *The Siboen and the Sibotre* [1976] 1 Lloyd's Rep. 293 at 336; *cf. Leyland Daf Ltd v Automotive Products* [1993] BCC 389.

[18] *CNT Cash & Carry Ltd v Gallagher Ltd* [1994] 4 All E.R. 714. There may have been an element of compromise in this case; *cf.* above, pp.87, 90; if so, the suggestions that the payment might have been recoverable on the ground that it was paid under a "mistaken belief" that it was legally due (at 720) is, with respect, open to doubt. *cf.* also *Smith v Charlick* (1923–24) 34 C.L.R. 38.

[19] *The Siboen and The Sibotre*, above, at 335; *cf.* below, p.575.

[20] [1966] 2 Q.B. 617; above, p.114. *cf. The Atlantic Baron* [1979] Q.B. 705, above, p.97; *Nixon v Furphy* (1925) 25 S.R. (N.S.W.) 151; *T. A. Sundell & Sons Pty Ltd v Emm Yannoulatos (Overseas) Pty Ltd* (1956) 56 S.R. (N.S.W.) 323; contrast *Smith v Charlick* (1923–4) 34 C.L.R. 38 (payment to avoid threat not to enter into *future* contracts); *Williams v Roffey Bros & Nicholls (Contractors) Ltd* [1991] 1 Q.B. 1 (where no threat was made and duress was not pleaded).

[21] In *The Siboen and The Sibotre*, above, at 335.

[22] [1984] I.C.R. 419; Palmer and Catchpole, 48 M.L.R. 102; *cf. The Alev* [1989] 1 Lloyd's Rep. 138; *Atlas Express Ltd v Kafco (Importers & Distributors) Ltd* [1989] Q.B. 833; Chandler, [1989] L.M.C.L.Q. 270; Flemming, [1989] C.L.J. 362; Phang, 53 M.L.R. 107.

that the payment had been made under duress and that the client was entitled to recover it back. Such cases must be contracted with *Pao On v Lau Yiu Long*,[23] where the claimants threatened to break a contract with a company unless the defendants, who were shareholders in the company, gave them a guarantee against loss resulting from the performance of that contract. The defendants, thinking that the risk of such loss was small, gave the guarantee in order to avoid the adverse publicity which the company might suffer if the contract were not performed. In these circumstances, it was held that there was no "coercion of the will", so that the guarantee was not voidable for duress. In deciding whether the threat actually coerced the person to whom it was addressed, the court will also consider what other courses of action (than submission to the threat) were reasonably available to that person: for example there will be no economic duress if it would have been reasonable for him to have resisted the threatened wrong by taking legal proceedings.[24]

The view that unlawful violence to the person was necessary to constitute duress had led in a number of nineteenth century cases to the conclusion that a contract could not be invalidated by "duress of goods". This meant that an agreement to pay money for the release of goods unlawfully detained, or to prevent their unlawful seizure, was valid.[25] But it had also been held that money which had actually been paid for such a purpose could be recovered back.[26] Parke B. in several cases stated this strange distinction with apparent complacency.[27] Its effect was not wholly clear. It could hardly have meant that a person who was successfully sued for money which he had agreed to pay for the release of his goods could then recover back what he had been compelled to pay in the first action. It seems to have meant that money which was simply paid for the release of the goods could be recovered back; while money to be paid under an agreement for their release could be sued for and could not (if paid) be recovered back. But if it meant this it was inconsistent with at least one case[28] in which money paid under such an agreement was recovered back; and if this was right it would have been very strange if the agreement to pay the money had been enforceable.[29] The authorities now support the view that the "duress of goods" cases are governed by the modern, flexible, test of duress, so that the question in each case is whether there had in fact been "coercion of the will"[30]; and that this test governs both the validity of the contract and the right to recover back money paid under it.[31]

The rule that money extorted by duress can be recovered back also applies where an unlawful charge is levied by unlawful threats, for example, where a carrier refuses to

---

[23] [1980] A.C. 614; cf. *Alec Lobb (Garages) Ltd v Total Oil (Great Britain) Ltd* [1983] 1 W.L.R. 87.

[24] e.g. *Hennessy v Craigmyle & Co* [1986] I.C.R. 461.

[25] *Skeate v Beale* (1841) 11 A. & E. 983; and see below, n.27. It is assumed that the seizure is not *known* to be unlawful, for, if this was known, there would be no consideration for the promise to pay: above, p.88, and see *Atlee v Backhouse* (1836) 3 M. & W. 633 at 650.

[26] *Astley v Reynolds* (1731) 2 Str. 915; *Valpy v Manley* (1845) 1 C.B. 594; *Green v Duckett* (1883) 11 Q.B.D. 275; *Maskell v Horner* [1915] 3 K.B. 106; *T D Keegan Ltd v Palmer* [1961] 2 Lloyd's Rep. 449 at 457.

[27] *Atlee v Backhouse* (1836) 3 M. & W. 633 at 650; *Oates v Hudson* (1851) 6 Ex. 346; *Parker v Bristol & Exeter Ry* (1851) 6 Ex. 702 at 705.

[28] *Tamvaco v Simpson* (1866) L.R. 1 C.P. 363, where the only question discussed by the Exchequer Chamber was whether the detention was lawful.

[29] cf. Beatson [1974] C.L.J. 97, *The Use and Abuse of Unjust Enrichment*, Chap.5, suggesting that the cases of valid agreements should be explained as compromises (above pp.88–89) or on similar grounds.

[30] *Pao On v Lau Yiu Long* [1980] A.C. 614 at 636; *Royal Boskalis Westminster NV v Mountain* [1997] 2 All E.R. 929.

[31] *The Universe Sentinel* [1983] 1 A.C. 366; cf. *The Atlantic Baron* [1979] Q.B. 705, (where the claim there failed on the ground of affirmation); *Lloyds Bank Ltd v Bundy* [1975] Q.B. 326 at 337; *The Alev* [1989] 1 Lloyd's Rep. 138.

carry goods unless he is paid more than he is legally entitled to charge.[32] Money paid by a citizen under an *ultra vires* demand for a tax or similar levy is also recoverable by the payor, irrespective of whether the demand amounts to duress[33]: this rule can be explained as resting either on the general principles of unjust enrichment[34] or on "common justice"[35] or on the ground that a payment made in response to such an invalid demand is analogous to one made for a consideration which has failed.[36] But where the demand is not of this kind, so that the only ground for recovery is duress, the claim for the return of the money will fail if the demand for the payment was not backed by any threat[37]; or where it is backed only by a threat to take legal proceedings[38]: if such a payment could be recovered back, no compromise would be secure.

As in the case of misrepresentation, it is not necessary to show that duress was the sole cause inducing the contract.[39] It is enough if it was *an* inducement; and once the fact of duress is established the burden is on the party exerting the duress to show that it did not in fact induce the contract.[40]

SECTION 2. UNDUE INFLUENCE IN EQUITY

A transaction can be set aside in equity if, because it has been procured by undue influence exerted by one party (A) on the other (B), it cannot "fairly be treated as the expression of [B's] free will."[41] The cases in which such relief is given are commonly divided into the two main groups to be discussed below; the second of these groups must, or may, have to be, further divided into two sub-groups. The law on this topic was extensively reviewed by the House of Lords in *Royal Bank of Scotland v Etridge (No.2)*[42] ("the *Etridge* case") and the following discussion attempts the far from easy task of stating the effects of that review.

1. Actual Pressure

The first group of cases in which equity gave relief on the ground of undue influence are those in which one party had induced the other to enter into the transaction by actual pressure which equity regarded as improper but which was formerly thought not to amount to duress at common law because no element of violence to the person was involved.[43] For example, a promise to pay money can be set aside if obtained by a threat

---

[32] *Parker v Bristol & Exeter Ry*, above. n.26; *Great Western Ry v Sutton* (1869) L.R. 4 H.L. 226; Winfield, 60 L.Q.R. 341.

[33] *Woolwich Equitable BS v IRC (No.2)* [1993] A.C. 70.

[34] *ibid.* at 197.

[35] *ibid.* at 172.

[36] *ibid.* at 197, 198.

[37] *Twyford v Manchester Corp* [1946] Ch. 236; discussed by Marsh, 62 L.Q.R. 333, and see next note.

[38] *Brown v M'Kinally* (1795) 1 Esp. 279; *William Whiteley Ltd v R* (1910) 101 L.T. 741. The *Twyford* and *William Whiteley* cases were doubted in the *Woolwich Equitable* case [1993] A.C. 70, but only in so far as they concerned unlawful demands for taxes and similar levies by public officials.

[39] See above, p.340.

[40] *Barton v Armstrong* [1976] A.C. 104.

[41] *Royal Bank of Scotland v Etridge (No.2)* [2001] UKHL 44; [2002] 2 A.C. 773, at [7]. *cf. ibid.* at [162]: no relief where B's "will had not been overborne".

[42] See above.

[43] *Turnbull & Co v Duvall* [1902] A.C. 429 at 434; but there seems to have been no actual pressure in that case: *Barclays Bank v O'Brien* [1994] 1 A.C. 180 at 191–192. *Chaplin & Co v Brammal* [1908] 1 K.B. 233; *Avon Finance Co v Bridger* [1985] 2 All E.R. 281 at 285.

to prosecute the promisor,[44] or his close relative, or his spouse, for a criminal offence.[45] Such threats might now constitute duress, but the equitable concept of "pressure" is still wider than that of duress at common law, for undue influence can be exercised without making illegitimate threats or indeed any threats at all.[46] The party who claims relief on the ground of actual undue influence must show that such influence existed and had been exercised,[47] and that the transaction resulted from that influence. There is no further requirement in cases of this kind that the transaction must be shown to be to the manifest disadvantage of the party seeking to set it aside[48] or that the transaction must be one that "calls for explanation"[49] by the other party.

2. Special Relationships: Presumed Undue Influence

The second group of cases in which equity gives relief for undue influence is that in which the relationship between the parties is such as to give rise to what has been called a "presumption of undue influence".[49a] This phrase contains an unfortunate element of ambiguity: it can mean either that such influence is presumed to *exist* or that it is presumed to have been *exercised*. It might be better if use of the phrase were abandoned; but as there is little prospect of such a development, we shall here continue to use it, drawing attention from time to time to its different shades of meaning.[50] At this stage, it suffices to say that, where the presumption applies, it is not necessary for the party claiming relief to show that the impugned transaction was in fact procured by undue influence.

Relief can be given on the ground of undue influence even though the person to whom the gift or promise was made obtained no personal benefit from it. Thus the rule applies where the head of a religious order uses a gift wholly for the purposes of the order and where a trustee extracts a promise from one beneficiary solely for the benefit of another.[51]

(1) Types of presumptions[52]

A presumption is a rule of law by which, on proof of a specified fact or facts (the basic fact(s)) another fact (the presumed fact) is taken to exist. There are many classifications of presumptions; for the present purposes it suffices to distinguish between so-called irrebuttable presumptions and rebuttable ones. Irrebuttable (or conclusive) presumptions are rules of substantive law which have nothing to do with ways of proving facts.[53] If the law says that, on proof of the basic fact, the presumed fact is irrebuttably taken to exist, this means that proof of the basic fact produces the same legal consequence as proof of the presumed fact, even though the latter fact may be shown not to exist. A

---

[44] Such a threat was formerly thought to be incapable of giving rise to duress at common law: *Flower v Sadler* (1882) 10 Q.B.D. 572.

[45] *Williams v Bayley* (1866) L.R. 1 H.L. 200; *Kaufman v Gerson* [1904] 1 K.B. 591; *Société des Hôtels Réunis (S.A.) v Hawker* (1913) 29 T.L.R. 578; *Mutual Finance Ltd v Wetton* [1937] 2 K.B. 389.

[46] *e.g. CIBC Mortgages v Pitt* [1994] 1 A.C. 200, where the claim failed for reasons stated on p.427 below.

[47] *Howes v Bishop* [1909] 2 K.B. 390; *Bank of Montreal v Stuart* [1911] A.C. 120 at 127.

[48] *CIBC Mortgages v Pitt* [1994] A.C. 200, disapproving *Bank of Credit & Commerce International SA v Aboody* [1990] 1 Q.B. 923 on this point; Cretney, 105 L.Q.R. 169; Dixon, [1989] C.L.J. 359.

[49] *cf.* below, p.410 at n.62.

[49a] *Barclays Bank plc v O'Brien* [1994] 1 A.C. 180 at 189; *Etridge* case, above n.41 at [16].

[50] See further below, p.413 at nn.3 and 4.

[51] *Allcard v Skinner*, above n.48; *Ellis v Barker* (1871) L.R. 7 Ch.App. 104; *cf. Bullock v Lloyds Bank* [1955] Ch. 317.

[52] For a full discussion, see *Cross on Evidence* (1st ed.), pp.86–91.

[53] Cross and Tapper on *Evidence* (9th ed.), p.66.

rebuttable presumption, by contrast, is a rule of law by which, on proof of the basic fact(s), the presumed fact is assumed to exist in the absence of evidence negativing (or "rebutting") its existence. Such presumptions may be subdivided into (i) those which require the person against whom the presumption operates to show (on a balance of probabilities) that the presumed fact does *not* exist; and (ii) those which merely require that person to introduce some evidence to that effect, leaving it up to the proponent of the presumption to show that (on a balance of probabilities) that fact does exist. Presumptions of the latter kind are sometimes called "evidential presumptions,"[54] though this phrase has no generally accepted technical meaning.

(2) The presumption of undue influence

(a) REQUIREMENTS. To give rise to the "presumption of undue influence",[55] two basic facts must be established by the party claiming relief.[56] The first is the existence of a relationship between A and B by virtue of which B either in fact reposed trust and confidence in A or is taken as a matter of law to have done so; the kinds of relationship which are capable of producing these effects are discussed below. The second basic fact relates nature of the impugned transactions; and conflicting views have been expressed on the question whether it was necessary for B to show that the transaction was "disadvantageous" or "manifestly disadvantageous" to him. The original view appears to have been that there was no such requirement and that, once a relationship of trust and confidence was established, the transaction could be set aside on grounds of public policy, even though it was not in fact disadvantageous to B.[57] Later it was said that the ground for relief was "not a vague 'public policy' but specifically the victimization of one party [B] by the other [A]" and that B had to show that the transaction was to his "manifest disadvantage".[58] But this view was later doubted,[59] especially on the ground that, where A stood in a fiduciary position to B, the impugned transaction would (on grounds of public policy) not be allowed to stand unless its fairness was affirmatively proved by A[60]; the requirement of "manifest disadvantage" also does not apply in cases of actual pressure.[61] In the *Etridge* case, the use of the words "manifest disadvantage" to describe the second requirement of the presumption was therefore discouraged and the requirement was restated in the form that the transaction must be one which "calls for explanation"[62] or that it must be one which "is not readily explicable by the relationship between the parties."[63] This formulation of the requirement differs significantly from that in terms of "manifest disadvantage" since a substantial transaction may call for an explanation from A even though B may benefit from it indirectly (so that the disadvantage, if any, to B would not be "manifest"). On the other hand, an ordinary (or moderate) Christmas or birthday gift from B to A would not (even where there was a

---

[54] This usage is adopted in the *Etridge* case, n.41 above, *e.g.* at [16].

[55] See above, at n.49.

[56] *Etridge* case, above, n.41, at [13].

[57] *Allcard v Skinner* (1887) 36 Ch.D. 145 at 171; *Lloyd's Bank Ltd v Bundy* [1975] Q.B. 326 at 342; *cf. Hylton v Hylton* (1745) 2 Ves. Sen. 547 at 549 ("public utility").

[58] *National Westminster Bank plc v Morgan* [1985] A.C. 686 at 706; *cf. Hart v O'Connor* [1985] A.C. 1000 at 1024.

[59] *CIBC Mortgages plc v Pitt* [1994] 1 A.C. 200 at 209.

[60] *ibid.*; see the authorities cited in n.81 below and in n.182 on p.419, below, and the reference to "public policy" in *Hammond v Osborn* [2002] EWCA Civ 885, [2002] W.T.L.R. 1125.

[61] *CIBC Mortgages plc v Pitt* [1994] 1 A.C. 200, disapproving *Bank of Credit & Commerce International SA v Aboody* [1990] 1 Q.B. 923 on this point.

[62] [2002] 2 A.C. 773 at [14] *per* Lord Nicholls, with whose speech Lords Bingham and Clyde agreed; *cf. ibid.* at [156], [158] *per* Lord Scott.

[63] *ibid.*, at [21].

relationship of trust and confidence between them) "call for explanation" and so could not be set aside for presumed undue influence.[64]

(b) EFFECT AND NATURE. Once the basic facts of the presumption (*i.e.*, a relationship between A and B of trust and confidence, and a transaction calling for explanation) are established, then the presumed fact is that "the transaction can only have been procured by undue influence."[65] This presumption has been described as "a rebuttable evidential presumption of undue influence".[66] As the first of the phrases just quoted shows, the presumed fact is that such influence has been *exercised* (or that the trust and confidence has been abused). In this respect, the present presumption differs from another presumption, to be discussed below,[67] which merely establishes (or dispenses with the need to establish) that a relationship of trust and confidence *exists*. The statement that the presumption with which we are here concerned is "rebuttable" refers to the point that it can be displaced in one of the ways to be more fully discussed below[68]: *e.g.* that B took independent legal advice before entering into the transaction; or by other evidence that the transaction was the "expression of [B's] free will".[69] The meaning of the statement that the presumption is "evidential"[70] seems to be that if, after proof of the basic facts the presumption, A introduces evidence which, on a balance of probabilities, makes it doubtful whether the transaction was procured by undue influence, then B will not be entitled to relief unless he can introduce further evidence, showing, on balance of probabilities, that the transaction was so procured.[71]

(c) RELATIONSHIPS IN WHICH THE PRESUMPTION APPLIES. These relationships have traditionally been divided into two categories which became known as "class 2A" and "class 2B" cases.[72] Considerable difficulty arises in determining whether this classification has survived (at all or in a modified form) after, the *Etridge* case. It will be convenient first to describe the traditional categories under headings (i) and (ii) below and then to consider the effect on the classification of that case. It should be emphasised that this discussion is concerned with only *one* of the basic facts which must be established before it can be presumed that the transaction "can only have been procured by undue influence".[73] Even if the requisite relationship is established, this presumption will arise only if it is *also* shown that the impugned transaction is one "which calls for explanation".[74]

(i) *Relationships of presumed trust and confidence (class 2A)*. Where one of the types of relationships to be listed below exists, it is settled by law or (what amounts to the same thing),[75] "the law presumes, irrebuttably, that [A] had influence over [B]".[76] This presumption has been held to apply where the relationship between A and B is that of

---

[64] *ibid.*, at [24], [156]; *cf. ibid.*, at [104] (reasonable fee paid to solicitor).

[65] *ibid.*, at [14].

[66] *ibid.*, at [16], [153], [194].

[67] Under heading (c)(i).

[68] See below, p.419.

[69] *Etridge* case [2002] 2 A.C. 773 at [7].

[70] See above, at n.66.

[71] See *ibid.*, at [158].

[72] This terminology goes back to *Bank of Credit & Commerce International SA v Aboody* [1990] 1 Q.B. 923 at 953 and was approved in *Barclays Bank plc v O'Brien* [1994] 1 A.C. 180 at 189–190. "Class 1" (not relevant to the present discussion) comprises cases of *actual* pressure (above, p.408; *Etridge* case, above, n.69, at [14]).

[73] *Etridge* case, above n.69, at [14].

[74] *ibid.*

[75] See above, p.409.

[76] *Etridge* case, above n.69, at [18]; *cf. ibid.* at [104].

parent and child,[77] guardian and ward,[78] religious adviser and disciple,[79] doctor and patient,[80] solicitor and client[81] and trustee and *cestui que trust*.[82] It applies to some, but not all, transactions between fiancé and fiancée: thus it has been applied to a settlement made before marriage by which the wife agreed, in return for a small immediate payment, to give up large sums which were to accrue to her as a widow; but it would not apply to the gift of an extravagant engagement ring.[83] The present presumption does not apply between husband and wife,[84] or between employer and employee.[85] Nor does it apply to all relationships which are fiduciary in the sense that they give rise to a duty of disclosure: thus it does not apply between agent and principal.[86] The presumption may apply even after the relationship has ceased if the influence continues, for example, between solicitor and ex-client[87]; and between parent and child for a "short" time[88] after the child has come of age, but not once the child is "emancipated" from parental control.[89] Even the marriage of a child does not invariably have this effect.[90]

The present presumption must be "distinguished sharply"[91] from the "evidential presumption"[92] described above. The first distinction between them is that the present presumption is irrebuttable, while the "evidential presumption" is rebuttable. Since an irrebuttable presumption is (as was pointed out above)[93] a rule of substantive law, rather than a means of establishing facts, the effect of the present presumption is that proof of the relationship (*e.g.* of parent and child) becomes, in cases of alleged undue influence, a *substitute* for the need to prove that B reposed trust and confidence in A. It is then, on the one hand, unnecessary for B to show that (s)he actually reposed trust and confidence in A and, on the other,[94] irrelevant for A to show that this was not the case. The second is that the presumed fact the "irrebuttable" presumption is quite different from that of

---

[77] *Bullock v Lloyds Bank*, above; *Cocking v Pratt* (1749) 1 Ves.Sen. 400; *Powell v Powell* [1900] 1 Ch. 243; *cf. Re T* [1993] Fam. 95.

[78] *Hylton v Hylton* (1754) 2 Ves.Sen. 547; *Hatch v Hatch* (1804) 9 Ves. 292; the *de facto* relation of guardian and ward suffices: *Archer v Hudson* (1846) 15 L.J.Ch. 211.

[79] *Allcard v Skinner*, above p.410 n.57; *Nottidge v Prince* (1860) 2 Giff. 246; *cf. Tufton v Sperni* [1952] 2 T.L.R. 516; *Roche v Sherrington* [1982] 1 W.L.R. 599 at 606.

[80] *Dent v Bennett* (1839) 4 My. & Cr. 269; *Radcliffe v Price* (1902) 18 T.L.R. 466; *cf. Re CMG* [1970] Ch. 574 (authorities in charge of mental hospital and patient residing there); *Claughton v Price* [1997] E.G.C.S. 51.

[81] *Wright v Carter* [1903] 1 Ch. 27; *cf. Wintle v Nye* [1959] 1 W.L.R. 284.

[82] *Ellis v Barker* (1871) L.R. 7 Ch.App. 104; *Thomson v Eastwood* (1877) 2 App.Cas. 215.

[83] *Zamet v Hyman* [1961] 1 W.L.R. 1442; qualifying *Re Lloyds Bank Ltd* [1931] 1 Ch. 289.

[84] *Howes v Bishop* [1909] 2 K.B. 390; *Bank of Montreal v Stuart* [1911] A.C. 120; *Mackenzie v Royal Bank of Canada* [1934] A.C. 468; *Gillman v Gillman* (1946) 174 L.T. 272. *National Westminster Bank plc v Morgan* [1985] A.C. 686 at 703; *Kings North Trust Ltd v Bell* [1986] 1 W.L.R. 119 at 127; *Coldunell Ltd v Gallon* [1986] 1 All E.R. 429 at 437; Andrews, [1986] C.L.J. 195; *Midland Bank plc v Shephard* [1988] 3 All E.R. 17; *Barclays Bank plc v Khaira* [1992] 1 W.L.R. 623 at 632.

[85] *Matthew v Bobbins* (1980) 256 E.G. 603.

[86] *Re Coomber* [1911] 1 Ch. 723.

[87] *McMaster v Byrne* [1952] 1 All E.R. 1362; *cf. Longstaff v Birtles* [2002] EWCA Civ 1219; [2002] 1 W.L.R. 470 (a case, not of presumed undue influence, but of breach of fiduciary duty: see at [40]); *Allison v Clayhills* (1907) 97 L.T. 709 at 711.

[88] See *Re Pauling's Settlement Trusts* [1964] Ch. 303 at 337.

[89] *Bainbrigge v Browne* (1881) 18 Ch.D. 188.

[90] *Lancashire Loans Ltd v Black* [1934] 1 K.B. 380.

[91] *Etridge* case [2002] 2 A.C. 773 at [18].

[92] ibid., at [16], [18] and above p.410 at nn.54, 411, n.70.

[93] See above, p.409 at n.53.

[94] *Etridge* case, above, at [18].

the "evidential" presumption: the former is that A "had influence over"[95] B; the latter is that "the transaction can only have been procured by undue influence".[96] The third difference relates to the respective legal consequences of the two presumptions. The "irrebuttable" presumption is not itself a ground for relief[97]: it is merely a way of establishing *one* of the basic facts of the "evidential" presumption. An ordinary or moderate Christmas or birthday present can no more be set aside where it is made by a child to a parent or by a client to his solicitor than where it is made by a wife to her husband.[98] It follows that even where the "irrebuttable" presumption applies, B will be entitled to relief only if he shows that the transaction was *also* one that called for explanation; and if this further fact is established, then the "evidential" presumption comes into operation. Thus the two presumptions will operate in the same case and the "evidential" presumption remains rebuttable[99] (*e.g.* by evidence that B was independently advised) even where the relationship between A and B was such as to give rise to the "irrebuttable" presumption. There is, therefore, no inconsistency between saying, on the one hand, that, in the special relationship cases, "the law presumes, *irrebuttably*, that [A] had influence over [B]"[1] and, on the other, that if (even in such cases) B in addition showed that the impugned transaction called for explanation, then a "*rebuttable* evidential presumption"[2] arises that the transaction was "procured by" that influence. The irrebuttable presumption relates to the *existence*[3] of the influence, the rebuttable evidential presumption to its *exercise*.[4] The distinction is obscured by the unfortunate use of the ambiguous phrase "presumption *of* undue influence",[5] which is capable of referring to either or both of these operations.

(ii) *Relationships of actual confidence (class 2B).* In this group of cases, the relationship between A and B must be one in which B has in fact reposed trust and confidence in A. It is necessary for B to establish this fact, or that A has acquired "domination" over him.[6] If B shows this, and that the transaction which B seeks to avoid was such as to call for explanation, then the rebuttable presumption will arise, that the transaction was procured by undue influence.[7]

It follows from the nature of the present group of cases that the question in each such case will be whether the party seeking to set the transaction aside has reposed sufficient trust and confidence in the other, rather than whether the relationship between the parties belongs to a particular type.[8] For example, the relation of banker and customer will not normally give rise to a presumption of undue influence,[9] but it can do so in exceptional cases if the customer has placed himself entirely in the hands of the bank (in

---

[95] *ibid.*

[96] *ibid.*, at [14].

[97] *ibid.* at [104] ("no presumption properly so called that the confidence has been abused").

[98] *ibid.*, at [24], [156]; *cf.* [104].

[99] This point accounts for the discussion by Lord Nicholls *ibid.* at [15] of *Bainbrigge v Brown* (1881) 18 Ch.D. 188 in the context of the "evidential" presumption, even though the relationship of the parties was that of father and "unemancipated" children (above, p.380) so that the "irrebuttable presumption"; would *also* have operated between them.

[1] *ibid.*, at [18].

[2] *ibid.*, at [219].

[3] *ibid.*, at [18].

[4] *ibid.*, at [14].

[5] See above, p.378 at nn.49 and 50.

[6] *Goldsworthy v Brickell* [1987] CL 378 at 404.

[7] *Barclays Bank plc v O'Brien* [1994] A.C. 180 at 189–190; *Etridge* case [2002] 2 A.C. 773 at [14].

[8] Cited with approval in the *Etridge* case at [10]; *cf. ibid.* at [80] ("cannot be exhaustively classified").

[9] *National Westminster Bank plc v Morgan* [1985] A.C. 686; Andrews, [1985] C.L.J. 192; Tiplady, 48 M.L.R. 579; *Bank of Baroda v Panessar* [1987] Ch. 335; *Lloyd's Bank v Egremont* [1990] 2 FLR 351.

giving the bank a guarantee secured on his home) and has not been given any opportunity to seek independent advice.[10]

The flexible character of the present group of cases is illustrated by *Tate v Williamson*,[11] where the defendant became financial adviser to an extravagant Oxford undergraduate who sold him his estate for half its value and then drank himself to death at the age of 24. His executors successfully claimed that the sale should be set aside. Lord Chelmsford said: "The jurisdiction exercised by courts of equity over the dealings of persons standing in certain fiduciary relations has always been regarded as one of the most salutary description. . . . The courts have always been careful not to fetter this jurisdiction by defining the exact limits of its exercise."[12] A modern illustration of the principle is provided by *O'Sullivan v Management Agency & Music Ltd*[13] where the relationship between the claimant (then a young and unknown composer and performer of music) and his manager was held to be such as to give rise to a presumption of undue influence; and transactions which turned out to be unfair to the claimant when he later became a celebrity were accordingly set aside. On the other hand, it has been held that no such presumption arose on the score of "family loyalty"[14] between brothers trading in partnership, nor on the ground that one of them suffered from alcohol or drug addiction, unless perhaps the other had assumed the role of guardian or adviser to the former party.[15]

(iii) *Effects of the Etridge Case.* It will be recalled that, before the *Etridge* case,[16] cases of presumed undue influence had been divided into two categories (discussed above) called "class 2A" and "class 2B".[17] This classification was adopted by the House of Lords in *Barclays Bank plc v O'Brien* where Lord Browne-Wilkinson, giving the leading speech, said that, where the relationship between A and B was such as to fall into class 2A, then a presumption arose "that undue influence had been exercised"[18] while if that relationship fell into class 2B, then proof of it raised "the presumption of undue influence".[19] Reference has already been made to the ambiguity of the latter phrase,[20] but, from the context, the two phrases (quoted above) in Lord Browne-Wilkinson's speech seem to mean the same thing—*i.e.*, that, on proof of the relationship, it was presumed that undue influence had been exercised. If the phrases mean this, they must be qualified in the light of the *Etridge* case: as already noted,[21] the existence of the relationship between the parties (whether in a class 2A or class 2B case) is only *one* of

---

[10] *Lloyd's Bank Ltd v Bundy* [1955] Q.B. 326, esp. at 342; Carr, 38 M.L.R. 463; Sealy [1975] C.L.J. 17. The case was said in *National Westminster Bank plc v Morgan* [1985] A.C. 686 at 698 to turn on its "very special facts." See also *ibid.* 709 approving the ratio of the majority, based on the presumption of undue influence in *Lloyd's Bank Ltd v Bundy. cf. Cornish v Midland Bank plc* [1985] 3 All E.R. 513 at 518.

[11] (1866) L.R. 2 Ch.App. 55. For similar relationships between the aged and their advisors or companions, see *Inche Noriah v Shaik Allie bin Omar* [1929] A.C. 127; *Re Craig* [1971] Ch. 95; contrast *Hunter v Atkins* (1834) 3 My. & K. 113; *Re Brocklehurst* [1978] 1 Ch. 14.

[12] At p.60; *cf. Tufton v Sperni* [1952] 2 T.L.R. 516; *National Westminster Bank plc v Morgan* [1985] A.C. 686 at 708–709; *Goldsworthy v Brickell* [1987] Ch. 378; *Cheese v Thomas* [1994] W.L.R. 129; *Simpson v Simpson* [1992] 1 FLR 601.

[13] [1985] Q.B. 428; *Elton John v Richard Leon James* [1991] F.S.R. 397; *cf.* also *Horry v Tate & Lyle Refineries Ltd* [1982] 2 Lloyd's Rep. 417; *Mahoney v Purnell* [1996] 3 All E.R. 61; *Credit Lyonnais Bank Nederland NV v Burch* [1997] 1 All E.R. 144 (employer and employee) (approved in the *Etridge* case [2002] 2 A.C. 773 at [83], [86]).

[14] *Irvani v Irvani* [2000] 1 Lloyd's Rep. 412 at 425.

[15] *ibid.*

[16] *Royal Bank of Scotland v Etridge (No.2)* [2002] 2 A.C. 773, above p.411.

[17] See above, p.411 at n.72; the classes are discussed under headings (i) and (ii) at pp.411 to 413 above.

[18] [1994] 1 A.C. 180 at 489.

[19] *ibid.*

[20] See above, pp.409 at nn.49a and 50; p.413 at n.5.

[21] See above, p.413 at nn.95–97.

the basic facts of the presumption that undue influence has been *exercised*. That presumption arises only if it is also shown that the transaction is one which "calls for explanation".[22]

In the *Etridge* case, the leading speech was given by Lord Nicholls. Lords Bingham and Clyde expressed their agreement with this speech, Lord Bingham also saying that it commanded "the unqualified support of all members of the House".[23] At the same time, Lord Clyde questioned "the wisdom . . . of attempting to make classifications of cases of undue influence"[24] while Lords Hobhouse and Scott appeared, at least at first sight, to reject or doubt the "class 2B" category.[25] The question thus arises whether that category has survived the *Etridge* case.

Lord Nicholls' speech in that case does not make any express reference to the distinction between class 2A and class 2B cases. But he does distinguish between cases in which there is "[p]roof that [B] has placed trust and confidence in [A]"[26] and those in which B "need not prove he actually reposed trust and confidence in" A because their relationship is such that "the law presumes, irrebuttably, that [A] had influence over [B]"[27]: *e.g.* where their relationship is that of parent and child. This distinction appears to resemble[28] the substance (though not the nomenclature) of the distinction between class 2A and class 2B cases. Lord Hobhouse, on the other hand, says that "the so-called class 2B presumption ought not to be adopted"[29] while Lord Scott says that he "doubt[s] the utility of the class 2B classification".[30] The question arises how these statements are to be reconciled with the distinction drawn by Lord Nicholls in the terms just quoted.[31]

One possible answer to this question is to say that in a class 2B case no presumption arises *merely* on proof that B has reposed trust and confidence in A since this is only *one* of the basic facts of the presumption that the transaction has been procured by undue influence,[32] the other basic fact being that the transaction was one that called for an explanation. But this is also true of class 2A cases,[33] the existence of which is recognised by Lords Hobhouse and Scott,[34] so that this reasoning can scarcely account for their apparent rejection of the class 2B category.

It is submitted that a preferable way of reconciling the apparent conflict of opinion is to have regard to the exact context in which it arose in the *Etridge* case. The appeals there before the House of Lords concerned a group of cases in which wives had provided security for their husbands' business debts, usually by means of a guarantee by the wife of those debts, supported by a charge on the matrimonial home owned either by the wife alone or by her and the husband jointly. On the principal debtor's default, the lender (usually a bank) would seek to enforce the security, typically by sale of the house. The question to what extent and in what circumstances such a third party is adversely affected by actual or presumed undue influence between husband and wife will be

---

[22] *Etridge* case, above, n.16 at [14].

[23] *ibid.*, at [4].

[24] *ibid.*, at [92].

[25] See below, at nn.29 and 30.

[26] *Etridge* case at [14].

[27] *ibid.*, at [18].

[28] Lord Nicholls' distinction only *resembles*, and is not *identical* with, that drawn in earlier cases between class 2A and class 2B: see below at nn.32 and 33 and p.417 at n.53.

[29] *Etridge* case, above, at [107].

[30] *ibid.*, at [161]; *cf. McGregor v Taylor* [2002] 2 Lloyd's Rep. 468 at [16] (but see also *ibid.* at [93]).

[31] At nn.26 and 27, above.

[32] *cf. Etridge* case, above, at [158].

[33] See above, p.413 at n.97.

[34] *Etridge* case, above, at [104], [107], [108].

discussed later in this Chapter.[35] Our present concern is with the question to what extent the presumption of undue influence operates in such cases between husband and wife. This way of putting the question assumes that the interests of these parties are opposed to each other; but in practice this may well not be true in the present context. In a realistic sense, husband and wife in the situations under discussion may well make common cause against the bank since, if this wife's case of undue influence succeeds against the husband, then the bank may not be able to evict the couple from their home. There is little doubt that this aspect of such cases has influenced the development of the branch of the law.

It has long been settled and is accepted in the *Etridge* case[36] that the relationship of husband and wife does not give rise to the class 2A or "irrebuttable" presumption described under heading (i) above.[37] The question then arises whether that relationship can nevertheless give rise to the "rebuttable evidential presumption"[38] that can arise in cases of the kind described under heading (ii) above, *i.e.* in cases formerly regarded as falling within the class 2B presumption. It is clear from the *Etridge* case that no such presumption (that the transaction was procured by undue influence) arises *merely* because the wife has reposed trust and confidence in her husband: this is, as we have seen, only *one* of the basic facts of the presumption; and so the statement that B (the wife) "will succeed in setting aside the transaction merely by proof that [she] reposed trust and confidence in the wrongdoer"[39] (*i.e.* A, the husband) would no longer be accepted.

To the extent that the class 2B presumption was previously thought to arise on proof of this one basic fact alone, it must be taken to have been rejected in all the speeches in the *Etridge* case,[40] which has made it clear that any such presumption arises only if it is also shown that the transaction is one which "calls for explanation"[41]; indeed (as noted above) this is true also in class 2A cases.[42] But the rejection in some of the speeches of the class 2B category may go further since the transactions under consideration in the *Etridge* case, being guarantees of substantial business debts, did call for explanation. The second basic fact of the rebuttable evidential presumption was therefore also satisfied; but that presumption nevertheless did not arise in a number of the cases there under appeal. The reason why it did not arise in those cases lies, it is submitted, in certain features of the relationship of husband and wife which are of special significance in the present context. These features are referred to by Lord Scott when he says that he is unable to accept "The proposition that, if a wife, who generally reposes trust and confidence in her husband, agrees to become surety to support his debts or business enterprises a presumption of undue influence arises"[43]; on the contrary, in such a "surety wife" case, "undue influence, though a possible explanation for the wife's agreement to become surety, is a relatively unlikely one".[44] Lord Nicholls seems to have

---

[35] See below, p.424. One of the cases under appeal concerned a different kind of dispute, *i.e.* one between the wife and her solicitor.

[36] *Etridge* case, at [19].

[37] See above, p.412 at n.84.

[38] *Etridge* case at [16].

[39] See *ibid.* at [105] citing *Barclays Bank plc v O'Brien* [1994] 1 A.C. 180 at 189–190.

[40] *Etridge* case, above n.16, at [14], [104], [158]. *Quaere* whether it may have been this point that Lord Hobhouse had in mind at [104].

[41] *ibid.*, at [14].

[42] See above, at n.33.

[43] *Etridge* case, above, n.16, at [159]; Lord Hobhouse's statement *ibid.* at [106] that "there is no legal relationship of trust and confidence" may be a reference to the fact that the relations between spouses does not give rise to the "irrebuttable" (or class 2A) presumption.

[44] *ibid.*, at [162].

much the same point in mind when he says that "there is nothing unusual or strange in a wife, from motives of affection or for other reasons, conferring substantial financial benefits on her husband"[45]; and that same is true "*in the ordinary course*"[46] where she guarantees and provides security for, her husband's business debts: she may well do this because she has, in practice, a common interest with her husband in the success of his business ventures.[47] In such cases, it is therefore arguable that, even though there is both a relationship of trust and confidence and a transaction calling for explanation, no presumption arises that the transaction has been procured by undue influence. The reason for this view is that the nature of the relationship between the husband and the wife provides an alternative and more plausible explanation for the transaction, namely that the wife entered into it from motives of common interest or affection or both. The statements of Lord Hobhouse and Lord Scott,[48] rejecting, or doubting the utility of, the class 2B presumption are therefore, with respect, entirely appropriate (and are indeed reflected in the speech of Lord Nicholls)[49] in the context in which they occur: that is, where the relationship of the relevant parties is that of spouses in an on-going marriage and the wife alleges that a guarantee by her of her husband's business debts has been procured by undue influence exercised by him. *In such cases*, it would normally be inappropriate to apply the class 2B presumption; and the same is probably true of the closely analogous situation of parties living together in a quasi-marital relationship without being married.[50] But it is submitted that the same reasoning does not apply to other situations in which there is a relationship of trust and confidence, a transaction calling for explanation, and *no* explanation more plausible than that it was procured by undue influence: *e.g.*, in cases such as *Tate v Williamson*.[51] In such cases, there is still scope for the presumption that the transaction was procured by undue influence, even though the relationship of the parties is not one in which (in Lord Nicholls' words) "the law presumes, irrebuttably, that one party had influence over the other".[52] To this extent, the structure of Lord Nicholls' speech recognises the continued existence in the law of undue influence of two distinct categories of cases and of two different kinds of presumptions which resemble the former classes 2A and 2B. But the division into two classes by Lord Nichols is not identical with the former classification since under that classification the presumed fact in both classes was thought to be the *same*, *i.e.* "the undue influence has been *exercised*".[53] This is, indeed, also the effect of Lord Nicholls' "rebuttable evidential presumption"[54]; but, as already noted,[55] the effect of his irrebuttable presumption is merely that, by virtue of one of the specified relationships (such as that between parent and child) influence (which may be undue) is taken to *exist*[56] and this fact is not of itself a ground for relief. The most probable conclusion to be drawn from speeches which are not easy to reconcile is that the distinction between the two classes of presumptions survives, but with two significant modifications: first, that the class 2A presumption is no longer that undue influence is taken to have been *exercised*;

---

[45] *ibid.*, at [19].
[46] *ibid.*, at [30].
[47] *cf. National Westminster Bank plc v Legatt*, *The Times*, November 16, 2000.
[48] See above, p.415 at nn.29 and 30.
[49] *Etridge* case above, n.16 at [30].
[50] *cf. ibid.*, at [47].
[51] (1866) L.R. 2 Ch.App. 55 above p.414 and other cases there cited.
[52] *Etridge* case above, n.16, at [18].
[53] *Barclays Bank plc v O'Brien* [1994] A.C. 180 at 189.
[54] *Etridge* case at [14], [17].
[55] See above, pp.412, 413.
[56] *Etridge* case, at [18].

and, secondly, that the class 2B presumption will not normally (*i.e.* "in the ordinary course")[57] apply between spouses or parties in closely analogous relationships.

In discussing the husband and wife cases, Lord Nicholls distinguished between "*the ordinary course*" of cases[58] (in which there was no scope for the rebuttable evidential presumption) and cases falling outside this "ordinary course" in which the wife's giving of the guarantee "does call for explanation"[59]: *e.g.* where one party takes "advantage of the other's vulnerability".[60] In this "minority of cases"[61] the law does provide protection for the latter party (usually the wife). This was, for example, said to be the case where a wife was "in a position of subservience and obedience to the wishes of her husband"[62] in relation to financial and other matters by virtue of the culture of the religious community to which both belonged. It seems that in such cases the wife's protection is based on actual rather than on presumed undue influence.[63] In one of the cases under appeal in the *Etridge* case,[64] the wife was in a position of such subservience and could therefore have set the transaction aside against her husband; but her claim for relief against the bank whose loan to him she had guaranteed failed on grounds to be discussed later in this Chapter.[65]

(iv) *Actual pressure and presumed undue influence.* A case for relief may be based in the alternative on (a) actual pressure[66] or (b) presumed undue influence. If the court finds as a fact that B was *not* the victim of actual undue influence, then B cannot succeed on the ground of presumed undue influence; for the former finding rebuts the presumed fact.[67] The position may be compared with the operation of the presumption of death[68]: if the person alleged to be dead is in fact proved to be alive, proof of the basic facts of the presumption (roughly, seven years' absence, unheard of) becomes irrelevant. Conversely, if actual undue influence is established, the presumption becomes irrelevant: in this sense "a finding of actual undue influence and a finding that there is a presumption are not alternatives to each other".[69] *Allegations* of actual and of presumed undue influence are alternative ways of presenting B's case; the same is not true (as the dictum just quoted states) of *findings* and presumptions since the effect of a presumption is to lead to a finding of such influence.

(d) BURDEN OF PROOF. Where the necessary relationship is alleged to exist, the burden of proving that it does exist is on the party seeking to set the transaction aside.[70] Once this burden has been discharged, it is up to the party benefiting from the transaction to rebut the presumption of undue influence[71] in one of the ways to be discussed below.

---

[57] *ibid.*, at [30].

[58] *ibid.*

[59] *ibid.*, at [31].

[60] *ibid.*, at [36]; *cf.* [163].

[61] *ibid.*, at [37].

[62] *ibid.*, at [283].

[63] *ibid.*, at [130] ("actual undue influence"); *cf. ibid.* at [36] ("such abuse does occur"); but contrast *ibid.* at [291] ("the presumption arose").

[64] *Barclays Bank plc v Coleman.*

[65] See below, p.427.

[66] See above, p.408.

[67] *Etridge* case above, n.16, at [281].

[68] Phipson on Evidence (15th ed.), §4.23.

[69] *Etridge* case, above, n.16 at [291].

[70] *Lloyds Bank Ltd v Bundy* [1975] Q.B. 326 at 342; *cf. Re Craig* [1971] Ch. 95; *Coldunell Ltd v Gallon* [1986] Q.B. 1184; *Allied Irish Bank v Byrne* [1995] 1 F.C.R. 430.

[71] *Allcard v Skinner* (1887) 36 Ch.D. 145; *Re Craig*, above n.70.

(e) SCOPE OF THE PRESUMPTION. The presumption does not apply, even though one of the special relationships exists, if it cannot possibly have influenced the particular transaction. Thus it has been suggested that the presumption would not apply if a solicitor bought a horse from a client who had retained him to conduct an action for slander.[72]

(f) REMEDY. The normal remedy in cases of undue influence is to set the impugned transaction aside; but subsequent events, such as dealings with the subject-matter, may make this process impossible. The court then has (as in cases of misrepresentation[73]) a wide discretion to do what is practically just. It can, for example, make an award in the nature of damages giving the victim of the undue influence the difference between the amount for which he parted with the subject-matter and its fair value at the time of the transaction.[74]

(2) Rebutting the presumption

The presumption of undue influence is rebutted if the party benefiting from the transaction shows that it was "the free exercise of independent will".[75] The most usual way of doing this is to show that the other party had independent advice before entering into the transaction.[76] But the mere fact that independent advice was given will not of itself save the transaction. The advice must be competent and based on knowledge of all the relevant facts.[77] It has been suggested that the independent adviser must also approve the transaction, and that his advice must be followed.[78] This may be necessary where the influence is particularly strong, or where a very large gift is made; but it is not necessary in every case.[79] There is indeed no invariable rule that independent advice is necessary to save the transaction[80]; but the beneficiary would lack elementary prudence if he did not ensure that such advice was given.

Particularly stringent rules apply where a solicitor buys from or sells to his client.[81] The solicitor must show that the client was fully informed of all the relevant facts; (generally) that the client was separately advised; and that the transaction was a fair one: thus a sale to the solicitor can be set aside simply on the ground of undervalue.[82] A solicitor must make full disclosure even where the presumption of undue influence has been rebutted.[83]

---

[72] *Allison v Clayhills* (1907) 97 L.T. 709 at 711.

[73] See above, p.380.

[74] *Mahoney v Purnell* [1996] 3 All E.R. 61.

[75] *Inche Noriah v Shaik Allie bin Omar* [1929] A.C. 127 at 136; *Mahoney v Purnell* [1996] 3 All E.R. 61 at 85; *Naidoo v Naidu*, The Times, November 1, 2000; *Royal Bank of Scotland v Etridge (No.2)* [2001] UKHL 44; [2002] 2 A.C. 773; [2001] 4 All E.R. 44, at [7] ("expression of . . . free will"); *cf. ibid.*, at [162] ("will . . . not . . . overborne"); *Hammond v Osborn* [2002] EWCA Civ 865, [2002] W.T.L.R. 1125.

[76] *Allcard v Skinner* (1887) 36 Ch.D. 145 at 190; *Bullock v Lloyds Bank* [1955] Ch. 317; *Horry v Tate & Lyle Refineries Ltd* [1982] 2 Lloyd's Rep. 417 at 421; *Claughton v Price* [1997] E.G.C.S. 51.

[77] *Inche Noriah v Shaik Allie bin Omar* [1929] A.C. 127.

[78] *Powell v Powell* [1900] 1 Ch. 243 at 246; *Wright v Carter* [1903] 1 Ch. 27; *Credit Lyonnais Bank Nederland v Burch* [1997] 1 All E.R. 144 at 155–156.

[79] *Re Coomber* [1911] 1 Ch. 723 at 730; *Banco Exterior Industrial SA v Thomas* [1997] 1 All E.R. 46.

[80] *Inche Noriah v Shaik Allie bin Omar* [1929] A.C. 127 at 135; *Re Brocklehurst* [1978] Ch. 14.

[81] *cf.* also the provisions of the Solicitors Act 1974, ss.56 at 57, for regulating the remuneration of solicitors.

[82] *Wright v Carter* [1903] 1 Ch. 27; *Longstaff v Birtles* [2001] EWCA Civ 1129; [2002] 1 W.L.R. 470 (a case of breach of fiduciary duty rather than of undue influence: see at [40]); the same rule applies where a trustee buys from his *cestui que trust*: *Thomson v Eastwood* (1877) 2 App.Cas. 215. Manifest disadvantage was never considered to be a necessary condition for relief in cases of this kind. *cf.* above, p.378 at n.49; *Bank of Credit & Commerce International SA v Aboody* [1990] 1 Q.B. 923 at 962.

[83] *Moody v Cox & Hatt* [1917] 2 Ch. 71.

The above discussion assumes that the dispute is between the person who has (or is presumed to have) exercised the undue influence and the victim of that influence. Further problems which arise where the dispute is between the victim and a third party will be discussed later in this Chapter.[84]

3. Unconscionable Bargains

Equity can give relief against unconscionable bargains[85] in certain cases in which one party is in a position to exploit a particular weakness of the other. The burden of justifying such a transaction is on the former party.[86]

(1) Catching bargains[87]

Equity can set aside or modify an agreement with an "expectant heir" made in anticipation of his expectations. The transaction need not amount to a sale of or charge on the expectation.[88] Thus equity can relieve against a *post-obit* bond, by which a debtor promises his creditor a certain sum if the debtor survives a named person and becomes entitled to a share in his estate.[89] Nor is the equitable jurisdiction confined to "heirs": relief can be given to a young man whose sole expectation of wealth is from his father, who is still alive.[90]

A person who sold a reversionary interest could at one time obtain relief by proving only that the sale was at an undervalue. The law was changed by the Sales of Reversions Act 1867, now re-enacted in s.174 of the Law of Property Act 1925. This provides that no sale of a "reversionary interest" (which includes a mere expectancy) shall be opened or set aside merely on the ground of undervalue; but the section expressly preserves the jurisdiction of the court to set aside or modify unconscionable bargains. Undervalue remains "a material element in cases in which it is not the sole equitable ground for relief",[91] and may form the sole ground for relief if it is "so gross as to amount of itself to evidence of fraud".[92] Fraud is not here used in its common law sense[93] but means "an unconscientious use of the power arising out of" the relative positions of the parties.[94]

(2) Dealing with poor and ignorant persons

In *Evans v Llewellin*[95] a poor man became entitled to a share of an estate worth £1,700. He sold it for 200 guineas cash, and was later able to set the transaction aside as it was "improvidently obtained". A modern illustration of the principle may be provided by a case in which an employee of modest financial means guaranteed her employer's overdraft for up to £270,000. The transaction was described as "harsh and unconscionable"[96] and set aside; but the actual ground for the decision was that the relationship

---

[84] See below, pp.423–427.
[85] Not against *gifts*, though these can be set aside for undue influence: *Langton v Langton* [1995] FLR 890.
[86] *Aylesford v Morris* (1873) L.R. 8 Ch.App. 484.
[87] Dawson, 45 Mich.L.Rev. 267–279.
[88] *Aylesford v Morris* (1873) L.R. 8 Ch.App. 484.
[89] See *Chesterfield v Janssen* (1750) 2 Ves.Sen. 125.
[90] *Nevill v Snelling* (1880) 15 Ch.D. 679.
[91] *O'Rorke v Bolingbroke* (1877) 2 App.Cas. 814 at 833.
[92] *Fry v Lane* (1888) 40 Ch.D. 312, 321.
[93] See above, p.343.
[94] *Aylesford v Morris* (1873) L.R. 8 Ch.App. 484, 491.
[95] (1787) 1 Cox C.C. 333; mentioned with approval in *Fry v Lane*, above; *Longmate v Ledger* (1860) 2 Giff. 157; *Clark v Malpas* (1862) 4 D.F. & J. 401; *Baker v Monk* (1864) 4 D.J. & S. 338; *Lloyds Bank Ltd v Bundy* [1975] Q.B. 326 at 337; *Watkin v Watson-Smith, The Times*, July 3, 1986.
[96] *Credit Lyonnais Bank Nederland NV v Burch* [1997] 1 All E.R. 144 at 151.

between employer and employee was such as to give rise to a presumption of undue influence. It seems that equity may, even in the absence of such influence, give such relief when unfair advantage is taken of a person who is poor, ignorant or weak-minded, or is for some other reason in need of special protection.[97] Specific performance may be refused on similar grounds.[98] The equitable rule is based on unconscientious conduct by the stronger party: relief will not be granted merely because the transaction is unfair[99] or improvident.[1] *A fortiori*, mere inadequacy of consideration is not a ground for relief where the parties have bargained on equal terms.[2]

(3) Inequality of bargaining power[3]

A number of judicial statements give some support to the view that one party to a contract may be entitled to relief if the other has taken unfair advantage of the fact that there is a marked inequality of bargaining power between them.

One group of such statements is concerned with the special problem of the validity of covenants in restraint of trade.[4] This depends on whether the covenant is "reasonable", and the adequacy of consideration is taken into account in determining the issue of reasonableness.[5] The fairness of the bargain (which to some extent depends on the relative bargaining positions of the parties) is therefore relevant to the validity of the restraint; but the fact that it is taken into account for this purpose scarcely supports a general principle of relief against harsh bargains on the ground of inequality of bargaining power.

Such a principle was, however, stated (as an alternative ground of decision) by Lord Denning M.R. in *Lloyds Bank Ltd v Bundy*.[6] He referred to a number of rules (discussed earlier[7] in this Chapter) under which relief was given against harsh or unfair contracts; and he derived from them the generalisation that " . . . English law gives relief to one who, without independent advice, enters into a contract upon terms which are very unfair or transfers property for a consideration which is grossly inadequate, when his bargaining power is grievously impaired by reason of his own needs or desires, or by his own ignorance or infirmity, coupled with undue influence or pressures brought to bear on him by or for the benefit of the other".[8] The other members of the Court of Appeal based their decision solely on the equitable doctrine of undue influence.[9] Thus, while

---

[97] *e.g. Creswell v Potter* (1968) [1978] 1 W.L.R 255n. (wife in course of divorce proceedings transferring her share in the matrimonial home to husband without getting independent advice and for inadequate consideration); *cf. Backhouse v Backhouse* [1978] 1 W.L.R. 243. Mere unfamiliarity with the English language is not a ground for relief: *Barclays Bank plc v Schwartz, The Times*, August 2, 1995.

[98] *e.g. Falcke v Gray* (1859) 4 Drew. 651: see below, p.1028.

[99] *Alec Lobb (Garages) Ltd v Total Oil (Great Britain) Ltd* [1985] 1 W.L.R. 173; *Hart v O'Connor* [1985] A.C. 1000; *Boustany v Pigott* (1995) 69 P.& C.R. 298. *Irvani v Irvani* [2000] 1 Lloyd's Rep. 412 at 425.

[1] *Kalsep v X-Flow BV, The Times*, May 3, 2001.

[2] See *Collier v Brown* (1788) 1 Cox C.C. 428; *Coles v Trecothick* (1804) 9 Ves. 234 at 246; *Western v Russell* (1814) 3 v & B. 187.

[3] Cartwright, *Unequal Bargaining*; Thal, 8 O.J.L.S. 17.

[4] *A. Schroeder Music Publishing Co v Macaulay* [1974] 1 W.L.R. 1308 at 1315; *cf. Clifford Davis Management v WEA Records* [1975] 1 W.L.R. 61; *Shell UK Ltd v Lostock Garages Ltd* [1976] 1 W.L.R. 1187 at 1197; Wooldridge, [1977] J.B.L. 312; *Panayiotou v Sony Music Entertainment (UK) Ltd, The Times*, June 30, 1994.

[5] See below, p.462.

[6] [1975] Q.B. 326; above, p.419.

[7] See above, pp.408–421.

[8] [1975] Q.B. 326 at 339. *cf.* the rules against "collateral advantages" in mortgages: Megarry and Wade, *Law of Real Property* (5th ed.), pp.968–971. And see Beatson, 1 O.J.L.S. 426.

[9] See above, p.419; *cf. Horry v Tate & Lyle Refineries Ltd* [1982] 2 Lloyd's Rep. 417 at 422.

expressing "some sympathy"[10] for Lord Denning's principle, they did not find it necessary to express a concluded opinion on it. It follows that the principle does not form the ground for the decision.[11]

In a number of later cases, Lord Denning has nevertheless repeated his view that the law recognised a principle of "inequality of bargaining power".[12] The scope of the alleged principle seems to be very wide: it can apparently apply to such disparate transactions or terms as the contract in *Lloyds Bank Ltd v Bundy,*[13] the renegotiation of a contract,[14] the settlement of a tort claim,[15] and the inclusion of an exemption clause in a cleaning contract made in standard form.[16] No clear limit to the principle is stated except that a bargain will not be upset if it is "the result of the ordinary interplay of forces".[17] Reference by Lord Denning to "the American policy of inadequate bargaining power"[18] is from his point of view scarcely reassuring; for the lengths to which American courts have gone in implementing this policy would hardly be acceptable in England without express legislative authority. It is, for example, hard to imagine an English court holding that a consumer could keep goods after paying only part of the price simply because the seller's profit on the full contract price would be excessive.[19] The regulation of these and similar matters is in England, by general consent, left to legislation.[20]

For these reasons, Lord Denning's principle has little judicial[21] support in England. On the contrary, in *Pao On v Lau Yiu Long*[22] the Privy Council, having held that the contract was not voidable for duress,[23] also rejected the argument that it was invalid as having been procured by "an unfair use of a dominant bargaining position".[24] To treat this as a ground of invalidity distinct from duress would, in Lord Scarman's words, "be unhelpful because it would render the law uncertain".[25] In *National Westminster Bank plc v Morgan* Lord Scarman again expressed similar views when questioning "whether there is any need in the modern law to erect a general principle of relief against inequality of bargaining power".[26] Legislation having dealt with a number of specific instances in which superior bargaining power might be abused,[27] he doubted "whether the courts should assume the burden of formulating further restrictions"[28]; and the need for them

---

[10] [1975] Q.B. 326 at 347 (Sir Eric Sachs, with whom Cairns L.J. agreed); *cf. Backhouse v Backhouse* [1978] 1 W.L.R. 243 at 251; *Credit Lyonnais Bank Nederland NV v Burch* [1997] 1 All E.R. 144.

[11] *National Westminster Bank Ltd v Morgan* [1985] A.C. 686 at 708–709.

[12] *Arrale v Costain Civil Engineering Ltd* [1976] 1 Lloyd's Rep. 98 at 102; *Levison v Patent Steam Carpet Cleaning Co Ltd* [1978] Q.B. 69 at 78.

[13] [1975] Q.B. 326; above, p.419 at n.10.

[14] *D & C Builders v Rees* [1966] 2 Q.B. 617.

[15] *Arrale v Costain Civil Engineering Ltd* [1976] 1 Lloyd's Rep. 98.

[16] *Levison v Patent Steam Carpet Cleaning Co Ltd* [1978] Q.B. 69.

[17] *Lloyds Bank Ltd v Bundy* [1975] Q.B. 326 at 336.

[18] *ibid.* at 333 (during argument).

[19] *Jones v Star Credit Corp* 298 N.Y.S. 2d 264 (1969).

[20] See *Lloyds Bank Ltd v Bundy* [1975] Q.B. at p.336; *cf.* below, at n.27 and pp.440–441.

[21] Inequality of bargaining power may also be relevant to the exercise of discretions conferred *by legislation* to control contract terms: see, for example Unfair Contract Terms Act 1977, Sch.2 para.(*a*) (above, p.259); Consumer Credit Act 1974, s.138(3)(b) and (4)(b) (below p.428); Matrimonial Causes Act 1973, s.23 (now amended by Family Law Reform Act 1996 Sch.2, para.4), as interpreted in *Edgar v Edgar* [1980] 1 W.L.R. 1410; Unfair Terms in Consumer Contracts Regulations 1999 (above, p.273 at n.33a). But such discretions do not seem to provide any basis for a general *common law* principle: see below at n.35.

[22] [1980] A.C. 614.

[23] See above, pp.406–407.

[24] [1980] A.C. 614 at 634.

[25] *ibid.*

[26] [1985] A.C. 686 at 708.

[27] See, n.21, above.

[28] [1985] A.C. 686 at 708; *cf. Lloyds Bank Ltd v Bundy* [1975] Q.B. 326 at 336.

to do so has also been reduced by the widening of the scope of duress.[29] Decisions of the lower courts have similarly rejected the argument that inequality of bargaining power is, of itself, a ground of invalidity[30]; and this is true even in the restraint of trade cases, in which the courts have traditionally taken the "fairness" of the bargain into account.[31]

4. Bars to Relief

The right to rescind[32] for undue influence is barred on grounds similar to those which limit the right to rescind for misrepresentation.

(a) IMPOSSIBILITY OF RESTITUTION. The party seeking rescission must restore benefits that he has obtained under the contract, and he may be allowed to rescind in spite of the fact that he cannot make *precise* restitution, so long as equity can achieve a result that is "practically just".[33] The point is illustrated by *O'Sullivan v Management Agency & Music Ltd*[34] where the claimant sought to set aside for undue influence a number of management, sole agency, recording and publishing agreements and transfers of copyrights. On the one hand the defendants argued that rescission should not be allowed as they could no longer be restored to their pre-contract position in view of the work which they had done to promote the claimant's success; on the other hand the claimant argued that rescission for undue influence was (unlike rescission for misrepresentation) not subject to any requirement of restitution at all. The court rejected both arguments, holding that, even though precise restitution was not possible, rescission could be ordered so long as the court could do substantial justice. This could be done by upholding the claim for rescission while allowing the defendants a reasonable remuneration for their work on behalf of the claimant.[35]

(b) AFFIRMATION. A claim to relief on the ground of undue influence is barred by affirmation[36] of the transaction after the influence (or the relationship giving rise to a presumption of influence) has ceased. It has been held that affirmation is effective though made without independent advice and in ignorance of the right to have the transaction set aside.[37] It is submitted that the law on this point should (as in cases of misrepresentation and breach) require the injured party to know, or to have obvious means of knowing, of the right to rescind.[38]

Where a wife had, under her husband's undue influence, joined him in charging the matrimonial home to a bank and later affirmed the transaction as against the husband, it was held that she had also lost the secondary right of avoidance against the bank[39]

---

[29] See above, p.405.

[30] *Burmah Oil Co v Bank of England, The Times*, July 4, 1981; *Horry v Tate & Lyle Refineries Ltd* [1982] 2 Lloyd's Rep. 417 at 422; *Alec Lobb (Garages) Ltd v Total Oil (Great Britain) Ltd* [1985] 1 W.L.R. 173; *CNT Cash & Carry Ltd v Gallagher Ltd* [1994] 4 All E.R. 714 at 717.

[31] The *Alec Lobb* case, above, concerned restraint of trade.

[32] Where rescission is no longer possible, an alternative remedy by way of equitable compensation may be available, as in *Longstaff v Birtles* [2001] EWCA Civ 1219; [2002] 1 W.L.R. 470 at [36] (a case of breach of fiduciary duty).

[33] *Erlanger v New Sombrero Phosphate Co* (1878) 3 App.Cas. 1218 at 1279; above, p.379; *Cheese v Thomas* [1994] 1 W.L.R. 129; *cf. Dunbar Bank plc v Nadeem* [1998] 3 All E.R. 876 (where the claim based on undue influence failed).

[34] [1985] Q.B. 428; above, p.419.

[35] *cf.* above, pp.397, 380 for similar relief in cases of misrepresentation.

[36] *cf.* (in cases of duress) *The Atlantic Baron* [1979] Q.B. 705.

[37] *Mitchell v Homfray* (1882) 8 Q.B.D. 587.

[38] See above, p.382; below, pp.814–815.

[39] *First National Bank plc v Walker* [2001] 1 F.L.R. 505.

which would, but for the affirmation, have been available to her under the rules stated later in this Chapter.[40]

(c) DELAY. The victim of undue influence must "seek relief within a reasonable time after the removal of the influence under which the gift was made".[41] If with knowledge or obvious means of knowledge of his rights he fails to seek relief he is assumed to have affirmed the transaction.

(d) THIRD PARTY RIGHTS. Two types of cases call for discussion. In the first, A acquires property from B under a transaction procured, or presumed to have been procured, by undue influence; and A then transfers that property to C. In the second, A by undue influence, or in circumstances in which undue influence may be presumed, induces B to enter into a contract with C. The question in each case is to what extent C is adversely affected by the undue influence exerted, or presumed to have been exerted, by A on B.

(i) *Property acquired by undue influence transferred to third party.* In this type of case, B can set the transaction aside if C did not give value for the transfer from A or if he took it "with notice of the equity . . . or with notice of the circumstances from which the court infers the equity".[42] In this context, "notice" refers not only to actual knowledge of those circumstances but also to cases in which it is alleged that C ought to have known of them, or (in other words) where he had constructive notice of them. The "circumstances," notice of which will prejudicially affect C are those that would, but for the transfer to him, have entitled B to relief against A on the ground of undue influence.[43] But B will not be entitled to set the transaction aside against C on this ground if C has in good faith (*i.e.*, without notice, actual or constructive) and for value acquired an interest for value in the subject-matter. For example, in *O'Sullivan v Management Agency & Music Ltd*[44] relief was not available against a company which had acquired some of the claimant's copyrights and tapes in good faith and for value.

(ii) *Undue influence inducing contract with third party.* Our concern here is with the situation in which A is alleged to have induced B to deal directly with C. The most common (though not the only)[45] illustration of this situation is provided by a large group of recent cases in which a loan was made by C (a bank or building society) to A for the purposes of A's business[46] and B (usually A's wife) guaranteed the loan and provided security for it, *e.g.* by a charge on the matrimonial home owned by B or by A and B jointly. On A's default, the question would arise whether C was adversely affected by undue influence exerted or presumed to have been exerted by A or B (or by some other vitiating factor, such as misrepresentation, that would have operated between A and B, had the impugned transaction been between them). Before the *Etridge* case, the answer to this question had been said to depend on whether C had "constructive notice"[47] of the circumstances that would (or would be presumed to have) vitiated the transaction between A and B. It followed that B could set the transaction with C aside if C had such

---

[40] See below, under heading (d).

[41] *Allcard v Skinner* (1887) 36 Ch.D. 145 at 187.

[42] *Bainbrigge v Browne* (1881) 18 Ch.D. 188 at 197.

[43] See above, pp.409–419.

[44] [1985] Q.B. 428 at 459–460; above, at n.34.

[45] See *Naidoo v Naidu, The Times,* November 1, 2000.

[46] The business may for this purpose be A's even though it is run through a company controlled by A and in spite of the fact that B also holds shares in, or is a director of, the company: see, for example, *Bank of Cyprus v Markou* [1999] 2 All E.R. 707; *Royal Bank of Scotland v Etridge (No.2)* [2001] UKHL 44, [2002] 2 A.C. 773 at [49].

[47] *Barclays Bank plc v O'Brien* [1994] 1 A.C. 180 at 186.

notice[48]; but that C could enforce the transaction against B if C had no such notice[49] and had taken steps (of the kind to be described later in this Chapter) to protect B.[50] In the *Etridge* case,[51] however, the House of Lords discouraged this use, in the present context, of the concept of "constructive notice" (which normally operates in the context of transfers of *property* by persons with a defective title).[52] Instead, the test is whether C, the bank, is "put on inquiry."[53] Even this is "strictly a misnomer"[54] since C is not bound to investigate the state of the relationship between A and B; but the phrase is a convenient one to indicate that C must take reasonable steps to reduce the risk of B's entering into the transaction as a result of undue influence (or other similar vitiating factor) exerted by A on B.[55] The circumstances in which such steps must be taken go far beyond those in which the vitiating factor actually exists or is presumed to exist. Thus "a bank is put on inquiry whenever a wife offers to stand surety for her husband's debts"[56] even though (as the discussion in an earlier part of this Chapter shows) in many such cases the wife will not be able to show that the guarantee was actually procured by undue influence or to rely on the presumption that it was so procured.[57] The law as to when C is "put on inquiry" or (in other words) required to take steps to protect B against the risk of B's consent having been improperly obtained) was extensively reviewed in the *Etridge* case, from which it appears that C's duty in this respect depends primarily on two factors.

The first is the nature of the impugned transaction. Thus C's duty will arise where B guarantees business debts incurred by A or by a company through which A runs his business.[58] But a bank is not "put on inquiry" where it makes a joint loan to a husband and wife (even if the loan is secured on their matrimonial home) "unless the bank is aware that the loan is being made for the husband's purposes, as distinct from their joint purposes."[59] The reason for the distinction is that a wife's guarantee of her husband's business debts is, on its face, disadvantageous to her (in the sense of her not deriving any direct benefit from it) and so "calls for explanation",[60] while this is not true of a joint loan to her and her husband.

The second is the relationship between A and B. In most of the reported cases, B was A's wife; but C's duty applies equally in the converse case where "the husband stands

---

[48] See above, n.47; an alternative ground for allowing B to set the transaction aside was that C had constituted A as his agent for the purpose of concluding the transaction with B, so that A's knowledge of the relevant circumstances was attributed to C: *e.g. Chaplin and Co Ltd v Brammall* [1908] 1 K.B. 223; *Avon Finance Co v Bridger* [1985] 2 All E.R. 281. But the reasoning has been described as "artificial" (*Barclays Bank plc v O'Brien* [1994] 1 A.C. 180 at 195) and is now unlikely to be followed unless A had acted as C's agent "in a real sense": *CIBC Mortgages plc v Pitt* [1994] 1 A.C. 200 at 211.

[49] *e.g. Bainbridge v Browne* (1881) 18 Ch.D. 188; this was also the outcome in *Barclays Bank plc v O'Brien*, above n.48, where the vitiating factor was misrepresentation by A.

[50] See below, p.426.

[51] *Royal Bank of Scotland v Etridge (No.2)* [2001] UKHL 44; [2002] 2 A.C. 773.

[52] *ibid.*, at [39].

[53] *ibid.*, at [44].

[54] *ibid.*

[55] *ibid.*, at [41].

[56] *ibid.*, at [44], [46]. The burden of proof is on B to show that C knew her to be A's wife living with him (or that there was an analogous relationship between them) and that the transaction was one calling for an explanation; it is then up to C to show that it took reasonable steps to ensure that B's consent was properly obtained: *Barclays Bank plc v Boulter* [1999] 1 W.L.R. 1919.

[57] See above, p.416.

[58] *Etridge* case, above n.51 at [48].

[59] *ibid.*, citing *CIBC Mortgages v Pitt* [1944] 1 A.C. 200; contrast *Goode Durrant Administration v Biddulph* [1995] F.C.R. 196 (loan made jointly to husband, wife and a company owned largely by husband); *Allied Irish Bank v Byrne* [1995] 2 F.L.R. 325 (joint loan to husband and wife for purposes of husband's business).

[60] *Etridge* case, above n.51, at [47]; above, p.378 at n.62.

surety for his wife's debts"[61] and to "the case of unmarried couples, whether heterosexual or homosexual".[62] It can apply even where the relationship is neither a marital nor a quasi-marital one but is one in which trust and confidence is in fact reposed by B in A.[63] According to a "wider principle" approved by Lord Nicholls in the *Etridge* case,[64] the bank's duty extends to all cases in which the relationship between the surety (B) and the principal debtor is a non-commercial one.[65] The advantage of this formulation of the principle is that it promotes certainty in the sense that the creditor's duty to take steps to protect the surety against the risks described above will arise in all such suretyship cases and will not depend on any investigation by the bank of the actual state of the relationship between A and B. The principle would not, on the other hand, apply where the relationship between A and B was a commercial one: *e.g.* where they were associated companies or where A paid B a fee for acting as surety.[66]

The steps that C (the bank) is required to take in performance of its duty were also reviewed in the *Etridge* case. As the duty is no more than one to take reasonable care to protect B (the surety) against the risk of undue influence, C is not required itself to investigate the question whether B was in fact subjected to such influence.[67] Nor is it necessary[68] for C to arrange for one of its representatives to hold a personal meeting with B.[69] It will (in future cases)[70] suffice for C to communicate directly[71] with B to the effect that C will require a solicitor acting for B[72] (who may also act for A or C (or both of them) in the transaction[73] to confirm to C in writing that the solicitor has explained to B the nature and effects of the documents to be signed by B, containing the transaction[74]; this explanation must be given in a face to face meeting between the solicitor and B, conducted in the absence of A.[75] The solicitor must also be supplied by C with the financial information that he needs for the purpose of this explanation.[76] If these steps are taken, C will normally be entitled to rely on the solicitor's confirmation that he has "advised the wife [B] appropriately".[77] The word "advised" here refers to the solicitor's duty to *explain* the transaction: it is no part of his duty "to veto the transaction"[78] merely because he thinks it is not in B's best interests.[79] If, indeed, it is "*glaringly*

---

[61] *Etridge* case, above n.51 at [47].

[62] *ibid.*, *Barclays Bank plc v O'Brien* [1994] A.C. 180 at 198; *Massey v Midland Bank plc* [1995] 1 All E.R. 929 at 933.

[63] *e.g. Avon Finance Co v Bridger* [1985] 2 All E.R. 281, approved in *Barclays Bank plc v O'Brien*, above, n.62; *Credit Lyonnais Bank Nederland NV v Burch* [1997] 1 All E.R. 144. *cf. Wright v Cherrytree Finance Ltd* [2001] EWCA Civ 449; [2001] 2 All E.R. (Comm) 877 (widow and her son-in-law); part of the reasoning of this case would no longer be acceptable after the *Etridge* case.

[64] *Etridge* case, above n.51, at [82], citing Birks in Rose (ed.), *Restitution and Banking Law*, p.185.

[65] *Etridge* case, above n.51, at [87].

[66] *ibid.*, at [88].

[67] *ibid.*, at [53].

[68] Though such a step may be sufficient if the required explanation and recommendation to seek independent legal advice are given: *ibid.*, at [50].

[69] *ibid.*, at [55].

[70] See the reference in *ibid.* [50] to "the future".

[71] *ibid.*, at [79].

[72] See *National Westminster Bank plc v Amin* [2002] UKHL 9; [2002] 1 F.L.R. 735, where it was not clear that this requirement had been satisfied.

[73] *Etridge* case, above n.51, at [74].

[74] *ibid.*, at [79].

[75] *ibid.*, at [76].

[76] *ibid.*, at [79].

[77] *ibid.*, at [56]; *Barclays Bank plc v Goff* [2001] 2 All E.R. (Comm) 847, [2001] EWCA Civ 634.

[78] *Etridge* case, above, n.51, at [61].

[79] *ibid.*

obvious that the wife (B) is being *grievously* wronged"[80] he should decline to act further; and it seems that, if he did not so decline, his confirmation would not protect C. But in cases falling outside this extreme range, C is not precluded from relying on the solicitor's confirmation merely because the solicitor is not satisfied that the transaction was one into which [B] "could sensibly be advised to enter"[81] nor even because the transaction was "one into which no competent solicitor could have advised the wife [B] to enter".[82] If C takes the required steps (outlined above), it will normally[83] be entitled to rely on the solicitor's confirmation that the solicitor has "advised the wife [B] appropriately."[84] If C fails to take the required steps, C runs the risk of not being able to enforce the transaction against B.

The above steps are designed to protect B against the *risk* of undue influence (or similar vitiating factors). The mere fact that they were not taken does not therefore provide grounds on which B will be entitled to set the transaction aside for undue influence. B will be so entitled, even if C has not taken the required steps, only if B can also establish either that the transaction was procured by undue influence or that the basic facts of the "evidential presumption"[85] that it was so procured exist and if the presumption is not otherwise rebutted. According to some of the older authorities, indeed, C was unable to enforce the transaction whenever the relationship between A and B was one of those giving rise to the irrebuttable presumption described in above[86] (*e.g.* that of parent and child) and if C knew, or ought to have known, of that relationship.[87] But these cases seems to have been based on the view that the mere existence of such a relationship gave rise to a presumption that undue influence had been *exercised*.[88] This view can no longer stand after the *Etridge* case, according to which the effect of the irrebuttable presumption is merely to dispense with the need that such influence *exists*,[89] and this is not, of itself, enough to entitle B to set the transaction aside.[90]

SECTION 3. MONEYLENDING AND CONSUMER PROTECTION

1. Extortionate Credit Bargains

The rate of interest which could be charged by moneylenders was at one time regulated by statute. After the Usury Laws Repeal Act 1854, the lender was free to charge such interest as he could get, and for nearly 50 years the activities of moneylenders were subject only to the equitable rules as to unconscionable bargains.[91] Statutory powers to control moneylending contracts were, however, given to the courts by the Moneylenders Acts 1900 and 1927, and are now contained in the Consumer Credit Act 1974. Under that Act, the court has power to "reopen" any "extortionate credit bargain".[92] The Act provides that a credit bargain is extortionate if the payments to be made under it are at

---

[80] *ibid.*, at [62] italics supplied.
[81] *ibid.*, at [58]–[59].
[82] *ibid.*, at [63].
[83] *ibid.*, at [61]; but not if C knows that the solicitor "has not duly advised" B: *ibid.*, at [57]; *cf. National Westminster Bank plc v Breeds* [2001] N.L.J. 170.
[84] *ibid.*, at [56]; *cf. ibid.*, at [292] where this requirement was held to have been complied with in *Barclays Bank plc v Coleman*, one of the cases under consideration in the *Etridge* case, above, n.62.
[85] See above, p.411.
[86] See above, p.411.
[87] *Maitland v Irving* (1846) 15 Sim. 437; *Lancashire Loans Ltd v Black* [1934] 1 K.B. 380.
[88] See above, p.414.
[89] *Etridge* case, above n.51 at [18].
[90] See above, p.413.
[91] See *Nevill v Snelling* (1880) 15 Ch.D. 679.
[92] Consumer Credit Act 1974, s.137(1); *cf.* Insolvency Act 1986, ss.244, 343.

the time of contracting[93] "grossly exorbitant" *or* if it "otherwise grossly contravenes the ordinary principles of fair dealing".[94] These are stringent requirements: a bargain is not "extortionate" merely because it is harsh or even unconscionable.[95] Factors to be taken into account in determining whether a credit bargain is extortionate include the prevailing level of interest rates; matters affecting the debtor (such as his age and business capacity, and the degree to which he was under financial pressure when he made the bargain); and the degree of risk accepted by the creditor.[96] Under these provisions, it has been held that payments were not "grossly exorbitant" where interest at an annual rate of 48 per cent was charged on a loan which was made with little security, and on the very day on which the borrower applied for it, so as to enable him to complete the purchase of a house already heavily encumbered with other charges[97]; and that a bargain did not "grossly contravene the principles of fair dealing" where (in accordance with the principles already discussed[98]) the lender's conduct was not affected by the exercise of undue influence over the borrower by a third person.[99]

In "reopening" the transaction, the court has a wide discretion "to do justice between the parties."[1] It can alter the terms of the bargain in order to relieve the debtor "from payment of any sum in excess of that fairly due and reasonable"; order repayment of excessive sums paid; and grant various other forms of relief to the debtor or to a surety.[2]

2. Consumer Trade Practices

Reference has been made in Chapter 7 to legislation which provides for administrative control of exemption clauses and of other unfair terms in consumer contracts.[3] It can also be argued that much legislation protects the consumer against a form of economic duress. A similar policy against such duress appears to underlie the statutory provisions giving consumers a "cooling-off" period in certain cases. For example a person who is induced to sign a regulated consumer credit agreement[4] at home is entitled to cancel it within such a period.[5] And the policy of protecting consumers against certain exemption clauses and unfair terms has been an important influence on the legislative controls of such terms which have been discussed in Chapter 7.[6]

---

[93] *Paragon Finance plc v Staunton* [2001] EWCA Civ 1466; [2001] 2 All E.R. (Comm) 1025 at [66]; *Broadwick Financial Services Ltd v Spencer* [2002] 1 All E.R (Comm) 466, at [56, 57].

[94] Consumer Credit Act 1974, s.138(1); if the debtor or any surety alleges that a credit bargain is extortionate, the burden is on the creditor to prove the contrary: *ibid.* s.171(7).

[95] *Davies v Directloans Ltd* [1986] 1 W.L.R. 823. Nor does it seem that such a term would be affected by Unfair Terms in Consumer Contracts Regulations 1999: see reg.4(2)(a) and reg.6(2)(a), above, pp.248, 253.

[96] Consumer Credit Act 1974, s.138(2)–(4); *Davies v Directloans Ltd*, above.

[97] *Ketley v Scott* [1981] I.C.R. 241; *cf. Petrou v Woodstead Finance Ltd* [1986] F.L.R. 158 (42.5 per cent not extortionate on short term loan).

[98] See above, pp.386–389.

[99] *Coldunell Ltd v Gallon* [1986] Q.B. 1184.

[1] Consumer Credit Act 1974, s.137(1).

[2] *ibid.* s.139(2).

[3] Above, p.283.

[4] See above, pp.177–178.

[5] Consumer Credit Act 1974, ss.67–68; *cf.* Consumer Protection (Distance Selling) Regulations 2000, SI 2000/2334, reg.10; Consumer Protection (Cancellation of Contracts concluded away from Business Premises) Order 1987 (SI 1987/2117); Timeshare Act 1992, ss.2–4.

[6] See above, pp.246–283.

CHAPTER ELEVEN

ILLEGALITY[1]

THE law may refuse to give full effect to a contract on the ground of illegality, *i.e.* because the contract involves the commission of a legal wrong or is in some other way contrary to public policy.

SECTION 1. THE PROBLEM OF CLASSIFICATION

English writers commonly divide the cases in which contracts are affected by illegality into a number of classes.[2] One object of this classification is to make it possible to generalise about the *effects* of illegality; but it is doubtful whether any of the suggested classifications achieve this object to any considerable extent. Another object of classification is purely expository, and this does no harm so long as it is not actually misleading.

One classification is based on the nature of the objectionable conduct. Thus Sir Frederick Pollock divided the cases into those where the contract was contrary to (1) positive law, (2) morals or good manners, and (3) public policy; but he admitted that this classification was "only approximate".[3] The main difficulty with it is that the second category is hard to define and that it may overlap with the third. For this reason the second category is not used in the present Chapter. It can also be argued that public policy is the ground for invalidating *all* contracts affected by illegality, so that the third category includes the other two. But if all illegal contracts fell into a single category, there would be no point in attempting to classify them, even for purposes of exposition.

A second classification is based on the source of the rule infringed. Thus it is sometimes said that a contract is more likely to be invalid for violation of a statute than for violation of a rule of common law. The distinction is appropriate where a statute expressly prohibits or invalidates a contract.[4] But it is not decisive where the statute contains no such express prohibition and the illegality consists only in the method of making or performing the contract.[5] In *St John Shipping Corp v Joseph Rank Ltd*[6] a shipowner committed a statutory offence by overloading his ship while performing a number of contracts for the carriage of goods. Devlin J. held that he was nonetheless entitled to freight, because the object of the statute was to prevent overloading and not to prohibit contracts. This object was to be achieved by imposing a fine, and not by subjecting the shipowner to the additional financial loss which would result from invalidating the contracts of carriage. It is submitted that this approach should not be

---

[1] Enonchong, *Illegal Transactions*; Buckley, *Illegality and Public Policy*; Furmston (1966) U. of Tor.L.J. 267.

[2] The fashion seems to have been started by Sir Frederick Pollock (below, n.3). It has not spread to the United States. Williston, *Contracts* (rev. ed.), s.1628, says: "There seems to be no importance to these distinctions."

[3] *Principles of the Law of Contract*, (13th ed.), Chap.8, p.261.

[4] *e.g.* Fair Trading Act 1973, Pt XI, as extended by Trading Schemes Act 1996 (pyramid selling). *cf.* below, pp.487, 513.

[5] See *Shaw v Groom* [1970] 2 Q.B. 540; *London & Harrogate Securities Ltd v Pitts* [1976] 1 W.L.R. 1063.

[6] [1957] 1 Q.B. 267.

confined to cases in which the offence is statutory.[7] It would have been just as appropriate, and would probably have led to the same result, had the shipowner been convicted of manslaughter committed in the course of the voyage.

Classification may proceed, thirdly, by the legal consequences of the contracts concerned. Thus Sir John Salmond distinguished between "illegal" and "nugatory" contracts[8]; and the same classification has been adopted by later writers who distinguish between "illegal" and "void" contracts. This classification cannot, of course, lead to any deductions about the legal effects of the contracts in question as it assumes that those consequences are already known. Unfortunately, those who use the classification cannot always agree on this vital point. Thus some regard an agreement by a married person to marry as "illegal",[9] while others regard it as "void".[10] Moreover, the classification tries to do the impossible. The nature of the illegality which may affect a contract varies almost infinitely in seriousness.[11] To classify these contracts by their effects into only two groups is likely to result in a misleading degree of oversimplification.

In Section 2 of this Chapter, 22 types of illegal contracts are listed; for purposes of exposition they are divided into two groups, namely contracts involving the commission of a legal wrong and contracts contrary to public policy. The second group includes one particularly important type of contracts, those in restraint of trade. Because of the complexity of the law relating to such contracts, they will be discussed under an independent heading. The exact effects of illegality should ideally be discussed separately in relation to each type of contract, but such treatment would be inordinately long. An attempt will therefore be made in Section 3 of this Chapter to provide a general discussion of the effects of illegality. This approach can be justified on the ground that many of the relevant rules apply to all types of illegal contracts; but it is also often true that the effects vary with the type of illegality. Where this is the case, the general propositions in Section 3 will be qualified accordingly.

SECTION 2. TYPES OF ILLEGALITY

1. Contracts Involving the Commission of a Legal Wrong

(1) Contracts amounting to a legal wrong

A contract is illegal[12] if the mere making of it is a legal wrong: *e.g.*, if legislation prohibits the making of the contract.[13] At common law, a contract to "rig the market" by offering inflated prices for shares in a particular company is similarly illegal as it is a criminal conspiracy.[14] A contract by which one person agrees to finance another's litigation in return for a share in the proceeds, the former having no genuine or substantial interest in the outcome,[15] used to amount to the crime and tort of champerty; and accordingly

---

[7] *Wetherell v Jones* (1832) 3 B. & Ad. 221, 225–226; *Coral Leisure Group v Barnett* [1981] I.C.R. 503 at 509. For a similar approach in case of a civil wrong, see *The Ypatianna* [1988] Q.B. 345 at 369–370.

[8] Salmond and Winfield, *Law of Contracts*, Chap.7; Salmond and Williams, *Law of Contracts*, Chap.14.

[9] Salmond and Winfield, above; Salmond and Williams, above. An agreement to marry is no longer a contract, but may have other legal consequences: below, p.441.

[10] Cheshire, Fifoot and Furmston, *The Law of Contract* (14th ed.), p.449.

[11] Corbin, *Contracts*, s.1373.

[12] Except to the extent that a statute provides the contrary: *e.g.* Sex Discrimination Act 1975, s.77; (as amended by Sex Discrimination Act 1986, s.6 and Trade Union Reform and Employment Rights Act 1993, s.39(2) and Sch.2); Race Relations Act 1976, s.72, as amended by Trade Union Reform and Employment Rights Act 1993 s.39(2) and Sch.6.

[13] See *Mohamed v Alaga & Co* [2000] 1 W.L.R. 1815; *Hughes v Kingston upon Hull CC* [1999] Q.B. 1193; see now n.29 below.

[14] *Scott v Brown* [1892] 2 Q.B. 724; *cf. Harry Parker Ltd v Mason* [1940] 2 K.B. 590.

[15] See below, pp.697–698.

the contract was illegal.[16] Although criminal and tortious liability for champerty have been abolished[17] a champertous agreement remains, as a general rule, illegal[18]; but the scope of this rule is restricted by the requirement that, to be champertous, the agreement must amount to "wanton or officious intermeddling with the disputes of others".[19] At common law agreements between a client and his legal advisers in litigation for the payment of either a "contingency" or a "conditional" fee are champertous and illegal.[20] Contingency fee agreements are those by which the legal adviser is remunerated by a share in the amount recovered: these remain illegal. Conditional fee agreements are those which provide that the legal adviser is to be paid his fee if he wins the case but not if he loses it. With respect to such agreements, legislation now provides[21] that, in most cases,[22] an agreement in writing can validly be made[23] by which a client promises to pay a "conditional fee" to a person who provides him with advocacy or litigation services in legal proceedings.[24] The condition may be that the litigation ends in the client's favour; and the fee may be a "success fee", that is, one which provides that, in that event, the provider's fee is to be increased above the amount of normal fee[25] by a percentage (not exceeding that specified by the Lord Chancellor).[26] Conditional fee agreements which are not in terms validated by this legislation are declared by it to be unenforceable[27] and are also illegal at common law[28]; they are also illegal to the extent to which they are prohibited by other legislation.[29]

---

[16] *Re Thomas* [1894] 1 Q.B. 747.

[17] Criminal Law Act 1967, ss.13(1), 14(1).

[18] *ibid.* s.14(2); *Trendtex Trading Corp v Crédit Suisse* [1982] A.C. 679; *McFarlane v EE Caledonia (No.2)* [1995] 1 W.L.R. 366 at 372. For statutory exceptions (and their limits) in bankruptcy and insolvency cases, see Insolvency Act 1986 ss.165, 166; *Grovewood Holdings plc v James Capel & Co Ltd* [1995] Ch. 80; *Re Oasis Merchandising Services* [1998] Ch. 170; *Norglen Ltd v Reeds Rains Prudential Ltd* [1996] 1 W.L.R. 945; *ANC Ltd v Clark Goldring & Page Ltd* [2001] B.C.C. 479.

[19] *Giles v Thompson* [1994] 1 A.C. 142 at 164 (where the decision was expressly restricted at 156 to the terms of the particular agreements under consideration).

[20] *Wallersteiner v Moir (No.2)* [1975] Q.B. 373; *Awwad v Geraghty & Co* [2001] Q.B. 570; *Callery v Gray* [2001] EWCA Civ 1117; [2001] 1 W.L.R. 2212, at [5, 6]; conditional fee agreements with surveyors are valid at common law: *Pickering v Sogex Services* (1982) 262 E.G. 700; *Picton Jones & Co v Arcadia Developments* [1989] 1 E.G.L.R. 43; *Factortame Ltd v S of S for the Environment, etc. (No.2)* [2002] EWCA Civ 932; [2002] 4 All E.R. 97 (contingency fee agreement with accountants rendering services relating to assessment of damages upheld).

[21] Courts and Legal Services Act 1990, ss.58 and 58A, as substituted by Access to Justice Act 1999, s.27; and see nn.23 and 24 below.

[22] Criminal proceedings and most family proceedings are excluded by s.58A(1) of the 1990 Act, (above, n.21).

[23] *ibid.*, s.58(3)a; for other requirements of such agreements, see Conditional Fee Agreements Regulations 2000, SI 2000/692, as amended by Collective Conditional Fee Agreements Regulations 2000 (SI 2000/2988).

[24] These need not be court proceedings: Courts and Legal Services Act 1990 s.58A(4) (above, n.21).

[25] Courts and Legal Services Act 1990, s.58(2)(a) (above, n.21) *i.e.*, the amount to which he would have been entitled if his right to payment had not been conditional on the success of the client's claim.

[26] *ibid.*, s.58(4)(c); Conditional Fee Agreements Order 2000, SI 2000/823, reg.4 (up to 100%).

[27] Courts and Legal Services Act 1990, s.58(1) (above, n.1).

[28] See the first two cases cited in n.20, above. The point is significant in relation to restitionionary remedies: below, pp.464–465.

[29] *British Waterways Board v Norman* (1993) 26 H.L.R. 232 and *Aratra Potato Co Ltd v Joynson Garrett* [1995] 4 All E.R. 695, approved in *Hughes v Kingston upon Hull CC* [1999] Q.B. 1193, disapproving *Thai Trading Co v Taylor* [1998] Q.B. as having been decided *per incuriam* since the Court of Appeal in that case was not made aware of the legislative status of the Solicitors Practice Rules, as established in *Swain v The Law Society* [1983] 1 A.C. 589; *Awwad v Geraghty* [2001] Q.B. 570, again disapproving the *Thai Trading* case but pointing out that the relevant Rule had since been amended: see also *Wells v Barnsley MBC, The Times,* November 12, 1999.

A contract to stifle a prosecution for treason is illegal as it amounts to compounding. It is also an offence for a person who knows that an arrestable offence has been committed, and that he has information which may help to secure the conviction of the offender, to accept or agree to accept any consideration (other than the making good of the loss or injury caused by the offence) for not disclosing the information.[30] The mere making of some contracts is expressly made criminal by statute: it is, for example, an offence to sell a flick-knife,[31] to agree to indemnify a surety in criminal proceedings against liability to forfeit a recognisance,[32] and to deal for payment in human organs.[33] Such contracts are no doubt illegal. And where the making or variation of a contract is prohibited by a court order, disobedience of the order amounts to contempt of court; and the prohibited contract, or variation, is illegal.[34]

(2) Contracts to commit a crime

A contract for the deliberate commission of a crime is obviously illegal.[35] Such a contract would also amount to conspiracy. But many statutory crimes can be committed without criminal intent[36]; and there are cases in which only one of the parties to a contract has any criminal intent. The exact effects of illegality on such contracts, where one or both parties act in good faith, will be considered later in this Chapter.[37]

(3) Contracts to commit a civil wrong

A contract is illegal where its object is the *deliberate* commission of a civil wrong. Thus contracts to assault[38] or defraud[39] a third party are illegal: and the same is true of a contract by an insolvent debtor to pay one of his creditors in fraud of the others.[40] Similarly a contract may be illegal if its object is to procure one party to break a contract known by both to be binding on him.[41]

Where a contract involves the *unintentional* commission of a civil wrong two types of cases call for discussion.

(a) ONE PARTY INNOCENT. One party may know that the performance of the contract will involve the commission of a civil wrong, while the other is innocent. In *Clay v Yates*[42] the plaintiff agreed with the defendant to print a book with a dedication. He

---

[30] Criminal Law Act 1967, s.5(1); "arrestable offence" is defined in Police and Criminal Evidence Act 1984, s.24(1) (as amended by Police Reform Act 2000, s.48), which applies by virtue of s.119 and Sch.6, para.17 for the purposes of the 1967 Act.

[31] Restriction of Offensive Weapons Act 1959, s.1(1)(a).

[32] Bail Act 1976, s.9.

[33] Human Organ Transplants Act 1989, s.1.

[34] *Clarke v Chadburn* [1985] 1 W.L.R. 78.

[35] *e.g. Bostel Bros Ltd v Hurlock* [1949] 1 K.B. 74 (evasion of building licensing regulations); *Bigos v Bousted* [1951] 1 All E.R. 92 (evasion of exchange control legislation); *cf. Ashton v Turner* [1981] Q.B. 137 (agreements, probably not contractual, to commit burglary); *Pitts v Hunt* [1991] 1 Q.B. 24 (agreement to drive motorcycle so as to frighten others). Ignorance of the law makes no difference: see *Belvoir Finance Co Ltd v Stapleton* [1971] 1 Q.B. 210.

[36] In such a case there is no criminal liability for conspiracy: Criminal Law Act 1977, s.1(2).

[37] See below, pp.484–490.

[38] *Allen v Rescous* (1676) 2 Lev. 174.

[39] *Begbie v Phosphate Sewage Co Ltd* (1875) L.R. 10 Q.B. 491; *cf. Customs & Excise Commissioners v Oliver* [1980] 1 All E.R. 355 (sale of goods stolen, or known to have been stolen, by seller); *Taylor v Bhail* [1995] C.L.C. 337.

[40] *Cockshott v Bennett* (1788) 2 T.R. 763; *Mallalieu v Hodgson* (1851) 16 Q.B. 689; *cf. Cadbury Schweppes plc v Somji* [2001] 1 W.L.R. 615.

[41] Lauterpacht, 52 L.Q.R. 494.

[42] (1856) 1 H. & N. 73.

refused to print the dedication on discovering that it was libellous, but claimed the cost of printing the book. The defendant did not plead illegality but argued that the obligation to print the book with the dedication was "entire",[43] and that the plaintiff could not recover anything as he had performed only in part. In rejecting this argument, Pollock C.B. said that there was an implied undertaking to pay "for so much of the work *as is lawful*"[44]; while Martin B. said that the defendant was liable "to pay the plaintiff for that part *which he has performed*".[45] If the plaintiff had printed the dedication without knowing the facts which made it libellous, it seems that he could not have recovered his charges on Pollock C.B.'s test but that he could have done so under Martin B.'s test; and it is submitted that the latter is the preferable view.[46]

(b) BOTH PARTIES INNOCENT. If neither party knows that performance of the contract involves the commission of a civil wrong the contract is not illegal.[47] A contract for the sale of goods belonging to a third party may make buyer and seller liable to that third party in tort[48] even though they believed that the goods belonged to the seller; but such a contract has never been held illegal.[49]

(4) Use of subject-matter for unlawful purpose

A contract which is in itself lawful may be illegal if its subject-matter is to be used for an unlawful purpose. In *Langton v Hughes*[50] Spanish juice, isinglass and ginger were sold to a brewer who, as the seller knew, intended to put them into his beer. The contract was held to be illegal because an Act of 1802 made it an offence to use anything except malt and hops to flavour beer. Later cases suggest that this rule applies only if the seller to some extent "participates" in the illegal purpose[51]; but it seems that such participation would readily be inferred if he knew of that purpose and made its achievement possible by delivering the goods.

(5) Unlawful method of performance

A contract which is lawful in itself may be performed in a way which involves one or both parties in criminal liability. It used to be thought that the contract was illegal[52] if its performance involved breach of a statute passed for the protection of the public; but that, if the statute was passed only for the protection of the revenue, the contract was not illegal.[53] But the distinction between these two types of statutes is by no means

---

[43] See below, p.782.

[44] *Clay v Yates*, above, at 79.

[45] *ibid.* at 80.

[46] *cf.* Williams, 8 C.L.J. at p.54; Martin B.'s view may be reconciled with *Frank W Clifford Ltd v Garth* [1956] 1 W.L.R. 570; below, p.506, on the ground that the builder in that case took a conscious risk of illegality. *cf. ZYX Music GmbH v King* [1995] 3 All E.R. 1 at 10.

[47] *Clarion Ltd v National Power Association* [2000] 1 W.L.R. 1888 at 1908.

[48] See below, p.1055.

[49] Sale of Goods Act 1979, s.12 (as amended by Sale and Supply of Goods Act 1994, s.7(1) and Sch.2) assumes that the contract is valid.

[50] (1813) 1 M. & S. 593; *cf. Gas Light & Coke Co v Turner* (1839) 6 Bing.N.C. 324.

[51] *Hodgson v Temple* (1813) 5 Taunt. 181; *Pellecat v Angell* (1835) 2 Cr.M. & R. 311; *cf. Foster v Driscol* [1929] 1 K.B. 470; for similar reasoning in a case involving unlawful method of performance, see *Ashmore, Benson Pease & Co Ltd v A V Dawson Ltd* [1973] 1 W.L.R. 828; below, p.484.

[52] *Little v Poole* (1829) 9 B. & C. 192; *Fergusson v Norman* (1838) 5 Bing.N.C. 76; *Cundell v Dawson* (1847) 4 C.B. 376; *Victorian Daylesford Syndicate v Dott* [1905] 2 Ch. 624; *Brightman & Co v Tate* [1919] 1 K.B. 463; *Anderson Ltd v Daniel* [1924] 1 K.B. 138 (actual decision reversed by Fertilisers and Feeding Stuffs Act 1926, s.1(2)).

[53] *Johnson v Hudson* (1805) 11 East 180; *Brown v Duncan* (1829) 10 B. & C. 93; *Smith v Mawhood* (1845) 14 M. & W. 452; *Learoyd v Bracken* [1894] 1 Q.B. 114; *cf. Wetherell v Jones* (1832) 3 B. & Ad. 221.

decisive.[54] Even where the object of the statute is to protect the public (or a section of it) a contract involving a breach of it is not invariably illegal. Thus a contract to grant (or to transfer) a lease is not illegal merely because the landlord has committed a statutory offence by receiving or demanding an illegal premium. The tenant can accordingly enforce the contract, though without having to pay the premium.[55] Similarly, a tenancy is not illegal merely because the landlord has committed a statutory offence by failing to give his tenant a rent-book. Here the illegality relates to a merely collateral matter, so that the contract can be enforced even by the offender: *i.e.* the landlord can sue for the rent.[56] On the other hand, a contract may be illegal although the statute which it violates was passed for the protection of the revenue.[57] The test for determining whether an otherwise lawful contract is illegal because its performance involved the breach of a statute is that laid down in *St John Shipping Corp v Joseph Rank Ltd*[58]: did the statute intend only to penalise *conduct* or also to prohibit *contracts*? Some statutes expressly solve this problem: a contract for the supply of goods is not, for example, to be void or unenforceable merely because, in performing it, the seller has committed an offence under the Trade Descriptions Act 1968.[59]

A statute may subject contracts to a licensing or similar requirement, so that they can be lawfully performed only with the consent of some public body. Such a statute may expressly prohibit (and so render illegal) a contract made in breach of its provisions[60]; and even where the statute does not expressly prohibit the contract, it may do so by implication. Such an implication is most likely to arise where *both* parties are prohibited from making or performing the contract; but the implication may arise even where the statutory prohibition is directed at only one of the parties. At common law, this was the position where an insurer committed a statutory offence by engaging in certain types of insurance business without government authorisation[61]; by statute, such contracts are no longer illegal, but only unenforceable against the other party.[62]

A licensing or similar requirement may also apply merely to the performance of a particular contract (as opposed to the carrying on of a business): *e.g.* where a licence is required for the erection of a building or for the export or import of goods. Such a

---

[54] *Cope v Rowlands* (1836) 2 M. & W. 149 at 157.

[55] *Ailion v Spiekermann* [1976] Ch. 158; for enforceability of a contract by an innocent third party (in spite of a formal defect making one of the parties liable to a fine) see *OTV Birwelco Ltd v Technical & General Guarantee Co Ltd* [2002] EWHC 2240; [2002] 4 All E.R. 668 at [55].

[56] *Shaw v Groom* [1970] 2 Q.B. 504; *cf. London & Harrogate Securities Ltd v Pitts* [1976] 1 W.L.R. 1063; *The Lion* [1990] 2 Lloyd's Rep. 144; *Yango Pastoral Co Ltd v First National Chicago Australia Ltd* (1978) 139 C.L.R. 410; *P & B (Run Off) Ltd v Woolley* [2002] EWCA Civ 65; [2002] 1 All E.R. (Comm) 577.

[57] *e.g.*, where the object of the contract is to evade or to delay the payment of income tax: *Napier v National Business Agency Ltd* [1951] 2 All E.R. 264; *cf. Miller v Karlinski* (1945) 62 T.L.R. 85; below, p.450.

[58] [1957] 1 Q.B. 267; above, p.429. *Credit Lyonnais v P T Barnard & Associates* [1976] 1 Lloyd's Rep. 557; *cf. Curragh Investments Ltd v Cook* [1974] 1 W.L.R. 1559; *Skilton v Sullivan, The Times*, March 25, 1994; *Hughes v Asset Management plc* [1995] 3 All E.R. 669 at 673; *Mohammed v Alaga & Co* [2000] 1 W.L.R. 1815 at 1824, applying the same test to legislation which prohibited the *making* of a contract.

[59] s.35; *cf.* Fair Trading Act 1973, s.26; and see below, pp.486–487. Such a legislative provision may also be implied: see *Currencies Direct Ltd v Ellis* [2002] EWCA Civ 779; [2002] 2 B.C.L.C. 482 (Companies Act 1985, s.341, by making a prohibited loan *voidable by the company*, by implication entitled company to enforce it).

[60] *cf. Re Mahmoud and Ispahani* [1921] 2 K.B. 716, below, p.486.

[61] *Bedford Ins Co Ltd v Instituto de Resseguros do Brazil* [1985] 1 Q.B. 966; *Phoenix General Ins Co of Greece v Halvanon Ins Co Ltd* [1988] Q.B. 216, where the statute was not contravened and where *Stewart v Oriental Fire & Marine Ins Co Ltd* [1986] 1 Q.B. 988 was disapproved; *Re Cavalier Ins Co Ltd* [1989] 2 Lloyd's Rep. 430; *Overseas Union Insurance Ltd v Incorporated General Insurance Ltd* [1992] 1 Lloyd's Rep. 439 at 444–445. Contrast *Fuji Finance Inc v Aetna Life Insurance Co Ltd* [1997] Ch. 713, where conflicting views were expressed as to the effect on contracts of statutory provisions *not* giving rise to criminal liability.

[62] Financial Services and Markets Act 2000, s.s.26(1), 27(1).

contract is not illegal if it is expressly or by implication made subject to the relevant consent.[63] It will be illegal only if it is performed without such licence or consent[64] or if the parties intend to perform it even though no licence or consent is obtained.[65] A party may, however, guarantee that the licence will be obtained; if so, the undertaking can be enforced against him as a collateral contract, even though the main contract is illegal.[66] He may also be liable in damages for failing to perform an express or implied promise to make reasonable efforts to obtain the licence.[67]

A contract which is initially lawful may become illegal if, in the course of performing it, the parties agree deliberately to commit a civil wrong: *e.g.*, to defraud a third person who had undertaken to provide the finance necessary for its performance.[68] But a contract which is in itself lawful does not become illegal merely because in the course of performing it one party commits a fraud on the other.[69] That fraud is, however, likely to be a repudiatory breach, so that the victim of the fraud will be entitled to rescind the contract and so to avoid further liability under it.[70]

(6) Contracts to indemnify against liability for unlawful acts

(a) CRIMINAL LIABILITY. A contract to indemnify a person against criminal liability is illegal if the crime is one which can only be, or in fact is, committed with guilty intent.[71] But the position is less clear where the crime is one of strict liability. In *Cointat v Myham & Sons*[72] the defendants sold to a butcher the carcass of a pig, which was unfit for food. The butcher innocently exposed it for sale and was consequently convicted and fined £20. It was held that he could recover this sum from the defendants; but the legality of their implied promise to indemnify him was not discussed. The case has been criticised on the ground that "punishment inflicted by a criminal court is personal to the offender" and is fixed "having regard to the personal responsibility of the offender in respect of the offence".[73] One object of imposing strict criminal liability is to make a person take care not to commit the offence; and this object might be defeated by allowing him to recover the fine from a third party. Nonetheless it seems that the courts will allow a person to recover an indemnity against criminal liability if they are satisfied that he is wholly innocent. For example, in *Osman v J Ralph Moss Ltd*[74] a motorist had been convicted of driving while uninsured. He was morally innocent, having been told by his insurance agent that he was properly insured, and it was held that his fine could be included in the damages recoverable from the agent for breach of contract.

(b) CIVIL LIABILITY. A contract to indemnify a person against civil liability may be illegal if the wrong is intentionally and knowingly committed: for example, a contract to

---

[63] *Michael Richards Properties Ltd v St Saviour's Parish* [1975] 3 All E.R. 416;

[64] *e.g. J Dennis & Co Ltd v Munn* [1949] 2 K.B. 327. For an exception, see *SA Ancien Maison Marcel Bauche v Woodhouse Drake & Carey (Sugar) Ltd* [1982] 2 Lloyd's Rep. 516.

[65] *e.g. Bigos v Bousted* [1951] 1 All E.R. 92.

[66] *Peter Cassidy Seed Co Ltd v Osuustukkukauppa* [1957] 1 W.L.R. 273, as explained in *Walton (Grain and Shipping) Ltd v British Trading Co* [1959] 1 Lloyd's Rep. 223 at 236; *cf.* below, p.489. Both cases concerned foreign licensing requirements.

[67] See above, p.65, below, p.842.

[68] *Birkett v Acorn Business Machines Ltd* [1999] 2 All E.R. (Comm) 429.

[69] *Broaders v Kalhare Property Maintenance* [1990] I.R.L.R. 421.

[70] See below, p.807.

[71] *Colburn v Patmore* (1834) 1 C.M. & R. 73; *Fitzgerald v Leonard* (1893) L.R. 33 Ir. 675.

[72] [1913] 2 K.B. 220; reversed on another ground [1914] W.N. 46.

[73] *Askey v Golden Wine Co* (1948) 64 T.L.R. 379 at 380; *cf. Simon v Pawsons & Leafs Ltd* (1932) 38 Com.Cas. 151 at 158; *Crage v Fry* (1903) 67 J.P. 240; *R Leslie Ltd v Reliable Advertising, etc. Agency Ltd* [1915] 1 K.B. 652.

[74] [1970] 1 Lloyd's Rep. 313.

indemnify a person against liability for deceit is illegal.[75] Similarly, a person who publishes what he knows to be a libel cannot recover an indemnity from the person who instigated the publication,[76] for the tendency of such an agreement might be to increase the circulation of the libel. On the other hand, a contract to keep a communication confidential, and to indemnify the maker against any liability resulting from its disclosure, has been held valid even where the communication contained a malicious libel[77]—apparently because the tendency of such an agreement is to restrict the circulation of the libel.

A contract to indemnify a person against civil liability is perfectly valid if the liability was incurred innocently or negligently.[78] Indeed, in many such cases promises to indemnify, far from being illegal, are actually implied in law. The general principle is that where A at B's request does an act which is not "manifestly tortious", B must indemnify A for any liability incurred by A if the act turns out to be injurious to C.[79] The cases provide many illustrations of the validity of such express or implied promises to indemnify. Thus the innocent publisher of a libel can recover an indemnity from the person who instigated the publication.[80] An agent can recover an indemnity from his principal if he is made liable in conversion for selling a third person's property on the principal's instructions.[81] An employer can insure himself against civil liability for the tort of his employee; and he may also be entitled to an indemnity against such liability from the employee under the contract of employment.[82] And where A holds property which is claimed by B and C, a promise by one of them to indemnify A against liability to the other if he delivers the property to the promisor is perfectly valid.[83]

(c) CIVIL LIABILITY ARISING OUT OF CRIMINAL ACTS. Where an act amounts both to a crime and to a civil wrong, a promise to indemnify the wrongdoer against civil liability incurred as a result of the act is often illegal. For example, in *Gray v Barr*[84] a husband shot and killed his wife's lover in circumstances amounting in the view of the Court of Appeal to manslaughter (though in the criminal proceedings he had been acquitted). It was held that the husband could not recover under an insurance policy (even if it covered the occurrence) the damages which he had had to pay to the lover's estate. The decision was based on the public interest in deterring armed violence; but it does not follow that promises to indemnify against civil liability are necessarily invalid merely because the act giving rise to that liability also amounts to a crime. There are, in particular, three situations in which they may be upheld.

First, a promise to indemnify a person against civil liability can be enforced, even though the act giving rise to that liability is criminal, if the crime is one of strict liability or is in fact committed without *mens rea*. Thus in *Gray v Barr* the possibility was left open that a person who committed manslaughter in circumstances amounting to little more than an error of judgment might be able to recover an indemnity from his

---

[75] *Brown Jenkinson & Co Ltd v Percy Dalton (London) Ltd* [1957] 2 Q.B. 621.

[76] *W H Smith & Sons v Clinton* (1909) 99 L.T. 840.

[77] *Weld-Blundell v Stephens* [1919] 1 K.B. 520; *Bradstreets British Ltd v Mitchell and Carpanayoti & Co Ltd* [1933] Ch. 190; contrast *Howard v Odham's Press Ltd* [1938] 1 K.B. 1. And see *Distillers Co Ltd v Times Newspapers Ltd* [1975] Q.B. 613.

[78] *Betts v Gibbins* (1834) 2 A. & E. 57; cf. *Yeung v Hong Kong & Shanghai Banking Corp* [1981] A.C. 787.

[79] *The Nogar Marin* [1988] 1 Lloyd's Rep. 412 at 417.

[80] *Daily Mirror Newspapers Ltd v Exclusive News Agency* (1937) 81 S.J. 924; Defamation Act 1952, s.11.

[81] *Adamson v Jarvis* (1827) 4 Bing. 66; *Betts v Gibbins* (1834) 2 A. & E. 57.

[82] *Lister v Romford Ice & Cold Storage Co Ltd* [1957] A.C. 555; above, p.209.

[83] e.g. *Betts v Gibbins* (1834) 2 A. & E. 57.

[84] [1971] 2 Q.B. 554; criticised (on another point) in *DPP v Newbury* [1977] A.C. 500. Flemming, 34 M.L.R. 177; cf. *Haseldine v Hosken* [1933] 1 K.B. 822; *R. v National Insurance Commissioner, Ex p. Connor* [1981] 1 Q.B. 758.

insurance company.[85] The view that such an indemnity is recoverable is supported by a dictum in a later case, according to which the test "is not the label which the law applies to the crime which has been committed, but the nature of the crime itself".[86] Similarly, if the butcher in *Cointat v Myham & Son*[87] had had to pay damages for breach of contract to a customer who was poisoned by the pork, he should have been able to claim an indemnity against this loss from the defendant.

The second situation arises in the law of motor insurance. In *Tinline v White Cross Insurance*[88] a motorist, who was insured against liability for "accidental personal injury" to third parties, killed a pedestrian by driving with criminal negligence, and was convicted of manslaughter. He successfully sued the insurers for the damages which he had had to pay to the deceased. The motorist has this right only where the crime is committed negligently—not where it is committed deliberately.[89] But even in the latter case the position of the innocent victim of the motorist's crime is protected by being given rights in certain circumstances against the insurer[90] or against the Motor Insurers' Bureau.[91] The existence of such rights is obviously necessary to maintain the effectiveness of the scheme of compulsory motor insurance.

Thirdly, the principle stated in *Gray v Barr* applies only to contracts to indemnify the wrongdoer *himself* against civil liability arising out of criminal conduct. That conduct may also make the wrongdoer's *employer* civilly liable to the victim; and the employer can validly insure against such liability, even to the extent that the wrong gives rise to a claim against him for exemplary (or punitive) damages.[92]

(7) Promises to pay money on the commission of an unlawful act

A contract may be illegal if it provides for the payment of money to a person in the event of his doing an unlawful act, *e.g.* if A promises B £5 if B breaks the speed limit. From a legal point of view, such a promise is not easy to distinguish from an insurance policy under which a driver (or the cost of one) is to be made available to a motorist if he should be disqualified for a driving offence. A recommendation that such contracts[93] should be declared by statute to be unenforceable and void[94] has been accepted in principle, but

---

[85] [1971] 1 Q.B. 544 at 581; *cf. Gregory v Ford* [1951] 1 All E.R. 121 (employment contract). It has been held that a person convicted of manslaughter cannot at common law take under his victim's will irrespective of his degree of moral culpability: *Re Giles* [1972] Ch. 544; *Re Royse* [1985] Ch. 22; Price 48 M.L.R. 723; *Jones v Roberts* [1995] 2 FLR 222; but in *Re H* [1990] 1 FLR 441 the court refused to apply this rule where the person so convicted had, by reason of his diminished responsibility, "no responsibility at all" for the offence. Moreover, the court has power under Forfeiture Act 1982, s.2 to modify the rule: see *Re K* [1986] Ch. 180; Cretney, 10 O.J.L.S. 289; *Dunbar v Plant* [1998] Ch. 412; *Re S* [1996] 1 W.L.R. 235 (discretion exercised in favour of offender's *son*).

[86] *R. v National Insurance Commissioner, Ex p. Connor* [1981] Q.B. 758, 765 (where a claim for widow's benefit under the Social Security Act 1975 was rejected as the claimant had been convicted of manslaughter by *deliberately* stabbing her husband to death). *Semble*, that on such facts the result would not be affected by Forfeiture Act, 1982, s.4. though by Social Security Act 1986, s.76, Social Security Commissioners have the same discretion as the High Court to modify the "forfeiture" rule (above, n.85).

[87] [1913] 2 K.B. 220, above, p.435.

[88] [1921] 3 K.B. 327; followed in *James v British General Insurance Co Ltd* [1927] 2 K.B. 311; doubted in *Haseldine v Hosken* [1933] 1 K.B. 822 but approved in *Marles v Philip Trant & Sons Ltd* [1954] 1 Q.B. 29 at 40, and in *Gray v Barr* [1971] 1 Q.B. 544 at 568, 581.

[89] *Gardner v Moore* [1984] A.C. 548, 560; *Pitts v Hunt* [1991] 1 Q.B. 24 at 30; *Charlton v Fisher* [2001] EWCA Civ 112; [2002] Q.B. 578.

[90] See below, p.669.

[91] See below, p.669; *Hardy v M.I.B.* [1964] 2 Q.B. 743; *Gardner v Moore* [1984] A.C. 548 at 560–561.

[92] *Lancashire CC v Municipal Mutual Insurance Ltd* [1997] Q.B. 897; for punitive damages, see below, p.935.

[93] See *DTI v St Christopher's Motorist Association* [1974] 1 W.L.R. 99.

[94] *Road Traffic Law Report*, HMSO 1988 (The North Report) paras 16.32–16.35.

legislation has not been introduced, as the insurance industry has agreed to discontinue the practice of issuing policies of this kind.[95]

A life insurance policy was never wholly illegal merely because it provided that the sum insured was to be paid even if the assured committed suicide (which was formerly a crime). It could clearly be enforced if he died in some other way. But in *Beresford v Royal Exchange Assurance*[96] it was, however, held that such a policy could not be enforced by the personal representatives of the assured if he did commit suicide; to allow a man, or his estate, to benefit from his own crime was said to be against public policy.[97] But if the assured assigned the policy and then committed suicide, the assignees were entitled to the policy moneys since it was they, and not the assured, who benefited from the crime.[98] It is hard to see the force of this distinction where, as in *Beresford's* case, the assured was bankrupt, so that the only people who could benefit were his creditors. The actual decision can now be regarded as resting on the alternative ground that, under ordinary principles of insurance law, the assured cannot recover if he by his own deliberate act causes the event on which the insurance money is payable.[99]

(8) Effect of changes in the law

In relation to contracts which involve the commission of a legal wrong it is necessary to consider the effect of changes in the law, both on contracts in existence at the time of the change and on contracts made after the change.

First, the law may change so that previously lawful conduct becomes a legal wrong. The effect of such a change may be to frustrate existing contracts[1] and to make future contracts illegal. Whether it actually has this effect will depend on principles stated in *St John Shipping Corp v Joseph Rank Ltd.*[2]

A second kind of change is one by which conduct previously amounting to a legal wrong ceases to be so; and *prima facie* the effect of such a change in the law is that future contracts involving such conduct will be valid. This would be the case where the conduct in question had been criminal under some regulatory statute (for example, one requiring certain work to be licensed) which was then repealed. But there are exceptions to this general rule. First, a statute abrogating a rule of law under which certain conduct was unlawful may expressly preserve a rule under which a contract involving such conduct was previously illegal: this is the position (in general[3]) with regard to champertous agreements.[4] Secondly, it is possible that, even after the conduct in question has ceased to be a legal wrong, a contract involving such conduct would still be contrary to

---

[95] *The Road User and the Law* Cm.576 (1989).

[96] [1938] A.C. 586; Goodhart, 52 L.Q.R. 575.

[97] This principle applies even though the contract is not illegal: it has been applied to prevent recovery on a policy of life insurance where the assured was executed for felony though the policy did not in terms refer to this contingency: *Amicable Soc v Bolland* (1830) 4 Bligh (N.S.) 194, criticised by Devlin, *The Enforcement of Morals* at p.53 and Furmston (1966) U. of Tor.L.J. at p.274. *cf. Davitt v Titcumb* [1989] 3 All E.R. 417: murderer not allowed to benefit indirectly from policy on joint lives of victim and himself; *Geismar v Sun Alliance* [1978] Q.B. 383: insurer not liable to pay for loss of goods smuggled into this country; liability for loss of *other* goods covered by the policies seems not to have been disputed; contrast *Euro-Diam Ltd v Bathurst* [1990] Q.B. 1, below, p.511.

[98] *White v British Empire, etc. Assurance Co* (1868) L.R. 7 Eq. 394; *Charlton v Fisher* [2001] EWCA Civ 112; [2002] Q.B. 518, at [13].

[99] [1938] A.C. 586 at 595; *Reeves v Commissioner of Police of the Metropolis* [2000] 1 A.C. 360 at 388 (*per* Lord Hobhouse, dissenting).

[1] See below, p.887.

[2] [1957] 1 Q.B. 267, above, p.429.

[3] For an exception, see Courts and Legal Services Act 1990, s2.58 and 58A, above, p.431.

[4] Criminal Law Act 1967, s.14(2), above, p.431.

public policy. Thus a contract to do a homosexual act which was formerly, but is no longer,[5] criminal would probably be regarded as illegal where it promoted sexual immorality,[6] and so fell within one of the established heads of contracts which are against public policy.[7] But where this is not the case it is submitted that contracts should not generally be regarded as contrary to public policy merely because they involve conduct which was formerly criminal. Thus it is submitted that a contract to render services in connection with a lawful abortion is valid even though it would have been a contract to commit a crime before the Abortion Act 1967. Similarly it is submitted that the reasoning of *Beresford's* case is obsolete now that suicide is no longer a crime.[8]

The effect of this second kind of change in the law on contracts already in existence when the law was changed is more problematical. Changes in the law made after action brought are generally disregarded[9] but there seems to be no authority on the effect of changes in the law between the making of the contract and the commencement of the action. One possible view is that the validity of the contract must be determined, once for all, when it is made. But it is submitted that, so long as the act in question is lawful *when it is done*, no useful purpose is served by holding the contract invalid. The statute may itself solve the problem by specifying whether, and if so to what extent, the change in the law has retrospective effect.

2. Contracts Contrary to Public Policy: in General[10]

A contract which does not involve the commission of a legal wrong may be illegal because its tendency is to bring about a state of affairs of which the law disapproves on grounds of public policy. A contract is illegal for this reason only if its harmful tendency is clear, that is, if injury to the public is its probable and not merely its possible consequence.[11]

Such contracts are often called "illegal".[12] It is sometimes said that they are only "void" or "unenforceable"[13]; but these statements only emphasise that no specific legal wrong is involved. So long as this point is borne in mind, no harm is done by using the traditional terminology in which these contracts are "illegal".[14]

(1) Agreements by married persons to marry

An agreement to marry was formerly regarded as a contract, the breach of which gave rise to an action for damages. It was, however, thought to be against public policy to allow such actions to be brought on a promise by a married person to marry. Such a promise might be one to commit bigamy, but even where this was not the case the promise was illegal. Thus in *Spiers v Hunt*[15] a promise by a man to marry the promisee after his wife's

---

[5] Sexual Offences Act 1967; as amended by Sexual Offences (Amendment) Act 2000, s.1.

[6] *cf.*, in criminal law, *R. v Ford* [1977] 1 W.L.R. 1083.

[7] See below, p.444; but *cf.* also below, p.445 (stable relationships not contrary to public policy).

[8] Suicide Act 1961; *cf. Gray v Barr* [1971] 2 Q.B. 544, 582. In practice, insurers may pay in such circumstances: see *Foskett v McKeon* [2001] 1 A.C. 102.

[9] *Hitchcock v Way* (1837) 6 A. & E. 943.

[10] Lloyd, *Public Policy*; Winfield, 42 Harv.L.R. 76.

[11] *Fender v St John Mildmay* [1938] A.C. 1, 13; *cf. Multiservice Bookbinding Ltd v Marden* [1979] Ch. 84 at 104.

[12] *e.g. Hermann v Charlesworth* [1905] 2 K.B. 123 at 136; *McEllistrim's Case* [1919] A.C. 548 at 571; *cf.* Criminal Law Act 1967, s.14(2) ("contrary to public policy or otherwise illegal").

[13] *e.g. Bennett v Bennett* [1952] 1 K.B. 249 at 260; *Pao On v Lau Yiu Long* [1980] A.C. 614 at 634–635. *O'Sullivan v Management Agency & Music Ltd* [1985] Q.B. 428 at 447, 448, 469; *Watson v Prager* [1991] 1 W.L.R. 726 at 742.

[14] *cf. Mogul SS Co Ltd v McGregor Gow & Co* [1892] A.C. 25 at 46.

[15] [1908] 1 K.B. 720; *Wilson v Carnley* [1908] 1 K.B. 729.

death was held to be illegal as it had a tendency to break up the marriage, to encourage sexual immorality and even to lead to crime. These arguments are far from convincing and in *Fender v St John Mildmay*[16] the House of Lords held that they did not apply where the promise was made by a married man after he had obtained a decree nisi of divorce. But the promise was against public policy where, when it was made, a divorce (which later took place) was merely contemplated,[17] and also where the promisor believed that he was entitled to have his marriage annulled because of his wife's impotence.[18]

Actions for breach of promise of marriage were abolished by s.1 of the Law Reform (Miscellaneous Provisions) Act 1970,[19] so that the cases just discussed are, strictly speaking, obsolete. However, s.2 of the Act provides that "where an agreement to marry is terminated" the formerly engaged couple is to be treated for the purpose of certain rights[20] in, and disputes about, property as if they had been married. Difficult problems with regard to rights in property can obviously arise when an ex-fiancée makes a claim under s.2 against a man who, when he promised to marry her, was already married to someone else. It has been held that a party to an agreement to marry which is later brought to an end can take the benefit of s.2 even though that party was already married and so before the Act could not have claimed damages for breach of the promise.[21] It seems, *a fortiori*, to follow that the other (unmarried) party to the dissolved engagement should also be entitled to rely on the section. In such a case care must, however, be taken to safeguard the rights of the other party to the marriage: *e.g.* where the property in question was a house in which a man had lived first with his wife and then with a fiancée from whom he had later parted.[22]

Under the old law, a promisee who did not know that the promisor was married could take advantage of the general rule allowing innocent parties in certain cases to sue on illegal contracts[23] and so recover damages for breach of promise of marriage.[24] Clearly, this cause of action has been abolished by the 1970 Act. But it was also held before the Act that a woman who had innocently gone through a ceremony of marriage with a man who, unknown to her, was married, could, after his death, recover damages from his estate for breach of an implied warranty that he was single.[25] The 1970 Act makes special provision for this situation by giving the innocent party certain rights against the other party's estate.[26] It does not in terms abolish the action for breach of the implied warranty, and it is arguable that such an action could still be brought by an innocent promisee.[27] But the implied warranty is based on the assumption that, if the promisor had been single, the promise would have been actionable. In destroying this assumption,

---

[16] [1938] A.C. 1.
[17] *Skipp v Kelly* (1926) 42 T.L.R. 258.
[18] See *Siveyer v Allison* [1935] 2 K.B. 403.
[19] Cretney, 33 M.L.R. 534.
[20] Not all: *Mossop v Mossop* [1989] Fam. 77.
[21] *Shaw v Fitzgerald* [1992] 1 FLR 357.
[22] *cf.* Family Law Act 1996 s.33(1)(b)(i) permitting the court to make an order relating to a "matrimonial home" in favour of an "associated" person; persons are "associated" if "they have agreed to marry one another (whether or not that agreement has been terminated)" (s.62(3)(e)). The 1996 Act does not deal with the question whether the validity of the agreement is affected by the fact that one of the parties to it was married when it was made.
[23] See below, pp.484–487.
[24] *Wild v Harris* (1849) 7 C.B. 999; *Millward v Littlewood* (1850) 5 Ex. 775.
[25] *Shaw v Shaw* [1954] 2 Q.B. 429.
[26] s.6.
[27] *cf.* below, pp.487–488.

the Act has removed the substratum of the implied warranty; and it is submitted that no action could now be brought on it.[28]

(2) Agreements between spouses for future separation

It was at one time thought that all separation agreements between spouses were inconsistent with the duties arising out of marriage and therefore invalid. This rule still applies if the agreement is made while the spouses are living together, or before marriage. In *Brodie v Brodie*[29] a man felt obliged to marry a woman who shortly afterwards gave birth to a child of which he was the reputed father. An agreement made before the marriage that the parties should not live together was held invalid. The result of the rule is that the husband cannot, while he is living with his wife or before marriage, make a binding promise to provide for her in the event of a separation.[30] But an agreement regulating the rights of spouses who are already separated is valid[31] as it does not encourage any breach of marital duty; at most, it creates favourable conditions for the continuance of a breach which has already taken place. And where spouses who are separated become reconciled, they can validly provide for future separation: the law recognises that, unless they could do this, reconciliation would be less likely.[32]

(3) Agreements in contemplation of divorce

At common law, an arrangement or agreement between parties to divorce proceedings (about such matters as the wife's maintenance) was invalid if it was made with a corrupt intention, for example, if it amounted to a bribe to institute, or carry on, the proceedings,[33] or to a conspiracy to deceive the court. But it was valid if it was an honest attempt to minimise the difficulties which had arisen between the parties.[34] The law on this topic was formerly influenced by the rule that collusion was a bar to divorce; but the abolition of this rule "completely alters the public policy on this point",[35] so that an agreement is no longer invalid merely because it is collusive.[36]

(4) Agreements inconsistent with parental responsibility

At common law a father had the custody of his legitimate child and a contract by which he purported to assign that custody to any person was contrary to public policy as it was "repugnant entirely to his parental duty".[37] By statute, both parents have "parental

---

[28] For a dispute on this point, see Thomson, (1971) 87 L.Q.R. 159; L.C.B.G., *ibid.* 314.

[29] [1917] P.271; *cf. Scott v Scott* [1959] P.103n. (*tamquam sororem* agreement before marriage invalid); *N v N* [1999] F.L.R. 745 (antenuptial agreement to submit marital disputes to arbitration invalid); there is no reference to the rule stated in the text above in *Uddin v Ahmed* [2000] EWCA Civ 204; [2001] 3 F.C.R. 300, where the claim was dismissed on other grounds: below, pp.582, 587.

[30] The rule does not apply where the marriage is a polygamous one contracted abroad, under which the husband can divorce the wife at will: see *Shahnaz v Rizwan* [1965] 1 Q.B. 390. The "arrangements for the future" dealt with by Family Law Act 1996, s.9 are arrangements sanctioned by court order as opposed to arrangements made by private agreement. *cf.* also *Xydhias v Xydhias* [1999] 2 All E.R. 386.

[31] *Wilson v Wilson* (1848) 1 H.L.C. 538; *Hart v Hart* (1881) 18 Ch.D. 670.

[32] *Harrison v Harrison* [1910] 1 K.B. 35; *Macmahon v Macmahon* [1913] 1 I.R. 428.

[33] *Hope v Hope* (1857) 8 D.M. & G. 731; *Churchward v Churchward* [1895] P. 7.

[34] *Scott v Scott* [1913] P. 52.

[35] *Sutton v Sutton* [1984] Ch. 184, 194; *cf. N v N* [1992] 1 F.L.R. 266.

[36] When Pt II of the Family Law Act 1996 is brought into force, the court will be able to make a divorce order or a judicial separation order only if certain "requirements about the parties' arrangements for the future" (s.3(1)(c)) are satisfied; and one way of satisfying these requirements will be to produce to the court "a negotiated agreement [between the parties] as to their financial arrangements" (s.9(2)(b)).

[37] *Vansittart v Vansittart* (1858) D. & J. 249, 259; *Walrond v Walrond* (1858) Johns 18; *cf. Cole v Gower* (1805) 6 East 110. *cf.* also Adoption Act 1976, ss.57, 57A and 58, as amended by Children Act 1989, ss.88(1) and 108(7) (prohibition of advertisements and regulation of payments in connection with adoption).

responsibility"[38] for their child if they were married to each other at the time of the child's birth; if they were not, the mother has parental responsibility.[39] In the latter case, the parents may enter into a "parental responsibility agreement" providing for the father to have parental responsibility for the child[40]; but freedom of contract in making such an agreement, and in bringing it to an end, is severely restricted so as to protect the interests of the child.[41] The effect of such an agreement seems to be that parental responsibility is vested in both parents: the mother does not lose such responsibility since "a person who has parental responsibility for a child may not surrender or transfer such responsibility to another".[42] This statutory provision resembles the common law principle stated above and seems to be based on similar grounds of public policy. The person with parental responsibility may "arrange for some or all of it to be met by one or more persons acting on his behalf".[43] In such a case the responsibility is not transferred but vicariously performed.[44]

(5) Agreements in restraint of marriage

A contract may be invalid on the ground that it unjustifiably restricts a person's freedom to marry. This is, for example, true of a promise by a widow to pay £100 if she remarries,[45] and of a promise not to marry anyone except a specified person (not amounting to a promise to marry that person).[46] It may be that such promises are valid if they are limited in duration or otherwise reasonable: e.g. if a limited restraint is imposed for the sake of a person's health or (conceivably) of his moral well-being.[47] It is also possible that a promise not to marry anyone except a member of a fairly large group (for example, some religious denomination) might be valid.

The above cases concern actual promises not to marry, or to pay a sum of money on marriage. It seems that a contract is not invalid merely because it may in some other way deter one of the parties from marrying. Thus a promise to pay an allowance, or to permit a person to occupy a house, until the promisee's marriage, is valid.[48] Such promises may tend to discourage marriage, but they do not impose any contractual liability on a person as a result of marriage.[49]

(6) Marriage brokage contracts[50]

A marriage brokage contract is one by which a person promises in return for a money consideration to procure the marriage of another. Until the eighteenth century such contracts were valid at common law, thus making it possible for servants of young

---

[38] As defined by Children Act 1989, s.3.
[39] ibid. s.2(1); and see s.2(4), abolishing the former common law rule.
[40] ibid. s.4(1)(b).
[41] ibid. ss.4(1) and (3), 1(1).
[42] ibid. s.2(9).
[43] ibid. cf. also Child Support Act 1991, s.9, providing for the legal effects of certain maintenance agreements in favour of children.
[44] cf. below, pp.758–759.
[45] Baker v White (1690) 2 Vern. 215; cf. Hartley v Rice (1808) 10 East 22.
[46] Lowe v Peers (1768) 2 Burr. 2225.
[47] cf. Denny v Denny [1919] 1 K.B. 583; below, p.452.
[48] Gibson v Dickie (1815) 3 M. & S. 463; the same point was assumed in Thomas v Thomas (1842) 2 Q.B. 851.
[49] Contrast the position in the restraint of trade cases, below, pp.463–464. It is perhaps thought that stipulations which deter persons from trading are more likely to prejudice the public than those which deter them from marrying.
[50] Powell, 6 C.L.P. 254.

heiresses to obtain payment for assisting their charges to elope with fortune-hunters.[51] Equity therefore prevented the enforcement of these contracts[52]; and this equitable principle is not restricted to contracts to procure a marriage between one of the contracting parties and a *particular* third person. Thus a contract by which a marriage bureau simply undertakes to make efforts to find a spouse for a client has been held invalid, because it involved "the introduction of the consideration of a money payment into that which should be free from any such taint".[53] The harmful tendencies of such contracts seem to be no greater than those of contracts between "computer dating" agencies and their clients; and it has not been suggested that such contracts are contrary to public policy.

(7) Contracts promoting sexual immorality

A contract may be illegal if its object is sexually immoral. The common law originally applied this principle to all cases in which a contract could be said to promote such an object. But a distinction is now drawn between contracts with purely meretricious purposes and those which are intended to regulate stable extra-marital relationships.

(a) MERETRICIOUS PURPOSES. A promise by a man to pay a woman money if she will become his mistress is illegal.[54] A promise to pay money to a woman with whom the promisor had illicitly cohabited in the past is not contrary to public policy since it does not *promote* immorality. It is simply void because the consideration for it is past,[55] and it will be valid if made in a deed.[56] The validity of a promise in a deed made *during* cohabitation depends on its purpose. If it is simply a gift, or voluntary bond, it is as valid as one given after cohabitation.[57] But if its object is to secure the continuance of cohabitation, it is illegal.[58] A bond given after cohabitation would also be invalid if it were merely given to secure the performance of a promise of payment made before cohabitation. A promise to pay must be distinguished from a completed gift. In *Ayerst v Jenkins*[59] a man settled property on a woman with whom he was cohabiting. A claim by his personal representatives to have the settlement set aside failed as "the voluntary gift of part of his own property by one *particeps criminis* to another is in itself neither fraudulent nor prohibited by law".[60]

A contract is also illegal if it indirectly promotes sexual immorality. Thus in *Pearce v Brooks*[61] a contract to hire out a brougham to a prostitute for the purposes of her profession was held to be illegal. The same would be true of a contract of employment

---

[51] *e.g. Goldsmith v Bruning* (1700) 1 Eq.Ca.Abr. 89, pl. 4.

[52] *Cole v Gibson* (1750) 1 Ves.Sen. 503 at 506.

[53] *Hermann v Charlesworth* [1905] 2 K.B. 123 at 130; below, p.504.

[54] *Franco v Bolton* (1797) 3 Ves. 368; *Benyon v Nettlefold* (1850) 3 Mac. & G. 94.

[55] *Beaumont v Reeve* (1846) 8 Q.B. 483; *Binnington v Wallis* (1821) 4 B. & Ald. 650 suggests that such a promise is binding if made by a man who was a seducer, but this is based on the wide view of the "moral obligation" theory of consideration, which no longer prevails: above, p.75 and see *Jennings v Brown* (1842) 9 M. & W. 496, 501.

[56] *Annadale v Harris* (1727) 2 P.Wms. 432; *affirmed* 1 Bro.P.C. 250; *Turner v Vaughan* (1767) 2 Wils.K.B. 339; *Knye v Moore* (1822) 1 S. & S. 61. It is stressed in some of the old cases that the promisor was the seducer and that the payment was promised as "*praemium pudicitiae.*" Thus it was doubtful whether the rule applied in favour of a common prostitute: *Bainham v Manning* (1691) 2 Vern. 242; *Whaley v Norton* (1687) 1 Vern. 483; *contra, Hill v Spencer* (1767) Amb. 641, 836.

[57] *Gray v Mathias* (1800) 5 Ves. 286; *Hall v Palmer* (1844) 3 Hare 532.

[58] *The Lady Cox's Case* (1734) 3 P.Wms. 339; *Walker v Perkins* (1764) 3 Burr. 1568.

[59] (1873) L.R. 16 Eq. 275.

[60] *ibid.* at 283.

[61] (1866) L.R. 1 Ex. 213; *cf. Upfill v Wright* [1911] 1 K.B. 506, a case viewed with some scepticism in *Heglibiston Establishment v Heyman* (1977) 36 P. & C.R. 351.

by which the employee undertook to procure prostitutes for the employer's clients.[62] On the other hand, a contract to let a room to a prostitute who practises her profession elsewhere is valid "because persons of that description must have a place to lay their heads".[63] In the somewhat questionable case of *Lloyd v Johnson*[64] a contract to wash a prostitute's linen was held valid even though the linen included a quantity of gentlemen's nightcaps.

In the cases on this subject "immorality" always means extra-marital sexual intercourse. A contract might promote some other form of activity that could be described as immoral and sexual. For example, a contract might be made to publish an indecent book whose publication did not amount to a crime. Such a contract might formerly have been regarded as invalid on account of its "grossly immoral" tendency.[65] "But at the present day the difficulty is to identify what sexual conduct is to be treated as grossly immoral"[66]; so that it is less likely that such a contract would now be struck down on this ground.

(b) STABLE RELATIONSHIPS. The traditional common law approach to immoral contracts no longer applies to persons live together in a common household as husband and wife without being married. It has for example been held that a licence under which such a couple occupied furnished accommodation was not contrary to public policy.[67] The law also recognises that legal effects can flow from agreements between such persons with respect to the house in which they live. Where the house is owned by one of them, the agreement can confer legally enforceable rights on the other, such as a contractual licence to remain there,[68] or a share in the value of the house in respect of the contribution made by the other to its acquisition, maintenance or improvement.[69] The opening of a bank account by one party to such a relationship with funds intended to belong to both jointly has been held (on proof of the appropriate intention) to amount to a declaration of trust in favour of the other.[70] It seems, although the point has not yet been decided in England, that an express contract between such persons to "pool" their earnings and acquisitions would not be regarded as contrary to public policy.[71] And "when an illegitimate child has been born, there is certainly nothing contrary to public

---

[62] See *Coral Leisure Group v Barnett* [1981] I.C.R. 503 at 508 (where no such undertaking had, on the facts, been established); *cf. The Siben* [1996] 1 Lloyd's Rep. 35 at 62; *R v Registrar of Companies, Ex p. Attorney-General* [1991] B.C.L.C. 476 (company formed "to carry on the business of prostitution" ordered to be struck off the register).

[63] *Appleton v Campbell* (1826) 2 C. & P. 347; *cf. Bowry v Bennett* (1808) 1 Camp. 348.

[64] (1798) 1 B. & P. 340.

[65] *cf. Glyn v Weston Feature Film Co* [1916] 1 Ch. 261 (refusal to protect copyright in immoral book) approved in *Attorney-General v Guardian Newspapers (No.2)* [1990] A.C. 109 at 262, 276 (refusal to protect copyright in book written in breach of fiduciary duty); contrast *ZYX Music GmbH v King* [1995] 3 All E.R. 1 at 10; *A v B* [2000] E.M.L.R. 1007.

[66] *Stephens v Avery* [1988] Ch. 449 at 453 (protection of confidential information concerning lesbian relationship); *Armhouse Lee Ltd v Chappel, The Times*, August 7, 1996 (contract to advertise telephone sex lines held enforceable).

[67] *Somma v Hazlehurst* [1979] 1 W.L.R. 1014 (disapproved on another point in *Street v Mountford* [1985] A.C. 809); *cf.* also *Watson v Lucas* [1980] 1 W.L.R. 1493.

[68] *Tanner v Tanner* [1975] 1 W.L.R. 1346; *Chandler v Kerley* [1978] 1 W.L.R. 693; *Tanner v Clerical Medical & General Life Insurance Society* [1992] 1 FLR 262 (rights to proceeds of endowment mortgage policy). *cf. Fitzpatrick v Sterling Housing Association* [2001] 1 A.C. 27 (homosexual partner part of "family" for purposes of Rent Act 1977); and see the court's power under Family Law Act 1996, ss.36 and 38 to exclude a "cohabitant" (as defined by s.62(1)(a)) from a dwelling-house.

[69] *Eves v Eves* [1975] 1 W.L.R. 1338.

[70] *Paul v Constance* [1977] 1 W.L.R. 527.

[71] *Marvin v Marvin* 557 P.2d 106 (1976); and see *The Times*, August 14, 1981. *cf. Latham v Latham* 547 P.2d 144 (1975).

policy in the parents coming to an agreement which they intend to be binding in law, for the maintenance of the child and mother".[72]

These illustrations[73] show that the law now recognises that "unmarried cohabitation, whether heterosexual or homosexual, is widespread"[74]; and they suggest that the old common law rule governing immoral contracts will in future be confined to meretricious relationships (of whatever sexual orientation). Where domestic arrangements between parties to the present group of stable relationships satisfy the requirement of contractual intention,[75] they will no longer be struck down on grounds of public policy.[76]

(8) Contracts interfering with the course of justice

A contract may be illegal because the mere making of it amounts to a conspiracy to pervert the course of justice: *e.g.* where a person promises another money for giving false evidence on his behalf in criminal proceedings[77] or where two men agree to bribe a prosecution witness to withdraw a charge of rape.[78] A contract may also (even though it does not amount to a criminal conspiracy) be illegal if its object is to interfere with the course of public justice. Before the distinction between felonies and misdemeanours was abolished, a contract to stifle a prosecution for a misdemeanour was not itself an offence but such contracts were often held illegal. Thus contracts to stifle prosecutions for perjury, riot, assault on a police officer, interfering with a public road, and obtaining by false pretences were held illegal.[79] But this rule was not applied where the misdemeanour was said to be of a "private" nature. Thus in *McGregor v McGregor*[80] it was held that a husband and wife who had taken out cross-summonses for assault against each other could validly compromise them in a separation agreement. It has similarly been held that a prosecution for trade-mark offences could be compromised by agreement between the owner and the offender[81]; and it has been said that the same principle applies to criminal libel.[82]

The old cases must now be read in the light of the abolition of the distinction between felonies and misdemeanours and of the creation of the offence of concealing an arrestable offence.[83] A person does not, however, commit this offence if he withholds information which may lead to the conviction of the offender in consideration only of the making good of the loss or injury caused by the offence[84]; and it is doubtful whether an agreement to this effect should now be held illegal.[85] One view is that the agreement may still be illegal, even though it does not itself amount to an offence, for this was precisely

---

[72] *Horrocks v Forray* [1976] 1 W.L.R. 230 at 239.

[73] *cf.* also below, p.711; *Heglibiston Establishment v Heyman* (1977) 36 P. & C.R. 351.

[74] *Barclays Bank plc v O'Brien* [1994] 1 A.C. 180 at 198; *Royal Bank of Scotland v Etridge (No.2)* [2001] UKHL 44; [2002] 2 A.C. 773, at [47].

[75] See above, p.165.

[76] Devlin, 39 M.L.R. 1 at 12; Dwyer, 93 L.Q.R. 386.

[77] *R. v Andrews* [1973] Q.B. 422.

[78] *R. v Panayiotou* [1973] 3 All E.R. 112; *cf. R. v Ali* [1993] Crim.L.R. 396.

[79] *Collins v Blantern* (1767) 2 Wils.K.B. 341; *Keir v Leeman* (1846) 9 Q.B. 371; *Windhill Local Board of Health v Vint* (1890) 45 Ch.D. 351; *Clubb v Huston* (1865) 18 C.B.(N.S.) 414 (embezzlement); *cf. Howard v Odham's Press Ltd* [1938] 1 K.B. 42 (contract not to disclose confession of fraud); and *cf.* below, p.455, n.89. Contracts to stifle a prosecution for a felony were sometimes held illegal on this ground (*e.g. Rawlings v Coal Consumers' Association* (1874) 43 L.J.M.C. 111; *Whitmore v Farley* (1881) 45 L.T. 99), but were also illegal as they formerly amounted to compounding.

[80] (1888) 21 Q.B.D. 424.

[81] *Fisher & Co v Apollinaris Co* (1875) L.R. 10 Ch.App. 297.

[82] *ibid.*, at 303.

[83] Criminal Law Act 1967, ss.1, 5(1), above, p.431.

[84] Criminal Law Act 1967, s.5(1).

[85] Hudson, 43 M.L.R. 532.

the position under the old law where an agreement was made to stifle a prosecution for a misdemeanour. A second view is that, where the only consideration is the making good of the loss, no public interest is harmed by upholding the agreement; and this view can be supported by reference to the old cases concerning misdemeanours of a "private" nature. A third view is that the legality of an agreement to stifle a prosecution (not amounting to a conspiracy to pervert the course of justice or to the offence of concealing an arrestable offence) should depend on the question whether it was in the public interest that the prosecution should be brought; and it is submitted that this is the best view.[86]

The principle of public policy is not confined to contracts to stifle a prosecution: thus a contract to indemnify a surety in criminal proceedings is illegal.[87] Nor is the principle restricted to contracts affecting criminal proceedings. Thus agreements to obstruct bankruptcy proceedings[88] and corrupt agreements relating to matrimonial proceedings[89] are illegal. It has also been said that a contract by which a witness promised one party to a civil dispute not to give evidence for the other would be contrary to public policy.[90] On the other hand, it has been held not to be contrary to public policy for one party to an agreement to undertake that he would not oppose the other's application for planning applications and not give evidence in support of a compulsory purchase order relating to the land in question.[91] An ordinary civil claim can, of course, be validly compromised, even though the facts giving rise to the claim also amount to a crime. But in such a case an agreement to abandon "any legal proceedings" may be illegal, as this phrase is wide enough to refer to possible civil *and* criminal proceedings.[92]

(9) Contracts purporting to oust the jurisdiction of the courts

A contract is at common law contrary to public policy if it purports to deprive the courts of a jurisdiction which they would otherwise have. For example, a clause in an insurance policy which provides that the policy is in certain events to become "incontestable"[93] does not prevent the court from deciding whether the assured had any insurable interest.[94] Such agreements are contrary to public policy because they would, if valid, make it possible to evade or contravene many peremptory rules of law. It follows that they are invalid only so far as they purport to exclude the jurisdiction of the courts on a point of *law*. An agreement is not invalid to the extent that it gives a non-judicial body power to make final and binding decisions on questions of *fact*.[95] Such a provision does not, moreover, normally[96] rule out the possibility of a legal challenge to the decision on the

---

[86] It might be relevant that the offence was a "serious arrestable offence" as defined by Police and Criminal Evidence Act 1984, s.116 (though the Act does not use the definition for this purpose).

[87] *Herman v Jeuchner* (1885) 15 Q.B.D. 561. It is now an offence to make such an agreement: Bail Act 1976, s.9 (as amended by Criminal Justice and Public Order Act 1994, s.44 and Sch.4, para.25).

[88] *Elliott v Richardson* (1870) L.R. 5 C.P. 744; *cf. Murray v Reeves* (1828) 8 B. & C. 421; *Hall v Dyson* (1852) 17 Q.B. 785; *Kearley v Thomson* (1890) 24 Q.B.D. 742; *Coppock v Bower* (1838) 4 M. & W. 361 (agreement to abandon election petition on ground of bribery illegal); *Norman v Cole* (1800) 3 Esp. 253 (money paid for help in procuring a pardon).

[89] See above, p.442.

[90] *Harmony Shipping Co SA v Saudi Europe Line Ltd* [1979] 1 W.L.R. 1380 at 1386.

[91] *Fulham Football Club Ltd v Cabra Estates* (1992) 56 P. & C.R. 284.

[92] *Lound v Grimwade* (1888) 39 Ch.D. 605.

[93] *Anctil v Manufacturers' Life Insurance Co* [1899] A.C. 604.

[94] But such clauses are effective to prevent the insurer from contesting certain matters of *fact*, *e.g.* that statements in the proposal form were true: *cf.* below at n.95.

[95] *The Glacier Bay.* [1996] 1 Lloyd's Rep. 370; and see below p.449 n.34.

[96] For a common law exception, see below p.450 at n.36.

ground of "unfairness, bad faith or perversity",[97] so that the provision does not wholly exclude the jurisdiction of the courts even on questions of fact.

(a) ILLUSTRATIONS. The rule against allowing parties by contract to oust the jurisdiction of the courts is further illustrated by the following cases:

(i) *Agreements for maintenance.* A husband may, as part of a separation agreement or in the course of matrimonial proceedings, promise to pay his wife an allowance in return for the wife's promise not to apply to the court for maintenance. In *Hyman v Hyman*[98] the House of Lords held that such an agreement did not prevent the wife from applying to the court for maintenance. The contract was illegal, since "The wife's right to future maintenance is a matter of public concern which she cannot barter away".[99] But this rule had one unfortunate result: if the husband failed to pay the promised allowance, the wife could not sue him for it, since a promise cannot be enforced if the sole or main consideration for it is illegal.[1] By statute, the wife can, if such an agreement is in writing, sue the husband for the promised allowance, in spite of the fact that her own promise not to apply to the court is void.[2]

(ii) *Arbitration clauses.* There is no doubt about the validity of such clauses if they merely provide that the parties are to resort to arbitration before going to court. In *Scott v Avery*[3] a clause of this kind was upheld as it did not purport to oust the jurisdiction of the court,[4] but simply to lay down at what stage the cause of action arose upon which that jurisdiction might be exercised. At common law such a clause did not prevent the courts from nevertheless determining the dispute, though the party who disregarded the clause and in breach of it brought an action was liable in damages.[5] The courts have, however, an inherent jurisdiction to stay an action brought in breach of an agreement to decide disputes in some way other than by bringing an action.[6] Moreover, the Arbitration Act 1996 provides that, where an arbitration agreement is in writing,[7] the court must stay an action brought in breach of the agreement[8] unless the agreement is "null and void, inoperative or incapable of being performed". Where the agreement is made

---

[97] *The Glacier Bay*, above, at 379.

[98] [1929] A.C. 601. The principle laid down in this case has survived the abolition of collusion as a bar to divorce: *cf. Dean v Dean* [1978] Fam. 161 at 167.

[99] [1929] A.C. 601 at 629. But such an agreement is not contrary to public policy if it only ousts the jurisdiction of a foreign court: *Addison v Brown* [1954] 1 W.L.R. 779; nor if it is sanctioned by order of the court: *L v L* [1962] P. 101; *Minton v Minton* [1979] A.C. 593. The court can, however, later increase periodical payments due to the wife under such an agreement: *Wright v Wright* [1970] 1 W.L.R. 1219; *Jessel v Jessel* [1979] 1 W.L.R. 1148. The court can also take the wife's promise into account when exercising its discretion whether to make an award in her favour: *Edgar v Edgar* [1980] 1 W.L.R. 1410.

[1] *Bennett v Bennett* [1952] 1 K.B. 249; *aliter* if only a subsidiary part of the consideration was illegal: *Goodinson v Goodinson* [1954] 2 Q.B. 118; *cf. Sutton v Sutton* [1984] Ch. 184 (where *each* party promised not to invoke the jurisdiction of the court); and see below, p.505.

[2] Matrimonial Causes Act 1973, s.34. For a dispute on this point, see Dew, 56 Law Soc. Gaz. 365; J. H. H., 101 S.J. 73; 78 *Law Notes* 177; Treitel, 77 L.Q.R. 93–95. In *Sutton v Sutton*, above, the agreement was oral, so that s.34 did not apply. Under the Child Support Act 1991, s.9 (as amended by Child Support Act 1995, s.18) similar rules apply to certain maintenance agreements in respect of children.

[3] (1855) 5 H.L.C. 811; *cf. Atlantic Shipping & Trading Co Ltd v Louis Dreyfus & Co* [1922] 2 A.C. 250; *Persson v London County Buses* [1974] 1 W.L.R. 569.

[4] See *Halifax Financial Services v Intuitive Systems Ltd* [1999] 1 All E.R. (Comm) 303 at 310, where the clause in question was a "dispute resolution" clause which failed for lack of certainty: above, p.60.

[5] *Doleman & Sons v Ossett Corporation* [1912] 3 K.B. 257 at 267.

[6] *Channel Tunnel Group Ltd v Balfour Beatty Construction Ltd* [1993] A.C. 334; *cf. Cott UK Ltd v F E Barber Ltd* [1997] 3 All E.R. 540, and *T&N Ltd v Sun Alliance plc* [2002] EWHC 2420, C.L.C. 1342 where a stay was refused.

[7] For this requirement, see s.5(1).

[8] s.9(4); *Halki Shipping Corp v Sopex Oils Ltd* [1998] 1 W.L.R. 726; this rule cannot be excluded by contract: see s.4 and Sch.1.

between a party acting in the course of a business and a consumer, it does not bind the consumer if the amount claimed is less than £5,000[9]; but it binds the other party.

The fact that an arbitration clause excluded the jurisdiction of the court might at common law make the clause invalid on one of two grounds. First, such a clause was invalid to the extent that it purported to deprive the parties of the right to go to court to sue on a completed cause of action, or to exclude the power granted to the courts by statute to control the decisions of arbitrators on points of law.[10] This rule was justified by the argument that, if such a clause were valid, an arbitrator who decided a dispute on principles at variance with the general law would be subject to no control at all[11]; and this would be particularly undesirable if he made an award enforcing a wholly illegal agreement.[12] A substantially similar risk could arise where the clause, though not in terms restricting the parties' right to ask the court to control the arbitrator's decision, laid down standards which made such control nugatory. This is a second ground of invalidity at common law, so that "a clause which purported to free arbitrators to decide without regard to law and according, for example, to their own notions of what would be fair would not be a valid arbitration clause".[13] But the parties can validly specify standards which, at least to some extent, guard against the risk of invalidity on this ground: it is, for example, not contrary to public policy to enforce an arbitration award based on "internationally accepted principles of law governing contractual relations".[14] An arbitration clause can also free arbitrators from the need to apply strict legal rules of construction, *e.g.* by empowering them to interpret a contract "as an honourable engagement rather than in accordance with a literal interpretation of the language".[15] And the courts can to some extent save an arbitration clause which transgresses such limits by striking out such parts of the clause as go "further than the law permits in freeing arbitrators from strict rules of law".[16] The Arbitration Act 1996 provides more generally that "the parties should be free to agree how their disputes are to be resolved",[17] but this general principle is expressly made "subject to such safeguards as are necessary in the public interest".[18] These words seem to leave it open to the courts to continue to apply standards of public policy to such agreements. The Act also provides that the court may refuse to recognise or enforce an arbitral award on grounds of public policy,[19] and this provision could be applied where such an award purported to enforce an illegal agreement.

The invalidity, at common law, of arbitration clauses which purported to exclude the powers of the court to control an arbitrator's decision on points of law was open to a

---

[9] s.91; Arbitration Agreements (Specified Amounts) Order 1999 (SI 1999/2167).

[10] *Czarnikow v Roth Schmidt & Co* [1922] 2 K.B. 478. For a different approach in New Zealand, see *CBI NZ Ltd v Badger Chiyoda* [1989] N.Z.L.R. 669.

[11] Clauses making an arbitrator's decision "final" do not have this effect: see *Ford v Clarkson's Holidays Ltd* [1971] 1 W.L.R. 1412; *P & M Kaye v Hosier & Dickinson Ltd* [1972] 1 W.L.R. 146; *cf. Jones v Sherwood Computer Services* [1992] 1 W.L.R. 227 ("final and conclusive" valuation reviewable for error of law).

[12] *cf. Soleimany v Soleimany* [1999] Q.B. 785 at 799. See now below, after n.20.

[13] *Home and Overseas Insurance Co Ltd v Mentor Insurance Co (UK) Ltd* [1989] 1 Lloyd's Rep. 473 at 485; and see below, n.16.

[14] *Deutsche Schachtbau-und Tiefbohrgesellschaft mbH v Ras Al Khaimah National Oil Co* [1990] 1 A.C. 295 at 315 (reversed on other grounds *ibid.* pp.329 *et seq.*).

[15] *Overseas Union Insurance Ltd v AA Mutual International Insurance Ltd* [1988] 2 Lloyd's Rep. 63; *Home and Overseas Insurance Co Ltd v Mentor Insurance Co (UK) Ltd*, above, n.13.

[16] *Home Insurance Co v Administrata Asigurarilor* [1983] 2 Lloyd's Rep. 674 at 677.

[17] s.1(b).

[18] *ibid.*

[19] s.81(1)(c); *cf.* above after n.11.

practical objection: the resulting impossibility of excluding judicial control tended to erode the virtues of speed and cheapness that were supposed to be characteristics of arbitration as a method of settling disputes. The Arbitration Act 1996 therefore, while retaining a degree of judicial control over arbitration proceedings,[20] reduces the scope of such control in two important respects. First, the parties to a written arbitration agreement[21] can exclude such judicial control by agreement.[22] Secondly, the Act imposes strict limits on the scope of judicial control. This will generally be exercised by way of appeal to the court on a question of law.[23] Such an appeal can be brought either with the consent of the parties or with the leave of the court,[24] and such leave can be given only if a number of statutory requirements[25] are satisfied. The point of law must be one which substantially affects the rights of one or more of the parties and which the arbitral tribunal was asked to determine; the decision of that tribunal must *either* be "obviously wrong" *or* raise a question of "general public importance" and be "at least open to serious doubt;" and it must, in spite of the parties' agreement to resolve the dispute by arbitration be "just and proper for the court to determine the question". These requirements are based on (but go slightly beyond[25a]) tests which had been developed by the courts under earlier legislation.[26] The overriding consideration remains that stated in the course of this judicial development: *i.e.* whether the decision of the court "would add significantly to the clarity and certainty of English commercial law".[27] Thus the court is more likely to grant leave if the issue is as to the true construction of a standard form commercial contract in common use,[28] or if it raises an important general question of law,[29] than if it relates merely to the construction of a "one-off" contract specially drafted for a particular transaction.[30] A similar distinction has been drawn in relation to *events* giving rise to the dispute, or interfering with the performance of a contract. Thus leave is more likely to be given where the event is one that may affect many contracts (such as the hostilities in the Persian Gulf, preventing the movement of shipping there,[31] or an embargo on the export of some commodity from a major exporting country) than where the event is not likely to have this effect (*e.g.* where it is a strike that affects only the export of goods from a particular port).[32]

An arbitration agreement may, finally, be invalid for illegality at common law on grounds other than its tendency to exclude the jurisdiction of the courts. Such invalidity could arise by reason of the nature of the underlying transaction: for example, the court "would not recognise an agreement between highwayman to arbitrate their differences

---

[20] See below at n.23.
[21] Arbitration Act 1996 s.5(1).
[22] See the opening words of ss.45(1) and 69(1).
[23] s.69; under s.45 the court also has powers to determine preliminary questions of law, *i.e.* of the law of England and Wales: s.82(1); *Reliance Industries Ltd v Enron Oil & Gas Co* [2002] 1 All E.R. (Comm) 59.
[24] s.69(2).
[25] s.69(3).
[25a] *CMA CGM SA & Beteiligungs-Kommanditgesellschaft mbH & Co* [2002] EWCA Civ 1878, [2003] 1 All E.R. (Comm) 204.
[26] *The Nema* [1982] A.C. 724 and other cases; for full citations of these cases, see the 9th ed. of this book at pp.408–409.
[27] *The Nema*, above, at 743. For other grounds of public interest that may lead the court to give leave, see *Bulk Oil (Zug) AG v Sun International* [1984] 1 W.L.R. 147.
[28] *The Rio Sun* [1981] 2 Lloyd's Rep. 489; see also [1982] 1 Lloyd's Rep. 404.
[29] *The Alaskan Trader* [1983] 1 Lloyd's Rep. 315.
[30] *The Nema*, above, at 743.
[31] *The Wenjiang* [1982] 1 Lloyd's Rep. 128.
[32] As in *The Nema*, above.

any more than it would recognise the original agreement to split the proceeds"[33]; and even if an arbitrator made an award in such a case, the court would not enforce it.[34]

(iii) *Construction of rules of associations.* A clause in the rules of an association such as a trade union may purport to give to the committee of the association exclusive jurisdiction to construe the rules. But, as the construction of the rules is a question of law, it has been held that any attempt to deprive the courts of their jurisdiction over it is invalid.[35] By contrast, the jurisdiction of the Visitor of a University to decide matters governed by the "internal laws" of the University is at common law[36] exclusive, so that his decisions on points of this kind cannot be challenged in the ordinary courts.[37]

(b) SCOPE OF THE RULE. Contracts purporting to exclude the jurisdiction of the courts must be distinguished from promises in honour only.[38] A provision that a promise "shall not be enforced in any court" makes the promise legally unenforceable, but does not purport to oust the jurisdiction of the court to say so. Similar reasoning applies to the compromise of a genuine dispute as to legal rights. Such a compromise may vary or supersede the legal rights of the parties; but it does not prevent the courts from determining what those rights are. It is therefore not contrary to public policy[39]; and this is true even though the public can be said to have some interest in the dispute, *e.g.* because it relates to the performance of duties under a charitable trust.[40]

(10) Contracts to deceive public authorities

In *Alexander v Rayson*[41] a landlord let a service flat to the defendant for £1,200. Two documents were executed: in the first the defendant agreed to pay £450 for the flat and certain services; in the second she agreed to pay £750 for the same services, plus the use of a refrigerator. The landlord's object in splitting up the contract in this way was to defraud the rating authorities by showing them the first document only. The contract was therefore held to be illegal. A contract by which an employee gets an expense allowance grossly in excess of the expenses he actually incurs is similarly illegal as a fraud on the Revenue.[42] The same is true where part of the employee's actual pay is

---

[33] *Soleimany v Soleimany* [1999] Q.B. 785, 797; [1999] 3 All E.R. at 857; contrast *Westacre Investments Inc v Jugoimport-SDPR Holdings Co Ltd* [1999] 2 Lloyd's Rep. 65; [1999] 3 All E.R. 864; [2000] Q.B. 288 and *Omnium de Traitment et de Valorisation SA v Hilmarton Ltd* [1999] 2 Lloyd's Rep. 222 (contract not illegal by its proper law nor enforcement contrary to English public policy).

[34] *Soleimany v Soleimany*, above, at 799; and see Arbitration Act 1996, s.81(1)(c), above p.448 at n.19.

[35] *Lee v Showmen's Guild of Great Britain* [1952] 2 Q.B. 329; *Baker v Jones* [1954] 1 W.L.R. 1005; *cf. Edwards v Aberayron Insurance Soc Ltd* (1876) 1 Q.B.D. 563; *Re Davstone Estate Ltd's Leases* [1969] 2 Ch. 378; *Leigh v N.U.R.* [1970] Ch. 326; *Edwards v SOGAT* [1971] Ch. 354. There is no objection to leaving questions of *fact* to the final determination of a private tribunal: *Brown v Overbury* (1856) 11 Exch. 715; *Cipriani v Burnett* [1933] A.C. 83. *cf.*, in the law of trusts, *Re Tuck's ST* [1976] Ch. 99. See also the Trade Union and Labour Relations (Consolidation) Act 1992, s.63 (right of union members to go to court after six months).

[36] For a statutory exception, see Education Reform Act 1988, s.206; *Pearce v University of Aston* [1991] 2 All E.R. 461.

[37] *Thomas v University of Bradford* [1987] A.C. 795 (for subsequent proceedings before the Visitor, see *Thomas v University of Bradford* [1992] 1 All E.R. 964); *R. v Lord President of the Privy Council, Ex p. Page* [1993] A.C. 682. Contrast *Clark v University of Lincolnshire and Humberside* [2000] 1 W.L.R. 1985 (complaint by student at charterless university with no visitor about breach of university rules having contractual force to a limited extent open to adjudication in the courts).

[38] See above, p.164.

[39] See above, p.87. For compromise of a claim known by the claimant to be invalid, see above, p.88; below, p.480.

[40] *Bradshaw v University College of Wales* [1988] 1 W.L.R. 190.

[41] [1936] 1 K.B. 169; *cf. Palaniappa Chettiar v Arunasalam Chettiar* [1962] A.C. 294; *Mitsubishi Corp v Aristidis I Alafouzos* [1988] 1 Lloyd's Rep. 191.

[42] *Miller v Karlinski* (1945) 62 T.L.R. 85; *Napier v National Business Agency Ltd* [1951] 2 All E.R. 264; *cf. Hyland v J Barber (North West)* [1985] I.C.R. 861.

fraudulently concealed from the Revenue, with a view to evading tax.[43] But the contract is illegal only if the scheme that it furthers is a fraudulent one. Thus it is perfectly lawful for a contract of employment to provide that the employee is to receive a specified amount "free of tax", so long as the employer accounts to the revenue authorities for the tax due.[44] And where a seller sent out a false invoice with the intention of merely postponing the payment of VAT, it was held that this did not turn an originally lawful sale into an illegal contract, it having been found as a fact that the seller had acted without dishonest intent.[45]

(11) Sale of offices and honours, lobbying, etc.

Certain contracts for the sale of public offices are prohibited by statute[46] while others are illegal at common law.[47] The same rule applies to contracts for the sale of commissions in the armed forces of the Crown.[48] Exceptionally, commissions in the Army could be sold[49] until this practice was prohibited by Royal Warrant in 1871.[50] Contracts of this kind are contrary to public policy because of their tendency to lead to corruption and inefficiency.

Similarly, it was held in *Parkinson v College of Ambulance Ltd*[51] that a contract to procure a knighthood was illegal as it might lead to corruption and as it was "derogatory to the dignity of the Sovereign".[52] It is now an offence to make such a contract.[53] And a contract by a Member of Parliament to vote in accordance with the direction of some body outside Parliament is invalid.[54]

Similar problems can arise from the practice of "lobbying" for government contracts. While in some cases the practice is "recognised and respectable",[55] it is in others contrary to public policy. This was, for example, held to be the case where the defendant promised large commissions to the claimant for using its influence to secure the renewal of contracts between the defendant and a foreign government. It was essential to the success of the scheme that the government should be kept in ignorance of the claimant's financial interest in the matter, while the claimant knew that the original contract provided that no commissions should be paid to third parties. The claim for the commission was therefore rejected on grounds of public policy.[56]

---

[43] *cf. Corby v Morrison* [1980] I.C.R. 564.

[44] See *Newland v Simmons & Willer (Hairdressers) Ltd* [1981] I.C.R. 521.

[45] *Skilton v Sullivan, The Times,* March 25, 1994; see further p.483, below.

[46] Sale of Offices Act 1551, extended by Sale of Offices Act 1809, as amended by Criminal Law Act 1967, s.10 and Sch.3.

[47] *Garforth v Fearon* (1787) 1 H.B.L. 327; *Hannington v Du-Chatel* (1781) 1 Bro.C.C. 124; *Law v Law* (1735) 3 P.Wms. 391; *Parsons v Thompson* (1790) 1 H.B. 322. *cf.* the rule against assignment of a public officer's salary: below, p.698.

[48] *Morris v McCullock* (1763) Amb. 432.

[49] *Berrisford v Done* (1682) 1 Vern. 98.

[50] An attempt to abolish purchase of Army commissions by statute having failed to get a majority in the House of Lords.

[51] [1925] 2 K.B. 1.

[52] *ibid.* at 14.

[53] Honours (Prevention of Abuses) Act 1925.

[54] *ASRS v Osborne* [1910] A.C. 87. The House of Commons has resolved that it is a breach of privilege to make such a contract: (1947) 440 HC Col. 365.

[55] *Lemenda Trading Co Ltd v African Middle East Petroleum Co* [1988] Q.B. 448 at 458; Collier [1988] C.L.J. 169.

[56] *Lemenda* case, above.

(12) Trading with the enemy

A contract made during a war to which this country is a party is illegal if it involves commercial intercourse with an enemy.[57] An enemy, for this purpose, is a person voluntarily resident or carrying on business in enemy-occupied territory.[58] Such contracts are illegal as they tend to aid the economy of the enemy country. A contract is not illegal if one of the parties to it is an "enemy" but its performance involves no further commercial intercourse with the enemy[59] and it can be enforced if this does not benefit the enemy.[60] It is a statutory offence to trade or to attempt to trade with an enemy.[61]

(13) Contracts which involve doing an illegal act in a friendly foreign country

In the interests of good foreign relations, the courts will not uphold a contract which involves the performance in a friendly foreign country of an act which is illegal by its law. Thus a loan to support an armed attack on such a country[62] and a contract to smuggle whisky into the USA during the Prohibition period have been held illegal.[63] A contract for the sale of goods was likewise held illegal where it required the goods to be illegally exported from their country of origin.[64] And in *Regazzoni v KC Sethia Ltd*[65] a contract was made for the export of Indian jute to Italy, with a view to re-export to South Africa. The House of Lords refused to enforce the contract as it contravened an Indian law prohibiting the export of goods produced in India to South Africa, and as it could be performed only by making false declarations in India.

(14) Contracts restricting personal liberty

A contract may be illegal if it so severely restricts the liberty of an individual as to reduce him to a quasi-servile condition. In *Horwood v Millar's Timber and Trading Co*[66] a clerk borrowed money from a moneylender and agreed that he would not without the lender's written consent leave his job, borrow money, dispose of his property or move house. The contract was held to be illegal as it unduly restricted the liberty of the borrower.

---

[57] *Sovfracht (V/O) v Van Udens Scheepvaart en Agentuur Maatschappij (NV Gebr.)* [1943] A.C. 203.
[58] *Porter v Freudenberg* [1915] 1 K.B. 857.
[59] *Tingley v Muller* [1917] 2 Ch. 144.
[60] *Rodriguez v Speyer Bros* [1919] A.C. 59.
[61] Trading with the Enemy Act 1939.
[62] *De Wutz v Hendricks* (1824) 2 Bing. 314.
[63] *Foster v Driscoll* [1929] 1 K.B. 470; *cf. Ralli Bros v Compañia Naviera Sota y Aznar* [1920] 2 K.B. 287 (supervening illegality of payment); contrast *Libyan Arab Foreign Bank v Bankers Trust Co* [1989] Q.B. 728 at 744–745 (where there was no intention to do or procure an illegal act abroad); *Bangladesh Export & Import Co Ltd v Sucden Kerry SA* [1995] 2 Lloyd's Rep. 1 at 6 (where there was no obligation to do such an act); *Royal Boskalis Westminster NV v Mountain* [1997] 2 All E.R. 929.
[64] See *Soleimany v Soleimany* [1999] Q.B. 785 at 797 (refusal to enforce arbitration award based on such a contract).
[65] [1958] A.C. 30. Contrast *Fox v Henderson Investment Fund Ltd* [1999] 2 Lloyd's Rep. 303 (no illegality merely because acts to be done *in England* in performance of the contract would involve breach of an order made by a *foreign* court).
[66] [1917] 3 K.B. 305; *cf. Hepworth Manufacturing Co v Ryott* [1920] 1 Ch. 1; *Gaumont-British Picture Corp v Alexander* [1936] 2 All E.R. 1686. See also *Tailby v Official Receiver* (1888) 13 App.Cas. 533; *King v Michael Faraday & Partners Ltd* [1939] 2 K.B. 753 (assignment of salary depriving assignor of his sole means of support invalid), and *Syrett v Egerton* [1957] 1 W.L.R. 1130 (whether assignment of *all* an individual's property is contrary to public policy). Under Human Rights Act 1998, s.1 and Sch.1, Pt I, Art.5, contractual restrictions on personal liberty of the kind described in the text above could be unlawful if imposed by a "public authority": see s.6 and p.480, below. Such restrictions do not appear to fall within Art.1 of Sch.1, Pt I.

But a case has to be extreme to fall within this principle. In *Denny v Denny*[67] a father promised to pay his son's debts and to make him an allowance if the son did not become a bankrupt; became and remained a reformed character; gave up some named associates (who were swindlers); did not go within 80 miles of Piccadilly Circus without his father's previous consent; did not borrow money, or bet or directly or indirectly have any business or personal relations with any moneylenders, bookmakers or turf accountants or their servants. This contract was upheld even though, taken literally, it prevented the son from having personal relations with a bookmaker's clerk, who might be perfectly honest. The court was mainly influenced by the fact that the father had imposed the restrictions for the son's benefit, while the moneylender in *Horwood's* case had acted from selfish motives.

3. Contracts in Restraint of Trade[68]

Contracts which prevent or regulate business competition were at one time regarded as invariably void[69]; and persons who made them were even threatened with imprisonment.[70] But it came to be recognised that this inflexible attitude might defeat its own ends. A master might be reluctant to employ and train apprentices if he could not to some extent restrain them from competing with him after the end of their apprenticeship. And a trader might be unable to sell the business he had built up if he could not bind himself not to compete with the purchaser. The courts therefore began to uphold contracts in restraint of trade, and in 1711 the subject was reviewed in *Mitchel v Reynolds*.[71] The effect of that case, as interpreted in later decisions, was that a restraint was *prima facie* valid if it was supported by adequate consideration and was not general—*i.e.* did not extend over the whole Kingdom.

Since then, the law has changed in three respects. First, restraints are no longer *prima facie* valid; they are *prima facie* void, but can be justified if they are reasonable and not contrary to the public interest.[72] Secondly, it is no longer essential that the consideration should be adequate,[73] "though . . . the quantum of consideration may enter into the question of the reasonableness of the agreement".[74] Thirdly, the rule that a restraint must not be general no longer applies. In *Nordenfelt v Maxim Nordenfelt Guns & Ammunition Co*[75] the owner of an armaments business sold it to a company and covenanted not to carry on such a business for 25 years except on behalf of the company. The covenant was held valid although it prevented competition anywhere in the world.

Most authorities support the view that the question whether a restraint is valid must be determined once for all by reference to the circumstances in existence when the

---

[67] [1919] 1 K.B. 583; *cf. Upton v Henderson* (1912) 28 T.L.R. 398.

[68] Heydon, *The Restraint of Trade Doctrine* and 50 A.L.J. 290; Trebilcock, *The Common Law of Restraint of Trade*.

[69] *Claygate v Batchelor* (1602) Owen 143.

[70] *Dyer's Case* (1414) Y.B. 2 Hen. V, Pasch. pl. 26.

[71] (1711) 1 P.Wms. 181.

[72] See below, pp.458–463.

[73] *Tallis v Tallis* (1853) 1 E. & B. 391.

[74] *Nordenfelt v Maxim Nordenfelt Guns and Ammunition Co* [1894] A.C. 535 at 565; *Esso Petroleum Ltd v Harper's Garage (Stourport) Ltd* [1968] A.C. 300 at 318, 323; *Amoco Australia Pty Ltd v Rocca Bros Motor Engineering Pty Ltd* (1973) 47 A.L.J.R. 681 (affirmed without reference to this point [1975] A.C. 561); *Alec Lobb (Garages) Ltd v Total Oil (Great Britain) Ltd* [1985] 1 W.L.R. 173 at 179; *Turner v Commonwealth Minerals Ltd* [2000] I.R.L.R. 114.

[75] [1894] A.C. 535. For a trace of the older view, see *Home Counties Dairies Ltd v Skilton* [1970] 1 W.L.R. 526 at 530 ("an agreement in restraint of trade may be upheld *if partial*").

contract was made.[76] The view that a restraint which satisfies the tests of validity at that time may become invalid or unenforceable in the light of subsequent events[77] has been generally rejected as it would give rise to an unacceptable degree of uncertainty.

Agreements which have been held to be within the doctrine of restraint of trade can be divided into a number of groups or categories which will be discussed below. We shall see that some agreements which are, or may be, within the doctrine do not fall readily within any of these categories; and that other agreements which can in a sense be said to restrain trade are not within the doctrine at all, and are therefore not subject to the conditions on which the validity of covenants in restraint of trade depends.[78] Our main concern will be with the common law rules on this topic. After discussing these rules, we shall consider the relationship between them and the legislation which governs European Community and United Kingdom competition law.[79]

(1) Sale of a business and employment

In this group of cases, a covenant in restraint of trade is invalid unless three conditions are satisfied: there must be an interest meriting protection; the restraint must be reasonable; and it must not be contrary to the public interest.

(a) THE INTEREST. The interest must arise from the relationship of the parties as buyer and seller or as employer and employee. In the absence of such a relationship, freedom from ordinary trade competition is not, of itself, an interest meriting protection.[80] Thus a bare promise to a shopkeeper not to open (or work for) a competing business would be void; such a promise is known as a covenant in gross. Normally the covenant must be contained in a contract of sale or employment, but this is not absolutely necessary. It is enough if the covenant is closely related to such a contract; for example, if it is contained in a contract made (shortly after the termination of an employment contract) to settle outstanding differences.[81]

(i) *Sale of a business.* Even in the absence of a covenant in restraint of trade, the purchaser of the goodwill of a business can restrain the vendor from canvassing the old customers of the business.[82] This rule would not prevent the vendor from competing in other ways (*e.g.* from dealing with his old customers if they spontaneously came to him); but the purchaser can validly stipulate against such competition by a covenant in restraint of trade. His right to do so is said to depend on his "proprietary interest" in the goodwill of the business which he has bought.[83]

It follows that the purchaser is entitled to protection only in respect of the business which he has bought, and not in respect of some other business which he already carries on or may carry on in the future. If a company which owns shops in all parts of the

---

[76] *Commercial Plastics Ltd v Vincent* [1965] 1 Q.B. 623 at 644 (citing earlier authorities); *Gledhow Autoparts Ltd v Delaney* [1985] 1 W.L.R. 1366 at 1377; *A Schroeder Music Publishing Co Ltd v Macaulay* [1974] 1 W.L.R. 1308 at 1309; *Shell UK Ltd v Lostock Garages Ltd* [1976] 1 W.L.R. 1187 at 1203; *Briggs v Oates* [1991] 1 All E.R. 407 at 417; *Watson v Prager* [1991] 1 W.L.R. 726 at 738; *Rock Refrigeration Ltd v Jones* [1997] I.C.R. 938 at 996; *TSC Europe (UK) Ltd v Massey* [1999] I.R.L.R. 22 at 26; *Symbian Ltd v Christensen* [2001] I.R.L.R. 77.

[77] *Shell UK Ltd v Lostock Garages Ltd* [1976] W.L.R. 1187 at 1198.

[78] See below, p.474.

[79] See below, p.475.

[80] *cf. Vancouver Malt & Sake Brewing Co v Vancouver Breweries Ltd* [1934] A.C. 181.

[81] *Stenhouse Australia Ltd v Phillips* [1974] A.C. 391.

[82] *Trego v Hunt* [1896] A.C. 7.

[83] There can be such an interest even though the goodwill is inalienable: see *Whitehill v Bradford* [1952] Ch. 236; *Kerr v Morris* [1987] Ch. 90; and even though the interest is not purely financial: *cf.*, in an analogous context, *Young v Evans-Jones* [2002] EWCA Civ 732; [2001] 1 P. & C.R. 176.

country buys a village shop it can restrain the seller from competing in or near that village, but not at other places where it happens to carry on business.[84] Similarly, in the *Nordenfelt* case[85] the covenant restrained the seller from engaging not only in the manufacture of armaments but also "in any other business competing or liable to compete with that for the time being carried on by" the buyer. The latter part of the covenant was invalid. Its effect would be to restrain the seller from competing with the company if it started to make ploughshares; and he had sold no such business.[86] But a person who buys a business which is about to expand may be able to take a covenant against competition covering the area of the proposed expansion.[87] And the rule that the buyer can restrain the seller from competing only with the business formerly carried on by the seller is subject to a common-sense exception. A person who sells shares in a company which he controls may covenant not to compete in respect of the business carried on by *the company*. Such a covenant may be valid if it was in substance the seller who, through his control of the company, carried on the business[88]; and even a seller of a minority shareholding can validly covenant with the buyer not to use confidential information which relates to the business of the company.[89] If, however, the *business* carried on by a company (as opposed to the *shares* in it) is sold, it may be hard to frame a suitable covenant to protect the buyer from competition by associated companies.[90]

(ii) *Employment*. Even in the absence of a covenant in restraint of trade, the law gives an employer some degree of protection against his employee. He can restrain the employee from (i) using or disclosing trade secrets (ii) using or disclosing confidential information[91] falling short of a trade secret[92] and (iii) soliciting the employer's customers. The restriction on the use or disclosure of trade secrets applies at any time[93]; that on the solicitation of customers applies only to solicitation during the period of employment[94]; while that relating to confidential information occupies an intermediate position. It is normally limited to the employee's conduct during employment[95]; but it can extend beyond that period: *e.g.* where, on leaving his job, the employee takes away,

---

[84] *cf. British Reinforced Concrete Engineering Co Ltd v Scheff* [1921] 2 Ch. 563.

[85] [1894] A.C. 535.

[86] *cf.* (between employer and employee) *Scully UK Ltd v Lee* [1998] I.R.L.R. 259.

[87] *Lamson Pneumatic Tube Co v Phillips* (1904) 91 L.T. 363; *TSC Europe (UK) Ltd v Massey* [1999] I.R.L.R. 22 at 27–28.

[88] *Connors Bros v Connors Ltd* [1940] 4 All E.R. 179; *cf. Kirby (Inspector of Taxes) v Thorn EMI* [1988] 1 W.L.R. 445 (covenant on sale by company of shares in its subsidiary).

[89] *Systems Reliability Holdings v Smith* [1990] I.R.L.R. 377.

[90] See *Doyle v Olby (Ironmongers) Ltd* [1969] 2 Q.B. 158.

[91] Except where disclosure would be in the public interest, *e.g.* where the employer has been guilty of misconduct which ought to be disclosed: *Initial Services Ltd v Putterill* [1968] 1 Q.B. 396; North [1968] J.B.L. 32; *cf. Malone v Metropolitan Police Commissioner* [1979] Ch. 344 at 361–362; *British Steel Corp v Granada Television Ltd* [1981] A.C. 1096 at 1168, 1177, 1201; *Lion Laboratories Ltd v Evans* [1985] Q.B. 526; *Attorney-General v Guardian Newspapers Ltd (No.2)* [1990] A.C. 109 at 268; *Re a Company* [1989] 2 All E.R. 248; *W v Edgell* [1990] Ch. 359. Contrast *Distillers Co Ltd v Times Newspapers Ltd* [1976] Q.B. 613; *Schering Chemicals Ltd v Falkman Ltd* [1982] Q.B. 1; *Stephens v Avery* [1988] Ch. 449; *Re Barlow Clowes Gilt Managers Ltd* [1992] Ch. 208. For proposals to widen the scope of the "public interest" exception see Law Com. No. 110, paras 6.84(i) and 6.134(iii).

[92] See below at n.8.

[93] *Printers & Finishers Ltd v Holloway* [1965] 1 W.L.R. 1; *Faccenda Chicken Ltd v Fowler* [1987] Ch. 117 at 136; *Lock International plc v Beswick* [1989] 1 W.L.R. 1268 at 1273; *Berkley Administration v McClelland* [1990] F.S.R. 565; *PSM International v Whitehouse* [1992] I.R.L.R. 279. *cf. Attorney-General v Barker* [1990] 3 All E.R. 257 (express covenant by employee of Royal Household); *Poly Lina Ltd v Finch* [1995] F.S.R. 751.

[94] *Wessex Dairies Ltd v Smith* [1935] 2 K.B. 60; *cf. Wallace Bogan & Co v Cove* [1997] I.R.L.R. 453. If the solicitation occurs during employment it is irrelevant that the actual contract with the customers is made thereafter: *Sanders v Parry* [1967] 1 W.L.R. 753.

[95] *cf. Murray v Yorkshire Food Managers Ltd* [1998] 1 W.L.R. 951.

copies or memorises lists of the employer's trade connections.[96] He can then be restrained from using such information for his own benefit (or for that of a third party) for so long as such use would give him (or the third party) an unfair competitive advantage over the employer.[97] A similar restriction may be imposed where the employee *sells* such information, as opposed to using it to earn his living.[98] Certain confidential information acquired by employees in the public service is also subject to a lifelong duty of confidentiality.[99] All these rights of the employer are once again said to constitute "proprietary interests" which the employer is entitled to protect by a covenant in restraint of trade; and such a covenant may (as in the cases between vendor and purchaser) afford somewhat greater protection[1] than that provided by law in the absence of a covenant. But the employer cannot justify a covenant in restraint of trade simply on the ground that the covenant would protect the business in which the employee has worked.

Thus the interest meriting protection is more narrowly defined between employer and employee than between buyer and seller,[2] and two reasons have been given for this distinction. First, buyer and seller may bargain on a more equal footing than employer and employee. The courts certainly attach importance to disparity of bargaining power in restraint of trade cases.[3] But this factor would scarcely be significant where the terms of employment were settled between an employer and a powerful trade union, or where the restraint was undertaken by a company director who, though technically an employee, was by no means in a weak bargaining position.[4] In such cases, it is better to fall back on the second justification for the distinction between the two types of contract. The buyer of a business pays for freedom from competition and would lose part of what he paid for if the seller began to compete with him.[5] An employer pays for his employee's services and would not be deprived of what he paid for if the employee competed with him after leaving his service.

Unlike the purchaser of a business, an employer cannot protect himself by a covenant in restraint of trade against his former employee's competition as such. He cannot restrain the employee from using his own skill even though that skill was learnt from the employer.[6] To establish that he has an interest meriting protection, the employer must show *either* that the employee has learnt the employer's trade secrets, *or* that he has acquired influence over the employer's clients or customers. Trade secrets include secret

---

[96] *Faccenda Chicken Ltd v Fowler* [1987] Ch. 117 at 139; Miller 102 L.Q.R. 359; *cf. Johnson & Blay (Holdings) Ltd v Wolstenholme Rink plc* [1989] F.S.R. 135; *Universal Thermosensors Ltd v Hibden* [1992] 1 W.L.R. 840 at 850.

[97] *Roger Bullivant Ltd v Ellis* [1987] I.C.R. 464.

[98] *Faccenda Chicken Ltd v Fowler* [1987] Ch. 117 at 139.

[99] *Attorney-General v Guardian Newspapers (No.2)* [1990] A.C. 109 at 264, 284; *Lord Advocate v Scotsman Publications Ltd* [1990] 1 A.C. 812 at 821. Contrast *Attorney-General v Blake* [1998] Ch. 439 at 454–455 where the information was no longer confidential and an injunction to restrain its use was said to be an unjustifiable restraint of trade; in the House of Lords, the defendant was held liable for breach of his *express* promise not to disclose the information: [2001] 1 A.C. 268, below, p.930.

[1] See *Attorney-General v Blake* n.99, above and below, p.458.

[2] *Mason v Provident Clothing & Supply Co* [1913] A.C. 724; *Bridge v Deacons* [1984] A.C. 705, 713; *Systems Reliability Holdings v Smith* [1990] I.R.L.R. 377.

[3] *A Schroeder Music Publishing Co Ltd v Macaulay* [1974] 1 W.L.R. 1308; *Clifford Davies Management v WEA Records Ltd* [1975] 1 W.L.R. 61; below, p.462.

[4] "A managing director can look after himself": *M & S Drapers v Reynolds* [1957] 1 W.L.R. 9 at 19.

[5] *Attwood v Lamont* [1920] 3 K.B. 571 at 590; *cf. Leather Cloth Co v Lorsont* (1869) L.R. 9 Eq. 345 at 354; *Herbert Morris Ltd v Saxelby* [1916] 1 A.C. 688 at 701.

[6] *Herbert Morris Ltd v Saxelby* [1916] 1 A.C. 688; *cf. Eastes v Russ* [1914] 1 Ch. 468; *Faccenda Chicken Ltd v Fowler* [1987] Ch. 117 at 137; *FSS Travel Systems Ltd v Johnson* [1998] I.R.L.R. 382. For a proposal to extend this principle to certain persons other than employees, see Law Com. No. 110, para.6.75.

formulae or processes, and certain other similar kinds of highly confidential information[7] (but not information which is merely confidential in the sense that the employee must not disclose it during employment).[8] It used to be thought that "know-how" could not be protected[9] but now that such expertise has become a saleable commodity[10] it is likely that the courts will recognise it as an interest meriting protection.[11] In respect of clients or customers, the employer is entitled to protection only if the nature of the employment was such as to enable the employee to acquire influence over them,[12] e.g. where the employee was a solicitor's managing clerk,[13] or a hairdresser's assistant[14] but not where he was a factory worker who never came into contact with customers. If the employee comes into contact with some customers, the employer may be able to protect himself also in respect of some others.[15]

The question whether there is any other interest which an employer can protect by a covenant in restraint of trade was raised in *Eastham v Newcastle United Football Club Ltd*.[16] The defendant club employed a professional footballer subject to the "retain and transfer" system.[17] Under that system, a player who was "retained"[18] by one club could not be employed by another; nor could he be transferred to another club without the consent of both clubs. The defendant club could not claim that this system protected either of the two traditional interests. But Wilberforce J. said that "it would be wrong to pass straight to the conclusion that no . . . interest . . . exists".[19] He considered other possible interests, such as the danger that, but for the "retain and transfer" system, all the best players might go to the richest clubs. He found that such consequences would not in fact follow if the system were abandoned; that there was thus no interest to be protected; and that the system was invalid. But his approach suggests that interests other than the traditional ones might be entitled to protection. A covenant by a film actor not to appear on the stage for three months, made with the object of furthering the success of a new film,[20] might be enforceable even though it did not protect either of the orthodox interests. Such new interests would differ from the traditional ones in that they would be protected *only* if there was a covenant, while the traditional ones are to some extent protected even if there is no covenant. For this reason the new interests may be called "commercial" rather than "proprietary" ones; and we shall see that in some categories of contracts in restraint of trade the law now recognises that such commercial interests may be protected by covenants.[21] It is possible that this recognition will help to

---

[7] *Caribonum Co Ltd v Le Couch* (1913) 109 L.T. 587; *cf. The Littlewoods Organisation Ltd v Harris* [1977] 1 W.L.R. 1472. And see *Lansing Linde Ltd v Kerr* [1991] 1 W.L.R. 251 at 259, 268, 270; *Balston v Headline Filters* [1990] F.S.R. 385 at 417. Trade secrets do not need to be disclosed by public authorities under the Freedom of Information Act 2000: see ss.2 and 43.

[8] *Faccenda Chicken Ltd v Fowler* [1987] Ch. 117 at 136; *Brooks v Olyslager Oms (UK) Ltd* [1998] I.R.L.R. 590; *Intelsec Systems Ltd v Grech-Cini* [2000] 1 W.L.R. 1190.

[9] *Herbert Morris Ltd v Saxelby*, above; *Sir W C Leng & Co v Andrews* [1909] 1 Ch. 763 at 768.

[10] Blanco White, 15 Conv. 89; 26 Conv. 366.

[11] In *Commercial Plastics Ltd v Vincent* [1965] 1 Q.B. 623 at 642 Pearson L.J. hints at this possibility.

[12] *Faccenda Chicken Ltd v Fowler* [1987] Ch. 117 at 137.

[13] *Fitch v Dewes* [1921] 2 A.C. 158; below, p.456.

[14] *Marion White Ltd v Francis* [1972] 1 W.L.R. 1423.

[15] *C W Plowman & Son Ltd v Ash* [1964] 1 W.L.R. 568; and see pp.458–459 below.

[16] [1964] Ch. 413; *cf. Greig v Insole* [1978] 1 W.L.R. 302.

[17] See further p.467 n.6, below.

[18] A player could be "retained" by giving him notice and paying him a reasonable wage (determined, in case of dispute, by the Football Association).

[19] *Eastham v Newcastle United Football Club Ltd*, above, at p.432.

[20] For this practice, see *Higgs v Olivier* [1951] Ch. 899; *cf. Vaughan-Neil v IRC* [1979] 1 W.L.R. 1283 (covenant by a barrister, on becoming an employee of a company, not to practise at the Bar).

[21] See below, pp.465, 470.

modify the strict insistence on the need for a "proprietary" interest in cases between vendor and purchaser, and between employer and employee.

(iii) *Doubtful cases.* The distinction between vendor-purchaser and employer-employee covenants is by no means exhaustive. Thus a covenant by a retiring doctor or solicitor not to compete with his former partners does not fall precisely into either category[22]; but the courts do not subject it to the strict tests of validity that they apply to employer-employee covenants.[23] Again, a person may sell his business to a company of which he then becomes managing director. It seems that a covenant by such a person not to compete should be treated in the same way as a vendor-purchaser covenant, whether it is contained in the sale agreement or in the service agreement[24] or in both.[25] On the other hand, a covenant by a writer or composer not to dispose of his work except to a particular publisher may for present purposes be treated in the same way as an employer-employee covenant, even though there was never any contract of employment between the parties.[26]

(b) REASONABLENESS. A restraint is valid only if it goes no further than is reasonably necessary for the protection of the covenantee's interest. Reasonableness is determined by looking at the relationship between that interest and the covenant.[27]

(i) *Area of restraint.* To be reasonable, the restraint need not be precisely co-terminous with the interest.[28] If there were such a requirement, there would be little point in taking a covenant, since a "proprietary interest" is (by definition) protected even in the absence of a covenant.[29] So long as the employer has trade secrets he can take a covenant which to some extent prevents the employee from using his own skill by restraining him from working in competition with the employer. And an employer who has a "proprietary" interest in his relations with clients or customers can restrain his employee from working in the *area* in which those clients or customers live, even though most of the inhabitants of the area have never dealt with the employer.[30] Such restraints may be necessary for the protection of the employer as the actual infringement of his proprietary interests could be very hard to establish: in particular it would, if the employee were allowed to work for a competitor, be hard to tell whether he was disclosing trade secrets.[31] The covenant may, moreover, be enforced even though the "proprietary interest" infringed is of little value to the employer. Thus a former employee can be restrained from dealing with a client who has decided to deal with the ex-employee, rather than with the

---

[22] *Bridge v Deacons* [1984] A.C. 705 at 714.

[23] *Whitehill v Bradford* [1952] Ch. 236; *Kerr v Morris* [1986] 3 All E.R. 217; *Espley v Williams* [1997] 1 E.G.L.R. 9; *cf. Kall Kwick Printing (UK) Ltd v Rush* [1996] F.S.R. 114 and *Convenience Co Ltd v Roberts* [2001] F.S.R. 35 (covenants in franchise agreements); *contra, Jenkins v Reid* [1948] 1 All E.R. 471—but the defendant's covenant seems to have been "in gross".

[24] See *Silverman Ltd v Silverman, The Times,* July 7, 1969. *cf. Blake v Blake* (1967) 111 S.J. 715 (restraints imposed, on dissolution of a company, on its major shareholders: these were treated in the same way as vendor-purchaser covenants); *Allied Dunbar (Frank Weisinger) Ltd v Frank Weisinger* [1988] I.R.L.R. 60; *Alliance Property Group plc v Prestwich* [1995] I.R.L.R. 25; *Dawnay Day & Co v D'Alphen* [1997] I.R.L.R. 442 (so far as it relates to the service agreement).

[25] *T & C Europe (UK) Ltd v Massey* [1999] I.R.L.R. 22 at 26.

[26] See *A Schroeder Music Publishing Co Ltd v Macaulay* [1974] 1 W.L.R. 1308.

[27] *Allied Dunbar (Frank Weisinger) Ltd v Frank Weisinger* [1988] I.R.L.R. 60, at 65.

[28] *cf. Systems Reliability Holdings v Smith* [1990] I.R.L.R. 377 at 384; *Marshall v NM Financial Management Ltd* [1997] 1 W.L.R. 1527 at 1533.

[29] See above, pp.454, 455.

[30] *Fitch v Dewes* [1921] 2 A.C. 158; *Scorer v Seymour-Johns* [1966] 1 W.L.R. 1419; contrast *Fellowes v Fisher* [1976] Q.B. 122.

[31] *Poly Lina Ltd v Finch* [1995] F.S.R. 751; *cf. Kall Kwick Printing (UK) Ltd v Rush* [1996] F.S.R. 114 (franchise agreement).

employer, since it is precisely this type of competition "against which the covenant is designed to give protection".[32]

On the other hand, such "area covenants" may operate to some extent as pure restraints on competition; and in a number of cases[33] the courts have distinguished them from "solicitation covenants" (against soliciting the employer's old clients or customers). On the facts of those cases the courts have held or said that only "solicitation covenants" would be regarded as reasonable. The cases do not absolutely rule out the possibility that an "area covenant" may be valid between employer and employee[34]; but such a covenant will be void if it covers a much larger area than is needed for the protection of the employer's interest. Thus in *Mason v Provident Clothing & Supply Co Ltd*,[35] a canvasser who was employed to sell clothes in Islington covenanted not to enter into similar business within 25 miles of London. The covenant was held void because the area of the restraint was about 1,000 times as large as that in which the canvasser had been employed. It was said that the employer could have protected himself by a covenant restricted to the area in which the canvasser had worked. But if that area is very large and the employee has only dealt with a small number of customers within it, an area covenant will not,[36] though a solicitation covenant might,[37] be upheld.

Between vendor and purchaser (and in analogous cases[38]) area covenants are commonly enforced; and a restraint may be reasonable even though it is *unlimited* as to area. In the *Nordenfelt* case[39] such a restraint was enforced against the vendor of an armaments business since that business extended over the whole world; and where an employer is entitled to protect trade secrets of a business which has no clear geographical limits, a covenant which is unlimited as to area may similarly be enforced against the employee.[40] A "solicitation covenant" in a contract of employment may likewise be enforced though it contains no express limitations as to area,[41] particularly if it is limited to customers with whom the employee came into contact in the course of his employment[42]; but such a limitation is not essential to the validity of the covenant.[43] A worldwide restraint against disclosing confidential information is unlikely to be upheld

---

[32] *John Michael Design plc v Cooke* [1987] I.C.R. 445 at 446.
[33] *S W Strange Ltd v Mann* [1965] 1 W.L.R. 629; *Macfarlane v Kent* [1965] 1 W.L.R 1019 at 1024 (doubted on another point in *Peyton v Mindham* [1972] 1 W.L.R. 8); *Gledhow Autoparts Ltd v Delaney* [1965] 1 W.L.R. 1366; *T Lucas & Co Ltd v Mitchell* [1974] Ch. 129; *Stenhouse Australia Ltd v Phillips* [1974] A.C. 391; *Spafax v Harrison* [1980] I.R.L.R. 442; *Dairy Crest Ltd v Pigott* [1989] I.C.R. 92; *cf. Bridge v Deacons* [1984] A.C. 705 (solicitation covenant in partnership agreement between solicitors upheld); *Hanover Insurance Brokers v Shapiro* [1994] I.R.L.R. 82.
[34] *e.g. Anscombe & Ringland v Butchoff* (1984) 134 N.L.J. 37.
[35] [1913] A.C. 724; *cf. Empire Meat Co Ltd v Patrick* [1939] 2 All E.R. 85; *Spencer v Marchington* [1988] I.R.L.R. 392; *Office Angels Ltd v Rainer-Thomas* [1991] I.R.L.R. 214; for conflicting dicta in a borderline case, see *Lyne-Pirkis v Jones* [1969] 1 W.L.R. 1293.
[36] *Marley Tile Co Ltd v Johnson* [1982] I.R.L.R. 75.
[37] *Gledhow Autoparts Ltd v Delaney* [1965] 1 W.L.R. 1366. Contrast *Office Angels Ltd v Rainer-Thomas*, above, n.35 and *Lapthorne v Eurofi Ltd* [2001] EWCA Civ 999; [2001] U.K.C.L.R. 999.
[38] *e.g. Kerr v Morris*, [1987] Ch. 90; *cf. Kall Kwick Printing (UK) Ltd v Bell* [1994] F.S.R. 674 (franchisee); *Alliance Property Group plc v Prestwich* [1996] I.R.L.R. 25.
[39] [1894] A.C. 535; *cf. Systems Reliability Holdings v Smith* [1990] I.R.L.R. 377 at 382; *Dawnay Day & Co v D'Alphen* [1997] I.R.L.R. 442. Contrast *Convenienc Co Ltd v Roberts* [2001] F.S.R. 35 (one-year convenant in franchise agreement not to compete in UK too wide in area).
[40] *Poly Lina Ltd v Finch* [1995] F.S.R. 751.
[41] *G W Plowman & Son Ltd v Ash* [1964] 1 W.L.R. 568; *cf. Morris Angel & Son Ltd v Hollande* [1993] I.C.R. 71.
[42] As in *Stenhouse Australia Ltd v Phillips* [1974] A.C. 391; contrast *Austin Knight (UK) v Hinds* [1994] F.S.R. 52 (covenant invalid as not so limited).
[43] *Plowman & Son Ltd v Ash*, above n.41.

if the information in question relates only to business done by the employer in a limited geographical area (*e.g.* to customers in one country).[44]

(ii) *Duration of the restraint.* The question whether a restraint is invalid for excessive duration depends on the nature of the business to be protected. If it is one to which customers or clients are likely to resort for a long time, a restraint for the lifetime of the covenantor may be valid. Thus in *Fitch v Dewes*[45] a lifelong restraint on a solicitor's managing clerk not to practise within seven miles of his principal's office was upheld. But in view of the more recently developed distinction between "area" and "solicitation" covenants, it is unlikely that a *lifelong* restraint in an "area" covenant would now be regarded as valid.[46] A more lenient view was taken of a "solicitation" covenant for a *fixed period* in *Bridge v Deacons*[47]: the Privy Council there upheld a covenant by a partner in a firm of solicitors not to act as solicitor in Hong Kong for any client of the firm for five years after ceasing to be a partner; and a one year "area" covenant operating within a 10-mile radius has likewise been enforced against an assistant solicitor.[48] Where the business to be protected is of a more fluctuating nature, long restraints are unlikely to be upheld whether they are contained in "area" or in "solicitation" covenants.[49] A maximum duration of two years is prescribed by legislation in the case of a restraint on a "commercial agent".[50]

An employee's covenant not to disclose confidential information relating to the employer need not be limited as to time: such a covenant has, for example, been upheld where an employee of the Royal Household undertook that he would not either during or after service disclose information concerning any member of the Royal Family (and certain other persons) without written authority.[51] Such a limited restraint does not prevent the former employee from working for others, and is therefore not objectionable on grounds of public policy.

(iii) *Scope of restraint.* A restraint must not extend to an activity which is irrelevant to the interest to be protected. Thus a restraint in a tailor's service contract against working as a hatter is unreasonable.[52] Nor can an employer use his proprietary interest in trade secrets and confidential information to support a covenant restraining an employee from disclosing any information whatsoever "relating to the company [*i.e.* the employer] or its customers of which [the employee] becomes possessed while acting as sales director"[53]; for much information of this kind will have nothing to do with the employer's proprietary interest.

(iv) *Drafting problems.* So long as there is an interest meriting protection, some restraint can be validly imposed, but the draftsman may, by drawing the restraint too widely, wholly fail to achieve his purpose.[54] An attempt to evade this difficulty was made in *Davies v Davies*,[55] where the covenant simply restrained competition "so far as the law

---

[44] *Lansing Linde Ltd v Kerr* [1991] 1 W.L.R. 251 at 259.
[45] [1921] 2 A.C. 158.
[46] See *Fellowes v Fisher* [1976] Q.B. 122.
[47] [1984] A.C. 705; the suggestion made *ibid.* at 717 that a covenant which is otherwise reasonable will not be struck down "solely because of its duration" is, with respect, hard to reconcile with *Esso Petroleum Co Ltd v Harper's Garage (Stourport) Ltd* [1968] A.C. 269 (below, p.469), so far as that case related to the 21-year tie; and with *Eastes v Russ* [1914] 1 Ch. 468. See further Spowart-Taylor and Hough, 47 M.L.R. 745.
[48] *Hollis & Co v Stocks* [2000] U.K.C.L.R. 685.
[49] *e.g.*, *M & S Drapers v Reynolds* [1957] 1 W.L.R. 9; *cf. Eastes v Russ* [1914] 1 Ch. 468.
[50] See below, p.709; SI 1993/3053, reg.20(2).
[51] *Attorney-General v Barker* [1990] 3 All E.R. 257.
[52] *Attwood v Lamont* [1920] 3 K.B. 571; *cf. Scully UK Ltd v Lee* [1998] I.R.L.R. 259.
[53] *Lawrence David v Ashton* [1989] I.C.R. 123; *cf. Intelsec Systems Ltd v Grech-Cini* [2000] 1 W.L.R. 1190.
[54] *cf.* below, p.508.
[55] (1887) 36 Ch.D. 359.

allows"; but this was held void for uncertainty. The draftsman is therefore forced to use more precise language and this may, if taken literally, impose an excessive restraint even though the parties may not have intended that meaning. For example, in *Lyne-Pirkis v Jones*[56] a covenant in a partnership agreement between doctors in *general practice* provided that a retiring partner should not (within certain limits of time and space) "engage in medical practice". The court here refused to construe these words so as to refer only to general practice and held the covenant invalid as it prohibited practice even as a *consultant*. On the other hand, in *Home Counties Dairies Ltd v Skilton*[57] a covenant in a milk roundsman's contract provided that he should not serve or sell "milk or dairy produce". It was argued that this would prevent him from serving cheese as a grocer's assistant, but the court refused to invalidate the covenant as the parties clearly did not intend it to bear this meaning. A similar approach was adopted in *Rock Refrigeration Ltd v Jones*[58] where a sales director's contract of employment contained a covenant which was to take effect on termination of the contract "however occasioned". The contract was in fact terminated as a result of his resignation; but he argued that the words just quoted made the covenant unreasonable as they would also cover the case in which termination occurred as a result of his wrongful dismissal.[59] The argument was rejected, the majority of the Court of Appeal taking the view that the covenant would not as a matter of law operate in such a case since the effect of the employee's acceptance of the employer's repudiation would be to release the employee from further performance of the covenant.[60]

(v) *Reasonableness and fairness.* The law of restraint of trade has long recognised two principles: that adequacy of consideration is relevant to the validity of a restraint[61] and that the law has regard to the relative bargaining strengths of the parties.[62] This does not mean that a restraint is invalid merely because it was undertaken by the weaker party; for the transaction may be a perfectly fair one, having regard to the benefits obtained by that party under it.[63] It is only where the stronger party makes unconscionable use of his superior bargaining power that the resulting bargain may be struck down on account of its unfairness.[64] To this extent, the fairness of the bargain is a *necessary* condition of the

---

[56] [1969] 1 W.L.R. 1293; *cf. Peyton v Mindham* [1972] 1 W.L.R. 8; *JA Mont (UK) Ltd v Mills* [1993] I.R.L.R. 172.

[57] [1970] 1 W.L.R. 526; *cf. G W Plowman Ltd v Ash* [1964] 1 W.L.R. 568; *Marion White Ltd v Francis* [1972] 1 W.L.R. 1423; *The Littlewoods Organisation Ltd v Harris* [1977] 1 W.L.R. 1472; (doubting *Commercial Plastics Ltd v Vincent* [1961] 1 Q.B. 623 on the issue of construction); *Edwards v Worboys* [1984] A.C. 724, note; *Clarke v Newland* [1991] 1 All E.R. 397; *Alliance Paper Group v Prestwich* [1996] I.R.L.R. 25; *International Consulting Services (UK) Ltd v Hart* [2000] R.L.R. 227; *Hollis & Co v Stocks* [2000] U.K.C.L.R. 685; *Turner v Commonwealth Minerals Ltd* [2000] I.R.L.R. 114.

[58] [1997] I.C.R. 938; *cf.* also *Kall Kwick Printing (UK) Ltd v Rush* [1996] F.S.R. 114.

[59] For the invalidity of a covenant operating in such circumstances, see *D v M* [1996] I.R.L.R. 192.

[60] On the principle of *General Billposting Co Ltd v Atkinson* [1909] A.C. 118, below p.849; Phillips L.J. based the same conclusion on the different ground that the possibility of the employer's repudiating the contract was no more than a "remote" one (at 960).

[61] See above, p.453.

[62] See above, p.456.

[63] *Alec Lobb (Garages) Ltd v Total Oil (Great Britain) Ltd* [1985] 1 W.L.R. 173; this case, and those cited in the next note, were concerned with the type of restraint discussed below, pp.468–472.

[64] *A Schroeder Music Publishing Co v Macaulay* [1974] 1 W.L.R. 1308 at 1315–1316 (where Lord Diplock did not distinguish between unfairness and unconscionability); *Clifford Davis Management Ltd v WEA Records Ltd* [1975] 1 W.L.R. 61; *Silverstone Records v Mountfield* [1993] E.M.L.R. 152. *Quaere* whether it is up to the stronger party to establish the fairness of the restraint (below, pp.466–467) or to the weaker party to establish its unfairness. The latter view perhaps derives some support from the comparison in *Barclays Bank plc v Caplan* [1998] F.L.R. 532 at 546 of restraint of trade with undue influence cases, in which the party seeking to impugn the transaction must establish either actual undue influence (above, p.408) or the basic facts of the presumption of undue influence (above, p.410).

validity of the restraint; but it is submitted that it is not a *sufficient* condition. It has indeed been said that a restraint cannot be unreasonable if the parties have freely agreed to it[65] or if it is to their mutual advantage. This is true in the sense that the agreement of the parties may determine how much the covenantee has bought, and hence how much he can protect. But once the interest has been defined, the restraint will be upheld only if it is necessary for the protection of that interest.[66] This will generally depend on the relation between the restraint and the interest.[67] A world-wide restraint in a contract for the sale of a village shop would not satisfy this test however much both parties wanted to enter into it and even if the buyer had paid a greatly enhanced price to secure the restraint. The same point can be made in relation to a partnership agreement. Thus in *Bridge v Deacons* one factor emphasised by the Privy Council was "the mutuality of the contract", by which the five-year restraint "applied equally to all partners".[68] But while this was relevant to the validity of a five year solicitation covenant it would not, it is submitted, have justified a life-time area covenant covering the whole of Hong Kong since that would have been wholly disproportionate to the interest recognised as meriting protection. The rule that the restraint must not go further than necessary for the protection of the recognised interest of the covenantee is one of public policy and accordingly cannot be excluded merely by the agreement of the parties.

(c) PUBLIC INTEREST. In one sense, the requirement of reasonableness can be said to raise issues of public interest. But even if the restraint is "reasonable" in relation to the interest which the covenantee is entitled to protect, it may still be invalid if it is likely to prejudice the public. Many dicta state this rule,[69] but there is little direct authority to support it. In *Wyatt v Kreglinger & Fernau*[70] the employers of a wool broker promised to pay him a pension on his retirement provided that he did not re-enter the wool trade and did nothing to their detriment (fair business competition excepted). Nine years later the Court of Appeal rejected his claim for arrears of pension. Three reasons can be found in the judgments: that the employers' promise to pay the pension was simply a gratuitous promise; that the stipulation against competition was void because it was unreasonable; and that the stipulation against competition was void because it was contrary to the public interest. The view that a restraint imposed on an elderly wool broker at the time of his retirement was likely to injure the public may be regarded with some scepticism,[71] especially in view of the countervailing public interest of encouraging young recruits to the profession.[72] Reaction against it has gone so far that it has sometimes been said that public interest was not an independent ground of invalidity at all.[73] But *Wyatt's* case was followed in a later similar case[74]; and it is arguable that a

---

[65] *NW Salt Co v Electrolytic Alkali Co Ltd* [1914] A.C. 461 at 471; *English Hop Growers Ltd v Dering* [1928] 2 K.B. 174 at 185. *cf. World Wide Fund for Nature v World Wrestling Federation* [2002] EWCA Civ 196; [2002] U.K.C.L.R. 388, at [42], as to which see further below, p.464.

[66] *cf. A Schroeder Music Publishing Co Ltd v Macaulay*, above at 1316 ("reasonably necessary for the protection of the legitimate interests of the promisee.").

[67] See above, p.458; *Allied Dunbar (Frank Weisinger) Ltd v Frank Weisinger* [1988] I.R.L.R. 60 at 65.

[68] [1984] A.C. 705 at 716.

[69] e.g. *Attorney-General for Australia v Adelaide SS Co* [1913] A.C. 781 at 796; *Herbert Morris Ltd v Saxelby* [1916] A.C. 688 at 700; *McEllistrim's Case* [1919] A.C. 548 at 562. *Bridge v Deacons* [1984] A.C. 705 at 713; *cf. Kerr v Morris* [1987] Ch. 90, where the covenant was admitted to be reasonable in area and duration and public interest was discussed as a *separate* issue.

[70] [1933] 1 K.B. 793.

[71] 49 L.Q.R. 465.

[72] *cf. Bridge v Deacons* [1984] A.C. 705 at 718.

[73] *Routh v Jones* [1947] 1 All E.R. 179 at 182; *cf. Systems Reliability Holdings v Smith* [1990] I.R.L.R. 377 at 382; but at p.384 reasonableness *and* public interest are stated as separate requirements of validity.

[74] *Bull v Pitney-Bowes Ltd* [1967] 1 W.L.R. 273; Koh, 30 M.L.R. 587.

restraint on persons whose services are in short supply may be contrary to the public interest, even though it is reasonable in relation to the interest which the covenantee is entitled to protect.[74a] This argument is not, it is submitted, inconsistent with cases holding that it was not contrary to the public interest to restrain a solicitor from acting for a particular client or group of clients *merely* because of the fiduciary relationship between solicitor and client.[75] For the present purpose, the decisive factor is not the nature of the services but the availability of alternative sources of supply: the public interest lies in their general availability and not in their being rendered by a particular individual. Thus a restraint on a former partner in a general medical practice would not be invalid merely because patients wished to continue to be treated by that partner,[76] but such restraint might be contrary to the public interest if there was a shortage of doctors in the area in question.

The principle of public interest may, equally, apply to covenants for the sale of a business. In the *Nordenfelt*[77] case it was said that, as the business sold was a foreign one, a restraint on the vendor would not injure "the public policy of this country"; and more recently the promotion of export sales has been mentioned as a head of public interest.[78] The principle of public interest has, moreover, become increasingly important in relation to other categories of contracts in restraint of trade[79]; and it now seems to be clear that it can be an independent ground of invalidity.

In the common law relating to restraint of trade, the "public interest" refers to legally recognised interests, and in particular to the interest of the public that a person should not be subjected to unreasonable restrictions on his freedom to work or trade. An agreement is unlikely to be invalidated by a common law court because it is alleged to infringe some wider public interest, *e.g.* because it might lead to an improper allocation of economic resources, or prove inflationary. Such allegations often lack precision, and courts of law are not well equipped to evaluate them.[80]

(d) NO ACTUAL COVENANT AGAINST COMPETITION. The restraint of trade doctrine may apply where the terms of the contract provide a party with a financial incentive not to compete, even though he makes no actual promise not to do so: this was the position in *Waytt v Kreglinger & Fernau* where the employee made no promise not to compete, but his right to his pension was conditional on his not doing so.[81] Similarly, in *Stenhouse Australia Ltd v Phillips*[82] the defendant undertook to pay to his former employers half the gross commission which he might receive in respect of business done with their clients. This was held to be in restraint of trade (though there was no covenant) since it was "in effect . . . likely to cause the employee to refuse business which otherwise he

---

[74a] *cf. Dranez Anstalt v Hayetz* [2002] EWCA Civ at [25].

[75] *Edwards v Worboys* [1984] A.C. 724, n.; *Bridge v Deacons* [1984] A.C. 705 at 720; disapproving contrary dicta in *Oswald Hickson Collier & Co v Carter-Ruck* [1984] A.C. 720, n.

[76] *Kerr v Morris* [1987] Ch. 90, overruling *Hensman v Traill* (1980) 124 S.J. 776.

[77] [1894] A.C. 535 at 550; *cf. ibid.* 574.

[78] *Bull v Pitney-Bowes Ltd* [1967] 1 W.L.R. 273 at 276.

[79] See below, pp.471–472.

[80] *Texaco Ltd v Mulberry Filling Station Ltd* [1972] 1 W.L.R. 814, 827, a case concerned with the type of restraint discussed at 468–472, below; contrast *Bull v Pitney-Bowes Ltd*, above, n.74.

[81] [1933] 1 K.B. 793, *per* Scrutton and Slesser L.JJ.; Greer L.J. interpreted the correspondence to mean that there *was* a covenant not to complete. *cf. Sadler v Imperial Life Assurance of Canada* [1988] I.R.L.R. 388, where the stipulation by the agent not to compete after the end of his agency was similarly not a promise but his entitlement to future commissions was conditional on his not doing so. This was also the position in *Marshall v NM Financial Management Ltd* [1997] 1 W.L.R. 1527 at 1533.

[82] [1974] A.C. 391.

would take . . . ".[83] On the other hand in *Alder v Moore*[84] a professional footballer was paid £500 for "permanent total disability". He made a "declaration" not to play professional football again "and in the event of infringing this condition I will be subject to a penalty of £500". He did infringe the "condition" and a majority of the Court of Appeal held that he was liable to repay the £500. The sole question discussed was whether the stipulation to repay was a penalty[85]; and no reference was made to the restraint of trade doctrine. *Prima facie*, the stipulation appears to fall within that doctrine, though it may have been perfectly reasonable and not contrary to the public interest.

(e) RESTRAINT OPERATING DURING EMPLOYMENT. In the employment cases so far discussed, the issue has been as to the validity of covenants operating *after* the end of the period of service. Restrictions on competition *during* that period are normally valid,[86] and indeed may be implied by law by virtue of the servant's duty of fidelity.[87] In such cases the restriction is generally reasonable, having regard to the interests of the employer, and does not cause any undue hardship to the employee, who will receive a wage or salary for the period in question. But the contract may be a long-term one, and the main purpose of the restraint may be, not to secure faithful service, but to protect the employer from competition by sterilising the employee's working capacity. In such a case the restraint may be invalid even though it operates only during the period in which the employee can be required to serve,[88] and even if it is valid, the court may refuse the remedy of an injunction to the employer.[89]

(f) ESTABLISHING VALIDITY OF RESTRAINT. The reasonableness of the restraint must be established by the person who seeks to enforce the contract; it is then up to the party resisting enforcement to establish that the restraint is contrary to the public interest.[90] Thus in the normal case, in which the covenantee sues to enforce the restraint, he must establish its reasonableness and the covenantor its tendency to injure the public. But where, as in *Wyatt v Kreglinger & Fernau*[91] the action is brought by the covenantor to enforce the promise for which the restraint constitutes the consideration, the roles are reversed: the person under the restraint must show that it is reasonable and the other party that it is contrary to the public interest. It has further been held that where a stipulation in restraint of trade is contained in an agreement for the settlement of a genuine dispute relating to intellectual property rights, then it is not up to the party seeking to enforce the settlement to show that it is "reasonable".[92] The public policy against restraint of trade here appears to come into conflict with that in favour of bona

---

[83] *ibid.* at 402–403.

[84] [1961] 2 Q.B. 57.

[85] See below, p.1004.

[86] *cf. GFI Group v Eaglestone, The Times,* October 29, 1993; *Credit Suisse Asset Management Ltd v Armstrong* [1996] I.C.R. 882 covenant operating during "garden leave" (below, p.833) valid; but see below at n.89.

[87] See above, p.206. *Faccenda Chicken Ltd v Fowler* [1987] Ch. 117 at 135–136; *cf. Evening Standard Co Ltd v Henderson* [1987] I.C.R. 588; *Provident Financial Group plc. v Hayward* [1989] I.C.R. 160.

[88] *cf. A Schroeder Music Publishing Co Ltd v Macaulay* [1974] 1 W.L.R. 1308; *Clifford Davis Management Ltd v WEA Records* [1975] 1 W.L.R. 61; *Zang Tumb Tuum Records v Johnson* [1993] E.M.L.R. 61; *Silverstone Records v Mountfield* [1993] E.M.L.R. 152. Contrast *Greig v Insole* [1978] 1 W.L.R. 302 at 326; *Panayiotou v Sony Music Entertainment (UK) Ltd, The Times,* June 30, 1994.

[89] *William Hill Organisation Ltd v Tucker* [1998] I.R.L.R. 313; *Symbian Ltd v Christenson* [2001] I.R.L.R. 37; below, p.1045.

[90] See *Herbert Morris Ltd v Saxelby* [1916] A.C. 589 at 700, 706–707; *Attwood v Lamont* [1920] 3 K.B. 571 at 587–588; *Kores v Kolok Manufacturing Co Ltd* [1959] Ch. 108 at 120.

[91] [1933] 1 K.B. 793; above, p.461.

[92] *World Wide Fund for Nature v World Wrestling Foundation* [2002] EWCA Civ 196; [2002] U.K.C.L.R. 388 at [42].

fide compromises and the latter prevails so that it is up to the party resisting enforcement of the compromise to show that there was no genuine dispute or claim. It seems that "reasonableness" here refers to the genuineness of the underlying dispute[93]; and this is a different issue from the "reasonableness" which is a requirement of the validity of covenants in restraint of trade.[94]

The questions of reasonableness and public interest are questions of law[95] so that it is strictly inaccurate to say that the party claiming enforcement has the *onus of proving* that the covenant is reasonable. What he must do is to prove the circumstances from which the court may conclude that the ratio between the restraint and the interest is reasonable.[96] The same principle applies to the question of public interest.

(2) Restrictive trading and similar agreements

Agreements between suppliers of goods or services restricting competition between them are at common law[97] subject to the restraint of trade doctrine, so that they are *prima facie* void, but valid if reasonable and not contrary to the public interest. They also give rise to a number of special problems.

(a) THE INTEREST. In *McEllistrim's* case Lord Birkenhead said that "in this class of case the covenantee is not entitled to be protected against competition *per se*".[98] But he evidently regarded "stability in their lists of customers"[99] as an interest which producers were entitled to protect; and it is not clear how this differs from protection against "competition *per se*". It seems that in this group of cases, as in another to be discussed below,[1] a "commercial" as opposed to a "proprietary" interest[2] may support a covenant.

(b) CONDITIONS OF VALIDITY. The broad definition of the interest meriting protection by agreements of the present kind made it relatively easier to establish their validity than that of restraints between vendor and purchaser or between employer and employee. In *English Hop Growers v Dering*,[3] for example, the court upheld an agreement by which hop growers undertook to deliver their crops to a central selling agency in order to avoid cut-throat competition at a time when it was feared that there would be a glut of hops on the market. But even agreements of this kind were held invalid if they were plainly unreasonable or contrary to the public interest: for example, where the effect of the agreement was to force one of the parties to close down his business altogether.[4] Similarly, in *McEllistrim's* case[5] an association of farmers in Ireland promised to buy all the milk produced by its members in its area; and the members in turn promised not to sell milk there produced by them to anyone except the association. The agreement was held invalid because it provided that no farmer could withdraw without the consent of the committee of the association, and this consent could be arbitrarily withheld. But for this factor, it seems that the agreement would have been valid.

---

[93] *cf.* above, pp.89–90.
[94] This difference may account for the fact that none of the authorities cited at nn.90 and 94 above is referred to in the *World Wide* case, above n.92.
[95] *Dowden & Pook Ltd v Pook* [1904] 1 K.B. 45.
[96] *Herbert Morris Ltd v Saxelby* [1916] 1 A.C. 688 at 707 ("no question of onus either way").
[97] For the effect of competition law on some such agreements, see below, pp.475–477.
[98] [1919] A.C. 548 at 564.
[99] *ibid.*
[1] *i.e.* at p.470, below.
[2] See above, p.454.
[3] [1928] 2 K.B. 174; *cf. NW Salt Co v Electrolytic Alkali Co Ltd* [1914] A.C. 461.
[4] *cf. Joseph Evans & Co v Heathcote* [1918] 1 K.B. 418.
[5] [1919] A.C. 548; see also *Collins v Locke* (1879) 4 App.Cas. 674.

(c) HARDSHIP TO A PARTICULAR GROUP. An agreement may cause hardship to a particular group of persons, without being contrary to the interests of the public at large. In *Kores Manufacturing Co Ltd v Kolok Manufacturing Co Ltd*[6] two manufacturers of carbon paper and typewriter ribbons agreed not to employ each others' former employees for five years after they had left their original employer. The Court of Appeal held that, although the parties were entitled to protect their trade secrets, the covenant was invalid, as it covered all employees, whether they knew trade secrets or not, and as it was of excessive duration. It was further argued that the parties were entitled to protect their labour supplies, but the court doubted whether "labour supplies" were an interest meriting protection. If they were, employers could, by contracting with each other, achieve what they could not do by contracting directly with the employees themselves. An undertaking by an employee not to work for another employer would be invalid for lack of a proper interest[7] if he knew no trade secrets and had no influence over customers. The same principle should apply where the restraint was contained in a contract between employers and indirectly prejudiced their employees' opportunities of finding work.[8] It seems that the court can take hardship to third parties into account and hold that it invalidates a contract of this kind by making it contrary to the public interest,[9] so that a covenant by which A promised B not to employ or to offer to employ B's employees would be invalid[10] (though one by which A merely promised "not to solicit or entice away" B's employees could be upheld since it would not preclude A from employing them if they came to him of their own accord).[11]

(d) REMEDIES OF THIRD PARTIES. Reasoning of the kind just considered can help a third party only where one of the parties to the agreement has challenged its validity. In practice, these restrictive agreements were rarely broken, because they were usually beneficial to the contracting parties, however much third parties might suffer from them; and at common law the contracting parties are at liberty to give effect to the agreement.[12] If they did so, the third parties could not claim damages for conspiracy at common law[13]; and it used to be thought that they had no standing at all to challenge such agreements. But in *Eastham v Newcastle United Football Club Ltd*[14] a professional footballer sought a declaration that the "retain and transfer" system was invalid. The remedy was granted, not only against his club, but also against the Football Association and the Football League, with whom the plaintiff had never been in any contractual relationship; and it was said to be available "whether or not the plaintiff has a legal cause of action against the defendants".[15] The weakness of this remedy by way of declaration is that it has no

---

[6] [1959] Ch. 108; *cf. Mineral Water, etc. Trade Protection Soc v Booth* (1887) 36 Ch.D. 465; Sales, 104 L.Q.R. 600.

[7] See above, p.456.

[8] See *TSC Europe (UK) Ltd v Massey* [1999] I.R.L.R. 22 at 29; *cf.* below, at n.16.

[9] See *Esso Petroleum Ltd v Harper's Garage (Stourport) Ltd* [1968] A.C. 269 at 300, 319.

[10] *Hanover Insurance Brokers v Shapiro* [1994] I.R.L.R. 82; *Dawnay Day & Co Ltd v D'Alphen* [1997] I.R.L.R. 442, so far as it relates to clause 12.1.2 of the service contract: see [1997] I.R.L.R. 285, 296 (contrast *Alliance Paper Group plc v Prestwich* [1996] I.R.L.R. 25, where the "no poaching" covenant referred only to *senior* employees).

[11] See the *Dawnay Day* case, above [1997] I.R.L.R. 442 at 448 so far as it relates to clause 12.1.1. of the contract.

[12] *Boddington v Lawton* [1994] I.C.R. 478.

[13] *Mogul SS. Co v McGregor, Gow & Co* [1892] A.C. 25 at 39, 42, 46, 51, 57, 58.

[14] [1964] Ch. 413; above, p.457; *cf. Greig v Insole* [1978] 1 W.L.R. 302; *Newport Association Football Club Ltd v Football Association of Wales Ltd* [1995] 2 All E.R. 87. The system has been held to contravene Art.48 (now Art.39) of the European Community Treaty (below, p.477): *Union Royale Belge des Sociétés de Football Association ASBL v Bosman* [1996] All E.R. (E.C.) 97.

[15] [1964] Ch. 413 at 426; *cf. R v Jockey Club, Ex p. RAM Racecourses* [1993] 2 All E.R. 225, 243.

coercive effect: it would not prevent the parties to the invalid agreement from continuing to act in accordance with it. The declaration could help the third party only by giving one of the contracting parties grounds for thinking that he could break the agreement with impunity if it suited him to do so.

Sometimes a third party may, even at common law, have a more effective remedy. There is some support for the view that a person can obtain an injunction against a professional association to restrain it from applying a rule under which he is excluded from membership, and so prevented from exercising the profession,[16] on grounds not relevant to his capacity to do so.[17] Whether such a remedy is available in cases of this kind to a plaintiff who has no "cause of action against the defendants"[18] is, however, open to doubt,[19] for normally an injunction will be granted only where there is such a cause of action.[20] In one case[21] it was held that this requirement was satisfied where football clubs claimed a declaration that a resolution passed by an association from which they had resigned was in restraint of trade. The mere availability of a declaration was said to be a "cause of action", so that an interlocutory injunction could be granted to the clubs to restrain the association from acting on the resolution until the action for a declaration came to trial. This conclusion is, however, hard to reconcile with that part of the reasoning of the *Eastham* case (quoted above[22]) which assumes that a declaration is available even though the plaintiff has *no* cause of action against the third party. The possibility of the third party's obtaining injunctive relief appears, in any event, to be restricted to cases in which the right to work (or perhaps the right to trade[23]) is arbitrarily restricted by a contract between others. It seems unlikely that a buyer of goods or services could at common law get an injunction against a price-ring merely because it operated to his prejudice.

(3) Trade unions and employers' associations

At common law the validity of the rules of a trade union depended nominally on the principles which governed other contracts in restraint of trade. But in practice there was at one time a strong judicial tendency to hold such rules illegal. The courts relied in particular on the fact that the rules of a trade union might require an employee to stop work against his will; and they were no doubt also influenced by the fear that they might be called on to enforce a strike by injunction. The common law position was changed by legislation as long ago as 1871[24]; and the matter is now dealt with by the Trade Union

---

[16] The rule would not be contrary to public policy unless it had this effect: *cf. Cheall v APEX* [1983] 2 A.C. 180 at 191 (expulsion from a trade union).

[17] See *Nagle v Feilden* [1966] 2 Q.B. 633; A.L.G. (1966) 82 L.Q.R. 319; Rideout, (1966) 29 M.L.R. 424. That case concerned discrimination now unlawful under the Sex Discrimination Act 1975; but the same principle might now apply to (for example) discrimination on religious or political grounds; or if there has been a denial of "natural justice": see *McInnes v Onslow-Fane* [1978] 1 W.L.R. 1520 (where there was no such denial). In *R. v Jockey Club, Ex p. RAM Racecourses Ltd* [1993] 2 All E.R. 225 at 247–248 it was suggested that the more appropriate remedy would be by way of judicial review; but this suggestion was doubted in *R. v Disciplinary Committee of the Jockey Club, Ex p. Aga Khan* [1993] 1 W.L.R. 909 at 933 as there was no sufficient "public law" element in cases of the kind here under discussion. Freedom of religion is protected by Human Rights Act 1998, Sch.1, Pt I, Art.9, but this provision would make unlawful only the acts of a "public authority": s.6, see further p.479, below.

[18] See above, at n.15.

[19] *R. v Disciplinary Committee of the Jockey Club, Ex p. Aga Khan* [1993] 1 W.L.R. 909 at 933, where the applicant did have a cause of action in contract.

[20] See below, p.1047.

[21] *Newport Association Football Club v Football Association of Wales Ltd* [1995] 2 All E.R. 87.

[22] At n.15, above.

[23] It was this right which was at stake in the *Newport* case, above n.21.

[24] Trade Union Act 1871, s.3.

and Labour Relations (Consolidation) Act 1992. A detailed analysis of this complicated Act cannot be attempted in this book; but the main point is that under s.11 the purposes of a trade union[25] are not, by reason only of the fact that they are in restraint of trade, to be unlawful so as to make void or voidable any agreement; nor is any rule of a union to be unenforceable by reason only of its being in restraint of trade.[26] The Act contains similar provisions with regard to the purposes and rules of employers' associations,[27] which are to the same extent excepted from the scope of the restraint of trade doctrine.[28] But an agreement or rule of a trade union may still be invalid for some other reason. In particular, an employee (or person seeking employment) has a statutory right not to be excluded or expelled from a trade union[29] except in certain specified circumstances; and union rules which restrict membership are unenforceable unless they satisfy one or more of a number of criteria laid down by the legislation: *e.g.*, they may validly restrict membership by reference to qualifications for the type of work in question.[30]

(4) Exclusive dealing

The original tendency of the common law was to regard exclusive dealing arrangements as valid. This attitude is illustrated by decisions upholding sole agency and exclusive service agreements,[31] agreements not to buy or sell goods except from or to a particular person,[32] and agreements not to use goods except with others made by the same manufacturer.[33] In other cases, the courts have upheld[34] a covenant on the purchase of land giving the vendor the exclusive right of supplying beer to any public house built on the land; a contract by which the owner of a restaurant agreed to buy all the burgundy sold there from the claimants[35]; and a contract by a purchaser of garage premises to buy from the vendor all petrol used in the business carried on there.[36] Very occasionally, an exclusive dealing agreement was held invalid: for example, where a brassfounder contracted to execute orders only for a particular firm, which did not bind itself to place any orders with him.[37] Where the agreements were upheld, the rules relating to restraint of

---

[25] As defined by s.1.

[26] The exact scope of s.11 depends on whether or not the union is a "special register body" as defined by s.117.

[27] As defined by s.122(1); *semble* that two employers who agree not to "poach" on each other's labour force (as in *Kores Manufacturing Co Ltd v Kolok Manufacturing Co Ltd* [1959] Ch. 108, above, p.466) are not, for that reason alone, an "organisation" within s.122.

[28] s.128: the exact scope of this section depends on whether the association is incorporated.

[29] Trade Union and Labour Relations (Consolidation) Act 1992, ss.174 to 177 (as substituted by Trade Union Reform and Employment Rights Act 1993, s.14). *cf.* also Disability Discrimination Act 1995, s.13.

[30] 1992 Act, above, s.174(3).

[31] See *Esso Petroleum Co Ltd v Harper's Garage (Stourport) Ltd* [1968] A.C. 269 at 294, 307, 336; the last dictum excepts restrictions which are "purely limitative or sterilising" as in *Young v Timmins* (1831) 1 C. & J. 331, below n.37 and *cf.* above, p.464.

[32] *Donnell v Bennett* (1883) 22 Ch.D. 835; *Metropolitan Electric Supply Co v Ginder* [1901] 2 Ch. 799; *Monkland v Jack Barclay Ltd* [1951] 2 K.B. 252; *BMTA v Gilbert* [1951] 2 All E.R. 641.

[33] *United Shoe Machinery Co of Canada v Brunet* [1909] A.C. 330, criticised in the *Esso* case, above, at p.297.

[34] *Catt v Tourle* (1869) L.R. 4 Ch.App. 654 (the actual decision is no longer law: Megarry and Wade, *The Law of Real Property* (5th ed.), p.772).

[35] *Bouchard Servais v Prince's Hall Restaurant Ltd* (1904) 20 T.L.R. 574; *Greenall's Management Ltd v Canavan, The Times,* August 20, 1997. See Supply of Beer (Tied Estates) Order 1989 (SI 1989/2390); Supply of Beer (Tied Estates) (Amendment) Order 1997 (SI 1997/1740); Supply of Beer (Loan Ties, etc.) Order 1989 (SI 1989/2258).

[36] *Foley v Classique Coaches* [1934] 2 K.B. 1.

[37] *Young v Timmins* (1831) 1 Cr. & J. 331; the reasoning (based on lack of *adequate* consideration) would no longer be accepted: *Esso Petroleum Co Ltd v Harper's Garage (Stourport) Ltd* [1968] A.C. 269 at 294; and *cf. ibid.* 336. The actual decision is also hard to reconcile with the principles stated below, pp.504–505.

trade were in some cases simply not mentioned, while in others the rules were mentioned but the contracts were nevertheless held valid. In these cases, it was not always clear whether the contracts were valid because the restraint of trade doctrine did not apply to them at all or because its requirements were satisfied. The distinction is crucial because if the doctrine did not apply at all it would be unnecessary for the person seeking to enforce the agreement to establish its reasonableness.

The older authorities must now be read subject to a line of cases concerned with the validity of "solus agreements" between oil companies and garage proprietors. These agreements were usually made when an oil company advanced money to help with the purchase or development of garage premises; in return, the garage proprietor would give three undertakings: a "tying covenant", to buy all petrol (and sometimes certain other products) from the oil company; a "compulsory trading covenant", to keep his garage open at all reasonable times for the sale of petrol; and a "continuity covenant", to extract similar undertakings from any person to whom he might sell the garage during the subsistence of the solus agreement. The leading *Esso* case[38] concerned solus agreements made in respect of two garages. One agreement was to last for about four and a half years, and the other for 21 years. The House of Lords held that the solus agreements were within the restraint of trade doctrine; that the four-and-a-half year agreement was valid; but that the 21 year agreement was invalid as it was unreasonable and contrary to the public interest. Undertakings with regard to solus petrol agreements were later given to the Government by oil companies in consequence of a report by the Monopolies Commission[39]; but the decision in the *Esso* case gives rise to a number of general problems which still require discussion.

(a) WHETHER SUCH AGREEMENTS ARE WITHIN THE RESTRAINT OF TRADE DOCTRINE. In the *Esso* case, where Lord Pearce distinguished between "those contracts which are in restraint of trade and . . . those which merely regulate the normal commercial relations between the parties and which are therefore free from the doctrine".[40] He regarded solus agreements as falling within the former class, principally on the ground that the oil company gave no assurance that it would provide a supply of petrol at a reasonable price.[41] Lord Wilberforce said that contracts were not within the doctrine of restraint of trade if they were "such . . . as, under contemporary conditions, may be found to have passed into the accepted and normal currency of contractual or conveyancing relations".[42] The agreements in the *Esso* case were not of a kind which had in this way "passed into acceptance . . . ; the solus system is both too recent and too variable for this to be said".[43] However, Lord Wilberforce reserved the powers of the court to subject even "accepted" contracts to scrutiny in the light of changing social or economic conditions or of special features in individual transactions.[44] Later decisions have, in particular, made it clear that a contract is not taken out of the restraint of trade doctrine merely because it is in standard form and contains only terms which are usual in that type of transaction.[45] This factor may take contracts out of the restraint of trade doctrine

---

[38] *Esso Petroleum Co Ltd v Harper's Garage (Stourport) Ltd* [1968] A.C. 269; Heydon, 85 L.Q.R. 229; P.V.B., 83 L.Q.R. 478; Koh [1967] C.L.J. 151; and see Whiteman, 29 M.L.R. 507.
[39] 1965, House of Commons Paper 264; further undertakings were given in 1976 and 1994: Borrie, L.S.Gaz. Jan. 26, 1977, pp.71–72.
[40] [1968] A.C. 269 at 327.
[41] *ibid.* at 329.
[42] *ibid.* at 332–333.
[43] *ibid.* at 337.
[44] *ibid.* at 333; *Watson v Prager* [1991] 1 W.L.R. 726 at 744.
[45] *Watson v Prager*, above.

if they have been freely negotiated,[46] but the position is different where there is great disparity of bargaining power and the terms are imposed by the stronger on the weaker party. In *A Schroeder Music Publishing Co v Macaulay*[47] it was accordingly held that a contract by which an unknown song-writer undertook to give his exclusive services to a publisher who made no promise to publish his work was subject to the doctrine. Lord Reid said: "Normally the doctrine of restraint of trade has no application to such restrictions: they require no justification. But if contractual restrictions appear to be unnecessary or to be reasonably capable of enforcement in an oppressive manner, then they must be justified before they can be enforced".[48] This may be the position even where the contract is made on terms settled by a professional association for the purpose of protecting the party subject to the restraint, and where both parties have no alternative but to make use of such terms.[49]

The tests proposed by Lords Pearce and Wilberforce in the *Esso* case, and by Lord Reid in the *Schroeder* case continue to recognise the possibility that some exclusive dealing and exclusive service agreements will not be subject to the doctrine of restraint of trade. Many of the earlier cases which support this view[50] were cited, and none was overruled, in the *Esso* case. At the same time, the tests are very vague and leave much discretion to the courts in defining the scope of the doctrine in relation to such contracts. It seems probable that in future the doctrine will apply to contracts of this kind if they present any novel or unusual features, or if they contain terms which are likely to operate harshly on a party of weak bargaining power.

(b) REQUIREMENTS OF VALIDITY. Where an exclusive dealing or service contract is subject to the doctrine of restraint of trade, the usual requirements must be satisfied before it can be enforced.

(i) *The interest.* We have distinguished elsewhere between "proprietary" and "commercial" interests[51]; and the *Esso* case shows that a "commercial" interest will suffice in the present group of cases. Lord Reid there said that the statement "that a person is not to be protected against mere competition" was "not . . . very helpful in a case like the present"[52] and Lord Pearce, after expressing substantially the same view, seems to have regarded the oil company's "network of outlets"[53] as the interest which they sought to protect. Some difficulty arises from Lord Morris' description of the covenants as "naked covenants or covenants in gross"[54]; but he obviously regarded this, not as a ground of invalidity[55] (for he upheld one of the covenants), but merely as a ground for subjecting the covenants to the doctrine of restraint of trade.

(ii) *Reasonableness and fairness.* To satisfy the test of reasonableness, the party seeking to enforce the restrictions must show that they were "no more than what was reasonably required to protect his legitimate interest".[56] Here, as elsewhere,[57] relevant factors include the length of the restraint[58] and the adequacy of the consideration provided for it. We have seen that in the *Esso* case a four-and-a-half year tie was upheld and a 21-year

---

[46] *A Schroeder Music Publishing Co Ltd v Macaulay* [1974] 1 W.L.R. 1308 at 1314.
[47] See above; *cf. O'Sullivan v Management Agency & Music Ltd* [1985] Q.B. 428; *Watson v Prager*, above.
[48] [1974] 1 W.L.R. 1308, 1314; *Watson v Prager*, above at p.747.
[49] *Watson v Prager* [1991] 1 W.L.R. 726.
[50] See above, p.468.
[51] See above, p.457.
[52] [1968] A.C. 269 at 301.
[53] *ibid.* at 329.
[54] *ibid.* at 309.
[55] *cf.* above, p.454.
[56] *A Schroeder Music Publishing Co Ltd v Macaulay* [1974] 1 W.L.R. 1308 at 1310.
[57] See above, pp.458–462.
[58] *Watson v Prager* [1991] 1 W.L.R. 726 at 748.

one struck down.[59] But in a later case a 21-year tie in a solus agreement contained in a lease was upheld since the premises were already, before the lease, subject to a valid three-year tie, since the tenant had the right to break the lease after seven and 14 years, and since the landlord had paid the tenant £35,000 under a previous transaction leading to the execution of the lease.[60]

The fairness of the contract is also a relevant factor, particularly where the restrictions are imposed on the weaker party to a relationship of unequal bargaining power. The point is well illustrated by agreements between musical performers and recording companies. In one case,[61] a long-term (though not exclusive) contract of this kind was made to settle differences which had arisen under an earlier contract between the parties; when the new contract was made, the performer's reputation was well established and he had the benefit of expert legal advice. In these circumstances, the new contract was regarded as reasonable in view of the benefits which the performer had received under it. By contrast, the restriction imposed on the composer in *A Schroeder Music Publishing Co Ltd v Macaulay*[62] was neither necessary nor fair. It extended over a period of five years, during which he had to submit all his compositions to the publishers, while they were under no obligation to promote his work and had to make no more than minimal payments if they failed to do so. The restriction was accordingly invalid as it went beyond the protection of the publishers' legitimate interests and operated harshly on the other party: "his work will be sterilised and he can earn nothing from his abilities as a composer".[63]

Terms may also be unfair because the party claiming the benefit of the restriction is under the contract put into a position where his interest conflicts with the duty that he owes to the other party. This was the position in *Watson v Prager*[64] where, a professional boxer, agreed to be "managed and directed exclusively" by the defendant, who was both a manager and a boxing promoter and who undertook to negotiate terms "as advantageous as possible" for the boxer; the agreement was for an initial period of three years, renewable for a further period of equal length. The main reason why the agreement was held to be contrary to public policy was that it was not fair to hold the boxer to an agreement of such long duration since under it the defendant's duty as manager was to negotiate the highest possible fees for the boxer, and this conflicted with his interest as promoter, since in that capacity he would have to meet the cost of these fees.

(iii) *Public interest.* Lord Reid in the *Schroeder* case based his decision partly on the ground that "The public interest requires in the interests both of the public and of the individual that everyone should be free so far as practicable to earn a livelihood and give to the public the fruits of his particular abilities".[65] The *Esso* case, too, is noteworthy for the stress placed on the element of public interest; indeed Lord Hodson bases the invalidity of the 21-year agreement "on the public interest rather than on that of the parties"[66]; Lord Pearce says that the ultimate ground for interference in all cases is public policy so that there is no real separation between "what is reasonable on grounds of public policy and what is reasonable as between the parties".[67] Lord Wilberforce

---

[59] See above, p.469.

[60] *Alec Lobb (Garages) Ltd v Total Oil (Great Britain) Ltd* [1985] 1 W.L.R. 173.

[61] *Panayiotou v Sony Music Entertainment (UK) Ltd, The Times,* June 30, 1994. *cf.* the *Alec Lobb* case, above.

[62] [1974] 1 W.L.R. 1308; above, p.470.

[63] *ibid.,* at 1314.

[64] [1991] 1 W.L.R. 726.

[65] [1974] 1 W.L.R. 1308 at 1313; Lord Diplock at 1315 seems to view this point with some scepticism.

[66] [1968] A.C. 269 at 321; and *cf.* above, p.463.

[67] [1968] A.C. 269 at 324.

appears to take the same view but adds that it is "important that the vitality of the second limb . . . of the wider aspects of a single public policy rule should continue to be recognised".[68] These statements show that the courts would in these cases reject the once fashionable argument[69] that, if an agreement was shown to be reasonable between the parties, the public interest would also be satisfied.

(5) Covenants affecting the use of land

Such covenants are commonly enforced although they no doubt restrain trade, *e.g.* by imposing restrictions on building, or on the carrying on of some particular business or trade, or by providing that the land shall be used for residential purposes only. In the *Esso* case a majority of the House of Lords explained these cases on the ground that "A person buying or leasing land had no previous right to be there at all, let alone to trade there, and when he takes possession of that land subject to a negative restrictive covenant he gives up no right or freedom which he previously had".[70] It has therefore been held that where a person enters into a solus agreement when he acquires land, and that agreement is a term of the conveyance by which the land is transferred, the doctrine of restraint of trade does not apply at all.[71] Nevertheless, it is submitted that the reasoning is hard to reconcile with the emphasis placed in the *Esso* case itself on the element of public interest[72]; for restrictions on the use of land may cause harm to the public where they are imposed at the time when the land is acquired, no less than where they are imposed later. Of course, generally speaking, the object of a restrictive covenant affecting land is to preserve amenities and not to restrain trade or to prevent competition; and in most cases such a covenant would in any event pass the test of reasonableness because it would affect only a small area. But sometimes covenants of this kind do expressly restrain the carrying on of a particular business on the land acquired[73]; and cases of this kind can be imagined in which the covenant would not be reasonable. A person who owned a garage business on a 1,000-acre estate might sell all the land except for the garage and take a covenant that the purchaser would not carry on a garage business on any part of the land bought. Such a covenant could offend public policy just as much as a covenant not to compete within a given radius of the garage. Moreover, we may vary the example by supposing the original owner sells the garage but keeps the rest of the land, and covenants not to carry on a garage business on it. This covenant would, according to the reasoning of the *Esso* case, be subject to the doctrine of restraint of trade, for the landowner would be giving up a right which he previously had, to carry on a garage business on the land which he kept.[74] It is hard to see why the doctrine of restraint of trade should not apply to the first as well as to the second of these hypothetical cases. Suppose, further that the owner of a garage sells or leases it to an oil company and then *leases it back* on terms that include a solus agreement. Here it would seem that he did have a "previous right to be there" so that the doctrine of restraint of

---

[68] [1968] A.C. 269 at 341.

[69] See above, p.463.

[70] [1968] A.C. 269 at 298; *cf. ibid.* at 309, 316–317, 325.

[71] *Cleveland Petroleum Ltd v Dartstone Ltd* [1969] 1 W.L.R. 116; Korah, 32 M.L.R. 323; below, p.473. See also *Re Ravenseft Properties Ltd's Application* [1978] Q.B. 52 (where exceptions are envisaged at 67–68).

[72] See above, at n.66.

[73] See, for example, *Holloway Bros v Hill* [1902] 2 Ch. 612; *Newton Abbott Cooperative Society Ltd v Williamson & Treadgold Ltd* [1952] Ch. 286; *cf. Rother v Colchester Corporation* [1969] 1 W.L.R. 720.

[74] *cf. Kerrick v Schoenberg*, 328 S.W. 2d 595, 602 (1959).

trade would apply.[75] Attempts have, indeed, been made to evade this result by inter-posing a company controlled by the garage owner into such an agreement. Thus there is some support for the view that, if the land is leased from a garage owner and leased back to a company controlled by him, then the restraint of trade doctrine should not apply because *the company* had no "previous right to be there".[76] But the distinction between this situation and that in which the two leases are between the same parties can hardly be justified in terms of public policy. Accordingly, it has been held that the restraint of trade doctrine did apply where garage premises were owned by a company controlled by a mother and son, leased by that company to an oil company and then leased back to the mother and son personally.[77] It was said that the court should "pierce the corporate veil" and not give effect to such a "palpable device"[78] for evading the restraint of trade doctrine.

In three further situations the restraint of trade doctrine applies to covenants affecting land. First, it applies where the covenant is given by A to B on the acquisition of land by A, not from B, but from a third party C, *e.g.* where (as in the *Esso* case itself) the oil company (B) takes the covenant as one of the terms of a loan to A to enable him to buy a garage from C.[79] Secondly, it applies where the owner of a garage mortgages his existing premises and the mortgage contains a solus agreement.[80] Thirdly, it applies where the restriction is imposed not in the conveyance itself but in a separate con-temporaneous agreement: this was the position in *Foley v Classique Coaches*[81] where it was assumed that the doctrine did apply and this assumption seems to have been accepted in the *Esso* case.[82] But it is once again by no means clear why, if the doctrine of restraint of trade can apply in these cases, it should not apply to a restrictive covenant forming part of a conveyance between the parties to the covenant. Perhaps similar principles can be applied, if not at common law, then by virtue of s.84 of the Law of Property Act 1925.[83] That section gives the Lands Tribunal a statutory power in certain cases to discharge or modify restrictive covenants affecting land if they have become obsolete by reason of changes in the character of the neighbourhood or because their continued existence "would impede some reasonable user of the land for private or public purposes". This enactment is, in effect, a statutory extension of the doctrine of public policy to these covenants.[84]

---

[75] *e.g. Amoco Australia Pty Ltd v Rocca Bros Motor Engineering Co Pty Ltd* [1975] A.C. 561; Bowman, 38 M.L.R. 571.

[76] *Cleveland Petroleum Ltd v Dartstone Ltd* [1969] 1 W.L.R. 116, where the claim to enforce the restraint was actually made against an assignee of the company's leasehold interest in the garage.

[77] *Alec Lobb (Garages) Ltd v Total Oil (Great Britain) Ltd* [1985] 1 W.L.R. 173 (where the restraint was held reasonable).

[78] *ibid.* at 178.

[79] Heydon, 85 L.Q.R. 229 at 233 (and *The Restraint of Trade Doctrine*, pp.58–59) argues that this makes the reasoning in the *Esso* case inconsistent with the decision: as A had "no previous right to be there," the restraint of trade doctrine should not have applied. But it is submitted that this part of the reasoning was intended only to apply where the agreement imposing the restriction was between the same parties as the disposition of the land. *cf.* also *Petrofina (Great Britain) Ltd v Martin* [1966] Ch. 146, where a solus agreement with an oil company on the purchase of a garage from a third party was also held invalid for restraint of trade.

[80] *Texaco Ltd v Mulberry Filling Station Ltd* [1972] 1 W.L.R. 814; *semble* the mortgage in the *Esso* case was similarly executed after the defendant company had acquired the Corner Garage (though it was executed in pursuance of an earlier agreement).

[81] [1934] 2 K.B. 1; above, p.468.

[82] See [1968] A.C. 269 at 296, 311, 316, 327, 339.

[83] As amended by s.28 of the Law of Property Act 1969.

[84] Under the section, the person seeking modification may be ordered to pay compensation. It is arguable that this practice should be extended to some other cases where a person seeks relief from a promise in restraint of trade for which he has received consideration.

(6) Other agreements

In the past the courts were reluctant to apply the doctrine of restraint of trade to new classes of contracts. Thus at common law price-maintenance agreements are valid,[85] though some such agreements may be void under the rules (to be discussed later in this Chapter) which prohibit certain anti-competitive agreements.[86] So, too, at common law an agreement between two persons not to bid against each other at an auction is not illegal[87] but if at least one of them is a dealer they may be guilty of a statutory offence under the Auctions (Bidding Agreements) Act 1927.[88] This Act also provides that the contract can be set aside by the owner of the property auctioned; and, although it does not explicitly invalidate the agreement not to bid as between the parties to it, such invalidity probably follows at common law from the criminality of the agreement.[89] In these cases legislative intervention has been necessary to extend the scope of the doctrine of restraint of trade, but there are signs that the courts are prepared to resume a more creative role in this field. In the *Esso* case Lord Wilberforce said that no exhaustive tests could be stated for defining or identifying contracts in restraint of trade[90]; and that, although such contracts might "be listed, provisionally, in categories . . . the classification must remain fluid and the categories can never be closed".[91]

Subsequent cases illustrate a number of new departures. It has, for example, been held that covenants in a joint venture agreement (not amounting to a partnership) were subject to the restraint of trade doctrine and so enforceable only to the extent to which they were reasonable, having regard to the covenantee's interest.[92] It seems that, where a dispute about intellectual property is settled, the doctrine can apply to terms of the settlement which restrict a party's right to make use of the property.[93] A further novel application of the doctrine is illustrated by *Pharmaceutical Society of Great Britain v Dickson*,[94] where the House of Lords held that a rule of the Society restricting the trading activities of chemists was invalid. One ground for the decision was that the rule was *ultra vires*[95]; but a majority of the House of Lords also held that it was invalid for restraint of trade.[96] The rule was held invalid on this ground even though it was no more than part of a professional code of ethics which was not legally binding (whether as a contract or otherwise). *A fortiori*, a rule of a professional association may be in restraint of trade if it *is* intended to have contractual force. It has, for example, been said that the rule of the International Tennis Federation by which its members are subject to disqualification for taking prohibited drugs is in restraint of trade, though reasonable and hence valid at common law.[97]

---

[85] *Palmolive Co (of England) v Freedman* [1928] Ch. 264. *cf. Re Dott's Lease* [1920] 1 Ch. 281 (covenant to maintain price of tickets at the Garrick Theatre).

[86] See below, p.476, esp. at n.16. Whether the agreement is actually void will depend on (*inter alia*) the factors referred to on p.476 at n.16.

[87] *Rawlings v General Trading Co Ltd* [1921] 1 K.B. 635; *Harrop v Thompson* [1975] 1 W.L.R. 545.

[88] As amended by the Auctions (Bidding Agreement) Act 1969.

[89] See above, p.430.

[90] [1968] A.C. 269 at 332.

[91] *ibid.* at 337; *cf. Petrofina (Great Britain) Ltd v Martin* [1966] Ch. 146 at 169.

[92] *Dawnay Day & Co Ltd v D'Alphen* [1997] I.R.L.R. 422.

[93] *World Wide Fund for Nature v World Wrestling Federation* [2002] EWCA Civ 196; [2002] U.K.C.L.R. 388 at [40–42], where the agreement was held valid.

[94] [1970] A.C. 403; Koh, 31 M.L.R. 70.

[95] See below, p.560.

[96] Contrast *R. v General Medical Council, Ex p. Coleman* [1990] 1 All E.R. 489 (refusal to allow advertising of holistic medical practice held not to be open to challenge for restraint of trade as the refusal was authorised by statute).

[97] *Wilander and Novacek v Tobin & Jude* [1997] 2 Lloyd's Rep. 295 at 297.

The doctrine of restraint of trade does not apply merely because a contract restricts a party's freedom to deal with its particular subject-matter, for every contract "necessarily limits the freedom to enter into another contract".[98] The essential feature of contracts within the doctrine is that of "fettering a person's freedom in the future to carry on his trade, business or profession".[99] Various further kinds of agreements or arrangements can be imagined which might have this effect: for example, an agreement by A not to manufacture a certain product in competition with B[1]; an agreement on the sale of a ship not to operate her on certain routes; an agreement by a buyer not to export goods to a particular country[2]; or an agreement, on the lease of a hall for an exhibition, not to hold a similar exhibition there for six months.[3] It is not suggested that all or any of such agreements will be held invalid; but they may require justification under the doctrine of restraint of trade.

(7) Competition law

Earlier in this Chapter, we saw that the common law relating to restrictive trading agreements[4] gave only limited protection to third parties who might be adversely affected by the willingness of the parties to such agreements to give effect to them. A more comprehensive attack on this problem has, since 1956,[5] been made by legislation. The relevant rules are now contained in the Competition Act 1998 and will be amplified by further rules to be made and decisions to be taken under it.

Chap.I of Pt I of this Act prohibits a number of anti-competitive practices; it does so in words which closely follow those of Art.81[6] of the European Community Treaty.[7] This prohibition (called "the Chapter 1 prohibition"[8]) is to be interpreted in accordance with the extensive case law on the interpretation and effects of that Article[9]; the main difference between the two sets of provisions lies in their geographical scope. The prohibitions apply to agreements[10] between undertakings,[11] decisions by associations of undertakings or concerted practices which (a) may affect trade (under Chap.I) within the United Kingdom or (under Art.81) between Member States, and (b) have as their object or effect the prevention, restriction or distortion of trade within (under Chap.I) the United Kingdom or (under Art.81) the common market.[12] Prohibited agreements (etc.) are void[13] unless exemption is granted by (under the 1998 Act) the Office of Fair

---

[98] *Shearson Lehman Hutton Inc v Maclaine Watson & Co* [1989] 2 Lloyd's Rep. 570 at 615.

[99] *Shearson Lehman Hutton Inc v Maclaine Watson & Co* [1989] 2 Lloyd's Rep. 570 at 615.

[1] *International Pediatric Products Ltd v Cuddle-King Products Ltd* (1964) 46 D.L.R. (2d) 581.

[2] As in *National Panasonic (UK) Ltd v Commission of the European Communities* [1981] I.C.R. 51.

[3] *cf. Modern Exhibition Services v Cardiff Corporation* (1965) 63 L.G.R. 316, where restraint of trade was not discussed.

[4] See above, p.466.

[5] When the first of the Restrictive Trade Practices Acts (now repealed) was passed.

[6] Formerly Art.85.

[7] Which has the force of law in the United Kingdom by virtue of the European Communities Act 1972, s.2. The European Communities (Amendment) Act 1993 does not affect the rules stated in the text.

[8] Competition Act 1998, s.2(8).

[9] This is the effect of s.60 of the 1998 Act.

[10] It has been held under what is now Art.81 that the agreement need not be legally binding: *Italian Flat Glass* case [1990] 4 C.M.L.R. 535; *Re Northern Europe-USA Freight Lines Agreement* [1990] 4 C.M.L.R. 518.

[11] An individual engaged in economic activity can for the purposes of what is now Art.81 be an "undertaking" *Re Unitel* [1978] 3 C.M.L.R. 306 (opera singers).

[12] Competition Act 1998 s.2(1); European Community Treaty Art.81(1).

[13] 1998 Act, s.2(4); Treaty, Art.81(2).

Trading[14] or (under the Treaty) the European Community authorities.[15] Examples of agreements covered by the prohibition include those which "directly or indirectly fix purchase or selling prices or any other trading conditions".[16] Under Art.81, this this prohibition applies, not only to so-called "horizontal" agreements (*i.e.* to those between parties operating at the same level of production or supply, such as agreements between manufacturers as to the prices which they will charge for their products), but also to so-called "vertical" agreements (*i.e.* to those between parties operating at different levels of supply, such as exclusive dealing agreements between producers and dealers[17]). Under the 1998 Act, its provisions (including the Chap.I prohibition) can be made to apply to "vertical" and to "land" agreements by delegated legislation[18] defining these terms,[19] alternatively, such legislation may exclude the application of these prohibitions to such agreements.[20] It is the latter power which has been exercised,[21] so that "vertical" and "land" agreements are in general[22] excluded from the category of agreements prohibited by the 1998 Act.[23] The Act further makes claims for monetary compensation available to persons who have suffered loss or damage as a result of an infringement of these prohibitions.[23a] Where such persons are consumers, such claims can be brought on their behalf by bodies to be specified for this purpose by the Secretary of State.[23b] Such claims could, for example, have been brought on behalf of consumers who had paid prices inflated by price-fixing agreements between suppliers.

No attempt can be made in a book of this nature even to summarise the extremely complex rules which govern the scope of the above prohibitions and of the exemptions from them which have been granted under European Community law[24]; but a number of points must be made about the relationship between the prohibitions and the common law rules relating to restraint of trade. First, an employee is not an "undertaking" within Art.81,[25] so that the prohibitions would not affect the common law rules relating to restraints in employment contracts.[26] Secondly, the Art.81 prohibitions apply only where the agreement (etc.) in question has an "appreciable" effect on competition and not where that effect is "insignificant".[27] The crucial factor in determining whether the effect is "appreciable" (as opposed to "insignificant") is the percentage of the share of the market affected by it: for example, the prohibitions have been held not to apply where that share was no more than 0.02 per cent[28]; and it seems that a share of less than

---

[14] See Enterprise Act 2002, s.2(3).

[15] 1998 Act, ss.4, 6; Treaty, Art.81(3).

[16] 1998 Act, s.2(2)(a); Treaty Art.85(1)(a).

[17] *Consten & Grundig v Commission* [1966] E.C.R. 299.

[18] s.50(1).

[19] s.50(5).

[20] s.50(2).

[21] Competition Act (Land and Vertical Agreements Exclusion) Order 2000 (SI 2000/310).

[22] The Order cited in n.21 reserves power to withdraw the exclusion from particular agreements.

[23] *i.e.* by s.2 of the 1998 Act; see above after n.8.

[23a] S.47A, as inserted by Enterprise Act 2002, s.18.

[23b] S.47B, as inserted by Enterprise Act 2002, s.19.

[24] See, *e.g.* Bellamy and Child, *Common Market Law of Competition* (4th ed.).

[25] See *Suiker Unie v Commission* [1975] E.C.R. 1663 at 2007, §539.

[26] See above, pp.455 *et seq.*

[27] *Völk v Vervaeke* [1969] C.M.L.R. 273.

[28] *ibid.*; *cf. Passmore v Morland plc* [1998] 4 All E.R. 468, affirmed, [1999] 3 All E.R. 1005; *Inntrepreneur Pub Co (CPC) Ltd v Price, The Times*, December 4, 1998. The question of "appreciable" effect is judged at the time, not of the agreement, but of the proceedings: *Passmore v Morland plc* [1999] 3 All E.R. 1005, so that an agreement which was invalid under Art.81 when made may become valid in the light of later events, and conversely. Contrast the position under the common law of restraint of trade: above, p.416.

five per cent would be treated in the same way.[29] In determining whether the effect of an agreement is "appreciable," the court can take account of other agreements made (for example) by the supplier with other distributors[30]; but the point remains that many of the agreements dealt with by the common law rules discussed earlier in this Chapter would not have a sufficiently "appreciable" effect to be prohibited by Art.81 or by Chap.I of the Act. The point appears to be that the purpose of the two sets of rules is different: the Art.81 and Chap.I prohibitions are concerned with the effect of agreements (etc.) on the economy as a whole, while under the common law rules an agreement may be void by reason of its adverse effect merely on the party restrained by it.[31] The common law rules therefore continue to operate alongside the Art.81 and Chap.I prohibitions, so that it is perfectly possible for an agreement to fall outside those prohibitions but nevertheless to be invalid for restraint of trade at common law. The same may also be true of agreements which fall outside Art.81 and Chap.I because of their geographical scope as described above[32]; e.g., of an agreement which affected trade only in South America.

Contracts in restraint of trade can also be affected by the prohibition contained in Chap.II of Pt I of the Competition Act 1998 and Art.82[33] of the European Community Treaty against abuse by an undertaking of a "dominant position".[34] Such an abuse can of course occur without any contract being made to give effect to it; but it could also invalidate certain types of contracts,[35] such as contracts obliging a buyer of goods to secure supplies of other goods or services from the same supplier.[36]

(8) Other aspects of European Community law

Other provisions of the European Community Treaty which may be relevant in the context of contracts in restraint of trade include those which relate to the free movement of goods,[37] the free movement of workers,[38] freedom of establishment[39] and freedom to provide services.[40] Discussion of these provisions is beyond the scope of this book; reference should be made to works on European Community law.[41]

4. Scope of the Doctrine of Public Policy[42]

Public policy is a variable notion, depending on changing manners, morals and economic conditions. In theory, this flexibility of the doctrine of public policy could provide a

---

[29] See, e.g., *Miller v Commission* [1978] E.C.R. 131; *AEG v Commission* [1983] E.C.R. 3151. *cf.* Competition Act 1998 s.39, relating to "small" agreements.
[30] *Delimitis v Henninger Bräu* [1991] I E.C.R. 935 (tied house beer supplies).
[31] *cf.* above, p.461 at n.64.
[32] See above, p.475 at n.12.
[33] Formerly Art.86.
[34] Competition Act 1998, s.18.
[35] It could also give rise to a remedy for refusal to enter into a contract: see above p.4.
[36] *e.g. Hilti v Commission* [1991] II E.C.R. 1439; *Elopak Italia Srl v Tetra Pak (No.2)* [1992] 4 C.M.L.R. 551.
[37] *e.g.*, Art.28 (formerly Art.30), prohibiting quantitative restrictions on imports; this was held not to have been contravened in *R. v Royal Pharmaceutical Soc. of G.B.* [1989] 2 All E.R. 758.
[38] Art.39 (formerly Art.48); see *Union Royale Belge des Sociétés de Football Association ASBL v Bosman* [1996] All E.R. (EC) 97.
[39] Art.43 (formerly Art.52).
[40] Art.49 (formerly Art.59); this was held not to have contravened in *Wilander and Novacek v Tobin and Jude* [1997] 2 Lloyd's Rep. 295 or in *Edwards v British Athletics Federation, The Times*, June 30, 1997.
[41] *e.g.*, Wyatt and Dashwood, *European Community Law* (3rd ed.).
[42] Shand [1972] C.L.J. 144.

judge with an excuse for invalidating any contract which he violently disliked. With this danger in mind judges have sometimes criticised the doctrine of public policy. In 1824 Burroughs J. described it as "a very unruly horse, and when once you get astride it you never know where it will carry you. It may lead you from the sound law".[43] And Lord Halsbury has denied that any court could "invent a new head of public policy".[44]

On the other hand, the law does adapt itself to changes in economic and social conditions, as can be seen particularly from the development of the rules as to contracts in restraint of trade. This point has often been recognised judicially. Thus Lord Haldane has said: "What the law recognises as contrary to public policy turns out to vary greatly from time to time".[45] And Lord Denning has put a similar point of view: "With a good man in the saddle, the unruly horse can be kept in control. It can jump over obstacles".[46]

The present attitude of the courts represents a compromise between the flexibility inherent in the notion of public policy and the need for certainty in commercial affairs.

In the interests of certainty the courts will in general refuse to apply the doctrine of public policy to contracts of a kind to which the doctrine has never been applied before. In *Printing & Numerical Registering Co v Sampson*,[47] for instance, an inventor assigned a patent to a company and also agreed to assign to the company any patent of a like nature thereafter to be acquired by him. He argued that this agreement was contrary to public policy as it tended to discourage inventors. In rejecting the argument, Jessel M.R. said: "You are not to extend arbitrarily those rules which say that a given contract is void as being against public policy".[48] The reason why the courts are less ready to apply the doctrine of public policy to new classes of contracts is that Parliament and its delegates have become more active in this field.[49]

But in some cases (particularly "where the subject-matter is 'lawyers' law' "[50]) judicial intervention may still as a last resort be desirable.[51] The courts may occasionally invalidate a contract even though it is of a kind to which the doctrine of public policy has not been applied before. Such novel applications of the doctrine of public policy are illustrated by decisions to the effect that a moneylending contract is illegal if it imposes

---

[43] *Richardson v Mellish* (1824) 2 Bing. 229 at 252; *McFarlane v Tayside Health Board* [2000] 2 A.C. 59 at 100–101.

[44] *Janson v Driefontein Consolidated Mines Ltd* [1902] A.C. 484 at 491; *cf. Texaco Ltd v Mulberry Filling Station Ltd* [1972] 1 W.L.R. 814 at 827; *Geismar v Sun Alliance & London Insurance* [1978] Q.B. 383 at 389; *Nickerson v Barraclough* [1981] Ch. 426; *Deutsche Schachtbau-und Tiefbohrgesellschaft mbH v Ras Al Khaima National Oil Co* [1990] 1 A.C. 295 at 316 (reversed on other grounds *ibid.* at 329 *et seq.*).

[45] *Rodriguez v Speyer Bros* [1919] A.C. 59 at 79; *cf. Evanturel v Evanturel* (1874) L.R. 6 P.C. 1 at 29; *Davies v Davies* (1887) 36 Ch.D. 359 at 364; *Nordenfelt v Maxim Nordenfelt Guns & Ammunition Co* [1894] A.C. 535 at 553; *Naylor, Benzon & Co v Krainische Industrie Gesellschaft* [1918] 1 K.B. 331 at 345, affirmed [1918] 2 K.B. 486; *Gray v Barr* [1971] 2 Q.B. 554 at 582; *Thai Trading Co v Taylor* [1998] Q.B. 781 at 786 (as to which see above, p.431); *Bevan Ashford v Geoff Yeandle (Contractors) Ltd* [1998] [1999] Ch. 239 at 250.

[46] *Enderby Town FC Ltd v The Football Association Ltd* [1971] Ch. 591 at 606.

[47] (1875) L.R. 19 Eq. 462.

[48] *ibid.* 465.

[49] See *D v NSPCC* [1978] A.C. 171 at 235; *Johnson v Moreton* [1980] A.C. 37 at 67; *Cheall v APEX* [1983] 2 A.C. 180 at 191; *Johnstone v Bloomsbury Health Authority* [1992] Q.B. 333 at 347, 349; *Lancashire CC v Municipal Mutual Insurance Ltd* [1997] Q.B. 897 at 909; *cf. Multiservice Bookbinding Ltd v Marden* [1979] Ch. 84 (Swiss franc uplift clause in mortgage); *Nationwide BS v Registry of Friendly Societies* [1983] 1 W.L.R. 1226 (index-linked mortgage). For a similar argument in relation to the limit of the courts' power to create new crimes, see *DPP v Withers* [1975] A.C. 842 at 858.

[50] *D v NSPCC*, above, at p.235.

[51] *cf. Monkland v Jack Barclay Ltd* [1951] 2 K.B. 252 at 265.

quasi-servile obligations on the borrower[52]; that a contract by which a trade journal promises not to comment on the affairs of a company is illegal as it may prevent the journal from exposing frauds perpetrated by the company[53]; that an attempt to contract out of certain statutory provisions governing the liquidation of companies is contrary to public policy[54]; and that the same is true of an attempt to deprive an agricultural tenant of security of tenure where he is entitled to it by statute.[55] There are also cases in which attempts to impeach agreements by reference to new heads of public policy have been rejected on the ground that the agreement in question did not in fact have any injurious tendency.[56] It may be possible to infer from this reasoning that, if such a tendency had been established, the attempt would not have failed merely because the alleged head of public policy was a novel one.

There have been occasional hints that the courts might extend the doctrine of public policy to strike down contracts furthering certain kinds of discrimination[57]; but this suggestion now gives rise to a difficult problem with regard to the relative functions of Parliament and the courts in matters of public policy. Parliament has made elaborate provisions against discrimination on grounds of sex, colour, race, nationality, ethnic or national origins and disability in certain carefully defined spheres of activity.[58] Religious discrimination[59] was deliberately omitted from the scope of the Acts[60]; and the courts might hesitate to intervene where Parliament had deliberately decided not to do so.[61] On the other hand the courts can take account of these other forms of discrimination in deciding whether a contract satisfies the requirements of validity laid down under an existing head of public policy. In *Nagle v Feilden*,[62] for instance, the Court of Appeal appeared to take the view that, even before the Sex Discrimination Act, a contract in restraint of trade would not be regarded as reasonable, or as consistent with the public interest, if its object was to discriminate against women; and the same might now be true if the object of the contract were to discriminate against some religious group.[63] It is also

---

[52] *Horwood v Millar's Timber & Trading Co* [1917] 1 K.B. 305; above, p.452.

[53] *Neville v Dominion of Canada News Co Ltd* [1915] 3 K.B. 556; *cf. Initial Services Ltd v Putterill* [1968] 1 Q.B. 396 at 410; *Slater v Raw, The Times*, October 15, 1977.

[54] *British Eagle International Airlines Ltd v Cie Nationale Air France* [1975] 1 W.L.R. 758.

[55] *Johnson v Moreton* [1980] A.C. 37; *Featherstone v Staples* [1986] 1 W.L.R. 861; *Gisborne v Burton* [1989] Q.B. 390. The statute in question did not specify the legal effects of attempts to "contract out" of its provisions: contrast the provisions of Rent Act 1977 cited on p.3, n.18, above.

[56] *e.g. Giles v Thompson* [1994] 1 A.C. 142 at 165 rejecting the argument that allegedly champertous car-hire agreements created "a risk of exploitation" of motorists, since no such risk was created.

[57] *Nagle v Feilden* [1966] 2 Q.B. 633 at 655 ("the colour of his hair"); *Edwards v SOGAT* [1971] Ch. 354 at 382 ("the colour of his skin"). See generally Garner, (1972) 35 M.L.R. 478.

[58] Sex Discrimination Act 1975, Pts 1, 2, 3 and 4; see also Equal Pay Act 1970, as amended by Employment Protection Act 1975, s.125 and Sch.16, para.13; Sex Discrimination Act 1986 (as amended by Employment Act 1989); Courts and Legal Services Act 1990, s.64(1); Race Relations Act 1976, Pts 1, 2, 3 and 4; Courts and Legal Services Act 1990, s.64(2); Disability Discrimination Act 1995.

[59] Clauses in wills are not void for religious discrimination: *Blathwayt v Cawley* [1976] A.C. 397; *Re Tuck's ST* [1978] Ch. 49. *cf.* Race Relations Act 1976, s.34(2) and (3), exempting certain charitable instruments and acts done for charitable purposes from the operation of Pts 2, 3 and 4; and see similar provisions in Sex Discrimination Act 1975, s.43(1) and (2).

[60] Contrast Fair Employment (Northern Ireland) Act 1976, s.16, as substituted by Fair Employment (Northern Ireland) Act 1989, s.49 ("religious belief or political opinions"), and *cf.* s.20 of the 1989 Act.

[61] *cf.* in another context, *La Pintada* [1985] A.C. 104, 129; below, p.963.

[62] [1966] 2 Q.B. 633.

[63] The statement in *Mandla v Dowell Lee* [1983] Q.B. 1, 8, 12 that discrimination on grounds which are not racial is "perfectly lawful" merely means that it does not amount to a contravention of the Race Relations Act 1976; the actual decision was reversed by the House of Lords [1983] 2 A.C. 548 on the ground that the discrimination did contravene the Act.

arguable that the courts might in this context take account of the fact that "freedom of . . . religion"[64] is one of the "freedoms" which have been "incorporated into the law of the United Kingdom"[65] by the Human Rights Act 1998. That Act does not in terms affect the validity of contracts between private persons,[66] but it is at least arguable that its enactment has altered the content of public policy in the United Kingdom and so left it open to the courts to declare that contracts are against public policy where their effects would be to infringe those freedoms.[67]

There are, finally, cases in which the courts may invalidate contracts or contractual provisions on what are essentially grounds of public policy without, as a general rule, making express reference to the doctrine of public policy, or to some established "head" of public policy. Some of the limitations on contractual capacity could be based on public policy: and indeed the former "incapacity"[68] of a barrister to make a contract with his client,[69] have been explained on this ground. At one time the invalidity of promises to pay extra wages to seamen who were already bound to serve[70] and of promises not to enforce claims which were known to be invalid[71] was explained on grounds of public policy; though it is now more common to base these rules on lack of consideration.[72] The rule against the assignment of "mere rights of action"[73] was not usually discussed under the heading of public policy, though it might well be considered to belong there.[74] The same is true of the rules under which penalty clauses are invalid,[75] and of some of the common law rules which limit the operation of exemption clauses.[76] All these rules could be regarded as disguised extensions or applications of the doctrine of public policy.

SECTION 3. EFFECTS OF ILLEGALITY

1. Enforcement

A contract affected by illegality is sometimes unenforceable by one party and sometimes unenforceable[77] by both. Where it is "wholly unenforceable because it is contrary to English law, it may . . . accurately be said to be void as a contract, that is, not to be a

---

[64] Human Rights Act 1998, Sch.1, Pt I, Art.9.

[65] *ibid.* s.1.

[66] See the reference to "public authorities" in s.6; and *cf.* above, p.4 n.31.

[67] The argument accordingly extends to the other freedoms referred to in Sch.1.

[68] *Kennedy v Broun* (1863) 13 C.B.(N.S.) 667 at 736.

[69] *Rondel v Worsley* [1969] 1 A.C. 191 at 264. See now Courts and Legal Services Act 1990, s.61. The disapproval of *Rondel v Worsley* in *Arthur J.S. Hall Ltd v Simons* [2002] 1 A.C. 615 does not affect the present point: see above, p.78, n.2.

[70] *Harris v Watson* (1791) Peake 102; above, p.94.

[71] *Wade v Simeon* (1846) 2 C.B. 548; 564 ("almost *contra bonos mores*"); *Edwards v Baugh* (1843) 11 M. & W. 641 at 646.

[72] *Stilk v Myrick* (1809) as reported in 2 Camp. 317; *Poteliakhoff v Teakle* [1938] 2 K.B. 816; above, pp.89, 94.

[73] See below, p.695.

[74] *Trendtex Trading Corp v Crédit Suisse* [1982] A.C. 679 at 694.

[75] See below, pp.964–972. In *Robophone Facilities Ltd v Blank* [1966] 1 W.L.R. 1428 at 1446 and *The Angelic Star* [1988] 1 Lloyd's Rep. 122, 127, the rules invalidating penalty clauses are said to be based on public policy.

[76] *e.g.* above, pp.241–244: see the reference to "public policy" in *HIH Casualty & General Insurance v Chase Manhattan Bank* [2000] EWCA Civ 1250; [2001] 2 Lloyd's Rep. 483, at [103].

[77] *Hall v Woolston Hall Leisure Ltd* [2001] 1 W.L.R. 225 at 234.

contract at all"[78]; or to be "illegal and void".[79] In the restraint of trade cases, the illegality often affects only the term which imposes the restraint, and generally its effect is not to make the contract wholly void: it only makes *the stipulation in restraint of trade* unenforceable or "void"[80] in so far as it has not been performed.[81] It follows that, where one party voluntarily performs[82] another term of such a contract by paying money to the other, the payment cannot be recovered back from the payee; nor, if the contract is between more than two parties, can any other party to it prevent the payor from voluntarily making the payment to the payee.[83] A contract in restraint of trade would only be "wholly unenforceable" and "void" (in accordance with the statements quoted above) where the restraint formed the sole or principal subject-matter of the contract[84]; and it would also be appropriate to describe it as void where the law provided a third party with a remedy to prevent the parties to the contract from acting in accordance with it.[85]

A court will never "enforce" an illegal contract in the sense of ordering a party actually to do something that is unlawful or contrary to public policy.[86] But if A promises B £10 in return for B's promise to do such an act the court may sometimes award damages to A if B fails to do the act, or allow B to claim the £10 if he has actually done it. The law on this question is complex and not very satisfactory.[87]

Where, under the rules to be discussed below, the contract is unenforceable by one or both parties, the court "may refuse to enforce it even if illegality is not pleaded or alleged".[88] The unenforceability of illegal contracts rests on overriding grounds of public interest[89] and the present rule ensures that these cannot be circumvented by the litigation tactics of the parties to such transactions.

(1) Position of guilty party

An illegal contract cannot be enforced by a guilty party. Thus a person who hires a hall to deliver blasphemous lectures cannot sue for possession[90]; a landlord who lets premises

---

[78] *Mackender v Feldia* [1967] 2 Q.B. 590 at 601; *cf. Arnhold Karberg & Co v Blythe, Green, Jourdain & Co* [1915] 2 K.B. 379 at 388 ("illegal and void"), affirmed [1916] 1 K.B. 49; *Customs & Excise Commissioners v Oliver* [1980] 1 All E.R. 353 at 354, 355 ("void"). *Clarke v Chadburn* [1985] 1 W.L.R. 78, 81 ("void for illegality").

[79] *Phoenix General Insurance Co of Greece SA v Halvanon General Insurance Co* [1988] Q.B. 216 at 249, 267, 268 (as to which see above, p.434); *Harbour Assurance (UK) Ltd v Kansa General International Insurance* [1993] Q.B. 701 at 703, 724; *Group Josi Re v Walbrook Insurance Co Ltd* [1996] 1 W.L.R. 1152 at 1172. The assumption that, if the contracts had been held illegal, they would have been void also underlies *Hughes v Asset Management plc* [1995] 3 All E.R. 996, where the actual decision was that the contracts were *not* illegal: see above, p.434.

[80] *Rock Refrigeration Ltd v Jones* [1997] I.C.R. 938 at 948, 953.

[81] *O'Sullivan v Management Agency & Music Ltd* [1985] Q.B. 428 at 469 at least "where, as here, the restriction is during the pendency of the agreement": *ibid.* at 447.

[82] See above, p.466.

[83] *Boddington v Lawton* [1994] I.C.R. 478.

[84] As in *Amoco Australia Pty v Rocca Bros. Motor Engineering Pty Ltd* [1975] A.C. 561, where acts done under the agreement were accordingly annulled with retrospective effect: below, p.509.

[85] See *Newport Association Football Club v Football Association of Wales Ltd* [1995] 2 All E.R. 87, above, p.466.

[86] *e.g.* to perform a contract if to do so would amount to a criminal offence: *cf.* above pp.432, 434.

[87] For an account of tentative proposals for reform, see below, p.472.

[88] *Birkett v Acorn Business Machines Ltd* [1999] 2 All E.R. (Comm) 429 at 433; *Snell v Unity Finance Co Ltd* [1964] Q.B. 203; *Charlton v Fisher* [2001] E.W.C.A. Civ 112; [2002] Q.B. 518 at [80]. But facts giving rise to illegality must be pleaded where the contract is not *ex facie* illegal: *Bank of India v Transcontinental Merchants Ltd* [1982] 1 Lloyd's Rep. 427.

[89] *Birkett's* case, above, at 435 ("the court's overriding duty to the public interest supersedes the interests of the parties in litigation"); *Awwad v Geraghty & Co* [2000] [2001] Q.B. 570 at 596.

[90] *Cowan v Milbourn* (1867) L.R. 2 Ex. 230.

with guilty intent cannot sue for rent[91]; and the owner of a brougham knowingly let to a prostitute for the purpose of her profession cannot sue for hire.[92] A guilty party cannot evade the rule by enforcing the contract indirectly.[93] Thus the court will set aside or refuse to enforce an arbitration award enforcing an illegal contract,[94] will refuse to order an account of money due under an illegal contract,[95] and will not administer the funds of an illegal association.[96] Nor, where an illegal contract purports to release rights under an earlier valid contract, will a guilty party be allowed to rely on the illegal contract by way of defence to a claim to enforce those rights.[97]

The traditional justification for the rule is that it exists, "not for the sake of the defendant, but because the courts will not lend their aid to such a plaintiff".[98] Thus it applies even though the defendant shares the plaintiff's guilt and even though its effect may be to allow the defendant to keep a substantial benefit for nothing. For example, where money has been lent under an illegal loan, a guilty lender cannot recover it from the borrower.[99] The rule is capable of producing harsh results,[1] particularly as a party may be "guilty" without being morally to blame[2]; and it has therefore been suggested that the rule should be displaced by a general principle that the courts will refuse to assist the plaintiff only where to do so "would be an affront to the public conscience."[3] This approach, and the difficulties inherent in it, are illustrated by *Howard v Shirlstar Container Transport Ltd*[4] where the defendants, who owned two aircraft which had been detained in Nigeria after a *coup d'état*, promised to pay $25,000 to the plaintiff if he flew the aircraft out of that country. The plaintiff did fly the aircraft out of Nigeria and in doing so he committed breaches of Nigerian air traffic control regulations; he did so in order to make good his escape, after he had been warned that his life and that of his wireless operator (who was also his fiancée) would be in danger if they stayed in Nigeria. It was held that the plaintiff's claim under the contract was not barred by illegality since "in the perilous and life-threatening circumstances . . . it would not amount to an affront to the public conscience to afford the plaintiff the relief he sought".[5] But it has been rightly said that such a vague test is "very difficult to apply"[6]; and the House of

---

[91] *cf. Alexander v Rayson* [1936] 1 K.B. 169; *Edler v Auerbach* [1950] 1 K.B. 359.

[92] *Pearce v Brooks* (1866) L.R. 1 Ex. 213; the court stressed that the owner knew of the use to which the brougham was to be put; *cf.* below, p.484.

[93] *The Angel Bell* [1981] Q.B. 65 at 72–73.

[94] *David Taylor & Sons Ltd v Barnett Trading Co* [1953] 1 W.L.R. 562; *Soleimany v Soleimany* [1999] Q.B. 785; and see above, p.450 at n.33. But this principle does not apply to findings of *fact* on which the legality of the contract depend: *Binder v Alachouzos* [1972] 2 Q.B. 151; nor does an arbitrator lack jurisdiction to determine whether a contract is illegal: *Harbour Assurance (UK) Ltd v Kansa General International Insurance Co Ltd* [1993] Q.B. 701; Arbitration Act 1996, s.30(1)(a); nor is he deprived of such jurisdiction merely because it is alleged that performance of an originally lawful contract subsequently became illegal: *Prodexport v E D & F Man Ltd* [1973] 1 Q.B. 389; *Soleimany v Soleimany* above, at 804.

[95] *Victorian Daylesford Syndicate Ltd v Dott* [1905] 2 Ch. 624.

[96] *Sykes v Beadon* (1879) 11 Ch.D. 170; disapproved in *Smith v Anderson* (1880) 15 Ch.D. 247, but not on this point; *Shaw v Benson* (1883) 11 Q.B.D. 563. The court can order repayment of such funds to the members or contributors: *Barclay v Pearson* [1893] 2 Ch. 154; *Greenberg v Cooperstein* [1926] Ch. 657.

[97] *Royal Boskalis Westminster NV v Mountain* [1997] 2 All E.R. 929 (Phillips L.J. dissenting on this point).

[98] *Holman v Johnson* (1775) 1 Cowp. 341 at 343; *Soleimany v Soleimany* [1999] Q.B. 785 at 800.

[99] *Boissevain v Weil* [1950] A.C. 372; *Spector v Ageda* [1973] Ch. 30. *cf. Shanshal v Al Kishtaini* [2001] EWCA Civ 264; [2001] 2 All E.R. (Comm) 601, also holding that his position is not affected by Human Rights Act 1998, Sch.1, Pt II.

[1] *Birkett v Avon Business Machines Ltd* [1999] 2 All E.R. (Comm) 429 at 434.

[2] See below, p.484.

[3] *Euro-Diam Ltd v Bathurst* [1990] Q.B. 1 at 35. *cf.* (in the context of recovery of property obtained illegally) *Thackwell v Barclays Bank plc* [1986] 1 All E.R. 676 at 687.

[4] [1990] 1 W.L.R. 1292.

[5] *ibid.* at 1301.

[6] *Pitts v Hunt* [1991] 1 Q.B. 24 at 56.

Lords has accordingly rejected the "public conscience" test as one which can determine whether a guilty party should be allowed to enforce an illegal contract.[7] *Howard v Shirlstar Container Transport Ltd* has been explained[8] instead as an illustration of the principle of *St John SS Corp v Joseph Rank Ltd*,[9] *i.e.* on the ground that the purpose of the legislation was not to invalidate contracts but only to prohibit conduct. In applying this principle, it may be relevant that in *Howard's* case there were no passengers on board the aircraft, and that it made its escape by flying low over the sea. A different view might have been taken if an aircraft with passengers on board had (in breach of air traffic regulations) been flown low over a densely populated area. To have allowed the pilot in such circumstances to enforce the contract might well have been thought to contravene the purpose of the legislation. The rule that a guilty party cannot enforce an illegal contract therefore survives; but its severity is mitigated in two ways.

First, the rule only prevents a guilty party from enforcing *the contract*: it does not prevent him from recovering damages in tort where the other party's conduct constitutes, not merely a breach of the illegal contract, but also an independent tort.[10] This was the position in *Saunders v Edwards*,[11] where a contract had been made for the sale of a flat and the furniture in it; the purchasers had been induced to enter into the contract by the vendor's fraudulent misrepresentation that the premises included a roof-garden. The contract was also illegal[12] in that £5,000 of the agreed price of £45,000 was attributed to the furniture, which was worth no more than £1,000: this was apparently done at the suggestion of the purchasers, with a view to saving them the relatively small sum of £300 in stamp duty. Their claim for damages of over £7,000 for the vendor's deceit was nevertheless upheld. One reason for this result was that the purchasers were "not seeking to enforce the contract"[13] but only to claim damages in tort.[14] Another was that, in deciding whether to allow the tort claim, the court could, and should, have regard to the "relative moral culpability"[15] of the parties: the purchasers' fairly moderate tax evasion was outweighed by the vendor's more serious fraud. It is an open question whether this reasoning can survive the rejection of the "public conscience" test[16]; and, even if it can, there will still be situations in which a guilty party to an illegal contract will not be able to succeed merely by formulating his claim in tort. Thus in *Ashton v Turner*[17] one of two persons who had agreed (when drunk) to commit burglary together

---

[7] *Tinsley v Milligan* [1994] 1 A.C. 340 at 358–361 and 363–364, *per* Lord Goff, who dissented in the result but with whose views on the present point all the other members of the House of Lords directly or indirectly expressed their agreement; *Webb v Chief Constable of Merseyside Police* [2000] Q.B. 427 at 445.

[8] *ibid.* at 360.

[9] [1957] 1 Q.B. 267, above, p.429.

[10] For similar principle governing claims for the recovery of money paid or property transferred under an illegal contract, see below, pp.492–493. *cf. Leighton v Michael & Charterhouse* [1995] I.C.R. 1091 and *Hall v Woolston Hall Leisure Ltd* [2001] 1 W.L.R. 225 (illegality of employment contract no bar to claim for unlawful sex discrimination). *Cf. Evans v Souls Garages Ltd, The Times*, January 23, 2001 (sale of petrol to minor prohibited by statute but seller liable to such a buyer in tort).

[11] [1987] 1 W.L.R. 1116. *cf. The Siben* [1996] 1 Lloyd's Rep. 35 at 63 ("because the plaintiff does not have to rely upon or plead the illegality").

[12] On the principle of *Alexander v Rayson* [1936] 1 K.B. 169, above, p.450.

[13] [1987] 1 W.L.R. 1116 at 1125.

[14] *cf.* the successful tort claim in *Edler v Auerbach* [1950] 1 K.B. 359 in respect of a bath wrongfully removed by the tenant of premises let under an illegal lease.

[15] [1987] 1 W.L.R. at p.1127.

[16] See above, p.482. In *Tinsley v Milligan* [1994] 1 A.C. 340 the House of Lords do not refer to *Saunders v Edwards*, above; while Ralph Gibson L.J. (whose views on this issue eventually prevailed) explained that case as turning on the first of the two reasons stated in the text above: [1992] Ch. 310 at 332. After *Tinsley v Milligan* dicta in *Saunders v Edwards* at 1134 cannot stand so far as they relate to the claim in contract.

[17] [1981] Q.B. 137; *semble* there was no *animus contrahendi* and hence no contract. *cf. Pitts v Hunt* [1991] 1 Q.B. 24; *Gala v Preston* (1991) 172 C.L.R. 243.

sued the other for injuries inflicted by the latter when negligently driving the get-away car. The action failed as it would have been obviously contrary to public policy to allow such a claim.

Secondly, there is some latitude in determining who is a "guilty" party where the illegality lies in the method of performance. For the present purpose, a party is not guilty merely because he performs a contract in an unlawful manner. Thus the shipowner in *St John Shipping Corp v Joseph Rank Ltd*[18] succeeded in his claim for freight although he had overloaded his ship; but he could not have enforced the contract if he had at the time of contracting intended to overload his ship.[19] Similarly, a seller of fish succeeded in his claim for the price even though, after the contract was made, he committed an offence by sending a false invoice to the buyer with the intention of postponing the payment of VAT on the sale[20]; but it seems that his claim would have failed if at the time of the sale he had already formed the intention of issuing the false invoice. The same rules apply where the offending conduct is not contrary to law, but (for example) immoral. Thus an employee would not be precluded from enforcing a contract of employment which was lawful in itself merely because he had, in the course of performing it, procured prostitutes for his employer's clients[21]; but if he had agreed to do this when entering into the contract he could not have enforced it.[22] Where the intention that one party should do an unlawful (or immoral) act exists at the time of contracting, even the other party may be unable to sue on the contract. In *Ashmore, Benson, Pease & Co Ltd v A V Dawson Ltd*[23] a contract to carry two 25-ton loads was performed by using lorries which could not lawfully carry loads of more than 20 tons. This was known both to the carrier and to the owner of the goods, whose claim for damage done to them in the course of transit was rejected as he not only knew of the illegality but "participated" in it. "Participation" here means that he assented to a method of performance which he knew to be illegal,[24] and that he hoped to benefit from it by saving the extra expense of having the goods carried on different vehicles.

(2) Position of innocent party

For the present purpose, a person may be "innocent" because he is mistaken, or ignorant, about either the law or the facts.

(a) IGNORANCE OR MISTAKE OF LAW. In general, this does not give a party the right to enforce a contract which is affected by illegality. In *Nash v Stevenson Transport Ltd*[25] A agreed to allow B to use goods vehicle licences taken out by A in his own name. This arrangement was made in good faith, but by statute it involved both parties in criminal liability. It was held that A could not sue for the money promised to him under the

---

[18] [1957] 1 Q.B. 267; cf. *Shaw v Groom* [1970] 2 Q.B. 504. *S.A. Ancien Maison Marcel Bauche v Woodhouse Drake & Carey (Sugar) Ltd* [1982] 2 Lloyd's Rep. 516 at 529; *Yango Pastoral Co Pty Ltd v First National Chicago Australia Ltd* (1978) 139 C.L.R. 410, as explained in *Phoenix General Ins Co of Greece SA v Halvanon General Ins Co Ltd* [1988] Q.B. 216 (as to which see above, p.434); *Euro-Diam Ltd v Bathurst* [1990] Q.B. 1.

[19] [1957] 1 Q.B. at p.283; cf. *Fielding & Platt Ltd v Najjar* [1969] 1 W.L.R. 357. *Quaere* whether in the *St John Shipping* case the test of intention would have been strictly subjective. If the shipowner had made a single contract for so much cargo that his ship would inevitably be overloaded, would the court have said that he "must have" intended at the time of contracting to break the law?

[20] *Skilton v Sullivan*, *The Times*, March 25, 1994.

[21] *Coral Leisure Group v Barnett* [1981] I.C.R. 503.

[22] *ibid.* at 509.

[23] [1973] 1 W.L.R. 828; Hamson [1973] C.L.J. 199.

[24] *Hall v Woolston Hall Leisure Ltd* [2001] 1 W.L.R. 215 at 234 ("knowingly participated . . . ").

[25] [1936] 2 K.B. 128; cf. *Corby v Morrison* [1980] I.C.R. 218; *Mohamed v Alaga & Co* [2000] 1 W.L.R. 1815 at 1820, 1824, 1827.

contract. Similarly a person could not enforce a contract in restraint of trade merely because he thought that such contracts were valid.

In these cases the performance or enforcement of the contract *necessarily* involves a breach of the law, or a result which is contrary to public policy. Where this is not the position, the effect of mistake of law is harder to determine. In *Waugh v Morris*[26] a ship was chartered to carry hay from a French port to London. The cargo was to be taken from the ship "alongside," and the master was orally instructed to deliver it to a wharf in Deptford Creek. This could not lawfully be done because, before the time of contracting, an order had, unknown to the parties, been made prohibiting the landing of hay from French ports in the United Kingdom. The hay was therefore transshipped and exported. It was held that the shipowner could sue on the charterparty as it could have been, and in fact had been, performed lawfully. But in *J M Allan (Merchandising) Ltd v Cloke*[27] a roulette wheel was let on hire for the purpose of enabling the hirer to play roulette royale at a country club. Both parties honestly thought that this game was lawful when it was not. It was held that the owner of the wheel could not sue for payment of the agreed hire. One reason for the decision was that the parties had a "common design to use the subject-matter for an unlawful purpose".[28] But it is equally true that in *Waugh v Morris* the parties had a common design to land the hay in Deptford, and that this was an unlawful purpose. Alternatively, there was in *Cloke's* case an actual contract that the wheel should be used for playing roulette royale[29]: the position was as it would have been in *Waugh v Morris*, had the contract there been to *land* the hay at Deptford and not deliver it "alongside". It is, of course, possible that the hirer could, without committing a breach of contract, have used the wheel to play some other game; but this would not alter the fact that the owner had contracted to provide facilities for playing roulette royale. Thus if one party cannot perform his obligations without committing or abetting a breach of the law he cannot enforce the contract even though he was "innocent" in the sense that he made a mistake of law.

(b) IGNORANCE OR MISTAKE OF FACT. A party may be innocent in the sense of being unaware of, or mistaken about, the facts which give rise to the illegality. The right of such a party to enforce the contract has been upheld in some cases but denied in others; even where it has been denied, other remedies may be available to the innocent party.

(i) *Cases upholding the innocent party's claim.* One such case has already been considered: a printer can probably recover his charges for printing a document containing statements which, as a result of facts unknown to him, are defamatory.[30] An actual decision in favour of the innocent party is *Bloxsome v Williams*[31] where a person sold a horse on a Sunday and thereby committed an offence under the Sunday Observance Act 1677,[32] as he was a dealer. The buyer did not know that the seller was a dealer and recovered the money he had paid for the horse as damages for breach of warranty. *Bloxsome v Williams* was doubted in the *Bedford Insurance*[33] case, where a company issued insurance policies in violation of a statutory prohibition against "the effecting and carrying out of [certain] contracts of insurance" without government authorisation. The policies were described as "illegal and void *ab initio*"; and it was said that the insured

---

[26] (1873) L.R. 8 Q.B. 202; *cf. Hindley & Co Ltd v General Fibre Co Ltd* [1940] 2 K.B. 217; *Lloyd v Popeley* [2001] C.L.Y. 743.
[27] [1963] 2 Q.B. 340.
[28] *ibid.* at 348.
[29] [1963] 2 Q.B. 340 at 351.
[30] *cf. Clay v Yates* (1856) 1 H. & N. 73; above, p.433.
[31] (1824) 3 B. & C. 232; *cf. Newland v Simons & Willer* [1981] I.C.R. 521.
[32] Repealed by Statute Law (Repeals) Act 1969 Sch. Pt IV.
[33] [1985] Q.B. 966.

person, though innocent, acquired no rights under the policies "for it would be an offence for the insurer to pay him."[34] In the case of such contracts, this result has been reversed by statute,[35] and, even if the reasoning is sound as a matter of common law, it does not follow that *Bloxsome v Williams* was wrongly decided; for the buyer in that case was claiming, not delivery of the horse, but the return of his money. In upholding this claim, the court was not ordering the defendant to do an act prohibited by statute. This was also the position in *Archbolds (Freightage) Ltd v Spanglett Ltd*,[36] where the defendants contracted to carry the claimants' whisky in a van which was not licensed to carry goods belonging to third parties. In carrying the whisky in this van, the defendants committed a statutory offence. The whisky was stolen and the claimants, who did not know that the van was not properly licensed, recovered the value of the whisky as damages for breach of the contract. And in *Fielding & Platt Ltd v Najjar*[37] an English seller of machinery agreed to give the foreign buyer an invoice in a form requested by the buyer so that he could use it to deceive the authorities in his own country. It was held that the seller could sue on the contract as he did not either know of the illegality or actively participate in it.

(ii) *Cases rejecting the innocent party's claim.* The leading case in this group is *Re Mahmoud and Ispahani*,[38] where a contract was made to sell linseed oil at a time when it was (under delegated legislation) an offence to buy or sell such oil without licence. The seller had a licence to sell to other licensed dealers and was induced to enter into the contract by the buyer's fraudulent representation that he also had a licence. The buyer later refused to accept the oil, and it was held that the seller could not claim damages for non-acceptance, even if his lack of *mens rea* would exonerate him from criminal liability. Similarly, it has been held that builders who did work in the bona fide but mistaken belief that the necessary licences had been obtained could not enforce the contracts under which the work was done.[39] And, although the point has not been decided, it seems that mistake of fact would not entitle an innocent person to enforce a contract in restraint of trade or one to trade with the enemy. Thus the buyer of a shop whose customers all lived within one mile of it could not enforce a covenant against competition within 20 miles merely because he believed that the customers lived within the larger area. And a person who made a contract with a resident of an enemy country could not enforce it merely because he did not know that war had just broken out between the United Kingdom and that country.[40]

(iii) *Tests for distinguishing the two groups of cases.* Various tests have been suggested for distinguishing between the cases in which the innocent party can, and those in which he cannot, enforce the contract. One is to say that the contract can be enforced by the innocent party so long as it is not *ex facie* illegal. But if the contract is *ex facie* illegal and one party is innocent his mistake is almost always one of law; and the mere fact that the contract is *ex facie* legal is certainly not enough to enable the innocent party to sue.[41]

---

[34] *ibid.* p.982; approved in *Phoenix General Insurance Co of Greece SA v Halvanon Insurance Co Ltd* [1988] Q.B. 216; *Re Cavalier Insurance Co Ltd* [1989] 2 Lloyd's Rep. 430, see above, p.434; see also *Fuji Finance Inc v Aetna Life Insurance Co Ltd* [1997] Ch. 173 (where conflicting views were expressed on the effects on contracts of the breach of a statute which did *not* amount to an offence) and *Parks v Esso Petroleum Co Ltd* [1999] 1 C.M.L.R. 445 (where on appeal it was held that there was no illegality: [2000] Eu.L.R. 25).

[35] See now Financial Services and Markets Act 2000, ss.26(1) and 32; above, p.434; below, p.488.

[36] [1961] 1 Q.B. 374.

[37] [1969] 1 W.L.R. 357.

[38] [1921] 2 K.B. 716; *cf. Yin v San* [1962] A.C. 304; Williams, 8 C.L.J. 51; Buckley, 38 M.L.R. 535; Treitel, in (ed. Tapper) *Essays in Memory of Sir Rupert Cross*, pp.96–99.

[39] *J Dennis & Co Ltd v Munn* [1949] 2 K.B. 327; and see below, p.489.

[40] For discharge by *supervening* illegality in such cases see below, p.887.

[41] e.g. *Re Mahmoud and Ispahani* [1921] 2 K.B. 716.

Another suggestion is that the innocent party can enforce the contract where it is illegal as performed but not where it is illegal as formed. But in *Bloxsome v Williams* the innocent party's claim was upheld even though the contract was illegal as formed. Moreover, in *Archbolds (Freightage) Ltd v S Spanglett Ltd* the Court of Appeal regarded it as irrelevant whether the contract was to carry the whisky in the particular van, and yet this fact would be crucial if enforceability depended on whether the contract was illegal as formed or as performed. A third suggestion is that the innocent party's claim will succeed in cases of common law but not of statutory illegality. But this again does not fit the cases: in *Bloxsome v Williams* and *Archbolds (Freightage) Ltd v S Spanglett Ltd* the innocent party succeeded although the illegality was statutory. And if the suggestions made at the end of the last paragraph are sound there are cases in which the innocent party will fail although the illegality is brought about by common law. It is, moreover, hard to see why the innocent party's rights should depend on the distinction between statutory and common law illegality.

That distinction can, of course, be decisive where the illegality is statutory and the statute expressly or by implication specifies its effect on contracts. On the one hand, the statute may expressly provide that the validity of the contract is not to be affected. It is, for example, an offence under s.65(1) of the Road Traffic Act 1988 to supply certain vehicles which do not comply with specified safety requirements; and s.65(4) provides that "nothing in subsection (1) . . . shall affect the validity of any contract or any rights arising under or in relation to a contract".[42] On the other hand, the statute may expressly or impliedly provide that even an innocent party is not to be entitled to enforce the contract. This possibility was formerly illustrated by the cases, already mentioned,[43] in which insurance policies were issued in the course of a business carried on without government authorisation, thus making the insurers who had issued them guilty of a statutory offence; the general view was that such policies could not be enforced even by an insured person who was quite innocent of the illegality. This result was thought[44] to follow from the wording of the statute, which was considered to have impliedly invalidated the contract by prohibiting the "carrying out" of the policies. But to deny a remedy to the innocent party certainly did not promote the policy of the statutory requirement,[45] which had been imposed on insurers for the protection of insured persons; and the law in cases of this kind has been changed by the Financial Services and

---

[42] *cf. ibid.*, s.75(7); Fair Trading Act 1973, s.26; Sex Discrimination Act 1975, ss.62(1), 77; (as amended by Sex Discrimination Act 1986, s.6 and Trade Union Reform and Employment Protection Act 1993 s.32); Race Relations Act 1976, ss.53(1), 72 (as amended by Trade Union Reform and Employment Protection Act 1993, s.39(2) and Sch.6); Energy Conservation Act 1981, s.18; Property Misdescriptions Act 1991, s.1(4); Timeshare Act 1992, s.4(2); Criminal Justice Act 1993, s.63(2), the effect of which appears to be to reverse this aspect of *Chase Manhattan Equities Ltd v Goodman* [1991] B.C.L.C. 897; Disability Discrimination Act 1995, s.26.

[43] *Viz.*, the *Bedford* case [1985] 1 Q.B. 966 and the *Phoenix* case, [1988] Q.B. 216, above, p.434. The statements were strictly obiter since in the *Bedford* case the action was by a *guilty* insurer against an innocent reinsurer while in the *Phoenix* case no offence had been committed. For cases following or approving reasoning of these cases see *Re Cavalier Ins Co Ltd* [1989] 2 Lloyd's Rep. 430; *Overseas Union Insurance Ltd v Incorporated General Insurance Ltd* [1992] 1 Lloyd's Rep. 439 at 444–445; *D.R. Insurance Co v Seguros America Banamex* [1993] 1 Lloyd's Rep. 120.

[44] Though with evident reluctance: see the *Phoenix* case [1988] Q.B. 216 at 249, 273; *Re Cavalier Ins Co Ltd* [1989] 2 Lloyd's Rep. 440 at 443 ("without enthusiasm").

[45] From this point of view, the result in *Stewart v Oriental Fire & Marine Ins Co Ltd* [1985] 1 Q.B. 988 (giving the innocent party a remedy on the contract against the guilty party) was preferable to the reasoning of the authorities cited in n.43, above. *cf.* Clarke [1987] L.M.C.L.Q. 201; *D.R. Insurance Co Ltd v Central National Insurance Co* [1996] 1 Lloyd's Rep. 74.

Markets Act 2000.[46] This lays down the general principle that, where A provides specified financial services to B without A's having the requisite authorisation, then the contract is unenforceable against (not by) B,[47] who is also entitled to the return of money paid or property transferred by him under it, and to compensation for loss suffered by him as a result of having parted with the money or property.[48] However, if A (no less than B) is innocent of the illegality, then the court may exceptionally allow the contract to be enforced and money or property transferred under it to be retained.[49]

Where the statute does not expressly or by implication specify the effects of the illegality on contracts,[50] those effects are, it is submitted, to be determined by reference to the purpose of the statute. This approach is suggested by Devlin L.J. in *Archbolds (Freightage) Ltd v S Spanglett Ltd*, where he said: "I think that the purpose of this statute is sufficiently served by the penalties prescribed for the offender; the avoidance of the contract would cause grave inconvenience and injury to members of the public *without furthering the object of the statute.*"[51] Although Devlin L.J. refers only to statutory illegality, it is submitted that the same approach would be appropriate where the illegality was due to a rule of common law[52]: the court has to consider how it would further the object of the relevant rule of law to invalidate the contract. Where the rule exists for the protection of a class of persons, its object will obviously not be promoted by rejecting a claim to enforce the contract made by an innocent member of that class.[53] In other cases, it is more difficult to strike a balance between the interests of the public (which the invalidating rule is meant to protect) and those of the innocent party. Of course specific performance of promise to do an act that is unlawful or against public policy will not be ordered. The questions are whether, if the guilty party has failed to perform such a promise, the innocent party should be entitled to damages; and whether, if the latter party has innocently done such an act, he should be entitled to enforce the guilty party's counter-promise (typically, one to pay the agreed sum[54]). In what way does it ever "further the object" of the invalidating rule to deny the innocent party such a remedy?

One possible answer to this question is that the denial of a remedy may induce the innocent party to take greater care not to enter into an illegal transaction. Another is that a remedy should be refused whenever the contract is executory, since the availability of such a remedy might induce the other (guilty) party to perform. But where these arguments are sound, the innocent party should have no remedy at all, or at least no

---

[46] For earlier similar provisions, see Financial Services Act 1986, s.132. That Act is repealed by Financial Services and Markets Act (Consequential Amendments and Repeals) Order 2001 (SI 2000/3649), Art.1(c).

[47] Financial Services and Markets Act 2000, ss.26(1), 27(1).

[48] *ibid.*, ss.26(2), 272(2); if B elects not to perform or claims restitution he must in turn restore benefits received by him under the contract: s.28(7).

[49] *ibid.*, s.28(3)–(6).

[50] There may be a provision which is incomplete: *e.g.* Trade Descriptions Act 1968, s.35, which deals only with contracts for the supply of goods and not with contracts for the supply of services, though both types of contracts may be affected by the Act.

[51] [1961] 1 Q.B. 374 at 390.

[52] *cf. Cope v Rowlands* (1836) 2 M. & W. 149 at 157 ("expressly forbidden by the common law or statute law"), cited in *Hughes v Asset Management plc* [1995] 3 All E.R. 669 at 674.

[53] See *Nash v Halifax Building Society* [1979] Ch. 584, so far as it relates to the enforcement of the security; *cf. Hughes v Asset Management plc* [1995] 3 All E.R. 669 at 674, 675, where, however, the actual decision that the contract was *not* illegal operated *against* the inocent party in that it led to the rejection of his claim for the recovery of money paid by him under the contract; if the contract had been illegal, such a claim by a member of the protected class might have succeeded under the rule stated at p.491 below. The contract cannot of course be enforced *against* a member of the protected class: *Johnson v Moreton* [1980] A.C. 37.

[54] It is assumed that the making of the payment is not prohibited.

remedy as good as the action on the contract. In fact the innocent party who cannot enforce the contract may have other remedies, and one of these seems to be no worse than an action on the contract. There are three such remedies.

(iv) *Other remedies of innocent party.* First, the innocent party may be able to recover damages for breach of "collateral warranty." In *Strongman (1945) Ltd v Sincock*[55] the defendant employed a firm of builders to modernise his house. He promised to get the necessary licences (without which it was illegal to do the work), but he got licences for only part of the work and refused to pay for the rest on the ground that the contract to do it was illegal. The builders could not enforce the contract although they had acted in good faith. But they recovered damages (amounting to the value of the unlicensed work) for breach of the defendant's collateral undertaking to get the necessary licences. This is a useful device for doing justice to the innocent party, and in *Strongman (1945) Ltd v Sincock* little harm was done to the public interest. For in that case the defendant was an architect so that the builders were not careless[56] in failing to ask to see the licence. And the work had been completed, so that it would have been futile to deny a remedy on the ground that to grant it might induce the performance of an illegal act. But to allow the innocent party to sue on a "collateral warranty" in a case like *Re Mahmoud and Ispahani*[57] would be quite inconsistent with the rationale of the rule denying him a remedy on the contract. It would be mere sophistry to say: we will protect the public interest by denying a remedy on the contract, but we will also protect the innocent claimant by giving him as good a remedy on a collateral warranty. This remedy should be granted only where it will provide no incentive to do the illegal act and where the innocent party was not careless. But if these conditions are satisfied there seems to be no reason why the innocent party should not be able to enforce on the contract itself. Alternatively, the innocent party could be given a restitutionary claim for the reasonable value of his services. This follows *a fortiori* from the suggestion (to be discussed later in this Chapter)[58] that such a remedy may sometimes be available even to the guilty party.

Secondly, the innocent party may be able to recover damages in tort for mis-representation. In *Shelley v Paddock*[59] the claimant was by the fraud of the defendant induced to enter into a contract to buy a house in Spain and to make payments under it which were illegal as they violated exchange control regulations. Since the claimant's breach of the law was innocent and resulted from the defendant's fraud, she was entitled to damages for that fraud. Even where the misrepresentation was *not* fraudulent, a person who had, as a result of it, innocently entered into an illegal contract might similarly be entitled to damages, either for negligence at common law[60] or under the Misrepresentation Act 1967; and he might also be able to rescind the contract. But these remedies could be less advantageous than an action on the contract as they would not give the innocent party damages for loss of his bargain.[61]

---

[55] [1955] 2 Q.B. 525.

[56] *ibid.* at 536.

[57] [1921] 2 K.B. 716; above, p.486.

[58] See below p.503.

[59] [1980] Q.B. 348; *cf. Burrows v Rhodes* [1899] 1 Q.B. 816 and *Saunders v Edwards* [1987] 1 W.L.R. 1116 (above, p.483), where even a "guilty" party recovered damages for a fraud unconnected with the illegality.

[60] *Mohammed v Alaga & Co* [2000] 1 W.L.R. 1815 at 1826.

[61] *cf.* above, p.359, below, p.513. In *Shelley v Paddock*, above, the damages did not include any element of compensation for loss of the claimant's bargain: see [1979] Q.B. 120. In *Mohamed v Alaga & Co* [2000] 1 W.L.R. 1815 at 1826 Lord Bingham C.J. said that he could not "conceive that the plaintiff could be regarded as recovering anything under this head [*i.e.*, in tort] as damages which he would be debarred from recovering under the contract".

Thirdly, innocence may be material in an action for the recovery of money paid or property transferred under an illegal contract.[62] The object of the invalidating rule is less likely to be defeated by this remedy than by an award of damages for breach of contract since it amounts rather to an undoing[63] than to an enforcement[64] of the contract. The remedy may, however, be less advantageous than any of those so far discussed, for under it the claimant can only get back what he gave: he cannot recover in respect of other losses incurred in reliance on the contract, or for loss of his bargain.

(3) De facto enforcement

A contract which is illegal may be enforced de facto in the sense that one party may secure compliance with its terms by using or threatening to use some form of economic pressure. Such measures may be taken in good faith, and the question then arises whether the party who is thus induced to perform a contract that was not binding on him has any remedy in respect of loss suffered in consequence. In *Shell U.K. Ltd v Lostock Garages Ltd*[65] a garage proprietor was in effect compelled to observe the terms of a solus agreement by the oil company's threats that, if other suppliers were to sell petrol to him, it would sue them for inducing a breach of the solus agreement. Lord Denning M.R. held that the solus agreement was unenforceable and that the garage proprietor was entitled to damages in respect of the loss he had suffered through being nevertheless compelled to observe it.[66] Ormrod L.J. held that no such damages were available,[67] while Bridge L.J. awarded them on the different ground that the oil company was in breach of an implied term of its contract with the garage proprietor.[68] Lord Denning held that no such term could be implied,[69] so that the damages awarded by him cannot have been for breach of contract. His award seems rather to have been based on the novel principle, that the *de facto* enforcement of an illegal contract can, if it causes loss, give rise to a claim for damages. The correctness of this principle, as well as its extent, await further judicial consideration.

The above discussion is based on the assumption that performance of the illegal contract has actually been secured. Before this has happened, the court may be able to intervene to prevent such performance: *e.g.* by an injunction to restrain a party from drawing on a letter of credit issued to secure payment under an illegal contract. Since the effect of such a remedy is to prevent illegality, it may be granted even to the guilty party.[70]

2. Restitution

A person who cannot enforce an illegal contract may instead claim restitution in respect of money paid, property transferred or services rendered by him under the contract.

---

[62] *cf.* below, pp.492–493.

[63] This was the outcome of *Bloxsome v Williams* (1824) 3 B. & C. 232 (above, p.485) where the buyer's claim was for "damages" but the amount that he recovered was the price paid by him.

[64] This was the nature of the claim unsuccessfully made by the seller in *Re Mahmoud and Ispahani* [1921] 2 K.B. 716 (above, p.486); if he had actually delivered the oil to the buyer he could no doubt have recovered it back: below, p.492.

[65] [1977] 1 W.L.R. 1187.

[66] *ibid.* at 1200; *cf.* under Art.81 of the EC Treaty, *Courage Ltd v Crehan* [2002] Q.B. 507.

[67] [1977] 1 W.L.R. 1187 at 1200–1201.

[68] *ibid.* at 1204.

[69] See above, p.205, Ormrod L.J. agreed with Lord Denning on this point.

[70] *Group Josi Re v Walbrook Insurance Co Ltd* [1996] 1 W.L.R. 1152 at 1164, where the actual decision was that the performance of the contracts was saved from illegality by legislation of the kind described at p.487, above after n.45 so that no injunction was available.

(1) General rule: no recovery of money or property

The general rule is that money paid or property transferred under an illegal contract cannot be recovered back.[71] At one time the rule could be justified by saying that the courts should not give any help to a willing party to an illegal transaction; and by the argument that, by leaving one party at the mercy of the other, the rule had a deterrent effect. The first of these arguments is no longer wholly convincing now that a person may in all innocence make a contract that is technically illegal; and the second overlooks the possibility that sometimes illegality may be more effectively discouraged by allowing than by denying recovery. If, for example, a person receives money in the course of conducting an illegal business, the illegality is more likely to be deterred by making him pay the money back, than by allowing him to rely on the rule of non-recovery.[72] It would be better if the law did not adopt a "general rule" but asked in relation to each type of illegality whether it was recovery or non-recovery that was the more likely to promote the purpose of the invalidating rule. In practice the present general rule is subject to so many exceptions that the law, taken as a whole, comes close to achieving this result.

(2) Exceptional cases: recovery of money or property possible

(a) CLASS-PROTECTING STATUTES. If a contract is made illegal by a statute passed for the protection of a class of persons, a member of that class can recover back money paid or property transferred by him under the contract.[73] Some statutes expressly provide that a member of a protected class shall be entitled to recover back money paid or property transferred under an illegal contract. For example, the Rent Act 1977 contains various provisions entitling a tenant to recover back money which he could not lawfully have been required to pay[74]; and in a case decided under an earlier Act it was held that he could recover back an illegal premium even though he was a willing party to a fraudulent scheme to evade the Act.[75] The Financial Services and Markets Act 2000 similarly provides that, where A provides specified financial services to B without A's having the required authorisation, B is *prima facie* entitled to the return of money paid or property transferred by him under the contract[76]; he is so entitled even though he also has the option of enforcing the contract.[77]

There was at one time some support for the view that the prevalence of such statutory provisions had made the old class-protecting rules obsolete.[78] But this view was rejected

---

[71] *e.g. Scott v Brown* [1892] 2 Q.B. 724; *Edler v Auerbach* [1950] 1 K.B. 359; *cf. Shaw v Shaw* [1965] 1 W.L.R. 537. See generally Grodecki, 71 L.Q.R. 254; Higgins, 25 M.L.R. 598; Rose in (ed. Rose), *Consensus ad Idem, Essays in the Law of Contract in Honour of Guenter Treitel*, p.202.

[72] *cf. Hermann v Charlesworth* [1905] 2 K.B. 123.

[73] *Browning v Morris* (1778) 2 Cowp. 790; *Barclay v Pearson* [1893] 2 Ch. 154; *Bonnard v Dott* [1906] 1 Ch. 740 (unlicensed moneylender); *One Life Ltd v Roy* [1996] 2 B.C.L.C. 608 (unlawful lottery). In *Lodge v National Union Investment Co* [1907] 1 Ch. 300 it was held that the borrower could not recover his securities unless he repaid the money actually lent to him; but this decision has been distinguished out of existence: *Chapman v Michaelson* [1908] 2 Ch. 612; [1909] 1 Ch. 238; *Cohen v J Lester Ltd* [1939] 1 K.B. 504; *Kasumu v Baba-Egbe* [1956] A.C. 539; *cf. Barclay v Prospect Mortgages* [1974] 1 W.L.R. 837. Under Consumer Credit Act 1974, s.40(1), a regulated agreement with an unlicensed moneylender is not illegal but only unenforceable against the debtor unless the Office of Fair Trading orders otherwise.

[74] *e.g.* ss.57, 95, 125.

[75] *Gray v Southouse* [1949] 2 All E.R. 1019. For enforcement of the remainder of the contract by "unwilling victims" see *Ailon v Spiekermann* [1976] Ch. 158 at 165.

[76] Financial Services Markets Act 2000 ss.26(2), 27(2); above, p.449; and see *ibid.* for the courts power under s.28(3)–(6) to deny B's claim for restitution.

[77] Under ss.26(1) and 27(1) of the 2000 Act, the contract is only "unenforceable *against*" (not by) B.

[78] *Green v Portsmouth Stadium* [1953] 2 K.B. 190, esp. at 195.

in *Kiriri Cotton Ltd v Dewani*,[79] where a landlord had, by accepting an illegal premium
from his tenant, committed an offence under a Rent Restriction Ordinance which did
not expressly say that such premiums could be recovered back. The Privy Council held
that the tenant could recover back the premium under the old rules relating to class-
protecting statutes. Similarly, premiums paid under an illegal insurance policy of the
kind described above could be recovered back by the innocent policy-holder at common
law,[80] even before such a right of recovery was expressly conferred on him by legislation
of the kind described in the preceding paragraph.[81]

(b) OPPRESSION. A person can recover back money paid or property transferred
under an illegal contract if he was forced by the other party to enter into that contract.
"Oppression" is here used in a somewhat broad sense. In *Atkinson v Denby*[82] an
insolvent debtor offered to pay his creditors a dividend of 5s. in the £. All the creditors
were willing to accept the dividend in full settlement of their claims, except the
defendant, who said he would accept it only if the debtor first paid him £50. The debtor
did so, but was later allowed to recover back the £50 on the ground that he had been
forced to agree to defraud the other creditors. To say that the debtor was oppressed may
not be very convincing; but it was a convenient way of avoiding the general rule of non-
recovery where that rule would have led to the undesirable result of enabling one
creditor to keep more than his fair share of the insolvent debtor's assets.

The "oppression" may be due, not to the conduct of the other party, but to extraneous
circumstances, and such "oppression" has been recognised as a ground of recovery
where the contract is made illegal by a statute passed for the protection of a class. Thus
in *Kiriri Cotton Co Ltd v Dewani* Lord Denning said that the tenant was not "so much
to blame" for evading the Rent Restriction Ordinance as the landlord, who was "using
his property rights so as to exploit those in need of a roof over their heads".[83] In an
American case oppression not caused by the defendant was recognised as a ground of
recovery where a person had paid a bribe to escape from the danger of being imprisoned
and put to death by the Nazis.[84] Less extreme forms of pressure have in England not
been regarded as a ground for recovery. In *Bigos v Bousted*[85] a father made an illegal
contract to acquire foreign currency in order to send his daughter to Italy as a cure for
her recurrent attacks of pleurisy. This "pressure" did not entitle him to recover back
property transferred under the contract.

(c) MISREPRESENTATION. A person can recover back money paid or property transferred under an illegal contract if he entered into the contract as a result of the other
party's fraudulent misrepresentation that the contract was lawful. Thus in *Hughes v
Liverpool Victoria Legal Friendly Soc*[86] the claimant effected a policy of insurance with
the defendants on a life in which he had no insurable interest. The contract was illegal,[87]

---

[79] [1960] A.C. 192; *cf. Nash v Halifax BS* [1979] Ch. 584, so far as it relates to the money lent; and see above,
p.488.
[80] *Re Cavalier Insurance Co Ltd* [1989] 2 Lloyd's Rep. 430 at 450 (and see above, p.434). For the position where
payments had been made by the insurer under the policy, see below, p.495, n.17.
[81] See above at n.76.
[82] (1862) 7 H. & N. 934; *cf. Smith v Bromley* (1760) 2 Dougl. 696 n.; *Smith v Cuff* (1817) 6 M. & S. 160; *Davies
v London & Provincial Marine Insurance Co* (1878) 8 Ch.D. 469. In *Osborne v Williams* (1811) 18 Ves. 379
it seems even to have been thought that a father "oppressed" a son by offering him the prospect of financial
independence.
[83] [1960] A.C. 190 at 205.
[84] *Liebman v Rosenthal* 57 N.Y.S. 2d 875 (1945).
[85] [1951] 1 All E.R. 92.
[86] [1916] 2 K.B. 482; *cf. Reynell v Sprye* (1852) 1 D.M. & G. 660.
[87] Life Assurance Act 1774, s.1.

but the claimant was able to recover back the premiums he had paid as he had been induced to make the contract by the fraudulent representation of the defendants' agent that the policy was valid. The decisive factor in such cases is the fraud of the defendant, and not the innocence of the claimant. The claimant would have failed if the representation that the policy was valid had been innocently made.[88] Similarly, where a tenant was induced by the landlord's misrepresentation to enter into an illegal lease, it was held that he could not recover back a payment of rent without alleging and proving fraud.[89]

The cases on this subject suggest that, where recovery is allowed, the basis for it is the invalidity of the contract on the ground of illegality, and not misrepresentation as such. It follows that the right of recovery is not necessarily limited by the bars to rescission for misrepresentation.[90] If no such bar has arisen, it seems that a person who has been induced by even an *innocent* misrepresentation[91] to enter into an illegal contract can rescind it for misrepresentation and so recover back his money or property.[92] The bars to rescission for misrepresentation will also be relevant where the misrepresentation relates to matters other than those which are the source of the illegality: *e.g.* where a contract for the sale of property is induced by the vendor's misrepresentations as to his title, and the contract is also illegal by reason of its including an immoral business.[93]

(d) MISTAKE. A party who enters into a contract under a mistake of fact as to its legality can sometimes enforce the contract.[94] In such a situation he should be equally entitled to recover back money paid or property transferred under the contract; for it is inconceivable that this remedy will defeat the object of the invalidating rule where enforcement of the contract is allowed because it will not have this effect. Mistake[95] can also be a ground for recovery of money or property even where it does not give the mistaken party the right to enforce the contract.[96] In *Oom v Bruce*[97] the claimant, as agent for the Russian owner of goods in Russia, took out a policy of insurance on the goods with the defendant. Neither party knew (or could have known) that Russia had declared war on this country before the contract was made. It was held that the claimant could get back his premium as he was not guilty of any fault or blame in entering into the illegal contract. Here again no useful purpose would be served by applying the general rule of non-recovery.

(e) REPUDIATION OF ILLEGAL PURPOSE.[98] A person may be able to reclaim money paid or property transferred under an illegal contract if he repudiates the illegal purpose

---

[88] *Harse v Pearl Life Assurance Co* [1904] 1 K.B. 558. *Semble*, that in such a case the object of the invalidating rule would have been better served by allowing recovery: *cf.* above, p.491.

[89] *Edler v Auerbach* [1950] 1 K.B. 359.

[90] See above, pp.377–385.

[91] In *Harse v Pearl Life Assurance Co*, above, the misrepresentation was one of law, and (for the reasons given at p.333, above) it is submitted that such a representation could now give rise to a right to rescind for misrepresentation and so to recover back premiums, on the analogy of the similar rule applied in *Kleinwort Benson Ltd v Lincoln City Council* [1999] 2 A.C. 349 to payments made under a *mistake* of law.

[92] This was assumed in *Edler v Auerbach* [1950] 1 K.B. 359, but in that case the right to rescind for innocent misrepresentation was barred by execution of the lease. This would no longer be a bar: above, p.378.

[93] *The Siben* [1996] 1 Lloyd's Rep. 35 at 62; above p.381. The purchaser was not left entirely without remedy since his claim for damages succeeded on the ground stated at p.483, n.11 above.

[94] See above, p.485.

[95] For mistake of law, see *Harse v Pearl Life Assurance Co*, and above n.91.

[96] *e.g.* on facts such as those of *Re Mahmoud and Ispahani* [1921] 2 K.B. 716; above p.490, n.64.

[97] (1810) 12 East 225; *cf. Edler v Auerbach* [1950] 1 K.B. 359 at 374–375, where mistake of the payor alone was said to be insufficient; *sed quaere.*

[98] Beatson, 91 L.Q.R. 313; Merkin, 97 L.Q.R. 420.

in time.[99] By giving a party this right, the law tries to encourage him to give up the illegal purpose. Two conditions must be satisfied to bring the rule into operation.

(i) *Repudiation in time.* A party who repudiates before anything has been done to perform the illegal purpose can recover back his money or property, while one who repudiates after the illegal purpose has been fully carried out cannot recover.[1] The difficult cases are those in which the repudiation takes place after steps have been taken towards the performance of the illegal purpose, but before it has been fully carried out.

One such case was *Taylor v Bowers*,[2] where a debtor was being pressed by his creditors. To prevent certain machinery from falling into their hands, he transferred it to one Alcock. He then called two meetings of creditors in an attempt to reach a settlement with them, but none was reached. The debtor successfully claimed the machinery back from the defendant, who was one of the creditors and had obtained the machinery from Alcock with notice of the fraudulent scheme and in the hope of benefiting from it. The decision is based on the fact that the illegal purpose had not been carried out: no creditor had been defrauded. A similar result was reached in *Tribe v Tribe*[3] where a father transferred shares in a company to his son in order to "safeguard his interests"[4] against claims for dilapidations by the lessors of shops of which the father was tennant and in which the company carried on business. The issue of dilapidations was later resolved without the father's having shown the share transfer to the lessors or to any other creditor. It was held that the father was entitled to the return of the shares since the illegal purpose had "not been carried into effect in any way".[5]

In the contrasting case of *Kearley v Thomson*[6] the friend of a bankrupt paid £40 to the defendants in return for their undertaking not to appear at the bankrupt's public examination and not to oppose his discharge. The defendants duly absented themselves from the public examination, but before any application had been made for the bankrupt's discharge the payor claimed back the £40. His claim failed. Fry L.J. said, first, that the rule permitting recovery on repudiation of the illegal transaction did not exist before *Taylor v Bowers* and he doubted the correctness of that decision. But the principle was at least twice stated in earlier cases[7] and has since been accepted as good law.[8] Secondly, he said that *Taylor v Bowers* was distinguishable from *Kearley v Thomson*, since in the latter case there had been "a partial carrying into effect of an illegal purpose in a substantial manner".[9] This distinction looks at first sight tenuous, but it must be remembered that it is not the *transaction* but "the [illegal] *purpose* which has to be carried into effect"[10] to preclude recovery, and that the illegal purposes in the two cases were quite different. The illegal purpose in *Taylor v Bowers* was to defraud creditors, and no creditor was defrauded; this was also true in *Tribe v Tribe*. The illegal purpose in *Kearley*

---

[99] *Harry Parker Ltd v Mason* [1940] 2 K.B. 590 at 608.

[1] *Palaniappa Chettiar v Arunasalam Chettiar* [1962] A.C. 294.

[2] (1876) 1 Q.B.D. 291: now a case of "frustration"? *cf.* below, at n.13; *Symes v Hughes* (1870) L.R. 9 Eq. 475.

[3] [1996] Ch. 107.

[4] *ibid.* at 113.

[5] *ibid.* at 121. For further problems which arose in this case because the relationship of transferor and transferee was that of father and son, see below, pp.500–501.

[6] (1890) 24 Q.B.D. 742.

[7] *Hastelow v Jackson* (1828) 8 B. & C. 221 at 226; *Bone v Eckless* (1860) 5 H. & N. 925 at 928.

[8] See *Hermann v Charlesworth* [1905] 2 K.B. 123; *Bigos v Bousted* [1951] 1 All E.R. 92. In *Tribe v Tribe* [1996] Ch. 107 at 125 Millett L.J. doubted part of the *reasoning*, but not the *result*, in *Taylor v Bowers*.

[9] (1890) 24 Q.B.D. at 747.

[10] See *Tribe v Tribe* [1996] Ch. 107 at 122, italics supplied.

v Thomson was to interfere with the course of public justice,[11] and some such interference took place when the defendants stayed away from the bankrupt's public examination. Thus it seems that the repudiation is in time if it takes place after mere preparation to achieve the illegal purpose, but that it is too late if it takes place after performance of the illegal purpose has actually begun.

There is also the more practical point that in *Taylor v Bowers* the success of the debtor's claim promoted the equal distribution of his property among his creditors; for if the claim had failed, one of the creditors (the defendant) would have benefited at the expense of the others.[12] In *Kearley v Thomson*, on the other hand, the creditors would not have benefited at all if the claim for repayment had succeeded; for the £40 would then have gone back to the payor, and not to the bankrupt's estate.

(ii) *Voluntary repudiation.* Repudiation must be voluntary: it must not be forced on the party claiming recovery by the intervention of the police, or of a third person, or by the other party's breach of the contract.[13] This requirement follows from the justification for the present exception to the general rule of non-recovery, which is its tendency to encourage a party to give up the illegal purpose. For this reason it is hard to accept the suggestion[14] that a party to an illegal contract can recover back money paid under it simply because there has been a "total failure of consideration"[15] brought about by the other party's refusal to perform. Where illegality is involved, recovery is often denied (under the general rule of non-recovery) even though there has been a total failure of consideration[16]: and may conversely be allowed (under some of the exceptions to the general rule) even though there is no failure of consideration.[17] In these cases, the need to further the object of the invalidating rule often excludes the ordinary rules that govern recovery on the ground of failure of consideration under lawful contracts.

(f) NO RELIANCE ON ILLEGAL TRANSACTION. A person may be entitled to recover money or property which has been transferred under an illegal contract, if he can establish his right or title to it without relying *on the contract* or *on its illegality.*[18] It follows that there are two situations in which the claim may succeed: those in which the claimant does not rely on the illegal contract at all, but claims the property simply because he was already owner of it before that contract was made; and those in which he does rely on the contract (since it was by virtue of that contract that he acquired title) but does not have to rely on the illegality to establish his claim for the recovery of the

---

[11] *cf.* above, pp.445–446.

[12] *cf.* above, pp.492–493.

[13] As in *Bigos v Bousted* [1951] 1 All E.R. 92.

[14] Made in *Shaw v Shaw* [1965] 1 W.L.R. 537 at 539.

[15] See below, p.1049.

[16] *e.g. Parkinson v College of Ambulance Ltd* [1925] 2 K.B. 1; *Bigos v Bousted* [1951] 1 All E.R. 92. In *Edler v Auerbach* [1950] 1 K.B. 359 at 373–374 recovery was denied on the ground that there was no total failure of consideration; but this aspect of the case is better explained as an application of the general rule of non-recovery.

[17] *e.g., Atkinson v Denby* (1862) 7 H. & N. 934; *Kiriri Cotton Co Ltd v Dewani* [1960] A.C. 192. The contrary decision in *Re Cavalier Insurance Co Ltd* [1989] 2 Lloyd's Rep. 430 at 450 scarcely seems to give effect to the object of the legislation which had been contravened but may be explicable on the ground that the "guilty" insurer had not intended to violate the law and was in liquidation (so that the effective contest was between policyholders who had been paid and the insurer's creditors). *cf.* now Financial Services and Markets Act 2000, ss.26(2) and 27(2); above, p.491, n.76.

[18] For the application of a similar principle to a claim for damages for deceit, see *Standard Chartered Bank v Pakistan National Shipping Co (No.2)* [2000] 1 Lloyd's Rep. 218 at 232 (reversed on another point [2002] UKHL 43; [2003] 1 All E.R. 173).

property.[19] Some judicial statements of the rule refer to both these possibilities[20]; while others refer only to one[21] but should not, it is submitted, be read as excluding the other.

(i) *Recovering back goods transferred under an illegal contract.* Where goods are sold under an illegal contract, the property in them can pass (in accordance with the usual rules as to passing of property) notwithstanding the illegality[22]; and it may do so even though the goods have not been delivered to the buyer.[23] If the property has passed and the goods have been delivered to the buyer, the seller will not be entitled to their return—a point of special importance where the sale is on credit and the price has not been paid. Similarly, if property has passed to the buyer and the goods have been delivered to a third party, the seller cannot get them back from the third party, having no longer any title on which he can rely. The extent to which the *buyer* can rely on the passing of property in goods which have not been delivered to him is discussed below.[24]

If a thing is pledged, hired or lent under an illegal contract, a "special property" (or right to retain possession) passes when possession is transferred. So long as that special property endures, the subject-matter cannot be recovered back by the transferor. Thus in *Taylor v Chester*[25] half of a £50 Bank of England note was pledged as security for the expenses of a debauch in a brothel. The effect of the pledge was to transfer a special property in the note to the pledgee, with the result that the pledgor could not recover back the note without tendering the amount due. It seems that the effect of such tender would have been to put an end to the pledgee's special property and to entitle the pledgor to recover back the note on the strength of his title; but before the tender the pledgee would be entitled to take the usual steps to enforce his security against the pledged property.[26] The same principles would apply where a thing is hired under an illegal contract: the owner cannot recover it back while the hirer's special property lasts, but he can do so after that special property has come to an end, *e.g.* because the period of hire has run out.

In *Bowmakers Ltd v Barnet Instruments Ltd*[27] machine tools had been let out under hire-purchase agreements which were illegal[28] as they contravened war-time maximum price and licensing regulations. The hirers failed to pay the instalments due under the agreements, sold some of the goods and kept the rest. The owners successfully claimed damages for the conversion of all the goods. They did not have to "found [their] claim on the illegal contract or . . . plead its illegality in order to support [their] claim,"[29] but

---

[19] *Tinsley v Milligan* [1994] 1 A.C. 340 at 370 ("does not need to rely on the illegal contract for any purpose other than providing the basis of his claim to a property right"); Enonchong, 111 L.Q.R. 135.

[20] *e.g.* the statement in *Bowmakers Ltd v Barnet Instruments Ltd* [1945] K.B. 65 at 71 quoted below at n.29.

[21] *e.g. Tinsley v Milligan* above, at 366 ("provided he does not require to found on the unlawful agreement"); *ibid.* at 369 ("provided that the plaintiff can establish such title without pleading or leading evidence of the illegality").

[22] *Simpson v Nichols* (1838) 3 M. & W. 240 at 244; *Scarfe v Morgan* (1838) 4 M. & W. 270 at 281; *Elder v Kelly* [1919] 2 K.B. 179; *Singh v Ali* [1960] A.C. 167; *The Glastnost* [1991] 1 Lloyd's Rep. 483 at 487.

[23] *Belvoir Finance Co Ltd v Stapleton* [1971] 1 Q.B. 210; *cf. Kingsley v Sterling Industrial Securities Ltd* [1967] 2 Q.B. 747 at 738; below, p.501.

[24] See below, pp.501–502.

[25] (1869) L.R. 4 Q.B. 309; the same principle would apply to a pledge of *goods*.

[26] *Norwich Union Life Ins Co Ltd v Qureshi* [1999] 2 All E.R. (Comm) 707 at 709, where no offence had in fact been committed by the pledgee.

[27] [1945] K.B. 65; Hamson, 10 C.L.J. 249; Coote, 35 M.L.R. 38; Stewart, 1 J.C.L. 134.

[28] The owners had acquired the goods from one Smith under a contract which was also illegal; for this aspect of the case, see below p.501, n.73.

[29] At 71.

relied simply on their title. As the period of hire had not run out, it is at first sight hard to see why the hirers could not resist the owners' claim by relying on their special property under the hire-purchase agreements. The reason why they could not do so seems to be that a hirer's right to possession may come to an end otherwise than by lapse of time. First, it can come to an end as a result of a repudiatory breach on the part of the hirer.[30] Since a hirer is guilty of such a breach if he sells the thing hired, the defendants' special property in the goods which they had *sold* had therefore come to an end.[31] But this does not explain why their special property in the goods which they *simply kept* had come to an end. Failure to pay instalments is a breach of contract, but it is not normally of itself a repudiatory one. A possible solution of the difficulty is that a hirer's special property may come to an end as a result of *any* breach *because the contract expressly so provides*; *i.e.* because it provides that, on failure by the hirer to pay instalments, the agreement should *ipso facto* determine and that the owner should be entitled to take back the goods. If the agreements in *Bowmakers'* case contained some such clause[32] the hirers' right to possess the goods ceased as soon as they defaulted in paying instalments. The case can be reconciled with *Taylor v Chester* by assuming that the agreements did contain such a clause.

The preceding discussion of *Taylor v Chester*[33] and *Bowmakers Ltd v Barnett Instruments Ltd*[34] attempts to analyse these cases in the light of the rules governing the transfer of property (general or special) in the subject-matter of illegal contracts. This approach is however open to the objection that it ignores the crucial question: whether to allow the owner to recover his property would tend to promote or to defeat the purpose of the rule of law which makes the contract illegal.[35] In *Taylor v Chester* that purpose was presumably to discourage the keeping of brothels; and the decision can perhaps be explained on the ground that it created a stalemate position: the pledge being of *half* a bank note, neither pledgor nor pledgee could enforce any rights under the note until its two halves were reunited. On the other hand, it can be argued that, by giving the pledgor an incentive to redeem his pledge, the decision made it more, rather than less, likely that the brothel-keeper would be paid, and so tended to defeat the purpose of the invalidating rule. In *Bowmakers'* case the purpose of the regulations was presumably to prevent profiteering and to regulate the allocation of scarce resources in time of war; and it is unlikely that these purposes were defeated by upholding the owners' claims, particularly in view of the fact that "their error was involuntary".[36] The position would have been different if the owners had been guilty of a deliberate violation of a regulation made for the purpose of protecting hirers. It is submitted that, if this had been the position, the rule in *Bowmakers'* case should not have been applied; for if it were applied one of the owners' most important remedies for non-payment (that of retaking the goods) would be available irrespective of the legality of the agreement. In the example just given, such a result would defeat, rather than promote, the policy of the invalidating rule.

---

[30] *N Central Wagon & Finance Co v Graham* [1950] 2 K.B. 7. Election by the owners to rescind on account of the breach seems to be assumed (*cf.* below, pp.844–849).

[31] *cf. Belvoir Finance Co v Harold G Cole Co* [1969] 1 W.L.R. 1877 (where the hirer had sold the entire subject-matter); *Union Transport Finance Ltd v British Car Auctions Ltd* [1978] 2 All E.R. 385.

[32] The terms of the agreements are not set out in any of the reports of the case, but such provisions were certainly common.

[33] (1869) L.R. 4 Q.B. 309.

[34] [1945] K.B. 65.

[35] Treitel in *Essays in Memory of Sir Rupert Cross* (Tapper, ed.) pp.99–104.

[36] *Bowmakers'* case [1945] K.B. 65 at 68. The owners themselves had not attempted to make "excess" profits out of the transactions, having been brought in only to provide finance after the hirers had decided to acquire the goods from their former owners.

Where goods are let out under a regulated agreement,[37] the owner cannot retake them unless he first serves a default notice; and in certain cases he must in addition obtain a court order.[38] Such steps seem to amount to a reliance on the agreement and thus not to be available if the agreement is illegal.

(ii) *Recovering back money paid under an illegal contract.* A person who pays money under an illegal contract cannot generally recover it back by relying on his title, since the effect of the payment is almost always to transfer the entire property in the notes or coins to the payee. Money can be recovered back under the present rule only in the rare cases in which it is not paid out-and-out, but is paid as a deposit. Thus a person who deposits money with a stakeholder under an illegal wager can recover it back, so long as the stakeholder has not paid it over, in accordance with his instructions, to the other party to the wager.[39]

(iii) *Illegal leases.* An illegal lease generally vests a term of years in the tenant.[40] Thus if the tenant has gone into possession the landlord cannot rely on his title so as to turn the tenant out during the currency of the lease[41]; but he can do so once the lease has expired. The further question arises whether the landlord could recover possession if the tenant failed to pay rent. If this were possible the rule that a tenant under an illegal lease is not liable for rent[42] would be of small practical importance, for such a tenant, like any other, could be turned out for non-payment of rent. It might be argued that the tenant's right to possession comes to an end if he fails to pay rent, just as the hirers' right to possession in *Bowmakers'* case came to an end when they failed to pay instalments. But the analogy between illegal leases and *Bowmakers'* case is imperfect if the explanation of that case was that the hirers' right to possession determined *ipso facto* on the hirers' breach of contract.[43] For a lease cannot determine *ipso facto* on the tenant's breach as the law does not recognise such a thing as a lease for an uncertain period.[44] It is possible to have a lease "for five years, subject to forfeiture if the tenant fails to pay rent", but not "for five years, or for so long as the tenant pays rent, whichever is the shorter period". If the tenant fails to pay rent the landlord's right to possession does not automatically revive. He can only attempt to enforce the forfeiture clause. Such an attempt will fail, as it is an attempt to enforce a term of an illegal contract. Hence a landlord cannot recover possession of premises let under an illegal lease simply because the tenant fails to pay rent. A tenancy may also be terminable by notice, quite irrespective of default. If it is determined in this way, it seems that the landlord can recover possession on the strength of his title when the period of notice has expired.[45]

---

[37] See above, pp.177–178.

[38] Consumer Credit Act 1974, ss.87, 90.

[39] *cf. O'Sullivan v Thomas* [1895] 1 Q.B. 698.

[40] The general rule does not apply if on the true construction of the relevant legislation no interest is intended to pass to a person who takes a lease in contravention of it, *e.g.* where occupation of the land is meant to be restricted to a particular class: *Amar Singh v Kulubya* [1964] A.C. 142; Hamson [1964] C.L.J. 20; Cornish, 27 M.L.R. 225. No legal interest vests in a person occupying land under an agreement amounting, not to a lease but to a licence: *Parks v Esso Petroleum Co Ltd* [1999] 1 C.M.L.R. 455, affirmed [2000] Eu. L.R. 25, where it was held that there was no illegality.

[41] *Feret v Hill* (1854) 15 C.B. 207; *semble* that this case would now be differently decided on the ground of fraud; and see *Grace Rymer Investments Ltd v Waite* [1958] Ch. 831.

[42] See above, pp.481–482.

[43] See above, at n.32.

[44] *Lace v Chandler* [1944] K.B. 368; but see Validation of Wartime Leases Act 1944; *Prudential Assurance Co Ltd v London Residuary Body* [1992] 2 A.C. 386, where Lord Browne-Wilkinson said at 396 that there was no "satisfactory rationale" for the rule.

[45] The contrary assumption seems to have been made in *Amar Singh v Kulubya* [1964] A.C. 142, but was not necessary for the decision.

(iv) *Equitable title.* In the cases so far discussed, the claimant succeeded where he was able to establish legal title to the property in question without relying on the illegality. There was formerly some authority for the view that the position was different where the claimant relied on an equitable, rather than a legal title, and that in such cases the claim would be rejected once it appeared, or was admitted, that the equitable title had been acquired under an illegal transaction.[46] But this view was rejected by a majority of the House of Lords in *Tinsley v Milligan*, where Lord Browne-Wilkinson said that, as a result of later developments in the law relating to illegal contracts, the former equitable principle had "become elided into the common law rule".[47] The dispute in that case arose out of an agreement between the claimant and the defendant relating to a house in which they lived as lovers and which they jointly ran as a lodging house. The house had been purchased with money provided by both parties; and, although the parties accepted that the house was to be owned by them jointly, it was conveyed into the sole name of the claimant. This was done to enable the defendant to make false claims for social security benefits on the footing that she did not own her home; and such claims were in fact made. The parties later quarrelled and it was held that the defendant was entitled to an order for the sale of the house and to a declaration that it was owned by the parties in equal shares. The defendant was entitled in equity to a half share in the house by virtue of the presumption which normally arises in equity where one party transfers property to another, or provides money for the acquisition of property by another, that the property is held by the latter party (to the appropriate extent) on a resulting trust for the former party. It was this presumption of resulting trust which gave rise to the defendant's equitable title.[48] To establish that title, she had no need to impeach the transaction by relying on its illegality. It was, on the contrary, the claimant who sought to impeach the transaction by relying on its illegality in order to deprive it of its normal effect of giving the defendant an equitable title. The defendant's position was in substance the same as that of the buyer of goods under an illegal contract: she had acquired her equitable title, just as such a buyer can acquire a legal title,[49] in spite of the illegality. It was, moreover, undesirable for the present purpose to treat equitable title differently from legal title, since to do so would lead to some entirely capricious distinctions: for example, to the conclusion that the cases on illegal leases[50] would have been differently decided if the contracts had been agreements for leases (which give rise only to an equitable interest[51]) as opposed to executed leases (which give rise to a legal term of years).[52]

The crucial factor in *Tinsley v Milligan* was that the defendant was able to rely on the normal presumption that property bought in part with her money was to that extent, or to the extent agreed upon by the parties, held in trust for her. That presumption could, of course, have been rebutted by proof that the defendant had intended to make a gift; and if the claimant had proved this, then the defendant's claim to a share in the property would have failed for it would then have been the defendant who would have relied on the illegality to defeat the gift.[53] In the case of certain relationships between the parties

---

[46] See *Curtis v Perry* (1802) 2 Ves. 739 at 744 and other authorities on the point discussed in *Tinsley v Milligan* [1994] 1 A.C. 340.

[47] *ibid.* at 376; Buckley, 110 L.Q.R. 3; Thornton [1993] C.L.J. 394; Stowe, 56 M.L.R. 441.

[48] *cf. Silverwood v Silverwood* (1997) 74 P. & C.R. D9; *Lowson v Coombes*, *The Times*, December 2, 1998; *Mortgage Express v Robson* [2001] EWCA Civ 887; [2001] 2 All E.R. (Comm) 886 (equitable title acquired under earlier fraudulent transaction).

[49] See above, p.495.

[50] *e.g. Feret v Hill* (1854) 15 C.B. 207, above, p.498.

[51] *Walsh v Lonsdale* (1882) 21 Ch.D. 9; above, p.177.

[52] See the discussion of *Feret v Hill*, above. in *Tinsley v Milligan* [1994] 1 A.C. 340 at 370.

[53] *Tribe v Tribe* [1996] Ch. 107 at 128–129.

to the transaction, such an intention to make a gift is, moreover, presumed, thus reversing the normal presumption of resulting trust. This is, for example, the position where a father transfers property (or pays for property to be transferred) to his child: in such cases there is said to be a "presumption of advancement",[54] or, in other words, a presumption that the transfer was intended as a gift to the child. It follows that, if the transfer in such a case is alleged to have been made for an illegal purpose, then the general rule will be that the father will not be able to claim the property by relying on his title; and that he will not be able to do so by impeaching the transfer by reference to the illegal purpose, for this would require him to rely on the illegality. This was the position in *Chettiar v Chettiar*,[55] where a father transferred land to his son by an instrument recording a payment by the son which was not in fact made. The object of the transfer was to deceive the public authorities into thinking that the father held less land than he did, and so to enable the father to evade certain legislative restrictions on the production of rubber. The Privy Council dismissed the father's claim that the son was trustee of the land for him; for in order to rebut the presumption of advancement the father would have had to disclose and to rely on his illegal purpose.

The result in *Chettiar v Chettiar*[56] amounted to an application of the general rule that property transferred under an illegal contract cannot be recovered back by the transferor.[57] But we have seen that this rule is subject to a number of *other* exceptions[58] than the one here under discussion (*i.e.* the one under which the claimant does not need to rely on the illegal transaction); and where one of those other exceptions applied, a claim for the recovery of property was upheld even though the property was transferred in circumstances giving rise to the presumption of advancement. This was the position in *Tribe v Tribe*,[59] the facts of which have been stated earlier in this Chapter.[60] The shares in that case were transferred from father to son, so that there was a presumption of advancement; but a claim for their return was made before the illegal purpose for which they had been transferred had been "carried into effect in any way".[61] Hence the case fell within the exception to the general rule of non-recovery which applies where the illegal purpose is repudiated[62]; and it was held that the father could invoke this exception so as to recover the shares even though the process of rebutting the presumption of advancement involved his relying on the illegality of the transaction to show that it was not intended to be by way of gift. It is submitted that the same result should have followed if that father had been able to invoke one of the other exceptions, considered earlier in this Chapter, to the general rule of non-recovery: *i.e.* if the transfer had been procured by oppression or by misrepresentation or made under a mistake,[63] or if the father had been a member of a protected class.[64]

It was suggested above that the analysis of cases involving the transfer of property in goods under illegal contracts was open to the objection that it could lead to results which failed to promote (and might defeat) the purpose of the prohibition giving rise to the

---

[54] A discussion of the relationships giving rise to the presumption of advancement is beyond the scope of this book. For such a discussion, see Snell's *Equity* (30th ed.) §§9–11 to 9–14.

[55] [1962] A.C. 294.

[56] See above.

[57] See above, p.491.

[58] See above, pp.491–495.

[59] [1996] Ch. 107.

[60] See above, p.494.

[61] [1996] Ch. 107 at 121.

[62] See above, p.494.

[63] See above, pp.492–493.

[64] See above, p.491—a perhaps unlikely but not impossible situation.

illegality[65]; and same danger arises in the present group of cases. Suppose, for example, that the transfer in *Chettiar v Chettiar* had not been from father to son, but from son to father to enable the son to evade the legislative restrictions. There would then have been no presumption to advancement but, on the contrary, a presumption of resulting trust; and it would seem to follow from the reasoning of *Tinsley v Milligan* that the son could have recovered the land on the strength of his equitable title. Such a conclusion would scarcely have promoted the purpose of the rule of law which was infringed in that case. Reasoning which is based on proprietary concepts no doubt has the advantage of predictability; its disadvantage in the present context is that pays insufficient regard to the policy considerations with which the courts are normally concerned in working out the effects of illegality on contracts. *Tribe v Tribe*[66] is, with respect, to be welcomed in allowing a policy-based exception to the general rule of non-recovery to prevail over the more abstract application of purely proprietary reasoning.[67]

(v) *Special cases.* There may be special cases in which a person cannot recover back money or property although his right or title to it can be established without reference to the contract or its illegality. It has been suggested that if the property is such that it is unlawful to deal with it at all (*e.g.* an obscene book) it cannot be recovered back.[68] There is also some support for the view that the price paid for such a book cannot be recovered back by the buyer,[69] though this is scarcely the best way of discouraging the trade in such things. A further suggestion is that there is no right of recovery if the object of the contract is to enable one party to commit a serious crime,[70] *e.g.* if a dagger is lent to commit murder. On the other hand, a person who undertakes the safe keeping of a burglar's house-breaking tools is apparently bound to give them up to the burglar on demand.[71]

(vi) *Recovery of money or property obtained under an illegal contract.* The mere fact that something has been obtained under an illegal contract does not deprive the recipient of the usual remedies for its recovery or protection. Thus if goods are sold and delivered under an illegal contract, and the property in them has passed to the buyer, he can recover them or their value if they are later taken away from him by the seller.[72] Such remedies are also available against third parties,[73] and even (subject to statutory exceptions) against the police.[74] They may, moreover, be available to a buyer who has acquired the property in goods under an illegal sale, even though the goods have never been in his

---

[65] See above, pp.497–498.

[66] [1996] Ch. 107; above, p.500.

[67] *cf.*, in Australia, *Nelson v Nelson* (1995) 132 A.L.R. 132.

[68] *Bowmakers Ltd v Barnet Instruments Ltd* [1945] K.B. 65 at 72; *Costello v Chief Constable of Derbyshire Constabulary* [2001] EWCA Civ 381; [2001] 1 W.L.R. 1437, at [33]. *Aliter* if the book is seditious? See *Elias v Pasmore* [1934] 2 K.B. 164 at 174.

[69] *The Siben* [1996] 1 Lloyd's Rep. 35, 62; above, p.381.

[70] Williams, 8 C.L.J. at p.62, n.54. *After* conviction of the offender, an order to deprive him of "his rights, if any, in the property" may be made by the court under Powers of Criminal Courts (Sentencing) Act 2000, s.143.

[71] *R. v Lomas* (1913) 110 L.T. 239, as explained in *R. v Bullock* [1955] 1 W.L.R. 1.

[72] *Singh v Ali* [1960] A.C. 167.

[73] See the discussion of *Bowmakers Ltd v Barnet Instruments Ltd* [1945] K.B. 65 in *Tinsley v Milligan* [1994] 1 A.C. 340 at 369: the owners succeeded in spite of the illegality not only of the hire-purchase agreements, but also of the contracts under which they had acquired the goods from their former owner.

[74] *Gordon v Chief Commr. of Metropolitan Police* [1910] 2 K.B. 1080; *Chief Constable of the West Midlands Police v White*, (1992) 142 New L.J. 458; *Slater v Commissioner of Police of the Metropolis*, The Times, January 23, 1996; *Porter v Chief Constable of Merseyside Police* [2000] Q.B. 427. For police powers in certain cases to seize and retain property for a limited time, see *Malone v Metropolitan Police Commissioner* [1980] Q.B. 49; Police and Criminal Evidence Act 1984, ss.19, 22; after the expiry of that time, the property must be returned to the person from whom it was seized: *Costello v Chief Constable of the Derbyshire Constabulary* [2001] EWCA

possession. In *Belvoir Finance Co Ltd v Stapleton*,[75] Belgravia wanted to acquire cars from Francis, finance being provided by Belvoir. In relation to each car, two contracts were made: a sale by Francis to Belvoir and a letting on hire-purchase by Belvoir to Belgravia. All these contracts were illegal. Belvoir never acquired possession of the cars, which were delivered by Francis straight to Belgravia. It was held that Belgravia's assistant manager was liable to Belvoir for conversion of the cars, since the property in them had passed to Belvoir as soon as the contracts of sale between them and Francis were "executed".[76] The decision is, however, concerned only with the relative rights of the buyer and a third person. *The seller* had no further interest in the cars and was not in possession of them. The case therefore does not support the proposition that a buyer to whom property in goods has passed under an illegal contract can claim them, or damages for their conversion, *from a seller who has never delivered them at all*. Such a claim would not differ in substance from a claim for the delivery, or for damages for the non-delivery, of the goods under the illegal contract. Its success would thus defeat the object of the rule against the enforcement of such a contract.

The right to recover money or property obtained under an illegal contract has been extended, sometimes with surprising results, to make an agent employed in an illegal transaction liable to account for its proceeds to his principal. Thus in *Tenant v Elliott*[77] a broker who effected an illegal insurance and later received the policy moneys was held accountable for them to his principal. Similarly, in *Farmer v Russell*[78] a carrier received the price of goods on behalf of his principal, to whom he was held liable to account even though the goods were counterfeit halfpence. The same principle was applied in *Bone v Eckless*,[79] where the captain of a ship was instructed to sell it to the Turkish Government, and told the owner that this could be done only if he paid bribes of £500 to Turkish officials. The owner agreed that the bribes should be paid, and the ship was duly sold for £6,500, of which the captain kept £500 to pay the bribes. He paid away only £300 in bribes, and it was held that the owner could recover the remaining £200 from the captain because he "makes out his title to recover £6,500 by proving the sale of his ship for that sum, and it is the [captain] who is relying on the illegal agreement to justify the non-payment of the money". In all these cases the illegality was in the transaction which the agent was employed to effect. The principle would probably not apply where the agency itself was illegal[80] and more recent authority casts some doubt on its validity in suggesting that a claimant could not recover damages from a third party for conversion

---

Civ 381; [2001] 1 W.L.R. 1437; unless it is of such a nature that it would be unlawful for the police to transfer it to him or for him to be in possession of it, as in the case of controlled drugs: *ibid.*, at [33]. For powers to restrain an offender from dealing with the fruits of his crime, see *Chief Constable of Kent v V* [1983] Q.B. 34; *Chief Constable of Hampshire v A Ltd* [1985] Q.B. 132 (where the means of identification had failed); and *Attorney-General v Blake* [1998] Ch. 439 at 464–465; contrast *Chief Constable of Leicestershire v M* [1989] 1 W.L.R. 20, 23, and *Chief Constable of Surrey v A*, *The Times*, October 27, 1988 (no common law power to prevent a person, who had been charged with obtaining money by deception, from dealing with *profits* made by use of the money; and see *Halifax BS v Thomas* [1996] Ch. 217). Many statutes confer powers on the courts to make forfeiture, confiscation or similar orders; a complete discussion or even list of such provisions is beyond the scope of this book. Recent examples include Powers of Criminal Courts (Sentencing) Act 2000, s.143 and Anti-terrorism, Crime and Security Act 2001, s.1 and Sch.1. Confiscation powers forming part of the criminal justice system are not in conflict with the Human Rights Act: *R. v Rezvi* [2002] UKHL 1; [2002] 1 All E.R. 801; *R. v Benjafield* [2002] UKHL 2, [2002] 1 All E.R. 815.

[75] [1971] 1 Q.B. 210; *cf. Kingsley v Sterling Industrial Securities Ltd* [1967] 2 Q.B. 747 at 783.

[76] [1971] 1 Q.B. 210 at 220.

[77] (1791) 1 B. & P. 3.

[78] (1798) 1 B. & P. 296 (approved in *Sykes v Beadon* (1879) 11 Ch.D. 170); *cf. Bousfield v Wilson* (1846) 16 L.J.Ex. 44; *Pye v BG Transport Service* [1966] 2 Lloyd's Rep. 300; *contra*, *Griffith v Young* (1810) 12 East 513 at 514.

[79] (1860) 5 H. & N. 925.

[80] See *Booth v Hodgson* (1795) 6 T.R 405; *Harry Parker Ltd v Mason* [1940] 2 K.B. 590.

of property obtained by fraud where the property was "the very proceeds of the fraudulent conduct".[81] Protection will not be denied to property rights merely because their acquisition involves the innocent commission of a civil wrong. For example, the copyright in a musical work may be protected even though its creation involved the innocent infringement of copyright in a previous work.[82]

(3) Scope of the general rule

The general rule that property transferred or money paid under an illegal contract is irrecoverable was not settled without a good deal of hesitation; and in particular equity at one time inclined to the opposite view.[83] Traces of the equitable view can be found in *Hermann v Charlesworth*.[84] The defendant ran a marriage bureau, and the claimant promised to pay him £250 if he could find her a husband. She also paid a "special client's fee" of £52, of which £47 was to be repaid if no marriage or engagement took place within nine months. After four months she repudiated the contract and claimed back the £52. One reason for allowing her claim was that equity gave relief against marriage brokage bonds, even after a marriage had taken place,[85] and that, similarly, money actually paid under a marriage brokage contract could be recovered back: in other words, the general rule of non-recovery does not in equity apply to marriage brokage contracts. At one time this equitable principle also applied to other types of contract: thus money paid under a contract to get the payor a commission in the marines could be recovered back.[86] There is no good modern authority for applying the equitable principle except to marriage brokage contracts; but the possibility of its wider application should perhaps not be wholly ruled out. It would enable the courts to allow recovery where this was more likely, than the general rule of non-recovery, to further the policy of the invalidating rule.[87]

(4) Restitution in respect of services

Work done under an illegal contract may (no less than money paid or property transferred) give rise to a restitutionary claim, that is, to one for a reasonable remuneration on a *quantum meruit* basis. This possibility is illustrated by a case[88] in which the claimant had done work under a contract signed by him on behalf of a company. The contract was void because the company no longer existed[89]; and by trading in the name of a company which no longer existed the claimant had also committed an offence under s.34 of the Companies Act 1985. It was held that his claim was "maintainable on a *quantum meruit* though not under a supposed contract".[90] One possible reason for this result is that the policy of s.34 was not contravened by allowing such a claim.[91] Another

---

[81] *Thackwell v Barclays Bank plc* [1986] 1 All E.R. 676 at 689.
[82] *ZYX Music GmbH v King* [1995] 3 All E.R. 1.
[83] *Neville v Wilkinson* (1782) 1 Bro.C.C. 547 at 548. The same view was sometimes taken at common law; *e.g. Munt v Stokes* (1792) 4 T.R. 561.
[84] [1905] 2 K.B. 123.
[85] *ibid.* at 134, 137, 138.
[86] *Morris v McCullock* (1763) Amb. 432.
[87] *cf.* above, p.491.
[88] *Cotronic (UK) Ltd v Dezonie/(t/a Wendaland Builders) Ltd* [1991] B.C.L.C. 721.
[89] See below, p.736.
[90] [1991] B.C.L.C. 721 at 726.
[91] This is suggested by the reference, *ibid.*, to *Shaw v Groom* [1970] 2 Q.B. 504, above, p.429.

is that (as in the cases allowing recovery of property) the claimant did "not need to rely on any illegality to found a claim in that form".[92] The reason why he had no such need was that the contract was void for some *other* reason than the illegality, *i.e.* on account of the non-existence of the company. Where the *only* ground of invalidity is illegality, a guilty party who had done work under the contract should not, it is submitted, have a *quantum meruit* claim merely because of that invalidity. To allow such a claim merely on the ground that the contract was invalid for illegality would, at least in most cases[93] be inconsistent with the policy of the invalidating rule.[94] It follows that a solicitor who cannot enforce a conditional fee agreement, because it is illegal under the rules stated earlier in this Chapter,[95] is also precluded from recovering the reasonable value of services rendered under it on a *quantum meruit* basis.[96] The same is not, however, necessarily true of a *quantum meruit* claim made against a guilty party by a party who is innocent of the illegality (in the sense of being unaware of the rule of law making the contract illegal) in respect of services not affected by the illegality. In one case of this kind, the claimant agreed to introduce clients to solicitors who, in return, promised to pay him a share of the fees paid by those clients; he did not know that such an arrangement was prohibited[97] and that the fee-sharing contract was therefore illegal. It was held that he could neither enforce that contract nor bring a *quantum meruit* claim in respect of the work of introducing clients[98]; but that such a claim was available in respect of other services rendered by him in acting as interpreter between the clients in question and the solicitors.[99]

3. Severance[1]

Where a contract is illegal only in part, two problems can arise. The first is the problem of severance of consideration: can a promise be enforced if it is lawful in itself but is in part supported by illegal consideration? The second is the problem of severance of promises: can a promise be enforced if it is lawful in itself but is coupled with an illegal promise?

(1) Severance of consideration

(a) DEPENDS ON WHETHER ILLEGAL PART IS SUBSTANTIAL OR SUBSIDIARY. A promise cannot be enforced if the whole or substantially the whole[2] of the consideration for it is illegal. In *Lound v Grimwade*[3] A, who had committed a fraud making him civilly and criminally liable, promised to pay B £3,000 in return for B's promise not to take "any legal proceedings" in respect of the fraud. B's claim for the £3,000 failed as a substantial

---

[92] [1991] B.C.L.C. 721 at 726, relying on the analogy of *Bowmakers'* case [1945] K.B. 65; above, p.496.
[93] *e.g.* in cases such as *Ashmore Benson Pease & Co Ltd v AV Dawson Ltd* [1973] 1 W.L.R. 828, above, p.484; and *cf.* the situation discussed below at p.506 at n.17.
[94] *cf. Taylor v Bhail* (1995) 50 Con. L.R. 70.
[95] See above, p.431.
[96] *Awwad v Geraghty & Co* [2001] Q.B. 570 at 596.
[97] By the Solicitors' Practice Rules, which have the force of law: *Swain v Law Society* [1983] A.C. 598 at 608.
[98] *Mohamed v Alaga & Co* [2000] 1 W.L.R. 1815 at 1824–1825.
[99] *ibid.*, at 1825–1827 as explained in *Awwad v Geraghty & Co*, above, n.96.
[1] Marsh, 64 L.Q.R. 230 at 347.
[2] *Marshall v NM Financial Management Ltd* [1997] 1 W.L.R. 1527 at 1532.
[3] (1888) 39 Ch.D. 605; *cf. Walrond v Walrond* (1858) Johns. 18.

part of the consideration for A's promise to pay it was B's own illegal promise to stifle a criminal prosecution.[4]

On the other hand, a promise can be enforced if the main consideration for it is lawful, although it is also supported by a subsidiary illegal consideration.[5] For example, an employee who enters into too wide a contract in restraint of trade can recover his wages.[6] The main consideration for the employer's promise to pay is the employee's promise to serve, or the performance of it; his promise not to compete is only subsidiary. The position is similar where an employee as a term of his contract of service enters into a pension scheme which contains an invalid stipulation in restraint of trade. That stipulation forms only a subsidiary part of the consideration which the employee provides for the various promises made by the employer under the contract as a whole; and if the stipulation is invalid it can be severed, so that the pension will be payable although the stipulation is not complied with.[7] But if the sole consideration for the promise to pay the pension is an invalid stipulation in restraint of trade the employee cannot recover the pension. This was the position in *Wyatt v Kreglinger & Fernau*[8] where the promise was made on the lawful termination of the contract of service and the employee provided no consideration for the promise except his assent to, or performance of, the invalid stipulation in restraint of trade.

Similar principles apply where the vendor of a business enters into too wide a contract in restraint of trade. If the price is promised mainly for the business premises and stock-in-trade, the illegal promise not to compete is only a subsidiary part of the consideration for the promise to pay, so that the vendor can recover the price. But if the purpose of the transaction, viewed objectively,[9] was the elimination of a competitor, rather than the purchase of business, it might be held that the vendor's promise not to compete formed a substantial part of the consideration for the purchaser's promise to pay; and that accordingly the vendor would not be entitled to the price.

The distinction so far drawn may, however, be displaced by the policy of the invalidating rule. In *Ailion v Spiekermann*[10] the vendor of a leasehold interest required the purchasers to pay an illegal premium. He thereby committed a statutory offence, but the purchasers (who were "unwilling victims"[11]) committed none by promising to pay the premium. It was held that they could specifically enforce the vendor's obligations without having to pay the premium. They were able to do this, whether or not their promise to pay the premium constituted a substantial part of the consideration; for such enforcement by them was the most effective way of promoting the legislative policy against illegal premiums.

---

[4] See above, p.446. For rejection on similar grounds of a claim to rescind a contract, see *The Siben* [1996] 1 Lloyd's Rep. 35 at 62.

[5] See *Goodinson v Goodinson* [1954] 2 Q.B. 118 (the actual decision is obsolete: Matrimonial Causes Act 1973, s.34, above, p.447); *cf. Kearney v Whitehaven Colliery Co* [1893] 1 Q.B. 700; *Fielding & Platt Ltd v Najjar* [1969] 1 W.L.R. 357 at 362.

[6] *McFarlane v Daniell* (1938) S.R. (N.S.W.) 337, approved in *Carney v Herbert* [1985] A.C. 301 at 311; *cf. Sadler v Imperial Life Assurance Co of Canada* [1988] I.R.L.R. 388 and *Marshall v NM Financial Management Ltd* [1997] 1 W.L.R. 1527 (similar principle applied to agent's claim for commission).

[7] *Bull v Pitney-Bowes Ltd* [1967] 1 W.L.R. 273; *semble* the stipulation was not a mere condition but formed part of the consideration for the employer's promise since it was entered into at the employer's request: see above, p.72.

[8] [1933] 1 K.B. 793; above, p.462.

[9] *Triggs v Staines Urban DC* [1969] 1 Ch. 10; above, p.462.

[10] [1979] Ch. 158.

[11] *ibid.* at 165.

(b) APPORTIONMENT OF PROMISE TO LEGAL PART. In the cases so far discussed, the claimant has either failed or succeeded in full. The claimant in *Lound v Grimwade*[12] got nothing, though part of the consideration provided by him was lawful; while an employee who enters into too wide a restraint of trade can recover his entire wages, though the employer loses one of the advantages for which he bargained.[13] It might be thought fairer to make the defendant liable in proportion to the legal part of the consideration. The objection to such a rule is that it would often be hard to apply as the court cannot easily tell what value the parties attributed to the legal and illegal parts of the consideration respectively. But it seems that where the legal and illegal parts can be precisely valued, the claimant can recover so much of the promised payment as can be attributed to the lawful part of the consideration. In *Frank W. Clifford Ltd v Garth*[14] a builder agreed to do building work for the defendant on a "cost plus" basis, so that the total cost of the work could not be known in advance. The bill for the completed work came to £1,911. The defendant refused to pay anything because work costing more than £1,000 was illegal unless licensed, and no licence had been obtained. But he was held liable to pay £1,000: his promise to pay was enforced to the extent to which it was supported by lawful consideration. A person who has done work under a contract which is only partly illegal may also be awarded a reasonable sum in respect of the lawful part of the work.[15] Such an award is based on restitutionary principles and does not strictly speaking amount to partial enforcement *of the contract*, but in practical terms the outcome will often quite closely resemble such enforcement.

(c) SPECIAL CASES. It has been said that the doctrine of severance does not apply where part of the consideration is criminal or immoral,[16] *e.g.* where it is a promise to commit robbery or adultery, or the performance of such a promise. But the fact that part of the consideration is criminal prevents severance only if the party who provides it is guilty of a deliberate violation of the law. Thus in *Frank W Clifford Ltd v Garth* the builder recovered £1,000 in spite of the fact that he had committed an offence by doing unlicensed work worth more than £1,000. He would however have recovered nothing if he had agreed to do the work without a licence, knowing from the start that it would cost over £1,000.[17]

(2) Severance of promises

Where the promises of one party to a contract are partly lawful and partly illegal, the court may cut out the illegal promises and enforce the lawful ones alone. It will do this only if the following three conditions are satisfied.

(a) THE PROMISE MUST BE OF SUCH A KIND AS CAN BE SEVERED. It has been said that there can be no severance of a criminal or immoral promise.[18] But although this may be generally true, it seems that a criminal promise could be severed if it was made without guilty intent.[19] It has also been said that there can be no severance of a promise to trade

---

[12] (1888) 39 Ch.D. 605.

[13] In this respect the analogy drawn in *Barclays Bank plc v Caplan* [1998] 1 FLR 532 at 536, between illegality and undue influence cases is imperfect since in cases of the latter kind benefits received by the victim must be restored as a condition of rescission.

[14] [1956] 1 W.L.R. 570; *cf. Ex p. Mather* (1797) 3 Ves. 373; *J Dennis & Co v Munn* [1949] 2 K.B. 327; and see *The American Accord* [1983] 1 A.C. 168.

[15] *Mohamed v Alaga & Co* [1999] 3 All E.R. 699 at 707 at 710; above p.504.

[16] *Bennett v Bennett* [1952] 1 K.B. 249 at 254.

[17] *Frank W. Clifford v Garth* [1956] 1 W.L.R. at 572; *cf.* above, p.483.

[18] *Bennett v Bennett* [1951] 1 K.B. 249 at 254.

[19] As in the case of severance of consideration: above, at nn.16, 17.

with the enemy[20] or of a promise to defraud the Revenue.[21] Promises are most frequently severed in contracts in restraint of trade; and it has been assumed that promises excluding the jurisdiction of the courts can be severed.[22] The question whether other illegal promises can be severed at all is still an open one.

(b) THE "BLUE PENCIL" TEST. Under this test, the court will sever only where this can be done by cutting words out of the contract (or by running a blue pencil through the offending words).[23] The court will not redraft the contract by adding or rearranging words, or by substituting one word for another.[24] Thus in *Mason v Provident Clothing & Supply Co Ltd*[25] the House of Lords refused to strike out of the contract the words "within 25 miles of London" and to substitute "in Islington"; to do so would be, not to sever, but to redraft the contract. The test does little to protect the party subject to the restraint since it can easily be satisfied by skilful draftsmanship, while on the other hand it may entirely prevent enforcement of a restraint drawn up by laymen where some degree of enforcement would be reasonable.[26] Where this is the case, the courts will apply the test with some latitude. In *T Lucas & Co Ltd v Mitchell*[27] a contract provided that a sales representative should not within a certain *area* "deal in any goods similar to" those allocated to him for sale; or "*solicit orders* for . . . any *such* goods". It was held that the area covenant was invalid while the solicitation covenant was valid; and that the area covenant could be severed. Strictly speaking, this left no point of reference for the word "such" in the solicitation covenant, but the deleted area covenant could be looked at to give the word meaning.

It used to be thought that promises could be severed merely because the "blue pencil" test was satisfied[28]; but this view no longer prevails. The test may restrict, but it does not determine, the scope of the doctrine of severance. Even if the legal and illegal promises are actually contained in separate documents,[29] the court will sever only if the third requirement is also satisfied.

(c) SEVERANCE MUST NOT ALTER THE NATURE OF THE COVENANT. The court will not sever if to do so alters the whole nature of the covenant.[30]

In *Goldsoll v Goldman*[31] the seller of an imitation jewellery business in New Bond Street undertook that he would not for two years deal in real or imitation jewellery in

---

[20] *Kuenigl v Donnersmarck* [1955] 1 Q.B. 515; *cf. Royal Boskalis Westminster NV v Mountain* [1999] Q.B. 674 at 693.

[21] *Miller v Karlinski* (1945) 62 T.L.R. 85; *Corby v Morrison* [1980] I.C.R. 564; the contrary was assumed in *Napier v National Business Agency* [1951] 2 All E.R. 265 but it was held that the contract was not severable as there was only one promise in substance. In the case of long-term employment, the contract is wholly invalid during the period in respect of which the illegal payments are made, but not in respect of the rest of its duration; *Hyland v J H Barber (North-West) Ltd* [1985] I.C.R. 861.

[22] *Re Davstone Estate Ltd's Leases* [1969] 2 Ch. 378; but severance failed because the "blue pencil" test (below) was not satisfied; *Home Insurance Co v Administratia Asigurarilor* [1983] 2 Lloyd's Rep. 674 at 677.

[23] *e.g. Kall Kwick Printing (UK) Ltd v Rush* [1996] F.S.R. 114.

[24] Contrast the court's statutory power to revise contracts: in the cases described at p.510 below.

[25] [1913] A.C. 724 (above, p.459).

[26] See *Commercial Plastics Ltd v Vincent* [1965] 1 Q.B. 623 at 647.

[27] [1974] Ch. 129.

[28] *Putsman v Taylor* [1927] 1 K.B. 637 at 640; the Court of Appeal held the covenant valid *in toto*, so that severance was not necessary: [1927] 1 K.B. 741.

[29] As in *Kenyon v Darwen Cotton Manufacturing Co Ltd* [1936] 2 K.B. 193.

[30] *Putsman v Taylor* [1927] 1 K.B. 637 at 646; *cf. Spector v Ageda* [1973] Ch. 30 at 45; *Silverstone Records v Mountfield* [1993] E.M.L.R. 152; *Royal Boskalis Westminster NV v Mountain* [1999] Q.B. 674 at 693. This requirement does not apply to an agreement partly invalid under the rules of competition law stated at pp.437–439, above: *Barrett v Inntrepreneur Pub Co (GL) Ltd* [1999] E.G.C.S. 93.

[31] [1915] 1 Ch. 292.

the United Kingdom or certain named places abroad. The covenant was too wide in *area* as the seller had not traded abroad, and in respect of *subject-matter* as he had scarcely dealt in real jewellery. But it was held that the references to the foreign places and to real jewellery could be severed, and that the restraint on dealing in imitation jewellery in the United Kingdom could be enforced. The only question discussed by the court was whether the "blue pencil" test was satisfied; but it can be argued that the object of the original covenant was to protect the business which the buyer had bought; that the object of the covenant after severance remained the same; and that severance had thus not altered the nature of the original covenant.

In the contrasting case of *Attwood v Lamont*[32] the plaintiffs had a general outfitters' business at Kidderminster. It was divided into several departments, each of which was supervised by one of their employees. The head of each department undertook that he would not after leaving the plaintiffs' service "be concerned in any of the following trades or businesses: that is to say, the trade or business of a tailor, dressmaker, general draper, milliner, hatter, haberdasher, gentlemen's, ladies' or children's outfitter" within ten miles of Kidderminster. In an action to enforce this covenant against the head of the tailoring department, the plaintiffs admitted that the covenant was too wide in point of subject-matter, but they argued that everything except the reference to tailoring should be severed, and that part alone enforced. This argument was rejected as severance would have altered the whole nature of the covenant. After severance, the covenant would protect only that part of the business in which the defendant had worked, whereas the original covenant was "part of a scheme by which every head of a department was to be restrained from competition with the plaintiffs, even in the business of departments with which he had no connection".[33] The valid and invalid covenants were thus interdependent and, where this is the relationship between them, the court will not sever the invalid ones.[34]

It was at one time thought that *Goldsoll v Goldman* and *Attwood v Lamont* could be reconciled simply on the ground that the covenant in the first case was between vendor and purchaser while that in the second was between employer and employee.[35] This view was supported by a dictum in *Mason v Provident Clothing & Supply Co Ltd* that in employment cases the courts should only sever where the excess was trivial,[36] and by the view expressed in *Attwood v Lamont* that in such cases the courts should be reluctant to sever at all.[37] But if the court is satisfied that there are, as a matter of construction, separate covenants, and that one of them can be removed without altering the nature of the covenant, it can sever a restraint in an employment contract,[38] and it may do so even though the excess was not merely trivial.[39] On the other hand, the court will not sever a covenant between vendor and purchaser merely because the "blue pencil" test is

---

[32] [1920] 3 K.B. 571.

[33] [1920] 3 K.B. 571 at 579–580.

[34] *Scully UK Ltd v Lee* [1998] I.R.L.R. 259.

[35] *Ronbar Enterprises Ltd v Green* [1954] 1 W.L.R. 814 at 820.

[36] [1913] A.C. 724 at 745.

[37] [1920] 3 K.B. 571 at 593–596. Contrast the attitude of the court in *Commercial Plastics Ltd v Vincent* [1965] 1 Q.B. 623 at 647 (above, p.507) and in *The Littlewoods Organisation Ltd v Harris* [1977] 1 W.L.R. 1472 (where no question of severance arose).

[38] *T Lucas & Co Ltd v Mitchell* [1974] Ch. 129; *Stenhouse Australia Ltd v Phillips* [1975] A.C. 391; *Business Seating (Renovations) Ltd v Broad* [1989] I.C.R. 729 at 734–735; *Dawnay Day & Co Ltd v D'Alphen* [1997] I.R.L.R. 285, 296; *ibid.* 422 *cf. Commercial Plastics Ltd v Vincent* [1965] 1 Q.B. 623 at 647. *Anscombe & Ringland v Butchoff* (1984) 134 New L.J. 37.

[39] *Putsman v Taylor* [1927] 1 K.B. 637; *Scorer v Seymour-Johns* [1966] 1 W.L.R. 1419; and see n.38 above.

satisfied. Even between such parties, severance will not be allowed where its effect would be to alter the nature of the covenant.[40]

(d) ALLEGED NECESSITY FOR SEPARATE CONSIDERATION. It is sometimes said that a promise can be severed only if it is supported by separate consideration.[41] But this view is inconsistent with the cases just considered. In *Goldsoll v Goldman*, for instance, no separate consideration was provided for the valid and the invalid parts of the covenant. Yet the invalid parts were severed.

(e) WHETHER OTHER PROMISES AFFECTED. In the restraint of trade cases discussed above, the covenant not to compete has formed part of a larger transaction; and the effect of holding that excessive parts of the restraint could not be severed was simply that *that covenant* was wholly void. *Other* promises or obligations of the covenantor under the contract as a whole may nevertheless be enforceable. For example, an employee who has entered into a wholly void covenant in restraint of trade may still be restrained from breaking his duty of fidelity.[42] And a person to whom money has been lent on terms which include an invalid covenant in restraint of trade is nevertheless liable to repay the loan and to pay interest.[43] In such cases, it can be said that the main purpose of the contract is to create the relationship of employer and employee or of lender and borrower; and the fact that the contract seeks to impose an invalid restraint on the employee or borrower does not vitiate the entire relationship.

On the other hand, where the main purpose of the contract is to impose the restraint, the invalidity of that restraint can lead to the nullity of the whole contract. In such cases, the issue is not whether one part of the restraint can be severed from another without altering the nature *of the covenant* in restraint of trade; it is, rather, whether the invalidity of the restraint has left *the contract as a whole* without subject-matter. Two cases which raise the latter question may be contrasted. Both were concerned with solus petrol agreements; in each case the garage proprietor had leased his garage to the oil company which had then leased it back by granting an underlease to the garage proprietor, the solus agreement being contained in the underlease.[44] In the *Amoco*[45] case, the underlease was at a nominal rent for a period just one day shorter than the original lease: in these circumstances it was held that the solus agreement "constituted the heart and soul of the underlease."[46] As the solus agreement was invalid, it followed that neither the underlease nor the original lease (which was part of the same arrangement) could remain in force. On the other hand, in the *Alec Lobb*[47] case the original lease was for a period of 51 years; the oil company had paid a premium of £35,000 (the fair market value) for it; the underlease was for only 21 years and yielded a rent of £2,250 per annum. The solus agreement was held valid[48]; but it was said that, even if it had been invalid, the lease and underlease would have remained in force since the transaction as a whole would not, merely because of the invalidity of that one term, have "so changed its character as not

---

[40] *British Reinforced Concrete Engineering Co Ltd v Schelff* [1921] 2 Ch. 563, a vendor and purchaser case in which *Attwood v Lamont* [1920] 3 K.B. 571 was followed on this point.

[41] *e.g.* in *Putsman v Taylor*, above n.39, at 640; *Kuenigl v Donnersmarck* [1955] 1 Q.B. at p.538.

[42] See above, p.206; *Commercial Plastics Ltd v Vincent* [1965] 1 Q.B. 623; *Royal Boskalis Westminster NV v Mountain* [1999] Q.B. 674 at 693.

[43] *cf. Cleveland Petroleum Co v Trinity Garage (Bexleyheath)*, The Times, September 8, 1965.

[44] See above, pp.472–473.

[45] *Amoco Australia Pty v Rocca Bros Motor Engineering Pty Ltd* [1975] A.C. 561.

[46] *ibid.* at 578.

[47] *Alec Lobb (Garages) Ltd v Total Oil (Great Britain) Ltd* [1985] 1 W.L.R. 173; *cf.* the *Amoco* case, above, at 579.

[48] See above, p.471.

to be the sort of contract that the parties intended to enter into at all."[49] The contract would have remained one "for letting a petrol station ... at a rent which was not nominal. It was therefore the sort of contract which the parties intended to enter into".[50]

The principle just stated is not restricted to cases in which the source of illegality is restraint of trade. In *Carney v Herbert*[51] a contract was made for the sale of shares by instalments; the sellers asked for security for the payment of these instalments, and the form of security agreed on and given was illegal. It was held that the contract as a whole was not vitiated, so that the buyer remained liable for the price since the illegal security "did not go to the heart of the transaction".[52] The sellers had only wanted *some* security and the invalidity of the particular security given did not change the essential character of the contract as one for the sale of the shares.

(3) Statutory severance

Acts of Parliament which make specific terms in certain contracts unlawful sometimes contain provisions which give rise to a kind of statutory severance. Under the legislation against discrimination on grounds of sex, race or disability,[53] for example, the court may make orders for "modifying or removing" certain discriminatory provisions in contracts. Similarly the inclusion of certain terms in a contract may be an offence[54]; but a contract for the supply of goods or services is not to be void or unenforceable "by reason only" of the commission of the offence.[55]

4. Collateral Transactions

Collateral transactions may be infected with the illegality of a principal contract if they help a person to perform an illegal contract, or if they would, if valid, make possible the indirect enforcement of an illegal contract. Thus a loan of money is illegal if it is made to enable the borrower to make or to perform an illegal contract,[56] or to make an illegal payment,[57] or to pay a debt contracted under an illegal contract.[58] Similarly, a policy of insurance on an illegal venture is illegal[59]; a bond, bill of exchange or pledge given to secure an illegal debt is illegal[60]; and a bank is not liable on a letter of credit[61] to the

---

[49] [1985] 1 W.L.R. 173 at 192, applying the test stated by Buckley L.J. in *Chemidus Wavin Ltd v Soc. pour la Transformation et l'Exploitation des Resines Industrielles* [1978] 3 C.M.L.R. 514 at 520.

[50] [1985] 1 W.L.R. 173 at 192. An alternative ground for the decision in the *Alec Lobb* case is suggested by the statement there made at 181 that "The tie provisions ... were not *either* the sole consideration for the tie *or* the sole object of the transaction" (italics supplied). While the second alternative here stated is (with respect) plainly correct, the first is hard to follow: it seems to suggest that the tie could in part be consideration for itself.

[51] [1985] A.C. 301; *cf.* below, p.511.

[52] [1985] A.C. 301 at 316.

[53] Sex Discrimination Act 1975, s.77(5) as amended by Sex Discrimination Act 1996 and by Trade Union and Employment Rights Act 1993, s.32 and Sch.6; Race Relations Act 1976 s.72(5), as amended by Trade Union and Employment Rights Act 1993, s.39(2) and Sch.6; *cf.* Disability Discrimination Act 1995, s.26(3).

[54] See above, p.284.

[55] Fair Trading Act 1973, s.26.

[56] *De Begnis v Armistead* (1833) 10 Bing. 107; *M'Kinnell v Robinson* (1838) 3 M. & W. 434.

[57] *Cannan v Bryce* (1819) 3 B. & Ald. 179, as explained in *Spector v Ageda* [1973] Ch. 30.

[58] *Spector v Ageda*, above.

[59] *Toulmin v Anderson* (1808) 1 Taunt. 227.

[60] *Fisher v Bridges* (1854) 3 E. & B. 642 (bond); *Clugas v Penaluna* (1791) 4 T.R. 466 (bill of exchange; as to the rights of a holder in due course, see below, p.692); *Taylor v Chester* (1869) L.R. 4 Q.B. 309 (pledge). Contrast *Sharif v Azad* [1967] 1 Q.B. 605 as explained in *Mansouri v Singh* [1986] 1 W.L.R. 1393.

[61] See above, p.152.

extent that[62] the underlying contract of sale is prohibited by statute.[63] But if it is the collateral transaction which is illegal, it does not follow that this illegality infects the otherwise lawful principal contract. Thus where an illegal security was in good faith taken to secure the performance of a legal agreement that agreement was not thereby invalidated.[64] Nor is a contract illegal merely because one of the parties to it is also a party to an illegal contract which is remotely connected with the first. Thus a policy of marine insurance on a voyage is not illegal merely because the master has incurred statutory penalties through failing to make the service contracts with his crew in proper form[65]; a policy of insurance on goods is not illegal merely because, in the course of acquiring the goods, the insured had committed a violation of a foreign revenue law[66]; nor is a promise by one solicitor to pay another's charges in respect of a particular transaction illegal merely because the latter solicitor's client intended (without that solicitor's knowledge) to use the transaction in question as a vehicle of fraud.[67] In such cases, the first contract is illegal only if its object was to assist one of the parties in achieving the unlawful purpose under the second contract.[68]

An innocent party to an illegal contract can sometimes recover damages for breach of a "collateral warranty" that the contract was lawful.[69] Such a collateral warranty is not really a separate collateral transaction, but a device invented by law for the protection of an innocent party to an illegal contract.

4. Criticism

The law relating to the effects of illegality on contracts is open to a number of criticisms. The most important of these relate to the question of the enforceability of such contracts by, and to other remedies available to, an innocent party,[70] to the rules governing the right to restitution of benefits conferred under such contracts. In particular, the rules allowing a party to claim restitution of money or property if he can do so without reliance on the contract or its illegality can lead to results which, though explicable on technical grounds, appear to do little to further the policies underlying the legal prohibitions which are the course of the illegality of the contract.[71] The Law Commission has tentatively recommended that, at least in some cases of illegal contracts, the present rules should be replaced by a "structured discretion"[72] to allow enforcement or

---

[62] See above, p.506.

[63] *The American Accord* [1983] 1 A.C. 168 (where the sale was not illegal but only unenforceable under the Bretton Woods Agreement Act 1945); *Group Josi Re v Walbrook Insurance Co Ltd* [1996] 1 Lloyd's Rep. 345 at 363–364. A cheque given in pursuance of such a transaction is likewise unenforceable between the parties to the transaction: *Mansouri v Singh* [1986] 1 W.L.R. 1393.

[64] *South Western Mineral Water Co Ltd v Ashmore* [1967] 1 W.L.R. 1110; *cf. Carney v Herbert* [1985] A.C. 301; above, p.510.

[65] *Redmond v Smith* (1844) 7 Man. & G. 457.

[66] *Euro-Diam Ltd v Bathurst* [1990] Q.B. 1; the violation of the foreign law did not benefit the insured but only benefited his supplier; Clarke, [1988] L.M.C. L.Q. 124; Tan, 104 L.Q.R. 523; Tettenborn, [1988] C.L.J. 338.

[67] *Rooks Rider v Steel* [1994] 1 W.L.R. 818.

[68] See *Re Trepca Mines Ltd* [1963] Ch. 199; A.L.G. 79 L.Q.R. 49; *cf.* [1974] 6 C.L. 266; see now above, p.430.

[69] See above, p.489.

[70] See above, pp.484–490.

[71] See above, pp.497, 500–501.

[72] *Illegal Transactions: The Effect of Illegality on Contracts and Trusts*, Law Commission Consultation Paper No.154, §7.3.

(as the case may be) restitution.[73] These proposals await further consideration. In their present form, they are open to the objections that they go further than necessary, in the sense that the defects in the present law are reasonably specific[74] and scarcely justify and across-the-board abolition of the present rules; that their scope calls for elaboration[75]; and that the guidelines[76] which are meant to provide "structure" to the proposed discretion are so vague as do little to dispel the uncertainty that would necessarily result from the introduction of the discretion. It is to be hoped that further work on the proposals will help to meet at least some of these objections. The difficulty of the task is in no small part due to the fact that the law on this topic has to resolve a conflict of policies: the need to do justice between the parties has to be balanced against the wider considerations of public interest which underlie the law's refusal to give effect to illegal contracts.

---

[73] The "enforcement" proposals are not, but the restitution proposals are, to apply to contracts which are illegal only on grounds of public policy: §§7.16, 7.17. The scope of this category is problematical: above, pp.477–480.

[74] See above, nn.70 and 71.

[75] See above, n.73.

[76] §§7.27 to 7.42; only the second of these guidelines ("the knowledge and intention of the plaintiff": §7.33) is reasonably specific.

CHAPTER TWELVE

STATUTORY INVALIDITY

SECTION 1. IN GENERAL

WHERE a statute prohibits or regulates the making or performance of a contract, breach of the statute may make the contract illegal, void or unenforceable, or leave it perfectly valid. If the breach of the statute amounts to a crime, the effects of its breach depend on the principles discussed in Chapter 11.[1] Apart from these principles, the effect of a breach of a statute depends primarily on its express provisions, which may, for example, make the contract (or the offending term[2]) void,[3] voidable[4] or unenforceable[5]; or state that the breach is not to affect the validity of the contract.[6] The difficult cases are those in which the statute gives no clear lead. They may be divided into three groups.

1. "Void" Contracts held to be Illegal

S.1 of the Life Assurance Act 1774 provides that "no insurance shall be made" by any person on the life of another, or on certain other risks, unless the assured has an interest in the subject-matter of the insurance. Contracts of insurance made in breach of this section are declared to be "void" but have repeatedly been held illegal.[7] Similarly, s.1 of the Marine Insurance Act 1745 provided that "no assurance shall be made" on the terms that no further proof of interest than the policy should be required and declared that policies made in breach of the section were to be "void"; and again such policies were held illegal.[8] But when the section was replaced by s.4(1) of the Marine Insurance Act 1906, which simply made such policies void, it was held that they were no longer illegal.[9] The reason for this distinction seems to be that the older Acts first prohibited the contracts (though without penalty) and then declared them void, while the Act of 1906 contains no prohibition but only a declaration of nullity.

---

[1] See above, pp.430–439.

[2] *e.g.* Sex Discrimination Act 1975, s.77(1) and (2); Race Relations Act 1977, s.72(1) and (2)—"void" but only "unenforceable against" the victim of unlawful discrimination: *Orphanos v Queen Mary College* [1985] A.C. 761; Disability Discrimination Act 1995, s.26(1), and above, pp.487–488.

[3] *e.g.* Matrimonial Causes Act 1973, s.34 (above, p.447); Pension Schemes Act 1993, s.160(1)(a) ("void"); Competition Act 1998, s.2(4) (making agreements prohibited by s.2(1) "void").

[4] Companies Act 1985, s.341(1); *Re Circo Citterio Menswear plc* [2002] EWCA Civ 293, Ch.; [2002] 2 All E.R. 717.

[5] Either in so many words (*e.g.* Consumer Credit Act 1974, s.40(1), Financial Services and Markets Act 2000, ss.26(1), 27(1) (unenforceable against one party only) or by saying that "no action shall be brought," or by use of similar expressions: *e.g.* Statute of Frauds 1677, s.4; above p.181; Pension Schemes Act 1993, s.160(1)(b) ("unenforceable").

[6] *e.g.* Financial Services and Markets Act 2000, s.20(2)(b).

[7] *Harse v Pearl Life Assurance Co* [1904] 1 K.B. 558; *Hughes v Liverpool Victoria Legal Friendly Society* [1916] 2 K.B. 482; *Re London County Commercial Reinsurance Office* [1922] 2 Ch. 67. *cf. Fuji Finance Inc. v Aetna Life Insurance Co Ltd* [1997] Ch. 173.

[8] *Lowry v Bourdieu* (1780) 2 Dougl. 468; *Allkins v Jupe* (1877) 2 C.P.D. 375; *Gedge v Royal Exchange Assurance* [1900] 2 Q.B. 214; *contra, Tasker v Scott* (1815) 6 Taunt. 234.

[9] *Re London County Commercial Reinsurance Office* [1922] 2 Ch. 67.

2. Consequences of Breach not Specified

A statute may prohibit the making of a contract without imposing a criminal penalty or specifying all the civil consequences of breach. Contracts which violated such a prohibition were held illegal[10]: if such a consequences was, in the court's view, necessary to give effect to the purpose of the prohibition.[11-13]

3. Formalities Required by Statute

A statute may require some formalities to be observed in making a contract, or require some specific terms to be inserted into the contract, and again fail to specify the consequences of failure to comply with the requirement.[14] The question then is whether the statutory requirement is to be construed as being "directory only or obligatory".[15] Failure to comply with the statute makes the contract void if the requirement is obligatory, but not if it is only directory. In the case in which the distinction was drawn, statutory requirements as to the execution of a mortgage of a ship were held to be obligatory. Failure to comply with them accordingly invalidated the transaction though this effect of the failure was not specified in the legislation.[16] It seems that in applying the distinction the court will ask whether it is necessary, to promote the object of the statute, to hold that failure to comply with its requirements should invalidate transactions.[17]

SECTION 2. GAMING AND WAGERING CONTRACTS

1. Definitions

(1) Wagering contracts

In *Carlill v Carbolic Smoke Ball Co*[18] Hawkins J. said: "A wagering contract is one by which two persons, professing to hold opposite views touching the issue of a future uncertain event, mutually agree that, dependent upon the determination of that event, one shall win from the other, and that other shall pay or hand over to him, a sum of money or other stake; neither of the contracting parties having any other interest in that contract than the sum or stake he will so win or lose, there being no other real consideration for the making of such contract by either of the parties." The following points arising out of this definition call for comment.

(a) FUTURE UNCERTAIN EVENT. A wager is generally made on a future event but can equally well be made on a past event which is not uncertain at all, *e.g.* which horse won the Derby last year[19]; or on some other question of fact, *e.g.* whether the earth is flat.[20]

---

[10] *Sykes v Beadon* (1897) 11 Ch.D. 170; disapproved in *Smith v Anderson* (1880) 15 Ch.D. 247, but not on this point: *Shaw v Benson* (1883) 11 Q.B.D. 563; *cf. Greenberg v Cooperstein* [1926] Ch. 657. The prohibition with which these cases were concerned is repealed by the Regulatory Reform (Removal of 20 Member Limit in Partnerships, etc.) Order 2002, SI 2002/3203.

[11-13] For conflicting views on the purpose of a statutory provision which failed to specify the civil consequences of a prohibition, see *Fuji Finance Ltd v Aetna Life Insurance Co Ltd* [1997] Ch. 173; *cf.* above, p.488.

[14] See *ante*, pp.179–180 for cases in which the statute does specify the effects of non-compliance.

[15] *Liverpool Borough Bank v Turner* (1860) 2 D.F. & J. 502 at 508.

[16] *Liverpool Borough Bank v Turner* (1860) 2 D.F. & J. 502 (actual decision reversed by Merchant Shipping Act 1894, s.57).

[17] *cf. St. John Shipping Corp. v Joseph Rank Ltd* [1957] 1 Q.B. 267; above, p.429.

[18] [1892] 2 Q.B. 484 at 490; affirmed [1893] 1 Q.B. 256.

[19] *cf. Pugh v Jenkins* (1841) 1 Q.B. 631; *Rourke v Short* (1856) 5 E. & B. 904 (below, p.517).

[20] *Hampden v Walsh* (1876) 1 Q.B.D. 189.

The event need only be "uncertain" in the sense that the parties profess to hold opposite views on it. It has been suggested that there cannot be a wager on an event which is wholly within the control of one party.[21] But if A says that he will wear a red tie tomorrow, it is perfectly possible for B to bet him that he will not do so; and it is hard to see why the resulting contract should not be described as a wager.

(b) ONE TO LOSE, OTHER TO WIN. A contract is not a wager if one party cannot win or if one party cannot lose. Thus in *Carlill v Carbolic Smoke Ball Co*[22] the defendants promised to pay £100 to anyone who, after using a smoke-ball manufactured by them, caught influenza. This was not a wager because the user of the smoke-ball could not lose anything if he failed to catch influenza. Similarly, in *Ellesmere v Wallace*[23] the defendant entered his horse for two races under contracts made with the Jockey Club. If he won the first race, he was entitled to £200 put up by the Club plus the stakes of the other nominators. If he won the second, he was entitled to £200 put up by the Club plus the right to sell his horse by auction for £300. These contracts were not wagers because the Club could lose nothing on the outcome of the races: it paid the £200 to the winner, whoever he was. Similarly, persons who contribute to a totalisator[24] or football pool[25] or who take part in a bingo competition[26] do not wager with the person who runs it,[27] since he merely distributes a predetermined proportion of the total stakes among the winners.[28] And persons who participate in a whist drive at which they can win prizes contributed by third parties do not wager because they cannot lose.[29]

(c) BETWEEN TWO PERSONS. It has been said that there can only be two parties to a wager, or that, if there are more than two, they must be divided into two sides.[30] Thus if A and B bet on the result of an election in which there are two candidates, the contract is a wager. But if A, B and C bet on the result of an election in which there are three candidates, each contributing his stake to a common fund to be paid over to the person whose forecast turns out to be correct, the contract is not a wager. The authorities seem to support this distinction, though it is hard to see why the two cases should be treated differently.

(d) NO OTHER INTEREST. A contract is not a wager if the party to whom money is promised on the occurrence of an event has an "interest" in its non-occurrence. Hence contracts of insurance are not wagers if the insured person has some enforceable right or interest (whether contractual or proprietary) in the subject-matter.[31] So long as the insured has an insurable interest, the contract is not a wager merely because the interest

---

[21] *Ellesmere v Wallace* [1926] 2 Ch. 1 at 29.

[22] [1893] 1 Q.B. 256. See also *Kloeckner & Co AG v Gatoil Overseas Inc* [1990] 1 Lloyd's Rep. 177 at 192 (agent could not lose as he was remunerated by commission payable in any event); contrast *Richards v Starck* [1911] 1 K.B. 296 (risk of losing interest on money sufficient to make transaction a wager).

[23] [1929] 2 Ch. 1.

[24] *cf. Tote Investors Ltd v Smoker* [1968] 1 Q.B. 509 (but Lord Denning M.R. and Lord Pearson said at 515, 520 that, apart from authority, they would have regarded such transactions as wagers).

[25] But where the agreements between the promoters of the pool and the participants contain honour clauses they are not legally binding: above, p.163. Contrast the treatment of football pools in Scots Law: *Ferguson v Littlewoods Pools* 1997 S.L.T. 309.

[26] See *Peck v Lateu* (1973) S.J. 185.

[27] Nor do they wager with each other: below, n.30.

[28] *Att.-Gen. v Luncheon & Sports Club Ltd* [1929] A.C. 400.

[29] *Lockwood v Cooper* [1903] 2 K.B. 428.

[30] *Ellesmere v Wallace* [1929] 2 Ch. at p.50; if this is right, contributors to a totalisator or football pool or participants in a bingo competition do not wager with each other.

[31] *cf. Wilson v Jones* (1867) L.R. 2 Ex. 139 at 150.

is insured for more than its true value.[32] If he has no such interest at all, the contract may be a wager, though this is not necessarily the case since insurer and insured do not necessarily profess to hold opposite views concerning the event insured against.[33] Whether the contract is a wager or not, an insurance without interest is void and may be illegal by statute.[34] Thus a person cannot make a valid contract to insure a third person's property, unless damage to or destruction of it would cause him loss because he has a proprietary interest in it (*e.g.* where it has been pledged to him for a debt) or because he has a right to use it (*e.g.* under licence granted to him by the owner).[35] But a person does not have an insurable interest in property merely because loss of or damage to it would indirectly prejudice his financial position: thus, the assets of a company cannot be insured by its principal or even by its sole shareholder.[36] A person cannot in theory insure a mere expectation of benefit, however strong it may be.[37] But "there are many risks which cannot be regarded as legal or equitable in character, but which are not the less real from a business point of view, and which it is therefore important to cover".[38] Policies covering such risks are binding in honour only, but insurers in practice pay on them in spite of the theoretical lack of interest.

Although a mere expectation of benefit in the commercial sense cannot be insured, it is possible to insure a hope of benefit if it is founded on a legal right. Thus the owner of an orchard can insure "next year's apple crop"[39]; and a person who holds shares in a company can insure against the failure of an enterprise in which the company is engaged.[40]

In cases of life insurance, the interest insured is not strictly proprietary. The assured has an interest in his own life[41] and in the life of any relation who is legally bound to support him[42]; and in the life of his debtor.[43] Spouses can also insure each other's lives.[44]

A contract may be a wager although it concerns the property of one of the parties. Thus it is a wager to bet on one's own horse in a race.[45] The owner has an interest, but it is not the object of the contract to protect that interest. There seems to be no objection in principle to the owner's insuring the prize which the horse may win: this is not essentially different from insuring a future crop.

(e) NO OTHER REAL CONSIDERATION. Attempts are sometimes made to pass off as valid contracts transactions which are in substance wagers. In *Brogden v Marriott*[46] the defendant sold a horse on the terms that if it trotted at 18 miles per hour within a month

---

[32] *The Maira (No.2)* [1984] 1 Lloyd's Rep. 660 at 662, reversed [1986] 2 Lloyd's Rep. 12, but not on this point: see *ibid.* at 17.

[33] Hence Marine Insurance Act 1906, s.4(2) provides that, where the insured has no insurable interest, "a contract of marine insurance is *deemed to be* a gaming and wagering contract."

[34] *e.g.* Marine Insurance (Gambling Policies) Act 1909; *cf.* above, p.513.

[35] *The Moonacre* [1992] 2 Lloyd's Rep. 501.

[36] *Macaura v Northern Assurance Co Ltd* [1925] A.C. 619.

[37] *Lucena v Craufurd* (1806) 2 B. & P.N.R. 269.

[38] Arnould, *Marine Insurance*, (16th ed.), p.15; *cf.* *Strass v Spillers & Bakers Ltd* [1911] 2 K.B. 759 at 768–9.

[39] *Thacker v Hardy* (1878) 4 Q.B.D. 685 at 695; *cf. Cook v Field* (1850) 15 Q.B. 460.

[40] *Wilson v Jones* (1867) L.R. 2 Ex. 139. Contrast *Newbury International Ltd v Reliance International Insurance Co* [1994] 1 Lloyd's Rep. 83 at 92–93 (no insurable interest under "prize indemnity" policy when there was no genuine liability to pay the prize).

[41] *Wainwright v Bland* (1835) 1 Moo. & Rob. 481; (1836) 1 M. & W. 32.

[42] *Chitty on Contracts* (28th ed.) §41–005.

[43] *Von Lindenau v Desborough* (1828) 3 C. & P. 353.

[44] *Griffiths v Fleming* [1909] 1 K.B. 805.

[45] *Carlill v Carbolic Smoke Ball Co* [1892] 2 Q.B. 484 at 492.

[46] (1836) 3 Bing.N.C. 88.

the price was to be £200; if not the price was to be 1s. This was a wager: in effect the defendant staked his horse against £200 on the result of a trotting match.[47] Similarly, in *Rourke v Short*[48] the parties to an agreement for the sale of rags began, in the course of fixing the price, to argue about the price of a previous lot of rags, the seller maintaining that it had been 5s. 9d. per cwt. and the buyer that it had been 6s. This dispute was referred to a third party (who was to receive one gallon of brandy for deciding it) and it was agreed that the price of the present lot was to be 6s. per cwt. if the seller was right, and 3s. per cwt. if the buyer was right. This was held to be a wager on the price of the previous lot. There could be a perfectly genuine bargain for the price of goods to be fixed by reference to that paid for a previous lot. But that was not the bargain here, "for the lower the former price was, the higher the present price is to be."[49]

These cases should be contrasted with the Irish case of *Crofton v Colgan*,[50] where the claimant exchanged his horse for the defendant's, who also agreed to pay the claimant half the former horse's winnings in its next two races. This was held to be a valid contract, in which the price was made to depend on the horse's profit-earning capacity.

It is, again, possible to contract to pay a reward to a person for making some discovery, or for proving a particular hypothesis. But in *Hampden v Walsh*[51] the claimant, who believed that the earth was flat, offered a reward of £500 to any person who could satisfactorily prove the curvature of the earth by actual measurement. This was held to be a wager since the claimant's object was not to establish a scientific fact but "to establish his own view in a marked and triumphant manner".[52]

The most important group of contracts which may in substance amount to wagers are contracts for differences.[53] A person may buy shares or commodities on the understanding that they are neither to be transferred nor paid for but that on settlement day one party shall pay to the other the difference between the price on that day and the price on the contract day. Such a contract has been held to be a wager.[54] But it is not a wager if a person who has genuinely bought resells to the original seller, and the parties then settle accounts by agreeing that only the difference resulting from the two transactions shall change hands.[55] Many contracts for differences are now binding by statute, even if they are wagers[56]; but our present concern is with the question whether such a contract is a wager.

In some of the above cases the question whether a contract is a wager or a genuine transaction depended on the intention of the parties. The parties may have different

---

[47] For an undisguised wager on such a match, see *Batson v Newman* (1876) 1 C.P.D. 573.
[48] (1856) 5 E. & B. 904.
[49] *ibid.* p.912.
[50] (1859) 10 Ir.C.L.R. 133.
[51] (1876) 1 Q.B.D. 189.
[52] *ibid.* p.197.
[53] Chaikin and Moher, [1986] L.M.C.L.Q. 390.
[54] *Universal Stock Exchange Ltd v Strachan* [1896] A.C. 166; *Re Gieve* [1899] 1 Q.B. 794; *cf. Re The Futures Index* [1985] F.L.R. 147. If the proceeds of the transaction are "winnings from betting" they are not subject to Capital Gains Tax: Taxation of Chargeable Gains Act 1992, s.51(1). Under Licensed Dealers (Conduct of Business) Rules (SI 1983/585), r.18(2), a licensed dealer (in securities) may not plead the Gaming Act.
[55] *Grizewood v Blane* (1851) 11 C.B. 526; *The Filipinas I* [1973] 1 Lloyd's Rep. 349 at 357; *Wilson, Smithett & Cope Ltd v Teruzzi* [1976] Q.B. 683 at 710; *Kloeckner A.G. v Gatoil Overseas Inc* [1990] 1 Lloyd's Rep. 177; *Morgan Grenfell & Co Ltd v Welwyn-Hatfield DC* [1995] 1 All E.R. 1 (interest rate swaps).
[56] See below, pp.521, 526; *cf.* the *Kloeckner* case, above, at p.193; *Morgan Grenfell* case, above, at 12–14.

intentions: for example, one may intend to make a contract for differences and the other a real sale. Such a contract is not a wager.[57]

(2) Gaming

(a) DEFINITIONS. "Gaming" has been judicially defined to mean the playing of any game for money or money's worth[58]; and for this purpose a "game" includes horse-racing.[59] Some form of contest between the parties is necessary to constitute a "game".[60] A gaming contract[61] is simply a contract to take part in such gaming. It is not necessarily a wager since there may be more than two parties to it. If persons other than the participants in a game bet on its outcome, their contract is not a gaming contract, but it may be a wager on a game.[62]

Many kinds of gaming and wagers on games are regulated by various statutes.[63] The Gaming Act 1968 defines "gaming" as "the playing of any game of chance for winnings in money or money's worth, whether any person playing the game is at risk of losing money or money's worth or not".[64] This definition is narrower than the judicial definition in that it is limited to games *of chance*.[65] The judicial definition still applies in relation to enactments which use the word "gaming" without defining it.[66]

(b) LAWFUL AND UNLAWFUL GAMING. The 1968 Act defines the circumstances in which gaming is *unlawful*. For this purpose it distinguishes between gaming on licensed or registered premises (which may be carried on for profit) and gaming elsewhere (which may not be carried on for profit).[67] The Act provides that "no gaming . . . shall take place" under certain conditions: *i.e.* if the game involves staking against a bank; or if the chances are not equally favourable to all the players; or if the chances lie between the player or players and some other person and are not as favourable to the player or players as they are to that person; or if a charge other than the stake is made in respect of the gaming; or if a levy is made on the stakes or winnings.[68] But these conditions are subject to a number of qualifications and exceptions; and in particular they may be relaxed in the case of gaming on licensed or registered premises so as to enable the gaming to be carried

---

[57] *Thacker v Hardy* (1878) 4 Q.B.D. 685; *Weddle, Beck & Co v Hackett* [1929] 1 K.B. 321; *Morgan Grenfell* case, above, n.55 at 12.

[58] *Ellesmere v Wallace* [1929] 2 Ch. 1 at 55 (but see also *ibid.* p.28); *Ankers v Bartlett* [1936] 1 K.B. 147.

[59] *Applegarth v Colley* (1842) 10 M. & W. 723; presumably other kinds of racing could also fall within the definition.

[60] *One Life Ltd v Roy* [1996] 2 B.C.L.C. 608 ("pyramid scheme" not a "game" but an unlawful lottery).

[61] There seems to be no difference between a gaming contract and a "contract by way of gaming" within s.18 of the Gaming Act 1845; below, p.520.

[62] This depends on whether the elements of the definition discussed at pp.514–518, above, are satisfied: *e.g.* the contract will not be a wager if there are more than two sides or if one party cannot lose.

[63] Particularly by the Betting, Gaming and Lotteries Acts 1963–1971, the Gaming Act 1968 (as amended by Gaming (Amendment) Act 1986, Gaming (Amendment) Act 1987 and Gaming Act 1990), the Lotteries and Amusements Act 1976 and the National Lottery, etc., Act 1993.

[64] s.52(1); the object of the concluding words ("whether . . . not.") was to reverse the decision in *McCollom v Wrightson* [1968] A.C. 522.

[65] Defined by s.52(1) to include "a game of chance and skill combined and a pretended game of chance or of chance and skill combined." The possibility that the element of chance may be eliminated by "superlative skill" is to be disregarded: s.52(6). An "athletic game or sport" is not a game of chance: s.52(1).

[66] *e.g.* Gaming Act 1845, s.18 (below, p.520); *cf.* Gaming Act 1710 (below, p.527).

[67] See s.1 and Pts 1 and 2 respectively. For the distinction between licensed and registered premises, see s.11 and Schs 3 and 4. Roughly speaking, licensed premises are casinos established principally for commercial gambling while registered premises are clubs established for other purposes which also wish to make a sessional charge for gambling but not to profit from it in other ways.

[68] See ss.2(1), 3(1), 4, 13(1), 14(1) and 15(1); and Regulations made under ss.13–15.

on at a profit.[69] Gaming in streets or public places is also prohibited.[70] The definition of *unlawful* gaming in the Act is exhaustive; the previous common law and statutory definitions of unlawful gaming no longer apply.[71]

The 1968 Act does not, except in one section,[72] affect the law as to gaming and wagering *contracts*; but it has indirect repercussions on the law of contract in that the effect of a gaming contract or of a wager on a game sometimes depends on the legality of the gaming.

2. Effects of Gaming and Wagering Contracts

(1) Enforcement

(a) AT COMMON LAW wagers were valid and could thus be enforced by the winner.[73] This rule was not much liked by the courts, who refused to enforce wagers on many grounds. Some wagers were illegal: these included wagers on unlawful games[74]; wagers that one of the parties would commit a legal wrong or do an immoral act; wagers which affected the interests and feelings of a third person so as to make a breach of the peace likely; and wagers which were "against sound policy".[75] Thus the following wagers were held void: a wager that peace between England and France would be concluded by September 1797[76]; a wager on the life of Napoleon in time of peace[77]; a wager tending to cause public disorder[78]; a wager with voters in a constituency as to the outcome of an election there—an obvious cloak for bribery[79]; and a wager on the sex of a living person suspected to be masquerading as a man.[80] The courts also sometimes simply refused to enforce a wager on the ground that it was an "idle wager" and that it was a waste of the court's time to entertain an action on it.[81] Thus the courts refused to enforce a wager "on the number of ways of nicking 7 on the dice"[82]; a wager, made between persons who had no pecuniary interest in the matter, that the next child of an unmarried woman would be a boy,[83] and a wager on an abstract question of law in which the parties had only an academic interest.[84]

---

[69] See ss.13(2), 14(2) and 15(2). See also s.6 for special exceptions with regard to certain games played in public houses.

[70] s.5.

[71] This is not expressly provided by any section of the 1968 Act but is the effect of s.32(1) of the Betting, Gaming and Lotteries Act 1963. The repeal of this subsection by s.53(1) of the 1968 Act does not revive the previous statutory and common law rules as to what constituted unlawful gaming: see Interpretation Act 1978, ss.15, 16.

[72] s.16 (as amended by Gaming (Amendment) Act 1986) below, pp.529–530, 534–535.

[73] *Micklefield v Hipgin* (1760) 1 Anst. 33; *Good v Elliott* (1790) 3 T.R. 693; *Hussey v Crickitt* (1811) 3 Camp. 168.

[74] See now above, pp.518–519. At common law, cock-fighting, card games other than those of mere skill and (probably) all games of chance were unlawful: *Jenks v Turpin* (1884) 13 Q.B.D. 505 at 524.

[75] *Good v Elliott* (1790) 3 T.R. 693 at 695.

[76] *Lacaussade v White* (1798) 2 Esp. 629 (as to recovery of money under illegal contract, overruled in *Vandyck v Hewitt* (1800) 1 East 96).

[77] *Gilbert v Sykes* (1812) 16 East 150: because this might lead to his assassination (which would be "against sound policy" in time of peace) or to his preservation (which would be "against sound policy" in time of war).

[78] *Eltham v Kingsman* (1818) 1 B. & Ald. 683.

[79] *Allen v Hearn* (1785) 1 T.R. 56.

[80] *Da Costa v Jones* (1778) 2 Cowp. 729.

[81] *Robinson v Mearns* (1825) 6 D. & R.K.B. 26 at 27.

[82] *Brown v Leeson* (1792) 2 H.Bl. 43.

[83] *Ditchburn v Goldsmith* (1815) 4 Camp. 152.

[84] *Henkin v Gerss* (1810) 2 Camp. 408.

(b) UNDER GAMING ACT 1845. S.18 of this Act provides that "All contracts or agreements . . . by way of gaming or wagering shall be null and void; and . . . no suit shall be brought or maintained in any court of law and equity for recovering any sum of money or valuable thing alleged to be won upon any wager. . . . "[85]

(i) *Effects of s.18.* The section clearly prevents the winner from enforcing the wager by action.[86] It used to be thought that this was the sole effect of the section, and that the loser could be sued if he made a fresh promise, supported by fresh consideration, to pay the amount of the lost bet. In *Hyams v Stuart King*[87] the loser of bets on horse-races made a fresh promise to pay in consideration of the winner's promise not to post him as a defaulter. The Court of Appeal held that the winner could enforce this promise. But this case was overruled by the House of Lords in *Hill v William Hill (Park Lane) Ltd.*[88] It was held, on similar facts, that the winner could not enforce the loser's fresh promise because the second limb of s.18 prevented the recovery of money alleged to have been won on a wager, whether or not the action was brought on the wagering contract. The fresh promise to pay, though not void by the first limb of the section, was unenforceable by its second limb.

(ii) *Gaming with chips.* For the purpose of s.18, it makes no difference that the gaming is carried on, not with cash, but with gaming chips supplied by a gambling club to its members; and this is true even though the chips are supplied on terms which entitle the member to use them either for gaming or to buy refreshments in the club. Whether or not there is a separate contract for the supply of the chips,[89] their use for the purpose of gaming is "simply a convenient mechanism for facilitating gambling with money"[90]; and the fact that chips are used does not affect the invalidity of the gaming contract. No doubt if it could be proved that the chips had been used for some purpose other than gaming (*e.g.* for the purchase of refreshments[91]) a separate contract would arise in respect of that transaction; and that contract would not be affected by the Gaming Acts.

(iii) *Attempts to evade s.18.* The courts have always resisted attempts indirectly to enforce the wagering contract itself, and have, since *Hill's* case, resisted attempts to evade the effect of that decision. Thus the winner cannot recover by suing on an account stated[92] or by getting a third party to promise to pay, in return for the winner's promise not to post the loser as a defaulter.[93] The use of such devices came to an abrupt stop after it was held that a solicitor who indorsed a writ (now called a claim form) based in

---

[85] See further below, pp.522, 526, 527. The EC Directive on Electronic Commerce (2000/31) provides in Art.1(5)(d) that it is not to apply to "gambling activities which involve wagering a stake with monetary value in games of chance, including lotteries and betting transactions"; and the Electronic Commerce (EC Directive) Regulations 2002 (SI 2002/2013), which implement most of the Directive, do not apply to "betting, gaming or lotteries which involve wagering a stake of monetary value" (reg.3(1)(d)(iii)).

[86] The court can take this point of its own motion, although the loser does not plead the section: *Luckett v Wood* (1908) 24 T.L.R. 617; *Société des Hôtels Réunis (SA) v Hawker* (1913) 29 T.L.R. 578. *Semble*, the loser could also obtain a declaration of invalidity.

[87] [1908] 2 K.B. 696.

[88] [1949] A.C. 530.

[89] In *Lipkin Gorman v Karpnale Ltd* [1991] 2 A.C. 548 at 562 Lord Templeman said that "there was only one contract and that was a gaming contract;" but Lord Goff at 576–577 appears to treat the transaction as consisting of two contracts.

[90] *Lipkin Gorman v Karpnale Ltd* [1991] 2 A.C. 548 at 575. The issue in that case was not whether the contract could be enforced but the point arose indirectly for the purpose of the question discussed at pp.536–538, below.

[91] In *Lipkin Gorman v Karpnale Ltd* [1991] 2 A.C. 548 there was no such evidence: see p.569.

[92] *Law v Dearnley* [1950] 1 K.B. 400.

[93] *Coral v Kleyman* [1951] 1 All E.R. 518.

substance on a wager as a claim on an account stated was guilty of contempt of court, and liable to be imprisoned for having tried to deceive the court.[94]

(iv) *Possible qualifications.* There are three types of cases which may not fall within s.18.

First, the loser may promise the winner to *sell him something at an undervalue* in return for the winner's promise not to post him as a defaulter. It would be a question of fact whether an action brought to enforce the loser's promise would be one to recover a valuable thing alleged to be won on a wager; and the court "will not be deceived by any specious attempt to conceal the real nature of the promise".[95] If A, having defaulted on a bet of £300 to B and been threatened with exposure, agrees to sell B a car worth £1,000 for £700, and the contract shows a deduction of the £300 lost on the bet, it is clear that B could not enforce the contract. But it does not follow that "there can never be a case where a promise by a defaulting backer given in consideration of a promise by the winner of the bet not to report the defaulter may be enforced".[96]

Secondly, the loser may *bargain for time to pay*, without asking to be released from the debt of honour incurred under the bet. Thus A, having lost a bet of £1,000 to B, may promise to pay B £50 in return for B's promise not to report A as a defaulter for one month. An action to recover this £50 might not be an action "for recovering any sum of money . . . alleged to be won upon any wager."

Thirdly, the first limb of s.18 makes void *all* contracts by way of gaming and wagering but the second limb only precludes the recovery of *money or a valuable thing*. If the loser, in consideration of the winner's promise not to post him as a defaulter, promises to render some *service* to the winner, this promise may not be within section 18.[97]

In the cases in which a new promise can still be enforced, this can only be done subject to the restrictions which, before *Hill's* case, had been placed on the rule in *Hyams v Stuart King*. The winner must *promise* not to post the loser as a defaulter; it is not enough for him simply to refrain from posting,[98] nor for him to promise not to *sue* the loser, for a promise not to sue on a claim known to be invalid is no consideration.[99] It is also clear that the new promise would not be enforced if it had been obtained by threats amounting to blackmail.[1]

(v) *Excepted transactions.* Certain dealings in investments by way of business are excepted from invalidity under s.18 of the Gaming Act 1845 even though they might amount to wagering contracts, *e.g.* because they were contracts for differences[2] or bets on stock market indices.[3]

---

[94] *R. v Weisz* [1951] 2 K.B. 611. See also *L.S.Gaz.* January 1952, p.17.

[95] *Hill's Case* [1949] A.C. 530 at 559; *cf.* 549 at 565; *Re Browne* [1960] 1 W.L.R. 692.

[96] [1949] A.C. at 559; *cf. Re Browne* [1904] 2 K.B. 133; discussed in *Hill's* case at 564–566, 573–574.

[97] The third limb of s.18 (below, p.526) makes it clear that services cannot be a "valuable thing" within s.18; for the "thing" must be of a kind that can be "deposited".

[98] *Bob Guiness Ltd v Salomonsen* [1948] 2 K.B. 42; the case may be reconciled with the rule that actual forbearance to *sue* (without a promise) is good consideration along the lines suggested at pp.90–91, above.

[99] *Poteliakhoff v Teakle* [1938] 2 K.B. 816. But there might be consideration if the validity of the claim was in doubt, *e.g.* because it was not clear whether the original transaction was a wager.

[1] As defined by Theft Act 1968, s.21.

[2] Financial Services and Markets Act 2000, s.412 and Sch.2, Pt II, para.19(a), referring to "a contract for differences"; for such contracts, see above, p.517. "Specified" activities and investments for the purpose of s.412 are defined by Financial Services and Markets Act 2000 (Gaming Contracts) Order 2001 (SI 2001/2510).

[3] *City Index Ltd v Leslie* [1992] Q.B. 98. For bets on stock market indices, see Financial Services and Markets Act 2000, s.412 and Sch.2, Pt II, para.19(b)(ii).

(c) DISTANCE CONTRACTS. The Consumer Protection (Distance Selling) Regulations 2000[4] provide that, in the case of a "distance contract" for the supply of goods or services by a commercial supplier to a consumer, the consumer is to have the "right to cancel"[5]; but that in a number of exceptional cases there is to be no such right. One such exception is stated in reg.13(f) to apply in the case of "contracts . . . for gaming, betting or lottery services". The assumption underlying this exception is that the contract is *valid* apart from the Regulations: for example, it may be one for betting services without being a wager because one or more of the elements of the definition of a wager discussed earlier in this Chapter[6] are not satisfied. Where the contract is *invalid* because it is a wager, the consumer does not need to cancel it to escape liability; nor do the restitutionary consequences of cancellation specified in the Regulations[7] appear to displace the rule that losses paid under a wagering contract cannot be recovered back by the loser.[8]

The "right to cancel" may also be excluded by reg.13(f) where the contract, though it is a wager, is valid because it is an excepted transaction of the kind described above[9] and therefore excepted from invalidity under s.18 of the Gaming Act 1845. In such cases, the "right to cancel" a "distance contract" may in addition be excluded by reg.13(b) which provides that there is no such right in the case of "contracts . . . for the supply of goods or services the price of which is dependent on fluctuations in the financial market which cannot be controlled by the supplier". This exception to the "right to cancel" could, for example, apply to contracts for differences or to bets on stock market indices where such contracts are valid in spite of being wagers.[10]

(2) Recovering back money paid

(a) AT COMMON LAW a loser could not recover back money paid under a lost bet.[11] Money paid under a valid or merely unenforceable contract clearly cannot be recovered back, and money paid under an illegal contract is, in general, irrecoverable,[12] although there are exceptions to this rule. But there is no reported case in which the loser was able to rely on any of these exceptions to recover back his losses from the winner.

(b) UNDER THE GAMING ACT 1845. *Prima facie* money paid under a void contract can be recovered back.[13] Thus in *Re London County Commercial Reinsurance Office*[14] it was held that premiums paid under marine policies which were, or were deemed to be, wagers, and void under s.4 of the Marine Insurance Act 1906, could be recovered back. But it is well settled that losses paid under a simple wager are irrecoverable.[15] One possible reason for this rule is that, under the second limb of s.18, a person cannot bring an action to recover "any sum of money . . . alleged to be won upon any wager." But it has been said that the second limb only prevents the winner from recovering, and does not apply to an action by the loser.[16] If this is so, then the reason for the present rule is

---

[4] SI 2000/2334; above, p.29.
[5] reg.10.
[6] See above, pp.514–518.
[7] reg.14.
[8] See below, under heading (3).
[9] At n.2.
[10] See above, p.521 at nn.2 and 3.
[11] *Howson v Hancock* (1800) 8 T.R. 575; *Vandyck v Hewitt* (1800) 1 East 96.
[12] See above, p.491.
[13] See below, p.1057.
[14] [1922] 2 Ch. 67.
[15] *Lipkin Gorman v Karpnale Ltd* [1991] 2 A.C. 548 at 561.
[16] *Varney v Hickman* (1847) 5 C.B. 271 at 280.

that the loser, by paying, "waives a benefit which the statute has given him and confers a good title to the money on the person to whom he pays it"[17]; or that the payment is in law regarded as a gift by the loser to the winner.[18] It makes no difference, for the purpose of this rule, that the loser's "payment" is made, not in cash, but with gaming chips supplied by a club to its members as a "mechanism for facilitating gambling with money".[19] But if the winner cheats, the loser can probably recover back his losses on the ground of fraud.[20]

(c) OVERPAYMENT. It has been held that an overpayment by a bookmaker to his client in respect of a wager cannot be recovered back.[21] But if the client knows when he receives the payment that it is excessive and decides to keep it, he is guilty of theft[22]; and the court by or before which he is convicted can presumably make a compensation order against him.[23]

(3) Recovering back money or property deposited

One party to a wager may deposit a sum of money or other valuable thing with the other before the determination of the wager, as security for the performance of his undertaking.[24]

(a) ILLEGAL WAGERS. Such a deposit is irrecoverable if it was made under an illegal wager,[25] because of the general rule that money paid under an illegal contract cannot be recovered back.[26] But it may be recoverable under one of the exceptions to that rule, e.g., if the depositor repudiates the wager in time.[27] Whether it is actually recoverable then depends on the rules applicable to lawful wagers, discussed below.

(b) LAWFUL WAGERS. Where the wager is lawful,[28] a deposit can, in general, be recovered back by the winner. Thus in *Re Cronmire*[29] Waud deposited £60 with Cronmire by way of "cover" for gambling transactions between them on the Stock Exchange, which resulted to Waud's advantage. It was held that he could recover back his £60.

The question whether a deposit can be recovered back by the loser raises more complicated issues, which may be illustrated by reference to the two *Strachan* cases, both of which arose out of the same transactions. Strachan engaged in gambling transactions on the Stock Exchange with a company. He deposited securities and £3,000 in cash by way of "cover," and lost heavily. The House of Lords held that he was entitled to recover back his *securities* since they were deposited to secure payment of a void debt.[30] But the

---

[17] *Bridger v Savage* (1884) 15 Q.B.D. 363 at 367; *cf. Richards v Stark* [1911] 1 K.B. 296 (losses paid in advance irrecoverable).
[18] *Lipkin Gorman v Karpnale Ltd* [1991] 2 A.C. 548 at 562, 577.
[19] *ibid.* p.575.
[20] This was the common law position: *Dufour v Ackland* (1830) 9 L.J.(O.S.) K.B. 3. For a review of conflicting American decisions, see *Berman v Riverside Casino Corp.*, 323 F. 2d 977 (1963), where it was alleged that loaded dice had been used in a Nevada casino.
[21] *Morgan v Ashcroft* [1938] 1 K.B. 49.
[22] *R. v Gilks* [1972] 1 W.L.R. 1341.
[23] Powers of Criminal Courts (Sentencing) Act 2000, s.130; above, p.369.
[24] For the position where the deposit is made with a third person as stakeholder, see below, p.526.
[25] See above, p.518.
[26] See above, p.491.
[27] See above, p.494; *Tappenden v Randall* (1801) 2 B. & P. 467; *Aubert v Walsh* (1810) 3 Taunt. 277.
[28] A wager is lawful unless it falls into one of the categories of illegal wagers described on p.518, above.
[29] [1898] 2 Q.B. 383.
[30] *Universal Stock Exchange Ltd v Strachan* [1896] A.C. 166.

Court of Appeal held, on another appeal,[31] that the £3,000 deposited *in cash* was irrecoverable as it had actually been appropriated by the company in discharge of Strachan's "indebtedness". It seems that Strachan could not have recovered the securities if the contract had authorised the company to realise them and if the company had done so and appropriated the proceeds in discharge of Strachan's "indebtedness". It seems also that Strachan could have recovered back the £3,000, if he had demanded it back before appropriation of it in discharge of any "indebtedness" under the gambling transactions, *e.g.* if he had made the demand before those transactions had been determined. Thus in *Re the Futures Index*,[32] a bookmaker took sums of money from a client on account of possible future losses. On the bookmaker's going into liquidation, it was held that the sums could be recovered back by the client in so far as they had not yet been appropriated to any wager.

(4) Principal and agent

(a) FAILURE TO OBEY INSTRUCTIONS. An agent who undertakes to make a bet on behalf of his principal is not liable for failing to do so.[33] In *Cohen v Kittell* the reason for this rule was said to be that the principal suffered "no real loss"[34] since he could not have enforced the bet even if it had been made. But the rule applies even though it is clearly proved that the bet would have been paid, had it been made and won. It seems that the better reason for the rule is that "A contract declared by the law to be null and void cannot be either directly or indirectly the basis of a legal claim".[35]

An agent is similarly not liable if he makes a bet in a way forbidden by his instructions. In *A R Dennis & Co Ltd v Campbell*[36] the manager of a licensed betting shop, contrary to his instructions, allowed a customer to place bets on credit to the extent of £1,000. On the customer's failure to pay the bets after he had lost them, it was held that the manager was not liable to his employers for the £1,000. Even if the employers could prove that they had lost this amount,[37] the action was barred by the second limb of s.18 of the Gaming Act 1845.

(b) AGENT'S INDEMNITY. The agent may make the bet, lose it, and pay the winner. It was held in *Read v Anderson*[38] that an agent who paid the winner could recover the sum so paid from his principal on the ground that the latter had impliedly contracted to indemnify his agent[39] against liabilities, whether legally enforceable or not, which arose in the ordinary course of business from the execution of his authority.

This decision provided an easy means of evading the Gaming Act 1845: wagers could be enforced against a loser by simply interposing an agent. It was therefore reversed by s.1 of the Gaming Act 1892, which provides: "Any promise, express or implied, to pay

---

[31] *Strachan v Universal Stock Exchange Ltd (No.2)* [1895] 2 Q.B. 697.

[32] [1985] F.L.R. 147.

[33] *Cohen v Kittell* (1889) 22 Q.B. 680.

[34] *ibid.* at 684.

[35] *Cheshire & Co v Vaughan Bros & Co* [1920] 3 K.B. 240 at 254. Where gaming or wagering is not involved an agent may well be liable for failing to make an invalid contract if it is unlikely that the third party would have repudiated: see *Fraser v B N Furman (Productions) Ltd* [1967] 1 W.L.R. 898; *Everett v Hogg, Robinson & Gardner Mountain Insurance* [1973] 2 Lloyd's Rep. 216; *Dunbar v A & B Painters Ltd* [1986] 2 Lloyd's Rep. 38. But the degree of likelihood of such repudiation may raise an issue of remoteness under the "reasonable contemplation" test discussed at pp. 965–968 below: *Bates v Barrow Ltd* [1995] 1 Lloyd's Rep. 680 at 691.

[36] [1978] Q.B. 365.

[37] If the credit had not been allowed, it is more probable that the customer would not have made the bet than that he would have made it for cash.

[38] (1884) 13 Q.B.D. 779.

[39] See below, p.744.

any person any sum of money paid by him under or in respect of any contract or agreement rendered null and void by the Gaming Act 1845, or to pay any sum of money by way of commission, fee, reward, or otherwise in respect of any such contract, or of any services in relation thereto or in connection therewith, shall be null and void, and no action shall be brought or maintained to recover any such sum of money."

In *Levy v Warburton*[40] an agent tried to evade this provision by suing his principal before paying the winner. But the court rejected his claim, holding that "paid" included "to be paid." In *Law v Dearnley*[41] it was held that an agent cannot evade the Act by suing on an account stated. Tucker L.J. also said that the principle in *Hill v William Hill (Park Lane) Ltd*[42] applied to cases falling within the 1892 Act. That Act, however, only deals with promises *to pay money*.[43] Thus it seems that if the principal promised to deliver some *valuable thing* to the agent in return for the latter's promise not to post him as a defaulter, the agent could[44] enforce the principal's promise.

(c) AGENT'S LIABILITY TO ACCOUNT. An agent who made a bet for his principal which the principal won is liable at common law to account to the principal if he has received the money won from the loser. This position is not altered by the 1892 Act: the agent is not sued on an implied promise to pay the principal "any sum of money *paid* by him" (the agent) but on an implied promise to pay over a sum of money *received* by him.[45] It was further held in *Bridger v Savage*[46] that the agent's liability to pay over winnings received by him was not affected by s.18 of the Gaming Act 1845. One reason given was that the section struck only at the wagering contract itself, and not at other transactions. But this reasoning is untenable after *Hill v William Hill (Park Lane) Ltd*[47] and it could plausibly be argued that the principal was suing to recover money "alleged to have been won upon any wager". On the other hand, it would certainly not defeat the policy of the Gaming Acts to force the agent to account to his principal for money actually received. The policy of the Acts is not to prevent the winner from getting his winnings but to prevent the loser from being *forced* to pay his losses. *Bridger v Savage* can be justified by saying that, once the loser has paid the bets, "any dispute as to their validity [is] gone".[48]

A person may be called an agent, but in fact bet *with* his "principal" and not *for* him. If so, he is an actual party to the bet and is not accountable under the rule in *Bridger v Savage*.[49]

It seems (although the point has not been decided) that the above principles would apply where several persons agreed to make a bet in the name of one of them and to share any winnings. Thus if the person in whose name the bet was made received any sum won he would have to account to the others, unless he had in fact bet with and not for them.[50]

(d) ADVANCE PAYMENT. An agent who makes a bet for his principal may account to the principal for his winnings before he has himself been paid by the loser. If the loser

---

[40] (1901) 70 L.J.K.B. 708.
[41] [1950] 1 K.B. 400.
[42] [1949] A.C. 530.
[43] Contrast "sum of money or valuable thing" in Gaming Act 1845, s.18.
[44] Subject to the exceptions stated above at p.521.
[45] *De Mattos v Benjamin* (1894) 63 L.J.Q.B. 248.
[46] (1884) 15 Q.B.D. 363.
[47] [1949] A.C. 530; above, p.520.
[48] (1884) 15 Q.B.D. 363 at 365. *Bridger v Savage* was treated as still good law in *The Vasso* [1979] 2 Lloyd's Rep. 412 at 419.
[49] *Higginson v Simpson* (1877) 2 C.P.D. 76; *Potter v Codrington* (1892) 9 T.L.R. 54.
[50] *cf. Higginson v Simpson*, above.

then defaults, the agent cannot recover back the winnings from the principal: the case falls within s.1 of the Act of 1892.[51]

(e) EXCEPTED TRANSACTIONS. The 1892 Act is subject to a statutory exception which applies where an agent by way of business conducts certain dealings in investments which might at common law amount to wagers, *e.g.* because they were contracts for differences or bets on stock market indices.[52]

(5) Stakeholders

A stakeholder is a person with whom the parties to a wager deposit their stakes under a "tripartite contract"[53] to the effect he will deliver the stakes to the winner on the determination of the wager. He is normally regarded as the agent of both parties, each of whom authorises him to hold his own stake, to receive the other party's and to dispose of the aggregate in accordance with the result of the wager.

The third limb of s.18 of the Gaming Act 1845 provides that no suit shall be brought or maintained "for recovering any sum of money or valuable thing . . . which shall have been deposited in the hands of any person to abide the event on which any wager shall have been made". In spite of the apparent generality of this provision, it has been held that it applies only "to the non-recovery by the winner of a sum deposited by the other party to abide the event, and not to the right of the depositor to recover back his deposit if demanded before the money was paid over".[54] Thus a loser can recover back his own stake, so long as he demands it back from the stakeholder before the latter has paid it over to the winner.[55] Similarly, the winner can recover back his own stake, but he cannot recover the entire stakes from the stakeholder.[56] These rules are not affected by s.1 of the Gaming Act 1892; this section refers to money "paid" out-and-out, and not to money *deposited* with a stakeholder.[57]

A stake deposited in pursuance of an illegal wager is, in general, irrecoverable as money paid under an illegal contract; but it can be recovered back by the payor if demanded back before execution of the illegal purpose. If the wager is illegal because it is a wager on an illegal game, the stake can thus be recovered back if its return is demanded before the game has taken place.[58] According to *Hastelow v Jackson*[59] the stake can be recovered back even though the illegal game has taken place so long as the *contract* has not been executed by payment of the stake to the winner. But it is submitted that the decisive question ought to be whether the *illegal purpose* has been carried into effect[60]; and that the stake should be irrecoverable once the illegal game has taken place. If the wager is illegal because of its intrinsic nature, *e.g.* because it is an illegal lottery, it could be said that the illegal purpose was not "executed" until the stake was paid over to the winner so that the loser could, till then, recover it back.[61]

---

[51] *cf. Simpson v Bloss* (1816) 7 Taunt. 246 (same rule at common law where wager illegal).
[52] Financial Services and Markets Act 2000, s.412; and see above, p.521, nn.2 and 3.
[53] *Rockeagle Ltd v Alsop Wilkinson* [1992] Ch. 47 at 50 (where the stakeholder held a deposit under a contract for the sale of land).
[54] *Hampden v Walsh* (1876) 1 Q.B.D. 189 at 196; *cf. Re The Futures Index* [1985] F.L.R. 147.
[55] *Varney v Hickman* (1874) 5 C.B. 271; *Hampden v Walsh*, above; *Diggle v Higgs* (1877) 2 Ex.D. 422; *Trimble v Hill* (1879) 5 App.Cas. 342.
[56] *Savage v Madder* (1867) 36 L.J.Ex. 178; a dictum that the winner could not recover even his own stake was unnecessary for the decision, and is not law: *Hampden v Walsh* (1876) 1 Q.B.D. 189 at 196.
[57] *O'Sullivan v Thomas* [1895] 1 Q.B. 698.
[58] *Martin v Hewson* (1855) 10 Exch. 737.
[59] (1828) 8 B. & C. 221.
[60] See above, pp.494–495.
[61] *cf. Barclay v Pearson* [1893] 2 Ch. 154 (not a wager, but a lottery).

(6) Prizes for lawful games

S.18 of the Gaming Act 1845 concludes: "Provided always that this enactment shall not be deemed to apply to any subscription or contribution or agreement to subscribe or contribute, for or towards any plate, prize or sum of money to be awarded to the winner or winners of any lawful game, sport, pastime or exercise."

In *Diggle v Higgs*[62] two persons agreed to enter into a walking match for £200 a side, to be deposited with a stakeholder and paid to the winner. It was held that this was a wager and not saved by the proviso since this only applied where the prize was due under a contract which was not a wager. This view would leave open the possibility that the proviso would apply where the prize was put up by a third party: the contract would not be a wager since the competitors could win, but not lose, money; nor would it be a gaming contract since no money was staked by the competitors. But since such a contract would in any case be valid it seems that the proviso has no effect at all.[63]

(7) Securities

A security given for the payment of money lost under a gaming or wagering contract, or of a debt incurred in connection with such a contract, has, between the parties to the bet, no greater validity than the principal contract. Thus if the loser gives the winner a cheque in payment, the winner cannot sue the loser on the cheque any more than on the original contract.[64] But the position is more complicated when a security which is negotiable[65] later comes into the hands of a third party. It was formerly common for cheques to be negotiable but they are now usually deprived of this quality by being crossed "a/c payee" or "a/c payee only".[66]

(a) NON-GAMING WAGERS. Where a negotiable security such as a bill of exchange, or promissory note is given in respect of a wager made void by the Gaming Act 1845, the security is also void between the parties as there is no consideration for it. But it can be enforced by a third party who becomes holder of it, if value has at any time been given for it; and, as such a third party will normally be presumed to be a holder in due course, and so to have given value,[67] he can sue on the instrument, unless the defendant proves that value has not been given.[68] It is immaterial that the holder knew that the security was originally given in connection with a wager.[69]

A security may be given in respect of a transaction which is a wager but which is nevertheless valid because it is excepted by statute[70] from invalidity under s.18 of the Gaming Act 1845. In such a case, the fact that the transaction was a wager would have no effect on the validity of the security which could therefore be enforced in the normal way, both between the parties and between one of them and a third party.

(b) GAMING AND WAGERS ON GAMES are governed by special legislation contained in the Gaming Acts of 1710, 1835 and 1968.[71]

(i) *The Acts of 1710 and 1835.* S.1 of the Gaming Act 1710 provided that all securities given wholly or in part for any money or valuable thing won by gaming or by playing at

---

[62] (1877) 2 Ex.D. 422; *cf. Parson v Alexander* (1855) 5 E. & B. 263; *Batson v Newman* (1876) 1 C.P.D. 573.

[63] *cf. Ellesmere v Wallace* [1929] Ch. 148, criticising the accepted interpretation.

[64] *Richardson v Moncrieffe* (1926) 43 T.L.R. 32.

[65] See below, p.691.

[66] Bills of Exchange Act 1882, s.81A, as inserted by Cheques Act 1992, s.1; below, pp.691–692.

[67] Bills of Exchange Act 1882, ss.27(2), 29, 30(2); below; p.692.

[68] *Fitch v Jones* (1855) 5 E. & B. 238.

[69] *Lilley v Rankin* (1886) 56 L.J.Q.B. 248.

[70] Financial Services and Markets Act 2000, s.412; above p.521 nn.2 and 3.

[71] As amended by Gaming (Amendment) Act 1986, below, p.529.

any game or by betting on any game,[72] or for repaying any money[73] lent for such gaming or betting or lent at the time and place of play to any person so gaming or betting, shall be "utterly void, frustrate and of none effect". The object of this enactment was to restrict gaming on credit; but it had the unfortunate effect of prejudicing third parties who in good faith gave value for securities within its scope. S.1 of the Gaming Act 1835 therefore provided that such securities should no longer be void, but that they should be "deemed and taken to have been . . . given . . . for an illegal consideration". Where, as a result of this Act, a bill of exchange is deemed to have been given for an illegal consideration, it still cannot be enforced by a third party who takes it with notice of the circumstances in which it was given, even though he gave value for it.[74] But it can be enforced by a holder in due course,[75] *i.e.* by one who took the bill (provided that it was regular on its face and not overdue) for value, in good faith, and without notice of the illegality[76]; it can also be enforced by a holder who derives his title from a holder in due course.[77] However, once it is admitted or proved that the bill is affected with illegality, a holder who sues on it cannot rely on the usual presumption that he is a holder in due course. He must show that, subsequent to the illegality, value has in good faith been given for the bill, either by him or by a previous holder through whom he derives title.[78] "In good faith" here means "without notice of the illegality".[79] The same rules would apply where the security was given in respect of an illegal wager which is not a gaming wager: in such a case the consideration would be illegal quite apart from the Acts of 1710 and 1835. This would also be true of a security given in respect of a wager on an illegal game.

The Acts of 1710 and 1835 apply (*inter alia*) to securities given for repaying money "lent for gaming." It has been held that securities given for money lent to enable the borrower to pay bets already lost are not within the Acts, as such money is not "lent for gaming."[80] The loan itself may be void under the Gaming Act 1892,[81] but a security given in respect of it is not "deemed and taken to have been given for an illegal consideration." The Acts of 1710 and 1835 would, however, apply to a security given for money lent if the lender knew that the money would be used to pay a lost bet[82] and either promised to advance the money before the bet was made[83] or stipulated that it should be used to pay the lost bet.[84]

---

[72] Including horse-racing: *Applegarth v Colley* (1842) 10 M. & W. 723, and (*semble*) other forms of racing: above, p.518, n.59.

[73] Including gaming chips: below, p.529. The 1710 Act seems to contemplate repayment *by the borrower*; but in *Ladup Ltd v Shaik* [1983] Q.B. 225 it seems to have been assumed that s.1 of that Act also applied to a cheque given by a casino to a loser on cashing in the remainder of his chips.

[74] *Hay v Ayling* (1851) 16 Q.B. 423 at 431; *Woolf v Hamilton* [1898] 2 Q.B. 337. Nor will an action lie on a fresh bill made in substitution if, when the holder acquired it, he had notice of the illegal consideration: *Hay v Ayling*, above; *Chapman v Black* (1819) 2 B. & Ald. 588.

[75] Bills of Exchange Act 1882, s.38(2).

[76] *ibid.* s.29(1) and (2).

[77] *ibid.* s.29(3); this subsection does not apply where the holder who derived title through a holder in due course is himself a party to any illegality.

[78] Bills of Exchange Act 1882, s.30(2).

[79] Bills of Exchange Act 1882, s.90 ("in fact done honestly"); and *cf. Tatam v Haslar* (1889) 23 Q.B.D. 345 at 348 (a case of fraud, not of illegality). It is submitted that a person who takes with notice of the illegality does not act "honestly".

[80] *Ex p. Pyke* (1878) 8 Ch.D. 754; the actual decision would now go the other way under the Gaming Act 1892.

[81] See below, p.531.

[82] *Humphery v Wilson* (1929) 141 L.T. 469.

[83] *Parker v Alcock* (1831) You. 361; contrast the position under the 1892 Act, where mere knowledge on the part of the lender is not enough: below, pp.530–531.

[84] *Hill v Fox* (1859) 4 H. & N. 359.

Although the Acts in terms deal only with securities given for *money* lent, it has been held that they also strike at a common gaming practice. In *Stuart v Stephen*[85] the defendant at a gambling party borrowed £150 worth of chips and lost them. He later[86] paid for the chips by cheque. The court held that the Acts of 1710 and 1835 applied even though no *money* was lent at the time of play. The same analysis of such a transaction applies for the purposes of s.18 of the Gaming Act 1845[87] and of s.16 of the Gaming Act 1968, to be discussed later in this Chapter.[88]

The Acts of 1710 and 1835 cannot be evaded by stating a fictitious consideration in the security. Thus in *William Hill (Park Lane) Ltd v Hofman*[89] a mortgage purported to have been given for money lent, but was really given for money lost at play. The court disregarded the false recital and deemed the mortgage to have been given for an illegal consideration.

There may be a loophole in this legislation. Suppose a person loses bets on horse-races and later promises to pay his losses in consideration of not being posted as a defaulter. This promise cannot be enforced because of s.18 of the Act of 1845.[90] But if the loser now gives a security in discharge of his liability *under the new promise* the security is not tainted with illegality. The reasoning of *Hill v William Hill (Park Lane) Ltd*[91] does not apply since s.18 of the Act of 1845, in providing that a promise to pay a lost bet cannot be enforced, does not refer to the consideration for the promise; while securities are only deemed to have been given for an illegal consideration under the Acts of 1710 and 1835 "where the whole or any part of the consideration shall be for money or other valuable thing won by gaming . . . or repaying any money knowingly lent . . . for such gaming."[92] Where the consideration for the security given by the loser is the winner's promise not to post the loser as a defaulter,[93] the security may thus not be deemed to have been given for an illegal consideration, since it is arguable that the consideration for the security is not "money . . . won by gaming". The security cannot be enforced between the original parties since between them it has no greater enforceability than the promise in respect of which it was given; and this promise could not be enforced by reason of the second limb of s.18 of the Gaming Act 1845. But if the security is negotiable, a third person may be able to enforce it, even though he knew of the circumstances in which it was given, unless the defendant proves that the third person did not give value.

(ii) *S.16 of the Gaming Act 1968*[94] was passed principally to limit credit for gaming on licensed premises[95]; and as part of that policy it restricts the circumstances in which the licensee may accept cheques in exchange for cash or tokens to be used for such gaming. Subs.(2) makes it an offence for him to take post-dated cheques and to take cheques at a discount.[96] Subs.(4) then provides that nothing in the Gaming Acts of 1710, 1835, 1845

---

[85] (1940) 56 T.L.R. 571.

[86] For the question whether there is a "loan" if the cheque is given at the time of the delivery of the chips, see below, p.532, n.22.

[87] *Lipkin Gorman v Karpnale Ltd* [1991] 2 A.C. 548, above, p.520.

[88] *Crockfords Club Ltd v Mehta* [1992] 1 W.L.R. 355, below, p.534.

[89] [1950] 1 All E.R. 1013.

[90] See above, p.520.

[91] [1949] A.C. 530.

[92] 1710 Act, s.1.

[93] The existence of such consideration would make the reasoning of *Lipkin Gorman v Karpnale Ltd* [1992] 2 A.C. 458 inapplicable so far as it related to consideration.

[94] As amended by Gaming (Amendment) Act 1986, below, at nn.1, 2.

[95] See further above, p.518, n.67 and below, p.535.

[96] Subs.(2) is clearly restricted to gaming on licensed premises, "the gaming" in the subsection referring back to gaming on licensed premises referred to in subs.(1).

and 1892 "shall affect the validity of, or any remedy in respect of, any cheque which is accepted in exchange for cash or tokens to be used by a player in gaming" on licensed or registered[97] premises. The effect of this appears to be that a cheque lawfully accepted for cash or tokens to be used for lawful gaming on licensed or registered premises is enforceable between the parties. It is true that subs.(4) is not in terms restricted to cheques lawfully accepted or to lawful gaming. But if the acceptance of the cheque, or the gaming, constituted an offence the cheque would be invalid at common law quite apart from the Acts of 1710, 1835, 1845 and 1892.[98] Such common law invalidity is not cured by subs.(4).[99] And the subsection does not affect the validity of any cheque lawfully accepted except in exchange for cash or tokens *to be* used by a player in gaming: it would not, for example, apply to a cheque given on registered premises to pay for a bet already lost.[1] Nor does the subsection apply to cheques accepted in connection with gaming on unlicensed or unregistered premises.

A player who has given a cheque which is enforceable under s.16(4) of the 1968 Act may later redeem that cheque and give the licensee a substitute cheque: *e.g.* where the player has paid for tokens worth £100 and has £40 worth left at the end of the playing session, he may redeem his original cheque in exchange for these tokens and a new cheque for £60. Provided that certain statutory conditions (designed to ensure that the restrictions on giving credit for gaming are not evaded) are satisfied,[2] s.16(4)[3] then allows the licensee to enforce the substitute cheque.

(8) Loans

We shall first discuss the general rules governing the validity of loans connected with gaming and wagering contracts and then consider certain special provisions with regard to credit for gaming on licensed premises.

(a) IN GENERAL. At common law, a loan made to enable a person to play an illegal game is irrecoverable.[4] The same is presumably true of a loan to enable a person to make any other kind of illegal wager, or to pay an illegal bet already lost. Where the wager is not illegal at common law, it may be a valid transaction because it is excepted by statute from invalidity under s.18 of the Gaming Acts of 1845. This is the position with regard to certain dealings in investments which may at common law be wagers, *e.g.* because they amount to contracts for differences.[5] In such a case, the fact that the transaction was a wager would have no effect on the validity of a loan made in connection with it. More commonly, lawful wagers would be void and unenforceable under s.18 of the 1845 Act; and loans for such lawful (but invalid) wagers give rise to two problems.

(i) *Loans to pay lost bets.* The loser of a bet may ask another person to pay it for him. If the latter then pays the money straight to the winner, he cannot sue the loser for it, since such a payment is made "in respect of" a wagering contract within s.1 of the

---

[97] Subs.(4) refers to "gaming to which this Part of this Act applies" and this includes gaming on registered premises: see s.9. The offences created by subs.(2), however, are restricted to licensed premises: see last note.

[98] See above, pp.431, 510.

[99] *Ladup Ltd v Shaik* [1983] Q.B. 225; *cf.* below, p.534.

[1] Acceptance of a cheque in such circumstances on *licensed* premises would be unlawful under s.16(1): below, p.534.

[2] Gaming Act 1968, s.16(2A), as inserted by Gaming (Amendment) Act 1986, s.1(2).

[3] As amended by Gaming (Amendment) Act 1986, s.1(6).

[4] *M'Kinnell v Robinson* (1838) 3 M. & W. 434.

[5] Financial Services and Markets Act 2000, s.412; and see above, p.521 nn.2 and 3.

Gaming Act 1892.[6] This reasoning was applied in *CHT Ltd v Ward*.[7] The owners of a gaming club advanced chips on credit[8] to the defendant to enable her to play poker. She lost chips worth nearly £200 and the owners paid these losses in cash to the winners. It was held that the payments were irrecoverable as they had been made "in respect of" gaming contracts.

But a payment is not necessarily made "in respect of" a wager simply because it enables the person for whose benefit it was made to pay betting debts. In *Re O'Shea*[9] a person guaranteed a gambler's overdraft for £500 which the guarantor ultimately had to pay to the bank. It was held that this payment was not made "in respect of" a wager: it was simply a contribution to the assets of a gambler which he could deal with as he pleased. But in *MacDonald v Green*[10] it was held that money had been lent "in respect of" a wager, even though it was paid into the hands of the loser, because the loan was made on the terms that it was to be used to pay the lost bet; and the same rule was said to apply where such a stipulation was to be implied.

In *Tatam v Reeve*[11] Wills J. said that a loan paid straight to the winner would be "in respect of" the wager even if the lender did not know that he was paying a betting debt. But this view has been doubted as it might cause grave hardship to the lender[12]; and it can no longer be supported after *MacDonald v Green*. The question whether a loan is made "in respect of" a wager depends, at least to some extent, on the intention of the lender, who cannot have the necessary intention if he is ignorant of the purpose of the loan.

It must be pointed out again that the 1892 Act invalidates only promises to pay money. If the borrower promises to deliver to the lender some valuable thing, or to render him some service in return for the loan, that promise seems to be perfectly valid. On the other hand, it seems clear from the concluding words of the section that the principle in *Hill v William Hill (Park Lane) Ltd*[13] applies. No action could be brought to enforce a promise supported by fresh consideration to repay a loan originally made "under or in respect of" a wager.

(ii) *Loans for future betting.* A loan to enable the borrower to make bets might be void under the Gaming Act 1892, if it was made subject to a stipulation that it should be used for betting. This seems to follow from *MacDonald v Green*,[14] though the point has not actually been decided.

A loan to enable the borrower to make *gaming* bets may also be affected by the Acts of 1710 and 1835.[15] It is uncertain whether these Acts only invalidate securities, or whether they also invalidate the consideration, *i.e.*, the original loan for which a security was given. Most of the cases decided under the Act of 1710 support the view that only the security is invalidated.[16] But in *Applegarth v Colley*[17] it was said that the Act of 1835

---

[6] *Tatam v Reeve* [1893] 1 Q.B. 44; *cf. Carney v Plimmer* [1897] 1 Q.B. 634 (money paid straight to stakeholder).

[7] [1965] 2 Q.B. 63; following *Woolf v Freeman* [1937] 1 All E.R. 178.

[8] To make such an advance on licensed premises would be an offence under s.16(1) of the Gaming Act 1968; below, pp.534–535.

[9] [1911] 2 K.B. 981.

[10] [1951] 1 K.B. 594.

[11] [1893] 1 Q.B. at 48.

[12] *Hyams v Stuart King* [1908] 2 K.B. 696 at 714; *cf. MacDonald v Green*, above, n.10, at p.605.

[13] [1949] A.C. 530; above, p.520.

[14] [1951] 1 K.B. 594.

[15] See above, pp.527–529.

[16] *Barjeau v Walmsley* (1746) 2 Stra. 1249; *Robinson v Bland* (1760) 2 Burr. 1077; *Wettenhall v Wood* (1793) 1 Esp. 18; a dictum in *Young v Moore* (1757) 2 Wils.K.B. 67 suggests the contrary, but as to this, see *CHT Ltd v Ward* [1965] 2 Q.B. at p.83.

[17] (1842) 10 M. & W. 723 at 732.

had by implication invalidated the consideration as well, since it was "impossible to impute to the legislature an intention so absurd as that the consideration should be good and capable of being enforced, until some security is given . . . and then that by the giving of security the consideration should become bad." The present position depends to some extent on cases in which loans were made in foreign countries for the purpose of gaming there. Three propositions can be deduced from the cases.

First: the lender cannot sue in England on a cheque drawn on an English bank even though the cheque was given to repay a loan made in a foreign country to enable the borrower to bet on a game that was legal there. In *Moulis v Owen*[18] money was lent to the defendant in Algiers to enable him to play baccarat there. The defendant gave the lender a cheque drawn on an English bank in payment of the loan. By French law (which then applied in Algiers) baccarat was a legal game, and both the loan and a cheque given in payment of it were valid. But it was held that the lender could not sue on the cheque in England since the cheque was governed by English law and was invalid under the Acts of 1710 and 1835.

Secondly: the lender can sue in England on a loan made in, and governed by the law of, a foreign country to enable the borrower to bet on a game that is legal there. In *Saxby v Fulton*[19] money was lent to one Brook in Monte Carlo to enable him to play roulette there. By the law of Monaco, roulette was a legal game, and the loan was valid. It was held that the lender could recover the loan. There were two reasons why the Acts of 1710 and 1835 did not apply: no security had been given upon which those Acts could operate; and the *loan* was wholly governed by the law of Monaco.

Thirdly: the lender can sue in England on a loan made in, and governed by the law of, a foreign country to enable the borrower to bet on a game that is legal there *even though* the borrower gives the lender a cheque drawn on an English bank. In *Baumgart's* case[20] the lender on such facts originally sued in England on the cheque and on the loan, but later abandoned the claim on the cheque. It was held that he could sue on the loan as this was governed by the law of the foreign country in which it had been made, and was valid by that law. It follows that *Saxby v Fulton* must now be explained on the ground that the loan was governed by foreign law.

The effect of these foreign gaming decisions on a case wholly governed by English law was considered in *Carlton Hall Club Ltd v Laurence*.[21] The Club advanced chips to the defendant to enable him to play at billiards and poker, and the defendant gave the Club a cheque for the amount of the chips at the time of the advance. This transaction was treated as a loan of money.[22] The Club claimed the amount of the loan, but did not rely on the cheque. The claim might have been resisted by arguing that poker was then an illegal game as it is a card game, and not one of mere skill.[23] But the question whether poker was such a game was of fact and the argument was not open to the defendant as

---

[18] [1907] 1 K.B. 746; *cf. Browne v Bailey* (1908) 24 T.L.R. 644.

[19] [1909] 2 K.B. 208; *cf. Quarrier v Colston* (1842) 1 Ph. 147.

[20] (1927) 96 L.J.K.B. 789.

[21] [1929] 2 K.B. 153.

[22] In *Cumming v Mackie*, 1973 S.L.T. 242, it was said that there was no "loan" if the cheque was given at the time of the advance but this view was disapproved in *R. v Knightsbridge Crown Court, Ex p. Marcrest Properties Ltd* [1983] 1 W.L.R. 300, where it was held that making an advance against a cheque amounts to a loan, even though the cheque is not post-dated; this view was approved in *Crockfords Club Ltd v Mehta* [1992] 1 W.L.R. 355. See also the analysis of a similar transaction as a loan to pay bets already lost in *CHT Ltd v Ward* [1965] 2 Q.B. 63; above, p.531. That analysis was not possible in the *Carlton Hall Club* case as there was no evidence that the defendant had lost his chips or that the Club had made any payments in respect of them to third parties who had won bets with the defendant.

[23] See above, p.519, n.74.

he had not raised it in the court of first instance.[24] The defendant chose, instead, to rely on the Acts of 1710 and 1835, and this defence succeeded. The question raised by the case, bearing in mind that the defendant could no longer allege that the money was lent for illegal gaming, was whether money lent to enable the borrower to play a game which was *lawful* in England could be recovered. But according to the *Law Reports* that was not the question answered. Shearman J. is reported to have said: "Having regard to the cases as a whole in regard to claims for money lent for the purpose of playing a game which is *unlawful* in this country one finds the law in this curious condition: that where the game is played in a foreign country in which it is lawful . . . the money can be sued for in . . . this country, but where the game is to be played in this country, the weight of opinion is in favour of the view that the money cannot be sued for here because the statute of Anne [*i.e.* of 1710] avoids not only the security but by implication the consideration also."[25] This suggests that the court held only that loans for *unlawful* games were invalid. But in the *Law Journal Reports* the corresponding passage reads as follows: "The curious position therefore arises that though the decisions on foreign gaming should logically apply to *legal games in this country*, the better authority is that the consideration cannot be sued on because it is avoided under the statute of Anne."[26] This version is preferable[27] to that in the *Law Reports* as it does at least make the court decide the question before it. The *Carlton Hall Club* case is thus authority for the proposition that if money is lent to enable the borrower to play in England a game which is lawful in England and if the borrower gives a cheque for the loan, then the lender cannot sue either on the cheque or on the loan. There are two possible criticisms of this decision.

The first is based on *Baumgart's* case[28]: if a person who has lent money abroad to enable the borrower to play a game that is legal there can disregard an English cheque which the borrower may have given him, why should not the lender have the same rights if the loan is made and the legal game played in England? But the crucial factor in the foreign gaming cases was the validity of the loan, rather than the legality of the game, under the foreign law. If in *Saxby v Fulton*[29] it had been proved that roulette was a legal game in Monte Carlo but that loans for the purpose of playing roulette were void there, the lender's claim would clearly have failed. The validity of the loan cannot, in a purely English case, be deduced from the legality of the game.

The second objection to the *Carlton Hall Club* case is based on the wording of s.1 of the Act of 1835. To say that a security is "*deemed* and taken to have been . . . given . . . for an illegal consideration" is not to say that the consideration for the security *is* illegal: if it really were illegal, there would be no need to *deem* it so.[30] But the 1835 Act was not drafted with modern precision. The draftsman probably did not intend to draw any distinction between a consideration which was illegal and one which was deemed to be so. The now repealed s.2 of the Act, in referring back to s.1, uses the words "such illegal consideration".

The decision in the *Carlton Hall Club* case is therefore consistent with the authorities and with the Acts. It could be said to give effect to the policy of the Acts of 1710 and 1835, which was to restrict credit for gaming. But the question is not in future likely to be of much practical importance. If the facts of *Carlton Hall Club Ltd v Laurence*

---

[24] This appears from the report in 45 T.L.R. 195.
[25] *Carlton Hall Club Ltd v Laurence* [1929] 2 K.B. at p.164 (italics supplied).
[26] L.J.K.B. 305, 307 (italics supplied); *cf.* 140 L.T. 534 at 536–537; 45 T.L.R. 195 at 196.
[27] *CHT Ltd v Ward* [1965] 2 Q.B. at 85; *Crockfords Club Ltd v Mehta* [1992] 1 W.L.R. 355 at 366.
[28] (1927) 96 L.J.K.B. 789, above, at n.20.
[29] [1909] 2 K.B. 208.
[30] Diamond, 54 L.Q.R. 418.

recurred and the premises on which the gaming took place were licensed or registered under the Gaming Act 1968, an action could be brought on the cheque.[31] If the gaming took place elsewhere, an action on the cheque would fail under the Acts of 1710 and 1835; and an action on the loan would probably fail under the Act of 1892 on the ground that there was an implied stipulation to use the loan for gaming.[32] The Acts of 1710 and 1835 would therefore rarely determine the validity of the loan.

Where no security is given for the loan, it seems that the Acts of 1710 and 1835 cannot apply for there is nothing to attract their operation. It has been said that in such a case the loan would be recoverable.[33] But if there is a stipulation that the loan is to be used for gaming or wagering, the loan will again be void under the Act of 1892.

(b) LOANS FOR GAMING ON LICENSED PREMISES. S.16(1) of the Gaming Act 1968 provides that where gaming takes place on licensed premises, the licensee shall not "make any loan or otherwise provide or allow to any person any credit, or release or discharge on another person's behalf, the whole or part of any debt (a) for enabling any person to take part in gaming, or (b) in respect of any losses incurred by any person in the gaming". Thus it is an offence for the licensee to advance money or tokens[34] on credit to enable a person to take part in the gaming, or to pay losses which a player has incurred in the gaming, or to give credit to a loser by paying the winner. But under s.16(2) a licensee who advances cash or tokens in exchange for a cheque will not be guilty of an offence (even though the advance may amount to giving credit) if he gives full value for the cheque and if it is not post-dated.[35] S.16(2) would not, however, exonerate the licensee where the cheque was a mere sham, e.g. where the advance was made against a "house-cheque" drawn on a bank at which the player was known to have no account and not intended to be enforced,[36] and where the licensee took large cheques which he agreed not to bank, and later accepted the smaller sums actually lost in satisfaction of those cheques.[37] An offence will also be committed if the cheque is accepted in payment partly of an advance for future gaming and partly of bets already lost.[38]

S.16 does not specify the civil consequences of the transactions which it prohibits; but a transaction which amounts to an offence under the section would be an illegal contract at common law.[39] It could clearly not be enforced by the lender; nor, probably, could the borrower claim damages if the lender failed to perform a promise to give credit, e.g. if he promised to pay a player's losses and then omitted to do so.[40] The borrower might, however, be able to recover property pledged by him in respect of the contract on the ground that subs.(1) was passed to protect gamblers on licensed premises as a class.[41] S.16(2) also (at least by implication) permits certain transactions and here s.16(4) does specify one of the civil effects by validating certain cheques accepted in exchange for

---

[31] See above, p.529; for the possible effect of the 1968 Act on actions on the loan, see below.

[32] See above, pp.530–531.

[33] *CHT Ltd v Ward* [1965] 2 Q.B. 63 at 86; *R. v Knightsbridge Crown Court, Ex p. Marcrest Properties Ltd* [1983] 1 W.L.R. 300 at 309.

[34] The provisions of the subsection are not restricted to loans of money. They would apply to a case like *CHT v Ward* [1965] 2 Q.B. 63 if the gaming took place on licensed premises: *R. v Knightsbridge Crown Court* above, at 309–310; *Crockfords Club Ltd v Mehta* [1992] 1 W.L.R. 355.

[35] See above, p.529.

[36] *R. v Knightsbridge Crown Court, Ex p. Marcrest Properties Ltd* [1983] 1 W.L.R. 300.

[37] *ibid.*

[38] *Ladup v Shaik* [1983] Q.B. 225.

[39] See above, p.430.

[40] The borrower would be "innocent" only in the sense that he might act under a mistake of law: see above, p.484.

[41] See above, p.491.

cash or tokens.[42] Where a cheque is thus validated, the reasoning of *Carlton Hall Club Ltd v Laurence*[43] would not invalidate the loan: on the contrary, "the implication appears . . . to be quite clear, that the giving of a cheque which does comply with the conditions laid down by s.16(2) results in the lawful grant of credit".[44]

The prohibitions in s.16 apply only where a licensee gives credit or accepts a cheque, for the purposes there specified, in respect of gaming on licensed premises. Other forms of credit for gaming remain subject to the previous law which therefore applies to gaming elsewhere than on licensed premises and may even apply to gaming on licensed premises, *e.g.* if a loan is made there by one player to another. However, a cheque may be validated by s.16(4) even though the gaming takes place on registered and not on licensed premises[45]; and where the cheque is thus validated it would once again seem that the loan could not be invalidated by the reasoning of *Carlton Hall Club Ltd v Laurence*, though it might be void under the Act of 1892.

(9) Gambling with stolen money

We have seen that, where a loser pays money lost under a wager, he cannot recover back the amount so paid from the winner.[46] That rule deals with the normal situation in which the payment is made with the loser's own money. But the loser may make such a payment with stolen money, and the victim of the theft may then seek to recover that money from the winner. Because of the negotiable[47] quality of money paid as currency, the victim cannot recover an equivalent sum, from the winner, if the winner has received the money in good faith, without notice of the theft and for valuable consideration. The following discussion is concerned largely with the difficulties which may arise in determining whether these conditions have been satisfied.

(a) ILLEGAL WAGERS. In *Clarke v Shee and Johnson*[48] a clerk stole money and negotiable notes from his employer and paid part of the amount so stolen to the defendant under a lottery[49] which had been made illegal and void by the Lotteries Act 1772. Lord Mansfield held that the employer was entitled to recover the amount so paid as it was "his property which has come into the hands of the defendant iniquitously and illegally and in breach of the Act of Parliament".[50] These words seem to indicate that the defendant was held liable because he had not received the money in good faith; though they do not make it clear whether his lack of good faith resulted from his awareness of the circumstances in which the money had come into the hands of the thief, or merely from his knowing participation in the violation of the 1772 Act. Later discussion of the case, however, treats it as authority for the view that the defendant had not provided any consideration for the payment, in the shape of the promise which he had made to the thief, since that promise was illegal and void under the Act of 1772.[51]

---

[42] See above, p.530. See also Gaming Act 1968, s.16(2A), above, p.530.

[43] [1929] 2 K.B. 153; above, p.532.

[44] *R. v Knightsbridge Crown Court, Ex p. Marcrest Properties Ltd* [1983] 1 W.L.R. 300 at 310; *Crockfords Club Ltd v Mehta* [1992] 1 W.L.R. 355; but the customer could escape liability on other grounds, *e.g.* by showing that he had not used the chips.

[45] See above, pp.529–530.

[46] See above, p.522.

[47] See below, p.691.

[48] (1774) 1 Cowp. 197.

[49] For the meaning of "lottery", see *Re Senator Hanseatische Verwaltungsgesellschaft mbH* [1997] 1 W.L.R. 515.

[50] (1774) 1 Cowp. at 199–200.

[51] *Lipkin Gorman v Karpnale Ltd* [1991] 2 A.C. 548 at 563, 575.

(b) LAWFUL WAGERS. In *Clarke v Shee and Johnson* the transaction in respect of which the payment was made was both illegal and void; but in *Lipkin Gorman v Karpnale Ltd*[52] the reasoning of the earlier case was held to apply even though the stolen money had been used for the purpose of wagers which were not illegal but only void under s.18 of the Gaming Act 1845, and even though the defendant had received the money in good faith. The facts of the *Lipkin Gorman* case were that one Cass, a salaried partner in the claimant firm of solicitors, wrongfully withdrew money from the firm's client account; after he had replaced part of the money, there was a shortfall of £222,908.98. He used this stolen money[53] (as well as some money of his own) in gambling at the defendants' club over a period of some 10 months. At the end of that time, his losses exceeded his winnings by £174,745, of which £20,050 was attributable to his own money, so that £154,695 of the losses was derived from the money which he had stolen from the firm. The club had throughout acted in good faith, without notice of the fact that the money used by Cass had been stolen, and it would have been entitled to retain the money if it had, in addition, been able to show that it had provided consideration for its receipt of the money. In holding that no such consideration had been provided, the House of Lords rejected two arguments advanced on behalf of the club.

(i) *Promise to pay or payment of winnings no consideration for receipt of the money.* The first of these arguments was that the club had provided consideration by allowing Cass to gamble and so to obtain the chance of winning, and of being paid in the event of his winning, or by actually paying his winnings on the bets which he had won. The first limb of this argument amounted to saying that the consideration for the payments to the club was its promise to pay Cass his winnings; and it was rejected on the ground that this promise was void under s.18 of the 1845 Act. This is in accord with the view that, *prima facie*, a void promise does not amount to consideration.[54] In cases unconnected with gaming, the law does, at least sometimes, regard the *performance* of a defective promise as constituting consideration[55] even where the mere making of the promise would not be so regarded. The possibility of so regarding the club's performance might seem to give some support to the second limb of the argument (*i.e.* that the club had provided consideration by making payments to Cass on the bets which he had won); but this limb, too, was rejected on the ground that any such payment to Cass was in law regarded as a gift by the club to him.[56] This may not be a very realistic view of the intention accompanying the payment[57]; but it appears to be derived from the rule that gambling losses which have actually been paid by the loser cannot be recovered back by him from the winner,[58] one rationalisation of this rule being that the payment is a gift from the loser to the winner.[59] It may, with respect, be doubted whether this is really an explanation of the rule, rather than a statement of its legal consequence.

(ii) *Supply of gaming chips no consideration for receipt of the money.* The second argument advanced by the club in the *Lipkin Gorman* case was based on the fact that the gambling had been carried on, not with cash, but with gaming chips. A majority of the Court of Appeal[60] had regarded the supply of chips as a transaction separate from

---

[52] [1991] 2 A.C. 548.
[53] The money so used consisted mainly of cash withdrawals but also included a banker's draft for £3,735 drawn on the client account and made out in favour of the solicitors. The solicitors' claim in respect of this amount succeeded on the basis that the defendants were liable for conversion of the draft.
[54] See above, p.149.
[55] See above, p.150.
[56] [1992] 2 A.C. 548 at 562, 577.
[57] See above, p.151; *cf.* below, p.538 at n.78.
[58] *Lipkin Gorman v Karpnale Ltd* [1991] 2 A.C. 548 at 561.
[59] See above, p.523.
[60] [1989] 1 W.L.R. 1340.

the wagering contracts and as one under which the club had provided consideration, not merely by parting with chips of little intrinsic value, but also by making a number of promises to the member: for example, to allow him to use the chips to take part in the gaming, and to use them for the purchase of refreshments. The House of Lords, however, rejected this view on a number of grounds. One was that the chips were "worthless and at all times remained the property of the club".[61] This reasoning might at first sight seem hard to reconcile with the rules that an object of little value (such as a peppercorn) can constitute consideration[62] and that parting with possession, no less than transfer of ownership, can constitute consideration.[63] But the decision of the House of Lords is nevertheless (with respect) justified, having regard to the context in which the issue of consideration arose. The House of Lords was concerned with the rule that a bona fide recipient of stolen money can retain it if he gives "valuable"[64] or "full"[65] consideration for it, and the object of that rule would be defeated if a technical consideration of the kind described above would (for the purpose of the rule) be allowed to suffice. Another reason, given by Lord Templeman, for rejecting the club's argument was that "there was only one contract and that was a gaming contract"[66] and that the "chips transaction was part of a single contract by virtue of which Cass gambled away money stolen from the solicitors".[67] Lord Goff, indeed, seems to regard the supply of chips as an "independent contract"[68] but this does not affect the issue of consideration where the chips are in fact used for gaming: in such a case they are "simply a convenient mechanism for gambling with money"[69]; and where the chips are so used the club is said not to provide consideration for their supply because it "is under no legal obligation to honour the bet."[70]

(iii) *Chips used for purposes other than gaming.* In the *Lipkin Gorman* case it was said that the use of chips for the purpose of buying refreshments in the club "appears to have been very rare" and there is no evidence that Cass ever used them for that purpose.[71] The effect of their use for that purpose was therefore left open; but Lord Templeman said that "neither the power to purchase refreshments nor the exercise of that power could constitute consideration for the receipt [by the club] of £154,693".[72] One possible interpretation of this passage is that the supply of refreshments could not constitute consideration for £154,693 (the net amount lost by Cass on the gambling transactions) since the disparity in value was too great; and that the rule that consideration need not be adequate[73] should not be applied in its full rigour in the context of an assertion by the recipient of stolen money that he has received the money for valuable consideration. But where the consideration is merely inadequate (as opposed to nominal)[74] this explanation could give rise to difficulty: *e.g.* if a bottle of champagne were to be supplied in exchange for chips given in return for £200 of stolen money. The preferable explanation for Lord Templeman's statement is that, as he says, the chips were "treated

---

[61] [1991] 2 A.C. 548 at 561.
[62] See above, pp.85–86.
[63] *Bainbridge v Firmstone* (1838) 8 A. & E. 743, above, p.156.
[64] [1991] 2 A.C. 548 at 577.
[65] *ibid.* at 560.
[66] *ibid.* at 562.
[67] *ibid.* at 567.
[68] [1991] 2 A.C. 548 at 576.
[69] *ibid.* at 575.
[70] [1991] 2 A.C. 548 at 577.
[71] *ibid.* at 569.
[72] *ibid.* at 567.
[73] See above, pp.73–74.
[74] See above, p.75.

as currency"[75] in the club and could there be used for a variety of purposes. The reason why refreshments would, if they had been supplied, not have been consideration for the money lost at play is that the gaming and the supply of refreshments were entirely separate transactions.

(c) PARTIAL DEFENCE OF CHANGE OF POSITION. The reasoning of *Lipkin Gorman's* case, as so far discussed, would have led to the result that the club was liable to return to the solicitors all the money stolen by Cass and not repaid by him into the client account, to the extent that it was used for gambling at the club, *i.e.* to the extent of £222,908.98. But that was not the result reached by the House of Lords, which held the club liable for no more than £154,695, this sum representing the net amount lost by Cass (deducting his winnings from his losses) over the period of 10 months during which he had gambled with the stolen money, after making allowance for the £20,050 attributable to his own money. The House of Lords was able to reach this conclusion by recognising that claims for the restitution of money were subject to the defence of change of position.[76] The club had changed its position by allowing Cass to enter into a series of transactions which "by laws of chance [yielded] the occasional winning bet"[77]; and although the club was not legally liable to pay these bets, they as a practical matter placed it under "an obligation which, in business terms, [it] had to comply with".[78] The end result of the case, therefore, was that the loss resulting from the theft was split between two innocent parties, and it was no doubt the desire of the House of Lords to reach such a conclusion which led to its rejection of the argument that the club had provided valuable consideration for the payments.[79] The reasoning of the speeches on the issue of consideration may be complex and difficult, but the conclusion is (with respect) justified by the loss-splitting result.

---

[75] [1991] 2 A.C. 548 at 561.
[76] See generally Goff and Jones, *The Law of Restitution*, 6th ed., pp.821 to 837.
[77] [1991] 2 A.C. 548 at 582.
[78] [1991] 2 A.C. 548 at 581.
[79] See above, pp.536–538.

CHAPTER THIRTEEN

CAPACITY

SECTION 1. MINORS[1]

IN the law of contract, persons below the age of majority were formerly called infants; and this expression is used in many of the older cases which deal with their contractual capacity. They are now more generally called minors; and, as this term is used in modern legislation on the subject,[2] it will also be used in this Chapter. When the age of majority was reduced from 21 to 18,[3] the practical importance of the rules which determine the extent to which minors are bound by their contracts was greatly reduced. If the decided cases are any guide, many of the legal problems in this area have in the past concerned the contracts of persons between 18 and 21, whose contractual capacity is now normal. But the question whether persons under 18 are bound by contracts can still arise today: for example, out of the contracts of young professional entertainers[4] or athletes, or out of hire-purchase agreements or contracts of employment involving minors. Legal problems can also arise where a claim is made by the minor against the other party, either to enforce the contract or to reclaim money or property with which the minor has parted under it.

The law on this topic is based on two principles. The first, and more important, is that the law must protect the minor against his inexperience, which may enable an adult to take unfair advantage of him, or to induce him to enter into a contract which, though in itself fair, is simply improvident.[5] This principle is the basis of the general rule that a minor is not bound by his contracts. The second principle is that the law should not cause unnecessary hardship to adults who deal fairly with minors. Under this principle certain contracts with minors are valid; others are voidable in the sense that they bind the minor unless he repudiates; and a minor may be under some liability in tort and in restitution.

1. Valid Contracts

(1) Necessaries

A contract for necessaries is binding "not for the benefit of the tradesman who may trust the infant, but for the benefit of the infant himself".[6] It is assumed, rightly or wrongly,[7] that the tradesman would not give credit to the minor unless the law imposed liability. In this connection it should be noted that parents are not liable on their child's contract

---

[1] For a comparative study, see Hartwig, 15 I.C.L.Q. 780.
[2] Family Law Reform Act 1969, s.12 says they "may" be called minors; they are so called in Sale of Goods Act 1979, s.3 and in Minors' Contracts Act 1987.
[3] Family Law Reform Act 1969, s.1; s.9 provides that a person attains 18 "at the commencement of the [18th] anniversary of his birth."
[4] *e.g. Mills v IRC* [1975] A.C. 38 at 53.
[5] *e.g.* if the minor for a fair price agrees to buy something that he cannot afford.
[6] *Ryder v Wombwell* (1868) L.R. 4 Ex. 32 at 38; *Zouch v Parsons* (1763) 3 Burr. 1794.
[7] *cf.* below, p.541.

unless the child acts as their agent[8]; and that in English law a minor's contract cannot be validated by the consent or authorisation of his parent or guardian.

Necessaries include goods supplied and services rendered to a minor. He is bound by a contract for necessaries only if it is on the whole for his benefit: not if it contains harsh and onerous terms.[9] Nor is he bound by an indivisible contract comprising necessaries and non-necessaries.[10]

(a) NECESSARY GOODS. Necessary goods are not confined to necessities: they include "such articles as are fit to maintain the particular person in the state, station and degree . . . in which he is".[11] In one case[12] a livery for a minor's servant was held to be a necessary; and in another[13] the court refused to disturb a verdict that rings, pins and a watch-chain supplied to the son of a rich man were necessaries. These "quaint examples of a bygone age"[14] are hardly cases in which liability was imposed "for the benefit of the infant himself".[15] The wide definition of necessaries was adopted rather for the protection of suppliers who reasonably gave credit to young men from wealthy families.

On the other hand the definition of necessaries was limited so as to exclude "mere luxuries." These were distinguished from "luxurious articles of utility",[16] which could be necessaries. Since few articles are so luxurious that they cannot be used at all, the real question was whether it was reasonable for the minor, however rich, to be supplied with articles of the kind in question. Thus it was said that if the son of the richest man in the kingdom bought a racehorse, it could not be a necessary[17] but where an apprentice bought a racing bicycle (which was no more expensive than an ordinary one) it was held to be a necessary.[18] It is doubtful whether goods bought by a minor to be given away can normally be necessaries.[19] But an engagement ring bought to be given to the minor's fiancée, whom he later marries, can be a necessary.[20]

Much difficulty was caused in the nineteenth century by the tendency of juries (consisting of 12 shopkeepers) to stretch the definition of necessaries beyond its legitimate limits. In one case "an Oxford jury held that champagne and wild ducks were necessaries to an infant undergraduate".[21] To counteract this tendency, the courts first distinguished between articles which could, and those which could not, as a matter of law, be necessaries.[22] They held, secondly, that the question whether goods were necessaries was "one of mixed law and fact; in so far as it is a question of fact it must be determined by the jury . . . ; but there is in every case . . . a preliminary question which is one of law, namely whether there is any evidence on which the jury could

---

[8] *Blackburn v Mackey* (1823) 1 C. & P. 1; *Law v Wilkin* (1837) 6 A. & E. 718; *Mortimore v Wright* (1840) 6 M. & W. 482.

[9] *Fawcett v Smethurst* (1914) 84 L.J.Ch. 473.

[10] *Stocks v Wilson* [1913] 2 K.B. 235.

[11] *Peters v Fleming* (1840) 6 M. & W. 42 at 46; *Bryant v Richardson* (1866) 14 L.T. 24 at 26.

[12] *Hands v Slaney* (1800) 8 T.R. 578. But a claim for the price of cockades for soldiers under the minor's command was disallowed.

[13] *Peters v Fleming*, above, n.11.

[14] *Allen v Bloomsbury Health Authority* [1993] 1 All E.R. 651 at 661.

[15] See above, p.539.

[16] *Chapple v Cooper* (1844) 13 M. & W. 252 at 258.

[17] *Wharton v Mackenzie* (1844) 5 Q.B. 606 at 612. Contrast *Barber v Vincent* (1680) Free.K.B. 581 (horse sold to a minor to carry him about his necessary business held a necessary).

[18] *Clyde Cycle Co v Hargreaves* (1898) 78 L.T. 296.

[19] *Ryder v Wombwell* (1868) L.R. 4 Ex. 32; *Hewlings v Graham* (1901) 84 L.T. 497.

[20] *Jenner v Walker* (1869) 19 L.T. 398.

[21] (1874) *Hansard*, Vol.219, ser.3, col.1225.

[22] *Ryder v Wombwell* (1868) L.R. 4 Ex. 32.

properly find the question for the party on whom the onus of proof lies".[23] The onus of proving that the goods are necessaries lies on the supplier. Thus in *Ryder v Wombwell*[24] the son of a deceased baronet bought jewelled cuff-links for £12 10s. apiece and an antique goblet to give to a friend. The jury found that these articles were necessaries. But the court set the verdict aside as there was no evidence on which it could properly be based.

The supplier must show both that the goods are capable of being necessaries and that they actually are necessaries. Thus in *Nash v Inman*[25] a tailor sued a minor for the price of clothes, including 11 fancy waistcoats. The action failed because the tailor had not adduced any evidence fit to be left to the jury that the clothes were suitable to the condition in life of the minor, *and* that the minor was not already adequately supplied with clothes. The courts have put on the claimant the burden of proving the difficult negative proposition that the minor was not adequately supplied. As a general rule a person is only required to prove a negative if such proof depends on facts peculiarly within his own knowledge; here the proof required of the supplier depends on facts peculiarly within the knowledge of the minor.

It was further held that the minor is not liable if he already had an adequate supply, even though the supplier did not know this.[26] Such a rule may help to protect minors; but it is difficult to reconcile with the view that minors are liable for necessaries because, if they were not, traders would not give them credit. For the rule makes it impossible for the supplier to tell, when the contract is made, whether the minor will indeed be bound by it.

(b) SERVICES RENDERED TO A MINOR. Certain services rendered to a minor may be necessaries. These include education (whether liberal or vocational)[27] and medical and legal advice.[28] The provision of a funeral for her deceased husband has been held a necessary for his widow, who was a minor.[29] It seems that any service can be a necessary if it satisfies the tests already stated in relation to necessary goods.

(c) EXECUTORY CONTRACTS.[30] It is disputed whether a minor is bound by an executory contract for necessary goods. Is he liable only if the goods have actually been delivered, or also if he wrongfully repudiates before delivery? Three main arguments have been used to support the view that the minor is liable only if the goods have been delivered.

First: in *Nash v Inman* Fletcher Moulton L.J. said that the minor was liable because he had been supplied, and not because he had contracted. "An infant, like a lunatic,[31] is incapable of making a contract . . . in the strict sense of the word: but if a man satisfies the need of the infant or lunatic by supplying to him necessaries, the law will imply an obligation to repay him for the services so rendered, and will enforce that obligation against the estate of the infant or lunatic".[32] But Buckley L.J. said that a contract for

---

[23] *Ryder v Wombwell* (1868) L.R. 4 Ex. 32 at 38.

[24] (1868) L.R. 4 Ex. 32; *cf. Wharton v Mackenzie* (1844) 5 Q.B. 606.

[25] [1908] 2 K.B. 1.

[26] *Foster v Redgrave* (1867) L.R. 4 Ex. 35n; *Barnes v Toye* (1884) 13 Q.B.D. 410; *Johnstone v Marks* (1887) 19 Q.B.D. 509.

[27] *Chapple v Cooper* (1844) 13 M. & W. 252 at 258; *Walter v Everard* [1891] 2 Q.B. 369; *Roberts v Gray* [1913] 1 K.B. 520. For contracts to pay school fees, see *Practice Direction* [1980] 1 W.L.R. 1441; *Practice Direction* [1983] 1 W.L.R. 800; *Sherdley v Sherdley* [1988] A.C. 213 at 225.

[28] *Huggins v Wiseman* (1690) Carth. 110; *Helps v Clayton* (1864) 17 C.B. (N.S.) 553.

[29] *Chapple v Cooper* (1844) 13 M. & W. 252.

[30] Miles, (1927) 43 L.Q.R. 389; Winfield, (1942) 58 L.Q.R. 83.

[31] Now called a mental patient: see below, pp.557 *et seq.*

[32] [1908] 2 K.B. 1 at 8; *cf. Re J* [1909] 1 Ch. 574.

necessaries was "such as the infant, notwithstanding infancy, could make" and that "an infant had a limited capacity to contract".[33] And the analogy of the "lunatic" is, with respect, imperfect. Sometimes the reason why such a person is "incapable of making a contract" may be that he cannot consent; and if he is then supplied with necessaries there is not even the shadow of an agreement to accept and pay for the goods. This may also be true when necessaries are supplied to a very young child.[34] But it is not true when a young man of 17 orders clothes and promises to pay for them. He can and does consent[35]: the only question is whether he ought as a matter of legal policy to be held to the agreement.

Secondly: the minor is liable only for a reasonable price, which may not be the same as the contract price. "That does not imply a consensual contract."[36] But the law often interferes with one or more of the terms of a transaction and this does not necessarily deprive it of its essential character as a contract.[37]

Thirdly: s.3(2) of the Sale of Goods Act 1979 provides that "Where necessaries are sold and delivered to a minor . . . he must pay a reasonable price for them". S.3(3) then defines " 'necessaries' in subsection (2) above" to mean "goods suitable to the condition in life of the minor . . . and to his actual requirements *at the time of sale and delivery.*" The words here italicised may seem to suggest that goods cannot be necessaries unless they have actually been delivered. But the definition is of necessaries "In subsection (2) above," and that subsection deals only with necessaries sold and delivered. The definition does not apply to goods sold but not yet delivered.

Thus the arguments in support of the view that the minor is not liable on an executory contract are inconclusive; and the contrary view is supported by *Roberts v Gray*.[38] The claimant, a famous billiards player, agreed to take a minor on a world billiards tour, and to pay for his board and lodging and travelling expenses. This was a contract for necessaries, mainly because its object was to teach the minor the profession of a billiards player. The minor repudiated the contract while it was still partly executory; and he was held liable in damages. Hamilton L.J. said: "I am unable to appreciate why a contract which is in itself binding . . . can cease to be binding merely because it is still executory".[39] It has been said that *Roberts v Gray* can be explained on the ground that contracts for education are more closely analogous to beneficial contracts of service[40] than to contracts for the supply of necessary goods.[41] But it is hard to see why any distinction should for this purpose be drawn between necessary goods and education; or between necessaries of either kind and beneficial contracts of service. The reasons for holding a minor liable, and for limiting his liability, are the same in all these cases. It is thought that the minor's overall position might be prejudiced if he could not bind himself, and also that liability should be imposed to protect the legitimate interests of the adult. These considerations have to be balanced against the need to protect the minor. If a balancing of all these factors justifies the view that the minor should be bound by an executory contract for education or of service, it is submitted that it can equally

---

[33] [1908] K.B. 1 at 12.

[34] See *Sherdley v Sherdley* [1988] A.C. 213 at 225. *R. v Oldham MBC, Ex p. Garlick* [1993] A.C. 509 at 517.

[35] For recognition of this requirement in other branches of the law see, *e.g.*, Family Law Reform Act 1969, s.8(1) (consent to medical treatment); *Gillick v West Norfolk Health Authority* [1986] A.C. 112 (consent to contraceptive advice).

[36] *Pontypridd Union v Drew* [1927] 1 K.B. 214 at 220.

[37] See above, p.3.

[38] [1913] 1 K.B. 520.

[39] *ibid.* at 530.

[40] See below, pp.543–545.

[41] Cheshire, Fifoot and Furmston, *Law of Contract* (14th ed.), p.481.

justify the view that he should be bound by an executory contract for the supply of necessary goods.[42]

(d) LEGISLATION AFFECTING THE MAINTENANCE OF CHILDREN. The common law rules relating to liability for necessaries are not directly affected by legislation imposing on an absent parent the duty to maintain a child[43] or empowering courts to make orders against parents for financial relief in respect of children.[44] Such legislation may, however, indirectly affect a minor's contractual liabilities for necessaries, in the sense that if, as a result of its operation, the minor is already adequately supplied with the goods or services in question, they will not fall within the common law definition of necessaries.

(e) LOANS FOR NECESSARIES. At common law a person who spends money in buying necessaries for a minor is entitled to recover it from the minor.[45] One who lends money to a minor to enable him to buy necessaries cannot recover it at law, but can in equity recover such part of the loan as was actually used by the minor to discharge his liability for necessaries supplied to him.[46] A promise in a mortgage deed to repay such a loan is ineffective since the minor is not bound by his deed.[47] The law leaves the lender for necessaries in a somewhat precarious position—perhaps because a loan of money can more easily be misapplied than an actual supply of necessaries.

(2) Service contracts

A minor[48] is bound by a service contract if it is on the whole for his benefit. He may be bound even though some of the terms of the contract are to his disadvantage. Thus in *Clements v L & NW Ry*[49] a minor who was a railway porter agreed to join an insurance scheme, to which his employers contributed, and to give up any claim for personal injury under the Employers' Liability Act 1880. His rights under the scheme were in some ways more, and in other ways less, beneficial than those under the Act; and it was held that the contract was on the whole beneficial, so that the minor was bound by it. But a term which simply limits or excludes the liability of the employer without giving the minor any rights in return is unlikely to be upheld.[50]

A minor is, *a fortiori*, not bound by a service contract which is on the whole harsh and oppressive to the minor.[51]

---

[42] The difficulties discussed above would be diminished if parents were liable for necessaries, or at least for necessities, supplied to a child. For an American case in which such liability was imposed, see *Greenspan v Slate*, 12 N.J. 426; 97 A. 2d. 390 (1953).

[43] Child Support Act 1991, s.1(1).

[44] Children Act 1989, s.15 and Sch.5.

[45] *Ellis v Ellis* (1689) Comb. 482; *Earle v Peale* (1712) 10 Mod. 67.

[46] *Marlow v Pitfeild* (1719) 1 P.Wms. 558; *Re National Permanent Benefit Building Society* (1869) L.R. 5 Ch.App. 309 at 313.

[47] *Martin v Gale* (1876) 4 Ch.D. 428.

[48] Contracts of service with children are to some extent regulated by statute: see, for example, Children and Young Persons Acts 1933, s.18; 1963, ss.34, 37; Employment of Children Act 1973 (as amended by Employment Act 1989 and Children Act 1989).

[49] [1894] 2 Q.B. 482; *Slade v Metrodent* [1953] 2 Q.B. 112; *Mills v IRC* [1975] A.C. 38 at 53.

[50] *Olsen v Corry and Gravesend Aviation Ltd* [1936] 3 All E.R. 241. Even if valid at common law, the term may be ineffective, or subject to the requirement of reasonableness, under Unfair Contracts Terms Act 1977, ss.2 or 3 (above, pp.248, 252–254), and see Sch.1 para.4 ("except in favour of the employee"). The Unfair Terms in Consumer Contracts Regulations, 1999 do not apply to contracts relating to employment: above, p.278.

[51] *De Francesco v Barnum* (1889) 43 Ch.D. 165; (1890) 45 Ch.D. 430. For an even more extreme case of this kind, in which there was said to be liability to the minor for intimidation (below, p.625), see *Goodwin v Uzoigwe*, *The Times*, June 18, 1992.

In deciding whether a service contract is on the whole beneficial the court is entitled to look at surrounding circumstances. For example, a service contract with a minor may contain a covenant in restraint of trade. Such a covenant, if otherwise valid,[52] does not invalidate the contract if the minor could not have got similar work on any other terms.[53] But it would invalidate a service contract with a minor if it was of a kind that was not usually found in service contracts in that trade and locality.[54] These principles also apply to contracts connected with service contracts. Thus they determine the validity of contracts to carry minors to work,[55] of compromises of industrial injury claims,[56] and of agreements to dissolve service contracts.[57]

The principles evolved in relation to service contracts also determine the validity of contracts under which a minor makes a living by the exercise of some profession, *e.g.* as an entertainer or author or athlete. In *Doyle v White City Stadium Ltd*[58] a professional boxer who was a minor made a contract to fight for £3,000, win, draw or lose, subject to the rules of the British Boxing Board of Control, under which a boxer who was disqualified forfeited his "purse". The minor was disqualified for hitting below the belt and his claim for the £3,000 was dismissed. Although in the circumstances the rules operated against him, he was bound by them: they were, on the whole, for his benefit as a professional boxer since they encouraged clean fighting. This case was followed in *Chaplin v Leslie Frewin (Publishers) Ltd*[59] where a minor contracted to give a firm of publishers the exclusive right to publish his memoirs. The Court of Appeal unanimously held that this was the sort of contract which could bind the minor if it was on the whole for his benefit.[60] Applying this test Lord Denning M.R. thought that, having regard to the contents of the memoirs, the contract was not binding, as it was not for the minor's good "that he should exploit his discreditable conduct for money".[61] But Danckwerts and Winn L.JJ. took the more materialistic view that "the mud may cling but the profits will be secured": thus the contract was on the whole beneficial, and bound the minor as it enabled him to "make a start as an author".[62]

The rule that a minor is bound by "beneficial" contracts is restricted to service or analogous contracts. There is no general principle that a minor is bound by a contract merely because it is for his benefit. For example, a minor would not be contractually liable to repay[63] a loan without interest. And it has long been settled that a minor is not bound by a trading contract. Thus he is not liable for goods supplied to him for the

---

[52] See above, p.454 *et seq.* The fact that the employee was a minor may be relevant to the issue of the reasonableness of the covenant: see *Sir W C Leng & Co Ltd v Andrews* [1909] 1 Ch. 763 at 771–772.

[53] *Bromley v Smith* [1909] 2 K.B. 235; *cf. Leslie v Fitzpatrick* (1877) 3 Q.B.D. 229; *Fellows v Wood* (1888) 59 L.T. 513.

[54] *Sir W C Leng & Co Ltd v Andrews* [1909] 1 Ch. 763.

[55] *Flower v London and North Western Ry* [1894] 2 Q.B. 65; in *Buckpitt v Oates* [1968] 1 All E.R. 1145 it seems to have been assumed that any contract to carry the minor (though not connected with his work) would be binding if on the whole for his benefit; *sed quaere.* The actual decision would now go the other way: Road Traffic Act 1988, ss.145, 149.

[56] *Stephens v Dudbridge Ironworks Co* [1904] 2 K.B. 225.

[57] *Waterman v Fryer* [1922] 1 K.B. 499.

[58] [1935] 1 K.B. 110. *cf.* also *Lumley v Wagner* (1852) 1 D.M. & G. 604, where a famous soprano was under age, as appears from 5 De G. & Sm. 485.

[59] [1966] Ch. 71; the case was later compromised: *The Times*, February 16, 1966.

[60] The same rule seems to apply to a contract between an entertainer who is under age and his agent: see *Denmark Productions Ltd v Boscobel Productions Ltd* (1967) 111 S.J. 715, reversed on other grounds [1969] 1 Q.B. 699, below, pp.749, 1016.

[61] [1966] Ch. 71 at 88.

[62] *ibid.* p.95. The majority may have been influenced by the fact that the minor had received considerable payments in advance of royalties. The publishers would have had considerable difficulties—both legal and practical—in getting these back.

[63] For liability to make restitution, see below, pp.551–557.

purpose of trade, nor for damages if he fails to deliver goods which he has sold as a trader.[64] Nor can he be made bankrupt for trade debts.[65]

It may be asked: why does the law distinguish between a minor who earns his living by the exercise of a profession and one who earns his living by trading? The traditional answer is that "the law will not suffer him to trade, which may be his undoing".[66] A minor who trades thereby necessarily risks his capital. If he exercises some profession or calling he may incur expense, but putting his capital at risk is not of the essence of the matter. Of course there are difficult borderline cases. A minor who is a haulage contractor is a trader,[67] but probably one who was a racing driver would not be so regarded. Similarly, it is probable that a minor who was a house painter would, while one who was a portrait painter would not, be regarded as a trader.[68] There is no precise definition of "trade" for this purpose.

Contracts of apprenticeship were governed by special rules. It was held in the seventeenth century that an apprentice who was under age was not liable in damages if, in breach of contract, he departed from service.[69] This rule was originally based on the fact that the master had other remedies such as having the minor ordered by a justice of the peace to return to work. These remedies no longer exist[70] and it seems that contracts of apprenticeship will now be governed by the normal rules. A minor is not bound by an apprenticeship deed as such, but he is bound by it as a simple contract. Thus he is liable to pay any premium which he has agreed to pay.[71] Similarly, a covenant in restraint of trade (if otherwise valid[72]) or an arbitration clause contained in the apprenticeship deed can be enforced against him so long as the deed is on the whole for his benefit.[73]

2. Voidable Contracts

(1) Cases of voidable contracts

In four cases a minor's contract is voidable: that is, it binds both parties but the minor can avoid liability by repudiating before majority or within a reasonable time thereafter. The other party cannot repudiate.[74]

(a) CONTRACTS CONCERNING LAND. A lessee who is under age is liable for rent unless he repudiates.[75] A minor who agrees to purchase freehold land is similarly bound unless he repudiates.[76] It seems that the same principle applies where a minor lets or agrees to

---

[64] *Mercantile Union Guarantee Corp Ltd v Ball* [1937] 2 K.B. 498; *Cowern v Nield* [1912] 2 K.B. 491; below, p.556.

[65] *Ex p. Jones* (1881) 18 Ch.D. 109; but he can be made bankrupt in respect of tax liability incurred in the course of trade: *Re a Debtor* [1950] Ch. 282. If a minor is made bankrupt as a result of a mistake as to his age, the court has a discretion to set the bankruptcy aside: *Re Davenport* [1963] 1 W.L.R. 817.

[66] *Whywall v Campion* (1738) 2 Stra. 1083.

[67] *Mercantile Union Guarantee Corp Ltd v Ball*, above, n.64.

[68] *Quaere* what the position would be if a minor agreed to sell a picture which he had painted without having been commissioned to paint it.

[69] *Gylbert v Fletcher* (1630) Cro.Car. 179.

[70] Family Law Reform Act 1969, s.11.

[71] *Walter v Everard* [1891] 2 Q.B. 369.

[72] See above, p.544, n.52.

[73] *Gadd v Thompson* [1911] 1 K.B. 304; *Slade v Metrodent* [1953] 2 Q.B. 112.

[74] *Clayton v Ashdown* (1714) 2 Eq.Ca.Abr. 516.

[75] *Keteley's Case* (1613) 1 Brownl. 120; *Davies v Benyon-Harris* (1931) 47 T.L.R. 424. A minor can no longer hold a legal estate in land: Law of Property Act 1925, s.1(b); *cf.* Trusts of Land and Apointment of Trustees Act 1996, s.2(6) and Sch.2; but these enactments do not affect the proposition in the text.

[76] *Whittingham v Murdy* (1889) 60 L.T. 956; *Thurstan v Notts PBBS* [1902] 1 Ch. 1 at 9, 13 (affirmed [1903] A.C. 6); *Orakpo v Manson Investments Ltd* [1978] A.C. 95 at 106, 113.

sell land.[77] Actual conveyances to and by minors give rise to special problems which are outside the scope of this book.

According to one case[78] a lessee who is under age is liable for rent only if the subject-matter of the lease is a necessary, but if this were so he could presumably not repudiate. The requirement is not elsewhere stated and is probably not law. On the contrary, it seems that a lessee who is under age is liable unless he repudiates even though the lease is disadvantageous to him.[79]

(b) SHARES IN COMPANIES. A minor who agrees to subscribe for shares in a company, or buys shares which are not fully paid, is liable for calls unless he repudiates. A mere plea that he has not ratified the transaction does not relieve him from liability.[80] If he repudiates he ceases to be liable and can have his name removed from the company's register.[81] If the minor buys shares from a previous owner and fails to repudiate liability for calls on them, *the company* cannot generally avoid the transaction and so make the transferor liable for the calls.[82] But if the company is being wound up while the buyer is still a minor, the liquidator can exercise the minor's right of repudiation for him and so make the transferor again liable for calls.[83]

The cases on this subject all concern the relations between the minor and the company or between the company and the person who has transferred shares to a minor. There appears to be no authority on the effect between buyer and seller of a sale of shares by or to a minor. Suppose that a minor buys shares, fails to pay for them when due, and then repudiates after majority. If the contract is voidable this repudiation may be too late,[84] so that the minor will be liable to pay. But he would not be liable if the contract had never been binding on him at all.[85]

(c) PARTNERSHIP. A minor can become a partner and is to some extent bound by the partnership agreement. He cannot be sued during minority by persons who give credit to the firm,[86] or be made liable for its losses.[87] But he is liable if after majority he fails to put an end to the partnership.[88] And he is not entitled to any share in the profits or assets of the partnership until its liabilities have been discharged.[89]

---

[77] *Slator v Trimble* (1861) 14 Ir.C.L.R. 342; Williams, *Vendor and Purchaser* (4th ed.), pp.847 *et seq.*

[78] *Lowe v Griffith* (1835) 4 L.J.C.P. 94.

[79] *North Western Ry v M'Michael* (1850) 5 Ex. 114 at 128; in *Keteley's Case*, sub nom. *Kirton v Eliot* (1613) 2 Bulst. 69, there is a conflict of opinion on this point. There would be no liability for necessaries in such a case: above, p.540 at n.9.

[80] *North Western Ry v M'Michael*, above; *Dublin & Wicklow Ry v Black* (1852) 8 Ex. 181; *Ebbett's Case* (1870) L.R. 5 Ch.App. 302. The rule was originally thought to be based simply on the provisions of the Act incorporating the company: *Cork & Bandon Ry v Cazenove* (1847) 10 Q.B. 935; but this reasoning was disapproved in *M'Michael's* case, above, and in *Leeds & Thirsk Ry v Fearnley* (1849) 4 Ex. 26. Thus the rule applies to shares in all companies, however incorporated.

[81] *Dublin & Wicklow Ry v Black*, above; *Steinberg v Scala (Leeds) Ltd* [1923] 2 Ch. 452.

[82] *Lumsden's Case* (1868) L.R. 4 Ch.App. 31; *Gooch's Case* (1872) L.R. 8 Ch.App. 266.

[83] *Capper's Case* (1868) L.R. 3 Ch.App. 458; *Castello's Case* (1869) L.R. 8 Eq. 504; *Symon's Case* (1870) L.R. 5 Ch.App. 298.

[84] See below, p.547.

[85] *i.e.* if it fell within the general rule stated at p.549, below.

[86] *Goode v Harrison* (1821) 5 B. & Ald. 147 at 157; *Lovell & Christmas v Beauchamp* [1894] A.C. 607.

[87] *Goode v Harrison*, above, at 159.

[88] *Goode v Harrison*, above.

[89] *Lovell & Christmas v Beauchamp* [1894] A.C. 607 at 611. *Semble*, the rules stated in this paragraph would apply to the relations between persons who became members of a limited liability partnership (below, p.563) if one or more of them were a minor: ss.4 and 5 of the Limited Liability Partnerships Act 2000 contain no reference to minority. Since under s.1 of the Act such a partnership is a body corporate, a minor would not (any more than a person of full age) be liable on its contracts; but his liability to contribute to the assets of the partnership would seem to be governed by the principles stated at nn.80 and 81 above.

(d) MARRIAGE SETTLEMENTS. It was once thought that a marriage settlement by a minor was binding to the extent to which it benefited him; but was otherwise not binding unless ratified after majority.[90] But the prevailing view is that such a settlement binds the minor unless he repudiates.[91] In certain cases a minor could, by statute, make an absolutely binding settlement with the consent of the court.[92] The statute has been repealed,[93] though not with retrospective effect.

(2) Loans for voidable contracts

A minor may borrow money to enable him to make a payment due from him under a voidable contract, and actually use the money borrowed to make the payment. The minor is not for this reason bound by the contract for the loan of the money[94]; but the lender has rights similar to those of a lender for necessaries.[95] In *Nottingham Permanent Benefit Building Society v Thurstan*[96] a minor borrowed money from a building society to buy land. She paid the money to the vendor and executed a mortgage to the society. The mortgage was void,[97] but the society was entitled to stand in the shoes of the vendor and to exercise the lien that he would have had over the property, if he had not been paid.

(3) Rules relating to repudiation

(a) TIME OF REPUDIATION. A voidable contract can be repudiated during minority, but such a repudiation can be withdrawn by the minor before, or within reasonable time of, majority.[98] If the minor repudiates during minority he need take no further steps to avoid liability on reaching full age.[99]

If the minor does not repudiate during minority, he must do so within a reasonable time of reaching full age. This is so even though he did not know of his right to repudiate, and even though his obligation under the contract had not yet matured. Thus a covenant by a minor in a marriage settlement to settle after-acquired property may not become operative for many years after the settlor comes of age. But it binds him unless he repudiates it within a reasonable time of majority. In *Edwards v Carter*[1] it was held that a settlement could not be repudiated nearly five years after the majority of the settlor, although he was for most of that time ignorant of his right to repudiate.

(b) EFFECTS OF REPUDIATION. Two points call for discussion.

(i) *Relief from future liabilities*. Repudiation relieves the minor from liabilities which would, but for the repudiation, have accrued after its date. There are conflicting dicta[2] on the question whether liabilities which have already accrued are extinguished by repudiation. According to an Irish case repudiation has no retrospective effect[3] thus a

---

[90] See *Simson v Jones* (1831) 2 Russ & My. 365; traces of this view remain in *Kingsman v Kingsman* (1880) 6 Q.B.D. 122 and in *Clements v London and North Western Ry* [1894] 2 Q.B. 482 at 493.

[91] *Duncan v Dixon* (1890) 44 Ch.D. 211; *Edwards v Carter* [1893] A.C. 360; [1892] 2 Ch. 278.

[92] Infant Settlements Act 1855.

[93] Family Law Reform Act 1969, s.11.

[94] It falls within the general rule stated at p.549, below.

[95] See above, p.543.

[96] [1903] A.C. 6.

[97] See above, p.543 at n.47.

[98] *North Western Ry v M'Michael* (1850) 5 Ex. 114 at 127; *Slator v Trimble* (1861) 14 Ir.C.L.R. 342.

[99] *Newry and Enniskillen Ry v Combe* (1849) 3 Ex. 565 at 575.

[1] [1893] A.C. 360.

[2] *North Western Ry v M'Michael*, above, n.96 at 125 (retrospective); *Keteley's Case* (1613) 1 Brownl. 120 (not retrospective); dicta in *Steinberg v Scala* (*Leeds*) *Ltd* [1923] 2 Ch. 452 at 463 can be cited on both sides.

[3] *Blake v Concannon* (1870) I.R. 4 C.L. 323.

lessee who is under age is liable for rent which has become payable before repudiation.

(ii) *No restitution of money or property.* A minor cannot recover back money paid under a voidable contract unless there has been a "total failure of consideration".[4] In *Steinberg v Scala (Leeds) Ltd*,[5] a minor applied for shares in a company but repudiated after allotment. She thus avoided liability for future calls, but her claim for the return of money already paid was rejected as there was no total failure of consideration: she had got the very shares she bargained for. Property transferred under a marriage settlement would similarly be irrecoverable once the marriage had taken place. On the other hand in *Corpe v Overton*[6] a minor agreed to enter into a partnership and paid a deposit of £100, to be forfeited if he failed to execute the partnership deed. No partnership deed was ever executed because the minor repudiated, and it was held that he could get his deposit back as there had been a total failure of consideration. An adult, too, can recover back money if there has been a total failure of consideration; but a minor (unlike an adult) can do so even though the failure of consideration is due to his own act in repudiating the contract.

(4) Why are these contracts voidable?

In general a minor is not bound by his contracts.[7] He need not repudiate to escape liability. Why must he do so in the four cases discussed above?[8]

The orthodox view is that the minor must repudiate because he has acquired an interest in a subject-matter of a permanent nature to which continuing obligations are attached: it would be unjust to allow him to retain the interest without fulfilling the obligations.[9] But this explanation is not wholly satisfactory. First, it is vague: what is meant by "permanent" here? Is a lease for one year permanent because land is virtually indestructible? Partnerships and shares in companies do not necessarily confer an interest in property which is permanent even in this sense. And marriage settlements can be brought within the explanation only by arguing that the marriage is permanent, whether the settled property is permanent or not. Secondly, the explanation does not cover all cases within the rule. It has been held that a minor's contract to buy freehold land to be paid for in instalments is voidable.[10] Nothing in the judgment suggests that it would have made any difference, had the price been payable in one lump sum. Yet in such a case the contract would not have created any "continuing" obligation between the parties. Thirdly, the explanation proves too much. It is admittedly unjust to allow a tenant who is a minor to retain possession of land without paying rent. But it is equally unjust to allow a minor to keep a car obtained under a hire purchase agreement without paying instalments. Yet the hire purchase agreement does not bind the minor[11]: he need repudiate.

There seems to be no satisfactory explanation for the existence of this separate class of voidable contracts. It perhaps provides the clearest illustration of the dilemma in which the law sometimes finds itself when it tries at the same time to protect minors and not to cause undue hardship to adults who deal with them. But this dilemma exists in all cases of contracts with minors and scarcely justifies special treatment of the four

---

[4] See below, p.1049.
[5] [1923] 2 Ch. 452.
[6] (1833) 10 Bing. 252; *Everett v Wilkins* (1874) 29 L.T. 846.
[7] See below, p.549, heading 3(1).
[8] See above, pp.545–547.
[9] See, *e.g.*, *Davies v Benyon Harris* (1931) 47 T.L.R. 424.
[10] *Whittingham v Murdy* (1889) 60 L.T. 956.
[11] *e.g. Mercantile Union Guarantee Corp Ltd v Ball* [1937] 2 K.B. 498.

classes of voidable contracts. Perhaps this is based on social and economic factors which have long since passed away.

3. Other Contracts

(1) Minor not bound

Contracts which are neither valid, nor voidable in the sense just discussed, do not bind the minor but have a number of legal effects.

(2) Other effects

(a) OTHER PARTY BOUND. Contracts in this group bind the other party.[12] However, the remedies available to the minor are somewhat restricted in that he cannot claim *specific* performance of the contract.[13]

(b) RATIFICATION. The minor as a general rule[14] becomes liable on the contract if he ratifies it after reaching full age.[15] Ratification may be express, or implied from conduct: the latter possibility is illustrated by the case in which the former minor continues after majority to act on the contract in such a way as to show that he regards it as binding on himself.[16] Because contracts in this group became binding as a result of ratification, they were sometimes called "voidable." But this is misleading as "voidable" normally means binding unless repudiated, whereas these contracts do not bind the minor unless he ratifies.

(c) EXECUTED CONTRACTS. Once the minor has actually performed the contract he cannot recover back money paid or property transferred by him under it merely on the ground that the contract did not bind him by reason of his minority.[17] He can recover back such money or property only in the same circumstances in which this remedy is available to an adult: for example, he can recover back money paid under the contract if there has been a total failure of consideration.[18] There is, indeed, some doubt as to the scope of the rule that property transferred in pursuance of contracts in this category cannot be recovered back. In *Chaplin v Leslie Frewin (Publishers) Ltd*[19] a majority of the Court of Appeal accepted the view that the minor would not be able to recover the copyright which he had transferred under the contract even if (contrary to the view of that majority) the contract did not bind him.[20] Lord Denning M.R., on the other hand, said that the rule, by which property could not be recovered back, applied only to transfers by delivery and not to those which require a written document: it would be

---

[12] *Farnham v Atkins* (1670) 1 Sid. 446; *Bruce v Warwick* (1815) 6 Taunt. 118; and see above, p.539.

[13] *Flight v Boland* (1828) 4 Russ. 298; *Lumley v Ravenscroft* [1895] 1 Q.B. 683; below; p.1037.

[14] Exceptionally, a penal bond is void so that it cannot be ratified: *Baylis v Dinely* (1815) 3 M. & S. 477.

[15] See *Williams v Moor* (1843) 11 M. & W. 256.

[16] This appears from cases which distinguished for the purpose of s.2 of the Infants Relief Act 1874 between a "ratification" (which under that section was not enforceable) and a fresh promise (which was enforceable): *e.g. Brown v Harper* (1893) 68 L.T. 488. Now that s.2 has been repealed by Minors' Contracts Act 1987, ss.1(a) and 4(2), a mere ratification is enforceable.

[17] *Wilson v Kearse* (1800) Peake Add. Cas. 196; *Corpe v Overton* (1833) 10 Bing. 252 at 259; *Ex p. Taylor* (1856) 8 D.M. & G. 254 at 256.

[18] See below, p.1049.

[19] [1966] Ch. 71; above, p.544.

[20] This view was based "on the authorities cited to us" (at p.94). But these were not strictly in point as the contract in one of them (*Steinberg v Scala (Leeds) Ltd* [1923] 2 Ch. 452) was truly voidable, while in the other two (*Valentini v Canali* (1889) 24 Q.B.D. 166; *Pearce v Brain* [1929] 2 K.B. 310) the contracts were "absolutely void" within s.1 of the Infants Relief Act 1874 (repealed by Minors' Contracts Act 1987, ss.1(a) and 4(2)). The majority's view is more appropriately supported by the authorities cited in n.17, above.

"absurd to hold that a contract to make a disposition is voidable and that the disposition is not".[21] But it is, with respect, hard to see why this is more absurd when the disposition has to be in writing than when it can, and does, take effect by delivery.[22]

(d) PASSING OF PROPERTY TO MINOR. It was said by Lush J. in *Stocks v Wilson*[23] that, where goods were delivered to a minor under a contract of sale, the property in them passed to him "by the delivery". The view that property can pass to a minor under a contract which does not bind him seems to be supported by s.3(1) of the Minors' Contracts Act 1987: this subsection[24] refers to "property acquired" by the minor under such a contract, and to the power of the court to order him to "transfer" such property.[25] The property, in the case put, seems to pass by delivery with intention to pass property. It may indeed be argued that the seller's intention to pass property is based on the assumption that the contract binds the minor and is nullified if this assumption is untrue, just as (in cases not involving minors) a seller's intention to pass property is nullified if the contract is void for mistake as to the identity of the buyer.[26] But delivery to the wrong person may well differ in legal effect from delivery for the wrong reason. In the first case there is no intention to pass the property to the person to whom the delivery is made; in the second there is such an intention, though possibly based on a mistaken assumption. Thus it is submitted that delivery of the goods to the minor can pass property to him. The attraction of this view is that it enables the law to protect an innocent third party who later buys the goods from the minor. It is an open question whether property can pass to the minor without delivery,[27] simply by virtue of the contract. The question is of small practical importance since property is unlikely to pass in this way until the price has been paid[28]; and in that case the seller generally has no interest in claiming that he still has the property in the goods.

(e) PASSING OF PROPERTY FROM MINOR. Cases such as *Chaplin v Leslie Frewin (Publishers) Ltd*[29] show that property can pass *from* the minor under a contract which does not bind him.[30] The same principle would apply where the minor made a pledge to secure a debt incurred under such a contract. The person taking the pledge would normally be guilty of an offence,[31] but this does not affect the civil consequences of the transaction.[32] Thus it seems that a special property in the thing pledged would pass to the pledgee and that the minor could not get the thing back without paying off the loan. This conclusion may be disadvantageous to the minor, but the argument that property passes by delivery seems to apply as much where the delivery is made *by*, as where it is made *to*, the minor.

---

[21] [1966] Ch. 71 at 90; *cf. G (A) v G (T)* [1970] 2 Q.B. 643 at 652.

[22] No such distinction is drawn where the contract is voidable for misrepresentation above, pp.369 *et seq.*

[23] [1913] 2 K.B. 235 at 246; *cf. Watts v Seymour* [1967] 2 Q.B. 647.

[24] See below, p.551; a similar assumption seems to underlie Criminal Justice Act 1988, s.141A(1), as inserted by Offensive Weapons Act 1996, s.6(1).

[25] See further below, pp.551–553.

[26] *Cundy v Lindsay* (1878) 3 App.Cas. 459; above, p.298.

[27] *e.g.* under Sale of Goods Act 1979, s.18, rule 1.

[28] See *R. v Ward Ltd v Bignall* [1967] 1 Q.B. 534 at 545.

[29] [1966] Ch. 71; above, pp.544, 549.

[30] Even Lord Denning accepted this view where the property was alleged to have passed by *delivery*: see above, at n.21.

[31] Consumer Credit Act 1974, s.114(2).

[32] *ibid.* s.170(1); *quaere* whether this excludes the rules stated at pp.491–492 above; *cf.* also pp.495–503, above.

4. Liability in Tort

The general rule is that minors are liable in tort in the same way as adults. One possible exception to this rule exists in the case of very young children. Our concern here, however, is with another exception, which exists where a cause of action in tort arises out of, or in connection with, a contract which does not bind the minor.

Conduct amounting to a breach of contract may also be a tort.[33] If a minor engages in such conduct and is sued in tort, he can sometimes set up the invalidity of the contract as a defence to the tort claim. He can do so where the tort consists of wrongfully doing an act authorised by the contract,[34] but not where it consists of doing an act forbidden by the contract.[35] The distinction between these two types of cases can be explained as the product of the law's two conflicting desires: to protect minors, but without causing unnecessary hardship to adults who deal with them.

The minor may be immune from liability in tort, not only where he commits a tort in breaking the invalid contract, but also where he commits a tort in procuring it. Thus it was held in *R Leslie Ltd v Sheill*[36] that a minor could not be sued in deceit for inducing an adult to lend him money by fraudulent misrepresentations as to his age. Similarly it was held in *Stocks v Wilson*[37] that a minor could not be sued in deceit for inducing an adult by such misrepresentations to sell and deliver goods to him. The practical effect of a judgment in tort in such cases would be to force the minor to repay the money lent or to pay the value of the goods obtained; and this would once again undermine the protection which the law gives to the minor by holding the contract invalid.

5. Liability in Restitution

Before the Minors' Contracts Act 1987, a minor could be held liable to restore certain benefits received by him under a contract which did not bind him. Such liability was imposed in equity if the minor was guilty of fraud,[38] and (probably) in certain other cases at common law.[39] S.3(1) of the 1987 Act now gives the court a discretion to order the minor to transfer to the adult party any property acquired by the minor under such a contract, or any property representing it. S.3(2) goes on to provide that nothing in s.3 "shall be taken to prejudice any other remedy available to the" adult party to the contract: thus in cases which fall outside s.3(1), or in which the court declines to exercise its discretion under that subsection, it remains open to the adult to seek restitution under the old rules of equity or common law. These therefore still call for discussion, even though generally claims for restitution are now likely to be made under s.3(1), since the conditions imposed by the subsection are less onerous than those imposed by the equitable or the common law rules.

(1) Minors' Contracts Act 1987, s.3(1)

(a) SCOPE. This subsection deals with the case where a contract has been made with a minor and the contract "is unenforceable against [the minor] (or he repudiates it)[40] because he was a minor when the contract was made". In such a case the court "may,

---

[33] See below, pp.983–984.
[34] *Jennings v Rundall* (1799) 8 T.R. 335; *cf. Fawcett v Smethurst* (1914) 84 L.J.K.B. 473.
[35] *Burnard v Haggis* (1863) 14 C.B. (N.S.) 45; *cf. Ballett Mingay* [1943] K.B. 281 (under-age bailee wrongfully disposing of the goods).
[36] [1914] 3 K.B. 607; *Johnson v Pye* (1665) 1 Sid. 258.
[37] [1913] 2 K.B. 235.
[38] See below, pp.554–556.
[39] See below, pp.556–557.
[40] This phrase refers to the "voidable" contracts discussed above, at pp.545–547.

if it is just and equitable to do so, require [the minor] to transfer to the [other party] any property acquired by the [minor] under the contract, or any property representing it".

(i) *Restoration of property acquired.* The subsection would most obviously apply to a case like *Nash v Inman*[41]: the minor could be ordered to return the fancy waistcoats to the seller. Such an order could be made even though the minor was not guilty of fraud, which is essential to liability in equity[42]; and even though there would, in the case put, be no liability in quasi-contract at common law.[43]

(ii) *Proceeds of property acquired.* S.3(1) goes beyond the simple case just put, in that the court can order the minor to transfer either the "property acquired . . . under the contract" or "any property representing it". Thus if the minor were to exchange the fancy waistcoats for a set of silver candlesticks, he could be ordered to transfer those to the seller of the fancy waistcoats. On the other hand, s.3(1) would not apply where the minor had dissipated the property acquired under the contract or its proceeds: *e.g.* where he had bought champagne and consumed it, or where he had sold property acquired under the contract for cash and had used the money to pay for a holiday. S.3(1) only empowers the court to order the minor to transfer either the property acquired under the contract or property representing it: the court cannot order him to pay either the price or the reasonable value of what he has obtained out of his other assets. The underlying principle seems to be that the minor should not be enriched by retaining "property" obtained under the contract. But his general assets (other than that "property") are not to be diminished as a result of the exercise of the court's discretion under the section.

The discretion will present few problems where the "property acquired . . . under the contract" is still in the minor's possession; but difficulty can obviously arise where the discretion is invoked in respect of "property representing it". The case in which the minor simply exchanges the "property acquired" for something else will be relatively uncommon. More usually, he will sell the "property acquired" and use the money to buy something else; that other thing may have been paid for wholly or in part with the money obtained from the sale of the property originally acquired. Further problems can arise where that money is paid by the minor into a bank account which is in credit and from which money is then drawn out to pay for the substitute purchase. In such a case it may be very hard to tell whether that substitute is indeed "property representing" the property acquired under the original contract. Even greater difficulties could arise if the substitute had been bought under another contract which was unenforceable against the minor, and if only part of the price due under that contract had been paid by the minor; in such a case claims under s.3 for the transfer of the same thing might be made by two sellers.

(iii) *Meaning of "property."* A final difficulty is to determine what is meant by "property" in the section; and in particular whether "property" includes money.[44] The difficulty arises because the cases decided before the Act displayed a somewhat greater reluctance to make a minor "restore" a sum of money than to return goods obtained by

---

[41] [1908] 2 K.B. 1; above, p.541.

[42] See below, pp.554–555.

[43] English law does not recognise any quasi-contractual claim for the recovery of chattels (as distinct from money): see *Power v Wells* (1778) 2 Cowp. 818. The only possible claim for chattels is in tort for wrongful interference with possession or with an immediate right to possession; and in the case put there would be no such claim as property in the goods would have passed to the minor.

[44] The Act contains no definition of property; contrast Theft Act 1968, s.4(1), expressly providing that "property" includes money. The 1987 Act refers to "property", not to "goods", so that the definitions referred to at pp.279–280 above are not relevant in the present context.

him under the contract[45]—apparently because a judgment against him to pay a sum of money was more likely than one for the return of goods to present the appearance of indirectly enforcing the contract. But those cases do not rule out the possibility of making the minor restore money,[46] at least where he was guilty of fraud, and s.3(1) seems to be intended to extend such liability to cases in which there was no fraud.[47] Moreover, it appears from the legislative history of the Act that s.3(1) is intended to produce the result that "the minor can be compelled to hand over the proceeds if he has sold the property[48]"; and, in the case of goods at least, the proceeds of a *sale*, by definition, consist of money.[49] This supports the view that the "property representing" the "property acquired" includes money; and if this is so, then it is submitted that the "property acquired" also includes money, since the word "property" must *prima facie* bear the same meaning in both the places in which it occurs in the subsection. Thus it is submitted that where a minor buys goods under a contract which is unenforceable against him by reason of his minority, and then sells them, he can be ordered to transfer the money to the seller; while if the minor borrows money under such a contract, and uses it to buy goods, he can be ordered to transfer those goods to the lender.

(b) DISCRETION OF THE COURT. S.3(1) does not entitle the other party to the transfer of the property as of right: it only provides that the court "may, if it is just and equitable to do so," order the transfer. Of the factors which the court can take into account in exercising this discretion, two call for comment. The first is the difficulty, where the minor has disposed of the property acquired, of determining whether assets still owned by him are indeed "property representing" what he originally acquired. The process of "tracing" assets into their product can be complex[50]; and the court may restrict the operation of s.3(1) to cases in which it is relatively clear that the property which the minor is ordered to restore does indeed represent that acquired under the contract. To extend the operation of the subsection beyond this point would increase the danger that an order to transfer property (especially in the form of money) would amount to indirect enforcement of the contract against the minor. The operation of the equitable doctrine of restitution in cases of the minor's fraud gave rise to a similar danger, and it was to avert this danger that the courts restricted the scope of that doctrine. The relevant equity cases are discussed below[51] (even though the equitable doctrine has lost much of its former practical importance) because it is submitted that they now provide guidance for the exercise of the statutory discretion. The second factor which the court might take into account is the fairness of the original contract: thus if the court regarded the price payable under the contract as too high it might order the minor to return the property unless he paid a reasonable price fixed by the court.[52] In failing to specify the circumstances and manner in which the discretion is to be exercised, the subsection no doubt gives rise to some uncertainty; but it avoids complexity. In the context, the balance that it thus strikes seems to be satisfactory, since the rules which govern a minor's liability in

---

[45] See *R Leslie Ltd v Sheill* [1914] 3 K.B. 607 (below, p.555); *Cowern v Neild* [1912] 2 K.B. 419 (below, p.556).

[46] See *Stocks v Wilson* [1913] 2 K.B. 235, below, p.555, and below, pp.556–557.

[47] See Law Com. No.134, para.4.21. The Act is based on this Report; for use of such materials to discover the mischief which the legislation was intended to cure, see *M/S Aswan Engineering Establishment Co v Lupdine Ltd* [1987] 1 W.L.R. 1 at 14. *Smith v Eric S Bush* [1990] 1 A.C. 831 at 857; *Pepper v Hart* [1993] A.C. 593 at 630, 635.

[48] Law Commission Report, above, n.47, para.4.21.

[49] Sale of Goods Act 1979, s.2(1) ("for a money consideration").

[50] See Goff and Jones, *The Law of Restitution* (6th ed.), §§2–021 to 2–053.

[51] See below, pp.554–556.

[52] See the reference in para.4.21 of the Law Commission's Report (above, n.47) to para.6.10 of the Commission's earlier Working Paper No.81 on Minors' Contracts.

restitution are not of a kind on which either party to the contract relies (or should be encouraged to rely) in conducting his business affairs.

(2) Effects of fraud

(a) COMMON LAW. At common law, a minor cannot be made liable on a contract merely because he has committed a fraud on the other party in inducing him to enter into the contract.[53] The other party can at most rely on the fraud as a defence or as a ground of rescission.[54]

(b) IN EQUITY. The common law rules just stated unduly favoured a class of minors that least deserved protection. Hence equity gave further relief against minors on the ground of fraud. For this purpose, it seems that fraud meant some misrepresentation by the minor as to his age, so that his mere failure to declare that he was under age did not amount to fraud[55]; nor was it fraud for him to keep, without paying, goods obtained by him under a contract which did not bind him.[56] Equitable relief on the ground of fraud took a number of forms.

(i) *Restoration of benefits.* Our principal concern is with the power of equity to order the fraudulent minor to restore benefits obtained under the contract.[57] The remedy, being equitable, was presumably discretionary,[58] and in this respect it resembles the statutory remedy now available under s.3(1) of the Minors' Contracts Act 1987.[59] On the other hand, the statutory remedy is in two respects more favourable to the adult than the old equitable remedy. First, the statutory remedy is available even though the minor was not guilty of fraud. Secondly, there is no doubt that the statutory remedy extends to the proceeds of the thing obtained under the contract,[60] while it was disputed whether the equitable remedy was available in respect of such proceeds.[61] Thus although the equitable remedy is one of those expressly preserved by the 1987 Act,[62] there seems to be no reason why the other party should wish to resort to it. It follows that questions as to the exact scope and extent of the equitable remedy no longer have any practical importance. The cases concerned with such questions are now useful only as providing illustrations of the factors that the courts may take into account in deciding whether to exercise their statutory discretion to order the minor to transfer property acquired under the contract, or property representing it. Two cases are of particular interest in this context.

---

[53] *Bartlett v Wells* (1862) 1 B. & S. 836; *De Roo v Foster* (1862) 12 C.B.(N.S.) 272; *Miller v Blankley* (1878) 38 L.T. 527; *Levene v Brougham* (1909) 25 T.L.R. 265; exceptionally a debt incurred by fraud can be proved in an uncontested bankruptcy: *Re King* (1858) 3 D. & J. 63.

[54] *e.g. Lemprière v Lange* (1879) 12 Ch.D. 675. No attempt seems to have been made in the cases to argue that the adult could, by rescinding the contract for fraud, avoid the minor's title *at law* (*cf.* above, pp.371–372). *Quaere* whether the court could award damages in lieu of rescission against a minor under s.2(2) of the Misrepresentation Act 1967 (above, p.357). To do this might amount to indirect enforcement of the contract in the sense discussed at p.555, below.

[55] For the definition of fraud, see above, p.343. In equity a person could be guilty of fraud even though he had no "actual intention to cheat": *Nocton v Ashburton* [1914] A.C. 932 at 954; but in the present context a number of cases state the requirement of a misrepresentation as to age: *Stikeman v Dawson* (1847) 1 De G. & Sm. 90 at 103; *Ex p. Jones* (1881) 18 CL.D. 109 at 120; *Re Hodson* [1894] 2 Ch. 421 at 427.

[56] This must have been assumed in *Nash v Inman* [1908] 2 K.B. 1; for the contrary view, see Atiyah, 22 M.L.R. 273 at 275. Because of the Minors' Contracts Act 1987, s.3(1), the point no longer has any practical importance: see below, after n.62.

[57] *e.g. Clarke v Cobley* (1789) 2 Cox 173.

[58] *cf.* above, pp.319, 321 and see p.378; below, pp.1026, 1040.

[59] See above, p.551.

[60] See the words "any property representing it" in s.3(1): above, p.552.

[61] See below, at nn.63 to 70.

[62] s.3(2).

The first is *Stocks v Wilson*[63] where a minor had obtained goods under a contract induced by fraud and had disposed of some of those goods. He was held liable to account[64] to the original seller for the proceeds of the goods. The second, contrasting, case is *R Leslie Ltd v Sheill*[65] where a minor had by fraud obtained a loan of £400 and was held not liable in equity to restore the money. Lord Sumner said: "the money was paid over to be used as the defendant's own and he has so used it, and, I suppose, spent it. There is no question of tracing it, no possibility of restoring the very thing got by fraud, nothing but compulsion through a personal judgment to pay an equivalent sum out of his present or future resources. . . . "[66]

The crucial point in *R Leslie Ltd v Sheill* was that there was no question of tracing the money, that is of showing that it, or some asset representing it, was still in the hands of the minor. If he had still got the £400 he could have been made to restore it in equity[67]; and if he had used the £400 to buy a car he could have been ordered to hand the car over to the lender.[68] An order to "transfer . . . property" could now be made in such circumstances under s.3(1) of the 1987 Act, even in the absence of fraud.[69] Conversely, in a case like *Stocks v Wilson* the minor could, under the subsection, be ordered to transfer the proceeds of sale if they could be identified as "property representing" the goods.[70] It is submitted that such an order could be made even if the minor had happened to resell the goods for the exact equivalent of the contract price. It is no objection to a claim for restitution that it leads to the same *measure* of recovery as an action on the contract. To order a minor to pay such an amount (or any amount) becomes objectionable only on account of the *nature* of the judgment: that is, if the judgment is, in Lord Sumner's words, "a personal judgment to pay an equivalent sum out of his present or future resources". The only type of order that can be made against the minor is one to *restore* the property acquired, or its proceeds, in equity, or to *transfer* it under s.3(1). He cannot be made liable to *pay* for the property acquired or to *account* for its proceeds by a personal judgment enforceable against his general assets. This point seems to have been overlooked in *Stocks v Wilson* where the court ordered the minor to *account for* the proceeds of sale without enquiring whether those proceeds were still in the hands of the minor.[71] The purpose of the equitable and statutory remedies is to ensure that the minor is not enriched as a result of the transaction which is not binding on him; but the remedy should not diminish such general resources as he had apart from the transaction. It follows that the remedies are limited by the value of the property in the hands of the minor at the time of judgment. If by then the minor has dissipated part of the property (or its proceeds) the remedy is available only in respect of the remainder.

(ii) *Other forms of relief.* Equity gives relief against fraudulent minors in a number of other ways. It has, for example, been held that a minor who obtained payment of a share in a trust fund by fraudulently pretending to be of age could not claim a second payment

---

[63] [1913] 2 K.B. 235.

[64] *ibid.* at 247—a passage criticised in *R Leslie Ltd v Sheill* [1914] 3 K.B. 607.

[65] See above.

[66] [1914] 3 K.B. 607 at 619.

[67] There would have been, in Lord Sumner's words (above, at n.66), a "possibility of restoring the very thing got by fraud."

[68] It is assumed that the money lent could be "traced" into the car, within Lord Sumner's words (above, at n.66).

[69] See above, pp.551–552.

[70] See above, pp.551–552.

[71] In *Westdeutsche Landesbank Girozentrale v Islington BC* [1996] A.C. 669 at 716 Lord Browne-Wilkinson refers with evident approval to *Stocks v Wilson* but treats it as a case in which the minor was "bound in equity to *restore*" property obtained by fraud.

on reaching full age[72]; and that a minor remainderman who by fraud enabled the tenant for life to mortgage the estate could not, when the estate vested in him, deny the validity of the charge.[73] These cases do not call for extended discussion here as they are not directly connected with the law of contract. It has been further suggested that equity recognised a broad principle of relief: *viz.* that if a minor sued without offering to pay he would be guilty of "fraud" which would give the adult an equitable defence,[74] even (apparently) where, under the contract, payment from the minor was not due until after the adult's performance. But the authorities do not support such a broad definition of "fraud": on the contrary, they support the view that, even in equity, relief is available to the other party only where the minor's "fraud" takes the form of a misrepresentation by him as to his age.[75]

(3) Liability in restitution at common law

In certain circumstances a minor who has obtained benefits at the expense of an adult may be liable to make restitution to the adult at common law. This remedy is available as of right, and it is expressly preserved by s.3(2) of the Minor's Contracts Act 1987.

It is illustrated by cases of so-called waiver of tort, in which the victim of a fraud (and of certain other torts) can claim restitution in respect of certain benefits obtained by the tortfeasor. Such an action lies against a minor if he would have been liable to the direct action in tort. Thus it was available in *Bristow v Eastman*,[76] where an apprentice, while under age, had embezzled[77] his master's property.

But the courts will not allow a minor's lack of contractual capacity to be circumvented by means of such a restitutionary action. Thus in *R Leslie Ltd v Sheill* the lenders made an alternative claim that the minor was liable to repay the money lent as money had and received to their use. This claim also failed as "the cause of action is in substance *ex contractu* and is so directly connected with the contract of loan that the action would be an indirect way of enforcing that contract".[78] Here again the decisive objection is not that the measure of liability may be the same in a restitutionary action as in one for breach of contract: the crucial point is that, where the money had been spent, the only possible effect of the judgment in either kind of action would be to impose personal liability on the minor, enforceable against his assets generally.[79]

Much difficulty is caused by *Cowern v Nield*.[80] A minor who was a trader sold hay and clover, and was paid in advance. He failed to deliver any hay, and the clover which he delivered was defective, so that the buyer justifiably rejected it. As the contract was a trading contract, the buyer's claim for damages failed; and his claim for the return of the money that he had paid was also rejected. The court took the view that such a claim could have succeeded if the minor had obtained the money by fraud, and therefore ordered a new trial on the issue of fraud. But this view is, with respect, open to doubt. A minor cannot be made liable in restitution if "the action would be an indirect way of enforcing [the invalid] contract".[81] If (contrary to the submission made above) this

---

[72] *Cory v Gertcken* (1816) 2 Madd. 40.
[73] *Watts v Cresswell* (1714) 2 Eq.Ca.Abr. 515.
[74] Atiyah, 22 M.L.R. 273.
[75] See above, p.554.
[76] (1794) 1 Esp. 172. "Even this has been doubted": *per* Lord Sumner in *R Leslie Ltd v Sheill* [1914] 3 K.B. 607 at 613.
[77] Such conduct would now be theft under Theft Act 1968, s.15.
[78] [1914] 3 K.B. at 621; *cf.* p.613.
[79] *cf.* above, p.555.
[80] [1912] 2 K.B. 419.
[81] *R Leslie Ltd v Sheill* [1914] 3 K.B. 607 at 621.

means that the judgment must not impose the same *measure* of liability as a judgment in action for breach of contract, then the action for the return of the price should have succeeded in *Cowern v Nield* irrespective of fraud. For the minor's duty under the contract was to deliver the goods, and the damages for their non-delivery might have been quite different from the price. But if (as seems more probable) indirect enforcement refers to the imposition of *personal* liability on the minor, the action should not have succeeded merely on proof of fraud. The minor should have been liable only to the extent that the money or its identifiable proceeds were still in his hands. Under s.3(1) of the Minors' Contracts Act 1987 the court could now order the minor to transfer such money, or property representing it, to the buyer, irrespective of fraud; but that remedy is discretionary, so that the buyer might prefer to pursue his restitutionary remedy at common law, as this is available as of right.

SECTION 2. MENTAL PATIENTS[82]

The law relating to contracts with persons suffering from mental disorder represents a compromise between two principles. The first is that such a person should not be liable on his contracts if he is incapable of intelligent consent. The second is that it might cause hardship to one contracting party to allow the other to "stultify himself".[83]

1. In General[84]

A contract with a mental patient is valid, except in two cases:

(1) Disability known to other party

If the other contracting party knows of the patient's disability, the contract is voidable at the patient's option.[85] The burden is on the patient to show that his disability prevented him from understanding the transaction,[86] and that the other party knew this. It seems that the patient becomes absolutely bound if he ratifies the contract after he is cured.[87] There is also some support for the view that the contract is binding so long as it was a fair one, even though the disability of one party was known to the other.[88]

Where the other party does not know of the patient's disability, the contract is valid: it cannot be attacked merely on the ground that it was "unfair" in the sense that its terms were more favourable to the other party than they were to the party under the disability.[89] The contract can be attacked on the ground of "unfairness" only (if at all) where if the circumstances are such that the party under the disability can rely, like a person of normal capacity, on the equitable rules relating to undue influence or unconscionable bargains.[90]

---

[82] A convenient, if slightly inaccurate, term to describe a person suffering from mental disorder within the Mental Health Act 1983.

[83] *Beverley's Case* (1603) 4 Co.Rep. 123b.

[84] Hudson [1984] Conv. 32.

[85] *Molton v Camroux* (1849) 4 Ex. 17; *Imperial Loan Co v Stone* [1892] 1 Q.B. 599.

[86] *Re K* [1988] Ch. 310, below, p.752.

[87] *Birkin v Wing* (1890) 63 L.T. 80; *Manches v Trimborn* (1946) 115 L.J.K.B. 305.

[88] *Dane v Kirkwall* (1838) 8 C. & P. 679.

[89] *Hart v O'Connor* [1985] A.C. 1000; *Irvani v Irvani* [2000] 1 Lloyd's Rep. 412 at 420.

[90] See above, pp.408–423.

(2) Property subject to control of the court[91]

If the patient is one whose property is subject to the control of the court[92] an attempt by him to dispose of the property does not bind him, since, if it did bind him, it would interfere with the court's control over the property.[93] But the contract binds the other party.[94]

The rule that the contract does not bind the patient clearly applies to any contract which purports to dispose of the patient's property. But it is not clear whether the rule applies *only* to such contracts, or whether it extends to *all* contracts with mental patients whose property is subject to the control of the court. On the one hand it can be argued that every contract creates a potential liability to pay money and thus interferes with the court's control over the property. On the other hand there are some negative contracts which can be enforced by injunction against the patient's person which need not interfere with his property. There is no reason, on principle, why such contracts should not be enforced in this way. The question is largely academic as the court only exercises control over the property in cases of serious disorder. The other party will generally know of such disorder and his claim will fail on this ground.

2. Necessaries

S.3(2) of the Sale of Goods Act 1979 provides that "where necessaries are sold and delivered . . . to a person who by reason of mental incapacity . . . is incompetent to contract, he must pay a reasonable price for them." As a mental patient is by no means always "incompetent to contract" two situations must be considered.

If the patient would be bound by the contract under the rules stated above, his liability for necessaries is not affected by s.3(2). Thus a person who sells and delivers necessaries to the patient without knowing of his disorder can enforce the contract[95]: he is not limited to an action for a reasonable price.

If the patient would not be bound by the contract under the rules stated above, he is liable under s.3(2). Thus a person who sells and delivers necessaries to the patient knowing of his disorder cannot enforce the contract: he can only recover a reasonable price.

S.3(2) applies "where necessaries are sold and delivered" to the patient. These words are scarcely appropriate where necessaries are simply supplied to a patient whose disorder is so serious that he has no capacity for rational thought; or where a patient in this condition is simply maintained at the expense of another person. In such cases the person who supplies or pays for the necessaries has a remedy at common law under the doctrine of agency of necessity[96] unless he acted gratuitously, without thought of recompense.[97]

We have seen that, in the case of minors, "necessaries" can include services no less than goods[98]; and the same principle can apply in the case of mental patients. For example, medical treatment supplied to such a person can be a necessary. Two questions arise in relation to such services. The first is, whether the treatment is lawful even

---

[91] Jennings, 23 M.L.R. 421; Fridman, 79 L.Q.R. 509–516.

[92] Under Part VII of the Mental Health Act 1983.

[93] *Re Walker* [1905] 1 Ch. 160; *Re Marshall* [1920] 1 Ch. 284.

[94] *cf. Baldwyn v Smith* [1900] 1 Ch. 588.

[95] *Baxter v Portsmouth* (1826) 5 B. & C. 170.

[96] *Brockwell v Bullock* (1889) 22 Q.B.D. 567; *Pontypridd Union v Drew* [1927] 1 K.B. 214 at 220; see also *Re Rhodes* (1889) 44 Ch.D. 94 and below, p.721.

[97] *Re Rhodes,* above.

[98] See above, p.541.

though the patient lacks the capacity to consent to it. This question arose in *Re F*[99] where it was held that a sterilisation operation could lawfully be carried on on a mental patient if it was necessary to save her life or to secure an improvement in (or to prevent deterioration of) her health. If the patient *refuses* the treatment, a higher degree of understanding of the nature and consequences of the treatment appears to be required to make the refusal effective (and hence the treatment unlawful) than would be required for the purpose of contractual capacity.[1] The second question is whether the person providing the treatment is entitled to be paid for it. This question does not normally arise where the treatment is carried out under the National Health Service[2]; but it seems that, if necessary services are rendered to a mental patient in circumstances in which a charge would normally be made for them, the person rendering them would be entitled to a reasonable remuneration for them.

A person who lends money to a mental patient knowing of his disorder cannot enforce the contract, but can recover so much of the money as has actually been spent on necessaries.[3]

SECTION 3. DRINK AND DRUGS

Extreme drunkenness is a defence to an action on a contract if it prevents the defendant from understanding the transaction, and if the claimant knows this.[4] The drunkard is liable if he ratifies the contract when he becomes sober.[5] He is also liable for necessaries[6] in the same way as a mental patient.

A defendant cannot rely at law on drunkenness which merely blurred his business sense: but such drunkenness is a ground on which equity may refuse to order specific performance.[7] Nor does a party's habitual drunkenness deprive him of contractual capacity[8] but it could be a ground for relief if the other party had taken over the position of guardian or adviser to the drunkard so as to give rise to a presumption of undue influence between them.[9]

The rules relating to drunkenness could perhaps be applied by analogy to the case of a person whose ability to understand the transaction was impaired by drugs.[10] Such impairment may, indeed, have been brought about by the illegal conduct of that party but this fact should not preclude reliance on the impairment (if known to the other party) since this course of action would not amount either to reliance on the illegality or to enforcement of the contract. Nor is there any good reason for denying a remedy to a supplier of necessaries to such a person, at least where (as will often be the case) the supplier has no connection with the illegality and seeks merely to alleviate the effect of the drugs.

---

[99] [1990] 2 A.C. 1; *cf. Simms v Simms* [2002] EWHC 2734 (Fam), [2003] 1 All E.R. 669.

[1] *Re C (Adult: Refusal of Medical Treatment)* [1994] 1 W.L.R. 290 at 295; *Re B (adult: refusal of medical treatment)* [2002] EWHC 429, Fam; [2000] 1 All E.R. 449, where the patients did have sufficient mental capacity to refuse consent.

[2] [1990] 2 A.C. at p.74. For statutory provisions relating to payment of National Health charges in respect of a "traffic casualty", see Road Traffic (NHS Charges) Act 1999, s.1.

[3] *Re Beavan* [1912] 1 Ch. 196.

[4] *Gore v Gibson* (1843) 13 M. & W. 623.

[5] *Matthews v Baxter* (1873) L.R. 8 Ex. 132.

[6] *Gore v Gibson*, above, at p.626; Sale of Goods Act 1979, s.3(2).

[7] See below, p.1027.

[8] *Irvani v Irvani* [2000] 1 Lloyd's Rep. 412 at 425.

[9] *ibid.*; above, pp.412–414.

[10] The mere fact that a person was an habitual drug addict does not suffice for this purpose: see *Irvani v Irvani*, above, at 425.

SECTION 4. CORPORATIONS

1. Common Law Corporations

Corporations are created at common law by Royal Charter. The orthodox view is that a common law corporation has the same contractual capacity as a natural person of full age and capacity. Although this view is based only on dicta,[11] which have been doubted,[12] it is probably good law. Thus a contract with such a corporation is binding although it is forbidden, or not authorised, by its charter. But if the corporation makes such a contract the Attorney-General can take proceedings for the revocation of its charter; and any member of the corporation can restrain it by injunction from carrying on a forbidden activity which may lead to the revocation of its charter,[13] or claim a declaration that the activity is *ultra vires*.[14]

2. Statutory Corporations

Statutory corporations can be created in two ways: first, by complying with the formalities required by statute; and secondly, by special statute, passed to create the particular corporation in question. Since 1862, most trading companies have been created in the first of these two ways; the principal Act now in force is the Companies Act 1985.

(1) Companies created under the Companies Acts

(a) INTRODUCTION. When a company is incorporated under the Companies Acts, the objects for which it is formed must be stated in its memorandum of association.[15] The contractual capacity of the company was formerly limited by the *ultra vires* doctrine, under which any act which was not authorised by the memorandum was void in law; and, being a nullity, it could not be ratified even by a unanimous vote of the company's shareholders.[16] It followed that the company was not liable on a contract which was not authorised by its memorandum. The primary purpose of the doctrine was to protect investors in the company by giving them some assurance that the assets of the company would not be used in some wholly unexpected way. On the other hand, a person who made a contract with the company was liable to be prejudiced by the doctrine, since he was unlikely to have read the company's memorandum, or (if he had read it) to have understood it. The doctrine could also prejudice the company itself by preventing it from taking advantage of business opportunities which (perhaps as a result of a defect in drafting) fell technically outside its objects. The company could to some extent avoid this prejudice by altering its objects, but its power to make such alterations could be exercised only for seven specified purposes.[17] It could also draw its objects clause in very

---

[11] *Case of Sutton's Hospital* (1613) 10 Co.Rep. 1, 30b; *Wenlock v River Dee Co* (1885) 36 Ch.D. 374 at 385; *British S Africa Co v De Beers Consolidated Mines* [1910] 1 Ch. 354 at 374; *Jenkin v Pharmaceutical Society* [1921] 1 Ch. 392 at 398; *Institution of Mechanical Engineers v Cane* [1961] A.C. 696 at 724; *Hazell v Hammersmith & Fulham LBC* [1992] 2 A.C. 1 at 39. Furmston, 24 M.L.R. 518. See also *Ayers v South Australia Banking Co* (1868) L.R. 3 P.C. 548, which appears to assume the correctness of the generally accepted view; the point is left open in *Crédit Suisse v Allerdale B.C.* [1997] Q.B. 306 at 336. For the possibility that the powers of a charter corporation may be restricted by special legislation, see below, p.564.

[12] *e.g.* Holdsworth, *History of English Law*, Vol.9, pp.55–66; Street, *Ultra Vires*, pp.18–22; Carden, 26 L.Q.R. 320.

[13] *Jenkin v Pharmaceutical Society* [1921] 1 Ch. 392.

[14] *Phamaceutical Society of Great Britain v Dickson* [1970] A.C. 403.

[15] Companies Act 1985, s.2(1)(c).

[16] *Ashbury Ry Carriage & Iron Co v Riche* (1875) L.R. 7 H.L. 653.

[17] Companies Act 1985, s.4 (original version), replaced by the provision referred to at n.22, below.

wide terms, enabling it to do almost any act which could be done by a company[18]; but such very widely drawn clauses tended to be restrictively interpreted by the courts,[19] since they made the protection which the *ultra vires* doctrine was intended to give to shareholders quite illusory.

(b) THE 1989 REFORMS. The effects of the *ultra vires* doctrine, as described above, were subjected to much criticism[20] and significant reforms were introduced by the Companies Act 1989, which inserted a number of new sections into the Companies Act 1985.

In discussing these reforms, two preliminary points should be noted. First, it is now possible to state the object of a company to be "to carry on business as a general commercial company". The object of the company will then be "to carry on any trade or business whatsoever" and also to do "all such things as are incidental or conducive to carrying on any trade or business by it".[21] The *ultra vires* doctrine can have very little scope in the case of a company with such an objects clause. Secondly, a company can now alter its objects for any purpose whatsoever, and not only for the seven purposes for which it could formerly do so.[22]

The legal effects of acts done by the company which are not authorised by its memorandum are dealt with by two new sections (35 and 35A) inserted in 1989[23] into the Companies Act 1985. These two sections are based on a distinction which was recognised in the previous English case law,[24] and was also drawn in an EC Council Directive,[25] implemented by the 1989 Act, between the *capacity* of the company and the *powers* of the board of directors to bind it. The new sections alleviate the hardship which the *ultra vires* doctrine formerly caused to persons who dealt with the company, while retaining some degree of protection for its shareholders.

(i) *The company's capacity.* So far as the company's capacity is concerned, the new s.35(1) of the 1985 Act provides that the validity of any act done by a company is not (as a general rule[26]) to be called into question on the ground of lack of the company's capacity by reason of anything in (or, presumably, not in) its memorandum. The argument that a contract is void for lack of capacity if it is not authorised by the memorandum is thus no longer available. S.35(1) will generally operate in favour of persons who enter into contracts with the company, which can no longer rely on its own lack of capacity (by reason of the provisions of the memorandum) against such persons. It is equally true that these persons cannot rely on such lack of capacity against the company.[27]

Members of the company are, in turn, protected by s.35(2), which gives them the right to bring proceedings to restrain the doing of an act which would (but for s.35(1)) be

---

[18] *Cotman v Brougham* [1918] A.C. 514; *Re Horsley & Weight Ltd* [1982] Ch. 442; *Brady v Brady* [1989] A.C. 755 at 772.

[19] *e.g. Rolled Steel (Holdings) Ltd v BSC* [1986] Ch. 246, drawing the distinction referred to at n.24, below.

[20] See especially Prentice, *Reform of the Ultra Vires Rule*, a consultative paper issued by the Department of Trade and Industry in 1986.

[21] Companies Act 1985, s.3A, as inserted by Companies Act 1989, s.110(1).

[22] Companies Act 1985, s.4, as substituted by Companies Act 1989, s.110(2). In the case of charitable companies, alterations of the memorandum, and of certain provisions of the articles, of association require the consent of the Charity Commissioners: Charities Act 1993, s.64.

[23] By Companies Act 1989, s.108(1).

[24] *Rolled Steel (Holdings) Ltd v BSC* [1986] Ch. 246.

[25] Dir.68/151 Art.9. For the construction of legislation based on such directives, see above p.267, n.29.

[26] For exceptions, see Companies Act 1985, s.35(4) (as substituted by Companies Act 1989, s.108(1) and amended by Charities Act 1993, s.98(1), and Sch.6, para.20) and Charities Act 1993, s.65 (charitable companies and certain transactions with directors).

[27] The phrase "shall not be called into question" in s.35(1) applies equally to both parties. Contrast the wording of s.35A(1), set out at n.31, below.

beyond the company's capacity.[28] But no such proceedings lie in respect of an act to be done in the fulfilment of a legal obligation arising from a previous act of the company, so that proceedings under subs.(2) cannot be brought to prevent the performance of a contract which cannot be called into question on the ground of lack of capacity by virtue of subs.(1). Members of the company are further protected by s.35(3), by which it remains the duty of directors to observe any limitation on their powers flowing from the company's memorandum. An act which transgresses these limitations can indeed be ratified by the company by special resolution, but a separate special resolution is required to relieve the directors from liability in respect of the act.[29]

(ii) *The powers of the directors.* Where a contract is not within the objects clause of the memorandum, the mere fact that it cannot be called into question on the ground of lack of capacity will not enable a person who deals with the company to enforce it; for the making of such an unauthorised contract is necessarily beyond the powers of the directors. Further protection to such a person is therefore given by the new s.35A(1) of the 1985 Act. This provides that, "In favour of a person dealing with a company in good faith, the power of the board of directors to bind the company, or to authorise others to do so, shall [as a general rule[30]] be deemed to be free of any limitation under the company's constitution".[31] The person who deals with the company is not bound to enquire whether the transaction is permitted by the memorandum or whether the power of the directors to bind the company or to authorise others to do so is limited.[32] He is presumed to have acted in good faith until the contrary is proved[33]; and he is not to be regarded as acting in bad faith "by reason *only* of his knowing that an act is beyond the powers of the directors under the company's constitution."[34] This provision allows for the possibility that it may be in the interests of the company to take advantage of a commercial opportunity by entering into a contract which is technically not within its objects. On the other hand, a person would presumably not be dealing with the company in good faith if the transaction in question was not only beyond the powers of the directors but also constituted a breach of their fiduciary duty to it, or was otherwise a collusive attempt on the part of the directors and the person dealing with the company to act in a way that was contrary to the interests of the company. In such a case the fact that a contract was not authorised by the company's memorandum would not, indeed, make it open to challenge on the ground of lack of capacity; but by reason of the element of bad faith the contract would be unenforceable as it was beyond the directors' powers, and it would not be saved by s.35A(1).

Persons who deal with the company are further protected by s.35A(5) which provides that s.35A(1) does not affect any liability incurred by the directors to persons other than members of the company by reason of the directors' exceeding their powers. Where the company is *liable* by virtue of subs.(1), such liability is unlikely to be incurred by the directors[35]; though it is possible for a director to undertake additional personal liability under a collateral contract. Where the company is *not* liable because the person dealing

---

[28] *cf.* the position in the case of charter corporations, above, p.560 at n.13.

[29] Companies Act 1985, s.35(3) (as substituted by Companies Act 1989, s.108(1)).

[30] *ibid.* s.35A(6) (as amended by Charities Act 1993, s.98(1) and Sch.6, para.20) and Charities Act 1993, s.65 (excepting charitable companies and certain transactions with directors).

[31] "Limitation under the company's constitution" is broadly defined in s.35A(3) and includes, *inter alia*, a limitation derived from a resolution of the company in general meeting.

[32] Companies Act 1985, s.35B, and see also s.711A (as substituted by Companies Act 1989, ss.108(1) and 142(1)).

[33] *ibid.* s.35A(2)(c).

[34] *ibid.* s.35A(2)(b) (italics supplied).

[35] *e.g.* the remedy for breach of warranty of authority (below, p.565) would not be available if the contract bound the company under s.35A(1): see below, p.739.

with it did so in bad faith, a claim against the directors is unlikely to succeed: it would probably be dismissed on the analogy of the rule that a contract to defraud a third party (*i.e.* the company) is illegal and void.[36]

Members of the company are protected in that they can bring proceedings to restrain the doing of an act which is beyond the powers of the directors.[37] But no such proceedings lie "in respect of an act to be done in fulfilment of a legal obligation arising from a previous act of the company".[38] Presumably it follows that proceedings cannot be brought to restrain a company from performing a contract which a person dealing with the company could enforce against it under s.35A(1). It seems that such a contract will, by virtue of that subsection, be deemed to be an "act of the company" even though the directors actually had no power to enter into it on the company's behalf.

S.35A(1) only operates "in favour of a person dealing with" the company. It therefore does not confer rights on the company. The company can however acquire such rights by ratifying the transaction.[39]

(2) Limited Liability Partnerships

The Limited Liability Partnerships Act 2000 makes provision[40] for the incorporation of limited liability partnerships by registration of specified documents. Such a partnership is "a body corporate (with legal personality separate from its members)"[41] and "has unlimited capacity".[42] The *ultra vires* doctrine therefore does not apply to it.

(3) Corporations incorporated by special statute

The *ultra vires* doctrine was originally established in relation to such corporations.[43] With respect to them, it is not affected by the reforms which have been described above,[44] though it has been mitigated with respect to certain contracts made by local authorities.[45] Before any of these reforms came into force, many of the rules which determine the scope and effects of the doctrine were laid down in cases arising out of contracts with companies incorporated under the Companies Acts (or with local authorities). These cases are obsolete now that the common law doctrine no longer invalidates such contracts (or has been mitigated with respect to them). But the principles stated in them can still (where appropriate) apply to transactions with other corporations which are created, or whose capacity is limited, by special statute. For this reason, the following account is to some extent based on such cases.

(a) THE ULTRA VIRES DOCTRINE. The contractual capacity of a corporation created by special statute continues, in general,[46] to be restricted by the *ultra vires* doctrine. The objects of such a corporation are set out in the statute by which it was created (or in rules made in pursuance of that statute). Any act done by or on behalf of the corporation which is not authorised by (or under) the incorporating statute is *ultra vires* and

---

[36] See above, p.432.
[37] s.35A(4).
[38] *ibid.*
[39] *Grant v U.K. Switchback Ry* (1888) 40 Ch.D. 135.
[40] Limited Liability Partnerships Act, s.2.
[41] *ibid.*, s.1(2). The general law relating to other partnerships (which do not have legal personality separate from their members) does not apply to limited liability partnerships: *ibid.*, s.1(5).
[42] *ibid.*, s.1(3).
[43] See *Eastern Counties Ry v Hawkes* (1855) 5 H.L.C. 331 at 347–348 (citing earlier cases).
[44] See above, pp.561–563; *Crédit Suisse v Allerdale Borough Council* [1997] Q.B. 306.
[45] Local Government (Contracts) Act 1997.
[46] For a statutory exception, see n.45, above.

ineffective. It follows that an *ultra vires* contract made by such a corporation does not bind the corporation. The corporation can also be restrained from doing *ultra vires* acts.[47] The same rules apply where the corporation has been created in some other way (*e.g.* by Royal Charter) but its capacity is nevertheless defined or limited by statute.[48]

(i) *Whether transaction is ultra vires.* The question whether a particular transaction falls within the powers of the corporation turns in the first place on the construction of the statute[49] by which it is incorporated, or which otherwise defines or limits its capacity. Particular difficulty can arise where the statute, after setting out the specific objects for which the corporation is created, goes on to confer a general power to do other acts which it is necessary or desirable for the company to do in order to achieve these objects. When the *ultra vires* doctrine applied to companies incorporated under the Companies Acts, the courts were faced with similar difficulties arising from analogous, broadly drafted, provisions in memoranda of association.[50] In deciding questions of this kind, they distinguished between the *objects* of a company and its *powers*. They went on to hold that, although powers could be exercised only for the purpose of the objects, their exercise for other purposes was not *ultra vires* but only beyond the powers of the directors; and that their exercise for other purposes could not confer rights on the other party to the transaction if he had notice of the fact that the powers had been so exercised.[51] It is arguable that the same distinction between objects and powers may apply where the officers of a corporation, whose capacity is defined by the incorporating statute, purport to exercise a general power (conferred by the statute) but do so for the purpose of achieving unauthorised objects: *e.g.* where they give a guarantee and it is alleged that the transaction in respect of which it is given is not an authorised object.[52] In the last resort, however, the question in cases of the present kind turns simply on the construction of the relevant legislation. Thus where the corporation was empowered to do "anything . . . which in its opinion is calculated to facilitate the proper discharge of its functions or is incidental or conducive thereto," it was held that a guarantee given by the corporation could not be challenged on the ground that it was *ultra vires*.[53]

(ii) *Incidental objects.* Even in the absence of widely drafted provisions of the kind just discussed, a corporation can do acts which it is not expressly authorised to do, if they are fairly incidental to the objects for which it was established. For example, in *Foster v London, Dover & Chatham Ry*[54] it was held that a railway company could validly grant short leases of the spaces under the arches of a viaduct, so long as those leases did not disable it from carrying on its railway business. But this rule does not enable the corporation to carry on activities substantially distinct from those authorised: thus a corporation authorised to run trams could not "incidentally" run buses.[55]

---

[47] *e.g. L.C.C. v Attorney-General* [1902] A.C. 165.

[48] *e.g. Hazell v Hammersmith and Fulham LBC* [1992] 2 A.C. 1.

[49] *Den Norske Creditbank v The Sarawak Economic Development Corp* [1988] 2 Lloyd's Rep. 616.

[50] See above, p.561, n.18.

[51] *Rolled Steel Products (Holdings) Ltd v BSC* [1986] Ch. 246; *cf.* above, p.561 at n.24. See also *Introductions Ltd v National Provincial Bank Ltd* [1970] Ch. 119; Wedderburn, 32 M.L.R. 563; 46 M.L.R. 204; Gregory, 48 M.L.R. 109.

[52] *Crédit Suisse v Allerdale BC* [1997] Q.B. 306; *Crédit Suisse v Waltham Forest LBC* [1997] Q.B. 362; *Sutton LBC v Morgan Grenfell & Co* (1997) 29 H.L.R. 608; in all these cases, the guarantees were held void.

[53] *Den Norske Creditbank v The Sarawak Economic Development Corp* [1988] 2 Lloyd's Rep. 616 (where the incorporating legislation was a Malaysian Ordinance).

[54] [1895] 1 Q.B. 711; *cf. Charles Roberts & Co v British Railways Board* [1965] 1 W.L.R. 396; and, in the case of certain companies incorporated under the Companies Acts, Companies Act 1985, s.3A(b), as substituted by Companies Act 1989, s.110(1).

[55] *LCC v Attorney-General* [1902] A.C. 165; *cf. Hazell v Hammersmith & Fulham LBC* [1992] 2 A.C. 1.

(iii) *Contracts ex facie intra vires.* A contract which is *ex facie* within the capacity of the corporation is not invalid merely because the corporation uses its proceeds for an *ultra vires* purpose: *e.g.* where an *intra vires* loan is spent on an *ultra vires* purpose.[56] But the corporation would not be bound by the contract if the lender knew that it intended to use the loan for such a purpose, or if he knew facts from which he could reasonably have deduced that the corporation had such an intention.[57]

(b) ALTERNATIVE REMEDIES. Where a transaction with a corporation is *ultra vires*, its invalidity can be a source of hardship to the other party: that party will, for example, have no remedy against the corporation if the corporation defaults on a transaction which has, by reason of market fluctuations, turned out to be disadvantageous to the corporation.[58] In theory, the other party can protect himself against this risk, before entering into the transaction, by reading the statute which defines or limits the corporation's powers. But in practice the other party is unlikely to take this step; and, even if he does take it, he runs the risk that his interpretation of the statute may, in legal proceedings on the contract, be held to have been erroneous. The law to some extent mitigates this hardship by making a number of alternative remedies available to the other party to the transaction.

(i) *Subrogation.* An *ultra vires* lender can recover so much of his loan as is used by the company to pay debts incurred under *intra vires* contracts.[59]

(ii) *Return of money.* Money paid under an *ultra vires* contract is normally recoverable as money paid under a void contract.[60] This remedy is more fully discussed in Chapter 22.[61]

(iii) *Remedy against officers.* A person who is induced to contract with a corporation by the false representation of a director that the contract is *intra vires* may be able to sue the director in tort for deceit or negligence,[62] or in contract for breach of implied warranty of authority.[63] The contractual action lies even though the representation was made innocently and in good faith.[64] It has been held that this remedy is not available if the misrepresentation is one of law[65]; though for reasons given in Chapter 9 the present status of this restriction on the scope of the remedy is open to question.[66] The construction of the company's incorporating statute is a matter of law,[67] so that a director who represents that, on the true construction of the statute, a contract is *intra vires*, makes a representation of law.

An *ultra vires* contractor may, finally, be able to show that the director is personally liable on the contract itself. Intention on the part of an agent to assume personal liability

---

[56] *Re David Payne & Co Ltd* [1904] 2 Ch. 608.
[57] *Re Jon Beauforte Ltd* [1953] Ch. 131; *cf. Introductions Ltd v National Provincial Bank Ltd* [1970] Ch. 199.
[58] *e.g. Hazell v Hammersmith and Fulham Borough Council* [1992] 2 A.C. 1.
[59] *Blackburn BS v Cunliffe, Brooks & Co* (1882) 22 Ch.D. 61; on appeal it was not necessary to decide this point: 9 App.Cas. 857.
[60] *Westdeutsche Landesbank Girozentrale v Islington LBC* [1996] A.C. 669 disagreeing with *Sinclair v Brougham* [1914] A.C. 938 so far as *contra*.
[61] See below, p.1057.
[62] At common law, but not under s.2(1) of the Misrepresentation Act 1967; see above, p.351 at n.98.
[63] See below, p.738.
[64] *Firbank's Executors v Humphreys* (1886) 18 Q.B.D. 54; *cf. Weeks v Propert* (1873) L.R. 8 C.P. 427; *Cherry v Colonial Bank of Australia* (1869) L.R. 3 P.C. 24.
[65] See below, p.739.
[66] See the discussion of *Kleinwort Benson Ltd v Lincoln CC* [1998] 4 All E.R. 513 at p.333 above.
[67] *Rashdall v Ford* (1866) L.R. 2 Eq. 750; *cf. Beattie v Ebury* (1872) L.R. 7 Ch.App. 777; affirmed L.R. 7 H.L. 102.

is readily inferred when the principal is non-existent.[68] Such an inference might also be drawn where the principal exists but lacks capacity to make the contract.

(c) ENFORCEMENT BY THE CORPORATION.[69] The *ultra vires* doctrine normally operates so as to prevent a contract from being enforced *against* the corporation. The authorities provide no clear answer to the question whether the doctrine also precludes enforcement of the contract *by* the corporation.

A similar problem used to arise where a contract with a corporation should have been, but was not, made under its common seal.[70] If such a contract was executory, the company could not enforce it because its own promise, being invalid, was no consideration for that of the other party[71]; but if the corporation actually performed its own invalid promise it thereby provided consideration and so became entitled to enforce the contract.[72] It can be argued that a similar distinction should be applied to *ultra vires* contracts; but it is submitted that the better approach is to ask whether the object of the statutory limitation on the corporation's capacity would be subverted by allowing it to enforce the contract (rather than to ask whether the corporation had provided consideration).[73] Where the corporation wishes to enforce the contract but has *not* yet performed its part, that the object is likely to be subverted by allowing such enforcement, at least if enforcement by the corporation were (as would often be the case)[74] conditional on performance by it. In such cases the corporation would be encouraged to engage in *ultra vires* activity so as to satisfy the condition; and since it should not be given any incentive to engage in such activity, the contract should not be enforceable by it.[75] Where, on the other hand, the corporation *has* performed its part, this argument has no force: enforceability by the corporation could not encourage it to engage in *future ultra vires* activity since (at least in relation to the transaction in question[76]) the *ultra vires* activity has already taken place; and this reasoning gives some support to the view that a corporation which has performed its part of the contract should be able to enforce that contract.[77] But it is submitted that this result should not necessarily follow and that a distinction should be drawn between cases in which the nature of the performance is such that it cannot, and those in which it is such that it can, be restored to the corporation. The first possibility is illustrated by the case in which the corporation has rendered services under an *ultra vires* contract. In such a case, the object of the rule making the contract *ultra vires* is hardly likely to be defeated by allowing the corporation to sue for the agreed price of the services so that there is no strong argument against allowing it to enforce the contract; though the injustice of denying it such a remedy would at least be mitigated by allowing it to claim a reasonable remuneration in respect

---

[68] *Kelner v Baxter* (1866) L.R. 2 C.P. 174; below, p.735.

[69] Furmston, 24 M.L.R. 215.

[70] This formal requirement was abolished by Corporate Bodies Contracts Act 1960.

[71] *Kidderminster Corp v Harwick* (1873) L.R. 9 Ex. 13, above, p.150.

[72] *Fishmongers' Co v Robertson* (1843) 5 Man. & G. 131.

[73] This approach would make it inappropriate to apply to *ultra vires* cases the further rule, laid down in *Ecclesiastical Commissioners v Merral* (1869) L.R. 4 Ex. 162, that a corporation could enforce a contract which should have been (but was not) under seal if the *other* party had done such acts of part performance as made the contract enforceable against the corporation.

[74] See below, pp.762–763; exceptions would be cases of independent promises (below, pp.763–764) and of accepted anticipatory breach (below, pp.767, 849, 863–864).

[75] See *Pellatt's Case* (1867) L.R. 2 Ch.App. 527; *Triggs v Staines Urban DC* [1969] Ch. 10; *Bell Houses Ltd v City Wall Properties Ltd* [1966] 1 Q.B. 207 (reversed [1966] 2 Q.B. 656 on the ground that the contract was *intra vires*).

[76] *Bell Houses Ltd v City Wall Properties Ltd* [1966] 2 Q.B. 656 at 694.

[77] Future *ultra vires* transactions could be restrained: above, p.562 at n.28.

of services rendered by it under a void contract.[78] The second possibility can be illustrated by supposing that the corporation has purported to sell an article which it was by its incorporating statute prohibited from selling,[79] and that it had actually delivered that article to the buyer. The object of the statute would, it is submitted, be more effectively promoted by allowing the corporation to sue for the return of the article than by allowing it to sue for the price, or for damages for non-acceptance of the subject-matter of the sale.[80] This argument is supported by a group of cases in which moneys had been paid both by and to corporations under *ultra vires* contracts and it was held that the payments must be returned to the corporation where it was the payor[81] and by the corporation where it was the payee.[82] It must follow from these cases that the corporation could not have enforced the contracts by claiming the money or damages for failure to pay it; and emphatic statements in them that the contracts were "wholly void"[83] and "devoid of any legal contractual effects"[84] lend further support to the view that an *ultra vires* contract cannot be enforced by, any more than against the corporation.

---

[78] On the principle of *Craven-Ellis v Cannons Ltd* [1936] 2 K.B. 403, below p.1063.

[79] *e.g.* British Museum Act 1963, s.3(4), as amended by Museums and Galleries Act 1992 s.11(2) and Sch.8, para.5.

[80] *cf.* the suggestion in the *Bell Houses* case, above, at first instance that the corporation's remedy should be in quasi contract (though this would not be a possible remedy for the recovery of goods in specie).

[81] *South Tyneside MBC v Svenska International plc* [1995] 1 All E.R. 545; *Kleinwort Benson Ltd v Lincoln CC* [1999] 2 A.C. 349 at 416.

[82] *e.g. Westdeutsche Landesbank Girozentrale v. Islington LBC* [1996] A.C. 669; *Guiness Mahon & Co Ltd v Kensington & Chelsea Royal Borough Council* [1999] Q.B. 215; *Kleinwort Benson Ltd v Lincoln CC* [1999] 2 A.C. 349 below, p.1059.

[83] *Morgan Grenfell & Co Ltd v Welwyn Hatfield DC* [1995] 1 All E.R. 1 at 4.

[84] *Guiness Mahon* case, above, n.82, at p.284.

CHAPTER FOURTEEN

PLURALITY OF PARTIES

A PROMISE may be made by or to more than one person. Such a promise must be distinguished from a multilateral contract.[1] If three persons agree to run a race subject to certain rules, there are three side to the contract, but each side consists of only one person.[2] If two persons promise to pay a third £10, or if one person promises to pay £10 to two others, there may only be two sides to the contract, one consisting of two persons and the other of one person. This Chapter is concerned with promises of this kind.

SECTION 1. PLURALITY OF DEBTORS[3]

1. Definitions

If A and B *each separately* promise to pay C £10 this does not amount to one promise by several to one, but to two independent promises. Thus C is entitled to £10 from A and a further £10 from B. This was, for example, the position where C granted licences to A and B under agreements providing for payment of a weekly sum by each of them,[4] and where a group of Lloyd's underwriters issued an insurance policy to an assured by which they bound themselves "each for his own part and not one for another".[5] There may be two such separate promises even where both are contained in the same document.[6]

If A and B *together* promise to pay £10, the promise may be join, or joint and several. It is joint if A and B make only one promise binding both of them; it is joint and several if they make one promise binding both of them and if in addition each makes a separate promise binding him alone. A joint and several promise is distinguishable from two entirely separate promises in that it does not involve the promisors in cumulative liability. If A and B jointly and severally promise to pay C £10, C is not entitled to more than £10 in all. It is a question of construction whether a promise is joint, or joint and several.[7] A promise by two persons together is deemed to be joint, unless it is qualified in some way.[8] To make a promise joint and several, it is advisable to say expressly "we promise jointly and severally," or "we, and each of us, will pay". But this is not the only way of creating joint and several liability. In *Tippins v Coates*[9] three persons executed a bond by which they bound themselves "jointly and our respective heirs." This was held to be a joint and several promise, since that was evidently the intention of the parties:

---

[1] See above, p.77.
[2] *cf. Rockeagle Ltd v Alsop Wilkinson* [1992] Ch. 47 at 50 ("tripartite agreement").
[3] Williams, *Joint Obligations.*
[4] *Mikeover v Brady* [1989] 3 All E.R. 618.
[5] *Touche Ross & Co v Colin Baker* [1992] 2 Lloyd's Rep. 207 at 209; *cf.* Lloyd's Act 1982, s.8.
[6] *Collins v Prosser* (1823) 1 B. & C. 682; *Gibson v Lupton* (1832) 9 Bing. 297; *Lee v Nixon* (1834) 1 A. & E. 201.
[7] *cf.* Bills of Exchange Act 1882, s.85(1) ("according to its tenour").
[8] *Levy v Sale* (1877) 37 L.T. 709; *White v Tyndall* (1888) 13 App.Cas. 263; *The Argo Hellas* [1984] 1 Lloyd's Rep. 296 at 300.
[9] (1853) 18 Beav. 401.

if it were held to be a joint bond, the *respective* heirs of the promisors would not be bound, but only the heir of the survivor.[10]

In some cases the question of whether liability is joint, or joint and several, is expressly dealt with by statute. For example, s.9 of the Partnership Act 1890, provides that "every partner in a firm is liable jointly with the other partners . . . for all debts and obligations of the firm incurred while he is a partner". On the other hand promissory notes made by a number of persons are deemed to be joint and several.[11]

2. Differences Between Joint, and Joint and Several, Promises

(1) Parties to the action

At common law, an action on a *joint* promise had to be brought against all the surviving joint debtors.[12] If this was not done the defendants could plead the non-joinder of their co-debtors in abatement. Although pleas in abatement no longer exist, it is still the general rule that the action must be brought against all the joint debtors.[13] But the court has a discretion to allow the action to proceed against one joint debtor if the other is out of the jurisdiction, or cannot be traced.[14] If one joint debtor is bankrupt, the other or others may be sued without him.[15]

An action on a *joint and several* promise could at common law be brought against one or all the co-debtors but not, it seems, against some (but not all). The creditor could either sue each debtor individually on his several promise or all on their joint promise; but he could not, by suing some, treat the contract as joint without also joining all the others.[16] It seems that in such a case the court now has a discretion to order all the other joint and several debtors to be joined to the action since it may order the names of persons to be joined to an action if their presence is "desirable . . . so that the court can resolve all matters in dispute in the proceedings".[17] The court might order such joinder so that the amount of the debt may be conclusively established for the purpose of the contribution[18] between all the debtors. It seems that the onus is on the debtor who is sued to bring his co-debtors before the court as third parties, with a view to claiming contribution from them.[19]

(2) Judgment

If one *joint* debtor is sued alone and does not plead non-joinder of the others, judgment may be given against him alone. After the creditor had recovered such a judgment, it was formerly the rule that he could not take further proceedings against any of the other joint debtors (even though the judgment remained unsatisfied) because the original cause of action was merged in the judgment.[20] This rule was, however, likely to cause hardship

---

[10] See below, p.570.

[11] Bills of Exchange Act 1882, s.85(2); see also Law of Property Act 1925, s.119; Landlord and Tenant (Covenants) Act 1995, s.13(1).

[12] *Cabell v Vaughan* (1669) 1 Wms.Saund. 291; *Richards v Heather* (1817) 1 B. & Ald. 29.

[13] *Norbury, Natzio & Co Ltd v Griffiths* [1918] 2 K.B. 369; it is up to the defendant to take the point; *Wegg-Prosser v Evans* [1895] 1 Q.B. 108. And see CPR, r.19.2(1).

[14] *Wilson, Sons & Co Ltd v Balcarres Brook SS Co Ltd* [1893] 1 Q.B. 422; *Robinson v Geisel* [1894] 2 Q.B. 685.

[15] Insolvency Act 1986 s.345(4).

[16] *Cabell v Vaughan* (1669) 1 Wms.Saund. 291, n.4.

[17] CPR, r.19.2(2)(a).

[18] See below, p.574.

[19] *cf. Wilson, Sons & Co Ltd v Balcarres Brook SS Co Ltd*, above, n.14, at p.428 (where the contract was joint).

[20] *Kendall v Hamilton* (1879) 4 App.Cas. 504.

to the creditor; and it has been abolished by statute,[21] so that a creditor is no longer precluded from suing one joint debtor merely because he has previously obtained a judgment against another.

Where the contract is *joint and several*, judgment against one debtor was never regarded as a bar to proceedings against another. Each is liable on his separate promise, as well as on the joint promise: hence there are several causes of action only some of which are merged in the first judgment.[22] A claim against joint and several debtors is barred only if one of them satisfies it, whether under a judgment or otherwise.

(3) Survivorship

At common law the liability of a *joint* debtor passed on his death to the surviving joint debtors.[23] The creditor therefore had no claim against the estate of the deceased, but only one against the surviving joint debtors. If they paid, they might be able to recover contribution from the estate of the deceased[24]; but the creditor himself had no direct right against the estate. On the death of the last surviving joint debtor, the creditor could recover the debt from his estate.[25]

On the death of a *joint and several* debtor, on the other hand, his several (though not his joint) liability remained enforceable against his estate.[26]

The rule that joint liability passed to the surviving debtors might be convenient where the debtors were engaged in administering a trust, but it was highly inconvenient in commercial affairs. If only one of a number of joint debtors was solvent, and that one happened to die, the creditor would lose all substantial remedy. The difficulty was particularly acute in partnership cases. Equity therefore treated partnership debts as joint and several to this extent, that they could be enforced against the estate of a deceased partner.[27] This rule is confirmed by s.9 of the Partnership Act 1890.[28]

The equitable right to enforce a joint debt against the estate of a deceased joint contractor was applied mainly in partnership cases, but there is some authority for saying that it was not confined to such cases, nor even to cases involving mercantile transactions.[29] It is therefore arguable that, on the question of survivorship, there was, before the Judicature Act 1873, a conflict between common law and equity, so that equity now prevails.[30] It is also arguable that the principle of survivorship has been abolished by s.1(1) of the Law Reform (Miscellaneous Provisions) Act 1934, which provides that all causes of action subsisting against a person at the time of his death shall (with certain exceptions) survive against the estate. The object of this provision was to abolish the common law rule that actions *in tort* could not be brought against the estate of a deceased tortfeasor; but its words seem apt to abolish the rule that the liability of a joint debtor

---

[21] Civil Liability (Contribution) Act 1978, ss.3, 7(1). For a situation not covered by these provisions, see *The Argo Hellas* [1984] 1 Lloyd's Rep. 296 at 304. S.3 also does not apply where a debt is discharged by an accord and satisfaction which is later embodied in a court order: *Morris v Molesworth* [1998] N.L.J. 1551. See also CPR, r.12.8 (default judgment).

[22] *Blyth v Fladgate* [1891] 1 Ch. 337.

[23] *Cabell v Vaughan* (1669) 1 Wms.Saund. 291, n.4(*f*); *Godson v Good* (1816) 6 Taunt. 587 at 594.

[24] *Batard v Hawes* (1853) 2 E. & B. 287; below, p.574.

[25] *Calder v Rutherford* (1822) 3 Brod. & B. 302.

[26] *Read v Price* [1909] 1 K.B. 577.

[27] See *Kendall v Hamilton* (1879) 4 App.Cas. 504 at 517. Lord Mansfield had anticipated the equitable rule: *Rice v Shute* (1770) 5 Burr. 2611 at 2613.

[28] But under this section separate debts of a deceased partner must be paid in priority to the partnership debts.

[29] *Thorpe v Jackson* (1837) 2 Y. & C. Ex. 553.

[30] Judicature Act 1873, s.25(11); now Supreme Court Act 1981, s.49(1).

passed on his death to the surviving joint debtors (so that it could no longer be enforced against his estate).

3. Similarities Between Joint, and Joint and Several, Promises

(1) Defence of one

If one of several co-debtors has a defence to the action, the question whether that defence also avails the others depends on its nature. If it goes to the root of the claim, and wholly destroys it, the other debtors can take advantage of it. Thus they can do so if one co-debtor can prove that the debt has been paid, or that the creditor is not entitled to payment because of his own breach of contract, or that a written contract is a forgery, or that the creditor was guilty of fraud.[31] But if the defence is personal to one co-debtor, *e.g.* that he was a minor or that he had been discharged as a result of bankruptcy proceedings, it does not avail the other as co-debtors.[32]

Special rules apply to contracts of guarantee, under which the guarantor generally undertakes joint and several liability with the principal debtor.[33] It has been held that the guarantor is not liable if the principal debt is illegal,[34] or if the principal debtor has been discharged as a result of the creditor's breach.[35] A guarantor of a debt that was unenforceable under the Moneylenders Acts was not liable on the guarantee[36]; and the Consumer Credit Act 1974 (which repeals those Acts) lays down a similar rule in the case of a guarantee given in respect of a regulated agreement.[37] These rules cannot be deduced from the general principles governing joint and several contracts, but appear to be based on considerations of policy.[38] It is obviously undesirable to allow a person who lends for an illegal purpose, or a lender who tries to evade the Consumer Credit Act, to recover his loan from any person whatsoever.

On the other hand, a guarantee may be valid where the principal debtor is a corporation acting *ultra vires*. Whether it is actually valid depends on its construction: did the guarantor undertake to pay only what the corporation could lawfully be required to pay, or what it had in fact promised to pay?[39] Where the principal debt is incurred by a company incorporated under the Companies Acts, the validity of that debt can no longer (as a general rule) be called into question on the ground of lack of the company's capacity by reason of anything in its memorandum[40]; it follows that the guarantee cannot be called into question on this ground. The position is the same where the principal debt arises out of a contract which is made by a person dealing with the company in good faith, but which is, under the company's constitution, beyond the power of the board of directors: in favour of the other contracting party, the power of the board is (as a general

---

[31] *Porter v Harris* (1663) 1 Lev. 63; *Gardner v Walsh* (1855) 5 E. & B. 83; *Pirie v Richardson* [1927] 1 K.B. 448.

[32] *Burgess v Merrill* (1812) 4 Taunt. 468; *Gillow v Lillie* (1835) 1 Bing.N.C. 695; *Lovell & Christmas v Beauchamp* [1894] A.C. 607; *King v Hoare* (1844) 3 M. & W. 494 at 506; *Pirie v Richardson* [1927] 1 K.B. 448, *cf. Chaplin v Leslie Frewin (Publishers) Ltd* [1966] Ch. 71.

[33] *e.g. Anderson v Martindale* (1801) 1 East 497; *Re W E A, a Debtor* [1901] 2 K.B. 642; *Read v Price* [1909] 1 K.B. 577.

[34] *Swan v Bank of Scotland* (1836) 10 Bli.(N.S.) 627; *Heald v O'Connor* [1971] 1 W.L.R. 497.

[35] *Unity Finance Ltd v Woodcock* [1963] 1 W.L.R. 455, explained on another ground in *Goulston Discount Co Ltd v Clark* [1967] 2 Q.B. 493.

[36] *Eldridge & Morris v Taylor* [1931] 2 K.B. 416; *Temperance Loan Fund Ltd v Rose* [1932] 2 K.B. 522.

[37] s.113(1) and (2); see above, p.178 for the meaning of "regulated" agreement.

[38] Mitchell, (1947) 63 L.Q.R. 354.

[39] *Yorks Ry & Wagon Co v McLure* (1882) 21 Ch.D. 309; *Garrard v James* [1925] Ch. 616, as explained in *Heald v O'Connor* [1971] 1 W.L.R. 497.

[40] Companies Act 1985, s.35(1) (as substituted by Companies Act 1989, s.108(1)); above, p.561.

rule) deemed to be free from any limitation under the company's constitution,[41] so that the contract giving rise to the debt, and consequently also the guarantee, cannot be challenged on the ground that it was beyond the powers of the board. The general rule is that the principal contract will be invalid only if the other party to it dealt with the company in bad faith; and mere knowledge of the fact that the contract was beyond the powers of the directors is not sufficient to constitute bad faith.[42] It seems that some kind of actual dishonesty is required to constitute bad faith; and if the principal transaction is invalid on this ground, then it is submitted that the guarantee should also be invalid. This submission is based on the analogy of the rule relating to illegal contracts,[43] for the principal contract in our last example would be, or would come close to being, one to defraud the company.[44] The only other situations in which the principal contract is now likely to be invalid on the ground that it is *ultra vires* are (i) those in which a statutory corporation was not incorporated under the Companies Act, so that the common law doctrine of *ultra vires* still applied to it,[45] and (ii) those in which, though the company was incorporated under those Acts, the statutory modifications of the *ultra vires* doctrine, described above, exceptionally do not apply.[46] If in such cases the creditor is induced to enter into the contract in reliance on a guarantee given by one of the corporation's directors or officers, it is submitted that the guarantor should be liable on the guarantee: there seems to be no ground of policy for allowing him to rely on the invalidity of the principal debt.

Similar policy considerations apply where the principal debtor is a minor: it would be wrong to allow the guarantor on this ground to escape from a liability deliberately undertaken since such a result would not be necessary for the protection of minors. It has therefore been provided by statute that the guarantee shall not be unenforceable against the guarantor merely because the principal obligation was unenforceable against the debtor because he was a minor when he incurred it.[47]

(2) Release of one

If the creditor releases one co-debtor, the release is available for the benefit of all the others since it wholly destroys the cause of action.[48] At first sight, the application of this rule to joint and several debtors looks illogical, since there are several causes of action against them; but it may be justified on the ground that it would make the release partly futile to hold that only one of the co-debtors was released. If the others could still be sued, they could claim contribution from the one who had been released, who would thus indirectly be made liable, notwithstanding the release.[49] But in spite of this

---

[41] *ibid.* s.35A(1), above, p.561.

[42] *ibid.* s.35A(2)(b).

[43] See above, at n.34.

[44] *cf.* above, p.432.

[45] See above, p.563; subject to the exceptions there stated relating to local authorities.

[46] Companies Act 1985, ss.35(4) and 35A(6) (as substituted by Companies Act 1989, s.108(1) and amended by Charities Act 1993 s.98(1) and Sch.6, para.20) and Charities Act 1993, s.65 (charitable companies and certain transactions with directors).

[47] Minors Contracts Act 1987, s.2 (reversing *Coutts & Co v Browne-Lecky* [1947] K.B. 104); and see s.4, amending Consumer Credit Act 1974, s.113(7).

[48] *Nicholson v Revill* (1836) 4 A. & E. 675; *Re E.W.A.* [1901] 2 K.B. 642; *Morris v Molesworth* [1998] N.L.J. 1551. For a statutory exception (the details of which are beyond the scope of this book), see Landlord and Tenant (Covenants) Act 1995, s.13(2). In tort, the rule applies where the liability is joint: *New Zealand Guardian Trust Ltd v Brooks* [1995] 1 W.L.R. 96; and where it is concurrent *Jameson v CEGB* [2000] 1 A.C. 455.

[49] *Jenkins v Jenkins* [1928] 2 K.B. 501 at 508.

argument, a covenant not to sue a single co-debtor releases him alone and does not release the other co-debtors.[50]

It used to be thought that a release granted to one co-debtor released the others even though it reserved the creditor's rights against them.[51] But the courts originally evaded this rule by distinguishing between a release and a covenant not to sue. The former released all the co-debtors; the latter released only the debtor with whom it was made.[52] The distinction turned on the construction of the document and the present approach is to go directly to the question of construction without first distinguishing between "release" and "covenant not to sue".[53] Accordingly, if the document releases one co-debtor but reserves the creditor's rights against the other or others, the courts will give effect to the intention of the parties as so expressed.[54] But a document which simply released one co-debtor without expressly or impliedly[55] reserving the creditor's rights against the others would still wholly extinguish those rights.[56]

The rules discussed above apply only to release by act of the parties. Where one co-debtor is released by operation of law (*e.g.* by an order of discharge in bankruptcy) the others are not released.[57] If the creditor appoints one co-debtor his executor, both the co-debtor and the others are released when probate is obtained. The reason for this rule is that "the debt is deemed to have been paid by the debtor [*qua* debtor] to himself as executor" and thus discharged.[58] In equity the executor is then deemed to have the amount of the debt in his hands as assets of the testator, and is thus accountable for it to the estate.[59]

Problems similar to those discussed above can arise where A and B are not joint, or joint and several, debtors but are persons who have entered into, and then broken, two entirely separate contracts with C.[60] The losses suffered by C in consequence of these breaches may be related: *e.g.* where A and B are associated companies and A's wrongful termination of an agency contract with C on the ground of C's alleged but unsubstantiated misconduct leads B wrongfully to terminate a similar (but not identical) contract, also with C.[61] An agreement by which C settles his claim against A may be expressed to release C's claim against A in respect of loss suffered by C by reason, not only of A's, but also of B's, wrongful termination of the contracts with C[62]; and the effect, if any, of this agreement of C's claim against B depends on its construction.[63] If

---

[50] See the authorities cited in n.52, below.

[51] *Nicholson v Revill* (1836) 4 A. & E. at p.683.

[52] *Hutton v Eyre* (1815) 6 Taunt. 289; *Kearsley v Cole* (1846) 16 M. & W. 128 at 136; *Webb v Hewitt* (1857) 3 K. & J. 438; *Ex p. Good* (1876) 5 Ch.D. 46; *Re Wolmerhausen* (1890) 62 L.T. 541. In *Duck v Mayeu* [1892] 2 Q.B. 511 and *Gardiner v Moore* [1969] 1 Q.B. 55 the same rule was applied in tort; the latter case also shows that reservation of the rights against one of the persons liable may be implied; for such an implied reservation, see also *Finley v Connell Associates* [1999] Lloyd's Rep. P.N. 895.

[53] *Johnson v Davies* [1999] Ch. 117 at 127–128, following *Watts v Aldington, The Times*, December 16, 1993.

[54] *Johnson v Davies*, above; for earlier cases reaching the same conclusion, see *Price v Barker* (1855) 4 E. & B. 760; *Appleby Estates Co v De Bernales* [1947] Ch. 217 (tort); *cf. Banco Santander SA v Bayfern Ltd* [2000] 1 All E.R. (Comm) 776 at 780 (release of one joint and several debtor by assignment of the creditor's right to that one).

[55] See *Gardiner v Moore*, above, n.52.

[56] *cf. Cutler v McPhail* [1962] 2 Q.B. 292; *cf. Deanplan Ltd v Mahmoud* [1993] Ch. 151 (where the liability of successive assignees of a lease was cumulative).

[57] Insolvency Act 1986, s.281(7); *Re Garner's Motors Ltd* [1937] Ch. 594.

[58] *Jenkins v Jenkins* [1928] 2 K.B. 501 at 509; Limitation (Amendment) Act 1980, s.10.

[59] *Jenkins v Jenkins*, above, at p.509; *Commissioner of Stamp Duties v Bone* [1977] A.C. 511.

[60] For the distinction between the two types of promises, see above, p.568.

[61] As in *Heaton v Axa Equity and Law Life Assurance Society plc* [2002] UKHL 15, [2002] 2 All E.R. 961.

[62] As in the *Heaton* case, above, where A's (unsubstantiated) allegations of misconduct may also have influenced B.

[63] *ibid.* at [8], [9], [27], [41].

it meant that the sum paid in pursuance of it were intended to represent the full amount of C's loss, resulting from both breaches, then C, having been fully compensated for that loss by A, would have no further claim in respect of it against B.[64] But such an agreement to release A from liability for A's breach will not bar C's claim against B in respect of other causes of action (than B's breach of contract) which C may have against B or in respect of loss caused by B's breach to the extent to which that loss was attributable to B's (rather than to A's) breach.[65] The only effect of C's settlement with A on such a claim results from the principle that C cannot recover twice over the same loss: that is, C must give credit to B for sums paid by A under the settlement so far as they represent the loss suffered by C as a result of B's breach[66] for which A nevertheless accepted liability on the ground that this breach was a consequence of A's prior breach.

(3) Contribution

If one co-debtor, being liable to pay the entire debt,[67] has paid it in full, he is entitled to recover contribution from the others.[68] *Prima facie*, he is entitled to recover from each co-debtor the amount of the debt divided by the number of co-debtors. If one of the co-debtors has died, his estate is liable to contribute, even if he was a joint debtor. The general rule may be varied by the terms of the contract or by the bankruptcy of one co-debtor.

(a) TERMS OF THE CONTRACT. The co-debtors can make any provision they like as to contribution. Where the co-debtors are principal debtor and surety, it is implied that the surety, if called on to pay, is entitled to be wholly indemnified by the principal debtor. Conversely, if the principal debtor pays the whole debt, he has no right of contribution against the surety. Several sureties for the same debt are *prima facie* entitled *inter se* to contribution in proportion to their number; but where one surety (A) promises to pay only if neither the debtor nor another surety (B) does so, and B pays on the debtor's default, then B will not be entitled to contribution from A.[69]

(b) BANKRUPTCY. At common law, the rule that the amount of contribution was the amount of the debt divided by the number of co-debtors prevailed even though some of the co-debtors were insolvent.[70] Equity adopted the fairer rule that the amount of contribution was the amount of the debt divided by the number of sureties who were *solvent* when the right to contribution arose.[71] This equitable rule now prevails.[72]

---

[64] *ibid.* at [8].

[65] This was the outcome in the *Heaton* case, above.

[66] In the *Heaton* case, C accepted the need to give credit for such sums (paid by A) in their claim against B and this concesssion was evidently regarded as correct by Lord Mackay at [47], with whose reasoning Lords Bingham, Steyn and Hutton agreed.

[67] For this requirement, see *Legal & General Assurance Society v Drake Insurance Co Ltd* [1992] Q.B. 887 where a debtor who was liable for only part of the debt, but had paid it in full, was held not to be entitled to contribution. Where a guarantee provided for payment on demand and one guarantor paid more than his share before any such demand had been made, he was nevertheless held entitled to contribution as the payment had not been made "officiously" and the making of the demand was said not to be a "condition precedent" of his liability: *Stimson v Smith* [1999] 2 All E.R. 833.

[68] *e.g. Davitt v Titcumb* [1990] Ch. 110 at 117.

[69] *Scholefield Goodman & Sons Ltd v Zyngier* [1986] A.C. 562.

[70] *Lowe v Dixon* (1885) 16 Q.B.D. 455 at 458.

[71] *Hitchman v Stewart* (1855) 3 Drew. 271.

[72] *Lowe v Dixon*, above. The rules as to assessment of contribution laid down in Civil Liability (Contribution) Act 1978, s.2 do not alter this position: they apply to *damages* but not to *debts*; for this distinction, *cf.* below, pp.1013–1014.

SECTION 2. PLURALITY OF CREDITORS

1. Definitions

If X promises to pay A and B £10, he may make two separate promises, under which A and B are entitled to £10 *each*, so that X's total liability is to pay £20. No special problems arise out of such promises. But if X makes only one promise to A and B, so that he is liable to pay only £10 in all, it becomes important to determine whether his promise to A and B is made to them jointly, or whether it is made to them severally. At common law, the question whether a contract was made with two persons jointly or with them severally depended on the wording of the contract, and on the interests of the parties in enforcing it.

If the contract was made with a number of persons "jointly" and their interests were joint, it was a joint contract[73]; if it was made with a number of persons severally, *i.e.* "with them and each of them" and their interests were several, it was a several contract.[74] If the contract was ambiguous, or did not state whether it was joint and several, then it was joint if the interests of the creditors were joint, and otherwise several.[75] The interests of the creditors were joint if each had the same interest in the performance of the contract, even though they had separate interests in the property affected. Hence a covenant to repair made with a number of lessors jointly was joint, though they did not hold the land jointly, but in common, so that their interests in it were several.[76] On the other hand, where land was sold by tenants in common and the purchaser promised to pay them the price in fixed proportions corresponding with their shares in the land, the promise was regarded as several.[77] The position was less clear where the contract was expressly joint and the interests several, or conversely; but the prevailing view appears to be that the court would give effect to the intention of the parties, as expressed in the agreement.[78] The common law did not originally recognise the possibility that a promise *to* a number of persons could be joint *and* several.[79] The possibility was, however, recognised in the late nineteenth century[80]; and the question is now of little importance as s.81 of the Law and Property Act 1925 provides that a covenant, and a contract made under seal[81] and a bond or obligation under seal made with two or more persons jointly, shall, if made after 1925, "be construed as being also made with each of them"[82] unless a contrary intention is expressed; where the instrument is executed by an individual, s.1 of the Law of Property (Miscellaneous Provisions) Act 1989 provides that it need no longer be sealed: execution as a deed in accordance with the requirements of that section is sufficient.[83] Such covenants, etc., are now *prima*

---

[73] *cf. Sorsbie v Park* (1843) 12 M. & W. 146 at 158.

[74] *James v Emery* (1818) 5 Price 529.

[75] *e.g. Anderson v Martindale* (1801) 1 East 487; *Palmer v Mallett* (1887) 36 Ch.D. 411.

[76] *Bradburne v Botfield* (1845) 14 M. & W. 559; *Thompson v Hakewill* (1865) 19 C.B.(N.S.) 713. For the position between the tenants in common *inter se*, see *Beer v Beer* (1852) 12 C.B. 60.

[77] *James v Emery* (1818) 5 Price 529.

[78] *Sorsbie v Park* (1843) 12 M. & W. 146 at 158; *Keightley v Watson* (1849) 3 Ex. 716; *Beer v Beer* (1852) 12 C.B. 60; for the earlier view that the interest of the parties was always decisive, see *Slingsby's Case* (1588) 5 Co. Rep. 18b; *Withers v Bircham* (1824) 3 B. & C. 254 at 256; *Hopkinson v Lee* (1845) 6 Q.B. 964.

[79] *Slingsby's Case*, above; *Anderson v Martindale*, above; *Bradburne v Botfield* (1854) 14 M. & W. 559 at 573; *Keightley v Watson*, above, at 723 (criticising the rule).

[80] *Thompson v Hakewill* (1865) 19 C.B.N.S., 713 at 726; *Palmer v Mallett* (1887) 36 Ch.D. 410 at 421.

[81] See now Law of Property (Miscellaneous Provisions) Act 1989, s.1(7).

[82] Re-enacting, with some changes, Conveyancing Act 1881, s.60. The section does not affect the law relating to joint *debtors*: *Johnson v Davies* [1999] Ch. 117 at 127.

[83] Law of Property (Miscellaneous Provisions) Act 1989, s.1(8) and Sch.1. And see above, pp.158–159 for execution of deeds by corporations.

facie joint and several.[84] S.81 of the 1925 Act applies only promises in deeds[85]; its object seems to have been to avoid in relation to such promises the common law rule that on the death of a joint creditor his rights passed by survivorship[86] to the other or others. In this respect, it resembles the rule under which a contract for the repayment of money lent by a number of lenders was presumed in equity to create a several right in each lender, even though under the common law rules the contract was joint.[87] The presumption could be rebutted, *e.g.* if the lenders were trustees[88]; here survivorship was administratively convenient, and created no substantive injustice. It seems that promises regarded as several under s.81 and under the equitable presumption will be so regarded not only for the purpose of limiting the doctrine of survivorship,[89] but also for the other purposes to be discussed below.

2. Parties to the Action

Where a promise is made to a number of persons *jointly*, all of them (if living) must be parties to the action.[90] If one joint creditor is unwilling to join, the one wishing to sue must offer him an indemnity as to costs; if he still refuses to join he can then be added as co-defendant.[91]

Where a promise is made to two or more persons *severally* an action can be brought by one or more of them: it is not necessary to join them all.[92]

3. Survivorship

On the death of a *joint* creditor, his rights pass to his surviving co-creditors.[93] On the death of a *several* creditor, his rights pass, not to his co-creditors, but to his personal representatives.[94]

4. Defence Against One

Where a contract is *joint*, a defence available against one creditor can be raised against the others if it goes to the root of the claim. For example, "when two persons are jointly insured and their interests are inseparably connected, so that a loss or gain necessarily affects them both, the misconduct of one is sufficient to contaminate the whole

---

[84] See *Josselson v Borst* [1938] 1 K.B. 723; for a statutory exception, see Law of Property Act 1925, s.119 (covenants with several mortgagees deemed to be joint).

[85] The primary meaning of "covenant" is a promise by deed: see *Rank Xerox Ltd v Lane* (*Inspector of Taxes*) [1981] A.C. 629 at 639. It seems that in Law of Property Act 1925, s.81, "covenant" refers to a promise which would not be binding unless it were under seal, and "contract . . . under seal" to one which would be binding even if it were not sealed.

[86] See below.

[87] *Steeds v Steeds* (1889) 22 Q.B.D. 537.

[88] *ibid.* at 542.

[89] This seems to have been the sole effect of Conveyancing Act 1881, s.60, but that section did not include the words quoted in the text at n.82, above.

[90] *Jell v Douglas* (1821) 4 B. & Ald. 374; *Sorsbie v Park* (1843) 12 M. & W. 146; *Thompson v Hakewill* (1865) 19 C.B.(N.S.) 713.

[91] *Cullen v Knowles* [1898] 2 Q.B. 380; no such indemnity need be offered to one joint creditor who is guilty of a fraud on the other: *Johnson v Stephens & Carter Ltd* [1923] 2 K.B. 857. If a joint creditor is added as co-defendant without being offered such an indemnity, the only person who can object is that joint creditor, and not the debtor; *Burnside v Harrison Marks Productions Ltd* [1968] 1 W.L.R. 728.

[92] *James v Emery* (1818) 5 Price 529; *Keightley v Watson* (1849) 3 Ex. 716; *Palmer v Mallett* (1887) 36 Ch.D. 411.

[93] *Anderson v Martindale* (1801) 1 East 497.

[94] *Withers v Bircham* (1824) 3 B. & C. 254.

insurance".[95] It seems, although there is no authority precisely in point, that a defence available against one joint creditor does not avail against the other if it is purely personal to the first. Thus, if the debtor can plead *ultra vires* against one joint creditor,[96] he may remain liable to the others.

Where a contract is *several*, a defence available against one creditor cannot be raised against the others. In *Hagedorn v Bazett*[97] an insurance of cargo covered goods some of which belonged to British subjects, some to neutrals and some to an alien enemy. It was held that the policy amounted to a number of separate policies, one with each owner, and was not wholly vitiated by the fact that one of the owners was an alien enemy. "There was no common or joint interest in the whole of the property insured subsisting in the different individuals, nor was there any fraud".[98] The reason why fraud would have vitiated the whole insurance is that the fraud referred to was that of the common agent of all the parties, and thus imputable to them all. It does not follow that the fraud of one several creditor is a defence against others to whom it cannot be imputed. Had the policy been joint (as it might have been if a single item jointly owned by the promisees had been its subject-matter), the fact that one of the owners was an alien enemy would have made it wholly illegal since it seems that this kind of illegal promise cannot be severed.[99]

Where a joint bank account is opened in the names of two persons, the amount standing to the credit of the account is owed to them jointly, so that neither of them can enforce the debt against the bank without joining the other.[1] But a promise by the bank to honour only instructions given by both account holders is made separately to each of them, so that, if the bank allows one of them to draw on the account without the knowledge or authority of the other, the latter can sue alone and recover damage from the bank for breach of this promise.[2]

5. Release by One

A release granted by one *joint* creditor discharges the debt. Unless this were so, the one who granted the release might be able, after the death of his co-creditor, to recover the debt in spite of his own release, under the rule of survivorship.[3] But if the release is given by one creditor in fraud of another, the latter can have it set aside.[4]

A release granted by one of a number of creditors entitled *severally* (whether at law or in equity) releases only the share of the grantor.[5]

6. Payment to One

The general rule is that payment to one of two *joint* creditors discharges the debt.[6] But this rule may be varied by the contract, and such variation may be implied from a course of dealing. Thus where persons have a joint account with a bank, and the usual course

---

[95] *P. Samuel & Co v Dumas* [1924] A.C. 432 at 445; *Arab Bank plc v Zurich Insurance Co* [1999] 1 Lloyd's Rep. 263 at 272.

[96] See above, p.563.

[97] (1813) 2 M. & S. 100; *State of the Netherlands v Youell and Hayward* [1997] 2 Lloyd's Rep. 440, affirmed on other grounds [1998] 1 Lloyd's Rep. 236.

[98] (1813) 2 M. & S. 100 at 105.

[99] See above, pp.506–507.

[1] *Brewer v Westminster Bank Ltd* [1952] 2 T.L.R. 568 (as to which, see next note).

[2] *Catlin v Cyprus Finance Corporation (London) Ltd* [1983] Q.B. 759 not following *Brewer's* case, above, on this point; Vroegop, 100 L.Q.R. 25.

[3] *Wallace v Kelsall* (1840) 7 M. & W. 264 at 274.

[4] *Jones v Herbert* (1817) 7 Taunt. 421.

[5] *Steeds v Steeds* (1889) 22 Q.B.D. 537.

[6] *Husband v Davies* (1851) 10 C.B. 645; *Powell v Broadhurst* [1901] 2 Ch. 160 at 164.

of dealing is to make payments only with the authority of them all, a payment made to one without the authority of the others does not discharge the bank.[7] Even where payment to one discharges the debt, it does not discharge any security which may have been given for the debt except to the extent of the payee's beneficial interest in the debt.[8]

Payment to one of a number of *several* creditors clearly does not discharge the whole debt since each is separately entitled to his share.

7. Consideration Moving from One[9]

Where a promise is made to A and B *jointly*, it can be enforced by both of them, even though the whole consideration was provided by A.[10] If this were not so, the promise could not be enforced at all; for, if A tried to sue alone, he would be defeated by the rule that all the promisees must be parties to the action.[11] It follows from the doctrine of survivorship[12] that B would be entitled to the entire benefit of the promise after A's death.

None of the above reasoning applies where a promise is made to A and B *severally*. Hence each promisee must provide consideration for the separate promise made to him.

It is, however, uncertain which of the above rules applies to the intermediate case of a promise made to two persons *jointly and severally*.[13] In *McEvoy v Belfast Banking Co*,[14] a father (A) deposited £10,000 in a bank; the deposit receipt stated that the money had been received from him and his son (B) and that it was payable "to either or the survivor". Lord Atkin said *obiter* that the contract was not by the bank with A for the benefit of B[15] but "with A and B, and I think with them jointly and severally. A purports to make a contract on behalf of B as well as himself, and the consideration supports such a contract."[16] Of course after A's death (which in *McEvoy's* case had occurred), B would be entitled to enforce any joint promise under the doctrine of survivorship.[17] But it is harder to see how he could sue on any several promise, for this is *ex hypothesi* an independent promise, and on the facts stated no consideration for it moved from B.[18] Indeed, the more probable view of such facts is that the bank makes no promise to B but only has authority to pay him. Hence it is discharged by a payment to B, but is not liable to him.[19] The bank would not, however, be discharged by such payment if it was *not* authorised by its contract with A to pay B. This possibility is illustrated by *Thavorn v Bank of Credit & Commerce SA*,[20] where A opened a bank account in the name of her nephew B (who was under age), stipulating that only A should operate the account. It

---

[7] *Husband v Davies* (1851) 10 C.B. 645 at 650.

[8] *Powell v Broadhurst* [1901] 2 Ch. 160 at 166.

[9] Cullity, 85 L.Q.R. 530; Winterton, 47 Can.Bar Rev. 483; Coote, [1978] C.L.J. 301.

[10] This proposition seems to have been accepted in *Coulls v Bagot's Executor and Trustee Co Ltd* [1967] A.L.R. 385; although the majority of the court held that no joint promise had in fact been made; below, p.605.

[11] See above, p.576.

[12] See above, p.576.

[13] For this type of promise, see above, p.576.

[14] [1935] A.C. 24.

[15] On this view, B would not be a "third party" for the purposes of the discussion in Chap.15.

[16] At p.43.

[17] *cf. Aroso v Coutts & Co* [2002] 1 All E.R. 241, where the contract expressly so provided.

[18] S.J.B., 51 L.Q.R. 419.

[19] See *Coulls v Bagot's Executor and Trustee Co Ltd* [1967] A.L.R. 385; below, p.605.

[20] [1985] 1 Lloyd's Rep. 259. The Contracts (Rights of Third Parties) Act 1999 (below, p.651) would not apply to such a case since it was not the intention of the contracting parties that B should be entitled to enforce the contract: see subs.1(2) of the Bill.

was held that B was a mere nominee and that the bank was not discharged by (or was liable in damages for) paying B at the sole request of B and without any instructions from A. As no promise to (or in favour of) B had been made by the bank, it follows that B could not have sued the bank on its promise to A.

CHAPTER FIFTEEN

THIRD PARTIES

SECTION 1. INTRODUCTION

OUR concern in this Chapter is with the extent to which persons can either take the benefit of, or be bound by, contracts to which they are not parties. At common law, the doctrine of privity states first, that a contract cannot confer rights and secondly that it cannot impose liabilities, on anyone except a party to it. The second of these propositions is generally regarded as just and sensible[1]; but the first was subjected to much criticism,[2] culminating in a Report, issued by the Law Commission in 1996, on *Privity of Contract: Contracts for the Benefit of Third Parties*.[3] The recommendations of this Report have (where legislation for this purpose was necessary[4]) been implemented by the Contracts (Rights of Third Parties) Act 1999. The Act does not precisely follow the wording of the Draft Bill attached to the Law Commission's Report, but the changes do not, in general,[5] reflect any major departures from the policy of the recommendations in that Report: their object has rather been to secure the clearer and more effective implementation of that policy. For this reason, it is submitted that reference can appropriately be made to the Report in discussing the 1999 Act; and such references will be made in this Chapter.

It is important at the outset to make a point about the nature of the reforms to be made by the 1999 Act, since this determines the present structure of the subject. A crucial passage in the Law Commission's Report states that "it is important to emphasise that, while our proposed reform will give some third parties the right to enforce contracts, there will remain many contracts where a third party stands to benefit and yet will not have a right of enforceability. Our proposed statute carves out a general and wide-ranging exception to the third party rule, but it leaves that rule intact for cases not covered by the statute".[6] The rights conferred on third parties by the 1999 Act therefore have the character of a new statutory exception[7] to the common law doctrine of privity;

---

[1] See below, p.606. The rule that a contract cannot in other respects bind third parties is, in the interests of convenience, subject to modifications: see below, pp.619–625, 638–645.

[2] See p.588, below.

[3] Law Com No. 242 (hereafter "Report"). For an earlier proposal, see Law Revision Committee, sixth Interim Report, Cmd. 5449 (1937), Section D.

[4] For a situation in which this was not necessary, see Report, §6.8 n.8, below, p.656.

[5] The exception is s.8 of the Act, subjecting the third party's rights to arbitration agreements, contrary to the views expressed in Report, §§14.14 to 14.19.

[6] Report §5.16; the importance of the point appears from the fact that it is repeated in almost identical terms in §13.2 of the Report.

[7] See Lord Bingham's reference in *Heaton v Axa Equity & Law Life Assurance plc* [2002] UKHL 15; [2002] 2 All E.R. 961 at [9] to "the limited class of contracts which either at common law or by virtue of the Contracts (Rights of Third Parties) Act 1999 was enforceable by... a third party". *cf. Alfred McAlpine Construction Ltd v Panatown Ltd* [2001] 1 A.C. 518 at 535 *per* Lord Clyde, saying that the 1999 Act had "made some inroads on the principle of privity" and Lord Browne-Wilkinson, *ibid.* at 575, saying that the Act had "fundamentally affected" the law on this topic. It is respectfully submitted that these are more accurate statements than Lord Goff's reference *ibid.* at 544 to the "abolition" by the Act of the doctrine of privity, and to his similar statement in *Johnson v Gore Wood & Co* [2002] 2 A.C. 1 at 40 ("recently abolished by statute").

and the Act is therefore treated as such an exception in this Chapter, though because of its importance a separate section will be devoted to it.[8] The new exception is, however, limited in two ways. First, a number of situations which have in the past been perceived as giving rise to problems resulting from the doctrine of privity are simply outside the scope of the exception and so are not affected by the provisions of the 1999 Act at all: this is, for example, true of many of the cases in which third parties who have suffered loss in consequence of the breach of a contract between others have sought a remedy in tort against the party in breach.[9] Secondly, the exception created by the 1999 Act is, in turn, under that Act subject to exceptions[10] to which the third party's new statutory rights do not extend; and the effect of this is that in some[11] of these cases the common law doctrine of privity continues to apply. The Act also does not affect any rights which the third party has apart from its provisions[12]: thus it does not deprive the third party of rights which he has because the case falls either outside the *scope* of the common law doctrine[13] or within one of the *exceptions* to it recognised either at common law, or in equity or under other legislation.[14] The scope of the doctrine and these other exceptions therefore continue to call for discussion, particularly because the content of rights available apart from the 1999 Act in some ways differs from that of the rights available under it.[15] The Act also (in accordance with the Law Commission's recommendations[16]) does not affect the common law rule that a contract cannot impose liabilities on a third party or (in general) otherwise bind him, so that this aspect of the common law doctrine, too, continues to call for discussion. Nor does the Act affect any rights of the promisee to enforce any term of the contract[17]: such questions as whether the promisee can recover damages in respect of the third party's loss will therefore continue to be governed by the rules which have been (and no doubt will further be) developed as a matter of common law. There is finally the point that the 1999 Act does not apply to contracts made before the end of the period of six months beginning on the day on which it was passed and came into force,[18] except where a contract made within that period expressly provides that the Act is to apply to it.[19] It is therefore likely that for some years to come the courts will be concerned with contracts subject to the rules of law established before the Act came into force. These rules will also, in a significant number of the situations described above, continue to apply even to contracts made after that date. These rules therefore still require discussion, even though a considerable number of the cases on which they are based would if their facts occurred now be decided differently (where they had denied the third party the right to enforce the contract) or be decided on different grounds (where they had given the third party such a right). The result of all these points is that the 1999 Act may have improved, but it has scarcely simplified, the law on this topic.

---

[8] See below, pp.651 *et seq.*
[9] For further discussion of this point, see below, pp.607 *et seq.*
[10] See s.6 of the Act, discussed at p.661, below.
[11] *e.g.* s.6(2) and 6(3); under some of the other exceptions, the third party will be able to get rights by another legal route: *e.g.* under those stated in s.6(1) and (5): see below, pp.661–662.
[12] s.7(1), below pp.662–663; Report, §12.12.
[13] See below, pp.606–619.
[14] See below, pp.645–651, 666–671.
[15] *e.g.* ss.2 and 3 of the 1999 Act do not apply where the third party has rights apart from the Act; below, pp.622–664.
[16] Report, §§10.32, 7.6.
[17] s.4; below, p.665.
[18] On November 11, 1999, when the Act received the Royal Assent: see s.10(2).
[19] See s.10(3).

SECTION 2. THE COMMON LAW DOCTRINE[20]

The common law doctrine of privity means that a contract cannot, as a general rule, confer rights or impose obligations arising under it on any person except the parties to it. Two questions arise from this statement: who are the parties to the agreement? and has the claimant provided consideration for the promise which he is seeking to enforce?

1. Parties to the Agreement

Normally, the parties to the agreement are the persons from whose communications with each other the agreement has resulted. There may, indeed, be factual difficulties in identifying these persons[21]; but such difficulties do not generally[22] raise any questions of legal principle. Problems as to the legal analysis of clearly established facts can, however, arise in situations in which there is clearly an agreement, while it is doubtful exactly who the parties to it are, or in which there are several contracts which affect the same subject-matter and involve more than two parties. The rights of all the parties to such contracts arise independently of the Contracts (Rights of Third Parties) Act 1999, and are not limited by its provisions.[23]

(1) Collateral contracts[24]

(a) ILLUSTRATIONS. A contract between two persons may be accompanied by a collateral contract between one of them and a third person relating to the same subject-matter. In *Shanklin Pier v Detel Products Ltd*,[25] the claimants employed contractors to paint a pier and instructed them for this purpose to buy and use paint made by the defendants. The instruction was given in reliance on a representation made by the defendants to the claimants that the paint would last for seven years. In fact it lasted for only three months. The main contract for the sale of the paint was between the contractors and the defendants, but it was held that there was also a collateral contract between the claimants and the defendants that the paint would last for seven years. The same reasoning can apply where a person buys goods from a dealer and is given a guarantee issued by the manufacturer. The main contract of sale is between the dealer and the customer, but it seems that the guarantee is a collateral contract between the manufacturer and the customer.[26] Special legislation applies to certain guarantees given to consumers in respect of goods sold or supplied to them. Where the requirements specified in this legislation are satisfied, such guarantees are to take effect as contractual

---

[20] Finlay, *Contracts for the Benefit of Third Persons*; Dold, *Stipulations for a Third Party*; Wilson, 11 Sydney L.Rev. 300; Flannigan, 105 L.Q.R. 564; Kincaid, [1989] C.L.J. 454; Andrews, 8 *Legal Studies* 14.

[21] *e.g. The Zinnia* [1984] 2 Lloyd's Rep. 211; *Empresa Lineas Maritimas Argentinas v The Oceanus Mutual Underwriting Association (Bermuda) Ltd* [1984] 2 Lloyd's Rep. 517; *Uddin v Ahmed* [2001] EWCA Civ 240; [2001] 3 F.C.R. 300; *The Starsin* [2003] UKHL 12, [2003] 2 W.L.R. 711, at [175].

[22] A highly specialised group of cases (beyond the scope of this book) concerns bills of lading issued in respect of goods shipped on a chartered ship: see *Carver on Bills of Lading* (1st ed.), §4–027 to 4–052; *The Starsin*, above, n.21.

[23] Contracts (Rights of Third Parties) Act 1999, s.7(1).

[24] Wedderburn [1959] C.L.J. 58.

[25] [1951] 2 K.B. 854; followed in *Wells (Merstham) Ltd v Buckland Sand & Silica Co Ltd* [1965] 2 Q.B. 170, even though no specific main contract was contemplated when the "collateral" undertaking was given. *cf.* also below, p.738.

[26] *cf.* above, p.77.

obligations[27] whether or not the requirements of a collateral contract[28] are satisfied; but these requirements continue to apply to manufacturers' guarantees not covered by this legislation: *e.g.*, where the person to whom the guarantee is given is not a "consumer".[29] Again, a contract for the execution of building work between A and B may be performed, wholly or in part, through the instrumentality of sub-contractor C, nominated by A but engaged by B. Such an arrangement usually gives rise to a contract between A and B and to one between B and C, but not to one between A and C[30]; but it is possible for a collateral contract to arise between these last two parties,[31] making C contractually liable to A. Yet a further situation in which a single transaction involves several contracts is that in which a supply of goods is paid for by the use of a cheque card or credit card. Such a transaction involves three contracts: one between the supplier and the customer, a second between the customer and the issuer of the card, and a third between the issuer of the card and the supplier of the goods.[32] The supplier therefore has a common law right of action against the issuer on this third contract.

The collateral contract device has also been used to solve a difficulty arising out of hire-purchase agreements. The customer may think of himself as "buying on hire-purchase" from the dealer on whose premises he selects the goods. Actually, the transaction may involve a sale of the goods by the dealer to a finance company which then hires them out to the customer and grants him an option to purchase them. Thus the main contract of hire-purchase is between the customer and the finance company. A representation by the dealer as to the quality of the goods used not to bind the finance company,[33] but it could be enforced against the dealer as a collateral contract.[34] If the transaction is a regulated agreement within the Consumer Credit Act 1974,[35] a dealer who conducts antecedent negotiations is deemed to do so as agent of the finance company as well as in his actual capacity.[36] His representations can therefore make the company liable under the main contract, while he himself may still be liable under a collateral contract.[37]

---

[27] Sale and Supply of Goods to Consumers Regulations 2002, SI 2002/3045; reg.15, implementing Dir.1999/44 Arts 2(e) and 6; for the meaning of "consumer" in this context, see reg.2.

[28] *i.e.*, those of consideration and contractual intention (below, p.584).

[29] *e.g.*, on facts such as those of the *Shanklin Pier* case, above, n.25.

[30] *e.g. Simaan General Contracting Co v Pilkington Glass Ltd (No.2)* [1988] Q.B. 758; *National Trust v Haden & Young* (1994) 72 B.L.R. 1.

[31] *Holland Hannen & Cubitts (Northern) v. Welsh Health Technical Services Ltd* (1987) 7 Con.L.R. 14; *cf. Welsh Health Technical Service Organisation v Haden Young* (1987) 37 Build.L.R. 130; *Greater Nottingham Co-operative Soc Ltd v Cementation Ltd* [1989] Q.B. 71; contrast *National Trust v Haden & Young*, above, where there was no such collateral contract; for C's possible liability to A in tort, see below, pp.607–608.

[32] *Re Charge Card Services* [1987] Ch. 150, affirmed [1989] Ch. 497; Tiplady, [1989] L.M.C.L.Q. 22; Jones, [1988] J.B.L. 457; *cf. Customs & Excise Commissioners v Diners Club Ltd* [1989] 1 W.L.R. 1196; *Metropolitan Police Commissioner v Charles* [1977] A.C. 177; *R. v Lambie* [1988] A.C. 449; *First Sport Ltd v Barclays Bank plc* [1993] 1 W.L.R. 1229 (where the card had been stolen and presented to the retailers by the thief); a different analysis probably applies where the card is issued by *the supplier*, as is the practice of some department stores: *Richardson v Worral* [1985] S.T.C. 693 at 720.

[33] *Campbell Discount Co Ltd v Gall* [1961] 1 Q.B. 431; reversed on other points in *Branwhite v Worcester Works Finance Ltd* [1969] 1 A.C. 552 and *United Dominions Trust Ltd v Western* [1976] Q.B. 513.

[34] *Brown v Sheen & Richmond Car Sales* [1950] 1 All E.R. 1102; *Andrews v Hopkinson* [1957] 1 Q.B. 229; Diamond, (1958) 21 M.L.R. 177; *cf. Astley Industrial Trust Ltd v Grimley* [1963] 1 W.L.R. 584; as to damages, see *Yeoman Credit Ltd v Odgers* [1962] 1 W.L.R. 215.

[35] See above, p.178.

[36] s.56(2); *cf.* also s.75, under which the finance company is liable for any breach of contract by the supplier, but entitled to an indemnity from him in respect of such liability.

[37] This follows from s.56(2), above.

(b) CONSIDERATION FOR COLLATERAL CONTRACTS. To be enforceable as a collateral contract, a promise must be supported by consideration,[38] and in the cases so far discussed this requirement was clearly satisfied. In the *Shanklin Pier* case the consideration was the instruction given by the claimants to their contractors[39]; in the guarantee case it is the purchase by the customer of the goods from the dealer[40]; in the building sub-contractor case, it is similarly the nomination of the sub-contractor by the client; in the cheque or credit card case it is the supply of goods by the supplier to the customer and the discount allowed by the supplier to the issuer of the card[41]; and in the hire-purchase case it is the entering by the customer into a hire-purchase agreement with the finance company. A case in which the problem of consideration gives rise to more difficulty is *Charnock v Liverpool Corporation*,[42] where a car was damaged and repaired under a contract between the owner's insurance company and a garage. It was held that there was also a collateral contract by which the garage promised the owner to do the repairs reasonably quickly. Although the owner did not pay or promise to pay the garage anything,[43] he had provided consideration by "leaving his car with the garage for repair".[44] This might not be a detriment to the owner, at least in the factual sense.[45] But it benefited the garage in giving it the opportunity of making a contract for the repair of the car with the insurance company; and this benefit constituted the consideration for the garage's promise to the owner.[46]

(c) CONTRACTUAL INTENTION. In the present context, as in others,[47] a promise will not amount to a collateral contract if it was made without contractual intention. For example, in *Independent Broadcasting Authority v EMI Electronics*[48] EMI had contracted to erect a television mast for the IBA, on the terms that the actual work was to be done by a sub-contractor, who was not a party to the main contract. The sub-contractor wrote to the IBA, saying: "We are well satisfied that the structure will not oscillate dangerously". The mast having later collapsed, it was held that this letter did not have contractual force as there was no *animus contrahendi*[49] (though the sub-contractor was held liable in negligence).

(2) Agency

Where an agent negotiates a contract with a third party on behalf of his princpal, that contract will generally be between the principal and the third party.[50] But it is sometimes

---

[38] *cf. Brikom Investments Ltd v Carr* [1979] Q.B. 467, (above, p.102), where no third party problem arose.

[39] [1951] 2 K.B. 854 at 856.

[40] *cf.* (in a different context) *Penn v Bristol & West BS* [1997] 1 W.L.R. 1356 at 1363 ("entering into some transaction with a third party").

[41] *Customs & Excise Commissioners v Diners Club Ltd* [1989] 1 W.L.R. 1196.

[42] [1968] 1 W.L.R. 1498.

[43] *cf. Godfrey Davies Ltd v Culling and Hecht* [1962] 2 Lloyd's Rep. 349; *Cooter & Green Ltd v Tyrell* [1962] 2 Lloyd's Rep. 377; *Brown & Davies v Galbraith* [1972] 1 W.L.R. 997.

[44] [1968] 1 W.L.R. 1498 at 1505.

[45] See above, p.69.

[46] *cf.* above, p.95. For similar reasoning, see *International Petroleum Refining & Supply Sociedad v Caleb Brett & Son Ltd* [1980] 1 Lloyd's Rep. 569 at 594.

[47] See above, pp.161–162, 179–180, 199–200, 356–357.

[48] (1980) 14 Build.L.R. 1; *cf. Alicia Hosiery Ltd v Brown Shipley Ltd* [1970] 1 Q.B. 195; *Lambert v Lewis* [1982] A.C. 225; *Law Debenture Trust Corp v Ural Caspian Oil Corp Ltd* [1993] 1 W.L.R. 138 at 142; for a successful appeal on another point, see [1995] Ch. 152, below, p.622.

[49] *cf.* also *Hannam v Bradford CC* [1970] 1 W.L.R. 937; *Construction Industry Training Board v Labour Force Ltd* [1970] 3 All E.R. 220.

[50] See below, pp.727 *et seq.*

doubtful whether a person acted as agent or on his own behalf.[51] Thus where a husband booked tickets on a cross-Channel ferry for himself, his wife and children, there was said to be a "contract of carriage between the [wife] and the [carriers]",[52] presumably made by the husband as agent of the wife. Where a husband and wife lunched together at a restaurant, it was again held that there was a contract between the wife and the proprietor, though on the different ground that husband and wife each made a separate contract with the proprietor.[53] But if there were no such separate contracts and the host on such an occasion did not act as agent it has been said that there would be a contract only between him and the restaurant proprietor.[54]

Similar problems arise where an agent employs a sub-agent. In some such cases there is a direct contract between principal and sub-agent; while in others the sub-agent is in a contractual relationship only with the agent who employed him.[55] In these cases it is again clear that there is a contract, but doubtful who the parties to it are.

(3) Multilateral contracts

When a person joins a club or other unincorporated association he may be in direct communication only with the secretary and be unaware of the identity of the other members. But his contract of membership is likely to be with them,[56] and not with the secretary.[57] It has similarly been held that an insurance policy, which was expressed to be between the assured and a syndicate of underwriters at Lloyd's, nevertheless constituted a number of separate contracts between the assured and each member of the syndicate.[58]

Problems of this kind can also arise where a number of persons agree to enter into a competition subject to rules laid down by the organising club. In *The Satanita*[59] it was held that the competitors in a regatta had contracted not only with the committee of the club but also with each other. But in *Ellesmere v Wallace*[60] it was held that persons who entered horses for races organised by the Jockey Club had contracted with the club, and not with each other.

---

[51] See below, pp.706–708; *P Samuel & Co Ltd v Dumas* [1923] 1 K.B. 593; [1924] A.C. 431. Similar problems commonly arise in relation to "forwarding agents": see, *e.g. Jones v European General Express* (1920) 25 Com.Cas. 296; *Elektronska, etc. v Transped, etc.* [1986] 1 Lloyd's Rep. 49.

[52] *The Dragon* [1979] 1 Lloyd's Rep. 257 at 262; affirmed [1980] 2 Lloyd's Rep. 415; *cf. Wilson v Best Travel Ltd* [1993] 1 All E.R. 353 at 355; *Bowerman v Association of British Travel Agents* [1995] N.L.J. 1815 (holiday booked for pupil by teacher).

[53] *Lockett v A M Charles Ltd* [1938] 4 All E.R. 170.

[54] *Jackson v Horizon Holidays Ltd* [1975] 1 W.L.R. 1468 at 1473 (where *Lockett v A M Charles Ltd supra*, was not cited).

[55] See below, p.747; contrast *Robbins v Fennell* (1847) 11 Q.B. 248 with *Collins v Brook* (1860) 5 H. & N. 700; *cf.* also *The Antama* [1982] 2 Lloyd's Rep. 112 (agent failing to specify which of two persons is the principal for the purpose of the transaction); *Henderson v Merrett Syndicates Ltd* [1995] 2 A.C. 145; and see the situation which arose for tax purposes in *Crossland v Hawkins* (1961) 39 T.C. 493.

[56] *Lee v Showmen's Guild* [1952] 2 Q.B. 329 at 341; but in *Anderton v Rowland, The Times*, November 5, 1999, it was held that breach of the rules by one member did not, as a matter of construction, give another member a right of action in damages against the member guilty of the breach.

[57] *Hybart v Parker* (1858) 4 C.B.(N.S.) 209; *Gray v Pearson* (1870) L.R. 5 C.P. 568; *Evans v Hooper* (1875) 1 Q.B.D. 45; *Nutting v Baldwin* [1995] 1 W.L.R. 201. But where a club was *owned by a company* of which the club's members were shareholders, the rules of the club were held to constitute contracts between each member and the company, and not between the members *inter se: Peskin v Anderson* [2000] 2 B.C.L.C. 1.

[58] *Touche Ross & Co v Colin Bank* [1992] 2 Lloyd's Rep. 207 at 209–210.

[59] [1895] P. 248; affirmed sub nom. *Clarke v Dunraven* [1897] A.C. 59, where only Lord Herschell dealt with the point here discussed; *cf. Meggeson v Burns* [1972] 1 Lloyd's Rep. 223; *White v Blackmore* [1972] 2 Q.B. 651 (where there was no contractual intention).

[60] [1929] 2 Ch. 1.

(4) Corporations

Under the Companies Acts[61] the memorandum and articles of association of a company[62] bind the company and its members as if they had been signed and sealed by each member and contained covenants by each member to observe the provisions of the memorandum and articles. The memorandum and articles amount to a "statutory contract"[63] between each member and the company[64]; and also to one between the members *inter se*.[65] But they only have the latter effect between the members in their capacity as members[66]; a director is not liable or entitled under them in his capacity as director simply because he happens also to be a member.[67]

In the case of a limited liability partnership (which is a body corporate),[68] the mutual rights and liabilities of the members *inter se* and between the members and the partnership are governed by agreement between the members or between them and the partnership[69]; or, in the absence of such agreement, by regulations made under the Act governing such partnerships.[70]

(5) Mortgage valuations

Problems as to parties may also arise where a house is valued at the instigation of a building society to which a prospective purchaser has applied for a loan which is to be secured by a mortgage on the house. Where the valuation is carried out by a full-time employee of the building society, there will usually be a contract between the society and its employee, and one between the society and the borrower (under which the society will be vicariously liable for the valuer's negligence) but none between the valuer and the borrower.[71] Where, on the other hand, the valuation is carried out by an independent valuer, there may be a contract between him and the borrower[72] but this is not necessarily the case. If, for example, the independent valuer were appointed and paid by the society and reported directly to it, there is unlikely to be any contractual relationship between borrower and valuer, though the valuer will be liable to the borrower in tort if as a result of his negligence his report is inaccurate or incomplete and the borrower suffers loss.[73]

The reason why there is no separate contract in the first of the above situations is presumably that the valuer has no intention to contract with the borrower since he

---

[61] See now Companies Act 1985, s.14(1); Goldberg, 48 M.L.R. 158. The reference to sealing seems (perhaps inadvertently) to have survived Law of Property (Miscellaneous Provisions) Act 1989, s.1.

[62] See above, p.560.

[63] *Soden v British Commonwealth Holdings* [1998] A.C. 298 at 323.

[64] *Hickman v Kent or Romney Marsh Sheepbreeders Association* [1915] 1 Ch. 881; *cf. Cumbrian Newspaper Group v Cumberland and Westmorland Herald Ltd* [1987] Ch. 1.

[65] *Rayfield v Hands* [1960] Ch. 1; *J H Rayner (Mincing Lane) Ltd v DTI* [1989] Ch. 72 at 190 (approved on this point [1990] 2 A.C. 418 at 515); *cf. Russell v Northern Bank Development Corp Ltd* [1992] B.C.L.C. 1016. But there is no contract between members on the one hand and third parties on the other: *Eley v Positive, etc., Assurance Co* (1876) 1 Ex.D. 88.

[66] For limitations on the scope of this contract, see *Soden v British and Commonwealth Holdings* [1998] A.C. 298. They are not affected by the Contracts (Rights of Third Parties) Act 1999: see s.6(2), below, p.662.

[67] *Beattie v E & F Beattie Ltd* [1938] Ch. 708; *Rayfield v Hands*, above, is difficult to reconcile with this principle: L.C.B.G., 21 M.L.R. 401.

[68] See above, p.563.

[69] Limited Liability Partnership Act 2000, s.5(1)(a).

[70] *ibid.*, s.5(1)(c).

[71] *Halifax Building Society v Edell* [1992] Ch. 436. Nor could the borrower enforce a term of the valuer's employment contract by virtue of the Contracts (Rights of Third Parties) Act 1999: see s.6(3), below, p.662.

[72] *Halifax Building Society v Edell*, above, at 454.

[73] See, *e.g. Smith v Eric S Bush* [1990] 1 A.C. 831.

believes that he is merely carrying out his duties under his contract with the society. The further suggestion that, in this situation, there is "seemingly no consideration for a contract by the valuer as principal"[74] is, with respect, harder to follow. It cannot mean that there is no consideration because the valuer is doing no more than performing his contract of employment, for it is now settled that performance of a contractual duty owed to a third party can constitute consideration[75]; and in any event the question is whether there is consideration for the valuer's promise, and this consideration must move, not from him, but from the purchaser. *Prima facie*, such consideration is provided by the payment of the survey fee by the purchaser to the society, or by his entering into the mortgage transaction; and it is immaterial that this consideration does not move (at least directly) to the valuer; for so long as consideration moves from the promisee it need not move to the promisor.[76] Nor would such consideration be past, even if the fee had been paid before the valuer had been engaged; for the test for deciding whether consideration is past is a functional (rather than a strictly chronological) one, which is satisfied in the situation discussed here since the consideration and the promise given in return are substantially one transaction.[77] Indeed, the assumption that it is so satisfied is supported by the view that there can be a contract between an independent valuer and the purchaser,[78] since the consideration which moves from the purchaser is exactly the same whether the valuer is an employee of the building society or an independent person.

2. Party to the Consideration

The common law rule that only a party to the agreement can enforce it will often lead to the same result as the rule that consideration must move from the promisee[79]; but the two rules appear to be distinct. They require the claimant to show (1) that the promise was made to him *and* (2) that the consideration for it moved from him. The statement that consideration must move *from the promisee* simply assumes that the first requirement has been satisfied. If the rule were stated to be that consideration must move *from the party seeking to enforce the promise* it would clearly be distinct from the common law rule that only a party to the agreement can sue. A father might, for example, promise his daughter to pay £1,000 to anyone who married her. A man who married the daughter with knowledge of and in reliance on such a promise might provide consideration for it, but could not enforce it, as it was not addressed to him.[80]

A decision which supports the view that the two rules are distinct is *Kepong Prospecting Ltd v Schmidt*,[81] where a third party made a claim to enforce a contract under the law of Malaysia, by which consideration need not move from the promisee. In rejecting the claim, the Privy Council said: "It is true that section 2(*d*) of the Contracts Ordinance gives a wider definition of 'consideration' than that which applies in England, particularly in that it enables consideration to move from another person than the promisee, but the appellant was unable to show how this affected the law as to enforcement of contracts by third parties".[82]

---

[74] *Halifax Building Society v Edell* [1992] Ch. 436 at 454.
[75] See above, pp.97–98.
[76] See above, p.81.
[77] See above, p.77.
[78] See above, at n.72.
[79] See *Price v Easton* (1833) B. & Ad. 433; *Tweddle v Atkinson* (1861) B & S. 393.
[80] *cf. Uddin v Ahmed* [2001] EWCA Civ 204, [2001] 3 F.C.R. 300, at [20].
[81] [1968] A.C. 810.
[82] *ibid.* at 826.

3. Reasons for the Doctrine

There are two aspects of the common law doctrine of privity: no one except a party to a contract can acquire rights under it; and no one except a party can be subjected to liabilities under it. The reason for the second aspect of the doctrine is obvious: a person should not, as a general rule, have contractual obligations imposed on him without his consent. The first aspect of the doctrine is harder to explain; indeed, Steyn L.J. has gone so far as to say that there is "no doctrinal, logical or policy reason"[83] for it. The rule that a third party cannot acquire rights under a contract can scarcely be justified by saying that a contract is, or gives rise to, a personal relationship, affecting only the parties to it; for this is rather a restatement of the rule than a reason for its existence. Nor is it satisfactory to say that it would be unjust to allow a person to sue on a contract on which he could not be sued[84]; for the law enforces unilateral contracts, to which the same argument applies.[85] A further possible reason is that, if third parties could enforce contracts made for their benefit, the rights of contracting parties to rescind or vary such contracts would be unduly hampered: this reasoning has certainly been influential in limiting the development of one of the judge-made exceptions to the doctrine.[86] Yet another possible reason is that the third party is often a mere donee. A system of law which does not give a right to enforce a gratuitous promise to the promisee may well be reluctant to give such as right to a gratuitous beneficiary who is not even a promisee. None of these reasons for the common law doctrine takes account of the inconvenience that can result from its practical operation. This factor accounts for the many exceptions to the doctrine which will be discussed later in this Chapter.[87]

4. Development

In the early authorities, there was considerable conflict on the question whether a person could enforce a contract to which he was not a party.[88] A negative answer to this question was given in 1861 in *Tweddle v Atkinson*,[89] where A promised B to pay a marriage portion to B's son C on C's marriage to A's daughter. It was held that C could not enforce this promise against A. This case was generally considered to have established the common law doctrine,[90] which was approved by the House of Lords in 1915, when the principle that "only a person who is a party to the contract can sue on it" was said to be a "fundamental"[91] one in English law. This view was, indeed, judicially doubted in a

---

[83] *Darlington BC v Wiltshier Northern Ltd* [1995] 1 W.L.R. 68 at 76.

[84] *Tweddle v Atkinson* (1861) 1 B. & S. at p.398.

[85] See above, pp.37–41, 151.

[86] See below, pp.645, 648. It is also reflected in s.2 of the Contracts (Rights of Third Parties) Act 1999.

[87] See below, pp.651 *et seq*; see also p.642–645.

[88] In *Crow v Rogers* (1724) 1 Str. 592; *Bourne v Mason* (1669) 1 Ventr. 6 and *Price v Easton* (1833) 4 B. & Ad. 433 the third party's claim failed; but it was upheld in *Thomas v ——* (1655) Sty. 461; *Dutton v Poole* (1678) 2 Lev. 210, affirmed T. Raym. 302 and approved in *Martyn v Hind* (1776) Cowp. 437 at 443; *Green v Horn* (1693) Comb. 219 (reversed (1694) 1 Salk. 197 on the ground that the third party must at least be mentioned in the deed) and *Marchington v Vernon* (1786) 1 B. & P. 101. n. (*c*); E.J.P., 70 L.Q.R. 467; Scammel, 8 C.L.P. 134–135; Palmer, 33 Am. Jl. of Legal History 3; Ibbetson in (ed.) Barton, *Towards a General Law of Contract*, 67, 96–99; Palmer, *The Paths to Privity: the History of Third Party Beneficiaries in English Law*; Andrews, 69 Tulane L.Rev. 69.

[89] (1861) 1 B. & S. 393.

[90] *Gandy v Gandy* (1884) 30 Ch.D. 57, at 69.

[91] *Dunlop Pneumatic Tyre Co Ltd v Selfridge & Co Ltd* [1915] A.C. 847 at 853; for a similar, earlier, statement, see *Keighley Maxsted & Co v Durant* [1901] A.C. 240 at 246.

number of cases.[92] But in 1961 the House of Lords once again affirmed the existence of the doctrine,[93] and this view of the law has been accepted in many later cases.[94]

The leading modern case is *Beswick v Beswick*.[95] A coal merchant transferred his business to his nephew who made various promises in return. One of these was that he would, after the uncle's death, pay £5 per week to the uncle's widow. The uncle died and the widow became his administratrix. She brought an action to enforce the nephew's promise, suing both in her own right and as administratrix. The House of Lords held that the widow could enforce the nephew's promise in her capacity as administratrix of the promisee and that she was entitled to an order of specific performance against the nephew, obliging him to make the payments to her for her personal benefit. In the Court of Appeal Lord Denning M.R. had said that the widow could also sue in her own right at common law,[96] because the doctrine of privity was "at bottom . . . only a rule of procedure"[97] and could be overcome by simply joining the promisee as a party to the action. The House of Lords found it unnecessary to express a concluded view on this point. But the speeches all assume the correctness of the generally accepted view that a contract can at common law be enforced only by the parties to it[98]; though the House of Lords has on a number of occasions indicated its willingness to reconsider this position.[99] Such reconsideration has indeed been undertaken by a majority of the High Court of Australia, but in a decision in which so many divergent views were expressed, that it provides no firm guidance for the development of the law.[1] The difficulties of

---

[92] In *Smith and Snipes Hall Farm Ltd v River Douglas Catchment Board* [1949] 2 K.B. 500 at 519; *Drive Yourself Hire Co (London) Ltd v Strutt* [1954] 1 Q.B. 250 at 274; *Pyrene Co Ltd v Scindia Steam Navigation Co Ltd* [1954] 2 Q.B. 402 at 426; *Rayfield v Hands* [1960] Ch. 1; Dowrick, 19 M.L.R. 375; *cf.* Andrews, 8 Legal Studies 14.

[93] *Scruttons Ltd v Midland Silicones Ltd* [1962] A.C. 446; below, p.628; see also *Green v Russell* [1959] 2 Q.B. 226.

[94] *Rookes v Barnard* [1964] A.C. 1129 (below, p.614); *Re Cook's Settlement Trust* [1965] Ch. 902 at 915; *Hepburn v A. Tomlinson (Hauliers) Ltd* [1966] A.C. 451; *The Eurymedon* [1975] A.C. 154 166; *The New York Star* [1981] 1 W.L.R. 138; *Woodar Investments & Development Ltd v Wimpey Construction UK Ltd* [1980] 1 W.L.R. 277; *Balsamo v Medici* [1984] 1 W.L.R. 951 at 959–960; *Southern Water Authority v Carey* [1985] 2 All E.R. 1077 at 1083; *The Forum Craftsman* [1985] 1 Lloyd's Rep. 291 at 295; *Singer (UK) Ltd v Tees & Hartlepool Port Authority* [1988] 2 Lloyd's Rep. 164 at 167; *J H Rayner. (Mincing Lane) Ltd v DTI* [1990] 2 A.C. 418 at 479, 506; *The Captain Gregos* [1990] 1 Lloyd's Rep. 310 at 318; *The Gudermes* [1993] 1 Lloyd's Rep. 311 at 314, *Siu Yin Kwan v Eastern Insurance* [1994] 2 A.C. 199 at 207; *Rhone v Stephens* [1994] 2 A.C. 310 at 321; *The Pioneer Container* [1994] 2 A.C. 324 at 335, *White v Jones* [1995] 2 A.C. 207 at 252, 266; *The Mahkutai* [1996] A.C. 650 at 658; *Amsprop Trading Ltd v Harris Distribution Ltd* [1997] 1 W.L.R. 1025 at 1028; *The Giannis N K* [1998] A.C. 605 at 616; the point is perhaps left open in *Esso Petroleum Ltd v Hall Russell & Co* [1989] A.C. 643 at 662.

[95] [1965] 2 All E.R. 858, [1966] Ch. 538; [1968] A.C. 58; Goodhart, 83 L.Q.R. 465; Fairest [1967] C.L.J. 149; Treitel, 29 M.L.R. 657; 30 M.L.R. 687.

[96] For the effect of Law of Property Act 1925, s.56, see below, pp.669–671.

[97] [1966] Ch. at 557.

[98] [1968] A.C. at 72, 81, 83, 92–93, 95.

[99] *ibid.* at 72; *Woodar Investment Development Ltd v Wimpey Construction UK Ltd* [1980] 1 W.L.R. 277 at 291, 297–298, 300; *Swain v Law Society* [1983] 1 A.C. 598 at 611; *cf. Williams v Natural Life Health Foods* [1998] 1 W.L.R. 830 at 837.

[1] *Trident Insurance Co Ltd v McNiece Bros Pty Ltd* (1988) 165 C.L.R. 107, where a claim under a liability insurance policy by a person who was not a party to it was upheld by a majority of five to two. But one member of the majority (Deane J.) was only prepared to allow the third party's claim under the well-established trust exception to the doctrine of privity (below, p.646), while another (Gaudron J.) based her decision in favour of the third party, not on contract, but on unjust enrichment (below, p.625), and said that this was "not an abrogation of the doctrine of privity of contract" (at 177). Only three of the seven members of the court can be said to have countenanced such abrogation, and even their view may be restricted to the special insurance context with which the case was concerned. See also Edgell, [1989] L.M.C.L.Q. 139;

reaching satisfactory results in this area through purely judicial reconsideration are formidable: they arise, particularly, in defining exactly what classes of third parties can acquire rights under the contract, and in determining how those rights are to be affected by attempts by the contracting parties to rescind the contract or to vary it, and by defences available between the contracting parties.[2] A satisfactory solution of such difficulties is more likely to be achieved by legislative reform,[3] such as that contained in the Contracts (Rights of Third Parties) Act 1999.[4] In a significant number of situations, however, third parties will not acquire rights by virtue of this Act[5]; and in many such situations the common law doctrine of privity will continue (at least for the time being[6]) to apply.

5. Operation of the Doctrine

Although at common law a third party cannot generally assert rights under a contract made for his benefit, the contract remains nevertheless binding between promisor and promisee. The fact that the contract was made for the benefit of a third party does, however, give rise to special problems so far as the promisee's remedies against the promisor are concerned. Actual performance of the contract may also lead to disputes between promisee and third party.

(1) Promisee's remedies

(a) SPECIFIC PERFORMANCE. The promisee (or those acting for his estate) may seek specific performance. If, as in *Beswick v Beswick*,[7] this remedy is granted, the third party will in fact receive the benefit contracted for. But the scope of the remedy of specific performance is limited in various ways; these limitations, and their applicability to cases involving third parties, will be discussed in detail in Chapter 21.[8] It is therefore necessary to consider what other remedies may be available to the promisee if the contract is broken.

(b) RESTITUTION. The promisee may claim restitution of the consideration provided by him. But part performance by the promisor[9] might defeat this remedy,[10] and it might also be unjust to restrict the promisee to such a claim: for example, return of premiums could be a quite inadequate remedy where a policy of life insurance had been taken out for the benefit of a third party and had matured.

Kincaid, 2 J.C.L. 160. For a different judicial approach in Canada, proceeding by means of the creation of an exception to the doctrine in the context of exemption clauses, see *London Drugs Ltd v Kuehne & Nagel International Ltd* [1992] 3 S.C.R. 299 (below, p.631); Waddams, 109 L.Q.R. 349; Adams and Brownsword, 56 M.L.R. 722. *Cf. Fraser River Pile and Dredge Ltd v Can-Drive Services Ltd* [2000] 1 Lloyds Rep. 199, where the Supreme Court of Canada, while refusing to engage in "wholesale abolition" of the doctrine of privity, continued to make "incremental changes" by holding that a third party could take the benefit of a "waiver of subrogation" clause in an insurance policy.

[2] See the elaborate discussion of these problems in American law (which in principle recognises the rights of third party beneficiaries) in Corbin on *Contracts*, Chaps 41–44. The effect of rescission or variation by the contracting parties gives rise to particular difficulties: *cf.* below, p.647.

[3] See Treitel, 29 M.L.R. 657, 665; Reynolds, 105 L.Q.R., 1, 3; contrast *Darlington BC v Wiltshier Northern Ltd* [1995] 1 W.L.R. 68 at 76, favouring judicial reform.

[4] See below, pp.651 *et seq.*

[5] See below, pp.654–655, 661–662.

[6] The passing of the 1999 Act will probably reduce the pressure for judicial reform.

[7] [1968] A.C. 58, above, p.589.

[8] See below, pp.1038–1040.

[9] As in *Beswick v Beswick* [1968] A.C. 68.

[10] As there would be no "total failure of consideration;" and as "rescission" for breach could probably not be allowed unless the third party was willing to restore any performance received: below, pp.1052–1053. For the suggestion that *the third party* may have a claim in restitution, see below, p.625.

(c) AGREED SUM. The promisee may claim payment to himself of the agreed sum. It can be objected that to allow such a claim would force the promisor to do something which he never contracted to do, *viz.* to pay the promisee when he contracted to pay the third party; and one view is therefore that the promisee cannot sue for the agreed sum,[11] save in the exceptional circumstances to be described later in this Chapter.[12] But the objection to allowing the promisee to claim payment to himself loses most of its force where the promisor would not in fact be prejudiced by having to pay the promisee rather than the third party (so long as by such payment gave him a good discharge). In such a case, the contract may, on its true construction, be one to pay the third party or as the promisee shall direct,[13] so that it would not be inconsistent with its terms to allow the promisee to claim payment for himself. The promisee is *a fortiori* so entitled where the contract is one to pay him (the promisee) as nominee for the third party[14]: such a contract is not one for the benefit of a third party[15] in the sense of one purporting to give that party a right against the promisor.

(d) DAMAGES IN RESPECT OF PROMISEE'S LOSS. The promisee may claim damages where he has suffered loss as a result of the promisor's failure to perform in favour of the third party. But in *Beswick v Beswick* the majority of the House of Lords evidently thought that no such loss had been or would be suffered and that the damages recoverable by the estate for breach of the nephew's promise would be merely nominal.[16] Lord Upjohn explained that this would be the case because the promisee "died *without any assets* save and except the agreement which he hoped would keep him and then his widow for their lives".[17] It seems from this that damages might have been substantial if the promisee had had other assets—either because the widow might then have had a claim against those assets if the promise was not performed[18] or because the promisee or his estate would in fact, even if not legally obliged to do so, have made some other, wholly voluntary, provision for the widow. The loss suffered by the promisee would be the cost of making an alternative provision, and there is some authority to support the view that damages for breach of contract may be recovered to compensate for such loss even though the provision is wholly voluntary.[19] *A fortiori* the promisee can recover substantial damages where he is under a legal obligation to make a payment to the third party and where this obligation would have been discharged if the promisor had paid in accordance with the contract.

---

[11] See *Coulls v Bagot's Executor and Trustee Co Ltd* [1967] A.L.R. 385 at 409–411; *cf. Beswick v Beswick* [1968] A.C. at 88, 101 (dealing with the remedy of damages).

[12] See *Cleaver v Mutual Reserve Fund Life Association* [1892] 1 Q.B. 147; *cf.* below, p.650.

[13] *The Spiros C* [2000] 2 Lloyd's Rep. 319 at 331; below, p.605.

[14] *The Turiddu* [1999] 2 Lloyd's Rep. 401 at 407.

[15] *ibid.*

[16] Lord Pearce, however, thought that damages would be substantial: [1968] A.C. at p.88. It is not entirely clear whether he had in mind an action for *damages* or one for the *agreed sum*: see his reference at p.87 to "separate actions as each sum falls due".

[17] [1968] A.C. at 102 (italics supplied).

[18] *e.g.* under the Inheritance (Family Provision) Act 1938, now Inheritance (Provision for Family and Dependants) Act 1975.

[19] *Admiralty Commissioners v SS Amerika* [1917] A.C. 38 at 61 (the actual decision was that payments voluntarily made to the victim of an alleged *tort* could not be recovered: on this point see also *Esso Petroleum Co Ltd v Hall Russell & Co Ltd* [1989] A.C. 643). For the possibility of recovering, as damages for breach of contract, voluntary payments to or benefits conferred on third parties, see also *Banco de Portugal v Waterlow & Sons Ltd* [1932] A.C. 452, below, pp.978–979. And see the discussion at pp.594 and 596, below of *Linden Gardens Trust Ltd v Lenesta Sludge Disposals Ltd* [1994] 1 A.C. 85 and of *Alfred McAlpine Construction Ltd v Panatown Ltd* [2001] 1 A.C. 518.

(e) DAMAGES IN RESPECT OF THIRD PARTY'S LOSS: GENERAL RULE. The starting point of the following discussion is the general principle that, in an action for damages, a claimant cannot recover more than the amount required to compensate him for his loss,[20] so that he cannot, in general, recover damages for breach of a contract made for the benefit of a third party[21] in respect of loss suffered, not by the promisee, but by that third party.[22] That principle was indeed doubted by Lord Denning M.R. in *Jackson v Horizon Holidays Ltd*,[23] where the defendants contracted with the claimant to provide holiday accommodation for the claimant, his wife and their two three-year-old children.[24] The accommodation fell far short of the promised standard, and the claimant recovered damages, including £500 for "mental distress".[25] Lord Denning M.R., said that this sum would have been excessive compensation for the claimant's own distress.[26] He nevertheless upheld the award on the ground that the claimant had made a contract for the benefit both of himself and of his wife and children[27]; and that he could recover damages in respect of their loss as well as in respect of his own. But the authorities cited in support of this conclusion seem to contradict rather than to favour it.[28] Moreover, in *Beswick v Beswick* the majority of the House of Lords said that the promisee's estate could have recovered no more than nominal damages as it had suffered no loss.[29] This is scarcely consistent with the view that the promisee under a contract for the benefit of a third party is, as a general rule, entitled to damages in respect of the third party's loss. James L.J. in *Jackson's* case seems to have regarded the £500 as compensation for the claimant's own distress.[30] No doubt this was increased by his witnessing the distress suffered by his wife and children, and if the promisee himself suffers loss he should not be prevented from recovering it in full merely because the contract was made partly for the benefit of third parties[31] who also suffered loss. In *Woodar Investment Development Ltd v Wimpey Construction Co Ltd*[32] the House of Lords disapproved Lord Denning's

---

[20] See below, p.927; *cf. White v Jones* [1995] 2 A.C. 207, below, p.616, where the damages recoverable by the estate of the other party to the contract would have been no more than nominal.

[21] *A fortiori*, a promisee cannot recover damages in respect of loss suffered by a third party *other* than one for whose benefit the contract was made. Thus if A agrees to buy goods from B which B intends to acquire from C, and A repudiates the contract so that B does not in turn buy the goods from C, then B cannot recover damages in respect of any loss suffered by C: *And so to Bed Ltd v Dixon*, Transcript November 21, 2000 at [46–49], [54], Ch D. Of course if B had *contracted* to acquire the goods from C and was in consequence of A's repudiation liable in damages to C, then B could recover the amount for which he was not liable from A as damages in respect of his (B's) *own* loss: see below, p.912.

[22] *The Albazero* [1977] A.C. 774 at 846; *Linden Gardens* case, above n.19 at p.114; *Alfred McAlpine Construction Co Ltd v Panatown Ltd* [2001] 1 A.C. 518, below, p.597 at nn.70 and 71.

[23] [1975] 1 W.L.R. 1468; Yates, 39 M.L.R. 202.

[24] It was assumed that the wife and children were not parties to the contract. Contrast, as to this, above, p.585 at n.52.

[25] [1975] 1 W.L.R. 1468 at 1472.

[26] [1975] 1 W.L.R. 1468 at 1474.

[27] *ibid.*; *cf. McCall v Abelesz* [1976] Q.B. 585 at 594.

[28] Lord Denning M.R. relied on a dictum of Lush L.J. in *Lloyd's v Harper* (1880) 16 Ch.D. 290 at 331 said to have been quoted by Lord Pearce in *Beswick v Beswick* "with considerable approval": [1975] 1 W.L.R. at 1473. In fact Lord Pearce said that the dictum "cannot be accepted without qualification and regardless of the context": [1968] A.C. at 88; *cf. ibid.* at 101; he agreed with the view expressed in *Coulls v Bagots Executor and Trustee Co Ltd* [1967] A.L.R. 385 at 411 that Lush L.J.'s dictum must be confined to the case in which the contract creates a trust in favour of the third party (below, p.646). This situation falls within the special exception stated at p.593, n.43 below.

[29] See above, p.591.

[30] At 1474.

[31] *cf. Radford v De Froberville* [1977] 1 W.L.R. 1262 (damages for failure to build a wall not reduced merely because claimant had entered into the contract, not only for his own benefit alone, but also for that of his tenants).

[32] [1980] 1 W.L.R. 277.

approach to the question of damages in *Jackson's case*, though the actual decision in the latter case was supported on the ground that the damages were awarded in respect of the claimant's own loss[33]; or alternatively on the ground that cases such as the booking of family holidays or ordering meals in restaurants[34] might "call for special treatment".[35] In the *Woodar* case itself a contract for the sale of land provided that, on completion, the purchaser should pay £850,000 to the vendor and also £150,000 to a third party. The vendor claimed damages on the footing that the purchaser had wrongfully repudiated the contract and the actual decision was that there had been no such repudiation,[36] so that the issue of damages did not arise. But the question what damages would have been recoverable in the *Woodar* case itself if there had been a wrongful repudiation was there described as "one of great doubt and difficulty"[37]: presumably it would turn on such factors as whether the vendor was under a legal obligation to ensure that the third party received the payment, or whether, on the purchaser's failure to make the payment, the vendor had himself made it, or procured it to be made, from other resources available to him.

The assumption underlying the *Woodar* case thus seems to be that, where a contract for the benefit of a third party has been broken, the promisee cannot generally recover damages in respect of a loss suffered only by the third party. But this position was there described as "most unsatisfactory"[38] and said to be in need of reconsideration, either by the legislature or by the House of Lords itself.[39] It is unsatisfactory because it can give rise to what has been called a "legal black hole"[40] that is, to a situation in which the promisor has committed a plain breach which has caused loss to the third party whom the contracting parties intended to benefit[41] but none to the promisee, and in which no other remedy[42] (than damages for the third party's loss) is available against the promisor.

(f) DAMAGES IN RESPECT OF THIRD PARTY'S LOSS: EXCEPTIONS IN GENERAL. Judicial awareness of the unsatisfactory results which can flow from the general rule that a promisee can recover damages only for his own loss has led to the creation of exceptions to that rule. For example, substantial damages for breach of contract can be recovered by a trustee even though the loss is suffered by his *cestui que trust*[43]; by an agent even though the loss is suffered by his undisclosed principal[44]; by a local authority even though the loss is suffered (ultimately) by its inhabitants[45]; and by the shipper of goods for breach

---

[33] [1980] 1 W.L.R. 277 at 283, 293, 297. Where a contract is made with a company and the breach causes loss to its subsidiary, damages can be recovered by the company since the value of its holding in the subsidiary will be reduced in consequence of the loss: *George Fischer (Great Britain) Ltd v Multi Construction Ltd* [1995] 1 B.C.L.C. 260.

[34] *cf. Lockett v AM Charles Ltd* [1938] 4 All E.R. 170, where agency reasoning was used in such a situation.

[35] [1980] 1 W.L.R. 277 at 283. *cf. Calabar Properties Ltd v Stitcher* [1984] 1 W.L.R. 287 at 290 where it was not disputed that a tenant's damages for her landlord's breach of his covenant to repair should include compensation for ill-health suffered by her husband.

[36] See below, p.808.

[37] [1980] 1 W.L.R. 277 at 284. See also below, p.602, n.31.

[38] *ibid.* at 291; *cf.* pp.297–298, 300–301; *cf. Forster v Silvermere Golf and Equestrian Centre* (1981) 125 S.J. 397 ("a blot on our jurisprudence").

[39] *cf. Beswick v Beswick* [1968] A.C. 58 at 72.

[40] *Darlington BC v Wiltshier (Northern) Ltd* [1995] 1 W.L.R. 68 at 79; for the origins of this metaphor, see *Alfred McAlpine Construction Ltd v Panatown Ltd* [2001] A.C. 518 at 529.

[41] See above, p.592 at n.21 for this requirement.

[42] *e.g.*, by way of specific performance, as in *Beswick v Beswick* [1968] A.C. 58.

[43] *cf.* below, p.646.

[44] See, for example, below, p.734.

[45] *cf. St Albans' CC v International Computers Ltd* [1996] 4 All E.R. 481.

of his contract of carriage with the shipowner even though the loss is suffered by a person to whom he has sold the goods, and to whom the risk and property in them had passed, but who has not himself acquired any rights to sue the shipowner under the contract of carriage[46]: it will be convenient to refer to this rule as "the *Albazero* exception", after the leading modern case in which it is recognised.[47] In all these exceptional cases a person recovers substantial damages for breach of contract even though the breach caused loss, not to him, but to a third party.[48]

(g) FURTHER EXCEPTIONS: BUILDING CONTRACTS. The list of exceptions just stated should not be regarded as closed and the possibility of extending them or of creating further exceptions is illustrated by a line of cases beginning with *Linden Gardens Trust v Lenesta Sludge Disposals Ltd*.[49] In that case, a building contract between parties described in it as employer and contractor provided for work to be done by the contractor by way of developing a site owned by the employer as shops, offices and flats. The site (but not the benefit of the contract) was later transferred by the employer to a third party, and it was assumed[50] for the purpose of the proceedings that the third party had suffered financial loss as a result of having to remedy breaches of the building contract committed after the transfer. In an action for breach of the building contract brought by the employer, the contractor argued that no loss had been suffered by the employer as he was no longer owner of the land when the alleged breaches occurred, and that the employer was therefore entitled to no more than nominal damages. In the House of Lords, this argument was rejected, and the employer's claim upheld,[51] on two distinct grounds.

Lord Griffiths upheld the employer's claim on what has become known as the "broader ground"[52] that the employer "ha[d] suffered financial loss because he ha[d] to spend money to give him the benefit of the bargain which the defendant had promised but failed to deliver".[53] He added that "the court will of course wish to be satisfied that the repairs have been or are likely to be carried out".[54] This approach is, it is submitted,

---

[46] *Dunlop v Lambert* (1839) 2 Cl. & F. 626 at 627 (as to which see *Alfred McAlpine Construction Ltd v Panatown Ltd* [2001] 1 A.C. 518 at 523 *et seq.*); *The Sanix Ace* [1987] 1 Lloyd's Rep. 465; *The Chanda* [1989] 2 Lloyd's Rep. 494. The rule was recognised in *The Albazero* [1977] A.C. 774, but held inapplicable as the buyer had acquired his own contractual rights against the shipowner under s.1 of the Bills of Lading Act 1855; (now repealed and replaced by Carriage of Goods by Sea Act 1992); Weir [1977] C.L.J. 24. In the case of contracts to which the Carriage of Goods by Sea Act 1992 applies, a special statutory exception is created by s.2(4) of the Act to the general rule that a person can recover damages only in respect of his own loss; for a full discussion of this subsection, see *Carver on Bills of Lading* (1st ed., 2001), §§5–067 to 5–073.

[47] *The Albazero*, above, n.46.

[48] For recognition of a similar possibility in the law of tort, see *Hunt v Severs* [1994] 2 A.C. 350 at 357.

[49] [1994] 1 A.C. 85; Duncan Wallace, 110 L.Q.R. 42.

[50] The case is reported on a preliminary issue of law, so that the alleged facts had not been proved.

[51] *cf. IMI Cornelius (UK) v Alan J Bloor* (1993) 57 Build L.R. 108.

[52] *Linden Gardens* case, above, at 96–97 (*per* Lord Griffiths); *Alfred McAlpine Construction Ltd v Panatown Ltd* [2001] 1 A.C. 518, *e.g.* at 532.

[53] [1994] 1 A.C. 85 at 97. In fact the third party had reimbursed the employer in respect of this expenditure: see *ibid.* at 97; but this did not affect the question of liability.

[54] *ibid.* This requirement has been doubted on the ground that, in general, the court is "not concerned with what the plaintiff proposes to do with his damages": *Darlington BC v Wiltshier Northern Ltd* [1995] 1 W.L.R. 68 at 80; and see below p.946. But it seems, with respect, that Lord Griffiths' requirement is concerned, not with the question what the plaintiff proposes to do with the damages, but with the question whether he has suffered any loss. In *Alfred McAlpine Construction Ltd v Panatown Ltd* [2001] 1 A.C. 518 at 592, Lord Millett (dissenting) rejects the above reasoning, apparently on the ground that the promisee is "bound to mitigate his loss" and "cannot increase it by entering into other arrangements". But, with respect, the mitigation rules only require the injured party to act reasonably (below, pp.978–979) and in cases of the present kind this requirement would normally be satisfied where he made alternative provision to secure for the third party the benefit which the promisor has, in breach of the contract, failed to provide.

consistent with the explanation given in *Beswick v Beswick*[55] of the fact that the damages there were regarded as no more than nominal: the court there could not be satisfied that the substitute provision for the widow was likely to be made, precisely because the promisee lacked the means to make it.[56] The essence of Lord Griffiths' reasoning is that the promisee recovers damages in respect of the loss which he himself has suffered in ensuring that the third party receives the intended benefit. The "broader ground" therefore cannot apply where there is no practical possibility of curing the breach and so of securing the intended benefit to the third party, as in the "family holiday" cases discussed above.

Although Lord Keith had "much sympathy"[57] with, and Lord Bridge was "much attracted by",[58] Lord Griffiths' reasoning, they (as well as Lord Ackner) preferred to base their decision on the narrower ground stated by Lord Browne-Wilkinson. This treats the loss as having been suffered by the third party rather than by the employer, but concludes that the employer could nevertheless recover substantial damages as the case fell within the rationale of the *Abazero* exception[59] to the general rule that a party can recover damages only in respect of his own loss. The rationale of this exception was that, in the carriage of goods cases to which it applies, the shipper and carrier must have contemplated that property in the goods might be transferred to third parties after the contract had been made, and that the shipper must therefore be treated in law as having made the contract of carriage for the benefit of all persons who might after the time of contracting acquire interests in the goods.[60] This rationale applied equally to the facts of the *Linden Gardens* case since the contractor could foresee that parts of the new development were going to be "occupied and possibly purchased by third parties" so that "it could be foreseen that damage caused by a breach would cause loss to later owners".[61] The contractor could also foresee that a later owner would not have acquired rights under the building contract against the contractor since that contract expressly prohibited assignment by the employer without the contractor's written consent, which had not been sought. The effect of the *Linden Gardens* case was thus to extend the *Albazero* exception to building (and possibly to other) contracts, but it was consistent with two factors which had restricted the scope of that exception: namely that (a) the loss or damage was caused to property which had been transferred by one of the contracting parties to the third party; and (b) the third party had not acquired any rights under the building contract[62] and it was foreseeable (by reason of the prohibition against assignment) that he would not do so. The significance of these factors is further considered in the two later cases discussed below.

(i) *No transfer of the subject-matter to third party.* In *Darlington BC v Wiltshier Northern Ltd*[63] where a local authority (the council) wished to develop land which it already owned. The building work was to be done by the defendant; finance was to be provided by a bank but this could not be done in the most obvious way, by a loan to the council from the bank, since such an arrangement would have violated government restrictions on local authority borrowing. The transaction was therefore cast in the form of two contracts: (1) a building contract in which the bank was the employer and the

---

[55] [1968] A.C. 58.
[56] *ibid.* at 102; above p.591.
[57] [1994] 1 A.C. 85 at 95.
[58] *ibid.* at 96.
[59] See above, at n.46.
[60] *The Albazero* [1977] A.C. 744 at 847.
[61] [1994] 1 A.C. 85 at 114.
[62] *cf.* above, p.594 at n.47.
[63] [1995] 1 W.L.R. 68.

defendant the building contractor; and (2) a contract between the council and the bank, by which the bank undertook to procure the erection of the buildings on the site, to pay all sums due under the building contract and to assign to the council the benefit of any rights against the defendant to which the bank might be entitled at the time of the assignment. Cl.4(5) of this second contract provided that the bank was not to be liable to the council "for any incompleteness or defect in the building work"; and it was this provision which was the principal source of the difficulties in the case. The bank duly assigned its rights against the defendant to the council which claimed damages as such assignee from the defendant in respect of defects in the work. Since an assignee cannot recover more than the assignor could have been done,[64] the question arose what the bank could have recovered; and it was argued that it could have recovered no more than nominal damages since it had suffered no loss, having no interest in the land (or buildings) on which the work had been done and being protected by cl.4(5) from any liability to the council for defects in the work.[65] But the Court of Appeal rejected this argument and held that the bank could have recovered substantial damages from the defendant in respect of the council's loss and that it was this right which had been assigned to the council. This amounted to an extension[66] of the *Linden Gardens* case to a situation in which there was *no* transfer of the property affected by the breach from the promisee to the third party. This extension was later approved by the House of Lords,[67] so that, at least in the context of defective performance of building contracts,[68] such a transfer is no longer a necessary condition of the promisee's right to recover damages in respect of the third party's loss.

(ii) *Third party with independent contractual right against promisor.* In *Alfred McAlpine Construction Ltd v Panatown Ltd*[69] the facts resembled those of the *Darlington* case in that a building contract was again made, not between the building contractor and the company which owned the site (the owner), but between that contractor and another company (the employer) associated with the owners; the object of adopting this tripartite structure was to avoid VAT. On the same day on which this building contract was made, a separate contract (the "Duty of Care Deed") was made between the owner and the contractor; the obligations imposed on the contractor by this deed were not precisely co-terminous with those imposed on him by the building contract; and the Deed did not, while the contract did, contain an arbitration clause. The employer alleged that the building work was seriously defective and in arbitration proceedings claimed damages from the contractor, who argued that the employer should recover no more than nominal damages since any loss resulting from the alleged defects in the work had been suffered, not by the employer (as the employer had never owned the property), but by the owner. The House of Lords, by a majority, upheld the contractor's argument and so rejected the

---

[64] See below, p.691.

[65] These difficulties are not, it is submitted, removed by Dillon L.J.'s alternative ground for decision, *viz.* that the bank was constructive trustee for the council of its contractual rights against the defendant: this reasoning merely pushes the enquiry back to the question what (if anything) the bank could have recovered from the defendant.

[66] [1995] 1 W.L.R. 68 at 79, *per* Steyn L.J. Dillon L.J. regarded the result in the *Darlington* case as a "direct application" of the *Linden Gardens* case: *ibid.*, at 75. Waite L.J. expressed his agreement with both the other judgments, though his reasoning seems to be closer to that of Dillon L.J. than to that of Steyn L.J. See also *John Harris Partnership v Groveworld Ltd* [1999] P.N.L.R. 697 (developer entitled to recover from architect retained by him loss suffered in part by a third party who had financed the building project).

[67] *Alfred McAlpine Construction Ltd v Panatown Ltd* [2001] A.C. 518 at 531, 566 *per* Lords Clyde and Jauncey; *ibid.*, at 545, 584 *per* Lords Goff and Millett (dissenting).

[68] *Quaere* whether this extension will be applied in the carriage by sea context in which the exception originated: see *Carver on Bills of Lading* (1st ed., 2001), §§5–057.

[69] [2001] 1 A.C. 518, discussed by Coote, 117 L.Q.R. 81, reversing (1998) 58 Const.L.R. 58, discussed by Treitel, 114 L.Q.R. 572; for further proceedings see (2001) 76 Con.L.R. 222.

employer's claim for substantial damages in respect of the owner's loss. It was accepted by the majority[70] and by one of the dissentients[71] that, as a general rule, a contracting party could not recover damages in respect of loss suffered, not by himself, but by a third party; and the question therefore arose whether the case could be brought within an exception to that general rule. This raised, in turn, the question whether either of the grounds for the decision in the *Linden Gardens* case[72] supported the employer's claim. It will be recalled that the "narrow" ground for that decision was derived from the "*Albazero* exception" under which a shipper of goods can sometimes recover damages in respect of a third party's loss.[73] That exception is, however, subject to the restriction that it does not apply where the third party had himself acquired contractual rights against the carrier,[74] usually by transfer to the third party of a bill of lading.[75] In the *Panatown* case, the majority held (and the dissentients accepted) that the case fell within this restriction, so that the "*Albazero* exception" (and hence the "narrow ground" in the *Linden Gardens* case) did not apply because the Duty of Care Deed gave the owner an independent contractual right against the contractor. This point was, moreover, decisive even though that right did not arise under a *building* contract, so that, in this respect the restriction was somewhat expanded: in the carriage by sea cases, the restriction normally[76] came into operation because the third party had acquired rights under a contract of *carriage*. Nevertheless it is respectfully submitted that this aspect of the *Panatown* case is consistent with the rationale of the restriction. In the carriage by sea cases, this could and did apply even though the *content* of the third party's contractual right against the carrier was not the same as that of the shipper's right[77]; and it was based on the reasoning that, where the third party had his own contractual rights against the carrier, the exception did not apply "because it was not needed".[78] It was not needed because, where the third party had his own contractual rights against the party in breach there was no risk of the "legal black hole"[79] which had driven judges to create exceptions to the general rule that a contracting party can recover damages only in respect of his own loss.

The majority in the *Panatown* case further held that the existence of the third party's rights against the contractor under the Duty of Care Deed also precluded the employer from recovering damages under the "broader ground"[80] given by Lord Griffiths in the *Linden Gardens* case. In view of the existence of those rights, the employer had no pecuniary interest in curing the defects in the contractor's work.[81] Hence he neither had suffered nor would suffer any loss of his own, in consequence of the contractor's breach,[82] and under the "broad ground" it is in respect of his *own* (not of the third party's) loss that the promisee recovers damages. This conclusion can, on the facts of the

---

[70] [2001] 1 A.C. 518 at 522, 563, 575.

[71] Lord Millett, *ibid.*, at 580–581; Lord Goff is more sceptical: see *ibid.* at 538–539.

[72] [1994] 1 A.C. 85, above, pp.551–552; referred to as the *St Martin* case throughout the speeches in the *Panatown* case.

[73] *The Albazero* [1977] A.C. 774; above pp.594, 595.

[74] This was the position in *The Albazero*, above, itself, where the exception accordingly did not apply.

[75] See above, p.594, n.46.

[76] The restriction could also apply where the third party's contractual right against the carrier were under an implied contract of the kind illustrated by *Brandt v Liverpool, etc., SN Co* [1924] 1 K.B. 575; see *The Albazero* [1977] A.C. 774 at 847.

[77] As in *The Albazero* [1977] A.C. 774.

[78] *Panatown* case [2001] 1 A.C. 518 at 575; *The Albazero*, above at 847–848.

[79] *Darlington BC v Wiltshier Northern Ltd* [1975] 1 W.L.R. 68 at 79; above, p.593 n.40.

[80] *Alfred McAlpine Construction Ltd v Panatown Ltd* [2001] 1 A.C. 518 at 532 all the other members of the House of Lords accepted and used in this terminology.

[81] *ibid.* at 574 and 577 (*per* Lords Jauncey and Browne-Wilkinson).

[82] *cf.* below, p.934.

Panatown case, be supported for two further reasons. First, the creation or extension of exceptions to the general rule that a party can recover damages only in respect of his own loss is and should be driven and limited by necessity[83]: that is, by the need to guard against the risk of "legal black holes" of the kind described above; and in the *Panatown* case there was no such risk.[84] Secondly, the decision gives effect to the "contractual scheme"[85] created by the parties; and this point, so far from being undermined by the fact that the contractor's obligations to the owner under the Duty of Care Deed were not precisely co-terminous with his obligations to the employer under the building contract, is reinforced by this fact. As the parties had taken the "plain and deliberate course"[86] of giving the owner a "distinct entitlement"[87] against the contractor in respect of defects in the work, and as this entitlement was to be governed by the terms of one contract (the Duty of Care Deed), it followed that there was no good practical reason for holding the contractor liable in respect of the same defects on the terms of another contract (the building contract) for substantial damages to the employer, to whom these defects had caused no loss of his own. The fact that the "general rule" has been the subject of frequent judicial disapproval no doubt gives rise to the temptation to continue the process of eroding it by creating new or extending existing exceptions to it. But that criticism has occurred mainly in cases in which the third party problem was an inescapable consequence of normal commercial factors such as those which existed in the *Linden Gardens* case. The pressure for eroding the unpopular general rule is much less strong where the third party problem is, so to speak, manufactured by the parties for an ulterior motive, such as Government restrictions on borrowing, as in the *Darlington* case, or avoiding tax,[88] as in the *Panatown* case, where, in the view of the majority any such pressure was eliminated for the further reason that the third party had his own contractual remedy against the party in breach under a separate contract between these parties.

(h) OUTSTANDING PROBLEMS. The *Panatown* case is significant not only for the points it decides, but also for some of those which it leaves open.

(i) *Status of the "broader ground"*. The first such point relates to the effect of the case on the status of Lord Griffiths' "broader ground" in the *Linden Gardens* case. This ground forms the basis of the two dissenting speeches[89] in the *Panatown* case, and it is not the subject of any adverse comment from the majority,[90] whose speeches do not rule out the possibility of its being applied in the, perhaps more common, situation in which the third party has *no* contractual rights of his own against the promisor in respect of loss suffered by him in consequence of the defective services rendered under the contract between promisor and promisee. It seems that, even in such a situation, the majority would deny the employer's right to recover substantial damages under the "broader ground" unless *either* the condition stated by Lord Griffiths is satisfied, *i.e.* "the repairs

---

[83] See the references given in n.78, above.

[84] *Panatown* case [2001] 1 A.C. 518 at 574, *per* Lord Jauncey.

[85] *ibid.*, at 577 *per* Lord Browne-Wilkinson; and see 76 Con. L.R. 224 at [38] ("made their contractual bed"). *Cf. Henderson v Merrett Syndicates Ltd* [1992] 2 A.C. 145 at 195, using the phrase "contractual structure" in the context of the faintly analogous question whether a contract between A and B can impose on a duty of care to C: see below, p.608, n.87; *cf. Greater Nottingham Co-operative Society Ltd v Cementation Piling and Foundation Ltd* [1989] Q.B. 71 (tort duty excluded by tripartite contractual structure); and *R M Turton & Co Ltd v Kerslake & Partners* [2000] Lloyd's Rep. P.N. 967 (New Zealand Court of Appeal).

[86] *Panatown* case [2001] 1 A.C. 518 at 536, *per* Lord Clyde.

[87] *ibid.*

[88] For the contrary view, see Lord Goff, dissenting, in the *Panatown* case, above, at 556–557.

[89] Of Lords Goff and Millett.

[90] Lords Clyde, Jauncey and Browne-Wilkinson.

have been or are likely to be carried out",[91] or the employer has entered into a separate contract with the owner undertaking liability in respect of defects in the contractor's work.[92] Where neither of these requirements is satisfied, the result of allowing the promisee to recover the cost of repairs as damages for his own loss would be "unattractive" in that it would enable him to "put the money in his own pocket"[93] without carrying out or paying for repairs: the technique of requiring him to hold the damages for the third party applies, on the authorities,[94] only where damages are recovered (under one of the exceptions to the general rule) in respect of the *third party's*, not in respect of the promisee's *own* loss. It follows that the requirements stated above[95] do not apply where the promisee's claim can succeed on the "narrow ground": in this respect, that ground is, paradoxically, broader than the "broader ground".

(ii) *Scope of the "broader ground"*. If the "broader ground" is accepted for cases in which the third party has no contractual rights of his own against the promisor, then a further problem arises as to its scope. The example given by Lord Griffiths in support of this ground is one in which loss is caused by reason of the *defective* performance of a contract to render *services*.[96] The case put by him[97] is that of a husband who contracts with a builder to have his wife's house repaired; if the builder does the work defectively the husband is (so long as the other requirements of the "broader ground" are satisfied) entitled (in the example) to substantial damages, *i.e.*, to the cost of putting the defects right. Two questions then arise. The first is whether the rationale of the "broader ground" applies to cases in which the breach consists of a simple *failure* or *refusal* to perform. And the second is whether it applies where the obligation which is not performed is one to do something other than to render services. The two questions come together in a case where, for a consideration provided or to be provided by A, a promise is made by B to A to pay a sum of money to C and B fails or refuses, wholly or in part to perform that promise. Those were, in substance, the facts of *Beswick v Beswick*[98] where the majority of the House of Lords took the view that the damages recoverable by the estate would be no more than nominal. That may not, indeed, amount to a direct rejection of the "broader ground" in such cases. The reason given in *Beswick v Beswick* for the view that the promisee's damages would there have been merely nominal was that the estate had no assets out of which it could make the payments to C which B had promised, but failed, to make.[99] But it is not clear whether in substance that reasoning is inconsistent with the "broader ground"; for, if the cost to A of securing the benefit intended for C is to be defrayed *out of the damages*, then it should not matter that A cannot provide that benefit out of his *other* assets, at least so long as A is solvent. The views expressed in *Beswick v Beswick* on the question of damages recoverable by the estate should, it is submitted, now be read subject to developments of the law as to damages in respect of a third party's loss in a number of later cases. The most directly relevant of these is the *Woodar* case[1] where it appears to be assumed that, as a general

---

[91] *Linden Gardens* case [1994] 1 A.C. 85 at 97; see further p.601 below at n.18.
[92] No such separate contract was established in the *Panatown* case: see 76 Con.L.R. 224 at [35].
[93] *Panatown* case [2001] 1 A.C. 518 at 571. This possible restriction on the scope of the broader ground is not considered in the discussion of that ground in the further proceedings in that case (76 Con. L.R. 244 at [20]) being unnecessary to the decision at this stage.
[94] See below, p.605.
[95] See above, at nn.91 and 92.
[96] Lord Millett's dissent is restricted to this situation: [2001] 1 A.C. 518 at 591; Lord Goff's dissent does not appear to be so restricted: see *ibid.* at 545, 552–553.
[97] *Linden Gardens* case [1994] 1 A.C. 85 at 97.
[98] [1968] A.C. 58, above, p.589.
[99] [1968] A.C. 58 at 102; above p.591.
[1] [1980] 1 W.L.R. 277, above p.593.

rule,[2] A cannot recover substantial damages from B for B's failure to perform his promise to A to pay a sum of money to C. This conclusion seems to be based on the assumptions that the loss is C's and that A cannot generally recover damages in respect of C's loss. It does not seem to preclude the possibility of A's recovering damages in respect of any loss which he himself might have suffered in consequence of B's breach: *e.g.* because A was under a contractual obligation to procure the payment to C or because A, acting reasonably, has made alternative provision for C.[3] Even in the absence of such factors, it is submitted that, in the light of the developments since the *Woodar* case,[4] the law should take account of the possibility that, unless B were held liable for substantial changes to A, then he might be under no substantial liability at all: in other words, that there would be a "legal black hole". In *Beswick v Beswick* and the *Panatown* case there were no such "black holes": in the former case, because of the availability of a satisfactory remedy for A against B by way of specific performance in favour of C[5]; in the latter because of the availability of a satisfactory remedy for C against B in damages under the separate contract between these parties.[6] If there is no such remedy and if the conditions in which A can (under the "broader ground") recover damages in respect of his *own* loss are not satisfied,[7] then the lack of any such remedy should, it is submitted be a ground for allowing A to claim damages in respect of C's loss. The need to avoid the "black hole" should generate this remedy; and, where A has suffered no loss himself, result of allowing him to recover damages in respect of C's loss (rather than in respect of A's own loss) would also have the advantage of ensuring that these damages were to be held for C,[8] thus avoiding the "unattractive" result of allowing A to "put the money in his own pocket".[9]

It is submitted that the same approach is also appropriate to the case where the contract between A and B is one for services for the benefit of C which B simply fails or refuses to perform, instead performing them defectively, as in Lord Griffiths' example,[10] in which it seems to be assumed that A has paid for the work. Lord Griffiths does not discuss the case of total non-performance by B, presumably assuming that in such a case B would not have been paid.[11] If A then gets another builder to do the work and that other builder charges no more than B would have done, A will (subject to questions of mitigation[12] and remoteness) be able to recover the difference as damages for his *own* loss. The position will be substantially the same where A has paid B in advance and B has done no part of the work: in that case A will be entitled to claim restitution of his payment[13] together with damages for his own loss in respect of any extra cost of employing a substitute builder.[14] So in none of these cases of total non-performance is there any "black hole" and hence no need to generate a new remedy at

---

[2] *i.e.* unless A can show that B's breach caused loss *to* A *himself.*

[3] See above, p.593.

[4] *i.e.*, in the *Linden Gardens* case [1994] A.C. 85, the *Darlington* case [1995] 1 W.L.R. 68 and the *Panatown* case [2001] 1 A.C. 518.

[5] See above, p.590.

[6] See above, p.590.

[7] See below, after n.18.

[8] See below, pp.605–606.

[9] *Panatown* case [2001] 1 A.C. 518 at 571.

[10] See above, at n.97.

[11] Performance of the work is in contracts of this kind *prima facie* a condition precedent of the right to be paid: below, p.762.

[12] *e.g.* damages on a "cost of cure" basis are not recoverable if the cost of cure is wholly disproportionate to the benefit to be derived from cure: below, p.944.

[13] There will be a "total failure of consideration": below, p.1049.

[14] See below p.942.

the suit of A in respect of C's loss. The most difficult case is that of an advance payment by A followed by *part* performance by B in circumstances in which A himself has suffered no loss: *e.g.* because A was under no obligation to C to secure completion of the performance that B was to render and has neither himself taken any steps to secure that completion nor is likely to do so.[15] In such a case of partial performance there might be considerable difficulty in holding B liable for partial restitution[16]; and if, in addition, the remedy of specific performance were not available (*e.g.* because the contract was one for personal services to be rendered by B[17]) then there would be at least a partial "black hole" and this fact should (it is again submitted) be a ground for allowing A to recover substantial damages from B in respect of C's loss.

(iii) *Use to which damages are put.* It will be recalled that, in his statement of the "broader ground" in the *Linden Gardens* case, Lord Griffiths said that the court would wish to be "satisfied that the repairs have been or are likely to be carried out".[18] In later cases, conflicting views have been expressed on the question whether this is an essential requirement for the operation of the "broader ground".

One view is that it is not, since (at least as a general rule[19]) a court in awarding damages is not concerned with the question of what the claimant intends to do with these damages[20]; that question is said to be relevant only to the issue of "reasonableness". This issue, however, arises, not for the purpose of determining the *existence* of a claim for substantial damages, but its *extent*: it may be relevant in determining whether damages in a two-party case are to be assessed on a difference in value or on a cost of cure basis,[21] or whether the claimant has failed to mitigate his loss[22]; but such questions arise only on the assumption that a claim for substantial damages does exist. A related argument in favour of the view that the claimant's intention with regard to the disposal of the damages is irrelevant is that he has been deprived by the defendant's breach of the benefit of his bargain, and this fact is, of itself, enough to support a claim for substantial damages.[23] This line of reasoning is, however, with respect, hard to reconcile with the principle that the victim of a breach has no claim to substantial damages if the breach has no adverse effect.[24] The assumption underlying this principle is that the mere failure to perform a contract does not suffice to sustain a claim for substantial damages: as Lord Clyde said in the *Panatown* case, "A breach of contract may cause a loss but is not in itself a loss in any meaningful sense".[25] In the cases here under consideration, the breach will have no adverse effect *on the claimant* (the promisee)[26] unless he has carried out or

---

[15] As in *Beswick v Beswick* [1968] A.C. 58, above, p.589.

[16] The "failure of consideration" would be only "partial": see below, pp.1050–1052.

[17] See below, pp.1029–1032.

[18] [1994] 1 A.C. 85 at 97; above, p.594; for further discussion, see below at nn.19–29.

[19] For a possible exception, see the discussion at pp.946–947 of the question whether cost of cure is recoverable where cure is not undertaken.

[20] See the *Darlington* case [1995] 1 W.L.R. 68 at 80; the *Panatown* case [2001] 1 A.C. 518 at 556, 592 *per* Lords Goff and Millett, dissenting; *Ruxley Electronics and Construction Co v Forsyth* [1966] A.C. 344 at 359 and 357; below, p.594 n.54.

[21] See below, pp.946–947.

[22] See below, p.977.

[23] See the references to the *Darlington* and *Panatown* cases in n.20, above.

[24] See below, p.934.

[25] [2001] 1 A.C. 518 at 534.

[26] Our concern here is with adverse *financial* effect on the claimant. A claim for damages for "loss of amenity" will generally be one for loss suffered by the claimant, though in the family holiday cases (above, pp.592–593) this loss may be increased by the claimaint's witnessing the sufferings of his family in comfortless hotels. *Cf.* also below, p.989.

intends to carry out cure; and the argument that he has been deprived of his bargain cannot answer the question whether it must be shown that this deprivation has had an adverse effect *on him*: it merely pushes this question back one stage.

The alternative view is that damages in respect of the cost of curing the breach (and so of securing the intended benefit for the third party) can be recovered only if cure has been, or is likely to be, carried out. The main practical argument in favour of this view is that (as noted above) it would be unattractive" to allow the promisee to recover the cost of cure as damages in respect of his own loss and then to "put the money in his own pocket".[27] It is respectfully submitted that this is the preferable view. In a two–party case it is indeed generally[28] no concern of the court's what the claimant intends to do with the damages; but the rationale of this rule does not necessarily apply in a three-party case. That rationale in a two–party case is that the defendant has, by reason of the breach, inflicted injury, loss or damage on the person or property *of the claimant* (or has failed to improve, or to transfer, an asset belonging to, or to be vested in, the claimant) who should therefore be able to deal in whatever way he pleases with the damages awarded to him in substitution of the interest *of his own* of which he has been deprived by the breach. For example, in the case of a contract to repair the claimant's own house, he could, but for the breach, have sold the house at a price reflecting the value of the repairs, had they been properly carried out, and then have disposed of the proceeds of the sale in any way he pleased; and so he should be able to dispose in the same way of the damages due to him for failure to carry out the repairs. Obviously, this reasoning cannot apply where the house is owned, not by the claimant, but by a third party. There is also the further point that, although in Lord Griffith's example the claimant as a matter of legal principle recovers damages in respect of his *own* loss, as a practical matter the purpose of the award is such a case is to protect the interests of the third party. Where damages are awarded in respect of a third party's loss (under one of the exceptions to the general rule) the court requires the promisee to hold these damages for the third party.[29] No such machinery is available where the damages are awarded in respect of the promisee's own loss; but a practical way of ensuring that the damages are in fact destined for the benefit of the third party is to require the promisee to show (as a condition of his entitlement to substantial damages) that they will be so used.

(i) RELATION TO THIRD PARTY'S RIGHT. Even where, in one of the exceptional situations discussed above, the promisee can recover damages in respect of the third party's loss, no right to enforce the contract is conferred directly on the third party, whose only claim will be to the fruits of any action which the promisee may decide to bring.[30] The third party will have a direct right against the promisor only under one of the exceptions to the doctrine of privity. On the facts of some[31] (though not of all[32]) of the cases discussed above, the third party would probably, if those facts recurred now, have such a right under the Contracts (Rights of Third Parties) Act 1999.[33] If the third party has such a right, then this very fact may restrict the number of situations in which the

---

[27] *Panatown* case [2001] 1 A.C. 158 at 571.

[28] See n.19, above.

[29] See below, pp.605–606.

[30] See below, pp.605–606.

[31] *e.g.* the *Woodar* case [1980] 1 W.L.R. 277 (above pp.592–593), see Law Com. No. 242, §7.49.

[32] *e.g.*, probably, the *Linden Gardens* case [1994] 1 A.C. 85 (above, p.594): see below, p.654.

[33] See below, pp.651 *et seq*. Subss 1(1)(a) and (3) of the 1999 Act will make it possible to draw up contracts, on facts similar to those of the *Linden Gardens* case, above, so as to confer a right of enforcement directly on the third party: see below, pp.651, 655.

promisee can recover damages in respect of the third party's loss[34]; and it will probably reduce the pressure on the courts to extend the range of such situations.[35] S.4 of the 1999 Act, however, preserves the promisee's rights under the contract.[36] The question of his right to recover damages in respect of the third party's loss will therefore continue to arise and to be of practical importance: *e.g.* where the promisor has a defence against the third party which is not available against the promisee.[37]

(j) NEGATIVE PROMISE. Where the promise is negative in nature, the promisee's most obvious remedy is an injunction to restrain the promisor's breach. This remedy would, for example, be available where A validly promised B not to compete with C.

One type of negative promise which gives rise to special difficulty is a promise by A to B *not to sue* C, *e.g.* for a debt owed by C to A. If, in breach of such a promise, A nevertheless did sue C, it would not be appropriate for B to start a second action for an injunction to restrain A from proceeding with the first action; for such a step would lead to undesirable multiplicity of legal proceedings.[38] B's remedy is to ask the court to exercise its discretion[39] to stay A's action against C. In *Gore v Van der Lann*[40] the Court of Appeal held that B could obtain a stay of A's action against C only if two conditions were satisfied: there must be a definite promise by A to B not to sue C, and B must have a sufficient interest[41] in the enforcement of A's promise. This last requirement would not be satisfied unless, as a result of A's breach, B were exposed to the risk of incurring legal liability to C: for example where B had *contracted with* C to procure his release from a debt or a liability to A, and would be put in breach of that contract by A's action against C.

Snelling v John G Snelling Ltd[42] goes even further in giving effect to a promise of this kind. Three brothers had lent money to a family company of which they were directors. They agreed that if one of them resigned he should "forfeit" any money due to him from the company. One of them did resign and sued the company for the amounts due to him. By way of defence the company relied on the agreement between the brothers, and, if matters had rested there, the defence would have failed as the company was not a party to the agreement.[43] But the other two brothers applied to be joined as defendants to the action, adopted the company's defence and counterclaimed for a declaration that the third brother's loan was forfeited. It was held that they were entitled to such a declaration by virtue of the contract between them and that brother.[44] Ormrod J. further held that they could obtain a stay of the action against the company and that the most convenient way of disposing of the action against the company was to dismiss it. So far as the granting of the stay is concerned, the judgment is hard to reconcile with the

---

[34] On the reasoning of *The Albazero* [1977] A.C. 774, above p.594 and of *Alfred McAlpine Construction Ltd v Panatown Ltd* [2001] 1 A.C. 518, above, p.596.

[35] The "legal black hole" referred to in the *Darlington* case [1995] 1 W.L.R. 68 at 79 would be much reduced in significance.

[36] See below, p.665.

[37] 1999 Act, s.3(4), below, p.660.

[38] Supreme Court Act 1981, s.49(2), replacing Supreme Court of Judicature (Consolidation) Act 1925, s.41 which expressly provided that no proceedings in the High Court could be restrained by injunction.

[39] Under Supreme Court Act 1981, s.49(3).

[40] [1967] 2 Q.B. 31; Davies, 1 *Legal Studies* 287; *European Asian Bank AG v Punjab and Sind Bank* [1982] 2 Lloyd's Rep. 356; *The Chevalier Roze* [1983] 2 Lloyd's Rep. 438; and see below, p.637.

[41] *Deepak Fertilisers & Petrochemical Corp v ICI Chemicals & Polymers Ltd* [1999] 1 Lloyd's Rep. 378 at 401.

[42] [1973] 1 Q.B. 87; Wilkie, 36 M.L.R. 214.

[43] [1973] Q.B. 87 at 95.

[44] *ibid.* at 96.

requirement of a sufficient interest as defined in *Gore v Van der Lann*[45]; but it is submitted that Ormrod J.'s decision is consistent with the spirit of *Beswick v Beswick*.[46] If *the promisee* takes steps specifically to enforce the contract the court should, wherever possible, grant such remedy as is most appropriate for that purpose. Normally this will be an order of specific performance or an injunction. The fact that the latter remedy is not appropriate to enforce a promise not to sue should not deter the court from granting other remedies that serve substantially to enforce the promise. Such a remedy is, again, available only if it is sought *by the promisee*.[47] If the two brothers in the *Snelling* case had not applied to be joined to the action, the company could not have relied on the agreement between them and the third brother by way of defence.[48]

(2) Position between promisee and third party

The promisor may be willing to perform, and may actually perform, in favour of the third party, *e.g.* by paying him the agreed sum. These possibilities give rise to further problems between the third party and the promisee. In discussing these problems we shall at this stage assume that the case does not fall within any of the exceptions to the doctrine of privity which will be considered later in this Chapter.[49]

(a) PROMISOR PAYS OR IS WILLING TO PAY. The first problem arises where the promisor has actually paid the third party or is willing to pay him, and the promisee claims that the third party is not entitled to keep the money for his own benefit but must hold it on behalf of the promisee. Such a claim is not likely to be made by the promisee himself, as he wants to benefit the third party. But it might be made by the promisee's trustee in bankruptcy, or by his personal representative on death. In *Beswick v Beswick* the House of Lords held that the third party (the widow) was entitled to keep the money which the promisor (the nephew) was ordered to pay her, simply because it appeared from the true construction of the contract that this was the intention of the contracting parties.[50] It seems that the position would be the same where payments were made willingly, *i.e.* without any order of the court.[51] Payments actually received by the third party can be claimed by the promisee only if, on the true construction of the contract, they were made to the third party as nominee for the promisee. Where the money has not yet been paid, the promisor and the promisee can agree to rescind or vary the contract; and if they vary it so as to provide for payment to the promisee, the third party has no claim under the contract. But the question whether the promisee can unilaterally (*i.e.* without the consent of the promisor) demand that payment should be made to himself depends once again on the construction of the contract. If the contract can be construed as one to pay the third party "or as the promisee shall direct", then the promisee is entitled to demand

---

[45] [1967] 2 Q.B. 31.

[46] [1968] A.C. 58; above, p.589.

[47] *cf. Heaton v Axa Equity and Law Life Assurance Society plc* [2002] UKHL 15; [2002] 2 All E.R. 961, at [9] ("is enforceable by B", *i.e.* the promisee. No such promise had been made: see above p.573).

[48] *Snelling v John G Snelling Ltd* [1973] Q.B. 87 at 95.

[49] See below, pp.645–671.

[50] *Beswick v Beswick* [1968] A.C. 58 at 71, 96, on this point overruling *Re Engelbach's Estate* [1924] 2 Ch. 348 and doubting *Re Sinclair's Life Policy* [1938] Ch. 799. Earlier cases supporting the view stated in the text include *Ashby v Costin* (1888) 21 Q.B.D. 401; *Harris v United Kingdom, etc., Society* (1889) 87 L.T.J. 272; *Re Davies* [1892] 3 Ch. 63.

[51] This appears from the treatment in *Beswick v Beswick* of *Re Engelbach's Estate* (above), where the money had in fact been paid to the third party: see 93 L.J.Ch. 616 at 617.

payment to himself.[52] But the contract is not likely to be construed in this way where it is a matter of concern to the promisor that payment should be made to the third party, *e.g.* because the third party is a close relative of the promisor and it matters to the promisor that the third party should be provided for.[53]

The rules just stated apply only if there is indeed a promise to pay the third party. In *Coulls v Bagot's Executor and Trustee Co Ltd*[54] an agreement between A and B provided for payment of royalties by B to A and concluded: "I [A] authorise . . . [B] to pay all money connected with this agreement to my wife [W] . . . and myself . . . as joint tenants". The document was signed by A, B and W. A majority of the High Court of Australia held that there was no *promise* by B to A to pay W but only a *mandate* by A authorising B to pay W (so that such payment would discharge B). This mandate was revocable and had been revoked by A's death. Consequently, the money (which B was willing to pay) belonged to A's estate and not to W. The third party would, *a fortiori*, not be entitled to the money if he were mentioned in the contract as a mere nominee in such a way as to indicate that no beneficial interest was intended to pass to him, and that payment to him without the request of the promisee should not discharge the promisor.[55]

(b) PROMISEE REFUSES TO SUE. The second problem arises where the promisee fails or refuses to take any action to enforce the promise. Lord Denning has suggested that, even at common law the third party could in such a case circumvent the doctrine of privity by suing the promisor and joining the promisee as co-defendant.[56] But Diplock and Salmon L.JJ. have said that the action can (in cases not falling within any of the exceptions to the doctrine of privity[57]) be brought only by the promisee[58]; and it is submitted that this is the correct view. Lord Denning's view is inconsistent with the common law doctrine of privity which was recognised in *Beswick v Beswick* and in later cases.[59] It is also inconsistent with the reasoning of the cases on trusts of promises to be discussed below,[60] for if the third party could always sue by joining the promisee to the action, it would be pointless to insist that he must in addition show the existence of a trust.

(c) PROMISEE SUES FOR DAMAGES OR RESTITUTION. The final problem arises where the promisee sues but claims some form of relief other than specific performance in favour of the third party: *i.e.* where he claims damages or recovery of the consideration provided by him. If such a claim succeeded, it would seem to lead to a judgment for payment to the promisee and not to the third party; and the question would arise whether the promisee could keep the payment for his own benefit or whether he would be bound to hold it for the third party. In tort, a person can sometimes recover damages for a loss suffered, not by himself, but by another: *e.g.* a husband may get damages for loss of earnings suffered by his wife in giving up her job to nurse him after an accident

---

[52] *The Spiros C* [2000] 2 Lloyd's Rep. 319 at 331. The same is true where a contract provides for some other performance to be rendered to a third party: *e.g. Mitchell v Ede* (1840) 11 Ad. & El. 888; *The Lycaon* [1983] 2 Lloyd's Rep. 548.

[53] As in *Re Stapleton-Bretherton* [1941] Ch. 482.

[54] [1967] A.L.R. 385; for a similar distinction, see below, p.679.

[55] *Thavorn v Bank of Credit & Commerce SA* [1985] 1 Lloyd's Rep. 259, as to which see above, p.578 n.20; *The Turridu* [1999] 2 Lloyd's Rep. 401.

[56] *Beswick v Beswick* [1966] Ch. at 557; *Gurtner v Circuit* [1968] 2 Q.B. 587 at 596.

[57] *ibid.* at 599, 606.

[58] See above, p.604 at n.49.

[59] See above, pp.588–590.

[60] See below, pp.646–651.

and such damages must then be held on trust for the other person.[61] Similarly, damages for breach of contract can in the exceptional situations discussed above be recovered in respect of loss suffered by another[62]; such damages must be held for that other person.[63] This may also be the position in the cases which call "for special treatment",[64] such as the booking of family holidays or ordering meals in restaurants; if, in such cases, the promisee can recover damages in respect of the third party's loss, it may be that those damages, when recovered, would be held by the promisee as money had and received for the use of the third party.[65] But apart from these exceptional or special cases there does not appear to be any similar possibility where the promisee claims damages for breach of a contract merely because the contract was made for the benefit of a third party. The general rule in such a case is that damages will be awarded only to compensate the promisee for his *own* loss[66]; and where that general rule applies, it does not seem that he can be under any obligation to pay those damages (or any part of them) over to the third party.[67]

SECTION 3. SCOPE

1. General

The common law doctrine of privity means that a person cannot acquire rights or be subjected to liabilities *arising under* a contract to which he is not a party. It does not mean that a contract between A and B cannot affect the legal rights of C indirectly. For example, an agreement between A and B under which A accepts from B part payment of a debt owed by C to A in full settlement of that debt can benefit C by precluding A from suing C for the balance of the debt[68]; and *a fortiori* full performance by B of C's obligation to A can discharge that obligation.[69] Conversely, a building contract between A and B may benefit C by defining his rights: *e.g.* by specifying the time at which payment becomes due to C under a subcontract between B and C for the execution of part of the work.[70] It is also possible for a contract between A and B to affect C

---

[61] *Hunt v Severs* [1994] 2 A.C. 350 at 363, following *Cunningham v Harrison* [1973] Q.B. 942 at 952 and rejecting the contrary view in *Donnelly v Joyce* [1974] Q.B. 454 at 461–462. *cf. Allen v Waters* [1935] 1 K.B. 200 and *Dennis v LTPB* [1948], All E.R. 779, as explained in 72 L.Q.R. 187; *Lowe v Guise* [2002] EWCA Civ 197; [2002] 3 All E.R. (Comm) 454 at [38]. No such damages can be recovered by the injured party (A) where the result of requiring A to hold the damages for the third party (X) would be indirectly to confer on X a right to recover payment rendered under a contract between A and X which was unenforceable by virtue of Consumer Credit Act 1974, s.127(3): see *Dimond v Lovell* [2002] 1 A.C. 384, above, p.179. It remains to be seen how (if at all) this conclusion will, in the present context, be effected by the view, taken in *Wilson v First County Trust Ltd (No.2)* [2001] EWCA Civ 633; [2002] Q.B. 74 that s.127(3) of the 1974 Act was incompatible with Human Rights Act 1998 Sch.1, Pt I, Art.6 and Pt II, Art.1.

[62] See above, pp.593–594.

[63] *The Albazero* [1977] A.C. 774 at 845; *O'Sullivan v Williams* [1992] 3 All E.R. 385 at 387, discussing *The Winkfield* [1902] P. 42; *cf.* below, p.634; *Linden Gardens* case [1994] 1 A.C. 85 (above, p.594); *John Harris Partnership v Groveland Ltd* [1999] P.N.L.R. 697; Carriage of Goods by Sea Act 1992, s.2(4).

[64] *Woodar Investment Development Ltd v Wimpey Construction UK Ltd* [1980] 1 W.L.R. 277 at 283; above, pp.592–593.

[65] This was the view of Lord Denning M.R. in *Jackson v Horizon Holidays Ltd* [1975] 1 W.L.R. 1468 at 1473. The strange result would be that the claimant was under quasi-contractual liability to his small children in respect of part of the £500 recovered as damages for distress.

[66] See above, pp.595, 599.

[67] *cf. Coulls v Bagot's Executor and Trustee Co Ltd* [1967] A.L.R. 385 at 411.

[68] *Hirachand Punamchand v Temple* [1911] 2 K.B. 330; above, p.129 (where the effects on such facts of the Contracts (Rights of Third Parties) Act 1999 are also discussed); *cf. Johnson v Davies* [1999] Ch. 117 at 130.

[69] For the conditions to be satisfied for such discharge, see below, pp.755–757.

[70] *Co-operative Wholesale Society Ltd v Birse Construction Ltd* (1997) 84 B.L.R. 58.

adversely.[71] Of course A and B cannot by a contract between them impose an obligation on C to perform duties arising under the contract. This aspect of the doctrine of privity is so obvious that it scarcely needs to be stated: if A and B agreed that C was to pay £100 to A, no one would suppose that this agreement could oblige C to make the payment. But a contract between A and B may in some other way restrict C's freedom of action: for example it may create rights in or over property, such as a lien[72] or a lease[73] or an equitable interest, or give rise to a constructive trust affecting property[74]; and such interests can affect the rights of third parties who later acquire the property.

The following situations, in which contracts can at common law indirectly affect the legal rights of third parties, call for more extended discussion.

2. Liability in Negligence to Third Parties

(1) Duty of care may be owed to third party

While the primary effect of a contract between A and B is to oblige them to perform their respective promises to each other, the contract may also impose on A a duty of care to C, the breach of which will enable C to sue A in tort for negligence. The contract may have this effect because it gives rise to a relationship in which A owes a duty of care to C: for example, to the relationship of passenger (or cargo-owner) and carrier,[75] of occupier of premises and visitor,[76] or of bailor and sub-bailee,[77] or of building owner and subcontractor.[78] In a number of cases persons providing professional services, such as

---

[71] *e.g. The Glacier Bay* [1996] 1 Lloyd's Rep. 370; *Banque Financière de la Cité v Parc (Battersea) Ltd* [1999] 1 A.C. 221; *cf.* below, pp.638–645.

[72] See *Faith v EIC* (1821) 4 B. & Ald. 630; *Tappenden v Artus* [1964] 2 Q.B. 185; contrast *Chellaram & Sons (London) Ltd v Butler's Warehousing & Distribution Ltd* [1978] 2 Lloyd's Rep. 412 (third party not bound by agreement purporting to confer on sub-bailee a lien more extensive than that which would, but for such agreement, have arisen at common law).

[73] As in *Ashburn Anstalt v Arnold* [1989] Ch. 1, overruled on another point in *Prudential Assurance Co Ltd v London Residuary Body* [1992] A.C. 386.

[74] See *Ashburn Anstalt v Arnold*, above, where the mere fact that C had notice of an earlier contract between A and B was said at 25–26 to be insufficient to give rise to a constructive trust on C's acquisition of the land affected by that contract; and where Fox L.J. (delivering the judgment of the Court) at 17 disapproved dicta in *Errington v Errington* [1952] 1 K.B. 290 (which had been followed in *Re Sharpe* [1980] 1 W.L.R. 219) to the effect that a contractual licence granted by A to B gave rise to an equitable interest binding third parties; Hill, 51 M.L.R. 226; Oakley [1988] C.L.J. 353; *cf.* also *Binions v Evans* [1972] Ch. 359; Smith, [1973] C.L.J. 81; Hornby, 93 L.Q.R. 568; *Pritchard v Briggs* [1980] Ch. 338 (option to purchase); *Lyus v Prowsa Developments Ltd* [1982] 1 W.L.R. 1044.

[75] *Austin v GW Ry* (1867) L.R. 2 Q.B. 442; *The Antonis P Lemos* [1985] A.C. 711.

[76] Occupiers' Liability Act 1957, s.3; Defective Premises Act 1972, ss.1(1)(b), 4.

[77] *Moukataff v BOAC* [1967] 1 Lloyd's Rep. 396; *Bart v BWIA* [1967] 1 Lloyd's Rep. 239 (where the claim failed as the sub-bailee's duty was limited to one to keep safely, and did not extend to transmission of the package); *The Kapetan Markos NL (No.2)* [1987] 2 Lloyd's Rep. 321. Such a sub-bailment may also operate to the disadvantage of C (the head bailor) in that he may be *bound* by an exemption clause in the contract between A (the head bailee) and B (the sub-bailee): see *Morris v CW Martin Ltd* [1996] 1 Q.B. 716 at 729 and *The Pioneer Container* [1994] 2 A.C. 324, below, p.641. But this principle does not enable B to take the *benefit* of a term in the contract between A and C: see *The Mahkutai* [1996] A.C. 650 at 667–668; it merely enables B to rely on the terms of B's *own* contract with A against C where C has authorised the relevant terms of the sub-bailment. No "sub-bailment" arises merely because a sub-agent has received the proceeds of sale of the principal's property: *Balsamo v Medici* [1984] 1 W.L.R. 951.

[78] *British Telecommunications plc v James Thomson & Sons (Engineers) Ltd* [1999] 1 W.L.R. 9 where the loss caused by the subcontractor's negligence was physical damage to property of the owner *other* than the very thing supplied by the sub-contractor, so that the various difficulties discussed in relation to the *Junior Books* case [1983] 1 A.C. 520 (below pp.608–609 and 614–616) did not arise.

solicitors,[79] insurance brokers[80] and safety consultants[81] have been held liable in tort to persons other than their immediate clients for negligence in the performance of contracts with those clients.[82] Surveyors, valuers, accountants and auditors can similarly be liable for negligent misrepresentation to third parties: the basis, and limits, of such liability have been discussed in Chapter 9.[83] Sometimes the provider of the services is liable in tort because his negligence in performing the contract with his client of itself causes loss to the third party: *e.g.*, where a solicitor's negligence in failing to carry out his client's testamentary instructions causes an intended gift to a prospective beneficiary to fail.[84] Sometimes the defendant's negligence results in his making a misrepresentation to the third party and the loss is suffered by the latter in consequence of his acting in reliance on the representation: *e.g.* where a valuer employed by A negligently makes a report on the structure of a house and the report is communicated to B and induces him to buy the house for more than its true value.[85]

A controversial extension of tort liability to a third party was made in *Junior Books Ltd v Veitchi Co Ltd*[86] where B had undertaken to build a factory for C by a contract which entitled C to nominate sub-contractors. C nominated A as flooring sub-contractor; B in consequence entered into a contract with A by which A undertook to lay the floor; but no contract came into existence between A and C.[87] The floor later cracked and, on the assumption that this was due to A's negligence in doing the work defectively, it was held that A was liable to C for the loss suffered by C in consequence of the fact that the work

---

[79] *Ross v Caunters* [1980] Ch. 287; *White v Jones* [1995] 2 A.C. 207; *cf. Smith v Claremont Haynes, The Times,* September 3, 1991; *Al Kandari v JR Brown & Co* [1988] Q.B. 665. Contrast *Clark v Bruce Lance* [1988] 1 All E.R. 364 (solicitor acting for testator in a different transaction held to owe no duty to beneficiary); *Worby v Rosser* [2000] P.N.L.R. 140 (solicitor engaged by testator to draw up a new will held to owe no duty to beneficiary under an earlier will). For earlier discussion of *Ross v Caunters*, above, see *Banque Keyser Ullmann SA v Skandia (UK) Insurance Co Ltd* [1990] Q.B. 659 at 794–796, affirmed on other grounds [1991] 2 A.C. 249; *Van Oppen v Clerk of the Bedford Charity Trustees* [1989] 1 All E.R. 273 at 289, affirmed [1990] 1 W.L.R. 235; *Caparo Industries plc v Dickman* [1990] 2 A.C. 605 at 635; *Murphy v Brentwood DC* [1991] 1 A.C. 398 at 486.

[80] *Punjab National Bank v de Boinville* [1992] 1 W.L.R. 1138 at 1152; *cf. Henderson v Merrett Syndicates Ltd* [1995] 2 A.C. 145; *Aiken v Stewart Wrightson Members Agency Ltd* [1995] 1 W.L.R. 1281; Cane in (Rose, ed.) *Consensus ad Idem, Essays in the Law of Contract in Honour of Guenter Treitel* p.96.

[81] *Driver v William Willett (Contractors) Ltd* [1969] 1 All E.R. 655; *cf. Dove v Banham's Patent Locks Ltd* [1983] 1 W.L.R. 1436; *Bailey v HSS Alarms Ltd, The Times,* June 20, 2000; *Bourne v McEvoy Timber Preservation* (1975) 237 E.G. 496 (timber preservation firm giving estimate of cost of work to vendor of a house held to owe a duty of care to purchaser). Contrast *The Nicholas H* [1996] 1 A.C. 211, below, p.612.

[82] See also *Knight v Lawrence* [1991] 1 E.G.L.R. 143.

[83] See above, pp.344–350.

[84] *e.g. Ross v Caunters* and *White v Jones,* above n.79; contrast *Gran Gelato Ltd v Richcliff Group Ltd* [1992] Ch. 650 (vendor's solicitor not liable to purchaser for negligently misrepresenting client's state of mind); Cane, 108 L.Q.R. 539; Tettenborn [1992] C.L.J. 415.

[85] *e.g. Smith v Eric S Bush* [1990] 1 A.C. 831, above, p.339; *cf. Niru Battery Manufacturing Co v Milestone Trading Ltd* [2002] EWHC 1425; [2002] 2 All E.R. (Comm) 705, at [60] (liability of certification company to third party).

[86] [1983] 1 A.C. 520; Jaffey [1983] C.L.J. 37; Palmer and Murdoch 46 M.L.R. 213. See further Jaffey, 5 *Legal Studies* 77; Reynolds (1985) 11 N.Z.U.L.R. 215; Stapleton, 104 L.Q.R. 213 and 389; Huxley, 53 M.L.R. 361; Beyleveld and Brownsword, 54 M.L.R. 48. The Contracts (Rights of Third Parties) Act 1999 probably does not apply on such facts: below, p.654.

[87] In *Greater Nottingham Co-operative Society Ltd v Cementation Piling & Foundations Ltd* [1989] Q.B. 71 there was a direct contract between A (the subcontractor) and C (the building owner) and it was held that A's duty to C was governed by that contract alone and not by the general law relating to the tort of negligence; *cf. Welsh Health Technical Services v Haden Young* (1987) 37 Build L.R. 310; *Sonat Offshore SA v Amerada Hess Development Co* [1988] 1 Lloyd's Rep. 145 at 159; *The Hellespont Ardent* [1997] 2 Lloyd's Rep. 547 at 593. But it was recognised that breaches of duty arising out of certain contractual relationships may be actionable

had to be done again. At first sight, this result represents a considerable encroachment on the common law doctrine of privity, but the following discussion will show that later decisions have taken a highly restrictive view of the scope of the *Junior Books* case.

In the situations just described, A's liability to C is in tort and not on the contract between A and B as such: both the standard and the basis of liability may differ according to whether A is being sued on the contract by B or in tort by C. Thus in the *Junior Books* case it does not seem that A would have been liable to C if A had unjustifiably repudiated his contract with B and done no work under it at all, with the result that completion of the building was delayed and C suffered loss.[88] In one group of cases, to be discussed later in this Chapter, A has indeed been held liable in tort to C for simple failure to take steps in the performance of his contract with B.[89] The cases in question hold that where a solicitor (A) fails to carry out his client's (B's) instructions to make a will in favour of C, then A can, after B's death, be held liable in tort to C for the value of the benefit lost by C. But one reason for this conclusion was that A's omission made him liable in tort, as well as for breach of contract, even to his own client, B.[90] This would not have been the position if, in the *Junior Books* case, A had wrongfully repudiated his contract with B or had simply failed to do any work under it: such a repudiation or omission would have made A liable to B only for breach of contract. The disappointed beneficiary cases are also distinguishable from the building contract cases for other reasons to be discussed later in this Chapter,[91] and they therefore do not support any general proposition that A's omission to perform his contract with B gives a cause of action in tort to C merely because, as a result of the omission, C suffers loss. Further differences between tort and contract liability are that the contract between A and B in the *Junior Books* case might have made A strictly liable to B,[92] without proof of negligence, while negligence was an essential element of C's cause of action in tort against A; in contract, B would have a cause of action against A as soon as the defective work was done, but in tort C's cause of action would accrue only when the resulting loss was suffered[93]; and in B's action on the contract B has to show only that the contract has been made and broken, while in C's action in tort, C must establish that there was a relationship between himself and A by virtue of which A owed him a duty of care.[94]

---

[88] in tort as well as in contract: see below, pp.983–984; *cf. Nitrigin Eirann Teoranta v Inco Alloys Ltd* [1992] 1 All E.R. 854 at 856–857; *The Volvox Hollandia (No. 2)* [1993] 2 Lloyd's Rep. 314 at 322; *Henderson v Merrett Syndicates Ltd* [1995] 2 A.C. 145; *Holt v Payne Skillington, The Times*, December 22, 1995; *Sumitomo Bank Ltd v Banque Bruxelles Lambert SA* [1997] 1 Lloyd's Rep. 487 at 512–514; *Weldon v GRE Linked Life Assurance Ltd* [2000] 2 All E.R. (Comm) 914 at 926–927; the same is true of the relationships described at nn.75 to 82, above.

[88] In *The Zephyr* [1984] 1 Lloyd's Rep. 58 at 85, it was said at first instance that even the law of torts can sometimes impose "positive duties . . . recognised . . . only because a party has voluntarily undertaken them." But this suggestion was disapproved on appeal: [1985] 2 Lloyd's Rep. 529; *cf. White v Jones* [1995] 2 A.C. 207 at 216. No issue of privity arose in *The Zephyr*; the dispute was as to contractual intention (above, pp.172–173).

[89] See below, p.616.

[90] *White v Jones*, above, n.79; *cf. Hooper v Fynmores* [2001] W.T.L.R. 1019; and see below, p.616.

[91] See below, p.618.

[92] See below, p.838. Similarly, on facts such as those of *Donoghue v Stevenson* [1932] A.C. 562 liability for breach of contract in respect of defects in the goods sold would be strict, while the tort liability of, or to, a third party would have depended on negligence. This difference between tort and contract liability in such cases is reduced in importance by Consumer Protection Act 1987, Pt I, introducing strict "product liability" to the ultimate consumer. But such liability is subject to important qualifications and will not extend to many of the situations with which the following discussion is concerned.

[93] *Dove v Banham's Safety Locks Ltd* [1983] 1 W.L.R. 1463; *cf. Bell v Peter Browne & Co* [1990] 2 Q.B. 495.

[94] For the elements of such a relationship, see above, pp.344–350.

(2) Restrictions on scope of the duty

(a) In GENERAL. A relationship giving rise to a duty of care,[95] is not established merely by showing that C has suffered foreseeable loss as a result of A's defective performance of his contract with B. In the *Junior Books* case, there were many special factors which could be said to have given rise to such a relationship: A were nominated as sub-contractors by C; A were specialists in flooring and knew of C's requirements; C relied on A's special skills in laying floors; and A must have known that defects in the work could necessitate repairs and lead to economic loss.[96] These special factors (and in particular the extent of C's reliance on A's special skills) may have given rise to a "special relationship" and hence to a duty of care in tort.[97] But such factors are unlikely to arise in the ordinary case where C suffers loss as a result of the defective performance by A of his contract with B. Accordingly later authorities[98] have emphasised the exceptional nature of the circumstances of the *Junior Books* case. It has been said that those circumstances were "unique"[99]; that the case "cannot now be regarded as a useful pointer to the development of the law"[1] or "as laying down any principle of general application in the law of tort"[2]; and that the statement of principle in Lord Brandon's dissenting speech is to be preferred to that of the majority.[3] The authority of the case is further undermined by the fact that the reasoning of the majority is to a considerable extent based on earlier decisions[4] which (so far as they hold the defendants liable for economic loss[5]) have since been overruled by the House of Lords.[6] In consequence of these developments, the decision in the *Junior Books* case has been described as "discredited"[7] and "virtually extinguished".[8]

The duty owed by A to C in tort may also be less extensive than that owed by A to the other contracting party. This was, for example, the position where A was employed as solicitor by B who was guarantor of C's mortgage. It was held[9] that, although A might owe a duty of care to C, this duty did not extend to requiring A to explain the implications of the mortgage to C, since the imposition of such an extensive duty might

---

[95] *ibid*; and *cf.* below p.612 at n.22.

[96] [1983] 1 A.C. 520 at 546.

[97] *Murphy v Brentwood DC* [1991] 1 A.C. 398 at 466, 481; see above, p.345.

[98] See below, p.616, nn.55 and 56.

[99] *D & F Estates Ltd v Church Commissioners for England* [1989] A.C. 177 at 202; *cf. Van Oppen v Clerk to the Bedford Charity Trustees* [1989] 1 All E.R. 273 at 289, affirmed [1990] 1 W.L.R. 235; *Duncan Stevenson MacMillan v A W Knott Becker Scott Ltd* [1990] 1 Lloyd's Rep. 98; *Nitrigin Eirann Teoranta v Inco Alloys Ltd* [1992] 1 W.L.R. 498 at 504.

[1] *Simaan General Contracting Co v Pilkington Glass Ltd (No.2)* [1988] Q.B. 758 at 784.

[2] *D & F Estates Ltd v Church Commissioners for England* [1989] A.C. 177 at 202; *cf. ibid.* at 215.

[3] *ibid.* at 202, 215; *Islander Trucking Ltd v Hogg Robinson & Gardner Mountain (Marine) Ltd* [1990] 1 All E.R. 826 at 829; *cf. Murphy v Brentwood DC* [1991] 2 A.C. 398 at 466, 469; and in Scotland, *Strathford East Kilbride Ltd v Film Design Ltd*, S.C.L.R. 877, 1997.

[4] *i.e. Anns v Merton London Borough* [1978] A.C. 728; *Dutton v Bognor Regis Urban DC* [1972] 1 Q.B. 373.

[5] See *Stovin v Wise* [1996] 3 All E.R. 801 at 824.

[6] *Murphy v Brentwood DC* [1991] 2 A.C. 398. Contrast in Australia *Bryan v Maloney* (1995) 182 C.L.R. 609; in New Zealand (as accepted by the Privy Council) *Invercargill City Council v Hamlin* [1996] A.C. 624; in Canada *Winnipeg Condominium Corp v Bird Construction Co Ltd* (1995) 121 D.L.R. (4th) 193 (where the defect made the building dangerous); and in Singapore *RSP Architects Planners & Engineers v Ocean Front Ltd* (1998) 14 Const.L.J. 139.

[7] *Société Commerciale de Réassurance v ERAS International Ltd* [1992] 1 Lloyd's Rep. 570 at 599.

[8] *The Volvox Hollandia (No.2)* [1993] 2 Lloyd's Rep. 315 at 322; *The Orjula* [1995] 2 Lloyd's Rep. 395 at 401.

[9] *Woodward v Wolfertrans, The Times*, April 8, 1997.

give rise to a conflict between A's duty to his own client (B) and the alleged duty to C.

The law finally restricts the range of persons to whom the duty may be owed. Where, for example, a valuer was requested by a borrower to address a valuation of the property on which the loan was to be secured to "the prospective lender", it was held that the valuer owed no duty to that lender's assignee.[10] Similarly, counsel who had given advice to his client in litigation has been held to owe no duty of care in respect of that advice to the other party to the litigation[11]; and a solicitor engaged by one party to a transaction will not normally owe a duty of care to the other party, since the imposition of such a duty could give rise to a conflict of interest.[12] Such a duty may, however, arise in exceptional circumstances: *e.g.* where, in relation to a loan to be secured on a leasehold flat, the borrower engaged defendants as his solicitors and they knew that the lender had not engaged and did not intend to engage his own solicitor. The defendants were held liable in tort to the lender for failing effectively to secure the loan on the flat.[13]

(b) ECONOMIC LOSS AND PHYSICAL HARM. Except where there is a "special relationship" between the parties (as in the misrepresentation cases,[14] and in cases in which the claim is based on the defendant's failure to perform a contract, such as one to perform professional services, which involves, in addition to his obligations under that contract to the other party to it, an assumption of responsibility to a third party[15]) a claimant cannot rely on the breach of a contract to which he was not a party merely because, as a result of the breach, he has suffered economic loss, that is, loss not taking the form of personal injury or of physical damage to his property.[16] The importance of this point is illustrated by *Simaan General Contracting Co v Pilkington Glass Ltd (No.2)*,[17] where the defendants had been nominated as suppliers of glass for incorporation in a building which was being erected by the claimants as main contractors for a client in Abu Dhabi. The glass had been sold by the defendants to a subcontractor engaged by the claimants, so that there was no contract between claimants and defendants; the glass was perfectly sound but was not of the colour specified in the contract of sale or in the main building contract. In consequence of this shortcoming, the claimants were not paid by their client and so suffered financial loss; but it was held that the defendants' breach of their contract with the subcontractors did not give the claimants any right of action in tort against the defendants merely because that breach had caused the claimants to suffer

---

[10] *Barex Brothers Ltd v Morris Dean & Co* [1999] P.N.L.R. 344.

[11] *Connolly-Martin v Davis* [1999] Lloyd's Rep. P.N. 790.

[12] *Dean v Allin & Watts* [2001] EWCA Civ 758; [2001] 2 Lloyd's Rep. 249, at [33].

[13] This was the actual result in *Dean v Allin & Watts*, above.

[14] See above, p.345.

[15] See above, pp.607–608 at nn.79–83; see especially *Henderson v Merret Syndicates Ltd* [1995] A.C. 145; *cf. Parkinson v St James & Seacroft University NHS Trust* [2002] EWCA Civ 530; [2002] Q.B. 266; *Rees v Darlington Memorial Hospital NHS Trust* [2002] EWCA Civ 88; [2003] Q.B. 20.

[16] *Tate & Lyle Industries Ltd v GLC* [1983] 2 A.C. 509 at 530–531; *cf. London Congregational Union Inc v Harriss* [1988] 1 All E.R. 15 at 25; *Simaan General Contracting Co Ltd v Pilkington Glass Ltd (No.2)* [1988] 1 Q.B. 758 at 781; *Greater Nottingham Co-operative Soc Ltd v Cementation Piling & Foundation Ltd* [1989] Q.B. 71 at 94; *Verderame v Commercial Union Assurance Co plc, The Times*, April 2, 1992; *Preston v Torfaen B.C.* [1993] EGCS 137. In *European Gas Turbines Ltd v MSAS Cargo International Ltd* [2001] C.L.C. 880 a cargo-owner (C) recovered damages from a sub-contracting carrier (A) for purely economic loss resulting from breach of A's subcontract with the contracting carrier (B) as to the mode of carriage. There was no contract between A and C so that this conclusion is at first sight hard to reconcile with the other authorities cited in this note. The case may be explicable on the ground that C's agent had notified A of the importance to C of carriage by the stipulated mode and that A had accepted this position so as to give rise to an "assumption of responsibility" (*cf.* above, p.347) to A to observe that stipulation.

[17] [1988] Q.B. 758.

financial loss. Similarly, it was held in *Balsamo v Medici*[18] that a sub-agent who had negligently paid over the proceeds of the sale of the principal's property to a fraudulent imposter was not liable in tort to the principal for such negligence in handling the money; nor was he liable to the principal in contract as there was no privity of contract between the sub-agent and the principal. To uphold a tort claim in such a situation would, it was said, "come perilously close to abrogating the doctrine of privity altogether".[19] A doctor employed by a company to assess replies of job applicants to medical questionnaires has likewise been held to owe no duty in tort to those applicants.[20] The existence of a duty of care to a person with whom the defendant was not in any contractual relationship may also be negatived by the fact that that person has an adequate remedy in respect of the loss in question under a contract with another potential defendant.[21]

The point that is emphasised in cases such as the *Simaan* and *Balsamo* cases is that the claimants in them suffered no physical harm as a result of the defendants' acts or omissions. It does not follow that the mere fact of the claimant's having suffered foreseeable harm of this kind is a *sufficient* condition of the defendant's liability in tort. The claimant must, in addition, show that the relationship between him and the defendant was one of "proximity", so that it was fair, just and reasonable to impose a duty of care on the defendant.[22] This requirement was held not to have been satisfied in *The Nicholas H*,[23] where a ship classification society had, in breach of its contract with shipowners, advised them that their ship could proceed on her current voyage until the cargo which she was then carrying had been discharged. In the course of that voyage the ship sank, and it was held that the owners of the cargo had no cause of action in tort against the society in respect of the loss of their cargo. The main reason given by the House of Lords for this conclusion was that the shipowners were, in turn, in breach of their contract of carriage with the cargo-owners; and that it was not fair, just or reasonable to impose on the classification society a liability to the cargo-owners in tort[24] since this would not be subject to the limitations of liability available to the shipowners under international Conventions[25] which have the force of law. The effect of holding

---

[18] [1984] 1 W.L.R. 951; Whittaker, 48 M.L.R. 86. It seems that on such facts the requirements of s.1(1), (2) and (3) of the Contracts (Rights of Third Parties) Act 1999 (below, pp.651–655) would not be satisfied.

[19] At 959–960; *cf. The Rebecca Elaine* [1999] 2 Lloyd's Rep. 1 at 8: "the dubious and lethal colonisation by the tort of negligence of the conceptual territory of contract" (engine manufacturer not liable in negligence for purely economic loss to owner of fishing boat with whom he was not in any contractual relationship); *Michael Sallis & Co v ECA Call* (1988) 4 Const. L.J. 125. The soundness of the cases discussed in this paragraph is not questioned in *Henderson v Merrett Syndicates Ltd* [1995] 2 A.C. 145, where the liability in tort of a subagent to a principal with whom he was in no contractual relationship was said at 195 to be based on the "most unusual" situation in that case.

[20] *Kapfunde v Abbey National plc* [1998] I.R.L.R. 583, disapproving *Baker v Kaye* [1997] I.R.L.R. 219 so far as it holds that a duty was owed by the doctor to the applicant.

[21] *Briscoe v Lubrizol Ltd* [2000] I.C.R. 694; the question whether the claimant might in such circumstances now have a right under s.1 of the Contracts (Rights of Third Parties) Act 1999 would depend on whether the requirements discussed at pp.651–656 were satisfied.

[22] For these requirements, see, *inter alia, Caparo Industries plc v Dickman* [1990] 2 A.C. 605 at 617–618; *Murphy v Brentwood DC* [1991] 1 A.C. 398 at 480, 486; *X (minors) v Bedfordshire CC* [1995] 2 A.C. 633 at 739; and pp.344–347 above.

[23] [1996] A.C. 211; *cf. Reeman v Dept. of Transport* [1997] 2 Lloyd's Rep. 648; *R M Turton & Co Ltd v Kerslake & Partners* [2000] Lloyd's Rep. P.N. (New Zealand CA).

[24] Nor had there been an "assumption of responsibility" (above, pp.347–348) since the cargo-owners were "not even aware of [the classification society's] examination of the ship:" [1996] A.C. 211 at 242.

[25] The Convention in question related to tonnage limitations; effect was given to it by Merchant Shipping Act 1979, s.17 and Sch.4, now superseded by Merchant Shipping Act 1995, s.185 and Sch.7, Pt I. The reasoning of the House of Lords is equally applicable to the contractual limitations and exceptions which protect the carrier by virtue of Carriage of Goods by Sea Act 1971 s.1(2) and Sch.: see *The Nicholas H* [1996] A.C. 211

classification societies liable in tort to cargo-owners would be to deprive shipowners of the benefits of these Conventions since the societies would pass this liability on to shipowners; and this would be an undesirable conclusion,[26] particularly as loss suffered by cargo-owners in excess of the Convention limits was "readily insurable".[27]

(c) DEFECTS IN THE VERY THING SUPPLIED NOT SUFFICIENT. Even where A's negligence in the performance of his contract with B has resulted in damage to "property", the scope of C's tort remedy is further restricted by the fact that "property" in this context normally refers to property belonging to C *other* than the very thing supplied by A under that contract. Thus where A sold goods to B who resold them to C, it was held that A would not be liable in tort to C merely because those goods disintegrated on account of a defect in them amounting to a breach of A's contract with B.[28] Nor, where goods are bought from a retailer, is the manufacturer liable to the buyer in tort[29] for negligence if the goods are defective and the defect is discovered before any injury, or harm to other property, has resulted. Even if the goods deteriorate by reason of the defect, the buyer's only loss is the financial or economic loss which he suffers because the defect has made them less valuable or because he discards them or incurs the cost of repairing them. Loss of this kind is not generally recoverable in tort,[30] though there may be an exception to this general rule where the defect is a source of danger in respect of which the claimant could become liable to third parties, so that money has to be spent in averting this danger.[31] The *Junior Books* case appears, indeed, to be inconsistent with the general rule; for the only "property" which could be said to have been damaged was the factory floor (which had cracked), and that damage was no more than a defect in the very thing supplied by A. The fact that A was nevertheless held liable in tort to C is now explicable (if at all) only by reference to the same special, or "unique", factors[32] which existed in that case.

(d) CLAIMANT HAVING NO TITLE TO THING DAMAGED. Even where A's breach of his contract with B does result in physical damage, the mere fact that the loss so occasioned falls on C will not necessarily give C a right of action in tort against A in respect of that loss. In *The Aliakmon*[33] A, a carrier, had contracted with B for the carriage of a quantity

---

at 238. In *Perrett v Collins* [1998] 2 Lloyd's Rep. 255 no such policy reasons were held to exist for protecting an aircraft inspection society for liability for *personal* injury to a passenger; *cf. Watson v British Boxing Board of Control Ltd* [2001] Q.B. 1134.

[26] *cf.* below, p.614 at nn.39 and 40.

[27] *The Nicholas H* [1996] A.C. 211 at 242.

[28] *Aswan Engineering Establishment Co v Lupine Ltd* [1987] 1 W.L.R. 1; *cf. D & F Estates Ltd v Church Commissioners for England* [1989] A.C. 177 at 202, 216; *Reid v Rush & Tompkins Group plc* [1990] 1 W.L.R. 212 at 224; *Warner v Basildon Development Corp* (1991) 7 Const. L.J. 146; *cf. Bacardi-Martini Beverages Ltd v Thomas Hardy Packaging Ltd* [2002] EWCA Civ 549; [2002] 2 All E.R. (Comm) 335 at [18] (contaminated ingredient used in manufacturing making finished product useless); for some extension of the principle, see *Bellefield Computer Services Ltd v E Turner & Sons* [2000] B.L.R. 97.

[29] For possible liability under a manufacturer's guarantee, see above, p.582.

[30] *Murphy v Brentwood DC* [1991] 1 A.C. 398 at 469; *Nitrigin Eirann Teoranta v Inco Alloys Ltd* [1992] 1 W.L.R. 498.

[31] *The Orjula* [1995] 2 Lloyd's Rep. 395 at 402, where it was also arguable that the defective thing supplied by the defendant had caused physical harm to *other* property in which the claimant had a prior interest as lessee.

[32] See above, p.610, n.99.

[33] [1986] A.C. 785; Treitel [1986] L.M.C.L.Q. 294; Markesinis, 103 L.Q.R. 354 at 384–390; Tettenborn [1987] J.B.L. 12; *cf. Transcontainer Express Ltd v Custodian Security Ltd* [1988] 1 Lloyd's Rep. 128; *The Ciudad de Pasto* [1988] 1 W.L.R. 1145; *The Filiatra Legacy* [1991] 2 Lloyd's Rep. 337 at 339; *The Gudermes* [1993] 1 Lloyd's Rep. 311 at 326; *The Hamburg Star* [1994] 1 Lloyd's Rep. 399 at 403–405; *The Seven Pioneer* [2001]

of steel coils which B had sold to C. The goods were damaged, as a result of A's negligent breach of the contract of carriage, after the risk in them had passed to C under the contract of sale, but while B remained owner of them. C had no claim under the contract of carriage as he was not a party to it[34]; and the House of Lords held that he also had no cause of action against A in tort in respect of the loss which he had suffered as a result of remaining liable for the full price of the goods in spite of the fact that they had been damaged in transit. This conclusion was based on a long line of authority[35] which had established the "principle of law that, in order to enable a person to claim in negligence for loss caused to him by reason of loss or damage to property, he must have had either the legal ownership of or a possessory title to the property concerned at the time when the loss or damage occurred[36]" or, where the loss is caused by a continuing process, at the time when the cause of action in respect of it first accrued.[37] It is not enough for him at the relevant time "to have only had contractual rights in relation to such property"[38] when the loss or damage occurred. The House of Lords refused to create an exception to this principle where (as in the present case) the contractual right, which C had under his contract of sale with B, was one to have property and possession of the goods transferred to him at a later date. The main reason for this refusal was that the contract of carriage between A and B was expressed to be subject to an international Convention[39] which gave A (as carrier) the benefit of certain immunities from, and limitations of, liability; and to have held A liable in tort to C would have produced the undesirable result of depriving A of the protection of that contract,[40] since C (being a stranger to it) was no more bound by its terms than entitled to assert rights under it.

(e) TORT AND CONTRACT DAMAGES CONTRASTED. Where a third party can recover damages in tort for the negligent performance of a contract between two others, the damages in such a tort action will not normally be assessed in the same way as they would be in a contractual action. In particular, certain kinds of "economic loss" are generally regarded as being recoverable only in a contractual action. This follows from the principle that the object of awarding damages in a contractual action is to put the claimant into the position in which he would have been, if the contract had been

---

2 Lloyd's Rep. 57 (High Court of New Zealand). For a possible qualification, see *The Kapetan Georgis* [1988] 1 Lloyd's Rep. 352, where A in breach of his contract with B caused physical harm to B in respect of which C became liable to indemnify B, and C was held to have an arguable case against A.

[34] On the facts of *The Aliakmon* rights under the contract of carriage would now be transferred to C by virtue of the Carriage of Goods by Sea Act 1992, s.2: see *White v Jones* [1995] 2 A.C. 207 at 265. But cases can still be imagined where this would not be the position: see *Carver on Bills of Lading* (1st ed., 2001) §5–098.

[35] Stretching from *Cattle v Stockton Waterworks Co* (1875) L.R. 10 Q.B. 453 through *The Wear Breeze* [1969] 1 Q.B. 219 to *The Mineral Transporter* [1986] A.C. 1.

[36] [1986] A.C. 785 at 809.

[37] *The Starsin* [2001] EWCA Civ 56; [2001] 1 Lloyd's Rep. 437 at [96] (*per* Rix L.J., whose judgment was on this point affirmed on appeal: [2003] UKHL 12, [2003] 2 W.L.R. at [40], [64], [90], [139].

[38] [1986] A.C 785 at 809. Griew (1986) 136 N.L.J. 1201 suggests that the principle may have been qualified by Latent Damage Act 1986, s.3; but there is no hint in the legislative history of s.3 that such a qualification was intended. It can in any event only apply where the damage was still latent when the claimant became owner: this was not the position in *The Aliakmon*. The point was left open in *The Starsin* [2001] EWCA Civ 56; [2001] 1 Lloyd's Rep. 437 at [119–128] (*per* Rix L.J., dissenting but not on this point), [134], [202, 203] and not discussed in the House of Lords (above, n.37).

[39] *i.e.* the Hague Rules set out in the Schedule to the Carriage of Goods by Sea Act 1924, now superseded in England by Carriage of Goods by Sea Act 1971.

[40] *cf.* below, pp.642–643; *Simaan General Contracting Co v Pilkington Glass Ltd (No.2)* [1988] Q.B. 758 at 782–783. For the suggestion that the position may be different where the potential tortfeasor has no such protection, see *Triangle Steel & Supply Co v Korean United Lines Inc* (1985) 63 B.C.L.R. 66 at 80 (the reasoning of which is in other respects inconsistent with that of *The Aliakmon*). For further discussion of this aspect of *The Aliakmon* see below p.639 n.65.

performed, while in an action in tort that object is to put him back into the position in which he was before the tort was committed.[41] The distinction is well illustrated by *Muirhead v Industrial Tank Specialities Ltd*[42] where the plaintiff, who owned a lobster farm, had entered into a contract for the installation of pumps which failed because of a defect in their electric motors. There was no contract between the plaintiff and the supplier of the motors but his claim against that supplier succeeded in tort in respect of the physical damage caused by the failure (*i.e.* the value of the lobsters which had died); and in respect of "any financial loss suffered by the plaintiff in consequence of that physical damage".[43] (*i.e.* the loss of profits on the sale of *those* lobsters). But a further claim "in respect of the whole economic loss suffered"[44] by the plaintiff (*i.e.* for loss of the profits that he would have made from the installation, had it not been defective) was rejected: such damages might have been recoverable from the installer of the pumps in contract but they could not be claimed from the suppliers of the motors in tort.

Considerable difficulty again arises in this connection from the *Junior Books* case.[45] The main question discussed in that case was whether damages for *any* economic or financial loss could be recovered in a tort action in the absence of any allegation that the cracks in the floor were a source of danger to persons or to other property. In the exceptional circumstances of the case, this question was answered in the affirmative and on that basis most of the items of loss, in respect of which damages were said to be recoverable, can be explained in terms of the principles governing the assessment of damages in tort: this is, for example, true of the profits lost and of the wages and overheads wasted while the factory was closed for repairs to the floor. But it was also said that the factory owners were entitled to the *cost of replacing the floor*[46] and such an award would, by putting them into the position in which they would have been if the sub-contractor's promise had been performed, amount to an award of contract damages in spite of the fact that there was no contract between them and the sub-contractors[47]: on the normal basis of assessment in tort, the damages for this item should not have included the cost of replacing the floor with a good one.[48] In the *Junior Books* case, Lord Keith explained this aspect of the case on the ground that, in replacing the floor, the factory owners had simply mitigated the loss of profit resulting from the defects in the floor originally provided[49]; and it is settled that expenses reasonably incurred in mitigation are recoverable.[50] But as this reasoning was not adopted by the other members of the House of Lords, an alternative explanation was given in the *Muirhead* case, namely that the same special (or "unique") factors in the *Junior Books* case, which gave rise to

---

[41] See above, p.359; below, pp.937–938.
[42] [1986] Q.B. 507; Whittaker, 49 M.L.R. 369; Oughton [1987] J.B.L. 370.
[43] [1986] Q.B. 507 at 533.
[44] *ibid.*
[45] [1983] 1 A.C. 520; Grubb [1984] C.L.J. 111; Holyoak, 99 L.Q.R. 591; Smith and Burns, 46 M.L.R. 147.
[46] This was one of the items claimed; the question whether the claim was proved was not before the House of Lords, which decided only that there was a cause of action in respect of it if negligence were established.
[47] The case was governed by Scots law, which recognises a *jus quaesitum tertio*, but the conditions giving rise to such a right were not satisfied.
[48] *cf. Murphy v Brentwood DC* [1991] 2 A.C. 398 at 469. Lord Roskill in the *Junior Books* case at p.545 discusses (without reaching a definite conclusion) the question whether the pursuer in *Donoghue v Stevenson* [1932] A.C. 562 could have recovered damages "for the diminished value of the ginger beer"—not for the cost of replacing the contaminated with pure ginger beer. Even the former basis of assessment is hard to reconcile with the authorities cited above, p.613, n.28.
[49] [1983] 1 A.C. 520 at 536.
[50] *cf.* below, pp.976–977, 978–979.

the duty of care there,[51] also explain the assessment of damages.[52] This narrow view of the *Junior Books* case is supported by dicta in the *Junior Books* case itself[53]; by the fact that there is no subsequent similar[54] case in which a third party has recovered damages in tort to put him into the position in which he would have been if the contract between two others *had been performed* (as opposed to that in which he was *before it was broken*); and by the fact that many later decisions[55] have made it highly unlikely that such damages will, in a future tort case of this kind, be awarded to a third party. On the contrary, two House of Lords decisions have specifically rejected such claims.[56] In each case, a lessee claimed damages in tort for the cost of remedying defects alleged to be due to the negligence of a building contractor in the performance of a contract to which the lessee was not a party. In each case, the contractor was held not liable in tort, even if he was negligent,[57] since the defects had been discovered before they had caused any personal injury, or damage to other property belonging to the lessees. To make the contractor liable for the purely economic loss suffered by the lessee in remedying the defect would "impose upon [the contractor] for the benefit of those with whom he had no contractual relationship the obligation of one who warranted the quality of"[58] his work. Such a result would have been inconsistent with the common law doctrine of privity; and these cases reinforce the view that liability in negligence to third parties has not wholly subverted (though it may have limited the scope of) that doctrine.

The general principle that a third party cannot recover damages in tort to put him into the position in which he would have been if a contract between two others had been performed is, at least at first sight, hard to reconcile with cases such as *White v Jones*,[59] where A had instructed his solicitor B to draw up a will containing bequests in favour of his daughters C and D, but B negligently and in breach of his contract with A had done nothing to carry out these instructions by the time of A's death. The House of Lords by a majority held that B was liable in tort to C and D, and that the damages to which they were entitled consisted of the amounts which they would have obtained under A's will, if B had duly carried out A's instructions. The case presented certain special features, namely that C had discussed A's testamentary intentions with B, and that the letter setting out A's wishes had been drafted by D's husband. The majority do

---

[51] See above, p.610.

[52] *Muirhead* case, [1986] Q.B. 507 at 523, 533–535.

[53] [1983] 1 A.C. 520 at 533 (*per* Lord Fraser, who took the same narrow view of the *Junior Books* case in *The Mineral Transporter* [1986] 1 A.C. at 24–25); and [1983] 1 A.C. at 546 (*per* Lord Roskill).

[54] For the different treatment of the "disappointed beneficiary" cases, see below, pp.616–618.

[55] *i.e. Tate & Lyle Industries Ltd v GLC* [1983] 2 A.C. 509; *Balsamo v Medici* [1984] 1 W.L.R. 951; *The Mineral Transporter* [1986] 1 A.C.; *Muirhead v Industrial Tank Specialities Ltd* [1986] Q.B. 507; *The Aliakmon* [1986] A.C. 785; *Aswan Engineering Establishment Co v Lupdine Ltd* [1987] 1 W.L.R. 1. *cf.* also *Smith v Littlewoods Organisation Ltd* [1987] A.C. 241 at 280; *Yuen Kun-yeu v Attorney-General of Hong Kong* [1988] A.C. 175; *Simaan General Contracting Co v Pilkington Glass Ltd (No.2)* [1988] Q.B. 758; *Greater Nottingham Co-operative Soc Ltd v Cementation Piling & Foundation Ltd* [1989] Q.B. 71 at 94; *Davies v Radcliffe* [1990] 1 W.L.R. 821; *Parker-Tweedale v Dunbar Bank plc* [1991] Ch. 12 at 24; *Deloitte Haskins & Sells v National Mututal Life Nominees* [1993] A.C. 774.

[56] *D & F Estates Ltd v Church Commissioners for England* [1989] A.C. 177; *Department of the Environment v Thomas Bates & Son Ltd* [1991] 1 A.C. 499.

[57] In the *D & F Estates* case, there was no such negligence as the builders had employed competent sub-contractors.

[58] [1989] A.C. 177 at 207; *cf. ibid.* at 211–212.

[59] [1995] 2 A.C. 207 (Lords Keith and Mustill dissenting), approving the result (though not the reasoning) in *Ross v Caunters* [1980] Ch. 287, where B's negligence took the form, not of simply failing to carry out A's instructions, but of carrying them out ineffectively. *cf. Esterhuizen v Allied Dunbar Assurance plc* [1998] 2 F.L.R. 668 (similar liability of company offering will-making services); and, in Australia, *Hill v van Erp* (1997) 142 A.L.R. 687 (also a case of actual misfeasance by the solicitor).

not seem to restrict the principle of liability to such special circumstances[60] though they accept that there must be "boundaries to the availability of the remedy" which "will have to be worked out . . . as practical problems come before the courts".[61] It is, for example, an open question whether such a remedy would be available to a prospective beneficiary who had no previous connection with the testator or knowledge of his intentions; and it seems that the solicitor would not be liable for the amount of the intended benefit where it would have been reasonable for the beneficiary to have secured this benefit by taking proceedings against the estate for rectification of the will.[62] But where the principle (whatever its precise scope may turn out to be) does apply, its effect is to put C into the position in which he would have been if the contract between A and B had been properly performed. Such cases are, however, distinguishable from those which hold that building contractors are not liable to third parties in respect of purely economic loss caused by defective work. In the building cases, the third party's complaint is that he has not received the benefit of the contractor's performance. In the disappointed beneficiary cases, the benefit of which the third party is deprived is not that of the solicitor's work: the lost benefit was to be provided, not by the solicitor, but by the testator; it was not to be created by the solicitor's work, but existed independently of it. The third party is not entitled to the cost of curing the defects in the solicitor's work (*e.g.* to the cost of employing another solicitor to give effect to the testator's intention). On the contrary, it has been held that, if the defect is discovered when cure is still possible, the solicitor owes no duty to the beneficiary.[63] There are also the points that, if any duty is to be imposed on the solicitor to the disappointed beneficiary, the only realistic measure of damages is the value of the lost benefit; and that no more than nominal damages could be recovered from the solicitor by the client's estate, since it would have suffered no loss. The negligent solicitor would thus escape all substantial liability if he were not held liable to the disappointed beneficiary for the value of the lost benefit. In the building contract cases, on the other hand, the employer will usually have a substantial remedy against the defaulting builder for damages amounting either to the cost of curing the defects in the work or to the difference between the value of the work which was done and that which should have been done[64]; and such a remedy may be available to the employer, not only in respect of his own loss, but also (in appropriate circumstances) in respect of loss suffered by the third party.[65] For these reasons, it is submitted that the building contract cases can be distinguished from disappointed beneficiary cases such as *White v Jones*.

The principle of that case extended to a number of closely analogous situations. One such extension was made in *Carr-Glynn v Frearsons*[66] where the solicitors' negligence took the form, not of failing to secure the proper execution of the will, but of failing to take steps to ensure that property specifically bequeathed to the beneficiary remained within the client's estate after her death.[67] Loss was thus suffered by the estate but the

---

[60] [1995] 2 A.C. 207 at 295.

[61] *ibid.*, at 269. The alleged beneficiary's claim clearly cannot succeed without proof of the requisite testamentary intention in his favour: see *Gibbons v Nelsons* [2000] Lloyd's Rep. P.N. 603.

[62] On the question whether it would have been reasonable for the beneficiary to have taken such proceedings, contrast *Walker v Geo H Medlicott & Son*, [1999] 1 W.L.R. 727, with *Horsfall v Hayward* [1999] 1 F.L.R. 1182.

[63] *Hemmens v Wilson Browne* [1995] Ch. 223.

[64] See below, p.945.

[65] See above, p.594.

[66] [1998] 4 All E.R. 225.

[67] The testatrix was joint owner of the property in question and the solicitors had negligently failed to advise her to sever the joint tenancy, so that on her death her share passed to the other co-owner by right of survivorship.

solicitors were nevertheless held liable to the intended legatee since the proceeds of any claim by the estate would have benefited, not that legatee, but the person entitled under the will to the residuary estate, thus defeating the intention of the testatrix.[68] The decision can be explained on the ground that "the estate" is something of a legal abstraction, the loss being in fact suffered by the individual who under the will would, but for the solicitors' negligence, have received the property which was lost to "the estate"; and that the court looked behind that abstraction[69] so as to fashion a remedy for that individual. The alternative possibility that the estate might have had a claim against the solicitors in respect of the intended legatee's loss[70] was not considered, nor was any attempt made to reconcile the result with those building contract cases (discussed above[71]) in which a third party was held to have no remedy in tort against the contractor for pure economic loss. The principle of the "disappointed beneficiary" cases has also been extended to the situation in which the benefit of which the claimant was deprived as a result of the defendant's negligence was one which would have arisen otherwise than *under a will*. In *Gorham v British Telecommunications plc*[72] an insurance company sold a policy to a customer who had made it clear to the company that he was buying the policy to provide for his wife and dependant children in the event of his predeceasing them. The company negligently failed to advise him that these dependants would have been better off if he had joined his employers' pension scheme; and it was held that the company was liable to the dependants for loss of benefits under the employers' scheme up to (but not beyond) the time when the company had corrected its original advice. The principle of *White v Jones*[73] applied because (as in that case) the customer had not himself suffered any loss, so that, if the dependants' claims had been rejected, then neither the persons who had suffered loss nor anyone else would have any claim for established negligence; and because the advice had been given "in a context in which the interests of the defendants were fundamental to the transaction".[74] In both these respects, the case was closely analogous to that of a disappointed testamentary beneficiary.[75]

The "disappointed beneficiary" cases go further than any other group of negligence cases in encroaching on the common law doctrine of privity of contract. Perhaps for this reason, they were described as "an unusual class of case" in *Goodwill v Pregnancy Advisory Service*.[76] In that case, the defendant had arranged for one M to have a vasectomy and, after the operation had been carried out, told him that it had been

---

[68] *cf. Corbett v Bond Pearce* [2001] EWCA Civ 531; [2001] 3 All E.R. 769, where a residuary gift in favour of a disappointed beneficiary was held invalid in legal proceedings the costs of which were paid out of the testatrix's estate. The solicitors whose negligence was the cause of the invalidity of that gift then settled the disappointed beneficiary's claim for the full value of the residuary estate, undiminished by those costs. It was held that the solicitors were not liable to the estate for such costs since to hold them so liable would (1) make them liable twice over for the same loss; and (2) result in benefiting persons whom the testatrix (in accordance with her final testamentary intentions as expressed in the invalid will) no longer wished to benefit.

[69] In a way somewhat reminiscent of the process, well known in company law, of "lifting the corporate veil."

[70] See above, pp.593 *et seq.*

[71] See above, n.56.

[72] [2000] 1 W.L.R. 2129.

[73] [1995] 2 A.C. 207, above, p.616.

[74] *Gorham's* case, above n.72, at 2142.

[75] *cf.* the reference in *Dean v Allin & Watts* [2001] EWCA Civ 758; [2001] 2 Lloyd's Rep. 249 (above p.563) at [69] by Robert Walker L.J. to the "very special problems" which had arisen in *White v Jones* and *Gorham's* case, evidently not sharing the view of Lightman J. in *Dean v Allin & Watts*, above at [40] that the decision there represented a further extension of the principle in *White v Jones*.

[76] [1996] 1 W.L.R. 1397 at 1403.

successful and that he no longer needed to use any other method of contraception. Some three years later, M formed a sexual relationship with the claimant, to whom he communicated the information given to him by the defendant relating to the vasectomy; she ceased to use any method of contraception after having consulted her own general practitioner who told her that there was only a minute chance of her becoming pregnant. The vasectomy having undergone a spontaneous reversal, the claimant became pregnant by M and one reason given for holding that the defendant was not liable to her in damages was that a doctor performing a vasectomy could not realistically be described as having been employed to confer a benefit on his patient's future sexual partners. The case was also said to be unlike the "disappointed beneficiary" cases in that dismissal of the claim would not produce the "rank injustice"[77] that would arise in those cases if in them the only person with a claim against the negligent solicitor were the testator's estate, and that estate had suffered no loss. In a sterilisation case, a substantial remedy for negligence (if established) would normally be available to the patient him (or her) self.

3. Interference With Contractual Rights

(1) In general

Although a contract primarily creates rights and duties enforceable by the contracting parties against each other, it also incidentally imposes on third parties the duty not to interfere with the contracting parties in performing the contract.[78] In the leading case of *Lumley v Gye*[79] it was held that a person who, knowing of a contract between two others, "maliciously"[80] induces one of them to refuse to perform it, is liable for what has since become known as the tort of wrongful interference with contractual, or other legal,[81] rights.

(2) Contracts affecting property

The principle just stated may help to solve the problem which arises when a person acquires property with notice of a contract concerning it, previously made between two other persons. The problem is: to what extent is the acquirer restricted[82] by the contract in the use which he is entitled to make of the property? Where the property is land, the law has developed complex rules as a result of which a third party may be bound by (and, indeed, entitled to enforce) the contract, by way of exception to the doctrine of privity.[83] But the law has been reluctant to admit that contracts concerning chattels can bind a

---

[77] [1996] 1 W.L.R. 1397 at 1403.
[78] For other effects on third parties, see *PSM International v Whitehouse* [1992] I.R.L.R. 279.
[79] (1853) 2 E. & B. 216. For further proceedings, see 23 L.T. 66, 18 Jur. 468n.; 23 L.J.Q.B. 116n; Waddams, 117 L.Q.R. 431.
[80] *i.e.* deliberately and with knowledge of the existence of the contract: *British Homophone Ltd v Kunz* (1935) 152 L.T. 589; *D C Thomson & Co Ltd v Deakin* [1952] Ch. 646 at 694; *Jones Bros (Hunstanton) Ltd v Stevens* [1955] 1 Q.B. 275 at 280. Such knowledge may be inferred from surrounding circumstances: *Merkur Island Shipping Corp v Laughton* [1983] 2 A.C. 570. Two dicta in *British Industrial Plastics Ltd v Ferguson* [1940] 1 All E.R. 479 at 483 suggesting that liability may be based on *constructive* knowledge were not necessary for the decision and run counter to the main stream of authority. See further, below, p.622, n.6. There is no tortious liability for inducing *unfair* dismissal (which is not a breach of contract): *Wilson v Housing Corp* [1997] I.R.L.R. 346.
[81] See *Law Debenture Trust Corp v Ural Caspian Oil Corp* [1995] Ch. 152 at 165; *cf. Royal Brunei Airlines Sdn Bhd. v Tan* [1995] 2 A.C. 378 and *Twinsectra Ltd v Yardley* [2002] UKHL 12; [2002] 2 A.C. 164, stating similar principles for liability for dishonestly interfering with a relationship arising by way of trust.
[82] For the possible effect of a *promise* by the acquirer to perform the contract, see below, p.702.
[83] See Megarry and Wade, *The Law of Real Property* (6th ed.), Chaps 15 and 16.

third party.[84] If a third party were bound by such contracts at all, he might (as in the land cases) be bound where he had merely constructive notice of them; and it is generally agreed that the doctrine of constructive notice should be kept, so far as possible, out of commercial affairs.[85] On the other hand, too rigid a refusal to allow contracts concerning chattels to affect third parties may itself prove commercially inconvenient.

Such contracts may be divided into four groups.[86] The first consists of contracts restricting the use or disposition of goods. Certain undesirable restrictions of this kind have been expressly invalidated by legislation.[87] But others may be perfectly reasonable business arrangements aimed at ensuring consistency of quality or stable markets: for example, contracts that goods shall be sold only in packets sealed by the manufacturer, or after a certain time has elapsed.[88] The second group of contracts consists of those requiring the use of *particular* chattels for their performance, without creating any proprietary or possessory interest in those chattels for example, a contract to carry cargo in a particular ship. The third group consists of contracts for the hire of a chattel: and the fourth of options to purchase a chattel. These last two groups are now very common; a hire-purchase agreement is a contract for the hire of a chattel, coupled with an option to purchase it.

(a) PROTECTION AGAINST THIRD PARTIES IN SPECIAL CASES. In a number of special cases, the courts protect the rights arising under such contracts against third parties with notice of them: for example, where restrictions are imposed by a patentee on the use or disposition of patented goods,[89] and where an option to purchase a chattel is specifically enforceable.[90] The same would be true where money was lent on the terms that the loan was to be repaid out of specific property. Since such an undertaking to repay is specifically enforceable, it would create a charge in equity over the property in favour of the lender, and this would prevail against a third party who later acquired an interest in it, unless he was a bona fide purchaser for value without notice.[91]

(b) GENERAL PRINCIPLE OF PROTECTION AGAINST THIRD PARTIES REJECTED. A more general principle was formulated in *De Mattos v Gibson*,[92] where Knight Bruce L.J. said:

---

[84] This aspect of the doctrine of privity is not affected by the Contracts (Rights of Third Parties) Act 1999: below, p.580.

[85] See *Manchester Trust Ltd v Furness* [1895] 2 Q.B. 539 at 545; *cf. Westdeutsche Landesbank Girozentrale v Islington BC* [1996] A.C. 669 at 704–705.

[86] See Chafee, 41 H.L.R. 945; *cf.* Wade, 44 L.Q.R. 51; Gardner, 98 L.Q.R. 278; Tettenborn [1982] C.L.J. 58; Cohen-Grabelsky, 45 M.L.R. 241.

[87] Patents Act 1977, s.44, to the extent to which this remains in force: see Competition Act 1998 (Transitional, Consequential and Supplemental Provisions) Order 2000, SI 2000/311, art.3.

[88] See *BMTA v Salvadori* [1949] Ch. 556; below, p.563; *semble* that in similar circumstances agreements of this kind would be likely to be exempted by virtue of Competition Act, s.4 or of *ibid.* Sch.3, para.7(1) from any potential invalidity under s.2.

[89] Subject to Patents Act 1977, s.44 (see above, n.87 formerly Patents Act 1949, s.57); *Dunlop Rubber Co Ltd v Long Life Battery Depot* [1958] 1 W.L.R. 1033. This position is not affected by Copyright, Designs and Patents Act 1988.

[90] *Falcke v Gray* (1859) 4 Drew. 651, as explained in *Erskine Macdonald Ltd v Eyles* [1921] 1 Ch. 631 at 641; *cf. The Stena Nautica (No.2)* [1982] 2 Lloyd's Rep. 336 (where specific enforcement was denied). For the special position of mortgages of ships, see *The Shizelle* [1992] 2 Lloyd's Rep. 444.

[91] *Swiss Bank Corp v Lloyd's Bank Ltd* [1982] A.C. 584 at 598, 613; the actual decision was that the contract of loan did *not* create an obligation to repay out of specific property so that there was no specifically enforceable agreement affecting it see below, p.1021, n.57. *cf. MacJordan Construction Ltd v Brookmount Erostin, The Times*, October 29, 1991.

[92] (1858) 4 D. & J. 276 at 282.

"Reason and justice seem to prescribe that, at least as a general rule, where a man, by gift or purchase, acquires property from another, with knowledge of a previous contract, lawfully and for valuable consideration made . . . with a third person, to use and employ the property . . . in a specified manner, the acquirer shall not, to the material damage of the third person, in opposition to the contract and inconsistently with it, use and employ the property in a manner not allowable to the giver or seller".

This principle came to be associated with the rule in *Tulk v Moxhay*[93] under which third parties are bound by restrictive covenants concerning land. That rule was later confined to cases in which the claimant's interest in enforcing the covenant consisted in the ownership of land capable of being benefited by the covenant. This usually meant adjacent land[94]; and since adjacency is hardly a satisfactory criterion of interest in the case of things that can be moved, the tendency of these developments of the rule in *Tulk v Moxhay* was to undermine Knight Bruce L.J.'s principle.[95] Nevertheless, in *Lord Strathcona SS Co v Dominion Coal Co*[96] the Privy Council relied on that principle to hold that the time charterer of a ship had an interest in the ship which he could enforce against a purchaser of the ship with notice of the charterparty; the purchaser was also said to be in the position of a constructive trustee, with obligations which a court of equity would not allow him to violate.[97] The decision provoked adverse criticism,[98] particularly because the land law analogies and the constructive trust reasoning on which it was based might lead to the third party's being made liable where he had only constructive notice of the earlier contract. Where that contract concerned the use or disposition of a chattel, such a conclusion was open to the objection that it might have the undesirable effect of introducing the doctrine of constructive notice into commercial affairs. When a similar problem arose in *Port Line Ltd v Ben Line Steamers Ltd*,[99] Diplock J. therefore refused to follow the Privy Council's decision. Alternatively, he was prepared to distinguish it: the buyer of the ship in the *Port Line* case knew that she was under charter to the claimant, but he did not have actual notice of the precise extent of the claimant's rights under the charterparty.[1] Thus the *Port Line* case rejects the principle stated by Knight Bruce L.J. so far as it relates to contracts concerning chattels; but it does not decide that a third party can always disregard such a contract. A number of possibilities must be considered.

(c) REMEDY. Later authorities have restricted the principle stated in *De Mattos v Gibson*[2] by emphasising that the remedy there sought was simply an injunction to restrain the acquirer, C, from using the property inconsistently with the terms of the

---

[93] (1848) 2 Ph. 774.
[94] *LCC v Allen* [1914] 3 K.B. 642; the actual decision was reversed by statute (see now Housing Act 1985, s.609), but the principle stated in the text remains unimpaired.
[95] See *Barker v Stickney* [1919] 1 K.B. 121 at 131; for criticism, see *Tito v Waddell (No.2)* [1977] Ch. at 300.
[96] [1926] A.C. 108.
[97] *ibid.* at 125.
[98] *e.g. Greenhalgh v Mallard* [1943] 2 All E.R. 234.
[99] [1958] Q.B. 146. The cases cited in n.74 at p.607, above, all apply the constructive trust reasoning to contracts concerning land and do not, it is submitted, undermine the rejection of that reasoning in the *Port Line* case so far as contracts affecting the use or disposition of chattels are concerned.
[1] Hence the buyer was not liable in tort: see below, n.6.
[2] See above p.621 at n.92.

contract between A and B, known to C.[3] The principle therefore cannot impose any positive obligation on C to perform the terms of the contract between A and B. Thus where A acquired shares from B, promising to make payments to B on the occurrence of specific events, which later happened, it was held that that promise could not be enforced against C who later acquired the shares from A with knowledge of the contract between A and B, nor against D who acquired them from C with such knowledge.[4] An injunction on the principle of *De Mattos v Gibson* was not available against C or D as they were not proposing to act inconsistently with the contract between A and B: "they [were] merely proposing . . . to do nothing whatever".[5]

(d) THIRD PARTY'S LIABILITY IN TORT. A third party who acquires a chattel with knowledge[6] of a contract affecting it may, if his acquisition or use of the chattel is inconsistent with that contract, be liable in tort for interfering with its performance.[7] Thus in *BMTA v Salvadori*[8] A bought a car and covenanted with B that he would not resell it for one year without first offering it to B. During the year, C bought the car from A with notice of the covenant, and was held liable to B for wrongfully interfering with B's contractual rights against A. It has been suggested that the decision of the Privy Council in the *Lord Strathcona* case[9] can be explained on the ground that the purchaser of the ship had committed this tort against the charterer.[10] The tort may be committed even though A was quite willing to break his contract with B. Thus it is immaterial whether A or C began the negotiations leading to the contract between them[11]; indeed, C's tort liability may arise precisely because he has colluded with A in an effort to get rid of a restriction imposed in favour of B by the contract between A and B.[12] The merit of this approach is that it avoids the danger of importing the doctrine of constructive notice into this branch of the law. On the other hand, it is subject to two limitations.

First, the tort is not committed if the defendant's interference was not the cause of the claimant's loss. In the *Lord Strathcona* case,[13] the purchasers of the ship (who were the defendants in the Privy Council proceedings) mortgaged her, but were too poor to put her to sea. The mortgage gave the mortgagees the right to sell the ship, and it was held that they were entitled to sell her free from the charterer's rights, though they had notice of those rights. The cause of the failure to perform the charterparty was the

---

[3] *Swiss Bank Corp v Lloyds Bank Ltd* [1979] Ch. 581 at 574 (as to which see also below, n.10).

[4] *Law Debenture Trust Corp v Ural Caspian Oil Corp Ltd* [1993] 1 W.L.R. 138; Tettenborn [1993] C.L.J. 382; for a successful appeal on another point see [1995] Ch.152; below, p.623, n.16.

[5] [1993] 1 W.L.R. 138 at 146.

[6] See *J T Stratford & Sons Ltd v Lindley* [1965] A.C. 269 at 332; *Emerald Construction Co Ltd v Lowthian* [1966] 1 W.L.R. 691; *Daily Mirror Newspapers Ltd v Gardner* [1968] 2 Q.B. 762; *Greig v Insole* [1978] 1 W.L.R. 302 at 336; and *cf. Distillers Co (Biochemicals) Ltd v Times Newspapers* [1975] Q.B. 613; *Merkur Island Shipping Corp v Laughton* [1983] 2 A.C. 570. But in the *Port Line* case (above, p.621) the defendant was not liable in tort as he had assumed that the charterparty with which he was alleged to have interfered was in the same terms as another charterparty which he had made with one of the contracting parties. This assumption was mistaken, but not, in the circumstances, unreasonable.

[7] Wade, 42 L.Q.R. 139.

[8] [1949] Ch. 556; *Rickless v United Artists Corp* [1988] Q.B. 40 at 58–59; *cf. Law Debenture Corp v Ural Caspian Oil Corp Ltd* [1993] 1 W.L.R. 138, where the fifth defendant admitted liability on this ground; for a successful appeal on another point, see [1995] Ch. 152.

[9] [1926] A.C. 108.

[10] *Swiss Bank Corp v Lloyd's Bank Ltd* [1979] Ch. 548 at 574; in the Court of Appeal it was conceded that there was "no substance" in the point in that case: see [1982] A.C. 584 at 598 and below, p.623 at n.25.

[11] *Sefton v Tophams Ltd* [1965] Ch. 1140 at 1161, 1167, reversed without reference to this point [1967] A.C. 50.

[12] *Esso Petroleum Co Ltd v Kingswood Motors (Addlestone) Ltd* [1974] Q.B. 142.

[13] [1926] A.C. 108; above, p.621.

shipowners' poverty, and not the mortgagees' sale of the ship.[14] Similarly, where breach of the contract has already been induced by C's acquisition of the property from A, there will be no tort liability for inducing breach of contract on D, who subsequently buys the property from C, even with knowledge of the contract between A and B, for D's conduct will not have played any part in inducing the original breach.[15] Nor is D in such a case liable for interference with the remedies arising out of the broken contract between A and B.[16]

Secondly, tort liability for interference with contractual rights is based on intentional wrongdoing. It follows that, if a defendant negligently damaged a ship which was subject to a time charterparty, he would not commit this tort against the charterer; nor would he be liable to the charterer in negligence for pecuniary loss, such as hire wasted or profits lost while the ship was, by reason of the damage, out of service.[17]

So far, in discussing the third party's liability for interference with contractual rights, it has been assumed that C either knew, or that he did not know, of the contract between A and B. In the former situation, he could, but in the latter he could not, be liable for the tort.[18] There is also an intermediate situation, in which C at the time of his contract with A had no more than constructive notice of A's earlier contract with B, but then acquired actual knowledge of that contract before calling for (or receiving) performance of his own contract with A.[19] The question then arises whether, on such facts, C is liable to B for the tort of interference with contractual rights. That tort is subject to the defence of "justification",[20] which is certainly available to C where he had contracted with A *before* B had done so.[21] The defence is a flexible one,[22] and the principle on which it is based appears to be equally applicable where C's contract with A was made *after* B's but in ignorance of it. The exercise by C of rights thus acquired in good faith against A should not, it is submitted, make C liable for the tort to B.[23] Even in such a situation, however, C may be liable to B (under the rules relating to special cases stated above[24]) if B's contract with A is specifically enforceable. Where the specific enforceability of this contract gives rise to an equitable interest, this can be asserted against C even though he had, when he contracted with A, only constructive notice of A's contract with B. In such a case, the tort claim would be "of no value"[25] if, as has been submitted above, it arises only where C, when he contracted with A, had actual knowledge of B's rights; but it

---

[14] *The Lord Strathcona* [1925] P. 143; judgment in this case was given four months before judgment in the Privy Council proceedings so that the injunction issued by the Privy Council never took effect. *De Mattos v Gibson* suffered a similar fate: (1858) 4 D. & J. 276. *cf. The Myrto* [1977] 2 Lloyd's Rep. 243; *Lyus v Prowsa Developments Ltd* [1982] 1 W.L.R. 1044 at 1049.

[15] *Law Debenture Trust Corp v Ural Caspian Oil Corp Ltd* [1993] 1 W.L.R. 138; and see next note.

[16] *Law Debenture Trust Corp v Ural Caspian Oil Corp Ltd* [1995] Ch. 152, reversing the decision at first instance (above) on this point.

[17] On the principle stated at p.611, above: *The Mineral Transporter* [1986] A.C. 1.

[18] See above, pp.619, 621.

[19] This was the position in *Swiss Bank Corp v Lloyds Bank Ltd* [1982] A.C. 584: see [1979] Ch. 548 at 568–569, and see below, n.23.

[20] See Salmond, *The Law of Torts* (21st ed.), pp.353–355.

[21] *Smithies v National Association of Operative Plasterers* [1909] 1 K.B. 310 at 337; *Edwin Hill & Partners v First National Finance Corp plc* [1989] 1 W.L.R. 225 at 230. For terms which may be imposed on C as a condition of obtaining relief against A, see *Guiness Peat Aviation (Belgium) NV v Hispania Lineas Aereas SA* [1992] 1 Lloyd's Rep. 190.

[22] *Glamorgan Coal Co v South Wales Miners' Federation* [1903] 2 K.B. 545 at 574–575.

[23] This was admitted in *Swiss Bank Corp v Lloyds Bank Ltd*, above, n.19: see [1979] Ch. 548 at 569–573.

[24] See above, p.620.

[25] *Swiss Bank Corp v Lloyds Bank Ltd* [1982] A.C. 584 at 598, where it was held, on construction, that the contract was *not* specifically enforceable; see below, p.1021, n.57.

would equally be unnecessary to rely on it,[26] since B could succeed against C on the different ground that B's contract with A was specifically enforceable and therefore conferred an equitable interest on B.

(e) PROTECTION OF "POSSESSORY RIGHTS". A final possibility relates to contracts under which possession of a chattel is, or is to be, transferred. The contracts in the *Strathcona* and *Port Line* cases were not of this kind: they were time charters, under which a shipowner undertakes to render services by the use of a particular ship, which remains in his possession.[27] Such charters must be contrasted with demise charters, which are contracts for the hire of a ship under which the shipowner does transfer, or undertake to transfer, possession of the ship to the charterer.[28] The nearest analogy in the land law to a contract for the hire of a chattel is a lease,[29] and not a restrictive covenant. Hence the development of the doctrine of *Tulk v Moxhay*, discussed above,[30] need not affect cases concerning such contracts. One reason given by Diplock J. for his decision in the *Port Line* case was that a time charterer had "no proprietary *or possessory* rights in the ship".[31] It can be inferred that a "possessory right" might have been protected. Where the hirer of a chattel is in actual possession of it he should certainly be protected against a third party who acquires the chattel with notice of the hirer's interest.

It is less clear whether, in this context, the words "possessory rights" refer only to rights *of* possession, or extend also to rights *to* possession, *i.e.* whether a person who has a contractual right to the *future* possession of a chattel would similarly be protected against the third party. In *The Stena Nautica (No.2)*[32] A had demise-chartered his ship to B under a contract which also gave B an option to purchase her. Later, while A was in possession of the ship, he granted a second demise charter of her to C who had no knowledge of the earlier contract. B exercised his option to purchase and it was held that his only remedy was by way of damages against A: since B's option to purchase was not specifically enforceable,[33] he could not assert rights to the ship against C. The question whether B could assert a *right to future possession as demise charterer* against C did not, strictly speaking, arise since B was suing to enforce, not that right, but rather his right as a person who had exercised an option to purchase. But it seems from the reasoning of the Court of Appeal that B's right to possession as demise charterer would have been protected only if the contract under which the right arose was one in respect of which the court was willing to make an order of specific performance. The argument of commercial convenience which justifies the decision in the *Port Line* case[34] would seem to apply as much where a contract creates a right to the future possession of a chattel as where it creates the right to have some particular use made of the chattel. In each case the right is hard to discover and should not be enforced against a third party *without*

---

[26] [1982] A.C. 584 at 598.
[27] *The Lancaster* [1980] 2 Lloyd's Rep. 497 at 500; *The Scaptrade* [1983] A.C. 694 at 702; *The Niizura* [1996] 2 Lloyd's Rep. 66 at 72; *The Starsin* [2003] UKHL 12, [2003] 2 W.L.R. 711, at [119].
[28] *Baumwoll Manufactur v Furness* [1893] A.C. 8; *The Giuseppe di Vittorio* [1998] 1 Lloyd's Rep. 136 at 156; *BP Operating Co Ltd v Chevron Transport (Scotland) Ltd* [2001] UKHL 50; [2003] A.C. 197, at [78, 79].
[29] *cf.* above, p.607 at n.73.
[30] See above, p.621.
[31] [1958] 2 Q.B. 146 at 166 (italics supplied).
[32] [1982] 2 Lloyd's Rep. 336.
[33] See below, p.1022. A licence to occupy *land* can be enforced against a trespasser even by a licensee not yet in possession: *Dutton v Manchester Airport plc* [1999] 2 All E.R. 675.
[34] See above, p.621.

actual knowledge of it; and adequate protection against a third party *with* such knowledge is provided by the rules relating to the tort of wrongful interference with contractual rights.

4. Intimidation

The tort of intimidation is committed where A induces B to act to the detriment of C by threatening B with some unlawful course of conduct. In *Rookes v Barnard*[35] the House of Lords decided that a threat by A to break his contract with B is for this purpose a threat to do an unlawful act. Such a threat may therefore entitle C to sue A for intimidation. It has been said that this view outflanks the common law doctrine of privity.[36] No doubt in such a case C bases his cause of action on the threat to break a contract to which he is not a party. But the doctrine of privity only prevents C from enforcing A's promise to B[37]; and in cases of intimidation C is certainly not doing that. If A induces B to dismiss C by threatening to defame B, C may be able to sue A for intimidation, but not for defamation. So, if A induces B to dismiss C by threatening to break A's contract with B, C may be able to sue A for intimidation, but not for breach of contract. In such a case C is not trying to enforce A's promise to B: "his ground of action is quite different".[38] C's complaint is not that A has broken his promise to B but that he has coerced B into acting to C's detriment.[39] The House of Lords has therefore rejected the argument that the doctrine of privity would be outflanked by holding that the tort of intimidation could be committed by threatening to commit a breach of contract.[40]

5. Restitution?

It has been suggested in Australia that the third party may have a claim in restitution where the promisor has received payment (or some other performance) from the promisee and has then failed or refused to perform the promise in favour of the third party; and that the measure of recovery on such a claim is the amount promised.[41] The suggestion was made where premiums under a policy of liability insurance for the benefit of a third party had been paid by the promisee to the promisor (the insurance company) which had then refused to pay the third party. The promisor's liability in restitution was said to be based on his unjust enrichment, and to arise in spite of the fact that there was no correlative impoverishment of the third party. But while it is true that liability in restitution is not based on loss to the claimant, it is (in the case put) based

---

[35] [1964] A.C. 1129. For restrictions on the scope of such liability where the unlawful conduct takes the form of acts done in the contemplation of furtherance of a trade dispute, see Trade Union and Labour Relation (Consolidation) Act 1992, s.219 as amended by Trade Union Reform and Employment Rights Act 1993 s.49(1) and Sch.8, para.72; for an extension of the principle in favour of an individual whose expected supply of goods or services is disrupted by unlawful acts inducing industrial action, see Trade Union and Labour Relations (Consolidation) Act 1992, s.235A, as inserted by Trade Union Reform and Employment Rights Act 1993, s.22.

[36] Wedderburn, 24 M.L.R. 572 at 577; in *Rookes v Barnard* the argument was accepted in the Court of Appeal: [1963] 1 Q.B. 623 at 695, but rejected by the House of Lords; below, at n.38.

[37] See above, p.582.

[38] *Rookes v Barnard* [1964] A.C. at 1168; *cf.* 1208; if C were trying to enforce the contract, the damages might be quite different.

[39] *Rookes v Barnard* [1964] A.C. at 1208.

[40] *ibid.* at 1168, 1200, 1208, 1235; Hamson [1961] C.L.J. 189; [1964] C.L.J. 159; Hoffmann, 81 L.Q.R. 116 at 124–128.

[41] *Trident Insurance Co Ltd v McNiece Bros Pty Ltd* (1988) 165 C.L.R. 107, *per* Gaudron J.; this view does not seem to be shared by any other member of the Court; Soh, 105 L.Q.R. 4.

on gain to the defendant and it is hard to see what justification there can be for wholly disregarding this *basis* of restitutionary liability in determining its *measure*. And the argument that, to hold the promisor liable to the third party was "not an abrogation of the doctrine of privity of contract",[42] merely because the liability was said to arise in restitution, is, it is submitted, inconsistent with the practical result of making the promisor so liable. We have seen that, in England, the promisor is not liable in tort where the practical effect of imposing such liability would be to abrogate the doctrine of privity[43]; and there seems to be no reason why the position should be different merely because the alleged basis of liability is restitution rather than tort. The suggestion that the promisor is liable in restitution to the third party for the amount promised, merely because the promisor has received performance from the promisee is also inconsistent with the reasoning of *Beswick v Beswick*,[44] where it was assumed that the third party had no common law right to sue the promisor in her own name, in spite of the fact that the promisor had received performance in full from the promisee. The view that claims of the kind here discussed fall outside the scope of the doctrine of privity of contract must therefore be regarded with scepticism. The argument based on restitution would in any event be of no avail to the third party where the promisor was willing to pay and the issue was merely whether it should pay the third party or the promisee[45]: in such cases the promisor would not be unjustly enriched so that there would be no basis for restitutionary liability.

The above discussion is based on the assumption that the promisor would be unjustly enriched if he were allowed to retain a payment received *from the promisee* in spite of his failure to perform his promise to pay the third party. There is the further possibility that the promisor may have received a benefit *from a third party*: for example, where A contracts to grant a development lease to B, a company controlled by C, and C incurs expense in improving A's land in anticipation of the development, which then fails to take place because of A's failure to perform his contract with B. In such a case, it is arguable that C may have a restitution claim against A.[46] To allow such a claim would not be inconsistent with the doctrine of privity since in such a case C's claim is not based on any promise made by A to B for the benefit of C; no such promise has been made. The basis and measure of any restitution claim which C may have against A is more closely analogous to cases in which restitution is granted in respect of benefits conferred under anticipated contracts which fail to come into existence.[47]

SECTION 4. EXEMPTION CLAUSES AND THIRD PARTIES

Where an exemption clause purports to affect a third party,[48] two questions arise. Can the third party take the benefit of the clause? Can he be bound by it? For the purpose

---

[42] 165 C.L.R. at 177.

[43] See above, p.612.

[44] [1968] A.C. 58; above, p.589.

[45] See above, p.604; *cf.* such cases as *Re Schebsman* [1944] Ch. 83 (below, p.647) and *Re Sinclair's Life Policy* [1938] Ch. 799 (below, p.648).

[46] *Brennan v Brighton BC, The Times,* May 15, 1997, where B was a company which had been wound up and so could no longer sue A for breach of the contract between them.

[47] See below, p.1062.

[48] A contract between A and B may by reference incorporate an exemption clause contained in a contract between B and C. If so, A is not for the present purpose a third party: see, for example, *The Coral* [1993] 1 Lloyd's Rep. 1.

of this discussion, it will be assumed that the clause is valid under the rules stated in Chapter 7.[49]

1. The Benefit

(1) Privity and exceptions

Originally, the courts held that a person could only take the benefit of an exemption clause in a contract which he did not make himself if one of the recognised exceptions to the doctrine of privity could be invoked in his favour: for example, if the contract was made through an agent acting either for him or for the other party.[50] Such agency reasoning might sometimes be artificial, but it at any rate saved the face of the doctrine of privity. A further exception has been created by the Contracts (Rights of Third Parties) Act 1999, under which third parties are, if the requirements of the Act are satisfied,[51] entitled to the benefit of exemption clauses in contracts between others.[52] But some of the cases with which the following discussion is concerned are[53] or may[54] not be, covered by that legislation; and in others it may be to the third party's advantage to rely, not on the new statutory exception, but on a common law exception,[55] since this is not limited by the provisions of the Act.[56]

Whether, in this context, the common law doctrine must be abandoned altogether depends on the effect of the decision of the House of Lords in *Elder, Dempster & Co v Paterson, Zochonis & Co*[57] A company agreed to carry the claimant's palm-oil from West Africa to Hull and time-chartered a ship for this purpose. The contract of carriage was evidenced by a bill of lading, the parties to which were the claimants and the company; this bill exempted "the shipowners, hereinafter called the company",[58] from liability for bad stowage. The oil was damaged by bad stowage and it was held that the shipowners were protected by the exemption clause, although there was no express contract directly made between them and the claimants. One possible ground for this decision was that the company had acted as the shipowners' agent for the purpose of making a contract between them and the claimants.[59] The inference that the company had so acted appears to have been based on the ground that the exemption clause expressly referred to, and

---

[49] Many of the cases discussed in this Section concern contracts for the international carriage of goods by sea and would not be affected by the Unfair Contract Terms Act 1977 or by the Unfair Terms in Consumer Contracts Regulations 1999; above, pp.266, 277. Others (*e.g.* those in which the claim was for personal injuries) would now often be differently decided, or decided on other grounds, under the Act or the Regulations; above, pp.249, 273.

[50] *Hall v NE Ry* (1875) L.R. 10 Q.B. 437; *cf. Barrett v Great Northern Ry* (1904) 20 T.L.R. 175; *The Kirkness* [1957] P. 51; *Texas Instruments Ltd v Nason (Europe) Ltd* [1991] 1 Lloyd's Rep. 146 (where the carrier's wilful misconduct deprived him of the benefit of an exempting provision having the force of law); *The Romina* [2002] EWHC 1759 (admty), [2003] 1 All E.R. (Comm) 129.

[51] See especially s.1(1), (2) and (3); below, pp.651–656.

[52] s.1(6).

[53] *e.g. Adler v Dickson* [1955] 1 Q.B. 158; *Scruttons Ltd v Midland Silicones Ltd* [1962] A.C. 446; see below, p.655.

[54] For the question whether *Elder, Dempster & Co v Paterson Zochonis & Co* [1924] A.C. 522 would be covered by the 1999 Act, see below p.656, n.34.

[55] s.7(1) of the Act preserves the third party's right to rely on such an exception.

[56] *e.g.* by ss.2 or 3: below, pp.657–661.

[57] [1924] A.C. 522; distinguished in *Gadsden Pty Ltd v Australian Coastal Shipping Commission* [1977] 1 N.S.W.L.R. 575, *The Golden Lake* [1982] 2 Lloyd's Rep. 632, *The Forum Craftsman* [1985] 1 Lloyd's Rep. 291 (especially at 295) and in *The Kapetan Markos NL (No.2)* [1987] 2 Lloyd's Rep. 321 at 331.

[58] It was admitted that these words were apt to protect the company: [1923] 1 K.B. 422.

[59] [1924] A.C. 522 at 534 (first sentence).

purported to protect, the shipowners[60]; and, although this fact would no longer of itself support such an inference,[61] the agency reasoning is consistent with the doctrine of privity in that it gives rise to a contract between the claimants and the shipowners. A second possible ground for the decision was that the act of the claimants in presenting the goods for carriage, followed by that of the captain in accepting them for this purpose on behalf of the shipowners,[62] gave rise to what Lord Sumner called a "bailment on terms"[63] between the claimants and the shipowners, that is, to one which incorporated the exemption clause by tacit reference.[64] "Bailment on terms" is, however, unfortunately an expression with more than one possible meaning. It has been judicially interpreted to refer *either* to a bailment into which terms were incorporated by virtue of an implied contract[65] arising from the conduct of the parties, *or* to a bailment operating irrespective of contract.[66] On the former view, the requirement of privity would be satisfied, while on the latter there would be no need to satisfy it, bailment being a relationship which can come into existence without any contract.[67] The bailment reasoning is thus again consistent with the doctrine of privity. But a third possible reason for the decision in the *Elder, Dempster* case is the so-called principle of vicarious immunity: this states that, where a person employs an agent to perform a contract, that agent is entitled, in performing the contract, to any immunity from liability which the contract confers on the principal.[68] Under this principle, the shipowners were protected by the exemption clause because, in carrying out the carriage *operation*, they had acted as agents for the company, even though the *contract* to perform that operation was between the company and the claimants. This reasoning is inconsistent with the doctrine of privity in the sense that it would enable an agent to rely by way of defence on the terms of a contract to which he was not a party; and it was rejected by the House of Lords in *Scruttons Ltd v Midland Silicones Ltd*.[69]

---

[60] *Quaere* whether the inference was realistic. The company usually carried goods in its *own* ships and may simply, as a result of an oversight, have used a form of bill of lading designed for this situation in the different one in which the carrying ship had been chartered from a third party.

[61] *Cosgrove v Horsfall* (1946) 62 T.L.R. 140; *Genys v Matthews* [1965] 3 All E.R. 24; *Gore v Van der Lann* [1967] 2 Q.B. 31; for the effect of the Contracts (Rights of Third Parties) Act 1999, see below, p.634.

[62] The charter being a time charter, the captain remained their employee and took possession of the goods on the shipowners' behalf: *cf.* the authorities cited in n.27 at p.624 above. This point is not affected by the fact that he signed the bill of lading (see *Scruttons Ltd v Midland Silicones Ltd* [1962] A.C. 446 at 455) on behalf of the charterers (see [1923] 1 K.B. 420 at 424).

[63] [1924] A.C. 522 at 564.

[64] Exactly how the exemption clause in the contract between the claimant and the company came to be incorporated into the bailment between the claimant and the shipowner is not made clear. Lord Sumner's reference ([1924] A.C. 522 and 564) to "the known and contemplated form of bill of lading" suggests the analogy of incorporation by custom or usage: above, p.213.

[65] *Adler v Dickson* [1955] 1 Q.B. 158 at 189, *per* Morris L.J.; *Pyrene Co Ltd v Scindia Navigation Co Ltd* [1954] 2 Q.B. 402 at 406, *per* Devlin J.; *Scruttons Ltd v Midland Silicones Ltd* [1959] 2 Q.B. 171 at 187, *per* Diplock J; *cf.* also *Sandeman Coprimar S.A. v Transitos y Transportes Integrales* [2003] EWCA Civ 113 at [62], [63], below, p.641, n.84a.

[66] *The Pioneer Container* [1994] 2 A.C. 324 at 335, 339–340, *per* Lord Goff ("notwithstanding the *absence of any contract*"); the question in this case was not whether a third party could take the *benefit* of a contract between others but whether he could be *bound* by such a contract: below, p.640. Lord Goff's reference in *The Mahkutai* [1996] A.C. 650 at 661 to the claimants in the *Elder, Dempster* case having "impliedly agreed that the goods were received by the shipowners, as bailees, subject to" the exemption clause could be read as supporting either the contractual or the non-contractual view. The latter view is supported by *The Starsin* [2003] UKHL 12, [2003] 2 W.L.R. 711, at [136].

[67] See above, p.156.

[68] [1924] A.C. 522 at 534 (second sentence), approving the view of Scrutton L.J. in the Court of Appeal [1923] 1 K.B. 420 at 441–442; *cf. Mersey Shipping & Transport Co v Rea* (1925) 21 Ll.L.R. 375 at 378.

[69] [1962] A.C. 446.

In that case a drum of chemicals had been shipped under a contract between shipper and carrier evidenced by a bill of lading which limited the liability of "the carrier" to $500. After the rights and duties under this contract had passed to the claimants by transfer of the bill of lading,[70] the drum was damaged by the negligence of a firm of stevedores who had been employed by the carrier to unload the ship. The House of Lords[71] held that the stevedores could not rely on the $500 limitation of liability as they were not parties to the contract of carriage; and that the principle of vicarious immunity was not the *ratio decidendi* of the *Elder, Dempster* case. Nor did any of the other reasons for that decision help the stevedores. It was not possible to infer that the carrier had intended to act as agent of the stevedores for the purpose of making a contract between them and the claimants so as to give the stevedores the benefit of the limitation clause in the bill of lading, for that term limited the liability only of *the carrier* and made no reference to the stevedores,[72] nor were there any circumstances extrinsic to the bill on which an inference of agency could be based.[73] Nor did any implied contract arise between the claimants and the stevedores since the claimants had not asked the stevedores to render any services that would normally be governed by contractual terms between them.[74] The claimants had merely applied to the carrier for delivery of the drum, which had been stored in a shed rented by the carrier from the port authority; and when the process of moving the drum from that shed into the lorry sent by the claimants to collect it was carried out through the instrumentality of the stevedores, the latter regarded this as no more than "the performance of their own obligations under the contract which they had made with"[75] the carrier. The implied contract argument thus failed for want of contractual intention.[76] Nor could the stevedores invoke the "bailment on terms" reasoning since, in the circumstances just described, they had not been entrusted with possession of the drum so as to become bailees of it.[77] Even if they had been such bailees (*e.g.* if the drum had been stored in a shed owned by them) it is far from clear that the mental element requisite for the incorporation of the limitation clause into the supposed bailment would have been satisfied. There would obviously be no requirement of *contractual* intention where the bailment was a non-contractual one, but it would appear that the *consent* of the claimants and of the stevedores was a necessary condition for the incorporation of the terms of the contract of carriage into the supposed

---

[70] See now Carriage of Goods by Sea Act 1992, ss.2 and 3, below, pp.675, 704.

[71] Lord Denning dissenting; his dissent was based, not on the ground that the stevedores were entitled to the *benefit* of the limitation provision in the contract of carriage, but on the ground that the cargo-owners were *bound* by a similar term (below, p.638) in the contract between carrier and stevedores: see [1962] A.C. 446 at 489 ("I must be wrong about all this"), 491. See also his judgments in *Adler v Dickson*, above n.65, *White v Warwick (John) & Co Ltd* [1953] 1 W.L.R. 1285 and *Morris v C W Martin & Sons Ltd* [1966] 1 Q.B. 716.

[72] [1962] A.C. 446 at 466, rejecting the argument that "carrier" could be construed so as to mean or include stevedores. For this reason, the stevedores would not, under the Contracts (Rights of Third Parties) Act 1999, be entitled to the benefit of a clause protecting only the carrier: below, pp.603–604. Contrast *South Australia Management Corp v Sheahan* [1995] ALM 3577 where, in another context, "carrier" was construed to include subcontractors of the carrier.

[73] For such extrinsic circumstances, see, for example, *The Kirkness* [1957] P. 51 at 66; *Raymond Burke Motors Ltd v Mersey Docks & Harbour Co* [1986] 1 Lloyd's Rep. 155; *Texas Instruments Ltd v Nason (Europe) Ltd* [1991] 1 Lloyd's Rep. 146 at 149.

[74] Diplock J. may have gone too far in saying that the claimants had not asked the stevedores to "do anything to their goods:" [1959] 2 K.B. at 188–189; but the mere moving of the goods from a store to a waiting lorry would not by itself normally be governed by contractual terms. See also [1962] 1 Q.B. 102 at 136.

[75] [1962] A.C. 446 at 496.

[76] For other cases in which contractual intention was negatived by a party's belief that he was merely performing a previously existing contract, see above, p.169.

[77] [1962] A.C. 446 at 470; *The Starsin* [2003] UKHL 12, [2003] 2 W.L.R. 711, at [146]. Contrast *The Rigoletto* [2000] 2 Lloyd's Rep. 532 at 540 (goods in stevedores' possession for six days before loss).

bailment[78]; and though the stevedores may be assumed to have consented to a limitation clause which could operate only in their favour,[79] there would have been nothing to show that the claimants had consented, not only to the hypothetical sub-bailment, but also to the inclusion of that clause in the sub-bailment so as to protect the stevedores.[80]

The reasoning of the *Midland Silicones* case may give the appearance of being merely a technical application of the doctrine of privity[81]; but the decision also reflects a conflict of policies. On one hand, there is the view that a "self-confessed tortfeasor" should not be allowed to "shelter behind a document that is no concern of his",[82] particularly where it is not clear that the injured party has agreed to the third party's having the benefit of the contractual exemptions from and limitations of liability. On the other hand, there is force in the argument that, if the third party were not protected, there would often be an "easy way round"[83] exemption and limitation clauses; it was this argument which was originally used to support the principle of vicarious immunity.[84] In rejecting that principle, the *Midland Silicones* case severely limited the effectiveness of such clauses. A person who suffered loss or injury as a result of a negligent breach of contract generally had a remedy against someone, if only against the workman who was negligent. In practice the employer would often feel morally obliged to pay the damages awarded against his employee,[85] and might be legally liable to do so.[86] Hence employers tried to protect their servants or agents by differently worded exemption clauses, and the cases to be discussed below make it clear that they can now do so by using appropriate words. There is no objection to this on policy grounds where the clause is itself valid[86a] and constitutes a legitimate device for allocating contractual risks and the burden of insurance. The Contracts (Rights of Third Parties) Act 1999 now provides a relatively simple drafting mechanism for giving third parties the benefit of exemption and limitation clauses[87]; and some statutes which limit the liability of carriers expressly extend these

---

[78] See *The Pioneer Container* [1994] 2 A.C. 324 at 339–340 where Lord Goff, in discussing the "bailment on terms" explanation of the *Elder, Dempster* case refers in turn to the state of mind of the shipowners ("the terms upon which the shipowners implicitly received the goods") and of the shippers ("the shippers . . . [having] impliedly consented" to the terms of the sub-bailment). *cf.* his use of the phrase "impliedly agreed" in the *The Mahkutai* [1996] A.C. 650 at 661.

[79] The requirement of the third party's consent is nevertheless significant, particularly where the term alleged to be incorporated in the bailment is one that can operate against him: *e.g.* an exclusive jurisdiction clause which the third party wished to contest: see *The Forum Craftsman* [1984] 2 Lloyd's Rep. 102 at 107.

[80] [1962] A.C. 446 at 474.

[81] *ibid.*, at 463, 473 and 494.

[82] *Wilson v Darling Island Stevedoring Co* [1956] 1 Lloyd's Rep. 349 at 359; *cf. Adler v Dickson* [1955] 1 Q.B. 158 at 187; in *Robert C Herd & Co v Krawill Machinery Corp* 359 U.S. 297, 303 (1959) this reasoning prevailed even in the United States, where the law *rejects* the doctrine of privity, so that the third party could have been protected by making him a "beneficiary" of the contract, even though he was not a "party" to it: *ibid.*, at 308.

[83] *Elder, Dempster & Co v Paterson Zochonis & Co* [1923] 1 K.B. 420 at 441, approved [1924] A.C. 522 at 534.

[84] The same argument continues to be used in support of that principle: see the *London Drugs* case [1992] 3 S.C.R. 299 (below at n.89) at 499.

[85] In *Adler v Dickson* [1955] 1 Q.B. 158, the employers said that they would satisfy any judgment which might be given against their servants. But, as the claimants had not made any promise to them not to sue the servants, the employers would not be entitled to have an action by the injured party against the servants stayed: *Gore v Van der Lann* [1967] 2 Q.B. 31.

[86] *i.e.* under an express contract to indemnify the servant or agent.

[86a] See *The Starsin* [2003] UKHL 12, [2003] 2 W.L.R. 711, below p.635, where this requirement was not complied with.

[87] See ss.1(1)(a) and (b) and 6(5) ("tailpiece"), below, pp.652–653, 654, 656, 661–662. A clause taking effect by virtue of these provisions will, however, do so only subject to the restrictions imposed by other provisions of the Bill: above, p.627, below pp.662–664; and these restrictions differ from those which may arise at common law by reason of defects in the main contract: see below pp.635–636.

limitations to the carriers' servants or agents.[88] This position is generally regarded as acceptable; and in Canada the courts have recognised an exception to the doctrine of privity precisely to protect employees of a contracting party by enabling them to rely on an exemption clause which is clearly intended to protect them, even though it does not expressly refer to them.[89] The doctrine of privity was never a satisfactory instrument for controlling undesirable exemption clauses,[90] and should no longer be used for this purpose now that the ability of a contracting party to exclude or restrict liability by means of such clauses is directly controlled by legislation.[91] Direct control of exemption clauses between the contracting parties is clearly preferable to indirect evasion by means of a claim against a third party whom the words of the clause seek to protect.

(2) Himalaya clauses

Granted, then, that on balance policy considerations support the view that a third party should, in appropriate cases, be able to take advantage of an exemption clause, the remaining question is how this result may be achieved. The most obvious possibility is by drafting the clause in such a way as to extend its protection to the third party; for the decision in the *Midland Silicones* case was partly based on the fact that the clause there did not refer to the stevedores at all, but only to the carrier. At common law, indeed, it would not suffice simply to say that the third party was to be protected,[92] or that he was to be deemed to be a party to the contract.[93] But a much more elaborate clause (known as a "Himalaya" clause[94]) was considered in *The Eurymedon*,[95] where it was held to be capable of protecting the third party. Our present concern is with the common law rules relating to such clauses: the effect on them of the Contracts (Rights of Third Parties) Act 1999 is considered later in this Chapter.[96]

(a) NATURE AND EFFECT. In that case a contract was made between a shipper and a carrier for the carriage of machinery from England to New Zealand. The machinery was damaged by employees of the stevedore while it was being unloaded; and the question was whether the stevedore was protected by the bill of lading issued by the carrier to the shipper as evidence of the contract. The relevant clause of the bill provided that no servant or agent (including independent contractor) of the carrier was to be liable for any

---

[88] *e.g.* Carriage by Air Act 1961, Sch.1, art.25A; Carriage of Goods by Sea Act 1971, Sch., art.4 *bis* (stevedores, being independent contractors rather than agents, would not be protected under this provision); Merchant Shipping Act 1995, s.183 and Sch.6, Pt I, art.11, and s.186(2) and (3).

[89] *London Drugs Ltd v Kuehne & Nagel International Ltd* [1992] 3 S.C.R. 299. The question whether English courts should in the present context develop a "fully fledged exception" to the doctrine of privity was left open in *The Mahkutai* [1996] A.C. 650 at 665; the creation of such an exception would involve the overruling of cases such as *Adler v Dickson* [1955] 1 Q.B. 158.

[90] *cf. Mason v Uxbridge Boat Centre* [1980] 2 Lloyd's Rep. 593 at 598.

[91] See above, pp.246–285. For example, in cases such as *Cosgrove v Horsfall* (1946) 62 T.L.R. 140, *Adler v Dickson* [1955] 1 Q.B. 158 and *Genys v Matthews* [1965] 3 All E.R. 24 the doctrine was used to allow recovery for personal injury against an employee of the party relying on the exemption clause. Its use for this purpose is no longer necessary where that party is prevented from relying on the clause by s.2 of the Unfair Contract Terms Act 1977 (above, p.249), and, in consumer contracts on standard terms, by the Unfair Terms in Consumer Contracts Regulations, 1999 (above, p.274).

[92] *Cosgrove v Horsfall* (1946) 62 T.L.R. 140; *Genys v Matthews* [1965] 3 All E.R. 24. Contrast the position in the United States: see above, n.82 and *The Hellespont Ardent* [1997] 2 Lloyd's Rep. 547 at 579, 592.

[93] *cf.* in another context, *Taddy v Sterious* [1904] 1 Ch. 354 (the agreement in that case might now be void under Competition Act 1998, s.2 if the conditions stated at p.476 above were satisfied).

[94] So named after the cruise ship in *Adler v Dickson* [1955] 1 Q.B. 155. For a fuller discussion of such clauses, see *Carver on Bills of Lading* (1st ed., 2001) §§7–047 to 7–063.

[95] [1975] A.C. 154; Reynolds, 90 L.Q.R. 301; Coote, 37 M.L.R. 453; Palmer [1974] J.B.L. 101, 220; Powles [1979] L.M.C.L.Q. 331; Davies & Palmer [1979] J.B.L. 337. And see below, p.640.

[96] See below, p.652.

act or default in the course of his employment[97]; that every limitation applicable to the carrier should be available to such persons; that for the purpose of the clause the carrier should be deemed to be acting as agent or trustee for such persons; and that they should to this extent be or be deemed to be parties to the contract. All the members of the Privy Council agreed that such third persons could be protected by an appropriately drawn clause; and a majority held that the clause in question did protect the stevedore. Lord Wilberforce said that the bill of lading "brought into existence a bargain initially unilateral but capable of becoming mutual, between the shipper and the [stevedore], made through the carrier as agent. This became a full contract when the [stevedore] performed the services by discharging the goods".[98] At this stage, a new contract arose[99] between the cargo-owner and the stevedore, separate from or collateral to the main contract of carriage, to which the stevedore was not a party.

A possible objection to this analysis is that stevedores (unlike carriers) might not be aware of the terms of bills of lading under which goods were carried, so that these could not amount to offers to them which they could accept by performing the services. On the facts of *The Eurymedon* this objection has little substance as the carrier was a subsidiary of the stevedore who probably did know of the terms of the bill of lading.[1] But the more important point is that it is by no means unknown for contracts to come into existence by a process which cannot be strictly analysed in terms of offer and acceptance.[2] The decision should therefore be evaluated, not in terms of such analysis, but by asking two questions: (1) was there any objection on grounds of policy to extending the protection of the clause to third parties such as the stevedores? and (2) did that extension give effect to the intention of the parties? It has already been suggested[3] that the first question should be answered in the negative, and this must have been the view even of the dissentients in *The Eurymedon*, for they accepted that a third party could be protected by an appropriately worded clause. The second question is harder to answer but it seems unlikely that the parties at the time of contracting made any conscious distinction between the shipper's rights against the carrier and against persons employed by the carrier in the performance of the contract of carriage; while it was no doubt the stevedore's intention to perform the work of unloading the goods only under the protective terms of the bill of lading. It is submitted that the majority's interpretation of an admittedly obscure clause did give effect to the intentions and commercial expectations of the parties; and that the decision is therefore to be welcomed. It has been both

---

[97] At common law, this part of the clause was crucial for the purpose of creating privity of contract between the cargo-owner and the third party; without it, the doctrine of privity would have prevented that party from relying on the clause: see above, p.631, n.92.

[98] At 167–168. More recently, it has been suggested that the contract would be regarded as "nowadays bilateral": *The Mahkutai* [1996] A.C. 650 at 664; but this description should not be understood as meaning that the contract granting the third party the limitation of or exemption from liability imposed executory obligations on the third party: see *Starsin* [2003] UKHL 12, [2003] 2 W.L.R. 711 at [34], [93], [152], [153] and [196], where the contract is described as "unilateral".

[99] See below, p.634 at n.24.

[1] He at least had means of knowledge since one original of the bill of lading had been delivered to him before the goods were unloaded, though only in his capacity as agent of the carrier; see [1975] A.C. 154 at 164.

[2] See *The Satanita* [1895] P. 248, affirmed sub nom. *Clarke v Dunraven* [1897] A.C. 59; above, p.47.

[3] See above, pp.630–631.

followed[4] and distinguished[5] in other jurisdictions.

Difficulty with regard to Himalaya clauses arises from a much-quoted passage in Lord Reid's speech in the *Midland Silicones* case. This states a number of requirements which must be satisfied before a third party, such as a stevedore, can at common law claim the protection of terms in the contract between shipper and carrier. Our present concern is with two of these requirements: first, the clause must make it clear that the carrier had contracted as agent of the stevedore for the purpose of securing the benefit of such terms for him; and secondly, the carrier must have had "authority from the stevedore to do so, or perhaps later ratification would suffice".[6] The first of these requirements is normally[7] satisfied simply by a declaration of agency in the Himalaya clause; but the second refers to factors extrinsic to the contract in which that clause is contained. In *The Eurymedon*, the relevant extrinsic factor was the previous connection between carrier and stevedore (as associated companies); and the reasoning of the case leaves open the possibility that, in the absence of some such previous connection, the requirement of "authority from the stevedore" would not be satisfied. In one case it was indeed held that the lack of any such connection made it impossible to regard the carrier as the stevedore's agent for the purpose of making a contract between him and the owner of the goods, so that the stevedore was not protected by virtue of the Himalaya clause.[8] But in *The New York Star*[9] the Privy Council followed *The Eurymedon* in unanimously holding that stevedores (who were regularly employed and partly owned by the carriers) were protected by virtue of a similarly worded clause. Lord Wilberforce said that stevedores would "normally and typically" be protected by such a clause and that "their Lordships would not encourage a search for fine distinctions which would diminish the general applicability, in the light of established commercial practice, of the principle".[10] In the later Privy Council case of *The Mahkutai* Lord Goff did, indeed, say that it was "inevitable that technical points of contract and agency law will continue to be invoked" and that counsel had acted "legitimately"[11] in raising such points. But he evidently did not regard the requirement of the third party's having authorised the carrier to act on his behalf as an obstacle to the enforceability of the Himalaya clause in that case, though reliance on it failed on grounds to be discussed below.[12] Similarly, in *The Pioneer Container* the actual decision was that a third party was protected by the terms of his *own* sub-bailment from the carrier, so that he did not have to rely on the Himalaya clause[13]; but it was also said that he could have

---

[4] *Ceres Stevedoring Co Ltd v Eisen und Metall AG* (1976) 72 D.L.R. (3d) 660 (where the third party's defence failed on another ground); *Miles International Corp v Federal Commerce & Navigation Co* [1978] 1 Lloyd's Rep. 285. *ITO International Terminal Operators Ltd v Miida Electronics Inc* [1986] 1 S.C.R. 752; *The Antwerpen* [1994] 1 Lloyd's Rep. 213; *cf.* the assumption evidently made in *The Zhi Jiang Kou* [1991] 1 Lloyd's Rep. 493, that an agent of the contracting party could rely on the clause.

[5] *Lummus Co Ltd v East African Harbours Corp* [1978] 1 Lloyd's Rep. 317; see also *Herrick v Leonnard and Dingley Ltd* [1975] 2 N.Z.L.R. 566 (discussed by Palmer and Rose, 39 M.L.R. 466), where a clause in different terms did not expressly refer to independent contractors.

[6] [1962] A.C. 446 at 474.

[7] For an exception, see *Quantum Corp Ltd v Plane Trucking Co* [2001] 1 All E.R. (Comm) 916 at [35], reversed on other grounds [2002] EWCA Civ 350; [2002] 2 Lloyd's Rep. 25.

[8] *The Suleymman Stalskiy* [1976] 2 Lloyd's Rep. 609; *cf. Southern Water Authority v Carey* [1985] 2 All E.R. 1077, at 1085, a building case where the sub-contractor could not for this reason take the benefit of an exemption clause in the main contract, but succeeded on another ground stated on p.587 at n.56.

[9] *The New York Star* [1981] 1 W.L.R. 138; Reynolds, 96 L.Q.R. 506; Coote, [1981] C.L.J. 13; Clarke [1981] C.L.J. 17; Rose, 44 M.L.R. 336. The reasoning of *The Eurymedon* was also approved in *The Starsin* [2003] UKHL 12, [2003] 2 W.L.R. 711, though in that case the third party was, for the reason given on p.635 below, not protected by the clause.

[10] [1981] 1 W.L.R. 138 at 144.

[11] [1996] A.C. 650 at 664.

[12] See below, pp.634–635.

[13] See below, p.640.

relied on that clause.[14] In both these cases, *The Eurymedon* and *The New York Star* were discussed with evident approval and with no direct reference to or emphasis on the special circumstances[15] of those cases; nor was there evidence of extrinsic circumstances from which previous authorisation could be inferred in *The Pioneer Container* and *The Mahkutai*. Moreover, while there are no doubt good reasons for requiring such previous authorisation where the contract arising by virtue of the Himalaya Clause[16] can impose obligations[17] on the third party,[18] it is hard to see what practice grounds there are for such a requirement where the only effect of that contract can be to *benefit* that party (by excluding his liability) and where that contract cannot, by reason of its nature as a unilateral contract,[19] impose any obligations on him. And even where the common law requirement of previous authorisation is not satisfied, the stevedore or other third party will "in the majority of cases"[20] be able to ratify the carrier's act and so by virtue of the Himalaya clause gain the protection of the exemptions from and limitations of liability available under the main contract of carriage to the carrier.

(b) SCOPE. The scope of the Himalaya Clause depends on its construction; and since typically such a clause is expressed to protect the third party only while he is engaged in the performance of the contract in which the clause is contained, he will not be protected by the clause in such terms, if he damages the goods before performance of that contract has begun[21] or after such performance has been completed.[22]

At common law, the part of the typical Himalaya Clause which purports to exclude or limit the third party's liability cannot *itself* produce the desired effect.[23] This can follow only from the separate contract[24] which arises or may arise from the agency provision of such a clause followed by the conduct of the third party and the injured party in relation to each other; the effect of this contract may be to extend to the third party the protection of, not only the Himalaya Clause itself, but also *other* terms of the contract in which that Clause is contained. Two further questions can therefore arise. The first is whether the provision which the third party seeks to invoke is covered by the wording of the Himalaya Clause. This question arose in *The Mahkutai*[25] where such a clause in a bill of lading provided that subcontracting carriers were to have the benefit of "all exceptions, limitations, provisions and liberties herein". It was held that these words did

---

[14] [1994] 2 A.C. 324 at 344.

[15] *i.e.* to the fact that stevedores and carriers were associated companies. *cf. Godina v Patrick Operations Ltd* [1984] 2 Lloyd's Rep. 333; *The Zinnia* [1984] 2 Lloyd's Rep. 211 at 217; for express authorisation by the third party of the carrier, see *Raymond Burke Motors Ltd v Mersey Docks & Harbour Co* [1986] 1 Lloyd's Rep. 155.

[16] *i.e.*, the new or separate contract referred to on pp.632 at n.99 and 634 at n.24.

[17] *e.g.* where it purports to be on the terms of an exclusive jurisdiction clause: *cf.* below at n.26. Such a clause is not normally within the scope of a Himalaya Clause: *ibid.*; but could be brought within it by express words to that effect.

[18] The "third party" to the main contract is of course an immediate party to the separate contract referred to in n.16 above.

[19] See above, p.582, at n.98.

[20] *The Mahkutai* [1996] A.C. 650 at 664, *per* Lord Goff. The phrase "in the majority of cases" is not amplified. It could refer to the requirement in the law relating to ratification that the stevedoring company must have been in *existence* when the carrier purported to act as its agent by issuing the bill of lading containing the Himalaya clause: for this requirement see below, p.724.

[21] *Raymond Burke Motors Ltd v Mersey Docks & Harbour Co* [1986] 1 Lloyd's Rep. 155; *cf. The Rigoletto* [2000] 2 Lloyd's Rep. 532 at 545, 547.

[22] This is implicit in the reasoning of *The New York Star* [1981] 1 W.L.R. 138, where the actual decision was that at the relevant time such performance had *not* been completed.

[23] See above, p.632, n.99.

[24] *The Starsin* [2003] UKHC 12, [2003] 2 W.L.R. 711, at [59] (dissenting, but not on this point), [93].

[25] [1996] A.C. 650.

not entitle the sub-contractors to rely on an exclusive jurisdiction clause in the bill of lading, since they referred only to those provisions in it which benefited *one* of the parties to it, while the exclusive jurisdiction clause was a "mutual agreement" creating "mutual obligations".[26] The second question is whether the terms of the clause, or of other provisions in the main contract to which it refers, do indeed protect the third party. The answer to this question depends on the rules relating to the construction and effectiveness of exemption clauses generally. These are discussed in Chapter 7; here it is necessary only to make the point that the third party would not be protected by a clause which, on its true construction, would not apply in the events which have happened or cover the loss which has occurred, or by a clause which was legally invalid.[27] The latter possibility is illustrated by *The Starsin*,[27a] where goods were damaged whilst being carried in a chartered ship under a bill of lading constituting a contract between charterer and shipper.[27b] The benefit of a Himalaya Clause in the bill of lading was claimed by the shipowner who was not a party to the contract of carriage and who relied on words in the clause exempting him from "any liability whatsoever to the shipper" for loss resulting from acts done by the shipowner in the course of his employment by the carrier.[27c] The Clause also provided that the shipowner was (to the extent to which it protected him) to be deemed to be a party to the bill of lading contract[27d]; and another term of that contract[27e] incorporated into it an international convention known as the Hague Rules. These rules specified certain obligations of a carrier of goods by sea, made available to him certain exemptions from and limitations of liability, and provided that any clause in the contract "lessening such liability otherwise than as provided in this convention shall be null and void."[27f] The House of Lords held[27g] that this provision of the Rules invalidated the wide words of the Himalaya Clause quoted above, so that the shipowner was not protected by these words.

The cases on Himalaya clauses assume that the third party seeking to invoke them is not in any contractual relationship with the claimant except for the collateral contract which may arise by virtue of such a clause. Where there is also an express contract between these parties on terms inconsistent with those of any such a collateral contract, then the terms of that express contract will prevail: *e.g.*, where a stevedore enters into an express contract with the cargo-owner making him liable to the cargo-owner for negligence but the bill of lading contains a Himalaya clause the effect of which would (if there were no such express contract) be to exonerate the stevedore from such liability.[29]

(c) DEFECT IN THE MAIN CONTRACT. In *The Eurymedon*[30] the Himalaya clause in the contract between shipper and carrier gave rise to a separate contract between shipper

---

[26] *ibid.* at 666; followed on this point in *Bougoyes Offshore SA v Caspian Shipping Co (No.2)* [1997] 2 Lloyd's Rep. 485 at 490.

[27] *e.g. Eisen and Metall AG v Ceres Stevedoring Co Ltd* [1977] 1 Lloyd's Rep. 665.

[27a] [2003] UKHL 12, [2003] 2 W.L.R. 711.

[27b] In this respect, the case resembles the *Elder Dempster* case [1924] A.C. 522, above, p.627.

[27c] Clause 5(1) of the bill of lading, in the numbering given by Lord Bingham in *The Starsin*, above, n.27a, as [20].

[27d] Clause 5(3), in the same numbering.

[27e] Clause 2: see *The Starsin*, above, n.27a, at [31].

[27f] Art III.8: see now the Hague Visby Rules, Art III.8, which have the force of law by virtue of Carriage of Goods by Sea Act 1971 s.1 and Sch.

[27g] Lord Steyn dissenting, Lord Hobhouse took the view that the contract between shipper and shipowner created by virtue of the Himalaya Clause was a "contract of carriage within the Rules": see at [153], [156]; but this view is rejected by Lord Millett at [203] and does not seem to be adopted by Lord Bingham or Lord Hoffmann.

[29] *The Rigoletto* [2000] 2 Lloyd's Rep. 532.

[30] *The Eurymedon* [1975] A.C. 154.

and stevedore collateral to the main contract of carriage.[31] This contract has what may be called certain parasitic qualities so that it may fail to protect the third party, at least in certain cases, where the main contract suffers from some legal defect. Thus in a South African case,[34] in which the relations of the parties were governed by English law,[35] the main contract between A and B contained a Himalaya clause by virtue of which C was *prima facie* entitled to the benefits of the exemptions from liability which the main contract conferred on A. The main contract was rescinded by B on account of A's misrepresentations and it was held that the Himalaya clause did not entitle C to the protection of the exemption clauses in the main contract since "once those . . . exemptions . . . fall away on rescission of the [main contract], nothing remains to exempt [C]".[36] This was so even though the Himalaya clause had given rise to a "separate contract" between A and C, since under the terms of that contract C took only "the benefits of the same exemptions which the carrier [A] receives, no more and no less".[37]

It is an essential part of this reasoning that the effect of misrepresentation on a contract is to "wipe it out altogether"[38] with retrospective effect. The position would be the same where the main contract was void for mistake at common law. On the other hand, the reasoning would not apply where the main contract was rescinded for A's breach, since this process brings the contract to an end only from the time of rescission and therefore does not deprive the guilty party of the protection of exemption and limitation clauses in respect of breaches occurring before such rescission[39]; consequently, it would not deprive the third party of this benefit where he was otherwise entitled to it by virtue of a Himalaya clause.[40] If the main contract were frustrated, the third party would likewise be deprived of its protection by virtue of such a clause only in respect of breaches of duty which had occurred after, and not in respect of those which had occurred before, the frustrating event: this follows from the principle that frustration discharges the contract only from the time of the frustrating event.[41] The most difficult cases would be those in which the main contract was affected by illegality. The source of the difficulty is that the effects of illegality vary widely[42]; and that the illegality of the main contract does not necessarily affect the validity of a collateral contract.[43] The guiding principle, it is submitted, should be that the illegality which affects the main contract should deprive the third party of the protection of the collateral contract which arises by virtue of the Himalaya clause only where such a result would in some way promote the policy of the rule of law, the violation of which had given rise to the illegality.[44] No doubt in applying this principle the court would have regard not only to the nature of the illegality but also to the third party's knowledge of or participation in the illegal purpose.

---

[31] See above, pp.632 at, n.99, p.634, n.24.

[34] *Bougoyes Offshore v Ultisol Transport Contractors* [1996] 2 Lloyd's Rep. 153, Note.

[35] *ibid.* at 154, 155. The circumstances underlying this case were the subject of much litigation both in South Africa and in England: see, for example, above n.26.

[36] [1996] 2 Lloyd's Rep. 153 at 165.

[37] *ibid.* For a similar restriction on the third party's right to rely on exemption clauses under the Contracts (Rights of Third Parties) Act 1999, see s.3(6) of that Act (below, p.661).

[38] *The Kanchenjunga* [1990] 1 Lloyd's Rep. 391 at 398; above, p.370.

[39] See above, p.239.

[40] Contracts (Rights of Third Parties) Act 1999, s.3(2) (below, p.660) would not apply to such a case: it deals with a different situation in which C sues A and A seeks to rely, against C, on B's repudiatory breach.

[41] See below, p.909.

[42] See above, pp.480–490.

[43] See above, p.510.

[44] *cf.* above, p.429.

3. Other drafting devices

The third party could also be protected by a form of words other than that used in *The Eurymedon*. For example, an exemption clause in a contract between A and B may contain an express promise by A to B not to sue C. Under the rules already considered, B can, even at common law,[45] enforce that promise by getting a stay of any action by A against C,[46] for example if there is a contract between B and C under which B is bound to indemnify C against liability to third parties incurred in the performance of his duties under that contract.[47] Alternatively, the contract between A and B might provide that A should be liable to pay over to B any sum that A might recover from C.[48]

4. Clauses defining duties

The preceding discussion is based on the assumptions that C is under a *prima facie* liability in tort to A and that C seeks to rely on a provision in a contract between A and B in order to exclude or restrict the liability. But it is arguable that the terms of that contract can be relevant at an earlier stage, namely in determining the extent of any duty of care owed to A by C. For example, work under a building contract between A and B may be done by a subcontractor C, who is a party to the sub-contract between himself and B, but not a party to B's main contract with A. If C does the work negligently and so causes harm to A (*e.g.* by damaging other property belonging to A[49]), then C may be liable in tort to A, and an exemption clause in the main contract between A and B will not, as such, at common law protect C. But in the *Junior Books* case, Lord Roskill suggested that a "relevant exclusion clause in the main contract" might "limit the duty of care"[50] of C and so indirectly provide him with a defence to a claim in tort by A. In *The Aliakmon*, this suggestion was doubted by Lord Brandon on the ground that the exemption clause in the example was contained "in a contract to which the plaintiff [was] a party but the defendant [was] not"[51]: in other words, because there was no privity of contract between them. *The Aliakmon* was, however, concerned with the converse of the situation discussed by Lord Roskill, namely with the case in which the exemption clause was contained in a contract to which the defendant was a party but the plaintiff was not.[52] Both situations raise issues of privity of contract but they are concerned with different aspects of that doctrine: the first with the question whether C can take the *benefit* of an exemption clause in a contract between A and B, and the second with the question whether A can be *bound* by an exemption clause in a contract between B and C. As a matter of policy, there is less objection to giving an affirmative answer to

---

[45] For the position under the Contracts (Rights of Third Parties) Act 1999, see below, p.656. C's rights at common law would not be subject to the provisions of the Act: *cf.* above, p.627, below, pp.662–663.

[46] *Snelling v John G Snelling Ltd* [1973] 1 Q.B. 87; above, p.603.

[47] See *Gore v Van der Lann* [1967] 2 Q.B. 31; above, p.591; *The Elbe Maru* [1978] 1 Lloyds's Rep. 206; contrast *The Starsin* [2003] 2 W.L.R. 711, where the House of Lords rejected the view that the words of the Himalaya Clause quoted on p.635 above at n.27g amounted only to a covenant not to sue. For the purpose of enforcement of such a covenant, it suffices that C has a claim for such an indemnity which is not "obviously bad": *Deepak Fertilisers & Petrochemicals Corp v ICI Chemicals & Polymers Ltd* [1999] 1 Lloyd's Rep. 378 at 401. Contrast *The Chevalier Roze* [1983] 2 Lloyd's Rep. 438 (where the contract between A and B had been fully performed before A's cause of action against C arose, and so did not protect C).

[48] *Quaere* whether this would be a penalty; see below, pp.999–1006. For further possible devices, see the *Midland Silicones* case [1962] A.C. 446, 473 and Hamson [1959] C.L.J. 150.

[49] In this respect the facts of the example given in the text differ from those of the *Junior Books* case [1983] 1 A.C. 520 and so do not give rise to the difficulties occasioned by that case (see above, p.613).

[50] [1983] 1 A.C. 520 at 546, applied in *Southern Water Authority v Carey* [1985] 2 All E.R. 1077, 1086.

[51] [1986] A.C. 785 at 817.

[52] See below, p.639. Lord Brandon's view (above, n.51) was accordingly questioned in *Pacific Associates Inc v Baxter* [1990] 1 Q.B. 993 at 1022.

the first question than to the second; for in the first situation A has assented to the clause while in the second no inference of such assent can be drawn merely from the presence of the clause in the contract between B and C.[53] Lord Roskill's suggestion has therefore been followed in a number of later cases in which exemption clauses in the main contract between A and B have been held to negative any duty of care which C might (but for such clauses) have owed to A.[54] In such cases, C is protected, in spite of the absence of privity of contract,[55] because the clause "destroys the duty of [C] if duty there ever was".[56] It follows that the clause may be available not only to C, but also to any other person whose hypothetical duty is in this way affected. It may thus protect C's employees as well as C himself: in one case of this kind it was said that if C owed no duty "then neither can any of their employees have done so".[57] Whether a clause affects the duty of persons other than C depends simply on its construction and not on the doctrine of privity.

Lord Roskill's statement refers only to "a *relevant* exclusion clause": that is, to one which can "limit *the duty of care*". A clause which merely imposed a financial limit on the *amount recoverable* would not be of this kind since such a clause would come into operation only on the assumption that a duty was owed and had been broken.[58] Similarly, the clause must refer to the duty of the person relying on it: thus if a contract between a building owner and a contractor contained a provision restricting the duty of subcontractors *nominated* by the owner, that provision would not protect *other* subcontractors (who had not been so nominated).[59]

2. The Burden

(1) General rule

The law starts with the principle that a person is not bound by an exemption clause in a contract to which he is not a party, unless one of the recognised exceptions to the doctrine of privity (such as agency) can be invoked against him.[60] In the *Midland Silicones* case[61] the contract between the carrier and the stevedores provided that the stevedores should have "such protection as is afforded by the terms of the bill of lading". The owners of the drum nonetheless recovered full damages from the stevedores. They were not bound by what was, in effect, a limitation clause in the contract between the

---

[53] For this reason, the suggestion, made in *Muirhead v Industrial Tank Specialties Ltd* [1986] Q.B. 507, 525, that Lord Roskill intended to refer to an exclusion clause in the *sub*-contract, may with respect be doubted. The suggestion is based on a passage in Lord Fraser's speech in the *Junior Books* case at 534, which is, however, not concerned with exclusion clauses at all but rather with the type of performance that C has agreed to render under his contract with B: see below, pp.642–643.

[54] *Southern Water Authority v Carey* [1985] 2 All E.R. 1077; *Norwich CC v Harvey* [1989] 1 W.L.R. 828; *Pacific Associates Inc v Baxter* [1990] 1 Q.B. 993; Adams and Brownsword [1990] J.B.L. 23.

[55] *Norwich CC v Harvey* [1989] 1 W.L.R. 828 at 837.

[56] *Pacific Associates Inc v Baxter* [1990] 1 Q.B. 993 at 1038.

[57] *Norwich CC v Harvey* [1989] 1 W.L.R. 828 at 834.

[58] *cf.* below, pp.642–643.

[59] *British Telecommunications plc v James Thomson & Sons (Engineering) Ltd* [1999] 2 All E.R. 241.

[60] *Delaurier v Wyllie* (1889) 17 R. (Ct. of Sess.) 167: *cf. The Kite* [1933] P. 164; *White v Warwick (John) & Co Ltd* [1953] 2 W.L.R. 1285 at 1294; *Chas Davis (Metal Brokers) Ltd v Gilyot & Scott Ltd* [1975] 2 Lloyd's Rep. 422; *The Eagle* [1977] 2 Lloyd's Rep. 70; *Twins Transport v Patrick Brocklehurst* (1983) 25 Build.L.R. 65. This rule applies even in systems of law under which a third party can take the *benefit* of a contract, as in the United States: see *The OOCL Bravery* [2000] 1 Lloyd's Rep. 394, 399. It follows that in England the rule survives the Contracts (Rights of Third Parties) Act 1999, s.1(6). For a statutory exception to the rule, see Congenital Disabilities (Civil Liability) Act 1976, s.1(6).

[61] [1962] A.C. 446, above, p.628.

stevedores and the carrier.[62] Similarly, in *The Aliakmon*[63] the buyers were not bound by exemption provisions in the contract of carriage since the only parties to that contract were the sellers and the shipowners.[64]

(2) Exceptions

The general rule stated above may be unsatisfactory in practice,[65] and is therefore subject to a number of exceptions.

(a) AGENCY AND IMPLIED CONTRACT. The first such exception is illustrated by *Pyrene Co Ltd v Scindia Navigation Co Ltd*,[66] where a fire tender which had been sold for export was to be shipped under a contract between buyer and carrier, which limited the latter's liability.[67] The seller presented the tender for loading to the carrier who, in carrying out this operation, damaged the tender while it was still at the seller's risk. It was held that the seller was bound by the limitation clause. The decision was partly based on the doubts which had been expressed in earlier cases as to the existence of the doctrine of privity.[68] It can no longer be supported on this ground; nor is the seller's tort claim against the carrier in such a case adversely affected by the Contracts (Rights of Third Parties) Act 1999, since under this Act a person will not, in general, be *bound* by terms of a contract to which he is not a party.[69] But the *Pyrene* case can still be justified either on the ground that the buyer was the seller's agent in making the contract with the carrier, at least so far as it concerned the seller[70]; or on the ground that an implied contract incorporating the limitation clause arose between seller and carrier when the tender was presented by the seller and accepted by the carrier for loading. The latter explanation is the one now generally accepted[71] though it is not entirely free from difficulty since the carrier may at this stage have intended merely to perform his contract of carriage with the buyer and so have lacked the contractual intention necessary for the creation of a new contract.[72]

---

[62] [1962] A.C. 446 at 474.

[63] [1986] A.C. 785, above, p.613.

[64] Paradoxically, it was the buyers who argued (unsuccessfully) that they *were* bound, their object being to establish that the undesirable consequence of depriving the shipowners of the benefit of those provisions (see above, p.614) would not follow if the shipowners were held liable to them in tort.

[65] *e.g.* if the buyers in *The Aliakmon*, above had been owners of the goods when they were damaged their tort claim would then have succeeded on the reasoning given at pp.613–614, above, but they might still not have been parties to the contract of carriage, so that the carriers would have been deprived of the protection of the international Convention known as the Hague Rules. Under the Conventions relating to the international carriage of goods by air, an owner of goods may have a right in tort against the carrier without depriving the latter of the protection of the Convention. Such protection may be retained by interpreting the relevant Convention so as either (i) to restrict the categories of persons entitled to sue the carrier to those specified in the Convention (*e.g.* as consignor or consignee, or as principals of the persons so specified) or (ii) to allow claims based on title to the goods (irrespective of contract) to be brought against the carrier only subject to the "scheme of liability" imposed by the Convention: see *Sidhu v British Airways plc* [1997] A.C. 430, 442–443, discussing *Gatewhite Ltd v Iberia Lineas de Espanea Sociedad* [1990] 1 Q.B. 326; *Herd v Clyde Helicopters* [1997] A.C. 437; *Western Digital Corp v British Airways plc* [2001] Q.B. 733 at 752, 755, 769. This reasoning would not affect *The Aliakmon* since the Hague Rules contain no equivalent provisions.

[66] [1954] 2 Q.B. 402.

[67] Under what is now Carriage of Goods by Sea Act 1971, Sch. art.IV. 5.

[68] At p.426; and see above, p.588.

[69] See above, p.582; for a qualification, not relevant in the present context of a third party's claim brought apart from the Act, see below, p.643.

[70] See [1954] 2 Q.B. at 423–425; *The Kite* [1933] P. 164 at 181 ("limited authority").

[71] *Scruttons Ltd v Midland Silicones Ltd* [1962] A.C. 446 at 471; *The Kapetan Markos NL (No.2)* [1987] 2 Lloyd's Rep. 321 at 331; *The Captain Gregos (No.2)* [1990] 2 Lloyd's Rep. 395 (claim by B.P.).

[72] *cf.* above, p.169.

Implied contract reasoning was also used in *The Eurymedon*,[73] to deal with the point that the action against the stevedore was brought, not by the shipper, but by the consignee, who (it was assumed) was not a party to the contract of carriage contained or evidenced in the bill of lading.[74] It was held that the consignee was nevertheless bound by the exclusion clause in that contract since an implied contract arose[75] between stevedore and consignee, as a result of the consignee's "acceptance of [the bill of lading] and request for delivery of the goods thereunder"[76]; and this implied contract incorporated the terms of the bill of lading (which protected the stevedore[77]). In the *Midland Silicones* case,[78] by contrast, there was no implied contract between the claimants and the stevedores incorporating the terms of the contract between the carrier and the stevedores. The case differs from *The Eurymedon* in that there the consignees had possession of the bill of lading and so knew, or at least had means of knowing, its terms, while in the *Midland Silicones* case there was nothing to indicate that the claimants knew anything about the contract between the carrier and the stevedores.[79] The implied contract argument may also fail on other grounds. In *The Aliakmon* the buyers had presented a bill of lading to which they were not parties, and took delivery of the goods; but no implied contract arose since they had there done these acts purely as agents of the sellers.[80]

Where an injured party is bound by the exemption clause in a contract between two others by virtue of agency or implied contract reasoning, the legal basis for his being so bound is not in doubt: it is that he is brought into a contractual relationship with the party relying on the clause. There are, however, a number of further grounds on which the injured party may be bound by an exemption clause in a contract to which he is not a party in spite of the fact that he has not come into any contractual relationship with the person relying on the clause; and it is with these grounds that the following discussion is concerned.

(b) BAILMENT ON TERMS. One such ground is that the injured party is so bound by virtue of a bailment on terms. Earlier in this Chapter, we saw that this concept could be invoked to enable a person to get the *benefit* of an exemption clause in a contract to which he was not a party.[81] Our present concern is with the use of the concept for the converse purpose of *binding* a person by such a clause in a contract between others. This possibility is illustrated by the case in which a customer sends goods to a cleaner or repairer and allows him to send the work out to a subcontractor. If the subcontract contains an exemption clause, the owner may be bound by it on the ground that he has "expressly or impliedly consented to the bailee making a sub-bailment containing those

---

[73] [1975] A.C. 154.

[74] It was assumed that the consignee had not become a party to the contract under the Bills of Lading Act 1855, s.1 since it was not clear that the requirements of the section had been satisfied. See now Carriage of Goods by Sea Act 1992, s.2, below, pp.675, 704.

[75] On the analogy of *Brandt v Liverpool etc. SN Co Ltd* [1924] 1 K.B. 575. The two cases raise different issues of consideration. In *Brandt's* case the issue was whether the owner of the goods could enforce an implied promise made *to* him, so that it was necessary to find consideration moving *from* him. In *The Eurymedon*, the issue was whether an implied promise not to sue made by the owner of the goods was supported by consideration, and this consideration would have to move *from the other parties* to that promise (or at least from the one seeking to rely on it).

[76] [1975] A.C. 154 at 168.

[77] See above, p.631.

[78] [1962] A.C. 446; above, p.628.

[79] [1962] A.C. 446 at 467, 493.

[80] [1986] A.C. 785 at 808; this fact was known to the carrier: see [1985] Q.B. 350 at 364.

[81] *Elder, Dempster & Co v Paterson Zochonis & Co* [1924] A.C. 522 at 564; above, p.627.

conditions, but not otherwise".[82] The same principle was applied in *The Pioneer Container*[83] where C had entered into a contract with B for the carriage of C's goods on terms which authorised B to sub-contract "on any terms". B did enter into a sub-contract with A (another carrier) on terms containing an exclusive jurisdiction clause and it was held that C was bound by this clause. Lord Goff said that the effect of the clause on C did "not depend for its efficacy either on the doctrine of privity of contract or on the doctrine of consideration"[84]; in other words. C was bound by it irrespective of contract.[84a] He was bound under the law of bailment, because he had consented to the making of the sub-bailment by B to A and to the terms of that sub-bailment. C's consent to those terms was thus essential[85]; though no doubt the law will here (as elsewhere) apply an objective test, so that C may be bound by terms of the sub-bailment, even though he has not actually consented to them, if he has so conducted himself as to induce A to believe that he has so consented.[86] The principle of such cases is, however, confined to situations in which there is a relationship of bailor and bailee (or sub-bailee) between the claimant and the defendant. In *The Aliakmon*, the exception did not apply as no such relationship there existed between the *buyers* and the shipowners: "The only bailment of the goods was one by the sellers to the shipowners".[87] Similarly, in the

---

[82] *Morris v C W Martin & Sons Ltd* [1966] 1 Q.B. 716 at 729; *cf. ibid.* 741; *Port Swettenham Authority v T W Wu & Co* [1979] A.C. 580; *The Kapetan Markos NL (No.2)* [1987] 2 Lloyd's Rep. 323 at 340; *Singer (UK) Ltd v Tees & Hartlepool Port Authority* [1988] 2 Lloyd's Rep. 164, 167–168; *The Captain Gregos (No. 2)* [1990] 2 Lloyd's Rep. 395 at 405; Palmer [1988] L.M.C.L.Q. 466; Phang, 8 O.J.L.S. 418. Carnegie, 3 Adelaide L.Rev 7. For a similar view, see *Fosbroke-Hobbs v Airwork Ltd* (1936) 53 T.L.R. 254 at 257 (carriage of persons), but contrast *Haseldine v C A Daw & Sons Ltd* [1941] 2 K.B. 343 at 379. *cf.* also Occupiers' Liability Act 1957, s.3; Defective Premises Act 1972, ss.11(b) and 4; *White v Blackmore* [1972] 2 Q.B. 651 at 676.

[83] [1994] 2 A.C. 324; *Lee Cooper Ltd v Jeakins & Son Ltd* [1964] 1 Lloyd's Rep. 300 (also reported [1967] 2 Q.B. 1, but not on this point); *Learoyd Bros & Co v Pope & Sons (Dock Carriers) Ltd* [1966] 2 Lloyd's Rep. 142; *Johnson Matthey & Co v Constantine Terminals Ltd* [1976] 2 Lloyd's Rep. 215; *Dresser UK Ltd v Falconbridge Management Ltd* [1992] Q.B. 502; *The Gudermes* [1993] 1 Lloyd's Rep. 311 at 328; *Spectra International plc v Hayesoak Ltd* [1997] 1 Lloyd's Rep. 153 (reversed on another ground [1998] 1 Lloyd's Rep. 162); *Sonicare International Ltd v EAFT Ltd* [1997] 2 Lloyd's Rep. 48; Coote [1977] C.L.J. 177; *The Starsin* [2003] UKHL 12, [2003] 2 W.L.R. 711, at [133–136]; *cf. The Agia Skepi* [1992] 2 Lloyd's Rep. 467 at 472; *The Termagent* (1914) 1 Com. Cas. 239, where no consent to the sub-bailment had been given. See also *The Rigoletto* [2000] 2 Lloyd's Rep. 532 at 546, though this aspect of the case seems to be concerned with the existence of the sub-bailee's *duty* to the owner rather than with any question of the availability against the owner of exemption clauses in the contract between sub-bailee and the head bailee.

[84] [1994] 2 A.C. 324 at 339.

[84a] C may be bound by reason *both* of a bailment on terms *and* of a contract between C and A made through the agency of B: see *Sandeman Coprimar SA v Transitos y Transportes Integrales SL* [2003] EWCA Civ 113 at [62], [63]. See also *East West Corp v DKBS 1912* [2003] EWCA Civ 83 at [24], [69] holding the same principle to be applicable to the case where the bailor was origianlly in a contractual relationship with the bailee and had lost his rights under the contract by transfer of the bill of lading which evidenced or contained the contract; but concluding that there were no relevant terms in that contract which protected the bailee: see *ibid.*, at [81], [85].

[85] [1994] 2 A.C. 324 at 340–342, rejecting the view that no such consent was necessary, which had been expressed by Donaldson J. in *Johnson Matthey & Co v Constantine Terminals Ltd* [1976] 2 Lloyd's Rep. 215 at 221. The need for such consent had also been stressed in *Chellaram & Sons (London) Ltd v Butler's Warehousing & Distribution Ltd* [1978] 2 Lloyd's Rep. 412, where the relevant clause in the sub-bailment was not an exemption, but a lien, clause.

[86] *cf.* Lord Goff's reference in *The Pioneer Container* [1994] 2 A.C. 324 at 342 to ostensible authority.

[87] [1986] A.C. 785 at 818; *cf. Swiss Bank Corp v Brink's-Mat Ltd* [1986] 2 Lloyd's Rep. 79 at 98; *The Captain Gregos (No.2)* [1990] 2 Lloyd's Rep. 395 (claim by PEAG), but the same case shows that a bailment incorporating the terms of the contract can arise by subsequent attornment of the carrier to the buyer (claim by B.P.). On the question whether a bailment relationship can arise between a carrier and a buyer of goods who is not an original party to the contract of carriage, see also *The Kapetan Markos NL (No.2)* [1987] 2 Lloyd's Rep. 321, where it was said at 332 that the existence of such a relationship was "not seriously disputed"; and *Sonicare International Ltd v EAFT* [1997] 2 Lloyd's Rep. 48 at 53.

Midland Silicones case the present exception did not apply since, for the reasons given earlier in this Chapter,[88] stevedores were not bailees of the drum.[89]

Where the present exception does apply, the head bailor, C, is bound by an exemption clause in the sub-bailment between the head bailee, B, and the sub-bailee, A, in spite of the fact that there is no contract between A and C. Some legal basis other than contract must therefore be found to explain this result. One view is that C is bound simply because he consented to the inclusion of the term in the contract between B and A.[90] But if this were the reason for the exception, then it would not be restricted, as on the authorities it is,[91] to cases of bailment. The reason for the restriction appears to be that (in cases of the present kind) C has consented, not only to the terms of the contract between B and A, but also to the creation of the very relationship of bailor and sub-bailee between C and A which is the sole source of the duty alleged to be owed by A to C and to have been broken.[92] It follows that the exception does not apply where C does not need to rely on the bailment to establish that A owed him a duty of care. This would be the position, not only where A was never a bailee of C's goods at all (as in the *Midland Silicones* case), but also where A was such a bailee and C's loss resulted, not from A's breach of his custodial duty as bailee, but from A's conduct causing damage to C's goods in breach of a duty which had arisen quite apart from the bailment, "simply by virtue of A's proximity to the goods".[93]

(c) CLAUSES DEFINING DUTIES. A distinction must here (as elsewhere[94]) be drawn between exemption clauses and clauses which define a party's duty. Clauses of the latter kind can adversely affect a claimant even though they are contained in a contract to which he is not a party. Breach of that contract may amount also to breach of a duty of care owed to a third party, giving that third party a remedy in tort[95] and the terms of the contract can be relevant to the scope of that duty of care. For example, where work in

---

[88] See above, pp.628–630.

[89] [1962] A.C. 446 at 470.

[90] This appears to have been the view of Denning L.J. in *Morris v CW Martin Ltd* [1966] 1 Q.B. 716 at 729 and in his dissenting speech in the *Midland Silicones* case [1962] A.C. 446 at 491.

[91] See the *Midland Silicones* case, above at nn.88 and 89 and the authorities cited in n.82 above and *The Mahkutai* [1996] A.C. 650 and n.92 below.

[92] See *The Pioneer Container* [1994] 2 A.C. 324 at 336; *The Starsin* [2003] UKHL 12, [2003] 2 W.L.R. 711 at [136]. The view that the exception may extend beyond cases of bailment derives some support from an *obiter dictum* in *Henderson v Merrett Syndicates Ltd* [1995] A.C. 145 at 196. This suggests that, where an owner enters into a building contract with a contractor who engages a sub-contractor, then the latter "may be protected from liability [to the owner] by a contractual exemption clause [apparently in the sub-contract] authorised by the building owner". The word "authorised" may indicate that the contractor acted as agent for the owner to create privity of contract between the owner and the sub-contractor; but even in the absence of such agency such an extension of the bailment exception could be supported on the grounds that the law now recognises that relationships other than bailment can be the source of a duty irrespective of contract; and that the rationale of the rule that a person cannot be bound by a contract to which he is not a party loses at least some of its force where he has consented to be so bound. The *Midland Silicones* case [1962] A.C. 446 could be distinguished from Lord Goff's example on the ground that the cargo-owner there had *not* consented to the terms of the contract between the carriers and the stevedores (though he must be taken to have consented to the carrier's employment of sub-contractors for the purpose of discharging the cargo and probably to have realised that such a sub-contract would contain exclusions and limitations of liability). The view that the exception is not confined to cases of bailment is also supported by Toulson J. in *Lukoil-Kalingradmorneft plc v Tata Ltd* [1999] 1 Lloyd's Rep. 365 at 375, affirmed without reference to this point [1999] 2 Lloyd's Rep. 129 (the actual issue was whether a lien was enforceable against a third party and the conclusion that it was so enforceable was based on agency reasoning).

[93] *The Kapetan Markos NL (No.2)* [1987] 2 Lloyd's Rep. 321 at 340; *cf. Johnson Matthey & Co v Constantine Terminals Ltd* [1976] 2 Lloyd's Rep. 215 at 222; this point is not affected by the disapproval of the case on another point, referred to in n.85 above.

[94] See above, pp.238, 637.

[95] See above, pp.607–611.

pursuance of a building contract between A and B is done by C under a roofing subcontract between B and C, the terms of the latter contract would clearly determine the type of work to be done by C.[96] If the sub-contract merely required C to tile the roof he would not be liable in tort to A on the ground that the main contract required the roof to be tiled and felted, or even on the ground that tiling and felting was standard practice for the type of building in question. It would not, in such a case, be "unfair"[97] to A to deprive him of a right in tort against C by a term in a contract over which A had no control; for A would not (even if B were authorised to sub-contract the work) be precluded from recovering damages for breach of contract from B if the work done by C was not in conformity with the contract between A and B.[98] Different reasoning would apply to a clause in the subcontract which merely limited C's liability (*e.g.*, to the cost of replacing defective tiles). Such a clause would not be relevant to the definition of C's duty to A in tort since it would not define what C had to do, but merely specify the legal consequences of failing to do it.[99] Hence such a clause would as a general rule not bind A contractually, since he was not a party to the contract in which it was contained.

(d) DERIVATIVE RIGHTS. Two points call for discussion.

(i) *Contracts (Rights of Third Parties) Act 1999.* Under this Act, a third party C is, in circumstances to be discussed later in this Chapter,[1] entitled to enforce a term in a contract between two others; but his right to do so is, in general, subject to defences which would have been available to the promisor A if the proceedings to enforce the term had been brought by the promisee B.[2] If, for example, a contract between A and B contained (1) a promise by A to B to render some service to C and (2) a term excluding or limiting A's liability for specified breaches, then, in an action by C under the 1999 Act to enforce the first of these terms, A would be entitled to rely on the second. In such a case, C's right, being derived from B's right, is subject to the restrictions which govern the latter right.[3] This statutory rule, however, applies only where C's claim against A is one to enforce a term of the contract between A and B under the 1999 Act. It does not apply where C's claim is not derived from that contract but arises independently of it and is made apart from the Act. This was the position in most of the cases with which the preceding discussion has been concerned. In them, the claim made by C against A was typically one in tort, and it was argued that C's right to sue A in tort was excluded or limited by the terms of a contract between A and B. That contract was not, in such cases, the basis of C's claim against A, but (at most) part of the history or chain of events giving rise to the circumstances in which A owed (or was alleged to owe) a duty of care to C. The 1999 Act expressly states that such common law claims are not to be affected by its provisions.[4]

(ii) *Transferred loss.* A more controversial way in which a person might, at common law, be adversely affected by an exemption clause in a contract to which he is not a party

---

[96] *Junior Books* case [1983] 1 A.C. 520 at 534; *cf. Simaan General Contracting Co v Pilkington Glass Ltd (No.2)* [1988] Q.B. 758 at 782–783.

[97] *ibid.* discussing a sale of goods example.

[98] See below, p.758.

[99] See *The Aliakmon* where the contract incorporated the Hague Rules which contained an intricate set of provisions some of which defined duties while others provided immunities and limitations; taken together, these could not be "synthesised into a standard of care": [1985] Q.B. 350 at 368, approved [1986] A.C. 785 at 818; *cf. Twins Transport Ltd v Patrick Brocklehurst* (1983) 25 Build.L.R. 65.

[1] See below, pp.651 *et seq.*

[2] 1996 Act, s.3(2); below, p.660.

[3] *cf.* Law Com. No.242, §10.24.

[4] 1999 Act, s.7(1); below, p.662.

has been said to arise under the so-called "principle of transferred loss".[5] The principle was, so far as English law is concerned, first stated by Robert Goff L.J. (as he then was) in *The Aliakmon*. It is said to apply where A, in breach of a duty of care in tort, causes physical damage to B's property but can reasonably foresee that the loss will fall on C, *e.g.* because B has sold the property to C and the risk under that contract has passed to C. The effect of the doctrine is then said to be that "C will be entitled, *subject to the terms of any contract restricting A's liability to B*, to bring an action in tort against A in respect of such loss or damage to the extent to which it falls upon him".[6] In *The Aliakmon* itself [7] the effect of the principle, on the assumption that the damage was due to the negligence of A,[8] would, in Robert Goff L.J.'s view, have been that C would have acquired a tort claim against A, and that this claim would have been subject to any terms in the bill of lading contract between A and B which restricted or excluded A's liability to B under that contract. But when the case reached the House of Lords, Lord Brandon[9] described the principle as "not only unsupported by authority, but . . . on the contrary inconsistent with it"[10] and declared himself unwilling to introduce it into English law. A more favourable view of the principle of transferred loss was, however, taken by Lord Goff in *White v Jones*,[11] the "disappointed beneficiary" case discussed earlier in this Chapter.[12] The actual decision in that case could not, indeed, be based on the principle since the solicitor's breach of duty had not caused any loss to his client[13]; but the analogy between cases covered by the principle and the facts of *White v Jones* was said to be "very close".[14] One point of resemblance between them is that, in Lord Goff's view, the solicitor's tort liability to an intended beneficiary would be "subject to any term of the contract between the solicitor and the testator which may exclude or restrict the solicitor's liability to the testator . . . ".[15] The fact that there is no support in the speeches of other members of the majority in *White v Jones* for this restriction on the beneficiary's tort claim[16] may be explicable on the ground that the restriction would be based on terms of a contract to which the beneficiary was not a party, to which he had not consented and which he had not authorised; for the principle of transferred loss, as formulated above,[17] does not contain any requirement that C should have consented to or authorised the exemption or limitation clauses in the contract between A and B. This position may be contrasted with the requirement of such consent which has been stated in a number of other contexts in which a person is or may be bound at common law by an exemption clause in a contract to which he is not a party: for example, in the sub-

---

[5] *The Aliakmon* [1986] A.C. 785 at 820; *White v Jones* [1995] 2 A.C. 207 at 264.

[6] [1985] Q.B. 350 at 399 (italics supplied).

[7] See above, p.613.

[8] Robert Goff L.J.'s conclusion was that A (the shipowner) was not liable since the person responsible for the damage was not A but the time charterer. Lord Donaldson M.R. and Oliver L.J. also held that A was not liable, but on the different ground that A owed no duty of care to C; this was also the view of the House of Lords: see above, pp.613–614.

[9] With whom all the other members of the House agreed.

[10] [1986] A.C. 785 at 820; see further p.614, above.

[11] [1995] 2 A.C. 207 at 264–265. In *Alfred McAlpine Construction Ltd v Panatown Ltd* [2001] 1 A.C. 518 at 529, the principle is referred to with apparent approval and, with some misgivings, by Lord Goff (dissenting) at p.557, citing Unberath, 115 L.Q.R. 535.

[12] See above, p.618.

[13] [1995] 2 A.C. 207 at 265.

[14] *ibid.*

[15] *ibid.* at 268; *cf. Trusted v Clifford Chance* (1999) [2000] W.T.L.R. 1219.

[16] There is no reference to the point in the speech of Lord Browne-Wilkinson, while Lord Nolan at 294 left the point open.

[17] At n.6.

bailment cases discussed above.[18] If the principle of transferred loss were to be accepted in English law, and if rights of a third party arising under it could be excluded or restricted by the terms of a contract between others, further judicial consideration would have to be given to the question whether there should, for the purpose of binding the third party by such terms, be a requirement of his authorisation of or consent to them. One possible view is that the bailment and other cases, in which such a requirement seems now to be firmly established, should be followed by analogy in cases in which the third party's right (if any) arose under the principle of transferred loss. The alternative view is that in those other cases the third party has an independent tort claim, of which he should not be deprived by terms of a contract over which he had no control, while a third party who relied on the principle of transferred loss would assert what is, in effect, a derivative claim which, in its nature, should not be more extensive than the claim of the person from whom it is derived.

SECTION 5. EXCEPTIONS

The doctrine of privity would, if inflexibly applied, give rise to considerable injustice and inconvenience. Many exceptions to it have therefore been developed by the courts and the legislature. The most important of these is the "general and wide ranging"[19] one which has been created by the Contracts (Rights of Third Parties) Act 1999. This Act preserves any right or remedy which the third party may have apart from its provisions.[20] The exceptions which were established before the Act came into force therefore still call for discussion, particularly because situations may arise in which it will be to the third parties' advantage to rely on one of these exceptions, rather than on the new one which has been created by the Act.[21]

1. Judge-made Exceptions

(1) Covenants concerning land

Covenants in a lease can benefit or bind persons, other than the original parties to the lease, who later acquire an interest in the property or the reversion; a person may be able to enforce a covenant affecting land made by his predecessor in title, and one who acquires land with notice that it is burdened by a restrictive covenant may be bound by it although he was not a party to the covenant. Detailed discussion of these topics will be found in works on the land law.[22]

(2) Agency

Agency is the relationship which arises when one person (the principal) authorises another (the agent) to act on his behalf and the agent agrees to do so. One legal consequence of this relationship is that the principal acquires rights and incurs liabilities under contracts made by the agent on his behalf with third parties. It is sometimes said that this is only an apparent exception to the doctrine of privity, since in such cases the

---

[18] See especially *The Pioneer Container* [1994] 2 A.C. 324; *cf.* also Lord Goff's dictum in *Henderson v Merrett Syndicates Ltd* [1995] 2 A.C. 145 at 196, discussed above, p.642 n.92.

[19] Law Com No 242, §5.16.

[20] s.7(1); this can apply not only to existing, but also to future, exceptions.

[21] See above, p.581; below, pp.653, 662–664.

[22] *e.g.* Megarry and Wade, *The Law of Real Property* (6th ed.), Chaps 15 and 16.

agent is only the instrument of the principal, who is the real contracting party.[23] This may be true where the agent acts within his actual authority. But it is only doubtfully true where the principal is liable under the doctrine of apparent authority although the agent's act is unauthorised, or where the principal ratifies.[24] And the principles of agency constitute a clear exception to the doctrine of privity where the agent acts without actual but within his "usual" authority,[25] where the principal is undisclosed,[26] and in certain cases of agency of necessity.[27] These matters are discussed in Chapter 17.

(3) Assignment

Assignment is a process whereby a contractual right is transferred to someone other than the original creditor without the consent of the original debtor. It is a clear exception to the doctrine of privity and is discussed in Chapter 16.

(4) Trusts of promises[28]

Equity developed a more general exception to the doctrine of privity by use of the concept of trust. A trust is an equitable obligation to hold property on behalf of another. It may be express or implied; and a person may be trustee not only of a physical thing or of a sum of money,[29] but also of a *chose in action*,[30] such as a debt owed to him. In Equity, a person could, moreover, be trustee of a promise to pay to money, not to himself, but to a third party; and where such a trust was established, the third party could enforce the promise against the promisor.[31] This device was applied in a number of eighteenth- and nineteenth-century cases[32] and was even recognised by the common law courts, who sometimes allowed the promisee to recover more than he had lost on the ground that he was bound to hold the surplus for a third party.[33] It was approved by the House of Lords in *Walford's* case,[34] where a broker (C) negotiated a charterparty by which the shipowner (A) promised the charterer (B) to pay the broker a commission. It was held that B was trustee of this promise for C, who could thus enforce it against A.[35] Many problems arise in determining the scope and effects of this trust device.

---

[23] *cf.* Pollock, *Principles of Contract* (13th ed.), p.163.

[24] See below, pp.712–716, 722–726.

[25] *Watteau v Fenwick* [1893] 1 Q.B. 346; below, pp.716–718.

[26] See below, pp.727–730.

[27] See below, pp.718–722.

[28] Corbin, 46 L.Q.R. 12; *Contracts*, Chap.46; Jaconelli [1998] Conv. 88.

[29] If A lends a sum of money to B and stipulates that the money is to be used only for paying a debt which B owes C, then B may hold the money on trust for C: see *Barclays Bank Ltd v Quistclose Investments Ltd* [1970] A.C. 567 (where the trust in favour of C failed and it was held that there was a resulting trust for A). In this case, the subject-matter of the trust was *the money* and not a *promise*. A made no promise to B to pay C; nor did B promise A to pay C: B promised only not to use the money for any other purpose.

[30] See below, p.672.

[31] *Tomlinson v Gill* (1756) Amb. 330. For the effectiveness of directions (not of a contractual nature) to executors in favour of a third party, see *Crowden v Aldridge* [1993] 1 W.L.R. 433.

[32] *e.g.* above, n.31; *Gregory v Williams* (1817) 3 Mer. 582; *Lloyd's v Harper* (1880) 16 Ch.D. 290.

[33] *e.g. Lamb v Vice* (1840) 6 M. & W. 467; *Robertson v Wait* (1853) 8 Ex. 299; *Prudential Staff Union v Hall* [1947] K.B. 685.

[34] *Les Affréteurs Réunis, SA v Leopold Walford (London) Ltd* [1919] A.C. 801; *The Panaghia P* [1983] 2 Lloyd's Rep. 653 at 655; *Atlas Shipping Agency (UK) Ltd v Suisse Atlantique Société d' Armement SA* [1995] 2 Lloyd's Rep. 188. Contrast *The Manifest Lipkowy* [1989] 2 Lloyd's Rep. 138, where an agreement for the sale of a ship provided for deduction of the broker's commission from the price, but seems to have contained no *promise* by the seller to pay the broker.

[35] Lord Finlay seems to have regarded the broker as a party to the contract.

(a) INTENTION TO CREATE A TRUST. A promisee will not be regarded as trustee for a third party unless he has the intention to create a trust.[36]

Such an intention can be made clear by using the word "trust" or "trustee"[37] though even where this is done the further question[38] may arise: in whose favour has the trust been created? In *Gandy v Gandy*[39] a husband entered into a separation agreement by which he promised trustees to pay them an annuity for the benefit of his wife, and to pay them money for the maintenance and education of his daughters. It was held that this agreement created no trust in favour of the daughters, since its sole object was to regulate the relations between husband and wife. Thus the wife could, but the daughters could not, enforce the agreement.[40]

A trust may be created without using any particular form of words, and where the word "trust" or "trustee" is not used, the question of intention to create a trust gives rise to great difficulty. Two cases may be contrasted. In *Re Flavell*[41] a partner retired and the continuing partners promised him that they would, after his death, pay an annuity to his widow. It was held that there was a trust in favour of the widow. But in *Re Schebsman*[42] a company promised one of its employees on his retirement that it would, after his death, pay annuities to his widow for a specified period, or (if she should die within that period) to his daughter. It was held that there was no trust in favour of the widow or daughter.[43]

Similarly, a life insurance policy expressed to be for the benefit of a third party has in some cases been held to create a trust in his favour,[44] but in others to confer no rights on him.[45] And in some cases concerning other types of insurance[46] the courts have held that a third party could take advantage of the policy under the trust device[47] while in others they have held that the third party had no rights because of the doctrine of

---

[36] *Swain v Law Society* [1983] 1 A.C. 598 at 620; Feltham, 98 L.Q.R. 17.

[37] *Fletcher v Fletcher* (1844) 4 Hare 67; *Bowskill v Dawson* [1955] 1 Q.B. 13.

[38] For the purpose of the present discussion, it is assumed that formal requirements, such as that imposed by Law of Property Act 1925, s.53(1)(b), have been satisfied. As to the effect on the rights of third parties of failure to satisfy such requirements, see Feltham [1987] Conv. 246.

[39] (1884) 30 Ch.D. 57.

[40] Fry L.J. held that the daughters had no claim because the trustees had a discretion as to their upbringing. But when the wife was joined to the action her claim succeeded even though enforcement by her could also be said to interfere with the trustees' discretion.

[41] (1883) 25 Ch.D. 89; see further, *cf. Page v Cox* (1852) 10 Hare 163; *Re Gordon* [1940] Ch. 851; *Drimmie v Davies* [1899] 1 I.R. 176.

[42] [1944] Ch. 83; see further, below, p.649, n.62; *cf. Re Stapleton-Bretherton* [1941] Ch. 482. In *Re Miller's Agreement* [1947] Ch. 615 and *Beswick v Beswick* [1968] A.C. 58 it was conceded that there was no trust.

[43] Paradoxically, the argument that there was a trust was advanced, not on behalf of the third parties, but on behalf of the promisee's trustee in bankruptcy. The point of the argument was to have the trust set aside under Bankruptcy Act 1914, s.42 (now superseded by Insolvency Act 1986, s.339): see [1944] Ch. 83 at 86. On p.104 the argument is attributed to "Mr. Denning," who appeared for the third parties. But this must be a mistake; the corresponding passage in [1943] 2 All E.R. 768 at 779 correctly attributes it to "counsel for the appellant," *i.e.* for the trustee in bankruptcy. As the company was willing to pay, the outcome of holding that there was *no* trust was that the third parties obtained the intended benefit. In *Re Flavell*, above, the same result followed from the decision that there *was* a trust.

[44] *Re Richardson* (1882) 47 L.T. 514; *Royal Exchange Assurance v Hope* [1928] Ch. 179; *Re Webb* [1941] Ch. 225; *Re Foster's Policy* [1966] 1 W.L.R. 222.

[45] *Re Burgess' Policy* (1915) 113 L.T. 443; *Re Clay's Policy of Assurance* [1937] 2 All E.R. 548; *Re Foster* [1938] 3 All E.R. 357; *Re Sinclair's Life Policy* [1938] Ch. 799; *Re Engelbach's Estate* [1924] 2 Ch. 348. For criticism of the last two cases in *Beswick v Beswick* [1968] A.C. 58 (but on another ground), see above, p.604, n.50.

[46] For statutory exceptions to the doctrine of privity in cases of insurance, see below, pp.666–669.

[47] *Williams v Baltic Insurance Co* [1924] 2 K.B. 282; *cf. Waters v Monarch Assurance Co* (1856) 5 E. & B. 870 at 881. See also Deane J. in *Trident General Ins Co Ltd v McNiece Bros Pty Ltd* (1988) 165 C.L.R. 107 (above, p.589).

privity.[48] There is no point in trying to reconcile all these cases. They represent different stages of development and show that the courts became, at one stage, reluctant to apply the trust device because, once a trust was held to have been created, the parties to the contract lost their right to rescind or vary that contract by mutual consent.[49] In this state of the authorities, the most that can be done is to try to extract from them a number of principles which will at any rate serve as guides to the solution of future problems.

(i) *There must be an intention to benefit the third party.* It follows from this requirement that, if the promisee intends the promise to be for his own benefit, there will be no trust in favour of the third party.[50] The same result may follow if it is as consistent with the facts that the promisee took the promise for his own benefit as for that of a third party.[51] Conversely, the fact that the promisee had *not* intended to take the promise for his own benefit can be relied on to support the argument that there was a trust in favour of the third party.[52]

(ii) *The intention to benefit the third party must be irrevocable.* It is now[53] settled that a contract will not normally[54] give rise to a trust in favour of a third party if, under the terms of the contract, the promisee is entitled to deprive the third party of the intended benefit by diverting it to himself. Thus in *Re Sinclair's Life Policy*[55] a policy of life insurance, taken out by the assured for the benefit of his godson, contained an option enabling the assured to surrender the policy for his own benefit.[56] This fact negatived the intention to create a trust. On the other hand, the existence of such a power to divert the benefit was held not to negative the intention to create the trust where the power was expressed to be exercisable only for a limited period and was not exercised within that period.[57] Nor will the existence of a trust necessarily be negatived where the contract names a group of beneficiaries but reserves to the promisee the power to alter the nature or destination of the benefit as between those beneficiaries.[58] And where a contract *by statute* creates a trust[59] a general provision in the contract entitling the promisee to divert the benefit to whom he pleases will not defeat the trust: on the contrary such power can be exercised only for the benefit of objects of the trust.[60] The court may conclude that there was no intention irrevocably to benefit the third party even though the contract contains no express provision entitling the promisee to divert the benefit away from the third party. It may do so on the ground that the contract would, if it were held to give rise to a trust, unduly limited the freedom of action of the parties or of one of them, *e.g.*

---

[48] *Vandepitte v Preferred Accident Insurance Corp* [1933] A.C. 70; *Green v Russell* [1959] 2 Q.B. 226, cited with approval in *McCamley v Cammell Laird Shipbuilders* [1990] 1 W.L.R. 963 at 969.

[49] See above, p.588; below, p.648.

[50] See *West v Houghton* (1879) 4 C.P.D. 197; criticised in *Re Flavell* (1883) 25 Ch.D. 89 at 98 and in *Lloyd's v Harper* (1880) 16 Ch.D. 290 at 311.

[51] *Vandepitte v Preferred Accident Ins Corp* [1993] A.C. 70, where one relevant factor for denying that a motor insurance policy created a trust in favour of a person authorised to drive the insured's car was that the insured was himself liable for the torts of that person. Contrast *Williams v Baltic Ins Co* [1920] 2 K.B. 283; for the statutory position relating to such policies, see below, p.667.

[52] *Lyus v Prowsa Developments Ltd* [1982] 1 W.L.R. 1044.

[53] For the earlier view that a trust may arise although the contracting parties can divert the benefit away from the third party, see *Hill v Gomme* (1839) 5 My. & Cr. 250; *Page v Cox* (1852) 10 Hare 163.

[54] For exceptions, see below, at nn.57 to 60.

[55] [1938] Ch. 799; criticised on another ground in *Beswick v Beswick* [1968] A.C. 58 at 96; above, p.604, n.50.

[56] A provision of this kind would not fall within Contracts (Rights of Third Parties) Act 1999, s.2 since this applies only to rescission or variation by *agreement*: see below, p.658.

[57] *Re Foster's Policy* [1966] 1 W.L.R. 432.

[58] *Re Webb* [1941] Ch. 225; *Re Flavell* (1883) 25 Ch. D. 89.

[59] See below, p.666.

[60] *Re a Policy of the Equitable Life Assurance of the United States and Mitchell* (1911) 27 T.L.R. 213; *Re Fleetwood's Policy* [1926] Ch. 48.

by restricting the promisee's freedom of movement[61] or by depriving the parties to the contract of their rights to vary it by mutual consent.[62]

(iii) *The intention to benefit is not, without more, sufficient.* An intention to create a trust must be distinguished from an intention to make a gift.[63] There are many cases in which the courts have refused to apply the trust device although the promisee clearly and without qualification intended to benefit the third party.[64] It seems that an intention to create a trust will readily be found where the contract for the benefit of the third party is made in performance of a previous contract between promisee and third party, *e.g.* where an employer promises to insure his employee against accident and then does so.[65] An intention to create a trust should, on principle, involve an intention on the part of the promisee to assume fiduciary responsibilities towards the third party.[66] But there is no clear definition of "fiduciary" for this purpose; and the courts did not at one time insist very strictly on proof of the intention to create a trust. The fact that they later came to do so is largely responsible for the present, more restricted, scope of the trust device.

The intention to create a trust may, finally, be negatived on the ground that a trust is not necessary to give rights to the third party because he is entitled to enforce the contract, even in the absence of a trust, under a statutory exception to the doctrine of privity.[67]

(b) EFFECTS OF THE TRUST. The effects of a trust in favour of a third party are as follows:

(i) *Third party can sue.* The third party is entitled to sue the promisor for the money or property which the promisor had promised to pay or to transfer to him.[68] He must join the promisee as a party to the action[69] since if this were not done the promisor might

---

[61] *e.g. Re Burgess' Policy* (1915) 113 L.T. 43 (policy to become void if insured went "beyond the boundaries of Europe" without previously notifying insurers).

[62] *e.g. Re Schebsman* [1944] 83 at 104 (parties "intended to keep alive their common law right consensually to vary the terms of the obligation"). The mere existence of such a right does not negative the statutory right of enforcement which a third party has under the Contracts (Rights of Third Parties) Act 1999: this is clear from s.2 of that Act, below pp.657–659.

[63] See *Richards v Delbridge* (1874) L.R. 18 Eq. 11.

[64] *Re Engelbach's Estate* [1924] 2 Ch. 348 (overruled on another point in *Beswick v Beswick* [1968] A.C. 58); *Re Clay's Policy of Assurance* [1937] 2 All E.R. 548; *Re Foster* [1938] 3 All E.R. 357; *Re Stapleton-Bretherton* [1941] Ch. 482; *Green v Russell* [1959] 1 Q.B. 28; *Re Cook's Settlement Trusts* [1965] Ch. 902; *cf. Cleaver v Mutual Reserve Fund Life Association* [1892] 1 Q.B. 147 at 152. Under the Contracts (Rights of Third Parties) Act 1999, s.1(1)(b) and (2) (below, pp.653–654) it will suffice for the term to purport to confer a benefit on the third party, so long as it is not shown that the contracting parties did not intend the term to be enforceable by the third party. For the reasons given at pp.581 above and 653, 662–664 below, however, it may be in the third party's interest to establish an intention to create a trust, so that he can rely on the trust exception rather than on the statutory right.

[65] See *Re Independent Air Travel Ltd, The Times*, May 20, 1961, where counsel, with the approval of the court, conceded this point.

[66] See *Harmer v Armstrong* [1934] Ch. 65, where the fact that the promisee was the third party's agent, and so under a fiduciary duty (below, p.745), helped to establish the necessary intention.

[67] *Swain v Law Society* [1983] 1 A.C. 598, esp. at 621.

[68] But where a trustee engages a professional adviser for the purpose of administering the trust, a claim for negligence against that adviser cannot be brought by the beneficiary since such a claim is not part of the trust property (though any damages recovered by the trustee would be): *Bradstock Trustee Services Ltd v Nabarro Nathanson* [1995] 1 W.L.R. 1405.

[69] *cf. Performing Right Society Ltd v London Theatre of Varieties* [1924] A.C. 1; *The Panaghia P* [1983] 2 Lloyd's Rep. 653 at 655; *Atlas Shipping Agency (UK) Ltd v Suisse Atlantique Société d' Armement* [1995] 2 Lloyd's Rep. 188 at 193; and below, pp.674–675.

be sued a second time by the promisee. As this rule as to joinder of parties exists for the benefit of the promisor, it can be waived by him.[70]

(ii) *Third party entitled to the benefit.* The third party is (as a general rule[71]) beneficially entitled to any money paid or payable under the contract; the promisee has no right to such money.[72] After *Beswick v Beswick*[73] the third party can generally keep money paid to him even if there is no trust.

(iii) *Failure of the trust.* There are exceptional cases in which the promisee may be entitled to the money even though there was a trust. In *Cleaver v Mutual Reserve Fund Life Association*[74] a husband insured his life for the benefit of his wife by a policy which, by statute, created a trust in her favour.[75] The wife was convicted of murdering the husband and was therefore disqualified from enforcing the trust. It was held that the executors of the husband were entitled to the policy moneys. It can be argued that the promisor should not have been held liable to pay the promisee when its promise was one to pay the third party.[76] But it seems that the destination of the payments was a matter of indifference to the insurance company and that there was nothing to show that the company would (even if there had been no conviction) have been in any way prejudiced by paying the husband's executors rather than the wife.[77] The actual decision may also turn on the interpretation of the statute creating the trust.[78]

(c) KINDS OF PROMISES WHICH CAN BE HELD ON TRUST. The trust device has so far been applied only to promises to pay money or to transfer property.[79] It is sometimes suggested that it might be applied to other kinds of promises, *e.g.* that an employer might hold the benefit of an exemption clause on trust for his employee.[80] But the present judicial tendency is to restrict the scope of the trust device; and the suggestion has therefore been rejected on the ground that "the conception of a trust attaching to a benefit under an exclusion clause extends far beyond conventional limits".[81] Other techniques for making the benefit of such clauses available to third parties have been discussed earlier in this Chapter.[82]

(d) RELATION BETWEEN TRUST DEVICE AND PRIVITY. The trust device has here been treated as an exception to the doctrine of privity, of limited if uncertain scope. It has, however, been argued that where a third party was enabled by this device to enforce a contract made for his benefit there was, before the Judicature Act 1873, a conflict between the rules of equity and those of common law; that the rules of equity now prevail[83]; and that therefore the third party generally has a right of action.[84] But this

---

[70] As in *Walford's* case [1919] A.C. 801; *cf. William Brandt's Sons & Co v Dunlop Rubber Co* [1905] A.C. 454.

[71] *i.e.* subject to the exception stated at n.74, below.

[72] *Re Flavell* (1883) 25 Ch.D. 89; *Re Gordon* [1940] Ch. 851; *cf. Paul v Constance* [1977] 1 W.L.R. 52.

[73] [1968] A.C. 58; see above, p.604.

[74] [1892] 1 Q.B. 147.

[75] Married Women's Property Act 1882, s.11; below, p.666.

[76] Ames, *Lectures*, 320; *Coulls v Bagot's Executor & Trustee Co Ltd* [1967] A.L.R. 385 at 410–411, *per* Windeyer J. (dissenting).

[77] *cf.* above, p.591.

[78] See [1892] 1 Q.B. 147 at 157.

[79] For a possible extension, see *Swain v Law Society* [1982] 1 A.C. 598, where a promise to provide indemnity insurance was evidently regarded as a possible subject-matter of a trust; though for the reason given at p.649, above, there was no intention to create a trust.

[80] See the clause in *The Eurymedon* [1975] A.C. 154; above, p.632.

[81] *Southern Water Authority v Carey* [1985] 2 All E.R. 1077 at 1083.

[82] See above, pp.631–638.

[83] Judicature Act 1873, s.25(11); now Supreme Court Act 1981, s.49(1).

[84] *Drimmie v Davies* [1899] 1 I.R. 176, 182 (the actual decision was that specific performance could be obtained by the executors of the promisee); Corbin, 46 L.Q.R. 12, 36; *cf.* Langbein, 105 Yale L.J. 625 at 646–647.

view has not been accepted.[85] Even in equity the third party did not succeed merely because the contract was expressed to have been made for his benefit: he had to show, in addition, that a trust had been created in his favour.[86] And the argument that third parties were entitled to enforce contracts made for their benefit has been rejected in many cases after the Judicature Act 1873. Some of these were admittedly argued entirely on common law principles,[87] but in others the equitable argument was considered and rejected.[88]

(5) Covenants in Marriage Settlements

A covenant to settle after-acquired property contained in a marriage settlement can be enforced by all persons "within the marriage consideration", *i.e.* the spouses and issue of the marriage, but not by anyone else.[89] For example, it cannot be enforced by either spouse's next-of-kin, who are regarded as volunteers.[90] The rule seems to be a relic from the days when it was thought that any stranger who provided consideration could enforce a promise.[91]

2. Contracts (Rights of Third Parties) Act 1999[92]

(1) Third party's right of enforcement

"A general and wide-ranging exception to"[93] the doctrine of privity is created by this Act, the central purpose of which is to enable a third party to acquire rights under a contract if, and to the extent that, the parties to the contract so intend. Subs.1(1) provides that a person who is not a party to the contract may in his own right enforce a term of the contract in the two situations to be described below. In discussing these situations and other provisions of the Act, it will be convenient to refer to the person who makes the promise which the third party is claiming to enforce (the promisor) as A, to the person to whom that promise is made (the promisee) as B[94] and to the third party as C.

(a) EXPRESS PROVISION. Under subs.1(1)(a) of the 1999 Act, C can enforce a term of the contract if "the contract expressly provides that he may": *e.g.* where a contract contains a promise by A to B to pay £1000 to C and also provides that C is to be entitled to enforce the term which contains this promise. If the contract contains such a provision, there is no further requirement (as there is under subs.1(1)(b), to be discussed

---

[85] *Re Schebsman* [1943] 1 Ch. at 370, approved [1944] Ch. at 104.

[86] *Colyear v Mulgrave* (1836) 2 Keen 81; the actual decision has been criticised, but the principle remains unimpaired. See *Page v Cox* (1852) 10 Hare 163; *Kekewich v Manning* (1851) 1 D.M. & G. 176.

[87] *e.g. Dunlop Pneumatic Tyre Co Ltd v Selfridge & Co Ltd* [1915] A.C. 847.

[88] *Re Burgess' Policy* (1915) 113 L.T. 443; *Re Clay's Policy of Assurance* [1937] 2 All E.R. 548; *Re Sinclair's Life Policy* [1938] Ch. 799; *Re Schebsman* [1944] Ch. 83; *Green v Russell* [1959] 1 Q.B. 28.

[89] *Hill v Gomme* (1839) 5 My. & Cr. 250 at 254; *Re D'Angibau* (1880) 15 Ch.D. 228 at 242; *Green v Patterson* (1886) 32 Ch.D. 95, 107; *Re Plumptre's Marriage Settlement* [1910] 1 Ch. 609 at 619. These cases, apart from constituting an exception to the doctrine of consideration, are also hard to reconcile with the modern definition of consideration: above, p.79.

[90] *Re Cook's Settlement Trusts* [1965] Ch. 902 at 915–918; Lee, 85 L.Q.R. 213; Barton, 91 L.Q.R. 326; Meagher and Lehane, 92 L.Q.R. 427.

[91] The statement in *Hill v Gomme*, above, that the children are "quasi-parties" to the contract is curiously reminiscent of the reasoning of *Dutton v Poole* (1678) 2 Lev. 210, above, p.588 n.88.

[92] See also above, pp.580–581.

[93] *ibid*; Law Commission Report on *Privity of Contract: Contracts for the Benefit of Third Parties*, Law Com No. 242, (1996), hereafter "Report"; Merkin & Faber (ed), *Privity—the Impact of the Contracts (Rights of Third Parties) Act 1999*.

[94] *cf.* the definitions of "promisor" and "promisee" in s.1(7) of the 1999 Act.

below) that the promise must have been made for C's own benefit: *e.g.* he can enforce the term even though the payment is to be made to him as trustee for D.[95] Express provisions in contracts of the kind just described, to the effect that C is to be entitled to enforce the term containing the promise made by A to B, have hitherto been rare, presumably because under the doctrine of privity they would at common law have been ineffective.[96] The 1999 Act provides a new drafting device to enable the contracting parties to give effect to their intention that C is to acquire an enforceable right against A. Apart from the Act, a similar result can be achieved by creating a trust of A's promise in favour of C[97] or by making him a joint promisee.[98] There is a procedural advantage in making use of the machinery of subs.1(1)(a) in that, if C sues under this provision, he will not (it seems) need to join B as a party to the action[99]; though the court could order B to be so joined where claims against A were made by both B and C, or where A relied against C on a defence available to A against B,[1] since in such cases B's presence before the court is likely to be "desirable . . . so that the court can resolve all the matters in dispute in the proceedings".[2] If C does have a claim apart from the Act as the beneficiary of a trust of A's promise or as joint promisee, it may, in spite of the need to join B to the action, be in C's interest to pursue that claim since it would not be subject to other provisions of the Act which may restrict his rights under it: *e.g.* to those relating to the rescission or variation of the contract between A and B, or to defences available to A against B.[3]

S.1(1)(a) is also likely to apply to terms such as Himalaya clauses,[4] by which A promises B that exemptions from or limitations of liability contained in a contract between A and B shall be available for the benefit of C, who typically will be an employee, agent or sub-contractor employed by B for the purpose of performing some or all of B's obligations under the contract. This follows from subs.1(6) of the 1999 Act, by which references to C's "enforcing" a term which "excludes or limits liability"[5] are to be "construed as references to his availing himself of the exclusion or limitation". Words in the contract to the effect that C is to be protected by the exemption or limitation clause therefore amount in themselves to an express provision that C may enforce the clause[6]; no further words will be necessary. C's protection under the Act will, however, be based on a theory different from that which accounts for the effectiveness of Himalaya clauses at common law. The common law theory is that such clauses, and the conduct of the relevant parties, can give rise to a separate or collateral contract between A and C.[7] Under the Act, by contrast, C enforces a term of a contract to which

---

[95] Report, §7.5.

[96] As in *Tweddle v Atkinson* (1861) 1 B. & S. 393, above, p.588.

[97] See above, p.646.

[98] See *McEvoy v Belfast Banking Co* [1935] A.C. 24, above, p.578.

[99] This appears to follow from the words "in his own right" in subs.1(1); *cf.* Report, §14.3.

[1] Under s.3 of the 1999 Act: see below, p.660.

[2] CPR, r. 19.2(2)(a); *cf.* above p.569.

[3] See ss.2 and 3 (below pp.657–660 and 660–661) and s.7(1) of the Act below, p.662. For the effect on one co-promisee of a defence available against, or of a release granted by, another, see above, pp.571–574.

[4] See above p.631. For the effect of the Act on such clauses, see further *Carver on Bills of Lading* (1st ed., 2000), §§7–073 to 7–079.

[5] This phrase would not include *other* terms in the contract on which C might wish to rely: *e.g.* not choice of forum clauses: see Report, §14.9; *cf.*, at common law, *The Mahkutai* [1996] A.C. 650, where the Himalaya clause in the bill of lading was held as a matter of construction not to cover the choice of forum clause in the same bill (above, pp.634–635). If, in a future case, a Himalaya clause were so drafted as to cover the choice of forum clause, the case would not fall within s.1(6) of the 1999 Act.

[6] Report, §7.10.

[7] See above, p.632.

he is *not* a party.[8] It follows that the agency requirements which exist at common law[9] are irrelevant for the purposes of the Act. On the other hand, under the Act C's right to "enforce" a Himalaya clause is subject to the provisions of the Act[10] while at common law the operation of such a clause is subject only to the common law rules discussed earlier in this Chapter[11]; and if C wishes to rely on his common law rights, in preference to those under the Act, it is open to him to do so.[12] For these (among other)[13] reasons, what may be called the old law relating to Himalaya clauses retains a considerable degree of practical importance, so that it would not be safe to rely exclusively on the simpler forms of words that can protect third parties under the Act.

(b) TERM CONFERRING BENEFIT ON THIRD PARTY. Under subs.1(1)(b) of the 1999 Act, C may enforce a term of the contract if "the term purports to confer a benefit on him"; but his right to do so in such a case is subject to subs.1(2), by which C has no such right "if on a proper construction of the contract it appears that [A and B] did not intend the term to be enforceable by" C. These will probably be the most significant provisions of the 1999 Act and their interpretation is likely to give rise to a number of difficulties. It seems that a "benefit" within subs.1(1)(b) can include any performance due under the contract between A and B: thus it can include a payment of money, a transfer of property, or the rendering of a service; it can also (by virtue of subs.1(6)) include the benefit of an exemption or limitation clause. The term must, moreover, purport to *confer* the benefit on C, so that it is not enough for C to show that he would happen to benefit from its performance. The question whether the term purported to confer a benefit on C would be one of construction. If, for example, A were employed by B "to cut my hedge adjoining C's land", performance by A might benefit C, but the term would not "purport to confer a benefit" on C. The question of construction could be particularly hard to answer where A was a sub-contractor employed by B to render services in relation to property owned by C. Assuming that the *term* does purport to confer a benefit on C, it is then necessary to construe the *contract* as a whole to determine the nature and extent of C's right to enforce the term. This follows from subs.1(4), under which "this section does not confer a right on [C] to enforce a term of a contract otherwise than subject to and in accordance with any other relevant terms of the contract". This provision would, for example, apply if the term which C was seeking to enforce provided for the payment to him of £1000, but another term of the contract provided that claims under the former term must be made within one year.

Yet a further and different question of construction arises (with regard to the intention of A and B) under subs.1(2) (quoted above) and it appears from the wording of this subsection that the burden of proof under it rests on A, or (in other words) that if the term purports to confer a benefit on C, then there is a rebuttable presumption that the term is intended by A and B to be enforceable by C.[14] To rebut the presumption, A must (in the words of subs.1(2)) show that "the parties" did not intend the term to be enforceable by C. This seems to mean that it is not enough for A to show that he did not so intend; he must show that neither he nor B had this intention. Nor is the presumption rebutted merely because in the contract A and B had reserved the right to rescind or vary the contract: this follows from the provisions with regard to such rescission or variation

---

[8] s.1(1) ("a person who is not a party . . . ").
[9] See above, p.633.
[10] s.1(1); see especially ss.2 and 3, below pp.657–661.
[11] See above, pp.634–636.
[12] 1999 Act, s.7(1).
[13] See n.5, above.
[14] Report, §§7.5. 7.17.

made in s.2 of the Act and discussed below.[15] As the question of intention put in subs.1(2) is there described as one of construction, it seems that the evidence which A will be allowed to adduce for this purpose will, in general, be limited by the rules which restrict the types of evidence admissible on other questions of construction.[16]

It is tempting to speculate how the provisions of the Act just discussed would apply to some of the leading cases in which the doctrine of privity was applied before the 1999 Act. To some extent, indeed, such an exercise is likely to be fruitless since the courts have not in the past directed their attention to the issues which will arise under the Act. In *Beswick v Beswick*,[17] for example, the contract no doubt purported to confer a benefit on C; but no finding of fact was made (because such a finding would have been irrelevant) as to the intention of A and B on the issue of legal enforceability by C: it is conceivable that A could succeed on this issue if, for example, he could show that A and B had, when the contract was made, instructed the solicitor who drafted it to do so in such a way as *not* to confer legally enforceable rights on C.[18] On the facts (if they now recurred) of a number of other cases, the position under the 1999 Act would, it is submitted, be clearer. Thus in the "disappointed beneficiary" cases such as *White v Jones*[19] C would not get a right under the Act against A, the negligent solicitor, since the terms of the solicitor's retainer (even if they identified C[20]) would not purport to confer a benefit on C: the intended benefit was to come, not from A, but from B.[21] It is similarly unlikely that cases such as the *Junior Books* case,[22] in which A is a subcontractor employed by B to enable B to perform his contract with C, would be covered, even if the subcontract named C, since the purpose of such a sub-contract would *prima facie* be to regulate the relations between A and B rather than to confer a benefit on C.[23] Cases such as the *Linden Garden* case[24] would likewise not be affected by s.1 of the Bill, since the mere possibility that land on which work is done by a building contractor might be transferred to purchasers from the owner would not be sufficient to show that the term relating to the quality of the work purported to "confer a benefit" on such purchasers; nor would the contract, without more, adequately "identify"[25] such purchasers as third parties for the purpose of subs.1(1)(b). Nor, in circumstances such as those in the *Panatown* case,[26] would the mere fact that the building contractor (A) knew that the property on which he was working in pursuance of his contract with B belonged to someone other than B suffice to show that the a benefit was to be conferred on that other person (C): the answer to the question whether the work was being done for the benefit of C or of B would depend on the contractual relations between B and C, of the details

---

[15] See below, pp.657–660.

[16] See above, pp.196–199; but the rule that evidence is not admissible to ascertain the "parties' intention" (*Prenn v Simmonds* [1971] 1 W.L.R. 1381 at 1385) can scarcely apply in the present context since the very purpose of the enquiry under s.1(2) is to determine what the parties intended.

[17] [1968] A.C. 58; above, p.589.

[18] It would have been easy for the solicitor to have drafted the contract so as to make it enforceable by C: *e.g.* by expressly making B trustee for C (above, p.647) or by making C a joint promisee with B (above, pp.576–578). We do not know whether the solicitor explained these possibilities to A and B or whether he received any instructions from them on the point.

[19] [1995] 2 A.C. 207; above p.616.

[20] See below p.655.

[21] Report, §7.25.

[22] [1983] 1 A.C. 520; above p.608.

[23] The case was a Scottish case and no claim was made in contract even though Scots law recognises a *jus quaesitum tertio* arising by way of contract.

[24] [1994] 1 A.C. 85; above p.594.

[25] Within subs.1(3), below.

[26] *Alfred McAlpine Construction Ltd v Panatown Ltd* [2001] 1 A.C. 518, above, p.596.

of which A might be wholly unaware. In the "family holiday" cases[27] the outcome under the Act would depend on the nature of the transaction. If the person making the booking supplied the names of other members of the family when the contract was made, those other members would probably acquire rights under subs.1(1); but no such rights are likely to be acquired if a person simply rented a holiday cottage without giving any information as to the number or names of the persons with whom he proposed to share the accommodation. In many of the situations which have here been discussed, the question whether the contract purports to confer a benefit on C will be closely related to the question, to be discussed in the following paragraph, whether C is adequately "identified" in the contract between A and B.

(c) IDENTIFICATION OF THIRD PARTY. Under subs.1(3) of the 1999 Act, it is a requirement of C's right to enforce A's promise that C must have been "*expressly* identified" in the contract between A and B, either "by name, as a member of a class or as answering a particular description"; it follows from this requirement that C could not rely for the purpose of subs.1(1) on the argument that the contract referred to him by implication.[28] So long as C is identified in accordance with these requirements, there is no need for C to be in existence when the contract was made: for example, a promise in favour of an unborn child, a future spouse or an unformed company could be enforced by[29] such a third party when it came into existence. Although it is a *necessary* condition for the creation of C's rights under subs.1 that he must be expressly identified in the contract between A and B, such identification is not a *sufficient* condition for this purpose, since a contract which identifies C does not necessarily purport to confer a benefit on him. If, for example, a portrait painter (A) were commissioned by a college (B) to paint a portrait of the head of the college (C) for display on its premises, the contract would not purport to confer a benefit on C, nor would A and B intend the contract to be enforceable by C. It would seem that C must be identified in such a way as to indicate that A and B intended to confer rights on C: thus the identification requirement would be satisfied where A promised B not to sue C for negligence but not where A promised B not to sue B for C's negligence.[30] The requirements of subs.1(3) are, in other words, *additional* to those of subs.1(2). Their operation may be illustrated by reference to the *Midland Silicones* case.[31] On the facts of that case, C would not be able to enforce the limitation clause since the contract between A and B contained no express reference to C (whether by name, by description or as a member of a class). In these circumstances, neither subsection would be satisfied: C would not be identified and this very fact would indicate that the contract did not purport to confer a benefit on him. Where a contract is (as it was in the *Midland Silicones* case) contained in or evidenced by a bill of lading, it is now likely to contain a Himalaya clause,[32] which would be likely adequately to identify C and confer a right on him to "enforce"[33] the limitation clause under subs.1(2). The question whether C is identified in such a way as to give him an enforceable right may itself raise a question of construction: *e.g.* where the words of the

---

[27] See above, pp.592–593.

[28] Thus cases such as *London Drugs Ltd v Kuehne & Nagel International Ltd* [1992] 3 S.C.R. 299 (above, p.631) would not appear to be covered by the Act.

[29] A company which did not at the time of the contract exist could, on coming into existence, by virtue of subs.1(3) enforce a term made for its benefit (within subs.1(2)); but the rules relating to contracts made on behalf of such a company stated at pp.735–736, below would continue to govern the extent to which such a company could be *bound* by a contract made on its behalf: Report §§8.9 to 8.16.

[30] As, for example, in *Adler v Dickson* [1955] 1 Q.B. 158.

[31] [1962] A.C. 446; above, p.628.

[32] See above, p.561.

[33] See s.1(6), above, p.652.

term are literally adequate to identify C but the term does not purport (or A and B do not intend) to confer a benefit on him.[34]

(d) REMEDIES. Where C has a right to enforce a term of the contract by virtue of subs.1(1) of the 1999 Act, he has this right in spite of the fact that he is not a party to the contract: the Act does not, in general, adopt the technique of transferring rights from B to C or of treating C as having acquired rights by means of the fiction that he has become a party to the contract.[35] It does, however, make use of such a fiction so far as C's *remedies* are concerned.[36] Subs.1(5) provides that "For the purpose of exercising his right to enforce a term of the contract, there shall be available to the third party any remedy that would have been available to him in an action for breach of contract if he had been a party to the contract (and the rules relating to damages, injunctions, specific performance and other relief shall apply accordingly)". It follows from this provision that C can invoke the same kinds of judicial remedies as would be available to B if no third party were involved, and that C can recover damages for loss of bargain (or "expectation" loss[37]) even though the bargain was made, not with him, but with B. It also follows that the same principles which would limit B's remedies in a two-party case apply to an action brought by C: for example, the principles of remoteness[38] and mitigation[39] and those which restrict the availability of specific relief.[40] The application of these principles may, however, lead to different practical results where the action is brought by C from those which would follow from them in an action brought by B. For example, in an action brought by C, the test of remoteness would be whether it was C's (not B's) loss which A ought reasonably have contemplated; the principles of mitigation would require the court to ask what steps C (not B) ought reasonably have taken to mitigate his loss; and the question whether specific relief should be refused on account of the conduct of the claimant could receive one answer where the action was brought by C and another if it were brought by B.

The contract containing the term which C seeks to enforce against A may also contain an arbitration clause amounting to a written arbitration agreement within the Arbitration Act 1996.[41] The 1999 Act provides that, if C seeks to enforce the former term against A, then C is to be treated as a party to the arbitration agreement.[42] It follows that, if C attempted to enforce that term *by action*, A could obtain a stay of that action under the 1996 Act and so secure compliance by C with the arbitration agreement. A contract between A and B may also provide that C is to be entitled to submit to arbitration some dispute between himself and A *other* than one concerning the enforcement by C against A of one of the other terms of the contract. Such an arbitration provision cannot compel C to resort to arbitration of (for example) a tort claim between himself and A. But if the provision is a term which C is entitled to enforce under s.1 of the 1999 Act and is also a written arbitration agreement within the Arbitration Act 1996 and C chooses to submit

---

[34] Such a question could arise on facts such as those in *Elder Dempster* [1924] A.C. 522, where the form of bill of lading used seems to have been based on the assumption that the goods would be carried by B but they were in fact carried by C and the words of the exemption clause in the bill happened to be apt to refer also to C: see above, p.627.

[35] 1999 Act, s.7(4). This refers only to other *legislation*, but the principle that C is not to be treated as a party to the contract appears also to apply for the purpose of rules of common law: see below at n.45.

[36] Also for a number of other purposes relating to defences available to A against C: see s.3(4) and (6), below, pp.660–661; and to arbitration provisions: see s.8, below, p.656.

[37] See below, p.944.

[38] See below, p.965.

[39] See below, p.976.

[40] See below, p.1020; and *cf.* above p.1013. Report, §§3.32, 3.33.

[41] See above, p.449.

[42] 1999 Act, s.8(1).

the dispute with A to arbitration, then C is treated for the purpose of the 1996 Act as a party to the arbitration agreement so that the arbitration proceedings will be governed by that Act.[43]

(e) NO REQUIREMENT OF CONSIDERATION MOVING FROM THIRD PARTY. The 1999 Act does not impose any requirement that consideration for A's promise must move from C. It does not contain any express provision to this effect[44]; but the consequence follows from the fact that the Act gives C the right to enforce the term and is further supported by the general principle that C is not to be treated as a party to the contract between A and B.[45] Since the promise in contracts of the kind in question is made to B, the fact that C need not provide any consideration for it is not strictly an exception to the rule that consideration need not move *from the promisee*, but it can be regarded as a quasi exception to that rule in the sense that C is a person in whose favour a promise is made and who can enforce it even though he may be no more than a gratuitous beneficiary.

(2) Right to rescind or vary the contract

Under the judge-made rules relating to contracts for the benefit of third parties, one objection to the creation of such rights has been that it would deprive the contracting parties of their right to rescind or vary the contract by mutual consent.[46] The 1999 Act deals with this problem by means of a compromise: it specifies the circumstances in which A and B *prima facie* lose this right, while it at the same time enables them so to draw up their contract so as to retain the right, or to change the *prima facie* rules laid down in the Act which specify when it is lost.

(a) GENERAL RULE: C's CONSENT REQUIRED. The general rule, stated in subs.2(1) of the 1999 Act, is that, once C has acquired the right to enforce a term of the contract between A and B "under section 1", then, if one of the circumstances to be described below has arisen, A and B may not, without C's consent, by agreement rescind or vary the contract, or vary it so as to "extinguish or alter" C's entitlement. Rescission calls for no further comment here; but with regard to variation it should be noted that A and B are, under the general rule, precluded from varying the contract not only so as to *extinguish* but also *so as to alter* C's rights. An alteration may of course operate, not only to C's prejudice, but also to his advantage: *e.g.* where it purports to increase payments to be made to C under the term in question. Such a variation is unlikely to give rise to any problems between A and C, since C will presumably consent to it as soon as he hears of it. But the argument that C is entitled to enforce a term of a contract between A and B can also give rise to problems between one of these parties and outside interests: *e.g.* creditors of B in the event of B's insolvency.[47] Such persons may seek to invoke subs.2(1) where the variation increases C's rights but where, on the crucial date for the assertion of their rights, C has either not yet acquired any knowledge of the variation or has not yet made any communication to A or done any other act from which his assent to the variation can be inferred.

(i) *C's assent to the term.* The first of the circumstances in which A and B may not, without C's consent, agree to rescind the contract, or vary it in the ways described above,

---

[43] 1999 Act, s.8(2).
[44] Report §6.8 n.8.
[45] See above, at n.35.
[46] This has been one reason for the restrictions on the scope of the equitable exception to the doctrine of privity by way of trusts of promises: above, p.648.
[47] As, for example, in *Re Schebsman* [1944] Ch. 83, above, p.647.

arises where C has communicated his assent to the term to A[48]; communication to B does not suffice for this purpose.[49] The assent may be by words or conduct[50]; and if it is "sent" to A by post or other means, it is not regarded as communicated to him "until received by him".[51] In other words, the "posting" rule, as developed in cases of contract formation[52] does not apply in the present context. "Sent" here seems to refer to some act done by C in order to communicate *words* of assent to A. The rule relating to an assent "sent" to A by post or other means is negative in nature: it states that the assent is not communicated to A until received by him. It thus leaves open the question whether an assent which has been so sent can take effect before it has actually come to A's notice: *e.g.* where it has been delivered to his address but not yet been read by him. If the overriding requirement is one of communication, it may not be satisfied in such a case. The expression "sent" also does not seem to be appropriate to refer to an assent by *conduct*; but it seems that such an assent must come to A's notice: this seems to follow from the general requirement that C's assent must be "communicated"[53] to A. No formality (such as writing) is required even for an assent in words,[54] so that an oral communication suffices.

(ii) *C's reliance.* The right to rescind or vary the contract is also barred where A is aware of C's having relied on the term,[55] or where A could reasonably have foreseen such reliance and it has actually taken place.[56] It would seem that, in such cases, C may be entitled, not merely to the promised performance, but also to damages in respect of his reliance loss: *e.g.* where he has travelled to the place specified in the contract for the receipt by him of the promised performance. This follows from the rule laid down by the 1999 Act with respect to C's remedies[57]; it also follows from this rule that C could not claim under both heads to the extent to which such a combination of claims would result in double recovery or in his being placed in a better position than that in which he would have been if A had performed his promise in accordance with its original terms.[58]

(b) CONSEQUENCES OF ATTEMPTED RESCISSION OR VARIATION WITHOUT C'S CONSENT. The general rule in subs.2(1) is that A and B "may not" by agreement rescind the contract, or vary it in the ways described above, without C's consent. The most obvious consequence of this provision is that a purported rescission or variation without C's consent is simply *ineffective*, so that C can, in spite of it, enforce the term in question *against A*. But such enforcement may, because of the rescission, become a practical impossibility (*e.g.* because A has in consequence of the rescission put it out of his power to perform); and it is arguable that the purported rescission is also *wrongful* so as to give C a remedy in damages *against B*, perhaps on the analogy of liability for wrongful interference with contractual rights.[59] This possibility could have practical significance in the event of A's insolvency.

---

[48] s.2(1)(a).
[49] This follows from the words "to the promisor" in s.2(1)(a).
[50] s.2(2)(a).
[51] s.2(2)(b).
[52] See above, p.24.
[53] s.2(1)(a).
[54] Contrast Law of Property Act 1925, s.136(1) (below, p.676) requiring written notice of an assignment.
[55] s.2(1)(b).
[56] s.2(1)(c).
[57] s.1(5); above p.656.
[58] *e.g.* where it would have been necessary for C to incur the reliance expenditure in order to secure the benefit—perhaps by travelling to the place where it was to be conferred. *cf.* below, p.942.
[59] See above, p.619.

(c) CONTRACT CONFERRING CHOICES ON PROMISEE. Subs.2(1) of the 1999 Act deals with the situation in which C has become entitled to enforce a term of the contract "under section 1" and A and B then attempt by agreement to rescind or vary the contract. This situation must be distinguished from that in which A promises B to perform in favour of C *or as B shall direct*. If, in such a case, B directs A to perform in favour of D (or of B himself) the contract is not varied. On the contrary, it is performed in accordance with its original terms, under which B has a choice as to the person to whom performance is to be rendered. The case therefore does not fall within subs.2(1), so that the requirement of C's consent, as there stated, does not apply.[60] Another way of explaining this conclusion is to say that, in the case put, the mere making of the promise was not intended to confer an indefeasible right on C; for the fact that B had power to divert the benefit away from C would indicate that A and B did not at this stage intend[61] the term to be enforceable by C if B exercised that power. A term of the present kind might, however, also limit B's power to divert the benefit away from C: *e.g.* by providing that the power was to be exercisable only for a specified period. After the end of the period, C could no longer be deprived of the benefit of A's promise by the unilateral act of B since the consent of A and B would then as a matter of common law be necessary to vary the contract; and any *such* variation would then be subject to the requirement of C's consent under subs.2(1).

(d) CONTRARY PROVISION IN THE CONTRACT. The general requirement of C's consent, imposed by subs.2(1), may be displaced by an express term of the contract. Two possibilities are envisaged.

The first, stated in subs.2(3)(a), is for such an express term to state that A and B may by agreement rescind or vary the contract without the consent of C. A and B can then rescind or vary the contract by agreement in spite of the fact that C has acquired a right under subs.1(1) and in spite of the fact that the circumstances specified in subs.2(1) have occurred: that is, even after communication of assent by C to A, or after reliance by C of which A is aware or which he could reasonably have been expected to foresee. It is not entirely clear whether it is enough for the express term to provide that A and B may by agreement rescind or vary the contract or whether it must go on to say in so many words that they may do so without the consent of C; but to be sure of achieving the desired result, A and B would be well advised to use the latter form of words.

The second possibility, stated in subs.2(3)(b), is for the express term to provide that the consent of C is required in circumstances other than those specified in subs.2(1). For example, the term might provide that such consent was required only for a specified period or that it must be given in a specified form (*e.g.* by registered letter). Again effect would be given to such provisions, so that in the first of our two examples C's consent would no longer be needed (even after the circumstances described in subs.2(1) had occurred) after the end of the period; and in the second it would be ineffective if not given in the specified form.

(e) JUDICIAL DISCRETION TO DISPENSE WITH CONSENT. Subs.2(4) give the court power, on the application of A and B, to dispense with the requirement of C's consent to a rescission or variation of the contract in two situations: (a) where C's consent cannot be obtained because "his whereabouts cannot reasonably be ascertained"; or (b) where he is mentally incapable of giving his consent. On a similar principle, the court has under subs.2(5) the same power where it is alleged that C's consent is required because A could

---

[60] *cf.* Report, §10.30.
[61] Within s.1(2).

reasonably have foreseen that C would rely on the term[62] but it cannot reasonably be ascertained whether he has in fact relied on it. Where the court under these provisions dispenses with C's consent, it may order compensation to be paid to him[63]; such an order may presumably be made against either A or B or both of them.

(3) Promisor's defences against third party

S.3 of the 1999 Act contains an elaborate set of provisions which specify matters on which A can rely by way of defence, set-off or counterclaim against C in an action by C for the enforcement, "in reliance on section 1",[64] of a term of the contract between A and B.

(a) GENERAL PRINCIPLE. The starting principle, stated in subs.3(2), is that A can rely by way of defence or set-off on any matter that "arises from or in connection with the contract [between A and B] and is relevant to the term" and would have been available to A if the proceedings (to enforce the term) had been brought by B. Under this principle, A could, for example, rely against C on a valid exemption clause in the contract between A and B[65]; and on the fact that the contract was void for mistake or voidable for misrepresentation, or that it had been frustrated or that A was justified in refusing to perform it on account of B's repudiatory breach.

(b) CONTRARY PROVISION. This general principle can, however, be excluded by a contrary provision in the contract: *i.e.* by a term in the contract between A and B that A is not to be entitled to rely on such matters against C[66]; though where the contract between A and B was wholly void such a term would appear to be of no more effect than the rest of the purported contract. The general principle can, conversely, be extended by an express term in the contract. Subs.3(3) provides that A can (in addition to the matters referred to in subs.3(2)) rely by way of defence or set-off against C on any matter if "an express term of the contract provides for it to be available to him in proceedings brought by" C and it would have been so available to A in proceedings brought by B. Under this provision, A could rely against C on debts owed by B to A even though the debts arose out of other transactions, if the contract containing the term which C was seeking to enforce contained an express term that A was to be entitled to rely on those debts also against C.

(c) DEFENCES AGAINST C ONLY. There is the further possibility that A may have defences or counterclaims against C which he would not have against B: *e.g.*, where A had been induced to enter into the contract by C's misrepresentation, or where C was indebted to A under another transaction. Subs.3(4) enables A to rely on such matters against C if they could have been so relied on if C had been a party to the contract; though this rule, like the general principle stated in subs.3(2), can be modified or excluded by an express term of the contract between A and B.[67]

(d) RELIANCE ON EXEMPTION CLAUSES. A rule analogous to the general principle of subs.3(2) applies where the "enforcement" of the term by C takes the form of his availing himself of an exemption or limitation clause in his favour in the contract

---

[62] See s.2(1)(c).
[63] s.2(6).
[64] s.3(1).
[65] *cf.* Report, §10.31.
[66] s.3(5).
[67] s.3(5) applies to subsection 3(4) as well as to subsection 3(2).

between A and B.[68] Subs.3(6) provides that C cannot in this way "enforce" the term if he could not have done so, had he been a party to the contract. This restriction on C's right to enforce the term would, for example, apply if, by reason of the Unfair Contract Terms Act 1977[69] the clause had been invalid or if it had not satisfied the requirement of reasonableness as imposed by that Act; or if C was guilty of a fraud on A and so could not have relied on the term (even though B might have been able to do so) by reason of the common law rule that an exemption clause does not protect a party from liability for his own fraud.[70]

(4) Exceptions to third party's entitlement

A number of situations which *prima facie* fall within s.1 of the 1999 Act are excepted by s.6 from the operation of s.1. These exceptions fall into two groups. In cases which fall within the first group, C has, or can acquire, rights under the contract between A and B by virtue of some other rule of law; and the purpose of excepting these cases from the operation of s.1 is to preserve the conditions under which C's rights arise or may arise under those other rules of law. In cases which fall within the second group, by contrast, C has *prima facie* no rights under other rules of law; and the purpose of excepting these cases from the operation of s.1 is to preserve in them the general rule of common law by which C acquires no rights under the contract between A and B. Such cases, in other words, continue to be governed by the common law doctrine of privity, subject to any limitations on its scope and to any exceptions to it that may exist at common law or under other legislation.

The first of the above group of exceptions includes contracts on bills of exchange, promissory notes and other negotiable instruments[71]: third parties can acquire rights under such contracts under the rules relating to negotiability, discussed elsewhere in this book, and it is not the purpose of the 1999 Act to extend these rights.[72] It also includes contracts for the carriage of goods by sea which are governed by the Carriage of Goods by Sea Act 1992, and corresponding electronic transactions to which that Act may be applied by Order.[73] The carefully regulated scheme of the 1992 Act[74] for the acquisition of rights under such contracts by third parties (such as transferees of bills of lading) would be seriously disrupted if such third parties could acquire rights under the 1999 Act in circumstances in which no such rights would be acquired under the 1992 Act. The same is (*mutatis mutandis*) true of contracts for the international carriage of goods by rail, road and air, which are governed by international conventions having the force of law in the United Kingdom,[75] so that these contracts are likewise excepted from the operation of s.1 of the 1999 Act.[76] The exception is, however, in turn, subject to an exception: C is not precluded from taking the benefit of an exemption or limitation clause in a contract for the carriage of goods governed by the 1992 Act or by the international conventions referred to above merely because such legislation applies to the contract.[77] Before the 1999 Act, C could in many cases take the benefit of an exemption or limitation clause in the contract of carriage *e.g.* where that contract

---

[68] See s.1(6), above p.653.
[69] See above, pp.246 *et seq.*; Report, §10.22.
[70] See above, p.242.
[71] s.6(1).
[72] See below, p.691; Report, §12.16.
[73] s.6(5).
[74] For details of this scheme, see *Carver on Bills of Lading* (1st ed.), §§5–008 *et seq.*
[75] See *Chitty on Contracts* (28th ed.), Vol.II, Chaps 35 and 36.
[76] s.6(5)(b) and 8.
[77] s.6(5), "tailpiece".

contained a Himalaya clause.[78] The legal reasoning on which this result was based was that a separate or collateral contract arose by virtue of such a clause between A and C.[79] Since C is a *party* to this contract, his right to "enforce" it does not depend (in the words of the present exception) on any "reliance on . . . section" 1.[80] The effectiveness of Himalaya clauses would therefore not be directly affected by the present exception[81] to a *third party's* entitlement under s.1 to "enforce" an exemption or limitation clause. But one of the objects of the 1999 Act appears to have been to simplify the drafting of Himalaya clauses and to remove obstacles to their efficacy which might be encountered in establishing the separate contract between A and C[82]; and it is for this reason that the present exception to the operation of s.1 does not apply to exemption and limitation clauses in contracts of carriage which, for other purposes, fall within that exception.

The second of the groups of exceptions described above includes the contract which binds a company and its members on the terms of the memorandum and articles of association, when these documents are registered, by virtue of s.14 of the Companies Act 1985. The purpose of this exception is presumably to preserve the established limitations of the scope of this "statutory contract"[83]: *e.g.* the rule that this contract confers no rights on a director of the company as such.[84] The second group also includes contracts of employment and certain analogous contracts to the extent that such a contract will not give the employer's customer any right under s.1 of the 1999 Act to enforce any term of the contract against the employee.[85]

(5) Third party's other rights unaffected

Subs.7(1) of the 1999 Act provides that "Section 1 does not affect any right or remedy of a third party that exists or is available apart from this Act". It follows that C will continue, after the coming into force of the Act, to be able to enforce rights and to rely on defences arising under a contract between A and B, if before then he could have done so under exceptions to the doctrine of privity established at common law, in equity or under other legislation, or if he could have done so because the case fell outside the scope of the doctrine of privity of contract: these possibilities are discussed elsewhere in this Chapter.[86] C will, for example, continue to be able to enforce a promise made by A to B if there is a trust of the promise in his favour[87]; he will be able to rely on Himalaya clauses and on other common law and statutory rules under which the benefit of an exemption clause in a contract between A and B is available to him[88]; and he will continue to be able to enforce collateral contracts between himself and A.[89] Indeed, in some such cases the person seeking to enforce the term is not truly a "third party" within the 1999 Act.[90] The whole point of the collateral contract device is to establish a direct contractual relationship between the parties that have here been called A and C;

---

[78] See above, p.631.

[79] See above, pp.632, 634.

[80] s.1(1) confers a right of enforcement only on a "person who is *not* a party" to the contract.

[81] *i.e.*, that contained in s.6(5) of the 1999 Act.

[82] See Report §§2.35, 12.10; for the complexity of the drafting of Himalaya clauses and the difficulties which arise, or are thought to arise, in satisfying the common law requirement of a separate contract between A and C, see above, pp.632–635.

[83] *Soden v British & Commonwealth Holdings* [1998] A.C. 298 at 323.

[84] See above, p.586.

[85] ss.6(3) and (4).

[86] See above, pp.606 *et seq*; below, pp.666 *et seq*.

[87] See above, pp.646 *et seq*.

[88] See above, p.631 *et seq*.

[89] See above, pp.582 *et seq*.

[90] s.1(1) ("not a party . . . ").

and the legal basis for the efficacy of Himalaya clauses is simlarly that a contract of some kind comes into existence between A and C, though this is not the same as "the contract" (*i.e.* that between A and B) containing the term which C is seeking to enforce.[91] Subs.7(1) also preserves any rights which C may have to sue A in tort in respect of loss suffered by C in consequence of A's breach of his contract with B; we have seen that in such cases C will often have no rights under the 1999 Act.[92] The subsection also leaves it open to the courts to develop new exceptions at common law to the doctrine of privity of contract.[93]

Although subs.7(1) in terms states only that "Section 1" does not affect other rights and remedies available to C, it follows from the structure of the 1999 Act that many of its other provisions will likewise not apply where C's rights against A arise apart from the Act. Of particular significance are the points that the rules as to rescission and variation, contained in s.2, and the rules as to defences and related matters, contained in s.3, will not so apply, since s.2 applies only "where a third party has a right *under section 1* to enforce a term of the contract"[94] and s.3 applies only "where, *in reliance on section 1*, proceedings for the enforcement of a term of a contract are brought by a third party".[95]

The structure resulting from the above distinctions is therefore a complex one. Four types of cases call for consideration. The first is that in which C has rights under the 1999 Act but none at common law because the case falls within the scope of the doctrine of privity of contract but not within any of the judge-made or other legislative exceptions to it. Here C's rights and remedies are clearly subject to the provisions of the Act. The second is the case in which C has no rights under the Act (either because the requirements of its s.1 are not satisfied or because one of the exceptions listed in its s.6 applies) but in which he does have rights apart from the Act, because the case falls either outside the scope of the doctrine of privity of contract or within one of the judge-made or other legislative exceptions to it. Here the rights and remedies to which C is entitled are clearly not subject to the provisions of the Act.[96] The third is the case in which C has rights both under the Act and apart from it (because the case falls outside the scope of the doctrine of privity of contract or within one of the judge-made or other legislative exceptions to it). It would seem that in such a case C can choose between making his claim under the Act (and so subject to its provisions) and apart from the Act (and so not subject to its provisions). If, for example, C has a cause of action against A in tort at common law, it may be to C's advantage to pursue that claim (rather than one which may also be *prima facie* available to him under s.1) since in making such a common law claim he would not, in general, be bound by an exemption clause in the contract between A and B, while he would be so bound if he made a claim under the Act.[97] The fourth is the case in which C has no rights under the Act and none under the existing rules of common law or under other legislative exceptions to the doctrine of privity of contract. Here, C's only hope is to induce the court to create a new exception to the doctrine of privity[98] or (in the House of Lords) to reject that doctrine altogether. If C's claim were

---

[91] See p.634, above.
[92] See above, p.654.
[93] See below, at n.98.
[94] s.2(1).
[95] s.3(1).
[96] *White v Jones* [1995] 2 A.C. 207 (above, p.616) illustrates this possibility.
[97] s.3(2), above, p.660.
[98] *e.g.* perhaps, to follow the Supreme Court of Canada's decision in *London Drugs Ltd v Kuehne & Nagel International Ltd* [1992] 3 S.C.R. 299 in recognising, at least to a limited extent, the principle of vicarious immunity: see above, p.631.

upheld on one of these grounds, it would plainly not be subject to the provisions of the 1999 Act.

(6) Nature of the third party's rights

Although the 1999 Act for a number of purposes[99] makes use of the fiction of treating C as if he were a party to the contract, it in general treats C's rights and defences as being *sui generis*. It does not, in other words, except for those purposes treat C as if he were or were deemed to be, or to have become, a party to the contract. In particular, the Act provides that C is not to be treated as a party to the contract between A and B for the purposes of other legislation.[1] For example, the references to a party or to the parties to a contract in the Law Reform (Frustrated Contracts) Act 1943[2] and in the Misrepresentation Act 1967[3] do not, under the Act include references to C. The same is true of the Unfair Contract Terms Act 1977. The point can be illustrated by supposing that a contract was made between A and B on A's standard terms of business, that a term of this contract conferred a benefit on C, that this term was enforceable by C by virtue of s.1 of the Act, and that the contract contained a term excluding or restricting A's liability for defects in the performance rendered to C. The requirement of reasonableness under s.3 of the 1977 Act[4] would not apply in favour of C since he was not one of the parties to the contract between A and B, or a party who had dealt on A's standard terms: the requirement would apply only in favour of B.[5] The justification given by the Law Commission for this position is that to apply the 1977 Act in a three-party case would raise complex policy issues going beyond those involved in reforming the doctrine of privity.[6]

(7) Effect on Unfair Contract Terms Act 1977, s.2

The relationship between the 1999 Act and the Unfair Contract Terms Act 1977 gives rise to the further difficulty that, under s.2(1) of that Act,[7] contract terms may be void if they purport to exclude or restrict liability for death or personal injury resulting from negligence; and that under s.2(2)[8] contract terms may be subject to the requirement of reasonableness if they purport to exclude or restrict liability for negligence in respect of other loss. Negligence here can include the breach of a contractual duty of care,[9] so that a claim by C affected by s.2 of the 1977 Act could be brought either under the 1999 Act or in tort, apart from the Act. Where it is brought under the latter Act, a compromise solution is adopted for cases of the kind here under discussion, *i.e.* for those in which C sues A for breach of a duty of care arising out of a contract between A and B, and A seeks

---

[99] See s.1(5), relating to C's remedies: above, p.656; s.3(4), relating to certain defences and s.3(6), relating to restrictions on the availability of exemption clauses: above, pp.660–661; for a different technique, see s.7(3), relating to limitation of actions and s.8, relating to arbitration agreements (above, p.604).

[1] 1999 Act, s.7(4). This provides that C is not to be so treated "by virtue of section 1(5) or 3(4) or 3(6)", above n.99. No reference is made in s.7(4) to s.8, above n.99, by virtue of which C *is* treated as a party to an arbitration agreement for the purposes of the Arbitration Act 1996: see above, p.656.

[2] See below, pp.911 *et seq.*

[3] See above, pp.350 *et seq.*

[4] See above, p.253.

[5] Report, §13.10; for B's right of enforcement, see below, p.665.

[6] Report, §13.10(vii) and (viii).

[7] See above, p.249.

[8] See above, pp.252–253.

[9] Unfair Contract Terms Act 1977, s.1(1)(a).

to rely on a term of that contract as excluding or restricting his liability for negligence.[10] Where C in consequence of the breach suffers death or personal injury, the strong policy considerations against contract terms excluding or restricting A's liability for such harm are to prevail, so that nothing in the 1999 Act will affect C's right to impugn the validity of a term excluding or restricting A's liability for such harm under s.2(1) of the 1977 Act. But where C suffers other loss, the case is regarded as more closely analogous to the situation (described above) that can arise under s.3 of the 1977 Act. Subs.7(2) of the 1998 Bill therefore provides that s.2(2) of the 1977 Act is not to apply where A's alleged negligence consists of the breach of an obligation arising from a term of a contract (between A and B) and the claim by C is brought in reliance on s.1 of the 1999 Act. In such an action, therefore, a term in that contract excluding or restricting A's liability for loss other than death or personal injury is not subject to the requirement of reasonableness under the 1977 Act.

(8) Promisee's rights

(a) IN GENERAL. At common law, the doctrine of privity of contract does not preclude the promisee from enforcing the contract[11] and this position is preserved by s.4 of the 1999 Act, by which "Section 1 does not affect any right of the promisee to enforce any term of the contract". The contract between A and B can thus be enforced by B even where the 1999 Act also gives C the right to enforce one of its terms against A. On A's failure to perform that term in favour of C, B can therefore make any claims for the agreed sum, for other specific relief or for damages that would have been available to him at common law apart from the Act. There is also nothing in the Act that affects B's right to restitution[12] against A in the event of the latter's non-performance of the term in favour of C, even though B's right to restitution would not normally be a "right of [B] to *enforce* a term of the contract" within s.4: it would have this character only where the contract provided for the return by A of the consideration provided by B to A in the event of A's failure to perform in favour of C. The 1999 Act also contains nothing to affect the common law rules which govern the relative rights of B and C where A has performed, or is willing to perform, in favour of C.[13]

(b) PROVISION AGAINST DOUBLE LIABILITY. At common law, A's failure to perform in favour of C may, in circumstances discussed earlier in this Chapter,[14] give B a right to recover damages in respect of C's loss or in respect of expenses incurred by B in making good A's default: *e.g.* in completing A's unfinished, or in repairing A's defective, work. If, after B had recovered such damages, C were to make a claim against A under s.1 of the 1999 Act, there would be a risk of A's being made liable twice over for the same loss. S.5 of the Act therefore directs the court in such circumstances "to reduce any award to [C] to such extent as it thinks appropriate to take account of the sum recovered by" B. Such a reduction would not prejudice C since, where damages had been recovered by B in respect of C's loss, these would have to be held by B for C[15]; and where B had incurred expense in curing A's breach, C's loss would be reduced in fact by his receipt

---

[10] See Report, §13.12.
[11] See above, p.590.
[12] See above, p.590.
[13] See above, pp.604 *et seq.*
[14] See above, pp.593 *et seq.*
[15] See above, p.605.

of the intended benefit,[16] though by a route other than that envisaged by the contract. S.5 of the Act applies only where B has recovered "a sum" (*i.e.* of money) in respect of C's loss or B's expense in making good A's default. Thus it will normally apply where B has recovered *damages*, though the possibility of its also applying where B has recovered *the agreed sum* or where he has made a successful claim for *restitution* does not appear to be excluded. It will not, however, apply where B has obtained an order for the specific performance of an obligation by A to render some performance to C other than the payment of money, or where B has obtained an injunction to enforce a negative promise made by A for the benefit of C. In such cases, C will obtain the performance due to him under the term made enforceable by him by virtue of s.1 and so will not have any right to damages for its non-performance. But C might, in addition to the receipt of the performance, claim damages from A, *e.g.*, in respect of delay in rendering the performance. Such a claim is not, and should not be, affected by s.5 of the 1999 Act since its success would not make A liable twice over for the *same* loss.

3. Other Statutory Exceptions

A number of other exceptions to the doctrine of privity have been created by statute[17] and will continue to be available to the third party after the coming into force of the Contracts (Rights of Third Parties) Bill 1998.[18] The most important of these are the following:

(1) Insurance

The doctrine of privity applies to contracts of insurance.[19] It was in practice much modified in this field by the trust device and by agency; but the inadequacy of these exceptions has led to the creation of further exceptions to the doctrine by statute.

(a) LIFE INSURANCE. S.11 of the Married Women's Property Act 1882[20] provides that where a man insures his life for the benefit of his wife or children, or where a woman insures her life for the benefit of her husband or children,[21] the policy "shall create a trust in favour of the objects therein named". This is a good provision so far as it goes, but it is subject to some odd limitations. It applies only where a person insures his or her own life, and not where the policy is on the life of the third party[22]; and it is restricted to policies for the benefit of spouses and children, so that it does not apply in favour of other dependants, such as informally adopted children.[23] These restrictions will not be affected by the Contracts (Rights of Third Parties) Act 1999[24]; but persons who have no rights under s.11 of the 1882 Act may, if the requirements of the 1999 Act are satisfied,

---

[16] *cf.* below, p.980.

[17] A statutory exception to the doctrine enabling price maintenance agreements to be enforced against third parties formerly existed by virtue of Resale Prices Act 1976, s.26; but that Act has been repealed by the s.1 of the Competition Act 1998 which makes no similar provision where such agreements are exempted (under ss.4 to 9) from *prima facie* invalidity under s.2.

[18] s.7(1).

[19] See *Boston Fruit Co v British & Foreign Marine Insurance Co* [1906] A.C. 336; *Yangtze Insurance Association v Lukmanjee* [1918] A.C. 585. Contrast, in Australia, *Trident General Ins Co Ltd v McNiece Bros Pty Ltd* (1988) 165 C.L.R. 107 (above, p.590).

[20] Replacing Married Women's Property Act 1870, s.10.

[21] Illegitimate children are included: Family Law Reform Act 1969, s.19(1).

[22] *Re Engelbach's Estate* [1924] 2 Ch. 348, overruled on another point in *Beswick v Beswick* [1968] A.C. 58.

[23] *Re Clay's Policy of Assurance* [1937] 2 All E.R. 548.

[24] Law Com. No. 242, §12.27.

acquire the more restricted[25] rights conferred on third parties by that Act. They may also have rights under the trust exception to the doctrine of privity.[26]

(b) MOTOR INSURANCE. In *Williams v Baltic Insurance Co*[27] it was held that the owner of a car may be trustee of his motor insurance policy for a person driving his car with his consent. By statute such a person can now take the benefit of the owner's insurance policy without having to prove that the owner intended to constitute himself trustee.[28]

(c) FIRE INSURANCE. Where a house which is insured is destroyed by fire, "any person . . . interested" may require the insurance money to be laid out towards reinstating the house[29]; thus a tenant may claim under his landlord's insurance,[30] and a landlord under his tenant's insurance.

(d) INSURANCE BY PERSONS WITH LIMITED INTERESTS. A person may insure property for its full value although he has only a limited interest in it. He may then be able to recover its full value from the insurers but be liable to pay over to the other persons interested any sum exceeding his own loss.[31] A number of real or supposed limitations on this principle have been removed by statute. Thus it has been provided that any person who has an interest in the subject-matter of a policy of marine insurance can insure "on behalf of and for the benefit of other persons interested as well as for his own benefit".[32] On a somewhat similar principle, where property is sold and suffers damage before the sale is completed, any insurance money to which the vendor is entitled in respect of the damage must be held by him for the purchaser, and be paid over to the purchaser on completion.[33]

(e) SOLICITORS' INDEMNITY INSURANCE. Under s.37 of the Solicitors Act 1974, a scheme has been established by the Law Society for the compulsory insurance of solicitors against liability for professional negligence or breach of duty. The scheme takes the form of a contract between the Society and insurers whereby the insurers undertake,

---

[25] *e.g.* powers of rescission or variation under s.2 of the 1999 Act do not apply where a trust has arisen under s.11 of the 1882 Act; *cf.* above, p.664.

[26] *Re Foster's Policy* [1966] 1 W.L.R. 222; above p.647.

[27] [1924] 2 K.B. 282.

[28] Road Traffic Act 1988, s.148(7), replacing Road Traffic Act 1930, s.36(4), discussed in *Tattersal v Drysdale* [1935] 2 K.B. 174; *Austin v Zurich, etc., Insurance Co* [1944] 2 All E.R. 243 at 248.

[29] Fires Prevention (Metropolis) Act 1774, s.83.

[30] *Portavon Cinema Co Ltd v Price and Century Insurance Co* [1939] 4 All E.R. 601; *Mark Rowlands Ltd v Berni Inns Ltd* [1986] Q.B. 211; *Lonsdale & Thompson Ltd v Black Arrow Group plc* [1993] Ch. 361.

[31] *Waters v Monarch Insurance Co* (1856) 5 E. & B. 870; *Hepburn v Tomlinson (Hauliers) Ltd* [1966] A.C. 451; *Lonsdale Thompson Ltd v Black Arrow Group plc*, above n.30; *Glengate Properties Ltd v Norwich Union Fire Insurance Society* [1996] 2 All E.R. 487 at 497; *Sumitomo Bank Ltd v Banque Bruxelles Lambert SA* [1997] 1 Lloyd's Rep. 487 at 495; *cf. Petrofina (UK) Ltd v Magnaload Ltd* [1984] Q.B. 127 (head contractor insuring for the benefit of himself and sub-contractors); contrast *Stone Vickers Ltd v Appledore Ferguson Shipbuilders Ltd* [1992] 2 Lloyd's Rep. 578, where the main contractors' insurance did not cover the subcontractors since the main contractors had no authority or intention to contract on behalf of the subcontractors; for similar reasoning, see *Colonia Versicherung AG v Amoco Oil Co* [1997] 1 Lloyd's Rep. 261 at 270–272; and see *Simon Container Machinery Ltd v Emba Machinery AB* [1998] 2 Lloyd's Rep. 428, at 437.

[32] Marine Insurance Act 1906, s.14(2).

[33] Law of Property Act 1925, s.47; reversing the rule in *Rayner v Preston* (1881) 18 Ch.D. 1; the section applies to all kinds of "property." For the definition of "property" see *ibid.* s.205(1) (xx). In contracts for the sale of land, s.47 appears to be commonly excluded: see Law Com. No. 191 para.3.2. *cf.* also Law of Property Act 1925, s.108 as to the application of insurance money where property is mortgaged.

on being paid the appropriate premiums, to provide indemnity insurance to solicitors. It has been held that the scheme gives rise to reciprocal rights and duties between the insurers and solicitors.[34] This result follows "by virtue of public law, not the ordinary English private law of contract"[35]; for in operating the scheme the Society acts, not in its private capacity as a professional association, but in its public capacity as a body one of whose functions is to protect members of the public against loss which they may suffer from dealings with solicitors.

(f) THIRD PARTIES' RIGHTS AGAINST INSURERS. Our concern here is not with insurance contracts which purport to confer benefits on third parties, but with those which insure the policy-holder against liability to third parties. By statute[36] such a third party may in certain circumstances[37] enforce the rights of the insured under the policy by proceeding directly against the insurance company. In the case of victims of motor accidents, these rights are supplemented by an agreement originally made between the Motor Insurers' Bureau and the Minister of Transport.[38] This provides that the Bureau will pay any judgment (to the extent to which it remains unsatisfied) "in respect of any liability which is required to be covered by a policy of insurance" under the statutory scheme of compulsory motor insurance. A person who is injured in a road accident cannot technically enforce the agreement as he is not a party to it. But the agreement may be specifically enforced by the Minister,[39] and, although "the foundations in jurisprudence" of the agreement "are better not questioned",[40] the Bureau's practice is

---

[34] *Swain v Law Society* [1983] 1 A.C. 598.

[35] *ibid.* at 611.

[36] Third Parties (Rights Against Insurers) Act 1930, s.1; Road Traffic Act 1988, ss.151–153, as amended by Road Traffic Act, s.48 and Sch.4, para.66 and s.83 and Sch.8 (giving rights to the third party against the insurer in respect of liability covered by the terms of the policy even though the insurer is entitled to avoid liability under it for breach of condition by the insured: see *Motor & General Insurance Co Ltd v Pavy* [1994] 1 Lloyd's Rep. 607, decided under similar, though not identical, legislation in force in Trinidad and Tobago); Michel, [1987] L.M.C.L.Q. 228; and see Policyholders Protection Act 1975, s.7 for the rights of such persons if the company is in liquidation.

[37] *Normid Housing Association v R John Ralphs* [1989] 1 Lloyd's Rep. 265; *Bradley v Eagle Star Insurance Co Ltd* [1989] A.C. 957 (third party unable to sue insurer where insured had gone into liquidation before liability was established); *Duncan Stevenson MacMillan v A W Knott Becker Scott Ltd* [1990] 1 Lloyd's Rep. 98; *Lefevre v White* [1990] 1 Lloyd's Rep. 569 at 577; *The Fanti and the Padre Island* [1991] 2 A.C. 1; *Cox v Bankside* [1995] 2 Lloyd's Rep. 437 at 457, 466–467; *Total Graphics Ltd v AGF Insurance Ltd* [1997] 1 Lloyd's Rep. 599 at 606; *Schiffahrtsgesellschaft Detlev von Appen GmbH v Alpine Intertrading GmbH* [1997] 2 Lloyd's Rep. 279 at 285; *cf. Eagle Star Insurance Co Ltd v Provincial Insurance plc* [1994] 1 A.C. 130, where the issue of contribution between insurers arose under legislation in force in the Bahamas giving third parties direct rights against insurers; *Nigel Upchurch Associates v Aldridge Estates Investment Co Ltd* [1993] 1 Lloyd's Rep. 53; (third party held to have no right against insurer until the latter's liability to insured had been established); *Charlton v Fisher* [2001] EWCA Civ 112; [2002] Q.B. 578 at [96] (third party has no claim under the 1930 Act where the insured's claim against the insurer would fail on grounds of public policy since "as statutory assignee under the 1930 Act the third party simply stands in the shoes of the insured"). This topic is not covered by the Contracts (Rights of Third Parties) Act 1999: see Law Com. No. 242, §12.21. For proposals for reform (relating largely to the procedure for enforcing such claims), see Law Com. Report No.272 (2001).

[38] For the text of the agreement and of a supplementary agreement, see *Hardy v MIB* [1964] 2 Q.B. 745 at 770; *White v London Transport* [1971] 2 Q.B. 721 at 729 *Evans v MIB*, The Times, November 10, 1997. The current agreements are published by HMSO under the titles *Motor Insurers' Bureau (Compensation of Victims of Untraced Drivers)* (1972) and *Motor Insurers' Bureau (Compensation of Victims of Uninsured Drivers)* (1988). For the interpretation of the 1998 agreement, see *White v White* [2001] UKHL 9; [2001] 1 W.L.R. 481; and see *ibid.* at [7] for a further "supplemental agreement" of August 13, 1999.

[39] See *Gurtner v Circuit* [1968] 2 Q.B. 587.

[40] *Gardner v Moore* [1984] A.C. 548 at 556.

not to rely on the doctrine of privity as a defence to claims by the injured parties themselves.[41]

(2) Law of Property Act 1925, s.56[42]

At common law a person could not take an immediate interest in property, or the benefit of any covenant, under an indenture purporting to be *inter partes*, unless he was named as a party to the indenture.[43] An indenture was a deed whose top was indented to match with a counterpart, as a precaution against fraud. It was said to be "*inter partes*" if it was expressed to be "between A of the first part, B of the second part . . . " etc. The common law rule did not apply to deeds poll (deeds with a smooth top) or to indentures not *inter partes*.[44] In the case of such deeds the grantee never had to be named *as a party*; and it was eventually settled that he need not be named at all, so long as he was sufficiently designated.[45] Deeds no longer have to be indented for any purposes,[46] but the law still distinguishes between deeds *inter partes* and other deeds and the distinction seems to retain some practical significance.[47]

The common law rule with regard to indentures *inter partes* was modified by s.5 of the Real Property Act 1845,[48] which was in turn replaced by s.56(1) of the Law of Property Act 1925, which provides: "A person may take an immediate or other interest in land or other property, or the benefit of any condition, right of entry, covenant or agreement over or respecting land or other property, although he may not be named as a party to the conveyance or other instrument". The 1925 Act further defines "property" to include "any thing in action".[49] In *Beswick v Beswick* Lord Denning M.R. and Danckwerts L.J. held that a promise in writing by A to B to pay a sum of money to C would, by virtue of this definition of "property", be within s.56(1) and so give C a right to sue A.[50] In their view, s.56(1) was a "clear" provision to this effect, doing away with the doctrine of privity where the contract is written. But the words "although he may not be *named as*

---

[41] *Persson v London County Buses* [1974] 1 W.L.R. 569; and see *Hardy v MIB*, above, n.38, at 757; *Randall v MIB* [1968] 1 W.L.R. 1900; *Porter v Addo* [1978] R.T.R. 503; for enforceability of the agreement by third parties, see also *Charlton v Fisher* [2001] EWCA Civ 112; [2002] Q.B. 578 at [25], [82]. As the Bureau is, therefore, interested in the outcome of litigation between the injured party and the driver, it may, at the court's discretion, be added as a party to such litigation: see *Gurtner v Circuit* [1968] 2 Q.B. 587; contrast *White v London Transport* [1971] 2 Q.B. 721. Notice of proceedings against the driver must be served on the Bureau in respect of claims against it: *Cambridge v Callaghan*, *The Times*, March 21, 1997.

[42] Elliot, 20 Conv. 43, 114; Andrews, 23 Conv. 179; Wade [1964] C.L.J. 66; Furmston, 23 M.L.R. 380–385; Ellinger, 26 M.L.R. 396; all these comments on s.56(1) must now be read in the light of the decision of the House of Lords, in *Beswick v Beswick* [1968] A.C. 58.

[43] *Scudamore v Vandenstene* (1587) 2 Colnst. 673; *Storer v Gordon* (1814) 3 M. & S. 308; *Berkeley v Hardy* (1826) 5 B. & C. 355; *Southampton v Brown* (1827) 6 B. & C. 718; *Gardner v Lachlan* (1836) 8 Sim. 123.

[44] *Cooker v Child* (1673) 2 Lev. 74; *Chelsea & Waltham Green Building Soc v Armstrong* [1951] Ch. 853.

[45] *Sunderland Marine Insurance Co v Kearney* (1851) 16 Q.B. 925; qualifying *Green v Horn* (1694) 1 Salk. 197. The old rule relating to indentures *inter partes* appears still to apply to deeds *inter partes* in cases falling outside s.56(1) of the Law of Property Act 1925; see *Beswick v Beswick* [1968] A.C. 58 at 104.

[46] Law of Property Act 1925, s.56(2).

[47] See n.45, above.

[48] Replacing s.11 of the Land Transfer Act 1844, which was not restricted to real property. For the history of this change, see Davidson's *Concise Precedents in Conveyancing* (2nd ed., 1845), pp.10 *et seq.*; Treitel, 30 M.L.R. 687, 688–689. S.5 of the 1845 Act applied only to real property: *Beswick v Beswick* [1968] A.C. 58, 87, 104, and, in the case of covenants, to those which run with the land: *Forster v Elvett Colliery Co Ltd* [1908] 1 K.B. 629 (in the House of Lords, Lord Macnaghten reserved the point: *Dyson v Forster* [1909] A.C. 98 at 102); *Grant v Edmonton* [1931] 1 Ch. 1.

[49] s.205(1)(xx).

[50] [1966] Ch. 538; see also *Smith and Snipes Hall Farm Ltd v River Douglas Catchment Board Ltd* [1949] 2 K.B. 500 and *Drive Yourself Hire Co (London) Ltd v Strutt* [1954] 1 Q.B. 250; criticised on this point by Wade [1954] C.L.J. 66.

a party" are far from clear. They could refer to a number of things: to a party who is not named but only described; to a person who is named but not as a party; and to a person who is neither named nor a party[51] (*e.g.* where A promises B to pay a pension "to any of your employees who is injured at work"). The House of Lords in *Beswick v Beswick* rejected the view of Lord Denning M.R. and Danckwerts L.J., principally on the ground that the definition of "property" in the Act was stated to apply "unless the context otherwise requires". The context in s.56(1) did otherwise require, since s.56(1) was part of a consolidating Act and was designed to reproduce s.5 of the 1845 Act, which admittedly did not have the wide effect suggested for s.56(1).[52] There was, moreover, nothing in the legislative history of s.56(1) to support the view that the subsection was intended to abolish the doctrine of privity in relation to written contracts.[53] Indeed, the legislative history gives some support to the view that no such change was intended.[54]

S.56(1) therefore does not apply to a bare promise in writing by A to B to pay a sum of money to C; and the correctness of a number of previous decisions to this effect[55] is reaffirmed by *Beswick v Beswick*. But the question, to what other cases the subsection does apply, remains one of great difficulty. There is support in *Beswick v Beswick* for four limitations on its scope: namely, that it applies only (1) to real property[56] (2) to covenants running with the land[57]; (3) to cases where the instrument is not merely for the benefit of the third party but purports to contain a grant to or covenant with him[58]; and (4) to deeds strictly *inter partes*.[59] But there is no clear majority in the speeches in favour of all, some or even one of these limitations, so that the scope of the subsection remains obscure. There appear to be only three reported cases in which s.56(1) has actually been applied. The first[60] is consistent with all four of the above limitations, the second[61] is consistent only with the last two and it is not clear whether the third is consistent with any of them.[62] The third limitation was regarded as the operative one in both these cases and also in a number of others in which the courts have refused to apply the subsection.[63] It seems probable that the subsection will be applied only where this limitation

---

[51] *cf.* the side-note to s.56: "Persons taking who are not parties."

[52] [1968] A.C. 58 at 77, 81, 87.

[53] [1968] A.C. 58 at 77, 81, 104; *cf.* Treitel, 29 M.L.R. 657, 661.

[54] Before the passing of the 1925 Act, a number of reforming measures had been enacted. None of these contained any provision from which the present s.56(1) is derived. In introducing one of the reforming Bills, which were consolidated, together with earlier Acts, in the 1925 property legislation, Lord Haldane L.C. said that no Parliamentary time would be needed for the consolidating Bills "because they do not change what will then be the law": (1924) 59 H.L. Deb. 125. In view of his speech in *Dunlop Pneumatic Type Co Ltd v Selfridge & Co Ltd* [1915] A.C. 847 at 853, Lord Haldane could hardly have taken this view of the 1925 legislation if the effect of s.56(1) had been to reverse (for written contracts) the "fundamental" principle that "only a person who is a party to a contract can sue on it".

[55] *Re Sinclair's Life Policy* [1938] Ch. 799 (criticised on another ground in *Beswick v Beswick* [1968] A.C. 58 at 90); *Re Foster* [1938] 3 All E.R. 357; *Re Miller's Agreement* [1947] Ch. 615.

[56] See [1968] A.C. 87 and 76; contrast p.105. See also *Southern Water Authority v Carey* [1985] 2 All E.R. 1077 at 1083.

[57] See [1968] A.C. 58 at 87; contrast 77, 93, 105.

[58] See [1968] A.C. 58 at 94, 106; *cf.* 74–75 and 87.

[59] See [1968] A.C. 58 at 107 and 94; *cf.* 76–77. See above, p.669.

[60] *Re Ecclesiastical Commissioners' Conveyance* [1936] Ch. 430; *cf. Re Windle* [1975] 1 W.L.R. 1628 at 1631 (not affected on this point by doubts expressed in *Re Kumar* [1993] 1 W.L.R. 224, 235).

[61] *Stromdale and Ball Ltd v Burden* [1952] Ch. 223.

[62] *OTV Birwelco Ltd v Technical & General Guarantee Co Ltd* [2002] EWHC 2240; [2002] 4 All E.R. 686 at [12]; the statement of facts leaves the point in doubt.

[63] See the cases cited in n.55, above; *White v Bijou Mansions* [1937] Ch. 610, affirmed [1938] Ch. 351; *Lyus v Prowsa Developments Ltd* [1982] 1 W.L.R. 1044 at 1049; *Amsprop Trading Ltd v Harris Distribution Ltd* [1997] 1 W.L.R. 1025. This is a more stringent requirement than those contained in Contracts (Rights of Third Parties) Act 1999, s.1(1) and (2), above, pp.651–654.

is satisfied. There is also much to be said on historical grounds for the fourth limitation, which is consistent with all the cases, though it does not form a ground of decision in any of them. The scope of s.56(1) is further limited by a rule which it was not necessary to consider in *Beswick v Beswick*, namely, that a person cannot take the benefit of a covenant under the subsection unless he, or his predecessor in title, was in existence[64] and identifiable in accordance with the terms of the instrument at the time when it was made.[65]

---

[64] *Kelsey v Dodd* (1883) 52 L.J.Ch. 34; *Westhoughton Urban DC v Wigan Coal Co* [1919] 1 Ch. 159 (both these cases were decided under s.5 of the Real Property Act 1845, but the position under s.56(1) of the 1925 Act seems to be the same); *White v Bijou Mansions*, above.

[65] There is no such requirement under the Contracts (Rights of Third Parties) Act 1999: see s.1(3), above, p.655.

CHAPTER SIXTEEN

ASSIGNMENT[1]

THE benefit of a contract may be transferred to a third party by a process called assignment. This is a transaction between the person entitled to the benefit of the contract (called the creditor or assignor) and the third party (called the assignee) as a result of which the assignee becomes entitled to sue the person liable under the contract (called the debtor). The debtor is not a party to the transaction and his consent is not necessary for its validity.

SECTION 1. AT COMMON LAW

The common law refused to give effect to assignments of "choses in action", that is, of rights which could be asserted only by bringing an action and not by taking possession of a physical thing. The early lawyers found it hard to think of a transfer of something intangible like a contractual right.[2] Later the rule was based on the fear that assignments of choses in action might lead to maintenance,[3] that is, to "intermeddling in litigation in which the intermeddler has no concern."[4] Such conduct was formerly a crime and a tort.[5]

Exceptionally, debts due to and by the Crown[6] and negotiable instruments[7] could be assigned at law. The common law also recognised that assignments were effective in equity: thus a promise by the assignee not to sue the debtor was good consideration for a promise by the debtor to pay the assignee.[8] And although an assignment did not at law entitle the assignee to sue the debtor, it might be binding as a contract between assignor and assignee, for breach of which the assignee could recover damages.[9]

The common law did give effect to three kinds of transactions which to some extent did the work of assignment.

---

[1] Marshall, *The Assignment of Choses in Action*; Bailey, 47 L.Q.R. 526; 48 L.Q.R. 248, 547.

[2] Pollock and Maitland, *History of English Law*, Vol.II, p.226.

[3] *Johnson v Collings* (1880) 1 East 98; *Wilson v Coupland* (1821) 5 B. & Ald. 228, 232; *Liversidge v Broadbent* (1859) 4 H. & N. 603; *Fitzroy v Cave* [1905] 2 K.B. 364, 372.

[4] *Neville v London Express Newspaper Ltd* [1919] A.C. 368, 385; *Re Oasis Merchandising Services* [1998] Ch. 170 at 174.

[5] Criminal and tortious liability for maintenance and champerty (bargaining for a share in the proceeds of the litigation) were abolished by Criminal Law Act 1967, ss.13(1) and 14(1), but under s.14(2) this has (in general) no effect on the validity of contracts: see p.430, above. For possible effects on the validity of certain assignments, see below, pp.695 *et seq.*

[6] *Miles v Williams* (1714) 1 P.Wms. 249 at 259.

[7] *Ryall v Rowles* (1750) 1 Ves.Sen. 348; below, p.691.

[8] *Forth v Stanton* (1681) 1 Wms.Saund. 210; *cf. Moulsdale v Birchall* (1772) 2 W.Bl. 820; *Master v Miller* (1791) 4 T.R. 320, 341 (for another explanation, see *Israel v Douglas* (1789) 1 H.Bl. 239). For other instances of recognition of assignment at common law, see *Winch v Keely* (1787) 1 T.R. 619; *Legh v Legh* (1799) 1 B. & P. 447; *Carpenter v Marnell* (1802) 3 B. & P. 40; *Crowfoot v Gurney* (1832) 9 Bing. 372.

[9] *Gerrard v Lewis* (1867) L.R. 2 C.P. 305.

1. Novation[10]

Novation is a contract between debtor, creditor and a third party that the debt owed by the debtor shall henceforth be owed to the third party. This is not assignment because the consent of all three parties,[11] including that of the debtor, is necessary, and because the original debt is not, strictly, transferred. The third party's right against the debtor is based on the new contract between him and debtor,[12] the consideration for the debtor's promise typically taking the form of some benefit (such as a payment of money) provided by the third party to the original creditor.[13] As the "third party" is thus a party to the tripartite contract of novation, it follows that he would not acquire any rights under the Contracts (Rights of Third Parties) Act 1999.[14] At common law, the third party's claim under the novation would fail if no consideration moved from him for the debtor's promise to pay him[15]; and this position is probably not affected by the 1999 Act.[16]

2. Acknowledgment[17]

If a creditor asks his debtor to pay a third party, and the debtor agrees to do so, and notifies the third party of his agreement, then the third party may be entitled to sue the debtor.[18] It was for long doubtful whether such a transaction had to be supported by consideration. In the second half of the nineteenth century, the following distinction was established: that consideration was, in general, necessary; but that it was not necessary where the debtor actually had in his hands (*e.g.* as banker) a fund belonging to the creditor.[19] But this distinction, which seems to have little merit, was disregarded in the later case of *Shamia v Joory*.[20] The defendant owed some £1,200 to his agent Youssuf, who asked him to pay £500 of this sum to the claimant, Youssuf's brother. The defendant agreed to do so and notified the claimant of this agreement. It was held that the claimant could sue the defendant for the £500, though no consideration moved from him. If this decision is right,[21] acknowledgment is in one respect more advantageous than assignment, since certain types of assignment have to be supported by consideration.[22] On facts such as those of *Shamia v Joory*, it is probable that the defendant's promise to Youssuf to pay the £500 to the claimant could now be enforced by the claimant against the defendant by virtue of the Contracts (Right of Third Parties) Act

---

[10] Ames, *Lectures*, p.298.

[11] See *The Aktion* [1987] 1 Lloyd's Rep. 283 at 309.

[12] *e.g. Rasbora Ltd v JCL Marine Ltd* [1977] 1 Lloyd's Rep. 645.

[13] Consideration need not move to the promisor (the original debtor): above, p.81.

[14] Rights are conferred by virtue of this Act only on "a person who is *not* a party" to the contract (s.1(1)).

[15] *Tatlock v Harris* (1789) 3 T.R. 174 at 180; *Cuxon v Chadley* (1824) 3 B. & C. 591; *Wharton v Walker* (1825) 4 B. & C. 163.

[16] A third party can make a claim under the Act even though he provided no consideration (above, p.657); but in the case put in the text the "third party" is a person to whom a promise has been made and the Act does not make it clear whether, if that promise is not enforceable, the person to whom it was made is to be regarded as a promisee or as a third party. *Prime facie* "promisee" in the Act means a "party to the contract by whom the term is enforceable against the promisor" (s.1(7)); but the Act also envisages the possibility of a person's being the promisee even though the term is *not* so enforceable because a "defence" is available to the promisor (s.3(2)(b)).

[17] Davies, 75 L.Q.R. 220; *cf.* Yates, 41 Conv. 49.

[18] *Wilson v Coupland* (1821) 5 B. & Ald. 228; *Hamilton v Spottiswoode* (1842) 4 Ex. 200; *Griffin v Weatherby* (1868) L.R. 3 Q.B. 753.

[19] *Liversidge v Broadbent* (1859) 4 H. & N. 603 at 612.

[20] [1958] 1 Q.B. 448.

[21] For criticism, see Goff and Jones, *The Law of Restitution* (5th ed.), pp.692–693.

[22] See below, pp.682 *et seq.*

1999[23]; and such a claim could succeed even though the claimant had not provided any consideration for that promise.[24]

3. Power of Attorney

A creditor can give a third party a power of attorney, authorising him to sue for the debt in the creditor's name, without any liability to account to creditor. But this device had many disadvantages from the third party's point of view. The most important of these was that a power of attorney could generally be revoked by the creditor, and was often revoked automatically by his death.[25]

SECTION 2. EQUITABLE ASSIGNMENTS

Equity regarded the common law's fear of maintenance as unrealistic[26] and took the view that choses in action were property[27] which ought, in the interest of commercial convenience, to be transferable, *e.g.* to provide security for a loan. Choses in action were therefore assignable in equity.[28] The phrase "choses in action" here refers to claims for the enforcement of a contract (*e.g.* for the sum due under it or for damages for its breach). These must be distinguished from *remedies* that are sometimes provided by law for purposes other than enforcement: for example, where a person who has entered into a transaction as a result of misrepresentation or undue influence is entitled to rescind it. It has been held that this remedy is not itself a chose in action and therefore cannot be assigned; but it is possible for the person to whom the remedy is available to agree to account to another person for any financial benefit which he may derive from its exercise.[29]

Where a chose in action is assigned, the machinery used for enforcing the assignment varied with the nature of the chose in action, which might be legal or equitable. A legal chose is one which could be sued for only in a common law court, *e.g.* a contract debt. An equitable chose is one which could be sued for only in the Court of Chancery, *e.g.* an interest in a trust fund.

1. Legal Choses

There were four reasons why equity could not simply allow the assignee of a legal chose to sue the debtor in the Court of Chancery. First, equity did not in general enforce purely legal debts. Secondly, the debtor might suffer hardship if he were later sued for a second payment at common law by the original creditor (the assignor): he would have to take separate proceedings in Chancery to make good his defence. Thirdly, the assignor might retain some interest in the debt, *e.g.* he might assign only part of it: in such a case, it was desirable to have him (as well as the assignee) before the court, so that the relative

---

[23] This would depend on whether (a) the agreement between the defendant and Youssuf had contractual force; and (b) the requirements of ss.1(1)(a) or (b) and (2) were satisfied: see above, pp.651 to 653 the reasoning in nn.13 and 16 above would not apply since the claimant was clearly not a party to the agreement between those parties nor a promisee in it.

[24] See above, p.657. Any such claim would not affect the claimant's common law rights as described in the text above: see 1999 Act, s7(1).

[25] See below, p.750.

[26] *Wright v Wright* (1750) 1 Ves.Sen. 409 at 411, ("very refined").

[27] *cf. Alloway v Phillips (Inspector of Taxes)* [1980] 1 W.L.R. 888 at 893.

[28] *Crouch v Martin* (1707) 2 Vern. 595; *Row v Dawson* (1749) 1 Ves.Sen. 331; *Ryall v Rowles* (1750) 1 Ves.Sen. 348; *Ex p. South* (1818) 3 Swanst. 392.

[29] *Investors Compensation Scheme Ltd v West Bromwich BC* [1998] 1 W.L.R. 896; for contrary dicta, see below, p.697.

rights of all the parties could be determined in a single action. Fourthly, the assignor might wish to dispute the validity of the assignment: this possibility again made it desirable to have him before the court at some stage.

These difficulties were solved by allowing the assignee to sue the debtor at common law in the name of the assignor. If the assignor refused to cooperate, equity could compel him to do so. In the resulting proceedings in Chancery, the rights of the assignor could be adequately safeguarded. Now that common law and equity are administered in the same courts, the first of the above two reasons for the original method of enforcing equitable assignments are of purely historical interest, but the third and fourth reasons may retain their force and sometimes make it important to have all the parties before the court.[30] But the action against the debtor need no longer be brought in the name of the assignor[31]: he is simply joined as co-claimant if he is willing to co-operate with the assignee, and as co-defendant if he is not,[32] *i.e.* if he wishes to dispute the validity of the assignment. The machinery of joining the assignor as a party to the action may, however, break down if the assignor has ceased to exist, *e.g.* because the assignor is a company which has been dissolved.[33] Where the assignor is a natural person and has died, it would seem to be possible for the assignee to sue, joining the assignor's legal personal representatives.

2. Equitable Choses

The assignee of an equitable chose could in his own name sue the trustee in the Court of Chancery.[34] The chose being equitable, the trustee was not exposed to the danger of a subsequent action in a different (common law) court by the assignor. It was necessary to make the assignor a party to the proceedings only if he retained some interest in the subject-matter. If he wished to dispute the validity of the assignment, he could take separate proceedings for that purpose.[35]

SECTION 3. STATUTORY ASSIGNMENTS

Certain specific contracts, such as life and marine insurance policies and bills of lading, were made assignable by statute during the nineteenth century.[36] A more general provision was made by the Judicature Act 1873, which fused the courts of common law and equity, and so made obsolete some of the reasons for the original method for enforcing equitable assignments of legal choses. There was no longer any difficulty in allowing the assignee to sue in any Division of the High Court; and a debtor who was successfully sued by the assignee no longer had to take separate proceedings if he were sued again by the assignor: he could simply rely on his payment to the assignee as a defence in the second action. Thus it was no longer necessary to have the assignor before

---

[30] *The Aiolos* [1983] 2 Lloyd's Rep. 25 at 33; *cf. Deposit Protection Board v Dalia* [1994] 2 A.C. 367 at 387, reversed on other grounds *ibid.* 391. See generally, Tolhurst, 118 L.Q.R. 98.

[31] *Weddell v J A Pearce & Major* [1988] Ch. 26 at 40.

[32] Conversely, if the assignor sues the debtor, the assignee must be joined as a party to the action: *Three Rivers DC v Bank of England*, [1996] Q.B. 292.

[33] See *M H Smith (Plant Hire) Ltd v D L Mainwaring (T/A Onshore) Ltd* [1986] 2 Lloyd's Rep. 244, where subrogation (below, p.696, n.26) was said at 246 in this respect to resemble equitable assignment.

[34] *Cator v Croydon Canal Co* (1841) 4 Y. & C. Ex. 405 at 593; *Donaldson v Donaldson* (1854) Kay 711.

[35] *e.g. Bridge v Bridge* (1852) 16 Beav. 315.

[36] *e.g.* Bills of Lading Act 1855, s.1 (now repealed and superseded by Carriage of Goods by Sea Act 1992); Policies of Assurance Act 1867 (life insurance); Marine Insurance Act 1868 (see now 1906 Act, s.50(1)).

the court unless he retained an interest in the subject-matter[37] or wished to dispute the validity of the assignment.

S.136(1) of the Law of Property Act 1925 (re-enacting s.25(6) of the Judicature Act 1873), therefore provides that an absolute assignment by writing under the hand of the assignor (not purporting to be by way of charge only) of any debt or other legal thing in action, of which express notice in writing has been given to the debtor or trustee, is effectual in law to pass the legal right to the debt or thing in action to the assignee. The effect of such an assignment is to enable the assignee to sue the debtor in his own name, and to sue alone, *i.e.*, without joining the assignor as a party to the action. The subsection finally makes provision for enabling the assignor to dispute the validity of the assignment; if he does so, the debtor can drop out of the proceedings and leave the dispute to be fought out between assignor and assignee.

1. Absolute Assignment

Under s.136(1), the assignee can sue alone only if the assignment is *absolute*; this requirement excludes cases in which the assignor retains an interest in the subject-matter so that it is still desirable to have him before the court. Absolute assignments are for this purpose contrasted with the following:

(1) Assignments by way of charge

In *Durham Bros v Robertson*[38] a builder to whom £1,080 was due under a building contract borrowed money and assigned the £1,080 to the lender as security for the loan "until the money [lent] . . . be repaid." This was held to be an assignment by way of charge. The builder had not assigned the £1,080 absolutely to the lender; he had only charged that sum with the repayment of the money he had borrowed. But an assignment may be absolute although it is made by way of mortgage, and does not transfer the subject-matter out-and-out. Thus in *Tancred v Delagoa Bay, etc., Ry*[39] a debt was assigned as security for a loan of money, with the proviso that, if the assignor repaid the loan, the debt should be reassigned to him. This was held to be an absolute assignment.

The distinction between these two cases can best be understood by taking the point of view of the debtor, and assuming that he wants to pay the debt. In *Tancred's* case, he can find out from documents in his own possession whether he ought to pay the assignor or the assignee; for even if the debt is reassigned to the assignor, the debtor can safely pay the assignee until he gets notice of the reassignment.[40] But in *Durham Bros. v Robertson* the debtor does not know whether to pay the assignee until it is settled whether the assignor still owes anything to the assignee. The debtor cannot find this out from documents in his own possession: he would have to investigate the state of accounts between the assignor and assignee. Similarly, if the assignee sued the debtor, the court could not determine whom the debtor should pay without investigating the state of accounts between assignor and assignee; and it cannot satisfactorily do this if the

---

[37] *The Mount I* [2001] EWCA Civ 68; [2001] 1 Lloyd's Rep. 597, at [60].

[38] [1898] 1 Q.B. 765; *cf. Jones v Humphreys* [1902] 1 K.B. 10; *Mercantile Bank of London Ltd v Evans* [1899] 2 Q.B. 613; *Colonial Mutual General Insurance Co v ANZ Banking Group (New Zealand)* [1995] 1 W.L.R. 1140 at 1144.

[39] (1889) 23 Q.B.D. 239; *cf. Hughes v Pump House Hotel Co Ltd* [1902] 2 K.B. 190; *The Cebu* [1983] Q.B. 1005 at 1016 (where nothing seems to have turned on the distinction between equitable and statutory assignments).

[40] See below, p.682.

assignor is not before the court. For similar reasons, an assignment of a debt to a bank was held to be by way of charge only where it was expressed to be made as security for a loan from the bank and was to become operative only on the assignor's failing to perform his obligations under the original contract which had given rise to the debt or under the loan agreement with the bank.[41]

In *Bank of Liverpool v Holland*[42] a creditor assigned a debt of £285 to a bank "to hold the same absolutely. And it is hereby agreed and declared that the amount recoverable by these presents shall not at any time exceed" £150. This was held to be an absolute assignment of the whole debt, with the proviso that, if the bank recovered more than £150, it was to hold the excess on trust for the assignor. This part of the arrangement did not concern the debtor: he could get a good discharge by paying the bank at any time.

(2) Assignments of part of a debt

An assignment of part of a debt (*e.g.* of £500 out of the £1,000 which X owes me; or of half of what X owes me) is not absolute.[43] In such a case a debtor who wants to pay may know perfectly well how much to pay to whom. But to hold such an assignment absolute might cause hardship to a debtor who wished to dispute the debt. If the assignment were absolute, the assignee would be able to sue alone. In this action, the debtor might be able to show that there was no debt. But he would have to prove this over again if he were later sued by the assignor for the balance of the alleged debt. And if the assignor split the debt up into a large number of small parts, the debtor might have to defend many actions arising out of the same transaction. Hence it is necessary, for the protection of the debtor, to have all the interested parties before the court. For the same reason, an assign*or* of part of a debt cannot sue for the part he retains without joining the assignee as a party to the action.[44]

The above reasoning does not apply to an assignment of the *balance* of a debt. Suppose A owes B £100 and pays off £25 of the debt. An assignment of the remaining £75 would be absolute since it would be an assignment of B's entire remaining interest in the debt.[45]

(3) Conditional assignments

S.136(1) of the Law of Property Act 1925 contrasts absolute assignments with assignments by way of charge; but some judgments also distinguish between absolute and conditional assignments.[46] Many assignments by way of charge are, in fact, assignments subject to the condition subsequent that they will cease to have effect when the assignor pays off the debt which he owes to the assignee. Assignments which are subject to some

---

[41] *The Halcyon The Great* [1984] 1 Lloyd's Rep. 283.

[42] (1926) 43 T.L.R. 29; *cf. Comfort v Betts* [1891] 1 Q.B. 737; *Fitzroy v Cave* [1905] 2 K.B. 364; *Ramsay v Hartley* [1977] 1 W.L.R. 686.

[43] *Forster v Baker* [1910] 2 K.B. 636; *Re Steel Wing Co* [1921] 1 Ch. 349; *Williams v Atlantic Assurance Co Ltd* [1933] 1 K.B. 81 at 100 (the actual decision seems to turn on Marine Insurance Act 1906, s.50(2)); *Deposit Protection Board v Dalia* [1994] 2 A.C. 367 at 392; *The Mount I* [2001] EWCA Civ 68; [2001] 1 Lloyd's Rep. 587, at [74].

[44] *Walter & Sullivan Ltd v J. Murphy & Sons Ltd* [1955] 2 Q.B. 584.

[45] *e.g. Harding v Harding* (1886) 17 Q.B.D. 442.

[46] *e.g. Durham Bros v Robertson* [1898] 1 Q.B. 765 at 773; *cf. The Balder London* [1980] 2 Lloyd's Rep. 489 at 495.

other condition (whether precedent or subsequent) should be treated in the same way.[47] Whatever the condition may be, the assignor retains a contingent interest in the debt, and is thus a desirable party to an action to recover it. Suppose that A assigns rent due under a lease "to my daughter until she marries". The assignment should not be absolute since it is desirable that A should be a party to an action brought by his daughter against the tenant for rent. If the daughter could sue alone, she might be able to prove that she was unmarried, and so entitled to the rent. But this would not prevent A, in a subsequent action against the tenant, from proving that the court in the first action had made a mistake in finding that the daughter was unmarried, so that the tenant would have to pay over again. What matters to the tenant is not whether the daughter is married but that the question should be decided, one way or the other, so as to bind both A and the daughter.[48]

2. Debt or Other Legal Thing in Action

A "debt" in s.136(1) is a sum certain due under contract or otherwise.[49] The phrase "other legal thing in action" has been broadly interpreted: it means any "debt or right which the common law looks on as not assignable by reason of its being a chose in action, but which a court of equity deals with as being assignable".[50] The phrase includes equitable choses in action,[51] though this point is of little practical importance since an assignment of an equitable chose is no more effective under the statute than it is in equity. The phrase also includes a debt not yet due but accruing due,[52] and the benefit of an obligation to do something other than to pay cash,[53] or of one to forbear from doing something.[54] It does not include choses in action which can be transferred *only*[55] by complying with some other statute; thus shares in a company cannot be assigned by statutory assignment under s.136, but only in the manner prescribed by the articles of association of the company.[56]

SECTION 4. GENERAL REQUIREMENTS

1. Formalities

A statutory assignment must be "by writing under the hand of the assignor". An assignment which for some reason fails to take effect as a statutory assignment may still be a good equitable assignment. Thus although an oral assignment cannot take effect

---

[47] e.g. *The Halcyon The Great* [1984] 1 Lloyd's Rep. 283; *Herkules Piling v Tilbury Construction* (1992) 61 Build.L.R. 107 at 117.

[48] cf. *The Aiolos* [1983] 2 Lloyd's Rep. 25 at 33.

[49] e.g. under statute: *Dawson v Great Northern & City Ry* [1905] 1 K.B. 260.

[50] *Torkington v Magee* [1902] 2 K.B. 427 at 430 (actual decision reversed on another ground: [1903] 1 K.B. 644); cf. *King v Victoria Insurance Co* [1896] A.C. 250 at 254; *Manchester Brewery v Coombs* [1901] 2 Ch. 608 at 619.

[51] *Re Pain* [1919] 1 Ch. 38 at 44.

[52] *Brice v Bannister* (1878) 3 Q.B.D. 569 at 574; *Walker v Bradford Old Bank* (1884) 12 Q.B.D. 511; *Re Green* [1979] 1 W.L.R. 1211 at 1219–1224. Contrast *Law v Coburn* [1972] 1 W.L.R. 1238, where the date on which the debt became due was crucial under the relevant legislation.

[53] *Torkington v Magee*, above.

[54] *Jacoby v Whitmore* (1883) 49 L.T. 335.

[55] s.136 may apply to a policy of marine insurance though such a policy is *also* assignable under Marine Insurance Act 1906, s.50: see *The Mount I* [2001] EWCA Civ 68; [2001] 1 Lloyd's Rep. 597, at [74].

[56] Companies Act 1985, s.182(1).

under the statute, it may be valid in equity.[57] The statute merely provides an alternative method of making assignments; it does not destroy the earlier method.

A disposition of an equitable interest "must be in writing signed by the person disposing of the same or by his agent thereunto lawfully authorised".[58] This rule is mandatory: an oral assignment of an equitable chose is therefore void.[59]

As a general rule, writing is not necessary for an equitable assignment of a legal chose in action. But a contract may provide that rights under it shall be assigned only by use of a specified form, such as writing. An attempt to assign such rights without using the stipulated form is probably not effective as an assignment, though it may amount to a contract to assign.[60]

For the protection of the assignor's creditors, provision has been made by various statutes for the registration of certain assignments. S.344 of the Insolvency Act 1986,[61] for example, requires general assignments of book debts (or any class of them) made by a person engaged in any business to be registered; if they are not registered they are void as against the trustee in bankruptcy to the extent specified in the section.

2. Intention to Assign

Although assignments must sometimes be in writing, no particular form of words has to be used to effect an assignment. The document need not on its face purport to be an assignment. As Lord Macnaghten said in *William Brandt's Sons & Co v Dunlop Rubber Co*[62] "An equitable assignment does not always take that form. It may be addressed to the debtor. It may be couched in the language of command. It may be a courteous request. It may assume the form of mere permission. The language is immaterial if the meaning is plain. All that is necessary is that the debtor should be given to understand that the debt has been made over by the creditor to some third person."[63] An assignment is not itself a contract between assignor and debtor: its legal nature is that of a direction amounting to the transfer of a right. It follows that an assignment does not confer rights on the assignee, under the Contracts (Rights of Third Parties) Act 1999.[64]

A creditor does not necessarily assign a debt by asking his debtor to pay a third party. The request may be intended only as a mandate (or instruction) to the debtor to pay the third party.[65] Such a mandate does not give the third party any rights against the debtor, and can be revoked by the creditor. Similarly, a person who draws a cheque on his bank

---

[57] *cf.* below, pp.682, 687–688.

[58] Law of Property Act 1925, s.53(1)(c), formerly Statute of Frauds 1677, s.9. The enactment applies to all "dispositions," whether they are assignments or not. But it does not apply to a transfer of the legal title which is intended to operate as a transfer of the equitable interest, even though before the transfer the legal title and the equitable interest were in different hands; *Vandervell v IRC* [1967] 2 A.C. 291; Strauss, 30 M.L.R. 461; Green, 47 M.L.R. 385. Nor does it apply to implied or constructive trusts: see s.53(2) and *Neville v Wilson* [1997] Ch. 144. As to joinder of documents, see above, pp.184–185.

[59] *Oughtred v IRC* [1960] A.C. 206; *cf. Grey v IRC* [1960] A.C. 1.

[60] *cf.* below, p.682.

[61] See also Companies Act 1985, ss.395, 396.

[62] [1905] A.C. 454.

[63] At 462. *cf.* also *Spellman v Spellman* [1961] 1 W.L.R. 921; *Palmer v Carey* [1926] A.C. 703; *The Kelo* [1985] 2 Lloyd's Rep. 85; *Re Marwalt* [1992] BCC 32 at 37; *Colonial Mutual General Insurance Co Ltd v ANZ Banking Group (New Zealand) Ltd* [1995] 1 W.L.R. 1140; and see *Swiss Bank Corp v Lloyd's Bank Ltd* [1982] A.C. 584 at 613 and *Kijowski v New Capital Properties* (1990) 15 Con.L.R. 1 (where there was no assignment).

[64] See above, pp.651 *et seq.*

[65] *Ex p. Hall* (1878) 10 Ch.D. 615; *cf. Re Williams* [1917] 1 Ch. 1; *Timpson's Executors v Yerbury* [1936] 1 K.B. 645; *Dalton v IRC* [1958] T.R. 45. For a similar distinction between a contract for the benefit of a third party and a mandate to pay a third party, see above, p.604.

in favour of a third person does not thereby assign part of his bank balance.[66] The bank is not liable to the third party, though if it fails to pay him it may be liable in damages to its own customer. The position is the same where the customer gives a standing order or direct debit instruction to his bank in favour of the third party.[67]

3. Communication to Assignee

An assignment has no effect unless it is communicated[68] to the assignee by the assignor, or by someone with his authority[69]; or unless it is made in pursuance of a prior agreement between assignor and assignee. The reason for the requirement is not immediately obvious since a person can have property transferred to him without his knowledge, subject to a right to repudiate the transfer when he becomes aware of it.[70] One possible reason for the requirement is that communication to the assignee is evidence of intention to assign[71]; but such an intention could equally well be proved by other evidence. Alternatively, communication to the assignee may be regarded as the equivalent of the delivery which is necessary to perfect a gift of a chattel made otherwise than by deed.[72] A final possible explanation of the requirement is that it is based on the nature of assignment as a transaction between assignor and assignee.

4. Notice to Debtor

(1) How to give notice '

Notice of an equitable assignment may be oral,[73] but if the chose assigned is equitable, oral notice will seldom be effective between successive assignees.[74] Notice of a statutory assignment under s.136 of the Law of Property Act 1925 must be in writing.[75] It need not be given by the assignor, nor at the time of the assignment: it may be given by the assignee and is effective so long as it is given before action brought.[76] There must, however, be a *notice* of assignment given by assignor or assignee: it is not enough to show that the debtor came to know of the assignment in some other way: *e.g.* as a result of discovery in legal or arbitral proceedings.[77] No particular form of words is necessary[78]; but the notice must clearly and unconditionally[79] tell the debtor to pay a third party *as assignee*, and not merely as agent for the creditor.[80] A notice which incorrectly states the

---

[66] Bills of Exchange Act 1882, s.53(1); *Schroeder v Central Bank of London Ltd* (1876) 34 L.T. 735; *Deposit Protection Board v Dalia* [1994] 2 A.C. 367 at 400. Thus if an account is overdrawn the bank is not concerned with the question of priorities between competing payees. See also *R. v Preddy* [1996] A.C. 815 (actual decision reversed by Theft (Amendment) Act 1996).

[67] *cf.*, in Scotland, *Mercedes-Benz Finance Ltd v Clydesdale Bank plc*, 1997 S.L.T. 905.

[68] According to *Alexander v Steinhardt, Walker & Co* [1903] 2 K.B. 208 posting is sufficient communication, but that case was doubted in *Timpson's Executors v Yerbury* [1936] 1 K.B. 645 at 657.

[69] *e.g.* by the debtor: *Burn v Carvalho* (1839) 4 My. & Cr. 690.

[70] *Standing v Bowring* (1885) 31 Ch.D. 282.

[71] See *Re Hamilton* (1921) 124 L.T. 737.

[72] See below, p.685.

[73] *Ex p. Agra Bank* (1868) L.R. 3 Ch.App. 555.

[74] See below, p.682.

[75] See above, p.622; there is no requirement of notice for an assignment under Marine Insurance Act 1906, s.50: *The Mount I* [2001] EWCA Civ 68; [2001] 1 Lloyd's Rep. 597.

[76] *Walker v Bradford Old Bank* (1884) 12 Q.B.D. 511; *Bateman v Hunt* [1904] 2 K.B. 530; *Re Westerton* [1919] 2 Ch. 104; *Holt v Heatherfield Trust Ltd* [1942] 2 K.B. 1.

[77] *Herkules Piling Ltd v Tilbury Construction Ltd* (1992) 61 Build.L.R. 107.

[78] *Smith v SS "Zigurds" Owners* [1934] A.C. 209.

[79] *The Balder London* [1980] 2 Lloyd's Rep. 489 at 495.

[80] *James Talcott Ltd v John Lewis & Co Ltd* [1940] 3 All E.R. 592.

date of the assignment or, it seems, the amount of the debt, is invalid.[81] But a notice which says nothing at all about these particulars appears to be valid, so long as it describes the debt with sufficient certainty. A notice is valid although it inaccurately states that another notice had been previously given.[82]

A notice sent through the post has been said to take effect when it is received by the debtor.[83] This is clearly right where a dispute arises between assignee and debtor, for it is unreasonable to make the debtor suffer for failing to act on a notice of which he is not yet aware. But where the dispute is between successive assignees, it is at least arguable that the first to post his notice should have priority over any other assignee who has not yet posted his notice (or otherwise communicated with the debtor) when the first notice was posted.[84]

(2) Effects of notice

Notice may affect the relative rights of assignor and assignee, of assignee and debtor, and of a number of successive assignees.

(a) BETWEEN ASSIGNOR AND ASSIGNEE. The rights of these parties may depend on whether the assignment is statutory[85]; and it can only have this character if notice is given.[86] If no notice is given, the assignment may still be effective in equity.[87] Notice to the debtor is not necessary to perfect the rights of an equitable assignee against the assignor.[88]

(b) BETWEEN ASSIGNEE AND DEBTOR. Notice is, however, necessary to perfect the title of an equitable assignee against the debtor,[89] since without such notice the debtor is entitled to assume that he remains liable to his original creditor (the assignor) and that he will get a good discharge by paying the assignor.[90] Notice may[91] also turn the assignment into a statutory assignment, in which case the debtor is liable to be sued by the assignee alone: he can no longer insist that the assignor be made a party to the action. Where the assignment is statutory, the debtor ceases, as soon as notice has been given, to be liable to the assignor[92] and becomes liable to the assignee. It is submitted that the same is true, where an assignment of part of a debt is valid in equity, to the extent of the amount assigned[93]; for it has been held that if the debtor in such a case ignores the notice and pays the assignor he is not discharged and will have to make a second payment to

---

[81] *Stanley v English Fibres Industries Ltd* (1889) 68 L.J.Q.B. 839; *W F Harrison & Co Ltd v Burke* [1956] 1 W.L.R. 419; criticised by R. E. M., 72 L.Q.R. 321.

[82] *Van Lynn Developments Ltd v Pelias Construction Ltd* [1969] 1 Q.B. 607.

[83] *Holt v Heatherfield Trust Ltd* [1942] 2 K.B. 1 at 6.

[84] *Holt v Heatherfield Trust Ltd, supra,* is not inconsistent with this suggestion since the order in which the two claimants communicated with the debtor is not stated in the report.

[85] See below, p.683.

[86] Law of Property Act 1925, s.136(1).

[87] *Holt v Heatherfield Trust Ltd* [1942] 2 K.B. 1.

[88] *Gorringe v Irwell India Rubber, etc., Works* (1886) 34 Ch.D. 128; *Re Trytel* [1952] 2 T.L.R. 32. Other aspects of the latter case are discussed in *Performing Rights Society v Rowland* [1997] 3 All E.R. 336.

[89] *Warner Bros Records Inc v Rollgreen Ltd* [1976] Q.B. 430; Kloss, 39 Conv.(N.S.) 261; *Herkules Piling v Tilbury Construction* (1992) 61 Build.L.R. 107 at 119.

[90] See *Stocks v Dobson* (1853) 4 D.M. & G. 11.

[91] *i.e.* if the assignment is in writing and is "absolute" (above, pp.676–678).

[92] *Cottage Club Estates Ltd v Woodside Estates (Amersham) Ltd* [1928] 2 Q.B. 463 at 467; *The Halcyon The Great* [1984] 1 Lloyd's Rep. 283 at 289.

[93] The contrary view was, indeed, taken by Simon Brown L.J. in *Deposit Protection Board v Dalia* [1994] 2 A.C. 367 at 382, but in a dissenting judgment; actual decision reversed but on other grounds [1994] 2 A.C. 391.

the assignee.[94] Nor, once notice of an equitable assignment had been given, could the assignor sue the debtor without joining the assignee[95]; and if he does join the assignee his claim will fail to the extent of the amount assigned.[96]

(c) BETWEEN SUCCESSIVE ASSIGNEES. A chose in action may be successively assigned by an insolvent assignor to several persons for more than it is worth. It is then necessary to decide in what order the assignees are to be paid. The rule is that successive assignments taken in good faith rank in the order in which notice is given to the debtor. Thus a later assignee may gain priority over an earlier one by giving notice first.[97] Notice of the assignment of an equitable chose should be given in writing, since oral notice of an assignment of such a chose does not give priority over later assignees in good faith and for value.[98]

SECTION 5. CONSIDERATION[99]

The question whether an assignment must be supported by consideration is one of great complexity. Two points must be made to clear the ground for the discussion. First, the dispute concerns only the relative rights of assignor and assignee. The debtor cannot refuse to pay the assignee on the ground that the assignment was gratuitous[1]; he is liable to pay the debt in any event and his only interest is to see that all possible claimants are before the court, so that he does not run the risk of having to pay twice over. So long as this possibility of prejudice to the debtor is removed by the joinder of all appropriate parties, it is only the assignor who can raise an issue as to the validity of the assignment on the ground that no consideration was given for it; indeed the only purpose of taking the point is to enable the assignor to claim payment of the debt for himself. In practice this most frequently happens if the assignor has died or become bankrupt: his representatives may, for the benefit of his estate or of his creditors, wish to challenge the validity of the assignment. Secondly, the discussion concerns all gratuitous assignments,

---

[94] *Jones v Farrell* (1857) 1 D. & J. 208; *Brice v Bannister* (1878) 3 Q.B.D. 569 (where the assignment was equitable: see *Durham Bros v Robertson* [1898] 1 Q.B. 765, 774); *Ex p. Nicholls* (1883) 22 Ch.D. 782 at 787. In view of these authorities it is hard to accept the suggestion in *Warner Bros Records Inc v Rollgreen Ltd*, [1976] Q.B. 430 at 443, 445 that an equitable assignment (of a legal chose) gives the assignee rights only against the assignor but none against the debtor. This suggestion may be true of an agreement to assign a chose in action in the future; but any historical support which may once have existed for it in the case of an actual present assignment seems to have been made obsolete by the developments outlined on pp.674–675 above. The suggestion seems, with respect, to be based on failure to distinguish between the substantive rights arising in equity out of assignments and the procedure for their enforcement: see *Three Rivers DC v Bank of England* [1996] Q.B. 292 at 315 and *ibid.* p.312, describing the requirement of joinder of the assignor to the action as "procedural and not substantive".

[95] See above, p.677.

[96] *Deposit Protection Board v Dalia*, [1994] 2 A.C. 367 at 386, 387, reversed on other grounds *ibid.* p.391.

[97] *Dearle v Hall* (1828) 3 Russ. 1; *cf. Stocks v Dobson* (1853) 4 D.M. & G. 11; *Mutual Life Assurance Society v Langley* (1886) 32 Ch.D. 460; *Ellerman Lines Ltd v Lancaster Maritime Co Ltd* [1980] 2 Lloyd's Rep. 497 at 503; *The Attika Hope* [1988] 1 Lloyd's Rep. 439 at 441; *Pfeiffer Weinkellerei-Weineinkauf GmbH & Co v Arbuthnot Factors* [1988] 1 W.L.R. 150. See also Goode, 92 L.Q.R. 554–559; Donaldson, 93 L.Q.R. 324; Goode, *ibid.* 487.

[98] Law of Property Act 1925, s.137(3).

[99] Megarry, 59 L.Q.R. 58; Hollond, *ibid.* 129; Hall [1959] C.L.J. 99; Sheridan, 33 Can. Bar Rev. 284.

[1] *Walker v Bradford Old Bank* (1884) 12 Q.B.D. 511; the question of consideration may also be relevant for revenue purposes, but the question in cases of this kind is always whether the assignor could have denied the validity of the assignment, as against the assignee: *e.g. Re Rose* [1952] Ch. 499; *Letts v IRC* [1957] 1 W.L.R. 201; *Dalton v IRC* [1958] T.R. 45. Nor is the assignor precluded from relying on want of consideration moving from the assignee by the Contracts (Rights of Third Parties) Act 1999 since in the relations between assignor and assignee the latter will not be a "third party" within subsection 1(1).

even those made by deed or for a nominal consideration.[2] The fact that an assignment is so made may make an assignor who disputes it liable in damages for breach of contract,[3] or make an agreement to assign binding contractually. But it does not, of itself, make the assignment effective as a transfer of the debt.

1. Assignments of Future Property

An assignment is the transfer of an existing right. There can be no assignment of rights which do not yet exist or belong to the assignor. Such rights are sometimes called "future property". An attempt to assign future property may operate as an agreement to assign which must be supported by consideration if it is to be binding.[4]

Money payable in the future under an existing contract is not necessarily future property, and a disposition of the right to receive such money may be an assignment and not an agreement to assign.[5] If the contingency on which the money is payable is within the control of the creditor, there is no difficulty in holding that the disposition is an assignment: thus a builder can assign instalments to become due to him under a building contract as the work progresses, for here the contingency on which the money will become due is simply his own performance.[6] If, however, the contingency is not within his control, the disposition is *prima facie* an agreement to assign: this would be the position where a person purported to assign future dividends in a company which was not under any obligation to him to declare any dividends.[7] But even where the rights of the assignor depend on a contingency outside his control, he may purport to assign *either* his present right to future income from a specified source *or* the future income itself. A disposition of the first kind may be regarded as an assignment[8] and a disposition of the second kind as an agreement to assign.[9] The question into which category it falls turns on the construction of the document purporting to effect the disposition.

2. Statutory Assignments

A statutory assignment, whether of a legal or of an equitable chose in action, is effective although it is made without consideration.[10] The reasons for this rule are discussed below.[11]

3. Equitable Assignments

The effects of a "voluntary" equitable assignment (*i.e.* one which is not supported by consideration) must be discussed historically.

---

[2] *Kekewich v Manning* (1851) 1 D.M. & G. 176 (deed); *Dillon v Coppin* (1839) 4 My. & Cr. 647 (nominal consideration).

[3] *Gerrard v Lewis* (1867) L.R. 2 C.P. 305; *Cannon v Hartley* [1949] Ch. 213.

[4] *Tailby v Official Receiver* (1888) 13 App.Cas. 523; *Glegg v Bromley* [1912] 3 K.B. 474; *Cotton v Heyl* [1930] 1 Ch. 510; *cf. Meek v Kettlewell* (1843) 1 Ph. 342; *The Annangel Glory* [1988] 1 Lloyd's Rep. 45 (actual decision reversed by Companies Act 1985, s.396(2)(g), as substituted by Companies Act 1989, s.93); *The Attika Hope* [1988] 1 Lloyd's Rep. 439 at 442 (where "*or* future chose" seems to be a misprint for "*of a* future chose"); *Wu Koon Tai v Wy Yau Loi* [1997] A.C. 179 at 189; *The Cebu (No.2)* [1993] Q.B. 1 (where it was not necessary to distinguish between an assignment and an agreement to assign); *The Mount I* [2001] EWCA Civ 68; [2001] 1 Lloyd's Rep. 597 at [80] ("for value"); *Smith v Smith* [2001] 1 W.L.R. 1937 at [11].

[5] *cf. Performing Rights Society v Rowland* [1997] 3 All E.R. 336 at 348.

[6] *e.g. Hughes v Pump House Hotel Co Ltd* [1902] 2 K.B. 190.

[7] *Norman v Commissioner of Taxation* (1963) 109 C.L.R. 9.

[8] *Shepherd v Commissioner of Taxation* [1966] A.L.R. 969; *The Mount I* [2001] EWCA Civ 68; [2001] 1 Lloyd's Rep. 597, at [80].

[9] *Williams v Commissioner of Inland Revenue* [1965] N.Z.L.R. 395.

[10] *Harding v Harding* (1886) 17 Q.B.D. 442; *Re Westerton* [1919] 2 Ch. 104.

[11] See below after n.13 and below, p.685 at n.26.

(1) Before the Judicature Act 1873

There are two main views as to the position in equity before 1873.

(a) PROCEDURAL VIEW. According to one view, the need for consideration depended on the procedure for enforcing the assignment. In *Re Westerton*[12] Sargant J. gave the following reason for holding that a statutory assignment was effective without consideration: "Apart from the Judicature Act . . . the want of consideration would have been fatal to [the assignee's] claim. Prior to the Judicature Act . . . a legal chose in action such as this debt could not be transferred at law, and the assignee of the debt could only have sued in the name of the assignor, and in the absence of consent . . . or of a binding contract by the assignor . . . the use of the assignor's name could only have been enforced by filing a bill in equity . . . and equity would not have granted that relief unless the assignment had been for valuable consideration".[13] Since a statutory assignee can now sue the debtor without the co-operation of the assignor, "there is no reason for continuing against the assignee those terms which were imposed by equity as a condition of granting relief".[14] In other words, consideration is necessary if the assignee needs the co-operation of the assignor to recover the debt, but is not necessary if the assignee does not need such co-operation. If this were true three things would follow.

First: consideration should not have been necessary in the rare cases in which the assignee could sue alone at law.[15] This assumption is to some extent supported by the rule that the voluntary transferee of a negotiable instrument could sue all the parties liable on it, except the transferor.[16] But this rule was based on commercial practice, and not on the fact that the transferee did not need the co-operation of the transferor. It is not clear whether assignments of debts due to and from the Crown had to be supported by consideration.

Secondly: consideration should not have been necessary for absolute assignments of equitable choses, since the assignee could sue without the co-operation of the assignor.[17] This assumption, too, is borne out by cases in which such assignments were upheld, though they were voluntary. But in most of these cases the fact that the assignee could sue alone is not even mentioned, let alone relied on.[18] The decisions were based on the view that the assignor had made a completed gift.[19] And in some cases voluntary assignments of equitable choses were held invalid as incomplete gifts[20]; these are hard to explain on the procedural view.

Thirdly: consideration should have been generally[21] necessary for the assignment of a legal chose, since the assignee could not sue the debtor without the co-operation of the

---

[12] [1919] 2 Ch. 104.

[13] *ibid.* at 111.

[14] *ibid.* at 114.

[15] See above, p.672.

[16] *Easton v Pratchett* (1835) 1 Cr.M. & R. 798 at 808. There is no reference to consideration in Carriage of Goods by Sea Act 1992, s.2, which deals with the transfer of rights arising under a contract contained in or evidenced by a bill of lading.

[17] See above, p.675.

[18] Exceptionally, the argument is mentioned in *Ward v Audland* (1845) 8 Beav. 201 (the actual decision was doubted in *Kekewich v Manning* (1851) 1 D.M. & G. 176).

[19] *Kekewich v Manning*, above; *Bentley v Mackay* (1851) 15 Beav. 12; *Voyle v Hughes* (1854) 2 Sm. & G. 18; *Donaldson v Donaldson* (1854) Kay 711; *Nanney v Morgan* (1887) 37 Ch.D. 346; *Re Way's Trust* (1864) 2 D.J. & S. 365.

[20] *e.g. Bridge v Bridge* (1852) 16 Beav. 315 (doubted but distinguished in *T Choithram International v Pagarani* [2001] 1 W.L.R. 1 at 12); *Beech v Keep* (1854) 18 Beav. 285.

[21] Except where the legal chose was, even before the Judicature Act, assignable by some special statute (above, p.675) or at common law (above, p.672).

assignor. Here the procedural view breaks down. Although some voluntary assignments of legal choses were held invalid, others were upheld.[22] The distinction between valid and invalid assignments was not based on procedural requirements. It depended on the question whether the assignor had made a completed gift.

(b) COMPLETED GIFT VIEW. A person may enter into a contract to dispose of his property, or make a gift of it, or create a trust of the property in favour of another.

Consideration (or a deed) is clearly necessary for the validity of a contract to dispose of property, including a contract to assign a chose in action.

It is equally clear that consideration is not necessary for the validity of a trust of a chose in action.[23] All that is necessary is that the settlor should clearly have expressed his intention to create a trust. As in the case of trusts of promises for the benefit of a third party,[24] a mere intention to benefit is not enough: there must be an intention to create a trust. The settlor must intend to undertake a legally binding obligation to hold the subject-matter for the beneficiary, or to persuade someone else to undertake such an obligation.[25]

Consideration is also unnecessary for the validity of a completed gift. Thus in *Harding v Harding*[26] a voluntary statutory assignment was held binding on the ground that it was a completed gift. In many cases, the law requires a gift to be made in a prescribed way: for example, the gift of a chattel must be made by delivery with intention to pass the property, or by deed of gift.[27] If a purported gift of a chattel is not made in one of these two ways, it is incomplete or imperfect; and equity refuses to complete an imperfect gift by ordering the donor to make it in the proper legal manner.[28]

In the same way, a voluntary assignment of a chose in action did not bind the assignor unless it was made in the manner, if any, required by law. In *Milroy v Lord*[29] the owner of shares in a company voluntarily assigned them by deed poll. This was held to be an imperfect gift since the legal title to the shares could not be transferred except by the execution of a proper instrument of transfer. Turner L.J. said: "In order to render a voluntary settlement valid and effectual, the settlor must have done everything which, according to the nature of the property comprised in the settlement, was necessary to be done in order to transfer the property and render the settlement binding upon him."[30] The assignment thus failed as a gift but the assignees argued that it could still take effect

---

[22] *Ex p. Pye* (1811) Ves. 140; *Fortescue v Barnett* (1834) 3 My. & K. 36; *M'Fadden v Jenkyns* (1842) 1 Ph. 153; *Paterson v Murphy* (1853) 11 Hare 88; *Richardson v Richardson* (1867) L.R. 3 Eq. 686; *Re King* (1879) 14 Ch.D. 179 (where the assignment was made before the Judicature Act); *cf. Re Patrick* [1891] 1 Ch. 82 and *Re Griffin* [1899] 1 Ch. 408, in which the provisions of the Judicature Act relating to assignment were not mentioned.

[23] *Ex p. Pye*, above; *Bentley v Mackay* (1851) 15 Beav. 12; *Paterson v Murphy*, above; *Richardson v Richardson*, above; *Re Richards* (1887) 36 Ch.D. 541; *Paul v Constance* [1977] 1 W.L.R. 527. A declaration of trust is not, strictly, an assignment: see *Grey v I.R.C.* [1958] Ch. 690; affirmed on other grounds: [1960] A.C. 1.

[24] See above, pp.648–649.

[25] *Bayley v Boulcott* (1828) 4 Russ. 345; *Smith v Warde* (1845) 15 Sim. 56; *Re Caplen's Estate* (1876) 45 L.J.Ch. 280.

[26] (1886) 17 Q.B.D. 442.

[27] *Re Breton's Estate* (1881) 17 Ch.D. 416; *Cochrane v Moore* (1890) 25 Q.B.D. 57; *Re Cole* [1964] Ch. 175.

[28] *Ellison v Ellison* (1802) 6 Ves. 656 at 662. For a special exception in cases of so-called *donatio mortis causa* see *Sen v Headley* [1991] Ch. 425 (land); *Woodward v Woodward* [1995] 3 All E.R. 980 (chattel).

[29] (1862) 4 D.F. & J. 264; *cf. Antrobus v Smith* (1805) 12 Ves. 39; *Dillon v Coppin* (1839) 4 My. & Cr. 647; *Jones v Lock* (1865) L.R. 1 Ch.App. 25; *Richards v Delbridge* (1874) L.R. 18 Eq. 11; *Heartley v Nicholson* (1875) L.R. 19 Eq. 233; *Re Shield* (1885) 53 L.T. 5; *Macedo v Stroud* [1922] 2 A.C. 330; *Re Wale* [1956] 1 W.L.R. 1346; *Pappadakis v Pappadakis* [2000] 1 W.L.R. 79; McKay, 40 Conv. 139.

[30] (1862) 4 D.F. & J. 264 at 274.

as a declaration of trust. This argument, too, was rejected, as the donor had no intention to create a trust, but only an intention to make a gift.

A gift is only incomplete under the rule in *Milroy v Lord* if something more has to be done *by the donor* to transfer the property. If the donor has done all that he needs to do to transfer the property, the gift is complete even though further steps to vest the property in the donee have to be taken by a third party,[31] or by the donee himself.[32] The rigour of rule has, moreover, been mitigated in a number of ways. It has been held that, where the gift takes the form of a declaration of trust, the vesting of its subject-matter in *one* of a number of trustees suffices to complete the gift[33]; and that a gift of shares in a company may be completed by the execution of a proper instrument of transfer (coupled with evidence of intention that this was to take effect of a gift and with circumstances making it unconscionable for the donor to resile from the gift) even without delivery of the instrument of transfer to either the donee or to the company.[34] Where further steps to complete the gift are capable of being taken by the donee, the donor may constitute himself the agent for the donee to take those steps: *e.g.*, by telling the donee that nothing more needs to be done by the donee to perfect the gift. Failure by the donor to take those steps will not then vitiate the gift if the donee has relied on the donor's statement so as to make it unconscionable for the donor to invoke that failure as a ground of invalidity.[35]

The rule in *Milroy v Lord* applied only to gifts which had, by law, to be made in a certain form. The only formal requirement for the assignment of an *equitable* chose was that it must be in writing.[36] Hence in *Kekewich v Manning*[37] a voluntary settlement in writing of an equitable interest in property was held binding on the settlor, since there was nothing more that he could have done to transfer the property. Again, in the absence of special rules, such as those governing the transfer of shares in companies, equity did not lay down any formal requirements for the transfer of *legal* choses. Thus in *Fortescue v Barnett*[38] a voluntary assignment by deed[39] of a life insurance policy[40] was held binding on the assignor, as there was nothing more that he could do to complete the transfer.

A gift may be imperfect for some reason other than failure to use the proper form. The donor may only have said that he would make a gift in the future, or subject to some condition which can only be satisfied by his doing some further act. Thus a gift "to my daughter when she marries a man of whom I approve" is imperfect until the donor gives his approval.

The "completed gift" view seems to be preferable to the "procedural" view in two respects. It is more consistent with the reasoning of the cases decided before the

---

[31] *Re Rose* [1952] Ch. 499; following *Re Rose* [1949] Ch. 78; *cf. Mascall v Mascall* (1985) P. & C.R. 119 (transfer of a house); contrast *Re Fry* [1946] Ch. 312.

[32] *cf. Re Paradise Motor Co Ltd* [1968] 1 W.L.R. 1125 (defective execution by transferee did not invalidate gift of shares).

[33] *T Choithram International SA v Pagarani* [2001] 1 W.L.R. 1.

[34] *Pennington v Waine* [2002] EWCA Civ 227; [2002] 4 All E.R. 215; the *execution* of the instrument of transfer by donor is essential for this purpose: *ibid.* at [69].

[35] *ibid.*, at [67].

[36] See above, p.678. *cf. Chinn v Collins* [1981] A.C. 533 at 548.

[37] (1851) 1 D.M. & G. 176; *cf. Re Way's Trusts* (1864) 2 D.J. & S. 365; *Nanney v Morgan* (1887) 37 Ch.D. 346, decided after the Judicature Act, but without reference to its provisions regarding assignments.

[38] (1834) 3 My. & K. 36; *cf. Edwards v Jones* (1836) 1 My. & Cr. 226; *Re King* (1879) 14 Ch.D. 179; *Re Patrick* [1891] 1 Ch. 82.

[39] This would not cure the want of consideration for the present purpose: above, p.682.

[40] See above, p.675: for assignment of life insurance policies.

Judicature Act. And it explains why voluntary assignments of legal choses were sometimes upheld.

(2) After the Judicature Act 1873

An assignment may now fail to be statutory, and so take effect (if at all) in equity, for one of three reasons.

(a) NO WRITTEN NOTICE. An assignment which fails to be statutory merely because written notice has not yet been given to the debtor is effective although it is not supported by consideration.[41] The assignor has done all that need be done *by him* to transfer the property, as notice can be given by the assignee. It would be futile to insist that the assignee must give consideration, since he could evade the requirement by simply writing to the debtor and so making the assignment statutory.

(b) NO WRITING. An oral assignment of an equitable chose is void, quite apart from the question of consideration.[42] It is more doubtful whether a voluntary oral assignment of a legal chose can be valid as a gift.

One view is that consideration is not now necessary in cases of this kind because the assignee no longer needs the co-operation of the assignor to sue the debtor: if the assignor refuses to join as co-claimant, he can simply be joined as co-defendant. But this argument is based on the untenable "procedural" view of the old rules of equity and it would fail even if that view were sound. It can make no difference whether the assignor is joined as co-claimant or as co-defendant. The important point is that he is joined at all. He is joined, not out of respect for history, but "to allow him to dispute the assignment."[43] One reason for disputing it might be that it was voluntary. If the assignor disputed the assignment on this ground, the debtor would in practice leave the assignor and assignee to fight out the dispute in which the debtor would have no interest. Thus in substance the assignor would be the sole defendant.[44] To argue that he will lose simply because he has been made defendant is to assume the very point in issue.

Another view is that an oral voluntary assignment of a legal chose in action fails as an imperfect gift under the rule in *Milroy v Lord*.[45] On this view, the proper way to transfer a debt is by making a statutory assignment. If the assignor does not put the assignment into writing, he has not done "everything which, according to the nature of the property . . . was necessary to be done [by him] to transfer the property". This view was adopted in the Australian case of *Olsson v Dyson*[46] where a voluntary oral assignment of a debt was accordingly held ineffective.

Under the first of the above views, all oral voluntary assignments of legal choses would be valid; under the second they would all be invalid. Neither of these conclusions can be accepted. The law may recognise two ways of making a gift of a chose in action, just as it recognises two ways of making a gift of a chattel.[47] Before the Judicature Act a gift of a chose in action could be made by equitable assignment and equity laid down no formal requirements for this purpose. The Act provided a second method of making such a gift, without necessarily affecting the first. Thus in *German v Yates*[48] a voluntary oral assignment of a debt was held binding on the personal representatives of the

---

[41] *Holt v Heatherfield Trust Ltd* [1942] 2 K.B. 1.
[42] See above, p.679.
[43] *Durham Bros v Robertson* [1898] 1 Q.B. 765 at 770.
[44] *cf.* above, p.675.
[45] (1862) 4 D.F. & J. 264; above, p.684.
[46] (1969) 120 C.L.R. 365.
[47] See above, p.685.
[48] (1915) 32 T.L.R. 52.

assignor. Lush J. rejected the argument that the gift was imperfect, and said that the Judicature Act had not "destroyed equitable assignments or impaired their validity in any way".[49]

The true position seems to be that oral voluntary assignments of legal choses can be valid so long as they are perfect gifts. They are not imperfect *merely* for want of writing, but they may be imperfect for some other reason. In particular, there may be room for doubt whether an oral statement was a completed gift, rather than a promise to make a gift in the future.

(c) NOT ABSOLUTE. There are three reasons why an assignment may not be absolute.[50]

(i) *Part of a debt.* An assignment of part of a debt may be effective without consideration. This can be deduced from *Re McArdle*.[51] A testator left his estate in equal shares to his five children. The wife of one of them, at her own expense, made improvements to a farm belonging to the estate. Thereafter, the children wrote to the wife: "In consideration of your carrying out certain alterations . . . we . . . hereby agree that the executors shall repay you [£488] from the estate." This promise was supported only by past consideration[52] and was held to be ineffective because it purported to be a contract and not a gift. It was further said that, even if the letter could be construed as a gift, it was not perfect, because something more had to be done by the donors; the executors could not have paid the wife without referring back to the children to find out whether the work had been done to their satisfaction.[53] On this reasoning, the result would have been different if the letter had on its face been a gift and had involved no reference back to the children. A letter simply saying "We hereby agree that the executors shall pay you £488 out of the estate" would have been a valid equitable assignment.

(ii) *By way of charge.* The question whether an assignment by way of charge must be supported by consideration is not likely to arise. Such an assignment is almost always made to secure a debt, so that there will generally be consideration for it in the shape of the assignee's advancing money or promising not to sue or actually forbearing to sue.[54] Moreover, such an assignment is usually intended to operate as a disposition by way of contract, and cannot be construed as a gift merely because, for some technical reason, there is no consideration. Even if the assignment were intended to operate as a gift, the fact that the amount assigned would fluctuate from time to time as the assignor increased or decreased his indebtedness to the assignee would show that the gift was not perfect.

(iii) *Conditional.* The validity of a voluntary conditional assignment depends on the nature of the condition. An assignment of rent due under a lease "to A until she marries" might well be a perfect gift, and so might an assignment "to A when she marries", unless it is construed as a promise to make a gift in the future. But a gift "to A when she marries a man of whom I approve"[55] would be imperfect as it could not take effect until some further act had been done by the donor.

---

[49] *ibid.* at 53. He also said that the assignor might have been able to revoke the assignment but that his personal representative could not do so; and that there might have been consideration for the agreement because the parties thought there was. No reasons were given for these puzzling statements. The decision is, however, consistent with the mitigations of the rule in *Milroy v Lord* described on p.632, above, at nn.33 and 34.

[50] See above, pp.676–678.

[51] [1951] Ch. 669; Stone, 14 M.L.R. 356.

[52] See above, p.77.

[53] For criticism of this reasoning, see R. E. M., 67 L.Q.R. 295.

[54] See above, pp.87–91.

[55] It is assumed that this is a condition and not consideration (*cf.* above, p.72).

SECTION 6. SUBJECT TO EQUITIES

An assignee takes "subject to equities",[56] *i.e.* subject to any defects in the assignor's title and subject to certain claims which the debtor has against the assignor. He takes subject to such defects and claims whether they arise at law or in equity, and whether or not he knew of their existence when he took his assignment.[57] And he cannot recover more than the assignor could have recovered. The object of these rules is to ensure that the debtor is not prejudiced by the assignment.[58]

1. Defects of Title

An assignor cannot confer any title if he had none himself. Thus if a builder assigns money to become due to him under a building contract, and then fails to perform the contract so that the money never becomes due, the assignee takes nothing.[59] Similarly, the assignee of a contract which is affected by mistake or illegality generally[60] takes no greater rights than the assignor would have had. And the assignee of a contract which is voidable for a misrepresentation made by the assignor takes subject to the right of the debtor to set the contract aside.[61] Defences available by the terms of the contract to the debtor against the assignor can similarly be raised against the assignee.[62] On the other hand payment of the debt to the assignor is a defence against the assignee only if made before notice of the assignment was given to the debtor[63] and the same is presumably true of rescission of the contract assigned by subsequent agreement between debtor and assignor.

2. Claims by Debtor against Assignor

The debtor may have claims[64] against the assignor which he could set up, if he were sued by the assignor, to diminish or extinguish his liability. Whether he can rely on such claims against the assignee depends on the way in which they arose.

(1) Claims arising out of the contract assigned

If the debtor has claims *arising out of the contract assigned*, on which he could have relied by way of defence or set off against the assignor, he can also rely on those claims against the assignee, and he can do so whether the claims have arisen before or after notice of the assignment is given to him.[65] Thus if a builder assigns money due to him under a

---

[56] *Ord v White* (1840) 3 Beav. 357; *Mangles v Dixon* (1852) 3 H.L.C. 702 at 731; Law of Property Act 1925, s.136(1).

[57] *Athenaeum Soc v Pooley* (1853) 3 D. & J. 294.

[58] *cf. Sinclair v British Telecommunications plc* [2001] 1 W.L.R. 38; (action by assignee stayed till an order for costs against assignor on an earlier action on the same contract had been satisfied).

[59] *Tooth v Hallett* (1869) L.R. 4 Ch.App. 242.

[60] An assignee for value may be able to enforce a life insurance policy though the estate of the assured could not do so because he died by his own hand: above, p.439.

[61] See above, pp.370 *et seq.*

[62] *The League* [1984] 2 Lloyd's Rep. 259 (arbitration clause); *Glencore International AG v Metro Trading International Inc* [1999] 2 All E.R. (Comm) 899 at 917 (exclusive jurisdiction clause).

[63] See above, p.681.

[64] For this purpose *legal* (as opposed to *equitable*) claims can be "equities": *Roxburghe v Cox* (1881) 17 Ch.D. 520; *Glencore Grain Ltd v Argos Trading Co* [1999] 2 Lloyd's Rep. 410 at 420.

[65] *Graham v Johnson* (1869) L.R. 8 Eq. 36; *William Pickersgill & Sons Ltd v London & Provincial Marine, etc., Insurance Co Ltd* [1912] 3 K.B. 614; *The Raven* [1980] 2 Lloyd's Rep. 266; contrast *The Dominique* [1987] 1 Lloyd's Rep. 239 at 251, (approved [1989] A.C. 1056 at 1109–1101), where the debtor's claim could *not* have been set up against the assignor (below, p.788, n.32) and was therefore not available against the assignee.

building contract, and then commits a breach of that contract, the debtor can set off against the assignee the amount of any damages which he could have recovered from the assignor.[66] If this amount exceeds the sum assigned, the assignee will not be entitled to anything; but he is not liable to the debtor for the excess[67] as he is not himself in breach of the contract. Nor, once the assignee has been paid, is he liable to return the payment merely because events later happen which make the assignor liable to return it to the debtor.[68]

If the debtor has been induced to enter into the contract by a misrepresentation on the part of the assignor, he can rely against the assignee on the right to rescind the contract on that ground[69]; but a further problem arises where that right has been lost. In *Stoddart v Union Trust Ltd*,[70] the defendants were induced by the fraud of one Price to buy a business from him. Price made an assignment of £800, part of the agreed price, and the assignees now claimed this sum from the defendants. Two defences were raised. First, the defendants counterclaimed for damages for Price's fraud, but such a claim could not be made against the assignees, as they were not themselves guilty of fraud, nor responsible for the fraud of Price. Secondly, the defendants pleaded that by reason of Price's fraud they had suffered loss exceeding £800, so that no money was due from them. This defence would have succeeded against Price; but it failed against the assignees as the claim for damages did not "arise out of the contract in question at all"[71] but was "something *dehors* the contract".[72] The decision seems to lead to the regrettable result that a contract may be worth more in the hands of the assignee than in the hands of the assignor, and so to defeat the purpose of the rule that an assignee takes "subject to equities". No attempt was made by the defendants to rely simply on their right to rescind the contract. They had disposed of the subject-matter and seem to have assumed that they could not rescind as they were unable to make restitution.[73] But the victim of a criminal fraud can rely on it by way of defence without making restitution.[74] This defence would seem to be an "equity" and should have been available against the assignee.

(2) Claims arising out of other transactions

(a) CLAIMS AGAINST ASSIGNOR. The debtor may have a claim against the assignor arising out of some transaction other than the contract assigned: *e.g.* a debtor may owe money under a building contract and in turn have a claim against the builder for the price of goods sold and delivered. Such a claim can only be set up against an assignee of the debt due under the building contract if it arose before notice of the assignment was given to the debtor.[75] If the claim arises later, the debtor is not prejudiced by being unable to raise it against the assignee. He knows that the assignor is no longer his creditor in respect of the debt assigned and cannot therefore expect to set off against it any claims which he may later acquire against the assignor.

---

[66] *cf. Govt of Newfoundland v Newfoundland Ry* (1888) 13 App.Cas. 199.

[67] *Young v Kitchin* (1878) 3 Ex.D. 127.

[68] *The Trident Beauty* [1994] 1 W.L.R. 161.

[69] See *Banco Santander SA v Bayfern Ltd* [2000] 1 All E.R. (Comm) 766.

[70] [1912] 1 K.B. 181; the decision is viewed with scepticism in the *Banco Santander* case, above, n.69.

[71] [1912] 1 K.B. 181 at 193.

[72] *ibid*. at 194.

[73] See above, pp.377 *et seq*.

[74] See above, pp.373–374.

[75] *Stephens v Venables* (1862) 30 Beav. 625; *cf. Watson v Mid Wales Ry* (1867) L.R. 2 C.P. 593; *Roxburghe v Cox* (1881) 17 Ch.D. 520; *Business Computers Ltd v Anglo-African Leasing Ltd* [1977] 1 W.L.R. 578.

(b) CLAIMS AGAINST INTERMEDIATE ASSIGNEE. Where a debt which has been assigned to one person is then assigned by him to another, the question may arise whether a claim or defence which the debtor has against the first assignee can be set up against the second assignee. Such a claim or defence should be available against the second assignee, if it arose after the first assignment,[76] but before notice of the second assignment had been given to the debtor. If the debtor *paid* the first assignee before the notice of the second assignment, he would clearly not have to make a second payment to the second assignee. The same rule should apply if the debtor supplied goods to the first assignee on the terms that the price was to be set off against the debt assigned.[77]

(c) PROVISIONS OF THE CONTRACT. The rule that claims arising before notice of the assignment can be set off against the assignee may be excluded by the express provisions of the contract creating the debt. Such provisions are often found in debentures issued by companies to secure loans, since the rule that an assignee takes subject to equities unduly restricts the transferability of such instruments.[78]

3. Assignee Cannot Recover More than Assignor

The assignee cannot recover more from the debtor than the assignor could have done. Thus in *Dawson v GN & City Ry*[79] a landowner had a statutory claim against a railway company for injuriously affecting his land. He sold the land and assigned the statutory claim to the buyer. It was held that the railway company's liability to the buyer must be measured by the loss which would have been suffered by the assignor and that any extra loss suffered by the buyer by reason of a trade carried on by him, but not by the assignor, must be disregarded.

SECTION 7. NEGOTIABILITY

Special rules apply to the assignment of certain written contracts, called negotiable instruments, such as bills of exchange, cheques and promissory notes. A bill of exchange is a written order made by one person (the drawer) requiring another (the drawee) to pay a sum of money either to, or to the order of, the drawer or a named third person, or simply to the bearer.[80] If the drawee accepts the bill, he becomes liable as acceptor of a bill. A cheque is a bill of exchange drawn on a banker payable on demand[81]; cheques are now usually deprived of negotiability by being crossed "a/c payee" or "a/c payee only".[82] A promissory note is an unconditional promise in writing to pay a person a sum of money.[83] The categories of negotiable instruments are not closed, so that instruments

---

[76] Not if it arose *before* then, since in that case the debtor can have had no expectation of being able to set it up in diminution of the debt assigned: *The Raven* [1980] 2 Lloyd's Rep. 266.

[77] According to a dictum in *Re Milan Tramways Co* (1884) 25 Ch.D. 587 at 593 an ultimate assignee takes "free from any equities which only attach on the intermediate assignee"; but this view could cause injustice to the debtor, and the actual decision can be explained on the ground that the intermediate assignee's liability to the debtor was not established until *after* the *second* assignment had been made (see *ibid.*, at 637). The actual decision in the *Milan Tramways* case was approved in *Fryer v Ewart* [1902] A.C. 187 at 192.

[78] Pennington, *Company Law* (7th ed.), pp.612–613.

[79] [1905] 1 K.B. 260.

[80] Bills of Exchange Act 1882, s.3.

[81] *ibid.* s.73.

[82] *ibid.* s.81A, as inserted by Cheques Act 1992; *Esso Petroleum Ltd v Milton* [1997] 1 W.L.R. 938 at 946, 954.

[83] Bills of Exchange Act 1882, s.83(1). A promissory note must be distinguished from an IOU, which is only evidence of a debt.

can still become negotiable by mercantile custom, that is, by being regularly so treated by businessmen.[84]

The transfer of a negotiable instrument differs from the assignment of an ordinary chose in action in the following ways.

1. Transfer

A negotiable instrument is actually or potentially transferable by delivery. A bill of exchange payable to bearer can be transferred by simply handing it to the transferee. If a bill of exchange is payable to the order of A, he can transfer it by indorsing it, *i.e.* by signing his name on it, and then handing it to the transferee. Notice of the transfer need not be given to the person or persons liable on the instrument.

2. Defects of Title

An ordinary assignee takes "subject to equities".[85] But negotiable instruments pass from hand to hand like cash, so that it is particularly important that those who deal with them should be able to rely on their apparent validity. The transferee of a negotiable instrument therefore takes it free from certain defects in the title of prior parties[86] and from defences available among them, if he is a "holder in due course".[87] Such a holder is a person in possession of the instrument who has in good faith given value for it, provided that it is complete and regular on its face, not overdue and that it has not, to his knowledge, been dishonoured.[88] Every holder is *prima facie* deemed to be a holder in due course[89] unless the instrument is affected by fraud, duress or illegality[90]; but even in such a case the holder can still enforce the instrument if he can prove that he in fact gave value for the instrument in good faith. The only cases in which his title is no better than that of the transferor are those in which a party's signature to the instrument is wholly void, *i.e.* for mistake or under statute.[91]

3. Consideration

The holder of a bill of exchange is deemed to be a holder for value if value[92] has at any time[93] been given for the bill. Thus he can enforce it against (for example) the acceptor even though he himself gave no consideration for it. This rule should be distinguished from the further rule that consideration is not necessary for the validity of a transfer of a negotiable instrument.[94] Suppose that A draws a bill of exchange on B who accepts it. If A transfers the bill to C, neither A nor B can deny the validity of the transfer on the ground that it was gratuitous. But B can escape liability by showing that his acceptance was gratuitous, and that C gave no consideration for the transfer. Want of consideration

---

[84] *Crouch v Crédit Foncier of England Ltd* (1873) L.R. 8 Q.B. 374.

[85] See above, p.689.

[86] Bills of Exchange Act 1882, s.38(2).

[87] *ibid.* s.29. And see Consumer Credit Act 1974, s.125, for special provisions designed to prevent evasions of that Act.

[88] Bills of Exchange Act 1882, s.29(1).

[89] *ibid.*, s.30(2).

[90] *ibid.*

[91] *Foster v Mackinnon* (1869) L.R. 4 C.P. 704; for contracts declared to be "void" by statute, see above, p.513.

[92] An antecedent debt or liability is sufficient by way of exception to the rule that consideration must not be past: Bills of Exchange Act 1882, s.27(1)(b); above, p.80.

[93] *ibid.* s.27(2).

[94] *Easton v Pratchett* (1835) 1 Cr.M. & R. 798 at 808. The transferee could not *sue* the transferor, but the transferor could not prevent the transferee from collecting the amount due from the other parties liable.

may enable the acceptor to resist an action *on the bill*. But it does not entitle the transferor to deny the validity of the *transfer*.

SECTION 8. RIGHTS WHICH ARE NOT ASSIGNABLE

1. Contracts Expressed to be Not Assignable

If a contract provides that the rights arising under it shall not be assigned, a purported assignment of such rights is not only a breach of that contract but is also ineffective, in the sense that it does not give the assignee any rights against the debtor.[95] For example, a hire-purchase agreement may provide that the rights of the hirer shall not be assignable; and if he nevertheless purports to assign them, the assignee cannot enforce them against the owner.[96] But an assignment of the benefit of a contract which is expressed to be not assignable may be binding as a contract or as a declaration of trust between assignor and assignee. Thus it has been held that a settlement of an insurance policy, expressed to be not assignable, could be enforced by the beneficiaries against the settlor.[97]

2. Personal Contracts

The benefit of a contract cannot be assigned if it is clear that the debtor is willing to perform only in favour of one particular creditor, and if it would be unjust to force him to perform in favour of another. In such cases it is sometimes said that the "personal" nature of the contract prevents assignment.

An important application of this principle is that an employer cannot assign the benefit of his employee's promise to serve. It has been said that the right of the employee to choose whom he would serve "constituted the main difference between a servant and a serf".[98] But in the case of an employee of a company, this right of choice will often depend on distinctions which are somewhat technical. If *the shares* in the company are sold, and its directors are replaced by others in the course of a take-over bid, the employee is, it seems, bound to go on serving the company. In law he still has the same employer[99] but his right of choice is in such cases of more theoretical than real importance. If, on the other hand, the company sells its *business*, then at common law the

---

[95] *Helstan Securities Ltd v Hertfordshire CC* [1978] 3 All E.R. 262; Munday [1979] C.L.J. 50; *Linden Gardens Trust Ltd v Lenesta Sludge Disposals Ltd* [1994] 1 A.C. 85 (rejecting the argument that such a prohibition is contrary to public policy); *Bawejem Ltd v MC Fabrications Ltd* [1999] 1 All E.R. (Comm) 377 at 328; *cf. Hendry v Chartsearch Ltd* [1998] C.L.C. 1382 (assignment invalid where contract required debtor's consent and that consent had not been sought); see generally Goode, 42 M.L.R. 453; Alcock [1983] C.L.J. 328. For the construction of clauses prohibiting assignment, see *Flood v Shand Construction Ltd* (1987) 81 B.L.R. 31.

[96] *United Dominion Trust Ltd v Parkway Motors* [1955] 1 W.L.R. 719 (disapproved as to the effect of such a provision on measure of damages in *Wickham Holdings Ltd v Brooke House Motors Ltd* [1967] 1 W.L.R. 295). Apart from such clauses prohibiting assignment, hire-purchase agreements are assignable: *Whiteley Ltd v Hilt* [1918] 2 K.B. 808.

[97] *Re Turcan* (1888) 40 Ch.D. 5. *cf. Don King Productions Inc. v Warren* [2000] Ch. 291; *Spellman v Spellman* [1961] 1 W.L.R. 921.

[98] *Nokes v Doncaster Amalgamated Collieries Ltd* [1940] A.C. 1014 at 1026; *cf. Denman v Midland Employer's Mutual Assurance Soc Ltd* [1955] 2 Q.B. 437; *Smith v Blandford Gee Cementation Ltd* [1970] 3 All E.R. 154 at 163; *O'Brien (Inspector of Taxes) v Benson's Hosiery (Holdings) Ltd* [1980] A.C. 562 at 572; *Don King* case, above n.97.

[99] *cf. Re Mack Trucks (Britain) Ltd* [1967] 1 W.L.R. 780; *Griffiths v S of S for Social Services* [1974] Q.B. 468; *Nicholl v Cutts* 1985 P.C.C. 311; (service contracts not determined by appointment of receiver); *cf. Gill & Duffus SA v Rionda Futures Ltd* [1994] 2 Lloyd's Rep. 67 at 83, 84 (guarantee not terminated by change of ownership of guarantor company).

effect of the sale is to terminate the contracts of employment.[1] This common law rule has in turn been modified by delegated legislation,[2] by which certain transfers of undertakings do not terminate the contracts of their employees. Each contract of employment is kept in being as if it had originally been made between the employee and the transferee of the undertaking.[3] It follows that the contract can be enforced by the transferee against the employee,[4] but the employee can avoid this consequence by giving notice to the transferor or to the transferee that he objects to becoming employed by the transferee[5]: hence his legal right to choose his employer is preserved.

The common law principle applies to all contracts involving personal confidence. Thus a publisher cannot assign the benefit of an author's contract to write a book if the author relied on the publisher's skill and judgment as a publisher.[6] And the holder of a motor insurance policy cannot assign it since the insurer relies on the holder's skill and record as a driver.[7] It may be that even the benefit of a builder's promise under a building contract cannot be assigned, since such contracts are "pregnant with disputes" so that the builder may intend to deal only "with the particular employer with whom he has chosen to enter into a contract"[8]

The principle may even apply to contracts for the sale of goods. Thus it has been held that the benefit of a contract to supply coal on credit to a retail coal merchant could not be assigned to his successor in the business. In making the contract, the sellers had relied on the original buyer's business experience; and to force them to give credit to his successor (who had no such experience) would subject them to quite a different business risk.[9] Again in *Kemp v Baerselman*[10] a farmer agreed to supply to a baker all the eggs which the latter should need in his business for one year; and the baker agreed not to buy eggs elsewhere during that period. The baker sold his business to a large company, to whom he purported to assign the benefit of his contract with the farmer. It was held that the farmer was justified in refusing to supply eggs to the company. One reason for the decision was that the baker's promise to deal exclusively with the farmer could not be enforced against the company.[11] Thus if the farmer were compelled to supply eggs to the company he would be subject to all the burdens of the original contract, but would lose the privilege of exclusive trading for which he had originally bargained.

---

[1] *Re Foster Clark Ltd's Indenture Trusts* [1966] 1 W.L.R. 125.

[2] Giving effect to EC Council Directive, 77/187/EEC.

[3] Transfer of Undertakings (Protection of Employment) Regulations 1981 (SI 1981/1794), reg.5(1), as amended by Trade Union Reform and Employment Rights Act 1993, s.33 and Collective Redundancies and Transfer of Undertakings (Protection of Employment) Regulations 1995 (SI 1995/2587). *cf.* also Learning & Skills Act 2000, s.95.

[4] *Morris Angel & Son Ltd v Hollande* [1993] I.C.R. 71; *cf. Newns v British Airways* [1992] I.R.L.R. 575. For enforcement by the employee against the transferee, see below, p.704.

[5] See the 1993 amendments of the 1981 Regulations (above n.3); *Humphreys v Oxford University* [2000] I.C.R. 405.

[6] *Stevens v Benning* (1854) 1 K. & J. 168; 6 D.M. & G. 223; *Hole v Bradbury* (1879) 12 Ch.D. 886; *Griffith v Tower Publishing Co* [1897] 1 Ch. 21.

[7] *Peters v GAFLAC* [1937] 4 All E.R. 628.

[8] *Linden Gardens Trust Ltd v Lenesta Sludge Disposals Ltd* [1994] 1 A.C. 85 at 105, where the point was put beyond doubt by an express provision prohibiting assignment by either party without the written consent of the other.

[9] *Cooper v Micklefield Coal & Lime Co Ltd* (1912) 107 L.T. 457.

[10] [1906] 2 K.B. 604.

[11] For the validity of such exclusive dealing arrangements, see above, pp.468–472. Where a *lease* contains such a covenant by the tenant (*e.g.* one to buy all the petrol that he needs for his business on the premises) it may "run with the land". If so, the principle in *Kemp v Baerselman* does not apply and the covenant is at common law enforceable against an assignee of the landlord's interest in the land by virtue of the rules referred to on p.645 above: *Clegg v Hands* (1890) 44 Ch. D. 503; *Caerns Motor Services Ltd v Texaco Ltd* [1994] 1 W.L.R. 1249. For the effect of the Competition Act 1998 see s.50 above, p.476.

But the benefit of a long-term contract for the sale of goods can be assigned if it was expressly or impliedly made with the buyer *or his assigns*. In *Tolhurst v Associated Portland Cement Co*[12] Tolhurst agreed that he would for 50 years supply to Imperial so much chalk as it should require for the manufacture of cement on certain land which was described in the contract. Imperial sold its business to Associated (a much larger concern), to which it purported to assign the benefit of its contract with Tolhurst. It was held that Tolhurst was not justified in refusing to supply chalk to Associated, since the contract was impliedly made between the parties and their respective assigns. The fact that Associated was a larger concern than Imperial did not increase Tolhurst's burden, since the contract obliged him only to supply so much chalk as was needed on the land originally occupied by Imperial.

It seems that the rule against the assignment of "personal" contracts does not apply where the creditor has an accrued right to a fixed sum of money. A person who is indebted to an indulgent creditor cannot apparently complain if the creditor assigns the debt to the debtor's trade rival (who may make him bankrupt), or to a debt-collecting agency.[13]

In cases of this kind, one party may be able to assign the benefit of the contract while the other cannot do so. Thus in *Kemp v Baerselman*[14] the farmer could no doubt have assigned the benefit of the baker's promise to pay for the eggs.

Where a purported assignment fails because of the "personal" nature of the debtor's obligation, the transaction may nevertheless take effect between assignor and assignee by way of contract between them or by way of trust.[15]

3. Mere Rights of Action

Equity in general[16] regarded the common law's fear that assignments would lead to maintenance as exaggerated. But where assignments in fact savoured of maintenance[17] or champerty,[18] equity refused to enforce them. The Criminal Law Act 1967 abolishes criminal and tortious liability for maintenance and champerty[19] but goes on to provide that this "shall not affect any rule of law as to the cases in which a contract[20] is to be treated as contrary to public policy or otherwise illegal".[21] The rule against the assignment of certain rights known as "mere rights of action" has therefore survived the 1967 Act.[22] But, partly as a result of the Act, and partly as a result of the current "more liberal attitude"[23] towards maintenance and champerty, the courts have considerably restricted the scope of the rule.

---

[12] [1903] A.C. 414; *cf. Shayler v Woolf* [1946] Ch. 320.

[13] *cf. Fitzroy v Cave* [1905] 2 K.B. 364. But the "personality" of the creditor may be material to the debtor: see *Gordon v Street* [1899] 2 Q.B. 641.

[14] [1906] 2 K.B. 604, above p.694.

[15] *Don King Productions Inc v Warren* [2000] Ch. 291; *cf.* above, p.693 at n.97.

[16] See above, p.674.

[17] *Rees v De Bernardy* [1896] 2 Ch. 437.

[18] *Laurent v Sale & Co* [1963] 1 W.L.R. 829; *Trendtex Trading Co v Crédit Suisse* [1982] A.C. 679 at 694–695; *Camdex International Ltd v Bank of Zambia* [1998] Q.B. 22 at 37. For a champerty, see above, p.430.

[19] ss.13(1) and (2).

[20] An assignment will often be a contract between assignor and assignee even though such a transaction may also be effective without consideration (above, pp.682–688) or even agreement: communication *to* the assignee is necessary, but not assent *by* him (above, p.680).

[21] s.14(2).

[22] *Trendtex Trading Corp v Crédit Suisse* [1982] A.C. 679.

[23] *ibid.* at 702. *cf. Giles v Thompson* [1994] 1 A.C. 142; see also Courts and Legal Services Act 1990, ss.58 and 58A, above, p.431.

(1) Claims in tort

A right of action in tort cannot generally be assigned.[24] A person who is defamed or assaulted cannot sell his right to sue the tortfeasor. He can, however, sue the tortfeasor and agree to assign any damages he may recover; this is unobjectionable as it does not give the assignee any right to interfere with the conduct of the action.[25] Exceptionally, a right of action in tort can be assigned to an insurance company which has compensated the victim of the tort[26] and by a trustee in bankruptcy or the liquidator of an insolvent company who is, by statute, entitled to sell all rights of action for the benefit of the bankrupt's or of the company's creditors.[27]

The generality of the rule against assignment of claims in tort is open to criticism. Such claims may be brought to assert rights of property; and it is hard to see why the assignment of a right of action in (for example) conversion is more likely to lead to maintenance than the assignment of a debt.[28] Some tort claims can be enforced by quasi-contractual (or restitutionary) actions,[29] and it is arguable that the assignment of these, at least, should be allowed.[30]

(2) Liquidated claims

A liquidated sum due under contract (e.g. for money lent, goods supplied, or services rendered) or otherwise[31] can be assigned in spite of the fact that the debtor denies liability. A debtor cannot destroy the assignability of a debt by refusing to pay it.[32] Nor is it relevant that such an assignment is made or taken with an oblique motive. An assignment of a debt is not invalid merely because its object is to enable the assignee to make the debtor bankrupt.[33]

(3) Unliquidated claims

If the benefit of a contract, e.g. to deliver goods, is assigned before breach, the assignee can claim damages for the seller's subsequent refusal to deliver the goods. But it is less

---

[24] *Defries v Milne* [1913] 1 Ch. 98.

[25] *Glegg v Bromley* [1912] 3 K.B. 474; *Trendtex Trading Corp v Crédit Suisse* [1982] A.C. 679 at 702.

[26] *King v Victoria Insurance Co* [1896] A.C. 250; *Compania Colombiana de Seguros v Pacific Steam Navigation Co* [1965] 1 Q.B. 101. Even if there is no assignment, the insurer is, to the extent that he has compensated the victim, entitled to be subrogated to the latter's rights against the tortfeasor: see *Hobbs v Marlowe* [1978] A.C. 16 at 37; *cf.* Marine Insurance Act 1906, s.79; *Napier & Ettrick v Kershaw* [1993] A.C. 713 at 732; *Caledonia North Sea Ltd v Norton (No.2) Ltd* [2002] UKHL 4; [2002] 1 All E.R. (Comm) 321. The insurer must in such a case sue in the name of the insured: see *The Aiolos* [1983] 2 Lloyd's Rep. 25 (where the claim was in contract); *M H Smith (Plant Hire) Ltd v D L Mainwaring (T/A Inshore)* [1986] 2 Lloyd's Rep. 244, where the insured was a company which had been wound up, so that the insurer lost his rights by way of subrogation; *Esso Petroleum Co Ltd v Hall Russell & Co Ltd* [1989] A.C. 643. Amounts recovered by the insurer in excess of those to which he is entitled must be held for the insured: *Lonrho Exports Ltd v ECGD* [1996] 2 Lloyd's Rep. 649.

[27] *Norglen Ltd v Reeds Rains Prudential Ltd* [1999] 2 A.C. 1 at 11–12.

[28] In *Three Rivers DC v Bank of England (No.1)* [1996] Q.B. 292 no objection seems to have been raised to the assignment on the ground that its subject matter was described at 305 as a claim "for a tortious wrong". *cf.*, in Australia, *South Australian Management Corp v Sheehan* [1995] A.L.M. 3577.

[29] i.e. in cases of so-called "waiver" of tort where the tort benefits the defendant, e.g. where he converts the claimant's property. See Goff & Jones, *The Law of Restitution* (6th ed.), Chap.36; Birks, *An Introduction to the Law of Restitution*, Chap.10.

[30] *cf. Re Berkeley Securities (Property) Ltd* [1980] 1 W.L.R. 1589 at 1611.

[31] *Dawson v Great Northern and City Ry* [1905] 1 K.B. 260.

[32] *County Hotel & Wine Co v London and North Western Ry* [1918] 2 K.B. 251 at 258; *Camdex International Ltd v Bank of Zambia* [1998] Q.B. 22.

[33] *Fitzroy v Cave* [1905] 2 K.B. 364; *Camdex* case, above, at p.32; for a different oblique motive, see *Deposit Protection Board v Dalia* [1994] 2 A.C. 367 and see below, p.698 at n.56.

clear whether the right to claim unliquidated damages for breach of contract can be assigned after the contract has already been broken.

One view is that such a right is a "mere" right of action and cannot be assigned.[34] But this view causes difficulty where the contract provides for the payment of a fixed sum in the event of its breach. Such a provision may be (i) invalid as a penalty, in which case no more than the actual loss is recoverable; or (ii) valid as a liquidated damages clause, in which case the fixed sum (no more and no less) is recoverable.[35] According to the present view, the assignment would be valid if the contractual provision were a liquidated damages clause, and invalid if the contractual provision were penal. But this distinction has no relevance to the tendency of the assignment to maintenance.

Another view is that a right to claim unliquidated damages for breach of contract can, generally,[36] be assigned. But this view in turn gives rise to difficulty where the claim which has been assigned could be framed in contract or in tort.[37] The assignability of the right to damages can hardly depend on the way in which it is described.

As both the views so far discussed are unsatisfactory, the law has adopted the intermediate view that a right to unliquidated damages for breach of contract may be validly assigned, so long as the assignment does not in fact savour of maintenance or champerty. If, for example, the assignee has a *proprietary* interest in the subject-matter, the assignment is valid since maintenance is committed only where a person interferes in another's litigation without having a genuine or substantial interest[38] in the outcome. Thus a vendor of land can assign to the purchaser the right to claim damages for breaches of covenant committed by the vendor's tenants before the sale[39]; and a buyer of goods which turn out to be defective can assign his claim in respect of the defect to a sub-buyer to whom he has resold the goods.[40] Similarly, "a conveyance of land can include the right to set aside an earlier transaction relating to it".[41] And a person can assign the benefit of a specifically enforceable contract, though the assignee elects, or is forced, to claim damages.[42]

Even where the assignee has no proprietary interest, the assignment may be valid if he has a "genuine commercial interest"[43] in the subject-matter of the action. Thus in *Trendtex Trading Ltd v Crédit Suisse*[44] a bank had financed a sale of cement by one of its customers. It was held that the bank could validly have taken an assignment from the

---

[34] *May v Lane* (1894) 64 L.J.Q.B. 236 at 237, 238.

[35] See below, pp.999–1007.

[36] In *County Hotel & Wine Co v London and North Western Ry*, above, at p.259, an exception is made for contracts which are "personal" in the sense discussed at pp.693–695, above.

[37] *e.g. Matthews v Kuwait Bechtel Corp* [1959] 2 Q.B. 57 at 77; and see below, pp.983–984.

[38] *Martell v Consett Iron Co Ltd* [1955] Ch. 363.

[39] *Williams v Protheroe* (1829) 5 Bing 309; *Defries v Milne* [1913] 1 Ch. 98; *Ellis v Torrington* [1920] 1 K.B. 399.

[40] *Total Liban SA v Vitol Energy SA* [2001] Q.B. 643.

[41] *Defries v Milne* [1913] 1 Ch. 98 at 110, citing *Dickinson v Burrell* (1866) L.R. 1 Eq. 337 (see especially p.342). The only point of these dicta is that such an assignment is not champertous. On the issue of the assignability of a right to rescind, they are hard to reconcile with *Investors Compensation Scheme Ltd v West Bromwich BC* [1998] W.L.R. 896 (above, p.674) where they were not cited.

[42] *Torkington v Magee* [1902] 2 K.B. 427; reversed on another ground: [1903] 1 K.B. 644.

[43] *Trendtex Trading Ltd v Crédit Suisse* [1982] A.C. 679 at 703; *cf. The Aiolos* [1983] 2 Lloyd's Rep. 25; *Brownton Ltd v Edward Moore Inbucon Ltd* [1985] 3 All E.R. 499 (where the same result could now be reached without assignment under the Civil Liability (Contribution) Act 1978, ss.1(1), 2(1)); *The Kelo* [1985] 2 Lloyd's Rep. 85; *SE Regional Health Authority v Lovell* (1985) 33 Build L.R. 127; *Weddell v J A Pearce & Major* [1988] Ch. 26, 43; *Murray v Young & Co's Brewery Co* [1997] 1 Lloyd's Rep. 236; *Tharros Shipping Co v Den Norske Bank plc* [1997] 1 Lloyd's Rep. 541; *Stocznia Gdanska v Latvian Shipping Co (No.2)* [1999] 3 All E.R. 822.

[44] See above; Thornely [1982] C.L.J. 29. For the requirement that the maintainer must accept liability for costs to the other party to the litigation, see *McFarlane v EE Caledonia Ltd* [1995] 1 W.L.R. 366.

customer of his claim for damages for wrongful failure to pay for the cement.[45] But the assignment actually made was held to be champertous and invalid because it was expressed to have been taken for the purpose of enabling the bank to resell the customer's right of action to a third party, so that the profit resulting from its enforcement (which was considerable)[46] could be divided between the third party and the bank. The crucial fact was that the assignee contemplated a further sale of the right, as opposed to its enforcement by himself. If he intends to pursue the latter course, the assignment is not champertous merely because he expects to improve his position by taking the assignment: unless this were so, few assignments would be valid.[47]

4. Public Policy

In English law, an assignment of wages or salary is generally valid,[48] so long as it does not deprive the employee of his sole means of support.[49] But a public officer cannot assign his salary.[50] This rule was originally based on two considerations of public policy.[51] First, it was thought that a public officer must not be deprived of the means to maintain the dignity of his office; but this argument now has little force, except, perhaps, in the case of ambassadors. Secondly, it was thought that public officers must have the means to pay damages for wrongs committed by them or by their order; but this is no longer important since the injured party can now sue the Crown.[52] It could perhaps be argued that to allow such assignments might lead to corruption. But this seems to be a remote contingency; and the argument proves too much. Officers who are paid out of local funds can assign their salaries,[53] but are presumably just as corruptible as officers paid out of national funds.

Maintenance and other similar payments to which a wife may become entitled as a result of matrimonial proceedings are inalienable, since to allow the wife to assign them might leave her destitute.[54] There are many other statutory restrictions on assignment, based on various considerations of public policy.[55]

An assignment is not contrary to public policy merely because it was made and taken with an oblique motive: for example, if its purpose was to enable the assignee to obtain legal aid when this would not have been available in an action brought by the assignor against the debtor.[56]

---

[45] The claim was not against the buyer for the price but against a bank for damages for failing to honour a letter of credit: cf. below, p.997.

[46] The bank paid $800,000 for the claim and sold it for $1,100,000 to the third party who settled it for $8,000,000.

[47] *Brownton Ltd v Edward Moore Inbucon Ltd* [1985] 3 All E.R. 499 at 506, 509, where the "profit" likely to be made by the assignee was (even proportionately) much more modest than that in the *Trendtex* case.

[48] For a statutory exception, see Merchant Shipping Act 1995, s.34(1)(c). See also Employment Rights Act 1996, s.14(4) for formal requirements to be satisfied before the amount assigned can be deducted from wages.

[49] *King v Michael Faraday & Partners Ltd* [1939] 2 K.B. 753.

[50] *Methwold v Walbank* (1750) 2 Ves.Sen. 238; *Barwick v Reade* (1791) 1 H.Bl. 267; *Liverpool Corp v Wright* (1859) 28 L.J.Ch. 868.

[51] Logan, 61 L.Q.R. 240.

[52] Under the Crown Proceedings Act 1947.

[53] *Re Mirams* [1891] 1 Q.B. 594.

[54] *Watkins v Watkins* [1896] P. 222.

[55] *e.g.* Army Act 1955, s.203(1); Superannuation Act 1972, s.5(1); Police Pension Act 1976, s.9; Social Security Administration Act 1992, s.187; Pension Schemes Act 1993 s.159; Pensions Act 1995, s.91.

[56] See *Norglen Ltd v Reeds Rains Prudential Ltd* [1999] 2 A.C. 1; *cf.* above p.696 at n.33.

SECTION 9. ASSIGNMENT BY OPERATION OF LAW

1. Death

On the death of a contracting party, his rights generally pass to his personal representatives, who can recover any sums due under the contract or damages for its breach. The representatives may sometimes recover less than the deceased would have done, and sometimes more. Thus, personal representatives cannot recover exemplary damages.[57] On the other hand, in *Otter v Church, Adams, Tatham & Co*[58] solicitors negligently advised a client that he had an absolute interest in property, when in fact he had an entailed interest. Had the mistake been discovered while the client was alive, he could have barred the entail, so that the solicitors would only have been liable for nominal damages. But the mistake was not discovered until after the client's death, with the result that the solicitors had to pay substantial damages as the entailed property was through their negligence lost to the client's estate.

Where at time of death the contract is still partly executory, the personal representatives are generally entitled to complete its performance and to claim the agreed remuneration. But they cannot do so if the contract is "personal" in the sense that one party places confidence in the skill, judgment or integrity of the other. Thus if either party to a contract of employment dies, his right to go on serving, or to be served (as the case may be), does not pass to his representatives: they can enforce only rights which had accrued before,[59] or which accrue on,[60] death. It is possible for one party, but not the other, to rely on such personal considerations. If a painter contracted to paint a house and died when the work was half-done, his representatives might not be entitled to finish the work and claim the contract price; but if the houseowner died, his representatives might well be able to demand further performance from the painter.

2. Bankruptcy

When a person is adjudged bankrupt, things in action forming part of his estate at the commencement of the bankruptcy[61] are "deemed to have been assigned" to his trustee in bankruptcy.[62] Thus the trustee can recover debts due to the bankrupt and claim damages for breach of any contract with the bankrupt. Where the contract is executory, the trustee may be entitled to perform it and claim payment from the other party. Certain "personal" rights do not pass to the trustee. The word "personal" is here used in two senses.

First: rights do not pass to the trustee if they are concerned with the person or personal affairs of the bankrupt. Thus a right to claim damages for injury to reputation does not pass,[63] nor does the benefit of a contract "to carry him [the bankrupt] in safety, [or] to cure his person of a wound or disease. . . . "[64] Such rights do not pass to the trustee, even though they have accrued before bankruptcy. The rule is based on the view that only the bankrupt's property is divisible between his creditors: they are not entitled to benefit from injuries to his person. The "property"[65] of the bankrupt that vests in his

---

[57] Law Reform (Miscellaneous Provisions) Act 1934, s.1(2)(a)(i), as amended by Administration of Justice Act 1982, s.4. Such damages are hardly ever (if at all) recoverable on a breach of contract: below, p.935.
[58] [1953] Ch. 280.
[59] *Stubbs v Holywell Ry* (1867) L.R. 2 Ex. 311.
[60] *e.g.* death benefits payable under a contract of employment.
[61] For after-acquired property, see Insolvency Act 1986, s.307.
[62] Insolvency Act 1986, s.311.
[63] *Wilson v United Counties Bank* [1920] A.C. 102.
[64] *Beckham v Drake* (1849) 2 H.L.C. 579 at 627.
[65] Insolvency Act 1986, s.283(1).

trustee[66] includes "things in action"[67] without qualification; it includes contractual rights even though the contract giving rise to them in terms prohibits their assignment.[68] But the definition has not changed the previous rules relating to "personal" rights of the kind just described.[69] The bankrupt may have a single cause of action giving rise to a right to damages in respect both of personal loss (such as pain and suffering resulting from personal injury) and economic loss (such as loss of earnings resulting from the same injury). The cause of action is then vested in his trustee but the trustee must account to the bankrupt for such part of the amount recovered as relates to the bankrupt's personal loss, and to earnings lost after the bankrupt's discharge.[70] The proceeds of insurance against permanent disability, on the other hand, do pass to the trustee since the purpose of such a policy is to protect the insured against economic loss by the payment of premiums which, had they not been used for this purpose, would have been available for the payment of his debts.[71] By statute, rights under certain pension schemes are excluded from the bankrupt's estate.[72]

Secondly: the benefit of an *executory* contract does not pass to the trustee if it was "personal" in the sense that the other contracting party relied on the skill and judgment of the bankrupt. In such a case the other party cannot be required to accept performance from the trustee or someone employed by him. Thus where a contract to build a house was "personal" in this sense, the trustee was not entitled to finish the house and then to demand payment.[73] But the trustee may employ the bankrupt to finish the work, and if the other party in this way gets precisely what he bargained for, the trustee can enforce the contract against him.[74]

Special rules apply to payments in the nature of income to which the bankrupt is from time to time entitled.[75] Such entitlement may not vest in the trustee because the bankrupt's right to the payment may not arise until after the commencement of the bankruptcy,[76] typically where the income consists of the bankrupt's earnings after the date of the bankruptcy. In respect of such earnings,[77] the trustee may apply to the court for an "income payments order"[78] requiring either the bankrupt or the person from whom the payments are due[79] to pay to the trustee so much of the income as may be specified in the order. In deciding what part (if any) of the income is to be paid over to the trustee, the court takes account of "what appears . . . to be necessary for meeting the reasonable domestic needs of the bankrupt and his family"[80]: an income payments order must not be made if its effect would be to reduce the income of the bankrupt below

---

[66] *ibid.* s.306.
[67] *ibid.* s.436; *Re Landau* [1998] Ch. 223; *Performing Rights Society v Rowland* [1997] 3 All E.R. 336 at 348.
[68] See *Re Landau* above; *Krasner v Dennison* [2001] Ch. 76; and see n.72.
[69] *Heath v Tang* [1993] 1 W.L.R. 1421, 1423; *Ord v Upton* [2000] Ch. 352 at 360; *Haigh v Aitken* [2001] Ch. 110 (bankrupt's personal correspondence not "property" for present purpose); *Cork v Rawlings* [2001] EWCA Civ 202; [2001] Ch. 792 at [21].
[70] *Ord v Upton* [2000] Ch. 352.
[71] *Cork v Rawlings* [2001] EWCA Civ 202; [2001] Ch. 792.
[72] Welfare Reform and Pensions Act 1999, s.11, dealing with situations such as those in the cases cited in n.68, above.
[73] *Knight v Burgess* (1864) 33 L.J.Ch. 727; *cf. Lucas v Moncrieff* (1905) 21 T.L.R. 683.
[74] *Oliphant v Wadling* (1875) 1 Q.B.D. 145; *Ex p. Shine* [1892] 1 Q.B. 522. To the extent that the right to the money had not yet vested in the bankrupt at the commencement of the bankruptcy, the trustee could claim it as after-acquired property under Insolvency Act 1986, s.307.
[75] Insolvency Act 1986, s.310(7).
[76] *ibid.*, s.283(1)(a).
[77] See *Krasner v Dennison* [2001] Ch. 76, at [33] (on such facts see now above, at n.70).
[78] *ibid.* s.310(1).
[79] *ibid.* s.310(3).
[80] *ibid.* s.310(2).

this level. These provisions are not based on the "personal" nature of the contract under which the income is earned (for *ex hypothesi* the bankrupt is himself still rendering the services) but on the need to allow the bankrupt to work to maintain himself and his family.[81]

A trustee in bankruptcy is in a less favourable position than an ordinary assignee in that he cannot gain priority over a previous assignee for value by being the first to give notice to the debtor.[82]

SECTION 10. ASSIGNMENT DISTINGUISHED FROM TRANSFER OF LIABILITIES

Assignment is the transfer of a *right* without the consent of the debtor. The common law does not recognise the converse process of the transfer of a contractual *liability* without the consent of the creditor: "the burden of a contract can never be assigned without the consent of the other party to the contract . . . "[83] If A has a contractual right against X, he cannot be deprived of that right merely because X and Y agree that X's duty under his contract with A is to be performed by Y and not by X.[84] The phrase "assignment of liabilities" is highly misleading and should be avoided.

It is of course possible for Y to perform X's obligation. The question whether the creditor is bound to accept such vicarious performance[85] (so as to discharge X) will be considered in Chapter 18. It is also possible, in the situations to be discussed below, for Y to become liable to perform the obligation originally undertaken by X; but in these situations there is generally[86] no true transfer of liability.

1. Novation

We have seen that it is possible by novation to substitute one creditor for another.[87] Similarly, one debtor may by novation be substituted for another. In *Miller's* case[88] the claimant insured his life with the X Co, which was later amalgamated with the Y Co, which agreed to become liable on the policy if the claimant paid future premiums to it. The claimant did so, and it was held that he could enforce the policy against the Y Co. It has been suggested that a similar analysis may apply where a customer pays by credit

---

[81] *cf. Re Roberts* [1900] 1 Q.B. 122, commenting on the position under earlier legislation.

[82] *Re Wallis* [1902] 1 K.B. 719. This rule does not seem to be affected by Insolvency Act 1986, s.311(4).

[83] *Linden Gardens Trust Ltd v Lenesta Sludge Disposals Ltd* [1994] 1 A.C. 85 at 103; *Don King Productions Inc v Warren* [1998] 1 All E.R. 609 at 631, affirmed [2000] Ch. 291; *cf. Baytur SA v Finagrain Holdings SA* [1991] 4 All E.R. 129 at 134; *Société Commerciale de Réassurance v ERAS International Ltd* [1992] 1 Lloyd's Rep. 570 at 595–596; *Weldon v GRE Linked Life Assurance Ltd* [2000] 2 All E.R. (Comm) 914 at 922.

[84] For statutory exceptions to this principle, by which either party to a lease may be released from liabilities under it in consequence of the assignment of his interest, see Landlord and Tenant (Covenants) Act 1995, ss.5, 6.

[85] See below, pp.755–758.

[86] For what seems to be an exception, see below p.704 at n.17.

[87] See above, p.673.

[88] (1876) 3 Ch.D. 391; *cf. Société Commerciale de Réassurance v ERAS International Ltd* [1992] 1 Lloyd's Rep. 570 at 596. Contrast *Re a Company (No. 0032314 of 1992), Duckwari plc v Offerventure Ltd* [1995] B.C.C. 89 where a purchaser of land (P) directed the vendor (V) to convey the land to a third party (X) but V did not agree to look to X (rather than to P) as the contracting purchaser and there was held to be no novation. A dictum at 97–98 that "novation requires a substitution of the obligor, not of the party who takes the benefit of the contract" should be read as descriptive of the context and should not be taken to *restrict* the process of novation to the substitution of an obligor (*i.e.* of a debtor). The latter interpretation would be inconsistent with the authorities cited earlier in this note and with those cited in n.90 below.

card[89] for goods supplied by a retailer: the customer's liability to the retailer is discharged and a new liability to the retailer is undertaken by the company issuing the card.[90] Such arrangements are binding only if they are made with the appropriate contractual intention,[91] and if they are supported by consideration. Usually the creditor provides consideration for the new debtor's promise to pay him by agreeing to release the original debtor or to accept a discount[92]; and the original debtor provides consideration for the creditor's promise to release him by providing a new debtor.[93] The effect of novation is not, in strict theory, to *transfer* a liability, but to extinguish it and put a new one in its place.

2. Benefit and Burden

Generally, a person to whom the benefit of a contract is assigned makes no promise to perform the obligations of the assignor; and in the ordinary case such an assignee does not become liable under the contract. Suppose, for example, that a builder assigns to a bank moneys due or to become due under a building contract. The bank is under no liability to the builder's client for any breach of contract by the builder; the most that the client can do is to rely on the builder's breach in diminution or extinction of the bank's claim.[94]

There are, however, exceptions, or apparent exceptions, to this general rule.[95] In particular, the discharge of a burden may be a condition of the enjoyment of the benefit, so that the burden can be said to be annexed to the benefit, or to the subject-matter of the contract. Where this is the case, a person (other than one of the original contracting parties) to whom the benefit is transferred must perform the burden, or at least forego the benefit if he fails to do so. If, for example, a right to extract minerals is subject to the duty to pay compensation if the surface of the land is let down, such compensation may have to be paid by the assignee of the mining right.[96] This exception, however, does not apply if the burden, though imposed in the same instrument which creates the right, is not a condition of its exercise but an independent obligation undertaken by the original grantee of the right.[97]

But even the burden of such independent obligations may have to be performed by an assignee under a second, and broader, exception to the general rule. This has been called by Megarry V.-C. the "pure principle of benefit and burden"[98]; it is "distinct from the conditional benefit cases, and cases of burdens annexed to property."[99] In *Tito v Waddell*

---

[89] See below, p.754.

[90] *Customs & Excise Commissioners v Diners Club Ltd* [1989] 1 W.L.R. 1196, citing *Re Charge Card Services* [1989] Ch. 497, 513 ("quasi-novation").

[91] A requirement not satisfied in *Tito v Waddell (No.2)* [1977] Ch. 106: see 287.

[92] *Customs & Excise Commissioners v Diners Club Ltd* [1988] 2 All E.R. 1016 at 1023, affirmed [1989] 1 W.L.R. 1196.

[93] See above, p.155.

[94] See *Young v Kitchin* (1878) 3 Ex.D. 127; *The Trident Beauty* [1994] 1 W.L.R. 161 at 165, 170; Tettenborn [1993] C.L.J. 220; above, p.689.

[95] For a statutory exception relating to covenants in leases, see Landlord and Tenant (Covenants) Act 1995, s.3.

[96] *e.g. Aspden v Seddon (No.2)* (1876) 1 Ex.D. 496 (for earlier proceedings see (1875) L.R. 10 Ch.App. 394); *cf. Chamber Colliery Co Ltd v Twyerould* (1893) [1915] 1 Ch. 268n; *Werderman v Société Générale d'Electricité* (1881) 19 Ch.D. 246; *Schiffahrtsgesellschaft Detlev von Appen GmbH v Voest Alpine Intertrading GmbH* [1997] 2 Lloyd's Rep. 279 at 286, 291.

[97] *Radstock Co-operative and Industrial Society v Norton-Radstock U.D.C.* [1967] Ch. 1094; [1968] Ch. 605. For independent obligations, *cf.* below, p.763.

[98] *Tito v Waddell (No.2)* [1977] Ch. 106 at 302.

[99] *ibid.*

(*No.2*)[1] a company that was engaged in mining phosphates on a Pacific island had acquired land there under contracts obliging it to return any worked out land to its former owners and to replant it. The rights under these contracts were transferred to commissioners "subject to . . . the covenants . . . therein contained"; and the commissioners undertook to keep the company indemnified against claims by the landowners under the original contracts. Many years after the company had been wound up, it was held that the commissioners were liable to the landowners for failing to perform the covenant to replant. Their liability was based on the "pure principle of benefit and burden".[2]

That principle had been recognised in a number of earlier cases[3]; but its existence does give rise to the problem how it is to be reconciled with the rule "that in general contractual burdens are not assignable, though contractual benefits are".[4] A person is certainly not subject to the burdens of a contract merely because he has taken benefits under it: it has, for example, been held that the equitable assignee of a licence to use a patent was not subject to the burdens imposed by the licence on the original licensee.[5] The "pure principle" is best regarded as a limited exception to this rule, restricted in scope by two factors. The first is that "the condition [which gives rise to the burden] must be relevant to the exercise of the right".[6] This limitation is illustrated by *Rhone v Stephens*[7] where the owner of a house covenanted to keep the common roof of the house and an adjoining cottage in repair and both properties were then sold. It was held that the "pure principle" did not entitle the purchaser of the cottage to enforce the repairing covenant against the purchaser of the house: the duty to repair the roof was not a "relevant" condition of the right to occupy the house as there was no necessary connection between them. The second factor which restricts the operation of the "pure principle" is the intention of the parties to the assignment.[8] An intention to subject the assignee of contractual rights to liabilities arising under the contract will not normally be inferred.[9] In particular, any such inference will be displaced where it is the assignor who has undertaken (in the contract between assignor and assignee) to discharge the burden[10]; where it is plainly the intention of both parties to the assignment that the assignee is *not* to be subject to the obligations imposed by the original contract on the assignor[11]; and where the assignment is of benefits acquired by the assignor under one instrument but the burden is imposed by another, recording a separate transaction.[12] Even where the "pure principle" does apply, its effect is not strictly to transfer a liability; for the assignor remains liable to the other contracting party.

---

[1] [1977] Ch. 106.

[2] *ibid.* at 307; the original contracts between the company and the landowners had not made the benefits conditional on discharge of the burdens.

[3] *Elliston v Reacher* [1908] 2 Ch. 665 at 669 (in argument); *Halsall v Brizell* [1957] Ch. 169 at 182 (but the point was conceded; see 180; and not necessary for the decision); *E R Ives Investment Ltd v High* [1967] 2 Q.B. 379 at 394, 399, 400 (where estoppel was another ground of decision).

[4] [1977] Ch. at p.291; *cf.* at 299; above, p.701.

[5] *Bagot Pneumatic Tyre Co v Clipper Pneumatic Tyre Co* [1902] 1 Ch. 146; *cf. Cox v Bishop* (1857) 8 D.M. & G. 815; *Barker v Stickney* [1919] 1 K.B. 121.

[6] *Rhone v Stephens* [1994] 2 A.C. 310 at 322.

[7] See above; see also *Amsprop Trading Ltd v Harris Distribution Ltd* [1997] 1 W.L.R. 1025 at 1034–1035.

[8] *Tito v Waddell (No.2)* [1977] Ch. 106 at 302.

[9] *ibid.*, at 291; *cf.* 299.

[10] *ibid.*, at 302.

[11] *Law Debenture Trust Corp v Ural Caspian Oil Corp Ltd* [1993] 1 W.L.R. 138 at 146–147; for a successful appeal on another point see [1995] Ch. 152, above, p.623.

[12] *Law Debenture Trust* case, [1993] 1 W.L.R. 138 at 146; and see previous note.

3. Operation of Law

In the following cases, a creditor may by operation of law be entitled to sue someone (other than the original debtor) who has not voluntarily undertaken such liability.

(1) Death

Contractual liabilities pass to the personal representatives of a deceased person in the sense that they must apply his assets in discharging those liabilities. They are not personally liable, so that there is no true transfer of liability.

(2) Bankruptcy and insolvency

Contractual liabilities of a bankrupt pass to his trustee in bankruptcy in the sense that the latter must distribute the bankrupt's assets among his creditors. Again there is no true transfer of liability as the trustee is not personally liable. He can also disclaim a contract which is wholly or partly executory if it is onerous or unprofitable, e.g. a lease at too high a rent.[13] Such disclaimer puts an end to the contract but does not relieve the bankrupt's estate from liability for breach of it.[14] An administrative receiver of a company may become liable on contracts by "adopting" them[15]; but this liability arises from a new contract taking effect on such adoption, rather than under a transfer of the company's liability, incurred before adoption, under the old contract.

(3) Legislation

Under legislation referred to earlier in this Chapter,[16] not only the benefit but also the burden of a contract of employment may be transferred as a result of the transfer of the undertaking, with the owner of which the original contract was made.[17] The transferor thus ceases to be liable on the contract,[18] while liabilities under it are imposed on the transferee, though the employee can take steps to avoid being bound to serve the transferee.[19] In this sense, the consent of all three parties to the transfer is necessary; and, perhaps for this reason, the process has been described as a "statutory novation"[20] of the contract.

Under the Carriage of Goods by Sea Act 1992, a person may acquire rights under a contract for the carriage of goods by sea to which he was not an original party: for example, by becoming the lawful holder of the bill of lading which contains or evidences the contract.[21] Such a person may also become subject to liabilities under the contract: for example, if he takes or demands delivery of the goods.[22] But the original party to the contract of carriage remains liable under it, so that there is no *transfer* of liability.[23]

---

[13] Insolvency Act 1986, s.315; cf. ibid. s.178. For exceptions, see Companies Act 1989, s.164.

[14] For the measure of such liability, see *Re Park Air Services plc* [2000] 2 A.C. 172.

[15] Insolvency Act 1986, s.44, as amended by Insolvency Act 1994; *Powdrill v Watson* [1995] 2 A.C. 394.

[16] Transfer of Undertakings (Protection of Employment) Regulations 1981 (S.I. 1981 No. 1794), reg. 5(1); for amendments, see, above, p.694.

[17] *Litster v Forth Dry Dock Co Ltd* [1990] A.C. 546 at 555.

[18] Reg.5(2); *Wilson v St Helen's BC* [1999] 2 A.C. 52 at 76, 83.

[19] See above, p.694.

[20] *Newns v British Airways* [1992] I.R.L.R. 575 at 577; *MRS Environmental Services v Dyke, The Times*, March 25, 1997.

[21] s.2(1)(a).

[22] s.3(1)(a); see *The Berge Sisar* [2001] UKHL 17, [2002] 2 A.C. 205.

[23] Carriage of Goods by Sea Act 1999, s.3(3).

CHAPTER SEVENTEEN

AGENCY[1]

SECTION 1. DEFINITION

AGENCY is a relationship which arises when one person, called the principal, authorises another, called the agent, to act on his behalf, and the other agrees to do so. Generally, the relationship arises out of an agreement[2] between principal and agent. Its most important effect, for the purpose of this book, is that it enables the agent to make a contract between his principal and a third party.

1. Agreement

(1) General

The agreement between principal and agent is often a contract. But agency may also arise out of an agreement which does not amount to a contract because one of the parties lacks contractual capacity[3] or because there is no consideration. Thus the committee of a club, though they act gratuitously, may be agents of the members.[4]

(2) Agency without agreement

There may be agency without agreement in the following cases:

(a) OPERATION OF LAW. The law may attribute an agent to a person: for example, when a company is first formed, its original directors are its agents by operation of law.[5] Public corporations created by statute are sometimes regarded as agents of the Crown[6]: such agency arises simply by virtue of the incorporating statute. Moreover, by statute, one person, or the court, may have power to appoint an agent to act on behalf of another: thus a mortgagee can in certain circumstances appoint an agent of the mortgagor[7]; an administrative receiver appointed by debenture holders is deemed to be the agent of the company[8]; and a person appointed by the court to manage the affairs of a mental patient has been held to be the patient's agent.[9] At common law, one person may be regarded as the agent of another, even against the latter's will, under the doctrine of agency of necessity.[10]

---

[1] The leading work on this subject is *Bowstead and Reynolds on Agency* (17th ed.).
[2] *Garnac Grain Co Inc v Faure & Fairclough Ltd* [1968] A.C. 1130 at 1137; Fridman, 84 L.Q.R. 224.
[3] See below, p.709.
[4] *cf. Flemyng v Hector* (1836) 2 M. & W. 172.
[5] *cf.* Companies Act 1985, s.282. But English law does not regard the company as agent for its shareholders: *J H Rayner (Mincing Lane) Ltd v DTI* [1989] Ch. 72 at 188 (approved on this point [1990] 2 A.C. 418 at 515). See also Limited Liability Partnerships Act 2000, s.6(1): members of a limited liability partnership (which is a body corporate: s.1(2)) are agents of the partnership.
[6] *e.g. Bank voor Handel en Scheepvaart NV v Administrator of Hungarian Property* [1954] A.C. 584.
[7] Law of Property Act 1925, s.109; see *Medforth v Blake* [2000] Ch. 86.
[8] Insolvency Act 1986, s.44(1)(a); *cf.* s.14(5).
[9] *Plumpton v Burkinshaw* [1908] 2 K.B. 572.
[10] See below, pp.718 *et seq.*

(b) APPARENT AND USUAL AUTHORITY. Under the doctrines of apparent and usual authority[11] a principal is liable on contracts made by his agent although he has not authorised the agent to make them.

2. Intention to Act on Behalf of Principal

Whether a person intends to act on behalf of another is a question of fact. Thus a person who agrees out of friendship to ferry another's car from one place to another can be regarded as the owner's agent,[12] so that his negligent driving may make the owner liable in tort; but a person who borrows another's car for his own purposes would not be so regarded.[13] Even where the owner is liable for the driver's torts, it does not follow that the driver is his agent for other purposes, such as pledging his credit for fuel or repairs. Where a person does intend to act on behalf of another, agency may arise although a contract between the parties declares that there is no such relationship[14]; conversely the mere fact that a person says he is an agent does not make him one if he intends to act on his own behalf and not on behalf of his alleged principal.[15]

The rule that an agent must intend to act on behalf of his principal distinguishes agency from other analogous relationships, and is helpful in cases where it is clear that a person acted as agent, but not clear whose agent he was.

(1) Agency distinguished from other relationships

(a) BUYER AND SELLER. A retailer or distributor may describe himself as the "agent" of the manufacturer whose products he sells. This description is legally accurate if he negotiates a contract between manufacturer and customer, accounts to the manufacturer for the price paid by the customer, and is remunerated by a commission or salary paid by the manufacturer[16]; it may be accurate even if he is remunerated by a "mark-up" on the price that he pays to the manufacturer.[17] But generally the retailer acts, not in this capacity,[18] but as a middleman who buys and resells on his own behalf. He is the manufacturer's "agent" only in a commercial, and not in the legal sense.[19] Thus if the goods are defective the customer can sue only the retailer, and not the manufacturer, on the contract of sale. The manufacturer may be liable to the customer on a separate contract if he gives a guarantee[20]; he may also be liable in tort[21] if the customer suffers loss or injury because of a defect in the goods. Again a manufacturer who contracts to make something for a customer is not the agent of the customer. Although he makes the

---

[11] See below, pp.712–718.

[12] e.g. *Ormrod v Crosville Motor Services Ltd* [1953] 1 W.L.R. 1120; *Vandyke v Fender* [1970] 2 Q.B. 292.

[13] e.g. *Hewitt v Bonvin* [1940] 1 K.B. 188; *Morgans v Launchbury* [1973] A.C. 127.

[14] *McLaughlin v Gentles* (1919) 51 D.L.R. 383.

[15] *Kennedy v De Trafford* [1897] A.C. 180 at 188.

[16] In *Triffit Nurseries v Salads, etc. Ltd* [2000] 2 Lloyd's Rep. 74 a contract between P and A authorised A to contract with customers "as principal" but required A to account to P for sums received from such customers. The contract was treated as giving rise to an agency relationship between P and A.

[17] cf. *Mercantile International Group plc v Chuan Soon Huat International Group Ltd* [2002] EWCA Civ 288; [2002] 1 All E.R.(Comm) 788.

[18] Similar problems can arise in determining whether a person who is asked to procure goods for another is his agent or a seller to him: see *Ireland v Livingston* (1871) L.R. 5 H.L. 395; Hill, 31 M.L.R. 623; *Kloekner & Co AG v Gatoil Overseas Inc* [1990] 1 Lloyd's Rep. 177; cf. *Customs & Excise Commissioners v Paget* [1989] S.T.C. 773; *The Coral Rose* [1991] 1 Lloyd's Rep. 563.

[19] cf. *AMB Imballaggi Plastici SRL v Pacflex Ltd* [1999] 2 All E.R.(Comm) 249.

[20] See above, pp.77, 582. "Consumer guarantees" under Sale and Supply of Goods to Consumers Regulations 2002 (SI 2002/3045), reg.15 take effect as "contractual obligations": see above, p.163 at n.7.

[21] For negligence at common law and irrespective of negligence under Consumer Protection Act 1987.

thing at the customer's request, he acts primarily for his own profit and on his own behalf.[22]

(b) HIRE-PURCHASE. A dealer who negotiates a hire-purchase agreement between a customer and a finance company is considered at common law to act primarily on his own behalf.[23] But he may be the agent of the company for some purposes, *e.g.* to accept offers on the terms of the company's proposal form.[24] And under the Consumer Credit Act 1974 he may be treated as the agent of the company when he makes any representation in the course of negotiations as to the quality of the goods,[25] and when he receives notice from the customer that the agreement has been cancelled or rescinded, or that the customer's offer has been withdrawn.[26]

(c) BANKER AND CUSTOMER. The relation of banker and customer is primarily that of debtor and creditor but may for certain purposes be that of agent and principal: for example, where a bank on the instructions of its customer makes a transfer of funds out of the customer's account.[27] Conversely, an ordinary agency agreement does not give rise to the relationship of banker and customer merely because funds belonging to or destined for the principal are held (and used to make payments under the agreement) by the agent.[28]

(d) PROVISION OF SERVICES. Persons who are engaged in the business or profession of supplying services may be described as "agents" in the commercial sense, without being agents in the legal sense: "To carry on the business of an 'agent' is not the same thing as saying that you are contracting as agent."[29] For example, where a "forwarding agent" is engaged to arrange for goods to be transported to a foreign destination, he may act as agent (in the legal sense) in making a contract between the exporter and a carrier[30]; but he may equally well act as principal in undertaking to get the goods to the specified destination.[31] Whether such persons act in the legal sense as agents depends on the responsibilities that they undertake in relation to the particular transaction. The same point may be illustrated by reference to two further examples.

(i) *Client and professional man.* In *Leicestershire CC v Michael Faraday & Partners Ltd*[32] it was held that a firm of valuers had not acted as agents for their clients. MacKinnon L.J. said that the case was "emphatically not one of principal and agent. It is the case of the relations between a client and a professional man to whom the client

---

[22] *Dixon v London Small Arms Co* (1876) 1 App.Cas. 632; *State of the Netherlands v Youell* [1998] 1 Lloyd's Rep. 236.

[23] *Mercantile Credit Co Ltd v Hamblin* [1965] 2 Q.B. 242 at 269; *cf. Woodchester Equipment (Leasing) Ltd v British Association of Canned Food Importers* [1995] C.C.L.R. 51; *Shogun Finance Ltd v Hudson* [2001] EWCA Civ 1000; [2002] Q.B. 834, at [42–44]. In *Branwhite v Worcester Works Finance Ltd* [1969] 1 A.C. 552 Lords Morris, Guest and Upjohn took the view stated in the text, but Lords Reid and Wilberforce said that the dealer would normally be the finance company's agent.

[24] *Northgran Finance Ltd v Ashley* [1963] 1 Q.B. 476.

[25] s.56(2); by s.56(3) a provision in a regulated agreement purporting to make the dealer the *customer's* agent is void.

[26] ss.69(6), 102(1), 57(3). See also s.175 for the "agent's" duty to transmit such notices.

[27] *Barclays Bank plc v Quinecare Ltd* [1992] 4 All E.R. 363.

[28] *Kingscroft Insurance Co Ltd v HS Weaver (Underwriting) Agencies Ltd* [1993] 1 Lloyd's Rep. 187 at 191.

[29] *Elektronska etc. v Transped etc.* [1986] 1 Lloyd's Rep. 49 at 52.

[30] *Lukoil-Kalingradmorneft plc v Tata Ltd* [1999] 2 Lloyd's Rep. 129 at 138.

[31] See *Jones v European General Express* (1920) 25 Com.Cas. 296; *cf. Poseidon Freight Forwarding Co Ltd* [1996] 2 Lloyd's Rep. 388 at 389.

[32] [1941] 2 K.B. 205. The question arose for the purpose of determining the ownership of documents created by the valuers, and this would not be in the client *merely* because the person creating the documents was his agent: *Formica Ltd v Secretary of State acting by the ECGD* [1995] 1 Lloyd's Rep. 692.

resorts for advice."[33] Some professional advisers, such as solicitors[34] and architects[35] often do act as agents for their clients. Other professional persons are engaged simply to produce specified results: for example, to prepare a report or to paint a picture. Such persons have no power to act on behalf of their clients; and it is to this type of "professional man" that MacKinnon L.J. refers in the *Leicester* case.

(ii) *Estate agents*.[36] An estate agent who is instructed to negotiate the sale of a house by private treaty has normally[37] no power to make a contract between his client and a prospective purchaser.[38] He may for certain purposes act on behalf of the client, *e.g.* for the purpose of making representations about the property[39]; and he also owes the client certain duties similar to those owed by an agent to his principal.[40] But "an estate agent, despite the style, is an independent person"[41] who for most purposes does not normally act in the legal sense as the vendor's agent. In particular, he does not so act when he receives a deposit from a person who has agreed, subject to contract, to buy the property.[42] So long as no contract of sale has been concluded, he must not pay the deposit over to his client. He holds the money in trust for the prospective purchaser,[43] and must return it to him on demand[44]; but if he fails to do so the client is not liable for the deposit unless he had expressly authorised the estate agent to receive it on his behalf.[45]

(2) Whose agent?

It may be clear that a person is an agent, but doubtful whose agent he is. Thus it has been held that a London agent employed by a country solicitor was the agent, not of the lay client, but that he is the agent of the country solicitor.[46] On the other hand counsel, though briefed by the solicitor, may be the client's agent.[47]

In other cases the question is whether a person who is undoubtedly the agent of P may not also for some purposes be the agent of Q. Thus persons employed by an insurance company to solicit proposals for insurance are generally the company's agents,[48] but may

---

[33] [1941] 2 K.B. at 216.

[34] *e.g. Tudor v Hamid* [1988] 1 E.G.L.R. 251 (vendor's solicitor vendor's agent in receiving deposit); contrast *Hastingwood Property Ltd v Sanders Bearman Anselm* [1991] Ch. 114 (solicitor receiving money as stakeholder).

[35] *e.g. Gibson v Pease* [1905] 1 K.B. 810.

[36] Murdoch, 91 L.Q.R. 357.

[37] *i.e.* unless specifically so authorised, as seems to have been the case in *Spiro v Lintern* [1973] 1 W.L.R. 1002 at 1006; *cf. Jawara v Cambian Airways* [1992] E.G.C.S. 54, where such authority was held to have been conferred on a solicitor. For a statutory definition of "estate agency work," see Estate Agents Act 1979, s.1(1).

[38] *Wragg v Lovett* [1948] 2 All E.R. 968.

[39] *Sorrell v Finch* [1977] A.C. 728 at 753.

[40] *e.g. Regier v Campbell-Stuart* [1939] Ch. 766 (agent engaged to *find* a property for the client). *cf.*, in the case of a commodity broker, *Brandeis (Brokers) Ltd v Black* [2001] 2 All E.R.(Comm) 98.

[41] *Sorrell v Finch* [1977] A.C. 728 at 753.

[42] *Sorrell v Finch*, above; *John McCann & Co v Pow* [1974] 1 W.L.R. 1643 at 1647; Reynolds, 92 L.Q.R. 484; Markesinis [1976] C.L.J. 237.

[43] Estate Agents Act 1979, s.13(1)(a).

[44] At common law, he is not liable for interest: *Potters v Loppert* [1973] Ch. 399; but regulations made under Estate Agents Act 1979, s.15 may impose such liability.

[45] *Ryan v Pilkington* [1959] 1 W.L.R. 403, as explained in *Sorrell v Finch*, above, at 750; *cf. Ojelay v Neosale* [1987] 2 E.G.L.R. 167.

[46] *Robbins v Fennell* (1847) 11 Q.B. 248.

[47] *Grindell v Bass* [1920] 2 Ch. 487.

[48] *Bawden v London Assurance* [1892] 2 Q.B. 534; *Stone v Reliance Mutual Insurance Soc Ltd* [1972] 1 Lloyd's Rep. 469; Reynolds, 88 L.Q.R. 462.

become the agents of the proposer when helping him to complete the proposal form.[49] On the other hand insurance brokers are for most purposes agents of the insured persons and not of the insurers.[50] But they may be agents of the insurers for some purposes, such as the provision of interim insurance cover until the policy is issued.[51] Again, directors of a company are primarily the agents of the company, and not of the shareholders; but they may for some purposes become agents of the shareholders, *e.g.* for the purpose of negotiating a sale of their shares.[52]

3. Commercial Agents

Our main concern in this chapter is with the common law principles of agency. Some of these are in effect restated, but others are modified, by Regulations which give effect to an EC Council Directive[53] governing the relations between "commercial agents" and their principals.[54] The Regulations define "commercial agent" to mean "a self-employed intermediary who has continuing authority to negotiate the sale or purchase of goods on behalf of [55] another person (the "principal"), or to negotiate and conclude the sale or purchase of goods on behalf of and in the name of the principal".[56] A detailed discussion of these Regulations is beyond the scope of this book, but their effect on the rules here under discussion will be noted at appropriate points in this Chapter.

SECTION 2. CAPACITY

1. Capacity to Act as Agent

As agency is a consensual but not necessarily a contractual relationship, any person who is capable of consenting can act as agent, although his contractual capacity may be limited. In the days when married women lacked contractual capacity they could nonetheless act as agents.[57] Similarly, a minor can, it seems, be an agent to make a contract which he has no capacity to make on his own behalf; and a corporation could probably act as agent in respect of a transaction which was *ultra vires*. But to say that a person of limited contractual capacity can act as agent does not mean that his agreement to do so gives rise to all the legal consequences that usually result from the relationship of principal and agent. It means that he can make a contract between his principal and a third party, but not that he acquires all the rights or is subject to all the liabilities of an agent towards his principal or the third party. The agent could not be made liable if to hold him liable would defeat the protection which the law means to give him by limiting his capacity. Thus he could not be made liable on the contract between principal and third party, even though the circumstances were such that an agent of full capacity

---

[49] *Biggar v Rock Life Assurance Co* [1902] 1 K.B. 516; *Newsholme v Road Transport Insurance Co* [1929] 2 K.B. 356; *cf.* above, pp.338–339.

[50] *Anglo-African Merchants v Bayley* [1970] 1 Q.B. 311 at 322; *McNealy v Pennine Ins Co* [1978] 2 Lloyd's Rep. 18; *John W. Pryke v Gibbs Hartley Cooper Ltd* [1991] 1 Lloyd's Rep. 602; *Winter v Irish Life Assurance plc* [1995] 2 Lloyd's Rep. 274. For criticism, see *Roberts v Plaisted* [1989] 2 Lloyd's Rep. 341 at 345.

[51] *Stockton v Mason* [1978] 2 Lloyd's Rep. 430 (except in cases of marine insurance: *cf.* above, p.181).

[52] *Briess v Woolley* [1954] A.C. 333.

[53] Dir.86/653.

[54] Commercial Agents (Council Directive) Regulations 1993 (SI 1993/3053), as amended by Commercial Agents (Council Directive) (Amendment) Regulations 1993 and 1998 (SI 1993/3173 and SI 1998/2868).

[55] These words do not cover the case of a person who, though an agent in the commercial sense (above, p.652), sells goods as principal: *Parks v Esso Petroleum Co Ltd* [2000] Eur.L.R. 25.

[56] reg.2(1); for excepted cases, see reg.2(1)(i) to (iii) and 2(2).

[57] *Stevenson v Hardie* (1773) 2 Wm.Bl. 872.

would be so liable.[58] On the other hand, there is no reason to suppose that he would be denied the ordinary agent's right of indemnity[59] against his principal.

2. Capacity to Act as Principal

Capacity to act as principal is determined by the rules governing contractual capacity generally. Thus a minor cannot make himself liable for luxuries merely by employing an agent; but he can appoint an agent to make a contract which would have bound him if he had made it personally.[60] This rule again applies primarily to determine the reciprocal rights and liabilities of principal and third party. It might also protect the principal from liability to the agent. Thus a principal who was under age would not be liable to indemnify an agent employed to buy luxuries. But the rule would not necessarily protect the agent: thus an under-age principal might well have a remedy against the agent if the latter accepted a bribe[61] from the third party.

SECTION 3. CREATION OF AGENCY

Agency may arise by express or implied agreement, or without agreement under the doctrines of apparent and usual authority, and where a person has authority of necessity. Finally, agency may arise *ex post facto* by ratification.

1. Agency by Agreement

(1) Express authority

An agent's authority is commonly conferred by express appointment. At common law, no formality is required. Oral appointment suffices even where the agent is appointed to make a contract which has to be in writing, or evidenced in writing.[62] Under the Regulations governing contracts with commercial agents,[63] such an agent and his principal are entitled, on request, to receive from the other a signed written document setting out the terms of the agency contract.[64] This provision does not require the contract to be *made* in writing; it only requires each party to provide the other with a written *record* of its terms. No sanction is specified for failure to comply with the request.

The extent of an agent's express authority depends on the true construction of the words of the appointment. If these are vague or ambiguous, the principal may be bound even though the agent, in good faith, interprets them in a sense not intended by the principal.[65] But in such cases the speed of modern communications will often make it reasonable for the agent to seek clarification of his instructions, and if he fails to do so he will not be able to rely on his own mistaken interpretation of his instructions.[66] Where

---

[58] See below, pp.732 *et seq.*

[59] See below, p.744.

[60] See Webb, 18 M.L.R. 861; R.E.M., 69 L.Q.R. 446; a contrary dictum in *Shephard v Cartwright* [1953] Ch. 728 at 755 (reversed without reference to this point [1955] A.C. 431) was later corrected in *G (A) v G (T)* [1970] 2 Q.B. 644 at 651–652.

[61] See below, p.746.

[62] *Heard v Pilley* (1869) L.R. 4 Ch. 548.

[63] See above, p.709.

[64] Commercial Agents (Council Directive) Regulations 1993 (SI 1993/3053), reg.13(1).

[65] *Weigall v Runciman* (1916) 85 L.J.K.B. 1187; *cf. Ireland v Livingston* (1871) L.R. 5 H.L. 395, as explained in *Woodhouse AC Israel Cocoa Ltd SA v Nigerian Produce Marketing Co* [1972] A.C. 741 at 757, 771–772; *Credit Agricole Indosuez v Muslim Commercial Bank Ltd* [2000] 1 Lloyd's Rep. 275 at 280.

[66] *European Asian Bank v Punjab & Sind Bank (No.2)* [1983] 1 W.L.R. 642 at 656 (where the claim succeeded on another ground).

the agent's instructions are clear, it makes no difference that the principal acted under a mistake in giving them: for example, if he instructed the agent to insure a ship for £3m he is liable to indemnify the agent for the premium even though his actual intention was to insure her for only £2m.[67]

(2) Implied authority

(a) EXISTENCE OF AUTHORITY IMPLIED. The very existence of agency may be implied, either from conduct, or from the relationship of the parties. Thus it has been held that a husband who lives with his wife impliedly authorises her to pledge his credit for necessary household expenses.[68] This authority is not a legal consequence of marriage, but depends on the inference of fact that the husband has permitted the wife to pledge his credit as manager of the household. The authority therefore does not arise where there is no household because the parties live in an hotel.[69] But where there is a household, the authority can arise even though the parties are not married.[70] As the authority is based on implied consent, it can be negatived if the husband forbids his wife to pledge his credit.[71] The wife's authority is also negatived if the husband gives her an adequate housekeeping allowance[72]; if the husband warns the tradesman not to supply goods to the wife on his credit; and if the wife already has an adequate supply of the goods in question.[73] The cases which lay down these rules are unlikely to be of much significance in modern conditions when household supplies are generally paid for either on delivery or on credit terms requiring the signature of the debtor personally[74]; but they could still have some practical importance in relation to services supplied to the household. A child has no implied authority to pledge his parents' credit; but such authority may be implied if the parent stands by and acquiesces in a purchase made by the child on his account.[75]

(b) INCIDENTAL AUTHORITY. An agent who is appointed for a particular purpose may have implied authority to do acts incidental to the execution of that authority. For example, a solicitor, or counsel engaged to conduct litigation, may have implied authority to compromise the suit.[76] On the other hand, an agent employed to sell a thing has generally no authority to receive payment for it.[77] The question whether he has authority to warrant its quality is one of fact, depending on the circumstances of each case.[78]

(c) CUSTOMARY AUTHORITY.[79] A principal who employs an agent to act for him in a particular market impliedly authorises the agent to act in accordance with the custom of

---

[67] *The Tzelepi* [1991] 2 Lloyd's Rep. 265.

[68] *Jewsbury v Newbold* (1857) 26 L.J.Ex. 247; *Phillipson v Hayter* (1870) L.R. 6 C.P. 38 at 42; *Gage v King* [1961] 1 Q.B. 188 (medical bills).

[69] *Debenham v Mellon* (1880) 6 App.Cas. 24.

[70] *Blades v Free* (1829) 9 B. & C. 167.

[71] *Jolly v Rees* (1864) 15 C.B.(N.S.) 628; *Miss Gray Ltd v Cathcart* (1922) 38 T.L.R. 562.

[72] *Morel Bros. v Westmorland* [1903] 1 K.B. 63; affirmed [1904] A.C. 11.

[73] *Miss Gray Ltd v Cathcart* (1922) 38 T.L.R. 562 at 565; *Seaton v Benedict* (1828) 5 Bing. 28.

[74] See Consumer Credit Act 1974, s.61(1)(a): the requirement of signature "*by* the debtor . . . and *by or on behalf* of the creditor" indicates that signature on behalf of the debtor is insufficient.

[75] *Law v Wilkin* (1837) 6 A. & E. 718; some dicta in this case are too sweeping: *Mortimore v Wright* (1840) 6 M. & W. 487.

[76] *Waugh v H B Clifford & Sons* [1982] Ch. 374.

[77] *Mynn v Jolliffe* (1834) 1 M. & Rob. 326; *Butwick v Grant* [1924] 2 K.B. 483. *cf.* above, p.708 as to deposits received by estate agents.

[78] Such authority was implied in *Alexander v Gibson* (1811) 2 Camp. 555; *Howard v Sheward* (1866) L.R. 2 C.P. 148; and *Baldry v Bates* (1885) 52 L.T. 620; contrast *Brady v Todd* (1861) 9 C.B.(N.S.) 592.

[79] *cf.* above, p.213, for the view that it is artificial to base such authority on actual agreement.

that market.[80] He is bound by the custom even if he is not aware of it.[81] But the inference that the principal authorises the agent to act in accordance with the custom cannot be drawn if the custom is inconsistent with the instructions given by the principal to the agent, or with the very relationship of principal and agent. The custom is then said to be "unreasonable" and the principal is not bound by it unless he knows of it.[82] Thus in *Robinson v Mollett*[83] there was a custom in the tallow market by which an agent employed by several principals was allowed to buy in bulk to satisfy the needs of all. The custom was held unreasonable since its effect was to turn an agent into a seller. This was inconsistent with the relationship of principal and agent since an agent must buy for his principal as cheaply as he can, while a seller sells at the highest price he can get. But in *Scott v Godfrey*[84] a custom of the Stock Exchange permitting stockbrokers to buy enough shares for several principals from a single seller was held reasonable because all the parties intended that contracts should be made between the seller and the various buyers.

2. Agency without Agreement

(1) Apparent authority

Where a person represents to a third party that he has authorised an agent to act on his behalf, he may, as against the third party, not be allowed to deny the truth of the representation, and be bound by the agent's act whether he in fact had authorised it or not. In *Summers v Solomon*,[85] for instance, the defendant employed a manager to run a jeweller's shop and regularly paid for jewellery ordered by the manager from the claimant for resale in the shop. The manager left the defendant's employment, ordered further jewellery in the defendant's name, and absconded with it. The defendant was held liable to pay for this jewellery since his conduct had led the claimant to believe that the manager had authority to pledge his credit, and he had not informed the claimant that that authority had come to an end.

The following conditions must be satisfied before apparent authority arises:

(a) THERE MUST BE A REPRESENTATION OF AUTHORITY. This may be express[86] but it is more frequently implied: for example, from a course of dealing, as in *Summers v Solomon*; or from placing the agent in such a position that it is reasonable for third parties to assume that he has the principal's authority to make a contract of the kind in question[87]; or from the known relationship of the parties, so that where a partner has

---

[80] *Graves v Legg* (1857) 2 H. & N. 210.

[81] *Pollock v Stables* (1848) 12 Q.B. 765; *Cropper v Cook* (1868) L.R. 3 C.P. 194; *Reynolds v Smith* (1893) 9 T.L.R. 494.

[82] *e.g. Perry v Barnett* (1885) 15 Q.B.D. 388 (custom to make contract without complying with statutory formalities and hence void); contrast *Seymour v Bridge* (1885) 14 Q.B.D. 460, where the principal knew of the custom.

[83] (1875) L.R. 7 H.L. 802; *cf. North & South Trust Co v Berkeley* [1971] 1 W.L.R. 471.

[84] [1901] 2 Q.B. 726.

[85] (1857) 7 E. & B. 879; *cf. Pole v Leask* (1862) 33 L.J.Ch. 155; *The Unique Mariner* [1978] 1 Lloyd's Rep. 438; *The Shamah* [1981] 1 Lloyd's Rep. 40; *Waugh v H B Clifford & Sons* [1982] Ch. 374; *John W Pryke v Gibbs Hartley Cooper Ltd* [1991] 1 Lloyd's Rep. 602 at 615; *First Sport Ltd v Barclays Bank plc* [1993] 1 W.L.R. 1229. The following discussion deals only with the extent to which the principal can as a result of the representation be held liable on an unauthorised contract. It is not concerned with any other form of liability for misrepresentation.

[86] *e.g. Gurtner v Beaton* [1993] 2 Lloyd's Rep. 369.

[87] *Panorama Developments (Guildford) Ltd v Fidelis Furnishing Fabrics Ltd* [1971] 2 Q.B. 711; *The Ocean Frost* [1986] A.C. 717 at 777; *United Bank of Kuwait v Hamoud* [1988] 1 W.L.R. 1051; *cf. Strover v Harrington* [1988] Ch. 390 at 409–410; contrast *Cleveland Manufacturing Co v Muslim Commercial Bank Ltd* [1981] 2 Lloyd's Rep. 646.

retired he continues to be liable to those who deal with the firm and know that he had been a partner but not that he had retired[88]; and conversely the firm will be liable to such third parties on contracts made by him, ostensibly on its behalf.[89] In such cases, the apparent authority is said to be *general* in character since it extends generally to all transactions which a person, in the position in which the principal has placed the agent, is normally regarded as having authority to conclude.[90] Even where the agent has no such apparent authority by virtue of his position, he may have *specific* apparent authority to enter into a particular transaction; but since in such cases it is (*ex hypothesi*) clear to the third party that the agent does not *normally* have authority to conclude a transaction of that kind, the principal will be liable on the basis of specific apparent authority only if the third party can show that the principal expressly represented that the agent had authority to enter into the particular contract on his behalf.[91]

(b) THE REPRESENTATION MUST BE OF FACT. A representation of law does not give rise to apparent authority.[92] Thus a third party cannot rely on the doctrine of apparent authority if he has read the terms of the agent's appointment, but has misconstrued them, since the construction of a document is a question of law. The rejection by the House of Lords of the former rule that mistake of law gives rise to no *restitutionary*[93] claim would not seem to affect the present rule, which is concerned with the *creation of contractual rights*.

(c) THE REPRESENTATION MUST BE THAT THE "AGENT" IS AUTHORISED TO ACT AS AGENT. Apparent authority does not arise if a person is represented to be the *owner* of a business or other property. In such cases the representor may be bound under the doctrine of usual authority, or under some analogous doctrine.[94] But the scope of these doctrines is limited, and where they do not apply, the representee can fall back on the more general doctrine of apparent authority only if the representation is one of *agency*.

(d) THE REPRESENTATION MUST BE MADE BY THE PRINCIPAL. Apparent authority can arise only out of a representation made by the principal: it cannot arise out of a representation made by some other person[95] or out of one made by the agent himself.[96] Of course, a principal may represent that the agent has authority to make further representations on his behalf; and the principal may make such a representation by conduct, for example, by placing the agent in a position in which he would normally have authority to enter into a transaction of the type in question or to communicate what purports to be the principal's approval of it[97] (even though the principal's instructions

---

[88] Partnership Act 1890, s.14(1); and *cf. Scarf v Jardine* (1882) 7 App.Cas. 345.

[89] *cf.* Limited Liability Partnerships Act 2000, s.6(3)(a).

[90] *The Ocean Frost* [1986] A.C. 717 at 777; contrast *The Suwalki* [1989] 1 Lloyd's Rep. 511 (shipbroker has no such authority); *Hirst v Etherington* [1999] Lloyd's P.N. 938 (solicitor not acting in usual course of business).

[91] *The Ocean Frost*, above, where the third party's claim on this basis failed.

[92] *cf.*, above, p.332; below, p.739.

[93] *Kleinwort Benson Ltd v Lincoln CC* [1999] 2 A.C. 349; below, p.1059.

[94] See below, pp.716–718.

[95] *The Rhodian River* [1984] 1 Lloyd's Rep. 373; *First Sport Ltd v Barclays Bank plc* [1993] 1 W.L.R. 1229 at 1240.

[96] *Lanyon v Blanchard* (1811) 2 Camp. 597; *Attorney-General for Ceylon v Silva* [1953] A.C. 461; *British Bank of the Middle East v Sun Life Assurance Co of Canada (U.K.) Ltd* [1983] 2 Lloyd's Rep. 9 at 17; *The Raffaela* [1985] 2 Lloyd's Rep. 36 at 43; *The Ocean Frost* [1986] A.C. 717 at 778; *The Suwalki* [1989] 1 Lloyd's Rep. 511; *Re Selectmove* [1995] 1 W.L.R. 474 at 478.

[97] *First Energy (UK) Ltd v Hungarian International Bank Ltd* [1993] 2 Lloyd's Rep. 195.

had negatived the agent's *actual* authority to take such steps).[98] In such a case, the agent may by his own representation enlarge an existing authority,[99] but such a representation cannot create an apparent authority out of nothing.[1]

(e) THE REPRESENTATION MUST BE MADE TO THE THIRD PARTY. The representation must be made to a third person or group of persons. The old notion of holding a person out as agent "to the world"[2] has long been discredited.[3] Nor can a representation made by principal to agent give rise to apparent authority.

(f) THE THIRD PARTY MUST HAVE RELIED ON THE REPRESENTATION. The third party must have been induced by the representation to deal with the agent in the belief that the principal had authorised the agent to enter into the transaction.[4] Two consequences flow from this requirement. First, the representation must actually be known to the third party; and this requirement cannot be satisfied if the representation is contained in a document which has not actually come to his attention.[5] Secondly, the third party is not allowed to say that he relied on the representation if he knew that it was untrue,[6] or if he had, but did not take, a reasonable chance of reading the agent's instructions and so of discovering the truth.[7]

These requirements have given rise to particular difficulties in cases in which a third party dealt with a corporation through an agent who had no actual authority to enter into the transaction. In the case of a company incorporated under the Companies Acts, these difficulties arose largely because the authority of such an agent might be set out in, or limited by, the company's memorandum or articles of association; and, before the changes in the law to be discussed below, the rule was that the third party had constructive notice of these documents.[8] This doctrine of constructive notice operated in favour of the company but not against it. Thus if the memorandum or articles *limited* the power of the company's officer, the third party was deemed to know of the limitation and could not rely on an appearance of authority inconsistent with it. But if they *conferred* power, the third party could not base a case of apparent authority on them, for he could not be said to have relied on something of which he was only deemed to know (but did not actually know).[9] This state of the law could cause considerable hardship to third parties, and two important changes in the law were made by the Companies Act 1989.

---

[98] *United Bank of Kuwait v Hamoud* [1988] 1 W.L.R. 1051.
[99] *The Raffaela* [1985] 2 Lloyd's Rep. 36 at 43.
[1] *The Ocean Frost* [1986] A.C. 717 at 778. *United Bank of Kuwait v Hamoud* [1988] 1 W.L.R. 1051 at 1064 ("cannot hold himself out"); *First Energy* case, above, n.97; *Suncorp Insurance & Finance v Milano Assicurazioni SpA* [1993] 2 Lloyd's Rep. 225 at 232; *Lukoil Kalingradmorneft plc v Tata Ltd* [1999] 2 Lloyd's Rep. 129 at 138; *cf. Hirst v Etherington* [1999] Lloyd's Rep. P.N. 938.
[2] *Whitehead v Tuckett* (1812) 15 East 400 at 411.
[3] *Dickinson v Valpy* (1829) 10 B. & C. 128 at 140.
[4] For cases in which this requirement was not satisfied, see *Kooragang Investments Pty Ltd v Richardson & Wrench Ltd* [1982] A.C. 462; *Bedford Insurance Co Ltd v Instituto de Ressaguros do Brasil* [1985] Q.B. 966; *The Ocean Frost* [1986] A.C. 717; *cf. Nationwide BS v Lewis* [1998] Ch. 482.
[5] *The Ocean Frost* [1986] A.C. 717 at 778.
[6] Similar restrictions apply where a member of a limited liability partnership enters into a transaction with a third party which is beyond the scope of the member's actual authority: see Limited Liability Partnerships Act 2000, s.6(2).
[7] *Jacobs v Morris* [1902] 1 Ch. 816; *Overbrooke Estates Ltd v Glencombe Properties Ltd* [1974] 1 W.L.R. 1335; Coote [1975] C.L.J. 17; *Rolled Steel (Holdings) Ltd v BSC* [1986] Ch. 246 at 295–296. The principle seems to have been overlooked in *Mendelssohn v Normand Ltd* [1970] 1 Q.B. 177.
[8] *Mahony v East Holyford Mining Co Ltd* (1875) L.R. 7 H.L. 869.
[9] See *Rama Corp v Proved Tin & General Investments Ltd* [1952] 2 Q.B. 147, discussing earlier authorities; for further discussion, see *Freeman & Lockyer v Buckhurst Properties (Mangal) Ltd* [1964] 2 Q.B. 480.

First, the doctrine of constructive or deemed notice of the company's registered documents has been abolished.[10] A third party may, indeed, still be "affected by notice of any matter by reason of a failure to make such inquiries as ought reasonably to be made".[11] But the latter provision is of limited importance in the present context because "a party to a transaction with a company is not bound to enquire as to whether it is permitted by the company's memorandum or as to any limitation on the powers of the board of directors to bind the company *or to authorise others to do so*."[12] The third party is thus not bound to inquire whether the directors actually had the power to authorise the agent, with whom he dealt, to enter into the transaction on behalf of the company.

Secondly, in favour of a person dealing in good faith with the company, the power of the board of directors to bind the company is "deemed to be free of any limitation under the company's constitution".[13] This provision has already been discussed[14]; here it is only necessary to repeat that a person does not act in bad faith merely because he knows that an act is beyond the powers of the directors under the company's constitution.[15] Liability under this provision may therefore arise even though the requirements of the doctrine of apparent authority are *not* satisfied because the third party knows of the limitation on the directors' authority.

The common law principles governing apparent authority can, however, still apply where the third party relies, not on the apparent *existence* of powers, but on their *exercise*. The point may be illustrated by supposing that the board of directors of a company has power under the articles to appoint a managing director, but that the person with whom the third party has dealt as such has not actually been appointed to the post. The third party cannot then rely simply on the fact that the board had power to make the appointment. But the third party's claim will be upheld if he can show that there has been a representation by the persons entitled to make the appointment, to the effect that it has in fact been made. Such a representation need not be express but may be implied from conduct: for example, from the action of the board in allowing the person with whom the third party dealt to act as managing director. The company will then be bound by contracts made by him (even though he has not actually been appointed managing director) so long as those contracts are within the scope of the authority normally conferred on managing directors.[16] A company may also be bound by contracts made by its officers on the ground that they were impliedly authorised to make them; but here the liability is based on actual (implied) and not on apparent authority.[17]

(g) FORGERIES BY AGENT. In two cases, company secretaries affixed the common seals of their companies to documents which they had forged. It was held that third parties who were taken in by the forgeries could not, against the companies, rely on them.[18] But in *Uxbridge PBS v Pickard*[19] a solicitor's clerk obtained money by way of mortgage on the strength of forged title deeds alleged to belong to a fictitious client. His principal was

---

[10] Companies Act 1985, s.711A(1) (as inserted by Companies Act 1989, s.142). Contrast Limited Liability Partnerships Act 2000, s.6(3)(b) under which the apparent authority of a member of such a body can be terminated by giving notice that he has ceased to be a member of the Registrar of Companies.

[11] Companies Act 1985, s.711A(2).

[12] *ibid.* s.35B (as inserted by Companies Act 1989, s.108(1)).

[13] *ibid.* s.35A(1).

[14] See above, p.562 (also listing cases excepted from s.35A).

[15] Companies Act 1985, s.35A(2)(b) (as inserted by Companies Act 1989, s.108(1)).

[16] *Freeman & Lockyer v Buckhurst Properties (Mangal) Ltd*, above, n.9.

[17] *Hely-Hutchinson v Brayhead Ltd* [1968] 1 Q.B. 549 at 573; Nock, 30 M.L.R. 705.

[18] *Bank of Ireland v Evan's Trustees* (1855) 5 H.L.C. 389; *Ruben v Great Fingall Consolidated* [1906] A.C. 439.

[19] [1939] 2 K.B. 248.

held liable. In the former cases, the secretaries had not been held out as having authority to execute the documents (respectively a power of attorney and a share transfer). In the latter case, the clerk had been held out as having authority to conclude mortgage transactions. Alternatively, the first two cases can be regarded as cases in which the agent had, in effect, forged the principal's signature. When this happens, the third party is induced to believe, not that the agent has his principal's authority, but that the signature is the act of the principal himself. Such a belief does not give rise to apparent authority.[20] The person whose signature is forged is, however, liable if he knew of the forgery and acquiesced in it.[21]

(h) SUBSEQUENT CONDUCT OF "PRINCIPAL". A person may be bound by a contract, even though the requirements of apparent authority are not satisfied, if he is precluded by his subsequent conduct from denying that the contract was made on his behalf. In *Spiro v Lintern*[22] a wife purported to enter into a contract for the sale of her husband's house. She had no actual authority to do so, nor had the husband before the transaction led the purchaser to believe that she was his agent for the purpose. But afterwards the husband met the purchaser, gave him the impression that there was a binding contract and allowed him to incur expenses in connection with the property. It was held that the husband was estopped[23] from denying his wife's authority to make the contract on his behalf.

(2) Usual authority

(a) MEANING. The phrase "usual authority" is used in a number of senses. First, it may mean implied authority, and, in particular, incidental authority.[24] Secondly, it may refer to cases in which an agent has apparent authority because he has been placed by his principal in a situation in which he would have had incidental authority, if this had not been expressly negatived by instructions given to him by the principal (and not communicated to the third party).[25] But the phrase will here be used in a third sense, to refer to cases in which a principal is bound by his agent's contracts although there is no express, implied or apparent authority. This usage is based on *Watteau v Fenwick*,[26] where the owner of a public-house was sued for the price of cigars bought without his authority by his manager for the purposes of the business. The manager had bought the cigars in his own name. Thus the seller could not rely on any appearance of authority since he believed, at the time of the contract, that the manager was contracting on his own behalf. But the defendant was nonetheless held liable. Wills J. said: "The principal is liable for all the acts of the agent which are within the authority usually confided to an agent of that character, notwithstanding limitations, as between the principal and the agent, put upon that authority. It is said that this is only so where there has been a holding out of authority. . . . But I do not think so."[27]

---

[20] *cf. Kooragang Investments Pty Ltd v Richardson & Wrench Ltd* [1982] A.C. 462.

[21] *Greenwood v Martins Bank Ltd* [1933] A.C. 51.

[22] [1973] 1 W.L.R. 1002; followed in *Worboys v Carter* [1987] 2 E.G.L.R. 1; *cf. Janred Properties Ltd v Ente Nazionale Italiano per il Turismo* [1989] 2 All E.R. 444.

[23] Detrimental reliance by the third party is necessary for this type of estoppel (above, p.403); while for the purposes of apparent authority, "the only detriment that has to be shown . . . is the entering into the contract": *The Tatra* [1990] 2 Lloyd's Rep. 51 at 59.

[24] See above, p.711.

[25] *The Raffaella* [1985] 2 Lloyd's Rep. 36 at 41; *First Energy (UK) Ltd v Hungarian International Bank Ltd* [1993] 2 Lloyd's Rep. 195 at 201.

[26] [1893] 1 Q.B. 346.

[27] *ibid.* at 348–349; *cf. The Ocean Frost* [1986] A.C. 717 at 734 (affirmed *ibid.* 773), where there was no holding out for the different reason stated at p.713, above.

This decision has been criticised,[28] and has been more often distinguished than followed, but later courts which have thought it necessary to distinguish it must have regarded it as still good law.[29] There are, moreover, other cases in which a principal is bound by his agent's acts done outside the scope of his express, implied or apparent authority. Thus if a principal gives his agent documents and authorises him to borrow a fixed sum on the security of them, he may be liable to a third party from whom the agent borrows more, even though the third party did not think that the agent had any authority to borrow.[30] Similarly, at common law a person was bound by an unauthorised sale of his goods by a factor, though the factor sold in his own name.[31] At common law, he was not bound by an unauthorised pledge, but under the Factors Act 1889, he is bound, if certain conditions are satisfied, by any disposition (though unauthorised) made by such an agent. These rules are, it is submitted, based on the same principle as *Watteau v Fenwick*. That principle seems to be more closely analogous to the doctrine of vicarious liability in tort (under which an employer may be liable even for forbidden acts if done by an employee in the course of employment[32]) than to the doctrine of apparent authority.

Two Privy Council decisions can be said to be inconsistent with the principle of usual authority, in that they simply did not consider it as a possible basis of liability where the requirements of apparent authority were not satisfied. But in the first[33] the question was whether a principal could be held *criminally* liable for his agent's unauthorised act in purporting to enter, on the principal's behalf, into a contract which the latter was by statute prohibited from making. The negative answer given to this question can be explained on the ground that the courts are reluctant to impose criminal liability without *mens rea*. And in the second case[34] the contract was a sale of Crown property made without actual or apparent authority. The conclusion that the Crown was not bound was supported on the ground that "The subject derives benefits . . . from property vested in the Crown, and its proper protection is necessary in the interests of the subject, though it may cause hardship to an individual."[35] But this reasoning proves too much, for the need to give "proper protection" to Crown property would seem to extend to *all* dispositions made without actual authority, *i.e.* even to those within the agent's apparent authority. And the only conclusion which follows from Privy Council's reasoning is that the Crown should not have been ordered to deliver the goods to the buyer, and such specific relief is not available against the Crown, even where it is bound by a contract.[36] The reasoning does not explain why the disappointed buyer should not receive damages or compensation; and in deciding whether such a remedy ought to be available it is submitted that the principle of usual (no less than that of apparent) authority should be taken into consideration.

(b) SCOPE. The extent of an agent's usual authority depends on the class of agent to which he belongs and on the common understanding of the trade concerning such

---

[28] See Montrose, 17 Can.Bar Rev. 693; Hornby [1961] C.L.J. 239; *The Rhodian River* [1984] 1 Lloyd's Rep. 373 at 379.

[29] See *Johnston v Reading* (1893) 9 T.L.R. 200; *Lloyds Bank v Swiss Bankverein* (1912) 107 L.T. 309; 108 L.T. 143; *Jerome v Bentley & Co* [1952] 2 T.L.R. 58.

[30] *Brocklesby v Temperance PBS* [1895] A.C. 173; *Fry v Smellie* [1912] 3 K.B. 282. For criticism of the reasoning of these cases, see *Bowstead and Reynolds on Agency* (17th ed.), pp.393–394.

[31] *Coles v NW Bank* (1875) L.R. 10 C.P. 354 at 362.

[32] *Limpus v LGOC* (1862) 1 H. & C. 526.

[33] *Miles v McIlwraith* (1883) 8 App.Cas. 120.

[34] *Attorney-General for Ceylon v Silva* [1953] A.C. 461; above, p.713.

[35] [1953] A.C. at 481.

[36] Crown Proceedings Act 1947, s.21(1)(a).

agents. *Watteau v Fenwick* should from this point of view be contrasted with *Daun v Simmins*,[37] where it was held that the manager of a tied public-house had no usual authority to order spirits from any person he chose. And where the agent does not belong to a well-known class of agents, but is simply appointed for an isolated transaction, the doctrine of usual authority does not apply. Thus in *Jerome v Bentley & Co*[38] a retired army officer to whom jewellery had been entrusted for sale was held not to have the usual authority which a mercantile agent would have had in the same circumstances.

A principal is liable under the doctrine of usual authority only if there is some dealing between the third party and the agent: the doctrine does not apply if the agent's involvement in the transaction has been concealed so that the third party thinks that he is dealing directly with the principal.[39] The contract must also be made in the course of the principal's business: in *Kinahan v Parry*[40] it was accordingly held that a hotel-owner was not liable for whisky bought without his authority by his manager, since it was not proved that the manager had bought it for use in the hotel rather than for his personal use. Similarly, where the manager of a tied house bought beer from outside suppliers and resold it on the premises on his own account, it was said that his employers could not have been sued for the price of the beer.[41] A person is, *a fortiori*, not liable under the doctrine of usual authority if the business in the course of which the contract was made was not his business at all. Thus in *MacFisheries Ltd v Harrison*[42] the owner of a public-house sold it as a going concern, but forgot to transfer the licence to the buyer. He was not liable for food supplied to his successor for consumption on the premises, since the latter was carrying on the business entirely on his own behalf.

(3) Authority of necessity[43]

Under this heading, we shall first discuss a number of situations in which one person acts to protect some interest of another without any previous authorisation from that other person. We shall then consider whether any useful purpose is served by attempting to bring all these, somewhat disparate, cases within the scope of a single doctrine.

(a) ACCEPTANCE OF A BILL OF EXCHANGE FOR THE HONOUR OF THE DRAWER. When a bill is not accepted by the person on whom it is drawn, a stranger may, with the consent of the holder, accept the bill for the honour of the drawer. If the stranger has to pay on this acceptance, he becomes entitled to the rights of the holder to sue the drawer on the bill.[44]

(b) SHIPMASTERS. Where it is necessary[45] to do so for the further prosecution of the voyage, the master of a ship has authority of necessity to borrow on the shipowner's

---

[37] (1879) 41 L.T. 783.
[38] [1952] 2 T.L.R. 58.
[39] *Kooragang Investments Pty Ltd v Richardson & Wrench Ltd* [1982] A.C. 462.
[40] [1911] 1 K.B. 459.
[41] *Attorney-General's Reference (No.1 of 1985)* [1986] Q.B. 491 at 506.
[42] (1924) 93 L.J.K.B. 811.
[43] Williston, 22 Can.Bar Rev. 492; Treitel, 3 W.A.A.L. Rev. 1; Wade, 19 Vanderbilt L.Rev. 1183; Birks, 10 C.L.P. 110; Matthews [1981] C.L.J. 340. The old rules under which a deserted wife had authority of necessity were abolished by Matrimonial Proceedings and Property Act 1970, s.41, and are not revived by the repeal of that section by Matrimonial Causes Act 1973: see Interpretation Act 1978, ss.15, 16; for a dispute on the point see 36 M.L.R. 638 at 642, 37 M.L.R. 480.
[44] See Bills of Exchange Act 1882, ss.65–68.
[45] See below, pp.720–721.

credit, to hypothecate the ship, cargo and freight, or the cargo alone, to sell part of the cargo,[46] and to enter into a salvage agreement on behalf of the cargo-owner.[47]

(c) SALVAGE. A person who goes to the aid of a ship in distress at sea[48] and saves life or property is entitled to a reward the amount of which is (subject to certain limitations), at the discretion of the court.

(d) OTHER CASES. The courts have been reluctant to extend the doctrine of agency of necessity, because it may deprive a person of his property, or subject him to an obligation, without his consent.[49] But the doctrine is not confined to the three situations described above. It extends to a number of other situations, in some (but not in all) of which the authority is based on some prior relationship between the parties.[50]

(i) *Powers of sale*. It has been held that land carriers can have authority of necessity to sell.[51] At common law, the courts were reluctant to hold that a bailee with whom goods had been left for storage or repair was entitled to sell them merely because the owner had failed to collect them and could not be traced. By statute, the bailee is now entitled to sell in a number of situations if he has given notice to the bailor of his intention to sell or if he has failed to trace the bailor after having taken reasonable steps to do so.[52] This statutory power extends to cases in which there was, at common law, no authority of necessity to sell.[53] There may also be cases in which, though the statutory requirements are not satisfied, a sale can be justified under the common law doctrine of agency of necessity. For example, a buyer of goods may justifiably reject them on the ground that they are not in conformity with the contract of sale; and if the seller refuses to accept their return, the buyer may then have authority of necessity to sell them for the account of the seller.[54]

(ii) *Preservation of another's property*. A number of cases raise the question whether a person who preserves another's property has any claim against the owner. Two eighteenth-century cases decided that such a person has no lien on the property saved[55]; but it does not necessarily follow that he has no claim for reimbursement. In *Tetley v British Trade Corp*[56] an agent who, contrary to his principal's express instruction, removed goods from Batum to Constantinople (to save them from seizure by an invading army) recovered the expense of the removal from his principal. In *The Winson*[57] a salvor of goods from a stranded ship took them to a place of safety and (to prevent them from deteriorating) had them stored in a warehouse there. It was held that the owner was liable to the salvor for the cost of warehousing the goods. And in *GN Ry v Swaffield*[58]

---

[46] See *Notara v Henderson* (1872) L.R. 7 Q.B. 225.
[47] *The Winson* [1982] A.C. 939. But where the conditions stated at pp.720–721, below are not satisfied, the master has no *implied* authority to enter into such an agreement: *The Choko Star* [1990] 1 Lloyd's Rep. 516.
[48] For this restriction, see *The Goring* [1988] A.C. 831.
[49] *Falcke v Scottish Imperial Assurance Co* (1886) 34 Ch.D. 234 at 248; *The Winson* [1982] A.C. 939 at 962.
[50] *Re F* [1990] 2 A.C. 1 at 75. *cf. Crantrave Ltd v Lloyd's Bank plc* [2000] Q.B. 917 at 922–923, where there was no "necessity".
[51] *Sims & Co v Midland Ry* [1913] 1 K.B. 103 at 112; *Springer v Great Western Ry* [1921] 1 K.B. 257 at 265, 267; *cf.* Carriage of Goods by Road Act 1965, Sch., Arts 14(2), 16(3), for statutory provisions in case of international carriage.
[52] Torts (Interference with Goods) Act 1977, ss.12, 13 and Sch.1.
[53] *e.g. Sachs v Miklos* [1948] 2 K.B. 23; *Munro v Wilmott* [1949] 1 K.B. 295.
[54] *Graanhandel T Vink BW v European Grain & Shipping Co* [1989] 2 Lloyd's Rep. 531 at 533 (where there was no such agency as the buyer had lost his right to reject); *cf. The Olib* [1991] 2 Lloyd's Rep. 108 at 114.
[55] *Binstead v Buck* (1776) 2 Wm.Bl. 1117; *Nicholson v Chapman* (1793) 2 H.Bl. 254.
[56] Cited in (1922) 10 Ll.L.R. at 678.
[57] [1982] A.C. 939; Samuel, 98 L.Q.R. 362.
[58] (1874) L.R. 9 Ex. 132.

a railway company claimed the cost of feeding and stabling a horse from the owner, who had failed to collect it on arrival at its destination and had not authorised the company to incur these expenses. The claim succeeded on the ground that the company "were bound from ordinary feelings of humanity to keep the horse safely and feed him."[59]

(iii) *Improvement of another's property.* A person who improves another's property may do so in the mistaken but honest belief that it is his own. In such a case there is no agency of necessity since the improver's intention is to act on his own behalf, and not on behalf of the owner. If the subject-matter is goods and the owner sues the improver for wrongful interference, the improver is by statute entitled to an allowance (against the owner's claim) in respect of the improvements.[60] A similar rule existed at common law, and presumably applies in relation to property other than goods.[61] It is more doubtful whether the improver has an independent claim in respect of the improvements,[62] *i.e.* one that he can assert even though no action has been brought against him by the owner.

If the improver knows that he has no title to the property he may again have certain limited rights in respect of the improvements. In *Munro v Wilmott*[63] the plaintiff with the defendant's permission left his car in the defendant's yard. Some years later, the defendant wanted to have the car moved, and, after trying unsuccessfully to contact the plaintiff, spent some £85 on making the car saleable, and sold it. He was held liable for conversion, but the damages were reduced by £85 "not from the point of view of payment for what he has done, but in order to arrive at . . . the true value of the property which the plaintiff had lost".[64] The case would now come within the statutory provisions authorising sales of uncollected goods,[65] so that the defendant would no longer be liable in conversion. Under the statutory provisions the bailee must account for the proceeds of sale to the bailor and is entitled to deduct items such as the costs of sale and sums due to him under the terms of the bailment[66]; but nothing is said about the value of improvements.[67] However, the bailee can apply to the court for an order authorising the sale "subject to such terms . . . as may be specified in the order".[68] These could perhaps give him the right to make a deduction in respect of improvements. Even this possibility would not be open to the bailee if he did not sell the goods but simply returned them to the bailor. In such a case he could perhaps invoke the doctrine of agency of necessity.

(iv) *Conditions to be satisfied.* In the sale, preservation and improvement cases just discussed, the common law doctrine of agency of necessity will apply only if certain conditions are satisfied.[69] It must be impossible to communicate with the owner of the goods in time to get his instructions or impossible to obtain such instructions because

---

[59] *ibid.* at 137.
[60] Torts (Interference with Goods) Act 1977, ss.6(1), 3(7).
[61] *Peruvian Guano Co v Dreyfus Bros.* [1892] A.C. 166 at 176; *Greenwood v Bennett* [1973] Q.B. 195.
[62] For a suggestion that there is such a claim, see *Greenwood v Bennett,* above at p.201 (but see p.203); Jones, 93 L.Q.R. 273.
[63] [1949] 1 K.B. 295.
[64] [1949] 1 K.B. 295 at 299.
[65] Torts (Interference with Goods) Act 1977, ss.12, 13 and Sch.1; Palmer [1987] L.M.C.L.Q. 43.
[66] Torts (Interference with Goods) Act 1977, s.12(5).
[67] s.6 of the Act (above, n.60) would not apply as the defendant knew that he had no title to the car.
[68] s.13(1)(a).
[69] See *Springer v GW Ry* [1921] 1 K.B. 257; *Prager v Blatspiel, Stamp & Heacock Ltd* [1924] 1 K.B. 566. These principles also apply to a shipmaster's authority of necessity: above, pp.718–719; *cf. The Winson* [1982] A.C. 939.

the owner (though he can be reached) fails to give them[70]; the agent must act reasonably, in good faith and in the interests of the owner; and his acts must have been commercially necessary. It is not "necessary" to sell goods merely because they are causing inconvenience,[71] for there may be a reasonable opportunity of storing them.[72]

(v) *Preservation of life or health.* The doctrine of agency of necessity may apply where one person preserves the life or health of another. Thus it is the basis on which a person can sue for the value of necessaries supplied to a mental patient who has no capacity for rational thought.[73] A doctor who gives medical attention to an unconscious person might recover a fee on the same ground[74]; the case for allowing him to do so would be particularly strong where the doctor's acts are not merely lawful but are done in the performance of a legal duty to render the services in question.[75] A right to payment would of course be negatived if the circumstances were such that the services would not normally be paid for: this would be the position where emergency treatment is given under the National Health Service. Special statutory provisions entitle the doctor to a fee where he gives emergency treatment to the victim of a road accident[76] and require National Health Service charges to be paid to the Secretary of State in respect of hospital treatment given by the Service to a "traffic casualty" if a "compensation payment" is made (normally by an insurer) in respect of injury or death suffered as a result of the use of a motor vehicle on a road.[77]

(e) SCOPE OF THE DOCTRINE. It will be seen from the situations discussed above that "agency of necessity" can produce three quite different results. First, it may enable the agent to create a contract between the principal and a third party[78]; secondly it may entitle the agent to dispose of the principal's property[79]; and thirdly it may entitle the agent to recompense or reimbursement in respect of the efforts that he has made, or the expense that he has incurred, to protect the interests of the principal.[80] It has been suggested that the expression "agency of necessity" should no longer be used in its traditional broad sense, to refer to all these consequences, but that it should be used in a narrower sense, to refer only to cases in which the question is whether the agent has, by reason of the necessity, the power to create a contract between his principal and a third party.[81]

The purpose of this suggested departure from the traditional terminology is to make the point that the three consequences described above do not necessarily depend on the

---

[70] *The Winson*, above at 962; *The Olib* [1991] 2 Lloyd's Rep. 108 at 104; the possibility that the owner may fail to give the instructions shows that the difficulty of obtaining them is not invariably "overcome to-day by modern means of communication" (*Re F* [1990] 2 A.C. 1 at 75); *cf. The Choko Star* [1990] 1 Lloyd's Rep. 516 at 524); it may also be impracticable for a shipmaster to obtain instructions from *all* the cargo-owners.

[71] *Sachs v Miklos* [1948] 2 K.B. 23, as to which see above, p.719, n.53.

[72] As in *Prager v Blatspiel, Stamp & Heacock Ltd* [1924] 1 K.B. 566. *Semble* the statutory power of sale referred to on p.719, above, would not extend to the facts of this case.

[73] See above, pp.558–559.

[74] *Cotnam v Wisdom*, 83 Ark. 601, 104 S.W. 164 (1907); *Re Crisan's Estate*, 102 N.W. 2d 907 (1961). For the right of an accident victim to recover damages in respect of loss suffered by a person who nurses him, *cf.* above, p.594 n.48.

[75] *Re F* [1990] 2 A.C. 1 at 55, where the issue was whether the treatment was *lawful* (see above, pp.558–559); *cf. Re T* [1993] Fam. 95; *Re M B (Caesarean Section)* [1997] 2 F.L.R. 426; *Re B (adult's refusal of medical treatment)* [2002] EWHC 429, Fam.; [2002] 2 All E.R. 449).

[76] Road Traffic Act 1988, ss.158, 159, as amended by Road Traffic (NHS Charges) Act 1999, s.18(2).

[77] Road Traffic (NHS Charges) Act 1999, s.1.

[78] *e.g.*, above, p.719 at n.47.

[79] *e.g.* above, p.719 at n.51.

[80] *e.g.* above, pp.719–720 at nn.56–59.

[81] *The Winson* [1982] A.C. 939 at 958.

same requirements.[82] Thus a person who, to prevent another's goods from deteriorating, arranges for them to be stored in a warehouse, may have a claim against the owner for reimbursement of the charges that he has paid to the warehouseman. It does not follow from this that he also has the power to make a contract between the owner and the warehouseman, so that the warehouseman can sue the owner directly for his charges.[83] On the other hand, the fact that both consequences depend on necessity makes it at least likely that similar factors will often be relevant to each of them. For example, the humanitarian considerations which enabled the railway company in *GN Ry v Swaffield*[84] to claim reimbursement might well have been used in support of the argument that the railway company had power to create a contract between the owner of the horse and a livery stable in which it was housed on his failure to collect it. Similarly, it is relevant for the purpose of both consequences to ask whether the agent acted in the interests of the owner or out of self-interest.[85]

Thus it is submitted that the question whether the label "agency of necessity" should be used in its traditional broad, or in a new narrow, sense is largely one of emphasis, or, as has been said, a "purely terminological"[86] one. It is part of the wider question as to the effects of non-consensual agency, to be discussed later in this Chapter.[87] Such agency scarcely ever produces *all* of the effects of agency based on agreement, but it generally does produce *some* of those effects. This is true of all forms of non-consensual agency; and it is submitted that, so long as the relationships discussed under the present heading produce at least some of the consequences that normally flow from agency by agreement, it is not inappropriate to say that they give rise to "agency of necessity".

3. Ratification

A principal may acquire rights and incur liabilities as a result of his agent's unauthorised act by ratifying it.

(1) What amounts to ratification

Ratification may be express or implied. It can be implied if the principal by conduct unequivocally affirms the agent's acts, even though he purports to repudiate them.[88] Mere passive acquiescence does not of itself amount to ratification,[89] but it may, when combined with other circumstances, have this effect: for example where the principal knows that the third party believes him to have accepted the agent's act as having been authorised and takes no steps within a reasonable time to repudiate the transaction.[90] Ratification will not generally be implied from conduct unless the principal has full knowledge of the agent's unauthorised act.[91] But a principal may be held to have ratified if he indicates that he will support whatever the agent has done on his behalf, even

---

[82] *ibid.*

[83] *ibid.*

[84] (1874) L.R. 9 Ex. 132; above, pp.719–720.

[85] *The Winson*, above at 962.

[86] *ibid.* at p.965; *cf. Re F* [1990] 2 A.C. 1 at 75 (using the expression to refer to the intervenor's right to reimbursement).

[87] See below, p.748.

[88] *Cornwall v Henson* (1750) 1 Ves.Sen. 509.

[89] *Moon v Towers* (1860) 8 C.B.(N.S.) 611; reversed on other grounds: (1860) 9 H.L.C. 78. Contrast the now doubtful case of *Waithman v Wakefield* (1807) 1 Camp. 120; and *Michael Elliott & Partners v UK Land* [1991] 1 E.G.L.R. 39.

[90] *Suncorp Insurance & Finance v Milano Assicurazioni SpA* [1993] 2 Lloyd's Rep. 225 at 241.

[91] *Lewis v Read* (1845) 13 M. & W. 834.

though he does not know exactly what the agent has agreed to: in such a case the principal takes the risk of the agent's having exceeded his authority.[92]

An act will be regarded as a ratification only if the principal had a free choice whether to do it or not. Merely taking back one's own property after a third party has, in reliance on unauthorised instructions, done work on it is not ratification.[93]

(2) When ratification possible

Ratification is effective only if the following conditions are satisfied.

(a) THE AGENT MUST PURPORT TO ACT ON BEHALF OF THE PRINCIPAL. A principal can only ratify acts which the agent purported to do on his behalf.[94] The most important consequence of this rule is that if the agent purports to act on his own behalf the principal cannot ratify; or, in other words, that an undisclosed principal[95] cannot ratify. Thus in *Keighley, Maxsted & Co v Durant*[96] an agent bought corn at a price above that at which he had been instructed to buy. He intended to buy for his principal, but did not disclose this fact to the seller. The undisclosed principal purported to ratify the purchase, but later refused to accept delivery. It was held that the ratification was ineffective and that the principal was not liable. Lord Macnaghten said that "Civil obligations are not to be created by or founded upon undisclosed intentions."[97] It could be objected that this reasoning would destroy the whole law relating to undisclosed principals. But the decision is nonetheless intelligible, having regard to the common law doctrine of privity of contract. Ratification and the undisclosed principal are two important exceptions to that doctrine. To allow both exceptions to operate on the same set of facts would go far towards overthrowing the doctrine of privity altogether.[98]

On the other hand, an unnamed principal[99] can ratify. Policies of marine insurance may be taken out "for and on behalf of any person interested"; and such persons can ratify although they are not named in the policy.[1]

The rule that the agent must *purport* to act on behalf of the principal does not mean that he must *intend* to do so. Thus the principal may ratify although the agent intended to defraud him.[2]

---

[92] *Fitzmaurice v Bayley* (1856) 6 E. & B. 868; *cf. Haseler v Lemoyne* (1858) 5 C.B.(N.S.) 530; *Suncorp* case, above, n.90, at p.234.

[93] *Foreman & Co Pty Ltd v The Liddesdale* [1900] A.C. 190.

[94] *Wilson v Tumman* (1843) 6 Man. & G. 236.

[95] For the definition of "undisclosed principal," below, p.727.

[96] [1901] A.C. 240; *cf. The Astyanax* [1985] 2 Lloyd's Rep. 109; *Welsh Development Agency v Export Finance Co* [1992] B.C.L.C. 148; *The Moonacre* [1992] 2 Lloyd's Rep. 501 at 515; *Siu Yin Kwan v Eastern Insurance* [1994] 2 A.C. 199 at 207; *Secured Residential Funding plc v Douglas Goldberg Hendeles & Co*, The Times, April 26, 2000.

[97] [1901] A.C. 240 at 247.

[98] Since an undisclosed principal is, by definition, not identified in the contract, the present rule is not affected by the Contracts (Rights of Third Parties) Act 1999: see s.1(3), above, p.655. A further reason why the Act would not apply on facts such as those of the *Keighley Maxsted* case, above, is that the issue there was whether the ratifier was *liable* under the contract; and the rule that a contract does not *bind* a third party is generally unaffected by the Act: above, p.581.

[99] For the definition of "unnamed principal," see below, p.727.

[1] *Hagedorn v Oliverson* (1814) 2 M. & S. 485. *Quaere* whether the requirement stated in *Watson v Swann* (1862) 11 C.B.(N.S.) 756 at 771, that the person seeking to ratify must be described at the time of the contract in such a way as to be ascertainable at that time is generally accepted: see *Boston Fruit Co v British & Foreign Marine Insurance Co* [1906] A.C. 336 at 338–339 (a case apparently overlooked in *Southern Water Authority v Carey* [1985] 2 All E.R. 1077 at 1085); Arnould, *Marine Insurance* (16th ed.), §243.

[2] *Re Tiedemann & Ledermann Frères* [1899] 2 Q.B. 66.

In *Brook v Hook*[3] an agent forged his principal's signature to a promissory note. The principal's later ratification was held to be ineffective. This case has given rise to a dispute on the question whether a forgery can ever be ratified. But it does not seem that this question arises in a case of this kind. If an agent forges his principal's signature he does not say "I am signing for my principal" but "this is my principal's signature". The principal cannot ratify because the agent did not purport to act on his behalf.[4] But if the principal stands by knowing that his agent will forge his signature he may be estopped from denying its genuineness.[5]

(b) THE PRINCIPAL'S CAPACITY. At common law, a corporation cannot ratify the unauthorised act of its agent in entering into an *ultra vires* contract.[6] There are two reasons why, in general,[7] this rule no longer applies in relation to companies incorporated under the Companies Acts. First, the validity of an act done by such a company can no longer be called into question on the ground of lack of capacity by reason of anything in the company's memorandum.[8] Secondly, an act can be ratified even though it was done by the directors in breach of their duty to observe limitations on their powers contained in the memorandum.[9] Such ratification would also prevent the company from impugning the transaction on the ground that it was beyond the power of the board of directors.[10]

A person can become liable on a contract made by him while he was a minor if he "ratifies" it after reaching full age.[11] "Ratification" here seems to refer to confirmation by a person of a contract made by himself; but there seems to be no reason why a person should not be similarly liable on a ratification after full age of a contract made on his behalf, but without his authority, while he was a minor. There are, however, cases in which a person is not liable on a ratification in the sense of a confirmation of a contract made during minority by himself[12]; and it is submitted that he would equally not be liable if, after full age, he ratified a contract of this kind which had during his minority been made on his behalf but without his authority.[13]

(c) THE PRINCIPAL MUST HAVE BEEN IN EXISTENCE WHEN THE ACT WAS DONE. This rule can give rise to inconvenience when promoters contract on behalf of a projected company. It was held in *Kelner v Baxter*[14] that the company could not, after its formation, ratify the promoters' contracts, since it was not in existence when those contracts were made. One way of evading this rule is for the promoter to enter into a draft agreement providing that the company, when formed, shall enter into a similar agreement with the third party and that the liability of the promoter shall thereupon cease. But the draft agreement creates no binding contract between company and third

---

[3] (1871) L.R. 6 Ex. 89.

[4] *Imperial Bank of Canada v Begley* [1936] 2 All E.R. 367.

[5] *Greenwood v Martins Bank Ltd* [1933] A.C. 51.

[6] *Ashbury Ry Carriage & Iron Co v Riche* (1875) L.R. 7 H.L. 653; *Mann v Edinburgh N Tramways* [1893] A.C. 69; *Rolled Steel Products (Holdings) Ltd v BSC* [1986] Ch. 246 at 304.

[7] For exceptions, see above, p.561.

[8] Companies Act 1985, s.35(1) (as inserted by Companies Act 1989, s.108(1)); above, p.561.

[9] Companies Act 1985 (above), s.35(3).

[10] *i.e.* under *ibid.* s.35A(1); it seems to follow that ratification can be effective even if the third party acted in bad faith, at least if the members of the company were aware of this fact when ratifying the contract.

[11] See above, p.549.

[12] A penal bond could not be ratified as it was considered to be wholly void: *Baylis v Dineley* (1815) 3 M. & S. 477.

[13] On the principle that a nullity cannot be ratified: below, p.725.

[14] (1866) L.R. 2 C.P. 174; *cf. Melhado v Porto Alegre Ry* (1874) L.R. 9 C.P. 503.

party, so that each can, with the collusion of the promoter, deprive the other of the expected benefit of the contract. The position is somewhat better in equity. The company may be able to enforce the contract against the third party by showing that the promoter acted as trustee for it,[15] and the third party may be able to claim a reasonable remuneration out of any sum which the company has paid, or bound itself to pay, to the promoter for initial expenses.[16] But the third party has no such right if the company has neither made nor promised any payment to the promoter[17]; nor has he any claim against the company on a purely executory contract. By statute, a contract which purports to be made by or on behalf of a company before it is formed has effect (subject to contrary agreement) as a contract between the third party and the person purporting to act for the company or as agent for it.[18] But it is still impossible to create a direct contract between the company and the third party by ratification after incorporation. It would be better if the rule in *Kelner v Baxter* were wholly repealed by legislation.[19] We shall see that legislation to some extent solves the problems which arise out of pre-incorporation contracts; but it does so by techniques other than ratification.[20]

(d) THE PRINCIPAL MUST RATIFY IN TIME. A contract cannot be ratified after the time fixed for its performance[21]; if no such time is fixed, it must be ratified within a reasonable time of the principal's acquiring notice of the unauthorised act.[22] Nor can a contract be ratified at a time when the principal could not validly have made it.[23] Thus it has been held that, where an agent, without authority, insures his principal's property, the latter cannot ratify the insurance after the destruction of the property,[24] since he could not at that time have insured it. But exceptionally a policy of marine insurance can be ratified after the destruction of the property insured[25] and it has been suggested that this rule should also be applied to other kinds of insurance.[26]

(e) A NULLITY CANNOT BE RATIFIED.[27] Although ratification is not confined to lawful acts, an act which is simply void in law cannot be validated by ratification. Similarly, a principal cannot become liable if the unauthorised contract was prohibited by statute: "life cannot be given by ratification to prohibited transactions".[28] This is an additional reason for saying that a forgery cannot be ratified.[29]

---

[15] See above, pp.646 *et seq.*

[16] *Touche v Metropolitan Ry* (1871) L.R. 6 Ch.App. 671; *cf. Re Hereford, etc., Engineering Co* (1876) 2 Ch.D. 621 (where the third party lost his rights because of the promoter's fraud); *Re Empress Engineering Co* (1880) 16 Ch.D. 125. *Spiller v Paris Skating Rink Co* (1878) 7 Ch.D. 368 states the equitable principle too widely.

[17] *Re Rotherham Alum & Chemical Co* (1883) 25 Ch.D. 103.

[18] Companies Act 1985, s.36C(1), as inserted by Companies Act 1989, s.130(4); below, p.735.

[19] The Companies Bill 1973 (which was lost at the dissolution of Parliament in February 1974) contained a provision (cl.6) to this effect. And see Gross, 87 L.Q.R. 367.

[20] See below, pp.730–731, 731–732, 735–736.

[21] *Metropolitan Asylums Board v Kingham* (1890) 6 T.L.R. 217; *Dibbins v Dibbins* [1896] 2 Ch. 348.

[22] *Re Portuguese Consolidated Copper Mines* (1890) 45 Ch.D. 16; *cf. Bedford Insurance Co Ltd v Instituto de Ressaguros do Brasil* [1985] Q.B. 966 at 987 (and see above, p.434).

[23] *cf. Bird v Brown* (1850) 4 Ex. 786 at 789, quoted with approval by Dillon L.J. in *Presentaciones Musicales SA v Secunda* [1994] Ch. 271; for another explanation of *Bird v Brown*, see below, p.726, n.35.

[24] *Grover & Grover Ltd v Matthews* [1910] 2 K.B. 401.

[25] *Williams v N China Insurance Co* (1876) 1 C.P.D. 757; Marine Insurance Act 1906, s.86.

[26] *NOW v DOL* [1993] 2 Lloyd's Rep. 587 at 607–608.

[27] For a discussion of this rule, see *Danish Mercantile Co v Beaumont* [1951] Ch. 680 (where the act was held not to be a nullity).

[28] *Bedford Insurance Co Ltd v Instituto de Ressaguros do Brasil* [1985] Q.B. 966 at 986 (and see above, p.434).

[29] See above, p.723.

(3) Effect of ratification

The effect of ratification is to put principal, agent and third party into the position in which they would have been, if the agent's acts had been authorised from the start: his authority is said to relate back to the time of the unauthorised act. Thus in *Bolton Partners v Lambert*[30] an agent without authority purported to buy a house for his principal from the defendant, who later repudiated the contract. The principal then ratified. It was held that the defendant was bound by the contract. His repudiation was ineffective as the principal's ratification related back to the time of the agent's unauthorised purchase. The same rule applies where the agent does some act other than the making of a contract. Where, for example, he without authority, begins legal proceedings on behalf of his principal, the principal can ratify even after the expiry of the period of limitation.[31] For the purpose of the doctrine of relation back, it is assumed that the unauthorised act is not a nullity: if it were, ratification would be ineffective either because a nullity cannot be ratified or on the ground that, when it took place, the principal could not himself have validly or effectively done the act in question.[32]

The rule that ratification relates back does not apply where the agent contracts "subject to ratification": in such a case the third party can withdraw at any time before ratification.[33] Nor does the rule apply where before ratification the agent and the third party have cancelled the unauthorised transaction by mutual consent.[34] And the doctrine of relation back will not be allowed to deprive a stranger to the contract of a right of property which had vested in him before ratification[35]; though it may deprive him of a right to sue the agent in tort if the agent's unauthorised act would have been lawful, had it been done with the principal's prior authorisation.[36]

The rule in *Bolton Partners v Lambert* has been criticised on the ground that it puts the third party at the mercy of the principal, who is free to ratify or not as he pleases.[37] But the hardship to the third party should not be exaggerated. If the principal does not ratify, the third party has his remedy against the agent for breach of implied warranty of authority.[38] If the principal does ratify, the third party will be liable to him; but since this is precisely what he expected, he cannot complain. The only hardship is that the principal may be able to keep the third party waiting while he decides whether to ratify. But he must ratify within reasonable time; and the extent of such time is considerably abridged if the third party tells the principal that he wishes to withdraw from the contract.[39] Moreover, a principal cannot ratify after he has, by words or conduct, intimated to the third party that he does not intend to do so[40]; and such an intention could probably be inferred from his remaining silent for more than a comparatively short time after notice of the third party's intention to withdraw. Thus the third party need not be kept indefinitely in suspense. He can, in effect, say to the principal: ratify quickly or not at all.

---

[30] (1888) 41 Ch.D. 295; *cf. Maclean v Dunn* (1828) 4 Bing. 722; *Koenigsblatt v Sweet* [1923] 2 Ch. 314.
[31] *Presentaciones Musicales SA v Secunda* [1994] Ch. 271.
[32] *ibid.* at 280.
[33] *Watson v Davies* [1931] 1 Ch. 455; *Warehousing & Forwarding Co of East Africa Ltd v Jafferali & Sons Ltd* [1964] A.C. 1.
[34] *Walter v James* (1871) L.R. 6 Ex. 124; *Pacific & General Insurance Co Ltd v Hazell* [1997] L.R.L.R. 65.
[35] *Bird v Brown* (1850) 4 Ex. 786, as explained in *Presentaciones Musicales SA v Secunda* [1994] Ch. 271 at 285; Tan Cheng Han, 117 L.Q.R. 626.
[36] *Whitehead v Taylor* (1839) 10 A. & E. 210.
[37] Wambaugh, 9 Harv.L.R. 60; and see *Fleming v Bank of New Zealand* [1900] A.C. 577.
[38] See below, pp.738–740.
[39] *Re Portuguese Consolidated Copper Mines* (1890) 45 Ch.D. 16.
[40] *McEvoy v Belfast Banking Co* [1935] A.C. 24.

SECTION 4. EFFECTS OF AGENCY

When an agent makes a contract on behalf of his principal with a third party, the transaction can give rise to legal effects between principal and third party, between agent and third party, and between principal and agent. In discussing these effects, we shall first assume that the agency has arisen by consent, and then consider to what extent the same effects result from non-consensual agency.

1. Between Principal and Third Party

(1) Rights of principal against third party

The rights of principal against third party depend in part on the distinction between disclosed and undisclosed principals. A *disclosed principal* is one of whose existence the third party is aware at the time of contracting. He is called a named principal if the third party also knew his name, and an unnamed principal if the third party did not know his name.[41] An *undisclosed principal* is one of whose existence the third party is unaware at the time of contracting. Where a person makes a contract "as agent" or "on behalf of my client" the principal will generally be disclosed. But such words may not make it clear that that person is acting as agent *in the legal sense*[42]; they may merely indicate that he is acting as agent in a commercial sense. If that is the position and the person described as "agent" actually has a principal in the legal sense, that principal may be undisclosed.[43]

(a) DISCLOSED PRINCIPAL. The general rule is that a disclosed principal can enforce the contract against the third party.[44] The third party is not discharged by settling with the agent unless the principal by his conduct induced the third party to do so, or unless the agent had authority to receive payment.[45] The third party cannot set off against the principal any debt which the agent may owe to the third party[46]; and a custom enabling the agent to receive payment by such set-off is unreasonable.[47]

A former usage of trade, by which the general rule did not apply where an English agent contracted on behalf of a foreign principal, is obsolete so that such a principal can now enforce the contract against the third party.[48]

(b) UNDISCLOSED PRINCIPAL. An undisclosed principal can also, in general, enforce the contract against the third party. Attempts have been made to reconcile this rule with the doctrine of privity. One view is that the contract is "in truth" made with the

---

[41] Reynolds in (Rose, ed.) *Consensus ad Idem, Essays in the Law of Contract in Honour of Guenter Treitel*, p.77.

[42] See above, p.706.

[43] See a difference of opinion on this point in *Teheran-Europe Co Ltd v S T Belton (Tractors) Ltd* [1968] 2 Q.B. 545 at 552, 556, 561.

[44] *Langton v Waite* (1868) L.R. 6 Eq. 165. The principal's right arises because he *is* a party, so that it is not governed by the Contracts (Rights of Third Parties) Act 1999: this creates rights only in favour of "a person who is *not* a party" (s.1(1)).

[45] *Yates v Freckleton* (1781) 2 Dougl. 623; *Linck, Moeller & Co v Jameson & Co* (1885) 2 T.L.R. 206; *Butwick v Grant* [1924] 2 K.B. 483.

[46] *Pratt v Willey* (1826) 2 C. & P. 350; *Fish v Kempton* (1849) 7 C.B. 687; *Mildred v Maspons* (1883) 8 App.Cas. 874; *Cooke v Eshelby* (1887) 12 App.Cas. 271; unless the agent has authority to receive payment in this way: *Stewart v Aberdein* (1838) 4 M. & W. 211 at 228.

[47] *Pearson v Scott* (1878) 9 Ch.D. 198.

[48] *Teheran-Europe Co Ltd v S T Belton (Tractors) Ltd* [1968] 2 Q.B. 545; Reynolds, 85 L.Q.R. 92 at 97–103; Hudson, 32 M.L.R. 207. *Semble* the rule also applies to undisclosed principals: above, n.43.

undisclosed principal,[49] but this is scarcely consistent with the rule that the agent is fully entitled and liable under the contract.[50] Other views recognise that the contract is between agent and third party but say that the principal can intervene because his contract with the agent entitles him to do so, or because he is a *cestui que trust* or a quasi-assignee.[51] But the better view seems to be that the undisclosed principal's right is not based on the theory that he has somehow acquired the agent's right. His right is an independent right,[52] established by way of exception to the common law doctrine of privity,[53] in the interests of commercial convenience.[54]

The undisclosed principal's right could prejudice a third party, who necessarily thought that he was dealing only with the agent. To avoid such prejudice, the undisclosed principal's right is limited in the following ways.

(i) *Consistency with the terms of the contract.* An undisclosed principal is not allowed to intervene where this would be inconsistent with the terms of the contract. In *Humble v Hunter*[55] a person signed a charterparty as "owner." This was held to mean that he and he alone was owner,[56] so that his undisclosed principal was not allowed to intervene. But in *F Drughorn Ltd v Rederiaktiebolaget Transatlantic*[57] the fact that an agent signed a charterparty as "charterer" did not exclude his undisclosed principal's right to enforce the contract; and in *Siu Yin Kwan v Eastern Insurance Co Ltd*[58] the fact that the agent was described in an employer's liability policy as the employer did not exclude the right of the undisclosed principal (who was in fact the employer) to intervene. It seems that the courts have become reluctant to hold that this right has been excluded by descriptive words in the contract, since such a conclusion would tend to defeat the considerations of commercial convenience on which the doctrine of the undisclosed principal is based.[59]

(ii) *Personal considerations.* If the third party can show that he wanted to deal with the agent *and with no one else*, the undisclosed principal cannot intervene. This will, for example, be the position where the third party wished to contract only with the agent because the nature of the contract was such as to show that the third party relied on the agent's business reputation or integrity[60]; or because the agent owed him money which was to be set off against the amount due from the third party under the contract which

---

[49] *Keighley Maxsted & Co v Durant* [1901] A.C. 240 at 261.

[50] See below, p.734.

[51] For discussions of the basis of the doctrine, see Ames, *Essays*, 453; Seavey, 29 Y.L.J. 859; Goodhart and Hamson, 4 C.L.J. 320; Montrose, 16 Can.Bar Rev. 757; Dowrick, 17 M.L.R. 25; Higgins, 28 M.L.R. 167; Reynolds, above, n.41, pp.89–90. *cf. The Astyanax* [1985] 2 Lloyd's Rep. 109 at 113 (where "*not* a settled part of our law" should probably read "*now* a settled part . . . ," etc.).

[52] *Pople v Evans* [1969] 2 Ch. 255; *The Havprins* [1983] 2 Lloyd's Rep. 356 at 362.

[53] *Welsh Development Agency v Export Finance Co Ltd* [1992] B.C.L.C. 173 at 182, describing the exception as "anomalous."

[54] *Siu Yin Kwan v Eastern Insurance Co Ltd* [1994] 2 A.C. 199 at 207. The Contracts (Rights of Third Parties) Act 1999 does not confer any rights on the undisclosed principal both for the reason given in n.44 above and because he is, by definition, not "expressly identified" within s.1(3) (above, p.655).

[55] (1842) 12 Q.B. 316; *Formby Bros v Formby* (1910) 102 L.T. 116; *cf. The Astyanax* [1985] 2 Lloyd's Rep. 109.

[56] For the construction in this context of phrases such as "disponent owner" or "operating owner," see *The Yanxilas* [1982] 2 Lloyd's Rep. 444. In the context of a bill of lading, "[ship]owner" can refer to the person with whom the shipper enters into the contract of carriage and so include a charterer: *The Stolt Loyalty* [1995] 1 Lloyd's Rep. 559.

[57] [1919] A.C. 203; *Danziger v Thompson* [1944] K.B. 654. Contrast *The Starsin* [2003] UKHL 12, [2003] 2 W.L.R. 711, at [84, 85].

[58] [1994] 2 A.C. 199.

[59] *ibid.* at 210. *cf. Epps v Rothnie* [1945] K.B. 562 at 565, doubting *Humble v Hunter*, above.

[60] *Collins v Associated Greyhound Racecourses Ltd* [1930] Ch. 1 (underwriting contract).

the principal sought to enforce.[61] But the third party will not be prejudiced by the undisclosed principal's right to intervene if (as may be the case in many commercial contexts) it is a matter of indifference to him whether his contract is with the agent or with the undisclosed principal.[62] This was held to be the position in the *Siu Yin Kwan*[63] case, where the Privy Council also rejected the argument that the undisclosed principal's right should be excluded merely because the contract was one of indemnity insurance. While in some such contracts the insurer may rely on personal considerations relating to the insured,[64] he had not done so here since the proposal form had given him all the information relating to the principal that was relevant to the risk.[65] Presumably, however, the principal could not have intervened if the insurer had proved that, in entering into the contract, he had in fact relied on personal considerations relating to the agent.

A third party who has no particular reason for wanting to deal with the agent may nevertheless not want to deal with the principal. If the agent expressly says that he is not acting for the principal, the third party can avoid the contract for fraud.[66] If he makes no such misrepresentation, the law is less clear.

In *Nash v Dix*[67] a committee of Roman Catholics wanted to buy a Congregational chapel from the defendants and to turn it into a place of Roman Catholic worship. The defendants refused to deal with the committee as they disapproved of the proposed user. The committee then told the claimant that if he could buy the chapel from the defendants they would buy it from him for £100 more than he had paid for it. The defendants sold the chapel to the claimant but repudiated the contract on discovering that he intended to resell to the committee. North J. held that the defendants were bound (1) because the claimant was not an agent, but simply a person who had bought for resale; and (2) because the claimant had not been guilty of any misrepresentation. It appears from the judgment that the claimant would have failed if he *had* been the agent of the committee.

In *Said v Butt*[68] the claimant wanted to go to the first night of a play, but knew that the proprietors of the theatre would not sell him a ticket as he had in the past strongly criticised their conduct. He therefore sent a friend to the box-office to buy a ticket for him without disclosing his name, but he was later refused admission by the manager of the theatre. In an action against the manager for inducing a breach of contract, McCardie J. held that there was no contract between the proprietors and the claimant: since the proprietors reserved the right to sell first-night tickets to specially selected persons, the "personality" of the other contracting party was a material element in the contract.

Both these cases were distinguished in *Dyster v Randall & Sons.*[69] The claimant wanted to buy land from the defendants, who, to his knowledge, would not deal with him as they distrusted him. He employed an agent to buy the land in the agent's own name, and then claimed that he was entitled to intervene as undisclosed principal. Lawrence J.

---

[61] *Greer v Downs Supply Co* [1927] 2 K.B. 28; *quaere* whether this decision was necessary for the protection of the third party since an undisclosed principal can intervene only subject to the third party's right of set-off against the agent: below, p.730.

[62] *Siu Yin Kwan v Eastern Insurance Co Ltd* [1994] 2 A.C. 199 at 210.

[63] *ibid.* The claim was by employees of the principal under the equivalent of the Third Parties (Rights Against Insurers) Act 1930, above, p.668.

[64] *cf.* above, p.694 for restrictions on the assignment of such policies on this ground.

[65] [1984] 2 A.C. 199 at 208.

[66] *Archer v Stone* (1898) 78 L.T. 34; *cf. Berg v Sadler & Moore* [1937] 2 K.B. 158; above, pp.373–374.

[67] (1898) 78 L.T. 445.

[68] [1920] 3 K.B. 497.

[69] [1926] Ch. 932; *cf. Smith v Wheatcroft* (1878) 9 Ch.D. 223; for a discussion of these cases, see Williams, 23 Can.Bar Rev. 397.

upheld the claim: he said that it would be futile to deny the claimant's right to sue since the agent could have assigned the benefit of the contract to him. But this reasoning does not satisfactorily distinguish *Said v Butt*: theatre tickets can (unless they expressly provide the contrary)[70] be assigned no less than contracts to buy land. Again it was said that "personal" consideration entered into the two earlier cases but not into *Dyster v Randall & Sons*. While this may distinguish *Said v Butt*, it does not satisfactorily explain why the action in *Nash v Dix* would have failed if the claimant had been an agent; for it is hard to see why an objection based on religious grounds is more "personal" than one based on distrust.

It is submitted that an undisclosed principal should not be allowed to intervene if he knows that the third party does not want to deal with him. If the principal directly concealed his identity, the contract would be void for mistake, or voidable for fraud; and the principal should not be able to improve his position by simply employing an agent. The position is the same where the agent knows, or should know, that the third party wanted to contract *only* with him.[71]

(iii) *Other safeguards.* The rights of the undisclosed principal against the third party are subject to any defences which the third party has against the agent.[72] This rule is necessary for the protection of the third party, who thinks that he is dealing with the agent alone. Thus if the agent owes money to the third party, the debt can be set off by the third party against the principal, and if the third party pays the agent he can rely on the payment against the principal.[73] This rule is based on the third party's belief that he is dealing with the agent alone: it therefore does not apply where the third party has no such belief. In *Cooke v Eshelby*[74] the third party had no belief one way or the other whether the person with whom he was dealing was principal or agent. He was in fact an agent. The third party was not allowed to set off against the principal a debt which the agent owed to the third party.

The principal may intend the agent to disclose his existence, but the agent may fail to do so because he wants to misappropriate the proceeds of the contract, or to induce the third party to accept the principal's property in discharge of a debt which the agent owes to the third party. In such cases the third party can only rely on his settlement with, or set-off against, the agent, in an action brought by the principal, if the latter has so conducted himself as to enable the agent to appear as principal in the transaction.[75]

(c) NON-EXISTENT PRINCIPAL. At common law, a principal cannot become a party to a contract made on his or its behalf before the principal came into existence. This is, for example, the position where a contract purports to be made on behalf of a corporation before its incorporation: such a contract is a nullity because one party to it does not exist.[76] The Contracts (Rights of Third Parties) Act 1999, however, makes it possible so to draw up the contract as to make the corporation a third party beneficiary; it will then, in the circumstances specified in the Act,[77] be entitled to enforce the relevant terms of the contract.[78] The Act expressly provides that, for this purpose, the third party "need

---

[70] The report of *Said v Butt* does not state whether the ticket contained a condition prohibiting its assignment or transfer.

[71] *Siu Yin Kwan v Eastern Insurance Co Ltd* [1994] 2 A.C. 199 at 207.

[72] *Browning v Provincial Insurance Co of Canada* (1873) L.R. 5 P.C. 263 at 272.

[73] *George v Clagett* (1797) 7 T.R. 359; *Rabone v Williams*, *ibid.* p.360n.; *Mann v Forrester* (1814) 4 Camp. 60; *Montague v Forwood* [1893] 2 Q.B. 350, Derham [1986] C.L.J. 384.

[74] (1887) 12 App.Cas. 271; Reynolds [1983] C.L.P. 119.

[75] *Drakeford v Piercey* (1866) 14 L.T. 403.

[76] See below, p.680, n.17.

[77] See especially ss.1(1) and (2), above, pp.651–653.

[78] s.1(1).

not be in existence when the contract is entered into."[79] Statutory provisions which deal with the contractual relations between the *agent* and the third party under pre-incorporation contracts are discussed later in this Chapter.[80]

(2) Liability of principal to third party

The general rule is that a principal, whether disclosed or undisclosed, is liable to the third party.[81] The limitations on the right of an undisclosed principal to intervene exist mainly for the protection of the third party. Hence they do not necessarily apply where the third party sues the principal. But a person who is alleged to have contracted on behalf of another may, on the true construction of the contract, have contracted solely on his own behalf. In that case he alone is liable on the contract[82]: the reason why the other is not liable is not that he is an undisclosed principal whose liability is excluded, but that he is not a principal in the transaction at all.

The principal cannot set off against the third party any money owed to the principal by the agent.[83] If the principal gives the agent the money with which to pay the third party, but the agent fails to pay it over, the principal remains liable to the third party: he must seek out his creditor and see that he is paid.[84] The principal is discharged by payment to the agent only if such payment is made at the third party's request,[85] or if the third party looked to the agent for payment and so induced the principal to settle with the agent.[86]

In *Heald v Kenworthy*[87] it was assumed that an undisclosed principal is not (any more than one who is disclosed) discharged by settling with his agent. But in *Armstrong v Stokes*[88] the court said that this rule produced "intolerable hardship",[89] and refused to follow it. Thus it was held that an undisclosed principal who settled with his agent was not liable to make a second payment to the third party if the agent failed to pay over the money. Of course, it is hard for the principal to have to pay twice over; but it is equally hard for the third party not to be paid at all. It could be argued that the law should, in this situation, have no sympathy for the third party since he did not rely on the credit of a principal of whose existence he was unaware at the time of contracting. But this proves too much: whenever an undisclosed principal is sued the third party gets a windfall of this kind. Thus the case for applying a special rule to undisclosed principals in this context is weak. *Armstrong v Stokes* was doubted by the Court of Appeal in *Irvine v Watson*[90]; and it is submitted that an undisclosed principal who settles with his agent should remain liable to the third party.

At common law, a contract purporting to be made with a non-existent principal, *e.g.* with a corporation before its incorporation, is a nullity[91] and so cannot impose liabilities, any more than it can confer rights, on the corporation. This position is not directly affected by the Contracts (Rights of Third Parties) Act 1999; for although a third party

---

[79] s.1(3).
[80] See below, p.736.
[81] See *Boyter v Thomson* [1995] 2 A.C. 629 at 632.
[82] *JH Rayner (Mincing Lane) Ltd v DTI* [1989] Ch. 72 at 190–191, approved on this point [1990] 2 A.C. 418 at 515.
[83] *Waring v Favenck* (1807) 2 Camp. 85.
[84] *Irvine v Watson* (1880) 5 Q.B.D. 414.
[85] *Smyth v Anderson* (1849) 7 C.B. 21.
[86] See *Wyatt v Hertford* (1802) 3 East 147.
[87] (1855) 10 Ex. 739; Reynolds (1983) C.L.P. 119.
[88] (1872) L.R. 7 Q.B. 598.
[89] *ibid.* at 610.
[90] See above, n.84.
[91] See below, p.736 at n.38.

can by virtue of this Act acquire *rights* under a contract, the Act does not impose any *liabilities* on the third party.[92] However, the third party's right to enforce the term conferring a benefit on that party is "subject to . . . any other terms of the contract".[93] Thus it is possible to draw up a pre-incorporation contract so as to make the corporation's right of enforcement (once it has come into existence) subject to its discharging liabilities undertaken by its agents on its behalf. Even if this is not done, the corporation's right of enforcement is under the Act subject to defences available against the promisee (*i.e.*, in the present context, the agent).[94] The result is that the corporation cannot enforce rights under the contract unless it discharges the relevant liabilities. But if it chooses not to enforce the rights, then the liabilities cannot be enforced against it merely because it is named as a third party beneficiary in the contract. By statute, this problem is now in part resolved in the case of an agreement made before the incorporation of a limited liability partnership between the persons who subscribe their names to the incorporation document.[95] Such an agreement "may impose obligations"[96] on the partnership to take effect after its incorporation. But even this provision does not extend to agreements made with *other* persons before the incorporation of the partnership and purporting to impose liabilities on it.[97]

Our concern in the preceding discussion has been with the liabilities of the non-existent principal in the case of pre-incorporation contracts. The *rights* of such a principal against the third party are discussed earlier,[98] and the contractual relations between the *agent* and the third party are discussed later,[99] in this Chapter.

2. Between Agent and Third Party

Agent and third party may incur reciprocal rights and liabilities either under the contract which the agent makes on behalf of his principal, or under a collateral contract. The agent may also be liable for breach of implied warranty of authority and for other misrepresentation.

(1) Under the contract

(a) GENERAL RULE. The general rule is that an agent is neither liable under,[1] nor entitled to enforce,[2] a contract he makes on behalf of his principal.

(b) EXCEPTIONS. An agent may enter into a contract on his own behalf as well as on behalf of the principal and so be liable or entitled under the contract. This possibility is illustrated by the following cases.

(i) *Agent contracting personally.* An agent is liable under the contract if he intended to undertake personal liability. Where the contract is in writing, the question whether he

---

[92] See above, p.581.
[93] Contracts (Rights of Third Parties) Act 1999, s.1(4).
[94] *ibid.*, s.3(2); *cf.* above, p.643, n.3.
[95] For the status of such a partnership as a body corporate, see Limited Liability Partnerships Act 2000, s.1(2).
[96] *ibid.*, s.5(2).
[97] Companies Act 1985, s.36C (above, p.724, below, p.734) applies (with appropriate modifications) to limited liability partnerships by virtue of Limited Liability Partnership Regulations 2001, SI 2001/1090, reg.4(1) and Sch.2, Pt I, but does not impose liabilities on the principal.
[98] See above, p.729.
[99] See below, p.734.
[1] *Robins v Bridge* (1837) 3 M. & W. 114; *Ferguson v Wilson* (1866) L.R. 2 Ch.App. 77; *N. & J. Vlassopulos v Ney Shipping Ltd* [1977] 2 Lloyd's Rep. 478; *Boyter v Thomson* [1995] 2 A.C. 629 at 632.
[2] *Lucas v Beale* (1851) 10 C.B. 739; *Fairlie v Fenton* (1870) L.R. 5 Ex. 169.

had this intention is one of construction.[3] An agent who is described in a written contract as a party to it and signs it without qualification is liable under it although the third party knew that he was acting as agent.[4] He may be liable even though such a contract also provides that it is signed on behalf of a third person, for such a provision may merely be intended to mean that that person is to be a party to the contract and not that the agent is to be absolved from liability under it.[5] At the other extreme, an agent who is described as agent in the contract and signs as agent is not liable.[6] But an agent may be described as agent in the body of the contract and sign without qualification; or he may be described as a party in the body of the contract and sign as agent.[7] A distinction has been drawn in such cases between words which merely describe the agent's profession, and words of representation, which show that he is acting as agent. The former do not, while the latter do, exonerate him from liability. Thus the words "we, as solicitors, undertake . . . " were held in *Burrell v Jones*[8] to be merely descriptive; and even the words "as agent" when used in their commercial, rather than their legal, sense have been held to be descriptive.[9] The words "on behalf of" or "*per procurationem*" are generally representative. But no particular formula is conclusive; and where the description is equivocal the court will rely on other relevant circumstances in order to determine, on an objective standard, whether an undertaking of personal liability may be inferred. Thus in one case[10] a company director ordered repairs to be done to a boat which the company had hired from him. He gave the order on the company's notepaper and signed it with the addition "Director." He was, nevertheless, held personally liable as he was the owner of the boat. But for this fact it seems that he would not have been personally liable.[11] An agent is no longer personally liable merely because he acts on behalf of a foreign principal.[12]

Just as the agent may on the true construction of the contract, be liable, so he may be entitled.[13] The courts will, if possible, hold that "the existence of the liability on the one hand involves the existence of the correlative right on the other"[14]; but words which indicate that the agent is not to be liable are not necessarily construed to mean that he is not to be entitled. Thus where an agent had contracted "on account of" his principal,

---

[3] *Punjab National Bank v de Boinville* [1992] 1 W.L.R. 1138 at 1155; *cf. Ignazio Messina & Co v Polskie Linie Oceaniczne* [1995] 2 Lloyd's Rep. 566 at 571.

[4] *Basma v Weekes* [1950] A.C. 441; *cf. Davies v Sweet* [1962] 2 Q.B. 300; *Sika Contracts v Gill* (1978) 9 Build.L.R. 11; *Kai Yung v Hong Kong & Shanghai Banking Corp* [1981] A.C. 787 at 795.

[5] *The Sun Happiness* [1984] 1 Lloyd's Rep. 381.

[6] *Mahony v Kekulé* (1854) 14 C.B. 390; *The Rialto (No.2)* [1998] 1 Lloyd's Rep. 322 at 328.

[7] As in *Gadd v Houghton* (1876) 1 Ex.D. 357; *Universal Steam Navigation Co Ltd v James McKelvie & Co* [1923] A.C. 492 (in these cases the agents were held not liable); *The Maria D* [1992] 1 A.C. 21.

[8] (1819) 3 B. & Ald. 47.

[9] *Parker v Winlow* (1857) 7 E. & B. 942; *cf.* above, pp.706–708.

[10] *The Swan* [1968] 1 Lloyd's Rep. 5; Reynolds, 85 L.Q.R. 92; Legh-Jones, 32 M.L.R. 325; *cf. Tudor Marine Ltd v Tradax Export SA* [1976] 2 Lloyd's Rep. 135; *The Primorje* [1980] 2 Lloyd's Rep. 74; *Ojjeh v Waller* [1999] C.L.Y. 4405; contrast *Astilleros Canarios SA v Cape Hatteras Shipping Co SA* [1982] 1 Lloyd's Rep. 518.

[11] *cf. The Riza Sun* [1997] 2 Lloyd's Rep. 314.

[12] *Miller, Gibb & Co v Smith & Tyrer Ltd* [1917] 2 K.B. 141; *J S Holt & Moseley (London) Ltd v Sir Charles Cunningham & Partners Ltd* (1949) 83 Ll.L.R. 141 at 145; Hudson, 23 M.L.R. 695; 29 M.L.R. 353; 35 Can.Bar Rev. 336.

[13] *Short v Spackman* (1831) 2 B. & Ad. 962; *Clay v Southern* (1852) 7 Ex. 717; *H O Brandt & Co v H N Morris & Co Ltd* [1917] 2 K.B. 784; *cf. The Yanxilas* [1982] 2 Lloyd's Rep. 444; *Fraser v Thames Television* [1984] Q.B. 44; *Transcontinental Underwriting Agency SRL v Grand Union Ins Co Ltd* [1987] 2 Lloyd's Rep. 409.

[14] *Repetto v Millar's Karri & Jarrah Forests Ltd* [1901] 2 K.B. 306 at 310.

it was held that the agent was not personally liable on the contract[15]; but where a policy of insurance described the assured as a bank "a/c [a named customer]" it was held to confer rights on the bank (the agent), the reference to the customer being merely intended to remind the bank which of its customers was concerned with the transaction in question.[16] It follows that the agent can be entitled without being liable or liable without being entitled, if that is the true meaning of the contract. In the first of these situations, there may indeed be some difficulty in seeing what consideration has been provided by the agent so long as the contract remains wholly executory, but there would be no such difficulty where the agent has actually performed, *e.g.* by making a payment under the contract on behalf of the principal. In the second situation there is no similar difficulty even if the contract is still executory; the third party provides consideration for the agent's promise by undertaking liability towards the principal and it is immaterial that the consideration does not move to the agent: consideration must move from the promisee (the third party) but need not move to the promisor (the agent).[17]

(ii) *Trade usage or custom.* An agent may be personally liable or entitled if that is the usual course of business either between particular parties or in relation to a particular class of agents. For example, "where one attorney does work for another, it is common practice for him to give credit to that other and not to the client".[18] A local or trade custom can have the same effect.[19]

(iii) *Principal undisclosed.* Where the principal is undisclosed the agent is both entitled and liable[20]; but this rule does not apply where the agent uses words of representation and the principal is only unnamed.[21] The agent's failure to name the principal may make it easy to infer that he intended to contract personally; but there is no general rule to that effect.[22]

(iv) *Agent in fact principal.* An agent may purport to act on behalf of a principal when he is in fact acting on his own behalf. If he purports to act for an unnamed principal, he can enforce the contract for his own benefit.[23] But if he purports to act for a named principal, he can enforce the contract only after giving due notice to the third party that he acted on his own behalf.[24] Even then the agent will not be allowed to enforce the contract if this would prejudice the third party.[25] These safeguards are necessary as the third party may have relied on the principal's solvency or other attributes when he made the contract. It follows that the agent cannot enforce the contract if he knew that, for some "personal" reason, the third party was unwilling to contract with him either at all,

---

[15] *Gadd v Houghton* (1876) 1 Ex. D. 357.

[16] *Punjab National Bank v de Boinville* [1992] 1 W.L.R. 1138.

[17] See above, p.81.

[18] *Scrace v Whittington* (1823) 2 B. & C. 11. The above dictum makes the agent *exclusively* liable: *cf.* below, p.737.

[19] *Fleet v Murton* (1871) L.R. 7 Q.B. 126; *cf. Cory Brothers Shipping Ltd v Baldan Ltd* [1997] 2 Lloyd's Rep. 58 (forwarding agent acting for unnamed principal liable, by custom, for freight).

[20] *Sims v Bond* (1833) 5 B. & Ad. 389 at 393; *Siu Yin Kwan v Eastern Insurance Co Ltd* [1994] 2 A.C. 199 at 207; *Boyter v Thomson* [1995] 2 A.C. 629 at 632.

[21] *e.g. Universal Steam Navigation Co v James McKelvie & Co* [1923] A.C. 492; *Benton v Campbell, Parker & Co Ltd* [1925] 2 K.B. 410.

[22] *N & J Vlassopulos v Ney Shipping Ltd* [1977] 2 Lloyd's Rep. 478.

[23] *Schmaltz v Avery* (1851) 16 Q.B. 655; *Harper & Co v Vigers Bros* [1909] 2 K.B. 549. See *Bowstead and Reynolds on Agency* (17th ed.), pp.517–518 for the suggestion that this rule should only be applied where it was not inconsistent with the terms of the contract to allow the agent to sue.

[24] *Bickerton v Burrell* (1816) 5 M. & S. 383; *aliter* if the other party knows that the "agent" is the real principal: *Rayner v Grote* (1846) 15 M. & W. 359.

[25] See *Fellowes v Gwydyr* (1829) 1 Russ. & M. 83.

or on the same terms as those on which he was willing to contract with the principal.[26] If the claimant in *Said v Butt*[27] had gone in person to buy a ticket, pretending that it was not for him but for a friend, he could not later have said that his friend was in fact himself.

The present exception to the general rule, that an agent acquires no rights under the contract, is based on the assumptions that he has (i) purported to contract as agent and (ii) in fact contracted as principal. The exception therefore did not apply where a father conducted negotiations for the purchase of a house and the resulting contract was drawn up in the name of his son (who was a minor). It was held that the father could not enforce the contract since the contract did not say that he had entered into it on behalf of the son, or indeed mention the father's name at all.[28]

(v) *Principal non-existent.* Where the alleged principal does not exist, it may be easy to infer that the agent intended to assume personal liability. At common law this inference was drawn in *Kelner v Baxter*[29] with the result that promoters were held personally liable on a contract made by them on behalf of a company which had not yet been formed. But such an inference is not necessarily drawn merely because the agent purports to act for a non-existent principal[30]: the question is one of intention in each case.[31] The agent was accordingly held not liable where the contract was with a non-existent company which was believed to form part of a group of companies, the third party's intention being merely to contract with a company within that group, and one such company having accepted responsibility under the contract.[32] Similarly, it is arguable that the agent should not be personally liable where, under the rules discussed earlier in this Chapter,[33] the principal can be held liable under the contract in spite of not having been in existence when the contract was made.

S.36C(l) of the Companies Act 1985[34] provides that "a contract which purports to be made . . . on behalf of a company[35] at a time when the company has not been formed has effect, subject to any agreement to the contrary, as one made with the person purporting to act . . . as agent for" the company. Under this subsection, the agent can no longer escape liability merely on the ground that he entered into the contract "as agent"[36]; it is up to him to establish that there was an "agreement to the contrary" exonerating him from liability. The subsection puzzlingly concludes with the words "and he [*i.e.* the agent, in our examples] is personally liable on the contract accordingly". It seems these

---

[26] *The Remco* [1984] 2 Lloyd's Rep. 205.

[27] [1920] 3 K.B. 497; above, p.729.

[28] *Hector v Lyons* (1989) 58 P. & C.R. 156. No such point arose in *Shogun Finance Ltd v Hudson* [2001] EWCA Civ 1000; [2002] Q.B. 834 (above, p.299) where any attempt by the rogue to enforce the contract would have failed by reason of his fraud.

[29] (1886) L.R. 2 C.P. 174; above, p.696; *cf. Phonogram Ltd v Lane* [1982] Q.B. 938; Green, 47 M.L.R. 671.

[30] *Holman v Pullin* (1884) Cab. & Fl. 254.

[31] *Black v Smallwood* [1966] A.L.R. 744; Baxt, 30 M.L.R. 328; Lücke, 3 Adelaide L.Rev. 102.

[32] *Coral (UK) Ltd v Rechtman* [1996] 1 Lloyd's Rep. 235.

[33] See above, p.732 at n.96.

[34] As substituted by Companies Act 1989, s.130(4) for the former s.36(4) of Companies Act 1985, which had in its turn replaced European Communities Act 1972, s.9(2). The effect of s.36C(1) seems to be the same as that of the earlier provisions, in spite of slight changes in the wording.

[35] *i.e.* one incorporated in the United Kingdom: *Rover International Ltd v Cannon Film Sales Ltd (No.3)* (1987) 3 B.C.C. 369, reversed in part on other grounds [1989] 1 W.L.R. 912. The section applies to limited liability partnerships: see above, p.735, n.97.

[36] *Phonogram Ltd v Lane* [1982] Q.B. 938 at 944; McMullen [1982] C.L.J. 47. And see above, n.34. Contrast *Badgerhill Properties v Cottrell* [1991] B.C.L.C. 805 (agent not liable merely because existing company's name was incorrectly stated in the contract).

words merely spell out *one* consequence of the previous words and do not limit their operation: *i.e.* the agent may be *entitled* as well as liable.

At common law, a distinction was drawn between the cases so far considered where the agent purported to *act on behalf* of the unformed company, and those in which he said that the contract *actually was that* of the company[37] and purported to affix the company's signature. In the latter case it was held that the resulting transaction was a complete nullity,[38] and that the agent could not acquire any rights under it.[39] But the distinction between the two situations was criticised as highly technical[40] and one which businessmen were unlikely to appreciate. The provisions of s.36C(1) of the Companies Act 1985[41] therefore extend also to "a contract which purports to be made by a company" before it is formed. Such a contract has effect (subject to contrary agreement) "as one made with the person purporting to act for the company"; *e.g.* by the officer purporting to affix the company's signature. The concluding words of the subsection again refer only to the *liability* of such a person, but it has been held that he is also *entitled* to enforce the contract, subject only to restrictions which may be imposed on his right to do so at common law[42]: *e.g.*, on the ground that, for "personal" reasons of the kind described above, the third party was willing to contract only with the company, or unwilling to contract with the person purporting to act on its behalf.[43] But the subsection does not apply where the contract purports to have been made by a company which had once existed and later been dissolved before the time of the putative contract. That contract is then a nullity and cannot be enforced either by the person purporting to have acted for the company or by a new company formed after the date of contracting to carry on the business of former company. The reason why such a case is not within s.36C(1) is that the agent purported to act for the old company rather than on behalf of the new company before it was formed.[44]

Our concern here has been with the rights and liabilities of the *agent* under pre-incorporation contracts; the rights and liabilities of the *principal* in such cases have been discussed earlier in this Chapter.[45]

(vi) *Deeds.* At common law, an agent who executed a deed was personally liable on it even though the deed said that he had executed it on behalf of his principal.[46] It seems, however, that this rule has been reversed by statute.[47]

(vii) *Statute.* An agent may be personally liable by statute: for example, an administrative receiver appointed by debenture holders, who is deemed to be the agent of the company,[48] is nevertheless personally liable on a contract into which he enters in

---

[37] For the concept of an act done by the company itself, see *Meridian Global Funds Management Asia Ltd v Securities Commission* [1995] 2 A.C. 500 at 506–507.

[38] *cf. Rover International Ltd v Cannon Film Sales Ltd (No.3)* [1989] 1 W.L.R. 912—a position described in earlier proceedings in the same case as "a blot on English jurisprudence": [1987] 1 W.L.R. 670 at 679.

[39] *Newborne v Sensolid (Great Britain) Ltd* [1954] 1 Q.B. 45.

[40] The defendants in Newborne's case escaped from a bad bargain on a technicality: see the comments of Lord Goddard C.J. reported in *The Times*, March 20, 1953. *cf.* Lord Denning M.R. in *Phonogram Ltd v Lane* [1982] Q.B. 938 at 944.

[41] See above, n.34.

[42] *Braymist Ltd v Wise Finance Co Ltd* [2002] EWCA Civ 127; [2002] Ch. 273.

[43] *ibid.*, at [63], [83]. The *Braymist* case was not of this kind.

[44] *Cotronic (UK) Ltd v Dezonie (t/a Wendaland Builders Ltd)* [1991] B.C.L.C. 721.

[45] See above, pp.730, 731–732.

[46] *Appleton v Binks* (1804) 5 East 148.

[47] Powers of Attorney Act 1971, s.7(1), as amended by Law of Property (Miscellaneous Provisions) Act 1989, ss.1(8) and 4 and Schs 1 and 2.

[48] Insolvency Act 1986, s.44(1)(a).

carrying out his functions, except in so far as the contract or legislation otherwise provides.[49]

(c) ELECTION.[50] Where an agent is liable on the contract, one possible interpretation of the transaction is that he is solely liable, or, in other words, that the contract is simply between him and the third party and not between the third party and the principal at all.[51] Another possibility is that the agent and the principal are both liable under the contract.[52] This is certainly the position where the principal is undisclosed[53] and it may also be true where an agent incurs personal responsibility under a contract made on behalf of a disclosed principal.[54]

Where both principal and agent are liable on the contract, the third party may lose his right to sue one of them on the ground that he has "elected" to hold the other liable. This doctrine is most commonly discussed in relation to cases involving undisclosed principals, though there is some authority for applying it in all cases in which both principal and agent are liable on the contract.[55] The reasons for the doctrine are obscure: it is hard to see why a principal should be released merely because the third party has "elected" to hold the agent liable. It might be more satisfactory to hold that the principal should be released only if he had relied on the third party's conduct in such a way that he would be prejudiced by being subsequently held liable: for example, if the principal had adjusted his accounts with the agent in reliance on the third party's conduct.[56] Election to hold the principal liable may similarly be a ground for releasing the agent if it has led to action in reliance by the agent: for example, to his giving up rights against the principal. Where there has been no action in reliance on the third party's conduct, the courts do not often apply the doctrine of election. What amounts to election is a question of fact; and in the decided cases the courts have been somewhat reluctant to find an election. Merely sending a bill to one of two parties liable has been held not to be an election[57]; and even the commencement of legal proceedings, though strong evidence of election,[58] is not necessarily conclusive.[59]

There was formerly a rule that, if the liability of principal and agent was joint, and the third party obtained judgment against one of them, he could not then sue the other, *even though the judgment was not satisfied*.[60] This rule has been abolished by statute,[61] so that the mere obtaining of a judgment against principal or agent will not bar proceedings against the other; though it might, presumably, still amount to an "election".

---

[49] *ibid.* s.44(1)(b) as amended by Insolvency Act 1994, s.2; *cf. Powdrill v Watson* [1995] 2 A.C. 394 (personal liability on "adopted" contracts of employment); for his right of indemnity, see 1986 Act s.45.

[50] Reynolds, 86 L.Q.R. 318.

[51] *e.g.* above, p.734 at n.18, below, n.55.

[52] See Reynolds, 85 L.Q.R. 92.

[53] See above, pp.727, 734.

[54] See *The Swan* [1968] 1 Lloyd's Rep. 5 at 12; *Teheran-Europe Co v S T Belton (Tractors) Ltd* [1968] 2 Q.B. 545 at 558; *The Kurnia Dewi* [1997] 1 Lloyd's Rep. 553 at 559.

[55] *Debenham v Perkins* (1925) 113 L.T. 252 at 254. Other cases which have been cited to support the doctrine of election where the principal was disclosed may turn rather on the point that he was never liable under the contract at all because it was made solely with the agent: *e.g. Addison v Gandasequi* (1812) 4 Taunt. 574; *Thomson v Davenport* (1829) 9 B. & C. 78; *Calder v Dobell* (1871) L.R. 6 C.P. 486.

[56] *Smethurst v Mitchell* (1859) 1 E. & E. 622; *Davison v Donaldson* (1882) 9 Q.B.D. 623.

[57] *Chesterton v Barone* [1987] 1 E.G.L.R. 15.

[58] See *Scarf v Jardine* (1882) 7 App.Cas. 345.

[59] *Curtis v Williamson* (1874) L.R. 10 Q.B. 57; *Clarkson Booker Ltd v Andjel* [1964] 2 Q.B. 775; *cf. The Scaplake* [1978] 2 Lloyd's Rep. 380.

[60] See above, p.569.

[61] Civil Liability (Contribution) Act 1978, s.3.

(2) Under a collateral contract

There may be a collateral contract between agent and third party, quite distinct from the main contract between principal and third party. Thus when goods are sold by auction, the auctioneer undertakes certain obligations towards the buyer,[62] but they are not co-extensive with those of the seller. The seller undertakes that he has the right to sell, but the auctioneer only undertakes to give the buyer possession[63] so that he is not liable for the seller's lack of title.[64] The collateral contract may confer rights, as well as impose liabilities, on the agent. Thus an auctioneer can sue the buyer for the price of the goods sold.[65] The liability of an auctioneer who refuses to knock goods down to the highest bidder at an auction sale without reserve[66] has also been explained on the ground of a "collateral agreement existing between the auctioneer and the bidder."[67]

(3) Implied warranty of authority

(a) NATURE OF LIABILITY. An agent who purports to act for a principal, knowing that he has no authority to do so, is liable to the third party in deceit, even if he believed that the principal would ratify.[68] It was at one time thought that if the agent honestly believed that he had authority when in fact he had none, he was under no liability.[69] But it was settled in *Collen v Wright*[70] that the agent was in such circumstances liable for breach of an implied warranty that he had the authority which he purported to have. It makes no difference that the agent has acted in good faith and with due diligence.[71]

The rule sometimes operates harshly on the agent, and it might be more reasonable to imply a warranty that the agent should not negligently exceed his authority.[72] The agent's position has been alleviated by legislation, so that an agent who acts under a power of attorney incurs no liability if the power of attorney has without his knowledge been revoked.[73]

The agent does not impliedly[74] warrant that the contract which he makes between principal and third party will be performed, but only that he has authority to make it.[75] This has an important bearing on damages. If the third party could have obtained full satisfaction from the principal, had the contract been binding on him, the agent is liable to the same extent.[75a] But if the principal is insolvent, the third party cannot recover more from the agent than he would have got from the principal, had the agent had

---

[62] *Woolfe v Horne* (1877) 2 Q.B.D. 355.

[63] *Wood v Baxter* (1883) 49 L.T. 45.

[64] *Benton v Campbell, Parker & Co* [1925] 2 K.B. 410.

[65] *Coppin v Walker* (1816) 7 Taunt. 237; cf. *Wilson v Pike* [1949] 1 K.B. 176; *Chelmsford Auctions Ltd v Poole* [1973] Q.B. 542.

[66] See above, pp.11, 142.

[67] *Barry v Davies* [2000] 1 W.L.R. 1962 at 1968 ([2001] 1 All E.R. at 950).

[68] *Polhill v Walter* (1832) 3 B. & Ad. 114.

[69] This was one basis of *Smout v Ilbery* (1842) 10 M. & W. 1; see also below, p.739. The view that fault is essential was still stated (wrongly) in *Salton v New Beeston Cycle Co* [1900] 1 Ch. 43.

[70] (1857) 8 E. & B. 647; approved by the House of Lords in *Starkey v Bank of England* [1903] A.C. 114 and followed in *V/O Rasnoimport v Guthrie & Co Ltd* [1966] 1 Lloyd's Rep. 1; Reynolds, 83 L.Q.R. 189.

[71] *Yonge v Toynbee* [1910] 1 K.B. 215; see below, pp.750–751, for survival of apparent authority in cases of the principal's insanity.

[72] Negligence may lead to liability in damages at common law or under the Misrepresentation Act 1967; but the measure of such damages could differ from that for breach of implied warranty of authority: cf. above, p.359.

[73] Powers of Attorney Act 1971, s.5(1).

[74] He may expressly do so as (for example) in *The Maria D* [1992] 1 A.C. 21.

[75] cf. *Nelson v Nelson* [1997] 1 W.L.R. 233.

[75a] cf. *Habton Farms v Nimms* [2003] EWCA Civ 68, [2003] 1 All E.R. 1136.

authority; and this may be very little, or nothing, according to the degree of the principal's insolvency.[76]

Normally, the effect of the warranty is to induce the third party to enter into a contract with the principal or supposed principal. But liability may also be incurred if the third party acts in reliance on the warranty in some other way: *e.g.* where the agent falsely represents to a building society that he is authorised to act for a vendor of property and the society in consequence makes a loan to the purchaser.[77]

(b) RESTRICTIONS ON LIABILITY. An agent is not, or may not be, liable for breach of implied warranty of authority in the following cases:

(i) *Want of authority known to third party.* The agent is not liable where the third party knew, or must be taken to have known, that the agent had no authority.[78] The agent may also not be liable where he and the third party had equal means of knowing that the agent had no authority; though the claim in the case[79] which supports this view was actually one for goods sold and delivered, *i.e.* on the main contract of sale. Thus the case may not be authoritative on an agent's liability for breach of implied warranty.[80]

(ii) *Representation of law.* The traditional view (which may be open for reconsideration[81]) is that the agent is not liable where the representation is one of law.[82] Accordingly, it has been held that, since the construction of a document is a matter of law, an agent who misrepresents its meaning is not liable for breach of implied warranty. Thus if the director of a statutory corporation[83] which has, on the true construction of its incorporating statute, no borrowing powers, purports to borrow on its behalf, he is not liable for breach of implied warranty.[84] But if such a corporation has a limited power to borrow up to, say, £10m., and the director purports to borrow on its behalf above that limit, he is liable for breach of implied warranty, for he has misrepresented a fact: namely, that the company has not yet borrowed £10m.[85] If a loan is made to a company incorporated under the Companies Acts by a lender dealing with the company in good faith, the contract of loan will normally be enforceable against the company even though the directors had, under the company's constitution, no power to enter into the contract.[86] The lender's claim for breach of warranty against the directors will therefore fail on the principle stated in the following paragraph. If the lender had *no* claim against the company because he had acted in bad faith, he would know that the loan was unauthorised. His claim for breach of warranty of authority would fail on the ground that he knew of the agent's want of authority.[87]

(iii) *Principal liable on main contract.* An agent who has no actual authority is probably not liable for breach of implied warranty if the principal is liable to the third party on the ground of apparent or usual authority. In *Rainbow v Howkins*[88] an auctioneer who

---

[76] See below, p.975.

[77] *Penn v Bristol & West BS* [1997] 1 W.L.R. 1356.

[78] *Jones v Hope* (1880) 3 T.L.R. 247n.; *Lilly, Wilson & Co v Smales, Eeles & Co* [1892] 1 Q.B. 456; *Halbot v Lens* [1901] 1 Ch. 344.

[79] *Smout v Ilberry* (1842) 10 M. & W. 1.

[80] See *Oliver v Bank of England* [1901] 1 Ch. 652 at 660.

[81] See the discussion of *Kleinwort Benson Ltd v Lincoln CC* [1999] 2 A.C. 349, at p.333, above.

[82] *Saffron Walden, etc. BS v Rayner* (1880) 14 Ch.D. 406.

[83] Such corporations remain subject to the *ultra vires* doctrine: above, p.563.

[84] *Rashdall v Ford* (1866) L.R. 2 Eq. 750.

[85] *Cherry v Colonial Bank of Australasia* (1869) L.R. 3 P.C. 24; *Weeks v Propert* (1873) L.R. 8 C.P. 427.

[86] Companies Act 1985, s.35A(1), as substituted by Companies Act 1989, s.108(1); above, p.562 (also stating exceptions to these provisions).

[87] See above, at n.78.

[88] [1904] 2 K.B. 322; criticised in *McManus v Fortescue* [1907] 2 K.B. 1 at 6, but that case can be explained on the ground that the third party knew of the agent's want of authority.

had authority to sell a horse, subject to a reserve price, sold it without reserve. It was held that he was not liable for breach of implied warranty, as the buyer could have enforced the main contract against the seller on the ground that the auctioneer had apparent authority to sell without reserve.[89] Similarly, an agent would not be liable for breach of implied warranty if he did an unauthorised act which the principal later ratified.

(iv) *Crown agent*. An agent of the Crown is probably not liable for breach of implied warranty of authority. The assumption that such an agent impliedly warrants his authority is "utterly inconsistent with the facts".[90] In view of the enormous value of some government contracts, it would be extremely harsh to impose liability on a civil servant who in good faith and without negligence had misrepresented his authority.

(4) Other liability for misrepresentation

The agent's liability for breach of warranty of authority arises where he misrepresents his authority; but he may also be liable to the third party in tort for other misrepresentations. This was, for example, held to be the case where an estate agent who had been engaged by the vendor of property negligently made misrepresentations about it to a prospective purchaser who, in reliance on those representations, entered into a contract with the vendor for the purchase of the property.[91] Under the Property Misdescriptions Act 1991, an agent who makes such a misrepresentation may also incur criminal liability. The Act provides that no right of action in civil proceedings is to arise "by reason *only*" of the commission of such an offence[92]; but this provision would not seem to preclude the agent's being held liable to the third party for negligence at common law.

3. Between Principal and Agent

(1) Rights of agent

(a) COMMISSION. Three questions arise in connection with an agent's right to commission.

(i) *Whether payable at all*. Whether an agent is entitled to any commission at all depends on the terms of the agreement between principal and agent. In *Taylor v Brewer*[93] an agent was to receive "such commission . . . as should be deemed right" by the principal. It was held that he had no legal right to commission. But where the agency is a commercial relationship the courts are reluctant to send the agent away empty-handed.[94] Thus if the agreement merely provides that the *amount* of commission is to be left to the principal's discretion, and he refuses to fix the amount, he may be liable to pay a reasonable sum.[95] On the other hand, the director of a company may agree to work for it "for such remuneration as the other directors may determine" on the understanding that he will receive nothing until the company has "got on its feet". If this never happens, he cannot claim a reasonable remuneration for his work.[96]

---

[89] cf. *Mitsui & Co Ltd v Marpo Industrial Ltd* [1974] 1 Lloyd's Rep. 386 at 393. *Quaere* whether this reasoning might have been applied in *Yonge v Toynbee* [1910] 1 K.B. 215; cf., below p.751, n.19.

[90] *Dunn v Macdonald* [1897] 1 Q.B. 555 at 558.

[91] *McCullagh v Lane Fox & Partners Ltd* [1994] 1 E.G.L.R. 48.

[92] Property Misdescriptions Act 1991, s.1(4).

[93] (1813) 1 M. & S. 290.

[94] See *Kofi Sunkersette Obu v A Strauss & Co Ltd* [1951] A.C. 243.

[95] *Bryant v Flight* (1839) 5 M. & W. 114; *British Bank for Foreign Trade Ltd v Novinex Ltd* [1949] 1 K.B. 623; *Powell v Braun* [1954] 1 W.L.R. 401.

[96] *Re Richmond Gate Property Co Ltd* [1965] 1 W.L.R. 335.

(ii) *When earned.* Commission is payable only in respect of a transaction which the agent was employed to bring about. In *Toulmin v Millar*[97] the owner of a house employed an agent to find a tenant. The agent found a tenant, who later bought the house. His claim for commission on the sale failed, since he was only employed to let the house.

The transaction must also be caused by the agent's efforts. In *Tribe v Taylor*[98] a principal employed an agent to raise a loan of money. The lender later entered into partnership with the principal and on this occasion made a further loan. The agent's claim for commission on this second loan failed, since it was not brought about by his efforts.

Unless otherwise agreed,[99] the agent is not entitled to commission in respect of transactions which take place after the termination of the agency.[1] A contract may, however, provide that commission is *earned* when the agent secures the order (so that nothing more need be done by him to perfect his entitlement to it) but that it is only to *become payable* at some later stage, *e.g.* when the order is executed. In such a case the agent is entitled to commission on orders obtained before, though not executed till after, the termination of the agency.[2] Under the Regulations which apply to "commercial agents",[3] such an agent has somewhat more extensive rights in respect of transactions concluded after the termination of the agency[4] and in respect of transactions not brought about by his efforts but concluded in breach of an exclusive agency agreement.[5]

A principal may engage more than one agent: *e.g.* where an owner instructs two estate agents to find a purchaser for his house.[6] Commission will then be due to the agent whose efforts have brought about the sale[7]; and where the efforts of both have contributed to this result, each may[8] be entitled to commission.[9] Where two "commercial agents" appointed in succession claim commission on the same transaction, the first agent is not normally entitled to commission, but the court may, if it is equitable to do so, order the commission to be shared between the two agents.[10]

The precise stage at which the agent becomes entitled to commission depends on the terms of the contract between principal and agent.[11] This question has given rise to

---

[97] (1887) 12 App.Cas. 746. For a fuller report, see 58 L.T. 96.

[98] (1876) 1 C.P.D. 505; *cf. Debenham, Tewson & Chinnocks plc v Rimington* [1989] 2 E.G.L.R. 26 (where, however, the agents were awarded a reasonable remuneration for their efforts); *Harwood v Smith, The Times,* December 8, 1997; contrast *Nahun v Royal Holloway and Bedford New Colleges Ltd, The Times,* November 19, 1998.

[99] *Levy v Goldhill* [1917] 2 Ch. 297; *cf. Brian Cooper & Co v Fairview Estates (Investments) Ltd* [1987] 1 E.G.L.R. 18; *Robert Bruce & Partners v Wynyard Developments* [1987] 1 E.G.L.R. 20; *Barnard Marcus & Co v Ashraf* [1988] 1 E.G.L.R. 7; *Marshall v N M Financial Management Ltd* [1997] 1 W.L.R. 1527 (so far as it relates to the "renewal commission"); *Harwood v Smith* [1998] 1 E.G.L.R. 5.

[1] *Crocker-Horlock v B Lang & Co Ltd* [1949] 1 All E.R. 526; *Bronester Ltd v Priddle* [1961] 1 W.L.R. 1294.

[2] *Sellers v London Counties Newspapers* [1951] 1 K.B. 784.

[3] See above, p.709. SI 1993/3053.

[4] *ibid.,* regs 7(1)(b), 8.

[5] *ibid.,* reg.7(2); at common law, the agent's remedy in such a case would be by way of damages: *cf. Alpha Trading Ltd v Dunshaw-Patten* [1981] Q.B. 290, below, pp.744, 749. For exclusive dealing agreements, see above p.468.

[6] Although estate agents are not "agents" for the purpose of enabling them to conclude contracts between their clients and third parties (above, p.708), they are treated in the same way as agents for the purpose of their right to commission.

[7] *John D Wood & Co v Dantata* (1985) 275 E.G. 1278; *Chasen Rider v Hedges* [1993] 1 E.G.L.R. 47.

[8] Depending on the terms of the contract: see the authorities cited at nn.13–19, below.

[9] *Lordgate Properties v Balcombe* (1985) 274 E.G. 493; *Anscombe & Ringland v Watson* [1991] 2 E.G.L.R. 28.

[10] SI 1993/3953, reg.9.

[11] See, *e.g. Fairvale v Sabharwall* [1992] 2 E.G.L.R. 27.

much litigation in cases concerning estate agents' commission.[12] In *Luxor (Eastbourne)
Ltd v Cooper*[13] the landowner undertook to pay the estate agent his commission "on completion of sale". No sale took place because the owner refused to deal with the prospective purchaser introduced by the agent. It was held that the agent was not entitled to commission. Again, a contract for the payment of commission on the agent's "introducing a person ready, willing and able to purchase" does not entitle him to commission if the prospective purchaser makes a conditional offer subject to contract and satisfactory survey; or if he makes an offer and withdraws it before the vendor accepts[14]; or if he signs a contract which cannot be completed because of a defect in the vendor's title[15]; or if, before the prospective purchaser is introduced, the owner has entered into a binding contract to sell the property to a purchaser introduced by another agent.[16] Nor does a promise to pay commission "in the event of your introducing . . . a person prepared to enter into a contract" entitle the agent to commission where the person introduced only agrees to sign a contract which is subject to conditions.[17] Even a contract for the payment of commission "in the event of securing for you an offer" does not entitle the agent to commission unless a firm, unconditional offer is made.[18] But where the contract was to pay commission as soon as "any person introduced by us enters into a legally binding contract to purchase" it was held that the agent was entitled when such a contract was made although the vendor later rescinded it on account of the purchaser's breach.[19]

The common law on this topic is far from satisfactory. On the one hand it is hard for the estate agent, who may have gone to much trouble and expense in advertising[20] a house and securing offers, to be deprived of all reward through the caprice of his client. On the other hand it is hard for the client to have to pay commission where it is not his fault that no sale takes place: the common understanding is that the commission should come out of the proceeds of sale. In this conflict of interests, the estate agents usually have the advantage of being able to submit a standard form of contract[21] to the client, who may accept its terms without question. The courts have to some extent redressed the balance in favour of the client. They have (as the above cases show) construed stipulations for commission strictly against the agents,[22] or held them to be ineffective for uncertainty or for misrepresentation.[23] But it remains possible for commission to be payable even though there is no sale. It would perhaps be better if the question when an

---

[12] Gower, 13 M.L.R. 490; Hardy-Ivamy (1951) C.L.P. 305.

[13] [1941] A.C. 108.

[14] *Dennis Reed Ltd v Goody* [1950] 2 K.B. 277; *Graham & Scott (Southgate) Ltd v Oxlade* [1950] 2 K.B. 257. Contrast *Christie Owen & Davies Ltd v Rapacioli* [1974] Q.B. 781 (where a vendor who withdrew after a firm offer had been made by the prospective purchaser was held liable for commission).

[15] *Dellafiora v Lester* [1962] 1 W.L.R. 1208; cf. *Blake & Co v Sohn* [1969] 1 W.L.R. 1412.

[16] *A A Dickinson & Co v O'Leary* (1979) 254 E.G. 731.

[17] *A L Wilkinson Ltd v Brown* [1966] 1 W.L.R. 1914.

[18] *Bennett, Walden & Co v Wood* [1950] 2 All E.R. 134; cf. *Christie, Owen & Davies Ltd v Stockton* [1953] 1 W.L.R. 1353.

[19] *Scheggia v Gradwell* [1963] 1 W.L.R. 1049; cf. *Midgeley Estates Ltd v Hand* [1952] 2 Q.B. 432; *Drewery & Drewery v Ware-Lane* [1960] 1 W.L.R. 1204; *aliter* if the contract goes off because of the agent's misrepresentation: *Peter Long & Partners v Burns* [1956] 1 W.L.R. 413 at 1083.

[20] The agent can expressly stipulate for reimbursement of advertising expenses, as in *Bernard Thorpe & Partners v Flannery* (1977) 244 E.G. 129.

[21] The Unfair Contract Terms Act 1977 does not affect the validity of the provisions discussed: they confer *rights* on the agent and do not exclude or restrict his liability. For possible application of the Unfair Terms in Consumer Contracts Regulations 1999, see below at n.27.

[22] See above, at nn.13–19.

[23] See *Jaques v Lloyd D George & Partners* [1968] 1 W.L.R. 625.

estate agent was entitled to commission ceased to be regarded purely as one of construction. Only legislation could now achieve this result[24]; but the Estate Agents Act 1979 (which regulates the activities of estate agents) does not lay down any rules for this purpose. It merely requires the agent, before a client enters into an agency contract with him, to give the client particulars of the circumstances in which the commission will become due.[25] Nor are the estate agency cases affected by the Regulations which apply to "commercial agents" since these Regulations apply only to agents who have continuing authority and who negotiate sales or purchases of *goods*.[26] If an agent acts for purposes relating to his trade, business or profession, the client is a consumer and the term in question is not individually negotiated, that term might not be binding on the consumer under the Unfair Terms in Consumer Contracts Regulations 1999[27]: *e.g.* if it provided for payment of the full commission even if no sale took place.[28] Even where the agent is not entitled to commission, he may have other rights against the client. He may be entitled to damages[29] where the sale goes off as a result of the client's fault.[30] If the sale goes off as a result of the purchaser's default, and the purchaser's deposit is forfeited to the client, it has been suggested that the agent should be entitled to a *quantum meruit* out of the sum so forfeited.[31]

Under the Regulations which apply to "commercial agents", commission becomes due when the principal has executed the transaction or when he should have done so or when the third party has done so[32]; and it becomes due at the latest when the third party has executed the transaction or would have done so if the principal had duly executed his part of it.[33] Where "execution" fails the Regulations give the agent the right to commission only if the failure is due to the principal's breach of his contract with the third party.[34] Except in this situation, the question whether the agent can become entitled to commission before "execution" of that contract is (under the Regulations, no less than at common law) one of construction of the agency agreement.

(iii) *Whether principal must give agent a chance to earn commission.* If a principal employs an agent for a fixed period he is not, in general, bound to stay in business merely to enable the agent to earn his commission.[35] But if, on the true construction of the

---

[24] Lord Denning's view in *Jaques v Lloyd D George*, above, n.23, at p.629, that an unreasonable stipulation will not be enforced, does not seem to have received any judicial support.

[25] s.18(2)(a); supplemented by Estate Agents (Provision of Information) Regulations 1993 (SI 1993/859).

[26] See above, p.709.

[27] See above, pp.267 *et seq.*

[28] Such a term is not included in the list of *prima facie* unfair terms set out in Sch.2 of the 1999 Regulations, but that list is "non-exhaustive": *ibid.* reg.5(5).

[29] Unless the contractual provision for commission is intended to be his *only* remedy, as in *Property Choice v Fronda* [1991] 2 E.G.L.R. 249.

[30] *Dennis Reed Ltd v Goody* [1950] 2 K.B. 277 at 285; for this purpose the default must be wilful, and not merely inability to complete on account of a defect of title: *Blake & Co v Sohn* [1969] 1 W.L.R. 1412.

[31] *Boots v E Christopher & Co* [1952] 1 K.B. 89 at 99; *cf. Debenham Tewson & Chinnock plc v Rimington* [1989] 2 E.G.L.R. 26. In the United States, there is authority for holding the prospective *purchaser* liable to the agent for commission where he defaults: *Ellsworth Dobbs Inc v Johnson* 236 A. 2d. 843 (1967). Contrast *The Manifest Lipkowy* [1989] 2 Lloyd's Rep. 138 (buyer's agent held to have no right to commission against defaulting seller).

[32] SI 1993/3053, reg.10(1); above, p.709.

[33] reg.10(2). This rule cannot be excluded to the detriment of the agent: reg.10(4).

[34] reg.10(2); this would seem to apply in a situation analogous to that in those estate agency cases in which completion was prevented by a defect in the vendor's title: above, p.742 at n.15. The actual estate agency cases fall outside the scope of the 1993 Regulations for the reason stated at n.26, above.

[35] *Rhodes v Forwood* (1876) 1 App.Cas. 256; *cf. Lazarus v Cairn Line Ltd* (1912) 106 L.T. 378; *L French & Co Ltd v Leeston Shipping Co Ltd* [1922] 1 A.C. 451; Burrows, 31 M.L.R. 390. Contrast the position of "commercial agents" (above, p.709) SI 1993/3053, reg.17(7): *Page v Combined Shipping & Trading Co* [1997] 3 All E.R. 656.

agency contract, the principal has undertaken to stay in business so as to enable the agent to earn his commission, then the principal is liable in damages if he fails to do so. This was the effect of the contract in *Turner v Goldsmith*,[36] where the principal employed the agent for five years to obtain orders for shirts "manufactured or sold" by the principal. It was held that he was not justified in putting an end to the agency agreement simply because the factory in which he manufactured shirts was burnt down. An agency agreement may, moreover, relate to a specific contract which is actually concluded between principal and third party. In such a case, a term may be implied into the agency agreement that the principal will not break *that contract* so as to deprive the agent of his commission.[37]

A client who employs an estate agent to sell a house is, in general, under no liability if he sells it himself or through a second agent.[38] If the agent is appointed "sole agent" the client cannot sell through another agent, but he can still sell the house himself unless he gives the agent "the sole and exclusive right to sell".[39] A manufacturer's "sole agent" may simply be a buyer and not an agent at all.[40] The manufacturer's undertaking to sell all his output to such a "sole agent" would bind him not to dispose of any of it himself,[41] so long as it was not invalid for restraint of trade.[42]

(b) INDEMNITY. A principal must indemnify his agent against all liabilities reasonably incurred or discharged by him in the execution of his authority.[43] This right of indemnity exists not only where the agent incurs contractual liability, but also where he incurs tortious liability, *e.g.* as a result of selling a third person's property under the instructions of his principal.[44] The agent is not entitled to any indemnity in respect of an obviously illegal transaction,[45] nor in respect of a liability due to his own breach of duty.[46]

An agent may even be entitled to an indemnity in respect of payments which he was not legally obliged to make[47] so long as the payment, though not legally due, was made in the usual course of business, or possibly if it was made under a strong moral obligation.

(c) LIEN. An agent is (unless otherwise agreed)[48] entitled to a lien on all property of the principal which has come into his possession in the course of the agency. Every agent has a *particular* lien: that is, he can hold the property until the principal satisfies all

---

[36] [1891] 1 Q.B. 544; *cf. Re Patent Floor Cloth Co* (1872) 26 L.T. 467.
[37] *Alpha Trading Ltd v Dunshaw-Patten* [1981] Q.B. 290; Carter, 45 M.L.R. 220; *cf.*, above, pp.62–64 and 743 at n.30; *George Moundreas & Co SA v Navimpex Centrala Navala* [1985] 2 Lloyd's Rep. 515; *The Energy Progress* [1993] 1 Lloyd's Rep. 355.
[38] *Luxor (Eastbourne) Ltd v Cooper* [1941] A.C. 108.
[39] *Bentall Horsley & Baldry v Vicary* [1931] 1 K.B. 253; *Hampton & Sons Ltd v George* [1939] 3 All.E.R. 627. *cf.* in the case of "commercial agents," SI 1993/3053, reg.7(2), above, p.741.
[40] See above, p.706.
[41] *W T Lamb & Sons v Goring Brick Co Ltd* [1932] 1 K.B. 710.
[42] See above, pp.468–472.
[43] *Thacker v Hardy* (1878) 4 Q.B.D. 685; *Reynolds v Smith* (1893) 9 T.L.R. 494; *cf.* Insolvency Act 1986, s.44(1)(c) and (3); contrast *Wilson v Avec Audio Visual Equipment Ltd* [1974] 1 Lloyd's Rep. 80 (payment made after termination of authority).
[44] *Adamson v Jarvis* (1827) 4 Bing. 66.
[45] *cf. Thacker v Hardy*, above, at 687.
[46] *cf. Lister v Romford Ice & Cold Storage Co Ltd* [1957] A.C. 555; above, p.209.
[47] *Read v Anderson* (1884) 13 Q.B.D. 779; the actual decision was reversed by Gaming Act 1892 (above, pp.524–525), but the principle would still apply to cases not concerned with wagering contracts: *cf. Adams v Morgan* [1924] 1 K.B. 751; 40 L.Q.R. 389.
[48] *Rolls Razor Ltd v Cox* [1967] 1 Q.B. 552.

claims of the agent arising out of the agency. An agent may by custom or by special contract also have a *general* lien, entitling him to hold the property until the principal satisfies all claims of the agent, whether they have arisen out of the agency or not.

(2) Duties of agent

(a) TO CARRY OUT HIS INSTRUCTIONS. An agent who is appointed under a contract binding him to carry out his instructions is obviously obliged to carry them out.[49] He may be liable for failing to do so even if the contract which he was instructed to make would not, if made, have been a binding one.[50] He will also be in breach of the contract if he acts in a way not authorised by the terms of his appointment.[51] An agent who acts gratuitously or under a unilateral contract[52] is not bound to do anything, but may be liable if he starts to perform and then leaves the task unfinished.

(b) TO ACT WITH DUE CARE AND SKILL. The degree of care and skill expected of an agent depends on the circumstances. A person who holds himself out as being skilled in some profession or trade[53] must show greater care and skill than one who merely offers to give what help he can as a friend. There is probably no rigid distinction between paid and gratuitous agents for this purpose. The fact that the agent is paid is taken into account, along with other circumstances, in determining the degree of the care and skill to be expected of him; but even a gratuitous agent may be liable in tort for acting negligently.[54]

(c) FIDUCIARY DUTY. Although the position of an agent in various respects differs from that of a trustee,[55] an agent does, because the principal places confidence in him, owe a fiduciary duty to the principal.[56] This duty is distinct from his duty to act with due care and skill: its breach "connotes disloyalty or infidelity" and not merely failure by the agent to do his "incompetent best".[57] Its most important consequences are the following.

(i) *Conflict of interest and duty.* The agent must not put himself into a position where his interest and duty conflict.[58] He must not, for instance, sell his own goods to the principal when he is employed to buy: his interest as a seller would be to get the highest possible price, whereas his duty as agent is to buy at the lowest possible price.[59] Similarly, he must not, if employed to sell, buy the principal's property for himself.[60] Again, he

---

[49] *cf.*, in the case of "commercial agents," (above, p.709) SI 1993/3053, reg.3(2)(a).

[50] See above, p.524, n.35.

[51] *County Ltd v Girozentrale Securities* [1996] 3 All E.R. 834.

[52] See above, pp.37–38, 152, 157–158; *The Zephyr* [1985] 2 Lloyd's Rep. 529 at 538.

[53] See above, p.206.

[54] *Hedley Byrne & Co Ltd v Heller & Partners Ltd* [1964] A.C. 465 at 495, 510, 526–527, 530, 538; approving *Wilkinson v Coverdale* (1793) 1 Esp. 75; above, p.157.

[55] See, for example, above, p.412; *Kingscroft Insurance Co Ltd v H S Weaver (Underwriting) Ltd* [1993] 1 Lloyd's Rep. 187 at 191.

[56] *Attorney-General of Hong Kong v Reid* [1994] 1 A.C. 324, below at n.67 and p.746. *cf.* in the case of "commercial agents" (above, p.709) SI 1993/3053, reg.3(1) (duty of good faith).

[57] *Bristol & West BS v Mothew* [1998] Ch. 1 at 18. *cf. Coulthard v Disco Mix Club* [2000] 1 W.L.R. 707: claim in respect of under-accounting by agent held (for limitation purposes) to be a simple contract claim and not one for breach of fiduciary duty).

[58] *Lamb v Evans* [1893] 1 Ch. 218; *cf. Reading v Attorney-General* [1951] A.C. 507.

[59] *Armstrong v Jackson* [1917] 2 K.B. 822; *Tetley v Shand* (1871) 25 L.T. 658; *Regier v Campbell-Stuart* [1939] Ch. 766; *Guiness plc v Saunders* [1990] 2 A.C 663; *cf.* Companies Act 1985, s.317.

[60] *McPherson v Watt* (1877) 3 App.Cas. 254.

must not subject himself to conflicting duties by acting as agent for both principal and third party,[61] unless he fully discloses the position to each of these persons.[62] But where the nature of the agent's business is such that he will normally act for more than one principal it is an implied term of the contract of agency that he should be free to do so, even though the interests of the various principals are likely to conflict. Thus an estate agent is entitled to accept instructions for the sale of properties from several principals, and where he does so he is both entitled and bound not to disclose confidential information received from any one of his clients to the other or others.[63]

A contract made in breach of this fiduciary duty is voidable at the option of the principal. The agent himself cannot avoid a transaction on the ground that it may conflict with his duties to his principal.[64]

(ii) *Bribes and secret profits.*[65] The agent must not without the principal's consent[66] accept a commission from a third party. Such a secret commission is called a "bribe" if the third party, at the time of paying it, knew that the payee was acting as agent for another: the payment is then regarded as "a gift accepted by a fiduciary as an inducement to betray his trust".[67] It is immaterial that the third party had no corrupt motive in making the payment.[68] The promise or payment of a bribe has drastic effects. The agent can (even if he has been appointed for a fixed period) be summarily dismissed[69]; he loses his right to commission on the tainted transaction[70]; and he holds the bribe in trust[71] for the principal, to whom it must be paid over, whether or not he has suffered loss.[72] The principal is entitled to any increase in the value of the bribe or of its product: thus if a cash bribe has been invested in assets which have increased in value, the principal is entitled in equity to those assets.[73] If the bribe has not yet been paid, the

---

[61] *Fullwood v Hurley* [1928] 1 K.B. 498 at 502; *Anglo-African Merchants v Bayley* [1970] 1 Q.B. 311 at 322–323; *North & South Trust Co v Berkeley* [1971] 1 W.L.R. 470.

[62] See *Harrods Ltd v Lemon* [1931] 2 K.B. 157 and *Clark v Boyce Mouat* [1994] 1 A.C. 428 (where full disclosure was made). *cf.* Estate Agents Act 1979, s.21 (imposing a statutory duty of disclosure on estate agents: the remedy is disqualification under s.3 of the Act).

[63] *Kelly v Cooper* [1993] A.C. 205.

[64] *Boulting v ACCT* [1963] 2 Q.B. 606.

[65] Needham, 95 L.Q.R. 536.

[66] See *Anangel Atlas Compania Naviera SA v Ishikawajima-Harima Heavy Industries Co* [1990] 1 Lloyd's Rep. 167 (where the principal knew of the payments).

[67] *Attorney-General of Hong Kong v Reid* [1994] 1 A.C. 324 at 330; *Allwood v Clifford* [2002] E.M.L.R. 3 (where there was no such knowledge).

[68] *Industries & General Mortgage Co v Lewis* [1949] 2 All E.R. 573.

[69] *Boston Deep Sea Fishing & Ice Co v Ansell* (1888) 39 Ch.D. 339. For the effect of such dismissal on the agent's rights to salary (or recompense for work actually done), see below, pp.784–785. In the case of "commercial agents," (above, p.709) this right of dismissal is preserved by SI 1993/3053, reg.16.

[70] *Solomon v Pender* (1865) 3 H. & C. 639; *Andrews v Ramsey* [1903] 2 K.B. 635 (but commission on other transactions remains payable if they are severable: *Nitedals Taenstickfabrik v Bruster* [1906] 2 Ch. 671); *cf. Boston Deep Sea Fishing & Ice Co v Ansell*, above, where the fact that the agent had made secret profits on two groups of contracts did not defeat a right to commission on a third group. However, the reason given for this result was not that the transactions were severable but that the right to commission accrued before dismissal; this reasoning is hard to reconcile with such cases as *Andrews v Ramsey*, above.

[71] *Attorney-General of Hong Kong v Reid* [1994] 1 A.C. 324.

[72] *Reading v Attorney-General* [1951] A.C. 507; Sealy [1963] C.L.J. 119 at 128–136; *Islamic Republic of Iran Shipping Lines v Denby*, Financial Times, October 28, 1986.

[73] *Attorney-General of Hong Kong v Reid*, above, n.71, where the Privy Council disapproved the contrary decision of the Court of Appeal in *Lister v Stubbs* (1890) 45 Ch.D. 1. Where the asset is acquired partly with the bribe and partly with the agent's own money, the principal appears to be entitled to a pro rata share in the asset, on the analogy of *Foskett v McKeown* [2001] 1 A.C. 102 (where the wrongdoer was a trustee, not an agent).

agent cannot recover it from the third party, but the principal can do so.[74] The principal can further set the tainted transaction aside and retain the bribe, if it has been paid over to him by the agent[75]; whether or not the bribe has been paid, the principal can, as an alternative to claiming the bribe,[76] claim damages from the agent and the third party for the loss suffered as a result of the bribery.[77] These claims are available even though the payment of the bribe did not induce the principal to enter into any contract with the third party.[78] If the principal was induced to enter into such a contract with the third party, that party is also liable to the principal for an account of the profits made by the third party from that contract, but only to the extent that these exceeded the profits that he would have made if the contract had not been induced by bribery and that the third party has not already been required to pay such amounts to the principal by way of damages.[79] Agent and third party may also incur criminal liability.[80] Where the secret profit is not a bribe, the third party is under no contractual or tortious liability. The agent is likewise not guilty of theft[81] though he can be summarily dismissed[82] and is civilly liable to account for the payment to the principal.

(d) PERSONAL PERFORMANCE. The general rule is that an agent cannot delegate the performance of his duties, unless the principal expressly or impliedly authorises him to appoint a sub-agent.[83] But an agent does not "delegate" by instructing his own employees to do various necessary acts in connection with the execution of his duty.

An agent may have authority to appoint a sub-agent and to make a contract between the sub-agent and the principal.[84] He may, alternatively, have authority to delegate (in the sense that he commits no breach of duty by performing through another) but have no authority to make a contract between principal and sub-agent.[85] In such a case the agent remains contractually liable to the principal if the sub-agent performs defectively,[86] while the sub-agent is under no contractual duty to the principal. The sub-agent may, however, be liable on other grounds, *e.g.* for breach of fiduciary duty or in tort if he

---

[74] *Harrington v Victoria Graving Dock Co* (1878) 3 Q.B.D. 549; *Industries & General Mortgage Co v Lewis*, above, n.68.

[75] *Logicrose v Southend United FC* [1988] 1 W.L.R. 1256; Jones [1989] C.L.J. 22.

[76] *T Mahesan S/O Thambiah v Malaysian Government Officers' Housing Society* [1979] A.C. 374; disapproving dicta in *Salford Corp v Lever* [1891] 1 Q.B. 168; Tettenborn, 95 L.Q.R. 68; *Arab Monetary Fund v Hashim* [1993] 1 Lloyd's Rep. 543; *Island Records Ltd v Tring International plc* [1996] 1 W.L.R. 1256 at 1257; *Fyffes Group Ltd v Templeman* [2000] 2 Lloyd's Rep. 643.

[77] *Salford Corp v Lever* [1891] 1 Q.B. 168.

[78] *Petrotrade Inc v Smith* [2000] 1 Lloyd's Rep. 486, where the "third party" had itself been appointed as agent but the bribes were paid by its employees to *another* of the principal's agents, *i.e.* to one of the latter's employees.

[79] *Fyffes Group Ltd v Templeman* [2000] 2 Lloyd's Rep. 643 at 672.

[80] Prevention of Corruption Acts 1906–1916; corrupt motive is necessary for this purpose.

[81] *R. v Cullum* (1873) L.R. 2 C.C.R. 28. This decision has survived the Theft Act 1968; see s.5(3); Criminal Law Revision Committee, 8th Report (1966) Cmnd. 2977, para.57(iii); *Attorney-General's Reference (No.1 of 1985)* [1986] Q.B. 491; *R. v Cooke* [1986] A.C. 909 at 934. For possible liability for false accounting, see *Lee Cheung Wing v R.* [1992] Crim.L.R. 400.

[82] *Neary v Dean of Westminster* [1999] I.R.L.R. 288.

[83] *e.g. John McCann & Co v Pow* [1974] 1 W.L.R. 1643.

[84] *De Bussche v Alt* (1878) 8 Ch.D. 286.

[85] *New Zealand & Australian Land Co v Watson* (1881) 7 Q.B.D. 374; *Calico Printers' Assoc v Barclays Bank* (1931) 145 L.T. 51; *Royal Products Ltd v Midland Bank Ltd* [1981] 2 Lloyd's Rep. 194 at 198; *Henderson v Merrett Syndicates Ltd* [1995] 2 A.C. 145 at 202; *Prentis Donegan & Partners v Leeds & Leeds plc* [1998] 2 Lloyd's Rep. 326.

[86] *Powell & Thomas v Evan Jones & Co* [1905] 1 K.B. 11 apparently disapproved, but on another point, in *Attorney-General of Hong Kong v Reid* [1994] 1 A.C. 324 at 337.

negligently causes damage to the principal's property.[87] But the sub-agent is not liable in tort merely because he has negligently paid over the proceeds of the principal's property to an impostor (so that the principal suffers financial loss)[88]; for such liability would be in practice indistinguishable from contractual liability and so be inconsistent with the absence of a contractual relationship between principal and sub-agent. The contract between agent and sub-agent could also be drawn up in such a way as to confer rights on the principal under the Contracts (Rights of Third Parties) Act 1999.[89]

(e) INDEMNITY. It is an implied term in a contract of employment that the employee will indemnify the employer against any liability to third parties incurred by reason of the employee's negligence in doing what he was employed to do.[90] A contract of agency will generally give rise to a similar liability to indemnify the principal.

4. Effects of Non-consensual Agency

It is a difficult and largely unsolved problem to what extent the effects of agency which have so far been discussed arise where the agency is not created by agreement between principal and agent, e.g. in cases of apparent and usual authority, and in cases of agency of necessity.

One effect of apparent or usual authority is to make the principal liable to the third party. But is the third party liable to the principal? When an agent acts within his apparent authority, the principal is liable because he is estopped from denying the agent's authority; but no similar estoppel need arise against the third party. If the principal wants to enforce the contract, he will usually ratify. But there may be some reason why he cannot do so,[91] and, if this is the case, it is far from clear that he could sue the third party simply because the third party can sue him. An agent who does an unauthorised act which binds his principal is clearly not entitled to commission, but is probably subject to the usual liabilities if he accepts a bribe or makes a secret profit.[92] An agent of necessity often acquires rights of recompense or reimbursement against his principal, but it is less common for him to be able to create a contract between principal and third party. Thus it is impossible to make any general statement about the effects of non-consensual agency. The problems which may arise must be considered in the light of the considerations of policy which underlie each type of non-consensual agency.

SECTION 5. TERMINATION

Agency as a contract is determined by any event which terminates a contract,[93] and also in certain special ways. After discussing these, we shall discuss the effects of termination and finally consider some cases of irrevocable agency.

---

[87] *Meyerstein v Eastern Agency* (1885) 1 T.L.R. 595; *cf. Stewart v Reavell's Garage* [1952] 2 Q.B. 545.

[88] *Balsamo v Medici* [1984] 1 W.L.R. 951; contrast *Henderson v Merrett Syndicates Ltd* [1995] 2 A.C. 145, where in a "most unusual" (at 195) situation a sub-agent was held liable in tort to the principal for negligently inflicted financial loss. See also *Aiken v Stewart Wrightson Members Agency*, [1995] 1 W.L.R. 1281.

[89] See above, pp.651, *et seq.*

[90] *Lister v Romford Ice & Cold Storage Co Ltd* [1957] A.C. 555; contrast *Harvey v R G O'Dell Ltd* [1958] 2 Q.B. 78.

[91] See above, pp.722, *et seq.*; *e.g.* it may be too late to ratify.

[92] *English v Dedham Vale Properties Ltd* [1978] 1 W.L.R. 93.

[93] *e.g.* by performance, rescission or frustration.

1. Modes of Termination

(1) Consensual agency

It will be convenient first to consider modes of termination at common law and then to deal with special rules applicable to "commercial agents".[94]

(a) NOTICE. An agent's authority can be determined by giving him notice: for instance, a wife's implied authority to pledge her husband's credit for necessary household expenses can be terminated in this way.[95] Where the agency is contractual it may be for a fixed term or specify a period of notice. If no term or period of notice is specified, the contract is determinable on reasonable notice.[96] A notice given in breach of contract is, in general,[97] nonetheless *effective*. It determines the agent's actual authority[98] and the relationship of principal and agent. Thus the agent cannot restrain the breach by injunction or obtain a declaration that his dismissal was void or claim his agreed remuneration in respect of periods after the wrongful termination.[99] His normal remedies are by way of damages for wrongful dismissal and a declaration that the dismissal was wrongful.[1] He may also be able to restrain by injunction the breach of a negative stipulation in the agency contract,[2] such as an undertaking by the principal not to appoint another agent to conduct the business in question.[3]

(b) INCONSISTENT CONDUCT. It seems that agency can be determined without notice by conduct inconsistent with its continuance, *e.g.* if the principal sells the subject-matter of the agency.[4] Such conduct may again be a breach of contract but nevertheless puts an end to the agency.

(c) INSANITY. At common law,[5] agency is determined by the supervening insanity of principal or agent if the insanity is inconsistent with the consensual nature of agency. The principal's insanity terminates agency even though the agent has no notice of it.[6]

---

[94] See above, p.709.

[95] See above, p.711.

[96] *Martin-Baker Aircraft Co Ltd v Canadian Flight Equipment Ltd* [1955] 2 Q.B. 556; *cf. Re Spenborough UDC's Agreement* [1968] Ch. 139; *Richardson v Koefod* [1969] 1 W.L.R. 1812 at 1814. The "presumption of perpetual duration" in contracts specifying no time limit, stated in *Llanelly Ry & Dock Co v L & NW Ry* (1875) L.R. 7 H.L. 550 (discussed by Carnegie, 85 L.Q.R. 392) does not apply to contracts of agency.

[97] For exceptions, see below, pp.1030–1031.

[98] *i.e.* the authority based on the wrongfully repudiated contract; as to apparent authority, usual authority and authority of necessity, see below, pp.750–751.

[99] *Denmark Productions Ltd v Boscobel Productions Ltd* [1969] 1 Q.B. 699; *Roberts v Elwells Engineering Co Ltd* [1972] 2 Q.B. 586; *Gunton v London Borough of Richmond upon Thames* [1981] Ch. 448; *R. v East Berkshire Health Authority, Ex p. Walsh* [1985] Q.B. 152 at 165; *Delaney v Staples* [1992] 1 A.C. 687 at 692; below, p.1016; Freedland, 32 M.L.R. 314; Drake [1969] J.B.L. 113. Remuneration earned before the dismissal but payable thereafter could be claimed on the principle of *Sellers v London County Newspapers* [1951] 1 K.B. 784. Remuneration can also be claimed where the termination is lawful because it is authorised by a contractual provision for notice or payment in lieu: *Abrahams v Performing Rights Society* [1995] I.C.R. 1028.

[1] As to damages, see *Denmark Productions Ltd v Boscobel Productions Ltd*, above; *Marsh v National Autistic Society* [1993] I.C.R. 453 and *Boyo v Lambeth LBC* [1994] I.C.R. 727; as to declaration, see *Taylor v NUS* [1967] 1 W.L.R. 532.

[2] See below, pp.1042–1044.

[3] *Decro-Wall International SA v Practitioners in Marketing Ltd* [1971] 1 W.L.R. 361.

[4] *E P Nelson & Co v Rolfe* [1950] 1 K.B. 139.

[5] For a statutory exception, see below, pp.751–752.

[6] *Yonge v Toynbee* [1910] 1 K.B. 215; above, p.738.

(d) DEATH. Death of principal or agent terminates agency, whether the survivor has notice of death or not.[7] Dissolution of a company has the same effect, and so has dissolution of a partnership, unless the contract is, on its true construction, with the partners constituting the firm from time to time.[8] However, in such a case dissolution may be a repudiatory breach, justifying rescission of the contract by the agent.[9]

(e) BANKRUPTCY. The principal's bankruptcy terminates the agent's authority.[10] The bankruptcy of the agent terminates his authority if it makes him unfit to perform his duties.[11]

(f) COMMERCIAL AGENTS. The Regulations governing "commercial agents"[12] specify minimum periods of notice (depending on the duration of the agency contract) which must be given to terminate the agency contract.[13] The relevant rules appear to apply only to the relationship of the parties to that contract. They do not seem to apply to the agent's authority: in other words, the position under the Regulations appears to resemble the common law position that failure to give proper notice makes the termination wrongful, but not ineffective. Even where proper notice is given, the agent is entitled under the Regulations to compensation or to an indemnity in respect of the termination.[14] The object of this rule appears to be to provide the agent with a sort of redundancy or severance payment, reflecting the commission that he would (but for the termination) have earned, the expenses that he has incurred, and the benefits that have accrued to the principal in consequence of the agent's activities.[15] The rights of compensation and indemnity can also apply where the agency contract is terminated by the death of the agent[16] or by notice given by himself on the ground of his age, illness or infirmity, or on account of the principal's breach.[17] But the agent has no such rights where termination is justified by his own breach.[18]

(2) Non-consensual agency

The events listed above terminate an agent's express or implied authority, but do not necessarily terminate apparent or usual authority, or authority of necessity. Notice to the agent obviously does not terminate apparent or usual authority: notice must be given to the third party to have this effect. Again, a principal's insanity terminates his agent's actual authority; but a third party who goes on dealing with the agent without notice of the principal's insanity may be able to hold the principal liable on the ground that the

---

[7] *Campanari v Woodburn* (1854) 15 C.B. 400; *Pool v Pool* (1889) 58 L.J.P. 67.
[8] *Salton v New Beeston Cycle Co* [1900] 1 Ch. 43. And see *Brace v Calder* [1895] 2 Q.B. 253; *Harold Fielding Ltd v Mansi* [1974] 1 All E.R. 1035; *Tunstall v Condon* [1980] I.C.R. 786; *Briggs v Oates* [1990] I.C.R. 473. Dissolution of a limited liability partnership incorporated under the Limited Liability Partnership Act 2000 (above p.563) seems for the present purpose to have the same effect as dissolution of a company.
[9] *Briggs v Oates*, above.
[10] *Elliott v Turquand* (1881) 7 App.Cas. 79.
[11] *McCall v Australian Meat Co Ltd* (1870) 19 W.R. 188.
[12] See above, p.709.
[13] SI 1993/3053, reg.15.
[14] *ibid.* reg.17. Rights under reg.17 may be more extensive than those which would be available at common law: see *Page v Combined Shipping & Trading Co* [1997] 3 All E.R. 656; for claims both under the Regulations and at common law, see *Duffen v FRABO SpA* [2000] 1 Lloyd's Rep. 180.
[15] See *Moore v Piretta PTA Ltd* [1999] 1 All E.R. 174 at 181.
[16] SI 1993/3053, reg.17(8).
[17] *ibid.* reg.18(b) (as amended by SI 1993/3173).
[18] *ibid.* reg.18(a).

agent still had apparent authority.[19] It is submitted that the position should be the same where (unknown to the third party) the agent's actual authority has been terminated by the principal's death.[20]

Agency of necessity can sometimes be terminated by notice, *e.g.* a shipmaster's authority would be terminated, just as it could be prevented from arising, in this way. But notice would not terminate such authority where the need to encourage the agent to act was particularly strong. In *GN Ry v Swaffield*,[21] for instance, the railway company's claim was not defeated merely because the owner of the horse had said that he would not be responsible for the cost of feeding and stabling it.

2. Irrevocable Agency

In the following cases agency is irrevocable in the sense that any attempt to revoke it is not merely a breach of contract but also ineffective. The agent's authority continues in spite of the attempt to revoke it.

(1) Authority coupled with an interest

An authority coupled with an interest is irrevocable. This does not mean that an authority is irrevocable simply because the agent can, by executing it, earn commission. The authority must be given for valuable consideration or by deed to secure some interest of the agent which exists independently of the agency. Thus in *Carmichael's* case[22] one Phillips promoted a company to buy a mine from him. Carmichael agreed to underwrite 1,000 shares in this company—*i.e.* to take up so many of these shares as could not be sold to the public—and authorised Phillips to apply for the shares on his behalf. This authority was held to be irrevocable; it was coupled with an "interest" because, if the shares were not taken up, Phillips would not get the purchase-money for the mine.

This rule only applies if the authority was intended for the protection of the interest.[23] It therefore cannot apply where the interest arises after the creation of the authority.[24]

(2) Irrevocable and enduring powers of attorney

At common law a power of attorney, even though coupled with an interest, was revoked by the death of the donor, *i.e.* of the principal.[25]

This rule might cause hardship both to the agent and to a person who bought from him in ignorance of the principal's death. The Powers of Attorney Act 1971 therefore provides that a power of attorney which is expressed to be irrevocable and is given to

---

[19] *Drew v Nunn* (1879) 4 Q.B.D. 661; *Yonge v Toynbee* [1910] 1 K.B. 215 is only concerned with the termination of the agent's *actual* authority and his consequent liability for breach of warranty of authority. Normally such liability would not arise if the third party could hold the principal liable on the footing that the agent still had *apparent* authority (above, p.739). The two cases can, perhaps, be distinguished on the ground that the acts done by the agent in *Yonge v Toynbee* (taking steps in litigation) were acts which the insane principal had no capacity to do at all; while the contract in *Drew v Nunn* was one which could validly be made with an insane principal in accordance with the rules stated at pp.557–558, above. However that may be, the court did not in *Yonge v Toynbee* consider the possibility that the principal might have been held liable on the footing of apparent authority.

[20] As in *Blades v Free* (1829) 9 B. & C. 167, where apparent authority was not discussed.

[21] (1874) L.R. 9 Ex. 142; above, pp.719–720.

[22] [1896] 2 Ch. 643; *cf. Walsh v Whitcomb* (1797) 2 Esp. 565.

[23] *Frith v Frith* [1906] A.C. 254.

[24] *Smart v Sandars* (1848) 5 C.B. 895.

[25] *Watson v King* (1815) 4 Camp. 272.

secure a proprietary interest of, or the performance of an obligation owed to, the donee shall not be revoked by the donor without the consent of the donee, or by the donor's death, incapacity or bankruptcy, so long as the interest or obligation secured by it remains in being.[26] The Act also protects third parties who deal in good faith with the donee of a power which is expressed to be irrevocable and to be given by way of security. Such persons are entitled to assume (unless they know the contrary) that the power cannot be revoked except by the donor acting with the consent of the donee, and that it has not been revoked in this way.[27]

The Enduring Powers of Attorney Act 1985[28] makes provision for powers of attorney executed in a prescribed form and expressed to continue in spite of the donor's supervening mental incapacity.[29] To create such an "enduring power" the donor need only have the capacity to understand the act of conferring authority on the donee: it is not necessary for the donor to have the mental capacity of managing his or her own affairs.[30] An enduring power is not revoked by the supervening incapacity of the donor,[31] but when such incapacity occurs the power is, in effect, suspended[32] until it is registered by the court.[33] Once an enduring power has been registered, it can no longer be revoked by the donor of the power; it can be revoked only with the consent of the court.[34] The Act further protects the donee of the power and third parties in a number of cases: if they act in good faith in ignorance of the donor's supervening mental incapacity[35]; if they act in good faith in pursuance of an instrument which is registered as an enduring power in spite of not being a valid power of attorney; if an enduring power is invalidly revoked (i.e. by the donor without the consent of the court); and if the instrument, though valid as a power of attorney, was not a valid *enduring* power though purporting to be one, and the power has been revoked by the donor's supervening mental incapacity.[36]

---

[26] s.4.

[27] s.5(3); special protection is provided for transferees under stock exchange transactions by s.6.

[28] Cretney and Lush, *Enduring Powers of Attorney* (4th ed.).

[29] s.2.

[30] *Re K* [1988] Ch. 310. For the burden of proof on this issue, see *Re W (Enduring Power of Attorney)* [2001] Ch. 609.

[31] s.1(1)(a).

[32] s.1(1)(b).

[33] Under s.6. Execution of a second power of attorney in favour of different donees from those named in the first is no bar to registration of the first: *Re E (Enduring Power of Attorney)* [2001] Ch. 364.

[34] ss.7(1)(a), 8(3).

[35] s.1(1)(c).

[36] s.9.

CHAPTER EIGHTEEN

PERFORMANCE

A PARTY who performs a contract in accordance with its terms is thereby discharged from his obligations under it. Such performance also normally entitles him to enforce the other party's undertakings. It is often possible to perform a contract vicariously, *i.e.* by procuring performance by a third party. The legal effects of failure to perform are complex: a discussion of them forms the bulk of this Chapter. Special rules govern the effects of failure to perform certain stipulations as to time.

SECTION 1. METHOD OF PERFORMANCE

1. When Performance is Due

The general rule is that performance is due without demand: a debtor must seek his creditor.[1] This rule can be varied by contrary agreement, by mercantile usage or by other rules of law. The first possibility is illustrated by a contract which provides for payment to be made "on demand." The effect of these words is that the debtor is not bound to pay before the demand is made,[2] and that normally he must pay within a reasonable time of receiving the demand.[3] The second possibility is illustrated by the rule that the holder of a bill of exchange is not entitled to payment unless he first presents the bill for payment.[4] A demand or notice of default may also have to be given where the party from whom performance is claimed cannot, without notice, reasonably be expected to know that performance is due. Thus "a landlord is not in breach of his covenant to repair [the demised premises[5]] until he has been given notice of the want of repair and a reasonable time has elapsed in which repair could have been carried out."[6] The third possibility is illustrated by a legislative provision by which a tenant under a long lease of a dwelling is not liable to make payment of rent under the lease unless the landlord has given him a notice relating to the payment.[7] In certain other cases, a demand or notice of default is also necessary to entitle the injured party to rescind,[8] though not to establish breach.

Where a contract provides that money is to be paid on, or by, a specified day, the debtor has the whole of that day to make the payment. The creditor cannot treat him as

---

[1] *Walton v Mascall* (1844) 13 M. & W. 452. *cf. Carne v Debono* [1988] 1 W.L.R. 1107.

[2] *Esso Petroleum Co Ltd v Alstonbridge Properties Ltd* [1975] 1 W.L.R. 1474; *Libyan Arab Foreign Bank v Bankers Trust Co* [1989] Q.B. 728 at 748–749. For the possibility of the debtor's waiving a contractual requirement of a "demand" (and so of acquiring rights, by virtue of a payment without the demand against a co-debtor), see *Stimson v Smith* [1999] Ch. 340, above, p.574.

[3] *Toms v Wilson* (1862) 4 B. & S. 442; *Bank of Baroda v Panessar* [1987] Ch. 335. If the debtor has made it clear that he cannot or will not pay, he will be in default as soon as the demand is made: *Sheppard & Cooper Ltd v TSB Bank* [1996] 2 All E.R. 654.

[4] Bills of Exchange Act 1882, ss.41(1)(a), 40(1).

[5] *British Telecommunications plc v Sun Life Assurance Society plc* [1996] Ch. 69 at 74 (where the want of repair was in *another* part of the building, so that the landlord was in immediate breach as soon as the want of repair occurred).

[6] *Calabar Properties Ltd v Stitcher* [1984] 1 W.L.R. 287 at 298.

[7] Commonhold and Leasehold Reform Act 2002, s.166.

[8] See below, pp.779–780, 829–830.

in default before the end of that day (*i.e.* before midnight) merely because the bank at which payment was, under the contract, to be made had already closed.[9] As a practical matter, the debtor therefore cannot be treated as in default until the day following that specified in the contract.

2. Tender

A tender of money is ineffective unless the money is actually produced, or unless production is dispensed with by the creditor.[10] It will not do for the debtor to offer to pay and then simply to put his hand in his pocket.[11] Tender of part of a debt is bad.[12] Conversely, tender of too large a sum, *requiring change*, is bad, as this might put an unreasonable burden on the creditor.[13]

Tender of goods due under a contract of sale must be made at a reasonable hour; what is a reasonable hour is a question of fact.[14]

Where a bad tender is rejected and is, within the time fixed for performance, followed by a good tender, the latter must generally be accepted.[15] But if the first tender amounts to a repudiation of the contract, the injured party can treat the contract as discharged,[16] and if he does so he will not be bound to accept the second tender.

3. Payment by Cheque or Credit Card

There is a presumption that payment by cheque or negotiable[17] security operates only as conditional payment: that is, the payer is not discharged until the cheque or security is honoured.[18] During the currency of the security, the creditor impliedly undertakes not to sue on the original debt.[19] But the presumption of conditional payment can be rebutted by proof of contrary intention *i.e.* by showing that the creditor had accepted the security unconditionally in payment of the debt.[20] The presumption that payment is merely conditional does not apply where a customer pays for goods or services by use of a charge or credit card. Use by the customer of such a card discharges his obligations under the contract with the supplier and makes the customer liable to reimburse the card

---

[9] *The Lutetian* [1982] 2 Lloyd's Rep. 140; *The Afovos* [1983] 1 W.L.R. 195.

[10] *Farquharson v Pearl Insurance Co Ltd* [1937] 3 All E.R. 124.

[11] *Finch v Brook* (1834) 1 Bing.N.C. 253.

[12] *Dixon v Clark* (1847) 5 C.B. 365.

[13] *Betterbee v Davis* (1811) 3 Camp. 70; *Robinson v Cook* (1815) 6 Taunt. 336.

[14] Sale of Goods Act 1979, s.29(5).

[15] *Tetley v Shand* (1871) 25 L.T. 658; *cf. Borrowman Phillips & Co v Free & Hollis* (1878) 4 Q.B.D. 500; *McDougall v Aeromarine of Emsworth* [1958] 1 W.L.R. 1126 at 1132; *Agricultores Federados Argentinos v Ampro SA* [1965] 2 Lloyd's Rep. 157; *Getreide Import Gesellschaft mbH v Itoh & Co (America) Ltd* [1979] 1 Lloyd's Rep. 592; *Bremer Handelsgesellschaft mbH v J H Rayner & Co* [1979] 2 Lloyd's Rep. 216 at 224–229; *The Playa Larga* [1983] 2 Lloyd's Rep. 171 at 186; *The Niizura* [1996] 2 Lloyd's Rep. 66 at 70; Apps, [1994] L.M.C.L.Q. 525.

[16] See below, p.860.

[17] Cheques are now rarely negotiable: above, p.691.

[18] Once it is honoured, payment is taken to have been made when the cheque was received: *Homes v Smith* [2000] Lloyd's Rep. Bank. 139.

[19] *Sayer v Wagstaff* (1844) 14 L.J.Ch. 116; *Re Romer & Haslam* [1893] 2 Q.B. 286; *cf. Maran Road Saw Mill v Austin Taylor & Co Ltd* [1975] 1 Lloyd's Rep. 156 and *EDF Man v Nigerian Sweets & Confectionery Co* [1977] 2 Lloyd's Rep. 50 (payment by letter of credit). Payment by direct debit has been treated as equivalent to payment by cheque, at least for the purpose of set-off: *Esso Petroleum Ltd v Milton* [1997] 1 W.L.R. 938. In *DPP v Turner* [1974] A.C. 357 at 367–368, and *Jameson v CEGB* [2000] 1 A.C. 455 at 478 it is suggested that giving a cheque amounts to payment but that the debt revives if the cheque is not met. However, in *Sayer v Wagstaff* (above) "payment" was held to have taken place when the promissory note was *paid*, not when it was *given*.

[20] *Sard v Rhodes* (1836) 1 M. & W. 153.

issuing company in accordance with the contract between these two parties. If the company should fail to pay the supplier (*e.g.* because it has become insolvent) the supplier's sole remedy is against the company.[21] He cannot claim the price from the customer; for to allow him to do so would make the customer liable to immediate full payment in cash for the goods or services supplied and so impose on him an obligation substantially more onerous than that to which he agreed when contracting with the supplier on the terms that payment was to be made by means of the card.

4. Alternatives[22]

A contract may provide for performance in one of several ways without stating which party is to have the power of choosing between them. In *Reed v Kilburn Co-operative Society*[23] the claimant lent £50 to the defendants at six per cent per annum "for six or nine months". The period of the loan was held to depend on the choice of the borrower. One reason given was that "the alternative was put in for the benefit of the borrower".[24] On this view the result could vary with the state of the market: the alternative might be for the benefit of the borrower if interest rates were thought likely to rise and for that of the lender if they were thought likely to fall. But this is not the law: the choice is always the borrower's, unless the contract expressly provides the contrary. Another reason given was that "the option is in the party who is to do the first act; here the borrower is to do the first act by paying".[25] But this test would not satisfactorily solve all cases. Quain J. during the argument said: "A lease for seven, fourteen, or twenty-one years, without saying at whose option, is at the option of the lessee."[26] Yet before one knows whose the option is, it is impossible to tell who is to do the first act, *i.e.* whether landlord or tenant must give notice of termination. No general rule is satisfactory where parties make such obscure contracts. One can only deal with the problem by laying down arbitrary rules in particular cases.[27]

SECTION 2. VICARIOUS PERFORMANCE

A contract may be performed by a third party on behalf of the debtor. The legal effects of such performance depend on whether it is made (or tendered) with or without the creditor's consent.

1. With the Creditor's Consent

If the creditor agrees to accept[27a] performance by a third party, such performance can discharge the contract, even though it is not the same as that stipulated for in the contract. In *Hirachand Punamchand v Temple*[28] a debt was held to have been discharged when the creditor accepted a smaller sum from the debtor's father in full settlement. Payment by a third party will, however, discharge the debtor only if it was made by the

---

[21] *Re Charge Card Services Ltd* [1989] Ch. 497; *cf. Richardson v Worrall* [1985] S.T.C. 693 at 717, 720; *Customs & Excise Commissioners v Diners Club Ltd* [1989] 1 W.L.R. 1196 at 1205–1206 rejecting the argument that the debt is not extinguished but assigned to the card-issuing company.

[22] *cf.* below, p.892.

[23] (1875) L.R. 10 Q.B. 264; *cf. Price v Nixon* (1813) 5 Taunt. 338.

[24] (1875) L.R. 10 Q.B. 264 at 265.

[25] *ibid.* at 264.

[26] *ibid.* at 265.

[27] *cf. Benjamin's Sale of Goods* (6th ed.).

[27a] *See Customs & Excise Commissioners v National Westminister Bank plc* [2002] EWHC 2204, [2003] 1 All E.R. (Comm) 327.

[28] [1911] 2 K.B. 330; above, p.129.

third party on behalf of the debtor and with the intention of discharging him. These requirements are illustrated by a case[29] in which a company made an *ex gratia* payment to a person who had been defrauded by its secretary. The victim of the fraud was nevertheless entitled to claim the whole of his loss from the secretary, since the company's payment was not made on the secretary's behalf. Similarly, part-payment by one of two persons who are both liable for a debt will not discharge the other, since it will be presumed to have been made on account of his own and not of his co-debtor's liability.[30] It is an open question whether the debt is discharged if payment by a third party is made without the knowledge or consent of the debtor.[31] Some dicta support the view that the debt is discharged[32]; and this consequence clearly results if the debtor adopts or ratifies the payment.[33] But if, before he has done so, the transaction between creditor and third party is cancelled and the payment is returned to the third party, there is no discharge[34]; nor will the payment discharge the debt if the third party made it in the mistaken belief (however genuine[35]) that he was authorised by the debtor to pay the debt on his behalf.[36] It follows that, where a bank without its customer's authority or ratification pays the customer's debt, then the debt is not discharged; nor is the bank entitled to debit the customer's account with the amount of the payment.[37]

The cases on this subject all concern the payment of debts; but presumably the same principles apply where a creditor agrees to accept vicarious performance of some other obligation, *e.g.* of one to deliver goods.

2. Without the Creditor's Consent

A creditor cannot object to vicarious performance where he is not prejudiced by the fact that the debtor does not perform personally. Thus a tradesman, to whom money is owed for goods, cannot object if the debtor procures full payment in cash to be made on his behalf by a third party. The same is often true of obligations to do something other than pay cash. Thus in *British Waggon Co v Lea & Co*[38] it was held that a contract to let out railway wagons and to keep them in repair for seven years could be vicariously performed: it did not matter to the hirer who kept the wagons in repair so long as the work was efficiently done by someone.

But a creditor may be entitled to object to vicarious performance either on account of the nature of the contract or because of its terms.

(1) Nature of the contract

When a contract is "personal" in the sense that one party relies on the skill and judgment of the other, the latter must perform personally. Thus duties under a contract

---

[29] *Re Rowe* [1904] 2 K.B. 483; *Pacific Associates Inc v Baxter* [1990] 1 Q.B. 993 at 1033–1034.

[30] *Jones v Broadhurst* (1850) 9 C.B. 173; *Cook v Lister* (1863) 13 C.B. (N.S.) 543 at 594; *Kemp v Balls* (1854) 10 Ex. 607.

[31] See generally Beatson, *The Use and Abuse of Unjust Enrichment*, Chap.7.

[32] *Cook v Lister* (1863) 13 C.B. (N.S.) 543 at 594; contrast *Guardian Ocean Cargoes Ltd v Banco do Brasil SA* [1991] 2 Lloyd's Rep. 68 at 88, affirmed [1994] 2 Lloyd's Rep. 152. A theoretical objection might be based on the doctrine of privity but it is submitted that cases of the present kind fall outside the scope of that doctrine as properly understood: see above, p.559. For the possible application of the Contracts (Rights of Third Parties) Act 1999 to cases of this kind, see above, p.118.

[33] See *Walter v James* (1871) L.R. 6 Ex. 124 at 127.

[34] This was the position in *Walter v James* itself; *cf.* above, p.726.

[35] *Crantrave Ltd v Lloyds Bank plc* [2000] Q.B. 917.

[36] *Barclays Bank Ltd v WJ Simms Son & Co (Southern) Ltd* [1980] Q.B. 677. Contrast *Lloyds Bank plc v Independent Insurance Co Ltd* [2000] Q.B. 110, where the payment was authorised.

[37] *Crantrave Ltd v Lloyds Bank plc* [2000] Q.B. 917.

[38] (1880) 5 Q.B.D. 149; *cf. Phillips v Alhambra Palace Co* [1901] 1 Q.B. 59.

of service cannot be vicariously performed; an estate agent who has been instructed to find a purchaser for a house cannot perform vicariously, since he "holds a position of discretion and trust"[39]; a contract under which building operations are to be supervised by an architect whose work is known to the client cannot be vicariously performed[40]; a person who agrees to store another's goods must perform personally, since the owner of the goods relies on his skill and integrity[41]; a person who enters into a promotion contract with a professional boxer cannot require the boxer to accept performance from a person to whom the promoter has purported to assign the benefit and burden of the contract[42]; and a shipowner must perform a charterparty personally in the sense that he cannot require the charterer to accept performance from a third party to whom the ship has been sold.[43] There are cases in which even a contract for the sale of goods must be personally performed by the seller, e.g. if the goods are to be manufactured by the seller and the buyer has relied on the seller's skill as a manufacturer[44] or if the buyer has in some other way relied on the personal integrity of the seller.[45] Perhaps the most extreme case is *Robson v Drummond*,[46] where it was held that a person who had agreed to keep a carriage in repair for five years and to paint it from time to time was not entitled to delegate performance of the contract to his partner.

(2) Terms of contract

It is obvious that a contract must be personally performed if it expressly so provides. A contract may also contain terms which impliedly rule out vicarious performance. In *Davies v Collins*[47] the defendant accepted a uniform for cleaning under a contract which provided: "Whilst every care is exercised in cleaning... garments, all orders are accepted at owners' risk." It was held that the defendant had broken the contract by sending the uniform to be cleaned by a sub-contractor (who had lost it); for the words "whilst every care is exercised in cleaning... " were inconsistent with the right to perform the cleaning operation vicariously. If however, the uniform had been properly cleaned, and returned, by the sub-contractor, the owner would not have been prejudiced by the fact of vicarious performance, and it is submitted that he should have been liable to make at any rate some payment.[48] Lord Greene M.R. said that the clause did not preclude every kind of sub-contracting: the cleaner might have employed a sub-contractor to perform some purely ancillary service, such as returning the uniform to the customer. It is arguable that the clause precluded only vicarious performance of the duty to take care of the goods, and that, so long as that duty remained unbroken, the owner was liable to pay the cleaning charges.

---

[39] *John McCann & Co v Pow* [1974] 1 W.L.R. 1643 at 1647; *cf.* above, p.747.

[40] *Southway Group v Wolff* (1991) 57 Build L.R. 33.

[41] *Edwards v Newland* [1950] 2 K.B. 534.

[42] *Don King Productions Inc v Warren* [2000] Ch. 291 at 335–336; the contract in this case was not assignable: see above, pp.693, 695.

[43] *Fratelli Sorrentino v Buerger* [1915] 3 K.B. 367 at 370, but that case shows that the charterer cannot object if, notwithstanding the sale, the shipowner can still perform personally, *i.e.* if he retains the control and management of the ship during the chartered period or voyage; *cf. Humble v Hunter* (1842) 12 Q.B. 310; above, p.728.

[44] *Johnson v Raylton, Dixon & Co* (1881) 7 Q.B.D. 438.

[45] *Dr Jaeger's Sanitary Woollen System Co Ltd v Walker & Sons* (1897) 77 L.T. 180.

[46] (1831) 2 B. & Ad. 303.

[47] [1945] 1 All E.R. 247; *cf. Kollerich & Cie SA v The State Trading Co of India* [1980] 2 Lloyd's Rep. 32; and see above, p.230.

[48] *cf.* below, p.820.

3. Vicarious Performance Distinguished from Assignment

The factors which determine whether a contract can be vicariously performed closely resemble those which determine whether the benefit of a "personal" contract is assignable.[49] For this reason, vicarious performance is sometimes called *assignment of liabilities*; but this is (as already noted) a concept which is not recognised by the common law.[50] Where vicarious performance is permitted no liability is *transferred*; the original debtor remains liable for the due performance of his obligations under the contract; and the sub-contractor does not at common law become liable in contract to the creditor.[51] In *Stewart v Reavell's Garage*[52] the owner of a 1929 Bentley motor-car took it to the defendants' garage to have the brakes relined. At the defendants' suggestion, the owner agreed that the work should be done by a sub-contractor, who did it so badly that the brakes failed, and the owner was injured. The defendants were clearly entitled to perform vicariously, as the owner had agreed to their doing so. But they were nonetheless held liable for the sub-contractor's defective workmanship: their liability was not transferred. Nor did the sub-contractor incur any contractual liability to the owner. He might have been liable to the owner in tort for doing the work negligently[53] but he would not have been liable to the owner in contract, had he failed to do the work at all. The Contracts (Rights of Third Parties) Act 1999,[54] makes it possible to draw up the sub-contract in such a way as to confer rights against the sub-contractor on the creditor; but even if this is done, the debtor will not be relieved from his liability to the creditor under the main contract.

The above discussion is based on the assumption that a contract contains an undertaking by A to B for the provision of some service and that the contract permits A to delegate the performance of the service to C. It is, however, also possible for A's undertaking to be, not one that he will *render* the service, but one that he will *arrange* for it to be rendered by another person (C) as his agent.[55] In that case, A's duty is merely to exercise reasonable care and skill in selecting the agent[56]; and if he performs that duty he will not (at common law[57]) be liable to B for defects in C's performance. Such a case is not one of *vicarious* performance at all: A will have *personally* performed the only duty which the contract imposed on him.

---

[49] See above, pp.693–695.

[50] See above, p.701.

[51] Unless the main contractor is the other party's agent for the purpose of making a contract between him and the sub-contractor; above, p.747.

[52] [1952] 2 Q.B. 545; cf. *Basildon DC v JE Lesser (Properties) Ltd* [1985] Q.B. 839; *The Superhulls Cover Case (No.2)* [1990] 2 Lloyd's Rep. 431 at 445; *Société Commerciale de Reassurance v ERAS International Ltd* [1992] 1 Lloyd's Rep. 570 at 596; *Wong Mee Wan v Kwan Kin Travel Services Ltd* [1996] 1 W.L.R. 38.

[53] cf. *Learoyd Bros v Pope & Sons* [1966] 2 Lloyd's Rep. 142; *British Telecommunications plc v James Thomson & Sons (Engineers) Ltd* [1999] 1 W.L.R. 9.

[54] See above, pp.651 *et seq.*

[55] *Wong Mee Wan v Kwan Kim Travel Services* [1996] 1 W.L.R. 38, where the contract was not of this kind, and A was held liable for C's defective performance.

[56] *Wong Mee Wan v Kwan Kim Travel Services Ltd*, above; *Raflatec Ltd v Eade* [1999] 1 Lloyd's Rep. 507 at 509. The same conclusion has been drawn where performance required specialist skills which A could not reasonably be expected to have: see *Investors in Industry Commercial Property Ltd v Bedfordshire CC* [1986] 1 All E.R. 787 at 807 (not reported on this point in [1986] Q.B. 1034); for a similar rule where the defendant's only liability to the claimant is in tort for negligence, see *D & F Estates Ltd v Church Commissioners for England* [1989] A.C. 177 at 209 (the claim for the "trivial sum" of £50 in respect of damage to carpets). cf. *Aiken v Stewart Wrightson Members Agency Ltd* [1995] 1 W.L.R. 1281.

[57] For a legislative exception, see Package Travel, Package Holidays and Package Tours Regulations 1992 (SI 1992/3228), reg.15(1).

SECTION 3. RESCISSION FOR FAILURE TO PERFORM[58]

1. Introduction

(1) Terminology

Failure to perform may (and often will) amount to breach of contract. Where this is the case the injured party can bring actions either for the specific enforcement of the contract, or for damages.[59] In such actions, the injured party seeks to be put (either actually or so far as money can do it) into the position in which he would have been if the contract had been *performed*. But he may also resort to another group of remedies, the object of which is to put him into the position in which he would have been, if the contract *had not been made*. These remedies are based on failure in performance rather than on breach,[60] so that they may be available even though the failure does not amount to a breach because there is some lawful excuse[61] for it. Where there is *no* breach, these remedies are, moreover, the only ones available to the "injured party"; it will be convenient to use this expression to refer to any party who by reason of a failure in performance (whether excused or not) does not get what he bargained for. One special excuse for non-performance arises where supervening events so fundamentally disrupt performance of the contract as to bring it automatically to an end under the doctrine of frustration. This doctrine is discussed in Chapter 20; our present concern is with cases in which the failure in performance is not such as to frustrate the contract.[62] In cases of this kind, a number of remedies are available to an injured party who wishes to "undo" rather than to "enforce" the contract. One such remedy is a simple refusal by the injured party to perform his own promise, *e.g.* he may refuse to pay for work on the ground that it was defectively done. This remedy is often combined with a refusal to accept further performance from the other party on account of a defect in the performance so far rendered, *e.g.* with a refusal to accept further deliveries under an instalment contract on the ground that one or more of the deliveries so far made are defective. Alternatively, the injured party may wish to undo the transaction by returning the defective performance and claiming back the consideration which he provided for it, *e.g.* he may return defective goods and sue for recovery of the money which he had paid for them.[63]

---

[58] Devlin [1966] C.L.J. 192; Reynolds, 79 L.Q.R. 534; Shea, 42 M.L.R. 623.

[59] See below, Chap.21, Sections 1 to 3.

[60] *e.g.* in *The Kathleen* (1874) L.R. 4 A. & E. 269, and in *Poussard v Spiers* (1876) 1 Q.B.D. 410; below, pp.775, 776, 783. In *Shell UK Ltd v Lostock Garages Ltd* [1976] 1 W.L.R. 1187 at 1199, Lord Denning M.R. suggests that one party's "unfair conduct," not amounting even to non-performance (let alone to breach), justifies the other's refusal to perform; but acceptance of this view could lead to great uncertainty. *cf.* Lord Denning's view in *Western Excavating (ECC) Ltd v Sharp* [1978] Q.B. 761 at 770 that for the purpose of constructive dismissal the test of "unreasonable conduct" would be "too indefinite by far."

[61] See below, pp.835–838.

[62] In *The Great Peace* [2002] EWCA Civ 1407; [2002] 4 All E.R. 689, at [82] reference is made to the test formulated by Diplock L.J. in the *Hong Kong Fir* case [1962] 2 Q.B. 26 at 65 for the purpose of determining whether an event is sufficiently serious to "discharge *one* of the parties from further performance of his undertakings" (italics supplied). This test is discussed at pp.791 and 795, below; in *The Great Peace*, above, it is said to be "applicable alike to both frustration and fundamental breach". But it is, with respect, submitted that an event may be sufficiently serious to satisfy Diplock L.J.'s test *without* frustrating the contract: *e.g.* on facts such as those of *Poussard v Spiers* (1876) 1 Q.B.D. 410, below, p.775. This point is reflected in Diplock L.J.'s reference, above, to an event which discharges only *"one of the parties"* (and does so only at that party's election: below, p.844) while a frustrating event automatically discharges *both* parties: below, pp.893, 909. There is no reference in Blackburn J.'s judgment in *Poussard v Spiers*, above, to his earlier judgment in *Taylor v Caldwell* (1863) 3 B. & S. 826, below, p.866, in which he laid the foundations of what is now known as the doctrine of frustration.

[63] This remedy is more fully discussed in Chap.21: below, pp.1049–1056.

The first difficulty in discussing this subject is the terminological one of finding a suitable word or phrase to refer to the remedies just described. For this purpose, the courts[64] (and contractual draftsmen[65]) have commonly used words such as "rescission" and "termination". This traditional terminology has attracted judicial criticism. In the *Photo Production* case, Lord Wilberforce said that the use of "rescission" in this sense "may lead to confusion"[66]; and Lord Diplock described the usage as "misleading" unless it was borne in mind that, in cases of breach, such rescission did not deprive the injured party of his right to claim damages for the breach.[67] The Sale of Goods Act 1979 avoids this difficulty by referring to a buyer's "right to reject the goods and treat the contract as repudiated".[68] But even this language is inappropriate where the failure in performance does not amount to a breach; and Devlin J. has described the buyer's right to reject as being "merely a particular form of the right to rescind".[69] The Sale of Goods Act itself, moreover, refers to a contract of sale as being "rescinded" by the seller on account of the buyer's breach; and it meets the point made by Lord Diplock by going on to provide that the rescission is "without prejudice to any claim the seller may have for damages".[70] Recent amendments to the Act likewise refer to the right of a buyer who deals as consumer to "rescind" the contract for breach of an express term and of certain implied conditions[71]; and judges[72] (including Lord Diplock)[73] have continued to use the same terminology since the *Photo Production* case. This usage is certainly more convenient than the somewhat clumsy circumlocution of "treating a contract as repudiated (or discharged) for breach (or excused non-performance)." In the following discussion we shall therefore continue to use the term "rescission" to refer to the remedies described above, bearing in mind that such rescission does not deprive the injured party of his claim for damages where the failure in performance amounts to a breach. In this respect rescission for breach differs fundamentally from rescission for misrepresentation, discussed in Chapter 9.[74]

(2) Policy Considerations

The law governing the right to rescind for failure in performance is complex and difficult; and in this it reflects the difficulty which the courts have experienced in

---

[64] *e.g. McDougall v Aeromarine of Emsworth Ltd* [1958] 1 W.L.R. 1126 at 1134; *The Hansa Nord* [1976] Q.B. 44 at 66; *Buckland v Farmar & Moody* [1979] 1 W.L.R. 221 at 231–232; *Johnson v Agnew* [1980] A.C. 367 at 392–393; *Stocznia Gdanska SA v Latvian Shipping Co* [1998] 1 W.L.R. 574 at 577, 600; *cf. Gunton v Richmond-upon-Thames LBC* [1981] Ch. 448 at 468 ("determination").

[65] See, for example, the terms of the contracts in *Woodar Investment Development Ltd v Wimpey Construction UK Ltd* [1980] 1 W.L.R. 227, *Hyundai Heavy Industries Ltd v Papadopoulos* [1980] 1 W.L.R. 1129 and the *Stocznia* case, above.

[66] *Photo Production Ltd v Securicor Transport Ltd* [1980] A.C. 827 at 844; *cf.* an earlier criticism in *Heyman v Darwins Ltd* [1942] A.C. 356 at 399.

[67] [1980] A.C. 827, 851; below, p.851.

[68] ss.11(3), 11(4) and 61(1) (definition of "warranty").

[69] *Kwei Tek Chao v British Traders Ltd* [1954] Q.B. 459 at 480.

[70] s.48(4).

[71] ss.48A(2)(b)(ii), 48C and 48F, as inserted by Sale and Supply of Goods to Consumers Regulations 2002, SI 2002/3045, reg.5; similar provisions are inserted by reg.9 into the Supply of Goods and Services Act 1982.

[72] *Bunge Corp v Tradax Export SA* [1981] 1 W.L.R. 711 at 719, 723, 724; *The Cleon* [1983] 1 Lloyd's Rep. 587 at 590; *The TFL Prosperity* [1984] 1 W.L.R. 48 at 58; *Peyman v Lanjani* [1985] Ch. 457 at 482; *Shine v General Guarabovee Corp* [1988] 1 All E.R. 911 at 916; *Nova Petroleum etc. v Tricon Trading Ltd* [1988] 1 Lloyd's Rep. 312 at 315; *Barber v NSW Bank* [1996] 1 W.L.R. 641 at 646, 647; *Stocznia Gdanska SA v Latvian Shipping Co* [1998] 1 W.L.R. 574 at 584.

[73] *The Scaptrade* [1983] 2 A.C. 694 at 702; *Gill & Duffus SA v Berger Co Inc* [1984] A.C. 382 at 390, 391; *Metro Meat Ltd v Fares Rural Co Pty Ltd* [1985] 2 Lloyd's Rep. 13 at 17.

[74] See above, pp.369–377, especially at 370.

balancing or reconciling the conflicting interests of the parties in respectively seeking, and resisting, the remedy of rescission.[75]

The interests of the injured party in seeking rescission may be grouped under three heads. First, rescission will be his only remedy where the failure in performance is not a breach. Secondly, rescission may, even where the failure is a breach, lead to a result which is more favourable to the injured party in monetary terms than a claim for damages. This will be true where the contract would have been a bad bargain for the injured party even if it had been duly performed[76]; and also where the loss or injury which he suffers is one for which he might not recover damages in an action for breach of contract: for example, if his loss (or part of it) is irrecoverable because it is too remote.[77] Thirdly, the injured party may, by rescinding, get a quicker and more efficacious remedy. A buyer who has not yet paid for defective goods will often prefer to "rescind" (in the sense of rejecting the goods and refusing to pay) than to perform his side of the bargain and be left to pursue a claim for damages. By rescinding he avoids the delays of litigation, and the risk that the seller's credit may fail. Even if he has already paid, an action for the return of the payment is in many ways more convenient than one for damages. It is an action for a liquidated sum, which avoids many of the difficulties (such as quantification, mitigation and causation) which can arise in an action for damages.[78]

On the other hand, the party who fails to perform in accordance with the contract may have equally strong interests in resisting rescission. He may have incurred expenses in the course of performance, for example by paying commission on a sale or by transporting goods to a distant place; and these expenses will be thrown away if the contract is rescinded. He may, in addition, have conferred benefits on the injured party who may be unjustly enriched by being allowed to rescind: rescission of partly performed building contracts may, for example, produce this result.[79] And he may suffer hardship if the injured party is allowed to rescind on a falling market: he may be left with goods whose value has diminished by an amount far in excess of the loss which the defect in his performance would have caused to the injured party.

In balancing these conflicting interests, the courts have developed a number of rules and distinctions which *prima facie* determine the availability of rescission as a remedy for failure to perform. Further rules specify that the right to rescind, even where it is *prima facie* available, may be limited or barred by certain supervening factors.

2. The Order of Performance

The order in which contracting parties must perform their respective obligations depends on the distinction between conditions precedent, concurrent conditions, and independent promises. Somewhat confusingly, English law also uses the expression "condition" in rules which deal with the *conformity* of one party's performance with that promised (as opposed to the *order* in which the two performances must be rendered). This usage, and the distinction between these two senses of "condition," are discussed later in this Chapter.[80]

---

[75] Honnold, 97 U. of Pa.L.Rev. 457.

[76] *e.g.* if he has agreed to pay £100 for something which would, because of a later fall in the market, be worth only £50 on delivery even if there had been no breach. This is a constantly recurring problem: see below, pp.777, 778, 787, 793–794, 794, 796, 809, n.31.

[77] See below, pp.965–974.

[78] See below, pp.944–965, 974–982.

[79] See below, pp.759–760.

[80] See below, pp.788–805, especially at pp.788–789.

(1) Condition precedent

Performance by one party, A, is a condition precedent to the liability of the other, B, when A has to perform before B's liability accrues. This will most obviously be the case if the contract expressly provides that A's act is to be done before B's.[81] Thus if A agrees to work for B at a weekly wage payable in arrear, B need not pay A until A has done a week's work.[82] Performance by A may also be a condition precedent to the liability of B even though the contract does not expressly state the order in which the two acts are to be done. In *Trans Trust SPRL v Danubian Trading Co*[83] A bought steel from B to be paid for by "cash against shipping documents from a confirmed credit to be opened by" an American company (to whom A had resold) in favour of B. A undertook that the credit would be opened "forthwith". Performance by A of his undertaking to procure the letter of credit was regarded as a condition precedent to the liability of B although the order in which their acts were to be done was not expressly laid down in the contract. A knew that B could not get supplies of steel unless the credit was made available. Hence the nature of the contract made it clear that A was to perform before B became liable.

In Chapter 2 we distinguished between contingent and promissory conditions, and noted that "condition" was used to refer either to an event or to a term of a contract.[84] Our present concern is with conditions as events. In this sense, a contingent condition is an event which neither party undertakes to bring about and on which the existence of a contract, or the binding force of its principal obligations, depends. A promissory condition, on the other hand, refers to an event which one party is obliged by the contract to bring about. In the *Trans Trust* case, A argued that the opening of the credit was a condition of the former kind, so that A was not liable when his sub-buyer failed to open the credit. But the court rejected the argument and held A liable on the ground that the opening of the credit was not a condition precedent to the existence of the contract, but only a condition precedent to the liability of B. In other words, it was not a contingent, but a promissory condition. In its contingent sense, condition precedent is contrasted with condition subsequent. In its promissory sense (with which we are here concerned), condition precedent is contrasted with concurrent condition and independent promise: these concepts are discussed below.

The distinction between a contingent and a promissory condition turns on the question whether the agreement purports to impose on A an obligation to bring about the stipulated event.[85] For example, in one case A undertook to erect buildings on B's land, and B undertook, when A had done so, to grant a lease of the land to A. This was held not to be a (contingently) "conditional contract," but a case in which performance by A was a (promissory) condition precedent to the liability of B.[86] The position is similar where A contracts to buy a house from B and to pay a deposit. As A promised

---

[81] *Société Générale de Paris v Milders* (1883) 49 L.T. 55 at 59; *cf. Pioneer Concrete (UK) Ltd v National Employers Mutual, etc.* [1985] 2 All E.R. 395; *Motor & General Insurance Co Ltd v Pavy* [1994] 1 Lloyd's Rep. 607 at 612; *Kazakstan Wool Processors (Europe) Ltd v Credietverzekering Madtschapping NV* [2002] 1 All E.R. (Comm) 708 at 720.

[82] *Morton v Lamb* (1797) 7 T.R. 125; *Cresswell v Board of Inland Revenue* [1984] I.C.R. 508; *Miles v Wakefield MDC* [1987] A.C. 539 at 561, 574; *Wiluszynski v Tower Hamlets LBC* [1989] I.C.R. 493, 498; see further p.821, below.

[83] [1952] 2 Q.B. 297. For a similar argument in a different context, see *Films Rover International v Cannon Film Sales Ltd* [1987] 1 W.L.R. 670 at 684; for further proceedings see [1989] 1 W.L.R. 912. Contrast *Clowes Development (UK) Ltd v Mulchinock* [1998] 1 W.L.R. 42.

[84] See above, p.62; *cf.* below, p.788.

[85] *cf. Albion Sugar Co Ltd v Williams Tankers Ltd* [1977] 2 Lloyd's Rep. 457 at 464; *The Fanti and the Padre Island* [1991] 2 A.C. 1 at 31.

[86] *Eastham v Leigh, London & Provincial Properties Ltd* [1971] 1 Ch. 871; *cf. Michaels v Harley House (Marylebone) Ltd* [1997] 1 W.L.R. 967.

to pay the deposit, that payment is not a contingent condition precedent to the existence of the contract[87] but a promissory condition precedent to the liability of B. If the deposit is not paid, B is, moreover, entitled to rescind the contract,[88] while A can be sued for the unpaid deposit, or for damages for failing to pay it.[89]

(2) Concurrent condition

The two performances are said to be concurrent conditions when the parties undertake to perform concurrently (or simultaneously). Thus in the case of a contract for the sale of goods delivery and payment are concurrent conditions: this means that the buyer cannot claim delivery unless he is ready and willing to pay, and the seller cannot claim the price unless he is ready and willing to deliver.[90] Of course this rule can be varied by contrary agreement: the seller may agree to give credit or the buyer to pay in advance. Similarly, under a charterparty, delivery of the goods by the shipowner and payment of the freight are (unless otherwise agreed[91]) concurrent conditions.[92]

(3) Independent promises

If promises are "independent" each party can enforce the other's promise although he has not performed his own. The remedy of the party sued is not to withhold performance, but to make a counterclaim to enforce the promise of the party suing. In the old case of *Pordage v Cole*[93] a purchaser promised to pay a vendor "£775 for all his lands . . . the money to be paid before Midsummer." In an action to recover the £775 it was held that the vendor need not aver conveyance or tender of conveyance. A contract for the sale of land would now generally require conveyance and payment to take place concurrently.[94] But a tenant's covenant to pay rent and a landlord's covenant to repair are still regarded as independent, so that the landlord is not entitled to refuse to perform his covenant to repair merely because the tenant is in arrears with his rent.[95] Similarly, in a separation deed the wife's covenant not to molest her husband and the husband's covenant to pay the wife an annuity are independent unless the deed otherwise provides: breach of the wife's covenant is therefore no answer to an action by her for the annuity.[96] And where goods carried on a chartered ship are damaged as a result of the shipowner's breach of the charterparty, before the time fixed for payment of freight, the charterer

---

[87] *Michael Richards Properties Ltd v St Saviour's Parish* [1975] 3 All E.R. 416 at 420; *Portara Shipping Co v Gulf Pacifica Navigation Co Ltd* [1981] 2 Lloyd's Rep. 180 at 184; *Millichamp v Jones* [1982] 1 W.L.R. 1422; *The Blankenstein* [1985] 1 W.L.R. 435. These authorities reject the contrary view stated in *Myton Ltd v Schwab-Morris* [1974] 1 W.L.R. 326 at 330.

[88] *Myton Ltd v Schwab-Morris* [1974] 1 W.L.R. 326 at 331, below, p.774. The contract may require B to give notice of termination before he is entitled to rescind, as in *Millichamp v Jones* [1982] 1 W.L.R. 1422 (where this requirement was not satisfied).

[89] See below, pp.852, 1011–1012.

[90] Sale of Goods Act 1979, s.28; *Morton v Lamb* (1797) 7 T.R. 125.

[91] e.g. *The Karin Vatis* [1988] 2 Lloyd's Rep. 330.

[92] *Paynter v James* (1867) L.R. 2 C.P. 348 at 355; cf. *Stanton v Richardson* (1872) L.R. 7 C.P. 421 at 433 (affirmed 45 L.J.Q.B. 78); *The Posidon* [2001] 1 Lloyd's Rep. 697.

[93] (1669) 1 Wms.Saund. 319; cf. *Campbell v Jones* (1796) 6 T.R. 570; *Christie v Borelly* (1860) 29 L.J. Ch. 153; *Leiston Gas Co v Leiston cum Sizewell Urban DC* [1916] 2 K.B. 428 at 434 ("independent contract").

[94] But for this, *Pordage v Cole* would probably have been overruled long ago; it was said to "outrage common sense" as long ago as 1792, in *Goodison v Nunn* (1792) 4 T.R. 761 at 764.

[95] *Taylor v Webb* [1937] 2 K.B. 283 at 290 (reversed, *ibid.*, on another ground which was disapproved in *Regis Property Co Ltd v Dudley* [1959] A.C. 370); cf. *Johnstone v Milling* (1886) 16 Q.B.D. 460 at 468; *Tito v Waddell (No.2)* [1977] Ch. 106 at 290; *The Aegnoussiotis* [1977] 1 Lloyd's Rep. 268 at 276; *Yorbrook Investments Ltd v Batten* (1986) P. & C.R. 51.

[96] *Fearon v Aylesford* (1884) 14 Q.B.D. 792.

must nevertheless make the payment when that time comes: his remedy is by way of a cross-action for damages.[97]

(4) Criteria for drawing the distinction

The distinction between conditions precedent, concurrent conditions and independent covenants is easily illustrated by reference to stereotyped situations, such as the employment, sale of goods and tenancy cases referred to in the preceding discussion. In those cases, the distinction is governed by well-settled rules, though these can be excluded by express or implied[98] agreement. But more difficulty arises in drawing the distinction in cases of first impression which fall outside these stereotyped situations. For this purpose the courts have regard to certain policy considerations, though these can be displaced by evidence of the intention of the parties.

The effect of holding promises to be independent is to expose each party to the risk of having to perform without any security for the performance of the other; the effect of holding performance by one party to be a condition precedent is to expose that party to the same risk. To reduce the first of these risks, the courts have long been reluctant to classify promises as independent[99] unless the intention of the parties to that effect was clear. Both risks would be eliminated if the two performances were held to be concurrent conditions; and for this reason the law should, in doubtful cases, favour such a classification whenever simultaneous performance by both parties is possible.[1] In a contract between a commercial seller or supplier and a consumer, a term which has not been individually negotiated and which makes the consumer's undertaking, (*e.g.* to pay the agreed price or charge) independent of the due performance of the other party's obligations is *prima facie* unfair under the Unfair Terms in Consumer Contracts Regulations 1999,[2] and if it is actually unfair it will not bind the consumer.[3]

Where simultaneous performance is not possible (as in the case of contracts to do work over a period of time) performance by one party must necessarily be a condition precedent to the liability of the other. Which party has to perform first depends on their relative bargaining power and on the court's view (right or wrong) as to which of them is more likely to default after the other has performed. These factors no doubt account for the general rule that work must precede pay.[4] The position of the person doing the work is in practice safeguarded by stipulating for interim payments, such as weekly or monthly remuneration under contracts of employment, or progress payments under building contracts.

Even where it is possible for the two performances to be rendered simultaneously, it does not follow that they should invariably be classified as concurrent conditions. There are, in particular, three situations in which it is more appropriate to classify promises as independent.

The first such situation arises where the promise which has not been performed is of only minor importance. This was the position in *Huntoon Co v Kolynos (Inc)*,[5] where an agreement was made by which the claimants licensed the defendants to use a patent. By cl.7 the claimants undertook to prosecute all claims for infringement of the patent if

---

[97] See below, pp.785, 788, n.32; the rule applies even though the shipowner's breach was repudiatory: see *The Dominique* [1989] A.C. 1056 (not a case of damage but of delay).
[98] As in the *Trans Trust* case [1952] 2 Q.B. 297, above, p.762.
[99] See *Kingston v Preston* (1773) Lofft. 194; and *Jones v Barkley* (1781) 2 Dougl. 648 at 689.
[1] This is the view taken by the Restatement 2d, *Contracts*, §234(1); *cf. ibid.* §233(2).
[2] See above, pp.267–283; SI 1999/2083, reg.5(5) and Sch.2, para.1(o).
[3] reg.8(1).
[4] See above, p.762.
[5] [1930] 1 Ch. 528.

requested to do so by the defendants; while by cl.9 the defendants undertook to stamp the number of the patent on all articles incorporating it. It was held that cl.7 was an independent promise, so that, although the claimants were in breach of it, they could enforce cl.9. Lawrence L.J. said: "Where a covenant goes only to part of the consideration on both sides and a breach of such covenant may be paid for in damages, it is an independent covenant . . . ."[6] Cl.7 might apply in relation to quite trivial, or only suspected, infringements: failure to prosecute claims for these would not substantially deprive the defendants of what they had bargained for.

The classification of promises as independent is, secondly, appropriate where the circumstances show that this was the intention of the parties. This was the position in *The Odenfeld.*[7] A charterparty provided that hire was to be assessed by a panel from time to time, but that, if it were assessed at less than some $3.50 per ton, this amount was nevertheless payable. However, the parties also agreed by a "side letter" that, if the amount assessed by the panel fell below the $3.50 per ton, any excess over the amount assessed was to be paid back by the shipowners to the charterers. The freight market having collapsed, the panel assessed the amount payable at $1.50 per ton, but the shipowners failed to perform their promise contained in the "side letter" to repay $2 per ton to the charterers. It was held that the "side letter" constituted an independent promise, so that its breach did not justify the charterers' refusal to perform their obligations under the charterparty. Kerr J. relied mainly on the way in which the transaction had been set up in two documents: this supported the view that the promises were "intended to be independent and not interdependent".[8]

Thirdly, promises may be classified as independent because of their commercial setting. This possibility arises where goods are sold for export on "c.i.f." terms, that is, for an inclusive price covering their cost, insurance and freight. Under such a contract the seller must ship goods that are in conformity with the contract and tender certain shipping documents to the buyer, while the buyer must pay the price on tender of the documents.[9] So long as the documents are in accordance with the contract, the buyer cannot refuse to pay against tender of those documents merely because the goods were not, when shipped, in conformity with the contract.[10] This is true even if the non-conformity of the goods is such that it would justify their rejection when the goods themselves (as opposed to the documents) later reach the buyer. The seller's undertaking with respect to the conformity of *the goods* can therefore be described as an independent promise in the sense that his failure to perform it does not prevent the buyer's duty to pay the price from arising on tender of *documents*. The buyer's remedies, in the case put, are to claim damages for the defects in the goods, or to reject them and reclaim the price if, on their arrival at the agreed destination, it turns out that they suffered, when they were shipped, from defects of a kind that justify their rejection.[11]

(5) Effects of the distinction

It follows from the nature of an independent promise that failure by one party (A) to perform such a promise does not justify rescission by the other party (B). The position

---

[6] *ibid.* at 558.

[7] [1978] 2 Lloyd's Rep. 357.

[8] [1978] 2 Lloyd's Rep. 357 at 371. He may also have been influenced by the fact that to hold the promises interdependent would have prejudiced a bank which had taken an assignment of the shipowner's rights under the charterparty without notice of the "side letter."

[9] See generally *Benjamin's Sale of Goods* (6th ed.), §§19–072 to 19–076.

[10] *Gill & Duffus SA v Berger & Co Inc* [1984] A.C. 382, more fully discussed in *Benjamin's Sale of Goods* (6th ed.), §§19–158 to 19–161.

[11] *e.g.* from defects amounting to a breach of condition: see below, pp.788–805.

where A fails to perform a condition precedent or a concurrent condition is more complex: such a failure justifies B's refusal to perform for so long as the failure continues, but it does not, of itself, justify rescission in the sense of an outright refusal by B to perform, or to accept further performance from A. If A, an employee, fails to perform the condition precedent of doing the agreed work, his employer, B, is *prima facie* entitled to refuse to pay A so long as that failure continues; and B's refusal to pay may be justified even though he does not dismiss A.[12] But it does not follow that B is entitled to rescind (in the sense of dismissing A) merely on account of A's failure to perform: he would, for example, generally not be so entitled where A's failure was due to a relatively brief temporary illness.[13] Similarly, if A, a buyer of goods, fails to perform the concurrent condition of paying or tendering the price when due, the seller, B, is *prima facie* justified in withholding delivery; but it again does not follow that B is, merely on account of the failure, entitled to rescind the contract: he may, for example, still be bound to deliver if A tenders the price on the day after that fixed by the contract. In other words, A's failure to comply with a stipulation as to the order of performance which is a condition precedent or a concurrent condition justifies B's refusal to perform for as long as A's failure continues; but it does not, of itself, justify rescission.[14] It has the latter effect only where A's failure is (in accordance with the principles to be discussed later in this Chapter[15]) *either* sufficiently serious to justify rescission *or* such that it falls within one of the exceptions to the requirement of serious failure.

(6) Wrongful refusal to accept performance

(a) AS A GROUND OF RESCISSION. In general, A's failure to perform a condition precedent or a concurrent condition justifies a refusal by B to perform. But this rule is displaced if, before performance from A has become due, B has repudiated the contract by wrongfully refusing to accept performance (or indicating that he would do so) and A has rescinded the contract on account of that repudiation.

(i) *Repudiation inducing victim's failure to perform.* Suppose that a contract for the sale of goods provides that the goods are to be manufactured by A to B's order. If, before anything has, or should have been, done by A, B wrongfully repudiates the contract A is entitled to rescind; and, if he does so, two things follow: A need no longer manufacture the goods, and he can claim damages from B.[16] It would be pointless to require A to manufacture and tender the goods when the tender was virtually certain to be rejected. His inability to deliver the goods at the agreed time is not allowed to prejudice his rights against B as it was induced by B's wrongful repudiation; another way of putting the point is to say that B is estopped from relying on A's inability to perform.[17] A buyer is similarly not entitled to rely on the seller's failure to deliver where that failure was

---

[12] *Wiluszynski v Tower Hamlets LBC* [1989] I.C.R. 493. *Ticehurst & Thompson v British Telecommunications* [1992] I.C.R. 383.

[13] See below, pp.776, 875.

[14] *cf.* Sale of Goods Act 1979, s.10(1), below, p.766.

[15] See below, pp.769–811.

[16] *e.g. Glencore Grain Rotterdam BV v LORICO* [1997] 2 Lloyd's Rep. 386, where a seller's refusal to load goods was justified by the buyer's refusal to operate the contractual payment mechanism unless unjustified demands by the buyer were met; *cf. Grant v Cigman* [1996] B.C.L.C. 24 (A's inability to perform induced by B's failure to co-operate). As to A's remedy in such cases, see *The Odenfeld* [1978] 2 Lloyd's Rep. 357, below, p.1018.

[17] *The Simona* [1989] A.C. 788 at 805–806. *Foran v Wight* (1989) 168 C.L.R. 385 is explicable on this relatively simple ground.

induced by the buyer's insistence on delivery at a place other than that specified by the contract.[18]

(ii) *Victim's inability not induced by the repudiation.* In the situations just described, it has been assumed that A could have performed, and would have done so, if B had not repudiated. But sometimes A can recover damages even though he cannot show that he would, but for B's repudiation, have been able to perform his part. In *British and Beningtons Ltd v N W Cachar Tea Co Ltd*[19] A sold tea to B who, before delivery was due, without justification stated that they would refuse to accept it. It was held that A was entitled to damages even though he could not show that he could have delivered the tea at the agreed time and place. B's wrongful refusal to accept was an anticipatory breach,[20] and, once this had been "accepted" by A so as to rescind the contract, later events affecting A's ability to perform did not deprive A of his right of action[21]; for, by rescinding the contract, A had been liberated from his duty of further performance.[22] The position would have been different if, at the time of B's refusal to accept, A had himself already committed a repudiatory breach,[23] for such a breach would have justified B's refusal. It is therefore crucial to determine which party committed the first breach,[24] whether that breach was repudiatory, and whether it was accepted by the other party so as to rescind the contract.

These questions are easy enough to formulate but they can raise difficult issues of fact and law where each party to a commercial dispute in good faith believes that he is acting in accordance with the contract, and that the other is not. The issue is further complicated by two rules. The first is that A is not necessarily in breach merely because he makes a defective tender; for it may be open to him to cure the defect by making a second (and good) tender within the time allowed for performance.[25] The second is that

---

[18] *Bulk Oil (Zug) AG v Sun International Ltd* [1984] 1 Lloyd's Rep. 531 at 546.

[19] [1923] A.C. 48; *cf. Cort v Ambergate Ry* (1851) 7 Q.B. 127; *Rightside Properties Ltd v Gray* [1975] Ch. 72 at 87; *Texaxo Ltd v Eurogolf Shipping Co Ltd* [1987] 2 Lloyd's Rep. 541.

[20] See below, pp.857–865.

[21] See below, pp.863–864; *Braithwaite v Foreign Hardwood Co* [1905] 2 K.B. 543, as explained in *The Simona* [1989] A.C. 788 at 805.

[22] *Gill & Duffus SA v Berger & Co Inc* [1984] A.C. 382 at 390; *cf. MSC Mediterranean Shipping Co SA v BRE Metro Ltd* [1985] 2 Lloyd's Rep. 239 at 240; *Glencore Grain Rotterdam BV v LORICO* [1997] 2 Lloyd's Rep. 386 at 394–395; *North Sea Energy Holdings NV v Petroleum Authority of Thailand* [1997] 2 Lloyd's Rep. 418 at 432, where the principle stated in the text above was held at first instance not to apply because the contract had become ineffective by reason of failure of a condition precedent, without default of the allegedly repudiating party, *before* acceptance of any repudiation by the other party; the decision was affirmed on appeal without further reference to the present point: [1999] 1 Lloyd's Rep. 483. Dawson, 96 L.Q.R. 239 argues that *Universal Cargo Carriers Corp v Citati* [1957] 2 Q.B. 401 is inconsistent with the explanation of the *British and Beningtons* case given in the text above. But the claim in the *Citati* case was made *against* the party alleged to be unable to perform (the charterer) while in the *British and Beningtons* case it was made *by* that party. Moreover, in the *Citati* case the charterer was already in breach (actual and anticipatory) at the time of the shipowner's refusal to perform while in the *British and Beningtons* case the sellers were not in breach at the time of the buyer's refusal. The crucial issue in the *Citati* case was simply whether the charterer's breach was sufficiently serious to justify the shipowner's rescission.

[23] *i.e.* one that satisfied the requirement of "substantial failure" (below, pp.769–778) or fell within an exception to that requirement (below, pp.778–811). In *Braithwaite's* case (above n.21) A had already shipped non-conforming goods before B's repudiation; but there are at least three possible reasons why this did not justify that repudiation: (1) A had not yet tendered the goods: *Taylor v Oakes Roncoroni & Co* (1922) 38 T.L.R. 349 at 351 (affirmed *ibid.* at 517); (2) A still had the opportunity to cure the breach (below, at n.25) and was induced by B's repudiation not to make use of it: *cf.* below p.769 at n.42; (3) as the contract was on c.i.f. terms (see 74 L.J.K.B. 688 at 694) A's shipment of non-conforming goods was a breach only of an independent covenant and hence did not justify B's repudiation: above, p.765. See further Benjamin's *Sale of Goods* (6th ed.), §§19–162 to 19–166.

[24] *Glencore Grain* case, above, n.18; *cf. The Energy Progress* [1993] 1 Lloyd's Rep. 355 at 358.

[25] See above, p.754.

B is not necessarily in breach merely because, at the time of his refusal to accept A's performance, he gives an inadequate reason for the refusal, or none at all; for if he actually had a lawful excuse he can (in general) rely on it later even though he did not state it, or even know of it, at the time of his refusal to accept performance.[26]

(iii) *Pre-rescission non-repudiatory breach by injured party.* Before rescinding the contract on account of B's repudiation, A may himself have committed a breach, but one which did not justify B's repudiation, *e.g.* a breach of an independent promise.[27] Rescission by A does not affect his liability for that pre-rescission breach[28]; so that the damages to which A is entitled on account of B's wrongful repudiation will be reduced by those for which he is liable in respect of his own pre-rescission breach.[29] Those damages will *prima facie* be the amount by which A's breach reduces the value of his performance.[30]

(b) INJURED PARTY DOES NOT RESCIND. The reason for the rule that A may be entitled to damages for B's repudiation, without having to show that he could have performed, is that, when A accepts B's repudiation, he is liberated from his own duty to perform.[31] That reasoning obviously cannot apply where A does not accept the repudiation. In such a case, A continues to be bound by his own duties under the contract, so that his failure to perform these duties, even after B's repudiation, can (if not induced by B's repudiation[32]) amount to a breach by A. Such a breach will make A liable in damages,[33] and, if it is repudiatory,[34] it will also justify B's refusal to perform and so absolve B from liability in damages to A.[35]

Where A does not accept B's repudiation and then commits a breach which does *not* justify B's refusal to perform (*e.g.* because it is a breach of an independent promise[36]), A's breach will nevertheless be relevant to the damages to which A is entitled on account of B's repudiation. At the least, those damages will (as in the case where A has rescinded) be reduced by the damages for which A is liable by reason of his own breach, *e.g.* by the amount by which the value of goods delivered by A is reduced by reason of a defect in them. There are, moreover, circumstances in which, if A has not rescinded, B can rely on A's breach so as to reduce still further the damages for which B is liable by reason of his repudiation. This possibility arises where A's breach, though not originally of such a kind as to justify B's repudiation, later acquires that character. We have seen that, where goods are sold on c.i.f. terms, the buyer is not justified in refusing to pay against *documents* merely because the *goods* were not, when shipped, in conformity with the contract; but that such non-conformity may give him the right to reject the goods, a right that he will usually exercise when the goods arrive at the contractual destination and are actually delivered to him.[37] That stage is never reached if the seller rescinds on

---

[26] See below, p.836.

[27] See above, p.763.

[28] See below, p.851.

[29] *Gill & Duffus SA v Berger & Co Inc* [1984] A.C. 382 at 390 (where "certification clause" in the contract excluded such liability).

[30] See below, p.950.

[31] See above, p.767.

[32] See above, p.766.

[33] *Regent OHG Aisenstadt und Barig v Francesco of Jermyn Street* [1983] 3 All E.R. 327 at 335.

[34] In the sense described in n.23 at p.767, above.

[35] See *The Simona* [1989] A.C. 788, where A's failure was not a breach but justified cancellation under an express cancelling clause in the contract; Marston [1988] C.L.J. 340; Carter [1989] L.M.C.L.Q. 81.

[36] See above, p.763.

[37] See above, p.765.

the buyer's wrongful refusal to pay against documents[38]; but if the seller does *not* rescind, and the defect in the goods is such as to give the buyer the right to reject them on arrival, then the buyer will be able to argue that he would, even if he had duly paid against documents, have rejected the goods on arrival and so have become entitled to the return of the money that he ought to have paid at the earlier stage of tender of documents.[39] The effect of this argument is that the seller's damages will be merely nominal: he will have lost nothing but the worthless right to be paid a sum of money which he would (had it been paid) have later become liable to repay.[40] Such an argument is not, however, available to the buyer where it was still open to the seller to have cured his breach[41] and his failure to do so was induced by the buyer's wrongful repudiation.[42] If the seller's failure to cure was induced in this way, the buyer cannot rely on it in reduction of damages, any more than he can rely on the seller's original failure to perform (when so induced) on the issue of liability.[43]

(c) EVALUATION. The rule that A is entitled to rescind and to recover damages where his own inability to perform is induced by B's repudiation is generally regarded as uncontroversial. But there is dispute about the merit of the rule that A has the same rights where he could not have performed even if B had not repudiated and where his inability to perform was not in any way induced by B's conduct. This aspect of the rule can be criticised by saying that B is made liable in damages for merely saying that he will not perform, even though he may not thereby cause any prejudice to A.[44] On the other hand, B can avoid this hardship by simply waiting till A's performance is due: if it is not forthcoming at that time it is A, not B, who will be liable in damages; and any hardship that the rule may cause to B if he repudiates before that time is mitigated by the qualifications on its scope that have been stated above.[45] For these reasons, it does not seem that the rule causes undue prejudice to B. It can be justified on the ground that it promotes certainty by discouraging premature repudiation.

3. General Requirement of Substantial Failure

A party may comply with the rules as to the order of performance, just discussed, but his performance or tender may be deficient in quality or quantity or it may be late, *i.e.* after the agreed time. The general principle is that any such defect in performance must attain a certain minimum degree of seriousness to entitle the injured party to rescind. In

---

[38] As in *Gill & Duffus SA v Berger & Co Inc* [1984] A.C. 382.

[39] See *Henry Dean & Sons (Sydney) Ltd v O'Day Pty Ltd* (1929) 39 C.L.R. 330 at 340, so far as it relates to the *seller's* claim; the disapproval of that decision in *Gill & Duffus SA v Berger & Co Inc*, above, relates to the *buyer's* claim only; and in the *Gill & Duffus* case itself the House of Lords treated the seller's rescission as crucial to the success of his claim.

[40] *cf. The Mihalis Angelos* [1971] 1 Q.B. 641, below, p.779. An alternative view is that the seller's damages are nominal only if the defect makes the goods worthless: see *Bunge Corp v Vegetable Vitamin Foods (Private) Ltd* [1985] 1 Lloyd's Rep. 613 at 620; but the buyer's case is not that *the goods* are worthless: it is that the seller's *right to have them accepted* is worthless because the buyer's option to reject them would certainly have been exercised.

[41] See above, p.767 at n.25.

[42] This is one possible explanation of *Braithwaite v Foreign Hardwood Co* [1905] 2 K.B. 543, above, p.767, n.21: *cf. Sheffield v Gonran* (1987) 22 Con L.R. 108.

[43] *cf.* above, pp.766–767.

[44] The rule does not seem to apply in the United States: see, for example *Caporale v Rubine*, 105 A. 226 (1918); *Corbin on Contracts*, §978; *Williston on Contracts*, §699; *Farnsworth on Contracts* (3rd ed.), §8.22.

[45] *i.e.* at nn.27–43, above.

the following discussion we shall refer to this principle as the requirement of "substantial failure" in performance. Our present concern is with the general principle; it is subject to many important exceptions which will be discussed later in this Chapter.[46]

(1) Historical introduction

In *Boone v Eyre*[47] the plaintiff conveyed to the defendant a plantation in the West Indies, together with the slaves on it, for £500 plus an annuity of £160. He covenanted that he had good title to the plantation and that he was lawfully possessed of the slaves. He later sued for arrears of the annuity and was met by the plea that he was not lawfully possessed of the slaves. Lord Mansfield rejected the plea, saying: "Where mutual covenants go to the whole of the consideration on both sides, they are mutual conditions. But where they only go to a part, where a breach may be paid for in damages, there the defendant has a remedy on his covenant and shall not plead it as a condition precedent. If this plea were allowed any one negro not being the property of the plaintiff would be a bar to the action." In later cases, the contrast between the *whole* and a *part* of the consideration was not, however, taken quite literally. In *Duke of St Albans v Shore*[48] a contract was made for the sale of land with the timber on it. Before conveyance the vendor cut down a considerable part of the timber, and, on the purchaser's refusal to perform, sued him for the penalty payable under the contract on breach. The action failed for a number of reasons, one of which was that the timber might have been the *chief* inducement to the purchaser to enter into the contract. The fact that the timber formed only *part* of the consideration to be provided by the vendor was not decisive. Later dicta state that the plaintiff in *Boone v Eyre* would have lost if he had had no title *to the land*,[49] or if he had been lawfully possessed only of a single one of the slaves.[50] These discussions of *Boone v Eyre*, rather than the terms of the judgment in that case, may be considered to have established the requirement that a party who has only partly performed his obligations may nevertheless enforce the contract if the failure in performance does not "substantially" deprive the other party of what he bargained for.

(2) When failure is substantial

The question when a failure in performance "substantially" deprives a party of what he bargained for, or (as it is sometimes put) "frustrates" his purpose in making the contract gives rise to very great difficulty. The frequent references in the cases to breaches which "substantially" deprive a party of what he bargained for or "go to the root" of a contract are not particularly helpful in analysing the law or in predicting the course of future decisions. It is submitted that the courts, in applying the general requirement of substantial failure,[51] generally classify a failure in performance with an eye on the consequences. On the one hand, they consider whether rescission (as opposed to damages) is necessary to protect the injured party and, on the other hand, they take into account the prejudice which rescission will cause to the other party. If, on balancing these factors, they conclude that the injured party should be allowed to rescind, they will classify the failure in performance as "substantial" in order to produce the desired result; and conversely.[52] An attempt will be made in the following pages to illustrate this

---

[46] See below, pp.778–811.
[47] (1777) 1 Hy.Bl. 273n.; 2 W.Bl. 1312.
[48] (1789) 1 Hy.Bl. 270.
[49] *Glazebrook v Woodrow* (1799) 8 T.R. 366 at 374.
[50] *Ellen v Topp* (1851) 6 Ex. 424 at 442.
[51] Different factors govern the exceptions discussed at below, pp.778–811.
[52] *Decro-Wall International SA v Practitioners in Marketing Ltd* [1971] 1 W.L.R. 361 at 380.

approach. The decisions are for the most part soundly based on practical considerations; though it must be admitted that these do not always appear very clearly from the judgments.

(a) UNJUST ENRICHMENT. Where the requirement of substantial failure applies,[53] the courts are reluctant to allow a party to refuse to perform if he has received a benefit from the other party's partial or defective performance and cannot, or will not, restore that benefit. The point may be illustrated by a further distinction between *Boone v Eyre* and *Duke of St Albans v Shore*. In the former case the plantation had actually been conveyed to the defendant,[54] and a judgment in his favour would have enabled him to escape liability for a part of the price which might have exceeded the value of the slaves. In the latter case, however, it was said that "this is not an action of covenant where one party has performed his part, but is brought for a penalty on the other party refusing to execute his contract".[55] In such a case the claimant "ought punctually, exactly and literally to perform his part".[56] These words may suggest that an action on an executory contract in a case like *Boone v Eyre* would have failed even if the vendor had lacked title to only a single slave; but if this was indeed ever the law it has been neutralised by the developments about to be discussed.

(b) ADEQUACY OF DAMAGES. Sometimes the main reason for allowing rescission is that damages would not adequately compensate the injured party.

(i) *General principle.* In *Vigers v Cook*[57] an undertaker had contracted to make arrangements for the funeral of the defendant's son, but so negligently constructed the coffin that it could not be taken into the church where the funeral service was held. He was not entitled to recover any part of his charges as it was "an essential part of the funeral that the body should be taken into the church so that the service might be read in its presence".[58] The breach was one for which a money payment could not compensate. But where the loss suffered in consequence of the breach can be valued with relative certainty, an award or allowance of the sum so assessed will be regarded as an adequate remedy, more suitable than rescission.[59] For example, in one case the fact that a party was persistently late in making payments under a long-term contract was held not to be a ground of rescission, since the other party suffered no prejudice except in having to pay a relatively small amount of interest on the outstanding sums, and this loss could easily have been recovered from the party in breach.[60]

(ii) *Specific performance with compensation.* The same principle is illustrated by the equitable jurisdiction to order specific performance of contracts for the sale of land with "compensation"—*i.e.* at a price reduced to take account of a deficiency or defect.[61] In

---

[53] In cases falling within an exception to the requirement, rescission often does lead to unjust enrichment, *e.g.* where one party's refusal to pay is justified by the other's failure to perform an "entire" obligation; below, pp.782–784.

[54] This is stressed by Ashurst J. in (1777) 2 W.Bl. 1312 at 1314n. (*e*).

[55] (1789) 1 Hy.Bl. 270 at 279; for a similar argument, see *Graves v Legg* (1854) 9 Ex. 709 at 717.

[56] (1789) 1 Hy.Bl. 270 at 279.

[57] [1919] 2 K.B. 475; *cf. Sinclair v Bowles* (1829) 9 B. & C. 92.

[58] [1919] 2 K.B. 475 at 479. Had the defendant claimed damages he would (at least as the law then stood) have recovered nothing for injury to his feelings: below, pp.987–994.

[59] *cf.* the rule that specific relief may be refused where the more appropriate remedy is in damages: below, pp.1020–1026.

[60] *Decro-Wall International SA v Practitioners in Marketing Ltd* [1971] 1 W.L.R. 361. The payments were due under bills of exchange, so that common law the rule by which interest is not recoverable as general damages for non-payment of money did not apply: see below, p.784. For another case in which rescission was not justified as damages were an adequate remedy, see *The Angelia* [1973] 1 W.L.R. 210. *cf.* also below, p.828.

[61] Harpum [1981] C.L.J. 47.

one case[62] compensation was allowed where the area of land sold was stated to be "about 1200 square yards" and was in fact 935 square yards. But the jurisdiction will not be exercised (so that specific performance will not be ordered) where the defect is "substantial"[63]; and the test for determining whether the defect is of this character appears to be whether adequate compensation can be made for it by a monetary adjustment.[64] The same test applies where the contract itself provides that errors and misdescriptions shall not annul the sale but shall give rise to a claim for compensation.[65] Such a clause can (unlike the equitable jurisdiction) be invoked even after the contract has been performed[66]; but (like the equitable jurisdiction) it is normally inapplicable where the defect is "substantial".[67] Cases concerning such clauses can be regarded as illustrating what later became known as the doctrine of fundamental breach. They would therefore now turn on the construction of the clause in question, rather than on any rule of substantive law making it impossible to exclude the right to rescind.[68] On the other hand, a clause of this kind is not subject to the test of reasonableness under ss.2 to 4 of the Unfair Contract Terms Act 1977 since those sections do not apply to any contract so far as it relates to the creation or transfer of an interest in land.[69] This could be an important point where a developer entered into a contract for the sale of a house on written standard terms which would otherwise be subject to the requirement of reasonableness under s.3 of the Act.[70] It is not entirely clear whether the Unfair Terms in Consumer Contracts Regulations 1999 would apply to clauses of the kind here under discussion in contracts for the sale of land.[71]

A misdescription may not form part of the contract but be a misrepresentation inducing it; or it may originate as such a misrepresentation and be later incorporated in the contract. Under the Misrepresentation Act 1967, there is, in such a case, a right to rescind for misrepresentation,[72] but this is subject to the discretion of the court to declare the contract subsisting and to award damages in lieu of rescission.[73] Where the defect is not "substantial" the court will probably uphold the contract and award "damages"; and it seems likely that these will be assessed in much the same way as that in which "compensation" for misdescription was assessed in equity. The main difference between the old equitable and the new statutory powers is that the latter can be exercised even after conveyance.[74] The further question then arises whether, in cases of the present kind, a contract term restricting remedies for misdescription would be ineffective on the ground that it failed to satisfy the test of reasonableness imposed by s.3 of the Misrepresentation Act 1967.[75] Before that Act, it was held that a term which excluded

---

[62] *Aspinalls to Powell and Scholefield* (1889) 60 L.T. 595.

[63] *Re Fawcett and Holmes' Contract* (1889) 42 Ch.D. 150; *Jacobs v Revell* [1900] 2 Ch. 858; *Watson v Burton* [1957] 1 W.L.R. 19; *Strover v Harrington* [1988] Ch. 390 at 411.

[64] *Cato v Thomson* (1882) 9 Q.B.D. 616, 618; *Rudd v Lascelles* [1900] 1 Ch. 815; if the defect is substantial the party prejudiced by it may, instead of rescinding, claim specific performance, but only without compensation: *Durham v Legard* (1865) 34 Beav. 611.

[65] Harpum [1992] C.L.J. 263.

[66] *Bos v Helsham* (1866) L.R. 2 Ex. 72; *Re Turner and Skelton* (1879) 13 Ch.D. 130; *Palmer v Johnson* (1884) 13 Q.B.D. 351.

[67] *Flight v Booth* (1834) 1 Bing.N.C. 370; *cf. Walker v Boyle* [1982] 1 W.L.R. 495 (above, p.386).

[68] See above, p.225.

[69] Unfair Contract Terms Act 1977, Sch.1, para.1(c). For attempts to exclude liability for misrepresentation, see above, p.385; below at n.75.

[70] See above, p.253.

[71] See above, pp.277–280.

[72] s.1(a); above, pp.375–376.

[73] s.2(2); above, p.357.

[74] s.1(b); above, p.377.

[75] As substituted by Unfair Contract Terms Act 1977, s.8; above, p.385.

the right to rescind *and* the right to compensation entitled the vendor to enforce the contract without compensation.[76] Now such a term might be regarded as unreasonable in so far as it excluded the purchaser's right to compensation, or his right to rescind for a misrepresentation relating to a matter of substantial importance.[77] But if that matter was of only minor importance and the term, while excluding the right to rescind, *provided* for compensation, it is submitted that the requirement of reasonableness would normally be satisfied; for in such a case the term would not prejudice the purchaser. It would merely give contractual effect to the right that the vendor would have had, even in the absence of the term, to specific performance with compensation, or to the result that the court would be likely to reach in the exercise of its discretion to declare the contract subsisting and to award damages in lieu of rescission.[78]

These rules as to "compensation" in sales of land should be contrasted with the rule that a quantitative defect in delivery under a contract for the sale of goods generally justifies rescission,[79] even though it causes little prejudice to the buyer, and even though compensation for it may be quite easy to assess. It is, however, unlikely that this rule applies where a specific parcel of goods is sold and is said to contain a different quantity from that which it in fact contains,[80] *e.g.* where the sale is of "a cargo of 1,000 tons" in a named ship which actually contains only 950 tons. Such cases constitute the closest analogy to the land cases, so that the treatment of the two types of contract is not so radically different as might at first sight appear.

(c) Ratio of failure to the performance undertaken. The higher the ratio of the failure is to the performance undertaken, the more likely it is that the court will regard the failure as substantial. Thus where a buyer of oil deliverable in two instalments without justification refused to accept one of them (and added that he would not accept any other delivery) it was held that the seller was entitled to rescind.[81] On the other hand, in the *Maple Flock* case[82] a contract provided for delivery of 100 tons of rag flock in instalments of $1\frac{1}{2}$ tons at the rate of three instalments a week. The sixteenth instalment contained an excessive amount of chlorine and one reason why the court held that this breach did not entitle the buyers to rescind was that it related to a single instalment which bore only a small quantitative ratio to the contract as a whole.[83] Similarly, in the *Hongkong Fir* case,[84] a ship began service under a 24 month time charterparty. She was later found to be unseaworthy and to need extensive repairs which took altogether 20 weeks to complete. The charterers purported to rescind on a number of grounds,[85] one

---

[76] *Re Courcier and Harrold's Contract* [1923] 1 Ch. 565.

[77] *Walker v Boyle* [1982] 1 W.L.R. 495; *Cremdean Properties Ltd v Nash* (1977) 244 E.G. 547; *South Western General Property Co v Marton* (1982) 263 E.G. 2631.

[78] See above, after n.73.

[79] See below, p.783.

[80] See *Levi v Berk* (1886) 2 T.L.R. 898 at 899; *Benjamin's Sale of Goods* (6th ed.), §21–033; *Ellis v Hodder & Tolley Ltd* (1914) 33 N.Z.L.R. 362.

[81] *Warinco AG v Samor SpA* [1979] 1 Lloyd's Rep. 450.

[82] *Maple Flock Co Ltd v Universal Furniture Products (Wembley) Ltd* [1934] 1 K.B. 148; *cf. Simpson v Crippin* (1872) L.R. 8 Q.B. 14 (failure by buyer to take delivery). For such instalment contracts, the vague language of Sale of Goods Act 1979, s.31(2) gives virtually no guidance on the question when a breach justifies rescission. Contrast the very rigid rule laid down by s.30(1) with respect to short delivery (modified, in the case of non-consumer sales, by s.30(2A) as inserted by Sale and Supply of Goods Act 1994, s.4(2)), below p.783.

[83] *cf. Financings Ltd v Baldock* [1963] 2 Q.B. 104; *Eshun v Moorgate Mercantile Credit Co Ltd* [1971] 1 W.L.R. 722; *The Seaflower* [2000] 2 Lloyd's Rep. 37 at 41; in further proceedings ([2001] 1 Lloyd's Rep. 341) the term in question was held to be a condition, so that its breach entitled the victim to rescind without having to show that the failure in performance was substantial.

[84] *Hong Kong Fir Shipping Co Ltd v Kawasaki Kisen Kaisha Ltd* [1962] 2 Q.B. 26.

[85] See also below, pp.774, 777, 795.

of which was that the delay caused by the unseaworthiness was such as to "frustrate" their purpose in entering into the contract. One reason why this argument was rejected was that the ship was still available, after the completion of repairs, for 17 out of the original 24 months of the charterparty.[86]

(d) UNCERTAINTY AS TO FUTURE PERFORMANCE. In the case of continuing contracts, calling for repeated acts of performance over a period of time, the courts are influenced by the need to remove the uncertainty which may result from failure to perform some of those acts. In *Bradford v Williams*,[87] for example, the defendant's ship was chartered for one year from May to May; but in September the charterers wrongfully refused to provide a cargo. This refusal justified the defendant in putting an end to the contract as "no cross-action for damages would have fully compensated him".[88] In such a cross-action it might be alleged that he had failed to mitigate[89] by finding substitute employment for the ship. It would be hard for him to know for how long such employment should be sought, since, if the original charterparty had remained in force, the charterers might later have demanded further performance, and the shipowner would be bound to have his ship available in response to such a demand. Again, the failure of a house-buyer to pay a deposit as required by the contract gives rise to uncertainty in depriving the vendor of an important safeguard against eventual default; and accordingly it justifies rescission by the vendor.[90]

By way of contrast, further reference may be made to the *Hongkong Fir*[91] case, where it was said that, once major repairs were begun, there was no reasonable ground for believing that the ship would not be available for service within a fairly short and predictable time.[92] In the *Maple Flock* case[93] the court similarly stressed that the sellers' business was well conducted, that the source of the defect could easily be tracked down, and that the likelihood of its recurrence was small. Such likelihood has also been stressed where a seller has sought to rescind an instalment contract because of the buyer's refusal to pay in accordance with its terms.[94] Similarly, the insolvency of a buyer who has failed to pay may justify the seller's refusal to perform (at least in the sense that he need no longer deliver *on credit*) if it is unlikely that the buyer or his trustee in bankruptcy will eventually be able to pay in accordance with the contract.[95] On the other hand, mere delay in payment will not of itself justify rescission. In the *Decro-Wall* case[96] an English company had been appointed "sole concessionaires" for the sale in the United Kingdom

---

[86] [1962] 2 Q.B. 26 at 40, *per* Salmon J. On this issue the Court of Appeal simply approved Salmon J.'s judgment without giving reasons of their own: see [1962] 2 Q.B. 26 at 61, 73.

[87] (1872) L.R. 7 Ex. 259; *The Sanko Iris* [1987] 1 Lloyd's Rep. 487.

[88] (1872) L.R. 7 Ex. 259 at 269.

[89] See below, p.976.

[90] *Myton Ltd v Schwab-Morris* [1974] 1 W.L.R. 331 (for disapproval of this case on another point, see above, p.763); *Millichamp v Jones* [1982] 1 W.L.R. 1422 at 1430 (where the claim to rescind failed on the ground that the vendor should first have given notice of default); *The Blankenstein* [1985] 1 W.L.R. 435 at 446.

[91] [1962] 2 Q.B. 26.

[92] *i.e.* by September 1957: [1962] 2 Q.B. 26 at 40. *cf. The Hermosa* [1982] 1 Lloyd's Rep. 570, where it was held that a charterer was not entitled to rescind even though his "demand for reassurance" (p.580) was not met. The case seems near the line; the American principle of "adequate assurance of performance" (U.C.C. ss.2–609, Restatement 2d, *Contracts* §251) would be useful in such a situation. See also *Rice v Great Yarmouth BC, The Times*, July 26, 2000.

[93] [1934] 1 K.B. 148.

[94] Contrast *Withers v Reynolds* (1831) 2 B. & Ad. 882 with *Mersey Steel and Iron Co v Naylor Benzon and Co* (1884) 9 App.Cas. 434 and *Freeth v Burr* (1874) L.R. 9 C.P. 208; below, pp.807–810.

[95] *Ex p. Chalmers* (1873) L.R. 8 Ch.App. 289; *Bloomer v Bernstein* (1874) L.R. 9 C.P. 588; Insolvency Act 1986, s.345(1) and (2); *Leyland Daf Ltd v Automotive Products plc, The Times*, April 6, 1993, affirmed, *The Times*, April 9, 1993.

[96] *Decro-Wall International SA v Practitioners in Marketing Ltd* [1971] 1 W.L.R. 361.

of decorative tiles manufactured by a French company. The English company was persistently (though only slightly) late in making payments under the contract. One reason[97] why this did not justify rescission by the French company was that the delays did not give it any reason to doubt that payment would be made as soon as the goods had been disposed of.

The need to remove uncertainty as to future performance is, again, one factor which helps to explain the distinction between *Poussard v Spiers*[98] and *Bettini v Gye*.[99] In the former case the defendants had engaged Mme Poussard to play the leading part of Friquette in a new opera which was to open at the Criterion Theatre on November 28, 1874; the engagement was to last for three months "providing the opera shall run for that period."[1] On November 23 Mme Poussard fell ill and on November 25 the defendants entered into a contract with a Miss Lewis. This provided that Miss Lewis was to be ready to play Friquette on November 28 if Mme Poussard had not recovered by then; and that, if Miss Lewis did perform on that day, she was to be engaged for four weeks, until December 25. On November 28 Mme Poussard "continued in bed and ill"[2] so that Miss Lewis performed and acquired the right to go on performing until December 25. On December 4 Mme Poussard had recovered and offered to take her place, but the defendants refused to take her back. The jury found that her illness was not so "material" as to entitle the defendants to rescind the contract; that the arrangement with Miss Lewis "as made" was reasonable; and that the defendants were liable in damages for their refusal to have Mme Poussard back at any time. But the court held that the defendants' refusal was justified and that they were not liable in damages. What chiefly influenced the court was that Mme Poussard's illness "was a serious one of uncertain duration"[3] and that the defendants could not put off the opening night till she had recovered. The court considered the alternative possibility that the defendants might have found a temporary substitute, but rejected it on the ground that "no substitute capable of performing the part adequately could be engaged except on the terms that she should be permanently engaged. . . . "[4] In fact Miss Lewis's engagement expired on December 25 and it would have been possible for the defendants to take Mme Poussard back after that date. This was (according to one of the reports)[5] the argument put forward by counsel for the claimant; and it evidently impressed the jury.[6] It is not at all clear from the judgment why it was rejected by the court.

---

[97] For another see above, p.771.

[98] (1876) 1 Q.B.D. 410.

[99] (1876) 1 Q.B.D. 183.

[1] It in fact ran for more than three months.

[2] (1876) 1 Q.B.D. 410 at 413.

[3] (1876) 1 Q.B.D. 410 at 415.

[4] *ibid.*

[5] (1876) 24 W.R. 819.

[6] The damages awarded by the jury amounted to £83 and it is possible to guess how this figure was reached. Mme Poussard was engaged for three months (or 13 weeks) at £11 per week. Miss Lewis was engaged for four weeks at £15 per week. £83 is the difference between (a) the amount which Mme Poussard would have earned in the remaining nine weeks (£99), and (b) the extra amount which the defendants had had to pay to Miss Lewis (£4 per week for four weeks, or £16). Of course, this method of assessment cannot be supported in law as it overlooks, on the one hand, the fact that Mme Poussard was not liable to the defendants for the extra expense of hiring Miss Lewis (see below, p.776); and, on the other, the possibility that Mme Poussard might have mitigated by accepting another engagement. According to the report of the trial in *The Times* (November 22, 1875, p.11) Mme Poussard refused an offer of another engagement in December "thinking that her agreement with the defendants was still in force"; perhaps she was advised by a French lawyer who took the view that the contract could be rescinded only by a court order: see French Civil Code, art.1184. She finally obtained another engagement in Paris on February 28, 1875—the very day on which her engagement with the defendants expired.

In *Bettini v Gye*[7] the defendant, who was director of the Royal Italian Opera at Covent Garden, engaged Bettini "to fill the role of primo tenor assoluto in the theatres, halls and drawing rooms . . . in Great Britain and Ireland" from March 30 to July 13, 1875, that being the period of the Covent Garden season in 1875. The contract provided that Bettini should sing "in concerts as well as in operas"; that he should not "sing anywhere out of the theatre" (*i.e.* Covent Garden) during 1875 without the written permission of the defendant "except at a distance of more than 50 miles from London *and* out of the season of the theatre"; and that he was "to be in London without fail at least six days before the commencement of his engagement for the purpose of rehearsals." Bettini was prevented by temporary illness from being in London until March 28. He gave no advance notice of this delay to the defendant, and when he arrived in London the defendant refused to accept his services. In holding that this refusal was unjustified the court stressed two factors: first, that Bettini had been engaged to sing in operas and concerts for a 15-week season and the failure to attend at rehearsals could affect only a small part of this period[8]; secondly, that he had been "deprived of the power of earning anything in London from January 1st to March 30th."[9] The court also said that the defendant "must . . . seek redress by a cross-claim for damages".[10] This carries at any rate a hint that such a cross-claim had some chance of success, though it is hard to reconcile with the statement in *Poussard v Spiers* that the failure to appear in that case "having been occasioned by sickness was not any breach".[11] But there are many other grounds for distinguishing between the two cases. Bettini was not engaged to play any particular part; there is no suggestion that any substitute was engaged to take his place; he was available when the season opened; there is nothing to show that his failure to arrive in London six days before then in any way affected the opening night; and once he did arrive, there was no uncertainty about his future availability. *Bettini v Gye* was decided on a demurrer, so that the facts were never established, and it is hard from the facts as stated to see any practical justification for the defendant's attitude.

Even where a breach does create uncertainty as to future performance, the need to remove it may be overcome by the desire to prevent unjust enrichment. Thus in one case[12] it was held that long delay in payment of the *final* instalment due on a sale of land did not justify rescission by the vendor.

(e) ULTERIOR MOTIVES FOR RESCISSION. It sometimes happens that a party's real motive for wishing to rescind is not that there has been some failure in performance, but that the contract was, or has because of market movements become, a bad bargain for him.[13] In such circumstances the courts will often (if the case is one to which the general requirement of substantial failure applies[14]) hold that the failure in performance is not sufficiently serious and so refuse to allow rescission. The underlying policy has been

---

[7] (1876) 1 Q.B.D. 183.

[8] It is this point rather than the fact that Bettini's engagement was to sing in *concerts* and operas which should be stressed, for it is clear from the contract read as a whole that its main purpose was to engage Bettini for the Covent Garden season of 1875. There are many indications of this: for example, the dates of the engagement and the fact that the contract, though made in Milan on December 14, 1874, was headed "Royal Italian Opera, Covent Garden, London Year 1875."

[9] At 188. *Quaere* whether this in fact prejudiced Bettini; he may well have been taking part in an opera season elsewhere during this period.

[10] (1876) 1 Q.B.D. 183 at 189.

[11] (1876) 1 Q.B.D. 410 at 414.

[12] *Cornwall v Henson* [1900] 2 Ch. 298.

[13] *cf.* above, p.761.

[14] Where exceptions to the requirement apply, refusal to perform has often been allowed even though the motive for it fairly clearly was to escape from a bad bargain, *e.g. Cunliffe v Harrison* (1851) 6 Exch. 901, below, p.787; *Arcos v Ronaasen* [1933] A.C. 470, below p.793.

stated by Roskill L.J.: "Contracts are made to be performed and not to be avoided according to the whims of market fluctuation."[15]

The point is illustrated by *Dakin v Oxley*[16] where a shipowner in breach of contract had damaged the cargo, which, on arrival, was worth less than the freight. It was held that the cargo-owner was not justified in abandoning the cargo and refusing to pay freight. One reason given was that "It would be unjust and almost absurd that . . . *the risk of a mercantile adventure should be thrown upon the shipowner* by the mere accident of the value of the cargo [when undamaged] being worth little more than the freight."[17]

Similar considerations may also have influenced the decision in the *Hongkong Fir* case.[18] By the time the ship had been repaired, there had been a "catastrophic fall in the freight market"[19] to 13s. 6d. per ton, as against the 47s. per ton reserved in the charterparty.[20] In a 24 month charterparty the risk of such a fall in the freight market would normally be on the charterer; and the court was probably reluctant to allow him to throw it back on the shipowner by putting an end to the charterparty. It may also be relevant that the shipowner's breaches did not (so far as appears from the report) cause the charterer any loss at all.[21] But if a charterer can show that the owner's breach *was* a source of serious prejudice to him, he will not be prevented from rescinding merely because there has been a steep fall in the freight market. This is particularly true if his conduct shows that his real motive for rescinding was to avoid the prejudice caused by the breach, and not to escape from what has turned out to be a bad bargain.[22]

(f) OTHER FACTORS. The factors influencing decisions as to the availability of rescission by reason of the effects of a failure in performance cannot be exhaustively classified. Even where none of the factors discussed above is present, rescission may nevertheless be justified. In *Aerial Advertising Co v Batchelor's Peas Ltd*,[23] for example, the claimants agreed to conduct an advertising campaign for the defendants. On Armistice Day 1937 one of the claimants' aeroplanes set out with a banner bearing the message "Eat Batchelor's Peas." Unfortunately the aeroplane towed the banner over the main square of Salford, Lancashire, at the precise time when a large crowd was gathered there observing the two-minute silence. The effect of this breach of contract was described as "disastrous",[24] and it was held that the defendants were justified in refusing to accept further performance of the contract. Again, where a contract presupposes the continuation of a relationship involving personal confidence, it is possible for some isolated act of one party to destroy that confidence and so to justify rescission by the other.[25] In some of the cases, rescission was held to be justified because the nature or effects of the breach were regarded as sufficiently "serious" in ways that are hard to explain or even to

---

[15] *The Hansa Nord* [1976] Q.B. 44 at 71; *cf. The Gregos* [1994] 1 W.L.R. 1465 at 1475.
[16] (1864) 15 C.B.(N.S.) 647.
[17] *ibid.* at 667–668; italics supplied.
[18] [1962] 2 Q.B. 26; above, p.773.
[19] *ibid.* at 39.
[20] [1961] 2 All E.R. at 261.
[21] On the contrary, the shipowner's breaches can be said to have benefited the charterer by relieving him for 20 weeks from the obligation to pay the high rate of hire reserved by the charterparty, since, while the ship was under repair, she was "off hire".
[22] *cf. Federal Commerce Navigation Co Ltd v Molena Alpha Inc* [1979] A.C. 757.
[23] [1938] 2 All E.R. 788.
[24] *ibid.* at 792.
[25] See *Denmark Productions Ltd v Boscobel Productions Ltd* [1969] 1 Q.B. 699, where it was held by a majority that rescission was not justified on the facts. *cf.* also the employers' right to rescind the original service agreement in *Bell v Lever Bros Ltd* [1932] A.C. 161 (above, p.289).

articulate.[26] Such a vague notion has its dangers, but it cannot be altogether eliminated from a discussion of this branch of the law.

4. Exceptions to the Requirement of Substantial Failure

The preceding discussion attempts to identify factors that influence decisions on the issue of substantial failure in performance; but it must be admitted that their practical operation is not easy to predict. In the interests of greater certainty, the law therefore recognises a number of exceptions[27] to the requirement of substantial failure. Inevitably, the resulting certainty has sometimes been achieved only at the expense of justice, so that these exceptions have attracted an increasing weight of criticism.

(1) Express provision for determination

(a) LITERAL ENFORCEMENT IN GENERAL. A contract may expressly provide that one party shall be entitled to rescind in the event of some specified failure by the other to perform. For example, a voyage charterparty may stipulate that the ship is expected to be ready to load at a named port on (or about) a specified date, and that if she fails to arrive there within (say) 10 days of that date the charterer shall be entitled to cancel; and a time charterparty may provide either that the owner shall be entitled to withdraw the ship if hire is not punctually paid, or that the charterer shall be entitled to cancel if the ship becomes unavailable for service for more than a specified number of days.[28] The purpose of such clauses is to prevent disputes from arising as to the often difficult question whether the failure in performance is sufficiently serious to justify rescission; and they take effect even though there is no substantial failure.[29] For example, under a clause in a time charterparty entitling the shipowner to withdraw the ship if the charter fails to pay hire by a specified day, the shipowner can exercise his right of withdrawal immediately on such failure[30]; and he can do this even though the charterer tenders payment very soon after it was due, even though the short delay in payment causes the shipowner little prejudice, and even though his motive for withdrawal is simply that the freight market has risen. Such clauses are literally enforced because, in cases of this kind, "certainty is of primary importance"[31]; while the charterer can mitigate the severity of the clause by insisting (if his bargaining position permits) on the inclusion of a so-called "anti-technicality" provision allowing days of grace or requiring notice of default before withdrawal.[32] The principle of literal enforcement similarly applies where a contract for the sale of land specifies a completion date and provides that, on the purchaser's failure

---

[26] See *Bright v Ganas*, 189 A. 427 (1936), where a servant forfeited all rights to pay for four-and-a-half years' service by writing a love-letter to his employer's wife.

[27] For a further special exception in the law of agency, see above, pp.745–747.

[28] *The Span Terza (No.2)* [1984] 1 W.L.R. 27; such a clause avoids the difficulties that arose in the *Hong Kong Fir* case [1962] 2 Q.B. 26, above p.773. For similar cancelling clauses in contracts for the sale of ships, see *The Solholt* [1983] 1 Lloyd's Rep. 605; *The Oro Chef* [1983] 2 Lloyd's Rep. 509; *cf.* also *Bettini v Gye* (1876) 1 Q.B.D. 183 at 187.

[29] Such clauses are probably not within s.3(2)(b)(ii) of the Unfair Contract Terms Act 1977 for the reasons given on p.254, above, and because rescission under such clauses terminates the primary obligations of *both* parties; *cf. The Super Servant Two* [1990] 1 Lloyd's Rep. 1 at 7, distinguishing between cancellation and exemption clauses.

[30] *The Brimnes* [1975] Q.B. 929; *The Laconia* [1977] A.C. 850; Rose, 30 C.L.P. 213; *cf. The Chikuma* [1981] 1 W.L.R. 314; Mann, 97 L.Q.R. 379–382.

[31] *The Laconia* [1977] A.C. 850 at 878; *The Lutetian* [1982] 2 Lloyd's Rep. 140 at 159; *cf. The Chikuma*, above, at p.322.

[32] As in *Libyaville* [1975] 1 Lloyd's Rep. 537; and in *Federal Commerce and Navigation Co Ltd v Molena Alpha Inc* [1979] A.C. 757. *cf. The Laconia*, above, at 878; *The Rio Sun* [1981] 2 Lloyd's Rep. 489; [1982] 1 Lloyd's Rep. 404; *The Afovos* [1983] 1 W.L.R. 195.

to comply with any of the terms of the contract, the vendor is to be entitled to rescind. In one such case[33] the vendor declared the contract rescinded one minute after the time fixed for completion and the rescission was held to be effective, so that the purchaser was not entitled to specific performance on tendering the purchase price a mere ten minutes after that time. Again this conclusion was supported on the ground that "the parties should know with certainty that the terms of the contract will be enforced".[34]

Although, for the reasons just given, the law normally gives literal effect to express provisions for determination, it does insist on compliance with three requirements. First, the party who relies on the express term as justifying rescission for a breach which is not serious must show that the term does, as a matter of construction, apply to that breach. Thus where a term in a four-year maintenance contract allowed one party to terminate in the event of the other's breach of "*any* of its obligations under the contract", it was held that even this emphatic language did not have this effect.[35] Secondly, the party seeking to terminate must act strictly in accordance with the terms of the clause. For example, a voyage charterparty may provide that the charterer can cancel if the ship is not at the port of loading by September 30. The charterer would not be entitled to cancel on September 29, even though at that time the ship was so far away from the port that she could not possibly get there the next day.[36] Conversely where a time charterparty gives the shipowner the right to give notice of withdrawal, if hire is not paid on the due day, he is not entitled to exercise that right before the end of that day, even though the bank at which payment was to be made had already closed so that the charterer could not possibly have made the payment in accordance with the contract.[37] Thirdly, the party relying on the express provision must terminate without undue delay. Thus, in cases of non-payment of hire by a time charterer it has been said that the shipowner must exercise his right to withdraw the ship "within a reasonable time after default".[38]

(b) RELIEF AGAINST FORFEITURE IN CERTAIN CASES.[39] The willingness of the courts to give effect to express provisions for determination is, in the cases so far discussed, based on the assumption that the parties have bargained on more or less equal terms.[40] Where this is not the case, the law has developed restrictions on the right of a party to rely on an express provision for determination. This is the position where a lease entitles the landlord to forfeit if the tenant breaks *any* covenant; and where a regulated hire-purchase agreement[41] entitles the owner to terminate it if the hirer defaults in the

---

[33] *Union Eagle Ltd v Golden Achievement Ltd* [1997] A.C. 514.

[34] *ibid.* at 519; *cf. ibid* at 523; *cf. Kazakstan Wool Processors (Europe) Ltd v Nederlandsche Credietverzekering Madtschappig NV* [2000] 1 All E.R. (Comm) 708 at 720.

[35] *Rice v Great Yarmouth BC, The Times*, July 26, 2000; it was admitted that the clause did not allow termination for a "trivial" breach. *Cf. Wickman Ltd v Schuler AG* [1974] A.C. 235, below, p.792.

[36] *The Mihalis Angelos* [1971] 1 Q.B. 164; *cf. The Madeleine* [1967] 2 Lloyd's Rep. 224 at 243.

[37] *The Afovos* [1983] 1 W.L.R. 195; *cf.* above, p.723. The form of a notice of default under an "anti-technicality" clause must similarly comply strictly with the requirements of that clause: *The Pamela* [1995] 2 Lloyd's Rep. 249.

[38] *The Laconia* [1977] A.C. 850 at 872; *The Balder London* [1980] 2 Lloyd's Rep. 489 at 892–893; *The Scaptrade* [1981] 2 Lloyd's Rep. 425 at 430, affirmed without reference to this point [1983] 2 A.C. 699; *The Oro Chef* [1983] 2 Lloyd's Rep. 509; *cf. The Great Marine* [1990] 2 Lloyd's Rep. 245 at 249 (right to cancel sale of ship, under an express term, lost by delay of one week). The rule is based either on waiver or on an implied term that the right to withdraw must be exercised within a reasonable time: see *The Antaios* [1985] A.C. 191. It seems to be restricted to cases of rescission under an express term: see *Nichimen Corp v Gatoil Inc* [1987] 2 Lloyd's Rep. 46 at 54.

[39] Smith [2001] C.L.J. 178 (written before the decision of the House of Lords in the *On Demand Information* case, below, n.50.

[40] See *The Scaptrade* [1983] Q.B. 529 at 539–540 approved [1983] 2 A.C. 699.

[41] See above, p.178.

payment of even a single instalment. In such cases the provision for determination would deprive a party who committed some quite minor breach of the benefit of a contract which he has for a long period performed satisfactorily; and the court may allow him a period of grace within which to make good his default.[42] Normally such "relief against forfeiture" only gives the party in breach extra time to perform[43]; but sometimes such relief is allowed even though the breach cannot be remedied at all. Thus where a tenant had innocently broken a covenant against subletting it was held that the landlord could not enforce a forfeiture clause, as the breach had not prejudiced him in any way.[44] Further statutory restrictions apply to a landlord's right to forfeit certain long leases of dwelling houses for non-payment by the tenant of rent or certain other charges.[45]

In some of the time charterparty cases discussed above, it was suggested that relief against forfeiture should be granted to a charterer who failed to pay hire on time, and that the exercise by the shipowner of his right to withdraw the ship under a withdrawal clause should be restricted accordingly.[46] But the House of Lords has rejected these suggestions[47] for two reasons. First, the courts should give effect to commercial agreements concluded (as time charters usually are) between parties who had bargained on equal terms. Secondly, the principle of relief against forfeiture was restricted to cases where the party in breach would, if the contract were literally enforced, be deprived of "proprietary or possessory rights",[48] while a time charter conferred only contractual rights, being merely a contract for services to be rendered by the shipowner.[49] The first of these lines of reasoning states a policy ground for restricting relief against forfeiture in commercial situations; the second specifies the legal technique for giving effect to that policy. In the charterparty cases both lines of reasoning supported the conclusion that there should be no relief against forfeiture. But in other situations the two lines of reasoning may tend to support diverging conclusions since a contract of a "commercial" nature may confer "proprietary or possessory rights" on the party in breach: for example where a finance lease is granted to that party of equipment used by him in the course of his business. It has been held that, in such a case, the court has power to grant relief against forfeiture and that such relief could be given even after the lessor had retaken possession of and resold the subject-matter of the lease.[50]

The distinction between terms which deprive a party of "proprietary or possessory rights" and those which deprive him only of contractual rights can, moreover, be a fine one. The point can be illustrated by contrasting two cases. In the *Sport International* case[51] it was held that relief against forfeiture was not available where A granted B a licence to use certain trade-marks and the contract provided that the licence was to determine on B's default. But in *BICC plc v Burndy Corp*[52] such relief was held to be available where an agreement by which certain patents were vested in A and B provided

[42] See Consumer Credit Act 1974, ss.88, 89; requiring formal notice of termination and giving the hirer at least seven days to make good his default; and the rules relating to relief against forfeiture of leases: Law of Property Act 1925, s.146. *cf.* also the rules as to damages, discussed on pp.853–855, below. Relief was denied to a hirer, who had been a persistent defaulter, in *Goker v NWS Bank plc* [1990] C.C.L.R. 34.

[43] See *Nutting v Baldwin* [1995] 1 W.L.R. 201 at 208.

[44] *Scala House & District Property Co Ltd v Forbes* [1974] Q.B. 575.

[45] Commonhold and Leasehold Reform Act 2002, ss.167–170.

[46] *The Afovos* [1980] 2 Lloyd's Rep. 477 at 479, reversed on other grounds [1983] 1 W.L.R. 195; *The Tropwind* [1982] 1 Lloyd's Rep. 232 at 234.

[47] In *The Scaptrade* [1983] 2 A.C. 694 and see the authorities cited above, p.778, n.31.

[48] *The Scaptrade* [1983] 2 A.C. 694 at 702; *cf. SCI (Sales Curve Interactive) v Titus SARL* [2001] EWCA Civ 591; [2001] 2 All E.R. (Comm) 416, at [47].

[49] *The Scaptrade*, above, at 702; *Jones v Society of Lloyd's*, *The Times*, February 2, 2000.

[50] *On Demand Information plc v Michael Gerson (Finance) plc* [2002] UKHL 13; [2002] 2 W.L.R. 919.

[51] *Sport International Bussum BV v Inter-Footwear Ltd* [1984] 1 W.L.R. 776; Harpum, 100 L.Q.R. 369.

[52] [1985] Ch. 232.

that, on B's default, he should assign his rights in the patents to A. No doubt the cases are technically distinguishable on the ground that the actual *assignment* of a patent involves a transfer of "property", while the *termination of a contractual licence* to use a trade-mark does not. But from a commercial point of view a licence to use such forms of "intellectual property" often serves the same purpose as an actual transfer; and the practical effect of the clause in each case was to deprive the party in default of the right to make use of the "property." Where, as in the *BICC* case, the courts have recognised the availability of relief against forfeiture in a commercial context, the *policy* stated in the charterparty cases (of giving effect to commercial agreements between parties bargaining on equal terms) has in effect been subordinated to the *legal technique* used in those cases to give effect to that policy. What was regarded in those cases as a *necessary* condition for the power to grant relief is regarded, in such cases as the *BICC* case, as a *sufficient* condition for the existence (though not for the exercise) of that power. It is, with respect, open to question whether this development is consistent with the emphasis on the requirements of commercial certainty in a number of House of Lords and Privy Council decisions concerned with express provisions for determination.[53]

The view that power to grant relief arises merely because forfeiture would deprive the party in breach of a proprietary or possessory interest is also hard to reconcile with the rules which apply where a purchaser of land fails to complete at the agreed time. By virtue of the conclusion of the contract, the purchaser acquires an equitable interest in the land; but if he fails to complete at the time stipulated in the contract and the vendor rescinds under an express term entitling him to do so on account of that breach, then the purchaser cannot get relief against forfeiture in the sense of obtaining an order of specific performance against the vendor.[54] At the most, he may be able to obtain "restitutionary . . . relief against forfeiture" by securing the return of a penal deposit.[55] The reason for this distinction is that the purpose of the express term is to "restore to the vendor his freedom to deal with the land as he pleases"[56] and relief by way of specific performance would (while restitutionary relief would not) make it impossible for the vendor to know with certainty when that freedom had indeed been restored.

(c) CONSUMER PROTECTION. An express cancellation clause in a standard contract between a commercial seller of goods or supplier of goods or services and a consumer may also be open to challenge under the Unfair Terms in Consumer Contracts Regulations 1999 on the ground that it is "unfair" to the consumer and hence not binding on him.[57] The list of *prima facie* invalid terms given in the Regulations indeed refers only to cancellation clauses in contracts "of indeterminate duration"[58]; but as the list is "non-exhaustive" this restriction would not preclude the court from holding that a cancellation clause in a fixed-term contract was also unfair.

(d) INVALIDITY ON OTHER GROUNDS. It is arguable that in exceptional circumstances an "oppressive" cancellation clause may be open to attack at common law in accordance with the principles discussed in Chapter 7, or at least restricted in its operation so that the power to cancel can be exercised only on reasonable grounds.[59] Provisions entitling

---

[53] See *The Laconia* [1977] A.C. 850; *The Chikuma* [1981] 1 W.L.R. 314; *The Scaptrade* [1983] 2 A.C. 694; *Union Eagle Ltd v Golden Achievement Ltd* [1997] A.C. 514.

[54] *Union Eagle Ltd v Golden Achievement Ltd* [1997] A.C. 514; the fact that the purchaser has been let into possession and has improved the land may entitle him to such relief: *ibid.* at 520.

[55] See below p.1008.

[56] *Union Eagle* case, above, at 520.

[57] SI 1999/2083, reg.8(1); above, pp.267–283.

[58] reg.5(5) and Sch.2, para.1(g).

[59] *Timeload Ltd v British Telecommunications plc* [1995] E.M.L.R. 459 at 467.

a party to refuse to make payments under a contract in default of exact performance by the other may also be invalid as penalties.[60]

(2) Entire and severable obligations[61]

(a) ENTIRE OBLIGATIONS. A contractual obligation is said to be "entire" when the contract requires it to be *completely* performed by one party (A) before the other (B) is to pay, or to render such other counter-performance as may have been agreed.[62] Complete performance by A is sometimes said to be a "condition precedent" to B's liability; but the cases are not necessarily concerned with disputes as to the *order* of performance.[63] Often the dispute arises because A's purported performance, though rendered in the stipulated order, is in some way incomplete or defective.

Where A fails to complete performance of an entire obligation, B is entitled to refuse to pay even though the deficiency in A's performance causes him little prejudice or none at all. At common law A is not even generally entitled to any other recompense for the partial performance which he has rendered. In *Cutter v Powell*[64] a seaman agreed to serve on a ship bound from Jamaica for Liverpool; he was to be paid 30 guineas "ten days after the ship arrives at Liverpool . . . provided he proceeds, continues and does his duty . . . from hence to the port of Liverpool." On August 2 the ship sailed from Jamaica; she arrived at Liverpool on October 9, but the seaman had died on September 20. It was held that his administratrix could not recover for the work he had done before his death; for the contract meant that nothing was to be paid unless and until he had served for the whole voyage. At the ordinary rates of pay then prevailing, he would have earned only £8 for such a voyage. The higher rate of pay seems to have been intended to throw the risk of his completing the voyage on him. Lord Kenyon C.J. said: "It was a kind of insurance".[65] The result was that the administratrix recovered neither the 30 guineas, nor a proportionate part of it, nor a reasonable sum for the six or seven weeks' service which the deceased had rendered. According to one case, the same rule applies even where a contract of employment is terminated by mutual consent.[66]

Similarly, where a contract for the carriage of goods by sea provides that freight is to become due on arrival of the goods at the agreed destination, the shipowner cannot recover either the stipulated freight, or freight *pro rata*, if he is compelled to abandon the voyage by perils of the sea and to discharge the cargo at an intermediate port.[67] The same

---

[60] See *Gilbert-Ash (Northern) Ltd v Modern Engineeering (Bristol) Ltd* [1974] A.C. 689; below, p.1006.
[61] Williams, (1941) 57 L.Q.R. 373 at 490. (This article must be read in the light of the Law Reform (Frustrated Contracts) Act 1943.)
[62] Such a term is not affected by Unfair Contract Terms Act 1977, s.3(2)(b)(ii) for the reason stated at p.254, above; and also because B is not claiming to be entitled to render no performance "in respect of his contractual obligation": his case is rather that, before A's performance, he is not under any relevant obligation. Nor are the Unfair Terms in Consumer Contracts Regulations 1999 (above, pp.267–283) likely to affect the effectiveness of such a term. Reg.8(1) applies to contracts between a commercial seller or supplier and a consumer and provides that unfair standard terms in such contracts do not bind *the consumer*. Any entire obligation which may be imposed by such a contract is likely to be that of the *supplier*. The Regulations do not apply to contracts relating to employment: see Dir.93/13, Recital 10, above, p.278, so that they would not apply to cases such as *Cutter v Powell*, below, n.64.
[63] cf. above, p.761.
[64] (1795) 6 T.R. 320; Stoljar, 34 Can.Bar.Rev. 288; Dockray, 117 L.Q.R. 626.
[65] (1795) 6 T.R. 320 at 324. *Quaere* whether it was really insurance against the death of members of the crew, or against their desertion. For possible effects of the Apportionment Act 1870 and of the Law Reform (Frustrated Contracts) Act 1943 in a case like *Cutter v Powell*, see below, pp.824, 914.
[66] *Lambourn v Cruden* (1841) 2 M. & G. 253.
[67] *Vlierboom v Chapman* (1844) 13 M. & W. 230; *St. Enoch Shipping Co Ltd v Phosphate Mining Co* [1916] 2 K.B. 624; cf. *The Fort Kip* [1985] 2 Lloyd's Rep. 168.

rule applies where a ship is abandoned at sea and later saved by third parties[68] and it applies even though the shipowner's failure to get to the agreed destination is due, not to his breach, but to an excepted peril or to the act of a third party for whom he is not responsible.[69] The rule can be excluded by contrary provision in the contract, *e.g.* by one to the effect that freight is to be deemed to have been *earned* on loading.[70] In such a case, the shipowner can recover the freight even though the contract provides that it is to be *paid* on or after unloading: that provision affects only the *time* of payment, not the creation of the obligation to pay.[71]

The same principle is again illustrated by *Sumpter v Hedges*[72] where a builder agreed to build two houses for the defendant on the latter's land for a lump sum of £565. When the houses were still unfinished the builder told the defendant that he had run out of money and could not finish the work; and the defendant later completed the houses himself. It was held that the builder could not recover the agreed sum; nor could he recover a reasonable remuneration for his work as there was no evidence of a "new contract" to pay such a sum.[73]

As a general rule, a contract for the sale of goods is considered to impose an entire obligation with regard to the quantity contracted for.[74] If the seller fails to deliver the correct quantity the buyer is not bound to accept and pay (though if he does accept he must pay at the contract rate).[75] The rule applies where the seller delivers *more* than the quantity contracted for just as much as where he delivers less.[76] The rule is, however, subject to a number of qualifications. First, it can be varied by the provisions of the contract, *e.g.* by one calling for delivery of "about" the stipulated quantity, or for "five per cent more or less"[77] (though such a margin must not be exceeded).[78] Secondly, the rule does not permit rejection for a wholly trivial discrepancy, *e.g.* for an excess of 55 lbs, in a contract calling for delivery of 4,950 tons of wheat.[79] Thirdly, the rule is subject to a statutory exception which applies where the buyer does *not* deal as a consumer: in such a case he may not reject the whole of the quantity actually delivered on account of a shortfall or excess which is "so slight that it would be unreasonable for him to do so".[80] It seems that a defect may be "slight" for the purpose of this exception even though it is not wholly trivial within the common law exception stated above. The statutory exception applies only where the discrepancy is slight *and* it would be unreasonable for the buyer to reject. Thus it does not apply merely because the discrepancy is "slight,"

---

[68] *The Kathleen* (1874) L.R. 4 A. & E. 269; *The Cito* (1881) 7 P.D. 5; contrast *Bradley v H Newsom, Sons & Co* [1919] A.C. 16 (where there was no abandonment).

[69] As in *The Kathleen* (1874) L.R. 4 A. & E. 269.

[70] *The Dominique* [1989] A.C. 1056; Crabtree [1989] L.M.C.L.Q. 289; *The Karin Vatis* [1988] 2 Lloyd's Rep. 330.

[71] See the authorities cited in n.70; contrast *The Lorna I* [1983] 1 Lloyd's Rep. 373 (where there was no stipulation as to when the freight was *earned*, but only one as to when it was to be *paid*).

[72] [1898] 1 Q.B. 673; *cf. Munro v Butt* (1858) 8 E. & B. 738; *Bolton v Mahadeva* [1972] 1 W.L.R. 1009.

[73] For this requirement, see below, pp.819–820.

[74] See *Oxendale v Wetherell* (1829) 9 B. & C. 386–387; *Reuter v Sala* (1879) 4 C.P.D. 239; *cf. Cobec Brazilian Trading & Warehousing Corp v Alfred C Toepfer* [1983] 2 Lloyd's Rep. 386.

[75] Sale of Goods Act 1979, s.30(1). (It is assumed that the goods are not "unsolicited" within Consumer Protection (Distance Selling) Regulations 2000, SI 2000/2334, reg.24, above, p.9.) Conversely, the buyer cannot insist on delivery of less than he agreed to accept: *Honck v Muller* (1881) 7 Q.B.D. 92.

[76] Sale of Goods Act 1979, s.30(2).

[77] *e.g. Re Thornett and Fehr and Yuills* [1921] 1 K.B. 219; Sale of Goods Act 1979, s.30(5).

[78] *Tamvaco v Lucas* (1859) 1 E. & E. 581.

[79] *Shipton Anderson & Co v Weil Bros* [1912] 1 K.B. 574.

[80] Sale of Goods Act 1979, s.30(2A), as inserted by Sale and Supply of Goods Act 1994, s.4(2) (giving effect to the Law Commission's recommendation in Law Com. No.160 (1987) para.6.20). Where *too much* is delivered, the buyer can in any event reject *the excess*.

for it may nevertheless be commercially reasonable for the buyer to reject[81]; nor, where the discrepancy is *not* "slight," does the exception apply merely because it would be unreasonable for the buyer to reject (*e.g.*, where his sole motive for rejection was to escape from a bad bargain[82]). The uncertainty caused by the vagueness of the statutory exception is mitigated by the fact that the exception can be excluded by contrary agreement[83]; and it is submitted that it would be so excluded where the contract had expressly stipulated for a margin and that margin had been exceeded. Finally, the rule entitling the buyer to reject merely on account of quantitative defects does not apply where the contract provides for delivery by instalments, so that, where short delivery is made of one instalment the buyer is not entitled to refuse to accept either future deliveries, or even the instalment in question.[84]

The rule that a party cannot recover anything for partial performance of an entire obligation also applies where that party was willing to complete performance but was justifiably prevented from completing by the other party, *e.g.* where an employee is dismissed for misconduct.

(b) SEVERABLE OBLIGATIONS. A contract imposes severable obligations if payment under it is due from time to time as performance of a specified part of the contract is rendered. This is the situation under contracts of employment, which typically provide for payment to be made at weekly or monthly intervals, even though the contract may be expressed to continue for longer periods. Similarly, in building contracts the rule in *Sumpter v Hedges*[85] is often excluded by provision for "progress payments", to be made as specified as stages of the work are completed. The principle can be further illustrated by contrasting *Cutter v Powell*[86] with the case in which a seaman agrees to serve at a fixed rate *per month*; under such a contract, he can recover his pay for each completed month although he fails to complete the voyage for which he was engaged.[87] This would be so even though no money was actually to be *paid over* until the end of the voyage. On the same principle, a piece-rate worker does not forfeit wages already earned simply because it was agreed that nothing should actually be paid out to him till the end of each working week and he left or was lawfully dismissed before the end of the week.[88] Similarly, a contract for the sale of goods may be made severable by providing for delivery and payment in instalments. In all these cases, no more than the specified part of the performance need be rendered before the corresponding payment can be claimed. It is also true that, as a general rule, the specified part must be rendered in full. Thus an employee cannot at common law[89] recover his current pay if he is justifiably dismissed for misconduct during the period at the end of which he is to be paid.[90]

---

[81] *e.g.*, because he has resold under a contract from which s.30(2A) is excluded: see below, at n.83.

[82] As in *Cunliffe v Harrison* (1851) 6 Ex. 901, below, p.787, where the excess (of 50 per cent) was far from "slight".

[83] Sale of Goods Act 1989, s.30(5).

[84] *Regent OHG Aisenstadt und Barig v Francesco of Jermyn Street* [1981] 3 All E.R. 327: such a case is governed by s.31(2) of the Sale of Goods Act 1979. For the contrast between s.31(2) and s.30(1), see above, p.773, n.82. *Quaere* whether s.30(1) should not apply to the short-delivered instalment itself.

[85] [1898] 1 Q.B. 673; above, p.783.

[86] (1795) 6 T.R. 320; above, p.782.

[87] *Taylor v Laird* (1856) 25 L.J.Ex. 329; *Button v Thompson* (1869) L.R. 4 C.P. 330.

[88] *Warburton v Heyworth* (1880) 6 Q.B.D. 1.

[89] For the position under the Apportionment Act 1870, s.2, see below, p.824.

[90] *Ridgway v Hungerford Market Co* (1835) 3 A. & E. 171; *Boston Deep Sea Fishing & Ice Co v Ansell* (1888) 39 Ch.D. 339. *Semble* that he can recover remuneration which became due before dismissal though it was earned after a breach of duty justifying dismissal: *Healey v SA Française Rubastic* [1917] 1 K.B. 947. As to commission on transactions tainted by bribes, see above, p.746. For the position where the employee is *not* dismissed see below, pp.821–822.

Where a contract imposes severable obligations, a party who has fully performed the specified part can recover the corresponding payment even though his failure to complete the whole of the promised performance is a breach of contract. In *Ritchie v Atkinson*[91] a shipowner agreed to carry a cargo at a stipulated rate *per ton*. He carried only part of the cargo, and was entitled to recover a corresponding proportion of the freight. But he was later held liable in damages for failing to carry the rest of the cargo.[92] There is a similar liability in damages where performance of one of the specified parts is completed but is defective because it in some way falls short of the performance promised. For example, an employee may serve for the full payment period but fail or refuse, in the course of that period, to carry out some task which he was contractually obliged to perform. The employer is then entitled to damages in respect of that failure or refusal even though he may be bound to pay the agreed remuneration.[93] Whether he is so bound, and what other remedies may be available to him, are matters to be discussed later in this Chapter.[94]

(c) DISTINCTION BETWEEN ENTIRE AND SEVERABLE OBLIGATIONS. In discussions of the cases so far considered, it is sometimes said that the *contracts* are entire or severable. But this is misleading: what is entire or severable is a particular *obligation*[95] arising under the contract. The point is most easily illustrated by reference to contracts for the carriage of goods by sea. Suppose a shipowner agrees to carry 1,000 tons at a stated rate, due on delivery, for each ton carried to London. If he carries 1,000 tons to Southampton he is not entitled to any freight[96]; if he carries 750 tons to London he is *prima facie* entitled to three quarters of the freight[97]; and if he carries 1,000 tons to London but the goods arrive damaged, he will be entitled to full freight[98] unless the damage is so serious that the description under which the goods have been shipped ceases to apply to them: for example, where cement solidifies as a result of being damaged by water.[99]

The same point may be illustrated by further reference to *Cutter v Powell*[1]: the obligation to serve for the whole voyage was entire, but it has been said that, if the

---

[91] (1808) 10 East 295.

[92] *Atkinson v Ritchie, ibid.* at 530.

[93] *Sim v Rotherham Metropolitan BC* [1987] Ch. 216, where the measure of damages was not in dispute. In *Miles v Wakefield Metropolitan DC* [1987] A.C. 539 at 560 the measure of damages in case of an employee's refusal to perform the specified contractual duties for part of the agreed working time is said to be the wages for the "lost hours of work." *cf. ibid.* at 568. But these dicta were *obiter* (no claim for damages having been made); and strictly speaking the measure of damages should be the loss suffered by the employer, which is not necessarily the same as the wages for the lost hours. *cf.* below, pp.944, 1056–1057.

[94] See below, pp.786, 821–822.

[95] *cf. Cobec Brazilian Trading & Warehousing Corp v Alfred C Toepfer* [1982] 1 Lloyd's Rep. 528 at 531 ("indivisible obligation"); affirmed [1983] 2 Lloyd's Rep. 386; *Baltic Shipping Co Ltd v Dillon* (1993) 176 C.L.R. 344 at 350.

[96] See above, pp.782–783; below, p.820.

[97] *Ritchie v Atkinson* (1808) 10 East 295. If the contract provides for a "lump sum" freight, the shipowner will, in such a situation, be entitled to the entire freight: *Merchant Shipping Co v Armitage* (1873) L.R. 9 Q.B. 99; *Thomas v Harrowing SS Co* [1915] A.C. 58. He will also be entitled to the whole freight if the contract provides for freight to be computed by reference to the quantity taken on board though it is only payable after discharge of the cargo: see *The Aries* [1977] 1 W.L.R. 185; *The Metula* [1978] 2 Lloyd's Rep. 5; unless the contract provides for a deduction to be made if the quantity delivered is less than that taken on board, as in *The Olympic Brilliance* [1982] 2 Lloyd's Rep. 205.

[98] *Dakin v Oxley* (1864) 15 C.B.(N.S.) 646; *The Brede* [1974] Q.B. 233 (no freight was allowed in respect of a part of the goods that was *lost:* see [1972] 2 Lloyd's Rep. at 514, 519; but the Court of Appeal was concerned only with the part of the goods that was *damaged:* [1974] Q.B. at 245).

[99] *Duthie v Hilton* (1868) L.R. 4 C.P. 138; *cf. The Caspian Sea* [1980] 1 W.L.R. 48; *Dakin v Oxley*, above, at p.664; below, p.817; contrast *Britannia Distribution Co Ltd v Factor Pace Ltd* [1998] 2 Lloyd's Rep. 420 at 423.

[1] (1795) 6 T.R. 320; above, p.782.

seaman had completed the voyage and had been guilty during it of occasional breaches of duty, then the administratrix could have enforced the contract,[2] subject to a deduction in respect of any loss caused by those breaches.[3] Again, a building contract may provide for payments as the work progresses, subject to a "retention fund" to be paid over on completion. There is then a series of severable obligations to complete each stage as well as an entire obligation to complete the whole.[4] In *Sumpter v Hedges*[5] the builder's obligation was entire with respect to the quantity of work to be done; but his claim would not have been dismissed merely because he had failed in some other way to comply with the contract, *e.g.* by completing a week late[6] or (unless the contract had expressly made his right to payment subject to his doing the work strictly in accordance with the contract)[7] by completing the buildings with minor defects. Thus in *Hoenig v Isaacs*[8] the claimant contracted to redecorate and furnish the defendant's flat for £750. There were minor defects in the furniture, which could have been made good for £55. The defendant argued that the claimant was entitled to no more than a reasonable remuneration for work done in accordance with the contract. But the court held that he was entitled to be paid at the full contract rate (less the cost of making the defects good), as he had substantially completed the work. The obligation of a seller of goods is, again, generally entire as to quantity, but if the correct quantity is delivered he may be able to enforce the contract in spite of the fact that the goods are defective in quality.[9] Of course failure to perform an obligation which is not entire may give the other party a right to rescind on some other ground, *e.g.* that the failure is substantial; but it does not give him this right under the present rule.

In the cases so far discussed the distinction between entire and severable obligations is clearly settled either by the express terms of the contract or by commercial practice recognised by law. But there may be no rule of law on the point and the contract may be silent or self-contradictory, *e.g.* where A employs B to paint A's house for £1,000 but fails to say when it is to be paid; or where the contract provides for payment of "£200 per room payable on completion." In such cases the question whether a particular obligation is entire or severable is one of construction; and where a party agrees to do work under a contract, the courts are reluctant to construe the contract so as to require complete performance before any payment becomes due. "Contracts may be so made; but they require plain words to shew that such a bargain was really intended".[10] If the contract contains contradictory provisions the courts tend to give greater weight to those making the obligation to work a severable one. Thus where a contract provided (1) for payment at a fixed rate per month, but (2) that nothing was to be paid till performance was complete, the first clause prevailed over the second, *i.e.* the contract was construed

---

[2] *Hoenig v Isaacs* [1952] 2 All E.R. 176 at 178.

[3] *cf. Sim v Rotherham Metropolitan BC* [1987] Ch. 216; *Miles v Wakefield Metropolitan DC* [1987] A.C. 539 at 570 (no right to withhold pay for "bad work" without proof of loss). (For statutory restrictions on the right to deduct damages from wages, see Employment Rights Act 1996, Pt II, below, p.788, n.32.)

[4] *Hoenig v Isaacs*, above, at 181.

[5] [1898] 1 Q.B. 673.

[6] *ibid.* at 676.

[7] *Eshelby v Federated European Bank* [1932] 1 K.B. 423.

[8] [1952] 2 All E.R. 176; approving *Dakin & Co Ltd v Lee* [1916] 1 K.B. 566, which had been doubted in *Eshelby v Federated European Bank* [1932] 1 K.B. 423; *Williams v Roffey Bros & Nicholls (Contractors) Ltd* [1991] 1 Q.B. 1; below, p.787, n.23.

[9] *e.g.* below, pp.795–796.

[10] *Button v Thompson* (1869) L.R. 4 C.P. 330 at 342; *cf. Roberts v Havelock*; (1832) 3 B. & Ad. 404; *Davidson v Jones-Fenleigh* (1980) 124 S.J. 204.

as imposing severable obligations.[11] In one type of case this hostility towards entire obligations has been reinforced by statute: an agreement by a seaman to abandon his right to wages in case the ship is lost is void.[12]

The reason why the courts are reluctant to construe obligations to do work as entire is that such a construction will often lead to the unjust enrichment of the party receiving the partial or defective performance.[13] There is no such reluctance in contracts for the sale of goods: we have seen that the buyer is not generally bound to accept a different quantity from that contracted for[14]; nor is he bound, unless the contract so provides,[15] to accept delivery in instalments.[16] This state of the law does not give rise to any danger of unjust enrichment: if a buyer of goods rejects delivery of the wrong quantity, the goods will be returned to the seller. But even in this type of case rejection may cause a different type of hardship to the seller, namely that of throwing back on him the risk of market fluctuations. In *Cunliffe v Harrison*[17] a seller of wine delivered more than the agreed quantity. It was held that the buyer was not bound to accept any part of the wine, "although it may be that the refusal to take the wine was not bona fide but grounded upon the fact that the wine had fallen in price".[18]

(d) SO-CALLED DOCTRINE OF SUBSTANTIAL PERFORMANCE.[19] Cases such as *Hoenig v Isaacs*[20] are sometimes explained on the ground that the claimant had "substantially" performed an "entire contract".[21] It is submitted that the explanation is unsatisfactory since it is based on the error that *contracts*, as opposed to particular *obligations*, can be entire.[22] The basis of *Hoenig v Isaacs* is that the builder, even if he was under an entire obligation as to the quantity of work to be done, was under no such obligation as to its quality.[23] Defects of quality therefore fell to be considered under the general requirement of substantial failure, and on the facts there was no such failure.[24] To say that an obligation is entire *means* that it must be completely performed before payment becomes due. Suppose a contract is made to carry goods from Melbourne to London and the freight is payable on delivery in London. If the goods are carried only to Southampton, the carrier may have "substantially" performed; but he is not entitled to the freight.[25]

---

[11] See *The Juliana* (1822) 2 Dods. 504.
[12] Merchant Shipping Act 1995, s.38(1) (reversing the common law rule that freight was the "mother of wages").
[13] See below, pp.819–820.
[14] See above, p.783.
[15] On this question of construction, contrast *Reuter v Sala* (1879) 4 C.P.D. 239 with *Brandt v Lawrence* (1876) 1 Q.B.D. 344.
[16] Sale of Goods Act 1979, s.31(1).
[17] (1851) 6 Ex. 901.
[18] *ibid.* at 907; of course it is possible that the seller was not acting bona fide either but that he was trying to unload an excessive quantity on a falling market.
[19] Beck, 38 M.L.R. 413.
[20] [1952] 2 All E.R. 176; above, p.786.
[21] *Geipel v Smith* (1872) L.R. 7 Q.B. 404 at 411; *cf. Dakin v Lee* [1916] 1 K.B. 566 at 598; *Sim v Rotherham MBC* [1987] Ch. 216 at 253; *Wiluszynski v Tower Hamlets L.B.C.* [1989] I.C.R. 493 at 499; *Williams v Roffey Bros & Nicholls (Contractors) Ltd* [1991] 1 Q.B. 1 at 8–10; no such view is in terms stated by the court in *Hoenig v Isaacs*, above.
[22] See above, p.785.
[23] *Williams v Roffey Bros & Nicholls (Contractors) Ltd* [1991] 1 Q.B. 1 (where a subcontractor recovered instalments subject to a "small deduction for defective and *incomplete* items" (*ibid.* at 17) purports to follow *Hoenig v Isaacs*, but that case was concerned only with defective, not with incomplete, items.
[24] Contrast *Lawson v Supasink* (1984) Tr.L. 37 (where qualitative defects in kitchen installations were sufficiently serious to justify rescission).
[25] See above, p.782; *cf. Metcalfe v Britannia Ironworks* (1877) 2 Q.B.D. 423.

In relation to "entire" obligations, there is no scope for any doctrine of "substantial performance".

(3) Conditions, warranties and intermediate terms

(a) STATEMENT OF THE DISTINCTION. English law has for some considerable time recognised a distinction between two classes of contractual terms: conditions and warranties. "Condition" is here used (in its promissory sense[26]) to refer to a contractual term, the breach of which gives the injured party the right to rescind the contract. Of course he need not rescind but may instead affirm; and he can claim damages whether he affirms[27] or rescinds.[28] A warranty, on the other hand, is a term "the breach of which gives rise to a claim for damages but not to a right . . . to treat the contract as repudiated,"[29] so that the injured party is not entitled to rescind merely[30] on account of such a breach.[31] The injured party can generally set up the damages to which he is entitled by reason of a breach of warranty in diminution or extinction of the price[32] and if they are equal to, or exceed, the price he will not have to pay anything. Such an outcome may seem to resemble rescission (in the sense of refusal to pay); but the process differs from rescission in that it requires the injured party to prove both the breach and his loss, while rescission requires him to prove no more than the breach.

(b) NATURE OF THE DISTINCTION. Earlier in this Chapter we saw that the phrases "condition precedent" and "concurrent condition" were used to make a point about the

---

[26] See above, p.62.

[27] e.g. Aruna Mills Ltd v Dhanrajmal Gobindram [1968] 1 Q.B. 655; the test of affirmation seems to be the same here as in the law of misrepresentation so that mere lapse of time will not suffice: Allen v Robles [1969] 1 W.L.R. 1193; cf. above, p.385.

[28] See, e.g. Millar's Machinery Co Ltd v David Way & Son (1935) 40 Com.Cas. 204; Lesters Leather & Skin Co Ltd v Home & Overseas Brokers Ltd (1949) 82 Ll.L.Rep. 203; Heaven & Kesterton Ltd v Et Francois Albiac & Cie [1956] 2 Lloyd's Rep. 316; New India Assurance Co Ltd v Yeo Beng Chao [1972] 1 W.L.R. 786; Microbeads AG v Vinshurst Road Markings Ltd [1975] 1 W.L.R. 218 at 225; cf. General Billposting Co v Atkinson [1909] A.C. 118; Kwei Tek Chao v British Traders and Shippers Ltd [1954] 2 Q.B. 459 at 473 (but see ibid. at 477); and cf. below, p.851.

[29] Sale of Goods Act 1979, s.61(1) (definition of "warranty").

[30] See below, pp.804–805.

[31] cf. United Scientific Holdings Ltd v Burnley BC [1978] A.C. 904, 945; and see below, p.796, n.13. For a possible statutory exception, see below, p.805.

[32] Sale of Goods Act 1979, s.53(1)(a); cf. the right of a buyer who "deals as consumer" (see s.61(5A) of the 1979 Act) in certain cases to "require the seller to reduce the price", as an alternative to rescission for breach of condition, under s.48C(1)(a) of the 1979 Act (as inserted by Sale and Supply of Goods to Consumers Regulations 2002 (SI 2002/3045, reg.5)). The measure of such price reduction is not, however, necessarily the same as the measure of damages under s.53(3): see below, p.952. For the right to set off damages against agreed sums to be paid under other types of contracts, see Gilbert-Ash (Northern) Ltd v Modern Engineering (Bristol) Ltd [1974] A.C. 689. Sim v Rotherham MBC [1987] Ch. 216; UCB Leasing v Holtom [1987] R.T.R. 362; Connaught Restaurants Ltd v Indoor Leisure Ltd [1994] 1 W.L.R. 501; Eller v Grovecrest Investments Ltd [1995] Q.B. 272; cf. Miles v Wakefield MDC [1987] A.C. 539; for statutory restrictions, see Employment Rights Act 1996, Pt. II. The process is not available against a claim for freight under a voyage charterparty: The Brede [1974] Q.B. 233; The Aries [1977] 1 W.L.R. 185. Although this rule was described as "anomalous" in James & Co Scheepvaart en Handelmij BV v Chinacrest Ltd [1979] 1 Lloyd's Rep. 126 at 129, and as "arbitrary" in Dole Dried Fruit and Nut Co v Trustin Kerwood Ltd [1990] 2 Lloyd's Rep. 309 at 310 it has been extended in various ways: The Cleon [1983] 1 Lloyd's Rep. 587; RH & D International Ltd v SAS Animal Air Services Ltd [1984] 2 All E.R. 203; The Elena [1986] 1 Lloyd's Rep. 425; The Khian Captain (No.2) [1986] 1 Lloyd's Rep. 429; The Dominique [1989] A.C. 1059 (applying the rule to a repudiatory breach on account of which the charterer rescinded); United Carriers Ltd v Heritage Food Group (UK) Ltd [1996] 1 W.L.R. 371 (domestic carriage); Britannia Distribution Co Ltd v Factor Pace Ltd [1998] 2 Lloyd's Rep. 420 at 423. For the similar position under time charterparties, see Federal Commerce Navigation Co Ltd v Molena Alpha Inc [1978] Q.B. 927; affirmed without deciding this point [1979] A.C. 997; The Kostas Melas [1981] 1 Lloyd's Rep. 18 at 25; The Cebu [1983] Q.B. 1005 at 1011–1012; The Aditya Vaibav [1991] 1 Lloyd's Rep. 573.

order of performance.[33] At this stage, the word "condition" is used to make a different point, namely, one about the *conformity*[34] of the performance rendered with that promised. In the first of these two senses, the *performance* by one party may be a "condition precedent" to the liability of the other; in the second it is a *term* of the contract which is described as the "condition". It is perfectly possible for a party to comply with a condition in one of these senses but not in the other: for example, a seller of goods by sample who has agreed to give credit may deliver the goods before being paid and so perform a "condition precedent," but if the goods turn out not to correspond with the sample he will be in breach of "condition".[35] The distinction was formerly obscured by use of the phrase "condition precedent" in cases concerned with conformity, rather than with order of performance[36]: thus "condition precedent" was used to refer both to a term of a contract and to an event, *i.e.* the prior or concurrent performance by one party before that of the other became due. The use of the same phrase in these two senses is, however, confusing since the effects of one party's failure to perform a "condition precedent" or a "concurrent condition" differ in two ways from those of breach of "condition" (as opposed to warranty). First, a failure of the former kind only justifies refusal by the injured party to perform for so long as the failure continues[37]; while breach of condition justifies rescission in the sense of an outright refusal[38] to perform and to accept further performance from the party in breach. Secondly, the injured party's right to refuse to perform so long as a condition precedent or concurrent condition remains unperformed can be exercised without any previous election by the injured party (whose position is simply that his performance is not yet due[39]); while such an election is required for the purpose of the more drastic remedy of rescission (in the sense of an outright refusal of the kind just described) for breach of condition.[40] Modern authority accordingly recognises the distinction between the two concepts[41] and tends[42] to use the phrase "condition" when discussing conformity, and "condition precedent" when discussing the order of performance. That usage is adopted in this Chapter so that "condition precedent" is contrasted with "concurrent condition" and "independent covenant"; while "condition" (without any qualifying adjective) is contrasted with "warranty" and "intermediate term".[43]

---

[33] See above, p.761.

[34] Conformity includes time of performance: it is possible for performance to be rendered at the wrong *time* but in the right *order: e.g.* where goods are sold for cash on delivery on January 1 but are delivered on January 8.

[35] See below, p.792.

[36] *e.g. Glaholm v Hays* (1841) 2 Man. & G. 257, 267; *Behn v Burness* (1863) 3 B. & S. 751 at 755: *Bentsen v Taylor* [1893] 2 Q.B. 274 at 281.

[37] See above, pp.765–766.

[38] It is assumed that the time for "curing" the breach, under the rule stated at p.698 above, has expired.

[39] See *The Good Luck*, [1992] 1 A.C. 233 at 262.

[40] See below, p.754.

[41] *e.g. State Trading Corporation of India v M Golodetz Ltd* [1989] 2 Lloyd's Rep. 277 at 284 treating "condition" and "condition precedent" as distinct concepts; Treitel, 106 L.Q.R. 185; *cf. Universal Bulk Carriers Ltd v Andre & Cie* [2001] EWCA Civ 588; [2001] 2 Lloyd's Rep. 65 at [42]: "not a condition of the contract *or* a condition precedent to the performance by either party" (italics supplied).

[42] But not invariably: see, *e.g. The Aktion* [1989] 1 Lloyd's Rep. 283 at 285; *Soon Hua Seng Co Ltd v Glencore Grain Ltd* [1996] 1 Lloyd's Rep. 398 at 402; *The Niizura* [1996] 2 Lloyd's Rep. 66 at 70. For failure to recognise the distinction, see also *Alfred McAlpine plc v BAI (Run-off) Ltd* [2000] 1 Lloyd's Rep. 437 at 441, 444; requirement that insured must give notice of claim "as soon as possible" held not to be a "condition precedent" so that *delay* in giving such notice was no bar to a claim; but clearly notice had to be given *before* insurer could be held liable.

[43] See below, p.795.

PERFORMANCE

(c) BASES OF THE DISTINCTION. The distinction between conditions and warranties was originally based on two factors. One was the intention of the parties, as expressed in the contract: hence the question into which category a stipulation fell was treated as one of construction.[44] But often the intention of the parties in this respect was not discoverable from the words used; and so the courts relied secondly on the general requirement of substantial failure in performance. If "performance of the stipulation [went] to the very root . . . of the contract",[45] then the stipulation was treated as a condition. We shall see that a term may also be treated as a condition on other grounds[46]; but the actually or potentially serious effects of breach are still taken into account in deciding, in cases of first impression, whether the term broken is to be classified as a condition.[47] If a contractual term[48] relates to "a substantial ingredient in the identity of the thing sold",[49] it will be classified as a condition, and its breach will entitle the victim to rescind, on the theory that it would be unjust to require him to accept and pay for something which differed in an important way from that for which he had contracted. A warranty, on the other hand, concerns some less important or subsidiary element of the contract. Its breach does not entitle the victim to rescind, on the theory that a minor breach can be adequately remedied by the payment of money.

This approach can be seen in a number of cases in which decisions were based on the commercial importance of the term to the injured party: for example, if a buyer said that he would not buy goods at all unless they had a certain quality, then this fact would tend to support the view that an undertaking with respect to that quality was a condition.[50] Where there is no such evidence of intention, the court will base its decision on its own view of the commercial importance of the term. The older authorities on this question must be treated with caution, because in them the word "warranty" was sometimes used to refer to what would now be called a "condition".[51] But the cases do establish that there are certain terms the breach of which *prima facie* gives rise to a right to rescind and which are therefore "conditions" in the terminology now current. In *Behn v Burness*[52] a ship was described in a charterparty as "now in the port of Amsterdam" when in fact she was elsewhere. It was held that the charterer was entitled to rescind: the statement was a condition because of the commercial importance which charterers usually attach to such descriptive statements. Similarly, a statement that a ship will sail on a certain day

---

[44] *Glaholm v Hays* (1841) 2 Man. & G. 257 at 266; Sale of Goods Act 1979, s.11(3); *cf. Tradax Export SA v European Grain & Shipping Co* [1983] 2 Lloyd's Rep. 100; *George Hunt Cranes Ltd v Scottish Boiler & General Insurance Co Ltd* [2001] EWCA Civ 1964; [2001] 1 All E.R. (Comm) 366, at [10, 11].

[45] *Glaholm v Hays*, above, at 268; *cf. Bentsen v Taylor* [1893] 2 Q.B. 274 at 281.

[46] See below, p.791.

[47] Thus the fact that the breach is *not* likely to cause serious prejudice can support the view that the term is not a condition: see *State Trading Corporation of India v M Golodetz Ltd* [1989] 2 Lloyd's Rep. 277, below, p.799; *Alfred McAlpine plc v BAI (Run-off) Ltd* [2000] 1 Lloyd's Rep. 437 at 444; *The Mercandian Continent* [2001] EWCA Civ 1275; [2001] 2 Lloyd's Rep. 563, at [14].

[48] See *Harlingdon & Leinster Enterprises Ltd v Christopher Hull Fine Art Ltd* [1991] 1 Q.B. 564 at 586 (where the statement was held *not* to be a contractual term: above, p.355).

[49] *Couchman v Hill* [1947] K.B. 544 at 559.

[50] *cf. Bannerman v White* (1861) 10 C.B.(N.S.) 844; above, p.354.

[51] *e.g.* in *Behn v Burness* (1863) 3 B. & S. 751 at 755: "a warranty, that is to say a condition . . . ". A similar (though not identical) usage has survived in insurance law: see, below, p.846; *cf. Hadenfayre Ltd v British National Insurance Society* [1984] 2 Lloyd's Rep. 393 at 401. See also Food Act 1984, s.102(1)(a); *Lambert v Lewis* [1982] A.C. 225 at 273, 276, where Lord Diplock refers to the implied terms classified as *conditions* in s.14 of the Sale of Goods Act 1979 as "warranties"; and see *The Evia (No.2)* [1983] 1 A.C. 736 at 765.

[52] (1863) 3 B. & S. 751; *cf. The New Prosper* [1991] 2 Lloyd's Rep. 93 (statement as to ship's ability to comply with load port regulations); *The Aegean Dolphin* [1992] 2 Lloyd's Rep. 178 (statement as to speed of cruise ship).

has been treated as a condition in a charterparty.[53] The same is true of a statement in a charterparty that the ship is "expected ready to load" on or about a certain day.[54] The commercial importance of such a statement is, indeed, reduced by the rule that the shipowner will not be in breach merely because the ship is not ready on or about the day named. The term is broken only if the statement was made dishonestly or without reasonable grounds,[55] so that it does not give the charterer any firm assurance as to the date of readiness. The classification of the statement as a condition can, however, be justified on the ground that a shipowner who has made such a statement dishonestly or without reasonable grounds, is in a poor position to complain of any prejudice which he may suffer as a result of rescission.[56]

The reasoning of the cases discussed above is based on the requirement of serious failure in performance; and emphasis on this requirement gave rise at one time to the view that a term could be a condition *only* if "every breach . . . [of it would] . . . deprive the party not in breach of substantially the whole benefit which it was intended that he should obtain from the contract".[57] But this view was rejected by the House of Lords in *Bunge Corp v Tradax Export SA*, where Lord Roskill said that there were "many cases . . . where terms the breaches of which do not deprive the innocent party of substantially the whole benefit which he was intended to receive from the contract were nonetheless held to be conditions any breach of which entitled the innocent party to rescind".[58] The statement that "conditions . . . have the property that any breach of them is treated as going to the root of the contract"[59] must similarly be viewed with caution. It is accurate only in the sense that a breach of condition, like one going to the root of the contract, gives rise to a right to rescind; but that right arises, in the two cases, for different reasons. Where the breach *actually* "goes to the root of the contract", the right to rescind is intended to protect the injured party from serious prejudice; where the breach is one of condition, that right is intended to promote certainty, "without regard to the magnitude of the breach".[60] For this reason, breach of condition is here treated as an exception to, and not as an application of, the requirement of substantial failure in performance.

(d) EXPRESS CLASSIFICATION BY THE PARTIES. One basis for distinguishing conditions from warranties is the intention of the parties[61]; and the courts continue to rely on this factor where that intention can be ascertained.[62] Thus if a contract expressly says that a particular term is a condition,[63] that term will generally be so regarded; and the same is true where the contract expressly states that rescission will be available on breach of

---

[53] *Glaholm v Hays* (1841) 2 Man. & G. 257; *cf. Bentsen v Taylor* [1893] 2 Q.B. 274 (statement that ship "now sailed or about to sail" held to be a condition).

[54] *The Mihalis Angelos* [1971] 1 Q.B. 164; Horton Rogers, 34 M.L.R. 190; Greig, 89 L.Q.R. 93; *cf. The Mavro Vetranic* [1985] 1 Lloyd's Rep. 580 at 584 (estimated time of ship's arrival); *The Baleares* [1993] 1 Lloyd's Rep. 215 at 225.

[55] *Scrutton on Charterparties and Bills of Lading* (20th ed.), pp.92–94.

[56] *The Mihalis Angelos*, above, at 205. The charterer could also rescind for misrepresentation: *ibid.* p.194.

[57] *Hongkong Fir Shipping Co Ltd v Kawasaki Kisen Kaisha Ltd* [1962] 2 Q.B. 26 at 69, *per* Diplock L.J.; *cf. United Scientific Holdings v Burnley BC* [1978] A.C. 904 at 928.

[58] [1981] 1 W.L.R. 711 at 724; *cf. ibid.* at 715–716, 718. On this point the House of Lords followed the reasoning of Megaw L.J. in the Court of Appeal: see [1980] 1 Lloyd's Rep. 294 at 305. Lord Diplock himself took a similar view in *Photo Production Ltd v Securicor Transport Ltd* [1980] A.C. 827 at 849. His earlier view is, perhaps, reflected in *Gill & Duffus SA v Berger & Co Inc* [1984] A.C. 382 at 391.

[59] *Lombard North Central plc v Butterworth* [1987] Q.B. 527 at 535.

[60] *ibid.* (referring, apparently, to terms which are conditions by express classification of the parties).

[61] See above, p.790.

[62] *Astley Industrial Trust Ltd v Grimley* [1963] 1 W.L.R. 584 at 590; *Bunge Corp v Tradax Export SA* [1981] 1 W.L.R. 711 at 716.

[63] *e.g. Dawson's Ltd v Bonnin* [1922] 2 A.C. 413.

the term.[64] But if a term can be broken in a way which will cause only trifling (if any) loss, the court may hold that such a breach will not justify rescission even though the term is called a "condition" in the contract. In *Wickman Ltd v Schuler AG*[65] it was a "condition" of a four-year distributorship agreement that the distributor should visit six named customers once a week. The House of Lords held that the contract could not be rescinded *merely* because this term had been broken. The parties could not have intended the agreement to mean that a failure to make only one out of an obligatory total of some 1,400 visits should have such drastic results. More probably they had used "condition" in a nontechnical sense, to mean simply a term of the contract (as in the phrase "conditions of sale"). This view was supported by the fact that another clause in the contract conferred an express power of "determination" for any "material" breach: such a power can be exercised only if the breach is a "serious" one, in the sense discussed earlier in this Chapter.[66]

A term may be classified as a condition either by the express agreement of the parties or by law (*i.e.* by a previous judicial decision[67] or by statute[68]). One possible explanation of the cases in which a term has been classified by law as a condition is that the parties "have agreed . . . by implication of law"[69] that any breach of the term should give rise to the right to rescind. But this does not differ in substance from saying that there is a rule of law giving the injured party the right to rescind for the breach[70]: rescission is allowed, in these cases, even though the parties have not actually agreed that breach of the term should have this effect and even though the breach has not prejudiced the injured party seriously, or at all.

(e) STATUTORY CLASSIFICATION. In some cases the question whether a particular term is a condition or a warranty is determined by statute. The outstanding example of statutory classification is to be found in ss.12 to 15 of the Sale of Goods Act 1979,[71] which lay down in some detail which of the implied terms in a contract for the sale of goods are conditions and which are warranties. A full discussion of these provisions will be found in works on the sale of goods; but it is interesting to note that most of them are implied *conditions* (thus favouring the buyer's right to reject[72]); and a few of them may be mentioned here to illustrate the distinction between conditions and warranties. It is an implied condition that goods sold by description shall correspond with the

---

[64] *Harling v Eddy* [1951] 2 K.B. 739; *George Hunt Cranes Ltd v Scottish Boiler & General Insurance Ltd* [2001] EWCA Civ 1964; [2002] 1 All E.R. (Comm) 366.

[65] [1974] A.C. 235; Baker [1973] C.L.J. 196; Brownsword, 37 M.L.R. 104.

[66] See above, pp.770 *et seq.*; *e.g. Glolite Ltd v Jasper Conran Ltd, The Times*, January 28, 1998.

[67] See above, p.790.

[68] See below.

[69] *Photo Production Ltd v Securicor Transport Ltd* [1980] A.C. 827 at 849.

[70] *cf.* the discussion of "terms implied in law" as legal duties at pp.206–211, above.

[71] As amended by Sale and Supply of Goods Act 1994, ss.1, 7(1) and Sch.2 para.5 and by Sale and Supply of Goods to Consumers Regulations 2002 (SI 2002/3045), reg.3.

[72] This is also true of the similar terms implied in other contracts for the supply of goods by Supply of Goods (Implied Terms) Act 1973, ss.8–11 (as substituted by Consumer Credit Act 1974, Sch.4, para.35 and amended by Sale and Supply of Goods Act 1994, s.7(1) and Sch.2, para.4) and by Supply of Goods and Services Act 1982, ss.2–5, 7–10, as amended by Sale and Supply of Goods Act 1994, s.7(1) and Sch.2, para.6. For further amendments of ss.4 and 9 of the 1982 Act and of s.10 of the 1973 Act (all of which deal with implied conditions as to the quality or fitness of goods), see Sale and Supply of Goods to Consumers Regulations 2002, above, regs 7, 10 and 13. Contrast the Vienna Convention on Contracts for the International Sale of Goods (above, p.29) which has not yet been ratified by the UK. The Convention does not distinguish between conditions and warranties, but in art.49(1) makes the buyer's right to "declare the contract avoided" depend (generally) on a "fundamental breach" (as defined by art.25), thus favouring the seller. A full discussion of the complex system or remedies under the Convention is beyond the scope of this book.

contractual description,[73] that goods sold by sample shall correspond with the sample,[74] and (in certain cases) that goods shall be of satisfactory quality and fit for a particular purpose.[75] The right to rescind for breach of these implied conditions is subject to a statutory restriction to be discussed later in this Chapter.[76] There is an implied condition that the seller has the right to sell the goods,[77] but only an implied warranty that they are free from charges or incumbrances in favour of third parties.[78] To allow the seller to enforce the contract, when he had no right to sell, would generally[79] cause hardship to the buyer, as he would have to give the goods up to the true owner. But there is less hardship if the goods are subject to third party charges; these can simply be paid off so that the buyer can adequately and conveniently be compensated by damages.

The distinction between conditions and warranties does not apply to *quantitative* defects in the performance of a contract for the sale of goods. Subject to restrictions already discussed,[80] such defects justify rescission even though they cause little or no prejudice to the buyer.[81]

(f) TECHNICAL APPLICATIONS OF THE DISTINCTION. In some cases, rescission is allowed simply because the term broken has previously been classified as a condition. It is allowed even though there is no indication in the contract that the parties intended the remedy to be available, and even though the breach causes little prejudice, or none at all, to the injured party. Cases of this kind give rise to the question why the injured party should, in such circumstances, be entitled to rescind.

Sometimes, this result is justified by an argument based on hypothetical hardship. Rescission is allowed because the breach *might* have caused serious prejudice, irrespective of the question whether it *actually* did so. In one case,[82] for example, a seller of tinned fruit said to be packed in cases of 30 tins delivered cases of 24 tins. There was no evidence that this had caused any prejudice to the buyer, whose real motive for rejecting the goods was that they had arrived late; but this was not a matter for which the seller was responsible. The rejection was nevertheless held to be justified. Scrutton L.J. said: "a man who has bought . . . 30 tins to the case may have resold under the same description, and may be placed in considerable difficulty by having goods tendered to him which do not comply with the description under which he bought or under which he has resold".[83]

In other cases, no attempt is made to justify the result even by reference to such hypothetical hardship. Thus in *Arcos Ltd v Ronaasen*[84] timber was bought for the purpose of making cement barrels and was described in the contract as half an inch thick. Most of the timber delivered was in fact $\frac{9}{16}$in. thick, but this did not in the least impair its usefulness for making cement barrels. It was held that the buyers were nevertheless entitled to reject and it seems probable that their motive for wishing to do so was not that the timber did not comply with the description but that the market price

---

[73] Sale of Goods Act 1979, s.13.

[74] *ibid.*, s.15.

[75] *ibid.*, s.14.

[76] See below, p.800.

[77] *ibid*, s.12(1); an *express* term to this effect is likewise a condition: *Barber v NSW Bank Ltd* [1996] 1 W.L.R. 641.

[78] Sale of Goods Act 1979, s.12(2).

[79] For an exception, see Sale of Goods Act 1979, s.12(3) (agreement to transfer only such title as seller or third party may have).

[80] See above, pp.783–784.

[81] Sale of Goods Act 1979, s.30(1) and (2).

[82] *Re Moore & Co Ltd and Landauer Co* [1921] 2 K.B. 519.

[83] *ibid.* at 525.

[84] [1933] A.C. 470.

of the timber had fallen. Similarly, goods may be sold on the terms that they will be (or have been) shipped within a particular month. Such a term is part of the description of the goods and if they are shipped by so much as a day before or after the stipulated period the buyer can reject.[85] He can do this even though the early or late shipment does not in the least affect the value of the goods or prejudice him in any way; and even though his motive for rejection is simply to escape from a bad bargain on a falling market. And it seems that a charterer can rescind for breach of the condition as to the position of the ship or as to the date when she will sail[86] even though the breach did not cause him any loss and even though his real motive for rescinding was that freight rates had fallen.[87]

Such decisions can perhaps be explained on the ground that they promote certainty. Once a term has been classified as a "condition", the injured party can safely rescind for breach of it, without having to consider the often difficult question whether the breach amounted to a "substantial" failure in performance. On the other hand, in some of the examples given above, the exercise of the right to rescind can occasion obvious hardship to the party in breach: it results in his having to bear a loss that was not caused by the breach at all, but by market movements. For this reason, there has been some judicial reaction against the authorities which give a wide scope to the right to rescind; and in contracts for the supply of goods that right has also been limited by legislation.

(g) RESTRICTIONS OF TECHNICAL APPLICATIONS. In *Reardon Smith Line Ltd v Hansen Tangen*[88] Lord Wilberforce[89] said that some of the authorities just discussed[90] were "excessively technical and due for fresh examination in this House"[91]; and that generally, where goods are sold by description, the court should "ask whether a particular item in a description constitutes a substantial ingredient in the identity of the thing sold, and only if it does . . . treat it as a condition".[92] However, he recognised a possible exception in the case of "unascertained future goods (*e.g.* commodities) as to which each detail of the description must be assumed to be vital".[93] Since such goods often pass rapidly through many hands, the argument of commercial certainty is in such cases particularly strong: it is important for each buyer to be able to tell at once whether some defect or misdescription justifies rejection.

The judicial reaction against the excessively technical use of the right to rescind is illustrated by *Reardon Smith Line Ltd v Hansen Tangen* itself. The case arose out of the subcharter of a tanker then under construction and therefore not yet named. In the contract, she was accordingly described as "Yard No. 354 at Osaka . . . " (the name of the shipbuilder). She was built elsewhere, but by a company under Osaka's control and in accordance with the physical specifications in the subcharter. The tanker market fell and the subcharterers sought to reject, but it was held that they were not entitled to do so. The phrase "Yard No. 354 at Osaka" was not part of the description but a mere substitute for a name: it was a means of identification, which, in the circumstances, had

---

[85] *Bowes v Shand* (1877) 2 App.Cas. 455. The duty to tender conforming shipping documents (*e.g.* in performance of a c.i.f. contract) is similarly a condition: *The Hansa Nord* [1976] Q.B. 40 at 70; *Soon Hua Seng Co v Glencore Grain Ltd* [1996] 1 Lloyd's Rep. 398; Benjamin's *Sale of Goods* (6th ed.), §19–142.

[86] *Behn v Burness* (1863) 3 B. & S. 751; *Glaholm v Hays* (1842) 2 Man. & G. 257.

[87] This seems to have been the position in *Glaholm v Hays*, above.

[88] [1976] 1 W.L.R. 989; *cf. Sanko SS Co Ltd v Kano Trading Co Ltd* [1978] 1 Lloyd's Rep. 156.

[89] With whom Lords Simon and Kilbrandon agreed.

[90] *i.e.* Re *Moore & Co Ltd and Landauer Co* [1921] 2 K.B. 519 and *Behn v Burness*, above, "as interpreted."

[91] [1976] 1 W.L.R. 989, 998. *cf.* the criticism of the effects of breach of "warranty" in insurance law (above, p.790, n.51) in *Forsikringsaktieselskapet Vesta v Butcher* [1989] A.C. 852 at 893–894.

[92] [1976] 1 W.L.R. 989 at 998.

[93] *ibid.*

not failed. The effect of the case is to reintroduce the requirement of substantial failure into this branch of the law by making it part of the definition of a "description"[94]; and by thus narrowing the scope of an implied term which is undoubtedly a condition, *i.e.* the term requiring the goods to correspond with the contractual description.

(h) INTERMEDIATE OR INNOMINATE TERMS. The courts have also achieved a result similar to that just described by reducing the number of terms which are to be classified as conditions. They have done so by recognising that the distinction between conditions and warranties is not exhaustive. As Diplock L.J. has said: "There are many... contractual undertakings... which cannot be categorised as being 'conditions' or 'warranties'.... Of such undertakings, all that can be predicated is that some breaches will and others will not give rise to an event which will deprive the party not in default of substantially the whole benefit which it was intended that he should obtain."[95] These "intermediate or innominate terms"[96] differ from conditions, in that their breach does not of itself give rise to a right to rescind; and from warranties in that the injured party's remedy is not even *prima facie* restricted to damages. He can rescind for breach of an intermediate term if, but only if, the requirement of substantial failure is satisfied.[97] Thus it has been held that a shipowner's undertakings in a charterparty to provide a seaworthy ship[98] and to use reasonable despatch[99] are not conditions, so that the *mere* fact that they are not performed will not entitle the charterer to rescind. The same is true of the charterer's obligation to load within the time stipulated in the charterparty, so that the mere fact of delay will not justify rescission by the shipowner.[1] Similarly, it has been held that a time-charterer's obligation to repair the ship before redelivery is not a condition, so that his failure to repair does not, of itself, justify the shipowner's refusal to accept redelivery[2]; and it is probable that his breach ordering the ship to embark on a voyage which is illegitimate (because it cannot be completed within the period of the charter) will not of itself entitle the shipowner to rescind.[3] Some terms implied by statute seem also to fall into the category of intermediate terms. This seems to be true of the terms implied by the Supply of Goods and Services Act 1982 into contracts for the supply of services, that the services will be carried out with due care and skill and in a reasonable time; for the Act describes them simply as "terms"[4] (as opposed to the "conditions" and "warranties" implied into contracts for the supply of goods by the same Act).[5]

There was formerly some doubt on the question whether the category of intermediate terms existed in relation to contracts for the sale of goods. One view was that, as the Sale

---

[94] See above at n.92.

[95] *Hongkong Fir Shipping Co Ltd v Kawasaki Kisen Kaisha Ltd* [1962] 2 Q.B. 26 at 70.

[96] *Bunge Corp v Tradax Export SA* [1981] 1 W.L.R. 711 at 714.

[97] *e.g. Freeman v Taylor* (1831) 8 Bing. 124; *cf. The Antaios* [1985] A.C. 191 at 200 ("fundamental breach of an innominate term"); *Federal Commerce & Navigation v Molena Alpha* [1979] A.C. 757, esp. at 779; *The Honam Jade* [1991] 1 Lloyd's Rep. 38. In insurance law there is the further possibility that breach by the insured of an intermediate term relating to a claim may entitle the insurer to reject that claim but not to avoid the whole policy: see *Alfred McAlpine plc v BAI (Run-off) Ltd* [2000] 1 Lloyd's Rep. 437 at 444; *The Mercadian Continent* [2001] EWCA Civ 1275 at [14]; [2001] 1 Lloyd's Rep. 563.

[98] *Hongkong Fir* case, above; *cf. The Ymnos* [1982] 2 Lloyd's Rep. 574; *The Torenia* [1983] 2 Lloyd's Rep. 210 at 217.

[99] *Clipsham v Vertue* (1843) 5 Q.B. 265; *MacAndrew v Chapple* (1886) L.R. 1 C.P. 643.

[1] *Universal Cargo Carriers Corp v Citati* [1957] 2 Q.B. 401; *The Angelia* [1973] 1 W.L.R. 210.

[2] *Attica Sea Carriers Corp v Ferrostaal Poseidon Bulk Reederei GmbH* [1976] 1 Lloyd's Rep. 250 at 253, 256.

[3] *The Gregos* [1994] 1 W.L.R. 1465 at 1476, where it was not necessary to decide the point as the owner was entitled to rescind on the ground stated at p.808, below.

[4] Supply of Goods and Services Act 1982, ss.13, 14.

[5] *ibid.* ss.2–5 and 7–10; for amendments, see above, p.792, n.72.

of Goods Act 1979 referred only to two classes of terms (conditions and warranties), the further category of intermediate terms was impliedly excluded. But this view was rejected in *The Hansa Nord*.[6] Citrus pulp pellets had been sold for £100,000 under a contract which provided for "shipment to be made in good condition." Part of the goods had not been so shipped; and this fact reduced by some £20,000 the market value of the whole which would, if the goods had been sound, have been £86,000 at the time of their arrival.[7] The buyers rejected the goods which were later resold pursuant to a court order and eventually reacquired by the original buyers for just under £34,000. The buyers then used the goods for the originally intended purpose of making cattle food, though the defective part of the goods yielded slightly lower extraction percentages than sound goods would have done. The Court of Appeal held that rejection was not justified. The provision as to shipment in good condition was neither a condition nor a warranty but an intermediate term; and there was no finding that the effect of its breach was sufficiently serious to justify rejection. The buyers seem to have tried to reject, not because the utility of the goods was impaired, but because they saw an opportunity of acquiring them at well below the originally agreed price. In these circumstances their only remedy was in damages: they were entitled to the difference in value between damaged and sound goods at the agreed destination.[8]

The category of intermediate terms is thus established and is of general application. Its existence does, however, give rise to two further problems:

(i) *Are there three categories of terms?* This is a largely terminological problem.[9] The general view is that there are three classes of contractual terms: conditions, the breach of which at common law[10] invariably gives rise to a right to rescind; warranties, the breach of which gives rise only to a right to damages; and intermediate terms, the breach of which gives rise to a right to rescind if it is sufficiently serious, but otherwise sounds only in damages. There is, however, some support for the alternative view that there are only two categories: conditions and other terms.[11] This view is based on the argument that the injured party may be entitled to rescind even for a breach of warranty, if the effect of the breach is sufficiently serious. There is, as we shall see, considerable force in this argument[12] and if it is correct a warranty may be said to resemble an intermediate term, in that the availability of rescission as a remedy for breach of either type of term depends on the seriousness of the breach. Nevertheless, the weight of authority supports the continued existence of the threefold division of contractual terms.[13] It is respectfully

---

[6] [1976] Q.B. 44; Reynolds, 92 L.Q.R. 17; Weir [1976] C.L.J. 33; *cf. The Aktion* [1987] 1 Lloyd's Rep. 283.

[7] [1976] Q.B. 44 at 55–56, 68.

[8] *ibid.* at 63–64.

[9] *The Ymnos* [1982] 2 Lloyd's Rep. 574 at 583.

[10] For statutory exceptions see below, p.800.

[11] *e.g.* in *The Hansa Nord* [1976] Q.B. 44 at 60 where Lord Denning M.R. says that the court has to ask only two questions: (i) is the term broken a condition; (ii) if not, did the breach go to the root? But he also recognises warranty as a separate category at 59–60 and at 61 he expressly distinguishes between the three categories of terms.

[12] See below, pp.807–808.

[13] *Bunge Corp v Tradax Export SA* [1981] 1 W.L.R. 711 at 725 (where Lord Roskill, with whom three of the other members of the House of Lords agreed, referred to a "third class of term"); *Regent OHG Aisenstadt und Barig v Francesco of Jermyn Street* [1981] 3 All E.R. 327 at 334; *The Mercadian Continent* [2001] EWCA Civ 1275; [2001] 1 Lloyd's Rep. 563, at [13]; *cf.* Lord Diplock's division of stipulations as to time into three categories in *United Scientific Holdings Ltd v Burnley BC* [1978] A.C. 904 at 943. His statement in *Photo Production Ltd v Securicor Transport Ltd* [1980] A.C. 827 at 849 of a general rule subject to two exceptions similarly amounts to a three-fold classification; for similar statements by Lord Diplock in other cases, see *Bremer Vulkan Schiffbau und Maschinenfabrik v South India Shipping Corp* [1981] A.C. 909 at 980–981; *The Nema* [1982] A.C. 724 at 744; *The Afovos* [1983] 1 W.L.R. 195 at 203; *The Mavro Vetranic* [1985] 1 Lloyd's Rep. 580 at 583.

submitted that this is the preferable view since the distinction between warranties and intermediate terms remains for practical purposes an important one. Even if, in extreme cases, rescission is available for breach of warranty, there is at least a *prima facie* rule that the normal remedy for such a breach is by way of damages. In relation to intermediate terms, there is no such *prima facie* rule; so that (to put the matter at its lowest) there is a greater likelihood that rescission will be available for breach of an intermediate term than for breach of warranty.

(ii) *Scope of the category of intermediate terms.* Granted that the threefold classification of terms does exist, the question then arises into which category particular terms should be placed. In discussing this question we shall assume that the parties have not expressly classified the term in the contract itself; and that the court will generally apply a previous judicial classification of the term.[14] Our concern here is therefore with previously unclassified terms. Since judicial classification of a term as a warranty is rare,[15] the important issue is whether a previously unclassified term is to be classified as a condition or as an intermediate term. This issue is a difficult one because it gives rise to a conflict between two policies.

The first of these policies is to restrict the right to rescind to cases in which the breach causes serious prejudice to the injured party, and so to prevent a party from rescinding for ulterior motives (such as his wish "of escaping from an unwelcome bargain"[16]) or on grounds that have been criticised as "excessively technical."[17] This policy favours the classification of terms as intermediate. It is illustrated by the *Hongkong Fir*[18] case, the *Hansa Nord*[19] and by a number of later decisions. In *Tradax Internacional SA v Goldschmidt SA*[20] the words "four per cent foreign matters" in a contract for the sale of barley were held to amount only to an intermediate term, so that the buyer was not allowed to reject merely because the goods were certified to contain 4.1 per cent foreign matters. Slynn J. said that "in the absence of any clear agreement or prior decision that this was to be a condition, the court should lean in favour of construing this provision as to impurities as an intermediate term, only a serious and substantial breach of which entitled rejection."[21] This policy can, indeed, be displaced by evidence of contrary intention.[22] But where there is no such evidence of the intention of the parties, the policy of leaning in favour of classifying stipulations as intermediate terms can be said to promote the interests of justice by preventing the injured party from rescinding on grounds that are technical or unmeritorious.

The second policy, by contrast, emphasises the requirement of commercial certainty; and it in turn favours the classification of terms as conditions. Such a classification makes it unnecessary to go into the difficult questions of fact and degree which arise in determining whether a breach is "serious and substantial."[23] And once a term has been

---

[14] Occasionally the court may wish to reconsider such a classification: *cf.* Lord Wilberforce's suggestion in *Reardon-Smith Line Ltd v Hansen Tangen* [1976] 1 W.L.R. 989 at 998, above, p.794.

[15] For an example of such a classification, see *The Captain George K* [1970] 2 Lloyd's Rep. 21.

[16] *The Gregos* [1994] 1 W.L.R. 1465 at 1475.

[17] *Reardon-Smith Line Ltd v Hansen Tangen* [1976] 1 W.L.R. 989 at 998; above, p.794.

[18] [1962] 2 Q.B. 26; above, p.795.

[19] [1976] Q.B. 44; above, p.796.

[20] [1977] 2 Lloyd's Rep. 604.

[21] *ibid.* at 612; *cf.* below, p.800, n.46; *Bremer Handelsgesellschaft mbH v Vanden Avenne-Izegem PVBA* [1978] 2 Lloyd's Rep. 109 at 113, and *Federal Commerce & Navigation v Molena Alpha* [1979] A.C. 757; *Nynehead Developments Ltd v Fibreboard Containers Ltd* [1999] 1 E.G.L.R. 7.

[22] The fact that there was evidence of such intention appears to be the best ground for distinguishing *Tradax International SA v Goldschmidt SA*, above, from *Tradax Export SA v European Grain & Shipping Co* [1983] 2 Lloyd's Rep. 100: see *Benjamin's Sale of Goods* (6th ed.), §18–238; see also *The Zeus V* [2002] 2 Lloyd's Rep. 587.

[23] *Tradax Internacional SA v Goldschmidt SA* [1977] 2 Lloyd's Rep. 604 at 612.

classified as a condition, the breach of such a term will, in a future case, enable the injured party to know, as soon as the breach has been committed, that he is entitled to rescind: he will not need to show anything about its effects. These considerations prevailed in *Bunge Corp v Tradax Export SA*.[24] A contract for the sale of soya bean meal provided that the goods were to be delivered during June. Delivery was to begin on a day in that month to be chosen by the buyers and was to be made free on board on a ship provided by the buyers at a US Gulf port to be selected by the sellers. The contract went on to require the buyers to give at least 15 days' notice of the ship's readiness to load the goods. It was held that this term was a condition, so that the sellers were entitled to rescind on the ground that the notice reached them five days too late. Two justifications for this classification were given. First, the sellers could not, as a practical matter, perform their own obligation of nominating a port until the buyers had given them notice of the ship's readiness to load[25]; but later cases show that, though this factor is relevant to the classification of the term,[26] it is not decisive, so that terms have been classified as conditions even where there was no such interdependence between the obligations of the parties.[27] The second, and more important, point was that the classification promoted certainty,[28] for it enabled the sellers to tell, immediately on receipt of the notice of the ship's readiness to load, whether they were bound to deliver.

Failure to adhere to similar time-tables laid down by commodity contracts and charterparties has, in a number of other cases, likewise been held to amount to a breach of condition.[29] One explanation for this special treatment of time clauses is that "as to such a clause there is only one kind of breach possible, namely to be late"[30]; while terms that have been classified as intermediate are typically such as might be broken in various ways, some trivial and some serious.[31] This is, for example, true of the shipowner's undertaking of seaworthiness in a charterparty; but it is equally true that delay may be trivial or serious; and the law does not always give the injured party the right to rescind for delay which is not serious: we have, for example, seen that a charterer is not in breach of condition merely because he has failed to load within the time stipulated in the charterparty.[32] Stipulations as to the time of performance can, however, be put into a separate category on the ground that breach by delay is particularly easy to establish: if the injured party has received no performance by the due day, there can be no doubt about the fact of delay; while qualitative breaches (such as unseaworthiness) can give rise

---

[24] [1981] 1 W.L.R. 711.

[25] *cf. Gill & Duffus SA v Société pour l'Exportation des Sucres SA* [1986] 1 Lloyd's Rep. 332.

[26] *Universal Bulk Carriers Ltd v Andre & Cie* [2001] EWCA Civ 588; [2001] 2 Lloyd's Rep. 65, at [40].

[27] *The Mavro Vetranic* [1985] 1 Lloyd's Rep. 580 at 583; *Michael J Warde v Feedex International Inc* [1985] 2 Lloyd's Rep. 289 at 298; *The Niizura* [1996] 2 Lloyd's Rep. 66 at 71; *The Seaflower* [2001] 1 All E.R. (Comm) 240.

[28] *ibid.*, at 254.

[29] *e.g. Krohn & Co v Mitsui & Co Europe GmbH* [1978] 2 Lloyd's Rep. 419; *Toepfer v Lenersan-Poortman NV* [1980] 1 Lloyd's Rep. 143; *cf. Bremer Handelsgesellschaft mbH v Vanden Avenne-Izegem PVBA* [1978] 2 Lloyd's Rep. 109 (so far as it relates to the notice under clause 22 of the contract); *Portara Shipping Co v Gulf Pacific Navigation Co Ltd* [1981] 2 Lloyd's Rep. 180; *Nichimen Corp v Gatoil Overseas Inc* [1987] 2 Lloyd's Rep. 46; *The Naxos* [1990] 1 W.L.R. 1337, Treitel [1991] L.M.C.L.Q. 147; for time stipulations in charterparties, see *The Niizura* [1996] 2 Lloyd's Rep. 66 (distinguished in the *Universal Bulk* case, above, n.26) and *The Seaflower*, above, n.27. And see the authorities cited in nn.25 and 27, above.

[30] *Bunge Corp v Tradax Export SA* [1981] 1 W.L.R. 711 at 715.

[31] *ibid. cf. The Ymnos* [1982] 2 Lloyd's Rep. 574 at 584.

[32] See above, p.795; *cf.* Lord Wilberforce's statement that a charterer's deliberate delay in loading of only one day "can appropriately be sanctioned by damages:" *Suisse Atlantique* case [1967] 1 A.C. 361 at 423 (below, p.806).

to many disputed issues of fact. Delay is also of obvious commercial importance in dealings with commodities, which can fluctuate rapidly in value. It is this combination of the ease of establishing the breach without legal proceedings and of its likely commercial importance which accounts for the readiness of the courts to treat stipulations as to the time of performance in contracts for the sale of commodities as conditions, so that *any* breach of them will justify rescission.

It follows from the above reasoning that a stipulation as to the time of performance will not invariably be treated as a condition. It may, for example, not be so treated precisely because the context shows that its due performance is *not* of vital importance[33]; or because to give the injured party the right to rescind for *any* breach of it would make the contract unworkable[34] or because the contract provides that damages are to be the sole remedy for failure to comply with the stipulation[35]; or because failure by one party to perform the stipulation did not create any uncertainty as to the time at which the other party would have to perform[36]; or because the stipulation did not specify a *precise* time for performance, or enable that time to be precisely ascertained in the light of later events,[37] so that its classification as a condition would not promote certainty. Thus the House of Lords has held that a stipulation requiring a seller to give notice "without delay" of the occurrence of circumstances entitling him to invoke a prohibition of export clause was an intermediate term only.[38] In a later decision at first instance, on the other hand, a term in a contract of sale required the seller to give the buyer a notice appropriating goods to the contract "as soon as possible after vessel's sailing".[39] This term was held to be a condition and the earlier decision[40] was distinguished on the ground that in it the House of Lords had been concerned with a stipulation governing the machinery of *termination* while the later case was concerned with a stipulation governing the machinery of *performance*.[41] But the explanation is not entirely convincing[42] since an important question in relation to either kind of term is whether the breach of it entitles the injured party to treat the contract as at an end. The main justification for classifying the term as a condition is that this will significantly promote certainty by enabling the buyer to know exactly when delay on the seller's part in giving the notice will justify him (the buyer) in rescinding the contract.[43] Vague expressions such as "without delay," or "as soon as possible" do not enable him to know this, and

---

[33] *State Trading Corporation of India v M Golodetz Ltd* [1989] 2 Lloyd's Rep. 277 (where the stipulation was contained in one contract but related to a different contract between the same parties which was not to be performed for six months and was relatively unimportant in terms of money); *The Ballenita* [1992] 2 Lloyd's Rep. 445 at 464–465; *The Gregos* [1994] 1 W.L.R. 1465 at 1475; *Alfred McAlpine plc v BAI (Run-off) Ltd* [2000] 1 Lloyd's Rep. 437 at 441 ("merely ancillary" time stipulation).

[34] As in *The Honam Jade* [1991] 1 Lloyd's Rep. 39 (where strict compliance with the timetable was impossible in chain contracts).

[35] As in *The Aragon* [1991] 1 Lloyd's Rep. 61.

[36] *Universal Bulk Carriers Ltd v Andre & Cie* [2001] EWCA Civ 588; [2001] 2 Lloyd's Rep. 65 at [40].

[37] For terms enabling the time so to be ascertained, see *Toepfer v Lenersan-Poortman NV* [1980] 1 Lloyd's Rep. 143; *The Naxos* [1990] 1 W.L.R. 1337.

[38] *Bremer Handelsgesellschaft mbH v Vanden Avenne-Izegem PVBA*, above, n.29, so far as it relates to the notice under cl.21 of the contract; *cf. Tradax Export SA v Italgrani di Francesco Ambrosio* [1986] 1 Lloyd's Rep. 112 at 120.

[39] *The Post Chaser* [1981] 2 Lloyd's Rep. 695.

[40] See above, at n.38.

[41] [1981] 2 Lloyd's Rep. 695 at 700; *cf. McDougall v Aeromarine of Emsworth Ltd* [1958] 1 W.L.R. 1126 (duty to deliver within a *reasonable time*).

[42] For the difficulty of reconciling the two cases here under discussion, see *Concordia Trading BV v Richco International Ltd* [1991] 1 Lloyd's Rep. 475 at 481.

[43] See *Tradax Export SA v Italgrani di Francesco Ambrosio* [1986] 1 Lloyd's Rep. 112 at 120.

stipulations containing such words should not be classified as conditions[44] in the absence of express provisions to that effect[45] or of other evidence that the parties clearly intended them to take effect as such.

The foregoing discussion shows that there is considerable support both for the view that the court should "lean in favour"[46] of classifying contractual stipulations as intermediate terms, and for the view that commercial certainty sometimes requires their classification as conditions. The second of these views was applied in *Bunge Corp v Tradax Export SA*[47]; but the first was not rejected: on the contrary, Lord Wilberforce said that "the courts should not be too ready to interpret contractual clauses as conditions"[48]; while Lord Roskill recognised "the modern approach of not being over-ready to construe terms as conditions unless the contract clearly requires the court to do so."[49] The effect of the decision is not to discard, but rather to qualify, that approach by emphasising the importance traditionally attached in certain commercial contracts to exact compliance with stipulations as to the time of performance.[50] Stipulations of this kind are now likely to be classified as conditions if they are sufficiently precise; and other terms may also be so classified if exact performance of them is regarded as commercially vital[51] or if there is evidence either from the commercial setting or from the course of negotiations that the parties intended them to have the force of conditions.[52-53] Where a term does not fall within any of these three categories, the judicial attitude continues to be one of not being "too ready" to classify it as a condition. Such other terms are therefore likely to be classified as intermediate, so that rescission will be allowed only where the breach causes serious prejudice to the injured party.

(i) STATUTORY RESTRICTION ON RIGHT TO RESCIND FOR BREACH OF CONDITION. As a result of amendments to the Sale of Goods Act 1979 made in 1994, the buyer's right to rescind a contract for the sale of goods is restricted where the buyer does *not* deal as consumer; further restrictions on that right where the buyer *does* deal as consumer are imposed by amendments of the 1979 Act made in 2002. Similar restrictions apply to

---

[44] *Alfred McAlpine Ltd v BAI (Run-off) Ltd* [2001] 1 Lloyd's Rep. 437; *The Beursgracht* [2001] EWCA Civ 2051; [2002] 1 Lloyd's Rep. 574, at [43, 44].

[45] As in *George Hunt Cranes Ltd v Scottish Boilers & General Insurance Co Ltd* [2001] 2 Lloyd's Rep. 65 at [28].

[46] *Tradax Internacional SA v Goldschmidt SA* [1977] 2 Lloyd's Rep. 604 at 612; *cf. Bremer Handelsgesellschaft mbH v Vanden Avenne-Izegem PVBA* [1978] 2 Lloyd's Rep. 109 at 113; *Federal Commerce & Navigation v Molena Alpha* [1979] A.C. 757; *State Trading Corporation of India v M Golodetz Ltd* [1989] 2 Lloyd's Rep. 277 at 283; *The Silva Plana* [1989] 2 Lloyd's Rep. 371 at 375; *The Gregos* [1994] 1 W.L.R. 1465 at 1475; *Alfred McAlpine Ltd v BAI (Run-off) Ltd* [1998] 2 Lloyd's Rep. 694 at 700, affirmed, above n.44; *Universal Bulk Carriers Ltd v Andre & Cie* [2001] 2 Lloyd's Rep. 65 at [28].

[47] [1981] 1 W.L.R. 714, above, p.798.

[48] [1981] 1 W.L.R. 714 at 715.

[49] [1981] 1 W.L.R. 714 at 727; *cf.* also *Toepfer v Lenersan Poortman NV* [1980] 1 Lloyd's Rep. 143 at 147; *The Ymnos* [1982] 1 Lloyd's Rep. 574 at 583; *The Gregos* [1994] 1 W.L.R. 1465 at 1475.

[50] *cf. Bowes v Shand* (1877) 2 App.Cas. 455; above, p.794.

[51] *The Post Chaser* [1981] 2 Lloyd's Rep. 695 may be explicable on this ground: see p.700 of the report; or on the ground of concessions made in that case: see *British & Commonwealth Holdings plc v Quadrex Holdings Inc* [1989] Q.B. 842 at 857. The arbitrators' finding as to the commercial importance of compliance with the stipulation was a second ground for the decision in *The Naxos* [1990] 1 W.L.R. 1337; *cf. The New Prosper* [1991] 2 Lloyd's Rep. 93 at 99; *Petrotrade Inc v Stinnes Handel GmbH* [1995] 1 Lloyd's Rep. 142 (place of delivery in f.o.b. contract vital to buyers as they had to provide a ship there); *Mamidoil-Jetoil Greek Petroleum Company SA v Okta Crude Oil Refinery AD* [2002] EWHC 2462 (Comm), [2003] 1 Lloyd's Rep. 1 at [34].

[52-53] e.g. *Tradax Export SA v European Grain & Shipping Co* [1983] 2 Lloyd's Rep. 100; *Bergerco USA v Vegoil Ltd* [1984] 1 Lloyd's Rep. 440; *cf.* also *Michael J Warde v Feedex International Inc* [1985] 2 Lloyd's Rep. 284 at 288.

other contracts for the supply of goods; but for the sake of brevity the following discussion will deal only with cases of sale.

(i) *Buyer not dealing as consumer.* S.15A[54] of the Sale of Goods Act 1979 applies where the buyer does not deal as consumer and where he would be entitled to reject by reason of a breach of condition implied into the contract under the Sale of Goods Act 1979 as to correspondence with description or sample and as to quality.[55] S.15A provides that if, in such cases, the seller can show[56] that the breach is "so slight that it would be unreasonable"[57] for the buyer to reject the goods, then the breach is "not to be treated as a breach of condition but may be treated as a breach of warranty"[58]; when it is so treated the buyer's remedy will therefore be in damages. This exception to the general common law rule that breach of condition automatically justifies rescission is "not intended as a major alteration in the law".[59] Its scope is, in particular, limited in the following ways.

First, it applies only to contracts for the supply of goods: the law relating to breach of condition, in for example, time or voyage charterparties,[60] is unaffected. Secondly, it applies only to breaches by the supplier: a case such as *Bunge Corp v Tradax Export SA*[61] would not be affected since the breach was committed by the buyer. Thirdly, it applies only to breach of certain *implied* terms: the right to reject for breach of an *express* condition[62] is not affected. Fourthly, it applies only to breach of the statutorily implied terms listed above.[63] It does not apply to any other terms which may be implied by statute,[64] nor to terms implied as a matter of common law. Fifthly, the exception is excluded where "a contrary intention appears in, or is to be implied from, the contract",[65] Such an implication may arise from the nature of the contract or from its commercial setting. It is, for example, envisaged that the exception will for this reason not apply to breaches of such time clauses in commercial contracts as have been classified as conditions[66] (though the wording of the new s.15A can scarcely be said to make this point clear). Sixthly, the exception does not apply where the buyer deals as consumer: such a buyer is not well placed to dispose of defective goods on the market, so that it is important to preserve his unqualified right to reject for breach of the statutorily implied conditions.[67]

Where a case falls within s.15A, two requirements must be satisfied[68] before the buyer is deprived of his right to reject for breach of condition: the breach must be "slight" and

---

[54] Inserted by Sale and Supply of Goods Act 1994, s.4(1) giving effect to recommendations of the Law Commission in Law Com. 160 (1987), para.4.21. For similar provisions relating to other contracts for the supply of goods, see Supply of Goods (Implied Terms) Act 1973, s.11A and Supply of Goods and Services Act 1982, s.5A, as inserted by Sale and Supply of Goods Act 1994, s.7(1) and Sch. 2, paras 4 and 6.

[55] *i.e.* the terms implied by ss.13, 14 and 15 of the 1979 Act: above p.792.

[56] The burden of proof is on the seller: Sale of Goods Act 1979, s.15A(3) (above n.54).

[57] *ibid.* s.15A(1)(b).

[58] *ibid.* s.15A(1).

[59] Law Com. No.160 para.4.21 (on which s.15A is based).

[60] See above, p.790.

[61] [1981] 1 W.L.R. 711, above, p.798.

[62] As, for example, in *Bremer Handelsgesellschaft mbH v Vanden Avenne-Izegem PVBA* [1978] 2 Lloyd's Rep. 109 (so far as it relates to cl.22).

[63] See above at n.55.

[64] *e.g.* by Sale of Goods Act 1979, s.12(1) (such a breach might be "slight" if it affected part only of the goods sold).

[65] Sale of Goods Act 1979 s.15A(2).

[66] Law Com. No.160, para.4.24; *e.g. Bowes v Shand* (1877) 2 App. Cas. 455, above, p.794.

[67] See Law Com. No.160, Scot. Law Com. No.104, §§4.09–4.15.

[68] Law Com. No. 160, para.4.21 ("slight *and* it is unreasonable . . . ").

it must be "unreasonable for [the buyer] to reject" the goods. The policy underlying these requirements is similar to that on which the development of the category of intermediate terms is based[69]: it is to prevent the buyer from rejecting on unmeritorious grounds (though his motives for rejection are said not to be relevant).[70] But it should not be thought that, where the section applies, it has the effect of turning the implied conditions to which it refers into intermediate terms. The section only precludes the buyer from rejecting where the breach is "slight"; and a breach which is too serious to be "slight" may nevertheless not be serious enough to deprive the buyer of substantially the whole benefit which it was intended that he should obtain from the contract.[71] Where the breach falls between these extremes, the buyer's right to reject for breach of condition is not affected by s.15A, even though a similar breach would not give him a right to reject for breach of an intermediate term. The question just when a breach is so slight as to make it unreasonable for the buyer to reject the goods remains to be settled by judicial decision; and the vagueness of s.15A on this point is a source of regrettable uncertainty. It is, for example, far from clear how a case such as *Arcos Ltd v Ronaasen*[72] would now be decided. The difference between half an inch and $\frac{9}{16}$ of an inch is by no means obviously "slight" (at least as a proportion); and if it were not slight the buyer would not be deprived of his right to reject merely because it was unreasonable for him to reject or because his motive for rejection was to escape from what had turned out to be a bad bargain because of a fall in the market.[73]

S.15A is, it is submitted, an unfortunate provision which manages to fall between two stools. On the one hand, the section undermines the certainty which classification of the implied terms in question as conditions was intended to provide. It is no answer to this argument to say that the limitation on the right to reject which the section imposes will not often apply: the point is that it is hard to predict when it will apply, so that a buyer's legal adviser will not be able to answer that question with certainty.[74] Nor is it an answer to say that the limitation can be excluded by implied agreement[75]: it is, again, impossible to predict with certainty when such an implication will be made. On the other hand, the section scarcely goes far enough to promote justice: for this purpose, the right to reject should be restricted to serious breaches[76] and not merely excluded if the breach is slight, If a case like *Arcos Ltd v Ronaasen*[77] would not be affected by s.15A, the right to reject could still be exercised so as to cause injustice. Even if the section did cover all cases in which it would be unjust to allow the buyer to reject, it would be extraordinarily partial in its operation. Rescission by a seller can lead to just as much injustice as rejection by the buyer; but the section does nothing to limit the exercise by a seller of a right to rescind. It is submitted that the section has sacrificed certainty without attaining justice.

---

[69] See above, p.795.

[70] Law Com. No.160, paras 4.18 and 4.19.

[71] This is the test for determing when a breach of an intermediate term gives rise to a right to rescind: *Hongkong Fir Shipping Co Ltd v Kawasaki Kisen Kaisha Ltd* [1962] 2 Q.B. 26 at 70.

[72] [1933] A.C. 470, above, p.793.

[73] See above, at n.70.

[74] For a similar view in an analogous context, see *Union Eagle Ltd v Golden Achievement Ltd* [1997] A.C. 514 at 519. The Law Commissions do not explain their statement that "the uncertainty will be more apparent than real:" Law Com. No.160, para.4.23.

[75] *ibid*.

[76] *cf.* The Vienna Convention on Contracts for the International Sale of Goods Acts ss.49(1) and 25 (above, p.792 n.72).

[77] [1933] A.C. 470; above at n.72.

(ii) *Buyer dealing as consumer.* Ss.48A to 48C[77a] of the Sale of Goods Act 1979 specify a number of "additional rights"[77b] available to a buyer who "deals as consumer"[77c] where the goods[77d] do not conform to the contract of sale at the time of delivery.[77e] For this purpose goods do not conform to the contract where the seller is in breach of the conditions implied into the contract under the Act as to correspondence with description or sample, or as to quality[77f]; or where he is in breach of an express term.[77g] The first of these "additional rights" (conferred by s.48B) is one to require the seller to repair or replace the goods,[77h] subject to specified limitations.[77i] Where these limitations apply, so that the right is not available, or where the seller has failed to comply with the buyer's requirement to repair or replace the goods within a reasonable time,[77j] then the buyer has the right (under these sections) to rescind the contract with regard to the non-conforming goods.[77k] The buyer's right to reject goods for breach of condition is also limited in that, if he requires the seller to repair or replace the non-conforming goods under the above provisions, then he must not reject the goods for breach of condition[77l] until he has given the seller a reasonable time to repair or replace the goods.[77m] The right of the buyer who deals as consumer to "rescind the contract" under ss.48A and 48C is also, in effect, subject to the discretion of the court. S.48E provides (*inter alia*) that, where the buyer has claimed to rescind under s.48C, then if the court decides that another remedy under s.48B or 48C, (*e.g.* price reduction) is appropriate, the court may give effect to that other remedy.[77n] These restrictions on the buyer's right to reject and to "rescind the contract" at first sight come into conflict with the policy underlying s.15A, of preserving the consumer's unqualified right to reject for breach of condition. The conflict is, however, more apparent than real since the rights here under discussion are "additional" to his right to reject for breach of condition under the provisions of the Act which governed that right before the "additional rights" were created.[77o] There is nothing in ss.48A to 48C to compel the consumer to require repair or replacement or to seek to rescind under these new sections; and the restrictions here discussed on his remedies do not extend to cases in which the buyer simply rejects for breach of condition under the rules stated earlier in this Chapter,[77p] without seeking to assert any of the "additional rights" given to him by those sections.

(j) OTHER RESTRICTIONS ON RESCISSION FOR BREACH OF CONDITION. The right to rescind for breach of condition may be limited in the following further ways.

[77a] Inserted into the Act by Sale and Supply of Goods to Consumers Regulations 2002 (SI 2002/3045), reg.5, implementing Directive 1999/44.
[77b] Heading to new Pt 5A of the 1979 Act.
[77c] Sale of Goods Act 1979, s.61(5A), cross-referring to the definition in the Unfair Contract Terms Act 1977 discussed at p.247, above.
[77d] Second hand goods and certain auction sales are excepted by amendments to s.12(2) of the 1977 Act made by reg.14; above p.247.
[77e] Sale of Goods Act 1979, s.48A(1)(b).
[77f] *ibid.* s.48F, referring to ss.13–15.
[77g] *ibid.* s.48F ("express term").
[77h] *ibid.* ss.48A(2)(a) and 48B.
[77i] *ibid.* s.48B(3) and (4).
[77j] *ibid.* s.48C(2).
[77k] *ibid.* s.48C(1)(b).
[77l] *ibid.* s.48D(1), (2)(a).
[77m] *ibid.* s.48D(1), (2)(a).
[77n] *ibid.* s.48E(3), (4).
[77o] *ibid.* s.48E, which in effect enables the court to override the buyer's choice of remedies provided by ss.48B and 48C, does not apply where the buyer's choice is to pursue a remedy other than any of these specified in those sections.
[77p] See p.788, above.

(i) *Exemption clauses.* The right to rescind may be excluded by a clause which validly excludes all liability for breach of condition; or by a "non-rejection" or "non-cancellation" clause which bars the right to rescind without affecting the right to damages.[78] This power to exclude the right to rescind is subject to the rules discussed in Chapter 7, which limit the effectiveness of exemption clauses. In a contract for the supply of goods, a clause purporting to deprive a person who deals as a consumer of the right to reject for breach of the conditions implied by the Sale of Goods Act 1979 will generally have no effect.[79] If the person to whom the supply is made does not deal as consumer, the effectiveness of a non-rejection clause in a contract for the supply of goods will commonly be subject to the test of reasonableness[80]; while in a contract between a commercial seller of goods or supplier of goods or services and a consumer a standard term excluding or limiting the consumer's right to reject or cancel will not bind the consumer if it is unfair.[81] It is submitted that, in applying these tests of reasonableness and fairness to non-rejection and non-cancellation clauses the courts may be influenced by the likely effects of the breach (as viewed at the time of contracting), and so take into account the factors which determine whether a failure in performance is sufficiently "substantial" to give rise to a right to rescind. A similar point can be made with regard to the process of strict construction which is applied to exemption clauses in certain cases of particularly serious breach.[82] If the effect of a breach of condition is wholly to frustrate the injured party's purpose in making the contract, the clause may be held not to apply to the breach at all[83]; and if it is so construed, the injured party will once again be entitled to rescind where the breach gives rise to a substantial failure in performance.

(ii) *Consumer sales.* Where a buyer who "deals as consumer" claims rescission under s.48C of the Sale of Goods Act 1979, the court may instead award him a price reduction. This discretion, and its limits, have already been discussed.[84]

(iii) *Misrepresentation incorporated as condition.* Where a person has been induced to enter into a contract by a false statement of *fact*, his right to rescind for misrepresentation is subject to the discretion of the court under s.2(2) of the Misrepresentation Act 1967,[85] to declare the contract subsisting and to award damages in lieu of rescission. It is arguable that this discretion can be exercised even where the misrepresentation which induced the contract is later incorporated in it as a condition. But the better view seems to be that the subsection applies only to the right to rescind a contract for misrepresentation, and that it has not affected the right to rescind for breach.[86]

(k) RESCISSION FOR BREACH OF WARRANTY? Once a term is classified as a "condition" any breach of it at common law gives right to a right to rescind. It might be thought, conversely, to follow from the definition of "warranty"[87] that, once a term had been classified as a warranty, then a claim for damages was the only remedy for its breach. But

---

[78] *e.g.*, *The Aegean Dolphin* [1992] 2 Lloyd's Rep. 178.

[79] See above, pp.251–252.

[80] See above, pp.254–255.

[81] Unfair Terms in Consumer Contracts Regulations 1999 (above, p.267), reg.5(1); *cf.* Sch.3, para.1(b) and (q).

[82] See *J Aron & Co (Inc) v Comptoir Wegimont* [1921] 3 K.B. 435 for the application of these principles to non-rejection clauses.

[83] See pp.225 *et seq.*, above.

[84] Above, p.803.

[85] See p.357, above.

[86] See above, p.377.

[87] Sale of Goods Act 1979, s.61(1) (below at n.91); *cf. ibid.* s.11(3); above, p.788.

there are three situations in which the injured party may be able to rescind for breach of warranty.

(i) *Misrepresentation incorporated as warranty.* A statement of *fact* made before the contract may give rise to a right to rescind the contract for misrepresentation, and this right will survive the subsequent incorporation of the statement in the contract as a warranty.[88] But if the breach is of relatively small importance, it seems likely that the court will exercise its discretion under s.2(2) of the Misrepresentation Act 1967[89] to declare the contract subsisting and to award damages in lieu of rescission.

(ii) *Substantial failure.* It has been suggested[90] that breach of warranty may justify rescission where it leads (or amounts) to a substantial failure in performance. There is at first sight some difficulty in applying this suggestion to contracts for the sale of goods. The difficulty arises because "warranty" is defined in the Sale of Goods Act 1979 as an agreement "collateral to the main purpose of [the] contract, the breach of which gives rise to a claim for damages but not to a right to reject the goods. . . . "[91] On the other hand, it is arguable that the rule allowing rescission for a "substantial" failure in performance is a rule of common law, preserved by s.62(2) of the Act "except in so far as . . . inconsistent with the express provisions of this Act". In *The Hansa Nord*[92] this subsection was invoked in support of the view that the statutory classification of terms into conditions and warranties was not exhaustive. It can similarly be used to support the view that the Act does not exhaustively state the effects of breach of warranty.[93] If in particular circumstances such a breach leads to a substantial failure in performance, the *prima facie* rule[94] that damages are the only remedy for breach of warranty should be displaced and rescission should be allowed.

(iii) *Consumer sales.* Under ss.48A and 48C of the Sale of Goods Act 1979, a buyer who deals as consumer has, in circumstances described earlier in this Chapter,[94a] a right to "rescind the contract"[94b] with regard to non-conforming goods. Goods which do not conform to the contract are those in relation to which there is a breach of *either* the terms implied by ss.13 to 14 of the 1979 Act *or* of "an express term".[94c] The former are necessarily breaches of condition but the latter may be a breach of warranty. Under these sections, the buyer may therefore have a "right to rescind" for breach of warranty. This right is, however, subject to the power of the court to proceed as if the buyer had instead sought another remedy (such as price reduction) made available by those sections.[94d]

(4) Breach of fundamental term

In the law relating to exemption clauses, a distinction is drawn between conditions and fundamental terms. Breach of a fundamental term and breach of condition both give rise

---

[88] Misrepresentation Act 1967, s.1(*a*); above, pp.375–376.
[89] See above, p.357.
[90] *Astley Industrial Trust Ltd v Grimley* [1963] 1 W.L.R. 584 at 599. The term broken in this example would now be a condition under Supply of Goods and Services Act 1982, s.9(4) if the party in breach acted in the course of a business.
[91] s.61(1).
[92] [1976] Q.B. 44.
[93] *ibid.* at 83.
[94] See above, p.797.
[94a] Above, p.803.
[94b] Sale of Goods Act 1979, ss.48A(2)(b)(ii) and 48C(1)(b).
[94c] *ibid.*, s.48F.
[94d] *ibid.*, s.48E(3) and (4).

to a right to rescind regardless of the actual effects of the breach.[95] The main differences between them are that (1) words which are sufficient to exclude liability for breach of condition will not necessarily cover breach of a fundamental term[96] and (2) some of the factors which limit the right to rescind for breach of condition may not similarly limit the right to rescind a fundamental term.[97] Neither of these points is directly relevant to the present discussion, which concerns the question whether any right to rescind ever existed at all.

Usually, the effect of breach of a fundamental term will be serious, so that in most cases the right to rescind for such a breach will amount to an *application* of the requirement of substantial failure. But this is not necessarily the case, for in this branch of the law a development has taken place resembling that discussed in relation to breach of condition.[98] Certain terms in particular contracts have been classified by authority as fundamental terms. Once this has happened, any breach of such a term gives rise to a right to rescind, irrespective of its consequences. For example, in contracts for the carriage of goods by sea[99] the term as to the route to be followed has been classified as fundamental.[1] Any unjustified departure from that route by the carrier amounts to deviation and justifies rescission by the injured party. This is so even though the deviation is "for practical purposes irrelevant".[2] The right to rescind here constitutes an exception to the requirement of serious failure in performance; it can be criticised[3] and defended[4] on similar grounds to those which have been discussed in relation to the corresponding exception in the case of breach of condition.

The possibility that breach of a fundamental term may justify rescission, even though it causes no prejudice to the injured party, is further illustrated by *Pilbrow v Peerless De Rougemont & Co*[5] where a client contracted with a firm of solicitors for the provision of legal services by a solicitor. The services provided were rendered by an employee who, unknown to the client was at the time not a solicitor,[6] but they were up to the standard of a competent solicitor and the client was "not . . . disadvantaged by what has happened". Nevertheless it was held that the case was not one of merely "defective performance" but one of "non-performance of a contract to provide legal services by a solicitor".[7] It followed that the client was not liable for the unpaid balance of the firm's fees. This harsh result can perhaps be accounted for by the need to encourage the highest standards of behaviour of solicitors in their relation with clients; and it was to

---

[95] For this reason "fundamental term" is sometimes used in the same sense as condition, *i.e.* to mean any term, the breach of which justifies rescission: see *Millichamp v Jones* [1982] 1 W.L.R. 1422 at 1427; *Metro Meat Ltd v Fares Rural Pty Ltd* [1985] 2 Lloyd's Rep. 13 at 17; *Hurst v Bryk* [1999] Ch. 1 at 9; and *cf.* below, n.1.

[96] See above, pp.226–232.

[97] See below, pp.817–818.

[98] See above, pp.793–794.

[99] And probably by land: above, p.229, n.36.

[1] *Hain SS Co Ltd v Tate & Lyle Ltd* (1936) 41 Com.Cas. 350. Lord Diplock in *Photo Production Ltd v Securicor Transport Ltd* [1980] A.C. 827 at 850, appears to classify deviation as a breach of condition; but, at least in the law relating to exemption clauses, the effect of deviation seems still to differ from that of an ordinary breach of condition: *cf.* above, p.229, n.46.

[2] *Suisse Atlantique* case [1967] 1 A.C. 361 at 423.

[3] See *Farr v Hain SS Co* 121 F.2d 940 at 944 (1941), *cf.* above, p.229.

[4] In that it promotes certainty (above, pp.797–798), and on grounds stated at pp.228–230, above.

[5] [1999] 3 All E.R. 355.

[6] The employee was not negligent in taking on the work: *ibid.*, at 360.

[7] *ibid.*; this amounts to the equivalent of saying that there was a breach of a fundamental term, though this phrase is not used in the judgment.

some extent mitigated by the fact that the client made no claim for the return of the part of the fee that he had already paid.[8]

(5) Deliberate breach

A breach will not justify rescission *merely* because it is deliberate. For example, a shipowner could not rescind a charterparty merely because the charterer had deliberately and in breach of contract delayed in loading for one day: such a breach "can appropriately be sanctioned by damages".[9] A deliberate breach may, indeed, represent a perfectly honest attempt by the "guilty" party to do his best in the interests of the other party: for example, where a builder who is unable to obtain some minor component called for by the specifications, and who cannot quickly get into touch with the owner, on his own initiative uses a substitute of equal quality. The deliberate nature of the breach is, therefore, not decisive[10]; but it is sometimes relevant to the existence of the right to rescind.

(a) FRAUD. A deliberate breach may amount to fraud and may justify rescission on that ground. This would be the position where a vendor of land knowingly overstated its area and the statement became a term of the contract. In such a case the purchaser can rescind[11] and the vendor cannot compel him to take the land with "compensation,"[12] even though the breach was not "substantial," so that the latter remedy would have been available, had the misdescription been made innocently.[13] Where, however, the fraud relates to a matter which is not in itself an essential part of the bargain, the right to rescind for fraud appears to be restricted by factors similar to the requirement of serious breach. Thus fraud on the part of an insured with regard to a minor matter not affecting the validity of his claim has been held not to give the insurer the right to rescind the policy for that fraud.[14]

(b) REPUDIATION. The fact that the breach is deliberate may justify rescission on the ground that it is evidence of "an intention no longer to be bound by the contract",[15] and so amounts to a repudiation, or to an offer to rescind the contract which the other party may accept and so terminate the contract.[16] Thus in *Withers v Reynolds*[17] an instalment contract provided for cash *on* delivery. The buyer announced his intention of paying *after* delivery for all future instalments, and it was held that this justified the seller's refusal to make further deliveries. Similarly, the buyer would have been entitled to rescind if the

---

[8] The claim was for £1,800; the amount already paid was £800. The question whether the client had a restitution claim for the latter sum was left open at p.361; see below, p.1053.

[9] *Suisse Atlantique* case [1967] A.C. 361 at 435; *cf. Rhymney Ry v Brecon & Merthyr Tydfil Junction Ry* (1900) 69 L.J.Ch. 813 at 819; *Decro-Wall International SA v Practitioners in Marketing Ltd* [1971] 1 W.L.R. 361 at 369.

[10] *Nynehead Developments Ltd v Fibreboard Containers Ltd* [1999] 1 E.G.L.R. 7.

[11] *Flight v Booth* (1834) 1 Bing.N.C. 370 at 376.

[12] *Re Terry & White's Contract* (1886) 32 Ch.D. 14 at 29; *Shepherd v Croft* [1911] 1 Ch. 521 at 531; *Re Belcham & Gawley's Contract* [1930] 1 Ch. 56.

[13] See above, p.772.

[14] *The Mercadian Continent* [2001] EWCA Civ 1275; [2001] 2 Lloyd's Rep. 563, at [35].

[15] *Freeth v Burr* (1874) L.R. 9 C.P. 208 at 213; *cf. Warinco AG v Samor SpA* [1979] 1 Lloyd's Rep. 450; *The Product Star (No.2)* [1993] 1 Lloyd's Rep. 397 at 407; *Thompson v Coroon* (1993) 66 P. & C.R. 445 at 449; *Cantor Fitzgerald International v Callaghan* [1999] 2 All E.R. 411 at 420. Contrast *The Aktion* [1987] 1 Lloyd's Rep. 283.

[16] *Bradley v H Newsom, Sons & Co* [1919] A.C. 16 at 52.

[17] (1831) 2 B. & Ad. 882.

seller had demanded payment *in advance* for all future deliveries.[18] Conversely, the *supplier* of a computer system was held to be guilty of a repudiation where, after a dispute had arisen between him and his customer, he fitted and activated a device which made the system unusable.[19] Again, unseaworthiness is not of itself a ground on which a charterer is entitled to rescind a charterparty: in general, it has this effect only if it produces a substantial failure in performance. But in the *Hong Kong Fir* case it was said that the charterer could have refused to accept the ship if the unseaworthiness had been discovered on or before her delivery and the shipowner had refused to comply with a request to put the matter right within a reasonable time.[20] Such refusal would have been evidence of the shipowner's intention to be no longer bound by the contract. Conversely, the giving by time charterers of an order for a voyage which is illegitimate because the voyage cannot be completed within the period of the charter will not of itself entitle the owner to rescind,[21] but he will become entitled to do so if the charterers' "persistence in it . . . showed that they did not intend to perform the charter."[22] After *The Hansa Nord*[23] a similar rule could, it is submitted, be applied where a seller of goods refused to put right a defect discovered before delivery, even though it did not amount to a breach of condition.[24]

On the other hand, the mere fact that a party has deliberately refused what the contract required him to do is not sufficient to show that he intended no longer to be bound by the contract; for he may have acted in good faith, honestly but mistakenly believing that the terms of the contract justified his refusal.[25] In *Woodar Investment Development Ltd v Wimpey Construction UK Ltd*[26] a purchaser of land purported to withdraw on a ground which, on the true construction of a somewhat obscure term in the contract, did not justify his withdrawal; but the House of Lords held that he had not repudiated, for he had acted in the bona fide belief that he was entitled to withdraw and had indicated throughout that he would perform if it should be decided that his interpretation of the contract was wrong.[27] The decision was not unanimous, but it is respectfully submitted that the view of the majority is to be preferred. To regard a refusal to perform as a repudiation in such circumstances would unduly hamper parties in negotiating the settlement of a contractual dispute; for it would expose each of them to the danger that any forthright assertion of his view of their relative rights and duties could, if it turned out to be wrong, justify rescission by the other party. The same principle can apply where a party makes a demand which goes beyond his rights: *e.g.* where a seller in good faith claims a price higher than that to which he is under the

---

[18] *Total Oil Great Britain Ltd v Thompson Garages (Biggin Hill) Ltd* [1972] 1 Q.B. 318 at 322; *cf. Nottingham BS v Eurodynamics Systems* [1995] F.S.R. 605 (so far as it holds the defendant guilty of wrongful repudiation).

[19] *Rubicon Computer Systems Ltd v United Paints Ltd* (2000) 2 T.C.L.R. 453.

[20] [1962] 2 Q.B. 26 at 56, 64; *cf. Stanton v Richardson* (1872) L.R. 7 C.P. 421, affirmed (1875) 45 L.J.C.P. 78. It is assumed that the breach is not purely trivial.

[21] See above, p.795.

[22] *The Gregos* [1994] 1 W.L.R. 1465 at 1476.

[23] [1976] Q.B. 44; above, p.796.

[24] *Mantovani v Carapelli SpA* [1978] 2 Lloyd's Rep. 63 at 72 ("persisted in and amounted to a refusal"); affirmed [1980] 1 Lloyd's Rep. 375.

[25] *Spettabile Consorzio Veneziano, etc., v Northern Ireland Shipbuilding Co Ltd* (1919) 121 L.T. 628 at 635; *James Shaffer Ltd v Findlay Durham & Brodie* [1953] 1 W.L.R. 106.

[26] [1980] 1 W.L.R. 277; Carter [1980] C.L.J. 256; Nicol and Rawlings, (1980) 43 M.L.R. 696; *cf. The Hazelmoor* [1980] 2 Lloyd's Rep. 351; *The Lutetian* [1982] 2 Lloyd's Rep. 140 at 159; *Spencer v Marchington* [1988] I.R.L.R. 392; *Nottingham BS v Eurodynamics Systems* [1995] F.S.R. 605 (in so far as it holds that the claimant had not repudiated).

[27] Contrast *Agrokor AG v Tradigrain* [2001] 1 Lloyd's Rep. 497 (unfounded assertion that performance was impossible said to amount to a repudiation).

contract entitled.[28] By way of contrast, a party's refusal to perform, unless his demand for a change in the terms of the contract are accepted by the other party, has been held to amount to a repudiation.[29]

One factor relevant to the issue of intention to be no longer bound by the contract is that the party alleged to have such an intention had acted on legal advice which was later held by the court to be mistaken. In *Mersey Steel & Iron Co v Naylor Benzon & Co*[30] a buyer of steel under an instalment contract refused, on the basis of such advice, to pay for one instalment. It was held that this refusal did not justify rescission by the seller since in these circumstances the buyer's refusal to pay was not evidence of his intention no longer to be bound by the contract.[31] But the fact that the party refusing to perform did so on the basis of legal advice is relevant only to his *intention* to be no longer bound. It therefore does not rule out the possibility that the refusal may give rise to a right to rescind on the grounds stated in the immediately following discussion.[32]

(c) SUBSTANTIAL BREACH. The injured party's right to rescind on account of the deliberate nature of the breach is not restricted to cases in which that breach is evidence of the other party's intention no longer to be bound by the contract. That party "may intend to fulfil [the contract] but may be determined to do so only in a manner substantially inconsistent with his obligations".[33] If so, the injured party can rescind: for example, a buyer can rescind a contract to deliver goods by instalments if over half the goods are seriously defective. He can do so even though the seller's breach is not deliberate or even negligent, and even though the seller protests that he intends to fulfil the contract.[34] Similarly, where a shipowner wrongfully refused to perform a charter-party except in such a way as made further performance useless to the charterer, the latter was entitled to rescind. It made no difference that the shipowner subjectively intended to perform his part (it being in his interest to do so as freight rates had fallen).[35] Thus if the breach has the effect of substantially depriving the injured party of what he bargained for, it is not necessary to show that the party in breach intended not to fulfil the contract. But proof of such intention may be sufficient to establish the right to rescind where the effect of the breach is less drastic[36]: for example, where an employer refused to honour part of the contractual salary package although the part in question "was not in the context of the overall package very great".[37]

---

[28] *Vaswani v Italian Motors (Sales and Services) Ltd* [1996] 1 W.L.R. 270.

[29] *Dymock v Todd* [2002] UKPC 50; [2002] 2 All E.R. (Comm) 849.

[30] (1884) 9 App.Cas. 434; *cf. Payzu Ltd v Saunders* [1919] 2 K.B. 581; *Peter Dumenil & Co Ltd v James Ruddin Ltd* [1953] 1 W.L.R. 815; *Sweet & Maxwell Ltd v Universal News Ltd* [1964] 2 Q.B. 699; *Panchaud Frères SA v R Pagnan & Fratelli* [1974] 1 Lloyd's Rep. 394; *Toepfer v Cremer* [1975] 2 Lloyd's Rep. 118; *Bunge GmbH v CCV Landbouwbeland* [1980] 1 Lloyd's Rep. 458. Contrast *Dymock v Todd*, above, where non-payment of a fee was expressly stated in the contract to be a "fundamental breach".

[31] Lord Blackburn also refers (9 App.Cas. at 443) to the fact that the market price of the steel bought "had risen above the contract price." *cf.* above, pp.761, 777.

[32] *Vaswani v Italian Motors (Sales and Services) Ltd* [1996] 1 W.L.R. 270 at 277; the breach may be "repudiatory" in the second, though not in the first, of the two senses distinguished at pp.853–854, below.

[33] *Smyth & Co v Bailey Son & Co* [1940] 3 All E.R. 60 at 72; *Peter Lind & Co Ltd v Constable Hart & Co Ltd* [1979] 2 Lloyd's Rep. 248 at 254; *The Splendid Sun* [1981] Q.B. 694 at 713; *Bliss v SE Thames Regional Health Authority* [1985] I.R.L.R. 308.

[34] *Millar's Karri & Jarrah Co (1902) v Weddell, Turner & Co* (1909) 100 L.T. 128; *cf. Robert A Munro & Co Ltd v Meyer* [1930] 2 K.B. 312.

[35] *Federal Commerce and Navigation v Molena Alpha* [1979] A.C. 757; Carter [1979] C.L.J. 270.

[36] *cf. Bowmakers (Commercial) Ltd v Smith* [1965] 1 W.L.R. 855, esp. at 858–859; *Cantor Fitzgerald International v Callaghan* [1999] 2 All E.R. 411.

[37] *ibid.*, at 421.

There was formerly some support for a special rule in contracts of employment that "wilful disobedience of any lawful order is . . . a good ground of discharge."[38] But a single act of disobedience no longer of itself justifies dismissal. The test is whether the employee's act "shows a determination to disregard any essential term of his contract"[39]: in other words, the courts now apply in employment cases the normal rules governing deliberate breaches. Under these rules a teacher's refusal to supervise school meals has been held sufficiently serious to justify dismissal[40]; but a secretary's refusal to stay at a board meeting when her immediate superior walked out did not have this effect.[41] Dismissal may of course, also be justified by a long course of unsatisfactory conduct[42] (as opposed to a single act of deliberate disobedience).

(6) Unilateral contracts and options

So far we have been concerned with the effects of one party's failure to perform a promise, whether or not the failure amounts to a breach. A further possibility is that a party may fail to perform some act which he has not promised to perform, but the performance of which is a contingent condition[43] of the other party's liability. Such a condition must be strictly complied with. The rule may be illustrated by the case of a unilateral contract.[44] If A promises B £100 if B walks from London to York, B must walk all the way to York before he is entitled to the £100.[45] The requirement of strict performance can be explained on the ground that A has no other remedy than to withhold performance. He cannot recover damages if B fails to complete the walk, since B has made no promise.

The distinction between promises and conditions can apply also in relation to particular terms in bilateral contracts and has, in relation to such terms, given rise to differences of judicial opinion.[46] The question in each case is whether the term, on its true construction, imposes an obligation on one of the parties to do an act (*e.g.* to give a specified notice to the other) or whether its effect is merely to make the performance of the act a prerequisite of the accrual of the other party's liability. The authorities give little guidance on this question of construction, but at least the effect of the resulting distinction is clear. If the term in question is construed as a condition, the party seeking to rescind need not show that the other's failure to comply with the term prejudiced him seriously or at all. Yet where a term is construed as a *promise* such prejudice must, as a general rule,[47] be shown by a party who seeks to rescind.[48]

---

[38] *Turner v Mason* (1845) 14 M. & W. 112 at 117.

[39] *Gorse v Durham CC* [1971] 1 W.L.R. 775 at 781.

[40] *Gorse v Durham CC* (above); *cf. Miles v Wakefield MDC* [1987] A.C. 539 at 559–560; *Wiluszynshki v Tower Hamlets LBC* [1989] I.C.R. 493; below, p.791. In none of these cases was the employee in fact dismissed.

[41] *Laws v London Chronicle (Indicator Newspapers) Ltd* [1959] 1 W.L.R. 698.

[42] *Pepper v Webb* [1969] 1 W.L.R. 514; 85 L.Q.R. 325.

[43] See above, p.62.

[44] See above, p.37.

[45] It is assumed that A has not attempted to withdraw before B reaches York: see above, p.38.

[46] *e.g. Shires v Brock* (1977) 247 E.G. 127 where the disputed term appears to have been treated by Goff and Buckley L.JJ. at 131 and 133 as a condition, but by Scarman L.J. at 133 as a promise; *cf. United Dominion Trust Ltd v Eagle Aircraft Ltd* [1968] 1 W.L.R. 74, criticised by Atiyah, 31 M.L.R. 332 but approved in *United Scientific Holdings Ltd v Burnley BC* [1978] A.C. 904 at 928, 945, 951. The contract in the *United Dominion Trust* case resembled one of suretyship; had it actually been one of suretyship, the claimants' delay in giving the specified notice would probably have discharged the defendants: *cf. Midland Counties Finance Motor Co Ltd v Slade* [1951] 1 K.B. 346.

[47] *i.e.* in cases falling within the general rule discussed at pp.769–778, above, as opposed to the exceptions discussed at pp.778–811.

[48] *e.g. Alfred McAlpine plc v BAI (Run-off) Ltd* [2000] 1 Lloyd's Rep. 437.

The requirement that conditions which are not promises must be strictly complied with also applies to options to purchase. If the grantee fails to comply in any respect with a condition to which the exercise of the option is subject, he cannot enforce the option.[49] It makes no difference that the failure causes only insignificant prejudice, or none at all, to the grantor. Moreover, in the case of an option the rule applies even though the condition is the performance by the grantee of an obligation under another term of the agreement in which the option is contained. Thus in *West Country Cleaners (Falmouth) Ltd v Saly*[50] a lease gave a tenant an option to renew "providing all covenants herein contained have been duly observed and performed." The tenant had committed minor breaches of his covenant to paint the interior of his premises; and it was held that he was not entitled to exercise the option, even though it did not appear that the landlord was seriously prejudiced by the breaches. This application of the rule has been explained on the ground that "an option of this character is a privilege—a right which has always been treated by the law as requiring complete compliance with the terms and conditions upon which the option is to be exercised".[51] The severity of the rule is, however, mitigated in a number of ways. Thus the rule does not apply where a tenant was at one time in breach but has cured that breach by the time of the exercise of the option: *e.g.* if by that time he has paid off rent which had at an earlier stage been overdue.[52] The rule may also be displaced by a strict construction of the term imposing the condition, leading to the conclusion that there has been no failure to comply with it.[53]

5. Limitations on the Right to Rescind

The right to rescind may be excluded by the terms of the contract, *e.g.* by a non-rejection clause which, in accordance with the rules discussed in Chapter 7, is valid and on its true construction covers the breach which has occurred.[54] In such a case, no right to rescind ever arises.[55] Our present concern is with cases in which a right to rescind had at one stage arisen but in which it was later lost or limited: for example by waiver (or election), by part performance of the contract, by voluntary acceptance of a benefit, or under the Apportionment Act 1870. Where there are several breaches, each giving rise to a right to rescind, the fact that one such right has been lost does not necessarily bar the other or others.[56]

(1) Waiver or election

(a) DIFFERENT SENSES OF "WAIVER." Waiver is used in a number of senses, of which two[57] are relevant to the present discussion.

(i) *Waiver in the sense of election.* A party who is entitled to rescind may indicate that he will nevertheless perform his part of the contract. He is then said to have waived his right to rescind, or to have elected[58] to affirm the contract. For example, in *Bentsen v*

---

[49] *Hare v Nicholl* [1966] 2 Q.B. 160. The rule may be excluded by the terms of the option: see *Millichamp v Jones* [1982] 1 W.L.R. 1422, where the term which the grantee failed to perform was not a condition of the exercise of the option, but a promissory condition of the contract resulting from that exercise: *cf.* above, p.762.
[50] [1966] 1 W.L.R. 1485.
[51] *ibid.* at 1486.
[52] *Bass Holdings Ltd v Morton Music Ltd* [1988] Ch. 493.
[53] *Little v Courage Ltd* (1995) 70 P. & C.R. 469.
[54] See above, pp.221–241.
[55] *e.g. The Aegean Dolphin* [1992] 2 Lloyd's Rep. 178.
[56] See *Kwei Tek Chao v British Traders* [1954] 2 Q.B. 459.
[57] For other senses, see above, pp.102–105.
[58] *The Kanchenjunga* [1990] 1 Lloyd's Rep. 391 at 397–398.

Taylor[59] a charterparty falsely described the ship as "now sailed or about to sail" from a specified port. This was a breach of condition[60] on account of which the charterer could have refused to load; but he said that he would nevertheless load, and then refused to do so. It was held that he was liable for failure to load as he had waived his right to rescind.[61] Conversely, in *The Kanchenjunga*[62] a charterer in breach of contract nominated a port which was unsafe because of the Gulf war between Iran and Iraq, but the shipowner nevertheless pressed him to load there, and then sailed away. It was held that the shipowner had waived the charterer's breach and that he would have been liable in damages, if he had not been protected from such liability by a "war clause" in the charterparty. On the same principle, a shipowner loses his right to put an end to a charterparty under an express term entitling him to withdraw the ship for late payment of hire if he accepts such a payment knowing that the time for making it has passed[63]; a landlord loses the right to forfeit a lease for breach of covenant by the tenant if, knowing of the breach, he makes a demand for rent[64]; and a buyer of goods may lose the right to reject for breach of *one* implied condition if he has agreed with the seller that he will reject *only* for a breach of a *different* implied condition.[65] An important characteristic of waiver in the sense of election is that it bars only the injured party's right to rescind: it does not deprive him of his right to damages for the breach. Thus the shipowner in *The Kanchenjunga* would have been entitled to damages if his ship had entered the port and suffered damage there as a result of the charterer's breach.[66]

(ii) *Distinguished from total waiver.* The expression "total waiver" will here be used to refer to the situation in which a contracting party purports wholly to abandon rights under the contract.[67] It differs from waiver in the sense of election in that the injured party indicates that he is giving up, not merely his right to rescind, but also his right to damages[68] or to performance. S.11(2) of the Sale of Goods Act 1979 recognises both types of waiver in providing that "where a contract of sale is subject to a condition to be fulfilled by the seller, the buyer may *waive* the condition, *or* may *elect* to treat the breach of condition as a breach of warranty and not as a ground for treating the contract as repudiated."[69] Here "waive" is used to refer to total waiver (*i.e.* an abandonment by the buyer of his rights to rescind and to claim damages); while "elect" refers to waiver in the sense of election (*i.e.* to the buyer's abandonment of the right to rescind, while

---

[59] [1893] 2 Q.B. 274.

[60] See above, p.790.

[61] [1893] 2 Q.B. at 283, 285.

[62] [1990] 1 Lloyd's Rep. 391.

[63] *The Brimnes* [1975] Q.B. 929 at 954–956; *The Libyaville* [1975] 1 Lloyd's Rep. 537 at 554; cf. *Modern Transport Co Ltd v Duneric SS Co* [1917] 1 K.B. 370 (submission of question whether hire was due to arbitration held to be a waiver of the right to withdraw). But there is no waiver if the late payment is made into the owner's bank and rejected by him as soon as he learns of the payment: *The Laconia* [1977] A.C. 850; cf. *John Lewis Properties v Viscount Chelsea* [1993] 2 E.G.L.R. 77; and acceptance of an underpayment does not amount to waiver if there is still a reasonable possibility that the balance may be paid in time: *The Mihalios Xilas* [1979] 1 W.L.R. 1018.

[64] *David Blackstone Ltd v Burnetts* [1973] 1 W.L.R. 1487; *Expert Clothing Service & Sales Ltd v Hillgate House Ltd* [1986] Ch. 340 at 359. For an illustration of waiver by a purchaser of leasehold land see *Aquis Estates Ltd v Minton* [1975] 1 W.L.R. 1452 at 1596. Contrast *Re a Debtor (No.13A–10–1995)* [1995] 1 W.L.R. 1127 (no waiver where rent is demanded before or on the breach in question).

[65] *S N Kurkjan (Commodity) Brokers Ltd v Marketing Exchange for Africa Ltd* [1986] 2 Lloyd's Rep. 614.

[66] [1990] 1 Lloyd's Rep. 391 at 393, 397, 401.

[67] cf. *Tufton Associates Ltd v Dilmun Shipping* [1992] 1 Lloyd's Rep. 71, where the requirement of full performance of an entire obligation (above p.782) was displaced by waiver.

[68] *Ets Soules & Cie v International Trade Development Co Ltd* [1980] 1 Lloyd's Rep. 129 at 137–138; cf. *Banning v Wright* [1972] 1 W.L.R. 972; *The Happy Day* [2002] EWCA Civ 1068; [2002] 2 Lloyd's Rep. 487, at [64]–[65], [67].

[69] Italics supplied.

keeping alive his right to damages). It might be better if the courts were to use "waiver" only to refer to total waiver, and to use some other term, such as "election" or "affirmation" to refer to waiver in the sense of election.[70] They have in fact used "waiver" to refer to them both, perhaps because of an important similarity between the two processes; but unfortunately this usage also obscures an equally important difference between them. It will be convenient, in discussing these points, to refer to the two processes respectively as "total waiver" and "waiver in the sense of election."

(b) REQUIREMENT OF REPRESENTATION. The similarity between the two processes is that the operation of each depends on a "clear and unequivocal" representation.[71] In relation to total waiver, this requirement is discussed in Chapter 3.[72] Our present concern is with waiver in the sense of election: this also requires "an unequivocal act or statement"[73] by which the injured party clearly indicates that he intends, not to rescind, but to affirm, the contract. The reference to an "unequivocal act" shows that the injured party need not make an express statement of his intention to affirm: it is enough if he does some positive act from which that intention can be inferred. If the intention does not clearly appear from his words or conduct, there is no waiver. This is, for example, often the position where the injured party accepts defective performance subject to an express reservation of his rights[74] (though where several grounds of rescission exist and the reservation refers to only some of these, it will not preclude waiver of the others[75]). It has, similarly, been held that the right to rescind was not lost by waiver where a vendor of land, after the purchaser should have performed, said that he would consider a request for an extension of time[76]; where a buyer to whom short delivery had been made called for a "full tender"[77]; where a landlord, after the tenant had committed a breach of covenant, sent him a "negotiating document" designed to resolve the dispute[78]; where an employee continued, after the employer's breach, to accept wages for such time as was reasonably necessary for him to consider his position[79]; and where the injured party merely called on the guilty party to reconsider his position and to withdraw his repudiation.[80] Nor is the right lost by mere failure to exercise it: such failure is not normally a sufficiently clear indication that the right will not be exercised.[81] But where, as a matter of business, it is reasonable to expect the injured party to act promptly,

---

[70] cf. *Kammins Ballroom Ltd v Zenith Investments (Torquay) Ltd* [1971] A.C. 850 at 882–883; *State Trading Corp of India v Cie Française d'Importation et de Distribution* [1983] 2 Lloyd's Rep. 679 at 681.

[71] *Peyman v Lanjani* [1985] Ch. 457 at 501; *The Kanchenjunga* [1990] 1 Lloyd's Rep. 391 at 399; *The Great Marine (No.1)* [1990] 2 Lloyd's Rep. 245 at 249.

[72] See above, pp.107–109.

[73] *The Mihalios Xilas* [1979] 1 W.L.R. 1018 at 1024; cf. *The Balder London* [1980] 2 Lloyd's Rep. 489; *Bremer Handelsgesellschaft mbH v Finagrain (etc.) SA* [1981] 2 Lloyd's Rep. 259 at 266; *Cobec Brazilian Trading & Warehousing Corp v Alfred C Toepfer* [1983] 2 Lloyd's Rep. 386 at 392.

[74] *Bremer Handelsgesellschaft mbH v Deutsche Conti Handelsgesellschaft mbH* [1983] 2 Lloyd's Rep. 45; cf. *Nova Petroleum International Establishment v Trican Trading Ltd* [1989] 1 Lloyd's Rep. 312.

[75] *The Wise* [1989] 2 Lloyd's Rep. 451.

[76] *Prosper Homes v Hambros Bank Executor & Trustee Co* (1979) 39 P. & C.R. 395.

[77] *Cobec Brazilian Trading & Warehousing Corp v Alfred C Toepfer* [1983] 2 Lloyd's Rep. 386.

[78] *Expert Clothing Services & Sales Ltd v Hillgate House Ltd* [1986] Ch. 340.

[79] *Bliss v SE Thames Regional Health Authority*, [1987] I.C.R. 700.

[80] *Yukong Line of Korea v Rendsburg Investments Co of Liberia* [1996] 2 Lloyd's Rep. 604; for further proceedings, see *The Times*, October 30, 1997.

[81] See *Tyrer & Co v Hessler & Co* (1902) 7 Com.Cas. 166; *Allen v Robles* [1969] 1 W.L.R. 1193; cf. *Bremer Handelsgesellschaft mbH v Deutsche Conti Handelsgesellschaft mbH*, above, n.74; *The Scaptrade* [1981] 2 Lloyd's Rep. 425 at 430 (affirmed without reference to this point [1983] 2 A.C. 694); *Cantor Fitzgerald International v Callaghan* [1999] 2 All E.R. 411 at 423.

unreasonable delay in exercising the right to rescind may give rise to the inference that the contract has been affirmed.[82]

(c) No requirement of action in reliance. We saw in Chapter 3 that total waiver operated only where the party, to whom the representation giving rise to the waiver was made, had acted in reliance on that representation.[83] There is no similar requirement for the operation of waiver in the sense of election. The distinction is recognised in a number of cases[84] and the explanation for it seems to be as follows. In cases of total waiver, the injured party makes a promise wholly to give up his right to some or all of the performance due to him under the contract. *Prima facie*, this cannot be any benefit to him or any detriment to the party in breach, so that the promise is unsupported by consideration.[85] Action in reliance on the promise is necessary as a substitute for, or alternative to, consideration so as to give at least some legal effect to the promise.[86] In cases of the kind here under discussion, *i.e.* of waiver in the sense of election, the injured party has indicated that he is giving up only one of his remedies (*i.e.* rescission) but not any of his other remedies (by way of enforced performance or damages). Even if such an indication can be said to amount to a promise not to rescind, the process has never been considered to give rise to any problems of consideration.[87] The injured party is not *necessarily* in a worse position if he elects, instead of rescinding, to keep the contract in being and to claim damages. This *may* be more beneficial to him than rescission; and this possibility is sufficient to satisfy the requirement of consideration.[88]

Thus it is submitted that the difference in the requirements for the two types of waiver is supported by both authority and principle. It is, however, obscured by a number of factors. The first of these is the unfortunate use of "waiver" to describe both processes. This has resulted in the requirement of reliance being sometimes unnecessarily stated where waiver in the sense of election was under discussion (though inapplicable for want of a sufficiently clear representation)[89]; and occasionally such cases have been argued as if all the requirements of total waiver (including that of reliance) had to be satisfied.[90] The second is that some cases raise issues as to both types of waiver[91]; and in these the issue of reliance tends to be discussed generally, even in relation to the type of waiver to which it is not strictly relevant. The third is that "waiver" is sometimes

---

[82] *The Scaptrade* (above, n.81) [1981] 2 Lloyd's Rep. 425 at 430 relying on the analogy of cases of fraudulent misrepresentation (above, p.385); *The Laconia* [1977] A.C. 850 at 872; *The Balder London* [1980] 2 Lloyd's Rep. 489 at 491–493; above, p.751.

[83] See above, p.109.

[84] *Edm JM Mertens & Co PVBA v Veevoeder Import Export Vimex BV* [1979] 2 Lloyd's Rep. 372 at 384; *The Athos* [1981] 2 Lloyd's Rep. 74 at 87–88, affirmed on this point [1983] 1 Lloyd's Rep. 127; *The Scaptrade* [1981] 2 Lloyd's Rep. 425 at 430, affirmed on this point [1983] A.C. 694; *Peter Cremer v Granaria BV* [1981] 2 Lloyd's Rep. 583 at 589; *Peyman v Lanjani* [1985] Ch. 457 at 493, 500–501; *The Uhenbels* [1986] 2 Lloyd's Rep. 294 at 297; *The Kanchenjunga* [1990] 1 Lloyd's Rep. 391 at 399; *Oliver Ashworth (Holdings) Ltd v Ballard (Kent) Ltd* [2000] Ch. 12 at 27; *The Happy Day* [2002] EWCA Civ 1068; [2002] 2 Lloyd's Rep. 487, at [67].

[85] See above, pp.99, 101–102.

[86] See above, pp.102–119.

[87] *The Kanchenjunga* [1990] 1 Lloyd's Rep. 391 at 398.

[88] *cf.* above, pp.101, 126–130.

[89] *e.g. The Eurometal* [1981] 1 Lloyd's Rep. 337 at 341; *cf. Bremer Handelsgesellschaft mbH v Finagrain (etc.) SA* [1981] 2 Lloyd's Rep. 259 at 265.

[90] See *The Post Chaser* [1981] 2 Lloyd's Rep. 695, esp. at 702 where Robert Goff J. points out the difference between the two doctrines; *The Manila* [1988] 3 All E.R. 843 at 854, where the point seems not to have been argued; *The Wise* [1989] 2 Lloyd's Rep. 451.

[91] *e.g. Bremer Handelsgesellschaft mbH v C Mackprang Jr* [1979] 1 Lloyd's Rep. 221; *Bremer Handelsgesellschaft mbH v Deutsche Conti Handelsgesellschaft mbH* [1983] 2 Lloyd's Rep. 45; *Peter Cremer v Granaria BV* [1981] 2 Lloyd's Rep. 583.

used interchangeably with "estoppel,"[92] the operation of which does depend on action in reliance. That requirement is therefore assumed to exist where the decision can be based on either of these grounds and the court is not prepared to distinguish between them.[93]

(d) WHETHER KNOWLEDGE REQUIRED. There is some conflict in the authorities on the question whether a party can be said to have "waived" a right to rescind if he does not actually know of the existence of the right. Since the basis of waiver in the sense of election is that the injured party must be "taken to have affirmed"[94] the contract, it should follow that this type of waiver does require knowledge[95] by the injured party of the existence of the right to rescind.[96] This view is supported by *Peyman v Lanjani*[97] where the defendant had obtained a leasehold interest in a restaurant by means of a fraudulent impersonation, and later agreed to sell that interest. By reason of the fraud, the defendant's title was defective and the buyer, with knowledge of the fraud but not of the fact that it gave him the right to rescind, paid £10,000 and went into possession of the restaurant as the defendant's manager. It was held that the buyer had not lost the right to rescind; and one reason[98] for this conclusion was that he could not have elected to affirm the contract until he had become aware, not merely of the *facts* giving rise to the right to rescind, but of the *existence of the right* itself.[99] This reasoning does not apply to "total" waiver[1] which, far from being an affirmation of the original contract, generally amounts to an abandonment, or at least to a variation, of it.[2] Statements to the effect that a person can "waive" rights without being aware of their existence are best regarded as referring to such "total" waiver,[3] which is based on action in reliance by the party *to* whom the representation is made rather than on the subjective intention of the (allegedly affirming) party *by* whom it is made.

It is, however, possible for one party (A) so to conduct himself as to give the other (B) reasonable grounds for thinking that A has affirmed the contract; and B may form this belief even though A does not know of his right to rescind. If B proceeds to act in reliance on A's apparent affirmation, A may (even though he has not actually affirmed)

---

[92] *cf.* above, p.115.

[93] See *The Wise* [1989] 2 Lloyd's Rep. 451 at 460.

[94] *Kwei Tek Chao v British Traders & Shippers Ltd* [1954] 2 Q.B. 459 at 477.

[95] *i.e.* "actual knowledge or knowledge which a person deliberately refrains from acquiring:" *Transcatalana de Commercio SA v Incrobasa Industrial e Commercio Brazileira SA* [1995] 1 Lloyd's Rep. 215 at 219.

[96] *Panchaud Frères SA v Etablissements General Grain Co Ltd* [1970] 1 Lloyd's Rep. 53 at 57; *The Mihalios Xilas* [1979] 1 W.L.R. 1018 at 1023; *Trustees of Henry Smith's Charity v Willson* [1983] Q.B. 316 at 328; *Cobec Brazilian Trading & Warehousing Corp v Alfred C Toepfer* [1983] 2 Lloyd's Rep. 386 at 392. *Chrisdell Ltd v Johnson* [1987] 19 H.L.R. 406; *The Manila* [1988] 3 All E.R. 843; *The Kanchenjunga* [1990] 1 Lloyd's Rep. 391 at 398; *The Happy Day* [2002] EWCA Civ 1068, [2002] 2 Lloyd's Rep. 487 at [68].

[97] [1985] Ch. 457; applied in *Transcatalana de Commercio SA v Incrobasa Industrial e Commercio Brazileira SA* [1995] 1 Lloyd's Rep. 215, discussing both "waiver in the sense of election" (219) and estoppel (220). *cf.* in another context, *Banner Industrial & Commercial Properties v Clark Paterson* [1990] 2 E.G.L.R. 139; *Fraser Shipping Ltd v Colton* [1997] 1 Lloyd's Rep. 586 at 594.

[98] A second was that there had been no unequivocal representation: see *ibid.* pp.501–502.

[99] *Yukong Line of Korea v Rendsburg Investments Corp* [1996] 2 Lloyd's Rep. 604 at 608, 609; *HB Property Development Ltd v S of S for the Environment, etc.* (1999) 78 P. & C.R. 108 at 114. Earlier decisions, discussed in *Peyman v Lanjani*, were in conflict on the question whether the injured party could affirm when he was aware only of the facts but not of the right. In *The Kanchenjunga* [1990] 1 Lloyd's Rep. 391 at 398 it was not necessary to discuss the conflict on this point since the injured party knew of the facts giving rise to the right to rescind *and* of the existence of the right.

[1] A point apparently overlooked in *The Superhulls Cover Case (No.2)* [1990] 2 Lloyd's Rep. 431 at 449.

[2] See above, pp.102–105.

[3] See *Bremer Handelsgesellschaft mbH v C Mackprang Jr* [1979] 1 Lloyd's Rep. 221 at 230; contrast *ibid.* p.229; the case involved *both* types of waiver.

be estopped from denying that he has waived the right to rescind.[4] The *effects* of such an estoppel are the same as those of waiver in the sense of election, and both require an unequivocal representation. Their *requirements* differ,[5] however, in that this type of waiver requires knowledge by the injured party of the existence of the right to rescind but no reliance on the representation by the party in breach, while an estoppel of the kind described above does not seem to require any such knowledge[6] but does require action in reliance.[7] A party who does not know of the existence of the right to rescind may also lose it on one of the other grounds to be discussed below.[8]

(2) Part performance of the contract

(a) GENERALLY NO BAR. The fact that the party in breach has partly performed the contract does not of itself bar the right to rescind. For example, rescission is available where there has been partial performance of an entire obligation, as in *Sumpter v Hedges*.[9] Similarly, express provisions for determination often operate after part performance of the contract.[10]

The above illustrations concern *exceptions* to the requirement of serious failure in performance. In cases to which that requirement *applies*, the courts do sometimes take the fact of part performance into account so as to conclude that the failure is not sufficiently serious to give rise to a right to rescind at all.[11] But once the failure is found to be of the required degree of seriousness, the injured party will not lose the right to refuse to perform or to accept further performance[12] merely because the other party has partly performed the contract: for example, in *Aerial Advertising Co v Batchelor's Peas Ltd*[13] rescission was allowed after such part performance.

(b) EFFECT OF ACCEPTANCE ON BREACH OF CONDITION. Although part performance does not usually bar the right to rescind, there is a rule that, where this right is based on a breach of condition, it may be lost by conduct of the injured party consequent on the other party's defective performance of the contract. This rule is most clearly illustrated by s.11(4) of the Sale of Goods Act 1979,[14] which provides that where a buyer has "accepted"[15] goods under a contract which is not severable[16] "the breach of a condition to be fulfilled by the seller can only be treated as a breach of warranty, and not as a ground for rejecting the goods and treating the contract as repudiated." This rule differs from waiver in the sense of election (discussed above) and voluntary acceptance

---

[4] See *Peyman v Lanjani* [1985] Ch. 457 at 495, 501.

[5] *The Happy Day* [2002] EWCA Civ 1068; [2002] 2 Lloyd's Rep. 487 at [64].

[6] *i.e.* of the existence of the right: see *Peyman v Lanjani*, above, at 495, 500. According to *National Westminster Bank v Hart* [1983] Q.B. 773, knowledge or notice of *the facts* is necessary; but in *The Kanchenjunga* [1990] 1 Lloyd's Rep. 391 at 399 there is said to be no need for "particular knowledge." See also *Transcatalana de Commercio SA v Incrobasa Industrial e Commercio Brasileira* [1995] 1 Lloyd's Rep. 215 at 219 ("Estoppel operates on a different principle though knowledge may still play a role").

[7] Or, in cases of estoppel by representation, *detrimental* reliance: above, p.403.

[8] *e.g.* below, after n.13.

[9] [1898] 1 Q.B. 673; above, p.836.

[10] *e.g.* above, p.779.

[11] *e.g.* in *Boone v Eyre* (1777) 1 Hy.Bl. 273n., above, p.770.

[12] For the effect of part performance on his right to recover back money paid, see below, pp.1050–1052.

[13] [1938] 2 All E.R. 786; above, p.777. *Thorpe v Fasey* [1949] Ch. 649 may at first sight suggest that there cannot be rescission after part performance; but the case is best explained on the ground that rescission was not available as the breach was not a serious one and time was not of the essence of the contract: below, p.827.

[14] As amended by Sale and Supply of Goods Act 1994, s.3(2).

[15] See above, p.384.

[16] See above, p.784.

of a benefit (to be discussed below) in that it can apply even though the injured party has no knowledge of the breach.[17] A buyer of defective goods is, for example, deemed to have accepted them if he retains them after the lapse of a reasonable time without intimating to the seller that he has rejected them.[18] In determining what is, for this purpose, a reasonable time, the court will consider whether the buyer has had a reasonable *opportunity* of examining the goods[19]; but he may have accepted them, and so have lost the right to reject, even though he has not actually discovered the defect.[20] The general rule, then, is clear: "acceptance" bars the right to rescind a contract for breach of condition. But the rule is subject to three, and may be subject to four, qualifications.

(i) *Partial rejection.* A buyer of goods may have the right to reject all the goods even though only some of them are not in conformity with the contract. If he accepts some of the goods, he does not thereby lose his right to reject the rest.[21]

(ii) *Incorporated misrepresentation.* If a misrepresentation made before the contract is incorporated in the contract as a condition, the right to rescind the contract *for misrepresentation* survives and may be exercised in spite of the fact that the contract has been performed.[22] A buyer of goods might be able to exercise this right even though his right to rescind *for breach*[23] was barred by "acceptance." But the right to rescind for misrepresentation is subject to the court's discretion[24] to declare the contract subsisting and to award damages in lieu of rescission. It seems probable that the court will generally follow this course where the right to rescind for breach has been lost by "acceptance," though there may be cases of hardship to a buyer in which the court would not wish to confine him to a remedy in damages.

(iii) *Serious breach.* In Chapter 7 we saw that there was a "strong, though rebuttable, presumption"[25] that exemption clauses were not to be construed to cover certain particularly serious breaches. The distinction between various kinds of breaches there drawn is also relevant in considering the scope of the rule that acceptance bars the right to rescind for breach of condition.

One type of serious breach is that which makes "performance totally different from that which the contract contemplates".[26] As a matter of general common law, "execution" of a contract does not bar the right to rescind for a breach of this kind. This appears from *Dakin v Oxley*,[27] where the actual decision was that a charterer could not refuse to pay freight, after the goods had been carried to their destination, merely because they had been damaged in transit; but the court added that he would not be liable where "a valuable picture had arrived as a piece of spoilt canvas, cloth in rags, or crockery in broken shreds, iron all or almost rust, rice fermented or hides rotten".[28] The same general principle applies where the seller's breach is a breach of condition and its effect is wholly to deprive the buyer of what he bargained for. In *Rowland v Divall*[29] the

---

[17] *The Kanchenjunga* [1990] 1 Lloyd's Rep. 391 at 398; *Transcatalana de Commercio SA v Incrobasa Industrial e Commercio Brasileira SA* [1995] 1 Lloyd's Rep. 215 at 220.

[18] Sale of Goods Act 1979, s.35(4) (as substituted by Sale and Supply of Goods Act 1994, s.2(1)).

[19] *ibid.*, s.35(5).

[20] *e.g. Bernstein v Pamson Motors (Golders Green) Ltd* [1987] 2 All E.R. 220; Reynolds, 104 L.Q.R. 16; *cf. Shine v General Guarantee Corp* [1988] 1 All E.R. 911 (hire-purchase).

[21] Sale of Goods Act 1979, s.35A, as inserted by Sale and Supply of Goods Act 1994, s.3(1).

[22] Misrepresentation Act 1967, s.1(a); above, pp.375–376.

[23] For the distinction between this right and the right to rescind for misrepresentation, see above, pp.369, 376.

[24] Misrepresentation Act 1967, s.2(2); above, pp.357, 377.

[25] *Suisse Atlantique* case [1967] 1 A.C. 361 at 427; above, p.234.

[26] *Suisse Atlantique* case, above, at 393.

[27] (1864) 15 C.B.(N.S.) 646; *Pilbrow v Pearless de Rougemont & Co* [1993] 3 All E.R. 355, above, p.806.

[28] *ibid.* at 667; *cf. The Caspian Sea* [1980] 1 W.L.R. 48.

[29] [1923] 2 K.B. 500; and see further below, p.1053.

defendant sold a car which, unknown to him or to the buyer, had been stolen. The defendant was in breach of the implied condition that he had a right to sell the car but the buyer did various acts amounting to "acceptance" of the car[30] before it was traced by the police. It was held that the buyer could nevertheless rescind the contract (and so recover back the price paid) as "he did not get what he paid for—namely a car to which he would have title."[31] It is submitted that the position would be the same where beans were delivered under a contract to sell peas.[32] In such a case the buyer will not lose his right to rescind *merely* because his conduct amounts to "acceptance",[33] or would have amounted to "acceptance" if the seller had delivered peas which were not in accordance with the contract. Of course if the buyer knows that beans have been delivered and decides to keep them it may be possible to infer a new contract to buy beans.[34] But "acceptance" can take place without any knowledge of the breach, and "acceptance" without such knowledge should not (it is submitted) deprive the buyer of his right to rescind where the seller has delivered something "totally different" from the thing which he has contracted to sell.

The rule of construction discussed in Chapter 7 can also apply where the breach is serious in the wider sense of causing *substantial* prejudice to the injured party without making the performance rendered *totally* different from that bargained for.[35] In such a case, the right to rescind may be lost by "acceptance" in spite of the fact that the breach is sufficiently serious to prevent the party in breach from relying on an exemption clause. For example, a defect in the quality of goods may be sufficiently serious to justify the buyer in rejecting and to deprive the seller (as a matter of construction) of the benefit of an exemption clause. But the breach may nevertheless not be serious enough to allow the buyer to rescind after "acceptance" so as to recover back the money which he has paid.[36]

There are, finally, cases in which a party is prevented from relying on an exemption clause, because he has broken a fundamental term,[37] even though the breach does not deprive the injured party of what he bargained for at all: this would be the position where goods are safely carried to their destination in a ship which has deviated.[38] There is no doubt that in such a case the cargo-owner can rescind the contract. But he may nevertheless have to make some payment to the carrier under the rules to be discussed below.[39]

(iv) *Consumer sales.* A buyer who deals as a consumer may (subject to certain restrictions) require the seller to repair or to replace goods which do not conform to the contract by reason of the seller's breach of certain implied conditions or of an express term.[39a] The seller then has a reasonable time within which to comply with the buyer's requirement.[39b] During that time the buyer may not reject the goods for breach of

---

[30] He had painted it and sold it to a third party. As the law then stood, this amounted (or would, in the case of a breach of the implied conditions as to quality, have amounted) to acceptance, even without an opportunity of discovering the truth; see now above, p.384.

[31] [1923] 2 K.B. 500 at 504.

[32] *Chanter v Hopkins* (1838) 4 M. & W. 399 at 404.

[33] For the meaning of "acceptance", see above, p.384.

[34] *Charterhouse Credit Co Ltd v Tolly* [1963] 2 Q.B. 683 at 710.

[35] See above, pp.226–227.

[36] cf. *Yeoman Credit Ltd v Apps* [1962] 2 Q.B. 508.

[37] See above, p.227.

[38] See above, p.228. cf. above, p.806.

[39] See below, pp.820–821.

[39a] Sale of Goods Act 1979, ss.48A, 48B and 48F; above, p.803.

[39b] *ibid.*, s.48B(2)(a).

condition[39c]; but if by the end of the reasonable time the seller has failed so to comply, then the buyer may rescind the contract.[39d] Nothing in these provisions precludes the application of the rule that the right to rescind for breach of condition is lost by acceptance; but their structure makes it clear that a buyer does not accept goods merely by exercising his statutory right to require the seller to repair or replace them.

(c) PART PAYMENT. The above discussion is concerned with cases in which the part performance consists of something other than a payment of money. The mere fact that part of a sum of money due under a contract has been paid clearly does not bar the right to rescind if the payor then commits a repudiatory breach in failing or refusing to pay the balance.[40] The exercise of the right to rescind may, however, then give rise to a duty to return the part payment, in accordance with the rules to be discussed in Chapter 21.[41]

(3) Voluntary acceptance of benefit

This idea does not strictly limit, but rather attenuates, the right to rescind. Under it, the person who receives partial or defective performance does not lose the right to rescind *the contract*; but if he "voluntarily" accepts the defective performance he must make some payment for it. Thus in *Christy v Row*[42] a contract was made to carry coal to Hamburg. The ship was prevented by restraints of princes from reaching Hamburg, and the master *at the request of the consignees* delivered some of the coal at Gluckstadt. It was held that the shipowner could recover freight in respect of the coal so delivered. In this case the shipowner recovered the full freight, but later cases state the rule that he is entitled only to freight *pro rata itineris*, *i.e.* for freight at the contract rate for the proportion of the voyage originally undertaken which was actually accomplished.[43]

The present principle applies only if the benefit is accepted "voluntarily." A person is not considered to accept a benefit "voluntarily" if he merely takes possession of his own property. Thus a shipowner who discharges cargo at an intermediate port cannot recover freight *pro rata* merely because the cargo-owner has under protest taken possession of his own goods there.[44] In *Sumpter v Hedges*[45] the builder's claim for the reasonable value of his work was dismissed on similar grounds. Such a claim would succeed only if a "new contract" to pay a reasonable sum could be inferred. No such inference could be drawn from the mere fact that the defendant had reoccupied his own land with the partly completed buildings on it; he had no real "option whether he will take the benefit of the work done or not."[46] He did, however, "voluntarily" make use of certain loose materials left by the builder on the site and was held liable for the reasonable value of these materials.

The object of the requirement of a "new contract" is, no doubt, to protect the party receiving the partial or defective performance, who may be prejudiced by having to pay

---

[39c] *ibid.*, s.48D(1) and (2)(a).
[39d] *ibid.*, s.48C(1)(b) and (2)(b).
[40] *Hillel v Christoforides* (1991) 63 P. & C.R. 301.
[41] See below p.1007.
[42] (1808) 1 Taunt. 300; *cf. Lambourn v Cruden* (1841) 2 M. & G. 253 at 256.
[43] See *Scrutton on Charterparties* (20th ed.), p.333. In exceptional circumstances the proper measure of recovery may be a reasonable sum, assessed independently of the contract rate: *Mitchell v Darthez* (1836) 2 Bing.N.C. 555. Obviously, a strict geographical apportionment would be inappropriate where part of the journey was much more expensive than the rest, *e.g.* because it led through the Panama Canal.
[44] *Metcalfe v Britannia Ironworks Co* (1877) 2 Q.B.D. 423; *cf.* above, p.782.
[45] [1898] 1 Q.B. 673; above, p.783.
[46] [1898] 1 Q.B. 673 at 676.

pro rata or a reasonable sum. He may have suffered loss in consequence of the failure in performance, and, if the failure does not amount to a breach, rescission may be his only remedy. Even if there has been a breach, the damages legally recoverable for it may fall short of the actual loss suffered. The victim may have stipulated for complete performance before payment precisely in order to protect himself against these risks.

On the other hand, the failure in performance may not cause any loss at all,[47] or it may cause a loss worth much less than the value of the partial or defective performance. In such cases the requirement of a "new contract" may lead to the unjust enrichment of the party by whom such performance has been received. Under the rule in *Sumpter v Hedges* a landowner may get nearly completed buildings for nothing. This did not actually happen in the leading case itself, in which considerable payments had been made to the builder on account of the work.[48] But in *Bolton v Mahadeva*[49] a builder recovered nothing for his defective performance of a contract to install a central heating system for £560, even though no part of this sum had been paid to him, the defects in his work cost only £170 to put right, and the house-owner's other damages were assessed at £15. Again, where a shipowner discharges goods at an intermediate port, the cargo-owner may get the benefit of having them carried a considerable distance for nothing. This possibility is strikingly illustrated by a case in which it was held that the cargo-owner was not bound to pay anything even though the failure to carry the goods to their destination apparently benefited him, the goods having been sold for *more* at the intermediate port than they were worth at the agreed destination.[50] At the same time the requirement of a new contract may bear very harshly on the party conferring the benefit; and therefore the requirement that acceptance of the benefit must be "voluntary" so as to support the inference of a new contract is, or may be, modified in a number of situations.

The clearest modification of the requirement can be seen in cases in which a seller of goods delivers the wrong quantity, *e.g.* a quantity less than that contracted for. In such a case the buyer can generally reject the goods[51] but if he "accepts" them he "must pay for them at the contract rate."[52] This acceptance need not be "voluntary" in the full sense, for the buyer may do acts amounting to "acceptance" before he knows of the defect in delivery.[53]

A second situation in which the requirement of "voluntary" acceptance may be modified arises where a carrier by sea deviates.[54] This undoubtedly gives the cargo-owner the right to rescind; but he may not exercise this right and may accept the goods after the carrier has carried them to their agreed destination. This acceptance of the goods is no more "voluntary" than taking possession of goods which have been discharged without their owner's consent at an intermediate port; but dicta in the House

---

[47] See below, at n.50.

[48] The value of the work done is stated to be "about £333" and the builder had received £219 (67 L.J.Q.B. 545) or £119 plus two horses worth £100 (46 W.R. 464). Hence the total enrichment of the defendant appears to have been at the most £114, against which any loss suffered by him should be set off. The actual result may not have been unjust; certainly the builder's claim for £230 (78 L.T. 378) or £222 (46 W.R. 464) seems excessive.

[49] [1972] 1 W.L.R. 1009.

[50] *Hopper v Burness* (1876) 1 C.P.D. 137; it was said that there was no hardship to the shipowner as "the proper remedy is by insurance of freight" (at 141).

[51] See above, p.783.

[52] Sale of Goods Act 1979, s.30(1). (It is assumed that the goods are not "unsolicited" within Consumer Protection (Distance Selling) Regulations 2000, SI 2000/2334, reg.24; above, p.9.)

[53] See above, pp.817–818.

[54] For deviation, see p.228.

of Lords in *Hain SS Co Ltd v Tate & Lyle Ltd*[55] support the view that the shipowner may in such a case be entitled to a reasonable freight. This is not necessarily the same as the stipulated freight, so that the risk of any fall in freight rates would be on the carrier; but it seems most unlikely that he would be allowed to rely on the deviation to secure the benefit of any rise in freight rates.

A third modification of the requirement that acceptance of the benefit must be "voluntary" may exist where breaches of a contract of employment are committed in the course of an industrial dispute. Such a breach may take the form, not only of an outright refusal to work, but also of a refusal merely to carry out certain specified tasks. If (as will often be the case) the refusal amounts to a repudiatory breach,[56] the employer is at common law entitled to dismiss the employee. But he may not exercise that power and instead follow one of three other courses of action. First, he may voluntarily accept such services as the employee is willing to render. In that case, he can at the very least deduct from the employee's wages, by way of damages, any loss which he has suffered as a result of the breach.[57] Even if he has not suffered any loss, he can deduct from the employee's pay such part of the agreed wages as is attributable to the work which the employee has refused to perform[58]: that amount (at least) will not have been earned by reason of the employee's failure to perform a condition precedent.[59] Secondly, he may tell the employee that he declines to accept the services (falling short of those due under the contract) which the employee is prepared to render, and actually does render. In that event, the employee is not entitled to pay for any period during which no services are rendered[60]; nor is he entitled to any pay for rendering services falling short of those due, even if the employer has not physically prevented him from rendering them.[61] Thirdly, the employer may accept the services which the employee is prepared to render, and do so, not voluntarily, but "of necessity"[62]: he may do this either because he has no practical choice (where he cannot in fact prevent the employee from gaining access to his place of work), or because he is required to accept the services offered in order to mitigate his loss.[63] In such a case there has been no "voluntary" acceptance of a benefit; but there is nevertheless some support for the view that the employer must pay a reasonable remuneration for the services actually rendered.[64] This view seems to be based on unjust enrichment rather than on a "new contract": the employer is liable because he has received a benefit, not because he has impliedly agreed to pay for it. The difficulty in accepting this view, however, arises precisely because in the case put the employer has *not*

---

[55] (1936) 41 Com.Cas. 350 at 358, 367, doubting contrary dicta in the Court of Appeal 34 Com.Cas. 259, 285. The dicta in the House of Lords are accepted in *Scrutton on Charterparties*, (20th ed.), p.260, and in Carver, *Carriage of Goods by Sea* (13th ed.), para.1197; for the basis of liability, see *Carver on Bills of Lading* (1st ed., 2001), §§9–046, 9–049. *cf. Bornman v Tooke* (1808) 1 Camp. 376. Contrast *Pilbrow v Pearless De Rougement & Co* [1999] 3 All E.R. 355 at 360 (above, p.806; no claim for the reasonable value of the services rendered was made in that case).

[56] See above, p.806; below, p.843.

[57] *Sim v Rotherham Metropolitan BC* [1987] Ch. 216, where the action was not for the agreed wages, but for a declaration that the employer was not entitled to deduct damages: see *Miles v Wakefield Metropolitan DC* [1987] A.C. 539 at 574–575; Napier, [1987] C.L.J. 44.

[58] *Miles v Wakefield Metropolitan DC*, above; McMullen, 51 M.L.R. 234; the contrary assumption made in *Sim v Rotherham Metropolitan BC*, above, at p.255) is no longer maintainable.

[59] See above, p.762.

[60] *Ticehurst & Thompson v British Telecommunications* [1992] I.C.R. 383.

[61] *Wiluszynski v Tower Hamlets LBC* [1989] I.C.R. 493; McLean [1990] C.L.J. 28; Mead, 106 L.Q.R. 192; *Macpherson v London Borough of Lambeth* [1988] I.R.L.R. 470.

[62] *Miles v Wakefield Metropolitan DC* [1987] A.C. 539 at 553.

[63] *ibid.* at 561; *cf.* below, p.978.

[64] *ibid.* at 553 (*per* Lord Brightman) and 561 (*per* Lord Templeman). The point is left open by Lord Brandon (at 552) and Lord Oliver (at 576).

rescinded the contract, so that *prima facie* the rights and duties of the parties continue to be governed by that contract.[65]

(4) Comparisons

It is interesting to compare the various liabilities of a party who receives partial or defective performance under the preceding qualifications of the right to rescind; of course, where the failure in performance amounts to a breach these liabilities are subject to his right to damages. A buyer who "accepts" goods which are defective in a way that amounts to a breach of condition is liable for the contract price. A buyer who accepts short delivery of goods is not liable for the contract price, but for payment at the contract rate. In neither case is it necessary for the "acceptance" to be fully "voluntary," as it may take place before the buyer knows of the failure in performance. A cargo-owner who takes delivery at an intermediate port is under no liability at all unless he acts "voluntarily"; and if he does act "voluntarily" he is liable for freight *pro rata itineris*, that is, not for the agreed freight but for a proportion of it at the contract rate. A landowner in a situation similar to that in *Sumpter v Hedges* is not liable at all unless he "voluntarily" accepts the benefit; but if this requirement is satisfied he is liable for a reasonable sum. A cargo-owner who takes delivery at the agreed destination after the carrier has deviated is liable (if at all) for a reasonable sum; and it seems that he is liable even though he did not act "voluntarily" but merely took possession of his own goods. An employer who accepts services falling short of those promised may similarly be liable for a reasonable sum, even though his acceptance of the services is not truly voluntary. The reasons for these distinctions have never been satisfactorily explained.

(5) Wrongful prevention of performance

A contract may provide that one party (A) is not to be paid until he completes performance. If, after A has begun to perform, the other party (B) wrongfully refuses to let him complete, A can, no doubt, claim damages for breach of contract.[66] Alternatively, he can claim a *quantum meruit* for the work he has done. In *Planché v Colburn*[67] A agreed to write a book on costume and ancient armour which was to appear in serial form in B's periodical. B stopped publishing the periodical when A had written the greater part of the work, and it was held that A was entitled to a *quantum meruit*. This rule differs from those just discussed[68] in that A's right to a reasonable remuneration does not depend on the receipt of any benefit by B. It applies only where B's refusal was wrongful. Thus an employee who is justifiably dismissed cannot at common law recover a *quantum meruit* or any part of his current salary[69]; and a contractor employed to do building work cannot recover anything for his work if it is done so badly as to justify the customer's refusal to allow him to complete.[70]

---

[65] *Miles v Wakefield Metropolitan DC* [1987] A.C. 539 at 552 (*per* Lord Bridge), and *cf.* below, pp.1062–1063.

[66] It is assumed here that A could have completed but for B's wrongful refusal, so that the problem discussed at pp.766–769 above does not arise.

[67] (1831) 8 Bing. 14; *cf. De Bernardy v Harding* (1853) 8 Exch. 822; *Inchbald v Western Neilgherry Coffee Co* (1864) 17 C.B.(N.S.) 733.

[68] *i.e.* at pp.819–822, above.

[69] *Ridgway v Hungerford Market Co* (1835) 3 A. & E. 171; *Boston Deep Sea Fishing & Ice Co v Ansell* (1888) 39 Ch.D. 339, where it is said at p.364 that he cannot sue for a reasonable remuneration either. For the possible application of the Apportionment Act 1870, see below, pp.823–825.

[70] *Whitaker v Dunn* (1887) 3 T.L.R. 602.

(6) Both parties in breach

Where both parties are alleged to have committed breaches, each of which is claimed to be a ground for rescission, the first question to be considered is the order in which the alleged breaches have occurred. If A's breach occurred before B's, the normal position is that A's breach gives B a right to rescind, and, if B exercises that right, his subsequent failure to perform does not amount to a breach at all (even though it would have done so, if A had not committed the earlier breach).[71] It is, however, also possible for both parties simultaneously to commit breaches, each of which, standing alone, would justify rescission: for example, because each is a breach of condition. The normal rule in such cases is that each party is entitled to rescind on account of the other's breach.[72] There is however some support for a different conclusion where the two breaches are inter-related in the sense that the second consists of failure to perform a duty to avoid the consequences of the first. This was said to be the position in a line of cases concerning agreements to submit claims to arbitration. Where a claimant had committed a breach of such an agreement by undue delay in prosecuting his claim after it had been brought, it was held to be the duty of the respondent to apply to the arbitrator for directions to put an end to that delay. It was said to follow that "both claimant and respondent were in breach of their contractual obligations to each other[73]; and neither can rely on the other's breach as giving him a right to treat the primary obligations of each to proceed with the reference as at an end".[74] This reasoning had the unfortunate practical consequence that an arbitration might be allowed to continue after so long a delay that a satisfactory trial was no longer possible. This problem has been discussed in Chapter 2, where a number of common law and statutory solutions to it were considered.[75] The present point is that the reasoning just quoted is, with respect, open to question; for if both parties are in breach it is by no means clear why it should follow that neither can rescind; it is equally possible to conclude that each party has the option to do so. Now that the reasoning of the arbitration cases has been made largely obsolete by statute,[76] it should no longer be regarded as justifying an exception to the general rule[77] that, where both parties are guilty of breaches justifying rescission, each should have the right to rescind. The justification for that general rule is, it is submitted, that no good purpose is served by holding parties to a contract after each of them has committed a repudiatory breach of it.

(7) Apportionment Act 1870

S.2 of this Act provides that "All rents, annuities, dividends and other periodical payments in the nature of income . . . shall . . . be considered as accruing from day to day, and shall be apportionable in respect of time accordingly." By s.5 "annuities" includes "salaries and pensions"; and by s.7 the Act does not apply where it is "expressly stipulated that no apportionment shall take place." The Act raises a number of problems, three of which are relevant in the context of this Chapter.

---

[71] See above, p.767.
[72] *State Trading Corporation of India v M. Golodetz Ltd* [1989] 2 Lloyd's Rep. 277 at 286.
[73] *cf.* Arbitration Act 1996, s.40(2)(b), stating a more restricted duty.
[74] *Bremer Vulkan u Maschinenfabrik v South India Shipping Co* [1981] A.C. 909 at 987; this reasoning was affirmed, and the decision followed, in *The Hannah Blumenthal* [1983] 1 A.C. 854; *cf. The Matja Gubec* [1981] 1 Lloyd's Rep. 31; *The Boucraa* [1944] 1 A.C. 486 at 521–522; *The Frotanorte* [1996] 2 Lloyd's Rep. 461, referring to criticisms of the rule.
[75] See above, pp.10, 35.
[76] Arbitration Act 1996, s.41.
[77] Stated at n.72, above.

The first is what is meant by a "periodical" payment. It seems that this expression refers to a sum or sums payable under a contract at the end of a stipulated time, or at fixed intervals of time. A single lump sum payable for a specific piece of work would not be a periodical payment; and this is one reason why the Act would not apply to a case like *Cutter v Powell*.[78] Nor would the payment be periodical merely because the contract stipulated the time within which the piece of work was to be done: thus the Act would not apply to a case like *Sumpter v Hedges*[79] even though the contract in that case contained a completion date.[80]

The second question is whether the Act entitles a person whose salary is payable at the end of a stipulated period to recover a proportionate part of the salary if he works for only part of the period. An Irish case supports the view that the Act does apply in such a case.[81] Similarly, in *Moriarty v Regent's Garage Co*,[82] the claimant was appointed director of the defendant company on the terms that "his fees for so acting shall be £150 per annum." Before the end of the year he ceased (without any breach of contract) to be a director, and the Divisional Court held that he could recover a proportionate part of his salary under the Act.[83] The Court of Appeal reversed this decision on procedural grounds and left open the question whether the Act would apply.[84] The point is of little practical importance because "the question of apportionment is now usually dealt with by using the words 'at the rate of' in the Articles".[85] Indeed, the Articles often go further and provide expressly that remuneration "shall be deemed to accrue from day to day".[86]

The third question is whether the Act can be invoked by a party in breach of contract, for example by an employee who leaves in breach of contract or who is lawfully dismissed (for breach of duty) during the period at the end of which he is to be paid. In several cases since the Act, claims by such employees for their current pay have failed, but the Act is not mentioned in any of them.[87] In *Clapham v Draper*[88] it was held that a landlord could not recover rent for part of a rent period during which he had wrongfully turned the tenant out. This might be thought to support the view that the Act could not be invoked by a party in breach of contract; but another possible explanation of the decision is that "The Act was never intended to deal with *tortious* interferences with the right of any person."[89] In *Moriarty v Regent's Garage Co* Lush J. said that he would "hesitate to agree"[90] with the view that an employee could base a claim on the Act if he were lawfully

---

[78] (1795) 6 T.R. 320; apportionment would also on such facts be excluded by the express terms of the contract: see above, p.782.

[79] [1898] 1 Q.B. 673.

[80] See 67 L.J.Q.B. 545; 78 L.T. 378; 46 W.R. 464.

[81] *Treacy v Corcorran* (1874) I.R. 8 C.L. 40.

[82] [1921] 1 K.B. 423.

[83] *cf. Thames Water Utilities v Reynolds* [1996] I.R.L.R. 186. In two contrary decisions the Act was not mentioned: *Re Central de Kaap Gold Mines* (1899) 69 L.J.Ch. 18; *McConnell's Claim* [1901] 1 Ch. 728. In two further cases the Act was mentioned but held inapplicable to a claim by a *single* director because the articles provided for payment to *all* the directors of an annual lump sum to be divided between them in such proportion as they thought fit: *Salton v New Beeston Cycle Co* [1899] 1 Ch. 775; *Inman v Ackroyd & Best* [1901] 1 K.B. 613.

[84] [1921] 2 K.B. 766.

[85] *ibid.* at 779. It seems to have been assumed that the Articles had been incorporated in the contract of employment since they would not otherwise form part of the contract between the director and the company; above, p.586.

[86] See Companies Act 1985, s.8 and SI 1985/805, Table A, para.82.

[87] *Boston Deep Sea Fishing and Ice Co v Ansell* (1888) 39 Ch.D. 339; *Healey v SA Française Rubastic* [1917] 1 K.B. 947.

[88] (1885) Cab. & El. 484.

[89] *Murphy v Wood* [1941] 4 D.L.R. 454 at 457 (italics supplied).

[90] [1921] 1 K.B. 432 at 434.

dismissed, or left in breach of contract. McCardie J., while expressing "no opinion" on the point, puts the case of an employee whose salary is payable at the end of six months and who is lawfully dismissed in the last fortnight of that period. And he asks: "Is it right that he should be deprived of remuneration for five and a half months' work because during the last fortnight he has done something for which he has been dismissed?"[91] It is submitted that a negative answer should be given to this question, and that there is nothing in the 1870 Act which makes it inapplicable to such a situation.[92]

6. Criticism[93]

The law relating to the effects of failure to perform is hard to state; and parts of it are still harder to justify.[94] Criticism can, in particular, be directed at some of the exceptions to the requirement that a failure in performance must be substantial if it is to justify rescission. A number of judicial restrictions[95] on the scope of these exceptions may have improved the law; but it is arguable that two major defects remain.

The first is that a party may still be entitled to rescind though the breach does not prejudice him seriously or at all, *e.g.* where the breach is of a term previously classified as a "condition," or where a seller fails to deliver the correct quantity.[96] In such cases, the right to rescind can simply provide a party with an excuse for escaping from a bad bargain.[97] It would, it is submitted, be more satisfactory as a general principle to focus attention on the question whether damages were an adequate remedy for the breach; and to restrict exceptions to this general principle to cases in which the interests of commercial certainty require a clear recognition of the right to rescind for certain breaches, irrespective of their effects.[98] Some of the legislative limitations on the right to rescind[99] may have mitigated the defect in the law under which that right can be exercised on unmeritorious or technical grounds. But they have failed wholly to remove that defect while they have, on the other hand, undermined the virtue of certainty precisely in those commercial cases in which exceptions to the requirement of substantial failure in performance are intended to promote that virtue.[1]

The second main defect in the law is the rule in *Sumpter v Hedges*,[2] under which a party who has failed to complete performance may have no rights at all against the other party to the contract. This rule can plainly lead to the unjust enrichment of the latter party, and seems to go further than necessary for his protection. He should normally be liable to make some payment for that benefit, though he should be entitled

---

[91] [1921] 1 K.B. 432 at 448–449; *cf. Sim v Rotherham Metropolitan BC* [1987] Ch. 216, 255.

[92] *cf.* Williams, 57 L.Q.R. 381–383; Goff & Jones, *The Law of Restitution* (5th ed.), p.548; but see Matthews, 2 Legal Studies 302.

[93] Treitel, 30 M.L.R. 139.

[94] See especially the distinction between quantitative and qualitative defects in contracts for the sale of goods (above, p.793); and the distinctions between the various rights of a party who has failed to perform, under the limitations on the right to rescind (above, p.822).

[95] Especially *Wickman Ltd v Schuler AG* [1974] A.C. 235; *The Hansa Nord* [1976] Q.B. 44 and *Reardon-Smith Line Ltd v Hansen-Tangen* [1976] 1 W.L.R. 989.

[96] See above, pp.783, 787.

[97] *e.g.* in *Cunliffe v Harrison* (1851) 6 Ex. 901; *Arcos Ltd v Ronaasen* [1933] A.C. 47; above, pp.787, 793.

[98] *e.g. Bunge Corp v Tradax Export SA* [1981] 1 W.L.R. 711 (above, p.798); *cf.* also *The Laconia* [1977] A.C. 850; *The Chikuma* [1981] 1 W.L.R. 314 (above, pp.778–779).

[99] Sale of Goods Act 1979, ss.15A and 30(2A), as inserted by Sale and Supply of Goods Act 1994, s.4; and other legislation referred to above, p.801, n.54.

[1] See above, p.802.

[2] [1898] 1 Q.B. 673; above, p.783.

to a deduction in respect of any loss that he has suffered as result of the failure in performance.[3]

SECTION 4. STIPULATIONS AS TO TIME

1. In General

Failure to perform a stipulation as to time does not differ intrinsically from any other failure to perform; indeed a number of cases already discussed in this Chapter concern stipulations of this kind.[4] But the subject has a history and terminology of its own; and for this, perhaps not very satisfactory, reason it is usually discussed separately. Certain stipulations as to time are said to be "of the essence" of a contract. Any failure to perform such a stipulation justifies rescission; it makes no difference that the failure is trivial and causes little or no prejudice to the injured party. Where, on the other hand, a stipulation as to time is *not* of the essence, only a substantial or serious failure to comply with it will justify rescission.

The question whether a stipulation as to time is of the essence may be resolved by the terms of the contract itself. Time will obviously be of the essence if the contract expressly so provides.[5] The same is true if the contract provides that, in the event of one party's failure to perform within the stipulated time, the other is to be entitled to rescind[6]; or that the stipulation as to time is to be a condition.[7] In the absence of any contractual provisions on the point, the question is often determined by rules of law which have classified certain commonly found stipulations as to time in certain types of contracts as either being, or not being, of the essence. We have, for example, seen that in a charterparty failure by the shipowner to comply with a stipulation as to the time of sailing[8] or as to the ship's expected readiness to load[9] of itself justifies rescission; while the charterer's failure to load within the agreed time only has this effect if the delay is so serious as to frustrate the purpose of the contract.[10] Similarly, in a contract for the sale of goods a stipulation as to the time at which the seller is to deliver the goods is treated as of the essence of the contract[11]; while a stipulation as to the time at which the buyer is to pay for them is not normally so regarded (presumably because it is thought, rightly or wrongly, that late payment is unlikely to cause serious prejudice to the seller).[12] To the latter rule there are, however, many exceptions: it will, for example, be displaced if the goods are perishable[13]; if the buyer fails to comply with a stipulation as to the time of

---

[3] See Law Com. 121; not to be implemented: Law Commission, 19th Annual Report, para.2.11. See also McFarlane and Stevens, 118 L.Q.R. 596.

[4] *e.g. Glaholm v Hays* (1841) 2 Man. & G. 257; *Bettini v Gye* (1876) 1 Q.B.D. 183.

[5] See below, p.828.

[6] *e.g.* above, pp.778–779.

[7] *i.e.* in the sense discussed at pp.788 *et seq.*, above; *The Scaptrade* [1983] 2 A.C. 694 at 703.

[8] *Glaholm v Hays* (1841) 2 Man. & G. 751; above, p.790.

[9] *The Mihalis Angelos* [1971] 1 Q.B. 164; above, p.791.

[10] *Universal Cargo Carriers Corp v Citati* [1957] 2 Q.B. 401; above, p.795; below, p.862.

[11] *Hartley v Hymans* [1920] 3 K.B. 475 at 484; *cf. Aruna Mills Ltd v Dhanrajmal Gobindram* [1968] 1 Q.B. 655; *Toepfer v Lenersan Poortman NV* [1980] 1 Lloyd's Rep. 143 (time of tender of shipping documents). See also *Bowes v Shand* (1877) 2 App.Cas. 455 (where *early* shipment by the seller justified rejection; above, p.794).

[12] *Martindale v Smith* (1841) 1 Q.B. 389; Sale of Goods Act 1979, s.10(1). For a similar rule as to the effect of delay in payment in a distributorship agreement, see *Decro-Wall International SA v Practitioners in Marketing Ltd* [1971] 1 W.L.R. 361; *cf. Figre Ltd v Mander* [1999] Lloyd's Rep. I.R. 193 (time of payment of reinsurance premium not of the essence).

[13] See *Maclean v Dunn* (1828) 4 Bing. 722 at 728; *Ryan v Ridley & Co* (1902) 8 Com.Cas. 105; *RV Ward Ltd v Bignall* [1967] 1 Q.B. 534 at 550; Sale of Goods Act 1979, s.48(3).

paying a deposit under a contract with "a very tight time scale"[14]; or if there are other indications of the intention of the parties to treat the stipulation as of the essence.[15] The position is similar with regard to stipulations as to the time of taking delivery: failure by the buyer to comply with such a stipulation will not normally entitle the seller to rescind[16]; but it will have this effect if the goods are perishable,[17] or if the buyer undertakes to provide the ship on which the goods are to be loaded but fails to do so within the agreed time,[18] or if he fails within the time specified by the contract to notify the seller of the ship's readiness to load.[19]

Attempts have been made to formulate some general principle governing the legal classification of stipulations as to time. Thus it has been said, on the one hand, that "In modern English law time is *prima facie* not of the essence of the contract"[20]; and, on the other hand, that "*Broadly speaking* time will be considered of the essence in mercantile contracts."[21] But the italicised words indicate the tentative nature of these generalisations; and (as a glance at the rules stated in the preceding paragraph shows) they are, with respect, of limited value.[22] The classification of stipulations as to time seems to be based on considerations of commercial convenience applicable in particular contexts, rather than on any general principle or presumption as to time being, or not being, of the essence.

2. Sale of Land

(1) At common law

At common law, stipulations which specified[23] the time of performance were normally regarded as "of the essence" of contracts for the sale of land.[24] Thus the purchaser could not enforce the contract if he was not ready to pay on the precise day fixed for payment; and the vendor could not enforce the contract if he was not ready to show good title on the precise day on which he had undertaken to do so.

(2) In equity

(a) GENERAL RULE. Equity did not follow the common law rule but took the view that stipulations as to time were not generally "of the essence" of contracts for the sale of land.[25] In one case, delay of as much as eight years was not considered fatal to the purchaser's claim for specific performance.[26] The equitable rule, which now prevails,[27] is an application of the general requirement of substantial failure in performance. It is

---

[14] *The Selene G* [1981] 2 Lloyd's Rep. 180 at 185. Contrast *Millichamp v Jones* [1982] 1 W.L.R. 1422 at 1431 (deposit paid late by "mere oversight").

[15] *e.g.*, where payment was to be by irrevocable letter of credit to be opened within a stipulated time: see *Bunge Corp v Tradax Export SA* [1981] 1 W.L.R. 711 at 725.

[16] *Woolfe v Horne* (1877) 2 Q.B.D. 355 (rags).

[17] *Sharp v Christmas* (1892) 8 T.L.R. 687 (potatoes).

[18] *The Osterbek* [1973] 2 Lloyd's Rep. 86.

[19] *Bunge Corp v Tradax Export SA* [1981] 1 W.L.R. 711; above, p.798.

[20] *United Scientific Holdings Ltd v Burnley BC* [1978] A.C. 904 at 940; *British and Commonwealth Holdings plc v Quadrex Holdings Inc.* [1989] Q.B. 842 at 857.

[21] *Bunge Corp v Tradax Export SA* [1981] 1 W.L.R. 711 at 716.

[22] *cf. ibid.* at p.729; *The Peter Schmidt* [1998] 2 Lloyd's Rep. 1 at 7.

[23] *cf.* below, p.828.

[24] *Parkin v Thorold* (1852) 16 Beav. 59 at 65; unless the contract, on its true construction, provided otherwise: *Rightside Properties Ltd v Gray* [1975] Ch. 72 at 89.

[25] *Parkin v Thorold* (1852) 16 Beav. 59; *cf. Cole v Rose* [1978] 3 All E.R. 1121; *Graham v Pitkin* [1992] 1 W.L.R. 423.

[26] *Williams v Greatrex* [1957] 1 W.L.R. 31.

[27] See below, p.830.

based on the view that delay in completing a contract for the sale of land does not normally deprive the injured party of the substance of his bargain, damages being an adequate remedy.[28] Hence the general rule is that delay will justify rescission only where it does cause serious prejudice to the other party.[29]

(b) EXCEPTIONS. The equitable rule just stated is subject to the following exceptions. For these exceptions to apply, the stipulation must specify a date or time for performance: they cannot apply where a contract merely provides for performance "as soon as practicable."[30]

(i) *Term of the contract.* If the contract expressly provides that time shall be of the essence, it must be performed within the stipulated time.[31] Where there is no such express provision the question whether time is of the essence of the contract is one of construction. A mere provision that the vendor shall produce an abstract of title within seven days has been held not to make time of the essence.[32] But in *Harold Wood Brick Co Ltd v Ferris*[33] a contract provided for completion by August 31 and added that "the purchase shall in any event actually be completed not later than September 15." This clause was held to make time of the essence of the contract.

(ii) *Nature of the property.* Time is of the essence in sales of short leaseholds[34] or reversionary interests;[35] since the former will depreciate and the latter appreciate rapidly with the passing of time. Generally, time will also be regarded as of the essence where the subject-matter of the contract is of a highly speculative nature.[36]

(iii) *Commercial contracts.* Under the general rules stated at the beginning of this section[37] time is often of the essence in commercial transactions. In such cases, equity does not interfere, as it does in contracts for the sale of land. But many contracts for the sale of land are nowadays regarded as "commercial"; and in such cases the general equitable rule that time is not of the essence of such contracts does not apply. Time has accordingly been held to be of the essence of a contract for the sale of a public-house as a going concern[38]; of a contract for the sale of land which the buyer wanted to develop quickly for business purposes[39]; and, it seems, of a contract for the sale of a brickfield.[40] On the other hand, it has been held that time was not of the essence of a contract to sell 34 plots of land as and when each was built on.[41] This result may be justified on the

---

[28] See above, p.771; *Chancery Land Development v Wade's Development Stores* (1987) 53 P. & C.R. 306.

[29] *United Scientific Holdings Ltd v Burnley BC* [1978] A.C. 904 at 942; cf. *Amherst v James Walker Goldsmith & Silversmith Ltd* [1983] Ch. 305; *Metrolands Investments Ltd v JH Dewhurst Ltd* [1986] 3 All E.R. 659. These cases were concerned, not with breach, but with a landlord's delay in serving notice to increase rent under rent review clauses: they apply the *prima facie* rule that the stipulated time was not of the essence of the contract.

[30] *British & Commonwealth Holdings plc v Quadrex Holdings Inc* [1989] Q.B. 842 (not followed, on another point, in *Behzadi v Shaftsbury Hotels Ltd* [1992] Ch. 1).

[31] e.g. *Steedman v Drinkle* [1916] 1 A.C. 275. cf. *Country & Metropolitan Homes Surrey Ltd v Topclaim Ltd* [1996] Ch. 307 at 313; *Union Eagle Ltd v Golden Achievement Ltd* [1997] A.C. 514, above, p.781.

[32] *Roberts v Berry* (1858) 3 D.M. & G. 284. cf., in the context of rent review clauses, *Starmark Enterprises Ltd v CPL Distribution Ltd* [2002] EWCA Civ 1252; [2002] 4 All E.R. 265.

[33] [1935] 2 K.B. 198.

[34] *Hudson v Temple* (1860) 29 Beav. 536.

[35] *Newman v Rogers* (1793) 4 Bro.C.C. 391; unless there is evidence of contrary intention: *Patrick v Milner* (1877) 2 C.P.D. 342.

[36] See *Hare v Nicholl* [1966] 2 Q.B. 130.

[37] See above, pp.826–827.

[38] *Coslake v Till* (1826) 1 Russ. 376; *Lock v Bell* [1931] 1 Ch. 35.

[39] *Bernard v Williams* (1928) 44 T.L.R. 436; cf. *Hargreaves Transport Ltd v Lynch* [1969] 1 W.L.R. 215.

[40] See *Harold Wood Brick Co Ltd v Ferris* [1935] 2 K.B. 198.

[41] *Williams v Greatrex* [1957] 1 W.L.R. 31.

ground that the completion date was "only a target."[42] But it is hard to accept the further suggestion that a contract under which land is to be developed as a building estate is not a "commercial" contract. Indeed, the notion that some contracts for the sale of land are, while others are not, "commercial" is questionable now that land is an article of commerce, subject to violent fluctuations in value.[43] The crucial question should be whether delay causes substantial prejudice to the injured party, not whether the contract is "commercial."

(iv) *Conditional contracts.* The performance by one party of some stipulated act may be a condition precedent either to the existence of the contract or to the obligation of the other party.[44] Where the very existence of the contract depends on a condition to be performed by one of the parties, that condition must be performed within the time expressly or impliedly fixed by the contract.[45] If no time is expressly fixed, the condition must be performed by the date fixed for completion[46]; if no date is fixed for completion, it must be performed within a reasonable time.[47] The equitable principle that time is not of the essence of a contract does not apply in these cases, for until the condition is performed the whole existence of the contract remains in doubt. For the same reason, an option can be exercised only within the time laid down in the agreement by which it was granted.[48]

(c) WAIVER. The general principle that the right to rescind may be lost by waiver[49] applies where time is (under the exceptions just discussed) of the essence of a contract for the sale of land. Accordingly the requirement of punctual performance may be waived by giving the party in breach a further period for performance after the expiry of the period specified in the contract. Such waiver only has the effect of substituting the extended time for the original time; it is "not an utter destruction of the essential character of time."[50] Moreover, the mere fact that the injured party has not accepted the guilty party's failure to perform as a repudiation does not amount to waiver. The fact that the contract has not been rescinded merely entitles the guilty party to "perform the contract according to its terms"[51]; and this is no longer possible after the expiry of the stipulated time.

3. Notice

Where, under the equitable rules, time is not of the essence of a contract for the sale of land, the injured party is not bound to wait indefinitely for performance: he can make

---

[42] *ibid.* at 35.

[43] *United Scientific Holdings Ltd v Burnley BC* [1978] A.C. 904 at 924; *Union Eagle Ltd v Golden Achievement Ltd* [1997] A.C. 514 at 519.

[44] See above, p.762.

[45] *cf. Hare v Nicholl* [1966] 2 Q.B. 130.

[46] *Re Sandwell Park Colliery Co* [1929] 1 Ch. 277; *Aberfoyle Plantations v Cheng* [1960] A.C. 115; *aliter* where the completion date is only a target date subject to the occurrence of the condition; *Hargreaves Transport Ltd v Lynch* [1969] 1 W.L.R. 215 at 220; and where the condition is subsequent (above, p.62) and time is expressly stated *not* to be of the essence, as in *29 Equities Ltd v Bank Leumi (UK) Ltd* [1986] 1 W.L.R. 1490.

[47] *Re Longlands Farm* [1968] 3 All E.R. 522.

[48] *Hare v Nicholl* [1966] 2 Q.B. 130; *United Dominions Trust (Commercial) Ltd v Eagle Aircraft Ltd* [1968] 1 W.L.R. 74; *United Scientific Holdings Ltd v Burnley BC* [1978] A.C. 904 at 936.

[49] *i.e.* waiver in the sense of election: above, p.811.

[50] *Barclay v Messenger* (1874) 43 L.J. Ch. 449; *Nichimen Corp v Gatoil Overseas Inc* [1987] 2 Lloyd's Rep. 46.

[51] *Union Eagle Ltd v Golden Achievement Ltd* [1997] A.C. 514 at 518.

time of the essence by giving notice, as soon as the other party is in default,[52] calling on the latter party to complete. The contract may specify the period of notice required for this purpose; if it fails to do so, the notice must allow a reasonable time for completion. What is a reasonable time is a question of fact.[53] If one party has constantly pressed the other to complete, he can rely on this fact to shorten the amount of time which must be allowed by the notice.[54] Once a proper notice has expired and not been complied with, the injured party can either sue to enforce the contract or rescind it. If the notice is invalid (or if none is given), the injured party can nevertheless seek specific performance, after lapse of a reasonable time,[55] but he can rescind the contract only if the delay is such as to amount to evidence of the other party's intention to repudiate the contract.[56] A notice, once given, binds *both* parties. Thus if one of them gives notice to complete but is not ready to do so when the notice expires, the other can rescind.[57]

Notice sometimes has similar effects at common law where the stipulation as to time is not of the essence.[58] For example, an unpaid seller of goods can make time of the essence by giving the buyer notice of his intention to resell the goods.[59] But it does not follow that notice is in all cases sufficient to give rise to a right to rescind. For example, under a charterparty, delay in providing a cargo is a ground for rescission only if it is so prolonged that it "frustrates" the injured party's object in entering into the contract.[60] The contract cannot be rescinded merely because the party in breach has failed to comply with a notice calling on him to perform within a reasonable time.[61] Similarly, a hire-purchaser's failure to pay instalments may not of itself be a ground for rescission; and it has been held that it could not be turned into such a ground by merely giving notice to the hirer that he would be assumed to have repudiated if he did not pay within a stated time.[62]

4. Law of Property Act 1925, s.41

This section, re-enacting s.25(7) of the Judicature Act 1873, provides: "Stipulations in a contract, as to time or otherwise, which according to rules of equity, are not deemed to be or to have become of the essence of the contract, are also construed and have effect at law in accordance with the same rules". It follows from the section that, in contracts for the sale of land, the equitable rules now prevail, so that stipulations as to time in such

---

[52] *Behzadi v Shaftsbury Hotels Ltd* [1992] Ch. 1 disapproving dicta in *British & Commonwealth Holdings plc v Quadrex Holdings Inc* [1989] Q.B. 842.

[53] A notice giving only seven days was held in *Behzadi's* case, above, to be too short.

[54] *Stickney v Keeble* [1915] A.C. 386.

[55] *Woods v Mackenzie Hill Ltd* [1975] 1 W.L.R. 613; *cf. Cole v Rose* [1978] 3 All E.R. 1121 (where the delay in performance was *held* not to be unreasonable).

[56] *Graham v Pitkin* [1992] 1 W.L.R. 403.

[57] *Finkielkraut v Monohan* [1949] 2 All E.R. 234; *Quadrangle Development and Construction Co Ltd v Jenner* [1974] 1 W.L.R. 68; *Oakdown Ltd v Bernstein & Co* (1985) 49 P. & C.R. 282.

[58] *i.e.* under the rules discussed on pp.826–827, above.

[59] Sale of Goods Act 1979, s.48(3), as explained in *R V Ward Ltd v Bignall* [1967] 1 Q.B. 534. The Vienna Convention on Contracts for the International Sale of Goods (above, p.29) makes extensive use of this technique: see, *e.g.* Arts 47, 49 (1)(b), 63, 64 (1)(b).

[60] *Universal Cargo Carriers Corp v Citati* [1957] 2 Q.B. 401; above, p.795; below, p.862.

[61] According to *Re Olympia & York Canary Wharf (No.2)* [1993] B.C.C. 159, notice can make time of the essence even with respect to the performance of an intermediate term, but failure to comply with the notice will not, in such a case, amount to a repudiatory breach unless it goes to the root of the contract. This reasoning reaches the same conclusion as that stated in the text, but by an unusual route. Normally, the statement that time is (or has become) of the essence *means* that failure to perform within the specified time justifies rescission; if the failure does not have this effect, the orthodox reason is that time is *not* (or has not been made) of the essence.

[62] *Eshun v Moorgate Mercantile Credit Co Ltd* [1971] 1 W.L.R. 722.

contracts are no longer *prima facie* of the essence. It has been held that the section is not restricted to cases in which equity would have intervened before the Judicature Acts; it enables the courts also to take into account the subsequent development of equitable principles.[63] The section has the following effects.

First, delay is no longer a ground for rescission merely because it would formerly have been so regarded at common law.[64]

Secondly, a person can now recover damages where formerly he could not have done so. For example, a vendor of land may purport to rescind on the ground that the purchaser was not ready with the purchase money on the completion date. At common law the rescission would have been justified as the time of performance was of the essence of the contract. Under s.41, this is no longer the case, so that the purported rescission is wrongful and the purchaser is entitled to damages.[65]

Thirdly, delay in performance is a breach giving rise to liability in damages; and this is true even where in equity time is not of the essence. The authorities on this point were formerly in some confusion. It was clear that damages for delay were recoverable where the defendant was guilty of negligent or wilful default[66]; and there was some support for the view that the right to damages was restricted to such cases.[67] But this view was rejected by the House of Lords in *Raineri v Miles*,[68] where it was held that the purchaser of a house was entitled to damages for the vendor's delay in completion, whether or not that delay amounted to wilful default.

---

[63] *United Scientific Holdings Ltd v Burnley BC* [1978] A.C. 904 at 925, 957; Baker, 93 L.Q.R. 529.

[64] *Raineri v Miles* [1981] A.C. 1050 at 1082–1083.

[65] *Stickney v Keeble* [1915] A.C. 386 at 404; *Rightside Properties Ltd v Gray* [1975] Ch. 72.

[66] e.g. *Jones v Gardiner* [1902] 1 Ch. 191; *Phillips v Lamdin* [1949] 2 K.B. 33.

[67] See *Lock v Bell* [1931] Ch. 35 at 44; e.g. *Thorpe v Fasey* [1949] Ch. 649; *Woods v Mackenzie-Hill Ltd* [1975] 1 W.L.R. 613 at 615; cf. *Babacomp Ltd v Rightside Properties Ltd* [1973] 3 All E.R. 873 at 875.

[68] [1981] A.C. 1050; Samuels, 44 M.L.R. 100.

CHAPTER NINETEEN

BREACH

SECTION 1. WHAT AMOUNTS TO BREACH

A BREACH of contract is committed when a party without lawful excuse fails or refuses to perform what is due from him under the contract, or performs defectively or incapacitates himself from performing. Repudiation *before* performance has become due gives rise to special problems which are discussed at the end of this Chapter.[1]

1. Failure or Refusal to Perform

Failure or refusal to perform a contractual promise when performance has fallen due is *prima facie* a breach. This point looks obvious enough, but it does raise a number of problems.

The first is whether the stipulation which has not been complied with is indeed a promise, or only a condition. In the standard case of a unilateral contract, where A promises B £100 if B will walk to York,[2] B has not promised to do anything: his walking to York is merely a condition[3] of A's liability. Hence B commits no breach if he does not start the walk, or if, having started, he fails to complete it. But the distinction between the two types of stipulations is sometimes hard to draw.[4] It is, for example, not clearly settled whether an estate agent who is engaged to find a buyer for a house makes any promise to do anything[5]; and it is also possible for a person to commit a breach by failing to complete performance of an act which he was not originally bound to do if, by beginning performance, he impliedly promised to complete it.[6]

The second problem is whether performance has become due. Obviously performance is not due before the stipulated time: a promise to pay £100 tomorrow is not broken by failing to pay today. But greater difficulty arises where the contract, or the liability of one party, is subject to a condition. Where the contract is subject to a *contingent* condition precedent,[7] failure to perform is not a breach if the condition has not occurred; nor does the principal obligation of either party become due if one of them fails to bring about the condition on which the binding force of that obligation depends. At most, that party may be liable for breach of some subsidiary duty: for example, he is often under a duty not actively to prevent the occurrence of the condition; and he may be under a duty to make reasonable efforts to bring its occurrence about.[8] On the other hand, where the liability of A is subject to a *promissory* condition[9] to be performed by B, failure by B to

---

[1] See below, pp.857 *et seq.*
[2] See above, p.37.
[3] *i.e.* in the contingent sense (above, p.62) as B makes no promise.
[4] *cf.* above, p.38; and see above, pp.810–811.
[5] See above, pp.40–41.
[6] See above, p.38.
[7] See above, p.62.
[8] See above, pp.62–66.
[9] See above, pp.762–763.

perform that promise not only puts B in breach[10] of his principal obligation, but also prevents A's obligation to perform his counter-promise from becoming due.

Thirdly, a contract may contain a promise by one party, but fail to make it clear exactly what (if anything) has been promised in return by the other. In *Churchward v R*[11] a contractor agreed with the Admiralty that he would for 11 years carry from Dover to Calais such mail as he should from time to time be asked to carry by the Admiralty or the Postmaster-General. He was not given any mail to carry and claimed damages. One reason why his claim failed was that the agreement did not oblige the Admiralty to employ him: it only obliged him to carry mail if the Admiralty asked him to do so. The agreement thus resembled a tender by the contractor and amounted to no more than an offer, which might be accepted by the Admiralty from time to time.[12] A document which in terms imposes an obligation on only one party may, indeed, by implication also oblige the other to do something which is not expressly stated. Thus it was said in *Churchward v R* that "Where there is an engagement to manufacture some article [for a customer] a corresponding engagement on the other party is implied to take it, for otherwise it would be impossible that the party bestowing his services could claim any remuneration."[13] Similarly, where a document is headed "contract of sale" and in terms only imposes an obligation on the seller to sell, the court might imply an obligation on the buyer to buy.[14] But no such implication will be made where the terms of the document or the surrounding circumstances negative any intention on the prospective buyer's part to give such an undertaking.[15]

Fourthly, a contract may clearly oblige a party to do something but fail to specify exactly what it obliges him to do. The question sometimes arises, for example, whether an employer is bound only to pay the agreed wages, or whether he must actually give the employee work. The traditional view is that generally the employer need only pay wages,[16] though this rule does not apply where one of the objects of the contract is to enable the employee to gain, or retain, a skill, or to keep his name before the public. Thus a person who employs a well-known actor must actually give him a part in the play for which he was engaged.[17] More recently, it has been said that the law in some cases recognises a "right to work"[18] and that the question whether the contract gives rise to such a right depends on its express or implied terms.[19] If the employee needs to work to acquire or retain a skill or reputation, this fact is likely to support an implication that the employer must actually give him work. It does not follow that this duty can be

---

[10] *e.g. Trans Trust SPRL v Danubian Trading Co* [1952] 2 Q.B. 297; above, p.762.

[11] (1865) L.R. 1 Q.B. 173; *cf. R. v Demers* [1900] A.C. 109. Where *neither* party is by the terms of the contract obliged to do anything, the arrangement is likely not to be a contract at all for want of contractual intention: *Carmichael v National Power plc* [1999] 1 W.L.R. 2042, above, p.167.

[12] *cf.* above, pp.21–22.

[13] *Churchward v R*, above, at 195. *cf. The Unique Mariner (No.2)* [1979] 1 Lloyd's Rep. 37 at 51–52.

[14] *Firstpost Homes Ltd v Johnson* [1995] 1 W.L.R. 1567 at 1574.

[15] *ibid.*

[16] *Turner v Sawdon* [1901] 2 K.B. 653; *cf. Delaney v Staples* [1992] 1 A.C. 687, 692 (discussing so called "garden leave"); *McClory v Post Office* [1992] I.C.R. 758 (no obligation to provide opportunities for working overtime); *Marshall (Cambridge) Ltd v Hamblin* [1994] I.R.L.R. 260 (where the employee had resigned, so that there was no breach); *Abrahams v Performing Rights Society* [1995] I.C.R. 1028 (where the employer was not in breach as the contract gave him the option of paying in lieu of notice).

[17] *Herbert Clayton & Jack Waller Ltd v Oliver* [1930] A.C. 209.

[18] *Langston v AUEW* [1974] 1 W.L.R. 185; *cf. Gunton v Richmond-upon-Thames LBC* [1981] Ch. 448 at 472 (exclusion from place of work an "immediate breach" though salary was paid for a further month). Even if the employer is not in breach by failing to provide work, he may be unable to restrain such an employee from working for others in breach of another term of the contract of employment: see *Provident Financial Group plc v Hayward* [1989] I.C.R. 160, below, p.1044. See also the "right to return to work" after maternity parental and paternity leave given by the legislation referred to on p.1030, below.

[19] *William Hill Organisation Ltd v Tucker* [1998] I.R.L.R. 313.

specifically enforced[20]; but an employer who breaks a duty to provide work may be liable in damages on that account.

Finally, there may be a breach if a party *in substance* refuses to perform, and paradoxically he may do this by insisting with too great literalness on the terms of the contract. "Working to rule" in order to disrupt the employer's business may therefore be a breach of a contract of employment.[21]

2. Defective Performance

The phrase "defective performance" arguably contains an element of self-contradiction, in the sense that a person who promises to do one thing does not perform if he does another. Where the "defect" in performance is of a particularly serious kind, the acts done by the party in breach may indeed amount or lead to non-performance rather than defective performance, as in the case of the seller who promises beans but delivers peas.[22] But where the performance rendered is of the same kind as that promised, differing from it only in point of time, quantity or quality, it is reasonable to refer to it as defective performance.[23] It undoubtedly amounts to a breach; but the effects of such a breach often differ from those of a complete failure or refusal to perform.[24]

3. Incapacitating Oneself

A person may break a contract by incapacitating himself from performing it. Thus a seller commits a breach of contract for the sale of a specific thing if he sells it to a third party[25]; and a shipowner commits a breach of a charterparty if he sells the ship to a third party "free from any . . . charter engagement".[26] But a person who is entitled to make a choice as to the method of performance does not incapacitate himself merely by declaring that he will perform in a way that is impossible. For example, a seller of generic goods does not put himself in breach merely by telling the buyer that he will make delivery from a source which does not exist.[27] He is normally[28] entitled and bound to deliver from another source, and is in breach only if he fails or refuses to do so.

A person is not incapacitated from performing a contract under which he is obliged to pay money, merely because he is insolvent.[29] If the contract is profitable, his trustee in bankruptcy will probably wish to enforce it and provide funds to discharge his obligations under it. Insolvency incapacitates a contracting party only if no assets are set aside out of his estate for the performance of the contract.[30] Where, after a contract has

---

[20] *Langston v AUEW (No.2)* [1974] I.C.R. 510; below, p.1029.

[21] *Secretary of State v ASLEF (No.2)* [1972] 2 Q.B. 455; contrast *Power Packing Casemakers Ltd v Faust* [1983] Q.B. 471 (ban on overtime not a breach).

[22] *Chanter v Hopkins* (1838) 4 M. & W. 399 at 404; *Pilbrow v Pearless De Rougemont & Co* [1999] 3 All E.R. 355, above, p.806.

[23] *The Stork* [1955] 2 Q.B. 68 at 76; *Leeds Shipping Co Ltd v Soc Française Bunge* [1958] 2 Lloyd's Rep. 124 at 145; *Pilbrow v Pearless De Rougemont & Co* above, at 360 (customer who "asks for a pint of one make of bitter but is mistakenly provided with a pint of another").

[24] See above, pp.759–811, below, pp.1049–1057.

[25] *Bowdell v Parsons* (1808) 10 East 359; *Lovelock v Franklyn* (1846) 8 Q.B. 371.

[26] *Omnium D'Entreprises v Sutherland* [1919] 1 K.B. 618.

[27] *The Vladimir Ilich* [1975] 1 Lloyd's Rep. 322 at 329.

[28] In *The Vladimir Ilich*, above, the seller would not have been entitled to do this under the contract, since this provided that he was to give a "notice of appropriation" and that a valid notice of appropriation, once given, could not be withdrawn. But by treating the notice as *invalid* the buyer had precluded himself from relying on this provision.

[29] *Re Agra Bank* (1867) L.R. 5 Eq. 160.

[30] *Ex p. Chalmers* (1873) L.R. 8 Ch.App. 289; *Bloomer v Bernstein* (1874) L.R. 9 C.P. 588; *cf. Sale Continuation Ltd v Austin Taylor & Co* [1968] 2 Q.B. 849.

been made, one party to it is adjudged bankrupt, the other party may apply to the court for an order discharging obligations under the contract; and the court may make such an order on such terms as to payment of damages by the bankrupt or by the other party as appear to the court to be equitable.[31]

4. Without Lawful Excuse

There is no breach when non-performance of a contract is justified by some lawful excuse.

(1) Illustrations

In one sense, such an excuse for non-performance exists where one party is entitled to refuse to perform because the other has failed to perform a promissory condition precedent or a concurrent condition. In such cases, performance of the former party's obligation has never become due. This topic has already been discussed[32]; our present concern is with cases in which *after* an obligation has accrued, an extraneous event occurs which interferes with its performance. The event may interfere so seriously with performance that both parties are discharged under the doctrine of frustration (to be discussed in the next Chapter). But even where its effects are less drastic, it may still provide a party with an excuse for non-performance. Thus an employee who does not go to work because he is ill is not in breach,[33] even though the illness is not so serious as to frustrate the contract (so that performance must be resumed when the illness is over). Other extraneous circumstances may similarly justify refusal to perform, or to accept performance, at least in part. In one case it was, for example, held that the owner of a London café, who had engaged the claimants to give cabaret performances there, was justified in refusing to allow such performances to take place on the day on which King George V died, and on the following day, but not on the four days after that.[34] Again, if a farmer agrees to sell 500 tons of wheat to be grown on his farm and, through no fault of his, only 200 are produced, he is not liable for failing to produce the other 300 tons, though he will be liable in damages if he fails to deliver the 200 tons.[35] And a tenant is not in breach of a convenant to redevelop a site by a specified date if such redevelopment is prevented by an order listing a building on the site as of special architectural interest.[36]

Excuses for non-performance may be provided by the contract itself, which may contain "exceptions" absolving a party from his duty to perform if he is prevented from doing so by specified circumstances, such as strikes or similar delays. Failure to perform, if brought about by such events, is not a breach at all. The function of the "exception" is not to exclude liability for an assumed breach but rather to define the scope of the contracting party's obligations.[37]

A party relying on an excuse for non-performance must show that the excuse existed at the time of his refusal to perform: it is not enough for him to show that it arose or would (if the other party had not rescinded on account of the refusal) have arisen at some

[31] Insolvency Act 1986, s.345(1) and (2).
[32] See above, pp.762–763.
[33] See above, p.776 at n.11; below, p.875, but contrast above, p.776 at n.10. The excuse may extend to prevention by other causes: see *Sim v Rotherham Metropolitan BC* [1987] Ch. 216 at 254 (teacher locked in school lavatory "through no fault of his own").
[34] *Minnevitch v Café de Paris (Londres) Ltd* [1936] 1 All E.R. 884.
[35] *Howell v Coupland* (1876) 1 Q.B.D. 258; *H R and S Sainsbury Ltd v Street* [1972] 1 W.L.R. 834; Thornely [1973] C.L.J. 15; Goldberg, 88 L.Q.R. 464; *cf.* below, p.816.
[36] *John Lewis Properties v Viscount Chelsea* [1993] 2 E.G.L.R. 77.
[37] *The Angelia* [1973] 1 W.L.R. 210; above, p.238.

later time.[38] Suppose, for example, that a seller of wheat of a certain description is about to deliver wheat of a different description. The buyer cannot at this stage rely on the non-conformity as a ground for rescinding the contract, for the seller is not actually in breach until he tenders non-conforming goods.[39] Once a defective tender has been made, the buyer is indeed entitled to reject it, but it still does not follow that he is entitled to rescind the contract; for if, within the time allowed for delivery, the seller can make a further good tender, the buyer is normally bound to accept it.[40]

(2) Whether excuse must be stated

The general rule is that a refusal to perform by a party who has an excuse for non-performance is not a breach, even though he did not state the excuse, or even know of it, at the time of the refusal. Thus an employer can lawfully dismiss an employee who has committed a breach of duty justifying dismissal, though he did not at the time of the dismissal know of the breach, and though at that time he gave some other, insufficient, reason, or no reason at all.[41] Similarly a buyer can reject goods, if there has been a breach of condition, even though he did not know of the breach; and the rejection will not be wrongful merely because at the time he mistakenly alleged breach of some other condition.[42]

The rule may sometimes be justifiable on the ground that it prevents the party in breach from benefiting from the concealment of his own wrong. But it can also cause surprise and even hardship to the party in breach, and it has therefore been limited in a number of ways. A party cannot rely on an excuse which he did not specify at the time of his refusal to perform "if the point which was not taken is one which if taken could have been put right."[43] This might be the position if the effect of a buyer's failure to state the ground which justified rejection was to deprive the seller of the opportunity of curing the defect and making a second good tender[44] within the time allowed for performance.[45] The case is even stronger if the buyer makes some groundless objection to the seller's tender and the seller incurs trouble or expense in investigating or seeking to cure that objection.[46] In such circumstances, an estoppel can arise, precluding the buyer from alleging the existence of another, sufficient, reason for his refusal to perform.

---

[38] *British & Beningtons Ltd v NW Cachar Tea Co* [1923] A.C. 48; above, pp.766–768; *cf. The Siboen and the Sibotre* [1976] 1 Lloyd's Rep. 293.

[39] *Braithwaite v Foreign Hardwood Co Ltd* [1905] 2 K.B. 543, as explained in *Taylor v Oakes, Roncoroni & Co* (1922) 38 T.L.R. 349 at 351; and see above, p.766.

[40] See above, p.754.

[41] *Ridgway v Hungerford Market Co* (1835) 3 A. & E. 171; *Baillie v Kell* (1838) 4 Bing.N.C. 638; *Spottswood v Barrow* (1850) 5 Ex. 110; *Boston Deep Sea Fishing & Ice Co v Ansell* (1888) 39 Ch.D. 339; *Taylor v Oakes, Roncoroni & Co* (1922) 38 T.L.R. 349 at 351 (affirmed *ibid.* 517); *Cyril Leonard & Co v Simo Securities Trust Ltd* [1972] 1 W.L.R. 80; *Glencore Grain Rotterdam BV v LORICO* [1997] 2 Lloyd's Rep. 386 at 394; *Stocznia Gdanska SA v Latvian Shipping Co (No.3)* [2002] EWCA Civ 889; [2002] 2 All E.R. (Comm) 768 at [32]. The rule does not apply in cases of *unfair* dismissal (which need not be a breach of contract at all): see *Earl v Slater & Wheeler (Airlyne) Ltd* [1973] 1 W.L.R. 51; and *cf. Polkey v AE Dayton Services Ltd* [1988] A.C. 344 at 355–356.

[42] *e.g. Arcos Ltd v E A Ronaasen & Sons* [1933] A.C. 470.

[43] *Heisler v Anglo-Dal Ltd* [1954] 1 W.L.R. 1273 at 1278; *André & Cie v Cook Industries Inc* [1987] 2 Lloyd's Rep. 463.

[44] See above, p.754.

[45] Hence the present exception does not apply where that time has expired by the time of the refusal: see *Glencore Grain Rotterdam BV v LORICO* [1997] 1 Lloyd's Rep. 386 at 395, where it was the buyer who was guilty of the wrongful repudiation.

[46] *cf. The Lena* [1981] 1 Lloyd's Rep. 68 at 79; *The Eurometal* [1981] 1 Lloyd's Rep. 337 at 341.

One controversial case goes further in holding that a buyer who failed to specify a defect in existence at the time of rejection could not later rely on it, even though the defect was one which the seller could *not* have cured and even though the seller did not in any way change his position in consequence of the buyer's original failure to specify it. This is the *Panchaud Frères* case,[47] where maize was sold under a contract which provided for shipment to be made in "June/July." The goods were shipped in August and the buyers could have rejected them on this ground. But they paid against documents which would, if carefully examined, have revealed the fact of late shipment; and when the goods arrived the buyers rejected them for defects of quality. This was a bad ground as the goods were sound when shipped and the sellers were not responsible for their subsequent deterioration. The buyers claimed their money back, and, three years after their rejection of the goods, they relied for the first time on the fact of late shipment. Their claim failed, no doubt because the court was impressed by the possibly harsh consequences of allowing the buyers at such a late stage to rely on an originally unstated excuse for non-performance. To allow the buyers to do this would, it was said, be inconsistent with a "requirement of fair conduct."[48] But the vagueness of this requirement makes it virtually impossible to tell which cases will be governed by it and which by the general rule that a party can rely on an originally unstated excuse for non-performance.[49] Hence other attempts have been made to explain the *Panchaud Frères* case. One suggestion is that the case was one of waiver[50] (in the sense of election)[51]; but this was rejected in the case itself on the ground that the buyers did not know of the late shipment when they accepted the documents.[52] Another view is that the buyers' conduct gave rise to an estoppel or equitable estoppel.[53] These doctrines, however, operate only if two requirements are satisfied: an unequivocal representation made by one party and reliance on it by the other.[54] In one later case[55] the argument based on estoppel accordingly failed on the ground that no such representation had been made; and in the *Panchaud Frères* case, even if the inference of a representation could be drawn from the buyers' acceptance of the documents, it is hard to see in what way the sellers had relied on that representation.[56] They certainly lost no chance of curing the defect in their tender, for when that tender was made such a cure was no longer possible. Probably the safest explanation of the case is that the buyers had lost their right to reject by acceptance[57] when they paid against documents which disclosed the fact of late shipment. It follows that the buyers could have relied on the fact of late shipment if they had

---

[47] *Panchaud Frères SA v Établissement General Grain Co* [1970] 1 Lloyd's Rep. 53.
[48] [1970] 1 Lloyd's Rep. 53 at 59.
[49] Perhaps for this reason, the decision is treated with some reserve in *The Proodos C* [1980] 2 Lloyd's Rep. 390 at 392.
[50] *V Berg & Son Ltd v Vanden Avenne-Izegem PVBA* [1977] 1 Lloyd's Rep. 499 at 502–503; *Intertradex SA v Lesieur-Torteaux* [1978] 2 Lloyd's Rep. 509 at 513; *Bremer Handelsgesellschaft mbH v C Mackprang Jr* [1979] 1 Lloyd's Rep. 221 at 225.
[51] See above, p.811.
[52] For the requirement of such knowledge, see above, p.815.
[53] This was the view of Lord Denning M.R. in the *Panchaud Frères* case itself: [1970] 1 Lloyd's Rep. 53 at 56; *cf. V Berg & Son Ltd v Vanden Avenne-Izegem*, above, n.50, at 502–503; *Intertradex SA v Lesieur-Torteaux*, above, at 515; *The Manila* [1988] 3 All E.R. 843 at 852.
[54] See above, pp.403, 107–110.
[55] *Glencore Grain Rotterdam BV v LORICO* [1997] 2 Lloyd's Rep. 386.
[56] *cf. Raiffeisen Hauptgenossenschaft v Louis Dreyfuss & Co* [1981] 1 Lloyd's Rep. 345 at 352, where the *Panchaud Frères* case was held inapplicable precisely because the requirement of reliance was not satisfied.
[57] *BP Exploration Co (Libya) Ltd v Hunt* [1979] 1 W.L.R. 783 at 810–811; affirmed without reference to this point [1983] 2 A.C. 352; *Glencore Grain Rotterdam BV v LORICO* [1997] 2 Lloyd's Rep. 386 at 396.

rejected the documents, even though they had, at the time of such rejection, given an inadequate reason, or none at all.[58]

5. Standard of Duty[59]

The question to be discussed under this heading is whether liability for breach of contract is strict, or whether it is based on fault in the sense of want of care, diligence or honesty.[60]

(1) Cases of strict liability

Many contractual duties are strict.[61] The most obvious illustration of this principle is provided by the case of a buyer who cannot pay the price because his bank has failed or because his expectation of raising a loan has not been fulfilled, or because he is prevented by exchange control regulations from remitting money to the place where he has agreed to pay,[62] or because his supply of the currency in which he has agreed to pay has become exhausted and cannot be replenished.[63] In such cases there is no doubt that he is liable[64]: inability to pay money, even if it occurs entirely without the fault of the party who was to make the payment, is not an excuse for failing to make the payment. The same principle of strict liability applies to the duty of a seller of generic goods to make delivery. It is no defence for him to say that he was prevented from making delivery because he was let down by his supplier[65] or because no shipping space was available to get the goods to their agreed destination.[66] A charterparty similarly imposes a strict duty on the charterer to provide a cargo, so that inability to find one is no excuse.[67] In all these cases, the principle of strict liability may be modified by the terms of the contract (for example, by a *"force majeure"* clause),[68] but unless this is done liability is quite independent of fault.

The principle of strict liability also applies to certain cases of defective performance. At common law, a carrier of goods by sea was held to give an "absolute" warranty of seaworthiness[69]: it was not enough for him to show that he had taken reasonable care to make the ship seaworthy. In practice, sea carriers often contracted out of this strict

---

[58] *cf. V Berg & Son Ltd v Vanden Avenne-Izegem PVBA* [1977] 1 Lloyd's Rep. 499.

[59] Treitel, in Bos and Brownlie (ed.), *Liber Amicorum for Lord Wilberforce*, p.185.

[60] When, in *Target Holdings Ltd v Redferns* [1996] A.C. 421 at 432, Lord Browne-Wilkinson said that liability was "fault-based," he was concerned, not with the *standard* of liability, but with the rule that the defendant was "only liable for the consequences of the legal wrong." That "wrong" might result from breach of a strict duty as well as from one of a duty based on "fault" in the sense described in the text.

[61] *Raineri v Miles* [1981] A.C. 1050 at 1086.

[62] *Universal Corp v Five Ways Properties Ltd* [1979] 1 All E.R. 552.

[63] *Congimex SARL (Lisbon) v Continental Grain Export Corp (New York)* [1979] 2 Lloyd's Rep. 346.

[64] *cf. Francis v Cowcliffe* (1977) 33 P. & C.R. 368; *Christy v Pilkington* 273 S.W. 2d 533 (1954).

[65] *Barnett v Javeri & Co* [1916] 2 K.B. 390; *P J van der Zijden Wildhandel v Tucker & Cross Ltd* [1975] 2 Lloyd's Rep. 240; *Intertradex SA v Lesieur Torteaux SARL* [1978] 2 Lloyd's Rep. 509; *cf. The Al Tawfiq* [1984] 2 Lloyd's Rep. 598 (late delivery).

[66] *Lewis Emanuel & Son Ltd v Sammut* [1952] 2 Lloyd's Rep. 629.

[67] *The Aello* [1961] A.C. 135 (overruled on another point in *The Johanna Oldendorff* [1974] A.C. 479); *The Zuiho Maru* [1977] 2 Lloyd's Rep. 552; *cf. Hills v Sughrue* (1846) 15 M. & W. 252 (where it was the shipowner who undertook to find the cargo); *The World Navigator* [1991] 2 Lloyd's Rep. 23 at 30, 31 (time of loading); *The Athenasia Comninos* [1990] 1 Lloyd's Rep. 277 at 282 and *The Giannis K* [1998] A.C. 605 at 619, 624 (shipper's "warranty" that cargo is not dangerous).

[68] There was such a clause in the *Wildhandel* case above, n.65 but in the circumstances it did not apply so as to protect the seller.

[69] *Steel v State Line SS Co* (1877) 3 App.Cas. 72 at 86.

liability; and in many cases the duty is now reduced by statute to one of due diligence.[70]

Liability is, again, strict where goods delivered under a contract of sale are defective: for example, because they do not comply with the seller's undertakings as to quality.[71] It is no defence for the seller to show that he took all reasonable care to see that there were no defects,[72] or that he could not have discovered the defects because he was a retailer selling goods in packages sealed by the manufacturer.[73] The position appears to be the same where goods are supplied under a contract for the supply of goods other than one of sale, *e.g.* under one of hire or hire-purchase.[74]

A contractor who executes repairs or building work is also strictly liable for defects in components fitted by him. He is not exonerated by showing that the components were supplied by a reputable manufacturer and that the defects were latent so that they could not have been discovered by the exercise of reasonable care.[75] Contracts of this kind contain both a supply of goods, and a service, element. Strict liability with regard to the supply element can be justified on the ground that this is closely analogous to sale; and also on the ground that it is the first link in a chain of contractual liability which will stretch back to the manufacturer, on whom the liability should properly rest. The customer has no rights against the manufacturer in contract, as there is no contract between them[76]; and, by making the contractor strictly liable to the customer, the law gives the contractor an incentive[77] to recoup the loss so incurred by claiming damages for breach of contract from the manufacturer from whom he had bought the components. The introduction of the manufacturer's strict "product liability"[78] directly to the customer weakens this argument for the contractor's strict liability in contract to the

---

[70] Carriage of Goods by Sea Act 1971, s.3.

[71] *e.g.* with those implied under Sale of Goods Act 1979, s.14, as amended by Sale and Supply of Goods Act 1994, ss.1 and 7(1) and Sch.2, para.5. For further amendments of s.14, see Sale and Supply of Goods to Consumers Regulations 2002 (SI 2002/3045), reg.3; an element of fault enters into these provisions by virtue of the new s.14(2E)(a) by which a seller is not liable in respect of a "public statement" about specific characteristics of the goods if he "was not, and could not reasonably have been, aware of the statement".

[72] *Frost v Aylesbury Dairy Co Ltd* [1905] 1 K.B. 608; *cf. Lockett v AM Charles Ltd* [1938] 4 All E.R. 170; *H Parsons (Livestock) Ltd v Uttley Ingham & Co Ltd* [1978] Q.B. 791 at 799–800.

[73] *Daniels v White & Son* [1938] 4 All E.R. 258.

[74] See Supply of Goods (Implied Terms) Act 1973, s.10 (as substituted by Consumer Credit Act 1974, s.192 and Sch.4, para.35 and Sale and Supply of Goods Act 1994, s.7(1) and Sch.2, para.4); Supply of Goods and Services Act 1982, ss.4 and 9, as substituted by Sale and Supply of Goods Act 1994, s.7(1) and Sch.2, para.6. The wording of these provisions is similar to that of Sale of Goods Act 1979, s.14, under which liability is clearly strict. *cf. Wettern Electric Ltd v Welsh Development Agency* [1983] Q.B. 796 (strict liability for breach of implied undertaking in licence to occupy factory that premises are fit for occupier's purpose). For further amendments of the provisions of the 1973 and 1982 Acts cited in this note, see Sale and Supply of Goods to Consumers Regulations 2002 (SI 2002/3045), regs 7, 10 and 13; an element of fault enters into these new provisions for reasons *mutatis mutandis* the same as those given in relation to sale of goods in n.71 above.

[75] *G H Myers & Co v Brent Cross Service Co* [1934] 1 K.B. 46; *Young & Marten Ltd v McManus Childs Ltd* [1969] 1 A.C. 454; *cf. Hancock v Brazier* [1966] 1 W.L.R. 1317; *Barclays Bank plc v Fairclough Builders Ltd* [1995] Q.B. 214. In *The Zinnia* [1984] 2 Lloyd's Rep. 211 at 218 the repairer's duty was said to be one to ensure that reasonable care in buying the components was exercised; but as he was found not to have taken such care the further question whether he might be strictly liable did not arise. It is not clear what standard of liability is imposed by Defective Premises Act 1972, s.1(1)(a).

[76] This position appears not to be affected by the Contracts (Rights of Third Parties) Act 1999 (above, p.581 at n.9) and p.655 at n.28.

[77] Even if the contractor were not liable to the customer, he might be able to claim damages in respect of the customer's loss under the principle applied in *Linden Gardens Trust Ltd v Lenesta Sludge Disposals Ltd* [1994] A.C. 85, above, p.594; but the customer would have no legal right to require him to make such a claim.

[78] Consumer Protection Act 1987, Pt I.

customer, but does not wholly deprive it of its force since "product liability" is subject to many important qualifications.[79] The "chain of liability" argument is also open to the objection that the chain may be broken by a valid exemption clause.[80] It has therefore been suggested that, if the manufacturer is willing to sell the components only on terms that exclude his liability, and this fact was known both to the contractor and to his customer, then the contractor would not be strictly liable to his customer for defects in those components.[81]

(2) Liability based on fault

Under the Supply of Goods and Services Act 1982, a person who supplies a service in the course of a business impliedly undertakes to "carry out the service with reasonable care and skill".[82] Such liability is clearly based on fault; but the Act also preserves "any rule of law which imposes on the supplier a stricter duty".[83] Hence the question whether the supplier's liability is strict or is based on fault will continue to depend on distinctions drawn at common law.

Where the contract is one for the supply of *services and components*, liability for defects in the components is (as we have just seen) generally strict[84]; but the contractor's liability with regard to other phases of his operation is often based on fault. For example, a car repairer's duty with regard to the safe-keeping of a customer's car is one of care only.[85] The standard of a building or repairing contractor's duty with regard to the actual carrying out of the work that he is employed to do is less clear. In one of the relevant cases,[86] a sharp distinction was drawn between the "supply of goods" and "service" elements of the contract, and it seems to have been accepted that, in respect of the "service" element, the contractor's duty was one of care only.[87] Similarly, a contract for the supply of goods may impose on the supplier a duty to supply not only the goods but also the service, or to repair defects in, them after they have been supplied. He will then be strictly liable in respect of defects in the goods when supplied, but his service or repair undertakings will impose duties of diligence only.[88]

Where the contract is one for the supply of *services alone*, liability is often based on fault. Thus the general rule is that contracts under which services are rendered by professional persons (such as solicitors, architects, accountants or doctors) impose duties

---

[79] *e.g.* those arising from the meaning given to "defect" by s.3 of the 1987 Act, the defences made available by s.4, and the definition of "damage" in s.5.

[80] As in *Helicopter Sales (Australia) Pty Ltd v Rotor Works Pty Ltd* (1974) 132 C.L.R. 1.

[81] In *Young & Marten Ltd v McManus Childs Ltd* [1969] 1 A.C. 454 at 467; the suggestion is perhaps based on the fact that the building contract specified tiles which could be obtained only from a single manufacturer.

[82] s.13; *Wilson v Best Travel Ltd* [1993] 1 All E.R. 353.

[83] s.16(3)(a).

[84] See above, p.839. s.12(3)(a) of the Supply of Goods and Services Act 1982 provides that such contracts are contracts for the supply of services for the purposes of the Act; but it does not specify the standard of liability.

[85] See *Hollier v Rambler Motors (AMC) Ltd* [1972] 2 Q.B. 71; *cf. Alderslade v Hendon Laundry Ltd* [1945] 1 K.B. 189; *Smith v Eric S Bush* [1990] 1 A.C. 831 at 843 (plumber).

[86] *Young & Marten Ltd v McManus Childs Ltd* [1969] 1 A.C. 454.

[87] *ibid.* at 465; *cf. H Parsons (Livestock) Ltd v Uttley Ingham & Co Ltd* [1978] Q.B. 791 at 800; *The Raphael* [1981] 2 Lloyd's Rep. 659 at 665. See also *BP Exploration (Libya) Ltd v Hunt* [1979] 1 W.L.R. 783 at 796 (affirmed [1983] 2 A.C. 352).

[88] *BHP Petroleum Ltd v British Steel plc* [1999] 2 All E.R. (Comm) 544 at 577, affirmed [2000] 2 All E.R. (Comm) 133.

of care only.[89] In some at least of such cases, the person rendering the services obviously does not guarantee to produce a result: this is particularly clear in the case of the lawyer engaged to conduct litigation since one party must inevitably lose, and of the doctor since a person who provides medical treatment is not normally understood to guarantee its success.[90] All that such persons undertake is to perform the promised services with reasonable care and skill. The same is true of the architect to the extent that he undertakes to supervise the work of others, or the supply of materials by them: in performing this function he cannot be expected to do more than exercise a reasonable degree of professional care and skill.

But the position is different where an architect commits an error, not of supervision, but of design: there is considerable support for the view that, where he designs a structure, he gives an "absolute warranty"[91] that it will be fit for his client's purposes. Similarly, a person who in the course of a profession or business undertakes to *design and supply* an article has been held strictly liable for defects in that article.[92] Some dicta, indeed, suggest that liability is strict *only* where the contract contains a "supply" as well as a "service" element[93]; but this limitation on the incidence of strict liability may, with respect, be doubted. In some of the relevant authorities no defect in the components or raw materials was alleged[94]; and where a defendant is thus held liable for defects in services alone it would be strange if the standard of that liability depended on the existence of another obligation (*i.e.* to supply materials) in respect of which he was not in breach.

---

[89] *e.g. Clark v Kirby-Smith* [1964] Ch. 506 (solicitor); *Bagot v Stevens, Scanlan & Co Ltd* [1966] 1 Q.B. 197 (architect); *O'Connor v Kirby* [1972] 1 Q.B. 90 (insurance broker); *McNealy v Pennine Insurance Co Ltd* [1978] 2 Lloyd's Rep. 18 (insurance broker); *Stafford v Conti Commodity Services* [1981] 1 All E.R. 691 (commodities broker); *Perry v Sidney Phillips & Son* [1982] 1 All E.R. 1005 at 1010, varied [1982] 1 W.L.R. 1287 (surveyor); *cf. Investors in Industry Commercial Property Ltd v South Bedfordshire DC* [1986] 1 All E.R. 787 at 806 (not reported on this point in [1986] Q.B. 1034); *Luxmoore-May v Messenger May Baverstock* [1990] 1 W.L.R. 1009; *Henderson v Merrett Syndicates Ltd* [1995] 2 A.C. 145 (underwriting agent); *Barclays Bank plc v Weeks, Legg & Dean* [1999] Q.B. 309 and *Midland Bank plc v Cox McQueen* [1999] 1 F.L.R. 1002 (solicitors); *UCB Corporate Services Ltd v Clyde & Co* [2000] 2 All E.R. (Comm) 259; *Hone v Going Places Leisure Travel Ltd* [2001] EWCA Civ 947; *The Times*, August 6, 2001 (package holiday). See below, p.983, n.55 as to the first two cases cited in this note.

[90] See *Eyre v Measday* [1986] 1 All E.R. 488 and *Thake v Maurice* [1986] Q.B. 644, where doctors were held not to have guaranteed that sterilisation operations would make patients permanently sterile; though it was recognised that such a guarantee *might* be given. In the latter case, the doctor was held liable in negligence for failing to warn the patient that sterility might not be permanent. Contrast *Gold v Haringey Health Authority* [1988] Q.B. 481, where there seems to have been no contractual relationship, and failure to warn of a very slight risk did not give rise to liability in negligence as it was normal not to give such a warning. The defendants' liability in *Allen v Bloomsbury Health Authority* [1993] 1 All E.R. 651 was also evidently regarded as arising in tort: see the reference to "tortfeasor" at 658. For the persons to whom the doctor's tort liability is owed in such cases, see *Goodwill v Pregnancy Advisory Service* [1996] 1 W.L.R. 1379; above, p.618.

[91] *Greaves & Co (Contractors) Ltd v Baynham Meikle & Partners* [1975] 1 W.L.R. 1095 at 1101; *IBA v EMI (Electronics) Ltd* (1980) 14 Build.L.R. 1, especially at 47–48 (where the contract contained a supply of goods element but no defect in the goods was alleged).

[92] *Samuels v Davies* [1943] K.B. 526 (dentist supplying false teeth: here the "supply" element predominated and du Parq L.J. regarded the contract as one of sale); *IBA v EMI (Electronics) Ltd* (1980) 14 Build.L.R. 1 (contract to design and erect a television mast).

[93] *Basildon DC v JE Lesser Properties* [1985] 1 All E.R. 20 at 26 (not reported on this point in [1985] Q.B. 839); *cf. Cynat Properties Ltd v Landbuild (Investments & Property) Ltd* [1984] 3 All E.R. 513 at 523; *Wimpey Construction UK Ltd v DV Poole* [1984] 2 Lloyd's Rep. 499 at 514 (no undertaking by *designer* as to quality and *execution* of the work); *George Hawkins v Chrysler (UK)* (1986) 38 Build.L.R. 36 (where the contract contained no supply element).

[94] There was no such allegation in the cases cited in n.92, above.

(3) Fault and excuses for non-performance

Failure to perform is not a breach where a supervening event either discharges a contract under the doctrine of frustration[95] or provides a party with an excuse for non-perform-ance.[96] An event has this effect only if it occurs without the fault of the party relying on it. In cases of frustration, this requirement is expressed by saying that frustration must not be "self-induced".[97] Similarly, a party generally[98] cannot rely as an excuse for non-performance on an event that is due to his fault; *e.g.* a farmer who agreed to sell a quantity of wheat to be grown on his land could not rely on the fact that less was produced if this was due to want of proper cultivation.[99]

Excuses for non-performance may be provided by "exceptions" in the contract itself, and such provisions must be distinguished from exemption clauses. Where performance is prevented by an event specified in an "exception", there is no breach at all, while an exemption clause excludes or restricts liability once a breach has been established. One factor tending to put a provision into the category of "exceptions" is that the specified event was beyond the control of the party relying on the provision, and occurred without fault.[1] Here again fault is relevant in determining whether non-performance is excused or amounts to a breach.

(4) Conditional contracts

Where a contract is subject to a contingent condition,[2] two rules apply which to some extent make fault relevant to the issue of contractual liability. First, a party may be in breach if he deliberately prevents the occurrence of the condition.[3] Secondly, a party may be under some degree of duty to bring about the occurrence of the condition: for example where goods are sold "subject to" export or import licence. In such a case the duty of the party who is to obtain the licence is normally one of diligence only,[4] so that fault is again relevant to the question whether a breach of contract has been com-mitted.

6. Breach Distinguished from Lawful Termination

A contract may give a party the right lawfully to terminate it by notice. If that party says to the other that he no longer intends to perform, it may be hard to tell whether he has broken or terminated the contract. In *Bridge v Campbell Discount Co Ltd*[5] a hire-purchase agreement gave the hirer the right to terminate it by notice. He wrote to the owners: "Owing to unforeseen circumstances I am sorry but I will not be able to pay any more payments . . . . Will you please let me know when and where I will have to return the car. I am very sorry regarding this, but I have no alternative." The House of Lords held (by a majority) that he had not terminated but broken the contract, apparently because that

---

[95] See below, Chap.20.
[96] See above, pp.835–836.
[97] See below, p.905.
[98] Illness preventing performance of a contract of personal service may be an exception: *cf.* below, p.906.
[99] Lack of fault is mentioned, apparently as an essential ingredient of the excuse, in the cases discussed at p.835, above.
[1] *The Angelia* [1973] 1 W.L.R. 210 at 230; above, p.238. *cf. The Xantho* (1877) 2 App.Cas. 503.
[2] See above, pp.62–66.
[3] See above, p.64.
[4] See above, p.65.
[5] [1962] A.C. 600; *cf. United Dominions Trust (Commercial) Ltd v Ennis* [1968] 1 Q.B. 54; *Marriott v Oxford & District Co-operative Society Ltd* [1970] Q.B. 186; *Comet Group v British Sky Broadcasting, The Times,* April 26, 1991.

was his intention. "Why should the hirer apologise so humbly, twice, if *he thought* that he was merely exercising an option given to him by the agreement?"[6]

The analogous question has been raised whether a strike or other "industrial action" amounts to a breach of a contract of employment.[7] This depends in the first place on the exact form taken by the conduct in question. While "working to rule" may be a breach,[8] no breach is committed merely because employees who usually work overtime (without being under any contractual obligation to do so) refuse to continue the practice.[9] In the more common case of a refusal by employees to perform their contractual obligation to work, there is clearly a breach if the contract contains a "no strikes" clause.[10] The same is true if an employee stops work (whether in the course of a strike or not) without giving the notice required by the terms of the contract. If the contract does not contain a "no strikes" clause and if due notice of the strike has been given, one view is that the notice terminates the contract; but this is said[11] to be unrealistic since both parties would expect a return to work under the old contract (suitably modified) after the strike was over. A second view is that a strike notice operates as a lawful suspension of the contract, at least if the notice is no shorter than that required for lawful termination of the contract.[12] This view in turn gives rise to difficulties, particularly as the notion of "suspending" a contract is one with which English law is unfamiliar[13] and which the courts have not favoured.[14] The prevailing view, therefore, is[15] that generally a strike is a breach of contract and that it is, moreover, a "repudiatory breach",[16] *i.e.* one which at common law[17] entitles the employer to dismiss the employee. The employer's other remedies by way of damages and withholding pay have already been discussed.[18]

SECTION 2. EFFECTS OF BREACH

A breach of contract may entitle the injured party to claim damages, the agreed sum, specific performance or an injunction, in accordance with the principles discussed in Chapter 21. In appropriate circumstances he may be entitled to more than one of these

---

[6] [1962] A.C. 600 at 615 (italics supplied); *cf.* p.674. Another reason for the decision may be that it was in the hirer's interest to establish that he was in breach: see below, p.1005.

[7] Foster, 34 M.L.R. 274.

[8] See above, p.834.

[9] *Tramp Shipping Corp v Greenwich Marine Inc* [1975] 1 W.L.R. 1042; *cf. Power Packing Casemakers v Faust* [1983] Q.B. 471.

[10] As in *Rookes v Barnard* [1964] A.C. 1129.

[11] By Donovan L.J. in *Rookes v Barnard* [1963] 1 Q.B. 623 at 682. The statement was approved in the House of Lords by Lord Devlin: [1964] A.C. 1129 at 1204, though the decision of the Court of Appeal was reversed. See also Wedderburn, 25 M.L.R. at p.258; 27 M.L.R. at p.268.

[12] *Morgan v Fry* [1968] 2 Q.B. 710 at 728 *per* Lord Denning M.R.; *cf. ibid.* p.733, *per* Davies L.J.; O'Higgins [1968] C.L.J. 223. Trade Union and Labour Relations (Consolidation) Act 1992, s.234A (as inserted by Trade Union Reform and Employment Rights Act 1993, s.21 and amended by Employment Relations Act 1999, s.4 and Sch.3, para.11) requires at least seven days' notice to be given.

[13] See *Daily Mirror Newspapers Ltd v Gardner* [1968] 2 Q.B. 762; *Gorse v Durham CC* [1971] 1 W.L.R. 775. A contract can only be "suspended" if it contains a provision to that effect, as, for example, in *Bird v British Celanese Ltd* [1945] K.B. 336.

[14] *Shell UK Ltd v Lostock Garages Ltd* [1976] 1 W.L.R. 1187.

[15] *Simmons v Hoover Ltd* [1977] Q.B. 284; Napier [1977] C.L.J. 34; *cf. Rookes v Barnard* [1963] 1 Q.B. 623, 682 *per* Donovan L.J. (above, n.11). In *Chappell v Times Newspapers Ltd* [1975] 1 W.L.R. 482 at 502 Lord Denning M.R. similarly said that going on strike "wilfully to disrupt the employer's undertaking" was a breach of contract.

[16] *Miles v Wakefield Metropolitan DC* [1987] A.C. 539 at 562; *Wiluszynki v Tower Hamlets LBC* [1989] I.C.R. 493 at 503.

[17] By statute, the dismissal may be *unfair*, even where it is not *wrongful* at common law: see Employment Rights Act 1996, s.94.

[18] See above, pp.821–822.

remedies: *e.g.* to an injunction and damages. Breach may also give the injured party the right to "rescind" the contract in circumstances which have been discussed in Chapter 18.[19] It is with this right and with the legal effects of its exercise that we are here concerned.

1. The Option to Rescind or Affirm

(1) No automatic termination

A breach which justifies rescission does not automatically determine the contract.[20] It only gives the victim the option either to rescind the contract or to affirm it and to claim further performance. This is generally the case, even if the contract says that it is to become "void" on breach.[21] Normally such a stipulation is construed[22] restrictively so as to prevent one party from relying on his own breach of duty to the other party.[23] The reason for the rule that termination depends on the injured party's election is that the guilty party should not be allowed to rely on his own wrong so as to obtain a benefit under the contract,[24] or to excuse his own failure of further performance, or in some other way to prejudice the injured party's legal position under the contract.[25] Thus the guilty party is not allowed to take advantage of the breach by arguing that the original contract is discharged, so as to be entitled to a *quantum meruit* for work done by him,[26] or that he need pay only at the market rate (below that fixed by the contract) for services rendered to him.[27] Nor is he allowed to rely on the breach so as to prevent the injured party from enforcing provisions in the contract which are advantageous to that party and which may operate after the breach (such as a valid exclusive dealing clause[28]); or so as

---

[19] See above, pp.759 *et seq.*

[20] *Michael v Hart & Co* [1902] 1 K.B. 482 at 490; *Howard v Pickford Tool Co* [1951] 1 K.B. 417 at 421; *Heyman v Darwins Ltd* [1942] A.C. 356 at 361; *Decro-Wall International SA v Practitioners in Marketing Ltd* [1971] 1 W.L.R. 361 at 368, 375, 381; *Mayfair Photographic Supplies Ltd v Baxter Hoare & Co Ltd* [1972] 1 Lloyd's Rep. 410 at 417; *Lakshmijit v Sherani* [1974] A.C. 605; *The Odenfeld* [1978] 2 Lloyd's Rep. 357 at 374; *Great Atlantic Insurance Co v Home Insurance Co* [1981] 2 Lloyd's Rep. 219 at 229; *The TFL Prosperity* [1984] 1 W.L.R. 48 at 58; *Lusograin Commercio Internacional de Cereas Ltda. v Bunge AG* [1986] 2 Lloyd's Rep. 654 at 658; *Evening Standard Ltd v Henderson* [1987] I.C.R. 588 at 593, 595; *The Simona* [1989] A.C. 788 at 800; *Fenton Insurance Ltd v Gothaer Versicherungsbank VVaG* [1991] 1 Lloyd's Rep. 172; *cf.* the overruling in *Photo Production Ltd v Securicor Transport Ltd* [1980] A.C. 827 of *Harbutt's "Plasticine" Ltd v Wayne Tank & Pump Co Ltd* [1970] 1 Q.B. 447. See Thompson, 41 M.L.R. 137, suggesting a possible reconsideration of the rule stated in the text.

[21] *cf. Davenport v R* (1877) 3 App.Cas. 115; *New Zealand Shipping Co v Société des Ateliers, etc., de France* [1919] A.C. 1; *Cerium Investments Ltd v Evans, The Times,* February 14, 1991. Automatic termination results only if the event on which the contract is expressed to come to an end occurs without breach of duty, as in *Brown v Knowsley BC* [1986] I.R.L.R. 102.

[22] *e.g. Alghussein Establishment v Eton College* [1988] 1 W.L.R. 587; for the status of the rule as one of construction, capable of being excluded by contrary provision, see *Cheall v Apex* [1983] 2 A.C. 180 at 189; *Gyllenhammar & Partners International v Sour Brodogradevna Industrial* [1989] 2 Lloyd's Rep. 403; *Micklefield v SAC Technology Ltd* [1990] 1 W.L.R. 1002 at 1007; *cf. The Bonde* [1991] 1 Lloyd's Rep. 136 at 148; *Thornton v Abbey National plc, The Times,* March 4, 1993.

[23] For the requirement that the duty must be owed to the other party, see *Thompson v ASDA-MFI Group plc* [1988] Ch. 241; contrast *Cheall v Apex,* above, (breach of duty to third party).

[24] See the *Alghussein* case, above, n.22.

[25] *ibid*; contrast *Cheall v APEX* [1983] 2 A.C. 180 (breach of agreement with third party).

[26] *Boston Deep Sea Fishing & Ice Co v Ansell* (1888) 39 Ch.D. 339 at 364.

[27] Example based on *Timber Shipping Co SA v London & Overseas Freighters Ltd* [1972] A.C. 1 (where there was no breach).

[28] *e.g. Decro-Wall International v Practitioners in Marketing Ltd* [1971] 1 W.L.R. 361; *cf. Thomas Marshall (Exports) Ltd v Guinle* [1979] Ch. 227; *cf. WPM Retail v Laing* [1978] I.C.R. 787 (employee preserving right to bonus after wrongful dismissal); *Lusograin Commercio Internacional de Cereas Ltda v Bunge AG* [1986] 2 Lloyd's Rep. 654 (seller's right to "carrying charges" (below, p.1004) after repudiation by buyer). For exclusion of the rule by contrary agreement, see above, n.22.

to deprive the injured party of the chance of claiming specific relief,[29] or of obtaining a lien on the guilty party's property.[30]

(2) Employment contracts

In some situations, the general rule, that a repudiatory breach does not of itself terminate the contract, clearly applies to employment contracts. For example, in *Rigby v Ferodo Ltd*[31] an employer had committed such a breach by imposing a wage-cut. The employee nevertheless continued to work and it was held that the contract had not been terminated by the employer's unaccepted repudiation. It followed that employee was entitled to recover the difference between the wages paid and those due under the contract.

But there is some support for the view that the position is different where the employee does *not* continue to work for the employer after the repudiatory breach,[32] either because he has been wrongfully dismissed or because he has left in breach of contract. In such cases, it is sometimes said that wrongful repudiation by one party automatically terminates the contract, without any need for the injured party to exercise the option to rescind. One argument in support of this view is that, where the employee is no longer working for the employer (in consequence of the repudiation), the employment *relationship* has plainly come to an end,[33] even against the wishes of the injured party. But it does not follow from this that the *contract* of employment is similarly terminated[34]: the argument that the repudiating party should not be allowed to rely on his own wrong to deprive the injured party of valuable rights under the contract has as much force where the contract is one of employment as it has in relation to other contracts. A further argument for the view that a contract of employment is automatically terminated by repudiatory breach is that, if the contract were not so terminated, a wrongfully dismissed employee would be entitled to sue for his wages until the time of his election to terminate; whereas it is settled that his remedy is in damages and not by action for the agreed wages.[35] But this argument fails to distinguish between the continued existence of the *contract*, and the *remedies* for its breach.[36] This point is by no means restricted to contracts of employment. Suppose, for example, that a buyer wrongfully repudiates an instalment contract for the sale of goods by refusing to accept further instalments. If the seller elects to treat the contract as remaining in existence, it

---

[29] See *Decro-Wall International SA v Practitioners in Marketing Ltd* [1971] 1 W.L.R. 361 (where it was held that there was no automatic termination); *Evening Standard Co Ltd v Henderson* [1987] I.C.R. 588.

[30] *G Barker v Eynon* [1974] 1 W.L.R. 462 (where again the view that termination is automatic was implicitly rejected).

[31] [1988] I.C.R. 29.

[32] *Sanders v Ernest A Neale* [1974] I.C.R. 565; *Kolatsis v Rockware Glass Ltd* [1974] 3 All E.R. 555 at 558; *Gannon v Firth* [1976] I.R.L.R. 415; *cf. Hare v Murphy Bros Ltd* [1974] I.C.R. 603 (where the contract seems to have been frustrated on the ground stated at p.844, below); *R. v East Berkshire Health Authority, Ex p. Walsh* [1985] Q.B. 152 at 161; Thomson, 38 M.L.R. 347; Napier [1975] C.L.J. 36.

[33] *Micklefield v SAC Technology* [1990] 1 W.L.R. 1002 at 1006; *Delaney v Staples* [1992] 1 A.C. 687 at 692; *Wilson v St Helen's BC* [1998] I.C.R. 1141 at 1152.

[34] *Gunton v Richmond-upon-Thames LBC* [1981] Ch. 448 at 474 (doubted on this point in *Ex p. Walsh*, above); followed, though with reluctance, in *Boyo v Lambeth LBC* [1995] I.C.R. 727; *cf.* above, p.693; *Micklefield v SAC Technology* [1990] 1 W.L.R. 1002; *Litster v Forth Dry Dock & Engineering Co Ltd* [1990] 1 A.C. 546 at 568. *Villella v MFI Furniture Centres Ltd* [1999] I.R.L.R. 468 at 474. Conversely, the *relationship* may continue after the *contract* has come to an end if, after having accepted the employer's repudiation, the employee continues to work for the employer "on an entirely different basis" from that of the old contract: *Eastbourne BC v Foster* [2001] EWCA Civ 1091; [2002] I.C.R. 234.

[35] *Gunton's* case, above [1981] Ch. 448 at 474; *Marsh v National Autistic Society* [1993] I.C.R. 453; *cf. Delaney v Staples* [1992] 1 A.C. 687 at 693; *cf. Cerberus Software Ltd v Rowley* [2001] EWCA Civ 78; [2001] I.C.R. 376.

[36] See below, p.1016, n.95.

does not follow that he can sue for *the price* of the undelivered instalments. His remedy is normally in damages, though the amount recoverable may depend on whether he elects to terminate.[37] Similarly, where a time charter is wrongfully repudiated by the charterer, the shipowner is not bound to accept the repudiation; but even if he elects to affirm his remedy may be in damages rather than for the agreed hire[38]: "It is . . . the range of remedies which is limited, not the right to elect."[39] The same is true of contracts of employment: it does not follow from the continued existence of the *contract* that a wrongfully dismissed employee's *remedy* is by action for the agreed sum.[40] Thus it is submitted that the general rule applies to such contracts, *i.e.*, that a repudiatory breach by either party does not lead to automatic termination, but only gives the injured party an option to rescind the contract.[41]

(3) Insurance Contracts

In the law of insurance, "warranty" is used in a sense similar to that now more usually given to "condition:" *i.e.* to refer to a term, the breach of which justifies the injured party's refusal to perform.[42] But the exact legal effects of a breach of "warranty" in insurance law are not identical with those elsewhere given to a breach of "condition": in particular, there is no requirement in insurance law that an insurer who is the victim of a breach of "warranty" must take any steps to exercise his option to avoid liability. A statutory statement of this position is given in s.33(3) of the Marine Insurance Act 1906, which provides that "A warranty is a condition which must be exactly complied with. If it be not so complied with, then . . . the insurer is discharged from liability as from the date of the breach of warranty." The effect of these words was considered in *The Good Luck*,[43] where a ship had been insured under a policy entitling the insurers to declare certain areas as prohibited and containing a "warranty" that the shipowner would comply with any such prohibition. The policy was assigned to a bank (to which the ship had been mortgaged) and the insurers undertook to notify the bank "promptly" if they "ceased to insure" the ship. Some months later the ship was struck by an Iraqi missile while trading in the Persian Gulf (which had been declared by the insurers to be a prohibited area) and became a constructive total loss. A claim on the policy having been rejected, it was held that the insurers were liable on their undertaking to the bank. They had "ceased to insure" the ship as soon as she had entered the prohibited area: this breach of "warranty" released the insurers automatically,[44] without any election on their

---

[37] See below, p.962.
[38] See below, pp.1017–1018.
[39] *The Alaskan Trader (No.2)* [1983] 2 Lloyd's Rep. 645 at 651.
[40] *e.g. Silvey v Pendragon plc* [2001] EWCA Civ 784; [2001] I.R.L.R. 685.
[41] *Simmons v Hoover Ltd* [1977] Q.B. 284; *Western Excavating (EEC) Ltd v Sharp* [1978] Q.B. 761 at 769; *Thomas Marshall (Exports) Ltd v Guinle* [1979] Ch. 227; *Gunton v Richmond-upon-Thames LBC* [1981] 1 Ch. 448; *Rasool v Hepworth Pipe Co* [1980] I.C.R. 494; *London Transport Executive v Clark* [1981] I.C.R. 355; *Burdett-Coutts v Hertfordshire CC* [1984] I.R.L.R. 91; *Evening Standard Co Ltd v Henderson* [1987] I.C.R. 586 at 593, 595; *Dietman v LB of Brent* [1987] I.C.R. 737 (affirmed without reference to this point [1988] I.C.R. 842); *cf.* also *Decro-Wall International SA v Practitioners in Marketing Ltd* [1971] 1 W.L.R. 361 at 369–370, 375–376, 380–381; *Marsh v National Autistic Society* [1993] I.C.R. 453 at 458; the same assumption seems to underlie *Miles v Wakefield MDC* [1987] A.C. 539, above, pp.792–793; Thompson, 97 L.Q.R. 8, 235; 98 L.Q.R. 423; 42 M.L.R. 91; McMullen [1982] C.L.J. 110.
[42] See above, p.788.
[43] [1992] 1 A.C. 233.
[44] *cf. Hussain v Brown* [1996] 1 Lloyd's Rep. 627 at 630, where, because of this "draconian" consequence of breach, the court refused to hold the "warranty" to be a *continuing* one.

part.[45] This followed from the wording of s.33(3), by which the insurer "is discharged from liability as from the date of the breach of warranty:" These words should be contrasted with those of the Sale of Goods Act 1979, giving a buyer, in cases of breach of condition, "a right to treat the contract as repudiated".[46] The principle of automatic discharge for breach of "warranty" in insurance law was explained by Lord Goff in *The Good Luck* on the ground that "fulfillment of the warranty is a condition precedent to the liability [or further liability] of the insurer".[47] At first sight this gives rise to some difficulty, for if performance of the warranty were a condition precedent it would follow that the insurer never became liable at all; while s.33(3) says that he is "discharged", thus suggesting that a pre-existing liability has been brought to an end. It may be that this difficulty can be resolved by reference to the special nature of an insurance contract. Such a contract differs from a more typical contract (such as one of sale) in which the parties bargain for an exchange of performances (*i.e.*, of the goods for the price). In a contract of indemnity insurance the position is that the performance of one party (*i.e.*, payment of the premium by the assured) is exchanged for the *promise* of the other[48] (*i.e.*, that of the insurer to indemnify against the loss), and in the great majority of cases this promise does not have to be performed at all because the event insured against does not occur. The occurrence of this event is thus a contingent condition precedent[49] of the insurer's liability *to pay*, while on breach of the "warranty" he is "discharged" from his conditional promise even before the event occurs.

(4) Restrictions on injured party's choice

Although rescission depends (except in the insurance situation just discussed) on the election of the injured party, that party's option is to some extent curtailed by the rule that the damages to which he is entitled may be reduced if he fails to take reasonable steps to mitigate his loss.[50] This rule will sometimes put pressure on the injured party to rescind, for one common way of mitigating loss is to make a substitute contract; and the effect of doing this will often be to put it out of the injured party's power to perform the old contract. Where this is the case, the making of the substitute contract will involve the rescission of the original one. Thus if a wrongfully dismissed employee mitigates his loss by taking another job he will thereby be "taken to have accepted his wrongful dismissal as a repudiatory breach leading to a determination of the contract of service".[51] The same would be true where a seller, on the buyer's repudiation, disposed elsewhere of the subject-matter. In these cases the injured party is not under any legal obligation to make the substitute contract[52]; so that in this sense he remains free to choose between affirmation and rescission. But his freedom of choice is limited in that, if he acts unreasonably in failing to make such a contract, he will suffer a reduction in the damages to which he is entitled by reason of breach of the original contract.

---

[45] It follows that an insurer setting up breach of warranty as a defence does not thereby "rescind" the contract within the meaning of an exemption clause in the policy: *HIH Casualty & General Insurance Ltd v New Hampshire Insurance Co* [2001] EWCA Civ 735; [2001] 2 All E.R. (Comm) 39 at [122].

[46] Sale of Goods Act 1979, s.11(3).

[47] [1992] 1 A.C. 233 at 263; the words in square brackets do not occur in this report but do occur in [1991] 3 All E.R. 1 at 16 and in [1991] 2 Lloyd's Rep. 191 at 202.

[48] *cf.* below, p.1050.

[49] See above, p.62.

[50] See below, p.977.

[51] *Gunton v Richmond-upon-Thames LBC* [1981] Ch. 448 at 468; *Dietman's* case, above, n.41. The same result can follow where the employee continues to work for the employer "on an entirely different basis" from that of the repudiated contract: *Eastbourne BC v Foster* [2001] EWCA Civ 1091; [2002] I.C.R. 234.

[52] See below, p.977.

Conversely, the mitigation rules may require the injured party to accept performance from the party in breach even though it is not in accordance with the contract: *e.g.* they may require a buyer to accept late delivery.[53] In such a case, the mitigation rules again do not, strictly speaking, restrict the injured party's right to rescind, but they do require him, having rescinded, to enter into a new contract for late performance at the original price (subject to damages for delay).[54] The injured party does not commit any breach of duty by failing to enter into such a new contract, but his failure to do so will reduce the damages to which he is entitled for breach of the original contract. Hence his freedom of choice will, as a practical matter, be restricted, this time in the direction of putting him under pressure to accept performance, though subject to relatively minor modifications.

(5) Exercise of the option

The question whether the option to rescind has been exercised has been described as one of fact[55]; but this description assumes that a number of legal requirements have been satisfied. The prime requirement is that the behaviour of the injured party must unequivocally indicate his intention to exercise the option. Normally mere "silence and inactivity"[56] will not suffice for this purpose, but there is no absolute rule to this effect. Thus in *Vitol SA v Norelf Ltd*[57] a contract for the sale of propane was wrongfully repudiated by the buyer and, after receiving the repudiation, the seller made no attempt to take any of the steps which he would have been expected to take for the purpose of performing the contract,[58] if he were treating it as still in force. The House of Lords held that an arbitrator's finding that the seller had accepted the repudiation was not wrong in law; for, even if the seller's reaction to the breach could be described as "inactivity," it was in the circumstances not equivocal since it clearly conveyed to the buyer that the seller was treating the contract as at an end. The option will commonly be exercised by giving notice to this effect to the party in breach, and sometimes such notice must be given: for example, where the injured party seeks the return of property with which he has parted under the contract.[59] But there is plainly no such requirement where "inactivity" suffices for the exercise of the option; nor does notice seem to be necessary where the injured party has put it out of his power to perform the original contract by making a substitute contract to satisfy the mitigation requirement.[60] The option can also be exercised in the legal proceedings brought on the contract.[61] Obviously the victim affirms the contract by claiming specific performance but there is no inconsistency between claiming damages for a prior breach, or for the breach in question, and

---

[53] *The Solholt* [1981] 2 Lloyd's Rep. 574 (affirmed, [1983] 1 Lloyd's Rep. 605).

[54] *The Solholt* [1983] 1 Lloyd's Rep. 605, criticising *Strutt v Whitnell* [1975] 1 W.L.R. 870 for failing to observe the distinction drawn in the text.

[55] *Kish v Taylor* [1912] A.C. 604 at 617; *Agrokor AG v Tradigrain SA* [2000] 1 Lloyd's Rep. 497 at 500.

[56] *State Trading Corp of India v M Golodetz Ltd* [1989] 2 Lloyd's Rep. 277 at 286; *Glencore Grain Rotterdam BV v LORICO* [1997] 2 Lloyd's Rep. 386 at 394. *cf.* below, pp.858–859.

[57] [1996] A.C. 800.

[58] Such as tendering shipping documents as "a precondition to payment of the price:" *ibid.* at 811. Contrast *Jaks (UK) Ltd v Cera Investment Bank SA* [1998] 2 Lloyd's Rep. 89 at 96 (failure to take steps to perform another contract with a third party not sufficient).

[59] *Lakshmijit v Sherani* [1974] A.C. 605.

[60] *Gunton v Richmond-upon-Thames LBC* [1981] Ch. 448 at 468.

[61] It can be exercised even after beginning of the proceedings: *Tilcons Ltd v Land & Real Estate Investments Ltd* [1987] 1 W.L.R. 46.

exercising the option to rescind.[62] There are, moreover, cases in which the victim merely refuses to perform until the other party either cures his breach or (in the case of contracts calling for continuing performance) resumes performance in conformity with the contract. For example, an employer may refuse to pay wages, or to pay them in full, for so long as his employee refuses (in the course of "industrial action") to perform his duties under the contract of employment. Such a temporary refusal on the employer's part does not amount to an exercise by him of the option to rescind.[63]

If the victim accepts further performance after breach, he may be held to have affirmed, so that he cannot later rescind the contract.[64] He must, moreover, rescind the contract as a whole: for example, a tenant cannot remain on premises and ignore a particular term of the lease on the ground that the landlord had, in the past, failed to perform his obligations under that term.[65]

2. Effects of Rescission or Affirmation

(1) Rescission

Rescission by the victim is sometimes said to terminate the contract. But this statement can mislead, and it is best to consider the precise effects of rescission on the obligations of each party.

(a) ON OBLIGATIONS OF THE VICTIM. After rescission, the victim is no longer bound to accept or pay for further performance.[66] He is also entitled to refuse to make payments which had not yet fallen due at the time of rescission, e.g. because the other party's performance was incomplete or defective[67]; and he is released from other obligations which, under the contract, were to be performed in the future: for example, a wrongfully dismissed employee is no longer bound by covenants in restraint of trade in his contract of employment.[68]

On the other hand, recission does not operate retrospectively,[69] in the sense of liberating the victim from his duty to perform obligations which had accrued before rescission. For example, where freight under a charterparty is deemed earned on loading, the charterer remains liable to pay it even though he later justifiably rescinds on account of the shipowner's repudiatory breach.[70] The victim may also himself have been in breach at the time of the other party's repudiation, but not in such a way as to justify

---

[62] *General Billposting Co Ltd v Atkinson* [1909] A.C. 118. Contrast *United Dominions Trust (Commercial) Ltd v Ennis* [1968] 1 Q.B. 54 at 65, where it was said that the victim affirms by claiming a sum due under a provision in the contract fixing the amount payable in the event of breach, even though that provision was penal; *sed quaere*.

[63] *Wiluszynski v Tower Hamlets LBC* [1989] I.C.R. 493; it is assumed that the breach justified rescission. For the different question whether failure to perform a condition precedent of itself *entitles* the injured party to rescind, see above, pp.765–766.

[64] *Davenport v R* (1877) 3 App.Cas. 115; *cf.* above, pp.811–816; an *unsatisfied demand* for performance does not have the same effect: below, p.856.

[65] *Total Oil Great Britain Ltd v Thompson Garages (Biggin Hill) Ltd* [1972] 1 Q.B. 318.

[66] *Photo Production Ltd v Securicor Transport Ltd* [1980] A.C. 827 at 849.

[67] *e.g.* above, p.783; *SCI (Sales Curve Interactive) v Titus SARL* [2001] EWCA Civ 591; [2001] 2 All E.R. (Comm) 416, at [28–33], [65].

[68] *General Billposting Co Ltd v Atkinson* [1909] A.C. 118; *Briggs v Oates* [1990] I.C.R. 473. *cf. Thompson v Coroon* (1993) 66 P. & C.R. 445; contrast *Lawrence David Ltd v Ashton* [1991] 1 All E.R. 384 (where it was not clear that the employer was in repudiatory breach).

[69] *Hurst v Bryk* [2002] 1 A.C. 185.

[70] *The Dominique* [1989] A.C. 1056; *cf. Hurst v Bryk* [2002] 1 A.C. 185 for a special application of this principle to a partner's obligation to pay his share of the partnership liabilities incurred before, but falling due after, rescission.

that repudiation.[71] In such a case, the victim is, in spite of his own breach, entitled to rescind, but he remains liable in damages for the breach which he had himself committed before rescinding.[72]

The victim also continues to be bound, after rescission, by ancillary obligations of the kind to be described below,[73] and even by primary obligations where the contract expressly so provides.[74]

If, at the time of rescission, the victim has already performed, he may be entitled to recover back that performance. For example, a buyer who justifiably rejects goods for breach of condition is normally entitled to the return of the price.[75] To this extent, rescission has a retrospective effect. It is submitted that, where the victim would thus be entitled, after he has rescinded, to recover back money paid before rescission, he should also be relieved from liability to pay sums which had become due (but had not been paid) before rescission; for it would make no practical sense to hold him liable in one action for a payment which he could then claim back in another.[76]

(b) ON THE OBLIGATIONS OF THE PARTY IN BREACH. For the purpose of stating the effects of rescission on the obligations of the party in breach, it is necessary to distinguish between primary and secondary obligations.[77] The primary obligation is one to render the actual performance promised; the secondary obligation is one to pay damages for failure to perform the primary obligation.

The effect of rescission on the primary obligations of the party in breach is exactly the same as its effect on those of the victim: normally the party in breach is released from primary obligations which had not yet fallen due at the time of rescission,[78] but he remains liable to perform those which had already fallen due at that time,[79] except where a payment which he should have made before rescission was one which he could, if he had so made it, have recovered back, even on rescission for his own breach.[80]

The rules stated in the preceding paragraph can be excluded by contrary provision in the contract or by other evidence of contrary intention.[81] Thus even a primary obligation

---

[71] e.g. where the victim's own breach is a breach of an independent covenant (above, p.763); or one which is not sufficiently serious to justify rescission (above, pp.769–778); or one which occurs simultaneously with the other party's breach, as in *State Trading Corp of India v M Golodetz* [1989] 2 Lloyd's Rep. 277 at 288.

[72] *Gill & Duffus SA v Berger & Co Inc* [1984] A.C. 382 at 390.

[73] See below, after n.83.

[74] See below, at n.81.

[75] See below, p.1052.

[76] cf. *McDonald v Denys Lascelles Ltd* (1933) 48 C.L.R. 457 (see below, p.1011) where a claim against the party in breach failed on similar reasoning, which should *a fortiori* protect the *victim* of the breach; and below, p.911.

[77] A distinction drawn by Lord Diplock in a number of cases, *e.g.* in *Lep Air Services v Rolloswin Investments Ltd* [1973] A.C. 331 at 354–355 and *Photo Production Ltd v Securicor Transport Ltd* [1980] A.C. 827 at 848–849. cf. also below, p.1013, n.78.

[78] cf. above, p.849. It follows that there can be no specific enforcement of those primary obligations: see *Walker v Standard Chartered Bank* [1992] B.C.L.C. 535.

[79] *Hyundai Shipbuilding & Heavy Industries Co v Pournaras* [1978] 2 Lloyd's Rep. 502; *Stocznia Gdanska SA v Latvian Shipping Co* [1998] 1 W.L.R. 574; cf. *Fielding & Platt Ltd v Najjar* [1969] 1 W.L.R. 357 at 361; *Lep Air Services v Rolloswin Investments Ltd* [1973] A.C. 331 at 354–355; *Photo Production Ltd v Securicor Transport Ltd* [1980] A.C. 827 at 844, 849; *Hyundai Heavy Industries Ltd v Papadopoulos* [1980] 1 W.L.R. 1129; below, p.1012; *The Trident Beauty* [1994] 1 W.L.R. 161 at 164; *SCI (Sales Curve Interactive) v Titus SARL* [2001] EWCA Civ 591; [2001] 2 All E.R. (Comm) 416, at [35].

[80] *McDonald v Denys Lascelles Ltd*, above, n.76.

[81] *Yasuda Fire & Marine Insurance Co of Europe v Orion Marine Insurance Underwriting Agency Ltd* [1995] 1 Lloyd's Rep. 525.

which has not yet fallen due can survive rescission if the contract so provides,[82] while liability for one which had fallen due will not survive if the contract validly provides that rescission is to be the sole remedy.[83]

Primary obligations must also be distinguished from ancillary ones, that is, those imposed by provisions which deal not with the performance to be rendered, but with such matters as the resolution of disputes arising out of the contract,[84] or the inspection by one party of records to be kept by the other for the purpose of ascertaining what rights and duties have come into existence under the contract.[85] Normally, such ancillary obligations are intended to survive rescission and are accordingly not released by it.[86]

The important difference between the effects of rescission on the obligations of the two parties is that the party in breach (unlike the victim) comes, as a result of rescission, under a secondary obligation to pay damages,[87] and that his liability in damages may relate both to breaches committed before rescission and to losses suffered by the victim as a result of the defaulting party's repudiation of future obligations.[88] Suppose, for example, that a hirer under a hire-purchase agreement fails to make the agreed payments in circumstances amounting to a wrongful repudiation and therefore giving the owner the right to terminate. If the owner does terminate, the hirer remains liable for instalments which had fallen due *before* termination, his primary obligation to pay these being unaffected[89]; but he is not liable for *subsequent* instalments, having been released by termination from his primary obligation to make these payments. On the other hand, the hirer is liable in damages for wrongful repudiation[90] and these may include compensation for loss suffered by the owner after, and as a result of, the premature termination of the agreement: for example, where he has to dispose of the goods elsewhere for less than the amount which would have been paid by the defaulting hirer if the agreement with him had run its full course.

For the purpose of these rules, it is important to distinguish between claims for *damages* (which can be brought in respect of future losses) and claims for *agreed sums*[91]

---

[82] *Harbinger UK Ltd v GE Information Services Ltd* [2000] 1 All E.R. (Comm) 166 (a case of lawful termination by notice; but there seems to be no reason why a similar express provision should not take effect after rescission for breach).

[83] *Malcolm-Ellis (Liverpool) v American Electronics Laboratory* (1984) N.L.J. 500.

[84] *Heyman v Darwins Ltd* [1942] A.C. 356; *cf.* Arbitration Act 1996, s.7.

[85] *The Yasuda Fire & Marine Insurance Co of Europe Ltd v Orion Marine Insurance Underwriting Agency Ltd* [1995] 1 Lloyd's Rep. 525.

[86] See the authorities cited in nn.84 and 85 above. The same view was taken by Phillips L.J. in *Rock Refrigeration Ltd v Jones* [1997] I.C.R. 938 of covenants in restraint of trade in an employment contract which had been wrongfully repudiated by the employer; but this is hard to reconcile with *General Billposting Ltd v Atkinson* [1908] A.C. 118 (above, p.849), on which the other two members of the court based their decision in the *Rock Refrigeration* case. For the different position where the contract is wrongfully repudiated *by* the person subject to the restraint, see *Kall Kwick Printing (UK) Ltd v Rush* [1996] F.S.R. 114.

[87] *RV Ward Ltd v Bignall* [1967] 1 Q.B. 534 at 548; Thornely [1967] C.L.J. 168; *Lep Air Services Ltd v Rollswin Investments Ltd* [1973] A.C. 331 esp. at 350; *Lakshmijit v Sherani* [1974] A.C. 605; *State Trading Corp of India v M Golodetz Ltd* [1989] 2 Lloyd's Rep. 277 at 286; Carter, 1 J.C.L. 113 and 249.

[88] *R Leslie Shipping Co v Welstead* [1921] 3 K.B. 420; *Yeoman Credit Ltd v Waragowski* [1961] 1 W.L.R. 1124; *Overstone Ltd v Shipway* [1962] 1 W.L.R. 117; *Bridge v Campbell Discount Co Ltd* [1962] A.C. 600; *Hyundai Heavy Industries Ltd v Papadopoulos* [1980] 1 W.L.R. 1129 at 1141; *Photo Production Ltd v Securicor Transport Ltd* [1980] A.C. 827 at 849 ("anticipatory secondary obligation"); *The Rijn* [1981] 2 Lloyd's Rep. 267; *Gill & Duffus SA v Berger Co Inc* [1984] A.C. 382 at 390; *Nova Petroleum International Establishment v Tricon Trading Co* [1989] 1 Lloyd's Rep. 312; *Malik v BCCI* [1998] A.C. 20 at 36.

[89] *Brooks v Beirnstein* [1909] 1 K.B. 98; *Chatterton v Maclean* [1951] 1 All E.R. 761; *cf. The Almare Seconda* [1981] 2 Lloyd's Rep. 443; and see below, p.1011, n.56.

[90] *cf. Stocznia Gdanska SA v Latvian Shipping Co* [2002] EWCA Civ 889; [2002] 2 All E.R. (Comm) 768 at [83] (damages in respect of failure to pay instalments which would have become due after rescission).

[91] See below, pp.1013–1014.

(which can be brought only in respect of sums that have become due at the time of rescission). The distinction is sometimes overlooked because there is a tendency to describe any claim for money as one for damages, even when it is actually a claim for the enforcement of a primary obligation to pay an agreed sum. The point can be illustrated by taking the common case of a contract of sale which requires the buyer to pay a deposit and which is rescinded by the seller after, and on account of, the buyer's breach in failing to pay that deposit. In such a case, the seller will be entitled to (i) the deposit as an agreed sum due at the time of rescission; and (ii) damages for the buyer's repudiatory breach,[92] e.g. for loss suffered because the seller can resell the property only for an amount which falls short of the contract price by more than the amount of the deposit. In such a case, it is not strictly accurate to say that the seller can "sue for damages *including* the amount of the unpaid deposit."[93] This statement is accurate only where the seller has rescinded on account of some *other* breach by the buyer *before* the buyer's primary obligation to pay the deposit had accrued. This was the position in *The Blankenstein*,[94] where a contract for the sale of three ships provided for the signing of a formal memorandum and for the payment of a deposit of $236,500 on such signing. The seller rescinded on account of the buyer's wrongful refusal to sign and resold the ships for $60,000 less than the original contract price. As the deposit was to be paid only on signing, the primary obligation to pay it never accrued.[95] But it was held that the seller was entitled to $236,500 as damages for the buyer's repudiation in wrongfully refusing to sign the memorandum. The majority of the Court of Appeal rejected the argument that the seller's damages should be no more than $60,000; and their view seems, with respect, to be correct. At the time of rescission, the seller had been deprived, by the buyer's breach, of his right to receive the full amount of the deposit. He thus became entitled to damages of a precisely ascertainable amount, and later events (*i.e.* the relatively favourable resale of the ships) should not be allowed to deprive him of that accrued right. Such events should be relevant to the assessment of damages only where, at the time of rescission, it is *not* possible to put an exact value on the injured party's loss.

It follows from the preceding discussion that there is no inconsistency between rescinding a contract for breach and at the same time claiming damages for that breach. Accordingly it has been held that damages can be recovered by a buyer who rejects goods because they are defective,[96] or delivered late[97]; by a wrongfully dismissed employee who has rescinded so as to free himself from a covenant in restraint of trade[98]; by a vendor of land who has rescinded because of the purchaser's failure to comply with a notice to complete[99]; and by a purchaser of land who has rescinded on account of the vendor's breach.[1] Rescission for breach differs in this respect from rescission for misrepresenta-

---

[92] See above, p.774.

[93] *Millichamp v Jones* [1982] 1 W.L.R. 1422 at 1430.

[94] [1985] 1 W.L.R. 435; Carter, 104 L.Q.R. 207.

[95] The doctrine of "fictional fulfilment" of a condition against a party preventing its occurrence would support the argument that the buyer should be liable for the deposit as such, but that doctrine was rejected in *Thompson v ASDA-MFI Group plc* [1988] Ch. 241, above, p.66.

[96] *Millar's Machinery Co Ltd v David Way & Son* (1935) 40 Com.Cas. 204. *cf.* also the right of an unpaid *seller* to rescind (by exercising his right of resale) and claim damages: Sale of Goods Act 1979, s.48(4).

[97] *The Al Tawfiq* [1984] 2 Lloyd's Rep. 598.

[98] *General Billposting Co Ltd v Atkinson* [1909] A.C. 118.

[99] *Buckland v Farmar & Moody* [1979] 1 W.L.R. 221; *Johnson v Agnew* [1980] A.C. 367.

[1] The contrary was held in *Horsler v Zorro* [1975] Ch. 302 but that decision was disapproved in *Buckland v Farmar & Moody*, above, and overruled in *Johnson v Agnew*, above. *Horsler v Zorro* had been convincingly criticised by Alberry in 91 L.Q.R. 337; *cf.* Gummow, 92 L.Q.R. 5; Oakley [1980] C.L.J. 58; but see Dawson, 39 M.L.R. 241; Hetherington, 96 L.Q.R. 401, disputed by Jackson, 97 L.Q.R. 26.

tion, the effect of which is to treat the contract as if it had never existed.[2]

In discussing the effect of rescission on the obligations of the guilty party, we have so far assumed that the right to rescind has arisen under the general rules of law governing that right. It may, however, also arise under an express contractual provision, and such a provision may give the victim the right to rescind for some possibly quite minor breach. So far as the guilty party's *primary* obligations to perform are concerned, the exercise of such a right has exactly the same effects as the exercise of a right to rescind which has arisen under the general law: that is, in general accrued obligations remain due, while future ones (other than "ancillary" ones) are released.[3] But there is an important difference between the effects of rescission under the general law, and rescission under an express contractual provision, on the guilty party's *secondary* obligation to pay damages. Where the victim rescinds under the general law, he can recover damages for wrongful repudiation in respect of any loss suffered by reason of the premature determination of the contract[4] but he has (unless the contract otherwise provides[5]) no such right where he rescinds for a minor breach under an express contractual provision entitling him to do so.[6] Suppose, for example, that a hire-purchase agreement provides that the owner can terminate for any failure by the hirer to pay an instalment. If the owner terminates for the hirer's failure to pay two out of 24 instalments, he can sue for the two unpaid instalments, but not for any further ones which would have accrued later if he had not terminated the agreement.[7] Moreover, it was held in *Financings Ltd v Baldock*[8] that he cannot recover damages in respect of loss suffered by reason of the premature termination of the agreement. The reason for this is that, in the case put, the hirer's *only* breach is his failure to pay the two instalments. He is not, in addition, guilty of a repudiation of the whole contract, for which the damages for premature termination are recoverable where the right to rescind is governed by the general law. This restriction on the right to damages can, it is submitted, be supported on the policy ground that it alleviates the sometimes harsh operation of express provisions which allow a party to rescind even for a minor breach.[9]

The distinction between cases in which the right to rescind arises under general rules of law, and those in which it arises under express provisions may, however, itself give rise to difficulty. The reason for the difficulty lies in the fact that the terms "repudiation" or "repudiatory breach" (which are often used to describe breaches giving rise to the right rescind under general rules of law) can bear at least two meanings.[10] They can refer,

---

[2] See above, p.370 and *cf. Johnson v Agnew* [1980] A.C. 367 at 395, 398, also disapproving the reasoning of *Barber v Wolfe* [1945] Ch. 187.

[3] See above, p.850 at nn.78–79; for exceptions, see *ibid.* at nn.80–86.

[4] See above, p.851 at n.88.

[5] As in *The Solholt* [1981] 2 Lloyd's Rep. 574 at 579 (affirmed without reference to this point, [1983] 1 Lloyd's Rep. 605).

[6] The crucial question is whether the injured party has a right to determine under the general law (as opposed to one specifically conferred by the contract). If he has such a right, he can recover damages for wrongful repudiation even though, in determining the contract, he relies on an expressly conferred contractual right: *Yeoman Credit Ltd v Waragowski* [1961] 1 W.L.R. 1124; *Hyundai Heavy Industries Ltd v Pournaras* [1980] 1 W.L.R. 1129; *The Almare Seconda* [1981] 2 Lloyd's Rep. 433; an apparently contrary dictum in *UCB Leasing Ltd v Holtom* [1987] R.T.R. 362 at 368 is best explained on the ground that repudiation was not established (*ibid.*) so that there was *no* right to terminate except under the express provisions of the contract.

[7] *Financings Ltd v Baldock* [1963] 2 Q.B. 104 at 110; *Brady v St Margaret's Trust* [1963] 2 Q.B. 494; *Charterhouse Credit Corp v Tolly* [1963] Q.B. 683; *UCB Leasing Ltd v Holtom* [1987] R.T.R. 362.

[8] See above; *Kalsep Ltd v X-Flow Ltd BV, The Times*, May 3, 2001; *Amer-UDC Finance Ltd v Austin* (1986) 162 C.L.R. 170 (discussing earlier Australian cases); Goode, 104 L.Q.R. 25; Beale, 104 L.Q.R. 355; Opeskin, 106 L.Q.R. 293.

[9] See above, p.779.

[10] *The Gregos* [1994] 1 W.L.R. 1465 at 1474.

first, to breaches which amount to an actual repudiation because they give rise to a substantial failure in performance[11] (and therefore to a right to rescind), or, secondly, to all breaches which give rise to a right to rescind, including those which have this effect under one of the many exceptions[12] to the requirement of substantial failure. In the second of these senses, a breach may be described as "repudiatory" (because it gives rise to a right to rescind) even though it does not amount to an actual repudiation: for example, a breach of condition[13] may be called "repudiatory" even though it does not cause serious (or indeed any) prejudice to the victim of the breach. Moreover, a term may be a condition on the sole ground that the parties have expressly classified it as such in their contract.[14] Where such a term is broken, it is just as plausible to say that the right to rescind has arisen under a general rule of law (*i.e.* the rule that breach of condition gives rise to a right to rescind) as to say that it has arisen under an express provision of the contract (*i.e.* the express classification by the parties of the term as a condition). A similar point can be made about stipulations as to the time of performance. Breach of such a stipulation justifies rescission if time is "of the essence" of the contract and this will be the position if (a) delay causes, or is likely to cause, serious prejudice to the victim of the breach,[15] or (b) the contract expressly provides that time is to be of the essence.[16] In the latter case it is, again, possible to say *either* that the right to rescind for failure to perform at the agreed time has arisen under a general rule of law (*i.e.* the rule giving rise to a right to rescind where time is of the essence) *or* that the right has arisen under an express provision of the contract (*i.e.* the provision making time of the essence). *Financings Ltd v Baldock*[17] may from this point of view be contrasted with *Lombard North Central plc v Butterworth*,[18] where a contract of hire provided (1) that the owner could terminate for any failure to pay instalments when due; and (2) that the time of payment was of the essence of the contract. It was held that the second of these provisions made the stipulation as to the time of payment a condition of the contract so that its breach entitled the owners not only to rescind but also to damages for the premature termination of the agreement. But the decision was reached with evident reluctance[19] since there was no substantial distinction between the facts of this case and those of *Financings Ltd v Baldock*.[20] In the *Lombard* case the two provisions summarised above were simply two ways of saying the same thing and the policy consideration of alleviating the harsh operation of express provisions for determination is no weaker where the contract contains two such provisions than where it contains only one. For this reason it is submitted that the earlier decision in *Financings Ltd v Baldock* is to be preferred[21]: *i.e.* that damages for premature determination should not be available

---

[11] See above, pp.769–778.

[12] See above, pp.778–811.

[13] See above, pp.788–805; *SCI (Sales Curve Interactive) v Titus SARL* [2001] EWCA Civ 591; [2001] 2 All E.R. (Comm) 416, at [19]; *Stocznia Gdanska SA v Latvian Shipping Co (No.3)* [2002] EWCA Civ 889; [2002] 2 All E.R. (Comm) 768 at [76] (where there was also an actual repudiation).

[14] See above, pp.791–792.

[15] See above, pp.828–829 at nn.34–43.

[16] See above, p.828 at n.31.

[17] See above, n.8.

[18] [1987] Q.B. 527; Treitel [1987] L.M.C.L.Q. 143; Bojczuk [1987] J.B.L. 353; Nicholson, 1 J.C.L. 64; *cf.* also *The Afovos* [1983] 1 W.L.R. 195 at 203.

[19] See [1987] Q.B. at 546 ("with considerable dissatisfaction") and at 540 ("not a result which I view with much satisfaction").

[20] [1963] 2 Q.B. 683, above, p.853.

[21] For the same reason, *Financings Ltd v Baldock*, above, is (it is submitted) to be preferred to the reasoning of the Supreme Court of Canada in *Keneric Tractor Sales Ltd v Langille* [1987] 2 S.C.R. 440; Ziegel [1988] L.M.C.L.Q. 277, and 104 L.Q.R. 513.

merely[22] because the injured party has rescinded under express provisions giving him the right to do so.

The rules stated above assume that the injured party has, and has exercised, an option to rescind. We have seen that in the law of insurance an insurer may be discharged from liability automatically, without any such election on his part[23]; and where he is so discharged it does not follow that even the *primary* obligations of the other party are similarly discharged. Thus the assured can remain liable for premiums even though his breach of "warranty" has discharged the insurer.[24]

(2) Affirmation or failure to rescind

The victim may positively affirm the contract, or simply fail to exercise his option to rescind.[25] In either of these cases, the contract remains in force,[26] so that each party is bound to perform his primary obligations when that performance falls due.[27] It must, however, be recalled that, under the rules relating to the order of performance,[28] the effect of one party's breach may be to prevent performance of the other's obligations from falling due. For example, an employee may, in breach of contract, refuse to perform his duty to work and so give the employer a right to dismiss him.[29] The mere fact that the employer does not exercise that right does not lead to the result that the employer must continue to pay the agreed wages. On the contrary, he is under no such liability since performance of the employee's duty to work is a condition precedent of the employer's duty to pay.[30] The position is more complex where the employee's breach takes the form, not of an outright refusal to work, but of a refusal merely to perform specified tasks while continuing to perform the remaining duties of his employment. This situation has already been discussed[31]; the only point which needs to be made here is that, if the employer voluntarily accepts such partial performance, he must pay for it at the contract rate,[32] while the employee is liable in damages for loss caused by his breach.[33] It is in this sense that the obligations of both parties "remain in force".

The statement just made relates only to the *obligations* of the parties, and not to the *remedies* for their enforcement. To say that a party remains bound under the contract to do or to abstain from doing some act does not mean that these obligations can be enforced by an order of specific performance or by an injunction; and similarly to say that a party remains bound to make certain payments does not mean that an action for

---

[22] The injured party may be entitled to such damages by virtue of an express term giving him *this* right, even on rescission for a minor breach; but such a term runs the risk of being void as a penalty (below, p.929), as it was in the *Lombard* case, above, n.18.

[23] See above, p.999.

[24] *The Good Luck* [1992] A.C. 233 at 263.

[25] Mere inaction does not necessarily amount to such failure: see this situation discussed on p.848 above, after n.56.

[26] e.g., *Segap Garages Ltd v Gulf Oil (Great Britain) Ltd*, *The Times*, October 24, 1989; *BMBF (No.12) v Harland & Wolff Shipbuilding & Heavy Industries Ltd* [2001] EWCA Civ 862; [2001] 2 All E.R. (Comm) 385. These were cases of *actual* breach. The same rule applies in cases of *anticipatory* breach: below, pp.864–865.

[27] For certain effects of victim's inability to perform, see above, pp.767–769.

[28] See above, pp.761–766.

[29] See above, p.810.

[30] See above, p.762.

[31] See above, p.821.

[32] i.e. he can make a *pro rata* deduction in respect of the unperformed services: *Miles v Wakefield Metropolitan DC* [1987] A.C. 539.

[33] *Sim v Rotherham Metropolitan BC* [1987] Ch. 216.

the agreed sum can be brought against him.[34] The circumstances in which these remedies are available are discussed in Chapter 21[35]; here it is necessary only to say that, in any of the cases just mentioned, the victim's only remedy may be an action for damages.

(3) Change of course

Once the victim has rescinded, he cannot later affirm and demand performance: this follows from the rule that rescission releases the defaulting party from his primary obligation to perform.[36] On the other hand, where the victim's original reaction to the breach is to press for performance, he plainly does not release the guilty party from any obligation; nor does he, by demanding performance after breach,[37] necessarily waive his right to rescind, since such a demand is not of itself a "clear and unequivocal" representation[38] that that right will not be exercised. So long as there are no other circumstances from which such a representation can be inferred, the victim can therefore still rescind if the other party does not comply with the demand for performance.[39]

A special application of the rule just stated is to cases in which the injured party has actually obtained an order of specific performance. If the defendant fails to comply with the order, one possible course of action open to the injured party is to apply to the court for enforcement of the order. There was formerly some support for the view that this was the only remedy available to him, and that he could not, after having obtained an order of specific performance, then rescind and claim damages.[40] But this view was rejected by the House of Lords in *Johnson v Agnew*.[41] In that case, vendors of land were (as the purchaser knew) relying on the proceeds of the sale to pay off a mortgage on the land. The purchaser failed to complete, even after specific performance had been ordered against her, with the result that the land was sold by the mortgagee. The vendors were therefore no longer able to enforce the order of specific performance (since they could no longer convey the land) and it was held that they were entitled to damages, not only under the special statutory power to award damages in lieu of specific performance,[42] but also at common law.[43] The reasoning of *Johnson v Agnew* is not, moreover, restricted to the situation in which failure to comply with the order of specific performance has disabled the party who had obtained it from performing his side of the bargain.

---

[34] *Telephone Rentals v Burgess Salmon, The Independent*, April 22, 1987.

[35] See especially below, pp.1013–1019.

[36] See above, p.851; *Johnson v Agnew* [1980] A.C. 367 at 393; *cf. Meng Leong Developments Pte Ltd v Jip Hong Trading Co* [1985] A.C. 511. The position may be different where the party in breach denies the breach and maintains the continued existence of the contract: see *Systems Control plc v Munro Corporate plc* [1990] B.C.L.C. 659 at 666.

[37] Our concern here is with the victim's reaction to an *actual* breach. For the position in cases of *anticipatory* breach, see below, p.864.

[38] See above, pp.813–814; *e.g. Yukong Line Ltd of Korea v Rendsburg Investments Co of Liberia* [1996] 2 Lloyd's Rep. 604.

[39] *cf. Tilcon Ltd v Land and Real Estate Investments Ltd* [1987] 1 All E.R. 615; *Safehaven Investments Inc v Springbok Ltd* (1995) 71 P. & C.R. 59 at [68]; *Stocznia Gdanska SA v Latvian Shipping Co* [2002] EWCA Civ 889; [2002] 2 All E.R. (Comm) 768 at [100].

[40] See *Capital & Suburban Properties Ltd v Swycher* [1976] Ch. 319 and the authorities there cited; Dawson (1977) 93 L.Q.R. 232; Oakley [1977] C.L.J. 20.

[41] [1980] A.C. 367, disapproving *Capital & Suburban Properties Ltd v Swycher*, above.

[42] See below, pp.1046–1047; such damages had been awarded in *Biggin v Minton* [1977] 1 W.L.R. 701.

[43] *Semble*, the position would be the same if the order for specific performance were obtained, and then not complied with, by the purchaser. The contrary was decided in *Singh v Nazeer* [1979] Ch. 474; but that case followed *Capital & Suburban Properties v Swycher*, above, which is now disapproved: above, n.41.

It is based on the general rules relating to the effects of repudiatory breach and therefore applies even where no such disability results. The right to damages is subject only to the qualification that, where an order of specific performance has not been complied with, the party who had obtained the order and now wishes to claim damages must apply to the court for the dissolution of the order "and ask the court to put an end to the contract".[44]

SECTION 3. REPUDIATION BEFORE PERFORMANCE IS DUE

1. Doctrine of Anticipatory Breach

An "anticipatory breach"[45] is said to occur when, before performance is due, a party *either* renounces the contract *or* disables himself from performing it.[46]

Renunciation requires a "clear" and "absolute"[47] refusal to perform; this need not be express but can take the form of conduct indicating that the party is unwilling, even though he may be able, to perform. A repudiation may even be inferred from silence where it is a "speaking silence"[48]: for example, the previous conduct of a party in refusing to perform another related contract may give rise to the inference that he will refuse to perform the contract in question. His silence or inactivity can then be a repudiation of that contract unless he takes positive steps to dispel that inference.[49] The conduct must indicate to the other party that the party alleged to have renounced the contract is about to commit a breach of it: an indication given to a third party of an intention to commit a breach at an unspecified time in the future has been held not to amount to a renunciation.[50]

Disablement need not be "deliberate",[51] in the sense that there may be an anticipatory breach even though it was not the party's intention to disable himself from performing; but the disablement must be due to the party's "own act or default".[52] Such disablement is most clearly illustrated by cases in which a party does a positive act which is certain to prevent performance, such as disposing elsewhere of the specific thing[53] which forms the subject-matter of the contract.

Disablement may, however, also take the form of an omission. For example, a contract may be made for the sale of goods for future delivery, to be manufactured by the seller, or to be acquired by him from a third party, and the seller may fail to take any steps to

---

[44] [1980] A.C. 367 at 394; *GKN Distributors v Tyne Tees Fabrication* (1985) 50 P. & C.R. 403; *Hillel v Christoforides* (1991) 63 P. & C.R. 301.

[45] For criticism of this terminology, see *Bradley v H Newsom, Sons & Co* [1919] A.C. 16 at 53; *The Mihalis Angelos* [1971] 1 Q.B. 164 at 196. And see Dawson [1981] C.L.J. 83; Mustill, *Butterworth Lectures, 1989–1990*, 1.

[46] *Universal Cargo Carriers Corp v Citati* [1957] 2 Q.B. 401 at 438; *cf. The Angelia* [1973] 1 W.L.R. 210; Tiplady, 89 L.Q.R. 465.

[47] *The Hermosa* [1982] 1 Lloyd's Rep. 570 at 572; *cf. The Gregos* [1994] 1 W.L.R. 1465; *Jaks (UK) Ltd v Cera Investment Bank SA* [1998] 2 Lloyd's Rep. 89 at 93.

[48] *Stocznia Gdanska SA v Latvian Shipping Co (No.3)* [2002] EWCA Civ 889; [2002] 2 All E.R. (Comm) 768, at [96].

[49] *ibid.*

[50] *Laughton and Hawley v BAPP Industrial Supplies* [1986] I.C.R. 245.

[51] *Universal Cargo Carriers Corp v Citati*, above, at 438; contrast *The Super Servant Two* [1989] 1 Lloyd's Rep. 149 at 155 ("deliberate or at least voluntary"), affirmed [1990] 1 Lloyd's Rep. 1.

[52] *Universal Cargo Carriers Corp v Citati*, above, at 441; or (as in that case) from the act or default of another person to whom he had delegated performance of his contractual duty.

[53] Disposing of a thing which is *not* specific does not amount to disablement, for the seller may be able to perform, by supplying another thing of the contract description out of stock or from another source: *Texaco Ltd v Eurogulf Shipping Co Ltd* [1987] 2 Lloyd's Rep. 541. *cf. Alfred C Toepfer International GmbH v Itex Itagrani Export SA* [1993] 1 Lloyd's Rep. 360 (applying the same principle to disablement by a buyer).

manufacture the goods or to acquire them from the supplier. The failure will then amount to his "own . . . default" in the sense that he will have failed to do something that he was obliged by the contract to do in order to put himself into the position of being able to perform on the due date. But if a seller of goods to be acquired from a third party had duly contracted with that third party to acquire the goods, he would not be in anticipatory breach merely because it became highly unlikely that the third party would deliver them under his contract with the seller, so that the seller himself would, in turn, be unable to perform his contract with the buyer. *A fortiori* a seller is not in anticipatory breach merely because the buyer *fears* that the subject-matter of the sale, when delivered, will turn out to be defective.[54] Nor would a buyer be in anticipatory breach merely because, before the time fixed for payment, some external cause (such as exchange control, or the failure of a bank) made it virtually certain that he would be unable to pay on the due date. In the last three examples there is no disablement by the party's "own . . . default": hence the prospective inability does not amount to an anticipatory breach,[55] even though it would, if it persisted up to the time when performance was due, then amount to an actual breach.[56] Difficulties can obviously arise in deciding whether a prospective inability resulting from an omission is due to the party's "own . . . default." The difficulty is illustrated by the very case in which this requirement is stated, *Universal Cargo Carriers Corp v Citati*.[57] In that case, a charterer was held to be in anticipatory breach of his obligation to provide a cargo, at the time fixed for loading, because of the prospective failure of a third party, with whom he had contracted for the supply of the goods, to deliver them within that time. This aspect of the case has been judicially described as "debatable"[58]; it can perhaps be explained on the ground that the charterer had failed to ensure that his supply contract was effective for the purpose of the performance of his own obligations under the charterparty.

Where one party has committed an anticipatory breach, the other has a choice. He can try to keep the contract alive by continuing to press for performance,[59] in which case the anticipatory breach will have the same effects as an actual breach. Alternatively, he can "accept" the breach, in which case his rights to damages and rescission are governed by the special rules to be discussed below.

2. Acceptance of the Breach

A breach can be accepted by bringing an action for damages; or by giving notice of intention to accept it to the party in breach. Conduct known to the party in breach will suffice even if no notice of it is given by the injured party.[60] Conversely, once the injured party has made it plain that he is treating the contract as at an end, he "does not need to *do* anything more".[61] Mere acquiescence or inactivity will often be equivocal and so fail to constitute an acceptance for this purpose.[62] But there is no absolute rule of law

---

[54] *The Veracruz I* [1992] 1 Lloyd's Rep. 356; *The P* [1992] 1 Lloyd's Rep. 470.

[55] *FC Shepherd & Co Ltd v Jerrom* [1987] Q.B. 301 at 327–328.

[56] This may be so even though the party in breach is in no way at fault, *e.g.* where his source of funds fails: see above, p.838.

[57] [1957] 2 Q.B. 401 and see below, p.862.

[58] *FC Shepherd & Co Ltd v Jerrom*, above, at 323.

[59] *Michael v Hart & Co* [1902] 1 K.B. 482; *Harvela Investments Ltd v Royal Trust of Canada (CI) Ltd* [1986] A.C. 207 at 227.

[60] *Vitol SA v Norelf Ltd* [1996] A.C. 800, as to which see also n.64, below.

[61] *Lefevre v White* [1990] 1 Lloyd's Rep. 569 at 574; statements in *Société Génerale de Paris v Milders* (1883) 49 L.T. 55 at 57, which refer to the need to act on the notice of acceptance, can be explained as merely descriptive of the usual course of events.

[62] *Cranleigh Precision Engineering Ltd v Bryant* [1965] 1 W.L.R. 1293; *State Trading Corp of India v M Golodetz Ltd* [1989] 2 Lloyd's Rep. 277 at 286; *Lefevre v White* [1990] 1 Lloyd's Rep. 569 at 574, 576–577.

to this effect: for example, the fact of the injured party's having failed, in response to the breach, to take the steps which he would normally have been expected to take in the further performance of the contract may (in circumstances described earlier in this Chapter)[63] unequivocally indicate his acceptance of the breach.[64]

Acceptance of the breach must be complete and unequivocal.[65] A party cannot accept an anticipatory breach of one term in a contract while treating the contract as still in existence for other purposes.[66]

3. Effects of Accepting the Breach

(1) Damages for anticipatory breach

The most striking feature of the doctrine of anticipatory breach is that acceptance of the breach entitles the victim to claim damages *at once*, before the time fixed for performance. This rule was established in *Hochster v De la Tour*[67] where the defendant had agreed to employ the plaintiff as courier for three months from June 1, and repudiated the contract on May 11. The plaintiff was able to claim damages at once: he did not have to wait until June 1 before beginning his action. The main reason for the decision was that "if the plaintiff has no remedy for breach of contract unless he treats the contract as in force and acts upon it down to the 1st of June 1852, it follows that, till then, he must enter into no employment".[68] This reasoning has been justly criticised,[69] for the court could have held that the defendant's repudiation gave the plaintiff *the option to rescind* at once but did not *entitle him to damages* until June 1: there is no necessary connection between these two consequences of the repudiation.

Where the interval between repudiation and the time fixed for performance is a long one, there are also practical objections to the rule in *Hochster v De la Tour*, and these are particularly strong where the trial takes place well before the time fixed for performance. One such objection is that the rule may lead to a wrong quantification of damages. If a seller of goods to be delivered in three years' time repudiates and the buyer claims damages at once, the quantification of those damages may depend on the market price at the time fixed for delivery[70]; but if the case is tried before that time the court can only guess what that price will be. Another objection to the rule is that it results in an acceleration of the defendant's obligation; he will have to pay damages now, even though under the contract he was not to perform until some future time.[71] Thus if a debtor repudiates liability to repay future instalments of a debt, the creditor can claim damages at once, even though the instalments, or some of them, are not payable until a future

---

[63] See above, p.848.

[64] *Vitol SA v Norelf Ltd*, above, n.60. The case was treated in the lower courts as one of anticipatory breach, but, except in quotations from the judgments of those courts, no reference to this aspect of the case was made in the House of Lords.

[65] *Harrison v Northwest Holt Group Administration* [1985] I.C.R. 668; *Jaks (UK) Ltd v Cera Investment Bank Ltd* [1998] 2 Lloyd's Rep. 89 at 94.

[66] This was one reason for the decision in *Johnstone v Milling* (1886) 16 Q.B.D. 460.

[67] (1853) 2 E. & B. 678.

[68] (1853) 2 E. & B. 678 at 689.

[69] See Williston, *Contracts* (3rd ed.), §§ 1300 *et seq.*; Corbin, *Contracts*, §§ 959 *et seq.*; Vold, 41 Harv.L.Rev. 340 suggests that anticipatory breach might be regarded as a tort; *cf.* Weir [1964] C.L.J. 231; but see Hoffmann, 81 L.Q.R. 116.

[70] See below, pp.959–960.

[71] If the injured party affirms the contract and sues for specific performance, the court may give judgment in his favour at once, but the judgment will not order the defendant to perform until the time fixed for performance arrives: see *Hasham v Zenab* [1960] A.C. 316.

day.[72] Of course in assessing those damages the court will allow the debtor "a discount for accelerated payment".[73] Even more strikingly, the defendant will have to pay damages at once although at the time of the action his liability is still contingent and might never mature at all. Thus damages have been recovered for anticipatory breach of a husband's promise to make a will leaving a life interest in property to his wife, although it was uncertain at the time of the action whether the wife would survive the husband.[74]

In spite of these objections, the rule in *Hochster v De la Tour* is well established[75] and at least two points can be made in its favour. First, the rule may help to minimise loss. In a case like *Hochster v De la Tour*, the injured party might in fact be more *likely* (whether or not he was *bound*) to keep himself ready to perform if he had no right to sue at once. The rule giving him that right provides at any rate some incentive for him to abandon the contract, and so to avoid this extra loss. Secondly, the rule may sometimes be necessary to protect the injured party: for example, if he has paid in advance for a promise of future performance which is then repudiated. In such a case the injured party could be seriously prejudiced if he had no claim against the other party until the time fixed for performance had arrived; for, having made the advance payment, he might lack the means to procure a substitute contract.

Acceptance of the breach affects not only the claimant's entitlement to damages, but also the way in which those damages are assessed. The latter point is discussed in Chapter 21.[76]

(2) Rescission for anticipatory breach

(a) TYPES OF BREACH JUSTIFYING RESCISSION. An anticipatory breach, like an actual breach, can give rise to a right to rescind and that right arises immediately, *i.e.* before performance is due. Whether it does give rise to such a right depends on the factors discussed in Chapter 18.[77] Generally, therefore, the right to rescind will arise only if the prospective effects of the anticipatory breach are such as to satisfy the requirement of substantial failure in performance.[78] Thus a charterer's advance announcement of a deliberate delay of one day in loading would not (any more than an actual delay of this kind[79]) justify rescission. In relation to actual breach, however, the requirement of substantial failure is subject to many exceptions[80]; and the question arises whether the right to rescind for anticipatory breach extends to cases falling within those exceptions.

---

[72] In the United States, the doctrine of anticipatory breach does not apply in this situation: see Williston, *Contracts* (3rd ed.), §1326; Restatement 2d, *Contracts*, §243 Ill. 4. The American rule is convincingly criticised by Corbin, *Contracts*, §962; and it seems that it would not be followed in England: see next note. There is some support for the American rule in Canada and Australia: see *Melanson v Dominion of Canada General Ins Co* [1934] 2 D.L.R. 459; *MacKenzie v Rees* (1941) 65 C.L.R. 1 at 16–18; *Progressive Mailing House Pty Ltd v Tabali Pty Ltd* (1985) A.L.J.R. 373 at 385.

[73] *Lep Air Services Ltd v Rolloswin Investments Ltd* [1973] A.C. 331 at 356; *Re Park Air Services* [1999] 1 All E.R. 673 at 676.

[74] *Synge v Synge* [1894] 1 Q.B. 466; *cf. Frost v Knight* (1872) L.R. 7 Ex. 111. The actual decision in the latter case has been made obsolete by Law Reform (Miscellaneous Provisions) Act 1970, s.1; but *quaere* whether it could still govern the time at which an order under s.2 could be made: *cf.* above, p.440.

[75] See *Lep Air Services Ltd v Rolloswin Investments Ltd* [1973] A.C. 331 at 356, 358; *Woodar Investments Development Ltd v Wimpey Construction UK Ltd* [1980] 1 W.L.R. 277 at 297; *Gunton v Richmond-upon-Thames LBC* [1981] Ch. 448 at 467; *The Hazelmoor* [1980] 2 Lloyd's Rep. 351.

[76] See below, pp.962–964.

[77] See above, pp.759–811.

[78] See above, pp.769–778.

[79] See above, p.807.

[80] See above, pp.778–811.

There is one type of case in which a negative answer must clearly be given to this question, namely that in which the right to rescind exists by reason only of an express provision in the contract for determination.[81] We have seen that under such provisions in charterparties charterers cannot exercise their rights to cancel for late arrival of the ship, nor owners withdraw for non-payment of hire, merely because it has become certain that the ship *will not* arrive, or that the hire *will not* be paid in time: they are only entitled to rescind when the specified day has gone by without performance being rendered.[82] In *The Afovos* a shipowner gave notice (under such an express provision) of his intention to rescind on account of the charterer's failure to pay hire in time, but he did so while the charterer's breach was merely anticipatory; and Lord Diplock, in holding the purported rescission to be wrongful, said: "it is to fundamental breaches alone that the doctrine of anticipatory breach is applicable".[83] On the facts, the conclusion that the notice of rescission was premature cannot be doubted, for it is clear that the right to rescind for anticipatory breach does not apply to *the particular* exception to the requirement of substantial failure with which *The Afovos* was concerned, *i.e.* the exception under which rescission for actual breach is allowed because of an express provision for determination. But the mere fact that the right to rescind for anticipatory breach does not apply to *one* such exception does not support the conclusion that it cannot apply to *any* of them. Indeed, Lord Diplock himself has recognised that there can be a right to rescind for "an anticipatory breach of a fundamental term".[84] Yet such a breach is not necessarily a "fundamental breach" for it may occur without giving rise to a total or substantial failure in performance.[85] The same is true of a breach of a "condition," in the sense of a term *any* actual breach of which justifies rescission[86]; and Lord Diplock's suggestion in *The Afovos*,[87] that there can be no right to rescind for an anticipatory breach of condition may, with respect, be doubted. In part, the question whether there can be such a right is one of terminology. Lord Diplock has elsewhere defined "conditions" as terms the breach of which gives rise to the right to rescind because the parties have so "agreed, whether by express words or by implication of law".[88] Under this definition, express provisions for determination on non-performance *are* "conditions"; but a term is often classified as a "condition" by statute or by judicial decision[89] even though the parties have not expressly agreed that *any* breach of it is to give rise to the right to rescind. This group of conditions is in practice the more important group of such terms: and it is submitted that the right to rescind for anticipatory breach does extend to conditions of this kind. Thus in one leading case[90] on anticipatory breach the court asked *first* whether the prospective breaches were breaches of condition and (having reached the conclusion that they were not[91]) proceeded *secondly*

---

[81] See above, pp.778–782.
[82] See above, p.789.
[83] [1983] 1 W.L.R. 195 at 203.
[84] *Harvela Investments Ltd v Royal Trust of Canada (CI) Ltd* [1986] A.C. 207 at 226.
[85] See above, p.806; in *Metro Meat Ltd v Fares Rural Co Pty Ltd* [1985] 2 Lloyd's Rep. 13 at 15 Lord Diplock seems to use "breach of a fundamental term" to refer simply to a breach evincing an intention not to perform in accordance with the agreed terms.
[86] See above, p.788. The exceptions, stated at p.800 above, to the right to rescind for breach of condition do not affect the present discussion.
[87] [1983] 1 W.L.R. 195 at 203.
[88] *Photo Production Ltd v Securicor Transport Ltd* [1980] A.C. 827 at 849; *cf.* above, pp.788–791.
[89] See above, pp.790–791.
[90] *Universal Cargo Carriers Corp v Citati* [1957] 2 Q.B. 401.
[91] See below, nn.98, 99.

to the question whether they were sufficiently serious to justify rescission for anticipatory breach.[92] The first enquiry would have been unnecessary if the doctrine of anticipatory breach could never apply to breaches of condition.

(b) PROSPECTIVE EFFECT OF BREACH. In cases of anticipatory breach, the right to rescind may depend on the prospective effects of the breach. A question therefore arises as to what the injured party has to show to justify rescission. Is it enough for him to show that, at the time of rescission, he *reasonably believed* that the breach would, by the time fixed for performance, have acquired the character of a breach giving rise to the right to rescind? Or must he show that, at the time of rescission, it was *already certain* that the breach was going to be of this kind? This depends on the form taken by the anticipatory breach.

(i) *Renunciation.* The first form of anticipatory breach is by renunciation, *i.e.* by a "clear" and "absolute"[93] refusal to perform. This may be inferred from conduct where the party in breach has "acted in such a way as to lead a reasonable man to conclude that [he] did not intend to fulfil [his] part of the contract".[94] Whether conduct has this effect "is to be considered as at the time when it is treated as terminating the contract, in the light of the then existing circumstances".[95] The court therefore looks to the time of rescission to determine whether the injured party reasonably took the view that the refusal was sufficiently clear and absolute to give him the right to rescind.[96]

(ii) *Prospective inability.* Where a party is alleged to have committed an anticipatory breach by disabling himself from performing, the question whether the other party is entitled to rescind will generally depend on the seriousness of the resulting failure in performance. That failure being wholly prospective, its seriousness is more than usually a matter of speculation; but the injured party may nevertheless seek to rescind before the time fixed for performance. The problem arose in *Universal Cargo Carriers Corp v Citati*[97] where a charterparty obliged the charterer to provide a cargo of 6,000 tons of scrap iron, to load it at the rate of 1,000 tons a day, and to complete the loading by July 21. He had failed to provide any cargo by July 18 and on that day the shipowners purported to rescind. The charterer's failure to provide a cargo was an actual breach, though not one which of itself justified rescission.[98] It seems that the charterer was also in breach of his obligation to load, for if loading were to be completed at the rate of 1,000 tons a day by July 21 it ought to have begun before July 18. However, perhaps because the obligation to complete loading still lay in the future, the breach was at least in part anticipatory[99]; and the question discussed[1] was whether this breach by the charterer, assuming it to be anticipatory, justified rescission by the shipowners on July 18. This depended on the seriousness of the breach: the shipowners had to show "that on July 18 the charterer was unable to load a cargo within such a time as would not have frustrated the venture".[2] It was not sufficient for them to show that on July 18 they had reasonable grounds for believing that such a frustrating delay would occur; they were justified in

---

[92] See below at n.2.

[93] *The Hermosa* [1982] 1 Lloyd's Rep. 570 at 572.

[94] *ibid.* at 580.

[95] *ibid.* at 572.

[96] *ibid.*, at 573; *Universal Cargo Carriers Corp v Citati* [1957] 2 Q.B. 401 at 439–440; *The Sanko Iris* [1987] 1 Lloyd's Rep. 487; Carter [1988] L.M.C.L.Q. 21.

[97] [1957] 2 Q.B. 401.

[98] [1957] 2 Q.B. 401 at 429. He was also in breach of his obligation to nominate a berth. Neither breach was one of condition: *ibid.* and *cf.* above, p.795.

[99] Devlin J. at 429 discusses whether *this* breach (which was also not one of condition) was actual or anticipatory and concludes that "it must be one or the other."

[1] See [1957] 2 Q.B. 401 at 436.

[2] [1957] 2 Q.B. 401 at 450.

rescinding only if they could prove that a delay of this kind would actually have occurred.[3]

This rule is likely to prove inconvenient in practice. It does not apply where the contract is alleged to be frustrated.[4] In one such case Scrutton J. said that "Commercial men must not be asked to wait till the end of a long delay to find out from what in fact happens whether they are bound by a contract or not; they must be entitled to act on reasonable commercial probabilities at the time when they are called upon to make up their minds."[5] In the *Citati* case Devlin J. held that this principle did not apply to "questions of breach of contract"[6]; and he added that "An anticipatory breach must be proved in fact and not in supposition."[7] One can to some extent justify the distinction between the two types of cases. Frustration leads only to discharge of the contract, while anticipatory breach can lead both to rescission and to liability in damages. It seems obviously unfair to hold one party (A) liable *in damages*, merely because the other (B) reasonably believed that A would be unable to perform, if it turns out that A is in fact able to perform at the appointed time. But it does not follow that B should not in these circumstances be entitled to rescind. On this point the reasoning of the *Citati* case is open to the same objection as that of *Hochster v De la Tour*[8]: it assumes that, in cases of anticipatory breach, the right to damages and the right to rescind necessarily arise at the same time. This is, however, no criticism of the actual decision in the *Citati* case, which appears to be consistent with the view here put forward; for the issue in the case was not whether the shipowners were liable for wrongful repudiation, but whether the charterer was liable in damages for an anticipatory breach of his obligation to load.

(iii) *Prospective effects of actual breach.* A reasonable belief that a substantial failure will occur is also sufficient to justify rescission where there has at the time of rescission been an actual breach which gives rise to uncertainty as to future performance. For example, where a ship is unseaworthy, "the charterer may rightly terminate . . . if the delay in remedying any breach is so long in fact, *or likely to be so long in reasonable anticipation*, that the commercial purpose of the contract would be frustrated".[9] In such a case the court need not fear that the shipowner will be held liable in damages merely because it was reasonably anticipated that he could not perform. His liability in damages is already established by reason of the actual breach; all that is in issue is the right of the injured party to rescind. *That right* should, it is submitted, depend on "reasonable anticipation" in cases of anticipatory, no less than of actual[10] breach.

(c) CONSEQUENCES OF RESCISSION. Where the injured party is entitled to, and does, rescind for anticipatory breach, two results follow. First, he is released from future obligations under the contract: this is so even though between acceptance of the anticipatory breach and the time fixed for performance the party in breach changes his

---

[3] *ibid.* at 449. The point appears to have been conceded.

[4] See below, pp.890–891.

[5] *Embiricos v Sydney Reid & Co* [1914] 3 K.B. 45 at 54.

[6] [1957] 2 Q.B. 401 at 449.

[7] *ibid.* at 450; Carter, 47 M.L.R. 422. *cf. BV Oliehandel Jongkind v Coastal International Ltd* [1983] 2 Lloyd's Rep. 463 where the contract to some extent modified the English rule stated by Devlin J. in the *Citati* case. Contrast the American doctrine of "adequate assurance of performance" contained in U.C.C. s.2–609 and somewhat similar rules in civil law systems, *e.g.* German Civil Code §321.

[8] (1853) 2 E. & B. 678 at 679; above, p.859.

[9] *Hongkong Fir Shipping Co Ltd v Kawasaki Kisen Kaisha Ltd* [1962] 2 Q.B. 26 at 57 (italics supplied); *Snia v Suzuki & Co* (1929) 29 Com.Cas. 284 (the *Citati* case itself may have been of this kind: see above, p.862); *cf. The Hermosa* [1982] 1 Lloyd's Rep. 570 at 580 (where a mere reasonable *suspicion*, as opposed to a reasonable *conclusion*, of future inability was held insufficient to justify rescission).

[10] See above, pp.774–776.

mind and offers after all to perform.[11] Secondly, the injured party is no longer bound to perform in order to establish his right of action on the contract; indeed he need not even show that he could at the time fixed for performance have performed a condition precedent to the other party's liability or a concurrent condition.[12]

4. Effects of Not Accepting the Breach

If the injured party does not accept the breach, he remains liable to perform,[13] and he retains the right to enforce the other party's primary obligations.[14] As a practical matter, he also keeps alive the possibility of securing actual performance of the contract without legal action. The fact that the injured party initially calls for performance does not prevent him from rescinding the contract on account of a later *actual* breach[15]; but there is a conflict of judicial opinion on the question whether, after the injured party has affirmed the contract, he can then change his mind while the breach remains anticipatory and still continues at the time of the injured party's later rescission. One view is that the injured party should not be allowed to change course in this way[16] since, if the guilty party had acted in reliance on the affirmation by making continued efforts to perform the contract, he would be prejudiced by that change of course.[17] But where no such prejudice is suffered,[18] it is hard to see why effect should not be given to the change of course in cases of anticipatory (as it is in cases of actual)[19] breach. Refusal to give it such effect could unduly prejudice the injured party. For one thing, such refusal could require that party to "engage in performance that is entirely pointless and wasteful"[20] while the other party's anticipatory breach continued. For another, the injured party's initial reaction to the anticipatory breach might well be to call on the guilty party to perform and this might be regarded as an affirmation of the contract. One way of protecting the injured party in such cases would be to hold that the demand did not of itself amount to an affirmation,[21] but this possibility might be ruled out on the facts: *e.g.* by the terms of the demand. In such cases the possible hardship to the guilty party has to be set against that to the injured party and it is submitted that, on balance, the preferable view[22] is that the injured party should not, as a general rule, be precluded by his initial affirmation from rescinding the contract, even while the breach remains anticipatory, if after the affirmation the guilty party persists in his refusal. Any hardship which this view might cause to the guilty party would be removed by holding that there could be no such

---

[11] *Danube, etc., Ry v Xenos* (1863) 13 C.B.(N.S.) 825; *cf. Decro-Wall International SA v Practitioners in Marketing Ltd* [1971] 1 W.L.R. 361 at 382.

[12] See above, pp.766–769.

[13] See above, p.855.

[14] *ibid.*

[15] *Stocznia Gdanska SA v Latvian Shipping Co* [1997] 2 Lloyd's Rep. 228 at 236; *cf.* above, pp.856–857.

[16] This was the point actually decided in the *Stocznia* case, above; Treitel, 114 L.Q.R. 22. The decision was later set aside by the House of Lords: [1998] 1 W.L.R. 574 at 594 but without final resolution of the point here under discussion and see below, n.22.

[17] *Stocznia* case [1997] 2 Lloyd's Rep. 228 at 235–236.

[18] No such prejudice could have been suffered in the *Stocznia* case, above, since the injured party had originally served notices of rescission; but as these were served *under* express provisions of the contract they formed (perhaps somewhat paradoxically) part of the process of affirmation.

[19] See above, p.856.

[20] *Stocznia Gdanska SA v Latvian Shipping Co (No.3)* [2001] 1 Lloyd's Rep. 537 at 565, affirmed [2002] EWCA Civ 889; [2002] 2 All E.R. (Comm) 786.

[21] See *Yukong Line Ltd of Korea v Rendsburg Investments Co of Liberia* [1996] 2 Lloyd's Rep. 604; above, p.795; *Stocznia Gdanska SA v Latvian Shipping Co (No.3)* [2001] 1 Lloyd's Rep. 537 at 563–564; affirmed on this ground, above n.20, at [87]–[92].

[22] Expressed in the *Stocznia* case, above n.21, affirmed [2002] E.W.C.A. Civ 889, [2002] 2 All E.R. (Comm) 768, leaving the present point open at [97]–[100] but inclining towards the view stated in the text above.

change of course where the original demand for performance was so expressed as to give rise to a waiver[23] of the right to rescind, or where it actually induced the guilty party to continue, in response to the demand, to make efforts to perform the contract.

A party who does not accept the breach cannot at common law get damages before the time fixed for performance[24]; and meanwhile he runs the risk of losing his right of action altogether. This could, for example, happen if the contract created a contingent right and events occurred to defeat that right between the time of the anticipatory breach and that fixed for performance.[25] The injured party will similarly lose his rights in respect of the anticipatory breach if he does not accept it and if, before performance from the guilty party has become due, that party withdraws his repudiation,[26] or lawfully puts an end to the contract, *e.g.* under an express cancelling clause.[27] The position is the same if, before that time, the contract was discharged by operation of law under the doctrine of frustration[28]; it would, in such a case, make no difference if the repudiating party had been unable to perform even if the frustrating event had not occurred.[29]

---

[23] *cf.* above, p.856.

[24] For a possible statutory power to award damages in such a case, if the contract was of a kind that is specifically enforceable, see below, pp.1046–1047.

[25] *e.g.* if in *Synge v Synge* [1894] 1 Q.B. 466, above, p.860, the wife had died before the husband without accepting the breach.

[26] *Harrison v Northwest Holt Group Administration* [1985] I.C.R. 668.

[27] *The Simona* [1989] A.C. 788; *cf.* above, p.778.

[28] *Avery v Bowden* (1855) 5 E. & B. 714; (1856) 6 E. & B. 953; *cf. The Playa Larga* [1983] 2 Lloyd's Rep. 171 at 186; for frustration, see below, Chap.20.

[29] *Continental Grain Export Corp v STM Grain Ltd* [1979] 2 Lloyd's Rep. 460 at 470.

CHAPTER TWENTY

FRUSTRATION[1]

UNDER the doctrine of frustration a contract may be discharged if after its formation events occur making its performance impossible or illegal, and in certain analogous situations.

SECTION 1. DEVELOPMENT

At one time most contractual duties were regarded as absolute, in the sense that supervening events provided no excuse for non-performance. In *Paradine v Jane*[2] a tenant was sued for rent and pleaded that he had for about two years of his tenancy been dispossessed by act of the King's enemies. This plea was held bad. "When the party by his own contract creates a duty or charge upon himself, he is bound to make it good, if he may,[3] notwithstanding any accident by inevitable necessity, because he might have provided against it by his contract".[4] This doctrine of absolute contracts works well enough (and continues to apply) where it would be reasonable, having regard to the nature of the contract or the circumstances in which it was made, to expect it to provide for the event.[5] But where this is not the case, the doctrine is no longer regarded as a satisfactory way of allocating the loss that is occasioned by supervening events.

The doctrine probably never applied where a contract called for personal performance by a party who died or was permanently incapacitated[6]; and another early exception to it was recognised in cases of supervening illegality.[7] In *Taylor v Caldwell*[8] Blackburn J. relied on the first of these exceptions, and on a number of others, as bases for formulating the general rule of discharge which has become known as the doctrine of frustration. The defendants in that case had contracted to hire out the Surrey Gardens and Music Hall "for the purpose of giving four grand concerts" on four designated days in the summer of 1861; the defendants were also to provide various side-shows and other entertainments in the gardens. The hirers agreed to pay £100 on the evening of each of the designated days and to provide "all the necessary artistes". Six days before the first concert was to have been given, the hall was destroyed by an accidental fire,[9] so that "it became impossible to give the concerts".[10] It was held that the defendants were not liable

---

[1] McElroy and Williams, *Impossibility of Performance*; Treitel, *Frustration and Force Majeure*; McKendrick, (ed.), *Force Majeure and Frustration* (2nd ed.).
[2] (1647) Aleyn 26; Ibbetson in *Consensus ad Idem, Essays in the Law of Contract in Honour of Guenter Treitel* (Rose, ed.), p.3.
[3] *i.e.* if performance has not become illegal: below, p.887.
[4] At p.27.
[5] *e.g.* in *Lewis Emanuel & Son Ltd v Sammut* [1959] 2 Lloyd's Rep. 629 (where the seller could reasonably have been expected to contract "subject to shipment," but did not do so); *The Zuiho Maru* [1977] 2 Lloyd's Rep. 552.
[6] *Taylor v Caldwell* (1863) 3 B. & S. 826 at 836.
[7] *Brewster v Kitchell* (1691) 1 Salk. 198; *Atkinson v Ritchie* (1809) 10 East 530 at 534–535.
[8] (1863) 3 B. & S. 826.
[9] Apparently caused by a careless plumber, who had left an unattended flame in the roof: *The Times*, June 12, 1861.
[10] (1863) 3 B. & S. 826 at 830.

in damages for the hirers' wasted advertising and other expenses. The contract had been discharged because, "the parties must from the beginning have known that it could not be fulfilled unless . . . some particular specified thing continued to exist", and in these circumstances it was "not to be construed as a positive contract, but as subject to an implied condition that the parties shall be excused in case, before breach, performance becomes impossible from the perishing of the thing without the fault of the contractor".[11]

After being established in *Taylor v Caldwell*, the doctrine of frustration entered into a period of growth. It was extended to cases in which performance became impossible otherwise than through the perishing of a specific thing; and even to cases where performance did not become impossible at all but the commercial object, or purpose, of the contract was frustrated. In *Krell v Henry*[12] the defendant hired a flat in Pall Mall for the days on which the processions planned for the coronation of King Edward VII were to take place. His object was to see the processions, though this was not expressly stated in the contract.[13] The contract was frustrated when the processions were postponed because of the illness of the King. Performance was not physically impossible: the defendant could have used and paid for the flat on the days in question. But frustration was not restricted to physical impossibility: it also applied "to cases where the event which renders the contract incapable of performance is the cessation or non-existence of an express condition or state of things, going to the root of the contract, and essential to its performance".[14]

It can fairly be said that the defendant in *Krell v Henry* would have suffered unacceptable hardship if he had been held to the contract in the altered circumstances. But the courts have refused to extend the doctrine beyond this point; for to do so might enable a party to claim relief merely because circumstances had changed so as to turn the contract, for him, into a very bad bargain. In the *British Movietonenews* case[15] the House of Lords rejected the view that a mere "uncontemplated turn of events"[16] (in that case, the cessation of war-time conditions in which the contract had been made) was a ground of frustration. Lord Simon said: "The parties to an executory contract are often faced, in the course of carrying it out, with a turn of events which they did not at all anticipate—a wholly abnormal rise or fall in prices, a sudden depreciation of currency, an unexpected obstacle to the execution, or the like. Yet this does not in itself affect the bargain which they have made".[17] More recently, Lord Roskill has similarly said that the doctrine of frustration was "not lightly to be invoked to relieve contracting parties of the normal consequences of imprudent commercial bargains".[18]

A less strict approach appears at first sight to have been taken by Lord Hailsham in *National Carriers Ltd v Panalpina (Northern) Ltd*, when he described the "proposition

---

[11] (1863) 3 B. & S. 826 at 833.

[12] [1903] 2 K.B. 740. See further p.885, below.

[13] In this respect *Krell v Henry* is unique among the "coronation seat" cases: the contracts in all the other reported cases expressly refer to one or both of the two planned processions.

[14] At p.748.

[15] *British Movietonenews Ltd v London and District Cinemas* [1952] A.C. 166.

[16] [1951] 1 K.B. at 201, *per* Denning L.J.

[17] [1952] A.C. 166 at 185; *cf. Multiservice Bookbinding Ltd v Marden* [1979] Ch. 84 at 112–113; *Watford BC v Watford RDC* (1988) 86 L.G.R. 524 at 529. Lord Denning continued to adhere to the views expressed by him (above, n.16) in the *British Movietonenews* case in spite of their disapproval in the House of Lords: see *Staffs Area Health Authority v S Staffs Waterworks* [1978] 1 W.L.R. 1387 at 1395 (decided by the majority of the court on other grounds: below, p.883); and *cf. The Nema* [1980] Q.B. 547 at 568, 127 (affirmed [1982] A.C. 724).

[18] *The Nema* [1982] A.C. 724 at 752; *Atisa S.A. v Aztec A.G.* [1983] 1 Lloyd's Rep. 579 at 584; *cf. Tsakiroglou & Co Ltd v Noblee Thorl GmbH* [1962] A.C. 93 at 115; *The Super Servant Two* [1990] 1 Lloyd's Rep. 1 at 8.

that the doctrine was not to be extended" as "untenable".[19] But the point of this observation was that the doctrine applied to contracts generally: thus suggestions that it did not apply to particular contracts, such as time charters, demise charters, and leases of land, have from time to time been rejected by the courts.[20] The actual decision in the *National Carriers* case was that events which temporarily prevented one of the parties from putting the subject-matter to its intended use were not sufficiently serious to frustrate the contract. In this respect, the case, so far from departing from, actually illustrates, the approach adopted in the *British Movietonenews* case.

Since that case, there seems to have been some narrowing in the scope of the doctrine of frustration. Many factors account for this trend: the reluctance of the courts to allow a party to rely on the doctrine as an excuse for escaping from a bad bargain; the difficulty of drawing the line between cases of frustration and cases where liability for breach of contract is strict; the tendency of businessmen to "draft out" possible causes of frustration by making their own express provisions for obstacles to performance; and the practical difficulties to be discussed in the paragraph that follows. The trend is illustrated by the fact that the Second World War gave rise to few[21] reported cases in which contracts were held to be frustrated otherwise than by supervening illegality.[22] The Suez crisis of 1956 produced only two reported English cases in which frustration was successfully pleaded. Both these cases were later overruled.[23] When the Suez Canal was again closed in 1967, pleas of frustration met with no more success[24]; and the "energy crisis" resulting from further hostilities in the Middle East in 1973 did not lead to any reported cases in England in which frustration was even raised as a defence.[25] All this is not to say that the doctrine will not be applied where performance is actually prevented, as it was in a number of charterparty cases in which ships were trapped for long periods after the outbreak of hostilities between Iran and Iraq in 1980,[26] so that performance of the agreed services became impossible. In the Suez cases there was (with one exception[27]) no such prevention: performance merely became more onerous for the party alleging frustration. There is now a marked reluctance to apply the doctrine in such circumstances.

From a practical point of view, the doctrine of frustration gives rise to two related difficulties. The first is that it may scarcely be more satisfactory to hold that the contract is totally discharged than to hold that it remains in full force: often some compromise may be a more reasonable solution. Thus in some of the coronation seat cases the

---

[19] [1981] A.C. 675 at 689; *cf. ibid.* at 694, 712.

[20] *Bank Line Ltd v Arthur Capel & Co* [1919] A.C. 435 (time charters); *Blane Steamships Ltd v Minister of Transport* [1951] 2 K.B. 965 (demise charters); *National Carriers Ltd v Panalpina (Northern) Ltd* [1981] A.C. 675 (leases of land).

[21] There were some, *e.g. Morgan v Manser* [1948] 1 K.B. 184.

[22] The *Fibrosa* case [1943] A.C. 32, the *Denny, Mott* case [1944] A.C. 265 and the *Cricklewood* case [1945] A.C. 221 were all cases of supervening illegality.

[23] *Carapanayoti & Co Ltd v ET Green Ltd* [1959] 1 Q.B. 131; overruled in the *Tsakiroglou* case [1962] A.C. 93; and *The Massalia* [1961] 2 Q.B. 278; overruled in *The Eugenia* [1964] 2 Q.B. 226.

[24] For the Suez cases, see further p.879, below.

[25] *cf. Sky Petroleum Ltd v VIP Petroleum Ltd* [1974] 1 W.L.R. 576, where the only dispute was as to the injured party's remedy; no attempt was made to rely on frustration. In a number of American cases, it was argued (generally without success) that the contracts were discharged by these events on the ground of "impracticability": *e.g.* in *Eastern Airlines Inc v Gulf Oil* 415 F. Supp. 429 (1975); for a case giving relief on this ground, see *Aluminum Corp of America v Essex Group Inc* 499 F. Supp. 53 (1980), below, p.884.

[26] *The Evia (No.2)* [1983] 1 A.C. 736; *The Agathon* [1982] 2 Lloyd's Rep. 211; *The Wenjiang (No.2)* [1983] 1 Lloyd's Rep. 400; *The Chrysalis* [1983] 1 Lloyd's Rep. 503.

[27] *i.e. The Eugenia* [1964] 2 Q.B. 226; but there the fact that the ship was trapped in the Canal did not lead to frustration as it was due to the charterer's prior breach of the contract: see below, p.904.

contracts provided that, if the procession were cancelled, the ticket-holder should be entitled to use the ticket on the day on which the procession eventually did take place.[28] Similarly, after 1956, contracts for the carriage or sale of goods began to specify which party was to bear any extra expense that might be incurred, should the Suez Canal again be closed.[29] In the absence of such express provisions, this kind of solution is not open to the courts: they have no power to *modify* contracts in the light of supervening events. The second difficulty is that the allocation of risks produced at common law by the doctrine of frustration is not always entirely satisfactory. In a case like *Taylor v Caldwell* it may be reasonable that neither party should be liable for loss of the benefit that the other expected to derive from performance, so that the one should not recover his loss of anticipated profits, nor the other the payments promised to him. But it does not follow that loss suffered by one party as a result of acting in reliance on the contract should equally lie where it falls. In *Taylor v Caldwell* the hirers' claim was not one for loss of profits, but only one for expenses thrown away in advertising and preparing for the concerts.[30] No doubt the defendants also incurred expenses on the side-shows and other facilities for entertainment, which the contract obliged them to provide.[31] It might be more satisfactory if such losses could be apportioned. At common law this was possible only where the contract expressly so provided: for example, in one of the coronation cases the contract provided that, if the procession was cancelled, the ticket-holder was to get his money back, less a percentage to cover the other party's expenses.[32] A more general, but still limited, power of adjustment now exists by statute, but it does not cover all cases in which some form of apportionment would seem to be desirable.[33]

SECTION 2. APPLICATIONS

1. Impossibility

Supervening impossibility of performance is the most obvious ground of frustration. The various ways in which it can arise are discussed below; but it must be emphasised at the outset that such impossibility is by no means invariably a ground of discharge. We shall see that even the destruction of the subject-matter of a contract does not necessarily discharge it[34]; and where liability for breach of contract is strict,[35] a party may be liable for failing to do the impossible. For example, a seller who has undertaken to ship goods to his buyer may be liable for failing to do so, even though the failure was due to lack

---

[28] For contracts containing such provisions, see *Clark v Lindsay* (1903) 19 T.L.R. 202 and *Victoria Seats Agency v Paget* (1902) 19 T.L.R. 16 (first contract).

[29] *Achille Laura v Total Societa Italiana per Azioni* [1969] 2 Lloyd's Rep. 65; *DI Henry Ltd v Wilhelm G Clasen* [1973] 1 Lloyd's Rep. 159.

[30] (1863) 3 B. & S. at 827.

[31] But these expenses do not seem to have been wholly wasted: it appears from *The Times*, June 12, 1861, that the defendants continued, after the fire, to charge for admission to the Gardens. It also appears from *The Times*, June 13 and December 19, 1861 that the defendants were lessees of the Hall and that it was insured, so that they were to some extent protected against loss.

[32] *Victoria Seats Agency v Paget*, above, n.28 (second contract); *cf. Elliott v Crutchley* [1904] 1 K.B. 565, affirmed [1906] A.C. 7 (where a contract for the supply of refreshments on a steamer on the day of the naval review provided that the defendants were not to be liable if the review were cancelled "before any expense is incurred by the contractor" *i.e.* the claimant). The rule that advance payments could not be recovered back (below, p.911) no doubt produced a sort of rough apportionment, but in a way that was quite unrelated to any expenses actually incurred.

[33] See below, pp.911–916.

[34] See the discussion of frustration and risk at p.871, below.

[35] See above, pp.838–840.

of shipping space caused by events entirely beyond his control.[36] By contrast, a shipowner may be excused from liability under a charterparty if, after the time of contracting, his ship is disabled by an explosion which is not proved to be due to his fault.[37] The distinction between the two situations is not easy to put into words. In neither of them is the party claiming excuse at fault, so that lack of fault is not sufficient (though it is necessary[38]) to discharge the contract. It could be said that lack of shipping space was a risk undertaken by the seller in our first example, while in the second the explosion was not within the contractual risk taken by the shipowner; but this seems to amount to a restatement of the distinction rather than to an explanation for it. Another way of expressing the distinction is that in the first case the seller *undertook* that shipping space would be available, while in the second the parties merely *assumed* that the particular ship would remain available; and that it is impossibility resulting from the failure of such a common assumption that leads to discharge.

(1) Destruction of a particular thing

(a) ILLUSTRATIONS. The clearest illustration of frustration by the destruction of a particular thing is *Taylor v Caldwell*[39] itself, where it was the subject-matter of the contract which was destroyed. An agreement for the sale of specific goods is similarly avoided if, without the fault of either party, the goods perish before the risk has passed to the buyer.[40] For the present purpose, destruction need not amount to total annihilation. In *Asfar & Co v Blundell*[41] a cargo of dates was sunk and so affected by water and sewage as to become "for business purposes something else",[42] though it was still sold for £2,400. The cargo-owner's liability to pay freight was discharged as the merchantable character of the cargo had been destroyed.

Taylor v Caldwell shows that a contract may be frustrated by the destruction of only part of the subject-matter. The contract related to "the Surrey Gardens and Music Hall" and was discharged though only the Hall was destroyed, while the gardens remained in use as a place of entertainment.[43] The contract was frustrated because its main purpose (the giving of the concerts) had been defeated.[44] Partial destruction which does not defeat the main purpose of the contract will not frustrate it, though it may provide one party with an excuse for not performing in full[45] or give the other party the option to rescind.[46]

A contract may be frustrated where what is destroyed is not its subject-matter but something essential for its performance. For example, a contract to install machinery in a particular factory can be frustrated by the destruction of the *factory*,[47] even though its subject-matter is the *machinery*. The question whether something is essential for performance depends on the terms of the contract. Thus where an agency agreement

---

[36] *Lewis Emanuel & Sons Ltd v Sammut* [1959] 2 Lloyd's Rep. 629.
[37] *Joseph Constantine SS Line v Imperial Smelting Corp Ltd* [1942] A.C. 154; below, p.908.
[38] See below, p.904.
[39] (1863) 3 B. & S. 826; above, p.866.
[40] Sale of Goods Act 1979, s.7; for risk, see p.871, below.
[41] [1896] 1 Q.B. 123.
[42] At p.128; *cf. The Badagry* [1985] 1 Lloyd's Rep. 395 at 399. Contrast *Horn v Minister of Food* [1948] 2 All E.R. 1036.
[43] See above n.31.
[44] *cf.* below, pp.873, 875, 879–880, 887, 890, 894–895.
[45] See above, p.835.
[46] See below, p.875.
[47] *Appleby v Myers* (1867) L.R. 2 C.P. 651.

related to goods to be "manufactured *or sold*" by the owner of a factory it was held that destruction of the factory did not frustrate the agreement.[48]

(b) FRUSTRATION AND RISK. Even the destruction of the subject-matter of the contract will not necessarily frustrate it. In certain types of contracts, it will instead be governed by rules which determine when the "risk of loss" passes from one party to the other. Where these rules apply, the contract will not be frustrated by the destruction of the subject-matter, though it may be frustrated by other events (such as delay or illegality[49]). The effects of the risk rules are radically different from those of frustration. The difference can be summed up by saying that where the destruction leads to frustration it discharges all the contractual obligations of both parties, while where it is governed by the rules as to risk it discharges only some of the obligations of one party. At this stage,[50] two types of contracts will serve to illustrate the distinction.

(i) *Sale of goods.* Under a contract for the sale of goods, the general rule is that (unless otherwise agreed) risk passes with property.[51] Property may pass before delivery,[52] so that it is possible for the risk in goods to have passed to the buyer while they are still in the hands of the seller.[53] If the goods are destroyed *after* the risk has passed, the contract is not frustrated: on the contrary, the statement that the risk has passed *means* that the buyer must still pay the price, while the seller is discharged from his duty to deliver. But the seller is not necessarily discharged from *all* his obligations: he may, for example, have expressly or impliedly undertaken to transfer the benefit of insurance on the goods to the buyer, and this obligation would survive their destruction.[54] If goods are destroyed *before* the risk has passed, the contract is frustrated if the goods are specific,[55] or if they are to be taken from a particular source and all the goods from that source are destroyed.[56] If, on the other hand, the sale is of unascertained goods by description, the contract is not frustrated merely because the particular goods which the seller intended to supply under the contract were destroyed before the risk had passed. On the contrary, to say that the risk has not passed in this situation means that the seller is bound to deliver other goods of the contract description; and if he does so the buyer must accept and pay.

(ii) *Building contracts.* Under a building contract, the risk of the work is (unless otherwise agreed) on the builder until the agreed work is completed. Thus a contract to build a house or a factory would not be frustrated by destruction of the buildings before completion. On the other hand, where a builder agrees to do work on an existing building, *e.g.* to install new machinery in a factory, a distinction must be drawn.[57] If, before the work is finished, the *factory* is destroyed, the contract is frustrated[58]; but if only the *machinery* is destroyed there is no frustration and the builder will remain bound to complete the installation without extra charge.[59]

---

[48] *Turner v Goldsmith* [1891] 1 Q.B. 544.

[49] See below, pp.872–873, 887–888, 895–896.

[50] For the passing of risk and related problems in contracts for the sale of land, see below, pp.895–897.

[51] Sale of Goods Act 1979, s.20(1).

[52] *e.g.* under Sale of Goods Act 1979, s.18, r.1.

[53] Where the buyer "deals as consumer", risk does not pass until the goods are delivered to the consumer: Sale of Goods Act 1979, s.20(4), as inserted by Sale and Supply of Goods to Consumers Regulations 2002 (SI 2002/3045), reg.4; for the definition of "deals as consumer", see s.61(5A) of the 1979 Act.

[54] *e.g. Manbré Saccharine Co Ltd v Corn Products Co Ltd* [1919] 1 K.B. 198.

[55] Sale of Goods Act 1979, s.7, above, p.870.

[56] See below, pp.875–876.

[57] Hudson, *Building Contracts* (11th ed.), §4.248; *cf.* in the United States, *Butterfield v Byron* 27 N.E. 667 (1891).

[58] *Appleby v Myers* (1867) L.R. 2 C.P. 651.

[59] *ibid.* at 660.

(2) Death or incapacity

Certain "personal" contracts, such as contracts of employment, apprenticeship or agency, are discharged by the death of either party.[60] Even a commercial contract may involve reliance by one party on the personal skill of the other[61]; in which case the death of that party (though not that of the other) can discharge the contract. The same rules apply where a party is permanently incapacitated from performing such a contract. Thus a contract to write a book would be frustrated by the supervening insanity of the author[62]; and a contract to render services would be frustrated if continued performance involved a serious risk to the health of the person who had agreed to render them.[63] A contract may likewise be frustrated where it is the capacity of a party to *receive* performance that is affected by the supervening event: *e.g.* where a person who had booked a course of dancing lessons was so seriously injured that he could no longer dance[64]; but in contracts governed by the Regulations which apply to package travel it is an implied term that a consumer who is "prevented from proceeding with the package"[65] can transfer the booking to a suitably qualified person, so that the contract is not discharged by the supervening event. A contract may also be frustrated by the death or incapacity of a third party: for example, a contract between A and B to paint a portrait of C could be frustrated if C died before work on the portrait had begun.

(3) Unavailability

(a) IN GENERAL. A contract may be frustrated if its subject-matter, or a thing or person essential for the purpose of its performance, though not ceasing to exist or suffering permanent incapacity, becomes unavailable for that purpose. Thus charter-parties have been frustrated where the ship was seized, detained[66] or requisitioned,[67] and where cargo was unavailable because of a strike at the port of loading[68]; a contract for the sale of goods has been frustrated where the goods were requisitioned[69]; a contract to operate and share in the profits of an oilfield has been frustrated where the interests of both parties were expropriated by the government of the country in which the oilfield was situated[70]; and contracts for personal services have been frustrated where one of the parties fell ill[71] or was interned or conscripted.[72]

(b) TEMPORARY UNAVAILABILITY. A person or thing essential for performance may, as a result of the supervening event, be unavailable at the time fixed for performance, but become available later. Such temporary unavailability will most obviously frustrate the contract where it is clear from the terms or nature of the contract that it was to be performed only at, or within, the specified time, and that the time of performance was of the essence[73] of the contract. Thus a contract to play in a concert on a particular day

---

[60] *cf. Cutter v Powell* (1795) 6 T.R. 320; *Whincup v Hughes* (1871) L.R. 6 C.P. 78; above, pp.750, 782.
[61] *cf.* above, p.694.
[62] *Jackson v Union Marine Insurance Co Ltd* (1874) L.R. 10 C.P. 125 at 145.
[63] *Condor v The Barron Knights Ltd* [1966] 1 W.L.R. 87.
[64] *Parker v Arthur Murray Inc* 295 N.E. 2d 487 (1973).
[65] Package Travel, Package Holidays and Package Tours Regulations 1992 (SI 1992/3288), reg.10(1).
[66] *e.g.* in the Gulf War cases (above, p.868, below, p.891), and in *The Adelfa* [1988] 2 Lloyd's Rep. 466.
[67] *e.g. Bank Line Ltd v Arthur Capel & Co* [1919] A.C. 435.
[68] *The Nema* [1982] A.C. 724.
[69] *e.g. Re Shipton, Anderson & Co* [1915] 3 K.B. 676.
[70] *BP Exploration (Libya) Ltd v Hunt* [1983] 2 A.C. 352; below, p.913.
[71] *e.g. Hart v AR Marshall & Sons (Bulwell) Ltd* [1977] 1 W.L.R. 1067.
[72] *e.g. Morgan v Manser* [1948] 1 K.B. 184.
[73] See above, p.826.

is frustrated by the performer's illness on that day.[74] Temporary unavailability may also frustrate a contract even though no fixed date is expressly specified for performance and even though a time is fixed but is not of the essence. In such cases, the contract may be frustrated, not by the mere *fact*, but by the *length*, of the delay in performance.

Ths possibility is illustrated by *Jackson v Union Marine Insurance Co*,[75] where a charterparty was made in November 1871 for the carriage of rails from Newport to San Francisco; it provided that the ship was to proceed to Newport with all possible despatch. On her way there she went aground in January 1872 and was not repaired until the following August. The contract was held to have been frustrated by the length of the delay, in consequence of which the voyage which the ship was capable of making was substantially different from that envisaged in the contract. It was as if a ship chartered "to go from Newport to St. Michael's . . . in time for the fruit season"[76] did not become available till after the season was over. Contracts in cases of this kind are frustrated because performance at the end of the delay is no longer of any use to the party to whom it was to be rendered, *i.e.* to the charterer.

In another group of cases, the contract is frustrated for the different reason that, after the delay, the performance to be rendered by one party would be significantly more onerous for that party. This possibility is illustrated by *Acetylene Co of GB v Canada Carbide Co*,[77] where shipment of goods under a contract of sale was delayed for three years by war-time requisitioning of all the available shipping space. When performance again became physically possible, it was held that the seller was no longer bound to deliver, as market conditions had radically changed. Similarly, in *Metropolitan Water Board v Dick, Kerr & Co*[78] war-time restrictions imposed an indefinite delay on the performance of a contract to build a reservoir. It was held that the contract was frustrated since it was likely that there would be a total change in conditions by the time that the restrictions might be lifted.

Even where delay does not increase the *costs* of the party whose performance is affected by it, that party may be prejudiced for the different reason that rates of pay for the service which he was to render have increased substantially between the time of contracting and the end of the delay. This was the position in an American case[79] in which an actor had contracted to make a number of films. Performance was then delayed for a number of years while he served in the armed forces during the Second World War; and contract was held to have been discharged. One reason for this result was that, by the end of the delay, rates of pay for such work had radically changed, so that the actor would have been prejudiced by having to perform at the originally agreed rates. Similar reasoning appears to explain *Bank Line Ltd v Arthur Capel & Co*,[80] where a ship was chartered for 12 months; it was contemplated, though not expressly provided, that the period would run from April 1915 to April 1916. She was requisitioned before delivery and the owners did not procure her release till September 1915. In an action by the charterer for damages for non-delivery, the House of Lords held the charterparty frustrated. The contract was, in substance if not in form, an April to April charter; and to hold the parties to a September to September charter would be to hold them to a contract which was "as a matter of business a totally different thing".[81] The reason for

---

[74] *Robinson v Davison* (1871) L.R. 6 Ex. 269.
[75] (1874) L.R. 10 C.P. 125.
[76] *ibid.* at 143.
[77] (1922) 8 Ll.L.Rep. 456.
[78] [1918] A.C. 119.
[79] *Autry v Republic Productions* 180 P. 2d 888 (1947).
[80] [1919] A.C. 435; *cf. Hirji Mulji v Cheong Yue SS Co Ltd* [1926] A.C. 497.
[81] At p.460.

this view cannot have been that the delay prejudiced the charterers (for they were claiming performance). It seems rather to have been that the shipowners would have been prejudiced by the delay (if the contract had not been discharged) because freight rates had risen[82] so that by September they could have charged considerably more for their services than the amount payable under the original contract.[83]

In the cases so far considered, it was claimed that performance should be rendered *in full* when the temporary unavailability ceased. In other cases, involving long-term contracts, the claim was that *the balance* of the contract should then be performed. Obviously such a claim cannot succeed if the delay lasts, or is likely to last, for so long that *no* part of the agreed performance remains possible. Thus in *Countess of Warwick SS Co v Le Nickel SA*[84] the war-time requisition of a ship was held to frustrate a one year charter which, at the time of the requisition, still had six months to run, because it was unlikely that the ship would be released in time to render any substantial services under the charter. For the same reason, charterparties were frustrated in a number of cases in which ships became unavailable for service as a result of being trapped for long periods in the course of the Gulf War between Iran and Iraq.[85]

If, on the other hand, performance for some balance of the contract period remains, or is likely to remain, possible, the outcome of claims for that balance depends on the proportion of the interruption, or likely interruption, to the contract period: the greater that proportion is, the more likely it is that the contract will be frustrated. Thus in *The Nema*[86] a charterparty for six or seven voyages to be made from April to December was frustrated when, after the first voyage, a long strike at the loading port made it impossible to accomplish more than a further two voyages within the contract period. By contrast, in *Tamplin SS Co Ltd v Anglo-Mexican Petroleum Co*[87] the war-time requisition of a ship in February 1915 did not frustrate a five year charter which was not due to expire till December 1917: the majority of the House of Lords took the view that "there may be many months during which the ship will be available before the five years have expired".[88] The effect of such requisition must theoretically be determined at or near the time when it takes place.[89] In practice, the courts no doubt take later events into account, but the *Tamplin* case was decided before the end of the chartered period. Thus the House of Lords had to speculate as to the probable length of the requisition and indirectly as to the probable duration of the war. In the light of later events, the majority may have speculated wrongly. But this is no criticism of the decision, which has also been supported on another ground to be discussed later in this Chapter.[90]

Events such as illness, conscription or internment may interfere temporarily with the performance of long-term contracts involving personal service. Here again one test of frustration is the proportion which the interruption, or likely interruption, bears to the period specified in the contract. Thus in *Morgan v Manser*[91] a music hall artiste

---

[82] *cf. Modern Transport Co Ltd v Duneric SS Co* [1917] 1 K.B. 370 at 376.

[83] This appears from the fact that £31,000 would have been awarded to the charterers by way of damages if the contract had not been discharged: see [1919] A.C. 435 at 441.

[84] [1918] 1 K.B. 372.

[85] *The Evia (No.2)* [1983] A.C. 736; *The Agathon* [1982] 2 Lloyd's Rep. 211; *The Wenjiang (No.2)* [1983] 1 Lloyd's Rep. 400; *The Chrysalis* [1983] 1 Lloyd's Rep. 503.

[86] [1982] A.C. 724.

[87] [1916] 2 A.C. 397; *cf. Port Line v Ben Line Steamers Ltd* [1958] 2 Q.B. 146.

[88] [1916] 2 A.C. 397 at 405.

[89] See below, p.891.

[90] See below, p.910.

[91] [1948] 1 K.B. 184 (where it is not clear what prejudice the artiste would have suffered by being held to the balance of the contract); *cf. Unger v Preston Corporation* [1942] 1 All E.R. 200 (a case very near the line).

employed a manager for ten years from 1938. He was conscripted in 1940 and demobilised in 1946. The contract was held to be frustrated since in 1940 it was likely that the artiste would remain in the Army for a very long time. On the other hand, in *Nordman v Rayner & Sturgess*[92] a long-term commission agency was not frustrated when the agent (an Alsatian with anti-German sympathies) was interned, since his internment was not likely to last long and in fact only lasted one month.

A contract of employment may be frustrated by the illness of the employee. This is true, not only where the contract is a long-term one, but also where it provides for determination by relatively short periods of notice, since even such a contract is often intended to give rise to an enduring relationship.[93] But temporary illness will not of itself frustrate a contract of employment[94]: it will have this effect only where it is so serious as to put an end to the possibility of performance "in a business sense",[95] *e.g.* by making resumption within a reasonable time a practical impossibility.[96] An illness which is not serious enough to frustrate the contract does, however, have a number of other legal effects. It gives the employee a *temporary* excuse for non-performance, and it may also give the employer an *option* to rescind.[97] Unless and until this option is exercised, the employee is *prima facie* entitled to wages during sickness.[98] This *prima facie* rule can be displaced by an express contrary provision, or by circumstances from which a contrary provision can be implied. To establish such an implied term, it is not necessary to show that the employee would, at the time of contracting, have agreed that he should not be paid during sickness.[99] The rule can be displaced by other circumstances: for example by the practice of the employers not to make such payments and the failure of the employee to claim them.[1]

(4) Failure of a particular source

A contract may be discharged where the subject-matter was to be obtained from a particular source which without the fault of either party becomes unavailable: *e.g.* where goods were to be taken from a particular crop which fails as a result of drought or disease; or where they are to be imported from a particular country and such import is prevented by war, natural disasters or prohibition of export. Such cases raise two questions: whether the failure frustrates the contract; and what is the position where the source only fails in part.

(a) WHETHER CONTRACT FRUSTRATED. The cases which raise this question can be divided into three groups.

(i) *Express reference to source.* Where the contract expressly provides that the goods are to be taken from the specified source, the contract is frustrated if that source fails. Thus

---

[92] (1916) 33 T.L.R. 87.

[93] *Notcutt v Universal Equipment Co (London) Ltd* [1986] 1 W.L.R. 641; Howarth [1987] C.L.J. 47.

[94] *Marshall v Harland & Wolff Ltd* [1972] 1 W.L.R. 899; *Williams v Watson's Luxury Coaches* [1990] I.C.R. 536; *cf. Mount v Oldham Corp* [1973] Q.B. 309.

[95] *Jackson v Union Marine Insurance Co Ltd* (1874) L.R. 10 C.P. 124 at 145.

[96] *e.g. Hart v A. R. Marshall & Sons (Bulwell) Ltd* [1977] 1 W.L.R. 1067; *Notcutt v Universal Equipment Co (London) Ltd* [1986] 1 W.L.R. 641.

[97] See above, pp.775–776, 835.

[98] *Marrison v Bell* [1939] 2 K.B. 187; *Mears v Safecar Securities Ltd* [1983] Q.B. 54 at 79. *cf.* Employment Rights Act 1996, s.64.

[99] *Mears v Safecar Securities Ltd* [1983] Q.B. 54 at 74, disapproving *Orman v Saville Sportswear Ltd* [1960] 1 W.L.R. 1065, and following *O'Grady v Saper* [1940] 2 K.B. 469.

[1] *Mears v Safecar Securities Ltd*, above.

in *Howell v Coupland* [2] a farmer sold 200 tons of potatoes to be grown on land specified in the contract. That crop largely[3] failed, and it was held that the contract was frustrated so that the farmer was not liable in damages for non-delivery. For this purpose it is assumed that the contract specifies an *exclusive* source of supply. Where it refers to several sources, the contract is not frustrated merely because one of them becomes unavailable.[4]

(ii) *Source intended by one party only.* Where the contract contains no reference to the source and only one of the parties intends to use that source, the failure of that source does not lead to frustration. Thus a contract for the sale of "Finland birch timber" was not frustrated merely because the seller expected to get supplies from Finland and could not do so because of the severing of trade routes after the outbreak of war in 1914. For all the buyer knew, delivery might have been made from stocks kept in England.[5] Nor is a contract frustrated merely because the seller is let down by his supplier. This is so even where that supplier is the sole producer of goods of the contract description, so long, at least, as the buyer was unaware of this fact.[6] The same rule applies where a buyer's source of payment fails. Thus a contract is not frustrated merely because the buyer intends (unknown to the seller) to pay with money to be remitted from a foreign country and the remittance is prevented or delayed by changes in that country's exchange control regulations.[7] *A fortiori*, a contract is not frustrated merely because of the buyer's supply of the currency in which payment was to be made has become exhausted.[8]

(iii) *Source intended by both parties.* The most difficult cases are those in which the contract makes no express reference to the source but *both* parties contemplate that it will be used. Such contracts are sometimes construed as containing an implied reference to the source[9]; but for this purpose it is not enough to show that the parties contemplated the source: they must have intended that that source (and no other), should be used.[10] There is little English authority on the question whether (in the absence of any evidence of such intention) the failure of a source which was merely contemplated by both parties will frustrate a contract. In one case, it was conceded that the partial failure of such a source released the seller in part.[11] The view that the total failure of a mutually contemplated source will frustrate the contract is sometimes said to be supported by *Re Badische Co*,[12] where a contract for the supply of chemicals was held to be frustrated by illegality on the outbreak of war in 1914 because both parties intended the goods to be obtained from Germany. But this was a special case: it would clearly be contrary to public policy to allow such a contract to subsist; and this would be so whether the parties had specified the source or merely contemplated that it should be used. The problems raised where the supervening event makes the contract illegal differ significantly from

---

[2] (1876) 1 Q.B.D. 258.

[3] Not entirely: for a discussion of this aspect of the case, see below, p.877.

[4] *e.g. Turner v Goldsmith* [1891] 1 Q.B. 544; *cf. The Super Servant Two* [1990] 1 Lloyd's Rep. 1; and see below, p.892.

[5] *Blackburn Bobbin Co Ltd v TW Allen Ltd* [1918] 2 K.B. 467.

[6] *Intertradex SA v Lesieur Torteaux SARL* [1978] 2 Lloyd's Rep. 509.

[7] *Universal Corp v Five Ways Properties Ltd* [1979] 1 All E.R. 552; *cf.* above, p.838. For an analogous situation, see *Hole & Pugsley v Sumption* [2001] N.L.J. 1851.

[8] *Congimex SARL (Lisbon) v. Continental Grain Export Corp (New York)* [1979] 2 Lloyd's Rep. 346 at 353; *cf. Janos Paczy v Haendler & Natermann GmbH* [1981] 1 Lloyd's Rep. 302.

[9] *e.g. Ockerby & Co Ltd v Murdock* (1916) 19 W.A.R. 1, affirmed (1916) 22 C.L.R. 420.

[10] See above, at n.4.

[11] *Lipton Ltd v Ford* [1917] 2 K.B. 647.

[12] [1921] 2 Ch. 331.

those which arise where it makes performance impossible[13]; and there is no clear English decision on the effect of failure of a mutually contemplated (but unspecified) source of supply. Where that source was contemplated by one party only, the courts have sometimes emphasised this fact in rejecting the defence of frustration[14]; and this may give some support to the view that the defence would succeed where the source was contemplated by both. On the other hand, in some such cases the commercial background may now be that it would be usual for the seller to protect himself against the contingency: *e.g.* by a prohibition of export clause. Where this is the position it is less likely that failure of even a mutually contemplated source would frustrate the contract.

(b) PARTIAL FAILURE. A contract for the sale of goods may specify the source from which the goods are to be taken, so that the total failure of that source would undoubtedly lead to frustration. Further problems can then arise if the source fails only in part.

(i) *Effects in general.* Such partial failure normally has three consequences. First, the seller is excused to the extent of the deficiency. This was the outcome in *Howell v Coupland*,[15] where the seller had delivered the small quantity actually produced,[16] and was held not to be liable for the rest of the quantity sold. Secondly, the seller is bound to deliver the quantity actually produced[17]; unless, perhaps, it is so small that it is uneconomical to harvest it.[18] Thirdly, the buyer is not generally bound to accept the quantity produced if it is less than that contracted for[19]; but as partial crop failures normally lead to a rise in prices this point is of little practical importance.

(ii) *More than one contract.* Additional complications arise where a seller has made a number of contracts to deliver goods from a specified source, and that source fails in part. For example, a farmer who reasonably expects his land to yield 1,000 tons agrees to sell 200 tons to each of five customers, and as a result of partial crop failure only 600 tons are produced; or a seller of goods to be taken from a foreign source similarly agrees to sell 200 tons to each of five customers, and, as a result of export restrictions, cannot obtain more than 600 tons. If total failure of the source would have frustrated the contracts,[20] what difference does it make that the failure was only partial?

One possible view is that it makes no difference, so that all the contracts are frustrated because the seller cannot perform them all in full. But this is unlikely to be accepted because it would enable the seller to keep the available goods and so to make a windfall profit from the rising prices likely to result from the shortage.[21] A second possibility is to say that none of the contracts is frustrated: if the seller delivered 200 tons to each of three buyers, his inability to deliver to the other two would be due to his voluntary act

---

[13] See below, p.887.

[14] *Blackburn Bobbin Co Ltd v TW Allen Ltd* [1918] 2 K.B. 467.

[15] (1876) 1 Q.B.D. 256; above, p.876.

[16] $79\frac{1}{2}$ tons; some of this was produced on land other than that specified in the contract and to this extent the seller did more than he was obliged to do.

[17] *HR and S Sainsbury Ltd v Street* [1972] 1 W.L.R. 834; above, p.835.

[18] The contrary seems to have been held in *International Paper Co v Rockefeller*, 146 N.Y.S. 371 (1914); *sed quaere*: such a case could be regarded as being, in substance, one of total failure of the source.

[19] Sale of Goods Act 1979, s.30(1). For qualifications of the buyer's right to reject, see above, pp.783–784.

[20] See *Bremer Handelsgesellschaft mbH v Continental Grain Co* [1983] 1 Lloyd's Rep. 269, where this requirement was not satisfied.

[21] The view that all the contracts are frustrated may at first sight seem to be supported by *Tennants (Lancashire) Ltd v CS Wilson & Co Ltd* [1917] A.C. 495; but the only point actually decided was that no single buyer was entitled to delivery *in full*; and the seller was a middleman who would himself have had to pay the higher prices and so could not have profited from frustration.

or "election" and would therefore be incapable of frustrating his contracts with these two.[22] This view derives some support from an analogous case[23]; but it will be submitted later in this Chapter that there is no true "election" where, after the supervening event, the seller's only choice is whether to perform one contract rather than another.[24] The argument that discharge is due to the seller's "election" could also be met by imposing legal restrictions on his choice. This possibility leads to the third view, that some of the contracts are discharged. If this view were interpreted to mean that the seller must deliver to such buyers as were designated by law (*e.g.* by reference to the order in which their contracts were made or to the standard of reasonableness) it would not be open to the objection that the seller's failure to deliver to the other buyers resulted from his "election". A fourth view adopts the principle of *pro rata* division, so that in our examples the contracts would not be frustrated, but each buyer would receive 120 tons.[25] The difficulty with this view is that, under it, the contracts would be modified, rather than discharged[26]; and at common law the doctrine of frustration appears to be capable only of leading to a total discharge of the contract.[27] The principle of *pro rata* division does, however, have considerable support in cases in which the seller has relied on the partial failure of the source as discharging him, not under the common law doctrine of frustration, but under an express provision of the contract, such as a *force majeure* or prohibition of export clause. In such cases, there is support for two versions of the *pro rata* principle. One states negatively that no buyer is entitled to delivery in full[28]; the other states affirmatively that each buyer is entitled to his *pro rata* share, so that he would be entitled to damages if he received no delivery at all.[29] But there is also support for the view that, if the seller allocates all his supplies to earlier buyers, he is not liable if he delivers nothing to later ones.[30] Probably, the overriding test is whether the seller acted reasonably in allocating the available supplies. In applying this test, the court can have regard to circumstances other than the order in which the contracts were made, *e.g.* to the fact that the available quantity was "too small to be sensibly apportioned among relevant purchasers".[31] *Pro rata* division is, of course, possible only where the subject-matter is physically divisible. Suppose that a farmer sold to each of five buyers "a calf to be born to my herd", expecting that at least five calves would be so born, and that (for reasons beyond his control) only three calves were born. In such a case, *pro rata* division

---

[22] See below, pp.906–907.

[23] *The Super Servant Two* [1990] 1 Lloyd's Rep. 1, below, p.907.

[24] See below, pp.907–908.

[25] *cf.* in the United States UCC s.2-615(b). The rule there stated, that the seller can take into account "regular customers not . . . under contract," does not seem to represent English law: see *Pancommerce SA v Veecheema BV* [1983] 2 Lloyd's Rep. 304. Much less are the English courts likely to accept the further rule stated in s.2-615(b) that the seller can take into account "his own requirements for further manufacture": this seems inconsistent with *Maritime National Fish Ltd v Ocean Trawlers Ltd* [1935] A.C. 524, below, p.906; see generally Hudson, 31 M.L.R. 535.

[26] *The Super Servant Two* [1989] 1 Lloyd's Rep. 148 at 158, affirmed [1990] 1 Lloyd's Rep. 1.

[27] See above, p.869; below, p.909.

[28] *Bremer Handelsgesellschaft mbH v Vanden Avenne-Izegem P v BA* [1978] 2 Lloyd's Rep. 109 at 115, 128, 131 (where the exact method of division is left open); *cf. Tennants (Lancashire) Ltd v CS Wilson & Co Ltd* [1917] A.C. 495 at 511–512.

[29] *Bremer Handelsgesellschaft mbH v C Mackprang Jr* [1979] 1 Lloyd's Rep. 221 at 224; the point is left open in *Continental Grain Export Corp v STM Grain Ltd* [1979] 2 Lloyd's Rep. 460 at 472.

[30] *Intertradex SA v Lesieur Torteaux SARL* [1978] 2 Lloyd's Rep. 509; *cf. Continental Grain Export Corp v STM Grain Ltd*, above, at p.473; *The Marine Star* [1993] 1 Lloyd's Rep. 329 at 332–333; and (in another context) *Cox v Bankside* [1995] 2 Lloyd's Rep. 434.

[31] *Bremer Handelsgesellschaft mbH v Continental Grain Co* [1983] 1 Lloyd's Rep. 269 at 293, citing *Westfalische Genossenschaft GmbH v Seabright Ltd*, unreported, *per* Robert Goff J.

would not work,[32] and it is submitted that, if the farmer delivered to the earliest three buyers, his contracts with the later two should be frustrated.[33]

(5) Method of performance impossible

(a) IN GENERAL. A contract may be discharged if it provides for a method of performance which becomes impossible. In *Nicholl & Knight v Ashton Edridge & Co*[34] a contract was made for the sale of cottonseed "to be shipped per steamship *Orlando* from Alexandria during . . . January". The *Orlando* later went aground in the Baltic so that she could not get to Alexandria in January. It was held that the contract was frustrated since, in the view of the majority of the Court of Appeal, it was to be construed as providing for performance *only* in the stipulated manner. If the stipulated method had not been regarded as exclusive, the seller might have been obliged to perform in a different way, *e.g.* by shipping the goods on a different ship or at a later time.[35] Whether he would actually have been obliged to do this would then have depended on whether the substituted method of performance differed fundamentally from that originally undertaken. This appears from the Suez cases to be discussed below.

(b) THE SUEZ CASES. These cases arose because an agreed or contemplated method of performance became impossible when the Suez Canal was closed as a result of hostilities in the Middle East in 1956 and again in 1967. The first question was whether the parties had actually stipulated for the particular method of performance, or had only expected that it would probably be used. In *Tsakiroglou & Co Ltd v Noblee Thorl GmbH*[36] a contract was made for the sale of Sudanese groundnuts at an inclusive price to cover the cost of the goods, insurance and carriage to Hamburg. When the contract was made both parties expected that shipment would be via Suez, but the contract did not so provide. It was held that the contract was not frustrated by the closure of the Suez Canal, so that the seller ought to have shipped the goods via the Cape of Good Hope. Although this would have taken two and a half times as long as shipment via Suez and would have doubled the cost of carriage, the difference between the two methods of performance was not sufficiently fundamental to frustrate the contract.[37] If the difference had been of this kind, it seems that the contract could have been frustrated even though the method of performance was not specified in the contract but only contemplated by both parties.[38]

---

[32] See I Kings 3: 25.

[33] *The Super Servant Two* [1990] 1 Lloyd's Rep. 1 is distinguishable on the ground that the defendant claimed discharge in respect of the *earlier* contract: see below, p.908.

[34] [1901] 2 K.B. 126; *cf. Maine Spinning Co v Sutcliffe & Co* (1918) 87 L.J.K.B. 382, discussed in Benjamin's *Sale of Goods* (6th ed.), §20–015.

[35] *cf.* in the United States, *Meyer v Sullivan*, 181 P. 847 (1919); U.C.C. s.2-614(1). This rule prevents the seller from making a profit out of frustration on a rising market: *cf.* below, pp.909–910.

[36] [1962] A.C. 93.

[37] See further below p.909, at n.28.

[38] *cf.*, in another context, *Florida Power & Light Company v Westinghouse Electric Corporation* 826 F.2d 239 (1987), where the contemplated method of performing an obligation to remove irradiated fuel from a nuclear power station was *by reprocessing* and when this became impossible the obligation could be performed only *by storing* the fuel. The difference between these modes was held to be sufficiently fundamental to discharge the obligation since reprocessing would have yielded a profit to the contractor of some $18 million while storing the fuel would have imposed costs on him in the region of $80 million. And see *Codelfa Construction Pty Ltd v State Rail Authority of NSW* (1982) 149 C.L.R. 337.

Where, on the other hand, there is no such fundamental difference, the contract may stand even if it does provide for performance by the method which becomes impossible. Thus it was suggested in the *Tsakiroglou* case[39] that the contract there would not have been frustrated even if it *had* provided for shipment via Suez. The same view is supported by a number of cases in which shipowners argued that voyage charters were frustrated because of the extra length and expense of the voyage via the Cape of Good Hope. In some of these cases the contracts expressly referred to Suez[40]; and even where there was no such reference it was no doubt an implied term that the ship should go via the Suez Canal as that was the usual and customary route when the contract was made.[41] Nevertheless the contracts were not frustrated,[42] so that the shipowners were bound to carry the goods at no extra charge by the longer, available, route. The difference between the two routes was not sufficiently fundamental, even though in one case[43] the voyage actually accomplished was twice as long as that originally contracted for and in another added nearly a third to the shipowner's anticipated costs.[44] The same principle can, on the other hand, favour the shipowner where the charterparty provides for payment by reference to the time taken to accomplish the voyage. In one such case[45] the charterer pleaded frustration but the plea was rejected: once again the court took the view that the voyage via the Cape was not fundamentally different from that via Suez, though exceeding it in length by about a third. To provide an illustration of frustration resulting from the closure of the Canal it is necessary to put a more extreme case, such as that of a contract to carry perishable goods from Port Sudan to Alexandria.

(6) Statute

A contract under which a person holds a public office can be discharged if the office is abolished by statute.[46]

(7) Impossibility and impracticability

(a) IMPRACTICABILITY DISTINGUISHED FROM IMPOSSIBILITY. The doctrine of frustration originated in cases where performance was said to have become "impossible". That is, in itself, something of a relative term. What is "impossible" depends partly on the current state of technology,[47] and partly on the amount of trouble and expense to which one is prepared to go to achieve it. It has been said that even *Taylor v Caldwell* was not a case of literal impossibility since "by the expenditure of huge sums of money" the music hall could probably have been rebuilt "in time for the scheduled concerts"[48]; but no reasonable businessman would have been expected to incur such expenditure. For this reason the current trend in the United States is to abandon the very words "impossible"

---

[39] [1962] A.C. 93 at 112; *cf. Congimex Companhia Geral, etc. v Tradax Export SA* [1981] 2 Lloyd's Rep. 687 at 692 (affirmed [1983] 1 Lloyd's Rep. 250).

[40] *e.g. The Captain George K* [1970] 2 Lloyd's Rep. 21; *The Washington Trader* [1972] 1 Lloyd's Rep. 463; 453 F. 2d. 939.

[41] *Scrutton on Charterparties* (20th ed.), p.256.

[42] See the authorities cited in n.40, above, and *Glidden v Hellenic Lines Ltd*, 275 F. 2d. 253 (1960); *Transatlantic Finance Corp v USA*, 363 F. 2d. 312 (1966).

[43] *The Captain George K*, above, n.40.

[44] *The Washington Trader*, above, n.40.

[45] *The Eugenia* [1964] 2 Q.B. 226.

[46] *Reilly v R.* [1934] A.C. 176.

[47] See the illustration of "absolute" impossibility given in *Corbin on Contracts* (1962), § 1325: "No-one can go to the moon."

[48] Fuller & Eisenberg, *Basic Contract Law* (3rd ed.), p.801.

and "impossibility" and to use instead the terms "impracticable" and "impracticability".[49] This change seems, moreover, to be intended to widen the scope of the doctrine
of discharge by supervening events.[50] "Impracticability" includes "extreme and unreasonable difficulty, expense, injury or loss"[51] to one of the parties. Examples include "A
severe shortage of raw materials or of supplies due to war, embargo, local crop failure,
unforeseen shutdown of major sources of supply or the like, which . . . causes a marked
increase in cost. . . ".[52] The caveat is entered that "Increased cost alone does not excuse
performance . . ."[53]—but it is suggested that a price increase "well beyond the normal
range"[54] could lead to discharge. In England, dicta to the effect that a contract may be
discharged if its performance becomes "impracticable" are occasionally found in
the cases.[55] But the weight of English authority rejects this view. Thus it has been said
in the House of Lords that "a wholly abnormal rise or fall in prices"[56] would not affect
the bargain; and that "The argument that a man can be excused from performance of his
contract when it becomes 'commercially' impossible seems to me a dangerous contention
which ought not to be admitted unless the parties have plainly contracted to that
effect".[57]

(b) IMPRACTICABILITY GENERALLY NO EXCUSE. A number of cases illustrate the view
that "impracticability" is not generally sufficient to frustrate a contract in English law.
In *Davis Contractors Ltd v Fareham Urban DC*[58] contractors agreed to build 78 houses
for a local authority in eight months for £94,000. Because of labour shortages, the work
took 22 months and cost the contractors £115,000. They claimed that the contract had
been frustrated and that they were therefore entitled to extra remuneration on a *quantum
meruit* basis.[59] But the House of Lords rejected the claim as the events which caused the
delays were within the ordinary range of commercial probability and had not brought
about a fundamental change of circumstances. Lord Radcliffe said: "It is not hardship
or inconvenience or material loss itself which calls the principle of frustration into play.
There must be as well such a change in the significance of the obligation that the thing
undertaken would, if performed, be a different thing from that contracted for".[60] The
Suez cases[61] similarly reject the argument that the greater expense caused to the party
prejudiced by the closure of the Canal was a ground of frustration. In the words of Lord

---

[49] U.C.C. s.2-615; Restatement 2d, *Contracts*, §261.
[50] *Neal-Cooper Grain Co v Texas Gulf Sulphur Co*, 508 F. 2d. 283, 293 (1974) ("less stringent test of impracticability"); *cf. Nora Springs Cooperative Co v Brandau*, 247 N.W. 2d. 744 at 748 (1976).
[51] Restatement, *Contracts*, §454; Restatement 2d, *Contracts*, §261 Comment d.
[52] *ibid.*; U.C.C. s.2-615 Comment 4.
[53] U.C.C. s.2-615 Comment 4.
[54] Restatement 2d, *Contracts*, §261 Comment d.
[55] *e.g. Horlock v Beal* [1916] A.C. 486 at 492; *The Furness Bridge* [1977] 2 Lloyd's Rep. 367 at 377; *Nile Co for the Export of Agricultural Crops v H & JM Bennett (Commodities) Ltd* [1986] 1 Lloyd's Rep. 555 at 581; *cf.* in another context, *Moss v Smith* (1859) 9 C.B. 94 at 103 (a dictum said to be of general application in *Robert H Dahl v Nelson Donkin* (1881) 6 App.Cas. 38 at 52); *The Badagry* [1985] 1 Lloyd's Rep. 395 at 399. See further Beatson in *Consensus ad Idem, Essays in the Law of Contract in Honour of Guenter Treitel* (Rose, ed.), p.123.
[56] *British Movietonenews Ltd v London and District Cinemas* [1952] A.C. 166 at 185.
[57] *Tennants (Lancashire) Ltd v CS Wilson & Co Ltd* [1917] A.C. 495 at 510 (where the sellers were excused by the express terms of the contract); *cf. Shearson Lehman Hutton Inc v Maclaine Watson & Co Ltd* [1989] 2 Lloyd's Rep. 570 at 508 (commodity contract not frustrated by closure of market); and see the cases discussed in the next paragraph.
[58] [1956] A.C. 696.
[59] See below, p.1064.
[60] [1956] A.C. 696 at 729; *cf. Multiservice Bookbinding Ltd v Marden* [1979] Ch. 84 at 113; *Chaucer Estates v Fairclough Homes* [1991] E.G.C.S. 65.
[61] See above, pp.879–880.

Simonds, "an increase of expense is not a ground of frustration".[62] Where performance would, in view of changed circumstances, cause not merely extra expense but acute personal hardship to one party, it has been said that "equitable relief may . . . be refused because of an unforeseen change of circumstances not amounting to legal frustration".[63] But in such cases the contract is not discharged: the defendant remains liable in damages even though specific performance is refused on the ground of severe hardship.[64]

(c) POSSIBLE EXCEPTIONS. Four types of cases to be discussed below may at first sight seem to give some support to the view that a contract can be frustrated by "impracticability". But it will be submitted that these cases are all explicable on other grounds and that they do not support the view that impracticability (in the sense of great financial or commercial hardship to one of the parties) is of itself sufficient to discharge a contract in English law.

First, there are the cases in which discharge is based, not on impracticability alone, but on this factor when it is combined with impossibility or illegality. One group of such cases is that already discussed,[65] in which long delays in performance resulted from war-time restrictions, and it was held that performance need not be resumed in the totally altered conditions which prevailed when those restrictions were removed. It could be said that performance at the later time was "impracticable"; but this was only one factor leading to discharge, the other being that, for a considerable period, the war-time conditions made performance actually impossible. Similar reasoning can apply where a supervening change in the law makes it illegal to perform a contract to render a service unless (for example) additional safety precautions are taken by the party who is to render it. The extra expense to be incurred by that party in taking those precautions may then be regarded as a kind of "impracticability", leading to discharge[66]; but this result will, more significantly, be based on the special considerations of public policy on which discharge is based in cases of supervening illegality[67]: in other words, it does not follow that the contract would be discharged if the same amount of extra expense were occasioned simply by commercial factors, without any element of supervening illegality.

---

[62] *Tsakiroglou & Co v Noblee Thorl GmbH* [1962] A.C. 93 at 115; *cf. Exportelisa SA v Guiseppe Figli Soc Coll* [1978] 1 Lloyd's Rep. 433; *Finland Steamship Co Ltd v Felixstowe Dock Ry Co* [1980] 2 Lloyd's Rep. 287, where no attempt was made to argue that a contract was frustrated by cost increases described at p.288 as "devastating"; and *The Mercedes Envoy* where no attempt was made to rely on frustration on the ground that a ship had been so severely damaged that it was "not commercially viable" to repair her: [1995] 2 Lloyd's Rep. 559 at 563. Extreme cost increases might, however, be relevant where all that a party was bound to do was to take reasonable steps to produce a specified result. For example, in *Brauer & Co (Great Britain) Ltd v James Clark (Brush Materials) Ltd* [1952] 2 All E.R. 497 at 501 it was said that a seller would not be liable for failure to get an export licence if the cost of getting it were 100 times the contract price; the seller's duty in that case would have been limited to one to take reasonable steps (above, p.65) even if the contract had not been expressly "subject to export licence."
[63] *Patel v Ali* [1984] Ch. 283 at 288.
[64] See below, p.1026. In *Patel v Ali*, above, the defendant was required to pay £10,000 into court as a condition of the discharge of the order of specific performance against her.
[65] *Metropolitan Water Board v Dick Kerr & Co* [1918] A.C. 119; *Acetylene Co of GB v Canada Carbide Co* (1922) 8 Ll.L.Rep. 456; above, p.873; *cf. Florida Power & Light Company v Westinghouse Electric Corporation* 826 F.2d 239 (1987): impracticability coupled with impossibility in the contemplated method of performance (above, p.879, n.38).
[66] It seems to have been so regarded in *William Cory v L.C.C.* [1951] 1 K.B. 8, affirmed [1951] 2 K.B. 476. Similar considerations may in part account for the American decision in *Florida Power & Light Co v Westinghouse Elec Corp* 826 F 2d 239 (1987).
[67] See below, p.887.

Secondly, there are cases in which contracts were discharged, not under the general doctrine of frustration, but under express contractual provisions (such as *force majeure* or prohibition of export clauses) which excuse one party, or both, if a specified event prevents performance. Such clauses do not protect a party merely because supervening events make performance more difficult or more expensive for him[68]; nor do they normally protect him where he can perform in alternative ways and only one of them becomes impossible: for example, a seller who cannot obtain the goods that he had undertaken to deliver from the source intended by him (*e.g.* because of being let down by his supplier or because of an export embargo) must obtain them from other sources that remain available.[69] But this rule is subject to an exception which applies where it would be unreasonable to require the seller to perform in this way, because attempts to do so by him, and by other sellers similarly situated, would drive prices up to "unheard of levels".[70] In one case of this kind, it was said that the seller need not make such an attempt where to require him to do so would be "impracticable and commercially unsuitable".[71] These cases are, however, concerned, not with discharge under the general doctrine of frustration, but with discharge under express contractual provisions for supervening events.[72] Such a provision often operates in circumstances falling short of frustration under the general law.[73] Thus the fact that it may, on its true construction, cover "impracticability" does not support the view that the same circumstances would frustrate a contract which contained no such provision.

Thirdly it is arguable that impracticability may be a ground of discharge where the contract is one of indefinite duration. In *Staffordshire Area Health Authority v South Staffordshire Waterworks Co*[74] a hospital had in 1919 contracted to give up to a Waterworks Company its right to take water from a well, and the Company had in return promised "at all times hereafter" to supply water to the hospital at a fixed price specified in the contract. In 1975 the cost to the Company of making the supply had risen to over 18 times that fixed price and the Company gave seven months' notice to terminate the agreement. It was held that this notice was effective. Lord Denning M.R. regarded the contract as frustrated by the change of circumstances which had occurred between 1919 and 1975. But this view is, with respect, open to question, as it was based on the very passage of his own judgment in the *British Movietonenews* case which had there been disapproved by the House of Lords.[75] The preferable reason for the decision in the *Staffordshire* case is therefore that of the majority, who held that the agreement was, on

---

[68] See, for example, *Brauer & Co (Great Britain) Ltd v James Clark (Brush Materials) Ltd* [1952] 2 All E.R. 497; *B & S Contracts & Designs Ltd v Victor Green Publications Ltd* [1984] I.C.R. 419.

[69] *e.g. PJ van der Zijden Wildhandel NV v Tucker & Cross Ltd* [1975] 2 Lloyd's Rep. 240; *Agrokar AG v Tradigrain SA* [2000] 1 Lloyd's Rep. 497. For the possibility of excluding this rule by the terms of the clause, see *The Morning Watch* [1996] 2 Lloyd's Rep. 383.

[70] *Tradax Export SA v André & Cie* [1976] 1 Lloyd's Rep. 416 at 423; *cf. André & Cie SA v Tradax Export SA* [1983] 1 Lloyd's Rep. 254; *Cook Industries v Tradax Export SA* [1983] 1 Lloyd's Rep. 327 at 344, affirmed without reference to this point [1985] 2 Lloyd's Rep. 454 and see generally *Benjamin's Sale of Goods* (6th ed.), §19–136.

[71] *Bremer Handelsgesellschaft mbH v Vanden Avenne-Izegem PV BA* [1978] 2 Lloyd's Rep. 109 at 115. *cf. Owners of Steamship Matheos v Louis Dreyfus* [1925] A.C. 654 at 666 ("commercially impracticable").

[72] The same is true of *Ford & Sons (Oldham) Ltd v Henry Leetham & Sons Ltd* (1915) 21 Com.Cas. 55, which is nevertheless cited in support of the general principle of discharge by "impracticability" in U.C.C. s.2-615 Comment 4.

[73] See below, pp.900–901. For the significance of the distinction between discharge by frustration and under an express term, *cf.* also *The Super Servant Two* [1989] 1 Lloyd's Rep. 148 at 149, [1990] 1 Lloyd's Rep. 1 at 8.

[74] [1978] 1 W.L.R. 1387; Rose, 96 L.Q.R. 177.

[75] [1952] A.C. 166, 185; above, p.867.

its true construction, intended to be of indefinite (and not of perpetual) duration[76]: hence the case fell within the general principle under which, in commercial agreements of indefinite duration, a term is often implied entitling either party to terminate by reasonable notice.[77] It follows from this reasoning that the decision would have gone the other way if the agreement had been for a fixed term, *e.g.* for 10 years. The agreement could then not have been terminated by notice before the end of the ten years, nor would an increase in the suppliers' costs during that period have been a ground of frustration. This view is supported by later authority[78] and seems also to be correct in principle: if parties enter into a fixed term fixed price contract they must be taken thereby to have allocated the risks of market fluctuations. If the parties are not prepared to accept these risks (or to accept them in full) they can adopt the now common practice of providing in the contract itself for flexible pricing.[79]

The three situations so far discussed should be distinguished from a fourth which arose in *The Playa Larga*.[80] Sugar had been sold by a Cuban state trading organisation to a buyer controlled by a state trading organisation in Chile. When the contract was made, Cuba and Chile were both ruled by Marxist governments; but before deliveries under the contract had been completed, the Marxist government in Chile was overthrown; diplomatic relations between the two countries were severed; and there was a complete breakdown of commercial relations between them. It was held that the contract was frustrated even though its performance had not become impossible in any of the senses discussed in this Chapter. The decision was, however, based, not on extreme hardship to the seller, but on the fact that, in the altered conditions, there was no possibility of the implementation of the contract on either side[81]; and the court concluded that, in these conditions, the contract was no longer intended to be binding. A breakdown of diplomatic and commercial relations between governments would not normally be a ground of discharge; but in *The Playa Larga* it had this effect because both contracting parties were controlled by the governments in question.

(d) INFLATION. In the cases so far discussed, increases in the cost of performing a particular contract have made that contract unprofitable to one party. A similar situation may arise where the general process of inflation reduces in real terms the benefit which that party expected to obtain under the contract. In the *British Movietonenews* case "a sudden depreciation of currency" is listed as one of the uncontemplated turns of events

---

[76] "At all times hereafter" was (obviously) not to be taken literally, but meant "at all times hereafter during the subsistence of the agreement." The majority view was followed in *Tower Hamlets LBC v British Gas Corp*, *The Times*, March 23, 1982, affirmed, *The Times*, December 14, 1983, and approved in *Watford DC v Watford Rural DC* (1988) 86 L.G.R. 524 at 529.

[77] *cf.* above, p.749; contrast *Watford DC v Watford Rural DC* (1988) 86 L.G.R. 524, where it was held that no such term could be implied in an agreement to contribute variable amounts towards the maintenance of cemeteries; *Islwyn BC v Newport BC* (1994) 6 Admin. L.R. 386. For exclusion of an implied term permitting termination on reasonable notice by other words in the contract, see also *Harbinger UK Ltd v GE Information Services Ltd* [2000] 1 All E.R. (Comm) 166 (software suppliers undertaking to provide maintenance services "in perpetuity": *i.e.*, for so long as the users required, and were willing to pay for, the services).

[78] *Kirklees MBC v Yorks Woollen District Transport Co* (1978) 77 L.G.R. 448.

[79] See *Superior Overseas Development Corp v British Gas Corp* [1982] 1 Lloyd's Rep. 262; *Wates v GLC* (1983) 25 Build L.R. 1 (below at n.84); *Watford DC v Watford Rural DC* (1988) 86 L.G.R. 524 at 548; *Queensland Electricity Generating Board v New Hope Collieries Pty Ltd* [1989] 1 Lloyd's Rep. 205. In the American case of *Aluminum Corp of America Inc v Essex Group Inc*, 499 F. Supp. 53 (1980) relief was given even where a fixed term contract contained such a clause, the court substituting its own price-fixing formula for that agreed by the parties; but this seems to be an undue interference with a contract between parties of equal bargaining power.

[80] [1983] 2 Lloyd's Rep. 171.

[81] *ibid* at 188.

which do *not* frustrate a contract.[82] The passage continues to make the general point that a contract would cease to bind if a "fundamentally different situation" were to emerge. This may refer back to the illustrations, previously given in the passage, of events (such as currency fluctuations) which are stated *not* to frustrate a contract[83]; but more probably the reference is to *other* (*i.e.* to frustrating) events. Again, in *Wates Ltd v GLC*[84] a building contract to some extent protected the builder against inflation, by means of a price-escalation clause; and it was said that the fact that "inflation increased not [at] a trot or at a canter but at a gallop . . . was not so radical a difference from the inflation contemplated and provided for as to frustrate the contract".[85] Thus the English authorities do not support the view that inflation is a ground of frustration, though the possibility that extreme (as opposed to merely severe) inflation may be capable of frustrating a contract cannot be wholly ruled out.[86] It is again open to a party who fears that he will be prejudiced by inflation to guard against this risk by an express term, *e.g.* by providing (if his bargaining position permits) for "index-linked" payments.[87]

(e) CURRENCY FLUCTUATIONS. A debtor whose obligations are defined by reference to a foreign currency cannot avoid liability to pay in full merely because the pound sterling has fallen in value in relation to that currency by an unexpectedly large amount.[88]

2. Frustration of Purpose

Frustration of purpose is, in a sense, the converse of impracticability. The two ideas resemble each other in that neither is concerned with cases in which performance has become impossible. Impracticability is normally[89] said to arise when a *supplier* of goods, services or other facilities alleges that supervening events have made performance of his own promise so much more burdensome to him that he should no longer be bound to render it. The argument of frustration of purpose, on the other hand, is normally put forward by the *recipient* of the goods, services or facilities[90]: it is that supervening events have so greatly reduced the value to him of the other party's performance that he should no longer be bound to accept it and to pay the agreed price. Such an argument succeeded in some of the cases which arose out of the postponement of the coronation of King Edward VII. We have seen that in *Krell v Henry*[91] the effect of the postponement was to discharge a contract for the hire of a flat overlooking the route of the proposed processions. The obvious danger of such a rule is that it can all too easily be invoked by a party for whom a contract has simply become a very bad bargain. *Krell v Henry* has

---

[82] [1952] A.C. 166 at 185.

[83] *cf.* Mann, *The Legal Aspects of Money* (5th ed.), pp.117–118.

[84] (1983) 25 Build.L.R. 1.

[85] *ibid* at 34.

[86] *cf.* Lord Roskill's reference in *National Carriers Ltd v Panalpina Northern Ltd* [1981] A.C. 675 at 712, to "inflation" as one of the "circumstances in which the doctrine [of frustration] has been invoked, sometimes with success, *sometimes without.*"

[87] See *Nationwide BS v Registry of Friendly Societies* [1983] 1 W.L.R. 1226.

[88] *Multiservice Bookbinding Ltd v Marden* [1979] Ch. 84.

[89] See next note.

[90] Occasionally, the normal positions are reversed so that a buyer relies on impracticability where the cost to him of taking delivery has risen sharply (as in *Mineral Park Land Co v Howard*) 156 P. 458 (1916)) or a seller relies on frustration of purpose where supervening events affect his ability to realise the financial instruments by which payment is to be made (as in *Re Comptoir Commercial Anversois and Power Sons & Co* [1920] 1 K.B. 868).

[91] [1903] 2 K.B. 740 (above, p.867); McElroy and Williams, 4 M.L.R. 241; 5 M.L.R. 1.

therefore attracted much criticism[92]; but the decision can be justified[93] on the ground that the contract was, on its true construction, not merely one for the hire of the flat, but one to provide facilities for viewing the coronation processions.[94] The actual decision may be contrasted with an example given in one of the judgments: a contract to take a cab to Epsom on Derby day "at a suitable enhanced price"[95] would not be frustrated if the Derby were cancelled. Here the contract was evidently regarded as one to get the passenger to Epsom—not as one to get him to the Derby.

Similar reasoning distinguishes *Krell v Henry* from *Herne Bay Steamboat Co v Hutton*,[96] another of the coronation cases. A pleasure boat was hired "for the purpose of viewing the naval review and for a day's cruise round the fleet". The review, which formed part of the proposed coronation celebrations, was cancelled when the King fell ill, but the contract was not frustrated. It was construed simply as a contract for the hire of a boat; and it could still be performed although one of the motives of the hirer[97]—to carry passengers at high prices to see the review—was defeated.

Although the actual decision in *Krell v Henry* appears to be justifiable on the grounds stated above, the case has scarcely ever been followed in England. Normally, a contract is not frustrated merely because supervening events have prevented one party from putting the subject-matter to the use intended by him, even though that use was also contemplated by the other. Thus a contract by which a gas company agreed with a local authority to "provide, maintain and light" street lamps was not frustrated when war-time black-out regulations prohibited the lighting of such lamps,[98] since performance of the maintenance obligation ("which cannot be regarded as . . . trivial"[99]) remained possible.[1] Similarly, a contract for the sale of goods is not frustrated merely because the buyer's purpose to export the goods from, or to import them into, a particular country is defeated by export or import restrictions.[2] Perhaps the most striking illustration of the reluctance of the courts to apply the principle of frustration of purpose is provided by the *Amalgamated Investment & Property*[3] case, where it was held that a contract for the purchase of property for redevelopment was not frustrated when the buildings on the

---

[92] *Blackburn Bobbin Co Ltd v TW Allen & Sons Ltd* [1918] 1 K.B. 540 at 542 (affirmed [1918] 2 K.B. 467); *Larrinaga v Société Franco-Américaine des Phosphates de Medulla* (1923) 92 L.J.K.B. 455 at 459; *cf. Maritime National Fish Ltd v Ocean Trawlers Ltd* [1935] A.C. 524 at 528; *Scanlan's New Neon Ltd v Toohey's Ltd* (1943) 67 C.L.R. 169 at 191–194; *Corbin on Contracts*, §1355 at pp.464–465; Landon, 52 L.Q.R. 168; Gordon, *ibid.* p.326.

[93] See *Codelfa Construction Pty Ltd v State Rail Authority of NSW* (1982) 149 C.L.R. 337 at 358.

[94] *cf. The Great Peace* [2002] EWCA Civ 1407; [2002] 4 All E.R. 869, at [66] (contract for "a room with a view").

[95] [1903] 2 K.B. 740 at 750.

[96] [1903] 2 K.B. 683.

[97] For the requirement that the purpose of *both* parties must be frustrated, see *The Siboen and the Sibotre* [1976] 1 Lloyd's Rep. 293.

[98] *Leiston Gas Co v Leiston-cum-Sizewell Urban DC* [1916] 2 K.B. 428; on the interpretation of express contractual provisions for such events, see *Williams v Mercer* [1940] 3 All E.R. 293 and contrast *Egham & Staines Electricity Co Ltd v Egham Urban DC* [1944] 1 All E.R. 107.

[99] *Leiston* case, [1916] 2 K.B. 428 at 433.

[1] For contrasting decisions on the effect of black-out regulations on contracts for the hire of electric advertising signs, see *Scanlan's New Neon Ltd v Toohey's Ltd* (1943) 67 C.L.R. 169 (contract not discharged); *20th Century Lites v Goodman*, 149 P. 2d. 88 (1944) (contract discharged).

[2] *e.g. D McMaster & Co v Cox McEwen & Co*, 1921 S.C. (HL) 1; *Congimex SARL (Lisbon) v. Continental Grain Export Corp (New York)* [1979] 2 Lloyd's Rep. 346; *Congimex Companhia Geral, etc., SARL v Tradax Export SA* [1983] 1 Lloyd's Rep. 250; *Bangladesh Export Import Co Ltd v Sucden Kerry SA* [1995] 2 Lloyd's Rep. 1, where an additional ground for rejecting the buyer's plea of frustration was that the contract in terms imposed an obligation to obtain an import licence on the buyer.

[3] *Amalgamated Investment & Property Co Ltd v John Walker & Son Ltd* [1977] 1 W.L.R. 164.

land were listed as being of special architectural or historic interest, so that redevelopment became more difficult or impossible and the property lost most of its value.[4]

Such cases show that "the frustrated expectations and intentions of one party to a contract do not necessarily, or indeed usually, lead to the frustration of that contract".[5] They make it difficult to establish the defence of frustration of purpose; but they do not make it impossible. In *Denny, Mott & Dickson v James B Fraser & Co Ltd*[6] an agreement for the lease of a timber yard was made for the purpose of enabling the parties to carry out a contract between them for the sale of timber. When performance of the contract of sale was prohibited by war-time regulations, the House of Lords held that the agreement for the lease of the yard was also frustrated. The actual decision may to some extent rest on special policy considerations applicable to cases of supervening illegality; but other situations can be imagined in which the principle of frustration of purpose might also apply. For example, if premises were leased as a warehouse and supervening events made their use as such impossible for the whole period of the lease, it seems that the contract might be frustrated.[7] In such a case, the contract would be discharged, even though performance had not become impossible, because the supervening event had destroyed "some basic, though tacit assumption on which the parties had contracted".[8]

3. Illegality

A contract may be discharged by a supervening prohibition if the prohibition would have made the contract illegal, had it been in force when the contract was made.[9]

The object of the doctrine of frustration in cases of supervening impossibility or of frustration of purpose is to provide a satisfactory method of allocating or distributing the loss caused by the supervening event. Where, however, a contract is affected by supervening illegality, the court has to take into account, not only the relative interests of the parties, but also the interests of the public in seeing that the law is observed[10]; and this public interest may sometimes outweigh the importance of achieving a fair distribution of loss. For this reason supervening illegality is a ground of discharge distinct from supervening impossibility, and is to some extent governed by special rules.

(1) Illustrations

(a) TRADING WITH THE ENEMY. The public interest considerations just mentioned are particularly strong where a contract becomes illegal as a result of the war-time prohibition against trading with the enemy. In the leading *Fibrosa* case[11] a contract for the sale of machinery to be shipped to Gdynia was frustrated when that port was occupied by the enemy during the Second World War. Although it might have been physically possible

---

[4] The listing was said to have reduced the value of the property to £200,000—against a contract price of £1,710,000.

[5] *Congimex Companhia Geral, etc., SARL v Tradax Export SA* [1983] 1 Lloyd's Rep. 250 at 253.

[6] [1944] A.C. 265.

[7] This seems to be assumed in *National Carriers Ltd v Panalpina (Northern) Ltd* [1981] A.C. 675 (below, pp.894–895), where the temporary nature of the interruption was stressed in rejecting the plea of frustration.

[8] *Sir Lindsay Parkinson Ltd v Commissioners of Works* [1949] 2 K.B. 632 at 665.

[9] See above, pp.438–439.

[10] This book deals only with discharge by supervening illegality which arises under English law. The justification for discharge where the illegality arises under *foreign* law (*e.g.* under a foreign prohibition of export or import) is somewhat different: see *Benjamin's Sale of Goods* (6th ed.), §§18-303, 25-112.

[11] *Fibrosa Spolka Ackcyjna v Fairbairn, Lawson Combe Barbour Ltd* [1943] A.C. 32.

to get the goods to the destination,[12] the contract was discharged because of the strong public interest in ensuring that no aid should be given to the enemy economy in time of war. The same principle applies where goods are to be imported from an enemy country: the contract is frustrated even though the enemy source is not specified in the contract but only contemplated by the parties.[13] The public interest principle is so strong in these cases that frustration by or as a result of the prohibition cannot be excluded even by an express provision in the contract.[14]

(b) OTHER PROHIBITIONS. The cases provide many illustrations of frustration by supervening prohibitions other than that against trading with the enemy. In the *Denny Mott*[15] case, for example, a contract for the sale of timber was frustrated by a war-time prohibition against dealing in goods of the contract description. Contracts can similarly be frustrated by prohibition of export or import, by restrictions on the movement of capital,[16] or by licensing requirements of the kinds to be discussed below. In these cases the public interest in seeing that the prohibition is observed is less strong than in the trading with the enemy cases[17]; and they differ from the trading with the enemy cases in two further ways. First, frustration results only if it is an actual term of the contract that the subsequently prohibited act is to be done. Thus a contract for the sale of goods may be frustrated by prohibition of export if it provides that the goods are to be exported,[18] but not merely because the buyer intended to export them, even though the seller knew this.[19] Secondly, frustration can be excluded by express contractual provisions. Thus provisions suspending performance in the event of prohibition of export are valid[20] since, so far from contravening the policy of the prohibition, they assume that it will be observed. Similar provisions in trading with the enemy cases are contrary to the public interest since they involve continuing relations with an enemy subject, and so may indirectly support the enemy economy.

(2) Supervening and antecedent prohibition

Under the rules stated above, frustration may result from a supervening prohibition, *i.e.* from one imposed by a law made after the contract was made.[21] If, at the time of contracting, the prohibition is already in force, the case is one of antecedent prohibition.

---

[12] The mere outbreak of war does not frustrate a contract: see *The Chrysalis* [1983] 1 W.L.R. 1469 (where the war was one to which the United Kingdom was not a party, so that no question of trading with the enemy could arise). The suggestion in *Stocznia Gdanska SA v Latvian Shipping Co* [1998] 1 W.L.R. 574 at 600 that in the *Fibrosa* case "the outbreak of war frustrated the contract" is, with respect, open to question: it was not the outbreak of war, but the enemy occupation of the port of destination, which was the ground of frustration.

[13] *Re Badische Co* [1921] 2 Ch. 331; above, p.876.

[14] *Ertel Bieber & Co v Rio Tinto Co Ltd* [1918] A.C. 260; below, p.902.

[15] [1944] A.C. 265; above, p.887; *cf Marsh v Glanvill* [1917] 2 K.B. 87 at 91.

[16] See *Libyan Arab Foreign Bank v Bankers Trust Co* [1989] Q.B. 728 at 749, though in that case there was no frustration: *ibid.* at 771–772; *cf. Wahda Bank v Arab Bank plc, The Times*, December 23, 1992; for further proceedings in this case, see [1996] 1 Lloyd's Rep. 470.

[17] *cf. Benjamin's Sale of Goods* (6th ed.), §§18-298 to 18-300.

[18] As in *Andrew Miller & Co v Taylor & Co Ltd* [1916] 1 K.B. 402 (see at 403, 417); but in that case the plea of frustration failed as the embargo was not permanent: as to this point see below, p.891, n.41.

[19] See above, p.886.

[20] See above, pp.65, 882; below, pp.900–901.

[21] For the present purpose, a prohibition is supervening if it was imposed after the contract even though the state of affairs on which it is based already existed when the contract was made, as in *Gamerco SA v ICM/Fair Warning (Agency) Ltd* [1995] 1 W.L.R. 1226, where a stadium in which a "rock concert" was to be given suffered *before* the contract was made from an undiscovered structural defect and use of the stadium for giving the concert was prohibited when the defect was discovered *after* the contract was made.

This may make the contract void *ab initio* for illegality,[22] but it will not bring about frustration. There is, however, also an intermediate situation in which at the time of contracting a law is in force under which the contract can be lawfully performed only with the consent of a public authority: *e.g.* if a licence to build, or to export or import goods, is obtained. Such a licence may be sought but refused *after* the contract is made; and it is then possible to regard the refusal as a supervening event which frustrates the contract.[23] But it is submitted that generally there will be no frustration in cases of this kind. The cases fall into three groups.

In the first, the parties intend to perform, or actually perform, without the required licence. In such cases, the contract is not frustrated but illegal *ab initio.*[24]

In the second, the parties intend to perform only if the required licence is obtained. Here the principal obligations under the contract are subject to the condition precedent that the licence will be obtained; and normally one of the parties (*e.g.* a seller of goods for export) will be under a duty to take reasonable steps to obtain the licence.[25] If he takes such steps but the licence is nevertheless refused, he is not liable in damages[26]; but the reason is not that he is prevented from performing (and so discharged) but that he *has* performed by doing all that was required of him. Equally, the buyer is not liable, but again the reason is not that his liability is discharged: it is that he never became liable because the seller was unable to deliver and so failed to perform a condition precedent to, or a concurrent condition of, the buyer's duty to accept and pay.[27] Thus although neither party is liable the contract is not frustrated.[28] An alternative possibility, in cases of this kind, is that the seller has undertaken absolutely to obtain a licence.[29] If he fails, he is liable in damages; and to avoid conflict with the rules as to illegal contracts it has been said that the seller's liability is based on a collateral contract that he will secure the licence.[30]

In the third group of cases the licensing requirement is in existence at the time of the contract and the parties intend to perform only if a licence is obtained; but afterwards there is a change in government policy with regard to the issue of such licences. If such a change leads to the refusal of licences which previously had been issued as a matter of course,[31] it is possible that the change of policy may be regarded as a supervening event

---

[22] See above, pp.433–435.

[23] This is a possible interpretation of a dictum in *AV Pound & Co Ltd v MW Hardy Inc* [1956] A.C. 588 at 604 that "further performance of the contract was excused"; for another interpretation, see n.28, below.

[24] See above, p.432.

[25] See above, p.65.

[26] *Benjamin's Sale of Goods* (6th ed.), §18-293.

[27] See above, pp.761–763.

[28] This is an alternative, and preferable, interpretation of the dictum in *AV Pound & Co Ltd v MW Hardy Inc,* cited above, n.23; the issue of frustration was specifically left open in that case. *cf. Benjamin's Sale of Goods* (6th ed.), §§181-294 to 181-296. The question whether the contract is frustrated, or whether the parties escape liability on other grounds, is of more than academic interest: if there is no frustration the Law Reform (Frustrated Contracts) Act 1943 (below, pp.911–916) does not apply.

[29] *Peter Cassidy Seed Co Ltd v Osuustukkukaupa Ltd* [1957] 1 W.L.R. 273; *Pagnan Spa v Tradax Ocean Transport SA* [1987] 3 All E.R. 565; *cf. Congimex Companhia Geral, etc. SARL v Tradax Export SA* [1983] 1 Lloyd's Rep. 250 (absolute duty to obtain licence undertaken by buyer). "Clear words" are required to impose such an absolute duty, especially where the law prohibiting performance is passed after the time of contracting: *The Playa Larga* [1983] 2 Lloyd's Rep. 171 at 191.

[30] *Walton (Grain and Shipping) Ltd v British Italian Trading Co* [1959] 1 Lloyd's Rep. 223 at 226; *Johnson Matthey Bankers Ltd v State Trading Co of India* [1984] 1 Lloyd's Rep. 427 at 434.

[31] *cf.* the example given in *C Czarnikow Ltd v Centrala Handlu Zagranicznego "Rolimpex"* [1979] A.C. 351 at 372 (dog and television licences); *Johnson Matthey Bankers Ltd v State Trading Corp of India* [1984] 1 Lloyd's Rep. 427 at 429; contrast *Atisa SA v Aztec AG* [1983] 2 Lloyd's Rep. 579 (where the foreign government simply broke its contract to supply the seller).

which is capable of frustrating the contract.[32]

(3) Partial and temporary illegality

Partial and temporary illegality gives rise to two problems.

The first is whether it frustrates the contract. This depends (as in cases of partial impossibility[33]) on whether it defeats the main purpose of the contract. Thus in the *Denny Mott* case[34] a long-term agreement for the sale of timber provided that "to enable the aforesaid agreement to be carried out" the buyer should let a timber yard to the seller. When dealings in timber under the agreement were prohibited, it was held that the whole contract was frustrated, since its main object, namely trading in timber, had become illegal. Hence the seller could not enforce the part of it that related to the letting of the yard. But in *Cricklewood Property Investment Trust Ltd v Leighton's Investment Trust Ltd*[35] temporary war-time restrictions on building did not frustrate a 99-year building lease; for the illegality did not destroy the main object of the lease as there would probably be ample time for building after the war-time restrictions were removed.

The second question is whether illegality which does not frustrate the contract but affects only some subsidiary obligation excuses non-performance of that obligation. On principle it should have this effect. For example, a charterparty might provide that a ship should call at ten ports. If one of them became an enemy port, the shipowner could hardly be made liable for failing to call there, even if it were physically possible for him to do so.[36] Where temporary illegality does not discharge the contract,[37] it has similarly been held to provide an excuse for non-performance for so long as the prohibition lasted.[38] But in *Eyre v Johnson*[39] a tenant was held liable in damages for breach of his covenant to repair even though war-time regulations made it illegal for him to do the work. The better view, however, is that the tenant ought not to be held liable for refusing to do an act which subsequent legislation has made illegal. Though the lease as a whole is not frustrated, the illegality should provide the tenant with an excuse for non-performance of the part that has become illegal.[40]

4. Prospective Frustration

A claim that a contract has been discharged may be made before there actually *has* been any (or any sufficiently serious) interference with performance, on the ground that

---

[32] This was assumed in *Maritime National Fish Ltd v Ocean Trawlers Ltd* [1935] A.C. 524 (where the plea of frustration failed for reasons discussed at pp.906–908, below); *cf.* also *Walton (Grain and Shipping) Ltd v British Trading Co* [1959] 1 Lloyd's Rep. 223 at 236 (where the seller was excused by a *force majeure* clause); *Congimex SARL (Lisbon) v Continental Grain Export Corp (New York)* [1979] 2 Lloyd's Rep. 386; *Nile Co for the Export of Agricultural Produce v H & JM Bennett (Commodities) Ltd* [1986] 1 Lloyd's Rep. 555 at 581–582.

[33] See above, p.870.

[34] [1944] A.C. 265; *cf. Nile Co for the Export of Agricultural Crops v H & JM Bennett (Commodities) Ltd* [1986] 1 Lloyd's Rep. 555 at 581 (foreign government imposing change on method of payment).

[35] [1945] A.C. 221.

[36] *cf. Hindley & Co Ltd v General Fibre Co Ltd* [1940] 2 K.B. 517.

[37] As in the *Cricklewood* case, above, n.35.

[38] *Libyan Arab Foreign Bank v Bankers Trust Co* [1989] Q.B. 728 at 772 ("suspended but not discharged"); *cf. John Lewis Properties v Viscount Chelsea* [1993] 2 E.G.L.R. 77 (where it was not necessary to distinguish between impossibility and illegality).

[39] [1946] K.B. 481.

[40] *Cricklewood* case, above n.35, at 233, 244; *Sturcke v SW Edwards Ltd* (1971) 23 P. & C.R. 185 at 190; *cf. Brewster v Kitchell* (1691) 1 Salk. 198 ("the statute repeals the covenant"); *Grimsdick v Sweetman* [1909] 2 K.B. 740.

supervening events have made it highly probable that there *will* be such interference. The general rule is that the effect of those events must then be determined, not by waiting to see how they actually affect performance, but by reference to the time when they occur. The point is well illustrated by *Embiricos v Sydney Reid & Co*[41] where a Greek ship had been chartered for a voyage involving passage of the Dardanelles. On the outbreak of war between Greece and Turkey, it was held that the charterer was justified in treating the contract as frustrated, even though later the Turkish authorities unexpectedly announced that Greek ships were to be allowed through the straits during an "escape period" which would have made performance of the contract voyage possible. Similarly, where requisition interferes with performance of a charterparty, the question whether it frustrates the contract is to be determined by reference to the time of requisition.[42] The reason for the rule is that rights should not be left indefinitely in suspense.[43]

The rule is based on the assumption that the event is of such a kind that a reasonable view of its probable effect on the contract can be taken as soon as it occurs. Where this cannot be done, because the event is one which may equally well cause slight or serious interference with performance, the rule is necessarily subject to some qualification. This is, for example, the position where a strike of dockworkers interferes with performance of a charterparty.[44] The contract is not frustrated at once, as soon as the strike begins. It is "necessary to wait upon events—"[45] not, indeed, until the strike is over,[46] but until it has gone on for so long that a reasonable person would conclude that it was likely to interfere fundamentally with performance. This test determines not only the question whether the contract is frustrated, but also the date of frustration. The point arose in a number of cases in which ships which had been time-chartered were detained in the Shatt al Arab in the course of the Gulf War between Iran and Iraq.[47] That war is generally regarded as having begun on September 22, 1980; but at that time commercial opinion was that the war would soon be brought to an end and that foreign vessels would be speedily released. Later events falsified these forecasts and there was no doubt that the length of the detention which occurred was sufficient to frustrate the charterparties. But it was held that the contracts could be frustrated before the detention had *actually* gone on for this length of time, and that they were frustrated as soon as "a sensible prognosis of the commercial probabilities"[48] could be made, that the delay *would* continue for so long as to prevent the resumption of substantial services under the charterparties.[49] Similarly, where an employee suffered from a heart attack, his contract of employment was not discharged at once, but only when the effects of his heart attack

---

[41] [1914] 3 K.B. 45; so far as *contra*, *Andrew Miller v Taylor & Co Ltd* [1916] 1 K.B. 402 is criticised in *Watts, Watts & Co Ltd v Mitsui & Co Ltd* [1917] 2 A.C. 227 at 245.

[42] *Bank Line Ltd v Arthur Capel & Co* [1919] A.C. 435; *cf.* also *National Carriers Ltd v Panalpina (Northern) Ltd* [1981] A.C. 675 at 706; *Wong Lai Ying v Chinachem Investment Co* (1979) 13 Build. L.R. 81.

[43] *Bank Line* case, above, at 454; *cf. Embiricos v Sydney Reid & Co* [1914] 3 K.B. 45 at 54, quoted above, p.863; *Total Gas Marketing Ltd v Arco British Ltd* [1998] 2 Lloyd's Rep. 209 at 222.

[44] As in *The Nema* [1982] A.C. 724.

[45] [1982] A.C. 724 at 753.

[46] *The Nema*, above, at 753 ("businessmen must not be required to await events too long"); *cf. Chakki v United Yeast Ltd* [1982] I.C.R. 140.

[47] *The Evia (No.2)* [1983] 1 A.C. 736; *The Wenjiang (No.2)* [1983] 1 Lloyd's Rep. 400; *The Chrysalis* [1983] 1 W.L.R. 1469.

[48] *The Evia (No.2)* [1982] 1 Lloyd's Rep. 334 at 346, affirmed [1983] 1 A.C. 736; *The Wenjiang (No.2)*, above, at 408; *cf. The Adelfa* [1988] 2 Lloyd's Rep. 466 (delay in unloading due to arrest of ship).

[49] Commercial arbitrators had fixed the date of frustration as October 4, 1980 in *The Evia (No.2)* above, and as November 24, 1980 in *The Wenjiang (No.2)*, above, and in *The Chrysalis*, above. The courts expressed no opinion of their own as to the dates of frustration, merely holding that the arbitrators had applied the correct principle of law in fixing those dates.

could be assessed and "both sides accepted that ... [he] was not going to work again".[50]

5. Alternatives

A contract is said to impose an alternative obligation when it gives a party the right to choose between two or more specified performances, (*e.g.* to deliver X or Y) or between two or more specified ways of rendering performance (*e.g.* to deliver X on any day in October[51]). The power of selection between the alternatives may be given to either party: for example, a contract providing for goods to be delivered during a specified month, or at a range of ports, may give the power to choose the date or place of delivery or shipment to either seller[52] or buyer.[53] The general rule is that if a supervening event makes one of such alternative performances impossible or illegal, the contract is not discharged so long as another remains possible and lawful.[54] For example, if a contract is to deliver goods at X or Y, delivery must be made at X if delivery at Y has become impossible; if shipment is to be made from X or Y, shipment must be made from X if shipment from Y has become impossible.[55] The general rule, and the qualifications of it to be discussed below, apply not only where the contract is alleged to have been frustrated, but also where a party relies on the supervening event as providing him with an excuse under an express term of the contract, such as a *force majeure* clause.[56]

The general rule can be excluded by an express provision in the contract, *e.g.* by a strike clause which on its true construction excuses a seller if the port from which he intended to ship becomes strikebound, even though shipment from other ports within the contractual range remains possible.[57] Nor does the general rule apply where the contract calls for performance X and gives the party who is to render it a liberty to substitute Y: *e.g.* where a charterparty names ship X as its subject-matter but entitles the shipowner to substitute another ship. Under such a contract, X is due unless the liberty to substitute another ship (Y) is exercised,[58] while in the case of a true alternative obligation one cannot at the time of contracting tell whether X or Y is due. Hence, in the case of a liberty to substitute, the destruction of X before Y had been substituted, or the destruction of Y after the substitution had been made, would discharge the contract.[59] The distinction is further illustrated by contrasting a case in which a charterparty required the charterer to load a cargo of wheat, and gave him an "option" of instead loading rye,[60] with one in which a charterparty required the charterer to load a cargo of wheat or rye.[61] A contract of the first kind is sometimes said to confer a

---

[50] *Notcutt v Universal Equipment Co (London) Ltd* [1986] 1 W.L.R. 641 at 644.

[51] *e.g. Ross T Smyth & Co (Liverpool) v WN Lindsay (Leith)* [1953] 1 W.L.R. 1280 at 1283.

[52] *ibid.*

[53] *e.g. David T Boyd & Co Ltd v Louis Louca* [1973] 1 Lloyd's Rep. 209 (where no issue of discharge arose).

[54] *Barkworth v Young* (1856) 1 Drew. 1 at 25; *Reardon Smith Line Ltd v Ministry of Agriculture Fisheries and Food* [1963] A.C. 691 at 730; *cf. The Super Servant Two* [1989] 1 Lloyd's Rep. 148 at 157, affirmed [1990] 1 Lloyd's Rep. 1; for further difficulties arising from this case, see below, pp.907–908.

[55] *The Furness Bridge* [1977] 2 Lloyd's Rep. 367; *cf. Warinco AG v Fritz Mauthner* [1978] 1 Lloyd's Rep. 151; *The Safeer* [1994] 1 Lloyd's Rep. 637 at 642.

[56] See above, p.883; *cf. Warinco* case, above, n.55.

[57] *Sociedad Iberica de Molturacion SA v Tradax Export SA* [1978] 2 Lloyd's Rep. 545.

[58] *The Marine Star* [1993] 1 Lloyd's Rep. 329; *The Fjord Wind* [1999] 1 Lloyd's Rep. 307 at 328, affirmed [2000] 2 Lloyd's Rep. 191.

[59] See *The Badagry* [1985] 1 Lloyd's Rep. 395.

[60] *Reardon Smith Line Ltd v Ministry of Agriculture Fisheries and Food* [1963] A.C. 691.

[61] *Brightman & Co v Bunge y Born Limitada Sociedad* [1924] 2 K.B. 619, affirmed on another ground [1925] A.C. 799.

"contractual option" while one of the second kind is said to give rise to a "performance option".[62] Whatever terminology may be used to express the distinction, its effect (in the context of frustration) is clear. Supervening impossibility of loading wheat will discharge the contract in the first case (if the option to load rye has not been exercised when it became impossible to load wheat)[63]; but it will not have this effect in the second case even if the charterer has indicated that he intends to load wheat.[64]

An alternative obligation must also be distinguished from a contingent obligation: *i.e.* from one to do X but, if X is not done, to do Y.[65] Under such a contract, the primary obligation is to do X[66] and Y becomes due only if X is not performed and without any notice of election on the debtor's part.[67] Clearly the obligation to do X is not affected if it becomes impossible to do Y. Whether supervening impossibility of doing X is a ground of discharge depends on the construction of the contract: the contract would be discharged if it meant that Y was to become due if the debtor in *breach of contract* failed to do X, but not if it meant that Y was to become due if *for any reason* X was not done.

6. Events Affecting only one Party's Performance

In *Taylor v Caldwell*[68] the court was directly concerned only with the liability of the defendants, the performance of whose obligation to supply the Music Hall was made impossible by the fire. Yet the court clearly regarded the hirers as also having been discharged,[69] even though their principal obligation (to pay the agreed hire) had in no way become impossible. This is a common situation: in a typical bilateral contract one party undertakes to perform some act or abstention, while the other undertakes to pay for it. Supervening impossibility normally affects only the former undertaking (though illegality may affect either or both[70]). This fact was at one time thought to support the view that a time charter could not be frustrated by the unavailability of the ship: "if the shipowner's object is to receive the chartered hire . . . he does not care how much the charterer's adventures are frustrated, so long as he is able to pay".[71] But the argument was rejected on the ground that the "common object"[72] of the parties was frustrated; for even the owner's object "is not only to get hire but to afford services".[73] The "common object" in all these cases is the *exchange* of the services or facilities to be provided by one party for the payment to be made by the other. The same reasoning applies to cases of frustration of purpose. In *Krell v Henry*[74] the common object of the parties was the

---

[62] *The Didymi and the Leon* [1984] 1 Lloyd's Rep. 583, 587 per Sir John Donaldson M.R.; Staughton J., *ibid.* p.585, uses similar phrases to draw the somewhat different distinction between what is owed and how it is to be performed. A contractual term may also impose an *obligation* on one party to notify the other as to the way in, or time at, which performance is to be required. Such a term is distinct from one merely giving the former party an *option*: see *Universal Bulk Carriers Ltd v Andre & Cie* [2001] EWCA Civ 588; [2001] 2 Lloyd's Rep. 65, at [17].

[63] This follows from the reasoning of the *Reardon Smith* case, above, n.60.

[64] *Brightman* case, above, n.61 [1924] 2 K.B. 619, 637; *cf. ibid.* 630.

[65] See *Deverill v Burnell* (1873) L.R. 8 C.P. 475, below, p.959.

[66] In this respect it differs from a "performance option" (above, at n.62).

[67] In this respect it differs from a "contractual option" (above, at n.62).

[68] (1863) 3 B. & S. 826; above, p.866.

[69] (1863) 3 B. & S. 826 at 840 ("both parties are excused").

[70] *cf. Libyan Arab Foreign Bank v Bankers Trust Co* [1989] Q.B. 728 at 749, recognising that "an obligation to pay money can be frustrated" by illegality.

[71] *Bank Line Ltd v Arthur Capel & Co* [1991] A.C. 435 at 452.

[72] *Hirji Mulji v Cheong Yue SS Co Ltd* [1926] A.C. 497 at 507; contrast *Scanlan's New Neon v Tooheys Ltd* (1943) 67 C.L.R. 169 at 196–197.

[73] *Bank Line Ltd v Arthur Capel & Co Ltd* [1919] A.C. 435 at 453.

[74] [1903] 2 K.B. 740; above, pp.867, 885.

provision of facilities for seeing the coronation processions: this was what one party intended to sell and the other to buy. It made no difference that the one expected to benefit by receiving a sum of money and the other by seeing the processions. Hence both parties are discharged even though the supervening event affects only the performance of one.

7. Special Factors Affecting Land

(1) Leases of land

It was formerly thought that a lease of land could not be frustrated[75] because, in giving the tenant the right to exclusive possession for the specified time, it created a legal estate in the land. This estate was regarded as the subject-matter of the contract and survived even if later events prevented the tenant from making any use of the premises. But the commercial reality is that, generally, the tenant bargains for use and occupation and not simply for a legal estate; and in *National Carriers Ltd v Panalpina (Northern) Ltd*[76] the House of Lords held that the doctrine of frustration could apply to leases of land.

At the same time it was emphasised that the frustration of a lease will be a very rare event.[77] One reason for this is that a lease for a long period of years is in the nature of a long-term speculation. Such a transaction is hard to frustrate since the parties must contemplate that circumstances may change radically during its currency, and so to a large extent take the risk of supervening events.[78] Nor would interruption of enjoyment which was likely to last for only a few years frustrate a lease for a long term, such as 99 years, since the ratio of the interruption to the whole would be too small.[79] Even the physical destruction of the premises would not usually frustrate since it would normally be covered by express provisions[80] in the lease, such as covenants to repair and to keep the premises insured. A further reason why frustration of leases is uncommon is that to hold a long-term lease frustrated by the destruction of the buildings on the land could, paradoxically, operate to the prejudice of *tenants*, especially in a period of rising land values. Frustration operates automatically,[81] so that its effect, in the case put, would be to deprive the tenant of a valuable site long before the end of the agreed term.

For these reasons, the House of Lords in the *National Carriers*[82] case did not disapprove any of the earlier decisions to the extent that they held that the leases in question *were not* frustrated.[83] In those cases it had been held that the leases were not discharged by the destruction of the premises by enemy action[84]; by the requisitioning of the premises[85]; by war-time legislation which prevented the tenant from residing on the premises[86] or from developing the land[87]; or by the death of the tenant of furnished

---

[75] See the authorities cited in nn.83–88, below.

[76] [1981] A.C. 675.

[77] *ibid.* at 692, 697.

[78] *cf.* below, p.898.

[79] *cf.* above, pp.874–875.

[80] *cf.* below, p.898.

[81] See below, p.909.

[82] [1981] A.C. 675.

[83] Though *ibid.* at 715 *Matthey v Curling* [1922] 2 A.C. 180 was described as "a singularly harsh decision from the tenant's point of view." But the harshness was mitigated by the tenant's receipt of insurance moneys, in respect of the destruction, after the requisition.

[84] *Redmond v Dainton* [1920] 2 K.B. 256; *Denman v Brise* [1949] 1 K.B. 22; *Cusack-Smith v London Corp* [1956] 1 W.L.R. 1368.

[85] *Whitehall Court Ltd v Ettlinger* [1920] 1 K.B. 680; *Matthey v Curling* [1922] 2 A.C. 180; *Swift v Macbean* [1942] 1 K.B. 375.

[86] *London & Northern Estates Ltd v Schlesinger* [1916] 1 K.B. 20.

[87] *Cricklewood Property and Investment Trust Ltd v Leighton's Investment Trust Ltd* [1945] A.C. 221.

rooms.[88] In the *National Carriers* case itself a tenant claimed that a ten-year lease of a warehouse had been frustrated when, four and a half years before the end of the term, the only access road to the premises had been closed by the local authority and had remained closed for 20 months. The claim was rejected on the ground that the interruption was not sufficiently serious to bring about frustration.[89]

The doctrine of frustration is most likely to apply where the lease is a short-term one for a particular purpose: *e.g.* where a holiday cottage which has been rented for a month is burnt down without the fault of either party. Similarly, the contracts in cases like *Taylor v Caldwell*[90] and *Krell v Henry*[91] could be frustrated, even if the transactions were expressed as leases and not (as they actually were) as licences. In Scotland the lease of a salmon fishery was held to be frustrated when construction of a nearby bombing range prevented the tenant from using the fishery[92]; and this case might now be followed in England. A lease could also be frustrated if "some vast convulsion of nature swallowed up the property altogether, or buried it in the depths of the sea"; or if, in the case of a building lease, "legislation were subsequently passed which permanently prohibited private building in the area or dedicated it as an open space for ever".[93]

The doctrine of frustration can apply to an agreement for a lease, no less than to an executed lease.[94]

Even where the lease is not frustrated, supervening events can nevertheless provide a party with an excuse for not performing a particular obligation imposed by the lease. In *Baily v De Crespigny*[95] a landlord covenanted that neither he nor his assigns would permit building on a paddock adjoining the land let. The paddock was then compulsorily acquired by a railway company, which built a station on it. It was held that the landlord was not liable in damages for breach of his covenant, first because on the true construction of the covenant "assigns" did not include assigns by compulsion of law, and secondly because it was impossible for him to secure performance of the covenant.[96] Similarly, a tenant who covenanted to build would not be liable in damages if war-time conditions or legislation made building impossible or illegal.[97]

(2) Sale of land

The doctrine of frustration applies to contracts for the sale of land,[98] but its operation in relation to such contracts is restricted by the rule that under such a contract risk of loss passes[99] (unless otherwise agreed) as soon as the contract is made. It follows that the

---

[88] *Youngmin v Heath* [1974] 1 W.L.R. 135.

[89] *cf.* above, p.868. See also, in the United States, *Lloyd v Murphy*, 153 P. 2d. 47 (1944).

[90] (1863) 3 B. & S. 826; above, p.866.

[91] [1903] 2 K.B. 740; above, pp.867, 885.

[92] *Tay Salmon Fisheries Co v Speedie*, 1929 S.C. 593.

[93] *Cricklewood* case [1945] A.C. 221 at 229; *cf.* at 240.

[94] *Denny, Mott & Dickson v James B Fraser & Co Ltd* [1944] A.C. 265 (a decision not confined to Scots Law: see the *National Carriers* case [1981] A.C. 675 at 704); *Rom Securities Ltd v Rogers (Holdings) Ltd* (1968) 205 E.G. 427; *cf. Property Discount Corp Ltd v Lyon Group Ltd* [1981] 1 W.L.R. 300 at 305.

[95] (1869) L.R. 4 Q.B. 180.

[96] The actual decision seems to be very unjust. The landlord presumably got compensation from the railway company and was able to keep this for himself though the tenant's interests were prejudiced by the erection of the station.

[97] *Cricklewood* case [1945] at 233; *Eyre v Johnson* [1946] K.B. 481, *contra*, is doubted at p.890, above.

[98] This is assumed in *Amalgamated Investment and Property Co Ltd v John Walker & Co Ltd* [1977] 1 W.L.R. 164, where, for reasons stated at pp.886–887, above, the contract was not frustrated.

[99] See above, p.871.

contract is not frustrated if the house or buildings on the land (for the sake of which it was bought) are destroyed or seriously damaged between contract and completion.[1]

The rule promoted certainty by making it unnecessary to ask whether partial destruction was sufficiently serious to bring about frustration.[2] On the other hand, it could cause hardship to the purchaser by making him bear the risk of losses occurring before he had possession and hence before he could take steps to safeguard the property. The hardship was mitigated by the fact that the purchaser had the benefit of the vendor's insurance[3]; but as he could not be sure of the adequacy of this insurance he would normally take out his own insurance as soon as contracts were exchanged. This position could lead to double insurance and hence to a windfall for insurers. The rule that risk passes on contract is therefore commonly varied by contract: for example, by provisions leaving the risk with the seller till completion, and giving a right to rescind the contract *either* to the purchaser if the property has become unusable for its purpose, *or* to the vendor if the property has been destroyed and he cannot get planning permission to rebuild it.[4]

The rule that risk passes on contract applies where the land is sold with buildings already on it. Where a developer sells land with a house *to be built* on it, the risk *of the work* remains (unless otherwise agreed) on the vendor until the work is completed, in accordance with the rules applicable to building contracts.[5] Hence destruction of the partly completed building does not frustrate the contract and the vendor must do the work again at no extra cost. But the contract may be frustrated on other grounds. Thus where a landslip not only destroyed a partly completed block of flats, but also delayed the construction work for two-and-a-half years, it was held that a contract for the sale of one of the flats was frustrated *by the delay*; for in the interval market conditions had changed to such an extent as to make performance at the end of the delay radically different from that originally undertaken.[6]

Specific performance of a contract for the sale of land can be ordered against the purchaser even though, after contract, a compulsory purchase order is made in respect of the land.[7] The contract is not frustrated because the risk of compulsory acquisition is on the purchaser from the time of the contract[8]; and because the court's order will result in the conveyance of the land to him, against payment of the price, so that he will in due course get the compensation payable by the acquiring authority. Where, in pursuance of the compulsory acquisition order, the land is taken over by the acquiring authority *after* completion has become due, but before the hearing, the court will not order *specific* performance, since it cannot order the vendor to convey, but the contract is not frustrated, so that the purchaser's failure to complete on the due day is a breach for which he is liable in damages.[9] The position is different where the land is sold with vacant possession and is actually requisitioned *before* completion is due. In such a case

---

[1] *Paine v Meller* (1801) 6 Ves. 349; *E Johnson & Co (Barbados) Ltd v NSR Ltd* [1991] A.C. 400 at 406. The rule is criticised by the Law Commission (see Law Com. No.191, para.4.2), but legislative reform is not recommended in view of the developments described at n.4, below.

[2] This is the test adopted in some of the United States: see *Skelly Oil Co v Ashmore*, 365 S.W. 2d. 582 (1963); Uniform Vendor and Purchaser Risk Act; Uniform Land Transactions Act, s.2-406. It may seem to be more just, but it is also less convenient, than the English rule.

[3] Law of Property Act 1925, s.47 (above, p.667).

[4] Law Society's Standard Conditions of Sale (1992) Conditions 5.1.1 to 5.1.4.

[5] See above, p.871.

[6] *Wong Lai Ying v Chinachem Investment Co* (1979) 13 Build. L.R. 81.

[7] *Hillingdon Estates Co v Stonefield Estate Co* [1952] Ch. 627. The mere making of such an order does not affect ownership of the land.

[8] See above, p.895.

[9] *E Johnson Co (Barbados) Ltd v NSR Ltd* [1997] A.C. 400.

it has been held, not only that the vendor cannot specifically enforce the contract[10] (since he cannot perform his obligation to give possession on the due date), but also that the purchaser can get back his deposit.[11] It must follow from this reasoning that the purchaser will not be liable in damages.

8. Fact or Law

The question whether frustration is a matter of fact or law used to be important in determining the respective functions of judge and jury. Trial by jury is now rare in civil cases; but the question whether frustration is a matter of fact or law is still important in determining whether a court can control an arbitrator's finding. Such a finding is generally conclusive on matters of fact,[12] but does not bind the court when determining appeals from arbitrators on points of law.

The point is illustrated by the Suez cases where such questions as the greater length and cost of a voyage round the Cape of Good Hope and its physical effect on the ship or the goods were clearly questions of fact. In the *Tsakiroglou* case[13] the arbitrator found, in general terms, that performance of the contract by shipping via the Cape was "not commercially or fundamentally different from" performance by shipping via Suez. The House of Lords agreed with this finding, but added that it did not bind the court as the question whether the difference was fundamental was one of law[14] or one of mixed law and fact.[15]

In *Jackson v Union Marine Insurance Co Ltd*[16] the jury found that the delay caused by the stranding of the ship was "so long as to put an end in a commercial sense to the commercial speculation"; and Bramwell B. described this finding as "all-important".[17] One possible distinction between this attitude and that of the House of Lords in the *Tsakiroglou* case is that the jury's finding related to the effect of a specific factor (delay) on the contract, whereas the arbitrator's findings were in general terms.[18] But a better distinction is that the relations between judge and jury differ from those between court and arbitrator. The question of frustration depends on the inference to be drawn from primary facts, *i.e.*, from proved or admitted physical circumstances. The drawing of similar inferences was often left to juries, and for some purposes these inferences are called facts, or secondary facts.[19] But inferences of this sort are not treated as "facts" for the purpose of limiting the appellate or supervisory function of the court over lower tribunals. Thus when issues of negligence were left to juries, they might have been thought of as issues of fact. But appeals lie from findings of negligence made by courts whose decisions are subject to appeals only on points of law[20]; and the same is true of issues of frustration.

---

[10] *Cook v Taylor* [1942] Ch. 349.

[11] *James Macara Ltd v Barclays Bank Ltd* [1945] K.B. 148.

[12] See, *e.g. Universal Petroleum Co Ltd v Handels und Transport Gesellschaft mbH* [1987] 1 Lloyd's Rep. 517.

[13] [1962] A.C. 93.

[14] *cf. Re Comptoir Commercial Anversois and John Power Sons & Co* [1920] 1 K.B. 168; *Court Line Ltd v Dant Russell Inc* [1939] 3 All E.R. 314 at 316; *The Captain George K* [1970] 2 Lloyd's Rep. 21; *Peter Lind & Co Ltd v Constable Hart & Co Ltd* [1979] 2 Lloyd's Rep. 248 at 253; *The Wenjiang* [1982] 2 All E.R. 437; *The Wenjiang (No.2)* [1983] 1 Lloyd's Rep. 400 at 402.

[15] [1962] A.C. at 116 at 123. *The Chrysalis* [1983] 1 W.L.R. 1469 at 1475.

[16] (1874) L.R. 10 C.P. 125, above, p.873.

[17] At 141.

[18] *Tsakiroglou* case above, n.13, at 130.

[19] See *Benmax v Austin Motor Co Ltd* [1955] A.C. 370; *National Carriers Ltd v Panalpina (Northern) Ltd* [1981] A.C. 675 at 688; *The Adelfa* [1988] 2 Lloyd's Rep. 466 at 471.

[20] Goodhart, 74 L.Q.R. 402.

It does not follow from the description of the issue of frustration as one of law that the court will substitute its own view for that taken by an arbitrator merely because it disagrees with his conclusion. It will do so only if the arbitrator has applied the wrong legal test or, while purporting to apply the correct test, has reached a conclusion which no reasonable person would have reached on the primary facts as found.[21]

SECTION 3. LIMITATIONS

Even if an event occurs which would normally frustrate a contract under the rules so far considered, the doctrine of frustration may be excluded if the contract provides for the event; if the event was foreseen or foreseeable; or if it was due to the "fault" of one of the parties.

1. Contractual Provision for the Event

(1) In general

The object of the doctrine of frustration is to find a satisfactory way of allocating the risk of supervening events. There is, however, nothing to prevent the parties from making their own provisions for this purpose. Thus they can expressly provide that the risk of supervening events shall be borne by one of them and not by the other[22] or they can apportion it or deal with it in various other ways.[23] Such provisions exclude frustration[24]; and the same is true of an express term which, though it does not precisely cover the supervening event, shows that the parties had contemplated it and allocated the risk of its occurrence.[25]

A provision that excludes frustration may also be implied: for example, where the nature of the contract makes it clear that the parties intended the risk of supervening events to lie where it falls. In *Larrinaga & Co v Société Franco-Américaine des Phosphates de Médulla*[26] a contract was made in 1913 for the carriage of six cargoes of phosphates between March 1918 and November 1920. After the end of the First World War, the carriers argued that the contract was frustrated because of the altered shipping conditions then prevailing. The argument was rejected by the House of Lords. A contract of this kind, not to be performed for many years, was essentially speculative,[27] since each party had consciously taken the risk that conditions might alter. An implied agreement to exclude frustration may also be based on other characteristics of a transaction. In *The Maira (No.2)* agents had undertaken to manage a ship which was subsequently lost. It was held that this did not frustrate the management contract since the parties could hardly have intended "that the managers should be entitled to wash their hands of all duties concerning the vessel as soon as [it] was lost[28]:" they would be expected to attend to such matters as the repatriation of the crew and the settlement of claims arising out

---

[21] *The Nema* [1982] A.C. 724 (disapproving on this point *The Angelia* [1973] 1 W.L.R. 210); *The Wenjiang (No.2)* [1983] 1 Lloyd's Rep. 400; *The Chrysalis* [1983] 1 W.L.R. 1469 at 1475; *The Safeer* [1994] 1 Lloyd's Rep. 637.

[22] *Budgett v Binnington & Co* [1891] 1 Q.B. 35 at 41; *Thiis v Byers* (1876) 1 Q.B.D. 244. For an extreme case of this kind, see *Claude Neon Ltd v Hardie* [1970] Qd.Rep. 93.

[23] *e.g.* by provisions of the type mentioned at p.869, above, or by provisions for flexible pricing (above, p.884), as in *Wates Ltd v GLC* (1983) 25 Build. L.R. 1.

[24] *Joseph Constantine SS Line Ltd v Imperial Smelting Corp Ltd* [1942] A.C. 154 at 163; *The Safeer* [1994] 1 Lloyd's Rep. 637.

[25] *Bangladesh Export Import Co Ltd v Sucden Kerry SA* [1995] 2 Lloyd's Rep. 1.

[26] (1923) 92 L.J.K.B. 455.

[27] *cf.* above, p.2.

[28] [1985] 1 Lloyd's Rep. 300 at 311, affirmed on other grounds [1986] 2 Lloyd's Rep. 12.

of the loss. It is finally possible for legislation to provide for the implication of a term which excludes frustration.[29]

The general rule that frustration can be excluded by provision for the supervening event is not seriously disputed[30]; but the rule is subject to a number of qualifications.

(2) Qualifications

(a) TRADING WITH THE ENEMY. A contract may be frustrated by supervening illegality on the ground that it involves trading with the enemy; and such frustration is not excluded by a contrary provision in the contract. In *Ertel Bieber & Co v Rio Tinto Co Ltd*[31] an English company contracted to deliver copper ore to a German company from 1911 to 1919. It was held that the contract was wholly frustrated on the outbreak of war in 1914 even though it provided that, in the event of war, certain obligations should only be suspended; for to give effect to this provision would, for reasons stated earlier in this Chapter, be contrary to public policy.[32] The rule is based on the particular strength of the policy against giving aid to the economy of an enemy in time of war. It does not apply to express provisions which deal with other kinds of supervening illegality, such as prohibition of export. If, for example, a contract provides for a payment to be made in the event of such a prohibition,[33] or for suspension of the contract, followed by its termination if the prohibition is not lifted by the end of a specified period,[34] frustration is effectively excluded. Clauses of this kind are not contrary to public policy[35] since they assume that the prohibition is going to be observed, and since the continuation of the contractual relationship in cases of this kind does not have any tendency to subvert the purpose of the prohibition.

(b) PROVISION NARROWLY CONSTRUED. A clause may be literally wide enough to cover the event, but be held on its true construction not to have this effect. In *Metropolitan Water Board v Dick, Kerr & Co*[36] contractors agreed in July 1914 to construct a reservoir in six years; in the event of delays "however occasioned", they were to be given an extension of time. In February 1916, the contractors were required by a Government Order to stop work, and to sell their plant. It was held that the contract was frustrated although the events which had happened were literally within the delay clause. That clause was meant to apply to temporary difficulties, such as labour shortages, bad weather, or failure of supplies. It did not "cover the case in which the interruption is of such a character and duration that it vitally and fundamentally changes the conditions of the contract, and could not possibly have been in the contemplation of the parties to the contract when it was made".[37] *A fortiori*, an express provision in a contract for *some*

---

[29] See above, p.872, at n.65.

[30] A dictum in *WJ Tatem Ltd v Gamboa* [1939] 1 K.B. 132 at 138 suggests the contrary, but is immediately contradicted on the same page and at 139; below, pp.903, 923.

[31] [1918] A.C. 260; such clauses may also be narrowly construed, so as not to refer to war between the countries to which the contracting parties belong: *Re Badische Co Ltd* [1921] 2 Ch. 331 at 379; *cf. Fibrosa* case [1943] A.C. 32.

[32] [1918] A.C. at 286; above, p.888.

[33] *e.g. Johnson Matthey Bankers Ltd v State Trading Corp of India* [1984] 1 Lloyd's Rep. 427.

[34] *e.g.* in the *Tsakiroglou* case [1962] A.C. 93 at 95.

[35] *Johnson Matthey* case, above, at 434.

[36] [1918] A.C. 119; *The Penelope* [1928] P. 180 (approved, though with some reservations, in *The Nema* [1982] A.C. 724 at 754); *cf. Pacific Phosphate Co Ltd v Empire Trading Co Ltd* (1920) 36 T.L.R. 750; *Fibrosa* case [1943] A.C. 32 at 40; *C Czarnikow Ltd v Centrala Handlu Zagranicznego Rolimpex* [1979] A.C. 351; *Wong Lai Ying v Chinachem Investment Co* (1979) 13 Build. L.R. 81; *The Playa Larga* [1983] 2 Lloyd's Rep. 171 at 189; *Notcutt v Universal Equipment Co (London) Ltd* [1986] 1 W.L.R. 641 at 647; *FC Shepherd & Co Ltd v Jerrom* [1987] Q.B. 301.

[37] [1918] A.C. 119 at 126.

events which might otherwise frustrate it does not exclude the possibility of frustration by *other* events.[38]

(c) PROVISION INCOMPLETE. A clause may make some provision for the event which happens, but fail to make complete provision for it. In *Bank Line Ltd v Arthur Capel & Co*[39] a shipowner was sued for damages for failing to deliver a ship due under a charterparty. He pleaded that the contract was frustrated by the requisition of the ship. The charterer argued that frustration was excluded by two clauses giving him, but not the owner, the option to cancel if the ship was commandeered by the Government or if she was not delivered by April 30, 1915. But the House of Lords held that the charterparty was frustrated. Lord Sumner said that a contract could not be frustrated by a contingency for which it made "full and complete"[40] provision; but he added: "A contingency may be provided for, but not in such terms as to show that the provision is meant to be all the provision for it. A contingency may be provided for, but in such a way as shows that it is provided for only for the purpose of dealing with one of its effects and not with all".[41] Requisition or delay might frustrate the charterparty, but would not necessarily have this effect, *e.g.* if performance were only delayed by one week. The cancelling clauses entitled the charterer to cancel even if the contract was *not* frustrated. He could *escape* liability in that event. It did not follow that the shipowner should *remain* liable if requisition or delay did amount to frustration.

This principle is further illustrated by *Jackson v Union Marine Insurance Co*[42] where a charterparty provided that the ship should proceed with all possible dispatch (dangers and accidents of navigation excepted) to Newport. On the way there she was so badly damaged that she was not ready for service for eight months. The charterparty was held to be frustrated in spite of the provision excepting dangers and accidents of navigation. One possible explanation is that these words were not intended to cover so long a delay as had actually occurred.[43] But the reason given by the court was that the words of the exception "excuse the shipowner, but give him no right".[44] A delay caused by dangers and accidents of navigation might (but for the exception) have amounted either to a breach or to a frustrating event. The effect of the exception was to prevent the delay from constituting a breach. It did not deal with the effect of such delay as a possible frustrating event, and thus did not rule out frustration. To say that the shipowner is not liable for a delay does not lead necessarily to the conclusion that he can enforce the contract in spite of the delay.

(3) Provision for non-frustrating events

In its practical operation, the doctrine of frustration can give rise to two problems. It can be a source of *uncertainty* because it is often hard to tell whether the effect of supervening events on the contract is indeed sufficiently serious to discharge it. And it can be a source of *hardship* because, as a result of its narrow scope, a party may remain bound by a contract in spite of the fact that supervening events have made it substantially more burdensome or less beneficial than he could reasonably have expected. To avoid these

---

[38] *Intertradex SA v Lesieur-Torteaux SARL* [1978] 2 Lloyd's Rep. 509 at 515.
[39] [1919] A.C. 435; *cf. BP Exploration (Libya) Ltd v Hunt* [1979] 1 W.L.R. 783 at 830 (affirmed [1983] 2 A.C. 352); *The Evia* [1982] 1 Lloyd's Rep. 334 (affirmed [1983] 1 A.C. 736 at 767).
[40] [1919] A.C. 435 at 455.
[41] *ibid.* at 456.
[42] (1874) L.R. 10 C.P. 125.
[43] *Sir Lindsay Parkinson & Co Ltd v Commissioners of Works* [1949] 2 K.B. 632 at 665.
[44] At 144. *cf. Blane Steamships Ltd v Minister of Transport* [1951] 2 K.B. 965, where the words of the charterparty excused the charterer but were held to give him no rights.

difficulties, the contract may provide for discharge on the occurrence of specified events (for example by prohibition of export, or by other events beyond the control of the parties or of one of them)[45] and such a provision may take effect whether or not the effect of the event is such as to frustrate the contract under the general law. Such a clause may either give one of the parties the option to cancel the contract,[46] or provide for its automatic determination.[47] A clause of the latter kind has been described as a "contractual frustration clause".[48] The point of this description is, however, simply that the *effect* of the clause resembles that of frustration, in giving rise to automatic discharge.[49] The question *whether* the clause operates in the events which have happened depends simply on its construction[50] and not on the tests of frustration developed by the general law; and, if the clause does come into operation, the contract is discharged under one of its express terms and not under the general doctrine of frustration.[51]

2. Foreseen and Foreseeable Events[52]

(1) In general

Where the parties can at the time of contracting foresee the risk that a supervening event may interfere with performance, the normal inference is that their contract was made with reference to that risk. If, for example, the event would make performance more expensive for one party, he is likely to increase his charges; if, on the other hand, it would frustrate the other's purpose, he is likely to reduce the amount that he is willing to pay. Having thus allocated the risk by their contract, the parties should not be discharged if the event indeed occurs[53]; the loss caused by the event should lie where it falls. As Vaughan Williams L.J. has said, "The test [of frustration] seems to be whether the event which causes the impossibility was or might have been anticipated . . . "[54] Many other dicta similarly support the view that a contract cannot be frustrated by foreseen or foreseeable events[55]; and in other jurisdictions pleas of frustration have been rejected on

---

[45] Such a clause is normally construed so as to protect the party relying on it only if he has taken all reasonable steps to avoid the operation of the event or to mitigate its results: see *Channel Island Ferries Ltd v Sealink UK Ltd* [1988] 1 Lloyd's Rep. 323; *The Kriti Rex* [1996] 2 Lloyd's Rep. 171 at 196; contrast (on the point of construction) *The Morning Star (No.2)* [1996] 2 Lloyd's Rep. 383.

[46] *e.g. Bank Line Ltd v Arthur Capel & Co* [1918] A.C. 119.

[47] *e.g.* in the *Tsakiroglou* case: [1962] A.C. 93 at 95.

[48] *Bremer Handelsgesellschaft mbH v Vanden Avenne-Izegem PVBA* [1978] 2 Lloyd's Rep. 109 at 112.

[49] See below, p.909.

[50] See, *e.g. Hoecheong Products Ltd v Cargill Hong Kong Ltd* [1995] 1 Lloyd's Rep. 584; *The Kriti Rex* [1996] 2 Lloyd's Rep. 171.

[51] *Agrokor AG v Tradigrain SA* [2000] 1 Lloyd's Rep. 497 at 504. Hence the Law Reform (Frustrated Contracts) Act 1943 (below, pp.911–916) will not apply. Nor would such clauses be subject to the Unfair Contract Terms Act 1977 since they are clauses defining duties rather than exemption clauses (above, pp.248–249). Nor would they normally be open to attack under the Unfair Terms in Consumer Contracts Regulations 1999 (above, p.267) since a term operating only in circumstances beyond control of the party relying on it would not normally be unfair: *cf.* Sch.2, para.1(g) ("except where there are serious grounds . . . ").

[52] Hall, 4 *Legal Studies*, 300.

[53] See *Comptoir Commercial Anversois v Power, Son & Co* [1920] 1 K.B. 868 at 895, 901.

[54] *Krell v Henry* [1903] 2 K.B. 740 at 752.

[55] *Baily v De Crespigny* (1869) L.R. 4 Q.B. 180 at 185; *Braemont SS Co Ltd v Andrew Weir* (1910) 15 Com. Cas. 101 at 110; *Tamplin* case [1916] 2 A.C. 397 at 424; *Bank Line* case [1919] A.C. 435 at 458; *Re Badische Co Ltd* [1921] 2 Ch. 331 at 379; *Cricklewood* case [1945] A.C. 221 at 228; *Fareham* case [1956] A.C. 696 at 731; *Denmark Productions Ltd v Boscobel Productions Ltd* [1969] 1 Q.B. 699 at 725; *The Hannah Blumenthal* [1983] 1 A.C. 854 at 909; *Gamerco SA v ICM (Fair Warning) Agency Ltd* [1995] 1 W.L.R. 1226 at 1231; *Bangladesh Export Import Co Ltd v Sucden Kerry SA* [1995] 1 Lloyd's Rep. 1 at 6; *Lloyd v Murphy* 153 P. 2d. 47, 50 (1944); *cf.*, in the context of setting aside consent orders in the light of supervening events, *S v S* [2002] N.L.J. 398.

this ground.[56] There is no English case in which this was the sole ground for rejecting the plea; but it has been held that a party cannot rely, as a ground of frustration, on an event which was, or should have been, foreseen by him but not by the other party. In *Walton Harvey Ltd v Walker & Homfrays Ltd*[57] the defendants granted the claimants the right to display an advertising sign on the defendants' hotel for seven years. Within this period the hotel was compulsorily acquired, and demolished, by a local authority acting under statutory powers. The defendants were held liable in damages. The contract was not frustrated because the defendants knew, and the claimants did not, of the risk of compulsory acquisition. "They could have provided against that risk, but they did not".[58]

There is thus considerable support both in principle and in the authorities for the view that foresight or foreseeability of the supervening event excludes frustration. Nevertheless, that proposition is subject to a number of significant qualifications.

(2) Qualifications

(a) TRADING WITH THE ENEMY. A contract may be frustrated by supervening illegality resulting from the war-time prohibition against trading with the enemy, in spite of the fact that the war was a foreseeable event. Even an express provision against frustration does not save the contract in such a case[59]; and the policy considerations which justify this rule apply just as strongly where the event was or should have been foreseen. Thus contracts made in the summer of 1939 could be frustrated as a result of the outbreak of war with Germany in September although this event was foreseeable.[60]

(b) DEGREE AND EXTENT OF FORESEEABILITY. The inference that the parties contracted with reference to the event (and so took the risk of its occurrence) can be drawn only if the event was either actually foreseen or if the degree of foreseeability was a very high one. It is not sufficient for the low degree of foreseeability which constitutes the test of remoteness in tort[61] to be satisfied. In this sense, it was no doubt "foreseeable" that King Edward VII (who was 60 years old at the time) might fall ill on the day fixed for his coronation.[62] To support the inference of risk-assumption, the event must be one which any person of ordinary intelligence would regard as likely to occur. Moreover, the event or its consequences must be foreseeable in some detail. It is not sufficient that *a* delay or *some* interference with performance can be foreseen if *the* delay or interference which occurs is wholly different in extent. We have seen that this distinction restricts the scope of express provisions for a supervening event[63]; and there is no reason why it should not equally apply in relation to events alleged to have been foreseeable or foreseen. It is submitted that the points made above as to the degree and extent of foreseeability provide the best explanation for cases, in which it was said that a contract could be frustrated by foreseen or foreseeable events.

---

[56] *Baetjer v New England Alcohol Co*, 66 N.E. 2d. 748 (1946); *Glidden v Hellenic Lines*, 275 F. 2d. 253 at 256 (1960).
[57] [1931] 1 Ch. 274.
[58] *ibid.* at 282.
[59] See above, p.899.
[60] But see Taylor, *The Origins of the Second World War.*
[61] See below, p.967.
[62] *cf.* the express provisions made in some of the contracts for the possibility of postponement: *e.g. Victoria Seats Agency v Paget* (1902) 19 T.L.R. 16. According to D.N.B., 2d Supp. p.591, "A few days before the date appointed for the great ceremony rumours of the King's ill-health gained currency and were denied."
[63] See above, pp.899–900.

One such case is *W. J. Tatem Ltd v Gamboa*.[64] During the Spanish Civil War, the defendant, as agent for the Republicans, chartered a ship for 30 days from July 1 "for the evacuation of civil population from North Spain". Hire was to be paid at the rate of £250 per day "until her redelivery to the owners", but was to cease if the ship was "missing". On July 14 the ship was seized by the Nationalists, who kept her until September 7, so that she was not redelivered to the owners till September 11. The charterers had paid hire in advance up to July 31, but the owners claimed further hire from August 1 to September 11. Goddard J. rejected the claim on the ground that the charterparty was frustrated. The actual decision can be justified on the ground that it was *not* foreseeable that the ship would be detained "not only for the period of her charter but for a long period thereafter".[65] But Goddard J. added that the contract would have been frustrated even if that risk had been foreseen. "If the true foundation of the doctrine [of frustration] is that once the subject-matter of the contract is destroyed or the existence of a certain state of facts has come to an end, the contract is at an end, that result follows whether or not the event causing it was contemplated by the parties".[66] But it is submitted that a contract is not necessarily at an end if the existence of a certain state of facts has come to an end; for the parties may have been engaged in a deliberate speculation on this point.[67] A similar objection applies to the more recent suggestion[68] that an event can frustrate a contract, even though it "was or ought to have been foreseen", if it was "outside the scope of the contract on its true construction". It is submitted that it would be wrong first to construe the contract and *then* to have regard to the fact that the event was foreseen; for that fact must be of crucial importance in determining "the scope of the contract", *i.e.* whether the parties took the risk of the occurrence of the event. Where they actually foresaw the event, the more natural inference is that each of them took that risk unless the contract expressly protected him. In *WJ Tatem Ltd v Gamboa* the contract did not expressly protect the defendant from liability if the ship were seized and detained. The inference that he accepted the risk of these events (to the extent to which they were foreseen[69]) is strengthened by the fact that the contract did expressly protect him against another foreseen risk, namely, that the ship might be lost; in that event his liability to pay hire was to cease.[70]

Another such case is *The Eugenia*.[71] In September 1956, the defendants wished to charter the owners' ship to carry iron goods from Russian Black Sea ports to India. At that time "mercantile men realised that there was a risk that the Suez Canal might be closed"[72] because of the Suez crisis. The agents of the parties appreciated this risk and each made a suggestion for dealing with it.[73] But when the charterparty was concluded on September 19, nothing was expressly said about the risk of closure. The reason may be that before November 16 "mercantile men would not have formed any conclusion as to whether the obstructions in the Canal were other than temporary".[74] The actual decision was that the contract was not frustrated by the closure of the Canal on October

---

[64] [1939] 1 K.B. 132.

[65] *ibid.* at 135.

[66] *ibid.* at 138; *cf. The Captain George K* [1970] 2 Lloyd's Rep. 21 at 31.

[67] *cf.* above, pp.2, 898.

[68] *Nile Co for the Export of Agriculture Crops v H & JM Bennett (Commodities) Ltd* [1986] 1 Lloyd's Rep. 555 at 582.

[69] See above, at n.65.

[70] The shipowners may have found it easier to insure against loss than against detention and have distinguished for this reason between the effect of the two events.

[71] [1964] 2 Q.B. 226.

[72] [1963] 2 Lloyd's Rep. at 159. The facts are more fully stated in this report.

[73] *ibid.*

[74] *ibid.* at 162.

31, resulting in the detention of the ship: the charterers could not rely on the detention as it was due to their prior breach of contract and thus "self-induced"[75]; nor on the extra length of the voyage as the difference between a voyage via the Canal and one via the Cape was not sufficiently fundamental.[76] But Lord Denning M.R. also seemed to reject the further argument that frustration might have been excluded on the ground that at the time of contracting the closure of the Canal was foreseeable. He said: "It has often been said that the doctrine of frustration only applies where the new situation is 'unforeseen' or 'unexpected' or 'uncontemplated' as if that were an essential feature. But it is not so. The only thing that is essential is that [the parties] should have made no provision for it in the contract".[77] But these remarks are *obiter* and it is respectfully submitted that this aspect of the decision can be explained on other grounds. At the time of contracting, the risk of the Canal's being closed for a *very considerable time* was not foreseen; nor was it foreseeable on the high standard of foreseeability[78] required to exclude frustration. To the extent that the parties did foresee the risk, they seem to have allocated it by the terms of the charterparty. This provided that the voyage was to be paid for by the time it took,[79] so indicating an intention to throw the risk of delay on the charterers. There seems to be no reason why the court should, by applying the doctrine of frustration to foreseen events, reverse such an allocation of risks deliberately made by the contracting parties.

(c) CONTRARY INDICATIONS. The inference that the parties have assumed the risk of foreseen (or readily foreseeable) events is only a *prima facie* one and can be excluded by evidence of contrary intention. The parties may foresee an event and intend, if it occurs, "to leave the lawyers to sort it out"[80]; or they may actually provide that if the event occurs they will then determine how it is to affect the contract.[81] If the lawyers cannot "sort it out" or if the parties cannot reach agreement, the contract may then be frustrated even though the event was foreseen.

Similar reasoning explains *Bank Line Ltd v Arthur Capel Ltd*[82] where a charterparty was frustrated although the parties foresaw that the ship might be requisitioned and actually made some provision for this event. But it is by no means clear that the parties foresaw a requisition of such long duration as would frustrate the contract. Even if they did foresee this, the very fact that they had made *some* provision for the event complicated the issue. The contract entitled the charterer to cancel on requisition (so that the risk of the event was clearly not meant to be on him); but it made no reference to the effect of requisition on the liability of the owner. One could infer from this silence that the parties had decided to throw the risk of requisition on him, or that they had not thought about its effect on his liability at all. If the latter inference is correct, the contract could be frustrated although requisition was foreseen, and the House of Lords so held. The normal inference that parties take the risk of foreseen events was displaced by the special terms of the contract.

---

[75] See below, p.905.
[76] See above, p.880.
[77] [1964] 2 Q.B. at 239; cf. *Transatlantic Finance Corp v US* 363 F. 2d. 312 at 318 (1966); *Opera Co of Boston v Wolf Trap Foundation for the Performing Arts* 817 F. 2d. 1094 at 1101–1102 (1986).
[78] See above, p.902.
[79] The contract was in the form of a "time charter trip" which has become common: see *The Cebu* [1983] 1 Lloyd's Rep. 302 at 305.
[80] *The Eugenia* [1964] 2 Q.B. 226 at 234.
[81] *Autry v Republic Productions* 180 P. 2d. 888 (1947).
[82] [1919] A.C. 435; above, p.900.

3. Self-induced Frustration

A party cannot rely on "self-induced frustration",[83] that is, on frustration due to his own conduct or to the conduct of those for whom he is responsible.[84]

(1) Events brought about by one party's conduct

The doctrine of frustration obviously does not protect a party whose own breach of contract actually is, or brings about, the frustrating event. Nor does it protect him if the breach is only one of the factors leading to frustration. Thus a charterer who in breach of contract orders a ship into a war-zone, so that she is detained, cannot rely on the detention as a ground of frustration.[85] Similarly, unseaworthiness amounting to a breach of contract may cause delays in the prosecution of the voyage; and if war intervenes, so that the voyage cannot be completed, the carrier will be liable in damages[86]; such cases show that even an omission (*i.e.* failure to make the ship seaworthy) can sometimes exclude frustration.[87] The doctrine likewise does not apply where the circumstances alleged to have brought it into operation result partly from the breach of one party and partly from that of the other, *e.g.* where both breaches contribute to an allegedly frustrating delay.[88]

Where the allegedly frustrating event results from one party's deliberate act, that party cannot rely on it as a ground of frustration, even though the act is not in itself a breach of the contract[89]; but the other party may be able to rely on it for this purpose. Thus where an employee has been prevented from performing the agreed work because he has been imprisoned for a criminal offence, the employer can rely on this circumstance as a ground of frustration, so as to defeat a claim by the employee for unfair dismissal; and he can do this even though the offence had no connection with the employment, so that its mere commission did not amount to a breach of the contract.[90] But an attempt by the employee to set up the imprisonment as a ground of frustration,

---

[83] *Bank Line* case, above, n.82, at p.452; *Sudbrook Trading Estate Ltd v Eggleton* [1983] 1 A.C. 444 at 497; Swanton, 2 J.C.L. 699.

[84] Frustration is not self-induced where the cause of the delay is the act of a third party for whom the defendant is *not* responsible: see *The Adelfa* [1988] 2 Lloyd's Rep. 466, 471; nor merely because one of the parties is an enterprise controlled by a State which has by some legislative or executive act prevented performance of the contract or made it illegal: *C Czarnikow Ltd v Centrala Handlu Zagranicznego "Rolimpex"* [1979] A.C. 351 at, 372; *The Playa Larga* [1983] 2 Lloyd's Rep. 171 at 192.

[85] *The Eugenia* [1964] 2 Q.B. 226; *The Lucille* [1984] 1 Lloyd's Rep. 244; *cf. Mertens v Home Freeholds Co* [1921] 2 K.B. 526.

[86] See *Monarch SS Co v A/B Karlshamns Oljefabriker* [1949] A.C. 196. The position is different where the breach has no causal connection with the frustrating event: *The Silver Sky* [1981] 2 Lloyd's Rep. 95 at 98.

[87] *cf. Amalgamated Investment & Property Co Ltd v John Walker & Sons Ltd* [1977] 1 W.L.R. 164 (failure to take any steps to obtain planning permission).

[88] *The Hannah Blumenthal* [1983] 1 A.C. 854, rejecting suggestions in *The Splendid Sun* [1981] Q.B. 694 at 703, *The Argonaut* [1982] 2 Lloyd's Rep. 214 at 221, and *The Kehera* [1983] 1 Lloyd's Rep. 29 that there could be frustration "by mutual default." In *The Hannah Blumenthal* the plea of frustration failed on the further ground that the delay did not produce a radically different state of affairs; *cf.*, on this point, *Stockport MBC v O'Reilly* [1983] 2 Lloyd's Rep. 70. And see above, p.10 for a statutory solution of the problem which arose in *The Hannah Blumenthal.*

[89] *Denmark Production Ltd v Boscobel Productions Ltd* [1969] 1 Q.B. 699; *Black Clawson International Ltd v Papierwerke Waldhof-Aschaffenburg AG* [1981] 2 Lloyd's Rep. 446 at 457.

[90] *Harrington v Kent CC* [1980] I.R.L.R. 353; *FC Shepherd & Co Ltd v Jerrom* [1987] Q.B. 301; *Hare v Murphy Bros* [1974] I.C.R. 603 at 607; *contra Norris v Southampton CC* [1982] I.C.R. 177. Whether the imprisonment actually frustrates the contract depends on such circumstances as the length of the sentence and the nature of the employment: see *Chakki v United Yeast Ltd* [1982] I.C.R. 140 and *FC Shepherd & Co Ltd v Jerrom*, above.

in an action against him by the employer on the contract, would fail[91] on the ground that the employee could not rely on self-induced frustration.

(2) Negligence

Lord Simon has put the case of a prima donna who failed to perform a contract because she had lost her voice through carelessly catching cold. He seemed to incline to the view that she could rely on frustration so long as the incapacity "was not deliberately induced in order to get out of the engagement".[92] This result can perhaps be justified by the difficulty of foreseeing the effect of conduct on one's health.[93] But it is submitted that generally negligence should exclude frustration: for example, the plea should have failed in *Taylor v Caldwell*[94] if the fire had been due to the negligence of the defendants, for in such a case it would be unjust to make the other party bear the loss. Similarly, a shipowner cannot rely on the loss of his ship as a ground of frustration of a contract to carry goods in her if the loss is due to his negligence.[95] These examples show that "negligence" in this context is not restricted to "breach of an actionable legal duty": it includes "an event which the party relying on it had means and opportunity to prevent but nevertheless caused or permitted to come about".[96]

(3) Choosing between several contracts

Where a party has entered into a number of contracts, supervening events may deprive him of the power of performing them all, without depriving him of the power of performing one or some of them. He may then claim that one or more of the contracts are frustrated because the supervening event was one for which he was not responsible; but in two cases such claims have failed.

The first is *Maritime National Fish Ltd v Ocean Trawlers Ltd*,[97] where the defendants operated a fleet of five trawlers for fishing with otter trawls. Three of the trawlers were owned by the defendants through their subsidiaries,[98] while two, of which one was the *St Cuthbert*, were chartered from other owners. The use of otter trawls without licence was illegal, and because of a change in government policy[99] the defendants secured only three out of the five licences for which they had applied. Having allocated two of these to two of their own trawlers and one to the other chartered trawler,[1] they argued that the charter of the *St Cuthbert* had been frustrated. The argument was rejected by the Canadian courts on the ground that the defendants had taken the risk of not getting licences for all five trawlers, the licensing requirement being known both to them and to the owners of the *St Cuthbert* at the time of contracting. The Privy Council, though not dissenting from this view, preferred to base its decision on the ground that frustration was self-induced: "it was the act and election of [the defendants] which prevented the

---

[91] *cf. Sumnall v Statt* (1984) 49 P. & C.R. 367 (imprisonment of tenant no excuse for failing to perform covenant to "reside constantly" at farmhouse).

[92] *Joseph Constantine SS Co v Imperial Smelting Corp Ltd* [1942] A.C. 154 at 166–167.

[93] Restatement 2d, *Contracts*, §262 Comment (a).

[94] (1863) 3 B. & S. 826. Lack of "fault" is mentioned in the passage at 833 quoted at p.867, above.

[95] See *The Super Servant Two* [1990] 1 Lloyd's Rep. 1.

[96] [1990] 1 Lloyd's Rep. 1 at 10.

[97] [1935] A.C. 524.

[98] See [1934] 1 D.L.R. 621 at 623; [1934] 4 D.L.R. 288 at 299.

[99] See above, p.889.

[1] See the references in n.98, above.

St Cuthbert from being licensed for fishing with an otter trawl".[2] On the facts, there clearly was such an election, for the defendants could have allocated one of the three licences to the *St Cuthbert* rather than to one of their own trawlers. But suppose that the defendants had operated only the two chartered trawlers, had obtained only one licence, and that the licensing requirement had been introduced after both charterparties were concluded. The question would then have arisen whether their choice to allocate their only licence to one of the trawlers would have been an "election", so as to exclude the doctrine of frustration in relation to the charter of the other.

An affirmative answer to a similar question was given in *The Super Servant Two*,[3] where a contract was made to carry the claimants' drilling rig in one of two ships, the *Super Servant One* or the *Super Servant Two*, at the carrier's option. The *Super Servant Two* was lost and the carrier claimed that the contract was frustrated by this event because the *Super Servant One* was the subject of another fixture and hence not available for the purposes of performing the carrier's contract with the claimants. The argument was rejected on the ground that the carrier's decision to use the *Super Servant One* for the purpose of performing the other contract amounted to an "election" by him, thus precluding his reliance on the loss of the *Super Servant Two* as a ground of frustration, even if that loss was in no way due to his fault. Three grounds for the decision appear from the judgments but it is submitted with great respect that none of them is wholly convincing. First, it was said that the *Maritime National Fish* case had established that a party could not rely on frustration where his failure or inability was due to his "election"; and that the Court in *The Super Servant Two* should follow that decision.[4] It is, however, submitted that the two cases are readily distinguishable: in the *Maritime National Fish* case it was possible for the charterer to perform *all* the contracts which he had made with the owners of the other trawlers, even though only three licences had been allocated to him; while in *The Super Servant Two* it was no longer possible, after the loss of the ship, for the carrier to perform all the contracts which he had made to carry drilling rigs during the period in question. Secondly, it was said that, if the carrier were given the choice which of the contracts he would perform, frustration of the other or others could come about only as a result of the exercise of that choice, and such a position would be inconsistent with the rule that frustration occurs automatically, *without* any election by either party.[5] Again, it is submitted that this line of reasoning is not conclusive since the rule that frustration operates automatically is subject to qualification precisely in cases of allegedly self-induced frustration[6]: we have seen, for example, that the imprisonment of an employee is a circumstance on which the employer, but not the employee, can rely as a ground of discharge,[7] so that discharge cannot in such cases be described as automatic. Even where the rule that frustration operates automatically does apply, we shall see that this rule forms one of the least attractive aspects of the doctrine of frustration,[8] so that it is one which should not be extended. Moreover, the element of "election" could be eliminated if the question which of the contracts was to be discharged were left to be determined, not by the free choice of the promisor, but by a rule of law: *e.g.* by a rule to the effect that the various contracts

---

[2] [1935] A.C. 524 at 529.
[3] [1990] 1 Lloyd's Rep. 1, affirming [1989] 1 Lloyd's Rep. 148; McKendrick [1990] L.M.C.L.Q. 153.
[4] [1990] 1 Lloyd's Rep. 1 at 10, 13 (rejecting the contrary submission made in earlier editions of this book).
[5] [1990] 1 Lloyd's Rep. 1 at 9, 14.
[6] See below, p.910.
[7] *Shepherd & Co Ltd v Jerrom* [1987] Q.B. 301, discussed at p.905, above.
[8] See below, pp.909–910.

should for this purpose rank in the order in which they were made.[9] It may, from this point of view, be relevant that, in *The Super Servant Two*, some of the contracts which the carrier chose to perform (by the use of his other ship during the relevant period) had not been made "at any rate finally"[10] until *after* the contract with the claimants, and that, even after the loss of the *Super Servant Two*, the carrier had continued to negotiate for extra fees to be paid under one of those contracts, "before finally allocating the *Super Servant One* to the performance of these contracts".[11] The third reason given for the decision is that "It is within the promisor's own control how many contracts he enters into and the risk should be his".[12] But this point seems to undermine the whole basis of the doctrine of frustration: it has just as much force where the promisor enters into a single contract as where he enters into two or more, with different contracting parties. This, indeed, is the fundamental objection to the reasoning of *The Super Servant Two*, and it is submitted that the rationale of the doctrine should lead to discharge of some of the contracts where the supervening event (which makes it impossible to perform them all) occurs without the fault of the party claiming discharge.[13] Consistency with the reasoning of the *Maritime National Fish* case could be preserved by holding that *which* contracts were to be discharged should depend, not on the election of the party who can no longer perform, but on a rule of law. On this view, the actual decision in *The Super Servant Two* could be justified by reference to the order in which the various contracts with the carrier were made.

(4) Burden of proof

The onus of proving that frustration is self-induced is on the party who alleges that this is the case. In *Joseph Constantine SS Line v Imperial Smelting Corp Ltd*[14] a ship was disabled by an explosion so that her owners were prevented from performing their obligations under a charterparty. The charterers' claim for damages was rejected: the House of Lords held that the shipowners were discharged by frustration without having to disprove fault and in spite of the fact that the cause of the explosion was never explained. A possible objection to the rule is that the charterers were much less likely than the owners to be able to show how the explosion occurred. This reasoning does, indeed, prevail in one group of cases: a person to whom goods have been bailed, and who seeks to rely on their destruction as a ground of frustration of the contract of bailment, must show that the destruction was not due to any breach of his duty as a bailee.[15] But, this special situation excepted, the rule as to burden of proof laid down in the *Joseph Constantine* case, can be defended on the ground that, more often than not, catastrophic events which prevent performance do occur without the fault of either party. To impose the burden of disproving fault on the party relying on frustration is therefore less likely than the converse rule to lead to the right result in the majority of cases.

---

[9] *cf.* above, p.878.

[10] [1990] 1 Lloyd's Rep. 1 at 9.

[11] *ibid.* at 13.

[12] [1989] 1 Lloyd's Rep. 148 at 158 (at first instance); the reasoning of this judgment was approved on appeal in [1990] 1 Lloyd's Rep. 1.

[13] *cf. Bremer Handelsgesellschaft mbH v Continental Grain Co* [1983] 1 Lloyd's Rep. 269 at 292–293; the treatment of the 92 tonnes in *Bremer Handelsgesellschaft mbH v Vanden Avenne-Izegem PVBA* [1978] 2 Lloyd's Rep. 109 at 115; and see above, p.878.

[14] [1942] A.C. 154; Stone, 60 L.Q.R. 262. A contrary dictum in *FC Shepherd & Co Ltd v Jerrom* [1987] Q.B. 301 at 319 seems to have been made *per incuriam*.

[15] *The Torrenia* [1983] 2 Lloyd's Rep. 210 at 216.

SECTION 4. EFFECTS OF FRUSTRATION[16]

1. General

Frustration terminates a contract automatically at the time of the frustrating event.[17] The court may therefore hold that the contract was frustrated even though the parties for some time after the event went on behaving as if the contract still existed.[18] "Whatever the consequences of the frustration may be upon the conduct of the parties, its legal effect does not depend on their opinions, or even knowledge, as to the event".[19] Accordingly, "what the parties may say or do" has been described as "only evidence, and not necessarily weighty evidence, of the view to be taken of the event by informed and experienced minds".[20] This does not mean that the courts disregard the views of the parties as to the effect of the event: thus in one case Lord Sumner said: "Both [parties] thought its result was to terminate their contractual relations . . . and as they must have known more about it than I do there is no reason why I should not think so too".[21] The true position is that "the parties' beliefs are not determinative, but nor are they irrelevant".[22]

As frustration operates automatically, it is generally thought to terminate the contract without any election by either party: in this respect it differs from breach, which enables the victim to choose whether to treat the contract as discharged.[23] It follows that frustration can be invoked by either party, and not only by the party likely to be adversely affected by the frustrating event. Suppose, for example, that a ship under charter is requisitioned so that the charterer does not receive the promised performance (*i.e.*, the services of the ship). Frustration may, paradoxically be claimed by the shipowner, even though the charterer is perfectly willing to pay the agreed hire[24]; for if the compensation paid by the Government for the requisition exceeds that hire, the shipowner will actually profit from frustration. The courts are understandably reluctant to allow the doctrine of frustration to be used in this way. Thus the rejection of the plea of frustration in the *Tamplin*[25] case has been explained precisely on the ground that the House of Lords saw no good reason why the shipowner should be allowed to make a profit of the kind just described.[26] It seems that the seller in the *Tsakiroglou*[27] case would have made a similar profit if his plea of frustration had been upheld, for the market price of the goods had risen by more than the extra cost of carriage via the Cape of Good Hope[28]; and this fact may have had some influence on the decision that the contract remained in force. But

---

[16] Williams, *The Law Reform (Frustrated Contracts) Act 1943*.
[17] *Hirji Mulji v Cheong Yue SS Co Ltd* [1926] A.C. 497 at 505; *BP Exploration (Libya) Ltd v Hunt* [1979] 1 W.L.R. 783 at 809 (affirmed [1983] 2 A.C. 352); *The Super Servant Two* [1990] 1 Lloyd's Rep. 1 at 8, 9, 14.
[18] *cf. The Agathon* [1982] 2 Lloyd's Rep. 211 at 213; *GF Sharp & Co v McMillan* [1998] I.R.L.R. 632.
[19] *Hirji Mulji* case, above, at 509; *cf. Morgan v Manser* [1948] 1 K.B. 184 at 191.
[20] *Hirji Mulji* case, above.
[21] *Bank Line Ltd v Arthur Capel & Co* [1919] A.C. 435 at 460. See also *Black Clawson International Ltd v Papierwerke Waldhof-Aschaffenburg AG* [1981] 2 Lloyd's Rep. 446 at 457 where the fact that a party had "affirmed the contract" was said to exclude frustration.
[22] *The Wenjiang (No.2)* [1983] 2 Lloyd's Rep. 400 at 408.
[23] *FC Shepherd Ltd v Jerrom* [1987] Q.B. 301 at 327.
[24] *e.g. Bank Line Ltd v Arthur Capel & Co* [1919] A.C. 435.
[25] [1916] 2 A.C. 397; above, p.874.
[26] *Metropolitan Water Board v Dick Kerr & Co* [1918] A.C. 119 at 129; *cf.* also *Port Line Ltd v Ben Line Steamers Ltd* [1958] 2 Q.B. 146.
[27] [1962] A.C. 93; above, p.879.
[28] Shortly after the end of the shipment period, the market price of the goods had risen by £18 15s. per ton above the contract price, while the cost of shipment via the Cape was only £7 10s. per ton more than the cost of shipment via Suez.

in other cases the rule of automatic termination has, no doubt, enabled a party to profit from frustration.[29] It is doubtful whether such a result is necessary, and it might be better if frustration only gave an option to terminate to any party who is prejudiced by the supervening event in the sense of not receiving the now impossible performance (or, in cases of frustration of purpose, of not being able to use the subject-matter for its intended purpose). There is, indeed, some support for this view in the cases relating to self-induced frustration. Where an event is brought about by the deliberate act of one party (not amounting in itself to a breach), that party cannot rely on it as frustrating the contract; but the other party may be able so to rely on it. This is, for example, the position where an employee is imprisoned for a criminal offence and so unable to perform his part of a contract of employment. The employer can invoke frustration in such circumstances[30]; but the employee cannot do so since a party cannot rely on self-induced frustration.[31]

2. Problems of Adjustment[32]

The common law starts with the principle that frustration discharges the parties only from duties of "future performance".[33] Rights accrued before frustration therefore remain enforceable while those which would, but for the frustrating event, have accrued after the time of discharge do not become due. These rules sometimes caused hardship which has been mitigated both by common law developments and by statute.

(1) Rights accrued before frustration

(a) COMMON LAW. The rule that rights which had accrued before frustration remain enforceable can be illustrated by supposing that in *Taylor v Caldwell*[34] the fire had occurred after the first, but before the second, of the four specified days. The rest of the contract would then have been discharged, while each party would have remained liable for any failure to perform obligations which had fallen due on the first day. But the application of this principle could lead to injustice where one party's performance under the contract had become due before the frustrating event while that of the other was only to be rendered thereafter; for in such a case the former party would have still to perform, without getting what he had bargained for in return. For example, in *Chandler v Webster*[35] a contract for the hire of a room overlooking the proposed route of King Edward VII's coronation processions provided for payment of £141 15s. in advance: this was due, and £100 of it had been paid, before the day on which the processions were cancelled. The hirer was held liable to pay the remaining £41 15s. as the payment had fallen due before the contract was frustrated; while his claim to recover back the £100 already paid on the ground of "total failure of consideration"[36] was rejected[37]: it was

---

[29] A striking illustration is *The Isle of Mull*, 278 F. 131 (1921); *cf.* also *Nickoll & Knight v Ashton Edridge & Co* [1901] 2 K.B. 126 (above, p.879) where the market price of the goods rose above the contract price so that the seller seems to have made a profit out of frustration.

[30] *FC Shepherd & Co v Jerrom* [1987] Q.B. 301; above, p.905.

[31] *ibid.*

[32] Stewart and Carter [1992] C.L.J. 66.

[33] *Joseph Constantine* case [1942] A.C. 154 at 187; *cf. The Super Servant Two* [1990] 1 Lloyd's Rep. 1 at 18 ("further liability").

[34] (1863) 3 B. & S. 826, above, p.866.

[35] [1904] 1 K.B. 493; *cf.* Buckland, 46 Harv.L.Rev. 1281.

[36] See below, p.1049.

[37] *cf. Blakeley v Muller & Co* [1903] 2 K.B. 760 n. (referred to in *The Great Peace* [2002] EWCA Civ 1407; [2002] 4 All E.R. 869 at [65], [76] under its alternative name of *Hobson v Pattenden & Co*); *Civil Service Co-operative Society v General Steam Navigation Co* [1903] 2 K.B. 756.

thought that the failure of consideration was not total as frustration released the parties only from further performance, and did not make the contract void *ab initio*. But this aspect of *Chandler v Webster* was overruled in the *Fibrosa* case.[38] An English company had agreed to sell machinery to a Polish company for £4,800, of which £1,600 was to be paid in advance. When £1,000 had been paid, the contract was frustrated by the German occupation of Gdynia after the outbreak of war in 1939. The House of Lords held that the Polish company could recover back the £1,000 since the consideration for the payment had wholly failed: no part of the machinery had been delivered. Liability to pay the outstanding £600 must likewise have been discharged, for it would have been futile to require the buyer to make a payment which he would then immediately have been entitled to recover.[39]

But this solution was defective in two ways. First, it applied only where the consideration had *wholly* failed.[40] In *Whincup v Hughes*[41] a father apprenticed his son to a watchmaker for six years at a premium of £25. After one year the watchmaker died. The father could not recover back any part of the premium as the failure of consideration was only partial. Secondly, to allow the payor to recover back the whole of his advance payment might in turn cause injustice to the payee, who might (and in the *Fibrosa* case did) use the advance payment to finance the initial stages of the contract. If, in consequence of frustration, that expenditure was wasted, the resulting loss would fall entirely on the payee.

(b) STATUTE. To remedy the defects just described, s.1(2) of the Law Reform (Frustrated Contracts) Act 1943 lays down three rules:

(i) *Sums payable.* All sums payable under the contract before the time of discharge cease to be payable on frustration: thus in *Chandler v Webster* the claim for the unpaid £41 15s. would now fail.

(ii) *Sums actually paid.* All sums actually paid in pursuance of the contract before the time of discharge are recoverable from the payee "as money received by him to the use of the" payor. As the subsection does not refer to "total failure of consideration", this statutory right to recover back money arises even where the failure is only partial, for example, in such cases as *Whincup v Hughes*.

(iii) *Expenses.* If the party to whom sums were paid or payable in pursuance of the contract has before the time of discharge incurred expenses in or for the purpose of the performance of the contract, the court may allow him to retain or recover the whole or any part of the sums so paid or payable; but the court cannot allow him to retain or recover more than the actual amount of his expenses. The court can make an award in respect of expenses under s.1(2) only if the contract contains a stipulation for prepayment; a party who incurs expenses without asking for a prepayment, or who incurs greater expenses than the amount of the prepayment, does so at his own risk.[42]

The court is not bound to make any award in respect of expenses and has a discretion as to the amount of the award. This discretion is subject to two upper limits: the award

---

[38] *Fibrosa Spolka Akcyjna v Fairbairn, Lawson, Combe, Barbour Ltd* [1943] A.C. 32; above, pp.887–888. This point seems to have been overlooked in *Re Goldcorp Exchange Ltd* [1995] A.C. 74 at 103, where the Privy Council repeats what is in substance the reasoning of *Chandler v Webster*, without referring either to that case or the *Fibrosa* case.

[39] *cf.*, in another context, *McDonald v Denys Lascelles Ltd* (1933) 48 C.L.R. 457, above, p.850; *Fibrosa* case [1943] A.C. 32 at 53.

[40] *cf.* below, pp.1049–1051.

[41] (1871) L.R. 6 C.P. 78.

[42] An award in respect of expenses can be made under s.1(2) only where a *sum of money* was paid or payable to the party who has incurred expenses. Where that party has received a "payment in kind" a similar result may be reached under s.1(3)(a): below, p.915.

must not exceed either the amount of the expenses incurred, or the amount of the stipulated prepayment.[43] No doubt in exercising its discretion the court will be influenced by the degree to which the expenses have been made useless by the frustrating event. If machinery made for one customer can easily be sold to another, very little will be awarded; if it cannot be disposed of except as scrap, the court is likely to make a substantial award. Even in such a case, however, the court will not necessarily award the maximum amount available under the Act. Suppose that in the *Fibrosa* case the seller had received a prepayment of £1,600 and had incurred expenses of exactly that amount. Under the common law rule he would have had to pay back the whole £1,600, and this was unjust because it left him to bear the entire loss of the wasted expenditure. If, under the Act, the court were to allow him to retain the whole £1,600, this could be equally unjust as it would leave the buyer to bear the whole of that loss. In the exercise of its discretion under s.1(2) the court could split the loss (instead of merely shifting it from one party to the other) in such proportions as it thought just.[44]

In exercising its discretion under s.1(2), the court can also take account of the fact that expenses have been incurred by the *payor*. This was the position in *Gamerco SA v ICM/ Fair Warning (Agency) Ltd*,[45] where the promoter of a "rock concert" had made an advance payment to the performers and the contract was then frustrated. Exercising a "broad discretion",[46] the court allowed the promoter to recover the payment in full, without any deduction in respect of expenses incurred by the performers for the purpose of the performance of the contract.[47] It did so on the grounds that the promoter had also incurred expenses which not only exceeded the prepayment[48] but also amounted to about nine times those incurred by the performers,[49] and that each set of expenses had been wholly wasted.

(2) Rights not yet accrued

(a) COMMON LAW. At common law, rights not yet accrued at the time of frustration are unenforceable.[50] If a builder agrees to build a house for £100,000 payable on completion he cannot recover the £100,000 if the contract is frustrated before completion. This rule is perfectly reasonable: it would be unjust to make the building-owner pay the full price for an unfinished house. But, further, at common law the builder could not recover anything at all for partial performance before frustration. He could not recover a *quantum meruit* as no agreement to pay a proportionate sum for doing part of the work could be implied in the teeth of an express agreement for payment on completion. Thus in *Cutter v Powell*[51] a seaman whose wages were to become due on completion of a voyage

---

[43] Proceeds of insurance payable to the claimant by reason of the frustrating events must be disregarded: s.1(5).

[44] s.1(2) refers to "the whole *or any part* of the sums so paid or payable." Legislation in other jurisdictions provides for *equal* division of the loss: British Columbia Frustrated Contracts Act 1974, s.5(3); New South Wales Frustrated Contracts Act 1978, s.11(2)(b)(ii) and *cf.* s.13; South Australian Frustrated Contracts Act 1988, ss.3(3), 7(2)(c); but equal division is not necessarily appropriate in all circumstances: New South Wales Act, above, s.15; South Australian Act, above, s.7(d).

[45] [1995] 1 W.L.R. 1226.

[46] *ibid.* at 1236.

[47] s.1(5), above, also required the court to disregard the fact that both parties had insured against cancellation and received payments under those policies.

[48] The promoter's expenses exceeded $450,000; the prepayment amounted to $412,500.

[49] The performers' expenses appear to have been about $50,000.

[50] *The M Vatan* [1987] 2 Lloyd's Rep. 416 at 426.

[51] (1795) 6 T.R. 320.

died during it: his executrix recovered nothing for the services he had rendered. And in *Appleby v Myers*[52] engineering contractors agreed "to make and erect the whole of the machinery" in the defendant's factory "and to keep the whole in order for two years from the date of completion". After part of the machinery had been erected, an accidental fire destroyed the factory with such of the machinery as was already in it, and frustrated the contract. It was held that the contractors could recover nothing for the machinery which they had erected. The general view is that this result is unsatisfactory[53] and that the builder should get something for his work.

(b) STATUTE. The common law rule stated above was modified by s.1(3) of the Law Reform (Frustrated Contracts) Act 1943, which provides that "Where any party to the contract has, by reason of anything done by any other party thereto in, or for the purpose of, the performance of the contract, obtained a valuable benefit (other than a payment of money to which [s.1(2)] applies) before the time of discharge, there shall be recoverable from him by the said other party such sum (if any), not exceeding the value of the said benefit to the party obtaining it, as the court considers just, having regard to all the circumstances of the case"[54] and in particular to (a) the amount of any expenses incurred by the benefited party before the time of discharge, and (b) "the effect, in relation to the said benefit, of the circumstances giving rise to the frustration of the contract". Thus if A agrees to decorate B's house for £2,500 payable on completion but dies after decorating half the house, A's estate can recover something.

(i) *Measure of recovery.* The measure of recovery under s.1(3) was the main issue in *BP (Exploration) Libya Ltd v Hunt.*[55] The case arose out of an elaborate agreement between BP and Mr Hunt for the exploitation of an oil concession in Libya belonging to Mr Hunt. BP were to do all the work of exploration and to provide the necessary finance; they were also to make certain "farm-in" payments in cash and oil. In return, they were to get a half share in the concession; and, as soon as the field began to produce oil, they were to receive "reimbursement oil" (to be taken out of Mr Hunt's share) until they had recouped 125 per cent of their initial expenditure. A large oil field was discovered and oil began to flow from it in 1967; but in 1971 the contract between BP and Mr Hunt was frustrated when their interests in the concession were expropriated by Libyan decrees. At this time, BP had received only about one-third of the "reimbursement oil" to which they were entitled in respect of their initial expenditure; and they brought a claim under s.1(3) of the 1943 Act. The claim was allowed by Robert Goff J., whose decision was (subject to relatively minor modifications[56]) upheld by the Court of Appeal and the House of Lords. The learned judge held that, in considering a claim under s.1(3), the court must proceed in two stages: it must first identify and value the benefit obtained, and then assess the just sum (not exceeding the value of the benefit) which it was proper to award. At the first stage, he held that "benefit", on the true construction of s.1(3), referred, not to the cost of performance incurred by the claimant,

---

[52] (1867) L.R. 2 C.P. 651.

[53] *cf.* above, pp.819–820 for criticism of the rule that nothing can be recovered for partial performance of an entire obligation. One practical justification for that rule in cases of *breach* may be that it puts pressure to perform on the party in breach, but that argument cannot apply where performance is prevented by an event for which neither party is responsible.

[54] But not to the proceeds of insurance payable to the claimant by reason of the frustrating event: s.1(5).

[55] [1979] 1 W.L.R. 783; affirmed [1981] 1 W.L.R. 236, [1983] 2 A.C. 352; Baker [1979] C.L.J. 266.

[56] Recovery of a "farm-in" payment of $2m in *cash* had been allowed under s.1(3) when it plainly should have been allowed under s.1(2): see [1981] 1 W.L.R. 236 at 240; [1983] 2 A.C. 352 at 370; and see below, n.59.

but to the end product received by the other party.[57] In the case before him, that end product was the enhancement of the value of Mr Hunt's share in the concession resulting from BP's work; but because s.1(3)(b) required the court to have regard to "the effect, in relation to the said benefit, of the circumstances giving rise to . . . frustration", the value of that benefit had to be reduced to take account of the expropriation. In view of this fact, the total benefit obtained by Mr Hunt was the net amount of oil he had received from the concession, plus the compensation paid to him by the Libyan government. Of this total, half was attributed to BP's efforts and half to Mr Hunt's original ownership of the concession. The value of this benefit was quantified at some $85m. In assessing the "just sum" to be awarded, however, Robert Goff J. adopted a criterion which he had rejected in valuing the benefit, viz. the cost to BP of the work to the extent that it was done for Mr Hunt. To this was added the value of the "farm in" oil[58] and the resulting total was then reduced by the amount of the reimbursement oil already received by BP. On this basis, the just sum was some $34.67m[59] and, as the valuable benefit exceeded this amount, BP recovered the just sum in full.

(ii) *Definition of "valuable benefit"*. It follows from the definition of valuable benefit as an "end product" that s.1(3) will not apply merely because the claimant has incurred trouble and expense for the purpose of the performance of the contract.[60] On the other hand, there can be a valuable benefit within s.1(3) even though no physical thing has been transferred by the claimant to the defendant. Thus in *BP Exploration (Libya) Ltd v Hunt* the services rendered by BP to Mr Hunt constituted at least part of the benefit. In the case of a contract to paint a house, there would similarly be a valuable benefit if the contract was frustrated by illegality after half the work had been done.[61] In such cases the improvement to the defendant's property can be said to be an "end product;" but there are other contexts in which the definition of "valuable benefit" as an "end product" would be inappropriate: e.g. where the contract was one of the hire of a chattel. Such a contract is not intended to leave any "end product" in the hands of the hirer, who can nevertheless be said to have benefited if he has had the use of the chattel for part of the agreed period before the contract is frustrated. It would be unfortunate if s.1(3) were held to be inapplicable in such a case merely because of the definition of valuable benefit adopted in the different context of *BP Exploration (Libya) Ltd v Hunt*. Similarly, it is submitted that s.1(3) should now apply on facts such as those in *Cutter v Powell*[62]: the defendants would have had the benefit of the seaman's services during part of the voyage, even though it might not be easy to identify any "end product" resulting from those services.

(iii) *Destruction of the benefit*. The machinery of the Act worked satisfactorily in *BP (Exploration) Libya Ltd v Hunt* because the valuable benefit, even when reduced in the light of the frustrating event, exceeded the just sum. But the position would have been

---

[57] For this reason a claim for the "time value of money"—i.e. for the use that Mr. Hunt could have made of the proceeds of the sale of the oil—was rejected for it was not shown that he did make such use. But interest on the award from the time of frustration was allowed under Law Reform (Miscellaneous Provisions) Act 1934, s.3; see now Supreme Court Act 1981, s.35A(1), below, p.995.

[58] This value seems also to be relevant to the identification of the benefit.

[59] [1981] 1 W.L.R. 236, 241; this contrasts with the figure of some $35.40m in [1979] 1 W.L.R. 783, 827. The difference is not explained and may be due to the adoption of different currency conversion factors at first instance and in the Court of Appeal.

[60] This was precisely the position in *Taylor v Caldwell* (1863) 3 B. & S. 826: see above, p.866. For the court's power to allow the *recipient* of the benefit to deduct expenses, see below, p.915.

[61] Illustration given by Lord Simon L.C. when introducing s.1(3): HL Deb., June 29, 1943, Col. 139.

[62] (1795) 6 T.R. 320, above, pp.912–913; unless the contract was literally one of insurance: see above, p.782 and below, pp.917–918. The "just sum" should not be based on the exceptionally high rate of pay contracted for, but on current market rates (see above, p.782).

different if the expropriation had occurred immediately before oil had begun to flow and if no compensation for expropriation had been paid. On the reasoning of the judgment, there would then have been no valuable benefit (beyond the "farm-in" oil); for that reasoning has regard to "the circumstances giving rise to the frustration" within s.1(3)(b) in *valuing the benefit* rather than in *assessing the just sum.* The same reasoning is adopted in an example which closely resembles *Appleby v Myers*[63]: "Suppose that a contract for work on a building is frustrated by a fire which destroys the building and which therefore destroys a substantial amount of the work already done by the plaintiff. Although *it might be thought just* to award the plaintiff a sum assessed on a *quantum meruit* basis, the effect of s.1(3)(b) will be to reduce the award to nil. . . . "[64] If this is right, *Appleby v Myers* would not be affected by the Act; but in view of the evident reluctance with which the learned judge reached this conclusion it is submitted that an alternative interpretation of s.1(3) is to be preferred. This would make the destruction of the benefit relevant, not to the identification of the benefit, but to the assessment of the just sum. Two points seem to support such an interpretation. First, s.1(3) applies where a valuable benefit has been obtained *before* the time of discharge: thus to identify the benefit in a case like *Appleby v Myers* the court must look at the facts as they were before, and not after, the fire. The partly completed installation would at least *prima facie* be a benefit, since completion of the installation would be likely to cost less after part of the work had been done. Secondly, there is the structure of the subsection. This begins by setting out the circumstances in which the court has power to make an award (*i.e.* when a valuable benefit has been obtained) and then provides guidelines for the exercise of that power. The guideline contained in s.1(3)(b) is introduced by the words "such sum as the court thinks just having regard to. . . "; and these words seem to link the guideline to the *exercise* rather than to the *existence* of the court's discretion. This interpretation cannot cause any injustice, for if the court thinks that very little or nothing should be awarded it can exercise its discretion to that effect; and for this purpose the court can take the destruction of the benefit into account so as to split the loss in such proportions as the court thinks just.[65] But if such destruction necessarily led to the conclusion that no valuable benefit had been obtained before frustration, the court would have no discretion to award anything at all. It would be a pity if this useful discretion were restricted in a way that is neither clearly required by the words of the subsection nor necessary to promote justice.

(iv) *Relationship between s.1(2) and 1(3).* The power to make an award in respect of a valuable benefit under s.1(3) is, in theory, additional to the power to make an award in respect of expenses under s.1(2). Thus if a party who has incurred expenses has also both conferred a valuable benefit and received (or stipulated for) a prepayment he can claim under both subsections. But any amount awarded in respect of expenses will be taken into account in deciding how much should be awarded in respect of valuable benefit, and vice versa.[66] If the party who has incurred expenses has *received* a valuable benefit other than money (for example, a "prepayment" in kind) he cannot make any claim in respect of expenses under s.1(2) as that subsection only applies where a *sum of money* is paid or

---

[63] (1867) L.R. 2 C.P. 651.

[64] [1979] 1 W.L.R. 783 at 801 (italics supplied); *cf. Parsons Bros Ltd v Shea* (1966) 53 D.L.R. 2d 36, decided under a Newfoundland Act in similar (but not identical) terms to those of the English Act. It may also be significant that in the illustration of the half-painted house given by Lord Simon L.C. (above, n.61) the ground of frustration was illegality so that the benefit of having "got your house half painted" was not destroyed.

[65] Under the British Columbia, New South Wales and South Australian Acts referred to on p.912, n.44, the loss would be split equally; but s.1(3) of the English Act gives a more flexible discretion.

[66] See s.1(3)(a).

payable. But the court can reach much the same result under s.1(3), for it can take the expenses into account in deciding how much the recipient of the valuable benefit should pay for it.[67]

(3) Casus omissus?

Under s.1(2), sums of money payable before frustration cease to be payable on frustration. The subsection is restricted to *payments of money*. S.1(3), by contrast, provides for restitution claims in respect of *other benefits*, e.g. where A renders services or transfers property to B before frustration. But nothing in s.1(3) in terms releases A where before frustration he ought to have performed an obligation to do something other than to pay cash, has failed to do so, and would, if he had performed, have been entitled to make a claim for restitution under s.1(3). Thus if A has promised to make an advance payment *in cash* and has failed before frustration to do so, he is released by s.1(2); but if the stipulated payment had been *in kind* he would not be released by s.1(3). Nor can he, in the latter case, neutralise his liability by making a claim under s.1(3), for B has not "by reason of anything done [by A] obtained a valuable benefit . . . *before* the time of discharge". On the contrary, B has failed to obtain an expected benefit by reason of something not done by A. B may *after* the time of discharge obtain a benefit by suing A, but this does not bring the case within s.1(3) as the benefit is obtained too late. Nor would it help A to argue that before the time of discharge B had a valuable benefit, namely, his right to sue A, for this benefit would not have been obtained "by reason of anything done [by A] in or for the purpose of the performance of the contract". It is hard to believe that these consequences were intended. The failure of the Act in these circumstances to provide for the release obligations other than those to pay money seems to be a *casus omissus*.

(4) Special cases

(a) SEVERABILITY. A contract may provide for one party to make payments from time to time in response to specified parts of the other's performance. The common law rule was that, if the contract was frustrated, such payments as were due at the time of frustration could be recovered. In *Stubbs v Holywell Ry*[68] a consulting engineer was appointed for 15 months for £500 payable in five equal quarterly instalments. After two quarters he died. His administrator successfully claimed the £200 due to him at the date of his death. But he could have recovered nothing more had the deceased worked for another two months in the next quarter. Under the 1943 Act he can do so. S.2(4) provides that if parts of a contract which have been wholly performed can properly be severed from the remainder, they are to be treated as separate contracts; and that the provisions of s.1 (discussed above) shall apply to the remainder of the contract.

S.2(4) also affects the rights of a person to recover back money paid under such a contract. At common law money could be recovered back if paid for some severable part of the consideration which had wholly failed, even though the consideration for the whole payment had not failed.[69] If in *Stubbs v Holywell Ry* the whole £500 had been paid in advance, £200 could have been recovered back as no work at all was done by the deceased in the last two quarters; but nothing could have been recovered back in respect of the third quarter, if the deceased had done so much as a week's work in it. Now money

---

[67] *ibid.*
[68] (1867) L.R. 2 Ex. 311.
[69] See *Tyrie v Fletcher* (1777) 2 Cowp. 666 at 668; Marine Insurance Act 1906, s.84(2) (divisible insurance policies); below, pp.1050–1051.

paid in respect of the third quarter could be recovered back, but the personal representative could claim under section 1(3) in respect of the work done by the deceased in that week. An obligation may also be severable by statute under the provisions of the Apportionment Act 1870.[70]

(b) CONTRARY AGREEMENT. The common law rule that money is recoverable on the ground of total failure of consideration can be excluded by contrary agreement: the money may be paid out-and-out, with the intention that the payee shall keep it in any event.[71] The provisions of the Act can similarly be excluded by contrary agreement[72]; whether a term has this effect depends on its construction. In *BP Exploration (Libya) Ltd v Hunt*[73] the contract provided that the defendant was not to be personally liable to repay any advances and that BP's rights were to be exercisable only against the defendant's share of the oil. This provision did not exclude the Act as, on its true construction, it was not intended to deal with the risk of expropriation but with the different risk that no oil might be found.

(c) EXCLUDED CONTRACTS. The Act does not apply to:

(i) *Voyage charterparties and other contracts for the carriage of goods by sea.*[74] The object of this exception is to preserve two rules which are well established and known in the trade: first, that freight which has become due or been paid before frustration remains due and (if paid) cannot be recovered back, even though the cargo is lost[75]; and, secondly, that a person who contracts to carry goods by sea to a specified port cannot recover freight *pro rata*, even if he is forced by events outside his control to discharge them at an intermediate port.[76]

(ii) *Contracts of insurance.*[77] This exception preserves the rule that there can, in general, be no apportionment of premiums under an insurance policy once the risk has begun to run. The essence of a contract of insurance is that "the contract is for the

---

[70] See above, p.823.

[71] *Fibrosa* case [1943] A.C. 32 at 43, 77. The common law rule could still apply: *e.g.* to contracts excluded from the operation of the Act by s.2(5)(c), below, p.918.

[72] s.2(3). Contract terms *excluding the common law rule* stated at n.71, above, would not be subject to the requirement of reasonableness under Unfair Contract Terms Act 1977, s.3(2)(b)(ii) (above, p.254) since in the case of a frustrated contract there would be *no* "contractual obligation" to perform. They might, however, in a standard consumer contract be subject to the requirement of fairness under Unfair Terms in Consumer Contracts Regulations 1999 (above, p.267): see Sch.2 para.1(o). Contract terms *excluding the 1943 Act* would not be subject to the Unfair Contract Terms Act 1977, being "authorised" by s.2(3) of the 1943 Act and so excepted from the 1977 Act by virtue of s.29(1)(a) of that Act (above, p.266); but they could be subject to the Unfair Terms in Consumer Contracts Regulations 1999, for although these Regulations do not apply to "mandatory statutory . . . provisions" (reg.4(2)(a)) the provisions of the 1943 Act are (by reasons of s.2(3)) not "mandatory". The fact that s.2(3) permitted the parties to exclude the provisions of the 1943 Act would, however, be relevant to the question whether a term to this effect was "unfair" for the purposes of the 1999 Regulations.

[73] [1983] 2 A.C. 352.

[74] s.2(5)(a) provides that the Act shall not apply "to any charterparty, except a time charterparty or a charterparty by way of demise, or to any contract (other than a charterparty) for the carriage of goods by sea." These words make it clear that the Act does not apply to voyage charterparties, but leave open the question whether it applies to a "time charter trip" (above, p.904). The answer may depend on the degree of particularity with which the contract describes the voyage.

[75] *Byrne v Schiller* (1871) L.R. 6 Ex. 319; unless the contract provides the contrary, as in *The Oliva* [1972] 1 Lloyd's Rep. 458; contrast *The Lorna I* [1983] 1 Lloyd's Rep. 373 where, on the true construction of the contract, freight was not to become due till after the frustrating event. Freight may be *earned* before it is *payable*: above, p.783.

[76] *St Enoch Shipping Co Ltd v Phosphate Mining Co* [1916] 2 K.B. 625; above, p.782.

[77] s.2(5)(b).

whole entire risk, and no part of the consideration shall be returned".[78] Thus if a ship is insured but lost in some way not covered by the policy after part of the period of insurance has run, no part of the premium can be recovered back. This is obviously in accordance with the intention of the parties, for such a contract is essentially speculative. Had the ship been lost by one of the perils insured against on the first day, the insurer would have had to bear the whole loss. Conversely, he can keep the whole premium if the ship is lost by a peril that is not covered by the policy at any time during the period of insurance.

(iii) *Certain contracts for the sale of goods.* S.2(5)(c)[79] provides that the 1943 Act shall not apply to two types of such contracts.

First, it does not apply to "any contract to which s.7 of the Sale of Goods Act 1979 . . . applies". Under s.7 of that Act, an agreement to sell specific goods is avoided if the goods perish without any fault on the part of the seller or buyer before the risk[80] has passed to the buyer. That is, the buyer is not liable for the price and neither party is liable in damages. The same result would normally follow from the common law rules of frustration, since the destruction of specific goods would frustrate the contract. The cases in which the 1943 Act would (if it were not excluded by s.2(5)(c)) make a difference are those in which there has been an advance payment or part-delivery.

If the buyer pays in advance but does not get any of the goods, he can recover back his payment on the ground of total failure of consideration.[81] The exclusion of the Act does not affect this right, but it does prevent the seller from setting off any expenses which he may have incurred, *e.g.* in putting the goods into a deliverable state.

Part-delivery followed by frustration raises two problems. First, a buyer of a specific parcel of goods may have paid the whole price in advance and received only part-delivery. He probably cannot recover back any part of the payment at common law as the failure of consideration is not total.[82] Nor can he rely on the 1943 Act, as that is excluded. It has been suggested that he may be able to recover back a proportionate part of the advance payment simply on the ground that the undelivered goods are still at the seller's risk,[83] but this suggestion would give rise to difficulty where the price was not readily apportionable between the delivered and the undelivered parts.[84] Secondly, a seller may have delivered part of the goods and been paid nothing. As the 1943 Act is excluded, he cannot rely on it to recover anything in respect of the valuable benefit obtained by the buyer. He may be able to recover something at common law if a new contract can be implied from the buyer's keeping the goods after frustration. But it would be hard to imply such a contract if the buyer no longer had the goods, *e.g.* because he had used or resold them before frustration.

The 1943 Act secondly does not appply to "any other contract for the sale, or the sale and delivery, of specific goods, where the contract is frustrated by reason of the fact that the goods have perished". These words seem to refer to a case which would not fall within s.7 of the Sale of Goods Act 1979, because the risk *has* passed to the buyer. It is difficult to imagine how in such a case the contract could be frustrated by the perishing of the goods. Perhaps the point of excepting such a case from the 1943 Act is to make

---

[78] *Tyrie v Fletcher* (1777) 2 Cowp. 666 at 668. For a contractual provision displacing the normal rule, see *The M Vatan* [1987] 2 Lloyd's Rep. 416.

[79] As amended by Sale of Goods Act 1979, s.63 and Sch.2, para.2.

[80] See above, p.871.

[81] *Logan v Le Mesurier* (1846) 6 Moo.P.C. 116.

[82] It is assumed that the value of the part undelivered is not readily apportionable to the whole: see below, p.1051.

[83] Atiyah, *Sale of Goods* (10th ed.), p.363.

[84] *e.g.* if a contract for the sale of specific machinery to be delivered in sections is frustrated after payment in full and part delivery.

it clear that the buyer is liable for the whole price and that there is no power to order restitution or to apportion expenses.

S.2(5)(c) can produce some entirely capricious distinctions. The 1943 Act is excluded only where the goods are specific. Suppose that a farmer agrees to sell 200 tons out of a crop to be grown on his land, and the crop is destroyed by events for which he is not responsible.[85] As the goods are not specific,[86] the 1943 Act is not excluded and the farmer can set off his expenses of cultivating the crop[87] against any advance payment made by the buyer. But if an agreement were made to sell an identified parcel of 200 tons after the crop had been lifted, the goods would be specific so that the 1943 Act would be excluded. Hence if the agreement in such a case had provided that the farmer was to put the goods into sacks, and if the goods had been destroyed before this operation had been completed, the farmer would have to return the whole of any advance payment made by the buyer,[88] and have no right to deduct any part of the expenses of packaging.

The 1943 Act is excluded only where the cause of frustration is the perishing of the goods. Thus the Act applies where the contract is frustrated by illegality or requisition.

The reason for these distinctions is far from clear; and one might ask why contracts for the sale of goods were singled out for separate treatment at all. As a matter of abstract justice, there seems to be no reason why the powers of restitution and apportionment provided by the Act should apply to a contract to build a house but not a contract to supply a specific piece of machinery. The main reason for not applying the Act to contracts for the sale of goods is that in such contracts certainty is more important than justice; and the certainty which the rules as to the passing of risk is meant to provide would be disrupted if their effects could be modified by the exercise of the discretionary powers conferred on the courts by the 1943 Act. But on this view contracts for the sale of goods should have been wholly excluded from the operation of the 1943 Act. Their partial exclusion does not satisfy the requirements of either certainty or justice.

(d) COMMERCIAL AGENTS. Under the Regulations which govern contracts between "commercial agents"[89] and their principals, certain rights to "compensation" or "indemnity" accrue to the agent or to his estate on his death or on his serious disability preventing further performance of the contract.[90] The content of these rights differs significantly from the consequences of frustration under the 1943 Act. They can, for example, take account of the agent's loss of commission and of expenses incurred by him

---

[85] See *Howell v Coupland* (1876) 1 Q.B.D. 258; above, p.876.

[86] Mellish L.J. in *Howell v Coupland* at 262 called the potatoes "specific things," but they were clearly not "specific goods" within the definition given in s.61(1) of the Sale of Goods Act 1979 ("identified and agreed upon at the time a contract of sale is made"): see *Re Wait* [1927] 1 Ch. 606 at 631; and *cf.* above, p.875: the agreement was for the sale of an unidentified *part* of a future crop. The point is not affected by the amendment of the definition of "specific goods" (above) by the Sale of Goods (Amendment) Act 1995, s.2(d): that amendment widens the definition so as to include "undivided share, specified *as a fraction or percentage*," of such goods. In the example given in the text, the goods were not specified in this way but as a fixed quantity out of the bulk.

[87] At least if incurred *after* the contract. In *Howell v Coupland* 25 of the 68 acres of the defendant's land at Whaplode had been sown *before* the contract; *quaere* whether such expenditure would be recoverable under the Act.

[88] Under the rule in the *Fibrosa* case [1943] A.C. 32; above, p.911.

[89] Commercial Agents (Council Directive) Regulations 1993 (SI 1993/3053), as amended by SI 1993/3173 and SI 1998/2868; above, p.709.

[90] regs 17 and 18. The effect of frustration by other events is governed under reg.16 by the general law of frustration.

or of loss suffered by him,[91] in circumstances in which no claim in respect of a valuable benefit or allowance in respect of expenses could be made under the Act[92]; and (unlike rights under the Act) they cannot be excluded by the contract.[93]

SECTION 5. JURISTIC BASIS[94]

1. Theories of Frustration

Much discussion is to be found in the cases as to the so-called theoretical or juristic basis of the doctrine of frustration. The first puzzle is why judges have devoted so much attention to this question. Perhaps the reason is that they have felt the need to justify in some way their departure from the doctrine of absolute contracts. The second puzzle is to know exactly what the discussion is about. Two questions have become, perhaps inevitably, intertwined: *why* are contracts frustrated, and *when?*[95] Discussions of the juristic basis of the doctrine of frustration attempt sometimes to justify the doctrine, and sometimes to evolve some general formula for describing the conditions in which it operates. The main theories of frustration found in the cases are as follows.

(1) Implied term

The first theory is that the contract is discharged because it impliedly provides that in the events which have happened it shall cease to bind. This theory is put forward by Lord Loreburn in the *Tamplin* case. "No court has absolving power"[96] but the court will not regard an obligation as absolute if the parties themselves did not intend it to be absolute. If they "must have made their bargain on the footing that a particular thing or state of things would continue to exist . . . a term to that effect will be implied".[97]

In a purely subjective sense this theory is clearly untenable. The implication would have to arise at the time of contracting and at that time the parties are unlikely to have any view as to the effects on the contract of the supervening event; and after the event has occurred, the parties might well have no *common* view as to its effects: for example, one party might well take the view that it should, and the other that it should not, discharge the contract. Even if the parties could reach some agreement on the point, they would probably not agree to total, unconditional discharge. As Lord Wright has said, "they would almost certainly on the one side or the other have sought to introduce reservations or qualifications or compensations".[98]

---

[91] reg.17(3)(a) (subject to a limit of one year's commission under reg.17(4)) and 17(7)).

[92] *e.g.* because no valuable benefit had been obtained by the principal or no stipulation for prepayment to the agent had been made.

[93] reg.19.

[94] McNair, 56 L.Q.R. 173; *Legal Effects of War*, pp.143, *et seq.*

[95] Thus in *Davis Contractors Ltd v Fareham Urban DC* [1956] A.C. 696 at 729 Lord Radcliffe said that "Frustration occurs *whenever*" the changed circumstances make performance "radically different from that which was undertaken." This seems to deal with the second of the questions put in the text; but it has also been regarded as providing an answer to the first: *e.g.* in *National Carriers Ltd v Panalpina (Northern) Ltd* [1981] A.C. 675 at 688, 717.

[96] *Tamplin* case [1916] 2 A.C. 397 at 404.

[97] *ibid.*, at 403.

[98] *Denny, Mott* case [1944] A.C. 265 at 275; *cf. Shell UK Ltd v Lostock Garages Ltd* [1976] 1 W.L.R. 1187 at 1196: *Atisa SA v Aztec AG* [1983] 2 Lloyd's Rep. 579 at 586 (describing the implied term theory as "now rejected."); *FC Shepherd & Co Ltd v Jerrom* [1987] Q.B. 301 at 322; *The Super Servant Two* [1989] 1 Lloyd's Rep. 145 at 154, affirmed [1990] 1 Lloyd's Rep. 1; *The Great Peace* [2002] EWCA Civ 1407; [2002] 4 All E.R. 869, at [73] ("not realistic"); *cf.* Trakman, 46 M.L.R. 39. For a possible power of the court to introduce "reservations" etc. by means of an implied term while holding the contract *not* frustrated, see *The Maira (No.2)* [1985] 1 Lloyd's Rep. 300 at 311 (affirmed on other grounds [1986] 2 Lloyd's Rep. 12).

In fact Lord Loreburn did not put forward a purely subjective version of the implied term theory. He said: "From the nature of the contract it cannot be supposed that the parties *as reasonable men* intended it to be binding on them under such altered conditions. . . . "[99] But in this form, the implied term theory loses its chief attraction, which is that frustration merely gives effect to the intention of the parties themselves. As Lord Radcliffe has said: "By this time it might seem that the parties themselves have become so far disembodied spirits that their actual persons should be allowed to rest in peace. In their place there rises the figure of the fair and reasonable man. And the spokesman of the fair and reasonable man, who represents after all no more than the anthropomorphic conception of justice, is and must be the court itself".[1]

(2) Just solution

Lord Sumner once described the doctrine of frustration as "a device by which the rules as to absolute contracts are reconciled with a special exception which justice demands".[2] Lord Wright in the *Denny, Mott* case, found "the theory of the basis of the rule"[3] in this statement; he added that the doctrine of frustration did not depend on the possibility of implying a term, but was "a substantive and particular rule which the common law has evolved".[4] And in the *Constantine* case he said: "The court is exercising powers, when it decides that a contract is frustrated, in order to achieve a result which is just and reasonable".[5] This "just solution" theory does not purport to explain why the courts sometimes abandon the doctrine of absolute contracts: it simply says that they do so. The theory should not, moreover, be interpreted to mean that the courts can do what they think just whenever a change of circumstances causes hardship to one party: it does not supersede the strict rules which determine the scope of the doctrine of frustration.[6] Nor does it determine the type of relief which can be given. When a contract is frustrated, both parties are at common law discharged, though the "just solution" might be an apportionment of loss.

(3) Foundation of the contract

This theory was stated by Lord Haldane in the *Tamplin* case. "When people enter into a contract which is dependent for the possibility of performance on the continued availability of a specific thing, and that availability comes to an end by reason of circumstances beyond the control of the parties, the contract is *prima facie* regarded as dissolved. . . . Although the words of the stipulation may be such that the mere letter would describe what has occurred, the occurrence itself may yet be of a character and extent so sweeping that the foundation of what the parties are deemed to have had in contemplation has disappeared, and the contract itself has vanished with that foundation".[7] In *WJ Tatem Ltd v Gamboa*[8] Goddard J. regarded this as "the surest ground on which to rest the doctrine of frustration".

---

[99] [1916] 2 A.C. 397 at 404.
[1] *Davis Contractors Ltd v Fareham Urban DC* [1956] A.C. 696 at 728.
[2] *Hirji Mulji v Cheong Yue SS Co Ltd* [1926] A.C. 497 at 510. In the *Bank Line* case [1919] A.C. 435 at 455 he had supported the implied term theory.
[3] [1944] A.C. 265 at 275.
[4] [1944] A.C. 265 at 274.
[5] [1942] A.C. 154 at 186; *cf. National Carriers Ltd v Panalpina (Northern) Ltd* [1981] A.C. 675 at 696; *The Super Servant Two* [1990] 1 Lloyd's Rep. 1 at 8.
[6] See above, pp.867, 881–882. *cf. The Fjord Wind* [1999] 1 Lloyd's Rep. 307 at 328, affirmed [2000] 1 Lloyd's Rep. 191.
[7] [1916] 2 A.C. 397 at 406. Lord Haldane's was a dissenting speech.
[8] [1939] 1 K.B. 132 at 137.

At first sight this theory has the merit of simplicity as it does not involve speculation as to the intention of the parties. It is particularly appropriate where performance depends on the continued availability of a specific thing. But in other cases the metaphor "foundation" is unhelpful. How can one tell whether passage through the Suez Canal is the "foundation" of a charterparty? What is the "foundation" of a contract in which the parties take a deliberate risk as to the continued availability of a specific thing or existence of some state of affairs? Such questions can, in the last resort, only be resolved by construing the contract. If this is so, there is no real difference between the "foundation" theory and the "implied term" theory in its objective sense. Indeed, exponents of one sometimes use the language of the other. Thus in the *Tamplin* case Lord Loreburn, after stating the implied term theory, said that the court "can infer from the nature of the contract and the surrounding circumstances that a condition which is not expressed was a foundation on which the parties contracted".[9]

(4) Construction

All the theories so far stated depend in the last resort on the construction of the contract: to this extent, they "shade into one another".[10] After stating the implied term theory, Lord Loreburn proposed, as the ultimate test: "what, in fact, is the true meaning of the contract?"[11] Similarly, in *Taylor v Caldwell*, Blackburn J. said "the contract is not to be *construed* as a positive contract, but as subject to an *implied condition* that the parties shall be excused in case, before breach, performance becomes impossible. . . ."[12] Construing the contract and implying a term are in these cases only alternative ways of describing the same process. Similarly, the "foundation" theory raises a question of construction whenever it is at all doubtful what the "foundation" of the contract is. And Lord Wright, in the course of stating the "just solution" theory, said: "What happens is that the contract is held on its true construction not to apply at all from the time when the frustrating circumstances supervene".[13] It seems that this is the most satisfactory explanation of the doctrine of frustration.

(5) Failure of consideration

This theory is sometimes used to explain why *both* parties are discharged in the situation (discussed earlier in this Chapter[14]) in which the supervening event makes the performance of only *one* party impossible. Thus destruction of a specific thing may make performance of the *supplier's* obligation impossible; but it has no such effect on the *recipient's* obligation to pay, and it can be said that the latter is discharged by failure of consideration,[15] *i.e.* because he does not receive the performance for which he bargained. In England, however, these cases are explained on the ground that the "common object" of the parties is frustrated.[16] Moreover, in so far as the present theory suggests that the

---

[9] [1916] 2 A.C. 397 at 404.

[10] *National Carriers Ltd v Panalpina (Northern) Ltd* [1981] A.C. 675 at 693.

[11] [1916] A.C. 397 at 404.

[12] (1863) 3 B. & S. 826 at 833.

[13] *Denny, Mott* case [1944] A.C. 265 at 274; *cf. The Eugenia* [1964] 2 Q.B. 226 at 239; *The Siboen and the Sibotre* [1976] 1 Lloyd's Rep. 293 at 235.

[14] See above, pp.893–894.

[15] This explanation is commonly given in the United States: *e.g. Earn Line SS Co v Sutherland SS Co Ltd*, 254 F. 126, 131 (1918); Corbin, *Contracts*, §§1320, 1322; Restatement 2d, *Contracts*, Introductory Note to Chap.11, p.310.

[16] *Hirji Mulji v Cheong Yue SS Co Ltd* [1926] A.C. 497 at 510; above, p.893.

failure of consideration must be total[17] it is plainly wrong since frustration can occur in cases of partial destruction or after part performance; and the theory has for this reason been rejected in the House of Lords.[18]

2. Practical Importance

It is sometimes asked whether the above theoretical discussion has any practical importance. It seems to have none.[19] A number of possibilities must be discussed.

(1) In *W. J. Tatem Ltd v Gamboa* Goddard J. said that the contract would be frustrated although the parties foresaw that the ship would be seized and detained. He even said: "If the foundation of the contract goes, it goes whether or not the parties have made a provision for it".[20] These statements could only be made by an adherent of the "foundation" theory. But the first has been doubted earlier in this Chapter,[21] while the second was qualified later in the judgment: "*Unless the contrary intention is made plain, the law imposes this doctrine of frustration*".[22]

(2) In the *Davis Contractors* case, Lord Reid said that no review was possible of the arbitrator's decision on the "foundation" theory, as the question whether the "foundation" had disappeared was one of fact; while such review was possible on the "implied term" or "construction" theories, as implication and construction were questions of law.[23] But a question of law would be involved even on the "foundation" theory if the question: what is the "foundation"? is itself one of construction. And after the *Tsakiroglou* case[24] it is difficult to argue that the right to review an arbitrator's decision is restricted by any particular theory.

(3) In the *Davis Contractors* case, Lord Reid said that there might be a further practical difference between the "implied term" and "construction" theories. On the latter theory "there is no need to consider what the parties thought or how they or reasonable men in their shoes would have dealt with the new situation if they had foreseen it. The question is whether the contract which they did make is, on its true construction, wide enough to apply to the new situation: if not, then it is at an end".[25] But in construing the contract the court does not wholly disregard the intention of the parties. The court may not have to ask: what would the parties have said, had they thought of the frustrating event? But it does have to ask: in what circumstances did the parties intend the contract to operate? In answering this question, the court no doubt applies an objective test[26]; but it is only after the question has been answered that the intention of the parties becomes irrelevant: that is, it is not necessary to go on and ask whether they would have agreed to discharge or to some compromise. But this question does not arise under the implied term theory either, as frustration at common law always results in total discharge of the contract.

---

[17] For total failure of consideration, see above, p.911; below, p.1049.
[18] *National Carriers Ltd v Panalpina (Northern) Ltd* [1981] A.C. 675 at 687, 702.
[19] This seems to be the view of Lords Wilberforce and Roskill in *National Carriers Ltd v Panalpina (Northern) Ltd* [1981] A.C. 675 at 693, 717. Lord Hailsham (*ibid.* at 687) regards "the theoretical basis of the doctrine as clearly relevant to the point under discussion"; but he does not specify in what respect it is relevant.
[20] [1939] 1 K.B. 132 at 138.
[21] See above, pp.899, n.30, 903.
[22] [1939] 1 K.B. 132 at 139.
[23] *Davis Contractors Ltd v Fareham Urban DC* [1956] A.C. 696 at 720; *cf.* above, pp.333–334.
[24] [1962] A.C. 93; see generally above, p.897.
[25] [1956] A.C. 696 at 721.
[26] *cf.* above, p.198.

3. Frustration and Mistake

Frustration is sometimes compared with mistake of the kind which nullifies consent[27] because the supposed subject-matter of the contract does not exist or is fundamentally different from the subject-matter as it was believed to be. Thus in *Krell v Henry*[28] a contract for the hire of a room overlooking the route of the coronation processions was frustrated when the processions were *later* cancelled; in *Griffith v Brymer*[29] a similar contract was held void for mistake when the processions had *already* been cancelled before the contract was made.

This analogy is interesting and sometimes helpful; but it should not be pressed too far. Mistake and frustration are "different juristic concepts",[30] the one relating to the formation and the other to the discharge of contracts. Their factual bases are different in that mistake requires the parties to entertain an *affirmative belief* in the existence of the subject-matter, or of a state of affairs, when it in fact no longer exists. In cases of frustration, the parties often have no affirmative belief as to the event: they need not *believe* that it *will not* occur. Moreover, events which frustrate a contract would not necessarily make it void for mistake if, unknown to the parties, they had already happened when the contract was made. It is, for example, open to doubt whether *Griffith v Brymer* has survived later developments in the law of mistake.[31] Again, parties may validly agree on a contractual term "requiring one of them to do the impossible",[32] *e.g.* on a term requiring a seller of goods to deliver them from a named ship at a specified port which the ship was incapable of entering. The seller would then be liable for failing to deliver in accordance with that term; but he could be discharged if *after* the time of contracting an event happened which made it impossible for the ship to get into the port, *e.g.* "if a sudden storm had silted up the harbour"[33] there. The law seems to be less ready to hold a contract void for mistake than discharged by frustration, perhaps because it is, in general, easier to be sure of present facts than to foresee future events,[34] or because a contracting party is more likely, on the true construction of the contract, to have undertaken responsibility for an existing, than for an unexpected future, state of affairs.[35]

---

[27] See above, pp.286–298. *Associated Japanese Bank (International) Ltd v Crédit du Nord SA* [1989] 1 W.L.R. 255 at 264 ("related areas"); *William Sindall plc v Cambridgeshire CC* [1994] 1 W.L.R. 1016 at 1039; *Grains & Fourrages SA v Huyton* [1997] 1 Lloyd's Rep. 628 at 630 ("analogous concepts"). See also the reference to *Krell v Henry* [1903] 2 K.B. 740 in *Bell v Lever Bros Ltd* [1932] A.C. 161 at 226 and the words "whether as to existing or future facts" *ibid.* at 226–227; and the reliance on frustration cases in the mistake case of *The Great Peace* [2002] EWCA Civ 1407; [2002] 4 All E.R. 689, at [61]–[76]. This view of the relationship between the two doctrines seems not to have been shared by Blackburn J., whose judgment in *Taylor v Caldwell* (1863) 3 B. & S. 826 is generally regarded as having established the doctrine of frustration. His judgment, given only four years later, in the mistake case of *Kennedy v Panama, etc. Royal Mail Co* (1867) L.R. 2 Q.B. 580 contains no reference to *Taylor v Caldwell* even though that case was cited to the court in *Kennedy's* case at 581. The extent to which frustration cases are a safe guide to the solution of problems of mistake was also qualified in *The Great Peace* itself: see below, n.31.

[28] [1903] 2 K.B. 740.

[29] (1903) 19 T.L.R. 434.

[30] *Constantine* case [1942] A.C. 154 at 186; *cf. Bell v Lever Bros Ltd* [1932] A.C. 161 at 237; *Fibrosa* case [1943] A.C. 32 at 77.

[31] See above, p.288. The view that the test for a mistake which nullifies consent is stricter than that of frustration appears to be supported by *The Great Peace* [2002] EWCA Civ 1407; [2002] 4 All E.R. 689 at [83] (test of frustration "may not be adequate in the context of mistake"). Hence the analogy between the two doctrines drawn in that case in the passages referred to at n.27 above is, at best, imperfect.

[32] *The Epaphus* [1987] 2 Lloyd's Rep. 215 at 218; *The New Prosper* [1991] 2 Lloyd's Rep. 93 at 99.

[33] *The Epaphus* [1987] 2 Lloyd's Rep. 215 at 220. *cf. Bell v Lever Bros Ltd* [1932] A.C. 161 at 218 *per* Lord Atkin, approving the formulation by counsel (Sir John Simon K.C.).

[34] *cf. McAlpine Humberoak Ltd v McDermott International* (1992) 58 Build.L.R. 1.

[35] *The Great Peace* [2002] EWCA Civ 1407; [2002] 4 All E.R. 689 at [85].

The legal effects of the two doctrines are also distinct. At common law, mistake makes a contract void *ab initio*, while frustration discharges it only from the time of the frustrating event.[36] In equity, indeed, the courts at one time claimed a power to set contracts aside for certain kinds of mistake which did not make them void at law.[37] But the Court of Appeal has recently held that there is no such power,[38] and even if this view were to be rejected by the House of Lords and the equitable jurisdiction were to be again recognised, its operation would still differ from that of frustration in two ways. First, the equitable power in cases of mistake was regarded as discretionary while frustration discharges a contract automatically, by operation of law, without any scope for judicial discretion; frustration moreover results in total discharge, while the equitable jurisdiction was to set the contract aside on terms.[39] It is, finally, clear from the wording[40] of the Law Reform (Frustrated Contracts) Act 1943 that the powers of adjustment conferred by that Act apply only to discharge by supervening (and not to invalidity on the ground of antecedent) events.[41]

---

[36] See above, pp.286, 909.
[37] See above, p.319.
[38] *The Great Peace* [2002] EWCA Civ 1407; [2002] 4 All E.R. 689.
[39] See above, pp.320, 909.
[40] s.1(1) ("where a contract . . . *has become* impossible of performance or *been* otherwise frustrated").
[41] Somewhat similar adjustments could perhaps have been made in the exercise of the former equitable jurisdiction to rescind on terms contracts affected by mistake not sufficiently fundamental to avoid the contracts at law. But in *The Great Peace* [2002] EWCA Civ 1407; [2002] 4 All E.R. 689 it was held that this jurisdiction no longer existed (above, pp.319–320) and recognised at [161] that the 1943 Act did not apply to cases of mistakes making contracts void.

CHAPTER TWENTY-ONE

REMEDIES[1]

A BREACH of contract is a civil wrong. To break a contract can also occasionally be a criminal offence[2]; and some statutes penalise dangerous or deceptive conduct which may amount[3] to a breach of contract. Conviction in such cases makes the offender liable not only to punishment, but also to an order requiring him to pay compensation for any personal injury, loss or damage resulting from the offence.[4] In most cases, however, a breach of contract will involve only civil liability; and our sole concern in this Chapter will be with remedies available in civil proceedings. In such proceedings, the injured party may claim either specific relief, or damages or restitution.

A claim for specific relief is one for the actual performance of the defaulting party's undertaking. Where that undertaking is one to pay a sum of money, a claim for specific relief is made by the common law action for an agreed sum; where the undertaking is one to do some other act, or to forbear from doing something, a claim for specific relief is made by the equitable remedies of specific performance or injunction. A claim for damages is one for compensation in money for the fact that the claimant has not received the performance for which he bargained. This is the remedy most frequently discussed in the reported cases, and the bulk of this Chapter is therefore devoted to it. A person who has performed his part of the contract but has not received the agreed counter-performance may, finally, claim back his performance or its reasonable value. These restitutionary remedies are not confined to cases of breach of contract; but as they are often available in such cases they can conveniently be considered in this Chapter.

SECTION 1. DAMAGES

The action for damages is always available, as of right, when a contract has been broken. It should, from this point of view, be contrasted with claims for specific relief and for restitution, which are either subject to the discretion of the court or only available if certain conditions (to be discussed later in this Chapter) are satisfied. An action for damages can succeed even though the victim has not suffered any loss: in that event, it will result in an award of nominal damages. The effect of such an award may simply be to establish what the rights and liabilities of the parties under a contract are, though for

---

[1] Beale, *Remedies for Breach of Contract*; Treitel, *Remedies for Breach of Contract: a Comparative Account*; Harris, Campbell and Halson, *Remedies in Contract and Tort* (2nd ed); Burrows, *Remedies for Torts and Breach of Contract*, 2nd ed.

[2] For example, cutting off a tenant's gas supply may be an offence: *McCall v Abelesz* [1976] Q.B. 585 (as to which see below p.988, n.98); the offence may be committed even though the tenant is not a contractual tenant, so that there is no breach of contract: Protection from Eviction Act 1977, s.1(1); *R. v Yuthiwattana* (1985) Cr.App.R. 55; *R. v Burke* [1991] 1 A.C. 135; *cf.* National Minimum Wage Act 1998, s.31. See further, Treitel in *Essays in Memory of Sir Rupert Cross*, pp.82–92.

[3] *e.g.* Trade Descriptions Act 1968, s.1; Consumer Protection Act 1987, Pt.II: under these provisions, offences may be committed even though no contract is ever made or broken. Sometimes, the law also provides administrative remedies in respect of conduct that may amount to a breach of contract: *e.g.* under Sex Discrimination Act 1975, s.67(1)(a).

[4] Powers of Criminal Courts (Sentencing) Act 2000, s.130; *cf.* also Consumer Protection Act 1987, s.41 and p.369, above.

this purpose the action for a declaration now provides a more convenient remedy. Generally the victim will claim damages for a substantial loss; and our concern is with the law governing the award of such damages. We shall consider, first, the general principles which govern awards of damages; secondly, the way in which damages are assessed or quantified; thirdly, certain rules limiting the damages which can be recovered; and finally, contractual provisions purporting to establish in advance the amount that can be recovered (or retained) by the victim.

1. General Principles

(1) Damages are compensatory

Damages are awarded to compensate the claimant.[5] Three aspects of this principle require discussion at this point.

(a) LOSS TO CLAIMANT[6] THE CRITERION. As a general rule, damages are based on loss to the claimant and not on gain to the defendant[7]; but there are significant exceptions to this rule.

(i) *Illustrations of the general rule*. In a Scottish case,[8] a financier broke a contract to invest £15,000 in the business of a timber merchant and instead invested the same sum in a distillery. It was held that the timber merchant's damages were based on the loss to his business and not on the much larger profits which the financier had derived from the distillery. Similarly, where a shipowner in breach of contract withdraws his ship from a charterparty, damages are based on the charterer's loss, and not on any profit that the shipowner may make from other employment of the ship.[9] Likewise, an employee who left in breach of contract to take up a better paid job would not be liable to account to his employer for the extra pay, but only to compensate him for any loss that he may have suffered. The same principle again applies where a person who has agreed to sell goods for future delivery for £x fails to deliver because he has disposed elsewhere of the goods for £x + 100. If the buyer can in fact gets goods of the same description for £x or less at the time fixed for delivery, he will have suffered no loss and will get no (substantial) damages: it is irrelevant that the seller has, in a sense, made a profit of £100 out of the breach.[10] It also follows from the general rule that damages are not awarded merely on the ground that the defendant has by the breach saved himself expense. Where, for example, the claimant had bargained and paid for a deluxe delivery service but had received only a standard service, it was held that damages were based, not on the extra amount paid for the former service, but on the difference between the market value of

---

[5] *Tai Hing Cotton Mill Ltd v Kamsing Knitting Factory* [1979] A.C. 95 at 104.

[6] For exceptional cases in which the claimant can recover damages in respect of a third party's loss see above, pp.593 *et seq.*

[7] *Tito v Waddell (No.2)* [1977] Ch.106 at 332; *The Solholt* [1983] 1 Lloyd's Rep. 605 at 608; *cf. The Ypatianna* [1987] 2 Lloyd's Rep. 286 at 297. The Law Commission, in its report on *Aggravated, Exemplary and Restitutionary Damages* Law Com. No.247 (1997), para.6.2.6 does not propose any legislative change in either the general common law rule or the exceptions to be discussed below in cases of breach of contract. The rest of the report is not to be implemented: see *Kuddus v Chief Constable of the Leicestershire Constabulary* [2001] UKHL 29; [2002] 2 A.C. 122, at [35]. See also Jones, 99 L.Q.R. 443, Friedmann, 80 Col.L.Rev. 504, Farnsworth, 94 Yale L.J. 1339; Birks, [1987] L.M.C.L.Q. 421; Friedmann, 104 L.Q.R. 383; Birks, 1990–1991 Butterworth Lectures 55; *cf.* Stoljar, 2 J.C.L. 1.

[8] *Teacher v Calder* (1889) 1 F.(H.L.) 39; see also *Transocean Maritime Agencies SA Monegasque v Pettit* 1997 S.C.L.R. 534.

[9] *The Siboen and the Sibotre* [1976] 1 Lloyd's Rep. 293 at 337.

[10] *Acmé Mills v Johnson* 133 S.W. 784 (1911); *cf. The Solholt* [1983] 1 Lloyd's Rep. 605, where the buyer's damages were nominal as he had failed to mitigate (below, p.978) and it was irrelevant that the seller (who was in breach) had made a profit on resale.

what was bargained for and what had been provided. It was up to the claimant to prove what this difference was, and in the absence of such proof he could recover no more than nominal damages.[11]

(ii) *Exceptions.* In some situations, there is no doubt that a contract breaker must hand over to the victim any gain resulting from the breach. If, for example, the subject-matter of a sale is land, the vendor is, after the conclusion of the contract, considered to hold the land as trustee for the purchaser; and if the vendor wrongfully resells the land to a third party, the purchaser is entitled to the proceeds of that sale, even though they may exceed his loss.[12] Again, an account of profits may be ordered against a person who wrongfully uses another's trade secret or confidential information[13]; and this remedy is, no doubt, available where the wrongful use amounts to a breach of a contract of (for example) employment.[14] Where a breach of contract amounts also to breach of a fiduciary obligation, damages may similarly be based on the defendant's profit.[15] For example, an agent who commits a breach of his fiduciary duty by taking a bribe,[16] or by selling his own property to a principal, when he has been employed to buy for him, is liable to account for any profit made in this way.[17]

The defendant's profit is also relevant where, in breach of contract, he uses, or interferes with, another's property without, at first sight, inflicting on the latter any loss. In one case[18] the buyer of a floating dock failed, in breach of contract, to remove it from its berth. He argued that no substantial damages should be awarded because the sellers would not have made any use of the berth. Lord Denning rejected the argument saying that "the test of the measure of damages is not what the plaintiffs have lost, but what benefit the defendant obtained by having the use of the berth". But the actual award was based on the fair rental value of the berth, and can be explained on the basis that the plaintiffs lost *the chance* of reletting it. It seems that if the defendant had made a *greater* profit, he would not have been liable for it[19]; conversely, he is liable for the reasonable rental value even though the profit that he has actually made from the premises is less.[20]

(iii) *Borderline cases.* One group of cases which gives rise to difficulty in the present context concerns breaches of contractual restrictions on the development or use of land.

---

[11] *White Arrow Express Ltd v Lamey's Distribution Ltd* [1995] N.L.J. 1504. According to *Samson & Samson v Proctor* [1975] N.Z.L.R. 665, a builder may be liable to his customer for expenses saved through failure to comply with the agreed specifications; but no reason is given for this departure from the general rule that damages are based on loss to the claimant.

[12] See *Lake v Bayliss* [1974] 1 W.L.R. 1073. *cf.* also Housing Act 1988, ss.27 and 28(1), under which damages in tort of wrongful eviction are based on benefit to landlord: *Tagro v Cafane* [1991] 1 W.L.R. 378, 385–387; such damages are not recoverable from the landlord's agent: *Sampson v Wilson* [1996] Ch. 39.

[13] *Peter Pan Mfg Corp v Corsets Silhouette Ltd* [1964] 1 W.L.R. 96; *Attorney-General v Guardian Newspapers (No.2)* [1990] A.C. 109 at 262, 288. *cf.* Law Com. No.110, paras 4.86 and 6.114(2)(b).

[14] *cf. Printers & Finishers Ltd v Holloway* [1965] 1 W.L.R. 1.

[15] *Mathew v TM Sutton Ltd* [1994] 1 W.L.R. 1455; *Tang Man Sit v Capacious Investments Ltd* [1996] A.C. 514 (where the claimant elected to claim damages for breach of trust rather than an account of profits); *cf. Nottingham University v Fishel* [2000] I.C.R. 1462 at 1489.

[16] *Attorney-General of Hong Kong v Reid* [1994] 1 A.C. 324; above, p.746.

[17] *Regier v Campbell-Stuart* [1939] Ch. 766; *cf.* now Estate Agents Act 1979, s.21 (above, p.746).

[18] *Penarth Dock Engineering Co Ltd v Pound* [1963] 1 Lloyd's Rep. 359; *cf.* in tort, *Swordheath Properties Ltd v Tabet* [1979] 1 W.L.R. 285; *Ministry of Defence v Ashman* [1993] 2 E.G.L.R. 102; *Ministry of Defence v Thompson* [1993] 2 E.G.L.R. 107; *Kuwait Airways Corp v Iraqi Airways Corp* [2002] UKHL 19; [2002] 1 All E.R. (Comm) 843, at [87] ("user principle") and see the payment which a court may order a person to make on obtaining an "access order" under Access to Neighbouring Land Act 1992, s.2(5)(a) (gain to applicant) and (b) (loss to respondent).

[19] *cf. Strand Electric and Engineering Co Ltd v Brisford Entertainments Ltd* [1952] 2 Q.B. 246 at 252, 256.

[20] *Tang Man Sit v Capacious Investments Ltd* [1996] A.C. 514 (above, n.15).

In the *Wrotham Park*[21] case, a developer had acquired land subject to a restrictive covenant which had been imposed for the benefit of an adjoining estate. In breach of the covenant, the developer built houses on the land; this did not diminish the value of the estate, but its owners nevertheless recovered substantial damages for the breach, amounting, not to the whole of the developer's profits on the sale of the houses, but to 5 per cent of that profit. This percentage was said to represent "such sum of money as might reasonably have been demanded by the plaintiffs from [the defendant] as a quid pro quo for releasing the covenant".[22] But a different result was reached in the later *Bredero Homes*[23] case, where a developer had bought land from two local authorities under a contract providing that no more than 72 houses were to be built on the land, and then, in breach of that contract, built 77 houses there. The breach caused no loss to the vendors and the Court of Appeal held that the defendant was liable for no more than nominal damages. At the same time, the *Wrotham Park* case was treated as having been correctly decided,[24] and the question arises, how the two cases are to be reconciled.

One possibility is to say that the award in the *Wrotham Park* was based on restitutionary rather than on compensatory principles,[25] that such restitutionary principles apply only if there is either a fiduciary relationship or an invasion of the claimant's proprietary interests, that neither of these conditions was satisfied in the *Bredero Homes* case, while the second may have been satisfied in the *Wrotham Park* case.[26] But the view that the award in this case was based on restitutionary grounds was rejected in *Jaggard v Sawyer*[27] where the compensatory principle stated in the *Wrotham Park* case was reaffirmed and damages were awarded on that principle (*i.e.*, for the loss of a bargaining opportunity[28]) against defendants who, in breach of covenant, used part of the garden of their house in a private road to obtain access to a house which they had built on adjoining land. The question then arises why no similar damages were available to the claimants in the *Bredero Homes* case. A possible answer to this question is that the damages in the *Wrotham Park* case were awarded, not at common law, but in equity, in lieu of the injunction[29] which the claimants sought as soon as they became aware of the breach but which the court in its discretion refused to grant.[30] In the *Bredero Homes* case, by contrast, no attempt was ever made to restrain the breach by injunction; five years went by after the breach before any proceedings in respect of it were taken; during that time the defendants had disposed of all the houses so that an injunction was no longer available against them[31]; and the only claim made was one for damages at common law.

---

[21] *Wrotham Park Estate Co v Parkside Homes Ltd* [1974] 1 W.L.R. 798, approved in *Stoke-on-Trent City Council v W & J Wass Ltd* [1988] 1 W.L.R. 1406. *cf. Bracewell v Appleby* [1975] Ch. 408 (tort); *General Tire & Rubber Co v Firestone Tyre & Rubber Co* [1975] 1 W.L.R. 819 (patent infringement—a claim for an account of profits was not pursued); Sharpe and Waddams, 1 O.J.L.S. 290.

[22] [1974] 1 W.L.R. 798, at 815.

[23] *Surrey CC v Bredero Homes Ltd* [1993] 1 W.L.R. 1361; Birks, 109 L.Q.R. 518; O'Dair, I.R.L.R. 31.

[24] This is clear from the judgments of Steyn and Rose L.JJ., while Dillon L.J. does not expressly dissent from this view.

[25] [1993] 1 W.L.R. 1361 at 1369–1370, *per* Steyn L.J.

[26] In that the defendant had violated a restrictive covenant that ran with the land; this could be described as a property interest "in the broadest sense:" [1993] 1 W.L.R. at 1371.

[27] [1995] 1 W.L.R. 269; followed in *Gafford v Graham* (1998) 76 P.& C.R. D18.

[28] For use (with approval) of this phrase, see *Attorney-General v Blake* [2001] 1 A.C. 268 at 281. The argument that the damages in *Jaggard v Sawyer* should have been nominal was, paradoxically, put forward by *the claimant*, whose object was to show that damages were an inadequate remedy and that she should therefore be granted specific relief: *cf.* below, p.1022.

[29] See below, p.1046.

[30] [1993] 1 W.L.R. 1361 at 1336, this was also the reasoning (expressly approved *ibid.* at 1368) of Ferris J. at first instance: [1992] 3 All E.R. 303.

[31] *Jaggard v Sawyer*, above, at 290. Specific relief would be unavailable on the principle stated at pp.1028–1029 below.

At first sight, the difficulty with this explanation is that the House of Lords has, since the *Wrotham Park* case, held that the principles governing the assessment of damages are the same whether the award is made in equity (in lieu of specific enforcement) or at common law.[32] This difficulty can be overcome by arguing that it is only when damages are claimed in respect of the same breach that the principles of assessment are the same at common law and in equity, and that, while equity can award damages in respect of future breaches which it has jurisdiction to restrain[33] (as in the *Wrotham Park* case), there was no similar possibility in the *Bredero Homes* case[34] where no further breaches could be committed by the defendants as they no longer owned any of the houses. It is also arguable that the very fact that an injunction was no longer available in the *Bredero Homes* case made the claimant's bargaining opportunity worthless and so justified the conclusion that damages at common law should be no more than nominal.[35] This reasoning, however, seems to be based on the assumption that the value of the bargaining opportunity is to be assessed as at the time of the hearing; *prima facie* the more appropriate time for assessing that value would seem to be the time of breach.[36]

In *Attorney-General v Blake* (to be more fully discussed below) three members of the majority of the House of Lords accordingly took the view that "so far as the *Bredero Homes Ltd* decision is inconsistent with the approach adopted in the *Wrotham Park* case, the latter is to be preferred".[37] This seems to mean that, in principle, damages for loss of claimants' bargaining opportunity could now be claimed on facts such as those of the *Bredero Homes* case; but the guarded nature of the statement leaves open the two questions (1) how much that opportunity would have been worth (given that an injunction was no longer available), and (2) by reference to what time that opportunity should be valued. If the relevant time is (as suggested above) the time of breach, then the effect of the views expressed in *Blake's* case on the *Bredero Homes* case would be to reverse the outcome in the latter case.

(iv) *Discretionary account of profits.* The compensatory principle was recognised but a discretionary exception to it was created in *Attorney-General v Blake*.[38] While employed as a member of the security services, Blake passed secret information to agents of the Soviet Union, in breach not only of the terms of his employment but also of the Official Secrets Act 1911; he was convicted of offences under that Act and sentenced to 42 years' imprisonment. He escaped from prison and fled to Moscow where, over 20 years later, he entered into an agreement with an English publisher for the publication of his autobiography. Although the information in the book was no longer confidential[39] at the time of the delivery of his manuscript and of the publication of the book, the disclosure of the information amounted to both a further offence under the 1911 Act and a further breach of Blake's contract with the Crown. This breach, however, caused no material loss to the Crown in respect of which compensatory damages could have been recovered and, after publication, the remedy by way of injunction, which could have been sought before

---

[32] *Johnson v Agnew* [1980] A.C. 367, below, p.1048.

[33] See below, p.1046.

[34] Even at common law, damages for future breaches can be recovered in cases of accepted anticipatory breach, but this possibility was not relevant in the *Bredero Homes* case, where the only breaches committed by the defendant lay in the past.

[35] *Jaggard v Sawyer* above, p.291.

[36] *cf.* below, p.959.

[37] [2001] 1 A.C. 268 at 283, *per* Lord Nicholls with whose speech Lords Goff and Browne-Wilkinson agreed; *cf. ibid.* at 298, *per* Lord Hobhouse dissenting; contrast *ibid.* at 291 *per* Lord Steyn.

[38] [2001] 1 A.C. 268.

[39] So that the case did not fall directly within the exception (to the general rule that damages are compensatory) referred to on p.928 above at n.13.

then, was no longer available; nor could the case be brought within any of the qualifications of the compensatory principle which have been described above.[40] The House of Lords nevertheless held, by a majority, that where (as in *Blake's* case) damages were not a "sufficient"[41] remedy, the court should "exceptionally" be able to "grant the discretionary remedy of requiring a defendant to account to the plaintiff for benefits derived from his breach of contract".[42] This development was based on the analogy of the discretionary remedies by way of specific relief in equity, which are available also where damages are not an adequate (or the most appropriate)[43] remedy for breach. Two questions arise in relation to such discretionary remedies: when does the discretion *exist* and when will it be *exercised?* In relation to the equitable remedies by way of specific relief, the uncertainty that could arise from their discretionary nature is much reduced by the accumulation of case-law which not only indicates which types of contracts can (and which cannot) be specifically enforced[44] but also lists factors to be taken into account in determining when the discretion to order specific relief will be exercised[45]: the overriding principle is that this discretion is "to be governed so far as possible by fixed rules and principles".[46] In relation to the new discretion created by *Blake's* case, there can be no guidance on the first of these points since that discretion applies to breaches of contract generally[47]; and with regard to the second point Lord Nicholls says that "no fixed rules can be prescribed"[48] with regard to the exercise of the discretion. He is prepared only to give the "general guide" that this depends on "whether the plaintiff had a legitimate interest in preventing the defendant's profit-making activity"[49]; but this formula does little to reduce the resulting uncertainty, since every contracting party can be said to have a "legitimate interest" in the performance of a contractual promise made to him.[50] Some further guidance of a negative nature is, however, provided. An account of profits is not to be available merely because the defendant is guilty of either "skimped performance"[51] (the difference in value between what was and what should have been provided being the normal measure of damages in such a case)[52] or of breach of a negative obligation "by doing the very thing he has promised not to do"[53]; nor merely because the breach was "cynical and deliberate" or "enabled the defendant to enter into a more profitable contact elsewhere"[54]; nor merely because, by entering into such a contract "the defendant put it out of his power to perform his contract with the plaintiff".[55] But as no positive indications are given as to when the new discretion to

---

[40] Under headings (ii) and (iii) on pp.928–929 above.
[41] [2001] 1 A.C. at 285.
[42] *ibid.*, at 284–285 *per* Lord Nicholls, who (*ibid.* 284) preferred the phrase "account of profits" to "the unhappy expression 'restitutionary damages'".
[43] See below, p.1025; *cf.* the use by Lord Nicholls in *Blake's* case of the phrase "most appropriate" at 285.
[44] See below, pp.1029–1037.
[45] See below, pp.1026–1029.
[46] See below, p.1026.
[47] It goes beyond the situations referred to at n.40 above.
[48] [2001] 1 A.C. 268, at 285.
[49] *ibid.*, at 285.
[50] In this respect, the "legitimate interest" in receiving performance differs from that in continuing performance, referred to in a different context at p.1017 below.
[51] [2001] 1 A.C. 268 at 286.
[52] *White Arrow Express Ltd v Lamey's Distribution Ltd* [1995] N.L.J. 1504, above, pp.927–928.
[53] [2001] 1 A.C. 268, at 286. In the Court of Appeal "restitutionary damages" (see n.42, above) were said to be available in this situation and in cases of "skimped performance". These suggestions were doubted in the 10th edition of this book at p.869 and were rejected in the House of Lords not only by Lord Nicholls (above) but also by Lord Steyn at 291.
[54] [2001] 1 A.C. 268 at 286.
[55] *ibid.*

order an account of profits *will* be exercised, the creation of that discretion remains a source of considerable uncertainty.[56]

With regard to this uncertainty, a number of points can, however, be made in relation to *Blake's* case. First, the facts of that case can fairly be described as not merely exceptional, but as extreme; and it is hard to take issue with the outcome on those facts. Secondly, on such facts there would normally be other ways (not available on the special facts) of stripping the wrongdoer of his profits: *e.g.* by a confiscation order[57] if Blake had at the relevant time been amenable to the jurisdiction of the English criminal courts, or by an injunction if that remedy had been sought in time. Thirdly, in the factual context the argument in favour of certainty lacks its usual force. Certainty in rules of contract law is intended to enable parties to *rely* on such rules in regulating their conduct; and there is little plausibility and even less merit in the argument that, in deciding to break his contract with the Crown, Blake relied (or should have been encouraged to rely) on the rule that damages were compensatory. But although these points may justify the actual decision in *Blake's* case, they cannot entirely dispell the concern caused by the ill-defined discretionary exception to the compensatory principle that was there created. Lord Hobhouse, in his dissent, referred to the "disruptive"[58] consequences that could follow from attempts "to extend the decision of the present exceptional case to commercial situations so as to introduce restitutionary rights beyond those presently recognised by the law of restitution".[59] Such consequences could, for example, follow where a party to a commercial contract decided to commit a breach of it with a view to making a profit even after he has compensated the other party for his loss. It is hard to see why in such a case the law should "confer a windfall on the injured party"[60] by awarding such profits to him in excess of his loss or, *a fortiori*, why it should make such an award where he has suffered no loss at all. It seems from the terms of Lord Nicholls' speech that the discretion created in *Blake's* case is not intended to extend to cases of this kind[61]; and it is further to be hoped that Lord Hobhouse's warning will be heeded and that the discretion will be confined within narrow limits.

One restriction on the scope of that discretion is inherent in its nature. It applies only where the defendant has made an actual profit and so does not extend to cases in which the defendant has made a losing bargain and his breach merely avoids or reduces that loss by an amount exceeding the compensatory damages recoverable by the injured party.

(b) WHAT CONSTITUTES LOSS. For the present purpose, loss includes any harm to the person or property of the claimant, and any other injury to his economic position. The question to what extent harm to the person includes injury to feelings is discussed later in this Chapter.[62] Harm to property covers damage to or destruction of particular things, while injury to the claimant's economic position includes any amount by which he is worse off than he would have been if the contract had been performed. For example, if a seller in breach of contract fails to deliver the goods, or to deliver them on time, the buyer *prima facie* suffers loss in not having the goods, or in not having them at the agreed time.

---

[56] *cf.* Beatson, 118 L.Q.R. 377.
[57] See above, p.502.
[58] [2001] 1 A.C. 268 at 299. *cf. Surrey CC v Bredero Homes Ltd* [1993] 1 W.L.R. 1361 at 1370.
[59] *ibid.*, at 299; Lord Hobhouse appears to have in mind cases of the kind referred to at n.40 above.
[60] *Surrey CC v Bredero Homes Ltd*, above, at 1370.
[61] See above, at n.54.
[62] See below, pp.987–991.

(i) *Overall position taken into account.* In determining whether the victim has suffered loss, his overall position is taken into account.[63] Relevant factors include any benefits which he may have obtained under the broken contract, and his release from obligations under it. If, for example, a buyer has not yet paid and is released from his obligation to do so by the seller's wrongful failure to deliver, his loss will *prima facie* be the value of the goods less the price; and if he has agreed to pay no more than the goods are worth he may have suffered no loss at all. Whether this is indeed the position may turn on disputed questions of fact and it is then up to the defendant to show that the claimant's position is no worse than it would have been if there had been no breach.[64]

The court will similarly take the claimant's overall position into account in determining the basis on which damages are to be assessed: it will not generally order the defendant to pay an amount which will actually make the claimant's position better than it would have been if the contract had been performed. The principle is illustrated by *Phillips v Ward*[65] where a surveyor in breach of contract failed to draw his client's attention to the fact that the roof timbers of a house, which the latter was about to buy, were rotten. It was held that the client was not entitled to damages based on the cost of making the defects good. Such an award would put him into a better position than that in which he would have been if the contract had not been broken; for it would enable him to have a new roof with new timbers, which would be less expensive to maintain than an old roof with sound timbers. Hence the client was entitled to recover only the difference between the price that he paid and the value of the house when he bought it[66]; or the difference between the price actually paid and that which would have been paid if the surveyor had made his report with due care.[67]

The principle that the claimant's overall position should not be made better than it would have been, if the contract had not been broken, is, however, subject to a number of qualifications. First, it is not inflexibly applied where costs are actually incurred by the claimant in remedying the breach.[68] In *Harbutt's "Plasticine" Ltd v Wayne Tank & Pump Co Ltd*[69] the claimant's factory was burnt down as a result of the defendant's breach of contract. It was held that the claimant could recover the cost of rebuilding the factory without making any allowance for the fact that he would then have a new (and therefore

---

[63] *e.g. The Baleares* [1990] 2 Lloyd's Rep. 130 (and see [1991] 2 All E.R. 110). *cf.* below, p.980.

[64] See *Featherstone v Wilkinson* (1873) L.R. 8 Ex. 122, as explained by Steyn L.J. in *The Baleares* [1993] 1 Lloyd's Rep. 215 at 232–234.

[65] [1956] 1 W.L.R. 471.

[66] See *Perry v Sidney Phillips & Son* [1982] 1 W.L.R. 1297 at 1305, 1306; Burrows, 47 M.L.R. 357; *Treml v Ernest W Gibson & Partners* (1984) 272 E.G. 68 *Westlake v Bracknell DC* (1987) 19 H.L.R. 375 (where it is not clear whether the damages were awarded in contract or in tort); *Cross v David Martin & Mortimer* [1989] 1 E.G.L.R. 154; *Stewart v Rapley* [1989] 1 E.G.L.R. 159; *Watts v Morrow* [1991] 1 W.L.R. 1421; *Heatley v William Brown* [1992] 1 E.G.L.R. 289; *Gardner v Marsh & Parsons* [1997] 1 W.L.R. 489; *Shaw v Fraser Southwell* [1999] Lloyd's Rep. P.N. 633; *Berry v Newport BC* [2000] 2 E.G.L.R. 26. Where the client pays *more* than the valuation, such excess may be irrecoverable: see *Lucas v Ogden* [1988] 2 E.G.L.R. 176.

[67] *Perry v Sidney Phillips & Son* [1982] 1 W.L.R. 1297 at 1302; on the facts of this case the two formulae stated in the text would have yielded the same result, for the actual value of the property was assumed to be the amount that the buyer would have paid, if the surveyor's report had been accurate. In appropriate circumstances, further damages may be recoverable for such a breach. Thus in *Patel v Hooper & Jackson* [1999] 1 All E.R. 992 the defect which the surveyor's report should have revealed made the house uninhabitable, and the client recovered the reasonable costs of extricating himself from the transaction and damages in respect of discomfort suffered in the course of this process (*cf.* above, p.987).

[68] See further, p.945, below.

[69] [1970] 1 Q.B. 447, followed on this point in *Bacon v Cooper Metals Ltd* [1982] 1 All E.R. 397, and *Dominion Mosaics & Tile Co Ltd v Trafalgar Trucking Co Ltd* [1990] 2 All E.R. 246, though overruled on another point in *Photo Production Ltd v Securicor Transport Ltd* [1980] A.C. 827.

more valuable) factory. The case can be explained on the ground that the claimant had no reasonable alternative but to rebuild, or that he did so in order to mitigate his loss.[70] Secondly, the principle was modified where a client had suffered loss in consequence of bad investment advice given by the defendant and had, before suffering the loss, spent some of the income produced by the investments on living expenses. This expenditure yielded no permanent benefit to the client and did not have to be brought into account since the very object of the contract was to produce an increased income for the client, so that it was foreseeable that he might spend that income, or part of it, in a way that left no product of permanent benefit to him.[71] Thirdly, the principle in *Phillips v Ward* does not require the court to take into account benefits derived by the claimant under some contract with the defendant, other than the one which has been broken. Thus if the claimant makes two contracts with the defendant, any profit made by the claimant in consequence of the performance of one of those contracts will not have to be brought into account in assessing his damages in respect of the breach of the other.[72]

(ii) *Intended use of subject-matter.* It is sometimes argued that a claimant has suffered no loss because, even if the contract had been performed, he would not have used the subject-matter profitably, or at all. In one case,[73] contractors were sued for agreed damages[74] for delay in delivering warships to the Spanish government. The delay being *prima facie* a source of loss, it was held to be no defence that warships are not put to profitable use, or that the ships, if delivered on time, would probably have been sunk in a naval battle in which the fleet which they were to have joined suffered defeat. However, his intended use of the subject-matter may affect the amount of his loss: this is, for example, the case where a buyer of goods has made a subsale of the very goods comprised in the original sale.[75] Similarly, by statute a landlord cannot recover damages for breach of his tenant's obligation to repair if the tenant can prove that the landlord was going to demolish the premises.[76]

(c) BREACH HAVING NO ADVERSE EFFECT. A further consequence of the compensatory principle is that the claimant cannot recover substantial damages if the breach has not adversely affected his position; for "damages are designed to compensate for an established loss and not to provide a gratuitous benefit to the aggrieved party".[77] Another way of putting the point is that "A breach of contract may cause a loss but is not iself a loss in any meaningful sense".[78] This aspect of the principle is most readily illustrated by the case in which a seller of goods wrongfully fails to deliver on a falling market. If the buyer has not paid and if, at the time fixed for delivery, he can buy substitute goods more cheaply elsewhere, the breach will *prima facie* have had no adverse effect on him, so that he will not be entitled to substantial damages. Similarly, a shipowner cannot get substantial damages for breach of the charterer's obligation to load if he finds alternative and more profitable employment for the ship.[79] Nor can a buyer recover substantial

---

[70] See below, p.978.
[71] *R. v Investors Compensation Scheme, Ex p. Bowden* [1995] Q.B. 107, reversed on other grounds [1996] A.C. 261.
[72] *Brown v KMR Services Ltd* [1995] 4 All E.R. 598 at 640.
[73] *Clydebank Engineering Co v Don Jose Ramos Isquierdo y Castaneda* [1905] A.C. 6.
[74] See below, pp.999 *et seq.*
[75] *Re R & H Hall Ltd and WH Pim Jr & Co's Arbitration* (1928) 139 L.T. 50; below, p.949.
[76] Landlord and Tenant Act 1927, s.18(1).
[77] *Ruxley Electronics and Construction Co Ltd v Forsyth* [1996] A.C. 344 at 357.
[78] *Alfred McAlpine Construction Ltd v Panatown Ltd* [2001] 1 A.C. 518 at 534.
[79] *Staniforth v Lyall* (1830) 7 Bing. 169.

damages merely because the seller delivers goods which are not of the contract description if they are in fact no less valuable than goods which are of the contract description.[80]

The same principle was applied in *Ford v White*[81] where the claimants bought a house and adjoining plot for £6,350 after being advised by their solicitors that they could build on the plot. The solicitors had negligently and in breach of contract overlooked a covenant against building on the plot. The property subject to the covenant was in fact worth £6,350 but it would have been worth an extra £1,250 if there had been no covenant. It was held that the solicitors were not liable for this sum.[82] The claimants would not have bought at all, had they been told of the covenant (so that they did not lose the chance of a good bargain); nor had they paid more for the property than it was actually worth.

So far it has been assumed that the claimant has suffered no loss at all. He similarly cannot recover in respect of a loss which he does suffer if he would have suffered the same loss, even if there had been no breach. This situation is discussed later in this Chapter[83]; it would have arisen in *Ford v White* if the property had, because of the covenant, been worth less than £6,350, but it had been shown that the claimants would nevertheless have paid that sum for it, even with knowledge of the covenant.[84]

(d) NO PUNITIVE DAMAGES. Punitive (or exemplary) damages can be awarded in certain tort cases.[85] The purpose of such damages is not to compensate the claimant, nor even to strip the defendant of his profit,[86] but to express the court's disapproval of the defendant's conduct,[87] *e.g.* where he has deliberately committed a wrong (such as defamation[88]) with a view to profit.

As a general rule punitive damages cannot be awarded in a purely contractual action,[89] since the object of such an action is not to punish the defendant but to compensate the claimant.[90] Punitive damages are not available even though the breach was committed deliberately and with a view to profit. If the court is particularly outraged by the

---

[80] *Taylor v Bank of Athens* (1922) 27 Com.Cas. 142.

[81] [1964] 1 W.L.R. 885.

[82] It seems that, if the property had been resold, the solicitors would have been liable for expenses incurred in connection with, and loss suffered on, resale: *cf. County Personnel (Employment Agency) Ltd v Pulver* [1987] 1 W.L.R. 916; *Hayes v James and Charles Dodd* [1990] 2 All E.R. 815.

[83] See below, p.974.

[84] *cf. Sykes v Midland Bank Executor & Trustee Co Ltd* [1971] 1 Q.B. 113; A.L.G., 87 L.Q.R. 10. *Semble*, it would not be enough to show that the claimants *might* have bought for the same price even if they had been told the truth: *cf. Brikom Investments Ltd v Carr* [1979] Q.B. 467 at 483.

[85] See Lord Devlin's speech in *Rookes v Barnard* [1964] A.C. 1129; *Kuddus v Chief Constable of the Leicestershire Constabulary* [2001] UKHL 29; [2002] 2 A.C. 122.

[86] In *Stoke-on-Trent City Council v W & J Wass Ltd* [1988] 1 W.L.R. 1406 at 1414 the damages in the *Wrotham Park* case [1974] 1 W.L.R. 798, were described as "something akin to . . . exemplary damages for breach of contract," perhaps because the defendant's profit was taken into account in assessing them; but the purpose of the award was compensatory: above, p.929.

[87] *cf.* CPR 1999, Glossary, definition of "exemplary damages," making the point that such damages "go beyond compensating" the victim.

[88] *Cassell & Co Ltd v Broome* [1972] A.C. 1027.

[89] *Perera v Vandiyar* [1953] 1 W.L.R. 672; *Paris Oldham & Gustra v Staffordshire BG* [1988] 2 E.G.L.R. 39; *Reed v Madon* [1989] Ch. 408; *Johnson v Unisys Ltd* [2001] UKHL 13; [2001] I.C.R. 480, at [15], *per* Lord Steyn, dissenting on the main issue in that case and see below, n.91. Law Com. No.247 (1997) para.6.3.19 recognises and recommends no change in the rule that punitive damages are not available for breach of contract. McBride, 1995 *Anglo-American Law Review* 369, questions the reasons for the rule.

[90] *Calabar Properties Ltd v Stitcher* [1984] 1 W.L.R. 287 at 297; *Ruxley Electronics and Construction Ltd v Forsyth* [1996] A.C. 344 at 352, 365, 373.

defendant's conduct, it can sometimes achieve much the same result by awarding damages for injury to the claimant's feelings.[91] In theory such damages are meant to compensate the claimant for mental suffering, rather than to punish the defendant. But in practice the distinction is often hard to draw and—from the defendant's point of view—to perceive.[92] However, where the claimant has a cause of action both in tort and for breach of contract, he may be able to recover punitive damages by framing the claim in tort. For example, a landlord who unlawfully evicts his tenant is guilty both of a breach of contract and of a trespass; and punitive damages have been awarded in such a case.[93] Another type of case in which a defendant seeks to profit from a deliberate wrong which is both a breach of contract and a tort is that in which he gives a fraudulent warranty as to the subject-matter of a contract of sale. In the United States, punitive damages have been awarded in such a case[94]; but in England conflicting views have been expressed on the question whether such damages can be awarded in an action based on fraud even if the action is brought in tort.[95] It can be argued, on the one hand that the tort of deceit is generally one from which the defendant seeks to profit, so that it falls into the category of wrongs for which punitive damages are available[96]; and, on the other, that deceit generally involves the wrongdoer in criminal liability and that he should not suffer double punishment by being in addition ordered to pay punitive damages.[97]

Punitive damages should be distinguished from multiple damages which may sometimes be awarded to coerce the defendant rather than to express disapproval of his conduct. This seems to be the purpose of the statutory provision by which a tenant who wrongfully holds over after having been given notice to quit can be held liable for *twice* the annual value of the land for the period of his wrongful occupation.[98]

(2) Compensation for what?

The principle that damages are compensatory gives rise to the question: for what is it that the victim of a breach of contract is entitled to be compensated? This question calls

---

[91] See below, pp.988–991. *cf.* the suggestion in *McCall v Abelesz* [1976] Q.B. 585, 594 that damages for injury to feelings could now be awarded in a case like *Perera v Vandiyar*, above; Law Com. No.247, para.6.1.2, preferring the phrase "damages for mental distress" to "aggravated damages" in cases of this kind. CPR 1999, Glossary, uses "aggravated damages" and treats them as "compensation."

[92] See, for example, *Chelini v Nieri* 196 P.2d 915 (1948) where damages of $10,000 for injury to feelings were awarded for breach of contract against a Californian embalmer.

[93] *Drane v Evangelou* [1978] 1 W.L.R. 455; *cf. Guppys (Bridport) v Brookling* (1984) 269 E.G. 846 (nuisance and landlord's breach of covenant to repair); *McMillan v Singh* (1984) 17 H.L.R. 120 (where the claim seems to have been in contract only, but the tenant was said at 125 also to have had a claim in tort); *Millington v Duffy* (1984) 17 H.L.R. 232. *Ramdath v Oswald Daley* [1993] 1 E.G.L.R. 82: exemplary damages for wrongful eviction awarded against landlord but not against his agent unless the latter stood to gain personally from the wrong.

[94] *Grandi v Le Sage* 399 P.2d 285 (1965).

[95] *Mafo v Adams* [1970] 1 Q.B. 548; *Cassell & Co Ltd v Broome*, above, n.85, at 1076, 1131; *Metall und Rohstoff AG v ACLI Metals (London) Ltd* [1984] 1 Lloyd's Rep. 598 at 612; *Smith Kline & French Laboratories Ltd v Long* [1989] 1 W.L.R. 1; *Kuddus v Chief Constable of the Leicestershire Constabulary* [2001] UKHL 29; [2002] 2 A.C. 122, at [43]; *ibid.*, at [84] leaves the point open.

[96] It is arguable that punitive damages for fraudulent warranties are no longer necessary in view of the recognition in *Attorney-General v Blake* [2001] 1 A.C. 268 (above, p.930) of the possibility of awarding an account of profits in certain cases in breach of contract; see *Kuddus v Chief Constable of the Leicestershire Constabulary* [2001] UKHL 29; [2002] 2 A.C. 122, at [109]; but in breach of contract cases the latter remedy is exceptional and discretionary.

[97] *Archer v Brown* [1985] Q.B. 401 at 418–423.

[98] Landlord and Tenant Act 1730, s.1. *cf. Oliver Ashworth (Holdings) Ltd v Ballard Kent Ltd* [2000] Ch. 12, discussing Distress for Rent Act 1737; National Minimum Wage Act 1998, s.21(3).

for an analysis of the various types of losses for which the victim of a breach of contract can recover damages[99]; and it also gives rise to certain related problems.

(a) LOSS OF BARGAIN. The object of damages for breach of contract is to put the victim "so far as money can do it . . . in the same situation . . . as if the contract had been performed".[1] In other words, the victim is entitled to be compensated for the loss of his bargain, so that his expectations arising out of or created by the contract are protected. This protection of the victim's expectations must be contrasted with the principle on which damages are awarded in tort: the purpose of such damages is simply to put the victim into the position in which he would have been, if the tort had not been committed.[2] Of course, in many tort actions the victim can recover damages for loss of expectations: *e.g.* for loss of expected earnings suffered as a result of personal injury, or for loss of expected profits suffered as a result of damage to a profit-earning thing. But these expectations exist quite independently of the tortious conduct which impairs them[3]: it is the nature of most torts to destroy or impair expectations of this kind, rather than to create new ones. Tortious misrepresentation does, indeed, create new expectations, but the purpose of damages even for that tort is to put the victim into the position in which he would have been, if the misrepresentation had not been made, and not to protect his expectations by putting him into the position in which he would have been, if the representation had been true.[4] Such damages may be awarded in respect of losses which the victim could have avoided if he had been told the truth, and here again there is a sense in which the victim will recover damages for "loss of a chance",[5] but it is the chance of avoiding loss rather than that of making a profit for which he will be compensated. He may even be compensated for loss of profit if the tort impairs expectations which exist independently of it. In *East v Maurer*[6] the claimant was interested in buying a hairdressing salon and was induced to buy one belonging to the defendant by the latter's fraudulent representation. It was held that the claimant could recover (*inter alia*) damages in respect of *another* such business in which he would have invested his money if the representation had not been made, but not the profits which he would have made out of the defendant's business, if the representation relating to it had been true. In a contractual action, on the other hand, damages are recoverable as a matter of course for loss of the expectations created by the very contract for breach of

---

[99] Fuller and Perdue, 46 Yale L.J. 52, 373; *cf.* Burrows, 99 L.Q.R. 217; Owen 4 O.J.L.S. 393. For judicial recognition of the distinctions drawn in the following discussion, see *The Alecos M* [1990] 1 Lloyd's Rep. 82 at 84 (reversed, without reference to this point, [1991] 1 Lloyd's Rep. 120).

[1] *Robinson v Harman* (1848) 1 Ex. 850, 855; *Senate Electrical Wholesalers Ltd v Alcatel Submarine Networks* [1999] 2 Lloyd's Rep. 423 at 430, citing other statements to the same effect. Atiyah's emphasis in 94 L.Q.R. 193 on reliance loss and restitution (discussed below), fails adequately to account for the principle stated in the dictum quoted in the text above; or indeed for the availability of the action for the agreed sum (below, pp.1013–1019) or other specific relief (below, pp.1013–1046).

[2] *cf.* above, p.7. For an exception (now severely restricted in scope) see the discussion at pp.608–616, above of *Junior Books Ltd v The Veitchi Co Ltd* [1983] 1 A.C. 520; and see next note.

[3] This is also true in the "disappointed beneficiary" cases such as *White v Jones* [1995] 2 A.C. 207, above pp.616–618.

[4] See above, pp.359–362.

[5] *John W Pryke v Gibbs Hartley Cooper Ltd* [1991] 1 Lloyd's Rep. 602 at 621.

[6] [1991] 1 W.L.R. 461; Marks, 108 L.Q.R. 387; Oakley, [1992] C.L.J. 9. *cf. Clef Aquitaine SARL v Laporte Materials (Barrow) Ltd* [2001] Q.B. 488, above, p.361 (damages in respect of more favourable terms which could, but for the representation, have been negotiated with the representor himself).

which the action is brought.[7] That is why damages of this kind are the distinctive feature of a contractual action.

It follows from the principle of compensating the victim for loss of his bargain that the first and crucial question is to determine exactly what had been bargained for, or, in other words, the exact scope of the duty broken by the defendant. This was the question discussed in *South Australia Asset Management Corp v York Montague Ltd*[8] ("the *SAAMCO* case"). Loans of money had been made on the security of properties which had been valued by the defendants who had been engaged by the lender to make these valuations. In breach of their duty to carry out the valuations with due care, the defendants had overvalued the properties, which then also fell in value, in line with the general weakness in the property market. On the borrowers' default, the lenders realised the securities but recovered less than the amounts that they had lent. The House of Lords held that the valuers were liable for loss suffered by the lenders to the extent of the overvaluation but not for any loss beyond this amount which had been suffered by reason of the fall in the market value of the properties after the making of the loan. The point can be illustrated by supposing that a sum of £8 million had been lent on the security of a property valued at £10 million but actually worth only £6 million and that, on the borrower's default, the property (having fallen in value after the loan) yielded no more than £1.5 million. In such a case, the valuers would be liable, not for the £6.5 million lost by the lender,[9] but only to the extent of the £4 million by which they had overvalued the security. This follows from the general principle[10] that a wrongdoer is liable only for "those consequences which are attributable to that which made the act wrongful"[11]; and in the case of a breach of contract the definition of what "made the act wrongful" necessarily depends on the way in which the contractual duty is defined. In the *SAAMCO* case, the duty was merely one to *provide information* (as to the value of the security) on which it was then up to the lenders to decide upon their course of action[12]; and the valuer was held liable for no more than the adverse consequences of his failure to take reasonable care as to the accuracy of that information. Such a duty was distinguished by Lord Hoffmann[13] from a duty to *advise* a client as to a course of action: a defendant who commits a breach of a duty of this kind (by failing to take reasonable care in giving the advice) will be liable for all foreseeable loss suffered in consequence of the client's taking the advice. Liability in such a case could therefore extend to loss suffered by reason of a fall in the market value of the subject-matter acquired in reliance

---

[7] In *The Unique Mariner* [1979] 1 Lloyd's Rep. 37 at 54 it is said that damages in contract are assessed "on the usual principle of *restitutio in integrum*." This might suggest that the claimant is to be restored to his pre-contract position; but the method of assessment actually adopted in that case was such as to put the claimant into the position in which he would have been if the contract had been *performed*.

[8] [1997] A.C. 191; for subsequent proceedings, see *Nykredit Bank v Edward Erdman Group* [1997] 1 W.L.R. 1627.

[9] Contrast *Kenny & Good Pty Ltd v MGICA* [2000] Lloyd's Rep. P.N. 25 (High Court of Australia).

[10] A possible exception, applicable where the wrong is a misrepresentation which is, or is to be treated as being, fraudulent is recognised in [1997] A.C. at 215 and discussed at p.362 above; for another possible explanation of these cases, see below at n.14.

[11] [1997] A.C. 191 at 213.

[12] *ibid.* at 214; the *extent* of liability for failure to provide accurate information obviously depends on the information that should have been provided: see *Bristol & West BS v Fancy & Jackson* [1997] 4 All E.R. 582 at 621 (distinguishing a solicitor's duty in this respect from that of a valuer).

[13] [1997] A.C. 191 at 214; all the other members of the House of Lords agreed with Lord Hoffmann's speech; *Nykredit* case, above n.8 at 1638; "advice" *ibid.* at 1631 seems to be used to refer to the *valuation. cf. Bristol & West BS v Mothew* [1998] Ch. 1 at 11 (case of failure by a solicitor to provide correct information).

on the advice.[14] The distinction follows from the way in which the defendant's duty is defined; it "has nothing to do with questions of causation[15] or any limit or 'cap' imposed upon damages which would otherwise be recoverable".[16] Those limits cut down liability for losses for which a defendant is *prima facie* responsible[17]; our present concern is with the extent of his duty and hence of his *prima facie* responsibility.

The distinction just drawn between limiting damages and defining a duty can give rise to difficulty, particularly in relation to liability in tort for negligence. Here the rule that a defendant is not liable for unforeseeable loss has been explained on the ground that such loss is too remote; but it can equally well be explained on the ground that the defendant is under no duty to cause unforeseeable loss.[18] In the present group of negligent valuation cases, however, the two issues are clearly distinct: the "scope of the duty" depends on the true meaning of the contract (which clearly imposes *some* duty) while the test of remoteness depends on what consequences the valuer could have contemplated as likely to result from failure to make the valuation with due care.[19] If that test were applied, the valuer would be liable for the market loss; the effect of the "scope of duty" test is that in the "information" (as opposed to the "advice") cases he is under no *prima facie* liability for that loss because he has undertaken no duty with regard to the desirability or prudence of the transaction.[20]

Considerable difficulty can also arise in distinguishing, for the present purpose, between "advice" and "information". This difficulty arises, in the first place, from the ambiguity of the word "advise": this may be used to mean either "advise that . . . " or "advise to . . . " In the former sense, its primary meaning is "to provide information" while in the latter sense it is "to recommend a course of action . . . " The duty to provide what is commonly called legal "advice" may, for example, be no more than one to provide information: *e.g.* to the existence of restrictions on the use of land. The giving of such information does not involve any recommendation as to the commercial prudence of proceeding with a transaction, such as a loan on the security, or a purchase, of the land in question.[21] The second source of the difficulty lies in the fact that a person who expressly undertakes to give information may, by performing that duty, also impliedly give advice.[22] If, for example, A says to B "the girders of this bridge are sound", that statement may well, in the context, mean "you can safely cross", and so amount to advice as well as to information. Similarly, in the *Aneco* case[23] brokers had

---

[14] The misrepresentation cases referred to in n.10, above, could be brought within this principle by arguing that the purpose of misrepresentation, like that of advice, was to induce the transaction leading to the loss. *cf. Intervention Board for Agriculture Products v Leidis* [2000] Lloyd's Rep. P.N. 144.

[15] In this respect the case differs from those discussed at pp.364–366, above and 951–952 below where the question of recoverability of damages in respect of falls in market value depended on factors other than the definition of the defendant's duty.

[16] *Nykredit Bank v Edward Erdman Group* [1997] 1 W.L.R. 1627 at 1638; *Platform Home Loans Ltd v Oyston Shipways Ltd* [2000] 2 A.C. 190 at 208, 213; though the same case may raise an issue both as to the definition of the duty and as to a "cap" on damages, as in *Bank of Credit & Commerce (Overseas) Ltd v Price Waterhouse (No.3)*, The Times, April 2, 1998.

[17] See below pp.964 *et seq.*

[18] See Lord Hobhouse's discussion in *Platform Home Loans Ltd v Oyston Shipways Ltd* [2000] 2 A.C. 190; [1999] 1 All E.R. 835 at 847 of *The Wagon Mound* [1961] A.C. 388; *cf. Aneco Reinsurance Underwriting Ltd v Johnson & Higgins Ltd* [2001] UKHL 51 at [10–12]; [2001] 2 All E.R. (Comm) 929.

[19] See below, p.965.

[20] *cf.* Lord Hobhouse's statement in the *Platform Home Loans* case, above, at 848 that the "development" in the *SAAMCO* case (above n.8) was to apply the "scope of duty" reasoning to "*quantification* of damages" as opposed to "kinds or categories of damage".

[21] See *Lloyds Bank plc v Crosse & Crosse* [2001] EWCA Civ 366; [2001] P.N.L.R. 34; *Dent v Davis Blank Furniss* [2001] Lloyd's Rep. P.N. 534.

[22] See the *Aneco* case, above, n.18 at [1], [17], [32]; Lord Millett dissented.

[23] See above, n.18.

wrongly told a client that reinsurance against the risk which the client was about to underwrite was available in the market. Their duty was held to be one to "advise on the availability of reinsurance cover in the market, without which the transaction would not have gone ahead"[24] and they were therefore liable for the full loss suffered by the client as a result of having entered into that transaction.

The above discussion is concerned only with one type of expectation, namely that of receiving the promised performance. A contract can, however, give rise to two quite separate expectations: that of receiving the promised performance and that of being able to put it to some particular use. For example, a buyer of goods (such as machinery or raw materials) may expect not only to receive the goods but also to use them for manufacturing purposes. If the seller fails to deliver, the buyer is entitled to damages based on the value of the goods that he should have received and also[25] to damages for loss of profits[26] suffered as a result of not receiving the promised delivery.

(b) RELIANCE LOSS. An alternative principle is to put the claimant into the position in which he would have been if the contract had never been made, by compensating him for expenses incurred (or other loss suffered) in reliance on the contract. Sometimes the expenses are of a kind which the claimant *must* incur if he is to perform his part of the contract: for example, a contract for the sale of goods may provide that the seller is to deliver the goods at the buyer's premises; and if the buyer wrongfully refuses to accept them when they are tendered there, the seller can recover the expenses of delivery as an element of reliance loss. But sometimes wasted expenses may be recoverable as reliance loss even though the claimant was *not*, under the contract, actually obliged to incur them: in *McRae v Commonwealth Disposals Commission*,[27] for example, the defendants were held liable for breach of a contract that there was a wrecked tanker lying in a specified position[28]; and the claimants recovered, *inter alia*, the £3,000 which it had cost them to send out a salvage expedition to look for the tanker.

So far it has been assumed that the reliance loss is incurred after the contract was made; but even expenditure incurred before then may be recoverable on this basis. In *Anglia Television Ltd v Reed*[29] the defendant broke his contract to take a leading part in the claimants' television play: and he was held liable for £2,750 spent by the claimants on the production before they had entered into the contract with him. Although the claimants had not incurred this expenditure in reliance on their contract with the defendant, it could be said that they had relied on that contract in allowing the expenditure to be wasted: in other words, in forbearing to look for another leading actor to take the part until it was too late. The pre-contract expenditure in such cases is recoverable because it leads to a loss which, after breach, can no longer be avoided.[30]

Pre-contract expenditure may also be recoverable if it was incurred in reliance on an *agreement* before that agreement had become a legally binding *contract*. In *Lloyd v Stanbury*[31] a person who had contracted to sell land was accordingly held liable for certain expenses incurred by the purchaser in reliance on the agreement while it was still subject to contract.[32]

---

[24] At [1].
[25] See *The "Ile aux Moines"* [1974] 1 Lloyd's Rep. 262 (where in fact loss of profits was not proved).
[26] Provided that these are not too remote: below, pp.964 *et seq.*
[27] (1951) 84 C.L.R. 377, esp. 411.
[28] See above, pp.295–296.
[29] [1972] 1 Q.B. 60; A.L.G., 88 L.Q.R. 168; Ogus, 35 M.L.R. 423; Clarke [1972] C.L.J. 22.
[30] *CCC Films (London) Ltd v Impact Quadrant Films Ltd* [1985] Q.B. 16; Owen [1985] C.L.J. 24; Burrows, 100 L.Q.R. 27.
[31] [1971] 1 W.L.R. 535.
[32] See above, p.52.

(c) RESTITUTION.[33] A claim for restitution is not strictly one for "damages"[34] since its purpose is not to compensate the claimant for a loss, but to deprive the defendant of a benefit. The simplest case of restitution arises where a seller has been paid in advance and then fails to deliver. He is bound to restore the price and the effect of this is to put *both parties* into the position in which they would have been if the contract had *not been made*. A restitution claim obviously differs from a loss of bargain claim, which is meant to put the claimant into the position in which he would have been if the contract had been performed. It also differs from a claim for reliance loss, which is meant to put the claimant into the position in which he would have been if the contract had not been made, and which will often leave the defendant in a worse position. In practice there is considerable overlap between reliance and restitution. Performance by the claimant is a form of reliance which often benefits the defendant; and the requirement in restitution claims that the defendant must have "benefited" from that performance is a somewhat elastic one.[35] There may also be an overlap between loss of bargain and restitution where the amount paid by the injured party is the only evidence of the value of what he ought to have received; and in such a case that amount, or an "appropriate proportion"[36] of it will be the *prima facie* measure of the expectation loss which he suffers as a result of the defendant's failure to perform, or to perform in full.

(d) RELATIONSHIP BETWEEN LOSS OF BARGAIN, RELIANCE LOSS AND RESTITUTION. The relationship between the three types of claim so far discussed is a complex one, but it seems to be governed by the following principles.

(i) *Claimant's choice.* Where more than one type of claim is available the choice between them (if it has to be made) is the claimant's, who cannot be forced by the defendant to make one of the available claims rather than another. Suppose that a seller has been paid in advance and then fails to deliver. The buyer can choose between claiming the return of his money (restitution) and the value of the goods at the time fixed for delivery (loss of bargain). Obviously he will take the former course if he has made a bad bargain and the latter if he has made a good bargain. If the seller could force him to choose restitution, the buyer could easily be deprived of the benefit of a good bargain.

(ii) *Limitations on claimant's choice.* It does not follow from the mere fact of breach that the three types of claim are always available, or that they are available in full.

The claim for loss of bargain damages is, in principle, always available. But to make good such a claim the injured party must prove the value of his expectations. If he cannot do so with reasonable certainty, he may be limited to his reliance and restitution claims. The point may be illustrated by further reference to *McRae v Commonwealth Disposals Commission*[37] where the claimants sought damages for loss of their bargain, alleging that the value of the supposed tanker and its contents (for which they had paid £285) would have been £300,000. This basis for quantifying damages was dismissed as "manifestly absurd"[38]; and the claimants recovered their payment of £285 (restitution) plus the £3,000 spent on their fruitless salvage expedition (reliance loss).

At the other extreme, the claimant's right to claim restitution is severely limited, in particular by the rule that he can (in general) recover back money paid under the contract only if there has been a *total* failure of consideration. This rule will be discussed

---

[33] See further, below, pp.1049–1064.
[34] *Portman BS v Hamlyn Taylor Neck* [1998] 4 All E.R. 202 at 205; *cf.* above p.931, n.42.
[35] See especially above, p.822; below, p.1062.
[36] *Peninsular & Orient SNCo v Youell* [1997] 2 Lloyd's Rep. 136 at 141; below, p.1057.
[37] (1951) 84 C.L.R. 377.
[38] *ibid.* at 411.

later in this Chapter[39]; but a point to be emphasised here is that, if restitution is available, it is no objection to such a claim that it will leave the claimant better off than he would have been, if the contract had been performed. Indeed, this will be the result of a successful restitution claim whenever the claimant has made a bad bargain, *e.g.* by paying more for goods than they are worth.

Claims for reliance loss occupy an intermediate position. The Court of Appeal has held that such claims are normally available when a reliance loss has been suffered; and that the injured party is entitled to choose between such a claim and one for loss of bargain damages.[40] One type of case in which he will claim reliance loss is where he cannot prove the value of his expectations. This is no doubt why reliance loss was claimed in *Anglia Television Ltd v Reed*[41]: the claimants could not prove what profit (if any) they would have made out of the play. Similarly, in *McRae*'s case the claimants could not prove the value of the supposed tanker, and nevertheless recovered £3,000 by way of reliance loss. But they should not have been awarded the *whole* of this reliance loss if the defendants could have proved that the tanker, had it existed, would have been worth only £2,000. In such a case the claimant would have lost £1,000, even if there had been no breach; and where the claimant has in this way made a bad bargain, the court will not shift that loss to the defendant by allowing the claimant to recover the whole of his wasted expenditure.[42] It has been held that the burden of proof on this issue is on the defendant: in other words, it is not up to the claimant to show that his venture would have been profitable but up to the defendant to show that it would have been unprofitable.[43] As much of the relevant information on this issue will usually be more readily available to the claimant than to the defendant, it is likely that the defendant will find this burden a hard one to discharge.

By contrast, a claimant who claims restitution can shift a loss flowing from the fact that he has made a bad bargain (and not from the breach) to the defendant. The reason for this result is that the defendant would otherwise be enriched; and there is no such enrichment merely because a claimant's reliance loss exceeds the value of his bargain.

(iii) *Whether claims can be combined.* There is sometimes said to be an inconsistency between combining the various types of claim so far discussed. An award which seeks to put the claimant into the position in which he would have been if the contract had been *performed* cannot, on this view, be combined with one which seeks to put him (or both parties) into the position which would have existed, if the contract *had not been made*. But the courts have not accepted this kind of reasoning and have, in appropriate cases, allowed the claims to be combined. In one case[44] machinery was bought, paid for and installed. The buyer rejected the machinery because it was not in accordance with the contract; and he recovered the price (restitution), installation expenses (reliance loss) and his net loss of profits resulting from the breach (loss of bargain).

The true principle is not that there is any logical objection to combining the various types of claim, but that the claimant cannot combine them so as to recover more than

---

[39] See below, pp.1049–1057.
[40] *Cullinane v British "Rema" Mfg Co* [1954] 1 Q.B. 292 at 303; *Anglia Television Ltd v Reed* [1972] 1 Q.B. 60 at 63–64; *CCC Films (London) Ltd v Impact Quadrant Films Ltd* [1985] Q.B. 16 at 32; *cf. Lloyd v Stanbury* [1971] 1 W.L.R. 535 at 547; *The Selda* [1999] 1 Lloyd's Rep. 729.
[41] [1972] 1 Q.B. 60.
[42] See *C & P Haulage v Middleton* [1983] 1 W.L.R. 1461; *Bowlay Logging v Domtar* [1978] 4 W.W.R. 105; *cf. CCC Films (London) Ltd v Impact Quadrant Films* [1985] Q.B. 16 at 38.
[43] *CCC (London) Films Ltd v Imperial Quadrant Films* [1985] Q.B. 16; *cf. Commonwealth of Australia v Amann Aviation Pty Ltd* (1991) 66 A.L.J.R. 123; Treitel, 108 L.Q.R. 226.
[44] *Millar's Machinery Co Ltd v David Way & Son* (1935) 40 Com.Cas. 204; *cf. Snia Soc. di Navigazione v Suzuki & Co* (1924) 18 Ll.L.R. 333 at 336–337; *Naughton v O'Callaghan* [1990] 3 All E.R. 191 at 198; and see above, p.852.

once for the same loss.[45] Suppose that a buyer has paid in advance for goods which are not delivered. He obviously cannot recover both his payment (restitution) and the full value of the goods at the time fixed for delivery (loss of bargain). The point has been well put by Corbin: "*full* damages and *complete* restitution . . . will not both be given for the same breach of contract".[46]

The principle against double recovery also applies where a claimant seeks both reliance loss and damages for the loss of his bargain. If the claimant in *McRae's*[47] case had been able to establish the value of the hypothetical tanker, he should clearly not have been entitled to that amount *and* to the £3,285, for he would have had to spend the latter amount to acquire the former. Similarly, in *Cullinane v British "Rema" Manufacturing Co Ltd*[48] the defendants sold a clay pulverising machine, warranting that it could process clay at six tons per hour. The buyer claimed damages for breach of this warranty under two heads: first, the capital cost of the machine and its installation and, secondly, loss of profits. It was held that the buyer could not recover under both of these heads as "a claim for loss of profits could only be founded upon the footing that the capital expenditure had been incurred".[49] To allow the buyer to recover the capital expenditure and also his *full* profit would give him damages twice over for the same loss. It was however not established that the profits which would have been derived from the machine over the whole of its useful "life" would have *exceeded* its capital cost. If this had been proved the buyer could, according to a decision of the High Court of Australia, have recovered (a) the capital cost of the machinery less its actual value; plus (b) the excess of the estimated profits over the sum calculated under (a).[50] This alone would put the buyer into as good a financial position as if the contract had been performed.

A problem of double recovery again arose in *George Mitchell (Chesterhall) Ltd v Finney Lock Seeds Ltd*,[51] where a seed merchant sold defective seed to a farmer so that the latter's crop failed. It was said that the damages included "all the costs incurred by the [farmer] in the cultivation of the worthless crop as well as the profit [he] would have expected to make from a successful crop if proper seeds had been supplied".[52] Here "profit" must mean the proceeds of a successful crop *less* the cost of cultivating such a crop, for that cost would have been incurred by the farmer even if the seed had not been defective, so that he would be over-compensated if it were not taken into account in computing the profit.

(e) INCIDENTAL AND CONSEQUENTIAL LOSS. The victim of a breach of contract can often recover loss which does not fit easily into the categories so far discussed.

First, he may incur expenses after a breach has come to his attention, such as the administrative costs of buying a substitute[53] or of sending back defective goods. Such expenses are hardly incurred in reliance *on the contract*; and they will in this Chapter be called "incidental" loss.[54]

---

[45] *Peninsular & Orient SN Co v Youell* [1997] 2 Lloyd's Rep. 136 at 141.
[46] Corbin on *Contracts*, § 1221. *cf. The Unique Mariner* [1979] 1 Lloyd's Rep. 37 at 53; *Tang Man Sit v Capacious Investment Ltd* [1996] A.C. 514; *Baltic Shipping Co v Dillon* (1993) 176 C.L.R. 344 at 345.
[47] (1951) 84 C.L.R. 377; *Salvage Association v CAP Financial Services* [1995] F.S.R. 654 at 683.
[48] [1954] 1 Q.B. 292; Macleod [1970] J.B.L. 19; Stoljar, 91 L.Q.R. 68.
[49] [1954] 1 Q.B. 292 at 302.
[50] *TC Industrial Plant Pty Ltd v Robert's (Queensland) Ltd* [1964] A.L.R. 1083.
[51] [1983] A.C. 803.
[52] *ibid.* at 812.
[53] See, *e.g. Robert Stewart & Sons Ltd v Carapanayoti* [1962] 1 W.L.R. 34.
[54] *cf.* U.C.C. s.2–715(1).

Secondly, the injured party may suffer "consequential" loss. This expression is used in the law of contract in a number of senses. It may mean simply loss of profits[55] (as opposed to the mere failure to obtain the thing contracted for): in this sense it is merely an element of expectation loss. Alternatively, it may refer to reliance loss: *e.g.* to the expense wasted by a seller in delivering goods which the buyer wrongfully refuses to accept. But the expression is also used (and will be used here) to refer to further harm, such as personal injury or damage to property, suffered as a result of breach: for example, where a cow is sold under a warranty of soundness but is diseased and infects other cattle of the buyer, which die. The seller is *prima facie* liable for the loss of the other animals,[56] even though, when the buyer put the cow with them, the possibility of disease, or the risk of its spreading, was not present to his mind at all. In this situation he cannot have relied on the cow's not being diseased, since reliance presupposes an affirmative belief. Nor can it be said that he *expected not* to lose the other animals; he simply *did not expect* to lose them, which is a wholly different state of mind.

2. Quantification

Damages always consist of a sum of money, so that the loss has to be quantified in terms of money. This process is variously referred to as "quantifying" or "measuring" or "assessing" damages; it gives rise to a number of problems.

(1) The bases of assessment

(a) RELIANCE AND RESTITUTION. Relatively little difficulty arises where the injured party claims reliance loss or restitution. In the first case, the basis of assessment is the cost to him of his action in reliance on the contract; and in the second it is generally[57] the benefit obtained by the defendant under the contract. These assessments are particularly straightforward where the claimant has expended or the defendant received a sum of money. Where the reliance loss or the benefit to be "restored" consists of goods or services, a reasonable value must be placed on them. This may give rise to practical difficulties, but there is no doubt about the principle on which such assessment proceeds.

(b) LOSS OF BARGAIN. Where the injured party claims to be put into "the same situation . . . as if the contract had been performed",[58] there are two distinct bases of assessment:

(i) *"Difference in value"* and *"cost of cure."* The distinction between these two bases is strikingly illustrated by an American case[59] in which a coal company took a mining lease of farmland, covenanting to restore the land to its original state at the end of the lease. The cost of doing the work would have been $29,000, but the result of not doing it was to reduce the value of the land by only $300. Damages for the company's failure to do the work were assessed at the latter sum. In English law damages for breach of a

---

[55] See *Hotel Services Ltd v Hilton International Hotels (UK) Ltd* [2000] 1 All E.R. (Comm) 750 at 755; *Watford Electronics Ltd v Sanderson Ltd* [2001] EWCA Civ 317; [2001] 1 All E.R. (Comm) 696, at [36], [43]; these cases discuss the meaning of "consequential loss" in exemption clauses.

[56] *Smith v Green* (1875) 1 C.P.D. 92; *cf. The Batis* [1990] 1 Lloyd's Rep. 345 (expenses incurred in complying with directions wrongfully given by party in breach).

[57] Not always: see, *e.g. Planché v Colburn* (1831) 8 Bing. 14 (above, p.822), where there is no evidence that the defendant benefited at all; and see below, p.1062.

[58] *Robinson v Harman* (1848) 1 Ex. 850 at 855.

[59] *Peevyhouse v Garland Coal Co* 382 P. 2d 109 (1962); *cf. Attica Sea Carriers Corp v Ferrostaal Poseidon Bulk Reederei GmbH* [1976] 1 Lloyd's Rep. 250. For compensation for mining subsidence (available independently of contract), see Coal Mining Subsidence Act 1991, ss.2, 10, 22, 26; Coal Industry Act 1994, s.42.

tenant's covenant to repair are by statute assessed on a "difference in value" basis.[60] Apart from such statutory provisions, the law starts with certain *prima facie* assumptions for choosing between the two bases[61]; but these assumptions can be displaced. The point can be illustrated by reference to contracts for the supply of goods and for the execution of building work.

Where a seller delivers goods which are not of the contract quality, the damages are *prima facie* assessed on a difference in value basis, so that the buyer can recover "the difference between the value of the goods . . . and the value they would have had"[62] if they had been in accordance with the contract. But the rule is only a *prima facie* one and if the defect in the goods is cured at a reasonable cost there is little doubt that the cost of such cure can be awarded.[63] This is the position in analogous hire-purchase cases[64] and there seems to be no reason for not applying the same rule to sales.[65] Even the cost of an attempted cure which fails—such as veterinary fees spent on a sick animal which nevertheless dies—can be recovered.[66]

A defendant who is in breach of an obligation to do building work is *prima facie* liable on a "cost of cure" basis: *i.e.* he must pay for the cost of putting the defects right or of completing the work.[67] This, again, is only a *prima facie* rule, which can be displaced where the cost of putting the defect right would be out of all proportion to the advantage which cure would confer on the injured party. This would, for example, be the position where components not in accordance with the contractual specifications had been built into a structure which would have to be substantially demolished to effect a cure[68]; where the cost of cure was greater than the value of the whole building[69]; or where execution of the promised building work would confer no economic benefit at all on the claimant.[70] In such cases, difference in value (if any[71]) would form the normal[72] basis of assessment.[73] This basis of assessment is, in turn, liable to be displaced by further

---

[60] Landlord and Tenant Act 1927, s.18; *Culworth Estates Ltd v Society of Licensed Victuallers* (1991) 62 P. & C.R. 211. But in the absence of evidence as to difference in value, cost of repairs is a "starting point": *Drummond v SU Stores* (1980) 258 E.G. 1293 at 1294; *cf.* below, n.65.

[61] *Watts v Morrow* [1991] 1 W.L.R. 1421 at 1441.

[62] Sale of Goods Act 1979, s.53(3) below, p.885; *The Athenian Harmony* [1998] 2 Lloyd's Rep. 410 at 419.

[63] Where a buyer who deals as consumer has a "right to reduce the purchase price" under ss.48A and 48C of the 1979 Act (as inserted by Sale and Supply of Goods to Consumers Regulations 2002, SI 2002/3045, reg.5), the measure of such reduction does not appear to be either difference in value or cost of cure: see below, p.952.

[64] *e.g. Charterhouse Credit Co Ltd v Tolly* [1963] 2 Q.B. 683 at 711–712.

[65] *Jacovides v Constantinous*, *The Times*, October 27, 1986 (a sale of land case where damages were awarded for misrepresentation apparently having contractual effect). In *Keeley v Guy McDonald* (1984) 134 New L.J. 522 the *cost of repairing* an unmerchantable car was awarded *as the difference in value* between the car as it was and as it would have been if it had been merchantable.

[66] *Harling v Eddy* [1951] 2 Q.B. 739.

[67] *Mertens v Home Freeholds* [1921] 2 K.B. 526; *Hoenig v Isaacs* [1952] 1 T.L.R. 1360; *William Cory & Sons v Wingate Investments Ltd* (1978) 248 E.G. 687; *cf. Radford v de Froberville* [1977] 1 W.L.R. 1262 (breach of covenant to build a boundary wall); *Calabar Properties Ltd v Stitcher* [1984] 1 W.L.R. 287; and see, in insurance law, *Pleasurama v Sun Alliance* [1979] 1 Lloyd's Rep. 389.

[68] *e.g. Jacob & Youngs v Kent* 129 N.E. 889 (1921).

[69] *cf. Morris v Redland Bricks Ltd* [1970] A.C. 652.

[70] *James v Hutton* [1950] 1 K.B. 9 (where performance of the defendant's promise to restore a shop front to its pre-contract appearance would not have affected its value).

[71] There being no such difference in *James v Hutton*, above, the damages were held to be nominal.

[72] For a possible exception in cases of "deliberate" breach, see *Glaer v Schwartz*, 176 N.E. 616 (1913).

[73] See *Jacob & Youngs v Kent*, above; McGregor on *Damages* (16th ed.), §1150; Hudson, *Building Contracts* (11th ed.), §8.120; Keating, *Building Contracts* (6th ed.), p.220; *The Rozel* [1994] 2 Lloyd's Rep. 160 (breach of charterer's undertaking to repair a ship); *GW Atkins Ltd v Scott* (1996) 46 Con. L.R. 14; analogous tort cases support the same view: *e.g. Jones v Gooday* (1841) 8 M. & W. 146; *Darbishire v Warran* [1963] 1 W.L.R. 1067; *RC Taylor (Wholesale) Ltd v Hepworth Ltd* [1977] 1 W.L.R. 659.

circumstances. There is some support in the authorities for the view that the claimant can recover damages on the higher cost of cure basis if he can show *either* that he has in fact incurred that cost *or* that he will incur it by getting the work done.[74] He is, however, required to act reasonably to mitigate his loss,[75] and it is submitted that he would have failed to do so if he had insisted on cure even though its cost was wholly disproportionate to the resulting benefit to him. Where this is the position, he should recover only on a difference in value basis.[76] For this purpose, the disproportion would have to be a clear one, since the mitigation rules only require the injured party to act reasonably. Cost of cure which is actually incurred or going to be incurred may therefore be recoverable where the effect of cure on the value of property is speculative[77]; and where the cost of cure, though not resulting in any improvement to the property, is not excessive in relation to the initial value of the property.[78]

Damages against a surveyor who fails to draw his client's attention to defects in a house which the client buys in reliance on the surveyor's report are *prima facie* based on difference in value and not on cost of cure.[79] The reason for this rule is that the surveyor gives no warranty as to the condition of the house: he undertakes only to conduct the survey with reasonable care and skill.[80] The rule may be displaced by special circumstances: *e.g.* cost of cure may be recoverable if cure is undertaken in a reasonable effort to mitigate loss[81]; and the client may also be able to recover costs reasonably incurred in extricating himself from the transaction.[82]

(ii) *Cases where cure is not undertaken.* Where the claimant is *prima facie* entitled to damages based on cost of cure, the further question arises whether he can recover this amount (where it exceeds difference in value) even though he does not undertake cure, or propose to do so. There is, at least apparently, some conflict in the authorities on this point. The starting principle is that the cost of cure can be recovered in such cases since, in general, the court is not concerned with the use which the claimant makes of his damages.[83] But this principle is subject to significant qualifications. First, the fact that the injured party has decided not to effect cure is relevant to the issue whether it would have been reasonable for him to do so; if not, cost of cure will be irrecoverable under the mitigation rules already discussed.[84] Secondly, the conduct of the injured party after the breach may affect the basis of assessment: for example, if he has disposed of the defective or damaged subject-matter without effecting cure, the court is likely to conclude that

---

[74] *Tito v Waddell* (*No.2*) [1977] Ch. 106, 332, 335; *Radford v De Froberville* [1977] 1 W.L.R. 1262. For the position in tort, see *Heath v Keys, The Times*, May 28, 1984; *Ward v Cannock Chase DC* [1986] Ch.546; *cf. Minscombe Properties v Sir Alfred McAlpine & Son* (1986) 279 E.G. 759 (where the development potential of the damaged property was taken into account). Contrast *Wigsell v School for Indigent Blind* (1882) 8 Q.B.D. 357 (difference in value); and, see Harris, Ogus and Phillips, 95 L.Q.R. 581. For the possible relevance of this factor to a claim for damages in respect of a *third party's* loss, see above, pp.594, 601.

[75] See below, pp.977–979.

[76] *cf.* for example *Darbishire v Warran*, above, n.73; *The Maersk Colombo* [2001] EWCA Civ 117; [2001] 2 Lloyd's Rep. 275 at [32] (also a tort case).

[77] *Sunshine Exploration Ltd v Dolly Varden Mines Ltd* (1969) 8 D.L.R. (3d) 441.

[78] Corbin on *Contracts*, §1091. The position may be the same even where the work would actually *reduce* the value of the property: *ibid.* §1089.

[79] See above, p.933.

[80] *Watts v Morrow* [1991] 1 W.L.R. 1421 at 1439.

[81] *Cross v David Martin & Mortimer* [1989] 1 E.G.L.R. 154.

[82] *Heatley v William Brown* [1992] 1 E.G.L.R. 289; *cf. County Personnel (Employment Agency) Ltd v Alan R Pulver & Co* [1987] 1 W.L.R. 916 (negligent solicitor).

[83] *Ruxley Electronics and Construction Co Ltd v Forsyth* [1996] A.C. 344 at 359; *cf. ibid.* at 372; and see the cases discussed at pp.947–948, below in which damages are based on market prices.

[84] *Ruxley Electronics* case, below; for this aspect of mitigation, see above, p.945.

what he has lost is difference in value rather than cost of cure.[85] In such cases, therefore, difference in value will be the more appropriate basis of assessment.

(iii) *Both bases may lead to same result.* The two bases of assessment will not invariably lead to diverging results. For example, in *Dean v Ainley*[86] a vendor of land broke her contractual undertaking to seal a patio so as to prevent water from leaking into a cellar. The purchaser recovered the cost of doing the promised work, and this sum was variously described as the "cost of the works",[87] or as the extent to which the property was "clearly less valuable"[88] as a result of the vendor's failure to perform her undertaking. Where the only reliable evidence of difference in value is cost of cure,[89] the two methods of assessment will lead to the same practical result.

Sometimes the process of assessment can with equal plausibility be described as being based on difference in value or cost of cure. This is the position where a buyer is entitled to the difference between the contract and the market price of goods which the seller has failed to deliver.[90] It makes no difference whether such damages are described as the cost of curing the seller's breach or as the difference in value between what the buyer has received (*i.e.* nothing) and what he should have received (*i.e.* the goods). The buyer is, moreover, entitled to such damages whether or not he has actually made the substitute purchase.[91]

(iv) *Other loss.* The "difference in value" and "cost of cure" bases are not the only possible ones on which loss of bargain damages may be assessed. The point is well illustrated by *Ruxley Electronics and Construction Ltd v Forsyth*,[92] where a builder had contracted to build a swimming pool in his customer's garden. The contract required the pool to have a maximum depth of seven feet, six inches but the pool actually built had a maximum depth of only six feet, nine inches. This breach of the contract did not significantly affect the value of the pool; nor, since the pool remained, in spite of the breach, perfectly safe and serviceable, would the cost of rebuilding it to the stipulated depth have been reasonably incurred, being wholly disproportionate to the benefit to be obtained by carrying out these operations. Thus the customer was entitled neither to "difference in value" nor to "cost of cure" damages; but it did not follow that he was not entitled to any substantial damages whatsoever. The trial judge had awarded him £2,500 for "loss of amenity" and this award was allowed to stand by the House of Lords,[93] even though it was recognised that in most building contract cases no such damages are available to the customer.[94] This aspect of the case is perhaps best explained

---

[85] *Calabar Properties Ltd v Stitcher* [1984] 1 W.L.R. 297 at 229; *cf. Hole & Hole (Sayers Common) Ltd v Harrisons Ltd* [1973] 1 Lloyd's Rep. 345 (damaged building not repaired but demolished for redevelopment purposes); *Leppard v Excess Insurance Co Ltd* [1979] 1 W.L.R. 512 (an insurance case in which it was clear that reinstatement was not going to be effected); *Charterhouse Credit Ltd v Tolly* [1963] 2 Q.B. 683, disapproving *Yeoman Credit Ltd v Apps* [1962] 2 Q.B. 508, so far as *contra*; *GW Atkins Ltd v Scott* (1996) 46 Con. L.R. 14. In *Perry v Sidney Phillip & Son* [1982] 1 W.L.R. 1297 it was conceded that cost of cure (which was not effected or intended to be effected) was not the appropriate basis for assessing damages against a negligent surveyor; for the proper basis of assessment in such a case, see above, p.933 at nn.66–67.

[86] [1987] 1 W.L.R. 1729; *cf. Watts v Morrow* [1991] 1 W.L.R. 1421 at 1435; *The Rozel* [1994] 2 Lloyd's Rep. 160 at 167.

[87] [1987] 1 W.L.R. 1729 at 1736.

[88] *ibid.* at 1738.

[89] *e.g. Stewart v Rapley* [1989] 1 E.G.L.R. 159.

[90] Sale of Goods Act 1979, s.51(3), below, p.947 at n.98.

[91] *cf. Shearson Lehman Hutton Inc. v Maclaine Watson & Co (No.2)* [1990] 1 Lloyd's Rep. 441 at 443 (seller's damages); and (in tort) *Dominion Mosaics & Tile Co Ltd v Trafalgar Trucking Co Ltd* [1990] 2 All E.R. 246.

[92] [1996] A.C. 344; Coote [1997] C.L.J. 537.

[93] At 359; *cf.* Lord Lloyd's scepticism at 374 as to the amount of the award.

[94] *ibid. per* Lord Lloyd; *cf.* below, pp.988, 990 at n.18.

either on the ground that the building contractor had not challenged this part of the award, or on the ground that, in contracts for making "home improvements", damages can (by way of exception to the general rule applicable to building contracts) include compensation for the customers "disappointed expectations"[95] arising from the contractor's failure to provide the degree of comfort or enjoyment which, to the contractor's knowledge, it was the customer's object to obtain.[96]

(2) Actual and market values

Where damages are based on difference in value (or on the cost of a substitute) they may be assessed by reference either to actual or to market values. There is said to be a "market" for goods if they can be freely bought or sold at a price fixed by supply and demand.[97]

(a) WHERE THERE IS A MARKET, the loss is *prima facie* quantified by reference to it; but other factors may also have to be taken into account.

(i) *Non-delivery.* If a seller of goods fails to deliver, the buyer can go into the market and buy substitute goods at the prevailing price. Thus his damages will *prima facie* be based on the amount (if any) by which the market price exceeds the contract price.[98] It is irrelevant that the seller has disposed of the goods to a third party for *less* than the market price.[99] Similarly, where breach by a carrier results in a failure of the goods to reach the agreed destination, the injured party's damages are based on the market value of the goods at that destination when they should have been delivered there.[1]

The principle of assessment by reference to the market price normally applies even though the injured party has resold an equivalent quantity of goods at a different price, in the expectation of receiving those due under the contract. Such a subsale does not reduce the damages if it is made below the market price[2] for the buyer is nevertheless "entitled to recover the expense of putting himself into the position of having those goods [*i.e.* those which the seller has failed to deliver], and this he can do by going into the market and purchasing them at the market price".[3] So long as the subsale was not of the identical goods bought under the main contract, the buyer might have been able to supply his sub-buyer from some other source before the market rose. He could then have resold the goods bought from the defendant to a third party and made a further profit. Conversely the subsale will not increase the damages if it was made above the

---

[95] [1996] A.C. 344 at 374.

[96] *ibid.* pp.360–361, *per* Lord Mustill; *cf. Freeman v Niroomand* (1996) 52 Con. L.R. 116; and see below, pp.989–991.

[97] *Dunkirk Colliery Co v Lever* (1878) 9 Ch.D. 20; *WL Thompson Ltd v Robinson (Gunmakers) Ltd* [1955] Ch. 177; *Charter v Sullivan* [1957] 2 Q.B. 117. A "black" market may be taken into account: *Mouatt v Betts Motors Ltd* [1959] A.C. 71; but not a "monopoly market" fixed by a government: *The Texaco Melbourne* [1992] 2 Lloyd's Rep. 303 at 312, reversed on other grounds [1994] 1 Lloyd's Rep. 473.

[98] Sale of Goods Act 1979, s.51(3); *cf. The Elena D'Amico* [1980] 1 Lloyd's Rep. 75 (failure to provide a ship under charterparty); *Murray v Lloyd* [1989] 1 W.L.R. 1060 (market cost of substitute accommodation awarded against negligent solicitor).

[99] *cf. Barry v Davis* [2001] 1 W.L.R. 1962, where s.51(3) was applied by analogy to the case of an auctioneer's wrongful refusal to knock goods down to the highest bidder (above, pp.11, 142).

[1] *Rodocanachi Sons & Co v Milburn Bros* (1876) 18 Q.B.D. 67; *The Texaco Melbourne* [1994] 1 Lloyd's Rep. 473 at 479; *cf. Watts, Watts & Co v Mitsui & Co Ltd* [1917] A.C. 227. Expenses saved by the shipper, such as the freight that he would have had to pay if the goods had duly arrived and (in case of failure to ship) insurance premiums are deducted from the amount recoverable on the principle of taking the claimant's overall position into account (above p.933).

[2] *Williams Bros. v ET Agius Ltd* [1914] A.C. 510; *cf. Rodocanachi, Sons & Co v Milburn Bros* (1886) 18 Q.B.D. 67; *Brading v F McNeill & Co Ltd* [1946] Ch. 145.

[3] *Williams Bros v ET Agius Ltd* above, at 531.

market price, even if the seller knew that the buyer intended to resell.[4] The buyer's extra loss is either not caused by the seller's breach, but by the buyer's failure to go into the market; or it is irrecoverable as the buyer ought to have mitigated by going into the market to buy a substitute to satisfy his sub-buyer.[5] Once again, however, the position would be different if the subsale had been "of the self-same thing"[6]; for in that case the buyer would not have been able to satisfy his sub-buyer with substitute goods. Consequently, he would have lost his profit on the subsale and could have recovered that loss, so long as it was not too remote.[7]

(ii) *Late delivery*. Where delay in delivery is a ground of rejection, and the right to reject is exercised, damages are assessed in the same way as for non-delivery.[8] But where late delivery is accepted, damages are assessed on a different basis, the contract price being irrelevant. The buyer's complaint in such a case is not that he has to go into the market to buy a substitute for more than he had originally agreed to pay. It is that he has got the goods at a time that was less advantageous to him than the delivery time fixed by the contract. If he intended, on receipt of the goods, to resell them in the market, he will accordingly have lost the amount by which their market value when they were delivered to him was less than their market value when they should have been delivered; and this amount will be recoverable provided that the chance of resale is not too remote a contingency.[9] It is, however, disputed whether a buyer's damages will be reduced if he has resold the goods for *more* than the market price at the time of actual delivery. In *Wertheim v Chicoutimi Pulp Co*[10] wood pulp was sold for delivery in September/November but not delivered till the following June. The market price per ton was 70s. at the time fixed for delivery and 42s. 6d. at the time of actual delivery. *Prima facie* the buyers' loss was therefore 27s. 6d. per ton. But they had resold the pulp at 65s. per ton and were able to pass it on to their sub-buyers at that price. The Privy Council held that the sellers could rely on the subsale to reduce the damages to 5s. per ton. To allow the buyers to recover 27s. 6d. would, it was said, enable them to make a profit out of the breach. But this is hard to fit in with the principles normally governing the assessment of damages.[11] Two possibilities exist in cases of this kind. First, the buyer has resold the very goods comprised in the main contract.[12] If so he has admittedly not lost 27s. 6d. per ton but it is difficult to see that he has lost anything at all; he would not have been free to sell the pulp in the market at 70s. per ton as he was bound to deliver it to his sub-buyer. Secondly, the buyer has resold an equivalent quantity. If so the subsale should be disregarded. Had the pulp been delivered in September/November it could have *then* been sold to a third party, and the sub-buyer could still have been satisfied with an

---

[4] *Kwei Tek Chao v British Traders Ltd* [1954] 2 Q.B. 459 at 489.
[5] *cf.* below, p.976; *Mobil North Sea Ltd v PJ Pipe & Valve Co* [2001] EWCA Civ 741; [2001] 1 All E.R. (Comm) 289 at [30] (mitigation and causation "closely allied" concepts). The burden of proof on the issue whether the injured party ought to have mitigated is on the party in breach, whichever of the above rationales of the "market rule" is adopted: see *Standard Chartered Bank v Pakistan National Shipping Co (No.3)* [2001] EWCA Civ 55; [2001] 1 All E.R. (Comm) 822, at [41].
[6] *Williams Bros v E T Agius Ltd* [1914] A.C. 510 at 523; *cf. Seven Seas Properties Ltd v Al-Essa* [1988] 1 W.L.R. 1272; *The Ines* [1995] 2 Lloyd's Rep. 144 at 159.
[7] See below, pp.965 *et seq.*; *Re R & H Hall Ltd and WH Pim Jr* (1928) 139 L.T. 50, where the contract itself expressly provided for resale, and it was not suggested that the resale prices were "out of the ordinary course of business": *ibid.* at 54; *The Honam Jade* [1991] 1 Lloyd's Rep. 38.
[8] *e.g. The Almare Seconda* [1981] 2 Lloyd's Rep. 433; *cf.* above, p.826.
[9] See below, pp.966–967, 974. In tort it has been held that this amount is not recoverable as damages for detention where the claimant's purpose was not to resell the goods but to use them for manufacturing purposes: *Brandeis Goldschmidt & Co Ltd v Western Transport Ltd* [1981] Q.B. 864.
[10] [1911] A.C. 301.
[11] *Slater v Hoyle & Smith* [1920] 2 K.B. 11 at 23.
[12] *cf. Williams Bros v ET Agius Ltd* [1914] A.C. 510 at 530.

equivalent quantity bought in June at 42s. 6d. per ton. It is improbable that the buyer would have kept the pulp throughout this period on a falling market. On the other hand, if (in view of the delay) the buyer "had bought other goods and used them for the sub-contract he would have been left with the goods delivered at the time when the market price was 42s. 6d. instead of when it was 70s".[13] Nor is it right to say that the buyer would make a profit *out of the breach* of contract if he were awarded 27s. 6d. a ton. He would make a profit *out of the advantageous subsale*.

(iii) *Defective delivery: in general.* Where defective goods are delivered, and are not (or can no longer be) rejected, the buyer's loss is *prima facie* the difference between the actual value of the goods that he has received and the value that they would have had if they had been in accordance with the contract.[14] As in cases of late delivery, the difference between the contract and the market price is not relevant[15]: the buyer's complaint is not that he will have to buy an equivalent elsewhere, but that he has got something of lower value than that which he should have received. A subsale is again ignored[16]; unless it is of the very goods comprised in the original contract.[17]

A case of defective delivery which gives rise to much difficulty is *Bence Graphics International Ltd v Fasson UK Ltd*.[18] Vinyl film had been sold for use in the buyers' business of manufacturing decals which their customers attached to containers used in the carriage of goods. It was a term of the contract of sale that the decals were to have a "life" of five years; and this term was broken so that the film delivered was "worthless".[19] The defect being not immediately apparent, the buyers used the film for making decals; these were in turn defective, so that the buyers were faced with many complaints from their customers, though only with one relatively minor[20] claim; this was settled by the buyers who were compensated in this respect by the sellers. At first instance, the buyers recovered the whole of the price that they had paid since the film delivered had no value and since there was no evidence, other than the price, of the value which it would have had, if it had been in conformity with the contract. On appeal it was held by a majority that the sellers were liable for no more than the price of a small quantity of film which the buyers had returned,[21] plus the amount of the buyers' liability to the ultimate users of the decals; any loss in excess of this amount was regarded as too remote.[22] It may, however, with respect be doubted whether the case gave rise to any issue of remoteness. If a seller contracts to deliver an ounce of gold for £210 (its market value) and instead delivers an ounce of base metal worth only £5, there is no doubt that he is liable for £205; and this liability is not subject to any test of remoteness.[23] That test would apply only if he had suffered some *further* loss as a result (for example) of his use of the subject-matter; but no such claim was in issue in the *Bence Graphics* case.[24] A pure "difference in value" claim could, indeed, sometimes be resisted on the ground that the

---

[13] *Slater v Hoyle & Smith* [1920] 2 K.B. 11 at 23–24.

[14] Sale of Goods Act 1979, s.53(3). For application of the same principle where goods arrive damaged as a result of a *carrier's* breach, see *Vinmar International Ltd v Theresa Navigation SA* [2001] 1 Lloyd's Rep. 1 at [56].

[15] *cf. Commercial Fibres (Ireland) Ltd v Zabiada* [1975] 1 Lloyd's Rep. 27.

[16] *Slater v Hoyle & Smith* [1920] 2 K.B. 11.

[17] As in *Champanhac Ltd v Waller Ltd* [1948] 2 All E.R. 724.

[18] [1998] Q.B. 87; Treitel, 113 L.Q.R. 188.

[19] [1998] Q.B. 87 at 108, where it is also said that the sellers "always accepted" this.

[20] Relating to 349 out of over 100,000 decals produced.

[21] Worth £22,000; £564,328 had been paid for the whole amount supplied.

[22] This follows from the reliance by the majority on the rule in *Hadley v Baxendale* (1854) 9 Ex. 341 (below p.965) and Sale of Goods Act 1979, s.53(2), which is thought to embody that rule.

[23] See below, p.972.

[24] It would have arisen if the buyers' customers had made unexpectedly large claims against them.

buyer had not lost that difference because he had passed the subject-matter on to a sub-buyer for a price which took no account of the defect. But this would be the position only where the subsale was of the very goods comprised in the contract and could be performed only by delivery of those goods.[25] In such a case the goods in the buyer's hands would be worth the amount for which he had resold them; but where the subsale is not of those very goods, the buyer does suffer the "difference in value" loss since he could have used *other* goods to satisfy his sub-buyer and would then have been left with the goods bought under the broken contract. If he succeeds in disposing of those goods under an advantageous subsale, then it should be "immaterial that by some good fortune with which the [sellers] have nothing to do he has been able to recoup himself what he paid for those goods".[26] This was the position in the *Bence Graphics* case, where the buyers were under no obligation to their customers to use the material supplied by the sellers.[27] From this point of view, the decision is open to the same criticisms as those which have been discussed above in relation to *Wertheim*'s case.[28] It is respectfully submitted that the buyers' claim in the *Bence Graphics* case should have been upheld[29] and that any "windfall" which they might in this way have obtained would have been obtained by the grace of those of their customers, who had made no claims against them. There seems to be no reason why this indulgence should benefit the sellers who in breach of contract had delivered goods which they admitted to be worthless and who had received a price based on the warranted quality of those goods.

Where the market value of the goods has fallen between the making of the contract and the defective delivery, the buyer will normally wish to reject; for in this way he will be able to avoid the loss resulting, not from the breach, but from the fall in the market. If, however, he has lost the right to reject, his only remedy will be in damages, and those damages are *prima facie* recoverable only in respect of the defect, and not in respect of the fall in the market. In one case,[30] a contract for the sale of beans stipulated for shipment by the end of August but the seller delivered a September shipment. By the time of breach the market value of the beans had fallen some £2,000 below the contract price, so that the buyer would certainly have rejected if he had known of the defect in time. But he had "accepted"[31] the goods and it was held that the damages to which he was entitled were no more than nominal as there was no difference between the market value of an August and a September shipment and as the fall in the value of the goods since the time of contracting was not a loss which had resulted[32] from the seller's breach. There may, however, in cases of this kind, be a defect, not only in the goods, but also in the documents which the seller is obliged by the contract to tender[33] and the buyer may have accepted the documents without knowing of the defects in them,[34] paid the price, and so have been deprived (whether as a matter of law or of business[35]) of the chance to

---

[25] See above, at n.17.

[26] *Slater v Hoyle & Smith* [1920] 2 K.B. 11 at 18.

[27] *per* Morland J. at first instance, unreported, December 14, 1994, Transcript, p.10.

[28] [1911] A.C. 301; above, p.949.

[29] Subject only to a deduction in respect of the claim referred to in n.21, above. In *The Selda* [1999] 1 Lloyd's Rep. 729 at 733, the *Bence Graphics* case was cited with approval, but not on the point here under discussion.

[30] *Taylor v Bank of Athens* (1922) 27 Com.Cas. 142.

[31] See above, pp.384, 816.

[32] Within Sale of Goods Act 1979, s.53(2).

[33] Especially under c.i.f. contracts, as to which see above, pp.675, 768.

[34] For the significance of this point, see *Vargas Pena v Peter Cremer GmbH* [1987] 1 Lloyd's Rep. 392, below, n.36.

[35] This was the position in *Kwei Tek Chao v British Traders* [1954] 2 Q.B. 459.

reject the goods. In such a case the buyer can get damages on the footing that the defect in the documents was the cause of his losing the chance to reject the goods on a falling market; and he can do so even though the fact that the goods are not of the contract description has in no way affected their value.[36] For this reason it has been rightly said that there is "little merit"[37] in such a claim; and it is available only where there is a defect both in the documents and in the goods, each giving rise to an independent right to reject.[38]

(iv) *Defective delivery: consumer sales.* Where non-conforming goods are delivered to a buyer who deals as consumer, the buyer has in certain circumstances the right to require the seller "to reduce the purchase price of the goods in question to the buyer by an appropriate amount".[39] This concept of a price reduction is taken from the Civil law, where the price of non-conforming goods is reduced in the proportion which the actual value of the goods bears to the value which they would have had, if they had been in conformity with the contract.[40] Such a reduction is not the same as the "difference in value" measure discussed above[41]: the Civil law price reduction would yield *more* than that measure if the buyer had agreed to pay more than the value of the goods if they had been in conformity with the contract, and *less* if the buyer had agreed to pay less than that value.[42] It remains to be seen whether the English courts will, in interpreting the phrase "an appropriate amount", apply the Civil law principle of proportionate price reduction. Even if they do apply it, the buyer will not be prejudiced where the price reduction would yield less than difference in value, since the right to a "price reduction" is *additional*[43] to his other rights in respect of the breach. For the same reason, a buyer who claims a price reduction is also not precluded from claiming damages for consequential losses[44] such as personal injury caused by defects in the goods.

(v) *Refusal to accept and pay.* If a buyer of goods refuses to accept and pay for goods sold to him, the seller can go into the market and sell the goods at the prevailing price. He will then *prima facie* lose the amount (if any) by which the contract price exceeds the

---

[36] *James Finlay & Co Ltd v NV Kwik Hoo Tong HM* [1929] 1 K.B. 400; *Kwei Tek Chao v British Traders Ltd* [1954] 2 Q.B. 459; *Kleinjan & Holst NV Rotterdam v Bremer Handelsgesellschaft mbH* [1972] 2 Lloyd's Rep. 11; *The Kastellon* [1978] 2 Lloyd's Rep. 203. Contrast *Vargas Pena v Peter Cremer GmbH* [1987] 1 Lloyd's Rep. 394 where such damages were held not to be available to a buyer who knew of the defect *in the documents* when he accepted them, for in that situation the loss was not caused by the breach but by the buyer's decision to accept the documents.

[37] *The Kastellon*, above, at 207 (where the seller was not to blame for the defect in the documents).

[38] *Benjamin's Sale of Goods* (6th ed.), §§19–182 to 19–193; *Procter & Gamble Philippine Manufacturing Corp v Kurt A Becher* [1988] 2 Lloyd's Rep. 21; Treitel [1988] L.M.C.L.Q. 457. The principle on which "market loss" damages were denied in the "negligent valuation" cases (such as the *South Australian Asset Management* case [1997] A.C. 191, above p.938) does not apply in the present group of cases in which (1) the question *is* one of causation, while in those cases *no* such question arises (above, p.939); and (2) the scope of the seller's duty is always the same (to tender conforming documents relating to conforming goods), while those cases turn entirely on the scope of the valuer's duty (*i.e.* on whether it is one to inform or one to advise): see *Benjamin, op.cit.*, §19–197.

[39] s.48C(1) and (2), as inserted by Sale and Supply of Goods to Consumers Regulations 2002, SI 2002/3045, reg.5, implementing Dir.1999/44.

[40] See German Civil Code (BGB) §472; Vienna Convention on Contracts for the International Sale of Goods, Art.50 lays down the same formula.

[41] *i.e.* in Sale of Goods Act 1979, s.53(3), above, p.950.

[42] Suppose that the goods would have been worth £15.00 if in conformity with the contract but because of their non-conformity they are worth only £10.00. Under the formula stated in n.40, above, price reduction would yield £2.00 if the price had been £6.00, and £7.00 if the price had been £21.00. Sale of Goods Act 1979, s.53(3) would yield £5.00 whatever the price was.

[43] Heading before Sale of Goods Act 1979, s.48A, as inserted by the Regulations referred to at n.39 above.

[44] See above, p.943.

market price[45]; and it is normally[46] irrelevant that the seller has actually resold for a different price.[47] If the market price exceeds the contract price, the seller generally suffers no loss. But this is not always true. The contract may provide for an advance payment without which the seller himself cannot get the goods. If the buyer fails to make this payment, the seller suffers loss even though the market price has risen above the contract price: he loses a good bargain because he is not in a position to take advantage of a rising market. Subject to the rules of remoteness,[48] the buyer will be liable for such a loss.[49] The market may also be relevant where the buyer's breach takes the form of *delay* in taking delivery. If the contract provides that the price is to depend on the market price at the time of taking delivery, and that price falls between the time when delivery should have been, and when it was, taken, the seller will be entitled to damages in respect of that difference.[50]

(b) WHERE THERE IS NO MARKET, the loss must be quantified in some other, and sometimes more speculative, way.[51]

(i) *Failure to deliver.* If a seller or carrier fails to deliver goods which cannot be replaced by buying in the market, the court must assess the loss as best it can: relevant factors include the cost of the goods and of their carriage, and a reasonable profit.[52] Where the goods have actually been resold, the resale price is evidence of their value, but not conclusive evidence. The weight of the evidence will depend on such factors as the interval between the wrong and the resale and the extent of fluctuctions in the market price of other similar goods.[53] When the court takes the latter factor into account, it may be said to have regard to a substitute market; and a similar process is sometimes adopted where there is no market at the place where delivery should have been made, but there is a market for goods of the kind in question elsewhere. It may be reasonable for the injured party to resort to that other market,[54] and damages may then be based on the cost of doing so at the time of breach.[55]

Where goods are bought for use, the cost of acquiring a substitute is in principle the correct measure. In one case this was assessed as the scrap value of the goods, and this assessment, though described in the Court of Appeal as "surprising"[56] was held not to be incorrect in principle. At first right, the scrap value might seem to be an inappropriate

---

[45] Sale of Goods Act 1979, s.50(3). For administrative expenses, see above, p.943.

[46] *i.e.* subject to the qualifications stated (in the converse case of breach by the seller) on p.884, above, at nn.6–7.

[47] *Campbell Mostyn Provisions Ltd v Barnett Trading Co* [1954] 1 Lloyd's Rep. 65; *Texaco Ltd v Eurogulf Shipping Co Ltd* [1987] 2 Lloyd's Rep. 541 at 546; *cf. Jamal v Moolla Dawood Son & Co* [1916] 1 A.C. 175 (shares).

[48] See below, pp.965–974.

[49] *cf. Trans Trust SPRL v Danubian Trading Co Ltd* [1952] 2 Q.B. 297.

[50] *cf. Addax Ltd v Arcadia Petroleum Ltd* [2000] 1 Lloyd's Rep. 493.

[51] *cf. Luxmoore–May v Messenger May Baverstock* [1990] 1 W.L.R. 1009 at 1027.

[52] *O'Hanlon v GW Ry* (1865) 6 B. & S. 484; *Schulze v GE Ry* (1887) 19 Q.B.D. 30; *The Texaco Melbourne* [1994] 1 Lloyd's Rep. 473 at 479; *cf. The Pegase* [1981] 1 Lloyd's Rep. 175 at 183 (late delivery); *Shearson Lehman Hutton Inc. v Maclaine Watson & Co (No.2)* [1990] 1 Lloyd's Rep. 441 at 443. *cf. Quorum A/S v Schramm* [2002] 2 All E.R. (Comm) 147 at [100] *et seq.* (assessment of reduction in value of work of art as a result of fire damage).

[53] Contrast *France v Gaudet* (1871) L.R. 6 Q.B. 196 and *Stroud v Austin & Co* (1883) Cab. & El. 119 with *The Arpad* [1934] p.189 and *The Athenian Harmony* [1998] 2 Lloyd's Rep. 410 at 416.

[54] The reasonableness of such action will depend on (*inter alia*) the distance of the market from the place where delivery was to have been made: see *Lesters Leather & Skin Co Ltd v Home Overseas Brokers Ltd* (1949) 82 Ll.L.Rep. 203 at 205.

[55] So that loss due to currency fluctuations *after* that time will not be taken into account: see *The Texaco Melbourne* [1994] 1 Lloyd's Rep. 473.

[56] *The Alecos M* [1991] 1 Lloyd's Rep. 120 at 125; Treitel, 107 L.Q.R. 364.

measure where goods were, to the seller's knowledge, bought for use, since it can hardly represent the cost of acquiring a substitute. But the case can perhaps be explained on the ground that the goods in question were a spare part which was not immediately needed by the buyer and might never have been needed by him. In these circumstances the purchase of a substitute by the buyer might have been an unreasonable augmentation of his loss[57] which would be irrecoverable under the mitigation rules.[58]

(ii) *Failure to accept and pay.* If there is no market, the seller's damages for non-acceptance would *prima facie* be quantified by reference to the actual proceeds of a substitute sale,[59] so long as that transaction was in all the circumstances a reasonable one. As in the case of failure to deliver, the substitute transaction would be evidence of the value of the goods at the time of breach only if it was concluded at, or close to, that time. If the seller did not resell, the value of the goods left on his hands would have to be assessed according to the general criteria stated above[60]; and his damages would *prima facie* be the amount (if any) by which the contract price exceeded that value.

(c) OTHER LOSS. The market and other related rules just stated do not form the limit of recovery. They deal only with the problem of valuing one element of the claimant's loss, namely his expectation of getting either the goods or the price. In addition, the claimant may be able to recover damages for loss of profits. Suppose that a seller has wrongfully failed to deliver goods which the buyer has subsold at a profit. Even if the resale price is *not* good evidence of value,[61] it may nevertheless be taken into consideration in assessing the buyer's damages for loss of profits. Under the rules of remoteness, however, the seller is liable for loss of resale profit only[62] if he knew or could have contemplated[63] that the goods were required for resale,[64] and even then he is not liable for loss of an extraordinary profit unless he is notified of the possibility that such a profit may accrue.[65] If, on the other hand, there is no market and the resale price *is* good evidence of the value of the goods the seller's liability is based on the amount of it, quite irrespective of his state of knowledge.[66] Where the seller is in breach by reason of a defect in the goods, the buyer may similarly (and subject to the rules of remoteness) be able to recover from the seller damages which he has paid, or for which he has become liable, to his sub-buyer in respect of the defect.[67]

The possibility of claiming additional damages for loss of profits also exists where a buyer wrongfully refuses to accept and pay for goods. Here the seller may expect both to get the price and to make a profit; and he may lose the profit even though he manages to resell the goods for exactly the same (or even a higher) price to another buyer. The point may be illustrated by cases in which car-dealers have claimed damages for loss of profits from customers who had agreed to buy cars and then in breach of contract

---

[57] *Ruxley Electronics and Construction Co Ltd v Forsyth* [1996] A.C. 344 at 321–372.
[58] See below, p.978.
[59] *Janred Properties Ltd v Ente Nazionale per il Turismo* [1989] 2 All E.R. 444; *cf. The Noel Bay* [1989] 1 Lloyd's Rep. 361 (damages for charterer's repudiation based on substitute voyage).
[60] At n.52.
[61] *e.g.* because the interval between the breach and the resale was too long, as in *The Arpad*, above, n.53.
[62] *Schulze v GE Ry* (1887) 19 Q.B.D. 30.
[63] See below, pp.965–974.
[64] *Borries v Hutchinson* (1865) 18 C.B.(N.S.) 445; *Grébert-Borgnis v Nugent* (1885) 15 Q.B.D. 85; *Patrick v Russo-British Grain Export Co Ltd* [1927] 2 K.B. 535; *Household Machines v Cosmos Exporters Ltd* [1947] 1 K.B. 217; *J Leavey & Co Ltd v GH Hirst & Co Ltd* [1944] K.B. 24.
[65] See below, p.969.
[66] See below, pp.973–974.
[67] *Total Liban SA v Vitol Energy SA* [2001] Q.B. 643.

refused to accept them. Three situations can be distinguished. First, the sale is of a new car and the supply of cars of the contract description at the dealer's disposal exceeds the demand. Here the dealer's claim will succeed[68]; for he would, if the original customer had not defaulted, have been able to make a sale both to him and to the second customer: hence he would have made two profits,[69] one of which has been lost. Secondly, the sale is of a new car and the demand for cars of the contract description exceeds the supply available to the dealer. Here his claim will fail[70]; for the number of sales that he can make depends on the number of cars that he can get and not on the number of customers that he can find. Hence the default of the original customer does not reduce the number of profits that he can earn. Thirdly, the sale is of a second-hand car. In *Lazenby Garages Ltd v Wright*,[71] it was held that a second-hand BMW car was a "unique" object; and as the car was resold for more than the original price to a second customer, the original customer (who had refused to take it) was not liable for loss of profit. No such loss had been suffered in respect of the car in question; and the possibility that the dealer might have sold a different car to the second customer was dismissed as too remote.[72] Whether it is too remote perhaps depends on the type of car concerned. If the car had been of a kind more commonly sold after use as a "fleet" car, the dealer's chance of selling another (virtually identical) car to a second customer might have been regarded as sufficiently great to satisfy the test of remoteness. Even where the original customer is not liable for loss of profits, any expense of negotiating the second sale can presumably be recovered from him as "incidental" loss.[73]

(3) Speculative damages

A contracting party can recover damages if he can show that the breach has caused[74] him to lose the chance of gaining benefit. So long as the contingencies on which that chance depends are not wholly within the control of the party in breach,[75] the injured party can recover damages for loss of such a chance; he need not show that it was certain that he would have got the benefit if the contract had been performed. Thus damages can be

---

[68] *WL Thompson Ltd v Robinson (Gunmakers) Ltd* [1955] Ch. 177; *cf. Re Vic Mill* [1913] 1 Ch. 465. For the application of similar principles to contracts other than sale, where supply exceeds demand, see *Inter-Office Telephones Ltd v Robert Freeman & Co Ltd* [1958] 1 Q.B. 190; *Robophone Facilities Ltd v Blank* [1966] 1 W.L.R. 1428; *Western Web Offset Printers Ltd v Media Ltd*, The Times, October 10, 1995.

[69] *cf. Jebson v E & W India Dock Co* (1875) L.R. 10 C.P. 300.

[70] *Charter v Sullivan* [1957] 2 Q.B. 117.

[71] [1976] 1 W.L.R. 459.

[72] See below, pp.965 *et seq.*

[73] See above, p.943.

[74] For the requirement of causation, see *Allied Maples Group Ltd v Simmons & Simmons* [1995] 1 W.L.R. 1602 at 1623; *North Sea Energy Holdings NV v Petroleum Authority of Thailand* [1999] 1 Lloyd's Rep. 483 at 494; *Bank of Credit and Commercial International v Ali (No.2)* [2002] EWCA Civ 82; [2002] I.C.R. 1258 esp. at [42], [65] and [97].

[75] See *Lavarack v Woods of Colchester Ltd* [1967] 1 Q.B. 278. *Quaere*, whether *Blackpool & Fylde Aero Club Ltd v Blackpool BC* [1990] 1 W.L.R. 1195 (above, p.15) was not a case of this kind. Where a payment such as an employee's bonus is at the employer's discretion, the decision whether to pay it is not *wholly* within the latter's control if the discretion must be exercised in good faith: *Clark v BET* [1997] I.R.L.R. 348. In *Commonwealth of Australia v Amann Aviation Pty Ltd* (1992) 66 A.L.J.R. 123, loss of profits on future contracts which the defendants would probably have awarded to the injured party (without being bound to do so) were taken into account in assessing damages. But the claim was *for reliance loss* and the lost chance was taken into account for the purpose of the rule that such loss is recoverable only to the extent to which it will not leave the injured party better off than he would have been, if the contract had been performed: above, pp.941–942. It does not follow that damages would have been awarded *for loss of the chance*.

recovered for loss of the chance of taking part in a beauty contest,[76] for loss of the chance of earning tips,[77] for loss of the chance of obtaining pension benefits which depend on the exercise of discretion by a government department[78]; for loss of the chance of appealing against an arbitration award[79]; for loss of the chance of avoiding or of successfully contesting a criminal prosecution[80]; and for loss of the chance (of which clients had been deprived by the negligence of solicitors acting for them in property transactions) of bringing a claim against a third party[81] or of negotiating terms which could have protected the clients from liabilities to third parties.[82] The concept of loss of a chance is also used where the chance is not one of gaining some *specific* benefit or of avoiding some *specific* harm. In this more generalised sense,[83] damages for loss of a chance can be recovered for loss of profits expected to arise from transactions not yet concluded at the time of breach. A carrier of samples who delays in delivering them may thus be liable for loss of profits on contracts which the owner might have made, had he got the samples in time.[84] And a person who breaks a contract to deliver a profit-earning thing may be liable for the profits which the other party might have made by using the thing.[85]

The quantification of damages in such cases is necessarily speculative.[86] It depends on the value of the expected benefit and the likelihood of the claimant's actually getting it. The chance of winning a beauty contest is obviously worth less than the full prize. In deciding how much the chance is worth the court will consider (1) the number of contingencies on which it depends: "the more contingencies, the lower the value of the chance"[87]; and (2) the likelihood of their being satisfied in the claimant's favour: the greater this likelihood, the higher the value of the chance.[88]

The injured party may, as a result of the breach, save the cost of getting the chance. That cost must then be deducted from the damages for loss of the chance, so that no such damages will be recoverable if the cost saved is equal to or greater than the value of the chance.[89]

---

[76] *Chaplin v Hicks* [1911] 2 K.B. 786, described in *Bank of Credit and Commerce International SA v Ali (No.2)* [2002] EWCA Civ 82; [2002] I.C.R. 1258 at [63] as "not ultimately a case of third party volition at all, but it seems to have been treated as if it was"; *cf. Watson v Ambergate, etc., Ry* (1851) 15 Jur. 448. Contrast *McClory v Post Office* [1992] I.C.R. 758 (no damages for loss of chance to work overtime); Reece, 59 M.L.R. 188.

[77] *Manubens v Leon* [1919] 1 K.B. 208.

[78] *Scally v Southern Health and Social Services Board* [1992] 1 A.C. 294.

[79] *Corfield v Bosher & Co* [1992] 1 E.G.L.R. 163.

[80] *Acton v Graham Pearce & Co* [1997] 3 All E.R. 909.

[81] *Harrison v Bloom Camillin (No.2)* [2000] Lloyd's Rep. P.N. 89.

[82] *Allied Maples Group Ltd v Simmons & Simmons* [1995] 1 W.L.R. 1602; *cf. Stovold v Barlows, The Times,* October 30, 1995 (loss of chance of concluding a sale).

[83] See *Bank of Credit and Commerce International SA v Ali (No.2)* [2002] EWCA Civ 82; [2002] I.C.R. 1258 at [64].

[84] *e.g. Simpson v L & NW Ry* (1876) 1 Q.B.D. 274; below, p.970.

[85] *e.g. Victoria Laundry (Windsor) Ltd v Newman Industries Ltd* [1949] 2 K.B. 528; below, pp.965–966.

[86] The requirement of causation stated at n.74 above is satisfied only if the chance lost is "a real or substantial" chance as opposed to a speculative one": see the authorities cited in that note. But the *value* of even a "real or substantial" chance is necessarily speculative, depending on the factors stated at nn.87 and 88, below.

[87] *Hall v Meyrick* [1957] 2 Q.B. 455, 471 (actual decision reversed on another ground, *ibid.* 474); *Obagi v Stanborough (Developments)* (1995) 69 P. & C.R. 573; *First Interstate Bank of California v Cohen Arnold & Co.* [1995] E.G.C.S. 188; *Ministry of Defence v Wheeler* [1998] 1 All E.R. 790.

[88] *e.g. Dickinson v Jones Alexander & Co* [1993] 2 FLR 521; *cf. Allied Maples Group Ltd v Simmons & Simmons* [1999] 1 W.L.R. 1602 at 1622–1623.

[89] *Sapwell v Bass* [1910] 2 K.B. 486, as explained in *Chaplin v Hicks* [1911] 2 K.B. 786 at 796 (foals to be born not shown to be worth more than stud fee).

The court will award speculative damages where no other course is, in the nature of things, open to it. It will not do so where the claimant could have provided evidence as to the value of the bargain that he has lost, and has simply failed to do so.[90]

(4) Taxation

The value of the claimant's loss may be affected by the incidence of taxation. In *BTC v Gourley*[91] a person who was injured by the negligence of the defendant's servants, and claimed damages for loss of earnings. It was estimated that, but for the accident, the injured party would have earned £37,000. Had he actually earned this sum, it would have been taxed and £6,000 would have been left to him. But had he been awarded damages of £37,000 he could have kept the whole amount, since damages for loss of earnings resulting from personal injury are not taxable. The House of Lords held that the proper measure of damages was £6,000, that being the amount of the injured party's actual loss. *Gourley*'s case was an action in tort, but the same principle can apply where the liability is contractual, *e.g.* in assessing damages for wrongful dismissal.[92]

The reason for the rule is that the injured party ought not to make a profit out of the wrong by getting tax-free damages to compensate for loss of a benefit which would have been taxable. Thus the rule applies only if two conditions are satisfied. First, the damages must be compensation for loss of a taxable income or gain, and not simply for loss of a capital asset. Thus the rule would probably not apply if a buyer of goods claimed the amount by which their market value exceeded the contract price. These damages are meant to compensate him for failure to obtain a capital asset (out of which he might make a profit or a loss.)[93] Secondly, the damages themselves must not be taxable in the hands of the victim of the breach.[94] Damages for wrongful dismissal are now taxable to the extent that they exceed £30,000.[95] Hence such damages must be reduced by reference to the claimant's income-tax liability where his loss of income is less than £30,000[96]; where it is more, the court will assess his net loss and then award such sum as, after tax on the sum so assessed, would be equal to that loss.[97]

The rule in *Gourley*'s case has been much criticised. It is said to involve a paradox: for revenue purposes damages for loss of earnings are treated as compensation for loss of a

---

[90] *Clark v Kirby-Smith* [1964] Ch. 506, 512.

[91] [1956] A.C. 185; Jolowicz [1959] C.L.J. 85; Tucker, *ibid.* 185; Hall, 73 L.Q.R. 212; Smith, 1956 S.L.T. 13; Baxter, 19 M.L.R. 373; Bishop and Kay, 103 L.Q.R. 211. *cf. Otter v Church, Adams, Tatham & Co* [1953] Ch. 280 (death duties). *Cooper v Firth Brown Ltd* [1963] 1 W.L.R. 418 (national insurance contributions); *Dews v NCB* [1988] A.C. 1 (compulsory pension contribution).

[92] *Beach v Reed Corrugated Cases Ltd* [1956] 1 W.L.R. 807; *Re Houghton Main Colliery* [1956] 1 W.L.R. 1219; *Phipps v Orthodox Unit Trusts Ltd* [1958] 1 Q.B. 314. Contrast the position in cases of breach of trust: *Bartlett v Barclays Bank Trust Co* [1980] Ch. 515; *Re Bell's Indenture* [1980] 1 W.L.R. 1217; *cf. John v James* [1986] S.T.C. 352 (liability to account for breach of fiduciary duty under contract).

[93] *cf. Spencer v MacMillan's Trustees*, 1958 S.C. 300; *Lim Foo Yong Ltd v Collector of Land Revenue* [1963] 1 W.L.R. 295. But if goods are *sold* by a trader, damages for non-acceptance are taxable as receipts of his trade and so not subject to reduction in respect of tax: *Deeny v Gooda Walker Ltd (No.2)* [1996] 1 W.L.R. 426 at 432.

[94] *Diamond v Campbell-Jones* [1961] Ch. 22; *PC Producers v Dalton* [1957] R.P.C. 199; *Herring v BTC* [1958] T.R. 401; *Raja's Commercial College v Gian Singh & Co Ltd* [1977] A.C. 312; *Dickinson v Jones Alexander & Co* [1993] 2 FLR 521. *Deeny v Gooda Walker Ltd (No.2)* [1996] 1 W.L.R. 426.

[95] Income and Corporation Taxes Act 1988, ss.148, 188(4), as amended by Finance Act 1988, s.74. Payments in lieu of damages for dismissal must be distinguished from payments made as part of an agreed variation of a contract which continues after the variation: such payments are taxable even if they are less than £30,000: see *McGregor v Randall* [1984] 1 All E.R. 1092.

[96] *Parsons v BNM Laboratories Ltd* [1964] 1 Q.B. 95.

[97] *Bold v Brough, Nicholson & Hall Ltd* [1964] 1 W.L.R. 201; *Shove v Downs Surgical plc* [1984] I.C.R. 582; Lee, 47 M.L.R. 471; *Stewart v Glentaggart* 1963 S.C. (Ct. of Sess.) 300.

capital asset, since otherwise they would be taxable; while in assessing damages they are treated as compensation for loss of income, since otherwise the claimant's tax liability would be irrelevant.[98] A possible solution of this paradox is to say that the damages compensate the claimant for loss of *earning capacity*, which is a capital asset whose value depends on (amongst other things) the incidence of taxation.[99] Other criticisms are concerned with the practical effects of the rule. It is said that the rule enables the defendant to take advantage of wholly extraneous circumstances (*e.g.* that the claimant has a large private income); that it makes the assessment of damages highly speculative; and that the rule may make it cheaper to break a contract than to perform it. But similar criticisms could be made of other rules relating to damages, which have so far remained immune from them. Thus a seller can sometimes take advantage of an extraneous event, such as a subsale made by the buyer, in reducing damages for non-delivery[1]; speculative damages are by no means uncommon[2]; and it may often be cheaper to break a contract than to perform it: for example, where damages are assessed on a difference in value basis amounting only to a small fraction of the cost of performance.[3] The rule in *Gourley*'s case has therefore survived the criticisms which have been levelled against it; and it can be supported[4] on the ground that it gives effect to the principle that damages are meant only to compensate the claimant for his actual loss.

A breach of contract may actually *reduce* the victim's tax liability. The amount of the reduction is then deducted from the damages for the breach, on the principle that the benefit of having to pay less tax in fact mitigates the victim's loss.[5]

(5) Alternatives

Where a contract entitles the party in breach to perform in alternative ways, damages are, as a general rule, assessed on the assumption that he would have performed in the way that is least burdensome to himself and least beneficial to the other party.[6] Thus if a voyage charterparty gives the charterer the power to choose between a number of different ports of discharge, damages for his failure to load will be assessed on the assumption that he would have chosen the most distant port and so have reduced the shipowner's profit.[7] Similarly, where a supplier of goods has an option as to the exact quantity to be delivered, damages for non-delivery will be based on the assumption that he would have delivered the smallest permissible quantity.[8]

---

[98] Jolowicz, above, n.91.

[99] Tucker, above, n.91. Damages for personal injury are not taxable as capital gains: Taxation of Chargeable Gains Act 1992 s.51(2).

[1] See above, p.949.

[2] See above, p.955.

[3] See above, p.944.

[4] See Law Reform Committee, 7th Report (1958) Cmnd. 501.

[5] *Levison v Farin* [1978] 2 All E.R. 1149; below, pp.980–982.

[6] *Abrahams v Herbert Reiach Ltd* [1922] 1 K.B. 477; *Withers v General Theatre Corp* [1933] 2 K.B. 536; *The Rijn* [1981] 2 Lloyd's Rep. 267; the rule may be excluded by express contrary stipulation: *Yeoman Credit Ltd v Waragowski* [1961] 1 W.L.R. 1124; *Bremer Handelsgesellschaft mbH v Bunge Corp* [1982] 1 Lloyd's Rep. 108, affirmed without reference to this point [1983] 1 Lloyd's Rep. 476.

[7] *Kaye SN Co Ltd v W & R Barnett Ltd* (1932) 48 T.L.R. 400; *The Rijn* [1981] 2 Lloyd's Rep. 267 at 270; *cf. Phoebus D Kypriamou Co v Wm H Pim Jr* [1977] 2 Lloyd's Rep. 570; *The World Navigator* [1991] 2 Lloyd's Rep. 23 at 33.

[8] *Re Thornett & Fehr and Yuills Ltd* [1921] 1 K.B. 219. *cf.* the statement of the common law position in *Page v Combined Shipping & Trading Co* [1997] 3 All E.R. 656 at 660 (where the rule was displaced by Commercial Agents (Council Directive) Regulations 1993, SI 1993/3053, reg.17(7)). Where the contract does not clearly specify the supplier's options, these will have to be determined by the court as a matter of construction, as in *Paula Lee Ltd v Robert Zehil Ltd* [1983] 2 All E.R. 390.

The general rule just stated is subject to a number of qualifications. A contract of sale may, for example, give the seller an option as to the time of delivery by allowing him to deliver at any time chosen by him in a stated month. In such a case, damages for non-delivery will *prima facie* be assessed by reference to the market price at the end of the period. They will not be assessed by reference to the time during it when the market was lowest[9]; for such a rule would give rise to too much uncertainty. Moreover, the party who has the option may declare before breach that he will exercise it in a particular way. Damages will then be assessed on that basis[10] if the effect of the declaration is to bind him contractually to perform in the specified way.[11]

The above rules only apply where the obligation of the defendant is truly alternative. In *Deverill v Burnell*[12] the defendant undertook to transmit the proceeds of certain drafts to the plaintiff if they were paid; "and if the drafts should not be paid, the defendant should either return the same to the plaintiff *or* pay him the amount". The drafts were not paid but the defendant neither returned them nor paid the amount. In an action for the amount of the drafts the defendant argued that the obligation was alternative; that he could perform by returning the drafts; and that, as these were worthless, he was liable only for nominal damages. But he was held liable for the full amount. His undertaking was "not in the strictest sense an alternative promise, but a promise that the defendant would return the bills, and if he did not return them he would pay the amount of them".[13] The distinction is between a promise by A to do "X or Y" and a promise to do "X but, if X is not done, to do Y". In the first case, it is not possible to tell whether X or Y is due till A has exercised his choice between them; in the second, X is due but if X is not done (whether as a result of A's choice or for some other reason), then Y becomes due.[14] The defendant's obligation to pay (*i.e.* to do Y) was of the second kind: it was a contingent, rather than an alternative, one and became absolute on the occurrence of the condition, *i.e.* on failure to return the bills.

(6) Time for assessment

In times of fluctuating costs and values, it is important to know by reference to what point of time damages will be assessed.

(a) TIME OF BREACH. The starting principle is, or is generally assumed to be, that damages are assessed by reference to the time of breach. For example, where a buyer of goods fails to accept and pay for them [or a seller fails to deliver] the damages are *prima facie* the difference between the contract price and the market price "at the time or times when the goods ought to have been accepted [or delivered], or (if no time was fixed for acceptance [or delivery]) at the time of the refusal to accept [or deliver]".[15] The same principle of assessment by reference to the time of breach has been applied where a vendor of land wrongfully refused to convey.[16] The theory behind the rule is that any

---

[9] *cf. Harlow & Jones Ltd v Panex (International) Ltd* [1967] 2 Lloyd's Rep. 509; *Phoebus D Kyprianou Co v William H Pim Jr*, above (buyer's breach); *Benjamin's Sale of Goods* (6th ed.), §§20–111, 20–129.
[10] See *The Delian Spirit* [1972] 1 Q.B. 103 at 111–112; *Shipping Co of India Ltd v Naviera Letasa SA* [1976] 1 Lloyd's Rep. 132; *Toprak Mahsulleri Ofisi v Finagrain Cie Commerciale* [1979] 2 Lloyd's Rep. 98.
[11] Contrast *The Rijn*, above, n.7, at 270 (where the declaration was not of this kind).
[12] (1873) L.R. 8 C.P. 475.
[13] *ibid.* at 477.
[14] *cf.* above, p.892.
[15] Sale of Goods Act 1979, ss.50(3), 51(3); *cf. Jamal v Moolla Dawood Sons & Co* [1916] 1 A.C. 175; *The "Ile aux Moines"* [1974] 1 Lloyd's Rep. 262; *Phillips v Ward* [1956] 1 W.L.R. 471 at 474, 475, 478; *Amerena v Barling* [1993] E.G.C.S. 28; *The Texaco Melbourne* [1994] 1 Lloyd's Rep. 473 at 476; and see above p.953, n.55.
[16] *Diamond v Campbell-Jones* [1961] Ch. 22 at 36; *Janred Properties Ltd v Ente Nazionale Italiano per il Turismo* [1989] 2 All E.R. 444 at 457.

loss suffered by reason of market movements after the time of breach is not caused by the breach, but rather by the injured party's failure to mitigate[17] by making a substitute contract. Since under the mitigation rules the claimant need only act reasonably, it follows that even the principle of assessment by reference to the time of breach is applied with some latitude. In *C Sharpe & Co Ltd v Nosawa*[18] a contract for the sale of peas required the seller to deliver on "about July 21" but no delivery was made. Goods of the precise contract quality were not available in the market. It was held that the buyers had "a reasonable time to consider their position"[19]; and accordingly the damages were assessed by reference to the market price of similar goods at the end of July.[20]

The principle of assessment by reference to the time of breach is based on two assumptions: that the injured party knows of the breach as soon as it is committed, and that he can at that time take steps to mitigate the loss which is likely to flow from it. Where the facts falsify these assumptions, the courts will depart from the principle, and assess the damages by reference to "such other date as may be appropriate in the circumstances".[21] In particular they will have regard to the time when the breach was, or could have been discovered; and to the question whether it was possible or reasonable for the injured party to make a substitute contract immediately on such discovery.

(b) TIME OF DISCOVERY OF BREACH. The injured party may not have known of the breach when it was committed and may have been unable, acting with reasonable diligence, to discover it at that time. The damages will then *prima facie*[22] be assessed by reference (at the earliest[23]) to the time when that party, so acting, could have made the discovery. For example, a seller may first "appropriate" goods to the contract by indicating which particular goods he intends to deliver under a contract for the sale of unascertained goods, and then deliver them. If those goods are not in conformity with the contract, the seller will be in breach at the time of appropriation, but the damages are *prima facie* assessed by reference to the later time of *delivery*.[24] Where goods are sent to the buyer in sealed packages, the damages may be assessed by reference to the even later time, at which it is reasonable to expect the packages to be opened and their contents examined.[25] Similarly, where a builder does defective work and damages are based on cost of cure, they will normally be assessed by reference to the time when the

---

[17] See below, p.977.
[18] [1917] 2 K.B. 814; *cf. The Good Friend* [1984] 2 Lloyd's Rep. 586 at 596; *Shearson Lehman Hutton Inc v Maclaine Watson & Co (No.2)* [1990] 2 Lloyd's Rep. 441 at 447.
[19] [1917] 2 K.B. 814 at 821; *cf. Techno Land Improvements Ltd v British Leyland (UK) Ltd* (1979) 252 E.G. 805 at 809; *The Playa Larga* [1983] 2 Lloyd's Rep. 171 at 181.
[20] For similar reasons of convenience, the contract itself may provide for assessment by reference to a date other than that of breach: see, for example *Bremer Handelsgesellschaft mbH v Vanden Avenne-Izegem PVBA* [1978] 2 Lloyd's Rep. 109 at 117; *Lusograin Comercio Internacional de Cereas Ltda v Bunge AG* [1986] 2 Lloyd's Rep. 654 at 658.
[21] *Johnson v Agnew* [1980] A.C. 367 at 401; *County Personnel (Employment Agency) Ltd v Pulver* [1987] 1 W.L.R. 916; *South Australia Asset Management Corp v York Montague Ltd* [1997] A.C. 191 at 221; *quaere*, whether time of breach was the appropriate time in *Mahoney v Purnell* [1996] 3 All E.R. 61 at 95–96. *cf. Habton Farms v Nimmo* [2003] EWCA Civ 68.
[22] The rule is only a *prima facie* one and will not apply to the extent that delay in discovering the breach had no adverse effect on the injured party's position: *cf.* above, p.934 and see *Re Bell's Indenture* [1980] 1 W.L.R. 1217 (a case of breach of trust).
[23] For assessment by reference to later times, see the following paragraphs (c) to (f) of the text.
[24] Sale of Goods Act 1979, s.53(3).
[25] *Van den Hurk v R Martens & Co Ltd* [1920] 1 K.B. 850; *cf. The Hansa Nord* [1976] Q.B. 44 (damages assessed by reference to time of *arrival*, though breach occurred on *shipment*); *cf.* above, pp.364–365 for similar principles governing damages in tort for misrepresentation.

customer, acting with reasonable diligence, could have discovered the defect.[26] Delay in discovering the defect may affect not only the time but also the very basis of assessment; for if at the time of discovery the cost of cure is disproportionately high in relation to the value of a sound building, or if cure has become as a practical matter impossible, the court will award damages on a difference in value basis.[27]

(c) POSSIBILITY OF ACTING ON KNOWLEDGE OF BREACH. Even if the injured party knows of the breach, it may be impossible for him to act on that knowledge by making a substitute contract so as to reduce the loss. For example, a buyer might wrongfully refuse to pay for goods after they had been despatched to him, and it might be impossible for the seller to resell them until they had reached their destination. In such a case the damages would be assessed by reference to the time at which the seller could reasonably resell, and not to the time of the buyer's refusal to pay.[28]

Impossibility of acting on knowledge of the breach may also be due to the fact that the buyer lacks the means to buy a substitute on a rising market. In *Wroth v Tyler*[29] the defendant had contracted to sell his house for £6,000. The sale was to be completed in October 1971, when the value of the house had risen to £7,500; but in July 1971 the defendant had wrongfully repudiated the contract. The buyers started proceedings for specific performance and damages; judgment was given in January 1973, when the house was worth £11,500. It was held that specific performance should not be ordered[30]; that damages should be awarded in lieu[31] and that these should be assessed by reference to the value of the house at the time, not of breach, but of judgment,[32] *i.e.* not at £1,500 but at £5,500. Since the buyers had (as the defendant knew)[33] no financial resources beyond the £6,000 they had raised to buy the house, they could not act on their knowledge of the breach by making a substitute purchase on a rapidly rising market.

(d) REASONABLENESS OF ACTING ON KNOWLEDGE OF BREACH. Even where it is possible for the injured party to make a substitute contract on discovering the breach, it may not be reasonable to expect him to do so because at that time there is still a reasonable probability that the defendant will make good his default. In such cases damages are *prima facie* assessed by reference to the time when that probability ceased to exist.[34] Thus if a seller of goods, after the delivery date has gone by, assures the buyer that he will deliver, but then declares his final inability to perform, the damages will be assessed by reference to the market at the date of that declaration.[35] Again, the injured

---

[26] *East Ham BC v Bernard Sunley Ltd* [1966] A.C. 406; subsequent increases in cost may be taken into account if it is reasonable to delay the work: see (in tort) *Dodd Properties (Kent) Ltd v Canterbury CC* [1980] 1 W.L.R. 433; *London Congregational Union Inc v Harriss* [1985] 1 All E.R. 334, varied on other grounds [1987] 1 All E.R. 15; and see Feldman and Libling, 75 L.Q.R. 271; Duncan Wallace, 96 L.Q.R. 101; Waddams, 97 L.Q.R. 445; Duncan Wallace, 98 L.Q.R. 406; Waddams, 1 O.J.L.S. 134.

[27] *Applegate v Moss* [1971] 1 Q.B. 406; *King v Victor Parsons Ltd* [1972] 1 W.L.R. 801.

[28] See *Benjamin's Sale of Goods* (6th ed.), §20–128; *cf. Shearson Lehman Hutton Inc v Maclaine Watson & Co Ltd* [1989] 2 Lloyd's Rep. 570 at 647 (dealings suspended at time of alleged breach).

[29] [1974] Ch. 30; for further discussion see below at n.37 and below, pp.972, 1048.

[30] See below, p.1026.

[31] See below, p.1047.

[32] For the possibility of assessment by reference to an even later time, see *Grant v Dawkins* [1973] 1 W.L.R. 1406.

[33] *Wroth v Tyler* [1974] Ch.30 at 57; but for this fact, the loss might (at least in part) have been too remote: below, p.972.

[34] *Radford v De Froberville* [1977] 1 W.L.R. 1262; *Johnson Matthey Bankers Ltd v State Trading Corp of India* [1984] 1 Lloyd's Rep. 427 at 437–438. *cf.* in tort, *IBL Ltd v Coussens* [1991] 2 All E.R. 133. *cf. Habton Farms v Nimmo* [2003] EWCA Civ 68.

[35] *Barnett v Javeri & Co* [1916] 2 K.B. 390.

party may continue to press for performance after the agreed time, but finally elect to terminate on account of the breach: in such a case damages are assessed by reference to the date of termination.[36] A similar principle applies where the injured party brings an action for specific performance: thus a further explanation of the decision in *Wroth v Tyler*[37] is that the buyers could not be expected to make a substitute contract so long as their claim for specific performance was being maintained.[38] The same is true where an order of specific performance has actually been made but is not complied with, so that the injured party is eventually driven to abandon his attempt to enforce performance and to seek his remedy in damages: these are then assessed "as at the date when . . . the contract is lost".[39]

(e) LATE PERFORMANCE. If the party in default performs late and the other party suffers loss by reason of the delay, the damages for that loss will be assessed by reference to the date when performance actually was (and not by reference to the date when it should have been) rendered.[40]

(f) DAMAGES FOR ANTICIPATORY BREACH. The victim of an anticipatory breach can either continue to press for performance, or "accept" the breach.[41]

(i) *Breach not accepted.* If the injured party does not accept the breach, the principles (discussed above) as to the time for assessment apply. Assuming that subsequent events have not deprived the injured party of his right to damages,[42] the general rule is that those damages will be assessed by reference to the time when the contract ought to have been performed[43] and not by reference to the time of repudiation. The injured party is under no obligation to "accept" the breach. It follows that if the market moves so as to increase his loss between the time of repudiation and the time fixed for performance, he is entitled to damages assessed by reference to the latter time.[44]

(ii) *Breach accepted.* Where the injured party does accept the breach, he can start his action before the time fixed for performance; but the principle of assessment by reference to that time applies even in this type of case.[45] If the action comes to trial before the time fixed for performance, the damages will therefore necessarily be speculative, as they will be based on forecasts or guesses as to future market movements.[46] But where the injured party accepts the breach, the principle of assessment by reference to the time fixed for performance is subject to an important qualification: his damages will be reduced if, after accepting the breach, he fails to take

---

[36] *Toprak Mahsulleri Ofisi v Finagrain Cie Commerciale* [1979] 2 Lloyd's Rep. 98; *The Aktion* [1987] 1 Lloyd's Rep. 283.

[37] [1974] Ch. 30.

[38] *Wroth v Tyler*, above, as explained in *Radford v De Froberville* [1977] 1 W.L.R. 1262 at 1285–1286; *Meng Leong Development Pty Ltd v Jip Hong Trading Co Pte Ltd* [1985] A.C. 511; *Domb v Isoz* [1980] Ch. 548 at 559, where the injured party had bought another house *before* abandoning his claim for specific performance. This was said (at 559) to be irrelevant—presumably because, so long as that party was pursuing his claim for specific performance, it could not be said that the second house had been bought as a *substitute* for the first.

[39] *Johnson v Agnew* [1980] A.C. 367 at 401; *cf. Suleman v Shahsavari* [1988] 1 W.L.R. 1181; *Johnson & Co (Barbados) Ltd v NSR Ltd* [1997] A.C. 400 at 411–412.

[40] *Ozalid Group (Export) Ltd v African Continental Bank Ltd* [1979] 2 Lloyd's Rep. 231.

[41] See above, pp.857–865. *Garnac Grain Co Inc v Faure & Fairclough Ltd* [1968] A.C. 1130 at 1140.

[42] See above, pp.864–865 and below under heading (iii).

[43] *Tai Hing Cotton Mill Ltd v Kamsing Knitting Factory* [1979] A.C. 91.

[44] *Tredegar Iron & Coal Co Ltd v Hawthorn Bros & Co* (1902) 18 T.L.R. 716; under U.C.C. s.2–610(a) the injured party may await performance only "for a commercially reasonable time."

[45] *Roper v Johnson* (1873) L.R. 8 C.P. 167; *Melachrino v Nicholl & Knight* [1920] 1 K.B. 693 at 699.

[46] As in *Roper v Johnson*, above.

reasonable steps to mitigate his loss.[47] Under this rule, the injured party may, and if there is a market generally will, be required to make a substitute contract; and his damages will be assessed by reference to the time when that contract should have been made. This will usually be the time of acceptance of the breach[48] (or such reasonable time thereafter as may be allowed under the rules stated above[49]). If it is disputed whether a substitute contract could indeed have been made, the burden of proving that the injured party could have made such a contract lies on the party in breach. If that burden is not discharged, the damages will *prima facie* be assessed by reference to the time fixed for performance.[50]

(iii) *Effect of events after repudiation.* Under the rules just stated, market movements after acceptance of an anticipatory breach may be relevant to the assessment of damages; but it is further possible for the very existence of the right to damages to depend on events (other than such a breach) that occur, or will probably occur, between acceptance of the breach and the time fixed for performance. This possibility is illustrated by cases in which charterparties gave charterers a right to cancel if the ship was not ready to load at a named port by a specified date, and the charterers then committed anticipatory breaches by purporting to cancel before that date. In *The Simona*[51] it was held that a shipowner who affirmed the contract in such circumstances was not entitled to damages if the charterer then lawfully cancelled again, after the cancelling date. From the emphasis placed in that case on the fact of affirmation,[52] it appears that the shipowner's claim could have succeeded if, instead of affirming, he had accepted the original wrongful cancellation as an anticipatory breach. But in *The Mihalis Angelos*[53] it was said that the shipowner's damages for such a wrongful[54] cancellation would (even if he had so accepted it) have been merely nominal, since in that case it was already clear at the time of that cancellation that the ship could not possibly have reached the port of loading by the specified date. Hence the charterer could have relied on the point that he would have been entitled to cancel on the ship's late arrival; and as it was found that he certainly would have exercised that right, the contract was of no value to the shipowner.[55] In *The Simona* it was, indeed, also accepted that the ship was not ready to load by the time of the second cancellation,[56] but it does not appear that this prospective inability was already clearly established at the time of the original (wrongful) cancellation. Hence if that cancellation had been accepted as an anticipatory breach, it would not at the time of that acceptance have been clear that the shipowner's rights under the contract were

---

[47] See below, p.977.

[48] *Roth & Co v Taysen Townsend & Co* (1895) 1 Com.Cas. 240; (1896) 12 T.L.R. 211.

[49] See *C Sharpe & Co Ltd v Nosawa* [1917] 2 K.B. 814; above p.960; *Kaines (UK) Ltd v Oesterreichische Warenhandelsgesellschaft Autowaren etc* [1993] 2 Lloyd's Rep. 1.

[50] *Roper v Johnson* (1873) L.R. 8 C.P. 167. *cf.*, in tort, *Geest plc v Lansiquot* [2002] UKPC 48; [2002] 1 W.L.R. 3111 at [13–14].

[51] [1989] A.C. 788.

[52] *ibid.* at 800–801; *cf.* above, p.865.

[53] [1971] 1 Q.B. 164; George [1971] J.B.L. 109.

[54] The actual decision was that the cancellation was justified by the shipowner's breach of condition: above, pp.790–791; *cf. Walkinshaw v Diniz* [2002] 2 Lloyd's Rep. 165.

[55] [1971] 1 Q.B. 164 at 209–210; *cf. ibid.* 196, 202–203; *cf. The Noel Bay* [1989] 1 Lloyd's Rep. 361 at 365; *The World Navigator* [1991] 2 Lloyd's Rep. 23 at 32; *North Sea Energy Holding NV v Petroleum Authority of Thailand* [1999] 1 Lloyd's Rep. 483 at 496.

[56] *The Simona* [1989] A.C. 788 at 800.

worthless[57]; and the charterer could not have relied on the fact that they *subsequently* became worthless, since this state of affairs could have been induced by his wrongful repudiation, which could have led the shipowner to abandon any efforts which he might (but for the repudiation) have made to get the ship ready for loading by the cancelling date.

An important feature of the cases just discussed is that a cancelling clause gives the charterer an "independent option" to cancel if the ship is not ready to load by the specified date: it does "not impose any contractual obligation on the owners to commence loading by the cancelling date".[58] In other words, the right to cancel under such a clause is exercisable on the occurrence or non-occurrence of an *event*, and does not depend on any *breach* by the shipowner. The reasoning of *The Mihalis Angelos* would not apply (so as to reduce damages to a nominal amount) where the charterer's case was that he would have been entitled to rescind on account of the shipowner's *future breach*; for once the shipowner had accepted the charterer's earlier repudiation and so rescinded the contract for that anticipatory breach,[59] the shipowner would be relieved of any further obligation to perform, so that his failure to perform on the due day could no longer be a breach.[60]

3. Methods of Limiting Damages

To compensate the injured party fully for all loss that can, in some sense, be said to flow from a breach of contract would often lead to undesirable results. The point can be illustrated by reference to a case, said to have been decided early in the 17th century, "where a man going to be married to an heiress, his horse having cast a shoe on the journey, employed a blacksmith to replace it, who did the work so unskilfully that the horse was lamed, and, the rider not arriving in time, the lady married another; and the blacksmith was held liable for the loss of the marriage".[61] This result has rightly been called absurd.[62] Such complete protection of the injured party's interests would either deter the other party from entering into the contract at all, or lead to an undue raising of charges. The law has therefore developed a number of rules for the purpose of limiting damages for breach of contract.

---

[57] The crucial date for this purpose is "the date of *acceptance* of the repudiation" (*The Mihalis Angelos*, above, at p.210, italics supplied): not, it is submitted, "the date of repudiation" (*The Seaflower* [2000] 2 Lloyd's Rep. 37 at 44) since it is only acceptance of a wrongful repudiation that rescinds a contract (above, p.783), so that, before such acceptance, the victim of the wrongful repudiation will not have freed himself from further obligations under the contract. There is nothing in the report of *The Seaflower* to indicate that the victim (the shipowner) had accepted the repudiation; he seems, on the contrary, to have continued to make efforts to perform, and the limitation on his right to damages in that case can be explained on this ground. The event, or non-event, giving rise to the charterer's right to cancel in this case (failure to obtain a third party's approval) was also a breach since the shipowner had *guaranteed* that he would obtain the approval. For further proceedings in this case, see [2001] 1 Lloyd's Rep. 341. The same principles were applied by analogy in *Chiemgauer Membran und Zelthau GmbH v New Millennium Experience Co Ltd*, *The Times*, January 16, 2001, to termination without cause under an express term of the contract.

[58] *The Simona* [1989] A.C. 788 at 795.

[59] *Gill & Duffus SA v Berger & Co Inc* [1984] A.C. 382 at 391, below, p.767. After this case, apparently contrary dicta in *Regent OHG Aisestadt und Barig v Francecso of Jermyn Street* [1981] 3 All E.R. 327 and *Bremer Handelsgesellschaft mbH v JH Rayner & Co* [1979] 2 Lloyd's Rep. 216 at 224, 229 can no longer be supported.

[60] *cf.* above, at n.57.

[61] Referred to in *British Columbia Saw-Mill Co Ltd v Nettleship* (1868) L.R. 3 C.P. 499 at 508.

[62] *ibid.*

(1) Remoteness

A defendant is not liable for loss which is "too remote". The test of remoteness is whether the loss was within the reasonable contemplation of the parties; the application of this test gives rise to many problems.

(a) THE "REASONABLE CONTEMPLATION" TEST IN GENERAL. The general rules on this topic were formulated in *Hadley v Baxendale*.[63] A shaft in the plaintiffs' mill broke and had to be sent to the makers at Greenwich to serve as a pattern for the production of a new one. The defendants agreed to carry the shaft to Greenwich but, as a result of their breach of the contract, its delivery was delayed so that there was a stoppage of several days at the mill. The plaintiffs claimed damages of £300 in respect of their loss of profits during this period. At the trial the case was left generally to the jury, who returned a verdict of £50 for the plaintiffs. The defendants successfully applied for a new trial on the ground of misdirection. Alderson B. stated the principles in accordance with which the jury should have been directed: "The damages . . . should be such as may fairly and reasonably be considered *either* arising naturally, *i.e.* according to the usual course of things, from such breach of contract itself, *or* such as may reasonably be supposed to have been in the contemplation of both parties at the time they made the contract as the probable result of the breach".[64] Here the stoppage was not the "natural" consequence of the delay: it could not have been contemplated by a carrier that delay in delivering the shaft would keep the mill idle. "In the great multitude of cases of millers sending off broken shafts to third persons by a carrier under ordinary circumstances, such consequences would not, in all probability, have occurred".[65] The plaintiffs might have had a spare shaft[66] or been able to get one.[67] Nor could the stoppage, though it was no doubt anticipated by the *plaintiffs*, have been contemplated by *both* parties at the time of contracting as the probable result of breach. "The only circumstances here communicated by the plaintiffs to the defendants at the time the contract was made were that the article to be carried was the broken shaft of a mill, and that the plaintiffs were the millers of that mill".[68] The defendants were not told that any delay by them would keep the mill idle. If they had been told this, they might have attempted to limit their liability "and of this advantage it would be very unjust to deprive them".[69]

These principles were reformulated in *Victoria Laundry (Windsor) Ltd v Newman Industries Ltd*.[70] The defendants sold a boiler to buyers who, as the defendants knew, wanted it for immediate use in their laundry business. The boiler was delivered some five months after the agreed date, so that the buyers suffered loss of profits. Asquith L.J. said that the test of remoteness was whether the loss was "reasonably foreseeable as liable to

---

[63] (1854) 9 Exch. 341; Simpson, 91 L.Q.R. 272–277; Danzig, 4 *Journal of Legal Studies* 249; Pugsley 126 N.L.J. 420; Barton, 7 O.J.L.S. 40.

[64] (1854) 9 Exch. 341 at 354.

[65] *ibid.* at 356.

[66] *ibid.*

[67] 23 L.J.Ex. at 180.

[68] (1854) 9 Exch. at 355. This statement is hard to reconcile with the account of the facts given at 344: "The plaintiffs' servant told the [defendants'] clerk that the mill was stopped and that the shaft must be sent immediately." In the *Victoria Laundry* case [1949] 2 K.B. 528 at 537 Asquith L.J. said that the court "rejected this evidence"; but it is hard to see how the court could do this on an application for a new trial on the ground of misdirection. The more likely explanation of the apparent discrepancy is that the defendants were not told the crucial fact that the mill would *remain* idle if the shaft was delayed. According to 18 Jur. 358, "Although there was evidence that the defendant knew that the mill was standing still, *he did not know that this was for want of the shaft.*"

[69] (1854) 9 Ex. 341 at 355.

[70] [1949] 2 K.B. 528.

result from the breach".[71] This depended on the state of the defendant's knowledge. Every defendant had imputed to him knowledge of what happens in the ordinary course of things. He might also have actual knowledge of special circumstances, which would enable a reasonable man to foresee extraordinary loss. Here the defendants knew that the buyers wanted the boiler for immediate use in their business: they were thus liable for loss of profits that would ordinarily result from such use. But they were not liable for loss of exceptionally lucrative government contracts, which the buyers would have been able to make if they had received the boiler in time: they knew nothing of these contracts and could not reasonably have foreseen such loss.[72] The same reasoning would apply in the converse case of a buyer's breach, so that the seller could not recover damages in respect of his loss of profit to the extent that this was exceptionally large by reason of his having secured a supply of the goods in question at an unusually low price.[73]

The judgment in this case, and in particular the phrase "reasonably foreseeable as liable to result" gave rise to the view that the same test of "reasonable foreseeability" that governs remoteness in tort applies also in contract. But this view can no longer be accepted after the decision of the House of Lords in *The Heron II*.[74] In that case a ship was chartered to carry sugar from Constanza to Basrah. At the time of contracting, the charterer intended to sell the sugar as soon as it reached Basrah. The shipowner did not actually know this; but he did know that there was a market for sugar at Basrah, and "if he had thought about the matter he must have realised that at least it was not unlikely that the sugar would be sold in the market at market price on arrival".[75] The shipowner in breach of contract deviated and reached Basrah nine days late. During these nine days the market price of sugar at Basrah fell; and it was held that the charterer was entitled to damages for the loss suffered by reason of the fall in the market.[76] On the one hand, the House of Lords rejected the argument that in contracts for the carriage of goods by sea damages for delay were governed by a special rule, under which losses were too remote unless they were "reasonably certain" to result.[77] On the other hand, the House also rejected the view that the test of remoteness in contract was "reasonable foreseeability", at least if this phrase referred to the very low degree of probability required to satisfy the test of remoteness in tort.[78] Lord Reid said that the *Victoria Laundry* case was wrong in laying down this test for contract.[79] But when Asquith L.J. there referred to "loss reasonably foreseeable *as liable to result*"[80] he may have had a higher degree of probability in mind; and in this sense his judgment was (subject to one qualification[81])

---

[71] *ibid.* at 539.

[72] *cf. Kpohraror v Woolwich BS* [1996] 4 All E.R. 119; *The Mass Glory* [2002] EWHC 27 (Comm); [2002] 2 Lloyd's Rep. 245, and, in the tort of conversion, *Saleslease Ltd v Davis* [1999] 1 W.L.R. 1664; *Sandeman Coprimar SA v Transitos y Transportes Integrales SL* [2003] EWCA Civ 113 at [31] (conversion and negligence).

[73] See *North Sea Energy Holdings NV v Petroleum Authority of Thailand* [1997] 2 Lloyd's Rep. 418, at 438, affirmed [1999] 1 Lloyd's Rep. 483; the actual decision was that there was *no* breach by the buyer as the contract was ineffective by reason of the failure without his default of a condition precedent.

[74] Sub nom. *Koufos v C Czarnikow Ltd* [1969] 1 A.C. 350; Pickering, 31 M.L.R. 203.

[75] [1969] 1 A.C. 350 at 382.

[76] That loss amounted to some £4,000, which was *less* than the freight charge of about £9,000. In *Hadley v Baxendale* and the *Victoria Laundry* case this relationship was reversed: the losses considerably exceeded the amounts paid under the contracts to the defendants.

[77] *The Parana* (1877) 2 P.D. 118 at 123, overruled in *The Heron II*.

[78] [1969] 1 A.C. 350 at 385, 411, 425; *cf.* 413; *The Rio Claro* [1987] 2 Lloyd's Rep. 173 at 175; *Seven Seas Properties Ltd v Al Essa (No.2)* [1993] 1 W.L.R. 1083 at 1088; Cartwright [1996] C.L.J. 488.

[79] [1969] 1 A.C. 350 at 389.

[80] A phrase also used in *Farley v Skinner* [2001] UKHL 49; [2002] 2 A.C. 732 at [84].

[81] At one point in the *Victoria Laundry* case ([1949] 2 K.B. 528 at 540) Asquith L.J. suggested that the test was whether the occurrence of the loss was "on the cards." This test was rejected in *The Heron II* [1969] 1 A.C. 350 at 390, 399, 415, 425.

approved by the other members of the House of Lords. Various expressions are used in *The Heron II* to describe the degree of probability required to satisfy the test of remoteness in contract. There must be a "serious possibility"[82] or a "real danger"[83] or a "very substantial"[84] probability of loss; it must be "not unlikely"[85] or "easily foreseeable"[86] that loss will occur. The result of the decision is that a higher degree of probability is required to satisfy the test of remoteness in contract than in tort. When used in contract cases, the word "foreseeability" refers to this higher degree of probability.

The distinction established in *The Heron II* between the tests of remoteness in contract and tort was further considered in *H. Parsons (Livestock) Ltd v Uttley Ingham & Co Ltd*.[87] The defendants in that case supplied to the claimants a hopper for storing pig food; they failed, in breach of contract, to provide for proper ventilation, so that the food became mouldy and many of the pigs died from a rare intestinal disease. Swanwick J. ordered damages to be assessed for the value of the pigs which had died, for the claimants' expenses in dealing with the infection, and for "loss of sales and turnover". This judgment was affirmed on appeal, but for divergent reasons which give rise to three main difficulties. The first is to determine exactly what test of remoteness was applied. Lord Denning M.R. said that the higher degree of foreseeability stated in *The Heron II* applied only where the claim was for purely financial loss; where it was for physical damage the test of remoteness was the same in contract as in tort. He accordingly found for the claimants on the ground that the tort test was satisfied, even though that laid down in *The Heron II* was not: it was enough that the defendants could have foreseen a "slight possibility"[88] that eating mouldy food might make the pigs ill. Orr and Scarman L.JJ., on the other hand, took the view that there neither was nor should be any distinction between financial loss and physical damage for the purpose of remoteness. Their decision was based on the view that the test of remoteness laid down in *The Heron II* was satisfied as the defendants could have contemplated a "serious possibility"[89] that the pigs might become ill as a result of the defect in the hopper. The second difficulty is to account for the way in which the Court of Appeal dealt with Swanwick J.'s award of damages for "loss of sales and turnover".[90] This award was upheld but, in what seems to be a reference to it, Lord Denning M.R. said that the claimants were not entitled to damages "for loss of profit on future sales or future opportunities of gain"[91]; while Orr and Scarman L.JJ. agreed with Lord Denning in the result, but "by a different route".[92] It is not easy to reconcile these positions with each other or with the different ways (discussed above) in which the members of the Court formulated and applied the test of remoteness. Lord Denning's views on these points might seem to lead to the conclusion that there should be no recovery at all for "loss of sales and turnover",[93] while the

---

[82] *ibid.* at 414–415; *Malik v BCCI* [1998] A.C. 20 at 37.
[83] [1969] 1 A.C. 350 at 425; *cf. Bates v Barrow* [1995] 1 Lloyd's Rep. 680 at 691; *The Kriti Rex* [1996] 2 Lloyd's Rep. 171 at 173.
[84] [1969] 1 A.C. 350 at 388.
[85] *ibid.* at 383.
[86] *ibid. cf. Berryman v Hounslow LBC, The Times*, December 16, 1996.
[87] [1978] Q.B. 791.
[88] [1978] Q.B. 791 at 804.
[89] *ibid.* 812; Orr L.J. expressed his agreement with the reasoning of Scarman L.J. In *Saleslease Ltd v Davis* [1999] 1 W.L.R. 1664 the foreseeability test was applied to financial loss resulting from conversion; there was no discussion of any relevant difference between tort and contract rules of remoteness.
[90] [1978] Q.B. 791 at 793.
[91] *ibid.* at 804.
[92] *ibid.* at 806.
[93] Since this loss was financial and the test in *The Heron II* was (in Lord Denning's view) not satisfied.

reasoning of Orr and Scarman L.JJ. makes it hard to understand why they agreed with Lord Denning's conclusion that there should be no recovery "for loss of profit on future sales".[94] The most plausible reconciliation of the apparent conflict is that the claimants recovered damages for loss of the profits that they would have made from the pigs which had died, but not for loss of further profits which they would have been able to make (if the hopper had not been defective) by rearing and selling additional animals. The third difficulty is to determine whether, in the view of Orr and Scarman L.JJ., the test of remoteness in contract differs from that in tort. At one point, Scarman L.J. said that it was "absurd that the test of remoteness of damage should, in principle, differ according to the legal classification of the cause of action"; and that the law did not "differentiate between contract and tort save in situations where the agreement, or the factual relationship, of the parties with each other requires it in the interests of justice".[95] But he also accepted that "the formulation of the remoteness test is not the same in tort and contract because the relationship of the parties in a contract situation differs from that in tort".[96] It differs because, as Lord Reid said in *The Heron II*, a contracting party "who wishes to protect himself against a risk which to the other party would appear to be unusual, . . . can direct the other party's attention to it before the contract is made. In tort, however, there is no opportunity for the injured party to protect himself in that way . . . ".[97] Perhaps one may conclude that, where the same facts give rise to liability in both contract and tort, the claimant will be entitled to damages in respect of loss falling within the (to him more favourable) tort test[98]; and that the same may be true even where the cause of action arises in contract alone but the claimant does not in fact have the opportunity of protecting himself to which Lord Reid refers in *The Heron II*. Subject to these qualifications, the distinction drawn in that case between the contract and tort tests of remoteness continues to apply.[99]

(b) LOSS OCCURRING IN THE ORDINARY COURSE OF THINGS. A defendant is (even without knowledge of special circumstances) liable if the loss occurs "in the ordinary course of things", that is, if the probability of its occurrence comes up to the standard described in *The Heron II*. On this ground it has, for example,[1] been held that a person who agrees to supply or repair an obviously profit-earning thing is liable for loss of profits resulting from delay[2]; that a seller of poisonous cattle-food is liable for loss of the cattle to which it is fed[3]; that a merchant who sells defective seed to a farmer is liable for loss of the expected crop[4]; that a supplier of defective components to a manufacturer is liable for loss of business suffered by the latter when customers, dissatisfied with the

---

[94] Since (in their view) the *Heron II* test was satisfied.

[95] *ibid.* at 806; *cf. Bates v Barrow Ltd* [1995] 1 Lloyd's Rep. 680 at 691.

[96] [1978] Q.B. 791 at 806.

[97] [1969] 1 A.C. 350 at 385–386, cited in the *Parsons* case [1978] Q.B. 791 at 806. Torts (such as wrongful interference with goods) may, where they are preceded by negotiations between the victim and the wrongdoer, constitute an exception to Lord Reid's general statement, quoted in the text above.

[98] *cf. Archer v Brown* [1985] Q.B. 401 at 418 (where both tests seem to have been satisfied).

[99] *The Pegase* [1981] 1 Lloyd's Rep. 175 at 181, where *H Parsons (Livestock) Ltd v Uttley Ingham & Co Ltd* [1978] Q.B. 791 does not seem to have been cited; *Henderson v Merrett Syndicates Ltd* [1995] 2 A.C. 145 at 185 ("less restricted in tort").

[1] For further examples, see *The Almare Seconda* [1981] 2 Lloyd's Rep. 433; *The Good Luck* [1992] 1 A.C. 233; *The Kriti Rex* [1996] 2 Lloyd's Rep. 171 at 192.

[2] *Fletcher v Tayleur* (1855) 17 C.B. 21; *Wilson v General Iron Screw Colliery Co Ltd* (1887) 47 L.J.Q.B. 239; *cf. Mira v Aylmer Square Investments Ltd* [1990] 1 E.G.L.R. 45.

[3] *Pinnock Bros v Lewis & Peat Ltd* [1923] 1 K.B. 690; *Ashington Piggeries Ltd v Christopher Hill Ltd* [1972] A.C. 441; *cf. Cointat v Myham & Son* [1913] 2 K.B. 220; above, p.435.

[4] *George Mitchell (Chesterhall) Ltd v Finney Lock Seeds Ltd* [1983] 2 A.C. 803; and see above, p.943.

end-product, do not place repeat orders[5]; and that a person who sells goods to which he has no title, and which are later taken away from the buyer, is liable for money spent on repairing the goods.[6] On the other hand, it has been held that money spent on *improvements* to a house could not be recovered from a vendor who refused to convey[7] or from a builder as a result of whose breach of contract the house collapsed.[8] The line between repairs and improvements can obviously be a fine one; and where property is bought for restoration or development expenses incurred for this purpose would not be too remote.[9] In the last resort, the question whether the present test of remoteness has been *satisfied* is one of fact[10]; though the question whether the correct test has been *applied* is one of law.[11]

A defendant is not normally liable for a loss which is likely to occur in the ordinary course of things if it is not suffered[12]; nor for a loss which is suffered if it is too remote. But these rules are qualified where the claimant actually suffers a loss which is too remote while the defendant could have anticipated that he would have suffered another, smaller, loss. In *Cory v Thames Ironworks Co*[13] the defendants agreed to sell the hull of a floating boom derrick, but delivered it six months late. The defendants expected the buyers to use the hull as a coal store, and, if it had been so used, the buyers would, as a result of the delay, have lost £420. But, unknown to the defendants, the buyers intended to use the hull for a revolutionary method of transferring coal from colliers to barges, and lost profits of £4,000. The buyers admitted that they could not recover £4,000 and claimed £420. The court held the defendants liable for the latter sum, rejecting their argument that, as the £420 represented a loss not actually suffered, they were not liable even to this extent. There was "no hardship or injustice"[14] in making the sellers liable for the smaller sum when the buyers had lost a larger amount.[15] It is more doubtful whether damages can be recovered if the loss actually suffered is different in kind from that which would have occurred in the ordinary course of things. Suppose A sells poisonous cattle-food to B, who eats it himself in the course of an unforeseeable nutritional experiment, and dies. Can his executor sue A for the loss of a cow?

(c) KNOWLEDGE OF SPECIAL CIRCUMSTANCES. In *Hadley v Baxendale* it was suggested that the defendants might have been liable for the mill owners' loss of profits if they had known, at the time of contracting, that their delay would keep the mill idle. But mere knowledge of special circumstances is no longer regarded as sufficient.[16] Something more must be shown; and attempts have been made in later cases to define that additional requirement. In one case, Blackburn J. said that "in order that the notice [of special circumstances] may have any effect, it must be given under such circumstances

---

[5] *GKN Centrax Gears Ltd v Matbro Ltd* [1976] 2 Lloyd's Rep. 555.
[6] *Mason v Burningham* [1949] 2 K.B. 545; *cf. Bunny v Hopkinson* (1859) 27 Beav. 565.
[7] *Lloyd v Stanbury* [1971] 1 W.L.R. 535.
[8] *King v Victor Parsons Ltd* [1972] 1 W.L.R. 801.
[9] *cf.* below, pp.970–971 as to loss of profit.
[10] *Bulk Oil (Zug) AG v Sun International Ltd* [1984] 1 Lloyd's Rep. 531 at 544.
[11] *The Yanxilas (No.2)* [1984] 1 Lloyd's Rep. 676 at 682.
[12] *Sunley (B) & Co Ltd v Cunard White Star Ltd* [1940] 1 K.B. 740; *North Sea Energy Holdings NV v Petroleum Authority of Thailand* [1999] 1 Lloyd's Rep. 483.
[13] (1868) L.R. 3 Q.B. 181.
[14] (1868) L.R. 3 Q.B. 181 at 190.
[15] *Building & Civil Engineering Holidays Scheme Management Ltd v Post Office* [1966] 1 Q.B. 247 at 261; the recovery of "ordinary" profits in the *Victoria Laundry* case (above, pp.965–966) illustrates the same point.
[16] *e.g. Kemp v Intasun Holidays Ltd* (1988) 6 Tr.L. 161 (package tour operator not liable for discomfort suffered by holiday-maker because of asthmatic condition of which his wife told travel agent in casual conversation while booking holiday).

as that an *actual contract* arises on the part of the defendant to bear the exceptional loss".[17] But it is now clear that there need be no *express* contract to bear the exceptional loss.[18] Liability for loss caused by known special circumstances can perhaps be based on an "implied undertaking . . . to bear it",[19] but the reference seems to be to an undertaking implied in law (and not in fact), and so to mean that the defendant is liable for the exceptional loss, irrespective of any actual agreement to bear it.[20]

Simpson v L & NW Ry[21] illustrates the circumstances in which such liability can arise. The defendants had contracted to carry samples of cattle-food from an agricultural show at Bedford to another at Newcastle. They had an agent on the showground at Bedford specifically to attract such custom; the goods were marked "must be at Newcastle by Monday certain" but no express reference was made in the contract of carriage to the Newcastle show. The samples failed to arrive "by Monday" and did not reach Newcastle until after the show there was over. It was held that the defendants were liable for loss of the profits which the owner of the samples would have made, had the samples reached Newcastle in time. This should be contrasted with an example given in a 19th century case: a barrister going to Calcutta, where he had briefs awaiting him, could not sue the carriers for getting him there late, even if they knew why he is going to Calcutta.[22] The distinction between the cases lies in the nature of the two contracts. In the first, the contract was in substance one to carry samples to the Newcastle show—not simply to Newcastle. In the second the contract was one to carry the barrister to Calcutta—not to the Calcutta law sittings. Liability depends on "some knowledge *and acceptance* by one party of the *purpose and intention* of the other in entering the contract".[23]

The party in breach may know only some of the circumstances which lead to extra loss. He may then be liable for so much of that loss as he could have anticipated on the basis of the facts known to him, but not for further loss which results from other circumstances of which he was unaware.[24] In such cases, there is no rigid separation between the two rules in *Hadley v Baxendale*[25] and the defendant's liability increases with his degree of knowledge. Thus one reason why some loss of profits was recovered in the *Victoria Laundry* case, but none in *Hadley v Baxendale*, was that in the former the defendants knew that the boiler was wanted for immediate use, while in the latter case they did not know that want of the shaft would keep the mill idle. In *The Heron II* the defendants' knowledge that there was a sugar market at Basrah sufficed to make them liable for loss due to market movements there. Similarly, delay in the arrival of a

---

[17] *Horne v Midland Ry* (1873) L.R. 8 C.P. 131 at 141 (where this requirement was not satisfied); *cf. Coastal International Trading Ltd v Maroil Ltd* [1988] 1 Lloyd's Rep. 92 at 97; contrast *Laceys Footwear (Wholesale) Ltd v Bowler International* [1997] 2 Lloyd's Rep. 369 at 377 (loss of *ordinary* profits within contemplation of parties).

[18] *Robophone Facilities Ltd v Blank* [1966] 1 W.L.R. 1428 at 1448; *cf. Hydraulic Engineeering Co Ltd v McHaffie, Goslett & Co* (1878) 4 Q.B.D. 670 at 674; *The Heron II* [1969] 1 A.C. 350 at 422; *The Pegase* [1981] 1 Lloyd's Rep. 175 at 182; *Panalpina International Transport Ltd v Densil Underwear Ltd* [1981] 1 Lloyd's Rep. 187.

[19] *Robophone Facilities Ltd v Blank*, above n.18.

[20] *cf.* above, p.207.

[21] (1876) 1 Q.B.D. 274; *Jameson v Midland Ry.* (1884) 50 L.T. 426.

[22] *BC Saw-Mill Co Ltd v Nettleship* (1868) L.R. 3 C.P. 499 at 510; *cf. The Panalpina* case, above, n.18, where a carrier knew that goods were wanted for the Christmas trade but delivered them too late.

[23] *Weld-Blundell v Stephens* [1920] A.C. 956 at 980; contrast *GKN Centrax Gears Ltd v Matbro Ltd* [1976] 2 Lloyd's Rep. 555 at 580.

[24] *Borries v Hutchinson* (1865) 18 C.B.(N.S.) 445; *cf. International Minerals & Chemicals Corp v Karl O Helm AG* [1986] 1 Lloyd's Rep. 81 at 102 (exchange loss recoverable as damages for late payment in a currency known not to be "the currency of [the seller]"); *Danecroft Jersey Mills v Criegee, The Times*, April 14, 1987; *The Forum Craftsman* [1991] 1 Lloyd's Rep. 81 at 85–86; *Jackson v Royal Bank of Scotland* [2000] C.L.C. 1457.

[25] *Kpohraror v Woolwich Building Society* [1996] 4 All E.R. 119 at 128; *Hotel Services Ltd v Hilton International (UK) Ltd* [2000] 1 All E.R. (Comm) 750 at 755.

chartered ship at a loading port may cause loss to a charterer who intended to *buy* a cargo there, if the market rises during the period of the delay: the shipowner's liability in respect of such loss will depend on the degree of his knowledge of the market and of the charterer's arrangements in relation to the buying of the cargo.[26] And where a bank wrongfully dishonoured a customer's cheque, it was held liable to the customer for injury to his business reputation since it knew him to be a trader, but not for the further loss suffered by the customer when the particular transaction in respect of which the cheque had been drawn, and further business opportunities, were lost, since these were circumstances of which the bank neither was, nor could have been, aware on the basis of the facts known to it.[27] The point is further illustrated by two cases in which vendors wrongfully refused to convey land which the purchasers intended to redevelop. In the first,[28] the vendor was held liable for loss of development profits as he knew that the purchaser intended himself to carry out the development; in the second,[29] the vendor was not liable for such loss as he knew only that the purchaser was a dealer in real estate and not that he intended to develop the land.

What the defendant should have deduced from the facts known to him is generally judged by the standard of the reasonable person. Thus in *Hadley v Baxendale* the defendants could not reasonably have deduced from the facts known to them[30] that their delay would keep the mill idle, as the millers might have had a spare shaft.[31] In the *Victoria Laundry* case it would have been mere fantasy to suppose that the buyers kept a spare boiler.

In deciding what the defendant should reasonably have deduced from the facts known to him, the court can also take into account the commercial capacity in which he contracted. Thus a supplier of electricity to a building contractor cannot be expected to foresee the full consequences of a power failure on a complex construction project on which the contractor is engaged.[32] Similarly, in *Hadley v Baxendale* the defendants were general carriers and less well able to foresee the effects of delay than the defendants in the *Victoria Laundry* case, who were qualified engineers and knew more than the uninstructed layman of the purposes for which boilers of the kind in question were likely to be used.[33] But even a carrier can be made liable for loss of the chance of making profits on resale[34] and for loss of profits suffered by a manufacturer through non-delivery of raw materials known to be wanted for manufacturing purposes.[35] Similarly, a carrier who specialises in a particular trade may have imputed to him "a greater knowledge of the relevant market than might have been appropriate in different circumstances",[36] and so be liable for loss suffered by the other contracting party in consequence of movements in that market.

---

[26] Contrast *The Rio Claro* [1987] 2 Lloyd's Rep. with *The Baleares* [1993] 1 Lloyd's Rep. 215. See also *The Eurus* [1998] 1 Lloyd's Rep. 351.

[27] *Kpohraror v Woolwich Building Society* [1996] 4 All E.R. 119.

[28] *Cottrill v Steyning & Littlehampton Building Society* [1966] 1 W.L.R. 753; *cf. G & K Ladenbau (UK) Ltd v Crawley & de Reya* [1978] 1 W.L.R. 266; *Seven Seas Properties Ltd v Al-Essa* [1988] 1 W.L.R. 1272.

[29] *Diamond v Campbell-Jones* [1961] Ch. 22; *cf. Seven Seas Properties Ltd v Al Essa (No.2)* [1993] 1 W.L.R. 1083.

[30] See above, p.965.

[31] *cf. Gee v Lancs. & Yorks. Ry.* (1860) H. & N. 211 (carrier ignorant that manufacturer had no stocks of raw material); *The Pegase* [1981] 1 Lloyd's Rep. 175.

[32] *Balfour Beatty Construction (Scotland) v Scottish Power*, 1994 S.L.T. 807 (H.L.).

[33] [1949] 2 K.B. 528 at 540.

[34] e.g. *The Heron II* [1969] 1 A.C. 350; *Panalpina International Transport Ltd v Densil Underwear Ltd* [1981] 1 Lloyd's Rep. 187.

[35] *Monte Video Gas Co v Clan Line Steamers Ltd* (1921) 37 T.L.R. 866; *The Pegase* [1981] 1 Lloyd's Rep. 175; *cf. The Ocean Dynamic* [1982] 2 Lloyd's Rep. 88.

[36] *The Baleares* [1993] 1 Lloyd's Rep. 215 at 227.

A claimant may suffer extra loss because his financial position is such that he cannot avoid the adverse consequences of the breach. Damages can be recovered for such loss if the defendant knew of the claimant's lack of means and if the extra loss resulting from it "was such as might reasonably be expected to be in the contemplation of the parties as likely to flow from a breach of the obligation undertaken".[37]

(d) WHAT MUST BE "CONTEMPLATED". In tort cases, it is often said that the defendant is liable if he could have foreseen the type or kind of loss suffered, even though he could not have foreseen its extent or quantum.[38] Similar reasoning was used in *Wroth v Tyler*.[39] The defendant argued that he should not be liable for the full difference between the contract price and the market price because, though he could have contemplated some rise in house prices, he could not have contemplated the exceptionally large rise which occurred between 1971 and 1973. In rejecting this argument Megarry J. said that a defendant might escape liability for a "type or kind of loss"[40] which he could not have contemplated; but that there was no support in the authorities "for the alleged requirement that the quantum should have been in contemplation".[41] The distinction between "type" and "quantum" is, however, an elusive one; and the *Victoria Laundry*[42] case is hard to reconcile with the view that contemplation of the "quantum" is necessarily irrelevant. The most obvious description of the "type" of loss there within the defendants' contemplation was "loss of business profits"; and for some such loss they were held liable. The reason why they were not held liable for all the lost profits appears to be that those on the government contracts exceeded ordinary profits to an unforeseeable extent. It has been said that "loss of ordinary profits" is "different in kind from that flowing from a particular contract"[43]; but this suggestion gives rise to the difficulty that, in the last resort, all profit arises from some "particular contract". *Wroth v Tyler* is, it is submitted, best explained on the ground that the problem posed by the increase in house prices was not one of remoteness at all but one of quantification. The same is true of a later case in which a member of Lloyd's recovered underwriting losses from his agent as damages for breach of contract committed by the agent in pursuing a "high risk" strategy. This *type* of loss was foreseeable and not too remote: its *amount* was a matter of quantification and so not subject to any requirements of foreseeability.[44]

---

[37] *Muhammed Issa el Sheik Ahmed v Ali* [1947] A.C. 414, as explained in *Monarch SS Co v Karlshamns Oljefabriker (A/B)* [1949] A.C. 196 at 224; *cf. Trans Trust SPRL v Danubian Trading Co Ltd* [1952] 2 Q.B. 297; *Wroth v Tyler* [1974] Ch. 30 (as explained at p.961, above). *Robbins of Putney Ltd v Meek* [1971] R.T.R. 345; *Perry v Sidney Phillips & Son* [1982] 1 W.L.R. 1297; contrast *Pilkington v Wood* [1953] Ch. 770 (where defendant did not know of claimant's overdraft), and *Ramwade Ltd v WJ Emson & Co, The Times*, July 11, 1986 (which may be explicable on the same ground).

[38] *e.g. Smith v Leech Brain & Co Ltd* [1962] 2 Q.B. 405 at 415; *cf. Muirhead v Industrial Tank Specialities Ltd* [1986] Q.B. 507 at 532.

[39] [1974] Ch. 30; above, p.961.

[40] [1974] Ch. at 61; *cf. GKN Centrax Gears Ltd v Matbro Ltd* [1976] 2 Lloyd's Rep. 555 at 568 ("loss of a certain kind").

[41] [1974] Ch. 30 at 61; *cf. The Rio Claro* [1987] 2 Lloyd's Rep. 173 at 175 (but the loss suffered was said at 176 to have been of a "different category" from that which could have been contemplated).

[42] [1949] 2 K.B. 528; above, p.965. *cf.* also *The Forum Craftsman* [1991] 1 Lloyd's Rep. 81 at 85–86; *The Marine Star (No.2)* [1994] 2 Lloyd's Rep. 629 at 636 (reversed on other grounds [1996] 2 Lloyd's Rep. 383).

[43] *Brown v KMR Services Ltd* [1995] 4 All E.R. 598 at 621; *North Sea Energy Holdings NV v Petroleum Authority of Thailand* [1997] 2 Lloyd's Rep. 418 at 438, affirmed [1999] 1 Lloyd's Rep. 483; *quaere* whether the loss in the *Victoria Laundry* case indeed flowed from inability to secure a "particular contract," as opposed to a type of business.

[44] This seems to be the view of Hobhouse L.J. (with whom Ralph Gibson L.J. agreed) in *Brown v KMR Services Ltd* [1995] 4 All E.R. 598 at 642–643. See below pp.973–974 for discussion of the scope of the reasonable contemplation test.

The view that a defendant is liable if he could contemplate the type of loss, as opposed to its degree, was again put forward in *H Parsons (Livestock) Ltd v Uttley Ingham & Co Ltd*.[45] The defendants were held liable for the loss of the pigs because they could have contemplated that, as a result of their breach, the pigs would become ill[46]: it was not necessary for them to have contemplated that the pigs would suffer from the particular disease which affected them, and which turned out to be fatal. One explanation for this aspect of the case is that, where physical harm is caused, there is no need to show that its degree should have been anticipated.[47] An alternative (and, it is submitted, preferable) explanation of the *Parsons* case is that the only thing which the defendants failed to foresee was the *manner* in which the injury to the pigs might be caused.[48] On this view, no issue arose as to the distinction between *type* and *degree* of loss.

(e) SCOPE OF THE "REASONABLE CONTEMPLATION" TEST. "Reasonable contemplation" is a test of remoteness and not one of quantification.[49] It determines whether a claimant is entitled to compensation for a particular item of loss, but not how that loss is to be translated into money terms. If a seller of goods fails to deliver them, there is no doubt that he is liable for the loss that the buyer has suffered in simply not having the goods. Where there is a market, the buyer's loss will *prima facie* be valued by reference to that market[50]; and this process of valuation does not raise any issue as to what was within the reasonable contemplation of the parties.[51] In such cases, it is sometimes said that market fluctuations are *always* foreseeable; but this is either a fiction[52] or just another way of saying that foreseeability is, for purposes of quantification, irrelevant. It follows that the damages are not affected by the fact that the rise or fall in the market has been an unusually sharp one, or that it was due to circumstances which were not within the contemplation of the parties.[53] The same reasoning applies where a seller delivers defective goods: the buyer is entitled to the amount by which the value of the goods is reduced by reason of the defect and no question of remoteness arises in relation to this loss. Such a question could arise only in respect of further consequential loss, such as loss suffered by the buyer through his use of the goods.[54] Yet another illustration of the distinction here drawn is provided by *Wroth v Tyler* where the buyer was undoubtedly entitled to compensation for his loss in not getting the house, and the question how much the house was worth at the relevant date was simply one of quantification. A question of remoteness might have been raised in that case if the buyer had, in addition, lost a profit that he could have made by reselling the house or by

---

[45] [1978] Q.B. 791; above, p.935; P.V.B., 94 L.Q.R. 171.
[46] [1978] Q.B. 791 at 812.
[47] *ibid.* at 813.
[48] See [1978] Q.B. 791 at 813.
[49] For this distinction, see *Re National Coffee Palace Co* (1883) 24 Ch.D. 367 at 372: *JD D'Almeida Araujo Lda v Sir Frederick Becker & Co Ltd* [1953] 2 Q.B. 329. The distinction is said to be between "remoteness" and "measure" of damages, but in view of the ambiguity of the latter term, this usage has given rise to difficulties: see *NV Handel etc. v English Exporters Ltd* [1955] 2 Lloyd's Rep. 69 at 72 (affirmed *ibid.* at 317).
[50] See above, p.948.
[51] *cf. The Marine Star (No.2)* [1994] 2 Lloyd's Rep. 629 at 635 (reversed on other grounds [1996] 2 Lloyd's Rep. 383).
[52] *i.e.* if it relates to *particular* fluctuations.
[53] *e.g. Kwei Tek Chao v British Traders Ltd* [1954] 2 Q.B. 459. Similar reasoning applies where there is no market, so that the loss has to be quantified by reference to the factors described at p.953, above.
[54] The distinction between the two situations here discussed is reflected in ss.53(3) and (2) of the Sale of Goods Act 1979; so far as *contra, Bence Graphics International Ltd v Fasson UK Ltd* [1998] Q.B. 87 is doubted at pp.950–951, above.

redeveloping the site; but no attempt was made to show that any such loss had been suffered.

All this is not to say that loss due to market movements can never be subject to the "reasonable contemplation" test. It was so subject in *The Heron II*[55] where the charterer had lost, not *the goods*, but *the chance of going into the market to sell them* on a particular day. The question was whether *that chance* was something that the shipowner could have contemplated; and, once this issue had been settled in the charterer's favour, no serious attempt seems to have been made to show that market fluctuations in general, or the particular fluctuations which occurred, were unpredictable, so as to make the loss too remote.[56] In two of the speeches, it is said that the fall in the market was not due to "any unusual or unpredictable factor"[57]; and it may be possible to infer that, had it been due to some such factor, this might have affected the result. But it is submitted that a similar argument should not prevail where the market rule is used simply as a test of quantification.

(2) Causation

The statement that a claimant cannot recover damages because the breach "caused him no loss" is sometimes found in the cases (already mentioned) in which a state of affairs was clearly brought about by the breach, but was not disadvantageous to the claimant.[58] Our present concern, however, is with cases in which there is a breach, followed by a state of affairs clearly disadvantageous to the claimant, but the defendant argues that the breach did not bring about that state of affairs. For example, a shipowner may be technically in breach of contract because his ship was not equipped with a proper medicine chest; but if the ship later foundered in a storm, the owners of goods on board could not claim that the breach was the cause of their loss.[59] Similarly, the mere fact that a company continues to trade in consequence of its auditor's breach of duty in auditing its accounts does not make the auditor liable for losses incurred in the course of such trading: the auditor's breach is not an effective cause of the loss[60]; and the stigma which an employee may suffer as a result of his employer's breach of contract[61] will not give him the right to damages in respect of loss of employment prospects if he fails to prove that the stigma was the cause of such loss.[62] Another reason why loss may be held not to have been caused by the breach is that it would have been suffered even if the breach had not been committed. This was, for example, the position where solicitors acting for a mortgage lender committed a breach of contract and a breach of trust by parting with the lender's money before they should have done so; and the lender later suffered loss, not because the money had been paid over too soon, but; because the security turned out to be inadequate. It was held that the solicitors were not liable for this loss since the

---

[55] [1969] 1 A.C. 350; *cf. The Ulyanovsk* [1990] 1 Lloyd's Rep. 425 at 433.

[56] Contrast dicta in *Smeed v Foord* (1859) 1 E. & E. 602 at 616 and (in argument) 608. It is submitted that these dicta would not now be followed. The actual decision can be explained on the ground that, at the time of contracting, the defendant could not have contemplated that his delay in delivering the threshing machine would deprive the claimant of the chance of going into the market to sell his crop; for the claimant might have been expected to hire a substitute.

[57] [1969] 1 A.C. 350 at 394, 417.

[58] See above, p.934.

[59] See *Monarch SS Co v Karlshamns Oljefabriker (A/B)* [1949] A.C. 196 at 226.

[60] *Galoo v Bright Grahame Murray* [1994] 1 W.L.R. 1360. *cf. Seddington v Coleys Professional Services, The Times*, June 2, 1995 (tort); *Bank of Credit & Commerce International (Overseas) Ltd v Price Waterhouse (No.3), The Times*, April 2, 1998; *Equitable Life Assurance Society v Ernst & Young, The Times*, February 24, 2003.

[61] Below, p.991.

[62] *BCCI v Ali (No.2)* [2002] EWCA Civ 82; [2002] I.C.R. 1258.

lender had got exactly the charge it had bargained for, and since it would have suffered exactly the same loss, even if the solicitors' breach had not been committed.[63] The same reasoning applies where an agent without authority purports to contract on behalf of his principal with a third party and is liable to that third party for breach of implied warranty of authority.[64] The normal measure of damages for this breach is the amount that the principal would have had to pay, had he been bound by the contract and not performed it. But if the principal is utterly insolvent the damages are no more than nominal. The third party has not lost anything through the breach of warranty, for, had the agent had authority, the third party would have acquired only an empty right against the principal.[65] The loss is not caused by the breach in such cases since it would not have been averted if the defendant had duly performed his contract.[66]

(a) CONCURRENT CAUSES GENERALLY. In all the above cases, the defendant is not liable for a loss which is not caused by the breach at all; but a claimant can often recover damages although the breach is not the *sole* cause of the loss. As Devlin J. has said: "If a breach of contract is one of two causes, both co-operating and both of equal efficacy, . . . it is sufficient to carry a judgment for damages".[67] One such situation has already been mentioned: the victim of a breach of contract can recover damages for a loss caused partly by the breach and partly by his own lack of means (so long as the loss is not too remote).[68] Again, unseaworthiness is hardly ever the sole cause of a maritime loss: the shipowner is liable though ordinary sea perils have co-operated with unseaworthiness to produce the loss.[69] But he would not be liable if the unseaworthiness led to a delay and the ship then ran into a typhoon as such a catastrophe may occur anywhere[70] and as the delay would not be causally "of equal efficacy" with the typhoon. Nor is the party in breach liable for a loss in fact wholly caused by an extraneous supervening event, even though, if that event had not occurred, the same loss, or part of it, would have been caused by the breach.[71] Further problems of mitigation and contributory negligence, which arise where the concurrent cause is the victim's own conduct, are discussed below.[72]

---

[63] *Target Holdings Ltd v Redferns* [1996] A.C. 421; *cf. Stratton Ltd v Weston, Financial Times*, April 11, 1990; *Banque Keyser Ullman SA v Skandia (UK) Ins Co Ltd* [1991] 2 A.C. 249; *The World Navigator* [1991] 2 Lloyd's Rep. 23; *Brown v KMR Services Ltd* [1995] 4 All E.R. 598 (the 22% reduction); *cf.* also *Sykes v Midland Bank Executor & Trustee Co Ltd* [1971] 1 Q.B. 113; A.L.G., 87 L.Q.R. 10; *County Natwest v Pinsent & Co* [1994] 3 Bank. L.R. 4; and *Swindle v Harrison* [1997] 4 All E.R. 705 (where damages were awarded for breach of fiduciary duty); *Freeguard v Rogers, The Times*, October 22, 1998.

[64] See above, p.738.

[65] *Richardson v Williamson* (1871) L.R. 6 Q.B. 276 at 279; *Weeks v Propert* (1873) L.R. 8 C.P. 427 at 439; *Re National Coffee Palace Co* (1883) 24 Ch.D. 367 at 372.

[66] *cf. Hilton v Barker Booth & Eastwood* [2002] EWCA Civ 723; *The Times*, June 6, 2002.

[67] *Heskell v Continental Express Ltd* [1950] 1 All E.R. 1033 at 1048; disapproved on another point in *Hedley Byrne & Co Ltd v Heller & Partners Ltd* [1964] A.C. 465 at 532; *cf. Vimar International Ltd v Theresa Navigation Co Ltd* [2001] 2 Lloyd's Rep. 1 at [43].

[68] See above, p.972. In tort the loss resulting from the claimant's lack of means has been said to arise from a "separate and concurrent cause": *Liesbosch Dredger v SS Edison* [1933] A.C. 449 at 460. But this position is viewed with some scepticism in *Perry v Sidney Phillips & Son* [1982] 1 W.L.R. 1297 at 1302, 1305, 1307 and is now much qualified even in tort cases: see *Dodd Properties (Kent) Ltd v Canterbury CC* [1980] A.C. 433; *Archer v Brown* [1985] Q.B. 401 at 417; *Matlock v Man* [1993] R.T.R. 13; for an application of *The Liesbosch* in contract, see: *Ramwade Ltd v Emson & Co, The Times*, July 11, 1986, as to which see above, p.972, n.37.

[69] *Smith, Hogg & Co Ltd v Black Sea Insurance Co Ltd* [1940] A.C. 997.

[70] *Monarch Steamship* case [1949] A.C. 196 at 215.

[71] *Beoco Ltd v Alfa Laval Co Ltd* [1995] Q.B. 137.

[72] See below, pp.977, 978, 980, 982–987.

(b) INTERVENING ACTS OF THIRD PARTY. Where loss results partly from the breach and partly from the act of a third party, the party in breach is nevertheless liable for the loss if (but only if)[73] the third party's act was "foreseeable" on the standard of probability which governs remoteness in contract.[74] Thus a shipowner who in time of impending war commits breach of a charterparty is liable for the resulting loss though it was aggravated by government action[75]; a person who in breach of contract recommends a dishonest stockbroker is liable for loss caused by the broker's dishonesty[76]; a solicitor engaged to advise on legal aspects of a commercial transaction is similarly liable for loss suffered by his client in consequence of the act or default of the other party to the transaction if the solicitor's negligence consisted precisely in failing to take steps to safeguard the client against the risk of such loss[77]; and a house-painter who in breach of contract leaves his client's house unlocked is liable for the value of goods taken from it by thieves.[78] These cases show that, although remoteness and causation are "quite different concepts"[79] (so that a loss may be too remote even though it is clearly caused by the breach)[80] nevertheless "some of the relevant considerations are the same".[81]

In *Weld-Blundell v Stephens*[82] a client employed an accountant to investigate the affairs of a company and wrote him a letter defaming two of the company's directors. The accountant's partner negligently dropped the letter in the company's office, where it was picked up by the manager and shown to the two directors. They recovered heavy damages for libel from the client who, in turn, claimed this amount from the accountant as damages for breach of contract. The House of Lords gave two reasons for dismissing the claim. First, the client's liability for defamation *existed* quite apart from the breach of contract, which simply brought that liability to the directors' attention.[83] Secondly, the loss was not caused by the breach, but by the act of the manager in showing the letter to the directors, and this act was *not* one which the defendant could have foreseen. The view that the manager's act was not foreseeable may be regarded with some scepticism, particularly as the jury found that it was the defendant's duty to keep the letter secret. But it forms one basis of *Weld-Blundell v Stephens*. The case does not support the proposition that a party who breaks a contract can escape liability for loss caused partly by his breach and partly by a *foreseeable* intervening act.

(3) Mitigation

Two ideas are usually discussed under this heading. The first is that the claimant cannot recover damages for a loss that he ought to have avoided. He is said to be under a "duty to mitigate". This expression will be used here even though it is open to the objection that breach of the "duty" gives rise to no legal liability[84] but only reduces the amount

---

[73] *The Silver Sky* [1981] 2 Lloyd's Rep. 95.
[74] See above, pp.965–968.
[75] *Monarch Steamship* case [1949] A.C. 196.
[76] *De la Bere v Pearson Ltd* [1908] 1 K.B. 280; *cf. T v Surrey CC* [1994] 4 All E.R. 577 (child-minder); *Partridge v Morris* [1995] E.G.C.S. 158 (architect recommending builder); *Sasea Finance Ltd v KPMG* [2000] 1 All E.R. 676 (auditor failing to warn company of senior executives' fraud).
[77] *British Racing Drivers' Club v Hextall Erskine & Co* [1996] 3 All E.R. 667.
[78] *Stansbie v Troman* [1948] 2 K.B. 48; *cf. Marshall v Rubypoint Ltd* [1997] E.G.C.S. 12.
[79] *cf. Fairchild v Glenhaven Funeral Services Ltd* [2002] UKHL 22, [2003] A.C. 32 at [54] ("unrelated to causation").
[80] As in *Bates v Barrow Ltd* [1995] 1 Lloyd's Rep. 680.
[81] *The Yanxilas (No.2)* [1984] 1 Lloyd's Rep. 676 at 682; *The Eurus* [1998] 1 Lloyd's Rep. 351 at 362.
[82] [1920] A.C. 956.
[83] *cf. Clark v Kirby-Smith* [1964] Ch.506.
[84] *The Solholt* [1983] 1 Lloyd's Rep. 605 at 608; Lomnicka, 99 L.Q.R. 495; *The Good Friend* [1984] 2 Lloyd's Rep. 586, 597; *The Alecos M* [1991] 1 Lloyd's Rep. 120 at 124.

that the claimant can recover. The second idea is that the claimant has to give credit for certain benefits accruing to him in consequence of the breach. Here it can be said that his loss is in fact mitigated.

(a) THE DUTY TO MITIGATE has two aspects: first, the claimant must take reasonable steps to minimise his loss; and secondly he must forbear from taking unreasonable steps that increase his loss.[85] It follows from the principle on which the "duty" to mitigate is based that the duty will normally arise only when the claimant has become aware of the breach.[86] It has been suggested that, where the claimant has not actually become aware of the breach, the duty will not arise merely because he was careless in failing to discover it; but that such carelessness might be relevant for other purposes: *e.g.* in making the loss (or part of it) too remote or in reducing the amount recoverable on the ground of contributory negligence.[87] These techniques would normally lead to much the same result as the principles of mitigation; but it is submitted that there is no compelling reason for holding that those principles can never apply where the claimant had, but failed to take, clear opportunities of discovering the breach: *e.g.* where a buyer is warned of the need to test the goods but fails to do so.

(i) *Minimising loss.*[88] If the claimant fails to take reasonable steps to minimise his loss, he cannot recover anything in respect of extra loss due to that failure. Commonly, he is required to make a substitute contract. For example, where a seller of goods fails to deliver, the buyer must go into the market[89] at the relevant time[90] to buy substitute goods. If he fails to do so he cannot recover any further loss that he may suffer because the market continues to rise or because he is deprived of the opportunity of making a profit out of the use or resale of the goods.[91] Conversely, a seller of shares who kept them after the buyer's breach could not recover any extra loss that he might suffer as a result of a later fall in the market.[92] On the same principle, a wrongfully dismissed employee must make reasonable efforts[93] to find a comparable job. The injured party is, however, required to mitigate in this way only if the new transaction would be a true substitute for the old one. Where, for example, a customer wrongfully repudiates a contract for the provision of services at a time when the injured party has spare capacity, then the possibility of that party's making another contract with a new customer will not be taken into account: such a new contract will not be a true substitute for the broken contract since the injured party would, but for the breach, have been able to perform both contracts.[94]

Where the breach has induced the injured party not to claim sums due to him from third parties, the mitigation rules may require him to assert these claims.[95] But this is

---

[85] For the burden of proof on this issue, see below, p.1018 at n.19.
[86] *The Superhulls Cover Case (No.2)* [1990] 2 Lloyd's Rep. 431 at 461.
[87] *ibid.* at 462; below, p.982.
[88] Bridge, 105 L.Q.R. 398.
[89] If there are several markets, a transaction in any market that it was reasonable for the injured party to use can form the basis of assessment: *Gebruder Metelmann GmbH & Co KG v NBR (London) Ltd* [1984] 1 Lloyd's Rep. 614, a case of buyer's breach.
[90] See above, pp.959–964.
[91] *Hussey v Eels* [1990] 2 Q.B. 227 at 233 ("deemed mitigation"); *cf. The Marine Star (No.2)* [1994] 2 Lloyd's Rep. 629 at 635 (reversed on another ground [1996] 2 Lloyd's Rep. 383); *The Elena D'Amico* [1980] 1 Lloyd's Rep. 75 at 79 (charterparty); and see above, p.948.
[92] *Jamal v Moolla Dawood Sons & Co* [1916] 1 A.C. 175 at 179; *cf. Bristol & West BS v Fancy & Jackson* [1997] 4 All E.R. 582 at 623 (delay in realising security).
[93] See *Clark v BET* [1997] I.R.L.R. 348 (senior employee unlikely to get other employment).
[94] *Western Web Offset Printers Ltd v Independent Media Ltd, The Times,* October 10, 1995; *cf.* above, pp.965–966.
[95] *St Albans City & District Council v International Computers Ltd* [1996] 4 All E.R. 481 (the £484,000 claim).

subject to the overriding rule that he need only take such steps as are reasonable: he therefore does not need to take steps which would involve him in complicated litigation[96] or which would ruin his commercial reputation[97] or which would involve him in unreasonable expense or inconvenience.[98]

Sometimes the injured party will be required to mitigate by accepting from the party in breach a performance which differs in some way from that originally bargained for. Thus where a charterer fails to load the agreed cargo, the shipowner may be bound to mitigate by accepting the charterer's reasonable offer of alternative cargo, even at a lower rate[99]; where a seller agrees to give credit and then refuses to deliver except for cash, the buyer may be bound to mitigate by accepting such delivery instead of buying against the seller on a rising market[1]; and where a seller cannot deliver at the agreed time the buyer may be required to mitigate by accepting late delivery.[2] In these cases, any loss suffered by the injured party by reason of the difference between the performance rendered and that originally bargained for can easily and adequately be allowed for in damages. He is not required to mitigate by accepting an offer of modified performance which purports to extinguish his right to such damages.[3] Nor is the injured party bound to mitigate by accepting an offer of modified performance if the modification causes him substantial prejudice: for example, a buyer of goods need not mitigate by accepting the seller's tender of goods of a lower quality than contracted for, even with an allowance for the inferiority.[4] On a somewhat similar principle, an employee who has been wrongfully dismissed need not accept an offer of re-employment involving a reduction in status,[5] or a lower grade of work[6]; nor need he accept the former employer's offer to take him back, even on the original terms, if the wrongful dismissal occurred in circumstances of personal humiliation, e.g. on a charge of misconduct made before others.[7]

(ii) *Not augmenting loss.* If the claimant acts unreasonably in attempting to mitigate, he cannot recover extra loss which he suffers as a result.[8] Thus in general he should not, for example, spend more on curing a defect in performance than the subject-matter without the defect would be worth[9]; nor should he continue to incur expense for the purpose of tendering performance after the other party has clearly indicated that he will refuse to accept it. But these are only general rules: the crucial question in each case is whether the claimant has acted reasonably. The point is strikingly illustrated by *Banco*

---

[96] *Pilkington v Wood* [1953] Ch. 770; *The Ines* [1995] 2 Lloyd's Rep. 144 at 159.

[97] *James Finlay & Co Ltd v NV Kwik Hoo Tong HM* [1929] 1 K.B. 400; *cf. London & South of England Building Society v Stone* [1983] 1 W.L.R. 1242 (building society not required to enforce borrower's *personal* covenant).

[98] *The Griparion* [1994] 1 Lloyd's Rep. 533; *Hussey v Eels* [1990] 2 Q.B. 227.

[99] *Harries v Edmonds* (1845) 1 Car. & K. 686.

[1] *Payzu Ltd v Saunders* [1919] 2 K.B. 581; contrast *Harlow & Jones Ltd v Panex International Ltd* [1967] 2 Lloyd's Rep. 509 at 530 (claimant "not bound to nurse the interests of the contract breaker").

[2] *The Solholt* [1983] 1 Lloyd's Rep. 605.

[3] *Shindler v Northern Raincoat Co Ltd* [1960] 1 W.L.R. 1038; *cf. Strutt v Whitnell* [1975] 1 W.L.R. 870 (said in *The Solholt* [1983] 1 Lloyd's Rep. 605 at 609 to turn "on its own special facts").

[4] *Heaven & Kesterton Ltd v Et François Albiac & Cie* [1956] 2 Lloyd's Rep. 316 at 321.

[5] *Yetton v Eastwood Froy Ltd* [1967] 1 W.L.R. 104.

[6] *cf. Edwards v SOGAT* [1971] 1 Ch. 354.

[7] *Payzu Ltd v Saunders* [1919] 2 K.B. 581 at 589; in the absence of such circumstances it was held in *Brace v Calder* [1895] 2 K.B. 253 that an offer of re-employment should have been accepted.

[8] *The Borag* [1981] 1 W.L.R. 274; *Seven Seas Properties Ltd v Al-Essa* [1988] 1 W.L.R. 1272 at 1276 (the reasoning of the case is obsolete on its facts in view of Law of Property (Miscellaneous Provisions) Act 1989, s.3, below, p.999).

[9] *cf.* above, pp.945–946; *Darbishire v Warran* [1963] 1 W.L.R. 1067—a tort case; *Grant v Dawkins* [1973] 1 W.L.R. 1406; for an exception see *O'Grady v Westminster Scaffolding Ltd* [1962] 2 Lloyd's Rep. 238—another tort case.

de Portugal v Waterlow & Sons Ltd.[10] The defendants had contracted to print banknotes for the Bank of Portugal, and in breach of contract delivered a large number of these to a criminal, who put them into circulation in Portugal. On discovering this, the Bank withdrew the issue and undertook to exchange all the notes in question for others. The defendants argued that they were liable only for the cost of printing the notes: any further loss was due to the Bank's own act.[11] But the House of Lords, by a majority, held the defendants liable for the full face value of the notes as the conduct of the Bank was reasonable, having regard to its commercial obligations towards the public.[12] A similar result was reached where a manufacturer of soft drinks had been supplied with contaminated ingredients. It was held that, in withdrawing and destroying products containing the ingredient, the manufacturer had acted reasonably to protect its reputation, even though the contamination posed only a negligible risk to health; and that the supplier of the ingredient was liable for the manufacturer's wasted costs.[13]

On the same principle, the claimant may be able to recover amounts paid in reasonable settlement of a liability to a third party incurred in consequence of the breach.[14] Conversely, if the claimant decides to resist a claim brought against him by a third party as a result[15] of the breach, he may be able to recover legal expenses incurred in the proceedings between him and the third party. Thus a buyer can recover from the seller costs reasonably incurred in defending an action brought against him by a sub-buyer on account of a defect for which the seller is liable.[16] Similarly a person who sues an agent for breach of implied warranty of authority can recover costs thrown away in a previous action brought against the principal on the assumption that the agent had the authority he claimed to have.[17] But the costs must be reasonably incurred: the claimant cannot recover them if he persists in litigating when it is clear that he has no chance of success.[18]

Finally, it is possible for steps taken in performance of the duty to mitigate to be reasonable, but actually to increase the loss. For example, a buyer who accepts a seller's anticipatory breach is bound to mitigate by buying a substitute in the market at the time of acceptance. If, when he makes the substitute purchase, the market price exceeds the contract price, he can recover the excess. This is so even though by the time fixed for delivery the market price has fallen below the contract price so that the buyer, if he had not performed the duty to mitigate, would have suffered no loss at all.[19]

---

[10] [1932] A.C. 452.

[11] Portuguese currency was not convertible into gold; the bank had a monopoly of issuing notes as legal tender; and, although the amount of notes it could issue was limited by law, the limit had not been reached.

[12] *cf.* above, p.978 at n.97; and see *Buildings and Civil Engineering Holidays Scheme Management Ltd v Post Office* [1966] 1 Q.B. 247 (where the claim was not in contract).

[13] *Britvic Soft Drinks Ltd v Messer UK Ltd* [2002] 1 Lloyd's Rep 20 at [114]; affirmed without reference to this point [2002] EWCA Civ 548; [2002] 2 All E.R. (Comm) 321.

[14] *Biggin & Co Ltd v Permanite Ltd* [1951] 2 K.B. 314; *Bulk Oil (Zug) AG v Sun International Ltd* [1984] 1 Lloyd's Rep. 531 at 544; *Royal Brompton NHS Trust v Hammond* [1999] N.L.J. 89; *General Foods Inc Panama v Slobodovna Plovidba Yougoslavia* [1999] 1 Lloyd's Rep. 688; *Britvic case*, above n.13 [2002] 1 Lloyd's Rep. 20 at [127]; contrast *Anglian Water Services Ltd v Crawshaw Robbins & Co* [2001] B.L.R. 173 (where loss of this kind was too remote).

[15] See *The Antaios* [1981] 2 Lloyd's Rep. 284 at 299.

[16] *Hammond & Co v Bussey* (1887) 20 Q.B.D. 79; *Agius v Great Western Ry* [1899] 1 Q.B. 413; *Lloyd's & Scottish Finance Ltd v Modern Cars & Caravans (Kingston) Ltd* [1966] 1 Q.B. 764; *Bowmaker (Commercial) Ltd v Day* [1965] 1 W.L.R. 1396; *cf. The Saragasso* [1994] 1 Lloyd's Rep. 412.

[17] *Hughes v Graeme* (1864) 33 L.J.Q.B. 335; *Godwin v Francis* (1870) L.R. 5 C.P. 295; *Farley Health Products v Babylon Trading Co, The Times*, July 29, 1987.

[18] *Pow v Davies* (1861) 1 B. & S. 220; *Baxendale v London, Chatham & Dover Ry* (1874) L.R. 10 Ex. 38.

[19] *Melachrino v Nicholl & Knight* [1920] 1 K.B. 693 at 697.

(b) MITIGATION IN FACT. Loss is sometimes said to be mitigated where some benefit in fact accrues[20] to the claimant as a result of the breach.[21] If, for example, he is released from his own obligation to perform, this fact is taken into account in deciding how much, if anything, he has lost.[22] Or he may benefit from performing his duty to mitigate, e.g. by finding a job comparable to that from which he was wrongfully dismissed.[23] Here again his earnings in the other job will be taken into account in assessing his damages for wrongful dismissal.[24] The principle underlying such cases is that the purpose of an award of damages is "to compensate [the claimant] for his loss, not to enrich him".[25]

There is a further group of cases in which the claimant benefits from doing something that he was *not required* to do in performance of his duty to mitigate: for example, a wrongfully dismissed employee may take a job involving a reduction in status. His actual earnings in that job are taken into account in assessing damages, even though it was a job that he was not required to take in performance of his duty to mitigate.[26] But some benefits of this kind are not taken into account; and the distinction between the two kinds of benefit is illustrated by *Lavarack v Woods of Colchester Ltd*.[27] The claimant was wrongfully dismissed from his employment with the defendants and so freed from a provision in his contract with them that he should not, without their written consent, be engaged or interested in any other concern (except as a holder of investments quoted on a stock exchange). After his dismissal, he (1) took employment with the X Co at a lower salary than he had earned with the defendants; (2) acquired half the shares in the X Co; and (3) invested money in shares in the Y Co The value of the shares in both companies having risen, it was held that the increase in the value of the X Co shares, but not that of the Y Co shares, must be taken into account in reducing the claimant's damages. The former was regarded as a disguised remuneration, while the latter was "not a direct result of his dismissal" but a "collateral benefit".[28]

The question whether a benefit is "collateral" or a "direct result" of the breach can give rise to difficult problems of causation. In *British Westinghouse Co v Underground Electric Rys Co of London*,[29] A agreed to supply B with turbines of a stated efficiency but supplied less efficient ones, which used more coal. B accepted and used them, reserving his right to claim damages. After some years, and before A's turbines were worn out, B replaced them with others. These were so much more efficient than A's would have been, even had they been in accordance with the contract, that, over the whole period

---

[20] *e.g. Platt v London Underground Ltd*, The Times, March 13, 2001. "Benefit" here includes avoided loss: *The Kriti Rex* [1996] 2 Lloyd's Rep. 171 at 203.

[21] This principle presupposes that loss has been suffered *in consequence of a wrong*. It does not apply to a restitution claim based, not on any wrongdoing, but simply on the fact that a payment has been made under a void contract (below, p.1057): *Kleinwort Benson Ltd v Birmingham CC* [1997] Q.B. 380.

[22] See above, p.869. See also *Levison v Farin* [1978] 2 All E.R. 1149; *C & P Haulage v Middleton* [1983] 1 W.L.R. 1461.

[23] *cf. Evans Marshall & Co v Bertola* [1976] 2 Lloyd's Rep. 17.

[24] *e.g. Cerebus Software Ltd v Rowley* [2001] EWCA Civ 74; [2001] I.C.R. 376; unless the contract otherwise provides, as in *Gregory v Wallace* [1998] I.R.L.R. 387. For the position in cases of unfair dismissal (which generally does not involve any breach of contract) see Employment Rights Act 1996, s.123(4).

[25] *Longden v British Coal Corp* [1998] A.C. 653 at 662; *cf.* in tort, *Dimond v Lovell* [2002] 1 A.C. 384.

[26] See above, p.978; see *Edwards v SOGAT* [1971] Ch. 354; *S of S for Employment v Wilson* [1978] 1 W.L.R. 568; *cf. Techno Land Improvements Ltd v British Leyland (UK) Ltd* (1979) 252 E.G. 805 at 809; *The Concordia C* [1985] 2 Lloyd's Rep. 55; *The Fanis* [1994] 1 Lloyd's Rep. 633; *cf. Mobil North Sea Ltd v PJ Pipe & Valve Co* [2001] EWCA Civ 741; [2001] 2 All E.R. (Comm) 289, at [30].

[27] [1967] 1 Q.B. 278.

[28] *ibid.* at 290; *cf. Aruna Mills Ltd v Dhanrajmal Gobindram* [1968] 1 Q.B. 655 at 669; *Hodge v Clifford Cowling & Co* [1990] 2 E.G.L.R. 89; *Mobil North Sea Ltd v PJ Pipe & Valve Co* [2001] EWCA Civ 741; [2001] 2 All E.R. (Comm) 289.

[29] [1912] A.C. 673; *cf. Erie County Natural Gas Co v Carroll* [1911] A.C. 105; *Levison v Farin* [1978] 2 All E.R. 1149; *Merrett v Capitol Indemnity Corp* [1991] 1 Lloyd's Rep. 169.

during which A's turbines might have been expected to last, B actually used less coal than he would have done with turbines of the efficiency stated in the contract. The House of Lords held that B was under no duty to mitigate by buying new turbines.[30] But as he had bought the new turbines in consequence of A's breach, the financial advantage he gained by using them had to be set off against the cost of buying them. As B's savings in coal exceeded that cost, he recovered nothing in respect of it. This was so even though it could be argued that the benefit thus obtained by B was only in part the result of the breach; for the turbines originally contracted for had become obsolete so that a reasonable businessman would have replaced them even if they had been in accordance with the contract.[31] On the other hand, B had also, *before* replacing the turbines, suffered loss because the cost of operating them was greater than it would have been if they had been in accordance with the contract. This loss was not diminished as a result of the purchase of the new turbines and was accordingly recoverable.[32]

In the *British Westinghouse* case, it was said that a benefit is taken into account only if it is "one arising from the consequences of the breach".[33] It follows from this requirement that damages will not be reduced by reason of any insurance taken out by the injured party against the consequences of the breach[34] (unless the contract provides that the injured party's sole remedy is to be against the insurer[35]); or by reason of the fact that the victim is compensated for the loss under some other contract with a third party,[36] or that gratuitous benefits have been conferred on the victim in respect of the

---

[30] In this respect the case differs from *Bellingham v Dhillon* [1973] Q.B. 304 (a tort case purporting to follow the *British Westinghouse* case and approved in *Dimond v Lovell* [2002] 1 A.C. 384).

[31] [1912] A.C. 675 at 691.

[32] *ibid.* at 688.

[33] *ibid.* at 690.

[34] *cf. Bradburn v Great Western Ry* (1874) L.R. 10 Ex. 1; *The Yasin* [1979] 2 Lloyd's Rep. 45; *Brown v KMR Services* [1994] 4 All E.R. 385, 399 (varied on other grounds [1995] 4 All E.R. 598); *Europe Mortgage Co v Halifax Estate Agencies* [1996] E.G.C.S. 84; *Bristol & West BS v Christie* [1996] E.G.C.S. 60. Other techniques for avoiding double recovery in such cases are illustrated by *Arab Bank plc v John D Wood* [2000] 1 W.L.R. 857 and *Amec Civil Engineering Ltd v Cheshire CC* [1999] B.L.R. 303. For other benefits, see *Foxley v Olton* [1965] 2 Q.B. 306 (national assistance); *Hewson v Downs* [1970] 1 Q.B. 73 (state retirement pension); *Basnett v J & A Jackson* [1976] I.C.R. 63 (redundancy payment); *McCamley v Cammell Laird Shipbuilders Ltd* [1990] 1 W.L.R. 963 (voluntary payment from employer for injury at work); *Smoker v London Fire and Civil Defence Authority* [1991] 2 All E.R. 449 (employee's contributory disability pension); *Hopkins v Norcross* [1994] I.C.R. 11 (occupational pension scheme); contrast *Parsons v BNM Laboratories* [1964] 1 Q.B. 95; and *Nabi v British Leyland (UK) Ltd* [1980] 1 W.L.R. 529 (unemployment benefit); *Gaskill v Preston* [1981] 3 All E.R. 427 (family income supplement); *Plummer v PW Wilkins* [1981] 1 W.L.R. 831 and *Lincoln v Hayman* [1982] 1 W.L.R. 488 (supplementary benefit); *Westwood v S of S for Employment* [1985] A.C. 20 (unemployment and earnings related benefit); *Hussain v New Taplow Paper Mills* [1988] A.C. 514 (sickness benefit under insurance paid for by employer); *Colledge v Bass Mitchells & Butler Ltd* [1988] I.C.R. 125 (voluntary payment which would not have been made but for the accident); *Baldwin v British Coal Corp, The Times*, May 11, 1994 (supplementary payment to compensate for inadequate notice of termination); Administration of Justice Act 1982, s.5; Social Security Administration Act 1992, s.82 (social security benefits to be deducted from victim's damages, but to be paid by wrongdoer to Secretary of State); *Beriello v Felixstowe Dock & Ry Co* [1989] 1 W.L.R. 695 (payments from foreign State benefit fund which were recoverable by the fund out of the damages); *Deeny v Gooda Walker Ltd (No.3)* [1995] 1 W.L.R. 1206 (liabilities discharged out of Lloyd's central funds). See generally *Parry v Cleaver* [1970] A.C. 1.

[35] *Mark Rowlands Ltd v Berni Inns Ltd* [1986] Q.B. 211, where the party in breach was a tenant who had paid for the insurance by way of an "insurance rent": hence the normal justification for disregarding insurance moneys (*viz.* that the *injured party* had paid for the insurance) did not apply. This was also the position in *Bristol & West BS v May, May & Merrimans (No.2)* [1998] 1 W.L.R. 306.

[36] *Gardner v Marsh Parsons* [1997] 1 W.L.R. 489. For a possible qualification of this principle where a settlement agreement between one of two wrongdoers and the victim on its true construction covers the loss resulting from both breaches, see the discussion at p.573 above of *Heaton v Axa Equity and Law Life Assurance Society plc* [2002] UKHL 15; [2002] 2 A.C. 329, where the agreement was held to release the other wrongdoer.

loss by a third party[37] who was under no legal obligation to act in this way.[38] Nor will damages be reduced merely because the injured party has resold the defective subject-matter for more than the contract price. In *Hussey v Eels*[39] the claimants had been induced to buy a house as their home by a misrepresentation[40] that there had been no subsidence. More than two years later, they decided to demolish the house and resold the site for one and a half times the price which they had paid, having obtained planning permission for two dwellings on the site. On the assumption that this resale yielded a profit[41] to the claimants, it was held that this was not to be taken into account: the wrong which had caused their loss had not also caused the gain as the resale was "not . . . part of a continuous transaction of which the purchase . . . was the inception".[42] Similarly, where a buyer is entitled to damages based on the market price, those damages will not normally be reduced on the ground that he has made a good bargain by buying a substitute below the market price. But if a buyer who has rightfully rejected goods then buys *those very same goods* from the seller below the market (and the contract) price, this fact will be taken into account to reduce or extinguish the seller's liability.[43]

(4) Contributory negligence[44]

Where the injured party fails to perform the "duty" to mitigate, his damages are reduced because it can be said that he is at fault in failing to avoid loss. He may also be at fault in the sense of actually helping to bring about the loss or the event causing it. In the law of tort, such conduct is called "contributory negligence". At common law, it in some cases totally barred the injured party's tort claim, while in others it was completely ignored, so that he recovered in full. The Law Reform (Contributory Negligence) Act 1945 now provides that, where a person suffers damage as a result partly of his own "fault" and partly of the "fault" of another person, his claim is not to be defeated, but his damages are to be reduced in proportion to his degree of responsibility. Two questions arise for discussion here.

The first is whether *the common law doctrine of contributory negligence* applied in contract at all. Usually it did not,[45] for a contracting party is not bound to guard against breach. He may, indeed, be required to take steps to avoid the consequences of a known breach; but this follows from the rules as to mitigation, or the maxim *volenti non fit injuria*, rather than from the doctrine of contributory negligence. Where, however, a breach of contract was also a tort, the doctrine of contributory negligence was not excluded merely because there was a contractual relationship between the parties. Thus

---

[37] Not where the benefit is conferred by the party in breach: *Williams v BOC Gases Ltd* [2000] I.C.R. 1181; *cf.*, in tort, *Hunt v Severs* [1994] 2 A.C. 350.

[38] *Merrett v Capitol Indemnity Corp* [1991] 1 Lloyd's Rep. 169; *cf.* (in tort) *Giles v Thompson* [1994] 1 A.C. 142 at 166, where the point is left open.

[39] [1990] 2 Q.B. 227.

[40] Not incorporated in the contract, so that the cause of action was in tort; but the judgment is based on earlier decisions in contract cases.

[41] This depended on the cost of comparable accommodation at the time of the resale, as "The plaintiffs were not property speculators but residents:" [1990] 2 Q.B. 227 at 233; *cf.* (in tort) *Dominion Mosaics & Tile Co Ltd v Trafalgar Trucking Co Ltd* [1990] 2 All E.R. 246 at 252.

[42] [1990] 2 Q.B. 227 at 241; *cf. Needles Financial Services v Taber* [2002] 3 All E.R. 501.

[43] R. *Pagnan Fratelli v Corbisa Industrial Agropacuaria Ltd* [1970] 1 W.L.R. 1306; this case differs from the *British Westinghouse* case (which it purports to follow) in that the opportunity to buy the goods more cheaply would have arisen but for the seller's breach.

[44] Williams, *Joint Torts and Contributory Negligence*, §59; Swanton, 55 A.L.J. 278.

[45] *The Shinjitsu Maru (No.5)* [1985] 1 W.L.R. 1270 at 1287 (where this was conceded); *cf. The Nogar Marin* [1988] 1 Lloyd's Rep. 412 (where the point was not argued).

a carrier, when sued for negligently injuring a passenger, could no doubt rely on the passenger's contributory negligence.

The second question is whether *the Act of 1945* applies in cases of breach of contract. This depends on the interpretation of the definition of "fault" in the Act as "negligence, breach of statutory duty, or other act or omission which gives rise to liability in tort or would, apart from this Act, give rise to the defence of contributory negligence".[46] It has been argued that this includes *all* negligence, whether contractual[47] or tortious, and all *other* acts giving rise to liability in tort.[48] But the word "other" supports the view that negligence is here used in its tortious sense.[49]

It does not, however, follow from this interpretation of "fault" that the Act can never apply to cases of breach of contract. Two further distinctions must be drawn. The first is between breaches of contract that are, and those that are not, negligent. Here the phrase "negligent breach of contract" refers to situations in which liability arises for breach of a contractual duty of care[50]—not to cases in which liability for breach of contract is strict,[51] but the breach happens to have been committed negligently.[52] The second distinction is between breaches of contract which amount also to torts and those which do not. The content of a contractual duty of care is often the same as that of the duty of care which the law of tort would impose, even if there were no contract between the parties; and in such cases the same careless conduct *prima facie* gives rise to liability both for breach of contract and in tort.[53] For example, a careless statement inducing a contract may give rise to liability in tort for misrepresentation and in contract for breach of collateral warranty.[54] The liability of many professional persons for breach of the duties of care that they owe to their clients similarly arises both in contract and tort.[55] The same is true of duties arising out of a number of other contractual relationships, such as those between carrier and passenger, employer and employee, bailor and bailee,

---

[46] s.4. For an extension to include "product liability" see Consumer Protection Act 1987, s.6.

[47] See below, at n.50 and 53–56.

[48] Williams, above (n.44).

[49] *Forsikringsaktieselskapet Vesta v Butcher* [1989] A.C. 852, CA, affirmed, without reference to this point, *ibid* at 880 *et seq.*; Newman, 53 M.L.R. 201. *cf.* (in another statutory context) *Société Commerciale de Réassurance v ERAS International Ltd* [1992] 1 Lloyd's Rep. 570.

[50] *Quinn v Burch Bros (Builders) Ltd* [1966] 2 Q.B. 370, 378–379 (affirmed on other grounds *ibid.* at 381).

[51] *cf.* above, pp.838–840.

[52] *Quinn v Burch Bros (Builders) Ltd*, above, at pp.378–379.

[53] *Henderson v Merrett Syndicates Ltd* [1995] 2 A.C. 145 at 193.

[54] *Esso Petroleum Co Ltd v Mardon* [1976] Q.B. 801, approved on the point that liability could, on such facts, arise in contract and tort in *The Maira (No.3)* [1990] 1 A.C. 637 at 650 (reversed on other grounds *ibid.* at 672, *et seq.*).

[55] *Esso Petroleum Co Ltd v Mardon* [1976] Q.B. 801 at 819 (disapproving on this point *Bagot v Stevens, Scanlan & Co* [1966] 1 Q.B. 197); *Arenson v Arenson* [1977] A.C. 405 at 420–421; *Batty v Metropolitan Realisations Ltd* [1978] Q.B. 554 (disapproved as to damages in *D & F Estates Ltd v Church Commissioners for England* [1989] A.C. 177). *The Zephyr* [1985] 2 Lloyd's Rep. 529 at 537; *Dunbar v A & B Painters* [1985] 2 Lloyd's Rep. 616 at 620 (affirmed [1986] 2 Lloyd's Rep. 38); *Forsikringsaktieselskapet Vesta v Butcher* [1989] A.C. 852 at 860 (affirmed on other grounds *ibid.* at 880 *et seq.*); *Duncan Stevenson Macmillan v AW Knott Becker Scott Ltd* [1990] 1 Lloyd's Rep. 98 at 101; *Islander Trucking Ltd v Hogg Robinson & Gardner Mountain (Marine) Ltd* [1990] 1 All E.R. 826; *Murphy v Brentwood DC* [1991] 1 A.C. 398 at 465; *The Superhulls Cover Case (No.2)* [1990] 2 Lloyd's Rep. 431; *Harvest Trucking Co Ltd v PB Davies* [1991] 2 Lloyd's Rep. 638 at 643; *Punjab National Bank v De Boinville* [1992] 1 W.L.R. 1138; *Barclays Bank plc v Quinecare Ltd* [1992] 4 All E.R. 363; *Société Commerciale de Réassurances v ERAS (International) Ltd* [1992] 1 Lloyd's Rep. 570 at 599; *Henderson v Merrett Syndicates Ltd* [1995] 2 A.C. 145; *First National Provincial Bank Ltd v Humberts* [1995] 2 All E.R. 673; *South Australia Asset Management Corp v York Montague Ltd* [1997] A.C. 191 at 211;

or occupier of premises and visitor.[56] The breach will not, however, amount to a tort where the imposition of a tortious duty would be "so inconsistent with the applicable contract that . . . the parties must be taken to have agreed that the tortious remedy is to be limited or excluded".[57] This possibility is illustrated by a case[58] in which a building subcontractor had entered into a direct contract with the building owner (and not merely into one with the main contractor[59]). The court inferred from the nature of this arrangement that the parties had intended the relationship between owner and subcontractor to be governed by the contract alone, so that the subcontractor was not liable to the owner in tort. It follows from these distinctions that three categories of cases must be considered in discussing the application of the 1945 Act to cases involving breach of contract.[60]

(i) The defendant without negligence commits a breach of a strict contractual duty; his conduct does not also amount to a tort; and the claimant is careless. For example, A contracts with B to repair B's car. In doing the work, A without negligence[61] fits components which are defective. B is injured as a result partly of the defect and partly of his own negligent driving. The Act does not apply: A's conduct, being neither negligent nor an act or omission giving rise to liability in tort, must fall outside the

---

[56] *Nykreditbank v Edward Erdman Group* [1997] 1 W.L.R. 1327 at 1368; *Holt v Payne Skillington* (1996) 77 B.L.R. 51, where it was said that the tort duty could be more extensive than the duty imposed by the contract, but the tort claim failed on the pleadings. After the *Henderson* case, it seems that a solicitor's liability for negligence will *prima facie* arise in both contract and in tort: see *Bristol & West BS v Mothew* [1998] Ch.1 at 25, 26; for earlier conflicting authorities on this point (many of which are discussed but none of which is expressly overruled in the *Henderson* case, above), see *Groom v Crocker* [1939] 1 K.B. 194; *Clark v Kirby-Smith* [1964] Ch. 506, disapproved on this point in *Esso Petroleum Co Ltd v Mardon* [1976] Q.B. 801 at 819; *Midland Bank Trust Co Ltd v Hett, Stubbs & Kemp* [1979] Ch. 384; *DW Moore & Co Ltd v Ferrier* [1988] 1 W.L.R. 276; *Lee v Thompson* [1989] 2 E.G.L.R. 151; *Bell v Peter Browne & Co* [1990] 2 Q.B. 495; *Rowe v Turner Hopkins & Co* [1980] N.Z.L.R. 550; Kaye 100 L.Q.R. 680.

[56] *Bagot v Stevens, Scanlan & Co Ltd*, above, at pp.204–205; *cf. Matthews v Kuwait Bechtel Corp* [1959] 2 Q.B. 57; *Sayers v Harlow Urban DC* [1958] 1 W.L.R. 623; *Johnson v Coventry Churchill International Ltd* [1992] 3 All E.R. 14 at 22–23; *The Agia Skepi* [1992] 2 Lloyd's Rep. 467 at 472; *The Angelic Grace* [1995] 1 Lloyd's Rep. 87 at 91; *Spring v Guardian Insurance plc* [1995] 2 A.C. 296 at 320, *cf.* 340. But where the same facts are alleged to give rise to a claim in contract and in tort, the injured party cannot, after failing in contract, succeed by simply reclassifying his claim as one in tort: *Tai Hing Cotton Mill Ltd v Liu Chong Hing Bank* [1986] A.C. 80 at 107; *The Maira (No.3)* [1990] 1 A.C. 637 at 650 (reversed on other grounds *ibid.* at 672 *et seq.*); *Reid v Rush and Tompkins Group plc* [1990] 1 W.L.R. 212; *The Good Luck* [1990] 1 Q.B. 818 at 900 (reversed on other grounds, [1992] 1 A.C. 233); *cf. McNerney Lambeth LBC* [1989] N.L.J.R. 114 (no claim in tort at common law where claim for breach of implied covenant under Landlord and Tenant Act 1985, s.11 failed).

[57] *Henderson v Merrett Syndicates Ltd* [1995] 2 A.C. 145 at 194.

[58] *Greater Nottingham Co-operative Society Ltd v Cementation Piling & Foundation Ltd* [1989] Q.B. 71; *cf. Tai Hing Cotton Mill Ltd v Liu Chong, Hing Bank* [1986] A.C. 80 at 107; *Welsh Technical Services v Haden Young* (1987) 37 Build.L.R. 130; *Sonat Offshore SA v Amerada Hess Development Co* [1988] 1 Lloyd's Rep. 145 at 159; *Parker-Tweedale v Dunbar Bank plc.* [1990] 2 All E.R. 577 at 587; *Johnstone v Bloomsbury Health Authority* [1992] Q.B. 333; *Scally v Southern Health & Social Services Board* [1992] 1 A.C. 294 at 303; *Ashmore v Corp of Lloyd's* [1992] 2 Lloyd's Rep. 563 at 568; *Aiken v Stewart Wrightson Members Agency Ltd* [1995] 1 W.L.R. 1281; *The Hellespont Ardent* [1997] 2 Lloyd's Rep. 547 at 593.

[59] *cf.* above, p.608.

[60] *Forsikringsaktieselshapet Vesta v Butcher* [1986] 2 All E.R. 488 at 508 (affirmed without reference to this point [1989] A.C. 852).

[61] This is no defence to an action for breach of contract; above, p.839.

definition of "fault".[62] Hence at common law the result will, in a contract case,[63] depend on which party's conduct caused the loss. Thus in *Lambert v Lewis*[64] a dealer supplied a defective trailer coupling to a customer who went on using it after it was obviously[65] broken. Eventually there was an accident when the coupling gave way. It was held that the dealer was not liable to the customer: the accident had been caused by the customer's continued use of the coupling with knowledge of its condition, and not by the fact that it was defective when sold.

(ii) The defendant commits a breach of a contractual duty of care; his conduct does not also amount to a tort, because the relations of the parties are intended to be governed by the contract alone[66]; and the claimant is also careless. In *De Meza v Apple*[67] an auditor carelessly made a mistake in completing certain certificates, with the result that the client suffered loss through being underinsured. The client was also careless and his damages were reduced under the Act. The case seems to have been regarded as falling into the present category[68]; but it is equally plausible to say that the auditor's liability for professional negligence arose in both contract and tort.[69] On that view, the case would belong to our third category: this was said to be the position in a more recent case involving a careless insurance broker, and it was further said that the Act would not apply to cases in the second category, where the defendant was liable only in contract but not in tort.[70]

(iii) The defendant commits a breach of a contractual duty of care; his conduct also amounts to a tort; and the claimant is also careless. The Act can apply to such a situation: for example, where the claimant is injured partly through his own carelessness and partly through circumstances amounting both to a breach of contract by the defendant and to a breach of his duties as an occupier of dangerous premises[71]; or where loss is caused partly by the professional negligence of the defendant, amounting both to a breach of

---

[62] *Basildon DC v JE Lesser Properties* [1985] Q.B. 839 (as explained in *Forsikringsaktieselskapet Vesta v Butcher* [1989] A.C. 852 at 865, affirmed *ibid.* at 880 *et seq.*, without reference to this point); *The Good Luck* [1990] 1 Q.B. 818 at 904; (where the actual decision was that the defendant was not liable either in contract or in tort, so that the issue of contributory negligence did not arise; reversed on other grounds [1992] 1 A.C. 233); *Tenant Radiant Heat Ltd v Warrington Development Corp* [1988] E.G.L.R. 41 at 43; *Barclays Bank plc v Fairclough Building Ltd* [1995] Q.B. 214; *UCB Corporate Services Ltd v Clyde & Co* [2000] 2 All E.R. (Comm) 257 at 268; *Anglian Water Services Ltd v Crawshaw Robbins & Co Ltd* [2001] B.L.R. 173.

[63] In tort cases the result depended at common law on the question who had the "last opportunity" of avoiding the accident: see Williams, *op. cit.* (above, p.983), Ch.9.

[64] [1982] A.C. 225. See also *Young v Purdy* [1996] 2 F.L.R. 795.

[65] Failure to discover a defect which could have been discovered by taking reasonable steps may also amount to contributory negligence: *Nitrigin Eirann Teoranta v Inco Alloys Inc* [1992] 1 W.L.R. 498 at 506.

[66] See nn.57 and 58 above.

[67] [1974] 1 Lloyd's Rep. 508 (affirmed [1975] 1 Lloyd's Rep. 498 where the applicability of the Act was left open); *Quinn v Burch Bros (Builders) Ltd* [1966] 2 Q.B. 370 at 380–383.

[68] *Forsikringsaktieselskapet Vesta v Butcher* [1986] 2 All E.R. 488 at 508, as to which see below, n.70.

[69] See above, n.55.

[70] *Forsikringsaktieselskapet Vesta v Butcher* [1989] A.C. 852 at 866 (affirmed without reference to this point *ibid.* at 880 *et seq.*) where *De Meza v Apple*, above, n.67 was cited at 861 without disapproval; *Raflatac v Eade* [1999] 1 Lloyd's Rep. 506; *Rowe v Turner Hopkins & Co* [1980] N.Z.L.R. 550. The Law Commission has recommended that in cases of this kind the claimant's damages should be reduced on account of his contributory negligence, except where the contract expressly or by implication excludes this defence. Law Com. No.219 (1993) paras.4.7–15, 23–25; the proposal does not extend to sums payable under a valid liquidated damages clause (below, p.999): *ibid.*, para.4.26–27.

[71] *Sayers v Harlow Urban DC*, above, n.56; *cf Targett v Torfaen BC* [1992] 3 All E.R. 27.

contract and to a tort against his client, and partly by that client's own carelessness[72]: *e.g.* where a mortgage lender suffers loss partly because of the negligence of a valuer engaged by him in overvaluing the security and partly because of the lender's own imprudent lending policy.[73] There was formerly some support for the view that, even in cases in this category, the Act applied only where the claim was framed in tort.[74] But this view has been rightly rejected[75] as it is not supported by the definition of "fault" in the Act, and as it would be unsatisfactory[76] in enabling an injured party to evade the Act by simply suing in contract where he also had a claim in tort. On the other hand the Act would not apply where, though both contracting parties were careless, the court took the view that the loss was entirely caused by the carelessness of one: *e.g.* that of the client[77] or that of his professional adviser.[78]

In the three situations so far discussed, the defendant is guilty of a breach of contract and the claimant's conduct is careless; but that conduct does not amount to a legal wrong against the defendant. Where the loss to each party results in part from a breach of contract committed by one of them (A) against the other (B) and in part by an independent legal wrong committed by B against A, then the losses may be apportioned[79] (quite apart from the Act) on the ground that they resulted from two independent actionable wrongs. Each party can then recover in respect of his own loss to the extent that it was caused by the other's wrongful act.[80] This was, for example, held to be the case where goods belonging to the tenant of part of a warehouse, and the warehouse itself, were damaged as a result partly of the tenant's breach of covenant to repair and partly of omissions of the landlord giving rise to liability in tort. Each party was held liable for the other's loss to the extent that it had been caused by his own

---

[72] *Forsikringsaktieselskapet Vesta v Butcher* [1989] A.C. 852, affirmed without reference to this point *ibid.* at 880 *et seq.* but not followed in Australia: *Astley v Austrust Ltd* [1999] Lloyd's Rep. P.N. 758; *The Superhulls Cover Case (No.2)* [1990] 2 Lloyd's Rep. 431; *cf. The Moonacre* [1992] 2 Lloyd's Rep. 501, where the plea of contributory negligence failed as the client was *not* careless; *Paul Tudor Jones Ltd v Crawley Colosso Ltd* [1996] 2 Lloyd's Rep. 619 at 638; *Maes Finance Ltd v AL Phillips & Co, The Times*, March 25, 1997; *Bristol & West BS v Fancy & Jackson* [1997] 4 All E.R. 582 at 625; *Sumitomo Bank Ltd v Banque Bruxelles Lambert SA* [1997] 1 Lloyd's Rep. 487; *Nationwide BS v JR Jones* [1999] Lloyd's Rep. P.N. 614.

[73] The reduction of damages on account of the claimant's contributory negligence is in such cases calculated on the loss actually suffered (the "basic loss") and not on the lower amount for which the defendant is responsible under the "scope of duty" test (above, pp.938–940). *Platform Home Loans v Oyston Shipways Ltd* [2000] 2 A.C. 190.

[74] *Sole v WJ Hallt* [1973] Q.B. 574; *The Shinjitsu Maru (No.5)* [1985] 1 W.L.R. 1270; *cf. Basildon DC v JE Lesser (Properties) Ltd* [1985] Q.B. 839 at 849, 30 (as to which see above, p.985 n.62); Andrews [1986] C.L.J. 8; Burrows, 101 L.Q.R. 161; Spowart-Taylor, 49 M.L.R. 102.

[75] *Forsikringsaktieselskapet Vesta v Butcher*, above; [1989] A.C. 852 (where at 875 in the Court of Appeal, Neill L.J. acknowledged the error of his former contrary view in *The Shinjitsu Maru (No.5)*, above); *cf. Wheeler v Copas* [1981] 3 All E.R. 405 (where no express reference to the Act is made in the report). The Law Commission's proposal (above at n.70) seems to extend to this situation, even though it is already covered by the 1945 Act.

[76] This was admitted in *The Shinjitsu Maru (No.5)*, above, at p.1288.

[77] *O'Connor v BD Kirby & Co* [1972] 1 Q.B. 90 where the trial court's view that the client should recover two-thirds of the loss was described at 99 as "somewhat novel"; *cf. Quinn v Burch Bros (Builders) Ltd* [1966] 2 Q.B. 370; *Mint Security Ltd v Blair* [1982] 1 Lloyd's Rep. 188, 201; *County Ltd v Girozentrale Securities* [1996] 3 All E.R. 834; *Kapur v JW Francis & Co (No.2)* [1999] Lloyd's Rep. P.N. 834.

[78] *UCB Corporate Services Ltd v Clyde & Co* [2000] 2 All E.R. (Comm) 256 at 265.

[79] It is an open question whether there can be such apportionment where B's loss is caused partly by A's legal wrong against B and partly by conduct by B amounting to a legal wrong against a third party (C): see *Standard Chartered Bank v Pakistan National Shipping Co (No.2)* [2000] 1 Lloyd's Rep. 218 at 230, 236 (reversed on another point [2002] UKHL 43; [2003] 1 All E.R. 173), where the wrongs committed by A against B and by B against C amounted, not to breach of contract, but to the tort of deceit.

[80] For a special exception to this principle in the law of carriage of goods by sea, see *The Fiona* [1994] 2 Lloyd's Rep. 506.

wrong.[81] The position would have been the same if the wrongs of both parties had been breaches of contract,[82] *e.g.* if the tenant had undertaken to do internal and the landlord external repairs and the damage had been due to the failure of both to perform their respective undertakings. But the present line of reasoning cannot apply where only one party (the defendant) was guilty of a legal wrong, while the conduct of the claimant which is alleged to have contributed to his loss did not amount to such a wrong.[83]

All the situations so far discussed must be distinguished from those in which the defendant's contractual undertaking is to compensate the claimant for a loss not brought about by any act or omission on the part of the defendant at all: for example, where a bank issues travellers' cheques to a customer and promises to compensate him for their face value in the event of his losing them. If the loss is due to the customer's failure to guard against loss, the bank may, if the contract so provides,[84] escape liability for the loss; but such cases raise no issues of contributory negligence as no wrong, leading to the loss, is committed by the bank.

(5) Other restrictions

(a) INJURED FEELINGS AND REPUTATION.[85] A claimant can sometimes[86] recover damages in tort for injury to his feelings, far exceeding any financial loss suffered by him. In *Hurst v Picture Theatres Ltd*[87] the claimant was forcibly ejected from a cinema seat for which he had paid 6d. He recovered £150 in an action for assault and false imprisonment. In substance this was compensation for the indignity he had suffered.

(i) *Injured feelings: general principle.* In a contractual action, the right to recover such damages is restricted by the decision of the House of Lords in *Addis v Gramophone Co Ltd*,[88] where a company wrongfully dismissed its manager in a way that was "harsh and humiliating".[89] He recovered damages for loss of salary and commission, but not for the injury to his feelings caused by the manner of his dismissal. One possible justification for

---

[81] *Tenant Radiant Heat Ltd v Warrington Development Corp* [1988] 1 E.G.L.R. 41; distinguished from contributory negligence cases in *The Good Luck* [1990] 1 Q.B. 818, 904 (revsd on other grounds [1992] 1 A.C. 233); applied in *W Lamb Ltd v J Jarvis & Sons plc* [1999] 60 Con. L.R. 1.

[82] Where each party commits a tort, the outcome was governed at common law by the "last opportunity" rule (above n.63) and is now governed by the 1945 Act.

[83] *Raflatac Ltd v Eade* [1999] 1 Lloyd's Rep. 507 at 510, where the defendant's wrong was also said at 511 to have been the "dominant cause" of the loss.

[84] *Braithwaite v Thomas Cook Travellers Cheques Ltd* [1989] Q.B. 553; contrast *El Awadi v Bank of Credit and Commerce International SA* [1990] 1 Q.B. 606.

[85] Jackson, 26 I.C.L.Q. 502; Enochong (1996) 16 O.J.L.S. 617.

[86] For a list of such cases, see McGregor, *Damages* (16th ed.), §90. They include assault, false imprisonment, malicious prosecution, defamation, deceit (*Archer v Brown* [1985] Q.B. 401), and trespass to land where it is deliberately committed with the intention to molest or annoy: *cf. Wilkes v Wood* (1763) Lofft 1. Such damages are also available for unlawful discrimination under Sex Discrimination Act 1975, s.66(4), Race Relations Act 1976, s.57(4) and Disability Discrimination Act 1995, ss.8(4), 25(2); *cf.* the position under Trade Union and Labour Relations Act 1992, s.149(2), but contrast that in cases of unfair dismissal, now governed by Employment Rights Act 1996, s.123(1); *Norton Tool Co Ltd v Tewson* [1972] I.C.R. 510. *Quaere* whether negligent or innocent torts or torts of strict liability give rise to a claim for injury to feelings. By s.1A of the Fatal Accidents Act 1976, as amended by Administration of Justice Act 1982, s.3, damages of up to £10,000 (Damages for Bereavement (Variation of Sum) (England and Wales) Order, SI 2002/644) for "bereavement" are available in certain cases in respect of the death of the claimant's spouse or unmarried minor child.

[87] [1915] 1 K.B. 1. *cf. Ministry of Defence v Cannock* [1995] I.C.R. 918 (tort damages for dismissal, contrary to EC Directive, on ground of pregnancy).

[88] [1909] A.C. 488.

[89] At 493.

the rule is that such injury is not within the contemplation of the parties and is thus too remote; but an employer considering the effects of *such* a dismissal could surely contemplate injury to the employee's feelings.[90] More probably the rule results from a failure to distinguish between punitive (or exemplary) damages (which are not generally available in a contractual action) and damages for injured feelings (which are meant to compensate the claimant for a loss, though it is not a pecuniary one).[91] Whatever may be the basis of the rule, it continues to restrict the damages recoverable in an action for wrongful dismissal.[92]

Such damages normally consist of the amount which the employee would have earned during the period of notice which the employer was legally obliged to give to bring the contract lawfully to an end.[93] By statute, further compensation may be recoverable for *unfair* dismissal even where such notice is given; and the relevant legislation[94] subjects awards of such compensation to specified financial limits. In *Johnson v Unisys Ltd*,[95] an employee who had recovered the maximum amount available under this legislation (some £11,600) then sought to recover further damages (of some £400,000) at common law, alleging that the manner of his dismissal constituted a separate breach of contract which had caused him to suffer a mental breakdown and consequent loss of earnings. The House of Lords rejected the claim on the ground that it would be wrong to allow the financial limit laid down by the statutory scheme for compensation for unfair dismissal to be evaded by giving the dismissed employee a "parallel remedy [at common law] which is subject to no such limit".[96] It seems that, in cases *not* governed by any such statutory scheme, the House of Lords would be prepared to review the principle in *Addis v Gramophone Co Ltd*[97]; and this is a point important because that case, though strictly an authority only on damages for wrongful dismissal, has also been regarded as the basis of the wider principle that damages for injured feelings cannot, in general, be recovered in a contractual action.[98] That principle has recently been applied so as to preclude the recovery of damages by a company director in respect of mental distress and anxiety suffered by him as a result of alleged breaches of duty by a firm of solicitors engaged by

---

[90] See below, p.992 at n.50.

[91] See above, p.935 and *Johnson v Unisys Ltd* [2001] UKHL 13; [2001] I.C.R. 480, at [15] *per* Lord Steyn, dissenting on the main issue in that case; for the distinction in tort cases, see *McCarey v Associated Newspapers Ltd* [1965] 2 Q.B. 86; *Joyce v Sengupta* [1993] 1 W.L.R. 337 at 347.

[92] *Shove v Downs Surgical plc* [1984] I.C.R. 532; *Bliss v S.E. Thames Regional Health Authority* [1987] I.C.R. 700, overruling *Cox v Phillips Industries Ltd* [1976] 1 W.L.R. 638; *Rae v Yorkshire Bank* [1988] F.L.R. 1 (so far as it relates to damages for "humiliation"); Carty, 49 M.L.R. 240. The rule is viewed with scepticism, even in the context of wrongful dismissal, in *Johnson v Unisys Ltd* [2002] 2 A.C. 1 at 50 *per* Lord Cooke, dissenting on this point. Under the proposals in Law Com. No.247 (1997), para.6.1(2), damages for mental distress to reflect the conduct of the defendant are to be available in contractual actions.

[93] *Johnson v Unisys Ltd* [2001] UKHL 13; [2001] I.C.R. 480, at [41]; *Boardman v Copeland BC* [2001] EWCA Civ 888.

[94] Employment Rights Act 1996, Pt X.

[95] See above, n.5.

[96] *ibid.*, at [56, 57]; *cf. ibid.*, at [2], [80], Lord Steyn dissenting on this point.

[97] See, apart from this criticism of *Addis'* case in Lord Steyn's dissent on this point, the views of Lord Nicholls at [2] and Lord Hoffmann at [43].

[98] *cf. Kenny v Preen* [1963] 1 Q.B. 499; *Watts v Morrow* [1991] 1 W.L.R. 1421 at 1444; *Branchett v Beany* [1992] 3 All E.R. 910 at 916; *The Italia Express* [1992] 2 Lloyd's Rep. 281 at 293; *French v Barclays Bank* [1998] I.R.L.R. 646; *Johnson v Unisys Ltd* [2001] UKHL 13; [2001] I.C.R. 480, at [69]; *Farley v Skinner* [2001] UKHL 49; [2002] 2 A.C. 732, at [16], [34], [47], [54]. *Semble* the conduct of the landlord in *Kenny v Preen*, above, would now be an offence under Protection from Eviction Act 1977, s.1 (replacing Rent Act 1965, s.30), but breach of that section gave rise at common law to no separate civil claim: *McCall v Abelesz* [1976] Q.B. 585. See now Housing Act 1988, s.27.

him and the company to carry through the purchase of development land by the company.[99]

(ii) *Exceptions.* The principle stated above is, however, only a general one; and it is subject to many qualifications. First, damages can be recovered for pain and suffering for a breach of contract which causes personal injury.[1] Such an award takes account of the claimant's mental anguish and to this extent includes damages for injured feelings.[2] Moreover, it seems that personal injury can include physical or mental illness resulting from injury to feelings and that damages for such illness can be recovered,[3] so long as they are not too remote.[4] Secondly, damages can be recovered for physical inconvenience. Thus in *Bailey v Bullock*[5] a solicitor who negligently failed to take proceedings for the recovering of his client's house was held liable for the inconvenience (but not the indignity) that the client suffered in having to live for nearly two years with his wife's parents. Similarly, damages for inconvenience, but not for distress, can be recovered from a surveyor who in breach of contract with his client fails to draw attention to defects in a house which the client, in reliance on the surveyor's report, buys for personal occupation[6]; and a lessor or premises for use as solicitors' offices has been held liable for the "discomfort" caused by his breach of a repairing covenant.[7] It is obviously not easy to distinguish sharply between these two kinds of injury[8]; and damages for distress resulting from the discomfort can be recovered in such cases.[9] Thirdly, damages for distress or vexation can be awarded in a group of cases in which at least one of the "major and important"[10] objects of the contract was to provide enjoyment, security, comfort or sentimental benefits. Such awards have, for example, been made against a travel agent who broke his contract to provide a couple with accommodation for their honeymoon[11]; against a package-tour operator who provided accommodation falling short of the standard promised and so spoilt his client's holiday[12]; against a carrier for breach of a contract to convey guests to a wedding[13]; against a photographer for breach

---

[99] *Johnson v Gore Wood & Co* [2002] 2 A.C. 1.

[1] *e.g. Godley v Perry* [1960] 1 W.L.R. 9.

[2] See *H West & Sons Ltd v Shephard* [1964] A.C. 326.

[3] *e.g. Chelini v Nieri* 196 P. 2d 915 (1948); and see below, p.993 at n.56.

[4] Remoteness would depend on the employer's knowledge of the employee's mental state (and so of the likelihood of his suffering mental illness in consequence of the breach) at the time of *contracting*, not at that of *breach*: see above p.965 at n.64. This point accounts for rejection of the claim in *Johnson v Unisys Ltd* [2001] UKHL 13; [2001] I.C.R. 480, at [29] by Lord Steyn on the ground of remoteness; the same view is taken by Lord Millett, *ibid.*, at [70].

[5] (1950) 66 T.L.R. (Pt. 2) 791; *Hobbs v London & South Western Ry* (1875) L.R. 10 Q.B. 111; *Mafo v Adams* [1970] 1 Q.B. 548; *Wallace v Manchester CC*, *The Times*, July 23, 1998.

[6] *Perry v Sidney Phillips & Son* [1982] 1 W.L.R. 1287; *Watts v Morrow* [1991] 1 W.L.R. 1421; *Patel v Hooper & Jackson* [1999] 1 W.L.R. 1792; *Heatley v William Brown* [1992] 1 E.G.L.R. 289 must be explained on the ground that the damages were awarded for inconvenience rather than for distress. "Inconvenience" seems here to refer to *physical* inconvenience: see the rejection of the claim for "inconvenience and humiliation" (the two being evidently regarded as distinct) in *Rae v Yorkshire Bank* [1988] F.L.R. 1 (wrongful dishonour of a cheque).

[7] *Larkhouse Investments Ltd v Temple House* [1999] B.L.R. 297.

[8] *Watts v Morrow*, above.

[9] *cf. McCall v Abelesz* [1976] Q.B. 585 at 594, where "mental upset and distress" and "inconvenience" seem to be used interchangeably.

[10] *Farley v Skinner* [2001] UKHL 49; [2002] 2 A.C. 737 at [24].

[11] *Cook v Spanish Holiday Tours Ltd*, *The Times*, February 6, 1960.

[12] *Jarvis v Swan Tours Ltd* [1973] Q.B. 233; *cf. Jackson v Horizon Holidays Ltd* [1975] 1 W.L.R. 1468; *Wings Ltd v Ellis* [1985] A.C. 272 at 287; *Spencer v Cosmos Air Holidays Ltd*, *The Times*, December 6, 1989; *Peninsular & Orient SN Co v Youell* [1997] 2 Lloyd's Rep. 136 at 141; *Baltic Shipping Co v Dillon* (1993) 176 C.L.R. 144; *Leitner v TUI Deutschland GmbH & Co AG* [2002] All E.R. (EC) 651; and (in tort) *Ichard v Frangoulis* [1977] 1 W.L.R. 556.

[13] *Chandle v East African Airways Corp* [1964] E.A. 78.

of a contract to take wedding photographs[14]; against a cemetery for breach of a contract to grant exclusive burial rights[15]; and against a landlord for breach of his covenant to repair, which left a flat so damp as to make it uninhabitable.[16] The award of damages for "loss of amenity" where a contract to build a swimming pool for the customer's personal use was broken by building the pool to less than the stipulated depth[17] can be explained on the same ground; and this explanation also accounts for the view that an architect who designs a house for his client's personal occupation is liable for failing to incorporate in the design agreed features, such as an impressive entrance hall and wide staircase, thus depriving the client of the pleasure which he expected to derive from these features.[18] The distinction between cases in which damages are awarded on the present ground and those in which they are awarded for physical inconvenience (under the second exception, discussed above) sometimes hard to draw. The point is illustrated by *Farley v Skinner*[19] where the claiment had, before buying a house as his retirement home, engaged a surveyor whom he had specifically instructed to report on the question whether the house would be affected by aircraft noise. The surveyor in breach of contract carelessly failed to provide accurate information on this point and the purchaser recovered damages in respect of the market adverse effect which such noise had on the peace and tranquillity of the property, even though the price paid for it by him did not exceed its market value. The main ground for the decision is that one important (though not the sole) object of the contract was to provide "pleasure, relaxation and peace of mind"[20]; but there is also support in the speeches for the view that the award could have been supported on the ground that the claimant had suffered physical inconvenience (and not merely distress or vexation) in having to put up with the unexpected level of noise.[21] The question whether one of the main objects of the contract is to provide "pleasure, relaxation and peace of mind" can also give rise to difficulty in borderline cases. Thus in one case damages for distress were awarded against the seller of a new car which broke down and would not restart, so that the buyer suffered "a totally spoilt day comprising nothing but vexation",[22] while in another it was held that no such damages were available for breach of a contract to repair a car.[23] Again, in *Farley v Skinner* it was said that the case was "not 'an ordinary surveyor's contract' "[24] and considerable emphasis was placed on the fact that the contract had specifically referred to aircraft noise. It seems that, but for this fact the surveyor would have been liable only for pecuniary consequences and inconvenience resulting from physical defects in the property itself, as opposed to the vexation caused by adverse environmental factors.[25] Fourthly, the same conduct may amount both to a breach of contract and to a tort; and

---

[14] *Diesen v Samson* 1971 S.L.T. (Sh.Ct.) 49.

[15] *Reed v Madon* [1989] Ch.408.

[16] *Calabar Properties Ltd v Sticher* [1984] 1 W.L.R. 287; cf. *Inglis v Cant* [1987] C.L.Y. 1132 (delay and defects in renovation of house); *Chiodi v De Marney* [1988] 2 E.G.L.R. 64 (breach of statutory repairing covenant).

[17] *Ruxley Electronics Ltd v Forsyth* [1999] A.C. 344 (above, p.947) described in *Johnson v Gore Wood Co* [2002] 2 A.C. 1 at 37 as an "unusual case" but applied in *Farley v Skinner* [2001] UKHL 49; [2002] 2 A.C. 732 where the damages in the *Ruxley* case were said at [21] to have been awarded for "disappointment".

[18] This follows from the overruling in *Farley v Skinner*, above, of *Knott v Bolton* (1995) 45 Con.L.R. 127.

[19] See above, n.17.

[20] *Farley v Skinner*, above, at [24].

[21] *ibid.*, at [30], [38], [54], [105].

[22] *Bernstein v Pamson Motors (Golders Green) Ltd* [1987] 2 All E.R. 220 at 231; the case was later compromised when *the manufacturers* agreed to compensate the buyer in full: see (1987) N.L.J. 1194. cf. *Jackson v Chrysler Acceptance Ltd* [1978] R.T.R. 474 (defects in car bought for touring holiday).

[23] *Alexander v Rolls Royce Motors Ltd* [1996] R.T.R. 95.

[24] See above, n.17 at [42], referring to *Watts v Morrow* [1991] 1 W.L.R. 1421 at 1442.

[25] See especially *Farley v Skinner*, above n.17, at [44], [54–57].

where this is the case the claimant can sometimes recover damages for distress by suing in tort even though such damages would not be available in an action for breach of contract. Thus a tenant cannot recover damages for distress in respect of his landlord's breach of covenant for "quiet enjoyment"[26] (this phrase referring here to the tenant's exercise of the right granted by the lease, rather than to his deriving pleasure from it)[27]; but if a landlord so terrifies and abuses his tenants that they leave the premises he can be held liable in tort for their distress.[28]

(iii) *Injury to reputation.* In *Addis v Gramophone Co Ltd*[29] it was further held that, in an action for wrongful dismissal, the employee could not recover damages for the loss that he might suffer because the dismissal made it more difficult for him to get another job. But the view that damages in such an action cannot be recovered for loss of employment prospects, or for injury to reputation, was hard to justify; and "may no longer be law".[30] In *Malik v BCCI*[31] the House of Lords held that such "stigma damages" were in principle recoverable by former employees of a bank which had collapsed in consequence of corruption and dishonesty in which the employees had not been involved; though the employees' claim ultimately failed as they were unable to establish that the stigma was the cause of the rejection of any job applications which had been made by them; or that any future ones had a sufficiently real chance of success to justify an award for damages for loss of a chance; or that, if such a chance existed, the stigma was the cause of its loss.[32] The damages which they could have recovered if they had been able to establish any of these points would have been recoverable in respect, not of injury to feelings, but in respect of financial loss[33]; and they would have been recoverable, not for wrongful dismissal, but for breach of the employer's implied undertaking not without reasonable cause so to conduct itself as to destroy the relationship of trust and confidence between itself and its employees.[34] According to a further distinction drawn in *Malik's* case, the employee can recover such damages where the effect of the breach is "positively to damage" his job prospects, but not where its effect is merely a "failure to improve them".[35] It is, however, respectfully submitted that the possibility of the employer's being held liable for loss of the latter kind should not be ruled out, particularly where the employment involves training or similar features intended to enhance the employee's prospects. It was, for example, established even before *Malik's* case that an apprentice who was wrongfully dismissed before the end of his period of training was entitled to damages for diminution of his future prospects since "the very object of an apprenticeship agreement is to enable the apprentice to fit himself to get better employment".[36]

There are many other situations in which damages can be awarded for loss of employment prospects or for injury to reputation resulting from a breach of contract.

---

[26] *Branchett v Beany* [1992] 3 All E.R. 910 at 916.

[27] *Kenny v Preen* [1969] 1 Q.B. 499 at 511.

[28] *Sampson v Floyd* [1989] 2 E.G.L.R. 49 as explained in *Branchett v Beany* [1992] 3 All E.R. 910 at 918. In *Johnson v Gore Wood & Co* [2002] 2 A.C. 1 (above p.920) no attempt seems to have been made to argue that the claim for damages for mental distress might have been made in tort. This may account for Lord Bingham's statement at 38 that "on the argument presented on this appeal" the general principle should not be "further restricted". The duty alleged to have been broken by the solicitors was claimed to have arisen "in contract and tort": see *ibid.*, at 18.

[29] [1909] A.C. 488.

[30] *Johnson v Unisys Ltd* [2001] UKHL 13; [2001] I.C.R. 480, at [70].

[31] [1998] A.C. 20.

[32] *BCCI v Ali (No.2)* [2002] EWCA Civ 82; [2002] I.C.R. 1258.

[33] See [1999] 4 All E.R. 83.

[34] See above, p.206.

[35] [1998] A.C. 20 at 37.

[36] *Dunk v George Waller & Sons Ltd* [1970] 2 Q.B. 163.

First, a trader can recover damages for injury to his business reputation, *e.g.* if his reputation suffers because his wholesaler supplies him with defective goods[37]; on the same principle a travel agent can recover damages for loss of "goodwill" from a shipowner who breaks his contract to supply accommodation for passengers on a pleasure cruise.[38] A similar rule applies where a bank wrongfully dishonours its customer's cheque. It has long been settled that, if the customer is a trader, he can recover general damages for the resulting injury to his business reputation.[39] A person who was not a trader was formerly thought to be entitled to no more than a nominal amount unless he proved special damages, *i.e.* particular items of loss resulting from the bank's breach.[40] But this view no longer prevails now that "the credit rating of individuals is as important for their personal transactions . . . as it is for those who are engaged in trade".[41] Hence such persons, too, can now recover general damages in respect of injury to what may be called their financial reputation[42] resulting from the wrongful dishonour of a cheque.[43] Secondly, an actor or author can recover damages for "loss of publicity", that is, for loss of the chance to enhance his reputation,[44] and also for injury to his existing reputation.[45] Thirdly, a person who is wrongfully expelled from a trade union can recover damages for the resulting loss of employment opportunities.[46] Finally, it has been suggested that a claimant should be entitled to damages for injury to reputation where the contract "had as its purpose, or one of its purposes, the protection of the claimant against the sort of damage suffered".[47] Thus damages of this kind were said to be recoverable for breach of a contract not to broadcast a programme concerning the activities of the claimants until after the publication of a report concerning those activities.[48]

(iv) *"Anxiety"*. There is a separate rule that damages cannot be recovered for the "anxiety" which a breach of contract may cause to the injured party.[49] The rule is "not . . . founded on the assumption that such reactions are not foreseeable, which they surely are or may be, but on considerations of policy".[50] The policy consideration here referred to seems to be that anxiety is an almost inevitable concomitant of expectations

---

[37] *Cointat v Myham & Son* [1913] 2 K.B. 220.

[38] *Anglo-Continental Holidays Ltd v Typaldos Lines (London) Ltd* [1967] 2 Lloyd's Rep. 61.

[39] *Rolin v Steward* (1854) 14 C.B. 595 at 605; *Wilson v United Counties Bank Ltd* [1920] A.C. 102 at 112.

[40] *Gibbons v Westminster Bank* [1939] 2 K.B. 882.

[41] *Kpohraror v Woolwich Building Society* [1996] 4 All E.R. 119 at 124. The claimant in this case was a trader, so that it was not strictly necessary to decide the present point.

[42] Not for "loss of reputation *simpliciter*": *Kpohraror*'s case, above, at 125. The phrase "financial reputation" is used in the text to avoid the awkwardness of referring to the "business reputation" of someone who is not in business.

[43] *Kpohraror*'s case, below, at 124.

[44] *Herbert Clayton & Jack Waller Ltd v Oliver* [1930] A.C. 209; *Joseph v National Magazine Co Ltd* [1959] Ch. 14; *Malcolm v Chancellor, Masters and Scholars of the University of Oxford, The Times,* December 19, 1990.

[45] *Malik v BCCI* [1998] A.C. 20, overruling *Withers v General Theatre Corp Ltd* [1933] 2 K.B. 536. For subsequent proceedings in *Malik's* case, see above, p.991 at n.32.

[46] *Edwards v SOGAT* [1971] Ch. 354 at 378–379.

[47] *Cambridge Nutrition Ltd v B.B.C.* [1990] 3 All E.R. 523 at 540.

[48] *Cambridge Nutrition* case, above; *cf. McLeish v Amoo-Guttfried & Co, The Times,* October 13, 1993.

[49] *Cook v Swinfen* [1967] 1 W.L.R. 457; *Hutchinson v Harris* (1978) 10 Build L.R. 19; *Reed v Madon* [1989] Ch. 408, 426 and, so far as it relates to "anxiety", *Johnson v Gore Wood & Co* [2002] 2 A.C. 1. In *Kemp v Sober* (1851) 1 Sim.(N.S.) 517 (where the running of a girls' school in breach of covenant was restrained) Lord Cranworth said at 520: "The feeling of anxiety is damage." But the better explanation is that an injunction to restrain breach of a negative stipulation can be granted *without* proof of damage: *Tipping v Eckersley* (1855) 2 K. & J. 254; *Doherty v Allman* (1878) 3 App.Cas. 709 at 729; below, p.1040.

[50] *Watts v Morrow* [1991] 1 W.L.R. 1421 at 1445; *Farley v Skinner* [2001] UKHL 49; [2002] 2 A.C. 732 at [82].

based on promises, so that a contracting party must be deemed to take the risk of it.[51] Damages for anxiety or mental stress cannot, therefore, be recovered for breach of a contract made in the course of, or in connection with, a business and resulting in the failure of that business,[52] or for breach of contract by a bank in wrongly debiting a customer's account[53]; or for breach of contract by a broker, causing financial loss to his client.[54] On the other hand, such damages can be recovered if the very purpose of the contract is to secure relief from an existing state of anxiety, e.g. where a solicitor in breach of contract failed to take necessary steps in non-molestation proceedings, so that the molestation of his client continued.[55] Moreover, if actual mental illness results from anxiety, damages can be recovered in respect of it, so long as it is not too remote.[56]

(v) *Nature of claims for non-pecuniary loss.* Where damages are recoverable for "disappointment" resulting from failure to perform an obligation to provide enjoyment, security or peace of mind, it is sometimes said that the basis of such recovery is that the claimant was, by the breach, "deprived of the contractual benefit to which he was entitled".[57] Such language is, with respect, entirely appropriate in the context of such awards, which compensate the claiment in respect of a loss which he has in fact suffered, though the loss is non-pecuniary in nature. But phrases such as that quoted above could, if taken out of that context, be read as supporting the view that the mere fact of breach of contract, even though no loss of any kind had flowed from it, gave rise to a claim for substantial damages; and this view would, with respect, be inconsistent with a number of the rules or principles on which such claims are based. One such principle is that just discussed, that damages for breach of contract cannot be recovered *merely* in respect of the "anxiety" or "disappointment" that may be caused by the breach.[58] Another, discussed earlier in this Chapter, is that damages cannot be recovered in respect of a breach which has no adverse effect[59]; and, in particular, the application of this principle to cases in which the injured party has made a losing bargain,[60] e.g. where he is a buyer who has agreed to pay (but has not yet paid) more than the subject-matter is worth; nor can a buyer recover substantial damages in respect merely of the non-conformity of the goods delivered to him if those goods are worth no less than they would have been, if he had been in conformity with the contract.[61] In none of these cases are damages recoverable *merely* because the injured party has not received the benefit of the promised performance; and it is submitted that they support the view that "damages should not be awarded, unless perhaps nominally, for the fact of a breach of contract as distinct from the consequences of breach".[62] Of course the adverse consequences need not be of a

---

[51] *Johnson v Unisys Ltd* [2001] UKHL 13; [2001] I.C.R. 480 at [70].

[52] *Hayes v James & Charles Dodd* [1990] 2 All E.R. 815; Soh, 105 L.Q.R. 43. *A fortiori*, such damages cannot be recovered by a *corporate* claimant: *Firsteel Cold Rolled Products v Anaco Precision Products, The Times,* November 21, 1994.

[53] *McConville v Barclays Bank, The Times,* October 13, 1993.

[54] *R. v Investors Compensation Scheme, Ex p. Bowden* [1994] 1 W.L.R. 17, reversed on other grounds [1995] Q.B. 107, in turn reversed without reference to the present point [1996] A.C. 261.

[55] *Heywood v Wellers* [1976] Q.B. 446; *cf. Dickinson v Jones Alexander & Co* [1993] 2 FLR 521; contrast *Hartle v Laceys* [1997] C.L.Y. 3839 (solicitor employed for conveyancing purposes).

[56] *Cook v Swinfen,* above, n.49 *Esso Petroleum Co Ltd v Mardon* [1976] Q.B. 801 at 822; *Attia v British Gas plc* [1988] Q.B. 304 (where it is not clear whether the claim was in contract or in tort).

[57] *Farley v Skinner* [2001] UKHL 49; [2002] 2 A.C. 732 at [106]; *cf. ibid.,* at [86].

[58] See above p.992 at nn.49 and 50.

[59] See above, pp.934–935.

[60] *ibid., cf.* above, pp.948–949.

[61] *Taylor v Bank of Athens* (1922) 27 Com. Cas. 142.

[62] *Farley v Skinner,* above n.57, at [40] *per* Lord Clyde. For the application of the same principle to cases where the breach causes loss to a third party but none (beyond the bare fact of breach) to the promisee, see *Alfred McAlpine Construction Ltd v Panatown Ltd* [2001] 1 A.C. 518 at 534, *per* Lord Clyde; above, p.601.

financial kind, as is shown by the many exceptions, discussed above[63] to the general rule that damages for breach of contract cannot be recovered for injured feelings; but these cases do not negative the requirement that some adverse consequence to the claimant (other than mere "anxiety" or "disappointment") must flow from the breach in order to sustain an award of substantial damages. Nor is the present point affected by the fact that even a losing bargain might (in appropriate circumstances)[64] be specifically enforceable, though it would be somewhat eccentric for the injured party to seek specific enforcement of such a contract. The award of specific relief would not be open to the objection that could be levelled at an award of damages in such a case, *i.e.* that such an award would result in a "gratuitous benefit to the aggrieved party",[65] since the order of specific performance would be conditional on his performing his part of the bargain (*i.e.*, on paying the "excessive" price) if he had not already done so.

(b) NON-PAYMENT OF MONEY. The general rule of common law was that interest could not be recovered as damages for failure to pay a debt when due. This rule applied both where the debtor wholly failed to pay and was sued for the debt, and where he paid voluntarily but after the due day.[66] At common law,[67] interest could be awarded only if the debt arose out of a mercantile security or if there was an agreement to pay interest[68] in the events which had happened.[69] Two major modifications of the common law rule have been made by legislation, but these have not abolished the rule, so that its operation still calls for discussion.

(i) *Statutory interest.* The first such modification is the right to "statutory interest" which arises under the Late Payments of Commercial Debts (Interest) Act 1998. The Act applies only[70] to contracts for the supply of goods and services where each party is acting in the course of a business[71] The rules laid down by the Act are highly complex; but its central provision is that it is an implied term of a contract to which it applies that "statutory interest" will be payable on any "qualifying debt" created by the contract (*i.e.* broadly, on the price payable under the contract).[72] Statutory interest starts to run from the day after the date agreed for payment in the contract or, in default of such agreement, 30 days after either the performance of the supplier's obligation or notice of the amount of the debt (whichever is later).[73] Since statutory interest is available by virtue of an implied term, the supplier is in principle entitled to it as of right; but where

---

[63] See above, pp.989–991.

[64] *i.e.*, subject to the restrictions discussed at pp.1019 *et seq.*, below.

[65] *Ruxley Electronics Ltd v Forsyth* [1996] A.C. 334 at 357.

[66] *London, Chatham & Dover Ry v South Eastern Ry* [1893] A.C. 429; *La Pintada* [1985] A.C. 104; *Alex Lawrie Factors Ltd v Modern Injection Moulds Ltd* [1981] 3 All E.R. 658 at 683; *The Lips* [1988] A.C. 395 at 423; *Janred Properties Ltd v Ente Nazionale Italiano per il Turismo* [1989] 2 All E.R. 444 at 456.

[67] Interest can be awarded by way of ancillary relief and for breach of fiduciary duty in equity, and on damages and on salvage in Admiralty: see *La Pintada* [1985] A.C. 104 at 115; *Mathew v TM Sutton Ltd* [1994] 1 W.L.R. 1455.

[68] *Higgins v Sargent* (1823) 2 B. & C. 348.

[69] See *Janred Properties Ltd v Ente Nazionale Italiano per il Turismo* [1989] 2 All E.R. 444 (where the event on which interest was to be paid was held not to have occurred).

[70] In this respect the Act falls short of implementing the Law Commission's recommendations in its Report on *Interest* (Law Com. 88).

[71] s.2(1); for definition of "business" see s.2(7); for definition of "goods and services", see s.2(2) and (3); contracts of service and apprenticeship are excluded by s.2(4). The Act was brought into force in stages: see now Late Payment of Commercial Debts (Interest) Act (Commencement No.5) Order (SI 2002/1673), listing earlier commencement orders.

[72] s.1(1) and (2); "qualifying debt" is defined in s.3; for the treatment of obligations to make an "advance payment," see s.11.

[73] s.4, especially subss. (2), (3) and (5). The rate of statutory interest is 8% above the Bank of England's official dealing rate: Late Payment of Commercial Debts (Rate of Interest) (No.3) Order 2002 (SI 2002/1675).

by reason of his conduct the interests of justice so require, the court can remit such interest wholly or in part.[74] The parties remain free, in general, to make their own contractual provisions with regard to interest and the Act does not place any restrictions on their power to do so after the debt has been created.[75] But their right to contract out of the Act before that time[76] is restricted in that contract terms are, to the extent to which they purport to exclude or restrict the right to statutory interest or to vary it, void unless they provide for a "substantial remedy" for late payment of the debt.[77] Moreover, no reliance can be placed on any contract term purporting to postpone the time at which a qualifying debt would otherwise be created unless that term satisfies the requirement of reasonableness under the Unfair Contract Terms Act 1977[78]; this provision applies whether the contract in which the term is contained was the contract creating the debt or one made before or after that contract.[79] The scope of the Act is, as its title indicates, restricted in that it applies only to contracts in which *each* party acts in the course of a business and only to contracts for the supply of "goods" and "services".[80] The latter expression may cover financial services; but consumer credit agreements and contracts intended to operate by way of mortgage, pledge, charge or other security are specifically excepted from the provisions of the Act.[81]

(ii) *Discretionary interest.* The second modification of the common law rule dates back to 1833, and is now contained in s.35A of the Supreme Court Act 1981. This gives the courts a discretionary power to award interest when giving judgment for a debt or damages[82]; and where proceedings are brought for recovery of a debt and the defendant pays the debt before judgment.[83] The court in exercising this discretion will look at the overall position of the injured party in consequence of the breach. Thus if he retains the income of property sold till payment, the court will not award him interest on the price, since this would amount to allowing double recovery.[84] Unlike the right to "statutory interest" under the 1998 Act, the discretion to award interest under the 1981 Act applies to all contracts; but it is subject to a number of limitations. If the contract has been rescinded by the injured party before payment under it from the party in breach has become due, no action for *debt* will be available to the injured party[85]; and in such a case the statutory discretion to award interest will be exercisable only in relation to the *damages* to which that party is entitled.[86] This restriction (which appears to apply also to the right to "statutory interest" under the 1998 Act[87]) is a significant one: the

---

[74] s.5.
[75] ss.7(2) and 8(5).
[76] s.7(2).
[77] s.8(1), (3) (4); for the definition of "substantial remedy," see s.9. The use of standard terms which would be void under these provisions may be restrained by injunction on the application of a "representative body", *i.e.* one representing the interests of "small and medium-sized enterprises": see Late Payment of Commercial Debt Regulations 2002, SI 2002/1674 (implementing Dir.2000/35), reg.3; and see Explanatory Note for definitions of the phrases quoted above.
[78] s.14, bringing such a term within Unfair Contract Terms Act 1977, s.3(2)(b) even where it is *not* contained in "written standard terms".
[79] This follows from the reference in s.14(3) to the definition of "contract term" in s.10(1).
[80] s.2(1).
[81] s.2(5).
[82] See Supreme Court Act 1981, s.35(A)(1) as amended by Administration of Justice Act 1982, s.15 and Sch.I, Pt I. Pts II and IV of the Schedule confer the same powers on county courts and arbitrators; see Practice Direction [1983] 1 All E.R. 934.
[83] Supreme Court Act 1981, above, s.35A(3); for power to award interest *on damages* under s.35A, see *Edmunds v Lloyds Italico* [1986] 1 W.L.R. 492.
[84] *Janred Properties Ltd v Ente Nazionale Italiano per il Turismo* [1989] 2 All E.R. 444 at 456.
[85] See above, pp.850–851.
[86] *Janred Properties* case, above, n.84.
[87] Since in the case put there can be no "qualifying *debt*" within ss.1(1) and 3 of the 1998 Act.

damages suffered on a purchaser's default in completing a contract for the sale of a house are *prima facie* the difference between the contract price and the proceeds of resale,[88] a much smaller sum than the contract price. The statutory discretion to award interest under the 1981 Act does not moreover, extend to the case where an overdue debt is paid *before* any proceedings for recovery of the debt have begun.[89]

(iii) *Interest and other loss as damages.* A person who is entitled to statutory interest under the 1998 Act is, in addition, entitled to a relatively modest fixed sum,[90] intended to compensate him for the cost incurred by reason of the delay in payment. Subject to this qualification, neither of the statutory provisions described above enables the courts to award *more* than interest; and at common law the general rule was formerly thought to be that a debtor who defaulted was not liable for any other loss even though he knew that the creditor would be ruined by his default.[91] Long ago this rule was described by Jessell M.R. as "not quite consistent with reason"[92]; and its scope is now considerably restricted in the light of two distinctions. The first is that between claims for interest and claims for other types of loss suffered in consequence of the delay in payment; the second is that between "general" and "special" damages. The latter distinction is, in turn, used (in the present context) in two senses.[93] In the first sense, "general" damages are those recoverable under the first rule in *Hadley v Baxendale*,[94] while "special" damages are those recoverable under the second rule in that case; in the second sense, "general" damages are those which can be recovered without proof of loss, while "special" damages are those which can be recovered only as compensation for loss which the claimant can show that he has actually suffered.[95]

Common law claims for interest are *prima facie* claims for "general" damages in both these senses: loss of interest clearly arises (in the words of the first rule in *Hadley v Baxendale*) "according to the usual course of things from such breach of contract itself"[96]; and, under the statutory provisions described above an award of interest can be made without proof that any loss of interest has been suffered. In *The Lips*[97] the House of Lords had limited the general common law rule (that interest was not normally recoverable as damages for delay in payment) to claims for interest by way of "general" damages in the two senses just described. It follows that damages for loss of interest can be recovered at common law if the claimant can show (i) that such loss has actually been suffered, and (ii) that this loss was at the time of contracting within the reasonable contemplation of the defendant, so as to satisfy the second rule in *Hadley v Baxendale*.[98] For example, in *Wadsworth v Lydall*[99] the defendant was late in making a payment of

---

[88] See above, p.954.
[89] As in *The World Symphony* [1991] 2 Lloyd's Rep. 251, affd without reference to the point [1992] 2 Lloyd's Rep. 115; *cf. IM Properties plc v Dalgleish* [1999] Q.B. 297 (same principle applied to damages). There is no such restriction on the right to "statutory interest" under the 1998 Act.
[90] Late Payment of Commercial Debt (Interest) Act 1998, s.5A, inserted by Late Payment of Commercial Debts Regulations 2002 (SI 2000/1674), reg.2(4) implementing Dir.2000/35; the fixed sum ranges from £40 where the debt is less than £1,000 to £100 where the debt is £10,000 or more.
[91] *Fletcher v Tayleur* (1855) 17 C.B. 21 at 29; *Williams v Reynolds* (1865) 6 B. & S. 495 at 505; *British Columbia Saw-Mill Co Ltd v Nettleship* (1868) L.R. 3 C.P. 499 at 506.
[92] *Wallis v Smith* (1882) 21 Ch.D. 243 at 257; Mann, 101 L.Q.R. 30; *Jobson v Johnson* [1989] 1 W.L.R. 1026 at 1041.
[93] *International Minerals & Chemical Corp v Karl O Helm AG* [1986] 1 Lloyd's Rep. 81 at 103.
[94] See above, p.965.
[95] *International Mineral & Chemical Corp v Karl O Helm AG* [1986] 1 Lloyd's Rep. 81 at 103.
[96] *Hadley v Baxendale* (1854) 9 Exch. 341 at 354.
[97] [1988] A.C. 395 at 423, 429.
[98] See above, p.965; *International Minerals & Chemical Corp v Karl O Helm AG* [1981] 1 Lloyd's Rep. 81 at 103–105; *Knibb v NCB* [1987] Q.B. 906 at 913; *Dods v Coopers Creek Vinyards* [1987] N.Z.L.R. 530.
[99] [1981] 1 W.L.R. 598; approved in *La Pintada* [1985] A.C. 104.

£10,000 due to the claimant and needed by him (as the defendant knew) for completing the purchase of a farm as his home. As a result, the claimant incurred interest (and other) charges; and it was held that these were recoverable as damages for late payment. The interest recovered in this way was interest *incurred* by the claimant[1]: not interest *forgone* by him. It is the latter type of loss which is irrecoverable at common law even though it occurs (as it normally does) "according to the usual course of things" within the first rule in *Hadley v Baxendale*.[2]

According to *The Lips*, the common law rule precluding recovery of interest applies *only* to claims *for interest* as damages for late payment of money.[3] Claims for other losses suffered as a result of late payment are therefore not affected by the rule; and such claims are claims for "special" damages in the sense that they can succeed only if the claimant proves his loss. On the other hand, such losses "are subject to the same rules as apply to claims for damages for breach of contract generally",[4] so that damages in respect of such losses can be recovered if *either* rule in *Hadley v Baxendale* is satisfied: they do not have to be "special" in the first of the two senses distinguished above, *i.e.* in the sense of falling within the *second* rule of remoteness laid down in that case. For example, late payment of money due in a foreign currency may cause loss to the claimant because of exchange rate fluctations. Such loss is recoverable even if only the first (and not the second) rule in *Hadley v Baxendale* is satisfied.[5]

Where the claimant can show that he has suffered loss (other than loss of interest) as a result of the defendant's failure to pay money when due, he will have suffered "special" damage in our second sense (*i.e.* of loss actually proved). Many cases in which the courts have awarded damages can be explained by saying that the damages were "special" in this sense, and that, being claims for damages other than interest, they were subject only to the ordinary rules of remoteness. Such damages can be recovered from a banker who wrongfully repudiates liability, or delays in making payments due, under a letter of credit,[6] or who wrongfully fails to honour a customer's cheque[7]; from a buyer of goods who fails to provide a confirmed credit in accordance with the terms of the contract of a sale[8]; from a person who breaks a contract to subscribe for debentures in a company or who fails to pay calls on shares[9]; from a hire-purchaser or instalment buyer whose wrongful failure to pay instalments amounts to a repudiation of the contract[10]; and perhaps from any person who breaks a contract to lend or advance money.[11]

The decision in *Wadsworth v Lydall*,[12] and the restriction in *The Lips* of the original common law rule to claims for interest by way of general damages, are welcome

---

[1] *cf. Nykreditbank v Edward Erdman Group* [1997] 1 W.L.R. 1627 at 1637.

[2] *e.g. The World Symphony*, above, n.89.

[3] [1988] A.C. 395 at 424; *cf. IM Properties plc v Cape & Dalgleish* [1999] Q.B. 297 at 307 (where no such claim was made).

[4] [1988] A.C. 395 at 424.

[5] *ibid. International Minerals & Chemical Corp v Karl O Helm AG* [1986] 1 Lloyd's Rep. 81.

[6] *Prehn v Royal Bank of Liverpool* (1870) L.R. 5 Ex. 92; *Larios v Bonany y Gurety* (1873) L.R. 5 P.C. 346; *Urquhart Lindsay & Co v Eastern Bank Ltd* [1922] 1 K.B. 318; *Ozalid Group (Export) Ltd v African Continental Bank Ltd* [1979] 2 Lloyd's Rep. 231.

[7] *Rolin v Steward* (1854) 14 C.B. 595.

[8] *Trans Trust SPRL v Danubian Trading Co Ltd* [1952] 2 Q.B. 297; *Urquhart Lindsay & Co v Eastern Bank Ltd* [1922] 1 K.B. 318, 323; above, p.762.

[9] *Wallis Chlorine Syndicate Ltd v American Alkali Co Ltd* (1901) 17 T.L.R. 565.

[10] *Yeoman Credit Ltd v Waragowski* [1961] 1 W.L.R. 1124 at 1128; *Overstone Ltd v Shipway* [1962] 1 W.L.R. 117; *cf.* p.851, above.

[11] See Sedgwick, *Damages* (9th ed.), s.622; Corbin, *Contracts*, §1065.

[12] [1981] 1 W.L.R. 598; above, at n.99.

developments: they both recognise and mitigate the unsatisfactory nature of that rule as it was formerly understood.[13] But even after the statutory and common law developments so far described, we are left with cases which could still fall within the common law rule that interest cannot be recovered for late payment of a debt. This could be the position where there was no right to "statutory interest" under the 1998 Act because the contract in question was not one for the supply of goods or services,[14] and where the statutory discretion to award interest under the 1981 Act could not be exercised because the debtor had paid late but before proceedings for recovery of the debt had been started. The common law rule which could lead to such a result was criticised in the very case in which the House of Lords first recognised its existence[15]; and that criticism was repeated when the House of Lords in 1984 reluctantly recognised the continued existence of the rule.[16] In times of high inflation or high interest rates, the rule can cause real hardship to a creditor; and it cannot be justified by reference to any of the general principles governing damages for breach of contract. No doubt the new right to "statutory interest" will remove that hardship in many cases; and in cases to which that right does not extend the creditor can protect himself by expressly stipulating for interest. In one case where a contract contained no such express stipulation the court nevertheless construed the contract as containing a promise to pay interest.[17] The decision is a further (and welcome) indication of the courts' dislike of the rule. Its abolition has been recommended by the Law Commission[18]; but in view of Parliament's failure to implement this recommendation in full,[19] it is unlikely that what remains of the rule will be reversed by judicial decision.[20]

(iv) *Late payment of damages.* The discussion so far has been concerned with damages for late payment of a *debt.* Where a defendant incurs liability in *damages* and unjustifiably delays in paying those damages, there is a statutory power to award interest on the damages[21]; but there is "no such thing as a cause of action in damages for late payment of damages".[22] This may be true even if the damages are a fixed sum payable under a valid liquidated damages clause.[23] Such a clause does not necessarily fix the *time* when the payment is to be made; and where no such time is fixed, delay in paying the fixed sum is not, of itself, a breach of contract. Where the clause fixes both the amount payable and the time of payment, it seems that special damages for late payment can be recovered, subject to the usual tests of remoteness.[24]

---

[13] See above, p.996 at nn.91 and 92.

[14] As in *Wadsworth v Lydall* [1981] 1 W.L.R. 598, where the payment was due under an agreement for the dissolution of a partnership.

[15] *London, Chatham & Dover Ry v South Eastern Ry* [1893] A.C. 429 at 437 (*per* Lord Herschell L.C.); Mann, 101 L.Q.R. 30.

[16] *La Pintada* [1985] A.C. 104; Bowles and Whelan, 48 M.L.R. 235. As the principal debt was paid after arbitration proceedings had commenced, interest could now be awarded on the facts of the case under the provisions of the Administration of Justice Act 1982, s.15 and Sch.I, Pt I; but at the relevant time those provisions were not yet in force.

[17] *FG Minter v Welsh Health Technical Services Organization* (1980) 13 Build. L.R. 1. Contrast *Alsabah Maritime Services v Philippine International Shipping Corp* [1984] 1 Lloyd's Rep. 291 where a provisions in an agency agreement that "no other *charges* will be made . . . " was held to exclude *interest.*

[18] *Report on Interest* (Law Com. 88) paras 35–44.

[19] See above, p.994 n.70.

[20] *La Pintada* [1985] A.C. 104.

[21] See above, p.995 at nn.82 and 83.

[22] *The Lips* [1988] A.C. 395 at 425; *Rammade Ltd v WJ Emson & Co Ltd*, [1987] R.T.R. 72; *The Arras and Hoegh Rover* [1989] 1 Lloyd's Rep. 131; *The Italia Express* [1992] 2 Lloyd's Rep. 281 at 292.

[23] This was the position in *The Lips*, above.

[24] *The Lips* [1988] A.C. 395 at 427.

(c) FAILURE TO MAKE TITLE TO LAND. A special rule formerly governed the damages recoverable by a purchaser of land if the contract went off through a defect in the vendor's title. In *Bain v Fothergill*,[25] the House of Lords held that the purchaser could only get damages in respect of his expenses in investigating the title. He could not get damages for loss of his bargain or for expenses incurred otherwise than in investigating the title. The rule was subjected to much criticism[26] and it was abolished by s.3 of the Law of Property (Miscellaneous Provisions) Act 1989 in relation to contracts made after September 27, 1990. It remains possible for the vendor by the terms of the contract to limit his liability for breach by reason of a defect in his title. The Unfair Contract Terms Act 1977 would not apply to such a term either (a) in the case of a private sale, because the vendor's liability would not be "business liability"[27]; or (b) in the case of a sale in the course of a business (*e.g.* by a property developer) because the relevant provisions[28] of the Act do not apply to "any contract so far as it relates to the creation or transfer of an interest in land".[29] The Unfair Terms in Consumer Contracts Regulations 1999 likewise do not apply against private sellers and it is doubtful whether they apply to a simple contract for the sale of land.[30] A term excluding or restricting the vendor's liability for making a misrepresentation as to his title could, however, be ineffective if it did not satisfy the requirement of reasonableness imposed by s.3 of the Misrepresentation Act 1967.[31]

4. Damages Fixed by Contract

A contract may provide for the payment of a fixed sum on breach. Such a provision may serve the perfectly proper purpose of enabling a party to know in advance what his liability will be; and of avoiding difficult questions of quantification and remoteness. On the other hand the courts are reluctant to allow a party, under such a provision, to recover a sum which is obviously and considerably greater than his loss. They have therefore divided such provisions into two categories: penalty clauses, which are invalid,[32] and liquidated damages clauses, which will generally be upheld.

(1) Distinction between penalty and liquidated damages

A clause is penal if it provides for "a payment of money stipulated as *in terrorem* of the offending party"[33] to force him to perform the contract. If, on the other hand, the clause is a genuine attempt by the parties to estimate in advance the loss which will result from the breach, it is a liquidated damages clause. This is so even though the stipulated sum is not precisely equivalent to the injured party's loss. It seems that, if the stipulated sum is a genuine pre-estimate of the *actual* loss, the clause is valid even though part of that loss is *irrecoverable* because it is too remote[34]; and that it is similarly not penal if it

---

[25] (1874) L.R. 7 H.L. 158.

[26] As long ago as *Day v Singleton* [1899] 2 Ch. 320 at 329 ("anomalous"); see generally Law Com. No.166.

[27] Unfair Contract Terms Act 1977, s.1(3); above, p.246.

[28] *i.e.* those of s.3, above, p.253.

[29] *ibid.* s.1(2) and Sch.1, para.1(b); above, p.264.

[30] See above, pp.278–279, 281.

[31] As amended by the Unfair Contract Terms Act 1977, s.8; above, p.385.

[32] Unless in a form which parties to the kind of contract are, by legislation, required to use: *Golden Bay Realty Pte Ltd v Orchard Twelve Investments Pte Ltd* [1991] 1 W.L.R. 981.

[33] *Dunlop Pneumatic Tyre Co Ltd v New Garage & Motor Co Ltd* [1915] A.C. 79 at 86.

[34] *Robophone Facilities Ltd v Blank* [1966] 1 W.L.R. 1428 at 1448.

stipulates for payment to a contracting party of an actual loss that is likely to be suffered, not by him, but by a third party.[35]

The question whether a clause is penal or a pre-estimate of damages depends on its construction and on the surrounding circumstances at the time of contracting (not at the time of breach).[36] In answering this question, the fact that the payment is described in the contract as a "penalty" or as "liquidated damages" is relevant, but not decisive.[37] Clauses in identical terms may be held penal or not, according to the subject-matter of the contracts and to the circumstances in which the contracts were made.[38]

In *Dunlop Pneumatic Tyre Co Ltd v New Garage & Motor Co Ltd*[39] Lord Dunedin formulated four rules of construction:

(a) "It will be held to be a penalty if the sum stipulated for is extravagant and unconscionable in amount in comparison with the greatest loss that could conceivably be proved to have followed from the breach": to quote a rather far-fetched example, a clause in a contract to do building work worth £50 would be penal if it provided that the builder should pay £1 million if he failed to do the work.[40]

(b) "It will be held to be a penalty if the breach consists only[41] in not paying a sum of money, and the sum stipulated is a sum greater than the sum which ought to have been paid". A clause making a debtor liable to pay £1,000 if he failed to pay £50 on the due day would thus be penal. One explanation formerly given for this rule was that the only amount recoverable, as damages for failure to pay money when due, was interest, when available by statute or by special agreement[42]; but this reasoning is no longer convincing now that *special* damages can be recovered for loss caused by such a breach.[43] Alternatively, it was suggested that the rule was based on an equitable jurisdiction to reform unconscionable bargains[44]; but this explanation, too, is suspect, for the rule applies even though the contract is fair.[45] Where the bargain is a fair one, the courts are reluctant to apply the present rule. In *Wallis v Smith*[46] £5,000 was payable "on any substantial breach" of a contract to develop land as a building estate; one of the terms of the contract was that the defendant should pay £500 on signing the agreement. When the defendant wholly repudiated the contract, he was held liable for the £5,000. The court was able to escape from the present rule by adopting a narrow construction of the clause and holding that failure to pay the £500 was not a "substantial" breach.

The rule does not apply merely because a contract under which a sum of money is payable in instalments provides that, on default of any payment, the whole balance is to

---

[35] See *Alfred McAlpine Construction Ltd v Panatown Ltd* (1998) 58 Const. L.R. 58 at 92, reversed, on other grounds [2001] 1 A.C. 518; that payment would have to be held by the payee for the third party, above, p.606.

[36] *Dunlop Pneumatic Tyre Co Ltd v New Garage & Motor Co Ltd* [1915] A.C. 79 at 87; *Philips Hong Kong v Attorney-General of Hong Kong* (1993) 61 Build.L.R. 41.

[37] *Kemble v Farren* (1829) 6 Bing. 141 ("liquidated damages" held penalty); *Elphinstone v Monkland Iron & Coal Co Ltd* (1886) 11 App.Cas. 332 ("penalty" held liquidated damages); *cf. Pagnan & Fratelli v Coprosol SA* [1981] 1 Lloyd's Rep. 283.

[38] Contrast *Phonographic Equipment* (1958) *Ltd v Muslu* [1961] 1 W.L.R. 1379 with *Lombank Ltd v Excell* [1964] 1 Q.B. 415.

[39] [1915] A.C. 79 at 87–88.

[40] *Clydebank Engineering Co v Don Jose Ramos Isquierdo y Castaneda* [1905] A.C. 6 at 10.

[41] See *Thos P Gonzales Corp v FR Waring (International) Pty Ltd* [1980] 2 Lloyd's Rep. 160 at 163 (rule inapplicable where breach consists of buyer's failure to *accept and* pay).

[42] [1915] A.C. 79 at 87.

[43] See above, pp.996–997.

[44] [1915] A.C. 79 at 87.

[45] As in *Betts v Burch* (1859) 4 H. & N. 506. This case was decided in a common law court before the Judicature Acts 1873–75; but the same rule was recognised, if reluctantly, in the Chancery Division after 1875: *Wallis v Smith* (1882) 21 Ch.D. 243.

[46] (1882) 21 Ch.D. 243.

become immediately due.[47] Such a clause is said to accelerate, and not to increase, the liability of the debtor. But early payment in fact is generally more expensive to the debtor; and a provision for an extra payment equal in value to this expense would be undeniably penal.[48] In strict logic, such acceleration clauses should therefore fall within Lord Dunedin's second rule; the fact that they have been held not to do so is a further indication of the courts' reluctance to apply that rule. The parties can also circumvent this rule by providing that a high sum is to be paid as the contract price, subject to a discount if payment is made by a specified date; or by providing for the payment to be made by a third party under a performance bond.[49] These provisions for acceleration, for discounts, and for payments by third parties may be perfectly fair; and the relative ease with which Lord Dunedin's second rule can, by use of them, be evaded suggests that it serves no useful purpose and should be abandoned. Cases of real extortion could still be dealt with under Lord Dunedin's first rule; and it seems that under this rule an acceleration clause may be penal.[50] The foregoing submissions derive support from the judicial treatment of clauses which increase the rate of interest payable by a borrower in default. Such clauses are not penal if they operate prospectively only and if the increase is no more than a "modest"[51] one. The reason for this view is that the very fact of the borrower's default makes him a less good credit risk from the time of default and therefore provides a "good commercial reason"[52] for the increase. Even though such a stipulation may not be a genuine estimate of damage, it will therefore not be "*in terrorem*" of the offending party and hence not penal except where the increase is an "exceptionally large"[53] one.

(c) There is a presumption (but no more than a presumption) that a clause is penal when "a single lump sum is made payable . . . on the occurrence of one or more or all of several events, some of which may occasion serious and others but trifling damage". Under this rule, a sum is not presumed to be penal if it is expressly proportioned to the seriousness of the breach, *e.g.* if a lease provides for payment of £100 *per acre*[54] of land not restored to its former condition, or if a contractor agrees to pay £500 *per week* for delay.[55] Such stipulations are only penal if extravagant.

On the other hand, a sum payable on one of several events will be treated as penal if one of those events is the non-payment of a smaller sum,[56] or if one event is *bound* to cause greater loss than another.[57] A sum may, therefore, be regarded as penal if it *might* have become due on a trifling breach, even though the breach which *actually* occurred

---

[47] *Protector Loan Co v Grice* (1880) 5 Q.B.D. 529; *Wallingford v Mutual Society* (1880) 5 App.Cas. 685; *cf. Sport International Bussum BV v Inter-Footwear Ltd* [1984] 1 W.L.R. 776 at 793, and *White & Carter (Councils) Ltd v McGregor* [1962] A.C. 413, where it was conceded that the acceleration clause was valid; *The Angelic Star* [1988] 1 Lloyd's Rep. 122; contrast *O'Dea v Allstates Leasing Systems (WA) Pty Ltd* (1983) 57 A.L.J.R. 172; Muir, 10 Sydney L.R. 503.

[48] A stipulation for accelerated payment of a loan *plus interest* for the whole contractual period was said to be penal in *The Angelic Star* [1988] 1 Lloyd's Rep. 122 at 125.

[49] See below, p.1004.

[50] This seems to be the best explanation for *Wadham Stringer Finance Ltd v Meany* [1981] 1 W.L.R. 39 at 48, where such a clause was said to be subject to the rules as to penalties, though it was not penal in effect.

[51] *Lordsvale Finance Ltd v Bank of Zambia* [1996] Q.B. 752 at 767.

[52] *ibid.* at 763.

[53] *ibid.* at 767.

[54] *Elphinstone v Monkland Iron & Coal Co* (1886) 11 App.Cas. 332.

[55] *Clydebank Engineering* case [1905] A.C. 6; *Philips Hong Kong v Attorney-General of Hong Kong* (1993) 61 Build.L.R. 41. Such a provision will not operate where the contract is totally abandoned (since if it did so operate the payments would have to go on for ever): *British Glanzstoff Mfg Co v General Accident, etc. Co* [1913] A.C. 143.

[56] As in *Kemble v Farren* (1829) 6 Bing. 141; *cf. Duffen v FRABO SpA* [2000] 1 Lloyd's Rep. 180 at 196.

[57] *Wilson v Love* [1896] 1 Q.B. 626 (on such facts, see now Agricultural Holdings Act 1986, s.24); *cf.* below, pp.1004–1005.

was quite a serious one, and one for which the sum could be regarded as a genuine pre-estimate.[58] In this way, the rule can invalidate perfectly fair bargains. The courts will do their best to avoid such results by construing the contract so as to make the sum payable only on major breaches, for which it is a valid pre-estimate.[59] Even where this construction is not possible, it is submitted that the validity of the clause should depend on what is likely to be its normal operation. It should not be struck down merely because, in extraordinary circumstances (which have not in fact occurred), the stipulated sum might greatly exceed the claimant's loss.[60]

(d) "It is no obstacle to the sum stipulated being a genuine pre-estimate of damage that the consequences of breach are such as to make precise pre-estimation an impossibility. On the contrary, that is just the situation when pre-estimated damage was the true bargain between the parties". Thus in *Dunlop Pneumatic Tyre Co Ltd v New Garage & Motor Co Ltd* itself the defendants bought tyres and agreed with the sellers that they would not (i) tamper with the manufacturer's marks; (ii) sell to the public below list price[61]; (iii) sell to any person "suspended" by the sellers; (iv) exhibit or export the tyres without the seller's written consent. They further agreed to pay £5 to the sellers for every tyre sold or offered in breach of the agreement. The defendants sold to the public below list price. It was held that the provision for payment of £5 per tyre was not penal. The presumption that a sum payable on several events was penal was "rebutted by the very fact that the damage caused by each and every one of those events, however varying in importance, [was] of such an uncertain nature that it cannot be accurately ascertained".[62] But even in such circumstances the sum will be penal if it is extravagant.[63]

(2) Effects of the distinction

Often the stipulated sum will exceed the claimant's loss. In such a case, the claimant can nevertheless recover that sum if the stipulation is a liquidated damages clause, while if it is a penalty he cannot recover the stipulated sum but only the amount to which he would have been entitled if the contract had not contained the penalty clause.[64] This follows from the nature of the distinction between the two kinds of provision. Two further possibilities, however, require discussion.

First, a clause may be intended to provide for payment of a sum below the estimated loss. Such a clause is not invalid as a penalty as its object is not to act *in terrorem*. In *Cellulose Acetate Silk Co Ltd v Widnes Foundry (1925) Ltd*[65] a contract for the construction of an acetone recovery plant provided that if completion was delayed the contractors were to pay "by way of penalty £20 per working week". The plant was completed 30 weeks late, during which period the owners suffered losses of £5,850. It was held that they could recover £600 only. Both parties must have known that the actual loss would exceed £20 per week, so that one object of the clause was to limit the contractors' liability. But it was not a pure limitation clause, for the contractors would still have had

---

[58] *Ariston SRL v Charly Records Ltd*, *Financial Times*, March 21, 1990.
[59] *Webster v Bosanquet* [1912] A.C. 394; cf. above, p.1000 at n.46.
[60] See *Philips Hong Kong Ltd v Attorney-General of Hong Kong* (1993) 61 Build.L.R. 41; *International Leasing Corp (Vic) Ltd v Aiken* (1966) 85 W.N. (Pt.1) N.S.W. 766.
[61] For the possible effect of Competition Act 1998, s.2 on such a price-maintenance agreement, see above, p.476.
[62] [1915] A.C. 79, 96; cf. *Robophone Facilities Ltd v Blank* [1966] 1 W.L.R. 1428. For the now discarded view that a sum payable on several different events was necessarily penal, see *Astley v Weldon* (1801) 2 B. & P. 346.
[63] *Ford Motor Co (England) Ltd v Armstrong* (1915) 31 T.L.R. 267.
[64] *Jobson v Johnson* [1989] 1 W.L.R. 1026 at 1038.
[65] [1933] A.C. 20.

to pay £20 per week even if the owners had lost less.[66] For this reason, liquidated damages clauses are probably not exemption clauses, and so not subject to the Unfair Contract Terms Act 1977,[67] though they may in certain circumstances be subject to the Unfair Terms in Consumer Contracts Regulations 1994.[68]

Secondly, the clause may be a penalty even though the stipulated sum falls short of the claimant's loss.[69] This apparently paradoxical situation can arise *either* because changing conditions have made an originally extravagant sum inadequate, *or* because a perfectly reasonable sum is nevertheless penal on technical grounds (*i.e.* under the second or third rules of construction stated above).[70] The question then arises whether the clause is nevertheless effective to limit the defendant's liability to the amount of the penalty. According to one view, the clause is effective for this purpose; for penalty clauses are struck down to prevent oppression[71] and the party in breach cannot be oppressed by the clause when it actually works in his favour. But this view can cut across the general principle that the validity of contractual provisions should be determined once for all by reference to the time of contracting[72]; for under it a term which was originally invalid as a penalty could become valid as a limitation clause simply by reason of a change of circumstances. Hence in *Wall v Rederiaktiebolaget Lugudde*[73] it was held that a shipowner could disregard a penalty clause in a charterparty and recover his actual loss, which exceeded the amount of the penalty. In the *Cellulose Acetate* case[74] the question whether a penalty clause could always be disregarded in this way was left open as it is possible for a clause on its true construction to be both a penalty and a limitation clause. But this is an implausible construction of a clause which provides for payment of a fixed sum irrespective of proof of loss; and it seems that generally such a clause would be disregarded under the rule in *Wall*'s case.

(3) Analogous provisions

The penalty clauses with which the foregoing discussion is concerned are all stipulations for the payment of *money*. It is equally possible for a clause which requires some other performance from the party in breach to be a penalty. This could, for example, be the position where the clause required that party to make a "payment in kind", or to transfer shares at an undervalue.[75]

A number of other commonly found contractual provisions resemble penalties in their commercial purpose of putting pressure on a party to perform, but are nevertheless valid. This is, for example, true of acceleration clauses, of discounts for punctual payment[76] and of express provisions for termination on breach[77]; it is also sometimes true of provisions as to the forfeiture of deposits and part payments to be discussed below.[78] Two further types of clauses, however, give rise to considerable dispute.

---

[66] See above, p.237.
[67] See above, p.248.
[68] See below, p.1006.
[69] Hudson, 90 L.Q.R. 30; Gordon, *ibid.* 296; Hudson, 91 L.Q.R. 20; Barton, 92 L.Q.R. 20.
[70] See above, pp.1000–1001.
[71] *Elsley v JG Collins Insurance Agencies* (1978) 3 D.L.R. (3d) 1; *cf. Philips Hong Kong v Attorney-General of Hong Kong* (1993) 61 Build.L.R. 41; Hudson, 101 L.Q.R. 480.
[72] See above, pp.258, 271, 453–454, 1000.
[73] [1915] 3 K.B. 66 (not cited in the *Elsley* case, above); *cf. Dingwall v Burnett* 1912 S.C. 1097; *W & J Investments Ltd v Bunting* [1984] 1 N.S.W.R. 331.
[74] See above, n.65.
[75] *Jobson v Johnson* [1989] 1 W.L.R. 1026, where it was conceded that such a clause was penal.
[76] See above, p.1001.
[77] See above, p.778.
[78] See below, pp.1008, 1010.

(a) Sums payable ohterwise than on breach. The distinction between penalties and liquidated damages normally applies to sums payable *on breach* of the contract in which the stipulation for payment is contained. A clause under which a sum is payable *only* on some other event is therefore not a penalty. In *Alder v Moore*[79] a professional footballer received £500 from an insurance company in respect of an injury which was thought to have disabled him permanently; and he undertook to repay the money in the event of his again playing professional football. This was not a penalty[80] since he committed no breach when he did play again, as he had made no promise not to do so. Again, a contract for the sale of goods may give the buyer the option of postponing the date on which he is to take delivery, on payment of a "carrying charge". Such a provision is not a penalty since the permitted delay is not a breach and the extra charge is simply the price which the buyer pays for exercising the option conferred on him by the contract.[81] Nor is a sum a penalty where the liability to pay it arises, not on the breach itself, but only on an event triggered by the breach. This is the position where a lease provides that, on a tenant's failure to perform his covenant to repair, the landlord is to be entitled to execute the repairs and to recover the cost of so doing from the tenant. A claim for that amount is not a claim for damages but one for the agreed sum,[82] and is not subject to the law relating to penalties.[83] A stipulation is, similarly, not penal if it provides for the payment of a sum of money on breach of another contract with a third party. In one case A had contracted to build a refinery for B; C had undertaken responsibilities as guarantor for the financing of the project; and A had promised C that, in the event of a breach of A's contract with B, A would pay to C sums equivalent to those which C would have to pay under the guarantee. It was held that the latter stipulation was not a penalty as it "provided for payment of money on a specified event other than a breach of a contractual duty owed by the contemplated payor to the contemplated payee".[84] Similar reasoning seems to apply to performance bonds by which C promises to pay a sum of money to A if B fails to perform his contract with A. Such a promise is independent of the contract between A and B[85] and can be enforced by A against C even if A cannot show that B's breach has caused him any loss, or if the loss which A has suffered is less than the amount payable by C.[86]

It is less clear whether a clause in a contract can be penal if it provides for a payment on several events one of which is a breach of that contract while another is not. The

---

[79] [1961] 2 Q.B. 57; 77 L.Q.R. 300; Goff, 24 M.L.R. 637.

[80] [1961] 2 Q.B. 57 at 76.

[81] *Thos P Gonzales Corp v FR Waring (International) Pty Ltd* [1980] 2 Lloyd's Rep. 160; *Toepfer v Sosimage SpA* [1980] 2 Lloyd's Rep. 397 at 402; *Fratelli Moretti SpA v Nidera Handelscompagnie BV* [1981] 2 Lloyd's Rep. 47; *Lusograin Commercio Internacional de Cereas Ltda. v Bunge AG* [1986] 2 Lloyd's Rep. 654; *The Bonde* [1991] 1 Lloyd's Rep. 136 at 145. But demurrage clauses in charterparties (above, pp.237, 238) assume that the detention of the ship is a breach and provide for the payment of liquidated damages: *The Lips* [1988] A.C. 395. In *Interfoto Picture Library Ltd v Stiletto Visual Programmes Ltd* [1988] Q.B. 433 (discussed above, p.245) the question whether the "holding fee" was a "disguised penalty clause" was left open at 445–446. *cf. John George Leigh (T/A Moor Land Videos) v Customs & Excise Commissioners* [1990] 2 VATTR 59 ("fines" for late return of hired videos); *Jones v Society of Lloyd's, The Times*, February 2, 2000 (revival of original debt on debtor's failure to perform settlement agreement).

[82] See below, p.1013.

[83] *Jervis v Harris* [1996] Ch. 195 at 203.

[84] *Export Credit Guarantee Department v Universal Oil Products Co* [1983] 1 W.L.R. 399 at 402.

[85] *Edward Owen Engineering Ltd v Barclays Bank International* [1978] Q.B. 159.

[86] If A recovers more from C than he has lost, B (who will normally have procured and paid for C's promise to A) can, in general, recover the excess from A: *Cargill International SA v Bangladesh Sugar & Food Industries Corp* [1998] 1 W.L.R. 461; *Comdel Commodities Ltd v Siporex Trade SA* [1997] 1 Lloyd's Rep. 424 at 431.

problem has arisen under so-called minimum payment clauses in hire-purchase agreements. Such a clause commonly provides that on premature determination of the agreement the hirer shall bring his payments under it up to a specified proportion of the hire-purchase price (or the whole of it) "by way of agreed compensation for depreciation". It then specifies the events on which the agreement may be determined. The owner is usually given the right to determine if the hirer commits a breach of the agreement, and in certain other events.[87] The hirer also often has a right to return the goods on bringing his payments up to the specified amount.

The question whether the law as to penalties applies to such clauses has given rise to much dispute. It is said, on the one hand, that only a sum payable on breach can be a penalty; and, on the other, that the whole law as to penalties could be evaded, if it did not apply to these clauses, by simply including, among the events on which the sum was payable, one event which was not a breach. The common law does not fully adopt either of these views. If the agreement is in fact determined on the ground of the hirer's breach, the law as to penalties applies.[88] If the agreement is determined on some ground other than the hirer's breach, e.g. because the hirer exercises his right to return the goods, the law as to penalties does not apply.[89] This compromise is unsatisfactory; for under it a hirer who wishes to return the goods may be better off if he simply defaults than he would be if he exercised his lawful right to determine the agreement.[90]

In the case of a regulated agreement within the Consumer Credit Act 1974,[91] the hirer has a statutory right to determine on payment of one-half of the hire-purchase price. But if the court is satisfied that a smaller sum will adequately compensate the owner for his loss, it may make an order for the payment of such smaller sum.[92] Under these provisions, a hirer who terminates lawfully will no longer be worse off than one who commits a breach. But where the agreement is not a regulated one (e.g. because the amount of credit exceeds £15,000 or because the hirer is not an "individual") the unsatisfactory rules of common law still prevail.

Where the law as to penalties applies, the question whether a minimum payment clause is penal is determined in accordance with the principles already discussed. In *Lamdon Trust Ltd v Hurrell*[93] a minimum payment clause providing for payment of about three-quarters of the hire-purchase price on determination was held to be penal, *inter alia*, because this sum was payable whether the hirer defaulted in payment of the first or of the last instalment: the loss caused by these two breaches would clearly be very different. As this factor is present in many cases of this kind, it seems that minimum payment clauses will often be penal, unless the minimum payment is very small.[94]

We have seen that a clause is not presumed to be penal if the sum payable is proportioned to the seriousness of the breach.[95] An attempt to use this principle to

---

[87] *e.g.* the hirer's bankruptcy. Provisions for termination on the hirer's death used to be common but are ineffective if the agreement is a regulated agreement (above, pp.177–178) within the Consumer Credit Act 1974, ss.86, 87.

[88] *Cooden Engineering Co Ltd v Stanford* [1953] 1 Q.B. 86; *Lamdon Trust Ltd v Hurrell* [1955] 1 W.L.R. 391.

[89] *Associated Distributors Ltd v Hall* [1938] 2 K.B. 83; *Re Apex Supply Co Ltd* [1942] Ch. 108; *Campbell Discount Co Ltd v Bridge* [1961] 1 Q.B. 445; reversed on other grounds [1962] A.C. 600, where the House of Lords was equally divided on the point discussed in the text.

[90] *cf.* Law Commission Working Paper No.61, para.22.

[91] See above, p.178.

[92] s.100(1) and (3). Probably these provisions displace the Unfair Terms in Consumer Contracts Regulations 1999 in cases of this kind: above, p.277.

[93] [1955] 1 W.L.R. 391; *cf. Anglo-Auto Finance Co Ltd v James* [1963] 1 W.L.R. 1042; *United Dominions Trust (Commercial) Ltd v Ennis* [1968] 1 Q.B. 54.

[94] See *Lombank Ltd v Kennedy* [1961] N.I. 192.

[95] See above, p.1001.

support a minimum payment clause was rejected in *Bridge v Campbell Discount Co Ltd.*[96] The sum payable under the clause was said to be compensation for depreciation. Yet it *decreased* with each payment made by the hirer, while the depreciation obviously increased the longer the hirer kept the goods. "It is a sliding scale of compensation, but a scale that slides in the wrong direction".[97] Hence the clause was held to be penal. If the scale slides in the right direction, the clause may be upheld[98]; but it will still be invalid if it may result in excessive payment for any particular breach.[99]

(b) WITHHOLDING PAYMENTS. Normally, a penalty clause requires the defaulting party to *make* a payment to the victim; but it has been suggested that a provision entitling the victim to *withhold* a payment can also be penal. In *Gilbert-Ash (Northern) Ltd v Modern Engineering (Bristol) Ltd*[1] a building sub-contract entitled the sub-contractor to the agreed payments on the issue of architect's certificates; and it then gave the main contractor the "right to suspend or withhold payment" if the sub-contractor failed "to comply with any of the provisions" of the contract. This was said to be invalid as a penalty.[2] But it seems that the contract could have achieved in substance the desired result by providing that nothing was to become due until performance precisely in accordance with its terms had been completed. Effect has been given to such provisions[3] without any reference to the law as to penalties. Somewhat similar reasoning was used where the rules of an association which had been formed for the enforcement of legal claims by its members provided that members who defaulted in the payment of subscriptions should not share in the proceeds of such claims. Their argument that this provision was a penalty was rejected on the ground that it was "an essential part of the pooling arrangement".[4]

(4) Unfair Terms in Consumer Contracts Regulations 1999

Under these Regulations, certain standard terms in contracts between commercial sellers of goods or suppliers of goods or services and consumers do not bind the consumer if they are unfair.[5] An illustration given in the Regulations of a term which is *prima facie* unfair[6] is one requiring "any consumer who fails to fulfil his obligation to pay a disproportionately high sum in compensation".[7] Such a term is likely also to be invalid as a penalty at common law, so that normally the common law rules and the Regulations would lead to the same result. There are, however, significant differences between these two sets of rules. On the one hand, the scope of the common law rules is perfectly general, while that of the Regulations is limited in that they apply only to standard terms in contracts between commercial sellers or suppliers and consumers, in that even within these categories certain types of contract are excepted, and in that certain terms are

---

[96] [1962] A.C. 600.

[97] [1962] A.C. 600 at 623.

[98] *Phonographic Equipment (1958) Ltd v Muslu* [1961] 1 W.L.R. 1379; *cf. Essenda Finance Corp Ltd v Plessnig* (1989) 63 A.L.J.R. 238; Wilkin [1990] L.M.C.L.Q. 16; Carter, 2 J.C.L. 78.

[99] *Lombank Ltd v Excell* [1964] 1 Q.B. 415; the Court of Appeal felt unable to overrule *Muslu's* case on the ground of inconsistency with *Bridge's* case. See Ziegel [1964] C.L.J. 108.

[1] [1974] A.C. 689.

[2] *ibid.* at 698, 703, 711, 723; *cf. The Vainqueur José* [1979] 1 Lloyd's Rep. 557.

[3] *e.g. Eshelby v Federated European Bank* [1932] 1 K.B. 423; above, p.786.

[4] *Nutting v Baldwin* [1995] 1 W.L.R. 201; *cf. SCI (Sales Curve Interactive) v Titus SARL* [2001] EWCA Civ 591; [2001] 2 All E.R. (Comm) 416, at [66].

[5] See above, pp.267 *et seq.*

[6] SI 1999/2083, reg.5(2).

[7] *ibid.* Sch.2, para.1(e).

excepted even in contracts within the scope of the Regulations.[8] On the other hand, the scope of the Regulations appears to be wider than that of the common law rules in that the Regulations may (at least in some cases) apply to sums payable otherwise than on breach. A consumer who, in the words of the illustration quoted above, "fails to fulfil his obligations" is not necessarily in breach: he may, for example, have an excuse for non-performance.[9] The Regulations might also apply to a term by which a sum of money became payable on an event which was not a failure in performance at all: for example where a buyer agreed to pay a "carrying charge" if he failed to take delivery on the specified day, or where a hirer agreed to pay a "holding charge" if he did not return the subject-matter at the end of the specified period.[10] If the rate at which these charges are fixed is disproportionately high in relation to the amount which would be payable under the contract but for the delay, the term imposing the charge might well be regarded as "unfair" within the Regulations.[11]

5. Deposit and Part-payment[12]

(1) In general

A contract may provide that one party shall make an advance payment but fail to specify what is to happen to the payment if the contract is not performed. Clearly, the money must be paid back if the *payee*, in breach of contract, fails to perform.[13] But the more difficult question (with which the following discussion is concerned) is whether the money must also be paid back where it is the *payor* who, in breach of contract, fails to perform and the contract is in consequence rescinded by the other party. This depends at common law on the intention with which the money was paid: it may have been paid as a deposit or as a part-payment. A deposit is a sum of money paid as "a guarantee that the contract shall be performed".[14] At common law,[15] it is generally[16] irrecoverable[17] unless the contract otherwise provides.[18] A part-payment is simply a payment of part of the contract price: it is generally[19] recoverable[20] unless the contract validly provides the contrary.

---

[8] See above, pp.276–280.

[9] See above, p.835.

[10] See above, p.1004 at n.81.

[11] Even though such a term can be said to fix the "price" of an option, it would not seem to be saved by reg.6(2)(a) (above p.248) since it does not define "the *main* subject-matter of the contract."

[12] Beatson, 97 L.Q.R. 389, *The Use and Abuse of Unjust Enrichment* Ch.3; Milner, 42 M.L.R. 508; Harpum [1984] C.L.J. 134.

[13] *Country & Metropolitan Homes Surrey Ltd v Topclaim Ltd* [1997] 1 All E.R. 254.

[14] *Howe v Smith* (1884) 27 Ch.D. 89, 95; *cf. Public Works Commissioners v Hills* [1906] A.C. 368 (so far as it relates to the retention fund); *The Selene G* [1981] 2 Lloyd's Rep. 180 at 185.

[15] For the position under Law of Property Act 1925, s.49(2) see below, p.1008; for possible effects of the Unfair Terms in Consumer Contracts Regulations 1999, see below p.1012.

[16] For an exception, see the discussion of deposits and penalties, below, p.1008.

[17] *Howe v Smith*, above; *Ex p. Barell* (1875) L.R. 10 Ch.App. 512; *Harrison v Holland* [1921] 3 K.B. 297; [1922] 1 K.B. 211; *Union Eagle Ltd v Golden Achievement Ltd* [1997] A.C. 514 at 518; *Omar v El Wakil* [2001] EWCA Civ 1090; *The Times*, November 2, 2001, at [36].

[18] *Palmer v Temple* (1839) 9 A. & E. 508. A *precontract* deposit is recoverable if the negotiations fail to lead to the conclusion of the contemplated contract: *Chillingworth v Esche* [1924] 1 Ch. 97; *Guardian Ocean Cargoes Ltd v Banco do Brazil* [1991] 2 Lloyd's Rep. 68; *idem (No.3)* [1992] 2 Lloyd's Rep. 193.

[19] For a suggested exception, see below, p.1012 at n.66.

[20] *Mayson v Clouet* [1924] A.C. 980; *Dies v British International Mining Corp* [1939] 1 K.B. 725; and see *Hillel v Christoforides* (1991) 63 P. & C.R. 301.

(2) Deposits and penalties

A deposit is distinguishable from a penalty on the ground that it is payable before, and not after breach.[21] But the function of the two devices is similar: the only difference between "a guarantee that the contract shall be performed"[22] and "a payment of money stipulated as *in terrorem* of the offending party"[23] lies in the emotive force of the words used. The law as to penalties can therefore apply to deposits. In the *Workers' Trust* case,[24] for example, a contract for the sale of land provided for the payment by the purchaser of a deposit of 25 per cent of the price and for forfeiture of that deposit in the event of the purchaser's default. After the purchaser had paid the deposit and then failed to complete on the due day, the vendor rescinded the contract and purported to forfeit the deposit; but the Privy Council held that the deposit was not a reasonable pre-estimate of the loss which the vendor was likely to suffer in consequence of the default, that the deposit was therefore penal, and that it must be paid back to the purchaser. On the other hand, where the deposit is reasonable in relation to the loss likely to be suffered, it can be forfeited, particularly if the loss is such that it cannot be accurately assessed in advance.[25]

There is a well-established exception to the general rule that a penal deposit must be paid back. In contracts for the sale of land, it is the normal practice for the purchaser to pay a deposit of 10 per cent of the price and for the contract to provide for forfeiture of that deposit in the event of the purchaser's default. It is generally agreed that such a provision is valid even though it does not, and does not purport to, bear any relation to the vendor's loss. In the *Workers' Trust* case, the Privy Council described the exception as anomalous[26] but nevertheless recognised its existence.

(3) Law of Property Act 1925, s.49(2)

This subsection gives the court power "if it thinks fit" to order the return of a deposit paid under a contract for the sale of land. Originally, the courts took the narrow view that the subsection applied only in the exceptional situation in which, though the purchaser was in breach,[27] the vendor could not, for some reason, have obtained specific performance.[28] This restriction on the scope of the subsection may have had some support in the legislative history.[29] But the restriction derives no support from the words of the subsection; nor does it have any other merit. It was, moreover, open to the objection that, on a rising market, the purchaser's breach might cause the vendor no loss at all; and to allow him nevertheless to keep the deposit could be said to enrich him unjustly, while

---

[21] *cf. Corpe v Overton* (1833) 10 Bing. 252 at 257.

[22] See above, at n.14.

[23] See above, p.999 at n.33.

[24] *Workers' Trust and Merchant Bank Ltd v Dojap Investments Ltd* [1993] A.C. 573; Harpum, [1993] C.L.J. 389 *cf. Public Works Commissioners v Hills* [1906] A.C. 368; *Starside Properties Ltd v Mustapha* [1974] 1 W.L.R. 816, 819; *Jobson v Johnson* [1989] 1 W.L.R. 1026 at 1036, 1041.

[25] *Pye v British Automobile Commercial Syndicate Ltd* [1906] 1 K.B. 425; *cf. Starside Properties Ltd v Mustapha* [1974] 1 W.L.R. 816 at 819.

[26] See above n.24 at p.578; *cf. ibid.* at 580 ("without logic").

[27] The subsection is not needed where it is the vendor (*i.e.* the *payee* of the deposit) who is in breach: see above, p.1007 at n.13.

[28] See *James Macara v Barclays Bank Ltd* [1944] 2 All E.R. 31 at 32, affirmed [1945] K.B. 148. See also *Michael Richards Properties Ltd v St. Saviour's Parish* [1975] 3 All E.R. 416 (where a contractual provision excluding the statutory power was relevant, though obviously not decisive); *Cole v Rose* [1978] 3 All E.R. 1121; and *Windsor Securities Ltd v Loreldal Ltd, The Times*, September 10, 1975 (where no attempt seems to have been made to invoke the power); *Zieme v Gregory* [1963] V.R. 214.

[29] It was thought that the subsection was intended to do no more than to reverse *Re Scott & Alvarez' Contract* [1895] 2 Ch. 603 (so far as it related to irrecoverability of the deposit).

causing considerable hardship to the purchaser. A number of later cases therefore take the broader view that the subsection is "designed simply to do justice between vendor and purchaser"[30] and that the discretion conferred by it is to be exercised "where justice requires it".[31] This rejection of the original, and unsatisfactory, restriction on the scope of the subsection is certainly to be welcomed; but unfortunately the cases give no clear indication of the circumstances in which the courts will exercise their discretion under the subsection.[32] That discretion is no longer needed where the deposit is penal in effect, now that the *Workers Trust* case has held such a deposit to be recoverable at common law. This development may have reduced the need to invoke the statutory discretion and may in part account for the recently expressed view that this discretion will be exercised in favour of a defaulting purchaser only in "exceptional circumstances".[33] Just when circumstances are, for this purpose, exceptional remains obscure; but the requirement is evidently not satisfied merely by the fact that the deposit substantially exceeds the normal 10 per cent of the price[34] or by the fact that the vendor has not established that the breach has caused him any loss.[35]

(4) Forfeiture of instalments

A contract of sale may provide for payment of the price in instalments and add that, on default in payment of any one instalment, those already paid shall be forfeited. In such cases equity can sometimes grant certain kinds of relief against forfeiture to the purchaser if he is able and willing to perform after the agreed time,[36] particularly where enforcement of the forfeiture provision would cause him some prejudice (such as the loss of the value of improvements he had made to the land) beyond merely depriving him of the benefit of his bargain[37]; that is, it might be able to extend the time for payment,[38] or order repayment of the forfeited instalments if the purchaser was able and willing to perform, but the vendor was for some reason justified in refusing to accept late performance.[39]

It is more doubtful whether equity could order the repayment of forfeited instalments to a purchaser who was *not* able and willing to perform. In *Mussen v Van Diemen's Land Co*[40] land was sold for £321,000 payable in instalments and the contract provided that the vendor was to have the right to rescind, and to forfeit any money paid, in the event

---

[30] *Universal Corp v Five Ways Properties Ltd* [1979] 1 All E.R. 552, 555; Oakley [1980] C.L.J. 24.

[31] *Schindler v Pigault* (1975) 30 P. & C.R. 328 at 336; for other examples of the exercise of the discretion, see *Maktoum v South Lodge Flats Ltd*, The Times, April 21, 1980; *Wilson v Kingsgate Mining Industries Ltd* [1973] 2 N.S.W.L.R. 713; *Yammouni v Condidorio* [1975] V.R. 479.

[32] Contrast the authorities cited in n.31 above with *Carne v De Bono* [1988] 1 W.L.R. 1107, where no attempt was made to rely on the subsection; and *Safehaven Investments Inc v Springbok Ltd* (1996) 71 P. & C.R. 59, where "fairness between the parties" was held not to require an order for the return of the deposit, and it was said that relief under s.49(2) would not normally be given against the exercise of a contractually reserved right to forfeit the deposit.

[33] *Omar v El-Wakil* [2001] EWCA Civ 1090 at [37]; [2002] P. & C.R. 3.

[34] *ibid.*, at [36]; the deposit was about 31% of the price, but it was not argued that it was penal: *ibid.*, at [31]. Perhaps for this reason, no reference was made to the *Workers Trust* case [1993] A.C. 573, above, p.1008.

[35] *ibid.*, at [37].

[36] See *Jobson v Johnson* [1989] 1 W.L.R. 1026, where the defendant failed to comply with this requirement; and *Goker v NWS Bank plc* [1990] C.C.L.R. 34, where relief was denied to a persistent defaulter.

[37] *Union Eagle Ltd v Golden Achievement Ltd* [1997] A.C. 514 at 520, above, p.781.

[38] *Re Dagenham (Thames) Dock Co* (1873) L.R. 8 Ch.App. 1022 and *Kilmer v BC Orchard Lands Ltd* [1913] A.C. 319, as explained in *Union Eagle Ltd v Golden Achievement Ltd* [1997] A.C. 514 at 521; *Starside Properties Ltd v Mustapha* [1974] 1 W.L.R. 816; *cf. Millichamp v Jones* [1982] 1 W.L.R. 1422 (time for payment of deposit extended); Lang, 100 L.Q.R. 427. For other applications of, and restrictions on, the principle of relief against forfeiture, see above, pp.779–781.

[39] *Steedman v Drinkle* [1916] 1 A.C. 275, as explained in *Mussen v Van Diemen's Land Co*, [1938] Ch. 253; but see *Stockloser v Johnson* [1954] 1 Q.B. 476.

[40] See n.39 above.

of the purchaser's default. Such default occurred after the purchaser had paid £40,200.[41] His claim for the return of the money was rejected as it was not "unconscionable on the part of the vendor, who has contracted to part with his land on agreed terms, to enforce the contract . . . ".[42] This case left open the possibility of ordering repayment when it *was* unconscionable for the vendor to keep the money. In *Stockloser v Johnson*[43] quarrying machinery was sold under a contract which provided for payment in instalments, and, in the event of the buyer's default, for forfeiture of instalments paid. The buyer failed to keep up the agreed payments and the actual decision was that he was not entitled to the return of the forfeited instalments as, in the circumstances, it was not unconscionable for the seller to keep them after rescinding the contract: the buyer had speculated on the success of the quarry, and lost. But Somervell and Denning L.JJ. said that repayment could have been ordered if the mere act of keeping the money had been unconscionable.[44] Romer L.J., on the other hand, said that repayment could be ordered only if the vendor was guilty of fraud, sharp practice or other unconscionable conduct; and that there was "nothing inequitable *per se* in a vendor, whose conduct is not open to criticism in other respects, insisting on his contractual right to retain instalments of purchase-money already paid".[45]

Later dicta, as well as a decision at first instance,[46] support Romer L.J.'s view, which is based on the principle that the law should not interfere with contracts freely made. But this principle is discarded in the law as to penalties, and in particular in the law relating to penal deposits. In the *Workers Trust* case[47] the Privy Council left open the question whether relief against forfeiture of instalments should be given to a purchaser who has been let into possession. This fact may, indeed, affect the amount of the vendor's loss; but subject to this practical consideration, it is submitted that, since forfeiture provisions often resemble penalties in their purpose and effect,[48] their validity should depend on the tests that differentiate penalties from liquidated damages clauses. The court should accordingly have power to grant relief where, on these tests, the forteiture provision is penal in nature.[49] In the cases discussed above, such relief would take the form of ordering repayment of the forfeited instalments; but *Jobson v Johnson*[50] illustrates the possible availability of other forms of relief. In that case a contract for the sale of shares to be paid for by instalments provided that, if the buyer defaulted, he should retransfer the shares for £40,000. It was admitted that this clause was penal in

---

[41] Land equal in value to other payments had been conveyed to him.

[42] At 262.

[43] [1954] 1 Q.B. 476; Diamond, 19 M.L.R. 498; Price, 20 M.L.R. 620; *cf.* Hodkinson, 3 O.J.L.S. 393, discussing *Legione v Hateley* (1983) 152 C.L.R. 406.

[44] [1954] Q.B. 476 at 483, 485, 489–490. According to *Hyundai Shipbuilding and Heavy Industries Co Ltd v Pournaras* [1978] 2 Lloyd's Rep. 502 at 508 Somervell L.J.'s views are limited to cases of "default" (*sc.* by the buyer), while Denning L.J. went "somewhat further"; but exactly how much further is not made clear, nor is it apparent from the report in *Stockloser's* case.

[45] [1954] 1 Q.B. 476 at 501; *cf. Kazakstan Wool Processors (Europe) Ltd v Nederlandsche Credietverzekering Madtshappig NV* [2001] 1 All E.R. (Comm) 708 at 720 (retention of premium on termination of policy for breach by insured).

[46] *Galbraith v Mitchenall Estates Ltd* [1965] 2 Q.B. 473, citing dicta from *Campbell Discount Co Ltd v Bridge* [1961] 1 Q.B. 445 (reversed on other grounds [1962] A.C. 600); *Else (1982) v Parkland Holdings* [1994] B.C.L.C. 130.

[47] *Workers Trust and Merchant Bank Ltd v Dojap Investments Ltd* [1993] A.C. 573 at 581–582, discussing *Stockloser v Johnson*, above, n.43.

[48] *Jobson v Johnson* [1989] 1 W.L.R. 1026 at 1041.

[49] *cf. Stockloser v Johnson* [1954] 1 Q.B. 476 at 491; Law Commission Working Paper No.61, paras 65, 66. For a special statutory provision giving the court a discretion to order repayment, see Consumer Credit Act 1974, s.132(1); this would now apply on the facts of *Galbraith's* case, above, n.46 and would in a case of this kind displace the Unfair Terms in Consumer Contracts Regulations 1999: above, p.226.

[50] [1989] 1 W.L.R. 1026; Harpum [1989] C.L.J. 370.

effect[51]; and, on the buyer's default, it was held that the seller was entitled to an order for *either* the sale of the shares and the payment out of the proceeds of sale of the unpaid instalments, *or* the transfer of the shares so long as their value did not exceed the unpaid instalments by more than £40,000. This amounted to putting the seller into the same position as that in which he would have been if the penal element of the clause had been struck out: in this respect it resembled the legal consequence of a penalty clause in the normal sense of that expression.[52]

The foregoing discussion is concerned with contracts of sale, in which, as a result of the buyer's default, the contract is rescinded and the subject-matter remains the property of, or is restored to, the seller. The position is different where the contract is one for services to be rendered over a period of time in return for payments to be made at stated intervals. If the recipient of the services fails to keep up the payments and the contract is rescinded on that ground, he will not be able to recover back payments made before rescission, at least if they "represent the agreed rate of hire [for the services] and not a penny more".[53] In such a case the reasoning even of the majority in *Stockloser v Johnson* cannot apply as the payor will have received (and be unable to restore) pro rata what he bargained for in exchange for his payments. The position might be different if those payments contained a heavy element of "front loading".

(5) Failure to pay

The preceding discussion of deposits and part-payments deals with the situation in which a payment has been made and the contract is *then* broken by the payor. The main issue in such cases is whether the payor can get back the payment that he has made. But the breach may also consist in failing to make the payment; and if the injured party rescinds the contract on account of this breach,[54] the question arises whether the payment can be sued for by the prospective payee. The view that it can be sued for is supported by the principle that rescission does not retrospectively release the party in breach from accrued obligations[55]; and, after some conflict of judicial opinion, this view has prevailed where the money was to have been paid as a *deposit*[56] which, if it had been duly paid, could not have been claimed back by the payor.[57] But acceptance of the same view in the case of a *part-payment* might lead to the absurdity that the prospective payee could sue for the money because it was due before breach, while the payor could then sue for its return because a part-payment can be recovered back by the payor.[58] Hence in cases involving contracts for the sale of land the position is that a part-payment which was due but remained unpaid at the time of rescission cannot be sued for by the prospective payee.[59] It is submitted that the same reasoning should apply even to a claim for an unpaid deposit where the case is one of those exceptional ones in which the deposit would, if paid, have been recoverable by the payor, either at common law[60] or

---

[51] See above, p.1003.
[52] See above, p.1002.
[53] *The Scaptrade* [1983] 2 A.C. 694 at 703; *cf.* above, pp.1000–1001 and below, p.1012.
[54] See above, pp.762–763, 774.
[55] See above, p.849.
[56] *Hinton v Sparkes* (1868) L.R. 3 C.P. 161; *Dewar v Mintoft* [1912] 2 K.B. 373; *Millichamp v Jones* [1982] 1 W.L.R. 1422 at 1428, 1430; Carter 99 L.Q.R. 503; *The Blankenstein* [1985] 1 W.L.R. 435 at 451, disapproving *Lowe v Hope* [1970] 1 Ch. 94, where the court may have been reluctant to enforce what it regarded as in substance a penalty. For a possible way of giving effect to that reluctance, see below, n.62.
[57] See above, p.1007.
[58] See above, p.1007, at n.20.
[59] *McDonald v Denys Lascelles Ltd* (1933) 48 C.L.R. 457, cited with approval in *Johnson v Agnew* [1980] A.C. 367 at 396 and in *Hyundai Heavy Industries Ltd v Papadopoulos* [1980] 1 W.L.R. 1129 at 1141.
[60] See above, p.1008.

under s.49(2) of the Law of Property Act 1925[61]; and that a claim by the prospective payee for the payment of such a deposit should therefore be rejected.[62]

In the cases just considered, the outcome can be justified on the ground that the seller will, as a result of rescission, keep or get back the land, which constituted the entire consideration for the promised part-payment. Hence if liability to make the payments is discharged, each party will be left in, or restored to, his pre-contract position (though the buyer will be liable in damages). This is also true where a part-payment is to be made *in advance*, for work to be done in the future, *i.e.* after the part-payment had become due. In *Rover International Ltd v Cannon Films Ltd (No.3)*[63] it was accordingly held that a payment in respect of services to be rendered in the future under an agreement for the distribution of films on television could not be sued for by the prospective payee, even though the payment had fallen due (but none of the services had been rendered) before rescission. But the position was different where part-payments under shipbuilding contracts became due from time to time (as the work progressed) and the builder rescinded for the other party's failure to make one of the payments when due.[64] It was held that the builder was entitled to sue for that part-payment since the consideration, for which the part-payment was to be made, was not merely the delivery of the finished product, but also the builder's work. So far as the work which he had done was concerned, he could not be restored to his pre-contract position: hence it was proper to uphold his claim for a part-payment due before rescission. For the same reason, instalments due under a hire-purchase agreement before rescission can be sued for after rescission[65]: their legal character is that of payment for the hire of the subject-matter, and the benefit of possession during each period for which such a payment was due is one that cannot be restored by the hirer to the owner. It is submitted that this reasoning should also apply where the part-payment has actually been made before rescission, and that, accordingly, the *prima facie* rule by which part-payments can be recovered back by the payor[66] should be restricted to cases in which, as a result of rescission, each party can be restored to his pre-contract position.

(6) Unfair Terms in Consumer Contracts Regulations 1999

Under these Regulations, certain standard terms in contracts between commercial sellers or suppliers and consumers do not bind the consumer if they are unfair.[67] An illustration given in the Regulations of a term which is *prima facie* unfair[68] is one "permitting the seller or supplier to retain sums paid by the consumer where the latter decides not to conclude or perform the contract, without providing for the consumer to receive compensation of an equivalent amount from the seller or supplier where the latter is the party cancelling the contract".[69] This illustration is based on the civil law

---

[61] See above, p.1008.

[62] In a case like *Lowe v Hope*, above, n.56, a court could justify its refusal to allow the prospective payee's claim on the ground that it would have ordered the return of the deposit (if paid) under s.49(2) of the 1925 Act.

[63] [1989] 1 W.L.R. 912; Beatson, 105 L.Q.R. 179; Andrews [1990] C.L.J. 15.

[64] *Hyundai Shipbuilding and Heavy Industries Co Ltd v Pournaras* [1978] 2 Lloyd's Rep. 502; *Hyundai Heavy Industries Ltd v Papadopoulos* [1980] 1 W.L.R. 1129 (Lords Russell and Keith *dubitante* on this point); *Stocznia Gdanska SA v Latvian Shipping Co* [1998] 1 W.L.R. 574. In the first two of these cases, as in *McDonald v Denys Lascelles Ltd* (1933) 48 C.L.R. 457, the action was against a guarantor, but the judgments fully discuss the principal debtor's liability.

[65] See above, p.851.

[66] See above, p.1007 at n.20.

[67] See above, pp.267 *et seq.*

[68] See above, p.274.

[69] SI 1999/2083, Sch.2, para.1(d).

institution (which has no counterparty in the common law) by which a contract can, in effect, be dissolved on forfeiture of a deposit or on the return by the payee of double the amount.[70] Thus forfeiture provisions of the kind discussed above do not correspond precisely with the illustration just quoted; but this fact would not prevent the court from holding that such a provision was unfair.[71] It seems to follow not only that the seller or supplier could not sue for the payment, but also that he would have to return the payment, if it had been made.[72] It is, however, an open question whether the Regulations apply to contracts for the sale of land,[73] and it is with such contracts that many of the English cases on deposits and part-payments are concerned. The Regulations also apply only to contract terms[74] and not to rights of forfeiture conferred by law. Once a payment is classified as a deposit, it can be forfeited even in the absence of a contract term to that effect; and in such a case there would appear to be no relevant contractual term[75] on which the Regulations can operate. The mere description of the payment as a "deposit" would not suffice for this purpose since the question whether a payment has the legal characteristics of a deposit or of a part-payment is one of substance; the use of a particular word or phrase is clearly not decisive.[76]

SECTION 2. ACTION FOR AN AGREED SUM

1. Distinguished from Damages

A contract commonly provides for the payment by one party of an agreed sum in exchange for some performance by the other. Goods are sold for a fixed price; work is done for an agreed remuneration, and so forth. An action for this price or other agreed remuneration is, in its nature, quite different from an action for damages.[77] It is a claim for the *specific* enforcement of the defendant's primary obligation to perform what he has promised[78]; though, as it is simply an action for money, it is not subject to those

---

[70] Treitel, *Remedies for Breach of Contract*, §182.

[71] The list of illustrations in Sch.3 is "non-exhaustive:" reg.5(5).

[72] Reg.8(1). merely makes the term "not binding on the consumer" but the word "retain" in Sch.2, para.1(d) suggests the availability to the consumer of a remedy for the recovery of the payment.

[73] See above, pp.278–279.

[74] See reg.4(1).

[75] See reg.5(1); *cf.* reg.8(1).

[76] If it were, the law as to part payments could be evaded by simply calling them deposits.

[77] *cf. Re Park Air Services* [1999] 1 All E.R. 673 at 682–683. The distinction is sometimes obscured by the fact that damages may be *equal to* the agreed sum, as in *The Blankenstein* [1985] 1 W.L.R. 435, above, p.852; and sometimes by the description of the claim as one for "damages equal to" the agreed sum, when it appears to be one for the agreed sum, *e.g.* in *UCB Leasing Ltd v Holtom* [1987] R.T.R. 362 at 366.

[78] See above, p.850. Where A (an insurer) promises B (the insured) to pay to B any damages for which B may become liable to C, B's claim against A for the amount of such damages has been described as being itself a claim for damages: see *Chandris v Argo Insurance Co Ltd* [1963] 2 Lloyd's Rep. 65, *cf. The Fanti and Padre Island* [1991] 2 A.C. 1, 35; *Hong Kong Borneo Services Ltd v Pilcher* [1992] 2 Lloyd's Rep. 593 at 597; *The Italia Express* [1992] 2 Lloyd's Rep. 281 at 285; *The Kyriaki* [1993] 1 Lloyd's Rep. 137 at 150. In *Phoenix General Insurance Co of Greece SA v Halvanon Insurance Co Ltd* [1988] Q.B. 216 at 233 (reversed on other grounds *ibid.* at 248 *et seq.*) it was said to follow from this view that the action against the insurer was not one to enforce his primary obligation. But in the case put A's only promise is to repay B the damages for which B is liable to C; hence A's primary obligation is to make that payment; and an action to recover it is, it is submitted, one for the specific enforcement of A's promise. It is an action for an agreed sum, in the sense of a sum determined by reference to the agreement, rather than one calculated by reference to the consequences of breach. *cf. Jervis v Harris* [1996] Ch. 195, where a lease provided that, on a tenant's breach of his covenant to repair, the landlord could himself execute the repairs and recover the costs of so doing from the tenant. It was held that the landlord's claim to recover these costs "sounds in debt, not damages" (at 202). The action was one for an agreed sum even though that sum was not ascertained when the contract was made: it was enough for it to be ascertained when payment became due. This reasoning is, with respect, preferable to that of the insurance cases discussed earlier in this note.

restrictions which equity imposes on the remedies of specific performance and injunction,[79] on the ground that it would be undesirable actually to force the defendant to perform certain acts (*e.g.* to render personal service) or that it would be difficult to secure compliance with the court's order. Obviously, these factors have no weight where the claim is simply one for a sum of money. Of the reasons given for refusing specific performance, only one calls for discussion in relation to an action for the agreed sum: this is the possibility that damages may be an "adequate" remedy.[80]

The action for the agreed sum differs from a claim for damages not only in its nature, but also in its practical effects. The claimant in an action for the agreed sum recovers that sum—neither more nor less; no questions of quantification or remoteness can arise.[81] It is irrelevant in an action for the price of goods to ask how much they are worth or how much they cost the seller. The argument that the claimant should have mitigated can, however, arise in an action for the agreed sum.[82] If successful, it will lead to the conclusion that the action is not available at all—not to recovery of a reduced price.

Where the agreed sum is not paid and the claimant also suffers additional loss, he may be entitled to bring *both* the action for the agreed sum *and* an action for damages.[83]

2. Availability of the Action

The availability of the action for an agreed sum depends on three factors.

(1) Duty to pay the price

Obviously an action for the agreed sum cannot be brought if the duty to pay it has not arisen. Whether it has arisen depends primarily on the terms of the contract. Suppose that a contract of employment provides that the employee is to be paid wages after working for a month and that he is wrongfully dismissed after a week. He cannot sue for his wages but only for damages for wrongful dismissal.[84] On the other hand, in *Mount v Oldham Corp*[85]; a local authority wrongfully withdrew boys from a school without giving the customary one term's notice. It was held that the headmaster was entitled to bring an action for the term's fees as it was an implied term of the contract that these should be paid in advance.

So far, we have assumed that the only breach is by the party who was to make the payment. There may also be a breach by the other party, *e.g.* where the employee commits a breach of duty or the seller appropriates defective goods to the contract. Such breaches may prevent the duty to pay from arising or discharge it: this topic is discussed in Chapter 18.[86]

(2) Rules of law

The *action* for the price is not available merely because the *duty* to pay the price has arisen. The contract specifies the *duties* of the parties, but the law determines their

---

[79] See below, pp.1026–1038, 1040–1046.
[80] See below, pp.1020–1026; *Attica Sea Carriers Corp v Ferrostaal Poseidon Bulk Reederei GmbH (The Puerto Buitrago)* [1976] Lloyd's Rep. 250.
[81] *Jervis v Harris* [1996] Ch.195 at 202.
[82] The relevance of mitigation in such an action was, indeed, denied in *Jervis v Harris* [1996] Ch.195 at 203, but without any reference to the issues (which did not arise in that case) discussed at pp.1017–1018, below.
[83] *Overstone Ltd v Shipway* [1962] 1 W.L.R. 117; *cf. The Halcyon Skies* [1977] Q.B. 857; *Lawlor v Gray* [1984] 3 All E.R. 345; and see above, pp.994–998.
[84] See above, pp.762, 845.
[85] [1973] Q.B. 309; *cf. Denman v Winstanley* (1887) 4 T.L.R. 127.
[86] See above, pp.759 *et seq.*

remedies. This is generally recognised when specific performance is sought,[87] and it is also true of the action for the agreed sum.

The distinction[88] appears clearly in the Sale of Goods Act 1979. The *duty* to pay the price arises when the seller is ready and willing to deliver the goods (unless, of course, the sale is on credit or stipulates for an advance payment[89]). But s.49 of the Act provides that the *action* for the price is available to the seller if either the property in the goods has passed to the buyer or the price is payable "on a day certain irrespective of delivery". In *Stein Forbes & Co Ltd v County Tailoring Co Ltd*[90] a contract for the sale of sheepskins provided for payment in cash "against documents on arrival of steamer". This provision did not name a "day certain"; and the buyer's wrongful refusal to pay on tender of documents prevented the property in the goods from passing to him. It was held that the seller could not claim the price, but only damages. The effect (and probable purpose) of this restriction on the seller's action for the price is to encourage him to dispose of the goods elsewhere and so to mitigate his loss.

The *Stein Forbes* case should be contrasted with *Workman Clark & Co v Lloyd Brasileno*[91] where a contract for the construction and sale of a boat provided for payments in instalments, the first of which was to become due when the keel was laid; and property was not to pass until this payment had been made. After the keel had been laid, the builder successfully sued for the first instalment. The case is hard to reconcile with the wording of s.49; but it nevertheless accurately reflects the underlying policy. At the stage which the work had reached it must have been hard for the builder to mitigate his loss by finding another customer for a boat built to the defendant's order—much harder, probably, than it was for the seller in the *Stein Forbes* case to resell the sheepskins.

(3) Conduct of the injured party

On wrongful repudiation of a contract, the injured party has a choice: he can either "terminate" the contract or keep it alive.

(a) ELECTS TO TERMINATE. If the injured party elects to terminate, he cannot sue for any sum which, under the contract, was to accrue to him only after the date of termination.[92] He can claim damages for wrongful repudiation, and in assessing these the court may take into account any sums which he should have received under the broken contract. For example, if a hire-purchase agreement is wrongfully repudiated by the hirer and terminated by the owner, the owner cannot sue for instalments which were to accrue after the date of termination. But his damages may be based on the difference between the amount which the repudiating hirer was to have paid and the benefits obtained by the owner as a result of termination, *e.g.* in regaining possession of the goods.[93]

(b) ELECTS TO KEEP THE CONTRACT ALIVE. Where the injured party elects to keep the contract alive, he can bring the action for the agreed sum if, at the time of

---

[87] See below, p.1026.
[88] The distinction drawn in the text is sometimes overlooked: *e.g.* in *Huyton SA v Peter Cremer GmbH* [1999] 1 Lloyd's Rep. 620 at 630 and 642.
[89] Sale of Goods Act 1979, ss.27, 28.
[90] (1916) 115 L.T. 215; *cf. Tradax Internacional SA v Goldschmidt SA* [1977] 2 Lloyd's Rep. 604; *Regent OHG Aisenstadt und Barig v Francesco of Jermyn Street* [1981] 3 All E.R. 327.
[91] [1908] 1 K.B. 968; this report differs in some significant respects from those in 77 L.J.K.B. 953; 99 L.T. 481; and 11 Asp.M.L.C. 126.
[92] See above, pp.849–850.
[93] See above, p.851.

repudiation, he has already done all that is required to make the action available: for example, if he is a seller of goods and has already transferred the property in them to the buyer.[94]

If at the time of repudiation the injured party has not yet done all that is required to make the action available, there are some cases in which he cannot bring the action for the agreed sum. This is the position where it is impossible for him to do the required acts without the co-operation of the guilty party, who refuses to give it. For example, if a singer wrongfully repudiates his contract with his agent, the latter cannot continue performance without the co-operation of the former; and the agent's only claim is for damages[95]; and where work is to be done by A on the land or goods of B, who wrongfully refuses to allow A to have access to or possession of the property then, A cannot do the work without some co-operation from B and so his only remedy is an action for damages.[96] A could only do the work without B's co-operation if he already had possession of the goods or if he could get them without B's co-operation (*e.g.* from a warehouseman who had been effectively directed to deliver them to A).[97]

It is disputed whether the action for the agreed sum is available to the injured party where, at the time of repudiation, that party has not yet done all that was required of him to make the action available, but where he can, and does, continue performance without the co-operation of the other party. In *White & Carter (Councils) Ltd v McGregor*[98] the appellants agreed to advertise the respondents' garage business for three years on plates attached to litterbins. Payment was to be at the rate of 2s. per week per plate, plus 5s. per annum towards the cost of each plate. The respondents repudiated the contract on the very day on which it was made but the appellants nevertheless prepared the plates, displayed them, and claimed the full amount due under the contract: £187 4s. for the space and £9 in respect of the plates. A majority of the House of Lords upheld the claim. The main reason given was that repudiation did not, of itself, bring a contract to an end. It only gave the injured party an option to determine the contract; and if he chose instead to affirm, the contract remained "in full effect".[99] But this reasoning does not, of itself, lead to any conclusion as to the *particular remedy* available to the injured party. This appears from the cases in which the injured party *cannot* perform without the co-operation of the other party. Even here, repudiation does not of itself bring the contract to an end[1]; but the injured party's only remedy is an action for damages.[2]

That is not, however, to deny the validity of the principle of *McGregor*'s case in appropriate circumstances. The problem in cases of this kind is whether an award of the agreed sum is, on the one hand, necessary to protect the injured party, and, on the other, likely to cause undue hardship to the party in breach. In some cases it may make no difference to the injured party whether he (1) incurs the expense of performance and recovers the agreed sum, or (2) saves that expense by not performing and recovers the

---

[94] Sale of Goods Act 1979, s.49(1); in *Mackay v Dick* (1881) 6 App.Cas. 251 (where there was no discussion as to the remedy) property had apparently passed to the buyer, so that the action for the price would now be available under s.49(1).

[95] *Denmark Productions Ltd v Boscobel Productions Ltd* [1969] 1 Q.B. 699; cf. *Roberts v Elliwells Engineering Ltd* [1972] Q.B. 586; above, p.749.

[96] *Hounslow (London Borough) v. Twickenham Garden & Builders Ltd* [1971] Ch. 233 at 252–254; cf. *Finelli v Dee* (1968) 67 D.L.R. (2d) 393; *Attica Sea Carriers Corp v Ferrostaal Poseidon Bulk Reederei GmbH* [1976] 1 Lloyd's Rep. 250 at 256.

[97] *e.g. George Barker Transport Ltd v Eynon* [1974] 1 W.L.R. 462 at 468.

[98] [1962] A.C. 413; Goodhart, 78 L.Q.R. 263; Nienaber [1962] C.L.J. 213.

[99] [1962] A.C. 413 at 427.

[1] See above, p.844.

[2] See the authorities cited in n.95, above; cf. *The Alaskan Trader* [1983] 2 Lloyd's Rep. 645 at 651 (quoted above, p.846).

difference between it and the agreed sum by way of damages. If this is the position, damages are a perfectly adequate remedy. But there are other situations in which the injured party would be prejudiced by discontinuing performance and claiming damages: *e.g.* where this leads to injury to his reputation, for which damages (so far as recoverable at all)[3] could not be accurately assessed; where the injured party has entered into commitments with third parties which he must honour as a matter of business[4]; or where part of the loss which the injured party would actually suffer is legally irrecoverable because it is too remote.[5] It is only in cases of this kind that the rule in *McGregor*'s case will be applied, for Lord Reid there said that, if the injured party has "no substantial or legitimate interest"[6] in completing performance, his only remedy will be in damages. "Legitimate interest" here means that "the innocent party must have reasonable grounds for keeping the contract open, bearing in mind also the interests of the wrongdoer",[7] and if these conditions are satisfied, it is hard to see why the injured party should not be entitled to complete his performance and claim the agreed sum. Three contrary arguments must, however, be considered.

(i) *Mitigation.* The first, and most important, argument is that the injured party should mitigate his loss. It has been said, in reply, that mitigation is relevant only to a claim for damages and not to a claim for an agreed sum[8]; and in many cases this is no doubt true. A seller of goods who claims damages for non-acceptance may be under a duty to mitigate by reselling the goods; but once he has acquired the right to sue for the price[9] there seems, in English law,[10] to be no suggestion that he must mitigate even though he can easily resell and even though he is in a much better position than the buyer to do so. But even if this rule always[11] applies in cases involving sale of goods, it does not follow that it must necessarily apply to cases involving other kinds of contracts. In particular, it is submitted that the policy of the mitigation rules (which is to prevent needless waste) should make those rules applicable, even in an action for the agreed sum, where at the time of repudiation the claimant has not yet done all that is required of him to make that action available. This submission is supported by the *Attica Sea Carriers*[12] case, where a demise charterparty imposed continuing obligations on both parties. The charterer undertook to execute certain repairs before redelivery of the ship and to pay

---

[3] See above, pp.991–992, *cf. The Odenfeld* [1978] 2 Lloyd's Rep. 357 (damages very hard to assess).

[4] See *Anglo-African Shipping Co of New York Inc v Mortner* [1962] 1 Lloyd's Rep. 81 at 94; affirmed on other grounds, *ibid.* 610; *The Odenfeld* [1978] 2 Lloyd's Rep. 357; below, p.1018.

[5] See above, pp.965–974.

[6] [1962] A.C. 413 at 431; *The Alaskan Trader* [1983] 2 Lloyd's Rep. at 651; the legitimate "interest" may be in acquiring a security in the subject-matter: *George Barker Transport Ltd v Eynon* [1974] 1 W.L.R. 462. The requirement of "legitimate interest" brings the English rule close to the American rule, with which it is said to conflict: under Restatement, *Contracts* s.338, Comment *c*: the innocent party must not "unreasonably" continue performance after breach; *cf.* Restatement 2d, *Contracts* §350 Comment *b*.

[7] *Stocznia Gdanska SA v Latvian Shipping Co* [1996] 2 Lloyd's Rep. 132 at 139; reversed on another ground: [1998] 1 W.L.R. 574.

[8] Scott [1962] C.L.J. 12.

[9] See above, p.1014.

[10] Contrast U.C.C. s.2–709(1)(b), by which the seller can sue for the price of goods identified to the contract only if he is "unable after reasonable effort to resell them at a reasonable price," or the circumstances indicate that such an effort would be unavailing.

[11] If the seller is "bound to do something to [specific] goods for the purpose of putting them into a deliverable state, the property does not pass until the thing is done and the buyer has notice that it has been done": Sale of Goods Act 1979, s.18, r.2. Thus before the seller does the required act the action for the price is not generally available: s.49(1). It is sometimes assumed that, if the buyer repudiates at this stage, the seller can nevertheless do the act and sue for the price, but there is no actual decision to this effect.

[12] [1976] 1 Lloyd's Rep. 250; Kerr, 41 M.L.R. 1, 20–21; *cf. The Alaskan Trader* [1983] 2 Lloyd's Rep. 645 where a shipowner had no legitimate interest in spending more money than the ship was worth on repairing her so as to keep her available for service; Carter and Marston [1985] C.L.J. 18.

the agreed hire till then; and for the present purpose it was assumed[13] that the contract did not require the owner to accept redelivery until the repairs had been done. On the charterer's refusal to do the repairs, it was nevertheless held that the owner's remedy was not an action for the agreed hire. As the cost of the repairs far exceeded the value of the ship when repaired,[14] the owner had no "legitimate interest" in insisting on continued performance. Hence the mitigation rules required him to accept redelivery of the unrepaired ship and to seek his remedy in damages.

It does not follow that, in cases of this kind, the mitigation rules will always require the injured party to take such a course, since they require him only to act reasonably.[15] In *The Odenfeld*[16] a time charterer wrongfully repudiated the charterparty by refusing to pay the agreed hire. It was held that the shipowners were not bound at once to accept the repudiation and seek their remedy in damages, but that they could sue for the agreed hire until they finally did accept the repudiation. They had acted reasonably in requiring continued performance since the ship remained available for service,[17] and since they had entered into an obligation to third parties (to whom they had assigned hire due under the charterparty) to keep the contract in existence.

The argument that the appellants should have mitigated by discontinuing performance was no doubt open to the respondents in *McGregor*'s case; but it is submitted that the result in that case was consistent with the mitigation rules. There are, as will be recollected,[18] two such rules. The first is that the appellants should have minimised loss by reletting the advertising space. But the burden of proving that they could indeed have done this was on the respondents[19] and does not seem to have been discharged.[20] The argument required proof that the demand for space exceeded the appellants' available supply[21] and no evidence seems to have been directed to this issue. The second rule is that the appellants should not have augmented loss by spending money on the preparation of the plates. This has to be considered on the assumption that the space could not have been relet, or that it was doubtful whether it could have been relet. As a matter of strict law, the appellants could (on this assumption) have abandoned the contract and recovered the difference between the agreed rental and any expenses thus saved by way of damages.[22] Hence it could be said that the expense of preparing the plates should not have been incurred as it did not benefit anyone. But the mitigation rules do not require the injured party to act in accordance with the strict law. They only require him to act reasonably[23]; and if there was no possibility of reletting the space, or only a doubtful one,

---

[13] The assumption was in fact regarded as ill-founded: above, p.795.

[14] *cf.* above, pp.945–946, 978.

[15] See above, p.978.

[16] [1978] 2 Lloyd's Rep. 357.

[17] *ibid.* at 374; the owners could perform without the charterer's co-operation by simply (in the absence of orders) laying up the ship; contrast, on this point, *The Alaskan Trader* [1983] 2 Lloyd's Rep. 645 at 652.

[18] See above, pp.977–979.

[19] *Roper v Johnson* (1873) L.R. 8 C.P. 187 above, p.963 n.50; *Regent OHG Aisenstadt und Barig v Francesco of Jermyn Street* [1981] 3 All E.R. 327 at 332; *The Kriti Rex* [1996] 2 Lloyd's Rep. 171 at 199 (in these cases, the claims were for damages, but there is no reason to suppose that a different rule as to burden of proof would apply in an action for the agreed sum); and see *Standard Chartered Bank v Pakistan National Shipping Co (No.3)* [2001] EWCA Civ 55; [2001] 1 All E.R. (Comm) 822, at [58] (where the claim was in deceit).

[20] Lord Morton [1962] A.C. 413 at 432, says that the appellants "made no effort" to relet the space. But there is nothing to show whether efforts to relet would have succeeded; *cf.* Roger, 93 L.Q.R. 168.

[21] Unless this were so, the appellants would be under no duty to relet the space originally let to the respondents: they would be entitled to let *other* space to other customers, *cf.* above, pp.954–955, 977–978.

[22] *cf. British and Beningtons Ltd v NW Cachar Tea Co Ltd* [1923] A.C. 48; above, p.922.

[23] See above, p.978.

it seems that the appellants did act reasonably in incurring the expense necessary to substantiate their claim for the agreed sum.

(ii) *Indirect specific performance.* The second argument against *McGregor*'s case is that the award of the agreed sum amounted to indirect specific performance[24] of a contract which was not specifically enforceable; but, even if this argument is doctrinally sound, it does not seem that any of the reasons for refusing direct specific performance of such a contract applied in the circumstances of the case. Possible reasons for such refusal are that enforcement of the decree would require "constant supervision"; that there was no "mutuality"; and that the contract involved "personal" service.[25] But the first two reasons do not apply where the contract has been fully performed by one party and the only outstanding liability of the other is to pay cash.[26] Nor does the third reason seem to apply (even if one makes the doubtful assumption that the services were "personal") where one party has been able to perform *without any co-operation from the other.*[27]

(iii) *Hardship.* A third argument against *McGregor*'s case is that it is hard on the party in breach to have to pay for a performance which he does not want. But the injured party will not be entitled to the agreed sum if he has no "substantial or legitimate interest"[28] in completing performance; and even if he has such an interest, his action for the agreed sum may still fail if he ought to have mitigated by discontinuing performance. When these qualifications are borne in mind, it is submitted that the rule in *McGregor*'s case represents a reasonable compromise between the interests of the two contracting parties.

SECTION 3. SPECIFIC RELIEF IN EQUITY[29]

1. Specific Performance[30]

The common law did not specifically enforce contractual obligations except those to pay money. Specific enforcement of other contractual obligations was available only in equity. It was (and is) subject to many restrictions. These are based partly on the drastic character of the remedy,[31] which leads (more readily than an award of damages or of the agreed sum) to attachment of the defendant's person.[32] But this is an important factor only where the contract calls for "personal" performance, *i.e.* for acts to be done by the defendant himself.[33] Where the contract is not of this kind, it can be specifically enforced without personal constraint: for example, by sequestration,[34] or by the execution of a formal document by an officer of the court.[35] Other reasons for restricting specific

---

[24] [1962] A.C. 413 at 433.

[25] See below, pp.1029–1034, 1037–1038.

[26] See below, pp.1032, 1037–1038. The contract in *McGregor*'s case was to display the advertisements for three years from November 1957 and the action was commenced in October 1958, the claim being brought under an acceleration clause (above, pp.1000–1001). In view of this clause nothing turned on the fact that performance had not been completed when the action was brought: see [1962] A.C. 413 at 426–427.

[27] [1962] A.C. 413 at 429.

[28] *ibid.* at 431.

[29] Spry, *Equitable Remedies* (4th ed.); Sharpe, *Injunctions and Specific Performance.*

[30] Fry, *Specific Performance* (6th ed.); Jones and Goodhart, *Specific Performance.*

[31] *cf. Co-operative Insurance Society Ltd v Argyll Stores (Holdings) Ltd* [1998] A.C. 1 at 12.

[32] *cf. Enfield LBC v Mahoney* [1983] 1 W.L.R. 749, where even imprisonment failed to induce compliance with an order for specific restitution. Imprisonment for debt has been abolished (subject to exceptions not here relevant) by Debtors Act 1869, ss.4, 5, and Administration of Justice Act 1970, s.11. "Lawful arrest or detention of a person for non-compliance with the lawful order of a court" is permitted by Human Rights Act 1998 Sch.1, Pt I, Art.5(1)(b).

[33] Corbin, *Contracts*, s.1138.

[34] *Miliangos v George Frank (Textiles) Ltd* [1976] A.C. 443 at 494, 497.

[35] *The Messianiki Tolmi* [1983] 2 A.C. 787.

enforcement are that this form of relief may be unnecessary, undesirable or impracticable on various grounds to be considered in the discussion that follows. In a number of later authorities, some of these reasons are no longer regarded as entirely convincing,[36] so that these cases support some expansion in the scope of the remedy.[37] The most recent decision of the House of Lords[38] on the point may, however, foreshadow some degree of return to a more restrictive view, though with modern justifications.

(1) Granted where damages not "adequate"

The traditional view is that specific performance will not be ordered where damages are an "adequate" remedy.[39] After illustrating this requirement, we shall see that it now requires some reformulation.

(a) AVAILABILITY OF SATISFACTORY EQUIVALENT. Damages are most obviously an adequate remedy where the claimant can get a satisfactory equivalent of what he contracted for from some other source. For this reason specific performance is not generally ordered of contracts for the sale of commodities, or of shares, which are readily available in the market.[40] In such cases the claimant can buy in the market and is adequately compensated by recovering the difference between the contract and the market price by way of damages. Indeed, he is required to make the substitute purchase in order to mitigate his loss.[41] If he fails to do so, he cannot recover damages for extra loss suffered because the market has risen after the date when the substitute contract should have been made. To award him specific performance in such a case would, in substance, conflict with the principles of mitigation[42] as well as being oppressive to the defendant.[43] Similar reasoning seems to underlie the rule that a contract to lend money cannot be specifically enforced by either party[44]: it is assumed that damages can easily be assessed by reference to current rates of interest.

Damages will, on the other hand, not be regarded as an adequate remedy where the claimant cannot obtain a satisfactory substitute. The law takes the view that a buyer of

---

[36] e.g. below, pp.1026, 1029–1033.

[37] A trend forecast by Lord Justice Fry in his work on *Specific Performance*: see (6th ed.), p.21; *cf.* Burrows, 4 Legal Studies 102.

[38] *Co-operative Insurance Society Ltd v Argyll Stores Ltd* [1998] A.C. 1; below, pp.1033–1034.

[39] *Co-operative Insurance Society Ltd v Argyll Stores (Holdings) Ltd* [1998] A.C. 1 at 11; *Bankers Trust Co v PT Jakarta International Hotels & Development* [1999] 1 Lloyd's Rep. 910 at 911.

[40] *Cud v Rutter* (1719) 1 P.Wms. 570; *Re Schwabacher* (1908) 98 L.T. 127 at 128; *cf. Fothergill v Rowland* (1873) L.R. 17 Eq. 137; *Garden Cottage Foods Ltd v Milk Marketing Board* [1984] A.C. 130; *aliter* if the shares are not readily available: *Duncuft v Albrecht* (1841) 12 Sim. 189; *Langen & Wind Ltd v Bell* [1972] Ch. 685; *Jobson v Johnson* [1989] 1 W.L.R. 1026; *Grant v Cigman* [1996] 2 B.C.L.C. 24; or if the contract is for the sale of shares giving a controlling interest in the company: *Harvela Investments Ltd v Royal Trust C of Canada (CI) Ltd* [1986] A.C. 207.

[41] See above, p.977.

[42] See *Buxton v Lister* (1746) 3 Atk. 383 at 384.

[43] See *Re Schwabacher* (1908) 98 L.T. 127, where shares rose in value after breach. In such a case the defendant could be given the option of transferring the shares or paying the difference between contract and market price on the day fixed for performance, as in *Colt v Nettervill* (1725) 2 P.Wms. 301. See also *Whiteley Ltd v Hilt* [1918] 2 K.B. 808; *MEPC v Christian Edwards* [1978] Ch. 281 at 293 (affirmed on other grounds [1981] A.C. 205); *Chinn v Hochstrasser* [1979] Ch. 447 (reversed on other grounds [1981] A.C. 533).

[44] *Rogers v Challis* (1859) 27 Beav. 175 (suit by lender); *Sichel v Mosenthal* (1862) 30 Beav. 371 (suit by borrower: decision based on lack of mutuality (below, p.1037) rather than adequacy of damages); *cf. Larios v Bonnany y Gurety* (1873) L.R. 5 C.P. 346. By statute the court can specifically enforce a contract to take debentures in a company, that is, to make a secured loan to the company: Companies Act 1985, s.195 reversing *South African Territories Ltd v Wallington* [1898] A.C. 109. A contract to subscribe for shares in a company is also specifically enforceable: *Odessa Tramways Co v Mendel* (1878) 8 Ch.D. 235; *Sri Lanka Omnibus Co v Perera* [1952] A.C. 76.

land or of a house[45] (however ordinary) is not adequately compensated by damages, and that he can therefore get an order of specific performance.[46] Even a contractual licence to occupy land, though creating no interest in the land,[47] may be specifically enforced.[48] A vendor of land, too, can get specific performance, though his only claim is for money.[49] One reason for this rule is that it is just to allow the remedy *to* him as it is available *against* him. Another is that damages will not adequately compensate him for not getting the whole price, as he may not easily be able to find another purchaser.[50] And he may be anxious to rid himself of burdens attached to the land.[51] But the rule seems to apply though the land is readily saleable to a third party; and it has even been applied where after contract but before completion a compulsory purchase order was made in respect of the land.[52] Yet in such a case damages (consisting of the amount by which the contract price exceeded the compensation payable on compulsory acquisition) would normally be an adequate remedy.

(b) DAMAGES HARD TO QUANTIFY. A second factor which is relevant (though not decisive[53]) in considering the adequacy of damages is the difficulty of assessing and recovering them. This is one reason why specific performance has been ordered of contracts to sell (or to pay) annuities,[54] and of a sale of debts proved in bankruptcy,[55] the value of such rights being uncertain. Similarly, a contract to execute a mortgage in consideration of money lent at, or before, the time of the contract can be specifically enforced,[56] since the value of obtaining security for a debt cannot be precisely quantified. The same is true of the right to have a loan repaid out of specific property; and a term in a contract of loan conferring such a right is therefore specifically enforceable.[57] Even

---

[45] Fry, *Specific Performance* (6th ed.), §62. Damages are, however, an adequate remedy for breach of a "lock-out" agreement relating to land (above, p.54) since such an agreement is intended merely to protect the prospective purchaser from wasting costs and does not give him any right to insist on conveyance of the land: *Tye v House* [1997] 2 E.G.L.R. 171.

[46] Unless he elects to claim damages, as in *Meng Leong Developments Pte Ltd v Jip Hong Trading Co Pte Ltd* [1985] A.C. 511.

[47] See *Ashburn Anstalt v Arnold* [1989] Ch. 1, overruled on another point in *Prudential Assurance Co Ltd v London Residuary Body* [1992] 2 A.C. 386.

[48] *Verrall v Great Yarmouth BC* [1981] Q.B. 202. *cf. Dutton v Manchester Airport plc* [1999] 2 All E.R. 675, where the licensee's claim was not against the licensor but against a trespasser.

[49] *e.g. Walker v Eastern Counties Ry* (1848) 6 Hare 594; *Miliangos v George Frank (Textiles) Ltd* [1976] A.C. 443 at 496; *cf. Amec Properties v Planning & Research Systems* [1992] 1 E.G.L.R. 70. Where the purchaser has been allowed to go into possession and has then failed to complete, and the vendor has not elected between rescission and specific performance, the court may (unless the contract otherwise provides) order the purchaser either to perform or to vacate the premises: see *Greenwood v Turner* [1891] 2 Ch. 144; *Maskell v Ivory* [1970] Ch. 502; *Attfield v DJ Plant Hire & General Contractors* [1987] Ch. 141.

[50] *Lewis v Lord Lechmere* (1722) 10 Mod. 503.

[51] Fry, *Specific Performance* (6th ed.), §72.

[52] *Hillingdon Estate Co v Stonefield Estates Ltd* [1952] Ch. 627. The contract is not frustrated by the making of the order: above, p.896; but after title to the land has vested in the acquiring authority by virtue of the compulsory purchase, the vendor's remedy is in damages and not by way of specific performance: *E. Johnson & Co (Barbados) v NSR Ltd* [1997] A.C. 400.

[53] *Soc des Industries Metallurgiques SA v Bronx Engineering Co Ltd* [1975] 1 Lloyd's Rep. 465.

[54] *Ball v Coggs* (1710) 1 Bro. P.C. 140; *Kenney v Wexham* (1822) 6 Madd. 355; *Adderley v Dixon* (1824) 1 C. & S. 607 at 611; *Clifford v Turrell* (1841) 1 Y. & C.C.C. 138; *Beswick v Beswick* [1968] A.C. 58; see however Fry, *Specific Performance* (6th ed.), pp.30, 111, 112; *Crampton v Varna Ry* (1872) L.R. 7 Ch.App. 562.

[55] *Adderley v Dixon* (1824) 1 C. & S. 607.

[56] *Ashton v Corrigan* (1871) L.R. 13 Eq. 76; *Swiss Bank Corp v Lloyds Bank Ltd* [1982] A.C. 584 at 595, affirmed *ibid.* at 610.

[57] *Swiss Bank Corp v Lloyds Bank Ltd* [1979] Ch. 548, reversed [1982] A.C. 584, but on the ground that the contract did not on its true construction contain any such term. *cf. Kingscroft Insurance Co Ltd v HS Weaver (Underwriting) Agencies Ltd* [1993] 1 Lloyd's Rep. 187 at 193; *Napier and Ettrick v Hunter* [1993] 1 A.C. 713 at 952.

where there is no such difficulty in *quantifying* the loss, damages may be an inadequate remedy because the claimant's loss is difficult to prove,[58] or because certain items of loss[59] may not be legally recoverable, or quite simply because the defendant may not be "good for the money".[60]

(c) DAMAGES NOMINAL. In *Beswick v Beswick*[61] specific performance was ordered of a contract to pay an annuity to a third party. A majority[62] of the House of Lords took the view that damages were an inadequate remedy because they would be purely nominal, the promisee or his estate having suffered no loss. The point here seems to be, not that the promisee would be inadequately compensated, but that the defendant would be unjustly enriched (if damages were the sole remedy) by being allowed to retain the entire benefit of the promisee's performance while performing only a small part of his own promise.

(d) SALE OF GOODS. S.52 of the Sale of Goods Act 1979 gives the court a discretion to order specific performance in an action for breach of a contract to deliver "specific or ascertained" goods.[63] Although the section deals only with cases in which this remedy is sought by the buyer, the court also has power to order specific performance at the suit of the seller.[64]

Section 52 is based on an earlier enactment, which had been passed to broaden the scope of the remedy.[65] This seemed to have been restricted to cases in which the buyer could not get a satisfactory substitute because the goods were "unique". Heirlooms, great works of art and rare antiques are regarded as "unique" for this purpose[66]; and it seems that the courts go some way towards recognising a concept of "commercial uniqueness". Thus they may order specific performance of a contract to supply a ship,[67]

---

[58] *Decro-Wall International SA v Practitioners in Marketing Ltd* [1971] 1 W.L.R. 361; *Hollis v Stocks* [2000] UKCLR 685.

[59] *Hill v C A Parsons Ltd* [1972] 1 Ch. 305; *Evans Marshall & Co Ltd v Bertola SA* [1973] 1 W.L.R. 349 (injury to employment prospects and reputation; formerly, but no longer, regarded as irrecoverable: see above, p.991).

[60] *Evans Marshall & Co Ltd v Bertola SA*, above, at 380; *cf. The Oakworth* [1975] 1 Lloyd's Rep. 531 at 583; *The Oro Chef* [1983] 2 Lloyd's Rep. 509 at 521; *Lawrence David Ltd v Ashton* [1989] I.C.R. 123 at 134; *Themehelp Ltd v West* [1996] Q.B. 84, below, p.1041; *Kall-Kwik Printing (UK) v Bell* [1994] F.S.R. 674.

[61] [1968] A.C. 58; above, p.589, below, pp.1038–1039. For the effects on such facts of the Contracts (Rights of Third Parties) Act 1999, see also above, p.654.

[62] For Lord Pearce's view, see below, p.1039, n.56.

[63] "Specific" primarily means "identified and agreed on at the time a contract of sale is made": s.61(1); for an extension of the definition, see below, p.1024 at n.78. "Ascertained" is not defined in the Act but seems to mean "identified in accordance with the agreement after the time a contract of sale is made": *Re Wait* [1927] 1 Ch. 606 at 630; or identified in any other way: *Thames Sack & Bag Co Ltd v Knowles* (1918) 88 L.J.K.B. 585 at 588.

[64] *The Messiniaki Tolmi* [1982] Q.B. 1248, affirmed without reference to this point [1983] 2 A.C. 787 (sale of ship). For earlier authorities on the availability of the remedy to the seller, contrast *Shell-Mex Ltd v Elton Copy Dyeing Co* (1928) 34 Com Cas. 39 at 47 with *Elliott v Pierson* [1948] 1 All E.R. 939 at 943. The practical effect of ordering specific performance at the suit of the seller is to enable him to get an order for the payment of the price in a case falling outside Sale of Goods Act 1979, s.49 (above, p.1015).

[65] s.2 of the Mercantile Law Amendment Act 1856; Treitel [1966] J.B.L. 211.

[66] *Pusey v Pusey* (1684) 1 Vern. 273; *Somerset v Cookson* (1735) 3 P.Wms. 390; *Lowther v Lowther* (1806) 13 Ves. 95; *Falcke v Gray* (1859) 4 Drew. 651 at 658.

[67] Which "in some respects the law of contract . . . treats as if she were a piece of realty:" *The Laconia* [1977] A.C. 850 at 874.

or machinery or other industrial plant which cannot readily be obtained elsewhere.[68] Another special factor which may induce the court to order specific performance of a contract for the sale of goods is that the goods form the contents of a house which is being sold by the same seller to the same buyer, either by the same contract or by a separate contemporaneous one.[69] The court is particularly ready to order specific performance in such a case if removal of the goods would damage the land, but the remedy is not limited to such circumstances.[70]

S.52 does not restrict the discretion to order specific performance to cases in which the goods are "unique"; but the courts nevertheless at one time took the view that the discretion should be sparingly exercised.[71] One reason for this view is that the specific enforceability of a contract for the sale of goods might give the buyer an equitable interest in the goods[72]; and this could adversely affect third parties who had only constructive (but no actual) notice of that interest: *e.g.* it could give the buyer priority over not only unsecured but also secured creditors if he had paid for the goods and the seller had then become insolvent.[73] But a restrictive view of the scope of specific performance has been taken even where this factor of insolvency was not present. For example, in *Cohen v Roche*[74] the court refused specific performance to a buyer of a set of Hepplewhite chairs, saying they were "ordinary articles of commerce and of no special value or interest".[75] It is hard to see what legitimate interest of the seller was protected by the court's refusal to grant specific performance in this case; nor is the notion that damages are necessarily an adequate remedy for breach of a contract to sell goods unless they are "unique" an easy one to defend. The buyer may not in fact be able to get a substitute; his loss may be hard to assess; and part of it may be irrecoverable (*e.g.* because it is too remote).

S.52 refers only to goods which are "specific or ascertained".[76] The section therefore does not apply where the goods are purely generic (*e.g.* where the sale is of "1,000 tons

---

[68] See *Nutbrown v Thornton* (1804) 10 Ves. 159; *North v GN Ry* (1860) 2 Giff. 64; *Behnke v Bede Shipping Co* [1927] 1 K.B. 649; *The Oro Chef* [1983] 1 Lloyd's Rep. 509 at 520–521; *The Star Gazer* [1985] 1 Lloyd's Rep. 370; *Batthyany v Bouch* (1881) 50 L.J.Q.B. 421; *cf. Lingen v Simpson* (1824) 1 S. & S. 600 (pattern books). Contrast *Soc des Industries Metallurgiques SA v Bronx Engineering Co Ltd* [1975] 1 Lloyd's Rep. 465 (machinery available from another source); *The Stena Nautica (No.2)* [1982] 2 Lloyd's Rep. 336; *Gyllenham-mar Partners International v Sour Brodogradevna* [1989] 2 Lloyd's Rep. 403 at 422.

[69] *Record v Bell* [1991] 1 W.L.R. 853 at 862.

[70] *ibid.*

[71] A little-noticed exception is *Rawlings v General Trading Co* [1921] 1 K.B. 635, where specific performance was graboved without argument as to the remedy.

[72] For the view that specific enforceability does not necessarily give rise to an equitable interest, see *Tailby v Official Receiver* (1888) 13 App. Cas. 523 at 548; *Re London Wine Co (Shippers)* [1986] P.C.C. 121 at 149. *cf.* also *Leigh & Sillivan Ltd v Aliakmon Shipping Co (The Aliakmon)* [1986] A.C. 785, where it was said at 812–813 that equitable "ownership" or "title" did not pass under a contract for the sale of unascertained goods on "appropriation" of particular goods to the contract; but damages for breach of the contract would clearly have been an adequate remedy (above, p.1020) so that the question whether an equitable interest in goods can pass under a specifically enforceable contract for the sale of goods remains an open one.

[73] It was the fear of giving the buyer priority over secured creditors that was the main reason why specific performance was refused in *Re Wait* [1927] 1 Ch. 606: see esp. at 640. The buyer's problems in that case arose from the general rule, laid down by Sale of Goods Act 1979, s.16, that property under a contract of sale cannot pass in goods which are unascertained: see *Re Goldcorp Exchange Ltd* [1995] 1 A.C. 74; contrast *Re Stapylton Fletcher* [1994] 1 W.L.R. 1181, where the goods were segregated from the seller's own stock after sale. The buyer's interests are now in turn protected by a statutory exception to the general rule in s.16: see s.20A, discussed after n.80, below. Insolvency of the defendant is not a ground for refusing specific performance where the remedy is normally available as a matter of course: *Amec Properties v Planning Research and Systems* [1992] 1 E.G.L.R. 70.

[74] [1927] 1 K.B. 169.

[75] *ibid.* at 181. Contrast *Phillips v Lamdin* [1949] 2 K.B. 33 (Adam-style door).

[76] See n.63, above.

of wheat"). Where the goods form an undifferentiated part of an identified bulk, a distinction must, as a result of amendments to the Sale of Goods Act made in 1995,[77] be drawn between two types of cases. The first consists of cases in which the part sold is expressed as a *fraction or percentage* of the bulk: *e.g.* half the cotton shipped on the *Peerless*. Such a contract is one for the sale of specific goods so long as the bulk was identified and agreed on when the contract was made[78]; and the court therefore has a discretion to order specific performance of it under section 52 of the 1979 Act. The second consists of cases in which the part sold is expressed as a *specified quantity* of unascertained goods to be taken from an identified bulk[79]: *e.g.* 5,000 bales out of the cargo of cotton shipped or to be shipped on the *Peerless*, on which 10,000 bales are shipped in bulk. In such a case[80] the buyer can become owner in common of the goods to the extent that he had paid for them[81] and so he would have less need[82] to seek specific performance to secure priority over other creditors in the event of the seller's insolvency. He would, however, acquire such ownership, not because the goods were specific or ascertained, but in spite of the fact they remained unascertained.[83] Cases of this kind are therefore not covered by the words of s.52, under which the court has a discretion to order specific performance of a contract for the delivery of "specific or ascertained" goods.

It is an open question whether the court may not in appropriate circumstances have a discretion to order a seller specifically to perform his undertaking to deliver goods even in cases which fall outside s.52. The section does not in terms say that specific performance can be ordered *only* where the goods are "specific or ascertained"; and it is arguable that the remedy should be available, even where the goods are not of this kind, if to grant it would give effect to the general principle governing its scope. This might, for example, be the position where a contract was made to supply a manufacturer with goods urgently needed by him for the purpose of his business. Damages might be an inadequate remedy in such a case, for they "would be a poor consolation if the failure of supplies forces a trader to lay off staff and disappoint his customers (whose affections may be transferred to others) and ultimately forces him towards insolvency . . . ".[84] The view that specific performance could be ordered on such grounds[85] seemed at one time to have been abandoned[86]; but later cases give it fresh support. During a steel strike in 1980 a manufacturer sought an order for the specific delivery of a quantity of steel belonging to him against a rail carrier who (in fear of strike action) refused to allow it to be moved. The court made the order because, during the strike, "steel [was] available

---

[77] By Sale of Goods (Amendment) Act 1995.

[78] Sale of Goods Act 1979, s.61(1), definition of "specific goods" as amended by s.2(a) of the 1995 Act; the bulk must (as in our example) be identified and agreed on what the contract was made.

[79] As in *Re Wait* [1927] 1 Ch. 606.

[80] Sale of Goods Act 1979, s.20A(1), as inserted by s.1(3) of the 1995 Act.

[81] Sale of Goods Act 1979, s.20A(2).

[82] The buyer's property acquired by virtue of s.20A(2) would not necessarily prevail against a competing interest such as that of a bank to which documents of title representing the goods had been pledged, as in *Re Wait*, above; and where it did not so prevail the court would be unlikely to order specific performance to disturb this state of affairs: see *Benjamin's Sale of Goods* (6th ed.), §§18–265, 19–198.

[83] Sale of Goods Act 1979, s.20A(1) refers to the goods (in a case of the present kind) as "a specified quantity of *unascertained* goods."

[84] *Howard E Perry & Co v British Railways Board* [1980] 1 W.L.R. 1375 at 1383.

[85] *Taylor v Neville*, unreported, cited with approval in *Buxton v Lister* (1746) 3 Atk. 383 and in *Adderley v Dixon* (1824) 1 S. & S. 607.

[86] See *Fothergill v Rowland* (1873) L.R. 17 Eq. 137; *Pollard v Clayton* (1885) 1 K. & J. 462; *Dominion Coal Co v Dominion Iron & Steel Co* [1909] A.C. 293. Contrast *Donnell v Bennett* (1883) 23 Ch.D. 835, taking a more liberal view.

only with great difficulty".[87] It is submitted that, in such circumstances, specific performance should similarly be available to a buyer. This view is supported by a case[88] in which, during the "energy crisis" in 1973, an interim injunction was granted to stop an oil company from cutting off supplies of petrol to a garage, since alternative supplies were not available. As the goods were not "specific or ascertained", the case gives some support to the view that an obligation to deliver goods may be specifically enforced in a case falling outside s.52.[89]

The concept of specific performance in s.52 is that of a remedy for *non-delivery* of goods; but there is the further possibility that specific relief may be sought in respect of *defective delivery, i.e.* delivery of goods which are not in conformity with the contract. This possibility is recognised by recent amendments[90] to the Sale of Goods Act 1979, by which a buyer who deals as a consumer and to whom goods are sold by a commercial seller may, if the goods are not in conformity with the contract, require the seller to repair or replace them.[91] The remedy of specific performance is made available to enforce the seller's duty to comply with such a requirement[92]; and this extension of the remedy is, it is submitted, consistent with the principles governing specific relief in English law. Damages are unlikely to be the most appropriate remedy for a consumer who has bought (for example) an appliance which malfunctions; while hardship to the seller is avoided by a number of restrictions on the remedies described above. Thus repair or replacement cannot be ordered if either remedy is impossible,[93] or can one of these remedies be ordered "disproportionate" to the other.[94] Specific performance can also be refused where another of the new remedies (such as price reduction) provided by the recent amendments[95] is "appropriate",[96] *i.e.,* more appropriate than specific relief.

(e) APPROPRIATENESS OF THE REMEDY. The extension of specific relief (in the cases discussed above)[97] to situations not within s.52, as well as its recent legislative extension to certain cases of defective delivery, represented a more satisfactory approach to the scope of the remedy than that of the older authorities according to which the remedy was available to a buyer of goods which were "unique" or in a similar category.[98] The more liberal view of the scope of the remedy is also reflected in dicta to the effect that the availability of specific performance depends on the *appropriateness* of that remedy in the

---

[87] *Howard E Perry & Co v British Railways Board,* above, at p.1383.
[88] *Sky Petroleum Ltd v VIP Petroleum Ltd* [1974] 1 W.L.R. 576; *cf. Total Oil (Great Britain) Ltd v Thompson Garage (Biggin Hill) Ltd* [1972] 1 Q.B. 318 at 324; *Redler Grain Silos Ltd v BICC Ltd* [1982] 1 Lloyd's Rep. 435. *Wake v Renault (UK) Ltd, The Times,* August 1, 1996, could be explained on the same ground, though the case gives rise to difficulties discussed at pp.1043, 1046, below.
[89] This possibility was doubted in *Re London Wine Co (Shippers)* [1986] p.C.C. 121 at 149 but it was not necessary in that case to reach a final conclusion on the specific enforceability of the contract: see above, p.1023, n.72.
[90] Made by Sale and Supply of Goods to Consumers Regulations 2002 (SI 2002/3045) implementing Dir.1999/44. The Regulations provide similar remedies where goods are supplied to a consumer under a contract other than one of sale: for the sake of brevity, the following discussion is confined to cases of sale.
[91] Sale of Goods Act 1979, ss.48A(2)(a) and 48B, as inserted by reg.5 of the above Regulations; for dealing as consumer, see Sale of Goods Act 1979, s.61(5A).
[92] Sale of Goods Act 1979, s.48E(2), as inserted by reg.5 of the above Regulations.
[93] Sale of Goods Act 1979, s.48B(3)(a); *cf.* below p.1029 (impossibility).
[94] Sale of Goods Act 1979, s.48B(3)(a); *cf.* below p.1026 (severe hardship).
[95] For price reduction, see the new s.48C, inserted by the Regulations referred to in n.90 above.
[96] Sale of Goods Act 1979, s.48E(3) and (4).
[97] See above, at nn.81–88.
[98] See above, pp.1022–1024, especially at nn.66, 67, and 74.

circumstances of each case.[99] The question is not whether damages are an "adequate" remedy, but whether specific performance will "do more perfect and complete justice than an award of damages".[1] The point was well put in a case concerned with the analogous question whether an injunction should be granted: "The standard question . . . , are damages an adequate remedy? might perhaps, in the light of the authorities in recent years, be rewritten: is it just in all circumstances that the plaintiff should be confined to his remedy in damages . . . ?"[2]

A similar approach has been adopted to the analogous question whether specific performance can be ordered where the action for the agreed sum is also available. At one time a negative answer was given to this question, apparently because the common law remedy was an "adequate" one.[3] The current view, however, is that specific performance can be ordered in such a case if it is, in the circumstances, the most appropriate remedy.[4]

(2) Discretionary

Specific performance is a discretionary remedy: the court is not bound to grant it merely because the contract is valid at law and cannot be impeached on some specific equitable ground such as misrepresentation or undue influence.[5] The discretion is, however, "not an arbitrary . . . discretion, but one to be governed as far as possible by fixed rules and principles".[6] The court will, in particular, have regard to the grounds to be discussed below. Its discretion to refuse specific performance on such grounds cannot be excluded by the terms of the contract.[7]

(a) SEVERE HARDSHIP. Specific performance can be refused on the ground of severe hardship to the defendant. Thus in *Denne v Light*[8] the court refused to order specific performance against the buyer of farming land wholly surrounded by land which belonged to others and over which there was no right of way. Specific performance may similarly be refused where the cost of performance to the defendant is wholly out of proportion to the benefit which performance will confer on the claimant.[9] The court is also "slow" to order specific performance against a person who can put himself into a position to perform only by taking legal proceedings against a third party, especially where the outcome of such proceedings is in doubt.[10] Severe hardship may be a ground for refusing specific performance even though it results from circumstances which arise after the conclusion of the contract, which affect the person of the defendant rather than

---

[99] *Beswick v Beswick* [1968] A.C. 58 at 88, 90–91, 102; *cf. Coulls v Bagot's Executor & Trustee Co Ltd* [1967] A.L.R. 385 at 412.

[1] *Tito v Waddell (No.2)* [1977] Ch. 106 at 322. *Rainbow Estates Ltd v Tokenhold* [1999] Ch. 64 at 72–73.

[2] *Evans Marshall & Co Ltd v Bertola SA* [1973] 1 W.L.R. 349 at 379.

[3] *e.g. Crampton v Varna Ry* (1872) L.R. 7 Ch.App. 562 at 567 ("a money contract not enforceable in this court").

[4] *e.g. Beswick v Beswick* [1968] A.C. 58. The burden is on the claimant to show that damages are not an adequate remedy: *The Stena Nautica (No.2)* [1982] 2 Lloyd's Rep. 336 at 348.

[5] *Stickney v Keeble* [1915] A.C. 386 at 419.

[6] *Lamare v Dixon* (1873) L.R. 6 H.L. 414 at 423; *Co-operative Insurance Society Ltd v Argyll Stores (Holdings) Ltd* [1998] A.C. 1 at 16.

[7] *Quadrant Visual Communications Ltd v Hutchison Telephone (UK)* [1993] B.C.L.C. 442.

[8] (1857) 8 D.M. & G. 774; *cf. Wedgwood v Adams* (1843) 6 Beav. 600; *Sullivan v Henderson* [1973] 1 W.L.R. 333; *Jaggard v Sawyer* [1995] 1 W.L.R. 269 (injunction); *Insurance Co v Lloyd's Syndicate* [1995] 1 Lloyd's Rep. 273 at 276 (injunction).

[9] *Tito v Waddell (No.2)* [1977] Ch. 106 at 326; *cf. Morris v Redland Bricks Ltd* [1970] A.C. 652.

[10] *Wroth v Tyler* [1974] Ch. 30, where an additional ground for refusing specific performance was that the proceedings would have to be between the defendant and his wife thus tending to split up the family. *cf. Watts v Spence* [1976] Ch. 165 at 173.

the subject-matter of the contract, and for which the claimant is in no way responsible. For example, in *Patel v Ali*[11] specific performance of a contract for the sale of a house was refused after a four-year delay (for which neither party was responsible), the vendor's circumstances having during this time changed disastrously as a result of her husband's bankruptcy and of an illness which had left her disabled. On the other hand, "mere pecuniary difficulties" would "afford no excuse".[12] Thus the purchaser of a house will not be denied specific performance merely because the vendor, on a rising market, finds it difficult to acquire alternative accommodation with the proceeds of the sale.[13] Nor will specific performance be refused merely because compliance with the order exposes the defendant to the risk of a strike by his employees.[14]

(b) UNFAIRNESS. The court may refuse specific performance of a contract which has been obtained by means that are unfair, even though they do not amount to grounds on which the contract can be invalidated. Thus in *Walters v Morgan*[15] the defendant agreed to grant the claimant a mining lease over land which the defendant had only just bought. Specific performance was refused because the defendant was "surprised and was induced to sign the agreement in ignorance of the value of his property".[16] But specific performance will not be refused merely because the claimant fails to disclose circumstances which affect the value of the property or the defendant's willingness to contract with him.[17] Something more must be shown: for example, that the claimant has taken unfair advantage of his superior knowledge: in *Walters v Morgan* the court relied on the fact that the claimant had produced a draft lease during the negotiations, and had hurried the defendant into signing it before he could discover the true value of the property. On the same principle specific performance may be refused if the claimant has taken advantage of the defendant's drunkenness, though it was not so extreme as to invalidate the contract at law.[18] The claimant failure to disclose his own breach of the contract, reducing the value of the subject-matter,[19] has also been held to be a ground for refusing specific performance, even though the non-disclosure was not a ground for setting the contract aside at law.[20]

(c) INADEQUACY OF CONSIDERATION. The authorities on inadequacy of consideration as a ground for refusing specific performance are not easy to reconcile. On the one hand *mere* inadequacy of consideration is not a ground for refusing specific performance.[21] On the other hand the statement that inadequacy of consideration is not a ground for refusing specific performance unless it is "such as shocks the conscience and amounts in itself to conclusive and decisive evidence of fraud"[22] is probably too narrow, even when allowance is made for the possibility that fraud may have had a wider meaning in equity than at law. The best view seems to be that specific performance may be refused where inadequacy of consideration is coupled with some other factor, not necessarily amounting to fraud or other invalidating cause at law—for example, mistake that is

---

[11] [1984] Ch. 283.
[12] *ibid.* at 288; *cf. Francis v Cowcliffe* (1977) 33 P. & C.R. 368.
[13] *Mountford v Scott* [1975] Ch. 258; *cf. Easton v Brown* [1981] 3 All E.R. 278.
[14] See *Howard E Perry v British Railways Board* [1980] 1 W.L.R. 1375.
[15] (1861) 3 D.F. & J. 718.
[16] 3 D.F. & J. at p.723.
[17] *cf.* above, pp.390, 391, 728–730.
[18] *Malins v Freeman* (1837) 2 Keen 25 at 34; above, p.559.
[19] *Quadrant Visual Communications v Hutchison Telephone (UK)* [1993] B.C.L.C. 442.
[20] See above, p.400.
[21] *Collier v Brown* (1788) 1 Cox C.C. 428; *Western v Russell* (1814) 3 V. & B. 187; *Haywood v Cope* (1858) 25 Beav. 140.
[22] *Coles v Trecothick* (1804) 9 Ves. 234 at 246.

operative only in equity,[23] surprise[24] or unfair advantage taken by the claimant of his superior knowledge or bargaining position.[25] Specific performance may be refused on the ground of inadequacy of consideration even though the circumstances do not justify rescission of the contract.[26]

(d) CONDUCT OF CLAIMANT. "The conduct of the party applying for relief is always an important element for consideration".[27] Thus specific performance can be refused if the claimant fails to perform a promise which induced the defendant to enter into the contract, but which is neither binding contractually, nor (because it relates to the future) operative as a misrepresentation.[28] A similar view may be taken where the claimant has made a misrepresentation but the right to rescind for that misrepresentation has been lost. If the right has been lost by reason of the defendant's affirmation of the contract,[29] he will not be allowed to rely on the misrepresentation as a defence to specific performance since he in turn would be guilty of "unconscionable inconsistency in conduct"[30] in seeking, after *affirmation*, to invoke the misrepresentation for this purpose. But his conduct would not be open to such criticism where the right to rescind had been lost by impossibility of *restitution* arising otherwise than from the defendant's conduct.[31] Hence in a case of this kind the misrepresentation, though no longer a ground for rescission, could be relied on as a defence to the equitable remedy of specific performance.[32] The remedy may similarly be refused if the claimant has acted unfairly in performing the contract, though he has not broken any promise. Specific enforcement of a solus agreement[33] has accordingly been denied to a petrol company on the ground that it had given discounts to other garages, making it impossible for the defendant garage to trade on the terms of the agreement except at a loss.[34]

An action could formerly be brought on a contract for the sale of land against a party who had provided written evidence of it by one who had not.[35] It had, however, been held that specific performance would not be granted to a purchaser of land if he refused to perform a stipulation to which he had agreed, but which could not be enforced against him for want of written evidence.[36] A contract for the sale of land must now be made (and not merely evidenced) in writing, and the writing must incorporate all the terms on which the parties have expressly agreed.[37] Hence if the stipulation in question was such a term, but was not contained in the documents, specific performance would now be refused on the different ground that no contract had come into existence. An alternative possibility is that the stipulation might have been intended to take effect as a collateral contract.[38] In that event, the main contract would be valid but the reasoning of the cases

---

[23] *Webster v Cecil* (1861) 30 Beav. 62.
[24] See above at n.16; *cf. Mortlock v Buller* (1804) 10 Ves. 292.
[25] *Falcke v Gray* (1859) 4 Drew. 651.
[26] See *Mortlock v Buller*, above.
[27] *Lamare v Dixon* (1873) L.R. 6 H.L. 414 at 423; *cf. Chappell v The Times Newspapers Ltd* [1975] 1 W.L.R. 482; *Wilton Group v Abrams* [1990] BCC 310, 317 ("commercially disreputable" agreement).
[28] *Lamare v Dixon*, above; and see also above p.331.
[29] See above, p.383.
[30] *Geest plc v Fyffes plc* [1999] 1 All E.R. (Comm) 672 at 694.
[31] See above, pp.378–383, 383–384.
[32] *Geest plc v Fyffes plc*, above.
[33] See above, p.469.
[34] *Shell UK Ltd v Lostock Garages Ltd* [1976] 1 W.L.R. 1187.
[35] Law of Property Act 1925, s.40, replacing part of Statute of Frauds 1677, s.4, and now repealed by Law of Property (Miscellaneous Provisions) Act 1989, ss.1(8) and 4 and Sch.2; and see above, p.184.
[36] See *Martin v Pycroft* (1852) 2 D.M. & G. 785 at 795; *Scott v Bradley* [1971] Ch. 850.
[37] Law of Property (Miscellaneous Provisions) Act 1989, s.2(1); above, p.178.
[38] See above, p.179.

referred to above might still lead the court to refuse specific performance to the purchaser if it considered that the vendor would not be adequately protected, after being ordered to perform, by his claim for damages for breach of the collateral contract.[39]

(e) IMPOSSIBILITY. Specific performance will not be ordered against a person who has agreed to sell land which he does not own and cannot compel the owner to convey to him,[40] "because the court does not compel a person to do what is impossible".[41] The position is the same where a person has agreed to assign a lease and the landlord withholds his consent, without which the assignment cannot lawfully be effected.[42] Impossibility of enforcing an order of specific performance (e.g. because the defendant is not, and has no assets, within the jurisdiction) may also be a reason for refusing to make such an order.[43]

(f) OTHER FACTORS. The factors so far discussed operate negatively, as grounds for refusing specific performance. Others may operate positively, as grounds for awarding the remedy. Thus specific performance has been ordered of a contract to grant a licence to use a hall for a political meeting, and one reason for making the order was that it would promote freedom of speech and assembly.[44]

(3) Contracts not specifically enforceable

(a) CONTRACTS INVOLVING PERSONAL SERVICE. It has long been settled that equity will not, as a general rule, enforce a contract of personal service.[45] Specific enforcement against the employee was thought to interfere unduly with his personal liberty; it is this ground of policy which accounts for the rule, so that "questions of the adequacy of damages are irrelevant to this issue".[46] Legislative force is given to the principle by the Trade Union and Labour Relations (Consolidation) Act 1992, s.236 of which provides that no court shall compel an employee to do any work by ordering specific performance of a contract of employment or by restraining the breach of such a contract by injunction.[47] Conversely, an employer could not be forced to employ: it was thought to be difficult or undesirable to enforce the continuance of a "personal" relationship between unwilling parties. This principle is reflected in the provisions of the Employment Rights Act 1996,[48] as to the remedies for "unfair" dismissal (which is not normally a breach of contract at all). Under the Act, a tribunal may order the reinstatement or

---

[39] i.e. on the principle of "mutuality" as now understood: below, pp.1037–1038.
[40] See *Castle v Wilkinson* (1870) L.R. 5 Ch.App. 534; *Watts v Spence* [1976] Ch. 165; cf. *Elliot & Elliot (Builders) Ltd v Pierson* [1948] Ch. 453 (where the vendor sold land owned by a company that he controlled).
[41] *Forrer v Nash* (1865) 35 Beav. 167 at 171.
[42] *Wilmott v Barber* (1880) 15 Ch.D. 96; *Warmington v Miller* [1973] Q.B. 877; cf. *Sullivan v Henderson* [1973] 1 W.L.R. 333. Contrast *Rose v Stravron, The Times*, June 23 (where the remedy sought was not specific performance but a declaration).
[43] *The Sea Hawk* [1986] 1 W.L.R. 657 at 665.
[44] *Verrall v Great Yarmouth BC* [1981] Q.B. 202. For the relevance of this factor, see also Human Rights Act 1998, s.12; *Imutran Ltd v Uncaged Campaigns Ltd* [2001] 2 All E.R. 385.
[45] *Johnson v Shrewsbury and Birmingham Ry* (1853) 3 D.M. & G. 358; *Brett v East India and London Shipping Co Ltd* (1864) 2 H. & M. 404; *Britain v Rossiter* (1883) 11 Q.B.D. 123 at 127; *Rigby v Connol* (1880) 14 Ch.D. 482 at 487. cf. *Taylor v NUS* [1967] 1 W.L.R. 532; *Chappell v Times Newspapers Ltd* [1975] 1 W.L.R. 482 (injunction); *The Scaptrade* [1983] 2 A.C. 694 at 700–701 (below, p.1032); *Wishart v National Association of Citizens Advice Bureaux* [1990] I.C.R. 794; *Wilson v St. Hellen's BC* [1998] I.C.R. 1141 at 1153.
[46] *Young v Robson Rhodes* [1999] 3 All E.R. 524 at 534.
[47] Injunctions in respect of industrial action may lie against the *organisers* of such action, e.g. under Trade Union and Labour Relations (Consolidation) Act 1992, ss.226 or 235A (inserted by Trade Union Reform and Employment Rights Act 1993, s.22), but not against *individual employees*.
[48] Pt X.

re-engagement of the employee; but if such an order is not complied with, the employer can, in the last resort, only be made to pay compensation.[49] In practice, reinstatement is "effected in only a tiny proportion of . . . cases"[50] so that it is compensation which is the employee's "primary remedy".[51] The remedy for infringement of the statutory right of a person not to be excluded or expelled from a trade union is likewise by way of declaration and compensation.[52] Where an employee is dismissed in breach of contract, his normal remedy is a claim for damages or a declaration that the dismissal was *wrongful*: not specific enforcement,[53] or a declaration that the dismissal was *invalid*.[54] The statutory right to return to work[55] after maternity, parental or paternity leave appears likewise not to be specifically enforceable.[56]

The arguments usually advanced in support of the equitable principle are no longer wholly convincing[57]; and the principle is subject to a growing list of exceptions. A person who is dismissed from a public office in breach of the terms of his appointment may be entitled to reinstatement[58]; and the Visitor of a University has power to order the reinstatement of a wrongfully dismissed lecturer (even when such a remedy would not be available in the ordinary courts),[59] such a dismissal being, if it amounts to a violation

---

[49] Employment Rights Act 1996, ss.113–117. Under ss.129(9) and 130 of the 1996 Act, orders may be made for the continuation of the contract, but these do not give rise to the remedy of specific performance. *cf.* also Sex Discrimination Act 1975, ss.65(1)(c), 65(3)(a), 71(1); Race Relations Act 1976, ss.56(1)(c), 56(4); Reserve Forces (Safeguard of Employment) Act 1985, ss.10, 17 and 18; Trade Union and Labour Relations (Consolidation) Act 1992, ss.152–167 (as amended by s.49 and Schs 7 and 8 of Trade Union Reform and Employment Rights Act 1993) (dismissal on grounds related to trade union membership or activities); Disability Discrimination Act 1995, s.8(5) and Sch.3, para.2(1).

[50] *Johnson v Unisys Ltd* [2001] UKHL 13; [2002] I.C.R. 408, at [78] *per* Lord Millett; Lord Steyn at [23] states the proportion to be "only about three per cent".

[51] *ibid.*

[52] Trade Union and Labour Relations (Consolidation) Act 1992, ss.174 to 177, as substituted by Trade Union Reform and Employment Rights Act 1993, s.14.

[53] See above, p.749, n.1; below, p.1042, n.85.

[54] *Francis v Kuala Lumpur Councillors* [1962] 1 W.L.R. 1411; *Vidyodaya University Council v Silva* [1965] 1 W.L.R. 77; *Gunton v Richmond-upon-Thames LBC* [1981] Ch. 448 (declaration that dismissal was "ineffective *lawfully* to determine the contract"); *Marsh v National Autistic Society* [1993] I.C.R. 453. A declaration may also be made that a decision of a disciplinary committee leading to a dismissal is void: *Stevenson v United Road Transport Union* [1977] I.C.R. 893; but this does not amount to a declaration that the *contract* remains in operation: *ibid.* 906.

[55] Employment Rights Act 1996, Pt VIII, as substituted by Employment Relations Act 1999, ss.7, 8 and 9 and Sch.4 and amended by Employment Act 2002, s.1, and see *ibid.*, s.7; Maternity and Parental Leave Regulations 1999 (SI 1999/3312), reg.18.

[56] The Regulations cited in n.55 above do not specify civil remedies for infringement of the right.

[57] See Clark, 32 M.L.R. 532.

[58] *Ridge v Baldwin* [1964] A.C. 40; Ganz, 30 M.L.R. 288; *Malloch v Aberdeen Corp* [1971] 1 W.L.R. 1578; *Chief Constable of the North Wales Police v Evans* [1982] 1 W.L.R. 1155; *Jones v Lee* (1979) 78 L.G.R. 213. The line between ordinary and public employment is by no means clear-cut: see criticisms of the *Vidyodaya University* case, above, in *Malloch v Aberdeen Corp*, above, at 1595. But the distinction is one factor which determines the availability of judicial review as a remedy for alleged wrongful dismissal of public employees: see *R. v East Berkshire Health Authority, Ex p. Walsh* [1985] Q.B. 152 (judicial review not available to senior nursing officer); *R. v Civil Service Appeal Tribunal Ex p. Bruce* [1989] I.C.R. 171 (judicial review available to Inland Revenue executive officer but refused as other, preferable remedies available); *R. v Secretary of State for the Home Department, Ex p. Broom* [1986] Q.B. 198; *R. v Derbyshire CC, Ex p. Noble* [1990] I.C.R. 808 (judicial review available to police surgeon); *cf. McClaren v Home Office* [1990] I.C.R. 824 (claim by prison officer raised no issue of public law); *Roy v Kensington, etc., Family Practitioner Committee* [1992] 1 A.C. 624 (private law remedy available to general practitioner in respect of practice allowance); *R. v Crown Prosecution Service, Ex p. Hogg, The Times*, April 14, 1994 (no judicial review of dismissal of employee of Crown Prosecution Service).

[59] *Thomas v University of Bradford* [1987] A.C. 795 at 824; for subsequent proceedings, see *Thomas v University of Bradford* [1992] 1 All E.R. 964, where it was held by the Visitor that the lecturer's removal would have been invalid for procedural irregularities if these had not been waived by the lecturer.

of the University's Statutes, not merely wrongful but also invalid.[60] The continuance or creation of a "personal" relationship may also be enforced where an injunction is granted against expulsion from a social club,[61] or against the refusal of a professional association to admit a person to membership.[62] The right to exclude persons from membership of certain charitable associations is also restricted; for though such bodies have the right to exclude persons whom they in good faith regard as likely to damage their objectives, they must not adopt arbitrary procedures to that end: they may, for example, be required to invite persons who are about to be excluded to give reasons why they should be admitted.[63] By way of contrast, it has been held that specific relief was not available against a fee-paying school to reinstate a pupil who had been excluded for alleged misconduct, since the "breakdown of trust" had made it undesirable to require the parties "to co-exist in a pastoral and educational relationship".[64]

More generally, the modern relationship of employer and employee is often much less personal than the old relationship of master and servant was believed to be; and there are signs that the courts are prepared to re-examine or qualify the old equitable principles in the light of this development.[65] Industrial conditions may in fact force an employer to retain an employee whom he would prefer to dismiss or to dismiss one whom he is perfectly willing to retain. For example, in *Hill v CA Parsons Ltd*[66] employers were forced by union pressure to dismiss an employee. The dismissal amounted to a breach of contract and the court issued an injunction to restrain the breach, thus in effect reinstating the employee. As the employers and the employee were perfectly willing to maintain their relationship, the decision does not seem to violate the spirit of the general equitable principle against the specific enforcement of employment contracts. An injunction to restrain dismissal can also be issued in respect of a period during which no services are to be rendered under the contract. Thus where an employee had been suspended on full pay while disciplinary proceedings against him were in progress, it was held that the employers could be restrained from dismissing him before the disciplinary proceedings had run their full course.[67]

The equitable principle applies to all contracts involving personal service even though they are not strictly contracts of service. Thus an agreement to allow an auctioneer to sell a collection of works of art cannot be specifically enforced[68] by either party, though specific enforcement would hardly be an undue interference with personal liberty, even in a suit against the auctioneer. Again, an agreement to enter into a partnership will not be specifically enforced as "it is impossible to make persons who will not concur carry

---

[60] *Pearce v University of Aston (No.2)* [1991] 2 All E.R. 469. The Visitor's decision on the interpretation of the University's statutes is not subject to judicial review: *R. v Hull University Visitor, Ex p. Page* [1993] A.C. 682 (where the Visitor had held the dismissal to be in accordance with those statutes).

[61] *Young v Ladies Imperial Club Ltd* [1920] 2 K.B. 522.

[62] *cf. Nagle v Feilden* [1966] 2 Q.B. 633, doubted on the availability of specific relief in *R. v Disciplinary Committee of the Jockey Club, Ex p. Aga Khan* [1993] 1 W.L.R. 909 at 933. See also Sex Discrimination Act 1975, s.71(1) and Race Relations Act 1976, s.62 (injunction against "persistent" discrimination).

[63] *Royal Society for the Prevention of Cruelty to Animals v Attorney-General* [2002] 1 W.L.R. 448.

[64] *R. v Incorporated Froebel Educational Institute, Ex p. L* [1999] E.L.R. 488 at 493. *cf. R. v Fernhill Manor School* [1993] F.L.R. 620 (no judicial review of expulsion from private school).

[65] See *CH Giles & Co Ltd v Morris* [1972] 1 W.L.R. 307. *cf.*, in Scotland, *Peace v Edinburgh CC* [1999] I.R.L.R. 417.

[66] [1972] Ch. 305; Hepple [1972] C.L.J. 47; *cf. Irani v Southampton, etc. Health Authority* [1985] I.C.R. 590 (where the employers retained confidence in an employee but had dismissed him because of differences between him and another employee); *Powell v Brent LBC* [1988] I.C.R. 176; *Hughes v Southwark LCB* [1988] I.R.L.R. 55; *Jones v Gwent CC* [1992] I.R.L.R. 521 at 526.

[67] *Robb v Hammersmith and Fulham BC* [1991] I.C.R. 514.

[68] *Chinnock v Sainsbury* (1861) 30 L.J.Ch. 409; *cf. Mortimer v Beckett* [1920] 1 Ch. 571; *Young v Robson Rhodes* [1999] 3 All E.R. 524.

on a business jointly, for their common advantage".[69] The court can, however, order the execution of a formal partnership agreement, and leave the parties to their remedies on the agreement.[70] Similarly, the court can order the execution of a service contract even though that contract, when made, may not be specifically enforceable.[71]

The equitable principle here under discussion applies only where the services are of a personal nature. There is no general rule against the specific enforcement of a contract merely because one party undertakes to provide services[72] under it. Thus specific performance can be ordered of a contract to publish a piece of music[73] and sometimes of contracts to build.[74] It has, indeed, been suggested that a time charterparty cannot be specifically enforced against the shipowner because it is a contract for services[75]; but the services that the shipowner undertakes under such a contract will often be no more personal than those to be rendered by a builder under a building contract. Denial of specific performance in the case of time charters is best explained on other grounds.[76]

(b) CONTRACTS REQUIRING CONSTANT SUPERVISION. Specific performance will not be ordered of continuous contractual duties, the proper performance of which might require constant supervision by the court.[77] In *Ryan v Mutual Tontine Association*[78] the lease of a service flat gave the tenant the right to the services of a porter who was to be "constantly in attendance". Specific enforcement of this right was refused on the ground that it would have required "that constant superintendence by the court, which the court in such cases has always declined to give".[79] For the same reason the courts have refused specifically to enforce an undertaking to cultivate a farm in a particular manner[80]; a contract to keep a shop open[81]; a contract to keep an airfield in operation[82]; a contract to deliver goods in instalments[83]; and obligations to operate railway signals[84] and to

---

[69] *England v Curling* (1844) 8 Beav. 129 at 137. On the same principle, specific performance has been refused of a house-sharing arrangement which had been made between members of a family who later quarrelled: *Burrows and Burrows v Sharp* (1991) 23 H.L.R. 82, where the basis of liability was not contract but proprietary estoppel; *cf. Internet Trading Clubs Ltd v Freeserve (Investments) Ltd* Transcript June 19, 2001 at [3] (refusal specifically "to enforce an ongoing business relationship").

[70] As in *England v Curling* (above), where the object of obtaining such a decree was to ascertain the exact terms that had been agreed, and then to prevent one of the contracting parties from competing in business with the other.

[71] *CH Giles & Co Ltd v Morris* [1972] 1 W.L.R. 307; *cf. Posner v Scott-Lewis* [1987] Ch. 25.

[72] *e.g. Regent International Hotels v Pageguide, The Times*, May 13, 1985 (injunction against preventing claimant company from managing a hotel); *Posner v Scott-Lewis* [1987] Ch. 25 (below, p.1033 at n.90).

[73] *Barrow v Chappell & Co* (1951), now reported in [1976] R.P.C. 355, and cited in *Joseph v National Magazine Co Ltd* [1959] Ch. 14; contrast *Malcolm v Chancellor Masters and Scholars of the University of Oxford, The Times*, December 19, 1990, where specific performance of a contract to publish a book was refused on the ground that continued co-operation between author and publishers would have been required. For further related proceedings, see [2002] EWHC 10; [2002] E.L.R. 277.

[74] See below, p.1035.

[75] *The Scaptrade* [1983] 2 A.C. 694 at 700–701.

[76] See below at n.86.

[77] The principle does not apply to continuous obligations to pay money: thus an agreement to pay an annuity can be specifically enforced (above, p.1021).

[78] [1893] 1 Ch. 116.

[79] *ibid.* at 123.

[80] *Rayner v Stone* (1762) 2 Eden 128; *Phipps v Jackson* (1887) 56 L.J.Ch. 350.

[81] *Braddon Towers Ltd v International Stores Ltd* [1987] 1 E.G.L.R. 209 (decided in 1959); *Co-operative Insurance Society Ltd v Argyll Stores (Holdings) Ltd* [1998] A.C. 1, below at n.91.

[82] *Dowty Boulton Paul Ltd v Wolverhampton Corp* [1971] 1 W.L.R. 204; for later proceedings see [1973] Ch. 94.

[83] *Dominion Coal Co v Dominion Iron & Steel Co* [1900] A.C. 293; but see above, p.1024.

[84] *Powell Duffryn Steam Coal Co v Taff Vale Ry* (1874) L.R. 9 Ch. 331.

provide engine power.[85] And it has been held that a voyage charterparty cannot be specifically enforced against the shipowner.[86]

This "difficulty" of supervision should, however, not be exaggerated. In most cases the mere existence of the court's order will suffice to deter a deliberate breach. No practical difficulty seems to have arisen in the cases in which the courts have specifically enforced contracts to do building work.[87] If the defendant were recalcitrant, the court could appoint an expert as its officer to supervise performance. This is no more "difficult" than appointing a person to run the business of a bankrupt or to manage the property of a mental patient. The court has appointed a receiver to run a mine in a rescission action[88]; the same thing could be done in an action for specific performance. Alternatively, the claimant could be empowered to appoint a person to act as agent of the defendant to supervise the enforcement of the order: this would not be radically different from the statutory power of a mortgagee to appoint a receiver to act as agent of the mortgagor.[89] Where the acts to be done under the contract are not to be done by the defendant personally, the court can order him simply to enter into a contract to procure those acts to be done. From this point of view, *Ryan v Mutual Tontine Association* may be contrasted with the later case of *Posner v Scott-Lewis*[90] where the lessor of a block of luxury flats covenanted, so far as lay in his power, to employ a resident porter to perform a number of specified tasks. It was held that the covenant was specifically enforceable in the sense that the lessor could be ordered to appoint a resident porter for the performance of the specified services.

This balancing of arguments for and against ordering specific performance in cases of this kind is well illustrated by *Co-operative Insurance Society Ltd v Argyll Stores (Holdings) Ltd*,[91] where a 31-year lease of premises for use as a food supermarket in a shopping centre contained a covenant by the tenant to keep the premises "open for retail trade during the usual hours of business". Some six years after the commencement of the lease, the supermarket was running at a loss and the tenant ceased trading there. The main reason given by the House of Lords for refusing to order specific performance was the difficulty of supervising the enforcement of the order since the question whether it was being complied with might require frequent reference to the court. For this purpose, Lord Hoffmann distinguished between orders (such as that sought here) "to carry on an activity" and orders "to achieve a result". In the latter case, "the court . . . only has to examine the finished work"[92] so that compliance with the order could be judged *ex post facto*: it was on this ground that the cases in which building contracts had been specifically enforced[93] were to be explained. Difficulty of supervision was, however, not the sole ground for the decision. Lord Hoffmann referred also to a number of other

---

[85] *Blackett v Bates* (1865) L.R. 1 Ch. 177.

[86] *De Mattos v Gibson* (1858) 4 D. & J. 276 (voyage charter). The view expressed in *The Scaptrade* [1983] 2 A.C. 694 at 700–701, that a time charter is not specifically enforceable, is best explained on the ground that such enforcement would require too much supervision.

[87] See below, p.1035; *cf. Storer v GW Ry* (1842) 2 Y. & C.C.C. 48 (specific performance ordered of an agreement "for ever . . . to maintain one neat archway"); *Kennard v Cory Bros & Co* [1922] 2 Ch. 1 (mandatory injunction ordering defendant to keep a drain open); *Rainbow Estates Ltd v Tokenhold Ltd* [1999] Ch. 64.

[88] *Gibbs v David* (1870) L.R. 20 Eq. 373.

[89] Law of Property Act 1925, s.101; *cf.* Insolvency Act 1986, s.44 (as amended by Insolvency Act 1994, s.2).

[90] [1987] Ch. 25.

[91] [1998] A.C. 1.

[92] *ibid.* at 13; all the other members of the House of Lords agreed with Lord Hoffmann's speech.

[93] See below, p.1035.

factors, such as the "heavy-handed nature of the enforcement mechanism"[94] by proceedings for contempt; the injustice of compelling the tenant to carry on business at a loss which might well exceed the loss which the landlord would be likely to suffer if the covenant were broken; and the fact that it was not "in the public interest for the courts to require someone to carry on business at a loss if there is any plausible alternative by which the other party can be given compensation",[95] *i.e.* by way of damages. Reliance on such factors suggests that, if the court attaches sufficient importance to the claimant's interest in specific enforcement, it will not be deterred from granting such relief merely on the ground that it will require constant supervision. The outcome in each case will depend on the "cumulative effect"[96] of this factor together with any others which favour[97] or (as in the *Co-operative Insurance* case) militate against specific relief.[98]

(c) CONTRACTS WHICH ARE TOO VAGUE. An agreement may be so vague that it cannot be enforced at all, even by an action for damages.[99] But although an agreement is definite enough to be enforced in some form of legal proceeding, it may still be too vague to be enforced specifically.[1] Thus specific performance has been refused of a contract to publish an article as to the wording of which the parties disagreed.[2] In such a case the court would find it difficult or impossible to state in its order exactly what the defendant was to do; and precision is essential[3] since failure to comply with the court's order may lead to attachment for contempt. An agreement is not, however, too vague to be specifically enforced merely because it is expressed to be subject to such amendments as may reasonably be required by one (or by either) party.[4]

The difficulty of precisely formulating the court's order was at one time thought to prevent the specific enforcement of contracts for the sale of goodwill alone (without business premises): it was considered impossible for the court in its decree to state precisely what the vendor was to do.[5] But in *Beswick v Beswick* it was said that such a contract could be specifically enforced.[6] The older, contrary, authorities were not cited; and it seems that they have been made obsolete by the growing legal and commercial precision of the concept of goodwill.[7]

---

[94] [1988] A.C. 1 at 12.
[95] *ibid.* at 15.
[96] *ibid.* at 16.
[97] *Luganda v Service Hotels* [1969] 2 Ch. 209 (mandatory injunction ordering defendants to allow a protected tenant, who had been wrongfully locked out of a room in a residental hotel, to resume his residence in the hotel); *cf. Films Rover International Ltd v Cannon Films Sales Ltd* [1987] 1 W.L.R. 670 at 682 (for further proceedings, see [1989] 1 W.L.R. 912); *Sutton Housing Trust v Lawrence* (1987) 19 H.L.R. 520.
[98] *cf. Shiloh Spinners Ltd v Harding* [1973] A.C. 691, 724, where difficulty of supervision is said to be no longer a bar to relief against forfeiture (as it had been in *Hill v Barclay* (1810) 16 Ves.Jun. 402); but the possibility is recognised that such difficulty sometimes "explains why specific performance cannot be granted . . . ." *cf.* also the interpretation of these remarks in *Co-operative Insurance Society Ltd v Argyll Stores (Holdings) Ltd* [1998] A.C. 1 at 14 as relating to relief against forfeiture rather than to the availability of specific performance and doubting their interpretation in *Tito v Waddel (No.2)* [1977] Ch. 106 at 322.
[99] See above, p.49; *Waring & Gillow v Thompson* (1912) 29 T.L.R. 154.
[1] *Tito v Waddell (No.2)* [1977] Ch. 106 at 322–323.
[2] *Joseph v National Magazine Co Ltd* [1959] Ch. 14; *cf. Slater v Raw, The Times,* October 15, 1977.
[3] *cf. Lock International plc v Beswick* [1989] 1 W.L.R. 1268; *Lawrence David Ltd v Ashton* [1989] I.C.R. 123 at 132.
[4] *Sweet & Maxwell Ltd v Universal News Services Ltd* [1964] 2 Q.B. 699; *Alpenstow Ltd v Regalian Properties plc* [1985] 1 W.L.R. 721.
[5] *Bozon v Farlow* (1816) 1 Mer. 459 at 472; *cf. Baxter v Connolly* (1820) 1 J. & W. 576; *Coslake v Till* (1826) 1 Russ. 376; *Thornbury v Bevill* (1842) 1 Y. & C.C.C. 554 at 565; *Darbey v Whitaker* (1857) 4 Drew. 134 at 139.
[6] [1968] A.C. 58 at 89, 97.
[7] *Trego v Hunt* [1896] A.C. 7.

(d) BUILDING CONTRACTS. The general rule is that a contract to erect a building cannot be specifically enforced.[8] There seem to be three reasons for this rule. First, damages may be an adequate remedy if the building owner can engage another builder to do the work. Secondly, the contract may be too vague if it fails to describe the building with sufficient certainty. Thirdly, specific enforcement of the contract may require more supervision than the court is willing to give.

But where the first two reasons do not apply, the third has not been allowed to prevail. Specific performance of a contract to erect or repair buildings can therefore be ordered if (i) the work is precisely defined with sufficient certainty; (ii) damages will not adequately compensate the claimant, and (iii) the defendant is in possession of the land on which the building is to be done,[9] since in that case the claimant cannot get the work done by employing another builder.

(e) CONTRACTS SPECIFICALLY ENFORCEABLE IN PART ONLY. In *Ryan v Mutual Tontine Association*[10] the court refused specifically to enforce a landlord's undertaking to have a porter "constantly in attendance"; and it seems unlikely that the court would, even now, order the landlord to enter into a contract with a porter *on such terms* (though it could make an order of a similar nature where the lease *specified the tasks* to be done by the porter[11]). A further claim that the landlord should be ordered simply to appoint a porter was also rejected on the ground that "when the court cannot grant specific performance of the contract as a whole, it will not interfere to compel specific performance of part of a contract".[12] This does not mean that the court cannot order specific performance of one individual obligation out of a number of imposed by a contract[13]: it means only that it will not make such an order in relation to one such obligation if it cannot so enforce the rest of the contract.[14] Even in this restricted sense, the rule is by no means an absolute one. Thus where a monetary adjustment can be made in respect of the unperformable part the court may order specific performance with compensation.[15]

(f) TERMINABLE AND CONDITIONAL CONTRACTS. If the party against whom specific performance is sought is entitled to terminate the contract, the order will be refused as the defendant could render it nugatory by exercising his power to terminate. This

---

[8] *Flint v Brandon* (1808) 3 Ves. 159; and see *Wolverhampton Corporation v Emmons* [1901] 1 Q.B. 515; *cf. Gyllenhammar Partners International v Sour Brodogradevna Industria* [1989] 2 Lloyd's Rep. 403 at 422 (contract to build a ship).

[9] *Wolverhampton Corporation v Emmons* [1901] 1 Q.B. 515 at 525, as modified by *Carpenters Estates Ltd v Davies* [1940] Ch. 160; *cf. Jeune v Queens Cross Properties Ltd* [1974] Ch. 97; *Calabar Properties Ltd v Stitcher* [1984] 1 W.L.R. 287; *Price v Strange* [1978] Ch. 337 at 357; Landlord and Tenant Act 1985, s.17; *Gordon v Selico* (1986) 278 E.G. 53; *Barrett v Lounova* [1990] 1 Q.B. 348; *Tustian v Johnsone* [1993] 2 All E.R. 675 at 681 (reversed in part on other grounds [1993] 3 All E.R. 534); *Hammond v Allen* [1994] 1 All E.R. 307 at 314; *Rainbow Estates Ltd v Tokenhold Ltd* [1999] Ch. 64 at 69, 75, and see *Channel Tunnel Group Ltd v Balfour Beatty Construction Ltd* [1993] A.C. 334, where the House of Lords took the view that it had jurisdiction to restrain a building contractor by injunction from stopping work, but refused such relief as a matter of discretion. For the converse question, whether a builder can, in effect, compel the owner to allow him to complete the work, contrast *Hounslow (London Borough) v Twickenham Garden & Builders Ltd* [1971] Ch. 233 with *Mayfield Holdings v Moana Reef* [1973] 1 N.Z.L.R. 309; and *cf. Finelli v Dee* (1968) 76 D.L.R. (2d.) 393.

[10] [1893] 1 Ch. 116, above, p.1032.

[11] As in *Posner v Scott-Lewis* [1988] Ch. 25 (above, p.1033).

[12] [1893] 1 Ch. 116 at 123.

[13] See *Odessa Tramways Co v Mendel* (1878) 8 Ch.D. 235, where such an order was made.

[14] *Rainbow Estates Ltd v Tokenhold Ltd* [1999] Ch. 64 at 65–67; *Odessa Tramways Co v Mendel* (1878) 8 Ch.D. 235 (where contract is severable, specific performance of each part can be separately ordered); *Internet Trading Clubs Ltd v Freeserve (Investments) Ltd*, Transcript June 19, 2001 at [30], where specific performance of an unseverable part was refused.

[15] See above, p.771.

principle applies whether the contract is terminable under its express terms[16] or on account of the conduct of the party seeking specific performance.[17] On a somewhat similar principle, an obligation which is subject to a condition precedent not within the control of the party seeking the remedy will not be specifically enforced before the condition has occurred[18]; here too the making of the order could turn out to be nugatory if the condition were not satisfied. The occurrence of the condition will remove this obstacle to specific performance.[19]

(g) PROMISES WITHOUT CONSIDERATION. On the principle that equity will not aid a volunteer,[20] specific performance will not be ordered of a gratuitous promise even though it is binding at law because it is made by deed or supported by nominal consideration,[21] so that damages or the agreed sum can be recovered by the promisee. Where such a promise is made to a trustee for the benefit of a third party, it has been held that the trustee ought not to enforce the promise at law against the promisor,[22] unless the promise can be regarded as constituting a trust which is "already perfect".[23] Under the Contracts (Rights of Third Parties) Act 1999, promises for the benefit of a third party are (if the statutory requirements are satisfied) be enforceable not only by the promisee, but also by the third party,[24] who has the right of enforcement even though he has not provided any consideration for the promise.[25] The third party, moreover, has available to him any remedy, including specific performance, that "would have been available to him in an action for breach of the contract if he had been a party to the contract".[26] Nothing in the Act, however, affects the principle that equity will not aid a volunteer. Hence it is clear that if, between promisor and promisee, the contract is binding at law only because it is contained in a deed or supported by no more than nominal consideration (moving from the promisee), then equity will not order specific performance at the suit of the third party, any more than it will do so at the suit of the promisee. It is less clear what the position would be in the more usual case in which substantial consideration is provided by the promisee but none is provided by the third party. One possible view is that, since the third party is in such a case a volunteer, specific performance will not be ordered in his favour. But this would make the reference to specific performance in the Act, as one of the remedies available to the third party, largely nugatory. The courts may, therefore, prefer to take the view that the equitable principle applies only to gratuitous promises and that specific performance can be ordered at the suit of the third party, even though he has not provided any consideration for the promise, so long as substantial consideration for it has been provided by the promisee.

---

[16] e.g. *Sheffield Gas Co v Harrison* (1853) 17 Beav. 294; but *cf. Allhusen v Borries* (1867) 15 W.R. 739.

[17] *Gregory v Wilson* (1851) 9 Hare 683.

[18] *Chattey v Farndale Holdings Inc* [1997] 1 E.G.L.R. 153.

[19] *cf. Wu Koon Tai v Wu Yau Loi* [1997] A.C. 179 at 189.

[20] See above, p.76.

[21] See *Re Parkin* [1892] 3 Ch. 510; *Cannon v Hartley* [1949] Ch. 213. Contrast *Gurtner v Circuit* [1968] 2 Q.B. 587 at 596 where an agreement by deed between the Minister and the Motor Insurer's Bureau was said to be specifically enforceable by the Minister. The fact that no consideration moved from him was not mentioned by the court. *cf.* above, p.668.

[22] *Re Pryce* [1917] 1 Ch. 234; *Re Kay* [1939] Ch. 239; Elliot, 76 L.Q.R. 100; Hornby, 78 L.Q.R. 288; Matheson, 29 M.L.R. 397; Lee, 85 L.Q.R. 213; Barton, 91 L.Q.R. 236; Meagher and Lehane, 92 L.Q.R. 427; Macnair, 8 Legal Studies 172. The rule does not apply where a promise for the benefit of a third party volunteer is made to a promisee who has provided consideration: *Beswick v Beswick* [1968] A.C. 58.

[23] *Fletcher v Fletcher* (1844) 4 Hare 67, 74.

[24] See above pp.651 *et seq.*

[25] See above, p.657.

[26] s.1(5) of the 1999 Act.

The principle that equity will not aid a volunteer does not apply where an option to buy land is granted by deed but without consideration, or for only a nominal consideration. Such an option is for the present purpose regarded as an offer coupled with a legally binding promise not to revoke[27]; and it may therefore be exercised in spite of an attempt to revoke it. The resulting contract of sale can then be specifically enforced[28] —always assuming that it is supported by substantial consideration. The equitable principle likewise does not affect the validity of a *completed gift*: it is concerned with the enforceability of gratuitous *promises*.[29]

(4) Mutuality of remedy

The court will sometimes refuse to order specific performance at the suit of one party if it cannot order it at the suit of the other. Thus a party who undertakes to render personal services or to perform continuous duties cannot get specific performance as the remedy is not available against him[30]; and for the same reason a minor cannot get specific performance.[31] Such cases were explained on the ground that the remedy of specific performance must be mutual; and it was said that this requirement had to be satisfied at the time when the contract was made.[32]

There are, however, many cases in which specific performance can be obtained by a party even though it could not at the time of contracting have been ordered against him. Thus, if A agrees to grant a lease of land to B, who agrees to build on it, B cannot normally be forced to build; but if he actually does build he can get specific performance of A's promise to grant the lease.[33] Specific performance cannot be ordered against a person who sells land which he does not own[34] but if he becomes owner before the purchaser repudiates[35] he can get specific performance.[36] Conversely a vendor with defective title may be ordered to convey for a reduced price although he could not himself have obtained specific performance.[37] It seems that a person of full age can get specific performance of a voidable contract made during minority even though he could have elected to repudiate the contract.[38] And a victim of fraudulent or innocent misrepresentation can get specific performance although he may be entitled to rescind the contract so that it could not be enforced against him.[39]

Such cases show that the requirement of mutuality does not have to be satisfied at the time of contracting; the crucial time is that of the hearing.[40] The rule was reformulated by Buckley L.J. in *Price v Strange*: the court "will not compel a defendant to perform his obligations specifically if it cannot at the same time ensure that any unperformed

---

[27] For the nature of an option, see above, p.153, n.74.

[28] *Mountford v Scott* [1975] Ch. 258.

[29] *T Choithram International SA v Pagarani* [2001] 1 W.L.R. 1; *Pennington v Waine* [2002] EWCA Civ 227; [2002] 1 W.L.R. 2075.

[30] *Ogden v Fossick* (1862) D. F. & J. 426; *Blackett v Bates* (1865) L.R. 1 Ch.App. 117; *cf. Page One Records Ltd v Britton* [1968] 1 W.L.R. 157 (injunction). A dictum in *Warren v Mendy* [1989] 1 W.L.R. 853 at 866 rejects the requirement of mutuality even in this situation (but specific enforcement was refused for reasons discussed on p.1043, below).

[31] *Flight v Bolland* (1828) 4 Russ. 298; *Lumley v Ravenscroft* [1895] 1 Q.B. 683.

[32] Fry, *Specific Performance* (6th ed.), pp.219, 386.

[33] *Wilkinson v Clements* (1872) L.R. 8 Ch.App. 96.

[34] See above, p.1029.

[35] *Halkett v Dudley* [1907] 1 Ch. 590 at 596; *Salisbury v Hatcher* (1842) 2 Y. & C.C.C. 54; *Cleadon Trust v Davies* [1940] 1 Ch. 940.

[36] *Hoggart v Scott* (1830) 1 Russ. & My. 293; *Wylson v Dunn* (1887) 34 Ch.D. 569.

[37] *Mortlock v Buller* (1804) 10 Ves. 292 at 315; *Wilson v Wilson* (1857) 3 Jur.(N.S.) 810.

[38] *Clayton v Ashdown* (1714) 9 Vin.Abr. 393 (G.4) 1.

[39] See above, Ch.9, Section 4.

[40] *cf. E Johnson & Co (Barbados) Ltd v NSR Ltd* [1997] A.C. 400 at 410–411.

obligations of the plaintiff will be specifically performed, unless perhaps damages would be an adequate remedy for any default on the plaintiff's part".[41] The defendant in that case had promised to grant an underlease to the plaintiff who had in return undertaken to execute certain internal and external repairs. It was admitted that the plaintiff's undertakings were not specifically enforceable; and it seems clear that he could not have obtained specific performance of the promise to grant the underlease before any of the repairs had been done. For in that case the only remedy available to the defendant for default on the plaintiff's part might have been in damages, and this might have been inadequate,[42] especially if the plaintiff was of doubtful solvency. But in fact the plaintiff had done the internal repairs and was wrongfully prevented from doing the external ones by the defendant, who later had these done at her own expense. As by the time of the hearing all the repairs had been completed, specific enforcement of the defendant's promise to grant the underlease would not expose her to the risk of having no remedy except damages in the event of the plaintiff's default; and specific performance was ordered on the terms that the plaintiff make an allowance in respect of the repairs done by the defendant. The principle that mutuality is judged by reference to the time of the hearing similarly accounts for the rule that a person who has been induced to enter into a contract by misrepresentation can specifically enforce it against the other; for by seeking this remedy he affirms the contract[43] and so gives the court power to hold him to it. The court has no such power when specific performance is claimed on behalf of a minor: "the act of filing the bill by his next friend cannot bind him".[44]

(5) Specific performance and third parties

Where A promises B to render some performance in favour of C, two problems can arise. The first is whether B can specifically enforce the promise against A; the second is whether C can do so.

(a) CLAIM BY PROMISEE. In *Beswick v Beswick*[45] A promised B to pay an annuity to C in consideration of B's transferring the goodwill of his business to A. It was held that, although the promise did not give C any right of action, it could be specifically enforced by B's personal representative[46] against A; with the result that A was ordered to make the promised payments to C. Under the Contracts (Rights of Third Parties) Act 1999,[47] C is in many such cases entitled in his own right to enforce against A the term in the contract containing the promise in favour of C; and where C takes this course, the need for B to seek specific performance in favour of C will be much reduced. But it will not be altogether eliminated since there may still be situations in which C will not have any such right against A because the legislative requirements for its acquisition have not been

---

[41] [1978] Ch. 337 at 367–368; adopting Ames, 3 Col.L.Rev. 1. *cf. Lyus v Prowsa Developments Ltd* [1982] 1 W.L.R. 1044, at 1053; *Rainbow Estates Ltd v Tokenhold Ltd* [1999] Ch. 64 at 69, 76. See also *Sutton v Sutton* [1984] Ch. 184 where the argument of lack of mutuality was rejected because one of the claimant's promises had been performed, even though another was not binding. Specific performance was refused on grounds of public policy, above, p.447.

[42] *cf. National Provincial BS v British Waterways Board* [1992] E.G.C.S. 149. If the claimant can be ordered to give additional, satisfactory security, he can obtain an order of specific performance even though he has not yet performed and is not ordered immediately to do so: *Langen & Wind Ltd v Bell* [1972] Ch. 685.

[43] See above, p.383.

[44] *Flight v Bolland*, above, at p.301.

[45] [1968] A.C. 58; above, p.589.

[46] Who happened to be C.

[47] See above, pp.651 *et seq.*

satisfied.[48] The Act also expressly preserves B's right to enforce any term of the contract against A even where C has acquired a right of enforcement against A.[49] The scope of B's remedy by way of specific performance therefore still calls for discussion.

In holding that this remedy was available to B, the House of Lords in *Beswick v Beswick* stressed three points: that B's remedy at law was inadequate as the damages which he could recover would be purely nominal[50]; that A had received the entire consideration for his promise as the business had been transferred to him[51]; and that the contract could have been specifically enforced by A, if B had failed to perform his promise to transfer the business.[52] It is also relevant to the issue of specific enforceability that A's promise, being one to pay an annuity, was of a kind which would have been specifically enforceable if it had been made to B for his own benefit[53]; and that, if the promise had been in these terms, none of the grounds for refusing specific performance which have been discussed in this Chapter would have applied.

It does not, however, follow from *Beswick v Beswick* that specific performance in favour of a third party will be granted to the promisee *only* if the circumstances are such that the remedy would have been available in a two-party case. Thus it seems that specific performance could be ordered of a promise to pay a single lump sum to a third party,[54] though in a two-party case such an obligation would more appropriately[55] be enforceable by a common law action for the agreed sum. Again, it seems that specific performance in favour of a third party would not be excluded merely because substantial damages, constituting an "adequate" remedy, were available to the promisee. As Lord Pearce[56] said in *Beswick v Beswick*, such damages "would be a less appropriate remedy since the parties to the agreement were intending an annuity . . . ; and a lump sum of damages does not accord with this".[57] On the other hand specific performance will obviously not be ordered in favour of B where A contracts with B to render personal services to C, for the policy of the rule against the specific enforcement of service contracts applies no less where the services are to be rendered to a third party than where they are to be rendered to the promisee. Again, A may contract with B to pay C £10,000 immediately in return for B's promise to serve A for one year. If A repudiates before B has performed the service, B's claim for specific performance in favour of C should probably be refused on the ground that the grant of the remedy would offend the mutuality requirement[58]: A would have no security for the performance of B's promise to serve except a common law action for damages.

The above examples show that specific performance should not be granted to the promisee merely because the contract provides for performance in favour of a third party, nor refused merely because it would not have been ordered had there been no third party in the case. As a general principle, it is submitted that specific performance

---

[48] *e.g.* because of the requirements of subsections 1(1) and (2) are not satisfied; see above p.654 for the question whether they would be satisfied on the facts of *Beswick v Beswick*, above.

[49] s.4 of the 1998 Act.

[50] [1968] A.C. 58 at 73, 81, 83, 102. Nor did B have any other more satisfactory remedy at law, *e.g.* he could not have sued for the amount to be paid to C, or for the return of the goodwill (above, p.591). For the question of whether B could recover damages in respect of C's loss, see above, p.599.

[51] [1968] A.C. at 83, 89, 97, 102; *cf.* above, p.1022.

[52] [1968] A.C. 58 at 89, 97.

[53] See above, p.1021.

[54] As in *Gurtner v Circuit* [1968] 2 Q.B. 587 (as to which see above, p.1036, n.21).

[55] See above, p.955.

[56] Who thought that the damages in *Beswick v Beswick* would be substantial: [1968] A.C. 58 at 88.

[57] [1968] A.C. 58 at 88; *cf. ibid.* at 102 and the citation at 90–91 with approval of a dictum of Windeyer J. in *Coulls v Bagot's Executor & Trustee Co Ltd* [1967] A.L.R. 385 at 412.

[58] See above, pp.1037–1038.

in favour of a third party should *prima facie* be available to the promisee when it is the *most appropriate* remedy for the enforcement of the contract. But it should be open to the defendant to resist specific enforcement by showing that this remedy would lead to one of the undesirable results against which the established limitations on the scope of the remedy are meant to provide protection.

(b) CLAIM BY THIRD PARTY. Under the Contracts (Rights of Third Parties) Act 1999, C is in many cases entitled in his own right to enforce against A the term in the contract between A and B containing A's promise in favour of C.[59] The Act expressly lists specific performance as one of the remedies available to C where it would have been available to him "if he had been a party to the contract"; and it states that the rules relating to specific performance "shall apply accordingly".[60] Some such rules will apply to a claim by C in the same way as they apply to one by B: *e.g.*, if A's promise is one to render personal service to C, it will not be specifically enforceable at the suit of either B or C. Other rules will obviously apply with some modification: *e.g.*, if A promises B to pay a lump sum to C, then the most appropriate remedy for B might be specific performance in equity, while for C it would be a common law action for the agreed sum. The application to claims by C of the limitations on the scope of specific performance will need to be worked out on a case by case basis in the light of the policies which have given rise to these limitations in two-party cases.

2. Injunction

(1) General

Where a contract is negative in nature, or contains a negative stipulation, breach of it may be restrained by injunction. In such cases, an injunction is normally granted as a matter of course; though, since it is an equitable (and thus in principle a discretionary) remedy, it may be refused on the ground that its award would cause such "particular hardship"[61] to the defendant as to be oppressive to him.[62] An injunction would not be "oppressive" merely because observance of the contract was burdensome to the defendant[63] or because its breach would cause little or no prejudice to the claimant[64]; for in deciding whether to restrain breach of a negative stipulation, the court is not normally concerned with "the balance of convenience or inconvenience".[65] This rule, however, applies only to a *prohibitory* injunction restraining a defendant from *future* breaches. Where the breach lies entirely in the past (*e.g.* where the defendant has fenced land that he had covenanted to leave open), the claimant may seek a *mandatory* injunction, ordering the breach to be undone. Such an order *is* subject to a "balance of convenience" test and may therefore be refused if the prejudice suffered by the defendant in having to restore the original position heavily outweighs the advantage that will be derived from

---

[59] See above, pp.651 *et seq.*
[60] s.1(5) of the 1999 Act.
[61] *Insurance Co v Lloyd's Syndicate* [1995] 1 Lloyd's Rep. 273 at 276 (where there was no such hardship); *cf.* above, p.1026.
[62] See below, pp.1041–1042.
[63] *cf.* above, p.1027.
[64] *Kemp v Sober* (1851) 1 Sim. (N.S.) 517; *Tipping v Eckersley* (1855) 2 K. & J. 264; *Marco Productions Ltd v Pagola* [1945] K.B. 111; *Hollier & Co v Stocks* [2000] U.K.C.L.R. 685.
[65] *Doherty v Allman* (1878) 3 App.Cas. 709 at 720; *cf. Warner Bros Pictures Inc v Nelson* [1937] 1 K.B. 209 at 217 and (in tort) *Kennaway v Thompson* [1981] Q.B. 88; *Attorney-General v Barker* [1990] 3 All E.R. 257 at 262.

such restoration by the claimant.[66] In applying the "balance of convenience" test, the court will also take the nature of the breach into account. Thus where the defendant in breach of a restrictive covenant erected a building so as to block the claimant's sea view, a mandatory injunction was granted as the breach had been committed deliberately, with full knowledge of the claimant's rights, and as damages would not be an adequate remedy.[67]

The "balance of convenience" test also applies to interim injunctions,[68] (except where there is "a plain and uncontested breach of a clear covenant not to do a particular thing"[69]). If, for example, the grant of an interim injunction would amount in substance to a final resolution of the dispute between the parties, the court will, in considering a claim for interim relief, take into account the likelihood of the claimant's success at the eventual trial.[70] The court can also take into account the financial prejudice which would be likely to be suffered either by the claimant if the injunction were refused,[71] or by the defendant if it were granted,[72] and if at the trial the dispute were resolved in that party's favour. An award of damages to that party might then be an "inadequate" remedy for reasons discussed earlier in this Chapter[73]: e.g. because there was an appreciable risk of the other party's not being able to pay the amount of the award.

We shall see later in this Chapter that the court has power, by statute, to award damages in lieu of specific performance or injunction.[74] This power is likely to be exercised if the injury to the claimant is small, if it can readily be estimated in money, if compensation in money would adequately compensate the claimant, and if the grant of an injunction would be oppressive to the defendant.[75] These conditions were satisfied, and an injunction was refused, in *Jaggard v Sawyer*,[76] where the defendants had built a house on land which could be reached only by committing a breach of covenant and a trespass against neighbouring house-owners, including the plaintiff. An injunction

---

[66] *Sharp v Harrison* [1922] 1 Ch. 502; *Shepherd Homes Ltd v Sandham* [1971] Ch. 340; for subsequent proceedings, see [1971] 1 W.L.R. 1062; *Sutton Housing Trust v Lawrence* (1988) 55 P. & C.R. 320 (mandatory and prohibitory injunction); *Reed v Madon* [1989] Ch. 408; *cf. Newport Association Football Club v Football Association of Wales* [1995] 2 All E.R. 87 at 97 (injunction "mandatory in effect").

[67] *Wakeham v Wood* (1982) 43 P. & C.R. 40; *Chelsea v Muscat* [1990] 2 E.G.L.R. 48.

[68] *Texaco Ltd v Mulberry Filling Station Ltd* [1972] 1 W.L.R. 814; *Evans Marshall & Co v Bertola* [1973] 1 W.L.R. 439; *Clifford Davis Management Ltd v WEA Records Ltd* [1975] 1 W.L.R. 61; *Mike Trading & Transport Ltd v R. Pagnan & Fratelli* [1980] 2 Lloyd's Rep. 546; *The Sea Hawk* [1986] 1 W.L.R. 657; *Kerr v Morris* [1987] Ch. 90 at 112; *Films Rover International v Cannon Film Sales Ltd* [1987] 1 W.L.R. 670 (for further proceedings, see [1989] 1 W.L.R. 912); *Evening Standard Co Ltd v Henderson* [1987] I.C.R. 588; *Provident Financial Group plc v Hayward* [1989] I.C.R. 160; *Lock International plc v Beswick* [1989] 1 W.L.R. 1268; *GFI Group Inc. v Eaglestone*, [1994] I.R.L.R. 119; *Series 5 Software v Clarke* [1996] 1 All E.R. 853; *Tate & Lyle Industries v Cia. Usina Bulhoes* [1997] 1 Lloyd's Rep. 355; *Channel Tunnel Group Ltd v Balfour Beatty Construction Ltd* [1993] A.C. 334. For the general principles governing such injunctions, see *American Cyanamid Co v Ethicon* [1975] A.C. 396; *Fellowes v Fisher* [1976] Q.B. 122; *Lawrence David Ltd v Ashton* [1989] I.C.R. 123.

[69] *Hampstead and Suburban Properties Ltd v Diomedous* [1969] 1 Ch. 248 at 259; *cf. Attorney-General v Barker* [1990] 3 All E.R. 257.

[70] *Cambridge Nutrition Ltd v BBC* [1990] 3 All E.R. 523; *Lansing Linde Ltd v Kerr* [1991] 1 W.L.R. 251, at 258; *Imutran v Uncaged Campaigns Ltd* [2001] 2 All E.R. 385.

[71] *Themehelp Ltd v West* [1996] Q.B. 84, doubted on another point in *Group Josi Re v Walbrook Ins Co Ltd* [1996] 1 W.L.R. 1152 at 1162.

[72] *Cambridge Nutrition Ltd v BBC* [1990] 3 All E.R. 523.

[73] See above, p.1022 at n.60.

[74] See below, p.1046.

[75] *Shelfer v City of London Electric Lighting Co* [1895] 1 Ch. 287 at 322–323 (a tort case). The requirements stated above do not apply where it is the *defendant* who claims that specific relief is the more appropriate remedy since in such a case the grant of the injunction cannot be oppressive to him: *Marcic v Thames Water Utilities (No.2)* [2001] 4 All E.R. 327.

[76] [1995] 1 W.L.R. 269.

restraining such access would have rendered the new house "landlocked and incapable of beneficial ownership"[77]; and this would have been oppressive as the defendants had acted "openly and in good faith",[78] and not "in blatant . . . disregard of the plaintiff's rights"[79] in building the house. The test is once again[80] one of oppression rather than one of balance of convenience: if the plaintiff had sought interlocutory relief before the house had been built, she "would almost certainly have obtained it".[81]

An injunction will not be granted to retrain breach of a restrictive covenant affecting land against a body which has acquired the land under statutory powers where the legislation has provided an exclusive remedy by way of statutory compensation.[82]

(2) No indirect specific performance

An injunction will not be granted if its effect is directly or indirectly to compel the defendant to do acts which he could not have been ordered to do by an order of specific performance. Thus an employee cannot be restrained from committing a breach of his positive obligation to work, for that would amount to specific enforcement of a contract of service.[83] Nor can an employer generally[84] be restrained from dismissing his employee in breach of contract.[85]

(a) EXPRESS NEGATIVE PROMISES. A contract of employment may contain negative promises which can be enforced by injunction without indirectly compelling the employee to work, or the employer to employ.[86] Covenants in restraint of trade contained in such contracts are commonly enforced by injunction: this does not compel the employee to work for the employer, as such covenants generally begin to operate after the period of service is over. But some negative stipulations are expressed to operate during that period. These may be enforceable by injunction if the injunction merely provides an inducement to perform the positive obligation, but not if it in effect compels the employee to do the agreed work.

Thus in *Lumley v Wagner*[87] Mlle Wagner undertook that for three months she would sing at Mr Lumley's theatre in Drury Lane on two nights a week and that during those three months she would not use her talents at any other theatre without Mr Lumley's written consent. She then agreed, for a larger payment, to sing for Mr Gye at Covent Garden, and to abandon her agreement with Mr Lumley. Lord St Leonards granted Mr Lumley an injunction to restrain her from singing for Mr Gye. Similarly, a manufacturer can be restrained from breach of a "sole distributorship" agreement, in the sense that he can be prevented from engaging a different distributor, even though the court might not order him specifically to perform the positive part of the contract to

---

[77] [1995] 1 W.L.R. 269 at 288.

[78] *ibid*. at 289.

[79] *ibid*. at 283.

[80] *cf.* above, p.1040 after n.62.

[81] [1995] 1 W.L.R. at 289; *cf.* p.283; and see the similar case of *Gafford v Graham* (1998) 76 P. & C.R. D18.

[82] *Brown v Heathlands Mental Health NHS Trust* [1996] 1 All E.R. 133.

[83] *Whitwood Chemical Co v Hardman* [1891] 2 Ch. 416; *cf.* above, p.1029.

[84] For an exception to the general rule, see *Hill v CA Parsons & Co Ltd* [1972] 1 Ch. 305; above, p.1031.

[85] *Chappell v Times Newspapers Ltd* [1975] 1 W.L.R. 482; Hepple [1975] C.L.J. 212; *cf. City & Hackney Health Authority v NUPE* [1985] I.R.L.R. 252; *Alexander v Standard Telephone and Cables Ltd* [1990] I.C.R. 291.

[86] *cf. Evans Marshall & Co Ltd v Bertola SA* [1973] 1 W.L.R. 349.

[87] (1852) 1 D.M. & G. 604.

keep up the original distributor's supplies.[88] But a promise by an employee not to work in *any capacity* except for the employer[89] cannot be enforced by injunction since the effect of the injunction would be "to drive the defendant either to starvation or to specific peformance of the positive covenants"[90] to work.

Lumley v Wagner has been much criticised,[91] particularly in relation to contracts of employment. An injunction may put so much economic pressure on the employee as in effect to force him to perform the positive part of the contract. In *Warner Bros Pictures Inc v Nelson*[92] a film actress agreed to act for the claimants for a period of time during which she undertook not to act for anyone else without the claimants' written consent. She was restrained by injunction from breaking this undertaking; and it was said that this would not force her to act for the claimants as she could earn a living by doing other work. But it might be quite unreasonable to expect her to do this; and more recent cases support the view that an injunction should not be granted except where it leaves the employee with some other *reasonable* means of earning a living. They have arisen where professional entertainers or athletes have entered into long-term exclusive contracts with managers, in whom they then lost confidence. It has been held that the managers could not obtain injunctions either against their clients,[93] or against third parties with whom those clients had entered into substitute management contracts,[94] if the effect of the injunction would "as a practical matter"[95] be to force the clients to make use of the services of the original manager; and this would commonly be the case since such persons cannot successfully work without a manager.

An injunction, in cases of this kind, will always put *some* pressure on the defendant to perform his positive obligation to render the agreed services; and the view that this factor is, of itself, a ground for refusing to grant the injunction[96] is, with respect, hard to reconcile with the reasoning of *Lumley v Wagner*.[97] The crucial question, in these cases, is whether the injunction would put *undue* pressure on an employee to perform his positive obligation to work; and this question can give rise to difficult issues of fact and degree. In one case[98] a newspaper reporter undertook during the term of his contract not

---

[88] *Decro-Wall International SA v Practitioners in Marketing Ltd* [1971] 1 W.L.R. 361; *Evans Marshall & Co Ltd v Bertola SA* [1973] 1 W.L.R. 349 (for subsequent proceedings, see [1976] 2 Lloyd's Rep. 17). So far as *contra*, *Wake v Renault (UK) Ltd, The Times*, August 1, 1996, is, with respect, open to question; the authority of the decision is also undermined to the extent that it was based on that of the Court of Appeal in *Co-operative Insurance Society Ltd v Argyll Stores (Holdings) Ltd*, which was later reversed by the House of Lords: [1998] A.C. 1, above, pp.1033–1034. Reg.7(2) of the Commercial Agents (Council Directive) Regulations 1993 (SI 1993/3053) (above p.709) entitle a "commercial agent" to *commission* in certain cases of breach of a sole agency agreement but the Regulations say nothing about enforceability by injunction.
[89] *Ehrman v Bartholomew* [1898] 1 Ch. 671.
[90] *Warner Bros Pictures Inc v Nelson* [1937] 1 K.B. 209 at 216.
[91] Stevens, 6 Cornell L.Q. 235; Ashley, 6 Col.L.Rev. 82; Clark, 17 Col.L.Rev. 687; and see below, n.94.
[92] [1937] 1 K.B. 209.
[93] *Page One Records Ltd v Britton* [1968] 1 W.L.R. 157.
[94] *Warren v Mendy* [1989] 1 W.L.R. 853, citing criticism of *Warner Bros Inc v Nelson* (above, n.90) in *Nichols Advance Vehicle Systems Inc v De Angelis* (1979, unrep.); McLean [1990] C.L.J. 15.
[95] *Page One Records Ltd v Britton* [1968] 1 W.L.R. 157 at 166. *Lumley v Wagner* was distinguished at 165 on the ground that Mr Lumley had no obligation except to pay money; but in fact he also made certain promises which were negative in substance: *e.g.* that certain parts were to "belong exclusively" to Mlle Wagner.
[96] *Young v Robson Rhodes* [1999] 3 All E.R. 524 at 534 ("to coerce the defendants . . . ").
[97] (1852) 1 D.M. & G 694. *Lumley v Wagner* was cited by counsel, but not referred to in the judgment, in *Young v Robson Rhodes*, above. It seems that the defendant in the former case was not in fact "coerced" into performing her positive obligation to sing at the claimant's theatre: see Waddams, 117 L.Q.R. 431 at 440. The two cases may be distinguishable on the ground that there was no express negative covenant in *Young v Robson Rhodes*, above.
[98] *Evening Standard Co Ltd v Henderson* [1987] I.C.R. 588.

to work for others; the contract provided for termination by twelve months' notice. The reporter gave only two months' notice of termination, and it was held that he could be restrained by injunction from breach of the negative stipulation. This was said not to subject him to undue pressure since the employers had undertaken to go on paying him, to allow him to go on working for them for the rest of the contract period, and not to claim damages if he should choose simply to draw his pay without doing such work. But the position might have been different if the employers had merely undertaken to go on paying him, without allowing him to work. In such cases, the court can balance the employee's interest in continuing to work (so as to maintain his skill and reputation) against any prejudice likely to be suffered by the employer if the employee works for a third party; and, where the remedy is discretionary,[99] the court may refuse to grant the injunction if it is satisfied that breach of the negative stipulation will not seriously prejudice the employer.[1] *A fortiori*, such relief will be denied to the employer where his refusal to allow the employee to work amounts to a breach of the contract of employment on the employer's part.[2]

(b) RESTRAINT OF TRADE. A further danger of the rule in *Lumley v Wagner*[3] is that the injunction may help to stifle competition. It is arguable that this was the purpose of the negative stipulation, and the effect of the injunction, in the leading case itself; for it might have been physically possible for Mlle Wagner to sing at Drury Lane for two nights a week and to sing elsewhere on other nights. Yet the question whether the contract was invalid for restraint of trade was not discussed at all. It used to be thought that this question arose only where the relevant contractual provisions came into effect *after* the period of employment. A possible reason for this view is that, where the period of employment is fairly short (as in *Lumley v Wagner*), the negative stipulation is reasonable (and therefore valid[4]) because of its limited duration.[5] But this reasoning loses much of its force where the employer has options to extend the term of service, sometimes for very long periods[6] or where long periods of notice have to be given to terminate the contract.[7] The present position is that stipulations which operate during employment (no less than those which operate thereafter) can sometimes have their validity tested under the restraint of trade doctrine[8]; but even where their *validity* is not subject to these tests, the *remedy* of injunction is likely to be granted only where these tests are satisfied.[9] If this were not so, the law as to restraint of trade could, to a considerable extent, be evaded by simply giving the employer options to extend the period of service or by requiring long periods of notice for the termination of the

---

[99] See above, p.1041 at n.66. *cf. Delaney v Staples* [1992] 1 A.C. 692–693 and *William Hill Organisation Ltd v Tucker* [1998] I.R.L.R. 313, discussing so-called "garden leave."

[1] *Provident Financial Group plc v Hayward* [1989] I.C.R. 160.

[2] *William Hill Organisation Ltd v Tucker* [1998] I.R.L.R. 313; above, pp.833–834.

[3] (1852) 1 D.M. & G. 604.

[4] See above, pp.460, 464.

[5] Though in *Lumley v Wagner* it was unlimited as to area; *cf. Evening Standard v Henderson* [1987] I.C.R. 588.

[6] As in *Warner Bros Pictures Inc v Nelson* [1937] 1 K.B. 209; *cf.* the contract in *Riley v Coglan* [1967] 1 W.L.R. 1300, where a rugby league player agreed to serve his club "for the remainder of his football career . . . if the club should so long require." Contrast *Eastham v Newcastle United Football Club Ltd* [1964] Ch. 413, where the argument that the contract gave the employers a series of options was rejected.

[7] *e.g.* in cases of "garden leave" (above, p.833).

[8] *Esso Petroleum Ltd v Harper's Garage (Stourport) Ltd* [1968] A.C. 269 at 294, 328–329, discussing *Young v Timmins* (1831) 1 Cr. & J. 331; *A Schroeder Music Publishing Co Ltd v Macaulay* [1974] 1 W.L.R. 1308; *cf.* Restatement, *Contracts*, s.380(2), where illustration 1 reproduces *Lumley v Wagner* while the next illustration reproduces the *Nordenfelt* case (above, p.453).

[9] *William Hill Organisation Ltd v Tucker* [1998] I.R.L.R. 313; *Symbian Ltd v Christensen* [2001] I.R.L.R. 77 at [52].

contract.[10] A converse suggestion may also be made. Even where a covenant in restraint of trade takes effect after the period of service and is valid, it may be appropriate not to enforce it *by injunction* (but only by action for damages) if the injunction would leave the employee with no other reasonable means of making a living: the grant of an injunction in such circumstances might well be regarded as oppressive.[11]

(c) IMPLIED NEGATIVE PROMISES. An injunction to restrain the breach by an employee of a stipulation in a contract of employment will be issued only if the contract contains an *express* negative promise.[12] The remedy has been restricted in this way because an injunction may put so much economic pressure on the employee as in effect to force him to perform his positive obligation to work; and this is traditionally regarded as undesirable.[13] But where the defendant's obligation is *not* one to render personal services, there is less objection to an injunction which puts pressure on him to perform his positive undertaking, even though that undertaking may not be specifically enforceable; and in cases of this kind the courts have *implied* negative stipulations and restrained their breach by injunction. Thus an injunction can be issued to restrain a shipowner from using a ship under charter inconsistently with the charterparty[14]; to restrain breach of a promise to give a "first refusal" to purchase land[15]; and to restrain breaches of various exclusive dealing agreements,[16] and of agreements to submit disputes to arbitration.[17] Similarly, a seller of uncut timber has been restrained from interfering with the contractual right of the buyer to enter the land to cut down the timber and take it away: this was "not specific performance in the sense of compelling the vendor to do anything. It merely prevents him from breaking his contract".[18]

In the above cases, a negative stipulation, though not express, can readily be implied. The position would be different where the vagueness of the positive part of the contract made it impossible to say precisely what the defendant had undertaken *not* to do[19]; and also where the only negative stipulation which could be implied was one that would embrace the whole positive obligation. For example, if a contract were made for the sale of unascertained generic goods (such as "100 tons of coal") an injunction "not to break the contract" or "not to withhold delivery" would be indistinguishable from an order of

---

[10] It is no answer to an attack on the validity of the clause say that the employee may get paid since (a) he will not be entitled to any payment if he refuses to work for the employer, unless the contract expressly so provides; and (b) the mere fact that he gets paid does not oust the principles of restraint of trade: *cf. Wyatt v Kreglinger and Fernau* [1933] 1 K.B. 793. If the covenant is valid, the fact that the employee goes on working and gets paid is relevant to the employer's *remedy*: above, p.1043 at n.98 and above p.1044 at n.99.

[11] *cf.* above, pp.1041–1042.

[12] *Mortimer v Beckett* [1920] 1 Ch. 571; but breaches of negative obligations *imposed by law* can be restrained by injunction even though there is no express negative stipulation: *e.g. Hivac v Park Royal Scientific Instruments* [1946] Ch. 169.

[13] See above, p.1029.

[14] *Sevin v Deslandes* (1860) 30 L.J. (Ch.) 457; *The Oakworth* [1975] 1 Lloyd's Rep. 581.

[15] *Manchester Ship Canal v Manchester Racecourse Co* [1901] 2 Ch. 37.

[16] *Donnell v Bennett* (1883) 22 Ch.D. 835; *Metropolitan Electric Supply Co v Ginder* [1901] 2 Ch. 799; *Decro-Wall International SA v Practitioners in Marketing Ltd* [1971] 1 W.L.R. 361; *Evans Marshall & Co v Bertola SA* [1973] 1 W.L.R. 349. *Fothergill v Rowland* (1873) L.R. 17 Eq. 132, *contra*, is surprising in view of the reluctance with which Jessel M.R. decided for the defendants. As to the validity of exclusive dealing agreements, see above, pp.468–472.

[17] *Bankers Trust Co v PT Jakarta International Development* [1999] 1 Lloyd's Rep. 910 at 911 (injunction against proceedings in foreign court; in respect of English proceedings, the remedy would be by way of a stay: above, p.447).

[18] *Jones & Sons Ltd v Tankerville* [1909] 2 Ch. 400 at 443; *cf. Hounslow (London Borough) v Twickenham Garden and Builders Ltd* [1971] Ch. 233; above, p.1035, n.9.

[19] *Bower v Bantam Investments Ltd* [1972] 1 W.L.R. 1120.

specific performance,[20] and would not normally[21] be granted. And the implication of a narrower negative stipulation (*e.g.* not to sell to anyone else) would not fairly arise from the contract.

(d) SEVERANCE. A negative stipulation which is too widely expressed may be severed and enforced in part. Severance is not here governed by the rules which govern severance of promises in illegal contracts[22]: the question is not (as it is in the restraint of trade cases) whether severance alters the nature of the contract, but simply whether an injunction to enforce such part of the negative stipulation as the claimant specifies amounts to indirect specific performance. Thus in *Warner Bros Pictures Inc v Nelson*[23] the actress undertook, not only that she would not *act* for third parties, but also that she would not "*engage in any other occupation*" without the employers' written consent. She could clearly not be restrained from breach of the latter undertaking as this would force her to choose between idleness and performance of her obligation to work. But as the injunction sought was only one to restrain her from acting for third parties the objection that the whole of her undertaking could not be enforced by injunction was "removed by the restricted form in which the injunction is sought".[24] Of course if the negative stipulation, though operating during employment, is as a whole invalid for restraint of trade, the question of severance will be determined by the principles governing severance of illegal promises in illegal contracts.

3. Damages and Specific Performance or Injunction[25]

Power to award damages in addition to or "in substitution for . . . specific performance" was conferred on the Court of Chancery by s.2 of the Chancery Amendment Act 1858 (also known as Lord Cairns' Act). That power is now vested in the High Court by s.50 of the Supreme Court Act 1981. It applies where the court has "jurisdiction to entertain an application for an injunction or specific performance". So long as the court has such jurisdiction,[26] it can award damages in lieu even though, in its discretion, it refuses to order specific relief.[27] But it cannot do so where no attempt is made to seek specific relief, where any chance of obtaining such relief has been lost (*e.g.* by lapse of time) and where the only claim made was one for damages at common law.[28] Under s.49 of the Act, common law damages can also be awarded where specific performance or an injunction

---

[20] *cf.* Fry, *Specific Performance* (6th ed.), s.857; *Whitwood Chemical Co v Hardman* [1891] 2 Ch. 416 at 426. *The Scaptrade* [1983] A.C. 694 at 701. The granting in *Wake v Renault (UK) Ltd, The Times*, August 1, 1996 of an injunction "not to terminate" a distributorship agreement for some years is, with respect, open to question as it amounted to specific enforcement of an obligation of which specific performance would not normally be ordered since such an order would require "constant supervision" (above, p.1032); see also above, p.1043, n.88.

[21] For exceptions, see above, p.1024.

[22] See above, pp.506–510.

[23] [1937] 1 K.B. 209.

[24] *ibid.* at 219; see above, p.1043 for the question whether an injunction in even these limited terms should be granted, *cf. William Robinson & Co Ltd v Hever* [1898] 2 Ch. 451; *Provident Financial Group plc v Hayward* [1989] I.C.R. 150 at 160; *Symbian Ltd v Christensen* [2001] I.R.L.R. 77. Where the contract is illegal, *e.g.* for restraint of trade, the objection that an unseverable restraint is too wide cannot be met by claiming part-enforcement: contrast *Warner Bros. Pictures Inc v Nelson* with *Gledhow Autoparts Ltd v Delaney* [1965] 1 W.L.R. 1366.

[25] Jolowicz [1975] C.L.J. 224; Pettit [1977] C.L.J. 369; [1978] C.L.J. 51.

[26] *Hipgrave v Case* (1885) 28 Ch.D. 356; *Lavery v Pursell* (1888) 39 Ch.D. 508; *Price v Strange* [1978] Ch. 337 at 359.

[27] *e.g. Wroth v Tyler* [1974] Ch. 30; above, p.1026, n.10; *Jaggard v Sawyer* [1995] 1 W.L.R. 269. *cf.*, in tort, *Marcic v Thames Water Utilities (No.2)* [2001] 4 All E.R. 327.

[28] *Surrey CC v Bredero Homes Ltd* [1993] 1 W.L.R. 1361. For conflicting views on the correctness of this case, see *Attorney-General v Blake* [2001] 1 A.C. 268 at 283, 291 and 298.

is claimed, even though the case is not one in which specific relief could have been ordered.[29]

Since claims for damages can now be combined with claims for specific performance or injunction,[30] it is normally unnecessary to resort to the special power to award damages in lieu of these remedies. But it may sometimes be to the claimant's advantage to invoke that power where he has no completed cause of action at law, and its exercise has also given rise to certain special problems with regard to the assessment of damages.

(1) No completed cause of action at law

Damages may be awarded in lieu of specific performance or injunction even though there is no completed cause of action at law. For example a court can issue an injunction in respect of a threatened tort which has not yet been committed; and damages can be awarded in lieu of such an injunction.[31] A similar possibility exists where an anticipatory breach of contract has been committed and *not* been accepted. In such a case, an order for specific performance may be made at once[32]; and damages can be awarded in lieu under the Act even though there was (when the proceedings were commenced) no right to damages at common law.[33] However, a party is not in anticipatory breach of contract merely because the other fears that he will commit a breach of it; and where there is neither a present breach nor a wrongful repudiation, an injunction is not available against the former party,[34] so that there can be no award of damages in lieu. Again, an injunction is sometimes available against a refusal to contract; and it may be that damages can be awarded in lieu even though the refusal gives rise to no cause of action at common law.[35] An injunction may also be available to a third party where a contract between two others is in restraint of trade[36]; and in such cases it is arguable that damages may be awarded in lieu even though the third party has no cause of action for breach of contract against the parties to the contract in question.[37]

(2) Assessment of damages

There was formerly some support for the view that the assessment of damages might be more favourable to the claimant under Lord Cairns' Act than at common law, particularly where the value of the subject-matter had risen between the time of breach and the time of judgment. It was assumed that, at common law, damages were necessarily

---

[29] As in *Dominion Coal Co Ltd v Dominion Iron & Steel Co* [1909] A.C. 293; *cf. Proctor v Bayley* (1889) 42 Ch.D. 390.

[30] This follows from Supreme Court Act 1981, s.49.

[31] *Leeds Industrial Co-operative Society Ltd v Slack* [1924] A.C. 851.

[32] *Hasham v Zenab* [1960] A.C. 316 (but the order will be for performance on the due day).

[33] *cf. Oakacre Ltd v Claire Cleaners (Holdings) Ltd* [1982] Ch. 197.

[34] *The Veracruz I* [1992] 1 Lloyd's Rep. 356; *The P* [1992] 1 Lloyd's Rep. 470; *cf. Zucker v Tyndall Holdings plc* [1992] 1 W.L.R. 1127; and see *Mercantile Group (Europe) AG v Aiyela* [1994] Q.B. 366 at 375.

[35] See above, p.4; *Garden Cottage Foods Ltd v Milk Marketing Board* [1984] A.C. 130 (where the right to damages was said at 141 to be based on breach of statutory duty); where the refusal is wrongful by statute, the right to damages will often be regulated by that statute, *e.g.* Sex Discrimination Act 1975, ss.65, 66; Race Relations Act 1976, ss.56, 57, as amended by Race Relations (Remedies) Act, 1994; Disability Discrimination Act 1995, ss.4, 5, 12 and 19.

[36] See above, p.466.

[37] According to *Newport Association Football Club v Football Association of Wales Ltd* [1995] 2 All E.R. 87, the mere availability to the third party of a declaration that the contract is in restraint of trade is a cause of action; for difficulties arising from this reasoning, see above, p.467.

based on the difference between the contract price and the value of the subject-matter *at the time of breach*. In *Wroth v Tyler*[38] one reason given for nevertheless assessing the damages by reference to the *time of judgment*[39] was that they were awarded, not at common law, but under the Act, "in substitution for . . . specific performance". Such damages must, it was said, "constitute a true substitute for specific performance",[40] and give "as nearly as may be what specific performance would have given".[41] But even at common law the aim of damages is to put the claimant "in the same position . . . *as if* the contract had been *performed*"[42]; and it is hard to see any difference in principle between the two phrases "as if . . . performed" and "in substitution for . . . specific performance". Both state the same general objective; neither is followed through to its logical conclusion. The judgment in *Wroth v Tyler* itself seems to recognise the possibility that part of the claimant's loss would have been irrecoverable if it had been too remote[43]; and the mitigation rules can also reduce the amount recoverable as damages in lieu of specific performance.[44] In *Johnson v Agnew*[45] the House of Lords accordingly expressed the view that the assessment of damages was governed by the same principles whether the damages were awarded at common law or in lieu of specific performance. Even at common law, damages are not invariably assessed by reference to the date of breach. This method of assessment is adopted where it would have been reasonable for the claimant, at that date, to have mitigated his loss, *e.g.* by making a substitute contract; but if, for some reason, this is not the case, the damages will be assessed by reference to some other date.[46] In *Wroth v Tyler* the claimants were not at the time of breach in a position to make a substitute contract; and, so far as the assessment of damages is concerned, the decision must now be explained on that ground.[47]

The general principle that there is no difference between the assessment of damages at common law and damages in lieu of specific performance is based on the assumption that the damages are claimed in respect of the same breach or cause of action. The principle obviously cannot apply where there is no cause of action at common law: *e.g.* where equitable relief is sought in respect of threatened future breaches.[48]

(3) Damages and specific performance

Damages may be awarded in addition to specific performance. For example, where a vendor is in breach because his title is subject to an encumbrance, the purchaser can get specific performance ordering the vendor to convey what title he has, plus damages

---

[38] [1974] Ch. 30; above, p.961, and see *Grant v Dawkins* [1973] 1 W.L.R. 1406; Pettit, 90 L.Q.R. 297.
[39] See above, p.895.
[40] [1974] Ch. 30 at 58.
[41] *ibid.* at 59.
[42] *Robinson v Harman* (1848) 1 Ex. 850 at 855; above, p.937.
[43] See above, p.972.
[44] See *Radford v De Froberville* [1977] 1 W.L.R. 1262 at 1286; *Malhotra v Choudhury* [1980] Ch. 52; the point was, in effect, conceded in *Grant v Dawkins*, above.
[45] [1980] A.C. 367 at 400. This decision also makes it hard to accept the suggestion that damages under the Act can, as a general rule be based on the defendant's gain (rather than, as at common law, on the claimant's loss): see *Surrey CC v Bredero Homes Ltd* [1993] 1 W.L.R. 1361; *Jaggard v Sawyer* [1995] 1 W.L.R. 269. For *other* grounds for basing an award on the defendant's gain and for criticism of the *Bredero* case, see above, p.930.
[46] [1980] A.C. at 401; above, pp.959–962.
[47] See above, p.961.
[48] *Jaggard v Sawyer* [1995] 1 W.L.R. 269 at 291–292.

based on the cost of discharging the encumbrance.[49] The court may also award damages for delay in completion in addition to specific performance.[50]

SECTION 4. RESTITUTION[51]

A party who has wholly or in part performed his side of the contract and has not received the agreed counter-performance in full may sometimes be entitled to restitution in respect of his own performance. Where this consists of a payment of money, the payor will simply seek to get it back; where it consists of some other benefit he will claim recompense (or a *quantum meruit*) in respect of it.

1. Recovery of Money Paid

An action lies, in the cases to be discussed below, to recover back money paid under a contract or purported contract. The action is also available in a number of other cases which have nothing to do with the law of contract, being only connected with it historically in that the form of action used in them was also used to enforce claims arising out of contracts. Our sole concern in this book is with the use of the action in its contractual context.

(1) "Total failure of consideration"[52]

(a) DEFINITION. A contracting party can recover back money paid under a contract if there is a "total failure of consideration", *i.e.* if no part of the performance for which he bargained has been rendered.[53] In the *Fibrosa*[54] case, for example, a buyer of goods recovered back an advance payment when frustration had prevented the delivery of any part of the goods. Lord Simon explained the meaning of "consideration" in this context: "In the law relating to the formation of contract, the promise to do a thing may often be the consideration, but when one is considering the law of failure of consideration and of the quasi-contractual right to recover money on that ground it is, generally speaking, not the promise which is referred to but the performance of the promise".[55] This is only "generally speaking" the case[56] because a party may bargain for the promise itself. Thus a person who insures against the destruction of a thing by fire bargains for the insurer's promise. If the thing is then destroyed by water the insured person cannot recover back his premium: there is no total failure of consideration as he had the benefit of the insurer's promise for some time.[57] He could recover back his premium only if the insurer

---

[49] *Grant v Dawkins* [1973] 1 W.L.R. 1406.

[50] *Ford-Hunt v Ragbhir Singh* [1973] 1 W.L.R. 738; *cf. Oakacre Ltd v Claire Cleaners (Holdings) Ltd* [1982] Ch. 197 (damages for delay in substitution for specific performance). For damages for delay see above, pp.830–831.

[51] Beatson, 2 J.C.L. 65.

[52] Stoljar, 75 L.Q.R. 53; Birks in *Consensus ad Idem, Essays in the Law of Contract in Honour of Guenter Treitel* (Rose ed.), p.179.

[53] *Stocznia Gdanska SA v Latvian Shipping Co* [1998] 1 W.L.R. 574 at 587, 600; above p.1012 (the test is whether performance has been *rendered*, not whether it has been *received*).

[54] [1943] A.C. 32; above, p.911.

[55] *ibid.* at 48; *cf. Rover International Ltd v Cannon Films Ltd (No.3)* [1989] 1 W.L.R. 912 at 923; *Goss v Chilcott* [1996] A.C. 788 at 797. The point seems to have been overlooked in *Re Goldcorp Exchange Ltd* [1995] 1 A.C. 74 at 103: see above, p.911, n.38.

[56] *cf.* Lord Goff (dissenting) in *Westdeutsche Landesbank Girozentrale v Islington BC* [1996] A.C. 669 at 683 ("need not be so narrowly confined").

[57] *cf. Tyrie v Fletcher* (1777) 2 Cowp. 666.

had never been at risk, *e.g.* if the thing had been destroyed the day before the policy had begun to run.[58]

It is also possible for A to buy the benefit of a promise made to B by C: *e.g.* where B contracts to assign[59] to A a debt owed by C to B. The actual assignment of the debt by B to A is then the *performance* of B's promise, even though the result of that performance is to confer on A a legal right to the performance of another promise, *i.e.* of that made by C to B. In such a case there would be a total failure of consideration if the contract between B and C were void in law, so that nothing was transferred from B to A; but this defect was said to have been cured where, as a result of a subsequent novation, A "got the substance of what they were paying for, a valid and enforceable contract with" C, so that "there was no failure of consideration at all".[60] It will be recalled that novation is a transaction involving all three parties,[61] so that B contributed to the end result that A became legally entitled to the benefit of C's promise. If this state of affairs had come about as a result of an independent subsequent transaction involving only A and C, then it would not have cured the defect in B's original performance or prevented the failure of consideration from being total.

(b) PARTIAL FAILURE. In the above cases, there is either a total failure of consideration or no failure at all. There is also an intermediate situation in which there has been a *partial* failure; and in such cases, the traditional view, or general rule, is that there is no right to recover back a proportionate part of the money paid.[62] If, for example, A employed B for a lump sum paid in advance to paint A's house, and B abandoned the job before it was finished, A could not recover back any part of the payment: the right to recover back money paid on account of failure of consideration is said to be restricted to cases in which the failure is "total". One reason for this requirement is that, in the example just given, A already has his remedy in damages. This is generally governed by the compensatory principle[63] under which A can recover no more than his loss; and to allow him to claim restitution in respect of *any* breach would cut across this principle, particularly where he had made a bad bargain by paying B more than B's performance was worth. If B had simply done nothing after receiving the advance payment, A's right to recover the payment could be justified on the ground that B would be unjustly enriched if he were allowed to keep money paid to him "for nothing but a broken promise".[64] But this reasoning loses much of its force where B has performed in part,[65]

---

[58] *cf. Stevenson v Snow* (1761) 3 Burr. 1237; and see Marine Insurance Act 1906, s.84.

[59] See above, Ch.16.

[60] *Kleinwort Benson Ltd v South Tyneside MBC* [1994] 4 All E.R. 972 at 989.

[61] See above, p.673. In the present case, all three parties were involved: see [1994] 4 All E.R. 972 at 989.

[62] *Whincup v Hughes* (1871) L.R. 6 C.P. 78; the actual decision is no longer law: above, p.911; *Salvage Association v CAP v Financial Services* [1995] F.S.R. 654 at 682; *Baltic Shipping Co v Dillon* (1993) 176 C.L.R. 344 (no return of part of the price paid for aborted holiday cruise; though the price may be relevant in assessing *damages: Peninsular & Orient SN Co v Youell* [1997] 2 Lloyd's Rep. 136; and see below p.1057). Proposals for reform, in Law Commission Working Paper 65, Pt III were later abandoned: Law Com. 121, para.3.11. In *DO Ferguson & Associates v Sohl* (1992) 62 Build.L.R. 95 an advance payment was made to a builder who failed to do some of the work for which the payment was made. There was said to be a total failure of consideration with regard to the part of the work left undone so that the builder was held liable to restore the amount of the payment attributable to that part. But the notion of "total failure of part" is, with respect, quite inconsistent with the requirement of total failure; the case can perhaps be justified on the analogy of the cases discussed at n.66 below. In *White Arrow Express Ltd v Lamey's Distribution Ltd* [1995] N.L.J. 1504 no attempt was made to pursue what was called "a claim in quasi-contract based on partial failure of consideration," while the claim for damages failed on the ground stated on p.928, above.

[63] See above, pp.927–930.

[64] Palmer, 20 Ohio State L.J. 264, 267; above, p.927.

[65] For the position where only a very small part has been performed, see below, pp.1052–1053.

particularly where only a small part remains unperformed. A second reason for the general rule is that it may not be easy for the law to apportion the amount of work actually done by B to the whole in respect of which the payment was made; and where this is the case the amount of restitution that he should be required to make is correspondingly hard to assess. But there are also cases in which neither of the above justifications for the general rule applies; and in such cases recovery of money has been allowed even though the failure of consideration is only partial. Thus where apportionment of the unperformed part is in fact easy, the law will allow partial recovery: for example, a buyer to 100 tons could get back half his money if only 50 tons were delivered.[66]

Apportionment is also easy where the promise which is performed only in part is one by a borrower to pay money, whether by way of interest or of repayment of capital, under a contract for the loan of money. Normally the lender's action in such a case will be one for the recovery of the agreed sum, but where this is for some reason not available,[67] the fact that some payments have been made by the borrower will not deprive the lender of a restitutionary remedy based on failure of consideration.[68] Indeed, the very fact that *no* contractual remedy is available to the promisee will make the court anxious to allow restitution since in such cases this is the *only* way in which unjust enrichment of the promisor can be avoided.[69] This point is also reflected in the statutory provision by which money paid in advance under a contract which is later frustrated can be recovered even though the failure of consideration is only partial.[70] Any difficulty of making an apportionment is again outweighed by the fact that restitution is the payor's only possible remedy, since frustration provides the payee with a defence to any claim for damages. Partial failure of consideration can also give rise to a right to the return of advance payments where the contract in terms confers such a right.[71] The requirement that the failure must be "total" is, finally, attenuated in the cases, to be discussed below,[72] in which restitution of money has been allowed in spite of the fact that benefits other than those contracted for had been received by the payor; though in some of those cases the grant of the restitutionary remedy is open to criticism precisely on the ground that it has led to the payor's being overcompensated.[73]

The above discussion shows that the requirement of a "total" failure of consideration, though it continues to be stated in the authorities,[74] is now much qualified. These qualifications support the view that it should be restricted to those cases in which the reasons for it, stated above, still have force. It should, in other words, no longer apply where the payor has *no* remedy, or no satisfactory remedy, for breach (*e.g.* by way of action for damages[75]) in respect of the part left unperformed by the payee, or where

---

[66] *Whincup v Hughes*, above, at p.81; *cf. Ebrahim Dawood Ltd v Heath Ltd* [1961] 2 Lloyd's Rep. 512; *Clough Mill Ltd v Martin* [1985] 1 W.L.R. 111 at 117–118.
[67] See nn.68 and 69 below for examples.
[68] *Goss v Chilcott* [1996] A.C. 788, where the borrowers had been discharged from their contractual liability by an alteration of the repayment dates in a mortgage made on behalf of the lender.
[69] Hence perhaps the reference in *Kleinwort Benson Ltd v Glasgow CC* [1997] 4 All E.R. 641 at 652 to "failure of consideration" (omitting "total") in the context of a claim for the recovery of money paid under a void contract.
[70] See above, p.911.
[71] *The Trident Beauty* [1994] 1 W.L.R. 161 at 164–165.
[72] See below, pp.1053–1056.
[73] *Butterworth v Kingsway Motors Ltd* [1954] 1 W.L.R. 1286 and *Barber v NSW Bank Ltd* [1996] 1 W.L.R. 641, below, pp.1054–1055.
[74] *e.g. The Trident Beauty* [1994] 1 W.L.R. 161 at 164–165; *Baltic Shipping Co v Dillon* (1993) 176 C.L.R. 344 at 350–351, 367, 376, 384, 388.
[75] Or, in the case of a loan of money, by way of action for the agreed sum.

there is in fact no difficulty in apportioning that part to the whole in respect of which the payor's advance payment had been made.

(c) RETURNABLE AND NON-RETURNABLE BENEFITS. A party who has received only partial or defective performance may, on that ground, be entitled to rescind the contract.[76] If he does rescind, and restores what he has received under the contract, he brings about a total failure of consideration and can therefore recover any money that he has paid. For example, a buyer who has paid in advance for goods may find, on delivery, that they suffer from a defect amounting to a breach of condition, or that they are not of the agreed quantity. In that case, he can generally reject the goods and get his money back.[77] Normally, he must restore the goods, but this requirement does not apply where his inability to restore them is due to the very defect which has given rise to the right to reject: e.g. if the goods were so defective that they disintegrated; or if they were taken away from the buyer because the seller had no title to them.[78] The position seems to be the same where restoration of the subject-matter is made impossible by some external cause for which neither party was responsible.[79]

Where, on the other hand, the partial or defective performance is of such a nature that it cannot be returned, the mere fact that it has been rendered prevents the failure of consideration from being total: for example, where work to be done under a lump sum building contract has been paid for in advance, but is left unfinished or is done defectively. In such cases, the client's remedy is in damages: he would be entitled to the return of his payment only if the builder's breach were so serious that the work was wholly useless to the client.[80] Similarly, an employee may commit breaches of duty justifying his dismissal; but if he is not dismissed and is paid his salary or wages, the employer will not, on subsequently discovering the breaches of duty, be able to recover back the payments[81]: his remedy is in damages.

Even if the subject-matter of the contract is returned (or if its return is not required under the rules stated above) the injured party may have derived some benefit from it: e.g. by using or occupying it. Use for the sole purpose of testing is disregarded and so does not impair the right of the injured party to get his money back.[82] But any further use or occupation may prevent the failure of consideration from being total. In *Hunt v Silk*[83] an agreement for a lease provided that possession was to be given immediately; that certain repairs were to be done by the landlord; that the lease was to be executed within 10 days; and that, on execution of the lease, the tenant was to pay £10. The tenant went into possession and paid the £10 before the execution of the lease, but the landlord failed to do the repairs, or to execute the lease within 10 days. After a few more days, the tenant vacated the premises and claimed the return of his £10. The claim was rejected,[84] and (although other explanations are possible[85]) the case has generally been taken to lay down the strict rule that, if a party has received any part of the benefit that he contracted

---

[76] See Ch.18, Section 3.

[77] e.g. *Bragg v Villanova* (1923) 40 T.L.R. 154; *Baldry v Marshall* [1925] 1 Q.B. 260. Contrast *Linz v Electric Wire Co of Palestine* [1948] A.C. 371 (where a buyer of shares forming part of an invalid issue had sold, and was therefore unable to restore, them).

[78] e.g. *Rowland v Divall* [1923] 2 K.B. 500.

[79] e.g. *Head v Tattersall* (1871) L.R. 7 Ex. 7.

[80] *Heywood v Wellers* [1976] Q.B. 446, 458.

[81] *Horcal v Gatland* [1984] I.R.L.R. 288. For the employer's right to withhold pay, see above, pp.821–822.

[82] e.g. *Baldry v Marshall*, above.

[83] (1804) 5 East 449.

[84] Contrast *Wright v Colls* (1848) 8 C.B. 149, where the premium was paid specifically for execution of the lease and was held recoverable when the landlord failed to execute it.

[85] e.g. Goff and Jones, *The Law of Restitution* (6th ed.), pp.507–508.

for,[86] there is no total failure of consideration. The rule is open to the objection that it may bar a claim for the recovery of money even though the benefit received is only slight or technical.[87] On the other hand, the actual decision in *Hunt v Silk* does not seem to be unreasonable; for there is nothing in the reported facts to suggest that the tenant did not have a perfectly adequate remedy in damages.

(d) BENEFITS OTHER THAN THOSE BARGAINED FOR. It does not follow from *Hunt v Silk* that the receipt of *any* benefit by the injured party will bar his right to get his money back. If the benefit received was *different in kind* from that bargained for,[88] there may be a total failure of consideration even though the benefit cannot be returned in specie: for example, where a computer is delivered without the software needed to make it work,[89] or where it is made useless by the supplier's deliberately activating a disabling device.[90] This idea has made it possible to temper the rigidity of the rule in *Hunt v Silk*, but it has led to rules and distinctions which have in turn attracted criticism.

In *Rowland v Divall*[91] the plaintiff, who was a car dealer, bought a car from the defendant for £334, repainted it and resold it to a customer for £400. Subsequently the car was seized by the police as it had (unknown to any of the above parties) been stolen. The plaintiff thereupon repaid his customer the £400[92] and sued the defendant for the return of the £334. Meanwhile the original owner of the car had been compensated by his insurance company, who "took over the car themselves and then sold it to the plaintiff for £260".[93] The defendant took the position that his liability was limited to this sum and paid it into court.[94] But the Court of Appeal held that there had been a total failure of consideration, so that the plaintiff could recover back his payment of £334. He had not "received any portion of what he agreed to buy. . . . He did not get what he paid for—namely a car to which he would have title".[95] As the plaintiff was a dealer, this seems (with respect) to be a reasonable view: he did not want to use, but to resell, the car. For this purpose he needed a marketable title and not mere possession,

---

[86] The same principle was applied in *Thorpe v Fasey* [1949] Ch. 649 to the converse situation where a vendor claimed rescission. But it is hard to see why he should be deprived of this remedy merely because the *purchaser* had had some benefit from the subject matter. Perhaps the case can be explained on other grounds: *cf.* above, p.816, n.13.

[87] A kind of statutory modification of the rule in *Hunt v Silk*, above is contained in amendments to the Sale of Goods Act 1979 made by the Sale and Supply of Goods to Consumers Regulations 2002 (SI 2002/3045, regs.5 and 6 (implementing Dir.1999/44). Under ss.48A and 48C, a buyer who deals as consumer has in certain circumstances the right to "rescind" the contract on account of non-conformity of the goods. His right to "reimbursement", consequent on the exercise of his right to "rescind", may be reduced "to take account of the use he has had of the goods since they were delivered to him", s.48E(5); but see also p.1054, n.1 below.

[88] For this concept, contrast *Wilkinson v Lloyd* (1845) 7 Q.B. 27 with *Stray v Russell* (1859) 1 E. & E. 889 at 916 and *Knowles v Bovill* (1870) 22 L.T. 70 with *Taylor v Hare* (1805) 1 B. & P.N.R. 260 and *Lawes v Purser* (1856) 6 E. & E. 930; *cf.* also *Pilbrow v Pearless De Rougemont & Co* [1999] 3 All E.R. 355 (above, p.806) where the victim of the breach made no restitution claim; and the question whether such a claim might be available was left open at 361; and see below, pp.1058–1059 for the view (there doubted) that there is a "total failure of consideration" for payments made under a void contract; and *Lipkin Gorman v Karpnale Ltd* [1991] 2 A.C. 548, above, p.535.

[89] *South West Water Services Ltd v International Computers Ltd* [1999] Build.L.R. 420.

[90] *Rubicon Computer Systems Ltd v United Paints Ltd* (2000) 2 T.C.L.R. 453.

[91] [1923] 2 K.B. 500. The new provisions of the Sale of Goods Act 1979 cited in n.87, above, would not now apply to such facts since (1) the buyer did not deal as consumer: s.48A(1)(a); and (2) the seller's breach, being one of the term implied by s.12, did not fall within ss.48A–48C; see s.48F.

[92] He could now reduce his liability to the customer for failure of consideration by any increase in value attributable to the repainting: Torts (Interference with Goods) Act 1977, s.6(3).

[93] This fact is stated in the report of the case in 129 L.T. 757.

[94] *ibid.*

[95] [1923] 2 K.B. 500 at 504.

which was wrongful against the owner. Moreover, the fact that he did not get title caused him serious prejudice beyond having to buy the car a second time; for it resulted in his losing a presumably profitable resale.[96]

The same rule has, however, also been applied in the absence of such circumstances. In *Butterworth v Kingsway Motors Ltd*[97] a car owned by a finance company was let out on hire-purchase to a hirer who wrongfully sold it before she had paid all the instalments. It passed through a number of hands until it was sold for £1,275 by the defendant to a buyer, both of whom acted in good faith. Nearly a year later, the finance company notified the buyer that the car was theirs and asked for its return. Alternatively, they offered to allow the buyer to acquire title for £175,[98] this being all that remained due under the hire-purchase agreement as the hirer had kept up her payments under it. Meanwhile, however, second-hand car prices had fallen, so that the car was worth only £800. Two days after hearing from the finance company, the buyer claimed the return of the £1,275. After another eight days, the original hirer paid off the £175 and acquired a good title which could at that stage have been passed to the buyer. In these circumstances, the court rightly described the buyer's claim as "somewhat lacking in merits"[99]—but nevertheless allowed it in full. The decision represents a regrettable extension of *Rowland v Divall*. It is hardly realistic to say that the buyer did not get any part of what he bargained for: he bought the car for use and did use it for nearly a year. Moreover, any prejudice to the buyer from the defendant's lack of title was removed when the amount outstanding under the hire-purchase agreement was paid off.

The same result was again reached in *Barber v NSW Bank plc*,[1] where the buyer entered into a conditional sale agreement with the defendants relating to a car which was (unknown to either party) the subject of an earlier finance agreement and to which the defendant therefore had no title. The buyer became aware of this fact when he attempted, some 20 months after entering into the agreement to resell the car; and after a further three months he rescinded the agreement and successfully claimed the return of all the payments he had made under it. Although he had had the use of the car for nearly two years "without let or hinderance",[2] it was said to be "not inequitable in all the circumstances"[3] for him to recover his payments in full. This result was based "on the established authorities"[4] which appear to have included *Rowland v Divall* and *Butterworth v Kingsway Motors*, both of which were cited to the Court though neither was referred to in the judgment.[5] It is, with respect, unfortunate that no attempt was made by the Court of Appeal in the *Barber* case to distinguish the former or to evaluate

---

[96] The eventual fate of the car is not known; *cf.* above, p.955.

[97] [1954] 1 W.L.R. 1286. For the second of the reasons given in n.91, above, the new provisions of the Sale of Goods Act 1979 cited in n.87, above, would not now apply on such facts.

[98] This was all that the finance company could recover as damages from the plaintiff: see *Wickham Holdings Ltd v Brook House Motors Ltd* [1967] 1 W.L.R. 295. If the value of the car had been *less* than the amount outstanding under the agreement, the company could not have recovered more than that value: *Chubb Cash Ltd v John Crilley & Son* [1983] 1 W.L.R. 599.

[99] [1954] 1 W.L.R. 1286 at 1291.

[1] [1996] 1 W.L.R. 641. It seems that the buyer dealt as consumer; and, as the seller's breach was of an *express* term as to title, the new provisions of the Sale of Goods Act 1979 could now apply on such facts: see the reference in s.48F to an "express term". But the buyer could avoid reduction of his restitution claim under s.48E(5) by basing that claim, not on the new "additional rights" conferred on him by Pt 5A of the Act, but on his right to reject for breach of condition under s.11; this right is not affected by s.48E(5), above n.87.

[2] [1996] 1 W.L.R. 641 at 647.

[3] *ibid.*

[4] *ibid.*

[5] The court relied principally on the authorities cited in n.9, below, though it accepted, at p.646, that it was not bound by these cases.

the latter decision. The car had been bought for use (though the breach came to light when the buyer attempted to resell it); and as the buyer had used the car for some 23 months it is hard to accept that he received no part of the benefit for which he had bargained. The court may have attached some weight to the fact that the defendants had become aware of the earlier finance agreement some six months before the buyer rescinded[6] and they had made no attempt to settle the third party's claim during that interval.[7] It is, however, not easy to see how even this fact could be said to have deprived the buyer of the whole of what he had bargained for, particularly as he had used the car for more than 16 months before the defendants had acquired any knowledge of the earlier agreement[8] and so had any opportunity of settling the true owner's claim.

A line of hire-purchase cases is open to similar criticisms. According to these, there is a total failure of consideration if the person letting a car out has no title, so that he cannot give the hirer a valid option to purchase.[9] But once a valid option has been conferred, there is no total failure because the hirer is for some reason prevented from exercising it[10]; or because the car suffers from defects which are so serious that it cannot, for practical purposes, be used at all.[11] It seems unrealistic to say that a hirer who actually uses the car for a substantial period is wholly deprived of what he bargained for merely because there was no valid option, while one who cannot use the car at all because of a physical defect is not so deprived.

The view that the buyer in *Rowland v Divall* itself did not get *the* benefit for which he bargained is (as has been suggested above) a perfectly reasonable one. But the decision has nevertheless been criticised on the ground that the buyer recovered the *whole* of the price even though he and his sub-buyer had had the use of the car for some months. One way of meeting this criticism would be to reduce the buyer's claim for the return of the price by giving the seller the right to an allowance in respect of the benefit obtained by the buyer from his use of the subject-matter.[12] But this suggestion in turn gives rise to the problem of valuing that benefit. It would clearly be unfair to the buyer to assess it at a "reasonable rental value" since a person who is buying or hire-purchasing a car would not want to incur the cost of hiring one. An alternative possibility would be to value the buyer's benefit, in general,[13] at the amount by which the cost of replacing the goods when the buyer was deprived of them was less than the contract price.[14]

---

[6] The defendants became aware of the third party's claim on February 12, 1991; the buyer rescinded on August 16, 1991.

[7] They settled it on September 2, 1991.

[8] *i.e.* from October 10, 1989, when the car was supplied to the buyer, till February 12, 1991.

[9] See *Karflex Ltd v Poole* [1933] 2 K.B. 251; *Warman v Southern Counties Car Finance Corp Ltd* [1959] 2 K.B. 576 (where the point arose on a counter-claim against the hirer).

[10] *Kelly v Lombard Banking Co* [1959] 1 W.L.R. 41; *cf. CCC Films (London) Ltd v Impact Quadrant Films* [1985] Q.B. 16 at 28.

[11] *Yeoman Credit Ltd v Apps* [1962] 2 Q.B. 508.

[12] Law Commission Working Paper 65, paras 56–57; for an earlier proposal for reform, see Law Reform Committee, Cmnd. 2958 (1966) para.56, discussed by Treitel, 30 M.L.R. 139, 147–149; Law Commission Working Paper 85, paras 6.11 to 6.13 lists various possible reforms without deciding between them. The Law Commissions (Law Com. No.160, Scot. Law Com. No.104, para.6.5) have concluded that the subject is too complex for legislative reform. Sale of Goods Act 1979, s.48E(5), which empowers the court to reduce the reimbursement to which a consumer becomes entitled on rescinding the contract under s.48C (above, p.1053, n.87) does not apply where the seller's only breach is of terms implied by s.12 of the Act: see s.48F; and see above nn.91 and 1.

[13] For a suggested exception where the buyer has made a bad bargain, see Law Commission Working Paper 65, paras 74–75; *quaere*, whether a special provision for this situation is desirable where (*ex hypothesi*) buyer and seller have both acted in good faith.

[14] *ibid.* para.73.

A further problem arises in cases of this kind because the true owner may have a claim in tort against either the buyer[15] or the seller[16] or both; he may be entitled not only to the return of the property or its value, but also its reasonable rental value.[17] If the owner has already claimed the rental value from the buyer, it seems clear that the seller should restore the *whole* price[18]; for if the buyer also had to give credit to the seller for the use of the goods, he would be required to pay twice over for the same benefit. Similar considerations apply where the true owner has not yet made his claim: if the buyer had to give credit to the seller he could later be sued for a similar sum by the owner. He might be able to claim that second payment back from the seller as damages; but by then the seller may have disappeared or the right to sue him may be barred by lapse of time. Of course the true owner may choose not to assert his claim for rental value; and in that case the buyer would no doubt be enriched by having had the use of the subject-matter and nevertheless being allowed to get back the whole price from the seller. But the enrichment would be at the expense of the *owner* and not at the expense of the seller, who accordingly should not have a claim in respect of it.[19] In view of the buyer's possible liability to the true owner, the buyer should only have to make an allowance to the seller for the benefit of the use of the goods if the claim of the true owner has first been satisfied.[20]

A final criticism of the rule in *Rowland v Divall* is based on the following example[21]: B in good faith buys whisky from a thief and sells it to A, who drinks it. Can A recover back the whole price? It seems clear that he cannot,[22] because he is unable to restore the whisky, and this is entirely due to his voluntary act in drinking it.[23] But then it is said to be unjust to A that he *cannot* recover back his money: the true owner may sue him in conversion so that he will (in effect) have to pay for the whisky twice over. But B has also converted the whisky and is also liable to the true owner in respect of that damage. Hence A can recover contribution from him (which may amount to a complete indemnity[24]) under the Civil Liability (Contribution) Act 1978.[25] The result is perfectly fair. A has paid for the whisky; the true owner has its value. B has admittedly lost the amount he paid the thief for the whisky, but that is a risk to which everyone who deals, even innocently, with a thief is exposed.

(e) RELATION TO DAMAGES.[26] In a number of cases it has been held or said that a claimant may be able to get back money paid under a contract *as damages* for the

---

[15] *Hilberry v Hatton* (1864) 2 H. & C. 822.

[16] *Martindale v Smith* (1841) 1 Q.B. 389.

[17] *Strand Electric & Engineering Co Ltd v Brisford Entertainments Ltd* [1952] 2 K.B. 246; *Hillesden Securities Ltd v Ryjack Ltd* [1983] 1 W.L.R. 959.

[18] As in *Newsome v Graham* (1829) 10 B. & C. 234 (where the subject matter was an interest in land). *cf. Hizzett v Hargreaves* [1987] C.L.Y 1164.

[19] See *Warman v Southern Counties Car Finance Corp Ltd* [1959] 2 K.B. 576 at 582–583; *Argens v Whitcomb* 147 P. 2d 501 at 504 (1944).

[20] Law Commission Working Paper No.65, paras 68–70.

[21] Atiyah, *Sale of Goods* (10th ed.), p.107.

[22] This seems to be admitted by Atiyah, above.

[23] *cf.* above, p.1052.

[24] Civil Liability (Contribution) Act 1978, s.2(2).

[25] *ibid.* s.1. The damage for which A and B are liable is the "same damage;" *cf.*, as to the meaning of this phrase, *Jameson v CEGB* [2002] 1 A.C. 455; *Royal Brompton Hospital NHS Trust v Hammond* [2002] UKHL 14; [2002] W.L.R. 1379; *Co-operative Retail Services Ltd v Taylor Young Partnerships Ltd* [2002] UKHL 17; [2002] 1 W.L.R. 1419. Thus, in the case put, the difficulty discussed in *Brise Construction Ltd v Plastic Ltd* [1996] 1 W.L.R. 675 (where the two wrongdoers were liable to different claimants) would not arise.

[26] A claim for the return of money paid on a total failure of consideration is not one *for damages* even though (as was held in *Friends' Provident Life Office v Hilier Parker May & Rowden* [1997] Q.B. 85) one "in respect of . . . damage" for the purpose of Civil Liability (Contribution) Act 1978, ss.1(1) and 6.

defendant's breach. For example, in one case a cow had been sold warranted healthy, but in fact she suffered from a disease from which she died; and the buyer recovered the price as one item of damages for breach of warranty.[27] Payments made under hire purchase agreements by hirers have likewise been recovered by them as damages where the goods were so defective that they were completely useless or rightfully rejected by the hirers.[28] Similar relief has been given to buyers and hire purchasers of stolen goods who elected to claim damages[29]; and to tenants who left premises which had been leased to them in consequence of abusive conduct on the part of their landlord, amounting to breach of his covenant for quiet enjoyment.[30] Strictly speaking, the injured party's damages in such cases should be the *value of the subject-matter* at the relevant date,[31] and not *the price* as such. The cases can perhaps be explained on the ground that in them the price was the best, and indeed the only, evidence of value. It is also possible for the price paid under one contract to be recoverable as reliance loss by way of damages for breach of a second contract between the same parties.[32]

In an action for damages the injured party can often recover more than the money he has paid to the defendant. For example, if in consequence of a breach he is deprived of goods, he may be able to recover, not only what he has paid for them, but also money spent on them[33] or loss of profits (subject to the normal limitations on damages, such as remoteness and mitigation). On the other hand, when the injured party claims damages, benefits obtained by him under the contract are, in principle, taken into account; and he will also recover less than the price if he has paid more for the subject-matter than it was worth, or than it would cost to replace. A claim for damages is also subject to practical difficulties, such as quantification and remoteness, which do not arise on a claim for the recovery of money. The question which action should be brought, where both are available,[34] requires a careful weighing of all these factors. It should certainly not be assumed that the action for the recovery of money is necessarily the better remedy.

(2) Money paid under a void contract

(a) IN GENERAL. The law starts with the assumption that money paid under a void contract can be recovered back.[35] Thus in *Bell v Lever Bros Ltd*[36] it was clearly assumed that the money paid by the claimants under the compensation agreements could have been recovered back, had those agreements been void for mistake. Where a hire-

---

[27] *Harling v Eddy* [1951] 2 K.B. 739; *cf. George Wills & Sons Ltd v Thomas Brown & Sons* (1922) 12 Ll.L.R. 292, where no discussion as to damages is reported.

[28] *Charterhouse Credit Co Ltd v Tolly* [1963] 2 Q.B. 683; *Farnworth Finance Facilities Ltd v Attryde* [1970] 1 W.L.R. 1053; *Doobay v Mohabeer* [1967] 2 A.C. 278.

[29] *Mason v Burningham* [1949] 2 K.B. 545; *Warman v Southern Counties Car Finance Corp Ltd* [1949] 2 K.B. 576.

[30] *Sampson v Floyd* [1989] 2 E.G.L.R. 49, doubted on another point in *Branchett v Beany* [1992] 3 All E.R. 910 at 916.

[31] See above, pp.937, 948 *et seq.*; *Greenwood v Bennett* [1973] Q.B. 195 at 201 ("the value of the car as he sold it to them"); *The Rio Sun* [1985] 1 Lloyd's Rep. 351 at 368 ("the value of the oil . . . on the date when [the buyers] received it."; *cf.*, in case of failure to render services *Miles v Wakefield MDC* [1987] A.C. 539 at 568, above, p.785, n.93; *White Arrow Express Ltd v Lamey's Distribution Ltd* [1995] N.L.J. 1504, above, p.928; *Peninsular & Orient SN Co v Youell* [1997] 2 Lloyd's Rep. 136 at 141).

[32] *CCC Films (London) Ltd v Impact Quadrant Films Ltd* [1985] Q.B. 16.

[33] See the authorities cited in nn.27 and 29 above.

[34] See above, p.941.

[35] *e.g. Re London County Commercial Reinsurance Office* [1922] 2 Ch. 67. *cf. Colesworthy v Collmain Services* [1993] C.C.L.R. 4; *aliter* if the contract or relevant term is only unenforceable: *Boddington v Lawton* [1994] I.C.R. 478. And see Arrowsmith, 9 Legal Studies 121 and 307.

[36] [1932] A.C. (above, p.289); Landon, 51 L.Q.R. 650; Tylor, 52 L.Q.R. 27; Landon, *ibid.* 478; Hamson, 53 L.Q.R. 118.

purchase agreement was wholly void for mistake it was accordingly held that the hirer could recover back his deposit[37]; and it does not seem that he was under any liability to pay for the use of the subject-matter of the agreement, which had been in his possession for over three months.[38] Where a contract was void because one of the parties was a company not yet in existence when the contract was made,[39] it was similarly held that instalments paid under it could be recovered back by the payor.[40] The same rule has been applied where money was paid under an *ultra vires* contract[41] and where money was paid under a contract which was void by statute.[42]

(b) BASES OF THE RULE. The general rule that money paid under a void contract can be recovered back is clearly established; but there has been some difference of opinion as to its legal basis. This has arisen in cases[43] involving "interest rate swap" contracts under which A (a bank) had made lump sum payments to B (a local authority) which had in turn made some or all of the payments to A which were expressed under the contracts to be due from B to A. The contracts were found to be *ultra vires* and void[44] because B had no legal power to enter into them and it was argued that A's claim for the recovery of the balance of its payments[45] was barred *either* on the ground that B had made some of the stipulated counter-payments, so that the failure of consideration for A's payments was no more than partial *or* on the ground that the contracts had been fully performed on both sides, so that there had been no failure of consideration at all. For the reasons to be discussed below, however, these arguments were rejected, so that A's claim was upheld in spite of partial performance by B or even full performance by both parties of the void promises.

(i) *Lack or failure of consideration.* One reason for allowing A's claim was that the principle on which money paid under a void contract is recoverable differs from that of recovery for "total failure of consideration" under a valid contract. Where the contract is void, the right to recover money paid under it is based, not on failure to perform a contractual obligation (since under a void contract there can be no duty to perform[46]), but on the ground that there is "no legal justification"[47] or "no consideration"[48] for the payment. A second, alternative, reason for upholding A's claim was that there *had* (in the interest rate swap cases) been a total failure of consideration. There are, in turn, two versions of this view. One is that all payments made in pursuance of a void contract are

---

[37] *Branwhite v Worcester Works Finance Ltd* [1969] 1 A.C. 552.
[38] No claim of this kind was made by the finance company in *Branwhite's* case.
[39] See above, p.736.
[40] *Rover International Ltd v Cannon Films Ltd (No.3)* [1989] 1 W.L.R. 912; Birks, 2 J.C.L. 227.
[41] *Westdeutsche Landesbank Girozentrale v Islington LBC* [1994] 1 W.L.R. 938.
[42] See the discussion in *Westdeutsche Landesbank Girozentrale v Islington B.C.* at first instance and in the Court of Appeal [1994] 4 All E.R. 890 at 921–924; [1994] 1 W.L.R. 938 at 946, 952 of the cases on contracts made void by the Grants of Life Annuities Act 1777 (17 Geo. 3 c.26), s.1. This is presumably the "annuity bill" to which Sir Peter Teazle refers in Sheridan's *The School for Scandal*, III.1 (first produced in 1777).
[43] See especially *Westdeutsche Landesbank Girozentrale v Islington B.C.* [1994] 4 All E.R. 890; [1994] 1 W.L.R. 938; [1996] A.C. 669 (reversing the decision below on the issue of compound interest only); Birks, 32 U.W.A.L.R. 195; Burrows [1995] R.L.R. 15.
[44] See *Hazell v Hammersmith & Fulham BC* [1992] A.C. 1.
[45] *i.e.* the amount by which A's payments exceeded B's.
[46] *cf. Guiness Mahon & Co Ltd v Kensington & Chelsea Royal BC* [1999] Q.B. 215 at 236.
[47] *Westdeutsche Landesbank Girozentrale v Islington BC* [1994] 1 W.L.R. 938 at 953; *cf.* [1994] 4 All E.R. 890 at 929 ("not contractual payments at all"); *Kleinwort Benson Ltd v Birmingham CC* [1997] Q.B. 380 at 394 ("no justification for the retention of the money").
[48] *South Tyneside MBC v Svenska International plc* [1995] 1 All E.R. 545 at 577; *cf. Westdeutsche* case above, n.43 [1994] 4 All E.R. 890 at 924 ("absence of consideration"); *Kleinwort Benson Ltd v Birmingham C.C.* [1997] Q.B. 380 at 386–387.

"necessarily made for a consideration which has totally failed".[49] But if there is *necessarily* such a total failure of consideration whenever the contract is void, then there is no *separate* requirement of total failure of consideration: recovery is allowed simply because the contract is void. The other version is that there is a total failure of consideration because A had bargained for B's "*obligation* . . . to make counter-payments"[50] and the benefit of B's having *in fact* made such payments was different in kind from the benefit for which A had bargained.[51] Again this will be true in all cases in which payments are made under void contracts, so that on this view, too, there is no *separate* requirement of total failure of consideration.

(ii) *Mistake.* Where money is paid under a void contract, the payment will often (though not always[52]) be made in the mistaken belief that the contract was valid. Such a mistake was not formerly a ground on which the payor was entitled to the return of his money since the mistake was one of law and it had been held that there was no right to recover back money paid under a mistake of law (as opposed to one of fact). The authorities which had supported this view[53] were, however, overruled by the House of Lords in *Kleinwort Benson Ltd v Lincoln CC*,[54] where moneys had been paid by a bank to local authorities under interest rate swap contracts which were believed to be valid but which were actually void.[55] It was held that the bank was entitled to recover the moneys on the ground that they had been paid under a mistake of law.[56] It was further held that this right was not barred by the fact that the contract had been fully performed by both parties. The cases which supported the latter proposition where the claim was based, not on mistake, but simply on the fact that the contract was void[57] were referred to with approval, thus further supporting the view that money paid under a void contract is recoverble by the payor even though the circumstances are not such as would have given rise, if the contract had been valid, to a total failure of consideration. The reason for this conclusion was that the policy of the rule making the contract void might be defeated if full or partial performance of the contract were a bar to recovery: *e.g.* if a local authority were precluded by such a bar from recovering *ultra vires* payments made in the mistaken belief that they were *intra vires* and hence legally due.[58]

(iii) *Practical considerations.* There are also practical grounds for not applying the "total failure of consideration" requirement to claims for the recovery of payments under void contracts. Where the contract is *valid*, a party who is denied the right to recover back payments because he has received partial performance will normally have a claim for damages in respect of the part left unperformed. Where, on the other hand,

---

[49] *Guiness Mahon & Co Ltd v Kensington & Chelsea Royal BC* [1999] Q.B. 215 at 230.
[50] *Westdeutsche* case, above, n.43 [1996] A.C. 669 at 711 (italics supplied) approving the reasoning of the Court of Appeal [1994] 1 W.L.R. 938 at 943 *per* Dillon L.J.; Legatt L.J., *ibid.* at 951–953 is more equivocal as to the basis of recovery; *cf. Kleinwort Benson Ltd v Glasgow CC* [1999] 1 A.C. 153 at 167, 171.
[51] In this respect these cases can be said to resemble *Rowland v Divall* [1923] 2 K.B. 500, above p.1053.
[52] *e.g.* not where payment is made under a wager.
[53] *Bilbie v Lumley* 1802) 2 East 469; *Brisbane v Dacres* (1813) 5 Taunt. 143; *Kelly v Solari* (1841) 9 M. & W. 54.
[54] [1999] 2 A.C. 349; *Nurdin & Peacock plc v DB Ramsden & Co Ltd* [1999] 1 All E.R. 941. For proposals for legislative reform, see Law Com. No.227 (1994); for the need for further legislation, see below, n.56.
[55] See above, at n.44.
[56] The bank's reason for relying on mistake was to enable it to take advantage of Limitation Act 1980, s.31(1) under which, in an action "for relief from the consequences of a mistake" the period of limitation did not begin to run until the plaintiff had, or with reasonable diligence could have, discovered the mistake. The result may be to extend the period indefinitely and it was recognised in the *Kleinwort Benson* case [1999] 2 A.C. 349 at 389, 401, 418 that legislation may be needed to deal with this point.
[57] *e.g. Westdeutsche Landesbank Girozentrale v Islington BC*, above, n.43; *Guiness Mahon & Co v Kensington & Chelsea Royal BC*, above, n.46.
[58] *Kleinwort Benson* case (above n.54) [1999] 2 A.C. 349 at 387, 415–416; *cf.* above, p.567.

the contract is *void*, denial of restitution of money paid on the ground that the payee has partly performed his void promise, would leave the payor without any remedy in respect of the unperformed part.[59] In the interest rate swap cases, there is the further point that there was no difficulty in apportioning the partial performance by B to the total performance for which A had bargained, so that one rationale of the requirement that the failure must be total did not exist and the cases could be brought within the exception to that requirement which exists in cases of such apportionability.[60] Moreover, where the partial or total performance which has taken place consists simply of payments and counter-payments of money under a void contract, there is no difficulty in restoring each party to its pre-contract position and hence no injustice is likely to result from allowing recovery of the balance. It follows from this reasoning that the right to recover might be barred where supervening events do make such mutual restoration impossible.[61] The interest rate swap cases also do not directly touch the problem which would arise where the performance rendered by one party to a void contract is of such a nature that it cannot literally be restored: *e.g.* where A had paid a sum of money in advance to B in return for B's promise to render services and after some of the services had been rendered it was discovered that B had no power to enter into the contract so that it was *ultra vires* and void. It is submitted that in such a case A should be entitled to recover its payment on the ground that the contract was void; but that this right should be subject to B's right to retain so much of that payment as B could have recovered by way of *quantum meruit* for work done under a void contract.[62]

(c) SPECIAL CASES. The rule that money paid under a void contract is recoverable is no more than a general one,[63] which may be displaced by the policy considerations underlying the rule of law which makes the contract void. It may, for example, be displaced under the rules (discussed earlier in this book) relating to illegal contracts, gaming and wagering contracts and minors' contracts.[64] An as yet unresolved question would arise where the contract was void for more than one reason. It may, for example, be both an *ultra vires* contract and a wager[65] or it may be both *ultra vires* and illegal; and in each of these situations money paid under the contract is *prima facie* recoverable on the first but irrecoverable on the second ground. The solution in such cases would appear to depend on the reason why the money is thus either recoverable or irrecoverable. For example, if A makes a wager with B who has no legal power to enter into it and pays money lost under it to B, then the argument that the money is irrecoverable because A intended to make a gift[66] of it to B might well prevail; but if the payment were made by B to A, then the policy of the *ultra vires* rule (which is to protect the assets of B against *ultra vires* ventures[67]) might well require that policy to prevail. Hence in the first case the money should be irrecoverable and in the second recoverable. Where the contract was both *ultra vires* and illegal, the policy of the rule making it illegal would normally prevail, so that (for example) a payment made by a local authority for the supply of prostitutes to its members would appear to be irrecoverable. But this can be no more than a general rule: illegality can vary widely in its seriousness so that the answer to the present question would depend in

---

[59] *cf.* above, p.1051.
[60] See above, p.1051.
[61] See *Kleinwort Benson Ltd v South Tyneside MBC* [1994] 4 All E.R. 972.
[62] See below, p.1063.
[63] *Guiness Mahon & Co Ltd v Kensington & Chelsea Royal BC* [1999] Q.B. 215 at 231.
[64] See above, pp.491–503, 522–523, 535–538, 550, 551–554, 556–557.
[65] See *Morgan Grenfell & Co Ltd v Welwyn Hatfield DC* [1995] 1 All E.R. 1 at 15 where this point was left open.
[66] See above, p.523.
[67] Usually to safeguard those interested in B's assets: *e.g.* taxpayers where B is a local authority.

each case on the factors more fully discussed in Chapter 11: *i.e.* on the nature of the illegality and on the states of mind of the parties.

2. Quantum Meruit

Here we are concerned with cases in which a party claims a reasonable recompense for some benefit (other than a payment of money) conferred, or for work done, by him under contract or purported contract. Many such cases have already been discussed and are mentioned here only for the sake of completeness.

(1) Where there is no express provision for remuneration[68]

Two situations must be distinguished.

(a) CONTRACTS NOT PROVIDING FOR REMUNERATION. A party can claim a *quantum meruit* for work done or goods delivered under a contract which does not expressly provide how much he is to be paid. This will be the case where the whole agreement is implied from conduct,[69] or where it is simply silent as to the rate of payment. Sometimes it may be clear from the terms of the agreement, or from the circumstances in which it was made, that the claimant was not intended to have any legal right to be paid at all.[70] But if he was intended to have such a right the court will award a reasonable sum. Thus if a contract for the sale of goods does not fix the price, the buyer must pay a reasonable price[71]; and if a contract for services does not fix the remuneration, a reasonable sum must be paid.[72]

A similar situation arises where the contract makes some, but not a full, provision for payment. In *Sir Lindsay Parkinson & Co Ltd v Commissioners of Works*[73] contractors agreed to erect works for a payment consisting of the cost of the works plus £300,000. It was thought that the works would cost about £5 million, but the Commissioners exercised their right under the contract to ask for additional works worth £1.5 million. It was held that the express provision as to payment only applied to works worth about £5 million and that the contractors were entitled to a *quantum meruit* in respect of the additional works.

(b) NO CONCLUDED CONTRACT. Work may be done where the parties believe that there is a contract but this is not the case because there was never a clear acceptance of an offer. In one such case a *quantum meruit* was awarded to the party who had done the work.[74] Such an award may also be made where work is done, under an agreement which lacks contractual force for want of contractual intention,[75] in anticipation of a formal contract which fails to materialise for want of execution of the requisite formal document[76]; and where one party does work at the request of the other during negotiations

---

[68] Birks, (1974) C.L.P. 13; Jones, (1977) 93 L.Q.R. 273.
[69] See above, pp.9, 18; *Paynter v Williams* (1833) 1 C. & M. 810; *cf. The Batis* [1990] 1 Lloyd's Rep. 345; *Fairvale v Sabharwall* [1992] 2 E.G.L.R. 27; *The Kurnia Dewi* [1997] 1 Lloyd's Rep. 553.
[70] See above, pp.167, 740.
[71] Sale of Goods Act 1979, s.8(2).
[72] Supply of Goods and Services Act 1982, s.15(1); *cf.* at common law *Way v Latilla* [1937] 3 All E.R. 759; and see above, p.741.
[73] [1949] 2 K.B. 632; *cf. Steven v Bromley & Son* [1919] 2 K.B. 722; *The Gregos* [1985] 2 Lloyd's Rep. 347; *The Saronikos* [1986] 2 Lloyd's Rep. 277; *Adams Holden & Pearson v Trent Regional Health Authority* (1989) 47 Build.L.R. 34.
[74] *Peter Lind & Co Ltd v Mersey Docks & Harbour Board* [1972] 2 Lloyd's Rep. 234; above, p.17; Arrowsmith, above, p.1057, n.35.
[75] *Galliard Homes Ltd v Jarvis Interiors Ltd* [2000] C.L.C. 411.
[76] This was accepted by both parties (though doubted by Evans L.J.); *cf.* above, p.157.

which are expected to lead to a contract between them but are broken off before its conclusion.[77] But no such award will be made where the party doing the work takes the risk that the negotiations may fail. This was held to be the position where one party to an agreement "subject to contract"[78] incurred expenses without any request from, and without benefiting, the other but solely for the purpose of securing (and then of performing) the contract.[79]

(2) Where there is an express provision for remuneration

The general rule is that where a contract expressly provides for a fixed remuneration on specified events, the court cannot award any other remuneration on those events, nor can it award any remuneration if they do not occur.[80] To allow *quantum meruit* claims in such cases would contradict the agreement reached by the parties, and the courts will do this only if there are special circumstances justifying such interference. Such circumstances exist in the following cases.

(a) INCAPACITY. Where necessaries are sold and delivered to a minor, he need only pay a reasonable price for them, although he may have agreed to pay more.[81] There are obvious reasons of policy for interfering with the agreement in such a case. There would be no such reasons where the minor had agreed to pay less than a reasonable price.

(b) WRONGFUL PREVENTION OF PERFORMANCE. If one party starts to perform a contract but is prevented from completing by the other party's breach, he can claim a *quantum meruit* at the contract rate[82] for work done, even though the unperformed obligation is entire.[83] The party in breach here cannot complain of having to pay in circumstances other than those provided for by the contract.

(c) OTHER PARTIAL PERFORMANCE. In Chapter 18 we saw that, in general, a person who failed to complete performance of an entire obligation could not recover anything[84]; but that this rule was subject to a number of exceptions.[85] Under some of these, there is a right to payment of the contract price or at the contract rate. Under others, there is a right to a *quantum meruit* (or reasonable remuneration): for example, where a benefit conferred by partial performance of services is "voluntarily" accepted by the other party.

---

[77] *William Lacey (Hounslow) Ltd v Davis* [1954] 1 Q.B. 428; *BSC v Cleveland Bridge & Engineering Co Ltd* [1984] 1 All E.R. 504; Ball, 99 L.Q.R. 572; *Marston Construction Co v Kigass* (1990) 15 Con.L.R. 116; Key, 111 L.Q.R. 576; *Countrywide Communications Ltd v ICL Pathways Ltd* [2000] C.L.C. 324.

[78] See above, p.52.

[79] *Regalian Properties plc v London Dockland Development Corp* [1995] 1 W.L.R. 212, where the *Marston Construction* case, above n.77 was at 229 described as a "surprising decision".

[80] *Britain v Rossiter* (1879) 11 Q.B.D. 123; *Gilbert & Partners v Knight* (1968) 112 S.J. 155; *Wiluszynski v Tower Hamlets LBC* [1989] I.C.R. 493.

[81] See above, p.542; the same is also sometimes true where necessaries are sold and delivered to a person incapacitated by other factors, such as mental illness, drink or drugs.: above, pp.557–559.

[82] *Lodder v Slowey* (1901) 20 N.Z.L.R. 321 at 356, affirmed [1904] A.C. 442; *Lusty v Finsbury Securities* (1991) 58 Build.L.R. 66; *Kehoe v Borough of Rutherford*, 27 A 912 (1893). According to *Boomer v Muir*, 24 P. 2d. 570 (1933) he can recover a reasonable sum even though it greatly exceeds the contract price; but it is submitted that this would not be followed in England, for it seems absurd that the injured party should recover more for partial, than he could recover for full, performance. Where one party, after the other's breach, does *extra* work, the reasonable sum recoverable for the work may exceed the damages recoverable for the breach: *The Batis* [1990] 1 Lloyd's Rep. 345.

[83] See above, p.822.

[84] See above, pp.782–784.

[85] See above, pp.819–822.

This rule can be explained on the ground that the parties have agreed to abandon the original contract, and that a new one is made when the benefit is accepted.[86] In a number of further exceptional cases, a reasonable sum is, or may be, payable for services rendered by the party in breach even though the services differ from, or fall short of, those bargained for, even though there has been no "voluntary" acceptance of them by the injured party, and even though the contract remains in force. For example, it has been said that a carrier by sea who deviates but carries the goods to the agreed destination can recover a reasonable freight[87]; and conflicting views have been expressed on the question whether an employer who "of necessity" accepts services falling short of those bargained for is liable to his employee for a *quantum meruit*.[88] Such exceptional cases are controversial precisely because they reveal a conflict between two policies. One is that the court should not unjustifiably contradict a subsisting contract by awarding a reasonable sum for services falling short of those promised; the other is that the court should not allow the injured party to have the benefit of those services for nothing, since this would lead to his being unjustly enriched. The exact scope and rationale of the present group of exceptional cases must therefore remain very much in doubt.

(d) CONTRACT VOID. In *Craven-Ellis v Canons Ltd*[89] the claimant worked for the defendant company as managing director. His service agreement with the company was void as neither he nor those who appointed him held the necessary qualification shares. Thus he could not recover his agreed pay.[90] But the Court of Appeal held that he was entitled to a *quantum meruit*. The position is the same where a contract with a company is void because the company was not yet in existence or had been dissolved[91] when the contract was made.[92] A similar principle may apply where goods have been supplied under a contract of sale which is void for a mistake as to the identity of the buyer.[93]

Where the express contract is a nullity, the argument that the court must not interfere with the bargain between the parties loses much of its force. It does not seem that liability in these cases is based on an agreement which can be implied from voluntary acceptance by the defendant of the claimant's services,[94] for the parties usually think that they are acting under an existing valid contract. In *Craven-Ellis v Canons Ltd* Greer L.J. said that the liability to pay a *quantum meruit* "is an inference which a rule of law imposes on the parties where work has been done or goods have been delivered under what purports to be a binding contract but is not so in fact".[95]

The principle just stated may, however, be displaced by countervailing policy considerations. In *Guinness plc v Saunders*[96] a company director did work for the company in the course of negotiations for a take-over bid which was being made by the company. The

---

[86] Similar reasoning may explain an analogous suggestion in *The Ballenita* [1992] 2 Lloyd's Rep. 455 at 466 that the market price must be paid for goods, delivery of which is taken by the buyer after his acceptance of the seller's repudiation by delay.

[87] *Hain SS Co Td v Tate & Lyle Ltd* (1936) 41 Com. Cas. 350 at 358, 367; above, p.821, n.55.

[88] *Miles v Wakefield Metropolitan DC* [1987] A.C. 539 at 552–553, 561; above p.822.

[89] [1936] 2 K.B. 403; Denning, (1939) 55 L.Q.R. 54.

[90] cf. *Re Bodega Co* [1904] 1 Ch. 276: if he is paid his contractual remuneration he must pay it back.

[91] See above, pp.735–736.

[92] *Rover International Ltd v Cannon Films Ltd (No.3)* [1989] 1 W.L.R. 912; *Cotronic (UK) Ltd v Dezonie* [1991] B.C.L.C. 721, above, p.736. For pre-incorporation contracts with limited liability partnerships, see Limited Liability Partnerships Act 2000, s.5(2), above, p.732.

[93] e.g. on the facts of *Boulton v Jones* (1857) 27 L.J. Ex. 117, for the exact nature of the appropriate remedy in such a situation, see above, p.305.

[94] *Contra*, Denning, above, n.89.

[95] At 410. cf. *Lawford v Billericay RDC* [1903] 1 K.B. 772 (the actual decision has been made obsolete by the Corporate Bodies Contracts Act 1960; above, p.566, n.70).

[96] [1990] 2 A.C. 663; Beatson and Prentice, 106 L.Q.R. 365.

agreement under which the work was done was void because those who purported to make it on behalf of the company had no authority to do so. It was held that the director was not entitled to *quantum meruit* since the terms of the agreement (by which his remuneration increased with the amount paid by the company) gave rise to a conflict between his own financial interest and his fiduciary duty to the company as one of its directors.

(e) CONTRACT FRUSTRATED. Work done under a contract *before* it is frustrated does not give rise to any *quantum meruit* claim at common law, though a claim in respect of a valuable benefit conferred by such work can be made under the Law Reform (Frustrated Contracts) Act 1943.[97] But if work is done under the contract *after* frustration, it may be possible to claim a *quantum meruit* on the principle of *Craven-Ellis v Canons Ltd.* The argument that the court must not interfere with the express contract is here met by the fact that the contract has no longer any legal force. A contract for the carriage of goods may be frustrated because the method of performance becomes impossible. The carrier may nonetheless get the goods to their destination in some other way. So long as he acts reasonably in doing so, he can claim a *quantum meruit*. It is irrelevant that a new contract cannot be implied from the mere fact that the cargo-owner accepts the cargo at its destination.[98]

---

[97] s.1(3), above, p.913. *cf.* also the rights of "commercial agents" under the legislation discussed at pp.919–920, above.

[98] *The Massalia* [1961] 2 Q.B. 278; overruled in *The Eugenia* [1964] 2 Q.B. 226, but not on this point.

INDEX

1065